GW01458535

Holy Bible

Presented to

_____

(Name)

By

_____

(Giver)

On

_____

(Occasion & Date)

The Father has loved us so much . . .
that we are called children of God.
~ 1 John 3:1

My Family History

_____
My Name

_____
When I Was Born

_____
My Father

_____
My Mother

_____
My Father's Parents

_____
My Mother's Parents

My Brothers and Sisters

Name		Born
Name		Born
Name		Born
Name		Born

My Favorite Bible Verses

Adam & Eve

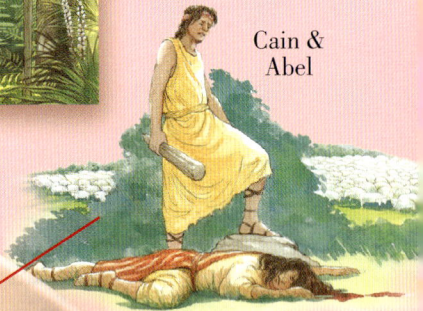

Cain & Abel

The Beginning

Creation

Tower of Babel

A Family Becomes a Nation— 2100 BC

Ur

Joseph in Egypt— 1900 BC

Noah & the Flood

The Exodus— 1450 BC

Bible

Time Line

Judges—
1380–1058 BC

Gideon

Deborah

Abraham & Isaac—
2000 BC

Moses &
the Law—
1450 BC

Joshua—
1399 BC

Tabernacle
Is Built—
1445 BC

Samson—
1070 BC

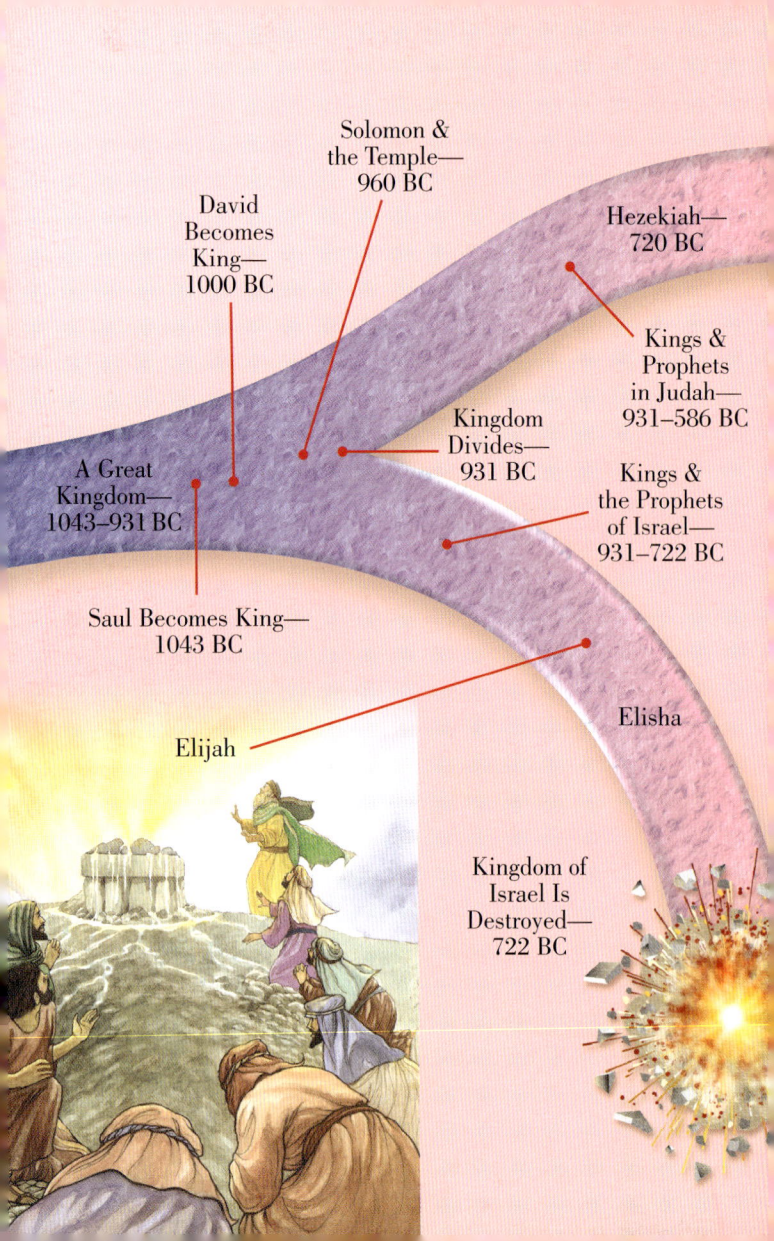

Solomon &
the Temple—
960 BC

David
Becomes
King—
1000 BC

Hezekiah—
720 BC

Kings &
Prophets
in Judah—
931–586 BC

Kingdom
Divides—
931 BC

A Great
Kingdom—
1043–931 BC

Kings &
the Prophets
of Israel—
931–722 BC

Saul Becomes King—
1043 BC

Elisha

Elijah

Kingdom of
Israel Is
Destroyed—
722 BC

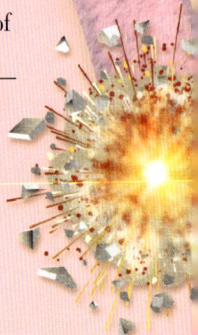

Josiah—
610 BC

Daniel—
605 BC

Jerusalem
Destroyed—
586 BC

Return
from Captivity—
458 BC

Birth of
Jesus—
4 BC

Death
of Jesus—
AD 30

The Church of Jesus—
AD 30

Letters to
Christians—
AD 45–90

*The church
continues until
the Lord returns*

THE
HOLY BIBLE

THE
HOLY BIBLE

CONTAINING THE OLD AND NEW TESTAMENTS

icb

International Children's Bible®

THOMAS NELSON
Since 1798

NASHVILLE   DALLAS   MEXICO CITY   RIO DE JANEIRO

PREFACE

The *International Children's Bible*® is not a storybook or a paraphrased Bible. It is a translation of God's Word from the original Hebrew and Greek languages. It is the first translation of the Holy Scriptures prepared specifically for children. Until now children have had to learn God's truths either from Bible storybooks or adult-language Bibles. Many words and concepts, readily understood by adults, may leave children mystified or even with false impressions.

Yet, God intended for everyone to be able to understand his Word. Earliest Scriptures were in Hebrew, ideally suited for a barely literate society because of its economy of words, acrostic literary form and poetic parallelism. The New Testament was first written in the simple Greek of everyday life, not in the Latin of Roman courts or the classical Greek of the academies. Even Jesus, the Master Teacher, taught spiritual principles by comparing them to such familiar terms as pearls, seeds, rocks, trees and sheep. It is for this same purpose of making the Scriptures intelligible, even to children, that this translation was created.

A Trustworthy Translation

Two basic premises guided the translation process. The first concern was that the translation be faithful to the manuscripts in the original languages. A team composed of the World Bible Translation Center and twenty-one additional, highly qualified and experienced Bible scholars and translators was assembled. The team included men with translation experience on such accepted versions as the *New International Version,* the *New American Standard Bible* and the *New King James Version.* The most recent scholarship and the best available Hebrew and Greek texts were used, principally the third edition of the United Bible Societies' Greek text and the latest edition of the Biblia Hebraica, along with the Septuagint.

A Clear Translation

The second concern was to make the language simple enough for children to read and understand it for themselves. In maintaining language simplicity, several guidelines were followed. Sentences have been kept short and uncomplicated. Vocabulary choice has been based upon *The Living Word Vocabulary* by Dr. Edgar Dale and Dr. Joseph O'Rourke (Worldbook-Childcraft International, 1981) which is the standard used by the editors of *The World Book Encyclopedia* to determine appropriate vocabulary. For difficult words which have no simpler synonyms, footnotes and dictionary references are provided. Footnotes appear at the bottom of the page and are indicated in the text by an [n] (for "note"). The dictionary is located at the back of the Bible with references indicated in the text by a [d].

Dr. Charles K. Kinzer of Peabody College of Education, Vanderbilt University, did a comparative study of this base text and four other versions commonly used by children. The results showed that the *International Children's Bible*® was clearly the easiest version for children to comprehend on the literal level. The word choice in this version was also judged to be the most appropriate for the youngest students. It was, in fact, the only version that could be comprehended on a third-grade instructional level (Kinzer, Ransom and Hammond, 1983).

The *International Children's Bible*® aids a child's understanding by putting concepts into natural terms. Modern measurements and geographical locations have been used as much as possible. For instance, the traditional "shekels" and "cubits" have been converted to modern equivalents of weights and measures.

Where geographical references are identical, the modern name has been used, such as the "Mediterranean Sea" instead of "Great Sea" or "Western Sea." Also, to minimize confusion, the most familiar name for a place is used consistently, instead of using variant names for the same place. "Lake Galilee" is used throughout rather than its variant forms, "Sea of Kinnereth," "Lake Gennesaret" and "Sea of Tiberias."

Ancient customs are often unfamiliar to modern readers. Customs such as shaving a man's beard to shame him or walking between the halves of a dead animal to seal an agreement are meaningless to children. So these are clarified either in the text or in a footnote.

Since *connotations* of words change with time, care has been taken to avoid potential misunderstandings. Instead of describing ancient citadels as "forts," which for modern children would likely conjure up pictures of wooden stockades in the Old West, the *International Children's Bible®* uses "strong, walled cities." Instead of using the phrase "God drove the nations out of Canaan," which could call up images in a child's mind of automobiles, the phrase is translated "forced them out of Canaan."

Rhetorical questions are obvious to adults, but not to children. To an adult, the implied answer to the psalmist's question, "Who is equal to our God?" is quite clear. To a child, the question remains unanswered. Therefore, rhetorical questions have been worded as statements, showing the implied meaning, as in this example: "No one is equal to our God."

Figures of speech can easily be misunderstood by children as literal statements. For instance, when Canaan is described as a land "flowing with milk and honey," children might literally see milk and honey running through the streets. To clarify, the *International Children's Bible®* has translated the meaning of the figures, while preserving the image as much as possible.

Idiomatic expressions of the biblical languages are translated to communicate the same meaning to today's child that would have been understood by the original audience. For example, the Hebrew idiom "he rested with his fathers" is translated by its meaning—"he died."

Every attempt has been made to maintain proper English style, while simplifying concepts and communications. The beauty of the Hebrew parallelism in poetry and the word plays have been retained. Images of the ancient languages have been captured in equivalent English images wherever possible.

Our Prayer

It is with great humility and prayerfulness that this Bible is presented to God's children. We acknowledge the infallibility of God's Word and our own human frailty. We pray that God has worked through us as his vessels so that his precious children might learn his truth for themselves and that it might richly grow in their lives. It is to his glory that this Bible is given.

THE PUBLISHER

CONTENTS

The
OLD TESTAMENT

The First Book of Moses Called
GENESIS

1 In the beginning God created the sky and the earth. [2]The earth was empty and had no form. Darkness covered the ocean, and God's Spirit[d] was moving over the water.

[3]Then God said, "Let there be light!" And there was light. [4]God saw that the light was good. So he divided the light from the darkness. [5]God named the light "day" and the darkness "night." Evening passed, and morning came. This was the first day.

[6]Then God said, "Let there be something to divide the water in two!" [7]So God made the air to divide the water in two. Some of the water was above the air, and some of the water was below it. [8]God named the air "sky." Evening passed, and morning came. This was the second day.

[9]Then God said, "Let the water under the sky be gathered together so the dry land will appear." And it happened. [10]God named the dry land "earth." He named the water that was gathered together "seas." God saw that this was good.

[11]Then God said, "Let the earth produce plants. Some plants will make grain for seeds. Others will make fruit with seeds in it. Every seed will produce more of its own kind of plant." And it happened. [12]The earth produced plants. Some plants had grain for seeds. The trees made fruit with seeds in it. Each seed grew its own kind of plant. God saw that all this was good. [13]Evening passed, and morning came. This was the third day.

[14]Then God said, "Let there be lights in the sky to separate day from night. These lights will be used for signs, seasons, days and years. [15]They will be in the sky to give light to the earth." And it happened.

[16]So God made the two large lights. He made the brighter light to rule the day. He made the smaller light to rule the night. He also made the stars. [17]God put all these in the sky to shine on the earth. [18]They are to rule over the day and over the night. He put them there to separate the light from the darkness. God saw that all these things were good. [19]Evening passed, and morning came. This was the fourth day.

[20]Then God said, "Let the water be filled with living things. And let birds fly in the air above the earth."

[21]So God created the large sea animals. He created every living thing that moves in the sea. The sea is filled with these living things. Each one produces more of its own kind. God also made every bird that flies. And each bird produces more of its own kind. God saw that this was good. [22]God blessed them and said, "Have many young ones and grow in number. Fill the water of the seas, and let the birds grow in number on the earth." [23]Evening passed, and morning came. This was the fifth day.

[24]Then God said, "Let the earth be filled with animals. And let each produce more of its own kind. Let there be tame animals and small crawling animals and wild animals. And let each produce more of its kind." And it happened. [25]So God made the wild animals, the tame animals and all the small crawling animals to produce more of their own kind. God saw that this was good.

[26]Then God said, "Let us make human beings in our image and likeness. And let them rule over the fish in the sea and the birds in the sky. Let them rule over the tame animals, over all the earth and over all the small crawling animals on the earth."

[27]So God created human beings in his image. In the image of God he created them. He created them male and female. [28]God blessed them and said, "Have many children and grow in number. Fill the earth and be its master. Rule over the fish in the sea and over the birds in the sky. Rule over every living thing that moves on the earth."

[29]God said, "Look, I have given you all the plants that have grain for seeds. And I have given you all the trees whose fruits have seeds in them. They will be food for you. [30]I have given all the green plants to all the animals to eat. They will be food for every wild animal, every bird of the air and every small crawling animal." And it happened. [31]God looked at everything he had made, and it was very good. Evening passed, and morning came. This was the sixth day.

2 So the sky, the earth and all that filled them were finished. [2]By the seventh day God finished the work he had been doing. So on the seventh day he rested from all his work. ³God blessed the seventh day and made it a holy day. He made it holy because on that day he rested. He rested from all the work he had done in creating the world.

⁴This is the story of the creation of the sky and the earth. When the Lord God made the earth and the sky, ⁵there were no plants on the earth. Nothing was growing in the fields. The Lord God had not yet made it rain on the land. And there was no man to care for the ground. ⁶But a mist often rose from the earth and watered all the ground.

⁷Then the Lord God took dust from the ground and formed man from it. The Lord breathed the breath of life into the man's nose. And the man became a living person. ⁸Then the Lord God planted a garden in the East, in a place called Eden. He put the man he had formed in that garden. ⁹The Lord God caused every beautiful tree and every tree that was good for food to grow out of the ground. In the middle of the garden, God put the tree that gives life. And he put there the tree that gives the knowledge of good and evil.

¹⁰A river flowed through Eden and watered the garden. From that point the river was divided. It had four streams flowing into it. ¹¹The name of the first stream is Pishon. It flows around the whole land of Havilah, where there is gold. ¹²That gold is good. Bdellium and onyxⁿ are also there. ¹³The name of the second river is Gihon. It flows around the whole land of Cush. ¹⁴The name of the third river is Tigris. It flows out of Assyria toward the east. The fourth river is the Euphrates.

¹⁵The Lord God put the man in the garden of Eden to care for it and work it. ¹⁶The Lord God commanded him, "You may eat the fruit from any tree in the garden. ¹⁷But you must not eat the fruit from the tree which gives the knowledge of good and evil. If you ever eat fruit from that tree, you will die!"

¹⁸Then the Lord God said, "It is not good for the man to be alone. I will make a helper who is right for him."

¹⁹From the ground God formed every wild animal and every bird in the sky. He brought them to the man so the man could name them. Whatever the man called each living thing, that became its name.²⁰The man gave names to all the tame animals, to the birds in the sky and to all the wild animals. But Adamⁿ did not find a helper that was right for him. ²¹So the Lord God caused the man to sleep very deeply. While the man was asleep, God took one of the ribs from the man's body. Then God closed the man's skin at the place where he took the rib. ²²The Lord God used the rib from the man to make a woman. Then the Lord brought the woman to the man.

²³And the man said,

"Now, this is someone whose bones
     came from my bones.
Her body came from my body.
I will call her 'woman,'
     because she was taken out of
     man."

²⁴So a man will leave his father and mother and be united with his wife. And the two people will become one body. ²⁵The man and his wife were naked, but they were not ashamed.

3 Now the snake was the most clever of all the wild animals the Lord God had made. One day the snake spoke to the woman. He said, "Did God really say that you must not eat fruit from any tree in the garden?"

²The woman answered the snake, "We may eat fruit from the trees in the garden. ³But God told us, 'You must not eat fruit from the tree that is in the middle of the garden. You must not even touch it, or you will die.'"

⁴But the snake said to the woman, "You will not die. ⁵God knows that if you eat the fruit from that tree, you will learn about good and evil. Then you will be like God!"

⁶The woman saw that the tree was beautiful. She saw that its fruit was good to eat and that it would make her wise. So she took some of its fruit and ate it. She also gave some of the fruit to her husband, and he ate it. ⁷Then, it was as if the man's and the woman's eyes were opened. They realized they were naked. So they sewed fig leaves together and made something to cover themselves.

⁸Then they heard the Lord God walking in the garden. This was during the cool part of the day. And the man and his wife hid from the Lord God among

2:12 **bdellium and onyx** Bdellium is an expensive, sweet-smelling resin like myrrh. And onyx is a gem. 2:20 **Adam** This is the name of the first man. It also means "humans," including men and women.

the trees in the garden. ⁹But the Lord God called to the man. The Lord said, "Where are you?"

¹⁰The man answered, "I heard you walking in the garden. I was afraid because I was naked. So I hid."

¹¹God said to the man, "Who told you that you were naked? Did you eat fruit from that tree? I commanded you not to eat from that tree."

¹²The man said, "You gave this woman to me. She gave me fruit from the tree. So I ate it."

¹³Then the Lord God said to the woman, "What have you done?"

She answered, "The snake tricked me. So I ate the fruit."

¹⁴The Lord God said to the snake,
"Because you did this,
   a curse will be put on you.
   You will be cursed more than any
      tame animal or wild animal.
You will crawl on your stomach,
   and you will eat dust all the days
      of your life.
¹⁵I will make you and the woman
      enemies to each other.
Your descendants[d] and her
      descendants
   will be enemies.
Her child will crush your head.
   And you will bite his heel."

¹⁶Then God said to the woman,
"I will cause you to have much
      trouble
   when you are pregnant.
And when you give birth to
      children,
   you will have great pain.
You will greatly desire your
      husband,
   but he will rule over you."

¹⁷Then God said to the man, "You listened to what your wife said. And you ate fruit from the tree that I commanded you not to eat from.

"So I will put a curse on the
      ground.
   You will have to work very hard
      for food.
In pain you will eat its food
   all the days of your life.
¹⁸The ground will produce thorns
      and weeds for you.
   And you will eat the plants of the
      field.
¹⁹You will sweat and work hard
   for your food.

Later you will return to the ground.
   This is because you were taken
      from the ground.
You are dust.
   And when you die, you will
      return to the dust."

²⁰The man named his wife Eve.[n] This is because she is the mother of everyone who ever lived.

²¹The Lord God made clothes from animal skins for the man and his wife. And so the Lord dressed them. ²²Then the Lord God said, "Look, the man has become like one of us. He knows good and evil. And now we must keep him from eating some of the fruit from the tree of life. If he does, he will live forever." ²³So the Lord God forced the man out of the garden of Eden. He had to work the ground he was taken from. ²⁴God forced the man out of the garden. Then God put angels on the east side of the garden. He also put a sword of fire there. It flashed around in every direction. This kept people from getting to the tree of life.

4 Adam had sexual relations with his wife Eve. She became pregnant and gave birth to Cain.[n] Eve said, "With the Lord's help, I have given birth to a man." ²After that, Eve gave birth to Cain's brother Abel. Abel took care of sheep. Cain became a farmer.

³Later, Cain brought a gift to God. He brought some food from the ground. ⁴Abel brought the best parts of his best sheep. The Lord accepted Abel and his gift. ⁵But God did not accept Cain and his gift. Cain became very angry and looked unhappy.

⁶The Lord asked Cain, "Why are you angry? Why do you look so unhappy? ⁷If you do good, I will accept you. But if you do not do good, sin is ready to attack you. Sin wants you. But you must rule over it."

⁸Cain said to his brother Abel, "Let's go out into the field." So Cain and Abel went into the field. Then Cain attacked his brother Abel and killed him.

⁹Later, the Lord said to Cain, "Where is your brother Abel?"

Cain answered, "I don't know. Is it my job to take care of my brother?"

¹⁰Then the Lord said, "What have you done? Your brother's blood is on the ground. That blood is like a voice that tells me what happened. ¹¹And now you

will be cursed in your work with the ground. It is the same ground where your brother's blood fell. Your hands killed him. [12]You will work the ground. But it will not grow good crops for you anymore. You will wander around on the earth."

[13]Then Cain said to the Lord, "This punishment is more than I can stand! [14]Look! You have forced me to stop working the ground. And now I must hide from you. I will wander around on the earth. And anyone who meets me can kill me."

[15]Then the Lord said to Cain, "No! If anyone kills you, I will punish that person seven times more." Then the Lord put a mark on Cain. It was a warning to anyone who met him not to kill him.

[16]Then Cain went away from the Lord. Cain lived in the land of Nod,[n] east of Eden. [17]Cain had sexual relations with his wife. She became pregnant and gave birth to Enoch. At that time Cain was building a city. He named it after his son Enoch. [18]Enoch had a son named Irad. Irad had a son named Mehujael. Mehujael had a son named Methushael. And Methushael had a son named Lamech.

[19]Lamech married two women. One wife was named Adah, and the other was Zillah. [20]Adah gave birth to Jabal. He was the first person to live in tents and raise cattle. [21]Jabal's brother was Jubal. Jubal was the first person to play the harp and flute. [22]Zillah gave birth to Tubal-Cain. He made tools out of bronze and iron. The sister of Tubal-Cain was Naamah.

[23]Lamech said to his wives:

"Adah and Zillah, hear my voice!
　You wives of Lamech, listen to
　　what I say.
I killed a man for wounding me.
　I killed a young man for hitting
　　me.
[24]Cain's killer may be punished 7
　times.
Then Lamech's killer will be
　punished 77 times."

[25]Adam had sexual relations with his wife Eve again. And she gave birth to a son. She named him Seth.[n] Eve said, "God has given me another child. He will take the place of Abel, who was killed by Cain." [26]Seth also had a son. They named him Enosh. At that time people began to pray to the Lord.

5 This is the family history of Adam. When God created human beings, he made them in God's likeness. [2]He created them male and female. And on that day he blessed them and named them human beings.

[3]When Adam was 130 years old, he became the father of another son. He was in the likeness and image of Adam. Adam named him Seth. [4]After Seth was born, Adam lived 800 years. During that time he had other sons and daughters. [5]So Adam lived a total of 930 years. Then he died.

[6]When Seth was 105 years old, he had a son named Enosh. [7]After Enosh was born, Seth lived 807 years. During that time he had other sons and daughters. [8]So Seth lived a total of 912 years. Then he died.

[9]When Enosh was 90 years old, he had a son named Kenan. [10]After Kenan was born, Enosh lived 815 years. During that time he had other sons and daughters. [11]So Enosh lived a total of 905 years. Then he died.

[12]When Kenan was 70 years old, he had a son named Mahalalel. [13]After Mahalalel was born, Kenan lived 840 years. During that time he had other sons and daughters. [14]So Kenan lived a total of 910 years. Then he died.

[15]When Mahalalel was 65 years old, he had a son named Jared. [16]After Jared was born, Mahalalel lived 830 years. During that time he had other sons and daughters. [17]So Mahalalel lived a total of 895 years. Then he died.

[18]When Jared was 162 years old, he had a son named Enoch. [19]After Enoch was born, Jared lived 800 years. During that time he had other sons and daughters. [20]So Jared lived a total of 962 years. Then he died.

[21]When Enoch was 65 years old, he had a son named Methuselah. [22]After Methuselah was born, Enoch walked with God 300 years more. During that time he had other sons and daughters. [23]So Enoch lived a total of 365 years. [24]Enoch walked with God. One day Enoch could not be found, because God took him.

[25]When Methuselah was 187 years old, he had a son named Lamech. [26]After Lamech was born, Methuselah lived 782 years. During that time he had other

---

4:16 Nod This name sounds like the Hebrew word for "wander." **4:25 Seth** This name sounds like the Hebrew word for "to give."

sons and daughters. [27] So Methuselah lived a total of 969 years. Then he died.

[28] When Lamech was 182, he had a son. [29] Lamech named his son Noah.[n] Lamech said, "Noah will comfort us from the pain of our work. The pain is because God has cursed the ground." [30] After Noah was born, Lamech lived 595 years. During that time he had other sons and daughters. [31] So Lamech lived a total of 777 years. Then he died.

[32] After Noah was 500 years old, he became the father of Shem, Ham and Japheth.

6 The number of people on earth began to grow. Daughters were born to these people. [2] The sons of God saw that these girls were beautiful. And they married any of them they chose. [3] The Lord said, "My Spirit[d] will not remain in human beings forever. This is because they are flesh. They will live only 120 years."

[4] The Nephilim[d] were on the earth in those days and also later. That was when the sons of God had sexual relations with the daughters of men. These women gave birth to children, who became famous. They were the mighty warriors of long ago.

[5] The Lord saw that the human beings on the earth were very wicked. He also saw that their thoughts were only about evil all the time. [6] The Lord was sorry he had made human beings on the earth. His heart was filled with pain. [7] So the Lord said, "I will destroy all human beings that I made on the earth. And I will destroy every animal and everything that crawls on the earth. I will also destroy the birds of the air. This is because I am sorry that I have made them." [8] But Noah pleased the Lord.

[9] This is the family history of Noah. Noah was a good man. He was the most innocent man of his time. He walked with God. [10] Noah had three sons: Shem, Ham and Japheth.

[11] People on earth did what God said was evil. Violence was everywhere. [12] And God saw this evil. All people on the earth did only evil. [13] So God said to Noah, "People have made the earth full of violence. So I will destroy all people from the earth. [14] Build a boat of cypress wood for yourself. Make rooms in it and cover it inside and outside with tar. [15] This is how big I want you to build the boat: 450 feet long, 75 feet wide and 45

feet high. [16] Make an opening around the top of the boat. Make it 18 inches high from the edge of the roof down. Put a door in the side of the boat. Make an upper, middle and lower deck in it. [17] I will bring a flood of water on the earth. I will destroy all living things that live under the sky. This includes everything that has the breath of life. Everything on the earth will die. [18] But I will make an agreement with you. You, your sons, your wife and your sons' wives will all go into the boat. [19] Also, you must bring into the boat two of every living thing, male and female. Keep them alive with you. [20] There will be two of every kind of bird, animal and crawling thing. They will come to you to be kept alive. [21] Also gather some of every kind of food. Store it on the boat as food for you and the animals."

[22] Noah did everything that God commanded him.

7 Then the Lord said to Noah, "I have seen that you are the best man among the people of this time. So you and your family go into the boat. [2] Take with you seven pairs, each male with its female, of every kind of clean[d] animal. And take one pair, each male with its female, of every kind of unclean animal. [3] Take seven pairs of all the birds of the sky, each male with its female. This will allow all these animals to continue living on the earth after the flood. [4] Seven days from now I will send rain on the earth. It will rain 40 days and 40 nights. I will destroy from the earth every living thing that I made."

[5] Noah did everything that the Lord commanded him.

[6] Noah was 600 years old when the flood came. [7] He and his wife and his sons and their wives went into the boat. They went in to escape the waters of the flood. [8] The clean animals, the unclean animals, the birds and everything that crawls on the ground [9] came to Noah. They went into the boat in groups of two, male and female. This was just as God had commanded Noah. [10] Seven days later the flood started.

[11] Noah was now 600 years old. The flood started on the seventeenth day of the second month of that year. That day the underground springs split open. And the clouds in the sky poured out rain. [12] The rain fell on the earth for 40 days and 40 nights.

5:29 **Noah** This name sounds like the Hebrew word for "rest."

[13] On that same day Noah and his wife, his sons Shem, Ham and Japheth and their wives went into the boat. [14] They had every kind of wild animal and tame animal. There was every kind of animal that crawls on the earth. Every kind of bird was there. [15] They all came to Noah in the boat in groups of two. There was every creature that had the breath of life. [16] One male and one female of every living thing came. It was just as God had commanded Noah. Then the Lord closed the door behind them.

[17] Water flooded the earth for 40 days. As the water rose, it lifted the boat off the ground. [18] The water continued to rise, and the boat floated on the water above the earth. [19] The water rose so much that even the highest mountains under the sky were covered by it. [20] The water continued to rise until it was more than 20 feet above the mountains.

[21] All living things that moved on the earth died. This included all the birds, tame animals, wild animals and creatures that swarm on the earth. And all human beings died. [22] So everything on dry land died. This means everything that had the breath of life in its nose. [23] So God destroyed from the earth every living thing that was on the land. This was every man, animal, crawling thing and bird of the sky. All that was left was Noah and what was with him in the boat. [24] And the waters continued to cover the earth for 150 days.

8 But God remembered Noah and all the wild animals and tame animals with him in the boat. God made a wind blow over the earth. And the water went down. [2] The underground springs stopped flowing. And the clouds in the sky stopped pouring down rain. [3-4] The water that covered the earth began to go down. After 150 days the water had gone down so much that the boat touched land again. It came to rest on one of the mountains of Ararat.[n] This was on the seventeenth day of the seventh month. [5] The water continued to go down. By the first day of the tenth month the tops of the mountains could be seen.

[6] Forty days later Noah opened the window he had made in the boat. [7] He sent out a raven. It flew here and there until the water had dried up from the earth. [8] Then Noah sent out a dove. This was to find out if the water had dried up from the ground. [9] The dove could not find a place to land because water still covered the earth. So it came back to the boat. Noah reached out his hand and took the bird. And he brought it back into the boat.

[10] After seven days Noah again sent out the dove from the boat. [11] And that evening it came back to him with a fresh olive leaf in its mouth. Then Noah knew that the ground was almost dry. [12] Seven days later he sent the dove out again. But this time it did not come back.

[13] Noah was now 601 years old. It was the first day of the first month of that year. The water was dried up from the land. Noah removed the covering of the boat and saw that the land was dry. [14] By the twenty-seventh day of the second month the land was completely dry.

[15] Then God said to Noah, [16] "You and your wife, your sons and their wives should go out of the boat. [17] Bring every animal out of the boat with you—the birds, animals and everything that crawls on the earth. Let them have many young ones and let them grow in number."

[18] So Noah went out with his sons, his wife and his sons' wives. [19] Every animal, everything that crawls on the earth and every bird went out of the boat. They left by families.

[20] Then Noah built an altar to the Lord. Noah took some of all the clean[d] birds and animals. And he burned them on the altar as offerings to God. [21] The Lord was pleased with these sacrifices. He said to himself, "I will never again curse the ground because of human beings. Their thoughts are evil even when they are young. But I will never again destroy every living thing on the earth as I did this time.

[22] "As long as the earth continues,
    there will be planting and harvest.
    Cold and hot,
    summer and winter,
    day and night
    will not stop."

9 Then God blessed Noah and his sons. He said to them, "Have many children. Grow in number and fill the earth. [2] Every animal on earth and every bird in the sky will respect and fear you. So will every animal that crawls on the ground and every fish in the sea respect and fear you. I have given them to you. [3] "Everything that moves, everything that is alive, is yours for food. Earlier I

8:3-4 Ararat The ancient land of Urartu, an area in Eastern Turkey.

gave you the green plants. And now I give you everything for food. [4]But you must not eat meat that still has blood in it, because blood gives life. [5]I will demand your blood for your lives. That is, I will demand the life of any animal that kills a person. And I will demand the life of anyone who takes another person's life.

[6]"Whoever kills a human being
    will be killed by a human being.
This is because God made humans
    in his own image.

[7]"Noah, I want you and your family to have many children. Grow in number on the earth and become many."

[8]Then God said to Noah and his sons, [9]"Now I am making my agreement with you and your people who will live after you. [10]And I also make it with every living thing that is with you. It is with the birds, the tame animals and the wild animals. It is with all that came out of the boat with you. I make my agreement with every living thing on earth. [11]I make this agreement with you: I will never again destroy all living things by floodwaters. A flood will never again destroy the earth."

[12]And God said, "I am making an agreement between me and you and every living creature that is with you. It will continue from now on. This is the sign: [13]I am putting my rainbow in the clouds. It is the sign of the agreement between me and the earth. [14]When I bring clouds over the earth, a rainbow appears in the clouds. [15]Then I will remember my agreement. It is between me and you and every living thing. Floodwaters will never again destroy all life on the earth. [16]When the rainbow appears in the clouds, I will see it. Then I will remember the agreement that continues forever. It is between me and every living thing on the earth."

[17]So God said to Noah, "That rainbow is a sign. It is the sign of the agreement that I made with all living things on earth."

[18]The sons of Noah came out of the boat with him. They were Shem, Ham and Japheth. (Ham was the father of Canaan.) [19]These three men were Noah's sons. And all the people on earth came from these three sons.

[20]Noah became a farmer and planted a vineyard. [21]He drank wine made from his grapes. Then he became drunk and lay naked in his tent. [22]Ham, the father of Canaan, looked at his naked father. Ham told his brothers outside. [23]Then Shem and Japheth got a coat and carried it on both their shoulders. They walked backwards into the tent and covered their father. They turned their faces away. In this way they did not see their father without clothes.

[24]Noah was sleeping because of the wine. Later he woke up. Then he learned what his youngest son, Ham, had done to him. [25]So Noah said,

"May there be a curse on Canaan!
    May he be the lowest slave to his
        brothers."

[26]Noah also said,

"May the Lord, the God of Shem,
    be praised!
May Canaan be Shem's slave.

[27]May God give more land to
    Japheth.
May Japheth live in Shem's tents,
    and may Canaan be their slave."

[28]After the flood Noah lived 350 years. [29]He lived a total of 950 years. Then he died.

10 This is the family history of the sons of Noah: Shem, Ham and Japheth. After the flood these three men had sons.

[2]The sons of Japheth were Gomer, Magog, Madai, Javan, Tubal, Meshech and Tiras.

[3]The sons of Gomer were Ashkenaz, Riphath and Togarmah.

[4]The sons of Javan were Elishah, Tarshish, Kittim[n] and Rodanim. [5]Those who lived in the lands around the Mediterranean Sea came from these sons of Japheth. All the families grew and became different nations. Each nation had its own land and its own language.

[6]The sons of Ham were Cush, Mizraim,[n] Put and Canaan.

[7]The sons of Cush were Seba, Havilah, Sabtah, Raamah and Sabteca.

The sons of Raamah were Sheba and Dedan.

[8]Cush also had a descendant[d] named Nimrod. Nimrod became a very powerful man on earth. [9]He was a great hunter before the Lord. That is why people say someone is "like Nimrod, a great hunter before the Lord." [10]At first Nimrod's kingdom covered Babylon, Erech, Akkad and Calneh in the land of Babylo-

10:4 Kittim His descendants were the people of Cyprus. **10:6 Mizraim** This is another name for Egypt.

nia. ¹¹From there he went to Assyria. There he built the cities of Nineveh, Rehoboth Ir and Calah. ¹²He also built Resen, the great city between Nineveh and Calah.

¹³Mizraim was the father of the Ludites, Anamites, Lehabites, Naphtuhites, ¹⁴Pathrusites, Casluhites and the people of Crete. (The Philistines came from the Casluhites.)

¹⁵Canaan was the father of Sidon his first son and of Heth. ¹⁶Canaan was also the father of the Jebusites, Amorites, Girgashites, ¹⁷Hivites, Arkites, Sinites, ¹⁸Arvadites, Zemarites and Hamathites. The families of the Canaanites scattered. ¹⁹The land of the Canaanites reached from Sidon to Gerar as far as Gaza. And it reached to Sodom, Gomorrah, Admah and Zeboiim, as far as Lasha.

²⁰All these people were the sons of Ham. All these families had their own languages, their own lands and their own nations.

²¹Shem, Japheth's older brother, also had sons. One of his descendants[d] was the father of all the sons of Eber.

²²The sons of Shem were Elam, Asshur, Arphaxad, Lud and Aram.

²³The sons of Aram were Uz, Hul, Gether and Meshech.

²⁴Arphaxad was the father of Shelah. Shelah was the father of Eber. ²⁵Eber was the father of two sons. One son was named Peleg[b] because the earth was divided during his life. Eber's other son was named Joktan.

²⁶Joktan was the father of Almodad, Sheleph, Hazarmaveth, Jerah, ²⁷Hadoram, Uzal, Diklah, ²⁸Obal, Abimael, Sheba, ²⁹Ophir, Havilah and Jobab. All these people were the sons of Joktan. ³⁰These people lived in the area between Mesha and Sephar in the hill country in the East.

³¹These are the people from the family of Shem. They are arranged by families, languages, countries and nations.

³²This is the list of the families from the sons of Noah. They are arranged according to their nations. From these families came all the nations who spread across the earth after the flood.

11 At this time the whole world spoke one language. Everyone used the same words. ²As people moved from the East, they found a plain in the land of Babylonia. They settled there to live.

³They said to each other, "Let's make bricks and bake them to make them hard." So they used bricks instead of stones, and tar instead of mortar. ⁴Then they said to each other, "Let's build for ourselves a city and a tower. And let's make the top of the tower reach high into the sky. We will become famous. If we do this, we will not be scattered over all the earth."

⁵The Lord came down to see the city and the tower that the people had built. ⁶The Lord said, "Now, these people are united. They all speak the same language. This is only the beginning of what they will do. They will be able to do anything they want. ⁷Come, let us go down and confuse their language. Then they will not be able to understand each other."

⁸So the Lord scattered them from there over all the earth. And they stopped building the city. ⁹That is where the Lord confused the language of the whole world. So the place is called Babel.[n] So the Lord caused them to spread out from there over all the whole world.

¹⁰This is the family history of Shem. Two years after the flood, when Shem was 100 years old, his son Arphaxad was born. ¹¹After that, Shem lived 500 years and had other sons and daughters.

¹²When Arphaxad was 35 years old, his son Shelah was born. ¹³After that, Arphaxad lived 403 years and had other sons and daughters.

¹⁴When Shelah was 30 years old, his son Eber was born. ¹⁵After that, Shelah lived 403 years and had other sons and daughters.

¹⁶When Eber was 34 years old, his son Peleg was born. ¹⁷After that, Eber lived 430 years and had other sons and daughters.

¹⁸When Peleg was 30 years old, his son Reu was born. ¹⁹After that, Peleg lived 209 years and had other sons and daughters.

²⁰When Reu was 32 years old, his son Serug was born. ²¹After that, Reu lived 207 years and had other sons and daughters.

²²When Serug was 30 years old, his son Nahor was born. ²³After that, Serug lived 200 years and had other sons and daughters.

²⁴When Nahor was 29 years old, his son Terah was born. ²⁵After that, Nahor

10:25 Peleg This name sounds like the Hebrew word for "divided."   **11:9 Babel** This name sounds like the Hebrew word for "confused."

lived 119 years and had other sons and daughters.

²⁶After Terah was 70 years old, his sons Abram, Nahor and Haran were born.

²⁷This is the family history of Terah. Terah was the father of Abram, Nahor and Haran. Haran was the father of Lot. ²⁸Haran died while his father, Terah, was still alive. This happened in Ur in Babylonia, where he was born. ²⁹Abram and Nahor both married. Abram's wife was named Sarai. Nahor's wife was named Milcah. She was the daughter of Haran. Haran was the father of Milcah and Iscah. ³⁰Sarai was not able to have children.

³¹Terah took his son Abram, his grandson Lot (Haran's son) and his daughter-in-law Sarai (Abram's wife). They moved out of Ur of Babylonia. They had planned to go to the land of Canaan. But when they reached the city of Haran, they settled there.

³²Terah lived to be 205 years old. Then he died in Haran.

12 Then the Lord said to Abram, "Leave your country, your relatives and your father's family. Go to the land I will show you.

²I will make you a great nation,
    and I will bless you.
I will make you famous.
    And you will be a blessing to
        others.
³I will bless those who bless you.
    I will place a curse on those who
        harm you.
And all the people on earth
    will be blessed through you."

⁴So Abram left Haran as the Lord had told him. And Lot went with him. At this time Abram was 75 years old. ⁵Abram took his wife Sarai, his nephew Lot and everything they owned. They took all the servants they had gotten in Haran. They set out from Haran, planning to go to the land of Canaan. In time they arrived there.

⁶Abram traveled through that land. He went as far as the great tree of Moreh at Shechem. The Canaanites were living in the land at that time. ⁷The Lord appeared to Abram. The Lord said, "I will give this land to your descendants."ᵈ So Abram built an altar there to the Lord, who had appeared to him. ⁸Then Abram traveled from Shechem to the mountain east of Bethel. And he set up his tent there. Bethel was to the west, and Ai was to the east. There Abram built another altar to the Lord and worshiped him. ⁹After this, he traveled on toward southern Canaan.

¹⁰At this time there was not much food in the land. So Abram went down to Egypt to live because there was so little food. ¹¹Just before they arrived in Egypt, Abram said to his wife Sarai, "I know you are a very beautiful woman. ¹²When the Egyptians see you, they will say, 'This woman is his wife.' Then they will kill me but let you live. ¹³Tell them you are my sister. Then things will go well with me. And I may be allowed to live because of you."

¹⁴So Abram went into Egypt. The people of Egypt saw that Sarai was very beautiful. ¹⁵Some of the Egyptian officers saw her also. They told the king of Egypt how beautiful she was. They took her to the king's palace. ¹⁶The king was kind to Abram because he thought Abram was Sarai's brother. He gave Abram sheep, cattle and male and female donkeys. Abram also was given male and female servants and camels.

¹⁷But the Lord sent terrible diseases on the king and all the people in his house. This was because of Abram's wife Sarai. ¹⁸So the king sent for Abram. The king said, "What have you done to me? Why didn't you tell me Sarai was your wife? ¹⁹Why did you say, 'She is my sister'? I made her my wife. But now here is your wife. Take her and leave!" ²⁰Then the king commanded his men to make Abram leave Egypt. So Abram and his wife left with everything they owned.

13 So Abram, his wife and Lot left Egypt. They took everything they owned and traveled to southern Canaan. ²Abram was very rich in cattle, silver and gold.

³He left southern Canaan and went back to Bethel. He went where he had camped before, between Bethel and Ai. ⁴It was the place where Abram had built an altar before. So he worshiped the Lord there.

⁵During this time Lot was traveling with Abram. Lot also had many sheep, cattle and tents. ⁶Abram and Lot had so many animals that the land could not support both of them together. ⁷Abram's herders and Lot's herders began to argue. The Canaanites and the Perizzites were living in the land at this time.

⁸So Abram said to Lot, "There should be no arguing between you and me. Your herders and mine should not argue

either. We are brothers. ⁹We should separate. The whole land is there in front of you. If you go to the left, I will go to the right. If you go to the right, I will go to the left."

¹⁰Lot looked all around and saw the whole Jordan Valley. He saw that there was much water there. It was like the Lord's garden, like the land of Egypt in the direction of Zoar. (This was before the Lord destroyed Sodom and Gomorrah.) ¹¹So Lot chose to move east and live in the Jordan Valley. In this way Abram and Lot separated. ¹²Abram lived in the land of Canaan. But Lot lived among the cities in the Jordan Valley. He moved very near to Sodom. ¹³Now the people of Sodom were very evil. They were always sinning against the Lord.

¹⁴After Lot left, the Lord said to Abram, "Look all around you. Look north and south and east and west. ¹⁵All this land that you see I will give to you and your descendants⁴ forever. ¹⁶I will make your descendants as many as the dust of the earth. If anyone could count the dust on the earth, he could count your people. ¹⁷Get up! Walk through all this land. I am now giving it to you."

¹⁸So Abram moved his tents. He went to live near the great trees of Mamre. This was at the city of Hebron. There he built an altar to the Lord.

14 Now Amraphel was king of Babylonia. Arioch was king of Ellasar. Kedorlaomer was king of Elam. And Tidal was king of Goiim. ²All these kings went to war against several other kings: Bera king of Sodom, Birsha king of Gomorrah, Shinab king of Admah, Shemeber king of Zeboiim and the king of Bela. (Bela is also called Zoar.)

³These kings who were attacked united their armies in the Valley of Siddim. (The Valley of Siddim is now the Dead Sea.⁴) ⁴These kings had served Kedorlaomer for 12 years. But in the thirteenth year, they all turned against him. ⁵Then in the fourteenth year, Kedorlaomer and the kings with him came and defeated the Rephaites⁴ in Ashteroth Karnaim. They also defeated the Zuzites in Ham and the Emites in Shaveh Kiriathaim. ⁶And they defeated the Horites in the mountains of Edom to El Paran. (El Paran is near the desert.) ⁷Then they turned back and went to En Mishpat (that is, Kadesh). They defeated all the Amalekites. They also defeated

the Amorites who lived in Hazazon Tamar.

⁸At that time the kings of Sodom, Gomorrah, Admah, Zeboiim and Bela went out to fight in the Valley of Siddim. (Bela is called Zoar.) ⁹They fought against Kedorlaomer king of Elam, Tidal king of Goiim, Amraphel king of Babylonia, and Arioch king of Ellasar. So there were four kings fighting against five. ¹⁰There were many tar pits in the Valley of Siddim. The kings of Sodom and Gomorrah and their armies ran away. Some of the soldiers fell into the tar pits. But the others ran away to the mountains.

¹¹Now Kedorlaomer and his armies took everything the people of Sodom and Gomorrah owned. They also took all their food. ¹²They took Lot, Abram's nephew who was living in Sodom. The enemy also took everything he owned. Then they left. ¹³One of the men who was not captured went to Abram, the Hebrew. He told Abram what had happened. At that time Abram was camped near the great trees of Mamre the Amorite. Mamre was a brother of Eshcol and a brother of Aner. And they had all made an agreement to help Abram.

¹⁴Abram learned that Lot had been captured. So he called out his 318 trained men who had been born in his camp. Abram led the men and chased the enemy all the way to the town of Dan. ¹⁵That night he divided his men into groups. And they made a surprise attack against the enemy. They chased them all the way to Hobah, north of Damascus. ¹⁶Then Abram brought back everything the enemy had stolen. Abram brought back the women and the other people. And he also brought back Lot and everything Lot owned.

¹⁷After defeating Kedorlaomer and the kings who were with him, Abram went home. As Abram was returning, the king of Sodom came out to meet him in the Valley of Shaveh. (That is now called King's Valley.)

¹⁸Melchizedek king of Salem also went to meet Abram. Melchizedek was a priest for God Most High. He brought bread and wine. ¹⁹Melchizedek blessed Abram and said,

"Abram, may God Most High give
    you blessings.
God made heaven and earth.
²⁰And we praise God Most High.
    He has helped you to defeat your
    enemies."

Then Abram gave Melchizedek a tenth of everything he had brought back from the battle.

²¹Then the king of Sodom said to Abram, "You may keep all these things for yourself. Just give me my people who were captured."

²²But Abram said to the king of Sodom, "I make a promise to the Lord. He is the God Most High, who made heaven and earth. ²³I promise that I will not keep anything that is yours. I will not keep even a thread or a sandal strap. That way you cannot say, 'I made Abram rich.' ²⁴I will keep nothing but the food my young men have eaten. But give Aner, Eshcol and Mamre their share of what we won. They went with me into battle."

15 After these things happened, the Lord spoke his word to Abram in a vision. God said, "Abram, don't be afraid. I will defend you. And I will give you a great reward."

²But Abram said, "Lord God, what can you give me? I have no son. So my slave Eliezer from Damascus will get everything I own after I die." ³Abram said, "Look, you have given me no son. So a slave born in my house will inherit everything I have."

⁴Then the Lord spoke his word to Abram. He said, "That slave will not be the one to inherit what you have. You will have a son of your own. And your son will inherit what you have."

⁵Then God led Abram outside. God said, "Look at the sky. There are so many stars you cannot count them. And your descendants*d* will be too many to count."

⁶Abram believed the Lord. And the Lord accepted Abram's faith, and that faith made him right with God.

⁷God said to Abram, "I am the Lord who led you out of Ur of Babylonia. I did that so I could give you this land to own."

⁸But Abram said, "Lord God, how can I be sure that I will own this land?"

⁹The Lord said to Abram, "Bring me a three-year-old cow, a three-year-old goat and a three-year-old male sheep. Also bring me a dove and a young pigeon."

¹⁰Abram brought them all to God. Then Abram killed the animals and cut each of them into two pieces. He laid each half opposite the other half. But he

did not cut the birds in half. ¹¹Later, large birds flew down to eat the animals. But Abram chased them away.

¹²As the sun was going down, Abram fell into a deep sleep. While he was asleep, a very terrible darkness came. ¹³Then the Lord said to Abram, "You can be sure that your descendants will be strangers and travel in a land they don't own. The people there will make them slaves. And they will do cruel things to them for 400 years. ¹⁴But I will punish the nation where they are slaves. Then your descendants will leave that land, taking great wealth with them. ¹⁵Abram, you will live to be very old. You will die in peace and will be buried. ¹⁶After your great-great-grandchildren are born, your people will come to this land again. It will take that long, because the Amorites are not yet evil enough to punish."

¹⁷The sun went down, and it was very dark. Suddenly a smoking firepot and a blazing torch passed between the halves of the dead animals.* ¹⁸So on that day the Lord made an agreement with Abram. The Lord said, "I will give this land to your descendants. I will give them the land between the river of Egypt and the great river Euphrates. ¹⁹This is the land of the Kenites, Kenizzites, Kadmonites, ²⁰Hittites, Perizzites, Rephaites,*d* ²¹Amorites, Canaanites, Girgashites and Jebusites."

16 Sarai, Abram's wife, had no children. She had a slave girl from Egypt named Hagar. ²Sarai said to Abram, "Look, the Lord has not allowed me to have children. So have sexual relations with my slave girl. If she has a child, maybe I can have my own family through her."

Abram did what Sarai said. ³This was after Abram lived ten years in Canaan. And Sarai gave Hagar to her husband Abram. (Hagar was her slave girl from Egypt.)

⁴Abram had sexual relations with Hagar, and she became pregnant. When Hagar learned she was pregnant, she began to treat her mistress Sarai badly. ⁵Then Sarai said to Abram, "This is your fault. I gave my slave girl to you. And when she became pregnant, she began to treat me badly. Let the Lord decide who is right—you or me."

⁶But Abram said to Sarai, "You are Hagar's mistress. Do anything you want

---

15:17 passed . . . animals This showed that God sealed the agreement between himself and Abram.

to her." Then Sarai was hard on Hagar, and Hagar ran away.

[7]The angel of the Lord found Hagar beside a spring of water in the desert. The spring was by the road to Shur. [8]The angel said, "Hagar, you are Sarai's slave girl. Where have you come from? Where are you going?"

Hagar answered, "I am running from my mistress Sarai."

[9]The angel of the Lord said to her, "Go home to your mistress and obey her." [10]The angel of the Lord also said, "I will give you so many descendants[d] they cannot be counted."

[11]The angel also said to her,

"You are now pregnant,
    and you will have a son.
You will name him Ishmael,[n]
    because the Lord has heard your
        cries.
[12]Ishmael will be like a wild donkey.
    He will be against everyone.
    And everyone will be against
        him.
He will attack all his brothers."

[13]The slave girl gave a name to the Lord who spoke to her. She said to him, "You are 'God who sees me.'" This is because she said to herself, "Have I really seen God who sees me?" [14]So the well there was called Beer Lahai Roi.[n] It is between Kadesh and Bered.

[15]Hagar gave birth to a son for Abram. And Abram named him Ishmael. [16]Abram was 86 years old when Hagar gave birth to Ishmael.

17 When Abram was 99 years old, the Lord appeared to him. The Lord said, "I am God All-Powerful. Obey me and do what is right. [2]I will make an agreement between us. I will make you the ancestor of many people."

[3]Then Abram bowed facedown on the ground. God said to him, [4]"I am making my agreement with you: I will make you the father of many nations. [5]I am changing your name from Abram[n] to Abraham.[n] This is because I am making you a father of many nations. [6]I will give you many descendants.[d] New nations will be born from you. Kings will come from you. [7]And I will make an agreement between me and you and all your descendants from now on: I will be your God

and the God of all your descendants. [8]You live in the land of Canaan now as a stranger. But I will give you and your descendants all this land forever. And I will be the God of your descendants."

[9]Then God said to Abraham, "You and your descendants must keep this agreement from now on. [10]This is my agreement with you and all your descendants: Every male among you must be circumcised.[d] You must obey this agreement. [11]Cut away the foreskin to show that you follow the agreement between me and you. [12]From now on when a baby boy is eight days old, you will circumcise him. This includes any boy born among your people or any who is your slave. (He would not be one of your descendants.) [13]So circumcise every baby boy. Circumcise him whether he is born in your family or bought as a slave. Your bodies will be marked. This will show that you are part of my agreement that lasts forever. [14]Any male who is not circumcised will be separated from his people. He has broken my agreement."

[15]God said to Abraham, "I will change the name of Sarai,[n] your wife. Her new name will be Sarah.[n] [16]I will bless her. I will give her a son, and you will be the father. She will be the mother of many nations. Kings of nations will come from her."

[17]Abraham bowed facedown on the ground and laughed. He said to himself, "Can a man have a child when he is 100 years old? Can Sarah give birth to a child when she is 90?" [18]Then Abraham said to God, "Please let Ishmael be the son you promised."

[19]God said, "No. Sarah your wife will have a son, and you will name him Isaac.[n] I will make my agreement with him. It will be an agreement that continues forever with all his descendants.[d] [20]You asked me about Ishmael, and I heard you. I will bless him. I will give him many descendants. And I will cause their numbers to grow very greatly. He will be the father of 12 great leaders. I will make him into a great nation. [21]But I will make my agreement with Isaac. He is the son whom Sarah will have at this same time next year." [22]After God

16:11 **Ishmael** The Hebrew words for "Ishmael" and "has heard" sound similar. 16:14 **Beer Lahai Roi** This means "the well of the Living One who sees me." 17:5 **Abram** This name means "honored father." 17:5 **Abraham** The end of the Hebrew word for "Abraham" sounds like the beginning of the Hebrew word for "many." 17:15 **Sarai** An Aramaic name meaning "princess." 17:15 **Sarah** A Hebrew name meaning "princess." 17:19 **Isaac** The Hebrew words for "he laughed" (vs. 17) and "Isaac" sound the same.

finished talking with Abraham, God rose and left him.

²³Then Abraham gathered Ishmael and all the males born in his camp. He also gathered the slaves he had bought. So that day Abraham circumcised every man and boy in his camp. This was what God had told him to do. ²⁴Abraham was 99 years old when he was circumcised. ²⁵And Ishmael, his son, was 13 years old when he was circumcised. ²⁶Abraham and his son were circumcised on that same day. ²⁷Also on that day all the men in Abraham's camp were circumcised. This included all those born in his camp and all the slaves he had bought from other nations.

18 Later, the Lord again appeared to Abraham near the great trees of Mamre. At that time Abraham was sitting at the door of his tent. It was during the hottest part of the day. ²He looked up and saw three men standing near him. When Abraham saw them, he ran from his tent to meet them. He bowed facedown on the ground before them. ³Abraham said, "Sir, if you think well of me, please stay awhile with me, your servant. ⁴I will bring some water so all of you can wash your feet. You may rest under the tree. ⁵I will get some bread for you, so you can regain your strength. Then you may continue your journey."

The three men said, "That is fine. Do as you said."

⁶Abraham hurried to the tent where Sarah was. He said to her, "Hurry, prepare 20 quarts of fine flour. Make it into loaves of bread." ⁷Then Abraham ran to his cattle. He took one of his best calves and gave it to a servant. The servant hurried to kill the calf and to prepare it for food. ⁸Abraham gave the three men the calf that had been cooked. He also gave them milk curds and milk. While the three men ate, he stood under the tree near them.

⁹The men asked Abraham, "Where is your wife Sarah?"

"There, in the tent," said Abraham.

¹⁰Then the Lord said, "I will certainly return to you about this time a year from now. At that time your wife Sarah will have a son."

Sarah was listening at the entrance of the tent which was behind him. ¹¹Abraham and Sarah were very old. Sarah was past the age when women normally have children. ¹²So she laughed to herself, "My husband and I are too old to have a baby."

¹³Then the Lord said to Abraham, "Why did Sarah laugh? Why did she say, 'I am too old to have a baby'? ¹⁴Is anything too hard for the Lord? No! I will return to you at the right time a year from now. And Sarah will have a son."

¹⁵Sarah was afraid. So she lied and said, "I didn't laugh."

But the Lord said, "No. You did laugh."

¹⁶Then the men got up to leave and started out toward Sodom. Abraham walked along with them a short time to send them on their way.

¹⁷The Lord said, "Should I tell Abraham what I am going to do now? ¹⁸Abraham's children will certainly become a great and powerful nation. And all nations on earth will be blessed through him. ¹⁹I have chosen him so he would command his children and his descendantsᵈ to live the way the Lord wants them to. I did this so they would live right and be fair. Then I, the Lord, will give Abraham what I promised him."

²⁰Then the Lord said, "I have heard many things against the people of Sodom and Gomorrah. They are very evil. ²¹So I will go down and see if they are as bad as I have heard."

²²So the men turned and went toward Sodom. But Abraham stood there before the Lord. ²³Then Abraham approached the Lord. Abraham asked, "Lord, do you plan to destroy the good persons along with the evil persons? ²⁴What if there are 50 good people in that city? Will you still destroy it? Surely you will save the city for the 50 good people living there. ²⁵Surely you will not destroy the good people along with the evil people. Then the good people and the evil people would be treated the same. You are the judge of all the earth. Won't you do what is right?"

²⁶Then the Lord said, "If I find 50 good people in the city of Sodom, I will save the whole city because of them."

²⁷Then Abraham said, "I am only dust and ashes. Yet I have been brave to speak to the Lord. ²⁸What if there are only 45 good people in the city? Will you destroy the whole city for the lack of 5 good people?"

The Lord said, "If I find 45 good people there, I will not destroy the city."

²⁹Again Abraham said to the Lord, "If you find only 40 good people there, will you destroy the city?"

The Lord said, "If I find 40 good people, I will not destroy the city."

[30] Then Abraham said, "Lord, please don't be angry with me. Let me ask you this. If you find only 30 good people in the city, will you destroy it?"

The Lord said, "If I find 30 good people there, I will not destroy the city."

[31] Then Abraham said, "I have been brave to speak to the Lord. But what if there are 20 good people in the city?"

The Lord answered, "If I find 20 good people there, I will not destroy the city."

[32] Then Abraham said, "Lord, please don't be angry with me. Let me bother you this one last time. What if you find 10 good people there?"

The Lord said, "If I find 10 good people there, I will not destroy it."

[33] When the Lord finished speaking to Abraham, he left. And Abraham returned home.

19 The two angels came to Sodom in the evening. Lot was sitting near the city gate and saw them. He got up and went to them and bowed facedown on the ground. [2] Lot said, "Sirs, please come to my house and spend the night. There you can wash your feet. Then tomorrow you may continue your journey."

The angels answered, "No, we will spend the night in the city's public square."

[3] But Lot begged them to come to his house. So they agreed and went to his house. Then Lot prepared a meal for them. He baked bread without yeast, and they ate it.

[4] Before bedtime, all the men of the city surrounded Lot's house. These men were both young and old and came from every part of Sodom. [5] They called to Lot, "Where are the two men who came to you tonight? Bring them out to us. We want to have sexual relations with them."

[6] Lot went outside to them, closing the door behind him. [7] He said, "No, my brothers! Do not do this evil thing. [8] Look! I have two daughters. They have never slept with a man. I will give them to you. You may do anything you want with them. But please don't do anything to these men. They have come to my house, and I must protect them."

[9] The men around the house answered, "Move out of the way!" Then they said to each other, "This man Lot came to our city as a stranger. Now he wants to tell us what to do!" They said to Lot, "We

will do worse things to you than to them." So they started pushing Lot back. They were ready to break down the door.

[10] But the two men staying with Lot opened the door and pulled him back inside the house. Then they closed the door. [11] The two men struck the men outside the door with blindness. So these men, both young and old, could not find the door.

[12] The two men said to Lot, "Do you have any other relatives in this city? Do you have any sons-in-law, sons, daughters or any other relatives? If you do, tell them to leave now. [13] We are about to destroy this city. The Lord has heard of all the evil that is here. So he has sent us to destroy it."

[14] So Lot went out and spoke to his future sons-in-law. They were pledged to marry his daughters. Lot said, "Hurry and leave this city! The Lord is about to destroy it!" But they thought Lot was joking.

[15] At dawn the next morning, the angels begged Lot to hurry. They said, "Go! Take your wife and your two daughters with you. Then you will not be destroyed when the city is punished."

[16] But Lot delayed. So the two men took the hands of Lot, his wife and his two daughters. The men led them safely out of the city. So the Lord was merciful to Lot and his family. [17] The two men brought Lot and his family out of the city. Then one of the men said, "Run for your lives! Don't look back or stop anywhere in the valley. Run to the mountains or you will be destroyed."

[18] But Lot said to one of them, "Sir, please don't force me to go so far! [19] You have been merciful and kind to me. You have saved my life. But I can't run to the mountains. The disaster will catch me, and I will die. [20] Look, that little town over there is not too far away. Let me run there. It's really just a little town. I'll be safe there."

[21] The angel said to Lot, "Very well, I will allow you to do this also. I will not destroy that town. [22] But run there fast. I cannot destroy Sodom until you are safely in that town." (That town is named Zoar,[n] because it is little.)

[23] The sun had already come up when Lot entered Zoar. [24] The Lord sent a rain of burning sulfur down from the sky on Sodom and Gomorrah. [25] So the Lord destroyed those cities. He also destroyed

19:22 **Zoar** This name sounds like the Hebrew word for "little."

the whole Jordan Valley, everyone living in the cities and even all the plants. ²⁶At that point Lot's wife looked back. When she did, she became a pillar of salt. ²⁷Early the next morning, Abraham got up and went to the place where he had stood before the Lord. ²⁸Abraham looked down toward Sodom and Gomorrah and all the Jordan Valley. He saw smoke rising from the land. It was like smoke from a furnace.

²⁹God destroyed the cities in the valley. But he remembered what Abraham had asked. So God saved Lot's life. But he destroyed the city where Lot had lived.

³⁰Lot was afraid to continue living in Zoar. So he and his two daughters went to live in the mountains. They lived in a cave there. ³¹One day the older daughter said to the younger, "Our father is old. Everywhere on the earth women and men marry. But there are no men around here for us to marry. ³²Let's get our father drunk. Then we can have sexual relations with him. We can use our father to have children. That way we can continue our family."

³³That night the two girls got their father drunk. Then the older daughter went and had sexual relations with him. But Lot did not know when she lay down or when she got up.

³⁴The next day the older daughter said to the younger, "Last night I had sexual relations with my father. Let's get him drunk again tonight. Then you can go and have sexual relations with him, too. In this way we can use our father to have children to continue our family." ³⁵So that night they got their father drunk again. Then the younger daughter went and had sexual relations with him. Again, Lot did not know when she lay down or when she got up.

³⁶So both of Lot's daughters became pregnant by their father. ³⁷The older daughter gave birth to a son. She named him Moab. Moab is the ancestor of all the Moabite people who are still living today. ³⁸The younger daughter also gave birth to a son. She named him Ben-Ammi. He is the father of all the Ammonite people who are still living today.

20 Abraham left Hebron and traveled to southern Canaan. He stayed awhile between Kadesh and Shur. Then he moved to Gerar. ²Abraham told people that his wife Sarah was his sister. Abimelech king of Gerar heard this. So he sent some servants to take her. ³But

one night God spoke to Abimelech in a dream. God said, "You will die. That woman you took is married."

⁴But Abimelech had not slept with Sarah. So he said, "Lord, would you destroy an innocent nation? ⁵Abraham himself told me, 'This woman is my sister.' And she also said, 'He is my brother.' I am innocent. I did not know I was doing anything wrong."

⁶Then God said to Abimelech in the dream, "Yes, I know that you did not realize what you were doing. So I did not allow you to sin against me. I did not allow you to sleep with her. ⁷Give Abraham his wife back. He is a prophet.ᵈ He will pray for you, and you will not die. But if you do not give Sarah back, you will die. And all your family will surely die."

⁸So early the next morning, Abimelech called all his officers. He told them everything that had happened in the dream. They were very much afraid. ⁹Then Abimelech called Abraham to him. Abimelech said, "What have you done to us? What wrong did I do against you? Why did you bring this trouble to my kingdom? You should not have done these things to me. ¹⁰What were you thinking that caused you to do this?"

¹¹Then Abraham answered, "I thought no one in this place respected God. I thought someone would kill me to get Sarah. ¹²And it is true that she is my sister. She is the daughter of my father. But she is not the daughter of my mother. ¹³God told me to leave my father's house and wander in many different places. When that happened, I told Sarah, 'You must do a special favor for me. Everywhere we go tell people I am your brother.'"

¹⁴Then Abimelech gave Abraham some sheep, cattle and male and female slaves. Abimelech also gave Sarah, his wife, back to him. ¹⁵And Abimelech said, "Look around you at my land. You may live anywhere you want."

¹⁶Abimelech said to Sarah, "I gave your brother Abraham 25 pounds of silver. I did this to make up for any wrong that people may think about you. I want everyone to know that you are innocent."

¹⁷Then Abraham prayed to God. And God healed Abimelech, his wife and his servant girls. Now they could have children. ¹⁸The Lord had kept all the women in Abimelech's house from having children. This was God's punishment on

Abimelech for taking Abraham's wife Sarah.

21 The Lord cared for Sarah as he had said. He did for her what he had promised. [2]Sarah became pregnant. And she gave birth to a son for Abraham in his old age. Everything happened at the time God had said it would. [3]Abraham named his son Isaac. Sarah gave birth to this son of Abraham. [4]Abraham circumcised[d] Isaac when he was eight days old as God had commanded.

[5]Abraham was 100 years old when his son Isaac was born. [6]And Sarah said, "God has made me laugh.[n] Everyone who hears about this will laugh with me. [7]No one thought that I would be able to have Abraham's child. But I have given Abraham a son while he is old."

[8]Isaac grew and became old enough to eat food. At that time Abraham gave a great feast. [9]But Sarah saw Ishmael making fun of Isaac. (Ishmael was the son of Abraham by Hagar, Sarah's Egyptian slave.) [10]So Sarah said to Abraham, "Throw out this slave woman and her son. When we die, our son Isaac will inherit everything we have. I don't want her son to inherit any of our things."

[11]This troubled Abraham very much because Ishmael was also his son. [12]But God said to Abraham, "Don't be troubled about the boy and the slave woman. Do whatever Sarah tells you. The descendants[d] I promised you will be from Isaac. [13]I will also make the descendants of Ishmael into a great nation. I will do this because he is your son, too."

[14]Early the next morning Abraham took some food and a leather bag full of water. He gave them to Hagar and sent her away. Hagar carried these things and her son. She went and wandered in the desert of Beersheba.

[15]Later, all the water was gone from the bag. So Hagar put her son under a bush. [16]Then she went away a short distance and sat down. Hagar thought, "My son will die. I cannot watch this happen." She sat there and began to cry.

[17]God heard the boy crying. And God's angel called to Hagar from heaven. He said, "What is wrong, Hagar? Don't be afraid! God has heard the boy crying there. [18]Help the boy up. Take him by the hand. I will make his descendants into a great nation."

[19]Then God showed Hagar a well of water. So she went to the well and filled her bag with water. Then she gave the boy a drink.

[20]God was with the boy as he grew up. Ishmael lived in the desert. He learned to shoot with a bow very well. [21]He lived in the Desert of Paran. His mother found a wife for him in Egypt.

[22]Then Abimelech came with Phicol, the commander of Abimelech's army. They said to Abraham, "God is with you in everything you do. [23]So make a promise to me here before God. Promise that you will be fair with me and my children and my descendants.[d] Be kind to me and to this land where you have lived as a stranger. Be as kind to me as I have been to you."

[24]And Abraham said, "I promise."

[25]Then Abraham complained to Abimelech about Abimelech's servants. They had captured a well of water.

[26]But Abimelech said, "I don't know who did this. You never told me about this before today."

[27]Then Abraham gave Abimelech some sheep and cattle. And they made an agreement. [28]Abraham also put seven female lambs in front of Abimelech.

[29]Abimelech asked Abraham, "Why did you put these seven female lambs by themselves?"

[30]Abraham answered, "Accept these lambs from me. That will prove that you believe I dug this well."

[31]So that place was called Beersheba[n] because they made a promise to each other there.

[32]So Abraham and Abimelech made an agreement at Beersheba. Then Abimelech and Phicol, the commander of his army, went back to the land of the Philistines.

[33]Abraham planted a tamarisk tree at Beersheba. There Abraham prayed to the Lord, the God who lives forever. [34]And Abraham lived as a stranger in the land of the Philistines for a long time.

22 After these things God tested Abraham's faith. God said to him, "Abraham!"

And he answered, "Here I am."

[2]Then God said, "Take your only son, Isaac, the son you love. Go to the land of Moriah. There kill him and offer him as a whole burnt offering. Do this on

---

21:6 laugh The Hebrew words for "he laughed" and "Isaac" sound the same.   **21:31 Beersheba** This name means "well of the promise" or "well of seven."

one of the mountains there. I will tell you which one."

³Early in the morning Abraham got up and saddled his donkey. He took Isaac and two servants with him. He cut the wood for the sacrifice. Then they went to the place God had told them to go. ⁴On the third day Abraham looked up and saw the place in the distance. ⁵He said to his servants, "Stay here with the donkey. My son and I will go over there and worship. Then we will come back to you."

⁶Abraham took the wood for the sacrifice and gave it to his son to carry. Abraham took the knife and the fire. So Abraham and his son went on together.

⁷Isaac said to his father Abraham, "Father!"

Abraham answered, "Yes, my son."

Isaac said, "We have the fire and the wood. But where is the lamb we will burn as a sacrifice?"

⁸Abraham answered, "God will give us the lamb for the sacrifice, my son."

So Abraham and his son went on together. ⁹They came to the place God had told him about. There, Abraham built an altar. He laid the wood on it. Then he tied up his son Isaac. And he laid Isaac on the wood on the altar. ¹⁰Then Abraham took his knife and was about to kill his son.

¹¹But the angel of the Lord called to him from heaven. The angel said, "Abraham! Abraham!"

Abraham answered, "Yes."

¹²The angel said, "Don't kill your son or hurt him in any way. Now I can see that you respect God. I see that you have not kept back your son, your only son, from me."

¹³Then Abraham looked up and saw a male sheep. Its horns were caught in a bush. So Abraham went and took the sheep and killed it. He offered it as a whole burnt offering to God. Abraham's son was saved. ¹⁴So Abraham named that place The Lord Gives. Even today people say, "On the mountain of the Lord it will be given."

¹⁵The angel of the Lord called to Abraham from heaven a second time. ¹⁶The angel said, "The Lord says, 'You did not keep back your son, your only son, from me. Because you did this, I make you this promise by my own name: ¹⁷I will surely bless you and give you many descendants.ᵈ They will be as many as the stars in the sky and the sand on the seashore. And they will capture the cities

of their enemies. ¹⁸Through your descendants all the nations on the earth will be blessed. This is because you obeyed me.'"

¹⁹Then Abraham returned to his servants. They all traveled back to Beersheba, and Abraham stayed there.

²⁰After these things happened, someone told Abraham: "Your brother Nahor and his wife Milcah have children now. ²¹The first son is Uz. The second son is Buz. The third son is Kemuel (the father of Aram). ²²Then there are Kesed, Hazo, Pildash, Jidlaph and Bethuel." ²³Bethuel became the father of Rebekah. Milcah was the mother of these eight sons, and Nahor was the father. Nahor was Abraham's brother. ²⁴Also Nahor had four other sons by his slave womanᵈ Reumah. Their names were Tebah, Gaham, Tahash and Maacah.

23 Sarah lived to be 127 years old. ²She died in Kiriath Arba (that is, Hebron) in the land of Canaan. Abraham was very sad and cried because of her. ³After a while Abraham got up from the side of his wife's body. And he went to talk to the Hittites. He said, ⁴"I am only a stranger and a foreigner here. Sell me some of your land so that I can bury my dead wife."

⁵The Hittites answered Abraham, ⁶"Sir, you are a great leader among us. You may have the best place we have to bury your dead. You may have any of our burying places that you want. None of us will stop you from burying your dead wife."

⁷Abraham rose and bowed to the people of the land, the Hittites. ⁸Abraham said to them, "If you truly want to help me bury my dead wife here, speak to Ephron for me. He is the son of Zohar. ⁹Ask him to sell me the cave of Machpelah. It is at the edge of his field. I will pay him the full price. You can be the witnesses that I am buying it as a burial place."

¹⁰Ephron was sitting among the Hittites at the city gate. Ephron answered Abraham, ¹¹"No, sir. I will give you the land and the cave that is in it. I will give it to you with these people as witnesses. Bury your dead wife."

¹²Then Abraham bowed down before the Hittites. ¹³He said to Ephron before all the people, "Please let me pay you the full price for the field. Accept my money, and I will bury my dead there."

¹⁴Ephron answered Abraham, ¹⁵"Sir, the land is worth ten pounds of silver.

Erudite Scholar

But I won't argue with you over the price. Take the land, and bury your dead wife."

[16] Abraham agreed and paid Ephron in front of the Hittite witnesses. Abraham weighed out the full price: ten pounds of silver. They counted the weight as the traders normally did.

[17-18] So Ephron's field in Machpelah, east of Mamre, was sold. Abraham became the owner of the field, the cave in it and all the trees that were in the field. The sale was made at the city gate, with the Hittites as witnesses. [19] After this, Abraham buried his wife Sarah in the cave. It was in that field of Machpelah, near Mamre. (Mamre was later called Hebron in the land of Canaan.) [20] Abraham bought the field and the cave on it from the Hittites. He used it as a burying place.

24 Abraham was now very old. The Lord had blessed him in every way. [2] Abraham's oldest servant was in charge of everything Abraham owned. Abraham called that servant to him and said, "Put your hand under my leg.[n] [3] Make a promise to me before the Lord, the God of heaven and earth. Don't get a wife for my son from the Canaanite girls who live around here. [4] Instead, go back to my country, to the land of my relatives. Get a wife for my son Isaac from there."

[5] The servant said to him, "What if this woman does not want to return with me to this land? Then, should I take your son with me back to your homeland?"

[6] Abraham said to him, "No! Don't take my son back there. [7] The Lord is the God of heaven. He brought me from the home of my father and the land of my relatives. But the Lord promised me, 'I will give this land to your descendants.'[d] The Lord will send his angel before you. The angel will help you get a wife for my son there. [8] But if the girl won't come back with you, you will be free from this promise. But you must not take my son back there." [9] So the servant put his hand under his master's leg. He made a promise to Abraham about this.

[10] The servant took ten of Abraham's camels and left. He carried with him many different kinds of beautiful gifts. He went to Northwest Mesopotamia to Nahor's city. [11] He made the camels kneel down at the well outside the city.

It was in the evening when the women come out to get water.

[12] The servant said, "Lord, you are the God of my master Abraham. Allow me to find a wife for his son today. Please show this kindness to my master Abraham. [13] Here I am, standing by the spring of water. The girls from the city are coming out to get water. [14] I will say to one of the girls, 'Please put your jar down so I can drink.' Then let her say, 'Drink, and I will also give water to your camels.' If that happens, I will know she is the right one for your servant Isaac. And I will know that you have shown kindness to my master."

[15] Before the servant had finished praying, Rebekah came out of the city. She was the daughter of Bethuel. (Bethuel was the son of Milcah and Nahor, Abraham's brother.) Rebekah was carrying her water jar on her shoulder. [16] She was very pretty. She was a virgin;[d] she had never had sexual relations with a man. She went down to the spring and filled her jar. Then she came back up. [17] The servant ran to her and said, "Please give me a little water from your jar."

[18] Rebekah said, "Drink, sir." She quickly lowered the jar from her shoulder and gave him a drink. [19] After he finished drinking, Rebekah said, "I will also pour some water for your camels." [20] So she quickly poured all the water from her jar into the drinking trough for the camels. Then she kept running to the well until she had given all the camels enough to drink.

[21] The servant quietly watched her. He wanted to be sure the Lord had made his trip successful. [22] After the camels had finished drinking, he gave Rebekah a gold ring weighing one-fifth of an ounce. He also gave her two gold arm bracelets weighing about four ounces each. [23] The servant asked, "Who is your father? Is there a place in his house for me and my men to spend the night?"

[24] Rebekah answered, "My father is Bethuel. He is the son of Milcah and Nahor." [25] Then she said, "And, yes, we have straw for your camels. We have a place for you to spend the night."

[26] The servant bowed and worshiped the Lord. [27] He said, "Blessed is the Lord, the God of my master Abraham. The Lord has been kind and truthful to him. He has led me to my master's relatives." [28] Then Rebekah ran and told her

24:2 Put . . . leg This showed that a person would keep the promise.

mother's family about all these things. [29]She had a brother named Laban. He ran out to Abraham's servant, who was still at the spring. [30]Laban had heard what he had said. And he had seen the ring and the bracelets on his sister's arms. So he ran out to the well. And there was the man standing by the camels at the spring. [31]Laban said, "Sir, you are welcome to come in. You don't have to stand outside. I have prepared the house for you and also a place for your camels."

[32]So Abraham's servant went into the house. Laban unloaded the camels and gave them straw and food. Then Laban gave water to Abraham's servant so he and the men with him could wash their feet. [33]Then Laban gave the servant food. But the servant said, "I will not eat until I have told you why I came."

So Laban said, "Then tell us."

[34]He said, "I am Abraham's servant. [35]The Lord has greatly blessed my master in everything. My master has become a rich man. The Lord has given him many flocks of sheep and herds of cattle. He has given Abraham silver and gold, male and female servants, camels and horses. [36]Sarah, my master's wife, gave birth to a son when she was old. My master has given everything he owns to that son. [37]My master had me make a promise to him. He said, 'Don't get a wife for my son from the Canaanite girls who live around here. [38]Instead you must go to my father's people and to my family. There you must get a wife for my son.' [39]I said to my master, 'What if the woman will not come back with me?' [40]But he said, 'I serve the Lord. He will send his angel with you and will help you. You will get a wife for my son from my family and my father's people. [41]Then you will be free from the promise. Or if they will not give you a wife for my son, you will be free from this promise.'

[42]"Today I came to this spring. I said, 'Lord, God of my master Abraham, please make my trip successful. [43]Look, I am standing by this spring of water. I will wait for a young woman to come out to get water. Then I will say, "Please give me water from your jar to drink." [44]Then let her say, 'Drink this water. I will also get water for your camels." By this I will know the Lord has chosen her for my master's son.'

[45]"Before I finished my silent prayer, Rebekah came out of the city. She had her water jar on her shoulder. She went down to the spring and got water. I said to her, 'Please give me a drink.' [46]She quickly lowered the jar from her shoulder. She said, 'Drink this. I will also get water for your camels.' So I drank, and she gave water to my camels also. [47]Then I asked her, 'Who is your father?' She answered, 'My father is Bethuel son of Milcah and Nahor.' Then I put the ring in her nose and the bracelets on her arms. [48]At that time I bowed my head and thanked the Lord. I praised the Lord, the God of my master Abraham. I thanked him because he led me on the right road to get the granddaughter of my master's brother for his son. [49]Now, tell me, will you be kind and truthful to my master? And if not, tell me so. Then I will know what I should do."

[50]Laban and Bethuel answered, "This is clearly from the Lord. We cannot change what must happen. [51]Rebekah is yours. Take her and go. Let her marry your master's son as the Lord has commanded."

[52]When Abraham's servant heard these words, he bowed facedown on the ground before the Lord. [53]Then the servant gave Rebekah gold and silver jewelry and clothes. He also gave expensive gifts to her brother and mother. [54]The servant and the men with him ate and drank. And they spent the night there. When they got up the next morning, the servant said, "Now let me go back to my master."

[55]Rebekah's mother and her brother said, "Let Rebekah stay with us at least ten days. After that she may go."

[56]But the servant said to them, "Do not make me wait. The Lord has made my trip successful. Now let me go back to my master."

[57]Rebekah's brother and mother said, "We will call Rebekah and ask her what she wants to do." [58]They called her and asked her, "Do you want to go with this man now?"

She said, "Yes, I do."

[59]So they allowed Rebekah and her nurse to go with Abraham's servant and his men. [60]They blessed Rebekah and said,

"Our sister, may you be the mother
    of thousands of people.
And may your descendants[d]
    capture the cities of their
    enemies."

[61]Then Rebekah and her servant girls got on the camels and followed the servant and his men. So the servant took Rebekah and left.

[62]At this time Isaac had left Beer Lahai Roi. He was living in southern Canaan. [63]One evening he went out to the field to think. As he looked up, he saw camels coming. [64]Rebekah looked and saw Isaac. Then she jumped down from the camel. [65]She asked the servant, "Who is that man walking in the field to meet us?"

The servant answered, "That is my master." So Rebekah covered her face with her veil.

[66]The servant told Isaac everything that had happened. [67]Then Isaac brought Rebekah into the tent of Sarah, his mother. And she became his wife. Isaac loved her very much. So he was comforted after his mother's death.

25 Abraham married again. His new wife was Keturah. [2]She gave birth to Zimran, Jokshan, Medan, Midian, Ishbak and Shuah. [3]Jokshan was the father of Sheba and Dedan. Dedan's descendants[d] were the people of Assyria, Letush and Leum. [4]The sons of Midian were Ephah, Epher, Hanoch, Abida and Eldaah. All these were descendants of Keturah. [5]Abraham left everything he owned to Isaac. [6]But before Abraham died, he did give gifts to the sons of his other wives. Abraham sent them to the East to be away from Isaac.

[7]Abraham lived to be 175 years old. [8]He breathed his last breath and died at an old age. He had lived a long and satisfying life. [9]His sons Isaac and Ishmael buried him in the cave of Machpelah. This cave is in the field of Ephron east of Mamre. Ephron was the son of Zohar the Hittite. [10]This is the same field that Abraham had bought from the Hittites. Abraham was buried there with his wife Sarah. [11]After Abraham died, God blessed his son Isaac. Isaac was now living at Beer Lahai Roi.

[12]This is the family history of Ishmael, Abraham's son. (Hagar, Sarah's Egyptian servant, was Ishmael's mother.) [13]These are the names of Ishmael's sons in the order they were born. The first son was Nebaioth. Then came Kedar, Adbeel, Mibsam, [14]Mishma, Dumah, Massa, [15]Hadad, Tema, Jetur, Naphish and Kedemah. [16]These were Ishmael's sons. And these are the names of the tribal leaders. They are listed according to their settlements and camps. [17]Ishmael lived 137 years. Then he breathed his last breath and died. [18]Ishmael's descendants lived from Havilah to Shur. This is east of Egypt stretching toward Assyria. Ishmael's descendants often attacked the descendants of his brothers.

[19]This is the family history of Isaac. Abraham had a son named Isaac. [20]When Isaac was 40 years old, he married Rebekah. Rebekah was from Northwest Mesopotamia. She was Bethuel's daughter and the sister of Laban the Aramean. [21]Isaac's wife could not have children. So Isaac prayed to the Lord for her. The Lord heard Isaac's prayer, and Rebekah became pregnant.

[22]While she was pregnant, the babies struggled inside her. She asked, "Why is this happening to me?" Then she went to get an answer from the Lord.

[23]The Lord said to her,

"Two nations are in your body.
Two groups of people will be
    taken from you.
One group will be stronger than the
    other.
The older will serve the younger."

[24]And when the time came, Rebekah gave birth to twins. [25]The first baby was born red. His skin was like a hairy robe. So he was named Esau.[n] [26]When the second baby was born, he was holding on to Esau's heel. So that baby was named Jacob.[n] Isaac was 60 years old when they were born.

[27]When the boys grew up, Esau became a skilled hunter. He loved to be out in the fields. But Jacob was a quiet man. He stayed among the tents. [28]Isaac loved Esau. Esau hunted the wild animals that Isaac enjoyed eating. But Rebekah loved Jacob.

[29]One day Jacob was boiling a pot of vegetable soup. Esau came in from hunting in the fields. He was weak from hunger. [30]So Esau said to Jacob, "Let me eat some of that red soup. I am weak with hunger." (That is why people call him Edom.[n])

[31]But Jacob said, "You must sell me your rights as the firstborn son."[n]

25:25 Esau This name may mean "hairy."   **25:26 Jacob** This name sounds like the Hebrew word for "heel." "Grabbing someone's heel" is a Hebrew saying for tricking someone.   **25:30 Edom** This name sounds like the Hebrew word for "red."   **25:31 rights . . . son** Usually the firstborn son had a high rank in the family. The firstborn son usually became the new head of the family.

[32]Esau said, "I am almost dead from hunger. If I die, all of my father's wealth will not help me."

[33]But Jacob said, "First, promise me that you will give it to me." So Esau made a promise to Jacob. In this way he sold his part of their father's wealth to Jacob. [34]Then Jacob gave Esau bread and vegetable soup. Esau ate and drank and then left. So Esau showed how little he cared about his rights as the firstborn son.

26 Once there was a time of hunger in the land. This was besides the time of hunger that happened during Abraham's life. So Isaac went to the town of Gerar. He went to see Abimelech king of the Philistines. [2]The Lord appeared to Isaac and said, "Don't go down to Egypt. Live in the land where I tell you to live. [3]Stay in this land, and I will be with you. I will bless you. I will give you and your descendants[d] all these lands. I will keep the agreement I made to Abraham your father. [4]I will give you many descendants. They will be as hard to count as the stars in the sky. And I will give them all these lands. Through your descendants all the nations on the earth will be blessed. [5]I will do this because your father Abraham obeyed me. He did what I said. He obeyed my commands, my teachings and my rules."

[6]So Isaac stayed in Gerar. [7]Isaac's wife Rebekah was very beautiful. The men of that place asked Isaac about her. Isaac said, "She is my sister." He was afraid to tell them she was his wife. He thought they might kill him so they could have her.

[8]Isaac lived there a long time. One day as Abimelech king of the Philistines looked out his window, he saw Isaac. Isaac was holding his wife Rebekah tenderly. [9]Abimelech called for Isaac and said, "This woman is your wife. Why did you say she was your sister?"

Isaac said to him, "I was afraid you would kill me so you could have her."

[10]Abimelech said, "What have you done to us? One of our men might have had sexual relations with your wife. Then we would have been guilty of a great sin."

[11]So Abimelech warned everyone. He said, "Anyone who touches this man or his wife will be put to death."

[12]Isaac planted seed in that land. And that year he gathered a great harvest. The Lord blessed him very much. [13]Isaac became rich. He gathered more wealth until he became a very rich man. [14]He had many slaves and many flocks and herds. The Philistines envied him. [15]So they stopped up all the wells the servants of Isaac's father Abraham had dug. (They had dug them when Abraham was alive.) The Philistines filled those wells with dirt. [16]And Abimelech said to Isaac, "Leave our country. You have become much more powerful than we are."

[17]So Isaac left that place. He camped in the Valley of Gerar and lived there. [18]Long before this time Abraham had dug many wells. After Abraham died, the Philistines filled them with dirt. So Isaac dug those wells again. He gave them the same names his father had given them. [19]Isaac's servants dug a well in the valley. From it a spring of water flowed. [20]But the men who herded sheep in Gerar argued with Isaac's servants. They said, "This water is ours." So Isaac named that well Argue because they argued with him. [21]Then Isaac's servants dug another well. The people also argued about it. So Isaac named that well Fight. [22]Isaac moved from there and dug another well. No one argued about this one. So he named that well Room Enough. Isaac said, "Now the Lord has made room for us. We will be successful in this land."

[23]From there Isaac went to Beersheba. [24]The Lord appeared to Isaac that night. The Lord said, "I am the God of your father Abraham. Don't be afraid because I am with you. I will bless you and give you many descendants.[d] I will do this because of my servant Abraham." [25]So Isaac built an altar and worshiped the Lord there. He made a camp there, and his servants dug a well.

[26]Abimelech came from Gerar to see Isaac. Abimelech brought with him Ahuzzath, who advised him, and Phicol, the commander of his army. [27]Isaac asked them, "Why have you come to see me? You were my enemy. You forced me to leave your country."

[28]They answered, "Now we know that the Lord is with you. We will make a promise to you. And we would like you to make one to us. We would like to make an agreement with you. [29]We did not hurt you. So promise you will not hurt us. And we were good to you, and we sent you away in peace. Now the Lord has blessed you."

[30]So Isaac prepared food for them, and they all ate and drank. [31]Early the

next morning the men made a promise to each other. Then Isaac sent them away, and they left in peace.

[32] That day Isaac's servants came and told him about the well they had dug. They said, "We found water in that well." [33] So Isaac named it Shibah[n] and that city is still called Beersheba even now.

[34] When Esau was 40 years old, he married two Hittite women. One was Judith daughter of Beeri. The other was Basemath daughter of Elon. [35] These women brought much sorrow to Isaac and Rebekah.

27 When Isaac was old, his eyes were not good. He could not see clearly. One day he called his older son Esau to him. Isaac said, "Son."

Esau answered, "Here I am."

[2] Isaac said, "I am old. I don't know when I might die. [3] So take your bow and arrows, and go hunting in the field. Kill an animal for me to eat. [4] Prepare the tasty food that I love. Bring it to me, and I will eat. Then I will bless you before I die." [5] So Esau went out in the field to hunt.

Rebekah was listening as Isaac said this to his son Esau. [6] Rebekah said to her son Jacob, "Listen, I heard your father talking to your brother Esau. [7] Your father said, 'Kill an animal. Prepare some tasty food for me to eat. Then I will bless you before the Lord before I die.' [8] So obey me, my son. Do what I tell you. [9] Go out to our goats and bring me two young ones. I will prepare them just the way your father likes them. [10] Then you will take the food to your father. And he will bless you before he dies."

[11] But Jacob said to his mother Rebekah, "My brother Esau is a hairy man. I am smooth! [12] If my father touches me, he will know I am not Esau. Then he will not bless me. He will place a curse on me because I tried to trick him."

[13] So Rebekah said to him, "If your father puts a curse on you, I will accept the blame. Just do what I said. Go and get the goats for me."

[14] So Jacob went out and got two goats and brought them to his mother. Then she cooked them in the special way Isaac enjoyed. [15] She took the best clothes of her older son Esau that were in the house. She put them on the younger son Jacob. [16] She took the skins of the goats. And she put them on Jacob's hands and neck. [17] Then she gave Jacob the tasty food and the bread she had made.

[18] Jacob went in to his father and said, "Father."

And his father said, "Yes, my son. Who are you?"

[19] Jacob said to him, "I am Esau, your first son. I have done what you told me. Now sit up and eat some meat of the animal I hunted for you. Then bless me."

[20] But Isaac asked his son, "How did you find and kill the animal so quickly?"

Jacob answered, "Because the Lord your God led me to find it."

[21] Then Isaac said to Jacob, "Come near so I can touch you, my son. If I can touch you, I will know if you are really my son Esau."

[22] So Jacob came near to Isaac his father. Isaac touched him and said, "Your voice sounds like Jacob's voice. But your hands are hairy like the hands of Esau." [23] Isaac did not know it was Jacob, because his hands were hairy like Esau's hands. So Isaac blessed Jacob. [24] Isaac asked, "Are you really my son Esau?"

Jacob answered, "Yes, I am."

[25] Then Isaac said, "Bring me the food. I will eat it and bless you." So Jacob gave him the food, and Isaac ate. Jacob gave him wine, and he drank. [26] Then Isaac said to him, "My son, come near and kiss me." [27] So Jacob went to his father and kissed him. Isaac smelled Esau's clothes and blessed him. Isaac said,

"The smell of my son
 is like the smell of the field
 that the Lord has blessed.
[28] May God give you plenty of rain
  and good soil.
 Then you will have plenty of
  grain and wine.
[29] May nations serve you.
 May peoples bow down to you.
 May you be master over your
  brothers.
 May your mother's sons bow
  down to you.
 May everyone who curses you be
  cursed.
 And may everyone who blesses
  you be blessed."

[30] Isaac finished blessing Jacob. Then, just as Jacob left his father Isaac, Esau came in from hunting. [31] Esau also prepared some tasty food and brought it to his father. He said, "Father, rise and eat

26:33 Shibah This name sounds like the Hebrew words for "seven" and "promise."

the food that your son killed for you. Then bless me."

[32]Isaac asked, "Who are you?"

He answered, "I am your son—your firstborn[d] son—Esau."

[33]Then Isaac trembled greatly. He said, "Then who was it that hunted the animals and brought me food before you came? I ate it, and I blessed him. And it is too late now to take back my blessing."

[34]When Esau heard the words of his father, he let out a loud and bitter cry. He said to his father, "Bless me—me, too, my father!"

[35]But Isaac said, "Your brother came and tricked me. He has taken your blessing."

[36]Esau said, "Jacob[n] is the right name for him. He has tricked me these two times. He took away my share of everything you own. And now he has taken away my blessing." Then Esau asked, "Haven't you saved a blessing for me?"

[37]Isaac answered, "I gave Jacob the power to be master over you. And all his brothers will be his servants. And I kept him strong with grain and wine. There is nothing left to give you, my son."

[38]But Esau continued, "Do you have only one blessing, Father? Bless me, too, Father!" Then Esau began to cry out loud.

[39]Isaac said to him,

"You will live far away from the best land,
    far from the rain.
[40]You will live by using your sword
    and be a slave to your brother.
But when you struggle,
    you will break free from him."

[41]After that Esau hated Jacob because of the blessing from Isaac. Esau thought to himself, "My father will soon die, and I will be sad for him. After that I will kill Jacob."

[42]Rebekah heard about Esau's plan to kill Jacob. So she sent for Jacob. She said to him, "Listen, your brother Esau is comforting himself by planning to kill you. [43]So, son, do what I say. My brother Laban is living in Haran. Go to him at once! [44]Stay with him for a while, until your brother is not so angry. [45]In time, your brother will not be angry. He will forget what you did to him. Then I will send a servant to bring you back. I don't want to lose both of my sons on the same day."

[46]Then Rebekah said to Isaac, "I am tired of Hittite women. If Jacob marries one of these Hittite women here in this land, I want to die."

28 Isaac called Jacob and blessed him. Then Isaac commanded him, "You must not marry a Canaanite woman. [2]Go to the house of Bethuel, your mother's father, in Northwest Mesopotamia. Laban, your mother's brother, lives there. Marry one of his daughters. [3]May God All-Powerful bless you and give you many children. May you become the father of many peoples. [4]May the Lord give you and your descendants[d] the blessing of Abraham. Then you may own the land where you are now living as a stranger. This is the land God gave to Abraham." [5]So Isaac sent Jacob to Northwest Mesopotamia. Jacob went to Laban, the brother of Rebekah. Bethuel, the Aramean, was the father of Laban and Rebekah. And Rebekah was the mother of Jacob and Esau.

[6]Esau learned that Isaac had blessed Jacob and sent him to Northwest Mesopotamia. Jacob went to find a wife there. Esau also learned that Isaac had commanded Jacob not to marry a Canaanite woman. [7]And Esau learned that Jacob had obeyed his father and mother. He had gone to Northwest Mesopotamia. [8]So Esau saw that his father Isaac did not want his sons to marry Canaanite women. [9]Now Esau already had wives. But he went to Ishmael son of Abraham. And he married Mahalath, Ishmael's daughter. Mahalath was the sister of Nebaioth.

[10]Jacob left Beersheba and set out for Haran. [11]He came to a place and spent the night there because the sun had set. He found a stone there and laid his head on it to go to sleep. [12]Jacob dreamed that there was a ladder resting on the earth and reaching up into heaven. And he saw angels of God going up and coming down the ladder. [13]And then Jacob saw the Lord standing above the ladder. The Lord said, "I am the Lord, the God of Abraham, your grandfather. And I am the God of Isaac. I will give you and your descendants[d] the land on which you are now sleeping. [14]Your descendants will be as many as the dust of the earth. They will spread west and east, north and

27:36 Jacob This name sounds like the Hebrew word for "heel." "Grabbing someone's heel" is a Hebrew saying for tricking someone.

south. All the families of the earth will be blessed through you and your descendants. ¹⁵I am with you, and I will protect you everywhere you go. And I will bring you back to this land. I will not leave you until I have done what I have promised you."

¹⁶Then Jacob woke from his sleep. He said, "Surely the Lord is in this place. But I did not know it." ¹⁷Jacob was afraid. He said, "This place frightens me! It is surely the house of God and the gate of heaven."

¹⁸Jacob rose early in the morning. He took the stone he had slept on and set it up on its end. Then he poured olive oil on the top of it. ¹⁹At first, the name of that city was Luz. But Jacob named it Bethel.ⁿ

²⁰Then Jacob made a promise. He said, "I want God to be with me and protect me on this journey. I want God to give me food to eat and clothes to wear. ²¹Then I will be able to return in peace to my father's house. If the Lord does these things, he will be my God. ²²This stone which I have set up on its end will be the house of God. And I will give God one-tenth of all he gives me."

29 Then Jacob continued his journey. He came to the land of the people of the East. ²He looked and saw a well in the field. Three flocks of sheep were lying nearby, because they drank water from this well. A large stone covered the mouth of the well. ³All the flocks would gather there. The shepherds would roll the stone away from the well and water the sheep. Then they would put the stone back in its place.

⁴Jacob said to the shepherds there, "My brothers, where are you from?"

They answered, "We are from Haran."

⁵Then Jacob asked, "Do you know Laban grandson of Nahor?"

They answered, "We know him."

⁶Then Jacob asked, "How is he?"

They answered, "He is well. Look, his daughter Rachel is coming now with his sheep."

⁷Jacob said, "But look, it is still the middle part of the day. It is not time for the sheep to be gathered for the night. So give them water and let them go back into the pasture."

⁸But they said, "We cannot do that until all the flocks are gathered. Then we will roll away the stone from the mouth of the well and water the sheep."

⁹While Jacob was talking with the shepherds, Rachel came with her father's sheep. It was her job to take care of the sheep. ¹⁰Then Jacob saw Laban's daughter Rachel and Laban's sheep. So he went to the well and rolled the stone from its mouth. Then he watered Laban's sheep. Now Laban was the brother of Rebekah, Jacob's mother. ¹¹Then Jacob kissed Rachel and cried. ¹²He told her that he was from her father's family. He said that he was the son of Rebekah. So Rachel ran home and told her father.

¹³When Laban heard the news about his sister's son Jacob, Laban ran to meet him. Laban hugged him and kissed him and brought him to his house. Jacob told Laban everything that had happened. ¹⁴Then Laban said, "You are my own flesh and blood."

So Jacob stayed there a month. ¹⁵Then Laban said to Jacob, "You are my relative. But it is not right for you to keep on working for me without pay. What would you like me to pay you?"

¹⁶Now Laban had two daughters. The older was Leah, and the younger was Rachel. ¹⁷Leah had weak eyes, but Rachel was very beautiful. ¹⁸Jacob loved Rachel. So he said to Laban, "Let me marry your younger daughter Rachel. If you will, I will work seven years for you."

¹⁹Laban said, "It would be better for her to marry you than someone else. So stay here with me." ²⁰So Jacob worked for Laban seven years so he could marry Rachel. But they seemed to him like just a few days. This was because he loved Rachel very much.

²¹After seven years Jacob said to Laban, "Give me Rachel so that I may marry her. The time I promised to work for you is over."

²²So Laban gave a feast for all the people there. ²³That evening Laban brought his daughter Leah to Jacob. Jacob and Leah had sexual relations together. ²⁴(Laban gave his slave girl Zilpah to his daughter to be her servant.) ²⁵In the morning Jacob saw that he had had sexual relations with Leah! He said to Laban, "What have you done to me? I worked hard for you so that I could marry Rachel! Why did you trick me?"

²⁶Laban said, "In our country we do not allow the younger daughter to marry

28:19 **Bethel** This name means "house of God."

before the older daughter. [27]But complete the full week of the marriage ceremony with Leah. I will give you Rachel to marry also. But you must serve me another seven years."

[28]So Jacob did this and completed the week with Leah. Then Laban gave him his daughter Rachel as a wife. [29](Laban gave his slave girl Bilhah to his daughter Rachel to be her servant.) [30]So Jacob had sexual relations with Rachel also. And Jacob loved Rachel more than Leah. Jacob worked for Laban for another seven years.

[31]The Lord saw that Jacob loved Rachel more than Leah. So the Lord made it possible for Leah to have children. But Rachel did not have any children. [32]Leah became pregnant and gave birth to a son. She named him Reuben,[n] because she said, "The Lord has seen my troubles. Surely now my husband will love me."

[33]Leah became pregnant again and gave birth to another son. She named him Simeon.[n] She said, "The Lord has heard that I am not loved. So he gave me this son."

[34]Leah became pregnant again and gave birth to another son. She named him Levi.[n] Leah said, "Now, surely my husband will be close to me. I have given him three sons."

[35]Then Leah gave birth to another son. She named him Judah.[n] Leah named him this because she said, "Now I will praise the Lord." Then Leah stopped having children.

30 Rachel saw that she was not giving birth to children for Jacob. So she envied her sister Leah. Rachel said to Jacob, "Give me children, or I'll die!"

[2]Jacob became angry with her. He said, "Can I do what only God can do? He is the one who has kept you from having children."

[3]Then Rachel said, "Here is my slave girl Bilhah. Have sexual relations with her so she can give birth to a child for me. Then I can have my own family through her."

[4]So Rachel gave Bilhah, her slave girl, to Jacob as a wife. And he had sexual relations with her. [5]She became pregnant and gave Jacob a son. [6]Rachel said, "God has declared me innocent. He has listened to my prayer and has given me a son." So Rachel named this son Dan.[n]

[7]Bilhah became pregnant again and gave Jacob a second son. [8]Rachel said, "I have struggled hard with my sister. And I have won." So she named that son Naphtali.[n]

[9]Leah saw that she had stopped having children. So she gave her slave girl Zilpah to Jacob as a wife. [10]Then Zilpah had a son. [11]Leah said, "I am lucky." So she named her son Gad.[n] [12]Zilpah gave birth to another son. [13]Leah said, "I am very happy! Now women will call me happy." So she named that son Asher.[n]

[14]During the wheat harvest Reuben went into the field and found some mandrake[n] plants. He brought them to his mother Leah. But Rachel said to Leah, "Please give me some of your son's mandrakes."

[15]Leah answered, "You have already taken away my husband. Now you are trying to take away my son's mandrakes."

But Rachel answered, "If you will give me your son's mandrakes, you may sleep with Jacob tonight."

[16]When Jacob came in from the field that night, Leah went out to meet him. She said, "You will have sexual relations with me tonight. I have paid for you with my son's mandrakes." So Jacob slept with her that night.

[17]Then God answered Leah's prayer, and she became pregnant again. She gave birth to a fifth son. [18]Leah said, "God has given me what I paid for, because I gave my slave girl to my husband." So Leah named her son Issachar.[n]

[19]Leah became pregnant again and gave birth to a sixth son. [20]She said, "God has given me a fine gift. Now surely Jacob will honor me, because I have given

---

29:32 Reuben This name sounds like the Hebrew word for "he has seen my troubles." **29:33 Simeon** This name sounds like the Hebrew word for "has heard." **29:34 Levi** This name sounds like the Hebrew word for "be close to." **29:35 Judah** This name sounds like the Hebrew word for "praise." **30:6 Dan** This name means "he has declared innocent." **30:8 Naphtali** This name sounds like the Hebrew word for "my struggle." **30:11 Gad** This name may mean "lucky." **30:13 Asher** This name may mean "happy." **30:14 mandrake** A plant which was believed to cause a woman to become pregnant. **30:18 Issachar** This name sounds like the Hebrew word for "paid for."

him six sons." So Leah named the son Zebulun.[n]

²¹Later Leah gave birth to a daughter. She named her Dinah.

²²Then God remembered Rachel and answered her prayer. God made it possible for her to have children. ²³She became pregnant and gave birth to a son. She said, "God has taken away my shame." ²⁴She named him Joseph.[n] Rachel said, "I wish the Lord would give me another son."

²⁵After the birth of Joseph, Jacob said to Laban, "Now let me go to my own home and country. ²⁶Give me my wives and my children, and let me go. You have earned them by working for you. You know that I served you well."

²⁷Laban said to him, "If I have pleased you, please stay. I know the Lord has blessed me because of you. ²⁸Tell me what I should pay you, and I will give it to you."

²⁹Jacob answered, "You know that I have worked hard for you. Your flocks have grown while I cared for them. ³⁰When I came, you had little. Now you have much. Every time I did something for you, the Lord blessed you. But when will I be able to do something for my own family?"

³¹Laban asked, "Then what should I give you?"

Jacob answered, "I don't want you to give me anything. Just do this one thing. Then I will come back and take care of your flocks. ³²Today let me go through all your flocks of white sheep and black goats. I will take every spotted or speckled lamb. I will take every black lamb and every spotted or speckled goat. That will be my pay. ³³In the future you can easily see if I am honest. You can come to look at my flocks. If I have any goat that isn't speckled or spotted or any sheep that isn't black, you will know I stole it."

³⁴Laban answered, "Agreed! We will do what you ask." ³⁵But that day Laban took away all the male goats that had streaks or spots. And he took all the speckled and spotted female goats (all those that had white on them). And he took all the black sheep. He told his sons to watch over them. ³⁶Laban took these animals to a place that was three days' journey away from Jacob. Jacob took care of all the animals that were left.

³⁷So Jacob cut green branches from poplar, almond and plane trees. He peeled off some of the bark so that the branches had white stripes on them. ³⁸He put the branches in front of the flocks at the watering places. When the animals came to drink, they also mated there. ³⁹So the goats mated in front of the branches. Then the young that were born were streaked, speckled or spotted. ⁴⁰Jacob separated the young animals from the others. And he made them face the streaked and dark animals in Laban's flock. Jacob kept his animals separate from Laban's. ⁴¹When the stronger animals in the flock were mating, Jacob put the branches before their eyes. This was so the animals would mate near the branches. ⁴²But when the weaker animals mated, Jacob did not put the branches there. So the animals born from the weaker animals were Laban's. And the animals born from the stronger animals were Jacob's. ⁴³In this way Jacob became very rich. He had large flocks, many male and female servants, camels and donkeys.

31 One day Jacob heard Laban's sons talking. They said, "Jacob has taken everything our father owned. Jacob has become rich in this way." ²Then Jacob noticed that Laban was not as friendly as he had been before. ³The Lord said to Jacob, "Go back to the land where your ancestors lived. I will be with you."

⁴So Jacob told Rachel and Leah to meet him in the field where he kept his flocks. ⁵He said to them, "I have seen that your father is not as friendly with me as he used to be. But the God of my father has been with me. ⁶You both know that I have worked as hard as I could for your father. ⁷But he cheated me. He has changed my pay ten times. But God has not allowed your father to harm me. ⁸At one time Laban said, 'You can have all the speckled goats as your pay.' After that, all the animals gave birth to speckled young ones. But then Laban said, 'You can have all the streaked goats as your pay.' After that, all the animals gave birth to streaked babies. ⁹So God has taken away from your father. And God has given them to me.

¹⁰"I had a dream during the season when the animals were mating. I saw

---

30:20 **Zebulun** This name sounds like the Hebrew word for "honor."   30:24 **Joseph** This name sounds like the Hebrew word for "he adds."

that the only male goats who were mating were streaked, speckled or spotted. [11]The angel of God spoke to me in that dream. He said, 'Jacob!' I answered, 'Yes!' [12]The angel said, 'Look! Only the streaked, speckled or spotted goats are mating. I have seen all the wrong things Laban does to you. [13]I am the God who appeared to you at Bethel. There you poured olive oil on the stone you set up on end. There you made a promise to me. Now I want you to leave here. Go back to the land where you were born.'"

[14]Rachel and Leah answered Jacob, "Our father has nothing to give us when he dies. [15]He has treated us like strangers. He sold us to you, and then he spent all of the money you paid for us. [16]God took all this wealth from our father, and now it belongs to us and our children. So you do whatever God told you to do."

[17]So Jacob put his children and his wives on camels. [18]Then they began their journey back to Isaac, his father. He lived in the land of Canaan. All the flocks of animals that Jacob owned walked ahead of them. He carried everything with him that he had gotten while he lived in Northwest Mesopotamia.

[19]Laban was gone to cut the wool from his sheep. While he was gone, Rachel stole the idols of false gods that belonged to him. [20]And Jacob tricked Laban the Aramean. He did not tell Laban he was leaving. [21]Jacob and his family left quickly. They crossed the Euphrates River and traveled toward the mountains of Gilead.

[22]Three days later Laban learned that Jacob had run away. [23]So Laban gathered his relatives and began to chase Jacob. After seven days Laban found him in the mountains of Gilead. [24]That night God came to Laban the Aramean in a dream. The Lord said, "Be careful! Do not say anything to Jacob, good or bad."

[25]So Laban caught up with Jacob. Now Jacob had made his camp in the mountains. So Laban and his relatives set up their camp in the mountains of Gilead. [26]Laban said to Jacob, "What have you done? Why did you trick me? You took my daughters as if you had captured them in a war. [27]Why did you run away without telling me? Why did you trick me? Why didn't you tell me? Then I could send you away with joy and singing. There would be the music of tambourines[d] and harps. [28]You did not even let me kiss my grandchildren and my daughters good-bye. You were very foolish to do this! [29]I have the power to harm you. But last night the God of your father spoke to me. He warned me not to say anything to you, good or bad. [30]I know you want to go back to your home. But why did you steal my idols?"

[31]Jacob answered Laban, "I left without telling you, because I was afraid! I thought you would take your daughters away from me. [32]If you find anyone here who has taken your idols, he will be killed! Your relatives will be my witnesses. You may look for anything that belongs to you. Take anything that is yours." (Now Jacob did not know that Rachel had stolen Laban's idols.)

[33]So Laban looked in Jacob's tent and in Leah's tent. He looked in the tent where the two slave women stayed. But he did not find his idols. When he left Leah's tent, he went into Rachel's tent. [34]Rachel had hidden the idols inside her camel's saddle. And she was sitting on them. Laban looked through the whole tent, but he did not find them.

[35]Rachel said to her father, "Father, don't be angry with me. I am not able to stand up before you. I am having my monthly period." So Laban looked through the camp, but he did not find his idols.

[36]Then Jacob became very angry. He said, "What wrong have I done? What law have I broken to cause you to chase me? [37]You have looked through everything I own. But you have found nothing that belongs to you. If you have found anything, show it to everyone. Put it in front of your relatives and my relatives. Then let them decide which one of us is right. [38]I have worked for you now for 20 years. During all that time none of the lambs and kids died during birth. And I have not eaten any of the male sheep from your flocks. [39]Any time a sheep was killed by wild animals, I did not bring it to you. I made up for the loss myself. You made me pay for any animal that was stolen during the day or night. [40]In the daytime the sun took away my strength. At night I was cold and could not sleep. [41]I worked like a slave for you for 20 years. For the first 14 years I worked to get your two daughters. The last 6 years I worked to earn your animals. And during that time you changed my pay ten times. [42]But the God of my father was with me. He is the God of Abraham and the God of Isaac. If God had not been with me, you would have

sent me away with nothing. But he saw the trouble I had and the hard work I did. And last night God corrected you."

43 Laban said to Jacob, "These girls are my daughters. Their children belong to me, and these animals are mine. Everything you see here belongs to me. But I can do nothing to keep my daughters and their children. 44 Let us make an agreement. Let us set up a pile of stones to remind us of our agreement."

45 So Jacob took a large rock and set it up on its end. 46 He told his relatives to gather rocks. So they took the rocks and piled them up. Then they ate beside the pile of rocks. 47 Laban named that place in his language A Pile to Remind Us. And Jacob gave the place the same name in Hebrew.

48 Laban said to Jacob, "This pile of rocks will remind us of the agreement between us." That is why the place was called A Pile to Remind Us. 49 It was also called Mizpah.ᵇ This was because Laban said, "Let the Lord watch over us while we are separated from each other. 50 Remember that God is our witness. This is true even if no one else is around us. He will know if you harm my daughters or marry other women. 51 Here is the pile of rocks that I have put between us. And here is the rock I set up on end. 52 This pile of rocks and this rock set on end will remind us of our agreement. I will never go past this pile to hurt you. And you must never come to my side of them to hurt me. 53 The God of Abraham is the God of Nahor and the God of their fathers. Let God punish either of us if we break this agreement."

So Jacob made a promise in the name of God. This was the God of his father Isaac. 54 Then Jacob killed an animal and offered it as a sacrifice on the mountain. And he invited his relatives to share in the meal. After they finished eating, they spent the night on the mountain. 55 Early the next morning Laban kissed his grandchildren and his daughters. He blessed them, and then he left to return home.

32 When Jacob also went his way, the angels of God met him. 2 When Jacob saw them, he said, "This is the camp of God!" So Jacob named that place Mahanaim.ᵇ

3 Jacob's brother Esau was living in the area called Seir in the country of Edom.

Jacob sent messengers to Esau. 4 Jacob told the messengers, "Give this message to my master Esau: 'This is what Jacob, your servant, says: I have lived with Laban and have remained there until now. 5 I have cattle, donkeys, flocks, and male and female servants. I send this message to you and ask you to accept us.'"

6 The messengers returned to Jacob and said, "We went to your brother Esau. He is coming to meet you. And he has 400 men with him."

7 Then Jacob was very afraid and worried. He divided the people who were with him into two camps. He also divided all the flocks, herds and camels into two camps. 8 Jacob thought, "Esau might come and destroy one camp. But the other camp can run away and be saved."

9 Jacob said, "God of my father Abraham! God of my father Isaac! Lord, you told me to return to my country and my family. You said that you would do good to me. 10 I am not worthy of the kindness and continual goodness you have shown me. The first time I traveled across the Jordan River, I had only my walking stick. But now I own enough to have two camps. 11 Please save me from my brother Esau. I am afraid he will come and kill all of us, even the mothers with the children. 12 You said to me, 'I will do good to you. I will make your children as many as the sand of the seashore. There will be too many to count.'"

13 Jacob stayed there for the night. He prepared a gift for Esau from what he had with him. 14 It was 200 female goats and 20 male goats, 200 female sheep and 20 male sheep. 15 There were 30 female camels and their young, 40 cows and 10 bulls, 20 female donkeys and 10 male donkeys. 16 Jacob gave each separate flock of animals to one of his servants. Then he said to them, "Go ahead of me and keep some space between each herd." 17 Jacob gave them their orders. To the servant with the first group of animals he said, "My brother Esau will come to you. He will ask you, 'Whose servant are you? Where are you going? Whose animals are these?' 18 Then you will answer, 'These animals belong to your servant Jacob. He sent them as a gift to you my master, Esau. And Jacob also is coming behind us.'"

19 Jacob ordered the second servant,

the third servant and all the other servants to do the same thing. He said, "Say the same thing to Esau when you meet him. [20]Say, 'Your servant Jacob is coming behind us.'" Jacob thought, "If I send this gift ahead of me, maybe Esau will forgive me. Then when I see him, perhaps he will accept me." [21]So Jacob sent the gift to Esau. But Jacob stayed that night in the camp.

[22]During the night Jacob rose and crossed the Jabbok River at the crossing. He took his 2 wives, his 2 slave girls and his 11 sons with him. [23]He sent his family and everything he had across the river. [24]But Jacob stayed behind alone. And a man came and wrestled with him until the sun came up. [25]The man saw that he could not defeat Jacob. So he struck Jacob's hip and put it out of joint. [26]Then the man said to Jacob, "Let me go. The sun is coming up."

But Jacob said, "I will let you go if you will bless me."

[27]The man said to him, "What is your name?"

And he answered, "Jacob."

[28]Then the man said, "Your name will no longer be Jacob. Your name will now be Israel,[n] because you have wrestled with God and with men. And you have won."

[29]Then Jacob asked him, "Please tell me your name."

But the man said, "Why do you ask my name?" Then he blessed Jacob there.

[30]So Jacob named that place Peniel.[n] He said, "I have seen God face to face. But my life was saved." [31]Then the sun rose as he was leaving that place. Jacob was limping because of his leg. [32]So even today the people of Israel do not eat the muscle that is on the hip joint of animals. This is because Jacob touched there.

33 Jacob looked up and saw Esau coming. With him were 400 men. So Jacob divided his children among Leah, Rachel and the two slave girls. [2]Jacob put the slave girls with their children first. Then he put Leah and her children behind them. And he put Rachel and Joseph last. [3]Jacob himself went out in front of them. He bowed down flat on the ground seven times as he was walking toward his brother.

[4]But Esau ran to meet Jacob. Esau put his arms around him and hugged him.

Then Esau kissed him, and they both cried. [5]Esau looked up and saw the women and children. He asked, "Who are these people with you?"

Jacob answered, "These are the children God has given me. God has been good to me, your servant."

[6]Then the two slave girls and their children came up to Esau. They bowed down flat on the earth before him. [7]Then Leah and her children came up to Esau. They also bowed down flat on the earth. Last of all, Joseph and Rachel came up to Esau. And they, too, bowed down flat before him.

[8]Esau said, "I saw many herds as I was coming here. Why did you bring them?"

Jacob answered, "They were to please you, my master."

[9]But Esau said, "I already have enough, my brother. Keep what you have."

[10]Jacob said, "No! Please! If I have pleased you, then please accept the gift I give you. I am very happy to see your face again. It is like seeing the face of God because you have accepted me. [11]So I beg you to accept the gift I give you. God has been very good to me. And I have more than I need." And because Jacob begged, Esau accepted the gift.

[12]Then Esau said, "Let us get going. I will travel with you."

[13]But Jacob said to him, "My master, you know that the children are weak. And I must be careful with my flocks and their young ones. If I force them to go too far in one day, all the animals will die. [14]So, my master, you go on ahead of me, your servant. I will follow you slowly. I will let the animals and the children set the speed at which we travel. I will meet you, my master, in Edom."

[15]So Esau said, "Then let me leave some of my men with you."

"No, thank you," said Jacob. "I only want to please you, my master." [16]So that day Esau started back to Edom. [17]But Jacob went to Succoth. There he built a house for himself. And he made shelters for his animals. That is why the place was named Succoth.[n]

[18]Jacob left Northwest Mesopotamia. And he arrived safely at the city of Shechem in the land of Canaan. He camped east of the city. [19]He bought a part of the field where he had camped. He bought

---

32:28 Israel This name means "he wrestles with God."   **32:30 Peniel** This name means "the face of God."   **33:17 Succoth** This name means "shelters."

it from the sons of Hamor father of She-chem for 100 pieces of silver. ²⁰He built an altar there and named it after God, the God of Israel.

34 Dinah was the daughter of Leah and Jacob. At this time Dinah went out to visit the women of that land. ²Shechem son of Hamor the Hivite, the ruler of that land, saw Dinah. He took her and forced her to have sexual relations with him. ³Shechem fell in love with Dinah, and he spoke kindly to her. ⁴He told his father, Hamor, "Please get this girl for me so I can marry her."

⁵Jacob learned how Shechem had dis-graced his daughter. But Jacob's sons were out in the field with the cattle. So Jacob said nothing until they came home. ⁶And Hamor father of Shechem went to talk with Jacob.

⁷When Jacob's sons heard what had happened, they came in from the field. They were very angry, because She-chem had done such a wicked thing to Israel. It was wrong for him to have sex-ual relations with Jacob's daughter. A thing like this should not be done.

⁸But Hamor talked to the brothers of Dinah. He said, "My son Shechem is deeply in love with Dinah. Please let him marry her. ⁹Marry our people. Give your women to our men as wives. And take our women for your men as wives. ¹⁰You can live in the same land with us. You will be free to own land and to trade here."

¹¹Shechem also talked to Jacob and to Dinah's brothers. He said, "Please ac-cept my offer. I will give anything you ask. ¹²Ask as much as you want for the payment for the bride. I will give it to you. Just let me marry Dinah."

¹³The sons of Jacob answered She-chem and his father with lies. They were angry because Shechem had disgraced their sister Dinah. ¹⁴The brothers said to them, "We cannot allow you to marry our sister. You are not circumcised.ᵈ That would be a disgrace to us. ¹⁵But we will allow you to marry her if you do this one thing: Every man in your town must be circumcised like us. ¹⁶Then your men can marry our women, and our men can marry your women. Then we will live in your land and become one people. ¹⁷If you refuse to be circumcised, we will take Dinah and leave."

¹⁸What they asked seemed fair to Ha-mor and Shechem. ¹⁹So Shechem went quickly to be circumcised because he loved Jacob's daughter.

Now Shechem was the most re-spected man in his family. ²⁰So Hamor and Shechem went to the gate of their city. They spoke to the men of their city. They said, ²¹"These people want to be friends with us. So let them live in our land and trade here. There is enough land for all of us. Let us marry their women. And we can let them marry our women. ²²But our men must agree to one thing. All our men must agree to be cir-cumcised as they are. Then they will agree to live in our land. And we will be one people. ²³If we do this, their cattle and their animals will belong to us. Let us do what they say, and they will stay in our land." ²⁴All the men who had come to the city gate heard this. And they agreed with Hamor and Shechem. And every man was circumcised.

²⁵Three days later the men who were circumcised were still in pain. Two of Jacob's sons, Simeon and Levi (Dinah's brothers), took their swords. They made a surprise attack on the city. And they killed all the men there. ²⁶Simeon and Levi killed Hamor and his son Shechem. Then they took Dinah out of Shechem's house and left. ²⁷Jacob's sons went among the dead bodies and stole every-thing that was in the city. This was to pay them back for what Shechem had done to their sister. ²⁸So the brothers took the flocks, herds and donkeys. And they took everything in the city and in the fields. ²⁹They took every valuable thing those people owned. They even took the wives and children and every-thing that was in the houses.

³⁰Then Jacob said to Simeon and Levi, "You have caused me a lot of trouble. Now the Canaanites and the Perizzites who live in the land will hate me. There are only a few of us. If they join together to attack us, my people and I will be destroyed."

³¹But the brothers said, "We will not allow our sister to be treated like a pros-titute."ᵈ

35 God said to Jacob, "Go to the city of Bethel and live there. Make an altar to the God who appeared to you there. This was when you were running away from your brother Esau."

²So Jacob said to his family and to all who were with him, "Put away the foreign gods you have. Make yourselves clean,ᵈ and change your clothes. ³We will leave here and go to Bethel. There I will build an altar to God. He has helped me during my time of trouble. He has

been with me everywhere I have gone." [4]So they gave Jacob all the foreign gods they had. And they gave him the earrings they were wearing. He hid them under the great tree near the town of Shechem. [5]Then Jacob and his sons left there. But God caused the people in the nearby cities to be afraid. So they did not follow the sons of Jacob. [6]And Jacob and all the people who were with him went to Luz. It is now called Bethel. It is in the land of Canaan. [7]There Jacob built an altar. He named the place Bethel, after God, because God had appeared to him there. That was when he was running from his brother.

[8]Deborah, Rebekah's nurse, died and was buried under the oak tree at Bethel. They named that place Oak of Crying.

[9]When Jacob came back from Northwest Mesopotamia, God appeared to him again. And God blessed him. [10]God said to him, "Your name is Jacob. But you will not be called Jacob any longer. Your new name will be Israel." So he called him Israel. [11]God said to him, "I am God All-Powerful. Have many children and grow in number as a nation. You will be the ancestor of many nations and kings. [12]I gave Abraham and Isaac land. I will give that same land to you and your descendants."[n] [13]Then God left him. [14]Jacob set up a stone on edge in that place where God had talked to him. And he poured a drink offering and olive oil on it to make it special for God. [15]And Jacob named the place Bethel.

[16]Jacob and his group left Bethel. Before they came to Ephrath, Rachel began giving birth to her baby. [17]But she was having much trouble with this birth. When Rachel's nurse saw this, she said, "Don't be afraid, Rachel. You are giving birth to another son." [18]Rachel gave birth to the son, but she died. As she lay dying, she named the boy Son of My Suffering. But Jacob called him Benjamin.[n]

[19]Rachel was buried on the road to Ephrath, a district of Bethlehem. [20]And Jacob set up a rock on her grave to honor her. That rock is still there today. [21]Then Israel, also called Jacob, continued his journey. He camped just south of Migdal Eder.

[22]While Israel was in that land Reuben had sexual relations with Israel's slave woman[d] Bilhah. And Israel heard about it.

Jacob had 12 sons. [23]He had 6 sons by his wife Leah. Reuben was his first son. Then Leah had Simeon, Levi, Judah, Issachar and Zebulun.

[24]He had 2 sons by his wife Rachel: Joseph and Benjamin.

[25]He had 2 sons by Rachel's slave girl Bilhah: Dan and Naphtali.

[26]And he had 2 sons by Leah's slave girl Zilpah: Gad and Asher.

These are Jacob's sons who were born in Northwest Mesopotamia.

[27]Jacob went to his father Isaac at Mamre near Hebron. This is where Abraham and Isaac had lived. [28]Isaac lived 180 years. [29]So Isaac breathed his last breath and died when he was very old. And his sons Esau and Jacob buried him.

36

This is the family history of Esau (also called Edom).

[2]Esau married women from the land of Canaan. He married Adah daughter of Elon the Hittite. And he married Oholibamah daughter of Anah. Anah was the son of Zibeon the Hivite. And he married [3]Basemath, Ishmael's daughter, the sister of Nebaioth.

[4]Adah gave Esau one son, Eliphaz. Basemath gave Esau Reuel. [5]And Oholibamah gave Esau Jeush, Jalam and Korah. These were Esau's sons who were born in the land of Canaan.

[6]Esau took his wives, his sons, his daughters and all the people who lived with him. He took his herds and other animals. And he took all the belongings he had gotten in Canaan. And he went to a land away from his brother Jacob. [7]Esau's and Jacob's belongings were becoming too many for them to live in the same land. The land where they had lived could not support both of them. They had too many herds. [8]So Esau lived in the mountains of Edom. (Esau is also called Edom.)

[9]This is the family history of Esau. He is the ancestor of the Edomites, who live in the mountains of Edom.

[10]Esau's sons were Eliphaz son of Adah and Esau, and Reuel son of Basemath and Esau.

[11]Eliphaz had five sons: Teman, Omar, Zepho, Gatam and Kenaz. [12]Eliphaz also had a slave woman[d] named Timna. Timna and Eliphaz gave birth to Amalek. These were Esau's grandsons by his wife Adah.

[13]Reuel had four sons: Nahath, Zerah,

35:18 Benjamin This name means "right-hand son" or "favorite son."

Shammah and Mizzah. These were Esau's grandsons by his wife Basemath.

[14]Esau's third wife was Oholibamah. She was the daughter of Anah. (Anah was the son of Zibeon.) Esau and Oholibamah gave birth to Jeush, Jalam and Korah.

[15]These were the leaders that came from Esau. Esau's first son was Eliphaz. From him came these leaders: Teman, Omar, Zepho, Kenaz, [16]Korah, Gatam and Amalek. These were the leaders that came from Eliphaz in the land of Edom. They were the grandsons of Adah.

[17]Esau's son Reuel was the father of these leaders: Nahath, Zerah, Shammah and Mizzah. These were the leaders that came from Reuel in the land of Edom. They were the grandsons of Esau's wife Basemath.

[18]Esau's wife Oholibamah gave birth to these leaders: Jeush, Jalam and Korah. These are the leaders that came from Esau's wife Oholibamah. She was the daughter of Anah. [19]These were the sons of Esau (also called Edom), and these were their leaders.

[20]These were the sons of Seir the Horite, who were living in the land: Lotan, Shobal, Zibeon, Anah, [21]Dishon, Ezer and Dishan. These sons of Seir were the leaders of the Horites in Edom.

[22]The sons of Lotan were Hori and Homam. (Timna was Lotan's sister.)

[23]The sons of Shobal were Alvan, Manahath, Ebal, Shepho and Onam.

[24]The sons of Zibeon were Aiah and Anah. Anah is the man who found the hot springs in the desert. He found them while he was caring for his father's donkeys.

[25]The children of Anah were Dishon and Oholibamah daughter of Anah.

[26]The sons of Dishon were Hemdan, Eshban, Ithran and Keran.

[27]The sons of Ezer were Bilhan, Zaavan and Akan.

[28]The sons of Dishan were Uz and Aran.

[29]These were the names of the Horite leaders: Lotan, Shobal, Zibeon, Anah, [30]Dishon, Ezer and Dishan.

These men were the leaders of the Horite families. They lived in the land of Edom.

[31]These are the kings who ruled in the land of Edom before the Israelites ever had a king.

[32]Bela son of Beor was the king of Edom. He came from the city of Dinhabah.

[33]When Bela died, Jobab son of Zerah became king. Jobab was from Bozrah.

[34]When Jobab died, Husham became king. He was from the land of the Temanites.

[35]When Husham died, Hadad son of Bedad became king. Hadad had defeated Midian in the country of Moab. Hadad was from the city of Avith.

[36]When Hadad died, Samlah became king. He was from Masrekah.

[37]When Samlah died, Shaul became king. He was from Rehoboth on the Euphrates River.

[38]When Shaul died, Baal-Hanan son of Acbor became king.

[39]When Baal-Hanan son of Acbor died, Hadad became king. He was from the city of Pau. His wife's name was Mehetabel daughter of Matred. Matred was the daughter of Me-Zahab.

[40]These Edomite leaders came from Esau. They are listed by their families and regions. Their names were Timna, Alvah, Jetheth, [41]Oholibamah, Elah, Pinon, [42]Kenaz, Teman, Mibzar, [43]Magdiel and Iram. These were the leaders of Edom. (Esau was the father of the Edomites.) The area where each of these families lived was named after that family.

37

Jacob lived in the land of Canaan, where his father had lived. [2]This is the family history of Jacob.

Joseph was a young man, 17 years old. He and his brothers cared for the flocks. His brothers were the sons of Bilhah and Zilpah, his father's wives. Joseph gave his father bad reports about his brothers. [3]Joseph was born when his father Israel, also called Jacob, was old. So Israel loved Joseph more than his other sons. He made Joseph a special robe with long sleeves. [4]Joseph's brothers saw that their father loved Joseph more than he loved them. So they hated their brother and could not speak to him politely.

[5]One time Joseph had a dream. When he told his brothers about it, they hated him even more. [6]Joseph said, "Listen to the dream I had. [7]We were in the field tying bundles of wheat together. My bundle stood up, and your bundles of wheat gathered around mine. Your bundles bowed down to mine."

[8]His brothers said, "Do you really think you will be king over us? Do you truly think you will rule over us?" His

brothers hated him even more now. They hated him because of his dreams and what he had said.

⁹Then Joseph had another dream. He told his brothers about it also. He said, "Listen, I had another dream. I saw the sun, moon and 11 stars bowing down to me."

¹⁰Joseph also told his father about this dream. But his father scolded him, saying, "What kind of dream is this? Do you really believe that your mother, your brothers and I will bow down to you?" ¹¹Joseph's brothers were jealous of him. But his father thought about what all these things could mean.

¹²One day Joseph's brothers went to Shechem to herd their father's sheep. ¹³Jacob said to Joseph, "Go to Shechem. Your brothers are there herding the sheep."

Joseph answered, "I will go."

¹⁴His father said, "Go and see if your brothers and the sheep are all right. Then come back and tell me." So Joseph's father sent him from the Valley of Hebron.

When Joseph came to Shechem, ¹⁵a man found him wandering in the field. He asked Joseph, "What are you looking for?"

¹⁶Joseph answered, "I am looking for my brothers. Can you tell me where they are herding the sheep?"

¹⁷The man said, "They have already gone. I heard them say they were going to Dothan." So Joseph went to look for his brothers and found them in Dothan.

¹⁸Joseph's brothers saw him coming from far away. Before he reached them, they made a plan to kill him. ¹⁹They said to each other, "Here comes that dreamer. ²⁰Let's kill him and throw his body into one of the wells. We can tell our father that a wild animal killed him. Then we will see what will become of his dreams."

²¹But Reuben heard their plan and saved Joseph. He said, "Let's not kill him. ²²Don't spill any blood. Throw him into this well here in the desert. But don't hurt him!" Reuben planned to save Joseph later and send him back to his father. ²³So when Joseph came to his brothers, they pulled off his robe with long sleeves. ²⁴Then they threw him into the well. It was empty. There was no water in it.

²⁵While Joseph was in the well, the brothers sat down to eat. When they looked up, they saw a group of Ishmael-ites. They were traveling from Gilead to Egypt. Their camels were carrying spices, balm[d] and myrrh.[d]

²⁶Then Judah said to his brothers, "What will we gain if we kill our brother and hide his death? ²⁷Let's sell him to these Ishmaelites. Then we will not be guilty of killing our own brother. After all, he is our brother, our own flesh and blood." And the other brothers agreed. ²⁸So when the Midianite traders came by, the brothers took Joseph out of the well. They sold him to the Ishmaelites for eight ounces of silver. And the Ishmael-ites took him to Egypt.

²⁹Reuben was not with his brothers when they sold Joseph to the Ishmael-ites. When Reuben came back to the well, Joseph was not there. Reuben tore his clothes to show he was sad. ³⁰Then he went back to his brothers and said, "The boy is not there! What will I do?" ³¹The brothers killed a goat and dipped Joseph's long-sleeved robe in its blood. ³²Then they brought the robe to their father. They said, "We found this robe. Look it over carefully. See if it is your son's robe."

³³Jacob looked it over and said, "It is my son's robe! Some savage animal has eaten him. My son Joseph has been torn to pieces!" ³⁴Then Jacob tore his clothes and put on rough cloth to show that he was sad. He continued to be sad about his son for a long time. ³⁵All of Jacob's sons and daughters tried to comfort him. But he could not be comforted. Jacob said, "I will be sad about my son until the day I die." So Jacob cried for his son Joseph.

³⁶Meanwhile the Midianites who had bought Joseph had taken him to Egypt. There they sold him to Potiphar. Poti-phar was an officer to the king of Egypt and captain of the palace guard.

38 About that time, Judah left his brothers. He went to stay with a man named Hirah. Hirah was from the town of Adullam. ²Judah met a Canaan-ite girl there and married her. Her father was named Shua. And Judah had sexual relations with her. ³She became preg-nant and gave birth to a son. Judah named him Er. ⁴Later she gave birth to another son. She named him Onan. ⁵Later she had another son. She named him Shelah. She was at Kezib when this third son was born.

⁶Judah chose a girl named Tamar to be the wife of his first son Er. ⁷Er was Judah's oldest son. But he did what the

Lord said was evil. So the Lord killed him. [8]Then Judah said to Er's brother Onan, "Go and have sexual relations with your dead brother's wife." It is your duty to provide children for your brother in this way."

[9]But Onan knew that the children would not belong to him. Onan was supposed to have sexual relations with Tamar. But he did not complete the sex act. This made it impossible for Tamar to become pregnant. So Er could not have descendants. [10]The Lord was displeased by this wicked thing Onan had done. So the Lord killed Onan also. [11]Then Judah said to his daughter-in-law Tamar, "Go back to live in your father's house. And don't marry until my young son Shelah grows up." Judah was afraid that Shelah also would die like his brothers. So Tamar returned to her father's home.

[12]After a long time Judah's wife, the daughter of Shua, died. After Judah had gotten over his sorrow, he went to Timnah. He went to his men who were cutting the wool from his sheep. His friend Hirah from Adullam went with him. [13]Tamar learned that Judah, her father-in-law, was going to Timnah to cut the wool from his sheep. [14]So she took off the clothes that showed she was a widow. Then she covered her face with a veil to hide who she was. She sat down by the gate of Enaim. It was on the road to Timnah. She did this because Judah's younger son Shelah had grown up. But Judah had not made plans for her to marry him.

[15]When Judah saw her, he thought she was a prostitute. This was because she had covered her face with a veil. [16]So Judah went to her and said, "Let me have sexual relations with you." He did not know that she was Tamar, his daughter-in-law.

She asked, "What will you give me if I let you have sexual relations with me?"

[17]Judah answered, "I will send you a young goat from my flock."

She answered, "First give me something to keep as a deposit until you send the goat."

[18]Judah asked, "What do you want me to give you as a deposit?"

Tamar answered, "Give me your seal and its cord, and give me your walking stick." So Judah gave these things to her. Then Judah and Tamar had sexual relations, and Tamar became pregnant. [19]Tamar went home. She took off the veil that covered her face. And she put on the clothes that showed she was a widow.

[20]Judah sent his friend Hirah with the young goat. Judah told Hirah to find the woman and get back his seal and the walking stick he had given her. But Hirah could not find her. [21]Hirah asked some of the men at the town of Enaim, "Where is the prostitute who was here by the road?"

The men answered, "There has never been a prostitute here."

[22]So he went back to Judah and said, "I could not find the woman. The men who lived there said, 'There has never been a prostitute here.'"

[23]Judah said, "Let her keep the things. I don't want people to laugh at us. I sent her the goat as I promised. But you could not find her."

[24]About three months later someone told Judah, "Tamar, your daughter-in-law, is guilty of acting like a prostitute. Now she is pregnant."

Then Judah said, "Bring her out and let her be burned to death."

[25]When the men went to bring Tamar out, she sent a message to her father-in-law. She said, "The man who owns these things has made me pregnant. Look at this seal and its cord and this walking stick. Tell me whose they are."

[26]Judah recognized them. He said, "She is more in the right than I. She did this because I did not give her to my son Shelah as I promised." And Judah did not have sexual relations with her again.

[27]When time came for Tamar to give birth, there were twins in her body. [28]While she was giving birth, one baby put his hand out. The nurse tied a red string on his hand. She said, "This baby came out first." [29]But he pulled his hand back in. So the other baby was born first. The nurse said, "So you are able to break out first." And they named him Perez. [30]After this, the baby with the

38:8 Go . . . wife It was a custom in Israel that if a man died without children, one of his brothers would marry the widow. If a child was born, it would be considered the dead man's child. 38:18 seal . . . cord A seal was used like a rubber stamp. People ran a string through it to tie around the neck. They wrote a contract, folded it, put wax or clay on the contract, and pressed the seal onto it as a signature. 38:29 Perez This name means "breaking out."

red string on his hand was born. They named him Zerah.

39 Now Joseph had been taken down to Egypt. An Egyptian named Potiphar was an officer to the king of Egypt. He was the captain of the palace guard. He bought Joseph from the Ishmaelites who had brought him down there. ²The Lord was with Joseph, and he became a successful man. He lived in the house of his master, Potiphar the Egyptian.

³Potiphar saw that the Lord was with Joseph. He saw that the Lord made Joseph successful in everything he did. ⁴So Potiphar was very happy with Joseph. He allowed Joseph to be his personal servant. He put Joseph in charge of the house. Joseph was trusted with everything Potiphar owned. ⁵So Joseph was put in charge of the house. He was put in charge of everything Potiphar owned. Then the Lord blessed the people in Potiphar's house because of Joseph. And the Lord blessed everything that belonged to Potiphar, both in the house and in the field. ⁶So Potiphar put Joseph in charge of everything he owned. Potiphar was not concerned about anything, except the food he ate.

Now Joseph was well built and handsome. ⁷After some time the wife of Joseph's master began to desire Joseph. One day she said to him, "Have sexual relations with me."

⁸But Joseph refused. He said to her, "My master trusts me with everything in his house. He has put me in charge of everything he owns. ⁹There is no one in his house greater than I. He has not kept anything from me, except you. And that is because you are his wife. How can I do such an evil thing? It is a sin against God."

¹⁰The woman talked to Joseph every day, but he refused to have sexual relations with her or even spend time with her.

¹¹One day Joseph went into the house to do his work as usual. He was the only man in the house at that time. ¹²His master's wife grabbed his coat. She said to him, "Come and have sexual relations with me." But Joseph left his coat in her hand and ran out of the house.

¹³She saw what Joseph had done. He had left his coat in her hands and had run outside. ¹⁴So she called to the servants in her house. She said, "Look! This Hebrew slave was brought here to shame us. He came in and tried to have sexual relations with me. But I

screamed. ¹⁵My scream scared him, and he ran away. But he left his coat with me." ¹⁶She kept his coat until her husband came home. ¹⁷And she told her husband the same story. She said, "This Hebrew slave you brought here came in to shame me! ¹⁸When he came near me, I screamed. He ran away, but he left his coat."

¹⁹When Joseph's master heard what his wife said Joseph had done, he became very angry. ²⁰So Potiphar arrested Joseph and put him into prison. This prison was where the king's prisoners were put. And Joseph stayed there in prison. ²¹But the Lord was with Joseph and showed him kindness. The Lord caused the prison warden to like Joseph. ²²The prison warden chose Joseph to take care of all the prisoners. He was responsible for whatever was done in the prison. ²³The warden paid no attention to anything that was in Joseph's care. This was because the Lord was with Joseph. The Lord made Joseph successful in everything he did.

40 After these things happened, two of the king's officers displeased the king. These officers were the man who served wine to the king and the king's baker. ²The king became angry with his officer who served him wine and his baker. ³So he put them in prison of the captain of the guard. This was the same prison where Joseph was kept. ⁴The captain of the guard put the two prisoners in Joseph's care. They stayed in prison for some time.

⁵One night both the king's officer who served him wine and the baker had a dream. Each had his own dream with its own meaning. ⁶When Joseph came to them the next morning, he saw they were worried. ⁷Joseph asked the king's officers who were with him, "Why do you look so unhappy today?"

⁸The two men answered, "We both had dreams last night. But no one can explain the meaning of them to us."

Joseph said to them, "God is the only One who can explain the meaning of dreams. So tell me your dreams."

⁹So the man who served wine to the king told Joseph his dream. He said, "I dreamed I saw a vine. ¹⁰On the vine there were three branches. I watched the branches bud and blossom, and then the grapes ripened. ¹¹I was holding the king's cup. So I took the grapes

and squeezed the juice into the cup. Then I gave it to the king."

¹²Then Joseph said, "I will explain the dream to you. The three branches stand for three days. ¹³Before the end of three days the king will free you. He will allow you to return to your work. You will serve the king his wine just as you did before. ¹⁴But when you are free, remember me. Be kind to me. Tell the king about me so that I can get out of this prison. ¹⁵I was taken by force from the land of the Hebrews. And I have done nothing here to deserve being put in prison."

¹⁶The baker saw that Joseph's explanation of the dream was good. So he said to Joseph, "I also had a dream. I dreamed there were three bread baskets on my head. ¹⁷In the top basket there were all kinds of baked food for the king. But the birds were eating this food out of the basket on my head."

¹⁸Joseph answered, "I will tell you what the dream means. The three baskets stand for three days. ¹⁹Before the end of three days, the king will cut off your head! He will hang your body on a pole. And the birds will eat your flesh."

²⁰Three days later it was the king's birthday. So he gave a feast for all his officers. In front of his officers, he let the chief officer who served his wine and the chief baker out of prison. ²¹The king gave his chief officer who served wine his old position. Once again he put the king's cup of wine into the king's hand. ²²But the king hanged the baker on a pole. Everything happened just as Joseph had said it would. ²³But the officer who served wine did not remember Joseph. He forgot all about him.

41 Two years later the king had a dream. He dreamed he was standing on the bank of the Nile River. ²He saw seven fat and beautiful cows come up out of the grass. They stood there, eating the grass. ³Then seven more cows came up out of the river. But they were thin and ugly. They stood beside the seven beautiful cows on the bank of the Nile. ⁴The seven thin and ugly cows ate the seven beautiful fat cows. Then the king woke up. ⁵The king slept again and dreamed a second time. In his dream he saw seven full and good heads of grain growing on one stalk. ⁶After that, seven more heads of grain sprang up. But they were thin and burned by the hot east wind. ⁷The thin heads of grain ate the seven full and good heads. Then the

king woke up again. And he realized it was only a dream. ⁸The next morning the king was troubled about these dreams. So he sent for all the magicians and wise men of Egypt. The king told them his dreams. But no one could explain their meaning to him.

⁹Then the chief officer who served wine to the king said to him, "I remember something I promised to do. But I had forgotten about it. ¹⁰There was a time when you were angry with me and the baker. You put us in prison in the house of the captain of the guard. ¹¹In prison we each had a dream on the same night. Each dream had a different meaning. ¹²A young Hebrew man was in the prison with us. He was a servant of the captain of the guard. We told him our dreams, and he explained their meanings to us. He told each man the meaning of his dream. ¹³Things happened exactly as he said they would: I was given back my old position, and the baker was hanged."

¹⁴So the king called for Joseph. The guards quickly brought him out of the prison. He shaved, put on clean clothes and went before the king.

¹⁵The king said to Joseph, "I have had a dream. But no one can explain its meaning to me. I have heard that you can explain a dream when someone tells it to you."

¹⁶Joseph answered the king, "I am not able to explain the meaning of dreams. God will do this for the king."

¹⁷Then the king said to Joseph, "In my dream I was standing on the bank of the Nile River. ¹⁸I saw seven fat and beautiful cows. They came up out of the river and ate the grass. ¹⁹Then I saw more cows come out of the river. They were thin and lean and ugly. They were the worst looking cows I have seen in all the land of Egypt. ²⁰And these thin and ugly cows ate the first seven fat cows. ²¹But after they had eaten the seven cows, no one could tell they had eaten them. They just looked as thin and ugly as they did in the beginning. Then I woke up.

²²"I had another dream. I saw heads full and good heads of grain growing on one stalk. ²³Then seven more heads of grain sprang up after them. But these heads were thin and ugly. They were burned by the hot east wind. ²⁴Then the thin heads ate the seven good heads. I told this dream to the magicians. But no one could explain its meaning to me."

²⁵Then Joseph said to the king, "Both of these dreams mean the same thing. God is telling you what he is about to do. ²⁶The seven good cows stand for seven years. And the seven good heads of grain stand for seven years. Both dreams mean the same thing. ²⁷The seven thin and ugly cows stand for seven years. And the seven thin heads of grain burned by the hot east wind stand for seven years of hunger. ²⁸This will happen as I told you. God is showing the king what he is about to do. ²⁹You will have seven years of good crops and plenty to eat in all the land of Egypt. ³⁰But after those seven years, there will come seven years of hunger. All the food that grew in the land of Egypt will be forgotten. The time of hunger will eat up the land. ³¹People will forget what it was like to have plenty of food. This is because the hunger that follows will be so great. ³²You had two dreams which mean the same thing. This shows that God has firmly decided that this will happen. And he will make it happen soon.

³³"So let the king choose a man who is very wise and understanding. Let the king set him over the land of Egypt. ³⁴And let the king also appoint officers over the land. They should take one-fifth of all the food that is grown during the seven good years. ³⁵They should gather all the food that is produced during the good years that are coming. Under the king's authority they should store the grain in the cities and guard it. ³⁶That food should be saved for later. It will be used during the seven years of hunger that will come on the land of Egypt. Then the people in Egypt will not die during the seven years of hunger."

³⁷This seemed like a very good idea to the king. All his officers agreed. ³⁸And the king asked them, "Can we find a better man than Joseph to take this job? God's spirit is truly in him!"

³⁹So the king said to Joseph, "God has shown you all this. There is no one as wise and understanding as you are. ⁴⁰I will put you in charge of my palace. All the people will obey your orders. Only I will be greater than you."

⁴¹Then the king said to Joseph, "Look! I have put you in charge of all the land of Egypt." ⁴²Then the king took off from his own finger his ring with the royal seal on it. And he put it on Joseph's finger. He gave Joseph fine linen clothes to wear. And he put a gold chain around Joseph's neck. ⁴³The king had Joseph ride in the second royal chariot. Men walked ahead of his chariot calling, "Bow down!" By doing these things, the king put Joseph in charge of all of Egypt.

⁴⁴The king said to him, "I am the king. And I say that no one in all the land of Egypt may lift a hand or a foot unless you say he may." ⁴⁵The king gave Joseph the name Zaphenath-Paneah. He also gave Joseph a wife named Asenath. She was the daughter of Potiphera, priest of On. So Joseph traveled through all the land of Egypt.

⁴⁶Joseph was 30 years old when he began serving the king of Egypt. And he left the king's court and traveled through all the land of Egypt. ⁴⁷During the seven good years, the crops in the land grew well. ⁴⁸And Joseph gathered all the food which was produced in Egypt during those seven years of good crops. He stored the food in the cities. In every city he stored grain that had been grown in the fields around that city. ⁴⁹Joseph stored much grain, as much as the sand of the seashore. He stored so much grain that he could not measure it.

⁵⁰Joseph's wife was Asenath daughter of Potiphera, the priest of On. Before the years of hunger came, Joseph and Asenath had two sons. ⁵¹Joseph named the first son Manasseh.[n] Joseph said, "God has made me forget all the troubles I have had and all my father's family." ⁵²Joseph named the second son Ephraim.[n] Joseph said, "God has given me children in the land of my troubles."

⁵³The seven years of good crops came to an end in the land of Egypt. ⁵⁴Then the seven years of hunger began, just as Joseph had said. In all the lands people had nothing to eat. But in Egypt there was food. ⁵⁵The time of hunger became terrible in all of Egypt. The people cried to the king for food. He said to all the Egyptians, "Go to Joseph. Do whatever he tells you to do."

⁵⁶The hunger was everywhere in that part of the world. And Joseph opened the storehouses and sold grain to the people of Egypt. This was because the time of hunger became terrible in Egypt.

41:51 Manasseh This name sounds like the Hebrew word for "made me forget." **41:52 Ephraim** This name sounds like the Hebrew word for "given me children."

⁵⁷And all the people in that part of the world came to Joseph in Egypt to buy grain. This was because the hunger was terrible everywhere in that part of the world.

42 Jacob learned that there was grain in Egypt. So he said to his sons, "Why are you just sitting here looking at one another? ²I have heard that there is grain in Egypt. Go down there and buy grain for us to eat. Then we will live and not die."

³So ten of Joseph's brothers went down to buy grain from Egypt. ⁴But Jacob did not send Benjamin, Joseph's brother, with them. Jacob was afraid that something terrible might happen to Benjamin. ⁵Along with many other people, the sons of Jacob, also called Israel, went to Egypt to buy grain. This was because the people in the land of Canaan were hungry also.

⁶Now Joseph was governor over Egypt. He was the one who sold the grain to people who came to buy it. So Joseph's brothers came to him. They bowed facedown on the ground before him. ⁷When Joseph saw his brothers, he knew who they were. But he acted as if he didn't know them. He asked unkindly, "Where do you come from?"

They answered, "We have come from the land of Canaan to buy food."

⁸Joseph knew they were his brothers. But they did not know who he was. ⁹And Joseph remembered his dreams about his brothers bowing to him. He said to them, "You are spies! You came to learn where this nation is weak!"

¹⁰But his brothers said to him, "No, my master. We come as your servants just to buy food. ¹¹We are all sons of the same father. We are honest men, not spies."

¹²Then Joseph said to them, "No! You have come to learn where this nation is weak!"

¹³And they said, "We are 10 of 12 brothers. We are sons of the same father. We live in the land of Canaan. Our youngest brother is there with our father right now. And our other brother is gone."

¹⁴But Joseph said to them, "I can see I was right! You are spies! ¹⁵But I will give you a way to prove you are telling the truth. As surely as the king lives, you will not leave this place until your youngest brother comes here. ¹⁶One of you must go and get your brother. The rest of you will stay here in prison. We will

see if you are telling the truth. If not, as surely as the king lives, you are spies." ¹⁷Then Joseph put them all in prison for three days.

¹⁸On the third day Joseph said to them, "I am a God-fearing man. Do this thing, and I will let you live: ¹⁹If you are honest men, let one of your brothers stay here in prison. The rest of you go and carry grain back to feed your hungry families. ²⁰Then bring your youngest brother back here to me. If you do this, I will know you are telling the truth. Then you will not die."

The brothers agreed to this. ²¹They said to each other, "We are being punished for what we did to our brother. We saw his trouble. He begged us to save him, but we refused to listen. That is why we are in this trouble now."

²²Then Reuben said to them, "I told you not to harm the boy. But you refused to listen to me. So now we are being punished for what we did to him."

²³When Joseph talked to his brothers, he used an interpreter. So they did not know that Joseph understood what they were saying. ²⁴Then Joseph left them and cried. After a short time he went back and spoke to them. He took Simeon and tied him up while the other brothers watched. ²⁵Joseph told his servants to fill his brothers' bags with grain. They were to put the money the brothers had paid for the grain back in their bags. They were to give them things they would need for their trip back home. And the servants did this.

²⁶So the brothers put the grain on their donkeys and left. ²⁷When they stopped for the night, one of the brothers opened his sack. He was going to get food for his donkey. Then he saw his money in the top of the sack. ²⁸He said to the other brothers, "The money I paid for the grain has been put back. Here it is in my sack!"

The brothers were very frightened. They said to each other, "What has God done to us?"

²⁹The brothers went to their father Jacob in the land of Canaan. They told him everything that had happened. ³⁰They said, "The master of that land spoke unkindly to us. He accused us of spying on his country. ³¹But we told him that we were honest men, not spies. ³²We told him that we were 10 of 12 brothers—sons of one father. We said that 1 of our brothers was gone. And we said that our

youngest brother was with our father in Canaan.

[33]"Then the master of the land said to us, 'Here is a way I can know you are honest men: Leave 1 of your brothers with me. Take back grain to feed your hungry families, and go. [34]And bring your youngest brother to me. Then I will know that you are not spies but honest men. And I will give you back your brother whom you leave with me. And you can move about freely in our land.'"

[35]Then the brothers emptied their sacks. And each of them found his money in his sack. When they and their father saw it, they were afraid.

[36]Their father Jacob said to them, "You are robbing me of all my children. Joseph is gone. Simeon is gone. And now you want to take Benjamin away, too. Everything is against me."

[37]Then Reuben said to his father, "You may put my 2 sons to death if I don't bring Benjamin back to you. Trust him to my care. I will bring him back to you."

[38]But Jacob said, "I will not allow Benjamin to go with you. His brother is dead. He is the only son left from my wife Rachel. I am afraid something terrible might happen to him during the trip to Egypt. Then I would be sad until the day I die."

43 Still no food grew in the land of Canaan. [2]Jacob's family had eaten all the grain they had brought from Egypt. So Jacob said to them, "Go to Egypt again. Buy a little more grain for us to eat."

[3]But Judah said to Jacob, "The governor of that country strongly warned us. He said, 'Bring your brother back with you. If you don't, you will not be allowed to see me.' [4]If you will send Benjamin with us, we will go down and buy food for you. [5]But if you refuse to send Benjamin, we will not go. The governor of that country warned us. He said we would not see him if we didn't bring Benjamin with us."

[6]Jacob, also called Israel, said, "Why did you tell the man you had another brother? You have caused me a lot of trouble."

[7]The brothers answered, "He questioned us carefully about ourselves and our family. He asked us, 'Is your father still alive? Do you have another brother?' We just answered his questions. How could we know he would ask us to bring our other brother to him?"

[8]Then Judah said to his father Jacob,

"Send Benjamin with me. Then we will go at once. Do this so that we, you and our children may live and not die. [9]I will guarantee you that he will be safe. I will be personally responsible for him. If I don't bring him back to you, you can blame me all my life. [10]If we had not wasted all this time, we could have already made two trips."

[11]Then their father Jacob said to them, "If it has to be that way, then do this: Take some of the best foods in our land in your packs. Give them to the man as a gift: some balm,[d] some honey, spices, myrrh,[d] pistachio nuts and almonds. [12]Take twice as much money with you this time. Take back the money that was returned to you in your sacks last time. Maybe it was a mistake. [13]And take Benjamin with you. Now leave and go to the man. [14]I pray that God All-Powerful will cause the governor to be merciful to you. I pray that he will allow Simeon and Benjamin to come back with you. If I am robbed of my children, then I am robbed of them!"

[15]So the brothers took the gifts. They also took twice as much money as they had taken the first time. And they took Benjamin. They hurried down to Egypt and stood before Joseph.

[16]In Egypt Joseph saw Benjamin with them. Joseph said to the servant in charge of his house, "Bring those men into my house. Kill an animal and prepare a meal. Those men will eat with me today at noon." [17]The servant did as Joseph told him. He brought the men to Joseph's house.

[18]The brothers were afraid when they were brought to Joseph's house. They thought, "We were brought here because of the money that was put in our sacks on the first trip. He wants to attack us, make us slaves and take our donkeys." [19]So the brothers went to the servant in charge of Joseph's house. They spoke to him at the door of the house. [20]They said, "Sir, we came here once before to buy food. [21]While we were going home, we stopped for the night and opened our sacks. Each of us found all his money in his sack. We brought that money with us to give it back to you. [22]And we have brought more money. It is to pay for the food we want to buy this time. We don't know who put that money in our sacks."

[23]But the servant answered, "It's all right. Don't be afraid. Your God, the God of your father, must have put the money

in your sacks. I got the money you paid me for the grain last time." Then the servant brought Simeon out to them.

²⁴The servant led the men into Joseph's house. He gave them water, and they washed their feet. Then he gave their donkeys food to eat. ²⁵The men prepared their gift to give to Joseph when he arrived at noon. They had heard they were going to eat with him there.

²⁶When Joseph came home, the brothers gave him the gift they had brought into the house. Then they bowed down to the ground to him. ²⁷Joseph asked them how they were doing. He said, "How is your aged father you told me about? Is he still alive?"

²⁸The brothers answered, "Your servant, our father, is well. He is still alive." And they bowed low before Joseph to show him respect.

²⁹Then Joseph saw his brother Benjamin, who had the same mother as he. Joseph asked, "Is this your youngest brother you told me about?" Then Joseph said to Benjamin, "God be good to you, my son!" ³⁰Then Joseph hurried off. He had to hold back the tears when he saw his brother Benjamin. So Joseph went into his room and cried there. ³¹Then he washed his face and came out. He controlled himself and said, "Serve the meal."

³²So they served Joseph at one table. They served his brothers at another table. And they served the Egyptians who ate with him at another table. This was because Egyptians did not like Hebrews and never ate with them. ³³Joseph's brothers were seated in front of him. They were in order of their ages, from oldest to youngest. And they looked at each other because they were so amazed. ³⁴Food from Joseph's table was taken to them. But Benjamin was given five times more food than the others. Joseph's brothers drank with him until they were very drunk.

44 Then Joseph gave a command to the servant in charge of his house. Joseph said, "Fill the men's sacks with as much grain as they can carry. And put each man's money into his sack with the grain. ²Put my silver cup in the sack of the youngest brother. Also put his money for the grain in that sack." The servant did what Joseph told him.

³At dawn the brothers were sent away with their donkeys. ⁴They were not far from the city when Joseph said to the servant in charge of his house, "Go after the men. When you catch up with them, say, 'Why have you paid back evil for good? ⁵The cup you have stolen is the one my master uses for drinking. And he uses it for explaining dreams. You have done a very wicked thing!'"

⁶So the servant caught up with the brothers. He said to them what Joseph had told him to say.

⁷But the brothers said to the servant, "Why do you say these things? We would not do anything like that! ⁸We brought back to you the money we found in our sacks. We brought it back from the land of Canaan. So surely we would not steal silver or gold from your master's house. ⁹If you find that silver cup in the sack of one of us, then let him die. And we will be your slaves."

¹⁰The servant said, "We will do as you say. But only the man who has taken the cup will become my slave. The rest of you may go free."

¹¹Then every brother quickly lowered his sack to the ground and opened it. ¹²The servant searched the sacks, going from the oldest brother to the youngest. He found the cup in Benjamin's sack. ¹³The brothers tore their clothes to show they were sad. Then they put their sacks back on the donkeys. And they returned to the city.

¹⁴When Judah and his brothers went back to Joseph's house, Joseph was still there. The brothers bowed facedown on the ground before him. ¹⁵Joseph said to them, "What have you done? Didn't you know that a man like me can learn things by signs and dreams?"

¹⁶Judah said, "Sir, what can we say? And how can we show we are not guilty? God has uncovered our guilt. So all of us will be your slaves, not just Benjamin."

¹⁷But Joseph said, "I will not make you all slaves! Only the man who stole the cup will be my slave. The rest of you may go back safely to your father."

¹⁸Then Judah went to Joseph and said, "Sir, please let me speak plainly to you. Please don't be angry with me. I know that you are as powerful as the king of Egypt himself. ¹⁹When we were here before, you asked us, 'Do you have a father or a brother?' ²⁰And we answered you, 'We have an old father. And we have a younger brother. He was born when our father was old. This youngest son's brother is dead. So he is the only one of his mother's children left alive. And our father loves him very much.' ²¹Then you said to us, 'Bring that brother to me. I

want to see him.' ²²And we said to you, 'That young boy cannot leave his father. If he leaves him, his father would die.' ²³But you said to us, 'You must bring your youngest brother. If you don't, you will not be allowed to see me again.' ²⁴So we went back to our father and told him what you had said.

²⁵"Later, our father said, 'Go again. Buy us a little more food.' ²⁶We said to our father, 'We cannot go without our youngest brother. Without our youngest brother, we will not be allowed to see the governor.' ²⁷Then my father said to us, 'You know that my wife Rachel gave me two sons. ²⁸One son left me. I thought, "Surely he has been torn apart by a wild animal." And I haven't seen him since. ²⁹Now you want to take this son away from me also. But something terrible might happen to him. Then I would be sad until the day I die.' ³⁰Now what will happen if we go home to our father without our youngest brother? He is the most important thing in our father's life. ³¹When our father sees that the young boy is not with us, he will die. And it will be our fault. We will cause the great sorrow that kills our father.

³²"I gave my father a guarantee that the young boy would be safe. I said to my father, 'If I don't bring him back to you, you can blame me all my life.' ³³So now, please allow me to stay here and be your slave. And let the young boy go back home with his brothers. ³⁴I cannot go back to my father if the boy is not with me. I couldn't stand to see my father that sad."

45 Joseph could not control himself in front of his servants any longer. He cried out, "Have everyone leave me." When only the brothers were left with Joseph, he told them who he was. ²Joseph cried so loudly that the Egyptians heard him. And the people in the king's palace heard about it. ³He said to his brothers, "I am Joseph. Is my father still alive?" But the brothers could not answer him, because they were very afraid of him.

⁴So Joseph said to them, "Come close to me." So the brothers came close to him. And he said to them, "I am your brother Joseph. You sold me as a slave to go to Egypt. ⁵Now don't be worried. Don't be angry with yourselves because you sold me here. God sent me here ahead of you to save people's lives. ⁶No food has grown on the land for two years now. And there will be five more

years without planting or harvest. ⁷So God sent me here ahead of you. This was to make sure you have some descendants[d] left on earth. And it was to keep you alive in an amazing way. ⁸So it was not you who sent me here, but God. God has made me the highest officer of the king of Egypt. I am in charge of his palace. I am the master of all the land of Egypt.

⁹"So leave quickly and go to my father. Tell him, 'Your son Joseph says: God has made me master over all Egypt. Come down to me quickly. ¹⁰Live in the land of Goshen. You will be near me. Also your children, your grandchildren, your flocks and herds and all that you have will be near me. ¹¹I will care for you during the next five years of hunger. In this way, you and your family and all that you have will not starve.'

¹²"Now you can see for yourselves. The one speaking to you is really Joseph. And my brother Benjamin can see this. ¹³So tell my father about how powerful I have become in Egypt. Tell him about everything you have seen. Now hurry and bring him back to me." ¹⁴Then Joseph hugged his brother Benjamin and cried. And Benjamin cried also. ¹⁵Then Joseph kissed all his brothers. He cried as he hugged them. After this, his brothers talked with him.

¹⁶The king of Egypt and his officers learned that Joseph's brothers had come. And they were very happy about this. ¹⁷So the king said to Joseph, "Tell your brothers to load their animals and go back to the land of Canaan. ¹⁸Tell them to bring their father and their families back here to me. I will give them the best land in Egypt. And they will eat the best food we have here. ¹⁹Tell them to take some wagons from Egypt for their children and their wives. And tell them to bring their father back also. ²⁰Tell them not to worry about bringing any of their things with them. We will give them the best of what we have in Egypt."

²¹So the sons of Israel did this. Joseph gave them wagons as the king had ordered. And he gave them food for their trip. ²²He gave each brother a change of clothes. But he gave Benjamin five changes of clothes. And Joseph gave him about seven and one-half pounds of silver. ²³Joseph also sent his father ten donkeys loaded with the best things from Egypt. And he sent ten female donkeys. They were loaded with grain,

bread and other food for his father on his trip back. ²⁴Then Joseph told his brothers to go. As they were leaving, he said to them, "Don't quarrel on the way home."

²⁵So the brothers left Egypt and went to their father Jacob in the land of Canaan. ²⁶They told him, "Joseph is still alive. He is the ruler over all the land of Egypt." Their father was shocked and did not believe them. ²⁷But the brothers told him everything Joseph had said. Then Jacob saw the wagons that Joseph had sent to carry him back to Egypt. Now Jacob felt better. ²⁸Jacob, also called Israel, said, "Now I believe you. My son Joseph is still alive. I will go and see him before I die."

46 So Jacob, also called Israel, took all he had and started his trip. He went to Beersheba. There he offered sacrifices to the God of his father Isaac. ²During the night God spoke to Israel in a vision. He said, "Jacob, Jacob."

And Jacob answered, "Here I am."

³Then God said, "I am God, the God of your father. Don't be afraid to go to Egypt. I will make your descendants^d a great nation there. ⁴I will go to Egypt with you. And I will bring you out of Egypt again. Joseph's own hands will close your eyes when you die."

⁵Then Jacob left Beersheba. The sons of Israel loaded their father, their children and their wives. They put them in the wagons the king of Egypt had sent. ⁶They also took their farm animals and everything they had gotten in Canaan. So Jacob went to Egypt with all his descendants. ⁷He took his sons and grandsons, his daughters and granddaughters. He took all his family to Egypt with him.

⁸Now these are the names of the children of Israel who went into Egypt. (They are Jacob and his descendants.^d)

Reuben was Jacob's first son. ⁹Reuben's sons were Hanoch, Pallu, Hezron and Carmi.

¹⁰Simeon's sons were Jemuel, Jamin, Ohad, Jakin, Zohar and Shaul. (Shaul was Simeon's son by a Canaanite woman.)

¹¹Levi's sons were Gershon, Kohath and Merari.

¹²Judah's sons were Er, Onan, Shelah, Perez and Zerah. (But Er and Onan had died in the land of Canaan.) Perez's sons were Hezron and Hamul.

¹³Issachar's sons were Tola, Puah, Jashub and Shimron.

¹⁴Zebulun's sons were Sered, Elon and Jahleel.

¹⁵These are the sons of Leah and Jacob born in Northwest Mesopotamia. His daughter Dinah was also born there. There were 33 persons in this part of Jacob's family.

¹⁶Gad's sons were Zephon, Haggi, Shuni, Ezbon, Eri, Arodi and Areli.

¹⁷Asher's sons were Imnah, Ishvah, Ishvi and Beriah. Their sister was Serah. Beriah's sons were Heber and Malkiel.

¹⁸These are Jacob's sons by Zilpah. She was the slave girl whom Laban gave to his daughter Leah. There were 16 persons in this part of Jacob's family.

¹⁹The sons of Jacob's wife Rachel were Joseph and Benjamin. ²⁰In Egypt, Joseph became the father of Manasseh and Ephraim by his wife Asenath. She was the daughter of Potiphera, priest of On.

²¹Benjamin's sons were Bela, Beker, Ashbel, Gera, Naaman, Ehi, Rosh, Muppim, Huppim and Ard.

²²These are the sons of Jacob by his wife Rachel. There were 14 persons in this part of Jacob's family.

²³Dan's son was Hushim.

²⁴Naphtali's sons were Jahziel, Guni, Jezer and Shillem.

²⁵These are Jacob's sons by Bilhah. She was the slave girl whom Laban gave to his daughter Rachel. There were 7 persons in this part of Jacob's family.

²⁶So the total number of Jacob's direct descendants who went to Egypt was 66. (The wives of Jacob's sons were not counted in this number.) ²⁷Joseph had 2 sons born in Egypt. So the total number in the family of Jacob in Egypt was 70.

²⁸Jacob sent Judah ahead of him to see Joseph in Goshen. Then Jacob and his people came into the land of Goshen. ²⁹Joseph prepared his chariot and went to meet his father Israel in Goshen. As soon as Joseph saw his father, he hugged his neck. And he cried there for a long time.

³⁰Then Israel said to Joseph, "Now I am ready to die. I have seen your face. And I know that you are still alive."

³¹Joseph said to his brothers and his father's family, "I will go and tell the king you are here. I will say, 'My brothers and my father's family have left the land of Canaan. They have come here to me. ³²They are shepherds and take care of farm animals. And they have brought their flocks and their herds and everything they own with

them.' ³³When the king calls you, he will ask, 'What work do you do?' ³⁴This is what you should tell him: 'We, your servants, have taken care of farm animals all our lives. Our ancestors did the same thing.' Then the king will allow you to settle in the land of Goshen. This is away from the Egyptians. They don't like to be near shepherds."

47 Joseph went in to the king and said, "My father and my brothers have arrived from Canaan. They have their flocks and herds and everything they own with them. They are now in the land of Goshen." ²Joseph chose five of his brothers to introduce to the king.

³The king said to the brothers, "What work do you do?"

And they said to him, "We, your servants, are shepherds. Our ancestors were also shepherds." ⁴They said to the king, "We have come to live in this land. There is no grass in the land of Canaan for our animals to eat. The hunger is very terrible there. So please allow us to live in the land of Goshen."

⁵Then the king said to Joseph, "Your father and your brothers have come to you. ⁶You may choose any place in Egypt for them to live. Give your father and your brothers the best land. Let them live in the land of Goshen. And if any of them are skilled shepherds, put them in charge of my sheep and cattle."

⁷Then Joseph brought in his father Jacob and introduced him to the king. And Jacob blessed the king.

⁸Then the king said to Jacob, "How old are you?"

⁹Jacob said to him, "My life has been spent wandering from place to place. It has been short, filled with trouble. I have lived only 130 years. My ancestors lived much longer than I." ¹⁰Then Jacob blessed the king and left.

¹¹Joseph obeyed the king. He gave his father and brothers the best land in Egypt. It was near the city of Rameses. ¹²And Joseph gave his father, his brothers and everyone who lived with them the food they needed.

¹³The hunger became worse, and there was no food anywhere in the land. The land of Egypt and the land of Canaan became very poor because of this. ¹⁴Joseph collected all the money that was to be found in Egypt and Canaan. People paid him this money for the grain they were buying. He brought that money to the king's palace. ¹⁵After some time, the people in Egypt and Canaan had no

money left. So they went to Joseph and said, "Please give us food. Our money is gone. If we don't eat, we will die here in front of you."

¹⁶Joseph answered, "Since you have no money, give me your farm animals. I will give you food in return." ¹⁷So people brought their farm animals to Joseph. And he gave them food in exchange for their horses, sheep, cattle and donkeys. So he kept them alive by trading food for their farm animals that year.

¹⁸The next year the people came to Joseph and said, "You know we have no money left. And all our animals belong to you. We have nothing left except our bodies and our land. ¹⁹Surely both we and our land will die here in front of you. Buy us and our land in exchange for food. And we will be slaves to the king, together with our land. Give us seed to plant. Then we will live and not die. And the land will not become a desert."

²⁰So Joseph bought all the land in Egypt for the king. Every Egyptian sold Joseph his field, because the hunger was very great. So the land became the king's. ²¹And Joseph made the people slaves from one end of Egypt to the other. ²²The only land he did not buy was the land the priests owned. They did not need to sell their land because the king paid them for their work. So they had money to buy food.

²³Joseph said to the people, "Now I have bought you and your land for the king. So I will give you seed. And you can plant your fields. ²⁴At harvest time you must give one-fifth to the king. You may keep four-fifths for yourselves. Use it as seed for the field and as food for yourselves, your families and your children."

²⁵The people said, "You have saved our lives. If you like, we will become slaves of the king."

²⁶So Joseph made a law in Egypt, which continues today: One-fifth of everything from the land belongs to the king. The only land the king did not get was the priests' land.

²⁷The Israelites continued to live in the land of Goshen in Egypt. There they got possessions. They had many children and grew in number.

²⁸Jacob, also called Israel, lived in Egypt 17 years. So he lived to be 147 years old. ²⁹Israel knew he soon would die. So he called his son Joseph to him. He said to Joseph, "If you love me, put

your hand under my leg.ⁿ Promise me you will not bury me in Egypt. ³⁰When I die, carry me out of Egypt. Bury me where my ancestors are buried."

Joseph answered, "I will do as you say."

³¹Then Jacob said, "Promise me." And Joseph promised him that he would do this. Then Israel worshiped as he leaned on the top of his walking stick.

48 Some time later Joseph learned that his father was very sick. So he took his two sons Manasseh and Ephraim and went to his father. ²When Joseph arrived, someone told Jacob, also called Israel, "Your son Joseph has come to see you." Jacob was weak. So he used all his strength and sat up on his bed.

³Then Jacob said to Joseph, "God All-Powerful appeared to me at Luz in the land of Canaan. God blessed me there. ⁴He said to me, 'I will give you many children. I will make you the father of many peoples. And I will give your descendantsᵈ this land forever.' ⁵Your two sons were born here in Egypt before I came. They will be counted as my own sons. Ephraim and Manasseh will be my sons just as Reuben and Simeon are my sons. ⁶But if you have other children, they will be your own. But their land will be part of the land given to Ephraim and Manasseh. ⁷When I came from Northwest Mesopotamia, Rachel died in the land of Canaan. We were traveling toward Ephrath. This made me very sad. I buried her there beside the road to Ephrath." (Today Ephrath is Bethlehem.)

⁸Then Israel saw Joseph's sons. He said, "Who are these boys?"

⁹Joseph said to his father, "They are my sons. God has given them to me here in Egypt."

Israel said, "Bring your sons to me so I may bless them."

¹⁰At this time Israel's eyesight was bad because he was old. So Joseph brought the boys close to him. Israel kissed the boys and put his arms around them. ¹¹He said to Joseph, "I thought I would never see you alive again. And now God has let me see you and also your children." ¹²Then Joseph moved his sons off Israel's lap. Joseph bowed face-down to the ground. ¹³He put Ephraim on his right side and Manasseh on his left. (So Ephraim was near Israel's left

hand, and Manasseh was near Israel's right hand.) Joseph brought the boys close to Israel. ¹⁴But Israel crossed his arms. He put his right hand on the head of Ephraim, who was younger. He put his left hand on the head of Manasseh. But he was the firstbornᵈ son. ¹⁵And Israel blessed Joseph and said,

"My ancestors Abraham and Isaac
    served our God.
And like a shepherd God has led
    me all my life.
¹⁶He was the Angel who saved me
    from all my troubles.
Now I pray that he will bless
    these boys.
May my name be known through
    these boys.
And may the names of my
    ancestors Abraham and Isaac
    be known through them.
May they have many descendantsᵈ
    on the earth."

¹⁷Joseph saw that his father put his right hand on Ephraim's head. Joseph didn't like it. So he took hold of his father's hand. He wanted to move it from Ephraim's head to Manasseh's head. ¹⁸Joseph said to his father, "You are doing it wrong, Father. Manasseh is the firstborn son. Put your right hand on his head."

¹⁹But his father refused and said, "I know, my son, I know. Manasseh will be great and have many descendants. But his younger brother will be greater. And his descendants will be enough to make a nation."

²⁰So Israel blessed them that day. He said,

"When a blessing is given in Israel,
    they will say:
'May God make you like Ephraim
    and Manasseh.'"

In this way he made Ephraim greater than Manasseh.

²¹Then Israel said to Joseph, "Look at me. I am about to die. But God will be with you. He will take you back to the land of your fathers. ²²I have given you something that I did not give your brothers. I have given you the land of Shechem that I took from the Amorite people. I took it with my sword and my bow."

49 Then Jacob called his sons to him. He said, "Come here to me. I will tell you what will happen to you in the future.

[2]"Come together and listen, sons of
Jacob.
   Listen to Israel, your father."

[3]"Reuben, my first son, you are my
strength.
   Your birth showed I could be a
father.
You have the highest position
among my sons.
   You are the most powerful.
[4]But you are uncontrolled like water.
So you will no longer lead your
brothers.
This is because you got into your
father's bed.
   You shamed me by having sexual
relations with my slave girl.

[5]"Simeon and Levi are brothers.
   They used their swords to do
violence.
[6]I will not join their secret talks.
   I will not meet with them to plan
evil.
They killed men because they were
angry.
   And they crippled oxen just for
fun.
[7]May their anger be cursed, because
it is too violent.
May their violence be cursed,
because it is too cruel.
I will divide them up among the
tribes[d] of Jacob.
   I will scatter them through all the
tribes of Israel.

[8]"Judah, your brothers will praise
you.
   You will grab your enemies by
the neck.
   Your brothers will bow down to
you.
[9]Judah is like a young lion.
   You have returned from killing,
my son.
Like a lion, he stretches out and
lies down to rest.
   No one is brave enough to wake
him.
[10]Men from Judah's family will be
kings.
   Someone from Judah will always
be on the throne.
Judah will rule until the real king
comes.
   And the nations will obey him.
[11]He ties his donkey to a grapevine.
   He ties his young donkey to the
best branch.

He can afford to use wine to wash
his clothes.
   He even uses grape juice to wash
his robes.
[12]His eyes are bright from drinking
wine.
   His teeth are white from drinking
milk.

[13]"Zebulun will live near the sea.
   His shore will be a safe place for
ships.
   His land will reach as far as
Sidon.

[14]"Issachar is like a strong donkey.
   He lies down while carrying his
load.
[15]He will see his resting place is
good.
   He will see how pleasant his land
is.
Then he will put his back to the
load.
   He will become a slave.

[16]"Dan will rule his own people
   like the other tribes in Israel.
[17]Dan will be like a snake by the side
of the road.
   He will be like a dangerous snake
lying near the path.
That snake bites a horse's leg.
   And the rider is thrown off
backward.

[18]"Lord, I wait for your salvation.

[19]"Robbers will attack Gad.
   But he will defeat them and drive
them away.

[20]"Asher's land will grow much good
food.
   He will grow food fit for a king.

[21]"Naphtali is like a female deer that
runs free.
   She has beautiful fawns.

[22]"Joseph is like a grapevine that
produces much fruit.
   He is like a healthy vine watered
by a spring.
   He is like a vine whose branches
grow over the wall.
[23]Men attack him violently with
arrows.
   They shoot at him angrily.
[24]But he aims his bow well.
   His arms are made strong.
He gets his power from the Mighty
God of Jacob.

He gets his strength from the
    Shepherd, the Rock[d] of Israel.
[25]Your father's God helps you.
    God All-Powerful blesses you.
He blesses you with rain from
    above.
He blesses you with water from
    springs below.
He blesses you with many babies
    born to your wives.
He blesses you with many young
    ones born to your animals.
[26]The blessings of your father are
    greater
    than the blessings of the oldest
    mountains.
They are greater than the good
    things of the long-lasting hills.
May these blessings rest on the
    head of Joseph.
May they rest on the forehead of
    the one who was separated
    from his brothers.

[27]"Benjamin is like a hungry wolf.
    In the morning he eats what he
    has caught.
    In the evening he divides what he
    has taken."

[28]These are the 12 tribes of Israel. And this is what their father said to them. He gave each son the blessing that was right for him. [29]Then Israel gave them a command. He said, "I am about to die. Bury me with my ancestors in the cave in the field of Ephron the Hittite. [30]That cave is in the field of Machpelah east of Mamre. It is in the land of Canaan. Abraham bought that field from Ephron the Hittite for a burying place. [31]Abraham and Sarah his wife are buried there. Isaac and Rebekah his wife are buried there. I buried my wife Leah there. [32]The field and the cave in it were bought from the Hittite people." [33]After Jacob finished talking to his sons, he lay down. He put his feet back on the bed, took his last breath and died.

50 When Jacob died, Joseph hugged his father and cried over him and kissed him. [2]He commanded the doctors who served him to prepare his father's body. So the doctors prepared Jacob's body to be buried. [3]It took the doctors 40 days to prepare his body. This was the usual time it took. And the Egyptians had a time of sorrow for Jacob. It lasted 70 days.

[4]When this time of sorrow had ended, Joseph spoke to the king's officers. He said, "If you think well of me, please tell this to the king: [5]'When my father was near death, I made a promise to him. I promised I would bury him in a cave in the land of Canaan. This is a burial place that he cut out for himself. So please let me go and bury my father. Then I will return.'"

[6]The king answered, "Keep your promise. Go and bury your father."

[7]So Joseph went to bury his father. All the king's officers, the older leaders and all the leading men of Egypt went with Joseph. [8]Everyone who lived with Joseph and his brothers went with him. And everyone who lived with his father also went. They left only their children, their flocks and their herds in the land of Goshen. [9]Men in chariots and on horses also went with Joseph. It was a very large group.

[10]They went to the threshing[d] floor of Atad, east of the Jordan River. There they cried loudly and bitterly for Jacob, also called Israel. Joseph's time of sorrow continued for seven days. [11]The people that lived in Canaan saw the sadness at the threshing floor of Atad. They said, "Those Egyptians are showing great sorrow!" So now that place is named Sorrow of the Egyptians.

[12]So Jacob's sons did what their father commanded. [13]They carried his body to the land of Canaan. They buried it in the cave in the field of Machpelah near Mamre. Abraham had bought this cave and field from Ephron the Hittite. He bought the cave to use as a burial place. [14]After Joseph buried his father, he returned to Egypt. His brothers and everyone who had gone with him to bury his father also returned.

[15]After Jacob died, Joseph's brothers said, "What if Joseph is still angry with us? We did many wrong things to him. What if he plans to pay us back?" [16]So they sent a message to Joseph. It said, "Your father gave this command before he died. [17]He said to us, 'You have done wrong. You have sinned and done evil to Joseph. Tell Joseph to forgive you, his brothers.' So now, Joseph, we beg you to forgive our wrong. We are the servants of the God of your father." When Joseph received the message, he cried.

[18]And his brothers went to him and bowed low before him. They said, "We are your slaves."

[19]Then Joseph said to them, "Don't be afraid. Can I do what only God can do? [20]You meant to hurt me. But God turned your evil into good. It was to save the

lives of many people. And it is being done. [21]So don't be afraid. I will take care of you and your children." So Joseph comforted his brothers and spoke kind words to them.

[22]Joseph continued to live in Egypt with all his father's family. He died when he was 110 years old. [23]During Joseph's life Ephraim had children and grandchildren. And Joseph's son Manasseh had a son named Makir. Joseph accepted Makir's children as his own.

[24]Joseph said to his brothers, "I am about to die. But God will take care of you. He will lead you out of this land. He will lead you to the land he promised to Abraham, Isaac and Jacob." [25]Then Joseph had the sons of Israel make a promise. He said, "Promise me that you will carry my bones with you out of Egypt."

[26]Joseph died when he was 110 years old. Doctors prepared his body for burial. Then they put him in a coffin in Egypt.

The Second Book of Moses Called
EXODUS

1 When Jacob, also called Israel, went to Egypt, he took his sons. And each son took his own family with him. These are the names of the sons of Israel: [2]Reuben, Simeon, Levi, Judah, [3]Issachar, Zebulun, Benjamin, [4]Dan, Naphtali, Gad and Asher. [5]There was a total of 70 people who were descendants[d] of Jacob. Jacob's son Joseph was already in Egypt.

[6]By some time later, Joseph and his brothers had died, along with all the people who had lived at that same time. [7]But the people of Israel had many children, and their number grew greatly. They became very strong, and the country of Egypt was filled with them.

[8]Then a new king began to rule Egypt. He did not know who Joseph was. [9]This king said to his people, "Look! The people of Israel are too many! And they are too strong for us to handle! [10]We must make plans against them. If we don't, the number of their people will grow even more. Then if there is a war, they might join our enemies. Then they could fight us and escape from the country!"

[11]So the Egyptians made life hard for the people of Israel. They put slave masters over the Israelites. The slave masters forced the Israelites to build the cities Pithom and Rameses for the king. These cities were supply centers in which the Egyptians stored things. [12]The Egyptians forced the Israelites to work even harder. But this made the Israelites grow in number and spread more. So the Egyptians became more afraid of them. [13]They forced the Israelites to work even harder. [14]The Egyptians made life hard for the Israelites.

They forced the Israelites to work very hard making bricks and mortar. They also forced them to do all kinds of hard work in the fields. The Egyptians were not merciful to them in all their hard work.

[15]There were two Hebrew nurses named Shiphrah and Puah. These nurses helped the Israelite women give birth to their babies. The king of Egypt said to the nurses, [16]"When you are helping the Hebrew women give birth to their babies, watch! If the baby is a girl, let the baby live. But if it is a boy, kill it!" [17]But the nurses feared God. So they did not do as the king told them. They let all the boy babies live. [18]Then the king of Egypt sent for the nurses. He said, "Why did you do this? Why did you let the boys live?"

[19]The nurses said to him, "The Hebrew women are much stronger than the Egyptian women. They give birth to their babies before we can get there." [20]God was good to the nurses. And the Hebrew people continued to grow in number. So they became even stronger. [21]Because the nurses feared God, he gave them families of their own.

[22]So the king commanded all his people: "Every time a boy is born to the Hebrews, you must throw him into the Nile River. But let all the girl babies live."

2 There was a man from the family of Levi. He married a woman who was also from the family of Levi. [2]She became pregnant and gave birth to a son. She saw how wonderful the baby was, and she hid him for three months. [3]But after three months, she was not able to hide the baby any longer. So she got a basket made of reeds and covered it with tar so that it would float. She put the baby in the basket. Then she put the basket among the tall grass at the edge of the Nile River. [4]The baby's sister stood a short distance away. She wanted to see what would happen to him.

[5]Then the daughter of the king of Egypt came to the river. She was going to take a bath. Her servant girls were walking beside the river. She saw the basket in the tall grass. So she sent her slave girl to get it. [6]The king's daughter opened the basket and saw the baby boy. He was crying, and she felt sorry for him. She said, "This is one of the Hebrew babies."

[7]Then the baby's sister asked the king's daughter, "Would you like me to find a Hebrew woman to nurse the baby for you?"

[8]The king's daughter said, "Yes, please." So the girl went and got the baby's own mother. [9]The king's daughter said to the woman, "Take this baby and nurse him for me. I will pay you." So the woman took her baby and nursed him. [10]After the child had grown older, the woman took him to the king's daughter. She adopted the baby as her own son. The king's daughter named him Moses,[n] because she had pulled him out of the water.

[11]Moses grew and became a man. One day he visited his people, the Hebrews. He saw that they were forced to work very hard. He saw an Egyptian beating a Hebrew man, one of Moses' own people. [12]Moses looked all around and saw that no one was watching. So he killed the Egyptian and hid his body in the sand. [13]The next day Moses returned and saw two Hebrew men fighting each other. He saw that one man was in the wrong. Moses said to that man, "Why are you hitting one of your own people?"

[14]The man answered, "Who made you our ruler and judge? Are you going to kill me as you killed the Egyptian?"

Then Moses was afraid. He thought, "Now everyone knows what I did."

[15]When the king heard about what Moses had done, he tried to kill Moses. But Moses ran away from the king and went to live in the land of Midian. There he sat down near a well.

[16]There was a priest in Midian who had seven daughters. His daughters went to that well to get water for their father's sheep. They were trying to fill the water troughs for their father's sheep. [17]But some shepherds came and chased the girls away. Then Moses defended the girls and watered their sheep.

[18]Then they went back to their father, Reuel, also called Jethro. He asked them, "Why have you come home early today?"

[19]The girls answered, "The shepherds chased us away. But an Egyptian defended us. He got water for us and watered our sheep."

[20]He asked his daughters, "Where is this man? Why did you leave him? Invite him to eat with us."

[21]Moses agreed to stay with Jethro. And he gave his daughter Zipporah to Moses to be his wife. [22]Zipporah gave birth to a son, and Moses named him Gershom.[n] Moses named him this because Moses was a stranger in a land that was not his own.

[23]After a long time, the king of Egypt died. The people of Israel groaned because they were forced to work very hard. They cried for help. And God heard them. [24]God heard their cries, and he remembered the agreement he had made with Abraham, Isaac and Jacob. [25]God saw the troubles of the people of Israel, and he was concerned about them.

3 One day Moses was taking care of Jethro's sheep. Jethro was the priest of Midian and also Moses' father-in-law. Moses led the sheep to the west side of the desert. He came to Sinai, the mountain of God. [2]There the angel of the Lord appeared to Moses in flames of fire coming out of a bush. Moses saw that the bush was on fire, but it was not burning up. [3]So Moses said, "I will go closer to this strange thing. How can a bush continue burning without burning up?"

[4]The Lord saw Moses was coming to look at the bush. So God called to him from the bush, "Moses, Moses!"

And Moses said, "Here I am."

[5]Then God said, "Do not come any closer. Take off your sandals. You are standing on holy ground. [6]I am the God

2:10 **Moses** The name Moses sounds like the Hebrew word for "to pull out." 2:22 **Gershom** This name sounds like the Hebrew word meaning "a stranger there."

of your ancestors. I am the God of Abraham, the God of Isaac and the God of Jacob." Moses covered his face because he was afraid to look at God.

[7]The Lord said, "I have seen the troubles my people have suffered in Egypt. And I have heard their cries when the Egyptian slave masters hurt them. I am concerned about their pain. [8]I have come down to save them from the Egyptians. I will bring them out of that land. I will lead them to a good land with lots of room. This is a land where much food grows. This is the land of these people: the Canaanites, Hittites, Amorites, Perizzites, Hivites and Jebusites. [9]I have heard the cries of the people of Israel. I have seen the way the Egyptians have made life hard for them. [10]So now I am sending you to the king of Egypt. Go! Bring my people, the Israelites, out of Egypt!"

[11]But Moses said to God, "I am not a great man! Why should I be the one to go to the king and lead the Israelites out of Egypt?"

[12]God said, "I will be with you. This will be the proof that I am sending you: You will lead the people out of Egypt. Then all of you will worship me on this mountain."

[13]Moses said to God, "When I go to the Israelites, I will say to them, 'The God of your fathers sent me to you.' What if the people say, 'What is his name?' What should I tell them?"

[14]Then God said to Moses, "I AM WHO I AM.[n] When you go to the people of Israel, tell them, 'I AM sent me to you.'"

[15]God also said to Moses, "This is what you should tell the people: 'The Lord is the God of your ancestors. He is the God of Abraham, the God of Isaac and the God of Jacob. And he sent me to you.' This will always be my name. That is how people from now on will know me.

[16]"Go and gather the older leaders and tell them this: 'The Lord, the God of your ancestors, has appeared to me. The God of Abraham, Isaac and Jacob spoke to me. He says: I care about you, and I have seen what has happened to you in Egypt. [17]I have decided that I will take you away from the troubles you are suffering in Egypt. I will lead you to the land of the Canaanites, Hittites, Amo-

rites, Perizzites, Hivites and Jebusites. This land grows much food.'

[18]"The older leaders will listen to you. And then you and the older leaders of Israel will go to the king of Egypt. You will tell him, 'The Lord, the God of the Hebrews, appeared to us. Let us travel three days into the desert. There we must offer sacrifices to the Lord our God.'

[19]"But I know that the king of Egypt will not let you go. Only a great power will force him to let you go. [20]So I will use my great power against Egypt. I will make miracles[d] happen in that land. After I do this, he will let you go. [21]And I will cause the Egyptian people to think well of the people of Israel. So when you leave, they will give gifts to your people. [22]Each Hebrew woman will ask her Egyptian neighbor and any Egyptian woman living in her house for gifts. Ask for silver, gold and clothing. You will put those gifts on your children when you leave Egypt. In this way you will take with you the riches of the Egyptians."

4Then Moses answered, "What if the people of Israel do not believe me or listen to me? What if they say, 'The Lord did not appear to you'?"

[2]The Lord said to him, "What is that in your hand?"

Moses answered, "It is my walking stick."

[3]The Lord said, "Throw it on the ground."

So Moses threw it on the ground. And it became a snake. Moses ran from the snake. [4]But the Lord said to him, "Reach out and grab the snake by its tail." So Moses reached out and took hold of the snake. When he did this, it again became a stick in his hand. [5]The Lord said, "When this happens, the Israelites will believe that the Lord appeared to you. I am the God of their ancestors. I am the God of Abraham, the God of Isaac and the God of Jacob."

[6]Then the Lord said to Moses, "Put your hand inside your coat." So Moses put his hand inside his coat. When he took his hand out, it was white with a harmful skin disease.

[7]Then the Lord said, "Now put your hand inside your coat again." So Moses put his hand inside his coat again. When he took it out, his hand was healthy again. It was like the rest of his skin.

3:14 I . . . I AM The Hebrew words are like the name "YAHWEH." This Hebrew name for God, usually called "Lord," shows that God always lives and is always with his people.

⁸Then the Lord said, "The people may not believe you or be convinced by the first miracle.ᵈ They may believe you when you show them this second miracle. ⁹After these two miracles they still may not believe or listen to you. Then take some water from the Nile River. Pour it on the dry ground. The water will become blood when it touches the ground."

¹⁰But Moses said to the Lord, "But Lord, I am not a skilled speaker. I have never been able to speak well. And now, even after talking to you, I am not a good speaker. I speak slowly and can't find the best words."

¹¹Then the Lord said to him, "Who made man's mouth? And who makes him deaf or not able to speak? Or who gives a man sight or makes him blind? It is I, the Lord. ¹²Now go! I will help you speak. I will tell you what to say."

¹³But Moses said, "Please, Lord, send someone else."

¹⁴The Lord became angry with Moses. He said, "Your brother Aaron, from the family of Levi, is a skilled speaker. He is already coming to meet you. And he will be happy when he sees you. ¹⁵I will tell you what to say. Then you will tell Aaron. I will help both of you know what to say and do. ¹⁶And Aaron will speak to the people for you. You will tell him what God says. And he will speak for you. ¹⁷Take your walking stick with you. Use it to do the miracles."

¹⁸Then Moses went back to Jethro, his father-in-law. Moses said to him, "Let me go back to my people in Egypt. I want to see if they are still alive."

Jethro said to Moses, "You may go. Have a safe trip."

¹⁹While Moses was still in Midian, the Lord said to him, "Go back to Egypt. The men who wanted to kill you are dead now."

²⁰So Moses took his wife and his sons and put them on a donkey. Then he started back to Egypt. He took with him the walking stick of God.

²¹The Lord said to Moses, "When you get back to Egypt, do all the miracles.ᵈ I have given you the power to do them. Show them to the king of Egypt. But I will make the king very stubborn. He will not let the people go. ²²Then say to the king: 'This is what the Lord says: Israel is my firstbornᵈ son. ²³And I told you to let my son go. Let him go so he may worship me. But you refused to let

Israel go. So I will kill your firstborn son.'"

²⁴As Moses was on his way to Egypt, he stopped at a resting place for the night. The Lord met him there and tried to kill him. ²⁵But Zipporah took a flint knife and circumcisedᵈ her son. She took the skin and touched Moses' feet with it. Then she said to him, "You are a bridegroom of blood to me." ²⁶Zipporah said this because she had to circumcise her son. So the Lord did not kill Moses.

²⁷Meanwhile the Lord said to Aaron, "Go out into the desert to meet Moses." When Aaron went, he met Moses at Sinai, the mountain of God, and kissed him. ²⁸Moses told Aaron everything the Lord had said to him when he sent him to Egypt. And Moses told him about the miracles which the Lord had commanded him to do.

²⁹So Moses and Aaron gathered all the older leaders of the Israelites. ³⁰Aaron told them everything that the Lord had told Moses. Then Moses did the miracles for all the people to see. ³¹So the Israelites believed. They heard that the Lord was concerned about them and had seen their troubles. Then they bowed down and worshiped him.

5 After Moses and Aaron talked to people, they went to the king of Egypt. They said, "This is what the Lord, the God of Israel says: 'Let my people go so they may hold a feast for me in the desert.'"

²But the king of Egypt said, "Who is the Lord? Why should I obey him and let Israel go? I do not know the Lord. And I will not let Israel go."

³Then Aaron and Moses said, "The God of the Hebrews has talked with us. Now let us travel three days into the desert. There we will offer sacrifices to the Lord our God. If we don't do this, he may kill us with a disease or in war."

⁴But the king said to them, "Moses and Aaron, why are you taking the people away from their work? Go back to your hard work! ⁵There are very many Hebrews. And now you want them to quit their hard work!"

⁶That same day the king gave a command to the slave masters and foremen. ⁷He said, "Don't give the people straw to make bricks as you used to do. Let them gather their own straw. ⁸But they must still make the same number of bricks as they did before. Do not accept fewer. They have become lazy. That is why they are asking me, 'Let us go to

offer sacrifices to our God.' [9]Make these people work harder. Keep them busy. Then they will not have time to listen to the lies of Moses."

[10]So the slave masters and foremen went to the Israelites and said, "This is what the king says: I will no longer give you straw. [11]Go and get your own straw wherever you can find it. But you must make as many bricks as you made before." [12]So the people went everywhere in Egypt looking for dry stalks to use for straw. [13]The slave masters kept forcing the people to work harder. They said, "You must make just as many bricks as you did when you were given straw." [14]The king's slave masters had chosen the Israelite foremen. They had made them responsible for the work the people did. The Egyptian slave masters beat these men and asked them, "Why aren't you making as many bricks as you made in the past?"

[15]Then the Israelite foremen went to the king. They complained and said, "Why are you treating us, your servants, this way? [16]You give us no straw. But we are commanded to make bricks. Our slave masters beat us. But it is your own people's fault."

[17]The king answered, "You are lazy! You don't want to work! That is why you ask to leave here and make sacrifices to the Lord. [18]Now, go back to work! We will not give you any straw. But you must make just as many bricks as you did before."

[19]The Israelite foremen knew they were in trouble. This was because the king had told them: "You must make just as many bricks each day as you did before." [20]As they were leaving the meeting with the king, they met Moses and Aaron. Moses and Aaron were waiting for them. [21]So they said to Moses and Aaron, "May the Lord punish you. You caused the king and his officers to hate us. You have given them an excuse to kill us."

[22]Then Moses returned to the Lord and said, "Lord, why have you brought this trouble on your people? Is this why you sent me here? [23]I went to the king and said what you told me to say. But ever since that time he has made the people suffer. And you have done nothing to save them."

6 Then the Lord said to Moses, "Now you will see what I will do to the king of Egypt. I will use my great power against him, and he will let my people go. Because of my power, he will force them out of his country."

[2]Then God said to Moses, "I am the Lord. [3]I appeared to Abraham, Isaac and Jacob by the name, God All-Powerful. But they did not know me by my name, the Lord. [4]I also made my agreement with them to give them the land of Canaan. They lived in that land, but it was not their own land. [5]Now I have heard the cries of the Israelites. The Egyptians are treating them as slaves. And I remember my agreement. [6]So tell the people of Israel that I say to them, 'I am the Lord. I will save you from the hard work the Egyptians force you to do. I will make you free. You will not be slaves to the Egyptians. I will free you by my great power. And I will punish the Egyptians terribly. [7]I will make you my own people, and I will be your God. You will know that I am the Lord your God. I am the One who saves you from the hard work the Egyptians force you to do. [8]I will lead you to the land that I promised to Abraham, Isaac and Jacob. I will give you that land to own. I am the Lord.'"

[9]So Moses told this to the people of Israel. But they would not listen to him. They were discouraged, and their slavery was hard.

[10]Then the Lord said to Moses, [11]"Go tell the king of Egypt that he must let the Israelites leave his land."

[12]But Moses answered, "The Israelites will not listen to me. So surely the king will not listen to me, either. I am not a good speaker."

[13]But the Lord told Moses and Aaron to talk to the king. He commanded them to lead the Israelites out of Egypt.

[14]These are the leaders of the families of Israel:

Israel's first son, Reuben, had four sons. They were Hanoch, Pallu, Hezron and Carmi. These are the family groups of Reuben.

[15]Simeon's sons were Jemuel, Jamin, Ohad, Jakin, Zohar and Shaul. Shaul was the son of a Canaanite woman. These are the family groups of Simeon.

[16]Levi lived 137 years. These are the names of his sons according to their family history: Gershon, Kohath and Merari.

[17]Gershon had two sons, Libni and Shimei, with their families.

[18]Kohath lived 133 years. The sons of

Kohath were Amram, Izhar, Hebron and Uzziel.

¹⁹The sons of Merari were Mahli and Mushi.

These are the family groups of Levi, according to their family history.

²⁰Amram married his father's sister Jochebed. Jochebed gave birth to Aaron and Moses. Amram lived 137 years.

²¹Izhar's sons were Korah, Nepheg and Zicri.

²²Uzziel's sons were Mishael, Elzaphan and Sithri.

²³Aaron married Elisheba. She was the daughter of Amminadab and the sister of Nahshon. Elisheba gave birth to Nadab, Abihu, Eleazar and Ithamar.

²⁴The sons of Korah were Assir, Elkanah and Abiasaph. These are the family groups of the Korahites.

²⁵Eleazar son of Aaron married a daughter of Putiel. And she gave birth to Phinehas.

These are the leaders of the family groups of the Levites.

²⁶This was the Aaron and Moses to whom the Lord spoke. He said, "Lead my people out of Israel in their divisions." ²⁷Aaron and Moses are the ones who talked to the king of Egypt. They told him to let the people of Israel leave Egypt.

²⁸The Lord spoke to Moses in the land of Egypt. ²⁹He said, "I am the Lord. Tell the king of Egypt everything I tell you."

³⁰But Moses answered, "I am not a good speaker. The king will not listen to me."

7 The Lord said to Moses, "I have made you like God to the king of Egypt. And your brother Aaron will be like a prophet^d for you. ²Tell Aaron your brother everything that I command you. Then let him tell the king of Egypt to let the Israelites leave his country. ³But I will make the king stubborn. Then I will do many miracles^d in Egypt. ⁴But he will still refuse to listen. So then I will punish Egypt terribly. And I will lead my divisions, my people the Israelites, out of that land. ⁵I will punish Egypt with my power. And I will bring the Israelites out of that land. Then they will know I am the Lord."

⁶Moses and Aaron did just as the Lord had commanded them. ⁷Moses was 80 years old, and Aaron was 83, when they spoke to the king.

⁸The Lord said to Moses and Aaron, ⁹"The king will ask you to do a miracle.^{d} When he does, Moses, you tell Aaron to throw his walking stick down in front of the king. It will become a snake."

¹⁰So Moses and Aaron went to the king as the Lord had commanded. Aaron threw his walking stick down in front of the king and his officers. And it became a snake.

¹¹So the king called in his wise men and his magicians. With their tricks the Egyptian magicians were able to do the same thing. ¹²They threw their walking sticks on the ground, and their sticks became snakes. But then Aaron's stick swallowed theirs. ¹³But the king was stubborn. He refused to listen to Moses and Aaron, just as the Lord had said.

¹⁴Then the Lord said to Moses, "The king is being stubborn. He refuses to let the people go. ¹⁵In the morning the king will go out to the Nile River. Go meet him by the edge of the river. Take with you the walking stick that became a snake. ¹⁶Tell him this: The Lord, the God of the Hebrews, sent me to you. He said, 'Let my people go worship me in the desert.' Until now you have not listened. ¹⁷This is what the Lord says: 'This is how you will know that I am the Lord. I will strike the water of the Nile River with this stick in my hand. And the water will change into blood. ¹⁸Then the fish in the Nile will die, and the river will begin to stink. And the Egyptians will not be able to drink the water from the Nile.'"

¹⁹The Lord said to Moses, "Tell Aaron to stretch the walking stick in his hand over the rivers, canals, ponds and pools in Egypt. The water will become blood everywhere in Egypt. There even will be blood in the wooden buckets and stone jars."

²⁰So Moses and Aaron did just as the Lord had commanded. Aaron raised his walking stick and struck the water in the Nile River. He did this in front of the king and his officers. So all the water in the Nile changed into blood. ²¹The fish in the Nile died, and the river began to stink. So the Egyptians could not drink water from it. Blood was everywhere in the land of Egypt.

²²Using their tricks, their magicians of Egypt did the same thing. So the king was stubborn and refused to listen to Moses and Aaron. This happened just as the Lord had said. ²³The king turned and went into his palace. He ignored what Moses and Aaron had done. ²⁴The Egyptians could not drink the water from the Nile. So all of them dug along

the bank of the river. They were looking for water to drink.

²⁵ Seven days passed after the Lord changed the Nile River.

8 Then the Lord told Moses, "Go to the king of Egypt and tell him, 'This is what the Lord says: Let my people go to worship me. ² If you refuse, then I will punish Egypt with frogs. ³ The Nile River will be filled with frogs. They will come from the river and enter your palace. They will be in your bedroom and your bed. The frogs will enter the houses of your officers and your people. They will enter your ovens and your baking pans. ⁴ The frogs will jump up all over you, your people and your officers.'"

⁵ Then the Lord said to Moses, "Tell Aaron to hold his walking stick in his hand over the rivers, canals and ponds. Make frogs come up out of the water onto the land of Egypt."

⁶ So Aaron held his hand over all the waters of Egypt. The frogs came up out of the water and covered the land of Egypt. ⁷ The magicians used their tricks to do the same thing. So even more frogs came up onto the land of Egypt.

⁸ So the king called for Moses and Aaron. He said, "Pray to the Lord to take the frogs away from me and my people. I will let your people go to offer sacrifices to the Lord."

⁹ Moses said to the king, "Please set the time that I should pray for you, your people and your officers. Then the frogs will leave you and your houses. They will remain only in the Nile."

¹⁰ The king answered, "Tomorrow."

Moses said, "What you want will happen. By this you will know that there is no one like the Lord our God. ¹¹ The frogs will leave you, your houses, your officers and your people. They will remain only in the Nile."

¹² Moses and Aaron left the king. Moses asked the Lord about the frogs he had sent to the king. ¹³ And the Lord did as Moses asked. The frogs died in the houses, in the yards and in the fields. ¹⁴ The Egyptians put them in piles. The whole country began to stink. ¹⁵ When the king saw that they were free of the frogs, he became stubborn again. He did not listen to Moses and Aaron, just as the Lord had said.

¹⁶ Then the Lord said to Moses, "Tell Aaron to raise his walking stick and strike the dust on the ground. Then everywhere in Egypt the dust will change into gnats." ¹⁷ They did this.

Aaron raised the walking stick that was in his hand and struck the dust on the ground. Then everywhere in Egypt the dust changed into gnats. The gnats got on the people and animals. ¹⁸ Using their tricks, the magicians tried to do the same thing. But they could not make the dust change into gnats. The gnats remained on the people and animals. ¹⁹ So the magicians told the king that the power of God had done this. But the king was stubborn and refused to listen to them. This happened just as the Lord had said.

²⁰ The Lord told Moses, "Get up early in the morning. Meet the king of Egypt as he goes out to the river. Tell him, 'This is what the Lord says: Let my people go so they can worship me. ²¹ If you don't let them go, I will send swarms of flies. I will send them into your houses. The flies will be on you, your officers and your people. The houses of Egypt will be full of flies. And they will be all over the ground, too. ²² But I will not treat the people of Israel the same as the Egyptian people. There will not be any flies in the land of Goshen, where my people live. By this you will know that I, the Lord, am in this land. ²³ I will treat my people differently from your people. This miracle⁴ will happen tomorrow.'"

²⁴ So the Lord did as he had said. Great swarms of flies came into the king's palace and his officers' houses. All over Egypt flies were ruining the land. ²⁵ The king called for Moses and Aaron. He told them, "Offer sacrifices to your God here in this country."

²⁶ But Moses said, "It wouldn't be right to do that. The Egyptians hate the sacrifices we offer to the Lord our God. They will see us offer sacrifices they hate. Then they will throw stones at us and kill us. ²⁷ Let us make a three-day journey into the desert. We must offer sacrifices to the Lord our God there. This is what the Lord told us to do."

²⁸ The king said, "I will let you go. Then you may offer sacrifices to the Lord your God in the desert. But you must not go very far away. Now go and pray for me."

²⁹ Moses said, "I will leave and pray to the Lord. He will take the flies away from you, your officers and your people tomorrow. But do not try to trick us again. Do not stop the people from going to offer sacrifices to the Lord."

³⁰ So Moses left the king and prayed to the Lord. ³¹ And the Lord did as Moses

asked. He removed the flies from the king, his officers and his people. Not one fly was left. ³²But the king became stubborn again and did not let the people go.

9 Then the Lord told Moses, "Go to the king of Egypt. Tell him, 'This is what the Lord, the God of the Hebrews, says: Let my people go to worship me. ²You might refuse to let them go and continue to hold them. ³Then the Lord will punish you. He will send a terrible disease on all your farm animals. He will cause all of your horses, donkeys, camels, cattle and sheep to become sick. ⁴But the Lord will treat Israel's animals differently from the animals of Egypt. None of the animals that belong to the Israelites will die. ⁵The Lord has set tomorrow as the time he will do this in the land.' " ⁶The next day the Lord did as he promised. All the farm animals in Egypt died. But none of the animals belonging to Israelites died. ⁷The king sent people to see what had happened to the animals of Israel. They found that not one of them had died. But the king was still stubborn. He did not let the people go.

⁸The Lord said to Moses and Aaron, "Fill your hands with the ashes from a furnace. Moses, throw the ashes into the air in front of the king of Egypt. ⁹The ashes will spread like dust through all the land of Egypt. The dust will cause boils to break out and become sores on the skin. These sores will be on people and animals everywhere in the land."

¹⁰So Moses and Aaron took ashes from a furnace. Then they went and stood before the king. Moses threw ashes into the air. It caused boils to break out and become sores on people and animals. ¹¹The magicians could not stand before Moses. This was because all the Egyptians had boils, even the magicians. ¹²But the Lord made the king stubborn. So he refused to listen to Moses and Aaron. This happened just as the Lord had said.

¹³Then the Lord said to Moses, "Get up early in the morning and go to the king of Egypt. Tell him, 'This is what the Lord, the God of the Hebrews, says: Let my people go to worship me. ¹⁴If you do not do this, this time I will punish you with all my power. I will punish you, your officers and your people. Then you will know that there is no one in the whole land like me. ¹⁵By now I could have used my power and caused a bad disease. It would have destroyed you

and your people from the earth. ¹⁶But I have let you live for this reason: to show you my power. In this way my name will be talked about in all the earth. ¹⁷You are still against my people. You do not want to let them go. ¹⁸So at this time tomorrow, I will send a terrible hailstorm. It will be the worst in Egypt since it became a nation. ¹⁹Now send for your animals and whatever you have in the fields. Bring them into a safe place. The hail will fall on every person or animal that is still in the fields. If they have not been brought in, they will die.' " ²⁰Some of the king's officers respected the word of the Lord. They hurried to bring their slaves and animals inside. ²¹But others ignored the Lord's message. They left their slaves and animals in the fields.

²²The Lord told Moses, "Raise your hand toward the sky. Then the hail will start falling over all the land of Egypt. It will fall on people, animals and on everything that grows in the fields of Egypt." ²³So Moses raised his walking stick toward the sky. And the Lord sent thunder and hail. And lightning flashed down to the earth. So he caused hail to fall upon the land of Egypt. ²⁴There was hail, and there was lightning flashing as it hailed. This was the worst hailstorm in Egypt since it had become a nation. ²⁵The hail destroyed everything that was in the fields in all the land of Egypt. The hail destroyed both people and animals. It also destroyed everything that grew in the fields. It broke all the trees in the fields. ²⁶The only place it did not hail was in the land of Goshen. The people of Israel lived there.

²⁷The king sent for Moses and Aaron. He told them, "This time I have sinned. The Lord is in the right. And I and my people are in the wrong. ²⁸Pray to the Lord. We have had enough of God's thunder and hail. I will let you go. You do not have to stay here any longer."

²⁹Moses told the king, "When I leave the city, I will raise my hands to the Lord in prayer. And the thunder and hail will stop. Then you will know that the earth belongs to the Lord. ³⁰But I know that you and your officers do not yet fear the Lord God."

³¹The flax was in bloom, and the barley had ripened. So these crops were destroyed. ³²But both wheat crops ripen later. So they were not destroyed.

³³Moses left the king and went outside the city. He raised his hands to the Lord. And the thunder and hail stopped. The

rain also stopped falling to the ground. [34]The king saw that the rain, hail and thunder had stopped. Then he sinned again. He and his officers became stubborn again. [35]The king became stubborn and refused to let the Israelites go. This happened just as the Lord had said through Moses.

10 The Lord said to Moses, "Go to the king of Egypt. I have made him and his officers stubborn. I did this so I could show them my powerful miracles.[d] [2]I also did this so you could tell your children and your grandchildren. Tell them how I made fools of the Egyptians. Tell them about the miracles I did among them. Then all of you will know that I am the Lord."

[3]So Moses and Aaron went to the king. They told him, "This is what the Lord, the God of the Hebrews, says: 'How long will you refuse to be sorry for what you have done? Let my people go to worship me. [4]If you refuse to let my people go, tomorrow I will bring locusts[d] into your country. [5]They will cover the land, and no one will be able to see the ground. They will eat anything that was left from the hailstorm. They will eat the leaves from every tree growing in the field. [6]They will fill your palaces and all your officers' houses. They will fill the houses of all the Egyptian people. There will be more locusts than your fathers or ancestors have ever seen. There will be more locusts than there have been since people began living in Egypt.'" Then Moses turned and walked away from the king.

[7]The king's officers asked him, "How long will this man make trouble for us? Let the Israelite men go to worship the Lord their God. Don't you know that Egypt is ruined?"

[8]So Moses and Aaron were brought back to the king. He said to them, "Go and worship the Lord your God. But tell me, just who is going?"

[9]Moses answered, "We will go with our young and our old people, our sons and daughters and sheep and cattle. This is because we are going to have a feast to honor the Lord."

[10]The king said to them, "The Lord really will have to be with you if ever I let you and all of your children leave Egypt. See, you are planning something evil. [11]No! Only the men may go and worship the Lord. That is what you have been asking for." Then the king forced Moses and Aaron out of his palace.

[12]The Lord told Moses, "Raise your hand over the land of Egypt, and the locusts will come. They will spread all over the land of Egypt. They will eat all the plants that the hail did not destroy."

[13]So Moses raised his walking stick over the land of Egypt. And the Lord caused a strong wind to blow from the east. It blew across the land all that day and night. When morning came, the east wind had brought the locusts. [14]Swarms of locusts covered all the land of Egypt and settled everywhere. There were more locusts than ever before or after. [15]The locusts covered the whole land so that it was black. They ate everything that was left after the hail. They ate every plant in the field and all the fruit on the trees. Nothing green was left on any tree or plant anywhere in Egypt.

[16]The king quickly called for Moses and Aaron. He said, "I have sinned against the Lord your God and against you. [17]Now forgive my sin this time. Pray to the Lord your God. Ask him to stop this punishment that kills."

[18]Moses left the king and prayed to the Lord. [19]So the Lord changed the wind. He made a very strong wind to blow from the west. It blew the locusts away into the Red Sea.[d] Not one locust was left anywhere in Egypt. [20]But the Lord caused the king to be stubborn again. And he did not let the people of Israel go.

[21]Then the Lord told Moses, "Raise your hand toward the sky, and darkness will cover the land of Egypt. It will be so dark you will be able to feel it." [22]So Moses raised his hand toward the sky. Then total darkness was everywhere in Egypt for three days. [23]No one could see anyone else. And no one could go anywhere for three days. But the Israelites had light where they lived.

[24]Again the king of Egypt called for Moses. He said, "All of you may go and worship the Lord. You may take your women and children with you. But you must leave your sheep and cattle here."

[25]Moses said, "You must let us have animals to use as sacrifices and burnt offerings. We have to offer them to the Lord our God. [26]So we must take our animals with us. Not a hoof will be left behind. We have to use some of the animals to worship the Lord our God. We do not yet know exactly what we will need to worship the Lord. We will know when we get there."

[27]But the Lord made the king stubborn

again. So he refused to let them go.
²⁸Then he told Moses, "Get out of here!
Don't come here again! The next time
you see me, you will die."

²⁹Then Moses told the king, "I'll do
what you say. I will not come to see you
again."

11 Now the Lord had told Moses, "I
have one more way to punish the
king and the people of Egypt. After this,
the king will send all of you away from
Egypt. When he does, he will force you
to leave completely. ²Tell the men and
women of Israel to ask their neighbors
for things made of silver and gold." ³The
Lord had caused the Egyptians to respect the Israelites. The king's officers
and the Egyptian people already considered Moses to be a great man.

⁴So Moses said to the king, "This is
what the Lord says: 'About midnight tonight I will go through all Egypt. ⁵Every
firstborn[d] son in the land of Egypt will
die. The firstborn son of the king, who
sits on his throne, will die. Even the firstborn of the slave girl grinding grain will
die. Also the firstborn farm animals will
die. ⁶There will be loud crying everywhere in Egypt. It will be worse than
any time before or after this. ⁷But not
even a dog will bark at the Israelites or
their animals.' Then you will know that
the Lord treats Israel differently from
Egypt. ⁸Then all your officers will come
to me. They will bow facedown to the
ground before me. They will say, 'Leave
and take all your people with you.' After
that, I will leave." Then Moses very angrily left the king.

⁹The Lord had told Moses, "The king
will not listen to you and Aaron. This is
so that I may do many miracles[d] in the
land of Egypt." ¹⁰Moses and Aaron did
all these great miracles in front of the
king. But the Lord made him stubborn.
And the king would not let the people of
Israel leave his country.

12 The Lord spoke to Moses and
Aaron in the land of Egypt: ²"This
month will be the first month of the year
for you. ³Both of you are to tell the whole
community of Israel: On the tenth day
of this month each man must get one
lamb. It is for the people in his house.
⁴There may not be enough people in his
house to eat a whole lamb. Then he must
share it with his closest neighbor. There
must be enough lamb for everyone to
eat. ⁵The lamb must be a one-year-old
male. It must have nothing wrong with
it. This animal can be either a young

sheep or a young goat. ⁶Keep the animal
with you to take care of it until the fourteenth day of the month. On that day all
the people of the community of Israel
will kill these animals. They will do this
as soon as the sun goes down. ⁷The people must take some of the blood. They
must put it on the sides and tops of the
doorframes. These are the doorframes
of the houses where they eat the lambs.
⁸On this night they must roast the lamb
over a fire. Then they must eat it with
bitter herbs and bread made without
yeast. ⁹Do not eat the lamb raw or boiled
in water. Roast the whole lamb over a
fire—with its head, legs and inner organs. ¹⁰You must not leave any of it until
morning. But if any of it is left over until
morning, you must burn it with fire.

¹¹"This is the way you must eat it: You
must be fully dressed as if you were going on a trip. You must have your sandals on, and you must have your
walking stick in your hand. You must
eat it in a hurry. This is the Lord's Passover.[d]

¹²"That night I will go through the
land of Egypt. I will kill all the firstborn[d]
of animals and people in the land of
Egypt. I will punish all the gods of
Egypt. I am the Lord. ¹³But the blood
will be a sign on the houses where you
are. When I see the blood, I will pass
over you. Nothing terrible will hurt you
when I punish the land of Egypt.

¹⁴"You are always to remember this
day. Celebrate it with a feast to the Lord.
Your descendants[d] are to honor the Lord
with this feast from now on. ¹⁵For this
feast you must eat bread made without
yeast for seven days. On the first day of
this feast, you are to remove all the yeast
from your houses. No one should eat
any yeast for the full seven days of the
feast. If anyone eats yeast, then that person will be separated from Israel. ¹⁶You
are to have holy meetings on the first
and last days of the feast. You must not
do any work on these days. The only
work you may do on these days is to
prepare your meals. ¹⁷You must celebrate the Feast[d] of Unleavened Bread.
Do this because on this very day I
brought your divisions of people out of
Egypt. So all of your descendants must
celebrate this day. This is a law that will
last from now on. ¹⁸You are to eat bread
made without yeast. Start this on the
evening of the fourteenth day of the first
month of your year. Eat this until the
evening of the twenty-first day. ¹⁹For

seven days there must not be any yeast in your houses. Anybody who eats yeast during this time must be separated from the community of Israel. This includes Israelites and non-Israelites. ²⁰During this feast you must not eat yeast. You must eat bread made without yeast wherever you live."

²¹Then Moses called all the older leaders of Israel together. He told them, "Get the animals for your families. Kill the animals for the Passover. ²²Take a branch of the hyssop plant and dip it into the bowl filled with blood. Wipe the blood on the sides and tops of the doorframes. No one may leave his house until morning. ²³The Lord will go through Egypt to kill the Egyptians. He will see the blood on the sides and tops of the doorframes. Then the Lord will pass over that house. He will not let the one who brings death come into your houses and kill you.

²⁴"You must keep this command. This law is for you and your descendants from now on. ²⁵Do this when you go to the land the Lord has promised to give to you. ²⁶When your children ask you, 'Why are we doing these things?' ²⁷you will say, 'This is the Passover sacrifice to honor the Lord. When we were in Egypt, the Lord passed over the houses of Israel. The Lord killed the Egyptians, but he saved our homes.'" So now the people bowed down and worshiped the Lord. ²⁸They did just as the Lord commanded Moses and Aaron.

²⁹At midnight the Lord killed all the firstborn sons in the land of Egypt. The firstborn of the king, who sat on the throne, died. Even the firstborn of the prisoner in jail died. Also all the firstborn farm animals died. ³⁰The king, his officers and all the Egyptians got up during the night. Someone had died in every house. So there was loud crying everywhere in Egypt.

³¹During the night the king called for Moses and Aaron. He said to them, "Get up and leave my people. You and your people may do as you have asked. Go and worship the Lord. ³²Take all of your sheep and cattle as you have asked. Go. And also bless me." ³³The Egyptians also asked the Israelites to hurry and leave. They said, "If you don't leave, we will all die!"

³⁴The people of Israel took their dough before the yeast was added. They wrapped the bowls for making dough in clothing and carried them on their shoulders. ³⁵The people of Israel did what Moses told them to do. They asked their Egyptian neighbors for things made of silver and gold and for clothing. ³⁶The Lord caused the Egyptians to think well of the Israelites. So the Israelites took rich gifts from the Egyptians.

³⁷The Israelites traveled from Rameses to Succoth. There were about 600,000 men walking. This does not include the women and children. ³⁸Many other people who were not Israelites went with them. A large number of sheep, goats and cattle went with them. ³⁹The Israelites used the dough they had brought out of Egypt. They baked loaves of bread without yeast. The dough had no yeast in it because they had been rushed out of Egypt. So they had no time to get food ready for their trip.

⁴⁰The people of Israel had lived in Egypt for 430 years. ⁴¹On the day the 430 years ended, the Lord's divisions of people left Egypt. ⁴²That night the Lord kept watch to bring them out of Egypt. So on this same night the Israelites are to keep watch. They are to do this to honor the Lord from now on.

⁴³The Lord told Moses and Aaron, "Here are the rules for Passover:ᵈ No foreigner is to eat the Passover. ⁴⁴Suppose a person buys a slave and circumcisesᵈ him. Then the slave may eat the Passover. ⁴⁵But no one who lives for a short time in your country may eat it. No hired worker may eat it.

⁴⁶"The meal must be eaten inside the house. None of the meat is to be taken outside the house. Don't break any of the bones. ⁴⁷The whole community of Israel must take part in this feast. ⁴⁸A foreigner who lives with you may share in the Lord's Passover. But first all the males in his house must be circumcised. Then, since he will be like a citizen of Israel, he may share in the meal. But a man who is not circumcised may not eat the Passover meal. ⁴⁹The same rules apply to an Israelite born in the country. And they apply to a foreigner living there."

⁵⁰So all the Israelites did just as the Lord had commanded Moses and Aaron. ⁵¹Then on that same day, the Lord led the Israelites out of Egypt. The people left by divisions.

13 Then the Lord said to Moses, ²"Give every firstbornᵈ male to me. Every firstborn male among the Israelites belongs to me, whether human or animal."

³Moses said to the people, "Remember this day, the day you left Egypt. You were slaves in that land. The Lord with his great power brought you out of it. You must not eat bread made with yeast. ⁴Today, in the month of Abib,ᵈ you are leaving Egypt. ⁵The Lord made a promise to your ancestors. The Lord promised to give you the land of these people: the Canaanites, Hittites, Amorites, Hivites and Jebusites. The Lord will lead you to this land where much food grows. There you must celebrate this feast during the first month of every year. ⁶For seven days you must eat bread made without yeast. On the seventh day there will be a feast to honor the Lord. ⁷So for seven days you must not eat any bread made with yeast. There must be no bread made with yeast anywhere in your land. ⁸On that day you should tell your son: 'We are having this feast because of what the Lord did for me when I came out of Egypt.' ⁹This feast will help you remember. It will be like a mark on your hand. It will be like a reminder on your forehead. This feast will remind you to speak the Lord's teachings. This is because the Lord used his great power to bring you out of Egypt. ¹⁰So celebrate this feast every year at the right time.

¹¹"The Lord will take you into the land of the Canaanites. He promised to give this land to you and your ancestors. ¹²Then you must give him every firstborn male. And every firstborn male animal must be given to the Lord. ¹³Buy back every firstborn donkey by offering a lamb. If you don't want to buy the donkey back, then break its neck. You must buy back from the Lord every firstborn of your sons.

¹⁴"From now on your son will ask you: 'What does this mean?' You will answer, 'With his great power, the Lord brought us out of Egypt. We were slaves in that land. ¹⁵In Egypt the king was stubborn. He refused to let us leave. But the Lord killed every firstborn male in Egypt, both human and animal. That is why I sacrifice every firstborn male animal to the Lord. And that is why I buy back each of my firstborn sons from the Lord.' ¹⁶This feast is like a mark on your hand. And it is like a reminder on your forehead. It will help you remember that the Lord brought us out of Egypt with his great power."

¹⁷The king sent the people out of Egypt. God did not lead them on the road through the Philistine country. That

road is the shortest way. But God said, "They might think they will have to fight. Then they might change their minds and go back to Egypt." ¹⁸So God led them through the desert toward the Red Sea.ᵈ The Israelites were dressed for fighting when they left the land of Egypt.

¹⁹Moses carried the bones of Joseph with him. Before Joseph died, he had made the sons of Israel promise to do this. He had said, "When God saves you, remember to carry my bones with you out of Egypt."

²⁰The people of Israel left Succoth and camped at Etham. Etham was on the edge of the desert. ²¹The Lord showed them the way. During the day he went ahead of them in a pillar of cloud. And during the night the Lord was in a pillar of fire to give them light. They could travel during the day or night. ²²The pillar of cloud was always with them during the day. And the pillar of fire was always with them at night.

14 Then the Lord said to Moses, ²"Tell the Israelites to turn back to Pi Hahiroth. Tell them to camp for the night between Migdol and the Red Sea. This is near Baal Zephon. ³The king will think, 'The Israelites are lost, trapped by the desert.' ⁴I will make the king stubborn again so he will chase after them. But I will defeat the king and his army. This will bring honor to me. Then the people of Egypt will know that I am the Lord." The people of Israel did just as they were told.

⁵The king of Egypt was told that the people of Israel had already left. Then he and his officers changed their minds about them. They said, "What have we done? We have let the people of Israel leave. We have lost our slaves!" ⁶So the king prepared his war chariot and took his army with him. ⁷He took 600 of his best chariots. He also took all the other chariots of Egypt. Each chariot had an officer in it. ⁸The Lord made the king of Egypt stubborn. So he chased the Israelites, who were leaving victoriously. ⁹The king of Egypt came with his horses, chariot drivers and army. And they chased the Israelites. They caught up with the Israelites while they were camped by the Red Sea.ᵈ This was near Pi Hahiroth and Baal Zephon.

¹⁰The Israelites saw the king and his army coming after them. They were very frightened and cried to the Lord for help. ¹¹They said to Moses, "What have

you done to us? Why did you bring us out of Egypt to die in the desert? There were plenty of graves for us in Egypt. ¹²We told you in Egypt, 'Let us alone! Let us stay and serve the Egyptians.' Now we will die in the desert."

¹³But Moses answered, "Don't be afraid! Stand still and see the Lord save you today. You will never see these Egyptians again after today. ¹⁴You will only need to remain calm. The Lord will fight for you."

¹⁵Then the Lord said to Moses, "Why are you crying out to me? Command the people of Israel to start moving. ¹⁶Raise your walking stick and hold it over the sea. The sea will split. Then the people can cross the sea on dry land. ¹⁷I have made the Egyptians stubborn so they will chase the Israelites. But I will be honored when I defeat the king and all of his chariot drivers and chariots. ¹⁸I will defeat the king, his chariot drivers and chariots. Then Egypt will know that I am the Lord."

¹⁹The angel of God usually traveled in front of Israel's army. Now the angel of God moved behind them. Also, the pillar of cloud moved from in front of the people and stood behind them. ²⁰So the cloud came between the Egyptians and the people of Israel. The cloud made it dark for the Egyptians. But it gave light to the Israelites. So the cloud kept the two armies apart all night.

²¹Moses held his hand over the sea. All that night the Lord drove back the sea with a strong east wind. And so he made the sea become dry ground. The water was split. ²²And the Israelites went through the sea on dry land. A wall of water was on both sides.

²³Then all the king's horses, chariots and chariot drivers followed them into the sea. ²⁴Between two and six o'clock in the morning, the Lord looked down from the pillar of cloud and fire at the Egyptian army. He made them panic. ²⁵He kept the wheels of the chariots from turning. This made it hard to drive the chariots. The Egyptians shouted, "Let's get away from the Israelites! The Lord is fighting for them and against us Egyptians."

²⁶Then the Lord told Moses, "Hold your hand over the sea. Then the water will come back over the Egyptians, their chariots and chariot drivers." ²⁷So Moses raised his hand over the sea. And at dawn the water became deep again. The Egyptians were trying to run from it. But

the Lord swept them away into the sea. ²⁸The water became deep again. It covered the chariots and chariot drivers. So all the king's army that had followed the Israelites into the sea was covered. Not one of them survived.

²⁹But the people of Israel crossed the sea on dry land. There was a wall of water on their right and on their left. ³⁰So that day the Lord saved the Israelites from the Egyptians. And the Israelites saw the Egyptians lying dead on the seashore. ³¹When the people of Israel saw the great power that the Lord had used against the Egyptians, they feared the Lord. And they trusted the Lord and his servant Moses.

15 Then Moses and the Israelites sang this song to the Lord:

"I will sing to the Lord
    because he is worthy of great
        honor.
He has thrown the horse and its
        rider
    into the sea.
²The Lord gives me strength and
        makes me sing.
    He has saved me.
He is my God,
    and I will praise him.
He is the God of my fathers,
    and I will honor him.
³The Lord is a great warrior.
    The Lord is his name.
⁴The chariots and soldiers of the
        king of Egypt
    he has thrown into the sea.
The king's best officers
    are drowned in the Red Sea.ᵈ
⁵The deep waters covered them.
    They sank to the bottom like a
        rock.
⁶Your right hand, Lord,
    is amazingly strong.
Lord, your right hand
    broke the enemy into pieces.
⁷In your great victory
    you destroyed those who were
        against you.
Your anger destroyed them,
    like fire burning straw.
⁸Just a blast of your breath,
    and the waters were blown back.
The moving water stood up like a
        wall.
    And the deep waters became
        solid in the middle of the sea.

⁹"The enemy bragged,
    'I'll chase them and catch them.
I'll take all their riches.

I'll take all I want.
I'll pull out my sword,
　and my hand will destroy them.'
[10]But you blew on them with your
　breath
　and covered them with the sea.
They sank like lead
　in the powerful water.

[11]"Are there any gods like you, Lord?
　No! There are no gods like you.
You are wonderfully holy.
You are amazingly powerful.
You do great miracles.d
[12]You reached out with your right
　hand,
　and the earth swallowed our
　enemies.
[13]You keep your loving promise.
　You lead the people you have
　saved.
With your strength you will guide
　them
　to your holy land.

[14]"The other nations will hear this
　and tremble with fear.
Terror will take hold of the
　Philistines.
[15]The leaders of the tribesd of Edom
　will be very frightened.
The powerful men of Moab will
　shake with fear.
The people of Canaan will lose all
　their courage.
[16]Those people will be filled with
　fear.
When they see your strength,
　they will be as still as a rock.
They will be still until your people
　pass by, Lord.
They will be still until the people
　you have bought from slavery
　pass by.
[17]You will lead your people and place
　them
　on your very own mountain.
Lord, that is the place that you
　made for yourself to live.
Lord, that is the temple that your
　hands have made.
[18]The Lord will rule forever!"

[19]The horses, chariot drivers and
chariots of the king of Egypt went into
the sea. And the Lord covered them with
water from the sea. But the Israelites
walked through the sea on dry land.
[20]Then Aaron's sister Miriam, who was
a prophetess,d took a tambourined in her
hand. All the women followed her, play-

ing tambourines and dancing. [21]Miriam
told them:

　"Sing to the Lord
　　because he is worthy of great
　　honor.
　He has thrown the horse and its
　　rider
　　into the sea."

[22]Moses led the people of Israel away
from the Red Sea.d The people went into
the Desert of Shur. They traveled for
three days in the desert but found no
water. [23]Then they came to Marah,
where there was water. But they could
not drink it because it was too bitter.
That is why the place was named Ma-
rah.n [24]The people grumbled to Moses.
They asked, "What will we drink?"
[25]Moses cried out to the Lord. So the
Lord showed him a tree. Moses threw
the tree into the water. And the water
became good to drink.

There the Lord gave the people a rule
and a law to live by. There he also tested
their loyalty to him. [26]He said, "You
must obey the Lord, your God. You must
do what the Lord said is right. You must
obey all his laws and keep his rules. If
you do these things, I will not give you
any of the sicknesses I gave the Egyptians. I am the Lord. I am the Lord who
heals you."

[27]Then the people traveled to Elim. At
Elim there were 12 springs of water and
70 palm trees. So the people camped
there near the water.

16 Then the whole Israelite community left Elim. They came to the
Desert of Sin. This place was between
Elim and Sinai. They came to this place
on the fifteenth day of the second month
after they had left Egypt. [2]Then the
whole Israelite community grumbled to
Moses and Aaron in the desert. [3]The Israelites said to them, "It would have
been better if the Lord had killed us in
the land of Egypt. There we had meat to
eat. We had all the food we wanted. But
you have brought us into this desert. You
will starve us to death here."

[4]Then the Lord said to Moses, "I will
cause food to fall like rain from the sky.
This food will be for all of you. Every
day the people must go out and gather
what they need for that day. I will do
this to see if the people will do what I
teach them. [5]On the sixth day of each
week, they are to gather twice as much

15:23 Marah This name means "bitter."

as they gather on other days. Then they are to prepare it."

⁶So Moses and Aaron said to all the Israelites: "This evening you will know that the Lord is the one who brought you out of Egypt. ⁷Tomorrow morning you will see the greatness of the Lord. He has heard you grumble against him. We are nothing. You are not grumbling against us, but against the Lord." ⁸And Moses said, "Each evening the Lord will give you meat to eat. And every morning he will give you all the bread you want. He will do this because he has heard you grumble against him. You are not grumbling against Aaron and me. You are grumbling against the Lord."

⁹Then Moses said to Aaron, "Speak to the whole community of the Israelites. Say to them, 'Meet together in front of the Lord because he has heard your grumblings.'"

¹⁰So Aaron spoke to the whole community of the Israelites. While he was speaking, they looked toward the desert. There the greatness of the Lord appeared in a cloud.

¹¹The Lord said to Moses, ¹²"I have heard the grumblings of the people of Israel. So tell them, 'At twilight you will eat meat. And every morning you will eat all the bread you want. Then you will know I am the Lord, your God.'"

¹³That evening, quail came and covered the camp. And in the morning dew lay around the camp. ¹⁴When the dew was gone, thin flakes like frost were on the desert ground. ¹⁵When the Israelites saw it, they asked each other, "What is that?" They asked this question because they did not know what it was.

So Moses told them, "This is the bread the Lord has given you to eat. ¹⁶The Lord has commanded, 'Each one of you must gather what he needs. Gather about two quarts for every person in your family.'"

¹⁷So the people of Israel did this. Some people gathered much, and some gathered little. ¹⁸Then they measured it. The person who gathered more did not have too much. The person who gathered less did not have too little. Each person gathered just as much as he needed.

¹⁹Moses said to them, "Don't keep any of it to eat the next day." ²⁰But some of the people did not listen to Moses. They kept part of it to eat the next morning. But it became full of worms and began to stink. So Moses was angry with these people.

²¹Every morning each person gath-

ered as much food as he needed. But when the sun became hot, it melted away.

²²On the sixth day the people gathered twice as much food. They gathered four quarts for every person. So all the leaders of the community came and told this to Moses. ²³Moses said to them, "This is what the Lord commanded. Tomorrow is the Sabbath,ᵈ the Lord's holy day of rest. Bake what you want to bake, and boil what you want to boil today. But save the rest of the food until tomorrow morning."

²⁴So the people saved it until the next morning, as Moses had commanded. And none of it began to stink or have worms in it. ²⁵Moses told the people, "Eat the food you gathered yesterday. Today is a Sabbath, the Lord's day of rest. So you will not find any out in the field today. ²⁶You should gather the food for six days. But the seventh day is a Sabbath day. On that day there will not be any food on the ground."

²⁷On the seventh day some of the people went out to gather food, but they couldn't find any. ²⁸Then the Lord said to Moses, "How long will all you people refuse to obey my commands and teachings? ²⁹Look, the Lord has made the Sabbath a day of rest for all of you. So on the sixth day he will give you enough food for two days. But on the Sabbath each of you must stay where you are. Do not leave your house." ³⁰So the people rested on the Sabbath.

³¹The people of Israel called the food manna.ᵈ The manna was like small white seeds. It tasted like wafers made with honey.

³²Then Moses said, "The Lord said, 'Save two quarts of this food for your descendants.ᵈ Then they can see the food that I gave you to eat. I did this in the desert when I brought you out of Egypt.'"

³³Moses told Aaron, "Take a jar and fill it with two quarts of manna. And save this manna for your descendants." ³⁴So Aaron did what the Lord had commanded Moses. Aaron put the jar of manna in front of the Boxᵈ of the Agreement. He did this so it could be kept. ³⁵The Israelites ate manna for 40 years. They ate it until they came to the land where they settled. They ate manna until they came to the edge of the land of

Canaan. [36]The measure they used for the manna was two quarts. It was one-tenth of an ephah.[n]

17 The whole Israelite community left the Desert of Sin. They traveled from place to place as the Lord commanded. They camped at Rephidim. But there was no water there for the people to drink. [2]So they quarreled with Moses. They said, "Give us water to drink."

But Moses said to them, "Why do you quarrel with me? Why are you testing the Lord?"

[3]But the people were very thirsty for water. So they grumbled against Moses. They said, "Why did you bring us out of Egypt? Was it to kill us, our children and our farm animals with thirst?"

[4]So Moses cried to the Lord, "What can I do with these people? They are almost ready to kill me with stones."

[5]The Lord said to Moses, "Go ahead of the people of Israel. And take some of the older leaders of Israel with you. Carry with you the walking stick that you used to strike the Nile River. Now go! [6]I will stand in front of you on a rock at Mount Sinai. Hit that rock with the stick, and water will come out of it. Then the people can drink." Moses did these things as the older leaders of Israel watched. [7]Moses named that place Massah[n] because the Israelites tested the Lord. They asked, "Is the Lord with us or not?" He also named it Meribah[n] because they quarreled.

[8]At Rephidim the Amalekites came and fought the Israelites. [9]So Moses said to Joshua, "Choose some men and go and fight the Amalekites. Tomorrow I will stand on the top of the hill. I will hold the stick God gave me to carry."

[10]Joshua obeyed Moses and went to fight the Amalekites. At the same time Moses, Aaron and Hur went to the top of the hill. [11]As long as Moses held his hands up, the Israelites would win the fight. But when Moses put his hands down, the Amalekites would win. [12]Later, Moses' arms became tired. So the men put a large rock under Moses, and he sat on it. Then Aaron and Hur held up Moses' hands. Aaron was on one side of Moses, and Hur was on the other side. They held his hands up like

this until the sun went down. [13]So Joshua defeated the Amalekites in this battle.

[14]Then the Lord said to Moses, "Write about this battle in a book so people will remember. And be sure to tell Joshua. Tell him because I will completely destroy the Amalekites from the earth."

[15]Then Moses built an altar. He named it The Lord is my Banner. [16]Moses said, "I lifted my hands toward the Lord's throne. The Lord will fight against the Amalekites forever."

18 Jethro, Moses' father-in-law, was the priest of Midian. He heard about everything that God had done for Moses and his people, the Israelites. Jethro heard how the Lord had led the Israelites out of Egypt. [2]Moses had sent his wife Zipporah to Jethro, his father-in-law. [3]Moses had also sent his two sons. The first son was named Gershom.[n] When he was born, Moses said, "I am a stranger in a foreign country." [4]The other son was named Eliezer.[n] When he was born, Moses said, "The God of my father is my help. He saved me from the king of Egypt."

[5]So Jethro, Moses' father-in-law, went to Moses. Moses was camped in the desert near Sinai, the mountain of God. Moses' wife and his two sons came with Jethro. [6]Jethro had sent a message ahead to Moses. He said, "I am Jethro, your father-in-law. I am coming to you with your wife and her two sons."

[7]So Moses went out to meet his father-in-law. Moses bowed down and then kissed him. The two men asked about each other's health. Then they went into Moses' tent. [8]Moses told his father-in-law everything the Lord had done to the king and the Egyptians. The Lord had done these things to help Israel. Moses told about all the problems they had faced along the way. And Moses told him how the Lord had saved them.

[9]Jethro was very happy when he heard all the good things the Lord had done for Israel. He was happy because the Lord had saved them from the Egyptians. [10]Jethro said, "Praise the Lord. He has saved all of you from the Egyptians and their king. He has saved the people from the power of the Egyptians. [11]Now I know the Lord is greater than all gods.

16:36 ephah An ephah was a measure that equaled 20 quarts.   **17:7 Massah** This name sounds like the Hebrew word for "testing."   **17:7 Meribah** This name sounds like the Hebrew word for "quarreled."   **18:3 Gershom** This name sounds like the Hebrew word for "a stranger there."   **18:4 Eliezer** This name sounds like the Hebrew word for "my help."

He did this to those who looked down on Israel." [12]Then Jethro, Moses' father-in-law, gave a whole burnt offering and other sacrifices to God. Aaron and all the older leaders of Israel came to Moses' father-in-law. They ate the holy meal together before God.

[13]The next day Moses solved disagreements among the people. So the people stood around Moses from morning until night. [14]Moses' father-in-law saw all that Moses was doing for the people. He asked, "What is all this you are doing for the people? Why are you the only one to solve disagreements? All the people are standing around you from morning until night!"

[15]Then Moses said to his father-in-law, "It is because the people come to me for God's help in solving their disagreements. [16]When people have a disagreement, they come to me. I decide who is right. And I tell them God's laws and teachings."

[17]Moses' father-in-law said to him, "You are not doing this right. [18]You and the people who come to you will get too tired. This is too much work for you. You can't do it by yourself. [19]Now listen to me. I will give you some advice. I want God to be with you. You must talk to God for the people. You must tell him about their disagreements. [20]You should tell them the laws and teachings. Tell them the right way to live and what they should do. [21]But choose some capable men from among the people. Choose men who respect God and who can be trusted. They will not change their decisions for money. Make these men officers over groups of 1,000, 100, 50 and 10 people. [22]Let these officers solve the disagreements among the people all the time. They can bring the hard cases to you. But they can decide the simple cases themselves. That will make it easier for you. These men will share the work with you. [23]Do this if it is what God commands. Then you will be able to do your job. And all the people will go home with their disagreements solved."

[24]So Moses listened to his father-in-law and did everything he said. [25]He chose capable men from all the Israelites. He made them leaders over the people. They were officers over groups of 1,000, 100, 50 and 10 people. [26]These officers solved disagreements among the people all the time. They brought the hard cases to Moses. But they decided the simple cases themselves.

[27]Then Moses let his father-in-law leave. And Jethro went back to his own home.

19 Exactly three months after the Israelites had left Egypt, they reached the Desert of Sinai. [2]They had left Rephidim and had come to the Desert of Sinai. The Israelites camped in the desert in front of Mount Sinai. [3]Then Moses went up on the mountain to God. The Lord called to him from the mountain. The Lord said, "Say this to the family of Jacob. And tell this to the people of Israel: [4]'Every one of you has seen what I did to the people of Egypt. You saw how I carried you out of Egypt. I did it as an eagle carries her young on her wings. And I brought you here to me. [5]So now obey me and keep my agreement. Do this, and you will be my own possession, chosen from all nations. Even though the whole earth is mine, [6]you will be my kingdom of priests. You will be a nation that belongs to me alone.' You must tell the Israelites these words."

[7]So Moses went down and called the older leaders of the people together. He told them all the words the Lord had commanded him to say. [8]And all the people answered together, "We will do everything he has said." Then Moses took their answer back to the Lord.

[9]And the Lord said to Moses, "I will come to you in a thick cloud. I will speak to you. The people will hear me talking to you. I will do this so the people will always trust you." Then Moses told the Lord what the people had said.

[10]The Lord said to Moses, "Go to the people and have them spend today and tomorrow preparing themselves. They must wash their clothes [11]and be ready by the day after tomorrow. On that day I, the Lord, will come down on Mount Sinai. And all the people will see me. [12]But you must set a limit around the mountain. The people are not to cross it. Tell the people not to go up on the mountain. Tell them not to touch the foot of it. Anyone who touches the mountain must be put to death. [13]He must be put to death with stones or shot with arrows. No one is allowed to touch him. Whether it is a person or an animal, he will not live. But the trumpet will make a long blast. Only then may the people go up on the mountain."

[14]So Moses went down from the mountain to the people. He made them prepare themselves for service to God.

And the people washed their clothes. ¹⁵Then Moses said to the people, "Be ready in three days. Do not have sexual relations during this time."

¹⁶It was the morning of the third day. There was thunder and lightning with a thick cloud on the mountain. And there was a very loud blast from a trumpet. All the people in the camp were frightened. ¹⁷Then Moses led the people out of the camp to meet God. They stood at the foot of the mountain. ¹⁸Mount Sinai was covered with smoke. This happened because the Lord came down on it in fire. The smoke rose from the mountain like smoke from a furnace. And the whole mountain shook wildly. ¹⁹The sound from the trumpet became louder. Then Moses spoke, and the voice of God answered him.

²⁰So the Lord came down on the top of Mount Sinai. Then he called Moses to come up to the top of the mountain. So Moses went up. ²¹The Lord said to Moses, "Go down and warn the people. They must not force their way through to see me. If they do, many of them will die. ²²Even the priests, who may come near me, must first prepare themselves. If they don't, I, the Lord, will punish them."

²³Moses told the Lord, "The people cannot come up Mount Sinai. You yourself told us to set a limit around the mountain. We made it holy."

²⁴The Lord said to him, "Go down and bring Aaron with you. But don't allow the priests or the people to force their way through. They must not come up to the Lord. If they do, I will punish them."

²⁵So Moses went down to the people and told them these things.

20 Then God spoke all these words: ²"I am the Lord your God. I brought you out of the land of Egypt where you were slaves.

³"You must not have any other gods except me.

⁴"You must not make for yourselves any idols. Don't make something that looks like anything in the sky above or on the earth below or in the water below the land. ⁵You must not worship or serve any idol. This is because I, the Lord your God, am a jealous God. A person may sin against me and hate me. I will punish his children, even his grandchildren and great-grandchildren. ⁶But I will be very kind to thousands who love me and obey my commands.

⁷"You must not use the name of the Lord your God thoughtlessly. The Lord will punish anyone who is guilty and misuses his name.

⁸"Remember to keep the Sabbath^d as a holy day. ⁹You may work and get everything done during six days each week. ¹⁰But the seventh day is a day of rest to honor the Lord your God. On that day no one may do any work: not you, your son or daughter, or your men or women slaves. Neither your animals nor the foreigners living in your cities may work. ¹¹The reason is that in six days the Lord made everything. He made the sky, earth, sea and everything in them. And on the seventh day, he rested. So the Lord blessed the Sabbath day and made it holy.

¹²"Honor your father and your mother. Then you will live a long time in the land. The Lord your God is going to give you this land.

¹³"You must not murder anyone.

¹⁴"You must not be guilty of adultery.^d

¹⁵"You must not steal.

¹⁶"You must not tell lies about your neighbor in court.

¹⁷"You must not want to take your neighbor's house. You must not want his wife or his men or women slaves. You must not want his ox or his donkey. You must not want to take anything that belongs to your neighbor."

¹⁸The people heard the thunder and the trumpet. They saw the lightning on the mountain and smoke rising from the mountain. They shook with fear and stood far away from the mountain. ¹⁹Then they said to Moses, "Speak to us yourself. Then we will listen. But don't let God speak to us, or we will die."

²⁰Then Moses said to the people, "Don't be afraid. God has come to test you. He wants you to respect him so you will not sin."

²¹The people stood far away from the mountain while Moses went near the dark cloud where God was. ²²Then the Lord told Moses to say these things to the Israelites: "You yourselves have seen that I talked with you from heaven. ²³You must not use gold or silver to make idols for yourselves. You must not worship these false gods in addition to me.

²⁴"Make an altar of dirt for me. Offer your whole burnt offerings and fellowship offerings on this altar as a sacrifice to me. Use your sheep and your cattle to do this. Worship me in every place that I choose. Then I will come and bless you. ²⁵You may use stones to make an altar

for me. But don't use stones that you have made smooth with tools. You must not use any tools on the stones. If you do, you make them unsuitable for use in worship. [26] And you must not make steps leading up to my altar. If you go up steps, people will be able to see under your clothes."

21 Then God said to Moses, "These are the laws for living that you will give to the Israelites:

[2] "If you buy a Hebrew slave, he will serve you for six years. In the seventh year you are to set him free. And he will have to pay nothing. [3] He might not be married when he becomes your slave. Then he must leave without a wife. The man might be married when he becomes your slave. Then he may take his wife with him. [4] The slave's master might give him a wife, and she might give birth to sons or daughters. Then the woman and her children will belong to the master. When the slave is set free, only he may leave.

[5] "But the slave might say, 'I love my master, my wife and my children. I don't want to go free.' [6] Then the slave's master will take him to God. The master will take him to a door or doorframe. And he will punch a hole through the slave's ear using a sharp tool. Then the slave will serve that master all his life.

[7] "A man might sell his daughter as a slave. There are rules for setting her free. They are different from the rules for setting the men slaves free. [8] Maybe the master wanted to marry her but then decided he was not pleased with her. He must let one of her close relatives buy her back. He has no right to sell her to foreigners. This is because he has treated her unfairly. [9] The man who bought her might promise to let the woman marry his son. Then he must treat her as a daughter. [10] The man who bought her might marry another woman. Then he must not keep his slave woman from having food or clothing or sexual relations. [11] If he does not give her these three things, she may go free. She owes him no money.

[12] "Anyone who hits a person and kills him must be put to death. [13] But if a person kills someone accidentally, God allowed that to happen. So the person must go to a place I will choose. [14] A person might plan and murder another person on purpose. Put him to death, even if he has run to my altar for safety.

[15] "Anyone who hits his father or his mother must be put to death.

[16] "A person might kidnap someone. Then he either sells him as a slave or still has him when he is caught. That person must be put to death.

[17] "Anyone who says cruel things to his father or mother must be put to death.

[18] "Two men might argue. And one might hit the other with a rock or with his fist. The hurt man might not be killed. But he might have to stay in bed. [19] Later he might be able to get up. And he might be able to walk around outside with his walking stick. The one who hit him is not to be punished. But he must pay the injured man for the loss of his time. And he must support the injured man until he is completely healed.

[20] "A man might beat his male or female slave with a stick. And the slave might die on the spot. Then the owner must be punished. [21] But the slave might get well after a day or two. Then that owner will not be punished since the slave belongs to him.

[22] "Two men might be fighting, and they might hit a pregnant woman so that the baby comes out. But there is no further injury. Then the man who caused the injury must pay money. He must pay what the woman's husband says and the court allows. [23] But if there is further injury, then the punishment is that life must be paid for life, [24] eye for eye, tooth for tooth. It is also hand for hand, foot for foot, [25] burn for burn, wound for wound and bruise for bruise.

[26] "A man might hit his male or female slave in the eye. And the eye might be blinded. Then the man is to free the slave to pay for the eye. [27] A master might knock out a tooth of his male or female slave. Then the man is to free the slave to pay for the tooth.

[28] "A man's bull might kill a man or woman. Then you must kill that bull with stones. You should not eat the bull. But the owner of the bull is not guilty. [29] But the bull might have hurt people in the past. The owner might have been warned. If he did not keep it in a pen and then it kills a man or woman, the bull must be killed with stones. And the owner must also be put to death. [30] But the family of the dead man might accept money. Then the man who owned the bull may buy back his life. But he must pay whatever is demanded. [31] Use this same law if the bull kills a

person's son or daughter. [32]But the bull might kill a male or female slave. Then the owner must pay the master the price for a new slave. That is 12 ounces of silver. And the bull must also be killed with stones.

[33]"A man might take the cover off a pit. Or he might dig one and not cover it. Another man's ox or donkey might come and fall into it. [34]The owner of the pit must pay the owner of the animal for his loss. The dead animal will belong to the one who pays.

[35]"One man's bull might kill another man's bull. Then they must sell the bull that is alive. Both men get half of the money. And both men will also get half of the bull that was killed. [36]A man's bull might have hurt other animals in the past. But the owner might not have kept it in a pen. Then that owner must pay bull for bull. And the dead animal is his.

22 "A man might steal a bull or a sheep and kill or sell it. Then he must pay back five bulls for the one bull he stole. Or he must pay back four sheep for the one sheep he stole.

[2-4]"The robber who is caught must pay back what he stole. He might own nothing. Then he must be sold as a slave to pay for what he stole. The stolen animal might be found alive with the robber. Then he must give the owner two animals for every animal he stole. He must pay, whether he stole a bull, donkey or sheep.

"A thief might be killed while breaking into a house at night. Then the one who killed him is not guilty of murder. But if this happens during the day, he is guilty of murder.

[5]"A person might let his farm animal graze in his field or vineyard. And it might wander into another person's field or vineyard. Then the owner of the animal must pay back the loss. The payment must come from the best of his crop.

[6]"A man might start a fire that spreads through the thornbushes to his neighbor's field. The fire might burn his neighbor's growing grain or grain that has been stacked. Or it might burn his whole field. Then the person who started the fire must pay for what was burned.

[7]"A man might give his neighbor money or other things to keep for him. Those things might be stolen from the neighbor's house. And the thief might be caught. Then he must pay back twice

as much as he stole. [8]But maybe the thief is never found. Then the owner of the house must make a promise before God. He must promise that he has not stolen his neighbor's things.

[9]"Two men might disagree about who owns something. It might be an ox, donkey, sheep or clothing. Or it might be something else that is lost. Each says, 'This is mine.' Each man must bring his case to God. God's judges will decide who is guilty. Then he must pay the other man twice as much as the thing is worth.

[10]"A man might ask his neighbor to keep his animal for him. This animal might be a donkey, ox, sheep or some other animal. And that animal might die, be hurt or be taken away. And no one saw what happened. [11]That neighbor must promise before the Lord that he did not harm or kill the other man's animal. The owner of the animal must accept his promise made before God. The neighbor does not have to pay the owner for the animal. [12]But the animal might have been stolen from the neighbor. Then he must pay the owner for it. [13]Wild animals might have killed the animal. Then the neighbor must bring the body as proof. He will not have to pay for the animal that was killed.

[14]"A man might borrow an animal from his neighbor. It might get hurt or die while the owner is not there. Then the one who borrowed it must pay the owner for the animal. [15]The owner might be with the animal. Then the one who borrowed it does not have to pay. If the animal was rented, the rental price covers the loss.

[16]"A man might find a woman who is not pledged to be married. She has never had sexual relations with a man. He might trick her into having sexual relations with him. Then he must give her family the payment to marry her. And she will be his wife. [17]But her father might refuse to allow his daughter to marry him. Then the man must still give the payment for a bride. He must pay the usual charge for a woman who has never had sexual relations.

[18]"Put to death any woman who does evil magic.

[19]"Put to death anyone who has sexual relations with an animal.

[20]"Destroy completely any person who makes a sacrifice to any god except the Lord.

[21]"Do not cheat or hurt a foreigner.

Remember that you were foreigners in the land of Egypt.

²²"Do not cheat a widow or an orphan. ²³If you do, they will cry out to me for help. I certainly will hear their cry. ²⁴And I will be very angry and kill you in war. Then your wives will become widows, and your children will become orphans.

²⁵"You might lend money to one of my people who is poor. Then do not treat him as a moneylender would. Charge him nothing for using your money. ²⁶Your neighbor might give you his coat as a promise. He is promising to pay you the money he owes you. But you must give it back to him by sunset. ²⁷That coat is the only cover to keep his body warm. He has nothing else to sleep in. If he cries out to me for help, I will listen because I am merciful.

²⁸"You must not speak against God. You must not curse a leader of your people.

²⁹"Do not hold back your offering from the first of your harvest. Give me the first grain that you harvest. Give me the first wine that you make. Also, you must give me your firstborn^d sons. ³⁰You must do the same with your bulls and your sheep. Let the firstborn males stay with their mothers for seven days. On the eighth day you must give them to me.

³¹"You are to be my holy people. You must not eat the meat of any animal that has been killed by wild animals. Instead, give it to the dogs.

23 "You must not tell lies. You might be a witness in court. Don't help a bad person by telling lies.

²"You must not do wrong just because everyone else is doing it. You might be a witness in court. Then you must not ruin a fair trial. You must not tell lies just because everyone else is. ³A poor man might be in court. You must not take his side just because he is poor.

⁴"You might see your enemy's ox or donkey wandering away. Then you must return it to him. ⁵You might see that your enemy's donkey has fallen because its load is too heavy. You must not leave it there. You must help your enemy get the donkey back on its feet.

⁶"You must not be unfair to a poor man when he is in court. ⁷You must not lie when you accuse someone in court. Never allow an innocent or honest person to be put to death as punishment.

This is because I will not treat guilty people as if they were innocent.

⁸"You must not accept money from a person who wants you to lie in court. Such money will not let you see what is right. Such money makes good people tell lies.

⁹"You must not mistreat a foreigner. You know how it feels to be a foreigner. You were foreigners in Egypt.

¹⁰"For six years you are to plant and harvest crops on your land. ¹¹Then during the seventh year, do not plow or plant your land. If any food grows there, allow the poor people to have it. And let the wild animals eat what is left. You should do the same with your vineyards and your orchards of olive trees.

¹²"You should work six days a week. But on the seventh day you must rest. This lets your ox and your donkey rest. This also lets the slave born in your house and the foreigner be refreshed.

¹³"Be sure to do all that I have said to you. You must not even say the names of other gods. The names of those gods must not come out of your mouth.

¹⁴"Three times each year you must hold a feast to honor me. ¹⁵You must celebrate the Feast^d of Unleavened Bread. Do this in the way I commanded you. For seven days you must eat bread that is made without yeast. You must do this at the set time during the month of Abib.^d This is the month when you came out of Egypt. No one is to come to worship me without bringing an offering.

¹⁶"You must celebrate the Feast^d of Harvest. Offer to God the first things you harvest. These are from the crops you planted in your fields.

"You must celebrate the Feast^d of Tents in the fall. Do this when you gather all the crops from your fields.

¹⁷"So three times during every year all men must come to worship the Lord God.

¹⁸"You must not offer animal blood along with anything that has yeast in it.

"You must not save any of the fat from the sacrifice for the next day.

¹⁹"You must bring the best of the firstfruits^d of your land. Bring them to the Holy Tentⁿ of the Lord your God.

"You must not cook a young goat in its mother's milk.

²⁰"I am sending an angel ahead of you. He will protect you as you travel. He will lead you to the place I have pre-

23:19 Holy Tent Literally, "house of the Lord your God." See Exodus 25:9.

pared. [21]Pay attention to the angel and obey him. Do not turn against him. He will not forgive such turning against him because my power is in him. [22]You must listen carefully to all he says. You must do everything that I tell you. If you do this, I will be an enemy to your enemies. I will fight all who fight against you. [23]My angel will go ahead of you. He will take you into the land of these people: the Amorites, Hittites, Perizzites, Canaanites, Hivites and Jebusites. And I will destroy them.

[24]"You must not bow down to their gods or worship those gods. You must not live the way those people live. You must destroy their idols. And you must break into pieces stone pillars they use in worship. [25]You must worship the Lord your God. If you do, I will bless your bread and your water. I will take away sickness from you. [26]None of your women will have her baby die before it is born. All women will have children. I will allow you to live long lives.

[27]"I will make your enemies afraid of me. I will confuse any people you fight against. I will make all your enemies run away from you. [28]I will send something like hornets ahead of you. They will force the Hivites, Canaanites and Hittites out of your way. [29]But I will not force all those people out in only one year. If I did, the land would become a desert. Then the wild animals would become too many for you. [30]Instead, I will force those people out of your land very slowly. I will wait until there are enough of you to take over the land. [31]"I will give you the land from the Gulf of Aqaba to the Mediterranean Sea. And I will give you the land between the desert and the Euphrates River. I will give you power over the people who now live in the land. You will force them out ahead of you. [32]You must not make an agreement with these people or with their gods. [33]You must not let them live in your land. If they live there, they will make you sin against me. If you worship their gods, you will be like someone caught in a trap."

24 The Lord told Moses, "You, Aaron, Nadab, Abihu and 70 of the older leaders of Israel must come up to me. You must worship me from a distance. [2]Then Moses alone must come near me. The other men must not come near. And the rest of the people must not come up the mountain with Moses."

[3]So Moses told the people all the Lord's words and laws for living. Then all of the people answered out loud together. They said, "We will do all the things that the Lord has said." [4]So Moses wrote down all the words of the Lord. And he got up early the next morning. He built an altar near the bottom of the mountain. He set up 12 stones, 1 stone for each of the 12 tribes[d] of Israel. [5]Then Moses sent young Israelite men to offer whole burnt offerings. They also sacrificed young bulls as fellowship offerings to the Lord. [6]Moses took the blood of these animals. He put half of it in bowls. And he sprinkled the other half of the blood on the altar. [7]Then Moses took the book with the agreement written in it. He read it so the people could hear him. And they said, "We will do everything that the Lord has said. We will obey."

[8]Then Moses took the blood from the bowls. He sprinkled it on the people. He said, "This is the blood that begins the agreement. This is the agreement which the Lord has made with you about all these things."

[9]Moses, Aaron, Nadab, Abihu and 70 of the older leaders of Israel went up the mountain. [10]They saw the God of Israel. Under his feet was a surface. It looked as if it were paved with blue sapphire stones. And it was as clear as the sky! [11]These leaders of the Israelites saw God. But God did not destroy them. Then they ate and drank together.

[12]The Lord said to Moses, "Come up the mountain to me. Wait there, and I will give you two stone tablets. On these are the teachings and the commandments. I have written these to teach the people."

[13]So Moses and his helper Joshua set out. Moses went up Sinai, the mountain of God. [14]Moses said to the older leaders, "Wait here for us until we come back to you. Aaron and Hur are with you. Anyone who has a disagreement with others can take it to them."

[15]When Moses went up on the mountain, the cloud covered it. [16]The greatness of the Lord came down on Mount Sinai. The cloud covered the mountain for six days. On the seventh day the Lord called to Moses from inside the cloud. [17]The Israelites could see the greatness of the Lord. It looked like a fire burning on top of the mountain. [18]Then Moses went into the cloud and went higher up the mountain. Moses was on the mountain for 40 days and 40 nights.

25 The Lord said to Moses, [2]"Tell the Israelites to bring me gifts. Receive for me the gifts each man wants to give. [3]These are the gifts that you should receive from them: gold, silver, bronze, [4]blue, purple and red thread, and fine linen. Receive cloth made of goat hair. [5]Receive the male sheep skins that are dyed red. Receive fine leather, acacia wood [6]and olive oil to burn in the lamps. And receive spices for sweet-smelling incense[d] and the special olive oil poured on a person's head to make him a priest. [7]Also accept onyx stones and other jewels to be put on the holy vest[d] and the chest covering.

[8]"The people must build a holy place for me. Then I can live among them. [9]Build this Holy Tent[d] and everything in it by the plan I will show you.

[10]"Use acacia wood and build a Holy Box.[d] It must be 45 inches long, 27 inches wide and 27 inches high. [11]Cover the Holy Box inside and out with pure gold. And put a gold strip all around it. [12]Make four gold rings for the Holy Box. Attach the gold rings to its four feet, two rings on each side. [13]Then make poles from acacia wood and cover them with gold. [14]Put the poles through the rings on the sides of the Box. Use these poles to carry the Holy Box. [15]These poles must always stay in the rings of the Holy Box. Do not take the poles out. [16]Then put the two flat stones in the Holy Box. I will give you these stones on which the commands are written.

[17]"Then make a lid of pure gold for the Holy Box. This lid is the mercy seat.[d] Make it 45 inches long and 27 inches wide. [18]Then hammer gold to make two creatures with wings. Put one on each end of the lid. [19]Put one creature with wings on one end of the lid. And put the other creature with wings on the other end. Attach the creatures with wings to the lid so that they will all be one piece. [20]The creatures' wings should be spread out over the lid. The creatures are to face each other across the lid. [21]Put this lid on top of the Holy Box. Also put in this Holy Box the agreement which I will make with you. [22]I will meet with you there, above the lid between the two creatures with wings. These are on the Box of the Agreement. There I will give you all my commands for the Israelites.

[23]"Make a table out of acacia wood. It must be 36 inches long, 18 inches wide and 27 inches high. [24]Cover it with pure gold. Put a gold strip around it. [25]Then make a frame three inches high that stands up all around the edge. Put a gold strip around the frame. [26]Then make four gold rings. Attach them to the four corners of the table where the four legs are. [27]Put the rings close to the frame around the top of the table. These rings will hold the poles for carrying the table. [28]Make the poles out of acacia wood and cover them with gold. Carry the table with these poles. [29]Make the plates and bowls for the table out of pure gold. Make the jars and cups out of pure gold. They will be used for pouring out the drink offerings. [30]On this table put the bread that shows you are in my presence. It must always be there in front of me.

[31]"Hammer pure gold to make a lampstand. Its base, stand, flower-like cups, buds and petals must all be joined together in one piece. [32]The lampstand must have three branches on one side and three branches on the other. [33]Each branch must have three cups shaped like almond flowers on it. Each cup must have a bud and a petal. [34]And there must be four more cups made like almond flowers on the lampstand itself. These cups must also have buds and petals. [35]Put a bud under each pair of branches that goes out from the lampstand. [36]The branches, buds and lampstand must be one piece of pure, hammered gold. [37]Then make seven small oil lamps and put them on the lampstand. They will give light to the area in front of the lampstand. [38]The wick trimmers and trays must be made of pure gold. [39]Use 75 pounds of pure gold to make the lampstand and everything with it. [40]Be very careful to make them by the plan I showed you on the mountain.

26 "Make the Holy Tent[d] with ten pieces of cloth. These pieces must be made of fine linen and blue, purple and red thread. Have a skilled craftsman sew designs of creatures with wings on the pieces of cloth. [2]Make each piece the same size. Each piece should be 42 feet long and 6 feet wide. [3]Sew five pieces of cloth together for one set. Sew the other pieces together for the second set. [4]Make loops of blue cloth down the edge of the end piece of each set. [5]Make 50 loops on the end piece of the first set. And make 50 loops on the end piece of the second set. These loops must be opposite each other. [6]And make 50 gold hooks. Use these to join the two sets of cloth. This will make the Holy Tent one piece.

⁷"Then make another tent that will cover the Holy Tent. Make this tent of 11 pieces of cloth made from goat hair. ⁸All these pieces of cloth must be the same size. They must be 45 feet long and 6 feet wide. ⁹Sew five of the pieces together into one set. Then sew the other six pieces together into the second set. Fold the sixth piece double over the front of the Tent. ¹⁰Make 50 loops down the edge of the end piece of one set. Do the same for the end piece of the other set. ¹¹Then make 50 bronze hooks. Put these in the loops to join the two sets of cloth. This will make the covering one piece. ¹²Let the extra half piece of cloth hang over the back of the Holy Tent. ¹³There will be 18 inches hanging over the sides of the Holy Tent. This will protect the Tent. ¹⁴Make two more coverings for the Holy Tent. One should be made from male sheep skins colored red. The outer covering should be from fine leather.

¹⁵"Use acacia wood to make upright frames for the Holy Tent. ¹⁶Each frame must be 15 feet long and 27 inches wide. ¹⁷Every frame must be made the same way. There must be two pegs side by side in each frame. ¹⁸Make 20 frames for the south side of the Holy Tent. ¹⁹Each frame must have 2 silver bases to go under it. A peg fits into each silver base. You must make 40 silver bases for the frames. ²⁰Make 20 more frames for the north side of the Holy Tent. ²¹Make 40 silver bases for them. Make 2 bases for each frame. ²²You must make 6 frames for the rear or west end of the Holy Tent. ²³Make 2 frames for each corner at the rear. ²⁴The 2 frames at each corner are to be joined together. Hold them together from bottom to top with a metal ring. Both corner frames must be made this way. ²⁵So there will be a total of 8 frames at the rear of the Tent. And there will be 16 silver bases—2 bases under each frame.

²⁶"Make crossbars of acacia wood to connect the upright frames of the Holy Tent. Make five crossbars to hold the frames together on one side. ²⁷Also make five crossbars to hold the frames together on the other side. And make crossbars to hold the frames together on the west end, at the rear. ²⁸The middle crossbar is to be set halfway up the frames. It is to run along the entire length of each side and rear. ²⁹Make gold rings on the sides of the frames. Pass the crossbars through the rings.

Cover the frames and the crossbars with gold. ³⁰Set up the Holy Tent by the plan shown to you on the mountain.

³¹"Make a curtain of fine linen and blue, purple and red thread. Have a skilled craftsman sew designs of creatures with wings on the curtain. ³²Hang the curtain by gold hooks on four posts of acacia wood. Cover these posts with gold and set them in four silver bases. ³³Hang the curtain from the hooks in the roof. Put the Holy Box^d containing the two flat stones behind the curtain. This curtain will separate the Holy Place from the Most Holy Place. ³⁴Put the lid on the Holy Box in the Most Holy Place.

³⁵"Outside the curtain, put the table on the north side of the Holy Tent. And put the lampstand on the south side of the Holy Tent. This will be across from the table.

³⁶"Then make a curtain for the entrance of the Tent.^{d} Make it with fine linen and blue, purple and red thread. Someone who can sew well is to sew designs on it. ³⁷Make five posts of acacia wood covered with gold. Make five gold hooks on which to hang the curtain from the posts. And make five bronze bases for the five posts.

27 "Make an altar for burnt offerings out of acacia wood. Make it 4½ feet high. It should be square: 7½ feet long and 7½ feet wide. ²Make each of the four corners of the altar stick out like a horn. The corners with their horns must be all one piece. Then cover the whole altar with bronze.

³"Use bronze to make all the tools and dishes that will be used on the altar. Make pots to remove the ashes. Make shovels, bowls for sprinkling blood, meat forks and pans for carrying the burning wood.

⁴"Make a large, bronze screen to hold the burning wood. And put a bronze ring at each of the four corners of the screen. ⁵Put the screen inside the altar, under its rim, halfway up from the bottom.

⁶"Make poles of acacia wood for the altar. And cover them with bronze. ⁷Put the poles through the rings on both sides of the altar to carry it. ⁸Make the altar out of boards and leave the inside hollow. Make it as you were shown on the mountain.

⁹"Make a wall of curtains to form a courtyard around the Holy Tent.^{d} The south side should have a wall of fine linen curtains 150 feet long. ¹⁰Hang the

curtain with silver hooks and bands. Put these on 20 bronze posts on 20 bronze bases. [11]The north side must also be 150 feet long. Hang its curtains on silver hooks and bands. Put these on 20 bronze posts on 20 bronze bases.

[12]"The west end of the courtyard must have a wall of curtains 75 feet long. It must have 10 posts and 10 bases on that wall. [13]The east end of the courtyard must also be 75 feet long. [14]On one side of the entry, there is to be a wall of curtains. It is to be 22½ feet long. It is to be held up by 3 posts on 3 bases. [15]On the other side of the entry, there is to be a wall of curtains. It is to be 22½ feet long. It is to be held up by 3 posts on 3 bases. [16]"The entry to the courtyard is to be a curtain 30 feet wide. It is to be made of fine linen with blue, purple and red thread. Someone who can sew well is to sew designs on it. It is to be held up by 4 posts on 4 bases. [17]All the posts around the courtyard must have silver bands and hooks and bronze bases. [18]The courtyard must be 150 feet long and 75 feet wide. The wall of curtains around it should be 7½ feet high. They must be made of fine linen. The bases in which the posts are set must be bronze. [19]All the things used in the Holy Tent must be made of bronze. And all the tent pegs for the Holy Tent and the wall around the courtyard must be made of bronze.

[20]"Command the people of Israel to bring you pure olive oil. It is to be made from pressed olives. This is to keep the lamps on the lampstand burning. [21]Aaron and his sons must keep the lamps burning before the Lord from evening till morning. This will be in the Meeting Tent.[d] It is outside the curtain which is in front of the Holy Box.[d] The Israelites and their descendants[d] must obey this rule from now on.

28 "Tell your brother Aaron to come to you. His sons Nadab, Abihu, Eleazar and Ithamar must come with him. Separate them from the other Israelites. These men must serve as priests. [2]Make holy clothes for your brother Aaron to give him honor and beauty. [3]Speak to all the people to whom I have given the ability to make clothes. Tell these skilled craftsmen to make the clothes for Aaron. Use these clothes to make him belong to me. Then he may serve me as a priest. [4]These are the clothes they must make: a chest covering, a holy vest,[d] an outer robe, a woven inner robe, a turban and a cloth belt. The craftsmen must make these holy clothes. They are for your brother Aaron and his sons. Then Aaron and his sons may serve me as priests. [5]The craftsmen must use gold and blue, purple and red thread, and fine linen.

[6]"Use gold and blue, purple and red thread, and fine linen to make the holy vest.[d] The craftsmen are to make this holy vest. [7]At each top corner of this holy vest there will be a pair of shoulder straps. These are to be tied together over each shoulder.

[8]"The craftsmen will very carefully weave a belt on the holy vest. Make the belt with gold and blue, purple and red thread, and fine linen.

[9]"Take two onyx stones. Write the name of the 12 sons of Israel on these jewels. [10]Write 6 names on one stone and 6 names on the other stone. Write the names in order, from the oldest son to the youngest. [11]Carve the names of the sons of Israel on these stones. Do this the same way a person carves words and designs on the seals.[d] Put gold around the stones to hold them on the holy vest. [12]Put the two stones on the two straps of the holy vest. These stones are reminders of the 12 sons of Israel. Aaron is to wear their names on his shoulders. They are before the Lord as reminders of the sons of Israel. [13]Make two gold pieces to hold the stones. [14]Then make two chains of pure gold. Twist them together like a rope. Attach the chains to the two gold pieces that hold the stones.

[15]"Make a chest covering to help in making decisions. The craftsmen should make it as they made the holy vest.[d] They must use gold and blue, purple and red thread, and fine linen. [16]The chest covering must be square. It should be nine inches long and nine inches wide. Fold it double to make a pocket. [17]Put four rows of beautiful gems on the chest covering. The first row of jewels must have a ruby, topaz and yellow quartz. [18]The second row must have turquoise, a sapphire and an emerald. [19]The third row must have a jacinth, an agate and an amethyst. [20]The fourth row must have a chrysolite, an onyx and a jasper. Put gold around these jewels to attach them to the chest covering. [21]There must be 12 jewels on the chest covering. That is 1 jewel for each of the names of the sons of Israel. Carve the name of one of the 12 tribes[d] on each of the stones. Carve them as you would carve a seal.[d]

²²"Make chains of pure gold for the chest covering. Twist them together like rope. ²³Make two gold rings. Put them on the two upper corners of the chest covering. ²⁴Attach the two gold chains to the two rings. These are at the upper corners of the chest covering. ²⁵Attach the other ends of the two chains to the two gold pieces on the shoulder straps. This will tie the chains to the shoulder straps in the front of the holy vest.

²⁶"Make two more gold rings. Put them at the two lower corners of the chest covering. Put them on the inside edge of the chest covering next to the holy vest. ²⁷Make two more gold rings. Attach them to the bottom of the shoulder straps in the front of the holy vest. Put the gold rings close to the seam above the woven belt of the holy vest. ²⁸Join the rings of the chest covering to the rings of the holy vest with blue ribbon. This will connect it to the woven belt. In this way the chest covering will not swing out from the holy vest.

²⁹"When Aaron enters the Holy Place, he will wear the names of the sons of Israel over his heart. These names are on the chest covering that helps in making decisions. This will be a continual reminder before the Lord. ³⁰And put the Urim and Thummim[d] inside the chest covering. These things will be on Aaron's heart when he goes before the Lord. They will help in making decisions for the Israelites. So Aaron will always carry them with him when he is before the Lord.

³¹"Make the outer robe to be worn under the holy vest, using only blue cloth. ³²Make a hole in the center for Aaron's head. And there must be a woven collar around the hole so it will not tear. ³³Make balls like pomegranates[d] of blue, purple and red thread. Hang these pomegranate balls around the bottom of the outer robe. And hang gold bells between them. ³⁴So all around the bottom of the outer robe there should be a gold bell and a pomegranate ball, a gold bell and a pomegranate ball. ³⁵Aaron must wear this robe when he serves as priest. The ringing of the bells will be heard. They will ring when he enters and leaves the Holy Place before the Lord. This way Aaron will not be killed.

³⁶"Make a strip of pure gold. Carve these words on the gold strip as you would carve on a seal:[d] 'Holy to the Lord.' ³⁷Use blue ribbon to tie a strip of gold to the turban. Put it on the front of the turban. ³⁸Aaron must wear this on his forehead. In this way, he will be blamed if anything is wrong with the gifts of the Israelites. Aaron must always wear this on his head so the Lord will accept the gifts of the people.

³⁹"Make the woven inner robe of fine linen. Make the turban of fine linen, also. Make the cloth belt with designs sewn on it. ⁴⁰Also make woven inner robes, cloth belts and headbands for Aaron's sons. This will give them honor and beauty. ⁴¹Put these clothes on your brother Aaron and his sons. Then pour olive oil on their heads to appoint them as priests. Make them belong to me so they may serve me as priests.

⁴²"Make for them linen underclothes to cover them from the waist to the upper parts of the legs. ⁴³Aaron and his sons must wear these underclothes when they enter the Meeting Tent.[d] And they must wear these clothes anytime they come near the altar to serve as priests in the Holy Place. If they do not wear these clothes, they will be guilty of wrong. And they will be killed. This will be a law that will last from now on for Aaron and all his descendants.[d]

29

"This is what you must do to appoint Aaron and his sons. Then they may serve me as priests. Take one young bull and two male sheep that have nothing wrong with them. ²Use fine wheat flour without yeast to make bread and cakes mixed with olive oil. Also use wheat flour without yeast to make wafers brushed with olive oil. ³Put these in one basket. Bring them in the basket along with the bull and two male sheep. ⁴Bring Aaron and his sons to the entrance of the Meeting Tent.[d] Then wash them with water. ⁵Take the clothes. Dress Aaron in the inner robe and the outer robe of the holy vest.[d] Then put on him the holy vest and the chest covering. Then tie the holy vest on him with its skillfully woven belt. ⁶Put the turban on his head. Put the holy crown, the strip of gold, on the turban. ⁷Take the special olive oil and pour it on his head to make him a priest.

⁸"Then bring his sons and put the inner robes on them. ⁹Put the headbands on their heads. Then tie the cloth belts around their waists. Aaron and his descendants[d] will be priests in Israel. This is by a rule that will continue from now on. This is how you will appoint Aaron and his sons as priests.

¹⁰"Bring the bull to the front of the

Meeting Tent. Aaron and his sons must put their hands on the bull's head. [11]Then kill the bull before the Lord at the entrance to the Meeting Tent. [12]Take some of the bull's blood and go to the altar. Use your finger to put some blood on the corners of the altar. Pour the blood that is left at the bottom of the altar. [13]Then take all the fat that covers the inner organs. Take the best part of the liver, and take both kidneys and the fat around them. Burn these on the altar. [14]Take the bull's meat, skin and intestines. Burn these things outside the camp. This is an offering to take away sin.

[15]"Take one of the male sheep. Have Aaron and his sons put their hands on its head. [16]Then kill that male sheep. Take its blood and sprinkle it on all four sides of the altar. [17]Then cut the male sheep into pieces. Wash its inner organs and its legs. Put them with its head and its other pieces. [18]Burn the whole male sheep on the altar. It is a burnt offering made by fire to the Lord. Its smell is pleasing to the Lord.

[19]"Take the other male sheep. Have Aaron and his sons put their hands on its head. [20]Kill that male sheep and take some of its blood. Put it on the bottom of the right ears of Aaron and his sons. Also put it on the thumbs of their right hands. And put it on the big toes of their right feet. Then sprinkle the rest of the blood against all four sides of the altar. [21]Then take some of the blood from the altar. Mix it with the special oil used in appointing priests. Sprinkle this on Aaron and his sons and their clothes. And sprinkle this on his sons and their clothes. This will show that Aaron and his sons and their clothes are given to my service.

[22]"Then take the fat from the male sheep. Take the fat tail and the fat that covers the inner organs. Take the best part of the liver. Take both kidneys and the fat around them and the right thigh. This is the male sheep to be used in appointing priests. [23]"Then take the basket of bread that you made without yeast. This is the basket you put before the Lord. From it take a loaf of bread, a cake made with olive oil and a wafer. [24]Put these in the hands of Aaron and his sons. Tell them to present these things in their hands before the Lord. This will be an offering presented to the Lord. [25]Then take them from their hands. Burn them on the altar with the whole burnt offering. This is an

offering made by fire to the Lord. Its smell is pleasing to the Lord. [26]Then take the breast of the male sheep used to appoint Aaron as priest. Present the breast of the male sheep before the Lord. It is an offering presented to the Lord. This part of the animal will be your share. [27]Then give to the service of the Lord the parts of the male sheep used to appoint them as priests. They belong to Aaron and his sons. They are the breast and the right thigh. These were presented to the Lord. [28]This is to be the regular share which the Israelites will always give to Aaron and his sons. This is the gift the Israelites must give to the Lord from their fellowship offerings.

[29]"The holy clothes made for Aaron will belong to his descendants. They must wear these clothes when they are appointed as priests. [30]Aaron's son will become high priest after Aaron. He will come to the Meeting Tent to serve in the Holy Place. He is to wear these clothes for seven days.

[31]"Take the male sheep used to appoint priests. Boil its meat in a place made holy for serving me. [32]Then Aaron and his sons must eat the meat of the male sheep. They must do that at the entrance of the Meeting Tent. And they must also eat the bread that is in the basket. [33]These offerings were used to remove their sins when they were made priests so they would belong to God. Now they should eat these offerings. But no one else is to eat these things because they are holy. [34]If any of the meat from that male sheep or any of the bread is left the next morning, it must be burned. It shall not be eaten because it is holy.

[35]"Do all these things that I commanded you to do to Aaron and his sons. You are to spend seven days appointing them. [36]Each day for seven days you are to offer a bull. This will remove the sins of Aaron and his sons so they will be given for service to the Lord. Make the altar ready for service to the Lord. Pour oil on it to make it holy. [37]Spend seven days making the altar ready for service to God and making it holy. Then the altar will become very holy. Anything that touches it must be holy.

[38]"Every day from now on, offer on the altar two lambs that are one year old. [39]Offer one lamb in the morning and the other in the evening. [40]In the morning, when you offer the first lamb, offer also two quarts of fine flour. Mix it with one quart of oil from pressed olives.

Pour out a quart of wine as a drink offering. ⁴¹Offer the second lamb in the evening. Also offer the same grain offering and drink offering as you did in the morning. This is an offering by fire to the Lord. And its smell is pleasing to the Lord.

⁴²"You must burn these things as an offering to the Lord every day. Do this at the entrance of the Meeting Tent[d] before the Lord from now on. When you make the offering, I, the Lord, will meet you there and speak to you. ⁴³I will meet with the people of Israel there. And that place will be holy because of my greatness.

⁴⁴"So I will make the Meeting Tent and the altar holy. And I will make Aaron and his sons holy so they may serve me as priests. ⁴⁵I will live with the people of Israel. I will be their God. ⁴⁶And they will know that I am the Lord their God. They will know that I am the one who led them out of Egypt. I did this so I could live with them. I am the Lord their God.

30 "Make an altar out of acacia wood for burning incense.[d] ²Make it square—18 inches long and 18 inches wide. It must be 36 inches high. Make the corners stick out like horns. These must be one piece with the altar. ³Cover its top, its sides and its corners with pure gold. And put a gold strip all around the altar. ⁴Make two gold rings beneath the gold strip on opposite sides of the altar. Slide poles through these gold rings to carry the altar. ⁵Make the poles from acacia wood and cover them with gold. ⁶Put the altar of incense in front of the curtain. This curtain is in front of the Box[d] of the Agreement. Put the altar in front of the lid that covers that Holy Box. There I will meet with you.

⁷"Aaron must burn sweet-smelling incense on the altar every morning. He will do this when he comes to take care of the oil lamps. ⁸He must burn incense again in the evening when he lights the lamps. So incense will burn before the Lord every day from now on. ⁹Do not use this altar for offering any other incense or burnt offering. Do not use this altar to offer any kind of grain offering or drink offering. ¹⁰Once a year Aaron must make the altar ready for service to God. He will do it by putting blood on its corners. This is blood of the animal offered to remove sins. He is to do this once a year from now on. This altar belongs completely to God's service."

¹¹The Lord said to Moses, ¹²"Count the people of Israel. At that time every person must pay to buy back his life from the Lord. Then no terrible things will happen to the people when you number them. ¹³Every person who is counted must pay one-fifth of an ounce of silver. This is set by the Holy Place measure, which weighs two-fifths of an ounce. This amount is a gift to the Lord. ¹⁴Every person who is counted and is 20 years old or older must give this amount to the Lord. ¹⁵A rich person must not give more than one-fifth of an ounce. And a poor person must not give less than one-fifth of an ounce. You are paying this to the Lord to buy back your lives. ¹⁶Gather from the people of Israel this money paid to buy back their lives. Spend it to buy things for the service in the Meeting Tent.[d] This payment will remind the Lord that the Israelites' lives have been bought back."

¹⁷The Lord said to Moses, ¹⁸"Make a bronze bowl for washing. Build it on a bronze stand. Put the bowl and stand between the Meeting Tent[d] and the altar. Put water in the bowl. ¹⁹Aaron and his sons must wash their hands and feet with the water from this bowl. ²⁰Each time, before they enter the Meeting Tent, they must wash with water. This way they will not die. They approach the altar to serve as priests. They offer a sacrifice to the Lord by fire. ²¹Each time they do this, they must wash their hands and their feet so they will not die. This is a rule which Aaron and his descendants[d] are to keep from now on."

²²Then the Lord said to Moses, ²³"Take the finest spices: 12 pounds of liquid myrrh,[d] half that amount (that is, 6 pounds) of sweet-smelling cinnamon, 6 pounds of sweet-smelling cane ²⁴and 12 pounds of cassia.[d] Weigh all these by the Holy Place measure. Also take 4 quarts of olive oil. ²⁵Mix all these things like a perfume to make a holy olive oil. This special oil must be put on people and things. Do this to make them ready for service to God. ²⁶Put this oil on the Meeting Tent[d] and the Holy Box[d] with my laws in it. ²⁷Put this oil on the table and all its dishes. And put this oil on the lampstand and all its tools. Put the oil on the incense[d] altar. ²⁸Also, put the oil on the altar for burning offerings and all its tools. Put this oil on the bowl and the stand under the bowl. Put oil on all these things to prepare them for service to God. ²⁹You will give these

things for service to God. They will be very holy. Anything that touches these things must also be holy.

30 "Put the oil on Aaron and his sons to make them priests. Give them for service to me. Then they may serve me as priests. 31 Tell the Israelites, 'This is to be my holy olive oil from now on. It is to be put on people and things to make them ready for service to God. 32 Do not pour it on the bodies of ordinary people. Do not make perfume the same way you make this oil. It is holy, and you must treat it as holy. 33 Someone might make perfume like it. Or he might put it on someone who is not a priest. Then that person must be separated from his people.'"

34 Then the Lord said to Moses, "Take these sweet-smelling spices: resin, onycha, galbanum and pure frankincense.d Be sure that you have equal amounts of each. 35 You must make incensed as a man who makes perfume would do. Add salt to it to keep it pure and holy. 36 Beat some of the incense into a fine powder. Put some of it in front of the Holy Boxd of the Agreement in the Meeting Tent.d There I will meet with you. You must use this incense powder only for its very special purpose. 37 Do not make incense for yourselves the same way you make this incense. Treat it as holy to the Lord. 38 Whoever makes incense like this to use as perfume must be separated from his people."

31 Then the Lord said to Moses, 2 "See, I have chosen Bezalel son of Uri from the tribed of Judah. Uri was the son of Hur. 3 I have filled Bezalel with the Spiritd of God. I have given him the skill, ability and knowledge to do all kinds of work. 4 He is able to design pieces to be made from gold, silver and bronze. 5 He is able to cut jewels and put them in metal. And he can carve wood. Bezalel can do all kinds of work. 6 I have also chosen Oholiab son of Ahisamach from the tribe of Dan. Oholiab will work with Bezalel. I have given skills to all skilled craftsmen. They will be able to make all these things I have commanded you: 7 the Meeting Tent,d the Boxd of the Agreement, the lid that covers the Holy Box and everything in the Tent. 8 This includes the table and everything on it, the pure gold lampstand and everything with it and the altar of incense.d 9 It also includes the altar for burnt offerings and everything used with it, the bowl and the stand under it.

10 They will make the woven clothes and the holy clothes for Aaron and the clothes for his sons to wear when they serve as priests. 11 They will also make the special olive oil used in appointing people and things to the service of the Lord, and the sweet-smelling incense for the Holy Place.

"These workers will make all these things just as I have commanded you."

12 Then the Lord said to Moses, 13 "Tell the Israelites, 'You must keep the rules about my Sabbaths.d This is because they will be a sign between you and me from now on. In this way you will know that I, the Lord, am making you holy. 14 "'Make the Sabbath a holy day. If anyone treats the Sabbath like any other day, that person must be put to death. Anyone who works on the Sabbath day must be separated from his people. 15 There are six days for working. But the seventh day is a day of rest. It is a day holy for the Lord. Anyone who works during the Sabbath day must be put to death. 16 The Israelites must remember the Sabbath day. It is an agreement between them and me that will continue from now on. 17 The Sabbath day will be a sign between me and the Israelites forever. This is because in six days I, the Lord, made the sky and the earth. And on the seventh day I did not work. I rested.'"

18 So the Lord finished speaking to Moses on Mount Sinai. Then the Lord gave him the two stone tablets with the agreement written on them. The finger of God wrote the commands on the stones.

32 The people saw that a long time had passed. And Moses had not come down from the mountain. So they gathered around Aaron. They said to him, "Moses led us out of Egypt. But we don't know what has happened to him. So make us gods who will lead us."

2 Aaron said to the people, "Take off the gold earrings that your wives, sons and daughters are wearing. Bring them to me." 3 So all the people took their gold earrings and brought them to Aaron. 4 Aaron took the gold from the people. Then he melted it and made a statue of a calf. He finished it with a tool. Then the people said, "Israel! These are your gods who brought you out of the land of Egypt!"

5 Aaron saw all this, and he built an altar before the calf. Then he made an announcement. He said, "Tomorrow

there will be a special feast to honor the Lord." [6] The people got up early the next morning. They offered whole burnt offerings and fellowship offerings. First the people sat down to eat and drink. Then they got up and sinned sexually.

[7] And the Lord said to Moses, "Go down from this mountain. Your people, the people you brought out of the land of Egypt, have done a terrible sin. [8] They have quickly turned away from the things I commanded them to do. They have made for themselves a calf of melted gold. They have worshiped that calf and offered sacrifices to it. The people have said, 'Israel, these are your gods who brought you out of Egypt.'"

[9] The Lord said to Moses, "I have seen these people. I know that they are very stubborn people. [10] So now do not stop me. I am so angry with them that I am going to destroy them. Then I will make you and your descendants[d] a great nation."

[11] But Moses begged the Lord his God. Moses said, "Lord, don't let your anger destroy your people. You brought these people out of Egypt with your great power and strength. [12] Don't let the people of Egypt say, 'The Lord brought the Israelites out of Egypt. But he planned to kill them in the mountains and destroy them from the earth.' So stop being angry. Don't destroy your people. [13] Remember the men who served you—Abraham, Isaac and Israel. You promised with an oath to them. You said, 'I will make your descendants as many as the stars in the sky. I will give your descendants all this land that I have promised them. It will be theirs forever.'" [14] So the Lord changed his mind. He did not destroy the people as he had said he might.

[15] Then Moses went down the mountain. In his hands he had the two stone tablets with the agreement on them. The commands were written on both sides of each stone, front and back. [16] God himself had made the stones. And God himself had written the commands on the stones.

[17] Then Joshua heard the noise of the people shouting. He said to Moses, "It sounds like war down in the camp."

[18] Moses answered:

"It is not an army's shout of victory.
　It is not an army's cry of defeat.
　It is the sound of singing that I
　　hear."

[19] When Moses came close to the camp, he saw the gold calf and the dancing. He became very angry. He threw down the stone tablets which he was carrying. He broke them at the bottom of the mountain. [20] Then he took the calf that the people had made. He melted it in the fire. And he ground the gold until it became powder. He threw the powder into the water. And he forced the Israelites to drink that water.

[21] Moses said to Aaron, "What did these people do to you? Why did you cause them to do such a terrible sin?"

[22] Aaron answered, "Don't be angry, master. You know that these people are always ready to do wrong. [23] The people said to me, 'Moses led us out of Egypt. But we don't know what has happened to him. So make us gods who will lead us.' [24] So I told the people, 'Take off your gold jewelry.' So they gave me the gold. I threw it into the fire and out came this calf!"

[25] Moses saw that the people were acting wildly. He saw that Aaron had let them get out of control. Their enemies would laugh at them. [26] So Moses stood at the entrance to the camp. He said, "Let anyone who wants to follow the Lord come to me." And all the people from the family of Levi gathered around Moses.

[27] Then Moses said to them, "The Lord, the God of Israel, says this: 'Every man must put on his sword and go through the camp from one end to the other. Each man must kill his brother, his friend and his neighbor.'" [28] The people from the family of Levi obeyed Moses. That day about 3,000 of the people of Israel died. [29] Then Moses said, "Today you have been given for service to the Lord. You were willing to kill your own sons and brothers. And God has blessed you for this."

[30] The next day Moses told the people, "You have done a terrible sin. But now I will go up to the Lord. Maybe I can do something so your sins will be removed. Then you will belong to God again." [31] So Moses went back to the Lord and said, "How terrible it is! These people have sinned horribly. They have made for themselves gods from gold. [32] Now, forgive them of this sin. If you will not, then erase my name. Erase it from the book in which you have written the names of your people."

[33] But the Lord told Moses, "I will erase from my book the names of the

people who sin against me. ³⁴So now, go. Lead the people where I have told you. My angel will lead you. When the time comes to punish, I will punish them for their sin."

³⁵So the Lord caused terrible things to happen to the people. He did this because of what they did with the calf Aaron had made.

33 Then the Lord said to Moses, "You and the people you brought out of Egypt must leave this place. Go to the land that I promised with an oath to give to Abraham, Isaac and Jacob. I said, 'I will give that land to your descendants.' ²I will send an angel to lead you. And I will force these people out of the land: the Canaanites, Amorites, Hittites, Perizzites, Hivites and Jebusites. ³Go up to the land where much food grows. But I will not go with you. This is because I might destroy you on the way. You are such a stubborn people."

⁴The people heard this bad news, and they became very sad. None of them put on jewelry. ⁵This was because the Lord had said to Moses, "Tell the Israelites, 'You are a stubborn people. If I were to go with you even for a moment, I would destroy you. So take off all your jewelry. Then I will decide what to do with you.'" ⁶So the people of Israel took off their jewelry at Mount Sinai.

⁷Moses took to take a tent and set it up a long way outside the camp. Moses called it the "Meeting Tent."ᵈ A person might want to ask the Lord about something. Then he would go to the Meeting Tent outside the camp. ⁸Anytime Moses went out to the Tent, all the people would rise. They stood at the entrances of their tents and watched Moses until he entered the Meeting Tent. ⁹When Moses went into the Tent, the pillar of cloud would always come down. It would stay at the entrance of the Tent while the Lord spoke with Moses. ¹⁰The people saw the pillar of cloud at the entrance of the Tent. Then they stood and worshiped, each person at the entrance of his own tent.

¹¹The Lord spoke to Moses face to face as a man speaks with his friend. Then Moses would return to the camp. But Moses' young helper, Joshua son of Nun, did not leave the Tent.

¹²Moses said to the Lord, "You have told me to lead these people. But you did not say whom you would send with me. You have said to me, 'I know you very well. I am pleased with you.' ¹³If I have

truly pleased you, show me your plans. Then I may know you and continue to please you. Remember that this nation is your people."

¹⁴The Lord answered, "I myself will go with you. And I will give you victory."

¹⁵Then Moses said to him, "If you yourself don't go with us, then don't send us away from this place. ¹⁶If you don't go with us, no one will know that you are pleased with me and your people. These people and I would be no different from any other people on earth."

¹⁷Then the Lord said to Moses, "I will do what you ask. This is because I know you very well, and I am pleased with you."

¹⁸Then Moses said, "Now, please show me your greatness."

¹⁹The Lord answered, "I will cause all my goodness to pass in front of you. I will announce my name, the Lord, so you can hear it. I will show kindness to anyone I want to show kindness. I will show mercy to anyone I want to show mercy. ²⁰But you cannot see my face. No one can see me and stay alive.

²¹"There is a place near me where you may stand on a rock. ²²My greatness will pass that place. I will put you in a large crack in that rock. And I will cover you with my hand until I have passed by. ²³Then I will take away my hand, and you will see my back. But my face must not be seen."

34 The Lord said to Moses, "Cut two more stone tablets like the first two. I will write the same words on them that were on the first two stones which you broke. ²Be ready tomorrow morning. Then come up on Mount Sinai. Stand before me there on the top of the mountain. ³No one may come with you. No one should even be seen any place on the mountain. Not even the sheep or cattle may eat grass near that mountain."

⁴So Moses cut two stone tablets like the first ones. Then early the next morning he went up Mount Sinai. He did this just as the Lord had commanded him. Moses carried the two stone tablets with him. ⁵Then the Lord came down in the cloud and stood there with Moses. And the Lord called out his name, the Lord. ⁶The Lord passed in front of Moses and said, "I am the Lord. The Lord is a God who shows mercy and is kind. The Lord doesn't become angry quickly. The Lord has great love and faithfulness. ⁷The Lord is kind to thousands of peo-

ple. The Lord forgives people for wrong and sin and turning against him. But the Lord does not forget to punish guilty people. The Lord will punish not only the guilty people. He will also punish their children, their grandchildren, their great-grandchildren and their great-great-grandchildren."

[8] Then Moses quickly bowed to the ground and worshiped. [9] Moses said, "Lord, if you are pleased with me, please go with us. I know that these are stubborn people. But forgive our evil and our sin. Take us as your own people."

[10] Then the Lord said, "I am making this agreement with you. I will do miracles[d] in front of all your people. These things have never before been done for any other nation on earth. The people with you will see my work. I, the Lord, will do wonderful things for you. [11] Obey the things I command you today, and I will force your enemies to leave your land. I will force out the Amorites, Canaanites, Hittites, Perizzites, Hivites and Jebusites ahead of you. [12] Be careful. Don't make any agreement with the people who live in the land where you are going. It will bring you trouble. [13] But destroy their altars. Break their stone pillars. Cut down their Asherah[d] idols. [14] Don't worship any other god. This is because I, the Lord, the Jealous One, am a jealous God.

[15] "Be careful. Don't make any agreements with the people who live in that land. They will worship their false gods. And they will invite you to join them. Then you will join them, and you will eat their sacrifices. [16] You might choose some of their daughters as wives for your sons. Those daughters worship false gods. They might lead your sons to do the same thing.

[17] "Do not make gods of melted metal.

[18] "Celebrate the Feast[d] of Unleavened Bread. For seven days you must eat bread made without yeast as I commanded you. Do this during the month I have chosen, the month of Abib.[d] This is because in that month you came out of Egypt.

[19] "Every firstborn[d] cow or sheep that is born to each animal belongs to me. [20] You may buy back a donkey by paying for it with a lamb. But if you don't want to buy back a donkey, you must break its neck. You must buy back all your firstborn sons.

"No one is to come before me without a gift.

[21] "You must work for six days. But on the seventh day you must rest. You must do this even during the planting season and harvest season.

[22] "Celebrate the Feast[d] of Weeks when you gather the first grain of the wheat harvest. And celebrate the Feast[d] of Harvest in the fall.

[23] "Three times each year all your men must come before the Master, the Lord, the God of Israel. [24] I will force out nations ahead of you. I will expand the borders of your land. You will go before the Lord your God three times each year. And at that time no one will try to take your land from you.

[25] "Do not offer the blood of a sacrifice to me with anything containing yeast. And do not leave any of the sacrifice of the Feast[d] of Passover. It must not be left until the next morning.

[26] "Bring the best first crops that you harvest from your ground. Bring those things to the Tent[d] of the Lord your God.

"You must not cook a young goat in its mother's milk."

[27] Then the Lord said to Moses, "Write down these words. This is because with these words I have made an agreement with you and Israel."

[28] Moses stayed there with the Lord 40 days and 40 nights. During that time he did not eat food or drink water. And Moses wrote the words of the agreement—the Ten Commandments—on the stone tablets.

[29] Then Moses came down from Mount Sinai. In his hands he was carrying the two stone tablets of the agreement. But Moses did not know that his face was shining because he had talked with the Lord. [30] Aaron and all the people of Israel saw that Moses' face was shining. So they were afraid to go near him. [31] But Moses called to them. So Aaron and all the leaders of the people returned to Moses. Moses talked with them. [32] After that, all the people of Israel came near him. And he gave them all the commands that the Lord had given him on Mount Sinai.

[33] When Moses finished speaking to the people, he put a covering over his face. [34] Anytime Moses went before the Lord to speak with him, Moses took off the covering until he came out. Then Moses would come out and tell the people of Israel the things the Lord had commanded. [35] The Israelites would see that Moses' face was shining. So he would cover his face again. He did this

until the next time he went in to speak with the Lord.

35 Moses gathered all the Israelite community together. He said to them, "These are the things the Lord has commanded you to do. ²You are to work for six days. But the seventh day will be a holy day, a Sabbath[d] of rest to honor the Lord. Anyone who works on that day must be put to death. ³On the Sabbath day you must not light a fire in any of your houses."

⁴Moses said to all the Israelites, "This is what the Lord has commanded: ⁵From what you have, take an offering for the Lord. Let everyone who is willing bring this offering to the Lord: gold, silver, bronze, ⁶blue, purple and red thread, and fine linen, goat hair ⁷and male sheep skins, colored red. And they may bring fine leather and acacia wood. ⁸They may also bring olive oil for the lamps, spices for the special olive oil used for appointing priests and for the sweet-smelling incense.[d] ⁹And they may bring onyx stones and other jewels to be put on the holy vest[d] and chest covering of the priests.

¹⁰"Let all the skilled workers come and make everything the Lord commanded: ¹¹the Holy Tent,[d] its outer tent and its covering, the hooks, frames, crossbars, posts and bases; ¹²the Box[d] of the Agreement, its poles, lid and the curtain in front of it; ¹³the table and its poles, all the things that go with the table and the bread that shows we are in God's presence; ¹⁴the lampstand for the light and all the things that go with it, the lamps and olive oil for the light; ¹⁵the altar of incense and its poles, the special oil and the sweet-smelling incense, the curtain for the entrance of the Meeting Tent; ¹⁶the altar of burnt offering and its bronze screen, its poles and all its tools, the bronze bowl and its base; ¹⁷the curtains around the courtyard, their posts and bases, and the curtain at the entry to the courtyard; ¹⁸the pegs of the Holy Tent and of the courtyard and their ropes; ¹⁹the special clothes that the priest will wear in the Holy Place. These are the holy clothes for Aaron the priest and his sons to wear when they serve as priests."

²⁰Then all the people of Israel went away from Moses. ²¹Everyone who wanted to give came and brought a gift to the Lord. These gifts were used for making the Meeting Tent, all the things in the Tent and the special clothes. ²²All

the men and women who wanted to give brought gold jewelry of all kinds. They brought pins, earrings, rings and bracelets. They all presented their gold to the Lord. ²³Everyone who had blue, purple and red thread, and fine linen came and gave it to the Lord. Anyone who had goat hair or male sheep skins colored red or fine leather brought them to the Lord. ²⁴Everyone who could give silver or bronze brought that as a gift to the Lord. Everyone who had acacia wood to be used in the work brought it. ²⁵Every skilled woman used her hands to make the blue, purple and red thread and fine linen. And they brought what they had made. ²⁶All the women who were skilled and wanted to help made thread of the goat hair. ²⁷The leaders brought onyx stones and other jewels. These stones and jewels were put on the holy vest and chest covering for the priest. ²⁸They also brought spices and olive oil. These were used for the sweet-smelling incense, the special oil and the oil to burn in the lamps. ²⁹All the men and women of Israel who wanted to help brought gifts to the Lord. They were used for all the work the Lord had commanded Moses and the people to do.

³⁰Then Moses said to the people of Israel, "Look, the Lord has chosen Bezalel. He is the son of Uri the son of Hur, from the tribe[d] of Judah. ³¹The Lord has filled Bezalel with the Spirit[d] of God. The Lord has given Bezalel the skill, ability and knowledge to do all kinds of work. ³²He is able to design pieces to be made of gold, silver and bronze. ³³He is able to cut stones and jewels and put them in metal. Bezalel can carve wood and do all kinds of work. ³⁴The Lord has given Bezalel and Oholiab the ability to teach others. Oholiab is the son of Ahisamach from the tribe of Dan. ³⁵The Lord has given them the skill to do all kinds of work. They are able to cut designs in metal and stone. They can plan and sew designs in the fine linen with the blue, purple and red thread. And they are also able to weave things.

36 "So Bezalel, Oholiab and every skilled person will do the work the Lord has commanded. The Lord gave these people the wisdom and understanding to do all the skilled work needed to build the Holy Tent."

²Then Moses called Bezalel, Oholiab and all the other skilled people to whom the Lord had given skills. And they came because they wanted to help with

the work. ³They received from Moses everything the people of Israel had brought as gifts to build the Holy Tent. The people continued to bring gifts each morning because they wanted to. ⁴So all the skilled workers left the work they were doing on the Holy Tent. And they went to speak to Moses. They said, ⁵"The people are bringing more than we need to do the work the Lord commanded."

⁶Then Moses sent this command throughout the camp: "No man or woman should make anything else as a gift for the Holy Tent." So the people were kept from giving more. ⁷What they had was already more than enough to do all the work.

⁸Then the skilled workers made the Holy Tent.ᵈ They made the ten pieces of blue, purple and red cloth. And they sewed designs of creatures with wings on the pieces. ⁹Each piece was the same size. It was 42 feet long and 6 feet wide. ¹⁰Five of the pieces were fastened together to make one set. The other five were fastened together to make another set. ¹¹Then they made loops of blue cloth along the edge of the end piece on the first set of five. They did the same thing with the other set of five. ¹²There were 50 loops on one piece and 50 loops on the other piece. The loops were opposite each other. ¹³Then they made 50 gold hooks to join the two pieces together. So the Holy Tent was joined together as one piece.

¹⁴Then the workers made another tent of 11 pieces of cloth made of goat hair. This was to put over the Holy Tent. ¹⁵All 11 pieces were the same size. They were 45 feet long and 6 feet wide. ¹⁶The workers sewed five pieces together into one set. Then they sewed six together into another set. ¹⁷They made 50 loops along the edge of the outside piece of one set. And they made 50 loops along the edge of the outside piece of the other set. ¹⁸Then they made 50 bronze rings to join the two sets of cloth together and make the tent one piece. ¹⁹Then they made two more coverings for the outer tent. One covering was made of male sheep skin colored red. The other covering was made of fine leather.

²⁰Then they made upright frames of acacia wood. ²¹Each board was 15 feet tall and 27 inches wide. ²²There were two pegs side by side on each frame. Every frame of the Holy Tent was made this same way. ²³They made 20 frames

for the south side of the Tent. ²⁴Then they made 40 silver bases that went under the 20 frames. There were two bases for every frame—one for each peg of each board. ²⁵They also made 20 frames for the north side of the Holy Tent. ²⁶They made 40 silver bases—2 to go under each frame. ²⁷They made 6 frames for the rear or west end of the Holy Tent ²⁸and 2 frames for the corners at the rear of the Holy Tent. ²⁹These 2 frames were joined together from the bottom to the top with a metal ring. They did this for each of these corners. ³⁰So there were 8 frames and 16 silver bases—2 bases under each frame.

³¹Then they made crossbars of acacia wood to connect the upright frames of the Holy Tent. Five crossbars held the frames together on one side of the Tent. ³²Five crossbars held the frames together on the other side. And five crossbars held the frames together on the west end, at the rear of the Tent. ³³They made the crossbar run along the entire length of each side and rear of the Tent. It was set halfway up the frames. ³⁴They made gold rings on the sides of the frames. They passed the crossbars through the rings. They covered the frames and the crossbars with gold.

³⁵Then they made the curtain with blue, purple and red thread, and fine linen. A skilled craftsman sewed designs of creatures with wings on it. ³⁶They made four posts of acacia wood and covered them with gold. Then they made gold hooks for the posts. And they made four silver bases in which to set the posts. ³⁷Then they made a curtain for the entrance to the Tent. They used blue, purple and red thread, and fine linen. A person who sewed well sewed designs on it. ³⁸Then they made five posts and hooks for it. They covered the tops of the posts and their bands with gold. And they made five bronze bases for the posts.

37 Bezalel made the Holy Boxᵈ of acacia wood. The Holy Box was 45 inches long, 27 inches wide and 27 inches high. ²He covered the inside and outside of the Holy Box with pure gold. Then he put a gold strip around it. ³He made four gold rings for it and attached them to its four feet. There were two rings on each side. ⁴Then he made poles of acacia wood and covered them with gold. ⁵He put the poles through the rings on each side of the Holy Box to carry it. ⁶Then he made a lid of pure gold. It was

45 inches long and 27 inches wide. [7]Then Bezalel hammered gold to make two creatures with wings. He attached them to each end of the lid. [8]He made one creature with wings on one end of the lid. He made the other creature with wings on the other end. He attached them to the lid so that it would be one piece. [9]The creatures' wings were spread out over the lid. The creatures faced each other across the lid.

[10]Then he made the table of acacia wood. The table was 36 inches long, 18 inches wide and 27 inches high. [11]He covered the table with pure gold. He put a gold strip around it. [12]Then he made a frame 3 inches high that stood up all around the edge. He put a gold strip around the frame. [13]Then he made four gold rings for the table. He attached them to the four corners of the table, where the four legs were. [14]The rings were put close to the frame around the top of the table. The rings held the poles that were used to carry the table. [15]The poles for carrying the table were made of acacia wood. They were covered with gold. [16]Then he made of pure gold all the things that were used on the table: the plates, bowls, cups and jars used for pouring the drink offerings.

[17]Then he made the lampstand of pure gold. He hammered out its base and stand. Its flower-like cups, buds and petals were joined together in one piece with the base and stand. [18]There were three branches on one side of the lampstand and three branches on the other. [19]Each branch had three cups shaped like almond flowers. Each cup had a bud and a petal. [20]There were four more cups shaped like almond flowers on the lampstand itself. Each cup had its buds and petals. [21]Three pairs of branches went out from the lampstand. A bud was under the place where each pair was attached to the lampstand. [22]The buds, branches and lampstand were all one piece of pure, hammered gold. [23]He made seven pure gold lamps for this lampstand. Then he made pure gold wick trimmers and trays. [24]He used about 75 pounds of pure gold to make the lampstand and all the things that go with it.

[25]Then he made the altar of incense[d] of acacia wood. The altar was square. It was 18 inches long, 18 inches wide and 36 inches high. Each corner stuck out like a horn. Each corner was joined into one piece with the altar. [26]He covered the top and all the sides and the corners with pure gold. Then he put gold trim around the altar. [27]He made two gold rings and put them below the trim on opposite sides of the altar. These rings held the poles for carrying the altar. [28]He made the poles of acacia wood and covered them with gold.

[29]Then he made the holy olive oil for appointing the priests. He also made the pure, sweet-smelling incense. He made them like a person who mixes perfumes.

38 Then he built the altar for burning offerings. He made the altar of acacia wood. The altar was square. It was 7½ feet long, 7½ feet wide and 4½ feet high. [2]He made each corner stick out like a horn. The horns and the altar were joined together in one piece. Then he covered the altar with bronze. [3]He made all the tools of bronze to use on the altar: the pots, shovels, bowls for sprinkling blood, meat forks and pans for carrying the fire. [4]He made a large bronze screen to hold the burning wood for the altar. He put the screen inside the altar, under its rim, halfway up from the bottom. [5]He made bronze rings for holding the poles for carrying the altar. He put the rings at the four corners of the screen. [6]Then he made poles of acacia wood and covered them with bronze. [7]He put the poles through the rings on both sides of the altar. They were used for carrying the altar. He made the altar of boards and left the inside hollow.

[8]He made the bronze bowl for washing. He built it on a bronze stand. He used the bronze of mirrors. These mirrors belonged to the women who served at the entrance to the Meeting Tent.[d]

[9]Then he made a wall of curtains to form a courtyard around the Holy Tent.[d] On the south side the curtains were 150 feet long and were made of fine linen. [10]The curtains hung on silver hooks and bands. These were on 20 bronze posts on 20 bronze bases. [11]On the north side the wall of curtains was also 150 feet long. It hung on silver hooks and bands on 20 posts with 20 bronze bases.

[12]On the west side of the courtyard, the wall of curtains was 75 feet long. It was held up by silver hooks and bands on 10 posts and 10 bases. [13]The east side was 75 feet wide. [14]On one side of the entry there was a wall of curtains that was 22½ feet long. It was held up by 3 posts and 3 bases. [15]On the other side of the entry there was a wall of curtains 22½ feet long. It was held up by 3 posts

and 3 bases. [16]All the curtains around the courtyard were made of fine linen. [17]The bases for the posts were made of bronze. The hooks and the bands on the posts were made of silver. The tops of the posts were covered with silver also. All the posts in the courtyard had silver bands.

[18]The curtain for the entry of the courtyard was made of blue, purple and red thread, and fine linen. It was sewn by a person who could sew well. The curtain was 30 feet long and 7½ feet high. It was the same height as the curtains around the courtyard. [19]The curtain was held up by 4 posts and 4 bronze bases. The hooks and bands on the posts were made of silver. The tops on the posts were covered with silver. [20]All the tent pegs for the Holy Tent and for the curtains around the courtyard were made of bronze.

[21]This is a list of the metals used to make the Holy Tent. This is where the two flat stones with the Ten Commandments are kept. Moses ordered the Levites to make this list. Ithamar son of Aaron was in charge of keeping the list. [22]Bezalel son of Uri made everything the Lord commanded Moses. Uri was the son of Hur of the tribe[d] of Judah. [23]Oholiab son of Ahisamach of the tribe of Dan helped him. Oholiab could cut designs into metal and stone. He was a designer. He was also skilled at sewing the blue, purple and red thread, and fine linen.

[24]The total amount of gold used to build the Holy Tent was presented to the Lord. It weighed over 2,000 pounds, as set by the Holy Place measure.

[25]The silver was given by the members of the community who were counted. It weighed 7,550 pounds, as set by the Holy Place measure. [26]All the men 20 years old or older were counted. There were 603,550 men, and each man had to pay ⅕ ounce of silver. This is the weight as set by the Holy Place measure. [27]Of this silver, 7,500 pounds was used to make the 100 bases. These bases were for the Holy Tent and for the curtain. There was 75 pounds of silver in each base. [28]The other 50 pounds of silver was used to make the hooks for the posts. It was also used to cover the tops of the posts and to make the bands on the posts.

[29]The bronze which was presented to the Lord weighed about 5,000 pounds. [30]They used the bronze to make the bases at the entrance of the Meeting Tent.

They also used the bronze to make the altar and the bronze screen. And this bronze was used to make all the tools for the altar. [31]This bronze was also used to make bases for the wall of curtains around the courtyard. It was used for the bases for the curtains at the entry to the courtyard. And this bronze was used to make the tent pegs for the Holy Tent and curtains that surrounded the courtyard.

39 They used blue, purple and red thread to make woven clothes for the priests. They were to wear these when they served in the Holy Place. They also made the holy clothes for Aaron as the Lord had commanded Moses.

[2]They made the holy vest[d] of gold and blue, purple and red thread, and fine linen. [3]They hammered the gold into sheets. Then they cut the gold into long, thin strips. They worked the gold into the blue, purple and red thread, and fine linen. This was done by a skilled craftsman. [4]They made the shoulder straps for the holy vest. These straps were attached to the top corners of the vest. Then the shoulder straps were tied together over each shoulder. [5]The skillfully woven belt was made in the same way. It was joined to the holy vest as one piece. It was made of gold and blue, purple and red thread, and fine linen. It was made the way the Lord commanded Moses.

[6]They put gold around the onyx stones. Then they wrote the names of the sons of Israel on these gems. They did that as a person carves words and designs on a seal.[d] [7]Then they attached the gems on the shoulder straps of the holy vest. These gems are reminders of the 12 sons of Israel. This was done the way the Lord had commanded Moses.

[8]The skilled craftsmen made the chest covering. It was made like the holy vest. It was made of gold and blue, purple and red thread, and fine linen. [9]The chest covering was square, nine inches long and nine inches wide. It was folded double to make a pocket. [10]Then they put four rows of beautiful jewels on it. In the first row there was a ruby, a topaz and a yellow quartz. [11]In the second row there was a turquoise, a sapphire and an emerald. [12]In the third row there was a jacinth, an agate and an amethyst. [13]In the fourth row there was a chrysolite, an onyx and a jasper. Gold was put around these jewels to attach them to the chest

covering. [14]The names of the sons of Israel were carved on these 12 jewels as a person carves a seal. Each jewel had the name of 1 of the 12 tribes[d] of Israel.

[15]They made chains of pure gold for the chest covering. They were twisted together like a rope. [16]The workers made two gold pieces and two gold rings. They put the two gold rings on the two upper corners of the chest covering. [17]Then they put two gold chains in the two rings. These are at the ends of the chest covering. [18]They fastened the other two ends of the chains to the two gold pieces. Then they attached these gold pieces to the two shoulder straps in the front of the holy vest. [19]They made two more gold rings and put them at the lower corners of the chest covering. They put them on the inside edge next to the holy vest. [20]Then they made two more gold rings on the bottom of the shoulder straps in front of the holy vest. These rings were near the seam, just above the woven belt of the holy vest. [21]They used a blue ribbon and tied the rings of the chest covering to the rings of the holy vest. This connected it to the woven belt. In this way the chest covering would not swing out from the holy vest. They did all these things the way the Lord commanded.

[22]Then they made the outer robe to be worn under the holy vest. It was woven of blue cloth. [23]They made a hole in the center of the outer robe. A woven collar was sewn around this hole so it would not tear. [24]Then they made balls like pomegranates[d] of blue, purple and red thread, and fine linen. They hung them around the bottom of the outer robe. [25]They also made bells of pure gold. They hung these around the bottom of the outer robe between the balls. [26]So around the bottom of the outer robe there was a bell and a pomegranate ball, a bell and a pomegranate ball. The priest wore this outer robe when he served as priest, just as the Lord had commanded Moses.

[27]They wove inner robes of fine linen for Aaron and his sons. [28]And they made turbans and underclothes of fine linen. [29]Then they made the cloth belt of fine linen and blue, purple and red thread. Designs were sewn onto the cloth. These things were made as the Lord had commanded Moses.

[30]They made a strip of pure gold, which is the holy crown. They carved these words in the gold: "Holy to the Lord." They did it as one might carve on a seal. [31]Then they tied this flat piece to the turban with a blue ribbon. This was done as the Lord had commanded Moses.

[32]So all the work on the Meeting Tent[d] was finished. The Israelites did everything just as the Lord had commanded Moses. [33]Then they brought the Holy Tent to Moses: the Tent and all its furniture, hooks, frames, crossbars, posts and bases; [34]the covering made of male sheep skins colored red, the covering made of fine leather and the curtain that covered the entrance to the Most Holy Place; [35]the Box[d] of the Agreement, its poles and lid; [36]the table, all its containers and the bread that showed they were in God's presence; [37]the pure gold lampstand with its lamps in a row, all its tools and the olive oil for the light; [38]the gold altar, the special olive oil used for appointing priests, the sweet-smelling incense,[d] and the curtain that covered the entrance to the Tent; [39]the bronze altar and its screen, its poles and all its tools, the bowl and its stand; [40]the curtains for the courtyard with their posts and bases, the curtain that covered the entry to the courtyard, the cords, pegs and all the things in the Meeting Tent. [41]They brought the clothes for the priests to wear when they served in the Holy Tent: the holy clothes for Aaron the priest and the clothes for his sons. They wore these when they served as priests.

[42]The Israelites had done all this work just as the Lord had commanded Moses. [43]Moses looked closely at all the work. He saw they had done it just as the Lord had commanded. So Moses blessed them.

40 Then the Lord said this to Moses: [2]"On the first day of the first month, set up the Holy Tent,[d] which is the Meeting Tent. [3]Put the Box[d] of the Agreement in the Meeting Tent. Hang the curtain in front of the Holy Box. [4]Then bring in the table. Arrange everything on the table that should be there. Then bring in the lampstand and set up its lamps. [5]Put the gold altar for burning incense[d] in front of the Box of the Agreement. Then put the curtain at the entrance to the Holy Tent.

[6]"Put the altar of burnt offerings in front of the entrance of the Holy Tent, the Meeting Tent. [7]Put the bowl between the Meeting Tent and the altar. Put water in the bowl. [8]Set up the courtyard

around the Holy Tent. Then put the curtain at the entry to the courtyard.

⁹"Use the special olive oil and pour it on the Holy Tent and everything in it. Give the Tent and all that is in it for service to the Lord. They will be holy. ¹⁰Pour the special oil on the altar for burning offerings. Pour it on all its tools. Give the altar for service to God. It will be very holy. ¹¹Then pour the special olive oil on the bowl and the base under it. When you do this, they will be given for service to God.

¹²"Bring Aaron and his sons to the entrance of the Meeting Tent. Wash them with water. ¹³Then put the holy clothes on Aaron. Pour the special oil on him, and give him for service to God. Then he may serve me as a priest. ¹⁴Bring Aaron's sons and put the inner robes on them. ¹⁵Pour the special oil on them to make them priests. Do this the same way that you appointed their father as priest. Then they may also serve me as priests. Pouring oil on them will make them a family of priests. They and their descendants[d] will be priests from now on." ¹⁶Moses did everything that the Lord commanded him.

¹⁷So the Holy Tent was set up. It was the first day of the first month during the second year after they left Egypt. ¹⁸When Moses set up the Holy Tent, he put the bases in place. Then he put the frames on the bases. Next he put the crossbars through the rings of the frames and set up the posts. ¹⁹After that, Moses spread the cloth over the Holy Tent. Then he put the covering over the Tent. He did these things just as the Lord commanded.

²⁰Moses put the flat stones into the Box of the Agreement. These had God's law written on them. Moses put the poles through the rings of the Holy Box. Then he put the lid on it. ²¹Next Moses brought the Holy Box into the Tent. He hung the curtain to cover the Holy Box. Moses did these things just as the Lord commanded him.

²²Moses put the table in the Meeting Tent. He put it on the north side of the Holy Tent in front of the curtain. ²³Then he put the bread on the table before the Lord. He did this just as the Lord commanded him. ²⁴Moses put the lampstand in the Meeting Tent. He put it on the south side of the Holy Tent across from the table. ²⁵Then he put the lamps on the lampstand before the Lord. He did this just as the Lord commanded him.

²⁶Moses put the gold altar for burning incense in the Meeting Tent. He put it in front of the curtain. ²⁷Then he burned sweet-smelling incense on it, just as the Lord commanded him. ²⁸Then he hung the curtain at the entrance to the Holy Tent.

²⁹He put the altar for burning sacrifices at the entrance to the Holy Tent, the Meeting Tent. Then Moses offered a whole burnt offering and grain offerings on that altar. He did these things just as the Lord commanded him. ³⁰Moses put the bowl between the Meeting Tent and the altar for burning sacrifices. Moses put water in the bowl for washing. ³¹Moses, Aaron and Aaron's sons used this water to wash their hands and feet. ³²They washed themselves every time they entered the Meeting Tent. They also washed themselves every time they went near the altar for burning sacrifices. They did these things just as the Lord commanded Moses.

³³Then Moses set up the courtyard around the Holy Tent. He put the altar for burning sacrifices in the courtyard. Then he put up the curtain at the entry to the courtyard. So Moses finished the work.

³⁴Then the cloud covered the Meeting Tent.[d] The greatness of the Lord filled the Holy Tent. ³⁵Moses could not enter the Meeting Tent. This was because the cloud had settled on it. And this was because the greatness of the Lord filled the Holy Tent.

³⁶When the cloud rose from the Holy Tent, the Israelites would begin to travel. ³⁷But as long as the cloud stayed on the Holy Tent, the people did not travel. They stayed in that place until the cloud rose. ³⁸So the cloud of the Lord was over the Holy Tent during the day. And there was a fire in the cloud at night. So all the Israelites could see the cloud while they traveled.

The Third Book of Moses Called
LEVITICUS

1 The Lord called to Moses and spoke to him from the Meeting Tent.[d] The Lord said, [2]"Tell the people of Israel: 'When you bring an offering to the Lord, bring as your offering one of the cattle. Or you may bring one of the sheep or goats.

[3]"'If anyone offers a whole burnt offering from the cattle, it must be a male. It must have nothing wrong with it. The person must take the animal to the entrance of the Meeting Tent. Then the Lord will accept the offering. [4]The person must put his hand on the animal's head. Then the Lord will accept that burnt offering. It will remove the person's sin so he will belong to God. [5]The person must kill the young bull before the Lord. Then the priests must bring its blood to the altar. They must sprinkle the blood on all sides of the altar. This is the altar at the entrance to the Meeting Tent. [6]The person will cut the skin from that animal. Then he will cut the animal into pieces. [7]The priests must put wood and fire on the altar. [8]They must lay the head, the fat and other pieces on the wood. That wood is on the fire on the altar. [9]The priest must wash the animal's inner organs and legs with water. Then the priest must burn all the animal's parts on the altar. It is a whole burnt offering, an offering made by fire. And its smell is pleasing to the Lord.

[10]"'The burnt offering may be a sheep or goat. It must be a male animal that has nothing wrong with it. [11]The person must kill the animal on the north side of the altar. This is to be before the Lord. Then the priests must sprinkle its blood on the altar. They must sprinkle it on all sides. [12]The person must cut the animal into pieces. Then the priest must lay the pieces with the head and fat on the wood. The wood is on the fire on the altar. [13]The person must wash the animal's inner organs and legs with water. Then the priest must burn all its parts on the altar. It is a burnt offering, an offering made by fire. And its smell is pleasing to the Lord.

[14]"'The whole burnt offering may be a bird. It must be a dove or a young pigeon. [15]The priest will bring the offering to the altar. He will pull off the bird's

head. Then he will burn it on the altar. The bird's blood must be drained out on the side of the altar. [16]The priest must remove the bird's crop[n] and its contents. He must throw them on the east side of the altar. This is where they put the ashes from the altar. [17]Then the priest must tear the bird open by its wings. But he must not divide the bird into two parts. Then the priest must burn the bird on the altar. He must place it on the wood which is on the fire. It is a burnt offering, an offering made by fire. Its smell is pleasing to the Lord.

2 "'When anyone offers a grain offering to the Lord, it must be made from fine flour. The person must pour oil on it and put incense[d] on it. [2]Then he must take it to Aaron's sons and the priests. The priest must take a handful of the fine flour, with the oil and all the incense. He must burn it on the altar as a memorial portion. It is an offering made by fire. Its smell is pleasing to the Lord. [3]The rest of the grain offering will belong to Aaron and the priests. This offering is a most holy part of the offerings made by fire to the Lord.

[4]"'If you bring a grain offering that was baked in the oven, it must be made from fine flour. It may be loaves made without yeast and mixed with oil. Or it may be wafers made without yeast. They are to have oil poured over them. [5]If your grain offering is cooked on a griddle, it must be made without yeast. It must be made of fine flour mixed with oil. [6]Crumble it and pour oil over it. It is a grain offering. [7]If your grain offering is cooked in a pan, it must be made from fine flour and oil. [8]Bring the grain offering made of these things to the Lord. Give it to the priest. He will take it to the altar. [9]He will take out the memorial portion from the grain offering. He will burn it on the altar. This is an offering made by fire. Its smell is pleasing to the Lord. [10]The rest of the grain offering belongs to Aaron and the priests. It is a most holy part of the offerings made to the Lord by fire.

[11]"'Every grain offering you bring to the Lord must be made without yeast. You must not burn yeast or honey in an offering made by fire to the Lord. [12]You

---

1:16 crop A small bag inside a bird's throat. When a bird eats, its food goes into this part first. There, the food is made soft before it goes into the stomach.

may bring yeast and honey to the Lord as an offering from the first harvest. But yeast and honey must not be burned on the altar as a pleasing smell. ¹³You must also put salt on all your grain offerings. Salt stands for your agreement with God that will last forever. Do not leave it out of your grain offering. You must add salt to all your offerings.

¹⁴"If you bring a grain offering from the first harvest to the Lord, bring crushed heads of new grain. They must be roasted in the fire. ¹⁵Put oil and incense on the grain. It is a grain offering. ¹⁶The priest will burn the memorial portion of the crushed grain and oil. It will have incense on it. It is an offering by fire to the Lord.

3 "'A person's fellowship offering to the Lord may be from the cattle. It may be a male or female animal. But it must have nothing wrong with it. ²The person must put his hand on the animal's head. He must kill it at the entrance to the Meeting Tent.ᵈ Then the priests must sprinkle the blood on all sides of the altar. ³This person must make a sacrifice from the fellowship offering. The sacrifice must be made by fire to the Lord. He must offer the fat of the animal's inner organs. This is both the fat that is in them and that covers them. ⁴He must also offer both kidneys and the fat on them. They are near the lower back muscle. He must also offer the best part of the liver. He will remove it with the kidneys. ⁵Then the priests will burn these parts on the altar. They will put them on the burnt offering that is on the wood on the fire. It is an offering made by fire. Its smell is pleasing to the Lord.

⁶"'A person's fellowship offering to the Lord may be a lamb or a goat. He may offer a male or female animal. But it must have nothing wrong with it. ⁷If he offers a lamb, he must bring it before the Lord. ⁸He must put his hand on its head. Then he must kill the animal in front of the Meeting Tent. The priests will sprinkle its blood on all sides of the altar. ⁹Then the person must make a sacrifice from the fellowship offering. The sacrifice must be made by fire to the Lord. The person must bring the fat and the whole fat tail. The tail must be cut off close to the backbone. He must also offer the fat of the inner organs. This is both the fat that is in them and that covers them. ¹⁰He must offer both kidneys and the fat on them. They are near the

lower back muscle. And he must offer the best part of the liver. He will remove it with the kidneys. ¹¹Then the priest will burn these parts on the altar as food. It will be an offering made by fire to the Lord.

¹²"'A person's fellowship offering may be a goat. He is to offer it before the Lord. ¹³He must put his hand on the goat's head. And he must kill it in front of the Meeting Tent. Then the priests must sprinkle its blood on all sides of the altar. ¹⁴From this fellowship offering the person must make a sacrifice. It will be an offering by fire to the Lord. The person must offer all the fat of the goat's inner organs. This is both the fat that is in them and that covers them. ¹⁵He must offer both kidneys and the fat on them. They are near the lower back muscle. And he must offer the best part of the liver. He will remove it with the kidneys. ¹⁶The priest will burn these parts on the altar as food. It is an offering made by fire. Its smell is pleasing to the Lord. All the fat belongs to the Lord.

¹⁷"'This law will continue for people from now on, wherever you live: You must not eat fat or blood.'"

4 The Lord said to Moses, ²"Tell the people of Israel this: 'A person might sin by accident. He might do some things the Lord has commanded not to be done. If so, that person must do these things:

³"'It may be the appointed priest who has sinned. If so, he has brought guilt on the people. So he must offer a young bull to the Lord. It must have nothing wrong with it. This will be a sin offering for the sin he has done. ⁴He will bring the bull to the entrance of the Meeting Tent.ᵈ He must bring it in front of the Lord. Then he will put his hand on the bull's head. And he will kill the bull before the Lord. ⁵Then the appointed priest must bring some of the bull's blood into the Meeting Tent. ⁶The priest is to dip his finger into the blood. He must sprinkle it seven times before the Lord in front of the curtain. This curtain is in front of the Most Holy Place. ⁷The priest must also put some of the blood on the corners of the altar of incense.ᵈ It stands before the Lord in the Meeting Tent. Then the priest must pour out the rest of the bull's blood. It must be poured at the bottom of the altar of burnt offering. That altar is at the door of the Meeting Tent. ⁸He must remove all the fat from the bull of the sin offer-

ing. He must remove the fat on and around the inner organs. ⁹He must remove both kidneys and the fat on them. They are near the lower back muscle. He must remove the best part of the liver with the kidneys. ¹⁰He must do this in the same way the fat is removed from the bull of the fellowship offering. Then the priest must burn the animal parts on the altar of burnt offering. ¹¹⁻¹²But the priest must carry out the skin of the bull and all its meat. He must take these with the rest of the bull—its head, legs, intestines and other inner organs. He must take it outside the camp to the special clean[d] place where the ashes are poured out. He must burn it on a wood fire on the pile of ashes.

¹³"The whole nation of Israel might sin without knowing it. They might do something the Lord has commanded not to be done. If this happens, they are guilty. ¹⁴When they learn about the sin they have done, a young bull must be offered. It is a sin offering for the whole nation. They must bring it and give it before the Meeting Tent. ¹⁵The older leaders of the group of people must put their hands on the bull's head. It must be done before the Lord. And the bull must be killed before the Lord. ¹⁶Then the appointed priest must bring some of the bull's blood into the Meeting Tent. ¹⁷The priest will dip his finger in the blood. He must sprinkle it seven times before the Lord in front of the curtain. ¹⁸Then he must put some of the blood on the corners of the altar. The altar is before the Lord in the Meeting Tent. The priest must pour out the rest of the blood. He must pour it at the bottom of the altar of burnt offering. That altar is at the entrance to the Meeting Tent. ¹⁹The priest must remove all the fat from the animal. And he must burn it on the altar. ²⁰He will do the same thing with this bull that he did with the first bull of the sin offering. In this way the priest removes the sins of the people so they will belong to the Lord. And the Lord will forgive them. ²¹Then the priest must carry the bull outside the camp and burn it. He must do this just as he did with the first bull. This is the sin offering for the whole community.

²²"A ruler might sin by accident. He might do something the Lord his God has commanded must not be done. If he does, he is guilty. ²³When he learns about his sin, he must bring a male goat. It must have nothing wrong with it. That will be his sin offering. ²⁴The ruler must put his hand on the goat's head and kill it. This must be done where they kill the whole burnt offering before the Lord. The goat is a sin offering. ²⁵The priest must take some of the blood of the sin offering on his finger. He must put it on the corners of the altar of burnt offering. He must pour out the rest of the blood at the bottom of the altar of burnt offering. ²⁶He must burn all the goat's fat on the altar. He must burn it in the same way he burns the fat of the fellowship offerings. In this way the priest removes the ruler's sin so he belongs to the Lord. And the Lord will forgive him.

²⁷"A person in the community might sin by accident. He might do something which the Lord has commanded must not be done. He is guilty of sin. ²⁸When the person learns about his sin, he must bring a female goat. It must have nothing wrong with it. That will be his sin offering. ²⁹He must put his hand on the animal's head. He must kill it at the place of the whole burnt offering. ³⁰Then the priest must take some of the goat's blood on his finger. He must put it on the corners of the altar of burnt offering. He must pour out the rest of the goat's blood at the bottom of the altar. ³¹Then the priest must remove all the goat's fat. He must do it in the same way the fat is removed from the fellowship offerings. He must burn it on the altar. Its smell is pleasing to the Lord. In this way the priest will remove that person's sin so he will belong to the Lord. And the Lord will forgive him.

³²"This person may bring a lamb as his sin offering. If he does, he must bring a female. It must have nothing wrong with it. ³³The person must put his hand on the animal's head. He must kill it as a sin offering. He must kill it where they kill the whole burnt offering. ³⁴The priest must take some of the blood from the sin offering on his finger. He must put it on the corners of the altar of burnt offering. Then he must pour out the rest of the lamb's blood at the bottom of the altar. ³⁵The priest must remove all the lamb's fat. He must do it in the same way that the lamb's fat is removed from the fellowship offerings. He must burn the pieces on the altar. They go on top of the offerings made by fire for the Lord. In this way the priest will remove that person's sins so he will belong to the Lord. And the Lord will forgive him.

5 " 'These are things for which a sin offering must be made:

" 'A person might be ordered to tell in court what he has seen or what he knows. If he does not tell the court, he is guilty of sin.

[2] " 'Or someone might touch something unclean.[d] It might be the dead body of an unclean wild animal or an unclean farm animal or an unclean crawling animal. He might not know that he touched it. But he will still be unclean and guilty of sin.

[3] " 'Many things come from a person which are not clean. Someone might touch one of these unclean things from a person and not know it. But when he learns about it, he will be guilty.

[4] " 'Or someone might make a promise before the Lord without thinking. He might promise to do something bad or good. The promise might be about anything. He might even make a promise before the Lord and forget about it. But when he remembers, he will be guilty.

[5] " 'When anyone is guilty of any of these things, he must tell how he sinned. [6] He must bring an offering to the Lord. It is a penalty for his sin. It must be a female lamb or goat from the flock. The priest will perform the acts to remove that person's sin so he will belong to the Lord.

[7] " 'But perhaps the person cannot afford a lamb. Then he must bring two doves or two young pigeons to the Lord. These will be the penalty for his sin. One bird must be for a sin offering. The other must be for a burnt offering. [8] He must bring them to the priest. First the priest will offer the one for the sin offering. He will pull the bird's head from its neck. But he will not pull it completely off. [9] He must sprinkle the blood from the sin offering on the side of the altar. Then he must pour the rest of the blood at the bottom of the altar. It is a sin offering. [10] Then the priest must offer the second bird as a burnt offering. This is what the law says. In this way the priest will remove the person's sin so he will belong to the Lord. And the Lord will forgive him.

[11] " 'The person might not be able to afford two doves or two pigeons. If not, he must bring about two quarts of fine flour. This will be an offering for his sin. He must not put oil on the flour. And he must not put incense[d] on it, because it is a sin offering. [12] He must bring the flour to the priest. The priest will take a hand-ful of the flour as a memorial offering. He will burn it on the altar. It goes on top of the offerings made by fire to the Lord. It is a sin offering. [13] In this way the priest will remove the person's sins so he will belong to the Lord. And the Lord will forgive him. What is left of the sin offering belongs to the priest. This is like the grain offering.' "

[14] The Lord said to Moses, [15] "A person might accidentally sin and do something against the holy things of the Lord. That person must bring a male sheep from the flock. It must have nothing wrong with it. This will be his penalty offering to the Lord. The value in silver of the male sheep must be correct. Use the proper value for silver as set by the Holy Place measure. [16] That person must pay for the sin he did against the holy thing. He must add one-fifth to its value. Then he must give it all to the priest. In this way the priest will remove the person's sin so he will belong to the Lord. The priest does it by means of the male sheep of the penalty offering. And the Lord will forgive the person.

[17] "A person might sin and do something the Lord has commanded not to be done. It does not matter if that person knew or not. He is guilty. He is responsible for his sin. [18] He must bring the priest a male sheep from the flock. It must have nothing wrong with it. It must be worth the correct amount. The male sheep will be a penalty offering. The person sinned without knowing it. But with this offering the priest will remove the sin so the person will belong to the Lord. And the Lord will forgive him. [19] The person is guilty of doing wrong against the Lord. So he must give the penalty offering to the Lord."

6 The Lord said to Moses, [2] "A person might sin against the Lord by doing one of these sins: He might lie about what happened to something he was taking care of for someone else. Or he might lie about a promise he made. Or he might steal something or cheat someone. [3] He might find something that had been lost and then lie about it. He might make a promise before the Lord about something and not mean it. Or he might do some other sin. [4] If he does any of these things, he is guilty of sin. He must bring back whatever he stole. Or he must bring back what he took by cheating. Or he must bring back the thing he took care of for someone else. Or he must bring back what he found and lied about. ⁵Or he must bring back what he made a false promise about. He must pay the full price. Then he must pay an extra one-fifth of the value of what he took. He must give the money to the true owner. This must be done on the day he brings his penalty offering. ⁶He must pay a penalty to the priest. It must be a male sheep from the flock. It must not have anything wrong with it. And it must be worth the correct amount. It will be a penalty offering to the Lord. ⁷Then the priest will perform the acts to remove that person's sin so he will belong to the Lord. And the Lord will forgive him for the sins that made him guilty."

⁸The Lord said to Moses, ⁹"Give this command to Aaron and the priests: 'These are the teachings about the whole burnt offering. The burnt offering must stay on the altar all night until morning. The altar's fire must be kept burning. ¹⁰The priest must put on his linen robe. He must put on linen underclothes next to his body. Then he will remove the ashes from the burnt offering on the altar. He will put these ashes beside the altar. ¹¹Then he must take off those clothes and put on others. He must carry the ashes outside the camp to a special cleanᵈ place. ¹²But the fire must be kept burning on the altar. It must not be allowed to go out. The priest must put more firewood on the altar every morning. He must place the whole burnt offering on the fire. He must burn the fat of the fellowship offerings. ¹³The fire must be kept burning on the altar all the time. It must not go out.

¹⁴"These are the teachings about the grain offering: The priests must bring it to the Lord in front of the altar. ¹⁵The priest must take a handful of fine flour. The oil and incenseᵈ must be on it. The priest must burn the grain offering on the altar. It will be a memorial offering to the Lord. Its smell is pleasing to him. ¹⁶Aaron and the priests may eat what is left. It must be eaten without yeast in a holy place. The priests must eat it in the courtyard of the Meeting Tent.ᵈ ¹⁷It must not be cooked with yeast. I have given it as their share of the offerings made to me by fire. It is most holy, like the sin offering and the penalty offering. ¹⁸Any male descendantᵈ of Aaron may eat it. It is his share of the offerings made to the Lord by fire. This will continue from now on. Whatever touches these offerings must be holy.'"

¹⁹The Lord said to Moses, ²⁰"This is the offering Aaron and the priests must bring to the Lord. They must do this on the day they appoint Aaron as high priest. They must bring two quarts of fine flour for a grain offering. They must bring half of it in the morning and half in the evening. ²¹The fine flour must be mixed with oil and cooked on a griddle. Bring it when it is well mixed. You must break it into pieces. It will be a smell that is pleasing to the Lord. ²²One of the priests will be appointed to take Aaron's place as high priest. He must make the grain offering to the Lord. It is a rule forever. The grain offering must be completely burned to the Lord. ²³Every grain offering made by a priest must be completely burned. It must not be eaten."

²⁴The Lord said to Moses, ²⁵"Tell Aaron and the priests: 'These are the teachings about the sin offering. The sin offering must be killed in front of the Lord. It must be killed in the same place the whole burnt offering is killed. It is most holy. ²⁶The priest who offers the sin offering must eat it. He must eat it in a holy place. It must be in the courtyard of the Meeting Tent.ᵈ ²⁷Whatever touches the meat of the sin offering must be holy. If the blood is sprinkled on any clothes, you must wash them in a holy place. ²⁸The clay pot the meat is cooked in must be broken. If a bronze pot is used, it must be scrubbed and rinsed with water. ²⁹Any male in a priest's family may eat the offering. It is most holy. ³⁰The blood of the sin offering may be taken into the Meeting Tent. It may be used to remove sin in the Holy Place. That sin offering must be burned with fire. It must not be eaten.

7 "'These are the teachings about the penalty offering. It is most holy. ²The penalty offering must be killed where the whole burnt offering is killed. Then the priest must sprinkle its blood on all sides of the altar. ³He must offer all the fat from the penalty offering. He must offer the fat tail and the fat that covers the inner organs. ⁴He must offer both kidneys and the fat on them. They are near the lower back muscle. And he must offer the best part of the liver. This is to be removed with the kidneys. ⁵The priest must burn all these things on the altar. They will be an offering made by fire to the Lord. It is a penalty offering. ⁶Any male in a priest's family may eat it. It is most holy. So it must be eaten in a holy place.

⁷"'The penalty offering is like the sin offering. The teachings are the same for both. The priest who offers the sacrifice to remove sins will get the meat for food. ⁸The priest who offers the burnt offering may also have the skin from it. ⁹Every grain offering belongs to the priest who offers it. This includes those baked in an oven, cooked on a griddle or baked in a dish. ¹⁰The grain offerings belong to the priests. They may be dry or mixed with oil. All priests will share alike.

¹¹"'These are the teachings about the fellowship offering a person may offer to the Lord: ¹²He may bring the fellowship offering to show his thanks. If he does, he should also bring loaves of bread. They must be made without yeast, mixed with oil. And he should bring wafers made without yeast. They must have oil poured over them. He should also bring loaves of fine flour mixed with oil. ¹³He must also offer loaves of bread made with yeast. These should be brought with his fellowship offering, which he gives to show thanks. ¹⁴One of each kind of offering will be for the Lord. It will be given to the priest who sprinkles the blood of the fellowship offering. ¹⁵The fellowship offering is to thank the Lord. The meat from it must be eaten the same day it is offered. None of it must be left until morning.

¹⁶"'A person might bring a fellowship offering just to give a gift to God. Or it may be done because of a special promise to God. Then, the sacrifice should be eaten the same day he offers it. If there is any left, it may be eaten the next day. ¹⁷If any meat from this sacrifice is left on the third day, it must be burned up. ¹⁸Any meat of the fellowship offering eaten on the third day will not be accepted. The Lord will not count the sacrifice for the person who offered it. It will become unclean.ᵈ Anyone who eats the meat will be guilty of sin.

¹⁹"'People must not eat meat that touches anything unclean. They must burn this meat with fire. But anyone who is clean may eat other meat. ²⁰But a person who is unclean might eat the meat from the fellowship offering that belongs to the Lord. If he does, he must be separated from his people.

²¹"'Someone might touch something unclean that comes from people. Or the unclean thing might be an animal or some hated thing. Touching it will make him unclean. If he then eats meat from the fellowship offering that belongs to the Lord, he must be separated from his people.'"

²²The Lord said to Moses, ²³"Tell the people of Israel: 'You must not eat any of the fat from cattle, sheep or goats. ²⁴If an animal is found dead or torn by wild animals, you may use its fat for other things. But you must not eat it. ²⁵Someone might eat fat from an animal offering made by fire to the Lord. That person must be separated from his people. ²⁶It does not matter where you live. You must not eat blood from any bird or animal. ²⁷Anyone who eats blood must be separated from his people.'"

²⁸The Lord said to Moses, ²⁹"Tell the people of Israel: 'Someone may bring a fellowship offering to the Lord. He must give part of it as his sacrifice to the Lord. ³⁰He must carry that part of the gift in his own hands. It will be an offering made by fire to the Lord. He must carry the fat and the breast of the animal to the priest. The breast must be presented to the Lord as the priests' share. ³¹Then the priest must burn the fat on the altar. But the breast of the animal will belong to Aaron and the priests. ³²You must also give the right thigh from the fellowship offering to the priest as a gift. ³³It will belong to the priest who offers the blood and fat of the fellowship offering. ³⁴I have taken the breast and the thigh of the fellowship offering. And I have given these parts to Aaron and the priests as their share from the Israelites.'"

³⁵This is the portion that belongs to Aaron and his sons. It is from the offerings made by fire to the Lord. Aaron and his sons were given this share on the day they were presented to the Lord as priests. ³⁶On the day the Lord appointed the priests, he commanded Israel to give this share to them. It is to be given to the priests as their share from now on.

³⁷These are the teachings about the whole burnt offering, the grain offering, the sin offering and the penalty offering. They are the teachings about the appointment of priests. And they are the teachings about the fellowship offerings. ³⁸The Lord gave these teachings to Moses on Mount Sinai. It was on the day he commanded the Israelites to bring their offerings to him in the Sinai Desert.

8 The Lord said to Moses, ²"Bring Aaron and his sons and their clothes. Bring the special olive oil used in appointing people and things to the service of the Lord. Also bring the bull of the sin offering and the two male sheep. And bring the basket of bread made without yeast. ³Then gather the people together at the entrance to the Meeting Tent."⁴ ⁴Moses did as the Lord commanded him. The people met together at the entrance to the Meeting Tent.

⁵Then Moses spoke to the people. He said, "This is what the Lord has commanded to be done." ⁶Then Moses brought Aaron and his sons forward. He washed them with water. ⁷He put the inner robe on Aaron. And he tied the cloth belt around Aaron. Then he put the outer robe on him. Next he put the holy vest⁴ on Aaron. Then he tied the skillfully woven belt around him. So the holy vest was tied to Aaron. ⁸Then Moses put the chest covering on him. And he put the Urim and the Thummim⁴ in the chest covering. ⁹He also put the turban on Aaron's head. He put the strip of gold on the front of the turban. This strip of gold is the holy crown. Moses did this as the Lord commanded him to do.

¹⁰Then Moses put the special oil on the Holy Tent⁴ and everything in it. In this way Moses made them holy for the Lord. ¹¹He sprinkled some oil on the altar seven times. He sprinkled the altar and all its tools. He also sprinkled special oil on the large bowl and its base. In this way he made them holy for the Lord. ¹²Then he poured some of the special oil on Aaron's head. In this way he made Aaron holy for the Lord. ¹³Then Moses brought Aaron's sons forward. And he put the inner robes on them. He tied cloth belts around them. Then he put headbands on them. He did these things as the Lord had commanded him.

¹⁴Then Moses brought the bull for the sin offering. And Aaron and his sons put their hands on its head. ¹⁵Moses killed the bull and took some of the blood. With his finger he put some of the blood on all the corners of the altar. In this way he made the altar pure. Then he poured out the rest of the blood at the bottom of the altar. So he made it holy and ready for service to God. ¹⁶Moses took all the fat from the inner organs of the bull. He took the best part of the liver. And he took both kidneys and the fat on them. Then he burned them on the altar. ¹⁷But he took the bull's skin, its meat and its intestines outside the camp. He burned them in a fire outside the camp. Moses did all these things as the Lord had commanded him.

¹⁸Next Moses brought the male sheep of the burnt offering. Aaron and his sons put their hands on its head. ¹⁹Then Moses killed it. He sprinkled the blood on all sides of the altar. ²⁰Moses cut the male sheep into pieces. And he burned the head, the pieces and the fat. ²¹He washed the inner organs and legs with water. Then he burned the whole sheep on the altar. It was a burnt offering made by fire to the Lord. Its smell was pleasing to the Lord. Moses did these things as the Lord had commanded him.

²²Then Moses brought the other male sheep. It was used in appointing Aaron and his sons as priests. They put their hands on its head. ²³Then Moses killed the sheep. He put some of its blood on the bottom of Aaron's right ear. He put some on the thumb of Aaron's right hand. And he put some on the big toe of his right foot. ²⁴Then Moses brought Aaron's sons close to the altar. He put some of the blood on the bottom of their right ears. He put it on the thumbs of their right hands. And he put it on the big toes of their right feet. Then he sprinkled blood on all sides of the altar. ²⁵He took the fat and the fat tail from the sheep. He took all the fat on the inner organs. He took the best part of the liver. He also took both kidneys, their fat and the right thigh. ²⁶A basket of bread made without yeast is put before the Lord each day. From the basket Moses took a loaf of bread. And he took a loaf made with oil and a wafer. He put these pieces of bread on the fat and right thigh of the male sheep. ²⁷He put all these things in the hands of Aaron and his sons. He presented the pieces as an offering before the Lord. ²⁸Then Moses took them from their hands. And he burned them on the altar on top of the burnt offering. So this was the offering for appointing Aaron and his sons as priests. It was an offering made by fire to the Lord. Its smell was pleasing to the Lord. ²⁹Moses took the breast and presented it as an offering before the Lord. It was Moses' share of the male sheep used in appointing the priests. This was as the Lord had commanded Moses.

³⁰Moses took some of the special oil and some of the blood which was on the altar. He sprinkled some of the oil on Aaron and Aaron's clothes. He also sprinkled some on Aaron's sons and their clothes. In this way Moses made Aaron, his clothes, his sons and their clothes holy for the Lord.

[31] Then Moses said to Aaron and his sons, "I gave you a command. I said, 'Aaron and his sons will eat these things.' So take the meat and basket of bread from the offering for appointing priests. Boil the meat at the door of the Meeting Tent. Eat it there with the bread. [32] If any of the meat or bread is left, burn it. [33] The time of appointing will last seven days. You must not go outside the entrance of the Meeting Tent until that time is up. Stay there until the time of your appointing is finished. [34] The Lord commanded the things that were done today. He commanded these things to remove your sins so you will belong to him. [35] You must stay at the entrance of the Meeting Tent. Stay there day and night for seven days. If you don't obey the Lord's commands, you will die! The Lord has given me these commands."

[36] So Aaron and his sons did everything the Lord had commanded through Moses.

9 On the eighth day after the time of appointing, Moses called for Aaron and his sons. He also called for the older leaders of Israel. [2] He said to Aaron, "Take a bull calf and a male sheep. There must be nothing wrong with these animals. The calf will be a sin offering. And the male sheep will be a whole burnt offering. Offer these animals to the Lord. [3] Tell the people of Israel, 'Take a male goat for a sin offering. And take a calf and a lamb for a whole burnt offering. The calf and the lamb must each be one year old. There must be nothing wrong with these animals. [4] Take a bull and a male sheep for fellowship offerings. Take with these animals a grain offering mixed with oil. Offer these things to the Lord. This is because the Lord will appear to you today.' "

[5] So all the people came to the front of the Meeting Tent.[d] They brought the things Moses had commanded them to bring. And they stood before the Lord. [6] Moses said, "You have done what the Lord commanded. So you will see the Lord's glory."

[7] Then Moses told Aaron, "Go to the altar. There offer sin offerings and whole burnt offerings. Do this to remove your sins and the people's sins so you will belong to God. Offer the sacrifices for the people. And perform the acts to remove their sins for them so they will belong to the Lord. Do this as the Lord has commanded."

[8] So Aaron went to the altar. He killed the bull calf as a sin offering for himself. [9] Then his sons brought the blood to him. Aaron dipped his finger in the blood and put it on the corners of the altar. Then he poured out the rest of the blood at the bottom of the altar. [10] Aaron took the fat, the kidneys and the best part of the liver from the sin offering. He burned these things on the altar. He did this the way the Lord had commanded Moses. [11] Aaron burned the meat and skin outside the camp.

[12] Then Aaron killed the animal for the whole burnt offering. Aaron's sons brought the blood to him. And he sprinkled it on all sides of the altar. [13] Aaron's sons gave the pieces and head of the burnt offering to Aaron. And he burned them on the altar. [14] Aaron also washed the inner organs and the legs of the burnt offering. And he burned them on the altar.

[15] Then Aaron brought the offering that was for the people. He took the goat of the people's sin offering. He killed and offered the goat of the sin offering. He did this just as he had done the first sin offering.

[16] Then Aaron brought the whole burnt offering and offered it. He did it as the Lord had commanded. [17] He also brought the grain offering to the altar. He took a handful of the grain and burned it on the altar. This was in addition to the morning's burnt offering.

[18] Aaron also killed the bull and the male sheep. These were the fellowship offerings for the people. Aaron's sons brought the blood from these animals to Aaron. He sprinkled it on all sides of the altar. [19] Aaron's sons also brought to Aaron the fat of the bull and the male sheep. They brought the fat tail and the fat covering the inner organs. They also brought the kidneys and the best part of the liver. [20] Aaron's sons put these fat parts on the breasts of the bull and sheep. Then Aaron burned these fat parts on the altar. [21] He presented the breasts and the right thigh before the Lord as the priests' share of the offering. He did this as Moses had commanded.

[22] Then Aaron lifted up his hands toward the people and blessed them. Aaron had finished offering the sin offering, the burnt offering and the fellowship offering. Then he stepped down from the altar.

[23] Moses and Aaron went into the Meeting Tent. Then they came out and

blessed the people. Then the Lord's glory came to all the people. [24]Fire came out from the Lord. It burned up the burnt offering and fat on the altar. When the people saw this, they shouted with joy. They bowed facedown on the ground.

10 Aaron's sons Nadab and Abihu took their pans for burning incense.[d] They put fire in them and added incense. But they did not use the special fire Moses had commanded them to use. [2]So fire came down from the Lord and destroyed Nadab and Abihu. They died in front of the Lord. [3]Then Moses said to Aaron, "This is what the Lord was speaking about when he said,

'I must be respected as holy
　　by those who come near me.
Before all the people
　　I must be given honor.'"

So Aaron did not say anything about the death of his sons.

[4]Aaron's uncle Uzziel had two sons named Mishael and Elzaphan. Moses said to them, "Come here. Pick up your cousins' bodies. Carry them outside the camp away from the front of the Holy Place." [5]So Mishael and Elzaphan obeyed Moses. They carried the bodies of Nadab and Abihu outside the camp. Nadab and Abihu were still wearing the special priest's inner robes.

[6]Then Moses spoke to Aaron and his other sons, Eleazar and Ithamar. Moses told them, "Don't show any sadness. Don't tear your clothes or leave your hair uncombed. If you do those things, you will die, and the Lord will be angry with all the people. All the people of Israel are your relatives. They may cry loudly about the Lord burning Nadab and Abihu. [7]But you must not even leave the Meeting Tent.[d] If you go out of the entrance, you will die! This is because the Lord has appointed you to his service." So Aaron, Eleazar and Ithamar obeyed Moses.

[8]Then the Lord said to Aaron, [9]"You and your sons must not drink wine or beer when you go into the Meeting Tent. If you do, you will die! This law will continue from now on. [10]You must keep what is holy separate from what is not holy. You must keep what is clean[d] separate from what is unclean. [11]The Lord gave his laws to Moses. And Moses gave them to the people. You must teach the people all the laws."

[12]Moses talked to Aaron and his remaining sons, Eleazar and Ithamar. Mo-

ses said, "Some of the grain offering is left from the sacrifices offered by fire to the Lord. Eat that part of the grain offering. But do not add yeast to it. Eat it near the altar because it is most holy. [13]The Law I gave you says this part belongs to you and your sons. But you must eat it in a holy place. It is part of the offerings made by fire to the Lord. I have been commanded to tell you this.

[14]"Also, you, your sons and daughters may eat the breast and thigh of the fellowship offering. They were presented to the Lord. You must eat them in a clean place. They are your share of the fellowship offerings given by the Israelites. [15]The people must bring the fat from their animals. It is part of the offering made by fire. They must also bring the thigh and the breast of the fellowship offering. These will be presented to the Lord. They will be the regular share of the offerings for you and your children. The Lord has commanded it."

[16]Moses looked for the goat of the sin offering. But it had already been burned up. So he became very angry with Eleazar and Ithamar, Aaron's remaining sons. He said, [17]"You were supposed to eat that goat in a holy place before the Lord! It is most holy! He gave it to you to take away the guilt of the people. The goat was for removing the sins of the people so they will belong to the Lord. [18]You didn't bring the goat's blood inside the Holy Place. So you were supposed to eat the goat in a holy place, as I commanded!"

[19]But Aaron said to Moses, "Today they brought their sin offering and burnt offering before the Lord. But these terrible things have still happened to me today! Do you think the Lord would be any happier if I ate the sin offering today?" [20]When Moses heard this, he was satisfied.

11 The Lord spoke to Moses and Aaron. [2]He said, "Tell the people of Israel this: 'These are the land animals you may eat: [3]You may eat any animal that has split hoofs completely divided and chews the cud. [4]Some animals only chew the cud or only have split hoofs. Don't eat these animals. The camel chews the cud but does not have a split hoof. It is unclean[d] for you. [5]The rock badger chews the cud but does not have a split hoof. It is unclean for you. [6]The rabbit chews the cud but does not have a split hoof. It is unclean for you. [7]Now the pig has a split hoof that is completely divided. But it does not chew the cud. It is unclean for you. [8]You must not eat the meat from these animals. Don't even touch their dead bodies. They are unclean for you.

[9]"'Some animals live in the sea or in a river. If the animal has fins and scales, you may eat it. [10]But some animals live in the sea or in a river and do not have fins and scales. This includes the things that fill the water. And it includes all other things that live in the water. You should hate them. [11]You must not eat any meat from them. Don't even touch their dead bodies. This is because you should hate them. [12]You must hate any animal in the water that does not have fins and scales.

[13]"'Also, some birds should not be eaten. They should be hated. You must not eat any of these birds: eagles, vultures, black vultures, [14]kites or any kind of falcon. [15]Don't eat any kind of raven, [16]horned owls, screech owls, sea gulls or any kind of hawk. [17]Don't eat little owls, cormorants, great owls, [18]white owls, desert owls or ospreys. [19]Don't eat storks, any kind of heron, hoopoes or bats.

[20]"'Don't eat insects that have wings and walk on all four feet. They are also to be hated.

[21]"'But you may eat certain insects that have wings and walk on four feet. You may eat those that have legs with joints above their feet so they can jump. [22]These are the insects you may eat: all kinds of locusts, winged locusts, crickets and grasshoppers. [23]But all other insects that have wings and walk on four feet are hated. [24]Those insects will make you unclean. Anyone who touches the dead body of one of these insects will become unclean until evening. [25]If someone picks up one of these dead insects, he must wash his clothes. He will be unclean until evening.

[26]"'Some animals have split hoofs. But the hoofs are not completely divided. And some animals do not chew the cud. They are unclean for you. Anyone who touches the dead body of one of these animals will become unclean. [27]Other animals do not have hoofs at all. They walk on their paws. These animals are unclean for you. Anyone who touches the dead body of one of these animals will become unclean. He will be unclean until evening. [28]Anyone who picks up their dead bodies must wash his clothes. He will be unclean until evening. These animals are unclean for you.

[29]"'These crawling animals are unclean for you: moles, rats, all kinds of great lizards, [30]geckos, crocodiles, lizards, sand reptiles and chameleons. [31]These crawling animals are unclean for you. Anyone who touches their dead bodies will be unclean until evening.

[32]"'If an unclean animal dies and falls on something, that thing will also become unclean. The animal might fall on a thing made from wood, cloth, leather or rough cloth. It does not matter what the thing was used for. Whatever the animal falls on must be washed with water. It will be unclean until evening. Then it will become clean again. [33]The dead, unclean animal might fall into a clay bowl. If it does, anything in the bowl will become unclean. And you must break the bowl. [34]If water from the unclean clay bowl gets on any food, that food will become unclean. [35]If any dead, unclean animal falls on something, that thing becomes unclean. The animal may fall on a clay oven or a clay baking pan. If so, it must be broken into pieces. These things will be unclean. They are unclean for you.

[36]"'A spring or well that collects water will stay clean. But anyone who touches the dead body of any unclean animal will become unclean. [37]A dead, unclean animal might fall on a seed to be planted. That seed is still clean. [38]But you might put water on some seeds. If a dead, unclean animal falls on those seeds, they are unclean for you.

[39]"'Also, an animal which you use for food may die. If it does, anyone who touches its body will be unclean until evening. [40]Anyone who eats meat from this animal's dead body must wash his clothes. He will be unclean until evening. Anyone who picks up the animal's dead body must wash his clothes. He will be unclean until evening.

[41]"'Every animal that crawls on the ground is one of the hated animals. It must not be eaten. Anyone who picks up the animal's dead body must wash his clothes. He will be unclean until evening. [42]You must not eat any of the animals that crawl on the ground. This includes animals that crawl on their stomachs. And it includes animals that walk on all four feet or on many feet. Those are hated animals to you. [43]Do not make yourself unclean by these hated animals. You must not become unclean by them. [44]I am the Lord your God. Keep yourselves holy for me because I am

holy. Don't make yourselves unclean with these hated, crawling animals. [46]I am the Lord who brought you out of Egypt. I did it so I could be your God. You must be holy because I am holy.

[46]"'These are the teachings about all of the cattle, birds and other animals on earth. These are the teachings about the animals in the sea. And these are the teachings about the animals that crawl on the ground. [47]These teachings help people know the difference between unclean animals and clean animals. They help people know which animals may be eaten and which ones must not be eaten.'"

12 The Lord said to Moses, [2]"Tell the people of Israel this: 'If a woman gives birth to a son, she will become unclean[d] for 7 days. This will be like her being unclean during her monthly period. [3]On the eighth day the boy must be circumcised.[d] [4]Then it will be 33 days before she becomes clean from her loss of blood. She must not touch anything that is holy. She must not enter the holy place until her time of cleansing is finished. [5]But a woman may give birth to a daughter. Then the mother will be unclean for 2 weeks. This is like her being unclean during her monthly period. It will be 66 days before she becomes clean from her loss of blood.

[6]"'After she has a son or daughter, she must have a time of cleansing. When it is over, the new mother must bring certain sacrifices to the Meeting Tent.[d] She must give the priest at the entrance a year-old lamb for a burnt offering. And she must bring a dove or young pigeon for a sin offering. [7]He will offer them before the Lord to make her clean so she will belong to the Lord again. Then she will be clean from her loss of blood. These are the teachings for a woman who gives birth to a boy or girl.

[8]"'If she cannot afford a lamb, she is to bring two doves or two young pigeons. One bird will be for a burnt offering and one for a sin offering. In this way the priest will make her clean so she will belong to the Lord again. And she will be clean.'"

13 The Lord said to Moses and Aaron, [2]"Someone might have a swelling on his skin. Or he might have a scab or a bright spot on his skin. If the sore looks like a harmful skin disease, the person must be brought to Aaron the priest. Or he must be brought to one of Aaron's sons, the priests. [3]The priest must look at the sore on the person's skin. The hair in the sore may have become white. And the sore may seem deeper than the person's skin. If so, it is a harmful skin disease. When he has finished looking at the person, the priest must announce that the person is unclean.[d]

[4]"'Sometimes there is a white spot on a person's skin, but the spot does not seem deeper than the skin. If that is true, and if the hair from the spot has not turned white, the priest must separate that person from other people for seven days. [5]On the seventh day the priest must look at the person again. He may see that the sore has not changed. It might not have spread on the skin. Then the priest must keep the person separated for seven more days. [6]On the seventh day the priest must look at the person again. The sore may have faded. And it may not have spread on the skin. If that is true, the priest must announce that the person is clean. The sore is only a rash. The person must wash his clothes. Then he will become clean again.

[7]"'But the sore may have spread again after the priest has announced him clean. Then the person must come again to the priest. [8]The priest must look at him. If the rash has spread on the skin, the priest must announce that person is unclean. It is a harmful skin disease.

[9]"'If a person has a harmful skin disease, he must be brought to the priest. [10]The priest must look at him. There might be a white swelling in the skin. And the hair may have become white. And the skin may look raw in the swelling. [11]If these things are true, it is a harmful skin disease. It is one that he has had for a long time. The priest must announce that the person is unclean. He will not need to separate that person from other people. This is because everyone already knows that the person is unclean.

[12]"'Sometimes skin disease spreads all over a person's body. The disease covers that person's skin from his head to his feet, as far as the priest can see. Then the priest must look at the person's whole body. [13]The priest might see that the disease covers the whole body. It might have turned all of the person's skin white. Then the priest must announce that the person is clean.

[14]"'But when the person has an open sore, he is not clean. [15]When the priest sees the open sore, he must announce that the person is unclean. The open

sore is not clean. It is a harmful skin disease. [16]If the open sore becomes white again, the person must come to the priest. [17]The priest must look at him. If the sores have become white, the priest must announce that the person with the sores is clean. Then he will be clean.

[18]"Someone may have a boil on his skin, but it is healed. [19]In the place where the boil was, there might be a white swelling. Or there might be a bright red spot. This place on the skin must be shown to the priest. [20]And the priest must look at it. The spot might seem deeper than the skin. And the hair on it might have become white. If these things are true, the priest must announce that the person is unclean. It has broken out from inside the boil. [21]But the priest must look at the spot. There might be no white hairs in it. The spot may not be deeper than the skin. And it may have faded. Then the priest must separate the person from other people for seven days. [22]If the spot spreads on the skin, the priest must announce that the person is unclean. It is a disease that will spread. [23]But the bright spot might not spread or change. Then it is only the scar from the old boil. Then the priest must announce that the person is clean.

[24]"A person might get a burn on his skin. If the open sore becomes white or red, [25]the priest must look at it. The white spot might seem deeper than the skin. And the hair at that spot might have become white. If these things are true, it is a harmful skin disease. The disease has broken out in the burn. Then the priest must announce that the person is unclean. It is a harmful skin disease. [26]But the priest must look at the spot. There might be no white hair in the bright spot. And the spot may be no deeper than the skin. It may have faded. Then the priest must separate the person from other people for seven days. [27]On the seventh day the priest must look at him again. If the spot has spread on the skin, the priest must announce that the person is unclean. It is a harmful skin disease. [28]But the bright spot may not have spread on the skin. It may have faded. Then it is the swelling from the burn. And the priest must announce that the person is clean. The spot is only a scar from the burn.

[29]"Someone might get a sore on his scalp or on his chin. [30]A priest must look at the sore. It may seem to be deeper than

the skin. And the hair around it may be thin and yellow. If these things are true, the priest must announce that the person is unclean. It is an itch, a harmful skin disease of the head or chin. [31]But when the priest looks at it, the sore might not seem deeper than the skin. There might not be any black hair in it. If that is true, the priest must separate the person from other people for seven days. [32]On the seventh day the priest must look at the sore. It may not have spread. There may be no yellow hairs growing in it. And the sore may not seem deeper than the skin. [33]If these things are true, the person must shave himself. But he must not shave the sore place. The priest must separate that person from other people for seven more days. [34]On the seventh day the priest must look at the sore. The sore may not have spread on the skin. And it may not seem deeper than the skin. If that is true, the priest must announce that the person is clean. So the person must wash his clothes and become clean. [35]But the sore might spread on the skin after the person has become clean. [36]Then the priest must look at him again. If the sore has spread on the skin, the priest doesn't need to look for the yellowish hair. The person is unclean. [37]But the priest might think the sore has stopped spreading. And black hair may be growing in it. Then the sore has healed. The person is clean. And the priest must announce that he is clean.

[38]"When a person has white spots on his skin, [39]a priest must look at them. If the spots on his skin are dull white, the disease is only a harmless rash. That person is clean.

[40]"A man might lose hair from his head and be bald. He is clean. [41]He might lose hair from the front of his head and have a bald forehead. He is clean. [42]But if there is a red-white sore on his scalp, it is a skin disease. [43]A priest must look at that person. The swelling of the sore might be red-white. It might look like a skin disease that spreads. [44]Then that person has a skin disease. He is unclean. And the priest must announce that the person is unclean because of the sore on his head.

[45]"If a person has a skin disease that spreads, he must warn other people. He must shout, 'Unclean, unclean!' His clothes must be torn at the seams. He must let his hair stay uncombed. And he must cover his mouth. [46]That person will

be unclean the whole time he has the disease. He is unclean. He must live alone outside the camp.

[47] "Some clothing might have mildew[d] on it. The cloth might be linen or wool. [48] It might be woven or knitted. The mildew might be on a piece of leather or on something made from leather. [49] The mildew might be in the clothing, leather or woven or knitted material. If the mildew is green or red, it is a spreading mildew. Then it must be shown to the priest. [50] The priest must look at the mildew. And he must put that thing in a separate place for seven days. [51] On the seventh day he must look at the mildew. It doesn't matter if the mildew is on leather or cloth. It doesn't matter if the cloth is woven or knitted. It doesn't matter what it was used for. If the mildew has spread, it is a mildew that destroys. [52] The priest must burn it. It does not matter if it is woven or knitted, wool or linen or a leather article. The mildew is spreading. The thing must be burned.

[53] "If the priest sees that the mildew has not spread, the cloth or leather must be washed. It does not matter if it is leather or cloth, knitted or woven. It must be washed. [54] The priest must order the people to wash that piece of leather or cloth. Then he must separate the clothing for seven more days. [55] After that time the priest must look at it again. If the mildew still looks the same, that thing is unclean.[d] It does not matter if the mildew has not spread. You must burn that cloth or piece of leather.

[56] "But when the priest looks at that piece of leather or cloth, the mildew might have faded. Then the priest must tear the mildew out of the piece of leather or cloth. It does not matter if the cloth is woven or knitted. [57] But the mildew might come back to that piece of leather or cloth. If that happens, the mildew is spreading. And that piece of leather or cloth must be burned. [58] The cloth, the woven or knitted material, or the leather may be washed. The mildew may then be gone. It must be washed again. Then it will be clean.

[59] "These are the teachings about mildew on pieces of leather or cloth. It doesn't matter if the cloth is woven or knitted."

14 The Lord said to Moses, [1] "These are the teachings for people who had a harmful skin disease and have become well. These teachings are for making that person clean.[d]

[3] "A priest must look at the person who had the skin disease. He must go to that person outside the camp. He must see if the skin disease is healed. [4] If the person is healthy, the priest will tell him to do these things: He must get two living, clean birds. He must also get a piece of cedar wood, a piece of red cloth and a hyssop plant. These things are for cleansing the person with the skin disease.

[5] "The priest must order one bird to be killed in a clay bowl containing fresh water. [6] Then he will take the other bird that is still alive. He will take the piece of cedar wood, the red cloth and the hyssop. He will dip the living bird and other things into the blood. (This is the blood of the bird that was killed over the fresh water.) [7] The priest will sprinkle the blood seven times on the person who had the skin disease. He must announce that the person is clean. Then the priest must go to an open field. He must let the living bird go free.

[8] "Next, that person must wash his clothes. He must shave off all his hair. And he must wash with water. Then he will be clean and may go into the camp. But at first he must stay outside his tent for seven days. [9] On the seventh day he must shave off all his hair. He must shave off his hair, his beard and his eyebrows. He must wash his clothes and bathe his body in water. Then he will be clean.

[10] "On the eighth day the person who had the skin disease must take two male lambs. They must have nothing wrong with them. He must also take a year-old female lamb. It must have nothing wrong with it. The person must take six quarts of fine flour mixed with oil. This is for a grain offering. He must also take two-thirds of a pint of olive oil. [11] A priest must announce that the person is clean. Then he must bring that person and his sacrifices before the Lord. This is at the entrance of the Meeting Tent.[d] [12] The priest will take one of the male lambs. He will offer it and the olive oil as a guilt offering. And he will present them before the Lord as an offering. [13] Then he will kill the male lamb in the holy place. He will kill it where they kill the sin offering and the whole burnt offering. The penalty offering is like the sin offering. It belongs to the priest. It is most holy.

[14] "The priest will take some of the blood of the penalty offering. He will

put some of it on the bottom of the right ear of the person to be made clean. He will put some of it on the thumb of the person's right hand. And he will put some on the big toe of the person's right foot. [15]The priest will also take some of the oil and pour it into his own left hand. [16]Then he will dip a finger of his right hand into the oil that is in his left hand. He will use his finger to sprinkle some of the oil seven times before the Lord. [17]The priest will put some oil from his hand on the bottom of the right ear of the person to be made clean. He will put some of it on the thumb of the person's right hand. And he will put some of it on the big toe of the person's right foot. The oil will go on these places on top of the blood for the penalty offering. [18]He will put the rest of the oil that is in his left hand on the head of the person to be made clean. In this way the priest will make that person clean so he can belong to the Lord again.

[19]"Next the priest will offer the sin offering. It will make that person clean so he can belong to the Lord again. After this the priest will kill the animal for the whole burnt offering. [20]Then he will offer the burnt offering and grain offering on the altar. In this way he will make that person clean so he can belong to the Lord again.

[21]"But the person may be poor and unable to afford these offerings. Then he must take one male lamb for a penalty offering. It will be presented to the Lord so the priest can make that person clean. Then he can belong to the Lord again. The person must take two quarts of fine flour mixed with oil. It will be used for a grain offering. He must also take two-thirds of a pint of olive oil. [22]He must take two doves or two young pigeons, which he can afford. One bird will be a sin offering. The other will be a whole burnt offering. [23]On the eighth day the person will bring them to the priest at the entrance of the Meeting Tent. The gifts will be offered before the Lord. This is so the person can become clean. [24]The priest will take the lamb for the penalty offering and the oil. He will present them as an offering before the Lord. [25]Then he will kill the lamb of the penalty offering. He will take some of the blood of the penalty offering. He will put it on the bottom of the right ear of the person to be made clean. The priest will put some of this blood on the thumb of the person's right hand. And he will

put some on the big toe of the person's right foot. [26]He will also pour some of the oil into his own left hand. [27]Then with a finger of his right hand, he will sprinkle some of the oil from his left hand. He will sprinkle it seven times before the Lord. [28]Then the priest will take some of the oil from his hand. He will put it on the bottom of the right ear of the person to be made clean. He will also put some of it on the thumb of the person's right hand. And he will put some on the big toe of the person's right foot. The oil will go on these places on top of the blood from the penalty offering. [29]The priest must put the rest of the oil that is in his hand on the head of the person to be made clean. In this way the priest will make the person clean so he can belong to the Lord again. [30]Then the priest will offer one of the doves or young pigeons. He must offer what the person can afford. [31]He must offer one of the birds as a sin offering. And he must offer the other bird as a whole burnt offering. He must offer them with the grain offering. In this way the priest will make the person clean so he can belong to the Lord again. The person will become clean.

[32]"These are the teachings for making a person clean. This is done after he has become well from a skin disease. These teachings are for people who cannot afford the regular sacrifices for becoming clean."

[33]The Lord also said to Moses and Aaron, [34]"I am giving the land of Canaan to your people. When they enter that land, I might cause mildew[d] to grow in someone's house. [35]The owner of that house must come and tell the priest. He should say, 'I have seen something like mildew in my house.' [36]Then the priest must order the people to empty the house. They must do this before he goes in to look at the mildew. This is so he will not have to say that everything in the house is unclean.[d] After the people have emptied the house, the priest will go in to look at it. [37]He will look at the mildew. The mildew on the walls of the house might be green or red. It might go into the wall's surface. [38]If these things are true, he must go out and close up the house for seven days. [39]On the seventh day the priest must come back and check the house. The mildew may have spread on the walls of the house. [40]If it has, the priest must order the people to tear out the stones with the mildew on

them. They should throw the stones away. They must put the stones at a certain unclean place outside the city. [41]Then the priest must have all the inside of the house scraped. The people must throw away the plaster they scraped off the walls. They must put the plaster at a certain unclean place outside the city. [42]Then the owner must put new stones in the walls. And he must cover the walls with new clay plaster.

[43]"A person may have taken away the old stones and plaster. He may have put in new stones and plaster. But mildew may again appear in his house. [44]If it does, the priest must come back and check the house again. If the mildew has spread in the house, it is a mildew that destroys things. So the house is unclean. [45]Then the owner must tear down the house. He must remove all its stones, plaster and wood. He must take them to the unclean place outside the city. [46]Anyone who goes into that house will be unclean until evening. [47]Anyone who eats in that house or lies down there must wash his clothes.

[48]"After new stones and plaster have been put in a house, the priest must check it again. The mildew may not have spread in the house. Then the priest will announce that the house is clean. This is because the mildew is gone.

[49]"Then, to make the house clean, the priest must take two birds. He must also take a piece of cedar wood, a piece of red cloth and a hyssop plant. [50]He will kill one bird in a clay bowl containing fresh water. [51]Then he will take the other bird that is still alive. He will also take the cedar wood, the hyssop and the red cloth. He will dip the living bird and other things into the blood. (This is the blood of the bird that was killed over the fresh water.) Then the priest will sprinkle the blood on the house seven times. [52]He will use the bird's blood, the fresh water and the live bird. And he will use the cedar wood, the hyssop and the red cloth. With these things he will make the house clean. [53]The priest will go to an open field outside the city. And he will let the living bird go free. This is how the priest makes the house clean and ready for service to the Lord."

[54]These are the teachings about any kind of skin disease. [55]These are the teachings for mildew on pieces of cloth or in a house. [56]These are also the teachings for swellings, rashes or bright spots on the skin. [57]They teach when things are unclean and when they are clean. These are the teachings about all these kinds of diseases.

15 The Lord also said to Moses and Aaron, [2]"Say to the people of Israel: 'When a fluid comes from a man's body, he is unclean.[d] [3]It doesn't matter if the fluid flows freely or if it is blocked from flowing.

[4]"'The man who discharges the body fluid may lie on a bed. If he does, that bed becomes unclean. Everything he sits on becomes unclean. [5]Also anyone who touches his bed must wash his clothes and bathe in water. This person will be unclean until evening. [6]Someone might sit on something that the man who discharges the fluid sat on. If he does, he must wash his clothes and bathe in water. He will be unclean until evening. [7]Anyone who touches the man who discharges the body fluid must wash his clothes and bathe in water. The person will be unclean until evening.

[8]"'The man who discharges the body fluid might spit on a clean person. If so, the person who was clean must wash his clothes. He must bathe in water. The person will be unclean until evening. [9]Everything on which the man who is unclean has ridden will become unclean. [10]Someone might touch something that was under the man who discharges a body fluid. If he does, he will be unclean until evening. Someone might carry these things that were under the man who discharges a body fluid. This person must wash his clothes and bathe in water. He will be unclean until evening.

[11]"'The man who discharges a body fluid may not have washed his hands in water. If he touches another person, that person must wash his clothes. That person must bathe in water. He will be unclean until evening.

[12]"'A man who discharges a body fluid may touch a clay bowl. That bowl must be broken. If he touches a wooden bowl, that bowl must be washed in water.

[13]"'A man who discharges a body fluid may be made clean. He must count seven days for himself for his cleansing. He must wash his clothes and bathe his body in fresh water. Then he will be clean. [14]On the eighth day he must take two doves or two young pigeons. He must come before the Lord at the entrance of the Meeting Tent.[d] He will give the two birds to the priest. [15]The priest will offer the birds. One bird is for a sin

offering. The other is for a burnt offering. So the priest will make that man clean so he can belong to the Lord again.

¹⁶"'If semenⁿ goes out from a man, he must bathe in water. He will be unclean until evening. ¹⁷If the fluid gets on any clothing or leather, it must be washed with water. It will be unclean until evening.

¹⁸"'If a man has sexual relations with a woman and semen comes out, both people must bathe in water. They will be unclean until evening.

¹⁹"'When a woman has her monthly period, she is uncleanᵈ for seven days. Anyone who touches her will be unclean until evening. ²⁰Anything she lies on during this time will be unclean. Everything she sits on during that time will be unclean. ²¹Anyone who touches her bed must wash his clothes and bathe in water. That person will be unclean until evening. ²²Anyone who touches something she has sat on must wash his clothes and bathe in water. That person will be unclean until evening. ²³It does not matter if the person touched the woman's bed or something she sat on. That person will be unclean until evening.

²⁴"'A man may have sexual relations with a woman during her monthly period. If he does, he will be unclean for seven days. Every bed he lies on will also be unclean.

²⁵"'A woman might have a loss of blood for many days. It may not be during her regular monthly period. Or she may continue to have a loss of blood after her regular period. If she does, she will be unclean, as she is during her monthly period. She will be unclean for as long as she continues to bleed. ²⁶Any bed she lies on during all the time of her bleeding will be like her bed during her regular monthly period. Everything she sits on will be unclean. It will be like during her regular monthly period.

²⁷"'If anyone touches those things, that person will be unclean. He must wash his clothes and bathe in water. He will be unclean until evening. ²⁸When the woman becomes clean from her bleeding, she must wait seven days. After this she will be clean. ²⁹Then on the eighth day she must take two doves or two young pigeons. She must bring them to the priest at the entrance of the Meeting Tent.ᵈ ³⁰Then the priest must offer one bird for a sin offering. He must offer the other bird for a whole burnt offering. So the priest will make her clean so she can belong to the Lord again.

³¹"'So you must warn the people of Israel to stay separated from things that make them unclean. If you don't warn the people, they might make my Holy Tentᵈ unclean. And then they would have to die!'"

³²These are the teachings for the man who discharges a body fluid. These are the teachings for men who become unclean from semenⁿ coming out of their bodies. ³³These are the teachings for women who become unclean from their monthly period. These are the teachings for anyone who becomes unclean by having sexual relations with another person who is unclean.

16 Now two of Aaron's sons had died while offering incenseᵈ to the Lord. At that time the Lord spoke to Moses. ²He said, "Talk to your brother Aaron. Tell him there are times when he cannot go behind the curtain into the Most Holy Place where the Holy Boxᵈ is. If he goes in when I appear in a cloud over the lid on the Holy Box, he will die.

³"Aaron may enter the Most Holy Place only on the Day of Cleansing. Before he enters, he must offer a bull for a sin offering. And he must offer a male sheep for a whole burnt offering. ⁴He must put on these clothes. He will put on the holy linen inner robe. The linen underclothes will be next to his body. His belt will be the cloth belt. And he will wear the linen turban. These are holy clothes. So he must wash his whole body with water before he puts them on.

⁵"Aaron must take from the people of Israel two male goats for a sin offering. And he must take one male sheep for a burnt offering. ⁶Then he will offer the bull for the sin offering. This sin offering is for himself. Then he will perform the acts to remove sins from him and his family so they will belong to the Lord.

⁷"Next Aaron will take the two goats. He will bring them before the Lord at the entrance to the Meeting Tent.ᵈ ⁸Aaron will throw lotsᵈ for the two goats. One lot will be for the Lord. The other lot will be for the goat that removes sin.

15:16 semen A man's body fluid by which he can make a woman pregnant. **15:32 semen** A man's body fluid by which he can make a woman pregnant.

⁹Then Aaron will take the goat that was chosen for the Lord by throwing the lot. He must offer this goat as a sin offering. ¹⁰The other goat was chosen by lot to remove the sin. It must be brought alive before the Lord. The priest will use it to perform the acts to remove Israel's sin so they will belong to the Lord. Then this goat will be sent out into the desert.

¹¹"Then Aaron will offer the bull as a sin offering for himself. This will remove the sins of him and his family so they will belong to the Lord. He will kill the bull for the sin offering for himself. ¹²Then he must take a pan full of burning coals from the altar before the Lord. Aaron must take two handfuls of sweet incense that has been ground into powder. He must bring it into the room behind the curtain. ¹³He must put the incense on the fire before the Lord. Then the cloud of incense will cover the lid on the Holy Box. Then when Aaron comes in, he will not die. ¹⁴Also, Aaron must take some of the blood from the bull. He must sprinkle it with his finger on the front of the lid. Then, with his finger he will sprinkle the blood seven times in front of the lid.

¹⁵"Then Aaron must kill the goat of the sin offering for the people. He must bring this goat's blood into the room behind the curtain. He must do with the goat's blood as he did with the bull's blood. He must sprinkle the goat's blood on the lid and in front of it. ¹⁶The people in Israel have been unclean.ᵈ So Aaron will perform the acts to make the Most Holy Place ready for service to the Lord. Then it will be clean from the sins and crimes of the people of Israel. He must do this because the Meeting Tent stays in the middle of unclean people. ¹⁷When Aaron makes the Most Holy Place ready for service to the Lord, no one is allowed in the Meeting Tent. No one must go in until Aaron comes out. So Aaron will perform the acts to remove sins from himself and his family so they will belong to the Lord. Then he will remove the sins of all the people of Israel so they will belong to the Lord. ¹⁸Afterward he will go out to the altar that is before the Lord. And he will make the altar ready for service to the Lord. Aaron will take some of the bull's blood and some of the goat's blood. He will put it on the corners of the altar on all sides. ¹⁹Then he will sprinkle some of the blood with his finger. He will sprinkle it on the altar seven times. In this way Aaron will

make the altar holy for the Lord. And it will be clean from all the sins of the people of Israel.

²⁰"Aaron will make the Most Holy Place, the Meeting Tent and the altar clean. Then he will bring the goat alive to the Lord. ²¹He will put both his hands on the head of the living goat. Then he will confess all the sins and crimes of Israel over the goat. In this way Aaron will put the people's sins on the goat's head. Then he will send the goat away into the desert. A man who has been appointed will lead the goat away. ²²So the goat will carry all the people's sins on itself. It will go to a lonely place in the desert. The man who leads the goat will let it loose there.

²³"Then Aaron will enter the Meeting Tent. He will take off the linen clothes. (He had put them on before he went into the Most Holy Place.) He must leave these clothes there. ²⁴He will wash his whole body with water in a holy place. Then he will put on his regular clothes. He will come out and offer the whole burnt offering for himself. And he will offer the whole burnt offering for the people. He will remove sins from himself and the people so they will belong to the Lord. ²⁵Then he will burn the fat of the sin offering on the altar.

²⁶"The person who led the goat into the desert must wash his clothes. Then he must wash his whole body with water. After that, he may come back into the camp.

²⁷"The bull and goat for the sin offerings must be taken outside the camp. The blood from these animals was brought into the Most Holy Place. It was to make the Holy Place ready for service to the Lord. The priests will burn the animals' skins, bodies and intestines in the fire. ²⁸Then the one who burns them must wash his clothes. And he must wash his whole body with water. After that, he may come back into the camp.

²⁹"This law will always continue for you: On the tenth day of the seventh month, you must not eat. You must not do any work. The travelers or foreigners living with you must not work either. ³⁰On this day the priests make you clean so you will belong to the Lord again. All your sins will be removed. ³¹This is a very important day of rest for you. And you must not eat. This law will continue forever.

³²"So the appointed priest will perform the acts for making things ready

for service to the Lord. He is the priest on whom oil was poured. He is appointed to take his father's place. That priest must put on the holy linen clothes. [33]He must make the Most Holy Place ready for service to the Lord. He must make the Meeting Tent and the altar ready for service to the Lord. He must remove the sins of himself and all the people of Israel so they will belong to the Lord. [34]That law for removing the sins of the Israelites so they will belong to the Lord will continue forever. You will do these things once a year."

So they did the things the Lord had commanded Moses.

17 The Lord said to Moses, [2]"Speak to Aaron, his sons and all the people of Israel. Tell them: 'This is what the Lord has commanded: [3]An Israelite might sacrifice an ox, a lamb or a goat. He might kill it inside the camp or outside it. [4]But he should have brought the animal to the entrance to the Meeting Tent.[d] He should have given the animal as a gift to the Lord. If he didn't, he is guilty of killing. He must be separated from his people. [5]This rule is so people will bring their sacrifices to the Lord. They have been sacrificing in the open fields. But they must bring those animals to the Lord at the entrance of the Meeting Tent. They must bring them to the priest and offer them as fellowship offerings. [6]Then the priest will sprinkle the blood from those animals on the Lord's altar. It is near the entrance to the Meeting Tent. And the priest will burn the fat from those animals on the altar. This smell will be pleasing to the Lord. [7]They must not offer any more sacrifices to their goat idols. They have chased after those other gods. In that way they have acted like prostitutes.[d] These rules will continue for people from now on.'

[8]"Tell the people this: 'Someone might offer a burnt offering or sacrifice. He might be a citizen of Israel. Or he might be a traveler or foreigner living with you. [9]That person must take his sacrifice to the entrance to the Meeting Tent. There he may offer it to the Lord. If he does not do this, he must be separated from his people.

[10]" 'I will be against anyone who eats blood. It does not matter if it is a citizen of Israel or a foreigner living with you. I will separate that person from his people. [11]This is because the life of the body is in the blood. And I have given you

rules for pouring that blood on the altar. You must do this to remove your sins so you will belong to the Lord. It is the blood that removes the sins from your life so you will belong to the Lord. [12]So I tell the people of Israel this: "None of you may eat blood. And no foreigner living among you may eat blood."

[13]" 'Someone may catch a wild animal or bird that can be eaten. The person may be a citizen of Israel or a foreigner living among you. He must pour the blood on the ground and cover it with dirt. [14]This is because if blood is still in the meat, the animal's life is still in it. So I give this command to the people of Israel: "Don't eat meat that still has blood in it. Anyone who eats blood must be separated from his people."

[15]" 'Someone may eat an animal that died by itself. Or he may eat an animal that was killed by another animal. The person may be a citizen of Israel or a foreigner living among you. If he eats the animal, he will be unclean until evening. He must wash his clothes and whole body with water. [16]If he does not wash his clothes and bathe his body, he will be guilty of sin.' "

18 The Lord said to Moses, [2]"Tell the people of Israel: 'I am the Lord your God. [3]In the past you lived in Egypt. You must not do what was done in that country. And you must not do as they do in the land of Canaan where I am bringing you. Do not follow their customs. [4]You must obey my rules and follow them. I am the Lord your God. [5]Obey my laws and rules. A person who obeys my laws and rules will live because of them. I am the Lord.

[6]" 'You must never have sexual relations with your close relatives. I am the Lord.

[7]" 'You must not shame your father by having sexual relations with your mother. She is your mother. Do not have sexual relations with her. [8]You must not have sexual relations with your father's wife. That would shame your father.

[9]" 'You must not have sexual relations with your sister. She may be the daughter of your father or your mother. It doesn't matter if she was born in your house or somewhere else.

[10]" 'You must not have sexual relations with your granddaughter. She may be your son's daughter or your daughter's daughter. That would bring shame on you.

[11]" 'If your father and his wife have a

daughter, she is your sister. You must not have sexual relations with her.

[12] "You must not have sexual relations with your father's sister. She is your father's close relative. [13] You must not have sexual relations with your mother's sister. She is your mother's close relative. [14] You must not have sexual relations with the wife of your father's brother. This would shame him. His wife is your aunt.

[15] "You must not have sexual relations with your daughter-in-law. She is your son's wife. Do not have sexual relations with her.

[16] "You must not have sexual relations with your brother's wife. That would shame your brother.

[17] "You must not have sexual relations with both a woman and her daughter. And do not have sexual relations with this woman's granddaughter. It may be the daughter of her son or her daughter. They are her close relatives. It is evil to do this.

[18] "While your wife is still living, you must not take her sister as another wife. Do not have sexual relations with her.

[19] "You must not go near a woman to have sexual relations with her during her monthly period. She is unclean[d] during this time.

[20] "You must not have sexual relations with your neighbor's wife and make yourself unclean with her.

[21] "You must not give any of your children to be sacrificed to Molech.[d] This will show that you do not respect your God. I am the Lord.

[22] "You must not have sexual relations with a man as you would a woman. That is a hated sin.

[23] "You must not have sexual relations with an animal and make yourself unclean with it. Also a woman must not have sexual relations with an animal. It is not natural.

[24] "Don't make yourself unclean by any of these wrong things. I am forcing nations out of their countries because they did these sins. And I am giving their land to you. [25] The land has become unclean. So I punished it for its sins. And the land is throwing out those people who live there.

[26] "You must obey my laws and rules. You must not do any of these hated sins. These rules are for the citizens of Israel. They are also for the people who live with you. [27] The people who lived in the land before you did all these hated

things. So the land became unclean. [28] If you do these things, you will also make the land unclean. And it will throw you out as it threw out the nations before you. [29] Anyone who does these hated sins must be separated from his people. [30] The people who lived in the land before you have done these hated sins. But you must not do them. You must obey my laws. Don't make yourself unclean by these hated sins. I am the Lord your God.' "

19 The Lord said to Moses, [2] "Tell all the people of Israel: 'I am the Lord your God. You must be holy because I am holy.

[3] "Each person among you must respect his mother and father. And you must keep my Sabbaths.[d] I am the Lord your God.

[4] "Do not worship idols. Do not make statues or gods for yourselves. I am the Lord your God.

[5] "You may sacrifice a fellowship offering to the Lord. If you do, you must offer it so you will be accepted. [6] You may eat it the same day you offer it. And you may also eat it on the next day. But if any is left on the third day, you must burn it up. [7] If any of it is eaten on the third day, it is unclean.[d] It will not be accepted. [8] Anyone who eats it then will be guilty of sin. This is because he did not respect the holy things that belong to the Lord. He must be separated from his people.

[9] "You harvest your crops on your land. But do not harvest all the way to the corners of your fields. If grain falls onto the ground, don't gather it up. [10] Don't pick all the grapes in your vineyards. And don't pick up the grapes that fall to the ground. You must leave those things for poor people. You must also leave them for people traveling through your country. I am the Lord your God.

[11] "You must not steal. You must not cheat people. You must not lie to each other. [12] You must not make a false promise by my name. If you do that, you will show that you don't respect your God. I am the Lord.

[13] "You must not cheat your neighbor. You must not rob him. You must not keep a hired worker's salary all night until morning. [14] You must not curse a deaf man. And you must not put something in front of a blind person to make him fall. But you must respect your God. I am the Lord.

[15] "Be fair in your judging. You must

not show special favor to poor people or great people. You must be fair when you judge your neighbor. ¹⁶You must not spread false stories against other people. You must not do anything that would put your neighbor's life in danger. I am the Lord.

¹⁷"'You must not hate your brother in your heart. If your neighbor does something wrong, tell him about it. If you do not, you will be partly to blame. ¹⁸Forget about the wrong things people do to you. You must not try to get even. Love your neighbor as you love yourself. I am the Lord.

¹⁹"'Obey my laws. You must not mate two different kinds of cattle. You must not sow your field with two different kinds of seed. You must not wear clothing made from two different kinds of material mixed together.

²⁰"'A man might have sexual relations with a slave girl of another man. But this slave girl has not been bought or given her freedom. If this happens, there must be punishment. But they are not to be put to death. This is because the woman was not free. ²¹The man must bring a male sheep as his penalty offering. He must bring it to the Lord at the entrance to the Meeting Tent.ᵈ ²²The priest will offer the male sheep as a penalty offering before the Lord. It will be for the man's sin. The priest will perform the acts to remove the sins of the man so he will belong to the Lord. Then the man will be forgiven for his sin.

²³"'In the future you will enter your country. You will plant many kinds of trees for food. After planting a tree, wait three years before using its fruit. ²⁴In the fourth year the fruit from the tree will be the Lord's. It will be a holy offering of praise to him. ²⁵Then in the fifth year, you may eat the fruit from the tree. The tree will then produce more fruit for you. I am the Lord your God.

²⁶"'You must not eat anything with the blood in it.

"'You must not try to tell the future by signs or black magic. ²⁷You must not cut the hair on the sides of your heads. And you must not cut the edges of your beard. ²⁸You must not cut your body to show sadness for someone who died. Do not put tattoo marks on yourselves. I am the Lord.

²⁹"'You must not make your daughter become a prostitute.ᵈ That only shows you do not respect her. If you do this,

the country will be filled with all kinds of sin.

³⁰"'Obey the laws about Sabbaths. You must respect my Most Holy Place. I am the Lord.

³¹"'Do not go to mediumsᵈ or fortune-tellers for advice. If you do, you will become unclean. I am the Lord your God.

³²"'Show respect to old people. Stand up when they come into the room. Show respect also to your God. I am the Lord.

³³"'Do not mistreat foreigners living in your country. ³⁴Treat them just as you treat your own citizens. Love foreigners as you love yourselves, because you were foreigners one time. That was in Egypt. I am the Lord your God.

³⁵"'Be fair when you judge people. And be fair when you measure and weigh things. ³⁶Your weighing baskets should be the right size. And your jars should hold the right amount of liquid. Your weights and balances should weigh correctly. I am the Lord your God. I brought you out of the land of Egypt.

³⁷"'Remember all my laws and rules, and obey them. I am the Lord.'"

20 The Lord said to Moses, ²"'You must also tell the people of Israel these things: 'A person in your country might give one of his children to Molech.ᵈ That person must be killed. It doesn't matter if he is a citizen or a foreigner living in Israel. You must throw stones at him and kill him. ³I will be against him. I will separate him from his people. This is because he gave his children to Molech. He showed that he did not respect my holy name. And he made my Holy Place unclean.ᵈ ⁴The people of the community might ignore that person. They might not kill the one who gave his children to Molech. ⁵But I will be against him and his family. I will separate him from his people. I will do this to anyone who is unfaithful to me and who worships Molech.

⁶"'I will be against anyone who goes to mediumsᵈ and fortune-tellers for advice. He is being unfaithful to me. So I will separate him from his people.

⁷"'Be my holy people. Be holy because I am holy. I am the Lord your God. ⁸Remember and obey my laws. I am the Lord, and I have made you holy.

⁹"'Anyone who curses his father or mother must be put to death. He has cursed his father or mother. So he must be punished.

¹⁰"'A man might have sexual relations with his neighbor's wife. If he does, both

the man and the woman are guilty of adultery.[d] So they must be put to death.
[11]A man might have sexual relations with his father's wife. If he does, both the man and his father's wife must be put to death. They have brought it on themselves. That man has shamed his father.

[12]"A man might have sexual relations with his daughter-in-law. If he does, both of them must be put to death. What they have done is not natural. It must be punished.

[13]"A man might have sexual relations with another man as a man does with a woman. If he does, these two men have done a hated sin. They must be put to death. They have brought it on themselves.

[14]"A man might have sexual relations with both a woman and her mother. This is evil. The people must burn that man and the two women in fire. Do this so that your people will not be evil.

[15]"A man might have sexual relations with an animal. If he does, he must be put to death. And you must also kill the animal. [16]A woman might have sexual relations with an animal. If she does, you must kill the woman and the animal. They must be put to death. They have brought it on themselves.

[17]"It is shameful for a brother to marry his sister and to have sexual relations with her. In front of everyone they must both be separated from their people. The man has shamed his sister. And he is guilty of sin.

[18]"A man might have sexual relations with a woman during her monthly period. If he does, both the woman and the man must be separated from their people. They sinned because they showed the source of her blood.

[19]"Do not have sexual relations with your mother's sister or your father's sister. That would shame a close relative. Both of you are guilty of this sin.

[20]"A man must not have sexual relations with his uncle's wife. That would shame his uncle. That man and his uncle's wife would die without children. They are guilty of sin.

[21]"It is unclean for a man to marry his brother's wife. That man has shamed his brother. They would have no children.

[22]"Remember all my laws and rules, and obey them. I am leading you to your own land. If you obey my laws and rules, that land will not throw you out. [23]I am

forcing the people who live there out of that country ahead of you. Because they did all these sins I have hated them. Do not live the way those people lived.

[24]"I have told you that you will get their land. I will give it to you as your very own. It is a land where much food grows. I am the Lord your God. I have set you apart from other people and made you my own. [25]So you must treat clean animals and birds differently from unclean animals. Do not make yourselves unclean by any of these unclean birds or animals or things that crawl on the ground. I have made them unclean for you. [26]I have set you apart from other people. So you must be holy to me. This is because I am the Lord, and I am holy.

[27]"A man or woman who is a medium[d] or a fortune-teller must be put to death. You must kill them with stones. They have brought it on themselves.'"

21

The Lord said to Moses, "Tell these things to Aaron's sons, the priests: 'A priest must not make himself unclean[d] by touching a dead person. [2]But if the dead person was one of his close relatives, he may touch him. The priest may make himself unclean if the dead person is his mother or father, son or daughter, brother or [3]unmarried sister. This sister is close to him because she has no husband. So the priest may make himself unclean for her if she dies. [4]But a priest must not make himself unclean if the dead person was only related to him by marriage.

[5]"Priests must not shave their heads. They must not shave off the edges of their beards. They must not cut their bodies. [6]Priests must be holy to their God. They must show respect for God's name. This is because they present the offerings made by fire to the Lord. This is the food of their God. So they must be holy.

[7]"A priest serves God in a special way. So he must not marry an unclean prostitute[d] or a divorced woman. [8]Treat the priest in a special way. Think of him as holy. This is because he offers up the food of your God. I am the Lord. I make you holy. And I am holy.

[9]"If a priest's daughter makes herself unclean by becoming a prostitute, she shames her father. She must be burned with fire.

[10]"The high priest was chosen from among his brothers. The special olive oil used in appointing people and things to the service of the Lord was poured on

his head. He was appointed to wear the priestly clothes. So he must not do things to show his sadness in public. He must not let his hair go uncombed. He must not tear his clothes. [11]He must not go into a house where there is a dead body. He must not make himself unclean, even if it is his own father or mother. [12]The high priest must not go out of the Holy Place. If he does and becomes unclean, he would make God's Holy Place unclean. The special oil used in appointing priests was poured on the high priest's head. This separated him from the rest of the people. I am the Lord.

[13]"'The high priest must marry a woman who is a virgin.[d] [14]He must not marry a widow, a divorced woman or a prostitute. He must marry a virgin from his own people. [15]This is so the people will respect his children as his own. I am the Lord. I have set the high priest apart for his special job.'"

[16]The Lord said to Moses, [17]"Tell Aaron: 'Some of your descendants[d] might have something wrong with them. If they do, they must never offer the special food of their God. [18]Anyone who has something wrong with him must not serve as priest. And he must not bring sacrifices to me. These people cannot serve as priests: blind men, crippled men, men with damaged faces, deformed men, [19]men with a crippled foot or hand, [20]hunchbacks, dwarfs, men who have something wrong with their eyes, men who have an itching disease or a skin disease or men who have damaged sex glands. [21]"'One of Aaron's descendants[d] might have something wrong with him. If he does, he cannot make the offerings made by fire to the Lord. He has something wrong with him. He cannot offer the food of his God. [22]But he is from the family of priests. So he may eat the most holy food. He may also eat the holy food. [23]But he may not go through the curtain into the Most Holy Place. He may not go near the altar. He has something wrong with him. He must not make my Holy Place unfit. I am the Lord. I make these things holy.'"

[24]So Moses told these things to Aaron, Aaron's sons and all the people of Israel.

22 The Lord said to Moses, [2]"Tell Aaron and his sons: 'The people of Israel will give offerings to me. These offerings are holy, and they are mine.

So you must respect these offerings. This will show that you respect my holy name. I am the Lord. [3]The people of Israel made the offerings holy for me. One of your descendants[d] might be unclean[d] and touch the offerings. From now on, anyone who does must be separated from appearing before me. I am the Lord.

[4]"'One of Aaron's descendants might have one of the harmful skin diseases. Or he might discharge a body fluid. He cannot eat the holy offerings until he becomes clean. He can become unclean from touching a dead body or from his own semen.[n] [5]He will become unclean if he touches any unclean crawling animal. He will become unclean if he touches an unclean person. It doesn't matter what made him unclean. [6]Anyone who touches those things will become unclean until evening. That person must not eat the holy offerings. But if he washes with water, he may eat the holy offerings. [7]He will be clean only after the sun goes down. Then he may eat the holy offerings. The offerings are his food.

[8]"'A priest might find an animal that died by itself. Or he might find one that was killed by some other animal. He must not eat that dead animal. If he eats it, he will become unclean. I am the Lord.

[9]"'The priests must keep all the rules I have given. That way they will not become guilty. If they are careful, they will not die. I am the Lord. I have made them holy. [10]Only people in a priest's family may eat the holy offerings. A visitor staying with the priest must not eat it. A hired worker must not eat it. [11]But the priest might buy a slave with his own money. If he does, that slave may eat the holy offerings. Slaves who were born in the priest's house may also eat the priest's food. [12]A priest's daughter might marry a person who is not a priest. If she does, she must not eat any of the holy offerings. [13]The husband of a priest's daughter might die. Or the daughter might become divorced. She might not have children to support her. So she might go back to her father's house where she lived as a child. If this happens, she may eat some of her father's food. But only people from a priest's family may eat this food. [14]"'Someone might eat some of the holy offering by mistake. That person must pay back the priest for that holy

22:4 semen A man's body fluid by which he can make a woman pregnant.

food. He must also pay the priest another one-fifth of the price of that food.

¹⁵ "The people of Israel will give offerings to the Lord. These gifts become holy. So the priest must not treat these holy things as though they were not holy. ¹⁶ The priests might allow someone who is not a priest to eat the holy offerings. If they do, they are treating those offerings as though they were not holy. The person who eats will become guilty. He will have to pay for it. I am the Lord. I make them holy.'"

¹⁷ The Lord said to Moses, ¹⁸ "Tell Aaron and his sons and all the people of Israel: 'A citizen of Israel or a foreigner living in Israel might want to bring a whole burnt offering. It might be for some special promise he has made. Or it might be a special gift he wanted to give to the Lord. ¹⁹ If he does, he must bring a male animal. It must have nothing wrong with it. The gift might be a bull, a sheep or a goat. This is so it might be accepted for him. ²⁰ He must not bring an animal that has something wrong with it. It will not be accepted for him.

²¹ "Someone might bring a fellowship offering to the Lord. That offering might be payment for a special promise the person made. Or it may be a special gift the person wanted to give the Lord. It might be a bull or a sheep. But it must be healthy. There must be nothing wrong with it. This is so it might be accepted for him. ²² You must not offer to the Lord any animal that is blind. It must not have broken bones or be crippled. It must not have running sores or any sort of skin disease. You must not offer any animals like these on the altar. They cannot be used as an offering by fire to the Lord.

²³ "Sometimes a bull or lamb is smaller than normal. Or it may not be perfectly formed. If someone wants to give that animal as a special gift to the Lord, it will be accepted. But it will not be accepted as payment for a special promise the person made.

²⁴ "An animal might have bruised, crushed, torn or cut sex glands. If it does, you must not offer that animal to the Lord in your own land. ²⁵ You must not take such animals from foreigners as sacrifices to the Lord. This is because the animals have been hurt in some way. They have something wrong with them. They will not be accepted for you.'"

²⁶ The Lord said to Moses, ²⁷ "When an ox, a sheep or a goat is born, it must stay seven days with its mother. But from the eighth day on, this animal will be accepted as a sacrifice. It may be offered by fire to the Lord. ²⁸ But you must not kill the animal and its mother on the same day. This rule is the same for an ox or a sheep.

²⁹ "You might want to offer some special offering of thanks to the Lord. But you must do it in a way that pleases the Lord. ³⁰ You must eat the whole animal that same day. You must not leave any of the meat for the next morning. I am the Lord.

³¹ "Remember my commands and obey them. I am the Lord. ³² Show respect for my holy name. You Israelites must remember that I am holy. I am the Lord. I have made you holy. ³³ I brought you out of Egypt. I became your God. I am the Lord."

23 The Lord said to Moses, ² "Tell the people of Israel: 'You will announce the Lord's appointed feasts as holy meetings. These are my special feasts.

³ "'There are six days for you to work. But the seventh day will be a special day of rest. It is a day for a holy meeting. You must not do any work. It is a Sabbath[d] to the Lord in all your homes.

⁴ "'These are the Lord's appointed feasts. You will announce the holy meetings at the times set for them. ⁵ The Lord's Passover[d] is on the fourteenth day of the first month. It begins at twilight. ⁶ The Feast[d] of Unleavened Bread begins on the fifteenth day of the same month. You will eat bread made without yeast for seven days. ⁷ On the first day of this feast you will have a holy meeting. On that day you must not do any work. ⁸ For seven days you will bring an offering made by fire to the Lord. There will be a holy meeting on the seventh day. And on that day you must not do any regular work.'"

⁹ The Lord said to Moses, ¹⁰ "Tell the people of Israel: 'You will enter the land I will give you. You will gather its harvest. At that time you must bring the first bundle of grain from your harvest to the priest. ¹¹ The priest will present the bundle before the Lord. Then it will be accepted for you. He will present the bundle on the day after the Sabbath.[d]

¹² "'On the day when you present the bundle of grain, offer a male lamb. It must be one year old. There must be nothing wrong with it. It will be a burnt offering to the Lord. ¹³ You must also offer a grain offering. It should be four

quarts of fine flour mixed with olive oil. It is an offering made by fire to the Lord. Its smell will be pleasing to the Lord. You must also offer a quart of wine as a drink offering. [14]First bring your offering to your God. Until you do this, do not eat the new grain, roasted grain or bread made from the new grain. This law will always continue for people from now on, wherever you live.

[15]"'Count seven weeks from the morning after the Sabbath.[d] (This is the Sabbath that you bring the bundle of grain to present as an offering.) [16]On the fiftieth day, you will bring a new grain offering to the Lord. This is the first day after the seventh week. [17]On that day bring two loaves of bread from your homes. That bread will be presented as an offering. Use yeast and four quarts of flour to make those loaves of bread. They will be your gift to the Lord from the first wheat of your harvest.

[18]"'Offer one bull, two male sheep and seven male lambs. The lambs must be one year old. There must be nothing wrong with them. Offer them with their grain offerings and drink offerings. They will be a burnt offering to the Lord. They will be an offering made by fire. And the smell will be pleasing to the Lord. [19]You must also offer one male goat for a sin offering. You must offer two male, one-year-old lambs as a fellowship offering.

[20]"'The priest will present the two lambs as an offering. He will present them with the bread from the first wheat of the harvest. They are holy to the Lord. They will belong to the priest. [21]On that same day you will call a holy meeting. You must not do any work that day. This law will continue for you from now on, wherever you live.

[22]"'You will harvest your crops on your land. But do not harvest all the way to the corners of your field. If grain falls onto the ground, don't gather it up. Leave it for poor people and foreigners in your country. I am the Lord your God.'"

[23]Again the Lord said to Moses, [24]"Tell the people of Israel: 'On the first day of the seventh month you must have a special day of rest. There will be a holy meeting. Blow the trumpet for a special time of remembering. [25]Do not do any work. And bring an offering made by fire to the Lord.'"

[26]The Lord said to Moses, [27]"The Day of Cleansing will be on the tenth day of the seventh month. There will be a holy meeting. You will give up eating and bring an offering made by fire to the Lord. [28]Do not do any work on that day. This is because it is the Day of Cleansing. On that day the priests will go before the Lord. They will perform the acts to make you clean[d] so you will belong to the Lord.

[29]"'If anyone refuses to give up food on this day, he must be separated from his people. [30]If anyone works on this day, I will destroy him from among his people. [31]You must not do any work at all. This law will continue for people from now on wherever you live. [32]It will be a special day of rest for you. And you must not eat. You will start this special day of rest on the evening after the ninth day of the month. It will continue from that evening until the next evening."

[33]Again the Lord said to Moses, [34]"Tell the people of Israel: 'On the fifteenth day of the seventh month is the Feast[d] of Shelters. This feast to the Lord will continue for seven days. [35]There will be a holy meeting on the first day. Do not do any work. [36]You will bring an offering made by fire to the Lord each day for seven days. On the eighth day you will have another holy meeting. And you will bring an offering made by fire to the Lord. This will be a holy meeting. Do not do any work.

[37]("'These are the Lord's special feasts. There will be holy meetings on these feast days. You will bring offerings made by fire to the Lord. They will be whole burnt offerings, grain offerings, sacrifices and drink offerings. You must bring these gifts at the right times. [38]You must bring these offerings in addition to those for the Lord's Sabbath[d] days. You must offer them in addition to offerings you give as payment for special promises. They are also in addition to special offerings you want to give to the Lord.)

[39]"'So on the fifteenth day of the seventh month, celebrate the Lord's festival for seven days. By then you will have gathered in the crops of the land. You must rest on the first day and the seventh day. [40]On the first day you will take good fruit from the fruit trees. And you will take branches from palm, poplars and other leafy trees. You will celebrate before the Lord your God for seven days. [41]Celebrate this festival to the Lord for seven days each year. This law will continue from now on. You will cele-

brate it in the seventh month. [42]Live in shelters for seven days. All the people born in Israel must live in shelters. [43]This is so that all your descendants[d] will know I made Israel live in shelters. It was during the time I brought them out of Egypt. I am the Lord your God.'"

[44]So Moses told the people of Israel about all of the Lord's appointed feast days.

24 The Lord said to Moses, [2]"Command the people of Israel to bring you pure oil from crushed olives. That oil is for the lamps. These lamps must never go out. [3]Aaron will keep the lamps burning in the Meeting Tent.[d] They will burn from evening until morning before the Lord. This will be in front of the curtain of the Box[d] of the Agreement. This law will continue from now on. [4]Aaron must always keep the lamps burning. They are on the lampstands of pure gold before the Lord.

[5]"Take fine flour and bake 12 loaves of bread with it. Use four quarts of flour for each loaf. [6]Put them in two rows on the golden table before the Lord. Six loaves will be in each row. [7]Put pure incense[d] on each row. This is the memorial portion to take the place of the bread. It is an offering made by fire to the Lord. [8]Every Sabbath[d] day Aaron will put the bread in order before the Lord. This agreement with the people of Israel will continue forever. [9]That bread will belong to Aaron and his sons. They will eat it in a holy place. This is because it is a most holy part of the offerings made by fire to the Lord. That bread is their share forever."

[10]Now there was a son of an Israelite woman and an Egyptian father. The son was walking among the Israelites. And a fight broke out in the camp between him and an Israelite. [11]The son of the Israelite woman began cursing and speaking against the Lord. So the people took him to Moses. (The mother's name was Shelomith. She was the daughter of Debri from the family of Dan.) [12]The people held him as a prisoner. They waited for the Lord's command to be made clear to them.

[13]Then the Lord said to Moses, [14]"Take the one who spoke against me outside the camp. Then bring together all the people who heard him. They must put their hands on his head.[n] Then all the

people must throw stones at him and kill him. [15]Tell the people of Israel this: 'If anyone curses his God, he is guilty of sin. [16]Anyone who speaks against the Lord must be put to death. All the people must kill him by throwing stones at him. Foreigners must be punished just like the person born in Israel. If someone speaks against the Lord, he must be put to death.

[17]"'If someone kills another person, he must be put to death. [18]Someone might kill an animal that belongs to another person. If he does, he must give that person another animal to take its place. [19]And someone might cause an injury to his neighbor. If he does, the same kind of injury must be given back to him. [20]A broken bone must be paid for a broken bone, an eye for an eye and a tooth for a tooth. In the same way someone injures another person, he must be injured in return. [21]So anyone who kills another person's animal must give that person another animal to take its place. But the person who kills another person must be put to death.

[22]"'The law will be the same for the foreigner as for those from your own country. I am the Lord your God.'"

[23]Then Moses spoke to the people of Israel. And they took the person who had cursed outside the camp. Then they killed him with stones. So the people of Israel did as the Lord had commanded Moses.

25 The Lord spoke to Moses at Mount Sinai. He said, [2]"Tell the people of Israel this: 'I will give you land. When you enter it, let it have a special time of rest. This will be to honor the Lord. [3]You may plant seed in your field for six years. You may trim your vineyards for six years and bring in their fruits. [4]But during the seventh year, you must let the land rest. This will be a special time to honor the Lord. You must not plant seed in your field or trim your vineyards. [5]You must not cut the crops that grow by themselves after harvest. You must not gather the grapes from your vines that are not trimmed. The land will have a year of rest.

[6]"'You may eat whatever the land produces during that year of rest. It will be food for your men and women servants. It will be food for your hired workers and the foreigners living in your country. [7]It will also be food for your cattle

and the wild animals of your land. Whatever the land produces may be eaten.

⁸"'Count off seven groups of 7 years. This will be 49 years. During that time there will be 7 years of rest for the land. ⁹On the Day of Cleansing,ᵈ you must blow the horn of a male sheep. This will be on the tenth day of the seventh month. You must blow the horn through the whole country. ¹⁰Make the fiftieth year a special year. Announce freedom for all the people living in your country. This time will be called Jubilee.ⁿ Each of you will go back to his own property. And each of you will go back to his own family and family group. ¹¹The fiftieth year will be a special time for you to celebrate. Don't plant seeds. Don't harvest the crops that grow by themselves. Don't gather grapes from the vines that are not trimmed. ¹²That year is Jubilee. It will be a holy time for you. You may eat the crops that come from the field. ¹³In the year of Jubilee each person will go back to his own property.

¹⁴"'Don't cheat your neighbor when you sell your land to him. And don't let him cheat you when you buy land from him. ¹⁵You might want to buy your neighbor's land. If you do, count the number of years since the last Jubilee. Use that number to decide the right price. If he sells the land to you, count the number of years left for harvesting crops. Use that number to decide the right price. ¹⁶If there are many years, the price will be high. If there are only a few years, lower the price. This is because your neighbor is really selling only a few crops to you. At the next Jubilee the land will again belong to his family. ¹⁷You must not cheat each other. You respect your God. I am the Lord your God.

¹⁸"'Remember my laws and rules, and obey them. Then you will live safely in the land. ¹⁹The land will give good crops to you. You will eat as much as you want. And you will live safely in the land.

²⁰"'But you might ask, "If we don't plant seeds or gather crops, what will we eat the seventh year?" ²¹Don't worry. I will send you a great blessing during the sixth year. That year the land will produce enough crops for 3 years. ²²When you plant in the eighth year, you will still be eating from the old crop. You will eat the old crop until the harvest of the ninth year.

²³"'The land really belongs to me. So you can't sell it forever. You are only foreigners and travelers living for a time on my land. ²⁴People might sell their land. But the family will always get its land back. ²⁵A person in your country might become very poor. He might be so poor that he must sell his land. So his close relatives must come and buy it back for him. ²⁶A person might not have a close relative to buy back his land for him. But he might get enough money to buy it back himself. ²⁷He must count the years since the land was sold. He must use that number to decide how much to pay for the land. Then he may buy it back. And the land will be his again. ²⁸But he might not find enough money to buy it back for himself. Then the one who bought it will keep it until the year of Jubilee.ᵈ But during that celebration, the land will go back to the first owner's family.

²⁹"'Someone may sell a home in a walled city. But, for a full year after he sold it, he has the right to buy it back. ³⁰But the owner might not buy back the house before a full year is over. If he doesn't, the house in the walled city will belong to the one who bought it. It will belong to his future sons. The house will not go back to the first owner at Jubilee. ³¹But houses in small towns without walls are like open country. They can be bought back. And they must be returned to their first owner at Jubilee.

³²"'The Levites may always buy back their houses. This is true in the cities which belong to them. ³³Someone might buy a house from a Levite. But that house in the Levites' city will again belong to the Levites in the Jubilee. This is because houses in Levite cities belong to the people of Levi. The people of Israel gave these cities to the Levites. ³⁴Also the fields and pastures around the Levites' cities cannot be sold. Those fields belong to the Levites forever.

³⁵"'Someone from your country might become too poor to support himself. Help him to live among you as you would a stranger or foreigner. ³⁶Do not charge him any interest on money you loan to him. Respect your God. And let the poor man live among you. ³⁷Don't lend him money for interest. Don't try to make a profit from the food he buys. ³⁸I am the Lord your God. I brought you out of the land of Egypt. I did it to give the land of Canaan to you and to become your God.

25:10 **Jubilee** This word comes from the Hebrew word for a horn of a male sheep.

Rewards for Obeying God 111 LEVITICUS 26:17

[39]" 'Someone from your country might become very poor. He might even sell himself as a slave to you. If he does, you must not make him work like a slave. [40]He will be like a hired worker. And he will be like a visitor with you until the year of Jubilee.[d] [41]Then he may leave you. He may take his children and go back to his family and the land of his ancestors. [42]This is because the Israelites are my servants. I brought them out of slavery in Egypt. They must not become slaves again. [43]You must not rule this person cruelly. You must respect your God.

[44]" 'You may buy men and women slaves from other nations around you. [45]Also you may buy children as slaves. These children must come from the families of foreigners living in your land. These child slaves will belong to you. [46]You may even pass these foreign slaves on to your children after you die. You can make them slaves forever. But you must not rule cruelly over your own brothers, the Israelites.

[47]" 'A foreigner or visitor among you might become rich. And someone in your country might become poor. The poor man might sell himself as a slave to a foreigner living among you. Or he might sell himself to a member of a foreigner's family. [48]The poor man has the right to be bought back and become free. One of his relatives may buy him back. [49]His uncle or his uncle's son may buy him back. One of his close relatives may buy him back. Or if he gets enough money, he may pay the money himself. Then he will be free again.

[50]" 'How do you decide the price? You must count the years from the time he sold himself to the foreigner. And count up to the next year of Jubilee. Use that number to decide the price. This is because the person really only hired himself out for a certain number of years. [51]There might still be many years before the year of Jubilee. If so, the person must pay back a large part of the price. [52]There might only be a few years left until Jubilee. If so, the person must pay a small part of the first price. [53]But he will live like a hired man with the foreigner every year. Don't let the foreigner rule cruelly over him.

[54]" 'That person will become free, even if no one buys him back. At the year of Jubilee, he and his children will become free. [55]This is because the people of Israel are my servants. I brought

them out of slavery in Egypt. I am the Lord your God.

26" 'Don't make idols for yourselves. Don't set up statues or memorials. Don't put stone statues in your land to bow down to. This is because I am the Lord your God.

[2]" 'Remember my Sabbaths,[d] and respect my Holy Place. I am the Lord.

[3]" 'Remember my laws and commands, and obey them. [4]If you do these things, I will give you rains at the right season. The land will produce crops. And the trees of the field will produce their fruit. [5]Your threshing[d] will continue until the grape harvest. And your grape harvest will continue until it is time to plant. Then you will have plenty to eat. You will live safely in your land. [6]I will give peace to your country. You will lie down in peace. No one will make you afraid. I will keep harmful animals out of your country. And armies will not pass through your country.

[7]" 'You will chase your enemies and defeat them. You will kill them with your sword. [8]Five of you will chase 100 men. And 100 of you will chase 10,000 men. You will defeat your enemies and kill them with your sword.

[9]" 'Then I will show kindness to you. I will let you have many children. I will keep my agreement with you. [10]You will have enough crops to last for more than a year. You will harvest the new crops. And you will have to throw out the old crops to make room for the new ones. [11]Also I will place my Holy Tent[d] among you. I will not turn away from you. [12]I will walk with you and be your God. And you will be my people. [13]I am the Lord your God. You were slaves in Egypt. You were bent low from the heavy weights you carried as slaves. But I broke the heavy weights that were on your shoulders. I let you walk proudly again.

[14]" 'But you must obey me. You must obey all my commands. [15]If you refuse to obey all my laws and commands, you have broken our agreement. [16]If you do that, I will cause terrible things to happen to you. I will cause you to have disease and fever. They will destroy your eyes and kill you. You will not have success when you plant your seed. And your enemy will eat your crops. [17]I will be against you, and your enemies will defeat you. These enemies hate you. And they will rule over you. You will run away even when no one is chasing you.

¹⁸"'If you still do not obey me, I will punish you seven times more for your sins. ¹⁹And I will also break the great cities that make you proud. The skies will not give rain. The earth will not produce crops. ²⁰You will work hard, but it will not help. Your land will not grow any crops. Your trees will not give their fruit.

²¹"'If you still turn against me and refuse to obey me, I will beat you seven times harder. The more you sin, the more you will be punished. ²²I will send wild animals to attack you. They will take your children away from you. They will destroy your cattle. They will make you so few in number the roads will be empty.

²³"'If you don't learn your lesson after all these things, and if you still turn against me, ²⁴I will also turn against you. I will punish you seven more times for your sins. ²⁵You broke my agreement, and I will punish you. I will bring armies against you. You will go into your cities for safety. But I will cause diseases to spread among you. Then your enemy will defeat you. ²⁶There will be very little bread to eat. Ten women will be able to cook all your bread in one oven. They will measure each piece of bread. You will eat, but you will still be hungry.

²⁷"'If you still refuse to listen to me, and if you still turn against me, ²⁸I will really show my anger. I will punish you seven more times for your sins. ²⁹You will eat the bodies of your sons and daughters. ³⁰I will destroy your places where false gods are worshiped. I will cut down your incenseᵈ altars. I will pile your dead bodies on the lifeless forms of your idols. I will hate you. ³¹I will destroy your cities. I will make your holy places empty. I will not smell the pleasing smell of your offerings. ³²I will make the land empty. Your enemies who come to live in it will be shocked at it. ³³I will scatter you among the nations. I will pull out my sword and destroy you. Your land will become empty. Your cities will become waste. ³⁴You will be taken to your enemy's country. So your land will finally get its rest. It will enjoy its time of rest all the time it lies empty. ³⁵During the time the land is empty, it will rest. It will have the rest you should have given it while you lived in it.

³⁶"'Those who are left alive will lose their courage in the land of their enemies. They will be frightened of everything. They will be frightened by even the sound of a leaf being blown by the wind. They will run as if someone were chasing them with a sword. They will fall even when no one is chasing them. ³⁷They will run as if someone were chasing them with a sword. They will fall over each other, even though no one is chasing them. You will not be strong enough to stand up against your enemies. ³⁸You will die among other nations. You will disappear in your enemies' countries. ³⁹So those who are left alive will rot away in their enemies' countries. They will rot away because of their sins and their ancestors' sins.

⁴⁰"'But maybe the people will confess their sins and the sins of their ancestors. Maybe they will admit they turned against me and sinned against me. ⁴¹That made me turn against them. So I sent them into the land of their enemies. These disobedient people might be sorry for what they did. They might accept punishment for their sin. ⁴²If they do, I will remember my agreement with Jacob. I will remember my agreement with Isaac and Abraham. And I will remember the land. ⁴³The land will be empty. It will enjoy its time of rest. Then those who are left alive will accept the punishment for their sins. They will learn that they were punished because they hated my laws. And they refused to obey my rules. ⁴⁴They truly sinned. But if they come to me for help, I will not turn away from them. I will listen to them even in the land of their enemies. I will not completely destroy them. I will not break my agreement with them. This is because I am the Lord their God. ⁴⁵For their good I will remember the agreement with their ancestors. I brought their ancestors out of the land of Egypt. I did it so I could become their God. The other nations saw these things. I am the Lord.'"

⁴⁶These are the laws, rules and teachings the Lord gave the people of Israel. He gave these laws to the Israelites through Moses. This was at Mount Sinai.

27 The Lord said to Moses, ²"Tell the people of Israel: 'Someone might make a special promise to the Lord. He might promise to give himself or another person as a servant to the Lord. That person will then begin to serve the Lord in a special way. The priest must set a certain price for that person. That is the price that would have to be paid to free the person from his special promise to the Lord. ³The price for a man 20 to 60 years old is about 1¼ pounds of silver. (You must use the measure as set by the Holy Place.) ⁴The price for a woman 20 to 60 years old is about 12 ounces of silver. ⁵The price for a man 5 to 20 years old is about 8 ounces of silver. The price for a woman 5 to 20 years old is about 4 ounces of silver. ⁶The price for a baby boy 1 month to 5 years old is about 2 ounces of silver. For a baby girl the price is about 1½ ounces of silver. ⁷The price for a man 60 years old or older is about 6 ounces of silver. The price for a woman 60 years old or older is about 4 ounces of silver.

⁸"A person might be too poor to pay the price. If he is, bring him to the priest. The priest will decide how much money the person can afford to pay.

⁹"Some animals may be used as sacrifices to the Lord. If someone promises to bring one of these animals, it will become holy. ¹⁰That person must not try to put another animal in its place. He must not try to exchange it for something else. He must not try to exchange a good animal for a bad animal. And he must not exchange a bad animal for a good animal. If he tries to exchange animals, both animals will become holy.

¹¹"'Unclean^d animals cannot be offered as sacrifices to the Lord. Someone might bring one of them to the Lord. If he does, that animal must be brought to the priest. ¹²The priest will decide a price for the animal. The price will be according to whether the animal is good or bad. If the priest decides a price, that is the price for the animal. ¹³If the person wants to buy back the animal, he must add an additional one-fifth to the price.

¹⁴"'A person might give his house as holy to the Lord. If he does, the priest must decide its value. The price will be according to whether the house is good or bad. If the priest decides a price, that is the price for the house. ¹⁵But the person who gives the house might want to buy it back. If he does, he must add an additional one-fifth to the price. Then the house will belong to him again.

¹⁶"'A person might give part of his fields to the Lord. The value of those fields will depend on how much seed is needed to plant them. It will cost about one and one-fourth pounds of silver for each six bushels of barley seed needed. ¹⁷The person might give his field at the year of Jubilee.^{d} Then its value will be what the priest decides. ¹⁸But he might give his field after the Jubilee. If he does,

the priest must decide the exact price. He must count the number of years to the next year of Jubilee. Then he will use that number to decide the exact price. ¹⁹The person who gave the field might want to buy it back. If he does, he must add one-fifth to that price. Then the field will belong to him again.

²⁰"'If he does not buy back the field, it will always belong to the priest. If it is sold to someone else, the first person cannot buy it back. ²¹But the person might not buy back the land. If he doesn't, at the year of Jubilee, it will remain holy to the Lord. It will belong to the priest forever. It will become the property of the priests.

²²"'Someone may give a field he has bought to the Lord. But it may not be a part of his family land. ²³If he gives a field, the priest must count the years to the next Jubilee. He must decide the price for the land. Then that land will belong to the Lord. ²⁴At the year of Jubilee, the land will go back to its first owner. It will go back to the family who sold the land.

²⁵"'You must use the measure as set by the Holy Place in paying these prices. It weighs two-fifths of an ounce.

²⁶"'People may give cattle and sheep to the Lord. But if an animal is the first one born to its parent, it already belongs to the Lord. So people may not give these animals again. ²⁷If the animal is unclean,^{d} the person must buy it back. The priest will decide the price of the animal. And the person must add one-fifth to that price. If he does not buy it back, the priest must sell it. He will sell it for the price he had decided.

²⁸"'There is a special kind of gift that people give to the Lord. It may be a person, animal or field from the family property. That gift cannot be bought back or sold. It is most holy to the Lord. ²⁹"'If a person is given for the purpose of being destroyed, he cannot be bought back. He must be put to death.

³⁰"'One-tenth of all crops belongs to the Lord. This includes the crops from fields and the fruit from trees. That one-tenth belongs to the Lord. ³¹A person might want to get back his tenth. If he does, he must add one-fifth to its price and buy it back.

³²"'The priest will take every tenth animal from a person's cattle or sheep. It will belong to the Lord. ³³The owner should not pick out the good animals from the bad. He should not exchange

one animal for another. If he does exchange it, both animals will become holy. They cannot be bought back.'"

[34]These are the commands the Lord commanded at Mount Sinai. They are for the people of Israel.

The Fourth Book of Moses Called
NUMBERS

1 The Lord spoke to Moses in the Meeting Tent.[d] This was in the Desert of Sinai. It was on the first day of the second month. This was in the second year after the people of Israel left Egypt. The Lord said to Moses: [2]"Count all the people of Israel. List the name of each man with his family and family group. [3]You and Aaron must count all the men of Israel 20 years old or older. They will serve in the army of Israel. List them by their divisions. [4]One man from each tribe[d] will help you. He is to be the leader of his family. [5]These are the names of the men who will help you:

from the tribe of Reuben—Elizur
    son of Shedeur;
[6]from the tribe of Simeon—
    Shelumiel son of Zurishaddai;
[7]from the tribe of Judah—Nahshon
    son of Amminadab;
[8]from the tribe of Issachar—
    Nethanel son of Zuar;
[9]from the tribe of Zebulun—Eliab
    son of Helon;
[10]from the tribe of Ephraim son of
    Joseph—Elishama son of
    Ammihud;
from the tribe of Manasseh son of
    Joseph—Gamaliel son of
    Pedahzur;
[11]from the tribe of Benjamin—
    Abidan son of Gideoni;
[12]from the tribe of Dan—Ahiezer son
    of Ammishaddai;
[13]from the tribe of Asher—Pagiel son
    of Ocran;
[14]from the tribe of Gad—Eliasaph
    son of Deuel;
[15]from the tribe of Naphtali—Ahira
    son of Enan."

[16]All these men were chosen by the people to be leaders of their tribes. They were the leaders of their family groups.

[17]Moses and Aaron took these men who had been picked. [18]And Moses and Aaron called all the people of Israel together. This was the first day of the second month. Then the people were listed by their families and family groups. All

the men who were 20 years old or older were listed by name. [19]Moses did exactly what the Lord had commanded. Moses listed the people while they were in the Desert of Sinai.

[20]The tribe of Reuben was counted. Reuben was the first son born to Israel. All the men 20 years old or older who were able to serve in the army were listed. They were each listed by name with their families and family groups. [21]The tribe of Reuben totaled 46,500 men.

[22]The tribe of Simeon was counted. All the men 20 years old or older who were able to serve in the army were listed. They were each listed by name with their families and family groups. [23]The tribe of Simeon totaled 59,300 men.

[24]The tribe of Gad was counted. All the men 20 years old or older who were able to serve in the army were listed. They were listed by name with their families and family groups. [25]The tribe of Gad totaled 45,650 men.

[26]The tribe of Judah was counted. All the men 20 years old or older who were able to serve in the army were listed. They were listed by name with their families and family groups. [27]The tribe of Judah totaled 74,600 men.

[28]The tribe of Issachar was counted. All the men 20 years old or older who were able to serve in the army were listed. They were listed by name with their families and family groups. [29]The tribe of Issachar totaled 54,400 men.

[30]The tribe of Zebulun was counted. All the men 20 years old or older who were able to serve in the army were listed. They were listed by name with their families and family groups. [31]The tribe of Zebulun totaled 57,400 men.

[32]The tribe of Ephraim was counted. (Ephraim was a son of Joseph.) All the men 20 years old or older who were able to serve in the army were listed. They were listed by name with their families and family groups. [33]The tribe of Ephraim totaled 40,500 men.

[34]The tribe of Manasseh was counted. (Manasseh was also a son of Joseph.) All the men 20 years old or older who were able to serve in the army were listed. They were listed by name with their families and family groups. [35]The tribe of Manasseh totaled 32,200 men.

[36]The tribe of Benjamin was counted. All the men 20 years old or older who were able to serve in the army were listed. They were listed by name with their families and family groups. [37]The tribe of Benjamin totaled 35,400 men.

[38]The tribe of Dan was counted. All the men 20 years old or older who were able to serve in the army were listed. They were listed by name with their families and family groups. [39]The tribe of Dan totaled 62,700 men.

[40]The tribe of Asher was counted. All the men 20 years old or older who were able to serve in the army were listed. They were listed by name with their families and family groups. [41]The tribe of Asher totaled 41,500 men.

[42]The tribe of Naphtali was counted. All the men 20 years old or older who were able to serve in the army were listed. They were listed by name with their families and family groups. [43]The tribe of Naphtali totaled 53,400 men.

[44]Moses, Aaron, and the 12 leaders of Israel counted these men. There was 1 leader from each of the families. [45]Every man of Israel 20 years old or older who was able to serve in the army was counted. Each man was listed with his family. [46]The total number of men was 603,550.

[47]The families from the tribe of Levi were not listed with the others. [48]The Lord had told Moses: [49]"Do not count the tribe of Levi or include them with the other Israelites. [50]But make the Levites responsible for the Holy Tent[d] of the Agreement. They must take care of it and everything that is with it. They must carry the Holy Tent and everything in it. They must take care of it and make their camp around it. [51]Any time the Holy Tent is moved, the Levites must take it down. Any time it is set up, the Levites must do it. If anyone else goes near the Holy Tent, he will be put to death. [52]The Israelites will make their camps in separate divisions, each man near his family flag. [53]But the Levites must make their camp around the Holy Tent of the Agreement. Then I will not be angry with the Israelites. The Levites will take care of the Holy Tent of the Agreement."

[54]So the Israelites did everything the Lord commanded Moses.

2 The Lord said to Moses and Aaron: [2]"The Israelites should make their camps around the Meeting Tent.[d] But they should not camp too close to it. Each person should camp under the flag of his division near the banner of his family group."

[3]The camp of Judah will be on the east side, where the sun rises. They will camp by divisions there under their flag. The leader of the people of Judah is Nahshon son of Amminadab. [4]There are 74,600 men in his division.

[5]Next to them the tribe[d] of Issachar will camp. The leader of the people of Issachar is Nethanel son of Zuar. [6]There are 54,400 men in his division.

[7]Next is the tribe of Zebulun. The leader of the people of Zebulun is Eliab son of Helon. [8]There are 57,400 men in his division.

[9]There are a total of 186,400 men in the camp of Judah. They are in their divisions. They will be the first to march out of camp.

[10]The divisions of the camp of Reuben will be south of the Holy Tent. They will camp under their flag. The leader of the people of Reuben is Elizur son of Shedeur. [11]There are 46,500 men in his division.

[12]Next to them the tribe of Simeon will camp. The leader of the people of Simeon is Shelumiel son of Zurishaddai. [13]There are 59,300 men in his division.

[14]Next is the tribe of Gad. The leader of the people of Gad is Eliasaph son of Deuel. [15]There are 45,650 men in his division.

[16]There are a total of 151,450 men in the camp of Reuben. They are in their divisions. They will be the second group to march out of camp.

[17]When the Levites move the Meeting Tent, they will be in between the other camps. The tribes will move in the same order as they camp. Each person will be with his family flag.

[18]The divisions of the camp of Ephraim will be on the west side. They will camp under their flag. The leader of the people of Ephraim is Elishama son of Ammihud. [19]There are 40,500 men in his division.

[20]Next to them the tribe of Manasseh will camp. The leader of the people of Manasseh is Gamaliel son of Pedahzur. [21]There are 32,200 men in his division.

[22]Next to them the tribe of Benjamin

will camp. The leader of the people of Benjamin is Abidan son of Gideoni. [23]There are 35,400 men in his division.

[24]There are a total of 108,100 men in the camp of Ephraim. They are in their divisions. They will be the third group to march out of camp.

[25]The divisions of the camp of Dan will be on the north side. They will camp under their flag. The leader of the people of Dan is Ahiezer son of Ammishaddai. [26]There are 62,700 men in his division.

[27]Next to them the tribe of Asher will camp. The leader of the people of Asher is Pagiel son of Ocran. [28]There are 41,500 men in his division.

[29]Next is the tribe of Naphtali. The leader of the people of Naphtali is Ahira son of Enan. [30]There are 53,400 men in his division.

[31]There are 157,600 men in the camp of Dan. They will be the last to march out of camp. They will travel under their own flag.

[32]These are the Israelites who were counted by families. The total number of Israelites in the camps, counted by divisions, is 603,550. [33]Moses did not count the Levites among the other people of Israel. This is what the Lord had commanded.

[34]So the Israelites obeyed everything the Lord commanded Moses. They camped under their flags. Each person traveled with his family and family group.

3 This is the family history of Aaron and Moses. This was at the time the Lord talked to Moses on Mount Sinai.

[2]Aaron had four sons. Nadab was the oldest. Then Aaron had Abihu, Eleazar and Ithamar. [3]Those were the names of Aaron's sons. They were appointed to serve as priests. [4]But Nadab and Abihu died when they sinned in the presence of the Lord. They made an offering to the Lord in the Desert of Sinai. But they used the wrong kind of fire. They had no sons. So Eleazar and Ithamar served as priests during the lifetime of their father Aaron.

[5]The Lord said to Moses, [6]"Bring the tribe[d] of Levi to Aaron the priest. They must help him. [7]They will help him and all the Israelites at the Meeting Tent.[d] They will do the work of the Holy Tent. [8]The Levites must take care of everything in the Meeting Tent. They will serve the people of Israel by doing the work in the Holy Tent. [9]Give the Levites

to Aaron and his sons. Of all the Israelites, the Levites are given completely to him. [10]Appoint Aaron and his sons to serve as priests. Anyone else who comes near the holy things must be put to death."

[11]The Lord also said to Moses, [12]"I am choosing the Levites from all the Israelites. They will take the place of all the firstborn[d] children of Israel. The Levites will be mine. [13]All the firstborn are mine. When you were in Egypt, I killed all the firstborn children of the Egyptians. I took all the firstborn of Israel to be mine. Firstborn animals and children are mine. I am the Lord."

[14]The Lord again talked to Moses in the Desert of Sinai. The Lord said, [15]"Count the Levites by families and family groups. Count every male one month old or older." [16]So Moses obeyed the Lord and counted them all.

[17]Levi had three sons. Their names were Gershon, Kohath and Merari. [18]The Gershonite family groups were Libni and Shimei. [19]The Kohathite family groups were Amram, Izhar, Hebron and Uzziel. [20]The Merarite family groups were Mahli and Mushi.

These were the family groups that belonged to the Levites.

[21]The family groups of Libni and Shimei belonged to Gershon. They were all the Gershonite family groups. [22]They had 7,500 males one month or older. [23]The Gershonite family groups camped on the west side, behind the Holy Tent. [24]The leader of the families of Gershon was Eliasaph son of Lael. [25]In the Meeting Tent the Gershonites were responsible for taking care of these things: the Holy Tent, its covering, the curtain at the entrance to the Meeting Tent, [26]the curtains in the courtyard, the curtain at the entry to the courtyard around the Holy Tent and the altar, the ropes and all the work connected with these things.

[27]The family groups of Amram, Izhar, Hebron and Uzziel belonged to Kohath. They were all the Kohathite family groups. [28]They had 8,600 males one month old or older. They were responsible for taking care of the Holy Place. [29]The Kohathite family groups camped south of the Holy Tent. [30]The leader of the Kohathite families was Elizaphan son of Uzziel. [31]They were responsible for the Holy Box,[d] the table, the lampstand, the altars, the tools of the holy place, the curtain and all the work con-

nected with these things. ³²The main leader of the Levites was Eleazar son of Aaron, the priest. Eleazar was in charge of all those responsible for the Holy Place.

³³The family groups of Mahli and Mushi belonged to Merari. They were all the Merarite family groups. ³⁴They had 6,200 males one month old or older. ³⁵The leader of the Merari families was Zuriel son of Abihail. They were to camp north of the Holy Tent. ³⁶The Merarites were responsible for the frame of the Holy Tent, the braces, the posts, the bases and all the work connected with these things. ³⁷They were also responsible for the posts in the courtyard around the Holy Tent and their bases, tent pegs and ropes.

³⁸Moses, Aaron and his sons camped east of the Holy Tent. They were in front of the Meeting Tent. They were responsible for the Holy Place. They did this for the Israelites. Anyone else who came near the Holy Place was to be put to death.

³⁹Moses and Aaron counted the Levite men. The Lord commanded this. There were 22,000 males one month old or older.

⁴⁰The Lord said to Moses, "Count all the firstborn⁴ sons in Israel one month old or older. List their names. ⁴¹Take the Levites for me instead of the firstborn sons of Israel. Take the animals of the Levites instead of the firstborn animals from the rest of Israel. I am the Lord."

⁴²So Moses did what the Lord commanded. Moses counted all the firstborn sons of the Israelites. ⁴³He listed all the firstborn sons one month old or older. There were 22,273 names.

⁴⁴The Lord also said to Moses, ⁴⁵"Take the Levites instead of all the firstborn sons of the Israelites. And take the animals of the Levites instead of the animals of the other people. The Levites are mine. I am the Lord. ⁴⁶There are 273 more firstborn sons than Levites. ⁴⁷So collect two ounces of silver for each of the 273 sons. Use the measure as set by the Holy Place. It weighs two-fifths of an ounce. ⁴⁸Give the silver to Aaron and his sons. It is the payment for the 273 Israelites."

⁴⁹So Moses collected the money for the people the Levites could not replace. ⁵⁰Moses collected the silver from the firstborn of the Israelites. He collected 35 pounds of silver, using the measure set by the Holy Place. ⁵¹So Moses obeyed

the Lord. He gave the silver to Aaron and his sons.

4 The Lord said to Moses and Aaron, ²"Count the Kohathites among the Levites. Count them by family groups and families. ³Count the men from 30 to 50 years old. They will serve in the Meeting Tent.ᵈ

⁴"They are responsible for the most holy things in the Meeting Tent. ⁵When the Israelites move, Aaron and his sons must go into the Holy Tent. They are to take down the curtain. Then they must cover the Holy Boxᵈ of the Agreement with it. ⁶Over this they must put a covering made from fine leather. Then they must spread the solid blue cloth over it. And they must put the poles in the rings on the Holy Box.

⁷"Then they must spread a blue cloth over the table. This is the table for the bread that shows we are in God's presence. They must put the plates, spoons, bowls and the jars for drink offerings on the table. They must leave the bread on the table. ⁸Then they must put a red cloth over all of these things. They must cover everything with fine leather. Then they must put the poles in place.

⁹"With a blue cloth they must cover the lampstand, its lamps, its wick trimmers and trays. They must cover all the jars for the oil used in the lamps. ¹⁰Then they must wrap everything in fine leather. They must put all these things on a frame for carrying them.

¹¹"They must spread a blue cloth over the gold altar. Then they must cover it with fine leather. They must put its poles in place.

¹²"They must gather everything used for serving in the Holy Place. They must wrap them in a blue cloth. Then they must cover that with fine leather. They must put these things on a frame for carrying them.

¹³"They must clean the ashes off the bronze altar. Then they must spread a purple cloth over it. ¹⁴They must gather all the things used for serving at the altar. These are the pans for carrying the fire, meat forks, shovels and bowls. They must put them on the bronze altar. Then they must spread a covering of fine leather over it. They must put the carrying poles in the rings on the altar.

¹⁵"When the camp is ready to move, have Aaron and his sons cover all the holy things. Then the Kohathites may go in and carry away those things. This way they won't touch the holy things

and die. It is the Kohathites' job to carry the things that are in the Meeting Tent.

16 "Eleazar son of Aaron, the priest, will be responsible for the Holy Tent. And he is responsible for everything in it: the oil for the lamp, the sweet-smelling incense,^d the continual grain offering and the oil used to appoint priests and things to the Lord's service."

17 The Lord said to Moses and Aaron, 18 "Don't let the Kohathites be destroyed from the Levites. 19 Do this for the Kohathites. Then they may go near the Most Holy Place and not die. Aaron and his sons must go in and show each Kohathite what to do. And they must show each man what to carry. 20 The Kohathites must not enter and look at the holy things, even for a second. If they do, they will die."

21 The Lord said to Moses, 22 "Count the Gershonites by families and family groups. 23 Count the men from 30 to 50 years old. Everyone has a job to do in the Meeting Tent.^d

24 "This is what the Gershonite family groups must do and what they must carry. 25 They must carry the pieces of cloth of the Holy Tent^d and Meeting Tent. They must also carry its covering and the covering made from fine leather. And they must carry the curtains for the entrance to the Meeting Tent. 26 They must carry the curtains of the courtyard that goes around the Holy Tent and the altar. They must carry the curtain for the entry to the courtyard and the ropes and all the things used with the curtains. They must do everything connected with these things. 27 Aaron and his sons are in charge of what the Gershonites do or carry. You tell them what they are responsible for carrying. 28 This is the work of the Gershonite family group at the Meeting Tent. Ithamar son of Aaron, the priest, will direct their work.

29 "Count the Merarite families and family groups. 30 Count the men from 30 to 50 years old. They will work at the Meeting Tent.^d 31 It is their job to carry the frame of the Meeting Tent, the cross-bars, the posts and bases. 32 They must also carry the posts that go around the courtyard. They must carry the bases, tent pegs and ropes. And they must carry everything that is used with the poles around the courtyard. Tell each man exactly what to carry. 33 This is the work the Merarites will do for the Meeting Tent. Ithamar son of Aaron, the priest, will direct their work."

34 Moses, Aaron and the leaders of Israel counted the Kohathites by families and family groups. 35 The men from 30 to 50 years old were to work at the Meeting Tent.^d 36 The family group had 2,750 men. 37 This was the total of the Kohath family group who worked at the Meeting Tent. Moses and Aaron counted them as the Lord had commanded Moses.

38 Also, the Gershon family group was counted by families and family groups. 39 The men from 30 to 50 years old were given work at the Meeting Tent. 40 The families and family groups had 2,630 men. 41 This was the total of the Gershon family group who worked at the Meeting Tent. Moses and Aaron counted them as the Lord had commanded.

42 Also, the men in the families and family groups of the Merari family were counted. 43 The men from 30 to 50 years old were to work at the Meeting Tent. 44 The family group had 3,200 men. 45 This was the total of the Merari family group. Moses and Aaron counted them as the Lord had commanded them.

46 So Moses, Aaron and the leaders of Israel counted all the Levites. They counted them by families and family groups. 47 The men from 30 to 50 were given work at the Meeting Tent. They also carried the Tent. 48 The total number of these men was 8,580. 49 Each man was counted as the Lord had commanded Moses. Each man was given his work and told what to carry. This was as the Lord had commanded Moses.

5 The Lord said to Moses, 2 "Command the Israelites to send away from camp anyone with a harmful skin disease. Send away anyone who gives off body fluid. And send away anyone who has touched a dead body. 3 Send both men and women away from camp. Then they won't spread the disease there. I am living among you." 4 So Israel obeyed God's command. They sent those people outside the camp as the Lord had told Moses.

5 The Lord said to Moses, 6 "Tell the Israelites: 'When a man or woman does something wrong to another person, that is really sinning against God. That person is guilty. 7 He must tell what he has done wrong. And he must fully pay for the wrong he has done. Then he must add one-fifth to it. And he must give it to the person he wronged. 8 But that person may be dead. That person may not have any close relatives to receive the payment. Then the one who did wrong owes

the Lord. That person must pay the priest. The priest must sacrifice a male sheep to remove the wrong so that person will belong to God. [9]When an Israelite brings a holy gift, he should give it to the priest. [10]No one has to give these holy gifts. But if someone does give them, they belong to the priest.'"

[11]Then the Lord said to Moses, [12]"Tell the Israelites: 'A man's wife might be unfaithful to him. [13]She might have sexual relations with another man. Her sin might be kept hidden from her husband. Her husband might not know about the wrong thing she did. Perhaps no one saw it, and she wasn't caught. [14]But her husband might have feelings of jealousy whether she has sinned or not. [15]He then should take her to the priest. The husband must also take an offering for her. This offering will be two quarts of barley flour. He must not pour oil or incense[d] on it. This is a grain offering for jealousy. It is to find out if she is guilty.

[16]"'The priest will bring in the woman and make her stand before the Lord. [17]He will take some holy water in a clay jar. Then he will put some dirt from the floor of the Holy Tent into the water. [18]The priest will make the woman stand before the Lord. Then he will loosen her hair. And he will hand her the grain offering for jealousy. He will hold the bitter water that brings a curse on her. [19]The priest will tell her what the oath says will happen to her. He will ask her, "Has another man had sexual relations with you? Have you been unfaithful to your husband? If you haven't, then this water that brings a curse won't hurt you. [20]But what if you have been unfaithful to your husband? What if you have had sexual relations with a man besides your husband?" [21]The priest will tell her the curse that the oath will bring. He will say, "If you are guilty, the Lord will make the people curse you. Your stomach will get big, and you will not be able to have another baby. [22]This water that brings a curse will go inside you. Your stomach will get big, and you will not be able to have another baby."

"'The woman must say, "I agree."

[23]"'The priest should write these curses on a scroll. Then he should wash the words off into the water. [24]Then he will make the woman drink the water that brings a curse. When she does, it may make her sick. [25]Then the priest will take the grain offering for jealousy from her. He will present it before the

Lord. Then he will bring it to the altar. [26]Then the priest will take a handful of the grain. This is a memorial offering. He will burn it on the altar. After that he will make the woman drink the water. [27]He will make her drink it to see if she is not pure. He will know if she has sinned against her husband. When it goes into her, her stomach may get big. And she may not be able to have another baby. Her people will turn against her. [28]But if the woman has not sinned, she is pure. She is not guilty. She will be able to have more babies.

[29]"'So this is the teaching about jealousy. This is what to do when a woman is unfaithful to her husband. [30]It also should be done if the man gets jealous because he suspects his wife. The priest will have her stand before the Lord. Then he will do all these things. This is the teaching. [31]If the husband is right, the woman will suffer.'"

6 The Lord said to Moses, [2]"Tell the Israelites: 'A man or a woman might want to promise to belong to the Lord in a special way. This person will be called a Nazirite. [3]During this time, he must not drink wine or beer. He must not drink vinegar made from wine or beer. He must not even drink grape juice or eat grapes or raisins. [4]While he is a Nazirite, he must not eat anything that comes from the grapevine. He must not even eat the seeds or the skin.

[5]"'During the time he promised to belong to the Lord, he must not cut his hair. He must be holy until this special time is over. He must let his hair grow long. [6]During his special time of belonging to the Lord, a Nazirite must not go near a dead body. [7]Even if his own father, mother, brother or sister dies, he must not touch them. This would make him unclean.[d] He must still keep his promise to belong to God in a special way. [8]While he is a Nazirite, he belongs to the Lord.

[9]"'If he is next to someone who dies suddenly, his hair has been made unclean. It was part of his promise. So he must shave his head seven days later to be clean. [10]Then on the eighth day, he must bring two doves or two young pigeons to the priest. The priest will be at the entrance to the Holy Tent.[d] [11]The priest will offer one as a sin offering. He will offer the other as a burnt offering. This removes sin so the man will belong to God. He had sinned because he was near a dead body. That same day he will

again promise to let his hair grow for the Lord. [12]He must give himself to the Lord for another special time. He must bring a male lamb a year old. It will be a penalty offering. The days of the special time before don't count. This is because he became unclean during his first special time.

[13]"This is the teaching for a Nazirite. When the promised time is over, he must go to the entrance of the Meeting Tent.[d] [14]There he will give his offerings to the Lord. He must offer a year-old male lamb as a burnt offering. It must have nothing wrong with it. He must also offer a year-old female lamb as a sin offering. There must be nothing wrong with it. And he must bring a male sheep for a fellowship offering. There must be nothing wrong with it. [15]He must also bring the grain offerings and drink offerings that go with them. And he must bring a basket of bread made without yeast. There must be loaves made with fine flour mixed with oil. And there must be wafers made without yeast spread with oil.

[16]"The priest will give these offerings to the Lord. He will make the sin offering and the burnt offering. [17]Then he will kill the male sheep as a fellowship offering to the Lord. Along with it, he will present the basket of bread. He will also make the grain offering and the drink offering along with it.

[18]"The Nazirite must go to the entrance of the Meeting Tent. There he must shave off his hair that he grew for his promise. The hair will be put in the fire that is under the sacrifice on the fellowship offering.

[19]"After the Nazirite cuts off his hair, the priest will give him a boiled shoulder from the male sheep. From the basket he will also give him a loaf and a wafer. Both are made without yeast. [20]Then the priest will present them to the Lord. This is an offering presented before the Lord. They are holy and belong to the priest. Also, he is to present the breast and the thigh from the male sheep to the Lord. They also belong to the priest. After that, the Nazirite may drink wine.

[21]"This is the teaching for the Nazirite promise. If a person makes the Nazirite promise, he must give all of these gifts to the Lord. If he promised to do more, he must keep his promise. That is also the teaching of the Nazirite promise.'"

[22]The Lord said to Moses, [23]"Tell Aaron and his sons, 'This is how you should bless the Israelites. Say to them:

[24]"May the Lord bless you and keep you.

[25]May the Lord show you his kindness.
    May he have mercy on you.

[26]May the Lord watch over you
    and give you peace."'

[27]"So Aaron and his sons will bless the Israelites with my name. And I will bless them."

7 When Moses finished setting up the Holy Tent,[d] he gave it for service to the Lord. Moses poured olive oil on the Tent and on everything used in the Tent. He also poured oil on the altar and all its tools. In this way he prepared them for service to the Lord. [2]Then the leaders of Israel made offerings. These were the heads of the families and leaders of each tribe.[d] They were the men who counted the people. [3]They brought to the Lord 6 covered carts and 12 oxen. Each leader gave an ox. Every two leaders gave a cart. They gave these to the Holy Tent.

[4]The Lord said to Moses, [5]"Accept these gifts from the leaders. Use them in the work of the Meeting Tent. Give them to the Levites as they need them."

[6]So Moses accepted the carts and the oxen. He gave them to the Levites. [7]He gave 2 carts and 4 oxen to the Gershonites. This is what they needed for their work. [8]Then Moses gave 4 carts and 8 oxen to the Merarites. This is what they needed for their work. Ithamar son of Aaron, the priest, directed the work of all of them. [9]Moses did not give any oxen or carts to the Kohathites. They were to carry the holy things on their shoulders. This was their job.

[10]The oil was poured on the altar. Then the leaders brought their offerings to it to give to the Lord's service. [11]The Lord had already told Moses, "Each day one leader must bring his gift. The gifts will make the altar ready for service to me."

[12-83]Each of the 12 leaders brought these gifts. Each leader brought 1 silver plate that weighed about 3¼ pounds. And each one brought 1 silver bowl that weighed about 1¾ pounds. These weights were set by the Holy Place measure. Each bowl and plate were filled with fine flour mixed with oil. This was for a grain offering. Each leader also brought a large gold dish that weighed

about 4 ounces. It was filled with incense.[d]

Each leader also brought 1 young bull, 1 male sheep and 1 male lamb a year old. These were for a burnt offering. Each leader also brought 1 male goat for a sin offering. Each leader brought 2 oxen, 5 male sheep, 5 male goats and 5 male lambs a year old. All of these were sacrificed for a fellowship offering.

On the first day Nahshon son of Amminadab brought his gifts. He was the leader of the tribe of Judah.

On the second day Nethanel son of Zuar brought his gifts. He was the leader of the tribe of Issachar.

On the third day Eliab son of Helon brought his gifts. He was the leader of the tribe of Zebulun.

On the fourth day Elizur son of Shedeur brought his gifts. He was the leader of the tribe of Reuben.

On the fifth day Shelumiel son of Zurishaddai brought his gifts. He was the leader of the tribe of Simeon.

On the sixth day Eliasaph son of Deuel brought his gifts. He was the leader of the tribe of Gad.

On the seventh day Elishama son of Ammihud brought his gifts. He was the leader of the tribe of Ephraim.

On the eighth day Gamaliel son of Pedahzur brought his gifts. He was the leader of the tribe of Manasseh.

On the ninth day Abidan son of Gideoni brought his gifts. He was the leader of the tribe of Benjamin.

On the tenth day Ahiezer son of Ammishaddai brought his gifts. He was the leader of the tribe of Dan.

On the eleventh day Pagiel son of Ocran brought his gifts. He was the leader of the tribe of Asher.

On the twelfth day Ahira son of Enan brought his gifts. He was the leader of the tribe of Naphtali.

[84] So these were the gifts from the Israelite leaders. Moses poured oil on the altar. And they brought their gifts to give the altar for service to the Lord. They brought 12 silver plates, 12 silver bowls and 12 gold dishes. [85] Each silver plate weighed about 3¼ pounds. And each bowl weighed about 1¾ pounds. All the silver plates and silver bowls together weighed about 60 pounds. This weight was set by the Holy Place mea-

sure. [86] The 12 gold dishes filled with incense weighed 4 ounces each. Together the gold dishes weighed about 3 pounds. [87] The total number of animals for the burnt offering was 12 bulls, 12 male sheep and 12 male lambs a year old. There was also a grain offering. And there were 12 male goats for a sin offering. [88] The total number of animals for the fellowship offering was 24 bulls, 60 male sheep, 60 male goats and 60 male lambs a year old. All these offerings were for giving the altar to the service of the Lord. This was after Moses had poured oil on it.

[89] Moses went into the Meeting Tent to speak with the Lord. He heard the Lord speaking to him. The voice was coming from between the two gold creatures with wings. They were above the lid of the Box[d] of the Agreement. And the Lord spoke with him.

8 The Lord said to Moses, [2] "Speak to Aaron. Tell him, 'Put the seven lamps where they can light the area in front of the lampstand.'"

[3] Aaron did this. He put the lamps so they lighted the area in front of the lampstand. He obeyed the command the Lord gave Moses. [4] The lampstand was made from hammered gold. It was gold from its base to the flowers. It was made exactly the way the Lord had showed Moses.

[5] The Lord said to Moses, [6] "Take the Levites away from the other Israelites and make them clean.[d] [7] This is what you should do to make them clean. Sprinkle the cleansing water on them. Have them shave their bodies and wash their clothes. Then they will be clean. [8] They must take a young bull and the grain offering that goes with it. The grain offering will be flour mixed with oil. Then take another young bull for a sin offering. [9] Bring the Levites to the front of the Meeting Tent.[d] And gather all the Israelites around. [10] Bring the Levites before the Lord. Then the Israelites should put their hands on them.[n] [11] Aaron will present the Levites before the Lord. They will be like an offering presented from the Israelites. Then the Levites will be ready to do the work of the Lord.

[12] "The Levites will put their hands on the bulls' heads. One bull will be a sin offering to the Lord. The other will be a burnt offering. This will remove the sins

---

8:10 put . . . them This showed that the people had a part in giving the Levites their special work.

of the Levites so they will belong to God. [13]Make the Levites stand in front of Aaron and his sons. Then present the Levites as an offering to the Lord. [14]In this way you must set apart the Levites from the other Israelites. The Levites will be mine.

[15]"So make the Levites pure. And present them as an offering. Then they may come to work at the Meeting Tent. [16]They will be given to me from the Israelites. I have taken them for myself. They are mine instead of the firstborn[d] son of every Israelite woman. [17]Every firstborn male in Israel—man or animal—is mine. I killed all the firstborn in Egypt. So now I set them aside for myself. [18]I have taken the Levites instead of all the firstborn sons in Israel. [19]I have chosen the Levites from all the Israelites. And I have given them to Aaron and his sons. They will serve all the Israelites at the Meeting Tent. They will help remove the Israelites' sins so they will belong to God. Then no disaster will strike the Israelites when they approach the Holy Place."

[20]So Moses, Aaron and all the Israelites obeyed the Lord. They did with the Levites what the Lord commanded Moses. [21]The Levites made themselves clean and washed their clothes. Then Aaron presented them as an offering to the Lord. Aaron also removed their sins so they would be pure for the Lord. [22]After that, the Levites came to the Meeting Tent to work. Aaron and his sons told them what to do. They did with the Levites what the Lord commanded Moses.

[23]The Lord said to Moses, [24]"This command is for the Levites. Every man 25 years old or older must come to the Meeting Tent. They all have a job to do in the work there. [25]At the age of 50, he must retire from his job. He doesn't have to work again. [26]He may help his fellow Levites with their work at the Meeting Tent. But he must not do the work himself. This is the way you are to give the Levites their jobs."

9 The Lord spoke to Moses in the Desert of Sinai. This was in the first month of the second year after the Israelites left Egypt. He said, [2]"Tell the Israelites to celebrate the Passover[d] at the appointed time. [3]That appointed time is the fourteenth day of this month. They should celebrate it at twilight. They must obey all the rules about it."

[4]So Moses told the Israelites to celebrate the Passover. [5]And so they did. It was in the Desert of Sinai at twilight. This was on the fourteenth day of the first month. The Israelites did everything just as the Lord commanded Moses.

[6]But some of the people could not celebrate the Passover on that day. They were unclean[d] because of a dead body. So they went to Moses and Aaron that day. [7]They said to Moses, "We are unclean because of a dead body. But why should we be kept from offering gifts to the Lord at this appointed time? Why can't we join the other Israelites?"

[8]Moses said to them, "Wait. I will find out what the Lord says about you."

[9]Then the Lord said to Moses, [10]"Tell the Israelites this: 'You or your descendants[d] might become unclean because of a dead body. Or, you might be away on a trip during the Passover. Still celebrate the Lord's Passover. [11]But celebrate it at twilight on the fourteenth day of the second month. Eat the lamb with bitter herbs and bread made without yeast. [12]Don't leave any of it until the next morning. Don't break any of its bones. When you celebrate the Passover, follow all the rules. [13]Anyone who is clean and is not away on a trip must eat the Passover. If he doesn't, he must be separated from his people. He did not give an offering to the Lord at the appointed time. He must be punished for his sin.

[14]"'A foreigner among you may celebrate the Lord's Passover. But he must follow all the rules. You must have the same rules for foreigners as you have for yourselves.'"

[15]On the day the Holy Tent[d] was set up, a cloud covered it. (The Holy Tent was also called the Tent of the Agreement.) From dusk until dawn the cloud above the Tent looked like fire. [16]The cloud stayed above the Tent. At night it looked like fire. [17]When the cloud moved from its place over the Tent, the Israelites moved. Wherever the cloud stopped, the Israelites camped. [18]So the Israelites moved at the Lord's command. And they camped at his command. While the cloud stayed over the Tent, they stayed in place. [19]Sometimes the cloud stayed over the Tent for a long time. The Israelites obeyed the Lord and did not move. [20]Sometimes the cloud was over it only a few days. At the Lord's command the people camped. And at his command they moved. [21]Sometimes the cloud stayed only from

dusk until dawn. When the cloud lifted the next morning, the people moved. When the cloud lifted, day or night, the people moved. ²²The cloud might stay over the Tent for two days, a month or a year. As long as it stayed, the people would camp. But when the cloud lifted, they moved. ²³At the Lord's command the people camped. And at his command they moved. They obeyed the Lord's order that he commanded through Moses.

10 The Lord said to Moses, ²"Make two trumpets of hammered silver. Use them to call the people together and to march out of camp. ³When both trumpets are blown, the people should gather. They should gather before you at the entrance to the Meeting Tent.^d ⁴If you blow only one trumpet, the leaders should meet before you. ⁵When you blow the trumpets once, the tribes^d camping on the east should move. ⁶When you blow them again, the tribes camping on the south should move. The sound will tell them to move. ⁷When you want to gather the people, blow the trumpets. But don't blow them the same way.

⁸"Aaron's sons, the priests, should blow the trumpets. This is a law for you and your descendants^d from now on. ⁹You might be fighting an enemy who attacks you in your own land. Blow the trumpets. The Lord your God will remember you. He will save you from your enemies. ¹⁰Also blow your trumpets at happy times. Blow them during your feasts and at New Moon^d festivals. Blow them over your burnt offerings and fellowship offerings. They will help you remember your God. I am the Lord your God."

¹¹The cloud lifted from the Tent^d of the Agreement. This was on the twentieth day of the second month of the second year. ¹²So the Israelites moved from the Desert of Sinai. They moved until the cloud stopped in the Desert of Paran. ¹³This was their first time to move. They did it as the Lord had commanded Moses.

¹⁴The divisions from the camp of Judah moved first under their flag. Nahshon son of Amminadab was the commander. ¹⁵Nethanel son of Zuar was over the division of the tribe^d of Issachar. ¹⁶Eliab son of Helon was over the division of the tribe of Zebulun. ¹⁷Then the Meeting Tent was taken down. The Gershonites and Merarites, who carried it, moved next.

¹⁸Then came the divisions from the camp of Reuben under their flag. Elizur son of Shedeur was the commander. ¹⁹Shelumiel son of Zurishaddai was over the division of the tribe of Simeon. ²⁰Eliasaph son of Deuel was over the division of the tribe of Gad. ²¹Then came the Kohathites. They carried the holy things. The Holy Tent was to be set up before they arrived.

²²Next came the divisions from the camp of Ephraim under their flag. Elishama son of Ammihud was the commander. ²³Gamaliel son of Pedahzur was over the division of the tribe of Manasseh. ²⁴Abidan son of Gideoni was over the division of the tribe of Benjamin.

²⁵The last ones were the rear guard for all the tribes. These were the divisions from the camp of Dan under their flag. Ahiezer son of Ammishaddai was the commander. ²⁶Pagiel son of Ocran was over the division of the tribe of Asher. ²⁷Ahira son of Enan was over the division of the tribe of Naphtali. ²⁸This was the order the Israelite divisions marched in when they moved.

²⁹Hobab was the son of Reuel the Midianite. Reuel, who is also called Jethro, was Moses' father-in-law. Moses said to Hobab, "We are moving to the land God promised to give us. Come with us. We will be good to you. The Lord has promised good things to Israel."

³⁰But Hobab answered, "No, I will not go. I will go back to my own land where I was born."

³¹But Moses said, "Please don't leave us. You know where we can camp in the desert. You can be our guide. ³²Come with us. We will share with you all the good things the Lord gives us." ³³So they left the mountain of the Lord. The Box^d of the Lord's Agreement went in front of the people. For three days they looked for a place to camp. ³⁴The Lord's cloud was over them during the day when they left their camp.

³⁵When the Holy Box left the camp, Moses always said,

> "Rise up, Lord!
>> Scatter your enemies.
>> Make those who are against you
>>> run from you."

³⁶And when the Holy Box was set down, Moses always said,

> "Return, Lord,
>> to the thousands of people of
>> Israel."

11 The people complained to the Lord about their troubles. When he heard them, he became angry. Fire from the Lord burned among the people. It burned the edge of the camp. ²So the people cried out to Moses. He prayed to the Lord, and the fire stopped burning. ³So that place was called Taberah.ⁿ The people named it that because the Lord's fire had burned among them.

⁴Some troublemakers among them wanted better food. Soon all the Israelites began complaining. They said, "We want meat! ⁵We remember the fish we ate for free in Egypt. We also had cucumbers, melons, leeks, onions and garlic. ⁶But now we have lost our appetite. We never see anything but this manna!"

⁷The manna was like small white seeds. ⁸The people would go to gather it. Then they ground it in handmills. Or they crushed it between stones. They cooked it in a pot or made cakes with it. It tasted like bread baked with olive oil. ⁹When the dew fell on the camp each night, so did the manna.

¹⁰Moses heard every family crying. They stood in the entrances of their tents. The Lord became very angry. And Moses got upset. ¹¹He asked the Lord, "Why have you brought me this trouble? I'm your servant. What have I done wrong? Why did you make me responsible for all these people? ¹²I am not the father of all these people. I didn't give birth to them. Why do you make me carry them to the land you promised to our ancestors? Must I carry them in my arms as a nurse carries a baby? ¹³Where can I get meat for all these people? They keep crying to me, 'We want meat!' ¹⁴I can't take care of all these people alone. It is too much for me. ¹⁵If you are going to continue doing this to me, then kill me now. If you like me, put me to death. Then I won't have any more troubles."

¹⁶The Lord said to Moses, "Bring me 70 of Israel's older leaders. Pick men you know are leaders among the people. Bring them to the Meeting Tent.ᵈ Have them stand there with you. ¹⁷I will come down and speak with you there. I will take some of the Spiritᵈ that is in you. And I will give it to them. They will help you care for the people. Then you will not have to care for them alone.

¹⁸"Tell the people this: 'Make yourselves holy. Tomorrow you will eat meat. The Lord heard you cry, "We want meat!

We were better off in Egypt!" So now the Lord will give you meat to eat. ¹⁹You will not eat it for just 1, 2, 5, 10 or even 20 days. ²⁰You will eat that meat for a whole month. You will eat it until it comes out your nose. You will hate it. This is because you have rejected the Lord. He is here with you. But you have cried to him. You said, "Why did we ever leave Egypt?"'"

²¹Moses said, "Lord, here are 600,000 men standing around me. And you say, 'I will give them enough meat to eat for a month!' ²²If we killed all the sheep and cattle, that would not be enough. If we caught all the fish in the sea, that would not be enough."

²³But the Lord said to Moses, "Do you think I'm weak? You will see if I can do what I say."

²⁴So Moses went out to the people. He told them what the Lord had said. Moses gathered 70 of the older leaders together. He had them stand around the Tent. ²⁵Then the Lord came down in the cloud and spoke to Moses. The Lord took some of the Spirit Moses had. And he gave it to the 70 leaders. With the Spirit in them, they prophesied,ᵈ but just that one time.

²⁶Two men named Eldad and Medad were also listed as leaders. But they did not go to the Tent. They stayed in the camp. The Spirit was given to them. So they prophesied in the camp. ²⁷A young man ran to Moses. He said, "Eldad and Medad are prophesying in the camp."

²⁸Joshua son of Nun said, "Moses, my master, stop them!" (Since he was a young boy, Joshua had been Moses' assistant.)

²⁹But Moses answered, "Are you afraid for me? I wish all the Lord's people could prophesy. I wish the Lord would give his Spirit to all of them!" ³⁰Then Moses and the leaders of Israel went back to the camp.

³¹The Lord sent a strong wind from the sea. It blew quail into the area all around the camp. The quail were about three feet above the ground. There were quail a day's walk in any direction. ³²The people went out and gathered quail. They gathered all that day, that night and the next day. Everyone gathered at least 60 bushels. Then they spread them around the camp. ³³But the Lord became very angry. He gave the people a terrible sickness. This came while the meat was

---

11:3 Taberah This name means "burning."

still in their mouths. [34]So the people named that place Kibroth Hattaavah.[n] They named it that because there they buried those who wanted other food.

[35]From Kibroth Hattaavah the people went to stay at Hazeroth.

12 Miriam and Aaron began to talk against Moses, who had married a Cushite. [2]They said to themselves, "Is Moses the only one the Lord speaks through? Doesn't he speak through us?" And the Lord heard this.

[3](Now Moses was very humble. He was the least proud person on earth.)

[4]So the Lord suddenly spoke to Moses, Aaron and Miriam. He said, "All three of you come to the Meeting Tent[d] now." So they went. [5]The Lord came down in a pillar of cloud. He stood at the entrance to the Tent. He called to Aaron and Miriam, and they both came near. [6]He said, "Listen to my words:

When a prophet[d] is among you,
I, the Lord, will show myself to
him in visions.
I will speak to him in dreams.
[7]But this is not true with my servant
Moses.
I trust him to lead all my people.
[8]I speak face to face with him.
I speak clearly, not with hidden
meanings.
He has even seen the form of the
Lord.
You should be afraid
to speak against my servant
Moses."

[9]The Lord was very angry with them, but he left.

[10]The cloud lifted from the Tent. Then Aaron turned toward Miriam. She was as white as snow. She had a harmful skin disease. [11]Aaron said to Moses, "Please, my master, forgive us for our foolish sin. [12]Don't let her be like a baby who is born dead. (Sometimes a baby is born with half of its flesh eaten away.)"

[13]So Moses cried out to the Lord, "God, please heal her!"

[14]The Lord answered Moses, "If her father had spit in her face, she would have been shamed for seven days. So put her outside the camp for seven days. After that, she may come back." [15]So Miriam was shut outside of the camp for seven days. And the people did not move on until she came back.

[16]After that, the people left Hazeroth. And they camped in the Desert of Paran.

13 The Lord said to Moses, [2]"Send men to explore the land of Canaan. I will give that land to the Israelites. Send one leader from each tribe."[d]

[3]So Moses obeyed the Lord's command. He sent the Israelite leaders out from the Desert of Paran. [4]These are their names: from the tribe of Reuben, Shammua son of Zaccur; [5]from the tribe of Simeon, Shaphat son of Hori; [6]from the tribe of Judah, Caleb son of Jephunneh; [7]from the tribe of Issachar, Igal son of Joseph; [8]from the tribe of Ephraim, Hoshea son of Nun; [9]from the tribe of Benjamin, Palti son of Raphu; [10]from the tribe of Zebulun, Gaddiel son of Sodi; [11]from the tribe of Manasseh (a tribe of Joseph), Gaddi son of Susi; [12]from the tribe of Dan, Ammiel son of Gamalli; [13]from the tribe of Asher, Sethur son of Michael; [14]from the tribe of Naphtali, Nahbi son of Vophsi; [15]from the tribe of Gad, Geuel son of Maki.

[16]These are the names of the men Moses sent to explore the land. (Moses gave Hoshea son of Nun the new name Joshua.)

[17]Moses sent them to explore Canaan. He said, "Go through southern Canaan and then into the mountains. [18]See what the land looks like. Are the people who live there strong or weak? Are there a few or many? [19]What kind of land do they live in? Is it good or bad? What about the towns they live in—do they have walls, or are they open like camps? [20]What about the soil? Is it fertile or poor? Are there trees there? Try to bring back some of the fruit from that land." (It was the season for the first grapes.)

[21]So they went up and explored the land. They went from the Desert of Zin all the way to Rehob by Lebo Hamath. [22]They went through the southern area to Hebron. That is where Ahiman, Sheshai and Talmai lived. They were the descendants[d] of Anak.[d] (The city of Hebron had been built seven years before Zoan in Egypt.) [23]In the Valley of Eshcol, they cut off a branch of a grapevine. It had one bunch of grapes on it. They carried that branch on a pole between two of them. They also got some pomegranates[d] and figs. [24]They call that place the Valley of Eshcol.[n] That is because the Israelites cut off the bunch of

11:34 **Kibroth Hattaavah** This name in Hebrew means "graves of craving." 13:24 **Eshcol** This name in Hebrew means "bunch."

grapes there. ²⁵After 40 days of exploring the land, the men returned to the camp.

²⁶They came back to Moses and Aaron and all the Israelites at Kadesh. This was in the Desert of Paran. The men reported to them and showed everybody the fruit from the land. ²⁷They told Moses, "We went to the land where you sent us. It is a land where much food grows! Here is some of its fruit. ²⁸But the people who live there are strong. Their cities are walled and large. We even saw some Anakites there. ²⁹The Amalekites live in the southern area. The Hittites, Jebusites and Amorites live in the mountains. The Canaanites live near the sea and along the Jordan River."

³⁰Then Caleb told the people near Moses to be quiet. Caleb said, "We should go up and take the land for ourselves. We can do it."

³¹But the men who had gone with him said, "We can't attack those people. They are stronger than we are." ³²And those men gave the Israelites a bad report about the land they explored. They said, "The land would eat us up. All the people we saw are very tall. ³³We saw the Nephilim[d] people there. (The Anakites come from the Nephilim people.) We felt like grasshoppers. And we looked like grasshoppers to them."

14 That night all the people in the camp began crying loudly. ²All the Israelites complained against Moses and Aaron. All the people said to them, "We should have died in Egypt. Or we should have died in the desert. ³Why is the Lord bringing us to this land? We will be killed with swords. Our wives and children will be taken away. We would be better off going back to Egypt." ⁴They said to each other, "Let's get a leader and go back to Egypt."

⁵Then Moses and Aaron bowed facedown in front of all the Israelites gathered there. ⁶Joshua son of Nun and Caleb son of Jephunneh were among those who had explored the land. They tore their clothes. ⁷They said to all of the Israelites, "The land we went to explore is very good. ⁸If the Lord is pleased with us, he will lead us into that land. He will give us that land where much food grows. ⁹Don't turn against the Lord! Don't be afraid of the people in that land! We will chew them up. They have no protection, but we have the Lord. So don't be afraid of them."

¹⁰Then all the people talked about killing them with stones. But the glory of the Lord appeared at the Meeting Tent[d] to the Israelites. ¹¹The Lord said to Moses, "How long will these people ignore me? How long will it be before they believe me? I have done miracles[d] among them. ¹²I will give them a terrible sickness. I will destroy them. But I will make you into a great nation. It will be stronger than they are."

¹³Then Moses said to the Lord, "The Egyptians will hear about it! You brought these people from there by your great power. ¹⁴And the Egyptians will tell this to those who live in this land. They have already heard about you, Lord. They know that you are with your people. And they know you were seen face to face. They know your cloud stays over your people. They know you lead your people with that cloud during the day and with fire at night. ¹⁵The nations have heard about your power. If you put to death your people all at once, the nations will talk. They will say, ¹⁶'The Lord was not able to bring them into the land he promised. So he killed them in the desert.'

¹⁷"So show your strength now, my Lord. Do what you said. You said: ¹⁸'The Lord doesn't become angry quickly. The Lord has great love. The Lord forgives sin and law breaking. He has great mercy. But the Lord does not forget to punish guilty people. When parents sin, he will also punish their children. He will punish their grandchildren, great-grandchildren and great-great-grandchildren.' ¹⁹Show your great love. Forgive these people's sin. Forgive them as you have from the time they left Egypt until now."

²⁰The Lord answered, "I have forgiven them as you asked. ²¹But, as surely as I live, I make this promise. As surely as my glory fills the whole earth, I make this promise. ²²All these men saw my glory. They saw the miracles I did in Egypt and in the desert. But they disobeyed me and tested me 10 times. ²³So not one will see the land I promised to their ancestors. No one who angered me will see that land. ²⁴But my servant Caleb has a different spirit. He follows me completely. So I will bring him into the land he has already seen. And his children will own that land. ²⁵The Amalekites and the Canaanites are living in the valleys. So leave tomorrow and go back. Follow the desert road toward the Gulf of Aqaba."

²⁶The Lord said to Moses and Aaron, ²⁷"How long will these evil people complain about me? I have heard these Israelites' grumbling and complaining. ²⁸So tell them, 'This is what the Lord says. I heard what you said. As surely as I live, I will do those things to you. ²⁹You will die in this desert. Every one of you who is 20 years old or older and who was counted with the people will die. You complained against me, the Lord. ³⁰Not one of you will enter and live in the land I promised to you. Only Caleb son of Jephunneh and Joshua son of Nun will go in. ³¹You said that your children would be taken away. But I will bring them into the land. They will enjoy what you refused. ³²As for you, you will die in this desert. ³³Your children will be shepherds here for 40 years. They will suffer because you were not loyal. They will suffer until you lie dead in the desert. ³⁴For 40 years you will suffer for your sins. That is a year for each of the 40 days you explored the land. You will know me as your enemy.' ³⁵I, the Lord, have spoken. I will certainly do these things to all these evil people. They have come together against me. So they will all die here in this desert."

³⁶The men Moses had sent to explore the land had returned. They had spread complaints among all the Israelites. They had given a bad report about the land. ³⁷They were responsible for the bad report. So the Lord killed them with a terrible sickness. ³⁸Only two of the men did not die. They were Joshua son of Nun and Caleb son of Jephunneh.

³⁹When Moses told these things to the Israelites, they were very sad. ⁴⁰Early the next morning they started to go toward the beginning of the mountains. They said, "We have sinned. We will go where the Lord told us."

⁴¹But Moses said, "Why are you disobeying the Lord's command? You will not win! ⁴²Don't go. The Lord is not with you. You will be beaten by your enemies. ⁴³You will run into the Amalekites and Canaanites. They will kill you with swords. You have turned away from the Lord. He will not be with you."

⁴⁴But they were proud. They went toward the beginning of the mountains. But Moses and the Box^d of the Agreement with the Lord did not leave the camp. ⁴⁵The Amalekites and the Canaanites who lived in those mountains came down. And they attacked the Israelites. They beat them back all the way to Hormah.

15 The Lord said to Moses, ²"Speak to the people of Israel. Say to them, 'You will enter a land that I am giving you as a home. ³There give the Lord offerings made by fire. These may be from your herds or flocks. And the smell will be pleasing to the Lord. These offerings may be burnt offerings or sacrifices for special promises. They may be offerings which are gifts to the Lord. Or they may be festival offerings. ⁴And the one who brings his offering shall also give the Lord a grain offering. It should be two quarts of fine flour mixed with one quart of olive oil. ⁵Each time you offer a lamb as a burnt offering or sacrifice, also prepare a quart of wine. This is a drink offering.

⁶"'If you are giving a male sheep, also prepare a grain offering. It should be four quarts of fine flour mixed with one and one-fourth quarts of olive oil. ⁷Also prepare one and one-fourth quarts of wine. This is a drink offering. Offer it to the Lord. Its smell is pleasing to him.

⁸"'You might prepare a young bull as a burnt offering or sacrifice. This might be for a fellowship offering or for a special promise to the Lord. ⁹Bring a grain offering with the bull. It should be six quarts of fine flour mixed with two quarts of olive oil. ¹⁰Also bring two quarts of wine as a drink offering. This offering is made by fire. And its smell will be pleasing to the Lord. ¹¹Prepare each bull or male sheep, lamb or young goat this way. ¹²Do this for every one of the animals you bring.

¹³"'All citizens must do these things in this way. And the smell of their offerings by fire will be pleasing to the Lord. ¹⁴From now on foreigners will live among you. They will make offerings by fire so the smell will be pleasing to the Lord. They must offer them the same way you do. ¹⁵The law is the same for you and for foreigners. It will be a law from now on. You and the foreigners are alike before the Lord. ¹⁶The teachings and rules are the same for you and for the foreigners among you.'"

¹⁷The Lord said to Moses, ¹⁸"Tell the Israelites: 'You are going to another land. I am taking you there. ¹⁹When you eat the food there, offer part of it to the Lord. ²⁰Offer a loaf of bread from the first of your grain. That will be your offering from the threshing^d floor. ²¹From

now on offer to the Lord the first part of your grain. [22]"'Now what if you forget to obey any of these commands the Lord gave Moses? [23]These are the Lord's commands given to you through Moses. They began the day the Lord gave them to you. And they will continue from now on. [24]But you might forget to obey one of these commands. The people might not remember the command. Then all the people must offer a young bull as a burnt offering. Its smell is pleasing to the Lord. By law you must also give the grain offering and the drink offering with it. And you must bring a male goat as a sin offering. [25]"'The priest will remove that sin for all the Israelites so they will belong to God. They are forgiven. They didn't know they were sinning. For the wrong they did they brought offerings to the Lord. They brought an offering by fire and a sin offering. [26]All of the people of Israel and the foreigners living among them will be forgiven. No one meant to do wrong.

[27]"'Just one person might sin without meaning to. He must bring a year-old female goat for a sin offering. [28]The priest will remove the sin of the person who sinned without meaning to. That person will belong to the Lord again. He will be forgiven. [29]The same teaching is for everyone who sins without meaning to. It is the same for those born Israelites and for foreigners living among you.

[30]"'But anyone who sins on purpose is against the Lord. That person must be separated from his people. It is the same for someone born among you or a foreigner. [31]That person has turned against the Lord's word. He has not obeyed the Lord's commands. He must surely be separated from the others. He is guilty.'"

[32]This happened when the Israelites were still in the desert. They found a man gathering wood on the Sabbath[d] day. [33]Those who found him gathering wood brought him to Moses and Aaron and all the people. [34]They held the man under guard. They did not know what to do with him. [35]Then the Lord said to Moses, "The man must die. All the people must kill him with stones outside the camp." [36]So the people took him outside the camp. They killed him with stones as the Lord commanded Moses.

[37]The Lord said to Moses, [38]"Speak to the Israelites. Tell them this: 'Tie several pieces of thread together. And tie them to the corners of your clothes. Put a blue thread in each one of these tassels. Wear them from now on. [39]You will have these tassels to look at. They will remind you of the Lord's commands. Then you will obey them. And you won't follow what your bodies want and what your eyes wish for. [40]Remember to obey all my commands. Then you will be God's holy people. [41]I am the Lord your God. I brought you out of Egypt to be your God. I am the Lord your God.'"

16

Korah, Dathan, Abiram and On turned against Moses. (Korah was the son of Izhar. Izhar was the son of Kohath, and Kohath was the son of Levi. Dathan and Abiram were brothers, the sons of Eliab. And On was the son of Peleth.) Dathan, Abiram and On were from the tribe[d] of Reuben. [2]These 4 men gathered 250 other Israelite men and challenged Moses. They were well-known leaders chosen by the community. [3]They came as a group to speak to Moses and Aaron. The men said, "You have gone too far. All the people are holy. Every one of them is holy. And the Lord is with them. So why do you put yourselves above all the people?"

[4]When Moses heard this, he bowed facedown. [5]Then he said to Korah and all his followers: "Tomorrow morning the Lord will show who belongs to him. The Lord will bring the one who is holy near to him. The Lord will bring to himself the person he chooses. [6]So Korah, you and all your followers do this: Get some pans for burning incense.[d] [7]Tomorrow put fire and incense in them. Then take them before the Lord. He will choose the man who is holy. You Levites have gone too far."

[8]Moses also said to Korah, "Listen, you Levites. [9]The God of Israel has separated you from the rest of the Israelites. He brought you near to himself. You do the work in the Lord's Holy Tent.[d] You stand before all the Israelites and serve them. Isn't that enough? [10]The Lord has brought you and all your fellow Levites near to himself. Now you want to be priests. [11]You and your followers have joined together against the Lord. Your complaint is not against Aaron."

[12]Then Moses called Dathan and Abiram, the sons of Eliab. But they said, "We will not come! [13]You have brought us out of a land where much food grows. You brought us to the desert to kill us. And now you want to order us around. [14]You haven't brought us into a land

where much food grows. You haven't given us any land with fields and vineyards. Will you put out the eyes of these men? No! We will not come!''

[15]Then Moses became very angry. He said to the Lord, "Don't accept their gifts. I have not taken anything from them, not even a donkey. I have not done wrong to any of them.''

[16]Then Moses said to Korah, "You and all your followers must stand before the Lord tomorrow. And Aaron will stand there with you and them. [17]Each of you must take your pan and put incense in it. Present these 250 pans before the Lord. You and Aaron must also present your pans.'' [18]So each man got his pan and put burning incense in it. Then they stood with Moses and Aaron at the entrance to the Meeting Tent. [19]Korah gathered all his followers who were against Moses and Aaron. And they stood at the entrance to the Meeting Tent. Then the glory of the Lord appeared to everyone.

[20]The Lord said to Moses and Aaron, [21]"Move away from these men. In a minute I will destroy them.''

[22]But Moses and Aaron bowed facedown. They cried out, "God, you are the God over the spirits of all people. Please don't be angry with this whole group. Only one man has really sinned.''

[23]Then the Lord said to Moses, [24]"Tell everyone to move away from the tents of Korah, Dathan and Abiram.''

[25]Moses stood and went to Dathan and Abiram. The older leaders of Israel followed him. [26]Moses warned the people, "Move away from the tents of these evil men! Don't touch anything of theirs. If you do, you will be destroyed because of their sins.'' [27]So they moved away from the tents of Korah, Dathan and Abiram. Dathan and Abiram were standing outside their tents with their wives, children and little babies.

[28]Then Moses said, "Now you will know that the Lord has sent me to do all these things. It was not my idea. [29]If these men die a normal death—the way men usually die—then the Lord did not really send me. [30]But if the Lord does something new, you will know they have insulted the Lord. The earth will open and swallow them. Alive, they will go to where the dead are. And everything that belongs to them will go with them.''

[31]When Moses finished saying these things, the ground under the men opened up. [32]The earth seemed to open its mouth and swallow them. All their families, all Korah's men and everything they owned went down. [33]They were buried alive, going to where the dead are. And everything they owned went with them. Then the earth closed over them. They died and were gone from the community. [34]The people of Israel around them heard their screams. They ran away and said, "The earth will swallow us, too!''

[35]Then a fire came down from the Lord. It destroyed the 250 men who had presented the incense.

[36]The Lord said to Moses, [37]"Tell Eleazar son of Aaron, the priest, to take all the incense pans out of the fire. Have him scatter the coals. But the incense pans are still holy. [38]These men sinned and lost their lives. Take their pans and hammer them into flat sheets. Cover the altar with them. They are holy because they were presented to the Lord. It will be a sign to the Israelites.''

[39]So Eleazar the priest gathered all the bronze pans. These were the pans brought by the men who were burned up. Eleazar had the pans hammered into flat sheets to put on the altar. [40]This is what the Lord had commanded him through Moses. These sheets were to remind the Israelites that only descendants[d] of Aaron should burn incense before the Lord. Anyone else would die like Korah and his followers.

[41]The next day all the Israelites complained against Moses and Aaron. They said, "You have killed the Lord's people.''

[42]The people gathered to complain against Moses and Aaron. But when they turned toward the Meeting Tent,[d] the cloud covered it. The glory of the Lord appeared. [43]Then Moses and Aaron went in front of the Meeting Tent.

[44]The Lord said to Moses, [45]"Move away from these people. In a minute I am going to destroy them.'' So Moses and Aaron bowed facedown.

[46]Then Moses said to Aaron, "Get your pan. Put fire from the altar and incense[d] in it. Hurry to the people and remove their sin. The Lord is angry with them. The sickness has already started.'' [47]So Aaron did as Moses said. He ran to the middle of all the people. The sickness had already started among them. So Aaron offered the incense to remove their sin. [48]He stood between the living and the dead. And the sickness stopped there. [49]But 14,700 people died from that

sickness. There were also those who died because of Korah. ⁵⁰Then Aaron went back to Moses at the entrance to the Meeting Tent. The terrible sickness had been stopped.

17 The Lord said to Moses, ²"Speak to the people of Israel. Get 12 walking sticks from them. Get 1 from the leader of each tribe.ᵈ Write the name of each man on his stick. ³On the stick from Levi, write Aaron's name. There must be 1 stick for the head of each tribe. ⁴Put them in the Meeting Tent.ᵈ Place them in front of the Boxᵈ of the Agreement, where I meet with you. ⁵I will choose one man. His stick will begin to grow leaves. And I will stop the Israelites from always complaining against you."

⁶So Moses spoke to the Israelites. Each of the 12 leaders gave him a walking stick. And Aaron's walking stick was among them. ⁷Moses put them before the Lord in the Tent of the Agreement.

⁸The next day Moses entered the Tent. He saw that Aaron's stick had grown leaves. (It stood for the family of Levi.) It had even budded, blossomed and produced almonds. ⁹So Moses brought out to the Israelites all the walking sticks from the Lord's presence. They all looked, and each man took back his stick.

¹⁰Then the Lord said to Moses, "Put Aaron's walking stick back. Put it in front of the Box of the Agreement. It will be a sign to these people who are always turning against me. This will stop their complaining against me. Now they won't die." ¹¹So Moses obeyed what the Lord commanded him.

¹²The people of Israel said to Moses, "We are going to die! We are lost. We are all lost! ¹³Anyone who even comes near the Holy Tent of the Lord will die. Will we all die?"

18 The Lord said to Aaron, "You, your sons and your family are now responsible for any wrongs done against the Holy Place. You and your sons are responsible for any wrongs done against the priests. ²Bring with you your fellow Levites from your tribe.ᵈ They will help you and your sons serve in the Tentᵈ of the Agreement. ³They are under your control. They will do all the work that needs to be done in the Tent. But they must not go near the things in the Holy Place or near the altar. If they do, both you and they will die. ⁴They

will join you. They will take care of the Meeting Tent. They must do the work at the Tent. No one else may come near you.

⁵"You must take care of the Holy Place and the altar. Then I won't become angry with the Israelites again. ⁶I myself chose your fellow Levites from among the Israelites. They are a gift given for you to the Lord. Their work is at the Meeting Tent. ⁷But only you and your sons may serve as priests. Only you may serve at the altar or go behind the curtain. I am giving you this gift of serving as a priest. Anyone else who comes near the Holy Place will be put to death."

⁸Then the Lord said to Aaron, "I myself make you responsible for the offerings given to me. All the holy offerings that the Israelites give to me, I give to you. They are for you and your sons as your share. They will be your continual portion. ⁹Your share of the holy offerings is that part which is not burned. The people will bring me gifts as most holy offerings. These are grain or sin or penalty offerings. These will be set apart for you and your sons. ¹⁰You must eat it in a most holy place. Any male may eat it. But you must respect it as holy.

¹¹"I also give you the offerings the Israelites present to me. I give these to you and your sons and daughters. This is your share. Anyone in your family who is cleanᵈ may eat it.

¹²"And I give you all the best olive oil and all the best new wine and grain. This is what the Israelites give to me, the Lord. These are the first things they harvest. ¹³They bring to the Lord all the first things they harvest. They will be yours. Anyone in your family who is clean may eat these things.

¹⁴"Everything in Israel that is given to the Lord is yours. ¹⁵The first one born to any family will be offered to the Lord. This is true for both men and animals. And that will be yours. But you must make a payment for every firstbornᵈ son and every firstborn animal that is unclean. ¹⁶When they are one month old, you must make a payment for them. The cost will be two ounces of silver as set by the Holy Place measure.

¹⁷"But you must not make a payment for the firstborn ox or sheep or goat. Those animals are holy. Sprinkle their blood on the altar and burn their fat. This is an offering made by fire. The smell is pleasing to the Lord. ¹⁸But the

meat will be yours. Also the breast that is presented and the right thigh will be yours. [19]Anything the Israelites present as holy gifts I, the Lord, give to you. It goes to you, your sons and daughters. It is your continual portion. This is a lasting promise before the Lord to you and your children forever."

[20]The Lord also said to Aaron, "You will not inherit any of the land. And you will not own any land among the other people. I will be yours. Out of all the Israelites, only you will inherit me.

[21]"The people of Israel will give a tenth of what they make. I give that tenth to the Levites. This is their payment for the work they do serving at the Meeting Tent. [22]But the other Israelites must never go near the Meeting Tent. If they do, they will die for their sin. [23]Only the Levites should work in the Meeting Tent. They are responsible for any sins against it. This is a rule from now on. The Levites will not get any land among the other Israelites. [24]But the Israelites will give a tenth of everything they make to me. And I will give that tenth to the Levites. That is why I said about the Levites: 'They will not get any land among the Israelites.'"

[25]The Lord said to Moses, [26]"Speak to the Levites. Tell them: 'You will receive a tenth of everything the Israelites make. I give that to you. But you must give a tenth of that back to the Lord. [27]I will accept your offering just as much as I accept the offerings from others. They give new grain or new wine. [28]In this way you will present an offering to the Lord as the other Israelites do. You will receive a tenth from the Israelites. Then you will give a tenth of that to Aaron the priest as the Lord's share. [29]Choose the best and holiest part from what you are given. This is the portion you must give to the Lord.'

[30]"Say to the Levites: 'When you present the best it will be accepted as much as the grain and wine from the other people. [31]You and your families may eat all that is left anywhere. This is your pay for your work in the Meeting Tent. [32]And if you always give the best part to the Lord, you will never be guilty. If you do not sin against the holy offerings of the Israelites, you will not die.'"

19 The Lord said to Moses and Aaron, [2]"These are the teachings that the Lord commanded. Tell the Israelites to get a young red cow. It must not have anything wrong with it. It must not

have been worked. [3]Give the cow to Eleazar the priest. He will take it outside the camp and kill it. [4]Then Eleazar the priest must put some of the blood on his finger. He must sprinkle it seven times toward the front of the Meeting Tent.[d] [5]Then the whole cow must be burned while he watches. The skin, the meat, the blood and the intestines must all be burned. [6]Then the priest must take a cedar stick, a hyssop branch and a red string. He must throw them onto the burning cow. [7]Then the priest must wash himself and his clothes with water. After that, he may come back into the camp. But he will be unclean[d] until evening. [8]The man who burns the cow must wash himself and his clothes in water. He will be unclean until evening.

[9]"Then someone who is clean will collect the ashes from the cow. He will put them in a clean place outside the camp. The Israelites will use these ashes in a special ceremony to cleanse away sin. [10]The man who collected the cow's ashes must wash his clothes. He will be unclean until evening. This is a lasting rule. It is for the Israelites and for the foreigners among them.

[11]"Whoever touches a dead body will be unclean for seven days. [12]He must wash himself with this water. He must do this on the third day and on the seventh day. Then he will be clean. But if he does not wash himself on the third day and the seventh day, he cannot be clean. [13]Whoever touches a dead body is unclean. If he stays unclean and goes to the Lord's Holy Tent, it becomes unclean. So he must be separated from Israel. If the cleansing water is not sprinkled on him, he will stay unclean.

[14]"This is the teaching about someone who dies in his tent. Anyone in the tent or who enters it will be unclean for seven days. [15]And every open jar or pot without a cover becomes unclean. [16]If anyone touches someone who was killed by a sword or who died a natural death, he is unclean. If he touches a human bone or a grave, he is unclean. He will be unclean for seven days.

[17]"So you must use the ashes from the burnt offering to make that person clean again. Pour fresh water over the ashes into a jar. [18]A clean person must take a hyssop branch and dip it into the water. Then he must sprinkle it over the tent and its objects. And he must sprinkle the people who were there. He must sprinkle anyone who touched a bone or

the body of someone who was killed. He must sprinkle anyone who touched a dead person or a grave. ¹⁹Then someone who is clean must sprinkle this water on the unclean person. He must do this on the third day and on the seventh day. On the seventh day that person becomes clean. He must wash his clothes and take a bath. He will be clean that evening. ²⁰If anyone who is unclean does not become clean, he must be separated from the community. He was not sprinkled with the cleansing water. He stays unclean. He could make the Holy Tent unclean. ²¹This is a lasting rule. Whoever sprinkles the cleansing water must also wash his clothes. Anyone who touches the water will be unclean until evening. ²²Anyone the unclean person touches becomes unclean. And whoever touches him will be unclean until evening."

20 In the first month all the people of Israel arrived at the Desert of Zin. They stayed at Kadesh. There Miriam died and was buried. ²There was no water for the people. So they came together against Moses and Aaron. ³They argued with Moses. They said, "We should have died in front of the Lord as our brothers did. ⁴Why did you bring the Lord's people into this desert? Are we and our animals to die here? ⁵Why did you bring us from Egypt to this terrible place? It has no grain, figs or pomegranates.ᵈ And there's no water to drink!"

⁶So Moses and Aaron left the people. Then they went to the entrance of the Meeting Tent.ᵈ They bowed facedown. And the glory of the Lord appeared to them. ⁷The Lord said to Moses, ⁸"You and your brother Aaron should gather the people. Also take your walking stick. Speak to that rock in front of them. Then water will flow from it. Give that water to the people and their animals."

⁹So Moses took the stick from in front of the Lord. He did as the Lord had said. ¹⁰He and Aaron gathered the people in front of the rock. Then Moses said, "Now listen to me, you complainers! Do you want us to bring water out of this rock?" ¹¹Then Moses lifted his hand and hit the rock twice with his stick. Water began pouring out. And the people and their animals drank it.

¹²But the Lord said to Moses and Aaron, "You did not believe me. You did

not honor me as holy before the people. So you will not lead them into the land I will give them."

¹³These are the waters of Meribah.ⁿ Here the Israelites argued with the Lord. And the Lord showed them he was holy.

¹⁴From Kadesh, Moses sent messengers to the king of Edom. He said, "Your brothers, the Israelites, say to you: You know about all the troubles we have had. ¹⁵Our ancestors went down into Egypt. And we lived there for many years. The people of Egypt were cruel to our ancestors. ¹⁶But we cried out to the Lord. He heard us and sent us an angel to bring us out of Egypt.

"Now we are here at Kadesh, a town on the edge of your land. ¹⁷Please let us pass through your country. We will not touch any fields of grain or vineyards. We will not drink water from the wells. We will travel only along the king's road. We will not turn right or left until we have passed through your country."

¹⁸But the king of Edom answered: "You may not pass through here. If you try, I will come and meet you with swords."

¹⁹The Israelites answered: "We will go along the main road. If our animals drink any of your water, we will pay for it. We only want to walk through. That's all."

²⁰But he answered: "You may not pass through here."

Then the Edomites went out to meet the Israelites with a large and powerful army. ²¹The Edomites refused to let them pass through their country. So the Israelites turned back.

²²All the Israelites moved from Kadesh to Mount Hor. ²³It was near the border of Edom. The Lord said to Moses and Aaron, ²⁴"Aaron will die. He will not enter the land that I'm giving to the Israelites. This is because you both acted against my command at the waters of Meribah. ²⁵Take Aaron and his son Eleazar up on Mount Hor. ²⁶Take off Aaron's special clothes. Put them on his son Eleazar. Aaron will die there. He will join his ancestors."

²⁷Moses obeyed the Lord's command. They climbed up Mount Hor. All the people saw them go. ²⁸Moses took off Aaron's clothes. He put them on Aaron's son Eleazar. Then Aaron died there on top of the mountain. And Moses and Eleazar came back down the mountain.

20:13 **Meribah** This name in Hebrew means "argument."

²⁹Then all the people learned that Aaron was dead. So everyone in Israel cried for him for 30 days.

21 The Canaanite king of Arad lived in the southern area. He heard that the Israelites were coming on the road to Atharim. So he attacked them and captured some of them. ²Then the Israelites made this promise to the Lord: "If you will help us defeat these people, we will completely destroy their cities." ³The Lord listened to the Israelites. And he let them defeat the Canaanites. The Israelites completely destroyed the Canaanites and their cities. So the place was named Hormah.ⁿ

⁴The Israelites left Mount Hor and went on the road toward the Gulf of Aqaba. They did this to go around the country of Edom. But the people became impatient on the way. ⁵They grumbled at God and Moses. They said, "Why did you bring us out of Egypt? We will die in this desert! There is no bread! There is no water! And we hate this terrible food!"

⁶So the Lord sent them poisonous snakes. They bit the people, and many of the Israelites died. ⁷The people came to Moses and said, "We sinned when we grumbled at you and the Lord. Pray that the Lord will take away these snakes." So Moses prayed for the people.

⁸The Lord said to Moses, "Make a bronze snake. And put it on a pole. If anyone is bitten, he should look at it. Then he will live." ⁹So Moses made a bronze snake. And he put it on a pole. Then when a snake bit anyone, he looked at the bronze snake and lived.

¹⁰The Israelites went and camped at Oboth. ¹¹They went from Oboth to Iye Abarim. This was in the desert east of Moab. ¹²From there they went and camped in the Zered Valley. ¹³From there they went and camped across the Arnon. This was in the desert just inside the Amorite country. The Arnon is the border between the Moabites and the Amorites. ¹⁴That is why the Book of the Wars of the Lord says:

"... and Waheb in Suphah, and the
    ravines,
 the Arnon, ¹⁵and the slopes of the
    ravines
that lead to the settlement of Ar.
 These places are at the border of
    Moab."

¹⁶The Israelites went from there to Beer. A well is there where the Lord said to Moses, "Gather the people. I will give them water."

¹⁷Then the Israelites sang this song:
"Pour out water, well!
    Sing about it.
¹⁸Princes dug this well.
    Important men made this hole.
    With their scepters^d and poles,
        they dug it."

The people went from the desert to Mattanah. ¹⁹From Mattanah they went to Nahaliel and on to Bamoth. ²⁰From Bamoth they went to the valley of Moab. There the top of Mount Pisgah looks over the desert.

²¹The people of Israel sent messengers to Sihon, king of the Amorites. They said to him, ²²"Let us pass through your country. We will not go through any fields of grain or vineyards. We will not drink water from the wells. We will travel only along the king's road. We will stay on it until we have passed through your country."

²³But King Sihon would not let the Israelites pass through his country. He gathered his army together. They marched out to meet Israel in the desert. At Jahaz they fought the Israelites. ²⁴Israel killed the king. Then they captured his land from the Arnon River to the Jabbok River. They took the land as far as the Ammonite border. That border was strongly defended. ²⁵Israel captured all the Amorite cities and lived in them. They took Heshbon and all the towns around it. ²⁶Heshbon was the city where Sihon, the Amorite king, lived. In the past he had fought with the king of Moab. Sihon had taken all the land as far as the Arnon.

²⁷That is why the poets say:
"Come to Heshbon
    and rebuild it.
    Rebuild Sihon's city.
²⁸A fire began in Heshbon.
    Flames came from Sihon's city.
    It destroyed Ar in Moab.
    It burned the Arnon highlands.
²⁹How terrible for you, Moab!
    The people of Chemosh^d are
        ruined.
His sons ran away.
    His daughters were captured
        by Sihon, king of the Amorites.
³⁰But we defeated those Amorites.

21:3 *Hormah* This name in Hebrew means "completely destroyed."

We ruined their towns from
Heshbon to Dibon.
We destroyed them as far as
Nophah, near Medeba."

³¹So Israel lived in the land of the Amorites.

³²Moses sent spies to the town of Jazer. Then they captured the towns around it. They forced out the Amorites who lived there.

³³Then the Israelites went up the road toward Bashan. Og, the king of Bashan, and his army marched out to meet the Israelites. They fought at Edrei.

³⁴The Lord said to Moses, "Don't be afraid of him. I will hand him, his whole army and his land over to you. Do to him what you did to Sihon, the Amorite king who lived in Heshbon."

³⁵So the Israelites killed Og and his sons and all his army. No one was left alive. And they took his land.

22 Then the people of Israel went to the plains of Moab. They camped near the Jordan River across from Jericho.

²Balak son of Zippor saw everything the Israelites had done to the Amorites. ³And Moab was scared of so many Israelites. Truly, Moab was terrified by them.

⁴The Moabites said to the older leaders of Midian, "This mob will take everything around us. It will be like an ox eating grass."

Balak son of Zippor was the king of Moab at this time. ⁵He sent messengers to Balaam son of Beor at Pethor. It was near the Euphrates River in the land of Amaw. Balak said, "A nation has come out of Egypt. They cover the land. They have camped next to me. ⁶They are too powerful for me. So come and put a curse on them. Maybe then I can defeat them and make them leave the area. I know that if you bless someone, the blessings happen. And if you put a curse on someone, it happens."

⁷The leaders of Moab and Midian went with payment in their hands. They found Balaam. Then they told him what Balak had said.

⁸Balaam said to them, "Stay here for the night. I will tell you what the Lord tells me." So the Moabite leaders stayed with him.

⁹God came to Balaam and asked, "Who are these men with you?"

¹⁰Balaam said to God, "The king of Moab, Balak son of Zippor, sent them. He sent me this message: ¹¹'A nation has come out of Egypt. They cover the land. So come and put a curse on them. Then maybe I can fight them and force them out of my land.'"

¹²But God said to Balaam, "Do not go with them. Don't put a curse on those people. I have blessed them."

¹³The next morning Balaam awoke and said to Balak's leaders, "Go back to your own country. The Lord will not let me go with you."

¹⁴So the Moabite leaders went back to Balak. They said, "Balaam refused to come with us."

¹⁵So Balak sent other leaders. He sent more leaders this time. And they were more important. ¹⁶They went to Balaam and said, "Balak son of Zippor says this: Please don't let anything stop you from coming to me. ¹⁷I will pay you well. I will do what you say. Come and put a curse on these people for me."

¹⁸But Balaam answered Balak's servants, "King Balak could give me his palace full of silver and gold. But I cannot disobey the Lord my God in anything, great or small. ¹⁹You stay here tonight as the other men did. I will find out what more the Lord tells me."

²⁰That night God came to Balaam. He said, "These men have come to ask you to go with them. Go. But only do what I tell you."

²¹Balaam got up the next morning. He put a saddle on his donkey. Then he went with the Moabite leaders. ²²But God became angry because Balaam went. So the angel of the Lord stood in the road to stop Balaam. Balaam was riding his donkey. And he had two servants with him. ²³The donkey saw the angel of the Lord standing in the road. The angel had a sword in his hand. So the donkey left the road and went into the field. Balaam hit the donkey to force her back on the road.

²⁴Later, the angel of the Lord stood on a narrow path between two vineyards. There were walls on both sides. ²⁵Again the donkey saw the angel of the Lord. So the donkey walked close to one wall. This crushed Balaam's foot against the wall. So he hit her again.

²⁶The angel of the Lord went ahead again. The angel stood at a narrow place. It was too narrow to turn left or right. ²⁷The donkey saw the angel of the Lord. So she lay down under Balaam. Balaam was very angry and hit her with his stick. ²⁸Then the Lord made the donkey talk. She said to Balaam, "What

have I done to make you hit me three times?"

²⁹Balaam answered the donkey, "You have made me look foolish! I wish I had a sword in my hand! I would kill you right now!"

³⁰But the donkey said to Balaam, "I am your very own donkey. You have ridden me for years. Have I ever done this to you before?"

"No," Balaam said.

³¹Then the Lord let Balaam see the angel. The angel of the Lord was standing in the road with his sword drawn. Then Balaam bowed facedown on the ground.

³²The angel of the Lord asked Balaam, "Why have you hit your donkey three times? I have stood here to stop you. What you are doing is wrong. ³³The donkey saw me. She turned away from me three times. If she had not turned away, I would have killed you by now. But I would let her live."

³⁴Then Balaam said to the angel of the Lord, "I have sinned. I did not know you were standing in the road to stop me. If I am wrong, I will go back."

³⁵The angel of the Lord said to Balaam, "Go with these men. But say only what I tell you." So Balaam went with Balak's leaders.

³⁶Balak heard that Balaam was coming. So he went out to meet him at Ar in Moab. It was beside the Arnon, at the edge of his country. ³⁷Balak said to Balaam, "I had asked you before to come quickly. Why didn't you come to me? I am able to reward you well."

³⁸But Balaam answered, "I have come to you now. But I can't say just anything. I can only say what God tells me to say."

³⁹Then Balaam went with Balak to Kiriath Huzoth. ⁴⁰Balak offered cattle and sheep as a sacrifice. He gave some meat to Balaam and the leaders with him.

⁴¹The next morning Balak took Balaam to Bamoth Baal. From there he could see the edge of the Israelite camp.

23 Balaam said, "Build me seven altars here. And prepare seven bulls and seven male sheep for me." ²Balak did what Balaam asked. Then they offered a male sheep and a bull on each of the altars.

³Then Balaam said to Balak, "Stay here beside your burnt offering. I will go. Maybe the Lord will come to me. I will tell you whatever he shows me." Then Balaam went to a higher place.

⁴God came to Balaam there. Balaam said to him, "I have prepared seven al-

tars. And I have offered a bull and a male sheep on each altar."

⁵The Lord told Balaam what he should say. Then the Lord said, "Go back to Balak and give him this message."

⁶So Balaam went back to Balak. Balak and all the leaders of Moab were still standing beside his burnt offering. ⁷Then Balaam gave them this message:

"Balak brought me here from
    Aram.
  The king of Moab brought me
    from the eastern mountains.
Balak said, 'Come, put a curse on
    the people of Jacob for me.
  Come, wish evil on the people of
    Israel.'
⁸But God has not cursed them.
  So I cannot curse them.
  The Lord has not wished evil on
    them.
  So I cannot wish evil on them.
⁹I see them from the mountains.
  I see them from the hills.
  I see a people who live alone.
  They think they are different
    from other nations.
¹⁰No one can number the people of
    Jacob.
  No one can count a fourth of
    Israel.
  Let me die like good men.
  Let me end up like them!"

¹¹Balak said to Balaam, "What have you done to me? I brought you here to curse my enemies. But you have only blessed them!"

¹²But Balaam answered, "I must say what the Lord tells me to say."

¹³Then Balak said to him, "Come with me to another place. There you can also see the people. But you can only see part of them, not all of them. Curse them for me from there." ¹⁴So Balak took Balaam to the field of Zophim. This was on top of Mount Pisgah. There Balak built seven altars. And he offered a bull and a male sheep on each altar.

¹⁵So Balaam said to Balak, "Stay here by your burnt offering. I will meet with God over there."

¹⁶So the Lord came to Balaam. He told Balaam what to say. Then he said, "Go back to Balak and say such and such."

¹⁷So Balaam went to Balak. Balak and the leaders of Moab were standing beside his burnt offering. Balak asked him, "What did the Lord say?"

¹⁸Then Balaam gave this message:

"Stand up, Balak, and listen.
　　Hear me, son of Zippor.
[19]God is not a man. He will not lie.
　　God is not a human being. He
　　　does not change his mind.
　What he says he will do, he does.
　　What he promises, he keeps.
[20]He told me to bless them.
　　So I cannot change the blessing.
[21]He has found no wrong in the
　　people of Jacob.
　He saw no fault in Israel.
　The Lord their God is with them.
　　They praise their King.
[22]God brought them out of Egypt.
　　They are as strong as a wild ox.
[23]No tricks will work on the people
　　of Jacob.
　No magic works against Israel.
　People now say this about them,
　　'Look what God has done!'
[24]The people are strong like a
　　lioness.
　They get up like a lion.
　Lions don't rest until they have
　　eaten.
　They drink their enemies' blood."

[25]Then Balak said to Balaam, "You
haven't cursed these people. So at least,
don't bless them!"

[26]Balaam answered Balak, "I told you
before. I can only do what the Lord tells
me."

[27]Then Balak said to Balaam, "Come,
I will take you to another place. Maybe
God will be pleased. He may let you
curse them from there." [28]So Balak took
Balaam to the top of Peor. This moun-
tain looks over the desert.

[29]Balaam told Balak, "Build me seven
altars here. Then prepare for me seven
bulls and seven male sheep." [30]Balak did
what Balaam asked. He offered a bull
and a male sheep on each altar.

24 Balaam saw that the Lord wanted
　to bless Israel. So Balaam did not
try to use any magic. He looked toward
the desert. [2]Balaam saw the Israelites
camped in their tribes.[d] Then the Spirit[d]
of God entered him. [3]And Balaam gave
this message:

"This is the message of Balaam son
　of Beor.
　This is the message of a man who
　　sees clearly.
[4]This is the message of a man who
　　heard the words of God.
　I see a vision from the
　　All-Powerful One.
　My eyes are open as I fall before
　　him.

[5]Your tents are beautiful, people of
　　Jacob!
　So are your homes, Israel!
[6]Your tents spread out like valleys.
　　They are like gardens beside a
　　　river.
　They are like spices planted by the
　　　Lord.
　They are like cedar trees growing
　　　by the water.
[7]Israel's water buckets will always
　　be full.
　Their crops will have plenty of
　　water.
　Their king will be greater than
　　Agag.
　Their kingdom will be very great.
[8]God brought them out of Egypt.
　　They are as strong as a wild ox.
　They will defeat their enemies.
　They will break their enemies'
　　bones.
　They will shoot them with
　　arrows.
[9]Like a lion, they lie waiting to
　　attack.
　No one would wake a sleeping
　　lion.
　Anyone who blesses you will be
　　blessed.
　And anyone who curses you will
　　be cursed."

[10]Then Balak was angry with Balaam.
Balak pounded his fist. He said to Balaam, "I called you here to curse my enemies. But you have blessed them three
times. [11]Now go home! I said I would
pay you well. But the Lord has made you
lose your reward."

[12]Balaam said to Balak, "You sent
messengers to me. I told them, [13]'Balak
could give me his palace filled with silver and gold. But I still cannot go
against the Lord's commands. I could
not do anything, good or bad, on my
own. I must say what the Lord says.'
[14]Now I am going back to my own people. But I will tell you what these people
will do to your people in the future."

[15]Then Balaam gave this message:
"This is the message of Balaam son
　of Beor.
　This is the message of a man who
　　sees clearly.
[16]This is the message of a man who
　　hears the words of God.
　I know the Most High God.
　I see a vision from the All-Powerful
　　One.
　My eyes are open as I fall before
　　him.

[17] I see someone who will come some day.
I see someone who will come, but not soon.
A star will come from Jacob.
A ruler will rise from Israel.
He will crush the heads of the Moabites.
He will smash the skulls of the sons of Sheth.
[18] Edom will be conquered.
His enemy Edom will be conquered.
But Israel will grow wealthy.
[19] The descendants[d] of Jacob will beat them down.
The Israelites will destroy those left in the city."
[20] Then Balaam saw Amalek and gave this message:
"Amalek was the most important nation.
But Amalek will be destroyed at last."
[21] Then Balaam saw the Kenites and gave this message:
"Your home is safe.
It is like a nest on a cliff.
[22] But you Kenites will be burned up.
Assyria will keep you captive."
[23] Then Balaam gave this message:
"No one can live when God does this.
[24] Ships will sail from the shores of Cyprus.
They will defeat Assyria and Eber.
But they will also be destroyed."
[25] Then Balaam got up and returned home. Balak also went on his way.

25 The people of Israel were still camped at Acacia. The men began sinning sexually with Moabite women. [2] The women invited them to their sacrifices to their false gods. The Israelites ate food there and worshiped these gods. [3] So the Israelites began to worship Baal[d] of Peor. And the Lord was very angry with them.

[4] The Lord said to Moses, "Get all the leaders of the people. Then kill them in open daylight in the presence of the Lord. Then the Lord will not be angry with the people of Israel."

[5] So Moses said to Israel's judges, "Each of you must put to death your men who have become worshipers of Baal of Peor."

[6] Moses and the Israelites were gathered at the entrance to the Meeting Tent.[d] They were crying there. Then an Israelite man brought a Midianite woman to his brothers. This was in plain sight of Moses and all the people. [7] Phinehas son of Eleazar, the son of Aaron, the priest, saw this. So he left the meeting and got his spear. [8] He followed the Israelite into his tent. And he drove his spear through both the Israelite man and the Midianite woman. Then the terrible sickness among the Israelites stopped.

[9] This sickness had killed 24,000 people.

[10] The Lord said to Moses, [11] "Phinehas son of Eleazar, the son of Aaron, the priest, has saved the Israelites from my anger. He is like I am in his concern for the people. He tried to save my honor among them. So I will not kill them. [12] So tell Phinehas that I am making my peace agreement with him. [13] He and all his descendants[d] will have an agreement. They will always be priests. This is because he had great concern for the honor of his God. He removed the sins of the Israelites so they would belong to God."

[14] The Israelite man who was killed with the Midianite woman was named Zimri son of Salu. He was the leader of a family in the tribe[d] of Simeon. [15] And the name of the Midianite woman who was put to death was Cozbi daughter of Zur. Zur was the chief of a Midianite family.

[16] The Lord said to Moses, [17] "The Midianites are your enemies. You should kill them. [18] They have already made you their enemies. They tricked you at Peor. Then there was Cozbi, the daughter of a Midianite leader. She was the woman who was killed when the sickness came. It came because the people were worshiping the false god at Peor."

26 After the great sickness, the Lord spoke to Moses and Eleazar son of Aaron, the priest. He said, [2] "Count all the people of Israel by families. Count all the men who are 20 years old or older. They will serve in the army of Israel." [3] Moses and Eleazar the priest spoke to the people. They were on the plains of Moab near the Jordan River, across from Jericho. They said, [4] "Count the men 20 years old or older. This is what the Lord commanded Moses."

Here are the Israelites who came out of Egypt:

[5] The tribe[d] of Reuben was counted. Reuben was the first son born to Israel. From Hanoch came the Hanochite family group. From Pallu came the Palluite

family group. [6]From Hezron came the Hezronite family group. From Carmi came the Carmite family group. [7]These were the family groups of Reuben. The total number of men was 43,730.

[8]The son of Pallu was Eliab. [9]Eliab's sons were Nemuel, Dathan and Abiram. Dathan and Abiram were the leaders who turned against Moses and Aaron. They followed Korah when he turned against the Lord. [10]The earth opened up and swallowed them and Korah. They died when the fire burned up the 250 men. This was a warning. [11]But the children of Korah did not die.

[12]These were the family groups in the tribe of Simeon. From Nemuel came the Nemuelite family group. From Jamin came the Jaminite family group. From Jakin came the Jakinite family group. [13]From Zerah came the Zerahite family group. From Shaul came the Shaulite family group. [14]These were the family groups of Simeon. The total number of men was 22,200.

[15]These were the family groups in the tribe of Gad. From Zephon came the Zephonite family group. From Haggi came the Haggite family group. From Shuni came the Shunite family group. [16]From Ozni came the Oznite family group. From Eri came the Erite family group. [17]From Arodi came the Arodite family group. From Areli came the Arelite family group. [18]These were the family groups of Gad. The total number of men was 40,500.

[19]Two of Judah's sons, Er and Onan, died in Canaan. [20]These were the family groups in the tribe of Judah. From Shelah came the Shelanite family group. From Perez came the Perezite family group. From Zerah came the Zerahite family group. [21]These were the family groups from Perez. From Hezron came the Hezronite family group. From Hamul came the Hamulite family group. [22]These were the family groups of Judah. The total number of men was 76,500.

[23]These were the family groups in the tribe of Issachar. From Tola came the Tolaite family group. From Puah came the Puite family group. [24]From Jashub came the Jashubite family group. From Shimron came the Shimronite family group. [25]These were the family groups of Issachar. The total number of men was 64,300.

[26]These were the family groups in the tribe of Zebulun. From Sered came the Seredite family group. From Elon came the Elonite family group. From Jahleel came the Jahleelite family group. [27]These were the family groups of Zebulun. The total number of men was 60,500.

[28]These were the family groups of Joseph through Manasseh and Ephraim.

[29]These were the family groups of Manasseh. From Makir came the Makirite family group. (Makir was the father of Gilead.) From Gilead came the Gileadite family group. [30]These were the family groups that came from Gilead. From Iezer came the Iezerite family group. From Helek came the Helekite family group. [31]From Asriel came the Asrielite family group. From Shechem came the Shechemite family group. [32]From Shemida came the Shemidaite family group. From Hepher came the Hepherite family group. [33](Zelophehad son of Hepher had no sons. He had only daughters. Their names were Mahlah, Noah, Hoglah, Milcah and Tirzah.) [34]These were the family groups of Manasseh. The total number of men was 52,700.

[35]These were the family groups in the tribe of Ephraim. From Shuthelah came the Shuthelahite family group. From Beker came the Bekerite family group. From Tahan came the Tahanite family group. [36]This was the family group from Shuthelah. From Eran came the Eranite family group. [37]These were the family groups of Ephraim. The total number of men was 32,500. These are the family groups that came from Joseph.

[38]These were the family groups in the tribe of Benjamin. From Bela came the Belaite family group. From Ashbel came the Ashbelite family group. From Ahiram came the Ahiramite family group. [39]From Shupham came the Shuphamite family group. From Hupham came the Huphamite family group. [40]These were the family groups from Bela through Ard and Naaman. From Ard came the Ardite family group. From Naaman came the Naamite family group. [41]These were the family groups of Benjamin. The total number of men was 45,600.

[42]This was the family group in the tribe of Dan. From Shuham came the Shuhamite family group. That was the family of Dan. [43]The total number of men in the Shuhamite family group of Dan was 64,400.

[44]These were the family groups in the tribe of Asher. From Imnah came the Imnite family group. From Ishvi came

the Ishvite family group. From Beriah came the Beriite family group. [45]These were the family groups that came from Beriah. From Heber came the Heberite family group. From Malkiel came the Malkielite family group. [46](Asher also had a daughter named Serah.) [47]These were the family groups of Asher. The total number of men was 53,400.

[48]These were the family groups in the tribe of Naphtali. From Jahzeel came the Jahzeelite family group. From Guni came the Gunite family group. [49]From Jezer came the Jezerite family group. From Shillem came the Shillemite family group. [50]These were the family groups of Naphtali. The total number of men was 45,400.

[51]So the total number of the men of Israel was 601,730.

[52]The Lord said to Moses, [53]"Divide the land among these people by the number of names. [54]A large tribe will get more land. And a small tribe will get less land. The amount of land each tribe gets will depend on the number of its people. [55]Divide the land by drawing lots.[d] And the land each tribe gets will be named for that tribe. [56]Divide the land by drawing lots. Divide it between large and small groups."

[57]The tribe of Levi was also counted. These were the family groups of Levi. From Gershon came the Gershonite family group. From Kohath came the Kohathite family group. From Merari came the Merarite family group. [58]These also were Levite family groups: the Libnite family group, the Hebronite family group, the Mahlite family group, the Mushite family group and the Korahite family group. (Kohath was the ancestor of Amram. [59]Amram's wife was named Jochebed. She was from the tribe of Levi. She was born in Egypt. She and Amram had two sons, Aaron and Moses, and their sister Miriam. [60]Aaron was the father of Nadab, Abihu, Eleazar and Ithamar. [61]But Nadab and Abihu died. They died because they made an offering before the Lord with the wrong kind of fire.)

[62]The total number of male Levites one month old or older was 23,000. But these men were not counted with the other Israelites. They did not receive any of the land that the Lord gave the other Israelites.

[63]Moses and Eleazar the priest counted all these people. They counted the Israelites on the plains of Moab across the Jordan River from Jericho. [64]Moses and Aaron the priest had counted them in the Desert of Sinai. But no one Moses counted on the plains of Moab was in the first counting. [65]The Lord had told the Israelites they would all die in the desert. The only two left were Caleb son of Jephunneh and Joshua son of Nun.

27 Zelophehad was the son of Hepher. Hepher was the son of Gilead. Gilead was the son of Makir. Makir was the son of Manasseh. Zelophehad's daughters belonged to the family groups of Manasseh son of Joseph. The daughters' names were Mahlah, Noah, Hoglah, Milcah and Tirzah. [2]They went to the entrance of the Meeting Tent.[d] There they stood before Moses, Eleazar the priest, the leaders and all the people. They said, [3]"Our father died in the desert. He was not one of Korah's followers who came against the Lord. Our father died because of his own sin. But he had no sons. [4]Our father's name will die out because he had no sons. Give us property among our father's relatives."

[5]So Moses brought their case to the Lord. [6]The Lord said to him, [7]"The daughters of Zelophehad are right. They should get what their father owned. Give them property among their father's relatives.

[8]"Tell the Israelites, 'If a man dies and has no son, then everything he owned should go to his daughter. [9]If he has no daughter, then everything he owned should go to his brothers. [10]If he has no brothers, then everything he owned should go to his father's brothers. [11]If his father had no brothers, then everything he owned should go to the nearest relative in his family group. This should be a rule among the people of Israel as the Lord has given this command to Moses.'"

[12]Then the Lord said to Moses, "Climb this mountain in the Abarim Mountains. Look at the land I have given to the Israelites. [13]After you have seen it, you will die as your brother Aaron did. [14]You both acted against my command in the Desert of Zin. You did not honor me as holy before the people at the waters of Meribah." (This was at Meribah in Kadesh in the Desert of Zin.)

[15]Moses said to the Lord, [16]"The Lord is the God of the spirits of all people. May he choose a good leader for these people. [17]He must go in and out before them. He must lead them out like sheep

and bring them in. The Lord's people must not be like sheep without a shepherd."

¹⁸So the Lord said to Moses, "Take Joshua son of Nun. My Spirit[d] is in him. Put your hand on him. ¹⁹Have him stand before Eleazar the priest and all the people. Then give him his orders as they watch. ²⁰Let him share your honor. Then all the Israelites will obey him. ²¹He must stand before Eleazar the priest. And Eleazar will get advice from the Lord by using the Urim.[d] At his command all the Israelites will go out. At his command they will all come in."

²²Moses did what the Lord told him. Moses had Joshua stand before Eleazar the priest and all the people. ²³Then Moses put his hands on him and gave him orders. This was just as the Lord had told him.

28 The Lord said to Moses, ²"Give this command to the Israelites. Tell them: 'Bring me food offerings made by fire. The smell is pleasing to me. Be sure to bring them at the right time.' ³Say to them: 'These are the offerings you must bring to the Lord. Bring two year-old lambs as a burnt offering each day. They must have nothing wrong with them. ⁴Offer one lamb in the morning and the other lamb at twilight. ⁵Also bring a grain offering of two quarts of fine flour. It must be mixed with one quart of oil from pressed olives. ⁶This is the daily burnt offering which began at Mount Sinai. The smell is pleasing to the Lord. ⁷Offer one quart of wine with each lamb as a drink offering. Pour it out to the Lord at the Holy Place. ⁸Offer the second lamb at twilight. As in the morning, also give a grain offering and a drink offering. This offering is made by fire. Its smell is pleasing to the Lord.

⁹"'On the Sabbath[d] day you must give two year-old lambs. They must have nothing wrong with them. Also give a drink offering and a grain offering. The grain offering must be four quarts of fine flour mixed with olive oil. ¹⁰This is the burnt offering for the Sabbath. It is in addition to the daily burnt offering and drink offering.

¹¹"'On the first day of each month bring a burnt offering to the Lord. This will be two young bulls, one male sheep and seven male lambs a year old. They all must have nothing wrong with them. ¹²Give a grain offering with each bull. It must be six quarts of fine flour mixed

with olive oil. Also give a grain offering with the male sheep. It must be four quarts of fine flour mixed with olive oil. ¹³Also give a grain offering with each lamb. It must be two quarts of fine flour mixed with olive oil. This is a burnt offering. And its smell is pleasing to the Lord. ¹⁴The drink offering with each bull will be two quarts of wine. With the male sheep it will be one and one-half quarts. And with each lamb it will be one quart of wine. This is the burnt offering that must be offered each month of the year. ¹⁵Besides the daily burnt offerings and drink offerings, bring a sin offering to the Lord. It must be one male goat.

¹⁶"'The Lord's Passover[d] will be on the fourteenth day of the first month. ¹⁷The Feast[d] of Unleavened Bread begins on the fifteenth day of that month. It lasts for seven days. You may eat only bread made without yeast. ¹⁸Have a holy meeting on the first day of the festival. Don't work that day. ¹⁹Bring these burnt offerings to the Lord: two young bulls, one male sheep and seven male lambs a year old. They all must have nothing wrong with them. ²⁰Also give a grain offering with each bull. It must be six quarts of fine flour mixed with olive oil. Give a grain offering with the male sheep. It must be four quarts of fine flour mixed with oil. ²¹Give a grain offering with each of the seven lambs. It must be two quarts of fine flour mixed with oil. ²²Bring one goat as a sin offering. It will remove your sins so you will belong to God. ²³Bring these offerings in addition to the burnt offerings you give every morning. ²⁴So bring food offerings each day for seven days. The offering is made by fire. And its smell is pleasing to the Lord. Do it in addition to the daily burnt offering and its drink offering. ²⁵On the seventh day have a holy meeting. Don't work that day.

²⁶"'On the day of firstfruits[d] offer new grain to the Lord. This is during the Feast[d] of Weeks. Have a holy meeting. Don't work that day. ²⁷Give this burnt offering to the Lord: two young bulls, one male sheep and seven male lambs a year old. This smell is pleasing to the Lord. ²⁸Also give a grain offering with each bull. It must be six quarts of fine flour mixed with oil. With the male sheep, it must be four quarts of flour. ²⁹With each of the seven lambs offer two quarts of flour. ³⁰Offer one male goat to remove your sins so you will belong to

God. ³¹Bring these offerings and their drink offerings. These are in addition to the daily burnt offering and its grain offering. The animals must have nothing wrong with them.

29 ¹ "Have a holy meeting on the first day of the seventh month. Don't work on that day. That is the day you blow the trumpets. ²Bring these burnt offerings to the Lord: one young bull, one male sheep and seven male year-old lambs. They all must have nothing wrong with them. Their smell will be pleasing to the Lord. ³Give a grain offering with the bull. It must be six quarts of fine flour mixed with oil. With the male sheep offer four quarts. ⁴And with each of the seven lambs offer two quarts. ⁵Offer one male goat for a sin offering. It will remove your sins so you will belong to God. ⁶These offerings are in addition to the monthly and daily burnt offerings. Their grain offerings and drink offerings must be done as you have been told. These offerings are made by fire to the Lord. And their smell is pleasing to him.

⁷ "Have a holy meeting on the tenth day of the seventh month. On that day do not eat and do not work. ⁸Bring these burnt offerings to the Lord: one young bull, one male sheep and seven male lambs a year old. They all must have nothing wrong with them. The smell will be pleasing to the Lord. ⁹Give a grain offering with the bull. It must be six quarts of fine flour mixed with oil. With the male sheep it must be four quarts. ¹⁰And with each of the seven lambs it must be two quarts. ¹¹Offer one male goat as a sin offering. This will be in addition to the sin offering which removes your sins. It will also be in addition to the daily burnt offering with its grain offering and the drink offerings.

¹² "Have a holy meeting on the fifteenth day of the seventh month. Do not work on that day. Celebrate a festival to the Lord for seven days. ¹³Give these burnt offerings to the Lord: 13 young bulls, 2 male sheep and 14 male lambs a year old. They all must have nothing wrong with them. The smell is pleasing to the Lord. ¹⁴Also offer a grain offering with each of the 13 bulls. It must be six quarts of fine flour mixed with oil. With each of the 2 male sheep it must be four quarts. ¹⁵And with each of the 14 lambs it must be two quarts. ¹⁶Offer 1 male goat as a sin offering. This must be in addition to the daily burnt offering with its grain and drink offerings.

¹⁷ "On the second day of this festival give an offering. Offer 12 bulls, 2 male sheep and 14 male lambs a year old. They all must have nothing wrong with them. ¹⁸Bring the grain and drink offerings for the bulls, sheep and lambs. ¹⁹Offer 1 male goat as a sin offering. This must be in addition to the daily burnt offering with its grain and drink offerings.

²⁰ "On the third day offer 11 bulls, 2 male sheep and 14 male lambs a year old. They all must have nothing wrong with them. ²¹Bring the grain and drink offerings for the bulls, sheep and lambs. ²²Offer 1 male goat as a sin offering. This must be in addition to the daily burnt offering with its grain and drink offerings.

²³ "On the fourth day offer 10 bulls, 2 male sheep and 14 male lambs a year old. They all must have nothing wrong with them. ²⁴Bring the grain and drink offerings for the bulls, sheep and lambs. ²⁵Offer 1 male goat as a sin offering. This must be in addition to the daily burnt offering with its grain and drink offerings.

²⁶ "On the fifth day offer 9 bulls, 2 male sheep and 14 male lambs a year old. They all must have nothing wrong with them. ²⁷Bring the grain and drink offerings for the bulls, sheep and lambs. ²⁸Offer 1 male goat as a sin offering. This must be in addition to the daily burnt offering with its grain and drink offerings.

²⁹ "On the sixth day offer 8 bulls, 2 male sheep and 14 male lambs a year old. They all must have nothing wrong with them. ³⁰Bring the grain and drink offerings for the bulls, sheep and lambs. ³¹Offer 1 male goat as a sin offering. This must be in addition to the daily burnt offering with its grain and drink offerings.

³² "On the seventh day offer 7 bulls, 2 male sheep and 14 male lambs a year old. They all must have nothing wrong with them. ³³Bring the grain and drink offerings for the bulls, sheep and lambs. ³⁴Offer 1 male goat as a sin offering. This must be in addition to the daily burnt offering with its grain and drink offerings.

³⁵ "On the eighth day have a closing meeting. Do not work on that day. ³⁶Bring a burnt offering. Its smell will be pleasing to the Lord. Offer 1 bull, 1 male

sheep and 7 male lambs a year old. They all must have nothing wrong with them. [37]Bring the grain and drink offerings for the bull, male sheep and lambs. [38]Offer 1 male goat as a sin offering. This must be in addition to the daily burnt offering with its grain and drink offerings.

[39]" 'At your festivals you should bring these to the Lord: your burnt offerings, grain offerings, drink offerings and fellowship offerings. These are in addition to other promised offerings and special gifts you want to give to the Lord.' "

[40]Moses told the Israelites everything the Lord had commanded him.

30 Moses spoke with the leaders of the Israelite tribes.[d] He told them these commands from the Lord.

[2]"A person might make a promise to the Lord. He might promise to do something special. If he does, he must keep his promise. He must do what he said. [3]A young woman still living at home might make a promise to the Lord. She might pledge to do something special. [4]Her father might hear about the promise or pledge and say nothing. Then she must do what she promised. She must keep her pledge. [5]But when her father hears about the promise or pledge, he might not allow it. Then the promise or pledge does not have to be kept. Her father would not allow them. So the Lord will free her from her promise.

[6]"A woman might make a pledge or a careless promise and then get married. [7]Her husband might hear about it and say nothing. Then she must keep her promise or the pledge she made. [8]But when her husband hears about it, he might not allow it. He cancels her pledge or the careless promise she made. The Lord will free her from keeping it.

[9]"A widow or divorced woman might make a promise. She must do whatever she promised.

[10]"A woman might make a promise or pledge while she was married. [11]When her husband hears about it, he might say nothing. He might not stop her. Then she must keep her promise or pledge. [12]But when her husband hears about it, he might cancel it. Then she does not have to do what she said. Her husband has canceled it. The Lord will free her from it. [13]A woman's husband may make her keep or cancel any promise or pledge she has made. [14]But her husband might say nothing to her about it for several days. Then she must keep her

promises. If he hears about them and says nothing, she must keep her promises. [15]But he might cancel them long after he heard about them. Then he is responsible if she breaks her promise."

[16]These are commands that the Lord gave to Moses. They are for husbands and wives. And they are for fathers with daughters living at home.

31 The Lord spoke to Moses. He said, [2]"Pay back the Midianites for what they did to the Israelites. After that you will die."

[3]So Moses said to the people, "Get some men ready for war. The Lord will use them to pay back the Midianites. [4]Send to war 1,000 men from each of the tribes[d] of Israel." [5]So 12,000 men got ready for war. There were 1,000 men from each tribe. [6]Moses sent those 1,000 men from each tribe to war. Phinehas son of Eleazar the priest was with them. He took with him the holy things and the trumpets. [7]They fought the Midianites as the Lord had commanded Moses. And they killed every Midianite man. [8]Among those they killed were Evi, Rekem, Zur, Hur and Reba. They were the five kings of Midian. They also killed Balaam son of Beor with a sword.

[9]The Israelites captured the Midianite women and children. They also took all their flocks, herds and goods. [10]Then they burned all the Midianite towns and camps. [11]They took all the people and animals and goods. [12]Then they went back to Moses and Eleazar the priest and all the Israelites. They brought back the captives, the animals and the goods. The camp was on the plains of Moab near the Jordan River. This was across from Jericho.

[13]Moses, Eleazar the priest and all the leaders of the people went outside the camp to meet them. [14]Moses was angry with the army officers who returned from war. He was angry with those commanders over 1,000 men and those over 100 men.

[15]He asked them, "Why did you let the women live? [16]They were the ones who followed Balaam's advice. They turned the Israelites from the Lord at Peor. Then a terrible sickness struck the Lord's people. [17]Kill all the Midianite boys. Kill all the Midianite women who have had sexual relations. [18]But save the girls for yourselves who have not had sexual relations with a man.

[19]"All you men who killed anyone or touched a dead body must stay outside

the camp for seven days. On the third and seventh days you and your captives must make yourselves clean.[d] [20]You must clean all your clothes. And you must clean anything made of leather, wool or wood."

[21]Then Eleazar the priest spoke to the soldiers who had gone to war. He said, "These are the teachings that the Lord gave to Moses. [22]Put any gold, silver, bronze, iron, tin or lead into the fire. [23]Put into the fire anything that will not burn. Then wash those things with the cleansing water. Then they will be clean. If something cannot stand the fire, wash it with the water. [24]On the seventh day wash your clothes. Then you will be clean. After that you may come into the camp."

[25]The Lord said to Moses, [26]"You, Eleazar the priest and the leaders should take a count. Count the goods, the men and the animals that were taken. [27]Then divide those things between the soldiers who went to war and the rest of the people. [28]Tax the soldiers who went to war. The Lord's share is 1 thing out of every 500 things. This includes people, cattle, donkeys, sheep or goats. [29]Take it from the soldiers' half. And give it to Eleazar the priest. It is the Lord's share. [30]And from the people's half, take 1 thing out of every 50. This includes people, cattle, donkeys, sheep, goats or other animals. Give that to the Levites. They take care of the Lord's Holy Tent."[d] [31]So Moses and Eleazar did as the Lord commanded Moses.

[32]There remained from what the soldiers had taken 675,000 sheep, [33]72,000 cattle, [34]61,000 donkeys [35]and 32,000 women. These were the women who had not had sexual relations with a man. [36]The soldiers who went to war got 337,500 sheep. [37]They gave 675 of the sheep to the Lord. [38]They got 36,000 cattle. They gave 72 of them to the Lord. [39]They got 30,500 donkeys. They gave 61 of them to the Lord. [40]They got 16,000 people. And they gave 32 of them to the Lord. [41]Moses gave the Lord's share to Eleazar the priest. This was what the Lord had commanded him.

[42]Moses separated the people's half from the soldiers' half. [43]The people got 337,500 sheep, [44]36,000 cattle, [45]30,500 donkeys [46]and 16,000 people. [47]From the people's half Moses took 1 thing out of every 50 for the Lord. This included the animals and the people. Then he gave them to the Levites. They took care of

the Lord's Holy Tent. This was what the Lord had commanded Moses.

[48]Then the officers of the army came to Moses. They were the commanders of 1,000 men and commanders of 100 men. [49]They told Moses, "We, your servants, have counted our soldiers under our command. Not one of them is missing. [50]So we have brought the Lord a gift. We have brought the gold things that each of us found: arm bands, bracelets, signet[d] rings, earrings and necklaces. These are to remove our sins so we will belong to the Lord."

[51]So Moses and Eleazar the priest took the gold things from them. [52]The commanders of 1,000 men and the commanders of 100 men gave the Lord the gold. All of it together weighed about 420 pounds. [53]Each soldier had taken something for himself. [54]Moses and Eleazar the priest took the gold from the commanders of 1,000 men and the commanders of 100 men. Then they put it in the Meeting Tent.[d] It was a memorial before the Lord for the people of Israel.

32 The people of Reuben and Gad had many cattle. They saw that the lands of Jazer and Gilead were good for cattle. [2]So they came to Moses, Eleazar the priest and the leaders of the people. [3-4]They said, "We, your servants, have many cattle. The Lord has captured for the Israelites a land that is good for cattle. This is the land around Ataroth, Dibon, Jazer, Nimrah, Heshbon, Elealeh, Sebam, Nebo and Beon. [5]If it pleases you, we would like this land to be given to us. Don't make us cross the Jordan River."

[6]Moses told the people of Gad and Reuben, "Shall your brothers go to war while you stay behind? [7]You will discourage the Israelites. They will not want to go over to the land the Lord has given them. [8]Your ancestors did the same thing. From Kadesh Barnea I sent them to look at the land. [9]They went as far as the Valley of Eshcol. They saw the land. And they discouraged the Israelites from going into the land the Lord had given them. [10]The Lord became very angry that day. He made this promise: [11]'None of the people who came from Egypt and who are 20 years old or older will see this land. I promised it to Abraham, Isaac and Jacob. But these people have not followed me completely. [12]Only Caleb son of Jephunneh the Kenizzite and Joshua son of Nun followed the Lord completely.'

[13]"The Lord was very angry with Israel. So he made them wander in the desert for 40 years. Finally all the people who had sinned against him had died. [14]And now you are acting just like your fathers! You sinful people are making the Lord even more angry with Israel. [15]If you quit following the Lord, it will add to their stay in the desert. So you will destroy all these people."

[16]But the Reubenites and Gadites came up to Moses. They said, "We will build pens for our animals. And we will build cities for our wives and children here. [17]Then our families will be in strong, walled cities. They will be safe from the people who live in this land. Then we will prepare for war. We will help the other Israelites get their land. [18]We will not return home until every Israelite has received his land. [19]We won't take any of the land west of the Jordan River. Our part of the land is east of the Jordan."

[20]So Moses told them, "You must do these things. You must go before the Lord into battle. [21]You must cross the Jordan River armed. The Lord will force out the enemy. [22]After the Lord helps us take the land, you may return home. You will have done your duty to the Lord and Israel. Then you may have this land as your own.

[23]"But if you don't do these things, you will be sinning against the Lord. And know for sure that you will be punished for your sin. [24]Build cities for your wives and children and pens for your animals. But then you must do what you promised."

[25]The Gadites and Reubenites said to Moses, "We are your servants. We will do what you, our master, command. [26]Our wives, children and all our cattle will stay in the cities of Gilead. [27]But we, your servants, will prepare for battle. We will go over and fight for the Lord, as you have said."

[28]So Moses gave orders about them to Eleazar the priest. And he gave them to Joshua son of Nun and the leaders of the tribes[d] of Israel. [29]Moses said to them, "The Gadites and Reubenites will prepare for battle. They will cross the Jordan River with you. They will go before the Lord and help you take the land. If they do that, give them the land of Gilead for their own. [30]But if they do not go over armed, they will not receive it. Their land will be in Canaan with you."

[31]The Gadites and Reubenites answered, "We are your servants. We will do as the Lord said. [32]We will cross over into Canaan. We will go before the Lord ready for battle. But our land will be east of the Jordan River."

[33]So Moses gave that land to the Gadites, Reubenites and the eastern half-tribe of Manasseh. (Manasseh was Joseph's son.) That land had been the kingdom of Sihon, the king of the Amorites. And it included the kingdom of Og, king of Bashan. It also included all the cities and the land around them.

[34]The Gadites rebuilt the cities of Dibon, Ataroth, Aroer, [35]Atroth Shophan, Jazer, Jogbehah, [36]Beth Nimrah and Beth Haran. These were strong, walled cities. And they built sheep pens.

[37]The Reubenites built Heshbon, Elealeh, Kiriathaim, [38]Nebo, Baal Meon and Sibmah. They renamed Nebo and Baal Meon when they rebuilt them.

[39]The descendants[d] of Makir son of Manasseh went and captured Gilead. They forced out the Amorites who were there. [40]So Moses gave Gilead to the family of Makir son of Manasseh. And they settled there. [41]Jair son of Manasseh went out and captured the small towns there. He called them the Towns of Jair. [42]Nobah went and captured Kenath and the small towns around it. Then he named it Nobah after himself.

33 These are the places the Israelites went as Moses and Aaron led them out of Egypt in divisions. [2]At the Lord's command Moses recorded the places they went. These are the places they went.

[3]On the fifteenth day of the first month, they left Rameses. That was the day after the Passover.[d] [4]The Israelites marched out boldly in front of all the Egyptians. [4]The Egyptians were burying their firstborn[d] sons. The Lord had killed them. He showed that the gods of Egypt were false.

[5]The Israelites left Rameses and camped at Succoth.

[6]They left Succoth and camped at Etham. It was at the edge of the desert.

[7]They left Etham and went back to Pi Hahiroth. This was east of Baal Zephon. They camped near Migdol.

[8]They left Pi Hahiroth. They walked through the sea into the desert. After going three days through the Desert of Etham, they camped at Marah.

[9]They left Marah and went to Elim. There were 12 springs of water and 70 palm trees where they camped.

[10]They left Elim and camped near the Red Sea.[d]

[11]They left the Red Sea and camped in the Desert of Sin.

[12]They left the Desert of Sin and camped at Dophkah.

[13]They left Dophkah and camped at Alush.

[14]They left Alush and camped at Rephidim. The people had no water to drink there.

[15]They left Rephidim and camped in the Desert of Sinai.

[16]They left the Desert of Sinai and camped at Kibroth Hattaavah.

[17]They left Kibroth Hattaavah and camped at Hazeroth.

[18]They left Hazeroth and camped at Rithmah.

[19]They left Rithmah and camped at Rimmon Perez.

[20]They left Rimmon Perez and camped at Libnah.

[21]They left Libnah and camped at Rissah.

[22]They left Rissah and camped at Kehelathah.

[23]They left Kehelathah and camped at Mount Shepher.

[24]They left Mount Shepher and camped at Haradah.

[25]They left Haradah and camped at Makheloth.

[26]They left Makheloth and camped at Tahath.

[27]They left Tahath and camped at Terah.

[28]They left Terah and camped at Mithcah.

[29]They left Mithcah and camped at Hashmonah.

[30]They left Hashmonah and camped at Moseroth.

[31]They left Moseroth and camped at Bene Jaakan.

[32]They left Bene Jaakan and camped at Hor Haggidgad.

[33]They left Hor Haggidgad and camped at Jotbathah.

[34]They left Jotbathah and camped at Abronah.

[35]They left Abronah and camped at Ezion Geber.

[36]They left Ezion Geber and camped at Kadesh in the Desert of Zin.

[37]They left Kadesh and camped at Mount Hor. This was on the border of Edom. [38]Aaron the priest obeyed the Lord and went up Mount Hor. There he died. He died on the first day of the fifth month. This was in the fortieth year af-ter the Israelites left Egypt. [39]Aaron was 123 years old when he died on Mount Hor.

[40]The king of Arad lived in the south-ern area of Canaan. He heard that the Israelites were coming.

[41]The people left Mount Hor and camped at Zalmonah.

[42]They left Zalmonah and camped at Punon.

[43]They left Punon and camped at Oboth.

[44]They left Oboth and camped at Iye Abarim. This was on the border of Moab.

[45]They left Iye Abarim and camped at Dibon Gad.

[46]They left Dibon Gad and camped at Almon Diblathaim.

[47]They left Almon Diblathaim and camped in the mountains of Abarim, near Nebo.

[48]They left the mountains of Abarim and camped on the plains of Moab. This was near the Jordan River across from Jericho. [49]They camped along the Jor-dan on the plains of Moab. Their camp went from Beth Jeshimoth to Abel Acacia.

[50]On the plains of Moab by the Jordan River across from Jericho, the Lord spoke to Moses. He said, [51]"Speak to the Israelites. Tell them, 'Cross the Jordan River and go into Canaan. [52]Force out the people who live there. Destroy all of their carved statues. Destroy their metal idols. Wreck all of their places of wor-ship. [53]Take over the land and settle there. I have given this land to you to own. [54]Throw lots[d] to divide up the land by family groups. Give larger portions to larger family groups. Give smaller portions to smaller family groups. The land will be given as the lots decide. Each tribe[d] will get its own land.

[55]"But if you don't force those people out of the land, they will bring you trou-ble. They will be like sharp hooks in your eyes. They will be like thorns in your sides. They will bring trouble to the land where you live. [56]I will punish you as I had planned to punish them.'"

34 The Lord said to Moses, [2]"Give this command to the people of Is-rael: 'You will soon enter Canaan. It will be yours. These shall be the borders. [3]On the south you will get part of the Desert of Zin. This is near the border of Edom. On the east side your southern border will start at the south end of the Dead Sea.[d] [4]It will cross south of Scorpion Pass. It will go through the Desert of Zin and south of Kadesh Barnea. Then it will go to Hazar Addar and over to Azmon. ⁵From Azmon it will go to the brook of Egypt. It will end at the Mediterranean Sea.

⁶"'Your western border will be the Mediterranean Sea.

⁷"'Your northern border will begin at the Mediterranean Sea and go to Mount Hor. ⁸From Mount Hor it will go to Lebo Hamath. Then it will go to Zedad. ⁹Then the border will go to Ziphron and end at Hazar Enan. This will be your northern border.

¹⁰"'Your eastern border will begin at Hazar Enan and go to Shepham. ¹¹From Shepham the border will go east of Ain to Riblah. It will go along the hills east of Lake Galilee. ¹²Then the border will go down along the Jordan River. It will end at the Dead Sea.

"'These are the borders around your country.'"

¹³So Moses gave this command to the Israelites: "This is the land you will receive. Throw lots[d] to divide it among the nine and a half tribes.[d] The Lord commanded that it should be theirs. ¹⁴The tribes of Reuben and Gad and the eastern half-tribe of Manasseh have already received their land. ¹⁵These two and a half tribes received land east of the Jordan River. It is across from Jericho."

¹⁶Then the Lord said to Moses, ¹⁷"These are the men who will divide the land: Eleazar the priest and Joshua son of Nun. ¹⁸Also take one leader from each tribe. They will divide the land. ¹⁹These are the names of the leaders: from the tribe of Judah, Caleb son of Jephunneh; ²⁰from the tribe of Simeon, Shemuel son of Ammihud; ²¹from the tribe of Benjamin, Elidad son of Kislon; ²²from the tribe of Dan, Bukki son of Jogli; ²³from the tribe of Manasseh son of Joseph, Hanniel son of Ephod; ²⁴from the tribe of Ephraim son of Joseph, Kemuel son of Shiphtan; ²⁵from the tribe of Zebulun, Elizaphan son of Parnach; ²⁶from the tribe of Issachar, Paltiel son of Azzan; ²⁷from the tribe of Asher, Ahihud son of Shelomi; ²⁸from the tribe of Naphtali, Pedahel son of Ammihud."

²⁹The Lord commanded these men to divide the land of Canaan among the Israelites.

35 The Lord spoke to Moses on the plains of Moab. This was across from Jericho by the Jordan River. He said, ²"Command the Israelites to give the Levites cities to live in. These will be cities in the land they receive. Also give the Levites the pastureland around these cities. ³Then the Levites will have cities where they may live. And they will have pastureland for their cattle, sheep and other animals. ⁴The pastureland you give the Levites will extend 1,500 feet from the city wall. ⁵Also measure 3,000 feet in each direction from the city wall. Measure 3,000 feet east of the city. Measure 3,000 feet south of the city. Measure 3,000 feet west of the city. And measure 3,000 feet north of the city. The city will be in the center. This will be pastureland for the Levites' cities.

⁶"Six of the cities you give the Levites will be cities of safety.[d] A person might accidentally kill someone. If he does, he may run to one of those cities for safety. You must also give 42 other cities to the Levites. ⁷Give the Levites a total of 48 cities and their pastures. ⁸The larger tribes[d] of Israel must give more cities. The smaller tribes must give fewer cities. Each tribe must give some of its cities to the Levites. The number of cities they give will depend on the size of their land."

⁹Then the Lord said to Moses, ¹⁰"Tell the Israelites these things: 'You will cross the Jordan River and go into Canaan. ¹¹You must choose cities to be cities of safety. If a person accidentally kills someone, he may run to them for safety. ¹²There he will be safe from the dead person's relative who has the duty of punishing the killer. He will not die before he is judged in court. ¹³The six cities you give will be cities of safety. ¹⁴Give three cities east of the Jordan River. And give three cities in Canaan as cities of safety. ¹⁵These six cities will be places of safety for citizens of Israel. And they will be for foreigners and other people living with you. Any of these people may run to one of these cities if he accidentally kills someone.

¹⁶"'If a person uses an iron weapon to kill someone, he is a murderer. He must be put to death. ¹⁷A person might take a rock that could kill someone. If he kills a person with it, he is a murderer. He must be put to death. ¹⁸A person might pick up a piece of wood that could kill someone. If he kills someone with it, he is a murderer. He must be put to death. ¹⁹A relative of the dead person must put the murderer to death. When he finds the murderer, he must kill him. ²⁰A person might shove someone and kill him.

Or he might throw something at someone and kill him. ²¹Or he might hit someone with his hand and kill him. If he did that from hate, he is a murderer. He must be put to death. A relative of the dead person must kill the murderer when he finds him.

²²"But a person might suddenly shove someone. He did not hate the person. Or he might accidentally throw something and hit someone. ²³Or he might drop a rock that could kill someone. It might fall on someone he did not see. And it might kill that person. He didn't plan to hurt anyone. He didn't hate the person he killed. ²⁴If that happens, the community must decide what to do. They must decide between the relative of the dead person and the killer. Here are the rules. ²⁵They must protect the killer from the dead person's relative. They must send the killer back to the city of safety that he ran to. He must stay there until the high priest dies. The high priest had the holy oil poured on him.

²⁶"That man must never go outside the limits of his city of safety. ²⁷If a relative of the dead person finds him outside the city, the relative may kill him. He will not be guilty of murder. ²⁸The killer must stay in his city of safety until the high priest dies. After the high priest dies, he may go back to his own land.

²⁹"These laws are for you from now on, wherever you live.

³⁰"A killer may be put to death only if he is a murderer. And there must be witnesses. No one may be put to death with only one witness.

³¹"A murderer should die. Don't take money to spare his life. He must be put to death.

³²"A person might run to a city of safety. Don't take money to let him go back home before the high priest dies.

³³"Don't let murder spoil your land. There is only one way to remove the sin of killing an innocent person. The murderer must be put to death. ³⁴I am the Lord. I live among the Israelites. I live

in that land with you. So do not spoil it with murder.'"

36 The leaders of Gilead's family group went to talk to Moses and the leaders of the families of Israel. (Gilead was the son of Makir. Makir was Manasseh's son, and Manasseh was Joseph's son.) ²They said, "The Lord commanded you, our master, to give the land to the Israelites by throwing lots.ᵈ And the Lord commanded you to give the land of Zelophehad, our brother, to his daughters. ³His daughters may marry men from other tribesᵈ of Israel. Then that land will leave our family. The people of the other tribes will get that land. So we will lose some of our land. ⁴The time of Jubileeᵈ will come for the Israelites. Then their land will go to other tribes. It will go to the tribes of the people they marry. So their land will be taken away from us. And that was land we received from our fathers."

⁵Then Moses gave the Israelites this command from the Lord: "These men from the tribe of Joseph are right. ⁶This is the Lord's command to Zelophehad's daughters: You may marry anyone you wish from your own tribe. ⁷In this way the Israelites' land will not pass from tribe to tribe. Each Israelite will keep the land in the tribe that belonged to his ancestors. ⁸A woman who inherits her father's land may marry. But she must marry someone from her own tribe. In this way every Israelite will keep the land that belonged to his ancestors. ⁹The land must not pass from tribe to tribe. Each Israelite tribe will keep the land it received from its ancestors."

¹⁰Zelophehad's daughters obeyed the Lord's command to Moses.

¹¹So Zelophehad's daughters—Mahlah, Tirzah, Hoglah, Milcah and Noah—married their cousins. These were their father's relatives. ¹²Their husbands were from the tribe of Manasseh son of Joseph. So their land stayed in their father's family group and tribe.

¹³These were the laws and commands that the Lord gave to the Israelites. He gave them through Moses. The Israelites were on the plains of Moab by the Jordan River, across from Jericho.

The Fifth Book of Moses Called
DEUTERONOMY

1 This is the message Moses gave the people of Israel. They were in the desert east of the Jordan River. They were in the Jordan Valley near Suph, between Paran and the towns of Tophel, Laban, Hazeroth and Dizahab. ²(The trip from Mount Sinai to Kadesh Barnea on the Mount Edom road takes 11 days.) ³But it was now 40 years after the Israelites had left Egypt. On the first day of the eleventh month, Moses spoke to the people. He told them everything the Lord had commanded him to tell them. ⁴This was after the Lord had defeated Sihon and Og. Sihon was king of the Amorite people and lived in Heshbon. Og was king of Bashan and lived in Ashteroth and Edrei.

⁵Now the Israelites were east of the Jordan River in the land of Moab. There Moses began to explain what God had commanded. Moses said:

⁶The Lord our God spoke to us at Mount Sinai. He said, "You have stayed long enough at this mountain. ⁷Get ready. Go to the mountain country of the Amorites. Go to all the places around there—the Jordan Valley, the mountains, the western slopes, the southern area, the seacoast, the land of Canaan and Lebanon. Go as far as the great river, the Euphrates. ⁸See, I have given you this land. Go in and take it for yourselves. The Lord promised it to your ancestors—Abraham, Isaac and Jacob and their descendants."ᵈ

⁹At that time I said, "I am not able to take care of you by myself. ¹⁰The Lord your God has made you grow in number. There are as many of you as there are stars in the sky. ¹¹I pray that the Lord, the God of your ancestors, will give you a thousand times more people. That's what he promised. ¹²But I cannot take care of your problems, your troubles and your arguments by myself. ¹³So choose some men from each tribe.ᵈ Choose wise men who have understanding and experience. I will make them leaders over you."

¹⁴And you said, "That's a good thing to do."

¹⁵So I took the wise and experienced leaders of your tribes. And I made them your leaders. I appointed commanders over 1,000 people, over 100 people, over 50 people and over 10 people. I made them officers over your tribes. ¹⁶Then I told your judges, "Listen to the arguments between your people. Judge fairly between two Israelites or between an Israelite and a foreigner. ¹⁷When you judge, be fair to everyone. Don't act as if one person is more important than another. Don't be afraid of anyone, because your decision comes from God. Bring the hard cases to me. I will judge them." ¹⁸At that time I told you everything you must do.

¹⁹Then, as the Lord our God commanded us, we left Mount Sinai. We went toward the mountain country of the Amorite people. We went through that large and terrible desert you saw. Then we came to Kadesh Barnea. ²⁰Then I said to you, "You have now come to the mountain country of the Amorites. The Lord our God will give us this land. ²¹Look, there it is! Go up. Take it. The Lord, the God of your ancestors, told you to do this. So don't be afraid. Don't worry."

²²Then all of you came to me. You said, "Let's send men before us to spy out the land. They can come back and tell us the way we should go. They can tell us about the cities we will find."

²³I thought that was a good idea. So I chose 12 of your men, 1 for each tribe.ᵈ ²⁴They left and went up to the mountains. They came to the Valley of Eshcol and explored it. ²⁵They took some of the fruit from that land. And they brought it down to us. They said, "It is a good land that the Lord our God is giving us."

²⁶But you refused to go. You would not obey the command of the Lord your God. ²⁷You grumbled in your tents. You said, "The Lord hates us. He brought us out of Egypt just to give us to the Amorites. They will destroy us. ²⁸Where can we go now? The spies we sent have made us afraid. They said, 'The people there are bigger and taller than we are. The cities are big. They have walls up to the sky. And we saw the Anakitesᵈ there!'"

²⁹Then I said to you, "Don't be frightened. Don't be afraid of those people. ³⁰The Lord your God will go ahead of you. He will fight for you as he did in Egypt. You saw him do it. ³¹And in the desert you saw how the Lord your God carried you. He was like a man carrying

his son. And he has brought you safely all the way to this place."

[32] But you still did not trust the Lord your God. [33] As you moved, he went before you. He found places for you to camp. He went before you in a fire at night and in a cloud during the day. He showed you which way to go.

[34] When the Lord heard what you said, he was angry. He made a promise. He said, [35] "I promised a good land to your ancestors. But none of you evil people will see it. [36] Only Caleb son of Jephunneh will see it. I will give him and his descendants[d] the land he walked on. I will do this because he followed me completely."

[37] Because of you, the Lord was also angry with me. He said to me, "You won't enter the land either. [38] But your assistant, Joshua son of Nun, will go there. Encourage Joshua, because he will lead Israel to take the land for their own."

[39] The Lord said to us, "You said your babies would be captured. But they will go into the land. They are too young to know right from wrong. So I will give the land to them. And they will take it for their own. [40] But you must turn around. Follow the desert road toward the Gulf of Aqaba."

[41] Then you said to me, "We have sinned against the Lord. But now we will go up and fight, as the Lord our God commanded us." Then all of you put on weapons. You thought it would be easy to go into the mountains.

[42] But the Lord said to me, "Tell them not to go up there and fight. I will not be with them. Their enemies will defeat them."

[43] So I told you, but you would not listen. You would not obey the Lord's command. You were proud. So you went on up into the mountains. [44] The Amorites who lived there came out and fought you. They chased you like bees. They defeated you from Edom to Hormah. [45] So you came back and cried to the Lord. But the Lord did not hear you. He refused to listen to you. [46] So you stayed in Kadesh a long time.

2 Then we turned around. And we traveled on the desert road toward the Gulf of Aqaba. That is what the Lord had told me to do. We traveled through the mountains of Edom for many days. [2] Then the Lord said to me, [3] "You have traveled through these mountains long enough. Turn north. [4] Tell the people this:

'You will soon go through the land of Edom. This land belongs to your relatives, the descendants[d] of Esau. They will be afraid of you. But be very careful. [5] Don't go to war against them. I am not giving you any of their land—not even a foot of it. I have given the mountains of Edom to Esau as his own. [6] You must pay them in silver for any food you eat or water you drink.'"

[7] The Lord your God has blessed everything you have done. He has protected you while you traveled through this large desert. The Lord your God has been with you for these 40 years. You have had everything you needed.

[8] So we passed by our relatives, the people of Esau who lived in Edom. We turned off the Jordan Valley road. It comes from the towns of Elath and Ezion Geber. And we traveled along the desert road of Moab.

[9] Then the Lord said to me, "Don't bother the people of Moab. Don't go to war against them. I am not giving you any of their land. I have given Ar to the descendants[d] of Lot." [10] (The Emites lived in Ar before. They were strong people, and there were many of them. They were very tall, like the Anakites.[d] [11] The Emites were thought to be Rephaites,[d] like the Anakites. But the Moabite people called them Emites. [12] The Horites also lived in Edom before. But the people of Esau forced them out. They destroyed the Horites and took their place. That is also what Israel did in the land the Lord gave them as their own.)

[13] And the Lord said to me, "Now get up and cross the Zered Valley." So we crossed the valley. [14] It had been 38 years since we left Kadesh Barnea until we crossed the Zered Valley. By then, all the fighting men from that time had died. This is what the Lord had promised would happen. [15] The Lord had continued to destroy them until they were all gone from the camp. [16] Now the last of those fighting men had died.

[17] Then the Lord said to me, [18] "Today you must go by Ar, on the border of Moab. [19] When you come near the people of Ammon, don't bother them. Don't go to war against them. I am not giving you their land. I have given that land to the descendants[d] of Lot."

[20] (That land was also thought to be a land of Rephaites. Those people used to live there. But the Ammonites called them Zamzummites. [21] They were strong

people, and there were many of them. They were very tall, like the Anakites. The Lord went before the Ammonites and destroyed the Zamzummites. The Ammonites forced them out of the land and took their place. ²²The Lord did the same thing for the descendants of Esau. They lived in Edom. He destroyed the Horites. The Edomites forced them out of the land and took their place. And they live there to this day. ²³The Caphtorite people came from Crete. They destroyed the Avvites. The Avvites lived in towns all the way to Gaza. But the Caphtorites destroyed them and took their place.)

²⁴The Lord said, "Get up. Cross the Arnon Ravine. See, I am giving you the power to defeat Sihon the Amorite. He is king of Heshbon. I am giving you his land. So fight against him and begin taking his land. ²⁵Today I will begin to make all the people in the world afraid of you. They will hear reports about you. And they will shake with fear. They will be terrified of you."

²⁶I sent messengers from the desert of Kedemoth to Sihon king of Heshbon. They offered him peace. They said, ²⁷"Let us pass through your country. We will stay on the road. We will not turn right or left. ²⁸We will pay you in silver for any food we eat or water we drink. We only want to walk through your country. ²⁹The descendants[d] of Esau in Edom let us go through their land. So did the Moabites in Ar. We want to cross the Jordan River into the land the Lord our God has given us." ³⁰But Sihon king of Heshbon would not let us pass. The Lord your God had made him stubborn. The Lord wanted you to defeat Sihon. And now this has happened.

³¹The Lord said to me, "See, I have begun to give Sihon and his country to you. Begin taking the land as your own." ³²Then Sihon and all his army came out. And they fought us at Jahaz. ³³But the Lord our God gave Sihon to us. We defeated him, his sons and all his army. ³⁴We captured all his cities. We completely destroyed them, the men, women and children. We left no one alive. ³⁵But we kept the cattle and valuable things from the cities for ourselves. ³⁶We defeated Aroer on the edge of the Arnon Ravine. And we defeated the town in the ravine, and even Gilead. No town was too strong for us. The Lord our God gave us all of them. ³⁷But you did not go near the land of the Ammonites. You did not go near the shores of the Jabbok River. You did not go near the towns in the mountains. This was what the Lord our God had commanded.

3 Then we turned and went up the road toward Bashan. Og king of Bashan and all his army came out to fight us at Edrei. ²The Lord said to me, "Don't be afraid of Og. I will hand him, his whole army and his land over to you. Do to him what you did to Sihon king of the Amorites, who ruled in Heshbon."

³So the Lord our God gave us Og king of Bashan and all his army. We defeated them and left no one alive. ⁴Then we captured all of Og's cities. We captured all 60 of them. We took the whole area of Argob, Og's kingdom in Bashan. ⁵All these were strong cities. They had high walls and gates with bars. And there were also many small towns with no walls. ⁶We completely destroyed them. We destroyed them just like the cities of Sihon king of Heshbon. We killed all the men, women and children. ⁷But we kept all the cattle and valuable things from the cities for ourselves.

⁸So at that time we took the land east of the Jordan River. We took it from these two Amorite kings. It went from the Arnon Ravine to Mount Hermon. ⁹(Hermon is called Sirion by the Sidonian people. The Amorites call it Senir.) ¹⁰We captured all the cities on the high plain and all of Gilead. We took all of Bashan as far as Salecah and Edrei. These were towns in Og's kingdom of Bashan. ¹¹(Only Og king of Bashan was left of the few Rephaites.[d] His bed was made of iron. It was more than 13 feet long and 6 feet wide! It is still in the Ammonite city of Rabbah.)

¹²At that time we took this land to be our own. I gave the people of Reuben and Gad the land from Aroer by the Arnon Ravine. And I gave them half of the mountain country of Gilead and the cities in it. ¹³To the eastern half-tribe of Manasseh I gave the rest of Gilead. And I gave them all of Bashan, the kingdom of Og. (The area of Argob in Bashan was called the land of the Rephaites.[d] ¹⁴Jair, a descendant[d] of Manasseh, took the whole area of Argob. It went to the border of the Geshurites and Maacathites. That land was named for Jair. So even today Bashan is called the Towns of Jair.) ¹⁵I gave Gilead to Makir. ¹⁶I gave the Reubenites and the Gadites the land that begins at Gilead. It goes from the Arnon Ravine to the Jabbok River. (The

middle of the Arnon is the border.) The Jabbok River is the Ammonite border. [17] The border on the west was the Jordan River in the Jordan Valley. It goes from Lake Galilee to the Dead Sea[d] west of Mount Pisgah.

[18] At that time I gave you this command: "The Lord your God has given you this land as your own. Now your fighting men must take their weapons. And you must lead the other Israelites across the river. [19] Your wives, your young children and your cattle may stay here. I know you have many cattle. They may stay here in the cities I have given you. [20] Some day your Israelite relatives will also have a place to rest. They will receive the land the Lord your God has given them. It is on the other side of the Jordan River. After that, you may each return to the land I have given you."

[21] Then I gave this command to Joshua: "You have seen for yourself what the Lord your God has done to these two kings. The Lord will do the same thing to all the kingdoms where you are going. [22] Don't be afraid of them. The Lord your God will fight for you."

[23] Then I begged the Lord: [24] "Lord God, you have begun to show me, your servant, how great you are. You have great strength. No other god in heaven or earth can do the powerful things you do. There is no other god like you. [25] Please let me cross the Jordan River. I want to see the beautiful mountains and Lebanon."

[26] But the Lord was angry with me because of you. He would not listen to me. The Lord said to me, "That's enough. Don't talk to me anymore about it. [27] Climb to the top of Mount Pisgah. Look west, north, south and east. You can look at the land. But you will not cross the Jordan River. [28] Appoint Joshua. Help him be brave and strong. He will lead the people across the river. He will give them the land that they are to inherit. You can only look at it." [29] So we stayed in the valley opposite Beth Peor.

4 Now, Israel, listen to the laws and commands I will teach you. Obey them so you will live. Then you will go over and take the land. The Lord, the God of your ancestors, is giving it to you. [2] Don't add to these commands. And don't leave anything out. But obey the commands of the Lord your God that I give you.

[3] You have seen for yourselves what the Lord did at Baal Peor. The Lord your God destroyed everyone among you who followed Baal[d] in Peor. [4] But you continued to follow the Lord your God. So you are still alive today.

[5] Look, I have taught you the laws and rules the Lord my God commanded me. Now you can obey the laws in the land you are entering. It is the land you will own. [6] Obey these laws carefully. This will show the other nations that you have wisdom and understanding. They will hear about these laws. And they will say, "This great nation of Israel is wise and understanding." [7] No other nation is as great as we are. Their gods do not come near them. But the Lord our God comes near when we pray to him. [8] And no other nation has such good teachings and commands. I am giving them to you today.

[9] But be careful! Watch out. Don't forget the things that you have seen. Don't forget them as long as you live. Teach them to your children and grandchildren. [10] Remember the day you stood before the Lord your God at Mount Sinai. He said to me, "Bring the people together to listen to what I say. Then they will respect me as long as they live in the land. And they will teach these things to their children." [11] Then you came and stood at the bottom of the mountain. It blazed with fire that reached to the sky. Black clouds made it very dark. [12] Then the Lord spoke to you from the fire. You heard the sound of words. But you did not see him. There was only a voice. [13] The Lord told you about his agreement. It was the Ten Commandments. And he told you to obey them. Then he wrote them on two stone tablets. [14] Then the Lord commanded me to teach you the laws and rules. You must obey them in the land you will own when you cross the Jordan River.

[15] The Lord spoke to you from the fire at Mount Sinai. But you did not see him. So watch yourselves carefully! [16] Don't sin by making idols of any kind. Don't make statues of men or women. [17] Don't make statues of animals on earth or birds that fly in the air. [18] Don't make statues of anything that crawls on the ground. Don't make statues of fish in the water below. [19] When you look up at the sky, you see the sun, moon and stars. You can see everything in the sky. But don't bow down and worship them. The Lord your God has made these things for all people everywhere. [20] Egypt tested

you like a furnace for melting iron. The Lord brought you out of Egypt. And he made you his very own people, as you are now.

²¹The Lord was angry with me because of you. He made a strong promise that I would not cross the Jordan River. I could not go into the good land the Lord your God is giving you to own. ²²I will die here in this land. I will not cross the Jordan. But you will soon go across and take that good land. ²³Be careful. Don't forget the agreement of the Lord your God that he made with you. Don't make any idols for yourselves. The Lord your God has commanded you not to do that. ²⁴The Lord your God is a jealous God. He is like a fire that burns things up.

²⁵You will live in the land a long time. You will have children and grandchildren. Even after that, don't do evil things. Don't make any kind of idol. Don't do what the Lord says is evil. That will make him angry. ²⁶I will ask heaven and earth to speak against you that day. Then you will quickly be removed from this land. You are crossing the Jordan River to take the land. But you will not live there long after that. You will be completely destroyed. ²⁷The Lord will scatter you among the other nations. Only a few of you will be left alive. And those few will be in other nations where the Lord will send you. ²⁸There you will worship gods made by men. They will be made of wood and stone. They cannot see, hear, eat or smell. ²⁹But even there you can look for the Lord your God. And you will find him if you look. But you must look for him with your whole being. ³⁰It will be hard when all these things happen to you. But after that you will come back to the Lord your God. You will obey him. ³¹The Lord your God is a merciful God. He will not leave you or destroy you. He will not forget the agreement he made with your ancestors. He made that agreement sure with his strong promise.

³²Nothing like this has ever happened before! Look at the past, long before you were even born. Go all the way back to when God made man on the earth. Look from one end of heaven to the other. Nothing like this has ever been heard of! ³³No other people have ever heard God speak from a fire and still lived. But you have. ³⁴No other god has ever taken for himself one nation out of another. But the Lord your God did this for you in Egypt. He did it right before your own eyes. He did it with tests, signs, miracles,ᵈ war and great sights. He did it by his great power and strength.

³⁵He showed you things so you would know that the Lord is God. There is no other God besides him. ³⁶He spoke to you from heaven to teach you. He showed you his great fire on earth. And you heard him speak from the fire. ³⁷The Lord loved your ancestors. That is why he chose you, their descendants.ᵈ He brought you out of Egypt himself by his great strength. ³⁸He forced nations out of their land ahead of you. And these nations were bigger and stronger than you were. But the Lord brought you into their land and gave it to you to own. And this land is yours today.

³⁹Know and believe today that the Lord is God. He is God in heaven above and on the earth below. There is no other god! ⁴⁰Obey his laws and commands, which I am giving you today. Obey them so that things will go well for you and your children. Then you will live a long time in this land. The Lord your God is giving it to you forever.

⁴¹Moses chose three cities east of the Jordan River. ⁴²A person who killed someone accidentally could go there. He did not hate the person he killed. So he could save his life by running to one of these cities. ⁴³These were the cities: Bezer in the desert high plain was for the Reubenites; Ramoth in Gilead was for the Gadites; Golan in Bashan was for the Manassites.

⁴⁴These are the teachings Moses gave to the people of Israel. ⁴⁵They are the rules, commands and laws he gave them when they came out of Egypt. ⁴⁶They were in the valley near Beth Peor. That is east of the Jordan River in the land of Sihon. Sihon was king of the Amorites. He ruled in Heshbon. He was defeated by Moses and the Israelites as they came out of Egypt. ⁴⁷The Israelites captured his land. They also took the land of Og king of Bashan. These were the two Amorite kings east of the Jordan River. ⁴⁸This land went from Aroer to Mount Hermon. Aroer is on the edge of the Arnon Ravine. ⁴⁹It included all the Jordan Valley east of the Jordan River. And it went as far as the Dead Seaᵈ below Mount Pisgah.

5 Moses called all the people of Israel together and said: Listen, Israel, to the commands and laws I give you today. Learn them and obey them carefully. [2]The Lord our God made an agreement with us at Mount Sinai. [3]He did not make this agreement with our ancestors. He made it with us. He made it with all of us who are alive here today. [4]The Lord spoke to you face to face. He spoke from the fire on the mountain. [5](At that time I stood between you and the Lord. I told you what the Lord said. You were afraid of the fire. So you would not go up on the mountain.) The Lord said:

[6]"I am the Lord your God. I brought you out of the land of Egypt where you were slaves.

[7]"You must not have any other gods except me.

[8]"You must not make for yourselves any idols. Don't make something that looks like anything in the sky above or on the earth below or in the water below the land. [9]You must not worship or serve any idol. This is because I, the Lord your God, am a jealous God. A person may sin against me and hate me. I will punish his children, even his grandchildren and great-grandchildren. [10]But I will be very kind to thousands who love me and obey my commands.

[11]"You must not use the name of the Lord your God thoughtlessly. The Lord will punish anyone who is guilty and misuses his name.

[12]"Keep the Sabbath[c] as a holy day. The Lord your God has commanded you to do this. [13]You may work and get everything done during six days each week. [14]But the seventh day is a day of rest to honor the Lord your God. On that day no one may do any work: not you, your son or daughter, or your men or women slaves. Neither your ox, your donkey nor any of your animals may work. The foreigners living in your cities may not work. That way your servants may rest as you do. [15]Remember that you were slaves in Egypt. The Lord your God brought you out of Egypt by his great power and strength. So the Lord your God has commanded you to rest on the Sabbath day.

[16]"Honor your father and your mother. The Lord your God has commanded you to do this. Then you will live a long time. And things will go well for you in the land. The Lord your God is going to give you this land.

[17]"You must not murder anyone.

[18]"You must not be guilty of adultery.[d]

[19]"You must not steal.

[20]"You must not tell lies about your neighbor in court.

[21]"You must not want to take your neighbor's wife. You must not want to take your neighbor's house or land. You must not want to take his men or women slaves. You must not want to take his ox or his donkey. You must not want to take anything that belongs to your neighbor."

[22]The Lord gave these commands to all of you on the mountain. He spoke them in a loud voice out of the fire. He spoke from the cloud and the deep darkness. He did not say anything else. Then he wrote them on two stone tablets. And he gave them to me.

[23]You heard the voice from the darkness. The mountain was blazing with fire. Then all your older leaders and leaders of your tribes[d] came to me. [24]And you said, "The Lord our God has shown us his glory and majesty. We have heard his voice from the fire. Today we have seen that a person can live even if God speaks to him. [25]But now, we will die! This great fire will burn us up. And we will die if we hear the Lord our God speak anymore. [26]No human being has ever heard the living God speaking from a fire and still lived. But we have. [27]Moses, you go near and listen to everything the Lord our God says. Then you tell us what the Lord our God tells you. We will listen and obey."

[28]The Lord heard what you said to me. And he said to me, "I have heard what the people said to you. Everything they said was good. [29]I wish their hearts would always respect me. I wish they would always obey my commands. Then things would go well for them and their children forever!

[30]"Go and tell the people to return to their tents. [31]But you stay here with me. I will give you all the commands, rules and laws. Teach the people to obey them in the land I am giving them to own."

[32]So be careful. Do what the Lord your God has commanded you. You must follow the commands exactly. [33]Live the way the Lord your God has commanded you. Then you will live and be successful. You will live a long time in the land you will own.

6 These are the commands, rules and laws of the Lord your God. He told me to teach them to you. Obey them in the land you are crossing the Jordan River to own. [2]You, your children and grandchildren must respect the Lord your God. You must do this as long as you live. Obey all his rules and commands I give you. Then you will live a long time. [3]Listen, Israel, and carefully obey these laws. Then all will go well for you. You will become a great nation in a land where much food grows. The Lord, the God of your ancestors, has promised it to you.

[4]Listen, people of Israel! The Lord is our God. He is the only Lord. [5]Love the Lord your God with all your heart, soul and strength. [6]Always remember these commands I give you today. [7]Teach them to your children. Talk about them when you sit at home and walk along the road. Talk about them when you lie down and when you get up. [8]Write them down and tie them to your hands as a sign. Tie them on your forehead to remind you. [9]Write them on your doors and gates.

[10]The Lord your God will bring you into the land. He promised it to your ancestors, to Abraham, Isaac and Jacob. He will give it to you. The land has large, growing cities you did not build. [11]The houses there are full of good things that you did not buy. They have wells you did not dig. There are vineyards and olive trees you did not plant. You will eat as much as you want. [12]But be careful! Do not forget the Lord. He brought you out of the land of Egypt where you were slaves.

[13]Respect the Lord your God. Serve only him. Make your promises in his name. [14]Do not worship other gods as the people around you do. [15]The Lord your God is a jealous God. He is present with you. If you worship other gods, he will become angry with you. And he will destroy you from the earth. [16]Do not test the Lord your God as you did at Massah. [17]Be sure to obey the commands of the Lord your God. Obey the rules and laws he has given you. [18]Do what the Lord says is good and right. Then things will go well for you. Then you may go in and take the good land the Lord promised to your ancestors. [19]He will force all your enemies out as you go in. This is what the Lord has said.

[20]In the future your son will ask you, "What do the laws, commands and rules the Lord our God gave us mean?" [21]Tell him, "We were slaves to the king of Egypt. But the Lord brought us out of Egypt by his great power. [22]The Lord showed us great and terrible signs and miracles.[d] He did them to Egypt, the king and his whole family. [23]The Lord brought us out of Egypt. He led us here.

And he will give us the land he promised our ancestors. [24]The Lord ordered us to obey all these commands. And we must respect the Lord our God. Then we will always do well and stay alive as we are today. [25]The right thing for us to do is this: Obey all these rules in the presence of the Lord our God. He has commanded it."

7 The Lord your God will bring you into the land. You are entering that land to own it. As you go in, he will force out these nations: the Hittites, Girgashites, Amorites, Canaanites, Perizzites, Hivites and Jebusites. These seven nations are stronger than you. [2]The Lord your God will hand these nations over to you. You will defeat them. You must destroy them completely. Do not make a peace treaty with them. Do not show them any mercy. [3]Do not marry any of them. Don't let your daughters marry their sons. And don't let your sons marry their daughters. [4]Those people will turn your children away from me. Your children will begin serving other gods. The Lord will be very angry with you. And he will quickly destroy you. [5]This is what you must do to those people: Tear down their altars. Smash their holy stone pillars. Cut down their Asherah[d] idols and burn their idols in the fire. [6]You are holy people. You belong to the Lord your God. He has chosen you from all the people on earth. You are his very own.

[7]The Lord did not care for you and choose you because there were many of you. You are the smallest nation of all. [8]But the Lord chose you because he loved you. And he kept his promise to your ancestors. So he brought you out of Egypt by his great power. He brought you back from the land of slavery. He bought you back from the power of the king of Egypt. [9]So know that the Lord your God is God. He is the faithful God. He will keep his agreement of love for a thousand lifetimes. He does this for people who love him and obey his commands. [10]But he will pay back those people who hate him. He will destroy them. And he will not be slow to pay back those who hate him. [11]So be careful to obey the commands, rules and laws I give you today.

[12]Pay attention to these laws. Obey them carefully. Then the Lord your God will keep his agreement and show his love to you. He promised your ancestors he would. [13]He will love and bless you.

He will make the number of your people grow. He will bless you with children. He will bless your fields with good crops. He will give you grain, new wine and oil. He will bless your cows with calves and your sheep with lambs. This is the way it will be in the land he promised your ancestors he would give you. [14] You will be blessed more than any other people. Every husband and wife will have children. All your cattle will have calves. [15] The Lord will take away all disease from you. You will not have the terrible diseases that were in Egypt. But he will give them to your enemies. [16] You must destroy all the people the Lord your God hands over to you. Do not feel sorry for them. Do not worship their gods. They will trap you.

[17] You might say to yourselves, "These nations are stronger than we are. We can't force them out." [18] But don't be afraid of them. Remember what the Lord your God did to all of Egypt and its king. [19] You saw for yourselves the troubles, signs and miracles[d] he did. You saw how the Lord's great power and strength brought you out of Egypt. The Lord your God will do the same thing to all the nations you now fear. [20] The Lord your God will also send hornets to attack them. Even those who are alive and hiding from you will die. [21] Don't be afraid of them. The Lord your God is with you. He is a great God and people are afraid of him. [22] The Lord your God will force those nations out of the land. They will leave little by little ahead of you. Don't destroy them all at once. Otherwise, the wild animals will grow too many in number. [23] But the Lord your God will hand those nations over to you. He will confuse them until they are destroyed. [24] The Lord will help you defeat their kings. The world will forget who they were. No one will be able to stop you. You will destroy them all. [25] Burn up their idols in the fire. Do not wish for the silver and gold on them. Don't take it for yourselves, or you will be trapped by it. The Lord your God hates it. [26] Do not bring one of those hated things into your house. If you do, you will be completely destroyed along with it. Hate and reject those things. They must be completely destroyed.

8 Carefully obey every command I give you today. Then you will live and grow in number. And you will enter and own the land the Lord promised your ancestors. [2] Remember how the Lord your God has led you in the desert for these 40 years. He took away your pride. He tested you. He wanted to know what was in your heart. He wanted to know if you would obey his commands. [3] He took away your pride. He let you get hungry. Then he fed you with manna.[d] Manna was something neither you nor your ancestors had ever seen. This was to teach you that a person does not live only by eating bread. But a person lives by everything the Lord says. [4] During these 40 years, your clothes did not wear out. And your feet did not swell. [5] Know in your heart that the Lord your God corrects you. He corrects you as a father does his son.

[6] Obey the commands of the Lord your God. Live as he has commanded you and respect him. [7] The Lord your God is bringing you into a good land. The land has rivers and pools of water. Springs flow in the valleys and hills. [8] The land has wheat and barley, vines, fig trees, pomegranates,[d] olive oil and honey. [9] It is a land where you will have plenty of food. You will have everything you need there. The rocks are iron. You can dig copper out of the hills.

[10] You will have all you want to eat. Then praise the Lord your God. He has given you a good land. [11] Be careful not to forget the Lord your God. Do not fail to obey his commands, laws and rules. I am giving them to you today. [12] You will eat all you want. You will build nice houses and live in them. [13] Your herds of cattle and flocks of sheep will grow large. Your silver and gold will grow. You will have more of everything. [14] Then your heart will become proud. You will forget the Lord your God. He brought you out of the land of Egypt, where you were slaves. [15] He led you through the large and terrible desert. It was dry and had no water. It had poisonous snakes and stinging insects. He gave you water from a solid rock. [16] He gave you manna to eat in the desert. Manna was something your ancestors had never seen. He did this to take away your pride and to test you. He did it so things would go well for you in the end. [17] You might say to yourself, "I am rich because of my own strength and power." [18] But remember the Lord your God! It is he who gives you the power to become rich. He keeps the agreement he promised to your ancestors. So it is today.

[19] Never forget the Lord your God. Do not follow other gods. Do not worship

them. Do not bow down to them. If you do, I warn you today that you will be destroyed. [20]The Lord destroyed the other nations for you. And you can be destroyed the same way if you do not obey the Lord your God.

9 Listen, Israel. You will soon cross the Jordan River. You will go in to force out nations that are bigger and stronger than you. They have large cities with walls up to the sky. [2]The people there are Anakites.[d] They are strong and tall. You know about them. You have heard it said: "No one can stop the Anakites." [3]But today remember that the Lord your God goes in before you. He will destroy them like a fire that burns things up. He will defeat them ahead of you. And you will force them out. You will destroy them quickly. It will happen just as the Lord has said.

[4]The Lord your God will force those nations out ahead of you. After that, don't say to yourself, "The Lord brought me here. I own this land because I am so good." No! It is because these nations are evil. That is why the Lord will force them out ahead of you. [5]You are going in to own the land. But it is not because you are good and honest. It is because these nations are evil. That is why the Lord your God will force them out ahead of you. The Lord will keep his promise to your ancestors, to Abraham, Isaac and Jacob. [6]The Lord your God is giving you this good land to own. But know this: It is not because you are good. You are a stubborn people.

[7]Remember this. Do not forget it. You made the Lord your God angry in the desert. You would not obey the Lord from the day you left Egypt until you arrived here. [8]At Mount Sinai you made the Lord angry. He was angry enough to destroy you. [9]I went up on the mountain to receive the stone tablets. The tablets were the agreement the Lord had made with you. I stayed on the mountain for 40 days and 40 nights. I did not eat bread or drink water. [10]The Lord gave me two stone tablets. God had written on them with his own finger. On them were all the commands of the Lord. He gave them to you on the mountain out of the fire. This was on the day you were gathered there.

[11]Then the 40 days and 40 nights were over. And the Lord gave me the two stone tablets. Those tablets had the agreement on them. [12]Then the Lord told me, "Get up. Go down quickly from here. The people you brought out from Egypt are ruining themselves. They have quickly turned away from what I commanded. They have made an idol for themselves."

[13]The Lord said to me, "I have watched these people. They are very stubborn! [14]Get away. I will destroy them. I will make the whole world forget who they are. Then I will make another nation from you. It will be bigger and stronger than they are."

[15]So I turned and came down the mountain. The mountain was burning with fire. And the two stone tablets with the agreement were in my hands. [16]When I looked, I saw you had sinned against the Lord your God. You had made an idol in the shape of a calf. You had quickly turned away from what the Lord had told you to do. [17]So I took the two stone tablets and threw them down. I broke them into pieces right in front of you.

[18]Then I again bowed facedown on the ground before the Lord. I did this for 40 days and 40 nights. I did not eat bread or drink water. You had sinned by doing what the Lord said was evil. You made him angry. [19]I was afraid of the Lord's anger and rage. He was angry enough with you to destroy you. But the Lord listened to me again. [20]And the Lord was angry enough with Aaron to destroy him. But then I prayed for Aaron, too. [21]I took that sinful calf idol you had made. And I burned it in the fire. I crushed it into a powder like dust. And I threw the dust into a stream that flowed down the mountain.

[22]You also made the Lord angry at Taberah, Massah and Kibroth Hattaavah.

[23]Then the Lord sent you away from Kadesh Barnea. He said, "Go up and take the land I have given you." But you would not obey the command of the Lord your God. You did not trust him or obey him. [24]You have refused to obey the Lord as long as I have known you.

[25]The Lord had said he would destroy you. So I threw myself down in front of him for those 40 days and 40 nights. [26]I prayed to the Lord. I said, "Lord God, do not destroy your people. They are your own people. You freed them and brought them out of Egypt by your great power and strength. [27]Remember your servants Abraham, Isaac and Jacob. Don't look at how stubborn these people are. Don't look at their sin and evil.

28Otherwise, Egypt will say, 'The Lord was not able to take his people into the land he promised them. He hated them. So he took them into the desert to kill them.' 29But they are your people, Lord. They are your own people. You brought them out of Egypt with your great power and strength."

10At that time the Lord said to me, "Cut two stone tablets like the first ones. Then come up to me on the mountain. Also make a wooden box. 2I will write on the tablets the same words that were on the first tablets, which you broke. Put the new tablets in the box."

3So I made the box out of acacia wood. And I cut out two stone tablets like the first ones. Then I went up on the mountain. I had the two tablets in my hands. 4The Lord wrote the same things on these tablets he had written before. He wrote the Ten Commandments. He had told them to you on the mountain from the fire. This was on the day you were gathered there. And the Lord gave them to me. 5Then I turned and came down the mountain. I put the tablets in the box I had made. That is what the Lord commanded. The tablets are still there in the box.

6(The people of Israel went from the wells of the Jaakanites to Moserah. There Aaron died and was buried. Aaron's son Eleazar became priest in Aaron's place. 7From Moserah they went to Gudgodah. From Gudgodah they went to Jotbathah, a place with streams of water. 8At that time the Lord chose the tribe^d of Levi. They were to carry the Box^d of the Agreement with the Lord. They were to serve the Lord. They were to bless the people in the Lord's name. They still do this today. 9That is why the Levites did not receive any land to own. Instead, they received the Lord himself as their gift. This is what the Lord your God told them.)

10I stayed on the mountain 40 days and 40 nights just like the first time. And the Lord listened to me this time also. He did not want to destroy you. 11The Lord said to me, "Go. Lead the people. They will go in and take the land I promised their ancestors."

12Now, Israel, this is what the Lord wants you to do. Respect the Lord your God. Do what he has told you to do. Love him. Serve the Lord your God with your whole being. 13And obey the Lord's commands and laws. I am giving them to you today for your own good.

14The Lord owns the world and everything in it. The heavens, even the highest heavens, are his. 15But the Lord cared for and loved your ancestors. And he chose you, their descendants.^d He chose you over all the other nations. And it is this way today. 16Give yourselves to serving the Lord. Do not be stubborn any longer. 17The Lord your God is God of all gods. He is the Lord of all lords. He is the great God. He is strong and wonderful. He does not take sides. And he will not be talked into doing evil. 18He helps orphans and widows. He loves foreigners. He gives them food and clothes. 19You also must love foreigners, because you were foreigners in Egypt. 20Respect the Lord your God and serve him. Be loyal to him. Make your promises in his name. 21You should praise him. He is your God. He has done great and wonderful things for you. You have seen them with your own eyes. 22There were only 70 of your ancestors when they went down to Egypt. Now the Lord your God has made you as many as the stars in the sky.

11Love the Lord your God. Obey his orders, rules, laws and commands. 2Remember today it was not your children who saw and felt the correction of the Lord your God. They did not see his majesty, his power and his strength. 3They did not see his signs and the things he did in Egypt to the king and his whole country. 4They did not see what he did to the Egyptian army, its horses and chariots. He drowned them in the Red Sea^d when they were chasing you. The Lord ruined them forever. 5They did not see what he did for you in the desert until you arrived here. 6They did not see what he did to Dathan and Abiram, the sons of Eliab the Reubenite. The ground opened up and swallowed them, their families and their tents. And it swallowed up everyone who stood with them in Israel. 7It was you who saw all these great things the Lord has done.

8So obey all the commands I am giving you today. Then you will be strong. Then you can go in and take the land you are going to own. 9Then you will live a long time in that land. The Lord promised to give it to your ancestors and their descendants.^d It is a land where much food grows. 10The land you are going to take is not like Egypt, where you were. There you had to plant your seed. Then you had to water it, like a vegetable garden, by using your feet.

¹¹But you will soon cross the Jordan River and take the land. It is a land of hills and valleys. It drinks rain from heaven. ¹²It is a land the Lord your God loves. His eyes are on it continually. He watches it from the beginning of the year to the end.

¹³Carefully obey the commands I am giving you today. Love the Lord your God. Serve him with your whole being. ¹⁴Then he will send rain on your land at the right time, in the fall and spring. You will be able to gather your grain, new wine and oil. ¹⁵He will put grass in the fields for your cattle. You will have plenty to eat.

¹⁶Be careful. Don't be fooled. Don't turn away and serve other gods. Don't worship them. ¹⁷If you do, the Lord will become angry with you. He will shut the heavens so it will not rain. Then the land will not grow crops. And you will soon die in the good land the Lord is giving you. ¹⁸Remember my words in your hearts and souls. Write them down and tie them to your hands as a sign. Tie them on your foreheads to remind you. ¹⁹Teach them well to your children. Talk about them when you sit at home and walk along the road. Talk about them when you lie down and when you get up. ²⁰Write them on your doors and gates. ²¹Then both you and your children will live a long time in the land. This is the land the Lord promised your ancestors. You will live there for as long as the skies are above the earth.

²²Be careful to obey every command I am giving you to follow. Love the Lord your God. Do what he has told you to do. And be loyal to him. ²³Then the Lord will force all those nations out of the land ahead of you. And you will take the land from nations that are bigger and stronger than you. ²⁴Everywhere you step will be yours. Your land will go from the desert to Lebanon. And it will go from the Euphrates River to the Mediterranean Sea. ²⁵No one will be able to stop you. The Lord your God will do what he promised. He will make the people afraid everywhere you go.

²⁶See, today I am letting you choose a blessing or a curse. ²⁷You will be blessed if you obey the commands of the Lord your God. I am giving them to you today. ²⁸But you will be cursed if you disobey the commands of the Lord your God. So do not disobey the commands I am giving you today. Do not worship other gods you do not know. ²⁹The Lord your God will bring you into the land you will own. Then you are to announce the blessings from Mount Gerizim. Announce the curses from Mount Ebal. ³⁰These mountains are on the other side of the Jordan River. They are west, toward the sunset. They are near the great trees of Moreh. They are in the land of the Canaanites who live in the Jordan Valley opposite Gilgal. ³¹You will soon cross the Jordan River. You will enter and take the land the Lord your God is giving you. You will take it over and live there. ³²Then be careful to obey all the commands and laws I am giving you today.

12 These are the commands and laws you must carefully obey in the land the Lord your God is giving you. Obey them as long as you live in the land. ²You will inherit the lands of these nations. You must completely destroy all the places where they serve their gods. These places are on high mountains and hills and under every green tree. ³Tear down their altars. Smash their holy stone pillars. Burn their Asherah*d* idols. Cut down their idols. Destroy their names from those places.

⁴Don't worship the Lord your God that way. ⁵But look for the place the Lord your God will choose. He will choose a place among your tribes*d* where he is to be worshiped. Go there. ⁶Bring to that place your burnt offerings and sacrifices. Bring a tenth of what you gain and your special gifts. Bring what you have promised and the special gifts you want to give the Lord. And bring the first animals born to your herds and flocks.

⁷There you will be together with the Lord your God. There you and your families will eat. And you will enjoy all the good things for which you have worked. The Lord your God has blessed you.

⁸Do not worship the way we have been doing today. Each person does what he thinks is right. ⁹You have not yet come to a resting place. The Lord your God will give you your own land. ¹⁰But you will soon cross the Jordan River. And you will live in the land the Lord your God is giving you to own. And he will give you rest from all your enemies. You will live in safety. ¹¹Then the Lord your God will choose a place where he is to be worshiped. To that place you must bring everything I tell you: your burnt offerings and sacrifices, your offerings of a tenth of what you gain, your special gifts and all your best

things you promised to the Lord. [12]There rejoice before the Lord your God. Everyone should rejoice: you, your sons and daughters, your male and female servants, and the Levites from your towns, who have no land of their own. [13]Be careful. Don't sacrifice your burnt offerings just anywhere you please. [14]Offer them only in the place the Lord will choose. He will choose a place in one of your tribes. And there you must do everything I am commanding you.

[15]But you may kill your animals in any of your towns. And you may eat as much of the meat as you want. Eat it as if it were a deer or a gazelle. This is the blessing the Lord your God is giving you. Anyone, clean or unclean, may eat this meat. [16]But do not eat the blood. Pour it out on the ground like water. [17]Do not eat in your own towns what belongs to the Lord: one-tenth of your grain, new wine or oil; the first animals born to your herds or flocks; whatever you have promised to give; the special gifts you want to give to the Lord, or any other gifts. [18]Eat these things when you are together with the Lord. Eat them in the place the Lord your God chooses to be worshiped. Everyone must do this: you, your sons and daughters, your male and female servants, and the Levites from your towns. Rejoice in the Lord's presence about the things you have worked for. [19]Be careful not to forget the Levites as long as you live in the land.

[20]The Lord your God will enlarge your country as he has promised. And you will want some meat. You will say, "I want some meat." Eat as much meat as you want. [21]The Lord your God will choose a place where he is to be worshiped. But it may be too far away from you. If it is, you may kill animals from your herds and flocks. The Lord has given them to you. I have commanded that you may do this. You may eat as much of them as you want in your own towns. [22]Eat them as you would eat gazelle or deer meat. Both clean and unclean people may eat this meat. [23]But be sure you don't eat the blood. The life is in the blood. Don't eat the life with the meat. [24]Don't eat the blood. Pour it out on the ground like water. [25]Don't eat it. Then things will go well for you and your children. You will be doing what the Lord says is right.

[26]Take your holy things and the things you have promised to give. And go to the place the Lord will choose. [27]Present your burnt offerings on the altar of the Lord your God. Offer both the meat and the blood. The blood of your sacrifices should be poured beside the altar. But you may eat the meat. [28]Be careful to obey all the rules I am giving you. Then things will always go well for you and your children. You will be doing what the Lord your God says is good and right.

[29]You will enter the land and take it away from the nations there. The Lord your God will destroy those nations ahead of you. You will force them out and live in their land. [30]They will be destroyed for you. Be careful not to be trapped by asking about their gods. Don't say, "How do these nations worship? I will do the same." [31]Don't worship the Lord your God that way. The Lord hates the evil ways they worship their gods. They even burn their sons and daughters as sacrifices to their gods!

[32]Be sure to do everything I have commanded you. Do not add anything to it. And do not take anything away from it.

13 A prophet[d] or someone who tells the future with dreams might come to you. He might say he will show you a miracle[d] or a sign. [2]The miracle or sign might even happen. Then he might say, "Let's serve other gods." (These are gods you have not known.) "And let's worship them." [3]But you must not listen to that prophet or dreamer. The Lord your God is testing you. He is finding out if you love him with your whole being. [4]Serve only the Lord your God. Respect him. Keep his commands and obey him. Serve him and be loyal to him. [5]That prophet or dreamer must be killed. He said you should turn against the Lord your God. The Lord brought you out of Egypt. He saved you from the land where you were slaves. That prophet tried to turn you from doing what the Lord your God commanded you to do. You must get rid of the evil among you.

[6]Some relative might try to lead you to serve other gods. It might be your brother, your son or daughter or the wife you love. Or it might be a close friend. He might say, "Let's go and worship other gods." (These are gods that neither you nor your ancestors have known. [7]They are gods of the people who live around you. Some are nearby, and some are far away. They are from one end of the land to the other.) [8]Do not give in to him. Do not listen. Do not feel sorry for

him. Do not let him go free or protect him. [9]You must put him to death. You must be the first one to start to kill him. Then everyone else must join in. [10]You must throw stones at him until he dies. He tried to turn you away from the Lord your God. The Lord brought you out of the land of Egypt, where you were slaves. [11]Then everyone in Israel will hear about this. And they will be afraid. No one among you will ever do such an evil thing again.

[12]The Lord your God is giving you cities in which to live. You might hear something about one of them. Someone might say [13]that evil men have moved in among you. And they might lead the people of that city away from God. They might say, "Let's go and worship other gods." (These are gods you have not known.) [14]Then you must ask about it. Look into the matter and check carefully. It might be true. It may be proved that a terrible thing has happened among you. [15]If it has, then you must kill with a sword everyone who lives in that city. Destroy the city completely. Kill everyone in it, as well as the animals, with a sword. [16]Gather up everything those people owned. Put it in the middle of the city square. Then completely burn the city and everything they owned. It will be a burnt offering to the Lord your God. That city should never be rebuilt. Let it be ruined forever. [17]Don't keep any of the things found in that city for yourselves. Then the Lord will not be angry anymore. He will give you mercy. He will feel sorry for you. And he will make your nation grow larger. He promised this to your ancestors. [18]You will have obeyed the Lord your God. You will be keeping all his commands. I am giving them to you today. And you will be doing what the Lord says is right.

14 You are the children of the Lord your God. When someone dies, do not cut yourselves or shave your heads to show your sadness. [2]You are holy people. You belong to the Lord your God. He has chosen you from all the people on earth to be his very own.

[3]Do not eat anything the Lord hates. [4]These are the animals you may eat: ox, sheep, goats, [5]deer, gazelle, roe deer, wild goats, ibex, antelope and mountain sheep. [6]You may eat any animal that has a split hoof and chews the cud.[d] [7]But you may not eat camels, rabbits or rock badgers. These animals chew the cud, but their feet are not divided. So they

are unclean[d] for you. [8]Pigs are also unclean for you. They have split hoofs, but they do not chew the cud. Do not eat their meat or touch their dead bodies.

[9]There are many things that live in the water. You may eat anything that has fins and scales. [10]But do not eat anything that does not have fins and scales. It is unclean for you.

[11]You may eat any clean bird. [12]But do not eat these birds: eagles, vultures, black vultures, [13]red kites, falcons, any kind of kite, [14]any kind of raven, [15]horned owls, screech owls, seagulls, any kind of hawk, [16]little owls, great owls, white owls, [17]desert owls, ospreys, cormorants, [18]storks, any kind of heron, the hoopoes or bats.

[19]All insects with wings are unclean for you. Do not eat them. [20]Other things with wings are clean. You may eat them.

[21]Do not eat anything you find that is already dead. You may give it to a foreigner living in your town. He may eat it. Or you may sell it to a foreigner. But you are holy people. You belong to the Lord your God.

Do not cook a baby goat in its mother's milk.

[22]Be sure to save one-tenth of all your crops each year. [23]Take it to the place the Lord your God will choose where he is to be worshiped. There you will be together with the Lord. There eat the tenth of your grain, new wine and oil. And eat the animals born first to your herds and flocks. Then you will learn to respect the Lord your God always. [24]But the place the Lord will choose to be worshiped might be too far away. And he may have blessed you so much you cannot carry a tenth. [25]If so, exchange your one-tenth for silver. Then take the silver with you to the place the Lord your God shall choose. [26]Use the silver to buy anything you wish. You may buy cattle, sheep, wine, beer or anything you wish. Then you and your family will eat and celebrate there before the Lord your God. [27]Do not forget the Levites in your town. They have no land of their own among you.

[28]At the end of every third year, everyone should bring one-tenth of that year's crop. Store it in your towns. [29]This is for the Levites so they may eat and be full. (They have no land of their own among you.) It is also for strangers, orphans and widows who live in your towns. All of them may eat and be full.

Then the Lord your God will bless you and all the work you do.

15 At the end of every seven years, you must forget about collecting what people owe you. [2]This is how you must do it: Everyone who has loaned money must forget the loan. He must not make his neighbor or brother pay it back. This is the Lord's time for canceling what people owe. [3]You may make a foreigner pay what he owes you. But you must not collect what your brother owes you. [4]But there should be no poor people among you. The Lord your God will richly bless you in the land he is giving you to own. [5]He will bless you if you obey him completely. But you must be careful to obey all the commands I am giving you today. [6]The Lord your God will bless you as he promised. You will lend to other nations. But you will not need to borrow from them. You will rule over many nations. But none will rule over you.

[7]There might be a poor man among you. He might be in one of the towns of the land the Lord your God is giving you. Do not be selfish or greedy toward your poor brother. [8]But give freely to him. Freely lend him whatever he needs. [9]Beware of evil thoughts. Don't think, "The seventh year is near. It's the year to forget what people owe." You might be mean to your needy brother. You might not give him anything. Then he will complain to the Lord about you. And the Lord will find you guilty of sin. [10]Give freely to the poor person. Do not wish that you didn't have to give. The Lord your God will bless your work and everything you touch. [11]There will always be poor people in the land. So I command you to give freely to your brothers. Give freely to the poor and needy in your land.

[12]One of your own people might sell himself to you as a slave. It may be a Hebrew man or woman. That person will serve you for six years. The seventh year you must let him go free. [13]And when you let him go, don't send him away without anything. [14]Give him some of your sheep, your grain and your wine. Give to him as the Lord has given to you. [15]Remember that you were slaves in Egypt. And the Lord your God saved you. That is why I am commanding this to you today.

[16]But your slave might say to you, "I don't want to leave you." He might love you and your family. He might have a good life with you. [17]If he does this, stick an awl[n] through his ear into the door. He will be your slave for life. Also do this to a woman slave.

[18]Do not think of it as a hard thing when you let your slave go free. After all, he served you six years. You paid him only half what a hired person would cost. The Lord your God will bless you in everything you do.

[19]Save all the first male animals born to your herds and flocks. They are for the Lord your God. Do not work the first calf born to your oxen. And do not cut off the wool from the first lamb born to your sheep. [20]Each year you and your family are to eat these animals. Eat them in the presence of the Lord your God. Eat them in the place he will choose to be worshiped. [21]An animal might have something wrong with it. It might be crippled or blind. It might have some other thing wrong with it. Do not sacrifice it to the Lord your God. [22]But you may eat that animal in your own town. Both clean[d] and unclean people may eat it. It would be like eating a gazelle or a deer. [23]But don't eat its blood. Pour it out on the ground like water.

16 Celebrate the Passover[d] of the Lord your God during the month of Abib.[d] It was during Abib that he brought you out of Egypt at night. [2]Offer a sacrifice for the Passover to the Lord your God. It should be an animal from your flock or herd. Offer it at the place the Lord will choose to be worshiped. [3]Do not eat it with bread made with yeast. But for seven days eat bread made without yeast. This is the bread of suffering because you left Egypt in a hurry. So all your life you will remember the time you left Egypt. [4]There must be no yeast anywhere in your land for seven days. Offer the sacrifice on the evening of the first day. Eat all the meat before morning. Do not leave it overnight.

[5]Do not offer the Passover sacrifice in just any town the Lord your God gives you. [6]Offer it in the place he will choose to be worshiped. Offer it in the evening as the sun goes down. That is when you left Egypt. [7]Roast the meat. Then eat it at the place the Lord your God will choose. The next morning go back to your tents. [8]Eat bread made without yeast for six days. On the seventh day have a special

15:17 awl A tool like a big needle with a handle at one end.

meeting for the Lord your God. Do not work that day.

⁹Count seven weeks from the time you begin to harvest the grain. ¹⁰Then celebrate the Feast[d] of Weeks for the Lord your God. Bring him an offering as a special gift to him. Give to him just as he has blessed you. ¹¹Rejoice before the Lord your God. Rejoice at the place he will choose to be worshiped. Everybody should rejoice: you, your sons and daughters, your male and female servants, the Levites in your town, the strangers, orphans and widows living among you. ¹²Remember that you were slaves in Egypt. And carefully obey all these laws.

¹³Celebrate the Feast[d] of Shelters for seven days. Do it after you have gathered your harvest from the threshing[d] floor and winepress.[d] ¹⁴Everybody should rejoice at your Feast: you, your sons and daughters, your male and female servants, the Levites and strangers who live in your towns, orphans and widows in your towns. ¹⁵Celebrate the Feast to the Lord your God for seven days. Celebrate it at the place he will choose. The Lord your God will bless all your harvest. He will bless all the work you do. And you will be completely happy.

¹⁶All your men must come before the Lord three times a year. They must come to the place he will choose. They must come at these times: the Feast[d] of Unleavened Bread, the Feast[d] of Weeks and the Feast of Shelters. No man should come before the Lord without a gift. ¹⁷Each of you must bring a gift. It should show how much the Lord your God has blessed you.

¹⁸Appoint judges and officers for your tribes.[d] Appoint them in every town the Lord your God is giving you. And they must judge the people fairly. ¹⁹Do not judge unfairly or take sides. Do not let people pay you to make wrong decisions. That kind of payment makes wise people seem blind. And it changes the words of good people. ²⁰Always do what is right. Then you will live and own the land the Lord your God is giving you.

²¹Do not set up a wooden Asherah[d] idol next to the altar you build for the Lord your God. ²²And do not set up holy stone pillars. The Lord your God hates them.

17An ox or sheep might have something wrong with it. Do not offer it as a sacrifice to the Lord your God. He would hate that.

²A man or woman might be found doing something evil in one of the towns the Lord gave you. That man or woman is breaking his agreement. ³That person may have served other gods. He may have bowed down to them, to the sun or moon or stars of the sky. I have commanded that should not be done. ⁴If someone has told you about it, you must look into the matter. It might be true. A terrible thing may have happened in Israel. ⁵If it is true, take the man or woman who has done the evil thing to the city gate. Throw stones at that person until he dies. ⁶There must be two or three witnesses that he did it. Then the person should be put to death. But if there is only one witness, the person should not be put to death. ⁷The witnesses must be the first to throw stones at the person. Then everyone else will follow. You must get rid of the evil among you.

⁸Some cases that come before you may be too difficult to judge. It may be a case of murder, quarreling or attack. Take these cases to the place the Lord your God will choose. ⁹Go to the priests who are Levites. And go to the judge who is on duty at that time. Ask them about the case, and they will decide. ¹⁰You must follow the decision they give you. They will be at the place the Lord your God will choose. Be careful to do everything they tell you. ¹¹Follow the teachings they give you. Do whatever they decide. Do exactly what they tell you. ¹²The person who does not show respect for the judge or priest must be put to death. They are there serving the Lord your God. You must get rid of that evil from Israel. ¹³Then everyone will hear about this. And they will be afraid. They will not show disrespect anymore.

¹⁴You will enter the land the Lord your God is giving you. You will take it as your own and live in it. Then you will say, "Let's appoint a king over us like the nations all around us." ¹⁵Be sure to appoint over you the king the Lord your God chooses. He must be one of your own people. Do not appoint a foreigner as your king. He is not a fellow Israelite. ¹⁶The king must not have too many horses for himself. He must not send people to Egypt to get more horses. The Lord has told you, "Don't return that

way again." ¹⁷The king must not have many wives. If he does, his heart will be led away from God. He must not have too much silver and gold.

¹⁸When he becomes king, he should write a copy of the teachings on a scroll for himself. He should copy it from the priests and Levites. ¹⁹He should keep it with him all the time. He should read from it every day of his life. Then he will learn to respect the Lord his God. And he will obey all the teachings and commands. ²⁰He should not think he is better than his brothers. He must not stop obeying the law in any way. Then he and his descendants[d] will rule the kingdom for a long time.

18 The priests are from the tribe[d] of Levi. That tribe will not receive a share of the land with the Israelites. They will eat the offerings made to the Lord by fire. That is their share. ²They will not inherit any of the land like their brothers. They will inherit the Lord himself. This is what he promised them.

³When you offer a bull or sheep as a sacrifice, you must share with the priests. Give them the shoulder, the cheeks and the inner organs. ⁴Give them the first of your grain, new wine and oil. Give them the first wool you cut from your sheep. ⁵The Lord your God has chosen the priests and their descendants[d] out of all your tribes. They are to stand and serve the Lord always.

⁶A Levite might move from one of your towns anywhere in Israel where he lives. He is sincere and comes to the place the Lord will choose. ⁷He may serve the Lord his God. He will be like his fellow Levites who serve there before the Lord. ⁸They all will have an equal share of the food. This is separate from what he has received from the sale of family possessions.

⁹You will enter the land the Lord your God is giving you. But don't learn to do the terrible things the other nations do. ¹⁰Don't let anyone among you offer his son or daughter as a sacrifice in the fire. Don't let anyone use magic or witchcraft.[d] No one should try to explain the meaning of signs. ¹¹Don't let anyone try to control others with magic. Don't let them be mediums[d] or try to talk with the spirits of dead people. ¹²The Lord hates anyone who does these things. The other nations do these things. That is why the Lord your God will force them out of the land ahead of you. ¹³You must

be innocent in the presence of the Lord your God.

¹⁴The nations you will force out listen to people who use magic and witchcraft.[d] But the Lord your God will not let you do those things. ¹⁵The Lord your God will give you a prophet[d] like me. He will be one of your own people. Listen to him. ¹⁶This is what you asked the Lord your God to do. You were gathered at Mount Sinai. You said, "Don't make us listen to the voice of the Lord our God again. Don't make us look at this terrible fire anymore. We will die."

¹⁷So the Lord said to me, "What they have said is good. ¹⁸So I will give them a prophet like you. He will be one of their own people. I will tell him what to say. And he will tell them everything I command. ¹⁹This prophet will speak for me. Anyone who does not listen when he speaks will answer to me. ²⁰But a prophet might say something I did not tell him to say. And he might say he is speaking for me. Or a prophet might speak in the name of other gods. That prophet must be killed."

²¹You might be thinking, "How can we know if a message is not from the Lord?" ²²What a prophet says in the name of the Lord might not happen. If it doesn't, it is not the Lord's message. That prophet was speaking his own ideas. Don't be afraid of him.

19 The Lord your God is giving you land that belongs to other nations. He will destroy those nations. You will force them out and live in their cities and houses. ²Then choose three cities. They must be in the middle of the land the Lord your God is giving you to own. ³Build roads to those cities. And divide the land the Lord is giving you into three parts. Then someone who kills another person may run to these cities.

⁴This is the rule for someone who kills another person. He may run to one of these cities to save his life. But he must have killed his neighbor without meaning to kill him. He did not hate his neighbor. ⁵A man might go into the forest with his neighbor to cut wood. The man swings his ax to cut down a tree. But the ax head flies off the handle. It hits his neighbor and kills him. The man who killed him may run to one of these cities to save his life. ⁶Otherwise, the dead man's relative who has the duty of punishing a murderer might be angry and chase him. And the relative might catch him if the city is far away. The relative

might kill the man. But the man should not be killed because he did not mean to kill his neighbor. [7]This is why I command you to choose these three cities.

[8-9]Carefully obey all these laws I'm giving you today. Love the Lord your God. Always do what he wants you to do. Then the Lord your God will enlarge your land as he promised your ancestors. He will give you the whole land he promised to them. After that, choose three more cities of safety. [10]This is so that innocent people will not be killed in your land. The Lord your God is giving it to you to own. By doing this you will not be guilty of murder.

[11]But a person might hate his neighbor. And he might hide and wait for him. He might attack and kill him and then run to one of these cities for safety. [12]The older leaders of his own city should send for him. They should bring him back from the city of safety. And they should hand him over to the relative who has the duty of punishing the murderer. [13]Give him no mercy. You must remove from Israel the guilt of murdering innocent people. Then things will go well for you.

[14]Do not move the stone that marks the border of your neighbor's land. People long ago set them in place. They mark what you inherit in the land the Lord your God is giving you to own.

[15]One witness is not enough to accuse a man of a crime or sin. A case must be proved by two or three witnesses.

[16]A witness might lie and accuse a person of a crime. [17]The two people who are arguing must stand before the Lord. They must stand before the priests and judges who are on duty. [18]The judges must check the matter carefully. The witness might be a liar. He might be lying about his fellow Israelite. [19]If so, he must be punished as he wanted his brother punished. You must get rid of the evil among you. [20]The rest of the people will hear about this and be afraid. No one among you will ever do such an evil thing again. [21]Give him no mercy. A life must be paid for a life. It must be an eye for an eye, a tooth for a tooth, a hand for a hand, a foot for a foot.

20 When you go to war against your enemies, you might see horses and chariots. Their army might be bigger than yours. But don't be afraid of them. The Lord your God will be with you. He brought you out of Egypt. [2]The priest must come and speak to the army

before you go into battle. [3]He should say, "Listen, Israel! Today you are going into battle against your enemies. Don't lose your courage or be afraid. Don't panic or be frightened. [4]The Lord your God goes with you. He will fight for you against your enemies. And he will save you."

[5]The officers should say to the army, "Has anyone built a new house but not given it to God? He may go home. He might die in battle. Then someone else would get to give his house to God. [6]Has anyone planted a vineyard and not begun to enjoy it? He may go home. He might die in battle. Then someone else would enjoy his vineyard. [7]Is any man engaged to a woman and not yet married to her? He may go home. He might die in battle. Then someone else would marry her." [8]Then the officers should also say, "Is anyone here afraid? Has anyone lost his courage? He may go home. Then he will not cause others to lose their courage, too." [9]When the officers finish speaking to the army, they should appoint commanders to lead it.

[10]You will march up to attack a city. First, make them an offer of peace. [11]They might accept your offer and open their gates to you. If that happens, all the people of that city will become your slaves. They will work for you. [12]But they might not make peace with you. They might fight you in battle. Then you should surround that city. [13]The Lord your God will give you the city. Then kill all the men with your swords. [14]You may take everything else in the city for yourselves. Take the women and children and animals. And you may use these things the Lord your God gives you from your enemies. [15]Do this to all the cities that are far away. They do not belong to the nations nearby.

[16]But leave nothing alive in the cities of the land. This is the land the Lord your God is giving you. [17]Completely destroy these people: the Hittites, Amorites, Canaanites, Perizzites, Hivites and Jebusites. The Lord your God has commanded you to do this. [18]Otherwise, they will teach you what they do for their gods. And if you do these terrible things, you will sin against the Lord your God.

[19]You might surround and attack a city for a long time, trying to capture it. But do not destroy its trees with an ax. You can eat the fruit from the trees. Do not cut them down. These trees are not the enemy. So don't make war against

them. 20But you may cut down trees that you know are not fruit trees. You may use them to build devices to attack the city walls. You may do this until the city is captured.

21 Someone might be found murdered. He might be lying in a field in the land the Lord your God is giving you to own. And no one knows who killed him. 2Your older leaders and judges should go to where he was found. And they should measure how far it is to the nearby cities. 3The older leaders of the city nearest the body are responsible. They must take a young cow that has never worked or worn a yoke.d 4And they must lead her down to a valley. It must never have been plowed or planted. It must have a stream flowing through it. There they must break the young cow's neck. 5The priests should come forward. They are the sons of Levi. They have been chosen by the Lord your God. They are to serve and give blessings in the Lord's name. And they are to decide cases of quarreling and attacks. 6Then all the older leaders of the city nearest the murdered man should wash their hands. They should do it over the young cow whose neck was broken in the valley. 7They should declare: "We did not kill this man. And we did not see it happen. 8Lord, remove this sin of your people Israel. You have saved them. Don't blame your people, the Israelites, for this innocent man's murder." And so the murder will be paid for. 9Then you will have removed from yourselves the guilt of murdering an innocent person. You will be doing what the Lord says is right.

10You will go to war against your enemies. The Lord will help you defeat them. You will take them captive. 11You might see a beautiful woman among the captives. And you might be attracted to her. You may take her as your wife. 12Bring her into your home. She must shave her head and cut her nails. 13She must change out of the clothes she was wearing when you captured her. And she must live in your house and cry for her parents for a month. After that, you may marry her. You will be her husband, and she will be your wife. 14But you might not be pleased with her. Then let her go anywhere she wants. You must not sell her for money. You must not make her a slave. You have taken away her honor.

15A man may have two wives. He might love one wife but not the other. Both wives might have sons by him. But the older son might be the son of the wife he does not love. 16Someday that man must will his property to his sons. But he must not give the son of the wife he loves what belongs to the older son. The older son is the son of the wife the man does not love. 17He must agree to give the older son two shares of everything he owns. The older son is from the wife he does not love. That son was the first to prove his father could have children. So he has the rights that belong to the older son.

18A man might have a son who is stubborn. The son turns against his father and mother and doesn't obey them. He will not listen when they correct him. 19His parents must take him to the older leaders at the city gate. 20They will say to the leaders, "Our son is stubborn and turns against us. He will not obey us. He eats too much. And he is always drunk." 21Then all the men in his town must throw stones at him until he dies. Get rid of the evil among you. All the people of Israel will hear about this and be afraid.

22A man might be guilty of a sin worthy of death. He must be put to death and his body displayed on a tree. 23But don't leave his body hanging on the tree overnight. Be sure to bury him that same day. Anyone whose body is displayed on a tree is cursed by God. You must not ruin the land the Lord your God is giving you to own.

22 You might see your fellow Israelite's ox or sheep wandering away. Don't ignore it. Take it back to its owner. 2The owner might not live close to you. Or you might not know who he is. Then take the animal home with you. Keep it until the owner comes looking for it. Then give it back to him. 3Do the same thing if you find his donkey or coat or anything he lost. Don't just ignore it.

4You might see your fellow Israelite's donkey or ox fallen on the road. Don't ignore it. Help him get it up.

5A woman must not wear men's clothes. And a man must not wear women's clothes. The Lord your God hates anyone who does that.

6You might find a bird's nest by the road. It might be in a tree or on the ground. And the mother bird might be sitting on the young birds or eggs. Do not take the mother bird with the young birds. 7You may take the young birds.

But you must let the mother bird go free. Then things will go well for you. And you will live a long time.

⁸When you build a new house, build a wall around the roof.ⁿ Then you will not be guilty of murder if someone falls off the roof.

⁹Don't plant two different kinds of seeds in your vineyard. Otherwise, both crops will be ruined.

¹⁰Don't plow with an ox and a donkey tied together.

¹¹Don't wear clothes made of wool and linen woven together.

¹²Tie several pieces of thread together. Then put these tassels on the four corners of your coat.

¹³A man might marry a girl and have sexual relations with her. But he might decide that he does not like her. ¹⁴So he might lie about her and give her a bad name. He might say, "I married this woman. But when I had sexual relations with her, I did not find that she was a virgin."ᵈ ¹⁵Then the girl's parents must bring proof that she was a virgin. They must bring it to the older leaders at the city gate. ¹⁶The girl's father will say to the leaders, "I gave my daughter to this man to be his wife. But now he does not want her. ¹⁷This man has told lies about my daughter. He has said, 'I did not find your daughter to be a virgin.' But here is the proof that my daughter was a virgin." Then her parents are to show the sheet to the city leaders. ¹⁸Then the leaders must take the man and punish him. ¹⁹They must make him pay about two and a half pounds of silver. The silver will go to the girl's father. This is because the man has given an Israelite girl a bad name. The girl must continue to be the man's wife. And he may not divorce her as long as he lives.

²⁰But the things the husband said about his wife might be true. And there might be no proof that she was a virgin. ²¹If so, the girl must be brought to the door of her father's house. Then the men of the town must put her to death by throwing stones at her. She has done a disgraceful thing in Israel. She had sexual relations before she was married. You must get rid of the evil among you.

²²A man might be found having sexual relations with another man's wife. Both the woman and the man who had sexual relations with her must die. Get rid of this evil from Israel.

²³A man might meet a virgin in a city and have sexual relations with her. But she might be engaged to another man. ²⁴You must take both of them to the city gate. Put them both to death by throwing stones at them. Kill the girl because she was in a city and did not scream for help. And kill the man for having sexual relations with another man's wife. You must get rid of the evil among you.

²⁵But a man might meet a girl out in the country. He might force her to have sexual relations with him. But she might be engaged to another man. Only the man who had sexual relations with her must be put to death. ²⁶Don't do anything to the girl. She has not done a sin worthy of death. This is like the person who attacks and murders his neighbor. ²⁷The man found the engaged girl in the country. And she screamed. But no one was there to save her.

²⁸A man might meet a virgin who is not engaged to be married. He might force her to have sexual relations with him. And people might find out about it. ²⁹The man must pay the girl's father about one and one-fourth pounds of silver. He must also marry the girl because he has dishonored her. And he may never divorce her for as long as he lives.

³⁰A man must not marry his father's wife. He must not dishonor his father in this way.

23 No man who has had part of his sex organ cut off may come into the worship meeting of the Lord's people.

²No one born to parents who were forbidden by law to marry may come into the meeting to worship the Lord. His descendants for ten generations may not come in either.

³No Ammonite or Moabite may come into the meeting to worship the Lord. And none of their descendants for ten generations may come in. ⁴This is because the Ammonites and Moabites did not give you bread and water when you came out of Egypt. And they hired Balaam to put a curse on you. He was the son of Beor from Pethor in Northwest Mesopotamia. ⁵But the Lord your God would not listen to Balaam. He turned the curse into a blessing for you. The

---

22:8 roof In Bible times houses were built with flat roofs. The roof was used for drying things such as flax and fruit. And it was used as an extra room, as a place for worship and as a place to sleep in the summer.

Lord your God loves you. [6]Don't wish for their peace or success as long as you live.

[7]Don't hate Edomites. They are your relatives. Don't hate Egyptians, because you were foreigners in their country. [8]The great-grandchildren of these two peoples may come into the meeting to worship the Lord.

[9]When you are camped in time of war, keep away from unclean[d] things. [10]A man might become unclean during the night. If he does, he must go outside the camp and not come back. [11]But when evening comes, he must wash himself. At sunset he may come back into the camp.

[12]Choose a place outside the camp where people may go to relieve themselves. [13]Carry a stick with you. When you relieve yourself, dig a hole. Cover up your dung. [14]The Lord your God moves around through your camp. He will protect you. He will help you defeat your enemies. So the camp must be holy. The Lord must not see anything unclean among you. Then he will not leave you.

[15]An escaped slave might come to you. Do not hand him over to his master. [16]Let the slave live with you anywhere he likes. He may live in any town he chooses. Do not mistreat him.

[17]No Israelite man or woman must ever become a temple prostitute.[d] [18]Do not bring a male or female prostitute's pay to the Temple[d] of the Lord your God to pay what you have promised to the Lord. The Lord your God hates prostitution.

[19]You may loan your fellow Israelite money or food or anything else. But don't make him pay back more than what you loaned him. [20]You may charge a foreigner, but not a fellow Israelite. Then the Lord your God will bless everything you do. He will bless you in the land you are entering to take as your own.

[21]You might make a promise to give something to the Lord your God. Do not be slow to pay it. The Lord your God demands it from you. Do not be guilty of sin. [22]But if you do not make the promise, you will not be guilty. [23]You must do whatever you say you will do. You chose to make the promise to the Lord your God.

[24]You might go into your neighbor's vineyard. You may eat as many grapes as you wish. But do not fill your basket with his grapes. [25]You might go into

your neighbor's grainfield. You may pick grain with your hands. But you must not cut down his grain with your sickle.

24 A man might marry a woman. But he might decide she doesn't please him. He has found something bad about her. He writes out divorce papers for her. He gives them to her and sends her away from his house. [2]After she leaves his house, she goes and marries another man. [3]But her second husband does not like her either. So he writes out divorce papers for her. He gives them to her and sends her away from his house. Or the second husband might die. [4]In either case, her first husband who divorced her must not marry her again. She has become unclean.[d] The Lord would hate this. Don't bring this sin into the land the Lord your God is giving you to own.

[5]A man who has just married must not be sent to war. And he must not be given any other duty. He should be free to stay home for a year to make his new wife happy.

[6]A man might owe you something. But do not take his two stones for grinding grain—not even the upper one—in place of what he owes. This is how he makes his living.

[7]A man might kidnap a fellow Israelite. He might make him a slave or sell him. The kidnapper must be killed. You must get rid of the evil among you.

[8]Be careful when someone has a harmful skin disease. Do exactly what the priests, the Levites, teach you. Be careful to do what I have commanded them. [9]Remember what the Lord your God did to Miriam on your way out of Egypt.

[10]You might make a loan to your neighbor. But don't go into his house to get something in place of it. [11]Stay outside. Let the man himself go in and get what he promised you. [12]A poor man might give you his coat to show he will pay the loan back. But don't keep his coat overnight. [13]Give his coat back to him at sunset. He needs his coat to sleep in. He will thank you. And the Lord your God will see that you have done a good thing.

[14]Don't cheat a hired servant who is poor and needy. He might be a fellow Israelite. Or he might be a foreigner living in one of your towns. [15]Pay him each day before sunset. He is poor and needs the money. Otherwise, he may complain

to the Lord about you. And you will be guilty of sin.

¹⁶Fathers must not be put to death when their children do wrong. And children must not be put to death when their fathers do wrong. Each person must die for his own sin.

¹⁷Do not be unfair to a foreigner or an orphan. Don't take a widow's coat in place of a loan. ¹⁸Remember that you were slaves in Egypt. And the Lord your God saved you from there. That is why I am commanding you to do this.

¹⁹You might be gathering your harvest in the field. You might not see a bundle of grain. Don't go back and get it. Leave it there for foreigners, orphans and widows. Then the Lord your God can bless everything you do. ²⁰You may beat your olive trees to knock the olives off. But don't beat the trees a second time. Leave what is left for foreigners, orphans and widows. ²¹You may harvest the grapes in your vineyard. But don't pick the vines a second time. Leave what is left for foreigners, orphans and widows. ²²Remember that you were slaves in Egypt. That is why I am commanding you to do this.

25 Two people may have an argument. They should go to the court. And the judges will decide the case. They will declare one person to be right. And they will punish the one who is guilty. ²The guilty person might have to be punished with a beating. If so, the judge will make him lie down. They will beat him in front of the judge. The number of lashes should match the crime. ³But don't hit him more than 40 times. If he is beaten more than that, it would disgrace him before others.

⁴When an ox is working in the grain, do not cover its mouth to keep it from eating.

⁵Two brothers might be living together. One of them might die without having a son. His widow must not marry someone outside her husband's family. Her husband's brother must marry her. This is his duty for her as a brother-in-law. ⁶The first son she has must be named for the dead brother. Then his name will not be forgotten in Israel.

⁷But a man might not want to marry his brother's widow. Then she should go to the older leaders at the town gate. And she should say, "My brother-in-law will not carry on his brother's name in Israel. He refuses to do his duty for me."

⁸Then the older leaders of the town must call for the man and talk to him.

But he might be stubborn and say, "I don't want to marry her."

⁹If he does, the woman must go up to him in front of the leaders. She must take off one of his sandals. She must spit in his face and say, "This is for the man who won't continue his brother's family!" ¹⁰Then that man's family shall be known in Israel as the Family of the Unsandaled.

¹¹Two men might be fighting. And one man's wife comes to save her husband from his attacker. And she grabs the attacker by his sex organs. ¹²You must cut off her hand. Give her no mercy.

¹³Don't carry two sets of weights with you, one heavy and one light. ¹⁴Don't have two different sets of measures in your house, one large and one small. ¹⁵You must have true and honest weights and measures. Then you will live a long time in the land the Lord your God is giving you. ¹⁶The Lord your God hates anyone who is dishonest and uses dishonest measures.

¹⁷Remember what the Amalekites did to you when you came out of Egypt. ¹⁸You were tired and worn out. And they met you on the road. They killed all those lagging behind. They were not afraid of God. ¹⁹The Lord your God will give you rest from all the enemies around you. It will be in the land he is giving you to own. Then you shall destroy any memory of the Amalekites on the earth. Do not forget!

26 Soon you will go into the land the Lord your God is giving you to own. You will take it over and live in it. ²Then you must take some of the first harvest of crops. It will grow from the land the Lord your God is giving you. Put the food in a basket. Then go to the place where the Lord your God will choose to be worshiped. ³Say to the priest on duty at that time, "Today I declare this before the Lord your God. I have come into the land the Lord promised to give us. He promised this to our ancestors." ⁴The priest will take your basket. He will set it down in front of the altar of the Lord your God. ⁵Then you shall announce before the Lord your God: "My father was a wandering Aramean. He went down to Egypt. He stayed there with only a few people. But they became a great, powerful and large nation there. ⁶But the Egyptians were cruel to us. They made us suffer and work very hard. ⁷So we prayed to the Lord, the God of our ancestors. He heard us.

He saw our trouble, hard work and suffering. [8]Then the Lord brought us out of Egypt. He did it with his great power and strength. He used great terrors, signs and miracles.[d] [9]Then he brought us to this place. He gave us this land where much food grows. [10]Now I bring you part of the first harvest from this land. Lord, you have given me this land." Then place the basket before the Lord your God. And bow down before him. [11]Then you and the Levites and foreigners among you should rejoice. The Lord your God has given good things to you and your family.

[12]Bring a tenth of all your harvest the third year. This is the year to give a tenth of your harvest. Give it to the Levites, foreigners, orphans and widows. Then they may eat in your towns and be full. [13]Then say to the Lord your God, "I have taken out of my house the part of my harvest that belongs to God. I have given it to the Levites, foreigners, orphans and widows. I have done everything you commanded me. I have not broken your commands. And I have not forgotten any of them. [14]I have not eaten any of the holy part while I was in sorrow. I have not removed any of it while I was unclean.[d] I have not offered it for dead people. I have obeyed you, the Lord my God. I have done everything you commanded me. [15]So look down from heaven, your holy home. Bless your people Israel. And bless the land you have given us. You promised it to our ancestors. It is a land where much food grows."

[16]Today the Lord your God commands you to obey all these rules and laws. Be careful to do them with your whole being. [17]Today you have said that the Lord is your God. You have promised to do what he wants you to do. You have promised to keep his rules, commands and laws. You have said you will obey him. [18]And today the Lord has said that you are his very own people. He has promised it. But you must obey his commands. [19]The Lord will make you greater than all the other nations he made. He will give you praise, fame and honor. And you will be a holy people to the Lord your God. This is what he said.

27 Moses and the older leaders of Israel commanded the people. They said, "Keep all the commands I have given you today. [2]Soon you will cross the Jordan River. You will go into the land the Lord your God is giving you.

On that day set up some large stones. Cover them with plaster. [3]When you cross over, write all the words of these teachings on them. Then you may enter the land the Lord your God is giving you. It is a land where much food grows. It is just as the Lord, the God of your ancestors, promised. [4]After you have crossed the Jordan River, set up these stones. Set them on Mount Ebal as I command you today. And cover them with plaster. [5]Build an altar of stones there to the Lord your God. But don't use any iron tool to cut the stones. [6]Build the altar of the Lord your God with stones from the field. Offer burnt offerings on it to the Lord your God. [7]Offer fellowship offerings there. Eat them and rejoice before the Lord your God. [8]Then write clearly all the words of these teachings on the stones."

[9]Then Moses and the Levites, who are the priests, spoke to all Israel. They said, "Be quiet, Israel. Listen! Today you have become the people of the Lord your God. [10]Obey the Lord your God. Keep his commands and laws that I give you today."

[11]That day Moses also gave the people this command:

[12]You will cross the Jordan River. Then these tribes[d] must stand on Mount Gerizim to bless the people: Simeon, Levi, Judah, Issachar, Joseph and Benjamin. [13]And these tribes must stand on Mount Ebal to announce the curses: Reuben, Gad, Asher, Zebulun, Dan and Naphtali.

[14]The Levites will say to all the people of Israel in a loud voice:

[15]"Anyone will be cursed who makes an idol or statue and secretly sets it up. The Lord hates idols made by man."

Then all the people will say, "Amen!"

[16]"Anyone will be cursed who dishonors his father or his mother."

Then all the people will say, "Amen!"

[17]"Anyone will be cursed who moves the stone that marks his neighbor's border."

Then all the people will say, "Amen!"

[18]"Anyone will be cursed who leads a blind person away from the road."

Then all the people will say, "Amen!"

[19]"Anyone will be cursed who is unfair to foreigners, orphans or widows."

Then all the people will say, "Amen!"

[20]"A man will be cursed who has sexual relations with his father's wife. It is a dishonor to his father."

Then all the people will say, "Amen!"

²¹"Anyone will be cursed who has sexual relations with an animal."

Then all the people will say, "Amen!"

²²"A man will be cursed who has sexual relations with his sister. She may be his father's daughter or his mother's daughter."

Then all the people will say, "Amen!"

²³"A man will be cursed who has sexual relations with his mother-in-law."

Then all the people will say, "Amen!"

²⁴"Anyone will be cursed who kills his neighbor secretly."

Then all the people will say, "Amen!"

²⁵"Anyone will be cursed who takes money to murder an innocent person."

Then all the people will say, "Amen!"

²⁶"Anyone will be cursed who does not agree with the words of these teachings and does not obey them."

Then all the people will say, "Amen!"

28 You must completely obey the Lord your God. And you must carefully follow all his commands I am giving you today. Then the Lord your God will make you greater than any other nation on earth. ²Obey the Lord your God. Then all these blessings will come and stay with you:

³You will be blessed in the city. You will be blessed in the country.

⁴Your children will be blessed. Your crops will be blessed. Your cattle will be blessed with calves and your sheep with lambs.

⁵Your basket and your kitchen will be blessed.

⁶You will be blessed when you come in and when you go out.

⁷The Lord will let you defeat the enemies that come to fight you. They will attack you from one direction. But they will run from you in seven directions.

⁸The Lord your God will bless you with full barns. He will bless everything you do. He will bless the land he is giving you.

⁹The Lord will make you his holy people, as he promised. But you must obey his commands. You must do what he wants you to do. ¹⁰Then everyone on earth will see that you are the Lord's people. They will be afraid of you. ¹¹The Lord will make you rich. You will have many children. Your cattle will have many calves. Your land will give good crops. It is the land that the Lord promised your ancestors he would give to you.

¹²The Lord will open up his storehouse. The skies will send rain on your land at the right time. And he will bless everything you do. You will lend to other nations. But you will not need to borrow from them. ¹³The Lord will make you like the head and not like the tail. You will be on top and not on bottom. But you must obey the commands of the Lord your God that I am giving you today. Be careful to keep them. ¹⁴Do not disobey anything I command you today. Do exactly as I command. Do not follow other gods or serve them.

¹⁵But you might not obey the Lord your God. You might not carefully follow all his commands and laws I am giving you today. Then all these curses will come upon you and stay:

¹⁶You will be cursed in the city. You will be cursed in the country.

¹⁷Your basket and your kitchen will be cursed.

¹⁸Your children will be cursed. Your crops will be cursed. The calves of your cattle will be cursed. And the lambs of your flocks will be cursed.

¹⁹You will be cursed when you go in and when you go out.

²⁰The Lord will send you curses, confusion and punishment in everything you do. You will be destroyed. You will suddenly be ruined. You did wrong when you left him. ²¹The Lord will give you terrible diseases. He will destroy you from the land you are going to take. ²²The Lord will punish you with disease, fever, swelling, heat, no rain, plant diseases and mildew.ᵈ Then you will die. ²³The sky above will look like bronze. And the ground below will be like iron. ²⁴The Lord will turn the rain into dust and sand. It will fall from the skies until you are destroyed.

²⁵The Lord will let your enemies defeat you. You will attack them from one direction. But you will run from them in seven directions. And you will become a thing of horror among all the kingdoms on earth. ²⁶Your dead bodies will be food for all the birds and wild animals. There will be no one to scare them away. ²⁷The Lord will punish you with boils like those the Egyptians had. You will have bad growths, sores and itches that can't be cured. ²⁸The Lord will give you madness, blindness and a confused mind. ²⁹You will have to feel around in the daylight like a blind man. You will fail in everything you do. People will hurt you and steal from you every day. There will be no one to save you.

³⁰You will be engaged to a woman. But

another man will force her to have sexual relations with him. You will build a house. But you will not live in it. You will plant a vineyard. But you will not get its grapes. [31]Your ox will be killed before your eyes. But you will not eat any of it. Your donkey will be taken away from you. And it will not be brought back. Your sheep will be given to your enemies. And no one will rescue them. [32]Your sons and daughters will be given to another nation. You will grow tired looking for them every day. But there is nothing you can do. [33]People you don't know will eat the crops your land and hard work have produced. You will be mistreated and abused all your life. [34]The things you will see will cause you to go mad. [35]The Lord will give you sore boils on your knees and legs. They cannot be cured. They will go from the soles of your feet to the tops of your heads.

[36]The Lord will send you and your king away to a nation you do not know. There you will serve other gods made of wood and stone. [37]You will become a hated thing to the nations where the Lord sends you. They will laugh at you and make fun of you.

[38]You will plant much seed in your field. But your harvest will be small. Locusts[d] will eat the crop. [39]You will plant vineyards and work hard in them. But you will not pick the grapes or drink the wine. The worms will eat them. [40]You will have olive trees in all your land. But you will not get any olive oil. The olives will drop off the trees. [41]You will have sons and daughters. But you will not be able to keep them. They will be taken captive. [42]Locusts will destroy all your trees and crops.

[43]The foreigners who live among you will get stronger and stronger. And you will get weaker and weaker. [44]Foreigners will lend money to you. But you will not be able to lend to them. They will be like the head. And you will be like the tail.

[45]All these curses will come upon you. They will chase you and catch you and destroy you. This will happen because you did not obey the Lord your God. You did not keep the commands and laws he gave you. [46]The curses will be signs and miracles[d] to you and your descendants[d] forever. [47]You had plenty of everything. But you did not serve the Lord your God with joy and a pure heart. [48]So you will serve the enemies the Lord sends against you. You will be hungry, thirsty,

naked and poor. The Lord will put a load on you until he has destroyed you.

[49]The Lord will bring a nation against you from far away. It will be from the end of the world. The nation will swoop down like an eagle. You won't understand their language. [50]They will look mean. They will not respect old people or feel sorry for the young. [51]They will eat the calves from your cattle and the harvest of your field. And you will be destroyed. They will not leave you any grain, new wine or oil. They will not leave you any calves from your herds or lambs from your flocks. You will be ruined. [52]That nation will surround and attack all your cities. You trust in your high, strong walls. But they will fall down. That nation will surround all your cities everywhere in the land the Lord your God is giving you.

[53]Your enemy will surround you. Those people will make you starve. You will eat your own babies. You will eat the bodies of the sons and daughters the Lord gave you. [54]Even the most gentle and kind man among you will become cruel. He will be cruel to his brother, his wife whom he loves and his children who are still alive. [55]He will not even give them any of the flesh of his children he is eating. It will be all he has left. Your enemy will surround you. Those people will make you starve in all your cities. [56]The most gentle and kind woman among you will become cruel. She is so gentle and kind she would hardly even walk on the ground. But she will be cruel to her husband whom she loves. And she will be cruel to her son and daughter. [57]She will give birth to a baby. But she will plan to eat the baby and what comes after the birth itself. She will eat them while the enemy surrounds the city. Those people will make you starve in all your cities.

[58]Be careful to obey everything in these teachings. They are written in this book. You must respect the glorious and wonderful name of the Lord your God. [59]The Lord will give terrible diseases to you and your descendants.[d] You will have long and serious diseases. You will have long and miserable sicknesses. [60]And the Lord will give you all the diseases of Egypt that you dread. And the diseases will stay with you. [61]The Lord will also give you every disease and sickness not written in this Book of the Teachings. Then you will be destroyed. [62]You people may have outnumbered the

stars. But only a few of you will be left. You did not obey the Lord your God. [63]Once the Lord was happy with you. He gave you good things. He made you grow in number. But now the Lord will be happy to ruin and destroy you. You will be removed from the land you are entering to own.

[64]Then the Lord will scatter you among the nations. He will scatter you from one end of the earth to the other. There you will serve other gods of wood and stone. They are gods that neither you nor your ancestors have known. [65]You will have no rest among those nations. You will have no place that is yours. The Lord will make your mind worried, your sight weak and your soul sad. [66]You will live with danger. You will be afraid night and day. You will not be sure that you will live. [67]In the morning you will say, "I wish it were evening." And in the evening you will say, "I wish it were morning." Terror will be in your heart because of the things you have seen. [68]The Lord will send you back to Egypt in ships. I, Moses, said you would never go back to Egypt. And there you will try to sell yourselves as slaves to your enemies. But no one will buy you.

29 The Lord commanded Moses to make an agreement with the Israelites in Moab. This agreement was in addition to the agreement he had made with them at Mount Sinai.

[2]Moses called all the Israelites together. And he said to them:

You have seen everything the Lord did to the king of Egypt. You saw what he did to the king's leaders and to the whole country. [3]With your own eyes you saw the great troubles, signs and miracles.[d] [4]But to this day the Lord has not given you a mind that understands. You don't really understand what you saw with your eyes or hear with your ears. [5]The Lord led you through the desert for 40 years. During that time neither your clothes nor sandals wore out. [6]You ate no bread. You drank no wine or beer. This was so you would understand that he is the Lord your God.

[7]You came to this place. Then Sihon king of Heshbon and Og king of Bashan came out to fight us. But we defeated them. [8]We captured their land. And we gave it to the Reubenites, the Gadites and the eastern half-tribe of Manasseh to own.

[9]You must carefully obey everything in this agreement. Then you will succeed in everything you do. [10]Today you are all standing here before the Lord your God. Here are your leaders and important men. Your older leaders, officers and all the other men of Israel are here. [11]Here are your wives and children and the foreigners who live among you. They chop your wood and carry your water. [12]You are all here to enter into an agreement and a promise with the Lord your God. The Lord is making this agreement with you today. [13]This will make you today the Lord's own people. He will be your God. This is what he told you. He promised it to your ancestors Abraham, Isaac and Jacob. [14]But the Lord is not just making this agreement and its promises with you. [15]You are standing here before the Lord your God today. But he is also making it with those who are not here today.

[16]You know how we lived in Egypt. You know how we passed through the countries when we came here. [17]You saw their hated idols made of wood, stone, silver and gold. [18]Make sure no man, woman, family group or tribe among you leaves the Lord. Don't let them go and serve the gods of those nations. That would be like a plant that grows bitter, poisonous fruit.

[19]That kind of person might hear these curses. But he blesses himself. And he thinks, "I will be safe. I will continue doing what I want to do." That person might destroy all of your land, both wet and dry. [20]The Lord will not forgive that person. His anger will be like a burning fire against that man. All the curses written in this book will come on him. And the Lord will destroy any memory of him on the earth. [21]The Lord will separate him from all the tribes of Israel for punishment. All the curses of the agreement will happen to him. They are written in this Book of the Teachings.

[22]Your children who will come after you will see this. And foreigners from faraway lands will see this. They will see the disasters that come to this land. And they will see the diseases the Lord will send on it. They will say, [23]"The land is nothing but burning cinders and salt. Nothing is planted. Nothing grows. Nothing blooms. It is like Sodom and Gomorrah, and Admah and Zeboiim. The Lord destroyed them because he was very angry." [24]All the other nations will ask, "Why has the Lord done this to the land? Why is he so angry?"

²⁵And the answer will be, "It is because the people broke the agreement of the Lord, the God of their ancestors. He made it with them when he brought them out of Egypt. ²⁶They went and served other gods. They bowed down to gods they did not even know. The Lord did not allow that. ²⁷So the Lord became very angry at the land. And he brought all the curses on it that are written in this book. ²⁸The Lord became angry and furious with them. So he took them out of their land. And he put them in another land where they are today."

²⁹There are some things the Lord our God has kept secret. But there are some things he has let us know. These things belong to us and our children forever. It is so we will do everything in these teachings.

30All these blessings and curses I have said will happen to you. The Lord your God will send you away to other nations. There you will think about these things. ²Then you and your children will return to the Lord your God. And you will obey him with your whole being. You will obey everything I command you today. ³Then the Lord your God will give you back your riches. He will feel sorry for you. And he will bring you back again from the nations where he sent you. ⁴He may send you to the ends of the earth. But he will gather you. He will bring you back from there. ⁵He will bring you back to the land that belonged to your ancestors. It will be yours. He will give you success. And there will be more of you than there were of your ancestors. ⁶The Lord your God will prepare you and your descendantsᵈ to serve him. You will love him with your whole being. Then you will live. ⁷The Lord your God will put all these curses on your enemies. They hate you and are cruel to you. ⁸And you will again obey the Lord. You will keep all his commands that I give you today. ⁹The Lord your God will make you successful in everything you do. You will have many children. Your cattle will have many calves. Your fields will produce good crops. He will again be happy with you, just as he was with your ancestors. ¹⁰But you must obey the Lord your God. You must obey his commands and rules that are written in this Book of the Teachings. You must follow the Lord your God with your whole being.

¹¹This command I give you today is not too hard for you. It is not beyond what you can do. ¹²It is not up in heaven. You do not have to ask, "Who will go up to heaven and get it for us? Then we can obey it and keep it." ¹³It is not on the other side of the sea. You do not have to ask, "Who will go across the sea and get it? Who will tell it to us? Then we can keep it." ¹⁴No, the word is very near you. It is in your mouth and in your heart. So, you may obey it.

¹⁵Look, today I offer you life and success, death and destruction. ¹⁶I command you today to love the Lord your God. Do what he wants you to do. Keep his commands, his rules and his laws. Then you will live and grow in number. And the Lord your God will bless you in the land you are going to take as your own.

¹⁷But you might turn away from the Lord. You might not obey him. You might be led to bowing down and serving other gods. ¹⁸I tell you today that you will be destroyed. And you will not live long in the land you are crossing the Jordan River to enter and own.

¹⁹Today I ask heaven and earth to be witnesses. I am offering you life or death, blessings or curses. Now, choose life! Then you and your children may live. ²⁰Love the Lord your God. Obey him. Stay close to him. He is your life. And he will let you live many years in the land. This is the land he promised to give your ancestors Abraham, Isaac and Jacob.

31Then Moses went and spoke these words to all the Israelites: ²"I am now 120 years old. I cannot lead you anymore. The Lord told me I would not cross the Jordan River. ³The Lord your God will lead you across himself. He will destroy those nations for you. You will take over their land. Joshua will also lead you across. This is what the Lord has said. ⁴The Lord will do to these nations what he did to Sihon and Og. They were the kings of the Amorites. He destroyed them and their land. ⁵The Lord will give those nations to you. Do to them everything I told you. ⁶Be strong and brave. Don't be afraid of them. Don't be frightened. The Lord your God will go with you. He will not leave you or forget you."

⁷Then Moses called Joshua and spoke to him in front of the people. Moses said, "Be strong and brave. Lead these people into the land the Lord promised to give their ancestors. Help the people take it as their own. ⁸The Lord himself will go

before you. He will be with you. He will not leave you or forget you. Don't be afraid. Don't worry."

⁹So Moses wrote down the teachings. He gave them to the priests and all the older leaders of Israel. The priests are the sons of Levi. They carried the Box[d] of the Agreement with the Lord. ¹⁰⁻¹¹Then Moses commanded them: "Read these teachings for all Israel to hear. Do it at the end of every seven years. That is the year to forget what people owe. Do it during the Feast[d] of Shelters. All the Israelites will come to appear before the Lord your God. They will stand at the place the Lord will choose. ¹²Gather all the people: the men, women, children and foreigners living in your towns. Then they can listen and learn to respect the Lord your God. Then they can carefully obey everything in this law. ¹³Their children do not know this law. They must hear it. They must learn to respect the Lord your God for as long as they live in the land. It is the land you are crossing the Jordan River to own."

¹⁴The Lord said to Moses, "Soon you will die. Get Joshua and come to the Meeting Tent.[d] I will command him." So Moses and Joshua went to the Meeting Tent.

¹⁵The Lord appeared at the Meeting Tent in a cloud. The cloud stood over the entrance of the Tent. ¹⁶And the Lord said to Moses, "You will soon die. Then these people will not be loyal to me. They will worship the foreign gods of the land they are entering. They will leave me. And they will break the agreement I made with them. ¹⁷Then I will become very angry at them. I will leave them. I will turn away from them. And they will be destroyed. Many terrible things will happen to them. Then they will say, 'God is not with us. That is why these terrible things are happening.' ¹⁸I will turn away from them then. They have done wrong. They have turned to other gods.

¹⁹"Now write down this song. And teach it to the Israelites. Then have them sing it. It will testify against them. ²⁰I will bring them into the land I promised to their ancestors. It is a land where much food grows. They will eat as much as they want and get fat. But then they will turn to other gods and serve them. They will reject me and break my agreement. ²¹Then many troubles and terrible things will happen to them. And this song will testify against them. The song will not be forgotten by their descen-

dants.[d] I know what they plan to do, even before I take them into the land I promised them." ²²So Moses wrote down the song that day. And he taught it to the Israelites.

²³Then the Lord gave this command to Joshua son of Nun: "Be strong and brave. Lead the people of Israel to the land I promised them. And I will be with you."

²⁴Moses wrote all the words of the teachings in a book. ²⁵Then he gave a command to the Levites. They carried the Box[d] of the Agreement with the Lord. ²⁶He said, "Take this Book of the Teachings. Put it beside the Box of the Agreement with the Lord your God. It must stay there as a witness against you. ²⁷I know how stubborn and disobedient you are. You have disobeyed the Lord while I am alive and with you. You will disobey even more after I die! ²⁸Gather all the older leaders of your tribes[d] and all your officers. I will say these things for them to hear. And I will ask heaven and earth to testify against them. ²⁹I know that after I die you will become completely evil. You will turn away from the commands I have given you. Then terrible things will happen to you in the future. You will do what the Lord says is evil. You will make him angry with the idols you have made."

³⁰And Moses spoke this whole song for all the people of Israel to hear:

32   Hear, heavens, and I will speak.
     Listen, earth, to what I say.
  ²My teaching will drop like rain.
     My words will fall like dew.
  They will be like showers on the
     grass.
  They will pour down like rain on
     young plants.
  ³I will announce the name of the
     Lord.
  Praise God because he is great!
  ⁴He is like a rock. What he does is
     perfect.
  He is always fair.
  He is a faithful God who does no
     wrong.
  He is right and fair.

  ⁵They have done evil against him.
  To their shame they are no longer
     his children.
  They are an evil and lying
     people.
  ⁶This is not the way to repay the
     Lord.
  You are foolish and unwise.

He is your Father and Maker.
He made you and formed you.
⁷Remember the old days.
Think of the years already
passed.
Ask your father. He will tell you.
Ask your older leaders. They will
inform you.
⁸The Most High God gave the
nations their lands.
He divided up the human race.
He set up borders for the people.
He even numbered the Israelites.
⁹The Lord took his people as his
share.
The people of Jacob were his
very own.

¹⁰He found them in a desert.
It was a windy, empty land.
He surrounded them and brought
them up.
He guarded them as those he
loved very much.
¹¹He was like an eagle building its
nest.
It flutters over its young.
It spreads its wings to catch them.
It carries them on its feathers.
¹²The Lord alone led them.
There were no foreign gods
among them.

¹³The Lord brought them to the
heights of the land.
He fed them the fruit of the
fields.
He gave them honey from the
rocks.
He brought oil from the solid
rock.
¹⁴There were milk curds from the
cows and milk from the sheep.
There were fat sheep and goats.
There were sheep and goats from
Bashan.
There was the best of the wheat.
You drank the juice of grapes.

¹⁵Israel grew fat and kicked.
They were fat and full and firm.
They left the God who made them.
They rejected the Rock^d who
saved them.
¹⁶They made God jealous with
foreign gods.
They made him angry with hated
idols.
¹⁷They made sacrifices to demons,^d
not God.

They were gods they had never
known.
They were new gods from
nearby.
Your ancestors did not fear them.
¹⁸You left God who is the Rock, your
Father.
You forgot the God who gave you
birth.

¹⁹The Lord saw this and rejected
them.
His sons and daughters had
made him angry.
²⁰He said, "I will turn away from
them.
I will see what will happen to
them.
They are evil people.
They are unfaithful children.
²¹They used things that are not gods
to make me jealous.
They used worthless idols to
make me angry.
So I will use those who are not a
nation to make them jealous.
I will use a nation that does not
understand to make them
angry.
²²My anger has started a fire.
It burns down to where the dead
are.
It will burn up the ground and its
crops.
And it will set fire to the
mountains.

²³"I will pile troubles upon them.
I will shoot my arrows at them.
²⁴They will be starved and sick.
They will be destroyed by terrible
diseases.
I will send them vicious animals
and gliding, poisonous snakes.
²⁵In the streets the sword will kill.
In their homes there will be
terror.
Young men and women will die.
So will babies and gray-haired
men.
²⁶I will scatter them as I said.
And no one will remember them.
²⁷But I didn't want their enemy to
brag.
Their enemy might
misunderstand.
They might say, 'We have won!
The Lord has done none of this.'"

²⁸Israel has no sense.
They do not understand.

²⁹I wish they were wise and
understood this.
I wish they could see what will
happen to them.
³⁰One person cannot chase 1,000
people.
And 2 people cannot fight 10,000.
This only happens if the Lord has
sold them.
Their Rock would have to give
them up.
³¹The rock of these people is not like
our Rock.
Our enemies agree to that.
³²Their vine comes from Sodom.
Their fields are like Gomorrah.
Their grapes are full of poison.
Their bunches of grapes are
bitter.
³³Their wine is like snake poison,
like the deadly poison of cobras.

³⁴"I have been saving this.
I have it locked in my storehouses.
³⁵I will punish those who do wrong. I
will repay them.
Sometime their foot will slip.
Their day of trouble is near.
And their punishment will come
quickly."

³⁶The Lord will defend his people.
He will have mercy on his
servants.
He will see that their strength is
gone.
He will see that nobody is left,
slaves or free.
³⁷Then he will say, "Where are their
gods?
Where is the rock they trusted?
³⁸Who ate the fat from their
sacrifices?
Who drank the wine of their
drink offering?
Let those gods come to help you!
Let them protect you!

³⁹"Now you will see that I am the one
God!
There is no god but me.
I send life and death.
I can hurt, and I can heal.
No one can escape from me.
⁴⁰I raise my hand toward heaven and
make this promise:
As surely as I live forever,
⁴¹I will sharpen my flashing sword.
And I will take it in my hand to
judge.
I will punish my enemies.
I will pay back those who hate me.

⁴²My arrows will be covered with
their blood.
My sword will eat their flesh.
The blood will flow from those who
are killed and the captives.
The heads of the enemy leaders
will be cut off."

⁴³Be happy, nations, with his people.
He will repay you for the blood of
his servants.
He will punish his enemies.
And he will remove the sin of his
land and people.

⁴⁴Moses came with Joshua son of Nun.
And they spoke all the words of this
song for the people to hear. ⁴⁵When Moses finished speaking these words to all
Israel, ⁴⁶he said to them: "Pay attention
to all the words I have said to you today.
Command your children to obey carefully everything in these teachings.
⁴⁷These should not be unimportant
words for you. They mean life for you!
By these words you will live a long time
in the land you are crossing the Jordan
River to own."

⁴⁸The Lord spoke to Moses again that
same day. He said, ⁴⁹"Go up the Abarim
Mountains. Go to Mount Nebo in the
country of Moab. It is across from Jericho. Look at the land of Canaan. I am
giving it to the Israelites to own. ⁵⁰You
will die on that mountain that you climb.
This is how your brother Aaron died on
Mount Hor. ⁵¹You both sinned against me
at the waters of Meribah Kadesh. That is
in the Desert of Zin. You did not honor
me as holy there among the Israelites.
⁵²So now you will only look at the land
from far away. You will not enter the
land I am giving the people of Israel."

33 Moses, the man of God, gave this
blessing to the Israelites before he
died. ²He said:
"The Lord came from Mount Sinai.
He rose like the sun from Edom.
He showed his greatness from
Mount Paran.
He came with thousands of angels.
He came from the southern
mountains.
³The Lord surely loves his people.
He takes care of all those who
belong to him.
They bow down at his feet.
And they are taught by him.
⁴Moses gave us the teachings.
They belong to the people of
Jacob.
⁵The Lord became king of Israel.

The leaders of the people
  gathered then.
The tribes[d] of Israel came
  together.

[6]"Let the people of Reuben live and
  not die.
But let the people be few."
[7]Moses said this about the people of
Judah:
"Lord, listen to Judah's prayer.
  Bring them back to their people.
They defend themselves with their
  hands.
  Help them fight their enemies!"
[8]Moses said this about the people of
Levi:
"Lord, your Thummim and Urim[d]
  belong
to Levi whom you love.
Lord, you tested him at Massah.
  You argued with him at the
    waters of Meribah.
[9]He said about his father and
  mother,
  'I don't care about them.'
He did not recognize his brothers.
  He did not know his children.
But he protected your word.
  And he guarded your agreement.
[10]He teaches your laws to the people
  of Jacob
and your teachings to the people
  of Israel.
He burns incense[d] before you.
  And he makes whole burnt
    offerings on your altar.
[11]Lord, make them strong.
  Be pleased with the work they do.
Defeat those who attack them.
  Don't let their enemies rise up
    again."
[12]Moses said this about the people of
Benjamin:
"The Lord's loved ones will lie
  down in safety.
The Lord protects them all day
  long.
The ones the Lord loves rest with
  him."
[13]Moses said this about the people of
Joseph:
"May the Lord bless their land with
  the best fruits.
Send rain from heaven above.
  And bring the water from the
    springs below.
[14]Let the sun produce the best fruits.
  Let each month bring its best
    fruits.

[15]Let the old mountains give the
  finest crops.
And let the everlasting hills give
  the best fruits.
[16]Let the full earth give the best
  fruits.
Let the Lord who lived in the
  burning bush be pleased.
May these blessings rest on the
  head of Joseph.
May they rest on the forehead of
  the one who was separated
    from his brothers.
[17]Joseph has the majesty of a
  firstborn[d] bull.
He is as strong as a wild ox.
He will stab other nations,
  even those nations far away.
These are the ten thousands of
  Ephraim.
And these are the thousands of
  Manasseh."
[18]Moses said this about the people of
Zebulun:
"Be happy when you go out,
  Zebulun.
And be happy in your tents,
  Issachar.
[19]They will call the people to the
  mountain.
And there they will offer the
  right sacrifices.
They will do well from all that is in
  the sea.
And they will do well from the
  treasures hidden in the sand on
    the shore."
[20]Moses said this about the people of
Gad:
"Praise God who gives Gad more
  land!
Gad lives there like a lion.
He tears off arms and heads.
[21]They chose the best land for
  themselves.
They received a large share, like
  that given to an officer.
When the leaders of the people
  gathered,
the people of Gad did what the
  Lord said was right.
And they judged Israel fairly."
[22]Moses said this about the people of
Dan:
"Dan is like a lion's cub,
  who jumps out of Bashan."
[23]Moses said this about the people of
Naphtali:
"Naphtali enjoys the Lord's special
  kindnesses.
They are full of his blessings.

Their land goes south to Lake
　　Galilee."
[24] Moses said this about the people of
Asher:

"Asher is the most blessed of the
　　sons.
He should be his brothers'
　　favorite.
Let him bathe his feet in olive oil.
[25] Your gates will have locks of iron
　　and bronze.
You will be strong as long as you
　　live.

[26] "There is no one like the God of
　　Israel.
He rides through the skies to
　　help you.
He rides on the clouds in his
　　majesty.
[27] The everlasting God is your place
　　of safety.
His arms will hold you up
　　forever.
He will force your enemy out ahead
　　of you.
He will say, 'Destroy the enemy!'
[28] The people of Israel will lie down in
　　safety.
Jacob's spring is theirs alone.
Theirs is a land full of grain and
　　wine.
There the skies drop their dew.
[29] Israel, you are blessed!
No one else is like you.
You are a people saved by the
　　Lord.
He is your shield and helper.
He is your glorious sword.
Your enemies will be afraid of you.
You will walk all over their holy
　　places."

34 Then Moses climbed up Mount
Nebo. He went from the plains of
Moab to the top of Mount Pisgah. It is
across from Jericho. From there the
Lord showed him all the land. He could
see from Gilead to Dan. [2] He could see
all of Naphtali and the lands of Ephraim
and Manasseh. He could see all the land
of Judah as far as the Mediterranean
Sea. [3] He could see the southern desert
and the whole Valley of Jericho up to
Zoar. Jericho is called the city of palm
trees. [4] Then the Lord said to Moses,
"This is the land I promised to Abraham, Isaac and Jacob. I said to them, 'I
will give this land to your descendants.'[d]
I have let you look at it, Moses. But you
will not cross over there."

[5] Then Moses, the servant of the Lord,
died there in Moab. It was as the Lord
had said. [6] The Lord buried Moses in
Moab in the valley opposite Beth Peor.
But even today no one knows where his
grave is. [7] Moses was 120 years old when
he died. His eyes were not weak. And
he was still strong. [8] The Israelites cried
for Moses for 30 days. They stayed in the
plains of Moab until the time of sadness
was over.

[9] Joshua son of Nun was then filled
with wisdom. Moses had put his hands
on Joshua. So the Israelites listened to
Joshua. And they did what the Lord had
commanded Moses.

[10] There has never been another
prophet[d] like Moses. The Lord knew
Moses face to face. [11] The Lord sent Moses to do signs and miracles[d] in Egypt.
He did them to the king, to all his officers and to the whole land of Egypt.
[12] Moses had great power. He did wonderful things for all the Israelites to see.

The Book of
JOSHUA

1 Moses was the servant of the Lord.
Joshua son of Nun was Moses' assistant. After Moses died, the Lord said to
Joshua: [2] "My servant Moses is dead.
Now you and all these people go across
the Jordan River. Go into the land I am
giving to the people of Israel. [3] I promised Moses I would give you this land.
So I will give you every place you go in
the land. [4] All the land from the desert in
the south to Lebanon in the north will

be yours. All the land from the great
river, the Euphrates, in the east, to the
Mediterranean Sea in the west will be
yours. This includes the land of the Hittites. [5] Just as I was with Moses, so I will
be with you. No one will be able to stop
you all your life. I will not leave you. I
will never leave you alone.

[6] "Joshua, be strong and brave! You
must lead these people so they can take
their land. This is the land I promised

their fathers I would give them. [7]Be strong and brave. Be sure to obey all the teachings my servant Moses gave you. If you follow them exactly, you will be successful in everything you do. [8]Always remember what is written in the Book of the Teachings. Study it day and night. Then you will be sure to obey everything that is written there. If you do this, you will be wise and successful in everything. [9]Remember that I commanded you to be strong and brave. So don't be afraid. The Lord your God will be with you everywhere you go."

[10]So Joshua gave orders to the officers of the people. He said, [11]"Go through the camp and tell the people, 'Get your supplies ready. Three days from now you will cross the Jordan River. You will go and take the land the Lord your God is giving you.'"

[12]Then Joshua spoke to the people of Reuben, Gad and the eastern half-tribe of Manasseh. Joshua said, [13]"Remember what Moses, the servant of the Lord, told you. He said the Lord your God would give you rest. And he said the Lord would give you this land. [14]Now the Lord has given you this land east of the Jordan River. Your wives, your children and your animals may stay here. But your fighting men must dress for war and cross the Jordan River ahead of your brothers. You must help your brothers. [15]The Lord has given you a place to rest. He will do the same for your brothers. But you must help them until they take the land. This is the land the Lord their God is giving them. Then you may return to your own land east of the Jordan River. That is the land that Moses, the servant of the Lord, gave you."

[16]Then the people answered Joshua, "Anything you command us to do, we will do. Any place you send us, we will go. [17]Just as we fully obeyed Moses, we will obey you. We ask only that the Lord your God be with you just as he was with Moses. [18]Then, if anyone refuses to obey your commands or turns against you, he will be put to death. Just be strong and brave!"

2 Joshua son of Nun secretly sent out two spies from Acacia. Joshua said to them, "Go and look at the land. Look closely at the city of Jericho."

So the men went to Jericho. They went to the house of a prostitute[d] and stayed there. This woman's name was Rahab.

[2]Someone told the king of Jericho, "Some men from Israel have come here tonight. They are spying out the land."

[3]So the king of Jericho sent this message to Rahab: "Bring out the men who came to you and entered your house. They have come to spy out our whole land."

[4]Now the woman had hidden the two men. She said, "They did come here. But I didn't know where they came from. [5]In the evening, when it was time to close the city gate, they left. I don't know where they went. Go quickly. Maybe you can catch them." [6](But the woman had taken the men up to the roof.[s] She had hidden them there under stalks of flax.[d] She had spread the flax out there to dry.) [7]So the king's men went out looking for the spies from Israel. They went to the places where people cross the Jordan River. The city gate was closed just after the king's men left the city.

[8]The spies were ready to sleep for the night. So Rahab went to the roof and talked to them. [9]She said, "I know the Lord has given this land to your people. You frighten us very much. Everyone living in this land is terribly afraid of you. [10]We are afraid because we have heard how the Lord helped you. We heard how he dried up the Red Sea[d] when you came out of Egypt. We heard how you destroyed Sihon and Og. They were the two Amorite kings who lived east of the Jordan. [11]When we heard this, we became very frightened. Now our men are afraid to fight you. This is because the Lord your God rules the heavens above and the earth below! [12]So now, make me a promise before the Lord. Promise that you will show kindness to my family just as I showed you kindness. Give me some proof that you will do this. [13]Promise me you will allow my family to live. Save my father, mother, brothers, sisters and all of their families from death."

[14]The men agreed. They said, "We will trade our lives for your lives. Don't tell anyone what we are doing. When the Lord gives us our land, we will be kind to you. You may trust us."

2:6 roof In Bible times houses were built with flat roofs. The roof was used for drying things such as flax and fruit. And it was used as an extra room, as a place for worship and as a place to sleep in the summer.

[15]The house Rahab lived in was built on the city wall. So she used a rope to let the men down through a window. [16]She said to them, "Go into the hills. The king's men will not find you there. Hide there for three days. After the king's men return, you may go on your way."

[17]The men said to her, "You must do as we say. If not, we cannot be responsible for keeping our promise. [18]You are using a red rope to help us escape. When we return to this land, you must tie it in the window through which you let us down. Bring your father, mother, brothers and all your family into your house. [19]We can keep everyone safe who stays in this house. If anyone in your house is hurt, we will be responsible. If anyone goes out of your house and is killed, it is his own fault. We cannot be responsible for him. [20]But you must not tell anyone about this agreement. If you do, we are free from it."

[21]Rahab answered, "I agree to this." So she sent them away, and they left. Then she tied the red rope in the window.

[22]The men left and went into the hills. There they stayed for three days. The king's men looked for them all along the road. But after three days, the king's men returned to the city without finding them. [23]Then the two men started back to Joshua. They left the hills and crossed the river. They went to Joshua son of Nun and told him everything that had happened to them. [24]They said to Joshua, "The Lord surely has given us all of the land. All the people in that land are terribly afraid of us."

3 Early the next morning Joshua and all the people of Israel left Acacia. They traveled to the Jordan River and camped there before crossing it. [2]After three days the officers went through the camp. [3]They gave orders to the people. They said, "You will see the priests and Levites carrying the Box[d] of the Agreement with the Lord your God. Then you should leave where you are and follow it. [4]That way you will know which way to go. You have never traveled this way before. But do not follow too closely. Stay about a thousand yards behind the Box of the Agreement."

[5]Then Joshua told the people, "Make yourselves holy for the Lord. Tomorrow the Lord will do amazing things among you."

[6]Joshua said to the priests, "Take the Box of the Agreement. Cross over the river ahead of the people." So the priests lifted the Holy Box and carried it ahead of the people.

[7]Then the Lord said to Joshua, "Today I will begin to make you a great man to all the Israelites. So the people will know I am with you just as I was with Moses. [8]The priests will carry the Box of the Agreement. Tell them this: 'Go to the edge of the Jordan River and stand in the water.'"

[9]Then Joshua said to the people of Israel, "Come here. Listen to the words of the Lord your God. [10]Here is proof that the living God is with you. Here is proof that he will drive out the Canaanites, Hittites, Hivites, Perizzites, Girgashites, Amorites and the Jebusites. [11]This is the proof: The Box of the Agreement will go ahead of you into the Jordan River. It is the Agreement with the Lord of the whole world. [12]Now choose 12 men from among you. Choose 1 from each of the 12 tribes[d] of Israel. [13]The priests will carry the Holy Box of the Lord, the Master of the whole world. They will carry it into the Jordan ahead of you. When they enter the water, the river will stop flowing. The water will be stopped. It will stand up in a heap as if a dam were there."

[14]So the priests carried the Box of the Agreement. And the people left the place where they had camped. Then they started across the Jordan River. [15]During harvest the Jordan is flooded. So the river was at its fullest. The priests who were carrying the Holy Box came to the edge of the river. And they stepped into the water. [16]Just at that moment, the water stopped flowing. It stood up in a heap a great distance away at Adam. This is a town near Zarethan. The water flowing down to the Sea of Arabah (the Dead Sea[d]) was completely cut off. So the people crossed the river near Jericho. [17]The ground there became dry. The priests carried the Box of the Agreement with the Lord to the middle of the river and stopped. They waited there while all the people of Israel walked across. They crossed the Jordan River on dry land.

4 All the people finished crossing the Jordan. Then the Lord said to Joshua, [2]"Choose 12 men from among the people. Choose 1 from each tribe.[d] [3]Tell the men to get 12 large rocks from the middle of the river. Take them from where the priests stood. Carry the rocks and put them down where you stay tonight."

⁴So Joshua chose 1 man from each tribe. Then he called the 12 men together. ⁵He said to them, "Go out into the river where the Holy Box[d] of the Lord your God is. Each of you should find 1 large rock. There will be 1 rock for each tribe of Israel. Carry the rock on your shoulder. ⁶They will be a sign among you. In the future your children will ask you, 'What do these rocks mean?' ⁷Tell them the Lord stopped the water from flowing in the Jordan. When the Holy Box of the Agreement with the Lord crossed the river, the water was stopped. These rocks will help the Israelites remember this forever."

⁸So the Israelites obeyed Joshua. They carried 12 rocks from the middle of the Jordan River. There was 1 rock for each of the 12 tribes of Israel. They did this the way the Lord had commanded Joshua. They carried the rocks with them. And they put them down where they made their camp. ⁹Joshua also put 12 rocks in the middle of the Jordan River. He put them where the priests had stood while carrying the Holy Box of the Lord. These rocks are still there today.

¹⁰The Lord had commanded Joshua to tell the people what to do. It was what Moses had said Joshua must do. So the priests carrying the Holy Box continued standing in the middle of the river until everything was done. And the people hurried across the river. ¹¹The people finished crossing the river. Then the priests carried the Holy Box of the Lord to the other side. As they carried it, the people watched. ¹²The men from the tribes of Reuben, Gad and the eastern half-tribe of Manasseh obeyed what Moses had told them. They were prepared for war. So they crossed the river ahead of the other people. ¹³About 40,000 soldiers were prepared for war. They passed before the Lord as they marched across the river. Then they went toward the plains of Jericho to go to war.

¹⁴That day the Lord made Joshua a great man to all the Israelites. They respected Joshua all his life, just as they had respected Moses.

¹⁵Then the Lord spoke to Joshua. ¹⁶He said, "Command the priests to bring the Box of the Agreement out of the river."

¹⁷So Joshua commanded the priests, "Come up out of the Jordan."

¹⁸So the priests carried the Box of the Agreement with the Lord out of the river. As soon as their feet touched dry land, the water began flowing again. The river again overflowed its banks. It was just as it had been before they crossed.

¹⁹The people crossed the Jordan on the tenth day of the first month. They camped at Gilgal, east of Jericho. ²⁰They carried with them the 12 rocks taken from the Jordan. And Joshua set them up at Gilgal. ²¹Then he spoke to the Israelites. He said, "In the future your children will ask you, 'What do these rocks mean?' ²²Tell them, 'Israel crossed the Jordan River on dry land. ²³The Lord your God caused the water to stop flowing. The river was dry until the people finished crossing it. The Lord did the same thing for us at the Jordan that he did for the people at the Red Sea.[d] Remember that he stopped the water at the Red Sea so we could cross. ²⁴The Lord did this so all people would know he has great power. Then they will always respect the Lord your God.'"

5 So the Lord dried up the Jordan River until the Israelites had crossed it. Now all the kings of the Amorites west of the Jordan heard about it. And the Canaanite kings living by the Mediterranean Sea heard about it. They were very scared. After that they were too afraid to face the Israelites.

²At that time the Lord spoke to Joshua. He said, "Make knives from flint stones. Circumcise[d] the Israelites again." ³So Joshua made knives from flint stones. Then he circumcised the Israelites at Gibeath Haaraloth.

⁴This is why Joshua circumcised the men: After the Israelites left Egypt, all the men old enough to serve in the army died. They died in the desert on the way out of Egypt. ⁵The men who had come out of Egypt had been circumcised. But many were born in the desert on the trip from Egypt. They had not been circumcised. ⁶The Israelites had moved about in the desert for 40 years. During that time all the fighting men who had left Egypt had died. This was because they had not obeyed the Lord. So the Lord swore they would not see the land. This was the land he had promised their ancestors to give them. It was a land where much food grows. ⁷So their sons took their places. But none of the sons born on the trip from Egypt had been circumcised. So Joshua circumcised them. ⁸After all the Israelites had been circum-

cised, they stayed in camp until they were healed.

[9]Then the Lord said to Joshua, "As slaves in Egypt you were ashamed. But today I have removed that shame." So Joshua named that place Gilgal. And it is still named Gilgal today.

[10]The people of Israel were still camped at Gilgal on the plains of Jericho. It was there, on the evening of the fourteenth day of the month, they celebrated the Passover[d] Feast. [11]The next day after the Passover, the people ate some of the food grown on that land: bread made without yeast and roasted grain. [12]The day they ate this food, the manna[d] stopped coming. The Israelites no longer got the manna from heaven. They ate the food grown in the land of Canaan that year.

[13]Joshua was near Jericho. He looked up and saw a man standing in front of him. The man had a sword in his hand. Joshua went to him and asked, "Are you a friend or an enemy?"

[14]The man answered, "I am neither one. I have come as the commander of the Lord's army."

Then Joshua bowed facedown on the ground. He asked, "Does my master have a command for me, his servant?"

[15]The commander of the Lord's army answered, "Take off your sandals. The place where you are standing is holy." So Joshua did.

6 Now the people of Jericho were afraid because the Israelites were near. So they closed the city gates and guarded them. No one went into the city. And no one came out.

[2]Then the Lord spoke to Joshua. He said, "Look, I have given you Jericho, its king and all its fighting men. [3]March around the city with your army one time every day. Do this for six days. [4]Have seven priests carry trumpets made from horns of male sheep. Tell them to march in front of the Holy Box.[d] On the seventh day march around the city seven times. On that day tell the priests to blow the trumpets as they march. [5]They will make one long blast on the trumpets. When you hear that sound, have all the people give a loud shout. Then the walls of the city will fall. And the people will go straight into the city."

[6]So Joshua son of Nun called the priests together. He said to them, "Carry the Box of the Agreement with the Lord. Tell seven priests to carry trumpets and march in front of it." [7]Then Joshua or-

dered the people, "Now go! March around the city. The soldiers with weapons should march in front of the Box of the Agreement with the Lord."

[8]So Joshua finished speaking to the people. Then the seven priests began marching before the Lord. They carried the seven trumpets and blew them as they marched. The priests carrying the Box of the Agreement with the Lord followed them. [9]The soldiers with weapons marched in front of the priests. And armed men walked behind the Holy Box. They were blowing their trumpets. [10]But Joshua had told the people not to give a war cry. He said, "Don't shout. Don't say a word until the day I tell you. Then shout!" [11]So Joshua had the Holy Box of the Lord carried around the city one time. Then they went back to camp for the night.

[12]Early the next morning Joshua got up. And the priests carried the Holy Box of the Lord again. [13]The seven priests carried the seven trumpets. They marched in front of the Holy Box of the Lord, blowing their trumpets. The soldiers with weapons marched in front of them. Other soldiers walked behind the Holy Box of the Lord. All this time the priests were blowing their trumpets. [14]So on the second day they marched around the city one time. Then they went back to camp. They did this every day for six days.

[15]On the seventh day they got up at dawn. They marched around the city seven times. They marched just as they had on the days before. But on that day they marched around the city seven times. [16]The seventh time around the priests blew their trumpets. Then Joshua gave the command: "Now, shout! The Lord has given you this city! [17]The city and everything in it are to be destroyed as an offering to the Lord. Only Rahab the prostitute[d] and everyone in her house should remain alive. They must not be killed. This is because Rahab hid the two spies we sent out. [18]Don't take any of the things that are to be destroyed as an offering to the Lord. If you take them and bring them into our camp, then you yourselves will be destroyed. You will also bring trouble to all of Israel. [19]All the silver and gold and things made from bronze and iron belong to the Lord. They must be saved for him."

[20]When the priests blew the trumpets, the people shouted. At the sound of the trumpets and the people's shout, the

walls fell. And everyone ran straight into the city. So the Israelites defeated that city. ²¹They completely destroyed every living thing in the city. They killed men and women, young and old. They killed cattle, sheep and donkeys.

²²Joshua spoke to the two men who had spied out the land. Joshua said, "Go into the prostitute's house. Bring her out. And bring out all the people who are with her. Do this because of the promise you made to her." ²³So the two men went into the house and brought out Rahab. They also brought out her father, mother, brothers and all those with her. They put all of her family in a safe place outside the camp of Israel.

²⁴Then Israel burned the whole city and everything in it. But they did not burn the things made from silver, gold, bronze and iron. These were saved for the Lord. ²⁵Joshua saved Rahab the prostitute, her family and all who were with her. He let them live. This was because Rahab had helped the men he had sent to spy out Jericho. Rahab still lives among the Israelites today.

²⁶Then Joshua made this important promise. He said:

"Anyone who tries to rebuild this
    city of Jericho
will be punished by a curse from
    the Lord.
The man who lays the foundation
    of this city
will lose his oldest son.
The man who sets up the gates
will lose his youngest son."

²⁷So the Lord was with Joshua. And Joshua became famous through all the land.

7 But the people of Israel did not obey the Lord. There was a man from the tribe^d of Judah named Achan. (He was the son of Carmi and grandson of Zimri. And Zimri was the son of Zerah.) Achan kept some of the things that were to be given to the Lord. So the Lord became very angry at the Israelites.

²Joshua sent some men from Jericho to Ai. (Ai was near Beth Aven, east of Bethel.) He told them, "Go to Ai and spy out the area." So the men went to spy on Ai.

³Later they came back to Joshua. They said, "There are only a few men in Ai to fight against us. So we will not need all our people to defeat them. Send 2,000 or 3,000 men to fight there. There is no need to send all of our people." ⁴So about 3,000 men went to Ai. But the

people of Ai beat them badly. ⁵The people of Ai chased the Israelites. They chased them from the city gate all the way to where stones were cut from the ground. They killed about 36 Israelites as they went down the hill. When the Israelites saw this, they became very afraid.

⁶Then Joshua tore his clothes to show how upset he was. He bowed facedown on the ground before the Box^d of the Lord. And he stayed there until evening. The leaders of Israel did the same thing. They also threw dirt on their heads to show they were upset. ⁷Then Joshua said, "Lord God, you brought our people across the Jordan River. Why did you bring us this far and then let the Amorites destroy us? We should have been happy to stay on the other side of the Jordan. ⁸Lord, there is nothing I can say now. Israel has been beaten by the enemy. ⁹The Canaanites and all the other people in this country will hear about this. They will surround and kill all of us! Then what will you do for your own great name?"

¹⁰The Lord said to Joshua, "Stand up! Why are you down on your face? ¹¹The Israelites have sinned. They have broken the agreement I commanded them to obey. They took some of the things I commanded them to destroy. They have stolen from me. They have lied. They have taken those things for themselves. ¹²That is why the Israelites cannot face their enemies. They turn away from the fight and run. I have commanded that they be destroyed. You must destroy everything I commanded you to destroy. I will not help you anymore unless you do this.

¹³"Now go! Have the people make themselves holy for me. Tell them, 'Set yourselves apart to the Lord for tomorrow. The Lord, the God of Israel, says some of you are keeping things he commanded you to destroy. You will never defeat your enemies until you throw away those things.

¹⁴"'Tomorrow morning you must all stand before the Lord. All the tribes will stand before him. The Lord will choose one tribe. And that tribe must stand alone before him. Then the Lord will choose one family group from that tribe. And that family group must stand alone before him. Then the Lord will choose one family from that family group. And it must stand alone before him. Then the Lord will look at that family man by

man. [15]The man who is keeping what should have been destroyed will himself be destroyed by fire. And everything he owns will be destroyed with him. He has broken the agreement with the Lord. He has done a disgraceful thing among the people of Israel!'"

[16]Early the next morning Joshua led all of Israel before the Lord. All of the tribes stood before him. And the Lord chose the tribe of Judah. [17]So all the family groups of Judah stood before the Lord. The Lord then chose the family group of Zerah. And all the families of Zerah stood before the Lord. Then the family of Zimri was chosen. [18]And Joshua told all the men in that family to come before the Lord. The Lord chose Achan son of Carmi. (Carmi was the son of Zimri. And Zimri was the son of Zerah.)

[19]Then Joshua said to Achan, "My son, you should tell the truth. Confess to the Lord, the God of Israel. Tell me what you did. Don't try to hide anything from me."

[20]Achan answered, "It is true! I have sinned against the Lord, the God of Israel. This is what I did: [21]Among the things I saw was a beautiful coat from Babylonia. And I saw about five pounds of silver and more than one and one-quarter pounds of gold. I wanted these things very much for myself. So I took them. You will find them buried in the ground under my tent. The silver is under the coat."

[22]So Joshua sent some men to the tent. They ran to the tent and found the things hidden there. The silver was under the coat. [23]The men brought them out of the tent. Then they took them to Joshua and all the Israelites. They spread them out on the ground before the Lord. [24]Then Joshua and all the people led Achan son of Zerah to the Valley of Trouble. They also took the silver, the coat and the gold. They took Achan's sons, daughters, cattle, donkeys, sheep, tent and everything he owned. [25]Joshua said, "I don't know why you caused so much trouble for us. But now the Lord will bring trouble to you." Then all the people threw stones at Achan until he died. They also killed his family with stones. Then the people burned them. [26]They piled rocks over Achan's body. And those rocks are still there today. That is why it is called the Valley of Trouble. After this the Lord was no longer angry.

8 Then the Lord said to Joshua, "Don't be afraid. Don't give up. Lead all your fighting men to Ai. I will help you defeat the king of Ai. I am giving you his people, his city and his land. [2]You will do to Ai and its king what you did to Jericho and its king. Only this time you may take all the wealth. You may keep it for yourselves. Now tell some of your soldiers to set up an ambush behind the city."

[3]So Joshua led his whole army toward Ai. Then he chose 30,000 of his best fighting men. He sent these men out at night. [4]Joshua gave them these orders: "Listen carefully. You must set up an ambush behind the city. Don't go far from it. Continue to watch and be ready. [5]I and the men who are with me will march toward the city. The men in the city will come out to fight us. Then we will turn and run away from them as we did before. [6]They will chase us away from the city. They will think we are running away from them as we did before. When we run away, [7]come out from your ambush and take the city. The Lord your God will give you the power to win. [8]After you take the city, burn it. See to it! You have your orders."

[9]Then Joshua sent them to their place of ambush to wait. They went to a place between Bethel and Ai, to the west of Ai. But Joshua stayed the night with his people.

[10]Early the next morning Joshua gathered his men together. He and the older leaders of Israel led them to Ai. [11]All of the soldiers who were with Joshua marched to Ai. They stopped in front of the city and made camp north of Ai. There was a valley between them and the city. [12]Then Joshua chose about 5,000 men. He set them in ambush in the area west of the city between Bethel and Ai. [13]So the people took their positions. The main camp was north of the city. The other men were hiding to the west. That night Joshua went down into the valley.

[14]Now the king of Ai saw the army of Israel. So he and his people got up early the next morning and hurried out to fight them. They went out to a place east of the city. The king did not know soldiers were waiting in ambush behind the city. [15]Joshua and all the men of Israel let the army of Ai push them back. Then they ran east toward the desert. [16]The men in Ai were called to chase Joshua and his men. So they left the city

and went after them. [17]All the men of Ai and Bethel chased the army of Israel. The city was left open. Not a man stayed to protect it.

[18]Then the Lord said to Joshua, "Hold your spear toward Ai. I will give you that city." So Joshua held his spear toward the city of Ai. [19]The men of Israel who were in ambush saw this. They quickly came out of their hiding place and hurried toward the city. They entered the city and took control of it. Then they quickly set it on fire.

[20]When the men of Ai looked back, they saw smoke rising from their city. At the same time the men of Israel stopped running. They turned against the men of Ai. The men of Ai could not escape in any direction. [21]Joshua and all his men saw that the army had taken control of the city. They saw the smoke rising from it. So they stopped running and turned to fight the men of Ai. [22]The men who were in ambush also came out of the city to help with the fight. The men of Ai were caught between the armies of Israel. The Israelites fought until not one of the men of Ai was left alive. None of the enemy escaped. [23]But the king of Ai was left alive. And Joshua's men brought him to Joshua.

[24]During the fighting the army of Israel chased the men of Ai into the fields and desert. So the Israelites killed all of them in the fields and desert. Then they went back to Ai and killed everyone there. [25]All the people of Ai died that day, 12,000 men and women. [26]Joshua had held his spear toward Ai. It was a sign to his people to destroy the city. And Joshua held out his spear until all the people of Ai were destroyed. [27]The people of Israel kept the animals for themselves. They also kept the other things the people of Ai had owned. This is what the Lord told them to do when he gave Joshua the commands.

[28]Then Joshua burned the city of Ai. It became an empty pile of ruins. And it is still like that today. [29]Joshua hung the king of Ai on a tree. He left him hanging there until evening. At sunset Joshua told his men to take the king's body down from the tree. He told them to throw it down at the city gate. Then they covered it with rocks. That pile of rocks is still there today.

[30]Then Joshua built an altar for the Lord, the God of Israel. He built it on Mount Ebal, as [31]Moses, the Lord's servant, had commanded. Joshua built the altar as it was explained in the Book of the Teachings of Moses. The altar was made from stones that were not cut. No tool was ever used on them. The Israelites offered burnt offerings to the Lord on that altar. They also offered fellowship offerings. [32]There Joshua wrote the teachings of Moses on stones. He did this for all the people of Israel to see. [33]The older leaders, officers, judges and all the Israelites were there. They were standing around the Box[d] of the Agreement with the Lord. They stood before the priests, the Levites who had carried the Holy Box. Israelites and non-Israelites were all standing there. Half of the people stood in front of Mount Ebal. The other half stood in front of Mount Gerizim. This was the way the Lord's servant Moses had earlier commanded the people to be blessed.

[34]Then Joshua read all the words of the teachings. He read the blessings and the curses. He read it exactly as they were written in the Book of the Teachings. [35]All the Israelites were gathered together. All the women and children were there. All the non-Israelites living with the Israelites were there. Joshua read every command that Moses had given.

9 All the kings west of the Jordan River heard about these things. These were the kings of the Hittites, Amorites, Canaanites, Perizzites, Hivites and Jebusites. They lived in the mountains and on the western mountain slopes. They also lived along the whole Mediterranean Sea coast. [2]All these kings gathered to fight Joshua and the Israelites.

[3]The people of Gibeon heard how Joshua had defeated Jericho and Ai. [4]So they decided to trick the Israelites. They gathered old leather wine bags that were cracked and mended. They put them on the backs of their donkeys. They also put old sacks on their donkeys. [5]The men put old sandals on their feet and wore old clothes. They took some dry, moldy bread. [6]Then they went to Joshua in the camp near Gilgal.

The men spoke to Joshua and the men of Israel. They said, "We have traveled from a faraway country. Make a peace agreement with us."

[7]The men of Israel said to these Hivites, "Maybe you live near us. How can we make a peace agreement with you?"

[8]The Hivites said to Joshua, "We are your servants."

But Joshua asked, "Who are you? Where do you come from?"

[9]The men answered, "We are your servants. We have come from a far country. We came because we heard of the fame of the Lord your God. We heard about what he has done. We heard about everything he did in Egypt. [10]We heard that he defeated the two kings of the Amorites. They were from the east side of the Jordan River: Sihon king of Heshbon and Og king of Bashan who was king in Ashtaroth. [11]So our older leaders and our people spoke to us. They said, 'Take food for your journey. Go and meet the Israelites. Tell them, "We are your servants. Make a peace agreement with us." '

[12]"Look at our bread. When we left home it was warm and fresh. But now it is dry and moldy. [13]Look at our leather winebags. When we left home they were new and filled with wine. Now they are cracked and old. Look at our clothes and sandals. The long journey has almost destroyed them."

[14]The men of Israel tasted the bread. But they did not ask the Lord what to do. [15]So Joshua agreed to make peace with the Gibeonites. He agreed to let them live. The leaders of the Israelites made a promise to keep the agreement.

[16]Three days later the Israelites learned that the Gibeonites lived nearby. [17]So the Israelites went to where they lived. On the third day the Israelites came to their cities. The cities were Gibeon, Kephirah, Beeroth and Kiriath Jearim. [18]But the Israelites did not attack those cities. They had made a promise to them before the Lord, the God of Israel.

All the Israelites grumbled against the leaders who had made the agreement. [19]But the leaders answered, "We have given our promise before the Lord, the God of Israel. We cannot attack them now. [20]This is what we must do. We must let them live. We cannot hurt them, or God's anger will be against us. We would be breaking the promise we made to them. [21]So let them live. But they will cut wood and carry water for our people." So the leaders kept their promise of peace to them.

[22]Joshua called for the Gibeonites. He said, "Why did you lie to us? Your land was near our camp. But you told us you were from a far country. [23]Now, you will be placed under a curse. You will be our slaves. You will have to cut wood and carry water for the people of the house of God."

[24]The Gibeonites answered Joshua, "We lied to you because we were afraid you would kill us. We heard that God commanded his servant Moses to give you all of this land. And God told you to kill all the people who lived in the land. That is why we did this. [25]Now you can decide what to do with us. You can do anything to us that you think is right."

[26]So Joshua saved their lives. He did not allow the Israelites to kill them. [27]But Joshua made the Gibeonites slaves to the Israelites. They cut wood and carried water for the Israelites. And they did it for the altar of the Lord—wherever he chose it to be. They are still doing this today.

10 At this time Adoni-Zedek was the king of Jerusalem. He heard that Joshua had defeated Ai and completely destroyed it. He learned that Joshua had done the same thing to Jericho and its king. The king also learned that the Gibeonites had made a peace agreement with Israel. And they lived very near Jerusalem. [2]So Adoni-Zedek and his people were very afraid because of this. Gibeon was not a little town like Ai. It was a large city. It was as big as a city that had a king. All its men were good fighters. [3]So Adoni-Zedek king of Jerusalem sent a message to Hoham king of Hebron. He also sent it to Piram king of Jarmuth, Japhia king of Lachish, and Debir king of Eglon. The king of Jerusalem begged these men, [4]"Come with me and help me attack Gibeon. Gibeon has made a peace agreement with Joshua and the Israelites."

[5]Then these five Amorite kings joined their armies. They were the kings of Jerusalem, Hebron, Jarmuth, Lachish and Eglon. These armies went to Gibeon, surrounded it and attacked it.

[6]The Gibeonites sent a message to Joshua in his camp at Gilgal. The message said: "We are your servants. Don't let us be destroyed. Come quickly and help us! Save us! All the Amorite kings from the mountains have joined their armies. They are fighting against us."

[7]So Joshua marched out of Gilgal with his whole army. His best fighting men were with him. [8]The Lord said to Joshua, "Don't be afraid of those armies. I will allow you to defeat them. None of them will be able to defeat you."

[9]Joshua and his army marched all night to Gibeon. So Joshua surprised

them when he attacked. [10]The Lord confused those armies when Israel attacked. So Israel defeated them in a great victory. They chased them from Gibeon on the road going to Beth Horon. The army of Israel killed men all the way to Azekah and Makkedah. [11]They chased the enemy down the road from Beth Horon to Azekah. While they were chasing them, the Lord threw large hailstones on them from the sky. Many of the enemy were killed by the hailstones. More men were killed by the hailstones than the Israelites killed with their swords.

[12]That day the Lord allowed the Israelites to defeat the Amorites. And that day Joshua stood before all the people of Israel and said to the Lord:

"Sun, stand still over Gibeon.
　Moon, stand still over the Valley
　　of Aijalon."
[13]So the sun stood still.
　And the moon stopped
　until the people defeated their
　　enemies.

These words are written in the Book of Jashar.

The sun stopped in the middle of the sky. It waited to go down for a full day. [14]That has never happened at any time before that day or since. That was the day the Lord listened to a man. Truly the Lord was fighting for Israel!

[15]After this, Joshua and his army went back to the camp at Gilgal.

[16]During the fight the five kings ran away. They hid in a cave near Makkedah. [17]But someone found them hiding in the cave and told Joshua. [18]So he said, "Cover the opening to the cave with large rocks. Put some men there to guard it. [19]But don't stay there yourselves. Continue chasing the enemy. Continue attacking them from behind. Don't let them get to their cities safely. The Lord your God has given you the victory over them."

[20]So Joshua and the Israelites killed the enemy. But a few were able to get back to their strong, walled cities. [21]After the fighting, Joshua's men came back safely to him at Makkedah. No one was brave enough to say a word against the Israelites.

[22]Joshua said, "Move the rocks that are covering the opening to the cave. Bring those five kings out to me." [23]So Joshua's men brought the five kings out of the cave. They were the kings of Jerusalem, Hebron, Jarmuth, Lachish and

Eglon. [24]They brought the five kings out to Joshua. He called all his men to come to that place. He said to the commanders of his army, "Come here! Put your feet on the necks of these kings." So they came close and put their feet on their necks.

[25]Then Joshua said to his men, "Be strong and brave! Don't be afraid. I will show you what the Lord will do to the enemies you will fight in the future." [26]Then Joshua killed the five kings. He hung their bodies on five trees. And he left them hanging on the trees until evening.

[27]At sunset Joshua told his men to take the bodies down from the trees. Then they threw their bodies into the same cave where they had been hiding. They covered the opening to the cave with large rocks. They are still there today.

[28]That day Joshua defeated Makkedah. He killed the king and completely destroyed all the people in that city. He killed them as an offering to the Lord. There was no one left alive. He did the same thing to the king of Makkedah as he had done to the king of Jericho.

[29]Then Joshua and all the Israelites traveled from Makkedah. They went to Libnah and attacked it. [30]The Lord allowed them to defeat it and its king. They killed every person in the city. No one was left alive. And they did the same thing to that king as they had done to the king of Jericho.

[31]Then Joshua and all the Israelites left Libnah and went to Lachish. They camped around Lachish and attacked it. [32]The Lord allowed them to defeat Lachish. On the second day Joshua defeated it. The Israelites killed everyone in that city. This was the same thing they had done to Libnah. [33]During this same time Horam king of Gezer came to help Lachish. But Joshua also defeated him and his army. There was no one left alive.

[34]Then Joshua and all the Israelites went from Lachish to Eglon. They camped around Eglon and attacked it. [35]That day they captured Eglon. They killed all its people and completely destroyed everything in it as an offering to the Lord. This is the same thing they had done to Lachish.

[36]Then Joshua and the Israelites went from Eglon to Hebron and attacked it. [37]They captured it and all the little towns near it. The Israelites killed everyone in

Hebron. No one was left alive there. This was the same thing they had done to Eglon. They completely destroyed the city and all its people as an offering to the Lord.

38 Then Joshua and the Israelites went back to Debir and attacked it. 39 They captured that city, its king and all the little towns near it. They completely destroyed everyone in Debir as an offering to the Lord. No one was left alive there. Israel did to Debir and its king the same thing they had done to Libnah and its king. This was what they had done to Hebron.

40 So Joshua defeated all the kings of the cities of these areas: the mountains, southern Canaan, the western mountain slopes and the eastern mountain slopes. The Lord, the God of Israel, had told Joshua to completely destroy all the people as an offering to the Lord. So he left no one alive in those places. 41 Joshua captured all the cities from Kadesh Barnea to Gaza. And he captured all the cities from Goshen to Gibeon. 42 He captured all these cities and their kings on one trip. He did it because the Lord, the God of Israel, was fighting for Israel.

43 Then Joshua and all the Israelites returned to their camp at Gilgal.

11 Jabin king of Hazor heard about all that had happened. He sent messages to Jobab king of Madon, to the king of Shimron and to the king of Acshaph. 2 He sent one to the kings in the northern mountains. Jabin also sent a message to the kings in the Jordan Valley south of Lake Galilee and in the western mountain slopes. He sent a message to the king of Naphoth Dor in the west. 3 Jabin also sent one to the kings of the Canaanites in the east and in the west. He sent messages to the Amorites, Hittites, Perizzites and Jebusites in the mountains. Jabin also sent one to the Hivites. They lived below Mount Hermon in the area of Mizpah. 4 So the armies of all these kings came together. There were many fighting men, horses and chariots. It was a huge army. It looked like there were as many men as grains of sand on the seashore.

5 All of these kings met together at the Waters of Merom. They joined their armies together into one camp. They made plans to fight against the Israelites.

6 Then the Lord said to Joshua, "Don't be afraid of them. At this time tomorrow I will allow you to defeat them. You will kill all of them. You will cripple their horses and burn all their chariots."

7 So Joshua and his whole army surprised the enemy. They attacked them at the Waters of Merom. 8 The Lord allowed Israel to defeat them. They chased them to Greater Sidon, Misrephoth Maim and the Valley of Mizpah in the east. Israel fought until none of the enemy was left alive. 9 Joshua did what the Lord said to do. He cut the legs of their horses and burned their chariots.

10 Then Joshua went back and captured the city of Hazor. He killed the king of Hazor. (Hazor had been the leader of all the kingdoms that fought against Israel.) 11 Israel killed everyone in Hazor. They completely destroyed them. There was nothing left alive. Then they burned Hazor itself.

12 Joshua captured all of these cities. He killed all of their kings. He completely destroyed everything in these cities. He did this the way Moses, the servant of the Lord, had commanded. 13 But the Israelites did not burn any cities that were built on their hills, except Hazor. That city alone was burned by Joshua. 14 The people of Israel kept for themselves everything they found in the cities. They kept all the animals they found. But they killed all the people there. They did not leave anyone alive. 15 Long ago the Lord had commanded his servant Moses to do this. Then Moses had commanded Joshua to do it. So Joshua obeyed God. He did everything the Lord had commanded Moses.

16 So Joshua defeated all the people in the land. He had control of the mountains and the area of southern Canaan. He controlled all the areas of Goshen, the western mountain slopes and the Jordan Valley. He controlled the mountains of Israel and all the hills near them. 17 Joshua controlled all the land from Mount Halak near Edom to Baal Gad. Baal Gad was in the Valley of Lebanon, below Mount Hermon. Joshua captured all the kings in the land and killed them. 18 He fought against them for many years. 19 The people of only one city in all the land had made a peace agreement with Israel. They were the Hivites living in Gibeon. All the other cities were defeated in war. 20 The Lord made those people stubborn so they would fight against Israel. This way he could completely destroy them without mercy. This is what the Lord had commanded Moses to do.

²¹Now Joshua fought the Anakites[d] who lived in the mountains of Hebron, Debir, Anab, Judah and Israel. And he completely destroyed them and their towns. ²²There were no Anakites left living in the land of the Israelites. Only a few Anakites were left in Gaza, Gath and Ashdod. ²³Joshua took control of all the land of Israel. This was what the Lord had told Moses to do long ago. He gave the land to Israel because he had promised it to them. Then Joshua divided the land among the tribes[d] of Israel. The fighting had finally ended. And there was peace in the land.

12 The Israelites took control of the land east of the Jordan River. They now had all the land from the Arnon Ravine to Mount Hermon. And they had all the land along the eastern side of the Jordan Valley. Here are all the kings the Israelites defeated to take this land:

²Sihon was the king of the Amorites. He lived in the city of Heshbon. He ruled the land from Aroer at the Arnon Ravine to the Jabbok River. His land started in the middle of the ravine. This was their border with the Ammonites. Sihon ruled over half the land of Gilead. ³He also ruled over the eastern side of the Jordan Valley from Lake Galilee to the Dead Sea.[d] And he ruled from Beth Jeshimoth south to the hills of Pisgah.

⁴Og king of Bashan was one of the last of the Rephaites.[d] He ruled the land in Ashtaroth and Edrei. ⁵He ruled over Mount Hermon, Salecah and all the area of Bashan. His land ended where the people of Geshur and Maacah lived. Og also ruled half the land of Gilead. It stopped at the border of Sihon king of Heshbon.

⁶The Lord's servant Moses and the Israelites defeated all these kings. And Moses gave that land to the tribes[d] of Reuben and Gad and to the eastern half-tribe of Manasseh. This land was to be their own.

⁷The Israelites also defeated kings in the land that was west of the Jordan River. Joshua led the people in this land. He gave the people this land and divided it among the 12 tribes. This was the land that was promised to them. It was between Baal Gad in the Valley of Lebanon and Mount Halak near Edom. ⁸This included the mountains, the western mountain slopes and the Jordan Valley. It also included the eastern mountain slopes, the desert and southern Canaan. This was the land where the Hittites,

Amorites, Canaanites, Perizzites, Hivites and Jebusites had lived. The people of Israel defeated the king of each of the following cities: ⁹Jericho, Ai (near Bethel), ¹⁰Jerusalem, Hebron, ¹¹Jarmuth, Lachish, ¹²Eglon, Gezer, ¹³Debir, Geder, ¹⁴Hormah, Arad, ¹⁵Libnah, Adullam, ¹⁶Makkedah, Bethel, ¹⁷Tappuah, Hepher, ¹⁸Aphek, Lasharon, ¹⁹Madon, Hazor, ²⁰Shimron Meron, Acshaph, ²¹Taanach, Megiddo, ²²Kedesh, Jokneam in Carmel, ²³Dor (in Naphoth Dor), Goyim in Gilgal, and ²⁴Tirzah.

The total number of kings was 31.

13 When Joshua was very old, the Lord spoke to him. He said, "Joshua, you have grown old. But there is still much land for you to take. ²You have not yet taken the land of Geshur and the land of the Philistines. ³You have not yet taken the area from the Shihor River at the border of Egypt to Ekron in the north. That belongs to the Canaanites. You must still defeat the five Philistine leaders. They are at Gaza, Ashdod, Ashkelon, Gath and Ekron. You must also defeat the Avvites. ⁴They live south of the Canaanite land. ⁵You have not yet defeated the Gebalites. And there is also the area of Lebanon east of Baal Gad below Mount Hermon to Lebo Hamath.

⁶"The Sidonians are living in the hill country from Lebanon to Misrephoth Maim. But I will force out all of them ahead of the Israelites. Be sure to remember this land when you divide the land among the Israelites. Do this as I told you.

⁷"Now divide the land among the nine tribes[d] and the western half-tribe of Manasseh."

⁸The eastern half-tribe of Manasseh and the tribes of Reuben and Gad had received their land. The Lord's servant Moses gave them the land east of the Jordan River. ⁹Their land started at Aroer at the Arnon Ravine. It continued to the town in the middle of the ravine. And it included the whole plain from Medeba to Dibon. ¹⁰All the towns that Sihon king of the Amorites ruled were in that land. He ruled in the city of Heshbon. The land continued to the area where the Ammonites lived. ¹¹Gilead was also there. And the area where the people of Geshur and Maacah lived was in that land. All of Mount Hermon and all of Bashan as far as Salecah was included. ¹²All the kingdom of Og king of Bashan was in the land. In the past he

ruled in Ashtaroth and Edrei. Og was one of the last of the Rephaites.*ᵈ* In the past Moses had defeated them and had taken their land. ¹³The Israelites did not force out the people of Geshur and Maacah. They still live among the Israelites today.

¹⁴The tribe of Levi was the only one that did not get any land. Instead, they were to be given all the burned sacrifices made to the Lord, the God of Israel. That is what the Lord had promised them.

¹⁵Moses had given each family group from the tribe of Reuben some land. This is the land they were given: ¹⁶It was the land from Aroer near the Arnon Ravine to the town of Medeba. This included the whole plain and the town in the middle of the ravine. ¹⁷The land continued to Heshbon. It included all the towns on the plain. These towns were Dibon, Bamoth Baal and Beth Baal Meon. ¹⁸They included Jahaz, Kedemoth, Mephaath, ¹⁹Kiriathaim, Sibmah and Zereth Shahar on the hill in the valley. ²⁰They also included Beth Peor, the hills of Pisgah and Beth Jeshimoth. ²¹So that land included all the towns on the plain and all the area that Sihon the king of the Amorites had ruled. He ruled from the town of Heshbon. But Moses had defeated him and the leaders of the Midianites. Those leaders included Evi, Rekem, Zur, Hur and Reba. All these leaders fought together with Sihon. And they lived in that country. ²²The Israelites killed many people during the fighting. They also killed Balaam of Beor. He tried to use magic to tell the future. ²³The land given to Reuben stopped at the shore of the Jordan River. So the land given to the family groups of Reuben included all these towns and their fields that were listed.

²⁴This is the land Moses gave to the tribe of Gad. He gave it to all the family groups: ²⁵He gave them the land of Jazar and all the towns of Gilead. He also gave them half the land of the Ammonites. It went as far as Aroer near Rabbah. ²⁶It included the area from Heshbon to Ramath Mizpah and Betonim. It included the area from Mahanaim to the land of Debir. ²⁷The land included the valley, Beth Haram, Beth Nimrah, Succoth and Zaphon. All the other land Sihon king of Heshbon had ruled was also included in it. This is the land on the east side of the Jordan River. It continued to the end of Lake Galilee. ²⁸All this is the land Mo-

ses gave to the tribe of Gad. It included all the towns that were listed. Moses gave it to all the family groups.

²⁹This is the land Moses had given to the eastern half-tribe of Manasseh. Half of all the family groups in the tribe of Manasseh were given this land: ³⁰The land started at Mahanaim. It included all of Bashan and the land ruled by Og king of Bashan. It also included all the Towns of Jair in Bashan. There were 60 cities in all. ³¹It also included half of Gilead, Ashtaroth and Edrei. (These were the cities where Og king of Bashan had ruled.) All this land had been given to the family of Makir son of Manasseh. Half of all his sons had been given this land.

³²Moses had given this land to these tribes on the plains of Moab. It was across the Jordan River east of Jericho. ³³But Moses had given no land to the tribe of Levi. The Lord, the God of Israel, promised that he himself would be the gift for the Levites.

14 Eleazar the priest, Joshua son of Nun and the leaders of all the tribes of Israel decided what land to give to the people. ²The Lord had commanded Moses long ago how he wanted the people to choose their land. The people of the nine-and-a-half tribes threw lots*ᵈ* to decide which land they would receive. ³Moses had already given the two-and-a-half tribes their land east of the Jordan River. But the tribe of Levi was not given any land like the others. ⁴The sons of Joseph had divided into two tribes—Manasseh and Ephraim. The tribe of Levi was not given any land. It was given only some towns in which to live. It was also given pastures for its animals. ⁵The Lord had told Moses how to give the land to the tribes of Israel. The Israelites divided the land as the Lord had commanded.

⁶One day some men from the tribe*ᵈ* of Judah went to Joshua at Gilgal. One of those men was Caleb son of Jephunneh the Kenizzite. He said to Joshua, "You remember what the Lord said at Kadesh Barnea. He was speaking to the prophet Moses about you and me. ⁷Moses, the Lord's servant, sent me to look at the land where we were going. I was 40 years old then. When I came back, I told Moses what I thought about the land. ⁸The other men who went with me told the people things that made them afraid. But I fully believed the Lord would allow us to take the land. ⁹So that day Moses

promised me, 'The land where you went will become your land. Your children will own it forever. I will give you that land because you fully believed in the Lord, my God.'

[10]"Now then, the Lord has kept his promise. He has kept me alive for 45 years from the time he said this to Moses. During that time we all wandered in the desert. Now here I am, 85 years old. [11]I am still as strong today as I was the day Moses sent me out. I am just as ready to fight now as I was then. [12]So give me the mountain country the Lord promised me that day long ago. Back then you heard that the Anakite[d] people lived there. And the cities were large and well protected. But now with the Lord helping me, I will force them out, just as the Lord said."

[13]Joshua blessed Caleb son of Jephunneh. He gave him the city of Hebron as his own. [14]And Hebron still belongs to the family of Caleb son of Jephunneh the Kenizzite. It still belongs to his people because he had faith. He obeyed the Lord, the God of Israel. [15](In the past it was called Kiriath Arba. It was named for the greatest man among the Anakites. He was named Arba.)

After this there was peace in the land.

15 The land that was given to the tribe[d] of Judah was divided among all the family groups. It went all the way to the Desert of Zin in the far south, at the border of Edom.

[2]The southern border of Judah's land started at the south end of the Dead Sea.[d] [3]It went south of Scorpion Pass to Zin. From there it passed to the south of Kadesh Barnea. It continued past Hezron to Addar. From Addar it turned and went to Karka. [4]It continued to Azmon, the brook of Egypt and then to the Mediterranean Sea. This was the southern border.

[5]The eastern border was the shore of the Dead Sea. It went as far as the area where the Jordan River flowed into the sea.

The northern border started at the area where the Jordan River flowed into the Dead Sea. [6]Then it went to Beth Hoglah and continued north of Beth Arabah. It continued to the stone of Bohan. Bohan was the son of Reuben. [7]Then the northern border went through the Valley of Achor to Debir. There it turned toward the north and went to Gilgal. Gilgal is across from the road that goes through the mountain of Adummim. It

is on the south side of the ravine. The border continued along the waters of En Shemesh. It stopped at En Rogel. [8]Then it went through the Valley of Ben Hinnom. This is next to the southern side of the Jebusite city. (That city was called Jerusalem.) There the border went to the top of the hill on the west side of Hinnom Valley. This was at the northern end of the Valley of Giants. [9]From there it went to the spring of the Waters of Nephtoah. Then it went to the cities near Mount Ephron. There it turned and went toward Baalah. (Baalah is also called Kiriath Jearim.) [10]At Baalah the border turned west and went toward Mount Edom. It continued along the north side of Mount Jearim (also called Kesalon) and came to Beth Shemesh. From there it went past Timnah. [11]Then it went to the hill north of Ekron. From there it turned toward Shikkeron and went past Mount Baalah. It continued on to Jabneel and ended at the sea.

[12]The Mediterranean Sea was the western border. Inside these borders lived the family groups of Judah.

[13]The Lord had commanded Joshua to give Caleb son of Jephunneh part of the land in Judah. So he gave Caleb the land God had commanded. He gave him the town of Kiriath Arba, also called Hebron. (Arba was the father of Anak.[d]) [14]Caleb forced out the three Anakite families living in Hebron. Those families were Sheshai, Ahiman and Talmai. They were descendants[d] of Anak. [15]Then he fought against the people living in Debir. (In the past Debir had been called Kiriath Sepher.) [16]Caleb said, "I want a man to attack and capture Kiriath Sepher. I will give him Acsah, my daughter, as a wife." [17]Othniel son of Kenaz defeated the city. So Caleb gave his daughter Acsah to Othniel to be his wife. [18]Acsah wanted Othniel to ask her father Caleb for more land.

So Acsah went to her father. When she got off her donkey, Caleb asked her, "What do you want?"

[19]Acsah answered, "I would like a special favor. The land you gave me is very dry. So also give me land with springs of water on it."

So Caleb gave her land with springs of water on the upper and lower part of it.

[20]The tribe of Judah got the land God had promised them. Each family group got part of the land.

[21]The tribe of Judah got all the towns

in the southern part of Canaan. These towns were near the border of Edom. Here is a list of the towns: Kabzeel, Eder, Jagur, ²²Kinah, Dimonah, Adadah, ²³Kedesh, Hazor and Ithnan; ²⁴Ziph, Telem, Bealoth, ²⁵Hazor Hadattah and Kerioth Hezron (also called Hazor); ²⁶Amam, Shema, Moladah, ²⁷Hazar Gaddah, Heshmon and Beth Pelet; ²⁸Hazar Shual, Beersheba, Biziothiah, ²⁹Baalah, Iim, Ezem, ³⁰Eltolad, Kesil and Hormah; ³¹Ziklag, Madmannah, Sansannah, ³²Lebaoth, Shilhim, Ain and Rimmon. There were 29 towns and all their fields.

³³The tribe of Judah got these towns in the western mountain slopes: Eshtaol, Zorah, Ashnah, ³⁴Zanoah, En Gannim, Tappuah and Enam; ³⁵Jarmuth, Adullam, Socoh, Azekah, ³⁶Shaaraim, Adithaim and Gederah (also called Gederothaim). There were 14 towns and all their fields.

³⁷Judah was also given these towns in the western mountain slopes: Zenan, Hadashah, Migdal Gad, ³⁸Dilean, Mizpah, Joktheel, ³⁹Lachish, Bozkath and Eglon; ⁴⁰Cabbon, Lahmas, Kitlish, ⁴¹Gederoth, Beth Dagon, Naamah and Makkedah. There were 16 towns and all their fields.

⁴²Judah was also given these towns in the western mountain slopes: Libnah, Ether, Ashan, ⁴³Iphtah, Ashnah, Nezib, ⁴⁴Keilah, Aczib and Mareshah. There were nine towns and all their fields.

⁴⁵The tribe of Judah also got the town of Ekron and all the small towns and fields near it. ⁴⁶They also got the area west of Ekron and all the fields and towns near Ashdod. ⁴⁷Ashdod and all the small towns around it were part of the land of Judah. They also got the fields and towns around Gaza. Their land continued to the brook of Egypt. And it went on along the coast of the Mediterranean Sea.

⁴⁸The tribe of Judah was also given these towns in the mountains: Shamir, Jattir, Socoh, ⁴⁹Dannah and Kiriath Sannah (also called Debir); ⁵⁰Anab, Eshtemoh, Anim, ⁵¹Goshen, Holon and Giloh. There were 11 towns and all their fields.

⁵²They were also given these towns in the mountains: Arab, Dumah, Eshan, ⁵³Janim, Beth Tappuah and Aphekah; ⁵⁴Humtah, Kiriath Arba (also called Hebron) and Zior. There were 9 towns and all their fields.

⁵⁵Judah was also given these towns in the mountains: Maon, Carmel, Ziph, Juttah, ⁵⁶Jezreel, Jokdeam, Zanoah,

⁵⁷Kain, Gibeah and Timnah. There were 10 towns and all their fields.

⁵⁸They were also given these towns in the mountains: Halhul, Beth Zur, Gedor, ⁵⁹Maarath, Beth Anoth and Eltekon. There were 6 towns and all their fields.

⁶⁰The people of Judah were also given the 2 towns of Rabbah and Kiriath Baal (also called Kiriath Jearim).

⁶¹Judah was given towns in the desert. Here are those towns: Beth Arabah, Middin, Secacah, ⁶²Nibshan, the City of Salt and En Gedi. There were 6 towns and all their fields.

⁶³The army of Judah was not able to force out the Jebusites living in Jerusalem. So the Jebusites still live among the people of Judah in Jerusalem to this day.

16 This is the land the tribeᵈ of Joseph received. It started at the Jordan River near Jericho. It continued to the waters of Jericho, just east of the city. The border went up from Jericho to the mountains of Bethel. ²Then it continued from Bethel (also called Luz) to the Arkite border at Ataroth. ³From there it went west to the border of the Japhletites. It continued to the area of the Lower Beth Horon. Then it went to Gezer and ended at the sea.

⁴So Manasseh and Ephraim received their land. They were sons of Joseph.

⁵This is the land that was given to the family groups of Ephraim: Their border started at Ataroth Addar in the east. It went to Upper Beth Horon ⁶and then to the sea. From Micmethath it turned eastward toward Taanath Shiloh and continued eastward to Janoah. ⁷Then it went down from Janoah to Ataroth and to Naarah. It continued until it touched Jericho and stopped at the Jordan River. ⁸The border went from Tappuah west to Kanah Ravine and went to the sea. This is all the land that was given to the Ephraimites. Each family group in the tribe got a part of this land. ⁹Many of the border towns of Ephraim were actually within Manasseh's borders. But the people of Ephraim got those towns and their fields. ¹⁰The Ephraimites could not force the Canaanites to leave Gezer. So the Canaanites still live among the Ephraimites today. But they became slaves of the Ephraimites.

17 Then land was given to the tribe of Manasseh. He was Joseph's first son. Manasseh's first son was Makir, the father of Gilead. Makir was a great soldier. So the lands of Gilead and Bashan were given to his family. ²Land was also given to the other family groups of Manasseh. They were Abiezer, Helek, Asriel, Shechem, Hepher and Shemida. These were all the other sons of Manasseh son of Joseph.

³Zelophehad was the son of Hepher. Hepher was the son of Gilead. Gilead was the son of Makir, and Makir was the son of Manasseh. But Zelophehad had no sons. He had five daughters. The daughters were named Mahlah, Noah, Hoglah, Milcah and Tirzah. ⁴The daughters went to Eleazar the priest. They also went to Joshua son of Nun and all the leaders. They said, "The Lord told Moses to give us land like the men received." So Eleazar obeyed the Lord and gave the daughters some land. These daughters received land just as the brothers of their father did. ⁵So the tribe of Manasseh had ten sections of land west of the Jordan River. They also had two more sections, Gilead and Bashan. These sections were on the other side of the Jordan River. ⁶The daughters of Manasseh got land just as the sons did. Gilead was given to the rest of the families of Manasseh.

⁷The lands of Manasseh were in the area between Asher and Micmethath. This is near Shechem. The border went south to the En Tappuah area. ⁸The land of Tappuah belonged to Manasseh. But the town of Tappuah did not. It was along the border of Manasseh's land and belonged to the sons of Ephraim. ⁹The border of Manasseh continued south to Kanah Ravine. The cities in this area of Manasseh belonged to Ephraim. Manasseh's border was on the north side of the ravine and went to the sea. ¹⁰The land to the south belonged to Ephraim. And the land to the north belonged to Manasseh. The Mediterranean Sea was the western border. The border touched Asher's land on the north. And it touched Issachar's land on the east.

¹¹In the areas of Issachar and Asher, the people of Manasseh owned Beth Shan and its small towns. They also owned Ibleam and its small towns. And they owned all the people who lived in Dor and its small towns. They owned the people in Naphoth Dor and its small towns. And they owned all the people who lived in Taanach and its small towns. Manasseh also owned the people in Megiddo and its small towns. ¹²Manasseh was not able to defeat those cities. So the Canaanites continued to live

there. ¹³But the Israelites grew strong. When this happened, they forced the Canaanites to work for them. But they did not force them to leave the land.

¹⁴The people from the tribes of Joseph spoke to Joshua. They said, "You gave us only one area of land. But we are many people. Why did you give us only one part of all the land the Lord gave his people?"

¹⁵And Joshua answered them, "You have many people. Go up to the forest. Make a place for yourselves to live there. This is in the land of the Perizzites and the Rephaites.ᵈ The mountain country of Ephraim is too small for you."

¹⁶The people of Joseph said, "It is true. The mountain country of Ephraim is not enough for us. But the land where the Canaanites live is dangerous. They are skilled fighters. They have powerful weapons in Beth Shan and all the small towns in that area. And they are also in the Valley of Jezreel."

¹⁷Then Joshua spoke to the people of Joseph—to Ephraim and to Manasseh. He said, "But there are many of you. And you have great power. You should be given more than one share of land. ¹⁸You also will have the mountain country. It is a forest. But you can cut down the trees and make it a good place to live. And you will own all of it. You will force the Canaanites to leave the land. You can defeat them even though they have powerful weapons and are strong."

18 All of the Israelites gathered together at Shiloh. There they set up the Meeting Tent.ᵈ The Israelites controlled that country. They had defeated all the enemies there. ²But there were still seven tribesᵈ of Israel that had not yet received the land God had promised them.

³So Joshua said to the Israelites: "Why do you wait so long to take your land? The Lord, the God of your fathers, has given this land to you. ⁴So each tribe should choose three men. I will send them out to study the land. They will describe in writing the land their tribe wants as its share. Then they will come back to me. ⁵They will divide the land into seven parts. The people of Judah will keep their land in the south. The people of Joseph will keep their land in the north. ⁶But you should divide the land into seven parts. Describe the seven parts in writing. Then bring what you have written to me. We will let the Lord our God decide which tribe will get

which land. [7]But the Levites do not get any part of these lands. They are priests, and their work is to serve the Lord. Gad, Reuben and the eastern half-tribe of Manasseh have received the land promised to them. They are on the east side of the Jordan River. Moses, the servant of the Lord, gave it to them."

[8]So the men who were chosen started into the land. Their plan was to describe it in writing and take it back to Joshua. Joshua told them, "Go and study the land. Describe it in writing. Then come back to me. Then I will ask the Lord to choose the land you should get. We will do this here in Shiloh." [9]So the men left and went into the land. They studied it and described it in writing for Joshua. They studied each town. They saw that the land had seven parts. They described it in writing and then came back to Joshua. He was still at the camp at Shiloh. [10]Then Joshua asked the Lord to help. He threw lots[d] to choose the lands that should be given to each tribe.

[11]The first part of the land was given to the tribe[d] of Benjamin. Each family group in the tribe of Benjamin received some land. They were given the land between the land of Judah and the land of Joseph. This is the land chosen for Benjamin:

[12]The northern border started at the Jordan River. It went along the northern edge of Jericho. Then it went west into the mountains. That boundary continued until it was just east of Beth Aven. [13]From there it went south to Luz (also called Bethel). Then it went down to Ataroth Addar. Ataroth Addar is on the hill south of Lower Beth Horon.

[14]There is a hill to the south of Beth Horon. At this hill the border turned and went south near the western side of the hill. It went to Kiriath Baal (also called Kiriath Jearim). This is a town where people of Judah lived. It was the western border.

[15]The southern border started near Kiriath Jearim and went to the Waters of Nephtoah. [16]Then it went down to the bottom of the hill. This was near the Valley of Ben Hinnom. It was the north side of the Valley of Rephaim. The border continued down the Hinnom Valley just south of the Jebusite city to En Rogel. [17]There it turned north and went to En Shemesh. It continued to Geliloth near the Adummim Pass in the mountains. Then it went down to the great Stone of Bohan. Bohan was the son of Reuben.

[18]The border continued to the northern part of Beth Arabah. Then it went down into the Jordan Valley. [19]From there it went to the northern part of Beth Hoglah. It ended at the north shore of the Dead Sea.[d] This is where the Jordan River flows into the sea. This was the southern border.

[20]The Jordan River was the border on the eastern side. So this was the land given to the family groups of Benjamin. These were the borders on all sides.

[21]Each family group of Benjamin received some of this land. And these are the cities they owned: Jericho, Beth Hoglah, Emek Keziz, [22]Beth Arabah, Zemaraim and Bethel; [23]Avvim, Parah, Ophrah, [24]Kephar Ammoni, Ophni and Geba. There were 12 towns and all their villages.

[25]The tribe of Benjamin also owned Gibeon, Ramah and Beeroth. [26]They owned Mizpah, Kephirah, Mozah, [27]Rekem, Irpeel and Taralah. [28]They also owned Zelah, Haeleph, the Jebusite city (Jerusalem), Gibeah and Kiriath. There were 14 towns and all their villages. All these areas are the lands the tribe of Benjamin was given.

19 The second part of the land was given to the tribe[d] of Simeon. Each family group received some of the land. It was inside the area of Judah. [2]They received Beersheba (also called Sheba), Moladah, [3]Hazar Shual, Balah, Ezem, [4]Eltolad, Bethul and Hormah. [5]They also received Ziklag, Beth Marcaboth, Hazar Susah, [6]Beth Lebaoth and Sharuhen. There were 13 towns and all their fields.

[7]They also received the towns of Ain, Rimmon, Ether and Ashan. There were 4 towns and all their fields. [8]They also received all the very small areas with people living in them as far as Baalath Beer. (This is the same as Ramah in southern Canaan.) So these were the lands given to the tribe of Simeon. Each family group received some of the land. [9]The land of the Simeonites was taken from part of the land of Judah. Judah had much more land than they needed. So the Simeonites received part of their land.

[10]The third part of the land was given to the tribe[d] of Zebulun. Each family group of Zebulun received some of the land. The border of Zebulun went as far as Sarid. [11]Then it went west to Maralah and came near Dabbesheth. Then it went near Jokneam. [12]Then it turned to

the east. It went from Sarid to the area of Kisloth Tabor. From there it went on to Daberath and to Japhia. [13]It continued eastward to Gath Hepher and Eth Kazin. Then it ended at Rimmon. Then the border turned and went toward Neah. [14]At Neah it turned again and went to the north. It went to Hannathon and continued to the Valley of Iphtah El. [15]Inside this border were the cities of Kattath, Nahalal, Shimron, Idalah and Bethlehem. There were 12 towns and all their fields.

[16]So these are the towns and the areas that were given to Zebulun. Each family group received some of the land.

[17]The fourth part of the land was given to the tribe[d] of Issachar. Each family group of Issachar received some of the land. [18]Their land included Jezreel, Kesulloth, Shunem, [19]Hapharaim, Shion and Anaharath; [20]Rabbith, Kishion, Ebez, [21]Remeth, En Gannim, En Haddah and Beth Pazzez.

[22]The border of their land touched the area called Tabor, Shahazumah and Beth Shemesh. It stopped at the Jordan River. There were 16 towns and their fields.

[23]These cities and towns were part of the land that was given to the tribe of Issachar. Each family group received part of this land.

[24]The fifth part of the land was given to the tribe[d] of Asher. Each family group of Asher received some of the land. [25]Their land included Helkath, Hali, Beten, Acshaph, [26]Allammelech, Amad and Mishal.

The western border touched Mount Carmel and Shihor Libnath. [27]Then it turned toward the east. It went to Beth Dagon. It touched Zebulun and the Valley of Iphtah El. Then it went north of Beth Emek and Neiel. It passed north to Cabul. [28]Then it went to Abdon, Rehob, Hammon and Kanah. It continued to Greater Sidon. [29]Then the border went back south toward Ramah. It continued to the strong, walled city of Tyre. Then it turned and went toward Hosah. It ended at the sea. This was in the area of Aczib, [30]Ummah, Aphek and Rehob. There were 22 towns and their fields.

[31]These cities and their fields were part of the land that was given to the tribe of Asher. Each family group in that tribe received some of this land.

[32]The sixth part of the land was given to the tribe[d] of Naphtali. Each family group of Naphtali received some of the

land. [33]The border of their land started at the large tree in the area of Zaanannim. This is near Heleph. Then it went through Adami Nekeb and Jabneel. It continued to the area of Lakkum and ended at the Jordan River. [34]Then it went to the west through Aznoth Tabor. It stopped at Hukkok. It went to the area of Zebulun on the south. And it went to the area of Asher on the west. It went to Judah, at the Jordan River, on the east. [35]There were some strong, walled cities inside these borders. Those cities were Ziddim, Zer, Hammath, Rakkath and Kinnereth; [36]Adamah, Ramah, Hazor, [37]Kedesh, Edrei and En Hazor; [38]Iron, Migdal El, Horem, Beth Anath and Beth Shemesh. There were 19 towns and all their fields.

[39]The cities and the towns around them were in the land that was given to the tribe of Naphtali. Each family group in that tribe got some of this land.

[40]The seventh part of the land was given to the tribe[d] of Dan. Each family group of Dan received some of the land. [41]Their land included Zorah, Eshtaol, Ir Shemesh, [42]Shaalabbin, Aijalon and Ithlah; [43]Elon, Timnah, Ekron, [44]Eltekeh, Gibbethon, Baalath, [45]Jehud, Bene Berak and Gath Rimmon; [46]Me Jarkon, Rakkon and the area near Joppa.

[47](But the Danites had trouble taking their land. There were strong enemies there. And the Danites could not easily defeat them. So the Danites went and fought against Leshem. They defeated Leshem and killed the people who lived there. So the Danites lived in the town of Leshem. They changed its name to Dan because he was the father of their tribe.) [48]All of these cities and towns were given to the tribe of Dan. Each family group got part of this land.

[49]So the Israelite leaders finished dividing the land and giving it to the different tribes.[d] After they finished, all the Israelites decided to give Joshua son of Nun some land, too. This was land that had been promised to him. [50]The Lord had commanded that he be given this land. So they gave Joshua the town of Timnath Serah in the mountains of Ephraim. This was the town that Joshua told them he wanted. So he built up the town and lived there.

[51]So all of these lands were given to the different tribes of Israel. Eleazar the priest, Joshua son of Nun and the leaders of each tribe worked together. They divided up the land while they were at

Shiloh. They met before the Lord at the entrance to the Meeting Tent[d] to do this. Now they had finished dividing the land.

20 Then the Lord said to Joshua: [2]"Tell the Israelites to choose the special cities of safety.[d] This is what I had Moses command you to do. [3]A person might kill someone accidentally and without meaning to kill him. He may go to a city of safety to hide. There he will be safe from the relative who has the duty of punishing a murderer.

[4]"This is what he must do. When he runs to one of those cities, he must stop at the entrance gate. He must stand there and tell the leaders of the people what happened. Then they will allow him to enter the city. They will give him a place to live among them. [5]But the one who is chasing him might follow him to that city. If this happens, the leaders of the city must not give him up. They must protect the person who came to them for safety. They must protect him because he killed that person accidentally. He was not angry and did not decide ahead of time to kill the person. [6]He should stay in the city until he has been judged by the court there. And he should stay until the high priest dies. Then he may go back to his own home in the town from which he ran away."

[7]So the Israelites chose some cities to be cities of safety. These cities were: Kedesh in Galilee in the mountains of Naphtali; Shechem in the mountains of Ephraim; Kiriath Arba (also called Hebron) in the mountains of Judah; [8]Bezer on the east side of the Jordan River near Jericho in the desert in the land of Reuben; Ramoth in Gilead in the land of Gad; and Golan in Bashan in the land of Manasseh. [9]Any Israelite or anyone living among them who killed someone accidentally was included. He was to be allowed to run to one of these cities of safety. Then he could be safe there and would not be killed by the relative who had the duty of punishing a murderer. He would be judged by the court in that city.

21 The heads of the Levite families went to talk to Eleazar the priest. They also talked to Joshua son of Nun and to the heads of the families of all the tribes[d] of Israel. [2]This happened at the town of Shiloh in the land of Canaan. The heads of the Levite families said to them, "The Lord commanded Moses that you give us towns where we may live. And he commanded that you give us pastures." [3]So the Israelites obeyed this commandment of the Lord. They gave the Levite people these towns and pastures: [4]The Kohath family groups were part of the tribe of Levi. Some of the Levites in the Kohath family groups were from the family of Aaron the priest. To these Levites were given 13 towns. These towns were in the areas that belonged to Judah, Simeon and Benjamin. [5]The other family groups of Kohath were given 10 towns. These 10 towns were in the areas of Ephraim, Dan and West Manasseh.

[6]The people from the Gershon groups were given 13 towns. They were in the land that belonged to Issachar, Asher, Naphtali and the eastern half-tribe of Manasseh in Bashan.

[7]The family groups of Merari were given 12 towns. These 12 towns were in the area that belonged to Reuben, Gad and Zebulun.

[8]So the Israelites gave the Levites these towns and the pastures around them. They did this to obey the commandment that the Lord had given Moses.

[9]These are the names of the towns that came from the lands of Judah and Simeon. [10]The first choice of towns was given to the Kohath family groups of the Levites. [11]They gave them Kiriath Arba (also called Hebron) and all its pastures. This was in the mountains of Judah. (Arba was the father of Anak.[d]) [12]But the fields and the small towns around the city of Kiriath Arba had been given to Caleb son of Jephunneh.

[13]So they gave the city of Hebron to the descendants[d] of Aaron. (Hebron was a city of safety.[d]) They also gave them these towns: Libnah, [14]Jattir, Eshtemoa, [15]Holon, Debir, [16]Ain, Juttah and Beth Shemesh. They also gave them all the pastures that were around these towns. There were 9 towns given to these two groups.

[17]They also gave the people of Aaron cities that belonged to the tribe of Benjamin. These cities were Gibeon, Geba, [18]Anathoth and Almon. They gave them these 4 towns and all the pastures around them.

[19]So these towns were given to the priests. These priests were from the family of Aaron. The total number of towns with their pastures was 13.

[20]The other Kohathite family groups of the Levites were given these towns

from the tribe of Ephraim: [21]They gave them the city of Shechem from the mountains of Ephraim. (Shechem was a city of safety.) They also gave them Gezer, [22]Kibzaim and Beth Horon. There were 4 towns and their pastures.

[23]The tribe of Dan gave them Eltekeh, Gibbethon, [24]Aijalon and Gath Rimmon. There were 4 towns and their pastures.

[25]The western half-tribe of Manasseh gave them Taanach and Gath Rimmon. They were also given all the pastures around these 2 towns.

[26]So this was 10 more towns and all the pastures around the towns. These were given to the rest of the Kohathite family groups.

[27]The Gershonite family groups of the Levite tribe were given these towns: The eastern half-tribe of Manasseh gave them Golan in Bashan. (Golan was a city of safety.) Manasseh also gave them Be Eshtarah. All the pastures around these two towns were also given to the Gershonites.

[28]The tribe of Issachar gave them Kishion, Daberath, [29]Jarmuth and En Gannim. Issachar also gave them all the pastures around these 4 towns.

[30]The tribe of Asher gave them Mishal, Abdon, [31]Helkath and Rehob. All the pastures around these 4 towns were also given to them.

[32]The tribe of Naphtali gave them Kedesh in Galilee. (Kedesh was a city of safety.) Naphtali also gave them Hammoth Dor and Kartan. All the pastures around these 2 towns were also given to the Gershonites.

[33]So the Gershonite family groups received 13 towns. They also received all the pastures around these towns.

[34]The Merarite family groups (the rest of the Levites) were given these towns: The tribe of Zebulun gave them Jokneam, Kartah, [35]Dimnah and Nahalal. All the pastures around these 4 towns were also given to the Merarites.

[36]The tribe of Reuben gave them Bezer, Jahaz, [37]Kedemoth and Mephaath. All the pastures around these 4 towns were also given to the Merarites.

[38]The tribe of Gad gave them Ramoth in Gilead. (Ramoth was a city of safety.) They also gave them Mahanaim, [39]Heshbon and Jazer. Gad also gave them all the pastures around these 4 towns.

[40]So the total number of towns given to the Merarite family groups was 12.

[41]A total of 48 towns with their pastures were given to the Levites. All these towns were in the land controlled by the Israelites. [42]Each town had pastures around it.

[43]So the Lord kept the promise he had made to the Israelites. He gave the people all the land he had promised. The people took the land and lived there. [44]The Lord allowed them to have peace on all sides of their land. This is what he had promised to their people who lived long ago. None of their enemies defeated them. The Lord allowed the Israelites to defeat every enemy. [45]He kept every promise he had made to the Israelites. No promises failed. Each one came true.

22 Then Joshua called a meeting of all the people from the tribes of Reuben, Gad and the eastern half-tribe of Manasseh. [2]He said to them, "You have obeyed everything Moses told you to do. He was a servant of the Lord. And also, you have obeyed all my commands. [3]All this time you have supported all the other Israelites. You have been careful to obey all the commands the Lord your God gave you. [4]The Lord your God promised to give the Israelites peace. Now he has kept his promise. Now you may go back to your homes. You may go to the land that Moses, the Lord's servant, gave you. It is the land on the east side of the Jordan River. [5]But continue to obey the teachings Moses gave you. That law is to love the Lord your God and obey his commands. Continue to follow him and serve him the very best you can."

[6]Then Joshua said good-bye to them, and they left. They went away to their homes. [7]Moses had given the land of Bashan to the eastern half-tribe of Manasseh. Joshua gave land on the west side of the Jordan River to the western half-tribe of Manasseh. And he sent them to their homes. He blessed them. [8]He said, "Go back to your homes and your riches. You have many animals, silver, gold, bronze and iron. And you have many beautiful clothes. Also, you have taken many things from your enemies. You should divide these among yourselves."

[9]So the people from the tribes of Reuben, Gad and the eastern half-tribe of Manasseh left the other Israelites. They left Shiloh in Canaan and went back towards Gilead. This was their own land. Moses gave it to them as the Lord had commanded.

[10]The people of Reuben, Gad and the

eastern half-tribe of Manasseh traveled to Geliloth. This was near the Jordan River in the land of Canaan. There they built a beautiful altar. [11]But the other Israelites still at Shiloh heard about the altar these three tribes had built. They heard that the altar was at the border of Canaan at Geliloth. It was near the Jordan River on Israel's side. [12]All the Israelites became very angry at these three tribes. They met together and decided to fight them.

[13]So the Israelites sent some men to talk to the people of Reuben, Gad and the eastern half-tribe of Manasseh. The leader of these men was Phinehas son of Eleazar the priest. [14]They also sent one leader of each of the ten tribes at Shiloh. Each of these men was a leader of his family group of Israelites.

[15]So these men went to Gilead. They went to talk to the people of Reuben, Gad and the eastern half-tribe of Manasseh. The men said to them: [16]"All the Israelites ask you: 'Why did you turn against the God of Israel? Why did you build an altar for yourselves? You know that this is against God's law. [17]Remember what happened at Peor? We still suffer today because of that sin. Because of it, God caused many of the Israelites to become very sick. [18]And now are you doing the same thing? Are you turning against the Lord? Will you refuse to follow the Lord?

"'If you don't stop what you're doing, the Lord will be angry with everyone in Israel. [19]Your land may not be a good enough place to worship. If not, come over into our land. The Lord's Tent is in our land. You may have some of our land and live there. But don't turn against the Lord by building another altar. We already have the altar of the Lord our God. [20]Remember Achan son of Zerah. He refused to obey the command about what must be completely destroyed. That one man broke God's law, but all the Israelites were punished. Achan died because of his sin. But many other people also died.'"

[21]The people from Reuben, Gad and the eastern half-tribe of Manasseh answered them. They said: [22]"The Lord is our God! Again we say that the Lord is our God! God knows why we did this. We want you to know also. You can judge what we did. If you believe we have done something wrong, you may kill us. [23]If we broke God's law, we ask the Lord himself to punish us. Do you

think we built this altar to offer burnt offerings? And did we build it to use for offerings of grain and fellowship?

[24]"No! We did not build it for that reason. We feared that some day your people would not accept us as part of your nation. Then they might say, 'You cannot worship the Lord, the God of Israel. [25]God gave you land on the other side of the Jordan River. It separates us from you people of Reuben and Gad. You cannot worship the Lord.' So we feared that your children might make our children stop worshiping the Lord.

[26]"So we decided to build this altar. But we did not plan to use it for burning sacrifices and making offerings. [27]It was really to show our people that we worship the same God as you. This altar is proof to you and us. And it will prove to all our children who will come after us that we worship the Lord. We give our whole burnt offerings, grain and fellowship offerings to the Lord. This was to keep your children from saying that our children could not worship the Lord.

[28]"In the future your children might say that we do not belong to Israel. Then our children could say, 'Look! Our fathers who lived before us made an altar. It is exactly like the Lord's altar. We do not use it for sacrifices. This altar shows that we are part of Israel.'

[29]"Truly, we don't want to be against the Lord. We don't want to stop following him. We know the only true altar is the one in front of the Holy Tent.[d] It belongs to the Lord our God."

[30]Phinehas the priest and the ten leaders heard these things. They listened to the people of Reuben, Gad and Manasseh. And they were pleased. [31]So Phinehas, son of Eleazar the priest, spoke. He said, "Now we know the Lord is with us. And we know you didn't turn against him. We're happy that the Israelites will not be punished by the Lord."

[32]Then Phinehas and the leaders went home. They left the people of Reuben and Gad in Gilead. And they went back to Canaan. There they told the Israelites what had happened. [33]They were also pleased. They were happy and thanked God. And they decided not to fight against the people of Reuben and Gad. They decided not to destroy those lands.

[34]And the people of Reuben and Gad gave the altar a name. They called it Proof that We Believe that the Lord Is God.

23 The Lord gave Israel peace from their enemies around them. He made Israel safe. Many years passed, and Joshua became very old. ²So he called a meeting of all the older leaders, heads of families, judges and officers of the Israelites. He said, "I am now very old. ³You have seen what the Lord has done to our enemies. He did it to help us. The Lord your God fought for you. ⁴Remember that your people have been given their land. It's the land between the Jordan River and the Mediterranean Sea in the west. It's the land I promised to give you. But you don't control that land yet. ⁵The Lord your God will make the people living there leave. You will enter the land. And the Lord will force them out ahead of you. He has promised you this.

⁶"Be strong. You must be careful to obey everything the Lord has commanded. Obey everything written in the Book of the Teachings of Moses. Do exactly as it says. ⁷There are still some people living among us who are not Israelites. They worship their own gods. Don't become friends with them. Don't serve or worship their gods. ⁸You must continue to follow the Lord your God. You have done this in the past. And you must continue to do it.

⁹"The Lord has helped you defeat many great and powerful nations. He has forced them to leave ahead of you. No nation has been able to defeat you. ¹⁰With his help, one Israelite could defeat a thousand enemies. This is because the Lord your God fights for you, as he promised to do. ¹¹So you must be careful to love the Lord your God.

¹²"Don't turn away from the way of the Lord. Don't become friends with these people who are not part of Israel. Don't marry them. If you do become their friends, ¹³the Lord your God will not help you defeat your enemies. So they will become like traps for you. They will cause you pain like a whip on your back and thorns in your eyes. And none of you will be left in this good land the Lord your God has given you.

¹⁴"It's almost time for me to die. You know and fully believe that the Lord has done great things for you. You know that he has not failed in any of his promises. He has kept every promise he has given. ¹⁵Every good promise that the Lord your God made has come true. And in the same way, his other promises will come true. He promised that evil

will come to you. He will destroy you from this good land that he gave you. ¹⁶This will happen if you don't keep your agreement with the Lord your God. You will lose this land if you go and serve other gods. You must not worship them. If you do, the Lord will become very angry with you. Then none of you will be left in this good land he has given you."

24 Then all the tribes[d] of Israel met together at Shechem. Joshua called them all together there. Then he called the older leaders, heads of families, judges and officers of Israel. These men stood before God.

²Then Joshua spoke to all the people. He said, "Here's what the Lord, the God of Israel, says to you: 'A long time ago your ancestors lived on the other side of the Euphrates River. I am talking about men like Terah, the father of Abraham and Nahor. They worshiped other gods. ³But I, the Lord, took your ancestor Abraham out of the land on the other side of the river. I led him through the land of Canaan. And I gave him many children. I gave him his son Isaac. ⁴And I gave Isaac two sons named Jacob and Esau. I gave the land around the mountains of Edom to Esau. But Jacob and his sons went down to Egypt. ⁵Then I sent Moses and Aaron to Egypt. I caused many terrible things to happen to the Egyptians. Then I brought you people out. ⁶When I brought your fathers out of Egypt, they came to the Red Sea.[d] And the Egyptians chased them. There were chariots and men on horses. ⁷So the people asked me, the Lord, for help. And I caused great trouble to come to the Egyptians. I caused the sea to cover them. You yourselves saw what I did to the army of Egypt. After that, you lived in the desert for a long time.

⁸"Then I brought you to the land of the Amorites. This was east of the Jordan River. They fought against you, but I gave you the power to defeat them. I destroyed them before you. Then you took control of that land. ⁹But the king of Moab, Balak son of Zippor, prepared to fight against the Israelites. The king sent for Balaam son of Beor to curse you. ¹⁰But I, the Lord, refused to listen to Balaam. So he asked for good things to happen to you! He blessed you many times. I saved you and brought you out of his power.

¹¹"'Then you traveled across the Jordan River and came to Jericho. The people in the city of Jericho fought against

you. Also, the Amorites, Perizzites, Canaanites, Hittites, Girgashites, Hivites and Jebusites fought against you. But I allowed you to defeat them all. [12]While your army traveled forward, I sent hornets ahead of them. These hornets made the people leave before you came. So you took the land without using your swords and bows. [13]It was I, the Lord, who gave you that land. I gave you land where you did not have to work. I gave you cities that you did not have to build. And now you live in that land and in those cities. You eat from vineyards and olive trees. But you did not have to plant them.'"

[14]Then Joshua spoke to the people. He said, "Now you have heard the Lord's words. So you must respect the Lord and serve him fully and sincerely. Throw away the false gods that your people worshiped. That happened on the other side of the Euphrates River and in Egypt. Now you must serve the Lord. [15]But maybe you don't want to serve the Lord. You must choose for yourselves today. You must decide whom you will serve. You may serve the gods that your people worshiped when they lived on the other side of the Euphrates River. Or you may serve the gods of the Amorites who lived in this land. As for me and my family, we will serve the Lord."

[16]Then the people answered, "No! We will never stop following the Lord. We will never serve other gods! [17]We know it was the Lord our God who brought our people out of Egypt. We were slaves in that land. But the Lord did great things for us there. He brought us out. He protected us while we traveled through other lands. [18]Then he helped us defeat the people living in these lands. He helped us defeat the Amorites who lived here. So we will continue to serve the Lord because he is our God."

[19]Then Joshua said, "You will not be able to serve the Lord well enough. He is a holy God. And he is a jealous God. If you turn against him and sin, he will not forgive you. [20]If you leave the Lord and serve other gods, he will cause great trouble to come to you. The Lord has been good to you. But if you turn against him, he will destroy you."

[21]But the people said to Joshua, "No! We will serve the Lord."

[22]Then Joshua said, "Look around at yourselves and the people with you here. Do you all know and agree that you have chosen to serve the Lord? Are you all witnesses to this?"

The people answered, "Yes, it's true! We all see that we have chosen to serve the Lord."

[23]Then Joshua said, "Now throw away the false gods that you have among you. Love the Lord, the God of Israel, with all your heart."

[24]Then the people said to Joshua, "We will serve the Lord our God. We will obey him."

[25]On that day Joshua made an agreement for the people. He made the agreement a law for them to follow. This happened at Shechem. [26]Joshua wrote these things in the Book of the Teachings of God. Then he found a large stone. He put the stone under the oak tree near the Lord's Holy Tent.[d]

[27]Then Joshua said to all the people, "See this stone! It will help you remember what we did today. It was here when the Lord was speaking to us today. It will help you remember what happened. It will stop you from turning against your God."

[28]Then Joshua told the people to go back to their homes. And everyone went back to his own land.

[29]After that, Joshua son of Nun died. He was 110 years old. [30]And they buried him in his own land at Timnath Serah. This was in the mountains of Ephraim, north of Mount Gaash.

[31]The Israelites had served the Lord during the time Joshua was living. And after he died, they continued to serve the Lord. They continued to serve him while their older leaders were still alive. These were the leaders who had seen what the Lord had done for the Israelites.

[32]When the Israelites left Egypt, they carried the bones of Joseph with them. They buried them at Shechem, in the land Jacob had bought from the sons of Hamor. (Hamor was the father of Shechem.) Jacob had bought the land for 100 pieces of silver. This land belonged to Joseph's children.

[33]And Eleazar son of Aaron died. He was buried at Gibeah in the mountains of Ephraim. Gibeah had been given to Eleazar's son Phinehas.

The Book of
JUDGES

1 Joshua died. Then the people of Israel prayed to the Lord. They said, "Who will be first to go and fight for us against the Canaanite people?"

[2] The Lord said to them, "The tribe[d] of Judah will go. I have given them the power to take this land."

[3] The men of Judah asked for help from the men of Simeon, their relatives. The men of Judah said, "Come and help us fight the Canaanites for our land. If you do, we will go and help you fight for your land." So the men of Simeon went with them.

[4] The Lord gave the men of Judah the victory over the Canaanites and the Perizzites. The men of Judah defeated 10,000 men at the city of Bezek. [5] There they found Adoni-Bezek, the ruler of the city, and fought him. The men of Judah defeated the Canaanites and the Perizzites. [6] So Adoni-Bezek ran away. But the men of Judah chased him. When they caught him, they cut off his thumbs and big toes.

[7] Then Adoni-Bezek said, "I cut off the thumbs and big toes of 70 kings. And those kings had to eat scraps that fell from my table. Now God has paid me back for what I did to them." The men of Judah took Adoni-Bezek to Jerusalem, and he died there.

[8] Then the men of Judah fought against Jerusalem and captured it. They used their swords to kill the people of Jerusalem. And they burned the city.

[9] Later, they went down to fight against more of the Canaanites. Some of the Canaanites lived in the mountains. Others lived in the dry country to the south. And still others lived in the western mountain slopes. [10] Then the men of Judah went to fight against the Canaanites in the city of Hebron. (Hebron used to be called Kiriath Arba.) The men of Judah defeated the descendants[d] of Sheshai, Ahiman and Talmai.

[11] Then the men of Judah left Hebron. They went to the city of Debir to fight against the people there. (Debir used to be called Kiriath Sepher.) [12] Before attacking the city, Caleb said, "I want a man to attack and capture the city of Kiriath Sepher. I will give him Acsah, my daughter, as a wife." [13] Caleb had a younger brother named Kenaz. Kenaz

had a son named Othniel. Othniel captured the city of Kiriath Sepher. So Caleb gave his daughter Acsah to Othniel to be his wife. [14] When Acsah came to Othniel, he told her to ask her father for some land. So she got down from her donkey, and Caleb said, "What do you want?"

[15] Acsah answered Caleb, "Do me a favor. You have put me in the dry land of southern Judah. Give me some land with springs of water." So Caleb gave her the upper and lower springs of water.

[16] The Kenite people left Jericho, the city of palm trees. They went with the men of Judah. The Kenites went to the Desert of Judah to live with the people there. This was in southern Judah near the city of Arad. (The Kenites were from the family of Moses' father-in-law.)

[17] Some Canaanite people also lived in the city of Zephath. So the men of Judah and the men of Simeon, their relatives, defeated those Canaanites. They completely destroyed the city. So they called the city Hormah.[n] [18] The men of Judah captured Gaza, Ashkelon and Ekron and all the lands around them.

[19] The Lord was on the side of the men of Judah. They took the land in the mountains. But they could not force out the people living on the plain. This was because those people had iron chariots. [20] As Moses had promised, Hebron was given to Caleb. Caleb forced out the three sons of Anak.[d] [21] But the people of Benjamin could not make the Jebusite people leave Jerusalem. Since that time the Jebusites have lived with the Benjaminites in Jerusalem.

[22] The men of Joseph went to fight against the city of Bethel. The Lord was on their side. [23] They sent some spies to Bethel. (Bethel used to be called Luz.) [24] The spies saw a man coming out of the city. They said to him, "Show us a way into the city. If you help us, we will be kind to you." [25] The man showed the spies the way into the city. The men of Joseph killed the people in Bethel. But the man who helped them and his family were allowed to go free. [26] He went to the land where the Hittite people lived, and he built a city. He named the city Luz, and it is called that today.

1:17 Hormah Hormah sounds like the Hebrew word meaning "to destroy completely."

[27] There were Canaanites living in the cities of Beth Shan, Taanach, Dor, Ibleam, Megiddo and the small towns around them. The people of Manasseh did not force those people out of their towns. The Canaanites were determined to stay there. [28] Later, the people of Israel grew strong. They forced the Canaanites to work as slaves for them. But the Israelites did not make all the Canaanites leave their land. [29] There were Canaanites living in Gezer. And the people of Ephraim did not make all of those Canaanites leave their land. So the Canaanite people continued to live in Gezer with the people of Ephraim. [30] Some Canaanites lived in the cities of Kitron and Nahalol. The people of Zebulun did not make them leave their land. They stayed and lived with the people of Zebulun. But Zebulun made them work as slaves.

[31] The people of Asher did not make the Canaanites leave the cities of Acco, Sidon, Ahlab, Aczib, Helbah, Aphek and Rehob. [32] The people of Asher did not make them leave their land. So the Canaanites continued to live with the people of Asher. [33] The people of Naphtali did not make the people leave the cities of Beth Shemesh and Beth Anath. So the people of Naphtali continued to live with the Canaanites in those cities. Those people worked as slaves for the people of Naphtali. [34] The Amorites forced the Danites back into the mountains. The Amorites would not let them come down to live in the plain. [35] The Amorites were determined to stay in Mount Heres, Aijalon and Shaalbim. But the Israelites grew stronger. Then they made the Amorites work as slaves for them. [36] The land of the Amorites was from Scorpion Pass to Sela and beyond it.

2 The angel of the Lord went up from Gilgal to Bokim. He spoke to the people of Israel there and said: "I brought you up from Egypt. I led you to the land I promised to give to your ancestors. I said, 'I will never break my agreement with you. [2] But in return, you must not make an agreement with the people who live in this land. You must destroy their altars.' But you did not obey me. How could you do this? [3] Now I will tell you this: 'I will not force out the people in this land. They will become your ene-

mies. Their gods will become a trap for you.'"

[4] After the angel gave Israel this message from the Lord, they cried loudly. [5] So they named the place Bokim.[n] There they offered sacrifices to the Lord.

[6] Then Joshua told the people they could go home. So each one went to take his own share of the land. [7] The people of Israel served the Lord as long as Joshua was alive. They continued serving the Lord during the lifetimes of the older leaders who lived on after Joshua. These men had seen all the great things the Lord had done for Israel. [8] Joshua son of Nun was the servant of the Lord. Joshua died at the age of 110. [9] So the Israelites buried him in the land he had been given. That land was at Timnath Heres. It was in the mountains of Ephraim, north of Mount Gaash.

[10] After those people had died, their children grew up. They did not know the Lord or what he had done for Israel. [11] So they did evil and worshiped the Baal[d] idols. They did what the Lord said was wrong. [12] The Lord had brought the people of Israel out of Egypt. And the ancestors of these people had worshiped the Lord. But the Israelites quit following the Lord. They began to worship the gods of the people who lived around them. That made the Lord angry. [13] The Israelites quit following the Lord and worshiped Baal and Ashtoreth.[d] [14] The Lord was angry with the people of Israel. So he let robbers attack them and take their possessions. He let their enemies who lived around them defeat them. They could not protect themselves from their enemies. [15] When the Israelites went out to fight, they always lost. They lost because the Lord was not on their side. The Lord had sworn to them this would happen. So the Israelites suffered very much.

[16] Then the Lord chose leaders called judges.[n] These leaders saved the people of Israel from the robbers. [17] But the Israelites did not listen to their judges. They were not faithful to God. They followed other gods instead. In the past the people of Israel obeyed the Lord's commands. But now the Israelites stopped obeying the Lord. [18] Many times the enemies of Israel hurt the Israelites. So the Israelites would cry for help. And each time the Lord felt sorry for them. Each

2:5 Bokim This name means "crying." **2:16 judges** They were not judges in courts of law, but leaders of the people in times of emergency.

time he sent a judge to save them from their enemies. The Lord was with those judges. [19]But when each judge died, the Israelites again sinned and worshiped the false gods. They became worse than their ancestors. The Israelites were very stubborn; they refused to change their evil ways.

[20]So the Lord became angry with the Israelites. He said, "These people have broken the agreement I made with their ancestors. They have not listened to me. [21]So I will no longer defeat the nations who were left when Joshua died. [22]I will use those nations to test Israel. I will see if Israel keeps the Lord's commands as their ancestors did." [23]In the past the Lord had permitted those nations to stay in the land. He did not quickly force them out. He did not help Joshua's army defeat them.

3 These are the nations the Lord did not force to leave. He wanted to test the Israelites who had not fought in the wars to take Canaan. [2]The only reason the Lord left those nations in the land was to teach the descendants[d] of the Israelites. He wanted to teach the people who had not fought in those wars how to fight. [3]These are the nations: the five rulers of the Philistines, all the Canaanites, the people of Sidon and the Hivites. The Hivites lived in the Lebanon mountains from Mount Baal Hermon to Lebo Hamath. [4]Those nations were in the land to test the Israelites. The Lord wanted to see if Israel would obey the commands he had given to their ancestors by Moses.

[5]The people of Israel lived with the Canaanites, Hittites, Amorites, Perizzites, Hivites and Jebusites. [6]The Israelites began to marry the daughters of those people. And the Israelites allowed their daughters to marry the sons of those people. Israel served the gods of those people.

[7]The people of Israel did what the Lord said was wrong. They forgot about the Lord their God. Instead, they served the idols of Baal[d] and Asherah.[d] [8]The Lord was angry with Israel. He allowed Cushan-Rishathaim king of Northwest Mesopotamia to rule over the Israelites. They were under that king's rule for eight years. [9]Then Israel cried to the Lord. So the Lord sent a man to save them. He was Othniel son of Kenaz. (Kenaz was Caleb's younger brother.) Othniel saved the Israelites. [10]The Spirit[d] of the Lord entered Othniel. And he be-

came Israel's judge and went to war. The Lord helped him to defeat Cushan-Rishathaim king of Northwest Mesopotamia. [11]So the land was at peace for 40 years. Then Othniel son of Kenaz died.

[12]Again the people of Israel did what the Lord said was wrong. So the Lord gave Eglon king of Moab power to defeat Israel. This was because of the evil Israel did. [13]Eglon got the Ammonite people and the Amalekite people to join him. Then he attacked Israel and took Jericho, the city of palm trees. [14]The people of Israel were under the rule of Eglon king of Moab for 18 years.

[15]So the people cried to the Lord. And he sent a man to save them. That man was Ehud, who was left-handed. Ehud was the son of Gera from the people of Benjamin. Israel sent Ehud to give Eglon king of Moab the payment he demanded. [16]Ehud made a sword for himself. The sword had two edges and was about 18 inches long. He tied the sword to his right upper leg under his clothes. [17]So Ehud came to Eglon king of Moab and gave him the payment he demanded. Eglon was a very fat man. [18]After he had given Eglon the payment, Ehud sent home the men who had carried it. [19]When he passed the statues near the city Gilgal, he turned around. Ehud said to Eglon, "I have a secret message for you, King Eglon."

The king said, "Be quiet!" Then he sent all of his servants out of the room. [20]Ehud went to King Eglon. Eglon was now sitting alone in the room on top of his summer palace.

Ehud said, "I have a message from God for you." As the king stood up from his chair, [21]Ehud reached with his left hand. He took out the sword that was tied to his right upper leg. Then he stabbed the sword deep into the king's belly! [22]The sword went into Eglon's belly so far that even the handle sank in. And the blade came out his back. The king's fat covered the whole sword. So Ehud left the sword in place. [23]He went out of the room and closed and locked the doors behind him.

[24]The servants returned just after Ehud left. They found the doors to the room locked. So they thought the king was relieving himself. [25]They waited for a long time. Finally they became worried because he still had not opened the doors. So they got the key and unlocked them. When they entered, they saw their king lying dead on the floor!

²⁶While the servants were waiting, Ehud had escaped. He passed by the statues and went to Seirah. ²⁷When he arrived there, he blew a trumpet in the mountains of Ephraim. The people of Israel heard it and went down from the hills with Ehud leading them.

²⁸He said to them, "Follow me! The Lord has helped us to defeat our enemies, the people of Moab." So Israel followed Ehud. They took control of the places where the Jordan River could easily be crossed. Israel did not allow the Moabites to come across the Jordan River. ²⁹Israel killed about 10,000 strong and able men from Moab. Not one Moabite man escaped. ³⁰So that day Moab was forced to be under the rule of Israel. And there was peace in the land for 80 years.

³¹After Ehud, another man saved Israel. His name was Shamgar son of Anath. Shamgar killed 600 Philistines with a sharp stick used to guide oxen.

4 After Ehud died, the people of Israel again did what the Lord said was wrong. ²So he let Jabin, a king of Canaan, defeat Israel. Jabin ruled in the city of Hazor. Sisera was the commander of Jabin's army. Sisera lived in Harosheth Haggoyim. ³He had 900 iron chariots and was very cruel to the people of Israel for 20 years. So they cried to the Lord for help.

⁴There was a prophetess[d] named Deborah. She was the wife of Lappidoth. She was judge of Israel at that time. ⁵Deborah would sit under the Palm Tree of Deborah. This was between the cities of Ramah and Bethel, in the mountains of Ephraim. And the people of Israel would come to her to settle their arguments.

⁶Deborah sent a message to a man named Barak. He was the son of Abinoam. Barak lived in the city of Kedesh, which is in the area of Naphtali. Deborah said to Barak, "The Lord, the God of Israel, commands you: 'Go and gather 10,000 men of Naphtali and Zebulun. Lead them to Mount Tabor. ⁷I will make Sisera, the commander of Jabin's army, come to you. Sisera, his chariots and his army will meet you at the Kishon River. I will help you to defeat Sisera there.'"

⁸Then Barak said to Deborah, "I will go if you will go with me. But if you will not go with me, I won't go."

⁹"Of course I will go with you," Deborah answered. "But you will not get credit for the victory. The Lord will let a woman defeat Sisera." So Deborah went with Barak to Kedesh. ¹⁰At Kedesh, Barak called the people of Zebulun and Naphtali together. From them, he gathered 10,000 men to follow him. Deborah went with Barak also.

¹¹Now Heber the Kenite had left the other Kenite people. (The Kenites were descendants[d] of Hobab, Moses' brother-in-law.) Heber had put up his tent by the great tree in Zaanannim. This is near Kedesh.

¹²Then Sisera was told that Barak son of Abinoam had gone up to Mount Tabor. ¹³So Sisera gathered his 900 iron chariots and all the men with him. They went from Harosheth Haggoyim to the Kishon River.

¹⁴Then Deborah said to Barak, "Get up! Today is the day the Lord will help you defeat Sisera. You know the Lord has already cleared the way for you." So Barak led 10,000 men down from Mount Tabor. ¹⁵He and his men attacked Sisera and his men. During the battle the Lord confused Sisera and his army and chariots. So Barak and his men used their swords to defeat Sisera's army. But Sisera left his chariot and ran away on foot. ¹⁶Barak and his men chased Sisera's chariots and army to Harosheth Haggoyim. They used their swords to kill all of Sisera's men. Not one of them was left alive.

¹⁷But Sisera himself ran away. He came to the tent where Jael lived. She was the wife of Heber, one of the Kenite family groups. Heber's family was at peace with Jabin king of Hazor. ¹⁸Jael went out to meet Sisera. She said to him, "Come into my tent, master! Come in. Don't be afraid." So Sisera went into Jael's tent, and she covered him with a rug.

¹⁹Sisera said to Jael, "I am thirsty. Please give me some water to drink." So she opened a leather bag in which she kept milk and gave him a drink. Then she covered him up.

²⁰Then Sisera said to Jael, "Go stand at the entrance to the tent. If anyone comes and asks you, 'Is anyone here?' say, 'No.'"

²¹But Jael, the wife of Heber, took a tent peg and a hammer. She quietly went to Sisera. Since he was very tired, he was sleeping. She hammered the tent peg through the side of Sisera's head and into the ground! And so Sisera died.

²²Then Barak came by Jael's tent, chasing Sisera. Jael went out to meet

him and said, "Come. I will show you
the man you are looking for." So Barak
entered her tent. There Sisera lay dead,
with the tent peg in his head.

[23]On that day God defeated Jabin king
of Canaan in the sight of Israel.

[24]Israel became stronger and stronger
against Jabin king of Canaan. Finally,
they destroyed him.

5 On that day Deborah and Barak son
of Abinoam sang this song:

[2]"The leaders led Israel.
　The people volunteered to go to
　　battle.
　Praise the Lord!
[3]Listen, kings.
　Pay attention, rulers!
　I myself will sing to the Lord.
　I will make music to the Lord, the
　　God of Israel.

[4]"Lord, in the past you came from
　　Edom.
　You marched from the land of
　　Edom,
　and the earth shook.
　The skies rained,
　and the clouds dropped water.
[5]The mountains shook before the
　　Lord, the God of Mount Sinai.
　They shook before the Lord, the
　　God of Israel!

[6]"In the days of Shamgar son of
　　Anath,
　in the days of Jael, the main
　　roads were empty.
　Travelers went on the back roads.
[7]There were no warriors in Israel
　　until I, Deborah, arose.
　I arose to be a mother to Israel.
[8]At that time they chose to follow
　　new gods.
　Because of this, enemies fought
　　us at our city gates.
　No one could find a shield or a
　　spear
　　among the 40,000 men of Israel.
[9]My heart is with the commanders
　　of Israel.
　They volunteered freely from
　　among the people.
　Praise the Lord!

[10]"You who ride on white donkeys
　　and sit on saddle blankets, listen!
　And you who walk along the
　　road, listen!
[11]Listen to the sound of the singers
　　at the watering holes.

　There they tell about the victories
　　of the Lord.
　They tell about the victories of
　　the Lord's warriors in Israel.
　Then the Lord's people went down
　　to the city gates.

[12]"Wake up, wake up, Deborah!
　Wake up, wake up, sing a song!
　Get up, Barak!
　Go capture your enemies, son of
　　Abinoam!

[13]"Then the men who were left came
　　down to the important leaders.
　The Lord's people came down to
　　me with strong men.
[14]They came from Ephraim in the
　　mountains of Amalek.
　Benjamin was among the people
　　who followed you.
　From the family group of Makir in
　　West Manasseh, the
　　commanders came down.
　And from Zebulun came those
　　men who lead with an officer's
　　staff.
[15]The princes of Issachar were with
　　Deborah.
　The people of Issachar were loyal
　　to Barak.
　They followed him into the
　　valley.
　The Reubenites thought hard
　　about what they would do.
[16]Why did you stay by the sheepfold?
　Was it to hear the music played
　　for your sheep?
　The Reubenites thought hard
　　about what they would do.
[17]The people of Gilead stayed east of
　　the Jordan River.
　People of Dan, why did you stay
　　by the ships?
　The people of Asher stayed at the
　　seashore.
　They stayed at their safe harbors.
[18]But the people of Zebulun risked
　　their lives.
　So did the people of Naphtali on
　　the battlefield.

[19]"The kings came, and they fought.
　At that time the kings of Canaan
　　fought
　at Taanach, by the waters of
　　Megiddo.
　But they took away no silver or
　　possessions of Israel.
[20]The stars fought from heaven.
　From their paths, they fought
　　Sisera.

²¹The Kishon River swept Sisera's
    men away,
  that old river, the Kishon River.
  March on, my soul, with strength!
²²Then the horses' hoofs beat the
    ground.
  Galloping, galloping go Sisera's
    mighty horses.
²³'May the town of Meroz be cursed,'
    said the angel of the Lord.
  'Bitterly curse its people,
  because they did not come to help
    the Lord.
  They did not fight the strong
    enemy.'
²⁴"May Jael, the wife of Heber the
    Kenite,
  be blessed above all women who
    live in tents.
²⁵Sisera asked for water,
  but Jael gave him milk.
  In a bowl fit for a ruler,
  she brought him cream.
²⁶Jael reached out and took the tent
    peg.
  Her right hand reached for the
    workman's hammer.
  And she hit Sisera! She smashed
    his head!
  She crushed and pierced the side
    of his head!
²⁷At Jael's feet he sank.
  He fell, and he lay there.
  At her feet he sank. He fell.
  Where Sisera sank, there he fell,
    dead!
²⁸"Sisera's mother looked out
    through the window.
  She looked through the curtains.
  She asked, 'Why is Sisera's chariot
    so late in coming?
  Why are sounds of his chariots'
    horses delayed?'
²⁹The wisest of her servant ladies
    answer her.
  And Sisera's mother says to
    herself,
³⁰'Surely they are taking the
    possessions of the people they
    defeated!
  Surely they are dividing those
    things among themselves!
  A girl or two is being given to each
    soldier.
  Maybe Sisera is taking pieces of
    dyed cloth.
  Maybe they are even taking
    pieces of dyed, embroidered cloth
    for the necks of the victors!'

³¹"Let all your enemies die this way,
    Lord!
  But let all the people who love you
    be powerful like the rising sun!"
So there was peace in the land for 40
years.

6 Again the people of Israel did what
the Lord said was wrong. So for
seven years the Lord let the people of
Midian rule Israel. ²The Midianites were
very powerful and were cruel to the Israelites. So the Israelites made hiding
places in the mountains. They also hid
in caves and safe places. ³Whenever the
Israelites planted crops, the Midianites,
Amalekites and other peoples from the
east would come and attack them.
⁴These people camped in the land. And
they destroyed the crops that the Israelites had planted. They did this as far
as the land near Gaza. The people left
nothing for Israel to eat. They left them
no sheep, cattle or donkeys. ⁵The Midianites came up and camped in the land.
They brought their tents and their animals with them. They were like swarms
of locusts!ᵈ There were so many people
and camels they could not be counted.
These people came into the land to ruin
it. ⁶Israel became very poor because of
the Midianites. So the Israelites cried
out to the Lord for help.
⁷The Israelites cried out to the Lord
for help against the Midianites. ⁸So the
Lord sent a prophetᵈ to them. The
prophet said, "This is what the Lord, the
God of Israel, says: I brought you out of
Egypt, the land of slavery. ⁹I saved you
from the people of Egypt. And I saved
you from all the people of Canaan. I
forced them out of their land. And I gave
it to you. ¹⁰Then I said to you, 'I am the
Lord your God. You will live in the land
of the Amorites, but you must not worship their gods.' But you did not obey
me."
¹¹The angel of the Lord came and sat
down under an oak tree at Ophrah. The
oak tree belonged to Joash, who was
one of the Abiezrite people. Joash was
the father of Gideon. Gideon was separating some wheat from the chaffᵈ in a
winepress.ᵈ Gideon did this to keep the
wheat from the Midianites. ¹²The angel
of the Lord appeared to Gideon and
said, "The Lord is with you, mighty warrior!"
¹³Then Gideon said, "Pardon me, sir.
If the Lord is with us, why are we having
so many troubles? Our ancestors told us
he did miracles.ᵈ They told us the Lord

brought them out of Egypt. But now he has left us. He has allowed the Midianites to defeat us."

[14] The Lord turned to Gideon and said, "You have the strength to save the people of Israel. Go and save them from the Midianites. I am the one who is sending you."

[15] But Gideon answered, "Pardon me, Lord. How can I save Israel? My family group is the weakest in Manasseh. And I am the least important member of my family."

[16] The Lord answered him, "I will be with you. It will seem as if you are fighting only one man."

[17] Then Gideon said to the Lord, "If you are pleased with me, give me proof. Show me that it is really you talking with me. [18] Please wait here. Do not go away until I come back to you. Let me bring my offering and set it in front of you."

And the Lord said, "I will wait until you come back."

[19] So Gideon went in and cooked a young goat. He also took about 20 quarts of flour and made bread without yeast. Then he put the meat into a basket. And he put the broth from the boiled meat into a pot. He brought out the meat, the broth and the bread without yeast. He brought the food to the angel of the Lord. Gideon gave it to him under the oak tree.

[20] The angel of God said to Gideon, "Put the meat and the bread without yeast on that rock over there. Then pour the broth on them." And Gideon did as he was told. [21] The angel of the Lord had a stick in his hand. He touched the meat and the bread with the end of the stick. Then fire jumped up from the rock! The meat and the bread were completely burned up! And the angel of the Lord disappeared! [22] Then Gideon understood he had been talking to the angel of the Lord. So Gideon cried, "Lord God! I have seen the angel of the Lord face to face!"

[23] But the Lord said to Gideon, "Calm down! Don't be afraid! You will not die!"

[24] So Gideon built an altar there to worship the Lord. Gideon named the altar The Lord Is Peace. It still stands at Ophrah, where the Abiezrites live.

[25] That same night the Lord spoke to Gideon. The Lord said, "Take the bull that belongs to your father and a second bull seven years old. Pull down your father's altar to Baal.[d] Cut down the Ashe-

rah[d] idol beside it. [26] Then build an altar to the Lord your God. Build it on this high ground. Lay its stones in the right order. Then kill and burn the bull on this altar. Use the wood from the Asherah idol to burn your offering."

[27] So Gideon got ten of his servants. And he did what the Lord had told him to do. But Gideon was afraid that his family and the men of the city might see him. So he did it at night, not in the daytime.

[28] The men of the city got up the next morning. They saw that the altar for Baal had been destroyed! And they saw that the Asherah idol beside it had been cut down! They also saw the altar Gideon had built. And they saw the bull that had been sacrificed on it. [29] The men of the city looked at each other and asked, "Who did this?" They asked many questions and looked for the person who had done those things.

Someone told them, "Gideon son of Joash did this."

[30] So they said to Joash, "Bring your son out. He has pulled down the altar of Baal. He has cut down the Asherah idol beside it. So your son must die!"

[31] But Joash spoke to the angry crowd around him. He said, "Are you going to take Baal's side? Are you going to defend Baal? Anyone who takes Baal's side will be killed by morning! If Baal is a god, let him fight for himself. It's his altar that has been pulled down." [32] So on that day Gideon got the name Jerub-Baal. The name means "let Baal fight against him." They named him this because Gideon pulled down Baal's altar.

[33] All the Midianites, the Amalekites and other peoples from the east joined together. They came across the Jordan River and camped in the Valley of Jezreel. [34] But the Spirit[d] of the Lord entered Gideon! Gideon blew a trumpet to call the Abiezrites to follow him. [35] He sent messengers to all of Manasseh. The people of Manasseh were called to follow Gideon. Gideon also sent messengers to the people of Asher, Zebulun and Naphtali. They also went up to meet Gideon and his men.

[36] Then Gideon said to God, "You said you would help me save Israel. [37] I will put some wool on the threshing[d] floor. Let there be dew only on the wool. But let all of the ground be dry. Then I will know what you said is true. I will know that you will use me to save Israel." [38] And that is just what happened. Gid-

eon got up early the next morning and squeezed the wool. He got a full bowl of water from the wool.

³⁹Then Gideon said to God, "Don't be angry with me. Let me ask just one more thing. Please let me make one more test. Let the wool be dry while the ground around it gets wet with dew." ⁴⁰That night God did that very thing. Just the wool was dry, but the ground around it was wet with dew.

7 Early in the morning Jerub-Baal and all his men set up their camp at the spring of Harod. (Jerub-Baal is also called Gideon.) The Midianites were camped north of them. The Midianites were camped in the valley at the bottom of the hill called Moreh. ²Then the Lord said to Gideon, "You have too many men to defeat the Midianites. I don't want the Israelites to brag that they saved themselves. ³So now, announce to the people, 'Anyone who is afraid may leave Mount Gilead. He may go back home.'" And 22,000 men went back home. But 10,000 remained.

⁴Then the Lord said to Gideon, "There are still too many men. Take the men down to the water, and I will test them for you there. If I say, 'This man will go with you,' he will go. But if I say, 'That one will not go with you,' he will not go."

⁵So Gideon led the men down to the water. There the Lord said to him, "Separate them. Those who drink water by lapping it up like a dog will be in one group. Those who bend down to drink will be in the other group." ⁶There were 300 men who used their hands to bring water to their mouths. They lapped it as a dog does. All the rest got down on their knees to drink.

⁷Then the Lord said to Gideon, "I will save you, using the 300 men who lapped the water. And I will allow you to defeat Midian. Let all the other men go to their homes." ⁸So Gideon sent the rest of Israel to their homes. But he kept 300 men. He took the jars and the trumpets of those who went home.

Now the camp of Midian was in the valley below Gideon. ⁹That night the Lord spoke to Gideon. He said, "Get up. Go down and attack the camp of the Midianites. I will allow you to defeat them. ¹⁰But if you are afraid to go down, take your servant Purah with you. ¹¹When you come to the camp of Midian, you will hear what they are saying. Then you will not be afraid to attack the camp."

So Gideon and his servant Purah went down to the edge of the enemy camp. ¹²The Midianites, the Amalekites and all the peoples from the east were camped in that valley. There were so many of them they seemed like locusts.ᵈ They had so many camels no one could count them. There were as many as there are grains of sand on the seashore!

¹³When Gideon came to the enemy camp, he heard a man talking. That man was telling his friend about a dream. He was saying, "Listen, I dreamed that a loaf of barley bread rolled into the camp of Midian. It hit the tent so hard that the tent turned over and fell flat!"

¹⁴The man's friend said, "Your dream is about the sword of Gideon son of Joash, a man of Israel. God will let Gideon defeat Midian and the whole army!"

¹⁵When Gideon heard about the dream and what it meant, he worshiped God. Then Gideon went back to the camp of Israel. He called out to them, "Get up! The Lord has defeated the army of Midian for you!" ¹⁶Then Gideon divided the 300 men into three groups. He gave each man a trumpet and an empty jar. A burning torch was inside each jar.

¹⁷Gideon told the men, "Watch me and do what I do. When I get to the edge of the camp, do what I do. ¹⁸Surround the enemy camp. I and everyone with me will blow our trumpets. When we blow our trumpets, you blow your trumpets, too. Then shout, 'For the Lord and for Gideon!'"

¹⁹So Gideon and the 100 men with him came to the edge of the enemy camp. They came just after the enemy had changed guards. It was during the middle watch of the night. Then Gideon and his men blew their trumpets and smashed their jars. ²⁰All three groups of Gideon's men blew their trumpets and smashed their jars. They held the torches in their left hands and the trumpets in their right hands. Then they shouted, "A sword for the Lord and for Gideon!" ²¹Each of Gideon's men stayed in his place around the camp. But inside the camp, the men of Midian began shouting and running away.

²²When Gideon's 300 men blew their trumpets, the Lord caused all the men of Midian to fight each other with their swords! The enemy army ran away to the city of Beth Shittah. It is toward Zererah. They ran as far as the border of the city of Abel Meholah. It is near the

city of Tabbath. ²³Then men of Israel from Naphtali, Asher and all of Manasseh were called out to chase the Midianites. ²⁴Gideon sent messengers through all the mountains of Ephraim. They said, "Come down and attack the Midianites. Take control of the Jordan River as far as Beth Barah. Do this before the Midianites can get to the river and cross it."

So they called out all the men of Ephraim. They took control of the Jordan River as far as Beth Barah. ²⁵The men of Ephraim captured two princes of Midian named Oreb and Zeeb. The men of Ephraim killed Oreb at the rock of Oreb. They killed Zeeb at the winepress[d] of Zeeb. And they continued chasing the Midianites. They cut off the heads of Oreb and Zeeb and took them to Gideon. He was now east of the Jordan River.

8 The men of Ephraim asked Gideon, "Why did you treat us this way? Why didn't you call us when you went to fight against Midian?" They were very angry at Gideon.

²But he answered them, "I have not done as well as you! The small part you did was better than all that my people of Abiezer did. ³God allowed you to capture Oreb and Zeeb, the princes of Midian. How can I compare what I did with what you did?" When the men of Ephraim heard Gideon's answer, they were not as angry anymore.

⁴Then Gideon and his 300 men came to the Jordan River. They were tired, but they chased the enemy across to the other side. ⁵Gideon said to the men of Succoth, "Please give my soldiers some bread. They are very tired. I am chasing Zebah and Zalmunna, the kings of Midian."

⁶But the leaders of Succoth said, "Why should we give your soldiers bread? You haven't caught Zebah and Zalmunna yet."

⁷Then Gideon said, "The Lord will help me capture Zebah and Zalmunna. After that, I will whip your skin with thorns and briers from the desert."

⁸Gideon left Succoth and went to the city of Peniel. He asked the men there for food. It was just as he had asked the men of Succoth. And the men of Peniel gave him the same answer as the men of Succoth. ⁹So Gideon said to the men of Peniel, "After I win the victory, I will come back here. And I will pull down this tower."

¹⁰Zebah and Zalmunna and their army were in the city of Karkor. Their army had about 15,000 men. They were all who were left of the army of the peoples of the east. Already 120,000 soldiers of that army had been killed. ¹¹Gideon used the road of those who live in tents. This road is east of Nobah and Jogbehah. Gideon attacked the enemy army when they did not expect it. ¹²Zebah and Zalmunna, the kings of Midian, ran away. But Gideon chased and captured them. Gideon and his men defeated the enemy army.

¹³Then Gideon son of Joash returned from the battle. He and his men returned by the Pass of Heres. ¹⁴Gideon captured a young man from Succoth and asked him some questions. The young man wrote down for Gideon the names of 77 men. They were the officers and older leaders of Succoth.

¹⁵Then Gideon came to Succoth. He said to the men of that city, "Here are Zebah and Zalmunna. You made fun of me by saying, 'Why should we give bread to your tired men? You have not caught Zebah and Zalmunna yet.'" ¹⁶So Gideon took the older leaders of the city. He punished them with thorns and briers from the desert. ¹⁷He also pulled down the tower of Peniel. Then he killed the men in that city.

¹⁸Gideon spoke to Zebah and Zalmunna. He said, "You killed some men on Mount Tabor. What were those men like?"

Zebah and Zalmunna answered, "They were like you. Each one of them seemed like a prince."

¹⁹Gideon said, "Those were my brothers, my mother's sons. As surely as the Lord lives, I would not kill you if you had spared them." ²⁰Then Gideon turned to Jether, his oldest son. Gideon said to him, "Kill them." But Jether was only a boy and was afraid. So he did not take out his sword.

²¹Then Zebah and Zalmunna said to Gideon, "Come on. Kill us yourself. As the saying goes, 'It takes a man to do a man's job.'" So Gideon got up and killed Zebah and Zalmunna. Then he took the decorations off their camels' necks.

²²The people of Israel said to Gideon, "You saved us from the Midianites. So now, rule over us. We want you, your son and your grandson to rule over us."

²³But Gideon told them, "The Lord will be your ruler. I will not rule over you. And my son will not rule over you."

²⁴He said, "I want you to do this one thing for me. I want each of you to give me a gold earring from the things you took in the fighting." (The Ishmaelite men wore gold earrings. And some Ishmaelites had been defeated in the battle.)

²⁵So the people of Israel said to Gideon, "We will gladly give you what you want." So they put a coat down on the ground. Each man threw an earring onto the coat. ²⁶The gold earrings weighed about 43 pounds. This did not count the weight of the other gifts the people gave to Gideon. They gave him decorations, necklaces and purple robes. These were things that the kings of Midian had worn. The people also gave him chains from the camels of the kings of Midian. ²⁷Gideon used the gold to make an idol. He put the idol in his hometown of Ophrah. All the people of Israel were unfaithful to God and worshiped the idol. It became a trap that caused Gideon and his family to sin.

²⁸So Midian was forced to be under the rule of Israel. Midian did not cause trouble anymore. And the land had peace for 40 years, as long as Gideon was alive.

²⁹Gideon son of Joash went to his home to live. ³⁰He had 70 sons of his own. He had many sons because he had many wives. ³¹Gideon had a slave woman[d] who lived in Shechem. He also had a son by her. He named that son Abimelech. ³²So Gideon son of Joash died at a good old age. He was buried in the tomb of Joash, his father. That tomb is in Ophrah, where the Abiezrites live.

³³As soon as Gideon died, the people of Israel were again unfaithful to God. They followed the Baal[d] gods. They made Baal-of-the-Agreement their god. ³⁴The Israelites did not remember the Lord their God. He had saved them from all their enemies who were living all around them. ³⁵And Jerub-Baal, also called Gideon, had done many good things for Israel. But Israel was not kind to the family of Gideon for these things.

9 Abimelech son of Jerub-Baal, also called Gideon, went to his uncles. They lived in the city of Shechem. He said to his uncles and all of his mother's family group, ²"Ask the leaders of Shechem this question: 'Is it better for you to be ruled by the 70 sons of Jerub-Baal or to be ruled by only 1 man?' Remember, I am your relative."

³Abimelech's uncles spoke to all the leaders of Shechem. They asked them that question. All the leaders decided to follow Abimelech. They said, "He is our brother." ⁴So the leaders of Shechem gave Abimelech about one and three-fourths pounds of silver. The silver was from the temple of the god Baal[d]-of-the-Agreement. Abimelech used the silver to hire some worthless, reckless men. They followed Abimelech wherever he went. ⁵Abimelech went to Ophrah, the hometown of his father. There Abimelech murdered his 70 brothers. They were the sons of Abimelech's father, Gideon. He killed them all on one stone. But Gideon's youngest son, Jotham, hid from Abimelech and escaped. ⁶Then all of the leaders of Shechem and Beth Millo came together. They gathered beside the great tree at the stone pillar in Shechem. There they made Abimelech their king.

⁷When Jotham heard this, he went and stood on the top of Mount Gerizim. Jotham shouted to the people: "Listen to me, you leaders of Shechem. Then God may listen to you! ⁸One day the trees decided to appoint a king to rule over them. They said to the olive tree, 'You be king over us!'

⁹"But the olive tree said, 'Men and gods are honored by my oil. Should I stop making it just to go and sway over the other trees?'

¹⁰"Then the trees said to the fig tree, 'Come and be our king!'

¹¹"But the fig tree answered, 'Should I stop making my sweet and good fruit? Should I stop just to go and sway over the other trees?'

¹²"Then the trees said to the vine, 'Come and be our king!'

¹³"But the vine answered, 'My wine makes men and gods happy. Should I stop making it just to go and sway over the trees?'

¹⁴"Then all the trees said to the thornbush, 'Come and be our king.'

¹⁵"But the thornbush said to the trees, 'If you really want to appoint me king over you, come and find shelter in my shade! But if you do not want to do this, let fire come out of the thornbush. Let the fire burn up the cedars of Lebanon!'

¹⁶"Now, were you completely honest and sincere when you made Abimelech king? Have you been fair to Gideon and his family? Have you treated Gideon as you should? ¹⁷Remember, my father fought for you. He risked his life to save you from the power of the Midianites.

[18]But now you have turned against my father's family. You have killed my father's 70 sons on one stone. You have made Abimelech king over the people of Shechem. He is the son of my father's slave girl! You have made Abimelech king just because he is your relative. [19]So then, if you have been honest and sincere to Gideon and his family today, be happy with Abimelech as your king. And may he be happy with you! [20]But if you have not acted right, may fire come out of Abimelech! May that fire completely burn you leaders of Shechem and Beth Millo! Also may fire come out of the leaders of Shechem and burn up Abimelech!"

[21]Then Jotham ran away. He escaped to the city of Beer. He lived there because he was afraid of his brother Abimelech.

[22]Abimelech ruled Israel for three years. [23]Then God sent an evil spirit to make trouble between Abimelech and the leaders of Shechem. So the leaders of Shechem turned against him. [24]Abimelech had killed Gideon's 70 sons. They were Abimelech's own brothers. And the leaders of Shechem had helped him kill them. So God sent the evil spirit to punish them. [25]The leaders of Shechem were against Abimelech then. They put men on the hilltops. These men attacked and robbed everyone who went by. Abimelech was told about these attacks.

[26]A man named Gaal and his brothers moved into Shechem. He was the son of Ebed. The leaders of Shechem decided to trust and follow Gaal. [27]The people of Shechem went out to the vineyards to pick grapes. They walked on the grapes to make wine. Then they had a feast in the temple of their god. The people ate and drank and cursed Abimelech. [28]Then Gaal son of Ebed said, "We are the men of Shechem. Why should we obey Abimelech? Who does he think he is? Isn't Abimelech one of Gideon's sons? Didn't Abimelech make Zebul his officer? We should not obey Abimelech! We should obey the men of Hamor, Shechem's father. Why should we obey Abimelech? [29]If you made me commander of these people, I would get rid of Abimelech! I would say to him, 'Get your army ready and come out to battle!'"

[30]Now Zebul was the ruler of Shechem. He heard what Gaal son of Ebed said. And Zebul became very angry. [31]He sent messengers to Abimelech in the city of Arumah. The message said, "Gaal son of Ebed and Gaal's brothers have come to Shechem. Gaal is turning the city against you! [32]So now you and your men should get up in the night. Then go lie in the fields outside the city. [33]When the sun comes up in the morning, attack the city. Gaal and his men will come out to fight you. Then do what you can to them."

[34]So Abimelech and all his soldiers got up during the night. They went near Shechem and separated into four groups. There they hid. [35]Gaal son of Ebed went out and was standing at the entrance to the city gate. As he was standing there, Abimelech and his soldiers came out of their hiding places.

[36]When Gaal saw the soldiers, he said to Zebul, "Look! There are people coming down from the mountains!"

But Zebul said, "You are seeing the shadows of the mountains. The shadows just look like people."

[37]But again Gaal said, "Look, there are people coming down from the center of the land. And there is a group coming from the fortune-tellers' tree!"

[38]Zebul said to Gaal, "Where is your bragging now? You said, 'Who is Abimelech? Why should we obey him?' You made fun of these men. Now go out and fight them."

[39]So Gaal led the men of Shechem out to fight Abimelech. [40]Abimelech and his men chased them. Many of Gaal's men were killed before they could get back to the city gate. [41]Then Abimelech stayed at Arumah. Zebul forced Gaal and his brothers to leave Shechem.

[42]The next day the people of Shechem went out to the fields. Abimelech was told about it. [43]So he separated his men into three groups. And he hid them in the fields. When he saw the people coming out of the city, he jumped up and attacked them. [44]Abimelech and his group ran to the entrance gate to the city. The other two groups ran out to the people in the fields and killed them. [45]Abimelech and his men fought the city of Shechem all day. They captured it and killed its people. Then Abimelech tore down the city. And he threw salt[n] over the ruins so nothing would ever grow there.

[46]The people who lived at the nearby

9:45 salt The salt would keep crops from growing there.

Tower of Shechem heard what had happened to Shechem. So the leaders gathered in the safest room of the temple of the god Baal[d]-of-the-Agreement. [47]Abimelech heard that all the leaders of the Tower of Shechem had gathered there. [48]So he and all his men went up to Mount Zalmon, near Shechem. Abimelech took an ax and cut some branches. Then he put them on his shoulders. He said to all his men with him, "Hurry! Do what I have done!" [49]So all those men cut branches and followed Abimelech. They piled the branches against the safest room of the temple. Then they set them on fire and burned the people in the room. So all the people who lived at the Tower of Shechem also died. There were about 1,000 men and women.

[50]Then Abimelech went to the city of Thebez. He surrounded the city, attacked it and captured it. [51]But inside the city was a strong tower. All the men and women of that city ran to the tower. When they got inside, they locked the door behind them. Then they climbed up to the roof of the tower. [52]Abimelech came to the tower and attacked it. He went up to the door of the tower to set it on fire. [53]As Abimelech came near, a woman dropped a large stone for grinding grain on his head. The stone crushed Abimelech's skull.

[54]He quickly called to the officer who carried his armor. He said, "Take out your sword and kill me. I don't want people to say, 'A woman killed Abimelech.'" So the officer stabbed Abimelech, and he died. [55]When the people of Israel saw Abimelech was dead, they all returned home.

[56]In that way God punished Abimelech for all the evil he had done. Abimelech had sinned against his own father by killing his 70 brothers. [57]God also punished the men of Shechem for the evil they had done. So the curse Jotham had spoken came true. (Jotham was the youngest son of Gideon.)

10 After Abimelech died, another judge came to save the people of Israel. He was Tola son of Puah. (Puah was the son of Dodo.) Tola was from the people of Issachar. He lived in the city of Shamir in the mountains of Ephraim. [2]Tola was a judge for Israel for 23 years. Then he died and was buried in Shamir.

[3]After Tola died, Jair became judge. He lived in the region of Gilead. He was a judge for Israel for 22 years. [4]Jair had 30 sons, who rode 30 donkeys. These 30 sons controlled 30 towns in Gilead. These towns are called the Towns of Jair to this day. [5]Jair died and was buried in the city of Kamon.

[6]Again the Israelites did what the Lord said was wrong. They worshiped the Baal[d] and Ashtoreth[d] idols. They also worshiped the gods of the peoples of Aram, Sidon, Moab and Ammon. And they worshiped the gods of the Philistines. The Israelites left the Lord and stopped serving him. [7]So the Lord became angry with them. He allowed the Philistines and the Ammonites to defeat them. [8]In the same year those people destroyed the Israelites who lived east of the Jordan River. This is in the region of Gilead, where the Amorites lived. The Israelites suffered for 18 years. [9]The Ammonites then crossed the Jordan River to fight the people of Judah, Benjamin and Ephraim. The Ammonites caused much trouble to the people of Israel. [10]So the Israelites cried out to the Lord, "We have sinned against you. We left our God and worshiped the Baal idols."

[11]The Lord answered the Israelites, "You cried to me when the Egyptians, the Amorites, the Ammonites and the Philistines hurt you. I saved you from these people. [12]You cried to me when the Sidonians, Amalekites and Maonites hurt you. I also saved you from those people. [13]But you have left me. You have worshiped other gods. So I refuse to save you again! [14]You have chosen those gods. So go call to them for help. Let them save you when you are in trouble!"

[15]But the people of Israel said to the Lord, "We have sinned. Do to us whatever you want, but please save us today!" [16]Then the Israelites threw away the foreign gods among them. And they worshiped the Lord again. So he felt sorry for them when he saw their suffering.

[17]The Ammonite people gathered for war and camped in Gilead. The Israelites gathered and camped at Mizpah. [18]The leaders of the people of Gilead said, "Who will lead us to attack the people of Ammon? He will become the head of all those who live in Gilead."

11 Jephthah was from the people of Gilead. He was a strong soldier. His father was named Gilead, and his mother was a prostitute.[d] [2]Gilead's wife had several sons. When they grew up, they forced Jephthah to leave his home. They said to him, "You will not get any of our father's property. You are the son of another woman." ³So Jephthah ran away from his brothers. He lived in the land of Tob. There some worthless men began to follow Jephthah.

⁴After a time the Ammonite people fought against Israel. ⁵The Ammonites made war against Israel. At that time the older leaders of Gilead came to Jephthah. They wanted him to come back to Gilead. ⁶They said to him, "Come and lead our army so we can fight the Ammonites."

⁷But Jephthah said to them, "Didn't you hate me? You forced me to leave my father's house! Why are you coming to me now that you are in trouble?"

⁸The older leaders of Gilead said to Jephthah, "That is the reason we come to you now. Please come with us and fight against the Ammonites! You will be the ruler over everyone who lives in Gilead."

⁹Then Jephthah answered, "Suppose you take me back to Gilead to fight the Ammonites. If the Lord helps me win, I will be your ruler."

¹⁰The older leaders of Gilead said to him, "The Lord is listening to everything we are saying. We promise to do all that you tell us to do." ¹¹So Jephthah went with the older leaders of Gilead. The people made him their leader and commander of their army. Jephthah repeated all of his words in front of the Lord at Mizpah.

¹²Jephthah sent messengers to the king of the Ammonites. The messengers asked the king, "What have you got against Israel? Why have you come to attack our land?"

¹³The king of the Ammonites answered the messengers of Jephthah. He said, "We are fighting Israel because you took our land when you came up from Egypt. You took our land from the Arnon River to the Jabbok River to the Jordan River. Now tell the people of Israel to give our land back to us in peace."

¹⁴Jephthah sent the messengers to the Ammonite king again. ¹⁵They took this message:

"This is what Jephthah says: Israel did not take the land of the people of Moab or Ammon. ¹⁶When the people of Israel came out of Egypt, they went into the desert. They went to the Gulf of Aqaba and then to Kadesh. ¹⁷Israel sent messengers to the king of Edom. They asked, 'Let the people of Israel go across your land.' But the king of Edom didn't

let us. We sent the same message to the king of Moab. But he would not let us go across his land either. So the Israelites stayed at Kadesh.

¹⁸"Then the Israelites went into the desert. They went around the borders of the lands of Edom and Moab. Israel walked east of the land of Moab. They camped on the other side of the Arnon River. It was the border of the land of Moab. They did not cross it to go into the land of Moab.

¹⁹"Then Israel sent messengers to Sihon king of the Amorites. Sihon was the king of the city of Heshbon. The messengers asked Sihon, 'Let the people of Israel pass through your land. We want to go to our land.' ²⁰But Sihon would not let the Israelites cross his land. He gathered all of his people and camped at Jahaz. Then the Amorites fought with Israel.

²¹"But the Lord, the God of Israel, helped the Israelites to defeat Sihon and his army. All the land of the Amorites became the property of Israel. ²²So Israel took all the land of the Amorites. It went from the Arnon River to the Jabbok River. It also went from the desert to the Jordan River.

²³"It was the Lord, the God of Israel, who forced out the Amorites ahead of the people of Israel. So do you think you can make the people of Israel leave this land? ²⁴Surely you can live in the land which your god Chemosh[d] has given you. So we will live in the land the Lord our God has given us!

²⁵"Are you any better than Balak son of Zippor? He was the king of Moab. Did he ever quarrel or fight with the people of Israel? ²⁶For 300 years the Israelites have lived in Heshbon and Aroer and the towns around them. They have lived for 300 years in all the cities along the Arnon River. Why have you not taken these cities back in all that time? ²⁷I have not sinned against you. But you are sinning against me by making war on me! May the Lord, the Judge, decide whether the Israelites or Ammonites are right."

²⁸But the king of the Ammonites ignored this message from Jephthah.

²⁹Then the Spirit[d] of the Lord entered Jephthah. Jephthah passed through Gilead and Manasseh. He came to the city of Mizpah in Gilead. From there, Jephthah passed through to the land of the Ammonites. ³⁰Jephthah made a promise to the Lord. He said, "If you will let me

defeat the Ammonites, [31] I will give you a burnt offering. I will sacrifice the first thing that comes out of my house to meet me when I return from the victory. It will be the Lord's."

[32] Then Jephthah went over to fight the Ammonites. The Lord helped him defeat them. [33] Jephthah defeated them from the city of Aroer to the area of Minnith. He defeated them as far as the city of Abel Keramim. He defeated 20 cities in this area. The defeat was great. So the Ammonites were defeated by the Israelites.

[34] When Jephthah returned home to Mizpah, his daughter came out to meet him. She was playing a tambourine[d] and dancing. She was his only child. Jephthah did not have any other sons or daughters. [35] When Jephthah saw his daughter, he tore his clothes to show how upset he was. He said, "My daughter! You have made me so sad! This is because I have made a promise to the Lord, and I cannot break it!"

[36] Then his daughter said, "Father, you made a promise to the Lord. So do to me just what you promised. The Lord helped you defeat your enemies, the Ammonites." [37] Then she said, "But let me do one thing. Let me be alone for two months to go to the mountains. I will never marry. So let me and my friends go and cry together."

[38] Jephthah said, "Go." He sent her away for two months. She and her friends stayed in the mountains. There they cried for her because she would never marry. [39] After two months she returned to her father. Jephthah did to her what he promised to the Lord. Now Jephthah's daughter had never had a husband.

So this became a custom in Israel. [40] Every year the women of Israel would go out for four days. They did this to remember the daughter of Jephthah from Gilead.

12 The men of Ephraim called all their soldiers together. Then they crossed the river to the town of Zaphon. They said to Jephthah, "Why didn't you call us to help you fight the Ammonites? We will burn your house down with you in it!"

[2] Jephthah answered them, "My people and I fought a great battle against the Ammonites. I called you, but you didn't come to help me. [3] I saw that you would not help me. So I risked my own life! I went over to fight against the Am-

monites. The Lord helped me to defeat them. Now why have you come to fight against me today?"

[4] Then Jephthah called the men of Gilead together. They fought the men of Ephraim. The men of Gilead attacked them because the Ephraimites had insulted them. They had said, "You men of Gilead are nothing but deserters from Ephraim and Manasseh." [5] The men of Gilead captured the crossing places of the Jordan River. Those places led to the country of Ephraim. A man from Ephraim trying to escape would say, "Let me cross the river." Then the men of Gilead would ask him, "Are you from Ephraim?" If he said, "No," [6] they would say to him, "Say the word 'Shibboleth.'" The men of Ephraim could not say that word correctly. They pronounced it "Sibboleth." If the man from Ephraim said, "Sibboleth," the men of Gilead would kill him at the crossing place. So 42,000 men from Ephraim were killed at that time.

[7] Jephthah was a judge for the people of Israel for six years. Then Jephthah, the man from Gilead, died. He was buried in a town in Gilead.

[8] After Jephthah died, Ibzan was a judge for Israel. He was from Bethlehem. [9] He had 30 sons and 30 daughters. He let his daughters marry men who were not in his family group. And he brought 30 women who were not in his tribe to be wives for his sons. Ibzan judged Israel for seven years. [10] Then he died and was buried in Bethlehem.

[11] After Ibzan died, Elon was a judge for Israel. He was from the tribe[d] of Zebulun. He judged Israel for ten years. [12] Then Elon, the man of Zebulun, died. He was buried in the city of Aijalon in the land of Zebulun.

[13] After Elon died, Abdon was a judge for Israel. He was the son of Hillel. Abdon was from the city of Pirathon. [14] He had 40 sons and 30 grandsons, who rode on 70 donkeys. He judged Israel for eight years. [15] Then Abdon son of Hillel died. He was buried in Pirathon in the land of Ephraim. This is in the mountains where the Amalekites lived.

13 Again the people of Israel did what the Lord said was wrong. So he let the Philistines rule over them for 40 years.

[2] There was a man named Manoah from the city of Zorah. Manoah was from the tribe[d] of Dan. He had a wife, but she could not have children. [3] The

angel of the Lord appeared to Manoah's wife. He said, "You have not been able to have children. But you will become pregnant and have a son! [4]Don't drink wine or beer. Don't eat anything that is unclean.[d] [5]You will become pregnant and have a son. You must never cut his hair because he will be a Nazirite.[d] He will be given to God from birth. He will begin the work of saving Israel from the power of the Philistines."

[6]Then Manoah's wife went to him and told him what had happened. She said, "A man from God came to me. He looked like an angel from God. His appearance was frightening. I didn't ask him where he was from. And he didn't tell me his name. [7]But he said to me, 'You will be pregnant and will have a son. Don't drink wine or beer. Don't eat anything that is unclean. The reason is that the boy will be a Nazirite to God. He will be that from his birth until the day of his death.'"

[8]Then Manoah said a prayer to the Lord: "Lord, I beg you to let the man of God come to us again. Let him teach us what we should do for the boy who will be born to us."

[9]God heard Manoah's prayer. The angel of God came to Manoah's wife again. This was while she was sitting in a field. But her husband Manoah was not with her. [10]So she ran to tell him, "He is here! The man who appeared to me the other day is here!"

[11]Manoah got up and followed his wife. When he came to the man, he said, "Are you the man who spoke to my wife?"

The man said, "I am."

[12]So Manoah asked, "When what you say happens, what kind of life should the boy live? What should he do?"

[13]The angel of the Lord said, "Your wife must do everything I told her to do. [14]She must not eat anything that grows on a grapevine. She must not drink any wine or beer. She must not eat anything that is unclean. She must do everything I have commanded her to do."

[15]Manoah said to the angel of the Lord, "We would like you to stay awhile. We want to cook a young goat for you."

[16]The angel of the Lord answered, "Even if I stay awhile, I would not eat your food. But if you want to prepare something, offer a burnt offering to the Lord." (Manoah did not understand that the man was really the angel of the Lord.)

[17]Then Manoah asked the angel of the Lord, "What is your name? We want to know. Then we may honor you when what you have said really happens."

[18]The angel of the Lord said, "Why do you ask my name? It is too wonderful for you to understand." [19]Then Manoah sacrificed a young goat on a rock. He also offered some grain as a gift to the Lord. The Lord did an amazing thing. Manoah and his wife watched what happened. [20]The flames went up to the sky from the altar. As the fire burned, the angel of the Lord went up to heaven in the fire! When Manoah and his wife saw that, they bowed facedown on the ground. [21]The angel of the Lord did not appear to them again. Then Manoah understood that the man was really the angel of the Lord. [22]Manoah said, "We have seen God! Surely we will die because of this!"

[23]But his wife said to him, "The Lord does not want to kill us. If he wanted to kill us, he would not have accepted our burnt offering or grain offering. He would not have shown us all these things. And he would not have told us all this."

[24]So the woman gave birth to a boy. She named him Samson. Samson grew, and the Lord blessed him. [25]The Spirit[d] of the Lord began to work in Samson. This was while he was in the city of Mahaneh Dan. It is between the cities of Zorah and Eshtaol.

14 Samson went down to the city of Timnah. There he saw a young Philistine woman. [2]When he returned home, he said to his father and mother, "I saw a Philistine woman in Timnah. I want you to get her for me. I want to marry her."

[3]His father and mother answered, "Surely there is a woman from Israel you can marry. Do you have to marry a woman from the Philistines? The Philistines are not even circumcised."[d]

But Samson said, "Get that woman for me! She is the one I want!" [4](Samson's parents did not know that the Lord wanted this to happen. He was looking for a way to start a fight with the Philistines. They were ruling over Israel at this time.) [5]Samson went down with his father and mother to Timnah. They went as far as the vineyard near there. Suddenly, a young lion came roaring toward Samson! [6]The Spirit[d] of the Lord entered Samson with great power. Samson tore the lion apart with his bare hands. For him it was as easy as tearing apart a young goat. But Samson did not tell his father or mother what he had done. [7]Then he went down to the city. There he talked to the Philistine woman, and he liked her.

[8]Several days later Samson went back to marry her. On his way he went over to look at the body of the dead lion. He found a swarm of bees in it. They had made some honey. [9]Samson got some of the honey with his hands. He walked along eating it. When he came to his parents, he gave some to them. They ate it, too. But Samson did not tell them he had taken the honey from the body of the dead lion.

[10]Samson's father went down to see the Philistine woman. The custom was for the bridegroom to give a feast. So Samson gave a feast. [11]When the people saw him, they sent 30 men to be with him.

[12]Then Samson said to the 30 men, "Let me tell you a riddle. This feast will last for seven days. Try to find the answer during that time. If you can, I will give you 30 linen shirts. I will also give you 30 changes of clothes. [13]But if you can't tell me the answer, you must pay me. You must give me 30 linen shirts and 30 changes of clothes."

So they said, "Tell us your riddle. We want to hear it."

[14]Samson said,

"Out of the eater comes something
    to eat.
Out of the strong comes
    something sweet."

The 30 men tried for three days to figure it out. But they could not find the answer.

[15]On the fourth[n] day, they came to Samson's wife. They said, "Did you invite us here to make us poor? Trick your husband into telling us the answer to the riddle. If you don't, we will burn you and everyone in your father's house!"

[16]So Samson's wife went to him and began crying. She said, "You hate me! You don't really love me! You told my people a riddle, but you won't tell me the answer."

Samson said, "I haven't even told my father or mother. Why should I tell you?"

[17]Samson's wife cried for the rest of the seven days of the feast. So he finally

gave her the answer on the seventh day. He told her because she kept bothering him. Then she told her people the answer to the riddle.

[18]Before sunset on the seventh day of the feast, the Philistine men had the answer. They came to Samson and said,

"What is sweeter than honey?
    What is stronger than a lion?"

Then Samson said to them,

"If you had not plowed with my
    little cow,
you would not have solved my
    riddle!"

[19]The Spirit[d] of the Lord entered Samson and gave him great power. Samson went down to the city of Ashkelon. He killed 30 of their men and took all their clothes and property. He gave those clothes to the men who had answered his riddle. Then he went to his father's house very angry. [20]And Samson's wife was given to his best man at the wedding.

15 At the time of the wheat harvest, Samson went to visit his wife. He took a young goat with him. He said, "I'm going to my wife's room." But her father would not let Samson go in.

[2]He said to Samson, "I thought you really hated your wife. So I gave her to the best man from the wedding. Her younger sister is more beautiful. Take her."

[3]But Samson said to him, "Now I have a good reason to hurt you Philistines. No one will blame me!" [4]So Samson went out and caught 300 foxes. He took 2 foxes at a time and tied their tails together. Then he tied a torch to the tails of each pair of foxes. [5]Samson lit the torches. Then he let the foxes loose in the grainfields of the Philistines. In this way he burned up their standing grain and the piles of grain. He also burned up their vineyards and their olive trees.

[6]The Philistines asked, "Who did this?"

Someone told them, "Samson, the son-in-law of the man from Timnah, did. He did this because his father-in-law gave his wife to his best man."

So the Philistines burned Samson's wife and her father to death. [7]Then Samson said to the Philistines, "Since you did this, I will hurt you, too! I won't stop until I pay you back!" [8]Samson attacked the Philistines and killed many of them.

14:15 **fourth** The Hebrew word is "seventh." Some old translations say "fourth," which fits the order of events better.

Then he went down and stayed in a cave. It was in the rock of Etam.

[9] Then the Philistines went up and camped in the land of Judah. They stopped near a place named Lehi. [10] The men of Judah asked them, "Why have you come here to fight us?"

They answered, "We have come to make Samson our prisoner. We want to pay him back for what he did to our people."

[11] Then 3,000 men of Judah went to the cave in the rock of Etam. They said to Samson, "What have you done to us? Don't you know that the Philistines rule over us?"

Samson answered, "I only paid them back for what they did to me!"

[12] Then they said to him, "We have come to tie you up. We will give you to the Philistines."

Samson said to them, "Promise me you will not hurt me yourselves."

[13] The men from Judah said, "We agree. We will just tie you up and give you to the Philistines. We will not kill you." So they tied Samson with two new ropes. Then they led him up from the cave in the rock. [14] When Samson came to the place named Lehi, the Philistines came to meet him. They were shouting for joy. Then the Spirit[d] of the Lord entered Samson and gave him great power. The ropes on him became weak like strings that had been burned. They fell off his hands! [15] Samson found a jawbone of a donkey that had just died. He took it and killed 1,000 men with it!

[16] Then Samson said,

"With a donkey's jawbone
    I have made donkeys out of them.
With a donkey's jawbone
    I have killed 1,000 men!"

[17] When he finished speaking, he threw away the jawbone. So that place was named Ramath Lehi.[n]

[18] Samson was very thirsty. So he cried out to the Lord. He said, "I am your servant. You gave me this great victory. Do I have to die of thirst now? Do I have to be captured by people who are not circumcised?"[u] [19] Then God opened up a hole in the ground at Lehi, and water came out. When Samson drank that water, he felt better. He felt strong again. So he named that spring Caller's Spring. It is still there in Lehi to this day.

[20] So Samson judged Israel for 20 years. That was in the days of the Philistines.

16 One day Samson went to Gaza. He saw a prostitute[d] there. He went in to spend the night with her. [2] Someone told the people of Gaza, "Samson has come here!" So they surrounded the place and hid and waited for him. Remaining very quiet, they stayed near the city gate all night. They said to each other, "When dawn comes, we will kill Samson!"

[3] But Samson only stayed with the prostitute until midnight. Then he got up and took hold of the doors and the two posts of the city gate. He tore them loose, along with the bar. Then he put them on his shoulders. And he carried them to the top of the hill that faces the city of Hebron!

[4] After this, Samson fell in love with a woman named Delilah. She lived in the Valley of Sorek. [5] The kings of the Philistines went to Delilah. They said, "Try to find out what makes Samson so strong. Try to trick him into telling you. Find out how we could capture him and tie him up. Then we will be able to control him. If you do this, each one of us will give you 28 pounds of silver."

[6] So Delilah said to Samson, "Tell me why you are so strong. How could someone tie you up and take control of you?"

[7] Samson answered, "Someone would have to tie me up. He would have to use seven new bowstrings that have not been dried. If he did that, I would be as weak as any other man."

[8] Then the kings of the Philistines brought seven new bowstrings to Delilah. They had not been dried. She tied Samson with them. [9] Some men were hiding in another room. Delilah said to Samson, "Samson, the Philistines are about to capture you!" But Samson easily broke the bowstrings. They broke like pieces of string burned in a fire. So the Philistines did not find out the secret of Samson's strength.

[10] Then Delilah said to Samson, "You've made me look foolish. You lied to me. Please tell me. How could someone tie you up?"

[11] Samson said, "They would have to tie me with new ropes that have not been used before. Then I would become as weak as any other man."

[12] So Delilah took new ropes and tied Samson. Some men were hiding in another room. Then she called out to him, "Samson, the Philistines are about to

---

15:17 Ramath Lehi This name means Jawbone Hill.

capture you!" But he broke the ropes as easily as if they were threads.

[13]Then Delilah said to Samson, "Until now, you have made me look foolish. You have lied to me. Tell me how someone could tie you up."

He said, "Use the loom.[n] Weave the seven braids of my hair into the cloth. Tighten it with a pin. Then I will become as weak as any other man."

Then Samson went to sleep. So Delilah wove the seven braids of his hair into the cloth. [14]Then she fastened it with a pin.

Again she called out to him, "Samson, the Philistines are about to capture you!" Samson woke up and pulled up the pin and the loom with the cloth.

[15]Then Delilah said to him, "How can you say, 'I love you,' when you don't even trust me? This is the third time you have made me look foolish. You haven't told me the secret of your great strength." [16]She kept bothering Samson about his secret day after day. He became so tired of it he felt he was going to die!

[17]So he told her everything. He said, "I have never had my hair cut. I have been set apart to God as a Nazirite[d] since I was born. If someone shaved my head, then I would lose my strength. I would become as weak as any other man."

[18]Delilah saw that he had told her everything sincerely. So she sent a message to the kings of the Philistines. She said, "Come back one more time. He has told me everything." So the kings of the Philistines came back to Delilah. They brought the silver they had promised to give her. [19]Delilah got Samson to go to sleep. He was lying in her lap. Then she called in a man to shave off the seven braids of Samson's hair. In this way she began to make him weak. And Samson's strength left him.

[20]Then she called out to him, "Samson, the Philistines are about to capture you!"

He woke up and thought, "I'll get loose as I did before and shake myself free." But he did not know that the Lord had left him.

[21]Then the Philistines captured Samson. They tore out his eyes. And they took him down to Gaza. They put bronze chains on him. They put him in prison and made him grind grain. [22]But his hair began to grow again.

[23]The kings of the Philistines gathered to celebrate. They were going to offer a great sacrifice to their god Dagon.[d] They said, "Our god has given us Samson our enemy." [24]When they saw him, they praised their god. They said,

"This man destroyed our country.
He killed many of us!
But our god helped us
capture our enemy."

[25]The people were having a good time at the celebration. They said, "Bring Samson out to perform for us." So they brought Samson from the prison. He performed for them. They made him stand between the pillars of the temple of Dagon. [26]A servant was holding his hand. Samson said to him, "Let me feel the pillars that hold up the temple. I want to lean against them." [27]Now the temple was full of men and women. All the kings of the Philistines were there. There were about 3,000 men and women on the roof.[n] They watched Samson perform. [28]Then Samson prayed to the Lord. He said, "Lord God, remember me. God, please give me strength one more time. Let me pay these Philistines back for putting out my two eyes!" [29]Then Samson held the two center pillars of the temple. These two pillars supported the whole temple. He braced himself between the two pillars. His right hand was on one, and his left hand was on the other. [30]Samson said, "Let me die with these Philistines!" Then he pushed as hard as he could. And the temple fell on the kings and all the people in it. So Samson killed more of the Philistines when he died than when he was alive.

[31]Samson's brothers and his whole family went down to get his body. They brought him back and buried him in the tomb of Manoah, his father. That tomb is between the cities of Zorah and Eshtaol. Samson was a judge for the people of Israel for 20 years.

17 There was a man named Micah. He lived in the mountains of Ephraim. [2]He said to his mother, "You remember the 28 pounds of silver that were taken from you. I heard you say a

---

16:13 loom A machine for making cloth from thread.   **16:27 roof** In Bible times houses were built with flat roofs. The roof was used for drying things such as flax and fruit. And it was used as an extra room, as a place for worship and as a place to sleep in the summer.

curse about it. I have the silver with me. I took it."

His mother said, "The Lord bless you, my son!"

[3]Micah gave the 28 pounds of silver to his mother. Then she said, "I will give this silver to the Lord. I will have my son make a carved idol and an idol of melted silver. So I will give the silver back to you."

[4]So he gave the silver back to his mother. She took about 5 pounds of the silver and gave it to a silversmith. He used it to make a carved idol and an idol of melted silver. The idols were put in Micah's house. [5]Micah had a temple for worshiping idols. He made a vest[d] for a priest and some household idols. Then Micah chose one of his sons to be his priest. [6]At that time the Israelites did not have a king. So everyone did what he thought was right.

[7]There was a young man who was a Levite.[n] He was from the city of Bethlehem in the land of Judah. He had been living with the people of Judah. [8]He left Bethlehem to look for another place to live. On his way he came to Micah's house. It was in the mountains of Ephraim. [9]Micah asked him, "Where have you come from?"

He answered, "I'm a Levite from Bethlehem in Judah. I'm looking for a place to live."

[10]Then Micah said to him, "Live with me. Be my father and my priest. I will give you 4 ounces of silver each year. I will also give you clothes and food." So the Levite went in. [11]The young Levite agreed to live with Micah. He became like one of Micah's own sons. [12]Micah made him a priest. And he lived in Micah's house. [13]Then Micah said, "Now I know the Lord will be good to me. I know this because I have a Levite as my priest!"

18 At that time the Israelites did not have a king. The people of Dan were still looking for a land where they could live. They wanted a land of their own. The other tribes[d] of Israel already had their own lands. But the Danites did not yet have their own land. [2]So they chose five soldiers from all their family groups. These five men were from the cities of Zorah and Eshtaol. They sent the men to spy out and explore the land. They were told, "Go, explore the land."

So they came to the mountains of Ephraim. They came to Micah's house, where they spent the night. [3]When they came near Micah's house, they recognized the voice of the young Levite. So they stopped at Micah's house. They asked the young Levite, "Who brought you to this place? What are you doing here? Why are you here?"

[4]He told them what Micah had done for him. "He has hired me. I am his priest."

[5]They said to him, "Please ask God something for us. Will our search for a place to live be successful?"

[6]The priest said to them, "Go in peace. The Lord is pleased with your journey."

[7]So the five men left. They came to the city of Laish. They saw that the people there lived in safety. They were like the people of Sidon. They lived in peace and were not afraid of others. They had plenty of everything. They lived a long way from the Sidonians. And they had no dealings with anyone else.

[8]The five men went back to Zorah and Eshtaol. Their relatives asked them, "What did you find?"

[9]They answered, "We have seen the land. And it is very good. We should attack them. Aren't you going to do something? Don't wait! Let's go and take that land! [10]When you go, you will see there is plenty of land. There is plenty of everything! The people are not expecting an attack. Surely God has given that land to us!"

[11]So 600 men of Dan left Zorah and Eshtaol. They were ready for war. [12]On their way they stopped near the city of Kiriath Jearim in Judah. They set up camp there. That is why the place is named Mahaneh Dan[n] to this very day. It is west of Kiriath Jearim. [13]From there they traveled on to the mountains of Ephraim. Then they came to Micah's house.

[14]So the five men who had explored the land around Laish spoke. They said to their relatives, "There is a vest[d] for a priest in one of these houses. And there are household gods in these houses. There are also a carved idol and an idol of melted silver in these houses. You know what to do." [15]So they stopped at

the Levite's house. This was also Micah's house. And they greeted the Levite. [16]The 600 men of Dan stood at the gate entrance. They wore their weapons of war. [17]The five spies went into the house. They took the carved idol, the vest for a priest, the household idols and the silver idol. The priest and the 600 men ready for war stood by the gate entrance.

[18]When the spies went into Micah's house and took the carved image, the vest for a priest, the household idols and the silver idol, the priest asked them, "What are you doing?"

[19]They answered, "Be quiet! Don't say a word. Come with us. Be our father and our priest. Is it better for you to be a priest for the people in one man's house? Or is it better for you to be a priest for a tribe[d] and family group in Israel?" [20]This made the Levite happy. So he took the vest for a priest, the household idols and the carved idol. And he went with the men of Dan. [21]They left Micah's house. They put their little children, their animals and everything they owned in front of them.

[22]The men of Dan went a long way from Micah's house. Then the men who lived near Micah were called out. They chased the men of Dan and caught up with them. [23]The men with Micah shouted at the men of Dan. The men of Dan turned around. They said to Micah, "What's the matter with you? Why have you called out your men to fight?"

[24]Micah answered, "You took my idols! I made those idols. You have also taken my priest. What do I have left? How can you ask me, 'What's the matter?' "

[25]The men of Dan answered, "You should not argue with us. Some of our men have hot tempers. If you shout at us, they might attack you. You and your family might be killed." [26]Then the men of Dan went on their way. Micah knew they were too strong for him. So he turned and went back home.

[27]So the men of Dan took what Micah had made. They also took his priest and went on to Laish. They attacked those peaceful people. The people of Laish had not expected an attack. The men of Dan killed them with their swords. Then they burned the city. [28]There was no one to save the people of Laish. They lived too far from Sidon. And they had no dealings with anyone else. Laish was in a valley near Beth Rehob.

The people of Dan rebuilt the city in that place. And they lived there. [29]They changed the name of Laish to Dan. They named it after their ancestor Dan. He was one of the sons of Israel.

[30]The people of Dan set up the idols in the city of Dan. They made Jonathan son of Gershom their priest. Gershom was the son of Moses. Jonathan and his sons were priests for the tribe of Dan. They served as priests until the Israelites were taken captive. [31]The people of Dan worshiped the idols Micah had made. They worshiped them as long as the Holy Tent[d] of God was in Shiloh.

19

At that time the people of Israel did not have a king.

There was a Levite who lived in the faraway part of the mountains of Ephraim. He had taken a slave woman.[d] She was from the city of Bethlehem in the land of Judah. [2]But she was unfaithful to him. She left him and went back to her father's house. It was in Bethlehem in Judah. She stayed there for four months. [3]Then her husband went to ask her to come back to him. He took with him his servant and two donkeys. The Levite came to her father's house. And she invited the Levite to come in. Her father was happy to see him. [4]The father-in-law, the young woman's father, asked him to stay. So he stayed for three days. He ate, drank and slept there.

[5]On the fourth day they got up early in the morning. The Levite was getting ready to leave. But the woman's father said to his son-in-law, "Refresh yourself by eating something. Then you may go." [6]So the two men sat down to eat and drink together. After that, the father said to him, "Please stay tonight. Relax and enjoy yourself." [7]When the man got up to go, his father-in-law asked him to stay. So he stayed again that night. [8]On the fifth day the man got up early in the morning to leave. The woman's father said, "Refresh yourself. Wait until this afternoon." So the two men ate together.

[9]Then the Levite, his slave woman and his servant got up to leave. His father-in-law, the young woman's father, said, "It's almost night. The day is almost gone. So spend the night here and enjoy yourself. Tomorrow morning you may get up early and go on your way home." [10]But the Levite did not want to stay another night. He took his two saddled donkeys and his slave woman. He traveled toward the city of Jebus. (Jebus is another name for Jerusalem.)

[11]The day was almost over. They were

near Jebus. So the servant said to his master, "Let's stop at this city. It's the city of the Jebusite people. Let's spend the night here."

[12] But his master said, "No. We won't go inside a strange city. Those people are not Israelites. We will go on to the city of Gibeah." [13] Then he said, "Come on. Let's try to make it to Gibeah or Ramah. We can spend the night in one of those cities." [14] So they went on. And the sun went down as they came near Gibeah. Gibeah belongs to the tribe[d] of Benjamin. [15] So they stopped there to spend the night. They came to the public square in the middle of the city and sat down. But no one invited them home to spend the night.

[16] That evening an old man came into the city from his work in the fields. His home was in the mountains of Ephraim. But now he was living in Gibeah. (The men of Gibeah were from the tribe of Benjamin.) [17] He saw the traveler, the Levite, in the public square. He asked, "Where are you going? Where did you come from?"

[18] The Levite answered, "We are traveling from Bethlehem in Judah. We're going to my home. I'm from a faraway part of the mountains of Ephraim. I have been to Bethlehem in Judah. Now I am going to the Holy Tent[d] of the Lord. No one has invited me to stay in his house. [19] We already have straw and food for our donkeys. There is bread and wine for me, the young woman and my servant. We don't need anything."

[20] The old man said, "You are welcome to stay at my house. Let me give you anything you need. But don't spend the night in the public square." [21] So the old man took the Levite into his house. He fed their donkeys, and they washed their feet. Then he gave them something to eat and drink.

[22] While they were enjoying themselves, some wicked men of the city surrounded the house. They beat on the door. They shouted to the old man who owned the house. They said, "Bring out the man who came to your house. We want to have sexual relations with him." [23] The owner of the house went outside. And he said to them, "No, my friends. Don't be so evil. This man is a guest in my house. Don't do this terrible thing! [24] Look, here is my daughter. She

has never had sexual relations before. And here is the man's slave woman. I will bring them out to you now. Do anything you want with them. But don't do such a terrible thing to this man."

[25] But the men would not listen to him. So the Levite took his slave woman and sent her outside to them. They had sexual relations with her even though she didn't want to. They treated her very badly all night long. Then, at dawn, they let her go. [26] She came back to the house where her master was staying. She fell down at the door and lay there until daylight.

[27] In the morning the Levite got up. He opened the door of the house. He went outside to go on his way. But there lay his slave woman. She had fallen down at the doorway of the house. Her hands were on the doorsill. [28] Then the Levite said to her, "Get up; let's go." But she did not answer. So he put her on his donkey and went home.

[29] When the Levite got home, he took a knife and cut his slave woman into 12 parts. Then he sent a part to each of the areas where the people of Israel lived. [30] Everyone who saw this said, "Nothing like this has ever happened before. It has never happened since the people of Israel came out of Egypt. Think about it. Tell us what to do."

20 So all the Israelites joined together. They came to stand before the Lord in the city of Mizpah. They came from as far away as the cities of Dan and Beersheba.[n] Even the Israelites from the land of Gilead were there. [2] The leaders of all the tribes[d] of Israel were there. They took their places in the meeting of the people of God. There were 400,000 soldiers with swords. [3] (The people of Benjamin heard that the Israelites had gone up to Mizpah.) Then the Israelites said to the Levite, "Tell us how this evil thing happened."

[4] So the husband of the murdered woman answered: "My slave woman[d] and I came to Gibeah in Benjamin to spend the night. [5] During the night the men of Gibeah came after me. They surrounded the house and wanted to kill me. They had sexual relations with my slave woman even though she didn't want to. And she died! [6] So I took her and cut her into parts. Then I sent one part to each area of Israel's land. I did

---

20:1 **Dan . . . Beersheba** Dan was the city farthest north in Israel. Beersheba was the city farthest south. So this means all the people of Israel.

it because the people of Benjamin have done this wicked and terrible thing in Israel. ⁷Now, all you men of Israel, speak up. Tell what you have decided we should do."

⁸Then all the people stood up at the same time. They said, "None of us will go home. Not one of us will go back to his house! ⁹Now this is what we will do to Gibeah. We will throw lots* so that God can show us what to do. ¹⁰We will choose 10 men from each 100 men. They will be from all the tribes of Israel. And we will choose 100 men from each 1,000. We will choose 1,000 men from each 10,000. These men will find supplies for the army. Then the army will go to the city of Gibeah of Benjamin. They will repay those people for the terrible thing they have done in Israel." ¹¹So all the men of Israel gathered against the city. They all agreed about what they were doing.

¹²The tribes of Israel sent men to all the family groups of Benjamin with a message. They said, "What is this evil thing some of your men have done? ¹³Give up the evil men in Gibeah so that we can put them to death. We must remove this evil from Israel."

But the Benjaminites would not listen to their relatives, the people of Israel. ¹⁴The Benjaminites left their own cities and met at Gibeah. They went to fight against the Israelites. ¹⁵In only one day the Benjaminites got 26,000 soldiers together. These soldiers were trained with swords. They also had 700 chosen men from Gibeah. ¹⁶Seven hundred of these trained soldiers were left-handed. Each of these left-handed soldiers could sling a stone at a hair and not miss!

¹⁷The Israelites, except for the Benjaminites, gathered 400,000 fighting men. These 400,000 men used swords and were trained soldiers.

¹⁸The Israelites went up to the city of Bethel. They asked God, "Which tribe shall be first to attack the Benjaminites?"

The Lord answered, "Judah shall go first."

¹⁹The next morning the Israelites got up. They made a camp near Gibeah. ²⁰Then the men of Israel went out to fight the Benjaminites. The Israelites got into battle position at Gibeah. ²¹Then the Benjaminites came out of Gibeah. They killed 22,000 Israelites during the battle that day. ²²⁻²³The Israelites went before the Lord. They cried until evening. They asked the Lord, "Shall we go to fight our relatives, the Benjaminites, again?"

The Lord answered, "Go up and fight them." The men of Israel encouraged each other. So they took the same battle positions they had taken the first day.

²⁴The Israelites brought their battle lines against the Benjaminites the second day. ²⁵The Benjaminites came out of Gibeah to attack the Israelites. This time, the Benjaminites killed 18,000 Israelites. All of these Israelites had been trained with swords.

²⁶Then the Israelites went up to Bethel. There they sat down and cried to the Lord. They went without food all day until evening. They also brought burnt offerings and fellowship offerings to the Lord. ²⁷The Israelites asked the Lord a question. (In those days the Box* of the Agreement with God was there at Bethel. ²⁸A priest named Phinehas served before the Box of the Agreement. He was the son of Eleazar, who was the son of Aaron.) The people of Israel asked, "Shall we again go to fight against our relatives the Benjaminites? Or shall we stop fighting?"

The Lord answered, "Go, because tomorrow I will help you defeat them."

²⁹Then the Israelites hid some men all around Gibeah. ³⁰They went to fight against the Benjaminites at Gibeah on the third day. They got into position for battle, as they had done before. ³¹Then the Benjaminites came out of the city to fight them. The Israelites backed up and led the Benjaminites away from the city. The Benjaminites began to kill some of the Israelites as they had done before. About 30 men from Israel were killed. Some of them were killed in the fields and some on the roads. One road led to Bethel. Another road led to Gibeah.

³²The Benjaminites said, "We are winning as before!"

But the Israelites said, "Let's run. Let's trick them into going farther away from their city and onto the roads."

³³All the men of Israel moved from their places. They got into battle positions at a place named Baal Tamar. Then the Israelites ran out from their hiding places west of Gibeah. ³⁴Ten thousand of the best trained soldiers from the army of Israel attacked Gibeah. The battle was very hard. The Benjaminites did not know disaster was about to come to them. ³⁵The Lord used the Israelites to defeat the Benjaminites. On that day the

Israelites killed 25,100 Benjaminites. All these men were armed with swords. [36]Then the Benjaminites saw that they were defeated.

The men of Israel had moved back. They backed up because they were depending on the surprise attack. They had set it up near Gibeah. [37]The men in hiding rushed into Gibeah. They spread out and killed everyone in the city with their swords. [38]Now the men of Israel had made a plan with the men in hiding. The men in the surprise attack were to send up a signal. It was to be a big cloud of smoke from the city. [39]So the army of Israel turned around in the battle.

The Benjaminites had killed about 30 Israelites. They were saying, "We are winning, as in the first battle!" [40]But then the big cloud of smoke began to rise from the city. The Benjaminites turned around and saw it. The whole city was full of smoke that went up into the sky. [41]Then the Israelites turned and began to fight. The Benjaminites were terrified. Now they knew that disaster was coming to them. [42]So the Benjaminites ran away from the Israelites. They ran toward the desert. But they could not escape the battle. And the Israelites who came out of the cities killed them. [43]They surrounded the Benjaminites and chased them. They caught them in the area east of Gibeah. So 18,000 brave and strong Benjaminite fighters were killed. [45]The Benjaminites ran toward the desert. They ran to a place called the rock of Rimmon. But the Israelites killed 5,000 Benjaminites along the roads. They kept chasing them as far as a place named Gidom. And they killed 2,000 more Benjaminites there.

[46]On that day 25,000 Benjaminites were killed. All of them had fought bravely with swords. [47]But 600 Benjaminites ran to the rock of Rimmon in the desert. They stayed there for four months. [48]Then the men of Israel went back to the land of Benjamin. They killed the people in every city. They also killed the animals. They destroyed everything they could find. And they burned every city they found.

21 At Mizpah the men of Israel had made a promise. This was their promise: "Not one of us will let his daughter marry a man from the tribe[d] of Benjamin."

[2]The people went to the city of Bethel. There they sat before God until evening, crying loudly. [3]They said, "Lord, you are the God of Israel. Why has this terrible thing happened to us? Why has one tribe of Israel been taken away?"

[4]Early the next day the people built an altar. They put burnt offerings and fellowship offerings to God on it.

[5]Then the Israelites asked, "Did any tribe of Israel not come here to meet with us before the Lord?" They asked this question because they had made a great promise. They had promised that anyone who did not meet with them at Mizpah would be killed.

[6]The Israelites felt sorry for their relatives, the Benjaminites. They said, "Today one tribe has been separated from Israel. [7]We made a promise before the Lord. We will not allow our daughters to marry a Benjaminite. How can we make sure that the men of Benjamin will have wives?" [8]Then they asked, "Which one of the tribes of Israel did not come here to Mizpah?" They found that no one from the city of Jabesh Gilead was there. [9]The people of Israel counted everyone, but no one from Jabesh Gilead was there.

[10]So the whole group of Israelites sent 12,000 soldiers to Jabesh Gilead. They told the soldiers to kill the people in Jabesh Gilead with their swords. Even the women and children were to be killed. [11]"This is what you must do: Kill every man in Jabesh Gilead. Also kill every woman who has had sexual relations with a man." [12]The soldiers found 400 young women in Jabesh Gilead who had never had sexual relations with a man. They brought these women to the camp at Shiloh in Canaan.

[13]Then the whole group of Israelites sent a message to the men of Benjamin. They offered to make peace with them. The men of Benjamin were at the rock of Rimmon. [14]So the men of Benjamin came back at that time. The Israelites gave them the women from Jabesh Gilead who had not been killed. But there were not enough women for all of them.

[15]The people of Israel felt sorry for the Benjaminites. This was because the Lord had separated the tribes of Israel. [16]The older leaders of the Israelites spoke. They said, "The women of Benjamin have been killed. Where can we get wives for the men of Benjamin who are still alive? [17]These men must have children to continue their families. This is so a tribe in Israel will not die out. [18]But we cannot allow our daughters to marry

them. We have made this promise: 'Anyone who gives a wife to a man of Benjamin is cursed.' [19]We have an idea! There is a yearly festival of the Lord at Shiloh. Shiloh is north of the city of Bethel. It is east of the road that goes from Bethel to Shechem. And it is south of the city of Lebonah."

[20]So the older leaders told the men of Benjamin about their idea. They said, "Go and hide in the vineyards. [21]Watch for the young women from Shiloh to come out. They will come to join the dancing. Then run out from the vineyards. Each of you take one of the young Shiloh women and go to the land of Benjamin. [22]The fathers or brothers of those young women will come to us. They will complain, but we will say: 'Be kind to the men of Benjamin. We did not get wives for Benjamin during the war. And you did not give the women to the men from Benjamin. So you are not guilty.'"

[23]So that is what the Benjaminites did. While the young women were dancing, each man caught one of them. They took them away and married them. Then they went back to the land God had given them. They rebuilt their cities and lived there.

[24]Then the Israelites went home. They went to their own tribes and family groups. They went to their own land that God had given them.

[25]In those days the Israelites did not have a king. Everyone did what he thought was right.

The Book of
RUTH

1 [1-2]Long ago the judges[n] ruled Israel. During their rule, there was a time in the land when there was not enough food to eat. A man named Elimelech left Bethlehem in Judah and moved to the country of Moab. He took his wife and his two sons with him. His wife was named Naomi, and his two sons were named Mahlon and Kilion. These people were from the Ephrathah district around Bethlehem in Judah. The family traveled to Moab and lived there.

[3]Later, Naomi's husband, Elimelech, died. So only Naomi and her two sons were left. [4]These sons married women from Moab. The name of one wife was Orpah. The name of the other wife was Ruth. Naomi and her sons lived in Moab about ten years. [5]Then Mahlon and Kilion also died. So Naomi was left alone without her husband or her two sons.

[6]While Naomi was in Moab, she heard that the Lord had taken care of his people. He had given food to them in Judah. So Naomi got ready to leave Moab and go back home. The wives of Naomi's sons also got ready to go with her. [7]So they left the place where they had lived. And they started back on the way to the land of Judah. [8]But Naomi said to her two daughters-in-law, "Go back home. Each of you go to your own mother's house. You have been very kind to me and to my sons who are now dead. I hope the Lord will also be kind to you in the same way. [9]I hope the Lord will give you another home and a new husband."

Then Naomi kissed the women. And they began to cry out loud. [10]Her daughters-in-law said to her, "No. We will go with you to your people."

[11]But Naomi said, "My daughters, go back to your own homes. Why do you want to go with me? I cannot give birth to more sons to give you new husbands. [12]So go back to your own homes. I am too old to have another husband. But even if I had another husband tonight and if I had more sons, it wouldn't help! [13]Would you wait until the babies were grown into men? Would you live for so many years without husbands? Don't do this thing. My life is much too sad for you to share. This is because the Lord is against me!"

[14]The women cried together again. Then Orpah kissed Naomi good-bye, but Ruth held on to her.

[15]Naomi said, "Look, your sister-in-law is going back to her own people and her own gods. Go back with her."

[16]But Ruth said, "Don't ask me to leave you! Don't beg me not to follow

---

1:1-2 judges They were not judges in courts of law, but leaders of the people in times of emergency.

you! Every place you go, I will go. Every place you live, I will live. Your people will be my people. Your God will be my God. [17]And where you die, I will die. And there I will be buried. I ask the Lord to punish me terribly if I do not keep this promise: Only death will separate us."

[18]Naomi saw that Ruth had made up her mind to go with her. So Naomi stopped arguing with her. [19]Naomi and Ruth went on until they came to the town of Bethlehem. When the two women entered Bethlehem, all the people became very excited. The women of the town said, "Is this Naomi?"

[20]But Naomi told the people, "Don't call me Naomi.ⁿ Call me Mara,ⁿ because God All-Powerful has made my life very sad. [21]When I left, I had all I wanted. But now, the Lord has brought me home with nothing. So why should you call me Naomi when the Lord has spoken against me? God All-Powerful has given me much trouble."

[22]So Naomi and her daughter-in-law Ruth, the woman from Moab, came back from Moab. They came to Bethlehem at the beginning of the barley harvest.

2 Now there was a rich man living in Bethlehem whose name was Boaz. Boaz was one of Naomi's close relatives from Elimelech's family.

[2]One day Ruth, the woman from Moab, said to Naomi, "Let me go to the fields. Maybe someone will be kind and let me gather the grain he leaves in his field."

Naomi said, "Go, my daughter."

[3]So Ruth went to the fields. She followed the workers who were cutting the grain. And she gathered the grain that they had left. It just so happened that the field belonged to Boaz. He was a close relative from Elimelech's family.

[4]When Boaz came from Bethlehem, he spoke to his workers: "The Lord be with you!"

And the workers answered, "May the Lord bless you!"

[5]Then Boaz spoke to his servant who was in charge of the workers. He asked, "Whose girl is that?"

[6]The servant answered, "She is the Moabite woman who came with Naomi from the country of Moab. [7]She said, 'Please let me follow the workers and gather the grain that they leave on the

ground.' She came and has remained here. From morning until just now, she has stopped only a few moments to rest in the shelter."

[8]Then Boaz said to Ruth, "Listen, my daughter. Stay here in my field to gather grain for yourself. Do not go to any other person's field. Continue following behind my women workers. [9]Watch to see which fields they go to and follow them. I have warned the young men not to bother you. When you are thirsty, you may go and drink. Take water from the water jugs that the servants have filled."

[10]Then Ruth bowed low with her face to the ground. She said to Boaz, "I am a stranger. Why have you been so kind to notice me?"

[11]Boaz answered her, "I know about all the help you have given to Naomi, your mother-in-law. You helped her even after your husband died. You left your father and mother and your own country. You came to this nation where you did not know anyone. [12]The Lord will reward you for all you have done. You will be paid in full by the Lord, the God of Israel. You have come to him as a little bird finds shelter under the wings of its mother."

[13]Then Ruth said, "You are very kind to me, sir. You have said kind words to me, your servant. You have given me hope. And I am not even good enough to be one of your servants."

[14]At mealtime Boaz told Ruth, "Come here! Eat some of our bread. Here, dip your bread in our vinegar."

So Ruth sat down with the workers. Boaz gave her some roasted grain. Ruth ate until she was full, and there was some food left over. [15]Ruth rose and went back to work. Then Boaz told his servants, "Let her gather even around the bundles of grain. Don't tell her to go away. [16]Drop some full heads of grain for her. Let her gather that grain, and don't tell her to stop."

[17]So Ruth gathered grain in the field until evening. Then she separated the grain from the chaff.ᵈ There was about one-half bushel of barley. [18]Ruth carried the grain into town. And her mother-in-law saw what she had gathered. Ruth also gave her the food that was left over from lunch.

[19]Naomi asked her, "Where did you gather all this grain today? Where did

1:20 Naomi This name means "happy" or "pleasant." **1:20 Mara** This name means "bitter" or "sad."

you work? Blessed be the man who noticed you!"

Ruth told her about whose field she had worked in. She said, "The man I worked with today is named Boaz."

[20] Naomi told her daughter-in-law, "The Lord bless him! The Lord still continues to be kind to all people—the living and the dead!" Then Naomi told Ruth, "Boaz is one of our close relatives,[n] one who will take care of us."

[21] Then Ruth said, "Boaz also told me to come back and continue working. He said, 'Keep close by my servants until they have finished the harvest.'"

[22] Then Naomi said to her daughter-in-law Ruth, "It is good for you to continue working with his women servants. If you work in another field, someone might hurt you." [23] So Ruth continued working closely with the women servants of Boaz. She gathered grain until the barley harvest was finished. She also worked there through the end of the wheat harvest. And Ruth continued to live with Naomi, her mother-in-law.

3 Then Naomi, Ruth's mother-in-law, said to her, "My daughter, I must find a suitable home for you. That would be good for you. [2] Now Boaz is our close relative. You worked with his women servants. Tonight he will be working at the threshing[d] floor. [3] Go wash yourself and put on perfume. Change your clothes, and go down to the threshing floor. But don't let him see you until he has finished eating and drinking. [4] Then he will lie down. Watch him so you will know the place where he lies down. Go there and lift the cover off his feet[a] and lie down. He will tell you what you should do."

[5] Then Ruth answered, "I will do everything you say."

[6] So Ruth went down to the threshing floor. She did all her mother-in-law told her to do. [7] After eating and drinking, Boaz was feeling good. He went to lie down beside the pile of grain. Then Ruth went to him quietly. She lifted the cover from his feet and lay down.

[8] About midnight Boaz woke up suddenly and rolled over. He was startled! There was a woman lying near his feet! [9] Boaz asked, "Who are you?"

She said, "I am Ruth, your servant girl. Spread your cover over me because you are the one who is to take care of me."

[10] Then Boaz said, "The Lord bless you, my daughter. Your kindness to me is greater than the kindness you showed to Naomi in the beginning. You didn't look for a young man to marry, either rich or poor. [11] Now, my daughter, don't be afraid. I will do everything you ask. All the people in our town know you are a very good woman. [12] And it is true, I am a relative who is to take care of you. But there is a man who is a closer relative to you than I. [13] But stay here tonight. In the morning we will see if he will take care of you. If he decides to take care of you, that is fine. If he refuses to take care of you, I myself will marry you. Then I will buy back Elimelech's land for you. As surely as the Lord lives, I promise to do this. So lie here until morning."

[14] So Ruth lay near his feet until the morning. She rose while it was still too dark to be recognized. Boaz said to his servants, "Don't tell anyone that the woman came here to the threshing[d] floor." [15] Then Boaz said to Ruth, "Bring me your shawl. Now, hold it open."

So Ruth held her shawl open, and Boaz poured six portions of barley into it. Boaz then put it on her back, and she went to the city.

[16] Ruth went to the home of her mother-in-law. And Naomi asked, "How did you do, my daughter?"

So Ruth told Naomi everything that Boaz did for her. [17] She said, "Boaz gave me these six portions of barley. He said, 'You must not go home without a gift for your mother-in-law.'"

[18] Naomi answered, "Ruth, my daughter, wait until you hear what happens. Boaz will not rest until he has finished doing what he should do this day."

4 Boaz went to the city gate. He sat there until the close relative he had mentioned passed by. Boaz called to him, "Come here, friend! Sit down here!" So the man came over and sat down. [2] Boaz gathered ten of the old men who were leaders of the city. He told them, "Sit down here!" So they sat down.

2:20; 3:2 close relatives In Bible times the closest relative could marry a widow without children so she could have children. He would care for this family, but they and their property would not belong to him. They would belong to the dead husband. **3:4 lift . . . feet** This showed Ruth was asking him to be her husband.

³Then Boaz spoke to the close relative. He said, "Naomi has come back from the country of Moab. She wants to sell the piece of land that belonged to our relative Elimelech. ⁴So I decided to say this to you: If you want to buy back the land, then buy it! Buy it in front of the people who live here and in front of the older leaders of my people. If you don't want to buy it, tell me. I am the only person after you who can buy back the land. If you don't buy it back, I will."

And the close relative said, "I will buy back the land."

⁵Then Boaz said, "When you buy the land from Naomi, you must marry Ruth, the dead man's wife. She is the woman from Moab. That way, the land will stay in her dead husband's family."

⁶The close relative answered, "Then I can't buy back the land. If I did, I might lose what I can pass on to my own sons. I cannot buy the land back. So you buy it yourself."

⁷Long ago in Israel when people traded or bought back something, one person took off his sandal and gave it to the other person. This was their proof of purchase.

⁸So the close relative said, "Buy the land yourself." And then he took off his sandal.

⁹Then Boaz spoke to the older leaders and to all the people. He said, "You are witnesses today of what I am buying from Naomi. I am buying everything that belonged to Elimelech and Kilion and Mahlon. ¹⁰I am also taking Ruth as my wife. She is the Moabite who was the wife of Mahlon. I am doing this so her dead husband's property will stay with his family. This way, his name will

not be separated from his family and his land. You are witnesses this day."

¹¹So all the people and older leaders who were at the city gate said, "We are witnesses. This woman will be coming into your home. We hope the Lord will make her like Rachel and Leah. They had many children. So the people of Israel grew in number. May you become powerful in the district of Ephrathah. May you become famous in Bethlehem! ¹²Tamar gave birth to Judah's son Perez.ⁿ In the same way, may the Lord give you many children through Ruth. And may your family be great like his."

¹³So Boaz took Ruth and married her. The Lord let her become pregnant, and she gave birth to a son. ¹⁴The women told Naomi, "Praise the Lord who gave you this grandson. And may he become famous in Israel. ¹⁵He will give you new life. And he will take care of you in your old age. This happened because of your daughter-in-law. She loves you. And she is better for you than seven sons. She has given birth to your grandson."

¹⁶Naomi took the boy, held him in her arms and cared for him. ¹⁷The neighbors gave the boy his name. These women said, "This boy was born for Naomi." The neighbors named him Obed. Obed was Jesse's father. And Jesse was the father of David.

¹⁸This is the family history of Perez. Perez was the father of Hezron. ¹⁹Hezron was the father of Ram. Ram was the father of Amminadab. ²⁰Amminadab was the father of Nahshon. Nahshon was the father of Salmon. ²¹Salmon was the father of Boaz. Boaz was the father of Obed. ²²Obed was the father of Jesse, and Jesse was the father of David.

The First Book of
SAMUEL

1 There was a man named Elkanah son of Jeroham. He was from Ramathaim in the mountains of Ephraim. Elkanah was from the family of Zuph. (Jeroham was Elihu's son. Elihu was Tohu's son. And Tohu was the son of Zuph from the family group of Ephraim.) ²Elkanah had two wives. One was named Hannah, and the other was named Peninnah. Peninnah had children, but Hannah had none.

³Every year Elkanah left his town Ramah and went up to Shiloh. There he worshiped the Lord of heaven's armies and offered sacrifices to him. Shiloh was where Hophni and Phinehas served as priests of the Lord. They were the sons of Eli. ⁴When Elkanah offered sacrifices, he always gave a share of the meat to his wife Peninnah. He also gave shares of the meat to her sons and

4:12 Perez One of Boaz's ancestors.

daughters. [5]But Elkanah always gave a special share of the meat to Hannah. He did this because he loved Hannah and because the Lord had made Hannah unable to have children. [6]Peninnah would upset Hannah and make her feel bad. She did this because the Lord had made Hannah unable to have children. [7]This happened every year when they went up to the Tent[d] of the Lord at Shiloh. Peninnah would upset Hannah until Hannah would cry and not eat anything. [8]Her husband Elkanah would say to her, "Hannah, why are you crying? Why won't you eat? Why are you sad? Don't I mean more to you than ten sons?"

[9]Once, after they had eaten their meal in Shiloh, Hannah got up. Now Eli the priest was sitting on a chair near the entrance to the Lord's Holy Tent. [10]Hannah was very sad. She cried much and prayed to the Lord. [11]She made a promise. She said, "Lord of heaven's armies, see how bad I feel. Remember me! Don't forget me. If you will give me a son, I will give him back to you all his life. And no one will ever use a razor to cut his hair.'"[n]

[12]While Hannah kept praying, Eli watched her mouth. [13]She was praying in her heart. Her lips moved, but her voice was not heard. So Eli thought she was drunk. [14]He said to her, "Stop getting drunk! Throw away your wine!"

[15]Hannah answered, "No, master, I have not drunk any wine or beer. I am a woman who is deeply troubled. I was telling the Lord about all my problems. [16]Don't think of me as an evil woman. I have been praying because of my many troubles and much sadness."

[17]Eli answered, "Go in peace. May the God of Israel give you what you asked of him."

[18]Hannah said, "I want to be pleasing to you always." Then she left and ate something. She was not sad anymore.

[19]Early the next morning Elkanah's family got up and worshiped the Lord. Then they went back home to Ramah. Elkanah had sexual relations with his wife Hannah. And the Lord remembered her. [20]So Hannah became pregnant, and in time she gave birth to a son. She named him Samuel.[n] She said, "His name is Samuel because I asked the Lord for him."

[21]Every year Elkanah went to Shiloh to offer sacrifices. He went to keep the promise he had made to God. He brought his whole family with him. So once again he went up to Shiloh. [22]But Hannah did not go with him. She told him, "When the boy is old enough to eat solid food, I will take him to Shiloh. Then I will give him to the Lord. He will become a Nazirite.[d] He will always live there at Shiloh."

[23]Elkanah, Hannah's husband, said to her, "Do what you think is best. You may stay home until the boy is old enough to eat. May the Lord do what you have said." So Hannah stayed at home to nurse her son until he was old enough to eat.

[24]When Samuel was old enough to eat, Hannah took him to the Tent[d] of the Lord at Shiloh. She also took a three-year-old bull, one-half bushel of flour and a leather bag filled with wine. [25]They killed the bull for the sacrifice. Then Hannah brought Samuel to Eli. [26]She said to Eli, "As surely as you live, my master, I am the same woman who stood near you praying to the Lord. [27]I prayed for this child. The Lord answered my prayer and gave him to me. [28]Now I give him back to the Lord. He will belong to the Lord all his life." And he worshiped the Lord there.

2 Hannah said:
　　"The Lord has filled my heart with
　　　　joy.
　　I feel very strong in the Lord.
　　I can laugh at my enemies.
　　I am glad because you have
　　　　helped me!

[2]"There is no one holy like the Lord.
　　There is no God but you.
　　There is no Rock[d] like our God.

[3]"Don't continue bragging.
　　Don't speak proud words.
　　The Lord is a God who knows
　　　　everything.
　　He judges what people do.

[4]"The bows of warriors break,
　　　　but weak people become strong.
[5]Those who once had plenty of food
　　　　now must work for food.
　　But people who once were
　　　　hungry now grow fat on food.
　　The woman who was unable to
　　　　have children now has had
　　　　seven.

1:11 And . . . hair People who made special promises not to cut their hair or to drink wine or beer were called Nazirites. These people gave their lives to the Lord. See Numbers 6:1-5.
1:20 Samuel This name sounds like the Hebrew word for "God heard."

But the woman who had many
  sons now is sad.

6"The Lord causes people to die,
  and he causes them to live.
He brings people down to where
  the dead are,
  and he raises them to life again.
7The Lord makes people poor,
  and he makes people rich.
He makes people humble,
  and he makes people great.
8The Lord raises the poor up from
  the dust.
And he picks needy people up
  from the ashes.
He lets the poor sit with princes,
He lets them sit on a throne of
  honor.

"The foundations of the earth
  belong to the Lord.
The Lord set the world upon
  them.
9He protects his holy people.
But those who do evil will be
  silenced in darkness.
Their power will not help them
  win.
10The Lord destroys his enemies.
He will thunder in heaven
  against them.
The Lord will judge all the earth.
He will give power to his king.
He will make his appointed king
  strong."

11Then Elkanah went home to Ramah.
But the boy continued to serve the Lord
under Eli the priest.
12Now Eli's sons were evil men. They
did not care about the Lord. 13This is
what the priests would do to the people:
Every time someone brought a sacrifice,
the meat would be cooked in a pot. The
priest's servant would then come with
a fork in his hand. The fork had three
prongs. 14He would plunge the fork into
the pot or the kettle. Whatever the fork
brought out of the pot belonged to the
priest. This is how they treated all the
Israelites who came to Shiloh to offer
sacrifices. 15But even before the fat was
burned, the priest's servant would come
to the person offering sacrifices. The
servant would say, "Give the priest some
meat to roast. The priest won't accept
boiled meat from you. He will only accept raw meat."
16But the man who offered the sacrifice might say, "Let the fat be burned up

first as usual. Then you may take anything you want."
If so, the priest's servant would answer, "No, give me the meat now. If you
don't, I'll take it by force."
17The Lord saw that the sin of the servants was very great. They did not show
respect for the offerings made to the
Lord.
18But Samuel obeyed the Lord. He wore
a linen holy vest.d 19Every year Samuel's
mother would make a little coat for him.
She would take it to him when she went
to Shiloh. She went there with her husband for the sacrifice. 20Eli would bless
Elkanah and his wife. Eli would say,
"May the Lord repay you with children
through Hannah. They will take the
place of the boy Hannah prayed for and
gave back to the Lord." Then Elkanah
and Hannah would go home. 21The Lord
was kind to Hannah. She became the
mother of three sons and two daughters.
And the boy Samuel grew up serving
the Lord.
22Now Eli was very old. He heard
about everything his sons were doing to
all the Israelites. He also heard about
how his sons had sexual relations with
the women who served at the entrance
to the Meeting Tent.d 23Eli said to his
sons, "The people here tell me about the
evil you do. Why do you do these evil
things? 24No, my sons. The Lord's people
are saying bad things about you. 25If
someone sins against another person,
God can help him. But if he sins against
the Lord himself, no one can help him!"
But Eli's sons would not listen to him.
This was because the Lord had decided
to put them to death.
26The boy Samuel kept growing. He
pleased God and the people.
27A man of God came to Eli. He said,
"This is what the Lord says: 'I clearly
showed myself to the family of your ancestor Aaron. This was when they were
slaves to the king of Egypt. 28I chose
them from all the tribesd of Israel to be
my priests. I wanted them to go up to
my altar, to burn incensed and to wear
the holy vest. I also let the family of your
ancestor have part of all the offerings
sacrificed by the Israelites. 29So why
don't you respect the sacrifices and
gifts? You honor your sons more than
me. You become fat on the best parts of
the meat the Israelites bring to me.'
30"Here's what the Lord, the God of
Israel, says: 'I promised that your family
and your ancestor's family would serve

me forever.' But now the Lord says this: 'That will never be! I will honor those who honor me. But I will take honor away from those who do not honor me. [31]The time is coming when I will destroy the descendants[d] of both you and your ancestors. No man will grow old in your family. [32]You will see trouble in my house. Good things will be done to Israel. But there will never be an old man in your family. [33]I will save one man to serve as priest at my altar. He will wear out his eyes and use up his strength. The rest of your descendants will die by the sword.

[34]"'I will give you a sign. Both your sons, Hophni and Phinehas, will die on the same day. [35]I will choose a loyal priest for myself. He will listen to me and do what I want. I will make his family strong. He will always serve before my appointed king. [36]Then everyone left in your family will come and bow down before him. They will beg for a little money or a little food. They will say, "Please give me a job as priest so I can have food to eat."'"

3 The boy Samuel served the Lord under Eli. In those days the Lord did not speak directly to people very often. There were very few visions.

[2]Eli's eyes were so weak he was almost blind. One night he was lying in bed. [3]Samuel was also in bed in the Lord's Holy Tent.[d] The Box[d] of the Agreement was in the Holy Tent. God's lamp was still burning.

[4]Then the Lord called Samuel. Samuel answered, "I am here!" [5]He ran to Eli and said, "I am here. You called me."

But Eli said, "I didn't call you. Go back to bed." So Samuel went back to bed.

[6]The Lord called again, "Samuel!"

Samuel again went to Eli and said, "I am here. You called me."

Again Eli said, "I didn't call you. Go back to bed."

[7]Samuel did not yet know the Lord. The Lord had not spoken directly to him yet.

[8]The Lord called Samuel for the third time. Samuel got up and went to Eli. He said, "I am here. You called me."

Then Eli realized the Lord was calling the boy. [9]So he told Samuel, "Go to bed. If he calls you again, say, 'Speak, Lord.

I am your servant, and I am listening.'"

So Samuel went and lay down in bed.

[10]The Lord came and stood there. He called as he had before. He said, "Samuel, Samuel!"

Samuel said, "Speak, Lord. I am your servant, and I am listening."

[11]The Lord said to Samuel, "See, I am going to do something in Israel. It will shock those who hear about it. [12]At that time I will do to Eli and his family everything I promised. I will not stop until I have finished. [13]I told Eli I would punish his family forever. I will do it because Eli knew his sons were evil. They spoke against me, but he did not control them. [14]So here is what I promised Eli's family: 'Your guilt will never be removed by sacrifice or offering.'"

[15]Samuel lay down until morning. Then he opened the doors of the Tent[d] of the Lord. He was afraid to tell Eli about the vision. [16]But Eli said to him, "Samuel, my son!"

Samuel answered, "I am here."

[17]Eli asked, "What did the Lord say to you? Don't hide it from me. May God punish you terribly if you hide from me anything he said to you." [18]So Samuel told Eli everything. He did not hide anything from him. Then Eli said, "He is the Lord. Let him do what he thinks is best."

[19]The Lord was with Samuel as he grew up. He did not let any of Samuel's messages fail to come true. [20]Then all Israel, from Dan to Beersheba,[n] knew Samuel was a prophet[d] of the Lord. [21]And the Lord continued to show himself to Samuel at Shiloh. He also showed himself to Samuel through his word.

4 News about Samuel spread through all of Israel.

At that time the Israelites went out to fight the Philistines. The Israelites camped at Ebenezer, and the Philistines camped at Aphek. [2]The Philistines went to meet the Israelites in battle. And as the battle spread, the Philistines defeated the Israelites. They killed about 4,000 soldiers of the Israelite army. [3]Then some Israelite soldiers went back to their camp. The older leaders of Israel asked, "Why did the Lord let the Philistines defeat us? Let's bring the Box[d] of the Agreement with the Lord here from Shiloh. In this way God will go with us into battle. He will save us from our enemies."

3:20 **Dan to Beersheba** Dan was the city farthest north in Israel. Beersheba was the city farthest south. So this means all the people of Israel.

[4]So the people sent men to Shiloh. They brought back the Box of the Agreement with the Lord of heaven's armies. Eli's two sons, Hophni and Phinehas, were there with the Holy Box. [5]The Box of the Agreement with the Lord came into the camp. And all the Israelites gave a great shout of joy. It made the ground shake. [6]The Philistines heard Israel's shout. They asked, "What's all this shouting in the Hebrew camp?"

Then the Philistines found out that the Holy Box of the Lord had come into the Hebrew camp. [7]They were afraid and said, "A god has come into the Hebrew camp! We're in trouble! This has never happened before! [8]How terrible it will be for us! Who can save us from these powerful gods? They are the ones who struck the Egyptians with all kinds of disasters in the desert. [9]Be brave, Philistines! Fight like men! In the past they were our slaves. So fight like men, or you will become their slaves."

[10]So the Philistines fought hard and defeated the Israelites. Every Israelite soldier ran away to his own home. It was a great defeat for Israel, because 30,000 Israelite soldiers were killed. [11]The Holy Box of God was taken by the Philistines. And Eli's two sons, Hophni and Phinehas, were killed.

[12]That same day a man from the tribe[d] of Benjamin ran from the battle. He tore his clothes and put dust on his head to show his great sadness. [13]When he arrived in Shiloh, Eli was by the side of the road. Eli was sitting there in a chair, watching. He was worried about the Holy Box of God. When the Benjaminite entered Shiloh, he told the bad news. Then all the people in town cried loudly. [14]Eli heard the crying and asked, "What's all this noise?"

The Benjaminite ran to Eli and told him what had happened. [15]Eli was now 98 years old, and he was blind. [16]The Benjaminite told Eli, "I have come from the battle. I ran all the way here today."

Eli asked, "What happened, my son?"

[17]The Benjaminite answered, "Israel ran away from the Philistines. The Israelite army has lost many soldiers. Your two sons are both dead. And the Philistines have taken the Holy Box of God."

[18]When he mentioned the Holy Box of God, Eli fell backward off his chair. He fell beside the gate and broke his neck, because he was old and fat. And Eli died. He had led Israel for 40 years.

[19]Eli's daughter-in-law, the wife of Phinehas, was pregnant. It was nearly time for her baby to be born. She heard the news that the Holy Box[d] of God had been taken. She heard also that Eli, her father-in-law, and Phinehas, her husband, were both dead. So she began to give birth to her child. The child was born, but the mother had much trouble in giving birth. [20]As she was dying, the women who helped her give birth said, "Don't worry! You've given birth to a son!" But she did not answer or pay attention. She named the baby Ichabod.[n] [21]She named him Ichabod and said, "Israel's glory is gone." She said this because the Holy Box of God had been taken. It was also because her father-in-law and husband were dead. [22]She said, "Israel's glory is gone, because the Holy Box of God has been taken away."

5 After the Philistines had captured the Holy Box[d] of God, they took it from Ebenezer to Ashdod. [2]They carried it into Dagon's[d] temple and put it next to Dagon. [3]The people of Ashdod rose early the next morning. They found that Dagon had fallen on his face on the ground. He was lying before the Holy Box of the Lord. So the people of Ashdod put Dagon back in his place. [4]The next morning the people of Ashdod rose from sleep. And again they found Dagon on the ground! He had fallen down before the Holy Box of the Lord. His head and hands had broken off and were lying in the doorway. Only his body was still in one piece. [5]So, even today, Dagon's priests and others who enter his temple at Ashdod refuse to step on the doorsill.

[6]The Lord punished the people of Ashdod and their neighbors. He gave them much trouble. He gave them growths on their skin. [7]The people of Ashdod saw what was happening. They said, "The Holy Box of the God of Israel can't stay with us. God is punishing us and Dagon our god." [8]The people of Ashdod called all five Philistine kings together. They asked them, "What should we do with the Holy Box of the God of Israel?"

The rulers answered, "Move the Holy Box of the God of Israel to Gath." So the Philistines moved it to Gath.

4:20 Ichabod This name means "Where is the glory?"

⁹But after they had moved it to Gath, the Lord punished that city also. He made the people very afraid. God troubled both old and young people in Gath. He caused them to have growths on their skin. ¹⁰Then the Philistines sent the Holy Box of God to Ekron.

But when it came into Ekron, the people of Ekron yelled. They said, "Why are you bringing the Holy Box of the God of Israel to our city? Do you want to kill us and our people?" ¹¹The people of Ekron called all the kings of the Philistines together. They said to the kings, "Send the Holy Box of the God of Israel back to its place. Do it before it kills us and our people!" They were very afraid. God's punishment was very terrible there. ¹²The people who did not die were troubled with growths on their skin. So the people of Ekron cried loudly to heaven.

6 The Philistines kept the Holy Box[d] of God in their land seven months. ²Then they called for their priests and magicians. They said, "What should we do with the Holy Box of the Lord? Tell us how to send it back home!"

³The priests and magicians answered them. They said, "If you send back the Holy Box of the God of Israel, don't send it away empty. You must offer a penalty offering so the God of Israel will forgive your sins. Then you will be healed. When God has forgiven you, he will stop punishing you."

⁴The Philistines asked, "What kind of penalty offering should we send to Israel's God?"

The priests and magicians answered, "Make five gold models of the growths on your skin. Also make five gold models of rats. The number of models must be the same as the number of Philistine kings. This is because the same sickness has come on you and your kings. ⁵Make models of the growths and the rats that are ruining the country. Give them to Israel's God and honor him. Then maybe Israel's God will stop punishing you, your gods and your land. ⁶Don't be stubborn like the king of Egypt and the Egyptians. God punished them terribly. That is why the Egyptians let the Israelites leave Egypt.

⁷"You must build a new cart. And get two cows that have just had calves. These must be cows that have never had yokes[d] on their necks. Then hitch the cows to the cart. Take the calves home. Don't let them follow their mothers. ⁸Put the Holy Box of the Lord on the cart.

And put the gold models in a box beside the Holy Box. They are your penalty offerings for God to forgive your sins. Send the cart straight on its way. ⁹Watch the cart. It may go toward Beth Shemesh in Israel's own land. If so, the Lord has given us this great sickness. But it may not go toward Beth Shemesh. Then we will know that Israel's God has not punished us. We will know that our sickness just happened by chance."

¹⁰The Philistines did what the priests and magicians said. They took two cows that had just had calves. They hitched them to the cart. But they kept their calves at home. ¹¹They put the Holy Box of the Lord on the cart. And they put the box with the gold rats and models of growths on the cart. ¹²Then the cows went straight toward Beth Shemesh. They stayed on the road, mooing all the way. They did not turn right or left. The Philistine kings followed the cows as far as the border of Beth Shemesh.

¹³Now the people of Beth Shemesh were harvesting their wheat in the valley. They looked up and saw the Holy Box of the Lord. They were very happy to see it again. ¹⁴The cart came to the field belonging to Joshua of Beth Shemesh. The cart stopped in this field near a large rock. The people of Beth Shemesh chopped up the wood of the cart. Then they killed the cows and sacrificed them to the Lord. ¹⁵The Levites took down the Holy Box of the Lord. They also took down the box that had the gold models. They put both on the large rock. That day the people of Beth Shemesh offered whole burnt offerings and made sacrifices to the Lord. ¹⁶The five Philistine kings watched them do all these things. Then they went back to Ekron the same day.

¹⁷The Philistines sent these gold models of the growths. They were penalty offerings to the Lord for their sins. They sent one model for each Philistine town. These towns were Ashdod, Gaza, Ashkelon, Gath and Ekron. ¹⁸And the Philistines also sent gold models of rats. The number of rats was the same as the number of towns belonging to the Philistine kings. These towns included strong, walled cities and country villages. The large rock on which they put the Holy Box of the Lord is still there. It is in the field of Joshua of Beth Shemesh.

¹⁹But some of the men of Beth Shemesh looked into the Holy Box of the

Lord. So God killed 70 of them. The people of Beth Shemesh cried because the Lord had punished them so terribly. [20]They said, "Who can stand before the Lord, this holy God? Where can the Holy Box go from here?"

[21]Then they sent messengers to the people of Kiriath Jearim. The messengers said, "The Philistines have brought back the Holy Box of the Lord. Come down and take it to your city."

7 The men of Kiriath Jearim came and took the Holy Box of the Lord. They took it to Abinadab's house on a hill. There they made Abinadab's son Eleazar holy for the Lord so he could guard the Holy Box.

[2]The Holy Box[d] stayed at Kiriath Jearim a long time—20 years in all. And the people of Israel began to follow the Lord again. [3]Samuel spoke to the whole group of Israel. He said, "If you're turning back to the Lord with all your hearts, you must remove your foreign gods. You must remove your idols of Ashtoreth.[d] You must give yourselves fully to the Lord and serve only him. Then he will save you from the Philistines."

[4]So the Israelites put away their idols of Baal[d] and Ashtoreth. And they served only the Lord.

[5]Samuel said, "All Israel must meet at Mizpah. I will pray to the Lord for you." [6]So the Israelites met together at Mizpah. They drew water from the ground and poured it out before the Lord. They did not eat that day. They confessed, "We have sinned against the Lord." And Samuel served as judge of Israel at Mizpah.

[7]The Philistines heard the Israelites were meeting at Mizpah. So the Philistine kings came up to attack them. When the Israelites heard they were coming, they were afraid. [8]They said to Samuel, "Don't stop praying to the Lord our God for us! Ask the Lord to save us from the Philistines!" [9]Then Samuel took a baby lamb. He offered the lamb to the Lord as a whole burnt offering. He called to the Lord for Israel's sake. And the Lord answered him.

[10]While Samuel was burning the offering, the Philistines came near. They were going to attack Israel. But the Lord thundered against the Philistines with loud thunder. They were so frightened they became confused. So the Israelites defeated the Philistines in battle. [11]The men of Israel ran out of Mizpah and chased the Philistines. They went almost to Beth Car, killing the Philistines along the way.

[12]After this happened Samuel took a stone. He set it up between Mizpah and Shen. He named the stone Ebenezer.[n] Samuel said, "The Lord has helped us to this point." [13]So the Philistines were defeated. They did not enter the Israelites' land again.

The Lord was against the Philistines all Samuel's life. [14]Earlier the Philistines had taken towns from the Israelites. But the Israelites won them back, from Ekron to Gath. They also took back from the Philistines the neighboring lands of these towns. There was peace also between Israel and the Amorites.

[15]Samuel continued as judge of Israel all his life. [16]Every year he went from Bethel to Gilgal to Mizpah. He judged the Israelites in all these towns. [17]But Samuel always went back to Ramah, where his home was. He also judged Israel there. And there he built an altar to the Lord.

8 When Samuel became old, he made his sons judges for Israel. [2]His first son was named Joel, and his second son was named Abijah. Joel and Abijah were judges in Beersheba. [3]But Samuel's sons did not live as he did. They tried to get money dishonestly. They took money secretly to be dishonest in their judging.

[4]So all the older leaders came together and met Samuel at Ramah. [5]They said to him, "You're old, and your sons don't live as you do. Give us a king to rule over us like all the other nations."

[6]When the older leaders said that, Samuel was not pleased. He prayed to the Lord. [7]The Lord told Samuel, "Listen to whatever the people say to you. They have not rejected you. They have rejected me from being their king. [8]They are doing as they have always done. When I took them out of Egypt, they left me. They served other gods. They are doing the same to you. [9]Now listen to the people. But give them a warning. Tell them what the king who rules over them will do."

[10]Samuel answered those who had asked him for a king. He told them all the words of the Lord. [11]Samuel said, "If you have a king ruling over you, this is what he will do: He will take your sons.

7:12 **Ebenezer** This name means "stone of help."

He will make them serve with his chariots and his horses. They will run in front of the king's chariot. [12]The king will make some of your sons commanders over 1,000 men or over 50 men. He will make some of your other sons plow his ground and reap his harvest. He will take others to make weapons of war and equipment for his chariots. [13]This king will take your daughters. Some of your daughters will make perfume. Others will cook and bake for him. [14]He will take your best fields, vineyards and olive groves. He will give them to his servants. [15]He will take one-tenth of your grain and grapes and give it to his officers and servants. [16]He will take your men servants and girl servants. He will take your best cattle and your donkeys. He will use them all for his own work. [17]He will take one-tenth of your flocks. And you yourselves will become his slaves. [18]When that time comes, you will cry out because of the king you chose. The Lord will not answer you then."

[19]But the people would not listen to Samuel. They said, "No! We want a king to rule over us. [20]Then we will be the same as all the other nations. Our king will judge us. He will go with us and fight our battles."

[21]Samuel heard all that the people said. Then he repeated all their words to the Lord. [22]The Lord answered, "You must listen to them. Give them a king."

Then Samuel told the people of Israel, "Everyone go back to his town."

9 Kish son of Abiel was from the tribe[d] of Benjamin. He was an important man. (Abiel was the son of Zeror. And Zeror was the son of Becorath. He was the son of Aphiah of Benjamin.) [2]Kish had a son named Saul. Saul was a fine young man. There was no Israelite better than he. Saul stood a head taller than any other man in Israel.

[3]Now the donkeys of Saul's father, Kish, were lost. So Kish said to Saul, his son, "Take one of the servants. Go and look for the donkeys." [4]Saul went through the mountains of Ephraim. And he went through the land of Shalisha. But he and the servant could not find the donkeys. They went into the land of Shaalim, but the donkeys were not there. They went through the land of Benjamin. But they still did not find the donkeys. [5]They arrived in the area of Zuph. Saul said to his servant, "Let's go back. My father will stop thinking about the donkeys. He will start worrying about us."

[6]But the servant answered, "A man of God is in this town. People respect him because everything he says comes true. Let's go into the town now. Maybe he can tell us something about the journey we have taken."

[7]Saul said to his servant, "If we go into the town, what can we give him? The food in our bags is gone. We have no gift to give him. Do we have anything at all to give him?"

[8]Again the servant answered Saul. "Look, I have one-tenth of an ounce of silver. Give it to the man of God. Then he will tell us about our journey." [9](In the past, someone in Israel might want to ask something from God. If so, he would say, "Let's go to the seer."[e] We call the person a man of God today. But in the past he was called a "seer.")

[10]Saul said to his servant, "That is a good idea. Come, let's go." So they went toward the town where the man of God was.

[11]Saul and the servant were going up the hill to the town. On the way they met some young women coming out to get water. Saul and the servant asked them, "Is the seer here?"

[12]The young women answered, "Yes, he's here. He's ahead of you. Hurry now. He has just come to our town today. This is because the people will offer a sacrifice at the place of worship. [13]When you enter the town, you will find him. He will be there before he goes up to the place of worship to eat. The people will not begin eating until the seer comes. He must bless the sacrifice. After that, the guests will eat. Go now, and you should find him."

[14]Saul and the servant went up to the town. Just as they entered the town, they saw Samuel. He was on his way up to the place of worship. So he was coming out of the city toward them.

[15]The day before Saul came, the Lord had told Samuel: [16]"About this time tomorrow I will send you a man. He will be from Benjamin. You must appoint him as leader over my people Israel. He will save my people from the Philistines. I have seen the suffering of my people. I have listened to their cry."

[17]When Samuel first saw Saul, the Lord spoke to Samuel. He said, "This is the man I told you about. He will rule my people."

[18]Saul came near Samuel at the gate. Saul said, "Please tell me where the seer's[d] house is."

[19] Samuel answered, "I am the seer. Go ahead of me to the place of worship. Today you and your servant are to eat with me. Tomorrow morning I will send you home. And I will answer all your questions. [20] Don't worry about the donkeys you lost three days ago. They have been found. Israel now wants you and all your father's family."

[21] Saul answered, "But I am from the tribe[d] of Benjamin. It's the smallest tribe in Israel. And my family group is the smallest in the tribe of Benjamin. Why do you say Israel wants me?"

[22] Then Samuel took Saul and his servant into a large room. He gave them a chief place at the table. About 30 guests were there. [23] Samuel said to the cook, "Bring the meat I gave you. It's the portion I told you to set aside."

[24] So the cook took the thigh and put it on the table in front of Saul. Samuel said, "This is the meat saved for you. Eat it because it was set aside for you for this special time. As I said, 'I have invited the people.'" So Saul ate with Samuel that day.

[25] After they finished eating, they came down from the place of worship. They went to the town. Then Samuel talked with Saul on the roof[n] of his house. [26] At dawn they got up, and Samuel called to Saul on the roof. He said, "Get up, and I will send you on your way." So Saul got up. He went out of the house with Samuel. [27] Saul, his servant and Samuel were getting near the edge of the city. Samuel said to Saul, "Tell the servant to go on ahead of us. I have a message from God for you."

10 Samuel took a jar of olive oil. He poured the oil on Saul's head. He kissed Saul and said, "The Lord has appointed you to be leader of his people Israel. You will rule over the people of the Lord. You will save them from their enemies all around. This will be the sign that the Lord has appointed you as leader of his people. [2] After you leave me today, you will meet two men. They will be near Rachel's tomb on the border of Benjamin at Zelzah. They will say to you, 'The donkeys you were looking for have been found. But now your father has stopped thinking about his donkeys. He is worrying about you. He is asking, "What will I do about my son?"'

[3] "Then you will go on until you reach the great tree at Tabor. There three men will meet you. They will be on their way to worship God at Bethel. One man will be carrying three young goats. The second man will be carrying three loaves of bread. And the third one will have a leather bag full of wine. [4] They will greet you and offer you two loaves of bread. You will accept the bread from them. [5] Then you will go to Gibeah of God. There is a Philistine camp there. When you come near this town, a group of prophets[d] will come out. They will be coming from the place of worship. And they will be playing harps, tambourines,[d] flutes and lyres.[d] And they will be prophesying. [6] The Spirit[d] of the Lord will enter you with power. You will prophesy with these prophets. You will be changed into a different man. [7] After these signs happen, do whatever you find to do. God will help you.

[8] "Go ahead of me to Gilgal. I will come down to you. Then I will offer whole burnt offerings and fellowship offerings. But you must wait seven days. Then I will come and tell you what to do."

[9] When Saul turned to leave Samuel, God changed Saul's heart. All these signs came true that day. [10] When Saul and his servant arrived at Gibeah, Saul met a group of prophets.[d] The Spirit[d] of God entered him. And he prophesied with the prophets. [11] People who had known Saul before saw him prophesying with the prophets. They asked each other, "What has happened to Kish's son? Is even Saul one of the prophets?"

[12] A man who lived there said, "Who is the father of these prophets?" This became a famous saying: "Is even Saul one of the prophets?" [13] When Saul finished prophesying, he went to the place of worship.

[14] Saul's uncle asked him and his servant, "Where have you been?"

Saul said, "We were looking for the donkeys. When we couldn't find them, we went to talk to Samuel."

[15] Saul's uncle asked, "Please tell me. What did Samuel say to you?"

[16] Saul answered, "He told us the donkeys had already been found." But Saul did not tell his uncle what Samuel had said about his becoming king.

[17] Samuel called all the people of Israel

9:25 **roof** In Bible times houses were built with flat roofs. The roof was used for drying things such as flax and fruit. And it was used as an extra room, as a place for worship and as a place to sleep in the summer.

to meet with the Lord at Mizpah. [18]He said, "This is what the Lord, the God of Israel, says: 'I led Israel out of Egypt. I saved you from Egypt's control. And I saved you from other kingdoms that were troubling you.' [19]But now you have rejected your God. He saves you from all your troubles and problems. But you said, 'No! We want a king to rule over us.' Now come, stand before the Lord in your tribes[d] and family groups."

[20]Samuel brought all the tribes of Israel near. And the tribe of Benjamin was chosen. [21]Samuel had them pass by in family groups, and Matri's family was chosen. Then he had each man of Matri's family pass by. And Saul son of Kish was chosen. But when they looked for Saul, they could not find him. [22]Then they asked the Lord, "Has Saul come here yet?"

The Lord said, "Yes. He's hiding behind the baggage."

[23]So they ran and brought him out. When Saul stood among the people, he was a head taller than anyone else. [24]Then Samuel said to the people, "See the man the Lord has chosen. There is no one like him among all the people."

Then the people shouted, "Long live the king!"

[25]Samuel explained the rights and duties of the king. He wrote the rules in a book and put the book before the Lord. Then he told the people to go to their homes.

[26]Saul also went to his home in Gibeah. God touched the hearts of certain brave men who went along with him. [27]But some troublemakers said, "How can this man save us?" They hated Saul and refused to bring gifts to him. But Saul kept quiet.

11 About a month later Nahash the Ammonite and his army surrounded the city of Jabesh in Gilead. All the people of Jabesh said to Nahash, "Make a treaty with us. And we will serve you."

[2]But he answered, "I will make a treaty with you. But I will only do it if I'm allowed to tear out the right eye of each of you. Then all Israel will be ashamed!"

[3]The older leaders of Jabesh said to Nahash, "Let us have seven days. We will send messengers through all Israel. If no one comes to help us, we will give ourselves up to you."

[4]The messengers came to Gibeah where Saul lived. When they told the people the news, the people cried loudly.

[5]Saul had finished plowing in the fields with his oxen. He was coming home when he heard the people crying. He asked, "What's wrong with the people? Why are they crying?" Then they told Saul what the messengers from Jabesh had said. [6]When Saul heard their words, God's Spirit[d] entered him with power. Saul became very angry. [7]So he took a pair of oxen and cut them into pieces. Then he gave the pieces of the oxen to messengers. He ordered them to carry the pieces through all the land of Israel.

The messengers made an announcement to the people. They said, "This is what will happen to the oxen of anyone who does not follow Saul and Samuel." So the people became very afraid of the Lord. They all came together as if they were one person. [8]Saul gathered the people together at Bezek. There were 300,000 men from Israel and 30,000 men from Judah.

[9]They spoke to the messengers who had come. They said, "Tell the people at Jabesh Gilead this: 'Before the day becomes hot tomorrow, you will be saved.'" So the messengers went and reported this to the people at Jabesh. They were very happy. [10]The people said to Nahash the Ammonite, "Tomorrow we will give ourselves up to you. Then you can do anything you want to us."

[11]The next morning Saul divided his soldiers into three groups. At dawn they entered the Ammonite camp. And they defeated the Ammonites before the heat of the day. The Ammonites who were left alive were scattered. Not even two of them were still together.

[12]Then the people said to Samuel, "Who was it that didn't want Saul as king? Bring them here, and we will kill them!"

[13]But Saul said, "No! No one will be put to death today. The Lord has saved Israel today!"

[14]Then Samuel said to the people, "Come, let's go to Gilgal. At Gilgal we will again promise to obey the king." [15]All the people went to Gilgal. And there, before the Lord, the people made Saul king. They offered fellowship offerings to the Lord. Saul and all the Israelites had a great celebration.

12 Samuel said to all Israel, "I have done everything you wanted me to do. I have put a king over you. [2]Now you have a king to lead you. I am old and gray, and my sons are here with you. I have been your leader since I was young. [3]Here I am. If I have done anything wrong, you must testify against me. Do this before the Lord and his appointed king. Did I steal anyone's ox or donkey? Did I hurt or cheat anyone? Did I ever secretly take money to pretend not to see something wrong? If I did any of these things, I will make it right."

[4]The Israelites answered, "You have not cheated us. You have not hurt us. You have not taken anything unfairly from anyone."

[5]Samuel said to them, "The Lord is a witness to what you have said. His appointed king is also a witness today. They are both witnesses that you did not find anything wrong in me."

"He is our witness," they said.

[6]Then Samuel said to the people, "The Lord is our witness. He chose Moses and Aaron. He brought your ancestors out of Egypt. [7]Now, stand there. And I will talk with you about all the good things the Lord did for you and your ancestors.

[8]"After Jacob entered Egypt, his descendants[d] cried to the Lord for help. So the Lord sent Moses and Aaron. They took your ancestors out of Egypt and brought them to live in this place.

[9]"But they forgot the Lord their God. So he let them become the slaves of Sisera. He was the commander of the army of Hazor. The Lord let them become the slaves of the Philistines and the king of Moab. They all fought against your ancestors. [10]Then your ancestors cried to the Lord. They said, 'We have sinned. We have left the Lord. We served the Baals[d] and the Ashtoreths.[d] But now save us from our enemies, and we will serve you.' [11]The Lord sent Gideon, who is also called Jerub-Baal. And he sent Barak, Jephthah and Samuel. Then he saved you from your enemies around you. And you lived in safety. [12]But then you saw Nahash king of the Ammonites coming against you. You said, 'No! We want a king to rule over us!' [13]Now here is the king you chose. The Lord has put him over you. [14]You must honor the Lord and serve him. You must obey his commands. Both you and the king ruling over you must follow the Lord your God. If you do, it will be well with you. [15]But if you don't obey the Lord, and if you fight against his commands, he will be

against you. He will do to you what he did to your ancestors.

[16]"Now stand still and see the great thing the Lord will do before your eyes. [17]It is now the time of the wheat harvest.[n] I will pray for the Lord to send thunder and rain. Then you will know what an evil thing you did against the Lord when you asked for a king."

[18]Then Samuel prayed to the Lord. That same day the Lord sent thunder and rain. And the people became very afraid of the Lord and Samuel. [19]They said to Samuel, "Pray to the Lord your God for us, your servants! Don't let us die! We've added to all our sins the evil of asking for a king."

[20]Samuel answered, "Don't be afraid. It's true that you did wrong. But don't turn away from the Lord. Serve the Lord with all your heart. [21]Idols are of no use. So don't worship them. They can't help you or save you. They are useless! [22]For his own sake, the Lord won't leave his people. Instead, he was pleased to make you his own people. [23]I will surely not stop praying for you. If I did, I would be sinning against the Lord. I will teach you what is good and right. [24]But you must honor the Lord. You must always serve him with all your heart. Remember the wonderful things he did for you! [25]But if you are stubborn and do evil, God will sweep you and your king away."

13 Saul was 30 years old when he became king. He was king over Israel 42 years.[n] [2]Saul chose 3,000 men from Israel. There were 2,000 men who stayed with him at Micmash in the mountains of Bethel. And 1,000 men stayed with Jonathan at Gibeah in Benjamin. Saul sent the other men in the army back home.

[3]Jonathan attacked the Philistine camp in Geba. And the other Philistines heard about it. Saul said, "Let the Hebrew people hear what happened." So he told the men to blow trumpets through all the land of Israel. [4]All the Israelites heard the news. The men said, "Saul has defeated the Philistine camp. Now the Philistines really hate us!" Then the Israelites were called to join Saul at Gilgal.

[5]The Philistines gathered to fight Israel. They had 3,000[n] chariots and 6,000

12:17 time . . . harvest This was a dry time in the summer when no rains fell. 13:1 Saul . . . years This is how the verse is worded in some early Greek copies. The Hebrew is not clear here. 13:5 3,000 Some Greek copies say 3,000. The Hebrew copies say 30,000.

men to ride in the chariots. Their soldiers were many in number, like the grains of sand on the seashore. The Philistines went and camped at Micmash which is east of Beth Aven. ⁶The Israelites saw that they were in trouble. So they went to hide in caves and bushes. They also hid among the rocks and in pits and wells. ⁷Some Hebrews even went across the Jordan River to the land of Gad and Gilead.

But Saul stayed at Gilgal. All the men in his army were shaking with fear. ⁸Saul waited seven days, because Samuel had said he would meet him then. But Samuel did not come to Gilgal. And the soldiers began to leave.

⁹So Saul said, "Bring me the whole burnt offering and the fellowship offerings." Then Saul offered the whole burnt offering. ¹⁰Just as he finished, Samuel arrived. Saul went to meet him. ¹¹Samuel asked, "What have you done?"

Saul answered, "I saw the soldiers leaving me, and you were not here. The Philistines were gathering at Micmash. ¹²Then I thought, 'The Philistines will come against me at Gilgal. And I haven't asked for the Lord's approval.' So I forced myself to offer the whole burnt offering."

¹³Samuel said, "You acted foolishly! You haven't obeyed God's command. If you had obeyed him, God would make your kingdom continue in Israel forever. ¹⁴But now your kingdom will not continue. The Lord has looked for the kind of man he wants. The Lord has appointed him to become ruler of his people. He is doing this because you haven't obeyed his command."

¹⁵Then Samuel left Gilgal and went to Gibeah in Benjamin. The rest of the army followed Saul into battle. Saul counted the men still with him, and there were about 600.

¹⁶Saul and his son Jonathan stayed in Geba in the land of Benjamin. The soldiers with them also stayed there. The Philistines made their camp at Micmash. ¹⁷Three groups went out from their camp to attack. One group went on the Ophrah road in the land of Shual. ¹⁸The second group went on the Beth Horon road. And the third group went on the border road. It overlooked the Valley of Zeboim toward the desert.

¹⁹The whole land of Israel had no blacksmith. This is because the Philistines had said, "The Hebrews might make swords and spears." ²⁰So all the Israelites went down to the Philistines. They went to have their plows, hoes, axes and sickles sharpened. ²¹The Philistine blacksmiths charged about one-fourth of an ounce of silver for sharpening plows and hoes. And they charged one-eighth of an ounce of silver for sharpening picks, axes and the sticks used to guide oxen.

²²So when the battle came, the soldiers with Saul and Jonathan had no swords or spears. Only Saul and his son Jonathan had them.

²³A group from the Philistine army had gone out to the mountain pass at Micmash.

14

One day Jonathan, Saul's son, spoke to the officer who carried his armor. Jonathan said, "Come, let's go over to the Philistine camp on the other side." But Jonathan did not tell his father.

²Saul was sitting under a pomegranateᵈ tree at the threshingᵈ floor near Gibeah. He had about 600 men with him. ³One man was Ahijah, who was a son of Ichabod's brother Ahitub. Ichabod was the son of Phinehas, Eli's son. Eli was the Lord's priest in Shiloh. He wore the holy vest.ᵈ No one knew Jonathan had left.

⁴There was a steep slope on each side of the pass. Jonathan planned to go through the pass to the Philistine camp. The cliff on one side was named Bozez. The other cliff was named Seneh. ⁵One cliff faced north toward Micmash. The other faced south toward Geba.

⁶Jonathan said to his officer who carried his armor, "Come. Let's go to the camp of those men who are not circumcised.ᵈ Maybe the Lord will help us. It doesn't matter if we have many people, or just a few. Nothing can keep the Lord from giving us victory."

⁷The officer who carried Jonathan's armor said to him, "Do whatever you think is best. Go ahead. I'm with you."

⁸Jonathan said, "Then come. We will cross over to the Philistines. We will let them see us. ⁹They may say to us, 'Stay there until we come to you.' If they do, we will stay where we are. We won't go up to them. ¹⁰But they may say, 'Come up to us.' If so, we will climb up. And the Lord will allow us to defeat them. This will be the sign for us."

¹¹Both Jonathan and his officer let the Philistines see them. The Philistines said, "Look! The Hebrews are crawling

out of the holes they were hiding in!"
[12]The Philistines in the camp shouted to Jonathan and his officer, "Come up to us. We'll teach you a lesson!"

Jonathan said to his officer, "Climb up behind me. The Lord has given the Philistines to Israel!" [13]So Jonathan climbed up, using his hands and feet. His officer climbed just behind him. Jonathan cut down the Philistines as he went. And his officer killed them as he followed behind Jonathan. [14]In that first fight Jonathan and his officer killed about 20 Philistines.

[15]All the Philistine soldiers panicked. Those in the camp and those in the raiding party were frightened. The ground itself shook! God caused the panic.

[16]Saul's guards were at Gibeah in the land of Benjamin. They saw the Philistine soldiers running in every direction. [17]Saul said to his army, "Check and find who has left our camp." When they checked, they learned that Jonathan and his officer were gone.

[18]So Saul said to Ahijah the priest, "Bring the Holy Box[d] of God." (At that time it was with the Israelites.) [19]While Saul was talking to the priest, the confusion in the Philistine camp was growing. Then Saul said to Ahijah, "Stop. There's not time to pray now!"

[20]Then Saul and the army with him gathered and entered the battle. They found the Philistines confused, even striking each other with their swords! [21]Earlier, there were Hebrews who had served the Philistines and had stayed in their camp. They now joined the Israelites with Saul and Jonathan. [22]All the Israelites hidden in the mountains of Ephraim heard that the Philistine soldiers were running away. They too joined the battle and chased the Philistines. [23]So the Lord saved the Israelites that day. And the battle moved on past Beth Aven.

[24]The men of Israel were miserable that day. This was because Saul had made an oath for all of them. He had said, "No one should eat food before evening and before I finish defeating my enemies. If he does, he will be cursed!" So no Israelite soldier ate food.

[25]Now the army went into the woods. There was some honey on the ground. [26]They came to where the honey was. But no one took any because they were afraid of the oath. [27]But Jonathan had not heard the oath Saul had put on the people. So Jonathan dipped the end of his stick into the honey. He pulled out the honey and ate it. Then he felt better. [28]So one of the soldiers told Jonathan, "Your father made an oath for all the soldiers. He said any man who eats today will be cursed! That's why they are weak."

[29]Jonathan said, "My father has made trouble for the land! See how much better I feel after just tasting a little of this honey! [30]It would have been much better for the men to eat the food they took from their enemies today. We could have killed many more Philistines!"

[31]That day the Israelites defeated the Philistines from Micmash to Aijalon. After they did this, they were very tired. [32]They had taken sheep, cattle and calves from the Philistines. Now they were so hungry they killed the animals on the ground and ate them. But the blood was still in the animals! [33]Someone said to Saul, "Look! The men are sinning against the Lord. They're eating meat that still has blood in it!"

Saul said, "You have sinned! Roll a large stone over here now!" [34]Then he said, "Go to the men. Tell them that each person must bring his ox and sheep to me. They must kill and eat their ox and sheep here. Don't sin against the Lord. Don't eat meat with the blood still in it."

That night everyone brought his animals and killed them there. [35]Then Saul built an altar to the Lord. It was the first altar Saul had built to the Lord.

[36]Saul said, "Let's go after the Philistines tonight. Let's take what they own. We won't let any of them live!"

The men answered, "Do whatever you think is best."

But the priest said, "Let's ask God." [37]So Saul asked God, "Should I chase the Philistines? Will you let us defeat them?" But that day God did not answer Saul. [38]That is why Saul said to all the leaders of his army, "Come here. Let's find what sin has been done today. [39]As surely as the Lord lives, even if my son Jonathan did the sin, he must die." But no one in the army answered.

[40]Then Saul said to all the Israelites, "You stand on this side. I and my son Jonathan will stand on the other side."

The men answered, "Do whatever you think is best."

[41]Then Saul prayed to the Lord, the God of Israel, "Give me the right answer."

And Saul and Jonathan were chosen by throwing lots.[d] The other men went free. [42]Saul said, "Throw the lot. It will show if it is I or Jonathan my son who is guilty." And Jonathan was chosen.

[43]Saul said to Jonathan, "Tell me what you have done."

So Jonathan told Saul, "I only tasted a little honey from the end of my stick. And must I die now?"

[44]Saul said, "Jonathan, if you don't die, may God punish me terribly!"

[45]But the soldiers said to Saul, "Must Jonathan die? Never! He is responsible for saving Israel today! As surely as the Lord lives, not even a hair of his head will fall to the ground! Today Jonathan fought against the Philistines with God's help!" So the army saved Jonathan, and he did not die.

[46]Then Saul stopped chasing the Philistines. And they went back to their own land.

[47]When Saul became king over Israel, he fought against Israel's enemies all around. He fought Moab, the Ammonites, Edom, the king of Zobah and the Philistines. Everywhere Saul went he defeated Israel's enemies. [48]He became strong. He fought bravely and defeated the Amalekites. He saved Israel from the enemies who had taken what the Israelites owned.

[49]Saul's sons were Jonathan, Ishvi and Malki-Shua. His older daughter was named Merab. His younger daughter was named Michal. [50]Saul's wife was Ahinoam daughter of Ahimaaz. The commander of his army was Abner son of Ner. Ner was Saul's uncle. [51]Saul's father Kish and Abner's father Ner were sons of Abiel.

[52]All Saul's life he fought hard against the Philistines. When he saw strong or brave men, he took them into his army.

15 Samuel said to Saul, "The Lord sent me to appoint you king over Israel. Now listen to his message. [2]This is what the Lord of heaven's armies says: 'The Israelites came out of Egypt. But the Amalekites tried to stop them from going to Canaan. I saw what they did. [3]Now go, attack the Amalekites. Destroy everything that belongs to them as an offering to the Lord. Don't let anything live. Put to death men and women, children and small babies. Kill the cattle and sheep, camels and donkeys.'"

[4]So Saul called the army together at Telaim. There were 200,000 soldiers and 10,000 men from Judah. [5]Then Saul went to the city of Amalek and set up an ambush in the ravine. [6]He said to the Kenites, "Go away. Leave the Amalekites so that I won't destroy you with them. You showed kindness to the Israelites when they came out of Egypt." So the Kenites moved away from the Amalekites.

[7]Then Saul defeated the Amalekites. He fought them all the way from Havilah to Shur, at the border of Egypt. [8]He took Agag king of the Amalekites alive. But he killed all of Agag's army with the sword. [9]But Saul and the army let Agag live. They also let the best sheep, fat cattle and lambs live. They let every good animal live. They did not want to destroy them. But when they found an animal that was weak or useless, they killed it.

[10]Then the Lord spoke his word to Samuel. [11]"Saul has stopped following me. And I am sorry I made him king. He has not obeyed my commands." Samuel was upset, and he cried out to the Lord all night long.

[12]Early the next morning Samuel got up and went to meet Saul. But the people told Samuel, "Saul has gone to Carmel. He has put up a monument in his own honor. Now he has gone down to Gilgal."

[13]Then Samuel came to Saul. And Saul said, "May the Lord bless you! I have obeyed the Lord's commands."

[14]But Samuel said, "Then why do I hear cattle mooing and sheep bleating?"

[15]Saul answered, "The soldiers took them from the Amalekites. They saved the best sheep and cattle to offer as sacrifices to the Lord your God. But we destroyed all the other animals."

[16]Samuel said to Saul, "Stop! Let me tell you what the Lord said to me last night."

Saul answered, "Tell me."

[17]Samuel said, "Once you didn't think much of yourself. But now you have become the leader of the tribes[d] of Israel. The Lord appointed you to be king over Israel. [18]And he told you to do something. He said, 'Go and destroy those evil people, the Amalekites. Make war on them until all of them are dead.' [19]Why didn't you obey the Lord? Why did you take the best things? Why did you do what the Lord said was wrong?"

[20]Saul said, "But I did obey the Lord. I did what the Lord told me to do. I destroyed all the Amalekites. And I brought back Agag their king. [21]The soldiers took the best sheep and cattle to sacrifice to the Lord your God at Gilgal."

²²But Samuel answered,
"What pleases the Lord more:
burnt offerings and sacrifices or
obedience?

It is better to obey God than to
offer a sacrifice.

It is better to listen to God than
to offer the fat of male sheep.

²³Refusing to obey is as bad as the
sin of sorcery.[d]

Being stubborn is as bad as the
sin of worshiping idols.

You have rejected the Lord's
command.

For this reason, he now rejects
you as king."

²⁴Then Saul said to Samuel, "I have
sinned. I didn't obey the Lord's commands. I didn't do what you told me. I
was afraid of the people, and I did what
they said. ²⁵Now I beg you, forgive my
sin. Come back with me so I may worship the Lord."

²⁶But Samuel said to Saul, "I won't go
back with you. You refused the Lord's
command. And now he rejects you as
king of Israel."

²⁷As Samuel turned to leave, Saul
caught his robe, and it tore. ²⁸Samuel
said to him, "The Lord has torn the kingdom of Israel from you today. He has
given it to one of your neighbors. He has
given it to one better than you. ²⁹The
Lord is the Eternal One of Israel. He
does not lie or change his mind. He is
not a man. So he does not change his
mind as men do."

³⁰Saul answered, "I have sinned. But
please honor me in front of my people's
older leaders. Please honor me in front
of the Israelites. Come back with me so
that I may worship the Lord your God."
³¹So Samuel went back with Saul, and
Saul worshiped the Lord.

³²Then Samuel said, "Bring me Agag
king of the Amalekites."

Agag came to Samuel in chains. Yet
Agag thought, "Surely the threat of
death has passed."

³³Samuel said to him, "Your sword
caused mothers to be without their children. Now your mother will have no
children." And Samuel cut Agag to
pieces before the Lord at Gilgal.

³⁴Then Samuel left and went to Ramah. But Saul went up to his home in
Gibeah. ³⁵And Samuel never saw Saul
again all the rest of his life. But he was
sorry for Saul. And the Lord was very
sorry he had made Saul king of Israel.

16The Lord said to Samuel, "How
long will you continue to feel sorry
for Saul? I have rejected him as king of
Israel. Fill your container with olive oil
and go. I am sending you to Jesse who
lives in Bethlehem. I have chosen one of
his sons to be king."

²But Samuel said, "If I go, Saul will
hear the news. And he will try to kill me."

The Lord said, "Take a young calf
with you. Say, 'I have come to offer a
sacrifice to the Lord.' ³Invite Jesse to the
sacrifice. Then I will show you what to
do. You must appoint the one I show
you."

⁴Samuel did what the Lord told him
to do. When he arrived at Bethlehem,
the older leaders of Bethlehem shook
with fear. They met him and asked, "Are
you coming in peace?"

⁵Samuel answered, "Yes, I come in
peace. I have come to make a sacrifice
to the Lord. Make yourselves holy for
the Lord and come to the sacrifice with
me." Then he made Jesse and his sons
holy for the Lord. And he invited them
to come to the sacrifice.

⁶When they arrived, Samuel saw
Eliab. Samuel thought, "Surely the Lord
has appointed this person standing here
before him."

⁷But the Lord said to Samuel, "Don't
look at how handsome Eliab is. Don't
look at how tall he is. I have not chosen
him. God does not see the same way
people see. People look at the outside
of a person, but the Lord looks at the
heart."

⁸Then Jesse called Abinadab and told
him to pass by Samuel. But Samuel said,
"The Lord has not chosen this man either." ⁹Then Jesse had Shammah pass
by. But Samuel said, "No, the Lord has
not chosen this one." ¹⁰Jesse had seven
of his sons pass by Samuel. But Samuel
said to him, "The Lord has not chosen
any of these."

¹¹Then he asked Jesse, "Are these all
the sons you have?"

Jesse answered, "I still have the youngest son. He is out taking care of the
sheep."

Samuel said, "Send for him. We will
not sit down to eat until he arrives."

¹²So Jesse sent and had his youngest
son brought in. He was a fine boy,
tanned and handsome.

The Lord said to Samuel, "Go! Appoint him. He is the one."

¹³So Samuel took the container of
olive oil. Then he poured oil on Jesse's

youngest son to appoint him in front of his brothers. From that day on, the Lord's Spirit[d] entered David with power. Samuel then went back to Ramah.

[14]But the Lord's Spirit[d] had gone out of Saul. And an evil spirit from the Lord troubled him.

[15]Saul's servants said to him, "See, an evil spirit from God is troubling you. [16]Give us the command. We will look for someone who can play the harp. When the evil spirit from the Lord enters you, he will play. Then the evil spirit will leave you alone. And you will feel better."

[17]So Saul said to his servants, "Find someone. If he plays well, bring him to me."

[18]One of the servants said, "Jesse of Bethlehem has a son who plays the harp. I have seen him play it. He is a brave man and fights well. He is a good speaker and handsome. And the Lord is with him."

[19]Then Saul sent messengers to Jesse. The message said, "Send me your son David, who is with the sheep." [20]So Jesse loaded a donkey with bread and a leather bag full of wine. He also took a young goat. He sent them all with his son David to Saul.

[21]When David came to Saul, he began to serve him. Saul loved David very much. And David became the officer who carried Saul's armor. [22]Saul sent a message to Jesse. He said, "Let David stay and serve me. I like him."

[23]When the evil spirit from God entered Saul, David would take his harp and play. Then the evil spirit would go out of him. And Saul would feel relief. He would feel better again.

17 The Philistines gathered their armies for war. They met at Socoh in Judah. Their camp was at Ephes Dammim between Socoh and Azekah. [2]Saul and the Israelites gathered in the Valley of Elah. And they camped there. They took their positions to fight the Philistines. [3]The Philistines controlled one hill. The Israelites controlled another. The valley was between them.

[4]The Philistines had a champion fighter named Goliath. He was from Gath. He was about nine feet four inches tall. He came out of the Philistine camp. [5]He had a bronze helmet on his head. And he wore a coat of scale armor. It was made of bronze and weighed about 125 pounds. [6]He wore bronze protectors on his legs. And he had a small spear of bronze tied on his back. [7]The wooden part of his larger spear was like a weaver's rod. And its blade weighed about 15 pounds. The officer who carried his shield walked in front of him.

[8]Goliath stood and shouted to the Israelite soldiers, "Why have you taken positions for battle? I am a Philistine, and you are Saul's servants! Choose a man and send him to fight me. [9]If he can fight and kill me, we will become your servants. But if I defeat and kill him, you will become our servants." [10]Then he said, "Today I stand and dare the army of Israel! Send one of your men to fight me!" [11]When Saul and the Israelites heard the Philistine's words, they were very afraid.

[12]Now David was the son of Jesse, an Ephrathite. Jesse was from Bethlehem in Judah. He had eight sons. In Saul's time Jesse was an old man. [13]His three oldest sons followed Saul to the war. The first son was Eliab. The second son was Abinadab. And the third son was Shammah. [14]David was the youngest son. Jesse's three oldest sons followed Saul. [15]But David went back and forth from Saul to Bethlehem. There he took care of his father's sheep.

[16]The Philistine Goliath came out every morning and evening. He stood before the Israelite army. This continued for 40 days.

[17]Now Jesse said to his son David, "Take this half bushel of cooked grain. And take ten loaves of bread. Take them to your brothers in the camp. [18]Also take ten pieces of cheese. Give them to the commander of your brothers' group of 1,000 soldiers. See how your brothers are. Bring back something to show me they are all right. [19]Your brothers are with Saul and the army in the Valley of Elah. They are fighting against the Philistines."

[20]Early in the morning David left the sheep with another shepherd. He took the food and left as Jesse had told him. When David arrived at the camp, the army was leaving. They were going out to their battle positions. The soldiers were shouting their war cry. [21]The Israelites and Philistines were lining up their men to face each other in battle. [22]David left the food with the man who kept the supplies. Then he ran to the battle line and talked to his brothers. [23]While he was talking with them, Goliath came out. He was the Philistine champion from Gath. He shouted things against Israel as usual, and David heard

it. ²⁴When the Israelites saw Goliath, they were very much afraid and ran away.

²⁵They said, "Look at this man Goliath. He keeps coming out to speak against Israel. The king will give much money to the man who kills Goliath. He will also give his daughter in marriage to whoever kills him. And his father's family will not have to pay taxes in Israel."

²⁶David asked the men who stood near him, "What will be done to reward the man who kills this Philistine? What will be done for whoever takes away the shame from Israel? Goliath is a Philistine. He is not circumcised.ᵈ Why does he think he can speak against the armies of the living God?"

²⁷The Israelites told David what they had been saying. They said, "This is what will be done for the man who kills Goliath."

²⁸David's oldest brother Eliab heard David talking with the soldiers. He became angry with David. He asked David, "Why did you come here? Who's taking care of those few sheep of yours in the desert? I know you are proud. Your attitude is very bad. You came down here just to watch the battle!"

²⁹David asked, "Now what have I done wrong? Can't I even talk?" ³⁰He then turned to other people and asked the same questions. And they gave him the same answer as before. ³¹Some men heard what David said and told Saul. Then Saul ordered David to be sent to him.

³²David said to Saul, "Don't let anyone be discouraged. I, your servant, will go and fight this Philistine!"

³³Saul answered, "You can't go out against this Philistine and fight him. You're only a boy. Goliath has been a warrior since he was a young man."

³⁴But David said to Saul, "I, your servant, have been keeping my father's sheep. When a lion or bear came and took a sheep from the flock, ³⁵I would chase it. I would attack it and save the sheep from its mouth. When it attacked me, I caught it by its fur. I would hit it and kill it. ³⁶I, your servant, have killed both a lion and a bear! Goliath, the Philistine who is not circumcised, will be like the lion or bear I killed. He will die because he has stood against the armies of the living God. ³⁷The Lord saved me from a lion and a bear. He will also save me from this Philistine."

Saul said to David, "Go, and may the Lord be with you." ³⁸Saul put his own clothes on David. He put a bronze helmet on David's head and armor on his body. ³⁹David put on Saul's sword and tried to walk around. But he was not used to all the armor Saul had put on him.

He said to Saul, "I can't go in this. I'm not used to it." Then David took it all off. ⁴⁰He took his stick in his hand. And he chose five smooth stones from a stream. He put them in his pouch and held his sling in his hand. Then he went to meet Goliath.

⁴¹At the same time, the Philistine was coming closer to David. The man who held his shield walked in front of him. ⁴²Goliath looked at David. He saw that David was only a boy, tanned and handsome. He looked down at David with disgust. ⁴³He said, "Do you think I am a dog, that you come at me with a stick?" He used his gods' names to curse David. ⁴⁴He said to David, "Come here. I'll feed your body to the birds of the air and the wild animals!"

⁴⁵But David said to him, "You come to me using a sword, a large spear and a small spear. But I come to you in the name of the Lord of heaven's armies. He's the God of the armies of Israel! You have spoken out against him. ⁴⁶Today the Lord will give you to me. I'll kill you, and I'll cut off your head. Today I'll feed the bodies of the Philistine soldiers to the birds of the air and the wild animals. Then all the world will know there is a God in Israel! ⁴⁷Everyone gathered here will know the Lord does not need swords or spears to save people. The battle belongs to him! And he will help us defeat all of you."

⁴⁸As Goliath came near to attack him, David ran quickly to meet him. ⁴⁹He took a stone from his pouch. He put it into his sling and slung it. The stone hit the Philistine on his forehead and sank into it. Goliath fell facedown on the ground.

⁵⁰So David defeated the Philistine with only a sling and a stone! He hit him and killed him. He did not even have a sword in his hand. ⁵¹David ran and stood beside the Philistine. He took Goliath's sword out of its holder and killed him. Then he cut off Goliath's head.

When the Philistines saw that their champion was dead, they turned and ran. ⁵²The men of Israel and Judah shouted and started chasing the Philistines. They chased them all the way to the entrance to the city of Gath. And they chased them to the gates of Ekron.

Many of the Philistines died. Their bodies lay on the Shaaraim road as far as Gath and Ekron. ⁵³The Israelites returned after chasing the Philistines. Then they took many things from the Philistine camp. ⁵⁴David took Goliath's head to Jerusalem. He also put Goliath's weapons in his own tent.

⁵⁵Saul had watched David go out to meet Goliath. Saul spoke to Abner, commander of the army. He said, "Abner, who is that young man's father?"

Abner answered, "As surely as you live, my king, I don't know."

⁵⁶The king said, "Find out whose son he is."

⁵⁷When David came back from killing Goliath, Abner brought him to Saul. David still held Goliath's head.

⁵⁸Saul asked him, "Young man, who is your father?"

David answered, "I am the son of your servant Jesse of Bethlehem."

18 When David finished talking with Saul, Jonathan felt very close to David. He loved David as much as he loved himself. ²Saul kept David with him from that day on. He did not let David go home to his father's house. ³Jonathan made an agreement with David. He did this because he loved David as much as himself. ⁴He took off his coat and gave it to David. He also gave David his uniform, including his sword, bow and belt.

⁵Saul sent David to fight in different battles. And David was very successful. Then Saul put David over the soldiers. When he did this, Saul's officers and all the other people were pleased.

⁶After David had killed the Philistine, he and the men returned home. Women came out from all the towns of Israel to meet King Saul. They sang songs of joy, danced and played tambourines[d] and stringed instruments. ⁷As they played, they sang,

> "Saul has killed thousands of his enemies.
> But David has killed tens of thousands!"

⁸The women's song upset Saul, and he became very angry. He thought, "The women say David has killed tens of thousands of enemies. But they say I killed only thousands of enemies. The only thing left for him to have is the kingdom!" ⁹So Saul watched David closely from then on. He was jealous of him.

¹⁰The next day an evil spirit from God entered Saul with power. And he prophesied[d] in his house. David was playing the harp as he usually did. But Saul had a spear in his hand. ¹¹He raised the spear and thought, "I'll pin David to the wall." But David got away from him two times.

¹²The Lord was with David but had left Saul. So Saul was afraid of David. ¹³He sent David away from him. He made David commander of 1,000 soldiers. So David led them in battle. ¹⁴He had great success in everything he did because the Lord was with him. ¹⁵Saul saw that David was very successful. And he became even more afraid of David. ¹⁶But all the people of Israel and Judah loved David. This was because he led them well in battle.

¹⁷Saul said to David, "You're a brave soldier. And you fight the Lord's battles. Here is my older daughter Merab. I will let you marry her." Saul had decided, "I won't have to kill David. The Philistines will do that!"

¹⁸But David said, "I am not good enough for this honor. And my family is not important enough for me to become the king's son-in-law." ¹⁹So when the time came for Saul's daughter Merab to marry David, Saul gave her instead to Adriel of Meholah.

²⁰Now Saul's other daughter Michal loved David. When they told Saul about Michal loving David, he was pleased. ²¹He thought, "I will let Michal marry David. Then she will become a trap for him. And the Philistines will defeat him." So Saul said to David a second time, "You may become my son-in-law."

²²And Saul gave an order to his servants. He told them, "Speak to David in private. Say, 'Look, the king is pleased with you. His servants like you. You should become his son-in-law.'"

²³Saul's servants said these words to David. But David answered, "Do you think it is easy to become the king's son-in-law? I'm only a poor man. Nobody knows me."

²⁴Then Saul's servants told him what David had said. ²⁵Saul said, "Say to David, 'The king doesn't want you to pay a large price for the bride. All he wants is 100 Philistine foreskins. Then he will be even with his enemies.'" Saul planned to let the Philistines kill David.

²⁶Saul's servants told David these words. David was pleased that he could

become the king's son-in-law. ²⁷So he and his men went out and killed 200 Philistines. David took all their foreskins and brought them to Saul. He wanted to become the king's son-in-law. Then Saul gave him his daughter Michal for his wife. ²⁸Saul saw that the Lord was with David. He also saw that his daughter Michal loved David. ²⁹So he became even more afraid of David. And he was David's enemy all his life.

³⁰The Philistine commanders continued to go out to fight the Israelites. But every time, David defeated them. He had more success than Saul's officers. And he became famous.

19 Saul told his son Jonathan and all his servants to kill David. But Jonathan cared very much for David. ²So he warned David, "My father Saul is looking for a chance to kill you. Watch out in the morning. Hide in a secret place. ³I will go out and stand with my father in the field where you are hiding. I'll talk to him about you. Then I'll let you know what I find out."

⁴Jonathan talked to Saul his father. He said good things about David. Jonathan said, "You are the king. Don't do wrong to your servant David. He did nothing wrong to you. What he did has helped you greatly. ⁵David risked his life when he killed Goliath the Philistine. The Lord won a great victory for all Israel. You saw it, and you were happy. Why would you do wrong against David? He's innocent. There's no reason to kill him!"

⁶Saul listened to Jonathan. Then he made this promise: "As surely as the Lord lives, David won't be put to death."

⁷So Jonathan called to David. And he told David everything that had been said. And he brought David to Saul. So David was with Saul as before.

⁸When war broke out again, David went out to fight the Philistines. He defeated them, and they ran away from him.

⁹But once again an evil spirit from the Lord entered Saul. He was sitting in his house, and he had his spear in his hand. David was playing the harp. ¹⁰Saul tried to pin David to the wall with his spear. But David moved away from him. So Saul's spear went into the wall. And David ran away that night.

¹¹Saul sent men to David's house. They watched it, wanting to kill him in the morning. But Michal, David's wife, warned him. She said, "Tonight you

must run away to save your own life. If you don't, you will be killed tomorrow morning." ¹²Then she let David down out of a window. So he ran away and escaped. ¹³Then Michal took an idol and laid it on the bed. She covered it with clothes and put goats' hair at its head.

¹⁴Saul sent messengers to take David prisoner. But Michal said, "He is sick."

¹⁵The men went and told Saul, but he sent them back to see David. He told them, "Bring him to me on his bed so I can kill him."

¹⁶But when the messengers entered David's house, they found it was just an idol on the bed. Its hair was goats' hair.

¹⁷Saul said to Michal, "Why did you trick me this way? You let my enemy go. He has run away!"

Michal answered Saul, "David told me if I did not help him escape, he would kill me."

¹⁸After David had escaped from Saul, he went to Samuel at Ramah. He told Samuel everything Saul had done to him. Then David and Samuel went to Naioth and stayed there. ¹⁹Saul heard that David was in Naioth at Ramah. ²⁰So he sent men to capture him. But they met a group of prophetsᵈ prophesying. Samuel was leading this group and was standing there. The Spiritᵈ of God entered Saul's men, and they also prophesied.

²¹Saul heard the news. So he sent other men, but they also prophesied. Then he sent men a third time, but they also prophesied. ²²Finally, Saul himself went to Ramah. He came to the well at Secu. He asked, "Where are Samuel and David?"

The people answered, "In Naioth at Ramah."

²³Then Saul went to Naioth at Ramah. But the Spirit of God also entered him. And he walked on, prophesying until he came to Naioth at Ramah. ²⁴He took off his robes and prophesied in front of Samuel. He lay that way all day and all night. That is why people ask, "Is even Saul one of the prophets?"

20 Then David ran away from Naioth in Ramah. He went to Jonathan and asked, "What have I done? What is my crime? How have I sinned against your father so that he's trying to kill me?"

²Jonathan answered, "No! You won't die! See, my father doesn't do anything without first telling me. It doesn't matter if it is very important or just a small

thing. Why would he refuse to tell me he wants to kill you? No, it's not true!"

³But David took an oath. He said, "Your father knows very well that I'm your friend. He has said to himself, 'Jonathan must not know about it. If he knows, he will tell David.' But as surely as the Lord lives and as you live, I am very close to death!"

⁴Jonathan said to David, "I'll do anything you want me to do."

⁵So David said, "Look, tomorrow is the New Moon[d] festival. I am supposed to eat with the king. But let me hide in the field until the third evening. ⁶Your father may notice I am gone. If he does, tell him, 'David begged me to let him go to his hometown of Bethlehem. Every year at this time, his family group offers a sacrifice.' ⁷If your father says, 'Fine,' I am safe. But if he becomes angry, you can believe he wants to hurt me. ⁸Jonathan, be kind to me, your servant. You have made an agreement with me before the Lord. If I am guilty, you may kill me yourself! Why hand me over to your father?"

⁹Jonathan answered, "No, never! If I learn that my father plans to harm you, I will warn you!"

¹⁰David asked, "Who will let me know if your father answers you unkindly?"

¹¹Then Jonathan said, "Come, let's go out into the field." So Jonathan and David went together into the field.

¹²Jonathan said to David, "I promise this before the Lord, the God of Israel: At this same time day after tomorrow, I will find out how my father feels. If he feels good toward David, I'll send word to you. I'll let you know. ¹³But my father may mean to hurt you. If so, I will let you know and send you away safely. May the Lord punish me terribly if I don't do this. And may the Lord be with you as he has been with my father. ¹⁴But show me the kindness of the Lord as long as I live. Do this so that I may not die. ¹⁵You must not stop showing your kindness to my family. Don't do this, even when the Lord has destroyed all your enemies from the earth."

¹⁶So Jonathan made an agreement with David. He said, "May the Lord punish David's enemies." ¹⁷And Jonathan asked David to repeat his promise of love for him. He did this because he loved David as much as he loved himself.

¹⁸Jonathan said to David, "Tomorrow is the New Moon festival. Your seat will be empty. So my father will notice you're gone. ¹⁹On the third day go to the place where you hid when this trouble began. Wait by the rock Ezel. ²⁰On the third day I will shoot three arrows to the side of the rock. I will shoot as if I am shooting at a target. ²¹Then I will send a boy and tell him to go find the arrows. I may say to him, 'Look, the arrows are on this side of you. Bring them here.' If so, you may come out of hiding. You may do this as surely as the Lord lives because you are safe. There is no danger. ²²But I may say to the boy, 'Look, the arrows are beyond you.' If I do, you must go, because the Lord has sent you away. ²³Remember what we talked about. The Lord is a witness between you and me forever."

²⁴So David hid in the field. And when the New Moon festival came, the king sat down to eat. ²⁵He sat where he always sat, near the wall. Jonathan sat across from him, and Abner sat next to him. But David's place was empty. ²⁶That day Saul said nothing. He thought, "Maybe something has happened to David so that he is unclean."[d] ²⁷But the next day was the second day of the month. And David's place was empty again. So Saul said to Jonathan, "Why hasn't the son of Jesse come to the festival yesterday or today?"

²⁸Jonathan answered, "David begged me to let him go to Bethlehem. ²⁹He said, 'Let me go, because our family has a sacrifice in the town. And my brother has ordered me to be there. Now if I am your friend, please let me go and see my brothers.' That is why he has not come to the king's table."

³⁰Then Saul became very angry with Jonathan. He said, "You son of an evil and disobedient woman! I know you are on the side of David son of Jesse! You bring shame on yourself and on your mother who gave birth to you. ³¹As long as Jesse's son lives, you'll never be king or have a kingdom. Now send for David and bring him to me. He must die!"

³²Jonathan asked his father, "Why should David be killed? What wrong has he done?" ³³Then Saul threw his spear at Jonathan, trying to kill him. So Jonathan knew that his father really wanted to kill David. ³⁴Jonathan was very angry and left the table. That second day of the month he refused to eat. He was upset about what his father wanted to do to David.

³⁵The next morning Jonathan went

out to the field. He went to meet David as they had agreed. He had a young boy with him. [36]Jonathan said to the boy, "Run and find the arrows I shoot." When he ran, Jonathan shot an arrow beyond him. [37]The boy ran to the place where Jonathan's arrow fell. But Jonathan called, "The arrow is beyond you!" [38]Then he shouted, "Hurry! Go quickly! Don't stop!" The boy picked up the arrow and brought it back to his master. [39](The boy knew nothing about what this meant. Only Jonathan and David knew.) [40]Then Jonathan gave his weapons to the boy. He told him, "Go back to town."

[41]When the boy left, David came out from the south side of the rock. He bowed facedown on the ground before Jonathan. He did this three times. Then David and Jonathan kissed each other. They cried together, but David cried the most.

[42]Jonathan said to David, "Go in peace. We have promised by the Lord that we will be friends. We said, 'The Lord will be a witness between you and me, and between our descendants[d] forever.'" Then David left, and Jonathan went back to town.

21 David went to Nob to see Ahimelech the priest. Ahimelech shook with fear when he saw David. He asked David, "Why are you alone? Why is no one with you?"

[2]David answered him, "The king gave me a special order. He told me, 'No one must know about the work I am sending you to do. And no one must know what I told you to do.' I told my men where to meet me. [3]Now, what food do you have with you? Give me five loaves of bread or anything you find."

[4]The priest said to David, "I don't have any plain bread here. But I do have some holy bread[n] here. You may eat it if your men have kept themselves from women."

[5]David answered, "Women have been kept from us. My men always keep their bodies holy, even when we do ordinary work. And this is especially true when the work is holy."

[6]There was no bread except the bread made holy for the Lord. So the priest gave David the bread that showed the people were in the presence of God. This was the bread the priests had taken from the holy table before the Lord.

Each day they took this bread away and put hot bread in its place.

[7]Now one of Saul's servants was there that day. He had been held there before the Lord. He was Doeg the Edomite, the chief of Saul's shepherds.

[8]David asked Ahimelech, "Do you have a spear or sword here? The king's business was very important. I had to leave quickly, and I didn't bring my sword or any other weapon."

[9]The priest answered, "The sword of Goliath the Philistine is here. He is the one you killed in the Valley of Elah. His sword is wrapped in a cloth. It is behind the holy vest.[d] If you want it, you may take it. There's no other sword here but that one."

David said, "There is no other sword like Goliath's. Give it to me."

[10]That day David ran away from Saul. He went to Achish king of Gath. [11]But the servants of Achish said to him, "This is David king of the Israelites. He's the man the Israelite women sing about when they dance. They sing:

'Saul has killed thousands of his
enemies.
But David has killed tens of
thousands.'"

[12]David paid attention to these words. And he was very much afraid of Achish king of Gath. [13]So he pretended to be insane in front of Achish and his servants. While he was with them, he acted like a madman. He made marks on the doors of the gate. He let spit run down his beard.

[14]Achish said to his servants, "Look at the man! He's insane! Why do you bring him to me? [15]I have enough madmen. I don't need you to bring him here to act like this in front of me! Don't leave him in my house!"

22 David left Gath and escaped to the cave of Adullam. His brothers and other relatives heard that he was there. And they went to see him. [2]Many people joined David. All those who were in trouble, who owed money or who were unsatisfied gathered around him. And he became their leader. He had about 400 men with him.

[3]From there David went to Mizpah in Moab. He spoke to the king of Moab. He said, "Please let my father and mother come and stay with you. Let them stay until I learn what God is going to do for

---

21:4 holy bread This was the bread that showed the people were in the presence of God. Normally only the priests should eat this bread.

me." ⁴So he left them with the king of Moab. And they stayed with the king as long as David was hiding in the protected place.

⁵But the prophet⁴ Gad said to David, "Don't stay in the protected place. Go to the land of Judah." So David left and went to the forest of Hereth.

⁶Saul heard that David and his men had been seen. He sat under the tamarisk tree on the hill at Gibeah. All his officers were standing around him. He had a spear in his hand. ⁷Saul said to them, "Listen, men of Benjamin! Do you think the son of Jesse will give all of you fields and vineyards? Will David make you commanders over thousands of men or hundreds of men? ⁸You have all made plans against me! No one tells me when my son makes an agreement with the son of Jesse! No one cares about me! No one tells me my son has encouraged my servant to ambush me! And David is doing this now!"

⁹Doeg the Edomite was standing there with Saul's officers. He said, "I saw the son of Jesse. He came to see Ahimelech son of Ahitub at Nob. ¹⁰Ahimelech prayed to the Lord for David. He also gave him food. And he gave him the sword of Goliath the Philistine."

¹¹Then the king sent for the priest Ahimelech son of Ahitub. He sent for all of Ahimelech's relatives who were priests at Nob. And they all came to the king. ¹²Saul said to Ahimelech, "Listen now, son of Ahitub."

Ahimelech answered, "Yes, master."

¹³Saul said, "Why have you and Jesse's son made plans against me? You gave him bread and a sword! You prayed to God for him. David is waiting to attack me. He is doing this now!"

¹⁴Ahimelech answered, "David is very loyal to you. You have no other servant who is as loyal as David. He is your own son-in-law and captain of your bodyguards. All the people in your house respect him. ¹⁵That was not the first time I prayed to God for David. Not at all! Don't blame me or any of my relatives. We are your servants. I know nothing about what is going on."

¹⁶But the king said, "Ahimelech, you and all your relatives must die!" ¹⁷Then he told the guards at his side, "Go and kill the priests of the Lord. Do this because they are on David's side. They knew he was running away, but they didn't tell me!"

But the king's officers refused to hurt the priests of the Lord.

¹⁸Then the king ordered Doeg, "Go and kill the priests." So Doeg the Edomite went and killed the priests. That day he killed 85 men who wore the linen holy vest.⁴ ¹⁹He also killed the people of Nob, the city of the priests. With the sword he killed men, women, children and small babies. And he killed cattle, donkeys and sheep.

²⁰But Abiathar escaped. He was a son of Ahimelech, who was the son of Ahitub. Abiathar ran away and joined David. ²¹He told David that Saul had killed the Lord's priests. ²²Then David told him, "Doeg the Edomite was there at Nob that day. I knew he would surely tell Saul. So I am responsible for the death of all your father's family. ²³The man who wants to kill you also wants to kill me. Stay with me. Don't be afraid. You will be safe with me."

23 Someone told David, "Look, the Philistines are fighting against Keilah. They are robbing grain from the threshing⁴ floors."

²David asked the Lord, "Should I go and fight these Philistines?"

The Lord answered him, "Go. Attack them, and save Keilah."

³But David's men said to him, "We're afraid here in Judah. We will be much more afraid if we go to Keilah where the Philistine army is."

⁴David again asked the Lord. And the Lord answered, "Go down to Keilah. I will help you defeat the Philistines." ⁵So David and his men went to Keilah. They fought the Philistines and took their cattle. David killed many Philistines and saved the people of Keilah. ⁶(Now Abiathar son of Ahimelech had brought the holy vest⁴ with him. He brought it when he came to David at Keilah.)

⁷Someone told Saul that David was now at Keilah. Saul said, "God has given David to me! He has trapped himself because he has entered a town with gates and bars." ⁸Saul called all his army together for battle. They prepared to go down to Keilah to attack David and his men.

⁹David learned Saul was making evil plans against him. So he said to Abiathar the priest, "Bring the holy vest."⁴ ¹⁰David prayed, "Lord, God of Israel, I have heard about Saul's plans. He is coming to Keilah to destroy the town because of me. ¹¹Will the people of Keilah give me to Saul? Will Saul come to

Keilah, as I heard? Lord, God of Israel, tell me, your servant!"

The Lord answered, "Saul will come down."

[12]Again David asked, "Will the people of Keilah give me and my men to Saul?"

The Lord answered, "They will."

[13]So David and his men left Keilah. There were about 600 men who went with him. And they kept moving from place to place. When Saul found that David had escaped from Keilah, he did not go there.

[14]David stayed in the protected places in the desert. He also stayed in the hills of the Desert of Ziph. Every day Saul looked for David. But the Lord did not let him take David.

[15]David was at Horesh in the Desert of Ziph. He was afraid because Saul was coming to kill him. [16]But Saul's son Jonathan went to David at Horesh. He helped David have stronger faith in God. [17]Jonathan told him, "Don't be afraid. My father won't touch you. You will become king of Israel, and I will be second to you. Even my father Saul knows this." [18]The two of them made an agreement before the Lord. Then Jonathan went home. But David stayed at Horesh.

[19]The people from Ziph went to Saul at Gibeah. They told him, "David is hiding in our land. He's at the protected places of Horesh. They are on the hill of Hakilah, south of Jeshimon. [20]Now, our king, come down anytime you want. It's our duty to give David to you."

[21]Saul answered, "The Lord bless you for helping me. [22]Go and learn more about him. Find out where he is staying. Find out who has seen him there. I have heard that he is clever. [23]Find all the hiding places he uses. And come back and tell me everything. Then I'll go with you. If David is in the area, I will find him. I will track him down among all the families in Judah."

[24]So they went back to Ziph ahead of Saul. David and his men were in the Desert of Maon.[n] This was in the desert area south of Jeshimon. [25]Saul and his men went to look for David. But people warned David that Saul was looking for him. David then went down to a rock and stayed in the Desert of Maon. Saul heard that David had gone there. So he went after him into the Desert of Maon. [26]Saul was going along one side of the mountain. David and his men were on the other side. They were hurrying to get away from Saul. Saul and his soldiers were closing in on David and his men. [27]But a messenger came to Saul. He said, "Come quickly! The Philistines are attacking our land!" [28]So Saul stopped chasing David and went to fight the Philistines. That is why people call this place Rock of Parting. [29]David left the Desert of Maon and lived in the protected places of En Gedi.

24
Now Saul had chased the Philistines away. Then he was told, "David is in the Desert of En Gedi." [2]So he chose 3,000 men from all Israel. He took these men and began looking for David and his men. They looked near the Rocks of the Wild Goats.

[3]Saul came to the sheep pens beside the road. A cave was there, and he went in to relieve himself. Now David and his men were hiding far back in the cave. [4]The men said to David, "Today is the day the Lord talked about! The Lord told you, 'I will give your enemy to you. You can do anything you want with him.'"

Then David crawled near Saul. He cut off a corner of Saul's robe. But Saul did not notice him. [5]Later David felt guilty because he had cut off a corner of Saul's robe. [6]He said to his men, "May the Lord keep me from doing such a thing to my master! Saul is the Lord's appointed king. I should not do anything against him, because he is the Lord's appointed king!" [7]David used these words to stop his men. He did not let them attack Saul. Then Saul left the cave and went his way.

[8]When David came out of the cave, he shouted to Saul, "My master and king!" Saul looked back, and David bowed facedown on the ground. [9]He said to Saul, "Why do you listen when people say, 'David plans to harm you'? [10]You have seen something with your own eyes today. You have seen how the Lord put you in my power in the cave. But I refused to kill you. I was merciful to you. I said, 'I won't harm my master, because he is the Lord's appointed king.' [11]My father, look at this piece of your robe in my hand! I cut off the corner of your robe, but I didn't kill you. Now understand and know I am not planning any evil against you. I did nothing wrong to you, but you are hunting me to kill me. [12]May the Lord judge between us. And may he punish you for the wrong you have done to me! But I won't fight you.

23:24 **Maon** Some early Greek copies say "Maon." The Hebrew copies say "Paran."

[13]There is an old saying: 'Evil things come from evil people.' So I won't hurt you. [14]Whom is the king of Israel coming out against? Whom are you chasing? You're not chasing someone who will hurt you! It's as if you are chasing a dead dog or a flea. [15]May the Lord be our judge and decide between you and me. May the Lord support me and show that I am right. May he save me from you!"

[16]David finished saying these words. Then Saul asked, "Is that your voice, David my son?" And he cried loudly. [17]He said, "You are right, and I am wrong. You have been good to me. But I have done wrong to you. [18]You told me what good things you did. The Lord brought me to you, but you did not kill me. [19]If a man finds his enemy, he won't send him away with goodness, will he? May the Lord reward you because you were good to me today. [20]I know you will surely be king. You will rule the kingdom of Israel. [21]Now make a promise to me. Promise in the name of the Lord that you will not kill my descendants.[d] Promise me that you won't wipe out my name from my father's family."

[22]So David made the promise to Saul. Then Saul went back home. David and his men went up to the protected place.

25 Now Samuel died. All the Israelites met and had a time of sadness for him. They buried him at his home in Ramah.

Then David moved to the Desert of Maon.[n] [2]A man in Maon who had land at Carmel was very rich. He had 3,000 sheep and 1,000 goats. He was cutting the wool off his sheep at Carmel. [3]His name was Nabal, and he was a descendant[d] of Caleb. His wife was named Abigail. She was a wise and beautiful woman. But Nabal was cruel and mean.

[4]David was in the desert. He heard that Nabal was cutting the wool from his sheep. [5]So he sent ten young men. He told them, "Go to Nabal at Carmel. Greet him for me. [6]Say to Nabal, 'May you and your family have good health! And may all who belong to you have good health. [7]I have heard that you are cutting the wool from your sheep. When your shepherds were with us, we did nothing wrong to them. All the time your shepherds were at Carmel, we stole nothing from them. [8]Ask your servants, and they will tell you. We come at a happy time. So for this reason, be kind to my young men. Please give them anything you can find for them. Please do this for your son David.'"

[9]When the men arrived, they gave the message to Nabal. But Nabal insulted them. [10]He answered them, "Who is David? Who is this son of Jesse? Many slaves are running away from their masters today! [11]I have bread and water. And I have meat that I killed for my servants who cut the wool. But I won't give it to men I don't know."

[12]David's men went back and told him all Nabal had said. [13]Then David said to them, "Put on your swords!" So they put on their swords, and David put on his also. About 400 men went with David. But 200 men stayed with the supplies.

[14]One of Nabal's servants spoke to Abigail, Nabal's wife. He said, "David sent messengers from the desert to greet our master. But Nabal insulted them. [15]These men were very good to us. They did nothing wrong to us. They stole nothing from us during all the time we were out in the field with them. [16]Night and day they protected us. They were like a wall all around us while we were with them caring for the sheep. [17]Now think about it, and decide what you can do. Terrible trouble is coming to our master and all his family. Nabal is such a wicked man that no one can even talk to him."

[18]Abigail hurried. She took 200 loaves of bread, 2 leather bags full of wine and 5 cooked sheep. She took about a bushel of cooked grain, 100 cakes of raisins and 200 cakes of pressed figs. She put all these on donkeys. [19]Then she told her servants, "Go on. I'll follow you." But she did not tell her husband.

[20]Abigail rode her donkey and came down into the mountain ravine. There she met David and his men coming down toward her.

[21]David had just said, "It's been useless! I watched over Nabal's property in the desert. I made sure none of his sheep were missing. I did good to him, but he has paid me back with evil. [22]May God punish me terribly if I let just one of Nabal's family live until tomorrow."

[23]When Abigail saw David, she quickly got off her donkey. She bowed facedown on the ground before David. [24]She lay at David's feet. She said, "My master, let the blame be on me! Please let me talk to you! Listen to what I say. [25]My master, don't pay attention to this

worthless man Nabal. He is the same as his name. His name means 'fool,' and he is truly foolish. But I, your servant, didn't see the men you sent. [26]The Lord has kept you from killing and punishing people yourself. As surely as the Lord lives and as surely as you live, may your enemies become like Nabal! [27]I have brought a gift to you. Please give it to the men who follow you. [28]Please forgive my wrong. The Lord will certainly let your family have many kings. He will do this because you fight his battles. As long as you live, people will find nothing bad in you. [29]A man might chase you to kill you. But the Lord your God will keep you alive. He will throw away your enemies' lives as he would throw a stone from a sling. [30]The Lord will keep all his promises about good things for you. He will make you leader over Israel. [31]Then you won't feel guilty. You won't have problems about killing innocent people and punishing them yourself. Please remember me when the Lord brings you success."

[32]David answered Abigail, "Praise the Lord, the God of Israel. He sent you to meet me. [33]May you be blessed for your wisdom. You have kept me from killing or punishing people today. [34]As surely as the Lord, the God of Israel, lives, he has kept me from hurting you. If you hadn't come quickly to meet me, no one belonging to Nabal would have lived until tomorrow."

[35]Then David accepted Abigail's gifts. He told her, "Go home in peace. I have heard your words, and I will do what you have asked."

[36]When Abigail went back to Nabal, he was in the house. He was eating like a king. He was very drunk and in a good mood. So she told him nothing until the next morning. [37]In the morning he was not drunk. Then his wife told him everything. His heart failed him, and he became like a stone. [38]About ten days later the Lord struck Nabal and caused him to die.

[39]When David heard that Nabal was dead, he said, "Praise the Lord! Nabal insulted me, but the Lord has supported me! He has kept me from doing wrong. And the Lord caused Nabal to die because he did wrong."

Then David sent a message to Abigail. He asked her to become his wife. [40]His servants went to Carmel and spoke to Abigail. They said, "David sent us to take you so you can become his wife."

[41]Abigail bowed facedown on the ground. She said, "I am your servant. I'm ready to serve you. I'm ready to wash the feet of my master's servants." [42]Abigail quickly got on a donkey and went with David's messengers. She had five maids following her. And she became David's wife.

[43]David also had married Ahinoam of Jezreel. So they were both David's wives. [44]Saul's daughter Michal was also David's wife. But Saul had given her to Paltiel son of Laish. Paltiel was from Gallim.

26

The people of Ziph went to see Saul at Gibeah. They said to him, "David is hiding on the hill of Hakilah opposite Jeshimon."

[2]So Saul went down to the Desert of Ziph. His 3,000 chosen men of Israel went with him. They looked for David in the Desert of Ziph. [3]Saul made his camp on the hill of Hakilah, beside the road opposite Jeshimon. But David stayed in the desert. He heard Saul had followed him. [4]So David sent out spies and learned that Saul had come to Hakilah.

[5]Then David went to the place where Saul had camped. He saw where Saul and Abner son of Ner were sleeping. Abner was the commander of Saul's army. Saul was sleeping in the middle of the camp with all the army around him.

[6]David talked to Ahimelech the Hittite and Abishai son of Zeruiah. Abishai was Joab's brother. He asked them, "Who will go down into Saul's camp with me?"

Abishai answered, "I'll go with you."

[7]So that night David and Abishai went into Saul's camp. Saul was asleep in the middle of the camp. His spear was stuck in the ground near his head. Abner and the army were sleeping around Saul. [8]Abishai said to David, "Today God has let you defeat your enemy! Let me pin Saul to the ground with the spear. I'll only do it once! I won't hit him twice."

[9]But David said to Abishai, "Don't kill Saul! No one can harm the Lord's appointed king and still be innocent! [10]As surely as the Lord lives, the Lord himself will punish Saul. Maybe Saul will die naturally. Or maybe he will go into battle and be killed. [11]But may the Lord keep me from harming his appointed king! Now pick up the spear and water jug that are near Saul's head. Then let's go."

¹²So David took the spear and water jug that were near Saul's head. They left, and no one saw them. No one knew about it or woke up. The Lord had made them stay asleep.

¹³David crossed over to the other side of the hill. He stood on top of the mountain far from Saul's camp. David's and Saul's camps were far apart. ¹⁴David shouted to the army and to Abner son of Ner, "Answer me, Abner!"

Abner answered, "Who is calling for the king? Who are you?"

¹⁵David said, "You're the greatest man in Israel. Isn't that true? Then why didn't you guard your master the king? Someone came into your camp to kill your master the king! ¹⁶What you have done is not good. As surely as the Lord lives, you and your men should die. You haven't guarded your master, the Lord's appointed king. Look! Where are the king's spear and water jug that were near his head?"

¹⁷Saul knew David's voice. He said, "Is that your voice, David my son?"

David answered, "Yes, it is, my master and king." ¹⁸David also said, "Why are you chasing me, my master? What wrong have I done? What evil am I guilty of? ¹⁹My master and king, listen to me. If the Lord caused you to be angry with me, let him accept an offering. But if men caused you to be angry with me, let the Lord curse them! They have made me leave the land the Lord gave me. They have told me, 'Go and serve other gods.' ²⁰Now don't let me die far away from the Lord's presence. The king of Israel has come out looking for a flea! You're like a man hunting a partridge bird in the mountains!"

²¹Then Saul said, "I have sinned. Come back, David my son. Today you respected my life. So I will not try to hurt you. I have acted foolishly. I have made a big mistake."

²²David answered, "Here is your spear. Let one of your young men come here and get it. ²³The Lord rewards every man for the things he does right and for his loyalty to him. The Lord put you into my power today. But I wouldn't harm the Lord's appointed king. ²⁴I respected your life today. Surely, in the same way, the Lord will respect my life. Surely he will save me from all trouble."

²⁵Then Saul said to David, "You are blessed, my son David. You will do great things and succeed."

So David went on his way, and Saul went back home.

27 But David thought to himself, "Saul will catch me someday. The best thing I can do is escape to the land of the Philistines. Then he will give up looking for me in Israel. That way I can get away from him."

²So David and his 600 men left Israel. They went to Achish son of Maoch. Achish was king of Gath. ³David, his men and their families made their home in Gath with Achish. David had his two wives with him. Their names were Ahinoam of Jezreel and Abigail of Carmel. Abigail was the widow of Nabal. ⁴Now Saul was told that David had run away to Gath. So he stopped looking for him.

⁵Then David said to Achish, "If you are pleased with me, give me a place in one of the country towns. I can live there. I don't need to live in the royal city with you."

⁶That day Achish gave David the town of Ziklag. That is why Ziklag has belonged to the kings of Judah ever since. ⁷David lived in the Philistine land a year and four months.

⁸David and his men went to raid the people of Geshur, Girzi and Amalek. (These people had lived for a long time in the land that reached to Shur and Egypt.) ⁹When David fought them, he killed all the men and women. He took sheep, cattle, donkeys, camels and clothes. Then he returned to Achish.

¹⁰Many times Achish would ask David, "Where did you go raiding today?" And David would tell him that he had gone to the southern part of Judah. Or he would say he had gone to the territory of the Jerahmeelites or of the Kenites. ¹¹David never brought a man or woman alive to Gath. He thought, "If we bring anyone alive, he may tell Achish, 'This is what David really did.'" David did this all the time he lived in the Philistine land. ¹²Achish trusted David. He said to himself, "David's own people, the Israelites, now hate David very much. So David will serve me forever."

28 Later, the Philistines gathered their armies to fight against Israel. Achish said to David, "You understand that you and your men must join with me in my army."

²David answered, "Certainly! Then you can see for yourself what I, your servant, can do!"

Achish said, "Fine, I'll make you my bodyguard for life."

[3]Now Samuel was dead, and all the Israelites had shown their sadness for him. They had buried Samuel in his hometown of Ramah.

And Saul had forced out the mediums[d] and fortune-tellers from the land of Israel.

[4]The Philistines came together and made camp at Shunem. Saul gathered all the Israelites and made camp at Gilboa. [5]When he saw the Philistine army, he was afraid. His heart pounded with fear. [6]He prayed to the Lord, but the Lord did not answer him through dreams, Urim[d] or prophets.[d] [7]Then Saul said to his servants, "Find me a woman who is a medium. I'll go and ask her what will happen."

His servants answered, "There is a medium in Endor."

[8]Then Saul put on other clothes so no one would know who he was. At night Saul and two of his men went to see the woman. Saul said to her, "Talk to a spirit for me. Call up the person I name."

[9]But the woman said to him, "Surely you know what Saul has done. He has forced the mediums and fortune-tellers out from the land of Israel. You are trying to trap me and kill me."

[10]Saul made a promise to the woman in the name of the Lord. He said, "As surely as the Lord lives, you won't be punished for doing this."

[11]The woman asked, "Whom do you want me to bring up for you?"

He answered, "Bring up Samuel."

[12]When the woman saw Samuel, she screamed loudly. She said, "Why have you tricked me? You are Saul!"

[13]The king said to the woman, "Don't be afraid! What do you see?"

The woman said, "I see a spirit coming up out of the ground."

[14]Saul asked, "What does he look like?"

The woman answered, "An old man wearing a coat is coming up."

Then Saul knew it was Samuel, and he bowed facedown on the ground.

[15]Samuel asked Saul, "Why have you disturbed me by bringing me up?"

Saul said, "I am greatly troubled. The Philistines are fighting against me. God has left me. He won't answer me anymore, either by prophets or in dreams. That's why I called you. I want you to tell me what to do."

[16]Samuel said, "The Lord has left you. He has become your enemy. So why do you call on me? [17]He has done what he said he would do. He said these things through me. He has torn the kingdom out of your hands. He has given it to one of your neighbors, David. [18]You did not obey the Lord. You did not show the Amalekites how angry he was with them. That's why he has done this to you today. [19]The Lord will give both Israel and you to the Philistines. Tomorrow you and your sons will be with me. The Lord will let the Philistines defeat the army of Israel."

[20]Saul quickly fell to the ground and lay there. He was afraid because of what Samuel had said. He was also very weak because he had eaten nothing all that day and night.

[21]Then the woman came to Saul. She saw that he was really frightened. She said, "Look, I, your servant, have obeyed you. I have risked my life and done what you told me to do. [22]Now please listen to me. Let me give you some food. Then you may eat and have enough strength to go on your way."

[23]But Saul refused. He said, "I won't eat."

His servants joined the woman in asking him to eat. And he listened to them. So he got up from the ground and sat on the bed.

[24]The woman had a fat calf at the house. She quickly killed it. She took some flour and mixed dough with her hands. Then she baked some bread without yeast. [25]She put the food before them, and they ate. Then that same night they got up and left.

29 The Philistines gathered all their soldiers at Aphek. Israel camped by the spring at Jezreel. [2]The Philistine kings were marching with their groups of 100 and 1,000 men. David and his men were marching at the back with Achish. [3]The Philistine commanders asked, "What are these Hebrews doing here?"

Achish told them, "This is David. He was an officer to Saul king of Israel. But he has been with me for over a year now. I have found nothing wrong in David since the time he left Saul and came to me."

[4]But the Philistine commanders were angry with Achish. They said, "Send David back! He must go back to the city you gave him. He can't go with us into battle. If he's here, we'll have an enemy in our own camp. He would please his king by killing our own men. [5]David is the one the Israelites sing about in their dances:

'Saul has killed thousands of his
enemies.
But David has killed tens of
thousands.' "

[6]So Achish called David. He said to
him, "As surely as the Lord lives, you
are loyal. I would be pleased to have
you serve in my army. Since the day you
came to me, I have found no wrong in
you. But the Philistine kings don't trust
you. [7]Go back in peace. Don't do anything to displease the Philistine kings."

[8]David asked, "What wrong have I
done? What evil have you found in me
from the day I came to you until now?
Why won't you allow me to fight your
enemies, my lord and king?"

[9]Achish answered, "I know you are as
pleasing to me as an angel from God.
But the Philistine commanders have
said, 'David can't go with us into battle.'
[10]Early in the morning you and your
master's servants, the Israelites, should
go back. Go back to the city I gave you.
Leave as soon as the sun comes up."

[11]So David and his men got up early
in the morning. They went back to the
country of the Philistines. And the Philistines went up to Jezreel.

30 On the third day David and his
men arrived at Ziklag. The Amalekites had raided southern Judah and
Ziklag. They had attacked Ziklag and
burned it. [2]They took the women and
everyone in Ziklag as prisoners, both
young and old. But they did not kill any
of the people. They only took them
away.

[3]When David and his men came to
Ziklag, they found the town had been
burned. Their wives, sons and daughters had been taken as prisoners. [4]Then
David and his army cried loudly until
they were too weak to cry anymore. [5]Da-
vid's two wives had also been taken.
They were Ahinoam of Jezreel and Abigail the widow of Nabal from Carmel.
[6]The men in the army were threatening
to kill David with stones. This upset David very much. Each man was sad and
angry because his sons and daughters
had been taken as prisoners. But David
found strength in the Lord his God. [7]Da-
vid said to Abiathar the priest, "Bring
me the holy vest."[d]

[8]Then David prayed to the Lord. He
said, "Should I chase the people who
took our families? Will I catch them?"

The Lord answered, "Chase them. You
will catch them. You will succeed in saving your families."

[9]David and the 600 men with him
came to the Besor Ravine. Some of the
men stayed there. [10]David and 400 men
kept up the chase. The other 200 men
stayed behind because they were too
tired and weak to cross the ravine.

[11]David's men found an Egyptian in a
field. They took him to David. They gave
the Egyptian some water to drink and
some food to eat. [12]They gave him a
piece of a fig cake and two clusters of
raisins. He felt better after eating. He
had not eaten any food or drunk any
water for three days and nights.

[13]David asked him, "Who is your master? Where do you come from?"

He answered, "I'm an Egyptian. I'm
the slave of an Amalekite. Three days
ago my master left me, because I became sick. [14]We attacked the southern
area of the Kerethites. We attacked the
land of Judah and the southern area belonging to Caleb. We burned Ziklag, as
well.

[15]David asked him, "Will you lead me
to the people who took our families?"

He answered, "Yes, if you will make a
promise to me before God. Promise that
you won't kill me or give me back to my
master. Then I will take you to them."

[16]So the Egyptian led David to the
Amalekites. They were lying around on
the ground, eating and drinking. They
were celebrating with the things they
had taken from the land of the Philistines and from Judah. [17]David fought
them from sunset until evening the next
day. None of them escaped, except 400
young men who rode off on their camels. [18]David got back his two wives. He
also got back everything the Amalekites
had taken. [19]Nothing was missing. David brought back everything: the young
and old people, the sons and daughters,
the valuable things and everything the
Amalekites had taken. [20]David took all
the sheep and cattle. His men made
these animals go in front. They said,
"They are David's prize."

[21]Then David came to the 200 men
who had been too tired and weak to follow him. He had made them stay at the
Besor Ravine. They came out to meet
David and the army with him. When he
came near, the men at the ravine greeted
David and his army.

[22]But there were evil men and troublemakers in the group that followed David. They said, "These 200 men didn't
go with us. So we won't give them any

of the things we took. But each man may take his wife and children and go." ²³David answered, "No, my brothers. Don't do that after what the Lord has given us. He has given us the enemy who attacked us. ²⁴Who will listen to what you say? The share will be the same for the man who stayed with the supplies as for the man who went into battle. All will share alike." ²⁵David made this an order and rule for Israel. This order and rule continues even today.

²⁶David arrived in Ziklag. Then he sent some of the things he had taken from the Amalekites to his friends, the leaders of Judah. He said, "Here is a present for you from the things we took from the Lord's enemies."

²⁷David sent some things from the Amalekites to the leaders in Bethel, Ramoth in the southern part of Judah, Jattir, ²⁸Aroer, Siphmoth, Eshtemoa ²⁹and Racal. He also sent some to the leaders of the cities of the Jerahmeelites and the Kenites, ³⁰to Hormah, Bor Ashan, Athach ³¹and Hebron. He sent some things to the people in all the other places where he and his men had been.

31 The Philistines fought against Israel, and the Israelites ran away from them. Many Israelites were killed at Mount Gilboa. ²The Philistines fought hard against Saul and his sons. They killed his sons Jonathan, Abinadab and Malki-Shua. ³The fighting became bad around Saul. When the archers shot at him, he was badly wounded. ⁴He said to the officer who carried his armor, "Pull out your sword and kill me. Then those uncircumcised[d] men won't make fun of me and kill me." But Saul's officer refused, because he was afraid. So Saul took his own sword and threw himself on it. ⁵The officer saw that Saul was dead. So he threw himself on his own sword. And he died with Saul. ⁶So Saul, his three sons and the officer who carried his armor died together that day.

⁷Now there were Israelites who lived on the other side of Jezreel Valley. And some lived across the Jordan River. They saw how the Israelite army had run away. And they saw that Saul and his sons were dead. So they left their cities and ran away. Then the Philistines came and lived there.

⁸The next day the Philistines came to take all the valuable things from the dead soldiers. They found Saul and his three sons dead on Mount Gilboa. ⁹They cut off Saul's head and took off his armor. Then they sent men to tell the news through all the land of the Philistines. They told it in the temple of their idols and to their people. ¹⁰They put Saul's armor in the temple of the Ashtoreths.[d] They also hung his body on the wall of Beth Shan.

¹¹The people living in Jabesh Gilead heard what the Philistines had done to Saul. ¹²So the brave soldiers of Jabesh marched all night and came to Beth Shan. They took the bodies of Saul and his sons off the wall of Beth Shan. Then they took them to Jabesh. There the people of Jabesh burned the bodies. ¹³They took their bones and buried them under the tamarisk tree in Jabesh. Then the people of Jabesh gave up eating for seven days.

The Second Book of

SAMUEL

1 Now Saul was dead. And after David had defeated the Amalekites, he returned to Ziklag. He stayed there two days. ²On the third day a young man came to Ziklag. He came from Saul's camp. To show his sadness his clothes were torn, and he had dirt on his head. He came and bowed facedown on the ground before David.

³David asked him, "Where did you come from?"

The man answered, "I escaped from the Israelite camp."

⁴David asked him, "What happened? Please tell me!"

The man answered, "The people have run away from the battle. Many of them have fallen dead. Saul and his son Jonathan are dead also."

⁵David said to him, "How do you know Saul and his son Jonathan are dead?"

⁶The young man answered, "I happened to be on Mount Gilboa. There I saw Saul leaning on his spear. The Philistine chariots and the men riding in

them were coming closer to Saul. ⁷When he looked back and saw me, he called to me. I answered him, 'Here I am!'

⁸"Then Saul asked me, 'Who are you?'

"I told him, 'I am an Amalekite.'

⁹"Then Saul said to me, 'Please come here and kill me. I am badly hurt and am almost dead already.'

¹⁰"So I went over and killed him. He had been hurt so badly I knew he couldn't live. Then I took the crown from his head and the bracelet from his arm. I have brought them here to you, my master."

¹¹Then David tore his clothes to show his sorrow. And all the men with him did also. ¹²They were very sad and cried. They did not eat until evening. They cried for Saul and his son Jonathan. And they cried for the Israelites who had been killed with swords.

¹³David asked the young man who brought the report, "Where are you from?"

The young man answered, "I am the son of a foreigner. I am an Amalekite."

¹⁴David asked him, "Why were you not afraid to kill the Lord's appointed king?"

¹⁵Then David called one of his men. David told him, "Go! Kill the Amalekite!" So the Israelite killed the Amalekite. ¹⁶David had said to the Amalekite, "You are responsible for your own death. You have spoken against yourself! You said, 'I have killed the Lord's appointed king.'"

¹⁷David sang a funeral song about Saul and his son Jonathan. ¹⁸David ordered that the people of Judah be taught this song. It is called "The Bow." This song is written in the Book of Jashar:

¹⁹"Israel, your leaders have been killed on the hills.
  How the mighty men have fallen in battle!
²⁰Don't tell it in Gath.
  Don't announce it in the streets of Ashkelon.
  If you do, the daughters of the Philistines will be happy.
  The daughters of the Philistines will rejoice.

²¹"May there be no dew or rain on the mountains of Gilboa.
  May their fields produce no grain.
  This is because there the mighty warrior's shield was dishonored.
  Saul's shield was no longer rubbed with oil.
²²Jonathan's bow killed its share of enemies.
  And Saul's sword killed its share, too.
  Their weapons are stained with the blood of dead men.
  Their weapons have stabbed the flesh of strong men.

²³"We loved Saul and Jonathan.
  We enjoyed them while they lived.
  Saul and Jonathan are together even in death.
  They were faster than eagles.
  They were stronger than lions.

²⁴"You daughters of Israel, cry for Saul.
  Saul clothed you with red dresses.
  He put gold decorations on your dresses.

²⁵"How the mighty men have fallen in battle!
  Jonathan is dead on Gilboa's hills.
²⁶I cry for you, my brother Jonathan.
  I enjoyed your friendship so much.
  Your love to me was wonderful, more wonderful than the love of women.

²⁷"How the mighty men have fallen in battle!
  The weapons of war are gone."

2 Later, David prayed to the Lord. David said, "Should I go up to any of the cities of Judah?"

The Lord said to David, "Go."

David asked, "Where should I go?"

The Lord answered, "To Hebron."

²So David went up to Hebron with his two wives. One was Ahinoam from Jezreel. The other was Abigail, the widow of Nabal in Carmel. ³David also brought his men and their families. They all made their homes in the cities of Hebron. ⁴Then the men of Judah came to Hebron. They appointed David king over Judah.

They told David that the men of Jabesh Gilead had buried Saul. ⁵So David sent messengers to the men of Jabesh Gilead. They told David's message to the men in Jabesh: "The Lord bless you. You have shown kindness to your master Saul by burying him. ⁶May the Lord now be kind and true to you. I will also be kind to you because you have done this. [7]Now be strong and brave. Saul your master is dead. The people of Judah have appointed me their king."

[8]Now Abner son of Ner was the commander of Saul's army. Abner took Saul's son Ish-Bosheth to Mahanaim. [9]There Abner made him king of Gilead, Ashuri, Jezreel, Ephraim, Benjamin and all Israel. [10]Saul's son Ish-Bosheth was 40 years old when he became king over Israel. He ruled two years. But the people of Judah followed David. [11]David was king in Hebron for seven years and six months.

[12]Abner son of Ner and the servants of Ish-Bosheth son of Saul left Mahanaim. They went to Gibeon. [13]Joab son of Zeruiah and David's men also went there. They met Abner and Ish-Bosheth's men at the pool of Gibeon. Abner's group sat on one side of the pool. Joab's group sat on the other side.

[14]Abner said to Joab, "Let's have the young men get up and have a contest here."

Joab said, "Yes, let them have a contest."

[15]Then the young men got up. The two groups counted their men for the contest. Twelve men were chosen from the people of Benjamin for Ish-Bosheth son of Saul. Twelve men were chosen from David's men. [16]Each man grabbed his enemy's head. Then he stabbed his enemy's side with a knife. And the men fell down together. So that place in Gibeon is called The Field of the Sharp Knives. [17]That day the contest became a terrible battle. And David's men defeated Abner and the Israelites.

[18]Zeruiah's three sons, Joab, Abishai and Asahel, were there. Now Asahel was a fast runner. He was as fast as a deer in the field. [19]Asahel chased Abner, going straight toward him. [20]Abner looked back and asked, "Are you Asahel?"

Asahel said, "Yes, I am."

[21]Then Abner said to Asahel, "Turn to your right or left. Catch one of the young men and take his armor." But Asahel refused to stop chasing him.

[22]Abner again said to Asahel, "Stop chasing me! If you don't stop, I'll have to kill you! Then I won't be able to face your brother Joab again!"

[23]But Asahel refused to stop chasing Abner. So Abner used the back end of his spear. He stabbed it into Asahel's stomach, and the spear came out of his back. Asahel died right there. Everyone stopped when they came to the place where Asahel's body lay.

[24]But Joab and Abishai continued chasing Abner. The sun was going down when they arrived at the hill of Ammah. This is near Giah on the way to the empty land near Gibeon. [25]The men of Benjamin came to Abner. They all stood together at the top of the hill.

[26]Abner shouted to Joab, "Must the sword kill forever? Surely you must know this will only end in sadness! Tell the people to stop chasing their own brothers!"

[27]Then Joab said, "If you had not said anything, the people would have chased their brothers until morning. This is as sure as God is alive." [28]Then Joab blew a trumpet, and his people stopped chasing the Israelites. They did not try to fight them anymore.

[29]Abner and his men marched all night through the Jordan Valley. They crossed the Jordan River. After marching all day, they arrived at Mahanaim.

[30]Joab came back after he had stopped chasing Abner. Then Joab gathered the people together. Asahel and 19 of David's men were missing. [31]But David's men had killed 360 Benjaminites who had followed Abner. [32]David's men took Asahel and buried him. They put him in the tomb of his father at Bethlehem. Then Joab and his men marched all night. The sun came up as they reached Hebron.

3 There was a long war between the people who supported Saul's family and those who supported David's family. The supporters of David's family became stronger and stronger. And the supporters of Saul's family became weaker and weaker.

[2]Sons were born to David at Hebron. The first son was Amnon. Amnon's mother was Ahinoam from Jezreel. [3]The second son was Kileab. Kileab's mother was Abigail, the widow of Nabal from Carmel. The third son was Absalom. Absalom's mother was Maacah daughter of Talmai. Talmai was king of Geshur. [4]The fourth son was Adonijah. His mother was Haggith. The fifth son was Shephatiah. His mother was Abital. [5]The sixth son was Ithream. His mother was Eglah, David's wife. These sons were born to David at Hebron.

[6]Abner made himself a main leader among the supporters of Saul. He did

this during the war between the supporters of Saul's family and the supporters of David's family.

⁷Now Saul had once had a slave womanᵈ named Rizpah. She was the daughter of Aiah. Ish-Bosheth said to Abner, "Why did you have sexual relations with my father's slave woman?"

⁸Abner was very angry because of what Ish-Bosheth said. Abner said, "I have been loyal to Saul and his family and friends! I didn't hand you over to David. I am not a traitor working for Judah! But now you are saying I did something wrong with this woman! ⁹May God punish me terribly if I don't help David. I will make sure that what God promised does happen! ¹⁰I will take the kingdom from the family of Saul. I will make David king of Israel and Judah! He will rule from Dan to Beersheba.'"ⁿ

¹¹Ish-Bosheth couldn't say anything to Abner. He was too afraid of Abner.

¹²Then Abner sent messengers to David. Abner said, "Who is going to rule the land? Make an agreement with me, and I will help you become the king of all Israel."

¹³David answered, "Good! I will make an agreement with you. But I ask you one thing. I will not meet with you unless you bring Saul's daughter Michal to me." ¹⁴Then David sent messengers to Saul's son Ish-Bosheth. David said, "Give me my wife Michal. She was promised to me. I killed 100 Philistines to get her."

¹⁵So Ish-Bosheth sent men to take Michal from her husband. He was Paltiel son of Laish. ¹⁶Michal's husband went with her, crying as he followed her to Bahurim. But Abner said to Paltiel, "Go back home." So he went home.

¹⁷Abner sent a message to the older leaders of Israel. He said, "You have been wanting to make David your king. ¹⁸Now do it! The Lord has spoken about David. The Lord said, 'I will save my people the Israelites. I will save them from the Philistines and all their enemies. I will do this through my servant David.'"

¹⁹Abner also said these things to the people of Benjamin. He then went to Hebron to tell David what the Benjaminites and Israel wanted to do. ²⁰Abner came with 20 men to David at Hebron. There David prepared a feast for them. ²¹Then Abner said to David, "My master and king, I will go and bring all the Israelites to you. Then they will make an agreement with you. You will rule over all Israel as you wanted." So David let Abner go, and he left in peace.

²²Just then Joab and David's men came from a battle. They had many valuable things they had taken from the enemy. David had let Abner leave in peace. So he was not with David at Hebron. ²³Joab and all his army arrived at Hebron. The army said to Joab, "Abner son of Ner came to King David. And David let him leave in peace."

²⁴Joab came to the king and said, "What have you done? Abner came to you. Why did you let him go? Now he's gone. ²⁵You know Abner son of Ner! He came to trick you! He came to learn about everything you are doing!"

²⁶Then Joab left David and sent messengers after Abner. They brought Abner back from the well of Sirah. But David did not know this. ²⁷When Abner arrived at Hebron, Joab took him aside into the gateway. Joab acted as though he wanted to talk with him in private. But Joab stabbed Abner in the stomach, and Abner died. Abner had killed Joab's brother Asahel. So Joab killed Abner to pay him back.

²⁸Later David heard the news. He said, "My kingdom and I are innocent forever. We did not kill Abner son of Ner. The Lord knows this. ²⁹Joab and his family are responsible for this. I hope many troubles will come to his family. May his family always have someone with sores or with a harmful skin disease. May they always have someone who must lean on a crutch. May some of his family be killed in war. May they always have someone without food to eat."

³⁰(Joab and his brother Abishai had killed Abner, because he had killed their brother Asahel. This was in the battle at Gibeon.)

³¹Then David spoke to Joab and to all the people with Joab. He said, "Tear your clothes and put on rough cloth to show how sad you are. Cry for Abner." King David himself followed behind the body of Abner. ³²So they buried Abner in Hebron. David and all the people cried at Abner's grave.

3:10 Dan to Beersheba Dan was the city farthest north in Israel. Beersheba was the city farthest south. So this means all the people of Israel.

[33]King David sang this funeral song for Abner.

"Did Abner die like a foolish man?
[34] His hands were not tied.
  His feet were not in chains.
He fell as a person falls before evil
  men."

Then all the people cried again for Abner. [35]They came to encourage David to eat while it was still day. But he made a promise. He said, "May God punish me terribly if I eat bread or any other food before the sun sets!"

[36]All the people saw what happened. They agreed with what the king was doing. [37]That day all the people of Judah and all the Israelites understood. They knew it was not David who had killed Abner son of Ner.

[38]David said to his officers, "You know that a very important leader died today in Israel. [39]Even though I am the appointed king, I am weak today. These sons of Zeruiah are too strong for me. May the Lord give them the punishment they should have."

4 Ish-Bosheth son of Saul heard that Abner had died at Hebron. Then Ish-Bosheth and all Israel became very frightened. [2]Two men who were captains in Saul's army came to Ish-Bosheth. One man was named Baanah, and the other was named Recab. They were the sons of Rimmon of Beeroth, who was a Benjaminite. (The town Beeroth belonged to the tribe[d] of Benjamin.) [3]The people of Beeroth ran away to Gittaim. And they still live there today.

[4](Now Jonathan son of Saul had a son who was crippled in both feet. His name was Mephibosheth. He was five years old when the news came from Jezreel that Saul and Jonathan were dead. Mephibosheth's nurse picked him up and ran away. But as she hurried to leave, he fell and became crippled.)

[5]Recab and Baanah, sons of Rimmon, were from Beeroth. They went to Ish-Bosheth's house at noon. [6-7]They came into the middle of the house. Recab and Baanah came as if they were going to get some wheat. Ish-Bosheth was lying on his bed in his bedroom. Recab and Baanah stabbed him in the stomach. Then they cut off his head and took it with them. They traveled all night through the Jordan Valley. [8]When they arrived at Hebron, they gave his head to David. They said to the king, "Here is the head of Ish-Bosheth son of Saul. He

was your enemy. He tried to kill you! Today the Lord has paid back Saul and his family for what they did to you!"

[9]David answered Recab and his brother Baanah sons of Rimmon of Beeroth. David said, "As surely as the Lord lives, he has saved me from all trouble! [10]Once a man thought he was bringing me good news. He told me, 'Look! Saul is dead!' But I took hold of him and killed him at Ziklag. That was the reward I gave him for his news! [11]So even more I must require your death. This is because evil men have killed an innocent man. And he was on his own bed in his own house!"

[12]So David commanded his men to kill Recab and Baanah. Then they cut off the hands and feet of Recab and Baanah. They hung their hands and feet over the pool of Hebron. Then they took Ish-Bosheth's head and buried it in Abner's tomb at Hebron.

5 Then all the tribes[d] of Israel came to David at Hebron. They said to him, "Look, we are your own family. [2]In the past Saul was king over us. But you were the one leading us in battle for Israel. The Lord said to you, 'You will be like a shepherd for my people, the Israelites. You will become their ruler.'"

[3]All the older leaders of Israel came to King David at Hebron. Then he made an agreement with them in Hebron in front of the Lord. Then they poured oil on David to make him king over Israel.

[4]David was 30 years old when he became king. He ruled 40 years. [5]He was king over Judah in Hebron for 7 years and 6 months. And he was king over all Israel and Judah in Jerusalem for 33 years.

[6]The king and his men went to Jerusalem to attack the Jebusites who lived there. The Jebusites said to David, "You can't come into our city. Even our people who are blind and crippled can stop you." They said this because they thought David could not enter their city. [7]But David did take the city of Jerusalem with its strong walls. It became the City of David.

[8]That day David said to his men, "To defeat the Jebusites you must go through the water tunnel. Then you can reach those 'crippled' and 'blind' enemies. This is why people say, 'The blind and the crippled cannot enter the palace.'"

[9]So David lived in the city with its strong walls. He called it the City of Da-

vid. David built more buildings around it. He began where the land was filled in on the east side of the city. He also built more buildings inside the city. [10]He became stronger and stronger, because the Lord of heaven's armies was with him.

[11]Hiram king of the city of Tyre sent messengers to David. He also sent cedar logs, carpenters and men to cut stone. They built a palace for David. [12]Then David knew the Lord really had made him king of Israel. And he knew the Lord had made his kingdom very important. This was because the Lord loved his people, the Israelites.

[13]In Jerusalem David took for himself more slave women[d] and wives. This was after he moved there from Hebron. More sons and daughters were born to David. [14]These are the names of the sons born to David in Jerusalem: Shammua, Shobab, Nathan, Solomon, [15]Ibhar, Elishua, Nepheg, Japhia, [16]Elishama, Eliada and Eliphelet.

[17]Now the Philistines heard that David had been made king over Israel. So all the Philistines went to look for him. But when David heard the news, he went down to a safe place. [18]So the Philistines came and camped in the Valley of Rephaim. David asked the Lord, "Should I attack the Philistines? Will you help me defeat them?"

[19]The Lord said to David, "Go! I will certainly help you defeat them."

[20]So David went to Baal Perazim and defeated the Philistines there. David said, "Like a flood of water, the Lord has broken through my enemies." So David named the place Baal Perazim.[n] [21]The Philistines left their idols behind at Baal Perazim. And David and his men carried these idols away.

[22]Once again the Philistines came and camped at the Valley of Rephaim. [23]David prayed to the Lord. This time the Lord told David, "Don't attack the Philistines from the front. Instead, go around them. Attack them opposite the balsam trees. [24]You will hear the sound of marching in the tops of the balsam trees. Then you must act quickly. I, the Lord, will have gone ahead of you and defeated the Philistine army." [25]So David did what the Lord commanded. He defeated the Philistines and chased them all the way from Gibeon to Gezer.

6 David again gathered all the chosen men of Israel. There were 30,000 of them. [2]Then David and all his people went to Baalah in Judah.[n] They took the Holy Box[d] of God from Baalah in Judah and moved it to Jerusalem. The Holy Box is called by the Name, the name of the Lord of heaven's armies. His throne is between the gold creatures with wings that are on the Holy Box. [3]David's men put the Holy Box of God on a new cart. Then they brought the Holy Box out of Abinadab's house on the hill. Uzzah and Ahio, sons of Abinadab, led the new cart. [4]This cart had the Holy Box of God on it. Ahio was walking in front of it. [5]David and all the Israelites were playing all kinds of musical instruments before the Lord. They were made of pine wood. There were lyres,[d] harps, tambourines,[d] rattles and cymbals.

[6]When David's men came to the threshing[d] floor of Nacon, the oxen stumbled. The Holy Box of God began to fall off the cart. So Uzzah reached out and took hold of it. [7]The Lord was angry with Uzzah and killed him. Uzzah had not honored God when he touched the Holy Box. So Uzzah died there beside it. [8]David was angry because the Lord had killed Uzzah. So that place is called The Punishment of Uzzah even today.

[9]David was afraid of the Lord that day. He said, "How can the Holy Box of the Lord come to me now?" [10]So David would not move the Holy Box of the Lord to be with him in Jerusalem. Instead, he took it to the house of Obed-Edom, a man from Gath. [11]The Holy Box of the Lord stayed in Obed-Edom's house for three months. And the Lord blessed Obed-Edom and all his family.

[12]The people told David, "The Lord has blessed the family of Obed-Edom. And all his things are blessed. This is because the Holy Box of God is there." So David went and brought it up from Obed-Edom's house to Jerusalem with joy. [13]When the men carrying the Holy Box of the Lord had walked six steps, David sacrificed a bull and a fat calf. [14]Then David danced with all his might before the Lord. He had on a holy linen vest.[d] [15]David and all the Israelites shouted with joy. They blew the trumpets as they brought the Holy Box of the Lord to the city.

[16]Saul's daughter Michal was looking

5:20 Baal Perazim This name means "the Lord breaks through." **6:2 Baalah in Judah** Another name for Kiriath Jearim.

out the window. She watched as the Holy Box of the Lord came into the city. When she saw David jumping and dancing before the Lord, she hated him.

[17]David put up a tent for the Holy Box. Then the Israelites put it in its place inside the tent. David offered whole burnt offerings and fellowship offerings before the Lord. [18]When David finished offering the whole burnt offerings and the fellowship offerings, he blessed the people in the name of the Lord of heaven's armies. [19]David gave a loaf of bread, a cake of dates and a cake of raisins to everyone. He gave them to all the Israelites, both men and women. Then all the people went home.

[20]David went back to bless the people in his home. But Saul's daughter Michal came out to meet him. She said, "The king of Israel did not honor himself today! You took off your clothes in front of the servant girls of your officers. You were like a foolish man who takes off his clothes without shame!"

[21]Then David said to Michal, "I did it before the Lord. The Lord chose me, not your father. He didn't choose anyone from Saul's family. The Lord appointed me to be leader of his people, the Israelites. So I will celebrate in front of the Lord. [22]Maybe I will lose even more honor. And you may think little of me. But the girls you talk about will honor me!"

[23]And Saul's daughter Michal had no children to the day she died.

7 King David was living in his palace. And the Lord gave him peace from all his enemies around him. [2]David said to Nathan the prophet,[d] "Look, I am living in a palace made of cedar wood. But the Holy Box[d] of God is still kept in a tent!"

[3]Nathan said to the king, "Go and do what you really want to do. The Lord is with you."

[4]But that night the Lord spoke his word to Nathan. The Lord said, [5]"Go and tell my servant David, 'This is what the Lord says: You are not the person to build a house for me to live in. [6]I did not live in a house when I brought the Israelites out of Egypt. I have been moving around all this time with a tent as my home. [7]I have continued to move with the tribes[d] of Israel. But I have never asked their leaders who take care of them to build me a house of cedar wood.'

[8]"You must tell my servant David, 'This is what the Lord of heaven's armies says: I took you from the pasture when you were following the sheep. I took you to become leader of my people, the Israelites. [9]I have been with you everywhere you have gone. I have defeated your enemies for you. I will make you as famous as any of the great men on the earth. [10]Also I will choose a place for my people, the Israelites. I will plant them so they can live in their own home. They will not be bothered anymore. Wicked people will no longer make them suffer as they have in the past. [11]Wicked people continued to do this even when I appointed judges. But I will give you peace from all your enemies. I also tell you that I will make your descendants[d] kings of Israel after you.

[12]"'Your days will come to an end, and you will die. At that time I will make one of your sons the next king. [13]He will build a temple[d] for me. I will make his kingdom strong forever. [14]I will be his father, and he will be my son. When he sins, I will use other people to punish him. They will be my whips. [15]But I will not stop loving him. I took away my love and kindness from Saul. I removed Saul when I turned to you. [16]But your family and your kingdom will continue forever before me. Your rule will last forever.'"

[17]Nathan told David everything he had heard.

[18]Then King David went in the tent and sat in front of the Lord. David said, "Lord God, why have you made me so important to you? Why have you made my family important? [19]But that was not enough for you, Lord God. You have also said these kind things about my future family. I am your servant. Lord God, this is not the usual way you talk to people.

[20]"What more can I say to you? Lord God, you love me, your servant, so much! [21]You have done this wonderful thing because you said you would. You have done it because you wanted to. And you have decided to let me know all these great things. [22]This is why you are great, Lord God! There is no one like you. There is no God except you. We have heard all this ourselves! [23]And there are no others like your people, the Israelites. They are the one nation on earth that God chose to be his people. You used them to make your name well-known. You did great and wonderful miracles[d] for them. You went ahead of them and forced other nations and their

gods out of the land. You freed your people from slavery in Egypt. ²⁴You made the people of Israel your very own people forever. And, Lord, you became their God.

²⁵"Now, Lord God, keep the promise you made about my family and me, your servant. Do what you have promised. ²⁶Then you will be honored forever. And people will say, 'The Lord of heaven's armies is God over Israel!' And the family of your servant David will continue before you.

²⁷"Lord of heaven's armies, the God of Israel, you have shown things to me. You have said, 'I will make your family great.' So I, your servant, am brave enough to pray to you. ²⁸Lord God, you are God, and your words are true. And you have promised these good things to me, your servant. ²⁹Please, bless my family. Let it continue before you forever. Lord God, you have said these wonderful things. With your blessing let my family be blessed forever."

8 Later, David defeated the Philistines. And he took control of their capital city.

²He also defeated the people of Moab. He forced them to lie on the ground. Then he used a rope to measure them. When two men were measured, David ordered them killed. But every third man was allowed to live. So the people of Moab became servants of David. They gave him the payments he demanded.

³As David went to take control again at the Euphrates River, he defeated Hadadezer. Hadadezer son of Rehob was king of Zobah. ⁴David took from Hadadezer 1,700 men who rode in his chariots. He also captured 20,000 foot soldiers. David crippled all but 100 of the chariot horses. He saved those horses to pull chariots.

⁵Arameans from Damascus came to help Hadadezer king of Zobah. But David defeated those 22,000 Arameans. ⁶Then David put groups of soldiers in Damascus in Aram. The Arameans became David's servants and gave him the payments he demanded. The Lord gave David victory everywhere he went.

⁷David took the shields of gold that had belonged to Hadadezer's officers. He brought them to Jerusalem. ⁸David also took many things made of bronze from Tebah and Berothai. (They were cities that had belonged to Hadadezer.)

⁹Toi king of Hamath heard that David

had defeated all the army of Hadadezer. ¹⁰So Toi sent his son Joram to greet and congratulate King David. Joram congratulated David for defeating Hadadezer. (Hadadezer had fought wars against Toi before.) Joram brought things made of silver, gold and bronze. ¹¹David took these things and gave them to the Lord. He also had given other silver and gold to the Lord. He had taken it from the nations he had defeated. ¹²These nations were Edom, Moab, Ammon, Philistia and Amalek. David also defeated the king of Zobah who was Hadadezer son of Rehob.

¹³David was famous after he returned from the Valley of Salt. There he had defeated 18,000 Arameans. ¹⁴David put groups of soldiers through all the land of Edom. All the people of Edom became servants for him. The Lord gave David victory everywhere he went.

¹⁵David was king over all Israel. His decisions were fair and right for all his people. ¹⁶Joab son of Zeruiah was commander over the army. Jehoshaphat son of Ahilud was the recorder. ¹⁷Zadok son of Ahitub and Ahimelech son of Abiathar were priests. Seraiah was the royal assistant. ¹⁸Benaiah son of Jehoiada was over the Kerethites and Pelethites, the king's bodyguards. And David's sons were important leaders.

9 David asked, "Is there anyone still left in Saul's family? I want to show kindness to this person for Jonathan's sake!"

²Now there was a servant named Ziba from Saul's family. So David's servants called Ziba to him. King David said to him, "Are you Ziba?"

He answered, "Yes, I am Ziba, your servant."

³The king asked, "Is there anyone left in Saul's family? I want to show God's kindness to this person."

Ziba answered the king, "Jonathan has a son still living. He is crippled in both feet."

⁴The king asked Ziba, "Where is this son?"

Ziba answered, "He is at the house of Makir son of Ammiel in Lo Debar."

⁵Then King David had servants bring Jonathan's son from the house of Makir son of Ammiel in Lo Debar. ⁶Mephibosheth, Jonathan's son, came before David and bowed facedown on the floor.

David said, "Mephibosheth!"

Mephibosheth said, "I am your servant."

⁷David said to him, "Don't be afraid. I will be kind to you for your father Jonathan's sake. I will give you back all the land of your grandfather Saul. And you will always be able to eat at my table."

⁸Mephibosheth bowed to David again. Mephibosheth said, "You are being very kind to me, your servant! And I am no better than a dead dog!"

⁹Then King David called Saul's servant Ziba. David said to him, "I have given your master's grandson everything that belonged to Saul and his family. ¹⁰You, your sons and your servants will farm the land for Mephibosheth. You will harvest the crops. Then your master's grandson will have food to eat. But Mephibosheth, your master's grandson, will always be able to eat at my table."

(Now Ziba had 15 sons and 20 servants.) ¹¹Ziba said to King David, "I am your servant. I will do everything my master, the king, commands me."

So Mephibosheth ate at David's table as if he were one of the king's sons. ¹²Mephibosheth had a young son named Mica. Everyone in Ziba's family became Mephibosheth's servants. ¹³Mephibosheth was crippled in both feet. He lived in Jerusalem and always ate at the king's table.

10 Later Nahash king of the Ammonites died. His son Hanun became king after him. ²David said, "Nahash was kind to me. So I will be kind to his son Hanun." So David sent his officers to comfort Hanun about his father's death.

David's servants went to the land of the Ammonites. ³But the important men of Ammon spoke to Hanun, their master. They said, "Do you think David wants to honor your father by sending men to comfort you? No! David sent them to study the city and to spy it out. They plan to capture it!" ⁴So Hanun took David's officers and shaved off half their beards to shame them. He cut their clothes off at the hips to insult them. Then he sent them away.

⁵When the people told David, he sent messengers to meet his officers. He did this because these men were very ashamed. King David said, "Wait at Jericho until your beards have grown out. Then come back to Jerusalem."

⁶Now the Ammonites saw that they had become David's enemies. So they hired 20,000 Aramean foot soldiers from Beth Rehob and Zobah. They also hired

the king of Maacah with 1,000 men. And they hired 12,000 men from Tob.

⁷David heard about this. So he sent Joab with the whole army of warriors. ⁸The Ammonites came out and got ready for the battle. They stood at the city gate. The Arameans from Zobah and Rehob and the men from Tob and Maacah were out in the field. They were standing away from the Ammonites.

⁹Joab saw that there were enemies both in front of him and behind him. So he chose some of the best men from the Israelites. He got them ready for battle against the Arameans. ¹⁰Then Joab gave the other men to his brother Abishai to lead against the Ammonites. ¹¹Joab said to Abishai, "If the Arameans are too strong for me, come help me. If the Ammonites are too strong for you, I will come and help you. ¹²Be strong. Let us fight bravely for our people and for the cities of our God. The Lord will do what he decides is right."

¹³Then Joab and his men attacked the Arameans, and they ran away. ¹⁴The Ammonites saw that the Arameans were running away. So they ran away from Abishai and went back to their city. So Joab returned from the battle with the Ammonites and came to Jerusalem.

¹⁵The Arameans saw that the Israelites had defeated them. So they came together into one big army. ¹⁶Hadadezer sent messengers to bring the Arameans who lived on the other side of the Euphrates River. These Arameans went to Helam. Their leader was Shobach, the commander of Hadadezer's army.

¹⁷When David heard about this, he gathered all the Israelites together. They crossed over the Jordan River and went to Helam. There the Arameans prepared for battle and attacked. ¹⁸But David defeated the Arameans, and they ran away from the Israelites. David killed 700 Aramean chariot drivers and 40,000 Aramean horsemen. He also killed Shobach, the commander of the Aramean army.

¹⁹The kings who served Hadadezer saw that the Israelites had defeated them. So they made peace with the Israelites and served them. And the Arameans were afraid to help the Ammonites again.

11 In the spring the kings would go out to war. So in the spring David sent out Joab, his servants and all the Israelites. They destroyed the Ammonites and attacked the city of Rabbah. But David stayed in Jerusalem. [2] One evening David got up from his bed. He walked around on the roof[n] of his palace. While he was on the roof, he saw a woman bathing. She was very beautiful. [3] So David sent his servants to find out who she was. A servant answered, "That woman is Bathsheba daughter of Eliam. She is the wife of Uriah the Hittite." [4] David sent messengers to bring Bathsheba to him. When she came to him, he had sexual relations with her. (Now Bathsheba had purified herself from her monthly period.) Then she went back to her house. [5] But Bathsheba became pregnant. She sent word to David, saying, "I am pregnant."

[6] So David sent this message to Joab: "Send Uriah the Hittite to me." So Joab sent Uriah to David. [7] Uriah came to David. And David asked him how Joab was, how the soldiers were and how the war was going. [8] Then David said to Uriah, "Go home and rest."

So Uriah left the palace. The king also sent a gift to him. [9] But Uriah did not go home. He slept outside the door of the palace. He slept there as all the king's officers did.

[10] The officers told David, "Uriah did not go home."

Then David said to Uriah, "You came from a long trip. Why didn't you go home?"

[11] Uriah said to him, "The Holy Box[d] and the soldiers of Israel and Judah are staying in tents. My master Joab and his officers are camping out in the fields. It isn't right for me to go home to eat and drink and have sexual relations with my wife!"

[12] David said to Uriah, "Stay here today. Tomorrow I'll send you back to the battle." So Uriah stayed in Jerusalem that day and the next. [13] Then David called Uriah to come to see him. Uriah ate and drank with David. David made Uriah drunk, but he still did not go home. That evening Uriah went to sleep with the king's officers outside the king's door.

[14] The next morning David wrote a letter to Joab and sent it by Uriah. [15] In the letter David wrote, "Put Uriah on the front lines where the fighting is worst.

Then leave him there alone. Let him be killed in battle."

[16] Joab watched the city and saw where its strongest defenders were. He put Uriah there. [17] The men of the city came out to fight against Joab. Some of David's men were killed. And Uriah the Hittite was one of them.

[18] Then Joab sent a report to David about everything that had happened in the war. [19] Joab told the messenger, "Tell King David what happened in the war. [20] After you finish, the king may become angry. He may ask you, 'Why did you go so near the city to fight? Didn't you know they would shoot arrows from the city wall? [21] Do you remember who killed Abimelech son of Jerub-Besheth?[n] It was a woman on the city wall. She threw a large stone for grinding grain on Abimelech. She killed him there in Thebez. Why did you go so near the wall?' If King David asks that, you must answer, 'Your servant Uriah the Hittite also died.'"

[22] The messenger went in and told David everything Joab had told him to say. [23] The messenger told David, "The men of Ammon were winning. They came out and attacked us in the field. But we fought them back to the city gate. [24] The men on the city wall shot arrows at your servants. Some of your men were killed. Your servant Uriah the Hittite also died."

[25] David said to the messenger, "Say this to Joab: 'Don't be upset about this. The sword kills everyone the same. Make a stronger attack against the city and capture it.' Encourage Joab with these words."

[26] When Bathsheba heard that her husband was dead, she cried for him. [27] After she finished her time of sadness, David sent servants to bring her to his house. She became David's wife and gave birth to his son. But the Lord did not like what David had done.

12 The Lord sent Nathan to David. When Nathan came to David, Nathan said, "There were two men in a city. One man was rich, but the other was poor. [2] The rich man had very many sheep and cattle. [3] But the poor man had nothing except one little female lamb he had bought. The poor man fed the lamb. It grew up with him and his children. It

11:2 **roof** In Bible times houses were built with flat roofs. The roof was used for drying things such as flax and fruit. And it was used as an extra room, as a place for worship and as a place to sleep in the summer.   11:21 **Jerub-Besheth** Another name for Gideon.

shared his food and drank from his cup. It slept in his arms. The lamb was like a daughter to him.

⁴"Then a traveler stopped to visit the rich man. The rich man wanted to give food to the traveler. But he didn't want to take one of his own sheep or cattle to feed the traveler. Instead, he took the lamb from the poor man. The rich man killed the lamb and cooked it for his visitor."

⁵David became very angry at the rich man. He said to Nathan, "As surely as the Lord lives, the man who did this should die! ⁶He must pay for the lamb four times for doing such a thing. He had no mercy!"

⁷Then Nathan said to David, "You are the man! This is what the Lord, the God of Israel, says: 'I appointed you king of Israel. I saved you from Saul. ⁸I gave you his kingdom and his wives. And I made you king of Israel and Judah. And if that had not been enough, I would have given you even more. ⁹So why did you ignore the Lord's command? Why did you do what he says is wrong? You killed Uriah the Hittite with the sword of the Ammonites! And you took his wife to become your wife! ¹⁰So there will always be people in your family who will be killed by a sword. This is because you showed that you did not respect me! And you took the wife of Uriah the Hittite!'

¹¹"This is what the Lord says: 'I am bringing trouble to you from your own family. While you watch, I will take your wives from you. And I will give them to someone who is very close to you. He will have sexual relations with your wives, and everyone will know it. ¹²You had sexual relations with Bathsheba in secret. But I will do this so all the people of Israel can see it.'"

¹³Then David said to Nathan, "I have sinned against the Lord."

Nathan answered, "The Lord has taken away your sin. You will not die. ¹⁴But what you did caused the Lord's enemies to lose all respect for him. For this reason the son who was born to you will die."

¹⁵Then Nathan went home. And the Lord caused the son of David and Bathsheba, Uriah's widow, to become very sick. ¹⁶David prayed to God for the baby. David refused to eat or drink. He went into his house and stayed there. He lay

on the ground all night. ¹⁷The older leaders of David's family came to him. They tried to pull him up from the ground. But he refused to get up. And he refused to eat food with them.

¹⁸On the seventh day the baby died. David's servants were afraid to tell him that the baby was dead. They said, "Look, we tried to talk to David while the baby was alive. But he refused to listen to us. If we tell him the baby is dead, he may harm himself."

¹⁹But David saw his servants whispering. Then he understood that the baby was dead. So he asked them, "Is the baby dead?"

They answered, "Yes, he is dead."

²⁰Then David got up from the floor. He washed himself, put lotions on himself and changed his clothes. Then he went into the Lord's house to worship. After that, he went home and asked for something to eat. His servants gave him some food, and he ate.

²¹David's servants said to him, "Why are you doing this? When the baby was still alive, you refused to eat. You cried. But when the baby died, you got up and ate food."

²²David said, "While the baby was still alive, I refused to eat, and I cried. I thought, 'Who knows? Maybe the Lord will feel sorry for me and let the baby live.' ²³But now the baby is dead. So why should I go without food? I can't bring him back to life. Some day I will go to him. But he cannot come back to me."

²⁴Then David comforted Bathsheba his wife. He slept with her and had sexual relations with her. She became pregnant again and had another son. David named the boy Solomon. The Lord loved Solomon. ²⁵The Lord sent word through Nathan the prophet[d] to name the baby Jedidiah.[n] This was because the Lord loved the child.

²⁶Now Joab fought against Rabbah, a city of the Ammonites. And he was about to capture the royal city. ²⁷Joab sent messengers to David and said, "I have fought against Rabbah. I have captured its water supply. ²⁸Now bring the other soldiers together and attack this city. Capture it before I capture it myself. If I capture this city, it will be called by my name!"

²⁹So David gathered all the army and went to Rabbah. He fought against Rabbah and captured it. ³⁰David took the

12:25 Jedidiah This name means "loved by the Lord."

crown off their king's head. It was gold and weighed about 75 pounds. It also had gems in it. They put the crown on David's head. And David took many valuable things out of the city. ³¹He also brought out the people of the city. He made them work with saws, iron picks and axes. He also forced them to build with bricks. David did this to all the Ammonite cities. Then David and all his army went back to Jerusalem.

13 Now David had a son named Absalom and a son named Amnon. Absalom had a beautiful sister named Tamar. And Amnon loved her. ²Tamar was a virgin.ᵈ Amnon did not think he should do anything bad to her. But he wanted her very much. He made himself sick just thinking about her.

³Amnon had a friend named Jonadab son of Shimeah. (Shimeah was David's brother.) Jonadab was a very clever man. ⁴He asked Amnon, "Why do you look so sad day after day? You are the king's son! Tell me what's wrong!"

Amnon told him, "I love Tamar. But she is the sister of my half-brother Absalom."

⁵Jonadab said to Amnon, "Go to bed. Act as if you are sick. Then your father will come to see you. Tell him, 'Please let my sister Tamar come in and give me food to eat. Let her make the food in front of me. Then I will see it and eat it from her hand.'"

⁶So Amnon lay down in bed and acted as if he were sick. King David came in to see him. Amnon said to him, "Please let my sister Tamar come in. Let her make two of her special cakes for me while I watch. Then I will eat them from her hands."

⁷David sent messengers to Tamar in the palace. They told her, "Go to your brother Amnon's house and make some food for him." ⁸So Tamar went to her brother Amnon's house. He was in bed. Tamar took some dough and pressed it together with her hands. She made some special cakes while Amnon watched. Then she baked them. ⁹Next she took the pan and took out the cakes for Amnon. But he refused to eat.

He said to his servants, "All of you, leave me alone!" So all his servants left the room. ¹⁰Amnon said to Tamar, "Bring the food into the inner room. Then I'll eat from your hand."

Tamar took the cakes she had made. And she brought them to her brother Amnon in the inner room. ¹¹She went to

him so he could eat from her hands. But Amnon grabbed her. He said, "Sister, come and have sexual relations with me."

¹²Tamar said to him, "No, brother! Don't force me! This should never be done in Israel! Don't do this shameful thing! ¹³I could never get rid of my shame! And you will become like the shameful fools in Israel! Please talk with the king. He will let you marry me."

¹⁴But Amnon refused to listen to her. He was stronger than she was. So he forced her to have sexual relations with him. ¹⁵After that, Amnon hated Tamar. He hated her much more than he had loved her before. Amnon said to her, "Get up and leave!"

¹⁶Tamar said to him, "No! Sending me away would be an even greater evil. That would be worse than what you've already done!"

But he refused to listen to her. ¹⁷He called his young servant back in. Amnon said, "Get this girl out of here right now! Lock the door after her." ¹⁸So his servant led her out of the room. And he bolted the door after her.

Now Tamar was wearing a special robe with long sleeves. The king's virgin daughters wore this kind of robe. ¹⁹To show how upset she was Tamar took ashes and put them on her head. She tore her special robe. And she put her hand on her head. Then she went away, crying loudly.

²⁰Absalom, Tamar's brother, said to her, "Has Amnon, that brother of yours, forced you to have sexual relations with him? He is your brother. So for now, sister, be quiet. Don't let this upset you so much!" So Tamar lived in her brother Absalom's house. She was sad and lonely.

²¹When King David heard the news, he was very angry. ²²Absalom did not say a word, good or bad, to Amnon. He hated Amnon for forcing his sister Tamar to have sexual relations with him.

²³Two years later Absalom had some men come to Baal Hazor, near Ephraim. They were to cut the wool from his sheep. Absalom invited all the king's sons to come also. ²⁴Absalom went to the king and said, "I have men coming to cut the wool. Please come with your officers and join me."

²⁵King David said to Absalom, "No, my son. We won't all go. It would be too much trouble for you." Absalom begged

David to go. David did not go, but he did give his blessing.

²⁶Absalom said, "If you don't want to go, then please let my brother Amnon go with me."

King David asked Absalom, "Why should he go with you?"

²⁷Absalom kept begging David. Finally, David let Amnon and all the king's sons go with Absalom.

²⁸Then Absalom gave a command to his servants. He said, "Watch Amnon. When he is drunk, I will tell you, 'Kill Amnon.' Right then, kill him! Don't be afraid. I have commanded you! Be strong and brave!" ²⁹So Absalom's young men killed Amnon as Absalom commanded. But all of David's other sons got on their mules and escaped.

³⁰While the king's sons were on their way, the news came to David. The message was, "Absalom has killed all of the king's sons! Not one of them is left alive!" ³¹King David tore his clothes and lay on the ground to show his sadness. All his servants standing nearby tore their clothes also.

³²Jonadab was the son of Shimeah, David's brother. Jonadab said to David, "Don't think all the young men, your sons, are killed. No, only Amnon is dead! Absalom planned this because Amnon forced his sister Tamar to have sexual relations with him. ³³My master and king, don't think that all of the king's sons are dead. Only Amnon is dead!"

³⁴In the meantime Absalom had run away.

There was a guard standing on the city wall. He saw many people coming from the other side of the hill. ³⁵So Jonadab said to King David, "Look, I was right! The king's sons are coming!"

³⁶As soon as Jonadab had said this, the king's sons arrived. They were crying loudly. David and all his servants began crying also. They all cried very much. ³⁷David cried for his son every day.

But Absalom ran away to Talmai[n] son of Ammihud. Talmai was king of Geshur. ³⁸After Absalom ran away to Geshur, he stayed there for three years. ³⁹When King David got over Amnon's death, he missed Absalom greatly.

14 Joab son of Zeruiah knew that King David missed Absalom very much. ²So Joab sent messengers to Te-

koa to bring a wise woman from there. Joab said to her, "Please pretend to be very sad for someone. Put on clothes to show your sadness. Don't put lotion on yourself. Act like a woman who has been crying many days for someone who died. ³Go to the king. Talk to him using the words that I tell you." Then Joab told the wise woman what to say.

⁴So the woman from Tekoa talked to the king. She bowed facedown on the ground to show respect. She said, "My king, help me!"

⁵King David asked her, "What is the matter?"

The woman said, "I am a widow. My husband is dead. ⁶I had two sons. They were out in the field fighting. No one was there to stop them. So one son killed the other son. ⁷Now all the family group is against me. They said to me, 'Bring the son who killed his brother. Then we will kill him for killing his brother. That way we will also get rid of the one who would receive what belonged to his father.' My son is like the last spark of a fire. He is all I have left. If they kill him, my husband's name and property will be gone from the earth."

⁸Then the king said to the woman, "Go home. I will take care of this for you."

⁹The woman of Tekoa said to him, "Let the blame be on me. My father's family and I are to blame, my master and king. But you and your throne are innocent."

¹⁰King David said, "Bring me anyone who says anything bad to you. Then he won't bother you again."

¹¹The woman said, "Please promise in the name of the Lord your God. Then my relative who has the duty of punishing a murderer won't add to the destruction. And he won't kill my son."

David said, "As surely as the Lord lives, no one will hurt your son. Not even one hair from your son's head will fall to the ground."

¹²The woman said, "Let me say something to you, my master and king."

The king said, "Speak."

¹³Then the woman said, "Why have you planned this? It is against the people of God. When you say this, you show that you are guilty. You have not brought back your son whom you forced to leave home. ¹⁴We will all die some day. We're like water spilled on the ground. No one

13:37 **Talmai** He was Absalom's grandfather.

can gather it back. But God doesn't take away life. Instead, he plans ways that those who have been sent away will not have to stay away from him! ¹⁵My master and king, I came to say this to you because the people have made me afraid! I thought, 'Let me talk to the king. Maybe he will do what I ask. ¹⁶Maybe he will listen. Perhaps he will save me from the man who wants to kill both me and my son. That man is trying to keep us from getting what God gave us.'

¹⁷"Now I say, 'May the words of my master the king give me rest. Like an angel of God, you know what is good and what is bad. May the Lord your God be with you!'"

¹⁸Then King David said, "You must answer the question I will ask you."

The woman said, "My master the king, please ask your question."

¹⁹The king said, "Did Joab tell you to say all these things?"

The woman answered, "As you live, my master the king, you are right. Your servant Joab did tell me to say these things. ²⁰Joab did it so you would see things differently. My master, you are wise like an angel of God. You know everything that happens on earth."

²¹The king said to Joab, "Look, I will do what I promised. Now please bring back the young man Absalom."

²²Joab bowed facedown on the ground. He blessed the king. Then he said, "Today I know you are pleased with me. I know because you have done what I asked."

²³Then Joab got up and went to Geshur. And he brought Absalom back to Jerusalem. ²⁴But King David said, "Absalom must go to his own house. He may not come to see me." So Absalom went to his own house. He did not go to see the king.

²⁵Now Absalom was greatly praised for his handsome appearance. No man in Israel was as handsome as Absalom. No blemish was on him from his head to his foot. ²⁶At the end of every year, Absalom would cut the hair on his head. He cut it because it became too heavy. He would weigh it, and it would weigh about five pounds by the royal measure.

²⁷Absalom had three sons and one daughter. His daughter's name was Tamar. She was a beautiful woman.

²⁸So Absalom lived in Jerusalem for two full years without seeing King David. ²⁹Then Absalom sent for Joab. Absalom wanted to send Joab to the king. But Joab would not come. Absalom sent a message a second time. But Joab still refused to come. ³⁰Then Absalom said to his servants, "Look, Joab's field is next to mine. He has barley growing there. Go burn it." So Absalom's servants set fire to Joab's field.

³¹Then Joab went to Absalom's house. Joab said to him, "Why did your servants burn my field?"

³²Absalom said to Joab, "I sent a message to you, asking you to come here. I wanted to send you to the king. I wanted you to ask him why he brought me home from Geshur. It would have been better for me to stay there! Now let me see the king. If I have sinned, he can kill me!"

³³So Joab went to the king and told him Absalom's words. The king called for Absalom, and Absalom came. He bowed facedown on the ground before the king. And the king kissed him.

15 After this, Absalom got a chariot and horses for himself. He got 50 men to run before him. ²Absalom would get up early and stand near the city gate.[n] If anyone had a problem he wanted the king to settle, he would come here. When he came, Absalom would call to the man. Absalom would say, "What city are you from?"

The man would answer, "I'm from one of the tribes[d] of Israel."

³Then Absalom would say to him, "Look, your claims are right. But the king has no one to listen to you." ⁴Absalom would also say, "I wish someone would make me judge in this land! Then I could help everyone who comes with a problem. I could help him get a fair decision for his problem!"

⁵People would come near Absalom to bow to him. When they did, Absalom would reach out his hand and take hold of them. Then he would kiss them. ⁶Absalom did that to all the Israelites who came to King David for decisions. In this way, Absalom won the hearts of all Israel.

⁷After four years Absalom said to King David, "Please let me go to Hebron. I want to carry out my promise that I made to the Lord. ⁸I made it while I was living in Geshur in Aram. I said,

---

15:2 city gate People came here to conduct business. Public meetings and court cases were also held here.

'If the Lord takes me back to Jerusalem, I will worship him in Hebron.'"

⁹The king said, "Go in peace."

So Absalom went to Hebron. ¹⁰But he sent secret messengers through all the tribes of Israel. They told the people, "When you hear the trumpets, say this: 'Absalom has become the king at Hebron!'"

¹¹Absalom had invited 200 men to go with him. So they went from Jerusalem with him. But they didn't know what he was planning. ¹²Ahithophel was one of the people who advised David. He was from the town of Giloh. While Absalom was offering sacrifices, he called Ahithophel to come from his hometown of Giloh. So Absalom's plans were working very well. More and more people began to support him.

¹³A man came in to tell the news to David. The man said, "The Israelites are beginning to follow Absalom."

¹⁴Then David spoke to all his officers who were with him in Jerusalem. He said, "We must leave quickly! If we don't, we won't be able to get away from Absalom. We must hurry before he catches us. He would destroy us and kill the people of Jerusalem."

¹⁵The king's officers said to him, "We will do anything you say."

¹⁶The king set out with everyone in his house. But he left ten slave women[d] to take care of the palace. ¹⁷The king left with all his people following him. They stopped at the last house. ¹⁸All the king's servants passed by him. All the Kerethites and Pelethites, the king's bodyguards, passed by him. All those from Gath, the 600 men who had followed him, passed by him.

¹⁹The king spoke to Ittai, a man from Gath. He said, "Why are you also going with us? Turn back and stay with King Absalom. You are a foreigner. This is not your homeland. ²⁰Only a short time ago you came to join me. Today should I make you go with us to other places? I don't even know where I'm going. Turn back, and take your brothers with you. May kindness and loyalty be shown to you."

²¹But Ittai said to the king, "As surely as the Lord lives and as you live, I will stay with you. I'll be with you wherever you are. I'll be with you whether it means life or death."

²²David said to Ittai, "Go, march on." So Ittai from Gath and all his people with their children marched on. ²³All the people cried loudly as everyone passed by. King David also crossed the Kidron Valley. Then all the people went on to the desert. ²⁴Zadok and all the Levites with him were carrying the Box[d] of the Agreement with God. They set down the Holy Box. And Abiathar offered sacrifices until all the people had left the city.

²⁵The king said to Zadok, "Take the Holy Box of God back into the city. If the Lord is pleased with me, he will bring me back. He will let me see both it and Jerusalem again. ²⁶But if the Lord says he is not pleased with me, I am ready. He can do what he wants with me."

²⁷The king also said to Zadok the priest, "You are a seer.[d] Go back to the city in peace. Take your son Ahimaaz and Abiathar's son Jonathan with you. ²⁸I will wait near the crossings into the desert until I hear from you." ²⁹So Zadok and Abiathar took the Holy Box of God back to Jerusalem and stayed there.

³⁰David went up the Mount of Olives[d] crying as he went. He covered his head and went barefoot. All the people with David covered their heads also. And they were crying as they went. ³¹Someone told David, "Ahithophel is one of the people with Absalom who made secret plans against you."

So David prayed, "Lord, please make Ahithophel's advice foolish."

³²David came to the top of the mountain. This was where he used to worship God. Hushai the Arkite came to meet him. Hushai's coat was torn, and there was dirt on his head to show how sad he was. ³³David said to Hushai, "If you go with me, you will be just one more person to take care of. ³⁴But if you return to the city, you can make Ahithophel's advice useless. Tell Absalom, 'I am your servant, my king. In the past I served your father. But now I will serve you.' ³⁵The priests Zadok and Abiathar will be with you. You must tell them everything you hear in the king's palace. ³⁶Zadok's son Ahimaaz and Abiathar's son Jonathan are with them. Send them to tell me everything you hear." ³⁷So David's friend Hushai entered Jerusalem. About that time, Absalom also arrived there.

16 David passed a short way over the top of the Mount of Olives.[d] There Ziba, Mephibosheth's servant, met David. Ziba had two donkeys with saddles on them. They carried 200 loaves of bread, 100 cakes of raisins and 100 cakes of figs. They also carried leather bags full of wine. ²The king asked Ziba, "What are these things for?"

Ziba answered, "The donkeys are for your family to ride. The bread and cakes of figs are for the servants to eat. And the wine is for anyone to drink who becomes weak in the desert."

³The king asked, "Where is Mephibosheth?"

Ziba answered him, "Mephibosheth is staying in Jerusalem. He thinks, 'Today the Israelites will give my father's kingdom back to me!'"

⁴Then the king said to Ziba, "All right. Everything that belonged to Mephibosheth, I now give to you!"

Ziba said, "I bow to you. I hope I will always be able to please you."

⁵As King David came to Bahurim, a man came out from there. He was from Saul's family group. His name was Shimei son of Gera. Shimei came out, cursing David as he came. ⁶He began throwing stones at David and his officers. But the people and soldiers gathered all around David. ⁷Shimei cursed David. He said, "Get out, get out, you murderer, you troublemaker. ⁸The Lord is punishing you for the people in Saul's family you killed! You took Saul's place as king! But now the Lord has given the kingdom to your son Absalom! Now you are ruined because you are a murderer!"

⁹Abishai son of Zeruiah said to the king, "Why should this dead dog curse you, the king? Let me go over and cut off his head!"

¹⁰But the king answered, "This does not concern you, sons of Zeruiah! If he is cursing me because the Lord told him to, who can question him?"

¹¹David also said to Abishai and all his officers, "My own son is trying to kill me! This man is a Benjaminite and has more right to kill me! Leave him alone. Let him curse me. The Lord told him to do this. ¹²Maybe the Lord will see my misery. Then maybe he will repay me with something good for the curses Shimei says today!"

¹³So David and his men went on down the road. But Shimei kept following David. Shimei walked on the hillside on the other side of the road. He kept cursing David and throwing stones and dirt at him. ¹⁴The king and all his people ar-

rived at the Jordan. They were very tired. So they rested there.

¹⁵Meanwhile, Absalom, Ahithophel and all the men of Israel arrived at Jerusalem. ¹⁶David's friend Hushai the Arkite came to Absalom. He said to Absalom, "Long live the king! Long live the king!"

¹⁷Absalom asked, "Why are you not loyal to your friend David? Why didn't you leave Jerusalem with your friend?"

¹⁸Hushai said, "I belong to the one chosen by the Lord and by these people and all the men of Israel. I will stay with you. ¹⁹In the past I served your father. So whom should I serve now? David's son! I will serve you."

²⁰Absalom said to Ahithophel, "Please tell us what we should do."

²¹Ahithophel said, "Your father left behind some of his slave women⁴ who give birth to his children. He left them here to take care of the palace. Have sexual relations with them. Then all the Israelites will hear that your father is your enemy. And all your people will be encouraged to give you more support."

²²So they put up a tent for Absalom on the flat roof of the palace. Everyone in Israel could see it. And Absalom had sexual relations with his father's slave women.

²³At that time people thought Ahithophel's advice was as reliable as God's own word. Both David and Absalom thought it was that reliable.

17 Ahithophel said to Absalom, "Let me choose 12,000 men. I'll chase David tonight. ²I'll catch him while he is tired and weak. I'll frighten him so all his people will run away. But I'll kill only King David. ³Then I'll bring everyone back to you. If the man you are looking for is dead, everyone else will return safely." ⁴This plan seemed good to Absalom and to all the leaders of Israel.

⁵But Absalom said, "Now call Hushai the Arkite. I also want to hear what he says." ⁶So Hushai came to Absalom. Absalom said to him, "This is the plan Ahithophel gave. Should we follow it? If not, tell us."

⁷Hushai said to Absalom, "Ahithophel's advice is not good this time." ⁸Hushai added, "You know your father and his men are strong. They are as angry as a bear that is robbed of its babies. Your

---

16:22 roof In Bible times houses were built with flat roofs. The roof was used for drying things such as flax and fruit. And it was used as an extra room, as a place for worship and as a place to sleep in the summer.

father is a skilled fighter. He won't stay all night with the people. ⁹He is probably already hiding in a cave or some other place. If your father attacks your men first, people will hear the news. And they will think, 'Absalom's followers are losing!' ¹⁰Then even the men who are as brave as a lion will become frightened. This is because all the Israelites know your father is a fighter. They know his men are brave!

¹¹"This is what I suggest: Gather all the Israelites from Dan to Beersheba.ⁿ There will be as many people as grains of sand by the sea. Then you yourself must go into the battle. ¹²We will catch David where he is hiding. We will fall on him as dew falls on the ground. We will kill him and all of his men. No one will be left alive. ¹³What if David escapes into a city? Then all the Israelites will bring ropes to that city. We'll pull that city into the valley. There won't be even a small stone left there!"

¹⁴Absalom and all the Israelites said, "The advice of Hushai the Arkite is better than that of Ahithophel." They said this because the Lord had planned to destroy the good advice of Ahithophel. In this way the Lord could bring disaster on Absalom.

¹⁵Hushai told these things to Zadok and Abiathar, the priests. He told them what Ahithophel had suggested to Absalom and the older leaders of Israel. He also reported to them what he himself had suggested. Hushai said, ¹⁶"Quickly! Send a message to David. Tell him not to stay tonight at the crossings into the desert. Tell him to cross over the Jordan River at once. If he crosses the river, he and all his people won't be caught."

¹⁷Jonathan and Ahimaaz were waiting at En Rogel. They did not want to be seen going into the town. So a servant girl would go out to them and give them messages. Then Jonathan and Ahimaaz would go and tell King David.

¹⁸But a boy saw Jonathan and Ahimaaz and told Absalom. So Jonathan and Ahimaaz ran away quickly. They went to a man's house in Bahurim. He had a well in his courtyard, and they climbed down into it. ¹⁹The man's wife spread a sheet over the opening of the well. Then she covered it with grain. No one could tell that Jonathan and Ahimaaz were hiding there.

²⁰Absalom's servants came to the woman at the house. They asked, "Where are Ahimaaz and Jonathan?"

She said to them, "They have already crossed the brook."

Absalom's servants then went to look for Jonathan and Ahimaaz. But they could not find them. So they went back to Jerusalem.

²¹After Absalom's servants had left, Jonathan and Ahimaaz climbed out of the well. Then they went to tell King David. They said, "Hurry, cross over the river! Ahithophel has said these things against you!" ²²So David and all his people crossed the Jordan River. By dawn, everyone had crossed the Jordan.

²³Now Ahithophel saw that the Israelites did not accept his advice. So he saddled his donkey and went to his hometown. He gave orders for his family and property. Then he hung himself. After Ahithophel died, he was buried in his father's tomb.

²⁴David arrived at Mahanaim. And Absalom and all his Israelites crossed over the Jordan River. ²⁵Now Absalom had made Amasa captain of the army instead of Joab. Amasa was the son of a man named Jether the Ishmaelite. Amasa's mother was Abigail daughter of Nahash and sister of Zeruiah. Zeruiah was Joab's mother. ²⁶Absalom and the Israelites camped in the land of Gilead.

²⁷Shobi, Makir and Barzillai were at Mahanaim when David arrived. Shobi son of Nahash was from the Ammonite town of Rabbah. Makir son of Ammiel was from Lo Debar. And Barzillai was from Rogelim in Gilead. ²⁸They brought beds, bowls and clay pots. They brought wheat, barley, flour, roasted grain, beans and small peas. ²⁹They also brought honey and milk curds, sheep, and cheese made from cows' milk. They brought these things for David and his people. They had said, "The people have become hungry and tired and thirsty in the desert."

18 David counted his men. He chose commanders over groups of 1,000 and commanders over groups of 100. ²He sent the troops out in three groups. Joab commanded one-third of the men. Joab's brother Abishai son of Zeruiah commanded another third. And Ittai from Gath commanded the last third.

17:11 Dan to Beersheba Dan was the city farthest north in Israel. Beersheba was the city farthest south. So this means all the people of Israel.

King David said to them, "I will also go with you."

3But the men said, "No! You must not go with us! If we run away in the battle, Absalom's men won't care. Even if half of us are killed, Absalom's men won't care. But you're worth 10,000 of us! It is better for you to stay in the city. Then, if we need help, you can send it."

4The king said to his people, "I will do what you think is best." So the king stood at the side of the gate as the army went out. They went out in groups of 100 and 1,000.

5The king gave a command to Joab, Abishai and Ittai. He said, "Be gentle with young Absalom for my sake." Everyone heard the king's orders about Absalom to the commanders.

6David's army went out into the field against Absalom's Israelites. They fought in the forest of Ephraim. 7There David's army defeated the Israelites. Many died that day—20,000 men. 8The battle spread through all the country. But that day more men died in the forest than in the fighting.

9Then Absalom happened to meet David's troops. As Absalom was riding his mule, it went under a large oak tree. The branches were thick, and Absalom's head got caught in the tree. His mule ran out from under him. So Absalom was left hanging above the ground.

10When one of the men saw it happen, he told Joab. He said, "I saw Absalom hanging in an oak tree!"

11Joab said to him, "You saw him? Why didn't you kill him and let him fall to the ground? I would have given you a belt and four ounces of silver!"

12The man answered, "I wouldn't try to hurt the king's son. I wouldn't even if you gave me 25 pounds of silver. We heard the king's command to you, Abishai and Ittai. The king said, 'Be careful not to hurt young Absalom.' 13If I had killed him, the king would have found out. And you would not have protected me!"

14Joab said, "I won't waste time here with you!" Now Absalom was still alive in the oak tree. So Joab took three spears and stabbed him in the heart. 15Ten young men who carried Joab's armor also gathered around Absalom. They struck him and killed him.

16Then Joab blew the trumpet. So the troops stopped chasing Absalom's Israelites. 17Then Joab's men took Absalom's body. They threw it into a large pit in the forest. Then they filled the pit with many stones. All the Israelites who followed Absalom ran away and went home.

18When Absalom was alive, he had put up a pillar in the King's Valley. It was a monument to himself. He said, "I have no son to keep my name alive." So he named the pillar after himself. That pillar is called Absalom's Monument even today.

19Ahimaaz son of Zadok spoke to Joab. He said, "Let me run and take the news to King David. I'll tell him the Lord has destroyed the enemy for him."

20Joab answered Ahimaaz, "No, you are not the one to take the news today. You may do it another time. But do not take it today, because the king's son is dead."

21Then Joab said to a man from Cush, "Go. Tell the king what you have seen." The Cushite bowed to Joab and ran to tell David.

22But Ahimaaz son of Zadok begged Joab again. He said, "No matter what happens, please let me go, along with the Cushite!"

Joab said, "Son, why do you want to carry the news? You won't get any reward for the news you bring!"

23Ahimaaz answered, "No matter what happens, I will run."

So Joab said to Ahimaaz, "Run!" Then Ahimaaz ran by way of the Jordan Valley and passed the Cushite.

24Now David was sitting between the inner and outer gates of the city. The watchman went up to the roof by the gate walls. As he looked up, he saw a man running alone. 25He shouted to tell King David.

The king said, "If he is alone, he is bringing good news!"

The man came nearer and nearer to the city. 26Then the watchman saw another man running. The watchman called to the gatekeeper, "Look! Another man is running alone!"

The king said, "He is also bringing good news!"

27The watchman said, "I think the first man runs like Ahimaaz son of Zadok."

The king said, "Ahimaaz is a good man. He must be bringing good news!"

28Then Ahimaaz called a greeting to the king. He bowed facedown on the ground to the king. He said, "Praise the Lord your God! The Lord has defeated the men who were against you, my king."

²⁹The king asked, "Is young Absalom all right?"

Ahimaaz answered, "When Joab sent me, I saw some great excitement. But I don't know what it was."

³⁰Then the king said, "Step over here and wait." So Ahimaaz stepped aside and stood there.

³¹Then the Cushite arrived. He said, "Master and king, hear the good news! Today the Lord has punished the people who were against you!"

³²The king asked the Cushite, "Is young Absalom all right?"

The Cushite answered, "May your enemies be like that young man. May all who come to hurt you be like that young man!"

³³Then the king knew Absalom was dead. He was very upset. He went to the room over the city gate and cried. As he went, he cried out, "My son Absalom, my son Absalom! I wish I had died for you. Absalom, my son, my son!"

19 People told Joab, "Look, the king is crying. He is very sad because of Absalom." ²David's army had won the battle that day. But it became a very sad day for all the people. This was because they heard, "The king is very sad for his son." ³The people came into the city quietly. They were like people who had been defeated in battle and had run away. ⁴The king covered his face and cried loudly, "My son Absalom! Absalom, my son, my son!"

⁵Then Joab went into the king's house. He said to the king, "Today you have shamed all your men. They saved your life today! They saved the lives of your sons, daughters, wives and slave women.ᵈ ⁶You have shamed them because you love those who hate you. And you hate those people who love you. Today you've made it clear that your commanders and men mean nothing to you. What if Absalom had lived and all of us were dead? I can see you would be very pleased. ⁷Now go out and encourage your servants. I swear by the Lord that if you don't go out, no man will be left with you by tonight! That will be worse than all the troubles you have had from your youth until today."

⁸So the king went to the city gate.ᵉ The news spread that the king was at the gate. So everyone came to see him.

All the Israelites who had followed Absalom had run away to their homes. ⁹People in all the tribesᵈ of Israel began to argue. They said, "The king saved us from the Philistines and our other enemies. But he left the country because of Absalom. ¹⁰We appointed Absalom to rule us, but now he has died in battle. We should make David the king again."

¹¹King David sent a message to Zadok and Abiathar, the priests. David said, "Speak to the older leaders of Judah. Say, 'Even in my house I have heard what all the Israelites are saying. So why are you the last tribe to bring the king back to his palace? ¹²You are my brothers, my own family. Then why are you the last tribe to bring back the king?' ¹³And say to Amasa, 'You are part of my own family. May God punish me terribly if I don't make you commander of the army in Joab's place!'"

¹⁴David touched the hearts of all the people of Judah. They agreed as if they were one man. They sent a message to the king. They said, "Return with all your men." ¹⁵Then the king returned as far as the Jordan River. The men of Judah came to Gilgal to meet him. They wanted to bring the king across the Jordan River.

¹⁶Shimei son of Gera was a Benjaminite. He lived in Bahurim. He hurried down with the men of Judah to meet King David. ¹⁷With Shimei came 1,000 Benjaminites. Ziba, the servant from Saul's family, also came. He brought his 15 sons and 20 servants with him. They all hurried to the Jordan River to meet the king. ¹⁸The people went across the Jordan River to help bring the king's family back to Judah. They did whatever the king wanted. As the king was about to cross the river, Shimei son of Gera came to him. Shimei bowed facedown on the ground in front of the king. ¹⁹He said to the king, "My master, don't hold me guilty. Don't remember the wrong things I did when you left Jerusalem! Don't hold it against me. ²⁰I know I have sinned. That is why I am the first person from Joseph's family to come down and meet you today, my master and king!"

²¹But Abishai son of Zeruiah said, "Shimei should die. He cursed you, the Lord's appointed king!"

²²David said, "This does not concern you, sons of Zeruiah! Today you're

---

19:8 city gate People came here to conduct business. Public meetings and court cases were also held here.

against me! No one will be put to death
in Israel today. Today I know I am king
over Israel!'' ²³Then the king said to
Shimei, ''You won't die.'' The king made
this promise to Shimei.

²⁴Mephibosheth, Saul's grandson,
also went down to meet King David. Mephibosheth had not cared for his feet,
cut his beard or washed his clothes
while David was gone. He had not done
this from the time the king had left Jerusalem until he returned safely. ²⁵Mephib-
osheth came from Jerusalem to meet the
king. The king asked him, ''Mephibosheth, why didn't you go with me?''

²⁶He answered, ''My master, my servant Ziba tricked me! I said to Ziba, 'I
am crippled. So saddle a donkey. Then
I will ride it so I can go with the king.'
²⁷But he lied about me to you. You, my
master and king, are like an angel from
God. Do what you think is good. ²⁸You
could have killed all my grandfather's
family. Instead, you put me with the people who eat at your own table. So I don't
have a right to ask anything more from
the king!''

²⁹The king said to him, ''Don't say
anything more. I have decided that you
and Ziba may divide the land.''

³⁰Mephibosheth said to the king, ''Let
Ziba take all the land. I'm just happy
that my master the king has arrived in
peace at his own house.''

³¹Barzillai of Gilead came down from
Rogelim to cross the Jordan River with
the king. ³²Now Barzillai was a very old
man. He was 80 years old. He had taken
care of the king when David was staying
at Mahanaim. Barzillai could do this, because he was a very rich man. ³³David
said to Barzillai, ''Cross the river with
me. Come with me to Jerusalem, and I
will take care of you.''

³⁴But Barzillai answered the king, ''Do
you know how old I am? Do you think I
can go with you to Jerusalem? ³⁵I am 80
years old! I am too old to taste what I
eat or drink. I am too old to hear the
voices of men and women singers. Why
should you be bothered with me? ³⁶I am
not worthy of a reward from you. But
I will cross the Jordan River with you.
³⁷Then please let me go back so I may
die in my own city. Let me die near the
grave of my father and mother. But here
is Kimham. Let him go with you, my
master and king. Do with him whatever
you want.''

³⁸The king answered, ''Kimham will
go with me. I will do for him anything

you wish. And I will do anything for you
that you wish.'' ³⁹The king kissed Barzillai and blessed him. Then Barzillai returned home. And the king and all the
people crossed the Jordan.

⁴⁰When the king crossed the Jordan to
Gilgal, Kimham went with him. All the
troops of Judah and half the troops of
Israel led David across the river.

⁴¹Soon all the men of Israel came to
the king. They said to him, ''Our
brothers, the men of Judah, stole you
away. They brought you and your family
across the Jordan River with your men!
Why did they do this?''

⁴²All the men of Judah answered the
Israelites, ''We did this because the king
is our close relative. Why are you angry
about it? We have not eaten food at the
king's expense! He did not give us any
gifts!''

⁴³The men of Israel answered the people of Judah, ''We have ten tribes in the
kingdom. So we have more right to David than you do! But you ignored us! We
were the first ones to talk about bringing our king back!''

But the men of Judah spoke even
more unkindly than the men of Israel.

20 It happened that a troublemaker
named Sheba son of Bicri was
there. Sheba was from the tribeᵈ of Benjamin. He blew the trumpet and said:

''We have no share in David!
  We have no part in the son of
    Jesse!
  People of Israel, let's go to our own
    homes!''

²So all the Israelites left David and
followed Sheba son of Bicri. But the men
of Judah stayed with their king all the
way from the Jordan River to Jerusalem.

³David came to his palace in Jerusalem. Earlier he had left there ten of his
slave womenᵈ who gave birth to his children. He had left them there to take care
of the palace. Now he put them in a
house where they would be guarded.
They were kept there for the rest of their
lives. David gave them food, but he did
not have sexual relations with them.
They lived like widows until they died.

⁴The king said to Amasa, ''Tell the
men of Judah to meet with me in three
days. And you must also be here.'' ⁵So
Amasa went to call the men of Judah
together. But he took longer than the
time the king had told him.

⁶David said to Abishai, ''Sheba son
of Bicri is more dangerous to us than
Absalom was. Take my men and chase

him. Hurry before he finds strong, walled cities. If he gets there, he will escape from us." ⁷So Joab's men, the Kerethites and the Pelethites, who were the king's bodyguards, and all the soldiers went with Abishai. They went out from Jerusalem to chase Sheba son of Bicri.

⁸When Joab and the army came to the great rock at Gibeon, Amasa came out to meet them. Joab was wearing his uniform. At his waist he wore a belt. It held his sword in its case. As Joab stepped forward, his sword fell out of its case. ⁹Joab asked Amasa, "Brother, is everything all right with you?" Then with his right hand he took Amasa by the beard to kiss him. ¹⁰Amasa did not guard against the sword that was in Joab's hand. So Joab pushed the sword into Amasa's stomach. This caused Amasa's insides to spill on the ground. Joab did not have to stab Amasa again. He was already dead. Then Joab and his brother Abishai continued to chase Sheba son of Bicri.

¹¹One of Joab's young men stood by Amasa's body. The young man said, "Everyone who is for Joab and David should follow Joab!" ¹²Amasa lay in the middle of the road, covered with his own blood. The young man saw that everyone was stopping to look at the body. So he dragged Amasa's body from the road and laid it in a field. Then he put a cloth over it. ¹³After Amasa's body was taken off the road, all the men followed Joab. They went with him to chase Sheba son of Bicri.

¹⁴Sheba went through all the tribes of Israel to Abel Beth Maacah. All the Berites also came together and followed him. ¹⁵So Joab and his men came to Abel Beth Maacah and surrounded it. They piled dirt up against the city wall so they could attack it. And they began digging under the city walls to make them fall down.

¹⁶But a wise woman shouted out from the city. She said, "Listen! Listen! Tell Joab to come here. I want to talk to him!"

¹⁷So Joab came near her. She asked him, "Are you Joab?"

He answered, "Yes, I am."

Then she said, "Listen to what I say!"

Joab said, "I'm listening."

¹⁸Then the woman said, "In the past people would say, 'Ask for advice at Abel.' Then the problem would be solved. ¹⁹I am one of the peaceful, loyal people of Israel. You are trying to destroy an important city of Israel. Why must you destroy what belongs to the Lord?"

²⁰Joab answered, "May I not destroy or ruin anything. ²¹That is not what I want. But there is a man here from the mountains of Ephraim. He is named Sheba son of Bicri. He has turned against King David. If you will bring him to me, I will leave the city alone."

The woman said to Joab, "His head will be thrown over the wall to you."

²²Then the woman spoke very wisely to all the people of the city. They cut off the head of Sheba son of Bicri. Then they threw it over the wall to Joab. So he blew the trumpet, and the army left the city. Every man returned home. And Joab went back to the king in Jerusalem.

²³Joab was commander of all the army of Israel. Benaiah son of Jehoiada led the Kerethites and Pelethites, the king's bodyguards. ²⁴Adoniram led the men who were forced to do hard work. Jehoshaphat son of Ahilud was the recorder. ²⁵Sheba was the royal assistant. Zadok and Abiathar were the priests. ²⁶And Ira the Jairite was David's priest.

21 During the time David was king, there was a time of hunger. It continued for three years. So David prayed to the Lord.

The Lord answered, "Saul and his family of murderers are the reason for this time of hunger. It has come because Saul killed the Gibeonites." ²(Now the Gibeonites were not Israelites. They were a group of Amorites who were left alive. The Israelites had promised not to hurt the Gibeonites. But Saul was very eager to help the people of Israel and Judah. So he tried to kill all the Gibeonites.)

King David called the Gibeonites together and talked to them. ³He asked them, "What can I do for you? What can I do to take away Israel's sin so you can bless the Lord's people?"

⁴The Gibeonites said to David, "Saul and his family don't have enough silver and gold to pay for what they did! And we don't have the right to kill anyone in Israel."

Then David asked, "What do you want me to do for you?"

⁵The Gibeonites said to him, "Saul made plans against us. He tried to destroy all our people who are left in the land of Israel. ⁶Saul was the Lord's chosen king. So bring seven of his sons to

us. Then we will kill them and hang them on stakes. We will put them in front of the Lord at Gibeah, Saul's hometown."

The king said, "I will give them to you." [7]But the king protected Jonathan's son Mephibosheth. (Jonathan was Saul's son.) David did this because of the promise he had made to Jonathan in the Lord's name. So the king did not let them hurt Mephibosheth. [8]But the king did take Armoni and Mephibosheth,[n] sons of Rizpah and Saul. (Rizpah was the daughter of Aiah.) And the king took the five sons of Saul's daughter Merab. Adriel was the father of Merab's five sons. (Adriel was the son of Barzillai the Meholathite.) [9]David gave these seven sons to the Gibeonites. Then the Gibeonites killed them and hung them on stakes on a hill before the Lord. All seven sons died together. They were put to death during the first days of the harvest season. (The barley harvest was just beginning.)

[10]Aiah's daughter Rizpah took the rough cloth that was worn to show sadness. Then she put it on a rock for herself. She stayed there from the beginning of the harvest until the rain fell on her sons' bodies. During the day she did not let the birds of the sky touch her sons' bodies. At night she did not let the wild animals touch them.

[11]People told David what Aiah's daughter Rizpah, Saul's slave woman,[d] was doing. [12]Then David took the bones of Saul and Jonathan from the men of Jabesh Gilead. (They had taken these bones secretly from the public square of Beth Shan. The Philistines had hung the bodies of Saul and Jonathan there after they had killed Saul at Gilboa.) [13]David brought the bones of Saul and his son Jonathan from Gilead. Then the people gathered the bodies of Saul's seven sons who were hanged on stakes. [14]The people buried the bones of Saul and his son Jonathan at Zela in Benjamin. They buried them in the tomb of Saul's father Kish. The people did everything the king commanded.

Then God answered the prayers of the people in the land.

[15]Again there was war between the Philistines and Israel. David and his men went out to fight the Philistines. But David became tired and weak.

[16]Ishbi-Benob was one of the sons of Rapha.[d] His bronze spearhead weighed about seven and a half pounds. Ishbi-Benob had a new sword, and he planned to kill David. [17]But Abishai son of Zeruiah killed the Philistine. So he saved David's life.

Then David's men made a promise to David. They said, "Never again will you go out with us to battle. If you were killed, Israel would lose its greatest leader."

[18]Later, at Gob, there was another battle with the Philistines. Sibbecai the Hushathite killed Saph, another one of the sons of Rapha.

[19]Later, there was another battle at Gob with the Philistines. Elhanan son of Jaare-Oregim from Bethlehem killed Goliath[n] from Gath. Goliath's spear was as large as a weaver's rod.

[20]At Gath another battle took place. A very large man was there. He had 6 fingers on each hand. And he had 6 toes on each foot. He had 24 fingers and toes in all. This man also was one of the sons of Rapha. [21]When he challenged Israel, Jonathan killed him. Jonathan was the son of Shimeah, David's brother.

[22]These four men were sons of Rapha from Gath. They all were killed by David and his men.

22

David sang this song to the Lord. He sang it when the Lord had saved him from Saul and all his other enemies. [2]He said:

"The Lord is my rock, my place of
   safety, my Savior.
[3]My God is my rock.
   I can run to him for safety.
He is my shield and my saving
   strength.
The Lord is my high tower and
   my place of safety.
The Lord saves me from those
   who want to harm me.
[4]I will call to the Lord.
   He is worthy of praise.
And I will be saved from my
   enemies.

[5]"The waves of death came around
   me.
   The deadly rivers overwhelmed
   me.
[6]The ropes of death wrapped around
   me.
   The traps of death were before
   me.

21:8 **Mephibosheth** This is not Jonathan's son but another man with the same name.
21:19 **Goliath** In 1 Chronicles 20:5 he is called Lahmi brother of Goliath.

⁷In my trouble I called to the Lord.
　I cried out to my God.
From his temple he heard my voice.
　My call for help reached his ears.

⁸"The earth trembled and shook.
　The foundations of heaven began
　　to shake.
They shook because the Lord
　was angry.
⁹Smoke came out of his nose.
　Burning fire came out of his
　　mouth.
Burning coals went before him.
¹⁰He tore open the sky and came
　down.
　Dark clouds were under his feet.
¹¹He rode a creature with wings and
　flew.
　He flew on the wings of the wind.
¹²He made darkness his shelter
　around him,
　surrounded by fog and clouds.
¹³Out of the brightness of his
　presence
　came flashes of lightning.
¹⁴The Lord thundered from heaven.
　The Most High God raised his
　　voice.
¹⁵He shot his arrows and scattered
　his enemies.
　His bolts of lightning confused
　　them with fear.
¹⁶The Lord spoke strongly.
　The wind blew from his nose.
The valleys of the sea appeared.
　The foundations of the earth
　　were seen.

¹⁷"The Lord reached down from
　above and took me.
　He pulled me from the deep
　　water.
¹⁸He saved me from my powerful
　enemies.
　Those who hated me were too
　　strong for me.
¹⁹They attacked me at my time of
　trouble.
　But the Lord supported me.
²⁰He took me to a safe place.
　Because he delights in me, he
　　saved me.

²¹"The Lord spared me because I did
　what was right.
　Because I have not done evil, he
　　has rescued me.
²²I have followed the ways of the
　Lord.
　I have not done evil by turning
　　from my God.

²³I remember all his laws.
　I have not broken his rules.
²⁴I have kept myself innocent before
　him.
　I have kept myself from doing
　　evil.
²⁵The Lord rescued me because I did
　what was right.
　I did what the Lord said was
　　right.

²⁶"Lord, you are loyal to those who
　are loyal.
　You are good to those who are
　　good.
²⁷You are pure to those who are pure.
　But you are against those who
　　are bad.
²⁸You save those who are not proud.
　But you make humble those who
　　are proud.
²⁹Lord, you give light to my lamp.
　The Lord brightens the darkness
　　around me.
³⁰With your help, I can attack an
　army.
　With God's help, I can jump over
　　a wall.

³¹"The ways of God are without fault.
　The Lord's words are pure.
He is a shield to those who trust
　him.
³²Who is God? Only the Lord.
　Who is the Rock?ᵈ Only our God.
³³God is my protection.
　He makes my way free from
　　fault.
³⁴He makes me like a deer, which
　does not stumble.
　He helps me stand on the steep
　　mountains.
³⁵He trains my hands for battle.
　So my arms can bend a bronze
　　bow.
³⁶You protect me with your saving
　shield.
　You have stooped to make me
　　great.
³⁷You give me a better way to live.
　So I live as you want me to.
³⁸I chased my enemies and destroyed
　them.
　I did not quit till they were
　　destroyed.
³⁹I destroyed and crushed them,
　so they couldn't rise up again.
　They fell beneath my feet.
⁴⁰You gave me strength in battle.
　You made my enemies bow
　　before me.

⁴¹You made my enemies turn back.
    I destroyed those who hated me.
⁴²They called for help,
    but no one came to save them.
They called to the Lord,
    but he did not answer them.
⁴³I beat my enemies into pieces.
    They were like dust on the
      ground.
I pounded them out and walked on
      them
    like mud in the streets.

⁴⁴"You saved me when my people
      attacked me.
    You kept me as the leader of
      nations.
People I never knew serve me.
⁴⁵Foreigners obey me.
    As soon as they hear me, they
      obey me.
⁴⁶They all become afraid.
    They tremble in their hiding
      places.

⁴⁷"The Lord lives!
    May my Rock be praised!
    Praise God, the Rock, who saves
      me!
⁴⁸God gives me victory over my
      enemies.
    He brings people under my rule.
⁴⁹He frees me from my enemies.

"You set me over those who hate
    me.
    You saved me from cruel men.
⁵⁰So I will praise you, Lord, among
      the nations.
    I will sing praises to your name.
⁵¹The Lord gives great victories to
      his king.
    He is loyal to his appointed king,
    to David and his descendants[d]
      forever."

23 These are the last words of David.
This is the message of David son
of Jesse.
    The man made great by the Most
      High God speaks.
He is the appointed king of the God
    of Jacob.
He is the sweet singer of Israel.

²"The Lord's Spirit[d] spoke through
    me.
    His word was on my tongue.
³The God of Israel spoke.
    The Rock[d] of Israel said to me:
'The person who rules fairly over
    people,

the person who rules with
    respect for God,
⁴he is like the morning light at
    dawn.
He is like a morning without
    clouds.
He is like sunshine after a rain.
    The sunshine makes the tender
      grass grow out of the ground.'

⁵"This is how God has cared for my
    family.
God made a lasting agreement
    with me,
    good in every way and strong.
This agreement is my salvation.
This agreement is all I want.
Truly, the Lord will make it grow.

⁶"But all evil people will be thrown
    away like thorns.
    People cannot hold on to thorns.
⁷Anyone who touches them
    uses a tool of iron or a spear.
They will be thrown in the fire and
    burned where they lie."

⁸These are the names of David's warriors:

Josheb-Basshebeth, the Tahkemonite, was head of the Three.[n] He killed 800 men at one time.

⁹Next there was Eleazar son of Dodai the Ahohite. Eleazar was one of the three soldiers who were with David when they challenged the Philistines. The Philistines were gathered for battle, and the Israelites drew back. ¹⁰But Eleazar stayed where he was. He fought the Philistines until he was so tired he could not let go of his sword. The Lord gave a great victory for the Israelites that day. The people came back after Eleazar had won the battle. But they came only to take weapons and armor from the enemy.

¹¹Next there was Shammah son of Agee the Hararite. The Philistines came together to fight. They stood where there was a field full of small peas. Israel's troops ran away from the Philistines. ¹²But Shammah stood in the middle of the field. He fought for the field and killed the Philistines. And the Lord gave a great victory.

¹³Once, three of the Thirty, David's chief soldiers, came down to him during harvest. Now David was at the cave of Adullam. The Philistine army had camped in the Valley of Rephaim. ¹⁴At that time David was in a protected place.

23:8 Three These were David's most powerful soldiers. See 1 Chronicles 11:11.

And some of the Philistine soldiers were in Bethlehem.

[15]David had a strong desire for some water. He said, "Oh, I wish someone would get me water from the well near the city gate of Bethlehem!" [16]So the three warriors broke through the Philistine army. They took water out of the well near the city gate of Bethlehem. Then they took it to David. But he refused to drink it. He poured it out on the ground before the Lord. [17]David said, "Lord, I can't drink this! It would be like drinking the blood of the men who risked their lives!" So David refused to drink the water. These were the brave things that the three warriors did.

[18]Abishai was the brother of Joab son of Zeruiah. He was captain of the Three. Abishai used his spear against 300 enemies and killed them. He became as famous as the Three. [19]Abishai received even more honor than the Three. He became their commander. But he was not a member of them.

[20]Benaiah son of Jehoiada was a brave fighter from Kabzeel. He did many brave things. He killed two of the best soldiers from Moab. He also went down into a pit when it was snowing. There he killed a lion. [21]Benaiah killed a big Egyptian. The Egyptian had a spear in his hand. But Benaiah only had a club. Benaiah grabbed the spear from the Egyptian's hand. Then Benaiah killed him with his own spear. [22]These were the brave things that Benaiah son of Jehoiada did. He was as famous as the Three. [23]He received more honor than the Thirty. But he did not become a member of the Three. David made him leader of his bodyguard.

[24]The following men were among the Thirty:

Asahel the brother of Joab;
Elhanan son of Dodo from Bethlehem;
[25]Shammah the Harodite;
Elika the Harodite;
[26]Helez the Paltite;
Ira son of Ikkesh (from Tekoa);
[27]Abiezer the Anathothite;
Mebunnai the Hushathite;
[28]Zalmon the Ahohite;
Maharai the Netophathite;
[29]Heled son of Baanah the Netophathite;

Ithai son of Ribai from Gibeah of the land of Benjamin;
[30]Benaiah the Pirathonite;
Hiddai from the ravines of Gaash;
[31]Abi-Albon the Arbathite;
Azmaveth the Barhumite;
[32]Eliahba the Shaalbonite;
the sons of Jashen;
Jonathan [33]son of Shammah the Hararite;
Ahiam son of Sharar the Hararite;
[34]Eliphelet son of Ahasbai the Maacathite;
Eliam son of Ahithophel the Gilonite;
[35]Hezro the Carmelite;
Paarai the Arbite;
[36]Igal son of Nathan of Zobah; the son of Hagri;
[37]Zelek the Ammonite;
Naharai the Beerothite, who carried the armor of Joab son of Zeruiah;
[38]Ira the Ithrite;
Gareb the Ithrite;
[39]and Uriah the Hittite.

There were 37 in all.

24

The Lord was angry with Israel again. He caused David to turn against the Israelites. David said, "Go, count the people of Israel and Judah."

[2]King David spoke to Joab, the commander of the army. David said, "Go through all the tribes[d] of Israel. Go from Dan to Beersheba[n] and count the people. Then I will know how many there are."

[3]But Joab said to the king, "May the Lord your God give you 100 times more people. And may you live to see this happen. But why do you want to do this?"

[4]But the king very strongly commanded Joab and the commanders of the army. So they left the king to count the people of Israel.

[5]After crossing the Jordan River, they camped near Aroer. They camped on the south side of the city in the ravine. They went through Gad and on to Jazer. [6]Then they went to Gilead and the land of Tahtim Hodshi. Next they went to Dan Jaan and around to Sidon. [7]They went to the strong, walled city of Tyre. They also went to all the cities of the Hivites and Canaanites. Finally, they went to southern Judah, to Beersheba. [8]After 9 months and 20 days, they had

---

24:2 Dan to Beersheba Dan was the city farthest north in Israel. Beersheba was the city farthest south. So this means all the people of Israel.

gone through all the land. Then they came back to Jerusalem.

⁹Joab gave the list of the people to the king. There were 800,000 men in Israel who could use the sword. And there were 500,000 men in Judah.

¹⁰David felt ashamed after he had counted the people. He said to the Lord, "I have sinned greatly in what I have done! Lord, I beg you, forgive my sin! I have been very foolish."

¹¹Before David got up in the morning, the Lord spoke his word to Gad. He was a prophet⁴ and David's seer.ᵈ ¹²The Lord told Gad, "Go and tell David, 'This is what the Lord says: I offer you three choices. Choose one for me to do to you.'"

¹³Gad went to David and told him. Gad said, "Choose one of these three things. Should three years of hunger come to you and your land? Or should your enemies chase you for three months? Or should there be three days of disease in your country? Think about it. Then decide which of these things I should tell the Lord who sent me."

¹⁴David said to Gad, "I am really in trouble. But the Lord is very merciful. So let the Lord punish us. Don't let my punishment come from people!"

¹⁵So the Lord sent disease on Israel. It began in the morning. And it continued until the chosen time to stop. From Dan to Beersheba 70,000 people died. ¹⁶The angel raised his arm toward Jerusalem to destroy it also. But the Lord felt very sorry about the terrible things that had happened. He said to the angel who was destroying the people, "That's enough! Put down your arm!" At this time the angel of the Lord was by the threshingᵈ floor of Araunah the Jebusite.

¹⁷David saw the angel that killed the people. Then he said to the Lord, "I've sinned! I've done wrong! But these people only followed me like sheep! They did nothing wrong! Please let your punishment be against me and my father's family!"

¹⁸That day Gad came to David. Gad told him, "Go and build an altar to the Lord. Build it on the threshing floor of Araunah the Jebusite." ¹⁹So David did what Gad told him to do. He obeyed the Lord's command and went to see Araunah.

²⁰Araunah looked and saw the king and his servants coming to him. So he went out and bowed facedown on the ground. ²¹He said, "Why has my master the king come to me?"

David answered, "To buy the threshing floor from you. I want to build an altar to the Lord. Then the disease will stop."

²²Araunah said to David, "My master and king, you may take anything you want for a sacrifice. Here are some oxen for the whole burnt offering. Here are the threshing boards and the yokesᵈ for the wood! ²³My king, I give everything to you!" Araunah also said to the king, "May the Lord your God be pleased with you!"

²⁴But the king answered Araunah, "No. I will pay you for the land. I won't offer to the Lord my God burnt offerings which cost me nothing!"

So David bought the threshing floor and the oxen for one and one-fourth pounds of silver. ²⁵Then he built an altar to the Lord there. And he offered whole burnt offerings and fellowship offerings. Then the Lord answered his prayer for the country. And the disease in Israel stopped.

The First Book of the
KINGS

1 At this time King David was very old. His servants covered him with blankets, but he could not keep warm. ²So they said to him, "We will find a young woman to care for you. She will lie close to you and keep you warm." ³So the king's servants looked everywhere in Israel for a beautiful young woman. They found a girl named Abishag from the Shunammite people. They brought her to the king. ⁴The girl was very beautiful. She cared for the king and served him. But King David did not have sexual relations with her.

⁵⁻⁶Adonijah was King David and Haggith's son. He was born next after Absalom. He was a very handsome man. He said, "I will be the king." So he got char-

iots and horses for himself. And he got 50 men to run ahead of him. Now David had never interfered with him by questioning what he did.

[7] Adonijah talked with Joab son of Zeruiah. He also talked with Abiathar the priest. They told him they would help him. [8] But several men did not join Adonijah. These men were Zadok the priest, Benaiah son of Jehoiada, Nathan the prophet,[d] Shimei, Rei and King David's special guard.

[9] Then Adonijah killed some sheep, cows and fat calves for sacrifices. He made these sacrifices at the Stone of Zoheleth near the spring, En Rogel. He invited all his brothers, the other sons of King David, to come. He invited all the rulers and leaders of Judah also. [10] But Adonijah did not invite Nathan the prophet, Benaiah, his father's special guard or his brother Solomon.

[11] When Nathan heard about this, he went to Bathsheba. She was the mother of Solomon. Nathan asked her, "Have you heard what Adonijah, Haggith's son, is doing? He has made himself king. And our real king, David, does not know it. [12] Your life and the life of your son Solomon may be in danger. But I will tell you how to save yourselves. [13] Go to King David and say to him, 'My master and king, you made a promise to me. You promised that my son Solomon would be the king after you. You said he would rule on your throne. So why has Adonijah become king?' [14] While you are still talking to him, I will come in. I will tell the king that what you have said about Adonijah is true."

[15] So Bathsheba went in to see the king in his bedroom. He was now very old. Abishag, the girl from Shunam, was caring for him there. [16] Bathsheba bowed down before the king.

He asked, "What do you want?"

[17] She answered, "My master, you made a promise to me in the name of the Lord your God. You said, 'Your son Solomon will become king after me. He will rule on my throne.' [18] But now Adonijah has become king. And you did not know it. [19] Adonijah has killed many cows, fat calves and sheep for sacrifices. And he has invited all your sons. He also has invited Abiathar the priest and Joab the commander of your army. But he did not invite Solomon, your son who serves you. [20] My master and king, all the people of Israel are watching you. They are waiting for you to decide who will be

king after you. [21] As soon as you die, Solomon and I will be treated as criminals."

[22] While Bathsheba was still talking with the king, Nathan the prophet arrived. [23] The servants told the king, "Nathan the prophet is here." So Nathan went to the king and bowed facedown on the ground before him.

[24] Then Nathan said, "My master and king, have you said that Adonijah will be the king after you? Have you decided he will rule on your throne after you? [25] Today he has sacrificed many cows, fat calves and sheep. And he has invited all your other sons, the commanders of the army and Abiathar the priest. Right now they are eating and drinking with him. They are saying, 'Long live King Adonijah!' [26] But he did not invite me, Zadok the priest, Benaiah son of Jehoiada or your son Solomon. [27] Did you do this? We are your servants. Why didn't you tell us whom you chose to be the king after you?"

[28] Then King David said, "Tell Bathsheba to come in!" So she came in and stood before the king.

[29] Then the king said, "The Lord has saved me from all trouble. As surely as he lives, I make this promise to you. [30] Today I will do what I promised you in the past. I made that promise in the name of the Lord, the God of Israel. I promised that your son Solomon would be king after me. I promised he would rule on my throne after me."

[31] Then Bathsheba bowed facedown on the ground before the king. She said, "Long live my master King David!"

[32] Then King David said, "Tell Zadok the priest, Nathan the prophet[d] and Benaiah son of Jehoiada to come in here." So they came before the king. [33] Then the king said to them, "Take my servants with you and put my son Solomon on my own mule. Take him down to the spring called Gihon. [34] There Zadok the priest and Nathan the prophet should pour olive oil on him and make him king over Israel. Blow the trumpet and shout, 'Long live King Solomon!' [35] Then come back here with him. He will sit on my throne and rule in my place. I have chosen him to be the ruler over Israel and Judah."

[36] Benaiah son of Jehoiada answered the king, "This is good! And may your God make it happen. [37] The Lord has always helped you, our king. Let the Lord also help Solomon. And let King Solomon be an even greater king than you."

[38]So Zadok the priest, Nathan the prophet and Benaiah son of Jehoiada went down. The Kerethites and Pelethites, the king's bodyguards, went with them. They put Solomon on King David's mule and went with him to the spring called Gihon. [39]Zadok the priest took with him the container of olive oil from the Holy Tent.[d] He poured the olive oil on Solomon's head to show he was the king. Then they blew the trumpet. And all the people shouted, "Long live King Solomon!" [40]All the people followed Solomon into the city. They were playing flutes and shouting for joy. They made so much noise the ground shook.

[41]At this time Adonijah and all the guests with him were finishing their meal. They heard the sound from the trumpet. Joab asked, "What does all that noise from the city mean?"

[42]While Joab was speaking, Jonathan son of Abiathar the priest arrived. Adonijah said, "Come in! You are an important man. So you must be bringing good news."

[43]But Jonathan answered, "No! Our master King David has made Solomon the new king. [44]King David sent Zadok the priest, Nathan the prophet, Benaiah son of Jehoiada and all the king's bodyguards with him. They put Solomon on the king's own mule. [45]And Zadok the priest and Nathan the prophet poured olive oil on Solomon at Gihon to make him king. Then they went into the city, shouting with joy. Now the whole city is excited. That is the noise you hear. [46]Solomon has now become the king. [47]All the king's officers have come to tell King David that he has done a good thing. They are saying, 'May your God make Solomon even more famous than you. And may your God make Solomon an even greater king than you.' " Jonathan continued, "And King David bowed down on his bed to worship God. [48]He said, 'Praise the Lord, the God of Israel. Today he has made one of my sons the king and allowed me to see it.' "

[49]Then all of Adonijah's guests were afraid, and they left quickly. [50]Adonijah was also afraid of Solomon. So he went and took hold of the corners of the altar.[n] [51]Then someone told Solomon, "Adonijah is afraid of you. He is at the altar, holding on to its corners. He says, 'Tell

King Solomon to promise me today that he will not kill me.' "

[52]So Solomon answered, "Adonijah must show that he is a man of honor. If he does, I promise that he will not lose even a hair from his head. But if he does anything wrong, he will die." [53]Then King Solomon sent some men to get Adonijah. They brought him to King Solomon. So Adonijah came before King Solomon and bowed down. Then Solomon said, "Go home."

2 It was almost time for David to die. So he talked to Solomon and gave him his last commands. [2]David said, "My time to die is near. Be a good and strong leader. [3]Obey everything that the Lord commands. Follow the commands he has given us. Obey all his laws, and do what he told us. Obey what is written in the teachings of Moses. If you do these things, you will be successful in all you do and wherever you go. [4]And if you obey the Lord, he will keep the promise he made to me. He promised: 'Your descendants[d] must live as I tell them. They must have complete faith in me. If they do this, then a man from your family will always be king over the people of Israel.'

[5]"Also, you remember what Joab son of Zeruiah did to me. He killed the two commanders of Israel's armies. He killed Abner son of Ner and Amasa son of Jether. He killed them as if he and they were at war. But this was in a time of peace. He killed innocent men. And their blood got on his belt and sandals. [6]You should punish him in the way you think is wisest. (But do not let him die peacefully of old age.)

[7]"Be kind to the children of Barzillai of Gilead. Allow them to eat at your table. They helped me when I ran away from your brother Absalom.

[8]"And remember, Shimei son of Gera is here with you. He is from the people of Benjamin in Bahurim. Remember he cursed me the day I went to Mahanaim. Then he came down to meet me at the Jordan River. I promised him before the Lord, 'Shimei, I will not kill you.' [9]But you should not leave him unpunished. You are a wise man. You will know what to do to him. But you must be sure he is killed."

[10]Then David died and was buried

1:50 corners of the altar If a person were innocent of a crime, he could run into the Holy Place. If he held on to the corners of the altar there, he would not be punished. The corners looked like horns.

with his ancestors in Jerusalem. [11]He had ruled over Israel 40 years. Seven years were in Hebron, and 33 years were in Jerusalem.

[12]Now Solomon became king after David, his father. And he was in control of his kingdom.

[13]At this time Adonijah son of Haggith went to Bathsheba, Solomon's mother. Bathsheba asked, "Do you come in peace?"

Adonijah answered, "Yes. This is a peaceful visit. [14]I have something to say to you."

"You may speak," she said.

[15]Adonijah said, "You remember that at one time the kingdom was mine. All the people of Israel thought I was their king. But things changed. Now my brother is the king because the Lord chose him. [16]So now I have one thing to ask you. Please do not refuse me."

Bathsheba answered, "What do you want?"

[17]Adonijah said, "I know King Solomon will do anything you ask him. So please ask him to give me Abishag the Shunammite woman to be my wife."

[18]"Very well," she answered. "I will speak to the king for you."

[19]So Bathsheba went to King Solomon to talk to him about Adonijah. When Solomon saw her, he stood up to meet her. Then he bowed down to her and sat on the throne. He told some servants to bring another throne for his mother. Then she sat down at his right side.

[20]Bathsheba said to him, "I have one small thing to ask you. Please do not refuse me."

The king answered, "Ask, mother. I will not refuse you."

[21]So she said, "Allow Abishag the Shunammite woman to marry your brother Adonijah."

[22]King Solomon answered his mother, "Why do you ask me to give him Abishag? Why don't you ask for him to become the king also since he is my older brother? Abiathar the priest and Joab son of Zeruiah will support him!"

[23]Then King Solomon made a promise in the name of the Lord. He said, "I promise Adonijah will pay for asking me this! May God punish me terribly if it doesn't cost Adonijah his life! [24]The Lord has given me the throne that be-

longed to my father David. The Lord has kept his promise and given the kingdom to me and my people. As surely as the Lord lives, Adonijah will die today!"

[25]So King Solomon gave orders to Benaiah son of Jehoiada. And he went out and killed Adonijah.

[26]Then King Solomon said to Abiathar the priest, "I should kill you. But I will allow you to go back to your home in Anathoth. I will not kill you now because you helped to carry the Holy Box[d] of the Lord God while marching with my father David. And I know you shared in all of the hard times with my father."

[27]So Solomon removed Abiathar from being a priest to the Lord. This happened as the Lord had said it would. He had said this about the priest Eli and his family in Shiloh.

[28]When Joab heard about this, he was afraid. He had supported Adonijah, but not Absalom. So Joab ran to the Tent[d] of the Lord and took hold of the corners of the altar.[n] [29]Someone told King Solomon that Joab had run to the Tent of the Lord and was beside the altar. So Solomon ordered Benaiah to go and kill him.

[30]Benaiah went into the Tent of the Lord and said to Joab, "The king says, 'Come out!'"

But Joab answered, "No, I will die here."

So Benaiah went back to the king and told him what Joab had said. [31]Then the king commanded Benaiah, "Do as he says! Kill him there and bury him. Then my family and I will be free of the guilt of Joab. Joab is guilty of killing innocent people. [32]He killed two men who were much better than he was. They were Abner son of Ner and Amasa son of Jether. Abner was the commander of Israel's army, and Amasa was the commander of Judah's army. My father David did not know that he killed them. So the Lord will pay him back for those men he killed. [33]He and his family will be forever guilty for their deaths. But there will be peace from God for David, his descendants,[d] his family and his rule forever."

[34]So Benaiah son of Jehoiada killed Joab. And he was buried near his home in the desert. [35]Solomon then made Benaiah son of Jehoiada commander of

---

2:28 corners of the altar If a person were innocent of a crime, he could run into the Holy Place. If he held on to the corners of the altar there, he would not be punished. The corners looked like horns.

the army in Joab's place. Solomon also made Zadok the new high priest in Abiathar's place.

[36] Next the king sent for Shimei. The king said to him, "Build a house for yourself here in Jerusalem. Live in the house, and don't leave the city. [37] If you leave and go past Kidron Valley, someone will kill you. And it will be your own fault."

[38] So Shimei answered the king, "What you have said is good. I will obey you, my master and king." So Shimei lived in Jerusalem for a long time.

[39] But three years later two of Shimei's slaves ran away. They went to Achish king of Gath. He was the son of Maacah. Shimei heard that his slaves were in Gath. [40] So he put his saddle on his donkey and left. He went to Achish at Gath to find his slaves. When he found them there, he brought them back to his home.

[41] Someone told Solomon that Shimei had gone from Jerusalem to Gath and had returned. [42] So Solomon sent for Shimei. Solomon said, "I made you promise in the name of the Lord not to leave Jerusalem. I warned you that if you went anywhere else you would die. And you agreed to what I said. You said you would obey me. [43] Why did you break your promise to the Lord? Why did you not obey my command? [44] You know the many wrong things you did against my father David. Now the Lord will punish you for those wrongs. [45] But the Lord will bless me. He will make the rule of David safe before the Lord forever."

[46] Then the king ordered Benaiah to kill Shimei, and he did. Now Solomon was in full control of his kingdom.

3 Solomon made an agreement with the king of Egypt by marrying his daughter. Solomon brought her to Jerusalem. At this time Solomon was still building his palace and the Temple[d] of the Lord. He was also building a wall around Jerusalem. [2] The Temple had not yet been finished. So people were still offering animal sacrifices at altars in many places of worship. [3] Solomon showed that he loved the Lord. He did this by following the commands his father David had given him. But Solomon still used the many places of worship to offer sacrifices and to burn incense.[d]

[4] King Solomon went to Gibeon to offer a sacrifice. He went there because it was the most important place of worship. He offered 1,000 burnt offerings on that altar. [5] While he was at Gibeon, the Lord came to him in a dream during the night. God said, "Ask for anything you want. I will give it to you."

[6] Solomon answered, "You were very kind to your servant, my father David. He obeyed you. He was honest and lived right. And you showed great kindness to him when you allowed his son to be king after him. [7] Lord my God, you have allowed me to be king in my father's place. But I am like a little child. I do not have the wisdom I need to do what I must do. [8] I, your servant, am here among your chosen people. There are too many of them to count. [9] So I ask that you give me wisdom. Then I can rule the people in the right way. Then I will know the difference between right and wrong. Without wisdom, it is impossible to rule this great people of yours."

[10] The Lord was pleased that Solomon had asked him for this. [11] So God said to him, "You did not ask for a long life. And you did not ask for riches for yourself. You did not ask for the death of your enemies. Since you asked for wisdom to make the right decisions, [12] I will give you what you asked. I will give you wisdom and understanding. Your wisdom will be greater than anyone has had in the past. And there will never be anyone in the future like you. [13] Also, I will give you what you did not ask for. You will have riches and honor. During your life no other king will be as great as you. [14] I ask you to follow me and obey my laws and commands. Do this as your father David did. If you do, I will also give you a long life."

[15] Then Solomon woke up. He knew that God had talked to him in the dream. Then he went to Jerusalem and stood before the Box[d] of the Agreement with the Lord. There he gave burnt offerings and fellowship offerings to the Lord. After that, he gave a feast for all of his leaders and officers.

[16] One day two women who were prostitutes[d] came to Solomon. They stood before him. [17] One of the women said, "My master, this woman and I live in the same house. I gave birth to a baby while she was there with me. [18] Three days later this woman also gave birth to a baby. No one else was in the house with us. There were only the two of us. [19] One night this woman rolled over on her baby, and it died. [20] So during the night she took my son from my bed while I

was asleep. She carried him to her bed. Then she put the dead baby in my bed. [21]The next morning I got up to feed my baby. But I saw that he was dead! Then I looked at him more closely. I saw that he was not my son."

[22]But the other woman said, "No! The living baby is my son. The dead baby is yours!"

But the first woman said, "No! The dead baby is yours, and the living one is mine!" So the two women argued before the king.

[23]Then King Solomon said, "Each of you says the living baby is your own. And each of you says the dead baby belongs to the other woman."

[24]Then King Solomon sent his servants to get a sword. When they brought it to him, [25]he said, "Cut the living baby into two pieces. Give each woman half of the baby."

[26]The real mother of the living child was full of love for her son. She said to the king, "Please, my master, don't kill him! Give the baby to her!"

But the other woman said, "Neither of us will have him. Cut him into two pieces!"

[27]Then King Solomon said, "Give the baby to the first woman. Don't kill him. She is the real mother."

[28]When the people of Israel heard about King Solomon's decision, they respected him very much. They saw he had wisdom from God to make the right decisions.

4 King Solomon ruled over all Israel. [2]These are the names of his leading officers:

Azariah son of Zadok was the priest;

[3]Elihoreph and Ahijah, sons of Shisha, recorded what happened in the courts;

Jehoshaphat son of Ahilud recorded the history of the people;

[4]Benaiah son of Jehoiada was commander of the army;

Zadok and Abiathar were priests;

[5]Azariah son of Nathan was in charge of the district governors;

Zabud son of Nathan was a priest and adviser to the king;

[6]Ahishar was responsible for everything in the palace;

Adoniram son of Abda was in charge of the slaves.

[7]Solomon placed 12 governors over the districts of Israel. They had to gather food from their districts. Then they were to give it to the king and his family. Each

governor was responsible for giving food to the king one month of each year. [8]These are the names of the 12 governors:

Ben-Hur was governor over the mountain country of Ephraim.

[9]Ben-Deker was governor over Makaz, Shaalbim, Beth Shemesh and Elon Bethhanan.

[10]Ben-Hesed was governor over Arubboth, Socoh and Hepher.

[11]Ben-Abinadab was governor over Naphoth Dor. (He was married to Taphath daughter of Solomon.)

[12]Baana son of Ahilud was governor over Taanach, Megiddo and all of Beth Shan next to Zarethan. (This was below Jezreel from Beth Shan to Abel Meholah across Jokmeam.)

[13]Ben-Geber was governor over Ramoth in Gilead. (He was governor over all the Towns of Jair in Gilead. Jair was the son of Manasseh. Ben-Geber was also over the district of Argob in Bashan. It had 60 large, walled cities with bronze bars on their gates.)

[14]Ahinadab son of Iddo was governor over Mahanaim.

[15]Ahimaaz was governor over Naphtali. (He was married to Basemath daughter of Solomon.)

[16]Baana son of Hushai was governor over Asher and Aloth.

[17]Jehoshaphat son of Paruah was governor over Issachar.

[18]Shimei son of Ela was governor over Benjamin.

[19]Geber son of Uri was governor over Gilead. (Gilead was the country where Sihon king of the Amorite people lived. Og king of Bashan also lived there.) But Geber was the only governor over the district.

[20]There were many people in Judah and Israel. There were as many people as there were grains of sand on the seashore. The people ate, drank and were happy. [21]Solomon ruled over all the kingdoms from the Euphrates River to the land of the Philistine people. His kingdom went as far as the border of Egypt. These countries brought Solomon the payments he demanded. And they obeyed him all his life.

[22]Solomon needed much food each day to feed himself and all the people who ate at his table. It took 185 bushels of fine flour and 375 bushels of meal. [23]It also took 10 cows that were fed good grain, 20 cows that were raised in the

fields and 100 sheep. And it took 3 different kinds of deer and fat birds.

[24] Solomon ruled over all the countries west of the Euphrates River. This was the land from Tiphsah to Gaza. And Solomon had peace on all sides of his kingdom. [25] During Solomon's life Judah and Israel, from Dan to Beersheba,[n] lived in peace. Each man was able to sit under his own fig trees and grapevines.

[26] Solomon had 4,000 stalls for his chariot horses. And he had 12,000 chariot soldiers. [27] Each month one of the district governors gave King Solomon all the food he needed. This was enough for every person who ate at the king's table. The governors made sure he had everything he needed. [28] They also gave the king enough barley and straw for the chariot and work horses. Each person brought this grain to the required places.

[29] God gave great wisdom to Solomon. Solomon could understand many things. His wisdom was as hard to measure as the sand on the seashore. [30] His wisdom was greater than the wisdom of all the men in the East. And his wisdom was greater than all the wisdom of the men in Egypt. [31] He was wiser than any other man on earth. He was even wiser than Ethan the Ezrahite. He was wiser than Heman, Calcol and Darda. They were the sons of Mahol. King Solomon became famous in all the countries around Israel and Judah. [32] During his life King Solomon spoke 3,000 wise teachings. He also knew 1,005 songs. [33] He taught about many different kinds of plants. He taught about everything from the great cedar trees of Lebanon to the hyssop that grows out of the walls. He also taught about animals, birds, crawling things and fish. [34] People from all nations came to listen to King Solomon's wisdom. The kings of all nations sent them to listen to him. These kings had heard of Solomon's wisdom.

5 Now King Hiram was the king of Tyre. He had always been a friend of David. Hiram heard that Solomon had been made king in David's place. So he sent his messengers to Solomon. [2] Then Solomon sent this message back to King Hiram: [3] "You remember that my father David had to fight many wars with the countries around him. So he was never able to build a temple for worship to the Lord his God. David was waiting until the Lord allowed him to defeat all his enemies. [4] But now the Lord my God has given me peace. There is peace on all sides of my country. I have no enemies now. My people are in no danger.

[5] "The Lord made a promise to my father David. The Lord said, 'I will make your son king after you. And he will build a temple for worship to me.' Now, I plan to build that temple for worship to the Lord my God. [6] And so I ask for your help. Send your men to cut down cedar trees for me from Lebanon. My servants will work with yours. I will pay your servants whatever wages you decide. We don't have anyone who can cut down trees as well as the people of Sidon can."

[7] When Hiram heard what Solomon asked, he was very happy. He said, "I thank the Lord today! He has given David a wise son to rule over this great nation!" [8] Then Hiram sent back this message to Solomon: "I received the message you sent. I will give you all the cedar and pine trees you want. [9] My servants will bring them down from Lebanon to the sea. There I will tie them together. Then I will float them down the shore to the place you choose. There I will separate the logs, and you can take them away. In return you will give food to all those who live with me." [10] So Hiram gave Solomon as much cedar and pine as he wanted. [11] And Solomon gave Hiram about 125,000 bushels of wheat each year. It was to feed all those who lived with Hiram. And Solomon gave him about 115,000 gallons of pure olive oil every year.

[12] The Lord gave wisdom to Solomon as he had promised. And there was peace between Hiram and Solomon. These two kings made a treaty between themselves.

[13] King Solomon forced 30,000 men of Israel to help in this work. [14] He put a man named Adoniram over them. Solomon sent a group of 10,000 men each month to Lebanon. So each group worked in Lebanon one month. Then it went home for two months. [15] Solomon forced 80,000 men to work in the hill country, cutting stone. And he had 70,000 men to carry the stones. [16] There were also 3,300 men who directed the workers. [17] King Solomon commanded

---

4:25 Dan to Beersheba Dan was the city farthest north in Israel. Beersheba was the city farthest south. So this means all the people of Israel.

them to cut large blocks of fine stone. These were to be used for the foundation of the Temple.[d] [18]Solomon's and Hiram's builders and the men from Byblos carved the stones. They prepared the stones and the logs for building the Temple.

6 So Solomon began to build the Temple.[d] This was 480 years after the people of Israel had left Egypt. (This was the fourth year of King Solomon's rule over Israel.) It was the second month, the month of Ziv.

[2]The Temple was 90 feet long and 30 feet wide. It was 45 feet high. [3]The porch in front of the main room of the Temple was 15 feet deep and 30 feet wide. The room ran along the front of the Temple itself. Its width was equal to the width of the Temple. [4]There were narrow windows in the Temple. These windows were narrow on the outside and larger on the inside. [5]Then Solomon built some side rooms against the walls of the main room of the Temple. These rooms were built on top of each other. [6]The rooms on the bottom floor were 7½ feet wide. The rooms on the middle floor were 9 feet wide. The rooms above that were 10½ feet wide. The Temple wall which made the side of each room was thinner than the wall in the room below. The rooms were pushed against the wall but did not have their main beams built into the wall.

[7]The stones were prepared at the same place they were cut from the ground. Only these stones were used to build the Temple. So there was no noise of hammers, axes or any other iron tools at the Temple.

[8]The entrance to the bottom rooms built beside the Temple was on the south side. From there, stairs went up to the second floor rooms. And from there, they went on to the third floor rooms. [9]Solomon put a roof made from beams and cedar boards on the Temple. So he finished building the Temple. [10]He also finished building the bottom floor that was beside the Temple. It was 7½ feet high. It was attached to the Temple by cedar beams.

[11]The Lord spoke his word to Solomon: [12]"Obey all my laws and commands. If you do, I will do for you what I promised your father David. [13]And I will live among the children of Israel in this Temple you are building. I will never leave the people of Israel."

[14]So Solomon finished building the Temple. [15]The inside walls were covered from floor to ceiling with cedar boards. The floor was made from pine boards. [16]A room 30 feet long was built in the back part of the Temple. It was divided from the rest of the Temple by cedar boards reaching from floor to ceiling. It was called the Most Holy Place. [17]The main room, the room in front of the Most Holy Place, was 60 feet long. [18]Inside the Temple was cedar. It was carved with pictures of flowers and plants. Everything inside was covered with cedar. So a person could not see the stones of the wall.

[19]He prepared the inner room at the back of the Temple to keep the Box[d] of the Agreement with the Lord. [20]This inner room was 30 feet long, 30 feet wide and 30 feet high. Solomon covered this room with pure gold. He built an altar of cedar and covered it also. [21]He covered the inside of the Temple with pure gold. And he placed gold chains across the front of the inner room. It was covered with gold. [22]So all the inside of the Temple was covered with gold. Also the altar in the Most Holy Place was covered with gold.

[23]Solomon made two creatures with wings from olive wood. Each creature was 15 feet tall. They were put in the Most Holy Place. [24]Each creature had two wings. Each wing was 7½ feet long. So it was 15 feet from the end of one wing to the end of the other wing. [25]The creatures were the same size and shape. [26]And each was 15 feet tall. [27]These creatures were put beside each other in the Most Holy Place. Their wings were spread out. So one creature's wing touched one wall. The other creature's wing touched the other wall. And their wings touched each other in the middle of the room. [28]The two creatures were covered with gold.

[29]All the walls around the Temple were carved. They were carved with pictures of creatures with wings, palm trees and flowers. This was true for both the main room and the inner room. [30]The floors of both rooms were covered with gold.

[31]Doors made from olive wood were put at the entrance to the Most Holy Place. The doors were made to fit into an area with five sides. [32]Creatures with wings, palm trees and flowers were carved on the two olive wood doors. Then the doors were covered with gold.

And the creatures and the palm trees were covered with gold. ³³At the entrance to the main room there was a door frame. It was square and was made of olive wood. ³⁴Two doors were made from pine. Each door had two parts so that the doors folded. ³⁵The doors were covered with pictures of creatures with wings, palm trees and flowers. And all of the carvings were covered with gold. The gold was smoothed over the carvings.

³⁶The inner courtyard was built and enclosed with walls. The walls were made of three rows of cut stones and one row of cedar boards.

³⁷Work began on the Temple in Ziv, the second month. This was during the fourth year Solomon ruled over Israel. ³⁸The Temple was finished during the eleventh year Solomon ruled. It was finished in the eighth month, the month of Bul. It was finished exactly as it was planned. Solomon had worked seven years to build the Temple.

7 King Solomon also built a palace for himself. It took him 13 years to finish building it. ²He built the Palace of the Forest of Lebanon. It was 150 feet long, 75 feet wide and 45 feet high. It had four rows of cedar columns. They supported the cedar beams. ³The ceiling was covered with cedar above the beams. There were 45 beams on the roof, with 15 beams in each row. ⁴Windows were placed in three rows facing each other. ⁵All the doors were square. The three doors at each end faced each other.

⁶Solomon also built the porch of pillars. It was 75 feet long and 45 feet wide. Along the front of the porch, there was a covering supported by pillars. ⁷Solomon also built a throne room where he judged people. He called this the Hall of Justice. The room was covered with cedar from the floor to the ceiling. ⁸The palace where Solomon was to live was behind the Hall of Justice. And it was built like the Hall of Justice. Solomon also built the same kind of palace for his wife. She was the daughter of the king of Egypt.

⁹All these buildings were made with blocks of carefully cut fine stone. Then they were trimmed with a saw in the front and back. These fine stones went from the foundations of the buildings to the top of the walls. Even the courtyard was made with blocks of stone. ¹⁰The foundations were made with large blocks of fine stone. Some of the stones were 15 feet long. Others were 12 feet long. ¹¹On top of those stones there were other cut blocks of fine stone and cedar beams. ¹²The palace courtyard, the courtyard inside the Templeᵈ and the porch to the Temple were surrounded by walls. All of these walls had three rows of cut stone blocks and one row of cedar beams.

¹³King Solomon sent to Tyre and had Huram brought to him. ¹⁴Huram's mother was a widow from the tribeᵈ of Naphtali. His father was from Tyre and had been skilled in making things from bronze. Huram was also very skilled and experienced in bronze work. So he came to King Solomon. And he did all the bronze work Solomon wanted.

¹⁵He made two bronze pillars. Each one was 27 feet tall and 18 feet around. ¹⁶He also made two bronze capitalsᵈ that were 7½ feet tall. He put them on top of the pillars. ¹⁷Then he made a net of seven chains for each capital. They covered the capitals on top of the two pillars. ¹⁸Then he made two rows of bronze pomegranatesᵈ to go on the nets. They were to cover the capitals at the top of the pillars. ¹⁹The capitals on top of the pillars in the porch were shaped like lilies. They were 6 feet tall. ²⁰The capitals were on top of both pillars. They were above the bowl-shaped section and next to the nets. At that place there were 200 pomegranates in rows all around the capitals. ²¹Huram put these two bronze pillars at the porch of the Temple.ᵈ He named the south pillar He Establishes. And he named the north pillar In Him Is Strength. ²²The capitals on top of the pillars were shaped like lilies. So the work on the pillars was finished.

²³Then Huram made a large round bowl from bronze, which was called the Sea. It was 45 feet around. It was 15 feet across and 7½ feet deep. ²⁴There was a rim around the outer edge of the bowl. Under this rim there were two rows of bronze plants surrounding the bowl. There were ten plants in every 18 inches. They were made in one piece with the bowl. ²⁵The bowl rested on the backs of 12 bronze bulls. They faced outward from the center of the bowl. Three bulls faced north, 3 faced east, 3 faced south and 3 faced west. ²⁶The sides of the bowl were 4 inches thick. The rim was like the rim of a cup or like a lily blossom. The bowl held about 11,000 gallons.

27Then Huram made ten bronze stands. Each one was 6 feet long, 6 feet wide and 4½ feet high. 28The stands were made from square sides, which were put on frames. 29On the sides were bronze lions, bulls and creatures with wings. On the frames above and below the lions and bulls there were designs of flowers hammered into the bronze. 30Each stand had four bronze wheels with bronze axles. At the corners there were bronze supports for a large bowl. The supports had designs of flowers. 31There was a frame on top of the bowls. It was 18 inches high above the bowls. The opening of the bowl was round, 27 inches deep. There were designs carved into the bronze on the frame. The frame was square, not round. 32The four wheels were under the frame. They were 27 inches high. The axles between the wheels were made as one piece with the stand. 33The wheels were like a chariot's wheels. Everything on the wheels was made of bronze. The axles, rims, spokes and hubs were made of bronze.

34The four supports were on the four corners of each stand. They were made as one piece with the stand. 35There was a strip of bronze around the top of each stand. It was 9 inches deep. It was made as one piece with the stand. 36The sides of the stand and the frames were totally covered with carvings. They were carved with pictures of creatures with wings, lions and palm trees. There were also flowers carved all around. 37So this is the way Huram made the ten stands. The bronze for each stand was melted and poured into a mold. So all of the stands were the same size and shape.

38Huram also made ten bronze bowls. There was one bowl for each of the ten stands. Each bowl was six feet across and could hold about 230 gallons. 39Huram put five of the stands on the south side of the Temple. And he put the other five stands on the north side. He put the large bowl in the southeast corner of the Temple. 40Huram also made bowls, shovels and small bowls.

So Huram finished making everything King Solomon wanted him to make. Here is a list of what Huram made for the Temple of the Lord:

41two pillars;

two large bowls for the capitals on top of the pillars;

two nets to cover the two large bowls for the capitals on top of the pillars;

42400 pomegranates for the two nets (there were two rows of pomegranates for each net covering the bowls for the capitals on top of the pillars);

43ten stands with a bowl on each stand;

44the large bowl with 12 bulls under it;

45the pots, shovels, small bowls and all the dishes for the Temple of the Lord.

Huram made everything King Solomon wanted. They were all made from polished bronze. 46The king ordered these things to be made near the Jordan River between Succoth and Zarethan. They were made by melting and pouring bronze into clay molds. 47Solomon never weighed the bronze used to make these things. There was too much to weigh. So the total weight of all the bronze was never known.

48Solomon also commanded that many things be made of gold for the Temple:

the golden altar;

the golden table which held the bread that shows God's people are in his presence;

49the lampstands of pure gold (five on the right side and five on the left side in front of the Most Holy Place);

the gold flowers, lamps and tongs;

50the pure gold bowls, wick trimmers, small bowls, pans and dishes used to carry coals;

the hinges for the doors of the Most Holy Place and the main room of the Temple.

51So the work King Solomon did for the Temple of the Lord was finished. David, Solomon's father, had saved silver, gold and other articles for the Temple. So Solomon brought these things into the Temple. And he put them into the treasuries of the Temple of the Lord.

8 Then King Solomon called for all the leaders of Israel to come to him in Jerusalem. He called for the older leaders, the heads of the tribes[d] and the leaders of the families. He wanted them to bring the Box[d] of the Agreement with the Lord from the older part of the city. 2So all the men of Israel came together with King Solomon. This was during a festival in the month of Ethanim. That is the seventh month. 3All of the older leaders of Israel arrived. Then the priests took up the Holy

Box. [4]They carried the Holy Box of the Lord, the Meeting Tent[d] and the holy things in it. The Levites helped the priests carry these things. [5]King Solomon and all the people of Israel gathered before the Box of the Agreement. They sacrificed so many sheep and cattle no one could count them all. [6]Then the priests put the Box of the Agreement with the Lord in its right place. This was inside the Most Holy Place in the Temple.[d] The Box of the Agreement was put under the wings of the golden creatures. [7]The wings of the creatures were spread out over the place of the Holy Box. So they covered it and its carrying poles. [8]The carrying poles were very long. Anyone standing in the Holy Place in front of the Most Holy Place could see the ends of the poles. But no one could see them from outside the Holy Place. The poles are still there today. [9]The only things inside the Holy Box were two stone tablets.[n] Moses had put them in the Holy Box at Mount Sinai. That was where the Lord made his agreement with the Israelites after they came out of Egypt.

[10]When the priests left the Holy Place, the cloud filled the Temple of the Lord. [11]The priests could not continue their work. This was because the Temple was filled with the glory of the Lord.

[12]Then Solomon said, "The Lord said he would live in a dark cloud. [13]Lord, I have truly built a wonderful Temple[d] for you. It is a place for you to live forever."

[14]While all the people of Israel were standing there, King Solomon turned to them and blessed them.

[15]Then he prayed: "Praise the Lord, the God of Israel. He himself has done what he promised to my father David. The Lord told my father, [16]'I brought my people Israel out of Egypt. But I have not yet chosen a city in any tribe[d] of Israel where a temple will be built for worshiping me. But I have chosen David to rule over my people Israel.'

[17]"My father David wanted to build a temple for worshiping the Lord, the God of Israel. [18]But the Lord said to my father David, 'I know you want to build a temple for worshiping me. And this is good. [19]But you are not the one to build the temple. It will be your son, who comes from your own body. He is the one who will build my temple.'

[20]"So the Lord has kept the promise that he gave. I am the king now in place of David my father. Now I rule Israel as the Lord promised. And I have built the Temple for worshiping the Lord, the God of Israel. [21]I have made a place in the Temple for the Holy Box. Inside that Box is the agreement the Lord made with our ancestors. He made that agreement when he brought them out of Egypt."

[22]Then Solomon stood facing the Lord's altar. All of the people of Israel were standing behind him. He spread out his hands and looked toward the sky. [23]He said:

"Lord, God of Israel, there is no god like you. There is no god like you in heaven above or on the earth below. You make agreements with your people because you love them. And you keep your agreements with those who truly follow you. [24]You have kept the promise you made to your servant David, my father. You made that promise with your own mouth. And with your great power you have made it come true today. [25]Now Lord, God of Israel, keep the other promises you made to your servant David, my father. You said, 'Your sons must be careful to obey me as you have obeyed me. If they do this, there will always be someone from your family ruling Israel.' [26]Again, Lord, God of Israel, I ask you. Please continue to keep that promise you made to my father.

[27]"But, God, can you really live here on the earth? Even the sky and the highest place in heaven cannot contain you. Certainly this house which I have built cannot contain you either. [28]But please listen to my prayer and my request. I am your servant, and you are the Lord my God. Hear this prayer I am praying to you today. [29]In the past you said, 'I will be worshiped there.' So please watch over this Temple[d] night and day. Hear the prayer I pray to you here. [30]Hear my prayers and the prayers of your people Israel. Please hear us when we pray facing this place. Hear us from your home in heaven. And when you hear us, forgive us.

[31]"If a person does something wrong against someone else, he will be brought to the altar in this Temple. If he swears an oath that he is not guilty, [32]then hear in heaven. Judge the man. Punish the guilty person for what he has done. And

8:9 stone tablets They were the two tablets on which God wrote the Ten Commandments.

declare that the innocent person is not guilty.

[33] "Sometimes your people of Israel will sin against you. Because of this their enemies will defeat them. Then the people will come back to you and praise you. They will pray to you in this Temple. [34] Please hear them in heaven. Forgive the sins of your people Israel. Allow them to have their land again. This is the land you gave to their ancestors.

[35] "Sometimes when they sin against you, you will stop the rain from falling on their land. Then they will pray, facing this place. They will praise you. They will stop sinning when you make them suffer. [36] When this happens, please hear their prayer in heaven. Then forgive the sins of your servant. And forgive the sins of the people of Israel. Teach them to do what is right. Then please send rain to this land you gave them.

[37] "At times the land will become so dry that no food will grow. Or, a great sickness will spread among the people. Sometimes all the crops will be destroyed by locusts[d] or grasshoppers. Your people will be attacked in their cities by their enemies. Your people will become sick. [38] When any of these things happen, the people will become truly sorry. If anyone of your people Israel spreads his hands in prayer toward this Temple, [39] please hear his prayer. Hear it from your home in heaven. Then forgive the people and help them. Only you know what people are really thinking. So judge each person, and do to him what is right. [40] Do this so your people will respect you all the time they live in this land. This is the land you gave to our ancestors.

[41-42] "People who are not Israelites, who come from other lands, will hear about your greatness and power. They will come from far away to pray at this Temple. [43] Please hear their prayers from your home in heaven. Please do whatever they ask you. Then people everywhere will know you and respect you, as your people in Israel do. Then everyone will know I built this Temple for worship to you.

[44] "Sometimes you will command your people to go and fight against their enemies. Then your people will pray to you facing this city which you have chosen. They will pray facing the Temple I have built for your worship. [45] When they pray, hear their prayers from your home in heaven. Then help them.

[46] "Everyone sins. So your people will also sin against you. And you will become angry with your people. You will let their enemies defeat them. Their enemies will make them prisoners and carry them away to their own countries. [47] Your people might be sorry for their sins when they are held as prisoners in another country. Perhaps they will be sorry and pray to you in the land where they are held as prisoners. They might say, 'We have sinned and done wrong.' [48] They may truly turn back to you in the land of their enemies. Perhaps they will pray to you, facing this land you gave their fathers. They may pray to you, facing this city you have chosen. They may face this Temple I have built for your worship. [49] If they do, then please hear them from your home in heaven. Hear their prayers and do what is right. [50] Forgive your people of all their sins. And forgive them for turning against you. Make those who have taken them as prisoners show them mercy. [51] Remember that they are your people. Remember that you brought them out of Egypt. It was as if you pulled them out of a blazing furnace!

[52] "Please give your attention to my prayers. And please give your attention to the prayers of your people Israel. Listen to their prayers anytime they ask you for help. [53] You chose them from all the nations on earth to be your very own people. This is what you promised through Moses your servant. You promised it when you brought our ancestors out of Egypt, Lord God."

[54] Solomon prayed this prayer to the Lord. He had been kneeling in front of the altar. And his arms had been raised toward heaven. When Solomon finished praying, he stood up. [55] Then, in a loud voice, he blessed all the people of Israel. Solomon said: [56] "Praise the Lord! He promised he would give rest to his people Israel. And he has given us rest! The Lord has kept all the good promises he gave through his servant Moses. [57] I ask that the Lord our God be with us. May he be with us as he was with our ancestors. May he never leave us. [58] May he cause us to turn to him and follow him. May we obey all the laws and commands he gave our ancestors. [59] I ask that the Lord our God always remember this prayer. I pray that he will help his servant and his people Israel. I pray he will help us every day as we need it. [60] Then all the people of the world will

know the Lord is the only true God. [61]So you must fully obey the Lord our God. You must follow all his laws and commands. You must continue to obey in the future as you do now."

[62]Then King Solomon and all Israel with him offered sacrifices to the Lord. [63]Solomon killed 22,000 cattle and 120,000 sheep. These were fellowship offerings. In this way the king and the Israelites showed they had given the Temple[d] to the Lord.

[64]Also that day King Solomon made the courtyard before the Temple holy. He offered whole burnt sacrifices and grain offerings. He also offered the fat from the fellowship offerings. He had to make these offerings in the courtyard. This was because the bronze altar before the Lord was too small. It could not hold all the offerings.

[65]So King Solomon and all the people of Israel also celebrated the other festival that came at that time. People came from as far away as Lebo Hamath in the north. And they came from as far as the brook of Egypt in the south. A great many people were there. They ate, drank and rejoiced before the Lord for a total of 14 days. [66]On the following day Solomon sent the people home. So they blessed the king and went home. They were happy because of all the good things the Lord had done for his servant David and for his people, Israel.

9 So Solomon finished building the Temple[d] of the Lord and his royal palace. Solomon finished building everything he wanted to build. [2]Then the Lord appeared to him again. This was just as he had done before, in Gibeon. [3]The Lord said to him: "I have heard your prayer. I have heard what you asked me to do. You built this Temple. And I have made it a holy place. So I will be worshiped there forever. I will watch over it and protect it always.

[4]"But you must serve me as your father David did. He was fair and sincere. You must obey my laws and do everything I command. [5]If you do these things, I will allow your family to rule Israel forever. I made this promise to your father David. I told him that someone from his family would always be king over Israel.

[6]"But you and your children must follow me. You must obey the laws and commands I have given you. You must

not go off to serve or worship other gods. [7]If you do, I will force Israel to leave the land I have given them. I made the Temple holy for people to worship me there. But if you don't obey me, I will tear it down. Then Israel will become a bad example, a joke, to other people. [8]If the Temple is destroyed, everyone who sees it will be shocked. They will make fun of you and ask, 'Why did the Lord do this? Why did he do this terrible thing to this land and this Temple?' [9]Other people will answer, 'This happened because they left the Lord their God. He brought their ancestors out of Egypt. But they decided to follow other gods. They worshiped and served those gods. That is why the Lord brought all this disaster to them.'"

[10]By the end of 20 years, King Solomon had built the Temple[d] of the Lord. And he had built the royal palace. [11]At that time King Solomon gave 20 towns in Galilee to Hiram king of Tyre. Solomon did this because Hiram had helped with the buildings. Hiram had given him all the cedar, pine and gold he wanted. [12]So Hiram traveled from Tyre to see the towns Solomon had given him. When Hiram saw them, he was not pleased. [13]He asked, "What are these towns you have given me, my brother?" So he named that land the Land of Cabul.[n] And it is still called that today. [14]Hiram had sent to King Solomon about 9,000 pounds of gold.

[15]King Solomon had forced slaves to build the Temple and the palace. Then he had them fill in the land on the east side of the city. And he had them build the wall around Jerusalem. He also had them rebuild the cities of Hazor, Megiddo and Gezer. [16](In the past the king of Egypt had attacked Gezer and captured it. He had burned it and killed the Canaanites who lived there. Then he gave it to his daughter as a wedding present. His daughter married Solomon. [17]So Solomon rebuilt it.) He also built the cities of Lower Beth Horon, [18]Baalath and Tadmor, which is in the Judean desert. [19]King Solomon also built cities where he could store grain and supplies. And he built cities for his chariots and chariot soldiers. Solomon built whatever he wanted in Jerusalem, Lebanon and everywhere he ruled.

[20]There were people in the land who were not Israelites. There were some

9:13 **Cabul** This name sounds like the Hebrew word for "worthless."

Amorites, Hittites, Perizzites, Hivites and Jebusites. [21]The Israelites had not been able to destroy them from the land. So Solomon forced them to work for him as slaves. And they are still slaves today. [22]But Solomon did not force any Israelites to be his slaves. The Israelites were his soldiers, government leaders, officers, captains and chariot commanders and drivers.

[23]There were 550 supervisors over Solomon's projects. They were supervisors over the men who did the work.

[24]The daughter of the king of Egypt moved from the old part of Jerusalem to the palace. This was the palace Solomon had built for her. Then Solomon filled in the land on the east side of the city.

[25]Three times each year Solomon offered whole burnt offerings and fellowship offerings on the altar. This is the altar he had built for the Lord. Solomon also burned incense[d] before the Lord. So he finished the work on the Temple.

[26]Solomon also built ships at Ezion Geber. This town is near Elath. It is on the shore of the Gulf of Aqaba, in the land of Edom. [27]King Hiram had sailors who knew much about the sea. So he sent them to serve in Solomon's ships with Solomon's men. [28]Solomon's ships sailed to Ophir. From there they brought back about 32,000 pounds of gold to King Solomon.

10 Now the queen of Sheba heard about Solomon's fame. So she came to test him with hard questions. [2]She traveled to Jerusalem with a very large group of servants. There were many camels carrying spices, jewels and much gold. She came to Solomon and talked with him about all that she had in mind. [3]Solomon answered all her questions. Nothing was too hard for him to explain to her. [4]The queen of Sheba learned that Solomon was very wise. She saw the palace he had built. [5]She saw his many officers and the food on his table. She saw the palace servants and their good clothes. She was shown the servants who served him at feasts. And she was shown the whole burnt offerings he made in the Temple[e] of the Lord. All these things amazed her.

[6]So she said to King Solomon, "I heard in my own country about your achievements and wisdom. And all of it is true. [7]I could not believe it then. But now I have come and seen it with my own eyes. I was not told even half of it! Your wisdom and wealth are much greater than I had heard. [8]Your men and officers are very lucky! In always serving you, they are able to hear your wisdom! [9]Praise the Lord your God! He was pleased to make you king of Israel. The Lord has constant love for Israel. So he made you king to keep justice and to rule fairly."

[10]Then the queen of Sheba gave the king about 9,000 pounds of gold. She also gave him many spices and jewels. No one since that time has brought more spices into Israel than the queen of Sheba gave King Solomon.

[11](Hiram's ships brought gold from Ophir. They also brought from there very much juniper wood and jewels. [12]Solomon used the juniper wood to build supports for the Temple of the Lord and the palace. He also used it to make harps and lyres[d] for the musicians. Such fine juniper wood has not been brought in or seen since that time.)

[13]King Solomon gave the queen of Sheba many gifts. He gave her gifts that a king would give to another ruler. Then he gave her whatever else she wanted and asked for. After this, she and her servants went back to her own country.

[14]Every year King Solomon received about 50,000 pounds of gold. [15]Besides that he also received gold from the traders and merchants. And he received gold from the kings of Arabia and governors of the land.

[16]King Solomon made 200 large shields of hammered gold. Each shield contained about seven and one-half pounds of gold. [17]He also made 300 smaller shields of hammered gold. They each contained about three and three-fourths pounds of gold. The king put them in the Palace of the Forest of Lebanon.

[18]Then King Solomon built a large throne of ivory. And he covered it with pure gold. [19]There were six steps leading up to the throne. The back of the throne was round at the top. There were armrests on both sides of the chair. And beside each armrest was a statue of a lion. [20]Twelve lions stood on the six steps. There was one lion at each end of each step. Nothing like this had ever been made for any other kingdom. [21]All of Solomon's drinking cups were made of gold. All of the dishes in the Palace of the Forest of Lebanon were pure gold. Nothing was made from silver. In Solomon's time people did not think silver was valuable.

²²King Solomon also had many trading ships at sea, along with Hiram's ships. Every three years the ships returned. They brought back gold, silver, ivory, apes and baboons.

²³So Solomon had more riches and wisdom than all the other kings on earth. ²⁴People everywhere wanted to see King Solomon. They wanted to hear the wisdom God had given him. ²⁵Every year everyone who came brought a gift. They brought things made of gold and silver, along with clothes, weapons, spices, horses and mules.

²⁶So Solomon had many chariots and horses. He had 1,400 chariots and 12,000 chariot soldiers. He kept some in special cities for the chariots. And he kept some with him in Jerusalem. ²⁷In Jerusalem silver was as common as stones while Solomon was king. Cedar trees were as common as the fig trees growing on the mountain slopes. ²⁸Solomon brought in horses from Egypt and Kue. His traders bought them in Kue and brought them to Israel. ²⁹A chariot from Egypt cost about 15 pounds of silver. And a horse cost about 3¾ pounds of silver. The traders also sold horses and chariots to the kings of the Hittites and the Arameans.

11 But King Solomon loved many women who were not from Israel. He loved the daughter of the king of Egypt. He also loved women of the Moabites, Ammonites, Edomites, Sidonians and Hittites. ²The Lord had told the Israelites, "You must not marry people of other nations. If you do, they will cause you to follow their gods." But Solomon fell in love with these women. ³He had 700 wives who were from royal families. He also had 300 slave women[d] who gave birth to his children. His wives caused him to turn away from God. ⁴As Solomon grew old, his wives caused him to follow other gods. He did not follow the Lord completely as his father David had done. ⁵Solomon worshiped Ashtoreth,[d] the goddess of the people of Sidon. And he worshiped Molech,[d] the hated god of the Ammonites. ⁶So Solomon did what the Lord said was wrong. He did not follow the Lord completely as his father David had done.

⁷On a hill east of Jerusalem, Solomon built two places for worship. He built a place to worship Chemosh,[d] the hated god of the Moabites. And he built a place to worship Molech, the hated god of the Ammonites. ⁸Solomon did the same thing for all of his foreign wives. So they burned incense[d] and gave sacrifices to their gods.

⁹The Lord had appeared to Solomon twice. But Solomon turned away from following the Lord, the God of Israel. So the Lord was angry with him. ¹⁰The Lord had commanded Solomon not to follow other gods. But Solomon did not obey the Lord's command. ¹¹So the Lord said to Solomon, "You have chosen to break your agreement with me. You have not obeyed my commands. So I promise I will tear your kingdom away from you. I will give it to one of your officers. ¹²But I will not take it away while you are alive. This is because of my love for your father David. I will tear it away from your son when he becomes king. ¹³But I will not tear away all the kingdom from him. I will leave him one tribe[d] to rule. I will do this because of David, my servant. And I will do it because of Jerusalem, the city I have chosen."

¹⁴Now Hadad was a member of the family of the king of Edom. And the Lord caused Hadad the Edomite to become Solomon's enemy. ¹⁵Earlier, David had defeated Edom. Joab, the commander of David's army, went into Edom to bury the dead. While he was there, he killed all the males. ¹⁶Joab and all the Israelites stayed in Edom for six months. During that time they killed every male in Edom. ¹⁷But at that time Hadad was only a young boy. So he ran away to Egypt with some of his father's officers. ¹⁸They left Midian and went to Paran. In Paran other men joined them. Then they all went to Egypt to see the king. He gave Hadad a house, some land and food to eat.

¹⁹The king liked Hadad so much he gave Hadad a wife. She was the sister of Tahpenes, the king's wife. ²⁰They had a son named Genubath. Queen Tahpenes allowed him to grow up in the royal palace. So he grew up with the king's own children.

²¹While he was in Egypt, Hadad heard that David had died. He also heard that Joab, the commander of the army, was dead. So Hadad said to the king, "Let me go home. Let me return to my own country."

²²But the king said, "Why do you want to go back to your own country? What haven't I given you here?"

Hadad answered, "Nothing. But please, let me go."

²³God also caused another man to be an enemy to Solomon. This man was

Rezon son of Eliada. Rezon had run away from his master, Hadadezer king of Zobah. ²⁴After David defeated the army of Zobah, Rezon gathered some men. He became the leader of a small army. They went to Damascus and settled there. And Rezon became king of Damascus. ²⁵Rezon ruled Aram, and he hated Israel. So he was an enemy of Israel all the time Solomon was alive. Rezon and Hadad caused some trouble for Israel.

²⁶Jeroboam son of Nebat was one of Solomon's officers. Jeroboam was one of the Ephraimite people. He was from the town of Zeredah. His mother was a widow named Zeruah. He turned against the king.

²⁷This is the story of how Jeroboam turned against the king. Solomon was filling in the land on the east side of Jerusalem. He was also repairing the wall of Jerusalem. It was the city of David, his ancestor. ²⁸Jeroboam was a capable man. Solomon saw that this young man was a good worker. So Solomon put him over all the workers from the tribes[d] of Ephraim and Manasseh.

²⁹One day Jeroboam was leaving Jerusalem. Ahijah, the prophet[d] from Shiloh, met him on the road. Ahijah was wearing a new coat. The two men were alone out in the country. ³⁰Ahijah took his new coat and tore it into 12 pieces. ³¹Then he said to Jeroboam, "Take 10 pieces of this coat for yourself. The Lord, the God of Israel, says: 'I will tear the kingdom away from Solomon. Then I will give you 10 tribes. ³²But I will allow the family of David to control 1 tribe. I will do this for my servant David and for Jerusalem. Jerusalem is the city I have chosen from all the tribes of Israel. ³³I will do this because Solomon has stopped following me. He worships the Sidonian god Ashtoreth[d] and the Moabite god Chemosh.[d] He also worships Molech,[d] the Ammonite god. Solomon has not obeyed me. He has not done what I said is right. He has not obeyed my laws and commands. He is not living the way his father David lived.

³⁴"'But I will not take all the kingdom away from Solomon. I will let him rule all his life. I will do this because of my servant David. I chose David, and he obeyed all my commands and laws. ³⁵But I will take the kingdom away from his son. Jeroboam, I will allow you to rule over the 10 tribes. ³⁶I will allow Solomon's son to continue to rule over 1 tribe. I will do this so that David, my servant, will always have a king before me in Jerusalem. It is the city where I chose to be worshiped. ³⁷But I will make you rule over everything you want. You will rule over all of Israel. ³⁸I will always be with you if you do what I say is right. You must obey all my commands. If you obey my laws and commands as David did, I will be with you. I will make your family a family of kings, as I did for David. I will give Israel to you. ³⁹I will punish David's children because of this. But I will not punish them forever.'"

⁴⁰Solomon tried to kill Jeroboam. But Jeroboam ran away to Egypt. He went to Shishak king of Egypt. And Jeroboam stayed there until Solomon died.

⁴¹Everything else Solomon did is written down. He showed much wisdom. It is written in the book of the history of Solomon. ⁴²Solomon ruled in Jerusalem over all Israel for 40 years. ⁴³Then he died and was buried in Jerusalem, the city of David, his father. And his son Rehoboam became king after him.

12 Rehoboam went to Shechem because all the Israelites had gone there to make him king. ²Jeroboam son of Nebat was still in Egypt. He had gone there to escape from Solomon. When Jeroboam heard about Rehoboam being made king, Jeroboam returned from Egypt. ³So the people sent for him. Then he and the people went to Rehoboam. They said to Rehoboam, ⁴"Your father forced us to work very hard. Now, make it easier for us. Don't make us work as hard as your father did. Then we will serve you."

⁵Rehoboam answered, "Come back to me in three days. Then I will answer you." So the people left.

⁶Some of the older leaders had helped Solomon make decisions during his lifetime. So King Rehoboam asked them what he should do. He said, "How do you think I should answer these people?"

⁷They answered, "You should be like a servant to them today. Serve them, and give them a kind answer. If you do, they will serve you always."

⁸But Rehoboam did not listen to this advice. He asked the young men who had grown up with him. They advised him in making decisions. ⁹Rehoboam said, "The people said, 'Don't make us work as hard as your father did.' How do you think I should answer them? What is your advice?"

¹⁰The young men answered, "Those people came to you and said, 'Your father forced us to work very hard. Now make our work easier.' So you should tell them, 'My little finger is bigger than my father's whole body. ¹¹My father forced you to work hard. But I will make you work even harder! My father beat you with whips. But I will beat you with whips that have sharp points.'"

¹²Rehoboam had told the people, "Come back to me in three days." So after three days all the people returned to Rehoboam. ¹³At that time King Rehoboam spoke cruel words to them. He did not listen to the advice that the older leaders had given him. ¹⁴He did what the young men had told him to do. Rehoboam said, "My father forced you to work hard. So I will give you even more work. My father beat you with whips. But I will beat you with whips that have sharp points." ¹⁵So the king did not do what the people wanted. The Lord caused this to happen. He did this to keep the promise he had made to Jeroboam son of Nebat. He had made this promise through Ahijah, the prophet[d] from Shiloh.

¹⁶All the people of Israel saw that the new king refused to listen to them. So they said to the king,

"We have no share in David!
We have no part in the son of Jesse!
People of Israel, let's go to our own homes!
Let David's son rule his own people!"

So the Israelites went home. ¹⁷But Rehoboam still ruled over the Israelites who lived in the towns of Judah.

¹⁸Adoniram was in charge of the people who were forced to work. King Rehoboam sent him to the people. But they threw stones at him until he died. But King Rehoboam ran to his chariot and escaped to Jerusalem. ¹⁹Since then, Israel has been against the family of David.

²⁰All the Israelites heard that Jeroboam had returned. So they called him to a meeting. And they made him king over all Israel. But the tribe[d] of Judah continued to follow the family of David.

²¹When Rehoboam arrived in Jerusalem, he gathered the tribes of Judah and Benjamin. This was an army of 180,000 men. Rehoboam wanted to fight against the people of Israel. He wanted to take back his kingdom.

²²But God spoke his word to Shemaiah, a man of God. The Lord said, ²³"Talk to Solomon's son Rehoboam, the king of Judah. Talk also to all the people of Judah and Benjamin and to the rest of the people. ²⁴Say to them, 'The Lord says you must not go to war against your brothers, the Israelites. Every one of you should go home. I made all these things happen!'" So the men in Rehoboam's army obeyed the Lord's command. They all went home as the Lord had commanded.

²⁵Then Jeroboam made Shechem a very strong city. It is in the mountains of Ephraim. And Jeroboam lived there. He also went to the city of Peniel and made it stronger.

²⁶Jeroboam said to himself, "The kingdom will probably go back to David's family. ²⁷The people will continue going to the Temple[d] of the Lord in Jerusalem. If they do, they will want to be ruled again by Rehoboam. Then they will kill me and follow Rehoboam king of Judah."

²⁸King Jeroboam asked his men for advice. So he made two golden calves. He said to the people, "It is too hard for you to go to Jerusalem to worship. Israel, here are your gods which brought you out of Egypt." ²⁹King Jeroboam put one golden calf in the city of Bethel. And he put the other in the city of Dan. ³⁰And this became a very great sin. The people traveled as far as Dan to worship the calf there.

³¹Jeroboam built temples on the places of worship. He chose priests from all the people. (He did not choose priests only from the tribe of Levi.) ³²And he started a new festival. It was the fifteenth day of the eighth month. This was like the festival in Judah. During that time the king offered sacrifices on the altar. He offered sacrifices to the calves in Bethel he had made. He also chose priests in Bethel to serve at the places of worship he had made. ³³So Jeroboam chose his own time for a festival for the Israelites. It was the fifteenth day of the eighth month. During that time he offered sacrifices on the altar he had built in Bethel. So he set up a festival for the Israelites. And he offered sacrifices on the altar.

13 The Lord commanded a man of God from Judah to go to Bethel. When he arrived, Jeroboam was standing by the altar to offer a sacrifice. ²The Lord had commanded the man of God to speak against the altar. The man said, "Altar, the Lord says to you: 'David's family will have a son named Josiah. He will kill the priests of the places of worship. They now make their sacrifices on you. But Josiah will sacrifice those priests on you. Human bones will be burned on you.'" ³The man of God gave proof that these things would happen. He said, "This is God's sign that this will happen. This altar will break apart. And the ashes on it will fall onto the ground."

⁴King Jeroboam heard what the man of God said about the altar in Bethel. So Jeroboam raised his hand from the altar and pointed at the man. "Capture him!" he said. But when the king said this, his arm became paralyzed. He could not move it. ⁵Also, the altar broke into pieces. All its ashes fell onto the ground. This was the sign the Lord had told the man of God to give.

⁶Then the king said to the man of God, "Please pray to the Lord your God for me. Ask him to heal my arm."

So the man of God prayed to the Lord. And the king's arm was healed. It became as it was before.

⁷Then the king said to the man of God, "Please come home and eat with me. I will give you a gift."

⁸But the man of God answered the king, "I will not go home with you! Even if you gave me half of your kingdom, I would not go! I will not eat or drink anything in this place. ⁹The Lord commanded me not to eat or drink anything. He also commanded me not to return on the same road by which I came." ¹⁰So he traveled on a different road. He did not return on the same road by which he had come to Bethel.

¹¹Now there was an old prophet[d] living in Bethel. His sons came and told him what the man of God had done there that day. They told their father what he had said to King Jeroboam. ¹²The father asked, "Which road did he use when he left?" So his sons showed him which road the man of God from Judah had taken. ¹³The prophet told his sons to put a saddle on his donkey. So they saddled the donkey, and he left.

¹⁴He went after the man of God. He found the man sitting under an oak tree. The prophet asked, "Are you the man of God who came from Judah?"

The man answered, "Yes, I am."

¹⁵So the prophet said, "Please come home and eat with me."

¹⁶But the man of God answered, "I can't go home with you. I can't eat or drink with you in this place. ¹⁷The Lord said to me, 'You must not eat or drink anything there. And you must not return on the same road by which you came.'"

¹⁸Then the old prophet said, "But I also am a prophet like you." Then he told a lie. He said, "An angel from the Lord came to me. He told me to bring you to my home. He said you should eat and drink with me." ¹⁹So the man of God went to the old prophet's house. And he ate and drank with him there.

²⁰While they were sitting at the table, the Lord spoke his word to the old prophet. ²¹The old prophet cried out to the man of God from Judah. He said, "The Lord said you did not obey him! He said you did not do what the Lord your God commanded you. ²²The Lord commanded you not to eat or drink anything in this place. But you came back and ate and drank. So your body will not be buried in your family grave."

²³The man of God finished eating. Then the prophet put a saddle on his donkey for him. And the man left. ²⁴As he was traveling on the road home, a lion attacked and killed him. His body lay on the road. The donkey and the lion stood near it. ²⁵Some men were traveling on that road. They saw the body and the lion standing near it. So they went to the city where the old prophet lived. And they told what they had seen.

²⁶The old prophet who had brought the man of God back heard about what had happened. He said, "It is the man of God who did not obey the Lord's command. So the Lord sent a lion to kill him. The Lord said he would do this."

²⁷Then the prophet said to his sons, "Put a saddle on my donkey." So they did. ²⁸The old prophet went out and found the body lying on the road. The donkey and the lion were still standing near it. The lion had not eaten the body. And it had not hurt the donkey. ²⁹So the prophet put the body on his donkey. And he carried it back to the city. There he would have a time of sadness for him and bury him. ³⁰The prophet buried the body in his own family grave. And he was sad for the man of God. He said, "Oh, my brother."

³¹So the prophet buried the body. Then he said to his sons, "When I die, bury me in this same grave. Put my bones next to his. ³²Through him the Lord spoke against the altar at Bethel. And he spoke against the places of wor-

ship in the towns of Samaria. And what the Lord spoke through him will certainly come true."

³³But King Jeroboam did not stop doing evil things. He continued to choose priests for the places of worship from all the people. Anyone who wanted to be a priest for the places of worship was allowed. ³⁴In this way the kingdom of Jeroboam sinned. And that sin caused its ruin and destruction from the earth.

14 At that time Jeroboam's son Abijah became very sick. ²So Jeroboam said to his wife, "Go to Shiloh. Go to see the prophetᵈ Ahijah. He is the one who said I would become king of Israel. But dress yourself so people won't know you are my wife. ³Give the prophet ten loaves of bread, some cakes and a jar of honey. Then ask him what will happen to our son. And he will tell you." ⁴So the king's wife did as he said. She went to Ahijah's home in Shiloh.

Now Ahijah was very old and had become blind. ⁵But the Lord had said to him, "Jeroboam's son is sick. So Jeroboam's wife is coming to ask you about him. When she arrives, she will pretend to be someone else." Then the Lord told Ahijah what to say.

⁶When Ahijah heard her walking to the door, he said, "Come in, wife of Jeroboam. Why are you pretending to be someone else? I have bad news for you. ⁷Go back and tell Jeroboam that this is what the Lord, the God of Israel, says: 'Jeroboam, I chose you from among all the people of Israel. I made you the leader of my people. ⁸I took the kingdom away from David's family. And I gave it to you. But you are not like my servant David. He always obeyed my commands. He followed me with all his heart. He did only the things I said were right. ⁹But you have done more evil things than anyone who ruled before you. You have quit following me. You have made other gods and idols of metal. This has made me very angry. ¹⁰So I will bring disaster to the family of Jeroboam. I will kill all of the men in your family, both slaves and free men. I will destroy your family as completely as fire burns up manure. ¹¹Anyone from your family who dies in the city will be eaten by dogs. And anyone from your family who dies in the fields will be eaten by the birds. The Lord has spoken!'"

¹²Then Ahijah said to Jeroboam's wife, "Now go home. When you enter your city gate, your son will die. ¹³All Israel will be sad for him and bury him. He will be the only one of Jeroboam's family who will be buried. This is because he is the only one in Jeroboam's family who pleased the Lord, the God of Israel.

¹⁴"The Lord will put a new king over Israel. That king will destroy Jeroboam's family. This will happen soon. ¹⁵Then the Lord will punish Israel. The people of Israel will be like grass moving in the water. The Lord will pull up Israel from this good land. This is the land he gave their ancestors. But he will scatter Israel beyond the Euphrates River. This will happen because the Lord is angry with the people. They made him angry when they made idols to worship Asherah.ᵈ ¹⁶Jeroboam sinned, and then he made the people of Israel sin. So the Lord will let the people of Israel be defeated."

¹⁷Then Jeroboam's wife traveled back to Tirzah. When she entered her home, the boy died. ¹⁸They buried him. And all Israel had a time of sadness for him. This happened as the Lord said it would. The Lord had said these things through his servant, the prophet Ahijah.

¹⁹Everything else Jeroboam did is written down. He fought wars and continued to rule the people. It is all written in the book of the history of the kings of Israel. ²⁰Jeroboam ruled as king for 22 years. Then he died, and his son Nadab became king in his place.

²¹Solomon's son Rehoboam was 41 years old when he became king of Judah. His mother was Naamah from the land of Ammon. Rehoboam ruled in Jerusalem for 17 years. (The Lord had chosen that city from all the land of Israel. He chose to be worshiped there.)

²²The people of Judah did what the Lord said was wrong. The people's sins made the Lord very angry at them. They made the Lord even more angry than their ancestors had done. ²³The people built stone pillars and places to worship false gods and Asherahᵈ idols. They built them on every high hill and under every green tree. ²⁴There were even male prostitutesᵈ at the places of worship to the gods. The people who had lived in the land before the Israelites had done many evil things. And God had taken the land away from them. Now the people of Judah were doing the same evil things.

²⁵During the fifth year Rehoboam was

king, Shishak attacked Jerusalem. Shishak was king of Egypt. [26]He took the treasures from the Temple[d] of the Lord and the king's palace. He took everything, even the gold shields Solomon had made. [27]So King Rehoboam made bronze shields to put in their place. He gave them to the men who were guarding the palace gates. [28]Whenever the king went to the Temple of the Lord, the guards carried the shields. After they were finished, they put the shields back in the guardroom.

[29]Everything else King Rehoboam did is written down. It is in the book of the history of the kings of Judah. [30]Rehoboam and Jeroboam were always fighting a war with each other. [31]Rehoboam died and was buried with his ancestors in Jerusalem. His mother was Naamah from Ammon. And Rehoboam's son Abijah became king in his place.

15 Abijah became king of Judah. This was during the eighteenth year Jeroboam son of Nebat ruled Israel. [2]And Abijah ruled in Jerusalem for three years. His mother was Maacah daughter of Abishalom. [3]He did all the same sins his father before him had done. Abijah was not faithful to the Lord his God. In this way he was not like David, his great-grandfather. [4]Because the Lord had loved David, the Lord gave Abijah a kingdom in Jerusalem. And the Lord allowed him to have a son to be king after him. The Lord also kept Jerusalem safe. [5]David had always done what the Lord said was right. All his life he had always obeyed the Lord's commands. There was only one time David did not obey the Lord. This was when he sinned against Uriah the Hittite.

[6]Now there was war between Abijah and Jeroboam during Abijah's lifetime. [7]Everything else Abijah did is written down. It is in the book of the history of the kings of Judah. During the time Abijah ruled, there was war between Abijah and Jeroboam. [8]And Abijah died and was buried in Jerusalem. Abijah's son Asa became king in his place.

[9]During the twentieth year Jeroboam was king of Israel, Asa became king of Judah. [10]Asa ruled in Jerusalem for 41 years. His grandmother's name was Maacah. She was the daughter of Abishalom.

[11]Asa did what the Lord said was right. This was as his ancestor David had done. [12]There were male prostitutes[d] at the places where false gods were worshiped. Asa forced them to leave the country. He also took away the idols that his ancestors had made. [13]His grandmother Maacah had made a terrible Asherah[d] idol. So Asa removed her from being queen. He cut down this idol and burned it in the Kidron Valley. [14]Asa was faithful to the Lord all his life. But he did not destroy the places where false gods were worshiped. [15]Asa and his father had given some things to God. They had given gifts of gold, silver and other objects. Asa put all these things in the Temple.[d]

[16]There was war between Asa and Baasha king of Israel. [17]Baasha fought against Judah. He wanted to stop people from leaving or entering Asa's country, Judah. So he made the city of Ramah very strong.

[18]Then Asa took all the silver and gold from the treasuries of the Temple of the Lord and his own palace. He gave it to his officers. And he sent them to Ben-Hadad king of Aram. (Ben-Hadad was the son of Tabrimmon. And he was the son of Hezion.) Ben-Hadad was ruling in the city of Damascus. [19]Asa sent this message: "My father and your father had a peace agreement. I am sending you a gift of gold and silver. Break your treaty with Baasha king of Israel so that he will leave my land."

[20]Ben-Hadad agreed with King Asa. So he sent his army to fight against the towns of Israel. He defeated the towns of Ijon, Dan and Abel Bethmaacah. And he defeated all the land near Lake Galilee and the area of Naphtali. [21]Baasha heard about these attacks. So he stopped building up Ramah and returned to Tirzah. [22]Then King Asa gave an order to all the people of Judah. Everyone had to help. They carried away all the stones and wood Baasha had been using in Ramah. King Asa used those things to build up Geba and Mizpah. (Geba was in the land of Benjamin.)

[23]Everything else Asa did is written down. His victories and the cities he built are written down. They are in the book of the history of the kings of Judah. When he became old, he got a disease in his feet. [24]Then Asa died. And he was buried with his ancestors in Jerusalem. It was the city of David, his ancestor. Then Jehoshaphat, Asa's son, became king in his place.

[25]Nadab son of Jeroboam became king of Israel. This was during the sec-

ond year Asa was king of Judah. And Nadab was king of Israel for two years. [26] He did what the Lord said was wrong. Jeroboam had caused the people of Israel to sin. Nadab sinned in the same way his father Jeroboam had sinned.

[27] Baasha son of Ahijah was from the tribe[d] of Issachar. He made plans to kill Nadab. Nadab and all Israel were attacking the Philistine town of Gibbethon. So Baasha killed Nadab there. [28] This happened during Asa's third year as king of Judah. And Baasha became the next king of Israel.

[29] As soon as Baasha became king, he killed all of Jeroboam's family. He left no one in Jeroboam's family alive. This happened as the Lord had said it would. The Lord had said this through his servant Ahijah from Shiloh. [30] This happened because King Jeroboam had sinned very much. And he had caused the people of Israel to sin. Jeroboam had made the Lord, the God of Israel, very angry.

[31] Everything else Nadab did is written down. It is in the book of the history of the kings of Israel. [32] There was war between Asa king of Judah and Baasha king of Israel all the time they were kings.

[33] Baasha son of Ahijah became king of Israel. This was during Asa's third year as king of Judah. And Baasha ruled in Tirzah for 24 years. [34] But Baasha did what the Lord said was wrong. Jeroboam had caused the people of Israel to sin. And Baasha sinned in the same way Jeroboam had sinned.

16 Then Jehu son of Hanani spoke the word of the Lord against King Baasha. [2] The Lord said, "You were nothing. Then I took you and made you a leader over my people Israel. But you have followed the ways of Jeroboam. You have caused my people Israel to sin. Their sins have made me angry. [3] So, Baasha, I will destroy you and your family. I will do to you what I did to the family of Jeroboam son of Nebat. [4] Anyone from your family who dies in the city will be eaten by dogs. And anyone from your family who dies in the fields will be eaten by birds."

[5] Everything else Baasha did and all his victories are written down. They are in the book of the history of the kings of Israel. [6] So Baasha died and was buried in Tirzah. His son Elah became king in his place.

[7] The Lord spoke his word through the prophet[d] Jehu son of Hanani. The Lord's message was against Baasha and his family. Baasha had done many things the Lord said were wrong. This made the Lord very angry. Baasha did the same things that Jeroboam's family had done before him. The Lord was also angry because Baasha killed all of Jeroboam's family.

[8] Elah son of Baasha became king of Israel. This was during Asa's twenty-sixth year as king of Judah. And Elah ruled in Tirzah for two years.

[9] Zimri was one of Elah's officers. He commanded half of Elah's chariots. But Zimri made plans against Elah.

Elah was in Tirzah, getting drunk at Arza's home. (Arza was the man in charge of the palace at Tirzah.) [10] So Zimri went into Arza's house and killed Elah. This was during Asa's twenty-seventh year as king of Judah. Then Zimri became king of Israel in Elah's place.

[11] As soon as Zimri became king, he killed all of Baasha's family. He did not let any man of Baasha's family or friends live. [12] So Zimri destroyed all of Baasha's family. This happened as the Lord had said it would. The Lord had spoken this against Baasha through the prophet[d] Jehu. [13] This happened because of all the sins of Baasha and his son Elah. They sinned and caused the people of Israel to sin. They also made the Lord, the God of Israel, angry because they had made worthless idols.

[14] Everything else Elah did is written down. It is in the book of the history of the kings of Israel.

[15] So Zimri became king of Israel. This was during Asa's twenty-seventh year as king of Judah. Zimri ruled in Tirzah seven days. This is what happened:

The army of Israel was camped near Gibbethon, a Philistine town. [16] The men in the camp heard that Zimri had made secret plans against the king. And they heard that Zimri had killed him. So that day in the camp they made Omri king over Israel. (Omri was commander of the army.) [17] So Omri and all the Israelites left Gibbethon and attacked Tirzah. [18] Zimri saw that the city had been captured. So he went into the palace and set it on fire. He burned the palace and himself with it. [19] So Zimri died because he had sinned. He did what the Lord said was wrong. Jeroboam had caused the people of Israel to sin. And Zimri sinned in the same way Jeroboam had sinned.

[20]Everything else Zimri did is written down. It is in the book of the history of the kings of Israel. The story of how Zimri turned against King Elah is also written there.

[21]The people of Israel were divided into two groups. Half of the people wanted Tibni to be king. He was the son of Ginath. The other half of the people wanted Omri. [22]But Omri's followers were stronger than the followers of Tibni son of Ginath. So Tibni died, and Omri became king.

[23]Omri became king of Israel. This was during the thirty-first year Asa was king of Judah. And Omri ruled Israel for 12 years. Six of those years he ruled in the town of Tirzah. [24]Omri bought the hill of Samaria from Shemer. He paid about 150 pounds of silver for it. Omri built a city on that hill. And he called it Samaria after the name of its earlier owner, Shemer.

[25]But Omri did what the Lord said was wrong. He did more evil than all the kings who were before him. [26]Jeroboam son of Nebat had caused the people of Israel to sin. And Omri sinned in the same way Jeroboam had sinned. So the Israelites made the Lord, the God of Israel, very angry. He was angry because they worshiped worthless idols.

[27]Everything else Omri did and all his successes are written down. They are all in the book of the history of the kings of Israel. [28]So Omri died and was buried in Samaria. His son Ahab became king in his place.

[29]So Ahab son of Omri became king of Israel. This was during Asa's thirty-eighth year as king of Judah. Ahab ruled Israel in the town of Samaria for 22 years. [30]Ahab did many things that the Lord said were wrong. He did more evil than any of the kings before him. [31]He sinned in the same ways that Jeroboam son of Nebat had sinned. But he did even worse things. He married Jezebel daughter of Ethbaal. (Ethbaal was king of the city of Sidon.) Then Ahab began to serve Baal[d] and worship him. [32]He built a temple in Samaria for worshiping Baal. And he put an altar there for Baal. [33]Ahab also made an idol for worshiping Asherah.[d] He did more things to make

the Lord, the God of Israel, angry than all the other kings before him.

[34]During the time of Ahab, Hiel from Bethel rebuilt the town of Jericho. It cost Hiel the life of Abiram, his oldest son, to begin work on the city. And it cost the life of Segub, his youngest son, to build the city gates. The Lord had said, through Joshua, that this would happen.[a] (Joshua was the son of Nun.)

17 Now Elijah was a prophet[d] from the town of Tishbe in Gilead. Elijah said to King Ahab, "I serve the Lord, the God of Israel. As surely as the Lord lives, I tell you the truth. No rain or dew will fall during the next few years unless I command it."

[2]Then the Lord spoke his word to Elijah: [3]"Leave this place. Go east and hide near Kerith Ravine. It is east of the Jordan River. [4]You may drink from the brook. And I have commanded ravens to bring you food there." [5]So Elijah did what the Lord told him to do. He went to Kerith Ravine, east of the Jordan, and lived there. [6]The birds brought Elijah bread and meat every morning and every evening. And he drank water from the brook.

[7]After a while the brook dried up because there was no rain. [8]Then the Lord spoke his word to Elijah, [9]"Go to Zarephath in Sidon. Live there. I have commanded a widow there to take care of you."

[10]So Elijah went to Zarephath. When he reached the town gate, he saw a widow there. She was gathering wood for a fire. Elijah asked her, "Would you bring me a little water in a cup? I would like to have a drink." [11]As she was going to get his water, Elijah said, "Please bring me a piece of bread, too."

[12]The woman answered, "As surely as the Lord your God lives, I tell you the truth. I have no bread. I have only a handful of flour in a jar. And I have only a little olive oil in a jug. I came here to gather some wood. I will take it home and cook our last meal. My son and I will eat it and then die from hunger."

[13]Elijah said to her, "Don't worry. Go home and cook your food as you have said. But first make a small loaf of bread from the flour you have. Bring it to me. Then cook something for yourself and your son. [14]The Lord, the God of Israel, says, 'That jar of flour will never become

16:34 The Lord . . . happen When Joshua destroyed Jericho, he said whoever rebuilt the city would lose his oldest and youngest sons. See Joshua 6:26.

empty. The jug will always have oil in it. This will continue until the day the Lord sends rain to the land.' "

¹⁵So the woman went home. And she did what Elijah told her to do. So Elijah, the woman and her son had enough food every day. ¹⁶The jar of flour and the jug of oil were never empty. This happened just as the Lord, through Elijah, said it would.

¹⁷Some time later the son of the woman who owned the house became sick. He grew worse and worse. Finally he stopped breathing. ¹⁸So the woman said to Elijah, "You are a man of God. What have you done to me? Did you come here to remind me of my sin? Did you come here to kill my son?"

¹⁹Elijah said to her, "Give me your son." So Elijah took the boy from her and carried him upstairs. Elijah laid the boy on the bed in the room where he was staying. ²⁰Then he prayed to the Lord. He said, "Lord my God, this widow is letting me stay in her house. Why have you done this terrible thing to her? Why have you caused her son to die?" ²¹Then Elijah lay on top of the boy three times. Elijah prayed to the Lord, "Lord my God, let this boy live again!"

²²The Lord answered Elijah's prayer. The boy began breathing again, and he was alive. ²³Elijah carried the boy downstairs. He gave the boy to his mother and said, "See! Your son is alive!"

²⁴The woman said to Elijah, "Now I know you really are a man from God. I know that the Lord truly speaks through you!"

18 During the third year without rain, the Lord spoke his word to Elijah. The Lord said, "Go and meet King Ahab. I will soon send rain." ²So Elijah went to meet Ahab.

By this time there was no food in Samaria. ³So King Ahab sent for Obadiah. Obadiah was in charge of the king's palace. (Obadiah was a true follower of the Lord. ⁴One time Jezebel was killing all the Lord's prophets.ᵈ So Obadiah took 100 of them and hid them in two caves. He put 50 in one cave and 50 in another cave. And he brought them food and water.) ⁵King Ahab said to Obadiah, "Let's look at every spring and valley in the land. Maybe we can find enough grass to keep our horses and mules alive. Then we will not have to kill our animals." ⁶So each one chose a part of the country to search. Ahab went in one di-

rection. Obadiah went in another direction.

⁷While Obadiah was walking along, Elijah met him. Obadiah knew who Elijah was. So he bowed down to the ground before Elijah. He said, "Elijah? Is it really you, master?"

⁸Elijah answered, "Yes. Go tell your master the king that I am here."

⁹Then Obadiah said, "If I tell Ahab that, he will kill me! I have done nothing wrong that I should be killed! ¹⁰As surely as the Lord your God lives, the king has looked everywhere for you! He has sent people to every country to look for you. If the ruler said you were not there, that was not enough. Ahab then forced the ruler to swear you could not be found in his country. ¹¹Now you want me to go to my master and tell him, 'Elijah is here'? ¹²The Spiritᵈ of the Lord may carry you to some other place after I leave. If I go tell King Ahab you are here, he will come. If he doesn't find you, he will kill me! I have followed the Lord since I was a boy. ¹³Haven't you heard what I did? When Jezebel was killing the Lord's prophets, I hid 100 of them. I put 50 prophets in one cave and 50 prophets in another cave. I brought them food and water. ¹⁴Now you want me to go and tell the king you are here. He will kill me!"

¹⁵Elijah answered, "I serve the Lord of heaven's armies. As surely as the Lord lives, I will stand before Ahab today."

¹⁶So Obadiah went to Ahab and told him where Elijah was. Then Ahab went to meet Elijah.

¹⁷When he saw Elijah, he said, "Is it you—the biggest troublemaker in Israel?"

¹⁸Elijah answered, "I have not caused trouble in Israel. You and your father's family have caused all this trouble. You have not obeyed the Lord's commands. You have followed the Baals.ᵈ ¹⁹Now tell all Israel to meet me at Mount Carmel. Also bring the 450 prophets of Baal there. And bring the 400 prophets of Asherah,ᵈ who eat at Jezebel's table."

²⁰So Ahab called all the Israelites and those prophets to Mount Carmel. ²¹Elijah stood before the people. He said, "How long will you try to serve both Baal and the Lord? If the Lord is the true God, follow him. But if Baal is the true God, follow him!"

But the people said nothing.

²²Elijah said, "I am the only prophet of the Lord here. But there are 450

prophets of Baal. ²³So bring two bulls. Let the prophets of Baal choose one bull. Let them kill it and cut it into pieces. Then let them put the meat on the wood. But they are not to set fire to it. Then I will do the same with the other bull. And I will put it on the wood. But I will not set fire to it. ²⁴You prophets of Baal, pray to your god. And I will pray to the Lord. The god who answers the prayer will set fire to his wood. He is the true God."

All the people agreed that this was a good idea.

²⁵Then Elijah said to the prophets of Baal, "There are many of you. So you go first. Choose a bull and prepare it. Pray to your god, but don't start the fire."

²⁶So they took the bull that was given to them and prepared it. They prayed to Baal from morning until noon. They shouted, "Baal, answer us!" But there was no sound. No one answered. They danced around the altar they had built.

²⁷At noon Elijah began to make fun of them. He said, "Pray louder! If Baal really is a god, maybe he is thinking. Or maybe he is busy or traveling! Maybe he is sleeping so you will have to wake him!" ²⁸So the prophets prayed louder. They cut themselves with swords and spears until their blood flowed. (This was the way they worshiped.) ²⁹The afternoon passed, and the prophets continued to act wildly. They continued until it was time for the evening sacrifice. But no voice was heard. Baal did not answer. No one paid attention.

³⁰Then Elijah said to all the people, "Now come to me." So they gathered around him. Elijah rebuilt the altar of the Lord because it had been torn down. ³¹He took 12 stones. He took 1 stone for each of the 12 tribes.ᵈ These 12 tribes were named for the 12 sons of Jacob. (Jacob was the man the Lord had called Israel.) ³²Elijah used these stones to rebuild the altar in honor of the Lord. Then he dug a small ditch around it. It was big enough to hold about 13 quarts of seed. ³³Elijah put the wood on the altar. He cut the bull into pieces and laid them on the wood. Then he said, "Fill four jars with water. Put the water on the meat and on the wood."

³⁴Then Elijah said, "Do it again." And they did it again.

Then he said, "Do it a third time." And they did it the third time. ³⁵So the water ran off of the altar and filled the ditch.

³⁶It was time for the evening sacrifice.

So the prophet Elijah went near the altar. He prayed, "Lord, you are the God of Abraham, Isaac and Israel. I ask you now to prove that you are the God of Israel. And prove that I am your servant. Show these people that you commanded me to do all these things. ³⁷Lord, answer my prayer. Show these people that you, Lord, are God. Then the people will know that you are bringing them back to you."

³⁸Then fire from the Lord came down. It burned the sacrifice, the wood, the stones and the ground around the altar. It also dried up the water in the ditch. ³⁹When all the people saw this, they fell down to the ground. They cried, "The Lord is God! The Lord is God!"

⁴⁰Then Elijah said, "Capture the prophets of Baal! Don't let any of them run away!" So the people captured all the prophets. Then Elijah led them down to Kishon Valley. There he killed all the prophets.

⁴¹Then Elijah said to Ahab, "Now, go, eat and drink. A heavy rain is coming." ⁴²So King Ahab went to eat and drink. At the same time Elijah climbed to the top of Mount Carmel. There he bent down to the ground with his head between his knees.

⁴³Then Elijah said to his servant, "Go and look toward the sea."

The servant went and looked. He said, "I see nothing."

Elijah told him to go and look again. This happened seven times. ⁴⁴The seventh time, the servant said, "I see a small cloud. It's the size of a man's fist. It's coming from the sea."

Elijah told the servant, "Go to Ahab. Tell him to get his chariot ready and to go home now. If he doesn't leave now, the rain will stop him."

⁴⁵After a short time the sky was covered with dark clouds. The wind began to blow. Then a heavy rain began to fall. Ahab got in his chariot and started back to Jezreel. ⁴⁶The Lord gave his power to Elijah. Elijah tightened his clothes around him. Then he ran ahead of King Ahab all the way to Jezreel.

19 King Ahab told Jezebel everything Elijah had done. Ahab told her how Elijah had killed all the prophetsᵈ with a sword. ²So Jezebel sent a messenger to Elijah. Jezebel said, "By this time tomorrow I will kill you. I will kill you as you killed those prophets. If I don't succeed, may the gods punish me terribly."

³When Elijah heard this, he was afraid. So he ran away to save his life. He took his servant with him. When they came to Beersheba in Judah, Elijah left his servant there. ⁴Then Elijah walked for a whole day into the desert. He sat down under a bush and asked to die. Elijah prayed, "I have had enough, Lord. Let me die. I am no better than my ancestors." ⁵Then Elijah lay down under the tree and slept.

Suddenly an angel came to him and touched him. The angel said, "Get up and eat." ⁶Elijah saw near his head a loaf baked over coals and a jar of water. So he ate and drank. Then he went back to sleep.

⁷Later the Lord's angel came to him a second time. The angel touched him and said, "Get up and eat. If you don't, the journey will be too hard for you." ⁸So Elijah got up and ate and drank. The food made him strong enough to walk for 40 days and nights. He walked to Mount Sinai, the mountain of God. ⁹There Elijah went into a cave and stayed all night.

Then the Lord spoke his word to him: "Elijah! Why are you here?"

¹⁰Elijah answered, "Lord, God of heaven's armies, I have always served you the best I could. But the people of Israel have broken their agreement with you. They have destroyed your altars. They have killed your prophets with swords. I am the only prophet left. And now they are trying to kill me, too!"

¹¹Then the Lord said to Elijah, "Go. Stand in front of me on the mountain. I will pass by you." Then a very strong wind blew. It caused the mountains to break apart. It broke apart large rocks in front of the Lord. But the Lord was not in the wind. After the wind, there was an earthquake. But the Lord was not in the earthquake. ¹²After the earthquake, there was a fire. But the Lord was not in the fire. After the fire, there was a quiet, gentle voice. ¹³When Elijah heard it, he covered his face with his coat. He went out and stood at the entrance to the cave.

Then a voice said to him, "Elijah! Why are you here?"

¹⁴Elijah answered, "Lord, God of heaven's armies, I have always served you the best I could. But the people of Israel have broken their agreement with you. They have destroyed your altars. They have killed your prophets with swords. I am the only prophet left. And now they are trying to kill me, too."

¹⁵The Lord said to him, "Go back on the road that leads to the desert around Damascus. Enter that city. There pour olive oil on Hazael to make him king over Aram. ¹⁶Then pour oil on Jehu son of Nimshi to make him king over Israel. Next, pour oil on Elisha son of Shaphat from Abel Meholah. He will be a prophet in your place. ¹⁷Jehu will kill anyone who escapes from Hazael's sword. And Elisha will kill anyone who escapes from Jehu's sword. ¹⁸But I have left 7,000 people living in Israel. Those 7,000 have never bowed down before Baal.ᵈ Their mouths have never kissed his idol."

¹⁹So Elijah left there and found Elisha son of Shaphat. He was plowing a field with a team of oxen. There were 11 teams ahead of him. Elisha was plowing with the twelfth team of oxen. Elijah came up to Elisha. Elijah took off his coat and put it on Elisha. ²⁰Then Elisha left his oxen and ran to follow Elijah. Elisha said, "Let me kiss my father and my mother good-bye. Then I will go with you."

Elijah answered, "That is fine. Go back. I won't stop you."

²¹So Elisha went back. He took his pair of oxen and killed them. He used the wooden yokeᵈ for the fire. Then he cooked the meat and gave it to the people. And they ate it. Then Elisha went and followed Elijah and became his helper.

20 Now Ben-Hadad was king of Aram. He gathered together all his army. There were 32 kings with their horses and chariots. They went with him and surrounded Samaria and attacked it. ²The king sent messengers into the city to Ahab king of Israel. ³This was his message: "Ben-Hadad says, 'You must give me your silver and gold and the best of your wives and children.'"

⁴Ahab king of Israel answered, "My master and king, I agree to what you say. I and everything I have belongs to you."

⁵Then the messengers came to Ahab again. They said, "Ben-Hadad says, 'I told you before that you must give me your silver and gold, your wives and your children. ⁶About this time tomorrow I am going to send my men to you. They are to search everywhere in your palace. And they are to search the

homes of the men who rule under you. My men will take anything they want.'"

[7] So Ahab called a meeting of all the older leaders of his country. He said, "Ben-Hadad is looking for trouble. First he said I had to give him my wives, my children, my silver and my gold. I agreed to that."

[8] But the older leaders and all the people said, "Pay no attention to him. Don't do what he says."

[9] So Ahab said to Ben-Hadad's messengers, "Tell my master the king this: 'I will do what you said at first. But I will not obey your second command.'" So King Ben-Hadad's men carried the message back to him.

[10] Then King Ben-Hadad sent another message to Ahab: "I will completely destroy Samaria. There won't be even enough left for each of my men to get a handful of dust. May the gods punish me terribly if I don't do this!"

[11] Ahab answered, "Tell Ben-Hadad this: 'The man who puts on his armor should not brag too soon. It's the man who lives long enough to take it off who has the right to brag.'"

[12] Now Ben-Hadad was drinking in his tent with the other rulers. The messengers came and gave him the message from Ahab. Ben-Hadad commanded his men to prepare to attack the city. So they moved into their places for the battle.

[13] At the same time a prophet[d] came to Ahab, king of Israel. The prophet said, "Ahab, the Lord says to you, 'Do you see that big army? I will let you defeat it today. Then you will know I am the Lord.'"

[14] Ahab said, "Who will you use to defeat them?"

The prophet answered, "The Lord says, 'The young officers of the district governors will defeat them.'"

Then the king asked, "Who will command the main army?"

The prophet answered, "You will."

[15] So Ahab gathered the young officers of the district governors. There were 232 of them. Then he called together the army of Israel. There were 7,000 of them.

[16] At noon Ben-Hadad and the 32 rulers helping him were getting drunk in their tents. At this time Ahab attacked them. [17] The young officers of the district governors attacked first.

Ben-Hadad's scouts told him that soldiers were coming from Samaria. [18] So

Ben-Hadad said, "They may be coming to fight. Or they may be coming to ask for peace. In either case capture them alive."

[19] The young officers of the district governors led the attack. The army of Israel followed them. [20] Then each officer of Israel killed the man who came against him. So the men from Aram ran away as Israel chased them. But Ben-Hadad king of Aram escaped on a horse with some of his horsemen. [21] Ahab king of Israel led the army. He captured the Arameans' horses and chariots. So King Ahab caused a great defeat of the Aramean army.

[22] Then the prophet went to Ahab king of Israel and said, "The king of Aram will attack you again next spring. So you should go home now and make your army stronger. Make plans to defend yourself."

[23] The officers of Ben-Hadad king of Aram said to him, "The gods of Israel are mountain gods. Since we fought in a mountain area, Israel won. So let's fight them on the flat land. Then we will win. [24] This is what you should do. Don't allow the 32 rulers to command the armies. Put commanders in their places. [25] Gather an army like the one that was destroyed. Gather as many horses and chariots as it had. We will fight the Israelites on flat land. Then we will win." Ben-Hadad agreed with their advice and did what they said.

[26] The next spring Ben-Hadad gathered the people of Aram. He went to Aphek to fight against Israel. [27] The Israelites also prepared for war. They marched out to meet the Arameans and camped opposite them. They looked like two small groups of goats. But the Arameans covered the area.

[28] A man of God came to the king of Israel with this message: "The Lord says, 'The people of Aram say that I, the Lord, am a god of the mountains. They think I am not a god of the valleys. So I will allow you to defeat this big army. Then you will know I am the Lord.'"

[29] The armies were camped across from each other for seven days. On the seventh day the battle began. The Israelites killed 100,000 Aramean soldiers in one day. [30] The rest of them ran away to the city of Aphek. There a city wall fell on 27,000 of them. Ben-Hadad also ran away to the city and hid in a room.

[31] His officers said to him, "We have heard that the kings of Israel are merci-

ful. Let's dress in rough cloth to show our sadness. And let's wear ropes on our heads as a sign of surrender. Then let's go to the king of Israel. Maybe he will let you live."

³²So they dressed in rough cloth and wore ropes on their heads. Then they went to the king of Israel. They said, "Your servant Ben-Hadad says, 'Please let me live.'"

Ahab answered, "Is he still alive? He is my brother."

³³Now Ben-Hadad's men had wanted a sign from Ahab. They wanted to know he would not kill Ben-Hadad. So when Ahab called Ben-Hadad his brother, they quickly said, "Yes! Ben-Hadad is your brother."

Ahab said, "Bring him to me." When Ben-Hadad came, Ahab asked him to join him in the chariot.

³⁴Ben-Hadad said to him, "Ahab, I will give you back the towns my father took from your father. And you may put shops in Damascus, as my father did in Samaria."

Ahab said, "If you agree to this, I will allow you to go free." So the two kings made a peace agreement. Then Ahab let Ben-Hadad go free.

³⁵One of the prophets[d] told another prophet, "Hit me!" He told him to do this because the Lord had commanded it. But the other prophet refused. ³⁶So the first prophet said, "You did not obey the Lord's command. So a lion will kill you as soon as you leave me." When the second prophet left, a lion found him and killed him.

³⁷The first prophet went to another man and said, "Hit me, please!" So the man hit him and hurt him. ³⁸Then the prophet wrapped his face in a cloth. This way no one could tell who he was. Then he went and waited by the road for the king. ³⁹As Ahab king of Israel passed by, the prophet called out to him. The prophet said, "I went to fight in the battle. One of our men brought an enemy soldier to me. Our man said, 'Guard this man. If he runs away, you will have to give your life in his place. Or, you will have to pay a fine of 75 pounds of silver.' ⁴⁰But I became busy doing other things. So the man ran away."

The king of Israel answered, "You have said what the punishment is. You must do what the man said."

⁴¹Then the prophet quickly took the cloth from his face. When the king of Israel saw him, he knew he was one of the prophets. ⁴²Then the prophet said to the king, "This is what the Lord says: 'You set free the man I said should die. So your life will be taken in his place. And the lives of your people will be taken in place of the lives of his people.'"

⁴³Then the king went back to his palace in Samaria. He was angry and upset.

21 A man named Naboth owned a vineyard. It was in Jezreel, near the palace of Ahab king of Israel. ²One day Ahab said to Naboth, "Give me your vineyard. It is near my palace. I want to make it into a vegetable garden. I will give you a better vineyard in its place. Or, if you prefer, I will pay you what it is worth."

³Naboth answered, "May the Lord keep me from ever giving my land to you. It belongs to my family."

⁴So Ahab went home, angry and upset. He did not like what Naboth from Jezreel had said. (Naboth had said, "I will not give you my family's land.") So Ahab lay down on his bed. He turned his face to the wall and refused to eat.

⁵His wife, Jezebel, came in. She asked him, "Why are you upset? Why do you refuse to eat?"

⁶Ahab answered, "I talked to Naboth, the man from Jezreel. I said, 'Sell me your vineyard. Or, if you prefer, I will give you another vineyard for it.' But Naboth refused."

⁷Jezebel answered, "Is this how you rule as king over Israel? Get out of bed. Eat something. Cheer up. I will get Naboth's vineyard for you."

⁸So Jezebel wrote some letters and signed Ahab's name to them. And she used his own seal[d] to seal them. Then she sent them to the older leaders and important men who lived in Naboth's town. ⁹The letter she wrote said: "Declare a day during which the people are to give up eating. Call the people together. And give Naboth a place of honor among them. ¹⁰Seat two troublemakers across from him. Have them say they heard Naboth speak against God and the king. Then take Naboth out of the city and kill him with stones."

¹¹So the older leaders and important men of Jezreel obeyed Jezebel's command. ¹²They declared a special day. On that day the people were to give up eating. They called the people together. And they put Naboth in a place of honor before the people. ¹³Then two troublemakers sat across from Naboth. They

said they had heard Naboth speak against God and the king. So the people carried Naboth out of the city. And they killed him with stones. ¹⁴Then the leaders sent a message to Jezebel. It said, "Naboth has been killed."

¹⁵When Jezebel heard that Naboth had been killed, she told Ahab. She said, "Naboth of Jezreel is dead. Now you may go and take for yourself his vineyard you wanted." ¹⁶When Ahab heard that Naboth was dead, he left. He went to the vineyard to take it for his own.

¹⁷At this time the Lord spoke his word to Elijah. (Elijah was the prophet⁴ from Tishbe.) The Lord said, ¹⁸"Go to Ahab king of Israel, who rules in Samaria. He is at Naboth's vineyard to take it as his own. ¹⁹Tell Ahab that I, the Lord, say to him, 'Ahab! You have murdered Naboth and have taken his land. So I tell you this! In the same place that Naboth died, you will also die. The dogs that licked up Naboth's blood will lick up your blood in the same place!'"

²⁰When Ahab saw Elijah, he said, "So you have found me, my enemy!"

Elijah answered, "Yes, I have found you. You have always chosen to do what the Lord says is wrong. ²¹So the Lord says to you, 'I will destroy you. I will kill you and every male in your family, both slave and free. ²²Your family will be like the family of King Jeroboam son of Nebat. And it will be like the family of King Baasha son of Ahijah. Both of these families were completely destroyed. I will do this to you because you have made me angry. And you have caused the people of Israel to sin.'

²³"And the Lord also says, 'Dogs will eat the body of Jezebel in the city of Jezreel.'

²⁴"Anyone in your family who dies in the city will be eaten by dogs. Anyone who dies in the fields will be eaten by birds."

²⁵There was no one like Ahab. No one had so often chosen to do what the Lord said was wrong. His wife Jezebel influenced him to do evil. ²⁶Ahab sinned terribly by worshiping idols. This was the same thing the Amorite people did. So the Lord took their land away from them. And he gave it to the people of Israel.

²⁷After Elijah finished speaking, Ahab tore his clothes. He put on rough cloth and refused to eat. He even slept in the rough cloth. He did this to show how sad and upset he was.

²⁸The Lord spoke his word to Elijah from Tishbe: ²⁹"I see that Ahab is now sorry for what he has done. So I will not cause the trouble to come to him during his life. I will wait until his son is king. Then I will bring this trouble to Ahab's family."

22For three years there was peace between Israel and Aram. ²During the third year Jehoshaphat king of Judah went to visit Ahab king of Israel.

³At this same time Ahab asked his officers, "Remember that the king of Aram took Ramoth in Gilead from us? Why have we done nothing to get it back?" ⁴So Ahab asked King Jehoshaphat, "Will you go with us? Will you fight against the army of Aram at Ramoth in Gilead?"

Jehoshaphat answered, "I will go with you. My soldiers and my horses are ready to join with your army. ⁵But first we should ask the Lord to guide us."

⁶So Ahab called the prophets⁴ together. There were about 400 men. He asked them, "Should I go to war against the army of Aram at Ramoth in Gilead? Or should I wait?"

The prophets answered, "Go, because the Lord will let you defeat them."

⁷But Jehoshaphat asked, "Isn't there a prophet of the Lord here? Let's ask him what we should do."

⁸King Ahab answered, "There is one other prophet. We could ask the Lord through him. But I hate him. When he prophesies, he never says anything good about me. He always says something bad. He is Micaiah, Imlah's son."

Jehoshaphat said, "King Ahab, you shouldn't say that!"

⁹So Ahab king of Israel told one of his officers to bring Micaiah to him at once.

¹⁰Ahab king of Israel and Jehoshaphat king of Judah had on their royal robes. They were sitting on their thrones at the threshing⁴ floor. This was near the entrance to the gate of Samaria. All the prophets were standing before them, speaking messages from the Lord. ¹¹One of the prophets was Zedekiah son of Kenaanah. He had made some iron horns. He said to Ahab, "This is what the Lord says, 'You will use these horns to fight the Arameans. And you will destroy them.'"

¹²All the other prophets said the same thing. They said, "Attack Ramoth in Gilead and win. The Lord will let you defeat the Arameans."

¹³The messenger who had gone to get

Micaiah found him. He said to Micaiah, "All the other prophets are saying the king will succeed. You should agree with them. Give the king a good answer."

[14] But Micaiah answered, "As surely as the Lord lives, I can tell him only what the Lord tells me."

[15] Then Micaiah came to Ahab. The king asked him, "Micaiah, should we attack Ramoth in Gilead or not?"

Micaiah answered, "Attack and win! The Lord will let you defeat them."

[16] But Ahab said to Micaiah, "Tell me only the truth in the name of the Lord. How many times do I have to tell you this?"

[17] So Micaiah answered, "I saw the army of Israel. They were scattered over the hills like sheep without a shepherd. The Lord said, 'They have no leader. They should go home and not fight.'"

[18] Then Ahab king of Israel said to Jehoshaphat, "I told you! This prophet never says anything good about me. He only says bad things about me."

[19] But Micaiah continued to speak. He said, "Hear the message from the Lord: I saw the Lord sitting on his throne. His heavenly army was standing near him on his right and on his left. [20] The Lord said, 'Who will trick Ahab into attacking Ramoth in Gilead? Do this so he will go and be killed.'

"The spirits did not agree about what they should do. [21] Then one spirit came and stood before the Lord. He said, 'I will trick him.'

[22] "The Lord asked, 'How will you trick Ahab?'

"The spirit answered, 'I will go to Ahab's prophets. I will make them tell lies.'

"So the Lord said, 'You will succeed in tricking him. Go and do it.'"

[23] Micaiah said, "Ahab, this has now happened. The Lord has caused your prophets to lie to you. The Lord has decided that great trouble should come to you."

[24] Then Zedekiah son of Kenaanah went up to Micaiah. And he hit Micaiah in the face. Zedekiah said, "Do you really believe the Lord's spirit has left me and is now speaking through you?"

[25] Micaiah answered, "You will find out on the day you go to hide in an inside room."

[26] Then Ahab king of Israel ordered, "Take Micaiah. Send him to Amon, the governor of the city, and to Joash, the king's son. [27] Tell them I said to put Micaiah in prison. Give him only bread and water for food. Keep him there until I come home from the battle."

[28] Micaiah said, "Ahab, if you come back safely from battle, the Lord has not spoken through me. Remember my words, all you people."

[29] So Ahab king of Israel and Jehoshaphat king of Judah went to Ramoth in Gilead. [30] Ahab said to Jehoshaphat, "I will go into battle. But I will change my appearance so that no one will recognize me. But you wear your royal clothes." So Ahab changed his appearance and went into battle.

[31] The king of Aram had 32 chariot commanders. He ordered them, "Don't fight with anyone but the king of Israel. It doesn't matter if they are important or unimportant." [32] When these commanders saw Jehoshaphat, they thought he was the king of Israel. So they turned to attack him. But Jehoshaphat began shouting. [33] Then the commanders saw he was not Ahab. So they stopped chasing him. [34] A soldier shot an arrow without aiming at anyone. But he hit Ahab king of Israel. The arrow hit him in a place not covered by his armor. King Ahab said to his chariot driver, "Turn the chariot around. Take me out of the battle. I am hurt!" [35] The battle continued all day. King Ahab was in his chariot, leaning against it to hold himself up. He was facing the Arameans. His blood flowed down and covered the bottom of the chariot. That evening he died. [36] Near sunset a cry went out through the army of Israel: "Each man go back to his own country and city."

[37] So in that way King Ahab died. His body was carried to Samaria and buried there. [38] The men cleaned Ahab's chariot at a pool in Samaria. This was a pool where prostitutes[d] bathed. And the dogs licked King Ahab's blood from the chariot. These things happened as the Lord had said they would.

[39] Everything else Ahab did is written down. It is in the book of the history of the kings of Israel. That book also tells about the palace Ahab built and decorated with ivory. And it tells about the cities he built. [40] So Ahab died, and his son Ahaziah became king in his place.

[41] Jehoshaphat son of Asa became king of Judah. This was during Ahab's fourth year as king over Israel. [42] Jehoshaphat was 35 years old when he became king. And he ruled in Jerusalem for 25

years. His mother was the daughter of Shilhi. She was named Azubah. [43]Jehoshaphat was good like his father before him. He did what the Lord said was right. But Jehoshaphat did not destroy the places where false gods were worshiped. So the people continued offering sacrifices and burning incense[d] there. [44]Jehoshaphat was at peace with the king of Israel. [45]Jehoshaphat fought many wars. These wars and his successes are written down. They are in the book of the history of the kings of Judah. [46]There were prostitutes[d] in the places where false gods were worshiped. Jehoshaphat's father, Asa, had not forced all of them out. But Jehoshaphat forced the rest of them to leave.

[47]During this time the land of Edom had no king. It was ruled by a governor.

[48]King Jehoshaphat built trading ships to sail to Ophir for gold. But the ships were destroyed at Ezion Geber. So they never set sail. [49]Ahaziah son of Ahab went to help Jehoshaphat. Ahaziah said he would give Jehoshaphat some men to sail with his men. But Jehoshaphat refused.

[50]Jehoshaphat died and was buried with his ancestors. He was buried in Jerusalem, the city of David, his ancestor. And his son Jehoram became king.

[51]Ahaziah son of Ahab became king of Israel in Samaria. This was during Jehoshaphat's seventeenth year as king over Judah. Ahaziah ruled Israel for two years. [52]Ahaziah did what the Lord said was wrong. He did the same things his father Ahab, his mother Jezebel and Jeroboam son of Nebat had done. All these rulers led the people of Israel into more sin. [53]Ahaziah worshiped and served the god Baal.[d] So Ahaziah made the Lord, the God of Israel, very angry. In these ways Ahaziah did what his father had done.

The Second Book of the
KINGS

1 After Ahab died, Moab broke away from Israel's rule. [2]Ahaziah fell down through the wooden bars in his upstairs room in Samaria. He was badly hurt. He sent messengers and told them, "Go. Ask Baal-Zebub god of Ekron if I will get well from my injuries."

[3]But the Lord's angel said to Elijah the Tishbite, "Get up. Go meet the messengers sent by the king of Samaria. Say to them, 'Why are you going to ask questions of Baal-Zebub god of Ekron? Is it because you think there is no God in Israel?' [4]So this is what the Lord says: 'You will not get up from the bed you are lying on. You will die.'" Then Elijah left.

[5]The messengers came back to Ahaziah. He asked them, "Why have you come back?"

[6]They said, "A man came to meet us. He said, 'Go back to the king who sent you. Tell him what the Lord says: "Why do you send men to ask questions of Baal-Zebub god of Ekron? Is it because you think there is no God in Israel? This is why you will not get up from your bed. You will die."'"

[7]Ahaziah asked them, "What did the man look like who met you and told you this?"

[8]They answered, "He wore a hairy coat and a leather belt around his waist."

Ahaziah said, "It was Elijah the Tishbite."

[9]Then he sent a captain with his 50 men to Elijah. The captain went to Elijah, who was sitting on top of the hill. He said to Elijah, "Man of God, the king says, 'Come down!'"

[10]Elijah answered the captain, "I am a man of God. So let fire come down from heaven and burn up you and your 50 men." Then fire came down from heaven. It burned up the captain and his 50 men.

[11]Ahaziah sent another captain and 50 men to Elijah. The captain said to him, "Man of God, this is what the king says: 'Come down quickly!'"

[12]Elijah answered, "I am a man of God. So let fire come down from heaven and burn up you and your 50 men!" Then fire came down from heaven. It burned up the captain and his 50 men.

[13]Ahaziah sent a third captain with his 50 men. The third captain came and fell down on his knees before Elijah. He

begged Elijah, "Man of God, I ask you. Please let my life and the lives of your 50 servants be valuable to you! ¹⁴See, fire came down from heaven. It burned up the first two captains of 50 with all their men. But now, let my life be valuable to you."

¹⁵The Lord's angel said to Elijah, "Go with him. Don't be afraid of him." So Elijah got up and went with him to see the king.

¹⁶Elijah told Ahaziah, "This is what the Lord says: 'You have sent messengers to ask questions of Baal-Zebub god of Ekron. Is it because you think there is no God in Israel to ask? Because of this, you will not get up from your bed. You will die.'" ¹⁷So he died, just as the Lord, through Elijah, had said he would.

Joram became king in Ahaziah's place. This was during the second year Jehoram son of Jehoshaphat was king of Judah. Joram ruled because Ahaziah had no son to take his place. ¹⁸The other things Ahaziah did are written down. They are in the book of the history of the kings of Israel.

2 It was near the time for the Lord to take Elijah. He was going to take him by a whirlwind up into heaven. Elijah and Elisha were at Gilgal. ²Elijah said to Elisha, "Please stay here. The Lord has told me to go to Bethel."

But Elisha said, "As the Lord lives, and as you live, I won't leave you." So they went down to Bethel. ³A group of the prophets^d at Bethel came to Elisha. They said to him, "Do you know the Lord will take your master away from you today?"

Elisha said, "Yes, I know. But don't talk about it."

⁴Elijah said to him, "Stay here, because the Lord has sent me to Jericho."

But Elisha said, "As the Lord lives, and as you live, I won't leave you."

So they went to Jericho. ⁵A group of the prophets at Jericho came to Elisha. They said, "Do you know that the Lord will take your master away from you today?"

Elisha answered, "Yes, I know. But don't talk about it."

⁶Elijah said to Elisha, "Stay here. The Lord has sent me to the Jordan River."

Elisha answered, "As the Lord lives, and as you live, I won't leave you."

So the two of them went on. ⁷Fifty men from a group of the prophets came. They stood far from where Elijah and Elisha were by the Jordan. ⁸Elijah took off his coat. Then he rolled it up and hit the water. The water divided to the right and to the left. Then Elijah and Elisha crossed over on dry ground.

⁹After they had crossed over, Elijah said to Elisha, "What can I do for you before I am taken from you?"

Elisha said, "Leave me a double share of your spirit."ⁿ

¹⁰Elijah said, "You have asked a hard thing. But if you see me when I am taken from you, it will be yours. If you don't, it won't happen."

¹¹Elijah and Elisha were still walking and talking. Then a chariot and horses of fire appeared. The chariot and horses of fire separated Elijah from Elisha. Then Elijah went up to heaven in a whirlwind. ¹²Elisha saw it and shouted, "My father! My father! The chariots of Israel and their horsemen!" Elisha did not see him anymore. Elisha grabbed his own clothes and tore them to show how sad he was.

¹³He picked up Elijah's coat that had fallen from him. Then Elisha returned and stood on the bank of the Jordan. ¹⁴Elisha hit the water with Elijah's coat. He said, "Where is the Lord, the God of Elijah?" When he hit the water, it divided to the right and to the left. Then Elisha crossed over.

¹⁵A group of the prophets at Jericho were watching. They said, "Elisha now has the spirit Elijah had." They came to meet him. And they bowed down to the ground before him. ¹⁶They said to him, "There are 50 strong men with us! Please let them go and look for your master. Maybe the Spirit^d of the Lord has taken Elijah up and set him down. He may be on some mountain or in some valley."

But Elisha answered, "No. Don't send them."

¹⁷The group of prophets begged Elisha until he hated to refuse them anymore. Then he said, "Send them." So they sent 50 men who looked for three days. But they could not find Elijah. ¹⁸Then they came back to Elisha at Jericho where he was staying. He said to them, "I told you not to go, didn't I?"

2:9 "Leave . . . spirit." By law, the first son in a family would inherit a double share of his father's possessions. Elisha is asking to inherit a share of his master's power. He is not asking for twice as much power as Elijah had.

¹⁹The men of the city said to Elisha, "Look, master, this city is a nice place to live. You can see that. But the water is bad. That's why the land cannot grow crops."

²⁰Elisha said, "Bring me a new bowl and put salt in it." So they brought it to him.

²¹Then Elisha went out to the spring of water and threw the salt in it. He said, "This is what the Lord says: 'I have healed this water. From now on it won't cause death. And it won't keep the land from growing crops.'" ²²The water was healed. It is still good today. It happened just as Elisha had said.

²³From there Elisha went up to Bethel. On the way some young men came out of the city. They made fun of Elisha. They said to him, "Go up, you baldhead! Go up, you baldhead!" ²⁴Elisha turned around and looked at them. He put a curse on them in the name of the Lord. Then two female bears came out of the woods. They tore to pieces 42 of the young men. ²⁵Then Elisha left and went on to Mount Carmel. From there he went back to Samaria.

3 Joram son of Ahab became king over Israel at Samaria. He began to rule in Jehoshaphat's eighteenth year as king of Judah. Joram ruled 12 years. ²Joram did what the Lord said was wrong. But he was not like his father and mother. He removed the stone pillars his father had made for Baal.ᵈ ³But he continued to do the same sins Jeroboam son of Nebat had done. Jeroboam had caused the people of Israel to sin. And Joram did not stop doing these same sins.

⁴Mesha king of Moab raised sheep. He had to give 100,000 lambs and the wool of 100,000 male sheep to the king of Israel. ⁵But when Ahab died, the king of Moab turned against the king of Israel. ⁶So King Joram went out from Samaria and gathered all Israel. ⁷He sent messengers to Jehoshaphat king of Judah. He said, "The king of Moab has turned against me. Will you go with me against Moab in battle?"

Jehoshaphat said, "I will go with you. I am ready to join you. My soldiers and my horses are ready to join with your army."

⁸Jehoshaphat asked, "Which way should we go to attack?"

Joram answered, "Through the Desert of Edom."

⁹So the king of Israel went with the king of Judah and the king of Edom. They marched seven days. There was no more water for the army or for their animals that were with them. ¹⁰The king of Israel said, "How terrible this is! Has the Lord called us three kings together so the Moabites can defeat us?"

¹¹But Jehoshaphat asked, "Is there a prophetᵈ of the Lord here? We can ask the Lord through a prophet."

An officer of the king of Israel answered, "Elisha son of Shaphat is here. He was Elijah's servant."

¹²Jehoshaphat said, "He speaks the Lord's truth." So the king of Israel and Jehoshaphat and the king of Edom went down to see Elisha.

¹³Elisha spoke to the king of Israel. He said, "I have nothing to do with you! Go to the prophets of your father and to the prophets of your mother!"

The king of Israel said to Elisha, "No. The Lord has called us three kings together to let the Moabites defeat us."

¹⁴Elisha said, "I serve the Lord of heaven's armies. As surely as he lives, I tell you the truth. I wouldn't even look at you or notice you if Jehoshaphat king of Judah were not here. I respect him! ¹⁵Now bring me someone who plays the harp."

While the harp was being played, the Lord gave Elisha power. ¹⁶Then Elisha said, "The Lord says to dig holes in the valley. ¹⁷He says that you won't see wind or rain. But the valley will be filled with water. Then you, your cattle and other animals will drink. ¹⁸This is easy for the Lord to do. He will also let you defeat Moab. ¹⁹You will destroy every strong, walled city and every important town. You will cut down every good tree. You will stop up all springs of water. You will ruin every good field with rocks."

²⁰The next morning, about the time the sacrifice was offered, there was water! It came from the direction of Edom and filled the valley.

²¹All the Moabites had heard that the kings had come up to fight against them. They gathered everyone old enough to put on armor. And they waited at the border. ²²But when the Moabites got up early in the morning, the sun was shining on the water. They saw the water across from them. It looked as red as blood. ²³The Moabites said, "This is blood! Surely the kings have fought and killed each other! Come, Moabites, let's take what is valuable from the dead bodies!"

²⁴The Moabites came to the camp of the Israelites. But the Israelites came out and fought them until they ran away. The Israelites went on into the land to fight the Moabites. ²⁵They tore down the cities. They threw rocks on every good field and filled it. They stopped up all the springs of water. And they cut down all the good trees. Kir Hareseth was the only city with its stones still in place. But the men with slings surrounded Kir Hareseth and conquered it, too.

²⁶The king of Moab saw that the battle was too strong for him. So he took 700 men with swords to break through to the king of Edom. But they could not break through. ²⁷Then the king of Moab took his oldest son, who would have become king after him. And he offered his son as a burnt offering on the wall. So there was great anger against the Israelites. They left and went back to their own land.

4 The wife of a man from a group of the prophets[d] came to Elisha. She said, "Your servant, my husband, is dead! You know he honored the Lord. But now the man he owes money to is coming to take my two boys. He will make them his slaves!"

²Elisha answered, "How can I help you? Tell me, what do you have in your house?"

The woman said, "I don't have anything except a pot of oil."

³Then Elisha said, "Go and get empty jars from all your neighbors. Don't ask for just a few. ⁴Then you must go into your house and close the door. Only you and your sons will be there. Then pour oil into all the jars. Set the full ones to one side."

⁵She left Elisha and shut the door. Only she and her sons were in the house. As they brought the jars to her, she poured the oil. ⁶When the jars were all full, she said to her son, "Bring me another jar."

But he said, "There are no more jars." Then the oil stopped flowing.

⁷She went and told Elisha. Elisha said to her, "Go. Sell the oil and pay what you owe. You and your sons can live on what is left."

⁸One day Elisha went to Shunem. An important woman lived there. She begged Elisha to stay and eat. So every

time Elisha passed by, he stopped there to eat. ⁹The woman said to her husband, "I know that Elisha is a holy man of God. He passes by our house all the time. ¹⁰Let's make a small room on the roof.[n] Let's put a bed in the room for Elisha. And we can put a table, a chair and a lampstand there. Then when he comes by, he can stay there."

¹¹One day Elisha came to the woman's house. He went to his room and rested. ¹²He said to his servant Gehazi, "Call the Shunammite."

When the servant called her, she stood in front of him. ¹³Elisha told his servant, "Now say to her, 'You have gone to all this trouble for us. What can I do for you? Do you want me to speak to the king or the commander of the army for you?'"

The woman answered, "I live among my own people."

¹⁴Elisha said, "But what can we do for her?"

Gehazi answered, "She has no son, and her husband is old."

¹⁵Then Elisha said, "Call her." So he called her, and she stood in the doorway. ¹⁶Then Elisha said, "About this time next year, you will hold a son in your arms."

The woman said, "No, master, man of God. Don't lie to me!"

¹⁷But the woman became pregnant. And she gave birth to a son at that time the next year as Elisha had told her.

¹⁸The child grew. One day he went out to his father, who was with the men harvesting grain. ¹⁹The boy said to his father, "My head! My head!"

The father said to his servant, "Carry him to his mother!" ²⁰The servant took him to his mother. He lay on his mother's lap until noon. Then he died. ²¹She took him up and laid him on Elisha's bed. Then she shut the door and went out.

²²She called to her husband. She said, "Send me one of the servants and one of the donkeys. Then I can go quickly to the man of God and come back."

²³The woman's husband said, "Why do you want to go to him today? It isn't the New Moon[d] or the Sabbath[d] day."

She said, "It will be all right."

²⁴Then she saddled the donkey and said to her servant, "Lead on. Don't

4:10 roof In Bible times houses were built with flat roofs. The roof was used for drying things such as flax and fruit. And it was used as an extra room, as a place for worship and as a place to sleep in the summer.

slow down for me unless I tell you." ²⁵So she went to Elisha at Mount Carmel.

He saw her coming from far away. So he said to his servant Gehazi, "Look, there's the Shunammite woman! ²⁶Run to meet her! Say to her, 'Are you all right? Is your husband all right? Is the child all right?'"

She answered, "Everything is all right."

²⁷Then she came to Elisha at the hill. She caught hold of his feet. Gehazi came near to pull her away. But Elisha said to him, "Let her alone. She's very upset, and the Lord has not told me about it. He has hidden it from me."

²⁸She said, "Master, I didn't tell you I wanted a son. I told you, 'Don't fool me.'"

²⁹Then Elisha said to Gehazi, "Get ready. Take my walking stick in your hand and go quickly. If you meet anyone, don't greet him. If anyone greets you, don't answer him. Lay my walking stick on the face of the boy."

³⁰But the child's mother said, "As surely as the Lord lives and as you live, I won't leave you!" So he got up and followed her.

³¹Gehazi went on ahead. He laid the walking stick on the child's face. But the child did not talk or move. Then Gehazi went back to meet Elisha. He told Elisha, "The child has not awakened."

³²Elisha came into the house. There was the child, lying dead on his bed. ³³When Elisha entered the room, he shut the door. Only he and the child were in the room. Then Elisha prayed to the Lord. ³⁴He went to the bed and lay on the child. He put his mouth on the child's mouth. He put his eyes on the child's eyes and his hands on the child's hands. He stretched himself out on top of the child. Then the child's skin became warm. ³⁵Elisha turned away and walked around the room. Then he went back and put himself on the child again. Then the child sneezed seven times and opened his eyes.

³⁶Elisha called Gehazi and said, "Call the Shunammite!" And he did. When she came, Elisha said, "Pick up your son." ³⁷She came in and fell at Elisha's feet. She bowed facedown to the floor. Then she picked up her son and went out.

³⁸Elisha came to Gilgal again. There was a time of hunger in the land. A group of prophets[d] was sitting in front of him. He said to his servant, "Put the large pot on the fire. Boil some stew for these men."

³⁹One of them went out into the field to gather plants. He found a wild vine. He picked fruit from the vine and filled his robe with it. Then he came and cut up the fruit into the pot. But they did not know what kind of fruit it was. ⁴⁰Then they poured out the stew for the men to eat. But when they began to eat it, they shouted out, "Man of God! There's death in the pot!" They could not eat it.

⁴¹Elisha told them to bring some flour. Then he threw it into the pot. He said, "Pour it out for the people to eat." And there was nothing harmful in the pot.

⁴²A man from Baal Shalishah came to Elisha. He brought 20 loaves of barley bread from the first harvest to Elisha. He also brought fresh grain in his sack. Then Elisha said, "Give it to the people to eat."

⁴³Elisha's servant said, "How can I feed 100 men with so little?"

But Elisha said, "Give the bread to the people to eat. This is what the Lord says: 'They will eat and will have food left over.'" ⁴⁴Then he gave it to them. The people ate and had food left over, as the Lord had said.

5 Naaman was commander of the army of the king of Aram. He was a great man to his master. He had much honor because the Lord had used him to give victory to Aram. He was a mighty and brave man. But he had a harmful skin disease.

²The Arameans had gone out to steal from the Israelites. And they had taken a little girl as a captive from Israel. This little girl served Naaman's wife. ³She said to her mistress, "I wish that my master would meet the prophet[d] who lives in Samaria. He would heal Naaman of his disease."

⁴Naaman went to the king. He told him what the girl from Israel had said. ⁵The king of Aram said, "Go now. And I will send a letter to the king of Israel." So Naaman left and took about 750 pounds of silver. He also took about 150 pounds of gold and ten changes of clothes with him. ⁶He brought the letter to the king of Israel. It read, "I am sending my servant Naaman to you. I'm sending him so you can heal him of his skin disease."

⁷The king of Israel read the letter. Then he tore his clothes to show how upset he was. He said, "I'm not God! I can't kill and make alive again! Why

does this man send someone with a harmful skin disease for me to heal? You can see that the king of Aram is trying to start trouble with me!"

[8]Elisha, the man of God, heard that the king of Israel had torn his clothes. So he sent a message to the king. It said, "Why have you become so upset that you tore your clothes? Let Naaman come to me. Then he will know there is a prophet in Israel!" [9]So Naaman went with his horses and chariots to Elisha's house. And he stood outside the door.

[10]Elisha sent a messenger to Naaman. The messenger said, "Go and wash in the Jordan River seven times. Then your skin will be healed, and you will be clean."

[11]Naaman became angry and left. He said, "I thought Elisha would surely come out and stand before me. I thought he would call on the name of the Lord his God. I thought he would wave his hand over the place and heal the disease! [12]Abana and Pharpar, the rivers of Damascus, are better than all the waters of Israel! Why can't I wash in them and become clean?" So Naaman went away very angry.

[13]But Naaman's servants came near and talked to him. They said, "My father, if the prophet had told you to do some great thing, wouldn't you have done it? Doesn't it make more sense just to do it? After all, he only told you, 'Wash, and you will be clean.'" [14]So Naaman went down and dipped in the Jordan seven times. He did just as Elisha had said. Then Naaman's skin became new again. It was like the skin of a little boy. And Naaman was clean!

[15]Naaman and all his group came back to Elisha. He stood before Elisha and said, "Look. I now know there is no God in all the earth except in Israel! Now please accept a gift from me."

[16]But Elisha said, "I serve the Lord. As surely as the Lord lives, I won't accept anything." Naaman urged him to take the gift, but he refused.

[17]Then Naaman said, "If you won't take the gift, then please give me some dirt. Give me as much as two of my mules can carry. From now on I'll not offer any burnt offering or sacrifice to any other gods. I'll only offer sacrifices to the Lord. [18]But let the Lord pardon me for this: My master goes into the temple of Rimmon[n] to worship. When

he goes, he will lean on my arm. Then I must bow in that temple. May the Lord pardon me when I do that."

[19]Elisha said to him, "Go in peace."

Naaman left Elisha and went a short way. [20]Gehazi was the servant of Elisha the man of God. Gehazi thought, "My master has not accepted what Naaman the Aramean brought. As surely as the Lord lives, I'll run after him. I'll get something from him." [21]So he went after him.

Naaman saw someone running after him. So he got off the chariot to meet Gehazi. He said, "Is everything all right?"

[22]Gehazi said, "Everything is all right. My master has sent me. He said, 'Two young men just came to me. They are from the group of the prophets in the mountains of Ephraim. Please give them 75 pounds of silver and two changes of clothes.'"

[23]Naaman said, "Please take 150 pounds." He urged Gehazi to take it. He tied 150 pounds of silver in two bags with two changes of clothes. Then he gave them to two of his servants. They carried them for Gehazi. [24]When they came to the hill, Gehazi took these things from Naaman's servants. And he put them in the house. He let Naaman's servants go, and they left.

[25]Then he came in and stood before his master. Elisha said to him, "Where have you been, Gehazi?"

Gehazi said, "I didn't go anywhere."

[26]But Elisha said to him, "My spirit was with you. I knew when the man turned from his chariot to meet you. This isn't a time to receive money, clothes, olives and grapes. It isn't a time to receive sheep, oxen, male servants and female servants. [27]Naaman's skin disease will come on you and your children forever." When Gehazi left Elisha, he had the disease. He was as white as snow.

6 The group of the prophets[d] said to Elisha, "The place where we meet with you is too small for us. [2]Let's go to the Jordan River. There every man can get a pole. And let's build a place there to live."

Elisha said, "Go."

[3]One of them said, "Please go with us."

Elisha said, "I will go." [4]So he went with them. When they arrived at the Jordan, they cut down some trees. [5] As one man was cutting down a tree, the head of his ax fell into the water. He yelled, "Oh, my master! I borrowed that ax!"

[6] Elisha asked, "Where did it fall?" The man showed Elisha the place. Then Elisha cut down a stick and threw it into the water. It made the iron head float. [7] Elisha said, "Pick up the axhead." Then the man reached out and took it.

[8] The king of Aram was at war with Israel. He had a council meeting with his officers. He said, "I will set up my camp in this place."

[9] But Elisha sent a message to the king of Israel. It said, "Be careful! Don't pass that place. The Arameans are going down there!"

[10] The king of Israel checked the place about which Elisha had warned him. Elisha warned him several times. So the king added guards in those places.

[11] The king of Aram was angry about this. He called his officers together. He said to them, "Tell me who of us is working for the king of Israel!"

[12] One of the officers of the king of Aram said, "No, my master and king. It's Elisha, the prophet from Israel. He can tell you what you speak in your bedroom."

[13] The king said, "Go and find him. Then I can send men and catch him."

The servants came back and reported, "He is in Dothan."

[14] Then the king sent horses, chariots and a large army to Dothan. They arrived at night and surrounded the city.

[15] The servant of Elisha got up early. When he went out, he saw an army with horses and chariots all around the city. The servant said to Elisha, "Oh, my master, what can we do?"

[16] Elisha said, "Don't be afraid. The army that fights for us is larger than the one against us."

[17] Then Elisha prayed, "Lord, open my servant's eyes. Let him see."

The Lord opened the eyes of the young man. And he saw that the mountain was full of horses and chariots of fire all around Elisha.

[18] As the enemy came down toward Elisha, he prayed to the Lord. He said, "Make these people blind." So the Lord made the Aramean army blind, as Elisha had asked.

[19] Elisha said to them, "This is not the right road. This is not the right city. Follow me. I'll take you to the man you are looking for." Then Elisha led them to Samaria.

[20] After they entered Samaria, Elisha said, "Lord, open these men's eyes so they can see." So the Lord opened their eyes. And the Aramean army saw that they were inside the city of Samaria!

[21] The king of Israel saw the Aramean army. He said to Elisha, "My father, should I kill them? Should I kill them?"

[22] Elisha answered, "Don't kill them. You wouldn't kill people whom you captured with your sword and bow. Give them food and water. And let them eat and drink. Then let them go home to their master." [23] So he prepared a great feast for the Aramean army. They ate and drank. Then the king sent them away. They went home to their master. The soldiers of Aram did not come anymore into the land of Israel.

[24] Later, Ben-Hadad king of Aram gathered all his army. He went to surround and attack Samaria. [25] There was a time of terrible hunger in Samaria. It was so bad that a donkey's head was sold for about two pounds of silver. Half of a pint of dove's dung sold for about two ounces of silver.

[26] The king of Israel was passing by on the wall. A woman yelled out to him, "Help me, my master and king!"

[27] The king said, "If the Lord doesn't help you, how can I? Can I get help from the threshing[d] floor or from the winepress?"[d] [28] Then the king said to her, "What is your trouble?"

She answered, "This woman said to me, 'Give up your son so we can eat him today. Then we will eat my son tomorrow.' [29] So we boiled my son and ate him. Then the next day I said to her, 'Give up your son so we can eat him.' But she had hidden him."

[30] When the king heard the woman's words, he tore his clothes to show how upset he was. He walked along the wall. The people looked and saw he had on rough cloth under his clothes. This was to show his sadness. [31] He said, "The head of Elisha son of Shaphat will be taken from his body today! May God punish me terribly if this doesn't happen!"

[32] The king sent a messenger to Elisha. Elisha was sitting in his house. And the older leaders were sitting with him. But before the messenger arrived, Elisha spoke to them. He said, "See, this murderer is sending men to take off my head. When the messenger arrives, shut

the door. Hold it and don't let him in. The sound of his master's feet is behind him."

[33] While Elisha was still talking with the leaders, the king came. He said, "This trouble has come from the Lord. Why should I wait for the Lord any longer?"

7 Elisha said, "Listen to the Lord's word. This is what he says: 'About this time tomorrow 7 quarts of fine flour will be sold for two-fifths of an ounce of silver. And 13 quarts of barley will be sold for two-fifths of an ounce of silver. This will happen at the gate of Samaria.'"

[2] Then the officer who was close to the king answered Elisha. He said, "Even if the Lord opened windows in heaven, that couldn't happen."

Elisha said, "Because you have said that, you will see it with your eyes. But you will not eat any of it."

[3] There were four men with a harmful skin disease at the entrance to the city gate. They said to each other, "Why do we sit here until we die? [4] A time of hunger is in the city. So if we go into the city, we will die there. If we stay here, we will die. So let's go to the Aramean camp. If they let us live, we will live. If they kill us, then we die."

[5] So they got up at twilight. And they went to the Aramean camp. But when they arrived, no one was there. [6] The Lord had caused the Aramean army to hear the sound of chariots, horses and a large army. They had said to each other, "The king of Israel has hired the Hittite and Egyptian kings to attack us!" [7] So they ran away in the twilight. They left their tents, horses and donkeys. They left the camp standing and ran for their lives.

[8] The men with the skin disease came to the edge of the camp. Then they went into one of the tents. They ate and drank. They carried silver, gold and clothes out of the camp and hid them. Then they came back and entered another tent. They carried things from this tent and hid them, also. [9] Then they said to each other, "We're doing wrong. Today we have good news, but we are silent. If we wait until the sun comes up, we'll be punished. Let's go now and tell the people in the king's palace."

[10] So they went and called to the gatekeepers of the city. They said, "We went to the Aramean camp. But no one is there. We didn't hear anyone. The horses and donkeys were still tied up, and the tents were still standing." [11] Then the gatekeepers shouted out and told the people in the palace.

[12] So the king got up in the night. He said to his officers, "I'll tell you what the Arameans are doing to us. They know we are hungry. They have gone out of the camp to hide in the field. They're saying, 'When the Israelites come out of the city, we'll capture them alive. Then we'll enter the city.'"

[13] One of his officers answered, "Let some men take five horses still left in the city. These men are like all the Israelites who are left. They are also about to die. Let's send them to see what has happened."

[14] So the men took two chariots with horses. The king sent them after the Aramean army. He told them, "Go and see what has happened." [15] The men followed the Aramean army as far as the Jordan River. The road was full of clothes and equipment. The Arameans had thrown these things away as they had hurried away. So the messengers came back and told the king. [16] Then the people went out and took valuable things from the Aramean camp. So 7 quarts of fine flour were sold for two-fifths of an ounce of silver. And 13 quarts of barley were sold for two-fifths of an ounce of silver. It happened just as the Lord had said.

[17] The king chose the officer who was close to him to guard the gate. But the people ran over the officer so that he died. This happened just as the man of God had told the king. Elisha had said it when the king came to his house. [18] He had said, "Thirteen quarts of barley and 7 quarts of fine flour will each sell for two-fifths of an ounce of silver. It will happen about this time tomorrow at the gate of Samaria."

[19] But the officer had answered, "Even if the Lord opened windows in heaven, that couldn't happen." And Elisha had told him, "Because you have said that, you will see it with your eyes. But you won't eat any of it." [20] It happened to the officer just that way. The people ran over him in the gate, and he died.

8 Elisha talked to the woman whose son he had brought back to life. He said, "Get up and go with your family. Stay any place you can. This is because the Lord has called for a time of hunger. It will last seven years." [2] So the woman got up and did as the man of God said.

She left with her family. And they stayed in the land of the Philistines for seven years. [3]After seven years she came back from the land of the Philistines. She went to beg the king for her house and land back. [4]The king was talking with Gehazi. He was the servant of the man of God. The king had said to Gehazi, "Please tell me all the great things Elisha has done." [5]Now Gehazi was telling the king how Elisha had brought a dead person back to life. Just then the woman whose son Elisha had brought back to life came and begged the king for her house and land.

Gehazi said, "My master and king, this is the woman. And this is the son Elisha brought back to life."

[6]The king asked the woman, and she told him about it. Then the king chose an officer to help her. The king said, "Give the woman everything that is hers. Give her all the money made from her land from the day she left until now."

[7]Elisha went to Damascus. Now Ben-Hadad king of Aram was sick. Someone told him, "The man of God has come here."

[8]Then the king said to Hazael, "Take a gift in your hand and go meet him. Ask the Lord through him if I will get well from my sickness."

[9]So Hazael went to meet Elisha. He took with him a gift. It was 40 camels loaded with every good thing in Damascus. He came and stood before Elisha. Hazael said, "Your son Ben-Hadad king of Aram sent me to you. He asks if he will get well from his sickness."

[10]Then Elisha said to Hazael, "Go and tell Ben-Hadad, 'You will surely get well.' But the Lord has told me he will really die." [11]Elisha stared at Hazael until Hazael felt ashamed. Then Elisha cried.

[12]Hazael asked, "Why are you crying, master?"

Elisha answered, "Because I know what evil you will do to the Israelites. You will burn their strong, walled cities with fire. You will kill their young men with swords. You will throw their babies to the ground. You will split open their pregnant women."

[13]Hazael said, "I, your servant, am only a dog. How could I do such things?"

Elisha answered, "The Lord has shown me that you will be king over Aram."

[14]Then Hazael left Elisha and came to his master. Ben-Hadad said to Hazael, "What did Elisha say to you?"

Hazael answered, "He told me that you will surely get well." [15]But the next day Hazael took a blanket and dipped it in water. Then he put it over Ben-Hadad's face, and he died. So Hazael became king in Ben-Hadad's place.

[16]Jehoram son of Jehoshaphat became king of Judah. This was during Joram's fifth year as king of Israel. Joram was the son of Ahab. [17]Jehoram was 32 years old when he began to rule. He ruled eight years in Jerusalem. [18]But Jehoram followed the ways of the kings of Israel. This was just as the family of Ahab had done. It was because Ahab's daughter was Jehoram's wife. Jehoram did what the Lord said was wrong. [19]But the Lord would not destroy Judah because of his servant David. The Lord had promised that David and his children would always have a kingdom.

[20]In Jehoram's time Edom broke away from Judah's rule. The people of Edom chose their own king. [21]So Jehoram and all his chariots went to Zair. At night the Edomites came around him and his chariot commanders. Jehoram got up and attacked the Edomites. But his army ran away to their tents. [22]So the Edomites broke away from the rule of Judah. And they are still separate today. At the same time Libnah also broke away from Judah's rule.

[23]The other acts of Jehoram and all the things he did are written down. They are in the book of the history of the kings of Judah. [24]Jehoram died and was buried with his ancestors in Jerusalem. Jehoram's son Ahaziah ruled in his place.

[25]Ahaziah son of Jehoram became king of Judah. This was during Joram's twelfth year as king of Israel. Joram was the son of Ahab. [26]Ahaziah was 22 years old when he became king. He ruled one year in Jerusalem. His mother's name was Athaliah. She was a granddaughter of Omri king of Israel. [27]Ahaziah followed the ways of Ahab's family. He did what the Lord said was wrong, as Ahab's family had done. He did this because he was a son-in-law in Ahab's family.

[28]Ahaziah went with Joram son of Ahab to Ramoth in Gilead. There they fought against Hazael king of Aram. The Arameans wounded Joram. [29]So King Joram returned to Jezreel to heal from the injuries. (He had been wounded

by the Arameans at Ramoth. This was when he fought Hazael king of Aram.) And Ahaziah son of Jehoram king of Judah went down to see Joram. He went to see Joram son of Ahab at Jezreel because he had been wounded.

9 Elisha called a man from the group of the prophets.[d] Elisha said, "Tighten your clothes around you. And take this small bottle of olive oil in your hand. Go to Ramoth in Gilead. [2]When you arrive, find Jehu son of Jehoshaphat. Jehoshaphat is the son of Nimshi. Go in and make Jehu get up from among his brothers. Take him to an inner room. [3]Take the bottle and pour the oil on Jehu's head. Say, 'This is what the Lord says: I have appointed you king over Israel.' Then open the door and run away. Don't wait!"

[4]So the young man, the prophet, went to Ramoth in Gilead. [5]When he arrived, he saw the officers of the army sitting together. He said, "Commander, I have a message for you."

Jehu asked, "For which one of us?"

The young man said, "For you, commander."

[6]Jehu got up and went into the house. Then the young prophet poured the olive oil on Jehu's head. He said to Jehu, "This is what the Lord of Israel says: 'I have appointed you king over the Lord's people, Israel. [7]You must destroy the family of Ahab your master. I will punish Jezebel for the deaths of my servants the prophets. And I will punish her for all the Lord's servants who were murdered. [8]So all Ahab's family will die. I will not let any male child in Ahab's family live in Israel. It does not matter if he is a slave or a free person. [9]I will make Ahab's family like the family of Jeroboam son of Nebat. They will be like the family of Baasha son of Ahijah. [10]The dogs will eat Jezebel in the portion of land at Jezreel. And no one will bury her.'"

Then the young prophet opened the door and ran away.

[11]Jehu went back to his master's officers. One of them said to Jehu, "Is everything all right? Why did this crazy man come to you?"

Jehu answered, "You know the man and how he talks."

[12]They answered, "That's not true! Tell us."

Jehu said, "He said, 'This is what the Lord says: I have appointed you to be king over Israel.'"

[13]Then the officers hurried. Each man took off his own coat. They put them on the stairs for Jehu. Then they blew the trumpet. They said, "Jehu is king!"

[14]So Jehu son of Jehoshaphat made plans against Joram. (Jehoshaphat was the son of Nimshi.) Now Joram and all Israel had been defending Ramoth in Gilead from Hazael king of Aram. [15]But King Joram had to return to Israel to heal from the injuries the Arameans had given him. He received these injuries when he fought against Hazael king of Aram.

Jehu said, "If you agree with this, don't let anyone leave the city. They might tell the news in Jezreel." [16]Then he got into his chariot and set out for Jezreel. Joram was resting there. And Ahaziah king of Judah had gone down to see him.

[17]The lookout was standing on the watchtower in Jezreel. He saw Jehu's troops coming. He said, "I see some soldiers!"

Joram said, "Take a horseman and send him to meet them. Tell him to ask, 'Do you bring good news?'"

[18]So the horseman rode out to meet Jehu. The horseman said, "This is what the king says: 'Do you bring good news?'"

Jehu said, "That's none of your business! Come along behind me."

The lookout reported, "The messenger reached them. But he is not coming back."

[19]So Joram sent out a second horseman. This rider came to Jehu's group and said, "This is what the king says: 'Do you bring good news?'"

Jehu answered, "That's none of your business! Come along behind me."

[20]The lookout reported, "The second man reached them. But he is not coming back. The man in the chariot is driving like Jehu son of Nimshi. He drives as if he were crazy!"

[21]Joram said, "Get my chariot ready." Then the servant got Joram's chariot ready. Joram and Ahaziah king of Judah went out. Each king went in his own chariot to meet Jehu. And they met him at the property of Naboth the Jezreelite.

[22]When Joram saw Jehu, he said, "Do you bring good news, Jehu?"

Jehu answered, "There will never be any good news as long as your mother Jezebel worships idols and uses witchcraft."[d]

[23]Joram turned the horses to run away.

He yelled to Ahaziah, "It's a trick, Ahaziah!"

²⁴Then Jehu drew his bow and shot Joram between his shoulders. The arrow went through Joram's heart. And he fell down in his chariot.

²⁵Jehu ordered Bidkar, his chariot officer, "Pick up Joram's body. Throw it into the field of Naboth the Jezreelite. Remember when you and I rode together with Joram's father Ahab. The Lord made this prophecy[d] against him: ²⁶'Yesterday I saw the blood of Naboth and his sons, says the Lord. So I will punish Ahab in his field, says the Lord.' So take Joram's body and throw it into the field, as the Lord has said."

²⁷When Ahaziah king of Judah saw this, he ran away toward Beth Haggan. Jehu chased him, saying, "Shoot Ahaziah, too!" Ahaziah was wounded in his chariot on the way up to Gur near Ibleam. Ahaziah got as far as Megiddo but died there. ²⁸His servants carried his body in a chariot to Jerusalem. They buried him with his ancestors in his tomb in Jerusalem. ²⁹(Ahaziah had become king over Judah in Joram's eleventh year as king. Joram was the son of Ahab.)

³⁰When Jehu came to Jezreel, Jezebel heard about it. She put paint on her eyes and fixed her hair. Then she looked out the window. ³¹Jehu entered the city gate. And Jezebel said, "Have you come in peace, you Zimri,[n] you who killed your master?"

³²Jehu looked up at the window. He said, "Who is on my side? Who?" Two or three eunuchs[d] looked out from the window at Jehu. ³³Jehu said to them, "Throw her down!" So they threw Jezebel down. And the horses ran over her body. Some of her blood splashed on the wall and on the horses.

³⁴Jehu went into the house and ate and drank. Then he said, "Now see about this cursed woman. Bury her, because she is a king's daughter."

³⁵The men went to bury Jezebel. But they could not find her body. They could only find the skull, feet and palms of her hands. ³⁶So they came back and told Jehu. Then Jehu said, "The Lord said this through his servant Elijah the Tishbite: 'The dogs will eat the body of Jezebel in the portion of land at Jezreel. ³⁷Her body will be like manure on the field in the land at Jezreel. Then people cannot say that the body is Jezebel.'"

10 Ahab's family had 70 sons in Samaria. Jehu wrote letters and sent them to Samaria. He sent them to the officers and older leaders of Jezreel. He also sent them to the guardians of the sons of Ahab. Jehu said, ²"You have chariots, horses and a city with strong walls. You also have weapons. When you get this letter, ³choose the best and most worthy person among your master's sons. Make him king. Then fight for your master's family."

⁴But the officers and older leaders of Jezreel were very frightened. They said, "The two kings could not stop Jehu. So, surely we can't either."

⁵The palace manager, the city governor, the older leaders and the guardians sent a message to Jehu. They said, "We are your servants. We will do everything you tell us to do. We won't make any man king. Do whatever you think is best."

⁶Then Jehu wrote a second letter. It said, "If you are on my side and will obey me, cut off the heads of your master's sons. And come to me at Jezreel tomorrow about this time."

Now there were 70 sons of the king's family. They were with the leading men of the city who were their guardians. ⁷The leaders received the letter. Then they took the king's sons and killed all 70 of them. They put their heads in baskets. And they sent them to Jehu at Jezreel. ⁸The messenger came to Jehu. He told Jehu, "They have brought the heads of the king's sons!"

Then Jehu said, "Lay the heads in two piles at the city gate until morning."

⁹In the morning, Jehu went out and stood before the people. He said to them, "You are innocent. Look, I made plans against my master. I killed him. But who killed all these? ¹⁰You should know that nothing the Lord said will fail. Everything the Lord said about Ahab's family will come true. The Lord has spoken through his servant Elijah. And the Lord has done what he said." ¹¹So Jehu killed everyone of Ahab's family in Jezreel who was still alive. He also killed all Ahab's leading men, close friends and priests. No one was left alive who had helped Ahab.

¹²Then Jehu left and went to Samaria. He went on the road to Beth Eked of

9:31 Zimri He was the man who killed Elah and the family of Baasha. Read 1 Kings 16:8-12.

the Shepherds. [13]There Jehu met some relatives of Ahaziah king of Judah. Jehu said, "Who are you?"

They answered, "We are relatives of Ahaziah. We have come down to visit the families of the king and the king's mother."

[14]Then Jehu said, "Take them alive!" So they captured Ahaziah's relatives alive. But they killed them at the well near Beth Eked. There were 42 of them. Jehu did not leave anyone alive.

[15]After Jehu left there, he met Jehonadab son of Recab. He was also on his way to meet Jehu. Jehu greeted him and said, "Are you as good a friend to me as I am to you?"

Jehonadab answered, "Yes, I am."

Jehu said, "If you are, then give me your hand." So Jehonadab gave him his hand, and Jehu pulled him into the chariot. [16]Jehu said, "Come with me. You can see how strong my feelings are for the Lord." So Jehu had Jehonadab ride in his chariot.

[17]When Jehu came to Samaria, he killed all of Ahab's family. He did this until he had destroyed all of those who were left. Jehu did what the Lord had told Elijah would happen.

[18]Then Jehu gathered all the people together. He said to them, "Ahab served Baal[d] a little. But Jehu will serve Baal much. [19]Now call for me all Baal's prophets and priests. Call all the people who worship Baal. Don't let anyone miss this meeting. I have a great sacrifice for Baal. Anyone who is not there will not remain alive." But Jehu was tricking them so he could destroy the worshipers of Baal. [20]He said, "Prepare a holy meeting for Baal." So they announced the meeting. [21]Then Jehu sent word through all Israel. All the worshipers of Baal came. Not one stayed home. They came into the temple of Baal. The temple was filled from one side to the other.

[22]Jehu spoke to the man who kept the robes. He said, "Bring out robes for all the worshipers of Baal." So he brought out robes for them. [23]Then Jehu and Jehonadab son of Recab went into the temple of Baal. Jehu said to the worshipers of Baal, "Look around. Be sure there are no servants of the Lord with you. Be sure there are only people here who worship Baal." [24]So the worshipers of Baal went in to offer sacrifices and burnt offerings.

But Jehu had 80 men waiting outside.

He told them, "Don't let anyone escape. If you let anyone escape, you must pay with your own life."

[25]Jehu finished offering the burnt offering. Then he spoke to the guards and the captains. He said, "Go in and kill the worshipers of Baal! Don't let anyone come out." So the guards and captains killed the worshipers of Baal with the sword. They threw the bodies of the worshipers of Baal out. Then they went to the inner rooms of the temple. [26]They brought out the pillars of the temple of Baal and burned them. [27]Then they tore down the stone pillar of Baal. They also tore down the temple of Baal. They made it into a sewage pit, and it is still one today.

[28]So Jehu destroyed Baal worship in Israel. [29]But he did not stop doing the sins Jeroboam son of Nebat had done. Jeroboam had caused Israel to sin. They worshiped the golden calves in Bethel and Dan.

[30]The Lord said to Jehu, "You have done well. You have done what I said was right. You have done to the family of Ahab as I wanted. Your descendants[d] as far as your great-great-grandchildren will be kings of Israel." [31]But Jehu was not careful to keep the teachings of the Lord with all his heart. He did not stop doing the same sins Jeroboam had done. Jeroboam had caused Israel to sin.

[32]At that time the Lord began to make Israel smaller. Hazael defeated the Israelites in all the land of Israel. [33]He took all the land on the east side of the Jordan. This was the land of Gilead. (It was the region of Gad, Reuben and Manasseh.) He took land from Aroer by the Arnon Ravine through Gilead to Bashan.

[34]The other things Jehu did are written down. Everything he did and all his victories are recorded. They are in the book of the history of the kings of Israel. [35]Jehu died and was buried in Samaria. Jehu's son Jehoahaz became king in his place. [36]Jehu was king over Israel in Samaria for 28 years.

11 Now Ahaziah's mother, Athaliah, saw that her son was dead. Then she killed all the royal family. [2]But Jehosheba took Joash, Ahaziah's son. She stole him from among the other sons of the king who were about to be murdered. (Jehosheba was King Jehoram's daughter and Ahaziah's sister.) She put Joash and his nurse in a bedroom. She hid Joash from Athaliah. So he was not killed. ³He was hidden with her in the Temple^d of the Lord for six years. During that time Athaliah ruled the land.

⁴In the seventh year Jehoiada sent for the commanders of groups of 100 men. He sent for guards and the Carites, the royal bodyguards. He brought them together in the Temple of the Lord. Then he made an agreement with them. There, in the Temple of the Lord, he made them promise loyalty. Then he showed them the king's son. ⁵He commanded them, "This is what you must do. A third of you who come in on the Sabbath^d will guard the king's palace. ⁶Another third of you will be at the Sur Gate. And another third will be at the gate behind the guard. This way you will guard the Temple. ⁷Two groups will go off duty on the Sabbath. They must protect the Temple of the Lord for the king. ⁸All of you must stand around the king. Each man must have his weapon in his hand. If anyone comes near, kill him. Stay close to the king when he goes out and when he comes in."

⁹The commanders over 100 men obeyed everything Jehoiada the priest had commanded. Each one took his men who were beginning their Sabbath duty. Each one also took those who were ending their Sabbath duty. Both groups came to Jehoiada the priest. ¹⁰And he gave spears and shields to the commanders. They used to belong to King David. They were kept in the Temple of the Lord. ¹¹Then each of the guards took his place. Each man had his weapon in his hand. There were guards from the south side of the Temple^d to the north side. They stood by the altar and the Temple and around the king. ¹²Jehoiada brought out the king's son. He put the crown on Joash. Then he gave Joash a copy of the Agreement with the Lord. They appointed him king and poured olive oil on him. They clapped their hands and said, "Long live the king!"

¹³Athaliah heard the noise of the guards and the people. So she came to the people at the Temple of the Lord. ¹⁴She looked, and there was the king. He was standing by the pillar, as the custom was. The officers and trumpeters were standing beside him. All the people of the land were very happy and were blowing trumpets. Then Athaliah tore her clothes to show how upset she was. She screamed, "Traitors! Traitors!"

¹⁵Jehoiada the priest gave orders to the commanders of 100 men who led the army. He said, "Surround her with soldiers. Kill with a sword anyone who follows her." He said this because he had said, "Don't put Athaliah to death in the Temple of the Lord." ¹⁶So they caught her when she came to where the horses enter the palace grounds. There she was put to death.

¹⁷Then Jehoiada made an agreement. It was between the Lord and the king and the people. They agreed to be the Lord's special people. He also made an agreement between the king and the people. ¹⁸All the people of the land went to the temple of Baal^d and tore it down. They smashed the altars and idols into small pieces. And they killed Mattan, the priest of Baal, in front of the altars.

Then Jehoiada the priest placed guards at the Temple of the Lord. ¹⁹He took with him the commanders of 100 men and the Carites, the royal bodyguards. He took the guards and all the people of the land. Together they took the king out of the Temple of the Lord. They went into the palace through the gate of the guards. Then the king sat on the royal throne. ²⁰So all the people of Judah were very happy. And Jerusalem had peace because Athaliah had been put to death with the sword at the palace.

²¹Joash was seven years old when he became king.

12 Joash became king of Judah in Jehu's seventh year as king of Israel. Joash ruled for 40 years in Jerusalem. His mother's name was Zibiah. She was from Beersheba. ²Joash did what the Lord said was right all the time Jehoiada the priest taught him. ³But the places where false gods were worshiped were not removed. The people still made sacrifices and burned incense^d there.

⁴Joash said to the priests, "Take all the money brought as offerings to the Temple^d of the Lord. This includes the money each person owes in taxes. It also includes the money each person promises or brings to the Lord because he wants to. ⁵Each priest must take the money from the people he serves. Then the priests must repair any damage they find in the Temple."

⁶But by the twenty-third year of Joash the priests still had not repaired the Temple. ⁷So King Joash called for Jehoiada the priest and the other priests. He said to them, "Why are you not repairing the damage of the Temple? Don't

take any more money from the people you serve. But hand over the money for the repair of the Temple." ⁸The priests agreed not to take any more money from the people. And they agreed not to repair the Temple themselves.

⁹But Jehoiada the priest took a box and made a hole in the top of it. Then he put it by the altar. It was on the right side as the people came into the Temple of the Lord. The priests guarding the doorway put all the money brought to the Temple of the Lord into the box.

¹⁰Each time the priests saw that the box was full of money, the king's royal assistant and the high priest came. They counted the money that had been brought to the Temple of the Lord. Then they put it into bags. ¹¹Next they weighed the money. They gave it to the men who were in charge of the work on the Temple. With it they paid the carpenters and the builders who worked on the Temple of the Lord. ¹²They also paid the stoneworkers and stonecutters. They used the money to buy timber and cut stone. The money was used to repair the damage of the Temple of the Lord. It paid for everything.

¹³The money brought into the Temple of the Lord was not used to make silver cups. It was not used for wick trimmers, bowls or trumpets. And it wasn't used for any gold or silver vessels. ¹⁴They paid the money to the workers. And the workers used it to repair the Temple of the Lord. ¹⁵They did not make the men tell how the money was spent. This was because the men were honest. ¹⁶The money from the penalty offerings and sin offerings was not brought into the Temple of the Lord. It belonged to the priests.

¹⁷About this time Hazael king of Aram attacked Gath and captured it. Then he went to attack Jerusalem. ¹⁸But Joash king of Judah took all the holy things his ancestors had given. His ancestors were the kings of Judah—Jehoshaphat, Jehoram and Ahaziah. He also took his own holy things. He took the gold that was found in the treasuries of the Templeᵈ of the Lord. And he took the gold from the palace. Joash sent all this treasure to Hazael king of Aram. Then Hazael turned away from Jerusalem.

¹⁹Everything else Joash did is written down. It is in the book of the history of the kings of Judah. ²⁰His officers made plans against him. They killed him at Beth Millo on the road to Silla. ²¹The officers who killed him were Jozabad son of Shimeath and Jehozabad son of Shomer. Joash was buried with his ancestors in Jerusalem. And Amaziah, his son, became king in his place.

13 Jehoahaz son of Jehu became king over Israel in Samaria. This was during Joash's twenty-third year as king of Judah. Joash was the son of Ahaziah. And Jehoahaz ruled 17 years. ²He did what the Lord said was wrong. Jehoahaz did the same sins Jeroboam son of Nebat had done. Jeroboam had caused Israel to sin. And Jehoahaz did not stop doing these same sins. ³So the Lord was angry with Israel. And he gave them into the power of Hazael king of Aram and his son Ben-Hadad.

⁴Then Jehoahaz begged the Lord, and the Lord listened to him. The Lord had seen the troubles of Israel. He saw how terribly the king of Aram was treating the Israelites. ⁵So he gave Israel a man to save them. And they escaped from the Arameans. So the Israelites lived in their own homes as they had before. ⁶But the Israelites still did not stop doing the same sins that the family of Jeroboam had done. He had caused Israel to sin. They continued doing those sins. The Asherahᵈ idol also was left standing in Samaria.

⁷Nothing was left of Jehoahaz's army except 50 horsemen, 10 chariots and 10,000 foot soldiers. The king of Aram had destroyed them. He had made them like dust at the time of threshing.ᵈ

⁸Everything else Jehoahaz did and all his victories are written down. They are in the book of history of the kings of Israel. ⁹Jehoahaz died and was buried in Samaria. His son Jehoash became king in his place.

¹⁰Jehoash son of Jehoahaz became king of Israel in Samaria. This was during Joash's thirty-seventh year as king of Judah. Jehoash ruled 16 years. ¹¹He did what the Lord said was wrong. He did not stop doing the same sins Jeroboam son of Nebat had done. Jeroboam had caused Israel to sin. And Jehoash continued to do the same thing. ¹²Everything else he did and all his victories are written down. This includes his war against Amaziah king of Judah. All this is written in the book of the history of the kings of Israel. ¹³Jehoash died, and Jeroboam took his place on the throne. Jehoash was buried in Samaria with the kings of Israel.

¹⁴At this time Elisha became sick.

(Later, he died from this illness.) Jehoash king of Israel went to Elisha and cried for him. Jehoash said, "My father, my father! The chariots of Israel and their horsemen!"

[15]Elisha said to Jehoash, "Take a bow and arrows." So he took a bow and arrows. [16]Then Elisha said to him, "Put your hand on the bow." So Jehoash put his hand on the bow. Then Elisha put his hands on the king's hands. [17]Elisha said, "Open the east window." So Jehoash opened the window. Then Elisha said, "Shoot," and Jehoash shot. Elisha said, "The Lord's arrow of victory over Aram! You will defeat the Arameans at Aphek until you destroy them."

[18]Elisha said, "Take the arrows." So Jehoash took them. Then Elisha said to him, "Hit the ground." So Jehoash hit the ground three times. Then he stopped. [19]The man of God was angry with him. Elisha said, "You should have hit five or six times! Then you would have defeated Aram until you had completely destroyed it! But now you will defeat it only three times."

[20]So Elisha died and was buried.

At that time groups of Moabites would rob the land in the springtime. [21]Once the Israelites were burying a man. Suddenly they saw a group of Moabites coming. The Israelites threw the dead man into Elisha's grave. When the man touched Elisha's bones, the man came back to life. And he stood up on his feet.

[22]During all the days Jehoahaz was king, Hazael king of Aram troubled Israel. [23]But the Lord was kind to the Israelites. He had mercy on them. And he helped them because of his agreement with Abraham, Isaac and Jacob. He did not destroy them or reject them.

[24]Hazael king of Aram died. And his son Ben-Hadad became king in his place. [25]During a war Hazael had taken some cities from Jehoahaz, Jehoash's father. But now Jehoash took back those cities from Hazael's son Ben-Hadad. He defeated Ben-Hadad three times and took back the cities of Israel.

14 Amaziah son of Joash became king of Judah. This was during the second year Jehoash son of Jehoahaz was king of Israel. [2]Amaziah was 25 years old when he became king. He ruled 29 years in Jerusalem. His mother was Jehoaddin. She was from Jerusalem. [3]Amaziah did what the Lord said

was right. Amaziah did everything his father Joash had done. But he did not do as David his ancestor had done. [4]The places where false gods were worshiped were not removed. The people still sacrificed and burned incense[d] there.

[5]Amaziah took strong control of the kingdom. Then he put the officers to death who had killed his father the king. [6]But he did not put to death the children of the murderers. This is because of the rule written in the Book of the Teachings of Moses. The Lord had commanded: "Fathers must not be put to death when their children do wrong. And children must not be put to death when their fathers do wrong. Each person must die for his own sins."[n]

[7]Amaziah killed 10,000 Edomites in the Valley of Salt. In a battle Amaziah took the city of Sela. He called it Joktheel, and it is still called that today.

[8]Amaziah sent messengers to Jehoash son of Jehoahaz. (Jehoahaz was the son of Jehu, king of Israel.) The message read, "Come, let's meet face to face in battle."

[9]Then Jehoash king of Israel answered Amaziah king of Judah. Jehoash said, "A little thornbush in Lebanon sent a message to a big cedar tree in Lebanon. It said, 'Let your daughter marry my son.' But then a wild animal from Lebanon came by. It walked on and crushed the thornbush. [10]Yes, you have defeated Edom. But you have become proud because of your victory over Edom. Stay at home and brag! Don't ask for trouble by fighting me. If you do, you and Judah will be defeated."

[11]But Amaziah would not listen. So Jehoash king of Israel went to attack. He and Amaziah king of Judah faced each other in battle at Beth Shemesh in Judah. [12]Israel defeated Judah. Every man of Judah ran away to his home. [13]At Beth Shemesh Jehoash king of Israel captured Amaziah king of Judah. Amaziah was the son of Joash, who was the son of Ahaziah. Then Jehoash went to Jerusalem. He broke down the wall of Jerusalem from the Gate of Ephraim to the Corner Gate. This part of the wall was about 600 feet long. [14]Then he took all the gold and silver and everything in the Temple[d] of the Lord. And he took the treasuries of the palace. He also took some hostages and returned to Samaria.

14:6 "Fathers . . . sins." See Deuteronomy 24:16.

[15]The other acts of Jehoash and his victories are written down. This includes his war against Amaziah king of Judah. All this is in the book of the history of the kings of Israel. [16]Jehoash died and was buried in Samaria with the kings of Israel. And his son Jeroboam became king in his place.

[17]Amaziah son of Joash was king of Judah. He lived 15 years after Jehoash king of Israel died. Jehoash was the son of Jehoahaz. [18]The other things Amaziah did as king are written down. They are in the book of the history of the kings of Judah. [19]The people made plans in Jerusalem against Amaziah. So he ran away to the town of Lachish. But they sent men after him to Lachish and killed him. [20]They brought his body back on horses. And he was buried with his ancestors in Jerusalem, the city of David.

[21]Then all the people of Judah chose Azariah[n] to be king. He became king in place of his father Amaziah. Azariah was 16 years old. [22]He rebuilt the town of Elath and made it part of Judah again. He did this after Amaziah died.

[23]Jeroboam son of Jehoash became king of Israel in Samaria. This was during the fifteenth year Amaziah was king of Judah. (Amaziah was the son of Joash.) And Jeroboam ruled 41 years. [24]He did what the Lord said was wrong. Jeroboam son of Nebat had caused Israel to sin. And Jeroboam son of Jehoash did not stop doing the same sins. [25]Jeroboam won back Israel's border from Lebo Hamath to the Dead Sea.[d] This happened as the Lord of Israel had said. He said it through his servant Jonah son of Amittai. He was the prophet[d] from Gath Hepher. [26]The Lord had seen how the Israelites, both slave and free, were suffering terribly. No one was left who could help Israel. [27]But the Lord had not said that he would completely destroy Israel from the world. So he saved the Israelites through Jeroboam son of Jehoash.

[28]Everything else Jeroboam did is written down. All his victories are recorded. He won back Damascus and Hamath for Israel. (They had belonged to Judah.) All this is written in the book of the history of the kings of Israel. [29]Jeroboam died and was buried with his ancestors, the kings of Israel. Jero-

boam's son Zechariah became king in his place.

15 Azariah son of Amaziah became king of Judah. This was during Jeroboam's twenty-seventh year as king of Israel. [2]Azariah was 16 years old when he became king. He ruled 52 years in Jerusalem. His mother was named Jecoliah, and she was from Jerusalem. [3]He did what the Lord said was right. He obeyed God just as his father Amaziah had done. [4]But the places where false gods were worshiped were not removed. So the people still made sacrifices and burned incense[d] there.

[5]The Lord struck Azariah with a harmful skin disease. He had this disease until the day he died. He lived in a separate house. Jotham, the king's son, was in charge of the palace. He governed the people of the land.

[6]All the other things Azariah did are written down. They are in the book of the history of the kings of Judah. [7]Azariah died and was buried near his ancestors in Jerusalem. And his son Jotham became king in his place.

[8]Zechariah son of Jeroboam was king over Israel in Samaria. He ruled for six months. This was during Azariah's thirty-eighth year as king of Judah. [9]Zechariah did what the Lord said was wrong. He did just as his ancestors had done. Jeroboam son of Nebat had caused the people of Israel to sin. And Zechariah did not stop doing the same sins.

[10]Shallum son of Jabesh made plans against Zechariah. He killed Zechariah in Ibleam. And Shallum became king in Zechariah's place. [11]The other acts of Zechariah are written down. They are in the book of the history of the kings of Israel. [12]Now the Lord had told Jehu: "Your sons down to your great-great-grandchildren will be kings of Israel." And the Lord's word came true.

[13]Then Shallum son of Jabesh became king. This was during Uzziah's thirty-ninth year as king of Judah. Shallum ruled for a month in Samaria. [14]Then Menahem son of Gadi came up from Tirzah to Samaria. He attacked Shallum son of Jabesh in Samaria. He killed him and became king in Shallum's place.

[15]The other acts of Shallum and his secret plans are written down. They are in the book of the history of the kings of Israel.

14:21; 15:1 Azariah Also called Uzziah in 2 Chronicles.

[16]Menahem started out from Tirzah and attacked Tiphsah. He destroyed the city and the area nearby. This was because the people had refused to open the city gate for him. So he defeated them and ripped open all their pregnant women.

[17]Menahem son of Gadi became king over Israel. This was during Azariah's thirty-ninth year as king of Judah. And Menahem ruled ten years in Samaria. [18]He did what the Lord said was wrong. Jeroboam son of Nebat had caused Israel to sin. And all the time Menahem was king, he did not stop doing the same sins.

[19]Pul king of Assyria came to attack the land. Menahem gave him about 74,000 pounds of silver. This was so Pul would support Menahem and make his hold on the kingdom stronger. [20]Menahem raised the money by taxing all the rich men of Israel. He taxed each man about 1¼ pounds of silver. Then he gave the money to the king of Assyria. So the king of Assyria left and did not stay in the land.

[21]Everything else Menahem did is written down. It is in the book of the history of the kings of Israel. [22]Then Menahem died. And his son Pekahiah became king in his place.

[23]Pekahiah son of Menahem became king over Israel in Samaria. This was during Azariah's fiftieth year as king of Judah. Pekahiah ruled two years. [24]He did what the Lord said was wrong. Jeroboam son of Nebat had caused Israel to sin. And Pekahiah did not stop doing the same sins.

[25]Pekah son of Remaliah was one of Pekahiah's captains. He made plans against Pekahiah. He took 50 men of Gilead with him and killed Pekahiah. They killed him, Argob and Arieh in the palace at Samaria. Then Pekah became king in Pekahiah's place.

[26]Everything else Pekahiah did is written down. It is in the book of the history of the kings of Israel.

[27]Pekah son of Remaliah became king over Israel in Samaria. This was during Azariah's fifty-second year as king of Judah. And Pekah ruled 20 years. [28]He did what the Lord said was wrong. Jeroboam son of Nebat had caused Israel to sin. And Pekah did not stop doing the same sins.

[29]Tiglath-Pileser, also called Pul, was king of Assyria. He attacked while Pekah was king of Israel. Tiglath-Pileser captured the cities of Ijon, Abel Beth Maacah, Janoah, Kedesh and Hazor. He also captured Gilead and Galilee. And he captured all the land of Naphtali. He sent the people from these places away to Assyria. [30]Then Hoshea son of Elah made plans against Pekah son of Remaliah. Hoshea attacked and killed Pekah. Then he became king in Pekah's place. This was during the twentieth year Jotham son of Uzziah was king.

[31]Everything else Pekah did is written down. It is in the book of the history of the kings of Israel.

[32]Then Jotham son of Uzziah became king of Judah. This was during the second year Pekah son of Remaliah was king of Israel. [33]Jotham was 25 years old when he became king. He ruled 16 years in Jerusalem. His mother's name was Jerusha daughter of Zadok. [34]Jotham did what the Lord said was right. He obeyed God just as his father Uzziah had done. [35]But the places where false gods were worshiped were not removed. And the people still made sacrifices and burned incense[d] there. Jotham rebuilt the Upper Gate of the Temple[d] of the Lord.

[36]The other things Jotham did while he was king are written down. They are in the book of the history of the kings of Judah. [37]At that time the Lord began to send Rezin king of Aram against Judah. He also sent Pekah son of Remaliah against them. [38]Jotham died and was buried with his ancestors in Jerusalem. It was the city of David, his ancestor. And Jotham's son Ahaz became king in his place.

16 Ahaz was the son of Jotham king of Judah. Ahaz became king of Judah in the seventeenth year Pekah was king of Israel. Pekah was the son of Remaliah. [2]Ahaz was 20 years old when he became king. He ruled 16 years in Jerusalem. He was not like his ancestor David. He did not do what the Lord his God said was right. [3]Ahaz did the same things the kings of Israel had done. He even sacrificed his sons by burning them in the fire. He did the same hated sins as the other nations had done. And the Lord had forced these nations out of the land ahead of the Israelites. [4]Ahaz offered sacrifices and burned incense[d] at the places where false gods were worshiped. And he did this on the hills and under every green tree.

[5]Rezin king of Aram and Pekah king of Israel came up to Jerusalem to attack

it. (Pekah was the son of Remaliah.) They surrounded Ahaz but could not defeat him. ⁶At that time Rezin king of Aram took back the city of Elath for Aram. He forced out all the people of Judah. Then Edomites moved into Elath. And they still live there today.

⁷Ahaz sent messengers to Tiglath-Pileser king of Assyria. Ahaz said, "I am your servant. Come and save me from the king of Aram and the king of Israel. They are attacking me." ⁸Ahaz took the silver and gold that was in the Temple[d] of the Lord. He also took the treasuries of the palace. He sent these as a gift to the king of Assyria. ⁹So the king of Assyria listened to Ahaz. He attacked Damascus and captured it. Then he sent all the people of Damascus to Kir. And he killed Rezin.

¹⁰Then King Ahaz went to Damascus to meet Tiglath-Pileser king of Assyria. Ahaz saw an altar at Damascus. He sent plans and a pattern of this altar to Uriah the priest. ¹¹So Uriah the priest built an altar. It was just like the plans King Ahaz had sent him from Damascus. Uriah finished the altar before King Ahaz came back from Damascus. ¹²When the king arrived from Damascus, he saw the altar. He went near and offered sacrifices on it. ¹³He burned his burnt offerings and grain offerings. He poured out his drink offering. He also sprinkled the blood of his fellowship offerings on the altar.

¹⁴Ahaz moved the bronze altar that was before the Lord at the front of the Temple. It was between Ahaz's altar and the Temple of the Lord. He put it on the north side of his altar. ¹⁵King Ahaz gave a command to Uriah the priest. Ahaz said, "Burn the morning burnt offering and the evening grain offering on the large altar. Also offer the king's burnt offering and his grain offering. Offer the whole burnt offering for all the people of the land. And offer their grain offering and drink offering. Sprinkle on the altar all the blood of the burnt offering and of the sacrifice. But I will use the bronze altar to ask questions of God." ¹⁶Uriah the priest did everything King Ahaz commanded him to do.

¹⁷Then King Ahaz took off the side panels from the bases. He took the washing bowls off the top of the bases. He also took the large bowl, which was called the Sea, off the bronze bulls that held it up. And he put it on a stone base. ¹⁸Ahaz took away the platform for the royal throne. It had been built at the Temple. He also took away the outside entrance for the king. He did these things because of the king of Assyria.

¹⁹The other things Ahaz did as king are written down. They are in the book of the history of the kings of Judah. ²⁰Ahaz died and was buried with his ancestors in Jerusalem. Ahaz's son Hezekiah became king in his place.

17 Hoshea son of Elah became king over Israel. This was during Ahaz's twelfth year as king of Judah. Hoshea ruled in Samaria nine years. ²He did what the Lord said was wrong. But he was not as bad as the kings of Israel who had ruled before him.

³Shalmaneser king of Assyria came to attack Hoshea. Hoshea had been Shalmaneser's servant. He had made the payments to Shalmaneser that he had demanded. ⁴But the king of Assyria found out that Hoshea had made plans against him. Hoshea had sent messengers to So, the king of Egypt. And Hoshea had quit giving Shalmaneser the payments he demanded. In the past Hoshea had paid him every year. So the king put Hoshea in prison. ⁵Then the king of Assyria came and attacked all the land of Israel. He surrounded Samaria and attacked it for three years. ⁶He defeated Samaria in the ninth year Hoshea was king. He took the Israelites away to Assyria. He settled some of them in Halah. Some were made to settle in Gozan on the Habor River. Others were settled in the cities of the Medes.

⁷All these things happened because the Israelites had sinned against the Lord their God. He had brought them out of Egypt. He had rescued them from the power of the king of Egypt. But the Israelites had honored other gods. ⁸They lived like the nations the Lord had forced out of the land ahead of them. They also lived as the evil kings had shown them. ⁹They secretly sinned against the Lord their God. They built places in all their cities where false gods were worshiped. They built them everywhere from the watchtower to the strong, walled city. ¹⁰They put up stone pillars for worshiping false gods. And they put up Asherah[d] idols on every high hill and under every green tree. ¹¹The Israelites burned incense[d] everywhere false gods were worshiped. The nations who lived there before them had done this. And the Lord had forced them out of the land. The Israelites did wicked

things that made the Lord angry. [12]They served idols. And the Lord had said, "You must not do this." [13]The Lord used every prophet[d] and seer[d] to warn Israel and Judah. He said, "Stop your evil ways. Obey my commands and laws. Follow all the teachings that I commanded your ancestors to obey. I sent you this law through my servants the prophets."

[14]But the people would not listen. They were stubborn, just as their ancestors had been. Their ancestors did not believe in the Lord their God. [15]They rejected the Lord's laws and the agreement he had made with their ancestors. And they refused to listen to his warnings. They worshiped useless idols and became useless themselves. They did what the nations around them did. And the Lord had warned them not to do this.

[16]The people disobeyed all the commands of the Lord their God. They made statues of two calves from melted metal. And they made an Asherah idol. They worshiped all the stars of heaven and served Baal.[d] [17]They sacrificed their sons and daughters in the fire. And they tried to find out the future by magic and witchcraft.[d] They always chose to do what the Lord said was wrong. And this made him angry. [18]So he was very angry with the people of Israel. He removed them from his presence. Only the tribe[d] of Judah was left.

[19]But even Judah did not obey the commands of the Lord their God. They did what the Israelites had done. [20]So the Lord rejected all the people of Israel. He punished them and let people destroy them. He threw them out of his presence. [21]The Lord separated them from the family of David. And the Israelites made Jeroboam son of Nebat their king. Jeroboam led the Israelites away from following the Lord. He caused them to sin greatly. [22]So they continued to do all the sins Jeroboam did. They did not stop doing these sins [23]until the Lord removed the people from his presence. This was just as he had said he would do. He had said this through all his servants the prophets.[d] So the Israelites were taken out of their land to Assyria. And they have been there to this day.

[24]The king of Assyria brought people from Babylon, Cuthah, Avva, Hamath and Sepharvaim. He put them in the cities of Samaria to replace the Israelites. These people took over Samaria and lived in the cities. [25]At first they did not

worship the Lord. So he sent lions among them. The lions killed some of them. [26]The king of Assyria was told this. It was said, "You sent foreigners into the cities of Samaria. They do not know the law of the god of the land. This is why that land's god has sent lions among them. The lions are killing them because they don't know what the god wants."

[27]Then the king of Assyria gave a command. He said, "You took Samaria's priests away. Send back one of the priests to live there. Let him teach them what the god wants." [28]So one of the priests who had been carried away from Samaria returned. He came to live in Bethel. And he taught the people how to worship the Lord.

[29]But each nation made gods of its own. They put them in the cities where they lived. They put them in the temples where false gods were worshiped. These temples had been made by the Samaritans. [30]The men from Babylon made Succoth Benoth their god. The men from Cuthah worshiped Nergal. The men of Hamath worshiped Ashima. [31]The Avvites worshiped Nibhaz and Tartak. And the Sepharvites burned their children in the fire. They sacrificed them to Adrammelech and Anammelech, the gods of Sepharvaim. [32]They also worshiped the Lord. But they chose priests for the places where false gods were worshiped. The priests were chosen from among themselves. And they made sacrifices for the people. [33]The people worshiped the Lord but also served their own gods. They served their gods as the nations did from which they had been brought. [34]Even today they do as they did in the past. They do not worship the Lord. They do not obey his rules and commands. They do not obey the teachings or the commands of the Lord. He gave these commands to the children of Jacob, whom the Lord had named Israel. [35]The Lord had made an agreement with them. He had commanded them, "Do not worship other gods. Do not bow down to them or serve them. Do not give sacrifices to them. [36]Worship the Lord who brought you up out of the land of Egypt. He did it with great power and strength. Bow to the Lord and make sacrifices to him. [37]Obey the rules, orders and the teachings. Obey the commands the Lord wrote for you. Obey and always do them. Do not worship other gods. [38]Do not forget the

agreement I made with you. And do not worship other gods. ³⁹Instead worship the Lord your God. He will save you from all your enemies."

⁴⁰But the Israelites did not listen. They kept on doing the same things they had done before. ⁴¹So these nations worshiped the Lord but served their idols. And their children and grandchildren still do as their ancestors did.

18 Hezekiah son of Ahaz king of Judah became king. This was during the third year Hoshea son of Elah was king of Israel. ²Hezekiah was 25 years old when he became king. And he ruled 29 years in Jerusalem. His mother's name was Abijah daughter of Zechariah. ³Hezekiah did what the Lord said was right. He did just as his ancestor David had done. ⁴He removed the places where false gods were worshiped. He broke the stone pillars they worshiped. He cut down the Asherahᵈ idols. Also the Israelites had been burning incenseᵈ to the bronze snake made by Moses. (It was called Nehushtan.) But Hezekiah broke it into pieces.

⁵Hezekiah trusted in the Lord, the God of Israel. There was no one like him among all the kings of Judah. There was no king like him, before him or after him. ⁶Hezekiah was loyal to the Lord. He did not stop following the Lord. He obeyed the commands the Lord had given Moses. ⁷And the Lord was with Hezekiah. He had success in everything he did. He turned against the king of Assyria and stopped serving him. ⁸Hezekiah defeated the Philistines all the way to Gaza and its borders. He defeated them everywhere, from the watchtower to the strong, walled city.

⁹Shalmaneser king of Assyria surrounded Samaria and attacked it. This was in the fourth year Hezekiah was king. And it was the seventh year Hoshea son of Elah was king of Israel. ¹⁰After three years the Assyrians captured Samaria. This was in the sixth year Hezekiah was king. And it was Hoshea's ninth year as king of Israel. ¹¹The king of Assyria took the Israelites away to Assyria. He put them in Halah and in Gozan on the Habor River. He also put them in the cities of the Medes. ¹²This happened because they did not obey the Lord their God. They broke his agreement. They did not obey all that Moses, the Lord's servant, had commanded. They would not listen to the commands or do them.

¹³During Hezekiah's fourteenth year as king, Sennacherib king of Assyria attacked Judah. He attacked all the strong, walled cities of Judah and defeated them. ¹⁴Then Hezekiah king of Judah sent a message to the king of Assyria at Lachish. He said, "I have done wrong. Leave me alone. Then I will pay anything you demand of me." So the king of Assyria told Hezekiah how much to pay. It was about 22,000 pounds of silver and 2,000 pounds of gold. ¹⁵Hezekiah gave him all the silver that was in the Templeᵈ of the Lord. And he gave him all the silver in the palace treasuries. ¹⁶Hezekiah cut off all the gold that covered the doors of the Temple of the Lord. He also removed the gold from the doorposts. Hezekiah had put gold on these doors himself. He gave it all to the king of Assyria.

¹⁷The king of Assyria sent out his supreme commander, his chief officer and his field commander. They went with a large army from Lachish to King Hezekiah in Jerusalem. When they came near the waterway from the upper pool, they stopped. The upper pool is on the road to the Washerman's Field. ¹⁸They called for the king. So Eliakim, Shebna and Joah went out to meet them. Eliakim son of Hilkiah was the palace manager. Shebna was the royal assistant. And Joah son of Asaph was the recorder.

¹⁹The field commander said to them, "Tell Hezekiah this:

"'The great king, the king of Assyria, says: You have nothing to trust in to help you. ²⁰You say you have battle plans and power for war. But your words mean nothing. Whom are you trusting for help so that you turn against me? ²¹Look, you are depending on Egypt to help you. Egypt is like a splintered walking stick. If you lean on it for help, it will stab you and hurt you. The king of Egypt will hurt those who depend on him. ²²You might say, "We are depending on the Lord our God." But Hezekiah destroyed the Lord's altars and the places of worship. Hezekiah told Judah and Jerusalem, "You must worship only at this one altar in Jerusalem."

²³"'Now make an agreement with my master, the king of Assyria: I will give you 2,000 horses if you can find enough men to ride them. ²⁴You cannot defeat one of my master's least important officers. So why do you depend on Egypt to give you chariots and horsemen? ²⁵I

have not come to attack and destroy this place without an order from the Lord. The Lord himself told me to come to this country and destroy it.'"

26 Then Eliakim son of Hilkiah, Shebna and Joah spoke to the field commander. They said, "Please speak to us in the Aramaic language. We understand it. Don't speak to us in Hebrew because the people on the city wall can hear you."

27 But the commander said, "No. My master did not send me to tell these things only to you and your king. My master sent me to tell them also to those people sitting on the wall. They will have to eat their own dung and drink their own urine like you."

28 Then the commander stood and shouted loudly in the Hebrew language. He said, "Listen to the word from the great king, the king of Assyria! 29 The king says you should not let Hezekiah fool you. Hezekiah can't save you from my power. 30 Don't let Hezekiah talk you into trusting the Lord. Hezekiah says, 'The Lord will surely save us. This city won't be given over to the king of Assyria.'

31 "Don't listen to Hezekiah. The king of Assyria says, 'Make peace with me. Come out of the city to me. Then everyone will be free to eat the fruit from his own grapevine and fig tree. Everyone will be free to drink water from his own well. 32 Then I will come and take you to a land like your own. It is a land with grain and new wine. It has bread and vineyards. It is a land of olives and honey. Then you can choose to live and not to die!'

"Don't listen to Hezekiah. He is fooling you when he says, 'The Lord will save us.' 33 The god of any other nation has not saved his people from the power of the king of Assyria. 34 Where are the gods of Hamath and Arpad? Where are the gods of Sepharvaim, Hena and Ivvah? They did not save Samaria from my power. 35 Not one of all the gods of these countries has saved his people from me. Then the Lord cannot save Jerusalem from my power."

36 The people were silent. They didn't answer the commander at all. This was because King Hezekiah had ordered, "Don't answer him."

37 Then Eliakim, Shebna and Joah tore their clothes to show how upset they were. (Eliakim son of Hilkiah was the palace manager. Shebna was the royal assistant. And Joah son of Asaph was the recorder.) The three men went to Hezekiah and told him what the field commander had said.

19 When King Hezekiah heard the message, he tore his clothes. And he put on rough cloth to show how sad he was. Then he went into the Temple[d] of the Lord. 2 Hezekiah sent Eliakim, Shebna and the older priests to Isaiah. Eliakim was the palace manager, and Shebna was the royal assistant. The men were all wearing the rough cloth when they came to Isaiah. He was a prophet,[d] the son of Amoz. 3 These men told Isaiah, "This is what Hezekiah says: Today is a day of sorrow and punishment and disgrace. It is sad, as when a child should be born, but the mother is not strong enough to give birth to it. 4 The king of Assyria sent his field commander to make fun of the living God. Maybe the Lord your God will hear what the commander said. Maybe the Lord your God will punish him for what he said. So pray for the few people of Israel who are left alive."

5 When Hezekiah's officers came to Isaiah, 6 he said to them, "Tell your master this: The Lord says, 'Don't be afraid of what you have heard. Don't be frightened by the words the servants of the king of Assyria said against me. 7 Listen! I am going to put a spirit in the king of Assyria. He will hear a report that will make him return to his own country. And I will cause him to die by the sword there.'"

8 The field commander heard that the king of Assyria had left Lachish. So the commander left and found the king fighting against the city of Libnah.

9 The king received a report that Tirhakah was coming to attack him. Tirhakah was the Cushite king of Egypt. When the king of Assyria heard this, he sent messengers to Hezekiah. The king said: 10 "Say this to Hezekiah king of Judah: Don't be fooled by the god you trust. Don't believe him when he says Jerusalem will not be defeated by the king of Assyria. 11 You have heard what the kings of Assyria have done. They have completely defeated every country. Do not think you will be saved. 12 The gods of those people did not save them. My ancestors destroyed them. My ancestors defeated the cities of Gozan, Haran and Rezeph. They defeated the people of Eden living in Tel Assar. 13 Where are the kings of Hamath and Arpad? Where is

the king of the city of Sepharvaim? Where are the kings of Hena and Ivvah?"

[14] Hezekiah received the letter from the messengers and read it. Then he went up to the Temple[d] of the Lord. Hezekiah spread the letter out before the Lord. [15] And he prayed to the Lord: "Lord, God of Israel, your throne is between the gold creatures with wings! Only you are God of all the kingdoms of the earth. You made the heavens and the earth. [16] Hear, Lord, and listen. Open your eyes, Lord, and see. Listen to the word Sennacherib has said to insult the living God. [17] It is true, Lord. The kings of Assyria have destroyed these countries and their lands. [18] These kings have thrown the gods of these nations into the fire. But they were only wood and rock statues that men made. So the kings have destroyed them. [19] Now, Lord our God, save us from the king's power. Then all the kingdoms of the earth will know that you, Lord, are the only God."

[20] Then Isaiah son of Amoz sent a message to Hezekiah. Isaiah said, "The Lord, the God of Israel, says this: I have heard your prayer to me about Sennacherib king of Assyria. [21] So this is what the Lord has said against Sennacherib:

'The people of Jerusalem
    hate you and make fun of you.
The people of Jerusalem
    laugh at you as you run away.
[22] You have insulted me and spoken
        against me.
    You have raised your voice
        against me.
    You have a proud look on your
        face.
    You disobey me, the Holy One of
        Israel!
[23] You have used your messengers to
        insult the Lord.
    You have said, "I have many
        chariots.
    With them I have gone to the tops
        of the mountains.
    I have climbed the highest
        mountains of Lebanon.
    I have cut down its tallest cedars.
    I have cut down its best pine
        trees.
    I have reached its farthest places.
    I have gone to its best forests.
[24] I have dug wells in foreign
        countries.
    I have drunk water there.
    By the soles of my feet,

    I have dried up all the rivers of
        Egypt."

[25] "'King of Assyria, surely you have
        heard.
    Long ago I, the Lord, planned
        these things.
Long ago I planned them.
    Now I have made them happen.
I allowed you to turn those strong,
        walled cities
    into piles of rocks.
[26] The people living in those cities
        were weak.
    They were frightened and put to
        shame.
    They were like grass in the field.
    They were like tender, young
        grass.
    They were like grass that grows on
        the housetop.
    It is burned by the wind before it
        can grow.

[27] "'I know when you rest and when
        you come and go.
    I know how you speak against
        me.
[28] You speak strongly against me.
    And I have heard your proud
        words.
    So I will put my hook in your nose.
    And I will put my bit in your
        mouth.
    Then I will force you to leave my
        country
    the same way that you came.'

[29] "Then the Lord said, 'Hezekiah, I will give you this sign:

This year you will eat the grain that
        grows wild.
    And the second year you will eat
        what grows wild from that.
But in the third year, plant grain
        and harvest it.
    Plant vineyards and eat their
        fruit.
[30] Some of the people in the family of
        Judah
    will be saved.
Like plants that take root,
    they will grow strong and have
        many children.
[31] A few people will come out of
        Jerusalem alive.
    There will be a few from Mount
        Zion[d] who will live.
The strong love of the Lord of
        heaven's armies
    will cause this to happen.'

[32] "So this is what the Lord says about the king of Assyria:

'He will not enter this city.
He will not even shoot an arrow here.
He will not fight against it with shields.
He will not build a ramp to attack the city walls.
[33] He will return to his country the same way he came.
He will not enter this city,'
says the Lord.
[34] The Lord says, 'I will defend and save this city.
I will do this for myself and for David, my servant.'"

[35] That night the angel of the Lord went out. He killed 185,000 men in the Assyrian camp. The people got up early the next morning. And they saw all the dead bodies! [36] So Sennacherib king of Assyria left. He went back to Nineveh and stayed there.

[37] One day Sennacherib was worshiping in the temple of his god Nisroch. While he was there, his sons Adrammelech and Sharezer killed him with a sword. Then they escaped to the land of Ararat. So Sennacherib's son Esarhaddon became king of Assyria.

20

At that time Hezekiah became very sick. He was almost dead. The prophet[d] Isaiah son of Amoz went to see him. Isaiah told him, "This is what the Lord says: You are going to die. So you should give your last orders to everyone. You will not get well."

[2] Hezekiah turned toward the wall and prayed to the Lord. He said, [3] "Lord, please remember that I have always obeyed you. I have given myself completely to you. I have done what you said was right." And Hezekiah cried loudly.

[4] Before Isaiah had left the middle courtyard, the Lord spoke his word to Isaiah: [5] "Go back and tell Hezekiah, the leader of my people: 'This is what the Lord, the God of your ancestor David, says: I have heard your prayer. And I have seen your tears. So I will heal you. Three days from now you will go up to the Temple[d] of the Lord. [6] I will add 15 years to your life. I will save you and this city from the king of Assyria. And I will protect the city for myself and for my servant David.'"

[7] Then Isaiah said, "Make a paste from figs." So they made it and put it on Hezekiah's boil. And he got well.

[8] Hezekiah asked Isaiah, "What will be the sign that the Lord will heal me? What is the sign that I will go up to the Temple[d] of the Lord on the third day?"

[9] Isaiah said, "The Lord will do what he says. This is the sign from the Lord to show you: Do you want the shadow to go forward ten steps? Or do you want it to go back ten steps?"

[10] Hezekiah answered, "It's easy for the shadow to go forward ten steps. Instead, let it go back ten steps."

[11] Then Isaiah the prophet called to the Lord. And the Lord brought the shadow back ten steps. It went back up the stairway of Ahaz that it had gone down.

[12] At that time Merodach-Baladan, son of Baladan, was king of Babylon. He sent letters and a gift to Hezekiah. He did this because he had heard that Hezekiah had been sick. [13] Hezekiah was happy to see the messengers. So he showed them what was in his storehouses: the silver, gold, spices and expensive perfumes. He showed them his swords and shields. He showed them all his wealth. He showed them everything in his palace and his kingdom.

[14] Then Isaiah the prophet[d] went to King Hezekiah. Isaiah asked him, "What did these men say? Where did they come from?"

Hezekiah said, "They came from a faraway country. They came to me from Babylon."

[15] So Isaiah asked him, "What did they see in your palace?"

Hezekiah said, "They saw everything in my palace. I showed them all my wealth."

[16] Then Isaiah said to Hezekiah, "Listen to the words of the Lord: [17] 'In the future everything in your palace will be taken away to Babylon. Everything your ancestors have stored up until this day will be taken away. Nothing will be left,' says the Lord. [18] 'Some of your own children will be taken away. Those who will be born to you will be taken away. And they will become eunuchs[d] in the palace of the king of Babylon.'"

[19] Hezekiah told Isaiah, "These words from the Lord are good." He said this because he thought, "There will be peace and security while I am king."

[20] Everything else Hezekiah did is written down. All his victories and his work on the pool are written down. And his work on the tunnel to bring water into the city is recorded. They are all written in the book of the history of the kings of Judah. [21] Then Hezekiah died.

And his son Manasseh became king in his place.

21 Manasseh was 12 years old when he became king. And he was king 55 years in Jerusalem. His mother's name was Hephzibah. [2]He did what the Lord said was wrong. He did the hated things the other nations had done. And the Lord had forced these nations out of the land ahead of the Israelites. [3]Manasseh's father, Hezekiah, had destroyed the places where false gods were worshiped. But Manasseh rebuilt them. He built altars for Baal.[d] And he made an Asherah[d] idol as Ahab king of Israel had done. Manasseh worshiped all the stars of heaven and served them. [4]The Lord had said about the Temple,[d] "I will be worshiped in Jerusalem." But Manasseh built altars in the Temple of the Lord. [5]He built altars to worship the stars in the two courtyards of the Temple of the Lord. [6]He burned his own son as a sacrifice. He practiced magic and told the future by explaining signs and dreams. He got advice from mediums[d] and fortune-tellers. He did many things that the Lord said were wrong. And this made the Lord angry.

[7]Manasseh carved an Asherah idol and put it in the Temple. The Lord had spoken to David and his son Solomon about the Temple. He had said, "I will be worshiped in this Temple and in Jerusalem forever. I have chosen Jerusalem from all the tribes[d] of Israel. [8]I will never again make the Israelites wander out of the land I gave their ancestors. But they must obey everything I have commanded them. And they must obey all the teachings my servant Moses gave them." [9]But the people did not listen. Manasseh led them to do wrong. They did more evil than the nations the Lord had destroyed ahead of the Israelites.

[10]The Lord spoke through his servants the prophets.[d] He said, [11]"Manasseh king of Judah has done these hated things. He has done more evil than the Amorites before him. Manasseh also has caused Judah to sin with his idols. [12]So this is what the Lord, the God of Israel, says: 'I will bring much trouble on Jerusalem and Judah. Anyone who hears about it will be shocked. [13]I will stretch the measuring line of Samaria over Jerusalem. And the plumb line[d] used against Ahab's family will be used on Jerusalem. I will wipe out Jerusalem as a man wipes a dish. He wipes it and turns it upside down. [14]I will go away from the rest of my people who are left. I will give them to their enemies. They will be robbed by all their enemies. [15]My people did what I said was wrong. They have made me angry from the day their ancestors left Egypt until now.'"

[16]Manasseh also killed many innocent people. He filled Jerusalem from one end to the other with their blood. This was besides the sin he caused Judah to do. He caused Judah to do what the Lord said was wrong.

[17]The other things Manasseh did as king are written down, even the sin he did. They are in the book of the history of the kings of Judah. [18]Manasseh died and was buried in the garden of his own palace. It is the garden of Uzza. Then Manasseh's son Amon became king in his place.

[19]Amon was 22 years old when he became king. He was king for two years in Jerusalem. His mother's name was Meshullemeth daughter of Haruz. She was from Jotbah. [20]Amon did what the Lord said was wrong. He did as his father Manasseh had done. [21]Amon lived in the same way his father had lived. He worshiped the idols his father had worshiped. And he bowed down before them. [22]Amon rejected the Lord, the God of his ancestors. He did not follow the ways of the Lord.

[23]Amon's officers made plans against him and killed him in his palace. [24]Then the people of Judah killed all those who had made plans to kill King Amon. And they made his son Josiah king in his place.

[25]Everything else Amon did is written down. It is in the book of the history of the kings of Judah. [26]He was buried in his grave in the garden of Uzza. And his son Josiah became king in his place.

22 Josiah was eight years old when he became king. He ruled 31 years in Jerusalem. His mother's name was Jedidah daughter of Adaiah. Adaiah was from Bozkath. [2]Josiah did what the Lord said was right. He did good things as his ancestor David had done. Josiah did not stop doing what was right.

[3]In Josiah's eighteenth year as king, he sent Shaphan to the Temple[d] of the Lord. Shaphan was the son of Azaliah, who was the son of Meshullam. Shaphan was the royal assistant. Josiah said, [4]"Go up to Hilkiah the high priest. Have him empty out the money the gatekeepers have gathered from the people. This is the money they have brought into

the Temple of the Lord. ⁵Have him give the money to the supervisors of the work on the Temple. They must pay the men who work to repair the Temple of the Lord. ⁶The workers are carpenters, builders and stoneworkers. Also use the money to buy timber and cut stone to repair the Temple. ⁷They do not need to report how they use the money given to them. They are working honestly."

⁸Hilkiah the high priest said to Shaphan the royal assistant, "I've found the Book of the Teachings. It was in the Temple^d of the Lord." He gave it to Shaphan, who read it.

⁹Then Shaphan the royal assistant went to the king and reported to Josiah, "Your officers have paid out the money that was in the Temple of the Lord. They have given it to the workers and supervisors at the Temple." ¹⁰Then Shaphan the royal assistant told the king, "Hilkiah the priest has given me a book." And Shaphan read from the book to the king.

¹¹The king heard the words of the Book of the Teachings. Then he tore his clothes to show how upset he was. ¹²He gave these orders to Hilkiah the priest and Ahikam son of Shaphan. He also gave them to Acbor son of Micaiah, Shaphan and Asaiah. Shaphan was the royal assistant. And Asaiah was the king's servant. These were the orders: ¹³"Go and ask the Lord about the words in the book that has been found. Ask for me and for all the people and for all Judah. The Lord's anger is burning against us because our ancestors did not obey the words of this book. They did not do all the things written for us to do!"

¹⁴So Hilkiah the priest, Ahikam, Acbor, Shaphan and Asaiah left. They went to talk to Huldah the prophetess.^d She was the wife of Shallum son of Tikvah, the son of Harhas. Harhas took care of the king's clothes. Huldah lived in Jerusalem, in the new area of the city.

¹⁵She said to them, "This is what the Lord, the God of Israel, says: Tell the man who sent you to me, ¹⁶'This is what the Lord says: I will bring trouble to this place and to the people living here. It is in the words of the book which the king of Judah has read. ¹⁷The people of Judah have left me. They have burned incense^d to other gods. They have made me angry by all the idols they have made. My anger burns against this place like a fire. It will not be put out.' ¹⁸Tell the king of Judah, who sent you to ask the Lord,

'This is what the Lord, the God of Israel, says about the words you heard: ¹⁹You heard my words against this place and its people. You became sorry in the Lord's presence for what you had done. I said they would become cursed and would be destroyed. Then you tore your clothes to show how upset you were. And you cried in my presence. This is why I have heard you, says the Lord. ²⁰So I will cause you to die. You will be buried in peace. You won't see all the trouble I will bring to this place.'"

So they took her message back to the king.

23 Then the king gathered all the older leaders of Judah and Jerusalem together. ²He went up to the Temple^d of the Lord. All the men from Judah and Jerusalem went with him. The priests, prophets^d and all the people—from the least important to the most important—went with him. He read to them all the words of the Book of the Agreement. That book was found in the Temple of the Lord. ³The king stood by the pillar. He made an agreement in the presence of the Lord. He agreed to follow the Lord and obey his commands, rules and laws with his whole being. He agreed to do what was written in this book. Then all the people promised to obey the agreement.

⁴The king gave a command to Hilkiah the high priest. He also gave it to the priests of the next rank and the gatekeepers. He told them to bring out of the Temple of the Lord everything made for Baal,^d Asherah^d and all the stars of heaven. Then Josiah burned them outside Jerusalem in the fields of the Kidron Valley. And he carried the ashes to Bethel. ⁵The kings of Judah had chosen priests for these gods. These priests burned incense^d on the places where false gods were worshiped. These places were in the cities of Judah and the towns around Jerusalem. The priests burned incense to Baal, the sun and the moon. And they burned incense to the planets and all the stars of heaven. But Josiah took those priests away. ⁶He removed the Asherah idol from the Temple of the Lord. He took it outside Jerusalem to the Kidron Valley. There he burned it and beat it into dust. And he threw the dust on the graves of the common people. ⁷Then he tore down the houses of the male prostitutes^d who were in the Temple of the Lord. This was

where the women did weaving for Asherah.

[8] King Josiah brought all the false priests from the cities of Judah. He made the places where false gods were worshiped impure. This is where the priests had burned incense. These places of worship were everywhere, from Geba to Beersheba. He destroyed the places of worship at the entrance to the Gate of Joshua. (Joshua was the ruler of the city.) This gate was on the left side of the city gate. [9] The priests at the places where false gods were worshiped were not allowed to serve at the Lord's altar in Jerusalem. But they could eat bread made without yeast with their brothers.

[10] Topheth was in the Valley of Ben Hinnom. Josiah made it impure so no one could sacrifice his son or daughter to Molech.[d] [11] Judah's kings had placed horses at the front door of the Temple of the Lord. This was in the courtyard near the room of Nathan-Melech, an officer. These horses were for the worship of the sun. But Josiah removed them. Then he burned the chariots that were for sun worship.

[12] The kings of Judah had also built altars on the roof[n] of the upstairs room of Ahaz. Josiah broke down these altars. He also broke down the altars Manasseh had made. These were in the two courtyards of the Temple of the Lord. He smashed them to pieces. Then he threw their dust into the Kidron Valley. [13] King Josiah made impure the places east of Jerusalem where false gods were worshiped. These were south of the Mount of Olives.[n] Solomon king of Israel had built these places. One was for Ashtoreth,[d] the hated goddess of the Sidonians. One was for Chemosh,[d] the hated god of Moab. And one was for Molech, the hated god of the Ammonites. [14] Josiah smashed into pieces the stone pillars they worshiped. He cut down the Asherah idols. And he covered the places with human bones.

[15] Josiah also broke down the altar at Bethel. This was the place of worship Jeroboam son of Nebat had made. Jeroboam had caused Israel to sin. Josiah burned that place. He broke the stones of the altar to pieces. Then he beat them into dust. And he burned the Asherah

idol. [16] When he turned around, he saw the graves on the mountain. He had the bones taken from the graves. Then he burned the bones on the altar to make it impure. This happened as the Lord had said it would through the man of God.

[17] Josiah asked, "What is that monument to the dead I see?"

The people of the city answered, "It's the grave of the man of God who came from Judah. This prophet announced the things you have done against the altar of Bethel."

[18] Josiah said, "Leave the grave alone. No person may move this man's bones." So they left his bones. And they left the bones of the prophet who had come from Samaria.

[19] The kings of Israel had built temples for worshiping false gods in the cities of Samaria. That had caused the Lord to be angry. Josiah removed all those temples. He did the same things as he had done at Bethel. [20] Josiah killed all the priests of those places of worship. He killed them on the altars. And he burned human bones on the altars. Then he went back to Jerusalem.

[21] The king gave a command to all the people. He said, "Celebrate the Passover[d] to the Lord your God. Do it as it is written in this Book of the Agreement." [22] No Passover like this one had been celebrated since the judges led Israel. Nor had one like it happened while there were kings of Israel and kings of Judah. [23] This Passover was celebrated to the Lord in Jerusalem. It was the eighteenth year of King Josiah's rule.

[24] Josiah destroyed the mediums,[d] fortune-tellers, house gods and idols. He destroyed all the hated gods seen in the land of Judah and Jerusalem. He did this to obey the words of the teachings. They were written in the book Hilkiah the priest had found in the Temple[d] of the Lord.

[25] There was no king like Josiah before or after him. He obeyed the Lord with all his heart, soul and strength. He followed all the Teachings of Moses.

[26] Even so, the Lord did not stop his strong and terrible anger. His anger burned against Judah. It was because of all that Manasseh had done to make him angry. [27] The Lord said, "I have taken Israel away. I will do the same to Judah.

23:12 roof In Bible times houses were built with flat roofs. The roof was used for drying things such as flax and fruit. And it was used as an extra room, as a place for worship and as a place to sleep in the summer. **23:13 Mount of Olives** Literally, "The Mountain of Ruin."

I will take them out of my sight. I will reject Jerusalem which I chose. I will take away the Temple about which I said, 'I will be honored there.'"

²⁸Everything else Josiah did is written down. It is in the book of the history of the kings of Judah.

²⁹While Josiah was king, Neco king of Egypt went to help the king of Assyria. Neco was at the Euphrates River. King Josiah marched out to fight against Neco. But at Megiddo, Neco faced Josiah and killed him. ³⁰Josiah's servants carried his body in a chariot from Megiddo. They brought him to Jerusalem and buried him in his own grave. Then the people of Judah chose Josiah's son Jehoahaz. They poured olive oil on him to appoint him king in his father's place.

³¹Jehoahaz was 23 years old when he became king. And he was king in Jerusalem for three months. His mother's name was Hamutal. She was the daughter of Jeremiah from Libnah. ³²Jehoahaz did what the Lord said was wrong. He did just as his ancestors had done.

³³King Neco took Jehoahaz prisoner at Riblah in the land of Hamath. He did this so Jehoahaz could not rule in Jerusalem. Neco made the people of Judah pay about 7,500 pounds of silver and about 75 pounds of gold.

³⁴King Neco made Josiah's son Eliakim the king in place of Josiah his father. Then Neco changed Eliakim's name to Jehoiakim. But Neco took Jehoahaz to Egypt, and he died there. ³⁵Jehoiakim gave Neco the silver and gold he demanded. But Jehoiakim taxed the land so he could pay the king. He took silver and gold from the people of the land. The amount he took from each person depended on how much he had.

³⁶Jehoiakim was 25 years old when he became king. He was king in Jerusalem for 11 years. His mother's name was Zebidah daughter of Pedaiah. She was from Rumah. ³⁷Jehoiakim did what the Lord said was wrong, just as his ancestors had done.

24 While Jehoiakim was king, Nebuchadnezzar king of Babylon attacked the land of Judah. So Jehoiakim became Nebuchadnezzar's servant for three years. Then Jehoiakim turned against Nebuchadnezzar. And he broke away from his rule. ²The Lord sent men from Babylon, Aram, Moab and Ammon against Jehoiakim. He sent them to destroy Judah. This happened the way the Lord had said it would through his servants the prophets.ᵈ

³The Lord commanded this to happen to the people of Judah. He did it to remove them from his presence. This was because of all the sins Manasseh had done. ⁴He had killed many innocent people. He had filled Jerusalem with their blood. And the Lord would not forgive these sins.

⁵The other things that happened while Jehoiakim was king and all he did are written down. They are in the book of the history of the kings of Judah. ⁶Jehoiakim died, and his son Jehoiachin became king in his place.

⁷The king of Egypt did not come out of his land again. This was because of the king of Babylon. He had captured all that belonged to the king of Egypt. He took all the land from the brook of Egypt to the Euphrates River.

⁸Jehoiachin was 18 years old when he became king. He was king three months in Jerusalem. His mother's name was Nehushta daughter of Elnathan. She was from Jerusalem. ⁹Jehoiachin did what the Lord said was wrong, just as his father had done.

¹⁰At that time the officers of Nebuchadnezzar king of Babylon came up to Jerusalem. They surrounded the city and attacked it. ¹¹Nebuchadnezzar himself came to the city while his officers were attacking it. ¹²Jehoiachin king of Judah surrendered to the king of Babylon. Jehoiachin's mother, servants, leaders and officers also surrendered. Then the king of Babylon made Jehoiachin a prisoner. This was in the eighth year Nebuchadnezzar was king. ¹³Nebuchadnezzar took all the treasures from the Templeᵈ of the Lord. He also removed the treasures from the palace. He took all the gold objects Solomon king of Israel had made for the Temple. This happened as the Lord had said it would. ¹⁴Nebuchadnezzar took away all the people of Jerusalem. This included all the leaders and all the wealthy people. He also took all the craftsmen and metal workers. There were 10,000 prisoners in all. Only the poorest people in the land were left. ¹⁵Nebuchadnezzar carried away Jehoiachin to Babylon. He took the king's mother and his wives. He also took the officers and leading men of the land. They were taken captive from Jerusalem to Babylon. ¹⁶The king of Babylon also took all 7,000 soldiers. These men were all strong and able to fight

in war. And 1,000 craftsmen and metal workers were taken, too. Nebuchadnezzar took them as prisoners to Babylon. [17] He made Mattaniah king in Jehoiachin's place. Mattaniah was Jehoiachin's uncle. He also changed Mattaniah's name to Zedekiah.

[18] Zedekiah was 21 years old when he became king. And he was king in Jerusalem for 11 years. His mother's name was Hamutal daughter of Jeremiah.[n] She was from Libnah. [19] Zedekiah did what the Lord said was wrong, just as Jehoiakim had done. [20] All this happened in Jerusalem and Judah because the Lord was angry with them. Finally, he threw them out of his presence.

Zedekiah turned against the king of Babylon.

25

Then Nebuchadnezzar king of Babylon marched against Jerusalem with his whole army. This happened during Zedekiah's ninth year, tenth month and tenth day as king. He made a camp around the city. Then he built devices all around the city walls to attack it. [2] The city was under attack until Zedekiah's eleventh year as king. [3] By the ninth day of the fourth month, the hunger was terrible in the city. There was no food for the people to eat. [4] Then the city wall was broken through. And the whole army ran away at night. They went through the gate between the two walls by the king's garden. The Babylonians were still surrounding the city. Zedekiah and his men ran toward the Jordan Valley. [5] But the Babylonian army chased King Zedekiah. They caught up with him in the plains of Jericho. All of his army was scattered from him. [6] So they captured Zedekiah and took him to the king of Babylon at Riblah. There he passed sentence on Zedekiah. [7] They killed Zedekiah's sons as he watched. Then they put out his eyes. They put bronze chains on him and took him to Babylon.

[8] Nebuzaradan was the commander of the king's special guards. This officer of the king of Babylon came to Jerusalem. This was on the seventh day of the fifth month. This was in Nebuchadnezzar's nineteenth year as king of Babylon. [9] Nebuzaradan set fire to the Temple[d] of the Lord and the palace. He also set fire to all the houses of Jerusalem. Every important building was burned.

[10] The whole Babylonian army broke

down the walls around Jerusalem. That army was led by the commander of the king's special guards. [11] Nebuzaradan, the commander of the guards, took captive the people left in Jerusalem. And he took captive those who had surrendered to the king of Babylon. The rest of the people were also taken away. [12] But the commander left behind some of the poorest people of the land. They were to take care of the vineyards and fields.

[13] The Babylonians broke up the bronze pillars, the bronze stands and the large bronze bowl, which was called the Sea. These were in the Temple of the Lord. Then they carried the bronze to Babylon. [14] They also took the pots, shovels, wick trimmers, dishes and all the bronze objects. These were used to serve in the Temple. [15] The commander of the king's special guards took away the pans for carrying hot coals. He also took the bowls and everything made of pure gold or silver. [16] There was so much bronze that it could not be weighed. There were two pillars and the large bronze bowl. There were also the movable stands which Solomon had made for the Temple of the Lord. [17] Each pillar was about 27 feet high. The bronze capital[d] on top of the pillar was about 4½ feet high. It was decorated with a net design and bronze pomegranates[d] all around it. The other pillar also had a net design. It was like the first pillar.

[18] The commander of the guards took some prisoners. He took Seraiah the chief priest, Zephaniah the priest next in rank, and the three doorkeepers. [19] The commander also took other people who were still in the city. He took the officer in charge of the fighting men. He also took five people who advised the king. And he took the royal assistant who selected people for the army. And he took 60 other men who were in the city. [20] Nebuzaradan, the commander, took all these people. And he brought them to the king of Babylon at Riblah. [21] There at Riblah, in the land of Hamath, the king had them killed. So the people of Judah were led away from their country as captives.

[22] Nebuchadnezzar king of Babylon left some people in the land of Judah. He appointed Gedaliah son of Ahikam as governor. (Ahikam was the son of Shaphan.)

[23] The army captains and their men

heard that the king of Babylon had made Gedaliah governor. So they all came to Gedaliah at Mizpah. They were Ishmael son of Nethaniah and Johanan son of Kareah. Also there were Seraiah son of Tanhumeth the Netophathite, Jaazaniah son of the Maacathite and their men. [24]Then Gedaliah made promises to these army captains and their men. He said, "Don't be afraid of the Babylonian officers. Live in the land and serve the king of Babylon. Then everything will go well for you."

[25]Ishmael was the son of Nethaniah. Nethaniah was the son of Elishama from the king's family. In the seventh month Ishmael came with ten men and killed Gedaliah. They also killed the men of Judah and Babylon who were with Gedaliah at Mizpah. [26]Then all the

people, from the least important to the most important, ran away to Egypt. The army leaders also went. This was because they were afraid of the Babylonians.

[27]Jehoiachin king of Judah was held in Babylon for 37 years. In the thirty-seventh year Evil-Merodach became king of Babylon. He let Jehoiachin out of prison on the twenty-seventh day of the twelfth month. [28]Evil-Merodach spoke kindly to Jehoiachin. He gave Jehoiachin a seat of honor. It was above the seats of the other kings who were with him in Babylon. [29]So Jehoiachin put away his prison clothes. For the rest of his life, he ate at the king's table. [30]Every day the king gave Jehoiachin an allowance. This lasted as long as he lived.

The First Book of the
CHRONICLES

1 Adam was the father of Seth. Seth was the father of Enosh. Enosh was the father of Kenan. [2]Kenan was the father of Mahalalel. Mahalalel was the father of Jared. Jared was the father of Enoch. [3]Enoch was the father of Methuselah. Methuselah was the father of Lamech. And he was the father of Noah.

[4]The sons of Noah were Shem, Ham and Japheth.

[5]Japheth's sons were Gomer, Magog, Madai, Javan, Tubal, Meshech and Tiras.

[6]Gomer's sons were Ashkenaz, Riphath and Togarmah.

[7]Javan's sons were Elishah, Tarshish, Kittim[n] and Rodanim.

[8]Ham's sons were Cush, Mizraim,[n] Put and Canaan.

[9]Cush's sons were Seba, Havilah, Sabta, Raamah and Sabteca.

Raamah's sons were Sheba and Dedan.

[10]Cush was the father of Nimrod. Nimrod grew up to become a mighty warrior on the earth.

[11]Mizraim was the father of the people living in Lud, Anam, Lehab and Naphtuh.

[12]Mizraim was also the father of the people living in Pathrus, Casluh and

Crete. (The Philistine people came from Casluh.)

[13]Canaan's first child was Sidon. Canaan was also the father of the Hittites, [14]Jebusites, Amorites and the Girgashites. [15]He was the father of the Hivites, Arkites, Sinites, [16]Arvadites, Zemarites and the Hamathites.

[17]Shem's sons were Elam, Asshur, Arphaxad, Lud and Aram.

Aram's sons were Uz, Hul, Gether and Meshech.

[18]Arphaxad was the father of Shelah. Shelah was the father of Eber.

[19]Eber had two sons. One son was named Peleg.[n] He was named this because the people on the earth were divided into different languages during his life. Peleg's brother was named Joktan.

[20]Joktan was the father of Almodad, Sheleph, Hazarmaveth, Jerah, [21]Hadoram, Uzal and Diklah. [22]He was also the father of Obal, Abimael, Sheba, [23]Ophir, Havilah and Jobab. All these were Joktan's sons. [24]The family line went from Shem to Abraham. It included Shem, Arphaxad, Shelah, [25]Eber, Peleg, Reu, [26]Serug, Nahor, Terah [27]and Abram, who is called Abraham.

1:7 Kittim His descendants were the people of Cyprus. **1:8 Mizraim** This is another name for Egypt. **1:19 Peleg** This name sounds like the Hebrew word for "divided."

[28] Abraham's sons were Isaac and Ishmael.

[29] These were the sons of Isaac and Ishmael. Ishmael's first son was Nebaioth. Ishmael's other sons were Kedar, Adbeel, Mibsam, [30] Mishma, Dumah, Massa, Hadad, Tema, [31] Jetur, Naphish and Kedemah. These were Ishmael's sons. [32] Keturah was Abraham's slave woman.[d] She gave birth to Zimran, Jokshan, Medan, Midian, Ishbak and Shuah.

Jokshan's sons were Sheba and Dedan.

[33] Midian's sons were Ephah, Epher, Hanoch, Abida and Eldaah. All these people were descendants[d] of Keturah.

[34] Abraham was the father of Isaac. Isaac's sons were Esau and Israel.

[35] Esau's sons were Eliphaz, Reuel, Jeush, Jalam and Korah.

[36] Eliphaz's sons were Teman, Omar, Zepho, Gatam, Kenaz, Timna and Amalek.

[37] Reuel's sons were Nahath, Zerah, Shammah and Mizzah.

[38] Seir's sons were Lotan, Shobal, Zibeon, Anah, Dishon, Ezer and Dishan.

[39] Lotan's sons were Hori and Homam. Lotan had a sister named Timna.

[40] Shobal's sons were Alvan, Manahath, Ebal, Shepho and Onam.

Zibeon's sons were Aiah and Anah.

[41] Anah's son was Dishon.

Dishon's sons were Hemdan, Eshban, Ithran and Keran.

[42] Ezer's sons were Bilhan, Zaavan and Akan.

Dishan's sons were Uz and Aran.

[43] There were kings ruling in Edom before there were kings in Israel. Bela son of Beor was king of Edom. Bela's city was named Dinhabah.

[44] When Bela died, Jobab son of Zerah became king. Jobab was from Bozrah.

[45] When Jobab died, Husham became king. He was from Teman.

[46] When Husham died, Hadad son of Bedad became king. Hadad's city was named Avith. Hadad defeated Midian in the country of Moab.

[47] When Hadad died, Samlah became king. He was from Masrekah.

[48] When Samlah died, Shaul became king. He was from Rehoboth by the River.

[49] When Shaul died, Baal-Hanan son of Acbor became king.

[50] When Baal-Hanan died, Hadad became king. Hadad's city was named Pau. Hadad's wife was named Mehetabel, and she was Matred's daughter. Matred was the daughter of Me-Zahab.

[51] Then Hadad died.

The leaders of the family groups of Edom were Timna, Alvah, Jetheth, [52] Oholibamah, Elah, Pinon, [53] Kenaz, Teman, Mibzar, [54] Magdiel and Iram. These were the leaders of Edom.

2 The sons of Israel, also called Jacob, were Reuben, Simeon, Levi, Judah, Issachar, Zebulun, [2] Dan, Joseph, Benjamin, Naphtali, Gad and Asher.

[3] Judah's sons were Er, Onan and Shelah. A Canaanite woman, the daughter of Shua, was their mother. Judah's first son, Er, did what the Lord said was wicked. So the Lord put him to death. [4] Judah's daughter-in-law Tamar gave birth to Perez and Zerah. Judah was the father. So Judah had five sons.

[5] Perez's sons were Hezron and Hamul.

[6] Zerah had five sons. They were Zimri, Ethan, Heman, Calcol and Darda.

[7] Carmi's son was Achan. He caused trouble for Israel because he took things that had been given to the Lord to be destroyed.

[8] Ethan's son was Azariah.

[9] Hezron's sons were Jerahmeel, Ram and Caleb.

[10] Ram was Amminadab's father. And Amminadab was Nashon's father. Nahshon was the leader of the people of Judah. [11] Nahshon was the father of Salmon. Salmon was the father of Boaz. [12] Boaz was the father of Obed. Obed was the father of Jesse.

[13] Jesse's first son was Eliab. His second son was Abinadab. His third son was Shimea. [14] His fourth son was Nethanel. His fifth son was Raddai. [15] Jesse's sixth son was Ozem, and his seventh son was David. [16] Their sisters were Zeruiah and Abigail. Zeruiah's three sons were Abishai, Joab and Asahel. [17] Abigail was the mother of Amasa. Amasa's father was an Ishmaelite named Jether.

[18] Caleb son of Hezron had children by his wife Azubah and by Jerioth. Caleb and Azubah's sons were Jesher, Shobab and Ardon. [19] When Azubah died, Caleb married Ephrath. They had a son named Hur. [20] Hur was the father of Uri. Uri was the father of Bezalel.

[21] Later, when Hezron was 60 years old, he married the daughter of Makir. Makir was Gilead's father. Hezron had sexual relations with Makir's daughter, and she had a son named Segub. [22] Se-

gub was the father of Jair. Jair controlled 23 cities in the country of Gilead. [23](But Geshur and Aram captured the Towns of Jair. They also captured Kenath and the small towns around it. There were 60 towns in all.) All these were descendants[d] of Makir, the father of Gilead.

[24]After Hezron died in Caleb Ephrathah, his wife Abijah had his son. He was named Ashur. Ashur became the father of Tekoa.

[25]Jerahmeel was Hezron's first son. Jerahmeel's sons were Ram, Bunah, Oren, Ozem and Ahijah. Ram was Jerahmeel's first son. [26]Jerahmeel had another wife, who was named Atarah. She was the mother of Onam.

[27]Jerahmeel's first son, Ram, had sons. They were Maaz, Jamin and Eker.

[28]Onam's sons were Shammai and Jada.

Shammai's sons were Nadab and Abishur.

[29]Abishur's wife was named Abihail. Abishur and Abihail's sons were Ahban and Molid.

[30]Nadab's sons were Seled and Appaim. Seled died without having children.

[31]Appaim's son was Ishi. Ishi was the father of Sheshan.

Sheshan was the father of Ahlai.

[32]Jada was Shammai's brother. Jada's sons were Jether and Jonathan. Jether died without having children.

[33]Jonathan's sons were Peleth and Zaza.

These were Jerahmeel's descendants.[d]

[34]Sheshan did not have any sons, only daughters. He had a servant from Egypt named Jarha. [35]Sheshan let his daughter marry his servant Jarha. Then she had a son named Attai.

[36]Attai was the father of Nathan. Nathan was the father of Zabad. [37]Zabad was the father of Ephlal. Ephlal was the father of Obed. [38]Obed was the father of Jehu. Jehu was the father of Azariah. [39]Azariah was the father of Helez. Helez was the father of Eleasah. [40]Eleasah was the father of Sismai. Sismai was the father of Shallum. [41]Shallum was the father of Jekamiah. And Jekamiah was the father of Elishama.

[42]Caleb was Jerahmeel's brother. Caleb's first son was Mesha. Mesha was the father of Ziph. And his son Mareshah was the father of Hebron.

[43]Hebron's sons were Korah, Tap-puah, Rekem and Shema. [44]Shema was the father of Raham. Raham was the father of Jorkeam. Rekem was the father of Shammai. [45]Shammai's son was Maon. Maon was the father of Beth Zur.

[46]Caleb's slave woman[d] was named Ephah. She was the mother of Haran, Moza and Gazez. Haran was the father of Gazez.

[47]Jahdai's sons were Regem, Jotham, Geshan, Pelet, Ephah and Shaaph.

[48]Caleb had another slave woman named Maacah. She was the mother of Sheber and Tirhanah. [49]She was also the mother of Shaaph and Sheva. Shaaph was the father of Madmannah. Sheva was the father of Macbenah and Gibea. Caleb's daughter was Acsah.

[50-51]These were Caleb's descendants:[d] Caleb's son Hur was the first son of his mother Ephrathah. Hur's sons were Shobal, Salma and Hareph. Shobal was the father of Kiriath Jearim. Salma was the father of Bethlehem. And Hareph was the father of Beth Gader.

[52]Shobal was the father of Kiriath Jearim. These were Shobal's descendants: Haroeh, half the Manahathites, [53]and the family groups of Kiriath Jearim. Shobal was also the ancestor of the Ithrites, Puthites, Shumathites and the Mishraites. The Zorathites and the Eshtaolites came from the Mishraite people.

[54]Salma's descendants were Bethlehem, the Netophathites, Atroth Beth Joab, half the Manahathites and the Zorites. [55]His descendants were also the families who lived at Jabez. These were the people who wrote and copied important papers. These people were the Tirathites, Shimeathites and Sucathites. They were from the Kenite family group who came from Hammath. He was the father of the people living in Recab.

3 These are David's sons who were born in Hebron. David's first son was Amnon. Amnon's mother was Ahinoam from the town of Jezreel. David's second son was Daniel. His mother was Abigail from Carmel. [2]David's third son was Absalom. His mother was Maacah, the daughter of Talmai king of Geshur. David's fourth son was Adonijah. His mother was Haggith. [3]David's fifth son was Shephatiah. His mother was Abital. David's sixth son was Ithream. David's wife Eglah was his mother. [4]These six sons of David were born to him in Hebron. David ruled there 7 years and 6 months.

David ruled in Jerusalem 33 years.

⁵These were David's children who were born in Jerusalem: David and Bathsheba, Ammiel's daughter, had four children. They were Shammua, Shobab, Nathan and Solomon. ⁶⁻⁸David's other nine children were Ibhar, Elishua, Eliphelet, Nogah, Nepheg, Japhia, Elishama, Eliada and Eliphelet. ⁹Those are all of David's sons, except for those born to his slave women.ᵈ David also had a daughter named Tamar.

¹⁰Solomon's son was Rehoboam. Rehoboam's son was Abijah. Abijah's son was Asa. Asa's son was Jehoshaphat. ¹¹Jehoshaphat's son was Jehoram. Jehoram's son was Ahaziah. Ahaziah's son was Joash. ¹²Joash's son was Amaziah. Amaziah's son was Azariah. Azariah's son was Jotham. ¹³Jotham's son was Ahaz. Ahaz's son was Hezekiah. Hezekiah's son was Manasseh. ¹⁴Manasseh's son was Amon. Amon's son was Josiah.

¹⁵These were Josiah's sons: Josiah's first son was Johanan. His second son was Jehoiakim. His third son was Zedekiah. His fourth son was Shallum.

¹⁶Jehoiakim was followed by Jehoiachin. Jehoiachin was followed by Zedekiah.

¹⁷Jehoiachin was taken as a prisoner. His sons were Shealtiel, ¹⁸Malkiram, Pedaiah, Shenazzar, Jekamiah, Hoshama and Nedabiah.

¹⁹Pedaiah's sons were Zerubbabel and Shimei.

Zerubbabel's sons were Meshullam and Hananiah. Their sister was Shelomith. ²⁰Zerubbabel also had five other sons. Their names were Hashubah, Ohel, Berekiah, Hasadiah and Jushab-Hesed.

²¹Hananiah's descendantsᵈ were Pelatiah and Jeshaiah, and the sons of Rephaiah, Arnan, Obadiah and Shecaniah. ²²Shecaniah's son was Shemaiah. Shemaiah's sons were Hattush, Igal, Bariah, Neariah and Shaphat. There were six in all.

²³Neariah had three sons. They were Elioenai, Hizkiah and Azrikam. ²⁴Elioenai had seven sons. They were Hodaviah, Eliashib, Pelaiah, Akkub, Johanan, Delaiah and Anani.

4 Judah's descendantsᵈ were Perez, Hezron, Carmi, Hur and Shobal. ²Reaiah was Shobal's son. Reaiah was the father of Jahath. Jahath was the father of Ahumai and Lahad. They were

the family groups of the Zorathite people.

³⁻⁴Hur was the oldest son of Caleb and his wife Ephrath. Hur was the leader of Bethlehem. Hur's three sons were Etam, Penuel and Ezer. Etam's sons were Jezreel, Ishma and Idbash. They had a sister named Hazzelelponi. Penuel was the father of Gedor. Ezer was the father of Hushah.

⁵Tekoa's father was Ashhur. Ashhur had two wives named Helah and Naarah.

⁶The sons of Ashhur and Naarah were Ahuzzam, Hepher, Temeni and Haahashtari. These were the descendants of Naarah.

⁷Helah's sons were Zereth, Zohar, Ethnan ⁸and Koz. Koz was the father of Anub and Hazzobebah. He was also the father of the Aharhel family group. Aharhel was the son of Harum.

⁹There was a man named Jabez. He was respected more than his brothers. His mother named him Jabez* because she said, "I was in much pain when I gave birth to him." ¹⁰Jabez prayed to the God of Israel. Jabez said, "Please do good things for me. Please give me more land. Stay with me, and don't let anyone hurt me. Then I won't have any pain." And God did what Jabez had asked.

¹¹Kelub was Shuhah's brother. Kelub was the father of Mehir. Mehir was the father of Eshton. ¹²Eshton was the father of Beth Rapha, Paseah and Tehinnah. Tehinnah was the father of the people from the town of Nahash. These people were from Recah.

¹³The sons of Kenaz were Othniel and Seraiah.

Othniel's sons were Hathath and Meonothai. ¹⁴Meonothai was the father of Ophrah.

Seraiah was the father of Joab. Joab was the ancestor of the people from Craftsmen's Valley. It is called Craftsmen's Valley because the people living there were craftsmen.

¹⁵Caleb was Jephunneh's son. Caleb's sons were Iru, Elah and Naam. Elah's son was Kenaz.

¹⁶Jehallelel's sons were Ziph, Ziphah, Tiria and Asarel.

¹⁷⁻¹⁸Ezrah's sons were Jether, Mered, Epher and Jalon. Mered married Bithiah, the daughter of the king of Egypt. The children of Mered and Bithiah were Miriam, Shammai and Ishbah. Ishbah

was the father of Eshtemoa. Mered also had a wife from Judah. She gave birth to Jered, Heber and Jekuthiel. Jered became the father of Gedor. Heber became the father of Soco. And Jekuthiel became the father of Zanoah.

19 Hodiah's wife was Naham's sister. The sons of Hodiah's wife were Eshtemoa and the father of Keilah. Keilah was from the Garmite people. And Eshtemoa was from the Maacathite people.

20 Shimon's sons were Amnon, Rinnah, Ben-Hanan and Tilon.

Ishi's sons were Zoheth and Ben-Zoheth.

21-22 Shelah was Judah's son. Shelah's sons were Er, Laadah, Jokim, the men from Cozeba, Joash and Saraph. Er was the father of Lecah. Laadah was the father of Mareshah and the family groups of linen workers at Beth Ashbea. Joash and Saraph ruled in Moab and Jashubi Lehem. The writings about this family are very old. 23 These sons of Shelah made things from clay. They lived in Netaim and Gederah. They stayed there and worked for the king.

24 Simeon's sons were Nemuel, Jamin, Jarib, Zerah and Shaul. 25 Shaul's son was Shallum. Shallum's son was Mibsam. Mibsam's son was Mishma. 26 Mishma's son was Hammuel. Hammuel's son was Zaccur. Zaccur's son was Shimei. 27 Shimei had 16 sons and 6 daughters. But his brothers did not have many children. So there were not as many people in their family group as there were in Judah.

28 Shimei's children lived in Beersheba, Moladah, Hazar Shual, 29 Bilhah, Ezem and Tolad. 30 They also lived in Bethuel, Hormah, Ziklag, 31 Beth Marcaboth, Hazar Susim, Beth Biri and Shaaraim. They lived in these cities until David became king. 32 The five villages near these cities were Etam, Ain, Rimmon, Token and Ashan. 33 There were also other villages as far away as Baalath. This is where they lived. And they wrote the history of their family.

34-38 This is the list of men who were leaders of their family groups. There were Meshobab, Jamlech, Joshah son of Amaziah, Joel and Jehu son of Joshibiah. (Joshibiah was the son of Seraiah, who was the son of Asiel.) There were also Elioenai, Jaakobah, Jeshohaiah, Asaiah, Adiel, Jesimiel, Benaiah and Ziza. (Ziza was the son of Shiphi, who was the son of Allon. Allon was the son

of Jedaiah, who was the son of Shimri. And Shimri was the son of Shemaiah.)

These men's families grew to be very large. 39 They went to the area outside the city of Gedor to the east side of the valley. They went there to look for pasture for their sheep. 40 They found good pastures with plenty of grass. The land was open country and peaceful and quiet. Ham's descendants[d] had lived there in the past.

41 These men listed above came to Gedor while Hezekiah was king of Judah. They fought against the Hamite people and destroyed their tents. They also fought against the Meunite people who lived there and completely destroyed them. So there are no Meunites there even today. Then these men began to live there, because there was pasture for their sheep. 42 Ishi's sons, Pelatiah, Neariah, Rephaiah and Uzziel, led 500 of the Simeonite people. They attacked the people living in the mountains of Edom. 43 They killed the few Amalekite people who were still alive. From that time until now these Simeonites have lived in Edom.

5 Reuben was Israel's first son. Reuben should have received the special privileges of the oldest son. But he had sexual relations with his father's slave woman.[d] So those special privileges were given to Joseph's sons. (Joseph was a son of Israel.) In the family history Reuben's name is not listed as the first son. 2 Judah became stronger than his brothers. And a leader came from his family. But Joseph's family received the privileges that belonged to the oldest son. 3 Reuben was the first son born to Israel. Reuben's sons were Hanoch, Pallu, Hezron and Carmi.

4 These were the children of Joel: Shemaiah was Joel's son. Gog was Shemaiah's son. Shimei was Gog's son. 5 Micah was Shimei's son. Reaiah was Micah's son. Baal was Reaiah's son. 6 Beerah was Baal's son. Beerah was a leader of the tribe[d] of Reuben. Tiglath-Pileser king of Assyria captured Beerah and took him away.

7 Joel's brothers and all his family groups are listed just as they are written in their family histories: Jeiel was the first, then Zechariah 8 and Bela. (Bela was the son of Azaz. Azaz was Shema's son. Shema was Joel's son.) They lived in the area of Aroer all the way to Nebo and Baal Meon. 9 Bela's people lived to the east. Their land went as far as the

edge of the desert, which is beside the Euphrates River. They lived there because they had too many cattle for the land of Gilead.

¹⁰When Saul was king, Bela's people fought a war against the Hagrite people. And they defeated the Hagrites. Then Bela's people lived in the tents that had belonged to the Hagrites. They lived in all the area east of Gilead.

¹¹The people from the tribe[d] of Gad lived near the Reubenite people. The Gadites lived in the area of Bashan all the way to Salecah. ¹²Joel was the main leader in Bashan. Shapham was the second leader. Then Janai and Shaphat were leaders.

¹³The seven relatives in their families were Michael, Meshullam, Sheba, Jorai, Jacan, Zia and Eber. ¹⁴They were the descendants[d] of Abihail. Abihail was Huri's son. Huri was Jaroah's son. Jaroah was Gilead's son. Gilead was Michael's son. Michael was Jeshishai's son. Jeshishai was Jahdo's son. Jahdo was the son of Buz. ¹⁵Ahi was Abdiel's son. Abdiel was Guni's son. Ahi was the leader of their family.

¹⁶The Gadite people lived in Gilead, Bashan and in the small towns around Bashan. They also lived on all the pasturelands in the Plain of Sharon all the way to the borders.

¹⁷All these people's names were written in the family history of Gad. This was done during the time Jotham was king of Judah and Jeroboam was king of Israel.

¹⁸There were 44,760 fighters from the tribes[d] of Reuben and Gad and the eastern half-tribe of Manasseh. They were brave men who could use shields and swords. They could use their bows well. They were skilled in war. ¹⁹They started a war against the Hagrites and the people of Jetur, Naphish and Nodab. ²⁰The men from the tribes of Manasseh, Reuben and Gad prayed to God in the war. They asked God to help them. So he helped them because they trusted him. He allowed them to defeat the Hagrites. And they also defeated all those who were with the Hagrites. ²¹They took the animals that belonged to the Hagrites. They took 50,000 camels, 250,000 sheep and 2,000 donkeys. They also captured 100,000 people. ²²Many Hagrites were killed. This is because God helped the people of Reuben, Gad and Manasseh. Then they lived there until Babylon captured them and took them away.

²³There were many people in the eastern half-tribe of Manasseh. They lived in the area of Bashan all the way to Baal Hermon, Senir and Mount Hermon.

²⁴These were the family leaders: Epher, Ishi, Eliel, Azriel, Jeremiah, Hodaviah and Jahdiel. They were all strong, brave and famous men. And they were leaders in their families. ²⁵But they sinned against the God that their ancestors had worshiped. They began worshiping the gods of the people in that land. And those were the people God was destroying. ²⁶So the God of Israel made Pul king of Assyria want to go to war. Pul was also called Tiglath-Pileser. He captured the people of Reuben, Gad and the eastern half-tribe of Manasseh. And he took them away to Halah, Habor, Hara and near the Gozan River. And they have lived there from that time until this day.

6 Levi's sons were Gershon, Kohath and Merari.

²Kohath's sons were Amram, Izhar, Hebron and Uzziel.

³Amram's children were Aaron, Moses and Miriam.

Aaron's sons were Nadab, Abihu, Eleazar and Ithamar. ⁴Eleazar was the father of Phinehas. Phinehas was the father of Abishua. ⁵Abishua was the father of Bukki. Bukki was the father of Uzzi. ⁶Uzzi was the father of Zerahiah. Zerahiah was the father of Meraioth. ⁷Meraioth was the father of Amariah. Amariah was the father of Ahitub. ⁸Ahitub was the father of Zadok. Zadok was the father of Ahimaaz. ⁹Ahimaaz was the father of Azariah. Azariah was the father of Johanan. ¹⁰Johanan was the father of Azariah. (Azariah was a priest in the Temple[d] Solomon built in Jerusalem.) ¹¹Azariah was the father of Amariah. Amariah was the father of Ahitub. ¹²Ahitub was the father of Zadok. Zadok was the father of Shallum. ¹³Shallum was the father of Hilkiah. Hilkiah was the father of Azariah. ¹⁴Azariah was the father of Seraiah. Seraiah was the father of Jehozadak.

¹⁵Jehozadak was forced to leave his home when the Lord sent Judah and Jerusalem into captivity. That was when Nebuchadnezzar captured them and took them away.

¹⁶Levi's sons were Gershon, Kohath and Merari.

¹⁷The names of Gershon's sons were Libni and Shimei.

¹⁸Kohath's sons were Amram, Izhar, Hebron and Uzziel.

[19] Merari's sons were Mahli and Mushi.

This is a list of the family groups of Levi. They are listed by the name of the father of each group.

[20] Gershon's son was Libni. Libni's son was Jehath. Jehath's son was Zimmah. [21] Zimmah's son was Joah. Joah's son was Iddo. Iddo's son was Zerah. And Zerah's son was Jeatherai.

[22] Kohath's son was Amminadab. Amminadab's son was Korah. Korah's son was Assir. [23] Assir's son was Elkanah. Elkanah's son was Ebiasaph. Ebiasaph's son was Assir. [24] Assir's son was Tahath. Tahath's son was Uriel. Uriel's son was Uzziah, and Uzziah's son was Shaul.

[25] Elkanah's sons were Amasai and Ahimoth. [26] Ahimoth's son was Elkanah. Elkanah's son was Zophai. Zophai's son was Nahath. [27] Nahath's son was Eliab. Eliab's son was Jeroham. Jeroham's son was Elkanah, and Elkanah's son was Samuel.

[28] Samuel's sons were Joel, the first son, and Abijah, the second son.

[29] Merari's son was Mahli. Mahli's son was Libni. Libni's son was Shimei. Shimei's son was Uzzah. [30] Uzzah's son was Shimea. Shimea's son was Haggiah, and Haggiah's son was Asaiah.

[31] David chose some men to be in charge of the music in the house of the Lord. They began their work after the Box[d] of the Agreement was put there. [32] They served by making music at the Holy Tent.[d] (It is also called the Meeting Tent.) And they served until Solomon built the Temple[d] of the Lord in Jerusalem. They followed the rules for their work.

[33] These are the musicians and their sons:

From Kohath's family there was Heman the singer. Heman was Joel's son. Joel was Samuel's son. [34] Samuel was Elkanah's son. Elkanah was Jeroham's son. Jeroham was Eliel's son. Eliel was Toah's son. [35] Toah was Zuph's son. Zuph was Elkanah's son. Elkanah was Mahath's son. Mahath was Amasai's son. [36] Amasai was Elkanah's son. Elkanah was Joel's son. Joel was Azariah's son. Azariah was Zephaniah's son. [37] Zephaniah was Tahath's son. Tahath was Assir's son. Assir was Ebiasaph's son. Ebiasaph was Korah's son. [38] Korah was Izhar's son. Izhar was Kohath's son. Kohath was Levi's son. Levi was Israel's son.

[39] There was Heman's helper Asaph. Asaph's group stood by Heman's right side. Asaph was Berekiah's son. Berekiah was Shimea's son. [40] Shimea was Michael's son. Michael was Baaseiah's son. Baaseiah was Malkijah's son. [41] Malkijah was Ethni's son. Ethni was Zerah's son. Zerah was Adaiah's son. [42] Adaiah was Ethan's son. Ethan was Zimmah's son. Zimmah was Shimei's son. [43] Shimei was Jahath's son. Jahath was Gershon's son. Gershon was Levi's son.

[44] Merari's family were the helpers of Heman and Asaph. Merari's family stood by Heman's left side. In this group was Ethan son of Kishi. Kishi was Abdi's son. Abdi was Malluch's son. [45] Malluch was Hashabiah's son. Hashabiah was Amaziah's son. Amaziah was Hilkiah's son. [46] Hilkiah was Amzi's son. Amzi was Bani's son. Bani was Shemer's son. [47] Shemer was Mahli's son. Mahli was Mushi's son. Mushi was Merari's son. Merari was Levi's son.

[48] The other Levites served by doing their own special work in the Holy Tent. It is the house of God. [49] Aaron and his descendants[d] offered the sacrifices on the altar of burnt offering. They also burned the incense on the altar of incense. They offered the sacrifices that removed the Israelites' sins so they could belong to God. They did all the work in the Most Holy Place. They followed all the laws that Moses, God's servant, had commanded.

[50] These were Aaron's sons: Eleazar was Aaron's son. Phinehas was Eleazar's son. Abishua was Phinehas' son. [51] Bukki was Abishua's son. Uzzi was Bukki's son. Zerahiah was Uzzi's son. [52] Meraioth was Zerahiah's son. Amariah was Meraioth's son. Ahitub was Amariah's son. [53] Zadok was Ahitub's son. Ahimaaz was Zadok's son.

[54] These are the places where Aaron's descendants[d] lived. Aaron's descendants from the Kohath family group were given this land to live in. They received the first share of the land that was given to the Levites.

[55] They were given the city of Hebron in Judah and the pastures around it. [56] But the fields farther from the city were given to Caleb son of Jephunneh. And the villages near Hebron were given to Caleb. [57] So the descendants of Aaron were given Hebron. It was one of

the cities of safety.[n] They also received the cities of Libnah, Jattir, Eshtemoa, [58]Hilen, Debir, [59]Ashan, Juttah and Beth Shemesh. They received all these cities and the pastures around them. [60]They also received cities from the tribe of Benjamin. They received Gibeon, Geba, Alemeth, Anathoth and their pastures.

The Kohath family groups received a total of 13 cities.

[61]The rest of the Kohath family group was given 10 cities. These cities were from the family groups of the western half-tribe of Manasseh. The cities were chosen by throwing lots.[d]

[62]The Gershon family group received 13 cities. They were from the tribes of Issachar, Asher, Naphtali and the part of Manasseh living in Bashan.

[63]The Merari family group received 12 cities from the tribes of Reuben, Gad and Zebulun. Those cities were chosen by throwing lots.

[64]So the Israelites gave these cities and their pastures to the Levites. [65]The cities from the tribes of Judah, Simeon and Benjamin were chosen by throwing lots. They are the cities named above.

[66]Some of the Kohath family groups received cities and pastures from the tribe of Ephraim. [67]They received Shechem in the mountains of Ephraim. It was one of the cities of safety. They also received the cities of Gezer, [68]Jokmeam, Beth Horon, [69]Aijalon and Gath Rimmon. They received the cities and the pastures around them.

[70]The rest of the people in the Kohath family group received cities from the western half-tribe of Manasseh. They received the cities of Aner and Bileam and their pastures.

[71]From the eastern half-tribe of Manasseh, the Gershon family received towns and pastures. They received Golan in Bashan, Ashtaroth and the pastures around them.

[72-73]From the tribe of Issachar, the Gershon family received towns and pastures. They received Kedesh, Daberath, Ramoth, Anem and their pastures.

[74-75]From the tribe of Asher, the Gershon family received towns and pastures. They received Mashal, Abdon, Hukok, Rehob and their pastures.

[76]From the tribe of Naphtali, the Gershon family received towns and pastures. They received Kedesh in Galilee, Hammon, Kiriathaim and their pastures.

[77]The rest of the Levites, the people from the Merari family, also received towns and pastures. They received Jokneam, Kartah, Rimmono and Tabor from the tribe of Zebulun. They also received the pastures around those cities.

[78-79]From the tribe of Reuben, the Merari family received towns and pastures. They received Bezer in the desert, Jahzah, Kedemoth, Mephaath and their pastures. (The tribe of Reuben lived east of the Jordan River, across from Jericho.)

[80-81]From the tribe of Gad, the Merari family received towns and pastures. They received Ramoth in Gilead, Mahanaim, Heshbon, Jazer and their pastures.

7 Issachar had four sons. Their names were Tola, Puah, Jashub and Shimron.

[2]Tola's sons were Uzzi, Rephaiah, Jeriel, Jahmai, Ibsam and Samuel. They were leaders of their families. In the family history of Tola's descendants,[d] 22,600 men were listed as fighting men. This was during the time David was king.

[3]Uzzi's son was Izrahiah.

Izrahiah's sons were Michael, Obadiah, Joel and Isshiah. All five of them were leaders. [4]Their family history shows they had 36,000 men ready to serve in the army. This was because they had many wives and children.

[5]The records of the family groups of Issachar show there were 87,000 fighting men.

[6]Benjamin had three sons. Their names were Bela, Beker and Jediael.

[7]Bela had five sons. Their names were Ezbon, Uzzi, Uzziel, Jerimoth and Iri. They were leaders of their families. Their family history shows they had 22,034 fighting men.

[8]Beker's sons were Zemirah, Joash, Eliezer, Elioenai, Omri, Jeremoth, Abijah, Anathoth and Alemeth. They all were Beker's sons. [9]Their family history listed the family leaders and 20,200 fighting men.

[10]Jediael's son was Bilhan.

Bilhan's sons were Jeush, Benjamin, Ehud, Kenaanah, Zethan, Tarshish and Ahishahar. [11]All these sons of Jediael were leaders of their families. They had

---

6:57 cities of safety A person who had accidentally killed someone could go to one of the six cities of safety. There he would receive protection and a fair trial.

17,200 fighting men ready to serve in the army.

[12] The Shuppites and Huppites were descendants[d] of Ir. And the Hushites were descendants of Aher.

[13] Naphtali's sons were Jahziel, Guni, Jezer and Shillem. They were Bilhah's grandsons.

[14] These are Manasseh's descendants:[d] Manasseh had an Aramean slave woman.[d] She was the mother of Asriel and Makir. Makir was Gilead's father. [15] Makir took a wife from the Huppites and Shuppites. His sister was named Maacah. His second son was named Zelophehad. Zelophehad had only daughters. [16] Makir's wife Maacah had a son whom she named Peresh. Peresh's brother was named Sheresh. Sheresh's sons were Ulam and Rakem.

[17] Ulam's son was Bedan.

These were the sons of Gilead. Gilead was Makir's son. Makir was Manasseh's son. [18] Makir's sister Hammoleketh gave birth to Ishhod, Abiezer and Mahlah.

[19] The sons of Shemida were Ahian, Shechem, Likhi and Aniam.

[20] These are the names of Ephraim's descendants.[d] Ephraim's son was Shuthelah. Shuthelah's son was Bered. Bered's son was Tahath. Tahath's son was Eleadah. Eleadah's son was Tahath. [21] Tahath's son was Zabad. Zabad's son was Shuthelah.

Ezer and Elead went to Gath to steal the people's cows and sheep. So some men who grew up in that city killed Ezer and Elead. [22] Their father Ephraim cried for them many days. And his family came to comfort him. [23] Then he had sexual relations with his wife again. She became pregnant and gave birth to a son. Ephraim named his son Beriah[n] because of the bad things that had happened to his family. [24] Ephraim's daughter was Sheerah. She built Lower Beth Horon and Upper Beth Horon and Uzzen Sheerah.

[25] Rephah was Ephraim's son. Resheph was Rephah's son. Telah was Resheph's son. Tahan was Telah's son. [26] Ladan was Tahan's son. Ammihud was Ladan's son. Elishama was Ammihud's son. [27] Nun was Elishama's son. Joshua was the son of Nun.

[28] Ephraim's descendants lived in these lands and cities: Bethel and the villages near it, Naaran on the east, Gezer and the villages near it on the west,

and Shechem and the villages near it. These villages went all the way to Ayyah and its villages. [29] Along the borders of Manasseh's land were the towns of Beth Shan, Taanach, Megiddo and Dor. There were also villages near them. The descendants of Joseph son of Israel lived in these towns.

[30] Asher's sons were Imnah, Ishvah, Ishvi and Beriah. Their sister was Serah.

[31] Beriah's sons were Heber and Malkiel. Malkiel was Birzaith's father.

[32] Heber was the father of Japhlet, Shomer and Hotham and their sister Shua.

[33] Japhlet's sons were Pasach, Bimhal and Ashvath. They were Japhlet's children.

[34] Japhlet's brother was Shomer. Shomer's sons were Rohgah, Hubbah and Aram.

[35] Shomer's brother was Hotham. Hotham's sons were Zophah, Imna, Shelesh and Amal.

[36] Zophah's sons were Suah, Harnepher, Shual, Beri, Imrah, [37] Bezer, Hod, Shamma, Shilshah, Ithran and Beera.

[38] Jether's sons were Jephunneh, Pispah and Ara.

[39] Ulla's sons were Arah, Hanniel and Rizia.

[40] All these men were descendants of Asher. They were leaders of their families. They were powerful warriors and outstanding leaders. Their family history lists that they had 26,000 soldiers ready to serve in the army.

8 Benjamin was the father of Bela. Bela was Benjamin's first son. Ashbel was his second son. Aharah was his third son. [2] Nohah was Benjamin's fourth son, and Rapha was his fifth son.

[3] Bela's sons were Addar, Gera, Abihud, [4] Abishua, Naaman, Ahoah, [5] Gera, Shephuphan and Huram.

[6] These were the descendants[d] of Ehud. They were leaders of their families in Geba. They were forced to leave their homes and move to Manahath. [7] Ehud's descendants were Naaman, Ahijah and Gera. Gera forced them to leave their homes. He was the father of Uzza and Ahihud.

[8-11] Shaharaim and his wife Hushim had sons named Abitub and Elpaal. In Moab Shaharaim divorced his wives Hushim and Baara. Shaharaim and his wife Hodesh had these children: Jobab, Zibia, Mesha, Malcam, Jeuz, Sakia and

7:23 Beriah This name sounds like the Hebrew word for "trouble."

Mirmah. These sons were leaders of their families.

¹²⁻¹³Elpaal's sons were Eber, Misham, Shemed, Beriah and Shema. Shemed built the towns of Ono and Lod and the villages around them. Beriah and Shema were leaders of the families living in Aijalon. These sons forced the people who lived in Gath to leave.

¹⁴Beriah's sons were Ahio, Shashak, Jeremoth, ¹⁵Zebadiah, Arad, Eder, ¹⁶Michael, Ishpah and Joha.

¹⁷Elpaal's sons were Zebadiah, Meshullam, Hizki, Heber, ¹⁸Ishmerai, Izliah and Jobab.

¹⁹Shimei's sons were Jakim, Zicri, Zabdi, ²⁰Elienai, Zillethai, Eliel, ²¹Adaiah, Beraiah and Shimrath.

²²Shashak's sons were Ishpan, Eber, Eliel, ²³Abdon, Zicri, Hanan, ²⁴Hananiah, Elam, Anthothijah, ²⁵Iphdeiah and Penuel.

²⁶Jeroham's sons were Shamsherai, Shehariah, Athaliah, ²⁷Jaareshiah, Elijah and Zicri.

²⁸The family histories show that all these men were leaders of their families. They lived in Jerusalem.

²⁹Jeiel lived in the town of Gibeon, where he was the leader. His wife was named Maacah. ³⁰Jeiel's first son was Abdon. His other sons were Zur, Kish, Baal, Ner, Nadab, ³¹Gedor, Ahio, Zeker ³²and Mikloth. Mikloth was the father of Shimeah. These sons also lived near their relatives in Jerusalem.

³³Ner was the father of Kish. Kish was the father of Saul. And Saul was the father of Jonathan, Malki-Shua, Abinadab and Esh-Baal.

³⁴Jonathan's son was Merib-Baal. Merib-Baal was Micah's father.

³⁵Micah's sons were Pithon, Melech, Tarea and Ahaz. ³⁶Ahaz was the father of Jehoaddah. Jehoaddah was the father of Alemeth, Azmaveth and Zimri. Zimri was the father of Moza. ³⁷Moza was the father of Binea. Raphah was Binea's son. Eleasah was Raphah's son. And Azel was Eleasah's son.

³⁸Azel had six sons. Their names were Azrikam, Bokeru, Ishmael, Sheariah, Obadiah and Hanan. All these were Azel's sons.

³⁹Azel's brother was Eshek. Eshek's first son was Ulam. Jeush was his second son, and Eliphelet was his third son. ⁴⁰Ulam's sons were mighty warriors who could use a bow and arrow well.

They had many sons and grandsons. There were 150 of them in all.

All these men were Benjamin's descendants.

9 The names of all the people of Israel were listed in their family histories. Those family histories were put in the book of the kings of Israel.

The people of Judah were captured and forced to go to Babylon. This is because they were not faithful to God. ²The first people to come back and live in their own lands and towns were some Israelites, priests, Levites and Templeᵈ servants.

³People from the tribesᵈ of Judah, Benjamin, Ephraim and Manasseh lived in Jerusalem. This is a list of those people.

⁴There was Uthai son of Ammihud. (Ammihud was Omri's son. Omri was Imri's son. Imri was Bani's son. Bani was a descendantᵈ of Perez. Perez was Judah's son.)

⁵Of the Shilonite people there were Asaiah and his sons. Asaiah was the oldest son in his family.

⁶Of the Zerahite people there were Jeuel and other relatives of Zerah. There were 690 of them in all.

⁷From the tribe of Benjamin there was Sallu son of Meshullam. (Meshullam was Hodaviah's son. Hodaviah was Hassenuah's son.) ⁸There was also Ibneiah son of Jeroham and Elah son of Uzzi. (Uzzi was Micri's son.) And there was Meshullam son of Shephatiah. (Shephatiah was Reuel's son, and Reuel was Ibnijah's son.) ⁹The family history of Benjamin lists 956 people living in Jerusalem. All these men were leaders of their families.

¹⁰Of the priests there were Jedaiah, Jehoiarib, Jakin and ¹¹Azariah son of Hilkiah. (Hilkiah was Meshullam's son. Meshullam was Zadok's son. Zadok was Meraioth's son. Meraioth was Ahitub's son. Ahitub was the officer who was responsible for the Temple of God.) ¹²Also there was Adaiah son of Jeroham. (Jeroham was Pashhur's son, and Pashhur was Malkijah's son.) And there was Maasai son of Adiel. (Adiel was Jahzerah's son. Jahzerah was Meshullam's son. Meshullam was Meshillemith's son, and Meshillemith was Immer's son.) ¹³There were 1,760 priests. They were leaders of their families. They were responsible for serving in the Temple of God.

¹⁴Of the Levites there was Semaiah

son of Hasshub. (Hasshub was Azrikam's son. Azrikam was Hashabiah's son. Hashabiah was from the family of Merari.) [15]There were also Bakbakkar, Heresh, Galal and Mattaniah son of Mica. (Mica was Zicri's son. Zicri was Asaph's son.) [16]There was also Obadiah son of Shemaiah. (Shemaiah was Galal's son, and Galal was Jeduthun's son.) And there was Berekiah son of Asa. (Asa was Elkanah's son. Elkanah lived in the villages of the Netophathite people.)

[17]Of the gatekeepers there were Shallum, Akkub, Talmon, Ahiman and their relatives. Shallum was their leader. [18]These gatekeepers from the tribe of Levi still stand next to the King's Gate on the east side of the city. [19]Shallum was Kore's son. Kore was Ebiasaph's son. Ebiasaph was Korah's son. Shallum and his relatives from the family of Korah were gatekeepers. They were responsible for guarding the gates of the Temple. Their ancestors had also been responsible for guarding the entrance to the Temple. [20]In the past Phinehas was in charge of the gatekeepers. He was Eleazar's son. The Lord was with Phinehas. [21]Zechariah was the gatekeeper at the entrance to the Temple. He was the son of Meshelemiah.

[22]In all, 212 men were chosen to guard the gates. Their names were written in their family histories in their villages. David and Samuel the seer[d] chose these men because they were dependable. [23]The gatekeepers and their descendants had the responsibility of guarding the gates of the Temple of the Lord. (The Temple took the place of the Holy Tent.[e]) [24]There were gatekeepers on all four sides of the Temple: east, west, north and south. [25]The gatekeepers' relatives who lived in the villages had to come and help them at certain times. Each time they came they helped the gatekeepers for seven days. [26]Because they were dependable, four gatekeepers were made the leaders of all the gatekeepers. They were Levites. They were responsible for the rooms and treasures in the Temple of God. [27]They stayed up all night guarding the Temple of God. And they opened it every morning.

[28]Some of the gatekeepers were responsible for the tools and dishes used in the Temple services. They counted these tools and dishes when people took them out. And they counted them when people brought them back. [29]Other gate-keepers were chosen to take care of the things in the Holy Place. They also took care of the flour, wine, oil, incense[d] and spices. [30]But some of the priests took care of mixing the spices. [31]There was a Levite named Mattithiah. Because he was dependable, he had the job of baking the bread used for the offerings. He was Shallum's first son. Shallum was from the family of Korah. [32]Some of the gatekeepers had the job of preparing the special bread. This was the bread that was put on the table every Sabbath.[d] These people were from the Kohath family.

[33]Some of the Levites were musicians in the Temple. The leaders of these families stayed in the rooms of the Temple. They were on duty day and night. So they did not do other work in the Temple.

[34]These are the leaders of the Levite families. Their names were listed in their family histories. They lived in Jerusalem.

[35]Jeiel lived in the town of Gibeon, where he was the leader. His wife was named Maacah. [36]Jeiel's first son was Abdon. His other sons were Zur, Kish, Baal, Ner, Nadab, [37]Gedor, Ahio, Zechariah and Mikloth. [38]Mikloth was Shimeam's father. Jeiel's family lived near their relatives in Jerusalem.

[39]Ner was Kish's father. Kish was Saul's father. And Saul was the father of Jonathan, Malki-Shua, Abinadab and Esh-Baal.

[40]Jonathan's son was Merib-Baal. Merib-Baal was Micah's father.

[41]Micah's sons were Pithon, Melech, Tahrea and Ahaz. [42]Ahaz was Jadah's father. Jadah was the father of Alemeth, Azmaveth and Zimri. Zimri was Moza's father. [43]Moza was Binea's father. Rephaiah was Binea's son. Eleasah was Rephaiah's son, and Azel was Eleasah's son.

[44]Azel had six sons. Their names were Azrikam, Bokeru, Ishmael, Sheariah, Obadiah and Hanan. They were Azel's sons.

10 The Philistine people fought against the people of Israel. The Israelites ran away from them. And many Israelites were killed on Mount Gilboa. [2]The Philistines continued chasing Saul and his sons. And they killed Saul's sons Jonathan, Abinadab and Malki-Shua. [3]The fighting became heavy around Saul. The archers shot him with their arrows and wounded him.

⁴Then Saul said to the officer who carried his armor, "Pull out your sword and kill me. If you don't, these men who are not circumcised will come and hurt me." But the officer was afraid. So he refused to kill Saul. Then Saul took his own sword and fell on it. ⁵The officer saw that Saul was dead. So he fell on his own sword and died. ⁶So Saul and three of his sons died. All his family died together.

⁷The Israelites living in the valley saw that their army had run away. And they saw that Saul and his sons were dead. So they left their towns and ran away. Then the Philistines came and lived in those towns.

⁸The next day the Philistines came to take valuable things from the dead bodies. On Mount Gilboa they found the bodies of Saul and his sons. ⁹The Philistines stripped Saul's body. And they took his head and his armor. They sent messengers through all their country to tell the news to their idols and their people. ¹⁰The Philistines put Saul's armor in the temple of their idols. And they hung his head in the temple of Dagon.ᵈ

¹¹All the people living in Jabesh Gilead heard what the Philistines had done to Saul. ¹²So all the brave men from Jabesh Gilead went and got the bodies of Saul and his sons. They brought them to Jabesh Gilead. Then they buried the bones of Saul and his sons under the large tree in Jabesh. And they gave up eating for seven days.

¹³Saul died because he was not faithful to the Lord. He did not obey the Lord. He even went to a mediumᵈ and asked her for advice. ¹⁴He did this instead of asking the Lord for help. This is why the Lord put Saul to death and gave the kingdom to Jesse's son David.

11 All the people of Israel came to David at the town of Hebron. They said, "We are your people. ²Even when Saul was king, you were the man who led Israel in battle. The Lord your God spoke to you. He said, 'David, you will be the shepherd of my people, the people of Israel. You will become their leader.'"

³All the leaders of Israel came to King David at Hebron. He made an agreement with them before the Lord in Hebron. The leaders poured olive oil on

David to appoint him king over Israel. The Lord had promised this would happen. He had made this promise through Samuel.

⁴David and all the Israelites went to the city of Jerusalem. At that time Jerusalem was called Jebus. The people living there were named Jebusites. ⁵They said to David, "You can't get inside our city." But David captured their strong city of Jerusalem, the City of David.

⁶David had said, "The person who leads the attack against the Jebusites will become the commander over all my army." Joab son of Zeruiah led the attack. So he became the commander of the army.

⁷Then David made his home in the strong, walled city. That is why it was named the City of David. ⁸David rebuilt the city. He started where the land was filled in and went to the wall that was around the city. Joab repaired the other parts of the city. ⁹David became more and more powerful. And the Lord of heaven's armies was with him.

¹⁰This is a list of the leaders over David's warriors. These warriors helped make David's kingdom strong. All the people of Israel also supported David's kingdom. These heroes and all the people of Israel made David king. This happened as the Lord had promised.

¹¹This is a list of David's warriors:

Jashobeam was from the Hacmonite people. He was the leader of the Three,ⁿ David's most powerful soldiers. He used his spear to fight 300 men at one time. And he killed them all.

¹²Next was Eleazar. He was one of the Three. Eleazar was Dodai's son. Dodai was from the Ahohite people. ¹³Eleazar was with David at Pas-Dammim. The Philistines came there to fight the Israelites. There was a field of barley at that place. The Israelites ran away from the Philistines. ¹⁴But they stopped in the middle of that field and fought the Philistines. And they killed the Philistines. The Lord gave Israel a great victory.

¹⁵Three of the 30 leaders went to David. He was at the rock by the cave near Adullam. At the same time a group from the Philistine army was camped in the Valley of Rephaim.

¹⁶David was in a protected place at that time. The Philistine army was staying in the town of Bethlehem. ¹⁷David had a strong desire for some water. He

said, "Oh, I wish someone would get me water from the well near the city gate of Bethlehem!" [18]So the Three fought their way through the Philistine army. And they took water out of the well near the city gate in Bethlehem. Then they took it back to David. But he refused to drink it. He poured it out before the Lord. [19]David said, "May God keep me from drinking this water! It would be like drinking the blood of the men who risked their lives to bring me this water." So David refused to drink it.

These were the brave things the Three did.

[20]Abishai brother of Joab was the leader of the Three. Abishai fought 300 men with his spear and killed them. He became as famous as the Three. [21]He was more honored than the Three. He became their commander even though he was not one of them.

[22]Benaiah son of Jehoiada was a brave fighter from Kabzeel. Benaiah did many brave things. He killed two of the best warriors from Moab. He also went down into a pit when it was snowing. There he killed a lion. [23]Benaiah also killed an Egyptian who was about seven and a half feet tall. The Egyptian had a spear as large as a weaver's rod. Benaiah had a club. But he grabbed the spear from the Egyptian's hand. And he used the Egyptian's own spear to kill him. [24]These were the things Benaiah son of Jehoiada did. Benaiah became as famous as the Three. [25]He received more honor than the Thirty, David's most powerful soldiers. But he did not become a member of the Three. David chose Benaiah to be the leader of his bodyguards.

[26]These were also mighty warriors:

Asahel brother of Joab;
Elhanan son of Dodo from Bethlehem;
[27]Shammoth from the Harorites;
Helez from the Pelonites;
[28]Ira son of Ikkesh from Tekoa;
Abiezer from the Anathothites;
[29]Sibbecai from the Hushathites;
Ilai from the Ahohites;
[30]Maharai from the Netophathites;
Heled son of Baanah from the Netophathites;
[31]Ithai son of Ribai from Gibeah in Benjamin.
Benaiah from the Pirathonites;
[32]Hurai from the ravines of Gaash;
Abiel from the Arbathites;
[33]Azmaveth from the Baharumites;
Eliahba from the Shaalbonites;
[34]the sons of Hashem from the Gizonites;
Jonathan son of Shagee from the Hararites;
[35]Ahiam son of Sacar from the Hararites;
Eliphal son of Ur;
[36]Hepher from the Mekerathites;
Ahijah from the Pelonites;
[37]Hezro from the Carmelites;
Naarai son of Ezbai;
[38]Joel brother of Nathan;
Mibhar son of Hagri;
[39]Zelek from the Ammonites;
Naharai, from the Berothites, the officer who carried the armor for Joab son of Zeruiah;
[40]Ira from the Ithrites;
Gareb from the Ithrites;
[41]Uriah from the Hittites;
Zabad son of Ahlai;
[42]Adina son of Shiza the Reubenite, who was the leader of the Reubenites, and his 30 soldiers;
[43]Hanan son of Maacah;
Joshaphat from the Mithnites;
[44]Uzzia from the Ashterathites;
Shama and Jeiel sons of Hotham from the Aroer;
[45]Jediael son of Shimri;
Joha, Jediael's brother, from the Tizites;
[46]Eliel from the Mahavites;
Jeribai and Joshaviah, Elnaam's sons;
Ithmah from the Moabites;
[47]Eliel, Obed and Jaasiel from the Mezobaites.

12 These were the men who came to David at Ziklag. David was hiding from Saul son of Kish at that time. These were the men who helped David in battle. [2]They came with bows for weapons. They could use either their right or left hands to shoot arrows or to sling rocks. They were Saul's relatives from the tribe[d] of Benjamin. [3]Ahiezer was their leader. And there was Joash. (Ahiezer and Joash were Shemaah's sons. He was from the town of Gibeah.) There were also Jeziel and Pelet the sons of Azmaveth. There were Beracah and Jehu from the town of Anathoth. [4]And there was Ishmaiah from the town of Gibeon. Ishmaiah was one of the Thirty. In fact, he was the leader of the Thirty. There were Jeremiah, Jahaziel, Johanan and Jozabad from Gederah. [5]There were Eluzai, Jerimoth, Bealiah and Shemariah. There was Shephatiah from Ha-ruph. [6]There were Elkanah, Isshiah, Azarel, Joezer and Jashobeam. They were from the family group of Korah. [7]And there were Joelah and Zebadiah the sons of Jeroham. They were from the town of Gedor.

[8]Part of the people of Gad joined David at his protected place in the desert. They were brave warriors trained for war. They were skilled with shields and spears. They were as fierce as lions. And they could run as fast as gazelles[d] over the hills.

[9]Ezer was the leader of Gad's army. Obadiah was second in command. Eliab was third. [10]Mishmannah was fourth, and Jeremiah was fifth. [11]Attai was sixth, and Eliel was seventh. [12]Johanan was eighth, and Elzabad was ninth. [13]Jeremiah was tenth, and Macbannai was eleventh in command.

[14]They were the commanders of the army from Gad. The weakest of these leaders was in charge of 100 soldiers. The strongest was in charge of 1,000 soldiers. [15]They crossed the Jordan River and chased away the people living in the valleys. They chased them to the east and to the west. This happened in the first month of the year when the Jordan floods the valley.

[16]Other people from the tribes[d] of Benjamin and Judah also came to David at his protected place. [17]David went out to meet them. He said to them, "If you have come peacefully to help me, I welcome you. Join me. But you might have come to turn me over to my enemies, even though I have done nothing wrong. If you do this, the God of our fathers will see this and punish you."

[18]Then the Spirit[d] entered Amasai, the leader of the Thirty. Amasai said:

"We belong to you, David.
We are with you, son of Jesse.
Success, success to you.
  Success to those who help you,
  because your God helps you."

So David welcomed these men. He made them leaders of his army.

[19]Some of the men from Manasseh also joined David. They joined him when he went with the Philistines to fight Saul. But David and his men did not really help the Philistines. After talking about it, the Philistine leaders decided to send David away. They said, "If David goes back to his master Saul, we will be killed!" [20]The men from Manasseh joined David when he went to Ziklag. These were the men: Adnah, Jozabad, Jediael, Michael, Jozabad, Elihu and Zillethai. Each of these men was a leader of a thousand men from Manasseh. [21]All these men of Manasseh were brave soldiers. They helped David fight against groups of men who went around the country robbing people. These soldiers became commanders in David's army. [22]Every day more men joined David. So his army became large. It was like the army of God.

[23]These are the numbers of the men who joined David at Hebron. They came ready for battle. They came to help turn the kingdom of Saul over to David. The Lord had said this would happen.

[24]There were 6,800 men with their weapons from the people of Judah. They carried shields and spears.

[25]There were 7,100 men from the people of Simeon. They were warriors ready for war.

[26]There were 4,600 men from the people of Levi. [27]Jehoiada, a leader from Aaron's family, was in that group. There were 3,700 with him. [28]Zadok was also in that group. He was a strong young warrior. He came with 22 leaders from his family.

[29]There were 3,000 men from the people of Benjamin. They were Saul's relatives. And most of them had remained loyal to Saul's family until then.

[30]There were 20,800 men from the people of Ephraim. They were brave warriors. They were famous men in their own family groups.

[31]There were 18,000 men from the western half-tribe of Manasseh. Each man was especially chosen to make David king.

[32]There were 200 leaders from the family of Issachar. They knew what Israel should do. And they knew the right time to do it. Their relatives were with them and under their command.

[33]There were 50,000 men from the people of Zebulun. They were trained soldiers. They were trained to use every kind of weapon of war. They followed David completely.

[34]There were 1,000 officers from the people of Naphtali. They had 37,000 men with them who carried shields and spears.

[35]There were 28,600 men from the people of Dan. They were ready for war.

[36]There were 40,000 trained soldiers from the people of Asher. They were ready for war.

[37]There were 120,000 men from the east side of the Jordan River. They were from the people of Reuben, Gad and the eastern half-tribe of Manasseh. They had every kind of weapon.

[38]All these fighting men were ready to go to war. They came to Hebron fully agreed to make David king of all Israel. All the other Israelites also agreed to make David king. [39]The men spent three days there with David. They ate and drank, because their relatives had prepared food for them. [40]Also, their neighbors brought food. They came from as far as the areas belonging to Issachar, Zebulun and Naphtali. They brought food on donkeys, camels, mules and oxen. They brought much flour, fig cakes, raisins, wine, oil, cows and sheep. This was because the people of Israel were very happy.

13 David talked with all the officers of his army. He talked with the commanders of 100 men and the commanders of 1,000 men. [2]Then David called the people of Israel together. He said, "If you think it is a good idea, and if it is what the Lord our God wants, let's send a message. Let's send it to our fellow Israelites in all the areas of Israel. Let's also send it to the priests and Levites living with them in their towns and pastures. Tell them to come and join us. [3]Let's bring the Holy Box[d] of our God back to us. We did not use it to ask God for help while Saul was king." [4]So all the people agreed with David. They all thought it was the right thing to do.

[5]So David gathered all the Israelites from the Shihor River in Egypt to Lebo Hamath. They were to bring the Holy Box of God back from the town of Kiriath Jearim. [6]David and all the Israelites with him went to Baalah of Judah. (Baalah is another name for Kiriath Jearim.) They went there to get the Holy Box of God the Lord. His throne is between the golden creatures with wings on the Holy Box. It is called by the Lord's name.

[7]The people moved the Holy Box of God from Abinadab's house. They put it on a new cart. And Uzzah and Ahio guided the cart. [8]David and all the Israelites were celebrating with all their strength before God. They were singing and playing harps, lyres,[d] tambourines,[d] cymbals and trumpets.

[9]They came to the threshing[d] floor of Kidon. The oxen pulling the cart stumbled. And Uzzah reached out his hand to steady the Holy Box. [10]The Lord became very angry with Uzzah. And he killed Uzzah because Uzzah had touched the Holy Box. So Uzzah died there in the presence of God.

[11]David became angry because the Lord had punished Uzzah in his anger. So even today that place is called the Punishment of Uzzah.

[12]David was afraid of God that day. David asked, "How can I bring the Holy Box of God home to me?" [13]So David did not take the Holy Box with him to Jerusalem. Instead, he took it to the house of Obed-Edom of Gath. [14]The Holy Box of God stayed with Obed-Edom's family in his house for three months. And the Lord blessed Obed-Edom's family and everything he owned.

14 Hiram king of the city of Tyre sent messengers to David. He also sent cedar logs, stonecutters and carpenters. He sent them to build a palace for David. [2]Then David knew that the Lord really had made him king of Israel. And he knew the Lord had made his kingdom very important. The Lord did this because he loved his people, the Israelites.

[3]David married more women in Jerusalem. And he had more sons and daughters. [4]These are the names of David's children born in Jerusalem: Shammua, Shobab, Nathan, Solomon, [5]Ibhar, Elishua, Elpelet, [6]Nogah, Nepheg, Japhia, [7]Elishama, Beeliada and Eliphelet.

[8]The Philistine people heard that David had been appointed king of all Israel. So all the Philistines went to look for him. When David heard about it, he went out to fight them. [9]The Philistines had attacked and robbed the people in the Valley of Rephaim. [10]David asked God, "Should I go and attack the Philistines? Will you let me defeat them?"

The Lord answered him, "Go. I will let you defeat them."

[11]So David and his men went up to the town of Baal Perazim. There he defeated the Philistines. David said, "Like a flood of water, God has broken through my enemies. He has done this through me." So that place was named Baal Perazim.[n] [12]The Philistines had left their idols there. So David ordered his men to burn them.

[13]Soon the Philistines attacked the

14:11 Baal Perazim This name means "the Lord breaks through."

people in the valley again. [14]So David prayed to God again, and God answered him. God said, "Don't attack the Philistines from the front. Instead, go around them. Attack them in front of the balsam trees. [15]You will hear the sound of marching in the tops of the balsam trees. Then quickly attack the Philistines. I, God, will have gone out before you to defeat the Philistine army." [16]David did what God commanded him to do. So David and his men defeated the Philistine army. They killed the Philistines all the way from Gibeon to Gezer.

[17]So David became famous in all the countries. And the Lord made all nations afraid of David.

15 David built houses for himself in Jerusalem. Then he built a place for the Holy Box[d] of God. And he set up a tent for it. [2]Then David said, "Only the Levites may carry the Holy Box of God. The Lord chose them to carry the Holy Box of the Lord. He chose them to serve him forever."

[3]David called all the people of Israel to come to Jerusalem. He wanted to bring the Holy Box of the Lord to the place he had made for it. [4]David called together the descendants[d] of Aaron and the Levites. [5]There were 120 people from Kohath's family group. Uriel was their leader. [6]There were 220 people from Merari's family group. Asaiah was their leader. [7]There were 130 people from Gershon's family group. Joel was their leader. [8]There were 200 people from Elizaphan's family group. Shemaiah was their leader. [9]There were 80 people from Hebron's family group. Eliel was their leader. [10]There were 112 people from Uzziel's family group. Amminadab was their leader.

[11]Then David asked the priests Zadok and Abiathar to come to him. He also asked these Levites to come: Uriel, Asaiah, Joel, Shemaiah, Eliel and Amminadab. [12]David said to them, "You are the leaders of the families of Levi. You and the other Levites must give yourselves for service to the Lord. Then bring up the Holy Box of the Lord, the God of Israel. Bring it to the place I have made for it. [13]The last time we did not ask the Lord how to carry it. You Levites didn't carry it. So the Lord our God punished us."

[14]Then the priests and Levites prepared themselves for service to the Lord. They did this so they could carry the Holy Box of the Lord, the God of Israel. [15]The Levites used special poles to carry the Holy Box of God on their shoulders. This was the way Moses had commanded. They carried it just as the Lord had said they should.

[16]David told the leaders of the Levites to appoint their brothers as singers. The singers were to play their lyres,[d] harps and cymbals. And they were to sing happy songs.

[17]So the Levites appointed Heman and his relatives Asaph and Ethan. Heman was Joel's son. Asaph was Berekiah's son. And Ethan, from the Merari family group, was Kushaiah's son. [18]There was also a second group of Levites. They were Zechariah, Jaaziel, Shemiramoth, Jehiel, Unni, Eliab, Benaiah, Maaseiah, Mattithiah, Eliphelehu, Mikneiah, Obed-Edom and Jeiel. They were the Levite guards.

[19]The singers Heman, Asaph and Ethan played bronze cymbals. [20]Zechariah, Jaaziel, Shemiramoth, Jehiel, Unni, Eliab, Maaseiah and Benaiah played the high-pitched lyres. [21]Mattithiah, Eliphelehu, Mikneiah, Obed-Edom, Jeiel and Azaziah played the low-pitched harps. [22]The Levite leader Kenaniah was in charge of the singing. He had this job because he was very good at singing.

[23]Berekiah and Elkanah were two of the guards for the Box of the Agreement. [24]The priests Shebaniah, Joshaphat, Nethanel, Amasai, Zechariah, Benaiah and Eliezer had the job of blowing trumpets. They did this in front of the Box of the Agreement. Obed-Edom and Jehiah were also guards for the Box of the Agreement.

[25]David, the leaders of Israel, and the commanders went to get the Box of the Agreement with the Lord. Each of the commanders was over a group of 1,000 soldiers. They all went to bring the Holy Box from Obed-Edom's house. And they were very happy. [26]God helped the Levites who carried the Box of the Agreement with the Lord. So they sacrificed seven bulls and seven male sheep. [27]All the Levites who carried the Holy Box wore robes of fine linen. Kenaniah, the man in charge of the singing, and all the singers wore robes of fine linen. David wore a robe of fine linen. And he also wore a holy vest[d] of fine linen. [28]So all the people of Israel brought up the Box of the Agreement with the Lord. They shouted and blew sheep horns and

trumpets. They played cymbals, lyres, and harps. ²⁹So the Box of the Agreement with the Lord entered Jerusalem. As it entered, Saul's daughter Michal watched from a window. When she saw King David dancing and celebrating, she hated him.

16 They brought the Holy Box of God and put it inside the tent. This was the tent David had set up for it. Then they offered burnt offerings and fellowship offerings to God. ²David finished giving the burnt offerings and fellowship offerings. Then he used the Lord's name to bless the people. ³He gave a loaf of bread, some dates and raisins to every Israelite man and woman.

⁴Then David appointed some of the Levites to serve before the Holy Box of the Lord. They had the job of leading the worship. They gave thanks and praise to the Lord, the God of Israel. ⁵Asaph was the leader. He played the cymbals. Zechariah was second to him. The other Levites were Jaaziel, Shemiramoth, Jehiel, Mattithiah, Eliab, Benaiah, Obed-Edom and Jeiel. They played the lyres and harps. ⁶Benaiah and Jahaziel were priests. They blew the trumpets regularly before the Box of the Agreement with God. ⁷That day David first gave Asaph and his relatives the job of singing praises to the Lord.

⁸Give thanks to the Lord and pray to him.
　Tell the nations what he has done.
⁹Sing to him. Sing praises to him.
　Tell about all the wonderful things he has done.
¹⁰Be glad that you are his.
　Let those who ask the Lord for help be happy.
¹¹Depend on the Lord and his strength.
　Always go to him for help.
¹²Remember the wonderful things he has done.
　Remember his miraclesᵈ and his decisions.
¹³You are the descendantsᵈ of Israel, the Lord's servant.
　You are the children of Jacob, his chosen people.
¹⁴He is the Lord our God.
　His laws are for all the world.
¹⁵He will keep his agreement forever.
　He will keep his promises always.

¹⁶He will keep the agreement he made with Abraham.
　He will keep the promise he made to Isaac.
¹⁷The Lord made it a law for the people of Jacob.
　He made it an agreement with Israel to last forever.
¹⁸The Lord said, "I will give you the land of Canaan. The promised land will belong to you."
¹⁹Then God's people were few in number.
　They were strangers in the land.
²⁰They went from one nation to another.
　They went from one kingdom to another.
²¹But the Lord did not let anyone hurt them.
　He warned kings not to harm them.
²²He said, "Don't hurt my chosen people.
　Don't harm my prophets."ᵈ

²³Sing to the Lord, all the earth.
　Every day tell how he saves us.
²⁴Tell the nations about the Lord's glory.
　Tell all peoples about his wonderful works.
²⁵The Lord is great; he should be praised.
　He should be honored more than all the gods.
²⁶All the gods of the nations are only idols.
　But the Lord made the skies.
²⁷The Lord has glory and majesty.
　He has power and joy in his Temple.ᵈ
²⁸Praise the Lord, all nations on earth.
　Praise the Lord's glory and power.
²⁹　Praise the Lord for the glory of his name.
　Bring your offering to him.
　Worship the Lord because he is holy.
³⁰The whole earth should tremble before the Lord.
　The earth is set, and it cannot be moved.
³¹Let the skies rejoice and the earth be glad.
　Let people everywhere say, "The Lord is king!"

³²Let the sea and everything in it
shout.
Let the fields and everything in
them show their joy.
³³Then the trees of the forest will
sing.
They will sing with joy before the
Lord.
They will sing because the Lord
is coming to judge the world.

³⁴Thank the Lord because he is good.
His love continues forever.
³⁵Say to him, "Save us, God our
Savior.
Bring us back and save us from
the nations.
Then we will thank you.
Then we will gladly praise you."
³⁶Praise the Lord, the God of Israel,
forever and forever.

All the people said, "Amen" and "Praise
the Lord."

³⁷Then David left Asaph and the other
Levites there in front of the Box[d] of the
Agreement with the Lord. They were to
serve there every day. ³⁸David also left
Obed-Edom and 68 other Levites to
serve with them. Hosah and Obed-Edom
son of Jeduthun were guards.

³⁹David left Zadok the priest and the
other priests who served with him in
front of the Tent of the Lord. This was at
the place of worship in Gibeon. ⁴⁰Every
morning and evening they offered burnt
offerings on the altar of burnt offerings.
They did this to follow the rules written
in the Teachings of the Lord. These were
the Teachings he had given Israel.
⁴¹With them were Heman and Jeduthun
and other Levites. They were chosen by
name to sing praises to the Lord because
the Lord's love continues forever. ⁴²He-
man and Jeduthun also had the job of
playing the trumpets and cymbals. They
also played other musical instruments
when songs were sung to God. Jeduthun's sons guarded the gates.

⁴³Then all the people left. Each person
went to his own home. And David also
went home to bless his family.

17 David moved into his palace. Then
he said to Nathan the prophet,
"Look, I am living in a palace made of
cedar. But the Box[d] of the Agreement
with the Lord sits in a tent."

²Nathan answered David, "Do what
you want to do. God is with you."

³But that night God spoke his word
to Nathan. God said, ⁴"Go and tell my
servant David: 'This is what the Lord

says: David, you are not the person to
build a house for me to live in. ⁵From
the time I brought Israel out of Egypt
until now I have not lived in a house. I
have moved from one tent site to another. I have gone from one place to another. ⁶I have moved with the Israelites
to different places. I commanded leaders to take care of my people. I never
said to any of those leaders, "Why
haven't you built me a house of cedar?" '

⁷"Now, tell my servant David: 'The
Lord of heaven's armies says: I took you
from the pasture and from tending the
sheep. I made you king of my people
Israel. ⁸I have been with you everywhere
you have gone. I have killed your enemies for you. Now I will make you one
of the most famous men on earth. ⁹I will
give this place to my people Israel. I
will settle them here. Then they will
have a home of their own. They won't
be bothered anymore. Evil people won't
hurt them as they have done since the
first. ¹⁰Evil people have hurt them since
I chose leaders for my people Israel. I
will also defeat all your enemies.

"'I tell you that the Lord will make
your descendants[d] kings of Israel after
you. ¹¹When you die and join your ancestors, I will let your child be the new
king. He will be one of your own sons.
And I will make his kingdom strong.
¹²He will build a house for me. And I will
let his family rule forever. ¹³I will be his
father, and he will be my son. I took
away my love from Saul, who ruled before you. But I will never stop loving
your son. ¹⁴I will put him in charge of my
house and kingdom forever. His family
will rule forever.'"

¹⁵Nathan told David everything God
had said in this vision.

¹⁶Then King David went in and sat in
front of the Lord. David said, "Lord
God, why have you made me so important to you? Why have you made my
family important? ¹⁷But that was not
enough for you, God. You have also said
these kind things about my future family. I am your servant, Lord God, you
have treated me like a very important
man.

¹⁸"What more can I say to you? You
have done so much for me, your servant.
You love me so much. ¹⁹Lord, you have
done this wonderful thing for me for my
sake. And you have done it because you
wanted to. You have let me know all
these great promises.

²⁰"There is no one like you, Lord.

There is no God except you. We have heard all this ourselves. [21]There is no one like your people, the Israelites. It is the one nation on earth that God chose to be his people. You used them to make your name well-known. You did great and wonderful things for them. You went ahead of them and forced other nations out of the land. You freed your people from slavery in Egypt. [22]You made the people of Israel your very own people forever. And, Lord, you became their God.

[23]"Lord, you made this promise about my family and me, your servant. Now, keep your promise forever. Do what you have promised. [24]Then people will know you and honor you forever. And people will say, 'The Lord of heaven's armies, the God over Israel, is Israel's God!' And the family of your servant David will continue before you.

[25]"My God, you have told me that you would make my family great. So I, your servant, am brave enough to pray to you. [26]Lord, you are God. You have promised these good things to me, your servant. [27]You have chosen to bless my family. Let it continue before you forever. Lord, you have blessed my family. So it will be blessed forever."

18 Later, David attacked the Philistine people and defeated them. He took Gath and the small towns around it from the Philistines.

[2]Then David defeated the country of Moab. So the Moabites became David's servants. And they brought the payments he demanded from them.

[3]David also fought against Hadadezer king of Zobah. David fought Hadadezer's army all the way to the town of Hamath. He did this because Hadadezer tried to spread his kingdom all the way to the Euphrates River. [4]David took from Hadadezer 1,000 chariots and 7,000 chariot drivers. And he took 20,000 soldiers on foot. David also crippled most of Hadadezer's horses used for pulling chariots. He saved only 100 of the chariot horses.

[5]The Aramean people from Damascus came to help Hadadezer king of Zobah. But David killed 22,000 of them. [6]Then David put camps of troops in Damascus in Aram. The Arameans became David's servants and brought him the payments he demanded. So the Lord gave David victory everywhere he went.

[7]David took the gold shields from Hadadezer's army leaders. And he brought them to Jerusalem. [8]David also took much bronze from the towns of Tebah and Cun. These towns belonged to Hadadezer. Later, Solomon used this bronze to make things for the Temple:[d] the large bronze bowl, which was called the Sea, the pillars and other bronze things.

[9]Toi was king of the city of Hamath. He heard that David had defeated the whole army of Hadadezer king of Zobah. [10]So Toi sent his son Hadoram to greet King David. Hadoram also congratulated David for fighting and defeating Hadadezer. Hadadezer had been at war with Toi before. Hadoram gave David all kinds of things made of gold, silver and bronze. [11]King David gave these things to the Lord. David had done the same thing with the silver and gold he had taken from these nations: Edom, Moab, the Ammonites, the Philistines and Amalek.

[12]Abishai son of Zeruiah killed 18,000 Edomite people in the Valley of Salt. [13]Abishai also put camps of troops in Edom. And all the Edomites became David's servants. The Lord gave David victory everywhere he went.

[14]David was king over all of Israel. He did what was right and fair for everyone. [15]Joab son of Zeruiah was commander of David's army. Jehoshaphat son of Ahilud was the recorder. [16]Zadok son of Ahitub and Ahimelech son of Abiathar were priests. Shavsha was the royal assistant. [17]Benaiah was responsible for leading the Kerethites and Pelethites, the king's bodyguards. Benaiah was Jehoiada's son. And David's sons were important officers. They served at King David's side.

19 Nahash was king of the Ammonite people. When Nahash died, his son became the king. [2]David said, "Nahash was kind to me. So I will be kind to Hanun son of Nahash." Then David sent a group to comfort Hanun about the death of his father.

David's men went to comfort Hanun in the country of Ammon. [3]But the Ammonite leaders said to Hanun, "Don't be fooled. David didn't send these men to comfort you. They are not here to honor your dead father. David sent his men to spy on you and your land. He wants to destroy your country." [4]So Hanun arrested David's men. To shame them he cut off their beards and cut off their clothes at the hips. Then he sent them away.

⁵David's men were too ashamed to go home. Some people came to David and told him what had happened to his men. So he sent messengers to meet them. He said, "Stay in Jericho until your beards have grown back. Then come home."

⁶The Ammonite people saw they had caused David to hate them. So Hanun and the Ammonites sent about 74,000 pounds of silver to hire chariots and chariot drivers. They hired Arameans from Northwest Mesopotamia, Aram Maacah and Zobah. ⁷The Ammonites hired 32,000 chariots and chariot drivers. They also hired the king of Maacah and his army. So he and his army came and set up camp near the town of Medeba. The Ammonites themselves came out of their towns and got ready for battle.

⁸David heard about this. So he sent out Joab and the whole army of Israel. ⁹The Ammonites came out and got ready for battle. They were near the city gate. The kings who had come to help stayed out in the fields by themselves.

¹⁰Joab saw that there were enemy troops in front of him and behind him. So Joab chose some of the best soldiers of Israel. And he sent them out to fight the Arameans. ¹¹Joab put the rest of the army of Israel under the command of Abishai, his brother. Then they went out to fight the Ammonites. ¹²Joab said to Abishai, "The Arameans may be too strong for me. If they are, then you must help me. Or, the Ammonites may be too strong for you. If they are, then I will help you. ¹³Let's be strong. We must fight bravely for our people and the cities of our God. The Lord will do what he thinks is right."

¹⁴Then Joab and the army with him went to attack the Arameans. And the Arameans ran away from them. ¹⁵The Ammonite army saw that the Arameans were running away. So they also ran away from Abishai and his army. The Ammonites went back inside their city. And Joab went back to Jerusalem.

¹⁶The Arameans saw that Israel had defeated them. So they sent messengers to bring other Arameans from east of the Euphrates River. Shophach the commander of Hadadezer's army led them. ¹⁷When David heard about this, he gathered all the Israelites. And he led them across the Jordan River. He lined them up for battle, facing the Arameans.

And they attacked the Arameans. ¹⁸But the Arameans ran away from the Israelites. David and his army killed 7,000 Aramean chariot drivers. And they killed 40,000 Aramean foot soldiers. They also killed Shophach, the commander of the Aramean army.

¹⁹Hadadezer's officers saw that Israel had defeated them. So they made peace with David. They became his servants. So the Arameans refused to help the Ammonites again.

20 In the spring Joab led the army of Israel out to battle. This was the time of year when kings went out to battle. But David stayed in Jerusalem. The army of Israel destroyed the land of Ammon. Then they went to the city of Rabbah. They surrounded it and attacked it until they destroyed it. ²David took the crown from the head of their king.ⁿ That gold crown weighed about 75 pounds. And it had valuable gems in it. The crown was put on David's head. Then David took many valuable things from the city. ³David brought out the people from Rabbah. And he forced them to work with saws, iron picks and axes. David did the same thing to all the Ammonite towns. Then David and all the army returned to Jerusalem.

⁴Later, war broke out between Israel and the Philistines at Gezer. At this time Sibbecai from Hushah killed Sippai. Sippai was one of the descendantsᵈ of the Rephaites.ᵈ So those Philistines were defeated.

⁵Another time, the Israelites again fought the Philistines. Elhanan son of Jair killed Lahmi, the brother of Goliath. Goliath was from the town of Gath. Lahmi's spear was as large as a weaver's rod.

⁶Later, the Israelites fought another war with the Philistines at Gath. In this town there was a very large man. He had 6 fingers on each hand and 6 toes on each foot. So he had 24 fingers and toes in all. He also was a descendant of Rapha.ᵈ ⁷When he made fun of Israel, Jonathan killed him. Jonathan was the son of Shimea, David's brother.

⁸These Philistines were descendants of Rapha from Gath. David and his men killed them.

21 Satan was against Israel. He encouraged David to count the people of Israel. ²So David gave an order to Joab and the commanders of the troops.

20:2 king Or, "Milcom," the god of the Ammonite people.

He said, "Go and count all the Israelites. Count everyone from Beersheba to Dan.ⁿ Then tell me so I will know how many people there are."

³But Joab answered, "May the Lord make the nation 100 times as large. My master the king, all the Israelites are your servants. Why do you want to do this, my master? You will make Israel guilty of sin."

⁴But King David made Joab follow his order. So Joab left and went through all Israel, counting the people. Then he returned to Jerusalem. ⁵He told David how many people there were. In Israel there were 1,100,000 men who could use a sword. And there were 470,000 men in Judah who could use a sword. ⁶But Joab did not count the tribesᵈ of Levi and Benjamin. He didn't count them because he didn't like King David's order. ⁷David had done something God had said was wrong. So God punished Israel.

⁸Then David said to God, "I have done something very foolish. It was a terrible sin. Now, I beg you to forgive me, your servant."

⁹Gad was David's seer.ᵈ The Lord said to Gad, ¹⁰"Go and tell David: 'This is what the Lord says: I am going to give you three choices. Choose one, and I will punish you in that way.'"

¹¹So Gad went to David and said to him, "This is what the Lord says: 'Choose which punishment you want. ¹²You may choose three years without enough food for the nation. Or choose three months of running from your enemies as they chase you with their swords. Or choose three days of punishment from the Lord. A terrible disease will spread through the country. The angel of the Lord will go through Israel destroying the people.' Now, David, decide which answer I will give to the Lord, who sent me."

¹³David said to Gad, "I am in trouble. I don't want some man to punish me. The Lord is very merciful. So let the Lord punish me."

¹⁴So the Lord sent a terrible disease on Israel, and 70,000 people died. ¹⁵God sent an angel to destroy Jerusalem. But when the angel started to destroy it, the Lord saw it and felt sorry. So he said to the angel who was destroying, "That is enough! Stop!" The angel of the Lord was then standing at the threshingᵈ floor of Araunah the Jebusite.

¹⁶David looked up and saw the angel of the Lord in the sky. The angel was holding his sword over Jerusalem. Then David and the older leaders bowed facedown on the ground. They were wearing rough cloth to show their sadness. ¹⁷David said to God, "I am the one who sinned. I gave the order for the people to be counted. I have done wrong. These people are only sheep. What wrong have they done? Lord my God, punish me and my family. But stop the terrible disease that is killing your people."

¹⁸Then the angel of the Lord gave an order to Gad. He told Gad to tell David to build an altar to worship the Lord. It was to be at the threshing floor of Araunah the Jebusite. ¹⁹Gad told David these things from the Lord. So David went to Araunah's threshing floor.

²⁰Araunah was separating the straw from the wheat. When he turned around, he saw the angel. Araunah's four sons who were with him hid. ²¹David went to Araunah. When Araunah saw David, he left the threshing floor. He bowed facedown on the ground before David.

²²David said to him, "Sell me your threshing floor. Then I can build an altar to worship the Lord here. Then the terrible disease will be stopped. Sell it to me for the full price."

²³Araunah said to David, "Take this threshing floor. You are my master the king. Do anything you want. Look, I will also give you oxen for the burnt offering. I will give you boards as wood for the fire. And I will give the wheat for the grain offering. I will give all this to you."

²⁴But King David answered Araunah, "No, I must pay the full price. I won't take anything that is yours and give it to the Lord. I won't give an offering that costs me nothing."

²⁵So David paid Araunah about 15 pounds of gold for the place. ²⁶David built an altar to worship the Lord there. He offered burnt offerings and fellowship offerings. David prayed to the Lord. And the Lord answered him by sending down fire from heaven. It came down on the altar of burnt offering. ²⁷Then the Lord commanded the angel to put his sword back into its holder.

²⁸David saw that the Lord had an-

21:2 Beersheba to Dan Beersheba was the city farthest south in Israel. Dan was the city farthest north. So this means all the people of Israel.

swered him on the threshing floor of Araunah. So he offered sacrifices to the Lord there. [29]The Holy Tent[d] and the altar of burnt offerings were in Gibeon. They were at the place of worship there. Moses had made the Holy Tent while the Israelites were in the desert. [30]But David could not go to the Holy Tent to speak with God. He was afraid of the angel of the Lord and his sword.

22 David said, "The Temple[d] of the Lord God will be built here. And the altar for burnt offerings for Israel will be built here."

[2]So David gave an order for all foreigners living in Israel to be gathered together. From that group David chose stonecutters. Their job was to cut stones to be used in building the Temple[d] of God. [3]David supplied a large amount of iron. It was used for making nails and hinges for the gate doors. He also supplied more bronze than could be weighed. [4]And he supplied more cedar logs than could be counted. Much of the cedar had been brought to David by the people from Sidon and Tyre.

[5]David said, "We should build a great Temple for the Lord. It should be famous everywhere for its greatness and beauty. But my son Solomon is young. He hasn't yet learned what he needs to know. So I will prepare for the building of it." So David got many of the materials ready before he died.

[6]Then David called for his son Solomon. He told Solomon to build the Temple for the Lord, the God of Israel. [7]David said to him, "My son, I wanted to build a temple for worshiping the Lord my God. [8]But the Lord spoke his word to me, 'David, you have killed too many people. You have fought too many wars. So you cannot build a temple for worship to me. You have killed too many people. [9]But, you will have a son. He will be a man of peace and rest. I will give him rest from all his enemies around him. His name will be Solomon.[n] And I will give Israel peace and quiet while he is king. [10]Solomon will build a temple for worship to me. He will be my son, and I will be his father. I will make his kingdom strong. Someone from his family will rule Israel forever.'"

[11]David also said, "Now, my son, may the Lord be with you. May you build a temple for the Lord your God, as he said you would. [12]The Lord will make you the king of Israel. May the Lord give you wisdom and understanding. Then you will be able to obey the teachings of the Lord your God. [13]Be careful to obey the rules and laws the Lord gave Moses for Israel. If you obey them, you will have success. Be strong and brave. Don't be afraid or discouraged.

[14]"Solomon, I have worked hard getting many of the materials for building the Temple of the Lord. I have supplied about seven and a half million pounds of gold. And I have supplied about seventy-five million pounds of silver. I have supplied so much bronze and iron it cannot be weighed. And I have supplied wood and stone. And you may add to them. [15]You have many workmen. You have stonecutters, stoneworkers and carpenters. You have men skilled in every kind of work. [16]They are skilled in working with gold, silver, bronze and iron. You have more craftsmen than can be counted. Now begin the work. And may the Lord be with you."

[17]Then David ordered all the leaders of Israel to help his son Solomon. [18]David said to them, "The Lord your God is with you. He has given you rest from our enemies. He helped me to defeat the people living around us. The Lord and his people are in control of this land. [19]Now give yourself completely to obeying the Lord your God. Build the holy place of the Lord God. Build the Temple for worship to the Lord. Then bring the Box[d] of the Agreement with the Lord into the Temple. And bring in the holy things that belong to God."

23 David had lived long and was old. Then he made his son Solomon the new king of Israel. [2]David gathered all the leaders of Israel, along with the priests and Levites. [3]David counted the Levites who were 30 years old and older. In all, there were 38,000 Levites. [4]David said, "Of these, 24,000 Levites will direct the work of the Temple[d] of the Lord. And 6,000 Levites will be officers and judges. [5]And 4,000 Levites will be gatekeepers. And 4,000 Levites will praise the Lord with musical instruments. I made these instruments for them to use for praise."

[6]David separated the Levites into three groups. These groups were led by Levi's three sons: Gershon, Kohath and Merari.

[7]From the people of Gershon, there were Ladan and Shimei.

22:9 **Solomon** This name sounds like the Hebrew word for "peace."

[8] Ladan had three sons. His first son was Jehiel. His other sons were Zetham and Joel.

[9] Shimei's sons were Shelomoth, Haziel and Haran. These three sons were leaders of Ladan's families. [10] Shimei had four sons. They were Jahath, Ziza, Jeush and Beriah. [11] Jahath was the first son, and Ziza was the second son. But Jeush and Beriah did not have many children. So they were counted as if they were one family.

[12] Kohath had four sons. They were Amram, Izhar, Hebron and Uzziel.

[13] Amram's sons were Aaron and Moses. Aaron and his descendants[d] were chosen to be special forever. They were chosen to prepare the holy things for the Lord's service. They were to offer sacrifices before the Lord. They were to serve him as priests. They were to give blessings in the Lord's name forever.

[14] Moses was the man of God. Moses' sons were counted as part of the tribe[d] of Levi. [15] Moses' sons were Gershom and Eliezer. [16] Gershom's first son was Shubael. [17] Eliezer's first son was Rehabiah. Eliezer had no other sons, but Rehabiah had many sons.

[18] Izhar's first son was Shelomith.

[19] Hebron's first son was Jeriah. His second son was Amariah. Jahaziel was the third son. And Jekameam was the fourth son.

[20] Uzziel's first son was Micah. And Isshiah was his second son.

[21] Merari's sons were Mahli and Mushi. Mahli's sons were Eleazar and Kish. [22] Eleazar died without having sons. He had only daughters. Eleazar's daughters married their cousins, the sons of Kish. [23] Mushi's three sons were Mahli, Eder and Jerimoth.

[24] These were Levi's descendants[d] listed by their families. They were the leaders of families. Each person who was 20 years old or older was listed. They served in the Lord's Temple.[d]

[25] David had said, "The Lord is the God of Israel. He has given rest to his people. He has come to live in Jerusalem forever. [26] So the Levites don't need to carry the Holy Tent.[d] They don't need to carry any of the things used in its services anymore." [27] David's last instructions were to count the Levites. All who were 20 years old and older were counted.

[28] The Levites had the job of helping Aaron's descendants. They helped in the service of the Temple of the Lord. They cared for the Temple courtyard and side rooms. They had the job of making all the holy things pure. Their job was to serve in the Temple of God. [29] They were responsible for putting the holy bread on the table. They also were responsible for the flour in the grain offerings. And they were responsible for the bread made without yeast. They were also responsible for the baking and mixing. And they did all the measuring. [30] The Levites also stood every morning and gave thanks and praise to the Lord. They also did this every evening. [31] The Levites offered all the burnt offerings to the Lord on the special days of rest. And they offered them at the New Moon[d] festivals and at all appointed feasts. They served before the Lord every day. They were to follow the rules for how many Levites should serve each time. [32] So the Levites took care of the Meeting Tent. They also took care of the Holy Place. And they helped their relatives, Aaron's descendants, with the services at the Temple of the Lord.

24

These were the groups of Aaron's sons:

Aaron's sons were Nadab, Abihu, Eleazar and Ithamar. [2] But Nadab and Abihu died before their father did. And they had no sons. So Eleazar and Ithamar served as the priests. [3] David separated the family groups of Eleazar and Ithamar into two different groups. Each group had certain duties it had been given. Zadok and Ahimelech helped David. Zadok was a descendant[d] of Eleazar. And Ahimelech was a descendant of Ithamar. [4] There were more leaders from Eleazar's family than from Ithamar's. There were 16 leaders from Eleazar's family. And there were 8 leaders from Ithamar's family. [5] Men were chosen from Eleazar's and Ithamar's families by throwing lots.[d] Some men from each family were chosen to be in charge of the Holy Place. And some men from each family were chosen to serve as priests.

[6] Shemaiah son of Nethanel was the secretary. He was from the tribe[d] of Levi. Shemaiah recorded the names of those descendants in front of King David and these officers: Zadok the priest, Ahimelech son of Abiathar, and the leaders of the families of the priests and Levites. The work was divided by lots among the families of Eleazar and Ithamar. The following men with their groups were chosen.

[7] The first one chosen was Jehoiarib.

The second was Jedaiah. [8]The third was Harim. The fourth was Seorim. [9]The fifth was Malkijah. The sixth was Mijamin. [10]The seventh was Hakkoz. The eighth was Abijah. [11]The ninth was Jeshua. The tenth was Shecaniah. [12]The eleventh was Eliashib. The twelfth was Jakim. [13]The thirteenth was Huppah. The fourteenth was Jeshebeab. [14]The fifteenth was Bilgah. The sixteenth was Immer. [15]The seventeenth was Hezir. The eighteenth was Happizzez. [16]The nineteenth was Pethahiah. The twentieth was Jehezkel. [17]The twenty-first was Jakin. The twenty-second was Gamul. [18]The twenty-third was Delaiah. The twenty-fourth was Maaziah.

[19]These were the groups chosen to serve in the Temple of the Lord. They obeyed the rules Aaron had given them. The Lord, the God of Israel, had given those rules to Aaron.

[20]These are the names of the rest of Levi's descendants:[d]

Shubael was a descendant of Amram. And Jehdeiah was a descendant of Shubael.

[21]Isshiah was the first son of Rehabiah.

[22]From the Izhar family group, there was Shelomoth. And Jahath was a descendant of Shelomoth.

[23]Hebron's first son was Jeriah. Amariah was his second son. Jahaziel was his third son, and Jekameam was his fourth.

[24]Uzziel's son was Micah. Micah's son was Shamir. [25]Isshiah was Micah's brother. Isshiah's son was Zechariah.

[26]Merari's descendants were Mahli and Mushi. Merari's son was Jaaziah. [27]Jaaziah son of Merari had sons named Shoham, Zaccur and Ibri. [28]Mahli's son was Eleazar. But Eleazar did not have any sons.

[29]Kish's son was Jerahmeel.

[30]Mushi's sons were Mahli, Eder and Jerimoth.

These are the Levites, listed by their families. [31]They were chosen for special jobs by throwing lots.[d] They did this just as their relatives, the priests, had done. The priests were Aaron's descendants. They threw lots in front of King David, Zadok and Ahimelech. The leaders of the families of the priests and Levites were also there. The families of the oldest brother and the youngest brother were treated the same.

25 David and the commanders of the army chose some men to preach. They chose some of the sons of Asaph, Heman and Jeduthun. They were to preach God's message and play harps, lyres[d] and cymbals. Here is a list of the men who served in this way:

[2]Asaph's sons who served were Zaccur, Joseph, Nethaniah and Asarelah. King David chose Asaph to preach. And Asaph directed his sons.

[3]Jeduthun's sons who served were Gedaliah, Zeri, Jeshaiah, Shimei, Hashabiah and Mattithiah. There were six of them, and Jeduthun directed them. He preached. And he used a harp to give thanks and praise to the Lord.

[4]Heman's sons who served were Bukkiah, Mattaniah, Uzziel, Shubael and Jerimoth. There were also Hananiah, Hanani, Eliathah, Giddalti and Romamti-Ezer. And there were Joshbekashah, Mallothi, Hothir and Mahazioth. [5]All these men were sons of Heman, David's seer.[d] God promised to make Heman strong. So Heman had many sons. God gave him 14 sons and 3 daughters. [6]Heman directed all his sons in making music for the Temple[d] of the Lord. They used cymbals, lyres and harps. That was their way of serving in the Temple of God. And King David was in charge of Asaph, Jeduthun and Heman. [7]These men and their relatives from the Levites were trained in music. They were skilled in making music for the Lord. There were 288 of them. [8]Everyone threw lots[d] to choose the time his family was to serve at the Temple. The young and the old had to throw lots. The teacher and the student had to throw lots.

[9]First, 12 men were chosen from Joseph, his sons and relatives. Joseph was from the family of Asaph.

Second, 12 men were chosen from Gedaliah, his sons and relatives.

[10]Third, 12 men were chosen from Zaccur, his sons and relatives.

[11]Fourth, 12 men were chosen from Izri, his sons and relatives.

[12]Fifth, 12 men were chosen from Nethaniah, his sons and relatives.

[13]Sixth, 12 men were chosen from Bukkiah, his sons and relatives.

[14]Seventh, 12 men were chosen from Jesarelah, his sons and relatives.

[15]Eighth, 12 men were chosen from Jeshaiah, his sons and relatives.

[16]Ninth, 12 men were chosen from Mattaniah, his sons and relatives.

[17] Tenth, 12 men were chosen from Shimei, his sons and relatives.

[18] Eleventh, 12 men were chosen from Azarel, his sons and relatives.

[19] Twelfth, 12 men were chosen from Hashabiah, his sons and relatives.

[20] Thirteenth, 12 men were chosen from Shubael, his sons and relatives.

[21] Fourteenth, 12 men were chosen from Mattithiah, his sons and relatives.

[22] Fifteenth, 12 men were chosen from Jerimoth, his sons and relatives.

[23] Sixteenth, 12 men were chosen from Hananiah, his sons and relatives.

[24] Seventeenth, 12 men were chosen from Joshbekashah, his sons and relatives.

[25] Eighteenth, 12 men were chosen from Hanani, his sons and relatives.

[26] Nineteenth, 12 men were chosen from Mallothi, his sons and relatives.

[27] Twentieth, 12 men were chosen from Eliathah, his sons and relatives.

[28] Twenty-first, 12 men were chosen from Hothir, his sons and relatives.

[29] Twenty-second, 12 men were chosen from Giddalti, his sons and relatives.

[30] Twenty-third, 12 men were chosen from Mahazioth, his sons and relatives.

[31] Twenty-fourth, 12 men were chosen from Romamti-Ezer, his sons and relatives.

26 These are the groups of the gatekeepers.

From the family of Korah, there was Meshelemiah and his sons. (Meshelemiah son of Kore was from Asaph's family.) [2] Meshelemiah had sons. Zechariah was his first son. Jediael was his second son. Zebadiah was his third son. Jathniel was his fourth son. [3] Elam was his fifth son. Jehohanan was his sixth son, and Eliehoenai was his seventh son.

[4] There were also Obed-Edom and his sons. Obed-Edom's first son was Shemaiah. Jehozabad was his second son. Joah was his third son. Sacar was his fourth son. Nethanel was his fifth son. [5] Ammiel was his sixth son. Issachar was his seventh son, and Peullethai was his eighth son. God had blessed Obed-Edom with children.

[6] Obed-Edom's son Shemaiah also had sons. They were leaders in their father's family because they were capable men. [7] Shemaiah's sons were Othni, Rephael, Obed, Elzabad, Elihu and Semakiah. Elihu and Semakiah were skilled workers. [8] All these men were Obed-Edom's descendants.[d] They and their sons and relatives were capable men. They were

strong enough to do the work. Obed-Edom had 62 descendants in all.

[9] Meshelemiah had sons and relatives. They were skilled workers. In all, there were 18 sons and relatives.

[10] These are the gatekeepers from the Merari family. Hosah had sons. Shimri was chosen to be in charge. He was not the oldest son, but his father chose him to be in charge. [11] Hilkiah was his second son. Tabaliah was his third son, and Zechariah was his fourth son. In all, Hosah had 13 sons and relatives.

[12] These were the leaders of the groups of the gatekeepers. They had jobs for serving in the Temple[d] of the Lord. Their relatives also had jobs in the Temple. [13] Each family was given a gate to guard. They were chosen by throwing lots.[d] Young and old threw lots.

[14] Meshelemiah was chosen by lot to guard the East Gate. Then lots were thrown for Meshelemiah's son Zechariah. He was a wise counselor. He was chosen for the North Gate. [15] Obed-Edom was chosen for the South Gate. And Obed-Edom's sons were chosen to guard the storehouse. [16] Shuppim and Hosah were chosen for the West Gate. They also were to guard the Shalleketh Gate on the upper road.

Guards stood side by side with guards. [17] Six Levites stood guard every day at the East Gate. Four Levites stood guard every day at the North Gate. Four Levites stood guard every day at the South Gate. And two Levites at a time guarded the storehouse. [18] There were two guards at the western court. And there were four guards on the road to the court.

[19] These were the groups of the gatekeepers. They were from the families of Korah and Merari.

[20] Other Levites were responsible for taking care of the treasuries of the Temple[d] of God. They were also responsible for the places where the holy things were kept.

[21] Ladan was Gershon's son. Ladan was the ancestor of several family groups. Jehiel was a leader of one of the family groups. [22] Jehiel's sons were Zetham and his brother Joel. They were responsible for the treasuries of the Temple of the Lord.

[23] Other leaders were chosen from the family groups of Amram, Izhar, Hebron and Uzziel. [24] Shubael was the leader responsible for the treasuries of the Temple of the Lord. Shubael was the de-

scendant[d] of Gershom, who was Moses' son. [25] These were Shubael's relatives from Eliezer: Eliezer's son Rehabiah, Rehabiah's son Jeshaiah, Jeshaiah's son Joram, Joram's son Zicri and Zicri's son Shelomith. [26] Shelomith and his relatives were responsible for everything that had been collected for the Temple. Things had been collected by King David and the heads of families. They had been collected by commanders of 1,000 men and of 100 men and other army commanders. [27] They also gave some of the things they had taken in wars. They gave them to be used in repairing the Temple of the Lord. [28] Shelomith and his relatives took care of all the holy things. Some had been given by Samuel the seer[d] and Saul son of Kish. Some had been given by Abner son of Ner and Joab son of Zeruiah.

[29] Kenaniah was from the Izhar family. He and his sons worked outside the Temple. They worked as officers and judges in different places in Israel.

[30] Hashabiah was from the Hebron family. He and his relatives were responsible for the Lord's work and the king's business in Israel west of the Jordan River. There were 1,700 skilled men in Hashabiah's group. [31] The history of the Hebron family shows that Jeriah was their leader. In David's fortieth year as king, the records were searched. Some capable men of the Hebron family were found living at Jazer in Gilead. [32] Jeriah had 2,700 relatives who were skilled men. They were leaders of families. King David gave them the responsibility of directing the tribes[d] of Reuben, Gad and the eastern half-tribe of Manasseh. They took care of the Lord's work and the king's business for them.

27 This is the list of the Israelite people who served the king in the army. Each division was on duty one month each year. There were leaders of families, commanders of 100 men, commanders of 1,000 men and other officers. Each division had 24,000 men.

[2] Jashobeam son of Zabdiel was in charge of the first division for the first month. There were 24,000 men in his division. [3] He was one of the descendants[d] of Perez. Jashobeam was leader of all the army officers for the first month.

[4] Dodai was in charge of the division for the second month. He was from the Ahohites. Mikloth was a leader in the division. There were 24,000 men in Dodai's division.

[5] The third commander was Benaiah son of Jehoiada the priest. He was the commander for the third month. There were 24,000 men in Benaiah's division. [6] He was the Benaiah who was one of the Thirty[n] soldiers. Benaiah was a brave warrior who led those men. Benaiah's son Ammizabad was in charge of Benaiah's division.

[7] The fourth commander was Asahel, the brother of Joab. He was the commander for the fourth month. Later, Asahel's son Zebadiah took his place as commander. There were 24,000 men in his division.

[8] The fifth commander was Shamhuth, from Izrah's family. He was the commander for the fifth month. There were 24,000 men in his division.

[9] The sixth commander was Ira son of Ikkesh. He was the commander for the sixth month. He was from the town of Tekoa. There were 24,000 men in his division.

[10] The seventh commander was Helez. He was the commander for the seventh month. He was from the Pelonites and a descendant of Ephraim. There were 24,000 men in his division.

[11] The eighth commander was Sibbecai. He was the commander for the eighth month. He was from Hushah and was from Zerah's family. There were 24,000 men in his division.

[12] The ninth commander was Abiezer, from the town of Anathoth. He was the commander for the ninth month. He was from the tribe[d] of Benjamin. There were 24,000 men in his division.

[13] The tenth commander was Maharai. He was the commander for the tenth month. He was from Netophah and was from Zerah's family. There were 24,000 men in his division.

[14] The eleventh commander was Benaiah. He was the commander for the eleventh month. He was from Pirathon and was from the tribe of Ephraim. There were 24,000 men in his division.

[15] The twelfth commander was Heldai. He was the commander for the twelfth month. He was from Netophah and was from Othniel's family. There were 24,000 men in his division.

[16] These were the leaders of the tribes[d] of Israel. Eliezer son of Zicri was over

27:6 **Thirty** These were David's most powerful soldiers. See 2 Samuel 23:24.

the tribe of Reuben. Shephatiah son of Maacah was over the tribe of Simeon. [17]Hashabiah son of Kemuel was over the tribe of Levi. Zadok was over the people of Aaron. [18]Elihu, one of David's brothers, was over the tribe of Judah. Omri son of Michael was over the tribe of Issachar. [19]Ishmaiah son of Obadiah was over the tribe of Zebulun. Jerimoth son of Azriel was over the tribe of Naphtali. [20]Hoshea son of Azaziah was over the tribe of Ephraim. Joel son of Pedaiah was over the western half-tribe of Manasseh. [21]Iddo son of Zechariah was over the eastern half-tribe of Manasseh. Jaasiel son of Abner was over the tribe of Benjamin. [22]Azarel son of Jeroham was over the tribe of Dan.

These were the leaders of the tribes of Israel.

[23]The Lord had promised to make the Israelites as many as the stars in the sky. So David only counted the men who were 20 years old and older. [24]Joab son of Zeruiah began to count the people. But he did not finish. God became angry with Israel for counting the people. So the number of the people was not put in the history book about King David's rule.

[25]Azmaveth son of Adiel was in charge of the royal storehouses.

Jonathan was in charge of the storehouses in the towns, villages and towers. He was the son of Uzziah.

[26]Ezri son of Kelub was in charge of the field workers. They farmed the land.

[27]Shimei was in charge of the vineyards. He was from the town of Ramah.

Zabdi was in charge of storing the wine that came from the vineyards. Zabdi was from Shepham.

[28]Baal-Hanan was in charge of the olive trees and sycamore trees in the western mountain slopes. He was from Geder.

Joash was in charge of storing the olive oil.

[29]Shitrai was in charge of the cows that fed in the Plain of Sharon. He was from Sharon.

Shaphat son of Adlai was in charge of the cows in the valleys.

[30]Obil was in charge of the camels. He was an Ishmaelite.

Jehdeiah was in charge of the donkeys. He was from Meronoth.

[31]Jaziz was in charge of the sheep. He was from the Hagrites.

All these men were the officers who took care of King David's property.

[32]Jonathan was David's uncle. He advised David. Jonathan was a wise man and a teacher of the law. Jehiel son of Hacmoni took care of the king's sons. [33]Ahithophel advised the king. Hushai was the king's friend. He was from the Arkite people. [34]Jehoiada and Abiathar later took Ahithophel's place in advising the king. Jehoiada was Benaiah's son. Joab was the commander of the king's army.

28 David commanded all the leaders of Israel to come to Jerusalem. There were the leaders of the tribes[d] and the commanders of the divisions serving the king. There were the commanders of 1,000 men and of 100 men. There were the leaders who took care of the property and animals that belonged to the king and his sons. There were the men over the palace, the powerful men and all the brave warriors.

[2]King David stood up and said, "Listen to me, my relatives and my people. I wanted to build a place to keep the Box[d] of the Agreement with the Lord. I wanted it to be God's footstool. And I made plans to build a temple for worship to God. [3]But God said to me, 'You must not build a temple for worship to me. You must not do that because you are a soldier. You have killed many men.'

[4]"But the Lord, the God of Israel, chose me from my whole family. He chose me to be king of Israel forever. The Lord chose the tribe of Judah to be a leader. And from the people of Judah, he chose my father's family. And from that family God was pleased to make me king of Israel. [5]The Lord has given me many sons. And from those sons he has chosen Solomon. Solomon will be the new king of Israel. Israel is the Lord's kingdom. [6]The Lord said to me, 'Your son Solomon will build my Temple.[d] And he will build the area around it. This is because I have chosen Solomon to be my son. And I will be his father. [7]He is obeying my laws and commands now. If he continues to obey them, I will make his kingdom strong forever.'"

[8]David said, "Now, in front of all Israel and God, I tell you these things: Be careful to obey all the commands of the Lord your God. Then you may keep this good land. And you may pass it on to your descendants[d] forever.

[9]"And you, my son Solomon, accept the God of your father. Serve him completely. Be happy to serve him. Do this because the Lord knows what is in every person's mind. He understands every-

thing you think. If you go to him for help, you will get an answer. But if you turn away from the Lord, he will leave you forever. [10]Solomon, you must understand this. The Lord has chosen you to build the Temple as his holy place. Be strong and finish the job."

[11]Then David gave his son Solomon the plans for building the Temple. Those plans were also for the porch around the Temple. They were for its buildings, its storerooms, its upper rooms and its inside rooms. They also were the plans for the place where the people's sins were removed. [12]David gave him plans for everything he had in mind. David gave him plans for the courtyards around the Lord's Temple and all the rooms around it. He gave him plans for the Temple treasuries. And he gave him plans for the treasuries of the holy things used in the Temple. [13]David gave Solomon directions for the groups of the priests and Levites. David told him about all the work of serving in the Temple of the Lord. He told him about the things to be used in the Temple service. [14]Many things made of gold or silver would be used in the Temple. David told Solomon how much gold or silver should be used to make each thing. [15]David told him how much gold to use for each gold lampstand and its lamps. He told him how much silver to use for each silver lampstand and its lamps. The different lampstands were to be used where needed. [16]David told how much gold should be used for each table that held the holy bread. And he told how much silver should be used for the silver tables. [17]He told how much pure gold should be used to make the forks, bowls and pitchers. He told how much gold should be used to make each gold dish. He told how much silver should be used to make each silver dish. [18]David told how much pure gold should be used for the altar of incense.[d] He also gave Solomon the plans for the chariot. This is where the golden creatures spread their wings over the Box[d] of the Agreement with the Lord.

[19]David said, "All these plans were written with the Lord guiding me. He helped me understand everything in the plans."

[20]David also said to his son Solomon, "Be strong and brave. Do the work. Don't be afraid or discouraged. The Lord God, my God, is with you. He will help you until all the work is finished.

He will not leave you. You will build the Temple of the Lord. [21]The groups of the priests and Levites are ready for all the work on the Temple of God. Every skilled worker is ready to help you with all the work. The leaders and all the people will obey every command you give."

29 King David spoke to all the Israelites who were gathered. He said, "God chose my son Solomon. Solomon is young and hasn't yet learned what he needs to know. But the work is important. This palace is not for people. It is for the Lord God. [2]I have done my best to prepare for building the Temple[d] of God. I have given gold for the things made of gold. I have given silver for the things made of silver. I have given bronze for the things made of bronze. I have given iron for the things made of iron. I have given wood for the things made of wood. I have given onyx for the settings and turquoise. I have given gems of many different colors. I have given valuable stones and white marble. I have given much of all these things. [3]I have already given this for the Temple. But now I am also giving my own treasures of gold and silver. I am doing this because I really want the Temple of my God to be built. [4]I have given about 220,000 pounds of pure gold from Ophir. And I have given about 520,000 pounds of pure silver. They will be used to cover the walls of the buildings. [5]They will also be used for all the gold and silver work. Skilled men may use the gold and silver to make things for the Temple. Now, who is ready to give himself to the service of the Lord today?"

[6]The family leaders and the leaders of the tribes of Israel gave their valuable things. The commanders of 1,000 men and of 100 men gave their valuable things. And the leaders responsible for the king's work gave their valuable things. [7]These are the things they gave for the Temple of God: about 380,000 pounds of gold, about 750,000 pounds of silver, about 1,350,000 pounds of bronze and about 7,500,000 pounds of iron. [8]People who had valuable gems gave them to the treasury of the Temple of the Lord. Jehiel, from the Gershon family, took care of the valuable gems. [9]The leaders gave freely and completely to the Lord. The people were happy to see their leaders give so gladly. King David was also very happy.

[10]David praised the Lord in front of

all of the people who were gathered. He said:

"We praise you, Lord.
You are the God of our father Israel.
We praise you forever and ever.
[11] Lord, you are great and powerful.
You have glory, victory and honor.
Everything in heaven and on earth belongs to you.
The kingdom belongs to you, Lord.
You are the ruler over everything.
[12] Riches and honor come from you.
You rule everything.
You have the power and strength to make anyone great and strong.
[13] Now, our God, we thank you.
And we praise your glorious name.

[14] "These things did not really come from me and my people.
Everything comes from you.
We have given you back what you gave us.
[15] We are like foreigners and strangers.
All our ancestors were also foreigners and strangers.
Our time on earth is like a shadow.
There is no hope.
[16] Lord our God, we have gathered all this to build your Temple.
We will build it for worship to you.
But everything has come from you.
Everything belongs to you.
[17] I know, my God, that you test people's hearts.
You are happy when people do what is right.
I was happy to give all these things.
I gave with an honest heart.
Your people gathered here are happy to give to you.
I am happy to see their giving.
[18] Lord, you are the God of our ancestors.
You are the God of Abraham, Isaac and Jacob.
Please help your people to want to serve you always.
And help them to want to obey you always.

[19] Give my son Solomon a strong desire to serve you.
Help him always obey your commands, laws and rules.
Help him build the Temple for which I have prepared."

[20] Then David said to all the people who were gathered, "Praise the Lord your God." So they all praised the Lord, the God their ancestors worshiped. They bowed to the ground to give honor to the Lord and the king.

[21] The next day the people made sacrifices to the Lord. They offered burnt offerings to him. They offered 1,000 bulls, 1,000 male sheep and 1,000 male lambs. They also brought drink offerings. Many sacrifices were made for all the people of Israel. [22] That day the people ate and drank with much joy. And the Lord was with them.

And they made David's son Solomon king for the second time. They poured olive oil on Solomon to appoint him king. And they poured oil on Zadok to appoint him as priest. They did this in the presence of the Lord. [23] Then Solomon sat on the Lord's throne as king. He took his father David's place. Solomon was very successful. And all the people of Israel obeyed him. [24] All the leaders and soldiers and King David's sons accepted Solomon as king. They promised to obey him. [25] The Lord made Solomon great before all the Israelites. The Lord gave Solomon much honor. No king of Israel before Solomon had such honor.

[26] David son of Jesse was king over all Israel. [27] He was king for 40 years. He ruled in the city of Hebron for 7 years. And he ruled in Jerusalem for 33 years. [28] David died when he was old. He had lived a good, long life. He had received many riches and honors. And David's son Solomon became king after him.

[29] Everything King David did as king, from beginning to end, is recorded. Those things are written in the records of Samuel the seer.[d] And they are in the records of Nathan the prophet and the records of Gad the seer. [30] Those writings tell what David did as king of Israel. They tell about his power and all that happened to him. And they tell what happened to Israel and all the kingdoms around them.

The Second Book of the
CHRONICLES

1 Solomon was David's son, and he became a powerful king. This was because the Lord his God was with him. The Lord made Solomon very great. ²Solomon spoke to all the people of Israel. He spoke to the commanders of 100 men and of 1,000 men. He spoke to the judges, to every leader in all Israel and to the leaders of the families. ³Then Solomon and all the people gathered with him went to the place of worship. This was at the town of Gibeon. God's Meeting Tent[d] was there. Moses, the Lord's servant, had made that Tent in the desert. ⁴David had brought the Box[d] of the Agreement with God from Kiriath Jearim to Jerusalem. David had made a place for it there. He had set up a tent for it in Jerusalem. ⁵Bezalel was Uri's son, and Uri was Hur's son. Bezalel had made a bronze altar. It was in Gibeon in front of the Holy Tent. So Solomon and the people worshiped the Lord there. ⁶Solomon went up to the bronze altar before the Lord at the Meeting Tent. He offered 1,000 burnt offerings on the altar.

⁷That night God appeared to Solomon. God said, "Solomon, ask for whatever you want me to give you."

⁸Solomon answered, "You have been very kind to my father David. You have chosen me to be the king in his place. ⁹Now, Lord God, may your promise to my father David come true. You have made me king of a very large nation. There are so many of them they are like the dust of the earth. ¹⁰Now give me wisdom and knowledge so I can lead these people in the right way. No one can rule them without your help."

¹¹God said to Solomon, "What you want is good. I have chosen you to be king of these people. You have not asked for wealth or riches or honor. You have not asked for your enemies to be killed. You have not asked for a long life. But you have asked for wisdom and knowledge to lead my people. ¹²So I will give you wisdom and knowledge. I will also give you more wealth, riches and honor than any king who has lived before you. And the kings who will live after you will not have as much."

¹³Then Solomon left the place of worship at Gibeon. He left the Meeting Tent and went back to Jerusalem. There King Solomon ruled over Israel.

¹⁴Solomon gathered horses and chariots. He had 1,400 chariots and 12,000 horses. He put some horses and chariots in the cities where the chariots were kept. And he kept some with him in Jerusalem. ¹⁵In Jerusalem, Solomon gathered much silver and gold. He got so much it was as common as rocks. He also gathered much cedar wood. It became as plentiful as the sycamore trees on the western mountain slopes. ¹⁶Solomon imported horses from Egypt and Kue. The king's traders bought the horses in Kue. ¹⁷They imported a chariot from Egypt for about 15 pounds of silver. And they imported a horse for nearly 4 pounds of silver. Then they sold the horses and chariots to all the kings of the Hittites and the Arameans.

2 Solomon decided to build a temple[d] as a place to worship the Lord. He also decided to build a palace for himself. ²He chose 70,000 men to carry things. He chose 80,000 men to cut stone in the mountains. And he chose 3,600 men to direct the workers.

³Then Solomon sent a message to Hiram king of the city of Tyre. Solomon said:

Help me as you helped my father David. You sent him cedar logs so he could build himself a palace to live in. ⁴I will build a temple as a place to worship the Lord my God. And I will give this temple to the Lord. There we will burn sweet-smelling spices in his presence. We will set out the bread that shows we are in God's presence. And we will burn sacrifices every morning and evening. We will worship him on Sabbath[d] days and New Moons.[d] And we will worship him on the other feast days the Lord our God has commanded us to celebrate. This is a rule for Israel to obey forever. ⁵The temple I build will be great. This is because our God is greater than all gods. ⁶But no one can really build a house for our God. Not even the highest of heavens can hold God. How then can I build a temple for him? I can only build a place to burn sacrifices to God.

⁷Now send me a man skilled in working with gold, silver, bronze and

iron. He must know how to work with purple, red and blue thread. He must know how to make engravings. He will work with my skilled craftsmen in Judah and Jerusalem. These are the men my father David chose.

⁸Also send me cedar, pine and juniper logs from Lebanon. I know your servants are experienced at cutting down the trees in Lebanon. My servants will help them. ⁹Send me a lot of wood. The temple I am going to build will be large and wonderful. ¹⁰I will give your servants who cut the wood 125,000 bushels of wheat. And I will give them 125,000 bushels of barley, 115,000 gallons of wine and 115,000 gallons of oil.

¹¹Then Hiram king of Tyre answered Solomon with this letter:

Solomon, the Lord loves his people. That is why he chose you to be their king.

¹²Hiram also said:

Praise the Lord, the God of Israel! He made heaven and earth! He gave King David a wise son. Solomon, you have wisdom and understanding. You will build a temple for the Lord and a palace for yourself.

¹³I will send you a skilled and wise man named Huram-Abi. ¹⁴His mother was from the people of Dan. And his father was from Tyre. Huram-Abi has skill in working with gold, silver, bronze, iron, stone and wood. He has skill in working with purple, blue and red thread and expensive linen. And he is skilled in making engravings. He can make any design you show him. He will help your craftsmen and the craftsmen of your father David.

¹⁵Now send my servants the wheat, barley, oil and wine you promised. ¹⁶We will cut as much wood from Lebanon as you need. We will use rafts to carry it by sea to Joppa. Then you may carry it to Jerusalem.

¹⁷Solomon counted all the foreigners living in Israel. This was after the time his father David had counted the people. There were 153,600 foreigners in the country. ¹⁸Solomon chose 70,000 of them to carry things. He chose 80,000 of them to cut stone in the mountains. And he chose 3,600 of them to direct the workers. They were to keep the people working.

3 Solomon began to build the Temple^d of the Lord. He built it in Jerusalem on Mount Moriah. This was where the Lord had appeared to David, Solomon's father. Solomon built the Temple on the place David had prepared. This place was the threshing^d floor of Araunah the Jebusite. ²Solomon began building in the second month of the fourth year he ruled Israel.

³Solomon used these measurements for building the Temple of God. It was 90 feet long and 30 feet wide. (Solomon used the old measurement.) ⁴The porch in front of the Temple was 30 feet long and 30 feet high.

Solomon covered the inside of the porch with pure gold. ⁵He put panels of pine on the walls of the main room. Then he covered them with pure gold. And he put designs of palm trees and chains in the gold. ⁶He put gems in the Temple for beauty. And he used gold from Parvaim.ⁿ ⁷Solomon put gold on the Temple's ceiling beams, doorposts, walls and doors. And he carved creatures with wings on the walls.

⁸Then Solomon made the Most Holy Place. It was 30 feet long and 30 feet wide. It was as wide as the Temple. He covered its walls with about 46,000 pounds of pure gold. ⁹The gold nails weighed over a pound. Solomon also covered the upper rooms with gold.

¹⁰He made two creatures with wings for the Most Holy Place. He made them out of hot liquid gold. ¹¹The wings of the gold creatures were spread out. Together, they were 30 feet across. One wing of one creature touched the Temple wall. The wing was 7½ feet long. The creature's other wing touched a wing of the second creature. This wing was also 7½ feet long. ¹²One wing of the second creature touched the other side of the room. It was also 7½ feet long. The second creature's other wing touched the first creature's wing. This wing was also 7½ feet long. ¹³Together, the creatures' wings were 30 feet across. The creatures stood on their feet. They looked inside toward the main room.

¹⁴Solomon made the curtain of blue, purple and red thread and expensive linen. And he put designs of creatures with wings in it.

¹⁵Solomon made two pillars to stand in front of the Temple. They were about 52 feet tall. The capital^d of each pillar

3:6 Parvaim There was much gold there. It may have been in the country of Ophir.

was over 7 feet tall. [16]Solomon made a net of chains. He put them on the tops of the pillars. He made 100 pomegranates[d] and put them on the chains. [17]Then Solomon put the pillars up in front of the Temple. One pillar stood on the south side. The other stood on the north. He named the south pillar He Establishes. And he named the north pillar In Him Is Strength.

4 Solomon made a bronze altar. It was 30 feet long, 30 feet wide and 15 feet tall. [2]Then Solomon used melted bronze to make a large bowl, which was called the Sea. It was round and measured 15 feet across from edge to edge. It was over 7 feet tall, and it measured 45 feet around. [3]There were carvings of bulls under the rim of the bowl. There were 10 bulls in every 1½ feet. They were put in two rows around the bowl when it was made.

[4]The bowl rested on 12 statues of bulls. Three bulls faced north, 3 faced west, 3 faced south and 3 faced east. The bowl was on top of them. They faced outward from the center of the bowl. [5]The bowl was 3 inches thick. Its rim was like the rim of a cup. It looked like a lily blossom. It could hold about 17,500 gallons.

[6]Solomon made 10 smaller bowls. He put 5 of them on the south side. And he put 5 of them on the north. They were to be used to wash the animals for the burnt offerings. But the large bowl was to be used by the priests for washing.

[7]Solomon made 10 lampstands of gold, following the plans for them. He put them in the Temple.[d] He put 5 on the south side and 5 on the north.

[8]Solomon made 10 tables and put them in the Temple. He put 5 on the south side and 5 on the north. And he used gold to make 100 other bowls.

[9]Solomon also made the priests' courtyard and the large courtyard. He made the doors that opened to the courtyard and covered them with bronze. [10]Then he put the large bowl on the south side. He put it in the Temple's southeast corner.

[11]He made the pots, shovels and bowls. So Huram finished his work for King Solomon on the Temple of God. He had made these things:

[12]two pillars;

two large bowls for the capitals on top of the pillars;

two nets to cover the two large bowls for the capitals on top of the pillars;

[13]400 pomegranates[d] for the two nets (there were two rows of pomegranates for each net covering the bowls for the capitals on top of the pillars);

[14]the stands with a bowl on each stand;

[15]the large bowl with 12 bulls under it;

[16]the pots, shovels, forks and all the things to go with them.

All the things Huram-Abi made King Solomon for the Temple of the Lord were made of polished bronze. [17]King Solomon first had these things poured into clay molds. The molds were made in the plain of the Jordan between Succoth and Zarethan. [18]Solomon had so many things made no one even tried to weigh all the bronze used.

[19]Solomon also made all the things for God's Temple. He made the gold altar. He made tables to hold the bread that shows we are in God's presence. [20]He made the lampstands and their lamps of pure gold. They were to burn in front of the Most Holy Place as planned. [21]Solomon used pure gold to make the flowers, lamps and tongs. [22]He used pure gold to make the wick trimmers. He used pure gold for the bowls, pans and dishes used to carry coals. He used pure gold to make the doors for the Temple. And he used pure gold for the inside doors for the Most Holy Place and the doors for the main room.

5 Then all the work Solomon had done for the Temple of the Lord was finished. He brought in everything his father David had given for the Temple. He brought in all the silver and gold and all the furniture. And he put everything in the treasuries of God's Temple.

[2]Then Solomon called for all the leaders of Israel. He asked them to come to him in Jerusalem. He called for all the older leaders, the heads of the tribes[d] and the leaders of the families. He wanted them to bring the Box[d] of the Agreement with the Lord from the older part of the city. [3]All the men of Israel came together with King Solomon. This was during the festival that was held in the seventh month.

[4]All the older leaders of Israel arrived. Then the Levites picked up the Holy Box. [5]The priests and the Levites carried the Box of the Agreement. They also

carried the Meeting Tent[d] and the holy things in it. [6]King Solomon and all the Israelites met in front of the Box of the Agreement. They sacrificed so many sheep and bulls no one could count them.

[7]Then the priests put the Box of the Agreement with the Lord in its place. This was inside the Most Holy Place in the Temple.[d] They put it under the wings of the gold creatures. [8]The wings of the creatures were spread out over the place for the Holy Box. They covered it and its carrying poles. [9]The carrying poles were very long. Anyone standing in the Holy Place in front of the Most Holy Place could see the ends of the poles. But no one could see the poles from outside the Holy Place. The poles are still there today. [10]The only things inside the Holy Box were two stone tablets.[n] Moses had put them in the Holy Box at Mount Sinai. That was where the Lord made an agreement with the Israelites after they came out of Egypt.

[11]Then all the priests left the Holy Place. All the priests from each group made themselves ready to serve the Lord. [12]All the Levite musicians stood on the east side of the altar. They were Asaph, Heman, Jeduthun and all their sons and relatives. They were dressed in white linen and played cymbals, lyres[d] and harps. With them were 120 priests who blew trumpets. [13]Those who blew the trumpets and those who sang together sounded like one person. They praised and thanked the Lord. They sang as they played their trumpets, cymbals and other instruments. They praised the Lord with this song:

"The Lord is good.
        His love continues forever."

Then the Temple of the Lord was filled with a cloud. [14]The priests could not continue their work because of the cloud. This was because the Lord's glory filled the Temple of God.

6 Then Solomon said, "The Lord said he would live in the dark cloud. [2]I have built a great Temple for you, Lord. It is a place for you to live forever."

[3]King Solomon turned around and blessed all the Israelites gathered in front of him. [4]He said, "Praise the Lord, the God of Israel. He has done what he promised my father David. The Lord said, [5]'I brought my people out of Egypt. But I have not yet chosen a city in any

tribe[d] of Israel for my temple.[d] This is where I have chosen to be worshiped. I have not chosen a man to lead my people, the Israelites. [6]But now I have chosen Jerusalem as the place I am to be worshiped. And I have chosen David to lead my people Israel.'

[7]"My father David wanted to build a temple as a place to worship the Lord, the God of Israel. [8]But the Lord said to my father, 'David, it was good that you wanted to build a temple as a place to worship me. [9]But you are not the one who will build the temple. Your own son will build my temple.'

[10]"Now the Lord has kept his promise. I have taken my father David's place. Now I am Israel's king. This is what the Lord promised. And I have built the Temple where the Lord, the God of Israel, will be worshiped. [11]I have put the Box[d] of the Agreement there. The agreement that the Lord made with the people of Israel is kept in the Holy Box."

[12]Solomon stood in front of the Lord's altar. He was standing before all the people gathered there. Then he spread his arms out. [13]He had made a bronze platform. It was 7½ feet long, 7½ feet wide and 7½ feet high. And he had placed it in the middle of the outer courtyard. Solomon stood on the platform. Then he kneeled in front of all the people of Israel who were gathered there. Solomon spread his hands out toward the sky. [14]He said, "Lord, God of Israel, there is no god like you in heaven or on earth. You keep your agreement of love with your servants who completely obey you. [15]You have kept your promise to my father David, your servant. With your words you made a promise. And with the work of your hands, you have made that promise come true today.

[16]"Now, Lord, God of Israel, also keep this promise you made to my father David, your servant. You said, 'David, you will always have someone from your family rule Israel. But this will happen only if they are careful to obey my teachings in everything they do. They must obey my teachings just as you have.' [17]Now, Lord, God of Israel, keep your promise. Let this promise to your servant David come true.

[18]"But, God, can you really live here on the earth with people? Not even the highest of heavens can hold you. And this Temple[d] I built cannot hold you.

5:10 stone tablets They were the two stone tablets on which God wrote the Ten Commandments.

¹⁹But pay attention to my prayer and my cry for mercy. Lord my God, listen to my cry. Listen to the prayer I, your servant, pray to you. ²⁰I pray that you will watch over this Temple day and night. You said you would make this the place to worship you. I pray that you will hear my prayers when I pray facing this Temple. ²¹Hear my prayers and the prayers of your people Israel. Hear us when we pray facing this Temple. Hear from your home in heaven. And when you hear our prayers, forgive us.

²²"A person might do something wrong against someone else. The person who did the wrong will have to swear he is innocent. He will come to swear this before your altar in the Temple. ²³When he does this, listen from heaven and act. Judge your servants. Punish the one who did wrong. Make him suffer the same things he made others suffer. Prove that the person who has done right is innocent.

²⁴"An enemy might defeat your people Israel because they have sinned against you. Then the people of Israel will return to you and say you are God. They will pray and beg you for help in this Temple. ²⁵When this happens, listen from heaven. Forgive the sin of your people, the Israelites. Bring them back into the land you gave to them and their ancestors.

²⁶"The sky might not let it rain because your people have sinned against you. Then they will pray, facing this Temple. They will say you are God. They will stop doing their sin because you are punishing them. ²⁷When that happens, then listen from heaven. Forgive the sins of your servants, the Israelites. Then teach them the right way to live. And send rain on your land. This is the land you gave your people as their own.

²⁸"There might be a time without food in the land. Or there might be terrible sicknesses, disease in the crops, mildew,ᵈ locustsᵈ or grasshoppers. Or enemies might attack Israel's cities. There might be a disaster in Israel. ²⁹Then one of your people, an Israelite, will pray or cry for help. Each person knows his own trouble and pain. He will spread his arms out, facing this Temple. ³⁰When that happens, then listen from heaven, your home. Forgive and treat each person as he should be treated. You know what is in his heart. (Only you know what is in a person's heart.) ³¹Then the people will fear and obey you as long as they live in this land. This is the land you gave our ancestors.

³²"A foreigner might come here from a country far away. He is not one of your people, the people of Israel. But he will come because he has heard about your greatness and power. He knows about the things you have done. When he comes and prays, facing this Temple, ³³then listen. Listen from heaven, your home. And do what he asks you to do. Then all the peoples of the earth will know you and respect you, just as your people Israel do. And they will know that this Temple I built is for worshiping you.

³⁴"You might send your people to fight their enemies. They will pray to you, facing this city you chose and the Temple I built for worshiping you. ³⁵If they do, then listen from heaven to their prayer. Listen to their cry and help them.

³⁶"People will sin against you. There is not a person who does not sin. And you will become angry with them. You will let an enemy defeat them. The enemy will capture them and take them away. It may be to a land far away or near. ³⁷But then they will be sorry for what they have done. As captives in that land, they will cry out to you. They will say, 'We have sinned. We have done wrong and acted wickedly.' ³⁸In the land where they are captives, they will come back to you. They will want to obey you completely. They will pray, facing their land, the land you gave their ancestors. They will pray, facing the city you chose and the Temple I built for you. ³⁹When this happens, listen from your home in heaven. Listen to their cries and help them. Forgive your people who have sinned against you.

⁴⁰"Now, my God, look at us. Listen to the prayers we will pray in this place.

⁴¹Now, rise, Lord God, and come to
  your resting place.
 Come with the Boxᵈ of the
   Agreement that shows your
   strength.
 Let your priests receive your
   salvation, Lord God.
 And may your holy people be
   happy because of your
   goodness.
⁴²Lord God, do not reject your
   appointed one.
 Remember your love for your
   servant David."

7 When Solomon finished praying, fire came down from the sky. It burned up the burnt offering and the sacrifices. The Lord's glory filled the Temple.[d] [2]The priests could not enter the Temple of the Lord because the Lord's glory filled it. [3]All the people of Israel saw the fire come down from heaven. They also saw the Lord's glory on the Temple. Then they bowed down on the pavement with their faces to the ground. They worshiped and thanked the Lord. They said,

"The Lord is good.

His love continues forever."

[4]Then King Solomon and all the Israelites offered sacrifices before the Lord. [5]King Solomon offered a sacrifice of 22,000 cattle and 120,000 sheep. So the king and all the people gave the Temple for the worship of God. [6]The priests stood ready to do their work. The Levites also stood with the instruments of the Lord's music. King David had made these instruments for praising the Lord. The priests and Levites were saying, "The Lord's love continues forever." The priests, who stood across from the Levites, blew their trumpets. And all the Israelites were standing.

[7]Solomon made the middle part of the courtyard holy for the Lord. That courtyard is in front of the Temple of the Lord. There Solomon offered burnt offerings and the fat of the fellowship offerings. He used the middle of the courtyard because the bronze altar he had made could not hold everything. It couldn't hold the burnt offerings, grain offerings and fat.

[8]Solomon and all the Israelites celebrated the festival for seven days. There were many people. They came from as far away as Lebo Hamath. And they came all the way from the brook of Egypt. [9]They had given the altar for the worship of the Lord. And they celebrated for seven days. Then they celebrated the festival for seven days. On the eighth day they had a meeting. [10]On the twenty-third day of the seventh month Solomon sent the people home. They were full of joy. They were happy because the Lord had been so good to David, Solomon and his people the Israelites.

[11]Solomon finished the Temple[d] of the Lord and the king's palace. He had success in doing everything he planned in the Temple of the Lord and his own palace. [12]Then the Lord appeared to Solomon at night. The Lord said, "Sol-

omon, I have heard your prayer. And I have chosen this place for myself to be a Temple for sacrifices.

[13]"I may stop the sky from sending rain. I may command the locusts[d] to destroy the land. I may send sicknesses to my people. [14]Then my people, who are called by my name, will be sorry for what they have done. They will pray and obey me and stop their evil ways. If they do, I will hear them from heaven. I will forgive their sin, and I will heal their land. [15]Now I will see them. And I will listen to the prayers prayed in this place. [16]I have chosen this Temple and made it holy. So I will be worshiped here forever. Yes, I will always watch over it and love it.

[17]"Solomon, obey me as your father David did. Obey all I have commanded. Obey my laws and rules. [18]If you do, I will make your kingdom strong. This is the agreement I made with your father David. I told him, 'David, someone from your family will always be king in Israel.'

[19]"But you must not turn away from me. You must not stop obeying the laws and commands I gave you. You must not serve and worship other gods. [20]If you do, I will take the Israelites out of my land, the land I gave them. And I will leave this Temple that I have made holy. All the nations will make fun of it and speak evil about it. [21]This Temple is honored now. But then, everyone who passes by will be surprised. They will say, 'Why has the Lord done this terrible thing to this land and this Temple?' [22]Then people will answer, 'It's because the Israelites left the Lord, the God their ancestors obeyed. He is the God who led them out of Egypt. But they accepted other gods and worshiped and served them. That is why the Lord brought this disaster on them.' "

8 It took Solomon 20 years to build the Temple[d] of the Lord and his own palace. [2]Then Solomon rebuilt the towns that Hiram had given him. And Solomon sent Israelites to live in them. [3]Then he went to Hamath Zobah and captured it. [4]Solomon also built the town of Tadmor in the desert. He built all the towns in Hamath as towns for storing things. [5]He rebuilt the towns of Upper Beth Horon and Lower Beth Horon. He made them protected towns with strong walls, gates and bars in the gates. [6]He also rebuilt the town of Baalath. And he built all the other towns where he stored things. He built all the cities where the chariots and horses were kept. Solomon built all he wanted in Jerusalem, Lebanon and in all the country he ruled.

⁷⁻⁸Many people who were not Israelites were left living in the country. These people were the Hittites, Amorites, Perizzites, Hivites and Jebusites. They were descendants^d of the people that the Israelites had not destroyed. Solomon forced all of them to be slave workers. This is still true today. ⁹But Solomon did not force any of the Israelites to be slave workers. They were his fighting men. They were the commanders of his army officers, his chariots and his chariot drivers. ¹⁰Some of them were his most important officers. There were 250 of them to direct the people.

¹¹Solomon brought the daughter of the king of Egypt from the older part of Jerusalem. He brought her to the palace he had built for her. Solomon said, "My wife must not live in King David's palace. This is because the places where the Box^d of the Agreement has been are holy places."

¹²Then Solomon offered burnt offerings to the Lord on the Lord's altar. Solomon built that altar in front of the Temple porch. ¹³He offered sacrifices every day as Moses had commanded. Sacrifices were to be offered on the Sabbath^d days, New Moons^d and the three yearly feasts. The three yearly feasts were the Feast^d of Unleavened Bread, the Feast of Weeks and the Feast of Shelters. ¹⁴Solomon followed his father David's instructions. Solomon chose the groups of priests for their service. He chose the Levites to lead the praise. And they were to help the priests do their daily work. And he chose the gatekeepers by their groups to serve at each gate. This is what David, the man of God, had commanded. ¹⁵They obeyed all of Solomon's commands to the priests and Levites. And they obeyed his commands about the treasuries.

¹⁶All Solomon's work was done. Everything was done as he had said from the day the Temple of the Lord was begun until it was finished. So the Temple was finished.

¹⁷Then Solomon went to the towns of Ezion Geber and Elath. They were near the Red Sea^d in the country of Edom. ¹⁸Hiram sent to Solomon ships commanded by his own men. They were skilled sailors. Hiram's men went with Solomon's men to Ophir. And they brought back about 34,000 pounds of gold to King Solomon.

9 The queen of Sheba heard about Solomon's fame. So she came to Jerusalem to test him with hard questions. She had a very large group of people with her. She had camels that carried spices, much gold and many gems. She came to Solomon and talked with him about all her questions. ²And Solomon answered all her questions. Nothing was too hard for him to explain to her. ³The queen of Sheba saw that Solomon was very wise. She also saw the palace he had built. ⁴She saw the food on his table and his many officers. She saw the palace servants and their good clothes. She saw the servants who served Solomon his wine. And she saw their good clothes. She saw the burnt offerings he made in the Temple^d of the Lord. All these things amazed her. ⁵So she said to King Solomon, "I heard in my own country about your achievements and wisdom. And all of it is true. ⁶I did not believe it then. But now I have come and seen it with my own eyes. Not even half of your great wisdom was told to me! You are much greater than I had heard. ⁷Your men and officers are very lucky! Since they are always serving you, they are able to hear your wisdom! ⁸Praise the Lord your God! He was pleased to make you king. He has put you on his throne to rule for the Lord your God. Your God loves Israel and supports Israel forever. So the Lord has made you king of Israel to keep law and order and to rule fairly."

⁹Then the queen of Sheba gave King Solomon about 9,000 pounds of gold. She also gave him many spices and gems. No one had ever given such fine spices as she gave to King Solomon.

¹⁰Hiram's men and Solomon's men brought in gold from Ophir. They also brought in juniper wood and gems. ¹¹King Solomon used the juniper wood to make steps for the Temple of the Lord and the palace. He also used it to make lyres^d and harps for the singers. No one in Judah had ever seen such beautiful things as these.

¹²King Solomon gave the queen of Sheba everything she wanted and asked for. He gave her more than she had brought to him. Then she and her servants left and returned to their own country.

¹³The amount of gold that Solomon received in one year weighed about

50,000 pounds. [14]Besides that, he also received gold from merchants and traders. All the kings of Arabia and the rulers of the land also brought gold and silver to Solomon.

[15]King Solomon made 200 large shields from hammered gold. Each shield contained about 7½ pounds of hammered gold. [16]Solomon also made 300 small shields of hammered gold. Each shield contained about 4 pounds of gold. King Solomon put them in the Palace of the Forest of Lebanon.

[17]Then he built a large throne of ivory. And he covered it with pure gold. [18]The throne had six steps on it. And it had a gold footstool on it. There were armrests on both sides of the chair. And beside each armrest was a statue of a lion. [19]Twelve lions stood on the six steps. There was one lion at each end of each step. Nothing like this had ever been made for any other kingdom. [20]All King Solomon's drinking cups were made of gold. All of the dishes in the Palace of the Forest of Lebanon were pure gold. In Solomon's time people did not think silver was valuable. So nothing was made of silver. [21]King Solomon had many ships that he sent out to trade. Hiram's men sailed Solomon's ships. Every three years the ships returned. They brought back gold, silver, ivory, apes and baboons.

[22]King Solomon had more riches and wisdom than all the other kings on earth. [23]All the kings of the earth came to see Solomon. They wanted to hear the wisdom God had given him. [24]Every year everyone who came brought a gift. They brought things made of silver and gold, clothes, weapons, spices, horses and mules.

[25]Solomon had 4,000 stalls to hold his horses and chariots. He had 12,000 horses. He kept them in special cities for the chariots. And he kept some with him in Jerusalem. [26]Solomon was king over all the kings from the Euphrates River to the Philistine country to the border of Egypt. [27]In Jerusalem silver was as common as stones while Solomon was king. Cedar trees were as common as the fig trees growing on the western mountain slopes. [28]Solomon imported horses from Egypt and all other countries.

[29]The other things Solomon did as king, from the beginning to the end, are written down. They are in the writings of Nathan the prophet.[c] And they are in the prophecy of Ahijah and the visions of Iddo. Ahijah was from Shiloh. Iddo was a seer[d] who wrote about Jeroboam, Nebat's son. [30]Solomon was king in Jerusalem over all Israel for 40 years. [31]Then Solomon died and was buried in Jerusalem. This was the city of his father David. And Solomon's son Rehoboam became king in his place.

10 Rehoboam went to Shechem because all the Israelites had gone there to make him king. [2]Jeroboam son of Nebat was in Egypt. He had gone there to run away from King Solomon. Jeroboam heard that Rehoboam was going to be the new king. So he returned from Egypt. [3]The people sent for Jeroboam. Then he and the people went to Rehoboam. They said to Rehoboam, [4]"Your father forced us to work very hard. Now, make it easier for us. Don't make us work as hard as your father did. Then we will serve you."

[5]Rehoboam answered, "Come back to me in three days." So the people left.

[6]There were some older leaders who had helped Solomon make decisions during his lifetime. So King Rehoboam asked them what he should do. He said, "How do you think I should answer these people?"

[7]They answered, "Be kind to these people. Please them and give them a kind answer. If you do, they will serve you always."

[8]But Rehoboam did not listen to the advice the older leaders gave him. He talked with the young men who had grown up with him. They advised him in making decisions. [9]Rehoboam asked them, "What is your advice? How should we answer these people? They said, 'Don't make us work as hard as your father did.'"

[10]Then the young men who had grown up with him said, "The people said to you, 'Your father forced us to work very hard. Now make our work easier.' But you should tell those people, 'My little finger is thicker than my father's waist. [11]My father forced you to work hard. But I will make you work even harder. My father beat you with whips. But I will beat you with whips that have sharp points.'"

[12]King Rehoboam had told the people, "Come back to me in three days." So three days later Jeroboam and all the people returned to Rehoboam. [13]Then King Rehoboam spoke to them in a cruel way. He did not take the advice of the

older leaders. [14]He followed the advice of the young men. He said, "My father forced you to work hard. But I will give you even more work. My father beat you with whips. But I will beat you with whips that have sharp points." [15]So King Rehoboam did not do what the people wanted. God caused this to happen. He did this so the Lord could keep his promise to Jeroboam son of Nebat. The Lord had made this promise through Ahijah, a prophet[d] from Shiloh.

[16]The people of Israel saw that King Rehoboam did not listen to them. So they said to the king,

"We have no share in David.
    We have no part in the son of Jesse.
People of Israel, let's go to our own homes!
    Let David's son rule his own people."

So all the Israelites went home. [17]But Rehoboam still ruled over the Israelites who lived in the towns of Judah.

[18]Adoniram was in charge of the people who were forced to work. Rehoboam sent him to the people. But they threw stones at Adoniram until he died. But King Rehoboam was able to run to his chariot and escape to Jerusalem. [19]Since then, Israel has always turned against the family of David.

11 When Rehoboam came to Jerusalem, he gathered 180,000 of the best soldiers. They were from the people of Judah and Benjamin. He gathered them to fight Israel. He wanted to bring the kingdom back under his control. [2]But the Lord spoke his word to Shemaiah, the man of God. The Lord said, [3]"Shemaiah, talk to Solomon's son Rehoboam, the king of Judah. Talk also to all the Israelites living in Judah and Benjamin. Say to them, [4]'The Lord says you must not go to war against your brothers. Every one of you should go home. I made all these things happen.'" So King Rehoboam and his army obeyed the Lord's command. They turned back and did not attack Jeroboam.

[5]Rehoboam lived in Jerusalem. He built strong cities in Judah to defend it against attacks. [6]He built up the cities of Bethlehem, Etam, Tekoa, [7]Beth Zur, Soco, Adullam, [8]Gath, Mareshah, Ziph, [9]Adoraim, Lachish, Azekah, [10]Zorah, Aijalon and Hebron. These were strong, walled cities in Judah and Benjamin. [11]When Rehoboam made those cities strong, he put commanders in them. He also put supplies of food, oil and wine in them. [12]Also, Rehoboam put shields and spears in all the cities. So he made them very strong. Rehoboam kept the peoples and cities of Judah and Benjamin under his control.

[13]The priests and the Levites from all over Israel joined Rehoboam. [14]The Levites even left their pasturelands and fields and came to Judah and Jerusalem. They did this because Jeroboam and his sons refused to let them serve as priests to the Lord. [15]Jeroboam chose his own priests to serve in the places of worship. He chose his own priests for the goat and calf idols he had made. [16]There were people from all the tribes[d] of Israel who wanted to obey the Lord, the God of Israel. They went to Jerusalem with the Levites. They went to sacrifice to the Lord, the God of their fathers. [17]These people made the kingdom of Judah strong. And they supported Solomon's son Rehoboam for three years. During this time they lived the way David and Solomon had lived.

[18]Rehoboam married Mahalath. She was the daughter of Jerimoth and Abihail. Jerimoth was David's son. Abihail was Eliab's daughter, and Eliab was Jesse's son. [19]Mahalath gave Rehoboam these sons: Jeush, Shemariah and Zaham. [20]Then Rehoboam married Absalom's daughter Maacah. And she gave Rehoboam these children: Abijah, Attai, Ziza and Shelomith. [21]Rehoboam loved Maacah more than his other wives and slave women.[d] Rehoboam had 18 wives and 60 slave women. He was the father of 28 sons and 60 daughters.

[22]Rehoboam chose Abijah to be the leader of his own brothers. He did this because he planned to make Abijah king. [23]Rehoboam acted wisely. He spread his sons through all the areas of Judah and Benjamin. He sent them to every strong, walled city. And he gave plenty of supplies to his sons. He also found wives for them.

12 Rehoboam became a strong king. He also made his kingdom strong. Then he and the people of Judah stopped obeying the teachings of the Lord. [2]Shishak was the king of Egypt. He attacked Jerusalem in the fifth year Rehoboam was king. This happened because Rehoboam and the people were unfaithful to the Lord. [3]Shishak had 1,200 chariots and 60,000 horsemen. He brought troops of Libyans, Sukkites and

Cushites from Egypt with him. There were so many they couldn't be counted. [4]Shishak captured the strong, walled cities of Judah. And he came as far as Jerusalem.

[5]Then Shemaiah the prophet[d] came to Rehoboam and the leaders of Judah. They had gathered in Jerusalem because they were afraid of Shishak. Shemaiah said to them, "This is what the Lord says: 'You have left me. So now I will leave you to face Shishak alone.'"

[6]Then the leaders of Judah and King Rehoboam were sorry for what they had done. They said, "The Lord does what is right."

[7]The Lord saw that they were sorry for what they had done. So the Lord spoke his word to Shemaiah. The Lord said, "The king and the leaders are sorry. So I will not destroy them but will save them soon. I will not use Shishak to punish Jerusalem in my anger. [8]But the people of Jerusalem will become Shishak's servants. Then they may learn that serving me is different than serving the kings of other nations."

[9]Shishak king of Egypt attacked Jerusalem. He took the treasures from the Temple[d] of the Lord and from the king's palace. He took everything, even the gold shields Solomon had made. [10]So King Rehoboam made bronze shields to take their place. He gave them to the commanders of the guards for the entrance to the king's palace. [11]Whenever the king entered the Temple of the Lord, the guards went with him. They would carry the shields. Later, they would put them back in the guard room.

[12]When Rehoboam was sorry for what he had done, the Lord held his anger back. So the Lord did not fully destroy Rehoboam. There was some good in Judah.

[13]King Rehoboam made himself a strong king in Jerusalem. He was 41 years old when he became king. And he was king in Jerusalem for 17 years. Jerusalem is the city that the Lord chose from all the tribes[d] of Israel. He chose to be worshiped in Jerusalem. Rehoboam's mother was Naamah from the country of Ammon. [14]Rehoboam did evil things because he did not want to ask the Lord for help.

[15]The things Rehoboam did as king, from the beginning to the end, are written down. They are in the records of Shemaiah the prophet. And they are in the records of Iddo the seer.[d] These men wrote family histories. There were wars between Rehoboam and Jeroboam all the time they ruled. [16]Rehoboam died and was buried in Jerusalem. Then Rehoboam's son Abijah became king.

13 Abijah became the king of Judah. This was during the eighteenth year Jeroboam was king of Israel. [2]Abijah was king in Jerusalem for three years. Abijah's mother was Maacah daughter of Uriel. Uriel was from the town of Gibeah.

And there was war between Abijah and Jeroboam. [3]Abijah led an army of 400,000 capable soldiers into battle. And Jeroboam prepared to fight him with 800,000 capable soldiers.

[4]Abijah stood on Mount Zemaraim in the mountains of Ephraim. He said, "Jeroboam and all Israel, listen to me! [5]You should know this: The Lord, the God of Israel, gave David and his sons the right to be king over Israel forever. God gave this right to David with an agreement which will last forever. [6]But Jeroboam turned against his master. Jeroboam was the son of Nebat, one of Solomon's officers. Solomon was David's son. [7]Then worthless, evil men became friends with Jeroboam. They were against Rehoboam, Solomon's son. Rehoboam was young and didn't know what to do. So he could not stop them.

[8]"Now you people are making plans against the Lord's kingdom. The Lord's kingdom belongs to David's sons! There are many of you. And you have the gold calves Jeroboam made for you as gods. [9]You have thrown out the Lord's priests and the Levites. The priests are Aaron's sons. You have chosen your own priests as people in other countries do. Anyone who comes to make himself ready to serve the Lord with a young bull and seven male sheep can become a priest. He may become a priest of idols that are not gods.

[10]"But as for us, the Lord is our God. We have not left him. The priests who serve the Lord are Aaron's sons. And the Levites help the priests serve the Lord. [11]They offer burnt offerings and sweet-smelling incense[d] to the Lord every morning and evening. They also put the bread on the special table in the Temple.[d] And they light the lamps on the gold lampstand every evening. We obey the command of the Lord our God. But you have left the Lord. [12]God himself is with us. He is our ruler, and his priests are with us. The priests blow the trum-

pet to call us to war against you. Men of Israel, don't fight against the Lord because you won't succeed. He is the God of your ancestors."

[13]But Jeroboam had sent some troops to sneak behind Abijah's army. So while Jeroboam was in front of Abijah's army, Jeroboam's soldiers were behind them. [14]The soldiers in Abijah's army looked around. Then they saw Jeroboam's army attacking both in front and back. They cried out to the Lord. And the priests blew the trumpets. [15]Then the men of Judah gave a battle cry. When they shouted, God defeated Jeroboam and the army of Israel. They ran away from Abijah and the army of Judah. [16]The men of Israel ran away from the men of Judah. God let the army from Judah defeat them. [17]Abijah's army killed many of Israel's men. Of Israel's best men 500,000 were killed. [18]So at that time the people of Israel were defeated. And the people of Judah won. They won because they depended on the Lord, the God of their ancestors.

[19]Abijah's army chased Jeroboam's army. Abijah's army captured from Jeroboam the towns of Bethel, Jeshanah and Ephron. They also captured the small villages near these towns. [20]Jeroboam never became strong again while Abijah was alive. The Lord struck Jeroboam, and he died.

[21]But Abijah became strong. He married 14 women. And he was the father of 22 sons and 16 daughters. [22]All the other things Abijah did as king are written down. What he said and did are recorded in what the prophet Iddo has written.

14 Abijah died and was buried in Jerusalem. Then Abijah's son Asa became king in his place. There was peace in the country for 10 years in Asa's time.

[2]Asa did what the Lord said was good and right. [3]He removed the foreign altars used for idol worship. He removed the places where false gods were worshiped. He smashed the stone pillars that honored false gods. And he tore down the Asherah[d] idols. [4]Asa commanded the people of Judah to obey the Lord, the God their ancestors followed. Asa commanded them to obey the Lord's teachings and commandments. [5]He also removed the places where false gods were worshiped and the incense altars from every town in Judah. So the kingdom had peace while Asa was king.

[6]Asa built strong, walled cities in Judah during the time of peace. He had no war in these years because the Lord gave him peace.

[7]Asa said to the people of Judah, "Let's build up these towns and put walls around them. Let's make towers, gates and bars in the gates. This country is ours because we have obeyed the Lord our God. We have tried to obey him, and he has given us peace all around." So they built and had success.

[8]Asa had an army of 300,000 men from the people of Judah. And he had 280,000 men from the people of Benjamin. The men from Judah carried large shields and spears. The men from Benjamin carried small shields and bows and arrows. All these men were brave fighting men.

[9]Then Zerah from Cush came out to fight Asa's army. Zerah had a large army and 300 chariots. They came as far as the town of Mareshah. [10]Asa went out to fight Zerah. Asa's army prepared for battle in the Valley of Zephathah at Mareshah.

[11]Asa called out to the Lord his God. He said, "Lord, only you can help weak people against the strong. Help us, Lord our God. We depend on you. We fight against this large army in your name. Lord, you are our God. Don't let anyone win against you."

[12]Then the Lord defeated the Cushites when Asa's army from Judah attacked them. And the Cushites ran away. [13]Asa's army chased them as far as the town of Gerar. So many Cushites were killed that the army could not fight again. They were crushed by the Lord and his army. Asa and his army carried many valuable things away from the enemy. [14]They destroyed all the towns near Gerar. The people living in these towns were afraid of the Lord. These towns had many valuable things. So Asa's army took these things away. [15]Asa's army also attacked the camps where the shepherds lived. And they took many sheep and camels. Then they went back to Jerusalem.

15 The Spirit[d] of God entered Azariah son of Oded. [2]Azariah went to meet Asa. Azariah said, "Listen to me, Asa and all you people of Judah and Benjamin. The Lord is with you when you are with him. If you obey the Lord, you will find him. But if you leave him, he will leave you. [3]For a long time Israel was without the true God. And they were without a priest to teach them and without the teachings. [4]But when they were in trouble, they turned to the Lord again. He is the God of Israel. They looked for the Lord and found him. [5]In those days no one could travel safely. There was much trouble in all the nations. [6]One nation would destroy another nation. And one city would destroy another city. This happened because God troubled them with all kinds of trouble. [7]But you should be strong. Don't give up, because you will get a reward for your good work."

[8]Asa felt brave when he heard these words and the message from Azariah. Azariah was the son of Oded the prophet.[d] So he removed the hated idols from all of Judah and Benjamin. And he removed them from the towns he had captured in the hills of Ephraim. He repaired the Lord's altar that was in front of the porch of the Temple[d] of the Lord.

[9]Then Asa gathered all the people from Judah and Benjamin. He also gathered the people of the tribes[d] of Ephraim, Manasseh and Simeon who were living in Judah. Many people came to Asa from Israel. They came because they saw that the Lord, Asa's God, was with him.

[10]Asa and these people gathered in Jerusalem. This was in the third month of the fifteenth year of Asa's rule. [11]At that time they sacrificed to the Lord 700 bulls and 7,000 sheep and goats. Asa's army had taken these animals and other valuable things from their enemies. [12]Then they made an agreement. They promised to obey the Lord with their whole being. He is the God their ancestors served. [13]Anyone who refused to obey the Lord, the God of Israel, was to be killed. It did not matter if that person was important or unimportant. It did not matter if that person was a man or woman. [14]Then Asa and the people made a promise before the Lord. They shouted with a loud voice. They also blew on trumpets and sheep's horns. [15]All the people of Judah were happy about the promise. They had promised with all their heart. They looked for God and found him. So the Lord gave them peace in all the country.

[16]King Asa also removed Maacah, his mother, from being queen mother. He did this because she had made an Asherah[d] idol, which the Lord hated. Asa cut down that idol and smashed it into pieces. Then he burned it in the Kidron

Valley. [17]The places of worship to false gods were not removed from Judah. Asa desired very much to obey the Lord all his life. [18]And Asa put the holy gifts that he and his father had given into the Temple of God. These things were made of silver and gold.

[19]There was no more war until the thirty-fifth year of Asa's rule.

16

In the thirty-sixth year of Asa's rule, Baasha king of Israel attacked Judah. He went to the town of Ramah and made it strong. He used it to keep people from going in or out of the country of Judah. [2]Asa took silver and gold out of the treasuries of the Temple[d] of the Lord. And he took silver and gold out of his own palace. Then he sent it with messengers to Ben-Hadad king of Aram. Ben-Hadad was living in Damascus. Asa's message said: [3]"Let's make an agreement between you and me. Let's make it like the agreement between your father and mine. See, I am sending you silver and gold. Now break your agreement with Baasha king of Israel. Then he will take his army away from my country."

[4]Ben-Hadad agreed with King Asa. So Ben-Hadad sent the commanders of his armies to attack the towns of Israel. These commanders defeated the towns of Ijon, Dan and Abel Beth Maacah. They also defeated all the towns in Naphtali where treasures were stored. [5]When Baasha heard about this, he stopped building Ramah. He left his work. [6]Then King Asa called all the men of Judah together. They went to Ramah and took away the rocks and wood that Baasha had used. And they used the rocks and wood to build up Geba and Mizpah.

[7]At that time Hanani the seer[d] came to Asa king of Judah. Hanani said to him, "You depended on the king of Aram to help you. You did not depend on the Lord your God. So the king of Aram's army escaped from you. [8]The Cushites and Libyans had a large and powerful army. They had many chariots and horsemen. But you depended on the Lord to help you. So he let you defeat them. [9]The Lord searches all the earth for people who have given themselves completely to him. He wants to make them strong. Asa, you did a foolish thing. From now on you will have wars."

[10]Asa was angry with Hanani the seer

because of what he had said. Asa was so angry that he put Hanani in prison. Asa was cruel with some of the people at that same time.

[11] The things Asa did as king, from the beginning to the end, are written down. They are in the book of the kings of Judah and Israel. [12] In the thirty-ninth year of his rule, Asa got a disease in his feet. His disease was very bad. But he did not ask for help from the Lord. He only asked for help from the doctors. [13] Then Asa died in the forty-first year of his rule. [14] The people buried Asa in the tomb he had made for himself in Jerusalem. They laid him on a bed. It was filled with spices and different kinds of mixed perfumes. And they made a large fire to honor Asa.

17 Jehoshaphat, Asa's son, became king of Judah in Asa's place. Jehoshaphat made Judah strong so they could fight against Israel. [2] He put troops in all the strong, walled cities of Judah. And he put troops in Judah and in the towns of Ephraim his father Asa had captured.

[3] The Lord was with Jehoshaphat because he did good things. He lived as his father Asa did when he first became king. Jehoshaphat did not ask for help from the Baal[d] idols. [4] He asked for help from the God his father had followed. He obeyed God's commands. He did not live as the people of Israel lived. [5] The Lord made Jehoshaphat a strong king over Judah. All the people of Judah brought gifts to Jehoshaphat. So he had much wealth and honor. [6] He wanted very much to obey the Lord. He also removed the places for worshiping false gods and the Asherah[d] idols from Judah.

[7] Jehoshaphat sent his officers to teach in the towns of Judah. This happened in the third year of his rule. These officers were Ben-Hail, Obadiah, Zechariah, Nethanel and Micaiah. [8] Jehoshaphat sent with them these Levites: Shemaiah, Nethaniah, Zebadiah, Asahel, Shemiramoth, Jehonathan, Adonijah, Tobijah and Tob-Adonijah. He also sent the priests Elishama and Jehoram. [9] These leaders, Levites and priests taught the people in Judah. They took the Book of the Teachings of the Lord with them. And they went through all the towns of Judah and taught the people.

[10] The nations near Judah were afraid of the Lord. So they did not start a war against Jehoshaphat. [11] Some of the Philistines brought gifts and silver to Jehoshaphat as forced payments. Some Arabs brought him flocks. They brought him 7,700 male sheep and 7,700 goats.

[12] Jehoshaphat became more and more powerful. He built strong, walled cities and storage towns in Judah. [13] He kept many supplies in the towns of Judah. And he kept trained soldiers in Jerusalem. [14] These soldiers were listed by families.

From the families of Judah, these were the commanders of groups of 1,000 men: Adnah was the commander of 300,000 soldiers. [15] Jehohanan was the commander of 280,000 soldiers. [16] And Amasiah was the commander of 200,000 soldiers. Amasiah son of Zicri had volunteered to serve the Lord.

[17] These were the commanders from the families of Benjamin: Eliada had 200,000 soldiers who used bows and shields. Eliada was a brave soldier. [18] And Jehozabad had 180,000 men armed for war.

[19] All these soldiers served King Jehoshaphat. The king also put other men in the strong, walled cities through all of Judah.

18 Jehoshaphat had much wealth and honor. He made an agreement with King Ahab through marriage.[a] [2] A few years later Jehoshaphat visited Ahab in Samaria. Ahab sacrificed many sheep and cattle as a great feast to honor Jehoshaphat and the people with him. He encouraged Jehoshaphat to attack Ramoth in Gilead. [3] Ahab king of Israel asked Jehoshaphat king of Judah, "Will you go with me to attack Ramoth in Gilead?"

Jehoshaphat answered, "I will be with you. And my soldiers will be like your own soldiers. We will join you in the battle." [4] Jehoshaphat also said to Ahab, "But first we should ask the Lord to guide us."

[5] So King Ahab called a meeting of the prophets.[d] There were 400 men. Ahab asked them, "Should we go to war against Ramoth in Gilead or not?"

They answered, "Go, because God will let you defeat it."

[6] But Jehoshaphat asked, "Is there a

18:1 agreement . . . through marriage Jehoshaphat's son Jehoram married Athaliah, Ahab's daughter. See 2 Chronicles 21:6.

prophet of the Lord here? If there is, let's ask him what we should do."

⁷Then King Ahab said to Jehoshaphat, "There is one other prophet. We could ask the Lord through him. But I hate him. When he prophesies, he never says anything good about me. He always says something bad. He is Micaiah, Imlah's son."

Jehoshaphat said, "King Ahab, you shouldn't say that."

⁸So King Ahab told one of his officers to bring Micaiah to him at once.

⁹King Ahab of Israel and King Jehoshaphat of Judah had on their royal robes. They were sitting on their thrones at the threshingᵈ floor. This was near the entrance to the gate of Samaria. All the prophets were speaking messages in front of the two kings. ¹⁰One of the prophets was Zedekiah son of Kenaanah. He had made some iron horns. He said to Ahab, "This is what the Lord says: 'You will use these horns to fight the Arameans. And you will destroy them.'"

¹¹All the other prophets said the same thing. They said, "Attack Ramoth in Gilead and win. The Lord will let you defeat the Arameans."

¹²The messenger who had gone to get Micaiah found him. He said to Micaiah, "All the other prophets are saying the same thing. They are saying that King Ahab will win against the Arameans. You had better agree with them. Give the king a good answer."

¹³But Micaiah said, "As surely as the Lord lives, I can tell him only what my God says."

¹⁴Then Micaiah came to King Ahab. The king asked him, "Micaiah, should we attack Ramoth in Gilead or not?"

Micaiah answered, "Attack and win. You will defeat it."

¹⁵King Ahab said to Micaiah, "Tell me only the truth by the power of the Lord. How many times do I have to tell you this?"

¹⁶Then Micaiah answered, "I saw the army of Israel. They were scattered over the hills like sheep without a shepherd. The Lord said, 'They have no leaders. Let each one go home and not fight.'"

¹⁷Then King Ahab of Israel said to Jehoshaphat, "I told you! This prophet never says anything good about me. He only says bad things about me."

¹⁸But Micaiah continued to speak. He said, "Hear the message from the Lord: I saw the Lord sitting on his throne. His

heavenly army was standing on his right and on his left. ¹⁹The Lord said, 'Who will trick King Ahab of Israel into attacking Ramoth in Gilead? Do this so he will go and be killed.' The spirits did not agree about what they should do. ²⁰Then a spirit came and stood before the Lord. He said, 'I will trick him.' The Lord asked, 'How will you do it?' ²¹The spirit answered, 'I will go to Ahab's prophets. I will make them tell lies.' So the Lord said, 'You will succeed in tricking him. Go and do it.'"

²²Micaiah said, "Ahab, this has now happened. The Lord has caused your prophets to lie to you. The Lord has decided that great trouble should come to you."

²³Then Zedekiah son of Kenaanah went up to Micaiah. And he slapped Micaiah in the face. Zedekiah said, "Do you really believe that the Lord's Spiritᵈ has left me and is now speaking through you?"

²⁴Micaiah answered, "You will find out on the day you go to hide in an inside room."

²⁵Then King Ahab ordered, "Take Micaiah. Send him to Amon, the governor of the city, and to Joash, the king's son. ²⁶Tell them I said to put Micaiah in prison. Give him only bread and water. Keep him there until I come back safely from the battle."

²⁷Micaiah said, "Ahab, if you come back safely from the battle, the Lord has not spoken through me. Remember my words, all you people!"

²⁸So Ahab king of Israel and Jehoshaphat king of Judah went to Ramoth in Gilead. ²⁹King Ahab said to Jehoshaphat, "I will go into battle. But I will wear other clothes so no one will know who I am. But you wear your royal clothes." So King Ahab of Israel wore other clothes and went into battle.

³⁰The king of Aram gave an order to his chariot commanders. He said, "Don't fight with anyone but the king of Israel. It doesn't matter if they are important or unimportant." ³¹When these commanders saw Jehoshaphat, they thought he was the king of Israel. So they turned to attack him. But Jehoshaphat called out, and the Lord helped him. God made the chariot commanders turn away from Jehoshaphat. ³²When they saw he was not King Ahab, they stopped chasing him.

³³By chance, a soldier shot an arrow. And it hit Ahab king of Israel. The arrow

went in between the pieces of his armor. King Ahab said to his chariot driver, "Turn around and get me out of the battle. I've been wounded." ³⁴The battle went on all day. King Ahab held himself up in his chariot. He faced the Arameans until evening. Then Ahab died at sunset.

19 Jehoshaphat king of Judah came back safely to his palace in Jerusalem. ²Jehu son of Hanani went out to meet him. Jehu was a seer.ᵈ He said to King Jehoshaphat, "Why did you help evil people? Why do you love those who hate the Lord? That is the reason the Lord is angry with you. ³But there is some good in you. You took the Asherahᵈ idols out of this country. And you have wanted to obey God."

⁴Jehoshaphat lived in Jerusalem. He went out again to be with the people. He went from Beersheba to the mountains of Ephraim. He brought these people back to the Lord, the God their ancestors followed. ⁵Jehoshaphat appointed judges in all the land. He appointed judges for each of the strong, walled cities of Judah. ⁶Jehoshaphat said to them, "Be careful in what you do. This is because you are not judging for people but for the Lord. He will be with you when you make a decision. ⁷Now let each of you fear the Lord. Be careful in what you do because the Lord our God wants people to be fair. He wants all people to be treated the same. And he doesn't want people to accept money to change their judgments."

⁸And in Jerusalem Jehoshaphat appointed some of the Levites, priests and leaders of Israelite families to be judges. They were to decide cases about the law of the Lord. And they were to settle problems between the people who lived in Jerusalem. ⁹Jehoshaphat gave them commands. He said, "You must always serve the Lord completely. You must fear him. ¹⁰You will have cases about killing, about the teachings, commands, rules or some other law. These cases will come from your people living in the cities. In all these cases you must warn the people not to sin against the Lord. If you don't, the Lord will be angry with you and your people. But if you warn them, you won't be guilty.

¹¹"Amariah is the leading priest. He will be over you in all cases about the Lord. Zebadiah son of Ishmael is a leader in the tribeᵈ of Judah. He will be over you in all cases about the king.

Also, the Levites will serve as officers for you. Have courage. May the Lord be with those who do what is right."

20 Later some people came to start a war with Jehoshaphat. They were the Moabites, Ammonites and some Meunites. ²Some men came and told Jehoshaphat, "A large army is coming against you from Edom. They are coming from the other side of the Dead Sea.ᵈ They are already in Hazazon Tamar!" (Hazazon Tamar is also called En Gedi.) ³Jehoshaphat was afraid. So he decided to ask the Lord what to do. He announced that no one in Judah should eat during this special time of prayer to God. ⁴The people of Judah came together to ask the Lord for help. They came from every town in Judah to ask for his help.

⁵The people of Judah and Jerusalem met in front of the new courtyard in the Templeᵈ of the Lord. Then Jehoshaphat stood up before them. ⁶He said, "Lord, you are the God of our ancestors. You are the God in heaven. You rule over all the kingdoms of the nations. You have power and strength. No one can stand against you. ⁷Our God, you forced out the people who lived in this land. You forced them out as your people Israel moved in. And you gave this land forever to the descendantsᵈ of your friend Abraham. ⁸They lived in this land and built a Temple for worshiping you. They said, ⁹'Trouble may come to us. It may be war, punishment, sickness or a time of hunger. If it comes, we will stand before you and before this Temple where you have chosen to be worshiped. We will cry out to you when we are in trouble. Then you will hear and save us.'

¹⁰"But now here are men from Ammon, Moab and Edom. You wouldn't let the Israelites enter their lands when the Israelites came from Egypt. So the Israelites turned away and did not destroy them. ¹¹But see how they repay us for not destroying them! They have come to force us out of your land. And you gave us this land as our own. ¹²Our God, punish those people. We have no power against this large army that is attacking us. We don't know what to do. So we look to you for help."

¹³All the men of Judah stood before the Lord. Their babies, wives and children were with them. ¹⁴Then the Spiritᵈ of the Lord entered Jahaziel. (Jahaziel was Zechariah's son. Zechariah was Benaiah's son. Benaiah was Jeiel's son,

and Jeiel was Mattaniah's son.) Jahaziel was a Levite and a descendant of Asaph. He stood up in the meeting. [15]And he said: "Listen to me, King Jehoshaphat! Listen, all you people living in Judah and Jerusalem! The Lord says this to you: 'Don't be afraid or discouraged because of this large army. The battle is not your battle. It is God's battle. [16]Tomorrow go down there and fight those people. They will come up through the Pass of Ziz. You will find them at the end of the ravine that leads to the Desert of Jeruel. [17]You won't need to fight in this battle. Just stand strong in your places. You will see the Lord save you. Judah and Jerusalem, don't be afraid. Don't be discouraged. The Lord is with you. So go out against those people tomorrow!'"

[18]Jehoshaphat bowed facedown on the ground. All the people of Judah and Jerusalem bowed down before the Lord. And they worshiped him. [19]Then some Levites from the Kohathite and Korahite people stood up and praised the Lord. They praised the God of Israel with very loud voices.

[20]Jehoshaphat's army went out into the Desert of Tekoa early in the morning. As they were starting out, Jehoshaphat stood and said, "Listen to me, people of Judah and Jerusalem! Have faith in the Lord your God. Then you will stand strong. Have faith in the Lord's prophets.[d] Then you will succeed." [21]Jehoshaphat listened to the people's advice. Then he chose men to be singers to the Lord. They were to praise the Lord because he is holy and wonderful. They marched in front of the army. They said,

"Thank the Lord.
His love continues forever."

[22]As they began to sing and praise God, the Lord set ambushes. He set them for the people of Ammon, Moab and Edom. They were the ones who came to attack Judah. And they were defeated. [23]The men of Ammon and Moab started to attack the men from Edom. They killed and destroyed them. After they had killed the men from Edom, they killed each other.

[24]The men from Judah came to a place where they could see the desert. They looked at the enemy's large army. But they only saw dead bodies lying on the ground. No one had escaped. [25]Jehosha-

phat and his army came to take valuable things from the dead bodies. They found many supplies, much clothing, and other valuable things. There was more than they could carry away. There was so much it took three days to gather it all. [26]On the fourth day Jehoshaphat and his army met in the Valley of Beracah. There they praised the Lord. That is why that place has been called the Valley of Beracah[b] to this day.

[27]Then Jehoshaphat led all the men from Judah and Jerusalem back to Jerusalem. The Lord had made them happy because their enemies were defeated. [28]They entered Jerusalem with lyres,[d] harps and trumpets and went to the Temple of the Lord.

[29]All the kingdoms of the lands around them heard how the Lord had fought Israel's enemies. So they feared the Lord. [30]So Jehoshaphat's kingdom was not at war. His God gave him peace from all the countries around him.

[31]Jehoshaphat ruled over the country of Judah. He was 35 years old when he began to rule. And he ruled 25 years in Jerusalem. His mother's name was Azubah daughter of Shilhi. [32]Jehoshaphat lived as his father Asa had lived. He followed what Asa had done. He did what the Lord said was right. [33]But the places where false gods were worshiped were not removed. And the people did not strongly desire to follow the God their ancestors had followed.

[34]The other things Jehoshaphat did as king, from the beginning to the end, are written down. They are in the writings of Jehu son of Hanani. These writings are in the book of the kings of Israel.

[35]Later, Jehoshaphat king of Judah made an agreement with Ahaziah king of Israel. It was wrong for him to do this. [36]Jehoshaphat agreed with Ahaziah to build trading ships. They built them in the town of Ezion Geber. [37]Then Eliezer son of Dodavahu spoke against Jehoshaphat. Eliezer was from the town of Mareshah. He said, "Jehoshaphat, because you joined with Ahaziah, the Lord will destroy what you have made." The ships were wrecked. So Jehoshaphat and Ahaziah could not send them out to trade.

21 Then Jehoshaphat died and was buried with his ancestors in Jerusalem. Jehoshaphat's son Jehoram became king in his place. [2]Jehoram's

20:26 **Beracah** This name means "blessing" or "praise."

brothers were Azariah, Jehiel, Zechariah, Azariahu, Michael and Shephatiah. They were the sons of Jehoshaphat king of Judah. ³Jehoshaphat gave his sons many gifts of silver, gold and valuable things. He also gave them strong, walled cities in Judah. But Jehoshaphat gave the kingdom to Jehoram because he was the first son.

⁴Jehoram took control of his father's kingdom. Then he killed all his brothers with a sword. He also killed some of the leaders of Israel. ⁵He was 32 years old when he began to rule. And he ruled eight years in Jerusalem. ⁶He lived as the kings of Israel had lived. He lived as Ahab's family had lived. This was because he married Ahab's daughter. Jehoram did what the Lord said was wrong. ⁷But the Lord would not destroy David's family. This was because of the agreement he had made with David. The Lord had promised that one of David's descendants*ᵈ* would always rule.

⁸While Jehoram was king, Edom turned against Judah's rule. The people of Edom chose their own king. ⁹So Jehoram went to Edom with all his commanders and chariots. The Edomite army surrounded Jehoram and his chariot commanders. But Jehoram fought his way out at night. ¹⁰From then until now the country of Edom has fought against Judah.

At the same time the people of Libnah also turned against Jehoram. This happened because Jehoram left the Lord, the God his ancestors followed. ¹¹Jehoram also had built places to worship false gods on the hills in Judah. He had led the people of Jerusalem into sinning. And he had led the people of Judah away from the Lord. ¹²Jehoram received a letter from Elijah the prophet. The letter said:

This is what the Lord says. He is the God your father David followed. The Lord says, "Jehoram, you have not lived as your father Jehoshaphat lived. You have not lived as Asa king of Judah lived. ¹³But you have lived as the kings of Israel lived. You have led the people of Judah and Jerusalem into sinning against God. That is what Ahab and his family did. You have killed your brothers. And they were better than you. ¹⁴So now the Lord is about to punish your people terribly. He will punish your children, wives and everything you own. ¹⁵You will

have a terrible disease in your intestines. It will become worse every day. Finally it will cause your intestines to come out."

¹⁶The Lord caused the Philistines and the Arabs to be angry with Jehoram. They lived near the Cushites. ¹⁷So the Philistines and Arabs attacked Judah. They took away all the wealth of Jehoram's palace, as well as his sons and wives. Only Jehoram's youngest son, Ahaziah, was left.

¹⁸After these things happened, the Lord gave Jehoram a disease in his intestines. It could not be cured. ¹⁹After he was sick for two years, Jehoram's intestines fell out because of the disease. He died in terrible pain. The people did not make a large fire to honor Jehoram as they had done for his ancestors.

²⁰Jehoram was 32 years old when he became king. And he ruled eight years in Jerusalem. No one was sad when he died. He was buried in Jerusalem, but not in the graves for the kings.

22 The people of Jerusalem chose Ahaziah to be king in Jehoram's place. Ahaziah was Jehoram's youngest son. The robbers who had come with the Arabs to attack Jehoram's camp had killed all of Jehoram's older sons. So Ahaziah began to rule Judah. ²He was 22 years old when he began to rule. And he ruled one year in Jerusalem. His mother's name was Athaliah, a granddaughter of Omri. ³Ahaziah also lived as Ahab's family had lived. This was because his mother encouraged him to do wrong things. ⁴Ahaziah did what the Lord said was wrong. That is what Ahab's family had done. And they gave advice to Ahaziah after his father died. Their bad advice led to his death. ⁵Ahaziah followed their advice when he went to fight King Hazael of Aram. King Joram of Israel, Ahab's son, went with him. They met Hazael at the town of Ramoth in Gilead. The Arameans wounded Joram in battle. ⁶So Joram returned to the town of Jezreel to get well. He was wounded at Ramoth when he fought Hazael king of Aram.

Then King Ahaziah of Judah, son of Jehoram, went to Jezreel. He went there to visit Joram son of Ahab because he was wounded.

⁷God caused Ahaziah's death when he went to visit Joram. Ahaziah arrived and went out with Joram to meet Jehu son of Nimshi. The Lord had appointed

Jehu to destroy Ahab's family. [8]While Jehu was punishing Ahab's family, he found the leaders of Judah. He also found Ahaziah's relatives who served Ahaziah. Jehu killed them all. [9]Then Jehu looked for Ahaziah. Jehu's men caught him hiding in Samaria. So they brought him to Jehu. Then they killed and buried him. They said, "Ahaziah is a descendant[d] of Jehoshaphat. And Jehoshaphat obeyed the Lord with all his heart." No one in Ahaziah's family had the power to take control of the kingdom of Judah.

[10]Now Ahaziah's mother, Athaliah, saw that her son was dead. Then she killed all the royal family in Judah. [11]But Jehosheba took Joash, Ahaziah's son. She stole him from among the other sons of the king. Those sons were going to be murdered. She put Joash and his nurse in a bedroom. Jehosheba was King Jehoram's daughter and Ahaziah's sister. She was also the wife of Jehoiada the priest. She hid Joash so Athaliah could not kill him. [12]Joash was hidden with them in the Temple[d] of God for six years. During that time Athaliah ruled the land.

23 In the seventh year Jehoiada decided to do something. He made an agreement with the commanders of the groups of 100 men. These were the commanders: Azariah son of Jeroham, Ishmael son of Jehohanan, Azariah son of Obed, Maaseiah son of Adaiah, and Elishaphat son of Zicri. [2]They went around in Judah and gathered the Levites from all the towns. They also gathered the leaders of the families of Israel. Then they went to Jerusalem. [3]All the people together made an agreement with the king in the Temple of God.

Jehoiada said to them, "The king's son will rule. That is what the Lord promised about David's descendants.[d] [4]Now this is what you must do: You priests and Levites go on duty on the Sabbath.[d] A third of you will guard the doors. [5]A third of you will be at the king's palace. And a third of you will be at the Foundation Gate. All the other people will stay in the courtyards of the Temple of the Lord. [6]Don't let anyone come into the Temple of the Lord. Only the priests and Levites who serve may come in. They may come because they have been made ready to serve the Lord. But all the other men must do the job the Lord has given them. [7]The Levites must stay near the king. Every man

must have his sword with him. If anyone tries to enter the Temple, kill him. You must stay with the king everywhere he goes."

[8]The Levites and all the people of Judah obeyed everything Jehoiada the priest had commanded. He did not excuse anyone from the groups of the priests. So each commander took the men who came on duty on the Sabbath with those who went off duty on the Sabbath. [9]Jehoiada gave the commanders of the groups of 100 men the spears and the large and small shields. They had belonged to King David. They were kept in the Temple of God. [10]Then Jehoiada told the men where to stand. Every man had his weapon in his hand. They stood around the king, near the altar and the Temple. They stood from the south side of the Temple to the north side.

[11]Jehoiada and his sons brought out the king's son. And they put the crown on him. They gave him a copy of the law. Then they appointed him king and poured olive oil on him. Then they shouted, "Long live the king!"

[12]Athaliah heard the noise of the people running and praising the king. So she went to them at the Temple of the Lord. [13]She looked and saw the king standing by his pillar at the entrance. The officers and the men who blew trumpets were near him. All the people of the land were happy and blowing trumpets. The singers were playing musical instruments and leading praises. Then Athaliah tore her clothes to show how upset she was. She shouted, "Traitors! Traitors!"

[14]Jehoiada the priest sent out the commanders of 100 men who led the army. He said to them, "Surround her with soldiers and take her out of the Temple area. Kill with a sword anyone who follows her." He had said, "Don't put Athaliah to death in the Temple of the Lord." [15]So they caught her when she came to the entrance of the Horse Gate near the palace. And they put her to death there.

[16]Then Jehoiada made an agreement with the people and the king. They agreed that they would be the Lord's special people. [17]All the people went to the temple of Baal[d] and tore it down. They smashed the altars and idols there. And they killed Mattan the priest of Baal in front of the altars.

[18]Then Jehoiada chose the priests to be responsible for the Temple of the

Lord. These priests were Levites. David had given them duties in the Temple of the Lord. They were to offer the burnt offerings to the Lord as the Teachings of Moses commanded. They offered the sacrifices with much joy and singing as David had commanded. [19]Jehoiada put guards at the gates of the Temple of the Lord. Then anyone who was unclean[d] in any way could not enter the Temple.

[20]Jehoiada took with him the commanders of 100 men, the important men, the rulers of the people and all the people of the land. They brought the king down from the Temple of the Lord. They went through the Upper Gate into the palace. Then they seated the king on the throne. [21]All the people of Judah were very happy. And Jerusalem had peace because Athaliah had been put to death with the sword.

24 Joash was seven years old when he became king. And he ruled 40 years in Jerusalem. His mother's name was Zibiah. She was from Beersheba. [2]Joash did what the Lord said was right as long as Jehoiada the priest was alive. [3]Jehoiada chose two wives for Joash. And Joash had sons and daughters.

[4]Later, Joash decided to repair the Temple[d] of the Lord. [5]He called the priests and the Levites together. He said to them, "Go to the towns of Judah. Gather the money all the Israelites have to pay every year. Use it to repair the Temple of your God. Do this now." But the Levites did not hurry.

[6]So King Joash called Jehoiada the leading priest. Joash said to him, "Why haven't you made the Levites bring in the tax money from Judah and Jerusalem? Moses the Lord's servant and the people of Israel used that money for the Holy Tent."[d]

[7]In the past the sons of wicked Athaliah had broken into the Temple of God. They had used its holy things for worshiping the Baal[d] idols.

[8]King Joash commanded that a box for contributions be made. It was to be put outside, at the gate of the Temple of the Lord. [9]Then the Levites made an announcement in Judah and Jerusalem. They told the people to bring the tax money to the Lord. Moses the servant of God had made the Israelites give it while they were in the desert. [10]All the officers and people were happy to give their money. They put it in the box until the box was full. [11]Then the Levites would take the box to the king's officers. They would see that it was full of money. Then the king's royal assistant and the leading priest's officer would come and take out the money. Then they would take the box back to its place. They did this often and gathered much money. [12]King Joash and Jehoiada gave the money to the people who worked on the Temple of the Lord. And they hired stoneworkers and carpenters to repair the Temple of the Lord. They also hired people to work with iron and bronze to repair the Temple.

[13]The people worked hard. And the work to repair the Temple went well. They rebuilt the Temple of God to be as it was before. And they made it stronger. [14]When the workers finished, they brought the money that was left to King Joash and Jehoiada. They used that money to make things for the Temple of the Lord. They made things for the service in the Temple and for the burnt offerings. They also made bowls and other things from gold and silver. Burnt offerings were given every day in the Temple of the Lord while Jehoiada was alive.

[15]Jehoiada grew old. He had lived many years. Then he died when he was 130 years old. [16]Jehoiada was buried in Jerusalem with the kings. He was buried there because he had done much good in Israel for God and his Temple.

[17]After Jehoiada died, the officers of Judah came and bowed down to King Joash. The king listened to them. [18]The king and these leaders stopped worshiping in the Temple[d] of the Lord. He is the God their ancestors obeyed. The king and the officers began to worship the Asherah[d] idols and other idols. Because they did wrong, God was angry with the people of Judah and Jerusalem. [19]The Lord sent prophets[d] to the people to turn them back to him. The prophets warned them, but the people refused to listen.

[20]Then the Spirit[d] of God entered Zechariah son of Jehoiada the priest. Zechariah stood before the people and said, "This is what God says: 'Why do you disobey the Lord's commands? You will not be successful. You have left the Lord. So the Lord has also left you.'"

[21]But the king and his officers made plans against Zechariah. The king commanded them to kill Zechariah. So they threw stones at him in the Temple court-yard until he died. [22]King Joash did not remember Jehoiada's kindness to him. So Joash killed Zechariah, Jehoiada's

son. Before Zechariah died, he said, "May the Lord see what you are doing and punish you."

²³At the end of the year, the Aramean army came against Joash. They attacked Judah and Jerusalem and killed all the leaders of the people. Then they sent all the valuable things to their king in Damascus. ²⁴The Aramean army came with only a small group of men. But the Lord let them defeat a very large army from Judah. He did this because the people of Judah had left the Lord. He is the God their ancestors followed. So Joash was punished. ²⁵When the Arameans left, Joash was badly wounded. His own officers made plans against him. They did this because he had killed Zechariah son of Jehoiada the priest. So they killed Joash in his own bed. He died and was buried in Jerusalem. But he was not buried in the graves of the kings.

²⁶The officers who made plans against Joash were Jozabad and Jehozabad. Jozabad was the son of Shimeath, a woman from Ammon. And Jehozabad was the son of Shimrith, a woman from Moab. ²⁷The story of Joash's sons, the great prophecies⁴ against him, and how he rebuilt the Temple of God are written down. They are in the book of the kings. Joash's son Amaziah became king in his place.

25 Amaziah was 25 years old when he became king. He ruled for 29 years in Jerusalem. His mother's name was Jehoaddin. She was from Jerusalem. ²Amaziah did what the Lord said was right. But he did not really want to obey the Lord. ³Amaziah took strong control of the kingdom. Then he put to death the officers who had murdered his father the king. ⁴But Amaziah did not put their children to death. He obeyed what was written in the Book of Moses. There the Lord commanded, "Fathers must not be put to death when their children do wrong. And children must not be put to death when their fathers do wrong. Each person must die for his own sins.'"

⁵Amaziah gathered the people of Judah together. He grouped all the people of Judah and Benjamin by families. And he put commanders over groups of 1,000 and over groups of 100. He counted the men who were 20 years old and older. In all there were 300,000 soldiers ready to fight. They were skilled with spears and shields. ⁶Amaziah also hired 100,000 soldiers from Israel. He paid about 7,500 pounds of silver for them. ⁷But a man of God came to Amaziah and said, "My king, don't let the army of Israel go with you. The Lord is not with Israel. He is not with the people from the tribes⁴ of Israel. ⁸You can make yourself strong for war. But God will defeat you. He has the power to help you or to defeat you."

⁹Amaziah said to the man of God, "But what about the 7,500 pounds of silver I paid to the Israelite army?"

The man of God answered, "The Lord can give you much more than that!"

¹⁰So Amaziah sent the Israelite army back home to Israel. They were very angry with the people of Judah. And they went home angry.

¹¹Then Amaziah became very brave and led his army to the Valley of Salt. It is in the country of Edom. There Amaziah's army killed 10,000 men from Edom. ¹²The army of Judah also captured 10,000 men. They took those men to the top of a cliff and threw them off. And they were broken to pieces.

¹³At the same time the Israelite army was robbing some towns in Judah. These were troops that Amaziah had not let fight in the war. They robbed towns from Samaria to Beth Horon. They killed 3,000 people and took many valuable things.

¹⁴Amaziah came home after he had defeated the Edomites. He brought back the idols they worshiped. And he started to worship them also. He bowed down to them and offered sacrifices to them. ¹⁵The Lord was very angry with Amaziah. The Lord sent a prophet⁴ to him. The prophet said, "Why have you asked their gods for help? They could not even save their own people from you!"

¹⁶As the prophet spoke, Amaziah said to him, "We never gave you the job of advising the king! Stop, or you will be killed."

The prophet stopped speaking. Then he said, "I know that God has decided to destroy you because you have done this. You did not listen to my advice."

¹⁷Amaziah king of Judah talked with his men who gave him advice. Then he sent a message to Jehoash son of Jehoahaz. (Jehoahaz was the son of Jehu king of Israel.) Amaziah said to Jehoash, "Come, let's meet face to face in battle."

25:4 "Fathers . . . sins." See Deuteronomy 24:16.

¹⁸Then Jehoash king of Israel answered Amaziah king of Judah. Jehoash said, "A little thornbush in Lebanon sent a message to a big cedar tree in Lebanon. It said, 'Let your daughter marry my son.' But then a wild animal from Lebanon came by. It walked on and crushed the thornbush. ¹⁹You say to yourself that you have defeated Edom. You are proud, and you brag. But you stay at home! Don't ask for trouble by fighting me. If you do, you and Judah will be defeated."

²⁰But Amaziah would not listen. God caused this to happen. He planned to let Jehoash of Israel defeat Judah. This was because Judah asked for help from the gods of Edom. ²¹So Jehoash king of Israel went to attack. He and Amaziah king of Judah faced each other in battle at Beth Shemesh in Judah. ²²Israel defeated Judah. Every man of Judah ran away to his home. ²³At Beth Shemesh Jehoash king of Israel captured Amaziah king of Judah. (Amaziah was the son of Joash, who was the son of Ahaziah.) Then Jehoash brought him to Jerusalem. Jehoash broke down the wall of Jerusalem from the Gate of Ephraim to the Corner Gate. This part of the wall was about 600 feet long. ²⁴Then he took all the gold and silver and everything in the Temple^d of God. Obed-Edom had taken care of these things. Jehoash also took the treasures from the king's palace. Then he took some hostages and returned to Samaria.

²⁵Amaziah son of Joash was king of Judah. He lived 15 years after Jehoash king of Israel died. Jehoash was the son of Jehoahaz. ²⁶The other things Amaziah did as king, from the beginning to the end, are written down. They are in the book of the kings of Judah and Israel. ²⁷When Amaziah stopped obeying the Lord, the people in Jerusalem made plans against him. So he ran away to the town of Lachish. But they sent men after him to Lachish and killed him there. ²⁸They brought his body back on horses. And he was buried with his ancestors in Jerusalem.

26 Then all the people of Judah chose Uzziah^n to be king. He became king in place of Amaziah, his father. Uzziah was 16 years old. ²He rebuilt the town of Elath and made it part of Judah again. He did this after Amaziah died.

³Uzziah was 16 years old when he became king. And he ruled 52 years in Jerusalem. His mother's name was Jecoliah, and she was from Jerusalem. ⁴He did what the Lord said was right. He obeyed God just as his father Amaziah had done. ⁵Uzziah obeyed God while Zechariah was alive. Zechariah taught Uzziah how to respect and obey God. As long as Uzziah obeyed the Lord, God gave him success.

⁶Uzziah fought a war against the Philistine people. He tore down the walls around their towns of Gath, Jabneh and Ashdod. He built new towns near Ashdod and in other places among the Philistines. ⁷God helped Uzziah fight the Philistines, the Arabs living in Gur Baal and the Meunites. ⁸The Ammonites made payments Uzziah demanded. Uzziah was very powerful. So his name became famous all the way to the border of Egypt.

⁹Uzziah built towers in Jerusalem and made them strong. He built them at the Corner Gate, the Valley Gate and where the wall turned. ¹⁰He also built towers in the desert and dug many wells. He had many cattle on the western mountain slopes and in the plains. He had people who worked his fields and vineyards. They worked in the hills and in the fertile lands. Uzziah loved the land.

¹¹He had an army of trained soldiers. They were counted and put in groups by Jeiel the royal assistant and Maaseiah the officer. Hananiah, one of the king's commanders, was their leader. ¹²There were 2,600 leaders over the soldiers. ¹³They were in charge of an army of 307,500 men. The army fought with great power. And they helped the king against the enemy. ¹⁴Uzziah gave his army shields, spears, helmets, armor, bows and stones for their slings. ¹⁵In Jerusalem Uzziah made devices that were invented by clever men. These devices were put on the towers and corners of the city walls. They were used to shoot arrows and large rocks. So Uzziah became famous in faraway places. He had much help until he became powerful.

¹⁶But when Uzziah became strong, his pride caused him to be destroyed. He was unfaithful to the Lord his God. He went into the Temple^d of the Lord to burn incense^d on the altar for incense. ¹⁷Azariah and 80 other brave priests who served the Lord followed Uzziah into the Temple. ¹⁸They told Uzziah he

26:1 **Uzziah** Also called Azariah in 2 Kings.

was wrong. They said to him, "You don't have the right to burn incense to the Lord. Only the priests, Aaron's descendants,[d] should burn the incense. They have been made holy for the Lord to do this special duty. Leave this holy place. You have been unfaithful to God. The Lord God will not honor you for this."

¹⁹Uzziah was standing beside the altar for incense in the Temple of the Lord. He had in his hand a pan for burning incense. He was very angry with the priests. As he was standing in front of the priests, a harmful skin disease broke out on his forehead. ²⁰Azariah the leading priest and all the other priests looked at him. They could see the harmful skin disease on his forehead. So they hurried him out of the Temple. Uzziah rushed out, because the Lord had punished him. ²¹So King Uzziah had the skin disease until the day he died. He had to live in a separate house. He could not enter the Temple of the Lord. His son Jotham was in charge of the palace. He governed the people of the land.

²²The other things Uzziah did as king were written down by the prophet Isaiah. Isaiah son of Amoz wrote about Uzziah's rule from beginning to end. ²³Uzziah died and was buried near his ancestors in a graveyard that belonged to the kings. This was because people said, "He had a harmful skin disease." And his son Jotham became king in his place.

27 Jotham was 25 years old when he became king. He ruled 16 years in Jerusalem. His mother's name was Jerusha daughter of Zadok. ²Jotham did what the Lord said was right. He obeyed God just as his father Uzziah had done. But Jotham did not enter the Temple[d] of the Lord to burn incense[d] as his father had. But the people continued doing wrong. ³Jotham rebuilt the Upper Gate of the Temple of the Lord. He did much building on the wall at the place named Ophel. ⁴He also built towns in the hill country of Judah. And he built walled cities and towers in the forests.

⁵Jotham also fought the king of the Ammonite people. And Jotham defeated the Ammonites. So each year for three years they gave Jotham about 7,500 pounds of silver. They also gave him about 62,000 bushels of wheat and about 62,000 bushels of barley. ⁶Jotham became powerful because he always obeyed the Lord his God.

⁷The other things Jotham did while he was king and all his wars are written down. They are in the book of the kings of Israel and Judah. ⁸Jotham was 25 years old when he became king. And he ruled 16 years in Jerusalem. ⁹Jotham died and was buried in Jerusalem. And Jotham's son Ahaz became king in his place.

28 Ahaz was 20 years old when he became king. And he ruled 16 years in Jerusalem. He was not like his ancestor David. He did not do what the Lord said was right. ²Ahaz did the same things the kings of Israel had done. He made metal idols to worship Baal.[d] ³He burned incense[d] in the Valley of Ben Hinnom. He sacrificed his own sons by burning them in the fire. He did the same terrible sins as the other nations had done. And the Lord had forced these nations out of the land ahead of the Israelites. ⁴Ahaz offered sacrifices and burned incense at the places where false gods were worshiped. And he did this on the hills and under every green tree.

⁵So the Lord his God let the king of Aram defeat Ahaz. The Arameans defeated Ahaz and took many people of Judah as prisoners. The Arameans took them to Damascus.

The Lord also let Pekah king of Israel defeat Ahaz. Pekah's army killed many soldiers of Ahaz. ⁶Pekah was the son of Remaliah. Pekah's army killed 120,000 brave soldiers from Judah in one day. Pekah defeated them because they had left the Lord. He is the God their ancestors obeyed. ⁷Zicri was a warrior from Ephraim. He killed King Ahaz's son Maaseiah. He also killed Azrikam, the officer in charge of the palace and Elkanah, second in command to the king. ⁸The Israelite army captured 200,000 of their own relatives. They took women, sons and daughters and many valuable things from Judah. Then they carried them back to Samaria. ⁹But a prophet[d] of the Lord named Oded was there. He met the Israelite army when it returned to Samaria. He said to them, "The Lord is the God your ancestors obeyed. He let you defeat Judah because he was angry with those people. But God has seen the cruel way you killed them. ¹⁰Now you plan to make the people of Judah and Jerusalem your slaves. But you also have sinned against the Lord your God. ¹¹Now listen to me. Send back your brothers and sisters whom you captured. Do this because the Lord is very angry with you."

¹²Then some of the leaders in Israel met the Israelite soldiers coming home from war. These leaders were Azariah son of Jehohanan, Berekiah son of Meshillemoth, Jehizkiah son of Shallum and Amasa son of Hadlai. ¹³They warned the soldiers, "Don't bring the prisoners from Judah here. If you do, we will be guilty of sin. That will make our sin and guilt even worse. And our guilt is already so much that the Lord is angry with Israel."

¹⁴So the soldiers left the prisoners and valuable things in front of the officers and people there. ¹⁵The leaders who were named took the prisoners. These four men got the clothes that the Israelite army had taken. And they gave them to these people who were naked. They gave the prisoners clothes, sandals, food, drink and medicine. They put the weak prisoners on donkeys. Then they took them back to their families in Jericho, the city of palm trees. Then they returned home to Samaria.

¹⁶⁻¹⁷At that same time the Edomites came again. They attacked Judah and carried away prisoners. So King Ahaz asked the king of Assyria for help. ¹⁸The Philistines also robbed the towns in the western mountain slopes and in southern Judah. They captured the towns of Beth Shemesh, Aijalon, Gederoth, Soco, Timnah and Gimzo. They also captured the villages around them. Then the Philistines lived in those towns. ¹⁹The Lord brought trouble on Judah because of Ahaz their king. Ahaz had caused the people of Judah to sin. And he had been unfaithful to the Lord. ²⁰Tiglath-Pileser king of Assyria came to Ahaz. But he gave Ahaz trouble instead of help. ²¹Ahaz took some valuable things from the Temple[d] of the Lord. He also took some from the king's palace and from the princes. Ahaz gave them to the king of Assyria, but it did not help.

²²In Ahaz's troubles he was even more unfaithful to the Lord. ²³He offered sacrifices to the gods the people of Damascus worshiped. These people had defeated him. So he thought, "The gods of the kings of Aram helped them. If I offer sacrifices to them, they will help me also." But this brought ruin to Ahaz and all Israel.

²⁴Ahaz gathered the things from the Temple of God and broke them into pieces. Then he closed the doors of the Temple of the Lord. He made altars and put them on every street corner in Jerusalem. ²⁵In every town in Judah, Ahaz made places for burning sacrifices to worship other gods. He made the Lord, the God his ancestors worshiped, very angry.

²⁶The other things Ahaz did as king, from the beginning to the end, are written down. They are in the book of the kings of Judah and Israel. ²⁷Ahaz died and was buried in the city of Jerusalem. But he was not buried in the graves of the kings of Israel. Ahaz's son Hezekiah became king in his place.

29 Hezekiah was 25 years old when he became king. And he ruled 29 years in Jerusalem. His mother's name was Abijah daughter of Zechariah. ²Hezekiah did what the Lord said was right. He did just as his ancestor David had done.

³Hezekiah opened the doors of the Temple[d] of the Lord and repaired them. He did this in the first month of the first year he was king. ⁴Hezekiah brought the priests and Levites together in a group. He met with them in the courtyard on the east side of the Temple. ⁵Hezekiah said, "Listen to me, Levites! Make yourselves ready for the Lord's service. And make the Temple of the Lord holy. He is the God your ancestors obeyed. Remove from the Temple the things that make it impure. ⁶Our ancestors were unfaithful to God. They did what the Lord said was wrong. They left the Lord. They stopped worshiping at the Temple where he lives. They rejected him. ⁷They shut the doors of the porch of the Temple. They let the fire go out in the lamps. They stopped burning incense[d] and offering burnt offerings in the holy place to the God of Israel. ⁸So the Lord became very angry with the people of Judah and Jerusalem. And he punished them. Other peoples are frightened and shocked by what the Lord did to Judah and Jerusalem. They insult the people of Judah. You know these things are true. ⁹That is why our ancestors were killed in battle. That is why our sons, daughters and wives were taken prisoner. ¹⁰So now I, Hezekiah, have decided to make an agreement with the Lord, the God of Israel. Then he will not be angry with us anymore. ¹¹My sons, don't waste any more time. The Lord chose you to serve him. You should serve him and burn incense to him."

¹²These are the Levites who started to

work. From the Kohathite family there were Mahath son of Amasai and Joel son of Azariah. From the Merarite family there were Kish son of Abdi and Azariah son of Jehallelel. From the Gershonite family there were Joah son of Zimmah and Eden son of Joah. [13]From Elizaphan's family there were Shimri and Jeiel. From Asaph's family there were Zechariah and Mattaniah. [14]From Heman's family there were Jehiel and Shimei. From Jeduthun's family there were Shemaiah and Uzziel.

[15]These Levites gathered their brothers together. Then they made themselves holy for service in the Temple. They obeyed the king's command that had come from the Lord. They went into the Temple of the Lord to purify it. [16]The priests went into the Temple of the Lord to purify it. They took out all the unclean[d] things they found in the Temple of the Lord. And they put them in the Temple courtyard. Then the Levites took these things out to the Kidron Valley. [17]They made the Temple holy for the Lord's service. They began on the first day of the first month. On the eighth day of the month, they came to the porch of the Temple. For eight more days they made the Temple of the Lord holy. They finished on the sixteenth day of the first month.

[18]Then they went to Hezekiah. They said to him, "We have purified all the Temple of the Lord. We have purified the altar for burnt offerings and its things. We have purified the table for the holy bread and all its things. [19]When Ahaz was king, he was unfaithful to God. He removed some things from the Temple. But we have put them back and made them holy for the Lord. They are now in front of the Lord's altar."

[20]Early the next morning King Hezekiah gathered the leaders of the city. They went up to the Temple of the Lord. [21]They brought seven bulls, seven male sheep, seven male lambs and seven male goats. These animals were an offering to remove the sin of the people and the kingdom of Judah. And this offering made the Temple ready for service to God. King Hezekiah commanded the priests to offer these animals on the Lord's altar. The priests were from the family of Aaron. [22]So the priests killed the bulls. Then they sprinkled the bulls' blood on the altar. They killed the male sheep and sprinkled their blood on the altar. Then they killed the lambs. And

they sprinkled the lambs' blood on the altar. [23]Then the priests brought the male goats before the king and the people there. The goats were for the sin offering. The king and the people put their hands on the goats. [24]Then the priests killed the goats. They made a sin offering with the goats' blood on the altar. They did this to remove the sins of the Israelites so they would belong to the Lord. The king had said that the burnt offering and sin offering should be made for all Israel.

[25]King Hezekiah put the Levites in the Temple of the Lord with cymbals, harps and lyres.[d] He did this as David, Gad and Nathan had commanded. (Gad was the king's seer,[d] and Nathan was a prophet.[d]) This command came from the Lord through his prophets. [26]So the Levites stood ready with David's instruments of music. And the priests stood ready with their trumpets.

[27]Then Hezekiah gave the order to sacrifice the burnt offering on the altar. When the burnt offering began, the singing to the Lord also began. The trumpets were blown. And the musical instruments of David king of Israel were played. [28]All the people worshiped, the singers sang, and the trumpet players blew their trumpets. They did this until the burnt offering was finished.

[29]When the sacrifices were finished, King Hezekiah and everyone with him bowed down and worshiped. [30]King Hezekiah and his officers ordered the Levites to praise the Lord. They were to use the words David and Asaph the seer used. They praised God with joy. And they bowed down and worshiped.

[31]Then Hezekiah said, "Now you people of Judah have given yourselves to the Lord. Come near to the Temple of the Lord. Bring sacrifices and offerings to show thanks to the Lord." So the people brought sacrifices and offerings to show thanks to the Lord. Anyone who wanted to also brought burnt offerings. [32]For burnt offerings they brought a total of 70 bulls, 100 male sheep and 200 lambs. All these animals were sacrificed as burnt offerings to the Lord. [33]The offerings made holy for the Lord totaled 600 bulls and 3,000 sheep and goats. [34]There were not enough priests to skin all the animals for the burnt offerings. So their relatives the Levites helped them. They helped until the work was finished and other priests could be made holy for the Lord's service. The

Levites had been more careful to make themselves holy for the Lord's service than the priests. [35]There were many burnt offerings. With them were the fat of fellowship offerings and drink offerings. So the service in the Temple of the Lord began again. [36]And Hezekiah and the people were very happy. They were happy that God had made it happen so quickly for his people.

30 King Hezekiah sent messages to all the people of Israel and Judah. He also wrote letters to the people of Ephraim and Manasseh. Hezekiah invited all these people to come to the Temple[d] of the Lord in Jerusalem. There they could celebrate the Passover[d] for the Lord, the God of Israel. [2]King Hezekiah, his officers and all the people in Jerusalem agreed to celebrate the Passover in the second month. [3]They could not celebrate it at the normal time. This was because not enough priests had made themselves ready to serve the Lord. And the people had not gathered yet in Jerusalem. [4]This plan satisfied King Hezekiah and all the people. [5]So they made an announcement everywhere in Israel, from Beersheba to Dan.[n] They told the people to come to Jerusalem. There they would celebrate the Passover for the Lord, the God of Israel. For a long time most of the people had not celebrated the Passover as the law commanded. [6]So the messengers took letters from the king and his officers all through Israel and Judah. This is what the letters said:

People of Israel, come back to obeying the Lord. He is the God that Abraham, Isaac and Israel obeyed. Then God will come back to you who are still alive. You have escaped from the kings of Assyria. [7]Don't be like your ancestors or your relatives. They turned against the Lord, the God their fathers obeyed. So the Lord caused other people to be disgusted with them. You know this is true. [8]Don't be stubborn as your ancestors were. Obey the Lord willingly. Come to the Temple, which the Lord has made holy for his service forever. Serve the Lord your God. Then he will not be angry with you. [9]Come back and obey the Lord. Then the people who captured your relatives and children will be kind to them. They will let them return to this land. The Lord your God is kind and merciful. He will not turn away from you if you come back to him.

[10]The messengers went to every town in Ephraim and Manasseh. They went all the way to Zebulun. But the people laughed at the messengers and made fun of them. [11]But some men from Asher, Manasseh and Zebulun were sorry for what they had done and went to Jerusalem. [12]And God caused all the people of Judah to agree to obey King Hezekiah and his officers. Their command had come from the Lord.

[13]A large crowd came together in Jerusalem to celebrate the Feast[d] of Unleavened Bread. This was in the second month. [14]The people removed the altars and incense[d] altars to false gods in Jerusalem. And they threw them into the Kidron Valley.

[15]They killed the Passover lamb on the fourteenth day of the second month. The priests and the Levites were ashamed. So they made themselves holy for the Lord. They brought burnt offerings into the Temple of the Lord. [16]They took their regular places in the Temple as the Teachings of Moses the man of God commanded. The Levites gave the blood of the sacrifices to the priests. Then the priests sprinkled the blood on the altar. [17]Many people in the crowd had not made themselves holy for the Lord. So they were not permitted to kill the Passover lambs. So the Levites were responsible for killing the Passover lambs for everyone who was not clean.[d] The Levites made each lamb holy for the Lord. [18-19]Many people from Ephraim, Manasseh, Issachar and Zebulun had not purified themselves for the feast. But they ate the Passover even though it was against the law. So Hezekiah prayed for them. He said, "Lord, you are good. You are the Lord, the God our ancestors obeyed. Please forgive everyone who tries to obey you. Forgive them even if they did not make themselves clean as the rules of the Temple command." [20]The Lord listened to Hezekiah's prayer, and he healed the people. [21]The Israelites in Jerusalem celebrated the Feast of Unleavened Bread for seven days. And they were very happy. The Levites and priests praised the Lord every day with loud music. [22]Some of

---

30:5 Beersheba to Dan Dan was the city farthest north in Israel. Beersheba was the city farthest south. So this means all the people of Israel.

the Levites understood well how to do their service for the Lord. And Hezekiah encouraged them. The people ate the feast for seven days. And they offered fellowship offerings. They praised the Lord, the God their ancestors worshiped.

²³Then all the people agreed to stay seven more days. So they celebrated the Passover with joy for seven more days. ²⁴Hezekiah king of Judah gave 1,000 bulls and 7,000 sheep to the people. The officers gave 1,000 bulls and 10,000 sheep to the people. Many priests made themselves holy for the Lord. ²⁵All the people of Judah, the priests, the Levites, those who came from Israel, the foreigners from Israel and the foreigners living in Judah were very happy. ²⁶There was much joy in Jerusalem. There had not been a celebration like this since Solomon's time. He was the son of David and king of Israel. ²⁷The priests and Levites stood up and blessed the people. And God heard them because their prayer reached heaven, which is his holy home.

31 The Passover^d celebration was finished. All the Israelites in Jerusalem went out to the towns of Judah. There they smashed the stone pillars used to worship false gods. They cut down the Asherah^d idols. They destroyed the altars and places for worshiping false gods. They destroyed all of them in the areas of Judah, Benjamin, Ephraim and Manasseh. They destroyed everything used for worshiping the false gods. Then all the Israelites returned to their own towns and homes.

²King Hezekiah appointed groups of priests and Levites for their special duties. They were to offer burnt offerings and fellowship offerings. They were to worship and to give thanks and praise at the gates where the Lord lives. ³Hezekiah gave some of his own animals for the burnt offerings. Burnt offerings were given every morning and evening. They were also given on Sabbath^d days and during New Moons^d and other feasts commanded by the Lord's Teachings.

⁴Hezekiah commanded the people living in Jerusalem to give the priests and Levites the portion that belonged to them. Then the priests and Levites could give all their time to the Lord's Teachings. ⁵Soon the king's command went out to the Israelites. And they gave quickly and freely. They gave the first

portion of their grain, wine, oil and honey. They gave the first portion of everything they grew in their fields. They brought a large amount, one-tenth of everything. ⁶The men of Israel and Judah who lived in Judah also gave. They brought one-tenth of their cattle and sheep. And they brought one-tenth of the holy things that were given to the Lord their God. They put all these things in piles. ⁷The people began bringing their things in the third month. And they finished in the seventh month. ⁸Hezekiah and his officers came and saw the piles. Then they praised the Lord and his people, the people of Israel. ⁹Hezekiah asked the priests and Levites about the piles. ¹⁰Azariah was the leading priest from Zadok's family. He answered Hezekiah, "Since the people began to bring their offerings to the Temple^d of the Lord, we have had plenty to eat. We have had plenty left over. The Lord has blessed his people. So we have all this left over."

¹¹Then Hezekiah commanded the priests to prepare the storerooms in the Temple of the Lord. So this was done. ¹²Then the priests brought the offerings and the things given to the Lord. They also brought the tenth of everything the people had given. All these things were put in the storerooms. Conaniah the Levite was in charge of these things. Conaniah's brother Shimei was second to him. ¹³Conaniah and his brother Shimei were over these supervisors: Jehiel, Azaziah, Nahath, Asahel, Jerimoth, Jozabad, Eliel, Ismakiah, Mahath and Benaiah. King Hezekiah and Azariah the officer in charge of the Temple of God chose those men.

¹⁴Kore was in charge of the special gifts the people wanted to give to God. He was responsible for giving out the contributions made to the Lord and the holy gifts. Kore was the son of Imnah the Levite. Kore was the guard at the East Gate. ¹⁵Eden, Miniamin, Jeshua, Shemaiah, Amariah and Shecaniah helped Kore. They served well in the towns where the priests lived. They gave from what was collected to the other groups of priests. They gave both to the young and the old.

¹⁶These men also gave from what was collected to the males 3 years old and older. These were males who had their names in the Levite family histories. They were to enter the Temple of the Lord for their daily service. Each group

had its own responsibilities. [17]The priests were given their part of the collection. This was done by families, as listed in the family histories. The Levites 20 years old and older were given their part of the collection. This was done by their responsibilities and by their groups. [18]The Levites' babies, wives, sons and daughters also got part of the collection. This was done for all the Levites who were listed in the family histories. This was because the Levites always kept themselves ready to serve the Lord.

[19]Some of Aaron's descendants,[d] the priests, lived on the farmland near the towns. Some also lived in the towns. Men were chosen by name to give part of the collection to these priests. All the males and those named in the family histories of the Levites received part of the collection.

[20]This is what King Hezekiah did in Judah. He did what was good and right and obedient before the Lord his God. [21]Hezekiah tried to obey God in his service of the Temple of God. He tried to obey God's teachings and commands. He gave himself fully to his work for God. So he had success.

32 Hezekiah did all these things to serve the Lord. Sennacherib king of Assyria came to attack Judah. He and his army surrounded and attacked the strong, walled cities. He wanted to take them for himself. [2]Hezekiah knew that Sennacherib had come to Jerusalem to attack it. [3]So Hezekiah talked to his officers and army commanders. They decided to cut off the waters from the springs outside the city. So the officers and commanders helped Hezekiah. [4]Many people came to help. They cut off all the springs and the stream that flowed through the land. They said, "The king of Assyria will not find much water when he comes here." [5]Then Hezekiah made Jerusalem stronger. He rebuilt all the broken parts of the wall. And he built towers on the wall. He also built another wall outside the first one. And he made the area that was filled in on the east side of the old part of Jerusalem stronger. He made many weapons and shields.

[6]Hezekiah put army commanders over the people. He met with these commanders at the open place near the city gate. Hezekiah encouraged them, saying, [7]"Be strong and brave. Don't be afraid or worried because of the king of

Assyria or his large army. There is a greater power with us than with him. [8]He only has men, but we have the Lord our God. He will help us. He will fight our battles." The people were encouraged by the words of Hezekiah king of Judah.

[9]King Sennacherib of Assyria and all his army surrounded and attacked Lachish. Then he sent his officers to Jerusalem with a message. The message was for King Hezekiah of Judah and all the people of Judah in Jerusalem. This was the message:

[10]Sennacherib king of Assyria says this: "You have nothing to trust in to help you. It is no use for you to stay in Jerusalem under attack. [11]Hezekiah says to you, 'The Lord our God will save us from the king of Assyria.' But he is fooling you. If you stay in Jerusalem, you will die from hunger and thirst. [12]Hezekiah himself removed your Lord's places of worship and altars. He told you people of Judah and Jerusalem that you must worship and burn incense[d] on only one altar.

[13]"You know what my ancestors and I have done to all the people in other nations. The gods of those nations could not save their people from my power. [14]My ancestors destroyed those nations. None of their gods could save them from me. So your god cannot save you from my power. [15]Do not let Hezekiah fool you or trick you. Do not believe him. No god of any nation or kingdom has been able to save his people from me or my ancestors. Your god is even less able to save you from me."

[16]Sennacherib's officers said worse things against the Lord God and his servant Hezekiah. [17]King Sennacherib also wrote letters insulting the Lord, the God of Israel. This is what his letters said: "The gods of the other nations could not save their people from me. In the same way Hezekiah's god won't be able to save his people from me." [18]Then the king's officers shouted out in Hebrew. They called out to the people of Jerusalem who were on the city wall. The officers wanted to scare the people away so they could capture Jerusalem. [19]They said evil things about the gods the people of the world worshiped. They are only things people have made with their

hands. In the same way the officers said evil things about the God of Jerusalem.

[20]King Hezekiah and the prophet[d] Isaiah son of Amoz prayed to heaven about this. [21]Then the Lord sent an angel to the king of Assyria's camp. That angel killed all the soldiers, leaders and officers of the Assyrian army. So the king of Assyria returned to his own country in disgrace. He went into the temple of his god. There some of his own sons killed him with a sword.

[22]So the Lord saved Hezekiah and the people in Jerusalem. He saved them from Sennacherib king of Assyria and from all other people. The Lord took care of Hezekiah and the people of Jerusalem. [23]Many people brought gifts for the Lord to Jerusalem. They also brought valuable gifts to King Hezekiah of Judah. From then on all the nations respected Hezekiah.

[24]At that time Hezekiah became very sick. He was almost dead. He prayed to the Lord. And the Lord spoke to him and gave him a sign.[n] [25]But Hezekiah was proud. So he did not thank God for his kindness. So the Lord was angry with him and the people of Judah and Jerusalem. [26]But later Hezekiah and the people of Jerusalem were sorry and stopped being proud. So the Lord did not punish them while Hezekiah was alive.

[27]Hezekiah had many riches and much honor. He made treasuries for his silver, gold, gems, spices, shields and other valuable things. [28]Hezekiah built storage buildings for grain, new wine and oil. He built stalls for all the cattle and pens for the sheep. [29]He also built many towns. He had many flocks of sheep and herds of cattle. God gave Hezekiah much wealth.

[30]It was Hezekiah who cut off the upper pool of the Gihon spring. He made those waters flow straight down on the west side of the older part of Jerusalem. And Hezekiah was successful in everything he did. [31]But one time the leaders of Babylon sent messengers to Hezekiah. They asked him about a strange sign that had happened in the land. When they came, God left Hezekiah alone to test him. He wanted to know everything that was in Hezekiah's heart.[n]

[32]Hezekiah's love for the Lord and the other things he did as king are recorded. They are written in the vision of the prophet[d] Isaiah son of Amoz. This is in the book of the kings of Judah and Israel. [33]Hezekiah died and was buried on a hill. It is where the graves of David's ancestors are. All the people of Judah and Jerusalem honored Hezekiah when he died. And Hezekiah's son Manasseh became king in his place.

33 Manasseh was 12 years old when he became king of Judah. And he was king for 55 years in Jerusalem. [2]He did what the Lord said was wrong. He did the hated things the other nations had done. And the Lord had forced these nations out of the land ahead of Israel. [3]Manasseh's father, Hezekiah, had torn down the places where false gods were worshiped. But Manasseh rebuilt them. Manasseh also built altars for the Baal[d] gods and made Asherah[d] idols. He bowed down to the stars and worshiped them. [4]The Lord had said about the Temple,[d] "I will be worshiped in Jerusalem forever." But Manasseh built altars for false gods in the Temple of the Lord. [5]He built altars to worship the stars in the two courtyards of the Temple of the Lord. [6]He burned his sons as sacrifices in the Valley of Ben Hinnom. He practiced magic and witchcraft.[d] He told the future by explaining signs and dreams. He got advice from mediums[d] and fortune-tellers. He did many things the Lord said were wrong. And this made the Lord angry.

[7]He carved an idol and put it in the Temple of God. God had spoken to David and his son Solomon about the Temple. He had said, "I will be worshiped in this Temple and in Jerusalem forever. I have chosen Jerusalem from all the tribes[d] of Israel. [8]I will never again make the Israelites leave the land I gave to their ancestors. But they must obey everything I commanded them. They must obey all the teachings, rules and commands I gave them through Moses." [9]But Manasseh led the people of Judah and Jerusalem to do wrong. They did more evil than the nations the Lord had destroyed ahead of the Israelites.

[10]The Lord spoke to Manasseh and his people, but they did not listen. [11]So the Lord brought the king of Assyria's army

32:24, 31 sign See Isaiah 38:1-8. It tells the story about the sign and how the Lord gave Hezekiah 15 more years to live. **32:31 God . . . heart** See 2 Kings 20:12-19.

commanders to attack Judah. They captured Manasseh and put hooks in him. They put bronze chains on his hands. They made him their prisoner and took him to Babylon. [12]As Manasseh suffered, he begged the Lord his God for help. He became very sorry for what he had done before the God of his ancestors. [13]When Manasseh prayed, the Lord heard him and had pity for him. So the Lord let him return to Jerusalem and to his kingdom. Then Manasseh knew that the Lord is the true God.

[14]After that happened, Manasseh rebuilt the outer wall for Jerusalem. It was in the valley on the west side of the Gihon spring. It went to the entrance of the Fish Gate and around the hill of Ophel. He also made the wall higher. Then he put commanders in all the strong, walled cities in Judah.

[15]Manasseh removed the idols of other nations. And he took the idol out of the Temple of the Lord. He removed all the altars he had built on the Temple hill and in Jerusalem. And he threw them out of the city. [16]Then he set up the Lord's altar. And he sacrificed on it fellowship offerings and offerings to show thanks to the Lord. Manasseh commanded all the people of Judah to serve the Lord, the God of Israel. [17]The people continued to offer sacrifices at the places of worship. But their sacrifices were only to the Lord their God.

[18]The other things Manasseh did as king are written down. His prayer to his God is recorded. And what the seers[d] said to him in the name of the Lord, the God of Israel, is recorded. They are all in the book of the history of the kings of Israel. [19]Manasseh's prayer and God's pity for him are written down. Also all of Manasseh's sins and how he was unfaithful to the Lord are recorded. The places he built for worshiping false gods and for the Asherah[d] idols are recorded. He did all these things but later became sorry for them. They are all in the book of the seers. [20]Manasseh died and was buried in his palace. Then Manasseh's son Amon became king in his palace.

[21]Amon was 22 years old when he became king. And he was king for two years in Jerusalem. [22]He did what the Lord said was wrong. He did as his father Manasseh had done. Amon worshiped and offered sacrifices to all the carved idols Manasseh had made. [23]Amon was not sorry for what he did wrong before the Lord. He was not sorry as his father Manasseh had been. Instead, Amon sinned even more. [24]Amon's officers made plans against him and killed him in his palace. [25]But the people of Judah killed all those who had made plans to kill King Amon. And they made his son Josiah to be king in his place.

34 Josiah was eight years old when he became king. He ruled 31 years in Jerusalem. [2]He did what the Lord said was right. He did good things as his ancestor David had done. Josiah did not stop doing what was right.

[3]In his eighth year as king, Josiah began to obey the God his ancestor David had followed. This was while Josiah was still young. In his twelfth year as king, Josiah began to remove the false gods from Judah and Jerusalem. He destroyed the places for worshiping false gods. He removed the Asherah[d] idols and the wooden and metal idols. [4]The people tore down the altars for the Baal[d] gods as Josiah directed. Then Josiah cut down the incense[d] altars that were above them. He broke up the Asherah idols and the wooden and metal idols. He beat them into powder. Then he sprinkled the powder on the graves of the people who had offered sacrifices to these gods. [5]He burned the bones of their priests on their own altars. So Josiah removed idol worship from Judah and Jerusalem. [6]He did the same for the towns in the areas of Manasseh, Ephraim and Simeon. He did this all the way to Naphtali. And he did the same for the ruins near these towns. [7]Josiah broke down the altars and Asherah idols. Then he beat the idols into powder. He cut down all the incense altars in all of Israel. Then he went back to Jerusalem.

[8]In Josiah's eighteenth year as king, he made Judah and the Temple[d] pure again. He sent Shaphan son of Azaliah, Maaseiah the city leader and Joah son of Joahaz the recorder. They were to repair the Temple of the Lord, the God of Josiah. [9]These men went to Hilkiah the high priest. They gave him the money the people had given for the Temple of God. The Levite doorkeepers had collected this money from the people of Manasseh, Ephraim and all the Israelites who were left alive. They also collected this money from all the people of Judah, Benjamin and Jerusalem. [10]Then the Levites gave it to the men who directed the work on the Temple of the Lord. And these supervisors paid the

workers that rebuilt and repaired the Temple. [11]They gave money to carpenters and builders to buy cut rocks and wood. The wood was used to rebuild the buildings and to make beams for them. The kings of Judah had let the buildings become ruins. [12]The men did their work well. Their supervisors were Jahath, Obadiah, Zechariah and Meshullam. Jahath and Obadiah were Levites from the family of Merari. Zechariah and Meshullam were from the family of Kohath. These Levites were all skilled musicians. [13]They were in charge of the workers who carried things and all the other workers. Some Levites worked as secretaries, officers and doorkeepers.

[14]The Levites brought out the money that was in the Temple[d] of the Lord. As they were doing this, Hilkiah the priest found the Book of the Lord's Teachings. These teachings had been given through Moses. [15]Hilkiah said to Shaphan the royal assistant, "I've found the Book of the Teachings. It was in the Temple of the Lord!" He gave it to Shaphan.

[16]Then Shaphan took the book to the king and reported to Josiah: "Your officers are doing everything you told them to do. [17]They have paid out the money that was in the Temple of the Lord. They have given it to the supervisors and the workers." [18]Then Shaphan the royal assistant told the king, "Hilkiah the priest has given me a book." And Shaphan read from the book to the king.

[19]The king heard the words of the Teachings. Then he tore his clothes to show how upset he was. [20]He gave these orders to Hilkiah, Ahikam son of Shaphan. He also gave them to Acbor son of Micaiah, Shaphan and Asaiah. Shaphan was the royal assistant. And Asaiah was the king's servant. These were the orders: [21]"Go and ask the Lord about the words in the book that was found. Ask for me and for the people who are left alive in Israel and Judah. The Lord is very angry with us because our ancestors did not obey the Lord's word. They did not do everything this book says to do."

[22]So Hilkiah and those the king sent with him left. They went to talk to Huldah the prophetess.[d] She was the wife of Shallum son of Tikvah, the son of Harhas. Harhas took care of the king's clothes. Huldah lived in Jerusalem, in the new area of the city.

[23]She said to them, "This is what the Lord, the God of Israel, says: Tell the man who sent you to me, [24]'This is what the Lord says: I will bring trouble to this place and to the people living here. I will bring all the curses that are written in the book that was read to the king of Judah. [25]The people of Judah have left me. They have burned incense[d] to other gods. They have made me angry by all the bad things they have made. So I will punish them in my anger. My anger will not be stopped.' [26]Tell the king of Judah who sent you to ask the Lord, 'This is what the Lord, the God of Israel, says about the words you heard: [27]You heard my words against this place and its people. And you became sorry for what you had done. You became sorry in my presence. You tore your clothes to show how upset you were. And you cried in my presence. This is why I have heard you, says the Lord. [28]So I will let you die. You will be buried in peace. You won't see all the trouble that I will bring to this place and the people living here.'"

So they took her message back to the king.

[29]Then the king gathered all the older leaders of Judah and Jerusalem together. [30]He went up to the Temple of the Lord. All the men from Judah and the people from Jerusalem went with him. The priests and the Levites and all the people—from the most important to the least important—went with him. He read to them all the words in the Book of the Agreement. That book was found in the Temple of the Lord. [31]Then the king stood by his pillar. He made an agreement in the presence of the Lord. He agreed to follow the Lord and to obey his commands, rules and laws with his whole being. And he agreed to obey the words of the agreement written in this book. [32]Then Josiah made all the people in Jerusalem and Benjamin promise to accept the agreement. The people of Jerusalem obeyed the agreement of God, the God their ancestors obeyed.

[33]And Josiah threw out the hated idols from all the land that belonged to the Israelites. He led everyone in Israel to serve the Lord their God. While Josiah lived, the people obeyed the Lord, the God their ancestors obeyed.

35 King Josiah celebrated the Passover[d] to the Lord in Jerusalem. The Passover lamb was killed on the fourteenth day of the first month. [2]Josiah chose the priests to do their duties. And he encouraged them as they served in the Temple[d] of the Lord. [3]The Levites taught the Israelites and were made holy for service to the Lord. Josiah said to them: "When David's son Solomon was king of Israel, he built the Temple. Put the Holy Box[d] in that Temple. Do not carry it from place to place on your shoulders anymore. Now serve the Lord your God and his people the Israelites. [4]Prepare yourselves by your family groups for service. Do the jobs that King David and his son Solomon gave you to do.

[5]"Stand in the holy place with a group of the Levites. Do this for each family group of the people so you may help them. [6]Kill the Passover lambs. Make yourselves holy to the Lord. And prepare the lambs for your relatives, the people of Israel. Do everything the Lord through Moses commanded us to do."

[7]Josiah gave the Israelites 30,000 sheep and goats to kill for the Passover sacrifices. He also gave them 3,000 cattle. They were all King Josiah's own animals.

[8]Josiah's officers also gave willingly to the people, the priests and the Levites. Hilkiah, Zechariah and Jehiel were the officers in charge of the Temple. They gave the priests 2,600 lambs and goats and 300 cattle for Passover sacrifices. [9]Also Conaniah, his brothers Shemaiah and Nethanel, and Hashabiah, Jeiel and Jozabad gave the Levites animals. They gave 5,000 sheep and goats and 500 cattle for Passover sacrifices. These men were leaders of the Levites.

[10]When everything was ready for the Passover service, the priests and Levites went to their places. This is what the king had commanded. [11]The Passover lambs were killed. Then the Levites skinned the animals and gave the blood to the priests. The priests sprinkled the blood on the altar. [12]Then they gave the animals for the burnt offerings to the different family groups. This was done so the burnt offerings could be offered to the Lord as the Law of Moses taught. They also did this with the cattle. [13]The Levites roasted the Passover sacrifices over the fire as they were commanded. And they boiled the holy offerings in pots, kettles and pans. Then they quickly gave the meat to the people. [14]After this was finished, the Levites prepared meat for themselves and for the priests. The priests were the descendants[d] of Aaron. The priests worked until night, offering the burnt offerings and burning the fat of the sacrifices.

[15]The Levite singers were from Asaph's family. They stood in the places King David had chosen for them. They were Asaph, Heman and Jeduthun, the king's seer.[d] The gatekeepers at each gate did not have to leave their places. This was because their fellow Levites had prepared everything for them for the Passover.

[16]So everything was done that day for the worship of the Lord. And it was done as King Josiah commanded. The Passover was celebrated, and the burnt offerings were offered on the Lord's altar. [17]The Israelites who were there celebrated the Passover and the Feast[d] of Unleavened Bread for seven days. [18]The Passover had not been celebrated like this in Israel since the prophet[d] Samuel was alive. None of the kings of Israel had ever celebrated a Passover like this. King Josiah, the priests and the Levites celebrated it. And the people of Judah and Israel who were there with the people of Jerusalem celebrated it. [19]This Passover was celebrated in the eighteenth year Josiah was king.

[20]So Josiah did all this for the Temple.[d] After this, King Neco of Egypt led an army to attack Carchemish. It was a town on the Euphrates River. And Josiah marched out to fight against Neco. [21]But Neco sent messengers to Josiah. They said, "King Josiah, there should not be war between us. I did not come to fight you, but my enemies. God told me to hurry, and he is on my side. So don't fight God, or he will destroy you."

[22]But Josiah did not go away. He wore different clothes so no one would know who he was. He refused to listen to what Neco said at God's command. So Josiah went to fight on the plain of Megiddo. [23]In the battle King Josiah was shot by arrows. He told his servants, "Take me away. I am badly wounded." [24]So they took him out of his chariot. And they put him in another chariot he had brought to the battle. Then they took him to Jerusalem where he died. He was buried in the graves where his ancestors were buried. All the people of Judah and Jerusalem were very sad because he was dead.

[25]Jeremiah wrote some sad songs about Josiah. Even to this day all the men and women singers remember and

honor Josiah with these songs. It became a custom in Israel to sing these songs. They are written in the collection of sad songs.

²⁶⁻²⁷The other things Josiah did as king, from the beginning to the end, are written down. They are in the book of the kings of Israel and Judah. It tells how he loved the Lord and obeyed the Lord's teachings.

36 The people of Judah chose Josiah's son Jehoahaz. They made him king in Jerusalem in his father's place.

²Jehoahaz was 23 years old when he became king. And he was king in Jerusalem for three months. ³Then King Neco of Egypt made Jehoahaz no longer a king in Jerusalem. Neco made the people of Judah pay about 7,500 pounds of silver and about 75 pounds of gold. ⁴The king of Egypt made Jehoahaz's brother Eliakim the king of Judah and Jerusalem. Then Neco changed Eliakim's name to Jehoiakim. But Neco took Eliakim's brother Jehoahaz to Egypt.

⁵Jehoiakim was 25 years old when he became king. And he was king in Jerusalem for 11 years. He did what the Lord his God said was wrong. ⁶King Nebuchadnezzar of Babylon attacked Judah. He captured Jehoiakim and put bronze chains on him. Then Nebuchadnezzar took him to Babylon. ⁷Nebuchadnezzar took some of the things from the Temple^d of the Lord. And he took them to Babylon and put them in his own palace.

⁸The other things Jehoiakim did as king are written down. The hated things he did and everything he was guilty of doing are recorded. They are in the book of the kings of Israel and Judah. Jehoiakim's son Jehoiachin became king in his place.

⁹Jehoiachin was 18 years old when he became king of Judah. And he was king in Jerusalem for three months and ten days. He did what the Lord said was wrong. ¹⁰In the spring King Nebuchadnezzar sent some servants to get Jehoiachin. They took him and some valuable treasures from the Temple^d of the Lord to Babylon. Then Nebuchadnezzar made Jehoiachin's relative Zedekiah the king of Judah and Jerusalem.

¹¹Zedekiah was 21 years old when he became king of Judah. And he was king in Jerusalem for 11 years. ¹²Zedekiah did what the Lord his God said was wrong. The prophet^d Jeremiah spoke messages from the Lord. But Zedekiah did not obey.

¹³Zedekiah turned against King Nebuchadnezzar. Nebuchadnezzar had forced Zedekiah to promise to be loyal to him. And Zedekiah had promised, using God's name. But Zedekiah became stubborn. He refused to obey the Lord, the God of Israel. ¹⁴Also, all the leaders of the priests and the people of Judah became more wicked. They followed the evil example of the other nations. The Lord had made the Temple^d in Jerusalem holy. But the leaders made the Temple unholy.

¹⁵The Lord, the God of their ancestors, sent prophets^d again and again to warn his people. He did this because he had pity for them and for his Temple. ¹⁶But they made fun of God's prophets. They hated God's messages. So they refused to listen to the prophets. Finally God became so angry with his people that he could not be stopped. ¹⁷So God brought the king of Babylon to attack them. The king killed the young men even when they were in the Temple. He did not have mercy on the people. He killed both young men and women. He even killed the old men and those who were sick. God permitted Nebuchadnezzar to punish the people of Judah and Jerusalem. ¹⁸Nebuchadnezzar carried away to Babylon all the things from the Temple of God, both large and small. He took all the treasures from the Temple of the Lord and from the king and his officers. ¹⁹Nebuchadnezzar and his army set fire to God's Temple. They broke down Jerusalem's wall. And they burned all the palaces. They took or destroyed every valuable thing in Jerusalem.

²⁰Nebuchadnezzar took captive to Babylon the people who were left alive. And he forced them to be slaves for him and his descendants.^d They remained there as slaves until the Persian kingdom defeated Babylon. ²¹And so what the Lord had told Israel through the prophet Jeremiah happened. The Lord had said that place would be an empty wasteland for 70 years. This happened to make up for the years of Sabbath rests^n that the people had not kept.

²²It was the first year Cyrus was king

36:21 Sabbath rests The Law said that every seventh year the land was not to be farmed. See Leviticus 25:1-7.

of Persia. The Lord caused Cyrus to write an announcement and send it everywhere in his kingdom. This happened so the Lord's message spoken by Jeremiah would come true. [23]This is what Cyrus king of Persia says:

"The Lord, the God of heaven, has given all the kingdoms of the earth to me. And he has appointed me to build a Temple for him at Jerusalem in Judah. Now all of you who are God's people are free to go to Jerusalem. May the Lord your God be with you."

The Book of
EZRA

1 It was the first year Cyrus was king of Persia. The Lord caused Cyrus to write an announcement and send it everywhere in his kingdom. And he also put it in writing. This happened so the Lord's message spoken by Jeremiah would come true. The announcement said:

[2]This is what Cyrus king of Persia says:

The Lord, the God of heaven, has given all the kingdoms of the earth to me. And he has appointed me to build a Temple[d] for him at Jerusalem in Judah. [3]Now all of you who are God's people are free to go to Jerusalem. May your God be with you. And you may build the Temple of the Lord. He is the God of Israel, who is in Jerusalem. [4]Those who stay behind should support anyone who wants to go. Give them silver and gold, supplies and cattle. And give them special gifts for the Temple of God in Jerusalem.

[5]Then the family leaders of Judah and Benjamin got ready to go to Jerusalem. So did the priests and the Levites. They were going to Jerusalem to build the Temple of the Lord. God made all these people want to go. [6]All their neighbors helped them. They gave them things made of silver and gold, along with supplies, cattle and valuable gifts. And they gave them the special gifts for the Temple. [7]Also, King Cyrus brought out the bowls and pans that belonged in the Temple of the Lord. Nebuchadnezzar had taken them from Jerusalem. And he had put them in the temple of his own god. [8]Cyrus king of Persia had Mithredath the treasurer get them out. So he made a list of the things for Sheshbazzar the prince of Judah.

[9]There were 30 gold dishes, 1,000 silver dishes, 29 silver pans, [10]30 gold bowls, 410 matching silver bowls and 1,000 other pieces. [11]There was a total of 5,400 pieces of gold and silver. Sheshbazzar brought all these things along when the captives went from Babylon to Jerusalem.

2 These are the people of the area who returned from captivity. Nebuchadnezzar king of Babylon had taken them captive to Babylon. Now they returned to Jerusalem and Judah. Each one went back to his own town. [2]These people returned with Zerubbabel, Jeshua, Nehemiah, Seraiah, Reelaiah, Mordecai, Bilshan, Mispar, Bigvai, Rehum and Baanah.

These are the men from Israel: [3]the descendants[e] of Parosh—2,172; [4]the descendants of Shephatiah—372; [5]the descendants of Arah—775; [6]the descendants of Pahath-Moab (through the family of Jeshua and Joab)—2,812; [7]the descendants of Elam—1,254; [8]the descendants of Zattu—945; [9]the descendants of Zaccai—760; [10]the descendants of Bani—642; [11]the descendants of Bebai—623; [12]the descendants of Azgad—1,222; [13]the descendants of Adonikam—666; [14]the descendants of Bigvai—2,056; [15]the descendants of Adin—454; [16]the descendants of Ater (through the family of Hezekiah)—98; [17]the descendants of Bezai—323; [18]the descendants of Jorah—112; [19]the descendants of Hashum—223; [20]the descendants of Gibbar—95.

[21]These are the men from the town of Bethlehem—123; [22]from Netophah—56; [23]from Anathoth—128; [24]from Azmaveth—42; [25]from Kiriath Jearim, Kephirah and Beeroth—743; [26]from Ramah and Geba—621; [27]from Micmash—122; [28]from Bethel and Ai—223; [29]from Nebo—52; [30]from Magbish—156; [31]from the other town of Elam—1,254; [32]from Harim—320; [33]from Lod, Hadid and

Ono—725; [34] from Jericho—345; [35] from Senaah—3,630.

[36] These are the priests: the descendants of Jedaiah (through the family of Jeshua)—973; [37] the descendants of Immer—1,052; [38] the descendants of Pashhur—1,247; [39] the descendants of Harim—1,017.

[40] These are the Levites: the descendants of Jeshua and Kadmiel (through the family of Hodaviah)—74.

[41] These are the singers: the descendants of Asaph—128.

[42] These are the gatekeepers of the Temple:[d] the descendants of Shallum, Ater, Talmon, Akkub, Hatita and Shobai—139.

[43] These are the Temple servants: the descendants of Ziha, Hasupha, Tabbaoth, [44] Keros, Siaha, Padon, [45] Lebanah, Hagabah, Akkub, [46] Hagab, Shalmai, Hanan, [47] Giddel, Gahar, Reaiah, [48] Rezin, Nekoda, Gazzam, [49] Uzza, Paseah, Besai, [50] Asnah, Meunim, Nephussim, [51] Bakbuk, Hakupha, Harhur, [52] Bazluth, Mehida, Harsha, [53] Barkos, Sisera, Temah, [54] Neziah and Hatipha.

[55] These are the descendants of the servants of Solomon: the descendants of Sotai, Hassophereth, Peruda, [56] Jaala, Darkon, Giddel, [57] Shephatiah, Hattil, Pokereth-Hazzebaim and Ami.

[58] The Temple servants and the descendants of the servants of Solomon numbered 392.

[59] Some people came to Jerusalem from these towns: Tel Melah, Tel Harsha, Kerub, Addon and Immer. But they could not prove that their families came from the family of Israel. Here are their names and their number: [60] the descendants of Delaiah, Tobiah and Nekoda—652.

[61] And these priests could not prove that their families came from Israel: the descendants of Hobaiah, Hakkoz and Barzillai. (He had married a daughter of Barzillai from Gilead and was called by her family name.)

[62] These people searched for their family records. But they could not find them. So they could not be priests because they were thought to be unclean.[d]

[63] The governor ordered them not to eat any of the food offered to God. First a priest had to settle this matter by using the Urim and Thummim.[d]

[64] The total number of those who returned was 42,360. [65] This is not counting their 7,337 male and female servants. They also had 200 men and women sing-

ers with them. [66] They had 736 horses, 245 mules, [67] 435 camels and 6,720 donkeys.

[68] That group arrived at the Temple of the Lord in Jerusalem. Some of the leaders of families gave special offerings. Those offerings were given to rebuild the Temple of God. It would be on the same site as before. [69] Those people gave as much as they could to the treasury. It was to rebuild the Temple. They gave about 1,100 pounds of gold, about 6,000 pounds of silver and 100 pieces of clothing for the priests.

[70] All the Israelites settled in their hometowns. The priests, Levites, singers, gatekeepers and temple servants, along with some of the other people, settled in their own towns.

3 By the seventh month, the Israelites were settled in their hometowns. They met together in Jerusalem. [2] Then Jeshua son of Jozadak and his fellow priests joined Zerubbabel son of Shealtiel. They began to build the altar of the God of Israel. That's where they offered burnt offerings just as it is written in the Teachings of Moses. Moses was the man of God. [3] They were afraid of the people living around them. But they still built the altar where it had been before. They offered burnt offerings on it to the Lord morning and evening. [4] Then, to obey what was written, they celebrated the Feast[d] of Shelters. They offered the right number of sacrifices for each day of the festival. [5] After the Feast of Shelters, they had regular sacrifices every day. They had sacrifices for the New Moon[d] and all the festivals commanded by the Lord. Also there were special offerings brought as gifts to the Lord. [6] On the first day of the seventh month they began to bring burnt offerings to the Lord. But the foundation of the Lord's Temple[d] had not yet been laid.

[7] Then they gave money to the stoneworkers and carpenters. They also gave food, wine and oil to the cities of Sidon and Tyre. This was so they would float cedar logs from Lebanon to the seacoast town of Joppa. Cyrus king of Persia had given permission for this.

[8] It was in the second year after their arrival at the Temple[d] of God in Jerusalem. In the second month Zerubbabel and Jeshua began the work. So did the rest of their fellow priests and Levites. And all who had returned from captivity to Jerusalem began to work. They chose Levites 20 years old and older to be in

charge of the building of the Temple of the Lord. [9]These men were in charge of the work of building the Temple of God: Jeshua and his sons and brothers; Kadmiel and his sons who were the descendants of Hodaviah; and the sons of Henadad and their sons and brothers. They were all Levites.

[10]The builders finished laying the foundation of the Temple of the Lord. Then the priests, dressed in their robes, got trumpets. And the Levites, the sons of Asaph, had cymbals. They all took their places. They praised the Lord just as David king of Israel had said to do. [11]With praise and thanksgiving, they sang to the Lord:

"He is good;
    his love for Israel continues
        forever."

And then all the people shouted loudly, "Praise the Lord! The foundation of his Temple has been laid." [12]But many of the older priests, Levites and family leaders cried aloud. They had seen the first Temple. Now they saw the foundation of this Temple. But most of the other people were shouting with joy. [13]The people made so much noise no one could tell the difference between the joyful shouting and the sad crying. It could be heard far away.

4 The people of Judah and Benjamin had enemies. They heard that the returned captives were building a Temple[d] for the Lord, the God of Israel. [2]So the enemies came to Zerubbabel and the leaders of the families. The enemies said, "Let us help you build. We are like you. We want to worship your God. We have been offering sacrifices to him since the time of Esarhaddon. He was king of Assyria, and he brought us here."

[3]But Zerubbabel, Jeshua and the leaders of Israel answered, "No. You people will not help us build a Temple to our God. We will build it ourselves. It is for the Lord, the God of Israel. This is what King Cyrus, the king of Persia, commanded us to do."

[4]Then the people around them tried to discourage the people of Judah. They tried to make them afraid to build. [5]Their enemies hired others to delay the building plans. This went on during the time Cyrus was king of Persia. And it continued to the time Darius was king of Persia.

[6]When Xerxes became king, those enemies wrote a letter against the people of Judah and Jerusalem.

[7]Later Artaxerxes became king of Persia. Then Bishlam, Mithredath, Tabeel and those with them wrote a letter to Artaxerxes. The letter was written in the Aramaic language.

[8]Also Rehum the governor and Shimshai the governor's assistant wrote a letter. It was to Artaxerxes the king. And it was against Jerusalem. It said:

[9]This letter is from Rehum the governor, Shimshai the assistant and others. They are judges and important officers. They are over the men who came from Tripolis, Persia, Erech and Babylon. They are over the Elamite people of Susa. [10]And they are over those whom the great and honorable Ashurbanipal forced out of their countries. He forced them to move and settle in the city of Samaria. And he forced them to settle in other places west of the Euphrates River.

[11](This is a copy of the letter they sent to Artaxerxes:)

To King Artaxerxes.
From your servants who live west of the Euphrates River.

[12]King Artaxerxes, you remember the Jews who came to us from you. You should know they have gone to Jerusalem. They are rebuilding that evil city that refuses to obey. They are fixing the walls and repairing the foundations of the buildings.

[13]Now, King Artaxerxes, you should know what could happen. If Jerusalem is built and its walls are fixed, Jerusalem will pay no taxes of any kind. Then the amount of money your government collects will be less. [14]Since we must be loyal to the government, we don't want to see the king dishonored. So we are writing to let the king know. [15]We suggest you search the records of the kings who ruled before you. You will find out that the city of Jerusalem refuses to obey. It makes trouble for kings and areas controlled by Persia. Since long ago it has been a place where disobedience started. That is why it was destroyed. [16]We want you to know this, King Artaxerxes. This city should not be rebuilt and its walls fixed. If it is, you will be left with nothing west of the Euphrates River.

[17]King Artaxerxes sent this answer:

To Rehum the governor and Shimshai the assistant. To all the people with them living in Samaria. And to those in other places west of the Euphrates.

Greetings.

[18]The letter you sent to us has been translated and read to me. [19]I ordered the records to be searched, and it was done. We found that Jerusalem has a long history of disobedience to kings. It has been a place of problems and trouble. [20]Jerusalem has had powerful kings. They have ruled over the whole area west of the Euphrates. Taxes of all kinds have been paid to them. [21]Now, give an order for those men to stop work. The city of Jerusalem will not be rebuilt until I say so. [22]Make sure you do this. If it continues, it will hurt the government.

[23]A copy of the letter that King Artaxerxes sent was read. It was read to Rehum and Shimshai the assistant and the others. Then they quickly went to the Jews in Jerusalem. They forced them to stop building.

[24]So the work on the Temple[d] of God in Jerusalem stopped. It stopped until the second year Darius was king of Persia.

5 Haggai and Zechariah son of Iddo were prophets.[d] They prophesied to the Jews in Judah and Jerusalem. They prophesied in the name of the God of Israel. [2]Then Zerubbabel son of Shealtiel and Jeshua son of Jozadak started working again. They worked to rebuild the Temple[d] of God in Jerusalem. The prophets of God were there, helping them.

[3]At that time Tattenai was the governor west of the Euphrates. He and Shethar-Bozenai and others went to the Jews. They asked, "Who gave you permission to rebuild this Temple and fix these walls?" [4]They also asked, "What are the names of these men working on this building?" [5]But their God was watching over the older leaders of the Jews. The builders were not stopped until a report could go to King Darius. And then his written answer had to be received.

[6]This is a copy of the letter that Tattenai, Shethar-Bozenai and the others sent to King Darius. Tattenai was governor west of the Euphrates River. The other people were important officers west of the Euphrates. [7]This is what the report they sent to him said:

To King Darius.

Greetings. May you have peace.

[8]King Darius, you should know that we went to the district of Judah. That is where the Temple of the great God is. The people there are building that Temple with large stones. They are putting timbers in the walls. The people are working very hard. And they are building very fast.

[9]We asked their older leaders, "Who gave you permission to rebuild this Temple and these walls?" [10]We also asked for their names. We wrote down the names of their leaders so you would know who they are.

[11]This is the answer they gave to us: "We are the servants of the God of heaven and earth. We are rebuilding the Temple that a great king of Israel built. He finished it many years ago. [12]But our ancestors made the God of heaven angry. So God let them be defeated by Nebuchadnezzar king of Babylon. He destroyed this Temple. And he took the people to Babylon as captives.

[13]"Later, Cyrus was in his first year as king of Babylon. He gave a special order for this Temple to be rebuilt. [14]And Cyrus brought out things from the temple in Babylon. They were the gold and silver bowls and pans that came from the Temple of God. Nebuchadnezzar had taken them from the Temple in Jerusalem. And he had put them in the temple in Babylon.

"Then King Cyrus gave them to Sheshbazzar. He had appointed Sheshbazzar as governor. [15]Cyrus said to him, 'Take these gold and silver bowls and pans. Put them back in the Temple in Jerusalem. And rebuild the Temple of God where it was.' [16]So Sheshbazzar came. He laid the foundations of the Temple of God in Jerusalem. From that day until now the work has been going on. But it is not yet finished."

[17]Now, if the king wishes, let a search be made. Search the royal records of Babylon to see if King Cyrus gave such an order. See if he gave an order to rebuild this Temple in Jerusalem. Then let the king write us and tell us what he has decided.

6 So King Darius gave an order to search the records. They were kept in the treasury in Babylon. [2] A scroll was found in the capital city, Ecbatana. It is in the area of Media. This is what was written on it:

Note:

[3] King Cyrus gave an order about the Temple[d] of God in Jerusalem. This was in the first year he was king. This was the order:

"Let the Temple be rebuilt. It will be a place to present sacrifices. Let its foundations be laid. The Temple should be 90 feet high and 90 feet wide. [4] It must have three layers of large stones, then one layer of timbers. The costs should be paid from the king's treasury. [5] The gold and silver things from the Temple of God should be put back in their places. Nebuchadnezzar took those things from the Temple in Jerusalem. And he brought them to Babylon. They are to be put back in the Temple of God in Jerusalem."

[6] Now then, I, Darius, give this order to you, Tattenai, governor west of the Euphrates. And I give it to Shethar-Bozenai and all the officers of that area. Stay away from there. [7] Do not bother or interrupt the work on that Temple of God. Let the governor of the Jews and the older Jewish leaders rebuild this Temple. Let them build it where it was before.

[8] Also, I order you to do this for those older leaders of the Jews. They are building this Temple. The cost of the building is to be fully paid from the royal treasury. The money will come from taxes collected west of the Euphrates River. Do this so the work will not stop. [9] Give those people anything they need. Give them young bulls, male sheep or male lambs for burnt offerings to the God of heaven. Give them wheat, salt, wine or olive oil. Give the priests in Jerusalem anything they ask for. Give it every day without fail. [10] Then they may offer sacrifices pleasing to the God of heaven. And they can pray for the life of the king and his sons.

[11] Also, I give this order: If anyone changes this order, a wood beam is to be pulled from his house. Drive one end of the beam through his body. And because he did this crime, make his house a pile of ruins. [12] God has chosen Jerusalem as the place he is to be worshiped. May he defeat any king or person who tries to change this order. May God destroy anyone who tries to destroy this Temple.

I, Darius, have given this order. Let it be obeyed quickly and carefully.

[13] So, Tattenai, the governor west of the Euphrates, Shethar-Bozenai and the others obeyed. They carried out King Darius' order quickly and carefully. [14] So the older Jewish leaders continued to build. And they were successful because of the preaching of Haggai the prophet[d] and Zechariah son of Iddo. They finished building the Temple[d] as the God of Israel had said. It was also done to obey the kings Cyrus, Darius and Artaxerxes of Persia. [15] The Temple was finished on the third day of the month Adar. It was the sixth year that Darius was king.

[16] Then the people of Israel celebrated. They gave the Temple to God to honor him. Everybody was happy: the priests, the Levites and the rest of the Jews who had returned from captivity. [17] This is how they gave the Temple to God for worshiping him: They offered 100 bulls, 200 male sheep and 400 male lambs as sacrifices. And as an offering to forgive the sins of all Israel, they offered 12 male goats. That is 1 goat for each tribe[d] in Israel. [18] Then they put the priests and the Levites into their separate groups. Each group had a certain time to serve God in the Temple at Jerusalem. This was done just as it is written in the Book of Moses.

[19] The Jews who returned from captivity celebrated the Passover.[d] This was on the fourteenth day of the first month. [20] The priests and Levites had made themselves clean.[d] The Levites killed the Passover lambs for all the Jews who had returned from captivity. They also did it for their relatives the priests and for themselves. [21] So all the people of Israel who returned from captivity ate the Passover lamb. So did those who had given up the unclean ways of their non-Jewish neighbors. They worshiped the Lord, the God of Israel. [22] For seven days they celebrated the Feast[d] of Unleavened Bread in a very joyful way. The Lord had made them happy by changing the mind of the King of Assyria. So the king had helped them in the work on the Temple of the God of Israel.

7After these things[n] during the rule of Artaxerxes king of Persia, Ezra came up from Babylon. Ezra was the son of Seraiah. Seraiah was the son of Azariah. Azariah was the son of Hilkiah. [2]Hilkiah was the son of Shallum. Shallum was the son of Zadok. Zadok was the son of Ahitub. [3]Ahitub was the son of Amariah. Amariah was the son of Azariah. Azariah was the son of Meraioth. [4]Meraioth was the son of Zerahiah. Zerahiah was the son of Uzzi. Uzzi was the son of Bukki. [5]Bukki was the son of Abishua. Abishua was the son of Phinehas. Phinehas was the son of Eleazar. Eleazar was the son of Aaron the high priest. [6]This Ezra came to Jerusalem from Babylon. He was a teacher. He knew the Teachings of Moses well. The Teachings had been given by the Lord, the God of Israel. Ezra received everything he asked for from the king. This was because the Lord his God was helping him. [7]In the seventh year of King Artaxerxes more Israelites came to Jerusalem. Among them were priests, Levites, singers, gatekeepers and Temple[d] servants.

[8]Ezra also arrived in Jerusalem. It was the fifth month of Artaxerxes' seventh year as king. [9]Ezra had left Babylon on the first day of the first month. And he arrived in Jerusalem on the first day of the fifth month. God was helping Ezra. [10]Ezra had worked hard to know and obey the Teachings of the Lord. He also taught the rules and commands of the Lord to the Israelites.

[11]King Artaxerxes had given a letter to Ezra. Ezra was a priest and teacher. He taught about the commands and laws the Lord gave Israel. This is a copy of the letter:

[12]From Artaxerxes, king of kings. To Ezra the priest, a teacher of the Law of the God of heaven.

Greetings.

[13]Now I give this order: Any Israelite in my kingdom who wishes may go with you to Jerusalem. This includes priests and Levites. [14]Ezra, you are sent by the king and the seven people who advise him. You are to ask about how Judah and Jerusalem are obeying the Law of your God, which you are carrying with you. [15]Also take with you the silver and gold the king and those who advise him have given

freely. It's for the God of Israel, whose Temple[d] is in Jerusalem. [16]Also take the silver and gold you receive from the area of Babylon. And take the offerings the Israelites and their priests have given as gifts to the Lord. They are for the Temple of their God in Jerusalem. [17]With this money buy bulls, male sheep and male lambs. Buy the grain offerings and drink offerings that go with those sacrifices. Then sacrifice them on the altar in the Temple of your God in Jerusalem.

[18]Then you and your fellow Jews may spend the silver and gold left over. Use it as you want and as God wishes. [19]Take to the God of Jerusalem all the things put in your care. They are for the worship in the Temple of your God. [20]And you may get anything else you need for the Temple of your God. Pay for it from the royal treasury.

[21]Now I, King Artaxerxes, give this order to all the men in charge of the treasury west of the Euphrates: Give Ezra anything he asks for right away. Ezra is a priest and a teacher of the Law of the God of heaven. [22]Give him up to 7,500 pounds of silver, 600 bushels of wheat, 600 gallons of wine and 600 gallons of olive oil. And give him as much salt as he wants. [23]Carefully give him whatever the God of heaven wants. Do it for the Temple of the God of heaven. We do not want God to be angry with the king and his sons. [24]Remember, you must not make these people pay taxes of any kind: priests, Levites, singers, gatekeepers, Temple servants and other workers in this Temple of God.

[25]And you, Ezra, use the wisdom you have from your God. Choose judges and lawmakers to rule the Jews west of the Euphrates. They know the laws of your God. And teach anyone who does not know them. [26]Whoever does not obey the law of your God or of the king must be punished. He will be killed or sent away. He will have his property taken away or be put in jail.

[27]Praise the Lord, the God of our ancestors. He caused the king to want to honor the Temple of the Lord in Jerusalem. [28]The Lord has shown me, Ezra, his love. He did this before the king, those who advise the king and the royal offi-

---

7:1 After these things There is a time period of about 60 years between chapters six and seven.

cers. The Lord my God was helping me. So I had courage. I gathered the leaders of Israel to return with me.

8 These are the leaders of the family groups who returned with me. And it is a listing of those who were with them. They came back from Babylon during the rule of King Artaxerxes.

²From the descendants[d] of Phinehas, there was Gershom.

From the descendants of Ithamar, there was Daniel.

From the descendants of David, there was Hattush ³of the descendants of Shecaniah.

From the descendants of Parosh, there was Zechariah. And 150 men came with him.

⁴From the descendants of Pahath-Moab, there was Eliehoenai son of Zerahiah, with 200 men.

⁵From the descendants of Zattu, there was Shecaniah son of Jahaziel, with 300 men.

⁶From the descendants of Adin, there was Ebed son of Jonathan, with 50 men.

⁷From the descendants of Elam, there was Jeshaiah son of Athaliah, with 70 men.

⁸From the descendants of Shephatiah, there was Zebadiah son of Michael, with 80 men.

⁹From the descendants of Joab, there was Obadiah son of Jehiel, with 218 men.

¹⁰From the descendants of Bani, there was Shelomith son of Josiphiah, with 160 men.

¹¹From the descendants of Bebai, there was Zechariah son of Bebai, with 28 men.

¹²From the descendants of Azgad, there was Johanan son of Hakkatan, with 110 men.

¹³From the descendants of Adonikam, these were the last ones: Eliphelet, Jeuel and Shemaiah. With them were 60 men.

¹⁴From the descendants of Bigvai, there were Uthai and Zaccur, with 70 men.

¹⁵I, Ezra, called all those people together at the canal. It flows toward Ahava. We camped there for three days. I checked all the people and the priests. But I did not find any Levites. ¹⁶So I called these leaders: Eliezer, Ariel, Shemaiah, Elnathan, Jarib, Elnathan, Nathan, Zechariah and Meshullam. And I called Joiarib and Elnathan, who were teachers. ¹⁷I sent those men to Iddo, the leader at Casiphia. I told them what to

say to Iddo and his relatives, who are the Temple[d] servants in Casiphia. I sent them to bring servants to us for the Temple[d] of our God. ¹⁸Our God was helping us. So Iddo's relatives gave us Sherebiah, a wise man from the descendants of Mahli. Mahli was the son of Levi. And Levi was the son of Israel. And they brought Sherebiah's sons and brothers. In all there were 18 men. ¹⁹And they brought to us Hashabiah and Jeshaiah from the descendants of Merari. And they also brought his brothers and nephews. In all there were 20 men. ²⁰They also brought 220 of the Temple servants. This is a group David and the officers had set up to help the Levites. All of those men were listed by name.

²¹There by the Ahava Canal, I announced we would all give up eating. We would make ourselves humble before our God. And we would ask God for a safe trip for ourselves, our children and all our possessions. ²²I was ashamed to ask the king for soldiers and horsemen. They could have protected us from enemies on the road. But we had said to the king, "Our God helps everyone who obeys him. But God is very angry with all who reject him." ²³So we gave up eating and prayed to our God about our trip. He answered our prayers.

²⁴Then I chose 12 of the priests who were leaders. They were Sherebiah and Hashabiah and 10 of their relatives. ²⁵I weighed the offering of silver and gold. And I weighed the things given for the Temple of our God. I gave them to the 12 priests I had chosen. The king, the people who advised him, his officers and all the Israelites there with us had given these things for the Temple. ²⁶I weighed out and gave them about 50,000 pounds of silver, about 7,500 pounds of silver objects and about 7,500 pounds of gold. ²⁷I gave them 20 gold bowls that weighed about 19 pounds. And I gave them 2 fine pieces of polished bronze that were as valuable as gold.

²⁸Then I said to the priests, "You and these things belong to the Lord for his service. The silver and gold are gifts to the Lord, the God of your ancestors. ²⁹Guard these things carefully. In Jerusalem, weigh them in front of the leading priests, Levites and the leaders of the family groups of Israel. Do this in the rooms of the Temple of the Lord."

³⁰So the priests and Levites took the silver, the gold and the special things that had been weighed out. They were to

Maaseiah, Mattaniah, Bezalel, Binnui and Manasseh.

[31]From the descendants of Harim, there were Eliezer, Ishijah, Malkijah, Shemaiah, Shimeon, [32]Benjamin, Malluch and Shemariah.

[33]From the descendants of Hashum, there were Mattenai, Mattattah, Zabad, Eliphelet, Jeremai, Manasseh and Shimei.

[34]From the descendants of Bani, there were Maadai, Amram, Uel, [35]Benaiah, Bedeiah, Keluhi, [36]Vaniah, Meremoth,

Eliashib, [37]Mattaniah, Mattenai and Jaasu.

[38]From the descendants of Binnui, there were Shimei, [39]Shelemiah, Nathan, Adaiah, [40]Macnadebai, Shashai, Sharai, [41]Azarel, Shelemiah, Shemariah, [42]Shallum, Amariah and Joseph.

[43]From the descendants of Nebo, there were Jeiel, Mattithiah, Zabad, Zebina, Jaddai, Joel and Benaiah.

[44]All these men had married non-Jewish women. And some of them had children by these wives.

The Book of
NEHEMIAH

1 These are the words of Nehemiah son of Hacaliah.

I, Nehemiah, was in the capital city of Susa. It was in the month of Kislev. This was in the twentieth year.[n] [2]One of my brothers named Hanani came from Judah. Some other men were with him. I asked them about the Jews who lived through the captivity. And I also asked about Jerusalem.

[3]They answered, "Nehemiah, those who are left from the captivity are back in the area of Judah. But they are in much trouble and are full of shame. The wall around Jerusalem is broken down. And its gates have been burned."

[4]When I heard these things, I sat down and cried for several days. I was sad and did not eat food. I prayed to the God of heaven. [5]I said, "Lord, God of heaven, you are the great God who is to be respected. You keep your agreement of love with those who love you and obey your commands. [6]Listen carefully. Look at me. Hear the prayer your servant is praying to you day and night. I am praying for your servants, the people of Israel. I confess the sins we Israelites have done against you. My father's family and I have sinned against you. [7]We have been wicked toward you. We have not obeyed the commands, rules and laws you gave your servant Moses.

[8]"Remember what you taught your servant Moses. You said, 'If you are unfaithful, I will scatter you among the nations. [9]But if you come back to me and obey my commands, I will gather your

people. I will gather them from the far ends of the earth. And I will bring them from captivity to where I have chosen to be worshiped.'

[10]"They are your servants and your people. You have saved them with your great strength and power. [11]Lord, listen carefully to my prayer. I am your servant. And listen to the prayers of your servants who love to honor you. Give me, your servant, success today. Allow this king to show kindness to me."

I was the one who served wine to the king.

2 It was the month of Nisan. It was in the twentieth year King Artaxerxes was king. He wanted some wine. So I took some and gave it to the king. I had not been sad in his presence before. [2]So the king said, "Why does your face look sad? You are not sick. Your heart must be sad."

Then I was very afraid. [3]I said to the king, "May the king live forever! My face is sad because the city where my ancestors are buried lies in ruins. And its gates have been destroyed by fire."

[4]Then the king said to me, "What do you want?"

First I prayed to the God of heaven. [5]Then I answered the king, "Send me to the city in Judah where my ancestors are buried. I will rebuild it. Do this if you are willing and if I have pleased you."

[6]The queen was sitting next to the king. He asked me, "How long will your trip take? When will you get back?" It

1:1 **twentieth year** This is probably referring to the twentieth year King Artaxerxes I ruled Persia.

pleased the king to send me. So I set a time.

⁷I also said to him, "If you are willing, give me letters for the governors west of the Euphrates River. Tell them to let me pass safely through their lands on my way to Judah. ⁸And may I have a letter for Asaph? He is the keeper of the king's forest. Tell him to give me timber. I will need it to make boards for the gates of the palace. It is by the Temple.ᵈ The wood is also for the city wall and the house I will live in." So the king gave me the letters. This was because God was showing kindness to me. ⁹So I went to the governors west of the Euphrates River. I gave them the king's letters. The king had also sent army officers and soldiers on horses with me.

¹⁰Sanballat the Horonite and Tobiah the Ammonite leader heard about this. They were upset that someone had come to help the Israelites.

¹¹I went to Jerusalem and stayed there three days. ¹²Then at night I started out with a few men. I had not told anyone what God had caused me to do for Jerusalem. There were no animals with me except the one I was riding.

¹³It was night. I went out through the Valley Gate. I rode toward the Dragon Well and the Trash Gate. I was inspecting the walls of Jerusalem. They had been broken down. And the gates had been destroyed by fire. ¹⁴Then I rode on toward the Fountain Gate and the King's Pool. But there was not enough room for the animal I was riding to get through. ¹⁵So I went up the valley at night. I was inspecting the wall. Finally, I turned and went back in through the Valley Gate. ¹⁶The officers did not know where I had gone or what I was doing. I had not yet said anything to the Jews, the priests, the important men or the officers. I had not said anything to any of the others who would do the work.

¹⁷Then I said to them, "You can see the trouble we have here. Jerusalem is a pile of ruins. And its gates have been burned. Come, let's rebuild the wall of Jerusalem. Then we won't be full of shame any longer." ¹⁸I also told them how God had been kind to me. And I told them what the king had said to me.

Then they answered, "Let's start rebuilding." So they began to work hard.

¹⁹But Sanballat the Horonite, Tobiah the Ammonite leader and Geshem the Arab heard about it. They made fun of us and laughed at us. They said, "What

are you doing? Are you turning against the king?"

²⁰But I answered them, "The God of heaven will give us success. We are God's servants. We will start rebuilding. But you have no share in Jerusalem. You have no claim or past right to it."

3 Eliashib the high priest and his fellow priests went to work. They rebuilt the Sheep Gate. They gave it to the Lord's service and set its doors in place. They worked as far as the Tower of the Hundred, and they gave it to the Lord's service. Then they went on to the Tower of Hananel. ²The men of Jericho built the part of the wall next to the priests. And Zaccur son of Imri built next to them.

³The sons of Hassenaah rebuilt the Fish Gate. They set the boards in place. And they put its doors, bolts and bars in place. ⁴Meremoth son of Uriah made repairs next to them. (Uriah was the son of Hakkoz.) Meshullam son of Berekiah worked next to Meremoth. (Berekiah was the son of Meshezabel.) And Zadok son of Baana worked next to Meshullam. ⁵The men from Tekoa made repairs next to them. But the leading men of Tekoa would not work under their supervisors.

⁶Joiada son of Paseah and Meshullam son of Besodeiah repaired the Old Gate. They set its boards in place. And they put its doors, bolts and bars in place. ⁷Next to them, men from Gibeon and Mizpah made repairs. Melatiah was from Gibeon, and Jadon was from Meronoth. These places were ruled by the governor west of the Euphrates River. ⁸Next to them, Uzziel son of Harhaiah made repairs. He was a goldsmith. And next to him, Hananiah made repairs. He was one of the people who made perfume. These men rebuilt Jerusalem as far as the Broad Wall. ⁹The next part of the wall was repaired by Rephaiah son of Hur. He was ruler of half of the district of Jerusalem. ¹⁰Next to him, Jedaiah son of Harumaph made repairs. He worked opposite his own house. And next to him, Hattush son of Hashabneiah made repairs. ¹¹Malkijah son of Harim and Hasshub son of Pahath-Moab repaired another part of the wall. And they repaired the Tower of the Ovens. ¹²Next to them, Shallum son of Hallohesh made repairs. He was ruler of half of the district of Jerusalem. His daughters helped him.

¹³Hanun and the people of Zanoah re-

paired the Valley Gate. They rebuilt it and put its doors, bolts and bars in place. They also repaired the 500 yards of the wall to the Trash Gate.

[14] Malkijah son of Recab repaired the Trash Gate. He was ruler of the district of Beth Hakkerem. He rebuilt that gate and put its doors, bolts and bars in place.

[15] Shallun son of Col-Hozeh repaired the Fountain Gate. He was ruler of the district of Mizpah. He rebuilt it and put a roof over it. And he put its doors, bolts and bars in place. He also repaired the wall of the Pool of Siloam. It is next to the King's Garden. He repaired the wall all the way to the steps. They went down from the older part of the city. [16] Next to Shallun, Nehemiah[n] son of Azbuk made repairs. He was ruler of half of the district of Beth Zur. He made repairs up to a place opposite the tombs of David. He made repairs as far as the man-made pool and the House of the Heroes.

[17] Next to him, the Levites made repairs. Some worked under Rehum son of Bani. Next to him, Hashabiah made repairs for his district. He was ruler of half of the district of Keilah. [18] Next to him, Binnui son of Henadad and his Levites made repairs. Binnui was the ruler of the other half of the district of Keilah. [19] Next to them, Ezer son of Jeshua worked. He was ruler of Mizpah. He repaired another part of the wall. He worked across from the way up to the storehouse for weapons. And he worked to the place where the wall turns. [20] Next to him, Baruch son of Zabbai worked very hard to repair another part of the wall. It went from the place where the wall turns to the entrance of the house of Eliashib. He was the high priest. [21] Next to him, Meremoth son of Uriah worked. (Uriah was the son of Hakkoz.) He repaired another part of the wall. It went from the entrance to Eliashib's house to the far end of it.

[22] Next to him worked the priests from the surrounding area. [23] Next to them, Benjamin and Hasshub made repairs in front of their own house. Next to them, Azariah son of Maaseiah made repairs beside his own house. (Maaseiah was the son of Ananiah.) [24] Next to him, Binnui son of Henadad repaired another part of the wall. It went from Azariah's house to the place where the wall turned. And it went to the corner. [25] Palal

son of Uzai worked across from the place where the wall turned. And he worked by the tower on the upper palace. That is near the courtyard of the king's guard. Next to Palal, Pedaiah son of Parosh made repairs. [26] The Temple[d] servants lived on the hill of Ophel. They made repairs as far as a point opposite the Water Gate. They worked toward the east and the tower that extends from the palace. [27] Next to them, the men of Tekoa made repairs. They worked on the wall from the great tower that extends from the palace to the wall of Ophel.

[28] The priests made repairs above the Horse Gate. Each worked in front of his own house. [29] Next to them, Zadok son of Immer made repairs across from his own house. Next to him, Shemaiah son of Shecaniah made repairs. He was the guard of the East Gate. [30] Next to him, Hananiah son of Shelemiah and Hanun, the sixth son of Zalaph, made repairs. They worked on another part of the wall. Next to them, Meshullam son of Berekiah made repairs. It was across from where he lived. [31] Next to him, Malkijah made repairs. He was one of the goldsmiths. He worked as far as the house of the Temple servants and the traders. That is across from the Inspection Gate. And he worked as far as the room above the corner of the wall. [32] The goldsmiths and the traders made repairs on another part of the wall. It was between the room above the corner of the wall and the Sheep Gate.

4 Sanballat heard we were rebuilding the wall. He was very angry, even furious. He made fun of the Jews. [2] He said to his friends and the army of Samaria, "What are these weak Jews doing? They think they can rebuild the wall. They think they will offer sacrifices. Maybe they think they can finish rebuilding it in only one day. They can't bring stones back to life. These are piles of trash and ashes."

[3] Tobiah the Ammonite was next to Sanballat. Tobiah said, "A fox could climb up on what they are building. Even it could break down their stone wall."

[4] I prayed, "Hear us, our God. We are hated. Turn the insults of Sanballat and Tobiah back on their own heads. Let them be captured and taken away like valuables that are stolen. [5] Do not hide their guilt. Do not take away their sins

3:16 Nehemiah This is a different Nehemiah than the one who wrote this book.

so you can't see them. The builders have seen them make you angry."

⁶So we rebuilt the wall until all of it went halfway up. The people were willing to work hard.

⁷But Sanballat, Tobiah, the Arabs, the Ammonites and the men from Ashdod were very angry. They heard that the repairs to Jerusalem's walls were continuing. And they heard that the holes in the wall were being closed. ⁸So they all made plans against Jerusalem. They planned to come and fight and stir up trouble. ⁹But we prayed to our God. And we appointed guards to watch for them day and night.

¹⁰The people of Judah said, "The workers are getting tired. There is too much dirt and trash. We cannot rebuild the wall."

¹¹And our enemies said, "The Jews won't know it or see us. But we will come among them and kill them. We will stop the work."

¹²Then the Jews who lived near our enemies came. They told us ten times, "Everywhere you turn, the enemy will attack us." ¹³So I put some of the people behind the lowest places along the wall. And I put some at the open places. I put families together with their swords, spears and bows. ¹⁴Then I looked around. I stood up and spoke to the important men, the leaders and the rest of the people. I said, "Don't be afraid of them. Remember the Lord. He is great and others are afraid of him. And fight for your brothers, your sons and daughters, your wives and your homes."

¹⁵Then our enemies heard that we knew about their plans. God had ruined their plans. So we all went back to the wall. Each person went back to his own work.

¹⁶From that day on, half my men worked on the wall. The other half was ready with spears, shields, bows and armor. The officers stood in back of the people of Judah ¹⁷who were building the wall. Those who carried materials did their work with one hand. They carried a weapon in the other hand. ¹⁸Each builder wore his sword at his side as he worked. The man who blew the trumpet to warn the people stayed next to me.

¹⁹Then I spoke to the important men, the leaders and the rest of the people. I said, "This is a very big job. We are spreading out along the wall. We are far apart. ²⁰So wherever you hear the sound

of the trumpet, assemble there. Our God will fight for us."

²¹So we continued to work. Half the men held spears. We worked from sunrise till the stars came out. ²²At that time I also said to the people, "Let every man and his helper stay inside Jerusalem at night. They can be our guards at night. And they can be workmen during the day." ²³Neither I, my brothers, my men nor the guards with me ever took off our clothes. Each person carried his weapon even when he went for water.

5 The men and their wives complained loudly against their fellow Jews. ²Some of them were saying, "We have many sons and daughters in our families. To eat and stay alive, we need grain."

³Others were saying, "We are borrowing money to get grain. There is not much food. We might not be able to pay back the money we've borrowed. Then we will have to pay with our fields, vineyards and homes."

⁴And still others were saying, "We are having to borrow money. We have to pay the king's tax on our fields and vineyards. ⁵We are just like our fellow Jews. Our sons are like their sons. But we have to sell our sons and daughters as slaves. Some of our daughters have already been sold. But there is nothing we can do. Our fields and vineyards already belong to other people."

⁶When I heard their complaints about these things, I was very angry. ⁷I thought about it. Then I accused the important people and the leaders. I told them, "You are charging your own brothers too much interest." So I called a large meeting to deal with them. ⁸I said to them, "Our fellow Jews had been sold to non-Jewish nations. But, as much as possible, we have bought them back. Now you are making your fellow Jews sell themselves to us!" The leaders were quiet. They had nothing to say.

⁹Then I said, "What you are doing is not right. You should live in fear of God. Don't let our non-Jewish enemies shame us. ¹⁰I, my brothers and my men are also lending money and grain to the people. But stop charging them too much for this! ¹¹Give back their fields, vineyards, olive trees and houses right now. Also give them back the extra amount you charged them. That is the hundredth part of the money, grain, new wine and oil."

¹²They said, "We will give it back. And

we will not demand anything more from them. We will do as you say."

Then I called for the priests. And I made the important men and leaders promise to do what they had said. [13]Also I shook out the folds of my robe. I said, "In this way may God shake out every man who does not keep his promise. May God shake him out of his house. And may he shake him out of the things that are his. Let that man be shaken out and emptied!"

Then the whole group said, "Amen." And they praised the Lord. So the people did what they had promised.

[14]I was appointed governor in the land of Judah. This was in the twentieth year of King Artaxerxes' rule. I was governor till his thirty-second year. So I was governor of Judah for 12 years. During that time neither my brothers nor I ate the food that was allowed for the governor. [15]But the governors before me placed a heavy load on the people. They took about one pound of silver from each person. And they took food and wine. The governors' helpers before me also controlled the people. But I did not do that because I feared God. [16]I worked on the wall. So did all my men who were gathered there. We did not buy any fields.

[17]Also, I fed 150 Jews and officers at my table. And I fed those who came from the nations around us. [18]This is what was prepared every day for me and those who ate with me: one ox, six good sheep, and birds. And every ten days there were all kinds of wine. But I never demanded the food that was allowed for the governor. This was because the people were already working very hard.

[19]Remember, my God, to be kind to me. Remember all the good I have done for these people.

6 Then Sanballat, Tobiah, Geshem the Arab and our other enemies heard that I had rebuilt the wall. There was not one gap in it. But I had not yet set the doors in the gates. [2]So Sanballat and Geshem sent me this message: "Come, Nehemiah, let's meet together in Kephirim on the plain of Ono."

But they were planning to harm me. [3]So I sent messengers to them with this answer: "I am doing a great work. I can't come down. I don't want the work to stop while I leave to meet you." [4]Sanballat and Geshem sent the same message to me four times. And I sent back the same answer each time.

[5]The fifth time Sanballat sent his helper to me with the message. And in his hand was an unsealed letter. [6]This is what was written:

A report is going around to all the nations. And Geshem says it is true. It says you and the Jews are planning to turn against the king. That's why you are rebuilding the wall. They say you are going to be their king. [7]They say you have appointed prophets[d] to announce in Jerusalem: "There is a king of Judah!" The king will hear about this. So come, let's discuss this together.

[8]So I sent him back this answer: "Nothing you are saying is really happening. You are just making it up in your own mind."

[9]Our enemies were trying to scare us. They were thinking, "They will get too weak to work. Then the wall will not be finished."

But I prayed, "God, make me strong."

[10]One day I went to the house of Shemaiah son of Delaiah. Delaiah was the son of Mehetabel. Shemaiah had to stay at home. He said, "Nehemiah, let's meet in the Temple[d] of God. Let's go inside the Temple and close the doors. Men are coming at night to kill you."

[11]But I said, "Should a man like me run away? Should I run into the Temple to save my life? I will not go." [12]I knew that God had not sent him. Tobiah and Sanballat had paid him to prophesy against me. [13]They paid him to frighten me so I would do this and sin. Then they could give me a bad name to shame me.

[14]I prayed, "Remember Tobiah and Sanballat, my God. Remember what they have done. Also remember the prophetess Noadiah and the other prophets who have been trying to frighten me."

[15]So the wall of Jerusalem was completed. It was on the twenty-fifth day of the month of Elul. It took 52 days to rebuild. [16]Then all our enemies heard about it. And all the nations around us saw it. So they were shamed. They understood that the work had been done with the help of our God.

[17]Also in those days the important men of Judah sent many letters to Tobiah. And Tobiah answered them. [18]Many Jews had promised to be faithful to Tobiah. This was because Tobiah was

the son-in-law of Shecaniah son of
Arah. And Tobiah's son Jehohanan had
married the daughter of Meshullam son
of Berekiah. ¹⁹Those important men
kept telling me about the good things
Tobiah was doing. Then they would tell
Tobiah what I said about him. So Tobiah
sent letters to frighten me.

7 After the wall had been rebuilt, I had
set the doors in place. Then the gatekeepers, singers and Levites were chosen. ²I put my brother Hanani, along
with Hananiah, in charge of Jerusalem.
Hananiah was commander of the palace. He was honest, and he feared God
more than most men. ³I said to them,
"The gates of Jerusalem should not be
opened until the sun is hot. While the
gatekeepers are still on duty, have them
shut and bolt the doors. Appoint people
who live in Jerusalem as guards. Put
some at guard posts and some near their
own houses."

⁴The city was large and full of room.
But there were few people in it. And the
houses had not yet been rebuilt. ⁵So my
God caused me to gather the people. I
gathered the important men, the leaders
and the common people. This was so I
could register them by families. I found
the family history of those who had returned first. This is what I found written
there:

⁶These are the people of the area who
returned from captivity. Nebuchadnezzar king of Babylon had taken them captive. Now they returned to Jerusalem
and Judah. Each one went back to his
own town. ⁷These people returned with
Zerubbabel, Jeshua, Nehemiah, Azariah, Raamiah, Nahamani, Mordecai,
Bilshan, Mispereth, Bigvai, Nehum and
Baanah.

These are the men from Israel: ⁸the
descendantsᵈ of Parosh—2,172; ⁹the descendants of Shephatiah—372; ¹⁰the
descendants of Arah—652; ¹¹the descendants of Pahath-Moab (through
the family of Jeshua and Joab)—2,818;
¹²the descendants of Elam—1,254; ¹³the
descendants of Zattu—845; ¹⁴the descendants of Zaccai—760; ¹⁵the descendants of Binnui—648; ¹⁶the descendants
of Bebai—628; ¹⁷the descendants of
Azgad—2,322; ¹⁸the descendants of Adonikam—667; ¹⁹the descendants of Bigvai—2,067; ²⁰the descendants of Adin—
655; ²¹the descendants of Ater (through
Hezekiah)—98; ²²the descendants of Hashum—328; ²³the descendants of Be-

zai—324; ²⁴the descendants of Hariph—
112; ²⁵the descendants of Gibeon—95.

²⁶These are the men from the towns
of Bethlehem and Netophah—188; ²⁷the
men from Anathoth—128; ²⁸the men
from Beth Azmaveth—42; ²⁹the men
from Kiriath Jearim, Kephirah and Beeroth—743; ³⁰the men from Ramah and
Geba—621; ³¹the men from Micmash—
122; ³²the men from Bethel and Ai—123;
³³the men from the other Nebo—52; ³⁴the
men from the other Elam—1,254; ³⁵the
men from Harim—320; ³⁶the men from
Jericho—345; ³⁷the men from Lod, Hadid and Ono—721; ³⁸the men from Senaah—3,930.

³⁹These are the priests: the descendants of Jedaiah (through the family
of Jeshua)—973; ⁴⁰the descendants of
Immer—1,052; ⁴¹the descendants of
Pashhur—1,247; ⁴²the descendants of Harim—1,017.

⁴³These are the Levites: the descendants of Jeshua (through Kadmiel
through the family of Hodaviah)—74.

⁴⁴These are the singers: the descendants of Asaph—148.

⁴⁵These are the gatekeepers: the descendants of Shallum, Ater, Talmon, Akkub, Hatita and Shobai—138.

⁴⁶These are the Templeᵈ servants: the
descendants of Ziha, Hasupha, Tabbaoth, ⁴⁷Keros, Sia, Padon, ⁴⁸Lebana, Hag-
aba, Shalmai, ⁴⁹Hanan, Giddel, Gahar,
⁵⁰Reaiah, Rezin, Nekoda, ⁵¹Gazzam,
Uzza, Paseah, ⁵²Besai, Meunim, Nephu-
sim, ⁵³Bakbuk, Hakupha, Harhur, ⁵⁴Baz-
luth, Mehida, Harsha, ⁵⁵Barkos, Sisera,
Temah, ⁵⁶Neziah and Hatipha.

⁵⁷These are the descendants of the servants of Solomon: the descendants of
Sotai, Sophereth, Perida, ⁵⁸Jaala, Darkon, Giddel, ⁵⁹Shephatiah, Hattil, Pokereth-Hazzebaim and Amon.

⁶⁰The Temple servants and the descendants of the servants of Solomon totaled
392 people.

⁶¹Some people came to Jerusalem
from these towns: Tel Melah, Tel Harsha, Kerub, Addon and Immer. But they
could not prove that their families came
from the family of Israel. Here are their
names and their number: ⁶²the descendants of Delaiah, Tobiah and Nekoda—
642.

⁶³And these priests could not prove
that their families came from Israel: the
descendants of Hobaiah, Hakkoz and
Barzillai. (He had married a daughter of
Barzillai from Gilead and was called by
her family name.)

[64]These people searched for their family records. But they could not find them. So they could not be priests because they were thought to be unclean.[d]
[65]So the governor ordered them not to eat any of the food offered to God. First a priest had to settle this matter by using the Urim and Thummim.[d]
[66]The total number of those who returned was 42,360. [67]This is not counting their 7,337 male and female servants. They also had 245 men and women singers with them. [68]They had 736 horses, 245 mules, [69]435 camels and 6,720 donkeys.
[70]Some of the family leaders gave to the work. The governor gave to the treasury about 19 pounds of gold. He also gave 50 bowls and 530 pieces of clothing for the priests. [71]Some of the family leaders gave about 375 pounds of gold to the treasury for the work. They also gave about 2,660 pounds of silver. [72]This is the total of what the other people gave: about 375 pounds of gold, about 2,250 pounds of silver and 67 pieces of clothing for the priests. [73]So these people all settled in their own towns: the priests, the Levites, the gatekeepers, the singers, the Temple servants and all the other people of Israel.

By the seventh month the Israelites were settled in their own towns.

8 All the people of Israel gathered together in the square by the Water Gate. They asked Ezra the teacher to bring out the Book of the Teachings of Moses. These are the Teachings the Lord had given to Israel.
[2]So Ezra the priest brought out the Teachings for the crowd. This was on the first day of the seventh month. Men, women and all who could listen and understand had gathered. [3]Ezra read the Teachings out loud. He read from early morning until noon. He was facing the square by the Water Gate. He read to the men, women and everyone who could listen and understand. All the people listened carefully to the Book of the Teachings.
[4]Ezra the teacher stood on a high wooden platform. It had been built just for this time. On his right were Mattithiah, Shema, Anaiah, Uriah, Hilkiah and Maaseiah. And on his left were Pedaiah, Mishael, Malkijah, Hashum, Hashbaddanah, Zechariah and Meshullam.
[5]Ezra opened the book. All the people

could see him because he was above them. As he opened it, all the people stood up. [6]Ezra praised the Lord, the great God. And all the people held up their hands and said, "Amen! Amen!" Then they bowed down and worshiped the Lord with their faces to the ground.
[7]These Levites taught the people the Teachings as they stood there: Jeshua, Bani, Sherebiah, Jamin, Akkub, Shabbethai, Hodiah, Maaseiah, Kelita, Azariah, Jozabad, Hanan and Pelaiah. [8]They read the Book of the Teachings of God. They read so the people could understand. And they explained what it meant. Then the people understood what was being read.
[9]Then Nehemiah the governor and Ezra the priest and teacher spoke up. And the Levites who were teaching spoke up. They said to all the people, "This is a holy day to the Lord your God. Don't be sad or cry." All the people had been crying as they listened to the words of the Teachings.
[10]Nehemiah said, "Go and enjoy good food and sweet drinks. Send some to people who have none. Today is a holy day to the Lord. Don't be sad. The joy of the Lord will make you strong."
[11]The Levites helped calm the people. They said, "Be quiet. This is a holy day. Don't be sad."
[12]Then all the people went away to eat and drink. They sent some of their food to others. And they celebrated with great joy. They finally understood what they had been taught.
[13]On the second day of the month, the leaders of all the families met with Ezra the teacher. The priests and Levites also met with him. They gathered to study the words of the Teachings. [14]This is what they found written in the Teachings: The Lord had commanded through Moses that the people of Israel were to live in shelters. This was during the feast of the seventh month. [15]The people were supposed to preach this message. They were to spread it through all of their towns and in Jerusalem: "Go out into the mountains. Bring back branches from olive and wild olive trees, myrtle trees, palms and shade trees. Make shelters with them. It is written in the Law."
[16]So the people went out and got tree branches. They built shelters on their

roofs[n] and in their courtyards. They built shelters in the courtyards of the Temple.[d] And they built them in the square by the Water Gate and the square next to the Gate of Ephraim. [17]The whole group that had come back from captivity built shelters. And they lived in them. The Israelites had not done this since the time of Joshua son of Nun. And they were very happy.

[18]Ezra read to them from the Book of the Teachings. He read every day, from the first day to the last. The people of Israel celebrated the feast for seven days. Then on the eighth day the people gathered as the law said.

9 It was on the twenty-fourth day of that same month. The people of Israel gathered together. They did not eat. And they put on rough cloth and put dust on their heads. This was to show their sadness. [2]Those people whose ancestors were from Israel had separated themselves from all foreigners. They stood and confessed their sins and their ancestors' sins. [3]For a fourth of the day they stood where they were. And they read from the Book of the Teachings of the Lord their God. Then they spent another fourth of the day confessing their sins. And they worshiped the Lord their God. [4]These Levites were standing on the stairs: Jeshua, Bani, Kadmiel, Shebaniah, Bunni, Sherebiah, Bani and Kanani. They called out to the Lord their God with loud voices. [5]And these Levites spoke: Jeshua, Kadmiel, Bani, Hashabneiah, Sherebiah, Hodiah, Shebaniah and Pethahiah. They said, "Stand up and praise the Lord your God. He lives forever and ever."

"Blessed be your wonderful name.
  It is more wonderful than all
    blessing and praise.
[6]You are the only Lord.
  You made the heavens, even the
    highest heavens.
  You made all the stars.
  You made the earth and everything
    that is on it.
  You made the seas and
    everything that is in them.
  You give life to everything.
  The heavenly army worships you.

[7]"You are the Lord God.
  You chose Abram.

You brought him out of Ur of the
    Babylonians.
  You named him Abraham.
[8]You found that he was faithful to
    you.
  So you made an agreement with
    him.
You promised to give his
    descendants[d] the land of the
    Canaanites,
  Hittites, Amorites,
  Perizzites, Jebusites and
    Girgashites.
You have kept your promise.
  You are fair.

[9]"You saw our ancestors suffering in
    Egypt.
  You heard them cry out at the
    Red Sea.[d]
[10]You did signs and miracles[d] against
    the king of Egypt.
  And you did them against all his
    officers and all the people of
    Egypt.
  You knew how proud they were.
You made everyone know your
    name.
  And it is still known today.
[11]You divided the sea in front of our
    ancestors.
  They walked through it on dry
    ground.
But you threw the people chasing
    them into the deep water.
  They were like a stone being
    thrown into mighty waters.
[12]You led our ancestors with a pillar
    of cloud in the daytime.
  And you led them with a pillar of
    fire at night.
It lit the way
  they were supposed to go.
[13]You came down to Mount Sinai.
  You talked to our ancestors from
    heaven.
  You gave them fair rules and true
    teachings.
  You gave them good orders and
    commands.
[14]You told them about your holy
    Sabbath.[d]
  You gave commands, orders and
    teachings to them
  through your servant Moses.
[15]When they were hungry, you gave
    them bread from heaven.

8:16 roofs In Bible times houses were built with flat roofs. The roof was used for drying things such as flax and fruit. And it was used as an extra room, as a place for worship and as a place to sleep in the summer.

When they were thirsty, you
brought them water from the
rock.
You told them to go into the land
and take it over.
You had promised to give it to
them.

[16] "But our ancestors were proud and
stubborn.
They did not obey your
commands.
[17] They refused to listen.
They forgot the miracles[d] you did
for them.
They became stubborn and turned
against you.
They chose a leader to lead them
back to their slavery.
But you are a forgiving God.
You are kind and full of mercy.
You do not become angry quickly.
And you have great love.
So you did not leave them.
[18] Our ancestors even made an idol of
a calf for themselves.
They said, 'This is your god,
Israel.
It brought you up out of Egypt.'
They spoke against you.

[19] "You have great mercy.
So you did not leave them in the
desert.
During the day the pillar of cloud
guided them on their way.
And the pillar of fire led them at
night.
It lit the way they were supposed
to go.
[20] You gave your good Spirit[d] to teach
them.
You gave them manna[d] to eat.
And you gave them water when
they were thirsty.
[21] You took care of them for 40 years
in the desert.
They needed nothing.
Their clothes did not wear out.
And their feet did not swell.

[22] "You gave them kingdoms and
nations.
You gave them more land.
They took over the country of
Sihon king of Heshbon.
And they took over the country
of Og king of Bashan.
[23] You made their children as many as
the stars in the sky.
And you brought them into the
land.

This was where you had told
their fathers to enter and take
over.
[24] So their children went into the land
and took over.
The Canaanites lived there.
But you defeated them for our
ancestors.
You handed over to them the
Canaanites, their kings and the
people of the land.
Our ancestors could do what they
wanted with them.
[25] Our ancestors captured strong,
walled cities and fertile land.
They took over houses full of
good things.
They took over wells that were
already dug.
They took vineyards, olive trees
and many fruit trees.
They ate until they were full and
became fat.
They enjoyed your great
goodness.

[26] "But they were disobedient and
turned against you.
They ignored your teachings.
Your prophets[d] warned them to
come back to you.
But they killed those prophets.
And they spoke against you.
[27] So you allowed their enemies to
defeat them.
Their enemies treated them
badly.
But in this time of trouble our
ancestors cried out to you.
And you heard from heaven.
You had great mercy.
You gave them saviors who saved
them from the power of their
enemies.
[28] But as soon as they had rest,
they again did what was evil.
So you left them to their enemies
who ruled over them.
But they cried out to you again.
And you heard from heaven.
Because of your mercy, you saved
them again and again.
[29] You warned them to return to
obeying your teachings.
But they were proud. They did
not obey your commands.
If a man obeys your laws, he will
live.
But they sinned against your
laws.

They were stubborn and disobedient.
They would not listen.
[30]You were patient with them for many years.
You warned them by your Spirit through the prophets.
But they did not pay attention.
So you allowed them to be defeated by other countries.
[31]But because your mercy is great, you did not kill them all.
You did not leave them.
You are a kind and merciful God.

[32]"And so, our God, you are the great and mighty and wonderful God.
You keep your agreement of love.
Do not let all our trouble seem unimportant in your eyes.
This trouble has come to us, to our kings and to our leaders.
It has come to our priests and prophets.
It has come to our ancestors and all your people.
This trouble has come to us since the days of the kings of Assyria.
And it has lasted until today.
[33]You have been fair in everything that has happened to us.
You have been loyal, but we have been wicked.
[34]Our kings, leaders, priests and ancestors did not obey your teachings.
They did not pay attention to the commands and warnings you gave them.
[35]Even when our ancestors were living in their kingdom, they did not serve you.
They were enjoying all the good things you had given them.
They were enjoying the land that was fertile and full of room.
But they did not stop their evil ways.

[36]"Look, we are slaves today in the land you gave our ancestors.
They were to enjoy its fruit and its good things.
But look, we are slaves here.
[37]The land's great harvest belongs to the kings you have put over us.
This is because of our sins.
Those kings rule over us and our cattle as they please.
And we are in much trouble.

[38]"Because of all this, we are making an agreement in writing. Our leaders, Levites and priests are putting their seals[d] on it."

10 These are the men who sealed the agreement:

Nehemiah the governor, son of Hacaliah, sealed it.

These men also sealed it: Zedekiah, [2]Seraiah, Azariah, Jeremiah, [3]Pashhur, Amariah, Malkijah, [4]Hattush, Shebaniah, Malluch, [5]Harim, Meremoth, Obadiah, [6]Daniel, Ginnethon, Baruch, [7]Meshullam, Abijah, Mijamin, [8]Maaziah, Bilgai and Shemaiah. These are the priests.

[9]These are the Levites who sealed it: Jeshua son of Azaniah, Binnui of the sons of Henadad, Kadmiel, [10]and their fellow Levites: Shebaniah, Hodiah, Kelita, Pelaiah, Hanan, [11]Mica, Rehob, Hashabiah, [12]Zaccur, Sherebiah, Shebaniah, [13]Hodiah, Bani and Beninu.

[14]These are the leaders of the people who sealed the agreement: Parosh, Pahath-Moab, Elam, Zattu, Bani, [15]Bunni, Azgad, Bebai, [16]Adonijah, Bigvai, Adin, [17]Ater, Hezekiah, Azzur, [18]Hodiah, Hashum, Bezai, [19]Hariph, Anathoth, Nebai, [20]Magpiash, Meshullam, Hezir, [21]Meshezabel, Zadok, Jaddua, [22]Pelatiah, Hanan, Anaiah, [23]Hoshea, Hananiah, Hasshub, [24]Hallohesh, Pilha, Shobek, [25]Rehum, Hashabnah, Maaseiah, [26]Ahiah, Hanan, Anan, [27]Malluch, Harim and Baanah.

[28]The rest of the people took an oath. They were the priests, Levites, gatekeepers, singers and Temple[d] servants. And they were all those who separated themselves from foreigners to keep the Teachings of God. It was also their wives and their sons and daughters who could understand. [29]They joined their fellow Israelites and their leading men. They took an oath, which was tied to a curse in case they broke the oath. They promised to follow the Teachings of God, which they had been given through Moses the servant of God. These people also promised to obey all the commands, rules and laws of the Lord our Master.
[30]They said:

We promise not to let our daughters marry foreigners. And we promise not to let our sons marry their daughters. [31]The foreigners might bring goods or grain to sell on the Sabbath.[d] But we will not buy on the Sabbath day or any holy day. Every seventh year we will not plant. And that year we will forget all that people owe us.

[32]We will be responsible for obeying the commands. We will pay for the service of the Temple of our God. We will give an eighth of an ounce of silver each year. [33]It is to pay for the bread that is set out on the table. It is to pay for the regular grain offerings and burnt offerings. It is for the offerings on the Sabbaths, New Moon[d] festivals and special feasts. It is for the holy offerings. And it is for the offerings to remove the sins of the Israelites so they will belong to God. It is for the work of the Temple of our God.

[34]We are the priests, the Levites and the people. We have thrown lots[d] to decide when each family must bring wood to the Temple. This is to be done at certain times each year. The wood is for burning on the altar of the Lord our God. We will do this as it is written in the Teachings.

[35]We also will bring the first fruits from our crops. And we will bring the first fruits of every tree to the Temple each year.

[36]We will bring our firstborn[d] sons and cattle to the Temple. We will bring the firstborn of our herds and flocks. We will do this as it is written in the Teachings. We will bring them to the priests who are serving in the Temple.

[37]We will bring things to the priests at the storerooms of the Temple. We will bring the first of our ground meal, our offerings, the fruit from all our trees and our new wine and oil. And we will bring a tenth of our crops to the Levites. The Levites will collect these things in all the towns where we work. [38]A priest of Aaron's family must be with the Levites when they receive the tenth of the people's crops. The Levites must bring a tenth of all they receive to the Temple of our God. Then they will put it in the storerooms of the treasury. [39]The people of Israel and the Levites are to bring their gifts to the storerooms. These are the gifts of grain, new wine and oil. The things for the Temple are kept in the storerooms. It is also where the priests, who are serving, the gatekeepers and singers stay.

We will not ignore the Temple of our God.

11 The leaders of Israel lived in Jerusalem. The rest of the people threw lots.[d] One person out of every ten was to come and live in Jerusalem. It was the holy city. The other nine could stay in their own cities. [2]The people blessed those who volunteered to live in Jerusalem.

[3]These are the area leaders who lived in Jerusalem. (Some people lived on their own land in the cities of Judah. These included Israelites, priests, Levites, Temple servants and descendants[d] of Solomon's servants. [4]Others from the families of Judah and Benjamin lived in Jerusalem.)

These are descendants of Judah who moved into Jerusalem. There was Athaiah son of Uzziah. (Uzziah was the son of Zechariah, who was the son of Amariah. Amariah was the son of Shephatiah, who was the son of Mahalalel. Mahalalel was a descendant of Perez.) [5]There was also Masseiah son of Baruch. (Baruch was the son of Col-Hozeh, who was the son of Hazaiah. Hazaiah was the son of Adaiah, who was the son of Joiarib. Joiarib was the son of Zechariah, who was a descendant of Shelah.) [6]All the descendants of Perez who lived in Jerusalem totaled 468 men. They were soldiers.

[7]These are descendants of Benjamin who moved into Jerusalem. There was Sallu son of Meshullam. (Meshullam was the son of Joed, who was the son of Pedaiah. Pedaiah was the son of Kolaiah, who was the son of Maaseiah. Maaseiah was the son of Ithiel, who was the son of Jeshaiah.) [8]Following him were Gabbai and Sallai. All together there were 928 men. [9]Joel son of Zicri was appointed over them. And Judah son of Hassenuah was second in charge of the new area of the city.

[10]These are the priests who moved into Jerusalem. There was Jedaiah son of Joiarib, Jakin [11]and Seraiah son of Hilkiah. (Hilkiah was the son of Meshullam, who was the son of Zadok. Zadok was the son of Meraioth, who was the son of Ahitub. Seraiah was the supervisor in the Temple.) [12]And there were others with them who did the work for the Temple. All together there were 822 men. Also there was Adaiah son of Jeroham. (Jeroham was the son of Pelaliah, who was the son of Amzi. Amzi was the son of Zechariah, who was the son of

Pashhur. Pashhur was the son of Malki-jah.) [13]And there were family heads with him. All together there were 242 men. Also there was Amashsai son of Azarel. (Azarel was the son of Ahzai, who was the son of Meshillemoth. Meshillemoth was the son of Immer.) [14]And there were brave men with Amashsai. All together there were 128 men. Zabdiel son of Hag-gedolim was appointed over them.

[15]These are the Levites who moved into Jerusalem. There was Shemaiah son of Hasshub. (Hasshub was the son of Azrikam, who was the son of Hasha-biah. Hashabiah was the son of Bunni.) [16]And there were Shabbethai and Joza-bad. They were two of the leaders of the Levites. They were in charge of the work outside the Temple. [17]There was Matta-niah son of Mica. (Mica was the son of Zabdi, who was the son of Asaph.) Mat-taniah was the director. He led the peo-ple in thanksgiving and prayer. There was Bakbukiah, who was second in charge over his fellow Levites. And there was Abda son of Shammua. (Shammua was the son of Galal, who was the son of Jeduthun.) [18]All together 284 Levites lived in the holy city of Jeru-salem.

[19]These are the gatekeepers who moved into Jerusalem. There were Ak-kub, Talmon and others with them. There was a total of 172 men. They guarded the city gates.

[20]The other Israelites, priests and Le-vites lived on their own land. They were in all the cities of Judah.

[21]The Temple servants lived on the hill of Ophel. Ziha and Gishpa were in charge of them.

[22]Uzzi son of Bani was appointed over the Levites in Jerusalem. (Bani was the son of Hashabiah, who was the son of Mattaniah. Mattaniah was the son of Mica.) Uzzi was one of Asaph's descen-dants. They were the singers. They were responsible for the service of the Tem-ple. [23]The singers took orders from the king. Those orders told the singers what to do each day.

[24]Pethahiah son of Meshezabel was the king's spokesman. Meshezabel was a descendant of Zerah, the son of Judah.

[25]Some of the people of Judah lived in villages with their surrounding fields. Some lived in Kiriath Arba and its sur-roundings. Some lived in Dibon and its surroundings. Some lived in Jekabzeel and its surroundings. [26]Others lived in Jeshua, Moladah, Beth Pelet, [27]Hazar

Shual, Beersheba and its surroundings. [28]Others were in Ziklag and Meconah and its surroundings. [29]Some people lived in En Rimmon, Zorah, Jarmuth, [30]Zanoah, Adullam and their villages. Some were in Lachish and the fields around it. Some lived in Azekah and its surroundings. So they settled from Be-ersheba all the way to the Valley of Hinnom.

[31]The descendants of the Benja-minites from Geba lived in Micmash, Aija, Bethel and its surroundings. [32]They lived in Anathoth, Nob, Ananiah, [33]Hazor, Ramah and Gittaim. [34]They lived in Hadid, Zeboim, Neballat, [35]Lod, Ono and in the Valley of the Craftsmen.

[36]Some groups of the Levites from Ju-dah settled in the land of Benjamin.

12 These are the priests and Levites who returned with Zerubbabel son of Shealtiel and with Jeshua. There were Seraiah, Jeremiah, Ezra, [2]Ama-riah, Malluch, Hattush, [3]Shecaniah, Rehum, Meremoth, [4]Iddo, Ginnethon, Abijah, [5]Mijamin, Moadiah, Bilgah, [6]Shemaiah, Joiarib, Jedaiah, [7]Sallu, Amok, Hilkiah and Jedaiah. They were the leaders of the priests and their rela-tives. This was in the days of Jeshua.

[8]The Levites were Jeshua, Binnui, Kadmiel, Sherebiah, Judah and also Mattaniah. He and his relatives were in charge of the songs of thanksgiving. [9]Bakbukiah and Unni, their relatives, stood across from them in the services.

[10]Jeshua was the father of Joiakim. Joiakim was the father of Eliashib. Elia-shib was the father of Joiada. [11]Joiada was the father of Jonathan. And Jona-than was the father of Jaddua.

[12]In the days of Joiakim, these priests were the leaders of the families of priests. Meraiah was over Seraiah's fam-ily. Hananiah was over Jeremiah's fam-ily. [13]Meshullam was over Ezra's fam-ily. Jehohanan was over Amariah's family. [14]Jonathan was over Malluch's family. Joseph was over Shecaniah's family. [15]Adna was over Harim's family. Helkai was over Meremoth's family. [16]Zechariah was over Iddo's family. Me-shullam was over Ginnethon's family. [17]Zicri was over Abijah's family. Piltai was over Miniamin's and Moadiah's families. [18]Shammua was over Bilgah's family. Jehonathan was over Shema-iah's family. [19]Mattenai was over Joia-rib's family. Uzzi was over Jedaiah's family. [20]Kallai was over Sallu's family. Eber was over Amok's family. [21]Hasha-

biah was over Hilkiah's family. Nethanel was over Jedaiah's family.

²²The leaders of the families of the Levites and the priests were written down. This was in the days of Eliashib, Joiada, Johanan and Jaddua. They were written down while Darius the Persian was king. ²³The family leaders among the Levites were written down in the history book. These were only up to the time of Johanan son of Eliashib. ²⁴The leaders of the Levites were Hashabiah, Sherebiah, Jeshua son of Kadmiel and their relatives. Their relatives stood across from them. They gave praise and thanksgiving to God. One group answered the other group. That is what David, the man of God, had commanded.

²⁵These were the gatekeepers who guarded the storerooms next to the gates: Mattaniah, Bakbukiah, Obadiah, Meshullam, Talmon and Akkub. ²⁶They served in the days of Joiakim son of Jeshua. (Jeshua was the son of Jozadak.) They also served in the days of Nehemiah the governor and Ezra the priest and teacher.

²⁷The wall of Jerusalem was offered as a gift to God. The Levites were found in the places where they lived. And they were brought to Jerusalem to celebrate with joy the giving of the wall. They were to celebrate with songs of thanksgiving and with the music of cymbals, harps and lyres.ᵈ ²⁸They also brought together singers. They came from all around Jerusalem and from the Netophathite villages. ²⁹They came from Beth Gilgal and the areas of Geba and Azmaveth. The singers had built villages for themselves around Jerusalem. ³⁰The priests and Levites made themselves pure. They also made the people, the gates and the wall of Jerusalem pure.

³¹I had the leaders of Judah go up on top of the wall. I appointed two large choruses to give thanks. One chorus went to the right on top of the wall. This was toward the Trash Gate. ³²Behind them went Hoshaiah and half the leaders of Judah. ³³Azariah, Ezra, Meshullam, ³⁴Judah, Benjamin, Shemaiah and Jeremiah also went. ³⁵Some priests with trumpets also went, along with Zechariah son of Jonathan. (Jonathan was the son of Shemaiah, who was the son of Mattaniah. Mattaniah was the son of Micaiah, who was the son of Zaccur. Zaccur was the son of Asaph.) ³⁶Zechariah's relatives also went. They were Shemaiah, Azarel, Milalai, Gilalai, Maai,

Nethanel, Judah and Hanani. These men played the musical instruments of David, the man of God. Ezra the teacher walked in front of them. ³⁷They went from the Fountain Gate straight up the steps to the older part of the city. They went on to the slope of the wall. They went above the house of David to the Water Gate on the east.

³⁸The second chorus went to the left. I followed them on top of the wall. Half the people were with me. We went from the Tower of the Ovens to the Broad Wall. ³⁹We went over the Gate of Ephraim to the Old Gate and the Fish Gate. We went to the Tower of Hananel and the Tower of the Hundred. We went as far as the Sheep Gate. We stopped at the Gate of the Guard.

⁴⁰The two choruses took their places at the Temple.ᵈ Half of the leaders and I did also. ⁴¹These priests were there with their trumpets: Eliakim, Maaseiah, Miniamin, Micaiah, Elioenai, Zechariah and Hananiah. ⁴²These people were also there: Maaseiah, Shemaiah, Eleazar, Uzzi, Jehohanan, Malkijah, Elam and Ezer. The choruses sang, led by Jezrahiah. ⁴³The people offered many sacrifices that day. They were happy because God made them very happy. The women and children were happy. The sound of happiness in Jerusalem could be heard far away.

⁴⁴At that time the leaders appointed men to be in charge of the storerooms. These rooms were for the gifts, the first fruits and a tenth of what the people gained. The Teachings said they should bring a share for the priests and Levites. These were to come from the fields around the towns. The people of Judah were happy to do this for the priests and Levites who served. ⁴⁵They performed the service of their God. They had the service of purifying things. The singers and gatekeepers also did their jobs as David had commanded his son Solomon. ⁴⁶Earlier, in the time of David and Asaph, there was a leader of the singers. There were songs of praise and thanksgiving to God. ⁴⁷So it was in the days of Zerubbabel and Nehemiah. All the people of Israel gave something to the singers and gatekeepers. They also set aside things for the Levites. The Levites set aside things for the descendantsᵈ of Aaron.

13 On that day they read the Book of Moses to the people. They found that it said no Ammonite or Moabite should ever be allowed in the meeting to worship. ²The Ammonites and Moabites had not welcomed the Israelites with food and water. Instead, they hired Balaam to put a curse on Israel. (But our God turned the curse into a blessing.) ³The people heard this teaching. So they separated all foreigners from Israel.

⁴Before that happened, Eliashib the priest was in charge of the Temple[d] storerooms. He was friendly with Tobiah. ⁵Eliashib let Tobiah use one of the large storerooms. That storeroom had been used for grain offerings, incense[d] and other things for the Temple. It was also used for the tenth offerings of grain, new wine and olive oil. These belonged to the Levites, singers and gatekeepers. It had also been used for gifts for the priests.

⁶I was not in Jerusalem when this happened. I had gone back to Artaxerxes king of Babylon. In the thirty-second year he was king. Finally I asked the king to let me leave. ⁷I came to Jerusalem. Then I found out the evil thing Eliashib had done. He had let Tobiah have a room in the Temple courtyard. ⁸I was very upset at this. I threw all of Tobiah's goods out of the room. ⁹I ordered the rooms to be purified. And I brought back the things for God's Temple, the grain offerings and the incense.[d]

¹⁰Then I found out the people were not giving the Levites their shares. So the Levites and singers who served had gone to their own farms. ¹¹So I argued with the officers. I said, "Why haven't you taken care of the Temple?" Then I gathered the Levites and singers. I put them back at their places.

¹²Then all the people of Judah brought a tenth of what they had gained in grain, new wine and olive oil. And they brought it to the storerooms. ¹³I put these men in charge of the storerooms: Shelemiah the priest, Zadok the teacher and Pedaiah a Levite. I made Hanan son of Zaccur their helper. (Zaccur was the son of Mattaniah.) Everyone knew they were honest men. They gave out the portions that went to their relatives.

¹⁴Remember me, my God, for this. Do not ignore my love for the Temple and its service.

¹⁵In those days I saw people in Judah working in the winepresses[d] on the Sabbath[d] day. People were bringing in grain and loading it on donkeys on the Sabbath day. People were bringing loads of wine, grapes and figs into Jerusalem on the Sabbath day. I warned them about selling food on that day. ¹⁶Men from the city of Tyre were living in Jerusalem. They brought in fish and other things. They sold them in Jerusalem on the Sabbath day to the people of Judah. ¹⁷I argued with the important men of Judah. I said to them, "What is this evil thing you are doing? You are ruining the Sabbath day. ¹⁸This is just what your ancestors did. So our God did terrible things to us and this city. Now you are making him even more angry at Israel. You are ruining the Sabbath day."

¹⁹So I ordered the doors shut at sunset before the Sabbath. The gates were not to be opened until the Sabbath was over. I put my servants at the gates. So no load could come in on the Sabbath. ²⁰Once or twice traders and sellers of all kinds of goods spent the night outside Jerusalem. ²¹So I warned them. I said, "Why are you spending the night by the wall? If you do it again, I will force you away." After that, they did not come back on the Sabbath. ²²Then I ordered the Levites to purify themselves. I told them to go and guard the city gates. They were to make sure the Sabbath remained holy.

Remember me, my God, for this. Have mercy on me because of your great love.

²³In those days I saw men of Judah who had married women from Ashdod, Ammon and Moab. ²⁴Half their children were speaking the language of Ashdod or some other place. They couldn't speak the language of Judah. ²⁵I argued with those people. I put curses on them. I hit some of them and pulled out their hair. I forced them to make a promise to God. I said, "Do not let your daughters marry the sons of foreigners. Do not take the daughters of foreigners as wives for your sons or yourselves. ²⁶Foreign women made King Solomon of Israel sin. There was never a king like him in any of the nations. God loved Solomon. God made him king over all Israel. But foreign women made Solomon sin. ²⁷And now you are not obedient when you do this evil thing. You are unfaithful to our God when you marry foreign wives."

²⁸Joiada was the son of Eliashib the high priest. One of Joiada's sons married a daughter of Sanballat the Horonite, who was not a Jew. So I forced Joiada's son away from me.

²⁹Remember them, my God. They made the priesthood unclean.[d] They

made the agreement of the priests and Levites unclean. [30]So I purified them of everything that was foreign. I appointed duties for the priests and Levites. Each man had his own job. [31]I also made sure wood was brought for the altar at regular times. And I made sure the first fruits were brought.

Remember, my God, to be kind to me.

The Book of
ESTHER

1 This is what happened during the time of King Xerxes. He was the king who ruled the 127 areas from India to Cush. [2]In those days King Xerxes ruled from his capital city of Susa. [3]In the third year of his rule, he gave a banquet. It was for all his important men and royal officers. The army leaders from the countries of Persia and Media were there. And the important men from all Xerxes' empire were there.

[4]The banquet lasted 180 days. All during that time King Xerxes was showing off the great wealth of his kingdom. And he was showing his own honor and greatness. [5]When the 180 days were over, the king gave another banquet. It was held in the courtyard of the palace garden for 7 days. It was for everybody in the palace at Susa, from the greatest to the least important. [6]The courtyard had fine white curtains and purple drapes. These were tied to silver rings on marble pillars by white and purple cords. And there were gold and silver couches. These were on a floor set with tiles of white marble, shells and gems. [7]Wine was served in gold cups of various kinds. And there was plenty of the king's wine because he was very generous. [8]The king commanded that each guest be permitted to drink as much as he wished. He had told the wine servers to serve each man what he wanted.

[9]Queen Vashti also gave a banquet. It was for the women in the royal palace of King Xerxes.

[10]On the seventh day of the banquet, King Xerxes was very happy because he had been drinking much wine. He gave a command to the seven eunuchs[d] who served him. They were Mehuman, Biztha, Harbona, Bigtha, Abagtha, Zethar and Carcas. [11]He commanded them to bring him Queen Vashti, wearing her royal crown. She was to come to show her beauty to the people and important men. She was very beautiful. [12]The eu-

nuchs told Queen Vashti about the king's command. But she refused to come. Then the king became very angry. His anger was like a burning fire.

[13]It was a custom for the king to ask advice from experts about law and order. So King Xerxes spoke with the wise men. They would know the right thing to do. [14]The wise men the king usually talked to were Carshena, Shethar, Admatha, Tarshish, Meres, Marsena and Memucan. They were seven of the important men of Persia and Media. These seven had special privileges to see the king. They had the highest rank in the kingdom.

[15]The king asked those men, "What does the law say must be done to Queen Vashti? She has not obeyed the command of King Xerxes, which the eunuchs took to her."

[16]Then Memucan spoke to the king and the other important men. He said, "Queen Vashti has not done wrong to the king alone. She has also done wrong to all the important men and all the people in all the empire of King Xerxes. [17]All the wives of the important men of Persia and Media will hear about the queen's actions. Then they will no longer honor their husbands. They will say, 'King Xerxes commanded Queen Vashti to be brought to him. But she refused to come.' [18]Today the wives of the important men of Persia and Media have heard about the queen's actions. And they will speak in the same way to their husbands. And there will be no end to disrespect and anger.

[19]"So, our king, if it pleases you, give a royal order. And let it be written in the laws of Persia and Media, which cannot be changed. The law should say Vashti is never again to enter the presence of King Xerxes. Also let the king give her place as queen to someone who is better than she is. [20]And let the king's order be announced everywhere in his large

kingdom. Then all the women will respect their husbands, from the greatest to the least important."

²¹The king and his important men were happy with this advice. So King Xerxes did as Memucan suggested. ²²He sent letters to all the areas of the kingdom. A letter was sent to each area, written in its own form of writing. And a letter was sent to each group of people, written in their own language. These letters announced that each man was to be the ruler of his own family. Also, each family was to speak the language of the man.

2 Later, King Xerxes was not so angry. Then he remembered Vashti and what she had done. And he remembered his order about her. ²Then the king's personal servants had a suggestion. They said, "Let a search be made for beautiful young virgins^d for the king. ³Let the king choose supervisors in every area of his kingdom. Let them bring every beautiful young virgin to the palace at Susa. These women should be taken to the women's quarters and put under the care of Hegai. He is the king's eunuch^d in charge of the women. And let beauty treatments be given to them. ⁴Then let the girl who most pleases the king become queen in place of Vashti." The king liked this advice. So he did as they said.

⁵Now there was a Jewish man in the palace of Susa. His name was Mordecai son of Jair. Jair was the son of Shimei. And Shimei was the son of Kish. Mordecai was from the tribe^d of Benjamin. ⁶Mordecai had been taken captive from Jerusalem by Nebuchadnezzar king of Babylon. Mordecai was part of the group taken into captivity with Jehoiachin king of Judah. ⁷Mordecai had a cousin named Hadassah, who had no father or mother. So Mordecai took care of her. Hadassah was also called Esther, and she had a very pretty figure and face. Mordecai had adopted her as his own daughter when her father and mother died.

⁸The king's command and order had been heard. And many girls had been brought to the palace in Susa. They had been put under the care of Hegai. When this happened, Esther was also taken to the king's palace. She was put into the care of Hegai, who was in charge of the women. ⁹Esther pleased Hegai, and he liked her. So Hegai quickly began giving Esther her beauty treatments and spe-

cial food. He gave her seven servant girls chosen from the king's palace. Then Hegai moved Esther and her seven servant girls to the best part of the women's quarters.

¹⁰Esther did not tell anyone about her family or who her people were. Mordecai had told her not to. ¹¹Every day Mordecai walked back and forth near the courtyard. This was where the king's women lived. He wanted to find out how Esther was and what was happening to her.

¹²Before a girl could take her turn with King Xerxes, she had to complete 12 months of beauty treatments. These were ordered for the women. For 6 months she was treated with oil and myrrh.^d And she spent 6 months with perfumes and cosmetics. ¹³Then she was ready to go to the king. Anything she asked for was given to her. She could take it with her from the women's quarters to the king's palace. ¹⁴In the evening she would go to the king's palace. And in the morning she would return to another part of the women's quarters. There she would be placed under the care of a man named Shaashgaz. Shaashgaz was the king's eunuch in charge of the slave women.^d The girl would not go back to the king again unless he was pleased with her. Then he would call her by name to come back to him.

¹⁵Esther daughter of Abihail, Mordecai's uncle, had been adopted by Mordecai. The time came for Esther to go to the king. She asked for only what Hegai suggested she should take. (Hegai was the king's eunuch who was in charge of the women.) And everyone who saw Esther liked her. ¹⁶So Esther was taken to King Xerxes in the royal palace. This happened in the tenth month, the month of Tebeth. It was in Xerxes' seventh year as king.

¹⁷And the king was pleased with Esther more than with any of the other girls. And he liked her more than any of the other virgins. So King Xerxes put a royal crown on Esther's head. And he made her queen in place of Vashti. ¹⁸Then the king gave a great banquet for Esther. He invited all his important men and royal officers. He announced a holiday in all the empire. And he was generous and gave everyone a gift.

¹⁹Now Mordecai was sitting at the king's gate. This was when the virgins^d were gathered the second time. ²⁰And Esther had still not told anyone about

her family or who her people were. That is what Mordecai had told her to do. She still obeyed Mordecai just as she had done when he was bringing her up.

²¹Now Bigthana and Teresh were two of the king's officers who guarded the doorway. While Mordecai was sitting at the king's gate, Bigthana and Teresh became angry at the king. And they began to make plans to kill King Xerxes. ²²But Mordecai found out about their plans and told Queen Esther. Then Queen Esther told the king. She also told him that Mordecai had found out about the evil plan. ²³When the report was investigated, it was found to be true. The two officers who had planned to kill the king were hanged. And all this was written down in the daily court record in the king's presence.

3 After these things happened, King Xerxes honored Haman son of Hammedatha the Agagite. He gave Haman a new rank that was higher than all the important men. ²And all the royal officers at the king's gate would bow down and kneel before Haman. This was what the king had ordered. But Mordecai would not bow down, and he did not kneel.

³Then the royal officers at the king's gate asked Mordecai, "Why don't you obey the king's command?" ⁴And they said this to him every day. When he did not listen to them, they told Haman about it. They wanted to see if Haman would accept Mordecai's behavior because Mordecai had told them that he was a Jew.

⁵Then Haman saw that Mordecai would not bow down to him or kneel before him. And he became very angry. ⁶He had been told who the people of Mordecai were. And he thought of himself as too important to try to kill only Mordecai. So he looked for a way to destroy all of Mordecai's people, the Jews, in all of Xerxes' kingdom.

⁷It was in the first month of the twelfth year of King Xerxes' rule. That is the month of Nisan. Pur (that is, the lot⁴) was thrown before Haman. The lot was used to choose a day and a month. So the twelfth month, the month of Adar, was chosen.

⁸Then Haman said to King Xerxes, "There is a certain group of people in all the areas of your kingdom. They are scattered among the other people. They keep themselves separate. Their customs are different from those of all the other people. And they do not obey the king's laws. It is not right for you to allow them to continue living in your kingdom. ⁹If it pleases the king, let an order be given to destroy those people. Then I will pay 375 tons of silver to those who do the king's business. They will put it into the royal treasury."

¹⁰So the king took his signet⁴ ring off and gave it to Haman. Haman son of Hammedatha, the Agagite, was the enemy of the Jews. ¹¹Then the king said to Haman, "The money and the people are yours. Do with them as you please."

¹²On the thirteenth day of the first month, the royal secretaries were called. They wrote out all of Haman's orders. They wrote to the king's governors and to the captains of the soldiers in each area. And they wrote to the important men of each group of people. The orders were written to each area in its own form of writing. And they were written to each group of people in their own language. They were written in the name of King Xerxes and sealed with his signet ring. ¹³Letters were sent by messengers to all the king's empire. They stated the king's order to destroy, kill and completely wipe out all the Jews. That meant young and old, women and little children, too. The order said to kill all the Jews on a single day. That was to be the thirteenth day of the twelfth month, which was Adar. And it said to take all the things that belonged to the Jews. ¹⁴A copy of the order was to be given out as a law in every area. It was to be made known to all the people so that they would be ready for that day.

¹⁵The messengers set out, hurried by the king's command. At the same time the order was given in the palace at Susa. And the king and Haman sat down to drink. But the city of Susa was in confusion.

4 Now Mordecai heard about all that had been done. To show how upset he was, he tore his clothes. Then he put on rough cloth and ashes. And he went out into the city crying loudly and very sadly. ²But Mordecai went only as far as the king's gate. This was because no one was allowed to enter that gate dressed in rough cloth. ³The king's order reached every area. And there was great sadness and loud crying among the Jews. They gave up eating and cried out loudly. Many Jews lay down on rough cloth and ashes to show how sad they were.

[4]Esther's servant girls and eunuchs[d] came to her and told her about Mordecai. Esther was very upset and afraid. She sent clothes for Mordecai to put on instead of the rough cloth. But he would not wear them. [5]Then Esther called for Hathach. He was one of the king's eunuchs chosen by the king to serve her. Esther ordered him to find out what was bothering Mordecai and why.

[6]So Hathach went to Mordecai. Mordecai was in the city square in front of the king's gate. [7]Then Mordecai told Hathach everything that had happened to him. And he told Hathach about the amount of money Haman had promised to pay into the king's treasury for the killing of the Jews. [8]Mordecai also gave him a copy of the order to kill the Jews, which had been given in Susa. He wanted Hathach to show it to Esther and to tell her about it. And Mordecai told him to order Esther to go into the king's presence. He wanted her to beg for mercy and to plead with him for her people.

[9]Hathach went back and reported to Esther everything Mordecai had said. [10]Then Esther told Hathach to say to Mordecai, [11]"All the royal officers and people of the royal areas know this: No man or woman may go to the king in the inner courtyard without being called. There is only one law about this. Anyone who enters must be put to death. But if the king holds out his gold scepter,[d] that person may live. And I have not been called to go to the king for 30 days."

[12]And Esther's message was given to Mordecai. [13]Then Mordecai gave orders to say to Esther: "Just because you live in the king's palace, don't think that out of all the Jews you alone will escape. [14]You might keep quiet at this time. Then someone else will help and save the Jews. But you and your father's family will all die. And who knows, you may have been chosen queen for just such a time as this."

[15]Then Esther sent this answer to Mordecai: [16]"Go and get all the Jews in Susa together. For my sake, give up eating. Do not eat or drink for three days, night and day. I and my servant girls will also give up eating. Then I will go to the king, even though it is against the law. And if I die, I die."

[17]So Mordecai went away. He did everything Esther had told him to do.

5 On the third day Esther put on her royal robes. Then she stood in the inner courtyard of the king's palace, facing the king's hall. The king was sitting on his royal throne in the hall, facing the doorway. [2]The king saw Queen Esther standing in the courtyard. When he saw her, he was very pleased. He held out to her the gold scepter[d] that was in his hand. So Esther went up to him and touched the end of the scepter.

[3]Then the king asked, "What is it, Queen Esther? What do you want to ask me? I will give you as much as half of my kingdom."

[4]Esther answered, "My king, if it pleases you, come today with Haman to a banquet. I have prepared it for him."

[5]Then the king said, "Bring Haman quickly so we may do what Esther asks."

So the king and Haman went to the banquet Esther had prepared for them. [6]As they were drinking wine, the king said to Esther, "Now, Esther, what are you asking for? I will give it to you. What is it you want? I will give you as much as half of my kingdom."

[7]Esther answered, "This is what I want and ask for. [8]My king, I hope you are pleased with me. If it pleases you, give me what I ask for and do what I want. Come with Haman tomorrow to the banquet I will prepare for you. Then I will answer your question about what I want."

[9]Haman left the king's palace that day happy and content. Then he saw Mordecai at the king's gate. And he saw that Mordecai did not stand up nor did he tremble with fear before him. So Haman became very angry with Mordecai. [10]But he controlled his anger and went home.

Then Haman called his friends and Zeresh, his wife, together. [11]And he told them about how wealthy he was and how many sons he had. He also told them about all the ways the king had honored him. And he told them how the king had placed him higher than his important men and his royal officers. [12]"And that's not all," Haman added. "I'm the only person Queen Esther invited to come with the king to the banquet she gave. And tomorrow also the queen has asked me to be her guest with the king. [13]But all this does not really make me happy. I'm not happy as long as I see that Jew Mordecai sitting at the king's gate."

¹⁴Then Haman's wife Zeresh and all his friends said, "Have a platform built to hang someone. Build it 75 feet high. And in the morning ask the king to have Mordecai hanged on it. Then go to the banquet with the king and be happy." Haman liked this suggestion. So he ordered the platform to be built.

6 That same night the king could not sleep. So he gave an order for the daily court record to be brought in and read to him. ²And it was found recorded that Mordecai had warned the king about Bigthana and Teresh. These men had planned to kill the king. They were two of the king's officers who guarded the doorway.

³Then the king asked, "What honor and reward have been given to Mordecai for this?"

The king's personal servants answered, "Nothing has been done for Mordecai."

⁴The king said, "Who is in the courtyard?" Now Haman had just entered the outer court of the king's palace. He had come to ask the king about hanging Mordecai on the platform he had prepared.

⁵The king's personal servants said, "Haman is standing in the courtyard."

So the king said, "Bring him in."

⁶So Haman came in. And the king asked him, "What should be done for a man that the king wants very much to honor?"

And Haman thought to himself, "Whom would the king want to honor more than me?" ⁷So he answered the king, "This is what you could do for the man you want very much to honor. ⁸Have the servants bring a royal robe that the king himself has worn. And also bring a horse with a royal crown on its head. The horse should be one the king himself has ridden. ⁹Then let the robe and the horse be given to one of the king's most important men. Let the servants put the robe on the man the king wants very much to honor. And let them lead him on the horse through the city streets. As they are leading him, let them announce: 'This is what is done for the man the king wants very much to honor!'"

¹⁰The king commanded Haman, "Go quickly. Take the robe and the horse just as you have said. And do all this for Mordecai the Jew who sits at the king's gate. Do not leave out anything that you have suggested."

¹¹So Haman took the robe and the horse. And he put the robe on Mordecai. Then he led him on horseback through the city streets. Haman announced before Mordecai: "This is what is done for the man the king wants very much to honor!"

¹²Then Mordecai went back to the king's gate. But Haman hurried home with his head covered. He was embarrassed and ashamed. ¹³He told his wife Zeresh and all his friends everything that had happened to him.

Haman's wife and the men who gave him advice said, "You are starting to lose power to Mordecai. Since he is a Jew, you cannot win against him. You will surely be ruined." ¹⁴While they were still talking, the king's eunuchs^d came to Haman's house. They made Haman hurry to the banquet Esther had prepared.

7 So the king and Haman went in to eat with Queen Esther. ²They were drinking wine. And the king said to Esther on this second day also, "What are you asking for? I will give it to you. What is it you want? I will give you as much as half of my kingdom."

³Then Queen Esther answered, "My king, I hope you are pleased with me. If it pleases you, let me live. This is what I ask. And let my people live, too. This is what I want. ⁴I ask this because my people and I have been sold to be destroyed. We are to be killed and completely wiped out. If we had been sold as male and female slaves, I would have kept quiet. That would not be enough of a problem to bother the king."

⁵Then King Xerxes asked Queen Esther, "Who is he? Where is he? Who has done such a thing?"

⁶Esther said, "A man who is against us! Our enemy is this wicked Haman!"

Then Haman was filled with terror before the king and queen. ⁷The king was very angry. He got up, left his wine and went out into the palace garden. But Haman stayed inside to beg Queen Esther to save his life. He could see that the king had already decided to kill him.

⁸The king came back from the palace garden to the banquet hall. And he saw Haman falling on the couch where Esther was lying. The king said, "Will he even attack the queen while I am in the house?"

As soon as the king said that, servants came in and covered Haman's face. ⁹Harbona was one of the eunuchs^d there serving the king. He said, "Look, a platform for hanging people stands near Haman's house. It is 75 feet high. This is the one Haman had prepared for Mordecai, who gave the warning that saved the king."

The king said, "Hang Haman on it!" [10]So they hanged Haman on the platform he had prepared for Mordecai. Then the king was not so angry anymore.

8 That same day King Xerxes gave Queen Esther everything Haman had left when he died. Haman had been the enemy of the Jews. And Mordecai came in to see the king. He came because Esther had told the king how he was related to her. [2]Then the king took off his signet[d] ring, which he had taken back from Haman. And he gave it to Mordecai. Then Esther put Mordecai in charge of everything Haman had left when he died.

[3]Once again Esther spoke to the king. She fell at the king's feet and cried. She begged the king to stop the evil plan of Haman the Agagite. Haman had thought up the plan against the Jews. [4]The king held out the gold scepter[d] to Esther. Esther got up and stood in front of the king.

[5]She said, "My king, I hope you are pleased with me. And maybe it will please you to do this. You might think it is the right thing to do. And maybe you are happy with me. If so, let an order be written to cancel the letters Haman wrote. [6]I could not stand to see that terrible thing happen to my people. I could not stand to see my family killed."

[7]King Xerxes answered Queen Esther and Mordecai the Jew. He said, "Because Haman was against the Jews, I have given his things to Esther. And my soldiers have hanged him. [8]Now write another order in the king's name. Write it to the Jews as it seems best to you. Then seal the order with the king's signet[d] ring. No letter written in the king's name and sealed with his signet ring can be canceled."

[9]At that time the king's secretaries were called. This was done on the twenty-third day of the third month, which is Sivan. The secretaries wrote out all of Mordecai's orders. They wrote to the Jews and to the governors and to the captains of the soldiers in each area. And they wrote to the important men of the 127 areas which reached from India to Cush. They wrote to each area in its

own form of writing. And they wrote to each group of people in their own language. They also wrote to the Jews in their own form of writing and their own language. [10]Mordecai wrote orders in the name of King Xerxes. And he sealed the letters with the king's signet ring. Then he sent the king's orders by messengers on horses. The messengers rode fast horses, which were raised just for the king.

[11]These were the king's orders: The Jews in every city have the right to gather together to protect themselves. They have the right to destroy, kill and completely wipe out the army of any area or people who attack them. And they are to do the same to the women and children of that army. The Jews also have the right to take by force the property of the enemies. [12]The one day set for the Jews to do this was the thirteenth day of the twelfth month. This was the month of Adar. They were allowed to do this in all the empire of King Xerxes. [13]A copy of the king's order was to be sent out as a law in every area. It was to be made known to the people of every nation living in the kingdom. This was so the Jews would be ready on that set day. The Jews would be allowed to pay back their enemies.

[14]The messengers hurried out, riding on the royal horses. They were blue manded those messengers to hurry. And the order was also given in the palace at Susa.

[15]Mordecai left the king's presence wearing royal clothes. They were blue and white. And he had on a large gold crown. He also had a purple robe made of the best linen. And the people of Susa shouted for joy. [16]It was a time of happiness, joy, gladness and honor for the Jews. [17]The king's order went to every area and city. And there was joy and gladness among the Jews. This happened in every area and city to which the king's order went. The Jews were having feasts and celebrating. And many people through all the empire became Jews. They did that because they were afraid of the Jews.

9 The order the king had commanded was to be done on the thirteenth day of the twelfth month. That was the month of Adar. That was the day the enemies of the Jews had hoped to defeat them. But that was changed. So the Jews themselves defeated those who hated them. [2]The Jews met in their cities in all the empire of King Xerxes. They met in order to attack those who wanted to harm them. And no one was strong enough to fight against them. This was because all the other people living in the empire were afraid of the Jews. [3]And all the important men of the areas, the governors, captains of the soldiers, and the king's officers helped the Jews. They helped because they were afraid of Mordecai. [4]Mordecai was very important in the king's palace. He was famous in all the empire. This was because he was becoming a leader of more and more people.

[5]And, with their swords, the Jews defeated all their enemies, killing and destroying them. And the Jews did what they wanted with those people who hated them. [6]In the palace at Susa, they killed and destroyed 500 men. [7]They also killed these men: Parshandatha, Dalphon, Aspatha, [8]Poratha, Adalia, Aridatha, [9]Parmashta, Arisai, Aridai and Vaizatha. [10]They were the ten sons of Haman, son of Hammedatha, the enemy of the Jews. But the Jews did not take their belongings.

[11]And on that day the number of the men killed in the palace at Susa was reported to the king. [12]The king said to Queen Esther, "The Jews have killed and destroyed 500 men in the palace at Susa. And they have also killed Haman's ten sons. What have they done in the rest of the king's empire! Now what else are you asking? I will do it! And what else do you want? It will be done."

[13]Esther answered, "If it pleases the king, give the Jews who are in Susa permission to do this. Let them do again tomorrow what the king ordered for today. And let the bodies of Haman's ten sons be hanged on the platform built for hanging people to death."

[14]So the king ordered that it be done. A law was given in Susa, and the bodies of the ten sons of Haman were hanged. [15]The Jews in Susa came together. It was on the fourteenth day of the month of Adar. And they killed 300 men in Susa. But they did not take their belongings.

[16]At that same time, the other Jews in the king's empire also met. They met in order to protect themselves and get rid of their enemies. And they killed 75,000 of those who hated them. But they did not take their belongings. [17]This happened on the thirteenth day of the month of Adar. And on the fourteenth day the Jews rested. They made it a day of joyful feasting.

[18]But the Jews in Susa met on the thirteenth and fourteenth days of the month of Adar. Then they rested on the fifteenth day. They made it a day of joyful feasting.

[19]This is why the Jews who live in the country and small villages celebrate on the fourteenth day. They keep the fourteenth day of the month of Adar as a day of joyful feasting. And it is also a day for giving presents to each other.

[20]Mordecai wrote down everything that had happened. Then he sent letters to all the Jews in all the empire of King Xerxes. He sent letters to places far and near. [21]Mordecai did this to have the Jews celebrate every year. They were to celebrate on the fourteenth and fifteenth days of the month of Adar. [22]It was to celebrate a time when the Jews got rid of their enemies. They were also to celebrate it as the month their sadness was turned to joy. It was the month when their crying for the dead was turned into celebration. Mordecai wrote letters to all the Jews. He wrote to tell them to celebrate those days as days of joyful feasting. It was to be a time of giving food to each other. And it was a time of giving presents to the poor.

[23]So the Jews agreed to do what Mordecai had written to them. And they agreed to hold the celebration every year. [24]Haman son of Hammedatha, the Agagite, was the enemy of all the Jews. He had made an evil plan against the Jews to destroy them. And Haman had thrown the pur (that is, the lot[d]) to choose a day to ruin and destroy the Jews. [25]But when the king learned of the evil plan, he sent out written orders. This was so the evil plans Haman had made against the Jews would be used against him. And those orders said that Haman and his sons should be hanged on the platform for hanging. [26]So these days were called Purim. The name Purim comes from the word "pur" (the lot). [27]And so the Jews set up this custom. They and their descendants[d] would celebrate these two days every year. The Jews and all those who join them are to celebrate these two days. They should do it without fail every year. They should do it in the right way and at the time Mordecai had ordered them in the letter. [28]These two days should be remembered and celebrated from now on in every family. And they must be cele-

brated in every area and every city. These days of Purim should never stop being celebrated by the Jews. And the descendants of the Jews should always remember to celebrate these two days of Purim.

²⁹So Queen Esther daughter of Abihail, along with Mordecai the Jew, wrote this second letter about Purim. Using the power they had, they wrote to prove the first letter was true. ³⁰And Mordecai sent letters to all the Jews in the 127 areas of the kingdom of Xerxes. Mordecai wrote a message of peace and truth. ³¹He wrote to set up these days of Purim. They are to be celebrated at their chosen times. Mordecai the Jew and Queen Esther had sent out the order for the Jews. They had set up for themselves and their descendants these two days. They set them up so the Jews would give up eat-

ing and cry loudly. ³²Esther's letter showed that these practices about Purim were correct. They were written down in the records.

10 King Xerxes made people pay taxes. Even the cities far away on the seacoast had to pay taxes. ²And all the great things that Xerxes did are written down. They tell of his power and strength. They are written in the record books of the kings of Media and Persia. Also written in those record books are all the things that Mordecai did. The king had made Mordecai a great man. ³Mordecai the Jew was second in importance to King Xerxes. He was the most important man among the Jews. And his fellow Jews respected him very much. They respected Mordecai because he worked for the good of his people. And they respected him because he spoke up for the safety of all the Jews.

The Book of
JOB

1 A man named Job lived in the land of Uz. He was an honest man and innocent of any wrong. He honored God and stayed away from evil. ²Job had seven sons and three daughters. ³He owned 7,000 sheep, 3,000 camels, 500 pairs of oxen and 500 female donkeys. And he had a large number of servants. He was the greatest man among all the people of the East.

⁴Job's sons took turns holding feasts in their homes. And they invited their sisters to eat and drink with them. ⁵After a feast was over, Job would send and have them made clean. Early in the morning Job would offer a burnt offering for each of them. He thought, "My children may have sinned and cursed God in their hearts." Job did this every time.

⁶One day the angels came to show themselves before the Lord. Satan also came with them. ⁷The Lord said to Satan, "Where have you come from?"

Satan answered the Lord, "I have been wandering around the earth. I have been going back and forth in it."

⁸Then the Lord said to Satan, "Have you noticed my servant Job? No one else on earth is like him. He is an honest man

and innocent of any wrong. He honors God and stays away from evil."

⁹But Satan answered God, "Job honors God for a good reason. ¹⁰You have put a wall around him, his family and everything he owns. You have blessed the things he has done. So his flocks of sheep and herds of cattle are large. They almost cover the land. ¹¹But reach out your hand and destroy everything he has. Then he will curse you to your face."

¹²The Lord said to Satan, "All right, then. Everything Job has is in your power. But you must not touch Job himself." Then Satan left the Lord's presence.

¹³One day Job's sons and daughters were eating and drinking wine together. They were at the oldest brother's house. ¹⁴A messenger came to Job and said, "The oxen were plowing. And the donkeys were eating grass nearby. ¹⁵And the Sabeans attacked and carried them away. They killed the servants with swords. And I am the only one who escaped to tell you!"

¹⁶The messenger was still speaking when another messenger came in. He said, "Lightning from God fell from the sky. It burned up the sheep and the ser-

vants. And I am the only one who escaped to tell you!"

¹⁷The second messenger was still speaking when another messenger came in. He said, "The Babylonians sent three groups of attackers. They swept down and stole your camels. They killed the servants. And I am the only one who escaped to tell you!"

¹⁸The third messenger was still speaking when another messenger came in. He said, "Your sons and daughters were eating and drinking wine together. They were at the oldest brother's house. ¹⁹Suddenly a great wind came in from the desert. It struck all four corners of the house at once. The house fell in on your sons and daughters. And they are all dead. I am the only one who escaped to tell you!"

²⁰When Job heard this, he got up. To show how sad he was he tore his robe and shaved his head. Then he bowed down to the ground to worship God. ²¹He said:

"I was naked when I was born.
   And I will be naked when I die.
The Lord gave these things to me.
   And he has taken them away.
   Praise the name of the Lord."

²²In all this Job did not sin. He did not blame God.

2 On another day the angels came to show themselves before the Lord. And Satan also came with them. ²The Lord said to Satan, "Where have you come from?"

Satan answered the Lord, "I have been wandering around the earth. I have been going back and forth in it."

³Then the Lord said to Satan, "Have you noticed my servant Job? No one else on earth is like him. He is an honest man, innocent of any wrong. He honors God and stays away from evil. You caused me to ruin him for no good reason. But he continues to be without blame."

⁴"One skin for another!" Satan answered. "A man will give all he has to save his own life. ⁵But reach out your hand and destroy his own flesh and bones. Then he will curse you to your face."

⁶The Lord said to Satan, "All right, then. Job is in your power. But you must let him live."

⁷So Satan left the Lord's presence. And he put painful sores all over Job's body. They went from the top of his head to the soles of his feet. ⁸Then Job took a piece of broken pottery. And he used it to scrape himself. He sat in ashes to show how upset he was.

⁹Job's wife said to him, "Are you still trying to stay innocent? You should just curse God and die!"

¹⁰Job answered, "You are talking like a foolish woman. Should we take only good things from God and not trouble?" In all this Job did not sin in what he said.

¹¹Now Job had three friends. They were Eliphaz the Temanite, Bildad the Shuhite and Zophar the Naamathite. These friends heard about the troubles that had happened to Job. So they agreed to meet and go see Job. They wanted to show him they were upset for him, too. And they wanted to comfort him. ¹²They saw Job from far away. But he looked so different they almost didn't recognize him. They began to cry loudly. They tore their robes and put dirt on their heads to show how sad they were. ¹³Then they sat on the ground with Job seven days and seven nights. No one said a word to him. This was because they saw how much he was suffering.

3 After seven days Job spoke. He cursed the day he had been born. ²Job said:

³"Let the day I was born be
     destroyed.
   And destroy the night when it
     was said, 'A boy is born!'
⁴Let that day turn to darkness.
   Let God not even care about it.
   Don't let light shine on that day.
⁵Let darkness and gloom have that
     day.
   Let a cloud hide that day.
   Let darkness cover its light.
⁶Let thick darkness capture that
     night.
   Don't count it among the days of
     the year.
   Don't put it in any of the months.
⁷Let that night be empty.
   Let no shout of joy be heard in it.
⁸Let the people who curse days
     curse that day.
   They know how to wake up the
     sea monster Leviathan.ᵈ
⁹Let that day's morning stars
     become dark.
   Let it wait for daylight, but don't
     let it come.
   Don't let it see the first light of
     dawn.

[10]This is because it allowed me to be born.
That day did not hide trouble from my eyes.

[11]"Why didn't I die as soon as I was born?
Why didn't I die when I came out of the womb?
[12]Why did my mother's knees receive me?
Why did my mother's breasts feed me?
[13]If they had not been there, I would be lying dead in peace.
I would be asleep and at rest.
[14]I would be asleep with kings and wise men of the earth.
They built places for themselves that are now ruined.
[15]I would be asleep with rulers who had gold.
They filled their houses with silver!
[16]Or why was I not buried like a child born dead?
I wish I were like a baby who never saw the light of day.
[17]In the grave the wicked stop causing trouble.
And people who are tired are at rest.
[18]In the grave there is rest for the captives.
They no longer hear the shout of the slave driver.
[19]People great and small are in the grave.
And the slave is freed from his master.

[20]"Why is life given to those who are in misery?
Why is it given to those who are so unhappy?
[21]Some people want to die, but death does not come.
They search for death more than for hidden treasure.
[22]They are very happy when they get to the grave.
[23]Life shouldn't be given to a man who doesn't know what will happen to him.
It shouldn't be given to a man who feels trapped by God.
[24]I make sad sounds as I eat.
My groans pour out like water.
[25]The thing I was afraid of has happened to me.
And the thing I dreaded has happened.
[26]I have no peace. I have no quietness.
I have no rest. I only have trouble."

4

Then Eliphaz the Temanite answered:

[2]"If someone tried to speak with you, would you be upset?
I cannot keep from speaking.
[3]Think about how many people you have taught.
Think about how you have made weak hands strong.
[4]Your words have comforted those who fell.
And you have given strength to those who could not stand.
[5]But now trouble comes to you. And you are discouraged.
Trouble hits you, and you are terrified.
[6]You should trust in your respect for God.
You should have hope because you are innocent.

[7]"Think about this now: A person who has not done wrong will not die.
Honest people were never destroyed.
[8]I have noticed that people who plow evil
and plant trouble harvest it.
[9]God's breath destroys them.
A blast of his anger kills them.
[10]The lions roar and growl.
But the teeth of great lions are broken.
[11]The lion dies because he can't find an animal to eat.
So the cubs of the female lion are scattered.

[12]"A word was brought to me in secret.
My ears heard a whisper of it.
[13]It was during troublesome dreams in the night
when men are in deep sleep.
[14]I was shaking with fear.
All my bones were shaking.
[15]A spirit glided past my face.
The hair on my body stood up in fear.
[16]The spirit stopped,
but I could not see what it was.
A shape stood before my eyes.
And I heard a quiet voice.

[17] It said, 'Can a man be holy in the presence of God?
Can a man be pure before the one who made him?
[18] God does not trust his servants.
He even blames his angels for mistakes.
[19] So he puts even more blame on people who live in clay houses.[n]
The foundations of these houses are made of dust.
They can be crushed more easily than a moth.
[20] Between dawn and sunset they are broken to pieces.
They are not noticed. They die and are gone forever.
[21] The ropes of their tents are pulled up.
And they die without wisdom.'

5 "Call if you want to, but no one will answer you.
You can't turn to any of the holy ones.
[2] Foolish anger kills a person.
And jealousy kills a weak-minded person.
[3] I have seen a fool have success like a tree taking root.
But suddenly his home was destroyed.
[4] His children are far away from safety.
They are crushed in court with no one to defend them.
[5] Hungry people eat this fool's harvest.
They even take what grew up among the thorns.
And thirsty people want his wealth.
[6] Hard times do not come up from the ground.
And trouble does not grow from the earth.
[7] But man is born to have trouble as surely as sparks fly upward.

[8] "But if I were you, I would call on God.
I would bring my problem before him.
[9] God does wonderful things that cannot be understood.
He does so many miracles[d] they cannot be counted.
[10] God gives rain to the earth.
He sends water on the fields.

[11] God makes the humble person important.
He lifts to places of safety those who are sad.
[12] God ruins the plans of those who trick others.
Then they have no success.
[13] He catches wise men in their own clever traps.
And the plans of those who try to trick others are swept away.
[14] Darkness covers them up in the daytime.
At noon they feel around in the dark.
[15] God saves needy people from their lies.
He saves them from the harm done by powerful people.
[16] So the poor people have hope.
And those who are unfair are silenced.

[17] "The person whom God corrects is happy.
So do not hate being corrected by God All-Powerful.
[18] God hurts, but he also bandages up.
He injures, but his hands also heal.
[19] He will save you from six troubles.
Even seven troubles will not harm you.
[20] God will buy you back from death in times of hunger.
And in battle he will save you from death by the sword.
[21] You will be hidden from the tongue that hits like a whip.
You will not need to be afraid when destruction comes.
[22] You will laugh at destruction and hunger.
You do not need to fear the wild animals.
[23] This is because you will have an agreement with the animals born in the wild.
And the wild animals will be at peace with you.
[24] You will know that your tent is safe.
You will check the things you own and find nothing missing.
[25] You will know that you will have many children.
Your descendants[d] will be as many as the blades of grass on the earth.
[26] You will come to the grave with all your strength.

4:19 clay houses This is probably talking about people's bodies.

You will be like bundles of grain
gathered at the right time.

²⁷"We have checked this, and it is
true.
So hear it and decide what it
means to you."

6 Then Job answered:

²"I wish my suffering could be
weighed.
And I wish my misery could be
put on the scales.
³My sadness would be heavier than
the sand of the seas.
No wonder my words seem
careless.
⁴The arrows of God All-Powerful are
in me.
My spirit drinks in their poison.
God's terrors are gathered
against me.
⁵A wild donkey does not bray when
it has grass to eat.
An ox is quiet when it has feed.
⁶Tasteless food is not eaten without
salt.
There is no flavor in the white
part of an egg.
⁷I refuse to touch it.
Such food makes me sick.

⁸"How I wish I might have what I
ask for.
How I wish God would give me
what I hope for.
⁹I wish God would be willing to
crush me
and reach out his hand to destroy
me.
¹⁰Then I would have this comfort.
I would be glad even in this
unending pain.
I would know I did not reject the
words of the Holy One.

¹¹"I do not have the strength to wait.
There is nothing to hope for so
how can I be patient?
¹²I do not have the strength of stone.
My flesh is not bronze.
¹³I have no power to help myself.
This is because success has been
taken away from me.

¹⁴"They say, 'A man's friends should
be kind to him when he is in
trouble.
This should be done even if he
stops fearing God
All-Powerful.'

¹⁵But my brothers cannot be counted
on.
They are like streams that do not
flow regularly,
streams that sometimes run over.
¹⁶They are like streams made dark
by melting ice,
that rise with melting snow.
¹⁷But they stop flowing when it is the
dry season.
They go away when it is hot.
¹⁸Groups of travelers turn away from
their paths.
They go into the desert and die.
¹⁹The groups of travelers from Tema
look for water.
The traders of Sheba who travel
look hopefully.
²⁰They are upset because they had
been sure.
But when they arrive, they are
disappointed.
²¹You also have been no help.
You see something terrible, and
you are afraid.
²²I have never said, 'Give me a gift.
Use your wealth to pay my debt.
²³Save me from the enemy's power.
Buy me back from the clutches of
cruel people.'

²⁴"Teach me, and I will be quiet.
Show me where I have been
wrong.
²⁵Honest words are painful!
But your arguments prove
nothing.
²⁶Do you mean to correct what I say?
Will you treat the words of a
troubled man as if they were
only wind?
²⁷You would even throw lots^d for
orphans.
And you would trade away your
friend.

²⁸"But now please look at me.
I would not lie to your face.
²⁹Change your mind. Do not be
unfair.
Think again, because my
innocence is being questioned.
³⁰What I am saying is not wicked.
I can tell the difference between
right and wrong.

7 "Man has a hard task on earth.
His days are like those of a hired
man.
²Man is like a slave wishing for the
evening shadows.

Or he is like a hired man who
wants his pay.
³But I am given months that are
empty.
Nights of misery have been given
to me.
⁴When I lie down, I think, 'How long
is it until I get up?'
The night is long, and I toss until
dawn.
⁵My body is covered with worms
and scabs.
My skin is broken and full of
running sores.

⁶"My days go by faster than a
weaver moves his tool.
And they come to an end without
hope.
⁷Remember, God, that my life is only
as long as a breath.
My eyes will never see happy
times again.
⁸Those who see me now will see me
no more.
You will look for me, but I will be
gone.
⁹A cloud disappears and is gone.
In the same way, a person who
goes where the dead are does
not return.
¹⁰He will never come back to his
house again.
His place will not know him
anymore.

¹¹"So I will not stay quiet.
I will speak out in the suffering
of my spirit.
I will complain because I am so
unhappy.
¹²I am not the sea or the sea monster.
So why have you set a guard over
me?
¹³Sometimes I think my bed will
comfort me.
Or I think my couch will stop my
complaint.
¹⁴Then you frighten me with dreams.
You terrify me with visions.
¹⁵My throat prefers to be choked.
My bones welcome death.
¹⁶I hate my life. I don't want to live
forever.
Let me alone. My days have no
meaning.

¹⁷"Why do you make man so
important?
Why do you give him so much
attention?

¹⁸Will you examine him every
morning?
Why do you test him every
moment?
¹⁹Will you never look away from me?
Will you not let me alone even
long enough to swallow?
²⁰If I have sinned, what have I done
to you,
you watcher of men?
Why have you made me your
target?
Have I become a heavy load for
you?
²¹Why don't you pardon my wrongs
and forgive my sins?
I will soon lie down in the dust and
die.
You will search for me, but I will
be no more."

8 Then Bildad the Shuhite answered:

²"How long will you say such
things?
Your words are no more than a
strong wind.
³God does not twist fairness.
God All-Powerful does not make
wrong what is right.
⁴Your children sinned against God.
And he punished them for their
sins.
⁵But you should ask God for help.
Pray to God All-Powerful for
mercy.
⁶You must be good and honest.
Then he will start doing
something for you.
And he will bring you back
where you belong.
⁷The place you began will seem
unimportant
because your future will be so
successful.

⁸"Ask old people
and find out what their ancestors
learned.
⁹We were only born yesterday and
know nothing.
Our days on earth are like only a
shadow.
¹⁰Those people will teach you and
tell you.
They will tell you what they
know.
¹¹Papyrus plants cannot grow tall
where there is no wet land.
Reeds cannot grow tall without
water.

¹²While they are still growing and not yet cut,
they will dry up more quickly than grass.
¹³That is what will happen to everyone who forgets God.
The hope of the person without God will be gone.
¹⁴What he trusts in is easily broken.
It is as easily broken as a spider's web.
¹⁵He leans on the spider's web, but it breaks.
He holds on to it, but it does not hold him up.
¹⁶He is like a well-watered plant in the sunshine.
The plant spreads its roots all through the garden.
¹⁷It wraps its roots around a pile of rocks.
And it looks for a place among the stones.
¹⁸But the plant may be torn from its place.
Then that place rejects it and says, 'I never saw you.'
¹⁹Then its life dries up.
And other plants grow up from the dirt in its place.

²⁰"Surely God does not reject innocent men.
He does not give strength to those who do evil.
²¹God will yet fill your mouth with laughter.
And he will fill your lips with shouts of joy.
²²Your enemies will be covered in shame.
And the tents of the wicked will be gone."

9 Then Job answered:

²"Yes, I know that this is true.
But how can man be right in the presence of God?
³A person might want to argue with God.
But he could not answer God one time out of a thousand.
⁴God's wisdom is deep, and his power is great.
No one can fight God without being hurt.
⁵God moves mountains without anyone knowing it.
He turns mountains over when he is angry.

⁶God shakes the earth out of its place.
And he makes the earth's foundations shake.
⁷God commands the sun not to shine.
He shuts off the light of the stars.
⁸God alone stretches out the skies.
And he walks on the waves of the sea.
⁹It is God who made the Bear, Orion and the Pleiades[n]
and the groups of stars in the southern sky.
¹⁰God does wonderful things that people cannot understand.
He does so many miracles[d] they cannot be counted.
¹¹When he passes me, I cannot see him.
When he goes by me, I cannot recognize him.
¹²If God snatches something away, no one can stop him.
No one can say to him, 'What are you doing?'
¹³God will not hold back his anger.
Even the helpers of the monster Rahab[d] lie at God's feet in fear.
¹⁴So how can I argue with God?
I cannot find words to argue with him.
¹⁵Even if I was right, I could not answer him.
I could only beg God, my Judge, for mercy.
¹⁶I might call to him. But even if he answered,
I still would not believe he would listen to me.
¹⁷God would crush me with a storm.
He would multiply my hurts for no reason.
¹⁸He would not let me catch my breath.
He would overwhelm me with misery.
¹⁹When it comes to strength, God is stronger than I.
And when it comes to justice, no one can accuse him!
²⁰Even if I were right, my own mouth would say I was wrong.
If I were innocent, my mouth would say I was guilty.

²¹"I am innocent.
But I don't think about myself.
I hate my own life.
²²It is all the same. That is why I say,

9:9 **Bear . . . Pleiades** Names of well-known groups of stars.

'God destroys both the innocent
and the evil people.'
²³A whip may bring sudden death.
And God will laugh when good
people suffer.
²⁴When land falls into the hands of
evil people,
God covers the judges' faces so
they can't see it.
If it is not God who does this,
then who is it?

²⁵"My days go by faster than a
runner.
They fly away without my seeing
even a little joy.
²⁶They glide past like boats made of
papyrus plants.
My days are like eagles that
swoop down on animals they
attack.
²⁷I might say, 'I will forget my
complaint.
I will change the look on my face,
and smile.'
²⁸But I will still dread all my
suffering.
I know you will hold me guilty.
²⁹I have already been found guilty.
So why should I struggle for no
reason?
³⁰I might wash myself with soap.
And I might even wash my hands
with strong soap.
³¹But you would push me into a dirty
pit.
And even my clothes would hate
me.

³²"God is not a man like me. So I
cannot answer him.
We cannot meet each other in
court.
³³I wish there was someone to make
peace between us.
I wish someone could decide our
case.
³⁴I wish someone could remove
God's punishment from me.
Then his terror would not
frighten me anymore.
³⁵Then I could speak up without
being afraid of God.
But I am not able to do that.

10 "I hate my own life.
So I will complain without
holding back.
And I will speak because I am so
unhappy.
²I will say to God: Do not hold me
guilty.

But tell me what you have
against me.
³Does it make you happy to trouble
me?
Don't you care about me, the
work of your own hands?
Are you happy with the plans of
evil people?
⁴Do you have human eyes?
Do you see as a man sees?
⁵Are your days like the days of
man?
Are your years like the years of a
man?
⁶You look for evil I have done
and search for my sin.
⁷But you know I am not guilty.
And you know no one can save
me from your power.

⁸"Your hands shaped me and made
me.
But now you turn around and
destroy me.
⁹Remember that you molded me like
a piece of clay.
Now will you turn me back into
dust?
¹⁰You formed me in my mother's
womb
as cheese is formed from milk.
¹¹You put skin and flesh on me like
clothing.
You sewed me together with
bones and muscles.
¹²You gave me life and showed me
kindness.
And in your care you watched
over my life.

¹³"But in your heart you hid other
plans.
I know this is what was in your
mind:
¹⁴If I sinned, you would be watching
me.
You would not let my sin go
unpunished.
¹⁵How terrible it will be for me if I
am guilty!
But even if I am right, I cannot
lift my head.
I am full of shame.
It is as if I am drowning in my
pain.
¹⁶If I hold up my head, you hunt me
like a lion.
And again you show your terrible
power against me.
¹⁷You bring new witnesses against
me.

You increase your anger against
me.
Your armies come against me
like waves of the sea.
¹⁸"So why did you allow me to be
born?
I wish I had died before anyone
saw me.
¹⁹I wish I had never been born.
Or I wish I had been carried
straight from birth to the
grave!
²⁰My few days of life are almost over.
Leave me alone so I can have a
moment of joy.
²¹Soon I will leave and not return.
I will go to the land of darkness
and gloom.
²²It is the land of darkest night.
It is the land of gloom and
confusion.
Even the light is darkness there."

11 Then Zophar the Naamathite answered:

²"All these words should not go
without an answer.
Is this talker to be judged as
right?
³Your talk should not make people
be quiet.
People should shame you when
you make fun of God.
⁴You say to God, 'My teachings are
right.
And I am clean^d in God's sight.'
⁵I wish God would speak.
I wish he would open his lips to
speak against you.
⁶I wish he would tell you the secrets
of wisdom.
This is because wisdom has two
sides.
Know this: God has even forgotten
some of your sin.

⁷"Can you understand the secrets of
God?
Can you search the limits of the
God All-Powerful?
⁸God's limits are higher than the
heavens. You cannot reach
them!
They are deeper than where the
dead are. You cannot know
them!
⁹His limits are longer than the earth
and wider than the sea.

¹⁰"God might come along and put
you in prison.

If he calls you into court, no one
can stop him.
¹¹God knows which men are evil.
And when he sees evil, he notices
it.
¹²A stupid person cannot become
wise.
That is as impossible as a wild
donkey being born tame.

¹³"You must give your whole heart to
him.
You must hold out your hands to
him for help.
¹⁴Put away the sin that is in your
hand.
Let no evil live in your tent.
¹⁵Then you can lift up your face
without shame.
You can stand strong without
fear.
¹⁶You will forget your trouble.
You will remember your troubles
only as water that has passed
by.
¹⁷Your life will be as bright as the
noonday sun.
And darkness will seem like
morning.
¹⁸You will feel safe because there is
hope.
You will look around and rest in
safety.
¹⁹You will lie down, and no one will
make you afraid.
Many people will want favor
from you.
²⁰But the wicked people will not be
able to see.
So they will not be able to find
the way to escape.
Their only hope will be to die."

12 Then Job answered:

²"You really think you are the
only wise people.
You think when you die wisdom
will die with you.
³But my mind is as good as yours.
You are not better than I am.
Everyone knows all these things.
⁴My friends all laugh at me
when I call on God and expect
him to answer me.
They laugh at me even though I
am right and innocent!
⁵People who are comfortable don't
care that others have trouble.
They think that people who are
in trouble should have more
troubles.

⁶The tents of robbers are not
bothered.
Those who make God angry are
safe.
They have their god in their
pocket.

⁷"But ask the animals, and they will
teach you.
Or ask the birds of the air, and
they will tell you.
⁸Speak to the earth, and it will teach
you.
Or let the fish of the sea tell you.
⁹Every one of these knows
that the hand of the Lord has
done this.
¹⁰The life of every creature
and the breath of all people are
in God's hand.
¹¹The ear tests words
as the tongue tastes food.
¹²Older people are supposed to be
wise.
Long life is supposed to bring
understanding.

¹³"But God has wisdom and power.
He has good advice and
understanding.
¹⁴What God tears down cannot be
rebuilt.
The man God puts in prison
cannot be let out.
¹⁵If God holds back the waters, there
is a time without rain.
But if he lets the waters go, they
flood the land.
¹⁶God is strong and victorious.
Both the person who fools others
and the one who is fooled
belong to him.
¹⁷God leads wise men away as
captives.
He turns wise judges into fools.
¹⁸God takes the royal belt off of
kings.
And he dresses them like
prisoners with only a cloth
around their waist.
¹⁹He leads priests away as captives.
He destroys the power of those
who have been powerful.
²⁰God makes trusted people be silent.
And he takes away the wisdom of
older leaders.
²¹God brings disgrace on important
people.
And he takes away the weapons
of the strong.

²²God uncovers the deep things of
darkness.
He brings dark shadows into the
light.
²³He makes nations great, and he
destroys them.
He makes nations large, and he
scatters them.
²⁴He takes understanding away from
the leaders of the earth.
He makes them wander through
a desert with no paths.
²⁵They feel around in darkness with
no light.
God makes them stumble around
like drunken people.

13 "My eyes have seen all this.
My ears have heard and
understood it.
²What you know, I also know.
You are not better than I am.
³But I want to speak to God
All-Powerful.
I want to argue my case with
God.
⁴But you smear me with lies.
You are worthless doctors, all of
you!
⁵I wish you would just stop talking.
Then you would really be wise!
⁶Listen to my argument.
Hear my lips begging.
⁷You should not speak for God by
saying evil things.
You cannot speak God's truth by
telling lies.
⁸You should not unfairly choose his
side against mine.
You should not argue the case for
God.
⁹You will not do well if he examines
you.
You cannot fool God as you
might fool men.
¹⁰God would surely scold you
if you unfairly took one person's
side.
¹¹His bright glory would scare you.
You would be very much afraid
of him.
¹²Your wise sayings are worth no
more than ashes.
Your arguments are as weak as
clay.

¹³"Be quiet and let me speak.
Then let things happen to me as
they will.
¹⁴I will put myself in danger
and take my life in my own
hands.

[15]He will kill me. I have no hope.[n]
But I still will defend my ways to
his face.
[16]This might really save me,
because a wicked man would not
be brave enough to come
before him.
[17]Listen carefully to what I say.
Let your ears hear what I say.
[18]See now, I have prepared my case.
I know I will be proved right.
[19]No one can blame me for doing
wrong.
If someone can, I will be quiet
and die.

[20]"God, please just give me these two
things.
Then I will not hide from you.
[21]Take your punishment away from
me.
And stop frightening me with
your terrors.
[22]Then call me, and I will answer.
Or let me speak and you answer.
[23]How many evil things and sins
have I done?
Show me my wrong and my sin.
[24]Don't hide your face from me.
Don't think of me as your enemy.
[25]Don't punish a leaf that is blown by
the wind.
Don't chase after dry chaff.[d]
[26]You write down cruel things
against me.
You make me suffer for sins I did
when I was young.
[27]You put my feet in chains.
You keep close watch on
everywhere I go.
And you mark the soles of my
feet.
[28]So man wears out like something
rotten.
He is like clothing that has been
eaten by moths.

14 "All of us born to women
live only a few days and have a
lot of trouble.
[2]We grow up like flowers and then
dry up and go away.
We are like a passing shadow
that does not last.
[3]Lord, do you need to watch
someone like this?
Do you need to bring him before
you to be judged?

[4]I wish something clean[d] could come
from something unclean.
But it never can!
[5]Our time is limited.
You have given us only so many
months to live.
You have set limits we cannot go
beyond.
[6]So look away from us and leave us
alone.
Leave us alone until we put in
our time like a hired man.

[7]"There is hope for a tree.
If you cut it down, it will grow
again.
It will keep sending out new
branches.
[8]Its roots may grow old in the
ground.
And its stump may die in the dirt.
[9]But at the smell of water it will bud.
It will put out new shoots like a
plant.
[10]But we die, and our bodies are laid
in the ground.
We take our last breath and are
gone.
[11]Water disappears from a lake.
And a river loses its water and
dries up.
[12]In the same way we lie down and
do not rise again.
We will not get up or be
awakened
until the heavens disappear.

[13]"I wish you would hide me where
the dead are.
Hide me until your anger is gone.
I wish you would set a time
and then remember me!
[14]If a man dies, will he live again?
I will wait, struggling hard
until things change for me.
[15]You will call, and I will answer you.
You will desire the creature your
hands have made.
[16]Then you will count my steps.
But you will not keep track of my
sin.
[17]My wrongs will be closed up in a
bag.
And you will cover up my sin.
[18]"A mountain washes away and
crumbles.
And a rock can be moved from
its place.
[19]Water washes over stones and
wears them down.

13:15 He . . . hope Or "Even if God kills me, I will still put my hope in him."

And rushing waters wash away
    the dirt.
  In the same way, you destroy my
    hope.
²⁰You defeat man forever, and he is
    gone.
  You change his appearance and
    send him away.
²¹His sons are honored, but he does
    not know it.
  His sons are disgraced, but he
    does not see it.
²²He only feels the pain of his body.
  And he feels sorry only for
    himself."

15 Then Eliphaz the Temanite an-
    swered:

²"A wise man would not answer
    with empty words.
  He would not fill his stomach
    with hot, east wind.
³He would not argue with useless
    words.
  He would not make speeches that
    have no value.
⁴But you even break down the
    worship of God.
  You stand in the way of those
    who pray to him.
⁵Your sin teaches your mouth what
    to say.
  You use the same words as
    people who trick others.
⁶It is your own mouth, not mine, that
    shows you are wicked.
  Your own lips speak as a witness
    against you.

⁷"You are not the first man ever born.
  You were not born before the
    hills were made.
⁸You cannot listen in on God's secret
    advice.
  You cannot limit wisdom to
    yourself.
⁹You don't know any more than we
    know.
  You don't understand any more
    than we understand.
¹⁰Old people with gray hair are on
    our side.
  They are men even older than
    your father.
¹¹The comfort God gives you is not
    enough for you,
  even when words are spoken
    gently to you.
¹²Your heart has carried you away
    from God.
  Your eyes flash with anger.

¹³You speak out your anger against
    God.
  And these words pour out of your
    mouth.

¹⁴"How can man be pure?
  How can a person born to a
    woman be good?
¹⁵God places no trust in his holy
    ones.
  Even the heavens are not pure in
    his eyes.
¹⁶And man is even less than they are.
  He is terrible and rotten.
  He drinks up evil as if it were
    water!

¹⁷"Job, listen to me, and I will tell
    you about it.
  I will tell you what I have seen.
¹⁸These are things wise men have
    told.
  Their fathers told them these
    things, and they have hidden
    nothing.
¹⁹(The land was given to their fathers
    only.
  No foreigner lived among them.)
²⁰The evil man suffers pain all his
    life.
  The cruel man suffers during all
    the years saved up for him.
²¹Terrible sounds fill his ears.
  When things seem to be going
    well, robbers attack him.
²²The evil person gives up trying to
    escape from the darkness.
  It has been decided that he will
    die by the sword.
²³He wanders around. He will
    become food for vultures.
  He knows death will soon come.
²⁴Worry and suffering terrify him.
  They overwhelm him. They seem
    like a king ready to attack.
²⁵This is because he shakes his fist at
    God.
  He tries to get his own way
    against God All-Powerful.
²⁶He stubbornly charges at God
  with a thick, strong shield.

²⁷"The evil person's face is covered
    with fat.
  His waist is fat with flesh.
²⁸He will live in towns that are
    ruined.
  He will live in houses where no
    one lives.
  They are houses that are
    crumbling into ruins.

²⁹The evil person will no longer get
rich.
And the riches he has will not
last.
The things he owns will no
longer spread over the land.
³⁰He will not escape the darkness.
A flame will dry up his branches.
God's breath will carry that evil
person away.
³¹The evil person should not fool
himself by trusting what is
useless.
If he does, he will get nothing in
return.
³²His branch will dry up before it
finishes growing.
It will not even become green.
³³He will be like a vine whose grapes
are pulled off before they are
ripe.
He will be like an olive tree that
loses its blossoms.
³⁴People without God can produce
nothing.
Fire will destroy the tents of
people who take money to do
evil.
³⁵They plan trouble and give birth to
evil.
Their hearts plan ways to trick
people."

16

Then Job answered:

²"I have heard many things like
these.
You are all painful comforters!
³Will your long, useless speeches
never end?
What makes you keep on arguing?
⁴I also could speak as you do
if you were in my place.
I could make great speeches
against you.
And I could shake my head at you.
⁵But, instead, my words would
encourage you.
I would speak words of comfort
to bring you relief.

⁶"But if I speak, my pain does not
become less.
And if I don't speak, it still does
not go away.
⁷God, you have surely taken away
my strength.
You have destroyed my whole
family.
⁸You have made me thin and weak.
And people feel that this shows I
have done wrong.

⁹God attacks me and tears me with
anger.
He grinds his teeth at me.
My enemy stares at me with his
angry eyes.
¹⁰People open their mouths to make
fun of me.
They hit my cheeks to insult me.
They join together against me.
¹¹God has turned me over to evil
men.
He has thrown me into the
clutches of the wicked.
¹²Everything was fine with me.
But then God broke me into
pieces.
He held me by the neck and
crushed me.
He has made me his target.
¹³   God's archers surround me.
He stabs my kidneys and has no
mercy.
He spills my blood on the
ground.
¹⁴Again and again God attacks me.
He runs at me like a soldier.

¹⁵"I have sewed rough cloth over my
skin to show my sadness.
I have buried my face in the dust.
¹⁶My face is red from crying.
I have dark circles around my
eyes.
¹⁷And yet my hands have never done
anything cruel.
And my prayer is pure.

¹⁸"Earth, please do not cover up my
blood.
Don't let my cry ever stop being
heard!
¹⁹Even now I have one who speaks
for me in heaven.
The one who is on my side is
high above.
²⁰The one who speaks for me is my
friend.
While he does this, my eyes pour
out tears to God.
²¹He begs God on behalf of a man
as a man begs for his friend.

²²"Only a few years will pass
before I go on the journey from
which I cannot return.

17

My spirit is broken.
The days of my life are almost
gone.
The grave is waiting for me.
²Those who laugh at me surround
me.
I watch them insult me.

³"God, make me a promise.
No one else will make a promise
for me.
⁴You have closed the minds of my
friends so they do not
understand.
So you will not let them win over
me.
⁵A man might speak against his
friends for money.
But if he does, the eyes of his
children go blind.

⁶"God has caused people to use my
name as a curse word.
People spit in my face.
⁷My sight has grown weak because
of my sadness.
My body is so thin it's like a
shadow.
⁸Honest people are upset about this.
Innocent people are upset with
people who do wrong.
⁹But people who do right will
continue to do right.
And those whose hands are not
dirty with sin will grow
stronger.

¹⁰"But, all of you, come and try
again!
I do not find a wise man among
you!
¹¹My days are gone, and my plans
have been destroyed.
The desires of my heart are also
destroyed.
¹²These men think night is day.
When it is dark, they say, 'Light
is near.'
¹³It might be that the only home I
hope for is where the dead are.
I might spread out my bed in
darkness.
¹⁴I might say to the grave, 'You are
my father.'
And I might say to the worm,
'You are my mother' or 'You
are my sister.'
¹⁵If these things are true, I have no
hope.
No one can see any hope for me.
¹⁶Hope will go down to the gates of
death.
We will go down together into
the dust."

18 Then Bildad the Shuhite answered:

²"When will you stop these
speeches?

Be sensible, and then we can
talk.
³You think of us as only cattle.
You think we are stupid.
⁴You tear yourself to pieces in your
anger.
Does everyone have to leave the
earth just for you?
Do the rocks have to be moved
from their place for you?

⁵"The lamp of the wicked person
will be put out.
The flame in his lamp will stop
burning.
⁶The light in his tent will become
dark.
The lamp by his side will go out.
⁷His footsteps will become weak
and lose their strength.
He will fall into his own evil trap.
⁸His feet are caught in a net
when he walks into its web.
⁹A trap will catch him by the heel.
And it will hold him tight.
¹⁰A trap for him is hidden on the
ground.
It lies in his path.
¹¹Terrible things startle him from
every side.
They chase him at every step.
¹²Hunger takes away his strength.
Disaster is at his side.
¹³Disease eats away parts of his skin.
The signs of death begin to eat
away at his arms and legs.
¹⁴The evil person is torn from the
safety of his tent.
He is dragged off to Death, the
King of Terrors.
¹⁵His tent is set on fire.
Burning sulfur is scattered over
his home.
¹⁶His roots dry up below ground,
and his branches above ground
die.
¹⁷People on earth will not remember
him.
His name will be forgotten in the
land.
¹⁸He will be driven from the light
into darkness.
He will be chased out of the
world.
¹⁹He has no children or descendantsᵈ
among his people.
No one will be left alive where he
once lived.
²⁰People of the west are shocked at
what has happened to him.

People of the east are very
frightened.
²¹This is surely what will happen to
the home of an evil person.
This is the place of one who does
not know God."

19

Then Job answered:

²"How long will you hurt me
and crush me with your words?
³You have insulted me ten times now.
You attack me without shame.
⁴If I have sinned,
it is my worry alone.
⁵Maybe you want to make
yourselves look better than I do
so you can blame me for my
suffering.
⁶Then know that God has wronged
me.
He has pulled his net around me.

⁷"I shout, 'I have been wronged!'
But I get no answer.
I call loudly for help,
but I receive no justice.
⁸God has blocked my way so I
cannot pass.
He has covered my paths with
darkness.
⁹He has taken away my honor.
He has removed the crown from
my head.
¹⁰He beats me down on every side
until I am gone.
He pulls up my hope as a tree is
pulled up by its roots.
¹¹His anger burns against me.
And he treats me as one of his
enemies.
¹²His armies gather.
They prepare a way to attack me.
They camp around my tent.

¹³"God has made my brothers my
enemies.
My friends have become
complete strangers.
¹⁴My relatives have gone away.
My friends have forgotten me.
¹⁵My guests and my women servants
think of me as a stranger.
They look at me as if I were a
foreigner.
¹⁶I call for my servant, but he does
not answer.
I even beg him with my own
mouth.
¹⁷My wife hates my breath.
My own family hates me.
¹⁸Even the little boys hate me.
When I leave, they talk about me.

¹⁹All my close friends hate me.
Even those I love have turned
against me.
²⁰I am nothing but skin and bones.
I have escaped with only the skin
of my teeth.
²¹Pity me, my friends. Pity me!
The hand of God has hit me.
²²Why do you chase me as God does?
Haven't you had enough of
hurting my body?

²³"How I wish my words were
written down.
I wish they were written on a
scroll.
²⁴I wish they were carved with an
iron pen into lead,
or carved into stone forever!
²⁵I know that my Defender lives.
And in the end he will come to
show that I am right.
²⁶Even after my skin has been
destroyed,
in my flesh I will still see God.
²⁷I will see him myself.
I myself will see him with my
own eyes.
How my heart wants that to
happen!

²⁸"You may say, 'We will continue to
trouble Job.
The problem lies with him.'
²⁹But you should be afraid of the
sword yourselves.
God's anger will bring
punishment by the sword.
Then you will know that there is
judgment."

20

Then Zophar the Naamathite answered:

²"My troubled thoughts cause me to
answer.
I am very upset.
³I hear you criticize, and I am
insulted.
But I understand how to answer
you.

⁴"You know how it has been for a
long time.
It has been this way since man
was put on the earth.
⁵The happiness of an evil person is
very short.
The joy of a person without God
lasts only a moment.
⁶His pride may be as high as the
heavens.
His head may touch the clouds.

⁷But he will be gone forever, like his
own dung.
People who knew him will say,
'Where is he?'
⁸He will fly away like a dream.
He will not be found again.
He will be chased away like a
vision in the night.
⁹Those who saw him will not see
him again.
The place where he lived will see
him no more.
¹⁰His children will have to make up
for how he mistreated the poor.
He will have to give his wealth
back with his own hands.
¹¹He has the strength of his youth in
his bones.
But it will lie with him in the dust
of death.

¹²"Evil may taste sweet in the evil
person's mouth.
He may hide it under his tongue.
¹³He cannot stand to let go of it.
So he keeps it in his mouth.
¹⁴But his food will turn sour in his
stomach.
It will be like the poison of a
snake inside him.
¹⁵He has swallowed riches, but he
will spit them out.
God will make the evil person's
stomach vomit them up.
¹⁶He will suck the poison of snakes.
The snake's poisonous fangs will
kill him.
¹⁷He will not admire the sparkling
streams
or the rivers flowing with honey
and cream.
¹⁸He must give back what he worked
for without eating it.
He will not enjoy the money he
made from his trading.
¹⁹This is because he has troubled the
poor people and left them with
nothing.
He has taken houses he did not
build.

²⁰"The evil person has no rest from
his desire.
Nothing escapes his selfishness.
²¹But nothing will be left for him to
eat.
His riches will not continue.
²²When he still has plenty, trouble
will catch up to him.
Great misery will come down on
him.

²³The evil person may eat until his
stomach is full.
But then God will send his
burning anger against him.
God will send blows of
punishment down on him like
rain.
²⁴The evil person may run away from
an iron weapon.
But then a bronze arrow will stab
him.
²⁵He will pull the arrow out of his
back.
He will pull its point out of his
liver.
Terrors will come over him.
²⁶ Total darkness waits for his
treasure.
A fire not fanned by people will
destroy him.
That fire will burn up what is left
of his tent.
²⁷The heavens will show his guilt.
The earth will rise up against
him.
²⁸A flood will carry his house away.
The rushing waters will come on
the day of God's anger.
²⁹This is what God plans for evil
people.
This is what he has decided they
will receive."

21 Then Job answered:

²"Listen carefully to my words.
Let this be the way you comfort
me.
³Be patient while I speak.
After I have finished, you may
continue to make fun of me if
you wish.

⁴"My complaint is not just against
people.
I have reason to be impatient.
⁵Look at me then and be shocked.
Put your hand over your mouth
in shock.
⁶When I think about this, I am
terribly afraid.
My body shakes!
⁷Why do evil people live a long time?
They grow old and become more
powerful.
⁸They see their children become
strong around them.
They watch their children grow
up.
⁹Their homes are safe and without
fear.
God does not punish them.

¹⁰Their bulls never fail to mate.
Their cows have healthy calves.
¹¹Their children run and play like
flocks of lambs.
Their little ones dance about.
¹²They sing to the music of
tambourines^d and harps.
The sound of the flute makes
them happy.
¹³Evil people enjoy success during
their lives.
Then they go down in peace to
where the dead are.
¹⁴But they say to God, 'Leave us
alone!
We don't want to know your
ways.
¹⁵Who is God All-Powerful that we
should serve him?
We would gain nothing by
praying to him.'
¹⁶But the wicked think they succeed
by their own strength.
Their way of thinking is not
godly.
¹⁷Yet how often is the lamp of evil
people turned off?
How often does trouble come to
them?
How often do they suffer the
punishment God plans in his
anger?
¹⁸How often are they like straw in the
wind
or like chaff^d that is blown away
by a storm?
¹⁹It is said, 'God saves up a man's
punishment for the man's
children.'
God should punish the evil
person himself so he will know
it.
²⁰His eyes should see his own
destruction.
He should suffer the anger of
God All-Powerful.
²¹He does not care about the family
he leaves behind
when his life has come to an end.

²²"No one can teach knowledge to
God.
He is the one who judges even
the most important people.
²³One man dies while he still has all
his strength.
He feels completely safe and
comfortable.
²⁴His body was well fed.
And his bones were strong and
healthy.

²⁵But another man dies with an
unhappy heart.
He never had any happiness.
²⁶These two men are buried next to
each other.
And worms cover both of them.

²⁷"I know very well what you are
thinking.
I know your plans to do wrong to
me.
²⁸You say about me, 'Now where is
this great man's house?
And where are the tents where
the evil men lived?'
²⁹You have never asked those who
travel.
You have not listened to their
stories.
³⁰On the day of God's anger and
punishment,
it is the evil man who is spared.
³¹Who will accuse him to his face?
No one pays him back for the evil
he has done.
³²He is carried to his grave.
And someone keeps watch over
his tomb.
³³The dirt in the valley will seem
sweet to him.
Everybody follows after him.
Many people go before him.

³⁴"So you cannot comfort me with
this nonsense.
Your answers are still only lies!"

22 Then Eliphaz the Temanite answered:

²"A man cannot be of any real use to
God.
Even a wise man does him no
good.
³It does not help God All-Powerful
for you to be good.
He gains nothing if you are
innocent.
⁴God does not punish you for
respecting him.
He does not bring you into court
for this.
⁵No! It is because your evil is
without limits.
And your sins have no end.
⁶You took your brothers' things to
pay a debt they didn't owe.
You took clothes from people and
left them naked.
⁷You did not give water to tired
people.
And you kept food away from the
hungry.

⁸You were a powerful man who
　　owned land.
　　You were honored and lived in
　　the land.
⁹But you sent widows away without
　　giving them anything.
　　You even mistreated orphans.
¹⁰That is why traps are all around
　　you.
　　That is why sudden danger
　　frightens you.
¹¹That is why it is so dark you cannot
　　see.
　　And that is why a flood of water
　　covers you.

¹²"God is in the highest part of
　　heaven.
　　See how high the highest stars
　　are!
¹³But you say, 'God knows nothing.
　　He cannot judge us through the
　　dark clouds.
¹⁴Thick clouds cover him so he
　　cannot see us.
　　He walks around high up in the
　　sky.'
¹⁵Are you going to stay on the old
　　path
　　where evil people walk?
¹⁶They were carried away before
　　their time was up.
　　Their foundations were washed
　　away by a flood.
¹⁷They said to God, 'Leave us alone!
　　God All-Powerful can do nothing
　　to us.'
¹⁸But it was God who filled their
　　houses with good things.
　　He did this even though their way
　　of thinking was not godly.

¹⁹"Good people can watch and be
　　glad.
　　Innocent people can laugh at
　　them and say,
²⁰'Surely our enemies are destroyed.
　　And fire burns up their wealth.'

²¹"Obey God, and then you will be at
　　peace with him.
　　This way you can be happy.
²²Accept teaching from his mouth.
　　Keep his words in your heart.
²³If you return to God All-Powerful,
　　you will be blessed again.
　　Remove evil from your house.
²⁴Throw your gold nuggets into the
　　dust.
　　Throw your fine gold to the rocks
　　in the ravines.

²⁵Then God All-Powerful will be your
　　gold.
　　He will be the best silver for you.
²⁶You will find pleasure in God
　　All-Powerful.
　　And you will look up to him.
²⁷You will pray to him, and he will
　　hear you.
　　And you will keep your promises
　　to him.
²⁸Anything you decide will be done.
　　And light will shine on your
　　ways.
²⁹When terrible things happen to
　　people, you will say, 'Have
　　courage.'
　　Then those who are humble will
　　be saved.
³⁰Even the guilty will escape.
　　They will be saved because your
　　hands are clean.'"ᵈ

23

Then Job answered:

²"My complaint is still strong
　　today.
　　God's hand is heavy against me
　　even though I am groaning.
³I wish I knew where to find God.
　　I wish I could go to where he
　　lives.
⁴I would present my case before
　　him.
　　I would fill my mouth with
　　arguments.
⁵I would know the words of his
　　answer.
　　And I would think about what he
　　would say.
⁶He would not come against me with
　　great power.
　　He would really listen to me.
⁷Then an honest person could
　　present his case to God.
　　And I would be saved forever
　　from my judge.

⁸"If I go to the east, God is not there.
　　And if I go to the west, I do not
　　see him there.
⁹When he is at work in the north, I
　　catch no sight of him.
　　And when he turns to the south, I
　　cannot see him.
¹⁰But God knows the way that I take.
　　When he has tested me, I will
　　come out pure as gold.
¹¹My feet have closely followed his
　　steps.
　　I have stayed in his way without
　　turning aside.

¹²I have never left the commands he
   has spoken.
  I have treasured his words more
   than my food.

¹³"But he is the only God.
  No one can come against him.
  He does anything he wants.
¹⁴He will do to me what he said he
   would do.
  And he has many plans like this.
¹⁵That is why I am so afraid before
   him.
  When I think of all this, I am
   afraid of him.
¹⁶God has made me afraid.
  God All-Powerful has made me
   terribly afraid.
¹⁷But I am not cut off by the
   darkness,
  by the thick darkness that covers
   my face.

24 "I wish God All-Powerful would
   set a time for judging.
  People who know God look for
   such a day, but they do not see
   it.
²Wicked people take other people's
   land.
  They steal flocks of sheep and
   take them to new pastures.
³They chase away the orphan's
   donkey.
  And they take the widow's ox
   when she cannot pay what she
   owes.
⁴They push needy people off the
   path.
  So all the poor people of the land
   hide from them.
⁵The poor become like wild donkeys
   in the desert.
  They go about their job of finding
   food.
  The desert gives them food for
   their children.
⁶They gather hay and straw in the
   fields.
  And they pick up leftover grapes
   from the evil man's vineyard.
⁷They spend the night naked,
   because they have no clothes.
  They have nothing to cover
   themselves in the cold.
⁸They are soaked from mountain
   rains.
  They stay near the large rocks
   because they have no shelter.
⁹The child who has no father is
   grabbed from its mother's
   breast.

They take a poor mother's baby
   to pay for what she owes.
¹⁰So the poor go around naked
   because they have no clothes.
  They carry bundles of grain for
   evil people, but they still go
   hungry.
¹¹They crush olives to get oil.
  And they crush grapes in the
   winepresses,ᵈ but they still are
   thirsty.
¹²Dying people groan in the city.
  People who are injured cry out
   for help.
  But God accuses no one of doing
   wrong.

¹³"There are people who fight
   against the light.
  God's ways are strange to them.
  And they do not stay in the
   lighted path.
¹⁴When the light of day is gone, the
   murderer gets up.
  He kills poor and needy people.
  At night he goes about like a
   thief.
¹⁵The person who is guilty of
   adulteryᵈ watches for the night.
  He thinks, 'No one will see me.'
  And he keeps his face covered.
¹⁶In the dark, evil people break into
   houses.
  But in the daytime they shut
   themselves up in their own
   houses.
  They want nothing to do with the
   light.
¹⁷Darkness is like morning to all
   these evil people.
  They make friends with the
   terrors of darkness.

¹⁸"They are like foam floating on the
   water.
  Their part of the land is cursed.
  No one uses the road that goes by
   their vineyards.
¹⁹Heat and dryness quickly take
   away the melted snow.
  In the same way, the place for the
   dead quickly takes away those
   who have sinned.
²⁰The evil person's mother will even
   forget him.
  The worms will eat his body.
  He will no longer be remembered.
  So wickedness is broken in
   pieces like a stick.

²¹These evil men are unfair to
women who cannot have
children.
    And they show no kindness to
widows.
²²God drags away strong men by his
power.
    But even though they seem
strong, they do not know how
long they will live.
²³God may let these evil people feel
safe.
    But he is watching their ways.
²⁴For a little while they are
important, and then they are
gone.
    They are made unimportant and
gathered up like everyone else.
    They are cut off like the tops of
stalks of grain.
²⁵If this is not true, who can prove I
am wrong?
    And who can show that my
words are worth nothing?"

25
Then Bildad the Shuhite answered:

²"God rules and must be honored.
    He set up order in his high
heaven.
³No one can count God's armies.
    His light shines on all people.
⁴So no man can be good in the
presence of God,
    No one born to a woman can be
pure.
⁵Even the moon is not bright,
    and the stars are not pure in his
eyes.
⁶Man is much less! He is like an
insect.
    He is only a worm!"

26
Then Job answered:

²"You are no help to a person
who has no strength!
    You have given no help to one
whose arm is weak!
³You have given advice to me as if I
had no wisdom!
    This is not great wisdom you
have shown!
⁴Who has helped you say these
words?
    And where did you get these
words you speak?

⁵"The spirits of the dead beneath the
waters shake.
    And so do those that live in the
waters.

⁶Death is naked before God.
    Destruction is uncovered before
him.
⁷God stretches the northern sky out
over empty space.
    And he hangs the earth on
nothing.
⁸God wraps up the waters in his
thick clouds.
    But the clouds do not break
under the weight of the water.
⁹God covers the face of the full
moon.
    He spreads his clouds over it.
¹⁰God draws the horizon like a circle
on the water
    at the place where light and
darkness meet.
¹¹Heaven's foundations shake
    when he thunders at them.
¹²God's power controls the sea.
    By his wisdom he destroyed
Rahab,ᵈ the sea monster.
¹³God breathes, and the sky becomes
clear.
    God's hand stabs the gliding
snake.
¹⁴And these are only a small part of
God's works.
    We only hear a small whisper of
him.
    So who can understand God's
thundering power?"

27
And Job continued speaking:

²"As surely as God lives, he has
taken away my rights.
    God All-Powerful has made me
unhappy.
³As long as I am alive
    and God's breath of life is in my
nose,
⁴My lips will not speak evil.
    And my tongue will not tell a lie.
⁵I will never agree you are right.
    Until I die, I will never stop
saying I was innocent.
⁶I will hold tightly to the right things
I said.
    My sense of right and wrong
does not bother me at all.

⁷"Let my enemies be like evil
people.
    Let them be like those who are
not fair!
⁸What hope does a wicked person
have when he dies?
    He has no hope when God takes
his life away.

⁹God will not listen to his cry
  when trouble comes to him.
¹⁰He will not find joy in God
    All-Powerful,
  even though he calls out to God
    all the time.

¹¹"I will teach you about the power
    of God.
  I will not hide the ways of God
    All-Powerful.
¹²You have all seen this yourselves.
  So why are we having all this
    talk that means nothing?

¹³"Here is what God has planned for
    evil people.
  This is what cruel people will get
    from God All-Powerful:
¹⁴They may have many children, but
    the sword will kill them.
  The children who are left will
    never have enough to eat.
¹⁵Then they will die and be buried.
  And the widows will not even cry
    for them.
¹⁶The evil person may heap up silver
    like piles of dirt.
  He may have so many clothes
    they are like piles of clay.
¹⁷But good people will wear what the
    evil person has gathered.
  And those who are not guilty of
    wrong will divide up his silver.
¹⁸The house the evil person builds is
    like a spider's web.
  It is like a hut that a guard builds.
¹⁹The evil person is rich when he
    goes to bed, but he is rich for
    the last time.
  When he opens his eyes,
    everything is gone.
²⁰Fears come over him like a flood.
  A storm snatches him away in
    the night.
²¹The east wind will carry him away,
    and then he is gone.
  It sweeps him out of his place.
²²The wind will hit the evil person
    without mercy
  as he tries to run away from its
    power.
²³It will be as if the wind is clapping
    its hands at him.
  It will whistle at him as he runs
    from his place.

28 "There are mines where people
    dig silver.
  And there are places where gold
    is made pure.
²Iron is taken out of the ground.
  And copper is melted out of
    rocks.
³Miners bring light into the mines.
  They search even the deepest
    parts of the mines.
  They look for metal in places of
    thick darkness.
⁴Miners dig a tunnel far away from
    where people live.
  They dig it where people never
    go.
  They work far away from people,
    swinging and swaying from
    ropes.
⁵Food grows on top of the earth.
  But below ground things are
    changed as if by fire.
⁶Sapphires are found in rocks.
  And the dust of the earth
    contains gold.
⁷No hawk knows the path.
  The falcon has not seen it.
⁸Proud animals have not walked on
    this path.
  And no lions cross over it.
⁹Men hit the rocks of flint.
  They dig away at the bottom of
    the mountains.
¹⁰Miners cut tunnels through the
    rock.
  They see all the treasures there.
¹¹They search the places where
    rivers begin.
  And they bring things hidden
    there out into the light.

¹²"But where can wisdom be found.
  Where does understanding live?
¹³People do not understand the value
    of wisdom.
  It cannot be found among living
    people.
¹⁴The deep ocean says, 'It's not in
    me.'
  The sea says, 'It's not in me.'
¹⁵Wisdom cannot be bought with the
    best gold.
  Its cost cannot be weighed in
    silver.
¹⁶Wisdom cannot be bought with fine
    gold.
  It cannot be bought with valuable
    onyx or sapphire gems.
¹⁷Gold and crystal are not as
    valuable as wisdom.

And you cannot buy it with
jewels of gold.
¹⁸Coral and jasper are not even
worth talking about.
The price of wisdom is much
greater than rubies.
¹⁹The topaz from Cush cannot
compare to wisdom.
It cannot even be bought with the
purest gold.

²⁰"So from where does wisdom
come?
And where does understanding
live?
²¹It is hidden from the eyes of every
living thing.
It is hidden even from the birds
of the air.
²²The places of destruction and death
say,
'We have only heard reports
about it.'
²³God understands the way to
wisdom.
And he is the only one who
knows where it lives.
²⁴This is because God sees to the
farthest parts of the earth.
And he sees everything under the
heavens.
²⁵Wisdom began when God gave
power to the wind.
It was when he measured the
water and put limits on it.
²⁶It was when God made rules for the
rain.
And he set a path for a
thunderstorm to follow.
²⁷Then God looked at wisdom and
decided its worth.
He set wisdom up and tested it.
²⁸Then he said to man,
'The fear of the Lord is wisdom,
and to stay away from evil is
understanding.'"

29 Job continued to speak:

²"How I wish for the months
that have passed.
I wish for the days when God
watched over me.
³I wish for the days when God's
lamp shined on my head.
And I wish for the time I walked
through darkness by his light.
⁴I wish for the days when I was at
my strongest,
when God's close friendship
blessed my house.

⁵That was when my children were
all around me.
And God All-Powerful was still
with me.
⁶Life was so good. It was as if my
path were covered with cream.
It was as if even the rocks poured
out streams of olive oil for me.
⁷I would go to the city gate
and sit in the public square.
⁸When the young men saw me, they
would step out of my way.
And the old men would stand up
in respect for me.
⁹The leading men stopped speaking
and covered their mouths with
their hands.
¹⁰The voices of the important men
were quiet.
It was as if each man's tongue
stuck to the roof of his mouth.
¹¹Anyone who heard me said good
things about me.
And those who saw me praised
me.
¹²This was because I saved the poor
who cried for help.
And I saved the orphan who had
no one to help him.
¹³The dying person blessed me.
And I made the widow's heart
sing.
¹⁴I put on right living as if it were
clothing.
I wore fairness as if it were my
robe and my turban.
¹⁵I tried to be eyes for the blind.
And I tried to be feet for those
who were crippled.
¹⁶I was like a father to needy people.
And I took the side of strangers
when they were in trouble.
¹⁷I broke the fangs of evil people.
And I snatched from their teeth
the people they wanted to hurt.
¹⁸I thought, 'I will live for as many
days as there are grains of
sand.
And I will die in my own house.
¹⁹I will be like a tree whose roots
reach down to the water.
The dew will lie on the branches
all night.
²⁰New honors will come to me
continually.
I will always have great strength.'

²¹"People listened to me carefully.
They waited quietly for my
advice.

22 After I finished speaking, they
spoke no more.
My words fell very gently on
their ears.
23 They waited for me as they would
for rain.
They drank in my words as if
they were spring rain.
24 I smiled at them when they
doubted.
And my approval was important
to them.
25 I chose the right way for them and
was their leader.
I lived like a king among his
army.
I was like a person who gives
comfort to sad people.

30 "But now men who are younger
than I
make fun of me.
I would not have even let their
fathers
sit with my sheep dogs.
2 Their hands had no strength to
help me.
They had even lost their strength
to work.
3 They were thin from being hungry
and in need.
They wandered through the dry
and ruined land at night.
4 They gathered desert plants by the
brush for food.
They even ate the root of the
broom tree.
5 They were forced to live away from
other people.
People shouted at them as if they
were thieves.
6 These young men had to live in
dried up streambeds.
They lived in caves and among
the rocks.
7 They howled like animals out
among the bushes.
And they huddled together in the
brush.
8 They are worthless people without
names.
They were forced to leave the
land.

9 "Now they make fun of me with
songs.
My name has become a joke
among them.
10 They hate me and stay far away
from me.
But they do not mind spitting in
my face.

11 God has taken away my strength
and made me suffer.
So they attack me with all their
anger.
12 On my right side they attack me
like a mob.
They lay traps for my feet.
They prepare to attack me.
13 They break up my road.
They work to destroy me
without anyone stopping them.
14 They go forward as if through a
hole in the wall.
They roll in among the ruins.
15 Great fears overwhelm me.
They blow my honor away as if
by a great wind.
My safety disappears like a
cloud.

16 "Now my life is almost over.
My days are full of suffering.
17 At night my bones ache.
Gnawing pains never stop.
18 In his great power God grabs hold
of my clothing.
He chokes me with the collar of
my coat.
19 He throws me into the mud.
And I become like dirt and ashes.

20 "I cry out to you, God, but you do
not answer.
I stand up, but you just look at
me.
21 You turn on me without mercy.
You attack me with your
powerful hand.
22 You snatch me up and throw me
into the wind.
You toss me about in the storm.
23 I know you will bring me down to
death.
You will bring me to the place
where all living people must
go.

24 "Surely no one would hurt a ruined
man
when he cries for help in his time
of trouble.
25 I have cried for those who are in
trouble.
My soul has been very sad for
poor people.
26 But when I hoped for good, only
evil came to me.
When I looked for light, darkness
came.
27 I never stop being upset inside.
Days of suffering are ahead of
me.

²⁸I have become black, but not by the sun.

I stand up in public and cry for help.

²⁹It is as if I have become a brother to wild dogs

and a friend to ostriches.

³⁰My skin becomes black and peels off.

My body burns with fever.

³¹My harp is tuned for singing a sad song.

And my flute is tuned for the sound of loud crying.

31 "But I made an agreement with my eyes

not to look with desire at a girl.

²What has God above promised those who do this?

What has God All-Powerful on high planned for them?

³It is ruin for the evil people.

It is disaster for those who do wrong.

⁴God sees my ways,

and he counts every step I take.

⁵"I have not been a dishonest person.

I have not lied to others.

⁶Let God weigh me on honest scales.

Then he will know I have done nothing wrong.

⁷I have not turned away from doing what is right.

My heart has not been led by my eyes to do wrong.

My hands have not been made unclean.ᵈ

⁸If I have done these things, then let other people eat what I have planted.

And let my crops be plowed up.

⁹"I have not desired another woman.

I have never waited at my neighbor's door to have sexual relations with his wife.

¹⁰If I have done these things, then let my wife grind another man's grain.

And let other men have sexual relations with her.

¹¹Sexual sin is shameful.

It is a sin which must be punished.

¹²It is like a fire that burns and destroys forever.

It would destroy all I have.

¹³"I have been fair to my male and female slaves

when they had a complaint against me.

¹⁴If I have not, how could I tell God what I did?

What will I answer when God asks me to explain what I've done?

¹⁵God made me in my mother's womb, and he also made them.

The same God formed both of us in our mothers' wombs.

¹⁶"I have never refused anything the poor wanted.

I have never let widows give up hope while looking for help.

¹⁷I have not kept my food to myself.

I have also given it to the orphans.

¹⁸Since I was young, I have been like a father to the orphans.

And from my birth I guided the widows.

¹⁹I have not let a person die because he had no clothes.

I have not let a needy person go without a coat.

²⁰That person's heart blessed me.

This was because I warmed him with the wool of my sheep.

²¹I have never hurt an orphan

even when I knew I could win in court.

²²If I have, then let my arm fall off my shoulder.

Let it be broken at the joint.

²³This is because I dread destruction from God.

I could not do such things because I fear his majesty.

²⁴"I have not put my trust in gold.

I have not said to pure gold, 'You are my safety.'

²⁵I have not celebrated my great wealth.

I have not celebrated that my hands had gained riches.

²⁶I have not thought about worshiping the sun in its brightness.

I have not admired the moon moving in glory

²⁷so that my heart was pulled away from God.

My hand has never offered the sun and moon a kiss of worship.

²⁸If I had, these also would have been sins to be punished.

I would have been unfaithful to
God if I had done these things.

²⁹"I have not been happy when my
enemy was ruined.
I have not laughed when he had
trouble.
³⁰I have not let my mouth sin
by cursing my enemy's life.
³¹The men of my house have always
said,
'Everyone has eaten all he wants
of Job's food.'
³²No stranger ever had to spend the
night in the street.
I always let the traveler stay in
my home.
³³I have not hidden my sin as other
men do.
I did not hide my guilt in my
heart.
³⁴I was not so afraid of the crowd.
I did not keep quiet and stay inside
because I feared being hated by
other families.
³⁵("How I wish a court would hear
my case!
Here I sign my name to show I
have told the truth.
Now let God All-Powerful answer
me.
Let the one who is against me
write down what he accuses
me of.
³⁶I would surely wear the writing on
my shoulder.
I would put it on like a crown.
³⁷I would explain to God every step I
took.
I would come near to God like a
prince.)
³⁸"My land did not cry out against
me.
Its plowed rows were not wet
with tears.
³⁹I did not take the land's harvest
without paying.
I did not break the spirit of those
who took care of the land.
⁴⁰If I did, then let thorns come up
instead of wheat.
And let weeds come up instead of
barley."
The words of Job are finished.

32 These three men stopped answering Job. This is because Job was so sure he was right. ²But Elihu son of Barakel the Buzite became very angry with Job. (Elihu was from the family of Ram.) He was angry because Job claimed he was right instead of God. ³Elihu was also angry with Job's three friends. They had no answer to show that Job was wrong. And yet they continued to blame him. ⁴Now Elihu had waited before speaking to Job. This is because the three friends were older than he was. ⁵But when Elihu saw that the three men had nothing more to say, he became very angry.

⁶So Elihu son of Barakel the Buzite said this:

"I am young,
and you are old.
That is why I was afraid
to tell you what I know.
⁷I thought, 'Older people should
speak.
Those who have lived many years
should teach wisdom.'
⁸But it is the spirit in a person that
gives him understanding.
It is the breath of God
All-Powerful in him.
⁹It is not just older people who are
wise.
Older people are not the only
ones who understand what is
right.
¹⁰So I say, listen to me!
I will also tell you what I know.
¹¹I waited while you spoke.
I listened to your explanations.
I waited while you looked for words
to use.
¹² I paid close attention to you.
But not one of you has proved Job
wrong.
Not one of you has answered his
arguments.
¹³Don't you say, 'We have found
wisdom.
Only God will show Job to be
wrong, not people.'
¹⁴Job has not spoken his words
against me.
So I will not use your arguments
to answer Job.

¹⁵"These three friends are defeated
and have no more to say.
Words have failed them.
¹⁶Now they are standing there with
no answer for Job.
Now that they are quiet, must I
wait to speak?
¹⁷No, I also will speak.
I will also tell what I know.
¹⁸I am full of words,

And the spirit in me causes me to speak.

¹⁹I am like wine that has been bottled up.
I am ready to burst like a new leather bag for holding wine.

²⁰I must speak. Then I will feel relief.
I must open my mouth and answer.

²¹I will be fair to everyone.
I will not flatter anyone.

²²I don't know how to flatter.
If I did, God, my Maker, would quickly take me away.

33 ¹"But now, Job, listen to my words.
Pay attention to everything I say.

²I open my mouth.
I am ready to speak.

³My words come from an honest heart.
I am sincere when I speak what I know.

⁴The Spirit^d of God created me.
The breath of God All-Powerful gave me life.

⁵Answer me if you can.
Get yourself ready and stand before me.

⁶I am just like you before God.
I was also made out of clay.

⁷Don't be afraid of me.
I will not be hard on you.

⁸"But I heard what you have said.
I heard every word.

⁹You said, 'I am pure and without sin.
I am innocent and free from guilt.

¹⁰But God has found fault with me.
He considers me his enemy.

¹¹He locks my feet in chains.
He closely watches everywhere I go.'

¹²"But I tell you, you are not right in saying this.
God is greater than we are!

¹³Why do you accuse God
of not answering man's complaints?

¹⁴God does speak—sometimes one way and sometimes another.
He speaks even though men may not understand it.

¹⁵God may speak in a dream or a vision of the night.
This is when men are in a deep sleep and lying in their beds.

¹⁶He may speak in their ears
and frighten them with warnings.

¹⁷He warns them to turn away from doing wrong.
And he warns them not to be proud.

¹⁸God does this to save a man's soul from death.
He does it to keep him from dying.

¹⁹A man may be corrected while on his bed in great pain.
He may have continual pain in his very bones.

²⁰He may be in such pain that he even hates food.
He may hate even the very best meal.

²¹His body becomes so thin there is almost nothing left of it.
And his bones that were hidden by flesh now stick out.

²²His soul is near the place of death.
His life is almost over.

²³"But there may be an angel on his side.
The angel may be one out of a thousand who will speak for the man.
He will tell the man what he should do.

²⁴The angel will beg for mercy and say:
'Save this man from the place of death.
I have found a way to pay for his life.'

²⁵Then his body is made new like a child's body.
It will be returned to the way it was when he was young.

²⁶That person will pray to God, and God will listen to him.
He will see God's face and will shout with happiness.
And God will set things right for him again.

²⁷Then the man will say to other people,
'I sinned and twisted what was right.
But I did not receive the punishment I should have received.

²⁸God bought back my life from death.
And I will continue to enjoy life.'

²⁹"God does all these things to a man.

He does them two times or even
three.
[30] He does them so a person won't die
as punishment for his sins.
He does it so the man may still
enjoy life.

[31] "Job, pay attention and listen to
me.
Be quiet, and I will speak.
[32] If you have anything to say, answer
me.
Speak up, because I want you to
be shown as right.
[33] But if you have nothing to say, then
listen to me.
Be quiet, and I will teach you
wisdom."

34

Then Elihu said:

[2] "Hear my words, you men who
think you are wise.
Listen to me, you men who think
you know a lot.
[3] The ear tests words
as the tongue tastes food.
[4] Let's decide for ourselves what is
right.
And let's learn together what is
good.

[5] "Job says, 'I am not guilty.
But God has refused me a fair
trial.
[6] Instead of getting a fair trial,
I am called a liar.
I have been seriously hurt,
even though I have not sinned.'
[7] There is no other man like Job.
He takes insults as if he were
drinking water.
[8] He is around people who do evil.
He spends time with wicked men.
[9] This is because he says, 'It does not
help a man
to try and please God.'

[10] "So listen to me, you who can
understand.
God All-Powerful can never do
wrong!
It is impossible for God to do evil.
[11] God pays a person back for what
he has done.
God gives him what his actions
deserve.
[12] Truly God will never do wrong!
God All-Powerful will never twist
what is right.
[13] No one chose God to rule over the
earth.

No one put him in charge of the
whole world.
[14] God could decide
to take away his spirit and
breath.
[15] If he did, all people would die
together.
And they would all turn back into
dust.

[16] "If you can understand, hear this.
Listen to what I have to say.
[17] Can anyone govern who hates what
is right?
How can you blame God who is
both fair and powerful?
[18] God is the one who says to kings,
'You are worth nothing.'
And he says to important people,
'You are evil.'
[19] God is not better to princes than
other people.
He is not better to rich people
than poor people.
This is because he made them all
with his own hands.
[20] They can die in a moment, in the
middle of the night.
The rich are struck down, and
then they pass away.
Powerful people die without
man's help.

[21] "God watches where people go.
He sees every step they take.
[22] There is no dark place or deep
shadow
where those who do evil can hide
from God.
[23] God does not need to watch people
more closely.
He does not need for men to
come before him for judging.
[24] Without asking questions, God
breaks powerful people into
pieces.
And he puts other people in their
place.
[25] This is because God knows what
people do.
He defeats them in the night, and
they are crushed.
[26] He punishes them for the evil
things they do.
He does it so that everyone else
can watch.
[27] This is because they stopped
following God.
They did not care about any of
his ways.

28God lets the cry of poor people
reach him.
He hears the cry of the needy.
29But if God keeps quiet, who can
blame him?
If he hides his face, no one can
see him.
But God still rules over both men
and nations.
30 He still keeps wicked men from
ruling.
And he keeps them from
trapping others.
31"But suppose such a man says to
God,
'I am guilty, but I will not sin
anymore.
32Teach me what I cannot see.
If I have done wrong, I will not
do it again.'
33So, Job, should God reward you the
way you want
when you will not change your
heart and life?
You must decide, not I.
So tell me what you know.

34"Men who understand speak.
And wise men who hear me say,
35'Job speaks without knowing what
is true.
His words show he does not
understand.'
36I wish Job would be tested
completely
because he answered like an evil
man!
37Job has sinned, and now he turns
against God.
He claps his hands as an insult.
And he speaks more and more
against God."

35 Then Elihu said:

2"Do you think this is fair?
You say, 'God will show that I am
right.'
3But you say to him, 'What good is it
to me?
I don't gain anything by not
sinning.'

4"I would like to answer you.
And I want to answer your
friends who are with you.
5Look up at the sky and see.
Look at the clouds so high above
you.
6If you sin, it does nothing to God.
Even if your sins are many, they
do nothing to God.

7If you are good, you give nothing to
God.
He receives nothing from your
hand.
8Your evil ways only hurt a man like
yourself.
And the good you do only helps
other human beings.

9"People cry out for help when they
are in trouble.
They beg for relief from powerful
people.
10But no one asks, 'Where is God, my
Maker?
He gives us songs in the night.
11He makes us more clever than the
animals of the earth.
He makes us wiser than the birds
of the air.'
12God does not answer evil people
when they cry for help.
This is because they are too
proud.
13He does not listen to their useless
begging.
God All-Powerful pays no
attention to them.
14He will listen to you even less
when you say you do not see him.
He will not listen when you say
your case is before him
and you must wait for him.
15He will not listen when you say his
anger never punishes
and that he doesn't notice evil.
16So Job is only speaking useless
words.
He says many words without
knowing what is true."

36 Elihu continued:

2"Listen to me a little longer.
Then I will show you
that there is more to be said for
God's side.
3What I know comes from far away.
I will show that God, my Maker,
is right.
4You can be sure that my words are
not false.
One who really knows is with
you.
5"God is powerful, but he does not
hate people.
He is powerful and sure of what
he wants to do.
6God will not keep evil people alive.
But he gives troubled people
their rights.

⁷God does not stop watching over
　　those who do right.
　He sets them on thrones with
　　kings.
　And he lifts them up on high
　　forever.
⁸People may be bound in chains.
　Or trouble may tie them up like
　　ropes around them.
⁹But then God tells them what they
　　have done.
　He tells them they have sinned by
　　being too proud.
¹⁰God makes them listen to his
　　warning.
　He commands them to change
　　from doing evil.
¹¹If they obey and serve him,
　the rest of their lives will be
　　successful.
　And the rest of their years will be
　　happy.
¹²But if they do not listen,
　they will die by the sword.
　And they will die without
　　knowing better.

¹³"People who have wicked hearts
　　hold on to anger.
　Even when God ties them down
　　with trouble, they do not cry
　　for help.
¹⁴They die while they are still young.
　They die among the male
　　prostitutes[d] at the places of
　　worship.
¹⁵But God will save suffering people
　　by their suffering.
　He gets them to listen through
　　their pain.

¹⁶"God is gently calling you from the
　　jaws of trouble.
　He is calling you to an open place
　　of freedom.
　There he has set your table full of
　　the best food.
¹⁷But now you are given the
　　punishment evil people should
　　have.
　Now you are being punished.
¹⁸Be careful! Don't be led away from
　　God by riches.
　Don't let a promise of much
　　money turn you away.
¹⁹Neither your wealth nor all your
　　great strength
　will keep you out of trouble.
²⁰Don't wish for the night.
　That is when people are taken
　　from their homes.

²¹Be careful not to turn to evil,
　which you seem to want more
　　than suffering.

²²"God does great things by his
　　power.
　No other teacher is like him.
²³No one has planned his ways for
　　him.
　No one has said to God, 'You
　　have done wrong.'
²⁴Remember to praise his work.
　Men sing about it.
²⁵Everybody has seen it.
　People look at it from far off.
²⁶God is so great! He is greater than
　　we can understand!
　No one can discover how many
　　years he has been alive.

²⁷"God takes up the drops of water
　　from the earth.
　And he turns them into drops of
　　rain.
²⁸Then the rain pours down from the
　　clouds.
　And showers fall on people.
²⁹No one understands how God
　　spreads out the clouds.
　No one understands how he
　　thunders from where he lives.
³⁰Watch how God scatters his
　　lightning around him.
　It even lights up the deepest parts
　　of the sea.
³¹This is the way God governs the
　　nations.
　This is how he gives us enough
　　food.
³²God fills his hands with lightning.
　And he commands it to strike its
　　target.
³³His thunder announces that a
　　storm is coming.
　Even the cattle show that the
　　storm is coming.

37 "At the sound of his thunder, my
　　heart pounds.
　It is as if my heart will jump out
　　of my chest.
²Listen! Listen to the thunder of
　　God's voice.
　Listen to the rumbling that comes
　　from his mouth.
³He turns his lightning loose under
　　the whole sky.
　And he sends it to the farthest
　　parts of the earth.
⁴After that you can hear the roar
　　when he thunders with a great
　　sound.

He does not hold back the flashing
  when his voice is heard.
⁵God's voice thunders in wonderful
    ways.
  He does great things we cannot
    understand.
⁶God says to the snow, 'Fall on the
    earth.'
  And he says to the rain shower,
    'Be a heavy rain.'
⁷With it, God stops everyone from
    working.
  That way, everyone knows it is
    the work of God.
⁸The animals take cover from the
    rain.
  They stay in their dens.
⁹The storm comes from where it was
    stored.
  The cold comes from the strong
    winds.
¹⁰The breath of God makes ice.
  And the wide waters become
    frozen.
¹¹God fills the clouds up with water.
  And he scatters his lightning
    through them.
¹²At God's command they swirl
    around
  over the whole earth.
  They do whatever he commands.
¹³God uses the clouds to punish
    people
  or to water his earth and show
    his love.

¹⁴"Job, listen to this.
  Stop and notice God's miracles.ᵈ
¹⁵Do you know how God controls the
    clouds
  and makes his lightning flash?
¹⁶Do you know how the clouds hang
    in the sky?
  They are the miracles of God,
    who knows everything.
¹⁷You suffer in your clothes
  when the land is made quiet by
    the hot, south wind.
¹⁸You cannot stretch out the sky like
    God
  and make it look as hard as
    polished bronze.
¹⁹Tell us what we should say to God.
  We cannot get our arguments
    ready because we do not have
    enough understanding.
²⁰Should God be told that I want to
    speak?
  A man might try to speak to God,
    but he would surely be
    swallowed up.

²¹No one can look at the sun
  when it is bright in the sky
  after the wind has blown all the
    clouds away.
²²God comes out of the north in
    golden light.
  He comes in overwhelming
    greatness.
²³God All-Powerful is too high for us
    to reach.
  He has great strength.
  He is always right and never
    punishes unfairly.
²⁴That is why people honor God.
  He does not respect those who
    say they are wise."

38 Then the Lord answered Job from
    the storm. He said:

²"Who is this that makes my
    purpose unclear
  by saying things that are not
    true?
³Be strong like a man.
  I will ask you questions,
    and you must answer me.
⁴Where were you when I made the
    earth's foundation?
  Tell me, if you understand.
⁵Who marked off how big it should
    be?
  Surely you know!
⁶What were the earth's foundations
    set on?
  Or who put its cornerstoneᵈ in
    place?
⁷Who did all this while the morning
    stars sang together?
  Who did this while the angels
    shouted with joy?

⁸"Who shut the doors to keep the
    sea in
  when it broke through and was
    born?
⁹This was when I made the clouds
    like a coat for the sea.
  And I wrapped the sea in dark
    clouds.
¹⁰It was when I put limits on the sea.
  And I put its doors and bars in
    place.
¹¹It was when I said to the sea, 'You
    may come this far, but no
    farther.
  This is where your proud waves
    must stop.'

¹²"Have you ever given orders for
    morning to begin?
  Or have you shown the dawn
    where its place was?

¹³The dawn takes hold of earth by its
edges
and shakes evil people out of it.
¹⁴At dawn the earth changes like clay
being pressed by a seal.ᵈ
The hills and valleys stand out
like folds in a coat.
¹⁵Light is not given to evil people.
Their arm is raised to do harm,
but it is broken.

¹⁶"Have you ever gone to where the
sea begins?
Or have you walked in the
valleys under the sea?
¹⁷Have the gates of death been
opened to you?
Or have you seen the gates of the
deep darkness?
¹⁸Do you understand the great width
of the earth?
Tell me, if you know all these
things.

¹⁹"What is the path to light's home?
And where does darkness live?
²⁰Can you take them to their places?
Do you know the way to their
homes?
²¹Surely you know, if you were
already born when all this
happened!
Have you lived that many years?

²²"Have you ever gone into the
storehouse where snow is
kept?
Or have you seen the storehouses
for hail?
²³I save the snow and hail for times
of trouble.
I save them for days of war and
battle.
²⁴How do you get to the place where
light comes from?
Or where is the place from which
the east winds are scattered
over the earth?
²⁵Who cuts a waterway for the heavy
rains?
And who sets a path for the
thunderstorm to follow?
²⁶Who waters the land where no one
lives?
Who waters the desert that has
no one in it?
²⁷Who sends rain to satisfy the
empty land
so the grass begins to grow?
²⁸Does the rain have a father?
Who is father to the drops of
dew?

²⁹Who is the mother of the ice?
Who gives birth to the frost from
the sky?
³⁰The waters become hard as stone.
Even the surface of the deep
ocean is frozen.

³¹"Can you tie up the stars of the
Pleiades?
Can you loosen the ropes of the
stars in Orion?
³²Can you bring out the stars at the
right times?
Or can you lead out the stars of
the Bear with its cubs?
³³Do you know the laws of the sky?
Can you understand their rule
over the earth?

³⁴"Can you shout an order to the
clouds
and cover yourself with a flood of
water?
³⁵Can you send lightning bolts on
their way?
Do the flashes of lightning report
to you and say, 'Here we are'?
³⁶Who put wisdom inside the mind?
Or who put understanding in the
heart?
³⁷Who has the wisdom to count the
clouds?
Who can pour water from the
jars of heaven?
³⁸Who can do this when the dust
becomes hard
and the clumps of dirt stick
together?

³⁹"Do you hunt food for the female
lion
to satisfy the hunger of the young
lions?
⁴⁰Do you hunt for them while they lie
in their dens
or hide in the bushes waiting to
attack?
⁴¹Who gives food to the birds
when their young cry out to God?
And who gives them food when
they wander about without
any?

39 "Do you know when the
mountain goats give birth?
Do you watch when the deer
gives birth to her fawn?
²Do you count the months until they
give birth?
Do you know when the time is
right for them to give birth?
³They lie down, and their young are
born.

Then the pain of giving birth is
over.

[4]Their young ones grow and become
strong in the wild country.
Then they leave their homes and
do not come back.

[5]"Who let the wild donkey go free?
Who untied his ropes?

[6]I am the one who gave the donkey
the desert as his home.
I gave him the desert lands as a
place to live.

[7]The wild donkey laughs at the
confusion in the city.
He does not hear the drivers
shout.

[8]He roams the hills looking for
pasture.
And he looks for anything green
to eat.

[9]"Will the wild ox agree to serve
you?
Will he stay by your feeding box
at night?

[10]Can you hold him to the plowed
row with a harness?
Will he plow the valleys for you?

[11]Will you depend on the wild ox for
his great strength?
Will you leave your heavy work
for him to do?

[12]Can you trust the ox to bring in
your grain?
Will he gather it to your
threshing[d] floor?

[13]"The wings of the ostrich flap
happily.
But the ostrich's wings are not as
beautiful as the feathers of the
stork.

[14]The ostrich lays her eggs on the
ground
and lets them warm in the sand.

[15]She does not stop to think that a
foot might step on them and
crush them.
She does not care that some
animal might walk on them.

[16]The ostrich is cruel to her young, as
if they were not even hers.
She does not care that her work
is for nothing.

[17]This is because God did not give
the ostrich wisdom.
God did not give her a share of
good sense.

[18]But when the ostrich gets up to run,
she is so fast

that she laughs at the horse and
its rider.

[19]"Job, are you the one who gives the
horse his strength?
Or do you put a flowing mane on
his neck?

[20]Do you make the horse jump like a
locust?[d]
He scares people with his proud
snorting.

[21]He paws wildly, enjoying his
strength.
And he charges into the battle.

[22]He laughs at fear and is afraid of
nothing.
He will not run away from the
sword.

[23]The bag of arrows rattles against
the horse's side.
It is there with the flashing
spears.

[24]With great excitement, the horse
races over the ground.
He cannot stand still when he
hears the trumpet.

[25]When the trumpet blows, the horse
snorts, 'Aha!'
He smells the battle from far
away.
He hears the thunder of
commanders and the shouts of
battle.

[26]"Is it through your wisdom that the
hawk flies?
Is this why he spreads his wings
toward the south?

[27]Are you the one that commands the
eagle to fly
and build his nest so high?

[28]The eagle lives on a high cliff and
stays there at night.
The rocky peak is his protected
place.

[29]From there he looks for his food.
His eyes can see it from far away.

[30]His young eat blood.
And where there is something
dead, the eagle is there."

40

The Lord said to Job:

[2]"Will the person who argues
with God All-Powerful
correct him?
Let the person who accuses God
answer him!"

[3]Then Job answered the Lord:

[4]"I am not worthy. I cannot answer
you anything.

I will put my hand over my mouth.
⁵I spoke one time, but I will not answer again.
I even spoke two times, but I will say nothing more.'"

⁶Then the Lord spoke to Job from the storm:

⁷"Be strong, like a man.
I will ask you questions.
And you must answer me.
⁸Would you say that I am unfair?
Would you blame me to make yourself look right?
⁹Are you as strong as God?
And can your voice thunder like his?
¹⁰If so, then decorate yourself with glory and beauty.
And put on honor and greatness as if they were clothing.
¹¹Let your great anger punish.
Look at everyone who is proud and make him feel unimportant.
¹²Look at everyone who is proud and bring him under your control.
Crush the wicked wherever they are.
¹³Bury them all in the dirt together.
Cover their faces in the grave.
¹⁴If you can do that, then I myself will praise you
because you are strong enough to save yourself.

¹⁵"Look at the behemoth.ⁿ
I made him just as I made you.
He eats grass like an ox.
¹⁶Look at the strength he has in his body.
The muscles of his stomach are powerful!
¹⁷His tail extends like a cedar tree.
The muscles of his thighs are woven together.
¹⁸His bones are like tubes of bronze metal.
His legs are like bars of iron.
¹⁹He is one of the first of God's works.
But God, his Maker, can destroy him.
²⁰The hills, where the wild animals play,
provide food for him.
²¹He lies under the lotus plants

hidden by the tall grass in the swamp.
²²The lotus plants hide him in their shadow.
The poplar trees by the streams surround him.
²³If the river floods, he will not be afraid.
He is not afraid even if the Jordan River rushes to his mouth.
²⁴Can anyone blind his eyes and capture him?
Can anyone put hooks in his nose?

41 "Can you catch the leviathanⁿ on a fishhook?
Or can you tie his tongue down with a rope?
²Can you put a cord through his nose
or put a hook in his jaw?
³Will he keep begging you for mercy?
Will he speak to you with gentle words?
⁴Will he make an agreement with you?
Will he let you take him as your slave for life?
⁵Can you make a pet of the leviathan as you would a bird?
Or can you put him on a leash for your girls?
⁶Will traders try to bargain with you for him?
Will they divide him up among the traders?
⁷Can you stick him with darts until his skin is full of them?
Or can you fill his head with fishing spears?
⁸If you put one hand on him,
you will never forget the battle.
And you will never do it again!
⁹There is no hope of defeating him.
Just seeing him overwhelms people.
¹⁰No one is brave enough to make him angry.
So who would be able to stand up against me?
¹¹No one has ever given me anything that I must pay back.
Everything under heaven belongs to me.

¹²"I can silence his bragging.

40:15 behemoth A large land animal. It could refer to the hippopotamus, the elephant or a monster.   **41:1 leviathan** Possibly a crocodile or a sea monster.

I can silence his brave words and powerful arguments.

[13] No one can tear off his outer hide. No one can poke through his double armor.

[14] No one can force open his great jaws. There are frightening teeth all around his jaws.

[15] He has rows of shields on his back. They are tightly sealed together.

[16] Each shield is so close to the next one that no air can go between them.

[17] They are joined strongly to one another. They hold on to each other and cannot be broken apart.

[18] When he snorts, flashes of light are thrown out. His eyes look like the light at dawn.

[19] Flames blaze from his mouth. Sparks of fire shoot out.

[20] Smoke pours out of his nose as if coming from a large pot over a hot fire.

[21] His breath sets coals on fire. And flames come out of his mouth.

[22] There is great strength in his neck. People are afraid and run away from him.

[23] The folds of his skin are tightly joined. They are set and cannot be moved.

[24] His chest is as hard as a rock. It is as hard as a stone used to grind grain.

[25] Powerful creatures fear his terrible looks. They draw back in fear as he moves.

[26] The sword that hits him does not hurt him. The darts and spears, small and large, do not hurt him.

[27] He treats iron as if it were straw. And he treats bronze metal as if it were rotten wood.

[28] He does not run away from arrows. Stones from slings are like chaff[d] to him.

[29] Clubs feel like pieces of straw to him. And he laughs when they shake a spear at him.

[30] The underside of his body is like broken pieces of pottery. It leaves a trail in the mud like a threshing[d] board.

[31] He makes the deep sea bubble like a boiling pot. And he stirs up the sea like a pot of oil.

[32] When he swims, he leaves a shining path in the water. It makes the sea look as if it had white hair.

[33] Nothing else on earth is equal to him. He is a creature without fear.

[34] He looks down on all those who are too proud. He is king over all proud creatures.''

42

Then Job answered the Lord:

[2] ''I know that you can do all things. No plan of yours can be ruined.

[3] You asked, 'Who is this that made my purpose unclear by saying things that are not true?' Surely I talked about things I did not understand. I spoke of things too wonderful for me to know.

[4] You said, 'Listen now, and I will speak. I will ask you questions. And you must answer me.'

[5] My ears had heard of you before. But now my eyes have seen you.

[6] So now I hate myself. I will change my heart and sit in the dust and ashes.''

[7] After the Lord had said these things to Job, he spoke to Eliphaz the Temanite. The Lord said to him, "I am angry with you and your two friends. This is because you have not said what is right about me. But my servant Job did. [8] So now take seven bulls and seven male sheep. Go to my servant Job. And offer a burnt offering for yourselves. My servant Job will pray for you. And I will listen to his prayer. Then I will not punish you for being foolish. You have not said what is right about me. But my servant Job did." [9] So Eliphaz the Temanite did as the Lord told him to do. Bildad the Shuhite and Zophar the Naamathite also did as the Lord said. And the Lord listened to Job's prayer.

[10] After Job had prayed for his friends, God gave him success again. God gave Job twice as much as he had owned before. [11] Job's brothers and sisters came

to his house. Everyone who had known him before came to his house. And they all ate with him there. They comforted Job and spoke kindly to him. They made him feel better about the trouble the Lord had brought on him. And each one gave Job a piece of silver and a gold ring. [12]The Lord blessed the last part of Job's life even more than the first part. Job had 14,000 sheep and 6,000 camels. He had 1,000 pairs of oxen and 1,000 female donkeys. [13]Job also had seven sons and three daughters. [14]He named the first daughter Jemimah. The second daughter he named Keziah. And his third daughter he named Keren-Happuch. [15]There were no other women in all the land as beautiful as Job's daughters. And their father Job gave them land to own along with their brothers.

[16]After this, Job lived 140 years. He lived to see his children, grandchildren, great-grandchildren and great-great-grandchildren. [17]Then Job died. He was old and had lived many years.

The Book of
PSALMS

Book 1

Psalms 1–41

PSALM 1

[1]Happy is the person who doesn't listen to the wicked.
　He doesn't go where sinners go.
　He doesn't do what bad people do.
[2]He loves the Lord's teachings.
　He thinks about those teachings day and night.
[3]He is strong, like a tree planted by a river.
　It produces fruit in season.
　Its leaves don't die.
Everything he does will succeed.

[4]But wicked people are not like that.
　They are like useless chaff[d]
　that the wind blows away.
[5]So the wicked will not escape God's punishment.
　Sinners will not worship God with good people.
[6]This is because the Lord protects good people.
　But the wicked will be destroyed.

PSALM 2

[1]Why are the nations so angry?
　Why are the people making useless plans?
[2]The kings of the earth prepare to fight.
　Their leaders make plans together against the Lord
　and his appointed king.
[3]"Let's break the chains that hold us prisoners.
　Let's throw off the ropes that tie us," the nations say.

[4]But the Lord in heaven laughs.
　He makes fun of them.
[5]Then the Lord warns them.
　He frightens them with his anger.
[6]He says, "I have appointed my own king!
　He will rule in Jerusalem on my holy mountain."

[7]Now I will tell you what the Lord has declared:
　He said to me, "You are my son.
　Today I have become your father.
[8]If you ask me, I will give you the nations.
　All the people on earth will be yours.
[9]You will make them obey you by punishing them with an iron rod.
　You will break them into pieces like pottery."

[10]So, kings, be wise.
　Rulers, learn this lesson.
[11]Obey the Lord with great fear.
　Be happy, but tremble.
[12]Show that you are loyal to his son.
　Otherwise you will be destroyed.
　He can quickly become angry.
　But happy are those who trust him for protection.

PSALM 3

David sang this when he ran away from his son Absalom.

[1]Lord, I have many enemies!
　Many people have turned against me.
[2]Many people are talking about me.
　They say, "God won't rescue him."
　　　　　　　　　　　　　　Selah[d]

³But, Lord, you are my shield.
    You are my wonderful God who
        gives me courage.
⁴I will pray to the Lord.
    And he will answer me from his
        holy mountain.   *Selah*

⁵I can lie down and go to sleep.
    And I will wake up again
        because the Lord protects me.
⁶Thousands of enemies may surround
        me.
    But I am not afraid.

⁷Lord, rise up!
    My God, come save me!
You have hit my enemies on the cheek.
    You have broken the teeth of the
        wicked.
⁸The Lord can save his people.
    Lord, bless your people.   *Selah*

PSALM 4

For the director of music. With stringed
instruments. A song of David.

¹Answer me when I pray to you,
    my God who does what is right.
Lift the load that I carry.
    Be kind to me and hear my prayer.

²People, how long will you turn my
        honor into shame?
    You love what is false, and you look
        for new lies.   *Selah*ᵈ
³You know that the Lord has chosen
        for himself those who are loyal to
        him.
    The Lord listens when I pray to
        him.
⁴When you are angry, do not sin.
    Think about these things quietly
        as you go to bed.   *Selah*
⁵Do what is right as a sacrifice to the
        Lord.
    And trust the Lord.

⁶Many people ask,
    "Who will give us anything good?
    Lord, be kind to us."
⁷But you have made me very happy.
    I am happier than they are,
        even with all their grain and wine.
⁸I go to bed and sleep in peace.
    Lord, only you keep me safe.

PSALM 5

For the director of music. For flutes. A song
of David.

¹Lord, listen to my words.
    Understand what I am thinking.
²Listen to my cry for help.
    My king and my God, I pray to you.

³Lord, every morning you hear my
        voice.
    Every morning, I tell you what I
        need.
    And I wait for your answer.

⁴You are not a God who is pleased
        with what is wicked.
    You do not live with those who do
        evil.
⁵Those people who make fun of you
        cannot stand before you.
    You hate all those who do wrong.
⁶You destroy liars.
    The Lord hates those who kill and
        trick others.

⁷Because of your great love,
    I can come into your Temple.ᵈ
Because I fear and respect you,
    I can worship in your holy Temple.
⁸Lord, since I have many enemies,
    show me the right thing to do.
    Show me clearly how you want me
        to live.

⁹With their mouths my enemies do not
        tell the truth.
    In their hearts they want to destroy
        people.
Their throats are like open graves.
    They use their tongues for telling
        lies.
¹⁰God, declare them guilty!
    Let them fall into their own traps.
Send them away because their sins
        are many.
    They have turned against you.

¹¹But let everyone who trusts you be
        happy.
    Let them sing glad songs forever.
Protect those who love you.
    They are happy because of you.
¹²Lord, you bless those who do what is
        right.
    You protect them like a soldier's
        shield.

PSALM 6

For the director of music. With stringed
instruments. By the sheminith.ᵈ A song of
David.

¹Lord, don't correct me when you are
        angry.
    Don't punish me when you are very
        angry.
²Lord, be kind to me because I am
        weak.
    Heal me, Lord, because my bones
        ache.

³I am very upset.
  Lord, how long will it be?

⁴Lord, return and save me.
  Save me because of your kindness.
⁵Dead people don't remember me.
  Those in the grave don't praise you.

⁶I am tired of crying to you.
  Every night my bed is wet with
    tears.
  My bed is soaked from my crying.
⁷My eyes are weak from so much
    crying.
  They are weak from crying about
    my enemies.

⁸Get away from me, all you who do
    evil.
  The Lord has heard my crying.
⁹The Lord has heard my cry for help.
  The Lord will answer my prayer.
¹⁰All my enemies will be ashamed and
    troubled.
  They will turn and suddenly leave
    in shame.

PSALM 7

A shiggaion[d] of David which he sang to the
Lord about Cush, from the tribe of Benjamin.
¹Lord my God, I trust in you for
    protection.
  Save me and rescue me
  from those who are chasing me.
²Otherwise, they will tear me apart
    like a lion.
  They will rip me to pieces, and no
    one can save me.

³Lord my God, what have I done?
  Have my hands done something
    wrong?
⁴Have I done wrong to my friend?
  Have I stolen from my enemy?
⁵If I have, let my enemy chase me and
    capture me.
  Let him trample me into the dust.
  Let him bury me in the ground.
                              Selah[d]

⁶Lord, rise up in your anger.
  Stand up against my enemies'
    anger.
  Get up and demand fairness.
⁷Gather the nations around you,
  and rule them from above.
⁸Lord, judge the people.
  Lord, defend me.
  Prove that I am right.
  Show that I have done no wrong,
    God Most High.
⁹God, you do what is right.

You know our thoughts and
    feelings.
Stop those wicked actions done by
    evil people.
And help those who do what is right.

¹⁰God Most High protects me like a
    shield.
  He saves those whose hearts are
    right.
¹¹God judges by what is right.
  And God is always ready to punish
    the wicked.
¹²If they do not change their lives,
  God will sharpen his sword.
  He will string his bow and take
    aim.
¹³He has prepared his deadly weapons.
  He has made his flaming arrows.

¹⁴There are people who think up evil.
  They plan trouble and tell lies.
¹⁵They dig a hole to trap other people.
  But they will fall into it themselves.
¹⁶They themselves will get into trouble.
  The violence they cause will hurt
    only themselves.

¹⁷I praise the Lord because he does
    what is right.
  I sing praises to the name of the
    Lord Most High.

PSALM 8

For the director of music. By the gittith.[d] A
song of David.
¹Lord our Master,
  your name is the most wonderful
    name in all the earth!
  It brings you praise in heaven
    above.
²You have taught children and babies
    to sing praises to you.
  This is because of your enemies.
  And so you silence your enemies
  and destroy those who try to get
    even.

³I look at the heavens,
  which you made with your hands.
  I see the moon and stars,
  which you created.
⁴But why is man important to you?
  Why do you take care of human
    beings?
⁵You made man a little lower than the
    angels.
  And you crowned him with glory
    and honor.
⁶You put him in charge of everything
    you made.
  You put all things under his control:

⁷all the sheep, the cattle
  and the wild animals,
⁸the birds in the sky,
  the fish in the sea,
  and everything that lives under
    water.
⁹Lord our Master,
  your name is the most wonderful
    name in all the earth!

PSALM 9

For the director of music. To the tune of "The
Death of the Son." A song of David.
¹I will praise you, Lord, with all my
    heart.
  I will tell all the miracles[d] you have
    done.
²I will be happy because of you.
  God Most High, I will sing praises
    to your name.
³My enemies turn back.
  They are overwhelmed and die
    because of you.
⁴You have heard what I complained to
    you about.
  You sat on your throne and judged
    by what was right.
⁵You spoke strongly against the
    foreign nations
  and destroyed the wicked people.
  You wiped out their names forever
    and ever.
⁶The enemy is gone forever.
  You destroyed their cities.
  No one even remembers them.

⁷But the Lord rules forever.
  He sits on his throne to judge.
⁸The Lord will judge the world by
    what is right.
  He will decide what is fair for the
    nations.
⁹The Lord defends those who suffer.
  He protects them in times of
    trouble.
¹⁰Those who know the Lord trust him.
  He will not leave those who come
    to him.
¹¹Sing praises to the Lord who is king
    on Mount Zion.[d]
  Tell the nations what he has done.
¹²He remembers who the murderers
    are.
  He will not forget the cries of those
    who suffer.
¹³Lord, be kind to me.
  See how my enemies hurt me.
  Do not let me go through the gates
    of death.

¹⁴Then, at the gates of Jerusalem, I will
    praise you.
  I will rejoice because you saved me.

¹⁵The nations have fallen into the pit
    they dug.
  Their feet are caught in the nets
    they laid.
¹⁶The Lord has made himself known by
    his fair decisions.
  The wicked get trapped by what
    they do.   *Higgaion.*[d] Selah[d]

¹⁷Wicked people will go to the grave.
  So will all those who forget God.
¹⁸Those who have troubles will not be
    forgotten.
  The hopes of the poor will not die.

¹⁹Lord, rise up and judge the nations.
  Don't let humans think they are
    strong.
²⁰Teach them to fear you, Lord.
  The nations must learn that they
    are only human.   *Selah*

PSALM 10

¹Lord, why are you so far away?
  Why do you hide when there is
    trouble?
²Proudly the wicked chase down those
    who suffer.
  The wicked set traps to catch them.
³They brag about the things they want.
  They bless the greedy but hate the
    Lord.
⁴The wicked people are too proud.
  They do not look for God.
  There is no room for God in their
    thoughts.
⁵They always succeed.
  They are far from keeping your
    laws.
  They make fun of their enemies.
⁶They say to themselves, "Nothing bad
    will ever happen to me.
  I will never be ruined."
⁷Their mouths are full of curses, lies
    and threats.
  They use their tongues for sin and
    evil.
⁸They hide near the villages.
  They look for innocent people to
    kill.
  They watch in secret for the
    helpless.
⁹They wait in hiding like a lion.
  They wait to catch poor people.
  They catch the poor in nets.
¹⁰The poor are thrown down and
    crushed.

They are defeated because the
others are stronger.
[11] The wicked think,
"God has forgotten us.
He doesn't see what is happening."

[12] Lord, rise up and punish the wicked.
Don't forget those who need help.
[13] Why do wicked people hate God?
They say to themselves, "God won't
punish us."
[14] Lord, surely you see these cruel and
evil things.
Look at them and do something.
People in trouble look to you for help.
You are the one who helps the
orphans.
[15] Break the power of wicked men.
Punish them for the evil they have
done.

[16] The Lord is King forever and ever.
Remove from your land those
nations that do not worship you.
[17] Lord, you have heard what the poor
people want.
Do what they ask. Listen to them.
[18] Protect the orphans. Put an end to
suffering.
Then they will no longer be afraid
of evil people.

PSALM 11

For the director of music. Of David.
[1] I trust in the Lord for protection.
So why do you say to me,
"Fly like a bird to your mountain.
[2] Like hunters, the wicked string their
bows.
They set their arrows on the
bowstrings.
They shoot from dark places
at those who are honest.
[3] When all that is good falls apart,
what can good people do?"

[4] The Lord is in his holy temple.
The Lord sits on his throne in
heaven.
And he sees what people do.
He keeps his eye on them.
[5] The Lord tests those who do right.
But he hates the wicked and those
who love to hurt others.
[6] He will send hot coals on the wicked.
Burning sulfur and a whirlwind is
what they will get.
[7] The Lord does what is right, and he
loves justice.
So honest people will see his face.

PSALM 12

For the director of music. By the sheminith.[d]
A song of David.
[1] Save me, Lord, because the good
people are all gone.
No true believers are left on earth.
[2] Everyone lies to his neighbors.
They say one thing and mean
another.

[3] The Lord will stop those lying lips.
He will cut off those bragging
tongues.
[4] They say, "Our tongues will help us
win.
We can say what we wish. No one
is our master."

[5] But the Lord says,
"I will now rise up
because the poor are being hurt.
Because of the moans of the helpless,
I will give them the help they
want."
[6] The Lord's words are pure.
They are like silver purified by fire,
like silver purified seven times
over.

[7] Lord, keep us safe.
Always protect us from such
people.
[8] The wicked are all around us.
Everyone loves what is wrong.

PSALM 13

For the director of music. A song of David.
[1] How long will you forget me, Lord?
How long will you hide from me?
Forever?
[2] How long must I worry?
How long must I feel sad in my
heart?
How long will my enemy win over
me?

[3] Lord, look at me.
Answer me, my God.
Tell me, or I will die.
[4] Otherwise my enemy will say, "I have
won!"
Those against me will rejoice that
I've been defeated.

[5] I trust in your love.
My heart is happy because you
saved me.
[6] I sing to the Lord
because he has taken care of me.

PSALM 14

For the director of music. Of David.

¹A wicked fool says to himself,
    "There is no God."
Fools are evil. They do terrible things.
    None of them does anything good.

²The Lord looked down from heaven
    at all the people.
    He looked to see if anyone was
      wise,
    if anyone was looking to God for
      help.
³But all have turned away.
    Together, everyone has become
      evil.
    None of them does anything good.

⁴Don't the wicked understand?
    They destroy my people as if they
      were eating bread.
    They do not ask the Lord for help.
⁵But the wicked are filled with terror
    because God is with those who do
      what is right.
⁶The wicked upset the plans of the
    poor.
    But the Lord will protect the poor.

⁷I pray that victory will come to Israel
    from Mount Zion!ᵈ
    May the Lord give them back their
      riches.
    Then the people of Jacob will
      rejoice.
    And the people of Israel will be
      glad.

PSALM 15

A song of David.

¹Lord, who may enter your Holy
    Tent?ᵈ
    Who may live on your holy
      mountain?

²Only a person who is innocent
    and who does what is right.
    He must speak the truth from his
      heart.
³ He must not tell lies about others.
    He must do no wrong to his
      neighbors.
    He must not gossip.
⁴He must not respect hateful people.
    He must honor those who honor
      the Lord.
    He must keep his promises to his
      neighbor,
    even when it hurts.
⁵He must not charge interest on
    money he lends.

And he must not take money to
    hurt innocent people.

Whoever does all these things will
    never be destroyed.

PSALM 16

A miktamᵈ of David.

¹Protect me, God,
    because I trust in you.
²I said to the Lord, "You are my Lord.
    Every good thing I have comes
      from you."
³There are godly people in the world.
    I enjoy them.
⁴But those who turn to idols will have
    much pain.
    I will not offer blood to those idols.
    I won't even speak their names.

⁵No, the Lord is all I need.
    He takes care of me.
⁶My share in life has been pleasant.
    My part has been beautiful.

⁷I praise the Lord because he guides
    me.
    Even at night, I feel his leading.
⁸I keep the Lord before me always.
    Because he is close by my side
    I will not be hurt.
⁹So I rejoice, and I am glad.
    Even my body has hope.
¹⁰This is because you will not leave me
    in the grave.
    You will not let your holy one rot.
¹¹You will teach me God's way to live.
    Being with you will fill me with joy.
    At your right hand I will find
      pleasure forever.

PSALM 17

A prayer of David.

¹Lord, hear me begging for fairness.
    Listen to my cry for help.
    Pay attention to my prayer.
    I speak the truth.
²You will judge that I am right.
    Your eyes can see what is true.
³You have examined my heart.
    You have tested me all night.
    You questioned me without finding
      anything wrong.
    I did not plan any evil.
⁴I have obeyed your commands.
    I have not done what evil people
      do.
⁵I have done what you told me to do.
    I have not failed.

⁶I call to you, God,
    and you answer me.

Listen to me now.
　Hear what I say.
[7] Your love is wonderful.
　By your power you save
　from their enemies those who trust
　　you.
[8] Protect me as you would protect your
　　own eye.
　Protect me as a bird hides her
　　young under her wings.
[9] Keep me from the wicked who attack
　　me.
　Protect me from my enemies who
　　surround me.
[10] They are selfish.
　They brag about themselves.
[11] They have chased me.
　Now they surround me.
　They plan to throw me to the
　　ground.
[12] They are like lions ready to kill.
　Like lions, they sit in hiding.
[13] Lord, rise up and face the enemy.
　Throw them down.
　Save me from the wicked
　　with your sword.
[14] Lord, save me from them by your
　　power.
　Their reward is in this life.
　They have plenty of food.
　They have many sons.
　They leave money to their children.

[15] Because I have lived right, I will see
　　your face.
　When I wake up, I will see your
　　likeness and be satisfied.

PSALM 18

For the director of music. By the Lord's
servant, David. David sang this song to the
Lord. He sang it when the Lord had saved
him from Saul and all his other enemies.

[1] I love you, Lord. You are my strength.

[2] The Lord is my rock, my protection,
　　my Savior.
　My God is my rock.
　I can run to him for safety.
　He is my shield and my saving
　　strength, my high tower.
[3] I will call to the Lord.
　He is worthy of praise.
　And I will be saved from my
　　enemies.
[4] The ropes of death bound me.
　The deadly rivers overwhelmed me.
[5] The ropes of death wrapped around
　　me.
　The traps of death were before me.

[6] In my trouble I called to the Lord.
　I cried out to my God for help.
　From his temple he heard my voice.
　My call for help reached his ears.

[7] The earth trembled and shook.
　The foundations of the mountains
　　began to shake.
　They shook because the Lord was
　　angry.
[8] Smoke came out of his nose.
　Burning fire came out of his mouth.
　Burning coals went before him.
[9] He tore open the sky and came down.
　Dark clouds were under his feet.
[10] He rode a creature with wings and
　　flew.
　He flew on the wings of the wind.
[11] He made darkness his covering, his
　　shelter around him,
　surrounded by fog and clouds.
[12] Out of the brightness of his presence
　　came clouds.
　They came with hail and lightning.
[13] The Lord thundered from heaven.
　God Most High raised his voice.
　And there was hail and lightning.
[14] He shot his arrows and scattered his
　　enemies.
　His many bolts of lightning
　　confused them with fear.
[15] Lord, you spoke strongly.
　The wind blew from your nose.
　The valleys of the sea appeared.
　The foundations of the earth were
　　seen.

[16] The Lord reached down from above
　　and took me.
　He pulled me from the deep water.
[17] He saved me from my powerful
　　enemies.
　Those who hated me were too
　　strong for me.
[18] They attacked me at my time of
　　trouble.
　But the Lord supported me.
[19] He took me to a safe place.
　Because he delights in me, he saved
　　me.
[20] The Lord spared me because I did
　　what was right.
　Because I have not done evil, he
　　has rewarded me.
[21] I have followed the ways of the Lord.
　I have not done evil by turning
　　away from my God.
[22] I remember all his laws.
　I have not broken his rules.
[23] I am innocent before him.
　I have kept myself from doing evil.

²⁴The Lord rewarded me because I did
  what was right.
  I did what the Lord said was right.

²⁵Lord, you are loyal to those who are
  loyal.
  You are good to those who are
  good.

²⁶You are pure to those who are pure.
  But you are against those who are
  bad.

²⁷You save those who are not proud.
  But you make humble those who
  are proud.

²⁸Lord, you give light to my lamp.
  My God brightens the darkness
  around me.

²⁹With your help I can attack an army.
  With God's help I can jump over a
  wall.

³⁰The ways of God are without fault.
  The Lord's words are pure.
  He is a shield to those who trust him.

³¹Who is God? Only the Lord.
  Who is the Rock?ᵈ Only our God.

³²God is my protection.
  He makes my way free from fault.

³³He makes me like a deer, which does
  not stumble.
  He helps me stand on the steep
  mountains.

³⁴He trains my hands for battle.
  So my arms can bend a bronze
  bow.

³⁵You protect me with your saving
  shield.
  You support me with your right
  hand.
  You have stooped to make me
  great.

³⁶You give me a wide path on which to
  walk.
  My feet have not slipped.

³⁷I chased my enemies and caught
  them.
  I did not quit till they were
  destroyed.

³⁸I crushed them so they couldn't rise
  up again.
  They fell beneath my feet.

³⁹You gave me strength in battle.
  You made my enemies bow before
  me.

⁴⁰You made my enemies turn back.
  I destroyed those who hated me.

⁴¹They called for help,
  but no one came to save them.
  They called to the Lord,
  but he did not answer them.

⁴²I beat my enemies into pieces.

They were like dust in the wind.
  I poured them out like mud in the
  streets.

⁴³You saved me when the people
  attacked me.
  You made me the leader of nations.
  People I never knew serve me.

⁴⁴As soon as they hear me, they obey
  me.
  Foreigners obey me.

⁴⁵They all become afraid.
  They tremble in their hiding places.

⁴⁶The Lord lives!
  May my Rock be praised.
  Praise the God who saves me!

⁴⁷God gives me victory over my
  enemies.
  He brings people under my rule.

⁴⁸He saves me from my enemies.

  You set me over those who hate me.
  You saved me from cruel men.

⁴⁹So I will praise you, Lord, among the
  nations.
  I will sing praises to your name.

⁵⁰The Lord gives great victories to his
  king.
  He is loyal to his appointed king,
  to David and his descendantsᵈ
  forever.

PSALM 19

For the director of music. A song of David.

¹The heavens tell the glory of God.
  And the skies announce what his
  hands have made.

²Day after day they tell the story.
  Night after night they tell it again.

³They have no speech or words.
  They don't make any sound to be
  heard.

⁴But their message goes out through
  all the world.
  It goes everywhere on earth.
  The sky is like a home for the sun.

⁵The sun comes out like a bridegroom
  from his bedroom.
  It rejoices like an athlete eager to
  run a race.

⁶The sun rises at one end of the sky,
  and it follows its path to the other
  end.
  Nothing hides from its heat.

⁷The Lord's teachings are perfect.
  They give new strength.
  The Lord's rules can be trusted.
  They make plain people wise.

⁸The Lord's orders are right.
  They make people happy.

The Lord's commands are pure.
They light up the way.
⁹It is good to respect the Lord.
That respect will last forever.
The Lord's judgments are true.
They are completely right.
¹⁰They are worth more than gold,
even the purest gold.
They are sweeter than honey,
even the finest honey.
¹¹They tell your servant what to do.
Keeping them brings great reward.

¹²No one can see all his own mistakes.
Forgive me for my secret sins.
¹³Keep me from the sins that I want to
do.
Don't let them rule me.
Then I can be pure
and free from the greatest of sins.

¹⁴I hope my words and thoughts please
you.
Lord, you are my Rock,ᵈ the one
who saves me.

PSALM 20

For the director of music. A song of David.
¹May the Lord answer you in times of
trouble.
May the God of Jacob protect you.
²May he send you help from his
Temple.ᵈ
May he support you from Mount
Zion.ᵈ
³May he remember all your offerings.
May he accept all your sacrifices.
Selahᵈ
⁴May he give you what you want.
May all your plans succeed.
⁵We will shout for joy when you
succeed.
We will raise a flag in the name of
our God.
May the Lord give you all that you
ask for.

⁶Now I know the Lord helps his
appointed king.
He answers him from his holy
heaven.
He saves him with his strong right
hand.
⁷Some trust in chariots, others in
horses.
But we trust the Lord our God.
⁸They are overwhelmed and defeated.
But we march forward and win.
⁹Lord, save the king!
Answer us when we call for help.

PSALM 21

For the director of music. A song of David.
¹Lord, the king rejoices because of
your strength.
He is so happy when you save him!
²You gave the king what he wanted.
You did not refuse what he asked
for.   *Selahᵈ*
³You put good things before him.
You placed a gold crown on his
head.
⁴He asked you for life.
And you gave it to him.
His years go on and on.
⁵He has great glory because you gave
him victories.
You gave him honor and praise.
⁶You always gave him blessings.
You made him glad because you
were with him.
⁷The king truly trusts the Lord.
Because God Most High always
loves him,
he will not be overwhelmed.
⁸Your hand is against all your
enemies.
Those who hate you will feel your
power.
⁹When you appear, you will burn them
like wood in a furnace.
In your anger you will eat them up.
Your fire will burn them up.
¹⁰You will destroy their families from
the earth.
Their children will not live.
¹¹They made evil plans against you.
But their traps won't work.
¹²You will make them turn their backs
when you aim your arrows at them.
¹³Be supreme, Lord, in your power.
We sing and praise your greatness.

PSALM 22

For the director of music. To the tune of "The
Doe of Dawn." A song of David.
¹My God, my God, why have you left
me alone?
You are too far away to save me.
You are too far away to hear my
moans.
²My God, I call to you during the day.
But you do not answer.
And I call at night.
I am not silent.

³You sit as the Holy One.
The praises of Israel are your
throne.
⁴Our ancestors trusted you.

They trusted you, and you saved
them.
5They called to you for help.
And they were rescued.
They trusted you.
And they were not disappointed.

6But I am like a worm instead of a
man.
Men make fun of me.
They look down on me.
7Everyone who looks at me laughs.
They stick out their tongues.
They shake their heads.
8They say, "Turn to the Lord for help.
Maybe he will save you.
If he likes you,
maybe he will rescue you."

9You had my mother give birth to me.
You made me trust you
while I was just a baby.
10I have leaned on you since the day I
was born.
You have been my God since my
mother gave birth to me.
11So don't be far away from me.
Now trouble is near,
and there is no one to help.
12Men have surrounded me like angry
bulls.
The strong bulls of Bashan are on
every side.
13Like hungry, roaring lions
they open their jaws at me.
14My strength is gone
like water poured out onto the
ground.
All my bones are out of joint.
My heart is like wax.
It has melted inside me.
15My strength has dried up like a piece
of a broken pot.
My tongue sticks to the top of my
mouth.
You laid me in the dust of death.
16Evil men have surrounded me.
Like dogs they have trapped me.
They have bitten my arms and legs.
17I can count all my bones.
People look and stare at me.
18They divided my clothes among
them,
and they threw lots[d] for my
clothing.

19But, Lord, don't be far away.
You are my power. Hurry to help
me.
20Save me from the sword.
Save my life from the dogs.

21Rescue me from the lion's mouth.
Save me from the horns of the
bulls.

22Then I will tell my fellow Israelites
about you.
I will praise you when your people
meet to worship you.
23Praise the Lord, all you who worship
him.
All you descendants[d] of Jacob,
honor him.
Fear him, all you Israelites.
24The Lord does not ignore
the one who is in trouble.
He doesn't hide from him.
He listens when the one in trouble
calls out to him.
25Lord, I praise you in the great
meeting of your people.
These worshipers will see me do
what I promised.
26Poor people will eat until they are
full.
Those who look to the Lord will
praise him.
May your hearts live forever!
27People everywhere will remember
and will turn to the Lord.
All the families of the nations
will worship him.
28This is because the Lord is King.
He rules the nations.

29All the powerful people on earth will
eat and worship.
Everyone will bow down to him.
30The people in the future will serve
him.
They will always be told about the
Lord.
31They will tell that he does what is
right.
People who are not yet born
will hear what God has done.

PSALM 23

A song of David.

1The Lord is my shepherd.
I have everything I need.
2He gives me rest in green pastures.
He leads me to calm water.
3He gives me new strength.
For the good of his name,
he leads me on paths that are right.
4Even if I walk
through a very dark valley,
I will not be afraid
because you are with me.

Your rod and your walking stick[n]
    comfort me.

[5] You prepare a meal for me
    in front of my enemies.
You pour oil on my head.[n]
    You give me more than I can hold.
[6] Surely your goodness and love will be
    with me
    all my life.
And I will live in the house of the
    Lord forever.

PSALM 24

A song of David.
[1] The earth and everything in it belong
    to the Lord.
    The world and all its people belong
    to him.
[2] He built it on the waters.
    He set it on the rivers.

[3] Who may go up on the mountain of
    the Lord?
    Who may stand in his holy
    Temple?[d]
[4] Only those with clean hands and pure
    hearts.
    They must not have worshiped
    idols.
    They must not have made promises
    in the name of a false god.
[5] It is they who will receive a blessing
    from the Lord.
    The God who saves them will
    declare them right.
[6] They try to follow God.
    They look to the God of Jacob for
    help.   *Selah*[d]

[7] Gates, open all the way.
    Open wide, aged doors.
    Then the glorious king will come
    in.
[8] Who is this glorious king?
    The Lord, strong and mighty.
    The Lord, the powerful warrior.
[9] Gates, open all the way.
    Open wide, aged doors.
    Then the glorious king will come
    in.
[10] Who is this glorious king?
    The Lord of heaven's armies—
    he is the glorious king.   *Selah*

PSALM 25

Of David.
[1] Lord, I give myself to you.
[2] My God, I trust you.

Do not let me be disgraced.
    Do not let my enemies laugh at me.
[3] No one who trusts you will be
    disgraced.
    But those who sin without excuse
    will be disgraced.

[4] Lord, tell me your ways.
    Show me how to live.
[5] Guide me in your truth.
    Teach me, my God, my Savior.
    I trust you all day long.
[6] Lord, remember your mercy and love.
    You have shown them since long
    ago.
[7] Do not remember the sins
    and wrong things I did when I was
    young.
But remember to love me always
    because you are good, Lord.

[8] The Lord is good and right.
    He points sinners to the right way.
[9] He shows those who are not proud
    how to do right.
    He teaches them his ways.
[10] All the Lord's ways are loving and
    true
    for those who follow the demands
    of his agreement.
[11] For the sake of your name, Lord,
    forgive my many sins.
[12] Is there someone who worships the
    Lord?
    The Lord will point him to the best
    way.
[13] He will enjoy a good life.
    His children will inherit the land.
[14] The Lord tells his secrets to those
    who respect him.
    He tells them about his agreement.
[15] My eyes are always looking to the
    Lord for help.
    He will keep me from any traps.
[16] Turn to me and be kind to me.
    I am lonely and hurting.
[17] My troubles have grown larger.
    Free me from my problems.
[18] Look at my suffering and troubles.
    Take away all my sins.
[19] Look at how many enemies I have!
    See how much they hate me!
[20] Protect me and save me.
    I trust you.
    Do not let me be disgraced.
[21] My hope is in you.
    So may goodness and honesty
    guard me.

23:4 **walking stick** The stick a shepherd uses to guide and protect his sheep. 23:5 **pour oil . . . head** This can mean that God gave him great wealth and blessed him.

²²God, save Israel from all their
    troubles!

PSALM 26

Of David.

¹Lord, defend me.
    I have lived an innocent life.
I trusted the Lord and never doubted.
²Lord, try me and test me.
    Look closely into my heart and
        mind.
³I see your love.
    I live by your truth.
⁴I do not spend time with liars.
    I do not make friends with people
        who hide their sin.
⁵I hate the company of evil people.
    I won't sit with the wicked.
⁶I wash my hands to show I am
        innocent.
    I come to your altar, Lord.
⁷I raise my voice in praise.
    I tell of all the miracles[d] you have
        done.
⁸Lord, I love the Temple[d] where you
        live.
    It is where your greatness is.
⁹Do not kill me with those sinners.
    Do not take my life with those
        murderers.
¹⁰Evil is in their hands.
    They do wrong for money.
¹¹But I have lived an innocent life.
    So save me and be kind to me.
¹²I stand in a safe place.
    Lord, I praise you in the great
        meeting.

PSALM 27

Of David.

¹The Lord is my light and the one who
        saves me.
    I fear no one.
The Lord protects my life.
    I am afraid of no one.
²Evil people may try to destroy my
        body.
    My enemies and those who hate me
        attack me.
But they are overwhelmed and
        defeated.
³If an army surrounds me,
    I will not be afraid.
If war breaks out,
    I will trust the Lord.

⁴I ask only one thing from the Lord.
    This is what I want:
Let me live in the Lord's house
    all my life.

Let me see the Lord's beauty.
    Let me look around in his Temple.[d]
⁵During danger he will keep me safe
        in his shelter.
    He will hide me in his Holy Tent.[d]
    Or he will keep me safe on a high
        mountain.
⁶My head is higher
        than my enemies around me.
    I will offer joyful sacrifices in his
        Holy Tent.
    I will sing and praise the Lord.

⁷Lord, hear me when I call.
    Be kind and answer me.
⁸My heart said of you, "Go, worship
        him."
    So I come to worship you, Lord.
⁹Do not turn away from me.
    Do not turn your servant away in
        anger.
    You have helped me.
    Do not push me away or leave me
        alone,
        God, my Savior.
¹⁰If my father and mother leave me,
    the Lord will take me in.
¹¹Lord, teach me your ways.
    Guide me to do what is right
    because I have enemies.
¹²Do not let my enemies defeat me.
    They tell lies about me.
    They say they will hurt me.

¹³I truly believe
    I will live to see the Lord's
        goodness.
¹⁴Wait for the Lord's help.
    Be strong and brave
    and wait for the Lord's help.

PSALM 28

Of David.

¹Lord, my Rock,[d] I call out to you for
        help.
    Do not be deaf to me.
    If you are silent,
    I will be like those in the grave.
²Hear the sound of my prayer,
    when I cry out to you for help.
I raise my hands
    toward your Most Holy Place.
³Don't drag me away with the wicked,
    with those who do evil.
They say, "Peace" to their neighbors.
    But evil is in their hearts.
⁴Pay them back for what they have
        done.
    They have done evil.

Pay them back for what they have
done.
Give them their reward.
[5]They don't understand what the Lord
has done
or what he has made.
So he will knock them down
and not lift them up.

[6]Praise the Lord.
He heard my prayer for help.
[7]The Lord is my strength and shield.
I trust him, and he helps me.
I am very happy.
And I praise him with my song.
[8]The Lord is powerful.
He gives power and victory to his
chosen one.
[9]Save your people.
Bless those who are your own.
Be their shepherd and carry them
forever.

PSALM 29

A song of David.
[1]Praise the Lord, you angels.
Praise the Lord's glory and power.
[2]Praise the Lord for the glory of his
name.
Worship the Lord because he is
holy.
[3]The Lord's voice is heard over the
sea.
The glorious God thunders.
The Lord thunders over the great
ocean.
[4]The Lord's voice is powerful.
The Lord's voice is majestic.
[5]The Lord's voice breaks the trees.
The Lord breaks the cedars of
Lebanon.
[6]He makes the land of Lebanon dance
like a calf.
He makes Mount Hermon jump like
a baby bull.
[7]The Lord's voice makes the lightning
flash.
[8]The Lord's voice shakes the desert.
The Lord shakes the Desert of
Kadesh.
[9]The Lord's voice shakes the oaks.
The leaves fall off the trees.
In his Temple[d] everyone says, "Glory
to God!"
[10]The Lord controls the flood.
The Lord will be King forever.
[11]The Lord gives strength to his people.
The Lord blesses his people with
peace.

PSALM 30

A song of David. A song for giving the
Temple[d] to the Lord.
[1]I will praise you, Lord,
because you rescued me.
You did not let my enemies laugh at
me.
[2]Lord, my God, I prayed to you.
And you healed me.
[3]You lifted me out of the grave.
You spared me from going down
where the dead are.

[4]Sing praises to the Lord, you who
belong to him.
Praise his holy name.
[5]His anger lasts only a moment.
But his kindness lasts for a lifetime.
Crying may last for a night.
But joy comes in the morning.

[6]When I felt safe, I said,
"I will never fail."
[7]Lord, in your kindness you made my
mountain safe.
But when you turned away, I was
frightened.

[8]I called to you, Lord.
I asked you to have mercy on me.
[9]I said, "What good will it do if I die
or if I go down to the grave?
Dust cannot praise you.
It cannot speak about your truth.
[10]Lord, hear me and be merciful to me.
Lord, help me."

[11]You changed my sorrow into dancing.
You took away my rough cloth,
which shows sadness, and
clothed me in happiness.
[12]I will sing to you and not be silent.
Lord, my God, I will praise you
forever.

PSALM 31

For the director of music. A song of David.
[1]Lord, I trust in you.
Let me never be disgraced.
Save me because you do what is
right.
[2]Listen to me.
Save me quickly.
Be my rock of protection,
a strong city to save me.
[3]You are my rock and my protection.
For the good of your name, lead me
and guide me.
[4]Set me free from the trap they set for
me.
You are my protection.

⁵I give you my life.
    Save me, Lord, God of truth.

⁶I hate those who worship false gods.
    I trust only in the Lord.
⁷I will be glad because of your love.
    You saw my suffering.
    You knew my troubles.
⁸You have not let my enemies defeat
        me.
    You have set me in a safe place.

⁹Lord, have mercy. I am in misery.
    My eyes are weak from so much
        crying.
    My whole being is tired from grief.
¹⁰My life is ending in sadness.
    My years are spent in crying.
    My troubles are using up my
        strength.
    My bones are getting weaker.
¹¹Because of all my troubles, my
        enemies hate me.
    Even my neighbors look down on
        me.
    When my friends see me,
        they are afraid and run.
¹²I am like a piece of a broken pot.
    I am forgotten as if I were dead.
¹³I have heard many insults.
    Terror is all around me.
    They make plans against me.
    They want to kill me.

¹⁴Lord, I trust you.
    I have said, "You are my God."
¹⁵My life is in your hands.
    Save me from my enemies' grasp.
    Save me from those who are
        chasing me.
¹⁶Show your kindness to me, your
        servant.
    Save me because of your love.
¹⁷Lord, I called to you.
    So do not let me be disgraced.
    Let the wicked be disgraced.
    Let them lie silent in the grave.
¹⁸With pride and hatred
        they speak against the righteous.
    So shut their lying lips.

¹⁹How great is your goodness!
    You have stored it up for those who
        fear you.
    You do good things for those who
        trust you.
    You do this for all to see.
²⁰You protect them by your presence
        from what people plan against
        them.
    You keep them safe in your shelter
        from evil words.

²¹Praise the Lord.
    His love to me was wonderful
        when my city was attacked.
²²In my distress, I said,
        "God cannot see me!"
    But you heard my prayer
        when I cried out to you for help.
²³Love the Lord, all you who belong to
        him.
    The Lord protects those who truly
        believe.
    But he punishes the proud as much
        as they have sinned.
²⁴All you who put your hope in the
        Lord
    be strong and brave.

PSALM 32

A maskil⁴ of David.
    ¹Happy is the person
        whose sins are forgiven,
        whose wrongs are pardoned.
    ²Happy is the person
        whom the Lord does not consider
            guilty.
        In that person there is nothing
            false.

³When I kept things to myself,
    I felt weak deep inside me.
    I moaned all day long.
⁴Day and night
    you punished me.
    My strength was gone
        as in the summer heat.   *Selah⁶*
⁵Then I confessed my sins to you.
    I didn't hide my guilt.
    I said, "I will confess my sins to the
        Lord."
    And you forgave my guilt.   *Selah*

⁶For this reason, all who obey you
        should pray to you while they still
        can.
    When troubles rise like a flood,
        they will not reach them.
⁷You are my hiding place.
    You protect me from my troubles.
    You fill me with songs of salvation.
                                   Selah

⁸The Lord says, "I will make you wise.
    I will show you where to go.
    I will guide you and watch over
        you.
⁹So don't be like a horse or donkey.
    They don't understand.
    They must be led with bits and reins,
        or they will not come near you."

¹⁰Wicked people have many troubles.

But the Lord's love surrounds those
who trust him.
[11] Good people, rejoice and be happy in
the Lord.
All you whose hearts are right,
sing.

PSALM 33

[1] Sing to the Lord, you who do what is
right.

Honest people should praise him.
[2] Praise the Lord on the harp.
Make music for him on the
ten-stringed lyre.[d]
[3] Sing a new song to him.
Play well and joyfully.

[4] God's word is true.
Everything he does is right.
[5] He loves what is right and fair.
The Lord's love fills the earth.

[6] The sky was made at the Lord's
command.
By the breath from his mouth, he
made all the stars.
[7] He gathered the water in the sea into
a heap.
He made the great ocean stay in its
place.
[8] All the earth should worship the
Lord.
The whole world should fear him.
[9] He spoke, and it happened.
He commanded, and it appeared.
[10] The Lord upsets the plans of nations.
He ruins all their plans.
[11] But the Lord's plans will stand
forever.
His ideas will last from now on.
[12] Happy is the nation whose God is the
Lord.
Happy are the people he chose for
his very own.
[13] The Lord looks down from heaven.
He sees every person.
[14] From his throne he watches
everyone who lives on earth.
[15] He made their hearts.
He understands everything they do.
[16] No king is saved by his great army.
No warrior escapes by his great
strength.
[17] Horses can't bring victory.
They can't save by their strength.
[18] But the Lord looks after those who
fear him.
He watches over those who put
their hope in his love.
[19] He saves them from death.

He spares their lives in times of
hunger.
[20] So our hope is in the Lord.
He is our help, our shield to protect
us.
[21] We rejoice in him.
We trust his holy name.
[22] Lord, show your love to us
as we put our hope in you.

PSALM 34

David's song from the time he acted crazy so
Abimelech would send him away. And David
did leave.

[1] I will praise the Lord at all times.
His praise is always on my lips.
[2] My whole being praises the Lord.
The poor will hear and be glad.
[3] Tell the greatness of the Lord with
me.
Let us praise his name together.

[4] I asked the Lord for help, and he
answered me.
He saved me from all that I feared.
[5] Those who go to him for help are
happy.
They are never disgraced.
[6] This poor man called, and the Lord
heard him.
The Lord saved him from all his
troubles.
[7] The Lord saves those who fear him.
His angel camps around them.

[8] Examine and see how good the Lord
is.
Happy is the person who trusts the
Lord.
[9] People who belong to the Lord, fear
him!
Those who fear him will have
everything they need.
[10] Even lions may become weak and
hungry.
But those people who go to the
Lord for help will have every
good thing.
[11] Children, come and listen to me.
I will teach you to worship the
Lord.
[12] You must do these things
to enjoy life and have many happy
days.
[13] You must not say evil things.
You must not tell lies.
[14] Stop doing evil and do good.
Look for peace and work for it.

[15] The Lord sees the good people.
He listens to their prayers.

16But the Lord is against those who do evil.
He makes the world forget them.
17The Lord hears good people when they cry out to him.
He saves them from all their troubles.
18The Lord is close to the brokenhearted.
He saves those whose spirits have been crushed.

19People who do what is right may have many problems.
But the Lord will solve them all.
20He will protect their very bones.
Not one of them will be broken.
21Evil will kill the wicked people.
Those who hate good people will be judged guilty.
22But the Lord saves his servants' lives.
No one who trusts him will be judged guilty.

PSALM 35

Of David.

1Lord, battle with those who battle with me.
Fight against those who fight against me.
2Pick up the shield and armor.
Rise up and help me.
3Lift up your spears, both large and small,
against those who chase me.
Tell me, "I will save you."

4Make those who want to kill me be ashamed and disgraced.
Make those who plan to harm me turn back and run away.
5Make them like chaff[d] blown by the wind.
Let the angel of the Lord chase them away.
6Let their road be dark and slippery as the angel of the Lord chases them.
7For no reason they spread out their net to trap me.
For no reason they dug a pit for me.
8So let ruin strike them suddenly.
Let them be caught in their own nets.
Let them fall into the pit and die.
9Then I will rejoice in the Lord.
I will be happy when he saves me.
10Even my bones will say,
"Lord, who is like you?
You save the weak from the strong.

You save the weak and poor from robbers."

11Men without mercy stand up to testify.
They ask me things I do not know.
12They repay me with evil for the good I have done.
They make me very sad.
13Yet when they were sick, I put on rough cloth to show my sadness.
I showed my sorrow by going without food.
But my prayers were not answered.
14 I acted as if they were my friends or brothers.
I bowed in sadness as if I were crying for my mother.
15But when I was in trouble, they gathered and laughed.
They gathered to attack before I knew it.
They insulted me without stopping.
16They made fun of me and were cruel to me.
They ground their teeth at me in anger.

17Lord, how long will you watch this happen?
Save my life from their attacks.
Save me from these people who are like lions.
18I will praise you in the great meeting.
I will praise you among crowds of people.
19Do not let my enemies laugh at me.
They hate me for no reason.
Do not let them make fun of me.
They have no reason to hate me.
20Their words are not friendly.
They think up lies about peace-loving people.
21They speak against me.
They say, "Aha! We saw what you did!"

22Lord, you have been watching. Do not keep quiet.
Lord, do not leave me alone.
23Wake up! Come and defend me!
My God and Lord, fight for me!
24Lord my God, defend me with your justice.
Don't let them laugh at me.
25Don't let them think, "Aha! We got what we wanted!"
Don't let them say, "We destroyed him."
26Let them be ashamed and embarrassed.
They were happy when I hurt.

Cover them with shame and disgrace.
They thought they were better than
I was.
27 May my friends sing and shout for
joy.
May they always say, "Praise the
greatness of the Lord.
He loves to see his servants do
well."
28 I will tell of your goodness.
I will praise you every day.

PSALM 36

For the director of music. Of David, the
servant of the Lord.

1 Sin speaks to the wicked man in his
heart.
He has no fear of or respect for
God.
2 He thinks too much of himself.
He doesn't see his sin and hate it.
3 His words are wicked lies.
He is no longer wise or good.
4 At night he makes evil plans.
What he does leads to nothing
good.
He doesn't refuse things that are
evil.

5 Lord, your love reaches to the
heavens.
Your loyalty goes to the skies.
6 Your goodness is as high as the
mountains.
Your justice is as deep as the great
ocean.
Lord, you protect both men and
animals.
7 God, your love is so precious!
You protect people as a bird
protects her young under her
wings.
8 They eat the rich food in your house.
You let them drink from your river
of pleasure.
9 You are the giver of life.
Your light lets us enjoy life.

10 Continue to love those who know
you.
And continue to do good to those
who are good.
11 Don't let proud people attack me.
Don't let the wicked force me away.
12 Those who do evil have been
defeated.
They are overwhelmed; they cannot
do evil any longer.

PSALM 37

Of David.

1 Don't be upset because of evil people.
Don't be jealous of those who do
wrong.
2 Like the grass, they will soon dry up.
Like green plants, they will soon
die away.

3 Trust the Lord and do good.
Live in the land and enjoy its
safety.
4 Enjoy serving the Lord.
And he will give you what you
want.
5 Depend on the Lord.
Trust him, and he will take care of
you.
6 Then your goodness will shine like
the sun.
Your fairness will shine like the
noonday sun.

7 Wait and trust the Lord.
Don't be upset when others get rich
or when someone else's plans
succeed.
8 Don't get angry.
Don't be upset; it only leads to
trouble.
9 Evil people will be sent away.
But people who trust the Lord will
inherit the land.
10 In a little while there will be no more
wicked people.
You may look for them, but they
will be gone.
11 People who are not proud will inherit
the land.
They will enjoy complete peace.

12 The wicked make evil plans against
good people.
They grind their teeth at them in
anger.
13 But the Lord laughs at the wicked.
He sees that their day is coming.
14 The wicked draw their swords.
They bend their bows.
They try to kill the poor and helpless.
They want to kill those who are
honest.
15 But their swords will stab their own
hearts.
Their bows will break.

16 It's better to have little and be right
than to have much and be wrong.
17 The power of the wicked will be
broken.
But the Lord supports those who do
right.

18The Lord watches over the lives of
the innocent.
Their reward will last forever.
19They will not be ashamed when
trouble comes.
They will be full in times of hunger.
20But the wicked will die.
The Lord's enemies will be like the
flowers of the fields.
They will disappear like smoke.
21The wicked people borrow but don't
pay back.
But those who do right give freely
to others.
22Those people the Lord blesses will
inherit the land.
But those he curses will be sent
away.

23When a man's steps follow the Lord,
God is pleased with his ways.
24If he stumbles, he will not fall,
because the Lord holds his hand.

25I was young, and now I am old.
But I have never seen the Lord
leave good people helpless.
I have never seen their children
begging for food.
26Good people always lend freely to
others.
And their children are a blessing.

27Stop doing evil and do good.
Then you will live forever.
28The Lord loves justice.
He will not leave those who
worship him.
He will always protect them.
But the children of the wicked will
die.
29Good people will inherit the land.
They will live in it forever.

30A good person speaks with wisdom.
He says what is fair.
31The teachings of his God are in his
heart.
He does not fail to keep them.
32The wicked watch for good people.
They want to kill them.
33The Lord will not take away his
protection.
He will not judge good people
guilty.

34Wait for the Lord's help
and follow him.
He will honor you and give you the
land.
And you will see the wicked people
sent away.

35I saw a wicked and cruel man.
He looked strong like a healthy tree
in good soil.
36But he died and was gone.
I looked for him, but he couldn't be
found.

37Think of the innocent person.
Watch the honest one.
The man who has peace
will have children to live after him.
38But sinners will be destroyed.
In the end the wicked will die.

39The Lord saves good people.
He is their strong city in times of
trouble.
40The Lord helps them and saves them.
He saves them from the wicked
because they trust in him for
protection.

PSALM 38

A song of David to remember.
1Lord, don't correct me when you are
angry.
Don't punish me when you are very
angry.
2Your arrows have wounded me.
Your hand has come down on me.
3My body is sick from your
punishment.
Even my bones are not healthy
because of my sin.
4My guilt has overwhelmed me.
Like a load it weighs me down.

5My sores stink and become infected
because I was foolish.
6I am bent over and bowed down.
I am sad all day long.
7I am burning with fever.
My whole body is sore.
8I am weak and faint.
I moan from the pain I feel.
9Lord, you know everything I want.
My cries are not hidden from you.
10My heart pounds, and my strength is
gone.
I am losing my sight.
11Because of my wounds, my friends
and neighbors leave me alone.
My relatives stay far away.
12Some people set traps to kill me.
Those who want to hurt me plan
trouble.
All day long they think up lies.

13I am like a deaf man; I cannot hear.
Like a mute, I cannot speak.
14I am like a person who does not hear.
I have no answer to give.

[15]I trust you, Lord.
    You will answer, my God and Lord.
[16]I said, "Don't let them laugh at me.
    Don't let them brag when I am
        defeated."
[17]I am about to die.
    I cannot forget my pain.
[18]I confess my guilt.
    I am troubled by my sin.
[19]My enemies are strong and healthy.
    Many people hate me for no
        reason.
[20]They repay me with evil for the good
        I did.
    They lie about me because I try to
        do good.

[21]Lord, don't leave me.
    My God, don't go away.
[22]Quickly come and help me,
    my Lord and Savior.

PSALM 39

For the director of music. For Jeduthun. A
song of David.

[1]I said, "I will be careful how I act.
    I will not sin by what I say.
I will be careful what I say
    around wicked people."
[2]So I kept very quiet.
    I didn't even say anything good.
    But I became even more upset.
[3]I became very angry inside.
    And the more I thought about it,
        the angrier I became.
    So I spoke:
[4]"Lord, tell me when the end will
        come.
    How long will I live?
    Let me know how long I have.
[5]You have given me only a short life.
    My lifetime is like nothing to you.
    Everyone's life is only a breath.
                                    Selah[d]
[6]A person is like a shadow moving
        about.
    All his work is for nothing.
    He collects things, but he doesn't
        know who will get them.

[7]"So, Lord, what hope do I have?
    You are my hope.
[8]Save me from all my sins.
    Don't let wicked fools make fun of
        me.
[9]I am quiet. I do not open my mouth.
    You are the one who has done this.
[10]Quit punishing me.
    Your beating is about to kill me.
[11]You correct and punish people for
        their sins.

Like a moth, you destroy what they
        love.
    Everyone's life is only a breath.
                                    Selah

[12]"Lord, hear my prayer.
    Listen to my cry.
    Do not ignore my tears.
I am like a visitor with you.
    Like my ancestors, I'm only here a
        short time.
[13]Leave me alone so I can be happy.
    Soon I will leave and be no more."

PSALM 40

For the director of music. A song of David.
[1]I waited patiently for the Lord.
    He turned to me and heard my cry.
[2]He lifted me out of the pit of
        destruction,
    out of the sticky mud.
He stood me on a rock.
    He made my feet steady.
[3]He put a new song in my mouth.
    It was a song of praise to our God.
Many people will see this and
        worship him.
    Then they will trust the Lord.

[4]Happy is the person
    who trusts the Lord.
He doesn't turn to those who are
        proud,
    to those who worship false gods.
[5]Lord our God, you have done many
        miracles.[d]
    Your plans for us are many.
If I tried to tell them all,
    there would be too many to count.

[6]You do not want sacrifices and
        offerings.
    But you have made a hole in my ear
    to show that my body and life are
        yours.
You do not ask for burnt offerings
    and offerings to take away sins.
[7]Then I said, "Look, I have come.
    It is written about me in the book.
[8]My God, I want to do what you want.
    Your teachings are in my heart."

[9]I will tell about your goodness in the
        great meeting of your people.
    Lord, you know my lips are not
        silent.
[10]I do not hide your goodness in my
        heart.
    I speak about your loyalty and
        salvation.

I do not hide your love and truth
    from the people in the great
    meeting.

[11] Lord, do not hold back your mercy
    from me.
    Let your love and truth always
    protect me.
[12] Troubles have gathered around me.
    There are too many to count.
My sins have caught me.
    I cannot see a way to escape.
I have more sins than hairs on my
    head.
    I have lost my courage.
[13] Please, Lord, save me.
    Hurry, Lord, to help me.
[14] People are trying to kill me.
    Shame them and disgrace them.
People want to hurt me.
    Let them run away in disgrace.
[15] People are making fun of me.
    Let them be shamed into silence.
[16] But let those who follow you
    be happy and glad.
They love you for saving them.
    May they always say, "Praise the
    Lord!"

[17] Lord, I am poor and helpless.
    But please remember me.
You are my helper and savior.
    My God, do not wait.

PSALM 41

For the director of music. A song of David.

[1] Happy is the person who thinks about
    the poor.
    When trouble comes, the Lord will
    save him.
[2] The Lord will protect him and spare
    his life.
    The Lord will bless him in the land.
    The Lord will not let his enemies
    take him.
[3] The Lord will give him strength when
    he is sick.
    The Lord will make him well again.

[4] I said, "Lord, be kind to me.
    Heal me because I have sinned
    against you."
[5] My enemies are saying bad things
    about me.
    They say, "When will he die and be
    forgotten?"
[6] Some people come to see me.
    But they lie.
They just come to get bad news.
    Then they go and gossip.
[7] All my enemies whisper about me.
    They think the worst about me.

[8] They say, "He has a terrible disease.
    He will never get out of bed again."
[9] My best and truest friend ate at my
    table.
    Now even he has turned against
    me.

[10] Lord, have mercy on me.
    Give me strength so I can pay them
    back.
[11] My enemies do not defeat me.
    That's how I know you are pleased
    with me.
[12] Because I am innocent, you support
    me.
    You will let me be with you forever.

[13] Praise the Lord, the God of Israel.
    He has always been,
    and he will always be.
        Amen and amen.

Book 2

Psalms 42–72

PSALM 42

For the director of music. A maskil[d] of the
sons of Korah.

[1] A deer thirsts for a stream of water.
    In the same way, I thirst for you,
    God.
[2] I thirst for the living God.
    When can I go to meet with him?
[3] Day and night, my tears have been
    my food.
People are always saying,
    "Where is your God?"
[4] When I remember these things,
    I speak with a broken heart.
I used to walk with the crowd.
    I led the happy crowd to God's
    Temple,[d]
    with songs of praise.

[5] Why am I so sad?
    Why am I so upset?
I should put my hope in God.
    I should keep praising him,
    My Savior and [6] my God.

I am very sad.
    So I remember you while I am in
    the land where the Jordan River
    begins.
I will remember you while I am near
    the Hermon mountains
    and on the mountain of Mizar.
[7] Troubles have come again and again.
    They sound like waterfalls.
Your waves are crashing
    all around me.

⁸The Lord shows his true love every
    day.
    At night I have a song,
    and I pray to my living God.
⁹I say to God, my Rock,^d
    "Why have you forgotten me?
Why am I sad
    and troubled by my enemies?"
¹⁰My enemies' insults make me feel
    as if my bones were broken.
They are always saying,
    "Where is your God?"

¹¹Why am I so sad?
    Why am I so upset?
I should put my hope in God.
    I should keep praising him,
    my Savior and my God.

PSALM 43

¹God, defend me.
    Argue my case against those who
        don't follow you.
    Save me from liars and those who
        do evil.
²God, you are my strength.
    Why have you rejected me?
Why am I sad
    and troubled by my enemies?
³Send me your light and truth.
    They will guide me.
Lead me to your holy mountain.
    Lead me to where you live.
⁴I will go to the altar of God,
    to God who is my joy and
        happiness.
I will praise you with a harp,
    God, my God.

⁵Why am I so sad?
    Why am I so upset?
I should put my hope in God.
    I should keep praising him,
    my Savior and my God.

PSALM 44

For the director of music. A maskil^d of the
sons of Korah.

¹God, we have heard about you.
    Our ancestors told us
what you did in their days,
    in days long ago.
²With your power you forced the
    nations out of the land.
    You placed our ancestors here.
You destroyed those other nations.
    But you made our ancestors grow
        strong.
³It wasn't their swords that took the
    land.

It wasn't their power that gave
    them victory.
But it was your great power and
    strength.
    You were with them because you
        loved them.

⁴My God, you are my King.
    Your commands led Jacob's people
        to victory.
⁵With your help we pushed back our
    enemies.
    In your name we walked on those
        who came against us.
⁶I don't trust my bow to help me.
    My sword can't save me.
⁷You saved us from Egypt.
    You made our enemies ashamed.
⁸We will praise God every day.
    We will praise your name forever.
                Selah^d

⁹But you have rejected and shamed
    us.
    You don't march with our armies
        anymore.
¹⁰You let our enemies push us back.
    Our enemies have taken our
        wealth.
¹¹You gave us away like sheep to be
    eaten.
    You scattered us among the
        nations.
¹²You sold your people for nothing.
    You made no profit on the sale.

¹³You made us a joke to our neighbors.
    The community laughs and makes
        fun of us.
¹⁴You made us a joke to the other
    nations.
    People shake their heads.
¹⁵I am always in disgrace.
    I am covered with shame.
¹⁶My enemy is getting even
    with insults and curses.

¹⁷All these things have happened to us,
    but we have not forgotten you.
    We have kept our agreement with
        you.
¹⁸Our hearts haven't turned away from
    you.
    We haven't stopped following you.
¹⁹But you crushed us in this place
    where wild dogs live.
    You covered us with deep darkness.
²⁰We did not forget our God.
    We did not lift our hands in prayer
        to foreign gods.
²¹God would have known if we had.
    He knows what is in our hearts.

²²But for you we are in danger of death
all the time.
People think we are worth no more
than sheep to be killed.

²³Wake up, Lord! Why are you
sleeping?
Get up! Don't reject us forever.

²⁴Why are you hidden from us?
Have you forgotten our pain and
troubles?

²⁵We have been pushed down into the
dirt.
We are flat on the ground.

²⁶Get up and help us.
Because of your love, save us.

PSALM 45

For the director of music. To the tune of
"Lilies." A maskil.ᵈ A love song of the sons of
Korah.

¹Beautiful words fill my mind.
I am speaking of royal things.
My tongue is like the pen of a
skilled writer.

²You are more handsome than anyone.
You are a very good speaker.
God has blessed you forever.

³Put on your sword, powerful warrior.
Show your glory and majesty.

⁴In your majesty win the victory.
Defend what is true and right.
Your power will do amazing things.

⁵Your sharp arrows will enter
the hearts of the king's enemies.
Nations will be defeated before
you.

⁶God, your throne will last forever and
ever.
You will rule your kingdom with
fairness.

⁷You love right and hate evil.
So God has chosen you to rule
those with you.
Your God has given you much joy.

⁸Your clothes smell like myrrh,ᵈ aloesᵈ
and cassia.ᵈ
From palaces of ivory
music comes to make you happy.

⁹Kings' daughters are among your
honored women.
Your bride stands at your right side
wearing gold from Ophir.

¹⁰Listen to me, daughter. Look and pay
attention.
Forget your people and your
father's family.

¹¹The king loves your beauty.

Because he is your master, you
should obey him.

¹²People from the city of Tyre have
brought a gift.
Wealthy people will want to meet
you.

¹³The princess is very beautiful.
Her gown is woven with gold.

¹⁴In her beautiful clothes she is brought
to the king.
Her bridesmaids follow behind her.
And they are also brought to him.

¹⁵They come with happiness and joy.
They enter the king's palace.

¹⁶You will have sons to take the place
of your ancestors.
You will make them rulers through
all the land.

¹⁷I will make your name famous from
now on.
People will praise you forever and
ever.

PSALM 46

For the director of music. By alamoth.ᵈ A
song of the sons of Korah.

¹God is our protection and our strength.
He always helps in times of trouble.

²So we will not be afraid if the earth
shakes,
or if the mountains fall into the sea.

³We will not fear even if the oceans
roar and foam,
or if the mountains shake at the
raging sea.   *Selah*ᵈ

⁴There is a river which brings joy to
the city of God.
This is the holy place where God
Most High lives.

⁵God is in that city, and so it will not
be shaken.
God will help her at dawn.

⁶Nations tremble, and kingdoms
shake.
God shouts, and the earth
crumbles.

⁷The Lord of heaven's armies is with
us.
The God of Jacob is our protection.
Selah

⁸Come and see what the Lord has
done.
He has done amazing things on the
earth.

⁹He stops wars everywhere on the
earth.
He breaks all bows and spears
and burns up the chariots with fire.

¹⁰God says, "Be quiet and know that I
    am God.
  I will be supreme over all the
    nations.
  I will be supreme in the earth."

¹¹The Lord of heaven's armies is with
    us.
  The God of Jacob is our protection.
                                    Selah

PSALM 47

For the director of music. A song of the sons
of Korah.
¹Clap your hands, all you people.
  Shout to God with joy.
²The Lord Most High is wonderful.
  He is the great King over all the
    earth!
³He defeated nations for us
  and put them under our control.
⁴He chose the land we would inherit.
  We are the children of Jacob, whom
    he loved.   *Selah*^d

⁵God has risen with a shout of joy.
  The Lord has risen as the trumpets
    sounded.
⁶Sing praises to God. Sing praises.
  Sing praises to our King. Sing
    praises.
⁷God is King of all the earth.
  So sing a song of praise to him.
⁸God is King over the nations.
  God sits on his holy throne.
⁹The leaders of the nations meet
  with the people of the God of
    Abraham.
  Even the leaders of the earth belong
    to God.
  He is supreme.

PSALM 48

A song of the sons of Korah.
¹The Lord is great; he should be
    praised
  in the city of our God, on his holy
    mountain.
²It is high and beautiful.
  It brings joy to the whole world.
  Mount Zion^d is like the high
    mountains of the north.
  It is the city of the Great King.
³God is within its palaces.
  He is known as its protection.
⁴Kings joined together
  and came together to attack the
    city.
⁵But when they saw it, they were
    amazed.
  They ran away in fear.

⁶Fear took hold of them.
  They hurt like a woman having a
    baby.
⁷You destroyed the large trading ships
  with an east wind.

⁸First we heard.
  And now we have seen that
  God will always keep his city safe.
  It is the city of the Lord of heaven's
    armies,
  the city of our God.   *Selah*^d

⁹God, we come into your Temple.^d
  There we think about your love.
¹⁰God, your name is known everywhere.
  Everywhere on earth people praise
    you.
  Your right hand is full of goodness.
¹¹Mount Zion is happy.
  All the towns of Judah rejoice
  because your decisions are fair.

¹²Walk around Jerusalem
  and count its towers.
¹³Notice how strong they are. Look at
    the palaces.
  Then you will be able to tell your
    children about them.
¹⁴This God is our God forever and ever.
  He will guide us from now on.

PSALM 49

For the director of music. A song of the sons
of Korah.
¹Listen to this, all you nations.
  Listen, all you who live on earth.
²Listen, both great and small,
  rich and poor together.
³What I say is wise.
  My heart speaks with
    understanding.
⁴I will pay attention to a wise saying.
  I will explain my riddle on the
    harp.

⁵Why should I be afraid of bad days?
  Why should I fear when evil men
    surround me?
⁶They trust in their money.
  They brag about their riches.
⁷No one can buy back the life of
    another person.
  No one can pay God for his own
    life.
⁸The price of a life is high.
  No payment is ever enough.
⁹Do people live forever?
  Don't they all face death?

¹⁰See, even wise men die.
  Fools and stupid people also die.
  They leave their wealth to others.

¹¹Their graves will always be their
  homes.
  They will live there from now on,
    even though they named places
    after themselves.
¹²Even rich people do not live forever.
  Like the animals, people die.

¹³This is what will happen to people
    who trust in themselves.
  And this will happen to their
    followers who believe them. *Selah*ᵈ
¹⁴Like sheep, they must die.
  And death will be their shepherd.
  Honest people will rule over them in
    the morning.
  Their bodies will rot in a grave far
    from home.
¹⁵But God will save my life.
  He will take me from the grave.
                                    Selah

¹⁶Don't be afraid of a rich man
    because his house is more
    beautiful.
¹⁷He won't take anything to the grave.
  His wealth won't die with him.
¹⁸He was praised when he was alive.
  (And people may praise you when
    you succeed.)
¹⁹But he will go to where his ancestors
    are.
  He will never see light again.
²⁰Rich people with no understanding
    are just like animals that die.

PSALM 50

A song of Asaph.

¹The God of gods, the Lord, speaks.
  He calls the earth from the rising to
    the setting sun.
²God shines from Jerusalem,
  whose beauty is perfect.
³Our God comes, and he will not be
    silent.
  A fire burns in front of him,
  and a storm surrounds him.
⁴He calls to the sky and to the earth
  to see him judge his people.
⁵He says, "You who worship me,
    gather around.
  You have made an agreement with
    me, using a sacrifice."
⁶God is the judge.
  Even the skies say he is right. *Selah*ᵈ

⁷God says, "My people, listen to me.
  Israel, I will testify against you.
  I am God, your God.
⁸I do not scold you for your sacrifices.
  You always bring me your burnt
    offerings.

⁹But I do not need the bulls from your
    stalls
  or the goats from your pens.
¹⁰Every animal of the forest is already
    mine.
  The cattle on a thousand hills are
    mine.
¹¹I know every bird on the mountains.
  Every living thing in the fields is
    mine.
¹²If I were hungry, I would not tell you.
  The earth and everything on it are
    mine.
¹³I don't eat the meat of bulls
  or drink the blood of goats.
¹⁴Give an offering to show thanks to
    God.
  Give God Most High what you have
    promised.
¹⁵Call to me in times of trouble.
  I will save you, and you will honor
    me."

¹⁶But God says to the wicked people,
  "Why do you talk about my laws?
  Why do you mention my
    agreement?
¹⁷You hate my teachings.
  You turn your back on what I say.
¹⁸When you see a thief, you join him.
  You take part in adultery.ᵈ
¹⁹You don't stop your mouth from
    speaking evil.
  Your tongue makes up lies.
²⁰You speak against your brother.
  You lie about your mother's son.
²¹I have kept quiet while you did these
    things.
  So you thought I was just like you.
  But I will scold you.
  I will accuse you to your face.

²²"Think about this, you people who
    forget God.
  Otherwise, I will tear you apart,
  and no one will save you.
²³Those people honor me
  who give me offerings to show
    thanks.
  And I, God, will save those who do
    that."

PSALM 51

For the director of music. A song of David
when the prophetᵈ Nathan came to David
after David's sin with Bathsheba.

¹God, be merciful to me
  because you are loving.
  Because you are always ready to be
    merciful,
  wipe out all my wrongs.

²Wash away all my guilt
and make me clean again.

³I know about my wrongs.
I can't forget my sin.
⁴You are the one I have sinned against.
I have done what you say is wrong.
So you are right when you speak.
You are fair when you judge me.
⁵I was brought into this world in sin.
In sin my mother gave birth to me.

⁶You want me to be completely
truthful.
So teach me wisdom.
⁷Take away my sin, and I will be clean.
Wash me, and I will be whiter than
snow.
⁸Make me hear sounds of joy and
gladness.
Let the bones you crushed be
happy again.
⁹Turn your face from my sins.
Wipe out all my guilt.

¹⁰Create in me a pure heart, God.
Make my spirit right again.
¹¹Do not send me away from you.
Do not take your Holy Spirit^d away
from me.
¹²Give me back the joy that comes
when you save me.
Keep me strong by giving me a
willing spirit.
¹³Then I will teach your ways to those
who do wrong.
And sinners will turn back to you.

¹⁴God, save me from the guilt of
murder.
God, you are the one who saves me.
I will sing about your goodness.
¹⁵Lord, let me speak
so I may praise you.
¹⁶You are not pleased by sacrifices.
Otherwise, I would give them.
You don't want burnt offerings.
¹⁷The sacrifice God wants is a willing
spirit.
God, you will not reject
a heart that is broken and sorry for
its sin.

¹⁸Do whatever good you wish for
Jerusalem.
Rebuild the walls of Jerusalem.
¹⁹Then you will be pleased with right
sacrifices and whole burnt
offerings.
And bulls will be offered on your
altar.

PSALM 52

For the director of music. A maskil^d of David.
When Doeg the Edomite came to Saul and
said to him, "David is in Ahimelech's house."

¹Mighty warrior, why do you brag
about the evil you do?
God's love will continue forever.
²You think up evil plans.
Your tongue is like a sharp razor,
making up lies.
³You love wrong more than right
and lies more than truth. *Selah*^d
⁴You love words that bite
and tongues that lie.

⁵But God will ruin you forever.
He will grab you and throw you out
of your tent.
He will tear you away from the land
of the living. *Selah*
⁶Those who do right will see this and
fear God.
They will laugh at you and say,
⁷"Look what happened to the man
who did not depend on God.
Instead, he depended on his money.
He grew strong by his evil plans."

⁸But I am like an olive tree
growing in God's Temple.^d
I trust God's love
forever and ever.
⁹God, I will thank you forever for what
you have done.
With those who worship you, I will
trust you because you are good.

PSALM 53

For the director of music. By mahalath.^d A
maskil^d of David.

¹A wicked fool says to himself,
"There is no God."
Fools are evil. They do terrible things.
None of them does anything good.

²God looked down from heaven at all
the people.
He looked to see if anyone was
wise,
if anyone was looking to God for
help.
³But everyone has turned away.
Together, everyone has become
evil.
None of them does anything good.

⁴Don't the wicked understand?
They destroy my people as if they
were eating bread.
They have not asked God for help.

⁵The wicked became filled with terror
  where there had been nothing to be
    terrified of.
  God will scatter the bones of your
    enemies.
 You will defeat them,
  because God has rejected them.

⁶I pray that victory will come to Israel
    from Mount Zion!ᵈ
  May God give them back their
    riches.
  Then the people of Jacob will
    rejoice.
  And the people of Israel will be
    glad.

PSALM 54

For the director of music. With stringed
instruments. A maskilᵈ of David when the
Ziphites went to Saul and said, "We think
David is hiding among our people."

¹God, save me because of who you
    are.
  By your strength show that I am
    innocent.
²Hear my prayer, God.
  Listen to what I say.
³Strangers turn against me.
  Cruel men want to kill me.
  They do not care about God.   *Selah*ᵈ

⁴See, God will help me.
  The Lord will spare my life.
⁵Let my enemies be punished with
    their own evil.
  Destroy them because you are loyal
    to me.

⁶I will offer a sacrifice as a special gift
    to you.
  I will thank you, Lord, because you
    are good.
⁷You have saved me from all my
    troubles.
  I have seen my enemies defeated.

PSALM 55

For the director of music. With stringed
instruments. A maskilᵈ of David.

¹God, listen to my prayer.
  Do not ignore my prayer.
²Pay attention to me and answer me.
  I am troubled and upset
³by what the enemy says
  and how the wicked look at me.
  They bring troubles down on me.
  In anger they attack me.

⁴I am frightened inside.
  The terror of death has attacked
    me.
⁵I am scared and shaking.
  Terror grips me.
⁶I said, "I wish I had wings like a
    dove.
  Then I would fly away and rest.
⁷I would wander far away.
  I would stay in the desert.   *Selah*ᵈ
⁸I would hurry to my place of escape,
  far away from the wind and storm."

⁹Lord, destroy and confuse their
    words.
  I see violence and fighting in the
    city.
¹⁰Day and night they are all around its
    walls.
  Evil and trouble are everywhere
    inside.
¹¹Destruction is everywhere in the city.
  Trouble and lying never leave its
    streets.

¹²It was not an enemy insulting me.
  I could stand that.
  It was not someone who hated me.
  I could hide from him.
¹³But it is you, a person like me.
  You were my companion and good
    friend.
¹⁴We had a good friendship.
  We went together to God's Temple.ᵈ

¹⁵Let death take away my enemies.
  Let them die while they are still
    young
  because evil lives with them.
¹⁶But I will call to God for help.
  And the Lord will save me.
¹⁷Morning, noon and night I am
    troubled and upset.
  But he will listen to me.
¹⁸Many are against me.
  But he keeps me safe in battle.
¹⁹God who lives forever
  will hear me and punish them.
  But they will not change.
  They do not fear God.   *Selah*

²⁰The one who was my friend attacks
    his friends.
  He breaks his promises.
²¹His words are slippery like butter.
  But war is in his heart.
  His words are smoother than oil,
  but they cut like knives.

²²Give your worries to the Lord.
  He will take care of you.
  He will never let good people down.
²³But, God, you will bring down
  the wicked to the grave.

Murderers and liars will live
  only half a lifetime.
But I will trust in you.

PSALM 56

For the director of music. To the tune of "The
Dove in the Distant Oak." A miktam[d] of
David when the Philistines captured him in
Gath.

[1] God, be merciful to me because
    people are chasing me.
  The battle has pressed me all day
    long.
[2] My enemies have chased me all day.
  There are many of them fighting
    me.
[3] When I am afraid,
  I will trust you.
[4] I praise God for his word.
  I trust God. So I am not afraid.
  What can human beings do to me?

[5] All day long they twist my words.
  All their evil plans are against me.
[6] They wait. They hide.
  They watch my steps.
  They hope to kill me.
[7] God, do not let them escape.
  Punish the foreign nations in your
    anger.
[8] You have recorded my troubles.
  You have kept a list of my tears.
  Aren't they in your records?

[9] On the day I call for help, my enemies
    will be defeated.
  I know that God is on my side.
[10] I praise God for his word to me.
  I praise the Lord for his word.
[11] I trust in God. I will not be afraid.
  What can people do to me?

[12] God, I must keep my promises to you.
  I will give you my offerings to
    thank you.
[13] You have saved me from death.
  You have kept me from being
    defeated.
  So I will walk with God
    in light among the living.

PSALM 57

For the director of music. To the tune of "Do
Not Destroy." A miktam[d] of David when he
escaped from Saul in a cave.

[1] Be merciful to me, God. Be merciful
    to me
  because I come to you for protection.
  I will come to you as a bird comes for
    protection under its mother's
    wings
  until the trouble has passed.

[2] I cry out to God Most High,
  to the God who does everything for
    me.
[3] He sends help from heaven and saves
    me.
  He punishes those who attack me.
                                    Selah[d]
  God sends me his love and truth.

[4] Enemies are like lions all around me.
  I must lie down among them.
  Their teeth are like spears and
    arrows.
  Their tongues are as sharp as
    swords.

[5] God is supreme over the skies.
  His greatness covers the earth.

[6] They set a trap for me.
  I am very worried.
  They dug a pit in my path.
  But they fell into it themselves. *Selah*

[7] My heart is right, God. My heart is
    right.
  I will sing and praise you.
[8] Wake up, my soul.
  Wake up, harp and lyre![d]
  I will wake up the dawn.
[9] Lord, I will praise you among the
    nations.
  I will sing songs of praise about
    you to all the nations.
[10] Your love is so great it reaches to the
    skies.
  Your truth reaches to the clouds.
[11] God, you are supreme over the skies.
  Let your glory be over all the earth.

PSALM 58

For the director of music. To the tune of "Do
Not Destroy." A miktam[d] of David.

[1] Do you rulers really say what is
    right?
  Do you judge people fairly?
[2] No, in your heart you plan evil.
  You think up violent crimes in the
    land.
[3] From birth evil men start doing bad
    things.
  They tell lies and do wrong as soon
    as they are born.
[4] They are like poisonous snakes,
  like deaf cobras that can't hear.
[5] They cannot hear the music of the
    snake charmer
  no matter how well he plays for
    them.
[6] God, break the teeth out of their
    mouths!

Tear out the fangs of those lions,
  Lord!
[7] Let them disappear like water that
    flows away.
  Let them be cut short like a broken
    arrow.
[8] Let them be like snails that melt as
    they move.
  Let them be like a child born dead
    who never saw the sun.
[9] His anger will blow them away alive.
  It will happen faster than burning
    thorns can heat a pot.
[10] Good people will be glad when they
    see him get even.
  They will wash their feet in the
    blood of the wicked.
[11] Then people will say,
  "There really are rewards for doing
    what is right.
  There really is a God who judges
    the world."

PSALM 59

For the director of music. To the tune of "Do
Not Destroy." A miktam[d] of David when Saul
sent men to watch David's house to kill him.

[1] God, save me from my enemies.
  Protect me from those who come
    against me.
[2] Save me from those who do evil.
  Save me from murderers.

[3] Look, men are waiting to attack me.
  Cruel men attack me.
  But I have not sinned or done
    wrong, Lord.
[4] I have done nothing wrong, but they
    are ready to attack me.
  Wake up to help me and look.
[5] You are the Lord God of heaven's
    armies, the God of Israel.
  Come and punish those people.
  Do not give those traitors any
    mercy.   *Selah*[d]

[6] They come back at night.
  Like dogs they growl and roam
    around the city.
[7] Notice what comes from their
    mouths.
  Insults come from their lips.
  They say, "Who's listening?"
[8] But, Lord, you laugh at them.
  You make fun of all of them.

[9] God, my strength, I wait for you.
  God, you are my protection.
[10] My God loves me, and he will be with
    me.
  He will help me defeat my enemies.

[11] Lord, our protector, do not kill them.
  If you do, my people will forget.
  With your power scatter them
    and defeat them.
[12] They sin by what they say.
  They sin with their words.
  They curse and tell lies.
  So let their pride trap them.
[13] Destroy them in your anger.
  Destroy them completely!
  Then they will know
    that God rules over Israel
    and to the ends of the earth.   *Selah*

[14] They come back at night.
  Like dogs they growl
    and roam around the city.
[15] They wander about looking for food.
  And they howl if they do not find
    enough.
[16] But I will sing about your strength.
  In the morning I will sing about
    your love.
  You are my protection,
    my place of safety in times of
      trouble.
[17] God, my strength, I will sing praises
    to you.
  God, my protection, you are the
    God who loves me.

PSALM 60

For the director of music. To the tune of "Lily
of the Agreement." A miktam[d] of David. For
teaching. When David fought the Arameans
of Northwest Mesopotamia and Zobah, and
when Joab returned and defeated 12,000
Edomites at the Valley of Salt.

[1] God, you have rejected us and
    scattered us.
  You have been angry, but please
    come back to us.
[2] You made the earth shake and crack.
  Fix its breaks because it is shaking.
[3] You have given your people trouble.
  You made us unable to walk straight,
    like people drunk with wine.
[4] You have raised a banner to gather
    those who fear you.
  Now they can escape the enemy.
                      Selah[d]
[5] Answer us and save us by your
    power.
  Then the people you love will be
    rescued.

[6] God has said from his Temple.[d]
  "When I win, I will divide Shechem
    and cut up the Valley of Succoth.
[7] Gilead and Manasseh are mine.
  Ephraim is like my helmet.
  Judah holds my royal scepter.[d]

⁸Moab is like my washbowl.
> I throw my sandals at Edom.
> I shout at Philistia."

⁹Who will bring me to the strong,
> walled city?
> Who will lead me to Edom?
¹⁰God, surely you have rejected us.
> You do not go out with our armies.
¹¹Help us fight the enemy.
> Human help is useless.
¹²But we can win with God's help.
> He will defeat our enemies.

PSALM 61

For the director of music. With stringed
instruments. Of David.

¹God, hear my cry.
> Listen to my prayer.
²I call to you from the ends of the
> earth.
> I am afraid.
> Carry me away to a high mountain.
³You have been my protection,
> like a strong tower against my
> enemies.

⁴Let me live in your Holy Tent[d] forever.
> Protect me as a bird protects its
> young under its wings.   *Selah[d]*
⁵God, you have heard my promises.
> You have given me the things that
> belong to those who fear you.

⁶Give the king a long life.
> Let him live many years.
⁷Let him rule in the presence of God
> forever.
> Protect him with your love and
> truth.
⁸Then I will praise your name forever.
> And every day I will keep my
> promises.

PSALM 62

For the director of music. For Jeduthun. A
song of David.

¹I wait patiently for God.
> Only he can save me.
²He is my rock, who saves me.
> He protects me like a strong, walled
> city.
> I will not be defeated.

³How long will you attack me?
> Will all of you throw me down?
> I am like a leaning wall, like a
> fence ready to fall.
⁴You are planning to make me fall.
> You enjoy telling lies about me.

With your mouth you bless me.
> But in your heart you curse me.
>   *Selah[d]*

⁵I wait patiently for God to save me.
> Only he gives me hope.
⁶He is my rock, who saves me.
> He protects me like a strong, walled
> city.
> I will not be defeated.
⁷My honor and salvation come from
> God.
> He is my mighty rock and my
> protection.

⁸People, trust God all the time.
> Tell him all your problems.
> God is our protection.   *Selah*

⁹People are only a breath.
> Even the greatest men are just a lie.
> On the scales, they weigh nothing.
> Together they are only a breath.
¹⁰Do not trust in force.
> Stealing is of no use.
> Even if you gain more riches,
> don't put your trust in them.

¹¹God has said this,
> and I have heard it over and over:
> God, you are strong.
¹²Lord, you are loving.
> You reward a person for what he
> does.

PSALM 63

A song of David when he was in the desert of
Judah.

¹God, you are my God.
> I want to follow you.
> My whole being
> thirsts for you,
> like a man in a dry, empty land
> where there is no water.
²I have seen you in the Temple.[d]
> I have seen your strength and glory.
³Your love is better than life.
> I will praise you.
⁴I will praise you as long as I live.
> I will lift up my hands in prayer to
> your name.
⁵I will be content as if I had eaten the
> best foods.
> My lips will sing. My mouth will
> praise you.

⁶I remember you while I'm lying in
> bed.
> I think about you through the night.
⁷You are my help.
> Because of your protection, I sing.
⁸I stay close to you.

You support me with your right
  hand.
⁹Some people are trying to kill me.
  But they will go down to the grave.
¹⁰They will be killed with swords.
  They will be eaten by wild dogs.
¹¹But the king will rejoice in his God.
  All who make promises in his name
    will praise him.
  But the mouths of liars will be shut.

PSALM 64

For the director of music. A song of David.

¹God, listen to my complaint.
  I am afraid of my enemies.
  Protect my life from them.
²Hide me from those wicked people,
  from that gang who does evil.
³They sharpen their tongues like
    swords.
  They shoot bitter words like
    arrows.
⁴They hide and shoot at innocent
    people.
  They shoot suddenly and are not
    afraid.
⁵They encourage each other to do
    wrong.
  They talk about setting traps.
  They think no one will see them.
⁶They plan wicked things and say,
  "We have a perfect plan."
  The mind of man is hard to
    understand.

⁷But God will shoot them with arrows.
  They will suddenly be struck down.
⁸Their own words will be used against
    them.
  All who see them will shake their
    heads.
⁹Then everyone will fear God.
  They will tell what God has done.
  They will learn from what he has
    done.
¹⁰Good people will be happy in the
    Lord.
  They will find protection in him.
  Let everyone who is honest praise
    the Lord.

PSALM 65

For the director of music. A song of David.

¹God, you will be praised in
    Jerusalem.
  We will keep our promises to you.
²You hear our prayers.
  All people will come to you.
³Our guilt overwhelms us.
  But you forgive our sins.

⁴Happy are the people you choose.
  You have them stay in your
    courtyards.
  We are filled with good things in your
    house,
  your holy Temple.ᵈ

⁵You answer us in amazing ways,
  God our Savior.
  People everywhere on the earth
    and beyond the sea trust you.
⁶You made the mountains by your
    strength.
  You have great power.
⁷You stopped the roaring seas,
  the roaring waves and the uproar of
    the nations.
⁸Even those people at the ends of the
    earth fear your miracles.ᵈ
  You are praised from where the sun
    rises to where it sets.

⁹You take care of the land and water
    it.
  You make it very fertile.
  The rivers of God are full of water.
  Grain grows because you make it
    grow.
¹⁰You cause rain to fall on the plowed
    fields.
  You soak them with water.
  You soften the ground with rain.
  And then you bless it.
¹¹You give the year a good harvest.
  You load the wagons with many
    crops.
¹²The desert is covered with grass.
  The hills are covered with
    happiness.
¹³The pastures are full of sheep.
  The valleys are covered with grain.
  Everything shouts and sings for joy.

PSALM 66

For the director of music. A song of praise.

¹Everything on earth, shout with joy to
    God!
²Sing about his glory!
  Make his praise glorious!
³Say to God, "Your works are
    amazing!
  Your power is great.
  Your enemies fall before you.
⁴All the earth worships you.
  They sing praises to you.
  They sing praises to your name."
                              *Selah*ᵈ

⁵Come and see what God has done.
  See what amazing things he has
    done for people.
⁶He turned the sea into dry land.

The people crossed the river on
foot.
So let us rejoice because of what he
did.
[7]He rules forever with his power.
He keeps his eye on the nations.
So people should not turn against
him.　　　*Selah*

[8]You people, praise our God.
Loudly sing his praise.
[9]He protects our lives
and does not let us be defeated.
[10]God, you have tested us.
You have purified us like silver.
[11]You let us be trapped.
You put a heavy load on us.
[12]You let our enemies walk on our
heads.
We went through fire and flood.
But you brought us to a place with
good things.

[13]I will come to your Temple[d] with
burnt offerings.
I will give you what I promised.
[14]I promised to give you these things
when I was in trouble.
[15]I will bring you offerings of fat
animals.
And I will offer male sheep, bulls
and goats.　　　*Selah*

[16]All of you who fear God, come and
listen.
I will tell you what he has done for
me.
[17]I cried out to him with my mouth.
I praised him with my tongue.
[18]If I had known of any sin in my heart,
the Lord would not have listened to
me.
[19]But God has listened.
He has heard my prayer.
[20]Praise God.
He did not ignore my prayer.
He did not hold back his love from
me.

PSALM 67

For the director of music. With stringed
instruments. A song of praise.
[1]God, have mercy on us and bless us.
Show your kindness to us.　　*Selah*[d]
[2]Then the world will learn your ways.
All nations will learn that you can
save.

[3]God, the people should praise you.
All people should praise you.

[4]The nations should be glad and sing
because you judge people fairly.
You guide all the nations on earth.
　　　Selah
[5]God, the people should praise you.
All people should praise you.

[6]The land has given its crops.
God, our God, blesses us.
[7]God blesses us
so people to the ends of the earth
will fear him.

PSALM 68

For the director of music. A song of David.
[1]Let God come and scatter his enemies.
Let those who hate him run away.
[2]Blow them away as smoke
is driven away by the wind.
As wax melts before a fire,
let the wicked be destroyed before
God.
[3]But those who do right should be
glad.
They should rejoice before God.
They should be happy and glad.

[4]Sing to God. Sing praises to his
name.
Prepare the way for him
who rides through the desert.
His name is the Lord.
Rejoice before him.
[5]God is in his holy Temple.[d]
He is a father to orphans.
He defends the widows.
[6]God gives the lonely a home.
He leads prisoners out with joy.
But those who turn against God
will live in a dry land.

[7]God, you led your people out.
You marched through the desert.
　　　Selah[d]
[8]The ground shook,
and the sky poured down rain
before God, the God of Mount Sinai,
before God, the God of Israel.
[9]God, you sent much rain.
You refreshed your tired land.
[10]Your people settled there.
God, in your goodness
you took care of the poor.

[11]The Lord gave the command.
And a great army told the news:
[12]"Kings and their armies run away.
The women at home divide the
wealth taken in war."
[13]Those who stayed behind by the
sheepfold
will get the riches taken in battle.

¹⁴God scattered kings
  like snow on Mount Zalmon.

¹⁵The mountains of Bashan are great
  mountains.
  Mount Bashan has many peaks.
¹⁶Why do you mountains with many
  peaks look down
  on Mount Zion,ᵈ which God chose
  for his home?
  The Lord will live there forever.
¹⁷God comes with millions of chariots.
  The Lord comes from Mount Sinai
  to his holy place.
¹⁸He went up to the heights.
  He led a parade of captives.
  He received the payment he
  demanded from the people,
  even from those who turned against
  him.
  And the Lord God will live there.

¹⁹Praise the Lord, day by day.
  God our Savior helps us.   *Selah*
²⁰Our God is a God who saves us.
  The Lord God saves us from death.

²¹God will crush his enemies' heads,
  the hairy skulls of those who
  continue to sin.
²²The Lord said, "I will bring the
  enemy back from Bashan.
  I will bring them back from the
  depths of the sea.
²³Then you can stick your feet in their
  blood.
  And your dogs can lick their
  share."

²⁴God, people have seen your victory
  march.
  God my King marched into the
  holy place.
²⁵The singers are in front, and the
  instruments are behind.
  In the middle are the girls with the
  tambourines.ᵈ
²⁶Praise God in the meeting place.
  Praise the Lord in the gathering of
  Israel.
²⁷There is the smallest tribe,ᵈ Benjamin,
  leading them.
  And there are the leaders of Judah
  with their group.
  There also are the leaders of
  Zebulun and of Naphtali.

²⁸God, order up your power.
  Show the mighty power you have
  used for us before.
²⁹Kings will bring their wealth to you,
  to your Temple in Jerusalem.

³⁰Punish Egypt, the beast among the
  tall grass along the river.
  Punish the leaders of nations, those
  bulls among the cows.
  Then they will bring you their silver.
  Scatter those nations that love war.
³¹Messengers will come from Egypt
  with forced payment.
  The people of Cush will pray to
  God.

³²Kingdoms of the earth, sing to God.
  Sing praises to the Lord.   *Selah*
³³Sing to the one who rides through the
  skies, which are from long ago.
  He speaks with a thundering voice.
³⁴Announce that God is powerful.
  He rules over Israel.
  His power is in the skies.
³⁵God, you are wonderful in your
  Temple.
  The God of Israel gives his people
  strength and power.

  Praise God!

PSALM 69

For the director of music. To the tune of
"Lilies." A song of David.
¹God, save me.
  The water has risen to my neck.
²I'm sinking down into the mud.
  There is nothing to stand on.
  I am in deep water.
  The flood covers me.
³I am tired from calling for help.
  My throat is sore.
  My eyes are tired from waiting
  for God to help me.
⁴There are more people who hate me
  for no reason
  than hairs on my head.
  Those who want to destroy me are
  powerful.
  My enemies are liars.
  They make me pay back
  what I did not steal.

⁵God, you know what I have done
  wrong.
  I cannot hide my guilt from you.
⁶Master, the Lord of heaven's armies,
  do not let those who hope in you be
  ashamed because of me.
  God of Israel,
  do not let your worshipers
  be disgraced because of me.
⁷For you, I carry this shame.
  My face is covered with disgrace.
⁸I am like a stranger to my brothers.
  I am like a foreigner to my
  mother's sons.

⁹My strong love for your Temple^d
  completely controls me.
    When people insult you, it hurts
      me.
¹⁰When I cry and go without food,
  they make fun of me.
¹¹When I wear rough cloth to show my
    sadness,
  they joke about me.
¹²They make fun of me in public places.
  The drunkards make up songs
    about me.

¹³But I pray to you, Lord.
  I pray that you will accept me.
  God, because of your great love,
    answer me.
  You are truly able to save.
¹⁴Pull me from the mud.
  Do not let me sink.
  Save me from those who hate me
    and from the deep water.
¹⁵Do not let the flood drown me.
  Do not let the deep water swallow
    me.
  Do not let the grave close its mouth
    over me.
¹⁶Lord, answer me because your love is
    so good.
  Because of your great kindness,
    turn to me.
¹⁷Do not hide from me, your servant.
  I am in trouble. Hurry to help me!
¹⁸Come near and save me.
  Rescue me from my enemies.

¹⁹You see my shame and disgrace.
  You know all my enemies and what
    they have said.
²⁰Insults have broken my heart.
  I am weak.
  I looked for sympathy, but there was
    none.
  I found no one to comfort me.
²¹They put poison in my food.
  They gave me vinegar to drink.

²²Let their own feasts cause their ruin.
  Let their feasts trap them and pay
    them back.
²³Let their eyes be closed so they
    cannot see.
  Let their backs be forever weak
    from troubles.
²⁴Pour your anger out on them.
  Show them how angry you are.
²⁵May their place be empty.
  Leave no one to live in their tents.
²⁶They chase after those you have hurt.
  They talk about the pain of those
    you have wounded.

²⁷Charge them with crime after crime.
  Do not let them have anything
    good.
²⁸Wipe their names from the book of
    life.
  Do not list them with those who do
    what is right.

²⁹I am sad and hurting.
  God, save me and protect me.

³⁰I will praise God in a song.
  I will honor him by giving thanks.
³¹That will please the Lord more than
    offering him cattle.
  It will please him more than the
    sacrifice of a bull with horns and
      hoofs.
³²People who are not proud will see
    this and be glad.
  Be encouraged, you who worship
    God.
³³The Lord listens to those in need.
  He does not look down on captives.

³⁴Heaven and earth should praise him.
  The seas and everything in them
    should also.
³⁵God will save Jerusalem.
  He will rebuild the cities of Judah.
  Then people will live there and own
    the land.
³⁶ The descendants^d of his servants
    will inherit that land.
  Those who love him will live there.

PSALM 70

For the director of music. A song of David.
To help people remember.

¹God, save me.
  Lord, hurry to help me.
²People are trying to kill me.
  Shame them and disgrace them.
  People want to hurt me.
  Let them run away in disgrace.
³People make fun of me.
  Stop them and make them
    ashamed.
⁴But let all the people who worship
    you
  rejoice and be glad.
  Let the people who love your
    salvation
  always say, "Praise the greatness of
    God."
⁵I am poor and helpless.
  God, hurry to me.
  You help me and save me.
  Lord, do not wait.

PSALM 71

¹In you, Lord, is my protection.
  Never let me be ashamed.
²Because you do what is right, save
    and rescue me.
  Listen to me and save me.
³Be my place of safety
  where I can always come.
Give the command to save me.
  You are my rock and my strong,
    walled city.
⁴My God, save me from the power of
    the wicked.
  Save me from the hold of evil and
    cruel people.
⁵Lord God, you are my hope.
  I have trusted you since I was
    young.
⁶I have depended on you since I was
    born.
  You have been my help from the
    day I was born.
  I will always praise you.

⁷I am an example to many people.
  You are my strong protection.
⁸I am always praising you.
  All day long I honor you.
⁹Do not reject me when I am old.
  Do not leave me when my strength
    is gone.
¹⁰My enemies have made plans against
    me.
  They meet together to kill me.
¹¹They say, "God has left him.
  Go after him and take him.
  No one will save him."

¹²God, don't be far off.
  My God, hurry to help me.
¹³Let them be ashamed.
  Destroy those who accuse me.
  They are trying to hurt me.
  Cover them with shame and
    disgrace.
¹⁴But I will always have hope.
  And I will praise you more and
    more.
¹⁵I will tell about how you do what is
    right.
  I will tell about your salvation all
    day long,
  even though it is more than I can
    tell.
¹⁶I will come and tell about your
    powerful works, Lord God.
  I will tell only about you and how
    you do what is right.

¹⁷God, you have taught me since I was
    young.

Even until today I tell about the
    miracles[d] you do.
¹⁸Even though I am old and gray,
  do not leave me, God.
  I will tell the children about your
    power.
  I will tell those who will live after
    me about your might.

¹⁹God, your justice reaches to the skies.
  You have done great things.
  God, there is no one like you.
²⁰You have given me many troubles
    and bad times.
  But you will give me life again.
  When I am almost dead,
    you will keep me alive.
²¹You will make me greater than ever.
  And you will comfort me again.

²²I will praise you with the harp.
  I trust you, my God.
  I will sing to you with the lyre.[d]
    You are the Holy One of Israel.
²³I will shout for joy when I sing
    praises to you.
  You have saved me.
²⁴I will tell about your justice all day
    long.
  And those who want to hurt me
    will be ashamed and disgraced.

PSALM 72

Of Solomon.
¹God, give the king your good
    judgment
  and the king's son your goodness.
²Help him judge your people fairly.
  Help him decide what is right for
    the poor.
³Let there be peace on the mountains
    and goodness on the hills.
⁴Help him be fair to the poor.
  Help him save the needy
  and punish those who hurt them.

⁵Help him live as long as the sun
    shines.
  Help him rule as long as the moon
    glows.
  Let him be king from now on!
⁶Let him be like rain on the grass,
  like showers that water the earth.
⁷Let goodness be plentiful while he
    lives.
  Let peace continue as long as there
    is a moon.

⁸Let his kingdom go from sea to sea,
  and from the Euphrates River to
    the ends of the earth.

⁹Let the people of the desert bow
down to him.
And make his enemies lick the dust.
¹⁰Let the kings of Tarshish and the
faraway lands
bring him gifts.
Let the kings of Sheba and Seba
bring their presents to him.
¹¹Let all kings bow down to him.
Let all nations serve him.

¹²He will help the poor when they cry
for help.
He will help the needy when no one
else will help them.
¹³He will be kind to the weak and poor.
He will save their lives.
¹⁴He will save them from cruel people
who try to hurt them.
Their lives are precious to him.

¹⁵Long live the king!
Let him receive gold from Sheba.
Let people always pray for him.
Let them bless him all day long.
¹⁶Let the fields grow plenty of grain.
Let the hills be covered with crops.
Let the land be as fertile as Lebanon.
Let the cities grow like the grass in
a field.
¹⁷Let the king be famous forever.
Let him be remembered as long as
the sun shines.
Let the nations be blessed because of
him.
And may they all bless him.

¹⁸Praise the Lord God, the God of
Israel.
Only he does such miracles.ᵈ
¹⁹Praise his glorious name forever.
Let his glory fill the whole world.
Amen and amen.
²⁰This ends the prayers of David son of
Jesse.

Book 3

Psalms 73–89

PSALM 73

A song of Asaph.
¹God is truly good to Israel,
to those who have pure hearts.
²But I had almost stopped believing
this truth.
I had almost lost my faith
³because I was jealous of proud
people.
I saw wicked people doing well.

⁴They are not suffering.
They are healthy and strong.

⁵They don't have troubles like the rest
of us.
They don't have problems like
other people.
⁶So they wear pride like a necklace.
They put on violence as their
clothing.
⁷They are looking for profits.
They do not control their selfish
desires.
⁸They make fun of others and speak
evil.
Proudly they speak of hurting
others.
⁹They brag to the sky.
Their mouths gossip on the earth.
¹⁰So their people turn to them
and give them whatever they want.
¹¹They say, "How can God know?
What does God Most High know?"
¹²These people are wicked,
always at ease and getting richer.

¹³So why have I kept my heart pure?
Why have I kept my hands from
doing wrong?
¹⁴I have suffered all day long.
I have been punished every
morning.

¹⁵God, if I had decided to talk about
this,
I would have let your people down.
¹⁶I tried to understand all this.
But it was too hard for me to see
¹⁷until I went to the Templeᵈ of God.
Then I understood what will
happen to them.
¹⁸You have put them in danger.
You cause them to be destroyed.
¹⁹They are destroyed in a moment.
They are swept away by terrors.
²⁰It will be like waking from a dream.
Lord, when you come, they will
disappear.

²¹When my heart was sad and
I was angry,
²²I was senseless and stupid.
I acted like an animal toward you.
²³But I am always with you.
You have held my hand.
²⁴You guide me with your advice.
And later you will receive me in
honor.
²⁵I have no one in heaven but you.
I want nothing on earth besides
you.
²⁶My mind and my body may become
weak.
But God is my strength.
He is mine forever.

²⁷Those who are far from God will die.
You destroy those who are
unfaithful.
²⁸But I am close to God, and that is
good.
The Lord God is my protection.
I will tell all that you have done.

PSALM 74

A maskil[d] of Asaph.

¹God, why have you rejected us for so
long?
Why are you angry with us, the
sheep of your pasture?
²Remember the people you bought
long ago.
You saved us. We are your very
own.
You live on Mount Zion.[d]
³Make your way through these old
ruins.
The enemy wrecked everything in
the Temple.[d]

⁴Those who were against you shouted
in your meeting place.
They raised their flags there.
⁵They came with axes raised
as if to cut down a forest of trees.
⁶They smashed the carved panels
with their axes and hatchets.
⁷They burned your Temple to the
ground.
They have made the place where
you live unclean.[d]
⁸They thought, "We will completely
crush them!"
They burned every place where
God was worshiped in the land.
⁹We do not see any signs.
There are no more prophets.
And no one knows how long this
will last.
¹⁰God, how much longer will the
enemy make fun of you?
Will they insult you forever?
¹¹Why do you hold back your power?
Bring your power out in the open
and destroy them!

¹²God, you have been our king for a
long time.
You have saved this country.
¹³You split open the sea by your power.
You broke the heads of the sea[a]
monster.
¹⁴You smashed the heads of the
monster Leviathan.[d]
You gave him to the desert
creatures as food.

¹⁵You opened up the springs and
streams.
And you made the rivers run dry.
¹⁶Both the day and the night are yours.
You made the sun and the moon.
¹⁷You made all the limits on the earth.
You created summer and winter.

¹⁸Lord, remember how the enemy
insulted you.
Remember how those foolish
people turned away from you.
¹⁹Do not give us, your doves, to those
wild animals.
Never forget your poor people.
²⁰Remember the agreement you made
with us
because violence fills every dark
corner of this land.
²¹Do not let your suffering people be
disgraced.
The poor and helpless people
praise you.

²²God, come and defend yourself.
Remember the insults that come
from those foolish people all day
long.
²³Don't forget what your enemies said.
Don't forget their roar as they rise
against you always.

PSALM 75

For the director of music. To the tune of "Do
Not Destroy." A song of Asaph.

¹God, we thank you.
We thank you because you are near.
We tell about the wonderful things
you do.

²You say, "I set the time for trial.
I will judge fairly.
³The earth with all its people may
shake.
I am the one who holds it steady.
Selah[d]
⁴I say to those who are proud, 'Don't
brag.'
I say to the wicked, 'Don't show
your power.
⁵Don't try to use your power against
heaven.
Don't be stubborn.' "

⁶No one from the east or the west
or the desert can judge you.
⁷God is the judge.
He judges one person as guilty, and
another as innocent.
⁸The Lord holds a cup of anger in his
hand.
It is full of wine mixed with spices.

He pours it out even to the last drop.
And the wicked drink it all.

⁹I will tell about this forever.
I will sing praise to the God of
Jacob.
¹⁰He will take all power away from the
wicked.
But the power of good people will
grow.

PSALM 76

For the director of music. With stringed
instruments. A song of Asaph.

¹People in Judah know God.
People in Israel know he is great.
²He lives in Jerusalem.
His home is on Mount Zion.ᵈ
³There God broke the flaming arrows,
the shields and swords of war. *Selah*ᵈ

⁴God, how wonderful you are!
You are more wonderful than the
hills full of animals.
⁵The brave soldiers were stripped
as they lay asleep in death.
Not one warrior
had the strength to stop it.
⁶God of Jacob, when you spoke
strongly,
horses and riders fell dead.
⁷You should be feared.
Who can stand against you when
you are angry?
⁸From heaven you gave the decision.
And the earth was afraid and silent.
⁹God, you stood up to judge
and to save the people of the earth
who were not proud.   *Selah*
¹⁰People praise you for your anger
against evil.
Those who live through your anger
are stopped from doing more evil.

¹¹Keep your promises to the Lord your
God.
From all around gifts should come
to the God we worship.
¹²God defeats great leaders.
The kings on earth fear him.

PSALM 77

For the director of music. For Jeduthun. A
song of Asaph.

¹I cry out loud to God.
I call to God, and he will hear me.
²I looked for the Lord on the day of
trouble.
All night long I reached out my
hands.
I cannot be comforted.

³When I remember God, I become
upset.
When I think, I become afraid.
*Selah*ᵈ

⁴You keep my eyes from closing.
I am too upset to say anything.
⁵I keep thinking about the old days,
the years of long ago.
⁶At night I remember my songs.
I think, and I ask myself:
⁷"Will the Lord reject us forever?
Will he never be kind to us again?
⁸Is his love gone forever?
Has he stopped speaking for all
time?
⁹Has God forgotten mercy?
Is he too angry to pity us?"   *Selah*
¹⁰Then I said, "This is what makes me
sad:
For years the power of God Most
High was with us."

¹¹I remember what the Lord did.
I remember the miraclesᵈ you did
long ago.
¹²I think about all the things you did.
I think about what you have done.

¹³God, your ways are holy.
No god is as great as our God.
¹⁴You are the God who did miracles.
You showed people your power.
¹⁵By your power you have saved your
people,
the descendantsᵈ of Jacob and
Joseph.   *Selah*

¹⁶God, the waters saw you.
They saw you and became afraid.
The deep waters shook with fear.
¹⁷The clouds poured down their rain.
The sky thundered.
Your lightning flashed back and
forth.
¹⁸Your thunder sounded in the
whirlwind.
Lightning lit up the world.
The earth trembled and shook.
¹⁹You made a way through the sea
and paths through the deep waters.
But your footprints were not seen.
²⁰You led your people like a flock of
sheep.
You led them by using Moses and
Aaron.

PSALM 78

A maskilᵈ of Asaph.

¹My people, listen to my teaching.
Listen to what I say.
²I will speak using stories.

I will tell things that have been
   secret since long ago.
[3] We have heard them and know them.
   Our fathers told them to us.
[4] We will not keep them from our
      children.
   We will tell those who come later
      about the praises of the Lord.
   We will tell about his power
      and the miracles[d] he has done.

[5] The Lord made an agreement with
      Jacob.
   He gave the teachings to Israel.
   And he commanded our ancestors
      to teach them to their children.
[6] Then their children would know
      them,
   even their children not yet born.
   And they would tell their children.
[7] So they would all trust God.
   They would not forget what God
      had done.
   Instead, they would obey his
      commands.
[8] They would not be like their
      ancestors
   who were stubborn and
      disobedient.
   Their hearts were not loyal to God.
   They were not true to him.

[9] The men of Ephraim had bows for
      weapons.
   But they ran away on the day of
      battle.
[10] They didn't keep their agreement
      with God.
   They refused to live by his
      teachings.
[11] They forgot what he had done
   and the miracles he had shown
      them.
[12] He did miracles while their ancestors
      watched,
   in the fields of Zoan in Egypt.
[13] He divided the Red Sea[d] and led them
      through.
   He made the water stand up like a
      wall.
[14] He led them with a cloud by day.
   And he led them at night by the
      light of a fire.
[15] He split the rocks in the desert.
   And he gave them much water, as if
      it were from the deep ocean.
[16] He brought streams out of the rock.
   The water flowed down like rivers.

[17] But the people continued to sin
      against him.

In the desert they turned against
   God Most High.
[18] They decided to test God
   by asking for the food they wanted.
[19] Then they spoke against God.
   They said, "Can God prepare food
      in the desert?
[20] When he hit the rock, water poured
      out.
   Rivers flowed down.
   But can he give us bread also?
   Will he provide his people with
      meat?"
[21] When the Lord heard them, he was
      very angry.
   His anger was like fire to the
      people of Jacob.
   His anger grew against the people
      of Israel.
[22] They had not believed God.
   They had not trusted him to save
      them.
[23] But he gave a command to the clouds
      above.
   The doors of heaven opened.
[24] He rained manna[d] down on them to
      eat.
   He gave them grain from heaven.
[25] So they ate the bread of angels.
   He sent them all the food they
      could eat.
[26] He sent the east wind from heaven.
   He led the south wind by his power.
[27] He rained meat on them like dust.
   The birds were as many as the sand
      of the sea.
[28] He made the birds fall inside the
      camp,
   all around the tents.
[29] So the people ate and became very
      full.
   God had given them what they
      wanted.
[30] While they were still eating,
   and while the food was still in their
      mouths,
[31] God became angry with them.
   He killed some of the healthiest of
      them.
   He struck down the best young
      men of Israel.

[32] But they kept on sinning.
   They did not believe even with the
      miracles.
[33] So he ended their days without
      meaning
   and their years in terror.
[34] Anytime he killed them, some would
   look to him for help.

They would come back to God and follow him.
[35] They would remember that God was their Rock,[d]
that God Most High had saved them.
[36] But their words were false.
Their tongues lied to him.
[37] Their hearts were not really loyal to God.
They did not keep his agreement.
[38] Still God was merciful.
He forgave their sins.
He did not destroy them.
Many times he held back his anger.
He did not stir up all his anger.
[39] He remembered that they were only human.
They were like a wind that blows and does not come back.
[40] They turned against God so often in the desert!
There they made him very sad.
[41] Again and again they tested God.
They brought pain to the Holy One of Israel.
[42] They did not remember his power or the time he saved them from the enemy.
[43] They forgot the signs he did in Egypt and his miracles in the fields of Zoan.
[44] He turned the rivers to blood.
So no one could drink the water.
[45] He sent flies that bit the people.
He sent frogs that destroyed them.
[46] He gave their crops to grasshoppers and what they worked for to locusts.[d]
[47] He destroyed their vines with hail and their sycamore trees with sleet.
[48] He killed their animals with hail and their cattle with lightning.
[49] He showed them his hot anger.
He sent his strong anger against them.
He sent his destroying angels.
[50] He found a way to show his anger.
He did not keep them from dying.
He let them die by a terrible disease.
[51] God killed all the firstborn[d] sons in Egypt,
the oldest son of each family of Ham.[n]
[52] But God led out his people like sheep.
He guided them like a flock through the desert.

[53] He led them to safety. They had nothing to fear.
But their enemies drowned in the sea.
[54] So God brought them to his holy land.
He brought them to the mountain country he took with his own power.
[55] He forced out the other nations.
And he had his people inherit the land.
He let the tribes[d] of Israel settle there in tents.

[56] But they tested God
and turned against the Most High.
They did not keep his rules.
[57] They turned away and sinned just like their ancestors.
They were like a crooked bow that does not shoot straight.
[58] They made God angry by building places to worship false gods.
They made him jealous with their idols.
[59] When God heard them, he became very angry.
And he rejected the people of Israel completely.
[60] He left his dwelling at Shiloh,
the tent where he lived among men.
[61] He let his Holy Box[d] be captured.
He let the Holy Box, which was his glory, be taken by enemies.
[62] He let his people be killed.
He was very angry with his children.
[63] The young men died by fire.
The young women had no one to marry.
[64] Their priests fell by the sword.
But their widows were not allowed to cry.

[65] Then the Lord got up as if he had been asleep.
He awoke like a man who was drunk with wine.
[66] He struck down his enemies.
He disgraced them forever.
[67] But God rejected the family of Joseph.
He did not choose the tribe of Ephraim.
[68] Instead, he chose the tribe of Judah and Mount Zion,[d] which he loves.
[69] And he built his Temple[d] high like the mountains.

78:51 Ham The people in Egypt were descendants of Ham, one of Noah's sons. See Genesis 10:6.

Like the earth, he built it to last
forever.
⁷⁰He chose David to be his servant.
He took him from the sheep pens.
⁷¹He brought him from tending the
sheep
so he could lead the flock, the
people of Jacob.
This flock was his own people, the
people of Israel.
⁷²And David led them with an innocent
heart.
He guided them with skillful hands.

PSALM 79

A song of Asaph.

¹God, nations have come against your
people.
They have ruined your holy
Temple.^d
They have turned Jerusalem into
ruins.
²They have given the bodies of your
servants
as food to the wild birds.
They have given the bodies of those
who worship you
to the wild animals.
³They have spilled blood like water
all around Jerusalem.
No one was left to bury the dead.
⁴We are a bad joke to the other
nations.
They laugh and make fun of us.

⁵Lord, how long will this last? Will you
be angry forever?
How long will your jealousy burn
like a fire?
⁶Be angry with the nations that do not
know you.
Be angry with the kingdoms that
do not honor you.
⁷They have destroyed the people of
Jacob.
Those nations have destroyed the
people's land.
⁸Don't punish us for the sins of our
ancestors.
Show your mercy to us soon.
We are helpless!
⁹God our Savior, help us
so people will praise you.
Save us and forgive our sins
so people will honor you.
¹⁰Why should the nations say,
"Where is their God?"
Tell the other nations in our presence
that you punish those who kill your
servants.
¹¹Hear the moans of the prisoners.

Use your great power
to save those sentenced to die.
¹²Repay those around us seven times
over
for their insults to you, Lord.
¹³We are your people, the sheep of your
flock.
We will thank you always.
Forever and ever we will praise
you.

PSALM 80

For the director of music. To the tune of
"Lilies of the Agreement." A song of Asaph.

¹Shepherd of Israel, listen to us.
You lead the people of Joseph like a
flock.
You sit on your throne between the
gold creatures with wings.
Show your greatness ²to the people
of Ephraim, Benjamin and
Manasseh.
Use your strength.
Come and save us.

³God, take us back.
Show us your kindness so we can
be saved.

⁴Lord God of heaven's armies,
how long will you be angry
at the prayers of your people?
⁵You have fed your people tears.
You have made them drink many
tears.
⁶You made those around us fight over
us.
Our enemies make fun of us.

⁷God of heaven's armies, take us back.
Show us your kindness so we can
be saved.

⁸You brought us out of Egypt as if we
were a vine.
You forced out other nations and
planted us in the land.
⁹You cleared the land for us.
Like a vine, we took root and filled
the land.
¹⁰We covered the mountains with our
shade.
We had limbs like the mighty cedar
tree.
¹¹Our branches reached the
Mediterranean Sea.
And our shoots went to the
Euphrates River.
¹²So why did you pull down our walls?
Now everyone who passes by steals
from us.

¹³Like wild pigs they walk over us.
　　Like wild animals they feed on us.
¹⁴God of heaven's armies, come back.
　　Look down from heaven and see.
　　Take care of us, your vine.
¹⁵　You planted this shoot with your
　　　　own hands.
　　You raised and strengthened this
　　　　child.
¹⁶Now it is cut down and burned with
　　　fire.
　　You destroyed us by your angry
　　　　looks.
¹⁷Help the man you have chosen.
　　Make this human being strong for
　　　　your service.
¹⁸Then we will not turn away from you.
　　Give us life again, and we will call
　　　　to you for help.
¹⁹Lord God of heaven's armies, take us
　　　back.
　　Show us your kindness so we can
　　　　be saved.

PSALM 81

For the director of music. By the gittith.ᵈ A
song of Asaph.
¹Sing for joy to God, our strength.
　　Shout out loud to the God of Jacob.
²Begin the music. Play the
　　　tambourines.ᵈ
　　Play pleasant music on the harps
　　　　and lyres.ᵈ
³Blow the sheep's horn at the time of
　　　the New Moon.ᵈ
　　Blow it when the moon is full,
　　　　when our feast begins.
⁴This is the law for Israel.
　　It is God's command to the people
　　　　of Jacob.
⁵He made this agreement with the
　　　people of Joseph
　　when they went out of the land of
　　　　Egypt.

I heard a language I did not know,
　　saying:
⁶"I took the load off your shoulders.
　　I let you put down your baskets.
⁷When you were in trouble, you called,
　　and I saved you.
　　I answered you with thunder.
　　I tested you at the waters of
　　　Meribah.　　　　　　　*Selah*ᵈ
⁸My people, listen. I am warning you.
　　Israel, please listen to me!
⁹You must not have foreign gods
　　　among you.
　　You must not worship any false
　　　god.

¹⁰I, the Lord, am your God.
　　I brought you out of Egypt.
　　Open your mouth, and I will feed
　　　　you.
¹¹"But my people did not listen to me.
　　Israel did not want me.
¹²So I let them go their stubborn way.
　　They followed their own advice.
¹³I wish my people would listen to me.
　　I wish Israel would live my way.
¹⁴Then I would quickly defeat their
　　　enemies.
　　I would turn my hand against those
　　　　who are against them.
¹⁵Those who hate the Lord would bow
　　　before him.
　　Their punishment would continue
　　　　forever.
¹⁶But I would give you the finest wheat.
　　I would fill you with honey from
　　　　the rocks."

PSALM 82

A song of Asaph.
¹God is in charge of the great meeting
　　　of his people.
　　He judges the judges.
²He says, "How long will you defend
　　　evil people?
　　How long will you show greater
　　　　kindness to the wicked?　　*Selah*ᵈ
³Defend the orphans and the weak.
　　Defend the rights of the poor and
　　　　suffering.
⁴Save the weak and helpless
　　　from the power of the wicked.

⁵"You know nothing. You don't
　　　understand.
　　You walk in the dark,
　　　while the world is falling apart.
⁶I said, 'You are gods.
　　You are all sons of the Most High
　　　　God.'
⁷But you will die like any other person.
　　You will die like all the leaders."

⁸God, come and judge the earth.
　　You own all the nations.

PSALM 83

A song of Asaph.
¹God, do not keep quiet.
　　God, do not be silent or still.
²Your enemies are making plans.
　　Those who hate you are getting
　　　　ready to attack.
³They are making plans against your
　　　people.
　　They plan to hurt those you love.

How Do I Pray?

We talk to our friends all day without a problem. But when it is time to pray, sometimes we don't know what to say. *How do I talk to God?* we may wonder. *How do I even begin?* Don't worry. Even Jesus' disciples asked these same questions. So Jesus taught them a simple prayer to help them understand how to talk to God. It might seem a little strange at first, speaking to someone you can't see. But God is right here, closer than you can even imagine. And He loves to hear what you have to say to Him. Praying is simply talking to your best friend, God.

Here's the prayer Jesus taught His disciples to pray:

Our Father in heaven,
we pray that your name will always be kept holy.
We pray that your kingdom will come.
We pray that what you want will be done,
here on earth as it is in heaven.
Give us the food we need for each day.
Forgive the sins we have done,
just as we have forgiven those who did wrong to us.
Do not cause us to be tested;
but save us from the Evil One.

~ Matthew 6:9–13

How Do I Know Jesus Loves Me?

Do you remember the song "Jesus Loves Me"? How can you know for sure that Jesus really loves you? There is proof! God the Father, Jesus the Son, and the Holy Spirit all show how much you are loved.

God created you in an amazing and wonderful way! Psalm 139 tells you all about it.

Jesus gave His life for us and died on the cross to take our sins so that we can live forever in heaven. The book of John tells this wonderful story.

The Holy Spirit lives in your heart and guides you to do God's will and live the wonderful life that God planned for you and Jesus sacrificed to give you.

There is not a single doubt that you are loved!

You made my whole being. You formed me in my mother's body. I praise you because you made me in an amazing and wonderful way.
~ Psalm 139:13–14

"For God loved the world so much that he gave his only Son. God gave his Son so that whoever believes in him may not be lost, but have eternal life."
~ John 3:16

Jesus answered, "I am the way. And I am the truth and the life. The only way to the Father is through me."
~ John 14:6

How Can I Know Jesus Better?

Many people in Bible times had heard about Jesus, and some were able to hear Him speak. But it was Jesus' disciples who knew Him best. Why? Because they lived with Him, ate with Him, and walked with Him all day long. We get to know people better the more we hang around them.

So how can we get to know Jesus even though He's in heaven and we're still on earth? We spend time with Him. We set aside time each day when we can read the Bible without other distractions. Then we talk to Jesus in prayer about the verses we've read and about the thoughts in our minds and hearts. Even after we've said "Amen," we can keep the conversation going all day long. For instance, when we see a beautiful sunset, we can tell Him thank You. When we're nervous about school, we can ask Him to make us brave. Whatever is happening in our lives, we can share it with Jesus. And when we do, we will soon see a beautiful friendship start to grow.

*"The thing you should want most
is God's kingdom and doing what God wants.
Then all these other things you need will be given to you."*

~ Matthew 6:33

Why Should I Read the Bible?

Imagine having a best friend who never listened to what you had to say. You had great and exciting things to share, but she didn't pay any attention to you. How well would she actually know you? How strong do you think your friendship would grow?

If we want to become best friends with God, we need to know what He has to say to us. He has written things that matter to Him in the pages of the Bible. When we take time to read it, we are not just reading another story. We are hearing God's heart and growing closer to the One who loves us! As we learn what is important to God, we begin to value those things too. We learn to live our lives by His directions and not our own thinking. God uses His Word to help us trust Him, obey Him, and love Him as we become more like Jesus.

> *All Scripture is given by God and is useful for teaching*
> *and for showing people what is wrong in their lives.*
> *It is useful for correcting faults and teaching how to live right.*
> ~ 2 Timothy 3:16

[4]They say, "Come, let's destroy them
     as a nation.
     Then no one will remember the
         name 'Israel' anymore."
[5]They are united in their plan.
     These have made an agreement
         against you:
[6]the families of Edom and the
     Ishmaelites,
     Moab and the Hagrites,
[7]the people of Byblos, Ammon,
     Amalek,
     Philistia and Tyre.
[8]Even Assyria has joined them
     to help Ammon and Moab, the
         descendants[d] of Lot.   *Selah*[d]

[9]God, do to them what you did to
     Midian.
     Do what you did to Sisera and
         Jabin at the Kishon River.
[10]They died at Endor.
     Their bodies rotted on the ground.
[11]Do to their important leaders what
     you did to Oreb and Zeeb.
     Do to their princes what you did to
         Zebah and Zalmunna.
[12]They said, "Let's take for ourselves
     the pasturelands that belong to
         God."
[13]My God, make them like the
     tumbleweed,
     like chaff[d] blown away by the wind.
[14]Be like a fire that burns a forest
     or like flames that blaze through
         the hills.
[15]Chase them with your storm.
     Frighten them with your wind.
[16]Cover them with shame.
     Then people will look for you,
         Lord.
[17]Make them afraid and ashamed
     forever.
     Disgrace them and destroy them.
[18]Then they will know that you are the
     Lord.
     They will know that only you are
         God Most High over all the earth.

PSALM 84

For the director of music. By the gittith.[d] A
song of the sons of Korah.
[1]Lord of heaven's armies,
     how lovely is your Temple![d]
[2]I want to be in
     the courtyards of the Lord's
         Temple.
My whole being wants
     to be with the living God.
[3]The sparrows have found a home.
     And the swallows have nests.

They raise their young near your
     altars,
     Lord of heaven's armies, my King
         and my God.
[4]Happy are the people who live at
     your Temple.
     They are always praising you. *Selah*[d]

[5]Happy are those whose strength
     comes from you.
     They want to travel to Jerusalem.
[6]As they pass through the Valley of
     Baca,
     they make it like a spring.
     The autumn rains fill it with pools
         of water.
[7]The people get stronger as they go.
     And everyone meets with God in
         Jerusalem.

[8]Lord God of heaven's armies, hear
     my prayer.
     God of Jacob, listen to me.   *Selah*
[9]God, look at our shield.
     Be kind to your appointed king.

[10]One day in the courtyards of your
     Temple is better
     than a thousand days anywhere
         else.
I would rather be a doorkeeper in the
     Temple of my God
     than live in the homes of the
         wicked.
[11]The Lord God is like our sun and
     shield.
     The Lord gives us kindness and
         glory.
He does not hold back anything good
     from those whose life is innocent.
[12]Lord of heaven's armies,
     happy are the people who trust
         you!

PSALM 85

For the director of music. A song of the sons
of Korah.
[1]Lord, you have been kind to your
     land.
     You gave the people of Jacob back
         their riches.
[2]You forgave the guilt of the people.
     You covered all their sins.   *Selah*[d]
[3]You stopped all your anger.
     You stopped your strong anger.

[4]God our Savior, bring us back again.
     Stop being angry with us.
[5]Will you be angry with us forever?
     Will you stay angry from now on?
[6]Won't you give us life again?
     Your people would rejoice in you.

⁷Lord, show us your love.
  Save us.

⁸I will listen to God the Lord.
  He has ordered peace for his
    people who worship him.
  Don't let them go back to
    foolishness.
⁹God will soon save those who respect
    him.
  And his greatness will be seen in
    our land.
¹⁰Love and truth will belong to God's
    people.
  Goodness and peace will be theirs.
¹¹On earth people will be loyal to God.
  And God's goodness will shine
    down from heaven.
¹²The Lord will give his goodness.
  And the land will give its crops.
¹³Goodness will go before God
  and prepare the way for him.

PSALM 86

A prayer of David.

¹Lord, listen to me and answer me.
  I am poor and helpless.
²Protect me, because I worship you.
  My God, save me, your servant.
  I trust in you.
³Lord, be merciful to me.
  I have called to you all day.
⁴Give happiness to me, your servant.
  Lord, I give my life to you.
⁵Lord, you are kind and forgiving.
  You have great love for those who
    call to you.
⁶Lord, hear my prayer.
  Listen when I ask for mercy.
⁷I call to you in times of trouble.
  You certainly will answer me.

⁸Lord, there is no god like you.
  There are no works like yours.
⁹Lord, all the nations you have made
    will come and worship you.
  They will honor you.
¹⁰You are great, and you do miracles.ᵈ
  Only you are God.

¹¹Lord, teach me what you want me to
    do.
  And I will live by your truth.
  Teach me to respect you completely.
¹²Lord, my God, I will praise you with
    all my heart.
  I will honor your name forever.
¹³You have great love for me.
  You have saved me from death.

¹⁴God, proud men turn against me.

A gang of cruel men are trying to
    kill me.
  They do not respect you.
¹⁵But Lord, you are a God who shows
    mercy and is kind.
  You don't become angry quickly.
  You have great love and
    faithfulness.
¹⁶Turn to me and be merciful.
  Give me, your servant, strength.
  Save me, the son of your female
    servant.
¹⁷Show me a sign of your goodness.
  When my enemies look, they will
    be ashamed.
  You, Lord, have helped me and
    comforted me.

PSALM 87

A song of the sons of Korah.

¹The Lord built Jerusalem on the holy
    mountain.
² He loves its gates
  more than any other place in Israel.
³City of God,
  wonderful things are said about
    you.   *Selah*ᵈ
⁴God says, "I will put Egypt and
    Babylonia
  on the list of nations that know me.
  People from Philistia, Tyre and Cush
    will be born there."

⁵They will say about Jerusalem,
  "This one and that one were born
    there.
  God Most High will strengthen her."
⁶The Lord will keep a list of the
    nations.
  He will note, "This person was
    born there."   *Selah*
⁷They will dance and sing,
  "All good things come from
    Jerusalem."

PSALM 88

A song of the sons of Korah. For the director
of music. By the mahalath leannoth.ᵈ A
maskilᵈ of Heman the Ezrahite.

¹Lord, you are the God who saves me.
  I cry out to you day and night.
²Accept my prayer.
  Listen to my cry.

³My life is full of troubles.
  I am nearly dead.
⁴They think I am on the way to my
    grave.
  I am like a man with no strength.
⁵I have been left as dead,
  like a body lying in a grave.

You don't remember dead people.
They are cut off from your care.
[6]You have brought me close to death.
I am almost in the dark place of the
dead.
[7]You have been very angry with me.
All your waves crush me.   *Selah*[d]
[8]You have taken my friends away from
me.
You have made them hate me.
I am trapped and cannot escape.
[9]   My eyes are weak from crying.
Lord, I have prayed to you every day.
I have lifted my hands in prayer to
you.

[10]Do you show your miracles[d] for the
dead?
Do their spirits rise up and praise
you?   *Selah*
[11]Will your love be told in the grave?
Will your loyalty be told in the
place of death?
[12]Will your miracles be known in the
dark grave?
Will your goodness be known in
the land where the dead are
forgotten?

[13]But, Lord, I have called out to you for
help.
Every morning I pray to you.
[14]Lord, why do you reject me?
Why do you hide from me?
[15]I have been weak and dying since I
was young.
I suffer from your terrors, and I am
helpless.
[16]You have been angry with me.
Your terrors have destroyed me.
[17]They surround me daily like a flood.
They are all around me.
[18]You have taken away my loved ones
and friends.
Darkness is my only friend.

PSALM 89

A maskil[c] of Ethan the Ezrahite.
[1]I will always sing about the Lord's
love.
I will tell of his loyalty from now
on.
[2]I will say, "Your love continues
forever.
Your loyalty goes on and on like
the sky."
[3]You said, "I made an agreement with
the man of my choice.
I made a promise to my servant
David.

[4]I told him, 'I will make your family
continue forever.
Your kingdom will continue from
now on.'"   *Selah*[d]

[5]Lord, the heavens praise you for your
miracles[d]
and for your loyalty in the meeting
of your holy ones.
[6]Who in heaven is equal to the Lord?
None of the angels is like the Lord.
[7]When the holy ones meet, it is God
they fear.
He is more frightening than all who
surround him.
[8]Lord God of heaven's armies, who is
like you?
Lord, you are powerful and
completely to be trusted.
[9]You rule the mighty sea.
You calm the stormy waves.
[10]You crushed the sea monster Rahab.[d]
By your power you scattered your
enemies.

[11]The skies and the earth belong to
you.
You made the world and everything
in it.
[12]You created the north and the south.
Mount Tabor and Mount Hermon
sing for joy at your name.
[13]Your arm has great power.
Your hand is strong. Your right
hand is lifted up.
[14]Your kingdom is built on what is right
and fair.
Love and truth are in all you do.

[15]Happy are the people who know how
to praise you.
Lord, let them live in the light of
your presence.
[16]In your name they rejoice all the
time.
They praise your goodness.
[17]You are their glorious strength.
In your kindness you honor our
king.
[18]Our king, our shield, belongs to the
Lord.
Our king belongs to the Holy One
of Israel.

[19]Once, in a vision, you spoke
to those who worship you.
You said, "I have given strength to a
warrior.
I have selected a young man from
my people.
[20]I have found my servant David.

I appointed him by pouring holy oil
on him.
[21] I will steady him with my hand.
I will strengthen him with my arm.
[22] No enemy will make him give forced
payments.
Wicked people will not defeat him.
[23] I will crush his enemies in front of
him.
I will defeat those who hate him.
[24] My loyalty and love will be with him.
Through me he will be strong.
[25] I will give him power over the sea
and control over the rivers.
[26] He will say to me, 'You are my father,
my God, the Rock,[d] the one who
saves me.'
[27] I will make him my firstborn[d] son.
He will be the greatest king on
earth.
[28] My love will watch over him forever.
My agreement with him will never
end.
[29] I will make his family continue.
His kingdom will last as long as the
skies.

[30] "But his descendants[d] might reject
my teachings
and not follow my rules.
[31] They might break my laws
and disobey my commands.
[32] Then I will punish their sins with a rod
and their wrongs with a whip.
[33] But I will not hold back my love from
David.
I will not stop being loyal.
[34] I will not break my agreement.
I will not change what I have said.
[35] It is certain that I am a holy God.
So it is certain I will not lie to
David.
[36] His family will continue forever.
His kingdom will continue before
me like the sun.
[37] It will last forever, like the moon,
like a lasting witness in the sky."
Selah

[38] But now, you have rejected your
appointed king.
You have been angry with him.
[39] You have broken the agreement with
your servant.
You threw his crown to the ground.
[40] You have torn down all the city walls.
You have turned his strong, walled
cities into ruins.
[41] Everyone who passes by steals from
him.
His neighbors insult him.

[42] You have given strength to his
enemies.
You have made them all happy.
[43] You have made his sword useless.
You did not help him stand in
battle.
[44] You have kept him from winning.
You threw his throne to the ground.
[45] You have cut his life short.
You have covered him with shame.
Selah

[46] Lord, how long will this go on?
Will you ignore us forever?
How long will your anger burn like
a fire?
[47] Remember how short my life is.
Why did you create us anyway?
[48] What man alive will not die?
Can he escape the grave? *Selah*

[49] Lord, where is your love from times
past?
With loyalty you promised it to
David.
[50] Lord, remember how they insulted
your servant.
Remember how I have suffered the
insults of the nations.
[51] Lord, remember how your enemies
insulted you.
Remember how they insulted your
appointed king wherever he
went.

[52] Praise the Lord forever!
Amen and amen.

Book 4

Psalms 90–106

PSALM 90

A prayer of Moses, the man of God.
[1] Lord, you have been our home
since the beginning.
[2] Before the mountains were born,
and before you created the earth
and the world,
you are God.
You have always been, and you will
always be.

[3] You turn people back into dust.
You say, "Go back into dust, human
beings."
[4] To you, a thousand years
is like the passing of a day.
It passes like an hour in the night.
[5] While people sleep, you take their
lives.
They are like weeds that grow in
the morning.

⁶In the morning they are fresh and
new.
But by evening they dry up and die.

⁷We are destroyed by your anger.
We are terrified by your hot anger.
⁸You have put the evil we have done
right in front of you.
You clearly see our secret sins.
⁹All our days pass while you are
angry.
Our years end with a moan.
¹⁰Our lifetime is 70 years.
If we are strong, we may live to be
80.
But the years are full of hard work
and pain.
They pass quickly, and then we are
gone.

¹¹Who knows the full power of your
anger?
Your anger is as great as our fear of
you should be.
¹²Teach us how short our lives really
are
so that we may be wise.

¹³Lord, how long before you return
and show kindness to your
servants?
¹⁴Fill us with your love every morning.
Then we will sing and rejoice all
our lives.
¹⁵We have seen years of trouble.
Now give us joy as you gave us
sorrow.
¹⁶Show your servants the wonderful
things you do.
Show your greatness to their
children.
¹⁷Lord our God, be pleased with us.
Give us success in what we do.
Yes, give us success in what we do.

PSALM 91

¹Those who go to God Most High for
safety
will be protected by God
All-Powerful.
²I will say to the Lord, "You are my
place of safety and protection.
You are my God, and I trust you."

³God will save you from hidden traps
and from deadly diseases.
⁴He will protect you like a bird
spreading its wings over its young.
His truth will be like your armor
and shield.
⁵You will not fear any danger by night
or an arrow during the day.

⁶You will not be afraid of diseases that
come in the dark
or sickness that strikes at noon.
⁷At your side 1,000 people may die,
or even 10,000 right beside you.
But you will not be hurt.
⁸You will only watch what happens.
You will see the wicked punished.

⁹The Lord is your protection.
You have made God Most High
your place of safety.
¹⁰Nothing bad will happen to you.
No disaster will come to your
home.
¹¹He has put his angels in charge of
you.
They will watch over you wherever
you go.
¹²They will catch you with their hands.
And you will not hit your foot on a
rock.
¹³You will walk on lions and cobras.
You will step on strong lions and
snakes.

¹⁴The Lord says, "If someone loves me,
I will save him.
I will protect those who know me.
¹⁵They will call to me, and I will
answer them.
I will be with them in trouble.
I will rescue them and honor them.
¹⁶I will give them a long, full life.
They will see how I can save."

PSALM 92

A song for the Sabbath[d] day.
¹It is good to praise the Lord,
to sing praises to God Most High.
²It is good to tell of your love in the
morning
and of your loyalty at night.
³It is good to praise you with the
ten-stringed lyre[d]
and with the soft-sounding harp.

⁴Lord, you have made me happy by
what you have done.
I will sing for joy about what your
hands have done.
⁵Lord, you have done such great
things!
How deep are your thoughts?
⁶Stupid people don't know these
things.
Fools don't understand.
⁷Wicked people grow like the grass.
Evil people seem to do well.
But they will be destroyed forever.
⁸But, Lord, you will be honored
forever.

⁹Lord, surely your enemies,
  surely your enemies will be
    destroyed.
  All who do evil will be scattered.
¹⁰But you have made me as strong as a
    wild ox.
  You have poured fine oils on me.
¹¹When I looked, I saw my enemies.
  I heard the cries of those who are
    against me.

¹²But good people will grow like palm
    trees.
  They will be tall like the cedar trees
    of Lebanon.
¹³They will be like trees planted in the
    courtyards of the Lord.
  They will grow strong in the
    courtyards of our God.
¹⁴When they are old, they will still
    produce fruit.
  They will be healthy and fresh.
¹⁵They will say that the Lord is good.
  He is my Rock,ᵈ and there is no
    wrong in him.

PSALM 93

¹The Lord is king. He is clothed with
    majesty.
  The Lord is clothed in majesty
    and armed with strength.
  The world is set,
    and it cannot be moved.
²Lord, your kingdom was set up long
    ago.
  You are everlasting.

³Lord, the seas rise up.
  The seas raise their voice.
  The seas lift up their pounding
    waves.
⁴The sound of the water is loud.
  The ocean waves are powerful.
  But the Lord above is much greater.

⁵Lord, your laws will stand forever.
  Your Templeᵈ will be holy
    forevermore.

PSALM 94

¹The Lord is a God who gives people
    what they should get.
  God, show your greatness and
    punish!
²Rise up, Judge of the earth.
  Give the proud what they should
    get.
³How long will the wicked be happy?
  How long, Lord?

⁴They are full of proud words.
  Those who do evil brag about what
    they have done.

⁵Lord, they crush your people.
  They make your children suffer.
⁶They kill widows and foreigners.
  They murder orphans.
⁷They say, "The Lord doesn't see.
  The God of Jacob doesn't notice."

⁸You stupid ones among the people,
    pay attention.
  You fools, when will you
    understand?
⁹Can't the creator of ears hear?
  Can't the maker of eyes see?
¹⁰Won't the one who corrects nations
    punish you?
  Doesn't the teacher of men know
    everything?
¹¹The Lord knows what people think.
  He knows they are just a puff of
    wind.

¹²Lord, those you correct are happy.
  You give them your teachings.
¹³You give them rest from times of
    trouble
  until a grave is dug for the wicked.
¹⁴The Lord won't leave his people.
  He will not give up his children.
¹⁵Judgment will again be fair.
  And all who are honest will follow
    it.

¹⁶Who will help me fight against the
    wicked?
  Who will stand with me against
    those who do evil?
¹⁷If the Lord had not helped me,
  I would have died soon.
¹⁸I said, "I am about to be
    overwhelmed."
  But, Lord, your love kept me safe.
¹⁹I was very worried.
  But you comforted me and made
    me happy.

²⁰Crooked leaders cannot be your
    friends.
  They use the law to cause suffering.
²¹They join forces against people who
    do right.
  They sentence to death the
    innocent.
²²But the Lord protects me like a
    strong, walled city.
  My God is the rock of my
    protection.
²³God will pay them back for their sins.
  He will destroy them for their evil.
  The Lord our God will destroy
    them.

PSALM 95

¹Come, let's sing for joy to the Lord.
Let's shout praises to the Rock[d]
who saves us.
²Let's come to him with thanksgiving.
Let's sing songs to him.
³The Lord is the great God.
He is the great King over all gods.
⁴The deepest places on earth are his.
And the highest mountains belong
to him.
⁵The sea is his because he made it.
He created the land with his own
hands.
⁶Come, let's bow down and worship
him.
Let's kneel before the Lord who
made us.
⁷He is our God.
And we are the people he takes
care of
and the sheep that he tends.

Today listen to what he says:
⁸ "Do not be stubborn, as your
ancestors were at Meribah,
as they were that day at Massah in
the desert.
⁹There your ancestors tested me.
They put me to the test even though
they saw what I did.
¹⁰I was angry with those people for 40
years.
I said, 'They are not loyal to me.
They have not understood my
ways.'
¹¹I was angry and made a promise,
'They will never enter my land of
rest.'"

PSALM 96

¹Sing to the Lord a new song.
Sing to the Lord, all the earth.
²Sing to the Lord and praise his name.
Every day tell how he saves us.
³Tell the nations of his glory.
Tell all peoples the miracles[d] he
does.
⁴The Lord is great; he should be
praised.
He should be honored more than
all the gods.
⁵All the gods of the nations are only
idols.
But the Lord made the skies.
⁶The Lord has glory and majesty.
He has power and beauty in his
Temple.[d]

⁷Praise the Lord, all nations on earth.
Praise the Lord's glory and power.
⁸Praise the glory of the Lord's name.
Bring an offering and come into his
Temple courtyards.
⁹Worship the Lord because he is holy.
The whole earth should tremble
before the Lord.
¹⁰Tell the nations, "The Lord is king."
The earth is set, and it cannot be
moved.
He will judge the people fairly.
¹¹Let the skies rejoice and the earth be
glad.
Let the sea and everything in it
shout.
¹²Let the fields and everything in them
show their joy.
Then all the trees of the forest will
sing for joy.
¹³ They will sing before the Lord
because he is coming.
He is coming to judge the world.
He will judge the world with fairness
and the nations with truth.

PSALM 97

¹The Lord is king. Let the earth
rejoice.
Faraway lands should be glad.
²Thick, dark clouds surround him.
His kingdom is built on what is
right and fair.
³A fire goes before him
and burns up his enemies all
around.
⁴His lightning flashes in the sky.
When the people see it, they
tremble.
⁵The mountains melt like wax before
the Lord.
He is Lord of all the earth.
⁶The skies tell about his goodness.
And all the people see his glory.

⁷Those who worship idols should be
ashamed.
They brag about their false gods.
All the gods should worship the
Lord.
⁸When Jerusalem hears this, she is
glad.
The towns of Judah rejoice.
They are happy because of your
judgments, Lord.
⁹You are the Lord Most High over all
the earth.
You are supreme over all gods.
¹⁰People who love the Lord should hate
evil.
The Lord watches over those who
follow him.

He frees them from the power of
the wicked.
¹¹Light shines on those who do right.
Joy belongs to those who are
honest.
¹²Rejoice in the Lord, you who do right.
Praise his holy name.

PSALM 98

A song.

¹Sing to the Lord a new song
because he has done miracles.ᵈ
By his right hand and holy arm
he has won the victory.
²The Lord has told about his power to
save.
He has shown the other nations his
victory for his people.
³He has remembered his love
and his loyalty to the people of
Israel.
All the ends of the earth have seen
God's power to save.

⁴Shout with joy to the Lord, all the
earth.
Burst into songs and praise.
⁵Make music to the Lord with harps,
with harps and the sound of singing.
⁶Blow the trumpets and the sheep's
horns.
Shout for joy to the Lord the King.

⁷Let the sea and everything in it shout.
Let the world and everyone on it
sing.
⁸Let the rivers clap their hands.
Let the mountains sing together for
joy.
⁹Let them sing before the Lord
because he is coming to judge the
world.
He will judge the world fairly.
He will judge the nations with
fairness.

PSALM 99

¹The Lord is king.
Let the nations shake with fear.
He sits between the gold creatures
with wings.
Let the earth shake.
²The Lord in Jerusalem is great.
He is supreme over all the nations.
³Let them praise your name.
It is great, holy and to be feared.

⁴The King is powerful and loves
justice.
Lord, you made things fair.
You have done what is fair and right
for the people of Jacob.

⁵Praise the Lord our God.
Worship at the Temple,ᵈ his footstool.
He is holy.

⁶Moses and Aaron were among his
priests.
And Samuel was among his
worshipers.
They called to the Lord,
and he answered them.
⁷He spoke to them from the pillar of
cloud.
They kept the rules and laws he
gave them.

⁸Lord our God, you answered them.
You showed them that you are a
forgiving God.
But you punished them for their
wrongs.
⁹Praise the Lord our God.
Worship at his holy mountain.
The Lord our God is holy.

PSALM 100

A song of thanks.

¹Shout to the Lord, all the earth.
² Serve the Lord with joy.
Come before him with singing.
³Know that the Lord is God.
He made us, and we belong to him.
We are his people, the sheep he
tends.

⁴Come into his city with songs of
thanksgiving.
Come into his courtyards with
songs of praise.
Thank him, and praise his name.
⁵The Lord is good. His love continues
forever.
His loyalty continues from now on.

PSALM 101

A song of David.

¹I will sing of love and fairness.
Lord, I will sing praises to you.
²I will be careful to live an innocent
life.
When will you come to me?

I will live an innocent life in my
house.
³ I will not look at anything wicked.
I hate those who turn against you.
They will not be found near me.
⁴Let those who want to do wrong stay
away from me.
I will have nothing to do with evil.
⁵If anyone secretly says things against
his neighbor,
I will stop him.

I will not allow people
  to be proud and look down on
    others.

⁶I will look for trustworthy people
  so I can live with them in the land.
Only those who live innocent lives
  will be my servants.
⁷No one who is dishonest will live in
  my house.
No liars will stay around me.
⁸Every morning I will destroy
  the wicked in the land.
I will rid the Lord's city
  of people who do evil.

PSALM 102

A prayer of a person who is suffering when
he is discouraged and tells the Lord his
complaints.

¹Lord, listen to my prayer.
  Let my cry for help come to you.
²Do not hide from me
  in my time of trouble.
Pay attention to me.
  When I cry for help, answer me
    quickly.

³My life is passing away like smoke.
  My bones are burned up with fire.
⁴My heart is like grass
  that has been cut and dried.
I forget to eat.
⁵Because of my grief,
  my skin hangs on my bones.
⁶I am like a desert owl.
  I am like an owl living among the
    ruins.
⁷I lie awake.
  I am like a lonely bird on a
    housetop.
⁸All day long enemies insult me.
  Those who make fun of me use my
    name as a curse.
⁹I eat ashes as my food.
  My tears fall into my drinks.
¹⁰Because of your great anger,
  you have picked me up and thrown
    me away.
¹¹My days are like a passing shadow.
  I am like dried grass.

¹²But, Lord, you rule forever.
  Your fame continues from now on.
¹³You will come and have mercy on
  Jerusalem.
The time has now come to be kind
  to her.
¹⁴Your servants love even her stones.
  They even care about her dust.
¹⁵Nations will fear the name of the
  Lord.

All the kings on earth will honor
  him.
¹⁶The Lord will rebuild Jerusalem.
  There his glory will be seen.
¹⁷He will answer the prayers of the
  needy.
He will not reject their prayers.

¹⁸Write these things for the future.
  Then people who are not yet born
    will praise the Lord.
¹⁹The Lord looked down from his holy
  place above.
From heaven he looked down at the
  earth.
²⁰He heard the moans of the prisoners.
  And he freed those sentenced to
    die.
²¹The name of the Lord will be heard in
  Jerusalem.
His praise will be heard in
  Jerusalem.
²²People will come together.
  Kingdoms will serve the Lord.

²³God has made me tired of living.
  He has cut short my life.
²⁴So I said, "My God, do not take me in
  the middle of my life.
Your years go on and on.
²⁵In the beginning you made the earth.
  And your hands made the skies.
²⁶They will be destroyed, but you will
  remain.
They will all wear out like clothes.
And, like clothes, you will change
  them.
  And they will be thrown away.
²⁷But you never change.
  And your life will never end.
²⁸Our children will live in your
  presence.
And their children will remain with
  you."

PSALM 103

Of David.

¹My whole being, praise the Lord.
  All my being, praise his holy name.
²My whole being, praise the Lord.
  Do not forget all his kindnesses.
³The Lord forgives me for all my sins.
  He heals all my diseases.
⁴He saves my life from the grave.
  He loads me with love and mercy.
⁵He satisfies me with good things.
  He makes me young again, like the
    eagle.

⁶The Lord does what is right and fair
  for all who are wronged by others.
⁷He showed his ways to Moses

and his miracles[d] to the people of Israel.

[8] The Lord shows mercy and is kind.
He does not become angry quickly,
and he has great love.

[9] He will not always scold us.
He will not be angry forever.

[10] He has not punished us as our sins
should be punished.
He has not repaid us for the evil we
have done.

[11] As high as the sky is above the earth,
so great is his love for those who
respect him.

[12] He has taken our sins away from us
as far as the east is from west.

[13] The Lord has mercy on those who
fear him,
as a father has mercy on his
children.

[14] He knows how we were made.
He remembers that we are dust.

[15] Human life is like grass.
We grow like a flower in the field.

[16] After the wind blows, the flower is
gone.
There is no sign of where it was.

[17] But the Lord's love for those who fear
him
continues forever and ever.
And his goodness continues to
their grandchildren

[18] and to those who keep his agreement
and who remember to obey his
orders.

[19] The Lord has set his throne in
heaven.
And his kingdom rules over
everything.

[20] You who are his angels, praise the
Lord.
You are the mighty warriors who
do what he says.
Listen to what he says.

[21] You, his armies, praise the Lord.
You are his servants who do what
he wants.

[22] Everything the Lord has made
should praise him in all the places
he rules.
My whole being, praise the Lord.

PSALM 104

[1] My whole being, praise the Lord.
Lord my God, you are very great.
You are clothed with glory and
majesty.

[2] You wear light like a robe.
You stretch out the skies like a tent.

[3] You build your room above the
clouds.
You make the clouds your chariot.
You ride on the wings of the wind.

[4] You make the winds your
messengers.
Flames of fire are your servants.

[5] You built the earth on its foundations.
So it can never be moved.

[6] You covered the earth with oceans.
The water was above the
mountains.

[7] But at your command, the water
rushed away.
When you gave your orders like
thunder, it hurried away.

[8] The mountains rose.
The valleys sank.
The water went to the places you
made for it.

[9] You set borders for the seas that they
cannot cross.
The water will never cover the
earth again.

[10] You make springs pour into the
ravines.
They flow between the mountains.

[11] They water all the wild animals.
The wild donkeys come there to
drink.

[12] Wild birds make nests by the water.
They sing among the tree branches.

[13] You water the mountains from above.
The earth is full of the things you
made.

[14] You make the grass for cattle
and vegetables for the use of man.
You make food grow from the
earth.

[15] You give us wine that makes happy
hearts.
And you give us olive oil that
makes our faces shine.
You give us bread that gives us
strength.

[16] The Lord's trees have plenty of water.
They are the cedar trees of
Lebanon, which he planted.

[17] The birds make their nests there.
The stork's home is in the fir trees.

[18] The high mountains belong to the
wild goats.
The rocks are hiding places for the
badgers.

[19] You made the moon to mark the
seasons.
And the sun always knows when to
set.

²⁰You make it dark, and it becomes night.
Then all the wild animals creep around.
²¹The lions roar as they attack.
They look to God for food.
²²When the sun rises, they leave.
They go back to their dens to lie down.
²³Then people go to work.
And they work until evening.

²⁴Lord, you have made many things.
With your wisdom you made them all.
The earth is full of your riches.
²⁵Look at the sea, so big and wide.
Its creatures large and small cannot be counted.
²⁶Ships travel over the ocean.
And there is the sea monster Leviathan,ᵈ
which you made to play there.

²⁷All these things depend on you
to give them their food at the right time.
²⁸When you give it to them,
they gather it up.
When you open your hand, they are filled with good food.
²⁹When you turn away from them,
they become frightened.
When you take away their breath,
they die and turn into dust.
³⁰When you breathe on them,
they are created.
You make the land new again.

³¹May the glory of the Lord be forever.
May the Lord enjoy what he has made.
³²He just looks at the earth, and it shakes.
He touches the mountains, and they smoke.

³³I will sing to the Lord all my life.
I will sing praises to my God as long as I live.
³⁴May my thoughts please him.
I am happy in the Lord.
³⁵Let sinners be destroyed from the earth.
Let the wicked people live no longer.

My whole being, praise the Lord.
Praise the Lord.

PSALM 105

¹Give thanks to the Lord and pray to him.
Tell the nations what he has done.
²Sing to him. Sing praises to him.
Tell about all the wonderful things he has done.
³Be glad that you are his.
Let those who ask the Lord for help be happy.
⁴Depend on the Lord and his strength.
Always go to him for help.
⁵Remember the wonderful things he has done.
Remember his miraclesᵈ and his decisions.
⁶You are descendantsᵈ of his servant Abraham,
the children of Jacob, his chosen people.
⁷He is the Lord our God.
His laws are for all the world.

⁸He will keep his agreement forever.
He will keep his promises always.
⁹He will keep his agreement he made with Abraham.
He will keep the promise he made to Isaac.
¹⁰He made it a law for the people of Jacob.
He made it an agreement that Israel to last forever.
¹¹The Lord said, "I will give you the land of Canaan.
The promised land will belong to you."

¹²Then God's people were few in number.
They were strangers in the land.
¹³They went from one nation to another.
They went from one kingdom to another.
¹⁴But the Lord did not let anyone hurt them.
He warned kings not to harm them.
¹⁵He said, "Don't hurt my chosen people.
Don't harm my prophets."ᵈ

¹⁶God ordered a time of hunger in the land.
And he destroyed all the food.
¹⁷Then he sent a man ahead of them.
It was Joseph, who was sold as a slave.
¹⁸They put chains around his feet
and an iron ring around his neck.
¹⁹Then the time he had spoken of came.

The Lord's words proved that
    Joseph was right.
20 The king of Egypt sent for Joseph
    and freed him.
The ruler of the people set him free.
21 He made him the master of his house.
    Joseph was in charge of his riches.
22 He could order the princes as he
    wished.
He taught the older men to be wise.
23 Then his father Israel came to Egypt.
    Jacob, also called Israel, lived in
    Egypt.[n]
24 The Lord made his people grow in
    number.
He made them stronger than their
    enemies.
25 And he caused the Egyptians to hate
    his people.
They made plans against the Lord's
    servants.
26 Then he sent his servant Moses,
    and Aaron, whom he had chosen.
27 They did many signs among the
    Egyptians.
They worked miracles in Egypt.
28 The Lord sent darkness and made the
    land dark.
But the Egyptians turned against
    what he said.
29 So he changed their water into blood
    and made their fish die.
30 Then their country was filled with
    frogs.
They were even in the bedrooms of
    their rulers.
31 The Lord spoke, and flies came.
    Gnats were everywhere in the
    country.
32 He made hail fall like rain.
    And he sent lightning through their
    land.
33 He struck down their grapevines and
    fig trees.
He destroyed every tree in the
    country.
34 He spoke, and grasshoppers came.
    The locusts[d] were too many to
    count.
35 They ate all the plants in the land.
    They ate what the earth produced.
36 The Lord also killed all the firstborn[d]
    sons in the land,
the oldest son of each family.

37 Then he brought his people out,
    and they carried with them silver
    and gold.
Not one of his people stumbled.

38 The Egyptians were glad when they
    left
because the Egyptians were afraid
    of them.
39 The Lord covered them with a cloud
    and lit up the night with fire.
40 When they asked, he brought them
    quail.
He filled them with bread from
    heaven.
41 God split the rock, and water flowed
    out.
It ran like a river through the
    desert.
42 He remembered his holy promise
    to his servant Abraham.
43 So God brought his people out with
    joy.
He brought out his chosen ones
    with singing.
44 He gave them lands that belonged to
    other nations.
They received what others had
    worked for.
45 This was so they would keep his
    orders
and obey his teachings.

Praise the Lord!

PSALM 106

1 Praise the Lord!
    Thank the Lord because he is good.
    His love continues forever.
2 No one can tell all the mighty things
    the Lord has done.
No one can speak all his praise.
3 Happy are those people who are fair,
    who do what is right at all times.

4 Lord, remember me when you are
    kind to your people.
Help me when you save them.
5 Let me see the good things you do for
    your chosen people.
Let me be happy along with your
    happy nation.
Let me join your own people in
    praising you.

6 We have sinned just as our ancestors
    did.
We have done wrong. We have
    done evil.
7 Our ancestors in Egypt
    did not learn from your miracles.[d]
They did not remember all your
    kindnesses.

105:23 Egypt Literally, "the land of Ham." Also in verse 27. The people in Egypt were descendants of Ham, one of Noah's sons. See Genesis 10:6.

So they turned against you at the Red Sea.[d]
[8]But the Lord saved them for his own sake,
to show his great power.
[9]He commanded the Red Sea, and it dried up.
He led them through the deep sea as if it were a desert.
[10]He saved them from those who hated them.
He saved them from their enemies.
[11]And the water covered their enemies.
Not one of them escaped.
[12]Then the people believed what the Lord said.
They sang praises to him.

[13]But they quickly forgot what he had done.
They did not wait for his advice.
[14]They became greedy for food in the desert.
And they tested God there.
[15]So he gave them what they wanted.
But he also sent a terrible disease among them.

[16]The people in the camp became jealous of Moses
and of Aaron, the holy priest of the Lord.
[17]Then the ground opened up and swallowed Dathan.
It closed over Abiram's group.
[18]Then a fire burned among their followers.
Flames burned up the wicked people.

[19]The people made a gold calf at Mount Sinai.
They worshiped a metal statue.
[20]They exchanged their glorious God for a statue of a bull, which eats grass.
[21]They forgot the God who saved them, who had done great things in Egypt.
[22]He did miracles in Egypt.[n]
He did amazing things by the Red Sea.
[23]So God said he would destroy them.
But Moses, his chosen one, stood before him.
He stopped God's anger from destroying them.

[24]Then they refused to go into the beautiful land of Canaan.

They did not believe what God promised.
[25]They grumbled in their tents
and did not obey the Lord.
[26]So he swore to them
that they would die in the desert.
[27]He said their children would be killed by other nations
and that they would be scattered among other countries.

[28]They joined in worshiping Baal[d] at Peor.
They ate meat that had been sacrificed to lifeless statues.
[29]They made the Lord angry by what they did.
So many people became sick with a terrible disease.
[30]But Phinehas prayed to the Lord, and the disease stopped.
[31]The Lord will remember that Phinehas did what was right.
And God will remember this from now on.

[32]The people also made the Lord angry at Meribah.
And Moses was in trouble because of them.
[33]The people turned against the Spirit[d] of God.
So Moses spoke without stopping to think.

[34]The people did not destroy the other nations
as the Lord had told them to do.
[35]Instead, they mixed with the other nations.
And they learned their customs.
[36]They worshiped other nations' idols.
And they were trapped by them.
[37]They even killed their sons and daughters
as sacrifices to demons.[d]
[38]They killed innocent people.
They killed their own sons and daughters
as sacrifices to the idols of Canaan.
So the land was made unholy by their blood.
[39]The people became unholy by their sins.
They were unfaithful to God in what they did.
[40]So the Lord became angry with his people.
He hated his own children.

106:22 Egypt Literally, "the land of Ham." The people in Egypt were descendants of Ham, one of Noah's sons. See Genesis 10:6.

⁴¹He let other nations defeat them.
  He let their enemies rule over them.
⁴²Their enemies were cruel to them.
  Their enemies kept them under
    their power.
⁴³The Lord saved his people many
    times.
  But they continued to turn against
    him.
  So they became even more wicked.

⁴⁴But God saw their misery.
  He heard their cry.
⁴⁵He remembered his agreement with
    them.
  And he felt sorry for them because
    of his great love.
⁴⁶He caused them to be pitied
  by those who held them captive.

⁴⁷Lord our God, save us.
  Bring us back from other nations.
  Then we will thank you.
  Then we will gladly praise you.

⁴⁸Praise the Lord, the God of Israel.
  He always was and always will be.
  Let all the people say, "Amen!"

  Praise the Lord!

Book 5

Psalms 107–150

PSALM 107

¹Thank the Lord because he is good.
  His love continues forever.
²That is what the people the Lord has
    saved should say.
  They are the ones he has saved
    from the enemy.
³He has gathered them from other
    lands,
  from east and west, north and
    south.

⁴Some people had wandered in the
    desert lands.
  They found no city to live in.
⁵They were hungry and thirsty.
  They were discouraged.
⁶In their misery they cried out to the
    Lord.
  And he saved them from their
    troubles.
⁷He led them on a straight road
  to a city where they could live.
⁸Let them give thanks to the Lord for
    his love
  and for the miraclesᵈ he does for
    people.
⁹He satisfies the thirsty.
  He fills up the hungry.

¹⁰Some sat in gloom and darkness.
  They were prisoners suffering in
    chains.
¹¹They had turned against the words of
    God.
  They had refused the advice of God
    Most High.
¹²So he broke their pride by hard work.
  They stumbled, and no one helped.
¹³In their misery they cried out to the
    Lord.
  And he saved them from their
    troubles.
¹⁴He brought them out of their gloom
    and darkness.
  He broke their chains.
¹⁵Let them give thanks to the Lord for
    his love
  and for the miracles he does for
    people.
¹⁶He breaks down bronze gates.
  And he cuts apart iron bars.

¹⁷Some became fools who turned
    against God.
  They suffered for the evil they did.
¹⁸They refused to eat anything.
  So they almost died.
¹⁹In their misery they cried out to the
    Lord.
  And he saved them from their
    troubles.
²⁰God gave the command and healed
    them.
  So they were saved from dying.
²¹Let them give thanks to the Lord for
    his love
  and for the miracles he does for
    people.
²²Let them offer sacrifices to thank
    him.
  With joy they should tell what he
    has done.

²³Others went out to sea in ships.
  They did business on the great
    oceans.
²⁴They saw what the Lord could do.
  They saw the miracles he did.
²⁵He spoke, and a storm came up.
  It blew up high waves.
²⁶The ships tossed as high as the sky
    and fell low in the waves.
  The storm was so bad the men lost
    their courage.
²⁷They stumbled and fell like men who
    were drunk.
  They did not know what to do.
²⁸In their misery they cried out to the
    Lord.

And he saved them from their
troubles.
²⁹He made the storm be still.
He calmed the waves.
³⁰They were happy that it was quiet.
And God guided them to the port
they wanted.
³¹Let them give thanks to the Lord for
his love
and for the miracles he does for
people.
³²Let them praise his greatness in the
meeting of the people.
They should praise him in the
meeting of the older leaders.

³³He changed rivers into a desert,
and springs of water into dry
ground.
³⁴He made fertile land salty
because the people there did evil.
³⁵He changed the desert into pools of
water
and dry ground into springs of
water.
³⁶He had the hungry settle there.
They built a city to live in.
³⁷They planted seeds in the fields and
vineyards.
And they had a good harvest.
³⁸God blessed them, and they grew in
number.
Their cattle did not become fewer.

³⁹Because of disaster, troubles and
sadness,
their families grew smaller and
weaker.
⁴⁰He showed he was displeased with
their important men.
He made them wander in a pathless
desert.
⁴¹But he lifted the poor out of their
suffering.
And he made their families grow
like flocks of sheep.
⁴²Good people see this and are happy.
But the wicked say nothing.

⁴³Whoever is wise will remember these
things.
He will think about the love of the
Lord.

PSALM 108

A song of David.
¹God, my heart is right.
I will sing and praise you with all
my being.
²Wake up, harp and lyre!ᵈ
I will wake up the dawn.

³Lord, I will praise you among the
nations.
I will sing songs of praise about
you to all the nations.
⁴Your love is so great that it is higher
than the skies.
Your truth reaches to the clouds.
⁵God, you are supreme over the skies.
Let your glory be over all the earth.

⁶Answer us and save us by your
power.
Then the people you love will be
rescued.
⁷God has said from his Temple,ᵈ
"When I win, I will divide Shechem
and cut up the Valley of Succoth.
⁸Gilead and Manasseh are mine.
Ephraim is like my helmet.
Judah holds my royal scepter.ᵈ
⁹Moab is like my washbowl.
I throw my sandals at Edom.
I shout at Philistia."
¹⁰Who will bring me to the strong,
walled city?
Who will lead me to Edom?
¹¹God, surely you have rejected us.
You do not go out with our armies.
¹²Help us fight the enemy.
Human help is useless.
¹³But we can win with God's help.
He will defeat our enemies.

PSALM 109

For the director of music. A song of David.
¹God, I praise you.
Do not be silent.
²Wicked people and liars have spoken
against me.
They have told lies about me.
³They have said hateful things about
me.
They attack me for no reason.
⁴They attacked me, even though I
loved them
and prayed for them.
⁵I was good to them, but they repay
me with evil.
I loved them, but they hate me in
return.

⁶They say about me, "Have the Evil
One work against him.
Let the devil accuse him.
⁷When he is judged, let him be found
guilty.
Let even his prayers show that he is
guilty.
⁸Let his life be cut short.
Let another man replace him as
leader.

⁹Let his children become orphans.
Let his wife become a widow.
¹⁰Make his children wander around,
    begging for food.
Let them be forced out of the ruins
    they live in.
¹¹Let the people he owes money to take
    everything he owns.
Let strangers steal everything he
    has worked for.
¹²Let no one show him love.
Let no one have mercy on his
    children.
¹³Let all his descendants⁴ die.
Let him be forgotten by people who
    live after him.
¹⁴Let the Lord remember how wicked
    his ancestors were.
Don't let the sins of his mother be
    wiped out.
¹⁵Let the Lord always remember their
    sins.
Then he will make people forget
    about them completely.

¹⁶"He did not remember to be loving.
He hurt the poor, the needy and
    those who were sad
until they were nearly dead.
¹⁷He loved to put curses on others.
So let those same curses fall on
    him.
He did not like to bless others.
So do not let good things happen to
    him.
¹⁸He cursed others as often as he wore
    clothes.
Cursing others filled his body and
    his life,
like drinking water and using olive
    oil.
¹⁹So let curses cover him like clothes.
Let them wrap around him like a
    belt."

²⁰May the Lord do these things to those
    who accuse me,
to those who speak evil against me.

²¹But you, Lord God,
    be kind to me so others will know
    you are good.
Because your love is good, save me.
²²I am poor and helpless.
And I am very sad.
²³I am dying like an evening shadow.
I am shaken off like a locust.⁴
²⁴My knees are weak from hunger.
I have become thin.
²⁵My enemies insult me.
They look at me and shake their
    heads.

²⁶Lord my God, help me.
Because you are loving, save me.
²⁷Then they will know that you have
    saved me.
They will know it was your power,
    Lord.
²⁸They may curse me, but you bless me.
They may attack me, but they will
    be disgraced.
Then I, your servant, will be glad.
²⁹Let those who accuse me be
    disgraced.
Let them be covered with shame
    like a coat.

³⁰I will thank the Lord very much.
I will praise him in front of many
    people.
³¹He defends the helpless.
He saved me from those who
    accuse me.

PSALM 110

A song of David.
¹The Lord said to my Master,
"Sit by me at my right side
until I put your enemies under your
    control."
²The Lord will make you king in
    Jerusalem over all nations.
And you will rule your enemies in
    their own countries.
³Your people will join you on the day
    you come to power.
You have been dressed in holiness
    from birth.
You have the freshness of a child.
⁴The Lord has made a promise
and will not change his mind.
He said, "You are a priest forever,
a priest like Melchizedek."
⁵The Lord is beside you to help you.
When he becomes angry, he will
    crush kings.
⁶He will judge those nations, filling
    them with dead bodies.
He will defeat rulers all over the
    world.
⁷The king will drink from the brook on
    the way.
Then he will be strengthened and
    win the battle.

PSALM 111

¹Praise the Lord!

I will thank the Lord with all my
    heart
in the meeting of his good people.
²The Lord does great things.

Those people who love them think
about them.
[3]What he does is glorious and
splendid.
His goodness continues forever.
[4]His miracles[d] are unforgettable.
The Lord is kind and merciful.
[5]He gives food to those who fear him.
He remembers his agreement
forever.
[6]He has shown his people his power
when he gave them the lands of
other nations.

[7]Everything he does is good and fair.
All his orders can be trusted.
[8]They will continue forever.
They were made true and right.
[9]He sets his people free.
He made his agreement everlasting.
He is holy and wonderful.

[10]Wisdom begins with respect for the
Lord.
Those who obey his orders have
good understanding.
He should be praised forever.

PSALM 112

[1]Praise the Lord!

Happy is the person who fears the
Lord.
He loves what the Lord commands.
[2]His descendants[d] will be powerful in
the land.
The children of honest people will
be blessed.
[3]His house will be full of wealth and
riches.
His goodness will continue forever.

[4]A light shines in the dark for honest
people.
It shines for those who are good
and kind and merciful.
[5]It is good to be kind and generous.
Whoever is fair in his business
[6]will never be defeated.
A good person will be remembered
from now on.
[7]He won't be afraid of bad news.
He is safe because he trusts the
Lord.
[8]That person is confident. He will not
be afraid.
He will look down on his enemies.
[9]He gives freely to the poor.
The things he does are right and
will continue forever.
He will be given great honor.

[10]The wicked will see this and become
angry.
They will grind their teeth in anger
and then disappear.
The wishes of the wicked will come
to nothing.

PSALM 113

[1]Praise the Lord!

Praise him, you servants of the Lord.
Praise the name of the Lord.
[2]The Lord's name should be praised
now and forever.
[3]The Lord's name should be praised
from where the sun rises to where
it sets.
[4]The Lord is supreme over all the
nations.
His glory reaches to the skies.

[5]No one is like the Lord our God.
He rules from heaven.
[6]He bends down to look
at the skies and the earth.
[7]The Lord lifts the poor from the dirt.
He takes the helpless from the
ashes.
[8]And he seats them with princes,
the princes of his people.
[9]He gives children to the woman who
has none.
He makes her a happy mother.

Praise the Lord!

PSALM 114

[1]The Israelites went out of Egypt.
The people of Jacob left that
foreign country.
[2]Then Judah became God's holy place.
Israel became the land he ruled.

[3]The Red Sea[d] looked and ran away.
The Jordan River turned back.
[4]The mountains danced like sheep
and the hills like little lambs.
[5]Sea, why did you run away?
Jordan, why did you turn back?
[6]Mountains, why did you dance like
sheep?
Hills, why did you dance like little
lambs?

[7]Earth, shake with fear before the
Lord.
Tremble in the presence of the God
of Jacob.
[8]He turned a rock into a pool of water.
He changed a hard rock into a
spring of water.

PSALM 115

[1] It does not belong to us, Lord.
　　The praise belongs to you
　　because of your love and loyalty.

[2] Why do the nations ask,
　　"Where is their God?"
[3] Our God is in heaven.
　　He does what he wants.
[4] Their idols are made of silver and
　　　gold.
　　They are made by human hands.
[5] They have mouths, but they cannot
　　　speak.
　　They have eyes, but they cannot
　　　see.
[6] They have ears, but they cannot hear.
　　They have noses, but they cannot
　　　smell.
[7] They have hands, but they cannot
　　　feel.
　　They have feet, but they cannot
　　　walk.
　　And no sounds come from their
　　　throats.
[8] The people who make idols and trust
　　　them
　　are all like them.

[9] Family of Israel, trust the Lord.
　　He is your helper and your
　　　protection.
[10] Family of Aaron, trust the Lord.
　　He is your helper and your
　　　protection.
[11] You people who fear the Lord should
　　　trust him.
　　He is your helper and your
　　　protection.

[12] The Lord remembers us and will
　　　bless us.
　　He will bless the family of Israel.
　　He will bless the family of Aaron.
[13] The Lord will bless those who fear
　　　him,
　　from the smallest to the greatest.

[14] May the Lord give you many
　　　children.
　　And may he give them children
　　　also.
[15] May the Lord bless you.
　　He made heaven and earth.

[16] Heaven belongs to the Lord.
　　But he gave the earth to people.
[17] Dead people do not praise the Lord.
　　Those in the grave are silent.
[18] But we will praise the Lord
　　now and forever.

　　Praise the Lord!

PSALM 116

[1] I love the Lord because he listens
　　to my prayers for help.
[2] He paid attention to me.
　　So I will call to him for help as long
　　　as I live.
[3] The ropes of death bound me.
　　The fear of death took hold of me.
　　I was troubled and sad.
[4] Then I called out the name of the
　　　Lord.
　　I said, "Please, Lord, save me!"

[5] The Lord is kind and does what is
　　　right.
　　Our God is merciful.
[6] The Lord watches over the foolish.
　　When I was helpless, he saved me.
[7] I said to myself, "Relax,
　　because the Lord takes care of
　　　you."
[8] Lord, you have saved me from death.
　　You have stopped my eyes from
　　　crying.
　　You have kept me from being
　　　defeated.
[9] So I will walk with the Lord
　　in the land of the living.
[10] I believed, so I said,
　　"I am completely ruined."
[11] In my distress I said,
　　"All people are liars."

[12] What can I give the Lord
　　for all the good things he has given
　　　to me?
[13] I will give him a drink offering for
　　　saving me.
　　And I will pray to the Lord.
[14] In front of all his people,
　　I will give the Lord what I
　　　promised.

[15] The death of one that belongs to him
　　is precious to the Lord.
[16] Lord, I am your servant.
　　I am your servant and the son of
　　　your female servant.
　　You have freed me from my chains.
[17] I will give an offering to show thanks
　　　to you.
　　And I will worship the Lord.
[18] In front of all his people,
　　I will give the Lord what I
　　　promised.
[19] I will do this in the Temple[d]
　　courtyards
　　in Jerusalem.

　　Praise the Lord!

PSALM 117

¹All you nations, praise the Lord.
All you people, praise him.
²The Lord loves us very much.
His truth is everlasting.

Praise the Lord!

PSALM 118

¹Thank the Lord because he is good.
His love continues forever.
²Let the people of Israel say,
"His love continues forever."
³Let the family of Aaron say,
"His love continues forever."
⁴Let those who fear the Lord say,
"His love continues forever."

⁵I was in trouble. So I called to the
Lord.
The Lord answered me and set me
free.
⁶I will not be afraid because the Lord
is with me.
People can't do anything to me.
⁷The Lord is with me to help me.
I will see my enemies defeated.
⁸It is better to trust the Lord
than to trust people.
⁹It is better to trust the Lord
than to trust princes.

¹⁰All the nations surrounded me.
But I defeated them in the name of
the Lord.
¹¹They surrounded me on every side.
But with the Lord's power, I
defeated them.
¹²They surrounded me like a swarm of
bees.
But they died as quickly as thorns
burn.
By the Lord's power, I defeated
them.
¹³They chased me until I was almost
defeated.
But the Lord helped me.
¹⁴The Lord gives me strength and
makes me sing.
He has saved me.

¹⁵Shouts of joy and victory
come from the tents of those who
do right:
"The Lord has done powerful things."
¹⁶The power of the Lord has won the
victory.
With his power the Lord has done
mighty things.

¹⁷I will not die, but live.
And I will tell what the Lord has
done.

¹⁸The Lord has taught me a hard
lesson.
But he did not let me die.

¹⁹Open for me the Temple^d gates.
Then I will come in and thank the
Lord.
²⁰This is the Lord's gate.
Only those who are good may enter
it.
²¹Lord, I thank you for answering me.
You have saved me.

²²The stone that the builders did not
want
became the cornerstone.^d
²³The Lord did this,
and it is wonderful to us.
²⁴This is the day that the Lord has
made.
Let us rejoice and be glad today!

²⁵Please, Lord, save us.
Please, Lord, give us success.
²⁶God bless the one who comes in the
name of the Lord.
We bless all of you from the Temple
of the Lord.
²⁷The Lord is God.
And he has shown kindness to us.
With branches in your hands, join the
feast.
Come to the corners of the altar.

²⁸You are my God, and I will thank you.
You are my God, and I will praise
your greatness.

²⁹Thank the Lord because he is good.
His love continues forever.

PSALM 119

¹Happy are the people who live pure
lives.
They follow the Lord's teachings.
²Happy are the people who keep his
rules.
They ask him for help with their
whole heart.
³They don't do what is wrong.
They follow his ways.
⁴Lord, you gave your orders
to be followed completely.
⁵I wish I were more loyal
in meeting your demands.
⁶Then I would not be ashamed
when I think of your commands.
⁷When I learned that your laws are
fair,
I praised you with an honest heart.
⁸I will meet your demands.
So please don't ever leave me.

⁹How can a young person live a pure
life?
He can do it by obeying your word.
¹⁰With all my heart I try to obey you,
God.
Don't let me break your
commands.
¹¹I have taken your words to heart
so I would not sin against you.
¹²Lord, you should be praised.
Teach me your demands.
¹³My lips will tell about
all the laws you have spoken.
¹⁴I enjoy living by your rules
as people enjoy great riches.
¹⁵I think about your orders
and study your ways.
¹⁶I enjoy obeying your demands.
And I will not forget your word.

¹⁷Do good to me, your servant, so I can
live,
so I can obey your word.
¹⁸Open my eyes to see the wonderful
things
in your teachings.
¹⁹I am a stranger on earth.
Do not hide your commands from
me.
²⁰I want to study
your laws all the time.
²¹You scold proud people.
Those who ignore your commands
are cursed.
²²Don't let me be insulted and hated
because I obey your rules.
²³Even if princes speak against me,
I, your servant, will think about
your demands.
²⁴Your rules give me pleasure.
They give me good advice.

²⁵I am about to die.
Give me life, as you have
promised.
²⁶I told you about my life, and you
answered me.
Teach me your demands.
²⁷Help me understand your orders.
Then I will think about your
miracles.ᵈ
²⁸I am sad and tired.
Make me strong again as you have
promised.
²⁹Don't let me be dishonest.
Be kind to me by helping me obey
your teachings.
³⁰I have chosen to obey you.
I have obeyed your laws.
³¹I hold on to your rules.
Lord, do not let me be disgraced.

³²I will obey your commands
because you have made me happy.

³³Lord, teach me your demands.
Then I will obey them until the
end.
³⁴Help me understand, so I can obey
your teachings.
I will obey them with all my heart.
³⁵Help me obey your commands
because that makes me happy.
³⁶Help me want to obey your rules
instead of selfishly wanting riches.
³⁷Keep me from looking at worthless
things.
Let me live by your word.
³⁸Keep your promise to me, your
servant,
so you will be feared.
³⁹Take away the shame I fear.
Your laws are good.
⁴⁰How I want to follow your orders.
Give me life because of your
goodness.

⁴¹Lord, show me your love.
Save me as you have promised.
⁴²Then I will have an answer for
people who insult me.
I trust what you say.
⁴³Never keep me from speaking your
truth.
I depend on your fair laws.
⁴⁴I will obey your teachings
forever and ever.
⁴⁵So I will live in freedom
because I want to follow your
orders.
⁴⁶I will discuss your rules with kings.
And I will not be ashamed.
⁴⁷I enjoy obeying your commands.
I love them.
⁴⁸I praise your commands, which I
love.
And I think about your demands.

⁴⁹Remember your promise to me, your
servant,
It gives me hope.
⁵⁰When I suffer, this comforts me:
Your promise gives me life.
⁵¹Proud people make fun of me all the
time.
But I do not reject your teachings.
⁵²I remember your laws from long ago.
They comfort me, Lord.
⁵³I become angry with wicked people.
They have not kept your teachings.
⁵⁴I sing about your demands
wherever I live.
⁵⁵Lord, I remember you at night.
I will obey your teachings.

⁵⁶This is what I do:
   I follow your orders.

⁵⁷Lord, you are my share in life.
   I have promised to obey your
      words.
⁵⁸I prayed to you with all my heart.
   Be kind to me as you have
      promised.
⁵⁹I thought about my life,
   and I decided to obey your rules.
⁶⁰I hurried and did not wait
   to obey your commands.
⁶¹Wicked people have surrounded me.
   But I have not forgotten your
      teachings.
⁶²In the middle of the night, I get up to
      thank you
   because your laws are right.
⁶³I am a friend to everyone who fears
      you.
   I am a friend to anyone who
      follows your orders.
⁶⁴Lord, your love fills the earth.
   Teach me your demands.

⁶⁵You have done good things for me,
      your servant,
   as you have promised, Lord.
⁶⁶Teach me wisdom and knowledge
   because I trust your commands.
⁶⁷Before I suffered, I did wrong.
   But now I obey your word.
⁶⁸You are good, and you do what is
      good.
   Teach me your demands.
⁶⁹Proud people have made up lies
      about me.
   But I will follow your orders with
      all my heart.
⁷⁰Those people have no feelings,
   but I love your teachings.
⁷¹It was good for me to suffer
   so I would learn your demands.
⁷²Your teachings are worth more to me
   than thousands of pieces of gold
      and silver.

⁷³You made me and formed me with
      your hands.
   Give me understanding so I can
      learn your commands.
⁷⁴Let those who fear you rejoice when
      they see me
   because I put my hope in your
      word.
⁷⁵Lord, I know that your laws are
      right.
   And it was right for you to punish
      me.
⁷⁶Comfort me with your love,
   as you promised me, your servant.

⁷⁷Have mercy on me so that I may live.
   I love your teachings.
⁷⁸Make the proud people ashamed
      because they lied about me.
   But I will think about your orders.
⁷⁹Let those who fear you come to me.
   They know your rules.
⁸⁰Let me obey your demands perfectly.
   Then I will not be ashamed.

⁸¹I am weak from waiting for you to
      save me.
   But I trust your word.
⁸²My eyes are tired from looking for
      your promise.
   When will you comfort me?
⁸³Even though I am like a leather wine
      bag going up in smoke,
   I do not forget your demands.
⁸⁴How long will I live?
   When will you judge those who are
      hurting me?
⁸⁵Proud people have dug pits to trap
      me.
   They have nothing to do with your
      teachings.
⁸⁶All of your commands can be
      trusted.
   Liars are hurting me. Help me!
⁸⁷They have almost put me in the
      grave.
   But I have not rejected your
      orders.
⁸⁸Give me life by your love
   so I can obey your rules.

⁸⁹Lord, your word is everlasting.
   It continues forever in heaven.
⁹⁰Your loyalty will continue from now
      on.
   You made the earth, and it still
      stands.
⁹¹All things continue to this day
      because of your laws.
   All things serve you.
⁹²If I had not loved your teachings,
   I would have died from my
      sufferings.
⁹³I will never forget your orders
   because you have given me life by
      them.
⁹⁴I am yours. Save me.
   I have wanted to know your
      orders.
⁹⁵Wicked people are waiting to destroy
      me.
   But I will think about your rules.
⁹⁶Everything I see has its limits.
   But your commands have none.

⁹⁷How I love your teachings!
   I think about them all day long.

⁹⁸Your commands make me wiser than
  my enemies
    because they are mine forever.
⁹⁹I am wiser than all my teachers
    because I think about your rules.
¹⁰⁰I have more understanding than the
  older leaders
    because I follow your orders.
¹⁰¹I have avoided every evil way
    so I could obey your word.
¹⁰²I haven't stopped obeying your laws
    because you yourself are my
      teacher.
¹⁰³Your promises are so sweet to me.
    They are like honey to my mouth!
¹⁰⁴Your orders give me understanding.
    So I hate lying ways.

¹⁰⁵Your word is like a lamp for my feet
    and a light for my way.
¹⁰⁶I will do what I have promised
    and obey your fair laws.
¹⁰⁷I have suffered for a long time.
    Lord, give me life by your word.
¹⁰⁸Lord, accept my willing praise.
    And teach me your laws.
¹⁰⁹My life is always in danger.
    But I haven't forgotten your
      teachings.
¹¹⁰Wicked people have set a trap for
  me.
    But I haven't disobeyed your
      orders.
¹¹¹I will follow your rules forever.
    They make me happy.
¹¹²I will try to do what you demand
    forever, until the end.
¹¹³I hate people who are not completely
  loyal to you.
    But I love your teachings.
¹¹⁴You are my hiding place and my
  shield.
    I trust your word.
¹¹⁵Get away from me, you people who
  do evil,
    so I can keep my God's commands.
¹¹⁶Support me as you promised so I can
  live.
    Don't let me be embarrassed
      because of my hopes.
¹¹⁷Help me, and I will be saved.
    I will always respect your
      demands.
¹¹⁸You reject everyone who ignores
  your demands.
    Their lies mislead them.
¹¹⁹You throw away the wicked of the
  world like trash.
    So I will love your rules.

¹²⁰I shake in fear of you.
    I fear your laws.

¹²¹I have done what is fair and right.
    Don't leave me to my enemies.
¹²²Promise that you will help me, your
  servant.
    Don't let proud people hurt me.
¹²³My eyes are tired from looking for
  your salvation
    and for your good promise.
¹²⁴Show your love to me, your servant.
    Teach me your demands.
¹²⁵I am your servant. Give me wisdom
    so I can understand your rules.
¹²⁶Lord, it is time for you to do
  something.
    People have disobeyed your
      teachings.
¹²⁷I love your commands
    more than the purest gold.
¹²⁸I respect all your orders.
    So I hate lying ways.

¹²⁹Your rules are wonderful.
    That is why I obey them.
¹³⁰Learning your words gives wisdom
    and understanding for the foolish.
¹³¹I want to learn your commands.
    I am like a person breathing hard
      and waiting impatiently.
¹³²Look at me and have mercy on me
    as you do for those who love you.
¹³³Guide my steps as you promised.
    Don't let any sin control me.
¹³⁴Save me from harmful people.
    Then I will obey your orders.
¹³⁵Show your kindness to me, your
  servant.
    Teach me your demands.
¹³⁶Tears stream from my eyes
    because people do not obey your
      teachings.

¹³⁷Lord, you do what is right.
    And your laws are fair.
¹³⁸The rules you commanded are right
    and completely trustworthy.
¹³⁹I am so upset I am worn out.
    This is because my enemies have
      forgotten your words.
¹⁴⁰Your promises are proven.
    I, your servant, love them.
¹⁴¹I am unimportant and hated.
    But I have not forgotten your
      orders.
¹⁴²Your goodness continues forever.
    And your teachings are true.
¹⁴³I have had troubles and misery.
    But I love your commands.
¹⁴⁴Your rules are good forever.
    Help me understand so I can live.

¹⁴⁵Lord, I call to you with all my heart.
    Answer me,
    and I will keep your demands.
¹⁴⁶I call to you. Save me
    so I can obey your rules.
¹⁴⁷I wake up early in the morning and
    cry out.
    I trust your word.
¹⁴⁸I stay awake all night
    so I can think about your
    promises.
¹⁴⁹Listen to me because of your love.
    Lord, give me life by your laws.
¹⁵⁰Those who love evil are near.
    They are far from your teachings.
¹⁵¹But, Lord, you are also near.
    And all your commands are true.
¹⁵²Long ago I learned from your rules
    that you made them to continue
    forever.

¹⁵³See my suffering and save me
    because I have not forgotten your
    teachings.
¹⁵⁴Argue my case and save me.
    Let me live by your promises.
¹⁵⁵Wicked people are far from being
    saved
    because they do not want to obey
    your demands.
¹⁵⁶Lord, you are very kind.
    Give me life by your laws.
¹⁵⁷Many enemies are after me.
    But I have not rejected your rules.
¹⁵⁸I see those traitors, and I hate them
    because they do not obey what you
    say.
¹⁵⁹See how I love your orders.
    Lord, give me life by your love.
¹⁶⁰Your words are true from the start.
    And all your laws will be fair
    forever.

¹⁶¹Leaders attack me for no reason.
    But I fear your law in my heart.
¹⁶²I am as happy over your promises
    as if I had found a great treasure.
¹⁶³I hate and despise lies.
    But I love your teachings.
¹⁶⁴Seven times a day I praise you
    for your fair laws.
¹⁶⁵Those who love your teachings will
    find true peace.
    Nothing will defeat them.
¹⁶⁶I am waiting for you to save me,
    Lord.
    I will obey your commands.
¹⁶⁷I keep your rules.
    I love them very much.

¹⁶⁸I keep your orders and rules.
    You know everything I do.

¹⁶⁹Hear my cry to you, Lord.
    Let your word help me understand.
¹⁷⁰Listen to my prayer.
    Save me as you promised.
¹⁷¹Let me speak your praise.
    You have taught me your demands.
¹⁷²Let me sing about your promises.
    All your commands are fair.
¹⁷³Always be ready to help me
    because I have chosen to obey
    your commands.
¹⁷⁴I want you to save me, Lord.
    I love your teachings.
¹⁷⁵Let me live so I can praise you.
    Your laws will help me.
¹⁷⁶I have wandered like a lost sheep.
    Look for your servant because I
    have not forgotten your
    commands.

PSALM 120

A song for going up to worship.
¹When I was in trouble, I called to the
    Lord.
    And he answered me.
²Lord, save me from liars
    and from those who plan evil.

³You who plan evil, what will God do
    to you?
    How will he punish you?
⁴He will punish you with the sharp
    arrows of a warrior
    and with burning coals of wood.

⁵How terrible it is to live in the land of
    Meshech.
    I have to live among the people of
    Kedar.
⁶I have lived too long
    with people who hate peace.
⁷I want peace and try to talk peace,
    but they want war.

PSALM 121

A song for going up to worship.
¹I look up to the hills.
    But where does my help come
    from?
²My help comes from the Lord.
    He made heaven and earth.

³He will not let you be defeated.
    He who guards you never sleeps.
⁴He who guards Israel
    never rests or sleeps.
⁵The Lord guards you.
    The Lord protects you as the shade
    protects you from the sun.

[6]The sun cannot hurt you during the
day.
And the moon cannot hurt you at
night.
[7]The Lord will guard you from all
dangers.
He will guard your life.
[8]The Lord will guard you as you come
and go,
both now and forever.

PSALM 122

A song for going up to worship. Of David.

[1]I was happy when they said to me,
"Let's go to the Temple[d] of the
Lord."
[2]Jerusalem, we are standing
at your gates.

[3]Jerusalem is built as a city
where friends can come together.
[4]The people from the tribes[d] go up
there.
The tribes belong to the Lord.
It is the rule to praise
the Lord at Jerusalem.
[5]There the descendants[d] of David
set their thrones to judge the
people.

[6]Pray for peace in Jerusalem:
"May those who love her be safe.
[7]May there be peace within her walls
and safety within her strong
towers."
[8]To help my relatives and friends,
I repeat, "Let Jerusalem have
peace."
[9]For the sake of the Temple of the
Lord our God,
I wish good for her.

PSALM 123

A song for going up to worship.

[1]Lord, I look up to you.
You live in heaven.
[2]Slaves depend on their masters.
And a female servant depends on
her mistress.
In the same way, we depend on our
God.
We wait for him to show us mercy.

[3]Be kind to us, Lord. Be kind to us
because we have been insulted.
[4]We have suffered many insults from
lazy people
and much cruelty from the proud.

PSALM 124

A song for going up to worship. Of David.

[1]What if the Lord had not been on our
side?
(Let Israel repeat this.)
[2]What if the Lord had not been on our
side
when men attacked us?
[3]When they were angry with us,
they would have swallowed us
alive.
[4]They would have been like a flood
drowning us.
They would have poured over us
like a river.
[5] They would have swept us away
like a mighty stream.

[6]Praise the Lord.
He did not let them chew us up.
[7]We have escaped like a bird
from the hunter's trap.
The trap has been broken,
and we have escaped.
[8]Our help comes from the Lord,
who made heaven and earth.

PSALM 125

A song for going up to worship.

[1]Those who trust the Lord are like
Mount Zion.[d]
It sits unmoved forever.
[2]The mountains surround Jerusalem.
And the Lord surrounds his people
now and forever.

[3]The wicked will not rule
over those who do right.
If they did, the people who do right
might use their power to do evil.

[4]Lord, be good to those who are good,
whose hearts are honest.
[5]But, Lord, when you punish those
who do evil,
also punish those who stop
following you.

Let there be peace in Israel.

PSALM 126

A song for going up to worship.

[1]When the Lord gave the riches back
to Jerusalem,
it seemed as if we were dreaming.
[2]Then we were filled with laughter,
and we sang happy songs.
Then the other nations said,
"The Lord has done great things
for them."

³The Lord has done great things for
us,
and we are very glad.
⁴Lord, give us back our riches again.
Do this as you bring streams to the
desert.
⁵Those who cry as they plant crops
will sing at harvesttime.
⁶Those who cry
as they carry out the seeds
will return singing
and carrying bundles of grain.

PSALM 127

A song for going up to worship. Of Solomon.
¹If the Lord doesn't build the house,
the builders are working for
nothing.
If the Lord doesn't guard the city,
the guards are watching for
nothing.
²It is no use for you to get up early
and stay up late,
working for a living.
The Lord gives sleep to those he
loves.
³Children are a gift from the Lord.
Babies are a reward.
⁴Sons who are born to a young man
are like arrows in the hand of a
warrior.
⁵Happy is the man
who has his bag full of arrows.
They will not be defeated
when they fight their enemies in
court.

PSALM 128

A song for going up to worship.
¹Happy are those who respect the
Lord
and obey him.
²You will enjoy what you work for.
You will be blessed with good
things.
³Your wife will give you many
children.
She will be like a vine that
produces a lot of fruit.
Your children will bring you much
good.
They will be like olive branches
that produce many olives.
⁴This is how the man who respects the
Lord
will be blessed.
⁵May the Lord bless you from Mount
Zion.ᵈ

May you enjoy the good things of
Jerusalem all your life.
⁶May you see your grandchildren.

Let there be peace in Israel.

PSALM 129

A song for going up to worship.
¹They have treated me badly all my
life.
(Let Israel repeat this.)
²They have treated me badly all my
life.
But they have not defeated me.
³Like farmers plowing, they plowed
over my back,
making long wounds.
⁴But the Lord does what is right.
He has set me free from those
wicked people.
⁵Let those who hate Jerusalem
be turned back in shame.
⁶Let them be like the grass on the roof.
It dries up before it has grown.
⁷There is not enough of it to fill a
man's hand
or to make into a bundle to fill his
arms.
⁸Let those who pass by them not say,
"May the Lord bless you.
We bless you by the power of the
Lord."

PSALM 130

A song for going up to worship.
¹Lord, I am in great trouble.
So I call out to you for help.
²Lord, hear my voice.
Listen to my prayer for help.
³Lord, if you punished people for all
their sins,
no one would be left.
⁴But you forgive us.
So you are respected.
⁵I wait for the Lord to help me.
I trust his word.
⁶I wait for the Lord to help me
more than night watchmen wait for
the dawn,
more than night watchmen wait for
the dawn.
⁷People of Israel, put your hope in the
Lord
because he is loving
and able to save.
⁸He will save Israel
from all their sins.

PSALM 131

A song for going up to worship. Of David.

[1]Lord, my heart is not proud.
    I don't look down on others.
  I don't do great things,
    and I can't do miracles.[d]
[2]But I am calm and quiet.
    I am like a baby with its mother.
  I am at peace, like a baby with its
    mother.

[3]People of Israel, put your hope in the
    Lord
  now and forever.

PSALM 132

A song for going up to worship.

[1]Lord, remember David
    and all his suffering.
[2]He made a promise to the Lord.
    He made a promise to the Mighty
    God of Jacob.
[3]He said, "I will not go home to my
    house.
  I will not lie down on my bed.
[4]I will not close my eyes
    or let myself sleep
[5]until I find a place for the Lord.
    I want to provide a home for the
    Mighty God of Jacob."

[6]We heard about the Box[d] of the
    Agreement in Bethlehem.
  We found it at Kiriath Jearim.
[7]Let's go to the Lord's house.
    Let's worship at his footstool.
[8]Rise, Lord, and come to your resting
    place.
  Come with the Holy Box that
    shows your strength.
[9]May your priests do what is right.
    May your people sing for joy.

[10]For the sake of your servant David,
    do not reject your appointed king.
[11]The Lord made a promise to David.
    It was a sure promise that he will
    not take back.
  He promised, "I will make one of
    your descendants[d]
    rule as king after you.
[12]But your sons must keep my
    agreement
  and the rules that I teach them.
  Then your sons after them will rule
    on your throne forever and ever."

[13]The Lord has chosen Jerusalem.
    He wants it for his home.
[14]He says, "This is my resting place
    forever.
  Here is where I want to stay.

[15]I will bless her with plenty of food.
    I will fill her poor with food.
[16]I will let her priests receive salvation.
    And those who worship me will
    really sing for joy.

[17]"I will make a king come from the
    family of David.
  I will provide my appointed one
    descendants[d] to rule after him.
[18]I will cover his enemies with shame.
    But his crown will shine."

PSALM 133

A song for going up to worship. Of David.

[1]It is good and pleasant
    when God's people live together in
    peace!
[2]It is like having perfumed oil poured
    on the priest's head
  and running down his beard.
  It ran down Aaron's beard
    and on to the collar of his robes.
[3]It is like the dew of Mount Hermon
    falling on the hills of Jerusalem.
  There the Lord gives his blessing
    of life forever.

PSALM 134

A song for going up to worship.

[1]Praise the Lord, all you servants of
    the Lord.
  You serve at night in the Temple[d] of
    the Lord.
[2]Raise your hands in the Temple
    and praise the Lord.

[3]May the Lord bless you from Mount
    Zion.[d]
  He made heaven and earth.

PSALM 135

[1]Praise the Lord!

Praise the name of the Lord.
    Praise him, you servants of the
    Lord.
[2]Praise him, you who stand in the
    Lord's Temple[d]
  and in the Temple courtyards.
[3]Praise the Lord, because he is good.
    Sing praises to him, because it is
    pleasant.
[4]The Lord has chosen the people of
    Jacob for himself.
  He has chosen the people of Israel
    for his very own.
[5]I know that the Lord is great.
    Our Lord is greater than all the
    gods.

⁶The Lord does what he wants,
   in heaven and on earth,
   in the seas and the deep oceans.
⁷He brings the clouds from the ends of
      the earth.
   He sends the lightning with the
      rain.
   He brings out the wind from his
      storehouses.

⁸He destroyed the firstborn^d sons in
      Egypt,
   the firstborn of both men and
      animals.
⁹He did many signs and miracles^d in
      Egypt.
   He did amazing things to the king
      and his servants.
¹⁰He defeated many nations
   and killed powerful kings:
¹¹Sihon king of the Amorites,
   Og king of Bashan
   and all the kings of Canaan.
¹²Then he gave their land as a gift.
   It was a gift to his people, the
      Israelites.

¹³Lord, your name is everlasting.
   Lord, you will be remembered from
      now on.
¹⁴You defend your people.
   You have mercy on your servants.

¹⁵The idols of other nations are made
      of silver and gold.
   They are made by human hands.
¹⁶They have mouths, but they cannot
      speak.
   They have eyes, but they cannot
      see.
¹⁷They have ears, but they cannot hear.
   They have no breath in their
      mouths.
¹⁸The people who make idols and trust
      them
   are all like them.

¹⁹Family of Israel, praise the Lord.
   Family of Aaron, praise the Lord.
²⁰Family of Levi, praise the Lord.
   You people who fear the Lord
   should praise him.
²¹You people of Jerusalem, praise the
      Lord on Mount Zion.^d
   Praise the Lord!

PSALM 136

¹Give thanks to the Lord because he is
      good.
   His love continues forever.
²Give thanks to the God over all gods.
   His love continues forever.

³Give thanks to the Lord of all lords.
   His love continues forever.

⁴Only he can do great miracles.^d
   His love continues forever.
⁵With his wisdom he made the skies.
   His love continues forever.
⁶He spread out the earth on the seas.
   His love continues forever.
⁷He made the sun and the moon.
   His love continues forever.
⁸He made the sun to rule the day.
   His love continues forever.
⁹He made the moon and stars to rule
      the night.
   His love continues forever.

¹⁰He killed the firstborn^d sons of the
      Egyptians.
   His love continues forever.
¹¹He brought the people of Israel out of
      Egypt.
   His love continues forever.
¹²He did it with his great power and
      strength.
   His love continues forever.
¹³He parted the water of the Red Sea.^d
   His love continues forever.
¹⁴He brought the Israelites through the
      middle of it.
   His love continues forever.
¹⁵But the king of Egypt and his army
      drowned in the Red Sea.
   His love continues forever.

¹⁶He led his people through the desert.
   His love continues forever.
¹⁷He defeated great kings.
   His love continues forever.
¹⁸He killed powerful kings.
   His love continues forever.
¹⁹He defeated Sihon king of the
      Amorites.
   His love continues forever.
²⁰He defeated Og king of Bashan.
   His love continues forever.
²¹He gave their land as a gift.
   His love continues forever.
²²It was a gift to his servants, the
      Israelites.
   His love continues forever.

²³He remembered us when we were in
      trouble.
   His love continues forever.
²⁴He freed us from our enemies.
   His love continues forever.
²⁵He gives food to every living creature.
   His love continues forever.
²⁶Give thanks to the God of heaven.
   His love continues forever.

PSALM 137

¹By the rivers in Babylon we sat and
cried
when we remembered Jerusalem.
²On the poplar trees nearby
we hung our harps.
³Those who captured us asked us to
sing.
Our enemies wanted happy songs.
They said, "Sing us a Temple[d] song
from Jerusalem!"

⁴But we cannot sing songs about the
Lord
while we are in this foreign
country!
⁵Jerusalem, if I forget you,
let my right hand lose its skill.
⁶Let my tongue stick to the roof of my
mouth
if I do not remember you.
Let these things happen if I do not
think about Jerusalem
as my greatest joy.

⁷Lord, remember what the Edomites
did
on the day Jerusalem fell.
They said, "Tear it down!
Tear it down to its foundations!"

⁸People of Babylon, you will be
destroyed.
The people who pay you back will
be happy.
They will punish you for what you
did to us.
⁹They will grab your babies
and throw them against the rocks.

PSALM 138

A song of David.
¹Lord, I will thank you with all my
heart.
I will sing to you before the false
gods.
²I will bow down facing your holy
Temple.[d]
And I will thank you for your love
and loyalty.
You have made your name and your
word
greater than anything.
³On the day I called to you, you
answered me.
You made me strong and brave.

⁴Lord, let all the kings of the earth
praise you.
They have heard the words you
speak.

⁵They will sing about what the Lord
has done
because the Lord's glory is great.
⁶Though the Lord is supreme
he takes care of those who are not
proud.
But he stays away from those who
are proud.
⁷Lord, even when I have trouble all
around me,
you will keep me alive.
When my enemies are angry,
you will reach down and save me
by your power.
⁸Lord, you do everything for me.
Lord, your love continues forever.
You made us. Do not leave us.

PSALM 139

For the director of music. A song of David.
¹Lord, you have examined me.
You know all about me.
²You know when I sit down and when
I get up.
You know my thoughts before I
think them.
³You know where I go and where I lie
down.
You know well everything I do.
⁴Lord, even before I say a word,
you already know what I am going
to say.
⁵You are all around me—in front and
in back.
You have put your hand on me.
⁶Your knowledge is amazing to me.
It is more than I can understand.

⁷Where can I go to get away from your
Spirit?[d]
Where can I run from you?
⁸If I go up to the skies, you are there.
If I lie down where the dead are,
you are there.
⁹If I rise with the sun in the east,
and settle in the west beyond the
sea,
¹⁰even there you would guide me.
With your right hand you would
hold me.
¹¹I could say, "The darkness will hide
me.
The light around me will turn into
night."
¹²But even the darkness is not dark to
you.
The night is as light as the day.
Darkness and light are the same to
you.

¹³You made my whole being.
  You formed me in my mother's
    body.
¹⁴I praise you because you made me in
    an amazing and wonderful way.
  What you have done is wonderful.
  I know this very well.
¹⁵You saw my bones being formed
    as I took shape in my mother's
    body.
  When I was put together there,
¹⁶ you saw my body as it was formed.
  All the days planned for me
    were written in your book
    before I was one day old.

¹⁷God, your thoughts are precious to me.
  They are so many!
¹⁸If I could count them,
  they would be more than all the
    grains of sand.
  When I wake up,
  I am still with you.

¹⁹God, I wish you would kill the
    wicked!
  Get away from me, you murderers!
²⁰These men say evil things about you.
  Your enemies use your name
    thoughtlessly.
²¹Lord, I hate those who hate you.
  I hate those who rise up against
    you.
²²I feel only hate for them.
  They are my enemies.

²³God, examine me and know my
    heart.
  Test me and know my thoughts.
²⁴See if there is any bad thing in me.
  Lead me in the way you set long
    ago.

PSALM 140

For the director of music. A song of David.
¹Lord, rescue me from evil people.
  Save me from cruel men.
²They make evil plans.
  They always start fights.
³They make their tongues sharp as a
    snake's.
  Their words are like snake poison.
                    Selah^d

⁴Lord, guard me from the power of
    wicked people.
  Save me from cruel men
  who plan to trip me up.
⁵Proud men have hidden a trap for me.
  They have spread out a net beside
    the road.
  They have set traps for me.   *Selah*

⁶I said to the Lord, "You are my God."
  Lord, listen to my prayer for help.
⁷Lord God, my mighty savior,
  you protect me in battle.
⁸Lord, do not give the wicked what
    they want.
  Don't let their plans succeed,
  or they will become proud.   *Selah*

⁹Those around me have planned
    trouble.
  Now let it come to them.
¹⁰Let burning coals fall on them.
  Throw them into the fire
  or into pits from which they cannot
    escape.
¹¹Don't let liars settle in the land.
  Let evil quickly hunt down cruel
    men.

¹²I know the Lord will get justice for
    the poor.
  He will defend the needy in court.
¹³Good people will praise his name.
  Honest people will live in his
    presence.

PSALM 141

A song of David.
¹Lord, I call to you. Come quickly.
  Listen to me when I call to you.
²Let my prayer be like incense^d placed
    before you.
  Let my praise be like the evening
    sacrifice.

³Lord, help me control my tongue.
  Help me be careful about what I
    say.
⁴Don't let me want to do evil
  or join others in doing wrong.
  Don't let me eat
  with those who do evil.

⁵If a good man punished me, that
    would be kind.
  If he corrected me,
  that would be like having perfumed
    oil on my head.
  I shouldn't refuse it.
  But I pray against those who do evil.
⁶ Let their leaders be thrown down
    the cliffs.
  Then people will know that I have
    spoken the truth:
⁷"The ground is plowed and broken
    up.
  In the same way, our bones have
    been scattered at the grave."

⁸Lord God, I look to you for help.
  I trust in you. Don't let me die.

⁹Protect me from the traps they set for
    me
   and from the net evil people have
    spread.
¹⁰Let the wicked fall into their own
    pits.
   And let me pass by safely.

PSALM 142

A maskil[d] of David when he was in the cave.
A prayer.

¹I cry out to the Lord.
   I pray to the Lord for mercy.
²I pour out my problems to him.
   I tell him my troubles.
³When I am afraid,
   you, Lord, know the way out.
In the path where I walk,
   a trap is hidden for me.
⁴Look around me and see.
   No one cares about me.
I have no place of safety.
   No one cares if I live.

⁵Lord, I cry out to you.
   I say, "You are my protection.
   You are all I want in this life."
⁶Listen to my cry
   because I am helpless.
Save me from those who are chasing
   me.
   They are too strong for me.
⁷Free me from my prison.
   Then I will praise your name.
Then the good people will surround
   me
   because you have taken care of me.

PSALM 143

A song of David.

¹Lord, hear my prayer.
   Listen to my cry for mercy.
Come to help me
   because you are loyal and good.
²Don't judge me, your servant,
   because no one alive is right before
    you.
³My enemies are chasing me.
   They have crushed me to the
    ground.
They have made me live in darkness
   like those who are long dead.
⁴I am afraid.
   My courage is gone.

⁵I remember what happened long ago.
   I recall everything you have done.
   I think about all you have made.
⁶I lift my hands to you in prayer.
   As a dry land needs rain, I thirst for
    you.   *Selah*[d]

⁷Lord, answer me quickly.
   I am getting weak.
Don't turn away from me,
   or I will be like those who are dead.
⁸Tell me in the morning about your
    love.
   I trust you.
Show me what I should do
   because my prayers go up to you.
⁹Lord, save me from my enemies.
   I come to you for safety.
¹⁰Teach me to do what you want,
   because you are my God.
Let your good Spirit[d]
   lead me on level ground.

¹¹Lord, let me live
   so people will praise you.
In your goodness
   save me from my troubles.
¹²In your love defeat my enemies.
   Destroy all those who trouble me
   because I am your servant.

PSALM 144

Of David.

¹Praise the Lord, my Rock.[d]
   He trains me for war.
   He trains me for battle.
²He gives me love and protects me like
    a strong, walled city.
He is my place of safety and my
    Savior.
He is my shield and my protection.
   He helps me rule my people.

³Lord, why is man important to you?
   Why do you even think about a
    human being?
⁴A man is like a breath.
   His life is like a passing shadow.

⁵Lord, tear open the sky and come
    down.
   Touch the mountains so they will
    smoke.
⁶Send the lightning and scatter my
    enemies.
   Shoot your arrows and force them
    away.
⁷Reach down from above.
   Pull me out of this sea of enemies.
   Rescue me from these foreigners.
⁸They are liars.
   They are dishonest.

⁹God, I will sing a new song to you.
   I will play to you on the
    ten-stringed harp.
¹⁰You give victory to kings.
   You save your servant David from
    cruel swords.

¹¹Save me, rescue me from these
   foreigners.
   They are liars.
   They are dishonest.

¹²Let our sons in their youth
   grow like strong trees.
   Let our daughters be
   like the decorated stones in the
   Temple.ᵈ

¹³Let our barns be filled
   with crops of all kinds.
   Let our sheep in the fields have
   thousands and thousands of lambs.

¹⁴ Let our cattle be strong.
   Let no one break in.
   Let there be no war.
   Let there be no screams in our
   streets.

¹⁵Happy are those who are like this.
   Happy are the people whose God is
   the Lord.

PSALM 145

A song of praise. Of David.

¹I praise your greatness, my God the
   King.
   I will praise you forever and ever.
²I will praise you every day.
   I will praise you forever and ever.
³The Lord is great. He is worthy of our
   praise.
   No one can understand how great
   he is.

⁴Parents will tell their children what
   you have done.
   They will retell your mighty acts,
⁵wonderful majesty and glory.
   And I will think about your
   miracles.ᵈ
⁶They will tell about the amazing
   things you do.
   I will tell how great you are.
⁷They will remember your great
   goodness.
   They will sing about your fairness.

⁸The Lord is kind and shows mercy.
   He does not become angry quickly
   but is full of love.
⁹The Lord is good to everyone.
   He is merciful to all he has made.
¹⁰Lord, everything you have made will
   praise you.
   Those who belong to you will bless
   you.
¹¹They will tell about the glory of your
   kingdom.
   They will speak about your power.

¹²Then everyone will know what
   powerful things you do.
   They will know about the glory and
   majesty of your kingdom.
¹³Your kingdom will continue forever.
   And you will be King from now on.

The Lord will keep his promises.
   With love he takes care of all he
   has made.
¹⁴The Lord helps those who have been
   defeated.
   He takes care of those who are in
   trouble.
¹⁵All living things look to you for food.
   And you give it to them at the right
   time.
¹⁶You open your hand,
   and you satisfy all living things.

¹⁷Everything the Lord does is right.
   With love he takes care of all he
   has made.
¹⁸The Lord is close to everyone who
   prays to him,
   to all who truly pray to him.
¹⁹He gives those who fear him what
   they want.
   He listens when they cry, and he
   saves them.
²⁰The Lord protects everyone who loves
   him.
   But he will destroy the wicked.

²¹I will praise the Lord.
   Let everyone praise his holy name
   forever.

PSALM 146

¹Praise the Lord!
   My whole being, praise the Lord.
²I will praise the Lord all my life.
   I will sing praises to my God as
   long as I live.

³Do not put your trust in princes
   or other people, who cannot save
   you.
⁴When people die, they are buried.
   Then all of their plans come to an
   end.
⁵Happy are those who are helped by
   the God of Jacob.
   Their hope is in the Lord their God.
⁶He made heaven and earth,
   the sea and everything in it.
   He remains loyal forever.
⁷The Lord does what is fair for those
   who have been wronged.
   He gives food to the hungry.
The Lord sets the prisoners free.
⁸ The Lord gives sight to the blind.

The Lord lifts up people who are in
trouble.
The Lord loves those who do right.
⁹The Lord protects the foreigners.
He defends the orphans and
widows.
But he overthrows the wicked.

¹⁰The Lord will be King forever.
Jerusalem, your God is everlasting.

Praise the Lord!

PSALM 147

¹Praise the Lord!

It is good to sing praises to our God.
It is good and pleasant to praise
him.
²The Lord rebuilds Jerusalem.
He brings back the scattered
Israelites who were taken
captive.
³He heals the brokenhearted.
He bandages their wounds.

⁴He counts the stars
and names each one.
⁵Our Lord is great and very powerful.
There is no limit to what he knows.
⁶The Lord defends those who are not
proud.
But he throws the wicked to the
ground.

⁷Sing praises to the Lord.
Praise our God with harps.
⁸He fills the sky with clouds.
He sends rain to the earth.
He makes grass grow on the hills.
⁹He gives food to cattle
and to the little birds that call.

¹⁰He is not pleased by the strength of a
horse
or the power of a man.
¹¹The Lord is pleased with those who
fear him,
with those who trust his love.

¹²Jerusalem, praise the Lord.
Jerusalem, praise your God.
¹³He makes your city gates strong.
He blesses the people inside.
¹⁴He brings peace to your country.
He fills you with the finest grain.

¹⁵He gives a command to the earth,
and it quickly obeys him.
¹⁶He spreads the snow like wool.
He scatters the frost like ashes.
¹⁷He throws down hail like rocks.
No one can stand the cold he sends.
¹⁸Then he gives a command, and it
melts.

He sends the breezes, and the
waters flow.

¹⁹He gave his word to Jacob.
He gave his laws and demands to
Israel.
²⁰He didn't do this for any other nation.
They don't know his laws.

Praise the Lord!

PSALM 148

¹Praise the Lord!

Praise the Lord from the heavens.
Praise him high above the earth.
²Praise him, all you angels.
Praise him, all you armies of
heaven.
³Praise him, sun and moon.
Praise him, all you shining stars.
⁴Praise him, highest heavens
and you waters above the sky.
⁵Let them praise the Lord
because they were created by his
command.
⁶He set them in place forever and ever.
He made a law that will never end.

⁷Praise the Lord from the earth.
Praise him, you large sea animals
and all the oceans.
⁸Praise him, lightning and hail, snow
and clouds,
and stormy winds that obey him.
⁹Praise him, mountains and all hills,
fruit trees and all cedar trees.
¹⁰Praise him, you wild animals and all
cattle,
small crawling animals and birds.
¹¹Praise him, you kings of the earth
and all nations,
princes and all rulers of the earth.
¹²Praise him, you young men and
women,
old people and children.

¹³Praise the Lord.
He alone is great.
He is greater than heaven and
earth.
¹⁴God has given his people a king.
He should be praised by all who
belong to him.
He should be praised by the
Israelites, the people closest to
his heart.

Praise the Lord!

PSALM 149

¹Praise the Lord!

Sing a new song to the Lord.
  Sing his praise in the meeting of
    his people.

²Let the Israelites be happy because of
    God, their Maker.
  Let the people of Jerusalem rejoice
    because of their King.
³They should praise him with dancing.
  They should praise him with
    tambourines[d] and harps.
⁴The Lord is pleased with his people.
  He saves those who are not proud.
⁵Let those who worship him rejoice in
    his glory.
  Let them sing for joy even in bed!

⁶Let them shout his praise
    with their two-edged swords in
    their hands.
⁷They will punish the nations.
  They will defeat the people.
⁸They will put those kings in chains

and those important men in iron
    bands.
⁹They will punish them as God has
    written.
  God is honored by all who worship
    him.

Praise the Lord!

PSALM 150

¹Praise the Lord!

Praise God in his Temple.[d]
  Praise him in his mighty heaven.
²Praise him for his strength.
  Praise him for his greatness.
³Praise him with trumpet blasts.
  Praise him with harps and lyres.[d]
⁴Praise him with tambourines[d] and
    dancing.
  Praise him with stringed
    instruments and flutes.
⁵Praise him with loud cymbals.
  Praise him with crashing cymbals.
⁶Let everything that breathes praise
    the Lord.

Praise the Lord!

The Book of
PROVERBS

1 These are the wise words of Solomon
  son of David. Solomon was king of
Israel.

²They teach wisdom and
    self-control.
  They give understanding.
³They will teach you how to be wise
    and self-controlled.
  They will teach you what is
    honest and fair and right.
⁴They give the ability to think to
    those with little knowledge.
  They give knowledge and good
    sense to the young.
⁵Wise people should also listen to
    them and learn even more.
  Even smart people will find wise
    advice in these words.
⁶Then they will be able to
    understand wise words and
    stories.
  They will understand the words
    of wise men and their riddles.

⁷Knowledge begins with respect for
    the Lord.

But foolish people hate wisdom
    and self-control.

⁸My child, listen to your father's
    teaching.
  And do not forget your mother's
    advice.
⁹Their teaching will beautify your
    life.
  It will be like flowers in your hair
    or a chain around your neck.

¹⁰My child, sinners will try to lead
    you into sin.
  But do not follow them.
¹¹They might say, "Come with us.
  Let's ambush and kill someone.
  Let's attack some harmless per-
    son just for fun.
¹²Let's swallow them alive, as death
    does.
  Let's swallow them whole, as the
    grave does.
¹³We will take all kinds of valuable
    things.
  We will fill our houses with what
    we steal.

¹⁴Come join us,
and we will share with you what
we steal."
¹⁵My child, do not go along with
them.
Do not do what they do.
¹⁶They run to do evil.
They are quick to kill.
¹⁷It is useless to spread out a net
right where the birds can see it!
¹⁸These men are setting their own
trap.
They will only catch themselves!
¹⁹All greedy people end up this way.
Greed takes away the life of the
greedy person.

²⁰Wisdom is like a good woman who
shouts in the street.
She raises her voice in the city
squares.
²¹She cries out in the noisy street.
She makes her speech at the city
gates:
²²"You foolish people! How long do
you want to stay foolish?
How long will you make fun of
wisdom?
How long will you hate
knowledge?
²³Listen when I correct you.
I will tell you what's in my heart.
I will tell you what I am thinking.
²⁴I called, but you refused to listen.
I held out my hand, but you paid
no attention.
²⁵You did not follow my advice.
You did not want me to correct
you.
²⁶So I will laugh when you are in
trouble.
I will make fun when disaster
happens to you.
²⁷Disaster will come over you like a
storm.
Trouble will strike you like a
whirlwind.
Pain and trouble will overwhelm
you.

²⁸"Then you will call out to me.
But I will not answer.
You will look for me.
But you will not find me.
²⁹You rejected knowledge.
You did not choose to respect the
Lord.
³⁰You did not accept my advice.
You rejected my correction.
³¹So you will get what you deserve.
You will get what you planned
for others.

³²Fools wander away and get killed.
They are destroyed because they
do not care.
³³But those who listen to me will live
in safety.
They will be safe, without fear of
being hurt."

2 My child, believe what I say.
And remember what I command
you.
²Listen to wisdom.
Try with all your heart to gain
understanding.
³Cry out for wisdom.
Beg for understanding.
⁴Search for it as you would for
silver.
Hunt for it like hidden treasure.
⁵Then you will understand what it
means to respect the Lord.
Then you will begin to know
God.
⁶Only the Lord gives wisdom.
Knowledge and understanding
come from him.
⁷He stores up wisdom for those who
are honest.
Like a shield he protects those
who are innocent.
⁸He guards those who are fair to
others.
He protects those who are loyal
to him.

⁹Then you will understand what is
honest and fair and right.
You will understand what is good
to do.
¹⁰You will have wisdom in your
heart.
And knowledge will be pleasing
to you.
¹¹Good sense will protect you.
Understanding will guard you.
¹²It will keep you from doing evil.
It will save you from people
whose words are bad.
¹³Such people do not do what is
right.
They do what is evil.
¹⁴They enjoy doing wrong.
They are happy to do what is
crooked and evil.
¹⁵What they do is wrong.
Their ways are dishonest.

¹⁶It will save you from the unfaithful
wife
who tries to lead you into
adultery[d] with pleasing words.

¹⁷Such women leave the husbands
they married when they were
young.
They forget the promise they
made before God.
¹⁸If you go to her house, you are on
your way to death.
What she does leads to death.
¹⁹No one who goes to her comes
back.
He will not continue to live.
²⁰But wisdom will help you be a good
person.
It will help you do what is right.
²¹Those who are honest will stay in
the land.
Those who are innocent will
remain in it.
²²But evil people will be removed
from the land.
The unfaithful will be thrown out
of it.

3 My child, do not forget my teaching.
    Keep my commands in mind.
²Then you will live a long time.
And your life will be successful.

³Don't ever stop being kind and
truthful.
Let kindness and truth show in
all you do.
Write them down in your mind as
if on a tablet.
⁴Then you will be respected
and pleasing to both God and
men.

⁵Trust the Lord with all your heart.
Don't depend on your own
understanding.
⁶Remember the Lord in everything
you do.
And he will give you success.

⁷Don't depend on your own wisdom.
Respect the Lord and refuse to
do wrong.
⁸Then your body will be healthy.
And your bones will be strong.

⁹Honor the Lord by giving him part
of your wealth.
Give him the firstfruits[d] from all
your crops.
¹⁰Then your barns will be full.
And your wine barrels will
overflow with new wine.

¹¹My child, do not reject the Lord's
discipline.
And don't become angry when he
corrects you.

¹²The Lord corrects those he loves,
just as a father corrects the child
that he likes.

¹³Happy is the person who finds
wisdom.
And happy is the person who
gets understanding.
¹⁴Wisdom is worth more than silver.
It brings more profit than gold.
¹⁵Wisdom is more precious than
rubies.
Nothing you want is equal to it.
¹⁶With her right hand wisdom offers
you a long life.
With her left hand she gives you
riches and honor.
¹⁷Wisdom will make your life
pleasant.
It will bring you peace.
¹⁸As a tree makes fruit, wisdom gives
life to those who use it.
Everyone who uses wisdom will
be happy.

¹⁹Using his wisdom, the Lord made
the earth.
Using his understanding, he set
the sky in place.
²⁰Using his knowledge, he made
rivers flow from underground
springs.
And he made the clouds drop
rain on the earth.

²¹My child, hold on to wisdom and
reason.
Don't let them out of your sight!
²²They will give you life.
Like a necklace, they will
beautify your life.
²³Then you will go on your way in
safety.
And you will not get hurt.
²⁴You won't need to be afraid when
you lie down.
When you lie down, your sleep
will be peaceful.
²⁵You won't need to be afraid of
trouble coming suddenly.
You won't need to fear the ruin
that comes to the wicked.
²⁶The Lord will keep you safe.
He will keep you from being
trapped.

²⁷Whenever you are able,
do good to people who need help.
²⁸If you have what your neighbor
asks for,
don't say to him,

"Come back later. I will give it to
you tomorrow."
[29] Don't make plans to hurt your
neighbor.
He lives nearby and trusts you.
[30] Don't accuse a man for no good
reason.
Don't accuse him if he has not
harmed you.
[31] Don't be jealous of men who use
violence.
And don't choose to be like them.
[32] The Lord hates those who do
wrong.
But he is a friend to those who
are honest.
[33] The Lord will put a curse on the
evil person's house.
But he will bless the home of
people who do what is right.
[34] The Lord laughs at those who
laugh at him.
But he is kind to those who are
not proud.
[35] Wise people will receive honor.
But foolish people will be
disgraced.

4

My children, listen to your father's
teaching.
Pay attention so you will understand.
[2] What I am telling you is good.
Do not forget what I teach you.
[3] I was once a young boy in my
father's house.
I was like an only child to my
mother.
[4] And my father taught me and said,
"Hold on to my words with all
your heart.
Keep my commands and you will
live.
[5] Get wisdom and understanding.
Don't forget or ignore my words.
[6] Use wisdom, and it will take care of
you.
Love wisdom, and it will keep
you safe.
[7] Wisdom is the most important
thing. So get wisdom.
If it costs everything you have,
get understanding.
[8] Believe in the value of wisdom, and
it will make you great.
Use it, and it will bring honor to
you.
[9] Like flowers in your hair, it will
beautify your life.
Like a crown, it will make you
look beautiful."

[10] My child, listen and accept what I
say.
Then you will have a long life.
[11] I am guiding you in wisdom.
And I am leading you to do what
is right.
[12] Nothing will hold you back.
You will not be overwhelmed.
[13] Always remember what you have
been taught.
Don't let go of it.
Keep safe all that you have learned.
It is the most important thing in
your life.
[14] Don't follow the ways of the
wicked.
Don't do what evil people do.
[15] Avoid their ways. Don't go near
what they do.
Stay away from them and keep
on going.
[16] They cannot sleep until they do
evil.
They cannot rest until they hurt
someone.
[17] They fill themselves with
wickedness and cruelty
as if they were eating bread and
drinking wine.
[18] The way of the good person is like
the light of dawn.
It grows brighter and brighter
until it is full daylight.
[19] But the wicked are like those who
stumble in the dark.
They can't even see what has
hurt them.

[20] My child, pay attention to my
words.
Listen closely to what I say.
[21] Don't ever forget my words.
Keep them deep within your
heart.
[22] These words are the secret to life
for those who find them.
They bring health to the whole
body.
[23] Be very careful about what you
think.
Your thoughts run your life.
[24] Don't use your mouth to tell lies.
Don't ever say things that are not
true.
[25] Keep your eyes focused on what is
right.
Keep looking straight ahead to
what is good.
[26] Be careful what you do.
Always do what is right.

²⁷Do not do anything unless it is
right.
Stay away from evil.

5 My son, pay attention to my wisdom.
Listen to my words of
understanding.
²Be careful to use good sense.
Watch what you say.
³The words of another man's wife
may seem sweet as honey.
Her words may be as pleasant as
olive oil.
⁴But in the end she will bring you
sorrow.
She will cause you pain like a
two-edged sword.
⁵She is on the way to death.
Her steps are headed straight to
the grave.
⁶She gives no thought to life.
She does not know that her ways
are wrong.
⁷Now, my sons, listen to me.
Don't ignore what I say.
⁸Stay away from such a woman.
Don't even go near the door of
her house.
⁹If you do, you will give your riches
to others.
And the best years of your life
will be given to someone who
is cruel.
¹⁰Strangers will enjoy your wealth.
And what you worked so hard for
will go to someone else.
¹¹You will groan at the end of your
life.
Then your health will be gone.
¹²Then you will say, "I hated
self-control!
I would not listen when I was
corrected!
¹³I would not listen to my teachers.
I paid no attention to what they
taught me.
¹⁴I have come very close to being
completely ruined
in front of a whole group of
people."

¹⁵Be faithful to your own wife.
She is like your own well of
water from which you drink.
¹⁶You wouldn't drink from streams
flowing in the city streets or
squares.
So be satisfied with your wife,
not those outside your home.
¹⁷These things are yours alone.
Don't share them with strangers.

¹⁸Be happy with the wife
you married when you were
young.
She gives you joys
as your fountain gives you water.
¹⁹She is as lovely and graceful as a
deer.
Let her love always make you
happy.
Let her love always hold you
captive.
²⁰My son, don't be held captive by a
woman who takes part in
adultery.[d]
Don't hold another man's wife.

²¹The Lord sees everything you do.
He watches where you go.
²²An evil man will be caught in his
evil ways.
He will be tied up by his sins as if
they were ropes.
²³He will die because he does not
control himself.
He will be held captive by his
own foolishness.

6 My child, be careful about giving a
guarantee for somebody else.
Be careful about promising to
pay what someone else owes.
²You might get trapped by what you
say.
You might be caught by your own
words.
³My child, you might do this and be
under somebody's control.
Then here is how to get free.
Go to your neighbor and don't be
proud.
Beg him to free you from your
promise.
⁴Don't go to sleep.
Don't even rest your eyes.
⁵But free yourself like a deer
running from a hunter.
Free yourself like a bird flying
away from a trapper.

⁶Go watch the ants, you lazy person.
Watch what they do and be wise.
⁷Ants have no commander.
They have no leader or ruler.
⁸But they store up food in the
summer.
They gather their supplies at
harvest.
⁹How long will you lie there, you
lazy person?
When will you get up from
sleeping?

[10]You sleep a little; you take a nap.
    You fold your hands and rest.
[11]So you will be as poor as if you had
        been robbed.
    You will have as little as if you
        had been held up.

[12]Some people are wicked and no
        good.
    They go around telling lies.
[13]They wink with their eyes and
        signal with their feet.
    They make signs with their
        fingers.
[14]They make evil plans in their
        hearts.
    They are always causing trouble.
[15]So trouble will strike them in an
        instant.
    Suddenly they will be hurt
        beyond cure.

[16]There are six things the Lord hates.
    There are seven things he cannot
        stand:
[17]   a proud look,
        a lying tongue,
        hands that kill innocent people,
[18]   a mind that thinks up evil
            plans,
        feet that are quick to do evil,
[19]   a witness who tells lies
        and a man who causes trouble
            among brothers.

[20]My son, keep your father's com-
        mands.
    Don't forget your mother's
        teaching.
[21]Remember their words forever.
    Let it be as if they were tied
        around your neck.
[22]They will guide you when you
        walk.
    They will guard you while you
        sleep.
    They will speak to you when you
        are awake.
[23]Their commands are like a lamp.
    Their teaching is like a light.
    And the correction that comes from
        them
    helps you have life.
[24]Such teaching will keep you from
        sinful women
    and from the pleasing words of
        another man's unfaithful wife.
[25]Don't want her because she is beau-
        tiful.
    Don't let her capture you by the
        way she looks at you.

[26]A prostitute[d] may leave you with
        only a loaf of bread.
    And a woman who takes part in
        adultery[d] may cost you your
        life.
[27]You cannot carry hot coals against
        your chest
    without burning your clothes.
[28]And you cannot walk on hot coals
    without burning your feet.
[29]The same thing happens if you
        have sexual relations with an-
        other man's wife.
    Anyone who does so will be pun-
        ished.

[30]People do not hate a thief
    when he steals because he is
        hungry.
[31]But if he is caught, he must pay
        back seven times what he stole.
    It may cost him everything he
        owns.
[32]A man who takes part in adultery
        doesn't have any sense.
    He will destroy himself.
[33]He will be beaten up and disgraced.
    And his shame will never go
        away.
[34]Jealousy makes a husband very
        angry.
    He will have no mercy when he
        gets even.
[35]He will accept no payment for the
        wrong.
    He will take no money, no matter
        how much it is.

7 My son, remember what I say.
    Treasure my commands.
[2]Obey my commands, and you will
        live.
    Protect my teachings as you
        would your own eyes.
[3]Remind yourself of them.
    Write them down in your mind as
        if on a tablet.
[4]Be good to wisdom as if she were
        your sister.
    Make understanding your closest
        friend.
[5]Wisdom and understanding will
        keep you away from adultery.[d]
    They will keep you away from
        the unfaithful wife and her
        pleasing words.

[6]I once was standing at the window
        of my house.
    I looked out through the shutters.

[7]I saw some foolish, young men.
  I noticed one of them who had no
    wisdom.
[8]He was walking down the street
    near the corner.
  He was on the road leading to
    her house.
[9]It was the twilight of the evening.
  The darkness of the night was
    just beginning.
[10]Then the woman approached him.
  She was dressed like a prostitute[d]
    and was planning to trick him.
[11]She was a loud and stubborn
    woman.
  She never stayed at home.
[12]She was always out in the streets or
    in the city squares.
  She was always waiting around
    on the street corners.
[13]She grabbed him and kissed him.
  Without shame she said to him,
[14]"I made my fellowship offering and
    have the meat at home.
  I have kept my special promises.
[15]So I have come out to meet you.
  I have been looking for you and
    have found you!
[16]I have covered my bed
    with colored sheets from Egypt.
[17]I have made my bed smell sweet
    with myrrh,[d] aloes[d] and
    cinnamon.
[18]Come, let's make love until
    morning.
  Let's enjoy each other's love!
[19]My husband is not home.
  He has gone on a long trip.
[20]He took a lot of money with him.
  And he won't be home for
    weeks."
[21]By her clever words she made him
    give in.
  By her pleasing words she led
    him into doing wrong.
[22]All at once he followed her.
  He was like an ox being led to
    the butcher.
  He was like a deer caught in a trap.
[23] But quickly an arrow shot
    through his liver.
  He was like a bird caught in a trap.
  He didn't know what he did
    would kill him.
[24]Now, my sons, listen to me.
  Pay attention to what I say.
[25]Don't let yourself be tricked by the
    woman who is guilty of
    adultery.
  Don't join her in her evil actions.

[26]She has ruined many good men.
  Many have died because of her.
[27]Going to her house is like taking
    the road to death.
  That road leads down to where
    the dead are.

8 Like a person, wisdom calls out to
    you.
  Understanding raises her voice.
[2]On the hilltops along the road
    and at the crossroads, she stands
    calling.
[3]She stands beside the city gates.
  At the entrances into the city, she
    calls out:
[4]"People, I'm calling out to you.
  I am shouting to all people.
[5]You who do not know better, get
    the ability to think.
  You who are foolish, get
    understanding.
[6]Listen. I have important things to
    say.
  What I tell you is right.
[7]What I say is true.
  I hate it when people speak evil.
[8]Everything I say is honest.
  Nothing I say is crooked or false.
[9]People with good sense know that
    what I say is true.
  People with knowledge know
    that my words are right.
[10]Choose my teachings instead of
    silver.
  Choose knowledge rather than
    the finest gold.
[11]Wisdom is more precious than
    rubies.
  Nothing you want is equal to it.

[12]"I am wisdom, and I have the
    ability to think.
  I also have knowledge and good
    sense.
[13]If you respect the Lord, you also
    will hate evil.
  It is wise to hate pride and
    bragging,
  evil ways and lies.
[14]I have good sense and advice.
  I have understanding and power.
[15]Kings use me to govern.
  And rulers use me to make fair
    laws.
[16]Princes use me to lead.
  So do important men and all
    good judges.
[17]I love those who love me.
  Those who want me find me.
[18]Riches and honor are mine.
  So are wealth and lasting success.

¹⁹What I give is better than the finest
gold.
What I give is better than pure
silver.
²⁰I do what is right.
I do what is fair.
²¹I give wealth to those who love me.
I fill them with treasures.

²²"I, wisdom, was with God when he
began his work.
This was before he made
anything else long ago.
²³I was appointed in the very
beginning,
even before the world began.
²⁴I began before there were oceans.
There were no springs
overflowing with water.
²⁵I began before the hills were there.
The mountains had not even
been put in place.
²⁶God still had not made the earth or
fields.
He had not even made the first
dust of the earth.
²⁷I was there when God put the skies
in place,
when he stretched the horizon
over the oceans.
²⁸I was there when he made the
clouds above.
I was there when he put the
fountains in the oceans.
²⁹I was there when he ordered the
sea
not to go beyond the borders he
had set for it.
I was there when he laid the earth's
foundation.
³⁰ I was like a child by his side.
I was happy every day
and enjoyed being in his
presence.
³¹I enjoyed the whole world.
And I was happy with all its
people.

³²"Now, my children, listen to me.
Those who follow my ways are
happy.
³³Listen to my teaching, and you will
be wise.
Do not ignore it.
³⁴Those who listen to me are happy.
They stand watching at my door
every day.
They are at my open doorway,
wanting to be with me.

³⁵Whoever finds me finds life.
And the Lord will be pleased
with him.
³⁶Whoever does not find me hurts
himself.
Those who hate me love death."

9 Wisdom has built her house.
She has made its seven columns.
²She has prepared her food and
wine.
She has set her table.
³She has sent out her servant girls.
She calls out from the highest
place in the city.
⁴She says to those who are not wise,
"Come in here, you foolish
people!
⁵Come and eat my food.
And drink the wine I have
prepared.
⁶Stop your foolish ways, and you
will live.
Be a person of understanding.

⁷"If you correct someone who
makes fun of wisdom, you will
get insulted.
If you correct an evil person, you
will get hurt.
⁸Do not correct someone who makes
fun of wisdom, or he will hate
you.
But correct a wise man, and he
will love you.
⁹Teach a wise man, and he will
become even wiser.
Teach a good man, and he will
learn even more.

¹⁰"Wisdom begins with respect for
the Lord.
And understanding begins with
knowing God, the Holy One.
¹¹If you live wisely, you will live a
long time.
Wisdom will add years to your
life.
¹²The wise person is rewarded by his
wisdom.
But a person who makes fun of
wisdom will suffer for it."

¹³Foolishness is like a loud woman.
She does not have wisdom or
knowledge.
¹⁴She sits at the door of her house.
It is at the highest place in the
city.
¹⁵She calls out to those who are
passing by.
They are minding their own
business.

¹⁶She says to those who are not wise,
"Come in here, you foolish
people!"
¹⁷Stolen water is sweeter.
Stolen food tastes better."
¹⁸But these people don't know that
everyone dies who goes there.
They don't realize that her guests
are deep in the grave.

10 These are the wise words of Solomon:

A wise son makes his father happy.
But a foolish son makes his
mother sad.

²Riches gotten by doing wrong have
no value.
But right living will save you
from death.

³The Lord does not let people who
live right go hungry.
But he does not let evil people get
what they hunger for.

⁴A lazy person will end up poor.
But a hard worker will become
rich.

⁵A son who gathers crops when they
are ready is wise.
But the son who sleeps through
the harvest is a disgrace.

⁶People who do what is right will
have rich blessings.
But the wicked will be
overwhelmed by violence.

⁷Good people will be remembered
as a blessing.
But evil people will soon be
forgotten.

⁸A wise person does what he is told.
But a talkative fool will be
ruined.

⁹The honest person will live safely.
But the one who is dishonest will
be caught.

¹⁰A wink may get you into trouble.
And foolish talk will lead to your
ruin.

¹¹Like a fountain of water, the words
of a good person give life.
But the words of the wicked
contain nothing but violence.

¹²Hatred stirs up trouble.
But love forgives all wrongs.

¹³You can expect smart people to
speak wisely.
But people without wisdom can
expect to be punished.

¹⁴Wise people don't tell everything
they know.
But a foolish person talks too
much and is ruined.

¹⁵Having lots of money protects the
rich.
But having no money destroys
the poor.

¹⁶Good people are rewarded with life.
But evil people are paid back
with punishment.

¹⁷The person who accepts correction
is on the way to life.
But the person who ignores
correction will be ruined.

¹⁸Whoever hides his hate is a liar.
Whoever tells lies is a fool.

¹⁹If you talk a lot, you are sure to sin.
If you are wise, you will keep
quiet.

²⁰The words of a good person are like
pure silver.
But an evil person's thoughts are
worth little.

²¹A good person's words will help
many others.
But a foolish person dies because
he doesn't have wisdom.

²²The Lord's blessing brings wealth.
And with it comes no sorrow.

²³A foolish person enjoys doing
wrong.
But a person with understanding
enjoys doing what is wise.

²⁴An evil person will get what he
fears most.
But a good person will receive
what he wants most.

²⁵A storm will blow the evil person
away.
But a good person will always be
safe.

²⁶A lazy person brings trouble to the
one he works for.
He bothers others like vinegar on
the teeth or smoke in the eyes.

²⁷Whoever respects the Lord will
have a long life.
But an evil person will have his
life cut short.

²⁸A good person can look forward to
    happiness.
        But an evil person can expect
        nothing.

²⁹The Lord will protect good people.
        But he will ruin those who do
        evil.

³⁰Good people will always be safe.
        But evil people will not remain in
        the land.

³¹A good person says wise things.
        But a liar's tongue will be
        stopped.

³²Good people say the right thing.
        But the wicked tell lies.

11 The Lord hates dishonest scales.
    But he is pleased with correct
    weights.

²Pride leads only to shame.
    It is wise not to be proud.

³Good people will be guided by
    honesty.
        But dishonesty will destroy those
        who are not trustworthy.

⁴Riches will not help when it's time
    to die.
        But doing what is right will save
        you from dying too soon.

⁵The goodness of an innocent
    person makes his life easier.
        But a wicked person will be
        destroyed by his wickedness.

⁶Doing what is right brings freedom
    to honest people.
        But those who are not
        trustworthy will be caught by
        their own desires.

⁷When a wicked person dies, his
    hope is gone.
        The hopes he placed in his riches
        will come to nothing.

⁸The good man is saved from
    trouble.
        It comes to the wicked instead.

⁹By his words an evil person can
    destroy his neighbor.
        But a good person will escape by
        being smart.

¹⁰When good people succeed, the city
    is happy.
        When evil people die, there are
        shouts of joy.

¹¹The influence of good people
    makes a city great.
        But the wicked can destroy it
        with their words.

¹²A person without good sense finds
    fault with his neighbor.
        But a person with understanding
        keeps quiet.

¹³A person who gossips can't keep
    secrets.
        But a trustworthy person can
        keep a secret.

¹⁴Without leadership a nation will be
    defeated.
        But when many people give
        advice, it will be safe.

¹⁵Whoever guarantees to pay what
    somebody else owes will suffer.
        It is safer to avoid such promises.

¹⁶A kind woman is respected.
        But cruel men get wealth.

¹⁷A kind person is doing himself a
    favor.
        But a cruel person brings trouble
        on himself.

¹⁸An evil person really gains nothing
    from what he earns.
        But a good person will surely be
        rewarded.

¹⁹Those who are truly good will live.
        But those who chase after evil
        will die.

²⁰The Lord hates those with evil
    hearts.
        But he is pleased with those who
        are innocent.

²¹You can be sure that evil people
    will be punished.
        But those who do what is right
        will not be punished.

²²A beautiful woman without good
    sense
        is like a gold ring in a pig's snout.

²³The wishes of those who do right
    will come true.
        But the hopes of the wicked will
        be defeated by God's anger.

²⁴Some people give much but get
    back even more.
        But others don't give what they
        should, and they end up poor.

²⁵A person who gives to others will
    get richer.

Whoever helps others will
himself be helped.

26 People curse someone who keeps
all the grain for himself.
But they bless a person who is
willing to sell it.

27 Whoever looks for good will find
kindness.
But whoever looks for evil will
find trouble.

28 Those who trust in riches will be
ruined.
But a good person will be as
healthy as a green leaf.

29 Whoever brings trouble to his
family will be left with nothing
but the wind.
And a foolish person will become
a servant to the wise.

30 As a tree makes fruit, a good
person gives life to others.
The wise person shows others
how to be wise.

31 Good people will be rewarded on
earth.
So the wicked and the sinners
will also be punished.

12 Anyone who loves learning
accepts being corrected.
But a person who hates being
corrected is stupid.

2 The Lord is pleased with a good
person.
But he will punish anyone who
plans evil.

3 Doing evil brings a person no
safety at all.
But a good person has safety and
security.

4 A good wife is like a crown for her
husband.
But a disgraceful wife is like a
disease in his bones.

5 The plans that good people make
are fair.
But the advice of the wicked will
trick you.

6 The wicked talk of killing people.
But the words of good people will
save them.

7 Wicked people die and leave
nothing behind.
But a good man's family goes on.

8 A wise person is praised.
But a stupid person is not
respected.

9 A person might not be important
but still have a servant.
He is better off than someone
who acts important but has no
food.

10 A good man takes care of his
animals.
But even the kindest acts of the
wicked are cruel.

11 The person who works his land will
have plenty of food.
But the one who chases useless
dreams isn't wise.

12 Evil people want what other evil
people have stolen.
But good people want to give to
others.

13 Evil people are trapped by their evil
talk.
But good people stay out of
trouble.

14 A person will be rewarded for what
he says.
And he will also be rewarded for
what he does.

15 A foolish person thinks he is doing
right.
But a wise person listens to
advice.

16 A foolish person quickly shows
that he is upset.
But a wise person ignores an
insult.

17 An honest witness tells the truth.
But a dishonest witness tells lies.

18 Careless words stab like a sword.
But wise words bring healing.

19 Truth will last forever.
But lies last only a moment.

20 Those who plan evil mean to lie.
But those who plan peace will be
happy.

21 No harm comes to a good person.
But an evil person's life is full of
trouble.

22 The Lord hates those who tell lies.
But he is pleased with those who
do what they promise.

23 A wise person keeps what he
knows to himself.

But a foolish person shows how
foolish he is.

24 Hard workers will become leaders.
But those who are lazy will be
slaves.

25 Worry makes a person feel as if he
is carrying a heavy load.
But a kind word cheers up a
person.

26 A good person takes advice from
his friends.
But an evil person is easily led to
do wrong.

27 A lazy person catches no food to
cook.
But a hard worker will have great
wealth.

28 Doing what is right is the way to
life.
But there is another way that
leads to death.

13 A wise son takes his father's
advice.
But a person who makes fun of
wisdom won't listen to
correction.

2 A person will be rewarded for what
he says.
But those who can't be trusted
want only violence.

3 Whoever is careful about what he
says protects his life.
But anyone who speaks without
thinking will be ruined.

4 The lazy person will not get what
he wants.
But a hard worker gets
everything he wants.

5 Good people hate what is false.
But wicked people do shameful
and disgraceful things.

6 Doing what is right protects the
honest person.
But evil ruins the sinner.

7 Some people pretend to be rich but
really have nothing.
Other people pretend to be poor
but really are wealthy.

8 A rich man may have to pay a
ransom for his life.
But a poor person will never have
to face such a danger.

9 Good people will live long like
bright flames.
But the wicked will die like a
flame going out.

10 Pride leads to arguments.
But those who take advice are
wise.

11 Money that comes easily
disappears quickly.
But money that is gathered little
by little will slowly grow.

12 It is sad when you don't get what
you hoped for.
But when wishes come true, it's
like eating fruit from the tree of
life.

13 Whoever rejects what he is taught
will pay for it.
But whoever does what he is told
will be rewarded.

14 The teaching of a wise person gives
life.
It is like a fountain of water that
can save people from death.

15 People with good understanding
will be liked.
But the lives of those who are not
trustworthy are hard.

16 Every wise person acts with good
sense.
But a foolish person shows how
foolish he is.

17 A wicked messenger brings
nothing but trouble.
But a trustworthy one makes
everything right.

18 A person who refuses correction
will end up poor and disgraced.
But a person who accepts
correction will be honored.

19 It is so good when wishes come
true.
But foolish people still refuse to
stop doing evil.

20 Whoever spends time with wise
people will become wise.
But whoever makes friends with
fools will suffer.

21 Trouble always comes to sinners.
But good people enjoy success.

22 Good people's wealth will be
inherited by their grandchildren.
And a sinner's wealth will be
saved for good people.

²³A poor man's field might have
plenty of food.
But unfair people steal it from
him.

²⁴If a person does not punish his
children, he does not love
them.
But the person who loves his
children is careful to correct
them.

²⁵Good people have enough to eat.
But the wicked will go hungry.

14 A wise woman strengthens her
family.
But a foolish woman destroys
hers by what she does.

²People who live good lives show
respect for the Lord.
But those who live evil lives show
no respect for him.

³A foolish person will be punished
for his proud words.
But a wise person's words will
protect him.

⁴When there are no oxen, there is no
food in the barn.
But with the strength of an ox,
much grain can be grown.

⁵A truthful witness does not lie.
But a false witness tells nothing
but lies.

⁶Those who make fun of wisdom
look for it but do not find it.
But the person with
understanding easily finds
knowledge.

⁷Stay away from a foolish person.
You won't learn anything from
him.

⁸What makes a person wise is
understanding what to do.
But what makes a person foolish
is dishonesty.

⁹Foolish people don't care if they
sin.
But honest people work at being
right with others.

¹⁰No one else can know your
sadness.
Strangers cannot share your joy.

¹¹The wicked person's house will be
destroyed.
But a good person's tent will still
be standing.

¹²Some people think they are doing
what's right.
But what they are doing will
really kill them.

¹³When someone is laughing, he may
be sad inside.
And when the laughter is over,
there is sorrow.

¹⁴Evil people will be paid back for
their evil ways.
And good people will be
rewarded for their good ones.

¹⁵A foolish person will believe
anything.
But a wise person thinks about
what he does.

¹⁶A wise person is careful and stays
out of trouble.
But a foolish person is quick to
act and careless.

¹⁷A person who quickly loses his
temper does foolish things.
But a person with understanding
remains calm.

¹⁸Foolish people get nothing for their
work but more foolishness.
But wise people are rewarded
with knowledge.

¹⁹Evil people will have to bow down
to good people.
The wicked will bow down at the
door of those who do right.

²⁰The poor are rejected, even by their
neighbors.
But rich people have many
friends.

²¹It is a sin to hate your neighbor.
But being kind to the needy
brings happiness.

²²Those who make evil plans will be
ruined.
But people love and trust those
who plan to do good.

²³Those who work hard make a
profit.
But those who only talk will be
poor.

²⁴Wise people are rewarded with
wealth.
But foolish people will only be
rewarded with more
foolishness.

²⁵A truthful witness saves lives.
But a false witness is a traitor.

²⁶A person who respects the Lord
  will have security.
  And his children will be
  protected.

²⁷Respect for the Lord gives life.
  It is like a fountain of water that
  can save people from death.

²⁸A king is honored when he has
  many people to rule.
  But a prince is ruined if he has
  none.

²⁹A person who does not quickly get
  angry shows that he has
  understanding.
  But a person who quickly loses
  his temper shows his
  foolishness.

³⁰Peace of mind means a healthy
  body.
  But jealousy will rot your bones.

³¹Whoever is cruel to the poor insults
  their Maker.
  But anyone who is kind to the
  needy honors God.

³²The wicked are ruined by their own
  evil.
  But those who do what is right
  are protected by their honesty.

³³The person who has understanding
  has wisdom.
  And even fools recognize it.

³⁴Doing what is right makes a nation
  great.
  But sin will bring disgrace to any
  people.

³⁵A king is pleased with a wise
  servant.
  But he will become angry with
  one who causes him shame.

15 A gentle answer will calm a
       person's anger.
       But an unkind answer will
       cause more anger.

²Wise people use knowledge when
  they speak.
  But fools speak only foolishness.

³The Lord's eyes see everything that
  happens.
  He watches both evil and good
  people.

⁴As a tree gives us fruit, healing
  words give us life.
  But evil words crush the spirit.

⁵A foolish person rejects his father's
  correction.
  But anyone who accepts
  correction is wise.

⁶There is much wealth in the houses
  of good people.
  But evil people are paid only with
  trouble.

⁷With their words wise people
  spread knowledge.
  But there is no knowledge in the
  thoughts of the foolish.

⁸The Lord hates the sacrifice that
  the wicked person offers.
  But he is pleased with an honest
  person's prayer.

⁹The Lord hates what evil people do.
  But he loves those who do what
  is right.

¹⁰The person who quits doing what is
  right will really be punished.
  The one who hates to be
  corrected will die.

¹¹The Lord knows what is happening
  where the dead people are.
  So he can surely know what
  living people are thinking.

¹²A person who laughs at wisdom
  does not like to be corrected.
  He will not ask advice from the
  wise.

¹³Happiness makes a person smile.
  But sadness breaks a person's
  spirit.

¹⁴Smart people want more
  knowledge.
  But a foolish person just wants
  more foolishness.

¹⁵Every day is hard for those who
  suffer.
  But a happy heart makes it like a
  continual feast.

¹⁶It is better to be poor and respect
  the Lord
  than to be wealthy and have
  much trouble.

¹⁷It is better to eat vegetables with
  those who love you
  than to eat meat with those who
  hate you.

¹⁸A person who quickly gets angry
  causes trouble.
  But a person who controls his
  temper stops a quarrel.

[19]A lazy person's life is as difficult as walking through a patch of thorns.
But an honest person's life is as easy as walking down a smooth highway.

[20]A wise son makes his father happy.
But a foolish person hates his mother.

[21]A man without wisdom enjoys being foolish.
But a man with understanding does what is right.

[22]Plans fail without good advice.
But plans succeed when you get advice from many others.

[23]People enjoy giving good answers!
Saying the right word at the right time is so pleasing!

[24]A wise person does things that will make his life better.
He avoids whatever would cause his death.

[25]The Lord will tear down the proud person's house.
But he will protect the property of a widow.

[26]The Lord hates evil thoughts.
But he is pleased with kind words.

[27]A greedy person brings trouble to his family.
But the person who can't be paid to do wrong will live.

[28]Good people think before they answer.
But the wicked simply give evil answers.

[29]The Lord does not listen to the wicked.
But he hears the prayers of those who do right.

[30]Good news makes you feel better.
Your happiness will show in your eyes.

[31]A wise person pays attention to correction
that will improve his life.

[32]A person who refuses correction hates himself.
But a person who accepts correction gains understanding.

[33]Respect for the Lord will teach you wisdom.
If you want to be honored, you must not be proud.

16 People make plans in their hearts.
But only the Lord can make those plans come true.

[2]A person may believe he is doing right.
But the Lord will judge his reasons.

[3]Depend on the Lord in whatever you do.
Then your plans will succeed.

[4]The Lord makes everything work the way he wants it.
He even has a day of disaster for evil people.

[5]The Lord hates those who are proud.
You can be sure that they will be punished.

[6]Love and truth bring forgiveness of sin.
By respecting the Lord you will avoid evil.

[7]A person should live so that he pleases the Lord.
If he does, even his enemies will make peace with him.

[8]It is better to be poor and do what is right
than to be wealthy and be unfair.

[9]A person may think up plans.
But the Lord decides what he will do.

[10]The words of a king are like a message from God.
So his decisions should be fair.

[11]The Lord wants honest balances and scales to be used.
He wants all weights to be honest.

[12]Kings hate those who do wrong because governments only last if they are fair.

[13]Kings are pleased with those who speak honest words.
They value a person who speaks the truth.

[14]If a king becomes angry, he may put someone to death.

So a wise man will try to keep
peace.

[15] A king's kindness can give people
life.
His kindness is like a spring
shower.

[16] It is better to get wisdom than gold.
It is better to choose
understanding than silver!

[17] A good person stays away from
evil.
A person who watches what he
does protects his life.

[18] Pride will destroy a person.
A proud attitude leads to ruin.

[19] It is better not to be proud and to
be with those who suffer
than to share stolen property
with proud people.

[20] Whoever pays attention to what he
is taught will succeed.
And whoever trusts the Lord will
be happy.

[21] A wise person is known for his
understanding.
He wins people to his side with
pleasant words.

[22] Understanding is like a fountain of
water which gives life to those
who use it.
But foolishness will cause foolish
people to be punished.

[23] A wise person's mind tells him
what to say.
This helps him to teach others
better.

[24] Pleasant words are like a
honeycomb.
They make a person happy and
healthy.

[25] Some people think they are doing
what's right.
But in the end it causes them to
die.

[26] The worker's hunger helps him.
His desire to eat makes him
work.

[27] An evil person makes evil plans.
And his words are like a burning
fire.

[28] An evil person causes trouble.
And a person who gossips ruins
friendships.

[29] A cruel man tricks his neighbor.
He leads him to do wrong.

[30] Someone who winks at you is
planning evil.
And the one who grins at you is
about to do something wrong.

[31] Gray hair is like a crown of honor.
You earn it by living a good life.

[32] Patience is better than strength.
Controlling your temper is better
than capturing a city.

[33] People throw lots[d] to make a
decision.
But the answer comes from the
Lord.

17 It is better to eat a dry crust of
bread in peace
than to have a feast where
there is quarreling.

[2] A wise servant will rule over his
master's disgraceful son.
And he will even inherit a share
of what the master leaves his
sons.

[3] A hot furnace tests silver and gold.
In the same way, the Lord tests a
person's heart.

[4] An evil person listens to evil words.
A liar pays attention to cruel
words.

[5] If you make fun of the poor,
you insult God, who made them.
If you laugh at someone's trouble,
you will be punished.

[6] Grandchildren are the reward of
old people.
And children are proud of their
parents.

[7] Foolish people should not be proud.
And rulers should not be liars!

[8] A person might think he can pay
people and they will do
anything he asks.
He thinks it will succeed every
time.

[9] Whoever forgives someone's sin
makes a friend.
But the one who tells about the
sin breaks up friendships.

[10] A wise man will learn more from a
warning
than a foolish person will learn
from 100 lashings.

¹¹A disobedient person is only
looking for trouble.
So a cruel messenger will be sent
against him.

¹²It is better to meet a bear robbed of
her cubs
than to meet a foolish person
doing foolish things.

¹³If a person gives evil in return for
good,
his house will always be full of
trouble.

¹⁴Starting a quarrel is like a leak in a
dam.
So stop the quarrel before a fight
breaks out.

¹⁵The Lord hates both these things:
letting guilty people go free and
punishing those who are not
guilty.

¹⁶It won't do a fool any good to try to
buy wisdom.
He doesn't really want to be wise.

¹⁷A friend loves you all the time.
A brother is always there to help
you.

¹⁸It is not wise to promise
to pay what your neighbor owes.

¹⁹Whoever loves to quarrel loves to
sin.
Whoever is proud is asking for
trouble.

²⁰A person with an evil heart will
find no success.
And the person whose words are
evil will get into trouble.

²¹It is sad to have a foolish son.
There is no joy in being the
father of a fool.

²²A happy heart is like good
medicine.
But a broken spirit drains your
strength.

²³A wicked person secretly accepts
money to do wrong.
Then there will be no fairness.

²⁴The person with understanding
looks for wisdom.
But a foolish person lets his mind
wander everywhere.

²⁵A foolish son makes his father sad.
And he causes his mother great
sorrow.

²⁶It is not good to punish those who
have done what is right.
Nor is it good to punish leaders
for being honest.

²⁷The person who has knowledge
says very little.
And a person with understanding
stays calm.

²⁸Even a foolish person seems to be
wise if he keeps quiet.
He appears to have
understanding if he doesn't
speak.

18

An unfriendly person cares only
about himself.
He makes fun of all wisdom.

²A foolish person does not want to
understand anything.
He only enjoys telling others
what he thinks.

³Do something evil, and people
won't like you.
Do something shameful, and they
will make fun of you.

⁴Understanding people's words is as
hard as getting water out of a
deep well.
But understanding wisdom is as
easy as getting water from a
flowing stream.

⁵It is not good to honor the wicked.
Nor is it good to be unfair to the
innocent.

⁶A fool's words start quarrels.
They make people want to give
him a beating.

⁷A fool's words will ruin him.
He will be trapped by his own
words.

⁸The words of a gossip are like tasty
bits of food.
People take them all in.

⁹A person who doesn't work hard
is just like a person who destroys
things.

¹⁰The Lord is like a strong tower.
Those who do what is right can
run to him for safety.

¹¹Rich people trust their wealth to
protect them.
They think it is like the high
walls of a city.

¹²People who are proud will be
ruined.
But those who are not proud will
be honored.

¹³A person who answers without
listening
is foolish and disgraceful.

¹⁴The will to live can get you through
sickness.
But no one can live with a broken
spirit.

¹⁵The mind of a smart person is
ready to get knowledge.
The wise person listens to learn
more.

¹⁶Taking a gift to an important
person
will help get you in to see him.

¹⁷The first person to tell his side of a
story seems right.
But that may change when
somebody comes and asks him
questions.

¹⁸Throwing lots^d settles arguments.
It keeps the two sides from
fighting.

¹⁹A brother who has been insulted is
harder to win back than a
walled city.
And arguments separate people
like the barred gates of a
palace.

²⁰What you say affects how you live.
You will be rewarded by how you
speak.

²¹What you say can mean life or
death.
Those who love to talk will be
rewarded for what they say.

²²A man who finds a wife finds
something good.
She shows that the Lord is
pleased with him.

²³Poor people beg for mercy.
Rich people give rude answers.

²⁴Some friends may ruin you.
But a real friend will be more
loyal than a brother.

19 It is better to be poor and honest
than to be foolish and tell lies.

²Enthusiasm without knowledge is
not good.

If you act too quickly, you might
make a mistake.

³A person's own foolishness ruins
his life.
But in his mind he blames the
Lord for it.

⁴Wealthy people are always finding
more friends.
But the poor lose their friends.

⁵A witness who lies will be
punished.
An untruthful person will not be
left unpunished.

⁶Many people want to please a
leader.
And everyone is friends with
those who give gifts.

⁷A poor person's relatives avoid
him.
Even his friends stay far away!
He runs after them, begging.
But they are gone.

⁸The person who gets wisdom is
good to himself.
And the one who has
understanding will succeed.

⁹A witness who lies will be
punished.
An untruthful person will die.

¹⁰No foolish person should live in
luxury.
No slave should rule over
princes.

¹¹A wise person is patient.
He will be honored if he ignores
a wrong done against him.

¹²A king's anger scares people like
the roar of a lion.
But his kindness is as pleasant as
the dew on the grass.

¹³A foolish son will ruin his father.
And a quarreling wife is as
bothersome as dripping water.

¹⁴Houses and wealth are inherited
from parents.
But a wise wife is a gift from the
Lord.

¹⁵Lazy people sleep a lot.
Idle people will go hungry.

¹⁶Whoever obeys the commands
protects his life.

Whoever is careless in what he does will die.

¹⁷Being kind to the poor is like lending to the Lord.
The Lord will reward you for what you have done.

¹⁸Correct your son while there is still hope.
Do not help him destroy himself.

¹⁹A person who is always getting angry will pay for it.
If you help him, you will have to do it again and again.

²⁰Listen to advice and accept correction.
Then in the end you will be wise.

²¹People can make many different plans.
But only the Lord's plan will happen.

²²People want others to be loyal.
So it is better to be poor than to be a liar.

²³Those who respect the Lord will live
and be content, unbothered by trouble.

²⁴The lazy person may put his hand in the dish,
but he won't lift the food to his mouth!

²⁵Whip a person who makes fun of wisdom, and then foolish people will learn how to think.
Just correct a smart man, and he will gain knowledge.

²⁶A son who robs his father and sends away his mother
brings shame and disgrace on himself.

²⁷Don't stop listening to correction, my child.
If you do, you will not obey what you have already learned.

²⁸An evil witness makes fun of fairness.
And wicked people love what is evil.

²⁹People who make fun of wisdom will be punished.
And the backs of foolish people will be beaten.

20 Wine and beer make people loud and uncontrolled.
It is not wise to get drunk on them.

²A king's anger is like the roar of a lion.
Making him angry may cost you your life.

³Foolish people are always getting into quarrels.
But avoiding quarrels will bring you honor.

⁴A lazy farmer doesn't plow when he should.
So at harvest time he has no crop.

⁵Understanding a person's thoughts is as hard as getting water from a deep well.
But someone with understanding can find the wisdom there.

⁶Many people claim to be loyal.
But it is hard to find someone who really can be trusted.

⁷The good person who lives an honest life
is a blessing to his children.

⁸A king sits on his throne and judges people.
He knows evil when he sees it.

⁹No one can say, "I am innocent. I have never done anything wrong."

¹⁰The Lord hates both these things: dishonest weights and dishonest measures.

¹¹Even a child is known by his behavior.
His actions show if he is innocent and good.

¹²The Lord has made both these things:
Ears that can hear and eyes that can see.

¹³If you love to sleep, you will be poor.
If you stay awake, you will have plenty of food.

¹⁴The buyer says, "This is bad. It's no good."
Then he goes away and brags about what he bought.

¹⁵There is plenty of gold, and there
  are many rubies.
  But there are only a few people
  who speak with knowledge.

¹⁶Take the coat of someone who
  promises to pay what a
  stranger owes.
  Keep it until he pays the
  stranger's bills.

¹⁷When a person gets food
  dishonestly, it may taste sweet
  at first.
  But later he will feel as if he has
  a mouth full of gravel.

¹⁸Get advice if you want your plans
  to work.
  If you go to war, get the advice of
  others.

¹⁹Gossips can't keep secrets.
  So avoid people who talk too
  much.

²⁰Whoever curses his father or
  mother
  will die like a light going out in
  darkness.

²¹Wealth that is gotten quickly in the
  beginning
  will do you no good in the end.

²²Don't say, "I'll pay you back for the
  evil you did."
  Wait for the Lord. He will make
  things right.

²³The Lord hates dishonest weights.
  And dishonest scales do not
  please him.

²⁴The Lord decides what a person
  does.
  So no one can understand what
  his life is all about.

²⁵It's dangerous to promise
  something to God too quickly.
  After you've thought about it, it
  may be too late.

²⁶A wise king finds out who the evil
  people are.
  Then he punishes them.

²⁷The Lord looks into a person's
  feelings.
  He searches through a person's
  thoughts.

²⁸Loyalty and truth keep a king in
  power.
  He continues to rule if he is loyal.

²⁹Young men are admired for their
  strength.
  Old men are honored for their
  experience.

³⁰Hard punishment will get rid of
  evil.
  Whippings can change the evil
  person's heart.

21 The Lord can control a king's
     mind as easily as he controls
     a river.
     He can direct it as he pleases.

²A person may believe he is doing
  right.
  But the Lord judges his reasons.

³Do what is right and fair.
  That is more important to the
  Lord than animal sacrifices.

⁴Proud looks, proud thoughts
  and evil actions are sin.

⁵Those who plan and work hard
  earn a profit.
  But those who act too quickly
  become poor.

⁶Wealth that comes from telling lies
  vanishes like a mist and leads to
  death.

⁷The violence of the wicked will
  destroy them
  because they refuse to do what is
  right.

⁸Guilty people live dishonest lives.
  But honest people do what is
  right.

⁹It is better to live in a corner on the
  roofⁿ
  than inside the house with a
  quarreling wife.

¹⁰An evil person only wants to harm
  others.
  His neighbor will get no mercy
  from him.

¹¹Punish a person who makes fun of
  wisdom, and he will become
  wise.
  But just teach a wise person, and
  he will get knowledge.

21:9 roof In Bible times houses were built with flat roofs. The roof was used for drying things
such as flax and fruit. And it was used as an extra room, as a place for worship and as a place
to sleep in the summer.

[12] God, who is always right, sees the
house of the wicked.
And he brings about the ruin of
every evil person.

[13] If you ignore the poor when they
cry for help,
you also will cry for help and not
be answered.

[14] A gift given secretly will calm an
angry man.
A present given in secrecy will
calm even great anger.

[15] When things are done fairly, good
people are happy,
but evil people are frightened.

[16] A person who does not use
understanding
will join the dead.

[17] Whoever loves pleasure will
become poor.
Whoever loves wine and rich
food will never be wealthy.

[18] Wicked people will suffer instead
of good people.
And those who cannot be trusted
will suffer instead of those who
can.

[19] It is better to live alone in the
desert
than with a quarreling and
complaining wife.

[20] Wise people store up the best foods
and olive oil.
But a foolish person eats up
everything he has.

[21] A person who tries to live right and
be loyal
finds life, success and honor.

[22] A wise person can defeat a city full
of strong men.
He can tear down the defenses
they trust.

[23] A person who is careful about what
he says
keeps himself out of trouble.

[24] People who act with stubborn pride
are called "proud" and
"bragger."

[25] The lazy person's desire for sleep
will kill him
because he refuses to work.

[26] All day long the lazy person wishes
for more.
But the good person gives
without holding back.

[27] The Lord hates sacrifices made by
evil people,
particularly when they make
them for the wrong reasons.

[28] The words of a lying witness will
die.
But the words of an obedient
man will always be
remembered.

[29] A wicked person is stubborn.
But an honest person thinks
carefully about what he does.

[30] There is no wisdom, understanding
or advice
that can succeed against the
Lord.

[31] You can get the horses ready for
battle.
But it is the Lord who gives the
victory.

22 Being respected is more
important than having great
riches.
To be well thought of is better
than owning silver or gold.

[2] The rich and the poor are alike
in that the Lord made them all.

[3] When a wise person sees danger
ahead, he avoids it.
But a foolish person keeps going
and gets into trouble.

[4] Respecting the Lord and not being
proud
will bring you wealth, honor and
life.

[5] The lives of evil people are like
paths covered with thorns and
traps.
People who protect themselves
don't have such problems.

[6] Train a child how to live the right
way.
Then even when he is old, he will
still live that way.

[7] The rich rule over the poor.
And borrowers become servants
to those who lend.

[8] A person who does evil things will
receive trouble in return.
Then he won't be cruel to others
any longer.

⁹A generous person will be blessed because he shares his food with the poor.

¹⁰Get rid of the person who makes fun of wisdom.
Then fighting, quarrels and insults will stop.

¹¹A person who loves innocent thoughts and kind words will have even the king as a friend.

¹²The Lord protects knowledge from being lost.
But he destroys false words.

¹³The lazy person says, "There's a lion outside!
I might get killed out in the street!"

¹⁴The words of an unfaithful wife are like a deep trap.
Those who make the Lord angry will get caught by them.

¹⁵Every child is full of foolishness.
But punishment can get rid of it.

¹⁶The one who gets rich by being cruel to the poor will become poor.
And so will the one who gives presents to the wealthy.

¹⁷Pay attention and listen to what wise people say.
Remember what I am teaching you.

¹⁸It will be good to keep these things in mind.
Be prepared to repeat them.

¹⁹I am teaching them to you now so that you will put your trust in the Lord.

²⁰I have written down 30 sayings for you.
They give knowledge and good advice.

²¹I am teaching you true and reliable words.
Then you can give true answers to anyone who asks.

²²Do not abuse poor people because they are poor.
And do not take away the rights of the needy in court.

²³The Lord will defend them in court.
And he will take the life of those who take away their rights.

²⁴Don't make friends with someone who easily gets angry.
Don't spend time with someone who has a bad temper.

²⁵If you do, you may learn to be like him.
Then you will be in real danger.

²⁶Don't promise to pay what someone else owes.
And don't give guarantees that you will pay what he owes.

²⁷If you cannot pay what he owes, your own bed will be taken and sold.

²⁸Don't move an old stone that shows where a person's land is.
These stones were set up by your ancestors.

²⁹Do you see a man skilled in his work?
That man will work for kings.
He won't have to work for ordinary people.

23 If you sit down to eat with a ruler, notice the food that is in front of you.
²Control yourself if you have a big appetite.
³Don't be greedy for his fine foods.
He might use that rich food to trick you.

⁴Don't wear yourself out trying to get rich.
Be wise enough to control yourself.

⁵Wealth can vanish in the wink of an eye.
It seems to grow wings and fly away like an eagle in the sky.

⁶Don't eat the food of a selfish person.
Don't be greedy for his fine foods.

⁷A selfish person is always worrying about how much the food costs.
He tells you, "Eat and drink."
But he doesn't really mean it.

⁸So you will feel like throwing up the little bit you have eaten.
And you will have wasted your kind words.

⁹Don't speak to a foolish person.
He will only ignore your wise words.

¹⁰Don't move an old stone that shows
  where somebody's land is.
  And don't take fields that belong
  to orphans.
¹¹God, their defender, is strong.
  He will take their side against
  you.

¹²Remember what you are taught.
  And listen carefully to words of
  knowledge.

¹³Don't fail to punish a child.
  If you spank him, you will keep
  him from dying.
¹⁴If you punish him with a spanking,
  you will save him from a fool's
  death.

¹⁵My child, if you are wise,
  then I will be happy.
¹⁶I will be so pleased
  if you speak what is right.

¹⁷Don't envy sinners.
  But always respect the Lord.
¹⁸If you do, you will have hope for
  the future.
  Your wishes will come true.

¹⁹Listen, my child, and be wise.
  Keep your mind on what is right.
²⁰Don't be one of those who drink
  too much wine
  or who eat too much food.
²¹Those who drink too much and eat
  too much become poor.
  They sleep too much and end up
  wearing rags.

²²Listen to your father, who gave you
  life.
  And do not forget your mother
  when she is old.
²³Learn the truth and never reject it.
  Get wisdom, self-control and
  understanding.
²⁴The father of a good child is very
  happy.
  The person who has a wise son is
  glad because of him.
²⁵Make your father and mother
  happy.
  Give your mother a reason to be
  glad.

²⁶My son, pay attention to me.
  And watch closely what I do.
²⁷A prostitute^d is as dangerous as a
  deep pit.
  And an unfaithful wife is like a
  narrow well.
²⁸They ambush you like robbers.

And they cause many men to be
  unfaithful to their wives.

²⁹⁻³⁰Some people drink too much
  wine.
  They try out all the different
  kinds of drinks.
So they have trouble. They are sad.
  They fight. They complain.
They have unnecessary bruises.
  They have bloodshot eyes.
³¹Don't stare at the wine's pretty, red
  color.
  It may sparkle in the cup.
  It may go down your throat
  smoothly.
³²But later it bites like a snake.
  Like a snake, it poisons you.
³³Your eyes will see strange sights.
  And your mind will be confused.
³⁴You will feel dizzy, as if you're out
  on the stormy ocean.
  You will feel as if you're on top of
  a ship's sails.
³⁵You will think, "They hit me, but
  I'm not hurt!
  They have beaten me up, but I
  don't remember it.
I wish I could wake up.
  Then I would get another drink."

24

¹Don't envy evil people.
  Don't try to be friends with
  them.
²In their minds they plan cruel
  things.
  And they always talk about
  making trouble.

³It takes wisdom to have a good
  family.
  It takes understanding to make it
  strong.
⁴It takes knowledge to fill a home
  with rare and beautiful treasures.

⁵A wise man has great power.
  And a man who has knowledge is
  very strong.
⁶So you need the advice of others
  when you go to war.
  If you have many people to give
  advice, you will win.

⁷A foolish person cannot
  understand wisdom.
  He has nothing to say in court.

⁸Whoever makes evil plans
  will be known as a troublemaker.
⁹Making foolish plans is sinful.
  And making fun of others is
  hateful.

¹⁰If you give up when trouble comes,
it shows that you have very little
strength.

¹¹Save those who are being led to
their death.
Rescue those who are about to be
killed.

¹²You may say, "We don't know
anything about this."
But God knows what is in your
mind, and he will notice.
He is watching you, and he will
know.
He will pay each person back for
what he has done.

¹³My child, eat honey because it is
good.
Honey from the honeycomb
tastes sweet.

¹⁴In the same way, wisdom is
pleasing to you.
If you find it, you have hope for
the future.
Your wishes will come true.

¹⁵Don't be like the wicked and attack
a good man's house.
Don't rob the place where he
lives.

¹⁶A good man may be bothered by
trouble seven times, but he
does not give up.
But the wicked are overwhelmed
by trouble.

¹⁷Don't be happy when your enemy
is defeated.
Don't be glad when he is
overwhelmed.

¹⁸The Lord will notice and be
displeased.
Then the Lord may not be angry
with him anymore.

¹⁹Don't envy evil people.
And don't be jealous of the
wicked.

²⁰An evil person has nothing to hope
for.
The wicked will die like a flame
that is put out.

²¹My child, respect the Lord and the
king.
Don't join those people who
refuse to obey them.

²²The Lord and the king will quickly
destroy such people.
Those two can cause great
trouble!

²³These are also wise sayings:

It is not good to take sides when
you are the judge.

²⁴Don't say that the wicked have
done right.
People will curse you, and
nations will hate you.

²⁵But things will go well for judges
who punish the guilty.
And they will receive good things
from God.

²⁶An honest answer is as pleasing
as a kiss on the lips.

²⁷First, you should work outside
and prepare your fields.
After that, you can start having
your family.

²⁸Don't testify against your neighbor
for no good reason.
Don't say things that are false.

²⁹Don't say, "I'll get even with that
man.
I'll do to him what he did to me."

³⁰I passed by a lazy person's field.
I went by the vineyard of a man
who had no sense.

³¹Thorns had grown up everywhere.
The ground was covered with
weeds.
And the stone walls had fallen
down.

³²I thought about what I had seen.
I learned this lesson from what I
saw.

³³You sleep a little; you take a nap.
You fold your hands and rest.

³⁴Soon you will be poor, as if you had
been robbed.
You will have as little as if you
had been held up.

25 These are more wise sayings of
Solomon. They were copied by the
men of Hezekiah king of Judah.

²God is honored for what he keeps
secret.
Kings are honored for what they
can discover.

³No one can measure the height of
the skies or the depth of the
earth.
So also no one can understand
the mind of a king.

⁴Remove the scum from the silver.
Then the silver can be used by
the silversmith.

⁵Remove wicked people from the
king's presence.

Then his government will be
honest and last a long time.

⁶Don't brag to the king.
Don't act as if you are a great
man.
⁷It is better for him to promote you
to a higher job
than to give you a less important
position.

Because of something you have
seen,
⁸ do not quickly take someone to
court.
What will you do later
when your neighbor proves you
are wrong?

⁹If you have an argument with your
neighbor,
don't tell other people what was
said.
¹⁰Whoever hears it might say bad
things about you.
And you might not ever be
respected again.

¹¹The right word spoken at the right
time
is as beautiful as gold apples in a
silver bowl.

¹²The warning of a wise person is
valuable to someone who will
listen.
It is worth as much as gold
earrings or fine gold jewelry.

¹³A trustworthy messenger refreshes
those who send him.
He is like the coolness of snow in
the summertime.

¹⁴People who brag about gifts they
never give
are like clouds and wind that
give no rain.

¹⁵With patience you can convince a
ruler.
And a gentle word can get
through to the hard-headed.

¹⁶If you find honey, don't eat too
much.
Too much of it will make you
sick.

¹⁷Don't go to your neighbor's house
too often.
Too much of you will make him
hate you.

¹⁸Anyone who lies about his neighbor
hurts him as a club, a sword or a
sharp arrow would.

¹⁹Don't trust unfaithful people when
you are in trouble.
It's like eating with a broken
tooth or walking with a
crippled foot.

²⁰Don't sing songs to someone who is
sad.
It's like taking off a coat on a
cold day
or pouring vinegar on soda.

²¹If your enemy is hungry, feed him.
If he is thirsty, give him a drink.
²²Doing this will be like pouring
burning coals on his head.
And the Lord will reward you.

²³The north wind brings rain.
In the same way, telling gossip
brings angry looks.

²⁴It is better to live in a corner on the
roof ⁿ
than inside the house with a
quarreling wife.

²⁵Hearing good news from a faraway
place
is like having a cool drink when
you are tired.

²⁶A good person who gives in to evil
is like a muddy spring or a dirty
well.

²⁷It is not good to eat too much honey.
In the same way, it is not good to
brag about yourself.

²⁸A person who does not control
himself
is like a city whose walls have
been broken down.

26 It shouldn't snow in summer or
rain at harvest.
Neither should a foolish person
ever be honored.

²Curses will not harm someone who
is innocent.
They are like sparrows or
swallows that fly around and
never land.

³A whip is used to guide a horse,
and a harness is used for a
donkey.

25:24 roof In Bible times houses were built with flat roofs. The roof was used for drying things
such as flax and fruit. And it was used as an extra room, as a place for worship and as a place
to sleep in the summer.

In the same way, a paddle is used
on a foolish person to guide
him.

⁴Don't give a foolish person a
foolish answer.
If you do, you will be just like
him.

⁵But answer a foolish person as he
should be answered.
If you don't, he will think he is
really wise.

⁶Don't send a message by a foolish
person.
That would be like cutting off
your feet or drinking poison.

⁷A wise saying spoken by a fool
does no good.
It is like the legs of a crippled
person.

⁸Giving honor to a foolish person
does no good.
It is like tying a stone in a
slingshot.

⁹A wise saying spoken by a fool
is like a thorn stuck in the hand
of a drunk.

¹⁰Someone might employ a foolish
person or anyone just passing
by.
That employer is like an archer
who shoots at anything he
sees.

¹¹A dog eats what it throws up.
And a foolish person repeats his
foolishness.

¹²Some people think they are wise.
There is more hope for a foolish
person than for them.

¹³The lazy person says, "There's a
lion in the road.
There's a lion in the streets!"

¹⁴The lazy person is like a door that
turns back and forth on its
hinges.
He stays in bed and turns over
and over.

¹⁵The lazy person may put his hand
in the dish.
But he's too tired to lift the food
to his mouth.

¹⁶The lazy person thinks he is wiser
than seven people who give
sensible answers.

¹⁷To grab a dog by the ears is asking
for trouble.
So is interfering in someone
else's quarrel if you're just
passing by.

¹⁸⁻¹⁹A person shouldn't trick his
neighbor
and then say, "I was just joking!"
That is like a madman shooting
deadly, burning arrows.

²⁰Without wood, a fire will go out.
And without gossip, quarreling
will stop.

²¹Charcoal and wood keep a fire
going.
In the same way, a quarrelsome
person keeps an argument
going.

²²The words of a gossip are like tasty
bits of food.
People take them all in.

²³Kind words from a wicked mind
are like a shiny coating on a clay
pot.

²⁴A person who hates you may fool
you with his words.
But in his mind he is planning
evil.

²⁵His words are kind, but don't
believe him.
His mind is full of evil thoughts.

²⁶He hides his hate with lies.
But his evil will be plain to
everyone.

²⁷Whoever digs a deep trap for
others will fall into it himself.
Whoever tries to roll a boulder
over others will be crushed
by it.

²⁸A liar hates the people he hurts.
And false praise can ruin others.

27 Don't brag about what will
happen tomorrow.
You don't really know what
will happen then.

²Don't praise yourself. Let someone
else do it.
Let the praise come from a
stranger and not from your
own mouth.

³Stone is heavy, and sand is hard to
carry.
But the complaining of a foolish
person causes more trouble
than either.

⁴Anger is cruel. It destroys like a
flood.
But who can put up with
jealousy!

⁵It is better to correct someone
openly
than to love him and not show it.

⁶The slap of a friend can be trusted
to help you.
But the kisses of an enemy are
nothing but lies.

⁷When someone is full, not even
honey tastes good.
But when he is hungry, even
something bitter tastes sweet.

⁸A man who leaves his home
is like a bird that leaves its nest.

⁹Perfume and oils make you happy.
And good advice from a friend is
sweet.

¹⁰Don't forget your friend or your
father's friend.
Don't always go to your brother
for help when trouble comes.
A neighbor close by is better
than a brother far away.

¹¹Be wise, my child, and you will
make me happy.
Then I can respond to any insult.

¹²When a wise person sees danger
ahead, he avoids it.
But a foolish person keeps going
and gets into trouble.

¹³Take the coat of someone who
promises to pay what a
stranger owes.
Keep it until he pays the
stranger's bills.

¹⁴Don't greet your neighbor loudly
early in the morning.
He will think of it as a curse.

¹⁵A quarreling wife is as bothersome
as a continual dripping on a
rainy day.

¹⁶Stopping her is like stopping the
wind.
It's like trying to grab oil in your
hand.

¹⁷Iron can sharpen iron.
In the same way, people can help
each other.

¹⁸The person who tends a fig tree will
eat its fruit.

And the person who takes care of
his master will be honored.

¹⁹As water shows you your face,
so your mind shows you what
kind of person you are.

²⁰People will never stop dying and
being destroyed.
In the same way, people will
never stop wanting more than
they have.

²¹A hot furnace tests silver and gold.
And people are tested by the
praise they receive.

²²Even if you ground up a foolish
person like grain in a bowl,
you couldn't remove his
foolishness.

²³Be sure you know how your sheep
are doing.
Pay close attention to the
condition of your cattle.

²⁴Riches will not continue forever.
Nor do governments continue
forever.

²⁵Bring in the hay. Let the new grass
appear.
Gather the grass from the hills.

²⁶Make clothes from the lambs' wool.
Sell some goats to buy a field.

²⁷There will be plenty of goat milk
to feed you and your family.
It will make your servant girls
healthy.

28 Evil people run even though no
one is chasing them.
But good people are as brave
as a lion.

²When a country is disobedient, it
has one ruler after another.
But when it is led by a man with
understanding and knowledge,
it continues strong.

³Rulers who are cruel to the poor
are like a hard rain that destroys
the crops.

⁴People who disobey what they have
been taught praise the wicked.
But those who obey what they
have been taught are against
the wicked.

⁵Evil people do not understand
fairness.
But those who follow the Lord
understand it completely.

⁶It is better to be poor and innocent
than to be rich and wicked.

⁷The son who obeys what he has
been taught
shows he is smart.
But the son who makes friends
with those who have no
self-control
disgraces his father.

⁸Some people get rich by
overcharging others.
But their wealth will be given to
those who are kind to the poor.

⁹If you refuse to obey what you have
been taught,
your prayers will not be heard.

¹⁰Those who lead honest people to do
wrong
will be ruined by their own evil.
But the innocent will be
rewarded with good things.

¹¹A rich man may think he is wise.
But a poor man who has
understanding knows the rich
man is wrong.

¹²When good people win, there is
great happiness.
But when the wicked get power,
everybody hides.

¹³If you hide your sins, you will not
succeed.
If you confess and reject them,
you will receive mercy.

¹⁴Those who always respect the Lord
will be happy.
But those who are stubborn will
get into trouble.

¹⁵A wicked ruler is as dangerous to
poor people
as a roaring lion or a charging
bear.

¹⁶A ruler who is cruel does not have
wisdom.
But the one who hates money
taken dishonestly will live a
long time.

¹⁷A man who is guilty of murder
will run until he dies.
So do not stop him.

¹⁸Innocent people will be kept safe.
But those who are dishonest will
suddenly be ruined.

¹⁹The person who works his land will
have plenty of food.

But the one who chases useless
dreams instead will end up
very poor.

²⁰A truthful man will have many
blessings.
But those eager to get rich will be
punished.

²¹It is not good for a judge to take
sides.
But some will sin for just a piece
of bread.

²²A selfish person is in a hurry to get
rich.
He does not realize his
selfishness will make him poor.

²³Those who correct others will later
be liked
more than those who give false
praise.

²⁴Some people rob their fathers or
mothers
and say, "It's not wrong."
Such people are just like those
who destroy things.

²⁵A greedy person causes trouble.
But the one who trusts the Lord
will succeed.

²⁶The person who trusts in himself is
foolish.
But the person who lives wisely
will be kept safe.

²⁷The person who gives to the poor
will have everything he needs.
But the one who ignores the poor
will have many curses put on
him.

²⁸When the wicked get power,
everybody hides.
But when the wicked die, the
good people do well.

29 Some people are still stubborn
after they have been
corrected many times.
But they will suddenly be hurt
beyond cure.

²When good people do well,
everyone is happy.
But when evil people rule,
everyone groans.

³Whoever loves wisdom makes his
father happy.
But the one who makes friends
with prostitutes^d wastes his
money.

[4] If a king is fair, he makes his
country strong.
But if he takes money
dishonestly, he tears his
country down.

[5] Anyone who gives false praise to
his neighbor
is setting a trap for him.

[6] An evil person is trapped by his
own sin.
But a good person can sing and
be happy.

[7] Good people are concerned that the
poor are treated fairly.
But the wicked don't care.

[8] People who make fun of others
cause trouble in a city.
But wise people calm anger
down.

[9] A wise man should not take a
foolish person to court.
The fool will only shout or laugh
at him. There will be no peace.

[10] Murderers hate honest people.
But those who do right try to
protect them.

[11] A foolish person loses his temper.
But a wise person controls his
anger.

[12] If a ruler pays attention to lies,
then all his officers will become
wicked.

[13] The poor person and the cruel
person are alike in this way:
The Lord gave eyes to both of
them.

[14] A king should judge poor people
fairly.
Then his government will
continue forever.

[15] Punishment and correction make a
child wise.
If he is left to do as he pleases, he
will disgrace his mother.

[16] When there are many wicked
people, there is much sin.
But those who do right will see
them destroyed.

[17] Correct your child, and you will be
proud of him.
He will give you pleasure.

[18] Where there is no word from God,
people are uncontrolled.

But those who obey what they
have been taught are happy.

[19] Words alone cannot correct a
servant.
Even if he understands, he won't
respond.

[20] Sometimes you see people who
speak too quickly.
There is more hope for a foolish
person than for them.

[21] Don't spoil your servant when he is
young.
If you do, he will bring you grief
later on.

[22] An angry person causes trouble.
A person who easily gets angry
sins a lot.

[23] A man's pride will ruin him.
But a person who is humble will
be honored.

[24] The partner of a thief is his own
worst enemy.
He has to testify in court, but he
is afraid to say anything.

[25] Being afraid of people can get you
into trouble.
But if you trust the Lord, you will
be safe.

[26] Many people want to be heard by a
ruler.
But fairness comes from the
Lord.

[27] Good people hate those who are
dishonest.
And the wicked hate those who
are honest.

30 These are the words of Agur son
of Jakeh. This is his message to
Ithiel and Ucal:

[2] "I am the most stupid person there
is.
I have no understanding.
[3] I have not learned to be wise.
And I don't know much about
God, the Holy One.
[4] Who has gone up to heaven and
come back down?
Who can hold the wind in his
hand?
Who can gather up the waters in
his coat?
Who has decided where the ends
of the earth will be?

What is his name? And what is his
son's name?
Surely, you know!

⁵"Every word of God can be trusted.
He protects those who come to
him for safety.
⁶Do not add to his words.
If you do, he will correct you and
prove that you are a liar.

⁷"I ask two things from you, Lord.
Don't refuse me before I die.
⁸Keep me from lying and being
dishonest.
And don't make me either rich or
poor.
Just give me enough food for
each day.
⁹If I have too much, I might reject
you.
I might say, 'I don't know the
Lord.'
If I am poor, I might steal.
Then I would disgrace the name
of my God.

¹⁰"Do not say bad things about a
servant to his master.
If you do, he will curse you, and
you will suffer for it.

¹¹"Some people curse their fathers.
And they do not bless their
mothers.
¹²Some people think they are pure.
But they are not really free from
evil.
¹³Some people have such a proud
look!
They look down on others.
¹⁴Some people have teeth like
swords.
It is as if their jaws are full of
knives.
They want to remove the poor
people from the earth.
They want to get rid of the needy.

¹⁵"Greed has two daughters.
Their names are 'Give me. Give
me.'
There are three things that are
never satisfied.
There are really four that never
say, 'I've had enough!'
¹⁶These things are the cemetery, the
childless mother,
the land that never gets enough
rain,
and fire that never says, 'I've had
enough!'

¹⁷"Don't make fun of your father.
Don't refuse to obey your mother.
If you do, your eye will be pecked
out by the birds of the valley.
You will be eaten by hawks.

¹⁸"There are three things that are too
hard for me.
There are really four that I don't
understand:
¹⁹the way an eagle flies in the sky,
the way a snake slides over a
rock,
the way a ship sails on the sea
and the way a man acts with a
girl.

²⁰"This is the way a woman who
takes part in adultery[d] acts:
She sins and doesn't care.
She says, 'I haven't done
anything wrong.'

²¹"There are three things that make
the earth tremble.
There are really four that it
cannot stand:
²²a servant who becomes a king,
a foolish person who has plenty
to eat,
²³a hateful woman who gets married
and a maid who replaces her
mistress.

²⁴"There are four things on earth that
are small.
But they are very wise:
²⁵Ants are not very strong.
But they store up food in the
summer.
²⁶Rock badgers are not powerful
animals.
But they can live among the
rocks.
²⁷Locusts[d] have no king.
But they all go out in formation.
²⁸And lizards can be caught in the
hand.
But they are found even in kings'
palaces.

²⁹"There are three things that strut
proudly.
There are really four that walk as
if they are important:
³⁰Lions are the proudest animals.
They are strong and run from
nothing.
³¹Roosters and male goats strut
proudly.
And so does a king when his
army is around him.

³²"You may have been foolish and
proud.
If you planned evil, cover your
mouth.
³³Stirring milk makes butter.
Twisting noses makes them
bleed.
And stirring up anger makes
trouble."

31 These are the words of King Lemuel. This is the message his
mother taught him:

²"My son, I gave birth to you.
You are the son I prayed for.
³Don't waste your strength on
women.
Don't waste your time on those
who ruin kings.
⁴"Kings should not drink wine,
Lemuel.
Rulers should not desire beer.
⁵If they drink, they might forget the
law.
They might keep the needy from
getting their rights.
⁶Give beer to people who are dying.
And give wine to those who are
sad.
⁷Let them drink and forget their
need.
Then they won't remember their
misery anymore.

⁸"Speak up for those who cannot
speak for themselves.
Defend the rights of all those
who have nothing.
⁹Speak up and judge fairly.
Defend the rights of the poor and
needy."

¹⁰It is hard to find an excellent wife.
She is worth more than rubies.
¹¹Her husband trusts her completely.
With her, he has everything he
needs.
¹²She does him good and not harm
for as long as she lives.
¹³She looks for wool and linen.
She likes to work with her hands.
¹⁴She is like a trader's ship.
She goes far to get food.

¹⁵She gets up while it is still dark.
She prepares food for her family.
She also feeds her servant girls.
¹⁶She looks at a field and buys it.
With money she has earned, she
plants a vineyard.
¹⁷She does her work with energy.
Her arms are strong.
¹⁸She makes sure that what she
makes is good.
She works by her lamp late into
the night.
¹⁹She makes thread with her hands
and weaves her own cloth.
²⁰She welcomes the poor.
She helps the needy.
²¹She does not worry about her family when it snows.
They all have fine clothes to keep
them warm.
²²She makes coverings for her bed.
Her clothes are made of linen
and other expensive material.
²³Her husband is recognized at the
city meetings.
He makes decisions as one of the
leaders of the land.
²⁴She makes linen clothes and sells
them.
She provides belts to the merchants.
²⁵She is strong and is respected by
the people.
She looks forward to the future
with joy.
²⁶She speaks wise words.
And she teaches others to be
kind.
²⁷She watches over her family.
And she is always busy.
²⁸Her children bless her.
Her husband also praises her.
²⁹He says, "There are many excellent
wives,
but you are better than all of
them."
³⁰Charm can fool you, and beauty
can trick you.
But a woman who respects the
Lord should be praised.
³¹Give her the reward she has
earned.
She should be openly praised for
what she has done.

The Book of
ECCLESIASTES

1 These are the words of the Teacher. He is a son of David, king in Jerusalem. [2] The Teacher says,

"Useless! Useless!
Completely useless!
All things are useless."

[3] What do people really gain
from all the hard work they do
here on earth?

[4] People live, and people die.
But the earth continues forever.
[5] The sun rises, and the sun sets.
Then it hurries back to the place
where it rises again.
[6] The wind blows to the south.
Then it blows to the north.
It blows from one direction and
then another.
Then it turns around and repeats
the same pattern, going nowhere.
[7] All the rivers flow to the sea.
But the sea never becomes full.
[8] Everything is boring.
It makes you so tired you don't
even want to talk about it.
Words come again and again to our
ears.
But we never can hear enough.
Nor can we ever really see all we
want to see.
[9] All things continue the way they
have been since the beginning.
The same things will be done that
have always been done.
There is nothing new here on
earth.
[10] A person might say,
"Look, this is new!"
But really it has always been here.
It was here before we were!
[11] People don't remember what happened long ago.
In the future, people will not remember what happens now.
And later, other people will not remember what was done before
them.

[12] I, the Teacher, was king over Israel in Jerusalem. [13] I decided to use my wisdom. I wanted to learn about everything that happens here on earth. I learned that God has given us terrible things to face here on earth. [14] I looked at everything done here on earth. I saw that it is all a waste of time. It is like chasing the wind.

[15] If something is crooked,
you can't make it straight.
If something is missing,
you can't say it is there.

[16] I said to myself, "I have become very wise. I am now wiser than anyone who ruled Jerusalem before me. I know that wisdom and knowledge really are." [17] So I decided to find out how wisdom and knowledge are better than foolish thinking. But I learned that trying to become wise is also like chasing the wind.

[18] With much wisdom comes much
disappointment.
The person who gains more
knowledge also gains more
sorrow.

2 I said to myself, "I will try having fun. I will enjoy myself." But I found that this is also useless. [2] It is foolish to laugh all the time. Having fun gets nothing done. [3] I decided to cheer myself up with wine. At the same time my mind was still thinking wisely. I wanted to find a way to enjoy myself. I wanted to see what was good for people to do during their few days of life.

[4] Then I did great things. I built houses, and I planted vineyards for myself. [5] I planted gardens, and I made parks. I planted all kinds of fruit trees in them. [6] I made pools of water for myself. And I used them to water my growing trees. [7] I bought men and women slaves. Slaves were also born in my house. I had large herds of cattle and flocks of sheep. I had more than anyone in Jerusalem before me. [8] I also gathered silver and gold for myself. I took treasures from kings and other areas. I had men and women singers. I had all the wives a man could ever want. [9] I became very famous. I was greater than anyone who had lived in Jerusalem before me. My wisdom helped me in all this.

[10] Anything I saw and wanted, I got
for myself.
I did not miss any pleasure I
desired.
I was pleased with everything I did.
And this pleasure was the reward
for all my hard work.

[11]But then I looked at what I had
done.
I thought about all the hard
work.
Suddenly I realized it was just a
waste of time, like chasing the
wind!
There is nothing to gain from
anything we do here on earth.

[12]Then I began to think again about
being wise.
And I thought also about being
foolish and doing crazy things.
But after all, what more can any
king do?
He can only do what some other
king has already done.

[13]I saw that being wise is certainly
better than being foolish,
just as light is better than
darkness.

[14]A wise man sees where he is going.
But a foolish person is like
someone walking around in the
dark.
Yet I saw that
both the foolish person and the
wise man end the same way.

[15]I thought to myself,
"What happens to a foolish person
will happen to me, too.
So what do I get for being so
wise?"
I said to myself,
"Being wise is also useless."

[16]The wise man and the foolish
person
will both die!
People will not remember either
one forever.
In the future, both will be
forgotten.

[17]So I hated life. It made me sad to
think that everything here on earth is
useless. It is like chasing the wind. [18]I
hated all the things I had worked for
here on earth. I hated them because I
must leave them to someone who will
live after me. [19]Someone else will control everything for which I worked so
hard here on earth. And I don't know if
he will be wise or foolish. This is also
useless. [20]So I became sad about all the
hard work I had done here on earth. [21]A
person can work hard using all his wisdom, knowledge and skill. But he will
die, and other people will get the things
he worked for. They did not do the work,
but they will get everything. This is also

unfair and useless. [22]What does a person
get for all his work and struggling here
on earth? [23]All his life his work is full of
pain and sorrow. Even at night his mind
doesn't rest. This is also useless.

[24]The best a person can do is eat, drink
and enjoy his work. I saw that even this
comes from God. [25]No one can eat or
enjoy life without God. [26]If a person
pleases God, God will give him wisdom,
knowledge and joy. But the sinner will
get only the work of gathering and storing wealth. Then he will have to give it
to the one who pleases God. So all his
work is useless. It is like chasing the
wind.

3 There is a right time for everything.
Everything on earth has its
special season.

[2]There is a time to be born
and a time to die.
There is a time to plant
and a time to pull up plants.
[3]There is a time to kill
and a time to heal.
There is a time to destroy
and a time to build.
[4]There is a time to cry
and a time to laugh.
There is a time to be sad
and a time to dance.
[5]There is a time to throw away
stones
and a time to gather them.
There is a time to hug
and a time not to hug.
[6]There is a time to look for
something
and a time to stop looking for it.
There is a time to keep things
and a time to throw things away.
[7]There is a time to tear apart
and a time to sew together.
There is a time to be silent
and a time to speak.
[8]There is a time to love
and a time to hate.
There is a time for war
and a time for peace.

[9]Does a person really gain anything
from his work? [10]I saw the hard work
God has given us to do. [11]God has also
given us a desire to know the future.
God certainly does everything at just the
right time. But we can never completely
understand what he is doing. [12]So I realize that the best thing for people is to be
happy. They should enjoy themselves as
long as they live. [13]God wants everyone
to eat and drink and be happy in his

work. These are gifts from God. [14]I know anything God does will continue forever. People cannot add anything to what God has done. And they cannot take anything away from it. God does it this way to cause people to honor him.

[15]What happens now has also
　happened in the past.
Things that will happen in the
　future have also happened
　before.
God makes the same things
　happen again and again.

[16]I also saw this here on earth:
Where there should have been
　justice, there was evil.
Where there should have been
　fairness, there was wickedness.
[17]I certainly believe that
God has planned a time for every
　thing and every action.
He will judge both good people
　and bad people.

[18]But I decided that God leaves it the way it is to test people. He wants to show them they are just like animals. [19]The same thing happens to animals and to people. They both have the same breath. So they both die. People are no better off than the animals. The lives of both are soon gone. [20]Both end up the same way. Both came from dust. And both will go back to dust. [21]Who can be sure that the spirit of man goes up to God? Or who can be sure that the spirit of an animal goes down into the ground? [22]So I saw the best thing a person can do is to enjoy his work. That is all he has. No one can help a person see what will happen in the future.

4 Again I saw all the people who were treated badly here on earth.
I saw their tears.
　I saw that they had no one to
　　comfort them.
Cruel people had all the power.
　There was no one to comfort the
　　people they hurt.
[2]I decided that the dead
　are better off than the living.
[3]But those who have never been
　born
　are better off still.
They have not seen the evil
　that is done here on earth.
[4]I realized the reason people work hard and try to succeed: They are jealous of each other. This, too, is useless. It is like chasing the wind.

[5]Some say that it is foolish to fold
　your hands and do nothing.
You will starve to death!
[6]Maybe so, but I say it is better to be
　content
with what little you have.
Otherwise, you will always be
　struggling for more.
That is like chasing the wind.

[7]Again I saw something here on
　earth that was senseless:
[8]I saw a person who had no family.
　He had no son or brother.
He always worked hard.
　But he was never satisfied with
　　what he had.
He never asked himself, "For whom
　am I working so hard?
Why don't I let myself enjoy
　life?"
This also is very sad and senseless.

[9]Two people are better than one.
　They get more done by working
　　together.
[10]If one person falls,
　the other can help him up.
But it is bad for the person who is
　alone when he falls.
　No one is there to help him.
[11]If two lie down together, they will
　be warm.
But a person alone will not be
　warm.
[12]An enemy might defeat one person,
　but two people together can
　　defend themselves.
A rope that has three parts
　wrapped together
is hard to break.

[13]A young person may be poor but wise. He is better than a foolish, old king who doesn't listen to advice. [14]I saw such a young person become king. He had been born poor in the kingdom. He had even gone to prison before becoming king. [15]I watched some of the people who live on earth follow him. They made him their king. [16]Yes, a great many people followed him at first. But later, they did not like him, either. So fame and power are shown to be useless. They are like chasing the wind.

5 Be careful when you go to worship at the Temple.[d] It is better to listen than to offer foolish sacrifices. People who do this don't even know they are doing wrong.

[2] Think before you speak.
Be careful about what you
promise to God.
God is in heaven,
and you are on the earth.
So say only a few words to God.
[3] The saying is true: Bad dreams
come from too much worrying.
So too many words come from
foolish people.

[4] If you make a promise to God, don't be slow to keep it. God is not happy with foolish people. Give God what you promised. [5] It is better not to promise anything than to promise something and not do it. [6] So don't let your words cause you to sin. Also, don't say to the priest at the Temple, "I didn't mean what I promised!" If you do, God will become angry with your words. He will destroy everything you have worked for. [7] Many empty promises are like many foolish dreams. They mean nothing. You should honor God.

[8] In some countries you will see poor people treated badly. They are not treated fairly or given their rights. Don't be surprised! One officer is cheated by a higher officer. They in turn are cheated by even higher officers. [9] The wealth of the country is divided up among them all. Even the king makes sure he gets his share of the profits.

[10] The person who loves money
will never have all the money he
wants.
The person who loves wealth
will not be satisfied when he gets
it.
This is also useless.
[11] The more wealth a person has,
the more friends he has to help
him spend it.
So what does he really gain?
He gains nothing except to look
at his riches.
[12] A man who works hard sleeps in
peace.
It is not important if he has little
or much to eat.
But a rich person worries about his
wealth.
He cannot sleep.

[13] I have seen something unfair here
on earth:
A person suffers harm from
saving up his money.

[14] Then he loses it all in a bad deal.
So he has nothing
to give to his son.
[15] A person comes into this world
with nothing.
And when he dies, he leaves with
nothing.
In spite of all his hard work,
he leaves exactly as he came.
[16] This, too, is unfair:
He leaves exactly as he came.
So what does he gain from
chasing the wind?
[17] All he gets are days filled with
sadness and sorrow.
He ends up sick, defeated and
angry.

[18] I have seen what is best for a person to do here on earth. He should eat and drink and enjoy his work. This is because the life God has given him on earth is short. [19] God gives some people the ability to enjoy the wealth and property he gives them. He also gives them the ability to accept their state in life and enjoy their work. [20] Such people do not worry much about how short life is. This is because God keeps them busy with the things they love to do.

6 I have seen something else unfair here on earth. It causes serious problems for people. [2] God gives some people great wealth, riches and honor. They have everything they want. But God does not let them enjoy such things. Someone else enjoys them instead. This is unfair and senseless. [3] It is sad when a person can't enjoy the good things God gives him. Such a person might have 100 children. He might live a long time. But what good is it if he can't enjoy the good God gives him? I say a baby who is born dead is better off than he is. [4] It is useless for such a baby to be born. It ends up in the darkness of the grave without even a name. [5] That baby never saw the sun. It never knew anything. But it finds more rest than the person who never gets to enjoy the good things God gives him. [6] Even if he lives 2,000 years, it is sad if a person can't enjoy the good things God gives him. After all, both he and the baby born dead go to the same place—the grave.
[7] A person works just to feed
himself.
But he never seems to get enough
to eat.

[8]In this way a wise man
    is no better off than a foolish
      person.
Then, too, it does a poor man little
    good
    to know how to get along in life.
[9]So it is better to be happy with
    what you have
    than always to be wanting more.
Always wanting more is useless—
    like chasing the wind.

[10]Everything that happens was
    planned long ago.
A man is only what he was
    created to be.
It is useless to argue with God
    about it.
    This is because God is more
      powerful than man is.
[11]The more you argue,
    the more useless it is.
    You gain nothing at all by
      arguing.

[12]A person has only a few days of life
on the earth. His short life passes like a
shadow. And who knows what is best
for him while he lives? Who can tell him
what will happen after his time on earth?

7It is better to have respect than
    good perfume.
    The day a person dies is better
      than the day he was born.
[2]It is better to go to a funeral
    than to a party.
We all must die.
    Everyone living should think
      about this.
[3]Sorrow is better than laughter.
    Sadness has a good influence on
      you.
[4]A wise man thinks about death,
    but a foolish person thinks only
      about having a good time.
[5]It is better to be criticized by a wise
    man
    than to be praised by a foolish
      person.
[6]The laughter of foolish people is
    useless.
    It is like heating a pot by burning
      straw.
    There is a lot of fire but no heat.

[7]Even a wise man will become
    foolish
    if he lets money change his
      thinking.

[8]It is better to finish something
    than to start it.

It is better to be patient
    than to be proud.
[9]Don't become mad quickly,
    because getting angry is foolish.

[10]Don't ask, "Why was life better in
    the 'good old days'?"
    It is not wise to ask such
      questions.

[11]Wisdom is as good to have as
    inheriting property.
    It helps people see what to do.
[12]Wisdom is like money.
    They both help a person.
But wisdom is better than money,
    because it can save a person's
      life.

[13]Stop and think about everything
    that God causes to happen.
You cannot change a thing,
    even if you think it is wrong.
[14]When life is good, enjoy it.
    But when life is hard, remember:
God gives us good times and hard
    times.
    And no one knows what
      tomorrow will bring.

[15]In my short life I have seen both of
    these:
I have seen good men die being
    good.
    And I have seen evil men living a
      long time.
[16]Don't try to be too right all the
    time.
    Don't try to be too wise, either.
    Why should you destroy yourself
      this way?
[17]Don't be too wicked.
    And don't be a foolish person.
    You will die young if you do so.
[18]Try to avoid going too far in doing
    anything.
    Those who honor God will avoid
      doing too much of anything.

[19]Wisdom gives a person strength.
    One wise man is stronger than
      ten leaders in a city.

[20]Surely there is not a good man on
    earth
    who always does good and never
      sins.

[21]Don't listen to everything people
    say.
    You might hear your servant
      insulting you.
[22]You know that many times
    you also have insulted others.

23 I used wisdom to test all these
  things.
   I wanted to be wise,
     but it was too hard for me.
24 I cannot understand why things are
  as they are.
   It is too hard for anyone to
     understand.
25 I studied and tried very hard to find
  wisdom.
   I tried to find some meaning for
     everything.
   I learned that it is foolish to be evil.
     And it is crazy to act like a fool.
26 I found that some women are worse
  than death.
   They are as dangerous as traps.
     Their love is like a net.
   Their arms hold men like chains.
   A man who follows God will run
     away from them.
   But a sinner will be caught by
     them.

27 The Teacher says, "This is what I
  learned:
   I added all these things together
     to see if I could find some
       meaning for everything.
28 I am still looking for it,
     but I have not found it.
   But I did discover that truly good
     people are hard to find.
   Such people are one in a million!
29 One thing I have learned:
   God made people good.
     But people have found all kinds
       of ways to be bad."

8 No one is like the wise man.
   He can understand what things
     mean.
   His wisdom makes him happy.
     It makes his sad face happy.

2 I advise you always to obey the king's
command. Do this because you made a
promise to God. 3 Don't be too quick to
quit the job the king gave you. But don't
support something that is wrong. Remember, the king does whatever he
pleases. 4 The king is the highest power.
No one can tell him what to do.

5 A person will be safe if he obeys
  the king's command.
   A wise man knows how to do the
     right thing at the right time.
6 And there is a right time and a
  right way for everything.
   Yet people often have many
     troubles.

7 They do not know what the future
  holds.
   No one can tell them what will
     happen.
8 No one has the power to keep the
  wind from blowing.
   No one has the power to stop his
     own death.
   During war a soldier cannot go
     home.
   So also, the person who does evil
     will not get away free.

9 I saw all of this as I studied. I considered all that is done here on earth. And
I saw men rule others and hurt them. 10 I
saw evil people being buried. They used
to go in and out of the holy place. Good
things were said about them in the same
towns where they had done evil. This is
senseless, too.
  11 Sometimes people are not punished
right away for the bad things they do.
That makes other people want to do bad
things, too. 12 A sinner might do a hundred evil things. And he might live a
long time. Even so, I know it will be better for those who honor God. They fear
him, and he sees it. 13 And I also know it
will not go well for evil people. Their
lives will be like a brief shadow. They
will not live very long. 14 But sometimes
something senseless happens on earth.
Bad things happen to good people.
Good things happen to bad people. This
is truly senseless. 15 So I decided it was
more important to enjoy life. The best
that people can do here on earth is to
eat, drink and enjoy life. These joys will
help people do the hard work God gives
them here on earth.
  16 I used my mind to learn about all
that happens on earth. I saw how busy
people are. They work day and night
and hardly ever sleep. 17 I also saw all
that God has done. Nobody can understand what God does here on earth. No
matter how hard a person tries to understand it, he cannot. Even if a wise man
says he understands, he really cannot.
No one at all can really understand it.
9 I thought about something else and
   tried hard to understand it. I saw that
God takes care of both good people and
wise people and what they do. But no one
knows if he will see good or bad times.

2 Both good and bad things happen
  to everyone.
   They happen to those who are
     fair and to those who are
       wicked.

They happen to those who are good
    and to those who are evil.
They happen to those who
    sacrifice and to those who do
    not.
The same things happen to a good
    person
    as happen to a sinner.
The same things happen to a
    person who makes promises to
    God
    as to one who does not.

[3]This is something unfair that happens here on earth. The same things happen to everyone. So men's minds are full of evil and foolish thoughts while they live. After that, they join the dead. [4]But anyone still alive has hope. Even a live dog is better off than a dead lion!

[5]The living know they will die.
    But the dead no longer think
    about such things.
Dead people have no more reward.
    People forget them.
[6]After a person is dead,
    he can no longer show love or
    hate or jealousy.
And he will never again share
    in the things that happen here on
    earth.
[7]So go eat your food and enjoy it.
    Drink your wine and be happy.
It is all right with God
    if you do this.
[8]Put on nice clothes
    and make yourself look good.

[9]Enjoy life with the wife you love. Enjoy all the days of this short life God has given you here on earth. It is all you have. So enjoy the work you have to do here on earth. [10]Whatever work you do, do your best. This is because you are going to the grave. There is no working, no planning, no knowledge and no wisdom there.

[11]I also realized something else here on earth that is senseless:
The fast runner does not always
    win the race.
The strong army does not always
    win the battle.
The wise man does not always have
    food.
The smart man does not always
    become wealthy.
And the man with special skills
    does not always receive praise.
Bad things happen to everyone.

[12]A person never knows what will
    happen to him next.
He is like a fish caught in a cruel
    net.
    He is like a bird caught in a trap.
In the same way, a person is
    trapped by bad things
    that suddenly happen to him.

[13]I also saw something wise happen here on earth. And it was very impressive to me. [14]There was a small town with only a few people in it. A great king fought against it and put his armies all around it. [15]Now there was a wise man in the town. He was poor, but he used his wisdom to save his town. But later on, everyone forgot about him. [16]I still think wisdom is better than strength. But those people forgot about the poor man's wisdom. And they stopped listening to what he said.

[17]The quiet words of a wise man are
    better
    than the shouts of a foolish ruler.
[18]Wisdom is better than weapons of
    war.
    But one sinner can destroy much
    good.

10 Dead flies will make even
    perfume smell bad.
In the same way, a little
    foolishness can ruin
    a wise man's fame for wisdom.
[2]A wise man's heart leads him in the
    right way.
But the heart of a foolish person
    leads him in the wrong way.
[3]A foolish person is not wise.
    It shows in everything he does.
Even as he walks along the road,
    he shows everyone how stupid he
    is.
[4]Don't leave your job
    just because the ruler is angry
    with you.
Remain calm.
    It will help correct your mistakes.

[5]Here is something else unfair that
    happens here on earth.
    It is the kind of mistake rulers
    make:
[6]Foolish people are given important
    positions
    while rich people are given less
    important ones.
[7]I have seen servants ride on horses
    while princes walk beside them
    on foot.

[8] Anyone who digs a pit might fall
   into it.
   Anyone who knocks down a wall
      might be bitten by a snake.
[9] Anyone who moves large stones
      might be hurt by them.
   And anyone who cuts logs might
      get hurt while doing it.
[10] Cutting logs with a dull ax
   makes you work harder.
   A wise man will sharpen his ax.
   In the same way, wisdom can
      make any job easier.
[11] Someone might know how to
      control snakes.
   But what good is such wisdom if
      the snake has already bitten
      him?

[12] A wise man's words bring him
      praise.
   But a foolish person's words will
      destroy him.
[13] A foolish person begins by saying
      something foolish.
   In the end he is saying even
      crazier things.
[14] A foolish person talks too much
      about what he will do.
   No one knows the future.
   No one can tell him what will
      happen after he dies.

[15] A foolish person doesn't know even
      the most obvious things.
   He can't even find his way back
      to town.
   So he has to wear himself out
      working.

[16] How terrible it will be for a country
      if its king is a child.
   How terrible it will be for that
      country
   if its leaders have parties all the
      time.
[17] A country is well off
   if its king comes from a good
      family.
   It is good for a country
   if its leaders control their eating
      and drinking.
   They should eat and drink for
      strength,
   not to get drunk.
[18] If a person is lazy and doesn't
      repair the roof,
   it will begin to fall.
   If he refuses to fix it,
   the house will leak.

[19] A party makes you feel good.
   And wine makes you feel happy.
   But both cost you a lot of money.
[20] Don't say or think bad things about
      the king.
   And don't say bad things about
      rich people even alone in your
      bedroom.
   A little bird might report it to others.
   A bird might fly to them and tell
      all you said.

11 Do good things everywhere you
      go.[n]
   After a while the good you do
      will return to help you.
[2] Invest what you have in several
      different businesses.
   You don't know what bad things
      might happen on earth.

[3] If clouds are full of rain,
   they will pour water on the earth.
   A tree can fall to the north or south.
   But it will stay where it falls.
[4] If a person waits for perfect
      weather,
   he will never plant his seeds.
   And if he is afraid that every cloud
      will bring rain,
   he will never harvest his crops.

[5] You don't know where the wind
      will blow.
   And you don't know how a baby
      grows in its mother's body.
   In the same way, God certainly
      made all things.
   But you can't understand what he
      is doing.
[6] Begin planting early in the
      morning,
   and don't stop working until
      evening.
   This is because you don't know
      which things you do will
      succeed.
   It is even possible that everything
      you do will succeed.

[7] It is good to be alive
   to enjoy the light of day.
[8] A person ought to enjoy every day
      of his life.
   This is true no matter how long
      he lives.
   But he should also remember this:
   You will be dead much longer
      than you live.
   After you are dead, you
      accomplish nothing.

11:1 Do good . . . go Literally, "Throw your bread upon the water."

[9] Young people, enjoy yourselves
      while you are young.
  Be happy while you are young.
Do whatever your heart desires.
  Do whatever you want to do.
But remember that God will judge
      you
  for everything you do.
[10] So avoid sorrow and sadness.
  Forget about all the bad things
      that happen to you.
  This is because the joys of youth
      pass quickly away.

12 Remember your Creator
      while you are young.
  Your old age is coming
      when you will have many troubles.
When that time comes,
  you won't have much to enjoy.
[2] When you become old,
      the light from the sun, moon and
      stars will seem dark to you.
  It will seem as if the rain clouds
      never go away.
[3] At that time your arms will lose
      their strength.
  Your strong legs will become
      weak and bent.
Your teeth will fall out so you
      cannot chew.
  Your eyes will not see clearly.
[4] Your ears will be deaf to the noise
      in the streets.
  You will barely hear singing.
The sound of the millstone grinding
      your grain will seem very quiet.
  But you'll wake up when a bird
      first starts singing!
[5] You will fear high places.
  And you will be afraid to go for a
      walk because you may fall.
Your hair will become white like
      the flowers on an almond tree.
  You will limp along like a
      grasshopper when you walk.
  Your desires will be gone.

Then you will go to your
      everlasting home.
  And people will go to your funeral.

[6] Remember God before your life is
      snapped like a silver chain.
  Remember God before your life
      is broken like a golden bowl.
It will be as useless as a broken
      bucket at the spring.
  It will be no good, like a broken
      wheel at a water well.
[7] Your body will become part of the
      dust of the earth again.
  But your spirit will return to God
      who gave it.

[8] Everything is useless!
  The Teacher says that everything
      is useless.

[9] The Teacher was very wise. He
taught the people what he knew. The
Teacher very carefully thought about,
studied and set in order many wise
teachings. [10] The Teacher looked for just
the right words. He wrote teachings that
are dependable and true.
[11] Words from wise men are like sharp
sticks used to guide animals. These words
are like nails that have been driven in
firmly. They are wise teachings that come
from God the Shepherd. [12] So be careful,
my son, about other teachings. People are
always writing books. And too much
study will make you very tired.

[13] Now, everything has been heard.
  Here is my final advice:
Honor God and obey his
      commands.
  This is the most important thing
      people can do.
[14] God knows everything people do,
  even the things done in secret.
He knows all the good and all the
      bad.
  He will judge everything people
      do.

The
SONG OF SOLOMON

1 Solomon's Greatest Song.
[2] Kiss me with the kisses of your
      mouth!
  Your love is better than wine.
[3] The smell of your perfume is
      pleasant.
  Your name is pleasant like
      expensive perfume!

That's why the young women
      love you.
[4] Take me with you; let's run.
  The king takes me into his rooms.

We will rejoice and be happy with
      you.
  We praise your love more than
      wine.

With good reason, the young
women love you, my lover.
[5]I'm dark but lovely,
women of Jerusalem.
I'm dark like the tents of Kedar,
like the curtains of Solomon.
[6]Don't look at how dark I am,
at how dark the sun has made me.
My brothers were angry with me.
They made me tend the
vineyards.
So I haven't tended my own
vineyard!
[7]Tell me, you whom I love,
where do you feed your sheep?
Where do you make them rest at
noon?
Why should I look for you near
your friend's sheep?
Am I like a woman who wears a
veil?[n]

[8]You are the most beautiful of women.
Surely you know to follow the
sheep.
Feed your young goats
near the shepherds' tents.
[9]My darling, you are like a mare
that pulls the king's chariots.
[10]Your cheeks are beautiful with
ornaments.
Your neck is beautiful with jewels.
[11]We will make for you gold earrings
with silver hooks.

[12]The smell of my perfume spreads
out
to the king on his couch.
[13]My lover is like a bag of myrrh[d]
that lies all night between my
breasts.
[14]My lover is like a bunch of flowers
from the vineyards at En Gedi.

[15]My darling, you are beautiful!
Oh, you are beautiful!
Your eyes are like doves!

[16]You are so handsome, my lover.
You are so pleasant!
Our bed is the grass.
[17]The boards of our house are cedar
trees.
And the wood of our ceiling is
juniper trees.

2 I am a rose in the Plain of Sharon.
I am a lily in the valleys.

[2]Among the young women, my
darling
is like a lily among thorns!

[3]Among young men, my lover
is like an apple tree among the
trees in the woods!
I enjoy sitting in his shadow.
His fruit is sweet to my taste.
[4]He brought me to the banquet
room.
His banner over me is love.
[5]Strengthen me with raisins.
Refresh me with apples,
because I am weak with love.
[6]My lover's left hand is under my
head.
And his right arm holds me tight!
[7]Women of Jerusalem, promise me
by the gazelles[d] and the deer.
Promise not to wake love.
Don't excite my feelings of love
until I'm ready.

[8]I hear my lover's voice.
He comes jumping across the
mountains.
He comes skipping over the hills!
[9]My lover is like a gazelle[d] or a
young deer.
Look, he stands behind our wall.
He stares in through the windows,
looking through the blinds.
[10]My lover spoke. He said to me,
"Get up, my darling.
Let's go away, my beautiful one.
[11]Look, the winter is past.
The rains are over and gone.
[12]Blossoms appear through all the
land.
The time has come to sing.
The cooing of doves is heard in
our land.
[13]There are young figs on the fig
trees.
The blossoms on the vines smell
sweet.
Get up, my darling.
Let's go away, my beautiful one."

[14]My beloved is like a dove that hides
in the cracks of the rock.
She hides in the secret places of
the cliff.
Show me your face.
Let me hear your voice.
Your voice is very sweet,
and your face is lovely.
[15]Catch the foxes for us—
the little foxes that ruin the
vineyards.
Our vineyards are in blossom.

1:7 veil This was the way a prostitute usually dressed.

¹⁶My lover is mine, and I am his.
   He feeds among the lilies
¹⁷until the day dawns
   and the shadows disappear.
Turn, my lover.
   Be like a gazelle[d] or a young deer
   on the rugged mountains.

3 At night on my bed,
   I looked for the one I love.
I looked for him, but I could not
   find him.
²I will get up now. I will go around
   the city,
   in the streets and squares.
I will look for the one I love.
   I looked for him, but I could not
   find him.
³The watchmen found me as they
   patrolled the city.
I asked, "Have you seen the one I
   love?"
⁴As soon as I had left them
   I found the one I love.
I held him. I would not let him go
   until I had brought him to my
   mother's house.
   I brought him into the room
   where I was born.
⁵Women of Jerusalem, promise me
   by the gazelles[d] and the deer.
Promise not to wake love.
   Don't excite my feelings of love
   until I'm ready.
⁶Who is this coming out of the
   desert
   like a cloud of smoke?
Who is this that smells like myrrh,[d]
   incense[d]
   and other spices?
⁷Look, it's Solomon's couch[n]
   with 60 soldiers around it.
   They are the finest soldiers of
   Israel.
⁸These soldiers all carry swords.
   They have been trained in war.
Every man wears his sword at his
   side.
   He is ready for the dangers of the
   night.
⁹King Solomon had a couch made
   for himself.
   It is made of wood from
   Lebanon.
¹⁰He made its posts of silver
   and its braces of gold.
   The seat was covered with purple
   cloth.

The women of Jerusalem wove it
   with love.
¹¹Women of Jerusalem, go out and
   see King Solomon.
He is wearing the crown his
   mother put on his head.
It was his wedding day,
   when his heart was happy!

4 How beautiful you are, my darling!
   Oh, you are beautiful!
Your eyes behind your veil are like
   doves.
   Your hair is like a flock of goats
   streaming down Mount Gilead.
²Your teeth are white like
   newly-sheared sheep
   just coming from their bath.
Each one has a twin.
   None of them is alone.
³Your lips are like red silk thread.
   Your mouth is lovely.
Your cheeks behind your veil
   are like slices of a pomegranate.[d]
⁴Your neck looks like David's tower.
   The tower was built with rows of
   stones.
A thousand shields hang on its
   walls.
   Each shield belongs to a strong
   soldier.
⁵Your breasts are like two fawns.
   They are like twins of a gazelle,[d]
   eating among the lilies.
⁶Until the day dawns
   and the shadows disappear,
I will go to that mountain of
   myrrh.[d]
   And I will go to that hill of
   incense.[d]
⁷My darling, everything about you is
   beautiful.
   There is nothing at all wrong
   with you.
⁸Come with me from Lebanon, my
   bride.
Come with me from Lebanon.
Come from the top of Mount
   Amana,
   from the tops of Mount Senir and
   Mount Hermon.
Come from the lions' dens
   and from the leopards' hills.
⁹My sister, my bride,
   you have thrilled my heart.
You have thrilled my heart
   with a glance of your eyes,
   with one jewel from your
   necklace.

3:7 **couch** Something like a bed carried by slaves on which the king lay or sat while traveling.

¹⁰Your love is so sweet, my sister, my
    bride!
  Your love is better than wine.
  Your perfume smells better than
      any spice.
¹¹My bride, your lips drip honey.
  Honey and milk are under your
      tongue.
  Your clothes smell like the cedars
      of Lebanon.
¹²My sister, my bride, you are like a
    garden locked up.
  You are like a spring with a wall
      around it, a fountain that is
      closed.
¹³Your limbs are like an orchard
    of pomegranates and all the best
      fruit.
  It is filled with flowers and nard.ᵈ
¹⁴It also has saffron,ᵈ calamusᵈ and
    cinnamon.
  It is filled with trees of incense,
      myrrh and aloesᵈ—
  all the best spices.
¹⁵You are like a garden fountain—
    a well of fresh water
    flowing down from the
      mountains of Lebanon.

¹⁶Awake, north wind!
  Come, you south wind!
  Blow on my garden.
  Let its sweet smells flow out.
  Let my lover enter the garden.
  And let him eat its best fruits.

5 I have entered my garden, my sister,
    my bride.
  I have gathered my myrrhᵈ with
    my spice.
  I have eaten my honeycomb and
    my honey.
  I have drunk my wine and my
    milk.

  Eat, friends, and drink.
  Yes, drink deeply, lovers.

²I sleep, but my heart is awake.
  I hear my lover knocking.
  "Open to me, my sister, my darling,
    my dove, my perfect one.
  My head is wet with dew.
  And my hair is wet with the
    dampness of the night."
³I have taken off my garment.
  I don't want to put it on again!
  I have washed my feet.
  I don't want to get them dirty
    again!
⁴My lover put his hand through the
    door opening.
  I felt excited inside.

⁵I got up to open the door for my
    lover.
  Myrrhᵈ was dripping from my
    hands.
  Myrrh was flowing from my
    fingers,
  onto the handles of the lock.
⁶I opened the door for my lover.
  But my lover had left. He was
    gone.
  When he had spoken, he had
    taken my breath away.
  I looked for him, but I could not
    find him.
  I called for him, but he did not
    answer me.
⁷The watchmen found me
    as they patrolled the city.
  They hit me; they hurt me.
  The guards on the wall took away
    my coat.
⁸I tell you, women of Jerusalem,
    if you find my lover,
  tell him I am weak with love.

⁹Is your lover better than other
    lovers,
  you, the most beautiful of
    women?
  Is your lover better than other
    lovers?
  Is that why you talk like this?

¹⁰My lover is clean and tanned.
  He's the best of 10,000 men.
¹¹His head is like the finest gold.
  His hair is wavy and black like a
    raven.
¹²His eyes are like doves
    by springs of water.
  They seem to be bathed in cream.
  They are set like jewels.
¹³His cheeks are like garden beds of
    spices.
  They smell like mounds of
    perfume.
  His lips are like lilies
    flowing with myrrh.ᵈ
¹⁴His hands are like gold hinges,
    filled with jewels.
  His body is like smooth ivory
    covered with sapphires.
¹⁵His legs are like large marble posts,
    standing on bases of fine gold.
  He is tall like a cedar of Lebanon—
    like the best cedar trees.
¹⁶His mouth is sweet to kiss.
  I desire him very much.

Yes, daughters of Jerusalem,
this is my lover.
This is my friend.

6 Where has your lover gone,
most beautiful of women?
Which way did your lover turn?
We will look for him with you.

²My lover has gone down to his
garden.
He has gone to the garden beds
of spices
to feed in the gardens
and to gather lilies.

³I belong to my lover.
And my lover belongs to me.
He feeds among the lilies.

⁴My darling, you are as beautiful as
the city of Tirzah.
You are as lovely as the city of
Jerusalem.
You are as wonderful as an army
flying flags.

⁵Turn your eyes from me.
They excite me too much!
Your hair is like a flock of goats
streaming down Mount Gilead.

⁶Your teeth are white like sheep
just coming from their bath.
Each one has a twin.
None of them is alone.

⁷Your cheeks behind your veil
are like slices of a pomegranate.[d]

⁸There may be 60 queens and 80
slave women[d]
and so many girls you cannot
count them.

⁹But there is only one like my dove,
my perfect one.
She is her mother's only
daughter,
the brightest of the one who gave
her birth.
The young women saw her and
called her happy.
The queens and the slave women
also praised her.

¹⁰Who is that young woman?
She shines with the dawn.
She's as pretty as the moon.
She's as bright as the sun.
And she's as wonderful
as an army flying flags.

¹¹I went down into the orchard of nut
trees.
I went to see the blossoms of the
valley.
I went to look for buds on the
vines,

to see if the pomegranate[d] trees
had bloomed.

¹²My desire for you makes me feel
like a prince in a chariot.

¹³Come back, come back, woman of
Shulam.
Come back, come back,
so we may look at you!

Why do you want to look at the
woman of Shulam
as you would at the dance of two
groups?

7 Your feet are beautiful in sandals,
you daughter of a prince.
Your round thighs are like jewels
shaped by an artist.

²Your navel is like a round drinking
cup
always filled with wine.
Your stomach is like a pile of wheat
with lilies around it like a fence.

³Your breasts are like two fawns.
They are like twins of a gazelle.[d]

⁴Your neck is like an ivory tower.
Your eyes are like the pools in
Heshbon
near the gate of Bath Rabbim.
Your nose is like a tower of
Lebanon
which looks toward Damascus.

⁵Your head is like Mount Carmel.
And your hair is like purple
cloth.
The king is captured in its folds.

⁶You are beautiful.
You are very pleasant.
My love, you are full of delights!

⁷You are tall like a palm tree.
Your breasts are like its bunches
of fruit.

⁸I said, "I will climb up the palm
tree.
I will take hold of its fruit."
Let your breasts be like bunches of
grapes.
Let the smell of your breath be
like apples.

⁹   And let your mouth be like the
best wine.

Let this wine go down sweetly for
my lover.
May it flow gently past the lips
and teeth.

¹⁰I belong to my lover,
and he desires only me.

¹¹Come, my lover.
Let's go out into the country.
Let's spend the night in the
fields.

¹²Let's go early to the vineyards.
  Let's see if the buds are on the
    vines.
Let's see if the blossoms have
    already opened
  and if the pomegranates^d have
    bloomed.
There I will give you my love.
¹³The mandrake flowers give their
    sweet smell.
  And at our gates there are all the
    best fruits.
I have saved them for you, my
    lover,
  the old delights and the new.

8 I wish you were like my brother
    who was fed at my mother's
    breasts!
  If I found you outside,
    I would kiss you.
  And no one would look down on
    me.
²I would lead you and bring you
    to my mother's house.
  She is the one who has taught
    me.
I would give you a drink of spiced
    wine
  from my pomegranates.

³My lover's left hand is under my
    head.
  And his right arm holds me tight!
⁴Women of Jerusalem, promise me.
  Promise not to wake love.
Don't excite my feelings of love
  until I'm ready.

⁵Who is this coming out of the
    desert,
  leaning on her lover?

I woke you under the apple tree.
  It was there that you were born.
  There your mother gave birth to
    you.
⁶Put me like a seal on your heart,
  like a seal on your arm.

Love is as strong as death.
  Desire is as strong as the grave.
Love bursts into flames.
  It burns like a very hot fire.
⁷Even much water cannot put out
    the flame of love.
  Floods cannot drown love.
If a man offered everything in his
    house for love,
  people would totally reject it.

⁸We have a little sister,
  and her breasts are not yet
    grown.
What should we do for our sister
  on the day she becomes
    engaged?
⁹If she is a wall,
  we will put silver towers on her.
If she is a door,
  we will protect her with cedar
    boards.

¹⁰I am a wall,
  and my breasts are like towers.
So I was to him,
  as one who brings happiness.
¹¹Solomon had a vineyard at Baal
    Hamon.
  He rented the vineyards for
    others to tend.
Everyone who rented had to pay
  25 pounds of silver for the fruit.
¹²But my own vineyard is mine to
    give.
  Solomon, the 25 pounds of silver
    are for you.
  And 5 pounds are for those who
    tend the fruit.

¹³You who live in the gardens,
  my friends are listening for your
    voice.
  Let me hear it!

¹⁴Hurry, my lover.
  Be like a gazelle^d
or a young deer
  on the mountains where spices
    grow.

The Book of
ISAIAH

1 This is the vision Isaiah son of Amoz
saw. God showed Isaiah what would
happen to Judah and Jerusalem. Isaiah saw these things while Uzziah, Jotham, Ahaz and Hezekiah were kings of
Judah.

²Heaven and earth, listen,
  because the Lord is speaking:
"I raised my children and helped
    them grow.
  But they have turned against me.
³An ox knows its master.

And a donkey knows where its
owner feeds it.
But the people of Israel do not
know me.
My people do not understand."

⁴Terrible times are coming for Israel,
a nation of sin.
The people are loaded down with
guilt.
They are like a group of children
doing evil.
They are full of evil.
They have left the Lord.
They hate God, the Holy One of
Israel.
They have turned away from him.

⁵Why should you continue to be
punished?
Why do you continue to turn
against him?
Your whole head is hurt.
And your whole heart is sick.
⁶There is no healthy spot
from the bottom of your foot to
the top of your head.
You are covered with wounds,
hurts and open sores.
Your wounds are not cleaned and
covered.
No medicine takes away the pain.

⁷Your land is ruined.
Your cities have been burned
with fire.
While you watch,
your enemies are stealing
everything from your land.
Your land is ruined like a country
destroyed by enemies.
⁸Jerusalem is left alone
like an empty shelter in a
vineyard.
It is like a hut left in a field of
melons.
It is like a city surrounded by
enemies.
⁹The Lord of heaven's armies
allowed a few of our people to
live.
Otherwise we would have been
completely destroyed
like the cities of Sodom and
Gomorrah.

¹⁰Jerusalem, your rulers are like
those of Sodom.
Your people are like those of
Gomorrah.
Hear the word of the Lord.

Listen to the teachings of our
God!
¹¹The Lord says,
"I do not want all these sacrifices
you give me.
I have had enough of your sacrifices
of male sheep and fat from fine
animals.
I am not pleased
by the blood of bulls, sheep and
goats.
¹²You come to meet with me.
But who asked you to do
all this running in and out?
¹³Don't continue bringing me
worthless sacrifices!
I hate the incense⁴ you burn.
I can't stand your New Moons,⁴
Sabbaths⁴ and other feast days.
I can't stand the evil you do in
holding your holy meetings.
¹⁴I hate your New Moon feasts
and your other yearly feasts.
They have become like heavy
weights on me.
I am tired of carrying them.
¹⁵You will raise your arms in prayer
to me.
But I will refuse to look at you.
Even if you say many prayers,
I will not listen to you.
It's because your hands are full of
blood.
¹⁶Wash yourselves and make
yourselves clean.⁴
Stop doing the evil things I see
you do.
Stop doing wrong!
¹⁷ Learn to do good.
Be fair to other people.
Punish those who hurt others.
Help the orphans.
Stand up for the rights of
widows."

¹⁸The Lord says,
"Come, we will talk these things
over.
Your sins are red like deep red
cloth.
But they can be as white as snow.
Your sins are bright red.
But you can be white like wool.
¹⁹If you will obey me,
you will eat good crops from the
land.
²⁰But if you refuse to obey and if you
turn against me,
you will be destroyed by your
enemies' swords."
The Lord himself said these things.

21The city of Jerusalem once
        followed the Lord.
    But she is no longer loyal to the
        Lord.
    She used to be filled with fairness.
    People there lived the way God
        wanted.
    But now, murderers live there.
22Jerusalem, you have become like
        the scum left when silver is
        purified.
    You are like wine mixed with
        water.
23Your rulers are rebels.
    They are friends of thieves.
    They all accept money for doing
        wrong things.
    They are paid to cheat people.
    They don't try to help the orphans.
    And they don't listen to the
        widows' needs.
24The Master, the Lord of heaven's
        armies,
    the Mighty One of Israel, says:
    "You, my enemies, will not cause
        me any more trouble.
    I will pay you back for what you
        did.
25I will turn against you.
    I will clean away all your wrongs
        as if with soap.
    I will take all the worthless
        things out of you.
26I will bring back judges as you had
        long ago.
    Your counselors will be like the
        ones you had in the beginning.
    Then you will be called the City
        That Is Right with God.
    You will be called the Loyal City."

27Because the Lord does what is fair,
    he will rescue Jerusalem.
    Because the Lord does what is right,
    he will save her people who come
        back to him.
28But sinners and those who turn
        against him will be destroyed.
    Those who have left the Lord will
        die.

29"You will be ashamed
    because you have worshiped
        false gods under the oak trees.
    You will be disgraced
    because you have worshiped
        idols in your gardens.
30You will be like an oak whose
        leaves are dying.
    You will be like a garden without
        water.
31Powerful people will be like small,
        dry pieces of wood.
    And what they do will be like
        sparks.
    The people and what they do will
        burn together.
    And no one will be able to stop
        that fire."

2 Isaiah son of Amoz saw this message
about Judah and Jerusalem.
2In the last days
    the mountain on which the Lord's
        Temple[d] stands
    will become the most important
        of all mountains.
    It will be raised above the hills.
    And people from all nations will
        come streaming to it.
3Many nations will come and say,
    "Come, let us go up to the
        mountain of the Lord.
    Let us go to the Temple of the
        God of Jacob.
    Then God will teach us his ways.
    And we will obey his teachings."
    The Lord's teachings will go out
        from Jerusalem.
    The Lord's message will go out
        from Jerusalem.
4Then the Lord will settle arguments
        among many nations.
    He will make decisions for strong
        nations that are far away.
    Then the nations will make their
        swords into plows.
    They will make their spears into
        hooks for trimming trees.
    Nations will no longer fight other
        nations.
    They will not even train for war
        anymore.

5Come, family of Jacob.
    We should follow the way of the
        Lord.

6Lord, you have left your people,
    the family of Jacob.
    They have become filled with
        wrong ideas from people in the
        East.
    Your people try to tell the future
        like the Philistines.
    They have completely accepted
        those foreign ideas.
7Their land has been filled with
        silver and gold.
    There are a great many treasures
        there.

Their land has been filled with
horses.
There are many chariots there.
⁸Their land is full of idols.
The people worship these idols
that they made with their own
hands.
They worship statues shaped by
their fingers.
⁹People will not be proud any
longer.
They will bow low with shame.
God, do not forgive them.

¹⁰Go into the caves of the cliffs.
Dig holes and hide in the ground.
Hide from the anger of the Lord
and from his great power!
¹¹Proud people will stop being proud.
They will bow low with shame.
At that time only the Lord will still
be praised.

¹²The Lord of heaven's armies has a
certain day planned.
On that day he will punish the
proud and those who brag.
They will no longer be important.
¹³He will bring down the tall cedar
trees from Lebanon.
He will destroy the great oak
trees of Bashan.
¹⁴He will destroy all the tall
mountains
and the high hills.
¹⁵He will knock down every tall tower
and every high, strong wall.
¹⁶He will sink all the trading ships.
And he will destroy the beautiful
ships.
¹⁷At that time proud people will stop
being proud.
They will bow low with shame.
And at that time only the Lord will
be praised.
¹⁸   But all the idols will be gone.

¹⁹People will run to caves in the
rocky cliffs.
They will dig holes and hide in
the ground.
They will hide from the anger of
the Lord
and his great power.
They will do this when the Lord
stands to shake the earth.
²⁰At that time people will throw away
their gold and silver idols.
They made these idols for
themselves to worship.
But they will throw them away to
the bats and moles.

²¹Then the people will hide in caves
and cracks in the rocks.
They will hide from the anger of
the Lord
and his great power.
They will do this when the Lord
stands to shake the earth.

²²You should stop trusting in people
to save you.
People are only human.
They aren't able to help you.

3 Understand what I am telling you.
The Master, the Lord of heaven's
armies,
will take away everything Judah
and Jerusalem need.
He will take away all the food
and water.
²He will take away all the heroes
and great soldiers.
He will take away all the judges,
prophets,ᵈ
people who do magic and older
leaders.
³He will take away the military
leaders and government
leaders.
He will take away the counselors,
the skilled craftsmen and those
who try to tell the future.
⁴The Lord says, "I will cause young
boys to be your leaders.
Foolish children will rule over
you.
⁵Everyone will be against everyone
else.
Young people will not respect
older people.
Common people will not respect
important people."
⁶At that time a man will grab one of
his brothers
from his own family and say,
"You have a coat. So you will be
our leader.
You will be the leader over all
these ruins."
⁷But that brother will stand up and
say,
"I cannot help you.
I do not have food or clothes in my
house.
You will not make me your
leader."
⁸This will happen because
Jerusalem has stumbled
and Judah has fallen.
The things they say and do are
against the Lord.
They sin openly against the Lord.

[9] The look on their faces shows they
are guilty of doing wrong.
Like the people of Sodom, they
are proud of their sin.
They don't care who sees it.
How terrible it will be for them!
They have brought much trouble
to themselves.

[10] Tell the good people that good
things will happen to them.
They will receive a reward for the
good they do.
[11] But how terrible it will be for
wicked people!
They will be punished for all the
wrong they have done.
[12] Children treat my people cruelly.
Women rule over them.
My people, your guides lead you in
the wrong way.
They turn you away from what is
right.

[13] The Lord takes his place in court.
He stands to judge the people.
[14] The Lord presents his case
against the older leaders and
other leaders of his people.
He says, "You have burned my
vineyard.
Your houses are full of what you
took from the poor.
[15] What gives you the right to crush
my people?
How can you grind the faces of
the poor into the dirt?"
The Master, the Lord of heaven's
armies, said this.

[16] The Lord says,
"The women of Jerusalem are
proud.
They walk around with their heads
held high.
They flirt with their eyes.
They take quick, short steps,
making noise with their ankle
bracelets."
[17] So the Lord will put sores on the
heads of those women in
Jerusalem.
He will make them lose all their
hair.

[18] At that time the Lord will take away
everything that makes them proud. He
will take away their beautiful ankle bracelets, their headbands and their necklaces
shaped like the moon. [19] He will take away
their earrings, bracelets and veils. [20] He
will take away their scarves, ankle chains,
the cloth belts worn around their waists,
their bottles of perfume and charms. [21] He
will take away their signet[d] rings, nose
rings, [22] their fine robes, capes, shawls
and purses. [23] And he will take away
their mirrors, linen dresses, turbans and
long shawls.

[24] Instead of having sweet-smelling
perfume, they will stink.
Instead of fine cloth belts, they
will have ropes of captives to
wear.
Instead of having their hair fixed in
fancy ways, they will be bald.
Instead of fine clothes, they will
have rough clothes of sadness.
Instead of having beauty, they
will have the brand of a
captive.
[25] At that time your men will be killed
with swords.
Your heroes will die in war.
[26] There will be crying and sadness in
the meeting places near the
city gates.
Jerusalem will be like a woman
who has lost everything and
sits on the ground.

4 At that time seven women
will grab one man.
They will say, "We will make our
own bread.
And we will make our own
clothes.
But please marry us!
Please, take away our shame."

[2] At that time the Lord's branch will
be very beautiful and great. The people
still living in Israel will be proud of what
the land grows. [3] All the people who are
still living in Jerusalem will be called
holy. This will be all the people whose
names are recorded among the living in
Jerusalem. [4] The Lord will wash away
the filth from the women of Jerusalem.
He will wash the bloodstains out of Jerusalem. He will clean Jerusalem with the
spirit of fairness and the spirit of fire.
[5] As he did when Israel left Egypt, the
Lord will cover them with a cloud of
smoke during the day. And he will cover
them with a bright, flaming fire at night.
These proofs will be over Mount Zion.[d]
They will be over every meeting of the
people there. There will be a covering
over every person. [6] This covering will be
a place of safety. It will protect the people
from the heat of the sun. It will be a safe
place to hide from the storm and rain.

5 Now I will sing a song to my friend.
This song is about his vineyard.
My friend had a vineyard
on a hill with very rich soil.
[2]He dug and cleared the field of
stones.
He planted the best grapevines
there.
And he built a tower in the middle
of it.
He cut out a winepress[d] as well.
He hoped good grapes would grow
there.
But only bad grapes grew.

[3]My friend says, "You people living
in Jerusalem,
and you men of Judah,
judge between me and my
vineyard.
[4]What more could I have done for
my vineyard?
I did everything I could.
I hoped for good grapes to grow.
But why were there only bad
grapes?
[5]Now I will tell you
what I will do to my vineyard:
I will remove the hedge,
and it will be burned.
I will break down the stone wall,
and it will be walked on.
[6]I will ruin my field.
It will not be trimmed or hoed.
Weeds and thorns will grow
there.
I will command the clouds
not to rain on it."

[7]The vineyard belonging to the Lord
of heaven's armies
is the nation of Israel.
The garden that the Lord loves
is the men of Judah.
The Lord looked for justice, but
there was only killing.
The Lord hoped for right living,
but there were only cries of
pain.

[8]How terrible it will be for you who
add more houses to your
houses
and more fields to your fields.
Finally there is no room left for
other people.
Then you are left alone in the
land.

[9]The Lord of heaven's armies said this
to me:

"The fine houses will be destroyed.
The large and beautiful houses
will be left empty.
[10]At that time a ten-acre vineyard will
make only six gallons of wine.
And ten bushels of seed will grow
only half a bushel of grain."

[11]How terrible it will be for people
who rise early in the morning
to look for strong drink.
They stay awake late at night,
becoming drunk with wine.
[12]At their parties they have lyres,[d]
harps,
tambourines,[d] flutes and wine.
They don't see what the Lord has
done.
They don't notice the work of his
hands.
[13]So my people will be captured and
taken away
because they don't really know
me.
All the great men will die of
hunger.
The common people will die of
thirst.
[14]So the place where the dead are
wants more and more people.
It opens its mouth wide.
Jerusalem's important men will go
down into it.
And the common people will go
down into it.
[15]So the common people and the
great people will be humbled.
Those who are proud will be
humbled.
[16]The Lord of heaven's armies will
receive glory by judging fairly.
The holy God will show himself
holy by doing what is right.
[17]Then the sheep will go anywhere
they want.
Lambs will feed on the land that
rich people once owned.

[18]How terrible it will be for those
people!
They pull their guilt and sins
behind them
as people pull wagons with
ropes.
[19]They say, "Let's see God hurry.
Let's see him do his work soon.
We want to see it.
Let's see the plan of the Holy One
of Israel happen soon.
Then we would know what it
really is."

20How terrible it will be for people
   who call good things bad
   and bad things good.
They think darkness is light
   and light is darkness.
They think sour is sweet
   and sweet is sour.

21How terrible it will be for people
   who think they are wise.
They think they are clever.

22How terrible it will be for people
   who are famous for drinking
   wine.
They are champions at mixing
   drinks.

23They take money to set the guilty
   free.
But they don't allow good people
   to be judged fairly.

24They will be destroyed
   just as fire burns straw or dry
   grass.
They will be destroyed
   like a plant whose roots rot
and whose flower dies and blows
   away like dust.
They have refused to obey the
   teachings of the Lord of
   heaven's armies.
They hated the message from the
   Holy God of Israel.

25So the Lord has become very angry
   with his people.
And he has raised his hand to
   punish them.
Even the mountains are frightened.
   Dead bodies lie in the streets like
   garbage.

But the Lord is still angry.
   His hand is still raised to strike
   down the people.

26God raises a banner for the nations
   far away.
He is whistling to call those
   people.
The enemy comes quickly!

27Not one of them becomes tired or
   falls down.
Not one of them gets sleepy and
   falls asleep.
Their weapons are close at hand.
   Their sandal straps are not
   broken.

28Their arrows are sharp.
   All of their bows are ready to
   shoot.
The horses' hoofs are hard as rock.

Their chariot wheels move like a
   whirlwind.

29Their shout is like the roar of a
   lion.
It is loud like a young lion.
The enemy growls as they grab
   their captives.
There is no one to stop them
   from taking their captives
   away.

30On that day they will roar
   like the waves of the sea.
And when people look at the land,
   they will see only darkness and
   pain.
All light will become dark in this
   thick cloud.

6 In the year that King Uzziah died, I
saw the Lord. He was sitting on a
very high throne. His long robe filled the
Temple.d 2Burning heavenly creatures
stood above him. Each creature had six
wings. They used two wings to cover
their faces. They used two wings to
cover their feet. And they used two
wings for flying. 3Each creature was
calling to the others:
   "Holy, holy, holy is the Lord of
      heaven's armies.
   His glory fills the whole earth."
4Their voices caused the frame around
the door to shake. The Temple filled
with smoke.

5I said, "Oh, no! I will be destroyed. I
am not pure. And I live among people
who are not pure. But I have seen the
King, the Lord of heaven's armies."

6On the altar there was a fire. One of
the burning heavenly creatures used a
pair of tongs to take a hot coal from the
fire. Then he flew to me with the hot
coal in his hand. 7The creature touched
my mouth with the hot coal. Then he
said, "Look. Your guilt is taken away
because this hot coal has touched your
lips. Your sin is taken away."

8Then I heard the Lord's voice. He
said, "Whom can I send? Who will go
for us?"

So I said, "Here I am. Send me!"

9Then the Lord said, "Go and tell this
to the people:
   'You will listen and listen, but you
      will not understand.
   You will look and look, but you
      will not learn.'

10Make these people stubborn.
   Make them not able to
      understand what they hear and
      see.

Otherwise, they might really
understand
what they see with their eyes
and hear with their ears.
They might really understand in
their minds.
If they did this, they would come
back to me and be forgiven."

[11] Then I asked, "Lord, how long
should I do this?"
He answered,
"Do this until the cities are
destroyed
and the people are gone.
Do this until there are no people
left living in the houses.
Do this until the land is destroyed
and left empty.
[12] I will send the people far away.
And the land will be left empty.
[13] One-tenth of the people will be left
in the land.
But the land will be destroyed
again.
These people will be like an oak
tree.
When the tree is chopped down,
a stump is left.
The people who remain will be
like a stump that will sprout
again."

7 Now Ahaz was the son of Jotham,
who was the son of Uzziah. When
Ahaz was king of Judah, Rezin and Pekah went up to Jerusalem to fight
against it. Rezin was king of Aram. And
Pekah son of Remaliah was king of Israel. But they were not able to defeat the
city. [2] A message was told to Ahaz king of
Judah. It said, "The armies of Aram and
Israel[n] have joined together."
When Ahaz heard this, he and the
people became very frightened. They
shook with fear like trees of the forest
blown by the wind. [3] Then the Lord told Isaiah, "You and
your son Shear-Jashub should go out
and talk to Ahaz. Go to the place where
the water flows into the upper pool. This
is on the road to the Washerman's Field.
[4] Tell Ahaz, 'Be careful. Be calm, and
don't be afraid. Don't let those two men,
Rezin and Remaliah's son Pekah, scare
you. Don't be afraid of their anger and

Aram's anger. Those two men are as
weak as two barely burning sticks that
are ready to go out. [5] They have made
plans against you. They said, [6]"Let's
fight against Judah and tear it apart. We
will divide Judah for ourselves. We will
make the son of Tabeel the new king of
Judah." [7] But I, the Lord God, say,
Their plan will not succeed.
It will not happen.
[8] That is because Aram is led by the
city of Damascus.
And Damascus is led by its weak
king, Rezin.
Within 65 years Israel will no
longer be a nation.
[9] Israel is led by the city of Samaria,
and Samaria is led by its weak
king, the son of Remaliah.
If your faith is not strong,
then you will not have strength to
last.'"

[10] Then the Lord spoke to Ahaz again.
[11] The Lord said, "Ask for a sign to prove
to yourself that these things are true. It
may be a sign from as deep as the place
where the dead are or as high as the
heavens."
[12] But Ahaz said, "I will not ask for a
sign. I will not test the Lord."
[13] Then Isaiah said, "Ahaz, descendant[d] of David, listen very carefully!
Isn't it bad enough that you wear out the
patience of people? Do you have to wear
out the patience of my God also? [14] But
the Lord himself will give you a sign:
The virgin[n] will be pregnant. She will
have a son, and she will name him Immanuel.[n] [15] He will be eating milk curds
and honey when he learns to reject what
is evil and to choose what is good. [16] You
are afraid of the kings of Israel and
Aram now. But before the child learns
what is good and what is evil, the lands
of Israel and Aram will be empty. [17] The
Lord will bring some troubled times to
you. Those troubles will come to your
people and to the people of your father's
family. The Lord will bring the king of
Assyria to fight against you.
[18] "At that time the Lord will whistle
to call for the Egyptians. And they will
come like flies from the streams of
Egypt. The Lord will call for the Assyrians. And they will come like bees from
the land of Assyria. [19] These enemies will

7:2 **Israel** Literally, "Ephraim." Isaiah often uses "Ephraim" to mean all of Israel.   7:14 **virgin**
The Hebrew word means "a young woman." Often this meant a girl who was not married
and had not yet had sexual relations with anyone.   7:14 **Immanuel** This name means "God is
with us."

camp in the deep ravines and in the cliffs. They will camp by the thornbushes and watering holes. [20] The Lord will use Assyria to punish Judah. Assyria will be hired and used like a razor. It will be as if the Lord is shaving the hair from Judah's head and legs and is shaving off Judah's beard.

[21] "At that time a person will be able to keep only one young cow and two sheep alive. [22] There will be only enough milk for that person to eat milk curds. All who remain in the land will go back to eating only milk curds and honey. [23] In this land there are now vineyards that have 1,000 grapevines. These grapevines are worth about 25 pounds of silver. But these fields will become full of weeds and thorns. [24] The land will become wild and useful only as a hunting ground. [25] People once worked and grew food on these hills. But at that time people will not go there. The land will be filled with weeds and thorns. Only sheep and cattle will go to those places."

8 The Lord told me, "Take a large scroll on which to write. Use a pen to write these words: 'Maher-Shalal-Hash-Baz.'" [2] I will gather some men to be reliable witnesses. They will be Uriah the priest and Zechariah son of Jeberekiah."

[3] Then I went to the prophetess.[d] She became pregnant and had a son. Then the Lord told me, "Name the boy Maher-Shalal-Hash-Baz. [4] The king of Assyria will take away all the wealth and possessions of Damascus and Samaria. This will happen before the boy learns to say 'my father' or 'my mother.'"

[5] Again the Lord spoke to me. [6] He said, "These people refuse to accept the slow-moving waters of the pool of Shiloah.
These people are terrified of Rezin and Remaliah's son Pekah.
[7] So I, the Lord, will bring the king of Assyria and all his power against them.
They will come like a powerful flood of water from the Euphrates River.
The Assyrians will be like water rising over the banks of the river,
flowing over the land.
[8] That water will flow into Judah and pass through it.
It will rise to Judah's throat.

Immanuel, this army will spread its wings like a bird
until it covers your whole country."

[9] Be broken, all you nations.
Be smashed to pieces.
Listen, all you faraway countries.
Prepare for battle and be smashed to pieces!
Prepare for battle and be smashed to pieces!
[10] Make your plans for the fight.
But your plans will be defeated.
Give orders to your armies.
But your orders will be useless.
This is because God is with us.

[11] The Lord spoke to me with his great power. He warned me not to follow the lead of the rest of the people. The Lord said,
[12] "People are saying that others make plans against them.
You should not believe those things.
Don't be afraid of the things they fear.
Do not dread those things.
[13] But remember that the Lord of heaven's armies is holy.
He is the one you should fear.
He is the one you should dread.
[14] Then he would be a place of safety for you.
But for the two families of Israel,
he will be like a stone that causes people to stumble.
He will be like a rock that makes them fall.
He will be like a trap for the people of Jerusalem.
He will catch them in his trap.
[15] Many people will fall over this rock.
They will fall and be broken.
They will be trapped and caught."

[16] Make an agreement.
Seal up the teaching while my followers are watching.
[17] I will wait for the Lord to help us.
The Lord is ashamed of the family of Israel.
I will trust the Lord.
[18] I am here. And with me are the children the Lord has given me. We are signs and proofs for the people of Israel.

8:1 Maher-Shalal-Hash-Baz This name means "there will soon be looting and stealing."

We have been sent by the Lord of heaven's armies. He lives on Mount Zion.[d]

[19] Some people say, "Ask the mediums[d] and fortune-tellers what to do. They whisper and mutter and ask dead people what to do." But I tell you that people should ask their God for help. Why should people who are still alive ask something from the dead? [20] You should follow the teachings and the agreement with the Lord. The mediums and fortune-tellers do not speak the word of the Lord. Their words are worth nothing.

[21] People will wander through the land troubled and hungry. When they become hungry, they will become angry. Then they will look up and curse their king and their God. [22] They will look around them at their land. And they will see only trouble and darkness and awful gloom. And they will be forced into the darkness.

9 But suddenly there will be no more gloom for the land that suffered. In the past God made the lands of Zebulun and Naphtali hang their heads in shame. But in the future that land will be made great. That land stretches from the way along the Mediterranean Sea to the land along the Jordan River. And it goes north to Galilee where the people who are not Israelites live.

[2] Now those people live in darkness.
    But they will see a great light.
They live in a place that is very dark.
    But a light will shine on them.
[3] God, you will cause the nation to grow.
    You will make the people happy.
    And they will show their happiness to you.
It will be like the joy during harvest time.
It will be like the joy of people taking what they have won in war.
[4] Like the time you defeated Midian, you will take away their heavy load.
You will take away the heavy pole from their backs.
    You will take away the rod the enemy uses to punish your people.
[5] Every boot that marched in battle will be destroyed.
    Every uniform stained with blood will be destroyed.
    They will be thrown into the fire.

[6] A child will be born to us.
    God will give a son to us.
He will be responsible for leading the people.
His name will be Wonderful Counselor, Powerful God,
    Father Who Lives Forever, Prince of Peace.
[7] Power and peace will be in his kingdom.
    It will continue to grow.
He will rule as king on David's throne
    and over David's kingdom.
He will make it strong,
    by ruling with goodness and fair judgment.
He will rule it forever and ever.
The Lord of heaven's armies will do this
    because of his strong love for his people.

[8] The Lord sent a message against the people of Jacob.
    That message says that God will judge Israel.
[9] Then everyone in Israel, even the leaders in Samaria,
    will know that God punished them.
Those people, who are proud and who brag now, say this:
[10] "These bricks have fallen,
    but we will build again with cut stones.
These small trees have been chopped down.
    But we will put great cedars there."
[11] But the Lord will make the enemies of Rezin strong against them.
    He will stir up their enemies against them.
[12] The Arameans come from the east and the Philistines from the west.
    They will eat up Israel with their armies.

But the Lord is still angry.
    His hand is still raised to punish the people.

[13] But the people do not return to the one who struck them.
    They do not follow the Lord of heaven's armies.
[14] So the Lord will cut off Israel's head and tail.
    He will take away both the branch and stalk in one day.

[15]The older leaders and important
   men are the head.
   The prophets[d] who speak lies are
     the tail.
[16]Those who lead the people lead
   them in the wrong direction.
   And those who follow them will
     be destroyed.
[17]So the Lord is not happy with the
   young men.
   He will not show mercy to the
     widows and orphans.
All the people are separated from
   God and are very evil.
   They all speak lies.

But the Lord is still angry.
   His hand is still raised to strike
     down the people.

[18]Evil is like a small fire.
   First, it burns weeds and thorns.
   Next, it burns the larger bushes in
     the forest.
   They all go up in a column of
     smoke.
[19]The Lord of heaven's armies is
   angry.
   So the land will be burned.
All the people will be burned in
   that fire.
   No one will try to save his
     brother.
[20]People will grab something on the
   right,
   but they will still be hungry.
They will eat something on the left,
   but they will not be filled.
Then each person will turn and eat
   his own children.
[21]The people of Manasseh will fight
   against the people of Ephraim.
   And Ephraim will fight against
     Manasseh.
   Then both of them will turn
     against Judah.

But the Lord is still angry.
   His hand is still raised to strike
     down the people.

10 How terrible it will be for the
     lawmakers who write evil
   laws.
   They write laws that make life
     hard for people.
[2]They are not fair to the poor.
   They rob my people of their
     rights.
   They allow people to steal from
     widows
   and to take from orphans what
     they should get.

[3]Lawmakers, how will you explain
   the things you have done?
   What will you do when your
     destruction comes from far
     away?
Where will you run for help?
   Where will you hide your money
     and your riches then?
[4]You will have to bow down among
   the captives.
   You will fall down among the
     dead bodies.

But the Lord is still angry.
   His hand is still raised to strike
     down the people.

[5]God says, "How terrible it will be
   for the king of Assyria.
   I use him like a stick.
   In anger I use Assyria like a club.
[6]I send it to fight against a nation
   that is separated from God.
   I am angry with those people.
   So I command Assyria to fight
     against them.
Assyria will take their wealth from
   them.
   Judah will become like dirt for
     them to walk on in the streets.
[7]But Assyria's king doesn't
   understand that I am using
   him.
   He doesn't know he is a tool for
     me.
He only wants to destroy other
   people.
   He plans to destroy many
     nations.
[8]The king of Assyria says to himself,
   'All of my commanders are like
     kings.
[9]The city Calno is like the city
   Carchemish.
   And the city Hamath is like the
     city Arpad.
   The city Samaria is like the city
     Damascus.
[10]I defeated those kingdoms that
   worship idols.
   And those idols were more than
     the idols of Jerusalem and
     Samaria.
[11]I defeated Samaria and her idols.
   So I will also defeat Jerusalem
     and her idols.'"

[12]The Lord will finish doing what he
planned to Mount Zion[d] and Jerusalem.
Then he will punish Assyria. The king
of Assyria is very proud. His pride made
him do these bad things. So God will

punish him. [13]The king of Assyria says this:

"By my own power I have done these things.
　By my wisdom I have defeated many nations.
I have taken their wealth.
　And like a mighty one, I have taken their people.
[14]I have taken the riches of all these people,
　like one who reaches into a bird's nest.
I have taken these nations,
　like a person taking eggs.
No one raised a hand against me.
　No one opened his mouth to stop me."

[15]An ax is not better than the person who swings it.
　A saw is not better than the person who uses it.
A stick cannot control the person who picks it up.
　A club cannot pick up the person!
[16]So the Master, the Lord of heaven's armies,
　will send a terrible disease against Assyria's soldiers.
The strength of Assyria will be burned up.
　It will be like a fire burning until everything is gone.
[17]God, the Light of Israel, will be like a fire.
　The Holy One will be like a flame.
He will be like a fire
　that suddenly burns the weeds and thorns.
[18]The fire burns away the great trees and rich farmlands.
　It will destroy everything.
　Things will be like a sick man who wastes away.
[19]Only a few trees will be left standing.
　There will be so few even a child will be able to count them.

[20]At that time some people will be left alive in Israel
　from the family of Jacob.
They will not continue to depend on the person who defeated them.
They will learn truly to depend on the Lord,
　the Holy One of Israel.

[21]The people who are left alive in Jacob's family
　will again follow the powerful God.
[22]Israel, your people are very many.
　They are like the grains of sand by the sea.
But only a few of them will be left alive to return to the Lord.
God has announced that he will destroy the land
　completely and fairly.
[23]The Master, the Lord of heaven's armies, will certainly destroy this land.
　He will destroy it as he has announced.

[24]This is what the Master, the Lord of heaven's armies, says:
"My people living in Jerusalem,
　don't be afraid of the Assyrians.
They beat you with a rod.
　They raise a stick to hurt you, as Egypt did.
[25]But after a short time my anger will stop.
　Then I will turn my anger to destroying them."

[26]Then the Lord of heaven's armies will beat the Assyrians with a whip.
　He will defeat them as he defeated Midian at the rock of Oreb.
He will raise his stick over the waters
　as he did in Egypt.
[27]Then the troubles that Assyria puts on you
　will be removed.
The load they make you carry
　will be taken away.

[28]The army of Assyria will enter near Aiath.
　They will walk through Migron.
　They will store their food in Micmash.
[29]The army will go over the pass.
　They will sleep at Geba.
The people of Ramah will be afraid.
　The people at Gibeah of Saul will run away.
[30]Cry out, Bath Gallim!
　Laishah, listen!
　Poor Anathoth!
[31]The people of Madmenah are running away.
　The people of Gebim are hiding.
[32]This day the army will stop at Nob.

And the army will shake their fist
at Mount Zion,[d]
at the hill of Jerusalem.
³³Watch! The Master, the Lord of
heaven's armies,
will chop them down like a great
tree.
He will do this with his great
power.
Those who are great will be cut
down.
Those who are important will fall
to the ground.
³⁴The Lord will cut them down
as a forest is cut down with an
ax.
And the great trees of Lebanon
will fall by the power of the
Mighty One.

11 A branch will grow
from a stump of a tree that was
cut down.
So a new king will come
from the family of Jesse.[n]
²The Spirit[d] of the Lord will rest
upon that king.
The Spirit gives him wisdom,
understanding, guidance and
power.
And the Spirit teaches him to
know and respect the Lord.
³This king will be glad to obey the
Lord.
He will not judge by the way things
look.
He will not judge by what people
say.
⁴He will judge the poor honestly.
He will be fair in his decisions for
the poor people of the land.
At his command evil people will be
punished.
By his words the wicked will be
put to death.
⁵Goodness and fairness will give
him strength.
They will be like a belt around
his waist.

⁶Then wolves will live in peace with
lambs.
And leopards will lie down to
rest with goats.
Calves, lions and young bulls will
eat together.
And a little child will lead them.
⁷Cows and bears will eat together in
peace.

Their young will lie down
together.
Lions will eat hay as oxen do.
⁸A baby will be able to play near a
cobra's hole.
A child will be able to put his
hand into the nest of a
poisonous snake.
⁹They will not hurt or destroy each
other
on all my holy mountain.
The earth will be full of the
knowledge of the Lord,
as the sea is full of water.

¹⁰At that time the new king from the
family of Jesse will stand as a banner
for the people. The nations will come
together around him. And the place
where he lives will be filled with glory.
¹¹At that time the Lord will again reach
out and take his people who are left
alive. These are God's people who are
left alive in Assyria, North Egypt, South
Egypt, Cush, Elam, Babylonia, Hamath
and all the islands of the sea.

¹²God will raise a banner as a sign
for all people.
He will gather the people of
Israel who were forced from
their country.
He will gather the scattered people
of Judah
from all parts of the earth.
¹³At that time Israel will not be
jealous anymore.
Judah will have no enemies left.
Israel will not be jealous of Judah.
And Judah will not hate Israel.
¹⁴But Israel and Judah will attack the
Philistines on the west.
Together they will take the riches
from the people of the east.
They will conquer Edom and Moab.
And the people of Ammon will be
under their control.
¹⁵The Lord will dry up
the Red Sea[d] of Egypt.
He will wave his arm over the
Euphrates River.
He will dry it up with a scorching
wind.
He will divide it into seven small
rivers.
And people will be able to walk
across them with their sandals
on.

11:1 Jesse King David's father.

16So God's people who are left alive
    will have a way to leave Assyria.
It will be like the time the Israelites
    went out of Egypt.

12 At that time you will say:
    "I praise you, Lord!
    You were angry with me.
    But you are not angry with me
        now!
    You have comforted me.
2God is the one who saves me.
    I trust him. I am not afraid.
The Lord, the Lord, gives me
        strength and makes me sing.
    He has saved me."
3You will receive your salvation with
        joy.
    You will take it as you would
        draw water from a well.
4At that time you will say,
    "Praise the Lord, and worship him.
    Tell everyone what he has done.
    Tell them how great he is.
5Sing praise to the Lord, because he
        has done great things.
    Let all the world know what he
        has done.
6Shout and sing for joy, you people
        of Jerusalem.
    The Holy One of Israel does great
        things before your eyes."

13 God showed Isaiah son of Amoz
    this message about Babylon:
2Raise a flag on the bare mountain.
    Call out to the men.
Raise your hand to signal them.
    Tell them to enter through the
        gates for important people.
3I myself have commanded those
        people
    whom I have separated as mine.
I have called those warriors to
        carry out my anger.
    They rejoice and are glad to do
        my will.

4Listen to the loud noise in the
        mountains.
    It sounds like many people.
Listen to the noise among the
        kingdoms.
    Nations are gathering together.
The Lord of heaven's armies is
        calling
    his army together for battle.
5This army is coming from a
        faraway land.
    It is coming from the edge of the
        horizon.

In anger the Lord is using this army
    like a weapon.
And it will destroy the whole
    country.
6Cry, because the Lord's day of
        judging is near.
    God All-Powerful is sending
        destruction.
7People will be weak with fear.
    Their courage will melt away.
8Everyone will be afraid.
    Pain and hurt will grab them.
    They will hurt like a woman
        giving birth to a baby.
They will look at each other in fear.
    Their faces will become red like
        fire.

9Look, the Lord's day of judging is
        coming.
    It will be a terrible day. God will
        be very angry,
and he will destroy the country.
    God will destroy the sinners who
        live in the land.
10The stars will not show their light.
    The skies will be dark.
The sun will grow dark as it rises.
    And the moon will not give its
        light.

11The Lord says, "I will punish the
        world for its evil.
    I will punish wicked people for
        their sins.
I will cause the proud people to
        lose their pride.
    I will destroy the pride of those
        who are cruel to others.
12People will be harder to find than
        pure gold.
    There will be fewer people than
        there is fine gold in Ophir.
13I will make the sky shake.
    And the earth will be moved from
        its place.
The Lord of heaven's armies will be
        very angry.
    His anger will burn at that time.

14"Then the people from Babylon will
        run away like hunted deer.
    They will run like sheep who
        have no shepherd.
Everyone will turn back to his own
        people.
    Each will run back to his own
        land.
15Anyone who is captured will be
        killed.

Everyone who is caught will be
killed with a sword.
[16]Their little children will be beaten
to death as their parents watch.
Everything in their houses will be
stolen.
And their wives will be raped.
[17]Look, I will cause the armies of
Media to attack Babylon.
They do not care about silver.
They do not delight in gold.
[18]Their soldiers will shoot the young
men with arrows.
The soldiers will show no mercy
on the children.
They will not feel sorry for the
little boys.
[19]Babylon is the most beautiful of all
kingdoms.
The Babylonians are very proud
of it.
But God will destroy it
like Sodom and Gomorrah.
[20]No one will ever live there.
No one will settle there again.
No Arab will put his tent there.
No shepherd will bring his sheep
there.
[21]Only animals from the desert will
live there.
The houses of Babylon will be
full of wild dogs.
Owls will live there.
Wild goats will leap about in the
houses.
[22]Wolves will howl within the strong
walls.
Wild dogs will bark in the
beautiful buildings.
The end of Babylon is near.
Its time is almost over."

14The Lord will again show mercy
to the people of Jacob. The Lord
will again choose the people of Israel.
He will settle them in their own land.
Then non-Israelite people will join the
Israelites. The non-Israelite people will
become a part of the family of Jacob.
[2]Nations will take the Israelites back to
their land. Those men and women from
the other nations will become slaves to
Israel. In the past the Israelites were
their slaves. But now the Israelites will
defeat those nations and rule over them.
[3]The Lord will take away the Israelites' hard work, and he will comfort
them. They will no longer have to work
as slaves. [4]On that day Israel will sing
this song about the king of Babylon:

The cruel king who ruled us is
finished.
His rule is finished!
[5]The Lord breaks the scepter[d] of evil
rulers.
He takes away their power.
[6]The king of Babylon beat people in
anger.
He beat them again and again.
He ruled the people in anger.
He kept on doing terrible things
to the people.
[7]But now, the whole land rests and
is quiet.
Now the people begin to sing.
[8]Even the pine trees are happy.
And the cedar trees of Lebanon
rejoice.
They say, "The king has fallen.
No one will ever cut us down
again."

[9]The place of the dead is excited
to meet you when you come.
It wakes the spirits of the dead to
greet you.
They were the leaders of the
world.
It makes dead kings stand up from
their thrones to greet you.
They were rulers of nations.
[10]All these leaders will make fun of
you.
They will say,
"Now you are weak, as we are.
Now you are just like us."
[11]Your pride has been sent down to
where the dead are.
The music from your harps goes
with it.
Flies are spread out like your bed
beneath you.
And worms cover your body like
a blanket.

[12]King of Babylon, morning star, you
have fallen from heaven,
even though you were as bright
as the rising sun!
In the past all the nations on earth
bowed down before you.
But now you have been cut down.
[13]You told yourself,
"I will go up to heaven.
I will put my throne
above God's stars.
I will sit on the mountain of the
gods.
I will sit on the slopes of the
sacred mountain.

¹⁴I will go up above the tops of the
clouds.
I will be like God Most High."
¹⁵But you were brought down to the
grave.
You were brought down to the
deep places where the dead
are.

¹⁶Those who see you stare at you.
They think about what has
happened to you.
They say, "Is this the same man
who caused great fear on
earth?
Is he the one who shook the
kingdoms?
¹⁷Is this the man who turned the land
into a desert?
Is he the one who destroyed its
cities?
Is he the one who captured people
in war
and would not let them go
home?"

¹⁸Every king of the earth has been
buried with honor.
Every king has his own grave.
¹⁹But you are thrown out of your
grave,
like an unwanted branch is cut
from a tree and thrown away.
You are covered by bodies
that died in battle.
You have been thrown into a rocky
pit.
And other soldiers walk on you.
²⁰ You will not be buried like other
people.
This is because you ruined your
own country.
And you killed your own people.
So your children will never
be mentioned again.

²¹Prepare to kill his children.
Kill them because their father is
guilty.
They will never again take control
of the earth.
They will never again fill the
world with their cities.

²²The Lord of heaven's armies says
this:
"I will fight against those people.
I will destroy Babylon and its
people.
I will destroy its people and their
descendants,"ᵈ says the Lord.

²³"I will make Babylon fit only for
owls.
It will become a swamp.
I will sweep Babylon as with a
broom of destruction,"
says the Lord of heaven's armies.

²⁴The Lord of heaven's armies has
made this promise:
"These things will happen exactly
as I planned them.
These things will happen exactly
as I set them up.
²⁵I will destroy the king of Assyria in
my country.
I will trample him on my
mountains.
He put a heavy load on my people.
But that weight will be removed.

²⁶"This is what I plan to do against
all the earth.
I will raise my hand to strike
down all nations."
²⁷When the Lord of heaven's armies
makes a plan,
no one can stop it.
When the Lord raises his hand to
punish people,
no one can stop him.

²⁸This message was given the year
King Ahaz died:
²⁹Country of Philistia, don't be so
happy.
The king who beat you is now
dead.
But he is like a snake that will give
birth to another dangerous
snake.
The new king will be like a quick,
dangerous snake to bite you.
³⁰Even the poorest of my people will
be able to eat safely.
People in need will be able to lie
down in safety.
But I will kill your family with
hunger.
And all your people who are left
will die.

³¹People near the city gates, cry out!
Philistines, be frightened!
A cloud of dust comes from the
north.
It is an army, full of men ready to
fight.
³²What shall we tell the messengers
from Philistia?

Say that the Lord has made
Jerusalem strong.
Say that his poor people will go
there for safety.

15 This is a message about Moab:
In one night armies took the
wealth from Ar in Moab.
That night the city was destroyed.
In one night armies took the wealth
from Kir in Moab.
That night the city was destroyed.
[2] The people of Dibon go to the
places of worship to cry.
The people of Moab cry for the
cities of Nebo and Medeba.
Everyone has shaved his head and
beard to show how sad he is.
[3] In the streets at Moab they wear
rough cloth to show their
sadness.
On the roofs[n] and in the public
squares,
they are crying loudly.
[4] People in the cities Heshbon and
Elealeh cry out loud.
You can hear their voices far
away in the city Jahaz.
Even the soldiers are frightened.
They are shaking from fear.

[5] My heart cries with sorrow for
Moab.
Its people run away to Zoar for
safety.
They run to Eglath Shelishiyah.
People are going up the mountain
road to Luhith.
They are crying as they go.
People are going on the road to
Horonaim.
They cry out loud over their
destruction.
[6] But the water of Nimrim has dried
up.
The grass has dried up.
All the plants are dead.
Nothing green is left.
[7] So the people gather up what they
have saved.
They carry those things and
cross the Ravine of the Poplars.
[8] Crying is heard everywhere in
Moab.
Their crying is heard as far away
as the city Eglaim.
Their crying is heard as far away
as Beer Elim.

[9] The water of the city Dibon is full
of blood.
And I, the Lord, will bring even
more troubles to Dibon.
A few people living in Moab have
escaped the enemy.
But I will send lions to kill them.

16 Send the king of the land
the payment he demands.
Send a lamb from Sela through the
desert
to the mountain of Jerusalem.
[2] The women of Moab
try to cross the river Arnon.
They are like little birds
that have fallen from their nest.

[3] They say: "Help us.
Tell us what to do.
Protect us from our enemies
as shade protects us from the
noon sun.
Hide us because we are running for
safety!
Don't give us to our enemies.
[4] Let those of us who were forced out
of Moab live in your land.
Hide us from our enemies."

The robbing of Moab will stop.
The enemy will be defeated.
The men who hurt others will
disappear from the land.
[5] Then a new loyal king will come.
This faithful king will be from the
family of David.
He will judge fairly.
He wants to do what is right.

[6] We have heard that the people of
Moab are proud
and very conceited.
They are very proud and angry.
But their bragging means
nothing.
[7] So the people of Moab will cry.
They will all be sad.
They will moan and groan
for the raisin cakes they had in
Kir Hareseth.
[8] But the fields of Heshbon and the
vines of Sibmah cannot grow
grapes.
Foreign rulers have destroyed the
grapevines.
The grapevines once spread as far
as the city of Jazer and into the
desert.

15:3 roofs In Bible times houses were built with flat roofs. The roof was used for drying things such as flax and fruit. And it was used as an extra room, as a place for worship and as a place to sleep in the summer.

They had spread as far as the
    sea.
⁹I cry with the people of Jazer
    for the grapevines of Sibmah.
I will cry with the people of
    Heshbon and Elealeh.
There will be no shouts of joy,
    because there will be no harvest
    or ripe fruit.
¹⁰There will be no joy and happiness
    in the orchards.
There will be no songs or shouts
    of joy in the vineyards.
No one makes wine in the
    winepresses.ᵈ
I have put an end to shouts of joy.
¹¹My heart cries for Moab like a harp
    playing a funeral song.
I am very sad for Kir Hareseth.
¹²The people of Moab will go to their
    places of worship.
They will try to pray.
But when they go to their temple to
    pray,
    they will not be able.

¹³The Lord said these things about
Moab before. ¹⁴And now the Lord says,
"In three years all those people and
what they are proud of will be hated.
(This is three years as a hired helper
would count time.) There will be a few
people left, but they will be weak."

17 This is the message for Damascus:
    "The city of Damascus will be
    destroyed.
Only ruins will be left there.
²People will leave the cities of Aroer.
    Flocks of sheep will wander
    freely in those empty towns.
There will be no one to bother
    them.
³The strong, walled cities of Israel
    will be destroyed.
The government in Damascus
    will end.
Those left alive of Aram will be
    like the glory of Israel," says the
    Lord of heaven's armies.

⁴"At that time Israel's wealth will all
    be gone.
Israel will be like a man who has
    lost much weight from sickness.
⁵That time will be like the grain
    harvest in the Valley of
    Rephaim.
The workers cut the wheat.
Then they cut the heads of grain
    from the plants.
And they collect the grain.

⁶That time will also be like the olive
    harvest,
when a few olives are left.
Two or three olives are left in the
    top branches.
Four or five olives are left on full
    branches," says the Lord, the
    God of Israel.

⁷At that time people will look to
    God, their Maker.
Their eyes will see the Holy One
    of Israel.
⁸They will not trust the altars they
    have made.
They will not trust what their
    hands have made.
They will not respect the Asherahᵈ
    idols
and altars they have made.
⁹In that day all their strong cities will
be empty. They will be like the cities that
the Hivites and the Amorites left. They
left their cities when the Israelites came
to take the land. Everything will be ruined.

¹⁰You have forgotten the God who
    saves you.
You have not remembered that
    God is your place of safety.
You plant the finest grapevines.
    You plant grapevines from
    faraway places.
¹¹You will plant your grapevines one
    day and try to make them
    grow.
The next day they will begin to
    grow.
But at harvest time everything will
    be dead.
A sickness will kill all the plants.

¹²Listen to the many people!
    They are crying loud like the
    noise from the sea.
Listen to the noise!
    The crying is like the crashing of
    great waves.
¹³The people roar like those waves.
But when God speaks harshly to
    them, they will run away.
They will be like chaffᵈ on the hills
    being blown by the wind.
They will be like tumbleweeds
    blown away by a storm.
¹⁴At night the people will be very
    frightened.
Before morning, no one will be
    left.

So our enemies will come to our
land,
but they will become nothing.

18 How terrible it will be for the
land beyond the rivers of
Cush.
It is filled with the sound of
wings.
[2] That land sends people across the
sea.
They go on the water in boats
made of reeds.

Quick messengers, go
to the people who are tall and
smooth-skinned.
They are feared everywhere.
They are a powerful nation with
strange speech.
They defeat the other nations.
Their land is divided by rivers.

[3] All you people of the world, look!
Everyone who lives in the world,
look!
You will see a banner raised on a
mountain.
You will hear a trumpet sound.
[4] The Lord said to me,
"I will quietly watch from where
I live.
I will be like heat in the sunshine.
I will be like the dew in the heat
of harvest time."
[5] The time will be after the flowers
have bloomed and before the
harvest.
The new grapes will be budding
and growing.
Then the enemy will cut the plants
with knives.
He will cut down the vines and
take them away.
[6] They will be left for the birds of the
mountains to eat.
They will be left for the wild
animals to eat.
Birds will feed on them all summer.
And that winter wild animals will
eat them.

[7] At that time gifts will be brought to
the Lord of heaven's armies.
They will come from the people
who are tall and
smooth-skinned.
They are feared everywhere.
They are a powerful nation with
strange speech.
Their land is divided by rivers.

These gifts will be brought to the
place of the Lord of heaven's
armies.
They will be brought to Mount
Zion.[d]

19 The message about Egypt:
Look, the Lord is coming on a
fast cloud.
He will enter Egypt.
And the idols of Egypt will tremble
before him.
Egypt's courage will melt away.

[2] The Lord says, "I will cause the
Egyptians to fight against
themselves.
Men will fight with their
brothers.
Neighbors will fight neighbors.
Cities will fight cities.
Kingdoms will fight kingdoms.
[3] The Egyptians will be afraid.
I will ruin their plans.
They will ask their idols and spirits
of the dead what they should
do.
They will ask their mediums[d] and
fortune-tellers."
[4] The Master, the Lord of heaven's
armies, says,
"I will give Egypt to a hard master.
A powerful king will rule over
them."

[5] The sea will become dry.
The water will disappear from
the Nile River.
[6] The canals will stink.
The streams of Egypt will
decrease and dry up.
All the water plants will rot.
[7] All the plants along the banks of
the Nile will die.
Even the planted fields by the Nile
will dry up, blow away and
disappear.
[8] The fishermen, all those who catch
fish from the Nile,
will groan and cry.
Those who depend on the Nile for
food will be sad.
[9] All the people who make cloth from
flax will be sad.
Those who weave linen will lose
hope.
[10] Those who weave cloth will be
broken.
All those who work for money
will be sad.
[11] The officers of the city of Zoan are
fools.

The wise men who advise the king
of Egypt give wrong advice.
How can they say to him they are
wise?
How can they say they are from
the old family of the kings?
[12]Egypt, where are your wise men?
Let them show you
what the Lord of heaven's armies
has planned for Egypt.
[13]The officers of Zoan have been
fooled.
The leaders of Memphis have
believed false things.
So the leaders of Egypt
lead her the wrong way.
[14]The Lord has made the leaders
confused.
They wander and lead Egypt in
the wrong ways.
They are like drunk people
stumbling in their own vomit.
[15]There is nothing Egypt can do.
No one in Egypt can help.

[16]In that day the people of Egypt will
be like frightened women. They will be
afraid of the Lord of heaven's armies.
He will raise his hand to strike them
down. [17]The land of Judah will bring
fear to the people in Egypt. Anyone in
Egypt who hears the name Judah will
be afraid. This will happen because the
Lord of heaven's armies has planned
terrible things for Egypt. [18]At that time
five cities in Egypt will speak Hebrew,
the language of Canaan. They will
promise to be loyal to the Lord of heav-
en's armies. One of these cities will be
named the City of Destruction. [19]At that
time there will be an altar for the Lord
in the middle of Egypt. At the border of
Egypt there will be a monument to the
Lord. [20]This will be a sign. It will show
that the Lord of heaven's armies is powerful. When the people cry to the Lord
for help, he will send help. He will send
someone to save and defend the people.
He will rescue them from those who
hurt them.
[21]So the Lord will show himself to the
Egyptians. Then they will say he is the
Lord. They will serve God and offer
many sacrifices. They will make promises to the Lord, and they will keep
them. [22]The Lord will punish the Egyptians. Then he will heal them. They will
come back to the Lord. He will listen to
their prayers and heal them.
[23]At that time there will be a highway

from Egypt to Assyria. Then people
from Assyria will go to Egypt. And the
Egyptians will go to Assyria. The Egyptians and Assyrians will worship God
together. [24]At that time Israel, Assyria
and Egypt will join together. This will
be a blessing for the earth. [25]The Lord
of heaven's armies will bless them. He
will say, "Egypt, you are my people. Assyria, I made you. Israel, I own you. You
are all blessed!"

20 Sargon was the king of Assyria.
He sent a military commander to
Ashdod to attack that city. So the commander attacked and captured it. [2]Then
the Lord spoke through Isaiah son of
Amoz. The Lord said, "Take the rough
cloth off your body. Take your sandals
off your feet." So Isaiah obeyed the
Lord. He walked around without his
clothes of rough cloth or his sandals.
[3]Then the Lord said, "Isaiah my servant has walked around without his
clothes of rough cloth or his sandals for
three years. This is a sign for Egypt and
Cush. [4]The king of Assyria will defeat
Egypt and Cush. Assyria will take prisoners and lead them away from their
countries. The old people and young
people will be led away naked. They will
go without clothes and without sandals.
So the Egyptians will be shamed. [5]Peo-
ple who looked to Cush for help will
be afraid. People who were amazed by
Egypt's glory will be shamed. [6]Those
people who live near the sea will say,
'We trusted those countries to help us.
We ran to them so they would save us
from the king of Assyria. But look at
them. They have been captured. So how
will we be able to escape?'"

21 The message about the Desert by
the Sea:[n]
Disaster is coming from the desert.
It is coming like wind blowing in
the south.
It is coming from a terrible
country.
[2]I have seen a terrible vision.
I see traitors turning against you.
I see people taking your wealth.

Elam, attack the people!
Media, surround the city and
attack it!
I will bring an end to the pain the
city causes.

[3]I saw those terrible things, and now
I am in pain.

21:1 **Desert by the Sea** Probably Babylon.

My pains are like the pains of
    giving birth.
What I hear makes me very afraid.
What I see causes me to shake
    with fear.
[4] I am worried,
    and I am shaking with fear.
My pleasant evening
    has become a night of fear.

[5] They set the table.
    They spread the rugs.
    They eat and drink!
Leaders, stand up.
    Prepare the shields for battle!

[6] The Lord said to me,
    "Go. Have a man be a lookout for
        the city.
    Have him report what he sees.
[7] If he sees chariots and teams of
        horses,
    donkeys or camels,
    he should pay very close attention."

[8] Then the lookout called out,
    "My Master, each day I stand in the
        watchtower watching.
    Every night I have been on guard.
[9] Look. I see a man coming in a chariot
        with a team of horses."
The man gives back the answer,
    "Babylon has fallen. It has fallen!
All the statues of her gods
    lie broken on the ground."

[10] My people are crushed like grain
        on the threshing[d] floor.
    My people, I tell you what I have
        heard from the Lord.
He is the Lord of heaven's armies,
    the God of Israel.

[11] The message about Dumah:[n]
Someone calls to me from Edom.
    He says, "Watchman, how much
        of the night is left?
    Watchman, how much longer will
        it be night?"
[12] The watchman answered,
    "Morning is coming, but then
        night will come again.
    If you have something to ask,
        then come back and ask."

[13] The message about Arabia:
A group of traders from Dedan
    spent the night near some trees
        in Arabia.

[14]   They gave water to thirsty
        travelers.
The people of Tema gave food
    to those who were escaping.
[15] They were running from swords.
    The swords were ready to kill.
They were running from bows
    ready to shoot.
They were running from a hard
    battle.

[16] This is what the Lord said to me: "In
one year all the glory of the country of
Kedar will be gone. (This is a year as a
hired helper counts time.) [17] At that time
only a few of the archers will be left.
Only a few of the soldiers of Kedar will
be left alive." The Lord, the God of Israel, has spoken.

22 The message about the Valley of
Vision:[n]
    What is wrong with you people?
        Why are you on your roofs?[n]
[2] This city was a very busy city.
    It was full of noise and wild
        parties.
But your people have been killed,
    but not with swords.
    They did not die in battle.
[3] All your leaders ran away together.
    But they all have been captured
        without using a bow.
All you who were captured
    tried to run away before the
        enemy came near.
[4] So I say, "Don't look at me.
    Let me cry loudly.
Don't hurry to comfort me
    about the destruction of
        Jerusalem."
[5] The Master, the Lord of heaven's
        armies, has chosen a special
        day.
    There will be riots and confusion.
    People will trample each other in
        the Valley of Vision.
The city walls will be knocked down.
    The people will cry out to the
        mountain.
[6] The soldiers from Elam will take
        their bags of arrows.
    Men in chariots and on horses
        will attack.
    Kir will prepare their shields.
[7] Your nicest valleys will be filled
        with chariots.

21:11 Dumah Another name for Edom. **22:1 Valley of Vision** This probably means a valley
near Jerusalem. **22:1 roofs** In Bible times houses were built with flat roofs. The roof was used
for drying things such as flax and fruit. And it was used as an extra room, as a place for
worship and as a place to sleep in the summer.

Horsemen will be ordered to
　　guard the gates of the city.
8　The walls protecting Judah will
　　fall.

At that time the people of
　Jerusalem depended on
the weapons kept at the Palace of
　the Forest.
9 You saw that the walls of Jerusalem
　　had many cracks that needed
　　repairing.
　　You stored up water in the lower
　　　pool.
10 You counted the houses of
　　Jerusalem.
　　You tore them down to fix the
　　　walls with their stones.
11 You made a pool between the two
　　walls.
　　It was to save water from the old
　　　pool.
But you did not trust the God who
　　made these things.
　　You did not respect the One who
　　　planned them long ago.

12 The Master, the Lord of heaven's
　　armies, told the people
　　to cry and be sad.
He told them to shave their heads
　　and wear rough cloth.
13 But look. The people are happy.
There are wild parties.
They kill the cattle and the sheep.
They eat the food and drink the
　　wine.
They say, "Let us eat and drink,
　　because tomorrow we will die."
14 The Lord of heaven's armies said to
me: "You people will die before this guilt
is forgiven." The Master, the Lord of
heaven's armies, said this.
15 This is what the Master, the Lord of
heaven's armies, says:
　　"Go to this servant Shebna.
　　He is the manager of the palace.
16 Say to him, 'What are you doing
　　here?
　　Who said you could cut out a
　　　tomb for yourself here?
　　Why are you preparing your tomb
　　　in a high place?
　　Why are you carving out a tomb
　　　from the rock?
17 Look, mighty man! The Lord will
　　throw you away.
　　He will take firm hold of you.
18 He will roll you tightly into a ball
　　and throw you into another
　　country.

There you will die.
　　Your fine chariots will remain
　　　there.
　　You are a disgrace to your
　　　master's house.
19 I will force you out of your
　　important job here.
　　You will be thrown down from
　　　your important place.'

20 "At that time I will call for my servant Eliakim son of Hilkiah. 21 I will take
your robe and put it on him. I will give
him your belt. I will give him the important job you have. He will be like a father
to the people of Jerusalem and the family of Judah. 22 I will put the key to the
house of David around his neck. If he
opens a door, no one will be able to close
it. If he closes a door, no one will be able
to open it. 23 He will be like an honored
chair in his father's house. I will make
him strong like a peg that is hammered
into a strong board. 24 All the honored
and important things of his family will
depend on him. All the adults and little
children will depend on him. They will
be like bowls and jars hanging on him.
25 "At that time," says the Lord of heav-
en's armies, "the peg hammered into the
strong board will weaken. It will break
and fall. And everything hanging on it
will be destroyed." The Lord says this.

23 The message about Tyre:
　　You ships of Tarshish, cry!
　　The houses and harbor of Tyre
　　　are destroyed.
This news came to the ships
　　from the land of Cyprus.
2 Be silent, you who live on the
　　island of Tyre.
　　You merchants of Sidon, be
　　　silent.
Seamen have made you rich.
3 They traveled the sea to bring grain
　　from Egypt.
　　The men of Tyre brought grain
　　　from the Nile Valley
　　and sold it to other nations.

4 Sidon, be ashamed.
　　Strong city of the sea, be
　　　ashamed. The sea says:
"I have not felt the pain of giving
　　birth.
　　I have not reared young men or
　　　women."
5 Egypt will hear the news about
　　Tyre.
　　And it will make Egypt hurt with
　　　sorrow.

⁶You ships should return to
Tarshish.
You people living near the sea
should be sad.
⁷Look at your once happy city!
Look at your old, old city!
People from that city have traveled
far away to live.
⁸Who planned Tyre's destruction?
Tyre made others rich.
Her merchants were treated like
princes.
Her traders were greatly
respected.
⁹It was the Lord of heaven's armies
who planned this!
He decided to make these proud
men unimportant.
He decided to disgrace those who
were greatly respected.
¹⁰Go through your land,
Tarshish, like the Nile goes
through Egypt.
There is no harbor for you now!
¹¹The Lord has stretched his hand
over the sea.
He makes its kingdoms tremble.
He commands that Canaan's
places of safety be destroyed.
¹²The Lord said, "Sidon, you will not
rejoice any longer.
You are destroyed.
Even if you cross the sea to Cyprus,
you will not find a place to rest."
¹³Look at the land of the
Babylonians.
Babylonia is not a country now.
Assyria has made it a place for
wild animals.
Assyria built towers to attack it.
The soldiers took all the treasures
from its cities.
They turned it into ruins.
¹⁴So be sad, you trading ships.
Your place of safety is destroyed.
¹⁵At that time people will forget about
Tyre for 70 years. That is the length of a
king's life. After 70 years, Tyre will be
like the prostitute[d] in this song:
¹⁶"Oh woman, you are forgotten.
Take your harp and walk through
the city.
Play your harp well. Sing your song
often.
Then people will remember you."

¹⁷After 70 years the Lord will deal
with Tyre. Tyre will again have trade. It
will be like a prostitute for all the nations of the earth. ¹⁸The profits will be
saved for the Lord. Tyre will not keep
the money she earns. It will give them

to the people who serve the Lord. So
they will have plenty of food and nice
clothes.

24

Look! The Lord will destroy the
earth and leave it empty.
He will ruin the surface of the
land and scatter its people.
²At that time the same thing will
happen to everyone:
to common people and priests,
to slaves and masters,
to women slaves and their
women masters,
to buyers and sellers,
to those who borrow and those
who lend,
and to bankers and those who
owe the bank.
³The earth will be completely empty.
The wealth will all be taken.
This will happen because the
Lord commanded it.
⁴The earth will dry up and die.
The world will grow weak and die.
The great leaders in this land will
become weak.
⁵The people of the earth have ruined
it.
They do not follow God's
teachings.
They do not obey God's laws.
They break their agreement with
God that was to last forever.
⁶A curse will destroy the earth.
The people of the world are
guilty.
So they will be burned up.
Only a few will be left.
⁷The new wine will be bad, and the
grapevines will die.
People who were happy will be
sad.
⁸The happy music of the
tambourines[d] will end.
The happy sounds of wild parties
will stop.
The joyful music from the harps
will end.
⁹People will no longer sing while
they drink their wine.
The beer will taste bitter to those
who drink it.
¹⁰The ruined city will be empty.
People will hide behind closed
doors.
¹¹People in the streets will ask for
wine.
But joy will have turned to
sadness.
All the happiness will have left.

¹²The city will be left in ruins.
  Its gates will be smashed to
    pieces.
¹³This is what will happen all over
    the earth.
  This will happen to all the
    nations.
The earth will be like an olive tree
    after the harvest.
  It will be like the few grapes left
    on a vine after harvest.

¹⁴The people shout for joy.
  From the west they praise the
    greatness of the Lord.
¹⁵People in the east, praise the Lord.
  People in the islands of the sea,
    praise the name of the Lord, the
    God of Israel.
¹⁶We hear songs from every part of
    the earth.
  These songs praise God, the
    Righteous One.

But I said, "I am dying! I am dying!
  How terrible it will be for me!
Traitors turn against people.
  With their dishonesty, they turn
    against people."
¹⁷There are terrors, holes and traps
    for the people of the earth.
¹⁸Anyone who tries to escape from
    the sound of terror
  will fall into a hole.
Anyone who climbs out of the hole
  will be caught in a trap.
The clouds in the sky will pour out
    rain.
  The foundations of the earth will
    shake.
¹⁹The earth will be broken up.
  And the earth will split open.
  The earth will shake violently.
²⁰The earth will stumble around like
    a man who is drunk.
  It will shake like a hut in a storm.
  Its sin is like a heavy weight on its
    back.
  The earth will fall and never rise
    again.

²¹At that time the Lord will punish
    the powers in the sky above
  and the rulers on earth below.
²²They will be gathered together.
  They will be thrown into a pit as
    prisoners.
They will be shut up in prison.
  After much time they will be
    punished.
²³The moon will be embarrassed.
  The sun will be ashamed.

This will happen because the Lord
  of heaven's armies will rule as
    king
on Mount Zion[d] in Jerusalem.
Jerusalem's leaders will see his
    greatness.

25 Lord, you are my God.
  I honor you and praise you.
You have done amazing things.
  You have always done what you
    said you would.
  You have done what you planned
    long ago.
²You have made the city a pile of
    rocks.
  You have destroyed her walls.
The city our enemies built with
    strong walls is gone.
  It will never be built again.
³People from powerful nations will
    honor you.
  Cruel people from strong cities
    will fear you.
⁴You help the poor people.
  You help the helpless when they
    are in danger.
You are like a shelter from storms.
  You are like shade that protects
    them from the heat.
The cruel people attack
  like a rainstorm beating against
    the wall.
⁵   The cruel people burn like the
    heat in the desert.
But you, God, stop their violent
    attack.
  As a cloud cools a hot day,
  Lord, you silence the songs of
    those who have no mercy.

⁶The Lord of heaven's armies will
  give a feast.
  It will be on this mountain for all
    people.
It will be a feast with the best food
    and wine.
  The meat and wine will be the
    finest.
⁷On this mountain God will destroy
    the veil that covers all nations.
  This veil, called "death," covers all
    peoples.
⁸But God will destroy death forever.
  The Lord God will wipe away
    every tear from every face.
God will take away the shame
  of his people from the earth.
The Lord has spoken.

⁹At that time people will say,
  "Our God is doing this!

We have trusted in him, and he has
come to save us.
We have been trusting our Lord.
So we will rejoice and be happy
when he saves us."
[10] The Lord will protect Jerusalem.
But the Lord will crush our
enemy Moab.
Moab will be like straw that is
trampled down in the manure.
[11] They will spread their arms in it
like a person who is swimming.
The Lord will bring down their
pride.
All the clever things they have
made will mean nothing.
[12] Moab's high walls protect them.
But the Lord will destroy these
walls.
The Lord will throw them down on
the ground.
The stones will lie in the dust.

26 At that time people will sing this
song in Judah:
We have a strong city.
God protects us with its strong
walls and defenses.
[2] Open the gates,
and the good people will enter.
They follow God's good way of
living.
[3] You, Lord, give true peace.
You give peace to those who
depend on you.
You give peace to those who trust
you.
[4] So, trust the Lord always.
Trust the Lord because he is our
Rock[d] forever.
[5] But the Lord will destroy the proud
city.
And he will punish the people
living there.
He will bring that high city down to
the ground.
He throws it down into the dust.
[6] Then those who were hurt by the
city will walk on its ruins.
Those who were made poor by
the city will trample it under
their feet.

[7] The path of life of the people who
are right with God is level.
Lord, you make the way of life
smooth for those people.
[8] But, Lord, we are waiting
for your way of justice.
Our souls want to remember
you and your name.

[9] My soul wants to be with you at
night.
And my spirit wants to be with
you at the dawn of every day.
When your way of justice comes to
the land,
people of the world will learn the
right way of living.
[10] An evil person will not learn to do
good
even if you show him kindness.
He will continue doing evil, even if
he lives in a good world.
He never sees the Lord's
greatness.
[11] Lord, you are ready to punish those
people.
But they do not see that.
Lord, show them your strong love
for your people.
Then the evil people will be
ashamed.
Burn them in the fire
you have prepared for your
enemies.
[12] Lord, all our success is because of
what you have done.
So give us peace.
[13] Lord, our God, other masters
besides you have ruled us.
But we honor only you.
[14] Those masters are now dead.
Their ghosts will not rise from
death.
You decided to destroy them.
And you destroyed any memory
of them.
[15] Lord, you multiplied the number of
your people.
You multiplied them and brought
honor to yourself.
You made the borders of the land
wide.
[16] Lord, people remember you when
they are in trouble.
They say quiet prayers to you
when you punish them.
[17] Lord, when we are with you,
we are like a woman giving birth
to a baby.
She cries and has pain from the
birth.
[18] In the same way, we had pain.
We gave birth, but only to wind.
We don't bring salvation to the
land.
We don't make new people for
the world.
[19] Your people have died, but they will
live again.
Their bodies will rise from death.

Dead people in the ground,
    get up and be happy!
The dew covering you is like the
    dew of a new day.
    The ground will give birth to the
      dead buried in it.

20 My people, go into your rooms.
    Shut your doors behind you.
Hide in your rooms for a short
    time.
    Hide until God's anger is
      finished.
21 The Lord will leave his place.
    He will punish the people of the
      world for their sins.
The earth will show the blood of
    the people who have been
    killed.
    It will not cover the dead any
      longer.

27 At that time the Lord will judge
    Leviathan,^{d} the gliding snake.
He will punish Leviathan, the
    coiled snake.
The Lord will use his great sword,
    his hard and powerful sword.
He will kill the monster in the sea.

2 In that day
    people will sing about the
      pleasant vineyard.
3 "I, the Lord, will care for that
    vineyard.
    I will water it at the right time.
No one will hurt it.
    I will guard it day and night.
4 I am not angry.
    If anyone builds a wall of
      thornbushes in war,
    I will march to it and burn it.
5 But if anyone comes to me for
    safety
    and wants to make peace with
      me,
    he should come and make peace
      with me."
6 In the days to come, the people of
    Jacob will be like a plant with
      good roots.
Israel will grow like a plant
    beginning to bloom.
    Then the world will be filled with
      their children.

7 The Lord has not hurt his people as
    he hurt their enemies.
His people have not been killed
    like those who tried to kill
    them.

8 The Lord will settle his argument
    with Israel by sending it far
    away.
    Like a hot desert wind, he will
      drive Israel away.
9 This is how Israel's guilt will be
    forgiven.
    This is how its sins will be taken
      away.
Israel will crush the rocks of the
    altar to dust.
    No statues or altars will be left
      standing for the Asherah^d
      idols.
10 At that time the strong, walled city
    will be empty.
    It will be like a desert.
Calves will eat grass there.
    They will lie down there.
    They will eat leaves from the
      branches.
11 The limbs will become dry and
    break off.
    Women will use them for
      firewood.
The people refuse to understand.
    So God will not comfort them.
    Their Maker will not be kind to
      them.

12 At that time the Lord will begin gathering his people one by one. He will gather all his people from the Euphrates River to the brook of Egypt. He will separate them from others as grain is separated from chaff.^{d} 13 Many of my people are now lost in Assyria. Some of my people have run away to Egypt. But at that time a great trumpet will be blown. And all those people will come back to Jerusalem. They will bow down before the Lord on that holy mountain.

28 How terrible it will be for
    Samaria, the pride of Israel's
      drunken people!
    That beautiful crown of flowers is
      just a dying plant.
It sits on a hill above a rich valley
    where drunkards live.
2 Look, the Lord has someone who is
    strong and full of power.
That person will come like a
    storm of hail and strong wind.
He will come like a sudden flood of
    water pouring over the country.
He will throw Samaria down to
    the ground.
3 That city, the pride of Israel's
    drunken people,
    will be trampled underfoot.

⁴That beautiful crown of flowers is
    just a dying plant.
  It sits on a hill above a rich
    valley.
  That city will be like the first fig of
    summer.
  When a person sees it,
    he quickly picks it and eats it.

⁵At that time the Lord of heaven's
    armies
  will be like a beautiful crown.
  He will be like a wonderful crown
    of flowers
  for his people who are left alive.
⁶Then the Lord will give wisdom
    to the judges who rule his people.
  The Lord will give strength
    to those who battle at the city
      gate.
⁷But now those leaders are drunk
    with wine.
  They stumble from drinking too
    much beer.
  The priests and prophets[d] are
    drunk with beer.
  They are filled with wine.
  They stumble from too much beer.
  The prophets are drunk when
    they see their visions.
  The judges stumble when they
    make their decisions.
⁸Every table is covered with vomit.
  There is not a clean place
    anywhere.

⁹The Lord is trying to teach the
    people a lesson.
  He is trying to make them
    understand his teachings.
  But the people are like little babies.
  They are like babies who just
    nursed at their mother's breast.
¹⁰So they make fun of the Lord's
    prophet and say:
  "A command here, a command
    there.
  A rule here, a rule there.
  A lesson here, a lesson there."
¹¹So the Lord will use strange words
    and foreign languages
  to speak to these people.
¹²God said to them,
  "Here is a place of rest.
  Let the tired people come and rest.
  This is the place of peace."
  But the people would not listen.
¹³So the words of the Lord will be,
  "A command here, a command
    there.
  A rule here, a rule there.
  A lesson here, a lesson there."
  They will fall back and will be
    defeated.
  They will be trapped and
    captured.

¹⁴You who brag should listen to the
    Lord's message.
  Pay attention, you leaders in
    Jerusalem.
¹⁵You say, "We have made an
    agreement with death.
  We have a contract with death.
  When punishment passes by,
    it won't hurt us.
  We will be safe with our lies.
  We will hide behind our tricks."

¹⁶Because of these things, this is what
  the Lord God says:
  "I will put a stone in the ground in
    Jerusalem.
  This will be a tested stone.
  Everything will be built on this
    important and precious rock.
  Anyone who trusts in it will
    never be disappointed.
¹⁷I will use justice as a measuring
    line.
  I will use goodness to measure
    by.
  The lies you hide behind will be
    destroyed as if by hail.
  They will be washed away as if in
    a flood.
¹⁸Your agreement with death will be
    erased.
  Your contract with death will not
    help you.
  When punishment comes,
    you will be crushed by it.
¹⁹Whenever punishment comes, it
    will take you away.
  It will come morning after
    morning.
  It will defeat you by day and by
    night.
  Those who hear of this punishment
    will be terrified."
²⁰You will be like the man who tried
    to sleep
  on a bed that was too short for
    him.
  And his blanket was too narrow
    to wrap around himself.
²¹The Lord will fight as he did at
    Mount Perazim.
  He will be angry as he was in the
    Valley of Gibeon.

Then the Lord will do his work, his
strange work.
He will finish his job, his strange
job.
²²Now, you must not make fun of
these things.
If you do, the ropes around you
will become tighter.
The Lord of heaven's armies has
told me these things.
He has told me how the whole
earth will be destroyed.

²³Listen closely to what I tell you.
Listen carefully to what I say.
²⁴A farmer does not plow his field all
the time.
He does not go on working the
soil.
²⁵He prepares the ground.
Then he plants the dill seed and
scatters the cummin seed.
He plants the wheat in rows.
He plants barley in its special
place,
and other wheat in its own field.
²⁶His God teaches him
and shows him the right way.
²⁷A farmer doesn't use heavy boards
to crush dill.
He doesn't use a wagon to crush
cummin.
He uses a small stick to break open
the dill.
With a stick he opens the
cummin.
²⁸The grain is ground to make bread.
People do not ruin it by crushing
it forever.
The farmer separates the wheat
from the chaff^d with his cart.
But he does not let his horses
grind it.
²⁹This lesson comes from the Lord of
heaven's armies.
He gives wonderful advice. He is
very wise.

29 How terrible it will be for you,
Jerusalem.
You are the city where David
camped.
Her festivals have continued
year after year.
²I will attack Jerusalem.
That city will be filled with
sadness and crying.
It will be like an altar to me.
³I will put armies all around you,
Jerusalem.
I will surround you with towers.

I will build devices around you to
attack you.
⁴You will be pulled down and will
speak from the ground.
I will hear your voice rising from
the ground.
It will sound like the voice of a
ghost.
Your words will come like a
whisper from the dirt.

⁵Your many enemies will become
like fine dust.
The groups of cruel people will
be like chaff^d that is blown
away.
Everything will happen very
quickly.
⁶ The Lord of heaven's armies will
come.
He will come with thunder,
earthquakes and great noises.
He will come with storms, strong
winds and a fire that destroys.
⁷Then all the nations that fight
against Jerusalem
will be like a dream.
All the nations that surround and
attack her
will be like a vision in the night.
⁸They will be like a hungry man
who dreams he is eating.
But when he wakes up, he is still
hungry.
They will be like a thirsty man who
dreams he is drinking.
But when he wakes up, he is still
weak and thirsty.
It will be the same way with all the
nations
who fight against Mount Zion.^d

⁹Be surprised and amazed.
Blind yourselves so that you
cannot see.
Become drunk, but not from wine.
Trip and fall, but not from beer.
¹⁰The Lord has made you go into a
deep sleep.
He has closed your eyes. (The
prophets are your eyes.)
He has covered your heads. (The
seers^d are your heads.)

¹¹This vision is like the words of a
book that is closed and sealed. You may
give the book to someone who can read.
And you may tell that person to read it.
But he will say, "I can't read the book.
It is closed, and I can't open it." ¹²Or
you may give the book to someone who
cannot read. You may tell him to read

the book. But he will say, "I can't read it
because I don't know how to read."

¹³The Lord says:
"These people say they love me.
    They show honor to me with
      words.
    But their hearts are far from me.
The honor they show me
    is nothing but human rules they
      have memorized.
¹⁴So I will continue to amaze these
    people
    by doing more and more
      miracles.ᵈ
Their wise men will lose their
    wisdom.
Their wise men will not be able
    to understand."

¹⁵How terrible it will be for those
    who try
    to hide things from the Lord.
How terrible it will be for those
    who do their work in darkness.
They think no one will see them
    or know what they do.
¹⁶You are confused.
    You think the clay is equal to the
      potter.
    You think that an object can tell the
      person who made it,
    "You didn't make me."
This is like a pot telling its maker,
    "You don't know anything."

¹⁷In a very short time, Lebanon will
    become rich farmland.
    And the rich farmland will seem
      like a forest.
¹⁸At that time the deaf will hear the
    words in a book.
    Instead of having darkness and
      gloom, the blind will see.
¹⁹The Lord will make the poor people
    happy.
    They will rejoice in the Holy One
      of Israel.
²⁰Then the people without mercy will
    come to an end.
    Those who do not respect God
      will disappear.
    Those who enjoy doing evil will
      be gone.
²¹Those who lie about others in court
    will be gone.
    Those who trap people in court
      will be gone.
    Those who lie and take justice
      from innocent people in court
      will be gone.

²²The Lord set Abraham free. This
Lord speaks to the family of Jacob.
    "Now the people of Jacob will not
      be ashamed.
    They will not be disgraced any
      longer.
²³They will see all their children,
    the children I made with my
      hands.
    And they will say my name is holy.
    The people will agree that the
      Holy One of Jacob is holy.
    They will respect the God of
      Israel.
²⁴People who do wrong will now
    understand.
    Those who complain will accept
      being taught."

30 The Lord said,
    "How terrible it will be for these
      stubborn children.
They make plans, but they don't
    ask me to help them.
    They make agreements with
      other nations, without asking
      my Spirit.ᵈ
    They are adding more and more
      sins to themselves.
²They go down to Egypt for help,
    but they didn't ask me about it
      first.
    They hope they will be saved by the
      king of Egypt.
    They want Egypt to protect them.
³But hiding in Egypt will bring you
    only shame.
    Egypt's protection will only
      disappoint you.
⁴Your officers have gone to Zoan.
    Your messengers have gone to
      Hanes.
⁵But they will be put to shame,
    because Egypt is useless to them.
    Egypt will give no help and be of
      no use.
    It will cause them only shame
      and embarrassment."

⁶This is the message about the animals in southern Judah:
    Southern Judah is a dangerous
      place.
    It is full of lions and lionesses,
      poisonous snakes and darting
      snakes.
The messengers travel through
    there with their wealth on
      donkeys' backs.
    They have put their treasure on
      the backs of camels.

They carry them to a nation that
cannot help them.
7 They go to Egypt whose help is
useless.
So I call that country Rahab[d] the
Do-Nothing.

8 Now write this on a sign for the
people.
Write this on a scroll.
Write these things for the days to
come.
Write them so they will last
forever.
9 These people are like children who
lie and refuse to obey.
They refuse to listen to the Lord's
teachings.
10 They tell the seers,[d]
"Don't see any more visions!"
They say to the prophets,[d]
"Don't tell us the truth!
Say things that will make us feel
good.
See only good things for us.
11 Stop blocking our path.
Get out of our way.
Stop telling us
about God, the Holy One of
Israel."

12 So this is what the Holy One of Israel
says:
"You people have refused to accept
this message from the Lord.
You depended on cruelty and lies
to help you.
13 You are guilty of these things.
So you are like a high wall with
cracks in it.
It will fall suddenly and break
into small pieces.
14 You will be like a clay jar that
breaks.
It breaks into many pieces.
Those pieces will be too small
to take coals from the fire
or to get water from a well."

15 This is what the Lord God, the Holy
One of Israel, says:
"If you come back to me and trust
me, you will be saved.
If you will be calm and trust me,
you will be strong."
But you don't want to do that.
16 You say, "No, we need horses to
run away on."
So you will run away on horses.
You say, "We will ride away on fast
horses."

So those who chase you will be
fast.
17 One enemy will make threats,
and 1,000 of your men will run
away.
Five enemies will make threats,
and all of you will run from them.
You will be left alone like a flagpole
on a hilltop.
You will be like a banner on a
hill.
18 The Lord wants to show his mercy
to you.
He wants to rise and comfort
you.
The Lord is a fair God.
And everyone who waits for his
help will be happy.

19 You people who live on Mount Zion[d]
in Jerusalem will not cry anymore. The
Lord will hear your crying, and he will
comfort you. The Lord will hear you,
and he will help you. 20 The Lord has
given you sorrow and hurt. It was like
the bread and water you ate every day.
But he is your teacher, and he will not
continue to hide from you. You will see
your teacher with your own eyes. 21 If
you go the wrong way—to the right or
to the left—you will hear a voice behind
you. It will say, "This is the right way.
You should go this way." 22 You have statues covered with silver and gold. But
you will ruin them for further use. You
will throw them away like filthy rags.
You will say, "Go away!"

23 At that time the Lord will send rain
for you. You will plant seeds in the
ground, and the ground will grow food
for you. The harvest will be very great.
You will have plenty of food in the fields
for your animals. There will be large
fields for your sheep. 24 Your oxen and
donkeys will work the soil. They will
have all the food they need. You will
have to use shovels and pitchforks to
spread all the food for your animals to
eat. 25 Every mountain and hill will have
streams filled with water. These things
will happen after many people are killed
and the towers are pulled down. 26 At
that time the light from the moon will
be bright like the sun. The light from the
sun will be seven times brighter than
now. The light from the sun in one day
will be like a full week. These things
will happen when the Lord bandages his
broken people and heals the hurts he
gave them.

27 Look! The Lord comes from far
away.
His anger is like a fire with thick
clouds of smoke.
His mouth is filled with anger,
and his tongue is like a burning
fire.
28 The Lord's breath is like a rushing
river.
It rises until it reaches the throat.
He will judge the nations as if he is
sifting them through the
strainer of destruction.
He will place in their mouths a
bit that will lead them the
wrong way.
29 You will sing happy songs
as on the nights you begin a
festival.
You will be happy as people
listening to flutes
as they go to the mountain of the
Lord.
The Lord is the Rock[d] of Israel.
30 The Lord will cause all people to
hear his great voice.
He will cause them to see his
powerful arm come down.
It will come with anger like a great
fire that burns everything.
It will be like a great storm with
much rain and hail.
31 Assyria will be afraid when it hears
the voice of the Lord.
The Lord will beat Assyria with a
rod.
32 The Lord will punish Assyria with
a rod.
He will beat them to the music of
tambourines[d] and harps.
The Lord will fight against them
with his mighty weapons.
33 Topheth[n] has been made ready for
a long time.
It is ready for the king.
It was made deep and wide.
There is much wood and fire
there.
And the Lord's breath will come
like a stream of burning sulfur
and burn it.

31 How terrible it will be for those
people who go down to
Egypt for help.
They think horses will save them.
They think their many chariots
and strong horsemen will save
them.

They don't trust God, the Holy One
of Israel.
They don't ask the Lord for help.
2 But it is the Lord who is wise and
who can bring them trouble.
He does not change his warnings.
He will rise up and fight against the
evil people.
And he will fight against those
who try to help evil people.
3 The Egyptians are only people and
are not God.
Their horses are only animals
and are not spirit.
The Lord will stretch out his arm,
and the one who helps will
stumble.
The people who wanted help will
fall.
All of them will be destroyed
together.

4 The Lord says this to me:
"When a lion or a lion's cub kills
an animal to eat,
it stands over the dead animal
and roars.
A band of shepherds
may be assembled against it.
But the lion will not be afraid of
their yelling.
It will not be upset by their noise.
So the Lord of heaven's armies will
come down
to fight on Mount Zion[d] and on
its hill.
5 The Lord of heaven's armies will
defend Jerusalem.
He will defend it like birds flying
over their nests.
He will defend and save it.
He will 'pass over' and save
Jerusalem."

6 You children of Israel, come back to
the God that you fought against. 7 The
time is coming when each of you will
stop worshiping the idols of gold and
silver that you made. You truly sinned
when you made them.

8 "Assyria will be defeated by a
sword, but not the sword of a
man.
Assyria will be destroyed, but not
by a man's sword.
Assyria will run away from the
sword of God.
But their young men will be
caught and made slaves.

30:33 Topheth Gehenna; the Valley of Hinnom. Here people burned the bodies of criminals and
animals, along with garbage.

[9]They will panic, and their place of
safety will be destroyed.
    Their commanders will be
      terrified when they see God's
      battle flag."
The Lord said all these things.
    The Lord's fire is in Jerusalem.
    His furnace is in Jerusalem.

32

A king will rule in a way that
    brings justice.
    Leaders will make fair decisions.
[2]Then each ruler will be like a
    shelter from the wind.
    He will be like a safe place in a
      storm.
He will be like streams of water in
    a dry land.
He will be like a cool shadow
    from a large rock in a hot land.

[3]People will look to the king for
    help.
    And they will truly listen to what
      he says.
[4]People who are now worried will be
    able to understand.
    Those who cannot speak clearly
      now will then be able to speak
      clearly and quickly.
[5]Fools will not be called great men.
    People will not respect wicked
      men.
[6]A fool says foolish things.
    And in his mind he plans to do
      evil things.
A fool wants to do things that are
    wrong.
    He says wrong things about the
      Lord.
A fool does not feed the hungry.
    He does not let thirsty people
      drink water.
[7]The wicked man uses evil like a
    tool.
    He plans ways to take everything
      from poor people.
He destroys the poor with lies,
    even when the poor man is in the
      right.
[8]But a good leader plans good
    things to do.
    And those good things make him
      a good leader.

[9]You women who are calm now,
    stand up and listen to me.
You women who feel safe now,
    hear what I say.
[10]You women feel safe now,
    but after one year you will be
    afraid.

There will be no grape harvest.
    There will not be any summer
      fruit to gather.
[11]Women, you are calm now, but you
    should shake with fear.
    Women, you feel safe now, but
      you should tremble.
Take off your nice clothes.
    Then put rough cloth around
      your waist to show your
      sadness.
[12]Beat your breasts in grief because
    the fields that were pleasant
      are now empty.
    Cry because the vines that once
      had fruit now have no more
      grapes.
[13]Cry for the land of my people.
    Cry because only thorns and
      weeds grow there now.
Cry for the city that once was
    happy.
    And cry for all the houses that
      once were filled with joy.
[14]The palace will be empty.
    People will leave the noisy city.
Strong cities and towers will be
    empty.
    Wild donkeys will love to live
      there. Sheep will go there to
      eat.
[15]This will continue until God puts
    his Spirit[d] from above into us.
    Then the desert will be like a
      fertile field.
    And the fertile field will be like a
      forest.
[16]Justice will be found even in the
    desert.
    And fairness will be found in the
      fertile fields.
[17]That fairness will bring peace.
    And fairness will bring calm and
      safety forever.
[18]My people will live in peaceful
    places.
    They will have safe homes.
    They will live in calm places of
      rest.
[19]Hail will destroy the forest.
    And the city will be completely
      destroyed.
[20]But you will be happy as you plant
    seeds near every stream.
    You will let your cattle and
      donkeys wander freely.

33

How terrible it will be for you
    who destroy others.
    But you have not been destroyed
      yet.

How terrible it will be for you,
  traitor.
  But no one has turned against
    you yet.
When you stop destroying,
  others will destroy you.
When you stop turning against
    others,
  they will turn against you.

²Lord, be kind to us.
  We have waited for your help.
Lord, give us strength every
    morning.
  Save us when we are in trouble.
³Your powerful voice makes people
    run away in fear.
  Your greatness causes the
    nations to run away.
⁴Like locusts,ᵈ your enemies will
    take away the things you stole
    in war.
  Like locusts rushing about, they
    will take your wealth.
⁵The Lord is very great. He lives in a
    high place.
  He fills Jerusalem with fairness
    and justice.
⁶The Lord will be your safety.
  He is full of salvation, wisdom
    and knowledge.
  Respect for the Lord is the
    greatest treasure.

⁷See, brave men are crying out in
    the streets.
  Those who tried to bring peace
    are crying loudly.
⁸There is no one on the roads.
  No one is walking in the paths.
  People have broken the agreements
    they made.
  People refuse to believe the proof
    from witnesses.
  No one respects other people.
⁹The land is sick and dying.
  Lebanon is ashamed and dying.
  The Plain of Sharon is dry like the
    desert.
  The trees of Bashan and Carmel
    are dying.

¹⁰The Lord says, "Now, I will stand
    up
  and show my greatness.
  Now, I will become important to
    the people.
¹¹You people do useless things.
  These things are like hay and
    straw.
  A destructive wind will burn you
    like fire.

¹²People will be burned until their
    bones become like lime.
  They will burn quickly like dry
    thornbushes."

¹³You people in faraway lands, hear
    what I have done.
  You people who are near me,
    learn about my power.
¹⁴The sinners in Jerusalem are
    afraid.
  The people who are separated
    from God shake with fear.
  They say, "Can any of us live
    through this fire that destroys?
  Who can live near this fire that
    burns on and on?"
¹⁵A person might do what is right.
  He might speak what is right.
  He might refuse to take money
    unfairly.
  He might refuse to take money to
    hurt others.
  He might not listen to plans of
    murder.
  He might refuse to think about
    evil.
¹⁶This is the kind of person who will
    be safe.
  He will be protected as he would
    be in a high, walled city.
  He will always have bread,
    and he will not run out of water.
¹⁷Your eyes will see the king in his
    beauty.
  You will see the land that
    stretches far away.
¹⁸You will think about the terror of
    the past.
  You will think, "Where is that
    officer?
  Where is the one who collected
    the taxes?
  Where is the officer in charge of
    our defense towers?"
¹⁹You will not see those proud people
    from other countries anymore.
  No more will you hear their
    strange language
  that you couldn't understand.

²⁰Look at Jerusalem, the city of our
    festivals.
  Look at Jerusalem, that beautiful
    place of rest.
  It is like a tent that will never be
    moved.
  The pegs that hold her in place
    will never be moved.
  Her ropes will never be broken.
²¹There the Lord will be our Mighty
    One.

That land is a place with streams
   and wide rivers.
But there will be no enemy boats
   on those rivers.
No powerful ship will sail on
   those rivers.
²²This is because the Lord is our
   judge.
The Lord makes our laws.
The Lord is our king.
He will save us.
²³You sailors from other lands, hear:
   The ropes on your boats hang
      loose.
   The mast is not held firm.
   The sails are not spread open.
The Lord will give us your wealth.
   There will be so much wealth
      even the crippled people will
      carry off a share.
²⁴No one living in Jerusalem will say,
   "I am sick."
The people who live there will
   have their sins forgiven.

34 All you nations, come near and
      listen.
      Pay attention, you peoples!
The earth and all the people in it
   should listen.
The world and everything in it
   should listen.
²The Lord is angry with all the
   nations.
He is angry with their armies.
He will destroy them and kill them
   all.
³Their bodies will be thrown
   outside.
The stink will rise from the
   bodies,
   and the blood will flow down the
      mountains.
⁴The sun, moon and stars will
   dissolve.
The sky will be rolled up like a
   scroll.
The stars will fall
   like dead leaves from a vine
   or dried-up figs from a fig tree.
⁵The Lord's sword in the sky is
   covered with blood.
It will cut through Edom.
He will destroy these people as
   an offering to the Lord.
⁶The Lord's sword will be covered
   with blood.
It will be covered with fat.
It is the blood from lambs and
   goats.

It is the fat from the kidneys of
   male sheep.
This is because the Lord decided
   there will be a sacrifice in
   Bozrah.
He has decided there will be
   much killing in Edom.
⁷The oxen will be killed.
And the cattle and the strong
   bulls will be killed.
The land will be filled with their
   blood.
The dirt will be covered with
   their fat.

⁸The Lord has chosen a time for
   punishment.
He has chosen a year when
   people must pay for the wrongs
   they did to Jerusalem.
⁹Edom's rivers will be like hot tar.
The dirt of Edom will be like
   burning sulfur.
The land of Edom will be like
   burning tar.
¹⁰The fires will burn night and day.
The smoke will rise from Edom
   forever.
Year after year that land will be
   empty.
No one will ever travel through
   that land again.
¹¹Birds and small animals will own
   that land.
Owls and ravens will live there.
God will make it an empty
   wasteland.
It will have nothing left in it.
¹²The important men will have no
   one left to rule them.
The leaders will all be gone.
¹³Thorns will take over the strong
   towers.
Wild bushes will grow in the
   walled cities.
Wild dogs will live there.
Owls will live in those homes.
¹⁴Desert animals will live with the
   hyenas there.
And wild goats will call to their
   friends.
Night animals will live there.
They will find a place of rest
   there.
¹⁵Owls will nest there and lay eggs.
When the eggs open, the owls
   will gather their young under
   their wings.
Hawks will gather
   with their own kind.

¹⁶Look at the Lord's scroll. Read what
is written there:
  None of these will be missing.
  Every one will have its mate.
  God said he will gather them
    together.
  So his Spirit[d] will gather them
    together.
¹⁷God has divided the land among
    them.
  And he has given them each their
    land.
  So they will own that land forever.
  They will live there year after
    year.

35 The desert and dry land will
    become happy.
  The desert will be glad and will
    produce flowers.
  Like a flower, ²it will have many
    blooms.
  It will show its happiness, as if it
    is shouting with joy.
  It will be beautiful like the forest of
    Lebanon.
  It will be as beautiful as the hill
    of Carmel and the Plain of
    Sharon.
  All people will see the glory of the
    Lord.
  They will see the splendor of our
    God.

³Make the weak hands strong.
  Make the weak knees strong.
⁴Say to people who are afraid and
    confused,
  "Be strong. Don't be afraid.
  Look, your God will come,
    and he will punish your enemies.
  He will make them pay for the
    wrongs they did.
  He will come and save you."

⁵Then the blind people will see
    again.
  Then the deaf will hear.
⁶Crippled people will jump like deer.
  And those who can't talk now
    will shout with joy.
  Springs of water will flow in the
    desert.
  Streams will flow in the dry land.
⁷The burning desert will have pools
    of water.
  The dry ground will have springs.
  Where wild dogs once lived,
    grass and water plants will grow.
⁸A road will be there.
  This highway will be called "The
    Road to Being Holy."

  Evil people will not be allowed to
    walk on that road.
  Only good people will walk on
    that road.
  No fools will go on it.
⁹No lions will be there.
  No dangerous animals will be on
    that road.
  They will not be found there.
  That road will be for the people
    God saves.
¹⁰ The people the Lord has freed
    will return there.
  They will enter Jerusalem with joy.
  Their happiness will last forever.
  Their gladness and joy will fill
    them completely.
  Sorrow and sadness will go far
    away.

36 During Hezekiah's fourteenth
    year as king, Sennacherib king of
Assyria attacked Judah. He attacked all
the strong, walled cities of Judah and
defeated them. ²The king of Assyria sent
out his field commander. He went with
a large army from Lachish to King Hezekiah in Jerusalem. When the commander came near the waterway from
the upper pool, he stopped. The upper
pool is on the road to the Washerman's
Field. ³Eliakim, Shebna and Joah went
out to meet him. Eliakim son of Hilkiah
was the palace manager. Shebna was
the royal assistant. And Joah son of
Asaph was the recorder.

⁴The field commander said to them,
"Tell Hezekiah this:

" 'The great king, the king of Assyria,
says: You have nothing to trust in to help
you. ⁵You say you have battle plans and
power for war. But your words mean
nothing. Whom are you trusting for help
so that you turn against me? ⁶Look, you
are depending on Egypt to help you.
Egypt is like a splintered walking stick.
If you lean on it for help, it will stab you
and hurt you. The king of Egypt will hurt
those who depend on him. ⁷You might
say, "We are depending on the Lord our
God." But Hezekiah destroyed the
Lord's altars and the places of worship.
Hezekiah told Judah and Jerusalem,
"You must worship only at this one
altar."

⁸" 'Now make an agreement with my
master, the king of Assyria: I will give
you 2,000 horses if you can find enough
men to ride them. ⁹You cannot defeat
one of my master's least important officers. So why do you depend on Egypt to

give you chariots and horsemen? [10]I have not come to attack and destroy this country without an order from the Lord. The Lord himself told me to come to this country and destroy it.'"

[11]Then Eliakim, Shebna and Joah spoke to the field commander. They said, "Please speak to us in the Aramaic language. We understand it. Don't speak to us in Hebrew because the people on the city wall can hear you."

[12]But the commander said, "No. My master did not send me to tell these things only to you and your king. My master sent me to tell them also to those people sitting on the wall. They will have to eat their own dung and drink their own urine like you."

[13]Then the commander stood and shouted loudly in the Hebrew language. He said, "Listen to the words from the great king, the king of Assyria! [14]The king says you should not let Hezekiah fool you. Hezekiah can't save you. [15]Don't let Hezekiah talk you into trusting the Lord. Hezekiah says, 'The Lord will surely save us. This city won't be given over to the king of Assyria.'

[16]"Don't listen to Hezekiah. The king of Assyria says, 'Make peace with me. Come out of the city to me. Then everyone will be free to eat the fruit from his own grapevine and fig tree. Everyone will be free to drink water from his own well. [17]Then I will come and take you to a land like your own. It is a land with grain and new wine. It has bread and vineyards.'

[18]"Don't let Hezekiah fool you. He says, 'The Lord will save us.' The god of any other nation has not saved his people from the power of the king of Assyria. [19]Where are the gods of Hamath and Arpad? Where are the gods of Sepharvaim? They did not save Samaria from my power. [20]Not one of all the gods of these countries has saved his people from me. Then the Lord cannot save Jerusalem from my power."

[21]The people were silent. They didn't answer the commander at all. This was because King Hezekiah had ordered, "Don't answer him."

[22]Then Eliakim, Shebna and Joah tore their clothes to show how upset they were. (Eliakim son of Hilkiah was the palace manager. Shebna was the royal assistant. And Joah son of Asaph was the recorder.) The three men went to Hezekiah and told him what the field commander had said.

37

When King Hezekiah heard the message, he tore his clothes. And he put on rough cloth to show how sad he was. Then he went into the Temple[d] of the Lord. [2]Hezekiah sent Eliakim, Shebna and the older priests to Isaiah. Eliakim was the palace manager, and Shebna was the royal assistant. The men were all wearing the rough cloth when they came to Isaiah. He was a prophet,[d] the son of Amoz. [3]These men told Isaiah, "This is what Hezekiah says: Today is a day of sorrow and punishment and disgrace. It is sad, as when a child should be born, but the mother is not strong enough to give birth to it. [4]The king of Assyria sent his field commander to make fun of the living God. Maybe the Lord your God will hear what the commander said. Maybe the Lord your God will punish him for what he said. So pray for the few people of Israel who are left alive."

[5]When Hezekiah's officers came to Isaiah, [6]he said to them, "Tell your master this: The Lord says, 'Don't be afraid of what you have heard. Don't be frightened by the words the servants of the king of Assyria said against me. [7]Listen! I am going to put a spirit in the king of Assyria. He will hear a report that will make him return to his own country. And I will cause him to die by the sword there.'"

[8]The field commander heard that the king of Assyria had left Lachish. So the commander left and found the king fighting against the city of Libnah.

[9]The king received a report that Tirhakah was coming to attack him. Tirhakah was the Cushite king of Egypt. When the king of Assyria heard this, he sent messengers to Hezekiah. The king said: [10]"Say this to Hezekiah king of Judah: Don't be fooled by the god you trust. Don't believe him when he says Jerusalem will not be defeated by the king of Assyria. [11]You have heard what the kings of Assyria have done. They have completely defeated every country. Do not think you will be saved. [12]The gods of those people did not save them. My ancestors destroyed them. My ancestors defeated the cities of Gozan, Haran and Rezeph. They defeated the people of Eden living in Tel Assar. [13]Where are the kings of Hamath and Arpad? Where is the king of the city of Sepharvaim? Where are the kings of Hena and Ivvah?"

[14]Hezekiah received the letter from the messengers and read it. Then he went up to the Temple[d] of the Lord. Hezekiah spread the letter out before the Lord. [15]And he prayed to the Lord: [16]"Lord of heaven's armies, you are the God of Israel. Your throne is between the gold creatures with wings. Only you are the God of all the kingdoms of the earth. You made the heavens and the earth. [17]Hear, Lord, and listen. Open your eyes, Lord, and see. Listen to all the words Sennacherib has said to insult the living God.

[18]"It is true, Lord. The kings of Assyria have destroyed all these countries and their lands. [19]These kings have thrown the gods of these nations into the fire. But they were only wood and rock statues that men made. So the kings have destroyed them. [20]Now, Lord our God, save us from the king's power. Then all the kingdoms of the earth will know that you, Lord, are the only God."

[21]Then Isaiah son of Amoz sent a message to Hezekiah. Isaiah said, "The Lord, the God of Israel, says this: 'You prayed to me about Sennacherib king of Assyria. [22]So this is what the Lord has said against Sennacherib:

The people of Jerusalem
hate you and make fun of you.
The people of Jerusalem
laugh at you as you run away.
[23]You have insulted me and spoken
against me.
You have raised your voice
against me.
You have a proud look on your
face.
You disobey me, the Holy One of
Israel!
[24]You have used your messengers to
insult the Lord.
You have said, "I have many
chariots.
With them I have gone to the tops
of the mountains.
I have climbed the highest
mountains of Lebanon.
I have cut down its tallest cedars.
I have cut down its best pine
trees.
I have gone to its greatest heights.
I have gone to its best forests.
[25]I have dug wells in foreign
countries.
I have drunk water there.
By the soles of my feet,
I have dried up all the rivers of
Egypt."

[26]"'King of Assyria, surely you have
heard.
Long ago I, the Lord, planned
these things.
Long ago I planned them.
Now I have made them happen.
I allowed you to turn those strong,
walled cities
into piles of rocks.
[27]The people living in those cities
were weak.
They were frightened and put to
shame.
They were like grass in the field.
They were like tender, young
grass.
They were like grass that grows on
the housetop.
It is burned by the wind before it
can grow.

[28]"'I know when you rest and when
you come and go.
I know how you speak against
me.
[29]You speak strongly against me.
And I have heard your proud
words.
So I will put my hook in your nose.
And I will put my bit in your
mouth.
Then I will force you to leave my
country
the same way that you came.'

[30]"Then the Lord said, 'Hezekiah, I will give you this sign:
This year you will eat the grain that
grows wild.
And the second year you will eat
what grows wild from that.
But in the third year, plant grain
and harvest it.
Plant vineyards and eat their
fruit.
[31]The people left alive in the family
of Judah
will be saved.
Like plants that take root,
they will grow strong and have
many children.
[32]A few people will come out of
Jerusalem alive.
There will be a few from Mount
Zion[d] who will live.
The strong love of the Lord of
heaven's armies
will cause this to happen.'

[33]"So this is what the Lord says about the king of Assyria:

'He will not enter this city.
He will not even shoot an arrow
here.
He will not fight against it with
shields.
He will not build a ramp to attack
the city walls.
[34] He will return to his country the
same way he came.
He will not enter this city,'
says the Lord.
[35] The Lord says, 'I will defend and
save this city.
I will do this for myself and for
David, my servant.' "

[36] Then the angel of the Lord went out.
He killed 185,000 men in the Assyrian
camp. When the people got up early the
next morning, they saw all the dead
bodies! [37] So Sennacherib king of Assyria left. He went back to Nineveh and
stayed there. [38] One day Sennacherib was worshiping in the temple of his god Nisroch.
While he was there, his sons Adrammelech and Sharezer killed him with a
sword. Then they escaped to the land of
Ararat. So Sennacherib's son Esarhaddon became king of Assyria.

38 At that time Hezekiah became
very sick. He was almost dead.
The prophet[d] Isaiah son of Amoz went
to see him. Isaiah told him, "This is what
the Lord says: You are going to die. So
you should give your last orders to
everyone. You will not get well."

[2] Hezekiah turned toward the wall and
prayed to the Lord. [3] He said, "Lord,
please remember that I have always
obeyed you. I have given myself completely to you. I have done what you said
was right." And Hezekiah cried loudly.

[4] Then the Lord spoke his word to Isaiah: [5] "Go to Hezekiah and tell him: 'This
is what the Lord, the God of your ancestor David, says: I have heard your
prayer. And I have seen your tears. I will
add 15 years to your life. [6] I will save you
and this city from the king of Assyria. I
will defend this city.' "

[21n] Then Isaiah said, "Make a paste
from figs. Put it on Hezekiah's boil.
Then he will get well."

[22] Hezekiah asked Isaiah, "What will
be the sign? What will show that I will
go up to the Temple[d] of the Lord?"

[7] Isaiah said, "The Lord will do what
he says. This is the sign from the Lord

to show you: [8] The sun has made a
shadow go down the stairway of Ahaz.
I will make it go back ten steps." So the
shadow made by the sun went back up
the ten steps it had gone down.

[9] After Hezekiah king of Judah got
well, he wrote this song:

[10] I said, "I am in the middle of my
life.
Do I have to go through the gates
where the dead are now?
Will I have the rest of my life
taken away from me?"
[11] I said, "I will not see the Lord
in the land of the living again.
I will not again see the people
who live on the earth.
[12] Like a shepherd's tent,
my home has been pulled down
and taken from me.
I am finished like the cloth
a weaver rolls up and cuts from
the loom.
In one day you brought me to this
end.
[13] All night I cried loudly.
Like a lion, he crushed all my
bones.
In one day you brought me to this
end.
[14] I cried like a bird.
I moaned like a dove.
My eyes became tired as I looked to
the heavens.
Lord, I have troubles. Please help
me."

[15] What can I say?
The Lord told me what would
happen and then made it
happen.
I have had these troubles in my
soul.
So now I will be humble all my
life.
[16] Lord, because of you, men live.
Because of you, my spirit also
lives.
You made me well and let me live.
[17] It was for my own good
that I had such troubles.
Because you love me very much,
you did not let me die.
You threw my sins
far away.
[18] People in the place where the dead
are cannot praise you.
Those who have died cannot sing
praises to you.

38:21-22 These verses are generally found at the end of chapter 38. But the same story in
2 Kings 20:6-9 shows the events happened in this order.

Those who die don't trust you
to help them.
[19]The people who are alive are the
ones who praise you.
They praise you as I praise you
today.
A father should tell his children
that you provide help.

[20]The Lord saved me.
So we will sing and play songs.
We will make music in the Temple
of the Lord
all the days of our lives.

39 At that time Merodach-Baladan son of Baladan was king of Babylon. He sent letters and a gift to Hezekiah. He did this because he had heard that Hezekiah had been sick and was now well. [2]Hezekiah was happy to see the messengers. So he showed them what was in his storehouses: the silver, gold, spices and expensive perfumes. He showed them his swords and shields. He showed them all his wealth. He showed them everything in his palace and in his kingdom.

[3]Then Isaiah the prophet[d] went to King Hezekiah. He asked Hezekiah, "What did these men say? Where did they come from?"

Hezekiah said, "They came from a faraway country. They came to me from Babylon."

[4]So Isaiah asked him, "What did they see in your palace?"

Hezekiah said, "They saw everything in my palace. I showed them all my wealth."

[5]Then Isaiah said to Hezekiah: "Listen to the words of the Lord of heaven's armies: [6]'In the future everything in your palace will be taken away to Babylon. Everything your ancestors have stored up until this day will be taken away. Nothing will be left,' says the Lord. [7]Some of your own children will be taken away. Those who will be born to you will be taken away. And they will become eunuchs[d] in the palace of the king of Babylon."

[8]Hezekiah told Isaiah, "These words from the Lord are good." He said this because he thought, "There will be peace and security while I am king."

40 Your God says,
"Comfort, comfort my people.
[2]Speak kindly to the people of
Jerusalem.
Tell them

that their time of service is finished.
Tell them that they have paid for
their sins.
Tell them that the Lord has
punished Jerusalem
twice for every sin they did."

[3]This is the voice of a man who calls
out:
"Prepare in the desert
the way for the Lord.
Make the road in the dry lands
straight for our God.
[4]Every valley should be raised up.
Every mountain and hill should
be made flat.
The rough ground should be made
level.
The rugged ground should be
made smooth.
[5]Then the glory of the Lord will be
shown.
All people together will see it.
The Lord himself said these
things."

[6]A voice says, "Cry out!"
Then I said, "What shall I cry
out?"

"Say all people are like the grass.
And all their strength is like the
flowers of the field.
[7]The grass dies, and the flowers fall.
This is because the breath of the
Lord blows on them.
Surely the people are like grass.
[8]The grass dies, and the flowers fall.
But the word of our God will live
forever."

[9]Jerusalem, you have good news to
tell.
Go up on a high mountain.
Jerusalem, you have good news to
tell.
Shout out loud the good news.
Shout it out and don't be afraid.
Say to the towns of Judah,
"Here is your God."
[10]Look, the Lord God is coming with
power.
He will use his power to rule all
the people.
Look, he will bring reward for his
people.
He will have their payment with
him.
[11]The Lord takes care of his people
like a shepherd.
He gathers the people like lambs
in his arms.
He carries them close to him.

He gently leads the mothers of the lambs.

¹²Who has measured the oceans in the palm of his hand?
Who has used his hand to measure the sky?
Who has used a bowl to measure all the dust of the earth?
Who has used scales to weigh the mountains and hills?
¹³Who has known the mind of the Lord?
Who has been able to give the Lord advice?
¹⁴Whom did the Lord ask for help?
Who taught him the right way?
Who taught the Lord knowledge?
Who showed him the way to understanding?

¹⁵The nations are like one small drop in a bucket.
They are no more than the dust on his measuring scales.
To him the islands are no more than fine dust on his scales.
¹⁶All the trees in Lebanon are not enough for the altar fires.
And all the animals in Lebanon are not enough for burnt offerings.
¹⁷Compared to the Lord all the nations are worth nothing.
To him they are less than nothing.

¹⁸Can you compare God to anything?
Can you compare him to an image of anything?
¹⁹An idol is formed by a man.
And another man covers it with gold.
And he makes silver chains for it.
²⁰A poor man cannot buy those expensive statues.
So he finds a tree that will not rot.
And he finds a skilled workman to make it into an idol that will not fall over.

²¹Surely you know. Surely you have heard.
Surely in the beginning someone told you.
Surely you understand how the earth was created.
²²God sits on his throne above the circle of the earth.
And compared to him, people are like grasshoppers.
He stretches out the skies like a piece of cloth.

He spreads them out like a tent to sit under.
²³He makes rulers unimportant.
He makes the judges of this world worth nothing.
²⁴They are like plants that are placed in the ground.
They are like seeds that are planted.
As soon as they begin to grow strong,
he blows on them and they die.
The wind blows them away like chaff.[d]

²⁵God, the Holy One, says, "Can you compare me to anyone?
Is anyone equal to me?"
²⁶Look up to the skies.
Who created all these stars?
He leads out all the army of heaven one by one.
He calls all the stars by name.
He is very strong and full of power.
So not one of them is missing.

²⁷People of Jacob, why do you complain?
People of Israel, why do you say,
"The Lord does not see what happens to me.
He does not care if I am treated fairly"?
²⁸Surely you know.
Surely you have heard.
The Lord is the God who lives forever.
He created all the world.
He does not become tired or need to rest.
No one can understand how great his wisdom is.
²⁹The Lord gives strength to those who are tired.
He gives more power to those who are weak.
³⁰Even boys become tired and need to rest.
Even young men trip and fall.
³¹But the people who trust the Lord will become strong again.
They will be able to rise up as an eagle in the sky.
They will run without needing rest.
They will walk without becoming tired.

41

The Lord says, "Faraway countries, listen to me.
Let the nations become strong.
Come to me and speak.

We will meet together to decide
who is right.

2"Who caused the man to come
from the east?
Who gives the man victories
everywhere he goes?
The one who brought him gives
nations over to him.
He defeats kings for him.
The man uses his sword, and the
kings become like dust.
He uses his bow, and they are
blown away like chaff.d
3He chases them and is never hurt.
He goes places where he has
never been before.
4Who caused this to happen?
Who has controlled history since
the beginning?
I, the Lord, am the one. I was here
at the beginning.
And I will be here when all
things are finished."

5All you faraway places, look and be
afraid.
All you places far away on the
earth, shake with fear.
Come close and listen to me.
6   The workers help each other.
They say to each other, "Be
strong!"
7The man who carves wood
encourages the man who
works with gold.
The workman who smooths the
metal with a hammer
encourages the man who
shapes the metal.
This last workman says, "This
metal work is good."
He nails the statue to a base so it
can't fall over.

8The Lord says, "People of Israel,
you are my servants.
People of Jacob, I chose you.
You are from the family of my
friend Abraham.
9You were far away on the earth.
I called you from a faraway
country.
I said, 'You are my servants.'
I have chosen you, and I have not
turned against you.
10So don't worry, because I am with
you.
Don't be afraid, because I am
your God.
I will make you strong and will
help you.

I will support you with my right
hand that saves you.

11"All those people who are angry
with you
will be ashamed and disgraced.
Those who are against you
will disappear and be lost.
12You will look for your enemies.
But you will not find them.
Those who fought against you
will vanish completely.
13I am the Lord your God.
I am holding your right hand.
And I tell you, 'Don't be afraid.
I will help you.'
14You few people of Israel who are
left,
do not be afraid even though you
are weak as a worm.
I myself will help you," says the
Lord.
"I am the one who saves you, the
Holy One of Israel.
15Look, I have made you like a
threshingd board.
You are new, with many sharp
teeth.
So you will walk on mountains and
crush them.
You will make the hills like
chaff.d
16You will throw them into the air.
And the wind will carry them
away.
A windstorm will scatter them.
Then you will be happy in the Lord.
You will be proud of the Holy
One of Israel.

17"The poor and needy people look
for water.
But they can't find any.
Their tongues are dry with thirst.
But I, the Lord, will answer their
prayers.
I, the God of Israel, will not leave
them to die.
18I will make rivers flow on the dry
hills.
I will make springs of water flow
through the valleys.
I will change the desert into a lake
of water.
I will change the dry land into
springs of water.
19I will make trees grow in the desert.
There will be cedars, acacia,
myrtle and olive trees.
I will put pine, fir and cypress trees
growing together in the desert.

²⁰People will see these things and understand.
Together they will think carefully about these things.
They will know that the Lord's power did this.
They will know that the Holy One of Israel made these things."

²¹The Lord says, "Present your case."
The Lord, the King of Jacob, says, "Tell me your arguments.
²²Bring in your idols to tell us what is going to happen.
Have them tell us what happened in the beginning.
Then we will think about these things.
Then we will know how they will turn out.
Tell us what will happen in the future.
²³ Tell us what is coming next.
Then we will believe that you are gods.
Do something, whether it is good or bad.
Make us afraid of you.
²⁴You false gods are less than nothing.
You can't do anything.
Those who worship you should be hated."

²⁵"I have brought someone to come out of the north.ⁿ
I have called by name a man from the east, and he knows me.
He walks on kings as if they were mud.
He walks on them as a potter walks on the clay.
²⁶Who told us about this before it happened?
Who told us ahead of time so we could say, 'He was right'?
None of you told us anything.
None of you told us before it happened.
No one heard you tell about it.
²⁷I, the Lord, was the first one to tell Jerusalem that the people were coming home.
I sent a messenger to Jerusalem with the good news.
²⁸I look at the idols, but there is not one that can answer.
None of them can give advice.

None of them can answer my questions.
²⁹Look, all these idols are false gods.
They cannot do anything.
They are worth nothing.

42 "Here is my servant, the one I support.
He is the one I chose, and I am pleased with him.
I will put my Spiritᵈ in him.
And he will bring justice to all nations.
²He will not cry out or yell.
He will not speak loudly in the streets.
³He will not break a crushed blade of grass.
He will not put out even a weak flame.
He will bring justice and find what is true.
⁴ He will not lose hope or give up until he brings justice to the world.
And people far away will trust his teachings."

⁵God, the Lord, said these things.
He created the skies and stretched them out.
He spread out the earth and everything on it.
He gives life to all people on earth.
He gives life to everyone who walks on the earth.
⁶The Lord says, "I called you to do right.
And I will hold your hand.
I will protect you.
You will be the sign of my agreement with the people.
You will be a light to shine for all people.
⁷You will help the blind to see.
You will free those who are in prison.
You will lead those who live in darkness out of their prison.

⁸"I am the Lord. That is my name.
I will not give my glory to another.
I will not let idols take the praise that should be mine.
⁹The things I said would happen have happened.
And now I tell you about new things.
Before those things happen, I tell you about them."

41:25 someone . . . north This probably means Cyrus, a king of Persia.

[10]Sing a new song to the Lord.
Sing his praise everywhere on
    the earth.
Praise him, you people who sail on
    the seas and you animals who
    live in them.
Praise him, you people living in
    faraway places.
[11]The deserts and their cities should
    praise him.
The settlements of Kedar should
    praise him.
The people living in Sela should
    sing for joy.
They should sing from the
    mountaintops.
[12]They should give glory to the Lord.
People in faraway lands should
    praise him.
[13]The Lord will march out like a
    strong soldier.
He will be excited like a man
    ready to fight a war.
He will shout out the battle cry.
    And he will defeat his enemies.

[14]The Lord says, "For a long time I
    have said nothing.
I have been quiet and held myself
    back.
But now I will cry out.
I will strain like a woman giving
    birth to a child.
[15]I will destroy the hills and
    mountains.
I will dry up all the plants that
    grow there.
I will make the rivers become dry
    land.
I will dry up the pools of water.
[16]Then I will lead the blind along a
    way they never knew.
I will guide them along paths
    they have not known.
I will make the darkness become
    light for them.
And I will make the rough
    ground smooth.
These are the things I will do.
I will not leave my people.
[17]But some people trust in idols.
They say to their statues,
'You are our gods.'
Those people will be rejected in
    disgrace.

[18]"You who are deaf, hear me.
You who are blind, look and see.
[19]No one is more blind than my
    servant Israel.
The messenger I send is the most
    deaf.

No one is more blind than the
    person I own.
No one is more blind than the
    servant of the Lord.
[20]Israel, you have seen much, but you
    have not obeyed.
You have heard, but you refuse to
    listen."
[21]The Lord made his teachings
    wonderful.
He did this because he is good.
[22]These people have been defeated
    and robbed.
They are trapped in pits.
They are locked up in prison.
Like robbers, enemies have taken
    them away.
There is no one to save them.
Enemies carried them off.
And no one said, "Bring them
    back."

[23]Will any of you listen to this?
Will you listen carefully in the
    future?
[24]Who let the people of Jacob be
    carried off?
Who let robbers take Israel
    away?
The Lord allowed this to happen
    because we sinned against him.
We did not live the way the Lord
    wanted us to live.
We did not obey his teaching.
[25]So the Lord became very angry
    with us.
He brought terrible wars against
    us.
It was as if the people of Israel had
    fire all around them.
But they didn't know what was
    happening.
It was as if they were burning.
But they didn't pay any attention.

43 Now this is what the Lord says.
He created you, people of
    Jacob.
He formed you, people of Israel.
He says, "Don't be afraid, because I
    have saved you.
I have called you by name, and
    you are mine.
[2]When you pass through the waters,
    I will be with you.
When you cross rivers, you will
    not drown.
When you walk through fire, you
    will not be burned.
The flames will not hurt you.
[3]This is because I, the Lord, am your
    God.

I, the Holy One of Israel, am your
Savior.
I gave Egypt to pay for you.
I gave Cush and Seba to make
you mine.
⁴You are precious to me.
I give you honor, and I love you.
So I will give other people in your
place.
I will give other nations to save
your life.
⁵So don't be afraid. I am with you.
I will gather your children from
the east.
I will gather you from the west.
⁶I will tell the north: Give my people
to me.
I will tell the south: Don't keep
my people in prison.
Bring my sons from far away.
Bring my daughters from
faraway places.
⁷Bring to me all the people who are
mine.
I made them for my glory.
I formed them; I made them."

⁸Bring out the people who have eyes
but don't see.
Bring out those who have ears
but don't hear.
⁹All the nations should gather
together.
All the people should come
together.
Which of their gods said that this
would happen?
Which of their gods can tell what
happened in the beginning?
They should bring their witnesses
to prove they were right.
Then others will say, "It is true."
¹⁰The Lord says, "You are my
witnesses.
You are the servant I chose.
I chose you so you would know and
believe me.
I chose you so you would
understand that I am the true
God.
There was no God before me,
and there will be no God after me.
¹¹I myself am the Lord.
I am the only Savior.
¹²I myself have spoken to you, saved
you and told you these things.
It was not some foreign god
among you.
You are my witnesses, and I am
God,"
says the Lord.

¹³ "I have always been God.
No one can save people from my
power.
When I do something, no one can
change it."

¹⁴This is what the Lord says.
He is the Holy One of Israel who
saves you.
He says, "I will send armies to
Babylon for you.
All the Babylonians will be
captured.
They will be taken away in their
ships they are proud of.
¹⁵I am the Lord, your Holy One.
I made Israel. I am your king."

¹⁶This is what the Lord says.
He is the one who made a road
through the sea.
Even through rough waters he
made a path for his people.
¹⁷He is the one who defeated the
chariots and horses.
He defeated the mighty armies.
They fell together, and they will
never rise again.
They were destroyed as a flame
is put out.
¹⁸The Lord says, "Forget what
happened before.
Do not think about the past.
¹⁹Look at the new thing I am going to
do.
It is already happening. Don't
you see it?
I will make a road in the desert.
I will make rivers in the dry land.
²⁰Even the wild animals will be
thankful to me.
The wild dogs and owls will
honor me.
They will honor me when I put
water in the desert.
They will honor me when I make
rivers in the dry land.
I will do this to give water to my
people, the ones I chose.
²¹ These are the people I made.
And they will sing songs to
praise me.

²²"People of Jacob, you have not
called to me.
People of Israel, you have
become tired of me.
²³You have not brought your
sacrifices of sheep to me.
You have not honored me by
bringing sacrifices to me.

I did not force you to give sacrifices
to me.
I did not force you to burn
incense[d] until you became
tired.
²⁴So you did not buy incense for me.
You did not freely bring fat from
your sacrifices to me.
Instead you have weighed me down
with your many sins.
You have made me tired of your
many wrongs.

²⁵"I, I am the One who forgives all
your sins.
I do this to please myself.
I will not remember your sins.
²⁶But you should remind me.
Let's meet and decide what is
right.
Tell what you have done and
show you are right.
²⁷Your first father sinned.
And your leaders have turned
against me.
²⁸So I will make your holy rulers not
holy.
And I will bring destruction on
the people of Jacob.
And I will let Israel be insulted."

44 The Lord says, "People of Jacob,
you are my servants. Listen
to me!
People of Israel, I chose you."
²This is what the Lord says. He
made you.
He formed you when you were in
your mother's body.
And he will help you.
The Lord says, "People of Jacob,
my servants, don't be afraid.
Israel, I chose you.
³I will pour out water for the thirsty
land.
I will make streams flow on dry
land.
I will put my Spirit[d] into your
children.
My blessing will be like a stream
of water flowing over your
family.
⁴Your children will grow like a tree
in the grass.
They will be like poplar trees
growing beside streams of
water.
⁵One person will say, 'I belong to the
Lord.'
Another will use the name Jacob.
Another will sign his name 'I am
the Lord's.'
And another will use the name
Israel.'"

⁶The Lord is the king of Israel.
The Lord of heaven's armies
saves Israel.
The Lord says, "I am the beginning
and the end.
I am the only God.
⁷There is no other God like me.
If there is, then that god should
come and prove it.
Who has announced coming events
from the beginning?
He should tell what will happen
in the future.
⁸Don't be afraid! Don't worry!
I have always told you what will
happen.
You are my witnesses.
There is no other God.
I know of no other Rock.[d] I am
the only One."

⁹Some people make idols, but they
are worth nothing.
People love them, but they are
useless.
Those people are witnesses for the
statues. But those people
cannot see.
They know nothing. They don't
know enough to be ashamed.
¹⁰Who made these false gods?
Who made these useless idols?
¹¹The workmen who made those
gods will be ashamed!
Those workmen are only human.
If they all would come together,
they would all be ashamed and
afraid.

¹²One workman uses tools to heat
iron.
He works over hot coals.
He uses his hammer to beat the
metal and make a statue.
He uses his powerful arms.
But when he becomes hungry, he
loses his power.
If he does not drink water, he
becomes tired.

¹³Another workman uses a line and a
compass
to draw lines on the wood.
Then he uses his chisels to cut a
statue from wood.
He uses his calipers to measure
the statue.
This way, the workman makes the
wood look exactly like a man.

And this statue of a man sits in
the house.
¹⁴A man cuts down cedar
or gets cypress or oak trees.
Those trees grew by their own
power in the forest.
Or he plants a pine tree, and the
rain makes it grow.
¹⁵Then he burns the tree.
He uses some of the wood for a
fire to keep himself warm.
He also starts a fire to bake his
bread.
But he uses part of the wood to
make a god. Then he worships
it!
He makes the idol and bows
down to it!
¹⁶The man burns half of the wood in
the fire.
He uses the fire to cook his meat.
And he eats the meat until he is
full.
He burns the wood to keep himself
warm. He says,
"Good! Now I am warm. I can
see because of the fire's light."
¹⁷But the man makes a statue from
the wood that is left. He calls it
his god.
He bows down to it and worships
it.
He prays to it and says,
"You are my god. Save me!"
¹⁸Those people don't know what they
are doing. They don't
understand!
It is as if their eyes are covered
so they can't see.
Their minds don't understand.
¹⁹They have not thought about these
things.
They don't understand.
They have never thought to
themselves,
"I burned half of the wood in the
fire.
I used the hot coals to bake my
bread.
I cooked and ate my meat.
And I used the wood that was left
to make this hated thing.
I am worshiping a block of
wood!"
²⁰He doesn't know what he is doing.
His confused mind leads him the
wrong way.
He cannot save himself.

He cannot say, "This statue I am
holding is a false god."

²¹The Lord says, "People of Jacob,
remember these things!
People of Israel, remember you
are my servants.
I made you. You are my servants.
So Israel, I will not forget you.
²²I have swept away your sins like a
big cloud.
I have removed your sins like a
cloud that disappears into the
air.
Come back to me because I saved
you."

²³Skies, sing for joy because the Lord
did great things!
Earth, shout for joy, even in your
deepest parts!
Sing, you mountains, with thanks
to God.
Sing, too, you trees in the forest!
The Lord saved the people of
Jacob.
The Lord showed his greatness
when he saved Israel.

²⁴The Lord saved you.
He formed you while you were
still in your mother's body.
The Lord says, "I, the Lord, made
everything!
I alone stretched out the skies.
I spread out the earth by myself.
²⁵I show that the lying prophets'^d
signs are false.
I make fools of those who do
magic.
I confuse even wise men.
They think they know much, but
I make them look foolish.
²⁶I make the messages of my
servants come true.
I make the advice of my
messengers come true.
I say to Jerusalem,
'People will live in you again!'
I say to the towns of Judah,
'You will be built again!'
I say to Jerusalem's ruins,
'I will repair you.'
²⁷I tell the deep waters, 'Become dry!
I will make your streams become
dry!'
²⁸I say of Cyrus,ⁿ 'He is my shepherd.
He will do all that I want him to
do.

44:28 Cyrus A king of Persia. He ruled from about 550-530 B.C.

He will say to Jerusalem, "You
will be built again!"
He will tell the Temple,[d] "Your
foundations will be rebuilt."'"

45 This is what the Lord says to Cyrus, his appointed king:
"I hold your right hand.
I will help you defeat nations.
I will help you take other kings'
power away.
I will open doors for you
so city gates will not stop you.
²I will go before you.
And I will make the mountains
flat.
I will break down the bronze gates
of the cities.
I will cut through the iron bars
on the gates.
³I will give you the wealth that is
stored away.
And I will give you hidden riches.
I will do this so you will know I am
the Lord.
I, the God of Israel, call you by
name.
⁴I do these things for my servants,
the people of Jacob.
I do these things for my chosen
people, the Israelites.
Cyrus, I call you by name.
I give you a title of honor even
though you don't know me.
⁵I am the Lord. There is no other
God.
I am the only God.
I will make you strong
even though you don't know me.
⁶I do these things so everyone will
know
there is no other God.
From the east to the west they will
know
I alone am the Lord.
⁷I made the light and the darkness.
I bring peace, and I cause
troubles.
I, the Lord, do all these things.

⁸"Sky above, make victory fall like
rain.
Clouds, pour down victory.
May the earth receive it.
May salvation grow.
May victory grow with it.
I, the Lord, have created it.

⁹"How terrible it will be for those
who argue with the God who
made them.

They are like one piece of broken
pottery among many pieces.
The clay does not ask the potter,
'What are you doing?'
The thing that is made doesn't say
to its maker,
'You have no hands.'
¹⁰How terrible it will be for the child
who says to his father,
'Why are you giving me life?'
How terrible it will be for the child
who says to his mother,
'Why are you giving birth to
me?'"

¹¹The Lord is the Holy One of Israel,
and its Maker.
He says this:
"You ask me about what will
happen.
You question me about my
children.
You give me orders about what I
have made.
¹²I made the earth.
And I made all the people living
on it.
With my own hands I stretched out
the skies.
I command all the armies in the
sky.
¹³I will bring Cyrus to do good
things.
And I will make his work easy.
Cyrus will rebuild my city,
and he will set my people free.
Cyrus has not been paid to do these
things.
The Lord of heaven's armies says
this."

¹⁴The Lord says,
"The things made in Egypt and
Cush
and the tall people of Seba
will come to you.
They will become yours.
The Sabeans will walk behind you.
They will come along in chains.
They will bow down before you.
They will pray to you, saying,
'God is with you.
And there is no other God.'"

¹⁵You are a God that people cannot
see.
You are the God and Savior of
Israel.
¹⁶All the people who make idols will
be put to great shame.
They will go off together in
disgrace.

[17]But Israel will be saved by the
Lord.
That salvation will continue
forever.
Never again will Israel be put to
shame.

[18]The Lord created the heavens.
He is the God
who formed the earth.
He made the earth.
But he did not want it to be empty.
He wanted life to be on the earth.
This is what the Lord says:
"I am the Lord. There is no other
God.
[19]I did not speak in secret.
I did not hide my words
somewhere in a dark place.
I did not tell the family of Jacob
to look for me in empty places.
I am the Lord, and I speak the
truth.
I say what is right.

[20]"You people have escaped from
other nations.
So gather together and come
before me.
Come near together.
People who carry idols of wood
don't know what they are
doing.
They pray to a god who cannot
save them.
[21]Tell these people to come to me.
Let them talk about these things
together.
Who told you long ago that this
would happen?
Who told about it long ago?
I, the Lord, said these things.
There is no other God besides
me.
I am the only good God. I am the
Savior.
There is no other God.

[22]"All people everywhere,
follow me and be saved.
I am God. There is no other God.
[23]I will make a promise by my own
power.
And my promise is true.
What I say will not be changed.
I promise that everyone will bow
before me.
Everyone will promise to follow
me.
[24]People will say, 'Goodness and
power
come only from the Lord.' "

Everyone who has been angry with
the Lord
will come to him and be
ashamed.
[25]But with the Lord's help, the people
of Israel
will be found to be good.
And they will praise him.

46

Bel[d] and Nebo[d] bow down.
Their idols are carried by
animals.
The statues are only heavy loads
that must be carried.
They only make people tired.
[2]These false gods will all bow down.
They cannot save themselves.
They will all be carried away like
prisoners.

[3]"Family of Jacob, listen to me!
All you people from Israel who
are still alive, listen!
I have carried you since you were
born.
I have taken care of you from
your birth.
[4]Even when you are old, I will take
care of you.
Even when your hair has turned
gray, I will take care of you.
I made you and will take care of
you.
I will carry you, and I will save
you.

[5]"Can you compare me to anyone?
No one is equal to me or like me.
[6]Some people are rich with gold.
They weigh their silver on the
scales.
They hire a goldsmith, and he
makes it into a god.
Then they bow down and
worship it.
[7]They put it on their shoulders and
carry it.
They set it in its place, and there
it stands.
It cannot move from its place.
People may yell at it, but it cannot
answer.
It cannot save people from their
troubles.

[8]"Remember this, and do not forget
it!
Think about these things, you
who turn against God.
[9]Remember what happened long
ago.
Remember that I am God. There
is no other God.

I am God. There is no one like
me.
[10]From the beginning I told you what
would happen in the end.
A long time ago I told you things
that have not yet happened.
When I plan something, it happens.
I do the things I want to do.
[11]I am calling a man from the east to
carry out my plan.
He will come like a hawk from a
country far away.
I will make what I have said come
true.
I will do what I have planned.
[12]Listen to me, you stubborn people.
You are far from what is right.
[13]I will soon do the things that are
right.
I will bring salvation soon.
I will save Jerusalem.
And I will bring glory to Israel."

47 The Lord says, "City of Babylon,
go down and sit in the dirt.
People of Babylon, sit on the
ground.
You are no longer the ruler.
You will no longer be called
tender or beautiful.
[2] You must use large stones to
grind grain into flour.
Remove your veil and your nice
skirts.
Uncover your legs and cross the
rivers.
[3]Men will see your nakedness.
They will see your shame.
I will punish you.
I will punish every one of you."

[4]Our Savior is named the Lord of
heaven's armies.
He is the Holy One of Israel.

[5]"Babylon, sit in darkness and say
nothing.
You will no longer be called the
queen of kingdoms.
[6]I was angry with my people.
So I rejected those people who
belonged to me.
I gave them to you,
but you showed them no mercy.
You even made the old people
work very hard.
[7]You said, 'I will live forever.
I will always be the queen.'
You did not think about these
things.
You did not think about what
would happen.

[8]"Now, listen, you lover of pleasure.
You think you are safe.
You tell yourself,
'I am the only important person.
I will never be a widow.
I will never lose my children.'
[9]Two things will happen to you
suddenly in a single day.
You will lose your children and
your husband.
These things will truly happen to
you.
All your magic and powerful
tricks
will not save you.
[10]You do evil things, but you feel
safe.
You say, 'No one sees what I do.'
Your wisdom and knowledge
have fooled you.
You say to yourself,
'I am God. No one is equal to me.'
[11]But troubles will come to you.
You will not know how to stop
them.
Disaster will fall on you.
And you will not be able to keep
it away.
You will be destroyed quickly.
You will not even see it coming.

[12]"Keep on using your tricks.
Continue doing all your magic.
You have done these things since
you were young.
Maybe they will help you.
Maybe you will be able to scare
someone.
[13]You are tired of the advice you have
received.
So let those who study the sky
come.
They tell the future by looking at
the stars.
So let them save you from what is
about to happen to you.
[14]But they are like straw.
Fire will quickly burn them up.
They cannot save themselves
from the power of the fire.
They are not like coals that give
warmth.
They are not like a fire you may
sit beside.
[15]You have worked with these
people.
They have been with you since
you were young.
But they will not be able to help
you.

Everyone will go his own way.
And there will be no one left to
save you."

48 The Lord says, "Family of Jacob,
listen to me.
You are called Israel.
You come from the family of
Judah.
You use the Lord's name to make
promises.
You praise the God of Israel,
but you are not honest or sincere.
²You call yourselves people of the
holy city.
You depend on the God of Israel.
He is named the Lord of heaven's
armies.
³Long ago I told you what would
happen.
I said these things and made
them known.
Suddenly I acted, and these
things happened.
⁴I did that because I knew you were
stubborn.
Your neck was like an iron
muscle.
It was as if your head were made
of bronze.
⁵So a long time ago I told you about
these things.
I told you about them before they
happened.
I did this so you couldn't say, 'My
idols did this.
My wooden and metal statues
made these things happen.'

⁶"You heard and saw all the things
that happened.
So you should tell this news to
others.
Now I will tell you about new
things.
These are hidden things that you
don't know yet.
⁷These things are happening now,
not long ago.
You have not heard about them
before today.
So you cannot say, 'We already
knew about that.'
⁸But you have not heard me. You
have not understood.
Even long ago you did not listen
to me.
I knew you would surely turn
against me.

You have fought against me since
you were born.
⁹But for my own sake I will be
patient.
People will praise me for not
becoming angry
and destroying you.
¹⁰I have made you pure, but not by
fire, as silver is made pure.
I have purified you by giving you
troubles.
¹¹I do this for myself, for my own
sake.
I will not let people speak evil
against me.
I will not let some false god take
my glory.

¹²"People of Jacob, listen to me.
People of Israel, I have called you
to be my people.
I am God.
I am the beginning and the end.
¹³I made the earth with my own
hands.
With my right hand I spread out
the skies.
When I call them,
they come together before me.

¹⁴"All of you, come together and
listen.
None of the false gods said these
things would happen.
I, the Lord, have chosen someone
to attack the Babylonians.
He will carry out my wishes
against Babylon.
¹⁵I have spoken. I have called him.ⁿ
I have brought him, and I will
make him successful.
¹⁶Come to me and listen to this.
From the beginning I have
spoken openly.
From the time it began, I was
there."

Now, the Lord God
has sent me with his Spirit.ᵈ

¹⁷The Lord is your close relative who
saves you, the Holy One of
Israel.
The Lord says,
"I am the Lord your God.
I teach you to do what is good.
I lead you in the way you should
go.
¹⁸If you had obeyed me,
you would have had peace like a
full-flowing river.

48:15 him This probably refers to Cyrus king of Persia.

Good things would have flowed
to you like the waves of the
sea.
¹⁹You would have had many children.
They would have been as many
as the grains of sand.
They would never have died out.
They would not have been
destroyed."

²⁰My people, leave Babylon!
Run from the Babylonians!
Tell this news with shouts of joy to
the people.
Spread it everywhere on earth.
Say, "The Lord has saved
his servants, the people of
Jacob."
²¹They did not become thirsty when
he led them through the
deserts.
He made water flow from a rock
for them.
He split the rock,
and water flowed out.
²²"There is no peace for evil people,"
says the Lord.

49 All of you people in faraway
places, listen to me.
Listen, all you nations far away.
Before I was born, the Lord called
me to serve him.
The Lord named me while I was
still in my mother's body.
²The Lord made my tongue like a
sharp sword.
He hid me in the shadow of his
hand.
The Lord made me like a sharp
arrow.
He hid me in the holder for his
arrows.
³The Lord told me, "Israel, you are
my servant.
I will show my glory through
you."
⁴But I said, "I have worked hard for
nothing.
I have used all my power, but I
did nothing useful.
But the Lord will decide what my
work is worth.
God will decide my reward."
⁵The Lord made me in the body of
my mother
so I would be his servant.
He made me to lead the people of
Jacob back to him.
He made me so that Israel might
be gathered to him.

The Lord will honor me.
I will get my strength from my
God.
⁶The Lord told me,
"You are an important servant to
me.
You will bring back the tribesᵈ of
Jacob.
You will bring back the people of
Israel who are left alive.
But, more importantly, I will make
you a light for all nations.
You will show people all over the
world the way to be saved."

⁷The Lord is your close relative who
saves you.
He is the Holy One of Israel.
He speaks to the one who is hated
by the people.
He speaks to the servant of
rulers.
The Lord says, "Kings will see you
and stand to honor you.
Great leaders will bow down
before you.
This is because the Lord can be
trusted.
He is the Holy One of Israel, who
has chosen you."

⁸This is what the Lord says:
"At the right time I will hear your
prayers.
On the day of salvation I will
help you.
I will protect you.
And you will be the sign of my
agreement with the people.
You will bring back the people to
the land.
You will give the land that is now
ruined back to its owners.
⁹You will tell the prisoners, 'Come
out of your prison.'
You will tell those in darkness,
'Come into the light.'
The people will eat beside the
roads.
They will find food even on bare
hills.
¹⁰They will not be hungry or thirsty.
Neither the hot sun nor the
desert wind will hurt them.
The God who comforts them will
lead them.
He will lead them by springs of
water.
¹¹I will make my mountains into
roads for my people.
And the roads will be raised up.

¹²Look, people are coming to me
from far away.
They are coming from the north
and from the west.
They are coming from Aswan in
southern Egypt."

¹³Heavens and earth, be happy.
Mountains, shout with joy.
Be happy because the Lord
comforts his people.
He will comfort those who suffer.

¹⁴But Jerusalem said, "The Lord has
left me.
The Lord has forgotten me."

¹⁵The Lord answers, "Can a woman
forget the baby she nurses?
Can she feel no kindness for the
child she gave birth to?
Even if she could forget her
children,
I will not forget you.
¹⁶See, I have written your name on
my hand.
Jerusalem, I always think about
your walls.
¹⁷Your children will soon return to
you.
And the people who defeated you
and destroyed you will leave.
¹⁸Look up and look around you.
All your children are gathering to
return to you."
The Lord says, "As surely as I live,
your children will be like jewels.
You will be as proud of them as a
bride is of her jewels.

¹⁹"You were destroyed and defeated.
Your land was made useless.
But now you will have more people
than the land can hold.
And those people who destroyed
you will be far away.
²⁰Children were born to you while
you were sad.
But they will say to you,
'This place is too small for us.
Give us a bigger place to live.'
²¹Then you will say to yourself,
'Who gave me all these children?
I was sad and lonely.
I was defeated and away from my
people.
So who reared these children?
I was left all alone.
Where did all these children
come from?'"

²²This is what the Lord God says:
"See, I will lift my hand to signal
the nations.
I will raise my banner for all
people to see.
Then they will bring your sons
back to you in their arms.
They will carry your daughters
on their shoulders.
²³Kings will teach your children.
Daughters of kings will take care
of those children.
They will bow down before you.
They will kiss the dirt at your
feet.
Then you will know I am the Lord.
Anyone who trusts in me will not
be disappointed."

²⁴Can the wealth a soldier wins in
war be taken away from him?
Can a prisoner be freed from a
powerful soldier?
²⁵But this is what the Lord says:
"The prisoners will be taken from
the strong soldiers.
What the soldiers have taken will
be saved.
I will fight your enemies.
I will save your children.
²⁶I will force those who trouble you
to eat their own flesh.
Their own blood will be the wine
that makes them drunk.
Then everyone will know
I, the Lord, am the One who
saves you.
I am the Powerful One of Jacob
who saves you."

50 This is what the Lord says:
"People of Israel, you say I
divorced your mother.
Then where is the paper that
proves it?
Or do you think I sold you to pay a
debt?
No! It was because of the evil
things you did that I sold you.
It was because of the times she
turned against me that your
mother was sent away.
²I came home and found no one
there.
I called, but no one answered.
Do you think I am not able to save
you?
Do I not have the power to save
you?
Look, I need only to shout, and the
sea becomes dry.
I change rivers into a desert.

Their fish rot because there is no
water.
The fish die of thirst.
³I can make the skies dark.
I can make them black like
clothes of sadness."

⁴The Lord God gave me the ability
to teach.
He has taught me what to say to
make the weak strong.
Every morning he wakes me.
He teaches me to listen like a
student.
⁵The Lord God helps me learn.
And I have not turned against
him.
I have not stopped following him.
⁶I offered my back to those who beat
me.
I offered my cheeks to those who
pulled my beard.
I won't hide my face from them
when they make fun of me and
spit at me.
⁷The Lord God helps me.
So I will not be ashamed.
I will be determined.
I know I will not be disgraced.
⁸The Lord shows that I am innocent,
and he is close to me.
So who can accuse me?
If there is someone, let us go to
court together.
If someone wants to prove I have
done wrong,
he should come and tell me.
⁹It is the Lord God who helps me.
So who can prove me guilty?
All those who try will become
useless like old clothes.
Moths will eat them.

¹⁰Who among you fears the Lord
and obeys his servant?
That person may walk in the dark
and have no light.
Then let him trust in the Lord.
Let him depend on his God.
¹¹But instead, some of you want to
light your own fires.
You want to make your own light.
So, go, walk in the light of your
fires.
Trust your own light to guide you.
But this is what you will receive
from me:

You will lie down in a place of
pain.

51 The Lord says, "Listen to me,
those of you who try to live
right and follow the Lord.
Look at the rock from which you
were cut.
Look at the stone quarry from
which you were dug.
²Look at Abraham, your ancestor.
Look at Sarah, who gave birth to
your ancestors.
Abraham had no children when I
called him.
But I blessed him and gave him
many descendants.^d
³So the Lord will comfort Jerusalem.
He will show mercy to those who
live in her ruins.
He will change her deserts into a
garden like Eden.
He will make her empty lands
like the garden of the Lord.
People there will be very happy.
They will give thanks and sing
songs.

⁴"My people, listen to me.
My nation, pay attention to me.
I will give the people my teachings.
And my decisions will be like a
light to all people.
⁵I will soon show I do what is right.
I will soon save you.
I will use my power and judge all
nations.
All the faraway places are waiting
for me.
They wait for my power to help
them.
⁶Look up to the heavens.
Look around you at the earth
below.
The skies will disappear like clouds
of smoke.
The earth will become useless
like old clothes.
Its people will die like flies.
But my salvation will continue
forever.
My goodness will never end.

⁷"You people who know what is
right should listen to me.
You people who follow my
teachings should hear what I
say.
Don't be afraid of the evil things
people say.
Don't be upset by their insults.

⁸Moths will eat those people as if
  they were clothes.
 Worms will eat them as if they
  were wool.
But my goodness will continue
  forever.
 My salvation will continue from
  now on."

⁹Wake up, wake up, and use your
  strength,
  powerful Lord.
Wake up as you did in the old times.
 Wake up as you did a long time
  ago.
With your own power, you cut
  Rahab[d] into pieces.
 You killed that sea monster.
¹⁰You caused the sea to become dry.
 You dried the waters of the deep
  ocean.
You made the deepest parts of the
  sea into a road.
 Your people crossed over on that
  road and were saved.
¹¹The people the Lord has freed will
  return.
 They will enter Jerusalem with
  joy.
 Their happiness will last forever.
They will have joy and gladness.
 All sadness and sorrow will be
  gone far away.

¹²The Lord says, "I am the one who
  comforts you.
 So why should you be afraid of
  people, who die?
 Why should you fear people who
  die like the grass?
¹³Have you forgotten that the Lord
  made you?
 He stretched out the skies.
 He made the earth.
Why are you always afraid
 of those angry people who
  trouble you?
 They want to destroy.
But where are those angry people
  now?
¹⁴ People in prison will soon be set
  free.
 They will not die in prison.
 They will have enough food.
¹⁵This is because I am the Lord your
  God.
 I stir the sea and make the waves
  roar.

My name is the Lord of heaven's
  armies.
¹⁶I will give you the words I want you
  to say.
 I will cover you with my hands
  and protect you.
I made the heavens and the earth.
 And I say to Jerusalem, 'You are
  my people.'"

¹⁷The Lord was very angry with you.
 Your punishment was like wine
  in a cup.
The Lord made you drink that wine
  until you stumbled.
¹⁸Jerusalem had many people.
 But there was not a person to
  lead her.
Of all the people who grew up there,
  no one was there to guide her.
¹⁹Troubles came to you in groups of
  two.
 No one will feel sorry for you.
There was ruin and disaster, great
  hunger and fighting.
 No one can comfort you.
²⁰Your people have become weak.
 They fall down and lie on every
  street corner.
 They are like animals caught in a
  net.
They have felt the full anger of the
  Lord.
 They have heard God's angry
  shout.

²¹So listen to me, poor Jerusalem,
  you who are drunk but not from
  wine.
²²Your God will fight for his people.
 This is what the Lord your God
  says:
"The punishment I gave you is like
  a cup of wine.
 You drank it and could not walk
  straight.
I am taking that cup of my anger
  away from you.
 You will never be punished by my
  anger again.
²³I will now give that cup of
  punishment to those who gave
  you pain.
They told you,
 'Bow down so we can walk over
  you.'
They made your back like dirt for
  them to walk on.
 You were like a street for them to
  travel on."

52

¹Wake up, wake up, Jerusalem!
  Become strong!
Be beautiful again,
  holy city of Jerusalem.
The people who do not worship
    God and who are not pure
  will not enter you again.
²Jerusalem, you once were a
    prisoner.
Now shake off the dust and stand
    up.
Jerusalem, you once were a
    prisoner.
But now free yourself from the
    chains around your neck.
³This is what the Lord says:
"You were not sold for a price.
  So you will be saved without
    cost."
⁴This is what the Lord God says:
"First my people went down to
    Egypt to live.
Later Assyria made them slaves.

⁵"Now see what has happened,"
    says the Lord.
"Another nation has taken away my
    people for nothing.
  This nation that rules them
    makes fun of me," says the
    Lord.
  "All day long they speak against
    me.
⁶But this has happened so my
    people will know who I am.
They will know I am God.
And they will know that I am the
    one speaking to them."

⁷How beautiful is the person
  who comes over the mountains to
    bring good news.
How beautiful is the one who
  announces peace.
He brings good news
  and announces salvation.
How beautiful are the feet of the
  one who says to Jerusalem,
  "Your God is king."
⁸Listen! Your guards are shouting.
  They are all shouting for joy!
They all will see with their own
    eyes
  when the Lord returns to
    Jerusalem.
⁹Jerusalem, your buildings are
    destroyed now.
But shout and rejoice together.
You can rejoice because the Lord
  has comforted his people.
He has saved Jerusalem.

¹⁰The Lord will show his holy power
  to all the nations.
Then everyone on earth
  will see the salvation of our God.

¹¹You people, leave, leave; get out of
    Babylon!
  Touch nothing that is unclean.ᵈ
You men who carry the things used
    in worship,
  leave there and make yourselves
    pure.
¹²You will not be forced to leave
    Babylon quickly.
You will not be forced to run
    away.
The Lord will go before you.
  And the God of Israel will guard
    you from behind.

¹³The Lord says, "See, my servant
  will act wisely.
People will greatly honor and
    respect him.
¹⁴Many people were shocked when
    they saw him.
His appearance was so changed
  he did not look like a man.
His form was changed so much
  they could barely tell he was
    human.
¹⁵But now he will sprinkle many
    people.
Kings will be amazed and shut
    their mouths.
They will see the things they had
    not been told about my
    servant.
They will understand the things
    they had not heard."

53

Who would have believed what
    we heard?
  Who saw the Lord's power in
    this?
²He grew up like a small plant
    before the Lord.
  He was like a root growing in a
    dry land.
He had no special beauty or form
  to make us notice him.
There was nothing in his
    appearance to make us desire
    him.
³He was hated and rejected by
    people.
He had much pain and suffering.
People would not even look at him.
  He was hated, and we didn't even
    notice him.

⁴But he took our suffering on him
  and felt our pain for us.

We saw his suffering.
We thought God was punishing
him.
5But he was wounded for the wrong
things we did.
He was crushed for the evil
things we did.
The punishment, which made us
well, was given to him.
And we are healed because of his
wounds.
6We all have wandered away like
sheep.
Each of us has gone his own way.
But the Lord has put on him the
punishment
for all the evil we have done.

7He was beaten down and punished.
But he didn't say a word.
He was like a lamb being led to be
killed.
He was quiet, as a sheep is quiet
while its wool is being cut.
He never opened his mouth.
8Men took him away roughly and
unfairly.
He died without children to
continue his family.
He was put to death.
He was punished for the sins of
my people.
9He was buried with wicked men.
He died with the rich.
He had done nothing wrong.
He had never lied.

10But it was the Lord who decided
to crush him and make him
suffer.
So the Lord made his life a
penalty offering.
But he will see his descendantsd
and live a long life.
He will complete the things the
Lord wants him to do.
11He will suffer many things in his
soul.
But then he will see life and be
satisfied.
My good servant will make many
people right with God.
He carried away their sins.
12For this reason I will make him a
great man among people.
He will share in all things with
those who are strong.
He willingly gave his life.
He was treated like a criminal.

But he carried away the sins of
many people.
And he asked forgiveness for
those who sinned.

54The Lord says, "Sing, Jerusalem.
You are like a woman who
never gave birth to children.
Start singing and shout for joy.
You never felt the pain of giving
birth.
But you will have more children
than the woman who has a
husband.
2Make your tent bigger.
Stretch it out and make it wider.
Do not hold back.
Make the ropes longer.
Make its stakes stronger.
3Do this because you will begin
growing very much.
Your children will take over other
nations.
And they will again live in cities
that once were destroyed.

4"Don't be afraid because you will
not be ashamed.
Don't be embarrassed because
you will not be disgraced.
You will forget the shame you felt
earlier.
You will not remember the shame
you felt when you lost your
husband.
5This is because the God who made
you is like your husband.
His name is the Lord of heaven's
armies.
The Holy One of Israel is the one
who saves you.
He is called the God of all the
earth.
6You were like a woman whose
husband left her.
And you were very sad.
You were like a wife who married
young
and then her husband left her.
But the Lord called you to be his,"
says your God.
7God says, "I left you, but only for a
short time.
But with great kindness I will
bring you back again.
8I became very angry
and hid from you for a short
time.
But I will show you mercy with
kindness forever,"
says the Lord your close relative
who saves you.

[9]The Lord says, "This is like the time of Noah.
I promised then
    that I would never flood the world again.
In the same way, I promise
    I will not be angry with you or punish you again.
[10]The mountains may disappear,
    and the hills may come to an end.
But my love will never disappear.
    My promise of peace will not come to an end,"
        says the Lord who shows mercy to you.

[11]"You poor city. Storms have hurt you,
    and you have not been comforted.
But I will rebuild you using turquoise stones.
    I will build your foundations with sapphires.
[12]I will use rubies to build your walls.
    I will use shining jewels for the gates.
    I will build all your outer walls from precious jewels.
[13]All your children will be taught by the Lord.
    And they will have much peace.
[14]I will build you using fairness.
You will be safe from those who would hurt you.
    So you will have nothing to fear.
    Nothing will come to make you afraid.
[15]I will not send anyone to attack you.
    And you will defeat those who do attack you.

[16]"See, I made the blacksmith.
He fans the fire to make it hotter.
    And he makes the kind of tool he wants.
In the same way I have made the destroyer to destroy.
[17]   So no weapon that is used against you will defeat you.
    You will show that those who speak against you are wrong.
These are the good things my servants receive.
    Their victory comes from me,"
        says the Lord.

55 The Lord says, "All you who are thirsty,
    come and drink.
Those of you who do not have money,
    come, buy and eat!
Come buy wine and milk.
    You don't need money; it will cost you nothing.
[2]Why spend your money on something that is not real food?
Why work for something that doesn't really satisfy you?
Listen closely to me, and you will eat what is good.
    You will enjoy the food that satisfies your soul.
[3]Come to me and listen.
    Listen to me so you may live.
I will make an agreement with you that will last forever.
    I will give you the blessings I promised to David.
[4]I made David a witness of my power for all nations.
    I made him a ruler and commander of many nations.
[5]You will call for nations that you don't yet know.
    And these nations will run to you.
This will happen because of the Lord your God.
    The Holy One of Israel honors you."

[6]So you should look for the Lord before it is too late.
    You should call to him while he is near.
[7]Evil people should stop being evil.
    They should stop thinking bad thoughts.
They should return to the Lord, and he will have mercy on them.
    They should come to our God, because he will freely forgive them.

[8]The Lord says, "Your thoughts are not like my thoughts.
    Your ways are not like my ways.
[9]Just as the heavens are higher than the earth,
    so are my ways higher than your ways.
    And my thoughts are higher than your thoughts.
[10]Rain and snow fall from the sky.
    They don't return without watering the ground.
They cause the plants to sprout and grow.

And the plants make seeds for
the farmer.
And from these seeds people
have bread to eat.
[11] The words I say do the same thing.
They will not return to me empty.
They make the things happen that I
want to happen.
They succeed in doing what I
send them to do.

[12] "So you will go out with joy.
You will be led out in peace.
The mountains and hills will burst
into song before you.
All the trees in the fields will clap
their hands.
[13] Large cypress trees will grow
where thornbushes were.
Myrtle trees will grow where
weeds were.
These things will be a reminder of
the Lord's promise.
And this reminder will never be
destroyed."

56 This is what the Lord says:
"Give justice to all people.
Do what is right.
Do this because my salvation will
come to you soon.
Soon everyone will know that I
do what is right.
[2] The person who obeys the law
about the Sabbath[d]
will be blessed.
And the person who does no evil
will be blessed."

[3] Foreigners have joined the Lord.
They should not say,
"The Lord will not accept me
with his people."
The eunuch[d] should not say,
"Because I cannot have children
the Lord will not accept me."
[4] This is what the Lord says:
"The eunuchs should obey the law
about the Sabbath.
They should do what I want.
They should keep my agreement.
[5] If they do, I will make their names
remembered
within my Temple[d] and its walls.
It will be better for them than
children.
I will give them a name that will
last forever.
It will never be forgotten.
[6] Foreigners will join the Lord to
serve him.
They will worship and love him.

They will worship him.
They will obey the law about the
Sabbath.
They will keep the agreement
with the Lord.
[7] I will bring these people to my holy
mountain.
I will give them joy in my house
of prayer.
The offerings and sacrifices
they place on my altar will please
me.
This is because my Temple will be
called
a house for prayer for people
from all nations."
[8] The Lord gathers the Israelites who
were forced to leave their
country.
This is what the Lord God says,
"I will bring other people to those
who are already gathered."

[9] All you animals of the field, come
to eat.
All you animals of the forest,
come to eat.
[10] The leaders who are to guard the
people are blind.
They don't know what they are
doing.
All of them are like quiet dogs.
They don't know how to bark.
They lie down and dream.
They love to sleep.
[11] They are like hungry dogs.
They are never satisfied.
They are like shepherds
who don't know what they are
doing.
They each have gone their own
way.
All they want to do is satisfy
themselves.
[12] They say, "Come, let's drink some
wine.
Let's drink all the beer we want.
And tomorrow we will do this
again.
Or, maybe we will have even a
better time."

57 Those right with God may die,
but no one pays attention.
Good people are taken away,
but no one understands.
The people who do right are being
taken away because of evil.
[2] But they are given peace.
The people who live the way God
wants them to
find rest in death.

³"Come here, you magicians!
Come here, you sons of
prostitutes[d] and those who take
part in adultery![d]
⁴Whom are you making fun of?
Whom are you insulting?
At whom do you stick out your
tongue?
You turn against God,
and you are liars.
⁵You have sexual relations under
every green tree
to worship your false gods.
You kill children in the ravines
and sacrifice them in the rocky
places.
⁶You take the smooth rocks from the
ravines.
They are your portion.
You pour drink offerings on them
to worship them.
You give grain offerings to them.
Do you think this makes me want
to forgive you?
⁷You make your bed on every hill
and mountain.
And there you offer sacrifices.
⁸You have hidden your idols
behind your doors and doorposts.
You have left me, and you have
uncovered yourself.
You have pulled back the covers
and climbed into bed.
You have made an agreement with
the ones whose beds you love.
And you have looked at their
nakedness.
⁹You use your oils and perfumes
to look nice for Molech.[d]
You have sent your messengers to
faraway lands.
You even tried to send them to
where the dead are.
¹⁰You have worked hard to do these
things.
But you never gave up.
You found new strength.
So you did not quit.

¹¹"Whom were you so afraid of
that you lied to me?
You have not remembered me
or even thought about me.
I have been quiet for a long time.
Is that why you are not afraid of
me?
¹²I will tell about your 'goodness' and
what you do.
And those things will do you no
good.
¹³When you cry out for help,

let the false gods you have
gathered help you.
The wind will blow them all away.
Just a puff of wind will take them
away.
But the person who depends on me
will receive the land.
He will have my holy mountain."

¹⁴The Lord says, "Build a road! Build
a road! Prepare the way!
Make the way clear for my
people."
¹⁵God lives forever and is holy.
He is high and lifted up, and he
says,
"I live in a high and holy place.
But I also live with people who
are sad and humble.
I give new life to those who are
humble.
I give new life to those whose
hearts are broken.
¹⁶I will not accuse forever.
I will not always be angry.
If I continued to be angry, man's
life would grow weak.
Man, whom I created, would die.
¹⁷I was angry because they were
dishonest in order to make
money.
I punished them and turned away
from them in anger.
But they continued to do evil.
¹⁸I have seen what they have done,
but I will heal them.
I will guide them and comfort
them.
And those who were sad will
praise me.
¹⁹I will give peace, real peace, to
those far and near.
And I will heal them," says the
Lord.
²⁰But evil people are like the angry
sea.
It cannot rest.
Its waves toss up waste and mud.
²¹"There is no peace for evil people,"
says my God.

58 The Lord says, "Shout out loud.
Don't hold back.
Shout out loud like a trumpet.
Tell the people about the things
they have done against God.
Tell the family of Jacob about
their sins.
²Then they will come every day
looking for me.
And they will want to learn my
ways.

They will become a nation that
does what is right.
They will obey the commands of
their God.
They will ask me to judge them
fairly.
They will want God to be near
them.
[3]They say, 'To honor you we had
special days when we gave up
eating.
But you didn't see.
We humbled ourselves to honor
you.
But you didn't notice.'"

But the Lord says, "You do what
pleases yourselves on these
special days.
And you are unfair to your
workers.
[4]On these special days when you do
not eat, you argue and fight.
You hit each other with your
fists.
You cannot do these things as you
do now
and believe I will listen to your
prayers.
[5]This kind of special day is not what
I want.
This is not the way I want people
to be sorry for what they have
done.
I don't want people just to bow
their heads like a plant.
I don't want them to wear rough
cloth and lie in ashes to show
their sadness.
This is what you do on your special
days when you do not eat.
But do you think this is what the
Lord wants?

[6]"I will tell you the kind of special
day I want.
I want you to free the people you
have put in prison unfairly.
Undo their chains.
Free those to whom you are unfair.
Free them from their hard labor.
[7]I want you to share your food with
hungry people.
I want you to bring poor,
homeless people into your own
homes.
When you see someone who has no
clothes, give him yours.
Don't refuse to help your own
relatives.

[8]If you do these things, your light
will shine like the dawn.
Then your wounds will quickly
heal.
Your God will walk before you,
and the glory of the Lord will
protect you from behind.
[9]Then you will call to the Lord, and
the Lord will answer you.
You will cry out to the Lord, and
he will say, 'Here I am.'

"You should stop making trouble
for others.
You should stop using cruel
words and pointing your finger
at others.
[10]You should feed those who are
hungry.
You should take care of the needs
of those who are troubled.
Then your light will shine in the
darkness.
And you will be bright like
sunshine at noon.
[11]The Lord will always lead you.
He will satisfy your needs in dry
lands.
He will give strength to your
bones.
You will be like a garden that has
much water.
You will be like a spring that
never runs dry.
[12]Your people will rebuild the old
cities that are now in ruins.
You will rebuild the foundations
of these ancient cities.
You will be known for repairing the
broken places.
You will be known for rebuilding
the roads and houses.

[13]"You must obey God's law about
the Sabbath.[d]
You must not do what pleases
yourselves on that holy day.
You should call the Sabbath a
joyful day.
You should honor the Lord's holy
day.
You should honor it by not doing
whatever you please on that
day.
You should not say whatever you
please on that day.
[14]Then you will find joy in the Lord.
And I, the Lord, will carry you to
the high places above the
earth.

I will let you eat the crops of the
land your ancestor Jacob had."
The Lord has said these things.

59 Surely the Lord's power is
enough to save you.
He can hear you when you ask
him for help.
[2] It is your evil that has separated
you from your God.
Your sins cause him to turn away
from you.
And then he does not hear you.
[3] With your hands you have killed
others.
Your fingers are covered with
blood from killing people.
With your lips you have lied.
With your tongue you say evil
things.
[4] People take each other to court
unfairly.
No one tells the truth in arguing
his case.
They accuse each other falsely and
tell lies.
They cause trouble and create
more evil.
[5] They hatch evil like eggs from
poisonous snakes.
If you eat one of those eggs, you
will die.
And if you break one open, a
poisonous snake comes out.
People tell lies as they would spin a
spider's web.
[6] The webs they make cannot be
used for clothes.
You can't cover yourself with
those webs.
The things they do are evil.
They use their hands to hurt
others.
[7] They eagerly run to do evil.
They are always ready to kill
innocent people.
They think evil thoughts.
Everywhere they go they cause
ruin and destruction.
[8] They don't know how to live in
peace.
There is no fairness in their lives.
They are dishonest.
Anyone who lives as they live
will never have peace.

[9] Fairness has gone far away.
Goodness is nowhere to be
found.
We wait for the light, but there is
only darkness now.
We hope for a bright light, but all
we have is darkness.
[10] We are like blind people feeling our
way along a wall.
We have to feel our way as if we
had no eyes.
In the brightness of day we trip as
if it were night.
We are like dead men among the
strong.
[11] All of us growl like the bears.
We call out sadly like the doves.
We look for justice, but there isn't
any.
We want to be saved, but
salvation is far away.

[12] We have done many wrong things
against our God.
Our sins show we are wrong.
We know we have turned against
God.
We know the evil things we have
done.
[13] We have sinned and turned against
the Lord.
We have turned away from our
God.
We have planned to hurt others and
to disobey God.
We have planned and spoken
lies.
[14] We have driven away justice.
We have kept away from what is
right.
Truth is not spoken in the streets.
What is honest is not allowed to
enter the city.
[15] Truth cannot be found anywhere.
And people who refuse to do evil
are attacked.

The Lord looked and could not find
any justice.
And he was displeased.
[16] He could not find anyone to help
the people.
He was surprised that there was
no one to help.
So the Lord used his own power to
save the people.
His own goodness gave him
strength.
[17] The Lord covered himself with
goodness like armor.
He put on the helmet of
salvation.
He put on the clothes of
punishment.
And he put on the coat of his
strong love.

¹⁸The Lord will pay back his enemies
for what they have done.
He will show his anger to those
who were against him.
He will punish the people in
faraway places.
He will give them the punishment
they should have.
¹⁹Then people from the west will fear
the Lord.
People in the east will fear his
glory.
The Lord will come quickly like a
fast-flowing river,
driven by the breath of the Lord.

²⁰"Then a close relative who will
save you will come to
Jerusalem.
He will come to the people of
Jacob who sinned but turned
back to God,"
says the Lord.

²¹The Lord says, "I will make an
agreement with these people. I promise
that my Spiritᵈ and my words that I give
you will never leave you. They will be
with your children and your grandchildren. They will be with you now and
forever."

60

"Jerusalem, get up and shine.
Your light has come.
The glory of the Lord shines on
you.
²Darkness now covers the earth.
Deep darkness covers her people.
But the Lord shines on you,
and people see his glory around
you.
³Nations will come to your light.
Kings will come to the brightness
of your sunrise.

⁴"Look around you.
People are gathering and coming
to you.
They are your sons coming from
far away.
And your daughters are coming
with them.
⁵When you see them, you will shine
with happiness.
You will be excited and full of
joy.
The wealth of the nations across
the seas will be given to you.
The riches of the nations will
come to you.
⁶Herds of camels will cover your
land.

Young camels will come from
Midian and Ephah.
People will come from Sheba
bringing gold and incense.ᵈ
And they will sing praises to the
Lord.
⁷All the sheep from Kedar will be
given to you.
The male sheep from Nebaioth
will be brought to you.
They will be pleasing sacrifices on
my altar.
And I will make my beautiful
Templeᵈ more beautiful.

⁸"The people are returning to you
like clouds.
They are like doves flying to
their nests.
⁹People in faraway lands are waiting
for me.
The great trading ships will come
first.
They are bringing your children
from faraway lands.
And with them they bring silver
and gold.
This will happen to honor the Lord
your God.
He is the Holy One of Israel.
And he does wonderful things for
you.

¹⁰"Jerusalem, foreigners will rebuild
your walls.
Their kings will serve you.
When I was angry, I hurt you.
But now I want to be kind to you
and comfort you.
¹¹Your gates will always be open.
They will not be closed day or
night
so the nations can bring their
wealth to you.
And their kings will be led to
you.
¹²If a nation or kingdom doesn't
serve you,
it will be destroyed.
It will be completely ruined.

¹³"The great trees of Lebanon will be
given to you.
Its pine, fir and cypress trees will
come to you.
You will use these trees to make my
Temple beautiful.
And I will give much honor to
this place where I rest my feet.
¹⁴The people who have hurt you will
bow down to you.

Those who hated you will bow
  down at your feet.
They will call you The City of the
  Lord.
They will call you Jerusalem, city
  of the Holy One of Israel.

[15] "You have been hated and left
  empty.
  No one has even passed through.
But I will make you great from now
  on.
  You will be a place of happiness
  forever and ever.
[16] Nations will give you what you
  need.
  It will be like a child drinking
  milk from its mother.
Then you will know that it is I, the
  Lord, who saves you.
  You will know that the Powerful
  One of Jacob protects you.
[17] I will bring you gold in place of
  bronze.
  I will bring you silver in place of
  iron.
I will bring you bronze in place of
  wood.
  I will bring you iron in place of
  rocks.
I will change your punishment into
  peace.
  And you will be ruled by what is
  right.
[18] There will be no more violence in
  your country.
  It will not be ruined or destroyed.
You will name your walls Salvation.
  And you will name your gates
  Praise.
[19] The sun will no longer be your light
  during the day.
  The light from the moon will no
  longer be your light.
This is because the Lord will be
  your light forever.
  Your God will be your glory.
[20] Your sun will never set again.
  Your moon will never be dark
  again.
This is because the Lord will be
  your light forever.
  And your time of sadness will
  end.
[21] All of your people will do what is
  right.
  They will receive the earth
  forever.
They are the plant I have planted.
  I made them with my own hands
  to show my greatness.

[22] The smallest family will grow to a
  thousand.
  The least important of you will
  become a powerful nation.
I am the Lord,
  and when it is time, I will make
  these things happen quickly."

61

The Lord God has put his Spirit[d]
  in me.
  This is because he has appointed
  me to tell the good news to the
  poor.
He has sent me to comfort those
  whose hearts are broken.
He has sent me to tell the captives
  they are free.
  He has sent me to tell the
  prisoners that they are
  released.
[2] He has sent me to announce the
  time when the Lord will show
  his kindness
  and the time when our God will
  punish evil people.
He has sent me to comfort all those
  who are sad.
[3] He has sent me to the sorrowing
  people of Jerusalem.
  I will give them a crown to
  replace their ashes.
I will give them the oil of gladness
  to replace their sorrow.
I will give them clothes of praise to
  replace their spirit of sadness.
Then they will be called Trees of
  Goodness.
  They will be like trees planted by
  the Lord and will show his
  greatness.

[4] They will rebuild the old ruins.
  They will build up the places
  destroyed long ago.
They will repair the ruined cities
  that were destroyed for so long.

[5] My people, foreigners will come to
  tend your sheep.
  People from other countries will
  tend your vineyards.
[6] You will be called priests of the
  Lord.
  You will be named the servants
  of our God.
You will have riches from all the
  nations on earth.
  And you will take pride in them.
[7] Instead of being ashamed, you will
  receive twice as much wealth.

Instead of being disgraced, you
    will be happy because of what
    you receive.
You will receive a double share of
    the land.
    So your happiness will continue
    forever.
[8]The Lord says, "I love justice.
    I hate stealing and everything
    that is wrong.
I will be fair and give my people
    what they should have.
I will make an agreement with
    them that will continue forever.
[9]Everyone in all nations will know
    the children of my people.
    And their children will be known
    among the nations.
Anyone who sees them will know
    that the Lord blesses them."

[10]The Lord makes me very happy.
    All that I am rejoices in my God.
The Lord has covered me with
    clothes of salvation.
He has covered me with a coat of
    goodness.
I am like a bridegroom dressed for
    his wedding.
I am like a bride dressed in
    jewels.
[11]The earth causes plants to grow.
    And a garden causes the seeds
    planted there to grow.
In the same way the Lord God will
    make grow what is right.
He will make praise come from
    all the nations.

62 Because I love Jerusalem, I will
    continue to speak for her.
For Jerusalem's sake I will not
    stop speaking.
I will speak until her goodness
    shines like a bright light.
I will speak until her salvation
    burns bright like a flame.
[2]Jerusalem, the nations will see your
    goodness.
    All kings will see your honor.
Then you will have a new name.
    The Lord himself will give you
    that new name.
[3]You will be like a beautiful crown
    in the Lord's hand.
    You will be like a king's crown in
    your God's hand.
[4]You will never again be called the
    People that God Left.
    Your land will never again be
    called the Land that God
    Destroyed.

You will be called the People God
    Loves.
    Your land will be called the Bride
    of God.
This is because the Lord loves you.
    And your land will belong to him
    as a bride belongs to her
    husband.
[5]As a young man marries a woman,
    so your children will marry your
    land.
As a man is very happy about his
    new wife,
    so your God will be happy with
    you.

[6]Jerusalem, I have put guards on the
    walls to watch.
    They must not be silent day or
    night.
You people who remind the Lord
    should never be quiet.
[7]You should not stop praying to the
    Lord until he builds up
    Jerusalem.
    Don't stop until he makes
    Jerusalem a city all people will
    praise.

[8]The Lord has made a promise.
    And by his power he will keep
    his promise.
He said, "I will never again give
    your grain
    as food to your enemies.
I will not let your enemies drink the
    wine
    that you have worked to make.
[9]The person who gathers food will
    eat it.
    And he will praise the Lord.
The person who gathers the grapes
    will drink the wine
    in the courts of my Temple."[d]

[10]Go through, go through the gates!
    Make the way ready for the
    people.
Build up, build up the road!
    Move all the stones off the road.
Raise the banner as a sign for the
    people.

[11]The Lord is speaking
    to all the faraway lands:
"Tell the people of Jerusalem,
    'Look, your Savior is coming.
He is bringing your reward to you.
    He is bringing his payment with
    him.'"
[12]His people will be called the Holy
    People.

They will be called the Saved
People of the Lord.
And Jerusalem will be called the
City God Wants.
It will be named the City God
Has Not Rejected.

63 Who is this coming from Edom?
He comes from the city of
Bozrah dressed in red.
Who is this dressed in fine clothes?
He marches forward with his
great power.

He says, "I, the Lord, speak what is
right.
I have the power to save you."

²Why are your clothes bright red
as if you had walked on the
grapes to make wine?

³The Lord answers, "I have walked
in the winepress[d] alone.
No one among the nations helped
me.
I was angry and walked on the
nations.
I crushed them because of my
anger.
Blood splashed on my clothes.
I stained all my clothing.
⁴I chose a time to punish people.
And the time has come for me to
save my people.
⁵I looked around, but I saw no one
to help me.
I was surprised that no one
supported me.
So I used my own power to save my
people.
My own anger supported me.
⁶While I was angry, I walked on the
nations.
In my anger I punished them
and poured their blood on the
ground."

⁷I will tell about the Lord's
kindness.
And I will praise him for what he
has done.
He has given many good things to
us.
He has been very good to the
people of Israel.
The Lord has shown mercy to us.
And he has been kind to us.
⁸The Lord said, "These are my
people.
My children will not lie to me."
So the Lord saved them.

⁹When they suffered, he suffered
also.
He sent his own angel to save
them.
Because of his love and kindness,
the Lord saved them.
Since long ago he has picked
them up and carried them.
¹⁰But they turned against the Lord.
They made his Holy Spirit[d] very
sad.
So the Lord became their enemy.
And he fought against them.

¹¹But then his people remembered
what happened long ago.
They remembered Moses.
Where is the Lord who brought the
people through the sea?
Where is the one who brought
them with the leaders of his
people?
Where is the one
who put his Holy Spirit among
them?
¹²The Lord led Moses by the right
hand.
The Lord led him by his
wonderful power.
The Lord divided the water before
them so the people could walk
through the sea.
And by this the Lord made his
name famous forever.
¹³The Lord led the people through
the deep waters.
Like a horse walking through a
desert,
the people did not stumble.
¹⁴Like cattle that go down to the
valley,
the Spirit of the Lord led the
people to a place of rest.
Lord, that is the way you led your
people.
And by this you made your name
wonderful.

¹⁵Lord, look down from the heavens
and see.
Look at us from your wonderful
holy home in heaven.
Where is your strong love and
power?
Why are you keeping your love
and mercy from us?
¹⁶You are our father.
Abraham doesn't know we are
his children.
Israel doesn't know who we are.
Lord, you are our father.

You are called "the one who has always saved us."

17 Lord, why are you making us wander from your ways?
Why do you make us stubborn so that we don't honor you?
For our sake come back to us.
We are your servants, and we belong to you.

18 Your people had your Temple[d] for a while.
But now our enemies have walked on your holy place and crushed it.

19 You have never ruled over some people.
They have never worn your name.
And we have become like those people.

64
Tear open the skies and come down to earth.
The mountains would tremble before you.

2 Be like a fire that burns twigs.
Be like a fire that makes water boil.
Do this so that your enemies will know who you are.
Then all nations will shake with fear when they see you.

3 You have done amazing things that we did not expect.
You came down, and the mountains trembled before you.

4 From long ago no one has ever heard of a God like you.
No one has ever seen a God besides you.
You help the people who trust you.

5 You help those who enjoy doing good.
You help those who remember how you want them to live.
But you were angry because we sinned.
For a long time we disobeyed.
How will we be saved?

6 All of us are dirty with sin.
All the right things we have done are like filthy pieces of cloth.
All of us are like dead leaves.
Like the wind our sins have carried us away.

7 No one worships you.
No one even asks you to help us.
So you have turned away from us.

And we are destroyed because of our sins.

8 But Lord, you are our father.
We are like clay, and you are the potter.
Your hands made us all.

9 Lord, don't continue to be angry with us.
Don't remember our sins forever.
Please, look at us
because we are your people.

10 Your holy cities are empty like the desert.
Jerusalem is like a desert;
Jerusalem is destroyed.

11 Our ancestors worshiped you
in our holy and wonderful Temple.
But now it has been burned with fire.
All our precious things have been destroyed.

12 When you see these things, will you hold yourself back from helping us, Lord?
Will you be silent and punish us beyond what we can stand?

65
The Lord says, "I made myself known to people who were not looking for me.
I was found by those who were not asking me for help.
I spoke to a nation that was not praying to me.
I said, 'Here I am. Here I am.'

2 All day long I stood ready to accept people who turned against me.
But the way they continue to live is not good.
They do anything they want to do.

3 Right in front of me they continue to do things that make me angry.
They offer sacrifices to their false gods in their gardens.
They burn incense[d] on altars of brick.

4 They sit among the graves.
They spend their nights waiting to get messages from the dead.
They eat the meat of pigs.
Their pots are full of soup made from meat that is wrong to eat.

5 But they tell others, 'Stay away.
Don't come near me.
I am too holy for you.'
These people are like smoke in my nose.

Like a fire that burns all the time,
they continue to make me
angry.

⁶"Look, it is written here before me.
I will not be quiet. Instead, I will
repay you in full.
I will punish you for what you
have done.
⁷I will punish you for your sins and
your ancestors' sins,"
says the Lord.
"They burned incense to false gods
on the mountains.
They shamed me on those hills.
So I will punish them as they
should be punished
for what they did."

⁸This is what the Lord says:
"When there is juice left in the
grapes,
people do not destroy them.
They know there is good left in
them.
I will do the same thing to my
servants.
I will not completely destroy
them.
⁹I will leave some of the children of
Jacob.
Some of the people of Judah will
receive my mountain.
I will choose the people who will
live there.
My servants will live there.
¹⁰Then the Plain of Sharon will be a
field for sheep.
The Valley of Achor will be a
place for cattle to rest.
They will be for the people who
want to follow me.

¹¹"But you who left the Lord will be
punished.
You forgot about my holy
mountain.
You worship the false god Luck.
You hold religious feasts for the
false god Fate.
¹²But I decide your fate, and I will
punish you with my sword.
You will all be killed.
This is because I called you, but
you refused to answer.
I spoke to you, but you wouldn't
listen.
You did the things I said were evil.
You chose to do things that
displease me."

¹³So the Lord God said these things:
"My servants will eat.
But you evil people will be
hungry.
My servants will drink.
But you evil people will be
thirsty.
My servants will be happy.
But you evil people will be
shamed.
¹⁴My servants will shout for joy
because of the goodness of their
hearts.
But you evil people will cry,
because you will be sad.
You will cry loudly because your
spirits will be broken.
¹⁵Your names will be like curses to
my servants.
And the Lord God will put you to
death.
But he will call his servants by
another name.
¹⁶People in the land who ask for
blessings
will ask for them from the
faithful God.
People in the land who make a
promise
will promise in the name of the
faithful God.
This is because the troubles of the
past will be forgotten.
I will make those troubles go
away.

¹⁷"Look, I will make new heavens
and a new earth.
And people will not remember
the past.
They will not think about those
things.
¹⁸My people will be happy forever
because of the things I will make.
I will make a Jerusalem that is full
of joy.
And I will make her people a
delight.
¹⁹Then I will rejoice over Jerusalem.
I will be delighted with my
people.
There will never again be
crying and sadness in that city.
²⁰There will never be a baby from
that city
who lives only a few days.
And there will never be an older
person
who doesn't have a long life.
A person who lives 100 years will
be called young.

And the person who dies before
he is 100 will be thought of as a
sinner.
²¹In that city the person who builds a
house will live there.
The person who plants vineyards
will get to eat grapes.
²²No more will one person build a
house and someone else live
there.
One person will not plant a
garden and someone else eat
its fruit.
My people will live a long time
as trees live long.
My chosen people will live there
and enjoy the things they make.
²³People will never again work for
nothing.
They will never again give birth
to children who die young.
All my people will be blessed by
the Lord.
My people and their children will
be blessed.
²⁴I will provide for their needs before
they ask.
I will help them while they are
still asking for help.
²⁵Wolves and lambs will eat together
in peace.
Lions will eat hay like oxen.
A snake on the ground will not hurt
anyone.
They will not hurt or destroy each
other
on all my holy mountain,"
says the Lord.

66 This is what the Lord says:
"The skies are my throne.
The earth is my footstool.
So do you think you can build a
house for me?
There is no place where I need to
rest.
²My hand made all things.
All things are here because I
made them,"
says the Lord.

"These are the people I am pleased
with.
They are those who are not
proud or stubborn.
They fear me and obey me.
³But those people who kill bulls as a
sacrifice to me
are like those who kill men.

Those who kill sheep as a sacrifice
to me
are like those who break the
necks of dogs.
Those who give me grain offerings
are like those who offer me the
blood of pigs.ⁿ
Those who burn incenseᵈ
are like those who worship idols.
These people choose their own
ways—not mine.
They love the terrible things they
do.
⁴So I will punish them.
I will punish them using what
they fear most.
I called to them, but they did not
listen.
I spoke to them, but they did not
hear me.
They did things I said were evil.
They chose to do things I did not
like."

⁵You people who obey the words of
the Lord,
listen to what he says:
"Your brothers hated you.
They turned against you because
you followed me.
Your brothers said, 'When the Lord
is honored,
we will come back and rejoice
with you.'
But they will be punished.
⁶Listen to the loud noise coming
from the city.
Hear the noise from the Temple.ᵈ
It is the Lord punishing his
enemies.
He is giving them the
punishment they should have.

⁷"A woman does not give birth
before she feels the pain.
She does not give birth to a son
before she feels the pain of
birth.
⁸No one has ever heard of that
happening.
No one has ever seen that
happen.
In the same way no one ever saw a
country begin in one day.
No one has ever heard of a new
nation beginning in one day.
But Jerusalem will give birth to her
children

66:3 dogs . . . pigs God did not want his people to offer dogs and pigs as sacrifices because they
were unclean animals.

just as soon as she feels the birth
pains.

[9] In the same way I will not cause
pain
without allowing something new
to be born," says the Lord.
"If I cause you the pain,
I will not stop you from giving
birth to your new nation," says
your God.
[10] "Jerusalem, rejoice.
All you people who love
Jerusalem, be happy.
Those of you who felt sad for
Jerusalem
should now feel happy with her.
[11] You will enjoy her good things and
be satisfied
as a child is nursed by its mother.
You will receive her good things
and enjoy her wealth."

[12] This is what the Lord says:
"I will give her peace that will flow
to her like a river.
The wealth of the nations will
come flowing to her.
Like babies you will be nursed and
held in my arms.
You will be bounced on my
knees.
[13] I will comfort you
as a mother comforts her child.
You will be comforted in
Jerusalem."

[14] When you see these things, you will
be happy.
You will grow like the grass.
The Lord's servants will see his
power.
But the Lord's enemies will see
his anger.
[15] Look, the Lord is coming with fire.
The Lord's armies are coming
with clouds of dust.
He will punish those people with
his anger.
He will punish them with flames
of fire.

[16] The Lord will judge the people with
fire.
He will destroy many people with
his sword.
He will kill many people.
[17] "These people make themselves holy
and pure to go to worship their false
gods in their gardens. They follow each
other into their special gardens. They
eat the meat of pigs and rats and other
hated things. But they will all be destroyed together," says the Lord.
[18] "I know they have evil thoughts and
do evil things. So I am coming to punish
them. I will gather all nations and all
people. All people will come together
and see my glory.
[19] "I will put a mark on some of the
people. And I will send some of these
saved people to the nations. I will send
them to Tarshish, Libya, Lud (the land
of archers), Tubal, Greece and all the
faraway lands. These people have never
heard about what I have done. They
have never seen my glory. So the saved
people will tell the nations about my
glory. [20] And they will bring all your fellow Israelites from all nations. They will
bring them to my holy mountain in Jerusalem. Your fellow Israelites will come
on horses, donkeys, camels and in chariots and wagons. They will be like the
grain offerings that the people bring in
clean containers to the Temple," says
the Lord. [21] "And I will choose some of
these people to be priests and Levites,"
says the Lord.
[22] "I will make new heavens and the
new earth. And they will last forever,"
says the Lord. "In the same way, your
names and your children will always be
with me. [23] All people will come to worship me. They will come to worship me
every Sabbath[d] and every New Moon,"[d]
says the Lord. [24] "They will go out and
see the dead bodies of the people who
sinned against me. The worms that eat
them will never die. The fires that burn
them will never stop. And everyone will
hate to see those bodies."

The Book of
JEREMIAH

1 These are the words of Jeremiah son of Hilkiah. He belonged to the family of priests who lived in the town of Anathoth. That town is in the land that belongs to the tribe[d] of Benjamin. ²The Lord spoke his word to Jeremiah. This happened during the thirteenth year that Josiah son of Amon was king of Judah. ³The Lord also spoke to Jeremiah while Jehoiakim son of Josiah was king of Judah. And the Lord spoke to Jeremiah during the 11 years and 5 months Zedekiah son of Josiah was king of Judah. After that, the people who lived in Jerusalem were taken away as captives out of their country.

⁴The Lord spoke these words to me:
⁵"Before I made you in your
    mother's womb, I chose you.
  Before you were born, I set you
    apart for a special work.
  I appointed you as a prophet[d] to
    the nations."

⁶Then I said, "But Lord God, I don't know how to speak. I am only a boy."

⁷But the Lord said to me, "Don't say, 'I am only a boy.' You must go everywhere that I send you. You must say everything I tell you to say. ⁸Don't be afraid of anyone, because I am with you. I will protect you," says the Lord.

⁹Then the Lord reached out with his hand and touched my mouth. He said to me, "See, I am putting my words into your mouth. ¹⁰Today I have put you in charge of nations and kingdoms. You will pull up and tear down, destroy and overthrow. You will build up and plant."

¹¹The Lord spoke this word to me: "Jeremiah, what do you see?"

I answered the Lord and said, "I see a stick of almond wood."

¹²The Lord said to me, "You have seen correctly! And I am watching to make sure my words come true."

¹³The Lord spoke his word to me again: "Jeremiah, what do you see?"

I answered the Lord and said, "I see a pot of boiling water. It is tipping over from the north!"

¹⁴The Lord said to me, "Disaster will come from the north. It will happen to all the people who live in this country. ¹⁵In a short time I will call all of the people in the northern kingdoms," said the Lord.

"Those kings will come and set up
    their thrones
  near the entrance of the gates of
    Jerusalem.
They will attack the city walls
    around Jerusalem.
  They will attack all the cities in
    Judah.
¹⁶And I will announce my judgments
    against my people.
  I will do this because of their evil
    in turning away from me.
They offered sacrifices to other
    gods.
  And they worshiped idols they
    had made with their own
    hands.

¹⁷"Jeremiah, get ready. Stand up and speak to the people. Tell them everything I tell you to say. Don't be afraid of the people. If you are afraid of them, I will give you good reason to be afraid of them. ¹⁸Today I am going to make you a strong city, an iron pillar, a bronze wall. You will be able to stand against everyone in the land: Judah's kings, officers, priests and the people of the land. ¹⁹They will fight against you. But they will not defeat you. This is because I am with you, and I will save you!" says the Lord.

2 The Lord spoke this word to me: ²"Go and speak to the people of Jerusalem. Say to them: This is what the Lord says:

'When you were a young nation,
    you were faithful to me.
  You loved me like a young bride.
You followed me through the
    desert.
  It was a land that had never been
    planted.
³The people of Israel were holy to
    the Lord.
  They were like the first fruits
    from his harvest.
Those who tried to hurt Israel were
    judged guilty.
  Disasters happened to them,'"
  says the Lord.

⁴Hear the word of the Lord, family
    of Jacob.
  Hear the message, all you family
    groups of Israel.

[5]This is what the Lord says:
"I was fair to your ancestors.
    Why did they turn away from me?
Your ancestors worshiped useless idols.
    And they became useless themselves.
[6]Your ancestors didn't say,
    'The Lord brought us out of Egypt.
He led us through the desert.
    He led us through a dry and rocky land.
He led us through a dark and dangerous land.
    He led us where no one travels or lives.
But where is he now?'
[7]I brought you into a fertile land.
    I did this so you could eat its fruit and produce.
But you came and made my land unclean.[d]
    You made it a hated place.
[8]The priests didn't ask,
    'Where is the Lord?'
The people who know the teachings didn't know me.
    The leaders turned against me.
The prophets[d] prophesied in the name of Baal.[d]
    They worshiped useless idols.

[9]"So now I will again tell what I have against you," says the Lord.
    "And I will tell what I have against your grandchildren.
[10]Go across the sea to the island of Cyprus and see.
    Send someone to the land of Kedar to look closely.
See if there has ever been anything like this!
[11]Has a nation ever exchanged their old gods for new ones?
    (Of course, their gods are not really gods at all.)
But my people have exchanged their glorious God
    for idols worth nothing!
[12]Skies, be shocked at the things that have happened.
    Shake with great fear!" says the Lord.
[13]"My people have done two sins.
    They have turned away from me.
And I am the spring of living water.

And they have dug their own wells.
    But they are broken wells that cannot hold water.
[14]Have the people of Israel become slaves?
    Have they become like someone who was born a slave?
Why was their wealth stolen?
[15]Enemies roar like lions at Israel.
    They growl at Israel.
They have destroyed the land of Israel.
    The cities of Israel have been burned,
and all the people have left.
[16]The men from the Egyptian cities of Memphis and Tahpanhes
    have disgraced you by shaving the top of your head.
[17]You have brought this on yourselves.
    You turned away from me, the Lord your God,
when I led you in the way.
[18]It did not help to go to Egypt
    and drink from the Shihor River.
It did not help to go to Assyria
    and drink from the Euphrates River.
[19]Your evil will bring punishment to you.
    The wrong you have done will teach you a lesson.
Think about it and understand.
It is a terrible evil to turn away
    from the Lord your God.
It is wrong not to fear me,"
    says the Lord, the Lord of heaven's armies.

[20]"A long time ago you refused to obey me as an ox breaks its yoke.[d]
    You broke the ropes I used to hold you to me.
You said to me, 'I will not serve you!'
In fact, on every high hill
    and under every green tree
you lay down as a prostitute.[d]
[21]I planted you as a special vine.
    You were like very good seed.
How then did you turn
    into a wild vine that grows bad fruit?
[22]You might wash yourself with cleanser.
    And you might use much soap.
But I can still see the stain of
    your guilt," says the Lord God.

²³"How can you say to me, 'I am not
   guilty.
I have not worshiped the Baalᵈ
   idols'?
Think about the things you did in
   the valley.
Think about what you have done.
You are like a she-camel in mating
   season
   that runs from place to place.
²⁴You are like a wild donkey that
   lives in the desert.
At mating time she sniffs the
   wind.
At that time no one can hold her
   back.
Any male who chases her will
   easily catch her.
At mating time, it is easy to find
   her.
²⁵Don't run until your feet are bare
   or until your throat is dry.
But you say, 'It's no use!
I love those other gods.
I must worship them!'

²⁶"A thief is ashamed when someone
   catches him stealing.
In the same way the family of
   Israel is ashamed.
The kings and the officers,
   the priests and the prophets are
   ashamed.
²⁷They say to things of wood, 'You
   are my father.'
They say to idols of stone, 'You
   gave birth to me.'
Those people won't look at me.
   They have turned their backs to
   me.
But when they get into trouble,
   they say,
'Come and save us!'
²⁸Where are the idols you have made
   for yourselves?
Let them come and save you
   when you are in trouble!
People of Judah, you have as many
   idols
   as you have towns!

²⁹"Why do you accuse me?
All of you have turned against me,"
   says the Lord.
³⁰"I punished your people, but it did
   not help.
They didn't come back when they
   were punished.
You killed with your swords the
   prophets who came to you.
You were like a dangerous lion.

³¹"People of Judah, pay attention to
the word of the Lord:
Have I been like a desert to the
   people of Israel?
Have I been like a dark and
   dangerous land to them?
Why do my people say, 'We are free
   to wander.
We won't come to you anymore'?
³²A young woman does not forget
   her jewelry.
A bride does not forget the
   decorations for her dress.
But my people have forgotten me
   for more days than can be
   counted!
³³You really know how to chase after
   love.
Even the worst women can learn
   evil ways from you.
³⁴You have blood on your clothes.
It is the blood of the poor and
   innocent people.
You killed them,
   but they weren't thieves you had
   caught breaking in.
You do all these things,
³⁵   but you say, 'I am innocent.
God is not angry with me.'
But I will judge you guilty of lying.
It is because you say, 'I have not
   sinned.'
³⁶It is so easy for you to change your
   mind.
Assyria let you down.
And Egypt will let you down, too.
³⁷You will eventually leave that place.
And, like captives, your hands
   will be on your head.
You trusted those countries.
But you will not be helped by
   them.
This is because the Lord has
   rejected them.

3 "Now a man might divorce his wife.
   And she might leave him and
   marry another man.
Should her first husband come
   back to her again?
If he went back to her, the land
   would become completely
   unclean.ᵈ
But you have acted like a
   prostituteᵈ with many lovers.
And now you want to come back
   to me?" says the Lord.
²"Look up to the bare hilltops,
   Judah.
Is there any place where you
   have not been a prostitute?

You have sat by the road waiting
for lovers.
You sat there like an Arab in the
desert.
You made the land unclean.
This was because you did evil
and were like a prostitute.
³So the rain has not come.
There have not been any spring
rains.
But your face still looks like the
face of a prostitute.
You refuse even to be ashamed of
what you did.
⁴But now you are calling to me.
You say, 'My father, you have
been my friend since I was
young.
⁵Will you always be angry at me?
Will your anger last forever?'
Judah, you say this,
but you do as much evil as you
can!"

⁶When King Josiah was ruling Judah,
the Lord spoke to me. He said: "Jeremiah, you saw what unfaithful Israel
did. She was guilty of adultery.ᵈ She had
idols on every hill and under every
green tree. ⁷I said to myself, 'Israel will
come back to me after she does this evil.'
But she didn't come back to me. And
Israel's wicked sister Judah saw what
Israel did. ⁸Unfaithful Israel knew that I
divorced her because of her adultery.
But that didn't make her wicked sister
Judah afraid. She also went out and
acted like a prostitute!ᵈ ⁹And she didn't
care that she was acting like a prostitute. So she made her country unclean.ᵈ
She was guilty of adultery. This was because she worshiped idols made of
stone and wood. ¹⁰Israel's wicked sister
didn't come back to me with her whole
heart. She only pretended to come back
to me," says the Lord.

¹¹The Lord said to me, "Unfaithful Israel had a better excuse than wicked
Judah. ¹²Go and speak this message toward the north:
'Come back, unfaithful people of
Israel,' says the Lord.
'I will stop frowning at you.
I am full of mercy,' says the Lord.
'I will not be angry with you
forever.
¹³All you have to do is admit your
sin.
You turned against the Lord your
God.
You worshiped the false gods of
other nations.

You worshiped them under every
green tree.
You didn't obey me,'" says the
Lord.

¹⁴"Come back to me, you unfaithful
people," says the Lord. "I am your husband. I will take one person from every
city. And I will take two people from
every family group. And I will bring you
to Jerusalem. ¹⁵Then I will give you new
rulers. They will be faithful to me. They
will lead you with knowledge and understanding. ¹⁶In those days there will
be many of you in the land," says the
Lord. "At that time people will no longer
say, 'I remember the Boxᵈ of the Agreement.' They won't even think about the
Holy Box anymore. They won't even remember or miss it or make another one.
¹⁷At that time Jerusalem will be called
The Throne of the Lord. All nations will
come together in Jerusalem to show respect to the Lord. They will not follow
their stubborn, evil hearts anymore. ¹⁸In
those days the family of Judah will join
the family of Israel. They will come together from a land in the north. They
will come to the land I gave to their ancestors.

¹⁹"I, the Lord, said,
'How happy I would be to treat you
as sons!
I would be glad to give you a
pleasant land.
It's a land more beautiful than
that of any other nation.'
I thought you would call me
'Father'
and not turn away from me.
²⁰But like a woman who is unfaithful
to her husband,
family of Israel, you have been
unfaithful to me," says the
Lord.

²¹You can hear crying on the bare
hilltops.
The people of Israel are crying
and praying for mercy.
They have become very evil.
They have forgotten the Lord
their God.

²²"Come back to me, you unfaithful
people of Israel.
Come back, and I will forgive you
for being unfaithful."

"Yes, we will come to you.
You are the Lord our God.

²³It was foolish to worship idols on
  the hills.
All the loud noises on the
  mountains were a lie.
Surely the salvation of Israel
  comes from the Lord our God.
²⁴Since we were young, shameful
  gods have eaten up in sacrifice
  everything our fathers worked
  for.
The shameful gods have taken our
  fathers' sheep and cattle.
They have taken our fathers' sons
  and daughters.
²⁵Let us lie down in our shame.
  And let our shame cover us like a
  blanket.
We have sinned against the Lord
  our God.
  Both we and our fathers have
  sinned.
Since we were children and until
  now,
  we have not obeyed the Lord our
  God."

4 "If you will come back, Israel,
  then come back to me," says the
  Lord.
"Throw away your idols that I hate.
  Don't wander away from me.
²Then you may say when you make
  a promise,
  'As surely as the Lord lives.'
And you can say it in a truthful,
  honest and right way.
Then the nations will be blessed by
  the Lord.
  And they will praise the Lord for
  what he has done."

³This is what the Lord says to the men
of Judah and Jerusalem:
"Plow your unplowed fields.
  Don't plant seeds among the
  thorns.
⁴Give yourselves to the service of
  the Lord.
  Decide to obey him.
Do this, men of Judah and people
  of Jerusalem.
If you don't, my anger will spread
  among you like a fire.
No one will be able to put it out
  because of the evil you have done.

⁵"Announce this message to Judah
  and say it in Jerusalem:
  'Blow the trumpet throughout the
  country!'
Shout out loud and say,
  'Come together!

Let's all escape to the strong,
  walled cities!'
⁶Raise the signal flag toward
  Jerusalem!
  Run for your lives! And don't
  wait!
Do this because I am bringing
  disaster from the north.
  It will be terrible destruction."

⁷A lion has come out of his den.
  A destroyer of nations has begun
  to march.
He has left his home
  to destroy your land.
Your towns will be destroyed.
  There will be no people left to
  live in them.
⁸So put on rough cloth,
  show how sad you are and cry
  loudly.
The terrible anger of the Lord
  has not turned away from us.

⁹"When this happens," says the
  Lord,
  "the king and officers will lose
  their courage.
The priests will be terribly afraid.
  And the prophets^d will be
  shocked!"

¹⁰Then I, Jeremiah, said, "Lord God,
you have tricked the people of Judah
and Jerusalem. You said, 'You will have
peace.' But now the sword is pointing at
our throats!"
¹¹At that time this message will be
given to Judah and Jerusalem: "A hot
wind blows from the bare hilltops. It
comes out of the desert toward the
Lord's people. It is not like the gentle
wind farmers use to separate grain from
chaff.^d ¹²It's a stronger wind than that.
And it comes from the Lord. Now he
will announce his judgment against the
people of Judah."

¹³Look! The enemy rises up like a
  cloud.
  His chariots come like a
  windstorm.
His horses are faster than eagles.
  How terrible it will be for us! We
  are ruined!
¹⁴People of Jerusalem, clean the evil
  from your hearts and be saved.
  Don't continue making evil plans.
¹⁵A voice from Dan makes an
  announcement.
  From the mountains of Ephraim
  someone brings bad news.

¹⁶"Report this to the nations.
Spread this news in Jerusalem:
'Enemies are coming from a
faraway country.
They are shouting words of war
against the cities of Judah.
¹⁷The enemy has surrounded
Jerusalem as men guard a
field.
This is because Judah turned
against me,'" says the Lord.
¹⁸"The way you have lived and acted
has brought this trouble to you.
This is your punishment.
How terrible it is!
The pain stabs your heart!"

¹⁹Oh, how I hurt! How I hurt!
I am bent over in pain.
Oh, the torture in my heart!
My heart is pounding inside me.
I cannot keep quiet.
This is because I have heard the
sound of the trumpet.
I have heard the words of war.
²⁰Disaster follows disaster.
The whole country has been
destroyed.
My tents are destroyed in only a
moment.
My curtains are torn down
quickly.
²¹How long must I look at the war
flag?
How long must I listen to the war
trumpets?

²²The Lord says, "My people are
foolish.
They do not know me.
They are stupid children.
They don't understand.
They are skillful at doing evil.
They don't know how to do
good."

²³I looked at the earth.
It was empty and had no shape!
I looked at the sky.
And its light was gone.
²⁴I looked at the mountains,
and they were shaking!
All the hills were trembling.
²⁵I looked, and there were no people!
Every bird in the sky had flown
away.
²⁶I looked, and the good, rich land
had become a desert!
All its towns had been destroyed.
The Lord and his great anger has
caused this.

²⁷This is what the Lord says:

"All the land will be ruined.
But I will not completely destroy
it.
²⁸So the people in the land will cry
loudly.
And the sky will grow dark.
This is because I have spoken and
will not change my mind.
I have made a decision, and I will
not change it."

²⁹The towns will hear the sound of
the horsemen and soldiers with
bows.
All the people will run away.
Some of them will hide in the thick
bushes.
Some will climb up into the
rocks.
All of the cities of Judah are empty.
No one lives in them.
³⁰Judah, you destroyed nation, what
are you doing?
Why do you put on your finest
dress?
Why do you put on your gold
jewelry?
Why do you put on your eye
shadow?
You make yourself beautiful, but
it is all useless.
Your lovers hate you.
They want to kill you.

³¹I hear a cry like a woman having a
baby.
It is a cry like a woman having
her first child.
It is the voice of Jerusalem gasping
for breath.
She lifts her hands in prayer and
says,
"Oh! I am about to faint.
They are about to murder me!"

5 The Lord says, "Walk up and down
the streets of Jerusalem.
Look around and think about
these things.
Search the public squares of the
city.
See if you can find one person who
does honest things.
Find just one who searches for
the truth.
If you can, I will forgive this city.
²The people say, 'As surely as the
Lord lives!'
But they don't really mean it."

³Lord, don't you look for truth in
people?

You hit the people of Judah.
  But they didn't feel any pain.
You crushed them,
  but they refused to learn what is
    right.
They became more stubborn than a
    rock.
  They refused to turn back to God.
[4]But I thought,
  "These are only the poor, foolish
    people.
They have not learned the way of
    the Lord.
  They do not know what their God
    wants them to do.
[5]So I will go to the leaders of Judah.
  I will talk to them.
Surely they understand the way of
    the Lord.
  They know what God wants them
    to do."
But the leaders had all joined
    together to break away from
    the Lord.
  They broke their ties with him.
[6]So a lion from the forest will attack
    them.
  A wolf from the desert will kill
    them.
A leopard is hiding and waiting for
    them near their towns.
  It will tear to pieces anyone who
    comes out of the city.
This will happen because the
    people of Judah have sinned
    greatly.
  They have wandered away from
    the Lord many times.
[7]The Lord said, "Tell me why I
    should forgive you.
  Your children have left me.
They have made promises to
    idols that are not gods at all.
I gave your children everything
    they needed.
  But they still were like an
    unfaithful wife to me.
They spent much time in houses
    of prostitutes.[d]
[8]They are like well-fed, male horses
    filled with sexual desire.
  Each one wants another man's
    wife.
[9]Shouldn't I punish the people of
    Judah for doing these things?"
    says the Lord.
  "I should give a nation such as
    this the punishment it
    deserves.

[10]"Go along and cut down Judah's
    vineyards.
  But do not completely destroy
    them.
Cut off all her people as if they
    were branches.
  Do it because they do not belong
    to the Lord.
[11]The families of Israel and Judah
    have been completely unfaithful
    to me," says the Lord!

[12]Those people have lied about the
    Lord.
  They have said, "The Lord will
    not do anything to us!
Nothing bad will happen to us.
  We will never see war or hunger.
[13]The prophets[d] are like an empty
    wind.
  The word of God is not in them.
  Let these bad things they say
    happen to them."

[14]So this is what the Lord of heaven's
armies says:
  "The people said I would not
    punish them.
So, Jeremiah, the words I give
    you will be like fire.
  And these people will be like
    wood the fire burns up.
[15]Listen, family of Israel," says the
    Lord.
  "I will soon bring a nation from
    far away to attack you.
It is an old nation that has lasted a
    long time.
  The people there speak a
    language you do not know.
  You cannot understand what they
    say.
[16]Their arrows bring death.
  All their men are strong warriors.
[17]They will eat your crops and your
    food.
  They will eat your sons and
    daughters.
They will eat your flocks and herds.
  They will eat your grapes and
    figs.
They will destroy with their swords
    the strong, walled cities you trust
    in!

[18]"Yet even then," says the Lord, "I
will not destroy you completely. [19]The
people of Judah will ask, 'Why has the
Lord our God done this terrible thing to
us?' Give them this answer: 'You have
left the Lord. You have served foreign
idols in your own land. So now you will

serve foreigners in a land that does not belong to you!'

20 "Announce this message to the family of Jacob.
And tell it to the nation of Judah.
21 Hear this message, you foolish people who have no sense.
You have eyes, but you don't really see.
You have ears, but you don't really listen.
22 Surely you are afraid of me," says the Lord.
"You should shake with fear in my presence.
I am the one who made the beaches to be a border for the sea.
They keep the water in its place forever.
The waves may pound the beach, but they can't win over it.
The waves may roar, but they cannot go beyond it.
23 But the people of Judah are stubborn and have turned against me.
They have turned aside and gone away from me.
24 They do not say to themselves, 'We should fear the Lord our God.
He gives us autumn and spring rains in their seasons.
He makes sure we have the harvest at the right time.'
25 But your evil has kept away both rain and harvest.
Your sins have kept you from enjoying good things.
26 There are wicked men among my people.
They are like men who make nets for catching birds.
But they set their traps to catch men instead of birds.
27 Like cages full of birds, their houses are full of lies.
They have become rich and powerful.
28 They have grown big and fat.
There is no end to the evil things they do.
They won't plead the case of the orphan.
They won't help the poor be judged fairly.
29 Shouldn't I punish the people of Judah for doing these things?" says the Lord.

"I should give a nation such as this the punishment it deserves.

30 "A terrible and shocking thing has happened in the land of Judah.
31 The prophets tell lies.
The priests take power into their own hands.
And my people love it this way.
But what will you do when the end comes?

6 "Run for your lives, people of Benjamin!
Run away from Jerusalem!
Blow the war trumpet in the town of Tekoa!
Raise the warning flag over the town of Beth Hakkerem!
Disaster is coming from the north.
Terrible destruction is coming to you.
2 Jerusalem, I will destroy you.
You are fragile and gentle.
3 Shepherds with their flocks will come against Jerusalem.
They will set up their tents all around her.
Each shepherd will take care of his own section."
4 They say, "Get ready to fight against Jerusalem!
Get up! We will attack at noon!
But it is already getting late.
The evening shadows are growing long.
5 So get up! We will attack at night.
We will destroy the strong towers of Jerusalem!"

6 This is what the Lord of heaven's armies says:
"Cut down the trees around Jerusalem.
Build an attack ramp to the top of Jerusalem's walls.
This city must be punished!
Inside this city is nothing but slavery.
7 Jerusalem pours out her evil as a well pours out its water.
The sounds of violence and destruction are heard within her.
I can see the sickness and hurts of Jerusalem.
8 Listen to this warning, Jerusalem.
If you don't listen, I will turn my back on you.

I will make your land an empty
desert.
No one will be able to live there!"

[9]This is what the Lord of heaven's armies says:
"Gather the few people of Israel
who are left alive.
Gather them as you would the
last grapes on a grapevine.
Check each vine again,
like someone who gathers
grapes."

[10]To whom can I speak? Whom can I
warn?
Who will listen to me?
The people of Israel have closed
ears!
So they cannot hear my
warnings.
They don't like the word of the
Lord.
They don't want to listen to it!
[11]But I am full of the anger of the
Lord.
I am tired of holding it in.

"Pour out the Lord's anger on the
children who play in the street.
Pour it out on the young men
gathered together.
A husband and his wife will both
be caught in his anger.
The very old people will be
caught in it.
[12]Their houses will be turned over to
others.
Their fields and wives will be
given away.
I will raise my hand
and punish the people of Judah,"
says the Lord.
[13]"Everyone, from the least
important to the greatest,
is greedy for money.
Even the prophets[d] and priests
all tell lies.
[14]They try to heal my people's
serious injuries
as if they were small wounds.
They say, 'It's all right, it's all
right!'
But really, it is not all right.
[15]They should be ashamed of the
terrible way they act.
But they are not ashamed at all.
They don't even know how to
blush about their sins.
So they will fall, along with
everyone else.

They will be thrown to the
ground when I punish them,"
says the Lord.

[16]This is what the Lord says:
"Stand where the roads cross and
look.
Ask where the old way is.
Ask where the good way is, and
walk on it.
If you do, you will find rest for
yourselves.
But you have said, 'We will not
walk on the good way!'
[17]I chose watchmen to watch over
you.
I told you, 'Listen for the sound
of the war trumpet!'
But you said, 'We will not listen.'
[18]So listen, all you nations.
Pay attention, you witnesses.
Watch what I will do to the
people of Judah.
[19]Hear this, people of the earth:
I am going to bring disaster to
the people of Judah!
It will happen because of the evil
they plan.
They have not listened to my
messages.
They have rejected my teachings.
[20]Why do you bring me offerings of
incense[d] from the land of
Sheba?
Why do you bring me
sweet-smelling cane from a
faraway land?
Your burnt offerings will not be
accepted.
Your sacrifices do not please
me."

[21]So this is what the Lord says:
"I will put problems in front of
Judah.
Fathers and sons will stumble
over them.
Neighbors and friends will die."

[22]This is what the Lord says:
"Look, an army is coming
from the land of the north.
A great nation is coming
from the far sides of the earth.
[23]The soldiers carry bows and
spears.
They are cruel and show no
mercy.
They sound like the roaring ocean
when they ride their horses.
That army is coming lined up for
battle.

It is coming to attack you,
Jerusalem."

[24] We have heard the news about that
army.
We are helpless from fear.
We feel trapped by our troubles.
We are in pain like a woman
having a baby.
[25] Don't go out into the fields.
Don't walk down the roads!
This is because the enemy has
swords.
There is terror on every side.
[26] My people, put on rough cloth
and roll in the ashes to show how
sad you are.
Cry loudly for those who are dead.
Cry as if your only son had died.
Do it because the destroyer
will soon come against us.
[27] "Jeremiah, I have made you like a
worker who tests metal.
And my people are like the ore
for the metal.
You must observe their ways.
And you must test them.
[28] My people have turned against me
and are stubborn.
They go around telling lies about
people.
They are like bronze and iron,
that became covered with rust.
[29] The fire is fanned to make it hotter.
But the lead does not melt.
The pure silver does not come out.
And the evil is not removed from
my people.
[30] My people will be called rejected
silver.
They will be given that name
because the Lord has rejected
them."

7 This is the word that the Lord spoke
to Jeremiah: [2] "Stand at the gate of
the Temple.[d] Preach this message there:
"'Hear the word of the Lord, all you
people of the nation of Judah! All you
who come through these gates to worship the Lord, listen to this message!
[3] This is what the Lord of heaven's armies, the God of Israel, says: Change
your lives and do what is right! If you
do, I will let you live in this place. [4] Don't
trust the lies that some people say! They
say, "This is the Temple of the Lord. This
is the Temple of the Lord. This is the
Temple of the Lord!" [5] You must change
your lives and do what is right. You must
be fair to each other. [6] You must not be

hard on the strangers, the orphans and
widows. Don't kill innocent people in
this place! Don't follow other gods, or
they will ruin your lives. [7] If you do
these things, I will let you live in this
land. This is the land I gave to your ancestors to keep forever.
[8] "'But look! You are trusting lies.
Such trust is useless. [9] Will you steal and
murder? Will you be guilty of adultery?[d]
Will you falsely accuse other people?
Will you worship the false god Baal?[d]
And will you follow other gods you have
not known? [10] If you do that, do you think
you can come before me? Can you stand
in this place where I have chosen to be
worshiped? Do you think you can say,
"We are safe!" Are you safe to do all
these hated things? [11] This is the place
where I have chosen to be worshiped. Is
it nothing more to you than a hideout
for robbers? I have been watching you,
says the Lord!
[12] "'You people of Judah, go now to the
town of Shiloh. It was there that I first
made a place to be worshiped. Go there
and see what I did because of the evil
things they had done. [13] You people of
Israel were doing all these evil things,
says the Lord. I spoke to you again and
again. But you did not listen to me. I
called you, but you did not answer. [14] So
I will destroy the place where I have chosen to be worshiped in Jerusalem. You
trust in that place. I gave it to you and
your ancestors. But I will destroy it just
as I destroyed Shiloh. [15] I will push you
away from me. I will do it just as I
pushed away your brothers, the people
of Israel!'
[16] "As for you, Jeremiah, don't pray for
these people. Don't cry out for them or
ask anything for them. Don't beg me to
help them. I will not listen to you.
[17] Don't you see what they are doing in
the towns of Judah? Don't you see what
they are doing in the streets of Jerusalem? [18] This is what the people of Judah
are doing: The children gather wood.
The fathers use the wood to make a fire.
The women make the dough for cakes of
bread. And they offer them to the Queen
Goddess.[d] They pour out drink offerings
to worship other gods. They do this to
make me angry. [19] But I am not the one
the people of Judah are really hurting,
says the Lord. They are only hurting
themselves. They are bringing shame
upon themselves.
[20] "'So this is what the Lord says: I will
pour out my anger on this place. I will

pour it out on man and animal. I will pour it out on the trees in the field. And I will pour it out on the crops in the ground. My anger will be like a hot fire. And no one will be able to put it out.

21"'This is what the Lord of heaven's armies, the God of Israel, says: Go and offer as many burnt offerings and sacrifices as you want! Eat the meat of those sacrifices yourselves! 22I brought your ancestors out of Egypt. I spoke to them. But I did not give them commands only about burnt offerings and sacrifices. 23I also gave them this command: Obey me, and I will be your God and you will be my people. Do all that I command, and good things will happen to you. 24But your ancestors did not listen or pay attention to me. They were stubborn and did whatever their evil hearts wanted. They went backward, not forward. 25Since the day your ancestors left Egypt, I have sent you my servants, the prophets.d I sent you to them again and again. 26But your ancestors did not listen or pay attention to me. They were very stubborn. And they did more evil than their ancestors.'

27"Jeremiah, you will tell these things to the people of Judah. But they will not listen to you! You will call to them, but they will not answer you. 28So say to them, 'This is the nation that has not obeyed the Lord its God. These people do nothing when I correct them. They do not tell the truth. It has disappeared from their lips.'

29"'Cut off your hair and throw it away. Go up to the bare hilltop and cry. Do it because I, the Lord, have rejected these people. I have turned my back on them. And in my anger I will punish them! 30The people of Judah have done what I said was evil, says the Lord. They have set up their hated idols in the place where I have chosen to be worshiped. They have made it unclean!d 31The people of Judah have built places of worship at Topheth in the Valley of Ben Hinnom. There the people offered their own sons and daughters as sacrifices. This is something I never commanded. It never even entered my mind! 32So, I warn you. The days are coming, says the Lord, when people will not call this place Topheth. They will not call it the Valley of Ben Hinnom anymore. They will call it the Valley of Killing. They will bury dead people in Topheth until there is no room to bury anyone else! 33Then the bodies

of the dead will lie on top of the ground. They will become food for the birds of the sky. Wild animals will eat the bodies. There will be no one left alive to chase the birds or animals away. 34I will end the happy sounds of the bride and bridegroom. There will be no happy sounds in Judah or in the streets of Jerusalem. The land will become an empty desert!

8 "'The Lord says: At that time the bones will be removed from the tombs. The bones of Judah's kings and officers, priests and prophetsd and the people of Jerusalem will be removed. 2The bones will be spread on the ground under the sun, moon and stars the people loved and served. They went after these gods, searched them out and worshiped them. No one will gather up the bones and bury them. So they will be like dung thrown on the ground. 3I will force the people of Judah to leave their homes and their land. Those of this evil family who are not dead will wish they were dead, says the Lord.'

4"Say to the people of Judah: 'This is what the Lord says:

When a man falls down, doesn't he
    get up again?
And when a man goes the wrong
    way, doesn't he come back
    again?
5Why, then, have the people of
    Judah gone the wrong way?
And why do the people of
    Jerusalem not turn back?
They believe their own lies.
    They refuse to turn around and
    come back.
6I have listened to them very
    carefully.
But they do not say what is right.
They do not feel sorry about their
    wicked ways.
    The people don't think about the
    bad things they have done.
Each person goes his own way.
    He is like a horse charging into a
    battle.
7Even the birds in the sky
    know the right times to do things.
The storks, doves, swifts and
    thrushes
    know when it is time to migrate.
But my people don't know
    what the Lord wants them to do!

8"'You keep saying, "We are wise.
    This is because we have the
    teachings of the Lord."

But actually, those who copy the Scriptures
have written lies with their pens.
⁹These wise men refused to listen to the word of the Lord.
So they are not really wise at all.
They will be ashamed.
They will be shocked and trapped.
¹⁰So I will give their wives to other men.
I will give their fields to new owners.
Everyone, from the least important to the greatest,
is greedy for money.
Even the prophets*d* and priests all tell lies.
¹¹They try to heal my people's serious injuries
as if they were small wounds.
They say, "It's all right, it's all right!"
But really, it is not all right.
¹²They should be ashamed of the terrible way they act.
But they are not ashamed at all.
They don't even know how to blush about their sins.
So they will fall, along with everyone else.
They will be thrown to the ground when I punish them,
says the Lord.

¹³"'I will take away their crops, says the Lord.
There will be no grapes on the vine.
There will be no figs on the fig tree.
Even the leaves will dry up and die.
I will take away what I gave them!'"

¹⁴"Why are we just sitting here?
Let's get together!
We have sinned against the Lord.
So he has given us poisoned water to drink.
Come, let's run to the strong, walled cities.
The Lord our God has decided that we must die.
So let's die there.
¹⁵We hoped to have peace.
But nothing good has come.
We hoped for a time when he would heal us.
But only disaster has come!
¹⁶From the land of the tribe*d* of Dan,

the snorting of the enemy's horses is heard.
The ground shakes from the neighing of their large horses.
They have come to destroy the land and everything in it.
They have come to destroy the city and all the people who live there."

¹⁷"Look! I am sending poisonous snakes to attack you.
These snakes cannot be charmed.
They will bite you," says the Lord.

¹⁸God, you are my comfort when I am very sad.
You are my comfort when I'm afraid.
¹⁹Listen to my people!
They are crying for help from a faraway land.
They say, "Is the Lord still in Jerusalem?
Is Jerusalem's king still there?"

But God says, "Why did the people make me angry by worshiping idols?
They worshiped their useless foreign idols."

²⁰And the people say, "Harvest time is over.
Summer has ended.
And we have not been saved."

²¹My people are crushed. So I am crushed.
I cry loudly, and I am afraid for them.
²²Surely there is a balm*d* in the land of Gilead.
Surely there is a doctor there.
So why aren't the hurts of my people healed?

9 I wish my head were like a spring of water.
And I wish my eyes were a fountain of tears!
Then I could cry day and night for my people who have been killed.
²I wish I had a place in the desert—
a house where travelers spend the night.
Then I could leave my people.
I could go away from them.
This is because they are all unfaithful to God.
They are all turning against him.

³"They use their tongues like a bow.
They shoot lies from their
mouths like arrows.
Lies, not truth,
have grown strong in the land.
They go from one evil thing to
another.
They do not know who I am,"
says the Lord.
⁴"Watch your friends.
Don't trust your own brothers.
This is because every brother is a
cheater.
And every friend tells lies about
you.
⁵Everyone lies to his friend.
No one speaks the truth.
The people of Judah have taught
their tongues to lie.
They become tired from sinning.
⁶Jeremiah, you live in the middle of
evil.
And lies follow lies.
The people have refused to know
me," says the Lord.

⁷So this is what the Lord of heaven's
armies says:
"I will test the people of Judah as a
person tests metal in a fire.
I have no other choice.
My people have sinned.
⁸Their tongues are like sharp
arrows.
Their mouths speak lies.
Everyone speaks nicely to his
neighbor.
But he is secretly planning to
attack him.
⁹Shouldn't I punish the people for
doing this?" says the Lord.
"Shouldn't I give them the
punishment they deserve?"

¹⁰I, Jeremiah, will cry loudly for the
mountains.
I will sing a funeral song for the
empty fields.
They are empty, and no one passes
through.
The mooing of cattle cannot be
heard.
The birds have flown away,
and the animals are gone.

¹¹"I, the Lord, will make the city of
Jerusalem a heap of ruins.
It will become a home for wild
dogs.
I will destroy the cities in the land
of Judah
so no one can live there."

¹²What man is wise enough to understand these things? Is there someone
who has been taught by the Lord who
can explain them? Why was the land
ruined? Why has it been made like an
empty desert where no one goes?

¹³The Lord answered, "It is because
Judah quit following my teachings that
I gave them. They have not obeyed me.
They have not done what I told them to
do. ¹⁴Instead, the people of Judah were
stubborn. They followed the false god
Baal.ᵈ Their fathers taught them to do
this!" ¹⁵So this is what the Lord of heav-
en's armies, God of Israel, says: "I will
soon make the people of Judah eat bitter
food. I will make them drink poisoned
water. ¹⁶I will scatter them through other
nations. They will live in strange nations
that they and their ancestors never
knew about. I will chase the people of
Judah with the sword until they are all
killed."

¹⁷This is what the Lord of heaven's armies says:
"Now, think about these things!
Call for the women who cry at
funerals.
Send for those women who are
good at that job.
¹⁸Let them come quickly
and cry loudly for us.
Then our eyes will fill with tears.
And streams of water will come
out of our eyes.
¹⁹The sound of loud crying is heard
from Jerusalem:
'We are truly ruined!
We are truly ashamed!
We must leave our land,
because our houses are in
ruins.'"

²⁰Now, women of Judah, listen to the
word of the Lord.
Open your ears to hear the words
of his mouth.
Teach your daughters how to cry
loudly.
Teach one another a funeral
song!
²¹Death has climbed in through our
windows.
It has entered our strong cities.
Death has taken away our children
who play in the streets.
It has taken the young men who
meet in the city squares.

²²Say, "This is what the Lord says:

'The dead bodies of men will lie
in the open field like dung.
They will lie on the ground like
grain a farmer has cut.
But there will be no one to gather
them.'"

²³This is what the Lord says:
"Wise men must not brag about
their wisdom.
Strong men must not brag about
their strength.
Rich men must not brag about
their money.
²⁴But if someone wants to brag, let
him brag about this:
Let him brag that he understands
and knows me.
Let him brag that I am the Lord.
Let him brag that I am kind and
fair.
Let him brag that I do things that
are right on earth.
This kind of bragging pleases me,"
says the Lord.

²⁵The Lord says, "The time is coming
when I will punish all those who are circumcised[d] only in the flesh. ²⁶That is the
people of Egypt, Judah, Edom, Ammon
and Moab. I will also punish the desert
people who cut their hair short. The men
in all those countries have not given
themselves to serving me. And the men
of Israel do not give themselves to serving me."

10 Family of Israel, listen to what the
Lord says to you. ²This is what he
says:
"Don't live like the people from
other nations.
Don't be afraid of special signs in
the sky,
even though the other nations are
afraid of them.
³The customs of other people are
worth nothing.
Their idols are nothing but wood
from the forest.
They are made by a worker with
his chisel.
⁴They decorate their idols with
silver and gold.
With hammers and nails they
fasten them down.
That keeps them from falling
over.
⁵Their idols are like scarecrows in
melon fields.
They cannot talk.

They cannot walk.
They must be carried.
Do not be afraid of those idols.
They can't hurt you.
And they can't help you either!"

⁶Lord, there is no one like you.
You are great.
Your name is great and powerful.
⁷Everyone should respect you, King
of all nations.
You deserve their respect.
There are many wise men among
the nations.
And there are wise men in all the
kingdoms.
But none of them are as wise as
you.
⁸Those wise men are stupid and
foolish.
Their teachings come from
worthless wooden idols.
⁹They use silver from Tarshish
and gold from Uphaz.
Their idols are made by craftsmen
and goldsmiths.
They put blue and purple clothes
on the idols.
All these things are made by
skilled workers.
¹⁰But the Lord is the only true God.
He is the only living God, King
forever.
The earth shakes when he is angry.
The nations cannot stand up to
his anger.

¹¹"Tell them this message: 'These false
gods did not make heaven and earth.
But they will be destroyed and disappear from heaven and earth.'"

¹²God made the earth by his power.
He used his wisdom to build the
world.
He used his understanding to
stretch out the skies.
¹³When he thunders, the waters in
the skies roar.
He makes clouds rise in the sky
all over the earth.
He sends lightning with the rain.
He brings out the wind from his
storehouses.

¹⁴People are so stupid and know so
little.
Goldsmiths are made ashamed
by their idols.
Those statues are only false gods.
They have no breath in them.
¹⁵They are worth nothing.
People make fun of them.

When they are judged, they will be
destroyed.
16But God, who is Jacob's Portion,d is
not like the idols.
God made everything.
And he made Israel to be his
special people.
The Lord of heaven's armies is
his name.

17Get everything you own and
prepare to leave.
You people of Judah are trapped
in the city by your enemies.
18This is what the Lord says:
"At this time I will throw out the
people of Judah who live in
this land.
I will bring pain and trouble to
them.
And they will really feel it."

19How terrible it will be for me
because of my injury.
I am injured and cannot be
healed.
Yet I told myself,
"This is my sickness; I must
suffer through it."
20My tent is ruined.
All its ropes are broken.
My children have gone away and
left me.
No one is left to put up my tent.
No one is left to set up a shelter
for me.
21The shepherds are stupid.
They don't ask the Lord.
So they do not have success.
Their flocks are scattered and
lost.
22Listen! The news is coming.
The loud noise is coming from
the north.
It will make the towns of Judah an
empty desert.
They will become a home for
wild dogs!

23Lord, I know that a person's life
doesn't really belong to him.
No one can control his own life.
24Lord, correct me, but be fair.
Don't punish me in anger.
If you do, you will destroy me.
25Pour out your anger on other
nations.
They do not know you.
They do not pray to you.

Those nations have destroyed
Jacob's family.
They have eaten him up.
They destroyed his homeland.

11 These are the words that the Lord
spoke to Jeremiah: 2"Listen to the
words of this agreement. Tell the people
of Judah about it. Tell it to those living
in Jerusalem. 3Tell them this is what the
Lord, the God of Israel, says: 'Trouble
will come to anyone who does not obey
this agreement. 4I am talking about the
agreement I made with your ancestors.
I made it with them when I brought
them out of Egypt. Egypt was like a furnace for melting iron!' I told them, 'Obey
me and do everything I command you.
If you do this, you will be my people.
And I will be your God. 5Then I will keep
the promise I made to your ancestors. I
promised to give them a land where
much food grows.' And you are living in
that country today!"
I, Jeremiah, answered, "Amen, Lord."
6The Lord said this to me: "Prophesyd
this message in the towns of Judah and
in the streets of Jerusalem: 'Listen to the
words of this agreement. Then obey
them! 7I warned your ancestors to obey
me when I brought them out of Egypt. I
have warned them again and again to
this very day! 8But your ancestors did
not listen to me. They were stubborn
and did what their own evil hearts
wanted. The agreement says curses will
come upon them if they don't obey it. So
I made all those curses come upon them!
I commanded them to obey the agreement, but they did not.'"
9Then the Lord said to me, "I know
the people of Judah and those living in
Jerusalem have made secret plans.
10They are doing the same sins their an-
cestors did! Their ancestors refused to
listen to my message. They followed and
worshiped other gods. The families of
Israel and Judah have broken the agreement I made with their ancestors. 11So
this is what the Lord says: 'I will soon
bring a disaster on the people of Judah.
They will not be able to escape! And
they will cry to me for help. But I will
not listen to them! 12The people living
in the towns of Judah and the city of
Jerusalem will pray to their idols for
help. They will burn incensed to their
idols. But those idols will not be able
to help when that terrible time comes!
13The people of Judah have as many
idols as there are towns in Judah. They

have built many altars for worshiping that shameful god Baal.[d] There are as many altars as there are streets in Jerusalem!'

14 "As for you, Jeremiah, don't pray for these people. Don't cry out for them or ask anything for them. I will not listen when they call to me in the time of their trouble.

15 "What is my lover, Judah, doing in my Temple?[d]
    She makes many evil plans.
Does she think animal sacrifices
    will stop her punishment?
When you do your evil, then you
    are happy."
16 The Lord called you "a leafy olive tree,
    with beautiful fruit to look at."
But with a strong storm
    the Lord will set that tree on fire.
    And its branches will be burned up.

17 The Lord of heaven's armies planted you. And he has announced that disaster will come to you. This is because the families of Israel and Judah have done evil things. They have made him angry by offering sacrifices to Baal.

18 The Lord showed me that men were making plans against me. The Lord showed me what they were doing. So I knew they were against me. 19 Before this, I was like a gentle lamb waiting to be butchered. I did not know they had made plans against me. They said:
    "Let us destroy the tree and its
        fruit!
    Let's kill him!
    Then people will forget him!"
20 But, Lord of heaven's armies, you
        are a fair judge.
    You know how to test peoples'
        hearts and minds.
I will tell you what I have against
        them.
And I will let you give them the
        punishment they should have!

21 So the Lord speaks about the men from Anathoth who were planning to kill Jeremiah. Those men say, "Don't prophesy[d] in the name of the Lord. If you do, we will kill you!" 22 So this is what the Lord of heaven's armies says: "I will soon punish the men from Anathoth. Their young men will die in war. Their sons and daughters will die from hunger. 23 No one from the city of Anathoth will be left alive. I will cause a disaster to happen to them that year."

12 Lord, if I complain to you,
        you are always right.
But I want to ask you about the
        justice you give.
    Why are evil people successful?
    Why do dishonest people have
        such easy lives?
2 You have put the evil people here.
    They are like plants with strong
        roots.
    They grow and produce fruit.
With their mouths they speak well
        of you.
    But their hearts are really far
        away from you.
3 But you know my heart, Lord.
    You see me and test my mind.
Drag the evil people away like
        sheep to be butchered.
    Set them aside for the day of
        killing.
4 How much longer will the land stay
        dried up?
    How long will the grass in every
        field be dead?
The animals and birds in the land
        have died.
    And it is because the people are
        evil.
Yet, they are saying,
    "God does not see what happens
        to us!"

5 "If you get tired racing against
        men,
    how can you race against horses?
You stumble in a country that is
        safe.
    What will you do in the thick
        thornbushes along the Jordan
        River?
6 These men are your own brothers.
    Members of your own family are
        making plans against you.
    People from your own family are
        crying out against you.
Don't trust them,
    even when they speak to you like
        friends!

7 "I have left Israel.
    I have left my people.
I have given the people I love
    to their enemies.
8 My people have become
    like a lion in the forest to me.
They roar at me.
    So I hate them.

⁹My people have become to me
  like a speckled bird attacked by
  hawks.

Go, gather the wild animals!
  Bring them to get something to
  eat.
¹⁰Many shepherds will ruin my
  vineyards.

They will walk on the plants in
  my field.

They will turn my beautiful field
  into an empty desert.
¹¹They will turn my field into a
  desert.

It will be wilted and dead.

The whole country is an empty
  desert.

This is because no one who lives
  there cares.
¹²Many soldiers will march over
  those barren hills.

The Lord will use the armies to
  punish that land.

People from one end of the land to
  the other will be punished.

No one will be safe.
¹³The people will plant wheat.

But they will harvest only thorns.

They will work hard until they are
  very tired.

But they will get nothing for all
  their work.

You will be ashamed of your poor
  harvest.

The Lord's terrible anger has
  caused this."

¹⁴This is what the Lord said to me:
"Here is what I will do to those wicked
people who take the land I gave my people, the Israelites. I will pull them up and
throw them out of their land. And I will
pull up the people of Judah from among
them. ¹⁵But after I pull them up, I will
feel sorry for them. I will bring each person back to his own property. And I will
bring him back to his own land. ¹⁶I want
them to learn their lessons well. In the
past they taught my people to use Baal's[d] name to make promises. Now I
want them to learn to use my name! I
want them to say, 'As surely as the Lord
lives . . .' If they do, I will allow them to
be successful. And I will let them live
among my people. ¹⁷But a nation might
not listen to my message. If it doesn't, I
will pull it up completely and destroy
it," says the Lord.

13 This is what the Lord said to me:
"Go and buy a linen belt. Then put
it around your waist. Don't let the belt
get wet."

²So I bought a linen belt, just as the
Lord told me. And I put it around my
waist. ³Then the Lord spoke his word to
me a second time: ⁴"Take the belt you
bought and are wearing. Go to Perath.
Hide the belt there in a crack in the
rocks." ⁵So I went to Perath and hid the
belt there, just as the Lord told me.

⁶Many days later the Lord said to me,
"Now go to Perath. Get the belt that I
told you to hide there." ⁷So I went to
Perath and dug up the belt. I took it from
where I had hidden it. But now it was
ruined. It was good for nothing.

⁸Then the Lord spoke his word to me.
⁹This is what the Lord said: "In the same
way I will ruin the pride of the people of
Judah and the great pride of Jerusalem.
¹⁰These evil people refuse to listen to my
warnings. They stubbornly do only
what they want to do. They follow other
gods to serve and worship them. So they
will become like this linen belt. They
will be good for nothing. ¹¹A belt is
wrapped tightly around a man's waist.
In the same way I wrapped the families
of Israel and Judah around me," says
the Lord. "I did that so they would be
my people. Then they would bring fame,
praise and honor to me. But my people
would not listen to me.

¹²"Say to them: 'This is what the Lord,
the God of Israel, says: All leather bags
for holding wine should be filled with
wine.' People will say to you: 'Of course,
we know all wine bags should be filled
with wine.' ¹³Then you will say to them,
'This is what the Lord says: I will make
everyone in this land like a drunken
man. I am talking about the kings who
sit on David's throne. I am also talking
about the priests and the prophets.[d] I am
talking about all the people who live in
Jerusalem. ¹⁴I will make the people of
Judah stumble and fall into one another.
Fathers and sons will fall into one another, says the Lord. I will not feel sorry
or have pity for them. My mercy will not
stop me from destroying them!'"

¹⁵Listen and pay attention.
  Don't be too proud.
  The Lord has spoken to you.
¹⁶Honor the Lord your God.
  Give him glory before he brings
  darkness.

Praise him before you fall
on the dark hills.
You hope for light.
But the Lord will turn it into
thick darkness.
He will change it into deep
gloom.
¹⁷If you don't listen to the Lord,
I will cry secretly.
Your pride will cause me to cry.
I will cry painfully.
My eyes will overflow with tears.
This is because the Lord's people
will be captured.

¹⁸Tell this to the king and queen
mother:
"Come down from your thrones.
Your beautiful crowns
have fallen from your heads."
¹⁹The cities in the desert of southern
Judah are shut up.
No one can open them.
All Judah will be taken as captives
to a foreign land.
They will be carried away
completely.

²⁰Jerusalem, look up and see.
Someone comes from the north.
Where is the flock God gave to you
to care for?
It is the flock you bragged about.
²¹What will you say when they
appoint as your heads
those you had thought were your
friends?
Won't you have much pain and
trouble?
Your pain will be like that of a
woman having a baby.
²²You might ask yourself,
"Why has this happened to me?"
It happened because of your many
sins.
Because of your sins, your skirt
was torn off
and your body has been treated
badly.
²³A black man from Cush cannot
change the color of his skin.
A leopard cannot change his
spots.
In the same way, Jerusalem, you
cannot change and do good.
You always do evil.

²⁴"I will scatter you like chaff^d that is
blown away by the desert wind.
²⁵This is what will happen to you.
This is your part in my plans,"
says the Lord.

"This will happen because you
forgot me.
You have trusted in false gods.
²⁶Jerusalem, I will pull your skirts up
over your face.
Everyone will see you, and you
will be ashamed.
²⁷I have seen the terrible things you
have done.
I know your acts of adultery^d and
your snorting.
I have seen you acting like a
prostitute.^d
I have seen your hated acts
on the hills and in the fields.
How terrible it will be for you,
Jerusalem.
How long will you continue being
unclean?"^d

14
These are the words that the Lord
spoke to Jeremiah about the time
when there was no rain:
²"The nation of Judah cries.
Her cities are dying.
They cry out for the land.
A cry goes up to God from
Jerusalem.
³The important men send their
servants to get water.
The servants go to the wells,
but they find no water.
So they return with empty jars.
They are ashamed and
embarrassed.
They cover their heads in shame.
⁴The ground is dry and cracked
open
because no rain falls on the land.
The farmers are upset and sad.
So they cover their heads in
shame.
⁵Even the mother deer in the field
leaves her fawn.
She does this because there is no
grass.
⁶Wild donkeys stand on the bare
hills.
They sniff the wind like wild
dogs.
But their eyes are dull because
there is no food."

⁷We know that we suffer because of
our sins.
Lord, do something to help us for
the good of your name.
We have left you many times.
We have sinned against you.
⁸God, you are the Hope of Israel.
You have saved Israel in times of
trouble.

But now you are like a stranger in
the land.
You are like a traveler who only
stays one night.
[9] You seem like a man who has been
attacked by surprise.
You seem like a warrior who is
not able to save anyone.
But you are among us, Lord.
And we are called by your name.
So don't leave us without help!

[10] This is what the Lord says about the
people of Judah:
"They really love to wander from
me.
They don't stop themselves from
leaving me.
So now I, the Lord, will not accept
them.
I will now remember the evil they
do.
I will punish them for their sins."

[11] Then the Lord said this to me: "Don't
pray for good things to happen to the
people of Judah. [12] Even if they give up
eating, I will not listen to their prayers.
Even if they offer burnt offerings and
grain offerings to me, I will not accept
them. I will destroy the people of Judah
with war, hunger and terrible diseases."

[13] But I said, "Oh! Lord God, the false
prophets[d] keep telling the people something different! They are saying, 'You
will not suffer from an enemy's sword.
You will never suffer from hunger. The
Lord will give you peace in this land.'"

[14] Then the Lord said to me, "Those
prophets are prophesying lies in my
name. I did not send them. I did not appoint them or speak to them. They have
been prophesying false visions, idola-
tries and worthless magic. And they
have been prophesying their own wishful thinking. [15] So this is what I say about
the prophets who are prophesying in my
name. I did not send them. They said,
'No enemy with swords will ever attack
this country. There will never be hunger
in this land.' Those prophets will die
from hunger. And an enemy's sword will
kill them. [16] And the people the prophets
spoke to will be thrown into the streets
of Jerusalem. They will die from hunger
and from an enemy's sword. No one will
be there to bury them. And no one will
bury their wives, their sons or their
daughters. I will punish them.

[17] "Speak this message to the people
of Judah:

'Let my eyes be filled with tears.
I will cry night and day, without
stopping.
I will cry for my people.
They have received a terrible blow.
They have been hurt very badly.
[18] If I go into the country,
I see people killed by swords.
If I go into the city,
I see much sickness because the
people have no food.
Both the priests and the prophets
have been taken to a foreign
land.'"

[19] Lord, have you completely rejected
the nation of Judah?
Do you hate Jerusalem?
Why have you hurt us so badly
that we cannot be made well
again?
We hoped for peace,
but nothing good has come.
We looked for a time of healing,
but only terror came.
[20] Lord, we admit that we are very
wicked.
We admit that our ancestors did
evil things.
We have sinned against you.
[21] For your sake, do not hate us.
Do not take away the honor from
your glorious throne.
Remember your agreement with us.
Do not break it.
[22] Do foreign idols have the power to
bring rain?
Does the sky itself have the power
to send down showers of rain?
No, it is you, Lord our God.
You are our only hope.
You are the one who made all
these things.

15 The Lord said to me: "I would not
feel sorry for the people of Judah
even if Moses and Samuel prayed for
them. Send the people away from me!
Tell them to go! [2] They might ask you,
'Where will we go?' You tell them this:
'This is what the Lord says:
Some people are meant to die.
And they will die.
Some are meant to die in war.
And they will die in war.
Some are meant to die from
hunger.
And they will die from hunger.
Some are meant to be taken as
slaves to a foreign country.
And they will become slaves in
that foreign country.'

[3]"I will send four kinds of destroyers against them," says the Lord. "I will send war to kill. I will send dogs to drag the bodies away. I will send birds of the air and wild animals. They will eat and destroy the bodies. [4]I will make the people of Judah hated by everyone on earth. I will do this because of what Manasseh did in Jerusalem. (Manasseh son of Hezekiah was king of the nation of Judah.)

[5]"Who will feel sorry for you,
      Jerusalem?
   Who will be sad and cry for you?
   Who will go out of his way to ask
      how you are?
[6]Jerusalem, you have left me," says
      the Lord.
   "You keep going farther and
      farther away.
So I will take hold of you and
      destroy you.
   I am tired of holding back my
      anger.
[7]I will separate the people of Judah
      with my pitchfork.
   I will scatter them at the city
      gates of the land.
My people haven't changed their
      ways.
   So I will destroy them.
   I will take away their children.
[8]Many women will lose their
      husbands.
   There will be more widows than
      the sand of the sea.
I will bring a destroyer at noontime
      against the mothers of the young
      men of Judah.
   I will suddenly bring pain and fear
      on the people of Judah.
[9]The enemy will attack.
   I will still hand over to the killers
      those who are left alive from
      Judah.
A woman might have seven sons,
      but they will all die.
   She will cry until she becomes
      weak and unable to breathe.
She will be upset and confused.
   Her bright day will become dark
      from sadness!" says the Lord.

[10]Mother, I am sorry that you gave
      birth to me.
   I am the one who must accuse
      and criticize the whole land.
I have not loaned or borrowed
      anything.
   But everyone curses me.
[11]The Lord said,
   "I will save you for a good reason.

I will make your enemies beg you
   in times of disaster and trouble.
[12]No one can smash a piece of iron
      or bronze.
   I mean the kind of iron and
      bronze that comes from the
      north.
[13]The people of Judah have wealth
      and treasures.
   But I will freely give those riches
      to others.
This is because the people of Judah
      have sinned
   throughout the country.
[14]I will make you slaves to your
      enemies.
   You will be slaves in a land that
      you have never known.
My anger is like a hot fire.
   And it will burn against you."

[15]Lord, you understand.
   Remember me and take care of
      me.
   Punish for me the people who are
      hurting me.
Don't destroy me while you remain
      patient with them.
   Think about the pain I suffer for
      you, Lord.
[16]Your words came to me, and I
      listened carefully to them.
   Your words made me very happy.
I was happy because I am called by
      your name.
   Your name is the Lord God of
      heaven's armies.
[17]I never sat with the crowd
      as they laughed and had fun.
   I sat by myself because you were
      there.
   You filled me with anger at the
      evil around me.
[18]I don't understand why my pain
      has no end.
   I don't understand why my injury
      is not cured or healed!
Lord, will you be like a brook that
      goes dry?
   Will you be like a spring whose
      water stops flowing?
[19]So this is what the Lord says:
"If you change your heart and
      come back to me, I will take
      you back.
   Then you may serve me.
You must speak things that have
      worth.
   You must not speak useless
      words.
   Then you may speak for me.

Let the people of Judah turn to you.
　But you must not change and be
　　like them.
[20] I will make you as strong as a wall
　　to this people.
　You will be as strong as a wall of
　　bronze.
They will fight against you.
　But they will not defeat you.
This is because I am with you.
　I will rescue you and save you,"
　　says the Lord.
[21] "I will save you from these evil
　　people.
　I will save you from these cruel
　　people."

16 Then the Lord spoke his word to
me: [2] "You must not get married.
You must not have sons or daughters in
this place."

[3] The Lord says this about the sons and
daughters born in this land. And he says
this about the mothers and fathers of
those children: [4] "They will die of terrible diseases. No one will cry for them.
No one will bury them. Their bodies will
lie on the ground like dung. They will
die in war, or they will starve to death.
Their dead bodies will be food for the
birds of the sky. And they will be food
for the wild animals."

[5] So this is what the Lord says: "Jeremiah, do not go into a house where there
is a funeral meal. Do not go there to cry
for the dead or to show your sorrow. Do
not do this because I have taken back
my blessing, my love and my pity from
these people," says the Lord. [6] "Important people and common people will die
in the land of Judah. No one will bury
them or cry for them. No one will cut
himself for them. And no one will shave
his head to show sorrow for them. [7] No
one will bring food to the people who
are crying for the dead. No one will comfort one whose mother or father has
died. No one will offer a drink to comfort them.

[8] "Do not go into a house where the
people are having a feast. Do not go
there and sit down to eat and drink.
[9] This is what the Lord of heaven's armies, the God of Israel, says: I will soon
stop the sounds of joy and gladness in
this place! I will stop the happy sounds
of brides and bridegrooms! This will
happen during your lifetime.

[10] "You will tell the people of Judah
these things. And they will ask you,
'Why has the Lord said these terrible

things to us? What have we done wrong?
What sin have we done against the Lord
our God?'

[11] "Then say to them: 'This is because
your ancestors quit following me,' says
the Lord. 'And they began to follow
other gods. They served and worshiped
other gods. Your ancestors left me. And
they quit obeying my teaching. [12] But you
have done even more evil than your ancestors. You are very stubborn. You do
only what you want to do. You have not
obeyed me. [13] So I will throw you out of
this country. You will go to a land that
you and your ancestors never knew.
There you can serve false gods day and
night. I will not help you or show you
any favors.'

[14] "People say, 'As surely as the Lord
lives, who brought the people of Israel
out of Egypt . . .' But the time is coming,"
says the Lord, "when people will not say
this anymore. [15] They will say instead,
'As surely as the Lord lives, who brought
the Israelites from the northern land
and from all the countries where he had
sent them . . .' And I will bring them
back to the land I gave to their ancestors.

[16] "I will soon send for many fishermen to come to this land," says the Lord.
"The fishermen will catch the people of
Judah. After that, I will send for many
hunters to come to this land. Those
hunters will hunt the people of Judah on
every mountain and hill. And they will
hunt Judah in the cracks of the rocks.
[17] I see everything they do. They cannot
hide the things they do from me. Their
sin is not hidden from my eyes! [18] I will
pay back the people of Judah for the evil
they have done. I will punish them two
times for every one of their sins. I will
do this because they have made my land
unclean.[d] They have done it with their
hated idols. They have filled my country
with them!"

[19] Lord, you are my strength and my
　　protection.
　You are a safe place for me to run
　　to in times of trouble.
　The nations will come to you from
　　all over the world.
　They will say, "Our fathers had
　　only false gods.
　They worshiped useless idols that
　　didn't help them.
[20] Can people make gods for
　　themselves?
　They will not really be gods!"

²¹The Lord says, "So I will teach
those who make idols.
Right now I will teach them
about my power and my strength.
Then they will know
that my name is the Lord.

17

"The sin of the people of Judah is
written with an iron tool.
Their sins were cut into stone
with a hard point.
That stone is their hearts.
Their sins were cut into the
corners of their altars.
²Even their children remember
their altars to idols and their
Asherah[d] idols.
They remember the altars under
the green trees
and on the high hills.
³They remember the altars on my
mountain and in the open
country.
I will give your wealth and
treasures
to other people.
And they will destroy the places of
worship in your country.
You sinned by worshiping at
those places.
⁴You will lose the land I gave you.
And it is your own fault.
I will let your enemies take you as
their slaves.
You will be slaves in a land you
have never known.
This is because you have made my
anger burn like a hot fire.
And it will burn forever."

⁵This is what the Lord says:
"A curse will be placed on those
who trust other people.
It will happen to those who
depend on people for strength.
Those are the ones who have
stopped trusting the Lord.
⁶They are like a bush in a desert.
It grows in a land where no one
lives.
It is in a hot and dry land with
bad soil.
They don't know about the good
things that God can give.

⁷"But the person who trusts in the
Lord will be blessed.
The Lord will show him that he
can be trusted.
⁸He will be strong, like a tree
planted near water.

That tree has large roots that find
the water.
It is not afraid when the days are
hot.
Its leaves are always green.
It does not worry in a year when no
rain comes.
That tree always produces fruit."

⁹"More than anything else, a
person's mind is evil.
It cannot be healed.
No one truly understands it.
¹⁰But I am the Lord, and I can look
into a person's heart.
I can test a person's mind.
So I can decide what each one
deserves.
I can give each one the right
payment for what he does."

¹¹Sometimes a bird will hatch an egg
that it did not lay.
That bird is like the man who
gets rich by cheating.
When that man's life is half
finished, he will lose his riches.
At the end of his life, it will be
clear he was a fool.

¹²From the beginning, our Temple[d]
has been honored
as a glorious throne for God.
¹³Lord, you are the hope of Israel.
Those who leave you will be
shamed.
A person who quits following the
Lord will be like a name
written in the dust.
That is because he has left the
Lord.
The Lord is the spring of living
water.

¹⁴Lord, heal me, and I will truly be
healed.
Save me, and I will truly be
saved.
Lord, you are the one I praise.
¹⁵The people of Judah keep asking
me,
"Where is the word from the
Lord?
Let's see that message come
true!"

¹⁶Lord, I didn't run away from being
the shepherd you wanted.
I didn't want the terrible day to
come.
You know everything I have said.
You see all that is happening.
¹⁷Lord, don't bring terror to me.

I run to you for safety in times of
trouble.
[18] Make those who are hurting me be
ashamed.
But don't bring shame to me.
Let them be terrified,
but keep me from terror.
Bring the day of disaster on my
enemies.
Destroy them, and destroy them
again.

[19] This is what the Lord said to me: "Go
and stand at the People's Gate of Jerusalem. This is where the kings of Judah go
in and out. And then go to all the other
gates of Jerusalem. [20] Say to them there:
'Hear the word of the Lord. Listen, kings
of Judah. Listen, all you people of Judah
and all who come through these gates
into Jerusalem! [21] This is what the Lord
says: Be careful not to carry a load on
the Sabbath[d] day. And don't bring it
through the gates of Jerusalem on the
Sabbath. [22] Don't take a load out of your
houses on the Sabbath. Don't do any
work on that day. Keep the Sabbath as
a holy day. I gave this same command
to your ancestors. [23] But your ancestors
did not listen. They did not pay attention
to me. They were very stubborn. I punished them, but it didn't do any good.
They did not listen to me. [24] But you must
be careful to obey me, says the Lord.
You must not bring a load through the
gates of Jerusalem on the Sabbath. You
must keep the Sabbath as a holy day.
You must not do any work on that day.
[25] 'If you obey this command, this is
what will happen: Kings who sit on David's throne will come through the gates
of Jerusalem with their officers. They
will come riding in chariots and on
horses. The people of Judah and Jerusalem will be with them. And the city of
Jerusalem will have people living in it
forever! [26] People will come to Jerusalem
from the villages around it and from the
towns of Judah. They will come from
the land of Benjamin. They will come
from the western mountain slopes and
from the mountains. And they will
come from southern Judah. They will all
bring burnt offerings, sacrifices, grain
offerings, incense[d] and offerings to
show thanks to God. They will bring
these to the Temple[d] of the Lord. [27] But
you must obey me and keep the Sabbath
day as a holy day. You must not carry
any loads into Jerusalem on the Sabbath. If you do, I will start a fire that

cannot be put out. It will start at the
gates of Jerusalem. And it will burn until
it burns even the strong towers!'"

18 This is the word the Lord spoke to
Jeremiah: [2] "Go down to the potter's house. I will give you my message
there." [3] So I went down to the potter's
house. I saw him working at the potter's
wheel. [4] He was making a pot from clay.
But something went wrong with it. So
the potter used that clay to make another pot. He used his hands to shape
the pot the way that he wanted it to be.
[5] Then the Lord spoke his word to me:
[6] "Family of Israel, can't I do the same
thing with you?" says the Lord. "You
are like the clay in the potter's hands.
[7] There may come a time when I will
speak about a nation or a kingdom. I
might say I will pull that nation up by
its roots. Or I might say I will pull that
nation down and destroy it. [8] But if the
people of that nation are sorry for the
evil they have done, I would change my
mind. I would not carry out my plans to
bring disaster to them. [9] There may come
another time when I will speak about a
nation. I might say that I will build up
and plant that nation. [10] But if I see it
doing evil by not obeying me, I would
change my mind. I would not carry out
my plans to do good for them.
[11] "So, say this to the people of Judah
and those who live in Jerusalem: 'This
is what the Lord says: I am preparing
disaster for you right now. I am making
plans against you. So stop doing the evil
you are doing. Change your ways and
do what is right.' [12] But the people of Judah will answer, 'It won't do any good
to try! We will continue to do what we
want. Each of us will do what his stubborn, evil heart wants!'"

[13] So this is what the Lord says:
"Ask the people in other nations
this question:
'Have you ever heard anything
like this?'
The people of Israel have done a
horrible thing.
[14] The snow on the mountains of
Lebanon
never melts from the rocks.
Its cool, flowing streams
do not dry up.
[15] But my people have forgotten me.
They make offerings to worthless
idols.
This makes them stumble in what
they do.

They stumble about in the old
    ways of their ancestors.
They walk along back roads
    and on poor highways.
[16]So Judah's country will become an
    empty desert.
People will not stop making fun
    of it.
They will shake their heads as they
    pass by.
They will be shocked at how the
    country was destroyed.
[17]I will scatter them before their
    enemies
as a strong east wind blows
    things away.
At that awful time they will not see
    me coming to help them.
They will see me leaving."

[18]Then the people said, "Come, let's
make plans against Jeremiah. Surely
the teaching of the law by the priest will
not be lost. And the advice from the wise
men will still be with us. We will still
have the words of the prophets.[d] So let's
ruin him by telling lies about him! We
won't pay attention to anything he
says."

[19]Lord, listen to me.
    Listen to what my accusers are
      saying!
[20]Good should not be paid back with
    evil.
But they have dug a pit in order
    to kill me.
Lord, remember that I stood before
    you
and asked you to do good things
    for these people.
I asked you to turn your anger
    away from them.
[21]So now, let their children starve.
Let their enemies defeat them
    with swords.
Let their wives lose their children
    and husbands.
Let the men from Judah be put to
    death.
Let the young men be killed in
    battle.
[22]Let them cry out in their houses.
Bring an enemy against them
    suddenly.
Let all this happen because my
    enemies have dug a pit to trap
    me.
And they have hidden traps for
    me to step in.
[23]Lord, you know
    about their plans to kill me.

Don't forgive their crimes.
    Don't erase their sins.
Make them fall from their places.
    Punish them while you are angry.

19 This is what the Lord said to me:
"Go and buy a clay jar from a potter. [2]Go out to the Valley of Ben Hinnom.
Go near the front of the Potsherd Gate.
Take some of the older leaders of the
people and priests with you. There
speak the words I tell you. [3]Say, 'King of
Judah and people of Jerusalem, listen to
this message from the Lord. This is what
the Lord of heaven's armies, the God of
Israel, says: I will soon bring a disaster
on this place! Everyone who hears about
it will be amazed and full of fear. [4]I will
do this because the people of Judah have
quit following me. They have made this
a place for foreign gods. They have
burned sacrifices to other gods. They
did not worship these gods long ago!
Their ancestors didn't worship these
gods. The kings of Judah filled this place
with the blood of the innocent people.
[5]The kings of Judah have built places
to worship Baal.[d] There they burn their
sons in the fire to Baal. I did not speak
about it or tell them to do that. I never
even thought of such a thing. [6]Now people call this place the Valley of Ben Hinnom or Topheth. But watch out! The
days are coming, says the Lord, when
people will call this place the Valley of
Killing.

[7]"'At this place I will ruin the plans of
the people of Judah and Jerusalem. The
enemy will chase them. And I will let the
people of Judah be killed with swords. I
will make their dead bodies food for the
birds and wild animals. [8]I will completely destroy this city. People will
make fun of it and hiss at it. And they
will shake their heads when they pass
by Jerusalem. They will be shocked
when they see how the city was destroyed. [9]An enemy army will surround
the city. They will not let anyone go out
to get food. The people will become so
hungry they will eat the bodies of their
own sons and daughters. And then they
will begin to eat each other.'"

[10]The Lord said, "While the people
with you are watching, break that jar.
[11]Then say this: 'The Lord of heaven's
armies says: I will break this nation and
this city just as someone breaks a clay
jar. It cannot be put back together again.
The dead people will be buried here in
Topheth. We will bury bodies until there

is no more room. [12]This is what I will do to these people and to this place, says the Lord. I will make this city like Topheth. [13]The houses in Jerusalem and the king's palaces will become as unclean[d] as this place, Topheth. This is because the people worshiped false gods on the roofs[n] of their houses. They worshiped the stars and burned incense[d] to honor them. They gave drink offerings to false gods.'"

[14]Then Jeremiah left Topheth where the Lord had told him to prophesy.[d] He went to the Lord's Temple,[d] stood in the courtyard and said to all the people: [15]"This is what the Lord of heaven's armies, the God of Israel, says: 'I said I would bring disaster to Jerusalem and the villages around it. I will make it happen soon! This is because the people are very stubborn. They do not listen at all to what I say.'"

20 Pashhur son of Immer was a priest. He was the highest officer in the Temple[d] of the Lord. He heard Jeremiah prophesying[d] in the Temple courtyard. [2]So he had Jeremiah the prophet beaten. And he had Jeremiah's hands and feet locked between large blocks of wood. This was at the Upper Gate of Benjamin of the Lord's Temple. [3]The next day Pashhur took Jeremiah out from between the blocks of wood. Then Jeremiah said to him, "The Lord's name for you is not Pashhur. Now the Lord's name for you is Terror on Every Side. [4]That is your name because this is what the Lord says: 'I will soon make you a terror to yourself and to all your friends. You will watch enemies killing your friends with swords. And I will give all the people of Judah to the king of Babylon. He will take them away as captives to Babylon. Then his army will kill them with swords. [5]I will give all the wealth of this city to its enemies. I will give them its goods and its valuables. I will give the treasures of the kings of Judah to their enemies. The enemies will carry Judah and all its valuables off to Babylon. [6]And Pashhur, you and everyone in your house will be taken away. You will be forced to go as a captive to Babylon. You will die and be buried there. Your friends you have prophesied lies to will also die and be buried in Babylon!'"

[7]Lord, you tricked me, and I was
 fooled.
 You are stronger than I am. So
  you won.
I have become a joke.
 Everyone makes fun of me all
  day long.
[8]Every time I speak, I shout.
 I am always shouting about
  violence and destruction.
I tell the people about the message
 I received from the Lord.
But this only brings me insults.
 The people make fun of me all
  day long.
[9]Sometimes I say to myself,
 "I will forget about the Lord.
 I will not speak anymore in his
  name."
But then the Lord's message
 becomes like a burning fire
  inside me.
 It feels like it burns deep within
  my bones.
I get tired of trying to hold the
 Lord's message inside of me.
 And finally, I cannot hold it in.
[10]I hear many people whispering
 about me:
 "Terror on every side!
 Let's tell the rulers about him."
My friends are all just waiting for
 me to make some mistake.
 They are saying,
"Maybe we can trick Jeremiah.
 Then we can defeat him.
 Then we can pay him back."

[11]But the Lord is with me like a
 strong warrior.
 So those who are chasing me will
  trip and fall.
 They will not defeat me.
They will be very disappointed and
 ashamed.
 Their shame will never be
  forgotten.

[12]Lord of heaven's armies, you test
 good people.
 You look deeply into the heart
  and mind of a person.
I have told you my arguments
 against these people.
 So let me see you give them the
  punishment they deserve.

[13]Sing to the Lord!
 Praise the Lord!

19:13 roofs In Bible times houses were built with flat roofs. The roof was used for drying things such as flax and fruit. And it was used as an extra room, as a place for worship and as a place to sleep in the summer.

He saves the life of the poor.
 He saves them from the power of
  wicked people.
[14]Let there be a curse on the day I
  was born.
 Let there be no blessing on the
  day when my mother gave
  birth to me.
[15]Let there be a curse on the man
  who brought my father the news:
 "You have a son!"
 This made my father glad.
[16]Let that man be like the towns
  the Lord destroyed without pity.
 Let that man hear loud crying in
  the morning.
 And let him hear battle cries at
  noon.
[17]This is because he did not kill me
  before I was born.
 Then my mother would have
  been my grave.
 I would never have been born.
[18]Why did I have to come out of my
  mother's body?
 All I have known is trouble and
  sorrow.
 And my life will end in shame.

21 This is the word that the Lord
spoke to Jeremiah. It came when
Zedekiah king of Judah sent Pashhur
son of Malkijah to Jeremiah. He also
sent the priest Zephaniah son of Maaseiah. [2]They said, "Ask the Lord for us
what will happen. We want to know because Nebuchadnezzar king of Babylon
is attacking us. Maybe the Lord will do
miracles[d] for us as he did in the past.
Maybe he will make Nebuchadnezzar
stop attacking us and leave."

[3]But Jeremiah answered them, "Tell
King Zedekiah this: [4]Here is what the
Lord, the God of Israel, says: You have
weapons of war in your hands. You are
using them to defend yourselves against
the king of Babylon and the Babylonians. But I will make those weapons
useless. The army from Babylon is all
around the outside of the city wall. Soon
I will bring that army into the center of
the city. [5]I myself will fight against you
with my great power and strength. I am
very angry with you. So I will fight
against you with my own powerful arm.
I will fight very hard against you in my
very great anger. [6]I will kill everything
living in Jerusalem—both people and
animals. They will die from terrible diseases. [7]Then, says the Lord, I'll give Zedekiah king of Judah to Nebuchadnezzar

king of Babylon. I will also give Zedekiah's officers to Nebuchadnezzar.
Some of the people in Jerusalem will not
die from the terrible diseases. Some will
not die in battle or from hunger. I will
give them also to Nebuchadnezzar king
of Babylon. I will let those win who want
to kill the people of Judah. So the people
of Judah and Jerusalem will be killed in
war. Nebuchadnezzar will not show any
mercy or pity or feel sorry for them!'

[8]"Also tell this to the people of Jerusalem: 'This is what the Lord says: I will
let you choose to live or die. [9]Anyone
who stays in Jerusalem will die. He will
die in war or from hunger or from a terrible disease. But anyone who goes out
of Jerusalem and surrenders to the Babylonians who are around the city will
live. Anyone who leaves the city will
save his life. [10]I have decided to make
trouble for this city and not to help it,
says the Lord. I will give it to the king
of Babylon. He will burn it with fire.'

[11]"Tell these things to Judah's royal
family: 'Hear the word of the Lord!
[12]Family of David, the Lord says these
things:

 You must judge people fairly every
  day.
 Protect from criminals
  the person who has been robbed.
 If you don't do that, I will become
  very angry.
 My anger will be like a fire that
  no one can put out.
 This will happen because you
  have done evil things.

[13]"'Jerusalem, I am against you.
 You sit on top of the mountain.
 You sit over this valley, says the
  Lord.
 You say, "No one can attack us.
 No one can come into our strong
  city."
[14]But I will give you the punishment
  you deserve, says the Lord.
 I will start a fire in your forests.
 It will burn up everything around
  you!' "

22 This is what the Lord says: "Go
down to the palace of the king of
Judah. Prophesy[d] this message there:
[2]Hear the word of the Lord, king of Judah. You rule from David's throne. You
and your officers, listen well! All of your
people who come through these gates,
listen! [3]This is what the Lord says: Do
what is fair and right. Protect those who
have been robbed from those who robbed

them. Don't do any wrong to the orphans or widows. Don't hurt them. Don't kill innocent people here. ⁴If you carefully obey these commands, this is what will happen: Kings who sit on David's throne will come through the gates of this palace. They will come with their officers and people. They will all come riding in chariots and on horses. ⁵But if you don't obey these commands, this is what the Lord says: I promise in my own name that this king's palace will become a ruin.'"

⁶This is what the Lord says about the palace where the king of Judah lives:

"This palace is tall like the forests of Gilead.
It is high like the mountains of Lebanon.
But I will truly make it like a desert.
It will be empty like towns where no one lives.
⁷I will send men to destroy the palace.
Each man will have his weapons with him.
They will cut up your strong, beautiful cedar beams.
And they will throw them into the fire.

⁸"People from many nations will pass by this city. They will ask each other, 'Why has the Lord done such a terrible thing to Jerusalem? This was such a great city.' ⁹And the answer will be: 'It was because the people of Judah quit following the agreement with the Lord their God. They worshiped and served other gods.'"

¹⁰Don't cry for the king who has died. Don't cry loudly for him.
But cry painfully for the king who is being taken away from here.
Cry for him because he will never come back again.
He will never see his homeland again.

¹¹This is what the Lord says about Jehoahaz son of Josiah. Jehoahaz became king of Judah after his father died. He has left this place. The Lord says, "He will never come back again. ¹²He will die where those who captured him have taken him. He will not see this land again."

¹³"How terrible it will be for him who builds his palace by doing evil.

He cheats people so he can build its upper rooms.
He is making his own people work for nothing.
He is not paying them for their work.
¹⁴He says, 'I will build a great palace for myself.
I will have large upper rooms.'
So he builds the palace with large windows.
He uses cedar wood for the walls.
And he paints it red.

¹⁵"Does having a lot of cedar in your house
make you a great king?
Your father was satisfied to have food and drink.
He did what was right and fair.
So everything went well for him.
¹⁶He helped those who were poor and needy.
So everything went well for him.
That's what it means to know God," says the Lord.

¹⁷"But your eyes only look for what you can get dishonestly.
You are always thinking about getting more for yourself.
You are even willing to kill innocent people to get it.
You are making it hard for people.
You even steal things from them."

¹⁸So this is what the Lord says to Jehoiakim son of Josiah king of Judah:

"The people of Judah will not cry loudly when Jehoiakim dies.
They will not say, 'Oh, my brother, I am so sad!
Oh, my sister, I am so sad!'
The people of Judah will not cry for him, saying:
'Oh, master, oh, my king.'
¹⁹The people of Jerusalem will bury him like a donkey.
They will just drag his body away.
Then they will throw it outside the gates of Jerusalem.

²⁰"Judah, go up to Lebanon and cry out.
Let your voice be heard in Bashan.
Cry out from Abarim.
All your friends are destroyed!
²¹Judah, when you were successful, I warned you.

But you refused to listen.
You have acted like this since you
    were young.
You have not obeyed me.
[22] My punishment will come like a
    storm.
And it will blow all your
    shepherds away.
Your friends will be taken away
    as captives.
Then you will really be ashamed.
You will be disgraced because of
    all the wicked things you did.
[23] King, you live in your palace.
You are cozy in your rooms of
    cedar.
But you will groan when your
    punishment comes.
You will hurt like a woman
    giving birth to a baby!

[24] "As surely as I live," says the Lord,
"I will do this to you, Jehoiachin son of
Jehoiakim king of Judah: Even if you
were a signet[d] ring on my right hand, I
would still pull you off. [25] Jehoiachin, I
will give you to Nebuchadnezzar king
of Babylon. And I will hand you over to
the Babylonians. Those are the people
you are afraid of because they want to
kill you. [26] I will throw you and your
mother into another country. Neither of
you was born there. But both of you will
die there. [27] You will want to come back.
But you will never be able to return."

[28] Jehoiachin is like a broken pot
    someone threw away.
He is like something no one
    wants.
Why will Jehoiachin and his
    children be thrown out?
Why will they be thrown into a
    foreign land?
[29] Land, land, land of Judah,
    hear the word of the Lord!
[30] This is what the Lord says:
    "Write this down about Jehoiachin:
He is a man who is to have no
    children.
He will not be successful in his
    lifetime.
And none of his children will be
    successful.
None of his children will sit on
    the throne of David.
They will not rule in Judah."

23 "How terrible it will be for the
leaders of Judah. They are destroying my people. They are making

them run in all directions," says the
Lord.
[2] They are responsible for the people.
And the Lord, the God of Israel, says to
them: "You have made my people run
away in all directions. You have forced
them away. And you have not taken care
of them. So I will punish you for the evil
things you have done," says the Lord.
[3] "I sent my people to other countries.
But I will gather my people who are left
alive. And I will bring them back to their
own country. When they are back in
their own land, they will have many
children. And they will grow in number.
[4] I will place new leaders over my people.
They will take care of my people. And
my people will not be afraid or terrified.
None of them will be lost," says the
Lord.
[5] "The days are coming," says the
    Lord,
    "when I will raise up a good
        descendant[d] in David's family.
This descendant will be a king who
    will rule in a wise way.
And he will do what is fair and
    right in the land.
[6] In his time Judah will be saved.
Israel will live in safety.
This will be his name:
    The Lord Does What Is Right.
[7] "So the days are coming," says the
Lord, "when people will not say: 'As
surely as the Lord lives, who brought
Israel out of Egypt . . .' [8] But people will
say something new: 'As surely as the
Lord lives, who brought Israel from the
land of the north and from all the countries where he had sent them away . . .'
Then the people of Israel will live in
their own land."

[9] A message to the prophets:[d]
My heart is broken.
    All my bones shake.
I'm like a man who is drunk.
    I'm like a man who has been
        overcome with wine.
This is because of the Lord
    and his holy words.
[10] The land of Judah is full of people
    who are guilty of adultery.[d]
Because of this, the Lord cursed
    the land.
And it has become very dry.
    The pastures have dried up.
The people are evil.
    They use their power in the
        wrong way.

[11]"Both the prophets and the priests
   are evil.
I have seen them doing evil
   things even in my own
   Temple,"[d] says the Lord.
[12]"So they will be in danger.
They will be forced into
   darkness.
There they will be defeated.
I will bring disaster on them.
   At that time I will punish those
   prophets and priests," says the
   Lord.

[13]"I saw the prophets of Samaria
   do something wrong.
I saw those prophets prophesy by
   the false god Baal.[d]
And they led my people, the
   Israelites, away.
[14]And I have seen the prophets of
   Jerusalem
do some terrible things.
These prophets are guilty of
   adultery
   and live by lies.
They encourage evil people to keep
   on doing evil.
So the people don't stop sinning.
All of those people are like the city
   of Sodom.
   The people of Jerusalem are like
   the city of Gomorrah to me!"

[15]So this is what the Lord of heaven's
armies says about the prophets:
   "I will make those prophets eat
   bitter food.
I will make them drink poisoned
   water.
This is because the prophets of
   Jerusalem spread wickedness
   through the whole country."

[16]This is what the Lord of heaven's armies says:
   "Don't pay attention to the things
   those prophets are saying to
   you.
They are trying to fool you.
Those prophets talk of visions from
   their own minds.
   But they did not get their visions
   from me.
[17]They say to those who hate me:
   'The Lord says: You will have
   peace.'
They say to those who are stubborn
   and do as they please:
   'Nothing bad will happen to you!'
[18]But none of these prophets has
   stood in the meeting of angels.

None of them has seen or heard
   the message of the Lord.
None of them has paid close
   attention to the Lord's
   message.
[19]Look, the punishment from the
   Lord
will come like a storm.
His anger will be like a hurricane.
It will come crashing down on
   the heads of those wicked
   people.
[20]The Lord's anger will not stop
   until he finishes what he plans to
   do.
When that day is over,
   you will understand this clearly.
[21]I did not send those prophets.
   But they ran to tell their message.
I did not speak to them.
   But they prophesied anyway.
[22]But if they had stood in the meeting
   of angels,
they would have told my message
   to my people.
They would have turned the people
   from their evil ways.
They would have turned them
   from doing evil.

[23]"I am a God who is near," says the
   Lord.
   "I am also a God who is far
   away."
[24]"No one can hide
   where I cannot see him," says the
   Lord.
   "I fill all of heaven and earth," says
   the Lord.

[25]"I have heard the prophets who
prophesy lies in my name. They say, 'I
have had a dream! I have had a dream!'
[26]How long will this continue in the
minds of these lying prophets? They
prophesy from their own wishful thinking. [27]They are trying to make the people
of Judah forget me. They are doing this
by telling each other these dreams. They
are trying to make my people forget me
in the same way that their ancestors forgot me. Their ancestors forgot me and
worshiped Baal. [28]Straw is not the same
thing as wheat!" says the Lord. "If a
prophet wants to tell about his dreams,
let him! But let the person who hears my
message speak it truthfully! [29]My message is like a fire," says the Lord. "It is
like a hammer that smashes a rock!
[30]"So I am against the false prophets,"
says the Lord. "These prophets keep

stealing words from each other. They say these words are from me. [31]I am against the false prophets," says the Lord. "They use their own words and pretend it is a message from me. [32]I am against the prophets who prophesy false dreams," says the Lord. "They mislead my people with their lies and false teachings! I did not send those prophets to teach the people. I never commanded them to do anything for me. They can't help the people of Judah at all," says the Lord.

[33]"The people of Judah, a prophet[d] or a priest may ask you: 'Jeremiah, what is the message from the Lord?' You will answer them and say, 'You are a heavy load to the Lord. And I will throw down this heavy load, says the Lord!' [34]A prophet or a priest or one of the people might say, 'This is a message from the Lord!' That person has lied. So I will punish him and his whole family. [35]This is what you will say to each other: 'What did the Lord answer?' or 'What did the Lord say?' [36]But you will never again say, 'The message of the Lord.' This is because the only message you speak is your own words. You used to change the words of our God. He is the living God, the Lord of heaven's armies. [37]This is how you speak to the prophets: 'What answer did the Lord give you?' or 'What did the Lord say?' [38]But don't say, 'What was the message from the Lord?' If you use these words, the Lord will say this to you: You should not have called it a message from the Lord. I told you not to use those words. [39]I will pick you up like a heavy load. And I'll throw you away from me. I gave the city of Jerusalem to your ancestors and to you. But I will throw you and that city away from me. [40]And I will make a disgrace of you forever. You will never forget your shame."

24 I saw a vision after Nebuchadnezzar king of Babylon took Jehoiachin son of Jehoiakim as a prisoner. Jehoiachin king of Judah and his officers were taken away from Jerusalem. They were taken to Babylon. Nebuchadnezzar also took away all the craftsmen and metalworkers of Judah. It was then that the Lord showed me these things: I saw two baskets of figs. They were arranged in front of the Temple[d] of the Lord. [2]One of the baskets had very good figs in it. They were like figs that ripen early in the season. But the other basket had rotten figs. They were too rotten to eat.

[3]The Lord said to me, "What do you see, Jeremiah?"

I answered, "I see figs. The good figs are very good. But the rotten figs are too rotten to eat."

[4]Then the Lord spoke his word to me. [5]This is what the Lord, the God of Israel, said: "I sent the people of Judah out of their country into Babylon. Those people will be like these good figs. I think of them as good. [6]I will look after them. I will bring them back to the land of Judah. I will not tear them down. I will build them up. I will not pull them up. I will plant them so they can grow. [7]I will make them want to know me. They will know that I am the Lord. They will be my people, and I will be their God. This is because they will return to me with their whole hearts.

[8]"But the bad figs are too rotten to eat," says the Lord. "Zedekiah king of Judah and his officers will be like those rotten figs. All the people from Jerusalem who are left alive will be like that. This will be true even if those people now live in Egypt. [9]I will make those people hated as an evil people by all the kingdoms of the earth. People will make fun of the people from Judah and tell jokes about them. People will point fingers at them. They will curse them everywhere I scatter them. [10]I will send war, hunger and disease against them. I will attack them until they have all been killed. Then they will no longer be in the land I gave to them and their ancestors."

25 This is the message that came to Jeremiah concerning all the people of Judah. It came in the fourth year that Jehoiakim son of Josiah was king of Judah. This was the first year Nebuchadnezzar was king of Babylon. [2]This is the message Jeremiah the prophet[d] spoke to all the people of Judah and Jerusalem:

[3]The Lord has spoken his word to me again and again for these past 23 years. I have been a prophet since the thirteenth year of Josiah. Josiah was the son of Amon king of Judah. I have spoken messages from the Lord to you from that time until today. But you have not listened.

[4]The Lord has sent his servants the prophets to you over and over again. But you have not listened to them. You have not paid any attention to them. [5]They have said, "Stop your evil ways. Stop doing what is wrong. Do this so you can stay in the land. This is the land that

the Lord gave to you and your ancestors long ago. He gave it to you to live in forever. [6]Don't follow other gods to serve them or to worship them. You must not worship idols that are the work of someone's hands. That makes the Lord angry, and he will punish you."

[7]"But you did not listen to me," says the Lord. "You worshiped idols that were the work of someone's hands. That made me angry. So I punished you."

[8]So this is what the Lord of heaven's armies says: "You have not listened to my messages. [9]So I will soon send for all the peoples of the north," says the Lord. "I will soon send for my servant Nebuchadnezzar king of Babylon. I will bring them all against Judah and all the nations around you, too. I will completely destroy all those countries. I will leave them in ruins forever. People will be shocked when they see how badly they will be destroyed. [10]I will bring an end to the sounds of joy and happiness. There will be no more happy sounds of brides and bridegrooms. I will take away the sound of people grinding meal. And I will take away the light of the lamp. [11]That whole area will be an empty desert. And these nations will be slaves of the king of Babylon for 70 years.

[12]"But when the 70 years have passed, I will punish the king of Babylon and his nation," says the Lord. "I will punish the Babylonians for their evil. I will make that land a desert forever. [13]I have said many terrible things will happen to Babylonia. All of them will happen. Jeremiah prophesied about those foreign nations. And the warnings are written in this book. [14]The Babylonians will have to serve many nations and many great kings. I will give them the punishment they deserve. They will be punished for all the things they do."

[15]The Lord, the God of Israel, said this to me: "My anger is like the wine in a cup. Take it from my hand. I am sending you to all the nations. Make them drink all of my anger from this cup. [16]They will drink my anger like wine. Then they will not be able to walk straight. They will act like madmen. They will do this because of the war that I am going to send among them."

[17]So I took the cup from the Lord's hand. I went to those nations. And I made them drink from the cup. [18]I poured this wine for the people of Jerusalem and the towns of Judah. I made the kings and officers of Judah drink from the cup. I did it so that they would become a ruin. People would be shocked when they saw how badly they were destroyed. People would insult them and speak evil of them. And it happened. Judah is like that now. [19]I also made these people drink from that cup of my anger: the king of Egypt, his servants, his officers and all his people; [20]all the Arabs, and all the kings of the land of Uz; all the kings of the Philistines (the kings of the cities of Ashkelon, Gaza, Ekron and the people left at Ashdod); [21]the people of Edom, Moab and Ammon; [22]all the kings of Tyre and Sidon; all the kings of the faraway countries; [23]the people of Dedan and Tema and Buz; all who cut their hair short; [24]all the kings of Arabia; and the kings of the people who live in the desert; [25]all the kings of Zimri, Elam and Media; [26]and all the kings of the north, near and far, one after the other. I made all the kingdoms on earth drink from the cup of the Lord's anger. But the king of Babylon will drink from this cup after all the others.

[27]"Then say this to them: 'This is what the Lord of heaven's armies, the God of Israel, says: Drink this cup of my anger. Get drunk from it and vomit. Fall down and don't get up. Don't get up because I am sending a war to kill you!'

[28]"They will refuse to take the cup from your hand. They will refuse to drink it. Then say this to them: 'The Lord of heaven's armies says this: You must drink from this cup. [29]I am already bringing disaster on Jerusalem. And it is the city that is called by my name. And do you think you will not be punished? You will be punished! I am sending war on all the people of the earth, says the Lord of heaven's armies.'

[30]"You will prophesy[d] against them with these words. Say to them:

'The Lord roars from heaven.
   He shouts from his Holy Temple.[d]
   He roars against his land.
He will shout like people who walk
     on grapes to make wine.
   He will shout against all who live
     on the earth.
[31]The noise will spread all over the
     earth.
   This is because the Lord is
     punishing all the nations.
He judges and tells what is wrong
     with all people.
   And he is killing the evil people
     with a sword,'" says the Lord.

[32]This is what the Lord of heaven's armies says:

"Disasters will soon spread
from nation to nation.
They will come like a powerful
storm
to all the faraway places on
earth."

[33]At that time the dead bodies will reach from one end of the earth to the other. No one will cry for them. No one will gather up their bodies and bury them. They will be left lying on the ground like dung.

[34]Cry, you leaders! Cry out loud!
Roll around in the dust, leaders
of the people!
It is now time for you to be killed.
You will fall and be scattered
everywhere, like pieces of a
broken jar.
[35]There will be no place for the
leaders to hide.
These leaders will not escape.
[36]I hear the leaders shouting.
I hear the leaders of the people
crying loudly.
This is because the Lord is
destroying their land.
[37]Those peaceful pastures will be like
an empty desert.
This happened because the Lord
is very angry.
[38]The Lord, like a lion, has left his
den.
Their land has been destroyed.
It is because of his destroying
anger.
It is because of his fierce anger.

26 This message came from the Lord. It was during the first year Jehoiakim son of Josiah was king of Judah. [2]This is what the Lord said: "Jeremiah, stand in the courtyard of the Temple[d] of the Lord. Give this message to all the people of the towns of Judah. They are coming to worship at the Temple of the Lord. Tell them everything I tell you to say. Don't leave out any part of my message. [3]Maybe they will listen and stop their evil ways. I have plans to bring disaster on them because of the evil they have done. But if they change, I will change my mind about bringing disaster on them. [4]Say to them: 'This is what the Lord says: I gave my teachings to you. You must obey me and follow my teachings. [5]You must listen to what my servants the prophets[d] say to you. I have

sent prophets to you again and again. But you did not listen to them. [6]If you don't obey me, I will destroy my Temple in Jerusalem. I will destroy it as I destroyed my Holy Tent[d] at Shiloh. People all over the world will curse Jerusalem.'"

[7]The priests, the prophets and all the people heard Jeremiah. He said all of these words in the Temple of the Lord. [8]Jeremiah finished speaking everything the Lord had commanded him to say. Then the priests, prophets and all the people grabbed Jeremiah. They said, "You must die! [9]How dare you prophesy such a thing in the name of the Lord! How dare you say that this Temple will be destroyed like the one at Shiloh! How dare you say that Jerusalem will become a desert without anyone to live in it!" All the people crowded around Jeremiah in the Temple of the Lord.

[10]Now the officers of Judah heard about what was happening. So they came out of the king's palace and went up to the Temple of the Lord. There they took their places at the entrance of the New Gate. [11]Then the priests and prophets spoke to the officers and all the other people. They said, "Jeremiah should be killed. He said bad things about Jerusalem! You heard him say it."

[12]Then Jeremiah spoke to all the officers of Judah and all the other people. He said, "The Lord sent me to say these things about this Temple and this city. Everything that you have heard is from the Lord. [13]Now change your lives! You must start doing good things. You must obey the Lord your God. If you do that, the Lord will change his mind. He will not bring on you the disaster he has told you about. [14]As for me, I am in your power. Do to me what you think is good and right. [15]But if you kill me, be sure of one thing. You will be guilty of killing an innocent person. You will make this city and everyone who lives in it guilty, too! The Lord sent me to you. The message you heard is from the Lord!"

[16]Then the officers and all the people spoke. They said to the priests and the prophets, "Jeremiah must not be killed. What he told us comes from the Lord our God."

[17]Then some of the older leaders stood up. They spoke to all the people. [18]They said, "Micah the prophet was from the city of Moresheth. He was a prophet during the time Hezekiah was king of Judah. Micah said these things to all the

people of Judah: 'This is what the Lord of heaven's armies says:

Jerusalem will be plowed like a field.

Jerusalem will become a pile of rocks.

The hill where the Temple stands will be covered with bushes.'

¹⁹"Hezekiah was the king of Judah. And he did not kill Micah. No one else in Judah killed him. You know that Hezekiah feared the Lord. He wanted to please the Lord. So the Lord changed his mind. He did not bring on Judah the disaster he had promised. If we hurt Jeremiah, we will bring a terrible disaster on ourselves!"

²⁰(Now there was another man who prophesied in the name of the Lord. His name was Uriah the son of Shemaiah. Uriah was from the city of Kiriath Jearim. He preached the same things against this city and land that Jeremiah did. ²¹King Jehoiakim, all his army officers and all the leaders of Judah heard Uriah preach. King Jehoiakim wanted to kill Uriah. But Uriah heard about it and was afraid. So he escaped to Egypt. ²²But King Jehoiakim sent Elnathan son of Acbor and some other men to Egypt. ²³They brought Uriah back from Egypt. Then they took him to King Jehoiakim. Jehoiakim ordered Uriah to be killed with a sword. His body was thrown into the burial place where poor people are buried.)

²⁴There was an important man named Ahikam son of Shaphan. Ahikam supported Jeremiah. So Ahikam kept Jeremiah from being killed by the people.

27 The Lord spoke his word to Jeremiah. This happened when Zedekiah son of Josiah was king of Judah. ²This is what the Lord said to me: "Make a yoke[d] out of straps and poles. Put it on the back of your neck. ³Then send messages to the kings of Edom, Moab, Ammon, Tyre and Sidon. Send the messages through the messengers of these kings. Those messengers have come to Jerusalem to see Zedekiah king of Judah. ⁴Tell them to give this message to their masters. Tell them, 'The Lord of heaven's armies, the God of Israel, says: "Tell your masters: ⁵I made the earth and everyone on it. I made all the animals on the earth. I did this with my great power and my strong arm. I can give the earth to anyone I want. ⁶Now I have given all these lands to Nebuchadnezzar king of Babylon. He is my ser-

vant. I will make even the wild animals obey him. ⁷All nations will serve Nebuchadnezzar and his son and grandson. Then the time will come for Babylon to be defeated. Many nations and great kings will make Babylon their servant.

⁸"'"But now some nations or kingdoms might refuse to serve Nebuchadnezzar king of Babylon. They might refuse to be under his control. If that happens, I will punish that nation with war, hunger and terrible sickness, says the Lord. I will do it until I destroy that nation. I will use Nebuchadnezzar to destroy the nation that fights against him. ⁹So don't listen to your false prophets.[d] Don't listen to people who use magic to tell what will happen in the future. Don't listen to those who say they can tell what dreams mean. Don't listen to mediums[d] or magicians. They all tell you, 'You will not be slaves to the king of Babylon.' ¹⁰They are telling you lies! They will only cause you to be taken far from your homeland. I will force you to leave your homes. And you will die in another land. ¹¹But some nations will put themselves under the control of the king of Babylon. They will serve him. I will let those nations stay in their own country, says the Lord. The people from those nations will live in their own land and farm it."'"

¹²I gave the same message to Zedekiah king of Judah. I said, "You must put yourself under the control of the king of Babylon and serve him. If you serve him and his people, you will live. ¹³Why should you and your people die like those who do not serve the king of Babylon? Why should you die because of war, hunger and sickness? The Lord said this will happen. ¹⁴But the false prophets are saying this: 'You will never be slaves to the king of Babylon.' Don't listen to them because they are prophesying lies to you! ¹⁵'I did not send them,' says the Lord. 'They are prophesying lies. And they are saying the message is from me. So I will send Judah away. You will die! And those prophets who prophesy to you will die also.'"

¹⁶Then I, Jeremiah, said to the priests and all the people, "This is what the Lord says: Those false prophets are saying that what the Babylonians took from the Temple[d] of the Lord will be brought back soon. Don't listen to them! They are prophesying lies to you. ¹⁷Don't listen to those prophets. But serve the king of Babylon, and you will live. There is

no reason for you to cause Jerusalem to become a ruin. [18]They might be prophets and have the message from the Lord. If so, let them pray to the Lord of heaven's armies. Let them pray about the things that are still in the Temple of the Lord. Let them pray about the things that are still in the king's palace and in Jerusalem. Let them pray that all this will not be taken away to Babylon.

[19]"This is what the Lord of heaven's armies says about those things left in Jerusalem. In the Temple there are the pillars, the large bronze bowl, which is called the Sea, the stands that can be moved and other things. Nebuchadnezzar king of Babylon left them in Jerusalem. [20]Nebuchadnezzar did not take these away when he took Jehoiachin king of Judah captive. Jehoiachin was the son of King Jehoiakim. Nebuchadnezzar also took other important people away from Judah and Jerusalem. [21]This is what the Lord of heaven's armies, the God of Israel, says about the things left in the Temple of the Lord and in the king's palace and in Jerusalem: 'All of this will also be taken to Babylon. [22]And they will stay there until the day I go to get them,' says the Lord. 'Then I will bring them back and return them to this place.'"

28 It was the fifth month of King Zedekiah's fourth year as king of Judah. This was at the beginning of the king's rule. At that time Hananiah the prophet[d] spoke to me. He was the son of Azzur. And he was from the town of Gibeon. He was in the Temple[d] of the Lord when he spoke to me. In front of the priests and all the people, Hananiah said: [2]"The Lord of heaven's armies, the God of Israel, says: 'I will break the yoke[d] the king of Babylon has put on Judah. [3]Before two years are over, I will bring back everything that Nebuchadnezzar king of Babylon took from the Lord's Temple. [4]I will also bring Jehoiachin son of Jehoiakim king of Judah back here. And I will bring back all the other people of Judah as captives to Babylon,' says the Lord. 'So I will break the yoke the king of Babylon put on Judah.'"

[5]Then the prophet Jeremiah answered the prophet Hananiah. They were standing in the Temple[d] of the Lord. The priests and all the people there could hear Jeremiah's answer. [6]He said, "Amen! Let the Lord really do that! May the Lord make the message you proph-

esy come true. May the Lord bring everything from the Lord's Temple back from Babylon. And may he bring back to their homes all the people who were taken as captives.

[7]"But listen to what I must say to you and all the people. [8]There were prophets long before we became prophets, Hananiah. They prophesied that war, hunger and terrible sicknesses would come. They would come to many countries and great kingdoms. [9]But a prophet might prophesy that we will have peace. The message of that prophet might come true. If it does, only then can he be recognized as one truly sent by the Lord!"

[10]Then the prophet Hananiah took the yoke off Jeremiah's neck and broke it. [11]Hananiah said in front of all the people, "This is what the Lord says: 'In the same way I will break the yoke of Nebuchadnezzar king of Babylon. He put that yoke on all the nations of the world. But I will break it before two years are over.'" After Hananiah had said that, Jeremiah left the Temple.

[12]Then the Lord spoke his word to Jeremiah. This was not long after the prophet Hananiah had broken the yoke off of the prophet Jeremiah's neck. [13]The Lord said, "Go and tell Hananiah, 'This is what the Lord says: You have broken a wooden yoke. But I will make a yoke of iron in the place of the wooden one! [14]The Lord of heaven's armies, the God of Israel, says: I will put a yoke of iron on the necks of all these nations. I will do that to make them serve Nebuchadnezzar king of Babylon. And they will be slaves to him. I will even give Nebuchadnezzar control over the wild animals.'"

[15]Then the prophet Jeremiah said to the prophet Hananiah, "Listen, Hananiah! The Lord did not send you. And you have made the people of Judah trust in lies. [16]So this is what the Lord says: 'Soon I will remove you from the earth. You will die this year. This is because you taught the people to turn against the Lord.'"

[17]Hananiah died in the seventh month of that same year.

29 Jeremiah the prophet[d] sent a letter to the people taken as captives to Babylon. He sent it to the older leaders who were among the captives, the priests and the prophets. And he sent it to all the other people Nebuchadnezzar had taken from Jerusalem to Babylon. [2](This letter was sent after all these people were taken away: Jehoiachin and the queen mother; the officers and leaders of Judah and Jerusalem; and the craftsmen and metalworkers.) ³Zedekiah king of Judah had sent Elasah son of Shaphan and Gemariah son of Hilkiah to King Nebuchadnezzar. So Jeremiah gave the letter to them to take to Babylon. This is what the letter said:

⁴This is what the Lord of heaven's armies, the God of Israel, says to all those people he sent away from Jerusalem as captives to Babylon: ⁵"Build houses and settle in the land. Plant gardens and eat the food you grow. ⁶Get married and have sons and daughters. Find wives for your sons. Let your daughters be married so they may also have sons and daughters. Have many children and grow in number in Babylon. Don't become fewer in number. ⁷Also do good things for the city where I sent you as captives. Pray to the Lord for the city where you are living. If there is peace in that city, you will have peace also." ⁸The Lord of heaven's armies, the God of Israel, says: "Don't let your prophets and the people who do magic fool you. Don't listen to their dreams. ⁹They are prophesying lies. And they are saying that their message is from me. But I did not send them," says the Lord.

¹⁰This is what the Lord says: "Babylon will be powerful for 70 years. After that time I will come to you who are living in Babylon. I will keep my promise to bring you back to Jerusalem. ¹¹I say this because I know what I have planned for you," says the Lord. "I have good plans for you. I don't plan to hurt you. I plan to give you hope and a good future. ¹²Then you will call my name. You will come to me and pray to me. And I will listen to you. ¹³You will search for me. And when you search for me with all your heart, you will find me! ¹⁴I will let you find me," says the Lord. "And I will bring you back from your captivity. I forced you to leave this place. But I will gather you from all the nations. I will gather you from the places I have sent you as captives," says the Lord. "And I will bring you back to this place."

¹⁵You might say, "The Lord has given us prophets here in Babylon."

¹⁶But the Lord says this about the king who is sitting on David's throne now. And I'm also talking about all the other people still in Jerusalem. These are your relatives who did not go to Babylon with you. ¹⁷The Lord of heaven's armies says: "I will soon send war, hunger and terrible diseases against those still in Jerusalem. I will make them like bad figs that are too rotten to eat. ¹⁸I will chase them with war, hunger and terrible diseases. I will make them a hated people by all the kingdoms of the earth. People will speak evil of them. They will be shocked when they hear what has happened. And people will use them as a shameful example wherever I make them go. ¹⁹This is because those in Jerusalem have not listened to my message," says the Lord. "I sent my message to them again and again. I used my servants, the prophets, to give my messages to them. But they did not listen," says the Lord.

²⁰You captives, I forced you to leave Jerusalem and go to Babylon. So listen to the message from the Lord. ²¹The Lord of heaven's armies says this about Ahab son of Kolaiah. And he says it about Zedekiah son of Maaseiah: "These two men have been prophesying lies to you. They have said that their message is from me. But I will hand over those two prophets to Nebuchadnezzar king of Babylon. And Nebuchadnezzar will kill them in front of you who are captives in Babylon. ²²Because of this, all the captives from Judah will use this curse: 'May the Lord treat you like Zedekiah and Ahab. The king of Babylon burned them with fire.' ²³They have done evil things among the people of Israel. They are guilty of adulteryᵈ with their neighbors' wives. They have also spoken lies. And they said those lies were a message from me, the Lord. I did not tell them to do that. I know what they have done. I am a witness!" says the Lord.

²⁴Also give a message to Shemaiah. He is from the Nehelamite family. ²⁵The Lord of heaven's armies, the God of Israel, says: "Shemaiah, you sent letters to all the people in Jerusalem. And you sent letters to the priest Zephaniah son of Maaseiah. You also sent letters to all the priests. You sent those letters in your own name. ²⁶You said to Zephaniah, 'The Lord has made you priest in place of Jehoiada. You are to be in charge of

the Temple[d] of the Lord. You should arrest any madman who acts like a prophet. You should lock the hands and feet of that person between wooden blocks. And put iron rings around his neck. [27]Now Jeremiah from Anathoth is acting like a prophet. So why haven't you arrested him? [28]Jeremiah has sent this message to us in Babylon: You will be there for a long time. So build houses and settle down. Plant gardens and eat what you grow.'"

[29]Zephaniah the priest read the letter to Jeremiah the prophet. [30]Then the Lord spoke his word to Jeremiah: [31]"Send this message to all the captives in Babylon: 'This is what the Lord says about Shemaiah the Nehelamite: Shemaiah has prophesied to you, but I did not send him. He has made you believe a lie. [32]Because Shemaiah has done that, this is what the Lord says: I will soon punish Shemaiah the Nehelamite. He will not see the good things I will do for my people, says the Lord. None of his family will be left alive among the people. This is because he has taught the people to turn against me.'"

30 These are the words that the Lord spoke to Jeremiah. [2]The Lord, the God of Israel, said: "Jeremiah, write in a book all the words I have spoken to you. [3]The days will come when I will make everything as good as it was before," says the Lord. "I will bring Israel and Judah back from captivity," says the Lord. "I will return them to the land I gave their ancestors. Then my people will own that land again!"

[4]The Lord spoke this message about the people of Israel and Judah. [5]This is what the Lord said:

"We hear people crying from fear.
    They are afraid. There is no peace.
[6]Ask this question, and consider it:
    A man cannot have a baby.
So why do I see every strong man
    holding his stomach in pain like a woman having a baby?
Why is everyone's face turning white like a dead man's face?
[7]This will be a terrible day!
    There will never be another time like this.
This is a time of great trouble for the people of Jacob.
    But they will be saved from it."

[8]The Lord of heaven's armies says, "At that time

I will break the yoke[d] from their necks.
And I will break the ropes holding them.
Foreign people will never again make my people slaves!
[9]They will serve the Lord their God.
And they will serve David their king.
    I will send that king to them.

[10]"So people of Jacob, my servants, don't be afraid!
    Israel, don't be frightened," says the Lord.
"I will save you from that faraway place where you are captives.
    I will save your family from that land.
The people of Jacob will be safe and have peace again.
    There will be no enemy to frighten them.
[11]I am with you and will save you," says the Lord.
"I scattered you among those nations.
    Even if I completely destroy all those nations,
    I will not destroy you.
You will be punished fairly.
    But I will punish you."

[12]This is what the Lord said:
"You people have a wound that cannot be cured.
    Your injury will not heal.
[13]There is no one to argue your case.
    There is no cure for your sores.
    So you will not be healed.
[14]All those nations who were your friends have forgotten you.
    They don't care about you.
I hurt you as an enemy would.
    I punished you very hard.
I did this because your guilt was so great.
    I did this because your sins were so many.
[15]Why are you crying about your injury?
    There is no cure for your pain.
I, the Lord, did these things to you because of your great guilt.
    I did these things because of your many sins.
[16]But those nations that destroyed you will now be destroyed.
    Your enemies will become captives.

Those who stole from you will have
their own things stolen.
Those who took things from you
in war will have their own
things taken.
[17] I will bring back your health.
And I will heal your injuries,"
says the Lord.
"This is because other people
forced you out from among
them.
Those people said about you, 'No
one cares about Jerusalem!'"

[18] This is what the Lord said:
"I will make the tents of Jacob's
people as they used to be.
And I will have pity on Israel's
houses.
The city will be rebuilt on its hill of
ruins.
And the king's palace will stand
in its proper place.
[19] People in those places will sing
songs of praise.
There will also be the sound of
laughter.
I will give them many children.
They will not be small.
I will bring honor to them.
No one will look down on them.
[20] Their descendants[d] will be like they
were in the old days.
I will make their people strong
before me.
And I will punish the nations who
have hurt them.
[21] One of their own people will lead
them.
Their ruler will come from
among them.
He will come near to me when I
invite him.
Who would dare to come
uninvited?" says the Lord.
[22] "So you will be my people,
and I will be your God."

[23] The Lord was very angry.
He punished the people.
And the punishment came like a
storm.
It came like a hurricane against
the evil people.
[24] The Lord will stay angry
until he finishes punishing the
people.
He will stay angry
until he finishes the punishment
he planned.

When that day comes,
you will understand this.

31 The Lord says, "At that time I will
be God of all Israel's family
groups. And they will be my people."
[2] This is what the Lord says:
"Some of the people were not killed
by the enemy's sword.
Those people will find help in the
desert.
I have come to give rest to
Israel."

[3] And from far away the Lord appeared to his people. He said,
"I love you people
with a love that will last forever.
I became your friend
because of my love and kindness.
[4] People of Israel, I will build you up
again,
and you will be rebuilt.
You will pick up your tambourines[d]
again.
You will dance with those who
are joyful.
[5] You will plant vineyards again
on the hills around Samaria.
The farmers will plant them
and enjoy their fruit.
[6] There will be a time when
watchmen in the mountains of
Ephraim shout this message:
'Come, let's go up to Jerusalem to
worship the Lord our God!'"

[7] This is what the Lord says:
"Be happy and sing for the people
of Jacob.
Shout for Israel, the greatest of
the nations.
Sing your praises and shout this:
'Lord, save your people!
Save those who are left alive
from the nation of Israel!'
[8] Look, I will bring Israel from the
country in the north.
I will gather them from the
faraway places on earth.
Some of the people are blind and
crippled.
Some of the women will be
pregnant and ready to give
birth.
A great many people will come
back.
[9] Those people will be crying as they
come back.
But they will pray as I bring them
back.

I will lead those people by streams
of water.
I will lead them on an even road
where they will not stumble.
This is because I am Israel's father.
And Israel is my firstborn[d] son.

[10] "Nations, listen to the message
from the Lord.
Tell this message in the faraway
lands by the sea:
'The one who scattered the people
of Israel will bring them back
together.
And he will watch over his
people like a shepherd.'
[11] The Lord will bring the people of
Jacob back.
The Lord will buy them back
from people stronger than they
were.
[12] The people of Israel will come to
the high points of Jerusalem.
There they will shout for joy.
Their faces will shine with
happiness about all the good
things from the Lord:
the grain, new wine, oil, young
sheep and cows.
They will be like a garden that has
plenty of water.
And the people of Israel will not
be troubled anymore.
[13] Then young women of Israel will be
happy and dance.
The young men and old men will
also dance.
I will change their sadness into
happiness.
I will give them comfort and joy
instead of sadness.
[14] The priests will have more than
enough sacrifices.
And my people will be filled with
the good things I give them!"
says the Lord.

[15] This is what the Lord says:
"A sound was heard in Ramah.
It was painful crying and much
sadness.
Rachel cries for her children.
And she cannot be comforted,
because her children are dead!"

[16] But this is what the Lord says:
"Stop crying.
Don't let your eyes fill with tears.
You will be rewarded for your
work!" says the Lord.
"The people will come back from
their enemy's land.

[17] So there is hope for you!" says the
Lord.
"Your children will come back to
their own land.

[18] "I have heard Israel moaning:
'Lord, you punished me, and I
have learned my lesson.
I was like a calf that had never
been trained.
Take me back, and I will come
back.
You truly are the Lord my God.
[19] Lord, I wandered away from you.
But I changed my heart and life.
Once I understood,
I beat my breast with sorrow.
I am ashamed and disgraced
because of the foolish things I did
when I was young.'

[20] "You know that Israel is my dear
son.
I love that child.
Yes, I often speak against Israel,
but I still remember him.
I love him very much.
And I want to comfort him," says
the Lord.

[21] "People of Israel, fix the road signs.
Put up the signs that show you
the way home.
Watch the road.
Pay attention to the road on
which you travel.
People of Israel, come home.
Come back to your towns.
[22] You are an unfaithful daughter.
How long will you wander before
you come home?
The Lord will make something new
happen in the land:
A woman will go seeking a man."

[23] The Lord of heaven's armies, the
God of Israel, says: "I will again do good
things for the people of Judah. At that
time the people in the land of Judah and
its towns will again say: 'May the Lord
bless you. You are a righteous dwelling.
You are a holy mountain.' [24] People in all
the towns of Judah will live together in
peace. Farmers and those who move
around with their flocks will live together in peace. [25] I will give rest and
strength to those who are weak and
tired."

[26] After hearing that, I, Jeremiah, woke
up and looked around. My sleep had
been very pleasant.
[27] The Lord says, "The days are com-

ing when I will help the families of Israel and Judah to grow. I will help their children and animals to grow, too. It will be like planting and caring for a plant. [28]In the past I watched over Israel and Judah, but I watched for the time to pull them up. I tore them down. I destroyed them. I brought disaster to them. But now I will watch over them to build them up and make them strong," says the Lord.

[29]"At that time people will no longer say:

'The fathers have eaten sour grapes.
And that caused the children to grind their teeth from the sour taste.'

[30]But each person will die for his own sin. The person who eats sour grapes will grind his own teeth.

[31]"Look, the time is coming," says the Lord,

"when I will make a new agreement.
It will be with the people of Israel and the people of Judah.
[32]It will not be like the agreement I made with their ancestors.
That was when I took them by the hand
to bring them out of Egypt.
I was a husband to them,
but they broke that agreement," says the Lord.

[33]"I will make this agreement with the people of Israel," says the Lord.
"I will put my teachings in their minds.
And I will write them on their hearts.
I will be their God,
and they will be my people.
[34]People will no longer have to teach their neighbors and relatives to know the Lord.
This is because all people will know me,
from the least to the most important," says the Lord.
"I will forgive them for the wicked things they did.
I will not remember their sins anymore."

[35]This is what the Lord says:
"The Lord makes the sun shine in the day.
And he makes the moon and stars shine at night.

He stirs up the sea so that its waves crash on the shore.
The Lord of heaven's armies is his name.
[36]"Only if these laws should ever fail,"
says the Lord,
"will Israel's descendants[d] stop being a nation before me."

[37]This is what the Lord says:
"There's only one way I will reject all the descendants of Israel.
That is if people can measure the sky above.
It is if they can learn the secrets of the earth below.
Then I will reject them because of what they have done," says the Lord.

[38]The Lord says, "The days are coming when Jerusalem will be rebuilt for me. Everything from the Tower of Hananel to the Corner Gate will be rebuilt. [39]The measuring line will stretch from the Corner Gate straight to the hill of Gareb. Then it will turn to the place named Goah. [40]There is the whole valley where dead bodies and ashes are thrown. It will be holy to the Lord. And all the terraces out to the Kidron Valley will be included. They are on the east as far as the corner of the Horse Gate. All that area will be holy to the Lord. The city of Jerusalem will never again be torn down or destroyed."

32

This is the word the Lord spoke to Jeremiah. It was in the tenth year that Zedekiah was king of Judah. The tenth year of Zedekiah was the eighteenth year of Nebuchadnezzar. [2]At that time the army of Babylon was surrounding Jerusalem. Jeremiah was under arrest in the courtyard of the guard. This courtyard was at the palace of the king of Judah.

[3]Zedekiah king of Judah had put Jeremiah in prison there. Zedekiah had asked, "Why have you prophesied[d] the things you have?" (Jeremiah had said, "This is what the Lord says: 'I will soon give the city of Jerusalem to the king of Babylon. Nebuchadnezzar will capture this city. [4]Zedekiah king of Judah will not escape from the army of the Babylonians. But he will surely be given to the king of Babylon. And Zedekiah will speak to the king of Babylon face to face. Zedekiah will see him with his own eyes. [5]The king of Babylon will take Zedekiah to Babylon. Zedekiah will stay

there until I have punished him,' says the Lord. 'If you fight against the Babylonians, you will not succeed.' ")

⁶While Jeremiah was prisoner, he said, "The Lord spoke his word to me. He said: ⁷Jeremiah, your cousin Hanamel will come to you soon. He is the son of your uncle Shallum. Hanamel will say to you, 'Jeremiah, you are my nearest relative. So buy my field near the town of Anathoth. It is your right and your responsibility to buy that field.'

⁸"Then it happened just as the Lord had said. My cousin Hanamel came to me in the courtyard of the guard. He said to me, 'Buy my field near Anathoth in the land of Benjamin. Buy that land for yourself. It is your right to buy it and own it.' So I knew this was a message from the Lord.

⁹"I bought the field at Anathoth from my cousin Hanamel. I weighed out seven ounces of silver for him. ¹⁰I signed the record that showed I now owned the field. And I had a copy of the record sealed up. Some men witnessed it and signed it also. And I weighed out the silver on the scales. ¹¹Then I took the sealed copy of the record of ownership. And I took the copy that was not sealed. ¹²And I gave them to Baruch son of Neriah. Neriah was the son of Mahseiah. The sealed copy of the record of ownership had all the demands and limits of my purchase. I gave this paper of ownership to Baruch. It was while my cousin Hanamel and the other witnesses were there. Those witnesses also signed the record of ownership. There were also many Jews sitting in the courtyard. And they saw me give the record of ownership to Baruch.

¹³"With all the people watching, I said to Baruch, ¹⁴'This is what the Lord of heaven's armies, the God of Israel, says: Take both copies of the record of ownership. Take both the sealed copy and the copy that was not sealed. And put them in a clay jar. Do this so that they will last a long time. ¹⁵This is what the Lord of heaven's armies, the God of Israel, says: In the future my people will once again buy houses. They will also buy fields for grain and vineyards in the land of Israel.'

¹⁶"I gave the record of ownership to Baruch son of Neriah. Then I prayed to the Lord. I said: ¹⁷'Oh, Lord God, you made the skies and the earth. You made them with your very great power. There is nothing too wonderful for you to do.

¹⁸Lord, you show love and kindness to thousands of people. But you also bring punishment to children for their fathers' sins. Great and powerful God, your name is the Lord of heaven's armies. ¹⁹You plan and do great things, Lord. You see everything that people do. You reward people for the way they live and for what they do. ²⁰Lord, you did miraclesᵈ and wonderful things in the land of Egypt. You have kept on doing them even until today. You did miracles in Israel and among the other nations. You have become well known. ²¹Lord, you used signs and miracles and brought your people, the Israelites, out of Egypt. You used your great power and strength to do those things. You brought great terror on everyone. ²²Lord, you gave this land to the people of Israel. This is the land you promised to their ancestors long ago. It's a land where much food grows. ²³The people of Israel came into this land and took it for their own. But those people did not obey you. They did not follow your teachings. They did not do the things you commanded. So you made all these terrible things happen to them.

²⁴"And now, the enemy has surrounded the city. They are building roads to the top of the walls. There will be war, hunger and terrible diseases. These will cause the city to be handed over to the Babylonians. They are attacking the city now. Lord, you said this would happen. And now you see it is happening. ²⁵But now, Lord God, you are telling me, 'Buy the field with silver. Choose some men to watch while I purchase it.' You are telling me this while the Babylonian army is ready to capture the city."

²⁶Then the Lord spoke his word to Jeremiah: ²⁷"I am the Lord. I am the God of every person on the earth. You know that nothing is impossible for me. ²⁸So this is what I say: I will soon give the city of Jerusalem to the Babylonian army. And I will give it to Nebuchadnezzar king of Babylon. That army will capture the city. ²⁹The Babylonian army is already attacking the city of Jerusalem. They will soon enter the city and start a fire to burn down the city. They will also burn down the houses. The people of Jerusalem made me angry. They offered

sacrifices to Baal[d] on the roofs[n] of their houses. And the people poured out drink offerings to other idols. [30]The people of Israel and Judah have done only the things I said were wrong. They have done this since they were young. They have made me angry by worshiping idols made with their own hands," says the Lord. [31]"From the day Jerusalem was built until now, they have made me very angry. Jerusalem has made me so angry I must remove it from my sight. [32]I will destroy it. This is because of the evil the people of Israel and Judah have done. The people, their kings and officers have made me angry. Their priests and prophets have made me angry. All the men of Judah and the people of Jerusalem have made me angry. [33]They turned their backs to me. I tried to teach them again and again. But they wouldn't listen to me. I tried to correct them, but they wouldn't listen. [34]They put their hated idols in the place where I have chosen to be worshiped. In this way they made it unclean.[d] [35]In the Valley of Ben Hinnom those people built places to worship Baal. They built them so they could burn their sons and daughters as sacrifices to Molech.[d] But I never commanded them to do such a hated thing. I never even thought of it! This would make Judah sin.

[36]"You are saying, 'There will be war, hunger and terrible diseases. So the city will be handed over to the king of Babylon.' But the Lord, the God of Israel, says: [37]I have forced the people of Israel and Judah to leave their land. I was very furious and angry with them. But I will gather them from the land where I forced them to go. I will bring them back to this place. I will let them live in peace and safety. [38]The people of Israel and Judah will be my people. And I will be their God. [39]I will make them want to be truly one people. They will have one goal. They will truly want to worship me all their lives. They will do this for their own good and for their children after them. [40]I will make an agreement with them. This agreement will last forever. And I will never turn away from them. I will always be good to them. I will make them want to respect me. Then they will never turn away from me. [41]I will enjoy

doing good to them. And I will surely plant them in this land and make them grow. I will do this with my whole being."

[42]This is what the Lord says: "I have brought this great disaster to the people of Israel and Judah. In the same way I will bring good things to them. I promise to do good things for them. [43]You are saying, 'This land is an empty desert. There are no people or animals here. The Babylonian army defeated this country.' But in the future, people will once again buy fields in this land. [44]They will use their money and buy fields. They will sign and seal their agreements. People will witness their signing records of ownership. They will again buy fields in the land of Benjamin and in the area around Jerusalem. They will buy fields in the towns of Judah and in the mountains. They will buy them in the western mountain slopes and in southern Judah. This is because I will make everything as good as it once was," says the Lord.

33

Now Jeremiah was still locked up in the courtyard of the guards. And the Lord spoke his word to him a second time: [2]"The Lord made the earth. He made it, and he keeps it safe. The Lord is his name. This is what the Lord says: [3]'Judah, pray to me, and I will answer you. I will tell you important secrets. You have never heard these things before.' [4]The Lord is the God of Israel. He says these things about the houses in Jerusalem and the royal palaces of Judah. They have been torn down to be used against the attack by the Babylonian army. [5]The Lord says, 'Some people will come to fight against the Babylonians. They will fill these houses with dead bodies. I killed those people in my hot anger. I have turned away from this city because of all the evil its people have done.

[6]"But then I will bring health and heal the people there. I will let them enjoy peace and safety. [7]I will make good things happen to Judah and Israel again. I will make them strong as in the past. [8]They sinned against me. But I will wash away that sin. They did evil and turned away from me, but I will forgive them. [9]Then Jerusalem will be a wonderful place! People who live there will

---

32:29 **roofs** In Bible times houses were built with flat roofs. The roof was used for drying things such as flax and fruit. And it was used as an extra room, as a place for worship and as a place to sleep in the summer.

be happy. And people from all nations will praise it. This will happen because they will hear about the good things I am doing there. They will be surprised and shocked at the good things and peace I will bring to Jerusalem.'

¹⁰"You are saying, 'Our country is an empty desert. There are no people or animals living there.' It is now quiet in the streets of Jerusalem and in the towns of Judah. There are no people or animals there either. But it will be noisy there soon! ¹¹There will be sounds of joy and gladness. There will be the happy sounds of brides and bridegrooms. There will be the sounds of people bringing their offerings to the Temple^d of the Lord. Their offerings will be to show thanks to the Lord. They will say,

'Praise the Lord of heaven's armies!
    The Lord is good!
    His love continues forever!'

They will say this because I will again do good things for Judah. It will be as in the beginning," says the Lord.

¹²This is what the Lord of heaven's armies says: "This place is empty now. There are no people or animals living here. But there will be shepherds in all the towns of Judah. And there will be pastures where they let their flocks of sheep rest. ¹³Shepherds will again count their sheep as the sheep walk in front of them. People will be counting their sheep all around the country. They will count them in the mountains and in the western mountain slopes. They will count them in southern Judah and the land of Benjamin. They will count them around Jerusalem and the other towns of Judah!"

¹⁴The Lord says, "The time is coming when I will do the things I promised. I made a special promise to the people of Israel and Judah.

¹⁵In those days and at that time,
    I will make a righteous branch
        sprout from David's family.
    He will do what is fair and right
        in the land.
¹⁶At this time Judah will be saved.
    The people of Jerusalem will live
        in safety.
    The branch will be named:
        The Lord Does What Is Right."

¹⁷This is what the Lord says: "Someone from David's family will always sit on the throne. And he will rule the family of Israel. ¹⁸And there will always be priests from the family of Levi. Those priests will always stand before me. And

they will offer burnt offerings and grain offerings. And they will offer sacrifices to me."

¹⁹The Lord spoke his word to Jeremiah. ²⁰"This is what the Lord says: I have an agreement with day and night. I agreed that they will continue forever. Day and night will always come at the right times. If you could change that agreement, ²¹you could also change my agreement with David and Levi. Only then would descendants^d from my servant David not be the kings on their thrones. And only then would the family of Levi not be priests serving me in the Temple.^d ²²But I will give many descendants to my servant David. And I will give them to the family group of Levi who serve me in the Temple. They will be as many as the stars in the sky that no one can count. And they will be as many as the grains of sand on the seashore that no one can count."

²³The Lord spoke his word to Jeremiah: ²⁴"Jeremiah, have you heard what the people are saying? They are saying: 'The Lord turned away from the two families of Israel and Judah. He chose those people. But now he doesn't think of them as a nation anymore!'"

²⁵This is what the Lord says: "If I had not made my agreement with day and night, and if I had not made the laws for the sky and earth, ²⁶only then might I turn away from Jacob's descendants. And only then I might not let the descendants of David my servant rule over the descendants of Abraham, Isaac and Jacob. And I will be kind to those people. I will cause good things to happen to them again."

34

The Lord spoke his word to Jeremiah. It came when Nebuchadnezzar king of Babylon was fighting against Jerusalem and all the towns around it. Nebuchadnezzar had with him all his army. And he had the armies of all the kingdoms and peoples he ruled. ²This is what the Lord, the God of Israel, said: "Jeremiah, go to Zedekiah king of Judah and tell him: 'This is what the Lord says: I will hand the city of Jerusalem over to the king of Babylon very soon. And he will burn it down! ³You will not escape from the king of Babylon. You will surely be caught and given to him. You will see the king of Babylon with your own eyes. He will talk to you face to face. And you will go to Babylon. ⁴But, Zedekiah king of Judah, listen to the promise of the Lord.

This is what the Lord says about you: You will not be killed with a sword. [5]You will die in a peaceful way. People made funeral fires to honor your ancestors, who ruled before you. In the same way, people will make a funeral fire to honor you. They will cry for you. They will sadly say, "Ah, master!" I myself make this promise to you, says the Lord.'"

[6]So Jeremiah the prophet[d] gave the message from the Lord to Zedekiah in Jerusalem. [7]This was while the army of the king of Babylon was fighting against Jerusalem. It was also fighting against the cities of Judah that had not been taken prisoners—Lachish and Azekah. These were the only strong, walled cities left in the land of Judah.

[8]King Zedekiah had made an agreement with all the people in Jerusalem. He agreed to give freedom to all the Hebrew slaves. After Zedekiah made that agreement, the Lord spoke his word to Jeremiah. [9]Everyone was supposed to free his Hebrew slaves. This included all male and female Hebrew slaves. No one was to keep a fellow Jew as a slave. [10]So the officers and all the people accepted this agreement. Everyone would free their male and female slaves. They would no longer keep them as slaves. So all the slaves were set free. [11]But after that, the people who had slaves changed their minds. So they took back the people they had set free. And they made them slaves again.

[12]Then the Lord spoke his word to Jeremiah: [13]"This is what the Lord, the God of Israel, says: I brought your ancestors out of Egypt where they were slaves. When I did that, I made an agreement with them. [14]I said to your ancestors: 'At the end of every seven years, each one of you must set his Hebrew slaves free. You might have a fellow Hebrew who has sold himself to you. You must let him go free after he has served you for six years.' But your ancestors did not listen or pay attention to me. [15]A short time ago you changed your hearts and did what is right. Each of you gave freedom to his fellow Hebrews who were slaves. And you even made an agreement before me. You made it in the place where I have chosen to be worshiped. [16]But now you have changed your minds. You have shown you do not

honor me. Each of you has taken back the male and female slaves you had set free. You have forced them to become slaves again.

[17]"So this is what the Lord says: You have not obeyed me. You have not given freedom to your fellow Hebrews. Because you have not kept the agreement, I will give freedom, says the Lord. I will give freedom to war. And I will give freedom to terrible diseases and to hunger to kill you. I will make you hated by all the kingdoms of the earth. [18]I will hand over the men who broke my agreement. They have not kept the promises they made before me. These men cut a calf into two pieces before me. And they walked between the two pieces.[n] [19]These people made the agreement before me: the leaders of Judah and Jerusalem; the officers of the court; the priests and all the people of the land. [20]So I will hand those people over to their enemies. I will hand them over to everyone who wants to kill them. Their bodies will become food for the birds of the air. And they will become food for the wild animals of the earth. [21]I will hand Zedekiah king of Judah and his officers over to their enemies. I will hand them over to everyone who wants to kill them. I will hand Zedekiah and his people over to the army of the king of Babylon. I will do this even though that army has left Jerusalem. [22]I will give the order, says the Lord, to bring the Babylonian army back to Jerusalem. That army will fight against Jerusalem. They will capture it, set it on fire and burn it down. I will destroy the towns in the land of Judah. And they will become empty ruins. No one will live there!"

35 When Jehoiakim son of Josiah was king of Judah, the Lord spoke his word to Jeremiah. This was his message: [2]"Jeremiah, go to the family of Recab. Invite them to come to one of the side rooms of the Temple[d] of the Lord. Offer them some wine to drink."

[3]So I went to get Jaazaniah son of Jeremiah.[n] Jeremiah was the son of Habazziniah. And I gathered all of Jaazaniah's brothers and sons. I gathered the whole family of the Recabites together. [4]Then I brought them into the Temple of the Lord. We went into the room of the sons of Hanan son of Igdaliah. Hanan was a

---

34:18 they walked . . . pieces This showed that the men were willing to be killed, like this animal, if they did not keep their agreement.   **35:3 Jeremiah** Not the prophet Jeremiah, but a different man with the same name.

man of God. The room was next to the one where the officers stay. It was over the room of Maaseiah son of Shallum. Maaseiah was the doorkeeper in the Temple. ⁵Then I put some bowls full of wine and some cups before the Recabite family. And I said to them, "Drink some wine."

⁶But the Recabite people answered, "We never drink wine. It is because of our ancestor Jonadab son of Recab. He gave us this command: 'You and your descendants[d] must never drink wine. ⁷Also you must never build houses, plant seeds or plant vineyards. You must never do any of those things. You must live only in tents. Then you will live a long time in the land where you are a wanderer.' ⁸So we Recabites have obeyed everything Jonadab our ancestor commanded us. We never drink wine. And our wives, sons and daughters never drink wine. ⁹We never build houses in which to live. And we never own fields or vineyards. And we never plant crops. ¹⁰We have lived in tents. And we have obeyed everything our ancestor Jonadab commanded us. ¹¹But Nebuchadnezzar king of Babylon attacked the country of Judah. We said to each other, 'Come, we must enter Jerusalem. This is so we can escape the Babylonian army and the Aramean army.' So we have stayed in Jerusalem."

¹²Then the Lord spoke his word to Jeremiah: ¹³"This is what the Lord of heaven's armies, the God of Israel, says: Jeremiah, go and tell the men of Judah and the people of Jerusalem: 'You should learn a lesson and obey my message,' says the Lord. ¹⁴'Jonadab son of Recab ordered his sons not to drink wine. And that command has been obeyed. Until today the descendants of Jonadab obeyed their ancestor's command. They do not drink wine. But I am the Lord. I have given you messages again and again. But you did not obey me. ¹⁵I sent my servants the prophets to you again and again. They said to you, "Each of you must stop doing evil. You must change and be good. Do not follow other gods to serve them. If you obey me, you will live in the land I have given to you and your ancestors." But you have not listened or paid attention to my message. ¹⁶The descendants of Jonadab obeyed the commands that their ancestor gave them. But the people of Judah have not obeyed me.'

¹⁷"So the Lord God of heaven's ar-

mies, the God of Israel, says: 'I said many disasters would come to Judah and on everyone living in Jerusalem. I will soon bring every one of those disasters on them. I spoke to those people, but they refused to listen. I called out to them, but they did not answer me.'"

¹⁸Then Jeremiah said to the Recabites, "This is what the Lord of heaven's armies, the God of Israel, says: 'You have obeyed the commands of your ancestor Jonadab. You have followed all of Jonadab's teachings. You have done everything he commanded.' ¹⁹So this is what the Lord of heaven's armies, the God of Israel, says: 'There will always be a descendant of Jonadab son of Recab to serve me.'"

36 The Lord spoke his word to Jeremiah. This was during the fourth year that Jehoiakim son of Josiah was king of Judah. This was his message: ²"Jeremiah, get a scroll. Write on it all the words I have spoken to you about Israel and Judah and all the nations. Write everything I have spoken to you since Josiah was king until now. ³Maybe the family of Judah will hear what disasters I am planning to bring on them. And maybe they will stop doing wicked things. Then I would forgive them for the sins and the evil things they have done."

⁴So Jeremiah called for Baruch son of Neriah. Jeremiah spoke the messages the Lord had given him. And Baruch wrote those messages on the scroll. ⁵Then Jeremiah said to Baruch, "I cannot go to the Temple[d] of the Lord. I must stay here. ⁶So I want you to go to the Temple of the Lord. Go there on a day when the people are giving up eating. Read to all the people of Judah from the scroll. These people come into Jerusalem from the towns where they live. Read the messages from the Lord. Read the words that you wrote on the scroll as I spoke them to you. ⁷Perhaps they will ask the Lord to help them. Perhaps each one will stop doing wicked things. The Lord has announced that he is very angry with them." ⁸So Baruch son of Neriah did everything Jeremiah the prophet[d] told him to do. He read aloud the scroll that had the Lord's messages written on it. He read it in the Lord's Temple.

⁹It was the ninth month of the fifth year that Jehoiakim son of Josiah was king. A special time to give up eating was announced. All the people of Jeru-

salem were supposed to give up eating to honor the Lord. And everyone who had come into Jerusalem from the towns of Judah was supposed to give up eating. [10] At that time Baruch read the scroll that contained Jeremiah's words. Baruch read the scroll in the Temple of the Lord to all the people there. He was in the room of Gemariah son of Shaphan. Gemariah was a royal assistant. That room was in the upper courtyard at the entrance of the New Gate of the Temple.

[11] A man named Micaiah son of Gemariah, the son of Shaphan, heard all the messages from the Lord. Baruch read them from the scroll. [12] Micaiah went down to the royal assistant's room in the king's palace. All of the officers were sitting there: Elishama the royal assistant; Delaiah son of Shemaiah; Elnathan son of Acbor; Gemariah son of Shaphan; Zedekiah son of Hananiah; and all the other officers. [13] Micaiah told those officers everything he had heard Baruch read from the scroll.

[14] Then the officers sent a man named Jehudi son of Nethaniah to Baruch. (Nethaniah was the son of Shelemiah, who was the son of Cushi.) Jehudi said to Baruch, "Bring the scroll that you read to the people and come with me."

So Baruch son of Neriah took the scroll and went with Jehudi to the officers. [15] Then the officers said to Baruch, "Sit down and read the scroll to us."

So Baruch read the scroll to them. [16] When the officers heard all the words, they became afraid. And they looked at one another. They said to Baruch, "We must certainly tell the king about these words." [17] Then the officers asked Baruch, "Tell us, Baruch, where did you get these words you wrote on the scroll? Did you write down what Jeremiah said to you?"

[18] "Yes," Baruch answered. "Jeremiah spoke, and I wrote down all the words with ink on this scroll."

[19] Then the officers said to Baruch, "You and Jeremiah must go and hide. Don't tell anyone where you are hiding." [20] Then the officers put the scroll in the room of Elishama the royal assistant. Then they went to the king in the courtyard and told him all about the scroll. [21] So King Jehoiakim sent Jehudi to get the scroll. Jehudi brought the scroll from the room of Elishama the royal assistant. Then Jehudi read the scroll to the king. And he read it to all the officers who stood around the king. [22] This hap-

pened in the ninth month of the year. So King Jehoiakim was sitting in the winter apartment. There was a fire burning in a small firepot in front of him. [23] Jehudi began to read from the scroll. But after he had read three or four columns, the king cut those columns off of the scroll with a pen knife. And he threw them into the firepot. Finally, the whole scroll was burned in the fire. [24] King Jehoiakim and his servants heard the message from the scroll. But they were not frightened! They did not tear their clothes to show their sorrow. [25] Elnathan, Delaiah and Gemariah tried to talk King Jehoiakim into not burning the scroll. But the king would not listen to them. [26] Instead, the king ordered some men to arrest Baruch the secretary and Jeremiah the prophet. Those men were Jerahmeel son of the king, Seraiah son of Azriel and Shelemiah son of Abdeel. But the Lord had hidden Baruch and Jeremiah.

[27] The Lord spoke his word to Jeremiah. This happened after King Jehoiakim had burned the scroll. This was the scroll where Baruch had written all the words Jeremiah had spoken to him. The Lord said: [28] "Jeremiah, get another scroll. Write all the words on it that were on the first scroll. That was the scroll that Jehoiakim king of Judah burned up. [29] Also say this to Jehoiakim king of Judah: 'This is what the Lord says: You burned up that scroll. You said, "Why did Jeremiah write that the king of Babylon will come and destroy this land? Why did he say the king of Babylon will destroy both men and animals in it?" [30] So the Lord says this about Jehoiakim king of Judah: Jehoiakim's descendants[d] will not sit on David's throne. When Jehoiakim dies, his body will be thrown out on the ground. It will be left out in the heat of the day. And it will also be left in the cold frost of the night. [31] I, the Lord, will punish Jehoiakim and his children. And I will punish his servants. I will do this because they have done evil things. I have promised to bring disasters upon them. And I will bring them upon all the people in Jerusalem and Judah, just as I promised. This is because they have not listened to me.'"

[32] So Jeremiah took another scroll and gave it to Baruch. Baruch son of Neriah was his secretary. As Jeremiah spoke, Baruch wrote on the scroll. He wrote the same words that were on the scroll Jehoiakim king of Judah had burned in

the fire. And many other words like those words were added to the second scroll.

37 Nebuchadnezzar was king of Babylon. He appointed Zedekiah son of Josiah as king of Judah. Zedekiah took the place of Jehoiachin son of Jehoiakim. [2]But Zedekiah, his servants and the people of Judah did not listen to the words of the Lord. The Lord had spoken his words through Jeremiah the prophet.[d]

[3]Now King Zedekiah sent Jehucal and Zephaniah with a message to Jeremiah the prophet. Jehucal was the son of Shelemiah. And Zephaniah the priest was the son of Maaseiah. This was the message: "Jeremiah, pray to the Lord our God for us."

[4]At that time Jeremiah had not yet been put into prison. So he was free to go anywhere he wanted. [5]The army of the king of Egypt had marched from Egypt toward Judah. Now the Babylonian army had surrounded the city of Jerusalem so they could attack it. Then they had heard about the Egyptian army marching toward them. So the Babylonian army left Jerusalem to fight the Egyptian army.

[6]The Lord spoke his word to Jeremiah the prophet: [7]"This is what the Lord, the God of Israel, says: Jehucal and Zephaniah, I know Zedekiah king of Judah sent you to ask me questions. Tell this to King Zedekiah: 'The army of the king of Egypt marched out of Egypt. They came here to help you against the Babylonian army. But that army will go back to Egypt. [8]After that, the Babylonian army will come back here. And they will attack Jerusalem. Then the Babylonian army will take and burn Jerusalem.'

[9]"This is what the Lord says: People of Jerusalem, do not fool yourselves. Do not say to yourselves: 'The Babylonian army will surely leave us alone.' They will not! [10]You might defeat all of the Babylonian army that is attacking you. But there would still be a few injured men left in their tents. Even those injured men would come from their tents and burn down Jerusalem!"

[11]So the Babylonian army left Jerusalem. They left to fight the army of the king of Egypt. [12]Now Jeremiah wanted to travel from Jerusalem to his home in the land of Benjamin. He was going there to get his share of the property that belonged to his family. [13]Jeremiah got to the Benjamin Gate of Jerusalem.

But then the captain in charge of the guards arrested him. The captain's name was Irijah son of Shelemiah son of Hananiah. So Irijah the captain arrested Jeremiah. Irijah said, "You are leaving us to join the Babylonian side!"

[14]Jeremiah said to Irijah, "That's not true! I am not leaving to join the Babylonians." But Irijah refused to listen to Jeremiah. So he arrested Jeremiah and took him to the officers of Jerusalem. [15]Those rulers were very angry with Jeremiah. They gave an order for him to be beaten. Then they put him in prison in the house of Jonathan the royal assistant. Jonathan's house had been made into a prison. [16]So those people put Jeremiah into a cell in a dungeon. And Jeremiah was there for a long time.

[17]Then King Zedekiah sent for Jeremiah and had him brought to the palace. Zedekiah talked to Jeremiah in private. He asked Jeremiah, "Is there any message from the Lord?"

Jeremiah answered, "Yes, there is a message from the Lord. Zedekiah, you will be handed over to the king of Babylon." [18]Then Jeremiah said to King Zedekiah, "What crime have I done against you? What crime have I done to your officers or the people of Jerusalem? Why have you thrown me into prison? [19]Where are your prophets now? Those prophets prophesied this message to you: 'The king of Babylon will not attack you or this land of Judah.' [20]But now, my master, king of Judah, please listen to me. And please do what I ask of you. Do not send me back to the house of Jonathan the royal assistant. If you do, I will die there!"

[21]So King Zedekiah gave orders for Jeremiah to be put under guard in the courtyard. And he ordered that Jeremiah be given bread from the street of the bakers. Jeremiah was to be given bread until there was no more bread in the city. So he stayed under guard in the courtyard.

38 Some of the officers heard what Jeremiah was prophesying.[d] They were Shephatiah son of Mattan, Gedaliah son of Pashhur, Jehucal son of Shelemiah and Pashhur son of Malkijah. Jeremiah was telling all the people this message: [2]"This is what the Lord says: 'Everyone who stays in Jerusalem will die in war. Or he will die of hunger or terrible diseases. But everyone who surrenders to the Babylonian army will live. They will escape with their lives and live.' ³And this is what the Lord says: 'This city of Jerusalem will surely be handed over to the army of the king of Babylon. He will capture this city!'"

⁴Then the officers said to the king, "Jeremiah must be put to death! He is making the soldiers who are still in the city become discouraged. He is discouraging everyone by the things he is saying. He does not want good to happen to us. He wants to ruin the people of Jerusalem."

⁵King Zedekiah said to them, "Jeremiah is in your control. I cannot do anything to stop you!"

⁶So the officers took Jeremiah and put him into the well of Malkijah, the king's son. That well was in the courtyard of the guards. The officers used ropes to lower Jeremiah into the well. It did not have any water in it, only mud. And Jeremiah sank down into the mud.

⁷But Ebed-Melech heard that the officers had put Jeremiah into the well. Ebed-Melech was a Cushite, and he was a eunuch*ᵈ* in the palace. King Zedekiah was sitting at the Benjamin Gate. ⁸So Ebed-Melech left the palace and went to the king. Ebed-Melech said, ⁹"My master and king, the rulers have acted in an evil way. They have treated Jeremiah the prophet badly! They have thrown him into a well! They have left him there to die! When there is no more bread in the city, he will starve."

¹⁰Then King Zedekiah commanded Ebed-Melech the Cushite: "Ebed-Melech, take 30 men from the palace with you. Go and lift Jeremiah the prophet out of the well before he dies."

¹¹So Ebed-Melech took the men with him. And he went to a room under the storeroom in the palace. He took some old rags and worn-out clothes from that room. Then he let those rags down with some ropes to Jeremiah in the well. ¹²Ebed-Melech the Cushite said to Jeremiah, "Put these old rags and worn-out clothes under your arms. They will be pads for the ropes." So Jeremiah did as Ebed-Melech said. ¹³The men pulled Jeremiah up with the ropes and lifted him out of the well. And Jeremiah stayed under guard in the courtyard.

¹⁴Then King Zedekiah sent someone to get Jeremiah the prophet.*ᵈ* He had Jeremiah brought to the third entrance to the Temple*ᵈ* of the Lord. Then the king said to Jeremiah, "I am going to ask you something. Do not hide anything from me. But tell me everything honestly."

¹⁵Jeremiah said to Zedekiah, "If I give you an answer, you will probably kill me. And even if I give you advice, you will not listen to me."

¹⁶But King Zedekiah made a secret promise to Jeremiah. He said, "As surely as the Lord lives who has given us breath and life, I will not kill you. And I promise not to give you to the officers who want to kill you."

¹⁷Then Jeremiah said to Zedekiah, "This is what the Lord God of heaven's armies, the God of Israel, says: 'You must surrender to the officers of the king of Babylon. Then your life will be saved. And Jerusalem will not be burned down. And you and your family will live. ¹⁸You must not refuse to surrender to the officers of the king of Babylon. If you do, Jerusalem will be given to the Babylonian army. They will burn Jerusalem down. And you will not escape from them.'"

¹⁹Then King Zedekiah said to Jeremiah, "I'm afraid of some of the Jews. They have already gone over to the side of the Babylonian army. I'm afraid the Babylonians may hand me over to them. And they will treat me badly."

²⁰But Jeremiah answered, "The Babylonians will not hand you over to the Jews. Obey the Lord by doing what I tell you. Then things will go well for you. And your life will be saved. ²¹But if you refuse to surrender to the Babylonians, the Lord has shown me what will happen. ²²All the women left in the palace of the king of Judah will be brought out. They will be taken to the important officers of the king of Babylon. Your women will make fun of you with this song:

'Your good friends led you the
        wrong way and were stronger
        than you.
    Those were friends that you
        trusted.
Your feet are stuck in the mud.
    Your friends have left you.'

²³"All your wives and children will be brought out. They will be given to the Babylonian army. You yourself will not even escape from them. You will be taken prisoner by the king of Babylon. And Jerusalem will be burned down."

²⁴Then Zedekiah said to Jeremiah, "Do not tell anyone that I have been talking to you. If you do, you will die. ²⁵Those officers might find out that I talked to you. Then they will come to you and say, 'Tell us what you said to King Zedekiah. And tell us what King

How Can I Let God's Love Shine Through Me?

What do we do with dirty clothes at the end of the day? Hopefully, we take them off and throw them in the laundry hamper. It's time to put on something fresh and new!

The Bible says that when we become Christians, it's time to take off all the old, bad habits of sin that we used to wear. Whenever sins such as complaining, disobedience, or disrespect pop up, we should admit our sins to God and ask Him for the strength to throw them out of our lives. Then we can put on the new clothes God gives us. They are sparkling clean robes made by God's Spirit.

Make no mistake. When we put our old desires aside and obey God instead, the world will notice. They will see the power of God working in us and will give Him the glory.

You were taught to leave your old self—to stop living the evil way you lived before. That old self becomes worse and worse because people are fooled by the evil things they want to do. But you were taught to be made new in your hearts. You were taught to become a new person. That new person is made to be like God—made to be truly good and holy.

~ Ephesians 4:22–24

How Do I Forgive?

Wouldn't it be nice if everyone was kind and got along? One day when we reach heaven, we will get to experience friendships that stay true and strong forever. But while we are here on earth, we have to deal with sin—in ourselves and in other people.

It's not easy when people don't treat us well. They may say something mean, leave us out, or serve themselves without even thinking about us. When that happens, we are tempted to fight back. We want to get even and maybe hurt them the same way they hurt us. But Jesus showed His children God's way. Even when the angry people were yelling at Jesus and insulting Him on the cross, Jesus asked His Father to forgive them.

And that's the true picture of forgiveness. When you choose to forgive others, you no longer hold their sin against them. You don't bring it up in future conversations or think of ways to get even anymore. Instead, you allow God to love them through your kind and loving response.

But if we confess our sins, he will forgive our sins.
We can trust God. He does what is right. He will make
us clean from all the wrongs we have done.

~ 1 John 1:9

Bible Verses to Know

In the beginning God created the sky and the earth.
~ Genesis 1:1

Remember that I commanded you to be strong and brave. So don't
be afraid. The Lord your God will be with you everywhere you go.
~ Joshua 1:9

The Lord is my shepherd. I have everything I need.
He gives me rest in green pastures. He leads me to calm water.
He gives me new strength.
For the good of his name, he leads me on paths that are right.
Even if I walk through a very dark valley, I will not be afraid
because you are with me.
Your rod and your walking stick comfort me.
You prepare a meal for me in front of my enemies.
You pour oil on my head. You give me more than I can hold.
Surely your goodness and love will be with me all my life.
And I will live in the house of the Lord forever.
~ Psalm 23

You made my whole being. You formed me in my mother's body.
I praise you because you made me in an amazing and wonderful way.
What you have done is wonderful. I know this very well.
~ Psalm 139:13–14

"I say this because I know what I have planned for you," says the
Lord. "I have good plans for you. I don't plan to hurt you. I plan
to give you hope and a good future."
~ Jeremiah 29:11

Bible Verses to Know

"For God loved the world so much that he gave his only Son. God gave his Son so that whoever believes in him may not be lost, but have eternal life." ~ John 3:16

So brothers, since God has shown us great mercy, I beg you to offer your lives as a living sacrifice to him. Your offering must be only for God and pleasing to him. This is the spiritual way for you to worship. ~ Romans 12:1

Love is patient and kind. Love is not jealous, it does not brag, and it is not proud. Love is not rude, is not selfish, and does not become angry easily. Love does not remember wrongs done against it. Love is not happy with evil, but is happy with the truth. Love patiently accepts all things. It always trusts, always hopes, and always continues strong. Love never ends. ~ 1 Corinthians 13:4–8

Children, obey your parents the way the Lord wants. This is the right thing to do. The command says, "Honor your father and mother." This is the first command that has a promise with it. ~ Ephesians 6:1–2

You are young, but do not let anyone treat you as if you were not important. Be an example to show the believers how they should live. Show them with your words, with the way you live, with your love, with your faith, and with your pure life. ~ 1 Timothy 4:12

Jesus answered, "Love the Lord your God with all your heart, soul and mind." ~ Matthew 22:37

Zedekiah said to you. Don't keep any secrets from us. If you don't tell us everything, we will kill you.' [26] If they ask you, tell them this: 'I was begging the king not to send me back to Jonathan's house to die.'"

[27] The officers did come to question Jeremiah. So he told them everything the king had ordered him to say. Then the officers said no more to Jeremiah. This was because no one had heard what Jeremiah and the king had discussed.

[28] So Jeremiah stayed under guard in the courtyard until the day Jerusalem was captured.

39 This is how Jerusalem was captured:

[1] Nebuchadnezzar king of Babylon marched against Jerusalem with his whole army. He surrounded the city to attack it. This was during the tenth month of the ninth year Zedekiah was king of Judah. [2] This lasted until the ninth day of the fourth month in Zedekiah's eleventh year. Then the city wall was broken through. [3] And all the officers of the king of Babylon came into Jerusalem. They sat down at the Middle Gate. They were Nergal-Sharezer of the district of Samgar; Nebo-Sarsekim, a chief officer; Nergal-Sharezer, an important leader; and all the other important officers.

[4] When Zedekiah king of Judah and all his soldiers saw them, they ran away. They left Jerusalem at night and went out from the king's garden. They went through the gate that was between the two walls. Then they headed toward the Jordan Valley. [5] But the Babylonian army chased them. They caught up with Zedekiah in the plains of Jericho. They captured him and took him to Nebuchadnezzar king of Babylon. Nebuchadnezzar was at Riblah in the land of Hamath. There Nebuchadnezzar passed his sentence on Zedekiah. [6] There at Riblah the king of Babylon killed Zedekiah's sons as he watched. And Nebuchadnezzar killed all the important officers of Judah as Zedekiah watched. [7] Then he put out Zedekiah's eyes. He put bronze chains on Zedekiah and took him to Babylon.

[8] The Babylonians set fire to the palace. And they set fire to the houses of the people of Jerusalem. And they broke down the walls around Jerusalem. [9] Nebuzaradan was commander of the king's special guards. He took the people left

in Jerusalem as captives. He also took those captives who had surrendered to him earlier. And he took the rest of the people of Jerusalem. He carried them all away to Babylon. [10] But Nebuzaradan, commander of the guard, left some of the poor people of Judah behind. They were the people who owned nothing. So on that day he gave them vineyards and fields.

[11] Nebuchadnezzar had given these orders about Jeremiah through Nebuzaradan, commander of the guard: [12] "Find Jeremiah and take care of him. Do not hurt him. Give him whatever he asks for." [13] So these men sent for Jeremiah: Nebuzaradan, commander of the guards; Nebushazban, a chief officer; Nergal-Sharezer, an important leader; and all the other officers of the king of Babylon. [14] They had Jeremiah taken out of the courtyard of the guard. They turned him over to Gedaliah son of Ahikam son of Shaphan. Gedaliah had orders to take Jeremiah back home. So they took him home, and he stayed among his own people.

[15] While Jeremiah was guarded in the courtyard, the Lord spoke his word to him: [16] "Jeremiah, go and tell Ebed-Melech the Cushite this message: 'This is what the Lord of heaven's armies, the God of Israel, says: Very soon I will make my words about Jerusalem come true. They will come true through disaster, not through good times. You will see everything come true with your own eyes. [17] But I will save you on that day, Ebed-Melech, says the Lord. You will not be handed over to the people you fear. [18] I will surely save you, Ebed-Melech. You will not die from a sword. But you will escape and live. This will happen because you have trusted in me, says the Lord.'"

40 The Lord spoke his word to Jeremiah. This was after Nebuzaradan, commander of the guards, had set Jeremiah free at the city of Ramah. He had found Jeremiah in Ramah bound in chains. He was with all the captives from Jerusalem and Judah. They were being taken away to Babylon. [2] When commander Nebuzaradan found Jeremiah, Nebuzaradan said to him, "The Lord your God announced this disaster would come to this place. [3] And now the Lord has done everything he said he would do. This disaster happened because the people of Judah sinned against the Lord. You people did not obey the Lord. [4]But now I will set you free. I am taking the chains off your wrists. If you want to, come with me to Babylon. And I will take good care of you. But if you don't want to come, then don't. Look, the whole country is open to you." [5]Before Jeremiah turned to leave, Nebuzaradan said, "Or go back to Gedaliah son of Ahikam, the son of Shaphan. The king of Babylon has chosen Gedaliah to be governor over the towns of Judah. Go and live with Gedaliah among the people. Or go anywhere you want."

Then Nebuzaradan gave Jeremiah some food and a present and let him go. [6]So Jeremiah went to Gedaliah son of Ahikam at Mizpah. And Jeremiah stayed with him there. He lived among the people who were left behind in Judah.

[7]There were some officers and their men from the army of Judah. These men were still out in the open country. They heard that the king of Babylon had put Gedaliah son of Ahikam in charge. He was put in charge of the people who were left in the land: the men, women and children who were very poor. They were the ones who were not carried off to Babylon as captives. [8]So these soldiers came to Gedaliah at Mizpah. They were Ishmael son of Nethaniah, and Johanan and Jonathan sons of Kareah. Also Seraiah son of Tanhumeth and the sons of Ephai the Netophathite came. And Jaazaniah son of the Maacathite and their men came.

[9]Gedaliah son of Ahikam, the son of Shaphan, made a promise to them. Gedaliah said, "Do not be afraid to serve the Babylonians. Live in the land and serve the king of Babylon. Then everything will go well for you. [10]I myself will live in Mizpah. I will speak for you before the Babylonians who come here. You harvest the wine, the summer fruit and the oil. Put what you harvest in your storage jars. Live in the towns you control."

[11]Some Jews were in Moab, Ammon, Edom and other countries. They heard that the king of Babylon had left a few Jews alive in the land. And they heard the king of Babylon had chosen Gedaliah as governor over them. (Gedaliah was the son of Ahikam, the son of Shaphan.) [12]When the people of Judah

heard this news, they came back to Judah. They came back to Gedaliah at Mizpah. They came from all the countries where they had been scattered. They gathered a large harvest of wine and summer fruit.

[13]Johanan son of Kareah came to Gedaliah at Mizpah. All the army officers of Judah still in the open country also came. [14]Johanan and the officers with him said to Gedaliah, "Don't you know that Baalis king of the Ammonite people wants you dead? He has sent Ishmael son of Nethaniah to kill you." But Gedaliah son of Ahikam did not believe them.

[15]Then Johanan son of Kareah spoke to Gedaliah in private at Mizpah. He said to Gedaliah, "Let me go and kill Ishmael son of Nethaniah. No one will know anything about it. We should not let Ishmael kill you. All the Jews gathered around you would be scattered to different countries again. Then the few people of Judah who are left alive would be lost."

[16]But Gedaliah son of Ahikam said to Johanan son of Kareah, "Do not kill Ishmael! The things you are saying about Ishmael are not true!"

41

In the seventh month Ishmael son of Nethaniah came to Gedaliah son of Ahikam. (Nethaniah was the son of Elishama.) Ishmael came with ten of his men to Mizpah. Now Ishmael was a member of the king's family. He had been one of the officers of the king of Judah. Ishmael and his men ate a meal with Gedaliah at Mizpah. [2]While they were eating together, Ishmael and his ten men got up. They killed Gedaliah son of Ahikam with a sword. Gedaliah was the man the king of Babylon had chosen as governor over Judah. [3]Ishmael killed all the Jews with Gedaliah at Mizpah, too. He also killed the Babylonian soldiers who were there with Gedaliah.

[4-5]The day after Gedaliah was murdered, 80 men came to Mizpah. They were bringing grain offerings and incense[d] to the Temple[d] of the Lord. Those 80 men had shaved off their beards, torn their clothes and cut themselves.[e] They came from Shechem, Shiloh and Samaria. None of them knew that Gedaliah had been murdered. [6]Ishmael son of Nethaniah went out from Mizpah to meet them. He cried as he walked. When

---

41:4-5 **shaved . . . themselves** The men did this to show they were sad about the Temple in Jerusalem being destroyed.

he met them, he said, "Come with me to meet Gedaliah son of Ahikam." [7] So they went into Mizpah. Then Ishmael son of Nethaniah and his men killed 70 of them! They threw the bodies into a deep well. [8] But the 10 men who were left alive said to Ishmael, "Don't kill us! We have wheat and barley. And we have oil and honey. We have hidden these things in a field." So Ishmael let those 10 men alone. He did not kill them with the others. [9] Now the well where he had thrown the bodies had been made by King Asa. Asa had made the well as a part of his defenses against Baasha king of Israel. But Ishmael son of Nethaniah put dead bodies in it until it was full.

[10] Ishmael captured all the other people in Mizpah. He captured the king's daughters and all the other people who were left there. They were the people whom Nebuzaradan commander of the guard had chosen Gedaliah son of Ahikam to take care of. So Ishmael son of Nethaniah captured those people. And he started to cross over to the country of the Ammonites.

[11] Johanan son of Kareah heard about all the evil things Ishmael son of Nethaniah had done. All the army officers with him heard it, too. [12] So Johanan and the army officers took their men and went to fight Ishmael son of Nethaniah. They caught him near the big pool of water at Gibeon. [13] The captives Ishmael had taken saw Johanan and the army officers. And they became very happy. [14] Then all the people Ishmael had taken captive turned around. They ran to Johanan son of Kareah. [15] But Ishmael son of Nethaniah and eight of his men escaped from Johanan. And they ran away to the Ammonites.

[16] So Johanan son of Kareah and all his army officers saved the captives. Ishmael son of Nethaniah had murdered Gedaliah son of Ahikam. Then he had taken those people from Mizpah. Among those left alive were soldiers, women, children and court officers. Johanan brought them back from the town of Gibeon.

[17-18] Johanan and the other army officers were afraid of the Babylonians. The king of Babylon had chosen Gedaliah son of Ahikam to be governor of Judah. But Ishmael son of Nethaniah had murdered Gedaliah. So Johanan was afraid that the Babylonians would be angry. They decided to run away to Egypt. On the way they stayed at Geruth Kimham, near the town of Bethlehem.

42 While there, Johanan son of Kareah and Jezaniah son of Hoshaiah went to Jeremiah the prophet. [6] All the army officers went with Johanan and Jezaniah. All the people, from the least important to the greatest, all went along, too. [2] They said to him, "Jeremiah, please listen to what we ask. Pray to the Lord your God. Pray for all the people left alive from the family of Judah. At one time there were many of us. You can see that there are few of us now. [3] So pray that the Lord your God will tell us where we should go. And pray he will tell us what we should do."

[4] Then Jeremiah the prophet answered, "I understand what you want me to do. I will pray to the Lord your God as you have asked. I will tell you everything he says. I will not hide anything from you."

[5] Then the people said to Jeremiah, "We will do everything the Lord your God tells us. If we don't, may the Lord be a true and loyal witness against us. We know he will send you to tell us what to do. [6] It does not matter if we like the message or not. We will obey the Lord our God. We are sending you to the Lord for a message from him. We will obey what he says. Then good things will happen to us."

[7] Ten days later the Lord spoke his word to Jeremiah. [8] Then Jeremiah called for Johanan son of Kareah and the army officers who were with him. Jeremiah also called all the other people, from the least important to the greatest. [9] Then Jeremiah said to them, "You sent me to ask the Lord for what you wanted. This is what the Lord, the God of Israel, says: [10] 'If you will stay in Judah, I will make you strong. I will not destroy you. I will plant you, and I will not pull you up. This is because I am sad about the disaster I brought on you. [11] Now you are afraid of the king of Babylon. But don't be afraid of him. Don't be afraid of the king of Babylon,' says the Lord. 'I am with you. I will save you. I will rescue you from his power. [12] I will be kind to you. And the king of Babylon will also treat you with mercy. He will bring you back to your land.'

[13] "But you might say, 'We will not stay in Judah.' If you say that, you will disobey the Lord your God. [14] Or you might

say, 'No, we will go and live in Egypt. We will not be bothered with war there. We will not hear the trumpets of war. And in Egypt we will not be hungry.' [15] If you say that, listen to the message of the Lord. It is to you who are left alive from Judah. This is what the Lord of heaven's armies, the God of Israel, says: 'If you make up your mind to go and live in Egypt, these things will happen: [16] You are afraid of war. But it will defeat you in the land of Egypt. And you are worried about hunger. But you will be hungry in Egypt. You will die there. [17] Everyone who goes to live in Egypt will die in war. Or he will die from hunger or terrible disease. No one who goes to Egypt will live. No one will escape the terrible things I will bring to them.'

[18] "This is what the Lord of heaven's armies, the God of Israel, says: 'I showed my anger against Jerusalem. I punished the people who lived in Jerusalem. In the same way I will show my anger against you when you go to Egypt. Other nations will speak evil of you. People will be shocked by what has happened to you. You will become a curse word. People will insult you. And you will never see Judah again.'

[19] "You who are left alive in Judah, the Lord has told you, 'Don't go to Egypt.' I warn you today. [20] You are making a mistake that will cause your deaths. You sent me to the Lord your God. You said to me, 'Pray to the Lord our God for us. Tell us everything the Lord says, and we will do it.' [21] So today I have told you the message from the Lord. But you have not obeyed the Lord your God. You have not done all that he sent me to tell you to do. [22] So now be sure you understand this: You want to go to live in Egypt. But you will die by war, hunger or terrible diseases."

43 So Jeremiah finished telling the people the message from the Lord their God. He told them everything the Lord their God had sent him to tell them.

[2] Azariah son of Hoshaiah, Johanan son of Kareah and some other men were too proud. They said to Jeremiah, "Jeremiah, you are lying! The Lord our God did not send you to say, 'You must not go to Egypt to live there.' [3] Baruch son of Neriah is causing you to be against us. He wants you to hand us over to the Babylonians. Then they will kill us. Or they will capture us and take us to Babylon."

[4] So Johanan, the army officers and all the people disobeyed the Lord's command. He had commanded them to stay in Judah. [5] But Johanan son of Kareah and the army officers took those who were left alive from Judah to Egypt. These were the people who had run away from the Babylonians to other countries. But they had come back to Judah. [6] Now Johanan and the army officers took the men, women and children. Among those people were the king's daughters. And they led them to Egypt. Nebuzaradan commander of the guard had put Gedaliah in charge of those people. (Gedaliah was the son of Ahikam son of Shaphan.) Johanan also took Jeremiah the prophet[d] and Baruch son of Neriah. [7] These people did not listen to the Lord. So they all went to Egypt to the town of Tahpanhes.

[8] In Tahpanhes the Lord spoke his word to Jeremiah: [9] "Take some large stones. Bury them in the clay in the brick pavement. This is in front of the king of Egypt's palace in Tahpanhes. Do this while the Jews are watching you. [10] Then say to them, 'This is what the Lord of heaven's armies, the God of Israel, says: I will send for my servant, Nebuchadnezzar king of Babylon. And I will set his throne over these stones I have buried. He will spread his covering for shade above these stones. [11] He will come here and attack Egypt. He will bring death to those who are supposed to die. He will make prisoners of those who are to be taken captive. And he will bring war to those who are to be killed with a sword. [12] Nebuchadnezzar will set fire to the temples of the gods of Egypt. He will burn those temples. And he will take the idols away. A shepherd wraps himself in his clothes. In the same way Nebuchadnezzar will wrap Egypt around him. Then he will safely leave Egypt. [13] He will destroy the stone pillars in the temple of the sun god in Egypt. And he will burn down the temples of the gods of Egypt.'"

44 Jeremiah received a message from the Lord. It was for all the Jews living in Egypt. It was for the Jews in Migdol, Tahpanhes, Memphis and southern Egypt. This was the message: [2] "The Lord of heaven's armies, the God of Israel, says: You saw the terrible things I brought on Jerusalem and the towns of Judah. Those towns are empty ruins today. [3] And it is because the people who lived there did evil. Those people burned incense[d] to other gods. And that made me angry! Your people and your ancestors did not worship those gods before. [4]I sent my prophets[d] to them again and again. Those prophets were my servants. They spoke my message and said to the people, 'Don't do this terrible thing. The Lord hates for you to worship other gods.' [5]But they did not listen to the prophets. They did not pay attention. They did not stop doing evil things. They did not stop burning incense to other gods. [6]So I showed my great anger against them. I punished the towns of Judah and the streets of Jerusalem. My anger made Jerusalem and the towns of Judah empty. They are only ruins and piles of stones today.

[7]"So the Lord of heaven's armies, the God of Israel, says: Why are you doing such great harm to yourselves by continuing to worship other gods? You are cutting off the men and women, children and babies from the family of Judah. So you leave yourselves without anyone from the family of Judah. [8]Why do you want to make me angry by making idols? Why do you burn incense to the gods of Egypt, where you have come to live? You will destroy yourselves. Other nations will speak evil of you. And all the other nations on the earth will make fun of you. [9]Have you forgotten about the evil things your ancestors did? And have you forgotten the evil the kings and queens of Judah did? Have you forgotten about the evil you and your wives did? They did these things in Judah and in the streets of Jerusalem. [10]Even to this day the people of Judah are still too proud. They have not learned to respect me. And they have not followed my teachings. They have not obeyed the laws I gave you and your ancestors!

[11]"So this is what the Lord of heaven's armies, the God of Israel, says: I am determined to bring disasters on you. I will destroy the whole family of Judah. [12]There were a few left alive from Judah. They were determined to go to Egypt and settle there. But they will all die in Egypt. They will be killed in war or die from hunger. From the least important to the greatest, they will be killed in war or die from hunger. Other nations will speak evil about them. People will be shocked by what has happened to them. They will become a curse word. People will insult them. [13]I will punish those people who have gone to live in Egypt. I will use swords, hunger and terrible

diseases to punish them. I will punish them just as I punished Jerusalem. [14]Of the people of Judah who were left alive and have gone to Egypt none will escape my punishment. They want to return to Judah and live there. But none of them will live to return to Judah. None of them will return to Judah, except a few people who escape."

[15]A large group of the people of Judah, who lived in southern Egypt, were meeting together. Among them were many women of Judah who lived in Egypt. They were burning incense to other gods, and their husbands knew it. All these people said to Jeremiah, [16]"We will not listen to the message from the Lord that you spoke to us. [17]We promised to make sacrifices to the Queen Goddess![d] And we will do everything we promised. We will burn incense and pour out drink offerings to worship her. We did that in the past. And our ancestors, kings and officers did that in the past. All of us did those things in the towns of Judah and in the streets of Jerusalem. At that time we had plenty of food. We were successful. Nothing bad happened to us. [18]But then we stopped making sacrifices to the Queen Goddess. And we stopped pouring out drink offerings to her. Since then we have had problems. Our people have been killed in war and by hunger."

[19]The women said, "Our husbands knew what we were doing. We had their permission to burn incense to the Queen Goddess! We had their permission to pour out drink offerings to her. Our husbands knew we were making cakes that looked like her and that we poured out drink offerings to her."

[20]Then Jeremiah spoke to all the people—men and women—who answered him. [21]He said to them, "The Lord remembered that you burned incense. You burned it in the towns of Judah and in the streets of Jerusalem. You and your ancestors, kings and officers did that. And the people of the land did that. The Lord remembered and thought about it. [22]Then he could not be patient with you any longer. He hated the terrible things you did. So he made your country an empty desert. No one lives there now. Other people curse that country. [23]All this happened because you burned incense to other gods. You sinned against the Lord. You did not obey him. You did not follow his teachings or the laws he gave you. You did not keep your part of

the agreement. This disaster has happened. It is there for you to see."

24Then Jeremiah spoke to all those men and also to the women. He said, "People of Judah who are now in Egypt, hear the word of the Lord. 25The Lord of heaven's armies, the God of Israel, says: You women did what you said you would do. You said, 'We will keep the promises we made. We promised to make sacrifices to the Queen Goddess. And we promised to pour out drink offerings to her.' So, go ahead. Do the things you promised you would do. Keep your promises. 26But hear the word of the Lord. Listen, all you Jews living in Egypt. The Lord says, 'I use my great name and make this promise: The people of Judah now living in Egypt will never again use my name to make promises. They will never again say, "As surely as the Lord God lives . . ." 27I am watching over them. I am not watching over them to take care of them, but to hurt them. The Jews who live in Egypt will die from swords or hunger until they are all destroyed. 28Some people will escape being killed by the sword. They will come back to Judah from Egypt. But there will only be a very few who escape. Then, of the people of Judah who came to live in Egypt, those who are left alive will know. They will know whether my word or their word came true. 29I will give you a sign that I will punish you here in Egypt,' says the Lord. 'Then you will know my promises to hurt you will really happen.' 30This is what the Lord says: 'Hophra king of Egypt has enemies who want to kill him. I will hand over King Hophra to his enemies. I will do this just as I handed Zedekiah king of Judah over to Nebuchadnezzar king of Babylon. Nebuchadnezzar wanted to kill Zedekiah.'"

45 It was the fourth year that Jehoiakim son of Josiah was king of Judah. Jeremiah the prophet[d] told these things to Baruch son of Neriah. And Baruch wrote them on a scroll. This is what Jeremiah said to Baruch: 2"This is what the Lord, the God of Israel, says to you: 3Baruch, you have said, 'How terrible it is for me! The Lord has given me sorrow along with my pain. I am tired because of my suffering. I cannot rest.'"

4The Lord said, "Say this to Baruch: 'This is what the Lord says: I will tear down what I have built. And I will pull up what I have planted. I will do that

everywhere in Judah. 5Baruch, you are looking for great things for yourself. Don't do that! Don't look for them because I will bring disaster on all the people. The Lord says these things! You will have to go many places. But I will let you escape alive wherever you go.'"

46 The Lord spoke this word to Jeremiah the prophet[d] about the nations:

2This message is about Egypt: This message is about the army of King Neco, king of Egypt. His army was defeated at the city of Carchemish on the Euphrates River. It was defeated by Nebuchadnezzar king of Babylon. This was in the fourth year that Jehoiakim son of Josiah was king of Judah. This is the Lord's message to Egypt:

3"Prepare your shields, large and
　　small.
　　March out for battle!
4Harness the horses.
　　Soldiers, get on your horses!
　　Go to your places for battle.
　　Put on your helmets!
Polish your spears.
　　Put on your armor!
5What do I see?
　　That army is terrified.
The soldiers are running away.
　　Their warriors are defeated.
They run away quickly.
　　They don't look back.
　　There is terror on every side!"
　　says the Lord.
6"The fast runners cannot run away.
　　The strong soldiers cannot
　　　　escape.
They will stumble and fall
　　in the north, by the Euphrates
　　　　River.
7Who is this, rising up like the Nile
　　River?
　　Who comes like that strong, fast
　　　　river?
8Egypt rises up like the Nile River.
　　It is Egypt that comes like that
　　　　strong, fast river.
Egypt says, 'I will rise up and cover
　　the earth.
　　I will destroy cities and the
　　　　people in them!'
9Horsemen, charge into battle!
　　Chariot drivers, drive hard!
March on, brave soldiers—
　　soldiers from Cush and Put who
　　　　carry shields.
　　March on, soldiers from Lydia
　　　　who use bows.

[10]"But that day belongs to the
Master, the Lord of heaven's
armies.
At that time he will give those
people the punishment they
deserve.
The sword will kill until it is
finished.
The sword will kill until it
satisfies its thirst for blood.
This is because the Master, the
Lord of heaven's armies, will
offer a sacrifice.
That sacrifice is Egypt's army in
the land of the north, by the
Euphrates River.

[11]"Go to Gilead and get some balm.[d]
Go up, people of Egypt!
You will make up many medicines,
but you will not be healed.
[12]The nations will hear of your shame.
Your cries will fill all the earth.
One warrior will run into another.
And both of them will fall down
together!'"

[13]This is the message the Lord spoke
to Jeremiah the prophet.[d] This message
is about Nebuchadnezzar king of Babylon as he came to attack Egypt:
[14]"Announce this message in Egypt,
and prophesy it in Migdol.
Preach this message also in
Memphis and Tahpanhes:
'Get ready for war.
The battle is all around you.'
[15]Egypt, why will your warriors be
killed?
They cannot stand because the
Lord will push them down.
[16]Those soldiers will stumble again
and again.
They will fall over each other.
They will say, 'Get up. Let's go back
to our own people and our
homeland.
We must get away from our
enemy's sword!'
[17]In their homelands those soldiers
will say,
'The king of Egypt is only a lot of
noise.
His time of glory is over!'"

[18]The King's name is the Lord of
heaven's armies.
He says, "As surely as I live,
a powerful leader will come.
He will be strong as great Mount
Tabor is higher than other
mountains.

He will be mighty as Mount
Carmel is higher than the sea.
[19]People of Egypt, pack your things
to be taken away as captives.
This is because Memphis will be
destroyed.
The cities will be ruins, and no
one will live there.

[20]"Egypt is like a beautiful young
cow.
But a horsefly is coming
from the north to attack her.
[21]The hired soldiers in Egypt's army
are like fat calves.
They will all turn and run away
together.
They will not stand strong
against the attack.
Their time of destruction is coming.
They will soon be punished.
[22]Egypt is like a hissing snake that is
trying to escape.
The enemy comes closer and
closer.
They will come against Egypt with
axes.
They are like men who cut down
trees.
[23]They will chop down Egypt's army
as if it were a great forest," says
the Lord.
"There are more enemy soldiers
than locusts.[d]
There are too many soldiers to
count.
[24]The people of Egypt will be
ashamed.
They will be handed over to the
enemy from the north."

[25]The Lord of heaven's armies, the
God of Israel, says: "Very soon I will
punish Amon, the god of Thebes. And I
will punish Egypt, her king and her
gods. And I will punish the people who
depend on the king. [26]I will let all those
people be defeated by their enemies.
And those enemies want to kill them. I
will give them to Nebuchadnezzar king
of Babylon and his officers. But in the
future, Egypt will live in peace as it once
did," says the Lord.

[27]"People of Jacob, my servants,
don't be afraid.
Don't be frightened, Israel.
I will surely save you from those
faraway places.
I will save your children from the
lands where they are captives.

The people of Jacob will have
    peace and safety again.
And no one will make them
    afraid.
[28] People of Jacob, my servants, do
    not be afraid.
I am with you," says the Lord.
"I scattered you to many different
    nations.
And I will completely destroy all
    those nations.
But I will not completely destroy
    you.
I will punish you fairly.
But I cannot let you escape your
    punishment."

47 The Lord spoke his word to Jeremiah the prophet.[d] This message is about the Philistine people. It came before the king of Egypt attacked the city of Gaza.

[2] This is what the Lord says:
"See, the enemy is gathering in the
    north like rising waters.
They will become like an
    overflowing stream.
They will cover the whole country
    like a flood.
They will cover the towns and
    the people living in them.
Everyone living in that country
    will cry for help.
The people will cry painfully.
[3] They will hear the sound of the
    running horses.
They will hear the noisy chariots.
They will hear the rumbling
    chariot wheels.
Fathers will not help their children
    to safety.
Those fathers will be too weak to
    help.
[4] The time has come
    to destroy all the Philistines.
It's time to destroy all who are left
    alive
who could help Tyre and Sidon.
The Lord will soon destroy the
    Philistines.
He will destroy those left alive
    from the island of Crete.
[5] The people from Gaza will be sad
    and shave their heads.
The people from Ashkelon will
    be made silent.
Those left alive from the valley,
    how long will you cut
    yourselves?[n]

[6] "You cry, 'Sword of the Lord,
    how long will you keep fighting?
Return to your holder.
    Stop! Be still.'
[7] But how can the sword of the Lord
    rest?
The Lord gave it a command.
The Lord has ordered it
    to attack the city of Ashkelon
    and the seacoast."

48 This message is about the country of Moab. This is what the Lord of heaven's armies, the God of Israel, says:
"How terrible it will be for Nebo.
    It will be ruined.
The town of Kiriathaim will be
    disgraced and captured.
The strong city will be disgraced
    and shattered.
[2] Moab will not be praised again.
    Men in the town of Heshbon plan
    Moab's defeat.
They say, 'Come, let us put an
    end to that nation!'
Town of Madmen, you will also be
    silenced.
The sword will chase you.
[3] Listen to the cries from the town of
    Horonaim.
They are cries of much confusion
    and destruction.
[4] Moab will be broken up.
    Her little children will cry for
    help.
[5] Moab's people go up the path to
    Luhith.
They cry loudly as they go.
On the road down to the town of
    Horonaim,
cries of pain and suffering can be
    heard.
[6] Run! Run for your lives!
    Go like a bush being blown
    through the desert.
[7] You trust in the things you do and
    in your wealth.
So you also will be captured.
The god Chemosh[d] will be taken
    into captivity.
And his priests and officers will
    be taken with him.
[8] The destroyer will come against
    every town.
Not one town will escape.
The valley will be ruined.
    The high plain will be destroyed.
    The Lord said this would happen.

47:5 sad and . . . yourselves? The people did these things to show their sadness.

[9] Spread salt[n] over the fields in
  Moab.
  The country will be an empty
    desert.
Moab's towns will become empty.
  No one will live in them.
[10] A curse will be on anyone who
    doesn't do what the Lord says.
  A curse will be on anyone who
    keeps back his sword from
    killing.

[11] "The people of Moab have never
    known trouble.
  They are like wine left to settle.
  They have never been poured like
    wine from one jar to another.
  They have not been taken into
    captivity.
  So they taste as they did before.
    And their smell has not changed.
[12] A time is coming," says the Lord.
  "And I will soon send men to
    pour you from your jars.
  Those men will empty Moab's jars.
    And they will smash their jugs.
[13] The people of Israel trusted that
    god in Bethel.
  They were ashamed when there
    was no help.
  In the same way Moab will be
    ashamed of their god
    Chemosh.

[14] "You cannot say, 'We are warriors!
    We are brave men in battle!'
[15] The enemy will attack Moab and
    destroy their towns.
  Their best young men will be
    killed!" says the King.
  The King's name is the Lord of
    heaven's armies.
[16] "The end of Moab is near.
  They will soon be destroyed.
[17] All you who live around Moab, cry
    for her.
  All you who know about her, cry
    for her.
  Say, 'The ruler's power is broken.
    Moab's power and glory are
    gone.'
[18] "You people living in Dibon, come
    down from your place of honor.
  Sit on the dry ground.
  This is because the destroyer of
    Moab is coming against you.
  And he will destroy your strong,
    walled cities.
[19] You people living in Aroer,
    stand next to the road and watch.

See the man running away and the
  woman escaping.
  Ask them what happened.
[20] Moab will be ruined and filled with
    shame.
  Cry, Moab, cry out!
  Announce at the Arnon River
    that Moab is destroyed.
[21] People on the high plain have been
    punished.
  Judgment has come to these
    towns:
  Holon, Jahzah and Mephaath;
[22] Dibon, Nebo and Beth
    Diblathaim;
[23] Kiriathaim, Beth Gamul and Beth
    Meon;
[24] Kerioth and Bozrah.
  Judgment has come to all the
    towns of Moab, far and near.
[25] Moab's strength has been cut off.
  Moab's arm is broken!" says the
    Lord.

[26] "The people of Moab thought they
    were greater than the Lord.
  So punish Moab until they act as
    if they are drunk.
  Moab will fall and roll around in
    their own vomit.
  People will make fun of them.
[27] Moab, you made fun of Israel.
  Israel was caught in the middle
    of a gang of thieves.
  You often spoke about Israel.
  And you shook your head and
    acted as if you were better than
    Israel.
[28] People in Moab, leave your towns
    empty.
  Go live among the rocks.
  Be like a dove that makes its nest
    at the entrance of a cave!

[29] "We have heard that the people of
    Moab are proud
    and very conceited.
  They are proud and think they are
    important.
  They were very proud in their
    hearts."
[30] The Lord says,
  "I know Moab's quick anger, but
    it is useless.
  Moab's bragging accomplishes
    nothing.
[31] So I cry sadly for Moab.
  I cry out for everyone in Moab.
  I moan for the men from Kir
    Haresheth.

48:9 salt The salt would keep crops from growing there.

[32] I cry with the people of Jazer
    for the grapevines of Sibmah.
In the past your vines spread all the
    way to the sea.
    They reached as far as the sea of
        Jazer.
But the destroyer has taken
    your fruit and grapes.
[33] Joy and happiness are gone
    from the large fields of Moab.
I have stopped the flow of wine
    from the winepresses.[d]
    No one walks on the grapes with
        shouts of joy.
There are shouts,
    but not shouts of joy.

[34] "Their crying can be heard
    from Heshbon to Elealeh and
        Jahaz.
It can be heard from Zoar as far
    away as Horonaim and Eglath
    Shelishiyah.
    Even the waters of Nimrim are
        dried up.
[35] I will stop Moab
    from making burnt offerings at
        the places of worship.
I will stop them from burning
    incense[d] to their gods," says
    the Lord.

[36] "My heart cries for Moab like a
    flute playing a funeral song.
It cries for the people from Kir
    Hareseth.
    Their money and riches have all
        been taken away.
[37] Everyone has a shaved head.
    Everyone's beard is cut off.
Everyone's hands are cut.
    Everyone wears rough cloth
        around his waist.[n]
[38] People are crying on every roof[n] in
    Moab
and in every public square.
There is nothing but sadness
    because I have broken Moab
like a jar no one wants," says the
    Lord.
[39] "Moab is shattered! The people are
    crying!
Moab turns away in shame!
People all around her make fun of
    her.
    The things that happened fill
        them with fear."

[40] This is what the Lord says:
    "Look! An eagle is diving down
        from the sky.
It spreads its wings over Moab.
[41] The towns of Moab will be
    captured.
The strong, walled cities will be
    defeated.
At that time Moab's warriors will
    be frightened.
    They will feel pain like a woman
        who is having a baby.
[42] The nation of Moab will be
    destroyed.
This is because they thought they
    were greater than the Lord.
[43] Fear, deep pits and traps wait for
    you,
    people of Moab," says the Lord.
[44] "People will run from fear.
    But they will fall into the pits.
Anyone who climbs out of the pits
    will be caught in the traps.
I will bring the year of punishment
    to Moab," says the Lord.

[45] "People have run from the powerful
    enemy.
    They ran to Heshbon for safety.
But fire started in Heshbon.
    A blaze broke out in Sihon's
        town.
And it burns the leaders of Moab.
    It destroys those proud people.
[46] How terrible it will be for you,
    Moab!
Chemosh's people are being
    destroyed.
Your sons and daughters are being
    taken away as captives.

[47] "But in days to come,
    I will make good things happen
        again to Moab," says the Lord.

This ends the judgment on Moab.

49 This message is about the Ammonite people. This is what the Lord says:
    "Do you think that Israel has no
        sons?
    Do you think there is no one to
        take the land when the parents
        die?
Maybe that is why Molech[d] took
    Gad's land.

48:37 shaved head . . . waist The people did these things to show their sadness for those who had died. **48:38 roof** In Bible times houses were built with flat roofs. The roof was used for drying things such as flax and fruit. And it was used as an extra room, as a place for worship and as a place to sleep in the summer.

Maybe that is why Molech's
people live in Gad's towns."
²The Lord says,
"The time will come when I will
make
the capital city of Rabbah
Ammon hear the battle cry.
It will be a hill covered with ruins.
And the towns around it will be
burned.
Those people forced Israel out of
that land.
But now the people of Israel will
force them out!" says the Lord.
³"People in Heshbon, cry because
the town of Ai is destroyed!
Those who live in Rabbah
Ammon, cry out!
Put on your rough cloth to show
your sadness, and cry loudly.
Run here and there for safety
inside the walls.
This is because the enemy will take
Molech away as a captive.
They will also take away his
priests and officers with him.
⁴You brag about your valleys.
You brag about the fruit in your
valleys.
You are like an unfaithful child.
You believe your treasures will
save you.
You think, 'Who would attack
me?'
⁵I will bring terror on you
from every side,"
says the Master, the Lord of
heaven's armies.
"You will all be forced away.
No one will be able to gather you.

⁶"But the time will come
when I will make good things
happen to the Ammonites
again,"
says the Lord.

⁷This message is about Edom. This is
what the Lord of heaven's armies says:
"Is there no more wisdom in
Teman?
Can the wise men of Edom no
longer give good advice?
Have they lost their wisdom?
⁸You people living in Dedan,
run away and hide in deep caves.
This is because I will punish
the people of Esau with disaster
for what they did.
⁹If workers came and picked the
grapes from your vines,

they would leave a few grapes
behind.
If robbers came at night,
they would steal only enough for
themselves.
¹⁰But I will strip Esau bare.
I will find all their hiding places.
They will not be able to hide
from me.
The children, relatives and
neighbors will die.
¹¹Leave the orphans, and I will take
care of them.
Your widows also can trust in
me."

¹²This is what the Lord says: "Some
people did not deserve to be punished.
But they had to drink from the cup of
suffering anyway. People of Edom, you
deserve to be punished. So you will not
escape punishment. You must drink
from the cup of suffering." ¹³The Lord
says, "I make this promise in my own
name. The city of Bozrah will become a
pile of ruins! People will be shocked by
what happened there. People will insult
that city and speak evil of it. And all the
towns around Bozrah will become ruins
forever."

¹⁴I have heard a message from the
Lord.
A messenger has been sent
among the nations, saying,
"Gather your armies to attack it!
Get ready for battle!"

¹⁵"Soon I will make you the smallest
of nations!
You will be greatly hated.
¹⁶Edom, you frightened other
nations.
Your pride has fooled you.
You live in the hollow places of the
cliff.
You live on the high places of the
hills.
Even if you build your home as
high as an eagle's nest,
I will bring you down from
there!" says the Lord.

¹⁷"Edom will be destroyed.
People will be shocked to see the
destroyed cities.
They will be amazed at the
injuries.
¹⁸Edom will be destroyed like the
cities of Sodom and Gomorrah
and the towns around them,"
says the Lord.

"No one will live there!
No man will stay in Edom."

¹⁹"A lion will come from the thick
bushes near the Jordan River.
And it will go into the rich
pastures where people feed
their flocks.
I am like that lion! I will suddenly
chase Edom from their land.
Who is the one I have chosen to
do this?
There is no one like me.
There is no one who can
challenge me.
None of their leaders can stand
up against me."

²⁰So listen to what the Lord has
planned to do against Edom.
Listen to what he has decided to
do to the people in Teman.
The Lord will surely drag away the
young ones of Edom.
Edom's pastures will surely be
destroyed because of them.
²¹At the sound of Edom's fall, the
earth will shake.
Their cry will be heard all the
way to the Gulf of Aqaba.
²²The Lord is like an eagle swooping
down.
He is like an eagle spreading its
wings over the city of Bozrah.
At that time Edom's soldiers will
become very frightened.
They will be crying from fear like
a woman having a baby.

²³This message is about the city of Damascus:
"The towns of Hamath and Arpad
are put to shame.
They are afraid because they
have heard bad news.
They are discouraged.
They are troubled like the tossing
sea.
²⁴The city of Damascus has become
weak.
The people want to run away.
The people are ready to panic.
The people feel pain and suffering
like a woman having a baby.
²⁵Damascus was a city of my joy.
Why have the people not left that
famous city yet?
²⁶Surely the young men will die in
the public squares of that city.
All of her soldiers will be killed
at that time," says the Lord of
heaven's armies.

²⁷"I will set fire to the walls of
Damascus.
The fire will completely burn the
strong cities of Ben-Hadad."

²⁸This message is about the tribe[d] of
Kedar and the kingdoms of Hazor. Neb-
uchadnezzar king of Babylon defeated
them. This is what the Lord says:
"Go and attack the people of Kedar.
Destroy the people of the East.
²⁹Their tents and flocks will be taken
away.
Their tents and all their things
will be carried off.
Their enemy will take away their
goods and camels.
Men will shout to them,
'Terror on every side!'

³⁰"Run away quickly!
People in Hazor, find a good
place to hide!" says the Lord.
"Nebuchadnezzar king of Babylon
has made plans against you.
He has made plans to defeat you!

³¹"There is a nation that is
comfortable.
It is sure that no one will defeat
it," says the Lord.
"That nation does not have gates or
fences to protect it.
Its people live alone.
Attack that nation!
³²The enemy will steal their camels
and their large herds of cattle.
I will scatter the Arabs to every
part of the earth.
And I will bring disaster on them
from everywhere," says the
Lord.
³³"Hazor will become a place where
wild dogs live.
It will become an empty desert
forever.
No one will live there.
No man will stay in it."

³⁴It was early in the time when Zedekiah was king of Judah. The Lord spoke
this word to Jeremiah the prophet.[d] This
message is about the nation of Elam.
³⁵This is what the Lord of heaven's armies says:
"I will break Elam's bow.
I will break its strength.
³⁶I will bring the four winds against
Elam.
I will bring them from the four
corners of the skies.

I will scatter the people of Elam
   everywhere the four winds
   blow.
   And its captives will go to every
   nation.
³⁷I will break Elam to pieces in front
   of their enemies.
   The enemies want to destroy
   Elam.
I will bring disaster to Elam.
   I will show them how angry I
   am!" says the Lord.
"I will send a sword to chase Elam.
   It will chase them until I have
   killed them all.
³⁸I will show Elam that I am king.
   And I will destroy her king and
   her officers!" says the Lord.

³⁹"But I will make good things
   happen to Elam again
in the future," says the Lord.

50 ¹This is the message the Lord
spoke about Babylon and the Babylonian people. He spoke this message
through Jeremiah the prophet.[d]
²"Announce this to the nations.
   Lift up a banner and tell them.
   Speak the whole message and
   say:
'Babylon will be captured.
   The god Bel[d] will be put to
   shame.
   The god Marduk[d] will be very
   afraid.
Babylon's idols will be put to
   shame.
   Her idols will be filled with
   terror!'
³A nation from the north will attack
   Babylon.
   That nation will make Babylon
   like an empty desert.
No people will live there.
   Both men and animals will run
   away from there."

⁴The Lord says, "At that time
   the people of Israel and Judah
   will be together.
   They will cry and look for the
   Lord their God.
⁵Those people will ask how to go to
   Jerusalem.
   They will start to go in that
   direction.
They will come and join themselves
   to the Lord.
   They will make an agreement
   that will last forever.

It will be an agreement that will
   never be forgotten.

⁶"My people have been like lost
   sheep.
   Their leaders have led them in
   the wrong way.
Their leaders made them wander
   around in the mountains and
   hills.
   They forgot where their resting
   place was.
⁷Whoever found my people hurt
   them.
   And those enemies said, 'We did
   nothing wrong.
Those people sinned against the
   Lord, their true resting place.
   He was the God their fathers
   trusted.'

⁸"Run away from Babylon.
   Leave the land of the Babylonians.
   Be like the goats that lead the
   flock.
⁹I will bring against Babylon
   many nations from the north.
This group of nations will take their
   places for war against Babylon.
   Babylon will be captured by
   people from the north.
Their arrows are like trained
   soldiers
   who do not return from war with
   empty hands.
¹⁰The enemy will take all the wealth
   from the Babylonians.
   Those enemy soldiers will get all
   they want!" says the Lord.

¹¹"Babylon, you are excited and
   happy.
   You took my land.
You dance around like a young cow
   in the grain.
   Your laughter is like the neighing
   of male horses.
¹²Your mother will be very ashamed.
   The woman who gave you birth
   will be disgraced.
Babylonia will be the least
   important of all the nations.
   She will be an empty, dry desert.
¹³The Lord will show his anger.
   No people will live there.
   Babylon will be completely
   empty.
Everyone who passes by Babylon
   will be afraid.
   They will shake their heads when
   they see how it has been
   destroyed.

¹⁴"Take your positions for war
against Babylon,
all you soldiers with bows.
Shoot your arrows at Babylon! Do
not save any of them.
This is because Babylon has
sinned against the Lord.
¹⁵Soldiers around Babylon, shout the
war cry!
Babylon has surrendered. Her
towers have fallen.
Her walls have been torn down.
The Lord is giving them the
punishment they deserve.
You nations should give Babylon
what she deserves.
Do to her what she has done to
others.
¹⁶Don't let the people from Babylon
plant their crops.
Don't let them gather the harvest.
The soldiers of Babylon treated
their captives cruelly.
Now, let everyone go back home!
Let everyone run to his own
country.

¹⁷"The people of Israel are like a
flock of sheep that are
scattered.
They are like sheep that have
been chased away by lions.
The first lion to eat them up
was the king of Assyria.
The last lion to crush their bones
was Nebuchadnezzar king of
Babylon."

¹⁸So this is what the Lord of heaven's
armies, the God of Israel, says:
"I will punish the king of Babylon
and his country.
I will punish him as I punished
the king of Assyria.
¹⁹But I will bring the people of Israel
back to their own pasture.
They will eat on Mount Carmel
and in Bashan.
They will eat and be full.
They will eat on the hills of
Ephraim and Gilead."
²⁰The Lord says,
"At that time people will try to
find Israel's guilt.
But there will be no guilt.
People will try to find Judah's sins.
But no sins will be found.
This is because I am saving the few
people left alive from Israel
and Judah.
And I am forgiving their sins.

²¹"Attack the land of Merathaim.
Attack the people who live in
Pekod.
Chase them, kill them and
completely destroy them.
Do everything I commanded
you!" says the Lord.

²²"The noise of battle can be heard
all over the country.
It is the noise of much
destruction.
²³Babylon was the hammer of the
whole earth.
But how broken and shattered
that hammer is now!
Babylon is truly the most ruined
of all the nations.
²⁴Babylon, I set a trap for you.
And you were caught before you
knew it.
You fought against the Lord.
So you were found and taken
prisoner.
²⁵The Lord has opened up his
storeroom.
He has brought out the weapons
of his anger.
This is because the Lord God of
heaven's armies has work to
do.
He has work to do in the land of
the Babylonians.
²⁶Come against Babylon from far
away.
Break open her storehouses of
grain.
Pile up her dead bodies like big
piles of grain.
Completely destroy Babylon
and do not leave anyone alive.
²⁷Kill all the young men in Babylon.
Let them be killed.
The time has come for their defeat.
How terrible it will be for them!
It is time for them to be
punished.
²⁸Listen to the people running from
the country of Babylon!
They are telling Jerusalem
how the Lord our God is punishing
Babylon as it deserves.
This is because Babylon
destroyed his Temple.ᵈ

²⁹"Call for the men who shoot arrows
to come against Babylon.
Tell them to surround the city.
Don't let anyone escape.
Pay her back for the bad things she
has done.

Do to her what she has done to
    other nations.
Babylon acted with pride against
    the Lord,
    the Holy One of Israel.
[30] So Babylon's young men will be
    killed in the streets.
All her soldiers will die on that
    day," says the Lord.
[31] "Babylon, you are too proud. And I
    am against you,"
    says the Master, the Lord of
    heaven's armies.
"This is because the time has come
    for you to be punished.
[32] Proud Babylon will stumble and
    fall.
And no one will help her get up.
I will start a fire in her towns.
    It will completely burn up
    everything around her."

[33] This is what the Lord of heaven's ar-
mies says:
    "The people of Israel
    and Judah both are slaves.
The enemy took them as prisoners.
    And they won't let them go.
[34] But God is strong and will buy
    them back.
His name is the Lord of heaven's
    armies.
He will defend them with power
    so he can give rest to their land.
But he will not give rest to those
    living in Babylon."

[35] The Lord says,
    "Let a sword kill the people living
    in Babylon!
Let a sword kill its officers and
    wise men!
[36] Let a sword kill its false prophets![d]
    They will become fools.
Let a sword kill Babylon's warriors!
    They will be full of terror.
[37] Let a sword kill its horses and
    chariots.
Let a sword kill all the soldiers
    hired from other countries!
They will be like frightened
    women.
Let there be a sword against
    Babylon's treasures!
    They will be taken away.
[38] Let there be a sword against its
    waters!
    They will be dried up.
It is a land of idols.
    Those idols will go crazy with
    fear.

[39] "Babylon will never be filled with
    people again.
Desert animals and hyenas will
    live there.
    Owls will live there.
But no people will live there ever
    again.
[40] God completely destroyed the cities
    of Sodom and Gomorrah
and the towns around them,"
    says the Lord.
"In the same way no people will
    live in Babylon.
    No man will stay there.

[41] "Look! An army is coming from the
    north.
    It comes from a powerful nation.
Many kings are coming together
    from all around the world.
[42] Their armies have bows and spears.
    The soldiers are cruel and have
    no mercy.
The soldiers come riding on their
    horses.
And the sound is loud like the
    roaring sea.
They stand in their places, ready
    for battle.
    They are ready to attack you, city
    of Babylon.
[43] The king of Babylon heard about
    those armies.
    And he became helpless because
    of his fear.
His fear is like pain.
    It is like the pain of a woman
    having a baby.

[44] "A lion will come from the thick
    bushes near the Jordan River.
It will go into the rich pastures
    where people feed their flocks.
I am like that lion! I will suddenly
    chase the people of Babylon
    from their land.
Who is the one I have chosen to
    do this?
There is no one like me.
    There is no one who can
    challenge me.
None of their leaders can stand
    up against me."

[45] So listen to what the Lord has
    planned to do against Babylon.
Listen to what he has decided to
    do to the people in Babylon.
He will surely drag away the young
    ones of Babylon.
Babylon's pastures will be
    destroyed because of them.

⁴⁶At the sound of Babylon's fall, the
earth will shake.
People in all nations will hear
about their destruction.

51 This is what the Lord says:
"I will cause a destroying wind to
blow.
It will blow against Babylon and
the Babylonian people.
²I will send foreign people to
destroy Babylon
like a wind that blows chaff^d away.
Those people will make Babylon
empty.
Armies will surround the city
when disaster comes upon her.
³The Babylonian soldiers will not
use their bows and arrows.
Those soldiers will not even put
on their armor.
Don't feel sorry for the young men
of Babylon.
Completely destroy her army.
⁴Babylon's soldiers will be killed in
Babylon.
They will be badly injured in
Babylon's streets.
⁵The Lord God of heaven's armies
did not leave Israel and Judah
alone.
They are fully guilty of leaving the
Holy One of Israel.
But he has not left them.

⁶"Run away from Babylon!
Run to save your lives!
Don't stay and be killed because
of Babylon's sins.
It is time for the Lord to punish
Babylon.
Babylon will get the punishment
it deserves.
⁷Babylon was like a gold cup in the
Lord's hand.
It made the whole earth drunk.
The nations drank Babylon's wine.
So they went crazy.
⁸Babylon will suddenly fall and be
broken.
Cry for her!
Get balm^d for her pain.
Maybe she can be healed.

⁹"Foreigners in Babylon say, 'We
tried to heal Babylon.
But she cannot be healed.
So let us leave her and each go to
his own country.
Babylon's guilt is as high as the
clouds.

Babylon's guilt reaches to the
sky.'

¹⁰"The people of Judah say, 'The
Lord has shown us to be right.
Come, let us tell about it in
Jerusalem.
Let us tell about what the Lord
our God has done.'

¹¹"Sharpen the arrows.
Pick up your shields!
The Lord has stirred up the kings
of the Medes.
He has stirred them up because
he wants to destroy Babylon.
The Lord will give the people of
Babylon the punishment they
deserve.
This is because Babylon
destroyed his Temple^d in
Jerusalem.
¹²Lift up a banner against the walls
of Babylon!
Bring more guards.
Put the watchmen in their places.
Get ready for a secret attack!
The Lord will do what he has
planned.
He will do what he said he would
do against the people of
Babylon.
¹³People of Babylon, you live near
much water.
You are rich with treasures.
But your end as a nation has come.
It is time for you to be destroyed.
¹⁴The Lord of heaven's armies has
promised in his own name:
'Babylon, I will surely fill you
with so many enemy soldiers
they will be like a swarm of
locusts.^d
They will stand over you and
shout their victory.'

¹⁵"The Lord made the earth by his
power.
He used his wisdom to build the
world.
He used his understanding to
stretch out the skies.
¹⁶When he thunders, the waters in
the skies roar.
He makes clouds rise in the sky
all over the earth.
He sends lightning with the rain.
He brings out the wind from his
storehouses.

¹⁷"People are so stupid and know so
little.

Goldsmiths are made ashamed
by their idols.
Those statues are only false gods.
They have no breath in them.
¹⁸They are worth nothing.
People make fun of them.
When they are judged, they will be
destroyed.
¹⁹But God, who is Jacob's Portion,ᵈ is
not like the idols.
God made everything.
And he made Israel to be his
special people.
The Lord of heaven's armies is
his name.

²⁰"You are my war club.
You are my battle weapon.
I use you to smash nations.
I use you to destroy kingdoms.
²¹I use you to smash horse and rider.
I use you to smash chariot and
driver.
²²I use you to smash men and
women.
I use you to smash old men and
young men.
I use you to smash young men
and young women.
²³I use you to smash shepherds and
flocks.
I use you to smash farmers and
oxen.
I use you to smash governors and
officers.

²⁴"But I will pay Babylon back, and I
will pay back all the Babylonians for all
the evil things they did to Jerusalem,"
says the Lord.

²⁵The Lord says,
"Babylon, you are a destroying
mountain.
And I am against you.
You have destroyed the whole
land.
I will put my hand out against you.
I will roll you off the cliffs.
I will make you a burned-out
mountain.
²⁶People will not find any rocks in
Babylon big enough for
cornerstones.ᵈ
People will not take any rocks
from Babylon to use for the
foundation of a building.
This is because your city will be
just a pile of ruins forever,"
says the Lord.

²⁷"Lift up the banner in the land!

Blow the trumpet among the
nations!
Get the nations ready for battle
against Babylon.
Call these kingdoms to come
fight against Babylon:
Ararat, Minni and Ashkenaz.
Choose a commander to lead the
army against Babylon.
Send so many horses that they
are like a swarm of locusts.
²⁸Get the nations ready for battle
against Babylon.
Get the kings of the Medes ready.
Get their governors and all their
officers ready.
Get all the countries they rule
ready for battle against
Babylon.
²⁹The land shakes and moves like it
is in pain.
It will shake when the Lord does
what he planned to Babylon.
His plan is to make Babylon into an
empty desert.
No one will live there.
³⁰Babylon's warriors have stopped
fighting.
They stay in their protected cities.
Their strength is gone.
They have become like
frightened women.
Babylon's houses are burning.
The bars of her gates are broken.
³¹One messenger follows another.
Messenger follows messenger.
They announce to the king of
Babylon
that his whole city has been
captured.
³²The river crossings have been
captured.
The swamplands are burning.
All of Babylon's soldiers are
terribly afraid."

³³This is what the Lord of heaven's armies, the God of Israel, says:
"The city of Babylon is like a
threshingᵈ floor,
where people crush the grain at
harvest time.
The time to harvest Babylon is
coming soon."

³⁴"Nebuchadnezzar king of Babylon
has destroyed us.
In the past he took our people
away.
And we became like an empty
jar.

He was like a giant snake that
   swallowed us.
He ate everything until he was
   full of our best things.
Then he spit us out.
35 Babylon did terrible things to hurt
   us.
Now let those things happen to
   Babylon,"
say the people of Jerusalem.
"The people of Babylon are guilty
   of killing our people.
Now let them be punished for the
   evil they did," says Jerusalem.

36 So this is what the Lord says:
"I will defend you, Judah.
I will make sure that Babylon is
   punished.
I will dry up Babylon's sea.
And I will make her springs
   become dry.
37 Babylon will become a pile of ruins.
Wild dogs will live there.
People will be shocked by what
   happened there.
No one lives there anymore.
38 Babylon's people are like roaring
   young lions.
They growl like baby lions.
39 While they are stirred up,
I will give a feast for them.
I will make them drunk.
They will shout and laugh.
And they will sleep forever and
   never wake up!" says the Lord.
40 "I will take the people of Babylon
   to be killed.
They will be like lambs,
like male sheep and goats
   waiting to be killed.

41 "How Babylon will be defeated!
The pride of the whole earth will
   be taken captive.
People from other nations will be
   shocked at what happened to
   Babylon.
And the things they see will
   make them afraid.
42 The sea will rise over Babylon.
Its roaring waves will cover her.
43 Babylon's towns will be ruined and
   empty.
Babylon will become a dry,
   desert land.
It will become a land where no one
   lives.
People will not even travel
   through Babylon.

44 I will punish the god Bel[d] in
   Babylon.
I will make him spit out what he
   has swallowed.
Nations will no longer come to
   Babylon.
And the wall around the city will
   fall.

45 "Come out of Babylon, my people!
Run for your lives!
Run from the Lord's great anger.
46 Don't lose courage.
Rumors will spread, but don't be
   afraid.
One rumor comes this year, and
   another comes the next year.
There will be rumors of terrible
   fighting in the country.
There will be rumors of rulers
   fighting against rulers.
47 The time will surely come
when I will punish the idols of
   Babylon.
And the whole land will be
   disgraced.
There will be many dead people
   lying all around.
48 Then heaven and earth and all that
   is in them
will shout for joy about Babylon.
They will shout because the army
   came from the north
and fought against Babylon,"
says the Lord.

49 "Babylon killed people from Israel.
Babylon killed people from
   everywhere on earth.
So Babylon must fall.
50 You people escaped being killed
   with swords.
You must hurry and leave
   Babylon.
Don't wait!
Remember the Lord in the
   faraway land where you are.
And think about Jerusalem."

51 "We people of Judah are disgraced.
We have been insulted.
We have been shamed.
This is because strangers have
   gone into
the holy places of the Lord's
   Temple!"[d]

52 The Lord says, "The time is coming
when I will punish the idols of
   Babylon.
Wounded people will cry with pain
   all over that land.

[53] Babylon might grow until she
touches the sky.
She might make her cities strong.
But I will send people to destroy
that city," says the Lord.

[54] "We can hear people crying in
Babylon.
We hear the sound of people
destroying things
in the land of the Babylonians.
[55] The Lord will destroy Babylon.
He will make the loud sounds of
the city become silent.
Enemies will come roaring in like
ocean waves.
People all around will hear that
roar.
[56] The army will come and destroy
Babylon.
Babylon's soldiers will be taken
captive.
Their bows will be broken.
This is because the Lord is a God
who punishes people for the
evil they do.
He gives them the full
punishment they deserve.
[57] I will make Babylon's rulers and
wise men drunk.
I will make her governors,
officers and soldiers drunk,
too.
Then they will sleep forever and
never wake up," says the King.
His name is the Lord of heaven's
armies.

[58] This is what the Lord of heaven's armies says:
"Babylon's thick wall will be pulled
down.
Her high gates will be burned.
The people will work hard, but it
won't help.
Their work will only become fuel
for the flames!"

[59] This is the message that Jeremiah
the prophet[d] gave to the officer Seraiah.
Seraiah was the son of Neriah, who was
the son of Mahseiah. Seraiah went to
Babylon with Zedekiah king of Judah.
This happened in the fourth year Zedekiah was king of Judah. [60] Jeremiah had
written on a scroll all the terrible things
that would happen to Babylon. He had
written all these words about Babylon.
[61] Jeremiah said to Seraiah, "Go to Babylon. Be sure to read this message so
all the people can hear you. [62] Then say,

'Lord, you have said that you will destroy this place. You will destroy it so
that no people or animals will live in it.
It will be an empty ruin forever.' [63] After
you finish reading this scroll, tie a stone
to it. And throw it into the Euphrates
River. [64] Then say, 'In the same way Babylon will sink. It will not rise again. It
will sink because of the terrible things I
will make happen here. Her people will
fall.'"

The words of Jeremiah end here.

52

Zedekiah was 21 years old when
he became king. And he was king
in Jerusalem for 11 years. His mother's
name was Hamutal daughter of Jeremiah.[a] She was from Libnah. [2] Zedekiah
did what the Lord said was wrong, just
as Jehoiakim had done. [3] All this happened in Jerusalem and Judah because
the Lord was angry with them. Finally,
he threw them out of his presence.

Zedekiah turned against the king of
Babylon.

[4] Then Nebuchadnezzar king of Babylon marched against Jerusalem with
his whole army. They made a camp
around the city. Then they built devices
all around the city walls to attack it. This
happened during Zedekiah's ninth year,
tenth month and tenth day as king. [5] The
city was under attack until Zedekiah's
eleventh year as king.

[6] By the ninth day of the fourth month,
the hunger was terrible in the city. There
was no food for the people to eat. [7] Then
the city wall was broken through. And
the whole army ran away at night. They
went through the gate between the two
walls by the king's garden. The Babylonians were still surrounding the city.
Zedekiah and his men ran toward the
Jordan Valley.

[8] But the Babylonian army chased
King Zedekiah. They caught up with
him in the plains of Jericho. All of his
army was scattered from him. [9] So they
captured Zedekiah and took him to the
king of Babylon at Riblah. Riblah is in
the land of Hamath. There he passed
sentence on Zedekiah. [10] There at Riblah
the king of Babylon killed Zedekiah's
sons as he watched. The king also killed
all the officers of Judah. [11] Then he put
out Zedekiah's eyes. He put bronze
chains on him and took him to Babylon.
And the king kept Zedekiah in prison
there until the day he died.

[12] Nebuzaradan was the commander

52:1 Jeremiah This is not the prophet Jeremiah but a different man with the same name.

of the king's special guards. This servant of the king of Babylon came to Jerusalem. This was on the tenth day of the fifth month. This was in Nebuchadnezzar's nineteenth year as king of Babylon. [13]Nebuzaradan set fire to the Temple[d] of the Lord and the palace. He also set fire to all the houses of Jerusalem. Every important building was burned. [14]The whole Babylonian army broke down the walls around Jerusalem. That army was led by the commander of the king's special guards. [15]Nebuzaradan, the commander of the guards, took captive some of the poorest people. And he took those who were left in Jerusalem. He took captive those who had surrendered to the king of Babylon. And he took away the skilled craftsmen who were left in Jerusalem. [16]But Nebuzaradan left behind the rest of the poorest people of the land. They were to take care of the vineyards and fields.

[17]The Babylonians broke up the bronze pillars, the bronze stands and the large bronze bowl, which was called the Sea. These were in the Temple of the Lord. Then they carried all the bronze to Babylon. [18]They also took the pots, shovels, wick trimmers, bowls, dishes and all the bronze objects. They were used to serve in the Temple. [19]The commander of the king's special guards took these things away: bowls, pans for carrying hot coals and large bowls; pots, lampstands, pans and bowls used for drink offerings. He took everything that was made of pure gold or silver.

[20]There was so much bronze that it could not be weighed. There were two pillars. There was the large bronze bowl with the 12 bronze bulls under it. And there were the movable stands, which King Solomon had made for the Temple of the Lord. [21]Each of the pillars was about 27 feet high. Each pillar was 18 feet around and hollow. The wall of each pillar was 3 inches thick. [22]The bronze capital[d] on top of the pillar was about 7½ feet high.

It was decorated with a net design and bronze pomegranates[d] all around it. The other pillar also had pomegranates. It was like the first pillar. [23]There were 96 pomegranates on the sides of the pillars. There was a total of 100 pomegranates above the net design.

[24]The commander of the guards took some prisoners. He took Seraiah the chief priest, Zephaniah the priest next in rank, and the three doorkeepers. [25]The commander also took other people who were still in the city. He took the officer in charge of the fighting men. He also took seven people who advised the king. He also took the royal assistant who selected people for the army. And he took 60 other men who were in the city. [26]Nebuzaradan, the commander, took all these people. And he brought them to the king of Babylon at Riblah. [27]There at Riblah, in the land of Hamath, the king had them killed.

So the people of Judah were led away from their country as captives. [28]This is how many people Nebuchadnezzar took away as captives: in the seventh year, 3,023 Jews; [29]in Nebuchadnezzar's eighteenth year, 832 people from Jerusalem; [30]in Nebuchadnezzar's twenty-third year, Nebuzaradan took 745 Jews as captives. Nebuzaradan was the commander of the king's special guards.

In all 4,600 people were taken captive. [31]Jehoiachin king of Judah was in prison in Babylon for 37 years. That year Evil-Merodach became king of Babylon. He let Jehoiachin king of Judah out of prison that year. He set Jehoiachin free on the twenty-fifth day of the twelfth month. [32]Evil-Merodach spoke kindly to Jehoiachin. He gave Jehoiachin a seat of honor. It was above the seats of the other kings who were with him in Babylon. [33]So Jehoiachin put away his prison clothes. For the rest of his life, he ate at the king's table. [34]Every day the king of Babylon gave Jehoiachin an allowance. This lasted as long as he lived, until Jehoiachin died.

The Book of
LAMENTATIONS

1 Jerusalem once was full of people.
But now the city is empty.
Jerusalem once was a great city
among the nations.
But now she[n] has become like a
widow.
She was like a queen of all the
other cities.
But now she is a slave.

[2] She cries loudly at night.
Tears are on her cheeks.
There is no one to comfort her.
All her lovers are gone.
All her friends have turned against
her.
They have become her enemies.

[3] Judah has gone into captivity.
She has suffered and worked
hard.
She lives among other nations.
But she has found no rest.
Those who chased her caught her.
They caught her when she was in
trouble.

[4] The roads to Jerusalem are sad.
No one comes to Jerusalem for
the feasts.
No one passes through her gates.
And her priests groan.
Her young women are suffering.
And Jerusalem suffers terribly.

[5] Her enemies have become her
masters.
Her enemies enjoy the wealth
they have won.
The Lord is punishing her
for her many sins.
Her children have gone away.
They are captives of the enemy in
a foreign land.

[6] The beauty of Jerusalem
has gone away.
Her rulers are like deer
that cannot find food.
They are weak and have run away
from those who chased them.

[7] Jerusalem is suffering and
homeless.
She remembers all the precious
things
she had in the past.
She remembers when her people
were defeated by the enemy.
There was no one to help her.
When her enemies saw her,
they laughed to see her ruined.

[8] Jerusalem sinned terribly.
So she has become unclean.[d]
Those who honored her hate her
now
because they have seen her
nakedness.
Jerusalem groans
and turns away.

[9] Jerusalem made herself dirty by
her sins.
She did not think about what
would happen to her.
Her defeat was surprising.
There was no one to comfort her.
She says, "Lord, see how I suffer.
The enemy has won."

[10] The enemy reached out and took
all her precious things.
She even saw foreigners
enter her Temple.[d]
Lord, you had commanded
that they should not enter the
meeting of your people.

[11] All of Jerusalem's people are
groaning.
They are looking for bread.
They are giving away their precious
things for food
so they can stay alive.
The city says, "Look, Lord, and see.
I am hated."

[12] Jerusalem says, "You who pass by
on the road don't seem to care.
Come, look at me and see.
Is there any pain like mine?
Is there any pain like that he has
caused me?
The Lord has punished me
on the day of his great anger.

[13] "The Lord sent fire from above.
It went down into my bones.
He stretched out a net for my feet.
He turned me back.
He made me sad and lonely.
I am weak all day.

[14] "He has noticed my sins.
They are tied together by his
hands.
They hang around my neck.

1:1 **she** In this poem the city of Jerusalem is described as a woman.

He has turned my strength into
　weakness.
The Lord has let me be defeated
　by those who are stronger than I
　am.

¹⁵"The Lord has rejected
　all my mighty men inside my
　　walls.
He brought an army against me
　to destroy my young men.
As if in a winepress,ᵈ the Lord has
　crushed
　the capital city of Judah.

¹⁶"I cry about these things.
　My eyes overflow with tears.
There is no one near to comfort me.
　There is no one who can give me
　　strength again.
My children are left sad and lonely
　because the enemy has won."

¹⁷Jerusalem reaches out her hands,
　but there is no one to comfort
　　her.
The Lord has commanded for the
　people of Jacob
　that their enemies surround
　　them.
Jerusalem has become unclean
　like those around her.

¹⁸Jerusalem says, "The Lord is right.
　But I refused to obey him.
Listen, all you people.
　Look at my pain.
My young women and men
　have gone into captivity.

¹⁹"I called out to my friends,
　but they turned against me.
My priests and my older leaders
　have died in the city.
They were looking for food
　so they could stay alive.

²⁰"Look at me, Lord. I am upset.
　I am troubled.
My heart is troubled
　because I have been so stubborn.
Out in the streets, the sword kills.
　Inside the houses, death destroys.

²¹"People have heard my groaning.
　There is no one to comfort me.
All my enemies have heard of my
　trouble.
　They are happy that you have
　　done this to me.
Now bring that day you have
　announced.
　Let my enemies be like me.

²²"Look at all their evil.
　Do to them what you have done
　　to me
　because of all my sins.
I groan over and over again,
　and I am afraid."

2 Look how the Lord in his anger
　has brought Jerusalem to shame.
He has thrown down the greatness
　of Israel
　from the sky to the earth.
He did not remember the Temple,ᵈ
　his footstool,
　on the day of his anger.

²The Lord swallowed up without
　mercy
　all the houses of the people of
　　Jacob.
In his anger he pulled down
　the strong places of Judah.
He threw her kingdom and its rulers
　down to the ground in dishonor.

³In his anger the Lord has removed
　all the strength of Israel.
He took away his power from Israel
　when the enemy came.
He burned against the people of
　Jacob like a flaming fire
　that burns up everything around
　　it.

⁴Like an enemy, the Lord prepared
　to shoot his bow.
　He took hold of his sword.
Like an enemy, he killed
　all the good-looking people.
He poured out his anger like fire
　on the tents of Jerusalem.

⁵The Lord has become like an
　enemy.
　He has swallowed up Israel.
He has swallowed up all her
　palaces.
　He has destroyed all her strong
　　places.
He has caused more moaning and
　groaning
　for Judah.

⁶He has destroyed his Temple as if it
　were a garden tent.
　He has destroyed the place where
　　he met with his people.
The Lord has made Jerusalem
　forget
　the set feasts and Sabbathᵈ days.
He has rejected the king and the
　priest
　in his great anger.

[7]The Lord has rejected his altar
and abandoned his Temple.
He has given to the enemy
the walls of Jerusalem's palaces.
The enemy shouted in the Lord's
Temple
as if it were a feast day.

[8]The Lord planned to destroy
the wall around Jerusalem.
He marked the wall off with a
measuring line.
He did not stop himself from
destroying it.
He made the walls and defenses
sad.
Together they have fallen.

[9]Jerusalem's gates have fallen to the
ground.
He destroyed and smashed the
bars of the gates.
Her king and her princes are sent
away among the nations.
The teaching of the Lord has
stopped.
The prophets[d] have not had
any visions from the Lord.

[10]The older leaders of Jerusalem
sit on the ground and are silent.
They pour dust on their heads
and put on rough cloth to show
how sad they are.
The young women of Jerusalem
bow their heads to the ground in
sorrow.

[11]My eyes are weak from crying.
I am troubled.
I feel as if I have been poured out
on the ground
because my people have been
destroyed.
Children and babies are fainting
in the streets of the city.

[12]They say to their mothers,
"Where is some bread and
wine?"
They faint like wounded soldiers
in the streets of the city.
They die in their mothers' arms.

[13]What can I say about you,
Jerusalem?
What can I compare you to?
What can I say you are like?
How can I comfort you,
Jerusalem?
Your ruin is as big as the sea.
No one can heal you.

[14]Your prophets saw visions about
you.
But they were false and worth
nothing.
They did not expose your sins.
They did not keep you from
being captured.
The messages they preached to you
were false.
They fooled you.

[15]All who pass by on the road
clap their hands at you.
They make fun and shake their
heads
at Jerusalem.
They ask, "Is this the city that
people called
the most beautiful city,
the happiest city on earth?"

[16]All your enemies open their mouths
to say things against you.
They make fun and grind their
teeth in anger.
They say, "We have swallowed
her up.
This is the day we were waiting for.
We have finally seen it happen."

[17]The Lord has done what he
planned.
He has carried out the order
that he commanded long ago.
He has destroyed without mercy.
He has made your enemies happy
because of what happened to
you.
He has strengthened your enemies.

[18]The people
cry out to the Lord.
Wall of Jerusalem,
let your tears flow
like a river day and night.
Do not stop.
Do not let your eyes rest.

[19]Get up, cry out in the night.
Cry all through the night.
Pour out your heart like water
in prayer to the Lord.
Lift up your hands in prayer to him.
Pray for the life of your children.
They are fainting with hunger
on every street corner.

[20]Jerusalem says: "Look, Lord, and
see.
You have never done this to
anyone else.
Women eat their own babies,
the children they have cared for.

Priests and prophets
  are killed in the Temple of the
    Lord.

²¹"Young men and old men
  lie on the ground in the streets of
    the city.
My young women and young men
  have been killed by the sword.
You, Lord, killed them on the day
    of your anger.
You killed them without mercy.

²²"You invited terrors to come
    against me on every side.
  It was as if you were inviting
    them to a feast.
No one escaped or remained alive
  on the day of the Lord's anger.
My enemy has killed
  those whom I gave birth to and
    brought up."

3 I am a man who has seen the
      suffering
    that comes from the rod of the
      Lord's anger.
²He led me
    into darkness, not light.
³He turned his hand against me
    again and again, all day long.

⁴He caused my flesh and skin to
      wear out.
  He broke my bones.
⁵He surrounded me and attacked me
    with sadness and grief.
⁶He made me sit in the dark,
    like someone who has been dead
      a long time.

⁷He shut me in so I could not get
      out.
  He put heavy chains on me.
⁸I cry out and beg for help.
  But he ignores my prayer.
⁹He has blocked my way with
      stones.
  He has made my life difficult.

¹⁰The Lord is like a bear ready to
      attack me.
  He is like a lion in hiding.
¹¹He led me the wrong way and tore
    me to pieces.
  He left me without help.
¹²He prepared to shoot his bow.
  He made me the target for his
      arrows.

¹³He shot me in the kidneys
    with the arrows from his arrow
      bag.

¹⁴I have become a joke to all my
      people.
  All day long they make fun of me
      with songs.
¹⁵The Lord filled me with misery.
  He filled me with suffering.
¹⁶The Lord broke my teeth with
      gravel.
  He crushed me into the dirt.
¹⁷I have no more peace.
  I have forgotten what happiness is.
¹⁸I said, "My strength is gone.
  I have no more hope that the
      Lord will help me."

¹⁹Lord, remember my suffering and
    how I have no home.
  Remember the misery and
      suffering.
²⁰I remember them well.
  And I am very sad.
²¹But I have hope
    when I think of this:

²²The Lord's love never ends.
  His mercies never stop.
²³They are new every morning.
  Lord, your loyalty is great.
²⁴I say to myself, "The Lord is what I
      have left.
  So I have hope."

²⁵The Lord is good to those who put
      their hope in him.
  He is good to those who look to
      him for help.
²⁶It is good to wait quietly
    for the Lord to save.
²⁷It is good for a man to work hard
    while he is young.

²⁸He should sit alone and be quiet
    because the Lord has given him
      hard work to do.
²⁹He should bow to the Lord with his
      face to the ground.
  Maybe there is still hope.
³⁰He should offer his cheek if
    someone wants to hit him.
  He should be filled with shame.

³¹The Lord will not reject
    his people forever.
³²Although the Lord brings sorrow,
    he also has mercy.
  His love is great.
³³The Lord does not like to punish
      people
    or make them sad.

³⁴The Lord sees if any prisoner of the
      earth
    is crushed under his feet.

[35] He sees if someone is treated
unfairly
before the Most High God.
[36] The Lord sees
if someone is cheated in his case
in court.

[37] Nobody can speak and have it
happen
unless the Lord commands it.
[38] Both bad and good things
come by the command of the
Most High God.
[39] No man should complain
when he is punished for his sins.

[40] Let us examine and look at what
we have done.
Then let us return to the Lord.
[41] Let us lift up our hands and pray
from our hearts.
Let us say to God in heaven,
[42] "We have sinned and turned
against you.
And you have not forgiven us.

[43] "You wrapped yourself in anger
and chased us.
You killed us without mercy.
[44] You wrapped yourself in a cloud.
No prayer could get through.
[45] You made us like scum and trash
among the other nations.

[46] "All of our enemies
open their mouths and say things
against us.
[47] We have been frightened and
fearful.
We have been ruined and
destroyed."
[48] Streams of tears flow from my eyes
because my people are destroyed.

[49] My tears flow continually,
without stopping,
[50] until the Lord looks down
and sees from heaven.
[51] I am sad when I see
what has happened to all the
women of my city.

[52] Those who are my enemies for no
reason
hunted me like a bird.
[53] They threw me alive into a pit.
They threw stones at me.
[54] Water came up over my head.
I said to myself, "I am going to
die."
[55] I called out to you, Lord,
from the bottom of the pit.

[56] You heard me calling, "Do not
close your ears.
Do not ignore my cry for help."
[57] You came close when I called out to
you.
You said, "Don't be afraid."

[58] Lord, you have taken my case.
You have given me back my life.
[59] Lord, you have seen how I have
been wronged.
Now judge my case for me.
[60] You have seen how my enemies
took revenge on me.
You have seen all their evil plans
against me.

[61] Lord, you have heard their insults
and all their evil plans against
me.
[62] The words and thoughts of my
enemies
are against me all the time.
[63] Look! In everything they do
they make fun of me with songs.

[64] Punish them as they should be
punished, Lord.
Pay them back for what they
have done.
[65] Make them stubborn.
Put your curse on them.
[66] Chase them in anger.
Destroy them from the Lord's
earth.

4 See how the gold has lost its shine!
See how the good gold has
changed!
The stones of the Temple[d] are
scattered
at every street corner.

[2] The precious people of Jerusalem
were more valuable than gold.
But now they are thought of as clay
jars
made by the hands of a potter.

[3] Even wild dogs give their milk
to feed their young.
But my people are cruel
like ostriches in the desert.

[4] The baby is so thirsty
that his tongue sticks to the roof
of his mouth.
Children beg for bread.
But no one breaks off a piece to
share with them.

[5] Those who once ate fine foods
are now starving in the streets.

The people who grew up wearing
   nice clothes
now pick through trash piles.

⁶My people have been punished
   more than Sodom was.
Sodom was destroyed suddenly.
   No hands reached out to help
   her.

⁷Our princes were purer than snow.
   They were whiter than milk.
Their bodies were redder than
   rubies.
   Their faces shined like sapphires.

⁸But now they are blacker than coal.
   No one even recognizes them in
   the streets.
Their skin is stretched over their
   bones.
   It is as dry as wood.

⁹Those people who were killed by
   the sword had it better
than those killed by hunger.
They starved in pain and died
   because there was no food from
   the field.

¹⁰With their own hands kind women
   cooked their own children.
The children became food for their
   parents.
   This happened when my people
   were destroyed.

¹¹The Lord turned loose all of his
   anger.
He poured out his strong anger.
He set fire to Jerusalem.
   It burned down to the
   foundations.

¹²Kings of the earth and people of
   the world
could not believe it.
They could not believe that enemies
   could come through the gates of
   Jerusalem.

¹³But it happened because her
   prophets[d] had sinned.
   And her priests had done evil.
They killed in the city
   the people who did what was
   right.

¹⁴They wandered in the streets
   like blind men.
They became dirty with blood.
   So no one could touch their
   clothes.

¹⁵"Go away! You are unclean,"[d]
   people shouted at them.
"Get away! Get away! Do not
   touch us!"
So they left and wandered around.
   The other nations said, "Don't
   stay here."

¹⁶The Lord himself scattered them.
   He did not look after them
   anymore.
He did not respect the priests.
   He showed no mercy to the older
   leaders.

¹⁷Also, our eyes grew tired
   looking for help that never came.
We kept watch from our towers
   for a nation to save us.

¹⁸Our enemies hunted us
   so we could not even walk in the
   streets.
Our end came near. Our time was
   up.
   Our end came.

¹⁹The men who chased us
   were faster than eagles in the
   sky.
They ran us into the mountains.
   They ambushed us in the desert.

²⁰The Lord's appointed king, who
   was our very breath,
was caught in their traps.
We had said about him, "We will be
   protected by him
   among the nations."

²¹Be happy and glad, people of
   Edom,
you who live in the land of Uz.
But the Lord's anger is like a cup of
   wine that you also will have to
   drink.
   Then you will get drunk on it and
   make yourselves naked.

²²Your punishment is complete,
   Jerusalem.
He will not keep you in captivity
   any longer.
But the Lord will punish your
   wrongs, people of Edom.
   He will uncover your sins.

5 Remember, Lord, what happened to
   us.
Look and see our disgrace.
²Our land has been turned over to
   strangers.
   Our houses have been given to
   foreigners.

³We have become orphans with no
father.
　Our mothers have become like
　widows.
⁴We have to buy the water we drink.
　We must pay for the wood for our
　fires.
⁵They work us hard as if we were
　animals with a yoke[d] on our
　necks.
　We get tired and have no rest.
⁶We made an agreement with Egypt
　and with Assyria to get enough
　food.
⁷Our ancestors sinned against you.
　But they are gone.
　Now we must suffer because of
　their sins.
⁸Slaves have become our rulers.
　There is no one who can save us
　from them.
⁹We risk our lives to get our food
　because there are men with
　swords in the desert.
¹⁰Our skin is hot like an oven.
　We burn with fever because of
　the terrible hunger.
¹¹The enemy attacked the women of
　Jerusalem
　and the girls in the cities of
　Judah.
¹²The enemy hung our princes by the
　hands.

　They do not honor our older
　leaders.
¹³The young men grind grain at the
　mill.
　Boys stumble while carrying
　loads of wood.
¹⁴The older leaders no longer sit at
　the city gates.
　The young men no longer make
　music.
¹⁵We have no more joy in our hearts.
　Our dancing has turned into
　sadness.
¹⁶The glory has gone from Jerusalem.
　How terrible it is for us because
　we have sinned.
¹⁷Because of this we are afraid.
　Because of these things our eyes
　are dim.
¹⁸Mount Zion[d] is empty.
　Now wild dogs wander around it.
¹⁹But you rule forever, Lord.
　You will be King from now on.
²⁰Why have you forgotten us for so
　long?
　Why have you left us for so long?
²¹Bring us back to you, Lord. We will
　return.
　Make our days as they were
　before.
²²Or have you completely rejected
　us?
　Will your anger never end?

The Book of
EZEKIEL

1 It was the thirtieth year, on the fifth
day of the fourth month of our captivity. I, Ezekiel, was by the Kebar River in
Babylon. I was among the people who
had been carried away as captives from
the land of Judah. The sky opened, and
I saw visions of God.

²It was the fifth year that King Jehoiachin had been a prisoner. It was on the
fifth day of the month. ³The Lord spoke
his word to Ezekiel son of Buzi. This
was in the land of the Babylonians by
the Kebar River. There he felt the power
of the Lord.

⁴When I looked, I saw a stormy wind
coming from the north. There was a
great cloud with a bright light around it.
Fire was flashing out of it. And there
was something that looked like glowing
metal in the center of the fire. ⁵Inside the

cloud were what looked like four living
creatures. They were shaped like men.
⁶Each of them had four faces. And each
of them had four wings. ⁷Their legs were
straight. Their feet were like a calf's
hoofs. And they sparkled like polished
bronze. ⁸The living creatures had men's
hands. They were under their wings on
their four sides. All four of them had
faces and wings. ⁹And their wings
touched each other. The living creatures
did not turn when they moved. Each
went straight ahead.

¹⁰Their faces looked like this: In front
each living creature had the face of a
man. Each one had the face of a lion on
the right side. Each one had the face of
an ox on the left side. And in back each
one had the face of an eagle. ¹¹This was
what their faces looked like. Their

wings were spread out above. Each had two wings that touched one of the other living creatures. Each living creature had two wings that covered its body. [12]Each went straight ahead. Wherever the spirit would go, the living creatures would also go. When they went, they did not turn. [13]The living creatures looked like burning coals of fire. They were like torches. Fire went back and forth among the living creatures. It was bright, and lightning flashed from it. [14]The living creatures ran back and forth like bolts of lightning.

[15]Now I looked at the living creatures. And I saw a wheel on the ground by each of the living creatures with its four faces. [16]The wheels and the way they were made were like this: They looked like sparkling chrysolite. All four of them looked the same. The wheels looked like one wheel crossways inside another wheel. [17]When they moved, they went in any one of the four directions. They did not turn as they went. [18]I saw the rims of the wheels. The rims were full of eyes all around.

[19]When the living creatures moved, the wheels moved beside them. When the living creatures were lifted up from the ground, the wheels also were lifted up. [20]Wherever the spirit would go, the living creatures would go. And the wheels were lifted up beside them. This is because the spirit of the living creatures was in the wheels. [21]When the living creatures moved, the wheels moved. When the living creatures stopped, the wheels stopped. And when the living creatures were lifted from the ground, the wheels were lifted beside them. This is because the spirit of the living creatures was in the wheels.

[22]Now there was something like a dome over the heads of the living creatures. It sparkled like ice and was frightening. [23]And under the dome the wings of the living creatures were stretched out straight toward one another. Each living creature also had two wings covering its body. [24]I heard the sound of their wings as they moved. It was like the roaring sound of the sea. It was like the voice of God All-Powerful. It was a roaring sound like a noisy army. When the living creatures stood still, they lowered their wings.

[25]And a voice came from above the dome over the heads of the living creatures. When the living creatures stood still, they lowered their wings. [26]Now

above the dome there was something that looked like a throne. It looked like a sapphire gem. And on the throne was a shape like a man. [27]Then I noticed what he looked like from the waist up. He looked like glowing metal with fire inside it. And from his waist down he looked like fire. I saw a bright light all around him. [28]The glow around him looked like the rainbow in the clouds on a rainy day. It seemed to look like the glory of the Lord. So when I saw it, I bowed facedown on the ground. And I heard a voice speaking.

2 He said to me, "Human being, stand up on your feet. Then I will speak with you." [2]While he spoke to me, the Spirit[d] entered me and put me on my feet. Then I heard the Lord speaking to me.

[3]He said, "Human being, I am sending you to the people of Israel. They are a nation of people who turned against me. They broke away from me. They and their ancestors have sinned against me until this very day. [4]And I am sending you to people who are stubborn. They do not obey. You will say this to them, 'This is what the Lord God says.' [5]The people may listen, or they may not. They are a people who turn against me. But whatever they do, they will know that a prophet[d] has been among them. [6]You, human being, don't be afraid of the people or their words. Thorny branches and thorns may be all around you. And you may live with insects that sting with poison. Don't be afraid of their words. Don't be afraid of their looks. They are a people who turn against me. [7]But speak my words to them. They may listen, or they may not, because they turn against me. [8]But you, human being, listen to what I say to you. Don't turn against me as those people do. Open your mouth and eat what I am giving you."

[9]I looked and saw a hand stretched out to me. A scroll was in the hand. [10]The Lord opened the scroll in front of me. The scroll was written on the front and back. Funeral songs, sad writings and troubles were written on the scroll.

3 Then the Lord said to me, "Human being, eat what you find. Eat this scroll. Then go and speak to the people of Israel." [2]So I opened my mouth, and the Lord gave me the scroll.

[3]The Lord said to me, "Human being, eat this scroll which I am giving you. Fill

your stomach with it." Then I ate it. And it was sweet like honey in my mouth.

⁴Then the Lord said to me, "Human being, go to the people of Israel. Speak my words to them. ⁵You are not being sent to people whose speech you can't understand. Their language is not difficult. You are being sent to Israel. ⁶You are not being sent to many nations whose speech you can't understand. The language of Israel is not difficult. You are not being sent to people whose words you cannot understand. If I had sent you to them, they would have listened to you. ⁷But the people of Israel are not willing to listen to you. This is because they are not willing to listen to me. Yes, all the people of Israel are stubborn and will not obey. ⁸See, I have made you as stubborn as they are. You will be as hard as they are. ⁹I have made you as hard as a diamond, harder than stone. Don't be afraid of them. Don't be frightened by them. They are a people who turn against me."

¹⁰Also, the Lord said to me, "Human being, believe all the words that I will speak to you. And listen carefully. ¹¹Go to the captives, your people. And speak to them, whether they listen or not. Tell them, 'The Lord God says this.'"

¹²Then the Spirit lifted me up. And I heard a loud rumbling sound behind me. A voice said, "Praise God in heaven." ¹³I heard the wings of the living creatures touching each other. And I heard the sound of the wheels by them. It was a loud rumbling sound. ¹⁴So the Spirit lifted me up and took me away. I was unhappy and angry. I felt the great power of the Lord. ¹⁵I came to the captives from Judah. They lived by the Kebar River at Tel Abib. I sat there seven days where these people lived. I was shocked.

¹⁶After seven days the Lord spoke his word to me again. He said, ¹⁷"Human being, I have made you a watchman for Israel. Any time you hear a word from my mouth, warn them for me. ¹⁸When I say to an evil person, 'You will surely die,' you must warn him. If you don't speak out to warn the evil person to leave his evil way, he will die in his sin. But I will hold you responsible for his death. ¹⁹You must warn the evil person. Then if he does not turn from his wickedness or his evil ways, he will die because of his sin. But you will have saved yourself.

²⁰"Again, a person who does right may turn away from his goodness. He may do evil. If I caused him to sin, he will die. Because you have not warned him, he will die because of his sin. And the good he did will not be remembered. But I will hold you responsible for his death. ²¹But if you do warn that good person not to sin, he may not sin. Then he will surely live. This is because he was warned. And you will save yourself."

²²Then I felt the power of the Lord there. He said to me, "Get up and go out to the plain. There I will speak to you." ²³So I got up and went out to the plain. I saw the glory of the Lord standing there. It was like the glory I saw by the Kebar River. And I bowed facedown on the ground.

²⁴Then the Spirit[d] entered me and made me stand on my feet. He spoke to me and said, "Go, shut yourself up in your house. ²⁵As for you, human being, the people will tie you up with ropes. They will tie you up, and you will not be able to go out among them. ²⁶Also, I will make your tongue stick to the roof of your mouth. Then you will be silent. And you will not be able to argue with the people, even though they turn against me. ²⁷But when I speak to you, I will open your mouth. And you will say, 'The Lord God says this.' Whoever will listen, let him listen. Whoever refuses, let him refuse. They are a people who turn against me.

4 "Now, human being, get yourself a brick. Put it in front of you and draw a map of Jerusalem on it. ²Then surround it with an army. Build battle works against the city. Build a road of earth to the top of the city walls. Set up camps around it. Put heavy logs in place to break down the walls. ³Then get yourself an iron plate. Put it up like an iron wall between you and the city. Turn your face toward the city as if to attack it. Then surround it and attack it. This is a sign to Israel.

⁴"Then lie down on your left side. Take the guilt of Israel on yourself. Their guilt will be on you for the number of days you lie on your left side. ⁵I have given you the same number of days as the years of the people's sin. So you will have the guilt of Israel's sin on you for 390 days.

⁶"When you have finished these 390 days, lie down a second time. This time lie on your right side. You will then have the guilt of Judah on you. I have given it to you for 40 days. This is a day for each

year of their sin. ⁷Then you will turn your face toward the army attacking Jerusalem. With your arm bare, you will prophesy[d] against Jerusalem. ⁸I will put ropes on you so you cannot turn from one side to the other. This will last until you have finished the days of your attack on Jerusalem.

⁹"Take wheat, barley, beans, small peas and millet seeds. And put them in one bowl. Make them into bread for yourself. You will eat it the 390 days you lie on your side. ¹⁰You will eat eight ounces of food every day. You will eat it at set times. ¹¹You will drink about two-thirds of a quart of water every day. Drink it at set times. ¹²Eat your food as you would eat a barley cake. Bake it over human dung where the people can see." ¹³Then the Lord said, "In the same way Israel will eat unclean[d] food. They will eat it among the nations where I force them to go."

¹⁴But I said, "No, Lord God! I have never been made unclean. From the time I was young until now I've never eaten anything that died by itself. And I've never eaten anything torn by animals. Unclean meat has never entered my mouth."

¹⁵"Very well," he said. "Then I will give you cow's dung instead of human dung. You may use it for your fire to bake your bread."

¹⁶Then the Lord said to me, "Human being, look! I am going to cut off the supply of bread to Jerusalem. They will eat the bread that is measured out to them. And they will worry as they eat it. They will drink water that is measured out to them. And they will be in shock as they drink it. ¹⁷This is because bread and water will be hard to find. And the people will be shocked at the sight of each other. They will become weak because of their sin.

5 "Now, human being, take a sharp sword. Use it like a barber's razor to shave your head and beard. Then take scales and weigh and divide the hair. ²Burn one-third with fire when the days of the attack on Jerusalem are over. Burn it in the middle of the city. Then take one-third and cut it up with the knife all around the city. And scatter one-third to the wind. This is how I will chase them with a sword. ³Also take a few of these hairs and tie them in the folds of your clothes. ⁴Take a few more and throw them into the fire and burn

them up. From there a fire will spread to all the people of Israel.

⁵"This is what the Lord says: This is Jerusalem. I have put her at the center of the nations with countries all around her. ⁶But she has refused to obey my laws. She has been more evil than the nations. She has refused to obey my rules even more than those around her. The people of Jerusalem have rejected my laws and have not lived by my rules. ⁷"So this is what the Lord God says: You caused more confusion than the nations around you. You did not follow my rules or obey my laws. You have not even obeyed the laws of the nations around you.

⁸"So this is what the Lord God says: I myself am against you. I will punish you and the nations will watch. ⁹I will do things among you that I have not done before. I will never do anything like them again. I will do them because you do the things I hate. ¹⁰So fathers among you will eat their children. And children will eat their fathers. I will punish you. I will scatter to the winds all who are left alive. ¹¹So the Lord God says: As surely as I live, you have made my Temple[d] unclean.[d] You have done it with all your evil idols and the hated things you do. Because of this I will cut you off. I will have no pity. I will show no mercy. ¹²A third of you will die by disease or be destroyed by hunger inside your walls. A third will fall dead by the sword outside your walls. And a third I will scatter in every direction. I will chase them with a sword. ¹³Then my anger will come to an end. I will use it up against them. Then I will be satisfied. Then they will know that I, the Lord God, have spoken. After I have carried out my anger against them, they will know how strongly I felt.

¹⁴"I will make you a ruin. And I will make you a shame among the nations around you. All who pass by will see this. ¹⁵Then you will be shamed by the nations around you. They will make fun of you. You will be a warning to them. They will be terrified. This will happen when I punish you in my great anger. I, the Lord, have spoken. ¹⁶I will send a time of hunger to destroy you. Then I will make your hunger get even worse. I will cut off your supply of food. ¹⁷I will send a time of hunger and wild animals against you. They will kill your children. Disease and death will sweep through your people. I will bring the sword

against you to kill you. I, the Lord, have spoken."

6 Again the Lord spoke his word to me. The Lord said, [2]"Human being, look toward the mountains of Israel. Prophesy[d] against them. [3]Say, 'Mountains of Israel, listen to the word of the Lord God. The Lord God says this to the mountains, the hills, the ravines and the valleys: I will bring a sword against you. I will destroy your places of idol worship. [4]Your altars will be destroyed. Your incense[d] altars will be broken down. Your people will be killed in front of your idols. [5]I will lay the dead bodies of the Israelites before their idols. And I will scatter your bones around your altars. [6]In all the places you live, cities will become empty. And the places of idol worship will be ruined. Your altars will become lonely ruins. Your idols will be broken and brought to an end. Your incense altars will be cut down. And the things you made will be wiped out. [7]Your people will be killed and fall among you. Then you will know that I am the Lord God.

[8]"But I will leave some people alive. Some will not be killed by the nations when you are scattered among the foreign lands. [9]Then those who have escaped will remember me. They will be living among the nations where they have been taken as captives. They will remember how I was hurt because they were unfaithful to me. They had turned away from me. They will remember how I was hurt because they desired to worship their idols. They will hate themselves because of the evil things they did that I hate. [10]Then they will know that I am the Lord. I did not bring this terrible thing on them for no reason.

[11]"This is what the Lord God says: Clap your hands, stamp your feet. Say, "Oh!" because the people of Israel have done terrible things. So they will die by war, hunger and disease. [12]The person who is far away will die by disease. The one who is nearby will die in war. The person who is still alive and has escaped these will die from hunger. So I will carry out my anger on them. [13]Their people will lie dead among their idols around the altars. They will be on every high hill, on all the mountain tops and under every green tree and leafy oak. These are the places where they offered sweet-smelling incense to their idols. Then you will know that I am the Lord. [14]I will use my power against them. I will

make the land empty and wasted from the desert to Diblah, wherever they live. Then they will know that I am the Lord.'"

7 Again the Lord spoke his word to me. He said: [2]"Human being, the Lord says this to the land of Israel: An end! The end has come on the four corners of the land. [3]Now the end has come for you. I will send my anger against you. I will judge you for the way you have lived. I will make you pay for your terrible actions. [4]I will have no pity on you. I will not hold back punishment from you. I will make you pay for your ways and for your terrible actions. Then you will know that I am the Lord.

[5]"This is what the Lord God says: Disaster on top of disaster is coming. [6]The end has come! The end has come! It has stirred itself up against you! Look! It has come! [7]The end has come for you who live in the land! The time has come. The day of confusion is near. There will be no happy shouting on the mountains. [8]Soon I will pour out my anger against you. I will carry out my anger against you. I will judge you for the way you have lived. I will make you pay for all the things you have done that I hate. [9]I will show no pity. I will not hold back punishment. I will pay you back for the way you have lived and the terrible things you have done. Then you will know that I am the Lord who punishes.

[10]"Look, the day is here. It has come. Destruction has come. Violence has grown. There is more pride than ever. [11]Violence has grown into a weapon for punishing wickedness. None of the people will be left. None of that crowd, none of their wealth, and nothing of value will be left among them. [12]The time has come. The day has arrived. Don't let the buyer be happy or the seller be sad. My burning anger is against the whole crowd. [13]Sellers will not return to the land they have sold as long as they live. This is because the vision against all that crowd will not be changed. Because of their sins, no one will save his life. [14]They have blown the trumpet, and everything is ready. But no one is going to the battle. My anger is against all that crowd.

[15]"The sword is outside. Disease and hunger are inside. The person who is in the field will die by the sword. Hunger and disease will destroy those in the city. [16]Those who are left alive and who escape will be on the mountains. They

will moan like doves of the valleys. Each person will groan about his own sin. [17]All hands will hang weakly. All knees will become as weak as water. [18]They will put on rough cloth to show how sad they are. They will tremble all over with fear. Their faces will show their shame. And all their heads will be shaved. [19]The people will throw their silver into the streets. Their gold will be like trash. Their silver and gold will not save them from the Lord's anger. It will not satisfy their hunger or fill their stomachs. It was what caused them to fall into sin. [20]They were proud of their beautiful jewelry. They used it to make their idols, which I hate, and their evil statues. So I will turn their wealth into something they hate. [21]And I will give it to the foreigners as treasures from war. I will give it to the evil people of the earth as treasure. These foreigners and evil people will dishonor the people's jewelry. [22]I will also turn away from the people of Israel. They will dishonor my treasured place. Then robbers will enter and dishonor it.

[23]"Make chains for captives. The land is full of bloody crimes. And the city is full of violence. [24]So I will bring the worst of the nations to take over the people's houses. I will also end the pride of the rich. And their holy places will be dishonored. [25]When the people are suffering greatly, they will look for peace. But there will be none. [26]Disaster will come on top of disaster. Rumor will be added to rumor. Then they will try to get a vision from a prophet.[d] Even the teachings of God from the priest will be lost. And advice from the older leaders will also be lost. [27]The king will cry greatly. The prince will give up hope. The hands of the people who owned land will shake with fear. I will punish them for the way they have lived. The way they have judged others is the way I will judge them. Then they will know that I am the Lord."

8 It was the sixth year, on the fifth day of the sixth month of our captivity. I was sitting in my house with the older leaders of Judah before me. There I felt the power of the Lord God. [2]I looked and saw something that looked like a man. From his waist down he looked like fire. From his waist up he looked like bright

glowing metal. [3]He stretched out the shape of a hand. And he caught me by the hair on my head. The Spirit[d] lifted me up between the earth and the sky. He took me in the visions of God to Jerusalem. He took me to the entrance to the north gate of the inner courtyard of the Temple.[d] The courtyard was where the idol was that caused God to be jealous. [4]The glory of the God of Israel was there. It was like what I had seen on the plain.

[5]Then God said to me, "Human being, now look toward the north." So I looked up toward the north. I saw an altar to the north of the gate. The idol that caused God to be jealous was in the entrance.

[6]The Lord said to me, "Human being, do you see what they are doing? Do you see how many hated things the people of Israel are doing here? This will drive me far away from my Temple. But you will see things more hated than these."

[7]Then the Lord brought me to the entry of the courtyard. When I looked, I saw a hole in the wall. [8]The Lord said to me, "Human being, dig through the wall." So I dug through the wall and saw an entrance.

[9]Then the Lord said to me, "Go in and see the terrible, evil things they are doing here." [10]So I entered and looked. And I saw pictures of every kind of crawling thing. I saw awful beasts and all the idols of the people of Israel. They were carved on the wall all around. [11]Seventy of the older leaders of Israel were standing there. They were in front of these carvings and idols. Jaazaniah son of Shaphan stood with them. Each man had his pan for burning incense[d] in his hand. A sweet-smelling cloud of incense was rising.

[12]Then the Lord said to me, "Human being, have you seen what the older leaders of Israel are doing in the dark? Have you seen each man in the room of his own idol? They say, 'The Lord doesn't see us. The Lord has left the land.'" [13]And he said to me, "You will see even more terrible things that they are doing."

[14]Then the Lord brought me to the opening of the north gate of the Temple. And I saw women sitting there crying for Tammuz.[n] [15]The Lord said to me, "Do

8:14 Tammuz Tammuz was a false god in Babylon. Every year people thought this god died when the plants died. After they cried for him, they believed he came back to life and the plants lived again.

you see, human being? You will see things even more terrible than these."

[16]Then the Lord brought me into the inner courtyard of the Temple. And I saw about 25 men. They were at the entrance to the Temple, between the porch and the altar. Their backs were turned to the Temple of the Lord. They faced east. They were worshiping the sun in the east.

[17]The Lord said to me, "Do you see, human being? Is it unimportant that the people of Judah are doing the terrible things they have done here? They have filled the land with violence. They continually make me angry. Look, they are insulting me every way they can. [18]So I will act in anger. I will have no pity. I will not show mercy. Even if they shout in my ears, I won't listen to them."

9 The Lord shouted with a loud voice in my ears. He said, "You who are chosen to punish this city, come near. Bring your weapon in your hand." [2]Then six men came from the direction of the upper gate, which faces north. Each had his powerful weapon in his hand. Among them was a man dressed in linen. At his side he had things to write with. The men went in and stood by the bronze altar.

[3]Then the glory of the God of Israel went up. It had been above the creatures with wings. It moved to the place in the Temple[d] where the door opened. Then the Lord called the man dressed in linen. He had the things to write with at his side. [4]The Lord said to him, "Go through Jerusalem. Put a mark on the foreheads of the people who groan and cry about all the terrible things being done among them."

[5]As I listened, the Lord spoke to the other men. He said, "Go through the city behind the man dressed in linen and kill. Don't pity anyone. Don't show mercy. [6]Kill and destroy old men, young men and women, little children and older women. But don't touch anyone who has the mark on him. Start at my Temple." So they started with the older leaders who were in front of the Temple.

[7]And the Lord said to the men, "Make the Temple unclean.[d] Fill the courtyards with those who have been killed. Go out!" Then the men went out and killed the people in the city. [8]While the men were killing the people, I was left alone. I bowed facedown on the ground. I cried out, "Oh, Lord God! Will you destroy

everyone left alive in Israel when you turn loose your anger on Jerusalem?"

[9]Then the Lord said to me, "The sin of the people of Israel and Judah is very great. The land is filled with people who murder. And the city is full of people who are not fair. The people say, 'The Lord has left the land. And the Lord does not see.' [10]But I will have no pity. I will show no mercy. But I will bring their evil acts back on their heads."

[11]Then the man dressed in linen reported to the Lord. He was the man who had things to write with at his side. He said, "I have done just as you have commanded me."

10 Then I looked and saw the sky above the heads of the living creatures. I saw something like a sapphire gem. It looked like a throne. [2]The Lord said to the man dressed in linen, "Go in between the wheels under the living creatures. And fill your hands with coals of fire from between the living creatures. Scatter the coals over the city."

As I watched, the man with linen clothes went in. [3]Now the living creatures were standing on the south side of the Temple[d] when the man went in. And the cloud from the Lord filled the inner courtyard. [4]Then the glory of the Lord went up from the living creatures. And it stood over the door of the Temple. The Temple was filled with the cloud. And the courtyard was full of the brightness from the glory of the Lord. [5]The sound of the wings of the living creatures was heard all the way to the outer courtyard. It was like the voice of God All-Powerful when he speaks.

[6]The Lord commanded the man dressed in linen, "Take fire from between the wheels, from between the living creatures." Then the man went in and stood by a wheel. [7]One living creature put out his hand to the fire that was among them. The living creature took some of the fire. And he put it in the hands of the man dressed in linen. The man took the fire and went out.

[8]Something that looked like a man's hand appeared under the wings of the living creatures. [9]I saw the four wheels by the living creatures. One wheel was by each living creature. The wheels looked like shining chrysolite. [10]All four wheels looked alike. Each looked like a wheel crossways inside another wheel. [11]When the wheels moved, they went in any of the directions that the four living creatures faced. The wheels did not turn

about. The living creatures did not turn their bodies as they went. But they followed wherever their faces pointed. [12]All their bodies, their backs, hands, wings and the wheels were full of eyes all over. Now each of the four living creatures had a wheel. [13]I heard the wheels being called "whirling wheels." [14]Each living creature had four faces. The first face was the face of a creature with wings. The second face was the face of a man. The third was the face of a lion. And the fourth was the face of an eagle.

[15]The living creatures flew up. They were the same living creatures I had seen by the Kebar River. [16]And when the living creatures moved, the wheels moved by their sides. The living creatures lifted their wings to fly up from the ground. And the wheels did not leave their sides. [17]When the living creatures stopped, the wheels stopped. When the creatures went up, the wheels went up also. This was because the spirit of the living creatures was in the wheels.

[18]Then the glory of the Lord left the door of the Temple[d] and stood over the living creatures. [19]The living creatures spread their wings. And they flew up from the ground while I watched. As they went up, the wheels stayed by their sides. They stood where the east gate of the Temple of the Lord opened. The glory of the God of Israel was over them. [20]These are the living creatures I had seen under the God of Israel. This was by the Kebar River. I knew they were called cherubim. [21]Each one had four faces. Each one had four wings. Things that looked like a man's hands were under their wings. [22]Their faces looked the same as the ones I had seen by the Kebar River. They each went straight ahead.

11 The Spirit[d] lifted me up. And he brought me to the front gate of the Temple[d] of the Lord. This gate faces east. I saw 25 men where the gate opens. I saw Jaazaniah son of Azzur and Pelatiah son of Benaiah. They were leaders of the people. They were among these 25 men. [2]Then the Lord said to me, "Human being, these are the men who plan evil. And they give wicked advice in this city of Jerusalem. [3]They say, 'It is almost time for us to build houses. This city is like a cooking pot. And we are like the best meat.' [4]So prophesy[d] against them. Prophesy, human being."

[5]Then the Spirit of the Lord entered me. He told me to say: "This is what the Lord says: You have said these things, people of Israel. But I know what is going through your mind. [6]You have killed many people in this city. You have filled its streets with their bodies.

[7]"So this is what the Lord God says: Those people you have killed and left in the middle of the city are like the best meat. And this city is like the cooking pot. But I will force you out of the city. [8]You have feared the sword. But I will bring a sword against you, says the Lord God. [9]I will force you out of the city. I will hand you over to strangers. I will surely punish you. [10]You will die by the sword. I will punish you at the border of Israel. Then you will know that I am the Lord. [11]This city will not be your cooking pot. You will not be the best meat in the middle of the city. I will punish you at the border of Israel. [12]Then you will know that I am the Lord. You did not live by my rules. You did not obey my laws. You did the same things that the nations around you do."

[13]As I prophesied, Pelatiah son of Benaiah died. Then I bowed facedown on the ground. I shouted with a loud voice and said, "Oh no, Lord God! Will you completely destroy the Israelites who are left alive?"

[14]The Lord spoke his word to me. He said, [15]"Human being, the people still in Jerusalem have spoken about your relatives. And they have spoken about all the people of Israel who are captives with you. The people still in Jerusalem have said, 'They are far from the Lord. This land was given to us as our property.'

[16]"So say, 'This is what the Lord God says: I sent the people far away among the nations. I scattered them among the countries. But for a little while I have become a Temple[d] to them in the countries where they have gone.'

[17]"So say: 'This is what the Lord God says: I will gather you from the nations. And I will bring you together from the countries where you have been scattered. Then I will give you back the land of Israel.'

[18]"They will come to this land. Then they will take away all the hated idols from the land. They will take all the terrible images from there. [19]I will give them a desire to respect me completely. I will put a new way to think inside them. I will take out the stubborn heart like stone from their bodies. Then I will give them an obedient heart of flesh.

[20]Then they will live by my rules. They will obey my laws and keep them. They will be my people, and I will be their God. [21]But some people will want to serve their evil statues and hated idols. And I will pay them back for their evil ways, says the Lord God."

[22]Then the living creatures lifted their wings. The wheels went beside them. And the glory of the God of Israel was above them. [23]The glory of the Lord went up from inside Jerusalem. And it stopped on the mountain on the east side of the city. [24]The Spirit[d] lifted me up. And he brought me to the captives who had been taken from Judah to Babylonia. He did this in a vision given by the Spirit of God. Then the vision I had seen ended. [25]And I told the things that the Lord had shown me. I told it to the captives from Judah.

12

Again the Lord spoke his word to me. He said: [2]"Human being, you are living among a people who refuse to obey. They have eyes to see, but they do not see. They have ears to hear, but they do not hear. This is because they are a family that refuses to obey.

[3]"So, human being, pack your things as if you will be taken away captive. And walk away like a captive. Do this in the daytime with the people watching. Move from your place to another with the people watching. Maybe they will understand, even though they are a people who refuse to obey. [4]Bring out the things you would pack as a captive. Do it during the day when the people are watching. At evening go out with the people watching. Go like those who are taken away as captives from their country. [5]Dig a hole through the wall while they watch. Bring your things out through the hole. [6]Lift them onto your shoulders with the people watching. Carry them out in the dark. Cover your face so you cannot see the ground. I have made you a sign to the people of Israel."

[7]I did these things as I was commanded. In the daytime I brought out my things. I was packed, ready to go away as a captive. Then in the evening I dug through the wall with my hands. I brought my things out in the dark. I carried them on my shoulders. And the people saw all this.

[8]Then in the morning the Lord spoke his word to me. He said: [9]"Human being, Israel refuses to obey. Didn't those people ask you, 'What are you doing?'

[10]"Say to them, 'This is what the Lord God says: This message is about the king in Jerusalem. And it is about all the people of Israel who live there.' [11]Say, 'I am a sign to you.'

"The same things I have done will be done to the people in Jerusalem. They will be taken away from their country as captives. [12]The king among them will put his things on his shoulder in the dark. And he will leave. The people will dig a hole through the wall to bring him out. He will cover his face so he cannot see the ground. [13]But I will spread my net over him. He will be caught in my trap. Then I will bring him to Babylon in the land of the Babylonians. He will not see that land, but he will die there. [14]All who are around the king I will scatter in every direction. I will scatter his helpers and all his army. I will chase them with a sword.

[15]"Then they will know that I am the Lord. I will scatter them among the nations. And I will spread them among the countries. [16]But I will save a few of them from the sword. I will save a few from hunger and disease. Then they can tell about their hated actions among the nations where they go. Then they will know that I am the Lord."

[17]The Lord spoke his word to me. He said: [18]"Human being, shake as you eat your food. Shake with fear as you drink your water. [19]Then say to the people of the land: 'This is what the Lord God says about the people who live in Jerusalem in the land of Israel: They will eat their food with fear. And they will drink their water in shock. This is because their land will be made empty. This is because of the violence of the people who live in it. [20]And the cities where people live will become ruins. The land will become empty. Then you will know that I am the Lord.'"

[21]The Lord spoke his word to me. He said: [22]"Human being, what is this saying you have in the land of Israel: 'The days go by and every vision comes to nothing'? [23]So say to them, 'This is what the Lord God says: I will make them stop saying this. Then nobody in Israel will use it anymore.' But tell them, 'The time is near when every vision will come true. [24]There will be no more false visions or pleasing prophecies[d] inside the nation of Israel. [25]This is because I, the Lord God, will speak. What I say will be done. It will not be delayed. You are a people who refuse to obey. And in your

time I will say the word and do it, says the Lord God.'"

²⁶The Lord spoke his word to me. He said: ²⁷"Human being, look! The people of Israel are saying this: 'The vision that Ezekiel sees is for a time many years from now. He is prophesying about times far away.'

²⁸"So say to them: 'The Lord God says this: None of my words will be delayed anymore. What I have said will be done, says the Lord God.'"

13 The Lord spoke his word to me. He said: ²"Human being, prophesy[d] against the prophets of Israel. Say to those who make up their own prophecies: 'Listen to the word of the Lord. ³This is what the Lord God says: How terrible it will be for the foolish prophets. They are the ones who follow their own ideas. And they have not seen a vision from me. ⁴People of Israel, your prophets have been like wild dogs hunting to kill and eat among ruins. ⁵Israel is like a house in ruins. But you have not gone up into the broken places. Your prophets have not repaired the wall. So how can Israel hold back the enemy in the battle on the Lord's day of judging? ⁶Your prophets see false visions. They prophesy lies. They say, "This is the message of the Lord." The Lord has not sent them. But they still hope their words will come true. ⁷You said, "This is the message of the Lord." But that is a false vision. Your prophecies are lies because I have not spoken.

⁸"So this is what the Lord God says: You prophets spoke things that are false. You saw visions that do not come true. That is why I am against you, says the Lord God. ⁹So I will punish the prophets who see false visions and prophesy lies. They will have no place among my people. Their names will not be written on the list of the people of Israel. They will not enter the land of Israel. Then you will know that I am the Lord God.

¹⁰"'It is because they led my people away. They said, "Peace!" but there is no peace. When the people build a weak wall, the prophets cover it with whitewash to make it look strong. ¹¹So tell those who cover a weak wall with whitewash that it will fall down. Rain will pour down. Hailstones will fall. And a stormy wind will break the wall down. ¹²When the wall has fallen, people will ask you, "Where is the whitewash you used on the wall?"

¹³"'So this is what the Lord God says: I will break the wall with a stormy wind. In my anger rain will pour down. And hailstones will destroy the wall. ¹⁴I will tear down the wall on which you put whitewash. I will level it to the ground. Then people will see the wall's foundation. And when the wall falls, you will be destroyed under it. Then you will know that I am the Lord. ¹⁵So I will carry out my anger on the wall and against those who covered it with whitewash. Then I will tell you, "The wall is gone. And those who covered it with whitewash are also gone. ¹⁶The prophets of Israel who prophesy to Jerusalem will be gone. And those who see visions of peace for Jerusalem will be gone also. There will be no peace, says the Lord God." '

¹⁷"Now, human being, reject the women among your people who make up their own prophecies.[d] Prophesy against them. ¹⁸Say, 'This is what the Lord God says: How terrible it will be for women who sew magic charms on their wrists. How terrible it will be for those who make veils of every length. These women do this to trap people. You ruin the lives of my people but try to save your own lives! ¹⁹And you have dishonored me among my people. You have done it for handfuls of barley and pieces of bread. You have killed people who should not die. And you have kept alive those who should die. You have done this by lying to my people. And my people are willing to listen to lies.

²⁰"'So this is what the Lord God says: I am against your magic charms. You use them to trap people as if they were birds. I will tear these charms off your arms. I will free those people you have trapped like birds. ²¹I will also tear off your veils. I will save my people from your hands. They will no longer be in your power. You will not trap them. Then you will know that I am the Lord. ²²By your lies you caused the heart of the person who did right to be sad. I did not make him sad. You have encouraged the evil person not to stop being evil. And that would have saved his life. ²³So you will not see any more false visions. You will not prophesy anymore. And I will save my people from your power. Then you will know that I am the Lord.'"

14 Some of the older leaders of Israel came to me and sat down before me. ²Then the Lord spoke his word to me. He said: ³"Human being, these men love to worship idols. They put up evil things that cause people to sin. Should I allow them to ask me for help? ⁴So speak to them. Tell them, 'This is what the Lord God says: Any person in Israel might want to worship idols. He might even put up evil things that cause people to sin. Then he might come to the prophet.ᵈ When he does, I, the Lord, will answer him. I will put him to death because he worshiped idols. ⁵Then I will win back my people Israel. They have left me because of all their idols.'

⁶"So say this to the people of Israel: 'This is what the Lord God says: Change your hearts and lives. Stop worshiping idols. Stop doing all the things I hate. ⁷Any Israelite or any foreigner in Israel can separate himself from me. He can do this by wanting to worship idols. Or he can put up the things that cause people to sin. Then if he comes to the prophet to ask me questions, I, the Lord, will answer him myself. ⁸I will reject him. I will make him a sign and an example. I will separate him from my people. Then you will know that I am the Lord.

⁹"'But the prophet may be tricked into giving a prophecy. Then it is because I, the Lord, have tricked that prophet to speak. Then I will use my power against him. I will destroy him from among my people Israel. ¹⁰The prophet will be as guilty as the one who asks him for help. They both will be responsible for their guilt. ¹¹Then the nation of Israel will not leave me anymore. And they will not make themselves uncleanᵈ anymore with all their sins. Then they will be my people. And I will be their God, says the Lord God.'"

¹²The Lord spoke his word to me. He said: ¹³"Human being, sometimes the people of a country will sin against me by not being loyal. When that happens, I will use my power against them. I will cut off their supply of food. I will send them a time of hunger. I will destroy both their people and animals. ¹⁴Three great men like Noah, Daniel and Job might be in that country. But their goodness could save only themselves, says the Lord God.

¹⁵"I might even send wild animals into that land. They would leave the land empty and without children. Then no one would pass through it because of the animals. ¹⁶As surely as I live, says the Lord God, not even Noah, Daniel and Job could help. Even if they were in

the land, they could not save their own sons or daughters. They could only save themselves. And that country would remain empty.

¹⁷"Or, I might bring a war against that country. I might say, 'Let a war be fought in that land. Let it destroy its men and animals.' ¹⁸As surely as I live, says the Lord God, not even these three men could help. Even if they were in the land, they could not save their sons or daughters. They could only save themselves.

¹⁹"Or, I might cause a disease to spread in that country. I might pour out my anger against that country, destroying and killing people and animals. ²⁰As surely as I live, says the Lord God, not even Noah, Daniel and Job could help. Even if they were in the land, they could not save their son or daughter. They could save only themselves because they did what was right.

²¹"This is what the Lord God says: I will send my four terrible punishments against Jerusalem. They are war, hunger, wild animals and disease. They will destroy people and animals from Jerusalem. ²²But some people will escape. Some sons and daughters will be led out. They will come out to you. You will see how they live. Then you will be comforted after the disasters I have brought against Jerusalem. You will be comforted after all the things I will bring against it. ²³You will be comforted when you see how they live. You will know there was a good reason for what I did to Jerusalem, says the Lord God."

15 The Lord spoke his word to me. He said: ²"Human being, what good is the wood of the vine? Is it better than the wood of a tree in the forest? ³Can wood be taken from the vine to make anything? Can you use it to make a peg on which to hang something? ⁴The vine is thrown into the fire for fuel. The fire burns up both ends and starts to burn the middle. Then is it useful for anything? ⁵When the vine was whole, it couldn't be made into anything. When the fire has burned it completely, it certainly cannot be made into anything."

⁶So this is what the Lord God says: "Out of all the trees in the forest, I gave the wood of the vine as fuel for fire. In the same way I have given up the people who live in Jerusalem. ⁷I will turn against them. They came through one fire. But fire will still destroy them. When I turn against them, you will

know that I am the Lord. ⁸So I will make the land empty. This is because the people have not been loyal, says the Lord God."

16 The Lord spoke his word to me. He said: ²"Human being, tell Jerusalem about her hated actions. ³Say, 'This is what the Lord God says to Jerusalem: Your beginnings and your ancestors were in the land of the Canaanites. Your father was an Amorite. And your mother was a Hittite. ⁴On the day you were born, your cord[n] was not cut. You were not washed with water for cleansing. You were not rubbed with salt. You were not wrapped in cloths. ⁵No one felt sorry for you. No one would do any of these things for you. No, you were thrown out into the open field. This is because you were hated on the day you were born.

⁶"'Then I passed by and saw you kicking about in your blood. I said to you, "Live!" ⁷I made you grow like a plant in the field. You grew up and became tall. You grew up and became like a beautiful jewel. Your breasts formed. Your hair grew. But you were naked and without clothes.

⁸"'Later I passed by you and looked at you. I saw that you were at the time for love. So I spread my robe over you and covered your nakedness. I also made a marriage promise to you. I entered into an agreement with you. Then you became mine, says the Lord God.

⁹"'Then I bathed you with water and washed all the blood off of you. I put oil on you. ¹⁰I put beautiful clothes made with needlework on you. I put sandals of fine leather on your feet. I wrapped you in fine linen and covered you with silk. ¹¹I put jewelry on you. I put bracelets on your arms and a necklace around your neck. ¹²I also put a ring in your nose and earrings in your ears. And I put a beautiful crown on your head. ¹³So you wore gold and silver. Your dress was made of fine linen, silk and beautiful needlework. You ate fine flour, honey and olive oil. You were very beautiful and became a queen. ¹⁴Then you became famous among the nations because you were so beautiful. Your beauty was perfect, because of the glory I gave you, says the Lord God.

¹⁵"'But you trusted in your beauty. You became a prostitute[d] because you were so famous. You had sexual rela-

tions with anyone who passed by. ¹⁶And you took some of your clothes and made your places of worship colorful. This is where you carried on your prostitution. These things should not have happened. They should never happen again. ¹⁷You also took your beautiful jewelry. It was made from gold and silver I had given you. Then you made for yourselves male idols. And you were a prostitute with them. ¹⁸Then you took your clothes with beautiful needlework and covered the idols. You gave my oil and incense[d] as an offering to them. ¹⁹Also, you took the bread I gave you. You took the fine flour, oil and honey I gave you to eat. And you offered them before the false gods as a pleasing smell. This is what happened, says the Lord God.

²⁰"'Also, you took your sons and daughters who were my children. And you sacrificed them to idols as food. Your sexual sins were not enough for you. ²¹You killed my children and offered them up in fire to idols. ²²You did all your hated acts and sexual sins. But you did not remember when you were young. At that time you were naked and had no clothes. You were left in your blood.

²³"'How terrible! How terrible it will be for you, says the Lord God. This is what you did after all these evil things. ²⁴You built yourself a place to worship false gods. You made for yourself a place of worship in every city square. ²⁵You built a place of worship at the head of every street. You made your beauty hateful. You offered your body for sex to anyone who passed by. Your sexual sins became worse and worse. ²⁶You also had sexual relations with the Egyptians. They were your neighbors and partners in sexual sin. Your sexual sins became even worse. And they caused me to be angry. ²⁷So then, I used my power against you. I took away some of your land. I let those who hated you defeat you. They were the Philistine women. Even they were ashamed of your evil ways. ²⁸Also, you had sexual relations with the Assyrians because you could not be satisfied. You had sexual relations with them, but you still were not satisfied. ²⁹You did even more sexual sins in the land of Babylonia. The Babylonians were traders. But you were not satisfied even with this.

³⁰"'Truly your will is weak, says the

16:4 **cord** The umbilical cord that gives the unborn baby food and air from its mother.

Lord God. You do all the things a stubborn prostitute does. [31] You built your place to worship false gods at the beginning of every street. And you made places of worship in every city square. But you were not like a prostitute because you refused payment.

[32] "You are a wife who is guilty of adultery.[d] You desire strangers instead of your husband. [33] Men pay prostitutes, but you pay all your lovers. You pay them to come to you. And they come from all around for sexual relations. [34] So you are different from other prostitutes. No one acts like a prostitute the same way you do. You give money, and no money is given to you. Yes, you are different.

[35] "So, prostitute,[d] hear the word of the Lord. [36] This is what the Lord God says: You showed your riches to other countries. And you uncovered your body in your sexual sins with your lovers. And you even did it with all your hated idols. You killed your children and offered their blood to your idols. [37] So I will gather all your lovers with whom you found pleasure. Yes, I will gather all those you loved and those you hated. Yes, I will gather them against you from all around. I will strip you naked in front of them. Then they will be able to see your nakedness. [38] So I will punish you as judges punish women guilty of adultery.[d] I will punish you as murderers are punished. I will put you to death because I am angry and jealous. [39] I will also hand you over to your lovers. They will tear down your places of worship. They will destroy the places where you worship false gods. They will tear off your clothes and take away your jewelry. They will leave you naked and bare. [40] They will bring a crowd against you. They will throw stones at you and cut you into pieces with their swords. [41] They will burn your houses with fire. They will punish you in front of many women. Then I will put an end to your sexual sins. And you will no longer pay your lovers. [42] Then I will rest from my anger against you. I will stop being jealous. I will be quiet and not angry anymore.

[43] "You didn't remember when you were young. So you have made me angry in all these ways. And I will repay you for what you have done, says the Lord God. Didn't you add sexual sins to all your other acts which I hate?

[44] "Everyone who uses wise sayings will say this about you: 'The daughter

is like her mother." [45] You are like your mother. She hated her husband and children. You are also like your sisters. They hated their husbands and children. Your mother was a Hittite. And your father was an Amorite. [46] Now your older sister is Samaria. She lived north of you with her daughters. And your younger sister Sodom lived south of you with her daughters. [47] You followed their ways. And you did what they did. But you were even worse than they were in everything you did. [48] As surely as I live, says the Lord God, this is true. Your sister Sodom and her daughters never did what you and your daughters have done.

[49] "This was the sin of your sister Sodom: She and her daughters were proud. They had plenty of food. They lived in great comfort. But she did not help the poor and needy. [50] So Sodom and her daughters were proud. And they did things I hate in front of me. So I got rid of them when I saw what they did. [51] Also, Samaria did not do half the sins you do. You have done more hated things than they did. So you make your sisters look good because of all the hated things you have done. [52] You will suffer disgrace because you have provided an excuse for your sisters. They are more right than you are. Your sins were even more terrible than theirs. Be ashamed and suffer disgrace because you made your sisters seem right.

[53] "But I will give Sodom and her daughters their riches back. I will give Samaria and her daughters their riches back. And with them I will also give you back your riches. [54] But you will have to suffer disgrace. You will feel ashamed for all the things you have done. You even gave comfort to your sisters in their sins. [55] Your sisters are Sodom with her daughters and Samaria with her daughters. They will return to what they were before. You and your daughters will also return to what you were before. [56] You would not even mention your sister Samaria when you were proud. [57] Nor would you mention her before your evil was uncovered. And now the Edomite women and their neighbors say bad things about you. Even the Philistine women say bad things about you. Those around you hate you. [58] You will be punished for your sexual sins and actions that I hate, says the Lord.

[59] "This is what the Lord God says: I will give you what you should have. You hated and broke the marriage agree-

ment. ⁶⁰But I will remember my agreement I made with you when you were young. I will make an agreement that will continue forever with you. ⁶¹Then you will remember what you have done. You will be ashamed when you receive your sisters—both your older and your younger sisters. I will give them to you like daughters. But it will not be because of my agreement with you. ⁶²I will set up my agreement with you. And you will know that I am the Lord. ⁶³You will remember and be ashamed. You will not open your mouth again because of your shame. This is because I will forgive you for all the things you have done, says the Lord God.' "

17 The Lord spoke his word to me. He said: ²"Human being, give a riddle. Tell a story to the people of Israel. ³Say, 'This is what the Lord God says: A great eagle came to Lebanon. He had great wings with long feathers of many different colors. The eagle took hold of the top of a cedar tree. ⁴He pulled off the top branch. And he brought it to a land of traders. The eagle planted it in a city of traders.

⁵" 'The eagle took a young plant from the land. And he planted it in a good field near plenty of water. He planted it to grow like a willow tree. ⁶The plant grew and became a low vine that spread over the ground. The vine's branches turned toward the eagle. The vine's roots were under the eagle. So the plant became a vine. And its branches grew, sending out leaves.

⁷" 'But there was another eagle with great wings and many feathers. The vine then bent its roots toward this eagle. The vine also sent out its branches toward the eagle so he could water it. The vine turned away from the area where it was planted. ⁸It was planted in a good field. It was by plenty of water so it could grow branches and give fruit. It could have become a fine vine.'

⁹"Say to them, 'This is what the Lord God says: The vine will not continue to grow. The first eagle will pull up the vine's roots and strip off its fruit. Then the vine will dry up. All its new leaves will dry up and die. It will not take a strong arm or many people to pull the vine up by its roots. ¹⁰It might be planted again. But it will not continue to grow. It will completely die when the east wind hits it. It will dry up in the area where it grew.' "

¹¹Then the Lord spoke his word to me.

He said: ¹²"Say now to the people who refuse to obey: 'Do you know what these things mean?' Say: 'The king of Babylon came to Jerusalem. He took the king and important men of Jerusalem and brought them to Babylon. ¹³Then he took a member of the family of the king of Judah. He made an agreement with him. The king of Babylon made this person promise to support him. The king also took away the leaders of Judah. ¹⁴He did this to make the kingdom of Judah weak so it would not be strong again. Then the kingdom of Judah could continue only by keeping its agreement with the king of Babylon. ¹⁵But the king of Judah turned against the king of Babylon. The king of Judah sent his messengers to Egypt. He asked the Egyptians for horses and many soldiers. Will the king of Judah succeed? Will the one who does such things escape? He cannot break the agreement and escape.

¹⁶" 'As surely as I live, says the Lord God, he will die in Babylon. He will die in the land of the king who made him king of Judah. The king of Judah hated his promise. He broke his agreement with the king of Babylon. ¹⁷The king of Egypt will not help the king of Judah in the war. He will not help with his mighty army and many people. The Babylonians will build devices to attack the cities and to kill many people. ¹⁸The king of Judah showed that he hated the promise by breaking the agreement. He promised to support Babylon, but he did all these things. So he will not escape.

¹⁹" 'So this is what the Lord God says: As surely as I live, this is true: I will pay back the king of Judah for hating my promise and breaking my agreement. ²⁰I will spread my net over him. He will be caught in my trap. Then I will bring him to Babylon. There I will judge him for the unfaithful acts he did against me. ²¹And all the best of his soldiers who escape will die by the sword. Those who live will be scattered to every wind. Then you will know that I, the Lord, have spoken.

²²" 'This is what the Lord God says: I myself will also take a young branch from the top of a cedar tree. And I will plant it. I will cut off a small twig. It will be from the top of the tree's young branches. I will plant it on a high and great mountain. ²³I will plant it on the high mountain of Israel. Then it will grow branches and give fruit. And it will become a great cedar tree. Birds of

every kind will build nests in it. They will live in the shelter of the tree's branches. [24]Then all the trees of the field will know that I am the Lord. I am the one who brings down the high tree. I make the low tree tall. I dry up the green tree. And I make the dry tree grow. I am the Lord. I have spoken, and I will do it.'"

18 The Lord spoke his word to me. He said: [2]"What do you mean by using this saying about the land of Israel:

'The fathers have eaten sour
    grapes.
    And that caused the children to
        grind their teeth from the sour
        taste'?

[3]"As surely as I live, says the Lord God, this is true: You will not use this saying in Israel anymore. [4]Every living thing belongs to me. The life of the father is mine. And the life of the son is mine. The person who sins will die.

[5]"There may be a good person. This person does what is fair and right. [6]He does not eat at the mountain places of worship. He does not look to the idols of Israel for help. He does not have sexual relations with his neighbor's wife. He does not have sexual relations with a woman during her time of monthly bleeding. [7]He does not mistreat anyone. But he returns what was given as a promise for a loan. He does not rob other people. He gives bread to hungry people. He gives clothes to those who have no clothes. [8]He does not lend money to get too much interest or profit. He keeps his hand from doing wrong. He judges fairly between men. [9]He lives by my rules and obeys my laws faithfully. The person who does all these things is good. He will surely live, says the Lord God.

[10]"But this person might have a wild son who murders people. This son may do any of these other bad things. [11](But the father himself has not done any of these things.) This son eats at the mountain places of worship. He has sexual relations with his neighbor's wife. [12]He mistreats the poor and needy. He steals things. He refuses to return what was promised for a loan. He looks to idols for help. He does things which I hate. [13]He lends money for too much interest and profit. Will this son live? No, he will not live! He has done all these hated things. He will surely be put to death. He will be responsible for his own sins.

[14]"But this son might have a son who has seen the sins his father did. But after seeing them, he does not do those things. [15]He does not eat at the mountain places of worship. He does not look to the idols of Israel for help. He does not have sexual relations with his neighbor's wife. [16]He does not mistreat anyone. He does not keep something promised for a loan. He does not steal. But he gives bread to the hungry people. He gives clothes to people without clothes. [17]He keeps his hand from doing wrong. He does not take too much interest or profit when he lends money. He obeys my laws and lives by my rules. He will not die for his father's sin. He will surely live. [18]But his father took other people's money unfairly. He robbed his brother. He did what was wrong among his people. So he will die for his own sin.

[19]"But you ask, 'Why is the son not punished for the father's sin?' The son has done what is fair and right. He obeys all my rules. So he will surely live. [20]It is the person who sins that will die. The son will not be punished for the father's sin. The father will not be punished for the son's sin. The person who does right is responsible for his own goodness. The evil person is responsible for his own evil.

[21]"But the evil person might stop doing all the sins he has done. And he might obey all my rules and do what is fair and right. Then he will surely live. He will not die. [22]His sins will be forgotten. Now he does what is right. So he will live. [23]I do not really want the evil person to die, says the Lord God. I want him to stop his bad ways and live.

[24]"But a person who does right might stop doing good and do wrong. And he might do the same hated things an evil person does. Will he live? All his good acts will be forgotten. This is because he became unfaithful. He has sinned. So he will die because of his sins.

[25]"But you say, 'What the Lord does isn't fair.' Hear now, people of Israel. I am fair. It is what you do that is not fair! [26]A good person might stop doing good. He might do wrong and die because of it. He will die because he did wrong. [27]An evil person might stop doing the evil things he has done. And he might do what is fair and right. He will save his life. [28]He thought about it and stopped doing all the sins he had done. He will surely live. He will not die. [29]But the peo-

ple of Israel still say, 'What the Lord does isn't fair.' People of Israel, I am fair. It is what you do that is not fair.

³⁰"So I will judge you, people of Israel. I will judge each person by what he does, says the Lord God. Change your hearts. Stop all your sinning. Then sin will not bring your ruin. ³¹Get rid of all the sins you have done. And get for yourselves a new heart and a new way to think. Why do you want to die, people of Israel? ³²I do not want anyone to die. So change your hearts and lives so you may live.

19 "Sing a funeral song for the leaders of Israel. ²Say:

'Your mother was like a female lion.
She lay down among the young lions.
She had many cubs.
³She brought up one of her cubs.
And he became a strong lion.
He learned to tear the animals he hunted.
And he ate people.
⁴The nations heard about him.
He was trapped in their pit.
And they brought him with hooks to the land of Egypt.

⁵" 'The mother lion waited and saw that there was no hope for her cub.
So she took another one of her cubs
and made him a strong lion.
⁶This cub roamed among the lions.
He was now a strong lion.
He learned to tear the animals he hunted.
And he ate people.
⁷He destroyed their strong places.
He destroyed their cities.
The land and everything in it were terrified by the sound of his roar.
⁸Then the nations came against him from areas all around.
And they spread their net over him.
He was trapped in their pit.
⁹Then they put him into a cage with chains.
And they brought him to the king of Babylon.
They put him into prison.
Then his roar could not be heard again
on the mountains of Israel.

¹⁰" 'Your mother was like a vine in your vineyard.
It was planted beside the water.
The vine had many branches and gave much fruit
because there was plenty of water.
¹¹The vine had strong branches.
They were good enough for a king's scepter.ᵈ
The vine became tall among the thick branches.
And it was seen because it was tall with many branches.
¹²But it was pulled up by its roots in anger.
It was thrown down to the ground.
The east wind dried it up.
Its fruit was torn off.
Its strong branches were broken off.
They were burned up.
¹³Now the vine is planted in the desert,
in a dry and thirsty land.
¹⁴And fire has spread from the vine's main branch.
It has destroyed its fruit.
There is not a strong branch left on it
that could become a scepter for a king.'

This is a funeral song. It is to be used as a funeral song."

20 It was the seventh year, in the fifth month of our captivity. It was the tenth day of the month. Some of the older leaders of Israel came to ask about the Lord. They sat down before me.

²The Lord spoke his word to me. He said: ³"Human being, speak to the older leaders of Israel. Say to them: 'This is what the Lord God says: Did you come to ask me questions? As surely as I live, I will not let you ask me questions.'

⁴"Will you judge them? Will you judge them, human being? Let them know the hated things their fathers did. ⁵Say to them: 'This is what the Lord God says: I chose Israel and made a promise to the descendantsᵈ of Jacob. At that time I made myself known to them in Egypt. I promised them, "I am the Lord your God." ⁶At that time I promised them I would bring them out of Egypt. I promised to bring them into a land I had chosen for them. This is a land where much food grows. It is the best of all lands. ⁷I said to them, "Each one of you must

throw away the hateful idols you have set your eyes on. Don't make yourselves unclean[d] with the idols of Egypt. I am the Lord your God."

[8] "But they turned against me and refused to listen to me. They did not throw away the hated idols which they saw and liked. They did not leave the idols of Egypt. Then I decided to pour out my anger against them in the land of Egypt. [9] But I acted to show who I am. I did not allow myself to be dishonored before the nations where the Israelites lived. I made myself known to the Israelites. I did this by bringing them out of Egypt while the nations were watching. [10] So I took them out of Egypt and brought them into the desert. [11] I gave them my rules. I told them about my laws. If a person obeys them, he will live. [12] I also gave them my Sabbaths.[d] They were to be a sign between us. Then they would know that I am the Lord. I make them holy.

[13] "But in the desert Israel turned against me. They did not follow my rules. They rejected my laws. But if a person obeys them, he will live. They dishonored my Sabbaths. Then I decided to pour out my anger against them and destroy them in the desert. [14] But I acted for the sake of my name. I did not allow it to be dishonored before the nations. As the nations watched, I had brought the Israelites out of Egypt. [15] But in the desert I had to make another promise to the Israelites. I had to promise I would not bring them into the land I had given them. It is a land where much food grows. It is the best of all the lands. [16] This is because they rejected my laws. They did not follow my rules. They dishonored my Sabbaths. They would rather worship their idols. [17] But I had pity on them. I did not destroy them. I did not put an end to them in the desert. [18] I said to their children in the desert, "Don't live by the rules of your fathers. Don't obey their laws. Don't make yourselves unclean with their idols. [19] I am the Lord your God. Live by my rules. Obey my laws and do them. [20] Keep my Sabbaths holy. They will be a sign between me and you. Then you will know that I am the Lord your God."

[21] "But the people turned against me. If a person obeys my laws, he will live. But they did not live by my rules. They were not careful to obey my laws. They dishonored my Sabbaths. So I decided to pour out my anger against them. I

decided to carry out my anger against them in the desert. [22] But I held back my anger. I acted for the sake of my name. Then my name would not be dishonored with the nations watching. As the nations watched, I had brought the Israelites out from Egypt. [23] Also in the desert I had to make a promise to the Israelites. I had to promise to scatter them among the nations and spread them among the countries. [24] This is because they did not obey my laws. They had rejected my rules and dishonored my Sabbaths. And they worshiped the idols of their ancestors. [25] I also allowed them to follow rules that were not good. And they followed laws by which they could not live. [26] I let the Israelites make themselves unclean by the gifts they brought to their false gods. They sacrificed their oldest children in the fire. This is how I shocked them so they would know that I am the Lord.'

[27] "So, human being, speak to the people of Israel. Say to them, 'This is what the Lord God says: Your ancestors spoke against me by being unfaithful to me in this way: [28] I had brought them into the land I promised to give them. They saw every high hill and every leafy tree. There they offered their sacrifices to false gods. They brought offerings that made me angry. There, also, they burned their incense.[d] There they poured out their drink offerings. [29] Then I said to them: What is this place where you go to worship false gods?'" (It is still called High Place today.)

[30] "So say to the people of Israel: 'This is what the Lord God says: Will you make yourselves unclean as your ancestors did? Will you be unfaithful and desire their hated idols? [31] You offer your children as gifts to the false gods. You sacrifice them in the fire. You make yourselves unclean with all your idols even today. So, people of Israel, should I let you ask me questions? As surely as I live, says the Lord God, I will not accept questions from you.

[32] "'What you want will not come true. You say, "We want to be like the other nations and the people in other lands. We want to worship idols made of wood and stone." [33] As surely as I live, says the Lord God, I will rule you. I will rule you with my great power and strength and anger. [34] I will bring you out from the foreign nations. I will gather you from the lands where you are scattered. I will do this with my great power and strength

and anger. ³⁵I will bring you among the nations as I brought your ancestors into the desert after Moses. There I will judge you face to face. ³⁶I will judge you the same way I judged your ancestors. That was in the desert of the land of Egypt. So I will judge you, says the Lord God. ³⁷I will take control of you. I will punish you by my agreement. ³⁸I will get rid of those who refuse to obey me and who turn against me. I will bring them out of the land where they are now living. But they will never enter the land of Israel. Then you will know that I am the Lord.

³⁹"'This is what the Lord God says: People of Israel, go serve your idols for now. But later you will listen to me. You will not continue to dishonor my holy name with your gifts and false gods. ⁴⁰My holy mountain is the high mountain of Israel. There all Israel will serve me in the land, says the Lord God. There I will accept you. There I will look for your offerings. I will look for the first harvest of your offerings and all your holy gifts. ⁴¹I will accept you like a pleasing smell. This will happen when I bring you out from the foreign nations. It will take place when I gather you from the lands where you are scattered. Then through you I will show how holy I am. The nations will see it. ⁴²When I bring you into the land of Israel, you will know that I am the Lord. I will bring you into the land I promised your ancestors. ⁴³There you will remember everything you did that made you unclean. Then you will hate yourselves for all the evil things you have done. ⁴⁴I will deal with you to show who I am. Then you will know I am the Lord, people of Israel. But it's not because of your evil ways or unclean actions, says the Lord God.'"

⁴⁵Now the Lord spoke his word to me. He said: ⁴⁶"Human being, look toward the south. Prophesy^d against the south. Prophesy against the forest of the southern area. ⁴⁷Say to that forest: 'Hear the word of the Lord. This is what the Lord God says: I am ready to start a fire in you. The fire will destroy all your green trees and all your dry trees. The flame that burns will not be put out. All the land from south to north will be burned by the fire. ⁴⁸Then all the people will see that I, the Lord, have started the fire. It will not be put out.'"

⁴⁹Then I said, "Ah, Lord God! The people are saying about me, 'He is only telling stories.'"

21 Then the Lord spoke his word to me. He said: ²"Human being, look toward Jerusalem and speak against their holy place. Prophesy^d against the land of Israel. ³Say to Israel: 'This is what the Lord says: I am against you. I will pull my sword out of its holder. I will separate you from both wicked people and those who do right. ⁴I am going to separate the wicked and those who do right. So my sword will come out from its holder. And it will come against all people from south to north. ⁵Then all people will know that I, the Lord, have pulled my sword out from its holder. My sword will not go back in again.'

⁶"So, human being, groan with breaking heart and great sadness. Make these sad sounds in front of the people. ⁷They will ask you, 'Why do you make these sad sounds?' Then you will say, 'Because of the news that is coming. Every heart will melt with fear. All hands will become weak. Everyone will be afraid. All knees will become weak as water. Look, it is coming. It will happen, says the Lord God.'"

⁸The Lord spoke his word to me. He said, ⁹"Human being, prophesy and say, 'This is what the Lord says:

A sword, a sword,
   made sharp and polished.
¹⁰It is made sharp for the killing.
   It is polished to flash like
     lightning.

"'You are not happy about this horrible punishment by the sword. But my son, Judah, you did not change when you were only beaten with a rod.
¹¹The sword should be polished.
   The sword is meant to be held in
     the hand.
It is made sharp and polished.
   It is made ready for the hand of
     the killer.
¹²Shout and yell, human being.
   This is because the sword is
     against my people.
   It is against all the rulers of
     Israel.
They will be killed by the sword,
   along with my people.
   So beat your chest in sadness.

¹³"'The test will come. And Judah, who is hated by the armies of Babylon, will not last, says the Lord God.'

¹⁴"So, human being, prophesy.
   And clap your hands.

Let the sword hit
two or three times.
It is the sword for killing.
It is the sword for much killing.
This sword surrounds the people.
[15]Their hearts will melt with fear.
And many people will die.
I have placed the killing sword
at all their gates.
Oh! The sword is made to flash like
lightning.
It is held, ready for killing.
[16]Sword, cut on the right side.
Then cut on the left side.
Cut anywhere your blade is
turned.
[17]I will also clap my hands.
Then my anger will rest.
I, the Lord, have spoken."

[18]The Lord spoke his word to me. He said: [19]"Human being, mark two roads that the king of Babylon and his sword can follow. Both of these roads will start from the same country. And make signs where the road divides and one way goes toward the city. [20]One sign shows the road he can take with his sword to Rabbah. It is in the land of the Ammonites. And the other sign shows the road he can take to Judah and Jerusalem. Jerusalem is protected with strong walls. [21]The king of Babylon will come to where the road divides into two. He will use magic. He will throw lots[d] with arrows. He will ask questions of his family idols. He will look at the liver of a sacrificed animal to learn where he should go. [22]The lots will tell him to go toward his right to Jerusalem. They will tell him these things: Use logs to break down the city gates. Shout the battle cry and give the order to kill. Build a dirt road to the top of the walls and devices to attack the walls. [23]The people of Jerusalem have made agreements with other nations to help them fight Babylon. So they will think this prediction is wrong. But the king of Babylon will remind them of their sin. And he will capture them.

[24]"So this is what the Lord God says: 'You have shown how sinful you are by turning against the Lord. Your sins are seen in all the things you do. So you will be taken captive by the enemy.

[25]"You unclean[d] and evil leader of Israel, you will be killed! The time of your final punishment has come. [26]This is what the Lord God says: Take off the turban. Take off the crown. Things will change. Those who are important now

will be made unimportant. And those who are unimportant now will be made important. [27]A ruin! A ruin! I will make it a ruin! This place will not be rebuilt until the one comes who has a right to be king. Then I will give it to him.'

[28]"And you, human being, prophesy[d] and say: 'This is what the Lord God says about the people of Ammon and their insults:

A sword, a sword
is pulled out of its holder.
It is polished to kill and destroy.
It will flash like lightning!
[29]Prophets[d] see false visions about
you
and prophesy lies about you.
The sword will be put on the necks
of these evil people who are to be
killed.
Their day has come.
The time of your final
punishment has come.
[30]Put the sword back in its holder.
I will judge you in the place
where you were created.
I will judge you in the land where
you were born.
[31]I will pour out my anger against
you.
I will breathe on you with the fire
of my anger.
I will hand you over to cruel men
who are skilled in destruction.
[32]You will be like fuel for the fire.
You will die in the land.
You will not be remembered.
I, the Lord, have spoken.'"

22 The Lord spoke his word to me. He said: [2]"And you, human being, will you judge? Will you judge the city of murderers? Then tell her about all her hated acts. [3]You will say: 'This is what the Lord God says: You are a city that kills those who come to live there. You make yourself unclean[d] by making idols. [4]You have become guilty of murder. And you have become unclean by your idols which you have made. So you have brought your time of punishment near. You have come to the end of your years. So I have made you a thing of shame to the nations. All lands will laugh at you. [5]Those near and those far away will laugh at you. You will have a bad name. You will be full of confusion.

[6]"'Jerusalem, see how each ruler of Israel in you has been trying to kill people. [7]The people in you hate their fathers and mothers. They mistreat the foreign-

ers in you. They wrong the orphans and widows in you. [8]You hate my holy things. You dishonor my Sabbaths.[d] [9]The men in you tell lies to cause the death of others. The people in you eat food offered to idols at the mountain places of worship. They do sexual sins in you. [10]The people in you have sexual relations with their fathers' wives. The men in you have sexual relations with women who are unclean, during their time of monthly bleeding. [11]One person in you does a hated act with his neighbor's wife. Another has shamefully made his daughter-in-law unclean sexually. And another forces his half sister to have sexual relations with him. [12]The people in you take money to kill people. You take unfair interest and profits. You make profits by mistreating your neighbor. And you have forgotten me, says the Lord God.

[13]"'So with my fists I will hit you who have stolen money and you who have murdered people. [14]Will you still be brave and strong when I punish you? I, the Lord, have spoken, and I will act. [15]I will scatter you among the nations. I will spread you through the countries. I will get rid of your uncleanness. [16]But you, yourself, will be dishonored in the sight of the nations. Then you will know that I am the Lord.'"

[17]The Lord spoke his word to me. He said: [18]"Human being, the people of Israel have become useless like scum to me. They are like the copper, tin, iron and lead left in the furnace. These are left when silver is purified by melting. [19]So this is what the Lord God says: 'You have become useless like scum. I am going to gather you into Jerusalem. [20]People gather silver, copper, iron, lead and tin into a furnace. Then they melt it in a blazing fire. In the same way I will gather you in my hot anger. I will put you in Jerusalem and melt you. [21]I will gather you. And I will make you feel the heat of my anger. You will be melted in the fire. [22]Silver is melted in the furnace. In the same way you will be melted in the city. Then you will know that I, the Lord, have poured out my anger against you.'"

[23]The Lord spoke his word to me. He said: [24]"Human being, say to the land, 'You are a land that has not had rain or showers in a day of anger.' [25]Israel's rulers make evil plans. They are like a roaring lion that tears the animal it has caught. They have destroyed lives. They

have taken treasure and valuable things. They have caused many women to become widows. [26]Israel's priests do cruel things to my teachings. They do not honor my holy things. They make no difference between holy and unholy things. They teach there is no difference between clean[d] and unclean things. They do not remember my Sabbaths.[d] So I am dishonored by them. [27]Jerusalem's leaders are like wolves tearing a dead animal. They have killed people for profit. [28]And the prophets[d] try to cover this up by false visions and by lying. They say, 'This is what the Lord God says' when the Lord has not spoken. [29]The people cheat others. They steal. They hurt people who are poor and needy. They cheat foreigners and don't treat them fairly.

[30]"I looked for someone to build up the walls. I looked for someone to stand before me where the walls are broken to defend these people. Then I would not have to destroy them. But I did not find anyone. [31]So I will let them see my anger. I will destroy them with an anger that is like fire. This is because of all the things they have done, says the Lord God."

23

The Lord spoke his word to me. He said: [2]"Human being, a woman had two daughters. [3]While they were young, they went to Egypt and became prostitutes.[d] They let men touch and hold their breasts. [4]The older girl was named Oholah, and her sister was named Oholibah. They were mine and had sons and daughters. Oholah is Samaria, and Oholibah is Jerusalem.

[5]"Samaria left me. She went to her lover, Assyria. The Assyrians were warriors. [6]They wore blue uniforms. And all of them—governors, commanders and horsemen—were handsome. [7]Samaria became a prostitute for all the important men in Assyria. And she made herself unclean[d] with all the idols of everyone she desired. [8]She continued the prostitution she began in Egypt. When she was young, she slept with men. They touched her breasts and had sexual relations with her.

[9]"So I gave her to her lovers, the Assyrians, that she wanted so badly. [10]They stripped her naked and took away her sons and daughters. Then they killed her with a sword. Women everywhere began talking about how she had been punished.

[11]"Her sister Jerusalem saw what hap-

pened to Samaria. And so Jerusalem became worse than her sister in her sexual desire and prostitution. ¹²She also desired the Assyrians. All of them—governors, commanders, warriors dressed in uniform, and horsemen—were handsome. ¹³I saw that both girls were alike. Both of them were prostitutes.

¹⁴"But Jerusalem went even further. She saw carvings of Babylonian men on a wall. They wore red ¹⁵and had belts around their waists. They wore turbans on their heads. They all looked like chariot officers born in Babylonia. ¹⁶When she saw them, she wanted to have sexual relations with them. So she sent messengers to them in Babylonia. ¹⁷So these Babylonian men came and had sexual relations with her. They made her unclean. After that, she became sick of them. ¹⁸But she continued her prostitution so that everyone knew about it. And I finally became sick of her, as I had her sister. ¹⁹But she remembered how she was a young prostitute in Egypt. So she took part in even more prostitution. ²⁰She wanted men who behaved like animals in their sexual desire. ²¹In the same way you desired to do the sinful things you had done in Egypt. There men touched and held your young breasts.

²²"So, Jerusalem, this is what the Lord God says: You have tired of your lovers. So now I will make them angry with you. And they will surround you. ²³Men from Babylon and all Babylonia and men from Pekod, Shoa and Koa will come against you. All the Assyrians will come against you. They are governors, commanders, chariot drivers and important men, all riding horses. ²⁴Those men will come with great armies. They will come with their weapons, chariots and wagons. They will surround you with large and small shields and with helmets. And I will hand you over to them for punishment. And they will punish you with their own kind of punishment. ²⁵Then you will see how strong my anger can be. They will punish you in their anger. They will cut off your noses and ears. They will take away your sons and daughters. Those who are left will be burned. ²⁶They will take off your clothes and steal your jewelry. ²⁷I will put a stop to the sinful life you began when you were in Egypt. You will not desire these things anymore. And you will not remember Egypt anymore.

²⁸"This is what the Lord God says: You became sick of your lovers. But I am giving you to those men you now hate. ²⁹They will treat you with hate and take away everything you worked for. They will leave you empty and naked. Everyone will know about the sinful things you did. Your sexual sins ³⁰have brought this on you. You have made yourselves unclean^d by worshiping their idols. ³¹You did the same things your sister did. So you will get the same punishment.

³²"This is what the Lord God says:
You will drink the same cup your
   sister did.
And that cup is deep and wide.
Everyone will make fun of you,
   because the cup is full.
³³It will make you miserable and
   drunk.
It is the cup of fear and ruin.
It is the cup of your sister
   Samaria.
³⁴You will drink everything in it.
Then you will smash it
   and tear at your breasts.
I have spoken, says the Lord God.

³⁵"So this is what the Lord God says: You have forgotten me and turned your back on me. So you will be punished for your sexual sins."

³⁶The Lord said to me: "Human being, will you judge Samaria and Jerusalem? Then show them their hated acts. ³⁷They are guilty of adultery^d and murder. They have taken part in adultery with their idols. They even offered their children as sacrifices in the fire. They were to be food for these idols. ³⁸They have also done this to me: They made my Temple^d unclean^d at the same time they dishonored my Sabbaths.^d ³⁹They offered their children to their idols. Then they entered my Temple at that very time to dishonor it. That is what they did inside my Temple.

⁴⁰"They even sent for men from far away. A messenger was sent to them, and they came. The two sisters bathed themselves for them, painted their eyes and put on jewelry. ⁴¹They sat on a fine bed with a table set before it. They put my incense^d and my oil on the table.

⁴²"There was the noise of a reckless crowd in the city. Common people gathered, and drunkards were brought from the desert. They put bracelets on the hands of the two sisters. And they put beautiful crowns on their heads. ⁴³Then I said about the one who was worn out

by her acts of adultery, 'Let them continue their sexual sins with her. She is nothing but a prostitute.'[d] [44]They kept going to her as they would go to a prostitute. So they continued to go to Oholah, which was Samaria, and Oholibah, which was Jerusalem. These were the shameful women. [45]But men who do right will judge them as they judge women who take part in adultery. And they will judge them as they judge women who murder people. This is because Samaria and Jerusalem are guilty of adultery and murder.

[46]"This is what the Lord God says: Bring together a mob against Samaria and Jerusalem. And hand them over to be frightened and robbed. [47]Let the mob kill them by throwing stones at them. Let the mob cut them down with their swords. Let them kill their sons and daughters and burn their houses with fire.

[48]"So I will put an end to sexual sins in the land. Then all women will be warned. And they will not do the sexual sins you have done. [49]You will be punished for your sexual sins and the sin of worshiping idols. Then you will know that I am the Lord God."

24

The Lord spoke his word to me. It was in the ninth year, in the tenth month of our captivity. It was on the tenth day of the month. He said: [2]"Human being, write for yourself this date, this very date. The king of Babylon has surrounded Jerusalem this very day. [3]And tell a story to the people who refuse to obey me. Say to them: 'This is what the Lord God says:

Put on the pot. Put it on
  and pour water in it.
[4]Put in the pieces of meat.
  Put in the best pieces—the legs
    and the shoulders.
  Fill it with the best bones.
[5] Take the best of the flock.
  Pile wood under the pot.
  Boil the pieces of meat
    until even the bones are cooked.

[6]"This is what the Lord God says:
How terrible it will be for the city
    of murderers!
How terrible it will be for the
    rusty pot!
  Its rust will not go away!
Take the meat out of it, piece by
    piece.
  Don't choose any special piece.

[7]"'The blood from her killings is
    still in the city.
  She poured the blood on the bare
    rock.
  She did not pour it on the ground
    where dust would cover it.
[8]To stir up my anger and revenge,
  I put the blood she spilled on the
    bare rock.
  So it will not be covered.

[9]"'So this is what the Lord God says:
How terrible it will be for the city
    of murderers!
  I will also pile the wood high for
    burning.
[10]Pile up the wood
    and light the fire.
  Finish cooking the meat.
    Mix in the spices.
    And let the bones burn.
[11]Then set the empty pot on the
    coals.
    It will become hot, and its copper
      sides will glow.
  The dirty scum stuck inside it may
      then melt
    and its rust burn away.
[12]But efforts to clean the pot have
    failed.
  Its heavy rust cannot be
      removed,
    even in the fire.

[13]"'In your sinful action there is shame. I wanted to cleanse you, but you are still unclean.[d] You will never be cleansed from your sin until my anger against you is carried out.

[14]"'I, the Lord, have spoken. The time has come for me to act. I will not hold back punishment. I will not feel pity. I will judge you by your ways and actions, says the Lord God.'"

[15]Then the Lord spoke his word to me. He said: [16]"Human being, I am going to take your wife from you. She is the desire of your eyes. She will die suddenly. But you must not be sad or cry loudly for her. You must not shed any tears. [17]Groan silently. Do not cry loudly for the dead. Tie on your turban, and put your sandals on your feet. Do not cover your face. And do not eat the food people eat when they are sad about a death."

[18]So I spoke to the people in the morning. Then my wife died in the evening. The next morning I did as I had been commanded. [19]Then the people asked me, "Tell us,

what do the things you are doing mean for us?"

²⁰Then I said to them, "The Lord spoke his word to me. He said, ²¹'Say to the people of Israel, This is what the Lord God says: I am going to dishonor my Temple.ᵈ You think it gives you strength. You are proud of it. You love to look at it. It makes you happy. But your sons and daughters that you left behind in Jerusalem will fall dead by the sword. ²²And you will do as I have done. You will not cover your face. You will not eat the food people eat when they are sad about a death. ²³Your turbans will be on your heads. And your sandals will be on your feet. You will not cry loudly. But you will rot away in your sins. You will groan to each other. ²⁴So Ezekiel will be a sign for you. You will do all the same things he did. When it happens, you will know that I am the Lord God.'

²⁵"And as for you, human being, this is how it will be. I will take away the Temple that gives them strength. It makes them happy and proud. They love to look at it. It makes them happy. And I will take away their sons and daughters also. ²⁶At that time the person who escapes will come to you. He will have information for you to hear. ²⁷At that time your mouth will be opened. You will speak and be silent no more. So you will be a sign for them. Then they will know that I am the Lord."

25 The Lord spoke his word to me. He said: ²"Human being, look toward the people of Ammon and prophesyᵈ against them. ³Say to them, 'Hear the word of the Lord God. This is what the Lord God says: You were glad when my Templeᵈ was dishonored. You were glad when the land of Israel was ruined. And you were glad when the people of Judah were taken away as captives. ⁴So I am going to give you to the people of the East to be theirs. They will set up their camps among you. They will make their homes among you. They will eat your fruit and drink your milk. ⁵And I will make the city of Rabbah a pasture for camels. And the land of Ammon will become a resting place for sheep. Then you will know that I am the Lord. ⁶This is what the Lord God says: You clapped your hands and stamped your feet. You are happy about all the insults you have made against the land of Israel. ⁷So I will use my power against you. I will give you to the nations as if you were

valuables taken in war. I will wipe you out of the lands so you will no longer be a nation. I will destroy you. And you will know that I am the Lord.'

⁸"This is what the Lord God says: 'Moab and Edom say, "The people of Judah are like all the other nations." ⁹So I am going to take away the cities that protect Moab's borders. They are the best cities in that land. They are Beth Jeshimoth, Baal Meon and Kiriathaim. ¹⁰Then I will give Moab, along with the Ammonites, to the people of the East. They will take over these people. Then along with the Ammonites, Moab will not be a nation anymore. ¹¹So I will punish the people of Moab. And they will know that I am the Lord.'"

¹²"This is what the Lord God says: 'Edom took revenge on the people of Judah. And the Edomites became guilty because of it. ¹³So this is what the Lord God says: I will use my power against Edom. I will kill every man and animal in Edom. And I will destroy Edom all the way from Teman to Dedan. The Edomites will die in battle. ¹⁴I will take revenge on Edom through my people Israel. So the Israelites will do to Edom what my hot anger demands. Then the Edomites will know my revenge, says the Lord God.'"

¹⁵"This is what the Lord God says: 'The Philistines have taken revenge with hateful hearts. Because of their strong hatred, they have tried to destroy Judah. ¹⁶So this is what the Lord God says: I will use my power against the Philistines. I will remove the Kerethites. I will destroy those people still alive on the coast of the Mediterranean Sea. ¹⁷I will punish them in my anger until they have had enough. They will know that I am the Lord when I punish them.'"

26 It was the eleventh year, on the first day of the month of our captivity. The Lord spoke his word to me. He said: ²"Human being, the city of Tyre has spoken against Jerusalem: 'The city that traded with the nations is destroyed. Now we can be the trading center. The city Jerusalem is ruined. Now we can make money.' ³So this is what the Lord God says: I am against you, Tyre. I will bring many nations against you. They will come like the sea beating its waves on your island shores. ⁴They will destroy the walls of Tyre and pull down her towers. I will also scrape away her ruins. I will make Tyre a bare rock. ⁵Tyre will be an island where fishermen dry their nets. I have spoken, says the Lord God. The nations will steal valuable things from Tyre. ⁶Also, her villages on the shore across from the island will be destroyed by war. Then they will know that I am the Lord.

⁷"This is what the Lord God says: I will bring a king from the north against Tyre. He is Nebuchadnezzar king of Babylon, the greatest king. He will bring horses, chariots, horsemen and a great army. ⁸He will fight a battle and destroy your villages on the shore across from the island. He will set up devices to attack you. He will build a road of earth to the top of the walls. He will raise his shields against you. ⁹He will bring logs to pound through your city walls. And he will break down your towers with his iron bars. ¹⁰His horses will be so many that they will cover you with their dust. Your walls will shake at the noise of horsemen, wagons and chariots. The king of Babylon will enter your city gates. He will enter as men enter a city where the walls are broken through. ¹¹The hoofs of his horses will run over your streets. He will kill your people with the sword. Your strong pillars will fall down to the ground. ¹²Also, his men will take away your riches. They will steal the things you sell. They will break down your walls and destroy your nice houses. They will throw your stones, wood and trash into the sea. ¹³So I will stop your songs. The music of your harps will not be heard anymore. ¹⁴I will make you a bare rock. You will be a place for drying fishing nets. You will not be built again. This is because I, the Lord, have spoken, says the Lord God.

¹⁵"This is what the Lord God says to Tyre: The people who live along the seacoast will shake with fear when they hear your defeat. Those of you who are injured and dying will groan. ¹⁶Then all the leaders of the seacoast will go down from their thrones. They will take off their beautiful needlework clothes. They will clothe themselves with fear. They will sit on the ground. They will shake with fear all the time. They will be shocked when they see you. ¹⁷They will begin singing a funeral song about you. They will say to you:

Tyre, you famous city, you have
been destroyed!
Once seamen lived in you.
You and your people
had great power on the seas.
All the people around you

were afraid of you.
¹⁸Now the people who live by the
coast
will shake with fear on the day
you fall.
The islands of the sea
will be afraid because you have
been defeated.'

¹⁹"This is what the Lord God says: I will make you an empty city. You will be like the cities that have no people living in them. I will bring the deep ocean waters over you. The Mediterranean Sea will cover you. ²⁰At that time I will send you down to the place of the dead. You will join the people who died long ago. I will make you live with the dead below the earth among old ruined places. You will not come back from there. People will never live in you again. ²¹Other people will be afraid of what happened to you. It will be the end of you. People will look for you. But they will never find you again, says the Lord God."

27 The Lord spoke his word to me. He said: ²"Human being, sing a funeral song for the city of Tyre. ³Speak to Tyre that is at the entrance to the Mediterranean Sea. For the people of many lands along the seacoast, Tyre is a place for trade. 'This is what the Lord God says:

Tyre, you have said,
"I am like a beautiful ship."
⁴You were at home on the high seas.
Your builders have made your
beauty perfect.
⁵Your builders made all your boards
of fir trees from Mount Hermon.
They have taken a cedar tree from
Lebanon.
They took it to make a ship's
mast for you.
⁶They made your oars
from oak trees in Bashan.
They made your deck
from cypress trees from the coast
of Cyprus.
Your deck has ivory set into it.
⁷Your sail of linen with designs
sewed on it came from Egypt.
Your sail became like a flag for
you.
Your cloth shades over the deck
were blue and purple.
They came from the island of
Cyprus.
⁸Men from Sidon and Arvad used
oars to row you.
Tyre, your skilled men were the
sailors on your deck.

⁹Workers of Byblos were on board
  ship with you.
  They put caulk[n] in your ship's
    seams.
All the ships of the sea and their
  sailors
  came alongside to trade with you.

¹⁰ "Men of Persia, Lydia and Put
  were soldiers in your army.
They hung their shields and
  helmets on your walls.
  Their victories made you famous.
¹¹Men of Arvad and Celicia
  guarded your city walls all
    around.
  Men of Gammad
  were in your watchtowers.
They hung their shields around
  your walls.
  They made your beauty perfect.

¹² " 'Tarshish traded with you for many
kinds of things. They paid for them with
silver, iron, tin and lead.
¹³ " 'People of Greece, Tubal and Meshech traded with you. They traded
slaves and bronze things for the things
you sell.
¹⁴ " 'People of Beth Togarmah traded
work horses, war horses and mules for
the things you sell.
¹⁵ " 'People of Rhodes traded with you.
You sold your things on many coastlands. They paid you with ivory tusks
and valuable black wood.
¹⁶ " 'Aram traded with you because you
had so many good things to sell. They
traded turquoise, purple cloth and cloth
with designs sewed on. They also traded
fine linen, coral and rubies for the things
you sell.
¹⁷ " 'Judah and Israel traded with you.
They paid for the things you sell with
wheat from Minnith. They also paid
with honey, olive oil and balm.[d]
¹⁸ " 'Damascus traded with you because you have many good things. They
paid for them with wine from Helbon
and wool from Zahar.
¹⁹ " 'The Greeks from Uzal traded for
the things you sold. They paid with
wrought iron, cassia[d] and sugar cane for
your good things.
²⁰ " 'Dedan traded saddle blankets to
you.
²¹ " 'Arabia and all the rulers of Kedar
traded with you. They traded lambs,
male sheep and goats to you.

²² " 'The traders of Sheba and Raamah
traded with you. They paid with all the
best spices, valuable gems and gold.
²³ " 'Haran, Canneh, Eden and the
traders of Sheba, Asshur and Kilmad
traded with you. ²⁴They paid with the
best clothes, blue cloth and cloth with
designs sewed on. They traded carpets
of many colors and tightly wound ropes.

²⁵ " 'Trading ships
  carried the things you sold.
You were like a ship full of heavy
  cargo
  in the middle of the sea.
²⁶The men who rowed you
  brought you out into the high
    seas.
But the east wind has broken you
  to pieces
  in the middle of the sea.
²⁷Your wealth, your trade and the
  things you sell will sink.
  Your seamen, your sailors and
    your workers will sink.
Your traders, your soldiers,
  and everyone else on board
  will sink into the sea.
  This will happen on the day your
    ship is wrecked.
²⁸The people on the shore will shake
  with fear
  when your sailors cry out.
²⁹All the men who row
  will leave their ships.
The seamen and the sailors of other
  ships
  will stand on the shore.
³⁰They will cry loudly about you.
  They will cry very much.
They will throw dust on their
  heads.
  They will roll in ashes to show
    they are sad.
³¹They will shave their heads for you.
  And they will put on rough cloth
    to show they are upset.
They will cry very much for you.
  They will cry loudly.
³²And in their loud crying
  they will sing a funeral song for
    you.
  "No one was ever destroyed like
    Tyre,
  surrounded by the sea."
³³The things you traded went out
  over the seas.
  You met the needs of many
    nations.

27:9 caulk Something like tar put between the boards of a ship to make it waterproof so it will
not sink.

With your great wealth and things
    you sold,
    you made kings of the earth rich.
³⁴But now you are broken by the sea.
    You have sunk to the bottom.
    The things you sell and all your
        people
    have gone down with you.
³⁵All those who live along the shore
    are shocked by what happened to
        you.
    Their kings are terribly afraid.
    Their faces show their fear.
³⁶The traders among the nations hiss
    at you.
    You have come to a terrible end.
    And you are gone forever.'"

28 The Lord spoke his word to me.
He said: ²"Human being, say to
the ruler of Tyre: 'This is what the Lord
God says:
    You are too proud.
    And you say, "I am a god.
    I sit on the throne of a god
        in the middle of the seas."
    You think you are as wise as a god.
    But you are a man, not a god.
³You think you are wiser than
        Daniel.
    You think you can find out all
        secrets.
⁴Through your wisdom and
        understanding
    you have made yourself rich.
    You have gained gold and silver.
    And you have saved it in your
        storerooms.
⁵Through your great skill in trading,
    you have made your riches grow.
    You are too proud
        because of your riches.

⁶"'So this is what the Lord God says:
    You think you are wise
        like a god.
⁷But I will bring foreign people
        against you.
    They will be the cruelest nation.
    They will pull out their swords
        and destroy all that your wisdom
        has built.
    And they will dishonor your
        greatness.
⁸They will kill you.
    You will die a terrible death
        like those who are killed at sea.
⁹While they are killing you,
    you will not be able to say
        anymore, "I am a god."
    You will be only a man, not a god,
        when your murderers kill you.

¹⁰You will die like an unclean[d]
        person.
    Foreigners will kill you.

I have spoken, says the Lord God.'"

¹¹The Lord spoke his word to me. He
said: ¹²"Human being, sing a funeral
song for the king of Tyre. Say to him:
'This is what the Lord God says:
    You were an example of what was
        perfect.
    You were full of wisdom and
        perfect in beauty.
¹³You had a wonderful life,
    like those in Eden, the garden of
        God.
    Every valuable gem was on you:
        ruby, topaz and emerald,
        yellow quartz, onyx and jasper,
        sapphire, turquoise and
            chrysolite.
    Your jewelry was made of gold.
    It was prepared on the day you
        were created.
¹⁴I appointed a living creature to
        guard you.
    I put you on the holy mountain of
        God.
    You walked among the gems of
        fire.
¹⁵Your life was right and good.
    This was from the day you were
        created,
    until evil was found in you.
¹⁶Because you traded with countries
        far away,
    you learned to be cruel, and you
        sinned.
    So I threw you down in disgrace
        from the mountain of God.
    And the living creature who
        guarded you
    forced you out from among the
        gems of fire.
¹⁷You became too proud
        because of your beauty.
    You ruined your wisdom
        because of your greatness.
    I threw you down to the ground.
    Your example taught a lesson to
        other kings.
¹⁸You dishonored your places of
        worship
    through your many sins and
        dishonest trade.
    So I set your city on fire.
    And it burned up.
    I turned you into ashes on the
        ground
    for all those watching to see.

¹⁹All the nations who knew you
   were shocked about you.
   Your punishment was so terrible.
   And you are gone forever.'"

²⁰The Lord spoke his word to me. He
said: ²¹"Human being, look toward the
city of Sidon and prophesy[d] against her.
²²Say: 'This is what the Lord God says:

I am against you, Sidon.
   I will show my greatness among
      you.
   Then people will know that I am
      the Lord
   when I have punished Sidon.
   I will show my holiness by
      defeating her.
²³I will send diseases to Sidon,
   and blood will flow in her streets.
   Those who are wounded in Sidon
      will fall dead.
   She will be attacked from all
      sides.
   Then they will know that I am the
      Lord.

²⁴"'No more will neighboring nations
be like thorny branches or sharp stick-
ers to hurt Israel. Then they will know
that I am the Lord God.
²⁵"'This is what the Lord God says: I
will gather the people of Israel from the
nations where they are scattered. I will
show my holiness when the nations see
what I do to my people. Then they will
live in their own land—the land I gave
to my servant Jacob. ²⁶Then they will
live safely in the land. They will build
houses and plant vineyards. They will
live in safety after I have punished all
the nations around who hate them. Then
they will know that I am the Lord their
God.'"

29 It was the tenth year, in the tenth
month of our captivity. It was on
the twelfth day of the month. The Lord
spoke his word to me. He said: ²"Human
being, look toward the king of Egypt.
And prophesy[d] against him and all
Egypt. ³Say: 'This is what the Lord God
says:

I am against you, king of Egypt.
   You are like a great crocodile that
      lies in the Nile River.
You say, "The Nile is mine.
   I made it for myself."
⁴But I will put hooks in your jaws.
   I will make the fish of the Nile
      stick to your sides.
I will pull you up out of your rivers,
   with all the fish sticking to your
      sides.

⁵I will leave you in the desert.
   I will leave you and all the fish
      from your rivers.
You will fall on the open field.
   You will not be picked up or
      buried.
I have given you to the wild
      animals.
   And I have given you to the birds
      of the sky for food.
⁶Then all the people who live in Egypt
will know that I am the Lord.

"'Israel tried to lean on you for help.
But you were like a crutch made out of a
weak stalk of grass. ⁷When their hands
grabbed you, you splintered and tore
open their shoulders. When they leaned
on you, you broke and made all their
backs twist.

⁸"'So this is what the Lord God says:
I will cause an enemy to attack you. He
will kill your men and animals. ⁹Then
Egypt will become an empty desert.
They will know that I am the Lord.

"'This is because you said, "The Nile
River is mine. And I have made it." ¹⁰So,
I am against you. I am against your rivers. I will destroy the land of Egypt. It
will be empty desert from Migdol in the
north to Aswan in the south. It will be
empty all the way to the southern border
of Cush. ¹¹No man or animal will walk
through it. No one will live in Egypt for
40 years. ¹²I will make the land of Egypt
the emptiest country of all. And her cities will be the emptiest of all ruined cities for 40 years. And I will scatter the
Egyptians among the nations. And I will
spread them among the countries.

¹³"'This is what the Lord God says:
After 40 years I will gather Egypt from
the nations where they have been scattered. ¹⁴I will bring back the Egyptian
captives. I will make the Egyptians return to southern Egypt. They will return
to the land that they came from. They
will become a weak kingdom there. ¹⁵It
will be the weakest kingdom. It will
never again rule other nations. I will
make it so weak it will never again rule
over the nations. ¹⁶The Israelites will
never again depend on Egypt. Egypt's
punishment will remind the Israelites of
their sin. They turned to Egypt for help
and not to God. Then they will know
that I am the Lord God.'"

¹⁷It was the twenty-seventh year of
our captivity, in the first month. It was
on the first day of the month. The Lord
spoke his word to me. He said: ¹⁸"Hu-

man being, Nebuchadnezzar king of
Babylon made his army fight hard
against Tyre. Every soldier's head was
rubbed bare. Every shoulder was
rubbed raw. But Nebuchadnezzar and
his army gained nothing from fighting
Tyre. ¹⁹So this is what the Lord God says:
I will give the land of Egypt to Nebuchadnezzar king of Babylon. And Nebuchadnezzar king of Babylon will take
away Egypt's people. He will take Egypt's wealth and
its valuable things as pay for his army.
²⁰I have given Nebuchadnezzar the land
of Egypt. It is a reward for working hard
to defeat Egypt for me. That is what the
Lord God says.

²¹"On that day I will make Israel grow
strong again. I will let you, Ezekiel,
speak to them. Then they will know that
I am the Lord God."

30 The Lord spoke his word to me. He
said, ²"Human being, prophesy[d]
and say, 'This is what the Lord God says:
Cry and say,
  "The terrible day is coming."
³The day is near.
  The Lord's day of judging is near.
It is a cloudy day.
  It is a time when the nations will
    be judged.
⁴An enemy will attack Egypt.
  And Cush will tremble with fear.
When the killing begins in Egypt,
  her wealth will be taken away.
Egypt's foundations will be torn
  down.

⁵Cush, Put, Lydia, Arabia, Libya and my
people will die. All these who made an
agreement with Egypt will fall dead in
war.
⁶"'This is what the Lord God says:
  Those who fight on Egypt's side
    will fall.
  The power she is proud of will go
    down.
  The people in Egypt will fall dead
    in war
    from Migdol in the north to
      Aswan in the south,
    says the Lord God.
⁷They will be
  the emptiest land.
  Egypt's cities will be
    like other cities that lie in ruin.
⁸Then they will know that I am the
  Lord.
  This will happen when I set fire
    to Egypt
  and when all those nations on
    her side are crushed.

⁹"'At that time I will send messengers
in ships. They will frighten Cush which
now feels safe. The people of Cush will
tremble with fear when Egypt is punished. And that time is sure to come.
¹⁰"'This is what the Lord God says:
  I will destroy great numbers of
    people in Egypt.
  I will do it through
    Nebuchadnezzar king of
    Babylon.
¹¹Nebuchadnezzar and his army
  are the cruelest army of any
    nation.
  They will be brought in to
    destroy the land.
  They will pull out their swords
    against Egypt.
  They will fill the land with those
    they kill.
¹²I will make the streams of the Nile
  River become dry land.
  Then I will sell the dry land to
    evil people.
  I will destroy the land and
    everything in it.
  I will do it through the power of
    strangers.

I, the Lord, have spoken.
  ¹³"'This is what the Lord God says:
  I will destroy the idols.
  And I will take away the statues
    of false gods from the city of
    Memphis.
  There will no longer be a leader in
    Egypt.
  And I will spread fear through
    the land of Egypt.
¹⁴I will make southern Egypt empty.
  I will start a fire in Zoan.
  I will punish Thebes.
¹⁵And I will pour out my anger
    against Pelusium,
  the strong place of Egypt.
  I will destroy great numbers of
    people in Thebes.
¹⁶I will set fire to Egypt.
  Pelusium will be in great pain.
  The walls of Thebes will be broken
    open.
  And Memphis will have troubles
    every day.
¹⁷The young men of Heliopolis and
    Bubastis
  will fall dead in war.
  And the people will be taken
    away as captives.
¹⁸In Tahpanhes the day will be dark
  when I break Egypt's power.
  A cloud will cover Egypt.

And her villages will be captured
  and taken away.
¹⁰So I will punish Egypt.
  And they will know I am the
    Lord.'"

²⁰It happened in the eleventh year of
our captivity, in the first month. It was
on the seventh day of the month. The
Lord spoke his word to me. He said:
²¹"Human being, I have broken the powerful arm of the king of Egypt. It has not
been tied up so it will not get well. It has
not been wrapped with a bandage. So
his arm will not be strong enough to
hold a sword in war. ²²So this is what the
Lord God says: I am against the king of
Egypt. I will break his arms. I will break
both the strong arm and the broken arm.
I will make the sword fall from his hand.
²³I will scatter the Egyptians among the
nations. And I will spread them among
the countries. ²⁴I will make the arms of
the king of Babylon strong. I will put my
sword in his hand. But I will break the
arms of the king of Egypt. Then he will
cry out in pain as a wounded man cries
out. ²⁵So I will make the arms of the king
of Babylon strong. But the arms of the
king of Egypt will fall. Then they will
know that I am the Lord. I will put my
sword into the hand of the king of Babylon. And he will use the sword in war
against Egypt. ²⁶Then I will scatter the
Egyptians among the nations. And I will
spread them among the countries. And
they will know that I am the Lord."

31 It happened in the eleventh year of
our captivity, in the third month. It
was on the first day of the month. The
Lord spoke his word to me. He said:
²"Human being, say to the king of Egypt
and his people:

'No one was like you in your
    greatness.
³Assyria was once like a cedar tree
    in Lebanon.
  It had beautiful branches that
    shaded the forest.
  It was very tall.
    Its top was among the clouds.
⁴Much water made the tree grow.
    The deep springs of water made
      the tree tall.
  Rivers flowed
    around the bottom of the tree.
  They sent their streams
    to all other trees of the field.
⁵So the tree was taller
    than all the other trees of the
      field.

Its branches became long and big
    because of so much water.
⁶All the birds of the sky
    made their nests in the tree's
      branches.
  And all the wild animals
    gave birth under the tree's
      branches.
  All great nations
    lived in the tree's shade.
⁷So the tree was great and beautiful,
    with its long branches.
  Its roots reached down to many
      waters.
⁸The cedar trees in the garden of
      God
    were not as great as it was.
  The pine trees
    did not have such great branches.
  The plane trees
    did not have such branches.
  No tree in the garden of God
    was as beautiful as this tree.
⁹I made it beautiful
    with many branches.
  And all the trees of Eden in the
      garden of God
    wanted to be like it.

¹⁰"'So this is what the Lord God says:
The tree has grown tall. Its top has
reached the clouds. And it has become
proud of its height. ¹¹So I have let a
mighty ruler of the nations take care of
the tree. The ruler will surely punish the
tree. Because it is evil I will get rid of it.
¹²The cruelest foreign nation cut it down
and left it. The tree's branches fell on
the mountains and in all the valleys. Its
broken branches were in all the ravines
of the land. All the nations of the earth
left the shade of that tree. ¹³The birds of
the sky live on the fallen tree. The wild
animals live among the tree's fallen
branches. ¹⁴Then the trees that grow by
the water will not be proud to be tall.
They will not put their tops among the
clouds. None of the trees that are watered well will grow that tall. They all
are meant to die and go under the
ground. They will be with those who
have died and have gone down to where
the dead are.

¹⁵"'This is what the Lord God says:
On the day when the tree went down to
where the dead are, I made people cry
loudly. I covered the deep springs and
held back their rivers. And the great
waters stopped flowing. I made Lebanon cry loudly for the great tree. All the
trees of the field dried up and died. ¹⁶I

made the nations shake with fear at the sound of the tree falling. I brought the tree down to where the dead are. It went with those who go down to the grave. Then trees of Eden and the best trees of Lebanon were comforted. All the well-watered trees were comforted in the earth below. ¹⁷But these trees also went down with the great tree to the place where the dead are. They went to join those who were killed in war. They had lived under the great tree's shade. They were its friends among the nations.

¹⁸"So no tree in Eden is equal to you in greatness and honor. But you will go down with the trees of Eden to the earth below. You will lie among unclean^d people who were killed in war.

"'This will happen to the king of Egypt and all his people, says the Lord God.'"

32 It happened in the twelfth year, in the twelfth month of our captivity. It was on the first day of the month. The Lord spoke his word to me. He said: ²"Human being, sing a funeral song about the king of Egypt. Say to him:

'You are like a young lion among the nations.
You are like a crocodile in the seas.
You splash around in your streams.
And you stir up the waters with your feet.
You make the rivers muddy.

³"'This is what the Lord God says:
I will spread my net over you.
And I will use a large group of people
to pull you up in my net.
⁴Then I will throw you on the land.
I will toss you into the open field.
I will let the birds of the sky rest on you.
And I will let the animals of the earth eat you until they are full.
⁵I will scatter your flesh on the mountains.
And I will fill the valleys with what is left of you.
⁶I will drench the land with your flowing blood.
I will soak the mountains,
and the ravines will be full of your flesh.
⁷I will make you disappear.
And I will cover the sky and make the stars dark.
I will cover the sun with a cloud.
And the moon will not shine.

⁸I will make all the shining lights in the sky
become dark over you.
I will bring darkness over your land,
says the Lord God.
⁹I will cause many people to be afraid
when I have another nation destroy you.
Nations you have not known will be afraid because of you.
¹⁰I will cause people to be shocked about you.
Their kings will tremble with fear because of you
when I swing my sword before them.
They will shake every moment
on the day you fall.
Each king will be afraid for his own life.

¹¹"'So this is what the Lord God says:
The sword of the king of Babylon will come on you.
¹²I will cause your people to fall
by the swords of mighty soldiers.
They are the most terrible of all the nations.
They will destroy the pride of Egypt.
All Egypt's people will be destroyed.
¹³I will also destroy all Egypt's cattle
which live alongside many waters.
The foot of man will not stir the waters.
And the hoofs of cattle will not muddy them anymore.
¹⁴So I will let the Egyptians' waters become quiet.
I will cause their rivers to run as smoothly as olive oil,
says the Lord God.
¹⁵I will make the land of Egypt empty.
I will take everything that is in the land.
I will destroy all those who live in Egypt.
Then they will know that I am the Lord.'

¹⁶"This is the funeral song people will sing for Egypt. The women of the nations will sing it for Egypt. They will sing a funeral song for Egypt and all its people, says the Lord God."

¹⁷It happened in the twelfth year of

our captivity. It was on the fifteenth day of the month. The Lord spoke his word to me. He said: [18]"Human being, cry for the people of Egypt. Bring down Egypt, together with the women of the powerful nations. Bring them down to the earth below. Bring them down with those who go to the place of the dead. [19]Say to them: 'Are you more beautiful than others? Go lie down in death with those who are unclean.'[d] [20]The Egyptians will fall among those killed by war. Egypt is going to be killed by the sword. The enemy will drag her and all her people away. [21]The leaders of the mighty ones will speak from the place of death. They will say about the king of Egypt and the nations which help him: 'The king and the nations which help him have come down here. They lie killed by the sword among those who are unclean.'

[22]"Assyria and all its army lie dead there. The graves of their soldiers are all around. All were killed in war. [23]Assyria's grave was put in the deep parts of the place where the dead are. And its army lies around its grave. When they lived, they frightened people in the land of the living. But now all of them have been killed in war.

[24]"The nation of Elam is there. And all its army is around its grave. All of them were killed in war. They had frightened people on earth and were unclean. So they went down to the lowest parts of the place where the dead are. And they must carry their shame with those who go down to the place where the dead are. [25]A bed is made for Elam with all those killed in war. They will be in the place where the dead are. The graves of her soldiers are all around her. Elam's people are unclean. So they have been killed in war. They also scared people who live on earth. But they must also carry their shame with those who go down to where the dead are. Their graves are with the rest who were killed. [26]"Meshech and Tubal are there. The graves of all their soldiers surround them. All of them are unclean. So they have been killed in war. They also frightened people who live on earth. [27]But they are not buried with the other unclean soldiers who have been killed in battle. They are not with those who went where the dead are with their weapons of war. These soldiers had their swords laid under their heads and their shields on their bodies. People who live on earth

used to be afraid of these mighty soldiers. [28]"You, king of Egypt, will be broken and lie among those who are unclean. You will be with those who were killed in war.

[29]"Edom is there also. Its kings and all its leaders are there. They were mighty. But now they lie in death with those killed in war. They will lie with those who are unclean. And they will be with those who go down to where the dead are. [30]"All the rulers of the north are there. And all the Sidonians are there. Their strength frightened people. These rulers of the north and the Sidonians have gone down in shame with those who were killed. They are unclean, lying with those killed in war. They have carried their shame with those who go down to where the dead are.

[31]"The king of Egypt and his army will see these who have been killed in war. Then the king and all his army will be comforted for all his soldiers killed in war, says the Lord God. [32]I made people who live on earth afraid of the king of Egypt. But he and his people will lie among those who are unclean. They will lie with those who were killed by the sword, says the Lord God."

33

The Lord spoke his word to me. He said: [2]"Human being, speak to your people. Say to them: 'I might bring a war against a land. The people of the land may choose one of their men. They may make him their watchman. [3]This watchman might see the enemy coming to attack the land. And he blows the trumpet and warns the people. [4]A person might hear the sound of the trumpet, but do nothing. Then the enemy will come and kill him. That person will be responsible for his own death. [5]He heard the sound of the trumpet. But he did not do anything. So he is to blame for his own death. If he had done something, he would have saved his own life. [6]But the watchman might see the enemy coming to attack and not blow the trumpet. So the people are not warned. Then the enemy comes and kills one of them. That person has died because of his own sin. But I will punish the watchman for the person's death.'

[7]"As for you, human being, I have made you a watchman for Israel. If you hear a message from me, you must warn them for me. [8]I might say to the wicked person: 'Wicked man, you will surely

die.' But you might not speak to warn the evil person to stop doing evil. Then he will die while still a sinner. But I will punish you for his death. [9]But you might warn a wicked person to stop doing evil. If he does not stop, he will die while still a sinner. But you have saved your life.

[10]"So you, human being, say to Israel: 'You have said: Surely our law-breaking and sins are hurting us. They will kill us. What can we do so we will live?' [11]Say to them: 'The Lord God says: As surely as I live, this is true. I do not want a wicked person to die. I want him to stop doing evil and live. Turn back! Turn back from your wicked ways! You don't want to die, people of Israel.'

[12]"And you, human being, say to your people: 'The goodness of a good person will not save him when he sins. The evil of the wicked person will not cause him to be punished if he turns from it. A good person will not be able to live by the good he did earlier if he sins.' [13]I might tell the good person, "You will surely live." But he might think he has done enough good and then do evil. Then none of the good things he did will be remembered. He will die because of the evil he has done. [14]Or, I might say to the wicked person, "You will surely die." But he might turn from his sin and do what is right and honest. [15]He returns what somebody gave him as a promise to repay a loan. He pays back what he stole. He lives by the rules that give life. He does not sin. Then that one will surely live. He will not die. [16]He will not be punished for any of his sins. He now does what is right and fair. He will surely live.

[17]"But your people say: 'The way of the Lord is not fair.' But it is their own way that is not fair. [18]The good person might turn from his goodness and do evil. Then he will die for his evil. [19]But the wicked person might stop doing evil and do what is right and fair. Then he will live. [20]You still say: 'The way of the Lord is not fair.' Israel, I will judge each of you by his own ways."

[21]It happened in the twelfth year of our captivity. It was on the fifth day of the tenth month. A person who had escaped from Jerusalem came to me. He said, "Jerusalem has been defeated." [22]Now I had felt the power of the Lord on me the evening before. The Lord had made me able to talk again. He did this before the person came to me in the

morning. I could speak. I was not without speech anymore.

[23]Then the Lord spoke his word to me. He said: [24]"Human being, people who live in the ruins in the land of Israel are saying: 'Abraham was only one person. Yet he was given the land as his own. Surely the land has been given to us, who are many, as our very own.' [25]So say to them: 'This is what the Lord God says: You eat meat with the blood still in it. You ask your idols for help. You murder people. Should you then have the land as your very own? [26]You depend on your sword. You do terrible things which I hate. Each of you has sexual relations with his neighbor's wife. So should you have the land?'

[27]"Say to them: 'This is what the Lord God says: As surely as I live, this is true. Those who are among the city ruins in Israel will be killed in war. Those who live in the country will be eaten by wild animals. People hiding in the strong places and caves will die of disease. [28]I will make the land an empty desert. The people's pride in the land's power will end. The mountains of Israel will become empty. No one will pass through them. [29]They will know that I am the Lord when I make the land an empty desert. This is because of the things they have done that I hate.'

[30]"But as for you, human being, your people talk against you. They talk by the walls and in the doorways of houses. They say to each other: 'Come now, and hear the message from the Lord.' [31]So they come to you as if they are still my people. They sit before you. They hear your words. But they will not do them. With their mouths they tell me they love me. But their hearts desire their selfish profits. [32]To your people you are nothing more than a singer who sings love songs. You are like one who has a beautiful voice. You are like one who plays a musical instrument well. They hear your words, but they will not do them. [33]"This will come true. It will surely happen. Then the people will know that a prophet[d] has been among them."

34 The Lord spoke his word to me. He said: [2]"Human being, prophesy[d] against the leaders of Israel, who are like shepherds. Prophesy and say to them: 'This is what the Lord God says: How terrible it will be for the shepherds of Israel who feed only themselves! Why don't the shepherds feed the flock? [3]You eat the milk curds from the sheep. You clothe yourselves with the wool from the sheep. You kill the fat sheep. But you do not feed the flock. [4]You have not made the weak strong. You have not healed the sick. You have not put bandages on those that were hurt. You have not brought back those who strayed away. You have not searched for the lost. You ruled the sheep with cruel force. [5]The sheep were scattered because there was no shepherd. Then they became food for every wild animal. [6]My flock wandered over all the mountains and on every high hill. They were scattered over all the face of the earth. And no one searched or looked for them.

[7]"So, you shepherds, hear the word of the Lord. This is what the Lord God says: [8]As surely as I live, my flock has been caught. It has become food for all the wild animals. This is because the flock has no shepherd. The shepherds did not search for my flock. No, they fed themselves instead of my flock. [9]So, you shepherds, hear the word of the Lord. [10]This is what the Lord God says: I am against the shepherds. I will blame them for what has happened to my sheep. I will not let them tend the flock anymore. Then the shepherds will stop feeding themselves. And I will take my flock from their mouths. My sheep will no longer be their food.

[11]"This is what the Lord God says: I, myself, will search for my sheep. I will take care of them. [12]A shepherd will take care of his scattered flock when it is found. In the same way I will take care of my sheep. I will save them from all the places where they are scattered. I will do this on a cloudy and dark day. [13]I will bring them out from the nations. I will gather them from the countries. I will bring them to their own land. I will pasture them on the mountains and in the ravines of Israel. And I will feed them in all the places where people live in the land. [14]I will feed them in a good pasture. They will eat grass on the high mountains of Israel. They will lie down on good ground where they eat grass. They will eat in rich grassland on the mountains of Israel. [15]I will feed my flock and lead them to rest, says the Lord God. [16]I will search for the lost. I will bring back those that were scattered. I will put bandages on those that were hurt. I will make the weak strong. I will destroy those sheep that are fat and strong. I will tend the sheep with fairness.

[17]"'This is what the Lord God says: And as for you, my flock, I will judge between one sheep and another. I will judge between the male sheep and the male goats. [18]Is it not enough for you to eat grass in the good land? Must you crush the rest of the grass with your feet? Is it not enough for you to drink clear water? Must you make the rest of the water muddy with your feet? [19]Must my flock eat what you crush? And must they drink what you make muddy with your feet?

[20]"'So this is what the Lord God says to them: I, myself, will judge between the fat sheep and the thin sheep. [21]You push with your side and with your shoulder. You knock down all the weak sheep with your horns. You do this until you have forced them away. [22]So I will save my flock. They will not be hurt anymore. I will judge between one sheep and another. [23]Then I will put one shepherd over them, my servant David. He will feed them. He will tend them and will be their shepherd. [24]Then I, the Lord, will be their God. And my servant David will be a ruler among them. I, the Lord, have spoken.

[25]"'And I will make an agreement of peace with my sheep. I will remove harmful animals from the land. Then the sheep will live safely in the desert. And they will sleep in the woods without danger. [26]I will bless them and let them live around my hill. I will cause the rains to come when it is time for them. There will be showers to bless them. [27]Also the trees of the field will give their fruit. The land will give its harvest. And the sheep will be safe on their land. Then they will know that I am the Lord. I will break the bars of their captivity. And I will save them from the power of those who made them slaves. [28]They will not be led captive by the nations again. The wild animals will not eat them. But they will live safely. No one will make them afraid. [29]I will give them a place famous for its good crops. Then they will no longer suffer from hunger in the land. They will not suffer the insults of other nations anymore. [30]Then they will know that I, the Lord their God, am with them. The nation of Israel will know that they are my people, says the Lord God. [31]And you, my sheep, are the sheep of my pasture. You are my people and I am your God, says the Lord God.'"

35 The Lord spoke his word to me. He said: [2]"Human being, look toward Mount Edom and prophesy[d] against it. [3]Say to it: 'This is what the Lord God says: I am against you, Mount Edom. I will stretch out my hand against you. And I will make you an empty desert. [4]I will destroy your cities. And you will become empty. Then you will know that I am the Lord.

[5]"'This is because you have always been an enemy of Israel. You let them be defeated in war when they were in trouble. It was the time of their final punishment. [6]So the Lord God says, As surely as I live, I will let you be murdered. Murder will chase you. You did not hate murdering people, so murder will chase you. [7]And I will make Mount Edom an empty ruin. And I will destroy everyone who goes in or comes out of it. [8]I will fill its mountains with those who are killed. Those killed in war will fall on your hills. They will fall in your valleys and in all your ravines. [9]I will make you a ruin forever. No one will live in your cities. Then you will know that I am the Lord.

[10]"You said, "These two nations, Israel and Judah, and these two lands will be ours. We will take them for our own." But the Lord was there. [11]So this is what the Lord God says: As surely as I live, this is true. I will treat you just as you treated them. When you were angry and jealous, you acted hatefully against them. I will punish you. And that is how I will show the Israelites who I am. [12]Then you will know that I, the Lord God, have heard all your insults. Those insults were against the mountains of Israel. You said, "They have been ruined. They have been given to us to eat." [13]You have not stopped your proud talk against me. I have heard you. [14]This is what the Lord God says: All the earth will be happy when I make you an empty ruin. [15]You were happy when the land of Israel was ruined. But I will do the same thing to you. Mount Edom and all Edom, you will become an empty ruin. Then you will know that I am the Lord God.'"

36 "Human being, prophesy[d] to the mountains of Israel and say: 'Mountains of Israel, hear the word of the Lord. [2]This is what the Lord God says: The enemy has said this against you: "Now the old places to worship false gods have become ours." [3]So prophesy and say: 'This is what the Lord

God says: They have made you an empty ruin. They have crushed you from all around. You belonged to the other nations. People talked and whispered against you. [4]So, mountains of Israel, hear the word of the Lord God. The Lord God speaks to the mountains, hills, ravines and valleys. The Lord God speaks to the empty ruins and abandoned cities that have been robbed and laughed at by the other nations. [5]This is what the Lord God says: I have spoken in hot anger against the other nations. I have spoken against Edom. The Edomites took my land for themselves. They did this with joy and with hate in their hearts. They forced out the people and took their pastureland.' [6]So prophesy about the land of Israel. Say to the mountains, hills, ravines and valleys: 'This is what the Lord God says: I speak in my jealous anger. This is because you have suffered the insults of the nations. [7]So this is what the Lord God says: I promise that the nations around you will also have to suffer insults.

[8]"'But you, mountains of Israel, you will grow branches and fruit for my people. My people will soon come home. [9]I am concerned about you. I am for you. You will be plowed, and seed will be planted in you. [10]I will multiply the people who live on you. All the people of Israel will come. The cities will have people living in them. The ruins will be rebuilt. [11]I will make the people and animals living on you increase in number. They will grow and be fruitful. You will have people living on you as you did before. I will make you better off than at the beginning. Then you will know that I am the Lord. [12]I will cause my people Israel to walk on you. Then they will take you, and you will belong to them. You will never again take their children away from them.

[13]"'This is what the Lord God says: People say about you: "You eat people and take children from your nation." [14]You will not destroy people anymore. You will not make your nation stumble anymore, says the Lord God. [15]I will not make you listen to insults from the nations anymore. You will not suffer shame from them anymore, says the Lord God.'"

[16]The Lord spoke his word to me again. He said: [17]"Human being, the nation of Israel was living in their own land. But they made it unclean[d] by their ways and the things they did. Their ways

were like a woman's uncleanness in her time of monthly bleeding. [18]So I poured out my anger against them. I did it because of the murders they did in the land. And I did it because they made the land unclean with their idols. [19]I scattered them among the nations. And they were spread through all the countries. I punished them for how they lived and the things they did. [20]They dishonored my holy name in the nations where they went. The nations said about them: 'These are the people of the Lord. But they had to leave the land which he gave them.' [21]But I felt bad about my holy name. The nation of Israel had dishonored it among the nations where they went.

[22]"So say to the people of Israel, 'This is what the Lord God says: Israel, I am going to act, but not for your sake. Israel, I will do something to help my holy name. You have dishonored it among the nations where you went. [23]I will prove the holiness of my great name. It has been dishonored among the nations. You have dishonored it among these nations. But the nations will know that I am the Lord. I will prove myself holy before their eyes, says the Lord God.

[24]"'I will take you from the nations. I will gather you out of all the lands. And I will bring you back into your own land. [25]Then I will sprinkle clean water on you, and you will be clean. I will cleanse you from all your uncleanness and your idols. [26]Also, I will teach you to respect me completely. I will put a new way to think inside you. I will take out the stubborn heart like stone from your bodies. And I will give you an obedient heart of flesh. [27]I will put my Spirit[d] inside you. And I will help you live by my rules. You will be careful to obey my laws. [28]Then you will live in the land I gave to your ancestors. So you will be my people, and I will be your God. [29]Also, I will save you from all your uncleanness. I will command the grain to come and grow. I will not allow a time of hunger to hurt you. [30]I will multiply the harvest of the field. You will never again suffer shame among the nations because of hunger. [31]And you will remember your evil ways and the things you did that were not good. Then you will hate yourselves because of your sins and terrible acts that I hate. [32]I want you to know that I am not doing this for your sake, says the

Lord God. Be ashamed and embarrassed about your ways, Israel.

[33]"'This is what the Lord God says: This is what will happen on the day I cleanse you from all your sins: I will cause the cities to have people living in them again. And the destroyed places will be rebuilt. [34]The empty land will be plowed. It will no longer be a ruin for everyone who passes by to see. [35]They will say: "This land was ruined. Now it has become like the garden of Eden. The cities were destroyed. They were empty and ruined. But now they are protected and have people living in them." [36]Then those nations still around you will know. They will know that I, the Lord, have rebuilt what was destroyed. And I have planted what was empty. I, the Lord, have spoken. And I will do it.'

[37]"This is what the Lord God says: I will again be asked by the people of Israel to do this thing for them. I will make their people grow to be as many as a flock of sheep. [38]They will be like the flocks brought to Jerusalem during her holy feasts. Her ruined cities will be filled with flocks of people. Then they will know that I am the Lord."

37
[1]I felt the power of the Lord was on me. He brought me out by the Spirit[d] of the Lord. And he put me down in the middle of a valley. It was full of bones. [2]The Lord led me around among the bones. There were many bones on the bottom of the valley. I saw the bones were very dry. [3]Then he asked me, "Human being, can these bones live?"

I answered, "Lord God, only you know."

[4]The Lord said to me, "Prophesy[d] to these bones. Say to them, 'Dry bones, hear the word of the Lord. [5]This is what the Lord God says to the bones: I will cause breath to enter you. Then you will live. [6]I will put muscles on you. I will put flesh on you. I will cover you with skin. Then I will put breath in you, and you will live. Then you will know that I am the Lord.'"

[7]So I prophesied as I was commanded. While I prophesied, there was a noise and a rattling. The bones came together, bone to bone. [8]I looked and saw muscles come on the bones. Flesh grew, and skin covered the bones. But there was no breath in them.

⁹Then the Lord said to me, "Prophesy to the wind.ⁿ Prophesy, human being, and say to the wind: 'This is what the Lord God says: Wind, come from the four winds. Breathe on these people who were killed so they can live again.'" ¹⁰So I prophesied as the Lord commanded me. And the breath came into them, and they came to life. They stood on their feet. They were a very large army.

¹¹Then the Lord said to me: "Human being, these bones are like all the people of Israel. They say, 'Our bones are dried up, and our hope has gone. We are destroyed.' ¹²So, prophesy, and say to them: 'This is what the Lord God says: My people, I will open your graves. And I will cause you to come up out of your graves. Then I will bring you into the land of Israel. ¹³This is how you, my people, will know that I am the Lord. I will open your graves and cause you to come up from them. ¹⁴And I will put my Spirit inside you. You will come to life. Then I will put you in your own land. And you will know that I, the Lord, have spoken and done it, says the Lord.'"

¹⁵The Lord spoke his word to me. He said, ¹⁶"Human being, take a stick of wood. Write on it, 'For Judah and all the Israelites with him.' Then take another stick of wood. Write on it, 'The stick of Ephraim, for Joseph and all the Israelites with him.' ¹⁷Then join them together into one stick. Then they will be one in your hand.

¹⁸"Your people will say to you, 'Explain to us what you mean by this.' ¹⁹Tell them, 'This is what the Lord God says: I will take the stick which is for Joseph and the tribesᵈ of Israel with him. This stick is in the hand of Ephraim. Then I will put it with the stick of Judah. And I will make them into one stick. And they will be one in my hand.' ²⁰Hold the sticks of wood on which you wrote these names. Hold them in your hands so the people can see them. ²¹Say to the people: 'This is what the Lord God says: I will take the people of Israel from among the nations where they have gone. I will gather them from all around. I will bring them into their own land. ²²I will make them one nation in the land, on the mountains of Israel. One king will rule all of them. They will never again be two nations. They will not be divided into two kingdoms anymore. ²³They will not

continue to make themselves uncleanᵈ by their idols, their statues of gods which I hate or their sins. But I will save them from all the ways they sin and turn against me. And I will make them clean. Then they will be my people. And I will be their God.

²⁴"'And my servant David will be their king. They will all have one shepherd. They will live by my rules and obey my laws. ²⁵They will live on the land I gave to my servant Jacob. It is the land in which your ancestors lived. They will all live on the land forever: they, their children and their grandchildren. David my servant will be their king forever. ²⁶And I will make an agreement of peace with them. It will be an agreement that continues forever. I will put them in their land. I will make them grow in number. Then I will put my Templeᵈ among them forever. ²⁷The place where I live will be with them. I will be their God, and they will be my people. ²⁸When my Temple is among them forever, the nations will know that I, the Lord, make Israel holy.'"

38 The Lord spoke his word to me. He said: ²"'Human being, turn toward Gog of the land of Magog. He is the chief ruler of the nations of Meshech and Tubal. Prophesyᵈ against him. ³Say, 'The Lord God says this: I am against you, Gog, chief ruler of Meshech and Tubal. ⁴I will turn you around. I will put hooks in your jaws. And I will bring you out with all your army, horses and horsemen. All of them will be finely dressed. They will be a large army with large and small shields. All of them will have swords. ⁵Persia, Cush and Put will be with them. All of them will have shields and helmets. ⁶There will also be Gomer with all its troops. And there will be the nation of Togarmah from the far north. It will have all its troops. There will be many other nations with you.

⁷"'Be prepared. Be prepared, you and all the armies that have come together to make you their commander. ⁸After many days you will be called for service. After many years you will come into a land that has been rebuilt from war. The people in the land will be gathered from many nations to the mountains of Israel. Those mountains were empty for a long time. These people were brought out from the nations. They will all be living in safety. ⁹And you will go up like a

storm. You will be like a cloud covering the land. It will be you, all your troops and many nations with you.

¹⁰ "'This is what the Lord God says: At that time ideas will come into your mind. You will think up an evil plan. ¹¹ You will say, "I will march against a land of towns without walls. I will attack those who are at rest and live in safety. All of them live without city walls. They have no gate bars or gates. ¹² I will capture valuable things and take good things. I will turn my power against the rebuilt ruins that now have people living in them. I will go against these people who have been gathered from the nations. They have become rich with farm animals and property. They live at the center of the world." ¹³ Sheba, Dedan and the traders of Tarshish, with all its villages, will say this to you: "Did you come to capture valuable things? Did you bring your troops together to take things? Did you bring them to carry away silver and gold? Did you bring them to take away farm animals and property?"'

¹⁴ "So prophesy, human being, and say to Gog: 'This is what the Lord God says: Now that my people Israel are living in safety, you will know about it. ¹⁵ You will come from your place in the far north. And many people will be with you. All of them will ride on horses. You will be a large group with a mighty army. ¹⁶ You will come against my people Israel like a cloud that covers the land. This will happen in the days to come. I will bring you against my land. Gog, then the nations will know me. They will see me show my greatness by what I do through you.

¹⁷ "'This is what the Lord God says: You are the one about whom I spoke in past days. I spoke through my servants the prophets of Israel. These prophets of Israel prophesied for many years. They said that I would bring you against them. ¹⁸ This is what will happen: On the day Gog comes against the land of Israel, my anger will become very great, says the Lord God. ¹⁹ With jealousy and great anger I tell you this. At that time there will surely be a great earthquake in Israel. ²⁰ The fish of the sea and the birds of the sky will shake with fear before me. The wild animals and everything that crawls on the ground will shake with fear. And all the people on the earth will shake with fear before me. Also the mountains will be thrown

down. And the cliffs will fall. Every wall will fall to the ground. ²¹ And I will call for a war against Gog on all my mountains, says the Lord God. Every man's sword will be against his brother. ²² I will punish Gog with disease and death. I will send a heavy rain, with hailstones and burning sulfur on Gog. I will send it on his army and on the many nations with him. ²³ Then I will show how great I am. I will show my holiness. And I will make myself known to the many nations that watch. Then they will know that I am the Lord.'

39 "Human being, prophesy[d] against Gog and say: 'This is what the Lord God says: I am against you, Gog, chief ruler of Meshech and Tubal. ² I will turn you around and lead you. I will bring you from the far north. I will send you to attack the mountains of Israel. ³ I will knock your bow out of your left hand. I will throw down your arrows from your right hand. ⁴ You will fall dead on the mountains of Israel. You, all your troops and the nations with you will fall dead. I will let you be food for every bird that eats meat and every wild animal. ⁵ You will die in the country. I have spoken, says the Lord God. ⁶ I will send fire on Magog and those who live in safety on the coastlands. Then they will know that I am the Lord.

⁷ "'And I will make myself known among my people Israel. I will not let myself be dishonored anymore. Then the nations will know that I am the Lord. They will know I am the Holy One in Israel. ⁸ It is coming! It will happen, says the Lord God. The day I talked about is coming.

⁹ "'Then those who live in the cities of Israel will go out. They will make fires with the enemy's weapons and burn them. They will burn both large and small shields. They will burn bows and arrows, war clubs and spears. They will use the weapons to burn in their fires for seven years. ¹⁰ They won't need to take wood from the field or chop firewood from the forests. This is because they will make fires with the weapons. They will take the valuable things of those who took their valuable things. They will grab the things of those who grabbed their things, says the Lord God.

¹¹ "'On that day I will give Gog a place to be buried in Israel. It will be the Valley of the Travelers, east of the Dead Sea.[d] It will block the road for travelers. This is because Gog and all his army will be

buried there. People will call it The Valley of Gog's Army.

[12] "The people of Israel will be burying them for seven months to make the land clean[d] again. [13] All the people of the land will bury them. The people of Israel will be honored on the day of my victory, says the Lord God.

[14] "They will choose men to work through the land to make it clean. With others they will bury Gog's soldiers still lying dead on the ground. After the seven months are finished, they will still search. [15] They will go through the land. If one person sees a human bone, he will put a marker by it. The sign will stay there until the gravediggers come. They will bury the bone in The Valley of Gog's Army. [16] A city will be there named Hamonah. So they will make the land clean again.'

[17] "Human being, this is what the Lord God says: Speak to every kind of bird and wild animal: 'Come together, come! Come together from all around to my sacrifice. I will prepare it for you. It is a great sacrifice on the mountains of Israel. Then you can eat flesh and drink blood. [18] You will eat the flesh of mighty men. You will drink the blood of the rulers of the earth. You will do it as people eat all the fat animals from Bashan: male sheep, lambs, goats and bulls. [19] You will eat and drink from my sacrifice which I have made ready for you. So you will eat fat until you are full. You will drink blood until you are drunk. [20] At my table you will eat until you are full of horses and riders and all kinds of soldiers,' says the Lord God.

[21] "And I will show my greatness among the nations. All the nations will feel my power when I punish them. [22] From that day on the people of Israel will know that I am the Lord their God. [23] And the nations will know Israel was taken away captive because they turned against me. So I turned away from them. And I let their enemies defeat them. All of them died in war. [24] I punished them for their uncleanness[d] and their sins. I turned away from them.

[25] "So this is what the Lord God says: Now I will bring the people of Jacob back from captivity. I will have mercy on the whole nation of Israel. I will not let them dishonor me. [26] The people will forget their shame. And they will forget how they rejected me. They will live in safety on their own land. No one will make them afraid. [27] I will bring the peo-

ple back from other lands. I will gather them from the lands of their enemies. That is how I will show that I am holy through my people. And many nations will see that I am holy. [28] Then my people will know that I am the Lord their God. This is because I sent them into captivity among the nations. But then I brought them back to their own land. And I didn't leave any behind. [29] I will not turn away from them anymore. I will put my Spirit[d] into the people of Israel, says the Lord God."

40 It was the twenty-fifth year of our captivity. It was at the beginning of the year, on the tenth day of the month. It was in the fourteenth year after Jerusalem was defeated. On that same day I felt the power of the Lord. He brought me to Jerusalem. [2] In the visions of God he brought me into the land of Israel. He put me on a very high mountain. On the south of the mountain there were some buildings that looked like a city. [3] The Lord took me closer to the buildings. I saw a man who looked as if he were made of bronze. He was standing in the gateway. He had a cord made of linen and a stick in his hand, both for measuring. [4] The man said to me, "Human being, look with your eyes and hear with your ears. And pay attention to all that I will show you. That's why you have been brought here. Tell the people of Israel all that you see."

[5] I saw a wall that surrounded the Temple.[d] The measuring stick in the man's hand was 10½ feet long. So the man measured the wall. It was 10½ feet thick and 10½ feet high.

[6] Then the man went to the east gate. He went up its steps and measured the opening of the gate. It was more than 10½ feet wide. [7] There were rooms for the guards. These were 10½ feet long and 10½ feet wide. The walls that came out between the guards' rooms were about 9 feet thick. And there was a gate next to the porch that faced the Temple. The opening of this gate was 10½ feet wide.

[8] Then the man measured the porch of the gate. [9] It was about 14 feet deep. And its doors were 3½ feet thick. The porch of the gate faced the Temple.

[10] There were three little rooms on each side of the last gate. These three rooms measured the same on each side. The walls between each room were the same thickness. [11] The man measured the width of the entrance to the gateway. It was 17½ feet wide. The length of the

gate was about 23 feet. [12]And there was a low wall about 21 inches high in front of each room. The rooms were 10½ feet on each side. [13]The man measured the gateway from the roof of one room to the roof of the opposite room. It was about 44 feet from one door to the opposite door. [14]The man also measured the porch. It was about 35 feet wide. The courtyard was around the porch. [15]From the front of the outer side of the gate to the front of the porch of the inner side of the gate was 87½ feet. [16]The rooms and porch had small windows on all sides. The windows were narrower on the side facing the gateway. Carvings of palm trees were on each inner wall of the rooms.

[17]Then the man brought me into the outer courtyard. I saw rooms and a pavement of stones. Thirty rooms were along the edge of the paved walkway. [18]The pavement ran alongside the gates. It was as long as the gates were wide. This was the lower pavement. [19]Then the man measured from the outer wall to the inner wall. The outer court between these two walls was 175 feet on the east and on the north.

[20]The man measured the length and width of the gate leading to the outer courtyard. It faced north. [21]It had three rooms on each side. Its inner walls and its porch measured the same as the first gate. It was 87½ feet long. And it was 44 feet wide. [22]Its windows, porch and carvings of palm trees measured the same as the east gate. Seven steps went up to the gate. And the gate's porch was opposite them. [23]The inner courtyard had a gate across from the northern gate like the one on the east. The man measured it and found it was 175 feet from inner gate to outer gate.

[24]Then the man led me south. I saw a gate facing south. He measured its inner walls and its porch. They measured the same as the other gates. [25]The gate and its porch had windows all around like the other gates. It was 87½ feet long and 44 feet wide. [26]Seven steps went up to this gate. Its porch was in front of them. It had carvings of palm trees on its inner walls. [27]A gate was on the south side of the inner courtyard. The man measured from gate to gate on the south side. It was 175 feet.

[28]Then the man brought me through the south gate to the inner courtyard. The inner south gate measured the same as the gates in the outer wall. [29]The inner southgate's rooms, inner walls and porch measured the same as the gates in the outer wall. There were windows all around the gate and its porch. The gate was 87½ feet long and 44 feet wide. [30]Each porch of each inner gate was about 44 feet long and about 9 feet wide. [31]The inner south gate's porch faced the outer courtyard. Carvings of palm trees were on its inside walls. Its stairway had eight steps.

[32]The man brought me into the inner courtyard on the east side. He measured the inner east gate. It measured the same as the other gates. [33]The inner east gate's rooms, inside walls and porch measured the same as the other gates. Windows were all around the gate and its porch. The inner east gate was 87½ feet long and 44 feet wide. [34]Its porch faced the outer courtyard. Carvings of palm trees were on its inner walls on each side. Its stairway had eight steps.

[35]Then the man brought me to the inner north gate. He measured it. It measured the same as the other gates. [36]Its rooms, inner walls and porch measured the same as the other gates. Windows were all around the gate. It was 87½ feet long and 44 feet wide. [37]Its porch faced the outer courtyard. Carvings of palm trees were on its inner walls on each side. And its stairway had eight steps.

[38]There was a room with a door that opened onto the porch of the inner north gate. In this room the priests washed animals for the burnt offerings. [39]There were two tables on each side of the room. Animals for burnt offerings, sin offerings and penalty offerings were killed on these tables. [40]On each side of the porch, outside the door to the room, were two tables. [41]So four tables were on one side of the gate. And four tables were on the other side of the gate. In all there were eight tables on which the priests killed animals for sacrifices. [42]There were four tables of cut stone for the burnt offering. These tables were about 3 feet long and 3 feet wide. And they were about 2 feet high. On these tables the priests put their tools. They used the tools to kill animals for burnt offerings and the other sacrifices. [43]Double hooks 3 inches long were put up on all the walls. The flesh for the offering was put on the tables.

[44]There were two rooms in the inner courtyard. One was beside the north gate. It faced south. The other room was beside the south gate. It faced north.

45The man said to me, "The room which faces the south is for the priests. They serve in the Temple.[d] 46And the room that faces north is for the priests who serve at the altar. These priests are descendants[d] of Zadok. They are the only descendants of Levi who can come near the Lord to serve him."

47The man measured the Temple courtyard. It was a perfect square. It was 175 feet long and 175 feet wide. The altar was in front of the Temple.

48The man brought me to the porch of the Temple.[d] And he measured each wall of the porch. It was about 9 feet on each side. The gate was 24½ feet wide. The walls of the gate were about 5 feet on each side. 49The porch was 35 feet long and 21 feet wide. Ten steps went up to the porch. Pillars were by the walls, one on each side of the entrance.

41 The man brought me to the Holy Place. He measured its walls. They were 10½ feet wide on each side. 2The entrance was 17½ feet wide. The walls alongside the entrance were about 9 feet wide on each side. The man measured the Holy Place. It was 70 feet long and 35 feet wide.

3Then the man went inside. And he measured the walls of the doorway. Each was 3½ feet wide. The doorway was 10½ feet wide. The walls next to it were more than 12 feet thick. 4Then the man measured the room at the end of the Holy Place. It was 35 feet long and 35 feet wide. The man said to me, "This is the Most Holy Place."

5Then the man measured the wall of the Temple.[d] It was 10½ feet wide. The side rooms were 7 feet wide all around the Temple. 6The side rooms were on three different stories, each above the other. There were 30 rooms on each story. The side rooms had ledges on the wall all around. The rooms rested on the ledges but were not attached to the walls. 7The side rooms around the Temple were wider on each higher story. So rooms were wider on the top story. A stairway went up from the lowest story to the highest through the middle story.

8I also saw that the Temple had a raised base all around. It was the foundation for the side rooms and was 10½ feet thick. 9The outer wall of the side rooms was about 9 feet thick. There was an open area between the side rooms of the Temple 10and the priests' rooms. It was 35 feet wide and went all around the Temple. 11The doors of the side rooms led to a paved base around the outside of the Temple. One door faced north. And the other door faced south. The paved base was about 9 feet wide all around.

12There was a building facing the Temple courtyard at the west side. It was 122½ feet wide. The wall of the building was about 9 feet thick all around. It was 157½ feet long.

13Then the man measured the Temple. The Temple was 175 feet long. This included the courtyard with the building and its walls. It was all 175 feet long. 14Also the eastern front of the Temple and its courtyard was 175 feet wide.

15The man measured the length of the building facing the courtyard on the west side, including its side rooms. Its walls from one side to the other were 175 feet.

The Holy Place, the Most Holy Place and the porch of the courtyard 16had wood panels on the walls. By the doorway, the Temple had wood panels on the walls. The wood covered all the walls from the floor up to the windows. The windows were covered with crossed strips of wood.

17In the space above the entrance to the Most Holy Place there were carvings. And on the outside and all the walls around the Most Holy Place and the Holy Place were carvings. 18The carvings were of creatures with wings and palm trees. A palm tree was between each carved creature. Every creature had two faces. 19One was a man's face looking toward the palm tree on one side. The other was a lion's face looking toward the palm tree on the other side. They were carved all around the Temple wall. 20This was from the floor to above the door. Palm trees and creatures with wings were carved on all the walls of the Holy Place. 21The walls of the Holy Place were square. In front of the Most Holy Place was something that looked like 22an altar of wood. It was more than 5 feet high and 3 feet wide. Its corners, base and sides were wood. The man said to me, "This is the table that is in the presence of the Lord." 23Both the Holy Place and the Most Holy Place had double doors. 24Each of the doors had two pieces that would swing open. 25Palm trees and creatures with wings were also carved on the doors of the Holy Place. They were like those carved on the walls. And there was a wood roof on the front Temple porch.

²⁶There were windows and palm trees on both side walls of the porch. The side rooms of the Temple were also covered by a roof.

42 Then the man led me north out into the outer courtyard. He led me to the rooms across from the Temple^d courtyard. The outer wall was north of these rooms. ²The building on the north side was 175 feet long and 87½ feet wide. ³There was 35 feet of the Temple courtyard between this building and the Temple. On the other side, this building faced the stone pavement of the outer courtyard. The building had rooms and balconies on three stories. ⁴There was a hallway on the north side of the rooms. It was 17½ feet wide and 175 feet long. Doors led into the rooms from this hallway. ⁵The top rooms were narrower. This was because the balconies took more space from them. The rooms on the first and second stories of the building were wider. ⁶The rooms were on three stories. They did not have pillars like the pillars of the courtyards. So the top rooms were farther back than those on the first and second stories. ⁷There was a wall outside parallel to the rooms and to the outer courtyard. It ran in front of the rooms for 87½ feet. ⁸The row of rooms along the outer courtyard was 87½ feet long. The rooms that faced the Temple were about 175 feet long. ⁹The lower rooms had an entrance on the east end of the building. This was so a person could enter them from the courtyard.

¹⁰There were rooms on the south side, parallel to the wall of the outer courtyard. They faced the Temple courtyard. ¹¹These rooms had a hallway in front of them. They were like the rooms on the north. They had the same length and width. And the doors were the same. ¹²The doors of the south rooms were like the doors of the north rooms. There was a door at the east end of a hall. This hall went to all the rooms.

¹³The man said to me, "The north and south rooms across from the Temple courtyard are holy rooms. There the priests who go near the Lord will eat the most holy offerings. There they will put the most holy offerings: the grain offerings, sin offerings and the penalty offerings. ¹⁴The priests who enter the Holy Place must leave their serving clothes there. Then they may go into the outer courtyard. This is because these clothes are holy. The priests must put on other clothes. Then they may go to the part of the Temple which is for the people."

¹⁵The man finished measuring inside the Temple.^d Then he brought me out through the east gate. He measured the area all around. ¹⁶The man measured the east side with the measuring stick. It was 875 feet by the measuring stick. ¹⁷He measured the north side. It was 875 feet by the measuring stick. ¹⁸He measured the south side. It was 875 feet by the measuring stick. ¹⁹He went around to the west side. And it measured 875 feet by the measuring stick. ²⁰So he measured the Temple on all four sides. The Temple had a wall all around it. It was 875 feet long and 875 feet wide. It separated the holy from that which is not holy.

43 The man led me to the outer east gate. ²And I saw the greatness of the God of Israel coming from the east. God's voice was like the roar of rushing water. His greatness made the earth shine. ³I saw a vision. It was like the vision I had seen when the Lord came to destroy the city. It was also like the vision I had seen by the Kebar River. I bowed facedown on the ground. ⁴The greatness of the Lord came into the Temple^d through the east gate.

⁵Then the Spirit^d picked me up. And he brought me into the inner courtyard. There the Lord's greatness filled the Temple. ⁶The man stood at my side. I heard someone speaking to me from inside the Temple. ⁷The voice from the Temple said to me, "Human being, this is my throne. And this is the place my feet rest. I will live here among the Israelites forever. The people of Israel will not make my holy name unclean^d again. Neither the people nor their kings will make it unclean by their sexual sins. Nor will they make it unclean with the dead bodies of their kings. ⁸They made my name unclean by putting their doorway next to my doorway. And they put their doorpost next to my doorpost. Only a wall separated me from them. When they did their acts that I hate, they made my holy name unclean. So I destroyed them in my anger. ⁹Now let them stop their sexual sins. And let them take the dead bodies of their kings far away from me. Then I will live among them forever.

¹⁰"Human being, tell the people of Israel about the Temple. Then they will be ashamed of their sins. Let them think about the plan of the Temple. ¹¹Then

they will be ashamed of all they have done. Let them know the design of the Temple. Let them know how it is built. Show them its exits and entrances. Show them all its designs, all its rules and all its teachings. And write the rules as they watch. Do this so they can obey all the Temple's teachings and rules. [12]This is the teaching of the Temple: All the area around the top of the mountain is most holy. This is the teaching of the Temple.

[13]"And these are the measurements of the altar, using the measuring stick. It is 21 inches long. The altar's base is 21 inches high and 21 inches long. Its rim is about 9 inches around its edge. And the altar is this tall: [14]From the ground up to the lower ledge, it measures 3½ feet. It is 21 inches wide. It measures 7 feet from the smaller ledge to the larger ledge and is 21 inches wide. [15]The place where the sacrifice is burned on the altar is 7 feet high. The four corners are shaped like horns and reach up above it. [16]It is square. It is 21 feet long and 21 feet wide. [17]The upper ledge is also square, 24½ feet long and 24½ feet wide. The border around it is 10½ inches wide. Its base is 21 inches around. Its steps are on the east."

[18]Then the man said to me, "Human being, this is what the Lord God says: These are the rules for the altar. When it is built, use these rules to offer burnt offerings and sprinkle blood on it. [19]You must give a young bull as a sin offering to the priests. These priests are the Levites from the family of Zadok. They come near me to serve me, says the Lord God. [20]Take some of the bull's blood and put it on the altar's four corners. Put it also on the four corners of the ledge. And put it on the border all around. This is how you will make the altar pure and ready for God's service. [21]Then take the bull for the sin offering and burn it in the proper place in the Temple[d] area. It will be outside the Holy Place.

[22]"On the second day offer a male goat. It must have nothing wrong with it. It will be for a sin offering. The priests will make the altar pure and ready for God's service. They will do it the same way they did with the young bull. [23]When you finish making the altar pure and ready, offer a young bull and a male sheep from the flock. They must also have nothing wrong with them. [24]You must offer them before the Lord. The priests will throw salt on them. Then

they will offer them as a burnt offering to the Lord. [25]"You must prepare a goat every day for seven days as a sin offering. Also, you must prepare a young bull and male sheep from the flock. They must have nothing wrong with them. [26]For seven days the priests will make the altar pure and ready for God's service. Then the priests will give the altar to God. [27]After these seven days, on the eighth day, the priests must present your offerings. They must offer your burnt offerings and your fellowship offerings on the altar. Then I will accept you, says the Lord God."

44

Then the man brought me back to the outer east gate of the Temple[d] area. The gate was shut. [2]The Lord said to me, "This gate will stay shut. It will not be opened. No one may enter through it. This is because the Lord God of Israel has entered through it. So it must stay shut. [3]Only the ruler himself may sit in the gateway to eat bread before the Lord. He must enter through the porch of the gateway and go out the same way."

[4]Then the man brought me through the outer north gate. He brought me to the front of the Temple. I looked and saw the greatness of the Lord. It was filling the Temple of the Lord. I bowed facedown on the ground.

[5]The Lord said to me, "Human being, pay attention. See this with your eyes. And hear this with your ears. See and hear everything I tell you about all the rules and teachings of the Temple of the Lord. Pay attention to the entrance to the Temple and to all the exits from the Temple area. [6]Then speak to those who refuse to obey. Say to the people of Israel, 'This is what the Lord God says: Stop doing all your acts that I hate, Israel! [7]You brought foreigners into my Holy Place. They were not circumcised[d] in the flesh. They had not given themselves to serving me. You dishonored my Temple when you offered me food, fat and blood. You broke my agreement by all your ways that I hate. [8]And you have not taken care of my holy things. You put foreigners in charge of my Temple. [9]This is what the Lord God says: Foreigners who are not circumcised in flesh and who do not give themselves to serving me may not enter my Temple. Even a foreigner living among the people of Israel may not enter.

[10]"'Some Levites stopped obeying me

when Israel left me and followed their idols. These Levites must be punished for their sin. [11]These Levites are to be servants in my Holy Place. They may guard the gates of the Temple. They may serve in the Temple. They may kill the animals for the burnt offering and the sacrifices for the people. They may stand before the people to serve them. [12]But these Levites helped the people worship their idols and caused the people of Israel to fall. So I have made this promise: They will be punished for their sin, says the Lord God. [13]They will not come near me to serve as priests. They will not come near any of my holy things or the most holy offerings. But they will be ashamed of the things they did that I hate. [14]But I will make them take care of the Temple. They will take care of everything that must be done in it.

[15]" 'But this is not true for priests who are Levites and descendants[d] of Zadok. They took care of my Holy Place when Israel left me. They may come near to serve me. They may stand in my presence. They will offer me the fat and blood of the animals they sacrifice, says the Lord God. [16]They are the only ones who may enter my Holy Place. They may come near my table to serve me. They may take care of the things I gave them.

[17]" 'When they enter the gates of the inner courtyard, they must wear linen robes. They must not wear wool to serve at the gates of the inner courtyard or in the Temple. [18]They will wear linen turbans on their heads and linen underclothes. They will not wear anything that makes them perspire. [19]At times they will go out into the outer courtyard to the people. But before they go, they must take off their serving clothes. They must put these clothes away in the holy rooms. And they must put on other clothes. Then they will not let their holy clothes hurt the people.

[20]" 'They must not shave their heads or let their hair grow long. They must keep the hair of their heads trimmed. [21]None of the priests may drink wine when they enter the inner courtyard. [22]The priests must not marry a widow or a divorced woman. They may marry only virgins[d] from the people of Israel. Or they may marry a widow of a priest. [23]They must teach my people the difference between what is holy and what is not holy. They must help my people

know what is unclean[d] and what is clean.

[24]" 'In court they will act as judges. When they judge, they will follow my teachings. They must obey my laws and my rules at all my special feasts. They must keep my Sabbaths[d] holy.

[25]" 'They must not go near a dead person, making themselves unclean.[d] But they are allowed to make themselves unclean if the dead person is a relative. It might be his father, mother, son, daughter, brother or a sister who has not married. [26]After the priest has been made clean again, he must wait seven days. [27]Then he may go into the inner courtyard to serve in the Temple. But he must offer a sin offering for himself, says the Lord God.

[28]" 'These are the rules about the priests and their property: They will have me instead of property. You will not give them any land to own in Israel. I am what they will own. [29]They will eat the grain offerings, sin offerings and penalty offerings. Everything Israel offers will be theirs. [30]And the best fruits of all the first harvests will be for the priests. And they will have all the special gifts offered to me. You will also give to the priests the first part of your grain that you grind. This will cause a blessing to come on your house. [31]The priests must not eat any bird or animal that died a natural death. And they must not eat one that has been torn by wild animals.

45" 'Divide the land for the Israelite tribes[d] by throwing lots.[d] At that time you will give a part of the land to belong to the Lord. It will be about 7 miles long and about 6 miles wide. All of this land will be holy. [2]An area of 875 feet square will be for the Temple.[d] There will be an open space around the Temple that is 87½ feet wide. [3]In the holy area you will measure a part about 7 miles long and 3 miles wide. The Most Holy Place will be in this holy area. [4]This holy part of the land will be for the priests who serve in the Temple. This is where they come near to serve the Lord. It will be a place for the priests' houses. And it will be the place for the Temple. [5]Another area will be about 7 miles long and more than 3 miles wide. It will be for the Levites, who serve in the Temple. It will belong to them so they will have cities in which to live.

[6]" 'And you will give the city an area that is about 1½ miles wide and about 7

miles long. It will be along the side of the holy area. It will belong to all the people of Israel.

⁷"The ruler will have land on both sides of the holy area and the city. On the west of the holy area, his land will reach to the Mediterranean Sea. On the east of the holy area, his land will reach to the eastern border. It will be as long as the land given to each tribe. ⁸This land will be the ruler's property in Israel. So my rulers will not be cruel to my people anymore. But they will give land to each tribe in the nation of Israel.

⁹"This is what the Lord God says: You have gone far enough, you rulers of Israel! Stop being cruel and hurting people. Do what is right and fair. Stop forcing my people out of their homes, says the Lord God. ¹⁰You must have honest scales, an honest dry measurement and an honest liquid measurement. ¹¹The dry measure and the liquid measure will be the same: The liquid measure will always be a tenth of a homer.ⁿ The ephah will always be a tenth of a homer. The measurement they follow will be the homer. ¹²The shekelⁿ will be worth 20 gerahs. A mina will be worth 60 shekels.

¹³"This is the gift you will offer: a sixth of an ephah from a homer of wheat; a sixth of an ephah from a homer of barley. ¹⁴The amount of oil you are to offer is a tenth of a bath from each cor. (Ten baths make a homer and also make a cor.) ¹⁵You should give 1 sheep from each flock of 200 from the watering places of Israel. They are to be offered with the grain offerings, burnt offerings and fellowship offerings. These offerings are to remove sins so you will belong to God, says the Lord God. ¹⁶All people in the land will give this special offering for the ruler of Israel. ¹⁷It will be the ruler's responsibility to supply the burnt offerings, grain offerings and drink offerings. These offerings will be given at the feasts and at the New Moons.ᵈ They will also be given on the Sabbathsᵈ and at all the other feasts of Israel. The ruler will supply the sin offerings, grain offerings and fellowship offerings. These offerings are to pay for the sins of Israel.

¹⁸"This is what the Lord God says: On the first day of the first month take a young bull that has nothing wrong with it. Use it to make the Templeᵈ pure and ready for God's service. ¹⁹The priest will take some of the blood from the sin offering. And he will put it on the doorposts of the Temple. He will put it on the four corners of the ledge of the altar. And he will put it on the posts of the gate of the inner courtyard. ²⁰You will do the same thing on the seventh day of the month. You will do it for anyone who has sinned by accident or without knowing it. This is how you make the Temple pure and ready for God's service.

²¹"On the fourteenth day of the first month you will celebrate the Feastᵈ of Passover. It will be a feast of seven days when you eat bread made without yeast. ²²On that day the ruler must offer a bull for himself and for all the people of the land. The bull will be a sin offering. ²³During the seven days of the feast the ruler must offer seven bulls. And he must offer seven male sheep. The bulls and sheep must have nothing wrong with them. They will be burnt offerings to the Lord. The ruler will offer them every day of the seven days of the feast. He must also offer a male goat every day as a sin offering. ²⁴The ruler must give as a grain offering a half bushel for each bull and a half bushel for each sheep. He must give a gallon of olive oil for each half bushel.

²⁵"Beginning on the fifteenth day of the seventh month, you will celebrate the Feastᵈ of Shelters. During the feast, the ruler will do the same things for seven days. He will supply the sin offering, burnt offering, grain offering and the olive oil.

46 "This is what the Lord God says: The east gate of the inner courtyard will be shut on the six working days. But it will be opened on the Sabbathᵈ day. And it will be open on the day of the New Moon.ᵈ ²The ruler will enter through the porch of the gateway. He will enter from outside and stand by the gatepost. Then the priests will offer the ruler's burnt offering and fellowship offerings. The ruler will worship at the entrance of the gate. Then he will go out. But the gate will not be shut until evening. ³The people of the land will worship at the entrance of that gateway. They will worship there in the presence

---

45:11 homer The Hebrew word means "donkey-load." It measured about 5 dry bushels or 175 liquid quarts. So an ephah was about one-half bushel. And a bath was about 18 quarts.
45:12 shekel In Ezekiel's time a shekel weighed about two-fifths of an ounce.

of the Lord on the Sabbaths and New Moons. [4]This is the burnt offering the ruler will offer to the Lord on the Sabbath day. It will be six male lambs that have nothing wrong with them. And it will be a male sheep that has nothing wrong with it. [5]He must give a half bushel grain offering with the male sheep. But he can give as much grain offering with the lambs as he pleases. He must also give a gallon of olive oil for each half bushel of grain. [6]On the day of the New Moon he must offer a young bull. It must have nothing wrong with it. He must also offer six lambs and a male sheep. They also must have nothing wrong with them. [7]The ruler must give a half bushel grain offering with the bull. And he must give the same with the male sheep. With the lambs, he can give as much grain as he pleases. But he must give a gallon of olive oil for each half bushel of grain. [8]And when the ruler enters, he must go in through the porch of the gateway. He must go out the same way.

[9]"'The people of the land must come before the Lord at the special feasts. Anyone who enters through the north gate to worship must go out through the south gate. Anyone who enters through the south gate must go out through the north gate. No one will return the same way he entered. Each person will go out straight ahead. [10]When the people go in, the ruler will go in with them. When they go out, the ruler will go out.

[11]"'At the feasts and regular times of worship a half bushel of grain must be offered. It will be offered with a young bull. And a half bushel of grain must be offered with a male sheep. But with an offering of lambs, the ruler may give as much grain as he pleases. He should give a gallon of olive oil for each half bushel of grain. [12]The ruler may give an offering as a special gift to the Lord. It may be a burnt offering or fellowship offering. When he gives it to the Lord, the inner east gate will be opened for him. He must offer his burnt offering and his fellowship offerings as he does on the Sabbath[d] day. Then he will go out. After he has gone out, the gate will be shut.

[13]"'Every morning you will give a year-old lamb that has nothing wrong with it. It will be for a burnt offering to the Lord every day. [14]Also, you must offer a grain offering with the lamb every morning. With it you will give three and a third quarts of grain and one and a third quarts of olive oil. This is to make the fine flour moist. It will be a grain offering to the Lord. This is a rule that must be kept from now on. [15]So they must always give the lamb, the grain offering and the olive oil every morning as a burnt offering.

[16]"'This is what the Lord God says: The ruler might give a gift from his land to one of his sons. Then that land will belong to that son's children. It is their property from their family. [17]But the ruler might give a gift from his land to one of his slaves. That land will belong to the slave only until the year of freedom. Then the land will go back to the ruler. Only the ruler's sons may keep a gift of land from the ruler. [18]The ruler must not take any of the people's land. He must not force them out of their land. He must give his sons land from his own land. Then my people will not be scattered out of their own land.'"

[19]The man led me through the entrance at the side of the gateway. He led me to the priests' holy rooms that face north. There I saw a place at the west end. [20]The man said to me, "This is where the priests will boil the meat of the penalty offering and sin offering. There the priests will bake the grain offering. Then they will not need to bring these offerings into the outer courtyard. That would hurt the people."

[21]Then the man brought me out to the outer courtyard. He led me to its four corners. In each corner of the courtyard was a smaller courtyard. [22]Small courtyards were in the four corners of the courtyard. Each small courtyard was 70 feet long and 52½ feet wide. All four corners measured the same. [23]A stone wall was around each of the four small courtyards. Places for cooking were built in each of the stone walls. The man said to me, "These are the kitchens. The Temple[d] priests will boil the sacrifices for the people here."

47 The man led me back to the door of the Temple.[d] I saw water coming out from under the doorway that faces east. (The Temple faced east.) The water flowed down from the south end of the Temple. It was south of the altar. [2]The man brought me out through the outer north gate. And he led me around outside to the outer east gate. The water was coming out on the south side of the gate.

[3]The man went toward the east with a

line in his hand. He measured about a third of a mile. Then he led me through water that came up to my ankles. ⁴The man measured about a third of a mile again. Then he led me through water that came up to my knees. Then he measured about a third of a mile again. And he led me through water up to my waist. ⁵The man measured about a third of a mile again. But it was now a river that I could not cross. The water had risen too high. It was deep enough for swimming. It was a river that no one could cross. ⁶The man asked me, "Human being, do you see this?"

Then the man led me back along the bank of the river. ⁷As I went back, I saw many trees on both sides of the water. ⁸The man said to me, "This water will flow toward the eastern areas. It will go down into the Jordan Valley. When the water enters the Dead Sea,ᵈ it will become fresh. ⁹And everywhere the river goes, there will be many animals and fish. Wherever this water goes the Dead Sea will become fresh. So where the river goes there will be many living things. ¹⁰Fishermen will stand by the sea. From En Gedi all the way to En Eglaim will become a place to spread fishing nets. There will be many kinds of fish in the Dead Sea. There will be as many kinds of fish as there are in the Mediterranean Sea. ¹¹But the swamps and marshes will not become fresh. They will be left for salt. ¹²All kinds of fruit trees will grow on both banks of the river. Their leaves will not dry and die. The trees will have fruit every month because the water for them comes from the Temple. The fruit from the trees will be for food. And their leaves will be for medicine."

¹³This is what the Lord God says: "These are the borders to divide the land among the 12 tribesᵈ of Israel. Joseph will have two parts of land. ¹⁴You will divide the land equally. I promised to give it to your ancestors. So this land will belong to you from your family.

¹⁵"This will be the border line of the land.

"On the north side it will start at the Mediterranean Sea. It will go by the Hethlon Road. This is where the road turns toward Lebo Hamath. And it will go to the cities of Zedad, ¹⁶Berothah and Sibraim. Sibraim is on the border between Damascus and Hamath. And it will go on to the city of Hazer Hatticon on the border of the country of Hauran.

¹⁷So the border line will go from the Mediterranean Sea east to the city of Hazar Enan. This is on the northern border of Damascus. And the country of Hamath will be on the north side of the border.

¹⁸"On the east side the border runs south from a point between Hauran and Damascus. It will go along the Jordan between Gilead and the land of Israel. It will continue to the city of Tamar on the Dead Sea.ᵈ This will be the east side of the land.

¹⁹"On the south side the border line will go east from Tamar. It will go all the way to the waters of Meribah Hadesh. Then it will run along the brook of Egypt to the Mediterranean Sea. This will be the south side of the land.

²⁰"On the west side the Mediterranean Sea will be the border line. It will go to a place across from Lebo Hamath. This will be the west side of your land.

²¹"So you will divide this land among the tribes of Israel. ²²You will divide it as a property for yourselves. And it will be for you and for the foreigners who live and have children among you. These foreigners will be like people born in Israel. You will divide some land for them among the tribes of Israel. ²³In whatever tribe the foreigner lives, you will give him some land," says the Lord God.

48 "These are the names of the tribes.ᵈ Dan will have one share. It will begin at the northern border. It will go from the sea and over the Hethlon Road. It will follow the road to Lebo Hamath. It will go all the way to Hazar Enan. This is on the northern border of Damascus. It will stop there next to Hamath. This will be Dan's northern border from the east side to the Mediterranean Sea on the west side.

²"South of Dan's border, Asher will have one share. It will go from the east side to the west side.

³"South of Asher's border, Naphtali will have one share. It will go from the east side to the west side.

⁴"South of Naphtali's border, Manasseh will have one share. It will go from the east side to the west side.

⁵"South of Manasseh's border, Ephraim will have one share. It will go from the east side to the west side.

⁶"South of Ephraim's border, Reuben will have one share. It will go from the east side to the west side.

⁷"South of Reuben's border, Judah

will have one share. It will go from the east side to the west side.

8 "South of Judah's border will be the holy area which you are to give. It will be about 7 miles wide. It will be as long and wide as one of the tribes' shares. It will run from the east side to the west side. The Temple[d] will be in the middle of this area.

9 "The share which you will give the Lord will be about 7 miles long and 3 miles wide. 10 The holy area will be divided among these people. For the priests on the north side, the land will measure about 7 miles. It will be 3 miles wide on the west side and 3 miles wide on the east side. It will be about 7 miles on the south side. The Temple of the Lord will be in the middle of it. 11 This land is for the priests who are given to serve the Lord. They are the descendants[d] of Zadok who did my work. They did not leave me. The other Levites left me when Israel did. 12 This share from the holy portion of the land will be a gift for these priests. It will be next to the land of the Levites.

13 "Alongside the land for the priests, the Levites will have a share. It will be about 7 miles long and 3 miles wide. Its full length will be about 7 miles. And its full width will be about 3 miles. 14 The Levites are not to sell or trade any of this land. They will not sell any of this best part of the land. It belongs to the Lord.

15 "The rest of the land will be an area about 1½ miles wide and 7 miles long. It will be for the other people's use. It will be for the city, for homes and for pastures. The city will be in the middle of it. 16 These are the city's measurements: the north side will be about a mile. The south side will be about a mile. The east side will be about a mile. And the west side will be about a mile. 17 The city's land for pastures will be about 437 feet on the north, 437 feet on the south, 437 feet on the east and 437 feet on the west. 18 Alongside the length of the holy area there will be left 3 miles on the east and 3 miles on the west. It will be used to grow food for the city workers. 19 The city workers will plow this land. The workers will be from all the tribes[d] of Israel. 20 This whole area will be square, 7 miles by 7 miles. You shall give to the Lord the holy share along with the city property.

21 "Land that is left over on both sides of the holy area and city property will belong to the ruler. That land will extend east of the holy area to the eastern border. And it will extend west of it to the Mediterranean Sea. Both of these areas run the length of the lands of the tribes. They belong to the ruler. The holy area with the Holy Place of the Temple[d] will be in the middle. 22 The Levites' land and the city property will be between the lands belonging to the ruler. The ruler's land will be between Judah's border and Benjamin's border.

23 "Here is what the rest of the tribes will receive: Benjamin will have one share. It will go from the east side to the Mediterranean Sea on the west side.

24 "South of Benjamin's land, Simeon will have one share. It will go from the east side to the west side.

25 "South of Simeon's land, Issachar will have one share. It will go from the east side to the west side.

26 "South of Issachar's land, Zebulun will have one share. It will go from the east side to the west side.

27 "South of Zebulun's land, Gad will have one share. It will go from the east side to the west side.

28 "The southern border of Gad's land will go east from Tamar on the Dead Sea[d] to the waters of Meribah Kadesh. Then it will run along the brook of Egypt to the Mediterranean Sea.

29 "This is the land you will divide among the tribes of Israel. These are to be their shares," says the Lord God.

30 "These will be the outside borders of the city: The north side will measure more than a mile. 31 There will be three gates facing north. They are Reuben's Gate, Judah's Gate and Levi's Gate. The city's gates will be named for the tribes[d] of Israel.

32 "The east side will measure more than a mile. There will be three gates facing east. They are Joseph's Gate, Benjamin's Gate and Dan's Gate.

33 "The south side will measure more than a mile. There will be three gates facing south. They are Simeon's Gate, Issachar's Gate and Zebulun's Gate.

34 "The west side will measure more than a mile. There will be three gates facing west. They are Gad's Gate, Asher's Gate and Naphtali's Gate.

35 "The city will measure about six miles around. From then on the name of the city will be The Lord God Is There."

The Book of
DANIEL

1 Nebuchadnezzar king of Babylon came to Jerusalem and surrounded it with his army. This happened during the third year that Jehoiakim was king of Judah. [2]The Lord allowed Nebuchadnezzar to capture Jehoiakim king of Judah. Nebuchadnezzar also took some of the things from the Temple[d] of God. He carried them to Babylonia and put them in the temple of his gods.

[3]Then King Nebuchadnezzar gave an order to Ashpenaz, his chief officer. He told Ashpenaz to bring some of the Israelite men into his house. He wanted them to be from important families. And he wanted those who were from the family of the king of Judah. [4]King Nebuchadnezzar wanted only healthy, young, Israelite men. These men were not to have anything wrong with their bodies. They were to be handsome and well educated. They were to be able to learn and understand things. He wanted those who were able to serve in his palace. Ashpenaz was to teach them the language and writings of the Babylonians. [5]The king gave the young men a certain amount of food and wine every day. That was the same kind of food that the king ate. They were to be trained for three years. Then the young men would become servants of the king of Babylon. [6]Among those young men were some from the people of Judah. These were Daniel, Hananiah, Mishael and Azariah.

[7]Then Ashpenaz, the chief officer, gave them Babylonian names. Daniel's new name was Belteshazzar. Hananiah's was Shadrach. Mishael's was Meshach. And Azariah's new name was Abednego.

[8]Daniel decided not to eat the king's food and wine because that would make him unclean.[d] So he asked Ashpenaz for permission not to make himself unclean in this way.

[9]God made Ashpenaz want to be kind and merciful to Daniel. [10]But Ashpenaz said to Daniel, "I am afraid of my master, the king. He ordered me to give you this food and drink. If you don't eat this food, you will begin to look worse than other young men your age. The king will see this. And he will cut off my head because of you."

[11]Ashpenaz had ordered a guard to watch Daniel, Hananiah, Mishael and Azariah. [12]Daniel said to the guard, "Please give us this test for ten days: Don't give us anything but vegetables to eat and water to drink. [13]Then after ten days compare us with the other young men who eat the king's food. See for yourself who looks healthier. Then you judge for yourself how you want to treat us, your servants."

[14]So the guard agreed to test them for ten days. [15]After ten days they looked very healthy. They looked better than all of the young men who ate the king's food. [16]So the guard took away the king's special food and wine. He gave Daniel, Hananiah, Mishael and Azariah vegetables instead.

[17]God gave these four men wisdom and the ability to learn. They learned many kinds of things people had written and studied. Daniel could also understand all kinds of visions and dreams.

[18]The end of the three years came. And Ashpenaz brought all of the young men to King Nebuchadnezzar. [19]The king talked to them. He found that none of the young men were as good as Daniel, Hananiah, Mishael and Azariah. So those four young men became the king's servants. [20]Every time the king asked them about something important, they showed much wisdom and understanding. He found they were ten times better than all the fortune-tellers and magicians in his kingdom. [21]So Daniel continued to be the king's servant until the first year Cyrus was king.

2 During Nebuchadnezzar's second year as king, he had some dreams. Those dreams bothered him, and he could not sleep. [2]So the king called for his fortune-tellers, magicians, wizards and wise men. The king wanted those men to tell him what he had dreamed. So they came in and stood in front of the king.

[3]Then the king said to them, "I had a dream that bothers me. I want to know what the dream means."

[4]Then the wise men answered the king in the Aramaic language. They said, "Our king, live forever! We are your servants. Please tell us your dream. Then we will tell you what it means."

[5]Then King Nebuchadnezzar said to them, "No! You must tell me the dream.

And then you must tell me what it means. If you don't do these things, I will have you torn apart. And I will turn your houses into piles of stones. [6]But if you tell me my dream and its meaning, I will reward you. I will give you gifts and great honor. So tell me the dream, and tell me what it means."

[7]Again the wise men said to the king, "Please, tell us the dream. And we will tell you what it means."

[8]King Nebuchadnezzar answered, "Now I know that you are trying to get more time. You know that I meant what I said. [9]If you don't tell me my dream, you will be punished. You have all agreed to tell me lies and wicked things. You are hoping things will change. Now, tell me the dream. Then I will know you can tell me what it really means!"

[10]The wise men answered the king. They said, "No one on earth can do what the king asks! Not even a great and powerful king has ever asked the fortune-tellers, magicians or wise men to do this. [11]The king is asking something that is too hard. Only the gods could tell the king this. But the gods do not live among people."

[12]When the king heard that, he became very angry. He gave an order for all the wise men of Babylon to be killed. [13]So King Nebuchadnezzar's order was announced. All the wise men were to be put to death. Men were sent to look for Daniel and his friends to kill them.

[14]Arioch was the commander of the king's guards. He was going to put to death the wise men of Babylon. But Daniel spoke to him with wisdom and skill. [15]Daniel asked, "Why did the king order such a terrible punishment?" Then Arioch explained everything to Daniel. [16]When Daniel heard the story, he went to King Nebuchadnezzar. Daniel asked him to give him some more time. Then he would tell the king what he had dreamed and what it meant.

[17]So Daniel went to his house. He explained the whole story to his friends Hananiah, Mishael and Azariah. [18]Daniel asked his friends to pray to the God of heaven. Daniel asked them to pray that God would show them mercy and help them understand this secret. Then Daniel and his friends would not be put to death with the other wise men of Babylon.

[19]During the night God explained the secret to Daniel in a vision. Then Daniel praised the God of heaven. [20]Daniel said:

"Praise God forever and ever.
    He has wisdom and power.
[21]He changes the times and seasons
        of the year.
    He takes away the power of
        kings.
    And he gives their power to new
        kings.
 He gives wisdom to people so they
        become wise.
    And he helps people learn and
        know things.
[22]He makes known secrets that are
        deep and hidden.
    He knows what is hidden in
        darkness,
        and light lives with him.
[23]I thank you and praise you, God of
        my ancestors.
    You have given me wisdom and
        power.
    You told me what we asked of you.
    You told us about the king's
        dream."

[24]Then Daniel went to Arioch. King Nebuchadnezzar had chosen Arioch to put to death the wise men of Babylon. Daniel said to Arioch, "Don't put the wise men of Babylon to death. Take me to the king. I will tell him what his dream means."

[25]So very quickly Arioch took Daniel to the king. Arioch said to the king, "I have found a man among the captives from Judah. He can tell the king what his dream means."

[26]The king asked Daniel (also called Belteshazzar) a question. He asked, "Are you able to tell me what I dreamed and what it means?"

[27]Daniel answered, "No person can explain to the king the secret he has asked about. No wise man, magician or fortune-teller can do this. [28]But there is a God in heaven who explains secret things. God has shown King Nebuchadnezzar what will happen at a later time. This is your dream. This is the vision you saw while lying on your bed: [29]My king, as you were lying there, you thought about things to come. God, who can tell people about secret things, showed you what is going to happen. [30]God also told this secret to me. It is not because I have greater wisdom than other men. It is so that you, my king, may know what it means. In that way

you will understand what went through your mind.

[31] "My king, in your dream you saw a large statue in front of you. It was huge, shiny and frightening. [32] The head of the statue was made of pure gold. Its chest and arms were made of silver. Its middle and the upper part of its legs were made of bronze. [33] The lower part of the legs were made of iron. Its feet were made partly of iron and partly of baked clay. [34] While you were looking at the statue, you saw a rock cut free. But no human being touched the rock. It hit the statue on its feet of iron and clay and smashed them. [35] Then the iron, clay, bronze, silver and gold broke to pieces at the same time. They became like chaff[d] on a threshing[d] floor in the summertime. The wind blew them away, and there was nothing left. Then the rock that hit the statue became a very large mountain. It filled the whole earth.

[36] "That was your dream. Now we will tell the king what it means. [37] My king, you are the greatest king. God of heaven has given you a kingdom. He has given you power, strength and glory. [38] God has given you power over people, wild animals and birds. Wherever they live, God has made you ruler over them all. King Nebuchadnezzar, you are the head of gold on that statue.

[39] "Another kingdom will come after you. But that kingdom will not be as great as yours. Next a third kingdom will rule over the earth. That is the bronze part. [40] Then there will be a fourth kingdom, strong as iron. Iron crushes and smashes things to pieces. In the same way the fourth kingdom will smash and crush all the other kingdoms. [41] You saw that the statue's feet and toes were partly baked clay and partly iron. That means the fourth kingdom will be a divided kingdom. It will have some of the strength of iron in it. As you saw, iron was mixed with clay. [42] The toes of the statue were partly iron and partly clay. So the fourth kingdom will be partly strong like iron and partly breakable like clay. [43] You saw the iron mixed with clay. But iron and clay don't mix completely together. In the same way the people of the fourth kingdom will be a mixture. Those people will not be united as one people.

[44] "During the time of those kings, the God of heaven will set up another kingdom. It will never be destroyed. And it will not be given to another group of people. This kingdom will crush all the other kingdoms. It will bring them to an end. But that kingdom itself will continue forever.

[45] "King Nebuchadnezzar, you saw a rock cut from a mountain. But no human being touched it. The rock broke the iron, bronze, clay, silver and gold to pieces. In this way the great God showed you what will happen. The dream is true, and you can trust this explanation."

[46] Then King Nebuchadnezzar fell facedown on the ground in front of Daniel. He honored him. He ordered that an offering and incense[d] be presented to Daniel. [47] Then the king said to Daniel, "Truly I know your God is the greatest of all gods. And he is the Lord of all the kings. He tells people about things they cannot know. I know this is true. You were able to tell these secret things to me."

[48] Then the king gave Daniel an important position in his kingdom. And he gave many gifts to Daniel. Nebuchadnezzar made him ruler over the whole area of Babylon. And he put Daniel in charge of all the wise men of Babylon. [49] Daniel asked the king to make Shadrach, Meshach and Abednego important leaders over the area of Babylon. And the king did as Daniel asked. Daniel himself became one of the important people who stayed at the royal court.

3 Now King Nebuchadnezzar had a gold statue made. That statue was 90 feet high and 9 feet wide. He set up the statue on the plain of Dura in the area of Babylon. [2] Then the king called the important leaders: the governors, assistant governors, captains of the soldiers, people who advised the king, keepers of the treasury, judges, rulers and all other officers in his kingdom. He wanted these men to come to the special service for the statue he had set up. [3] So they all came for the special service. And they stood in front of the statue that King Nebuchadnezzar had set up. [4] Then the man who made announcements for the king spoke in a loud voice. He said, "People, nations and men of every language, this is what you are commanded to do: [5] You will hear the sound of the horns, flutes, lyres,[d] zithers,[n] harps,

3:5 zithers Musical instruments with 30 to 40 strings.

pipes and all the other musical instruments. When this happens, you must bow down and worship the gold statue. This is the one King Nebuchadnezzar has set up. [6]Everyone must bow down and worship this gold statue. Anyone who doesn't will be quickly thrown into a blazing furnace."

[7]Now people, nations and men who spoke every language were there. And they heard the sound of the horns, flutes, lyres, zithers, pipes and all the other musical instruments. So they bowed down and worshiped the gold statue that King Nebuchadnezzar had set up.

[8]Then some Babylonians came up to the king. They began speaking against the men of Judah. [9]They said to King Nebuchadnezzar, "Our king, live forever! [10]Our king, you gave a command. You said that everyone would hear the horns, lyres, zithers, harps, pipes and all the other musical instruments. Then they would have to bow down and worship the gold statue. [11]Anyone who wouldn't do this was to be thrown into a blazing furnace. [12]Our king, there are some men of Judah who did not pay attention to your order. You made them important officers in the area of Babylon. Their names are Shadrach, Meshach and Abednego. They do not serve your gods. And they do not worship the gold statue you have set up."

[13]Nebuchadnezzar became very angry. He called for Shadrach, Meshach and Abednego. So those men were brought to the king. [14]And Nebuchadnezzar said, "Shadrach, Meshach and Abednego, is it true that you do not serve my gods? And is it true that you did not worship the gold statue I have set up? [15]Now, you will hear the sound of the horns, flutes, lyres, zithers, harps, pipes and all the other musical instruments. And you must be ready to bow down and worship the statue I made. That will be good. But if you do not worship it, you will be thrown quickly into the blazing furnace. Then no god will be able to save you from my power!"

[16]Shadrach, Meshach and Abednego answered the king. They said, "Nebuchadnezzar, we do not need to defend ourselves to you. [17]You can throw us into the blazing furnace. The God we serve is able to save us from the furnace and your power. If he does this, it is good. [18]But even if God does not save us, we want you, our king, to know this: We

will not serve your gods. We will not worship the gold statue you have set up."

[19]Then Nebuchadnezzar was furious with Shadrach, Meshach and Abednego. He ordered the furnace to be heated seven times hotter than usual. [20]Then he commanded some of the strongest soldiers in his army to tie up Shadrach, Meshach and Abednego. The king told the soldiers to throw them into the blazing furnace.

[21]So Shadrach, Meshach and Abednego were tied up and thrown into the blazing furnace. They were still wearing their robes, trousers, turbans and other clothes. [22]The king was very angry when he gave the command. And the furnace was made very hot. The fire was so hot that the flames killed the strong soldiers who took Shadrach, Meshach and Abednego there. [23]Firmly tied, Shadrach, Meshach and Abednego fell into the blazing furnace.

[24]Then King Nebuchadnezzar was very surprised and jumped to his feet. He asked the men who advised him, "Didn't we tie up only three men? Didn't we throw them into the fire?"

They answered, "Yes, our king."

[25]The king said, "Look! I see four men. They are walking around in the fire. They are not tied up, and they are not burned. The fourth man looks like a son of the gods."

[26]Then Nebuchadnezzar went to the opening of the blazing furnace. He shouted, "Shadrach, Meshach and Abednego, come out! Servants of the Most High God, come here!"

So Shadrach, Meshach and Abednego came out of the fire. [27]When they came out, the princes, assistant governors, governors and royal advisers crowded around them. They saw that the fire had not harmed their bodies. Their hair was not burned. Their robes were not burned. And they didn't even smell like smoke.

[28]Then Nebuchadnezzar said, "Praise the God of Shadrach, Meshach and Abednego. Their God has sent his angel and saved his servants from the fire! These three men trusted their God. They refused to obey my command. And they were willing to die rather than serve or worship any god other than their own. [29]So I now make this law: The people of any nation or language must not say anything against the God of Shadrach, Meshach and Abednego. Anyone who

does will be torn apart. And his house will be turned into a pile of stones. No other god can save his people like this." ³⁰Then the king promoted Shadrach, Meshach and Abednego in the area of Babylon.

4 King Nebuchadnezzar sent a letter. It went to the people, nations and those who speak every language in all the world. The letter said:

I wish you great wealth!

²The Most High God has done miracles[d] and wonderful things for me. I am happy to tell you about these things.

³The things he has done are great.
    His miracles are mighty.
  His kingdom continues forever.
    His rule will continue for all time.

⁴I, Nebuchadnezzar, was at my palace. I was happy and successful. ⁵I had a dream that made me afraid. As I was lying on my bed, I saw pictures and visions in my mind. Those things made me very afraid. ⁶So I gave an order. All the wise men of Babylon were to be brought to me. I wanted them to tell me what my dream meant. ⁷The fortune-tellers, magicians and wise men came. I told them about the dream. But those men could not tell me what it meant.

⁸Finally, Daniel came to me. (I called him Belteshazzar to honor my god. The spirit of the holy gods is in him.) I told my dream to Daniel. ⁹I said, "Belteshazzar, you are the most important of all the fortune-tellers. I know that the spirit of the holy gods is in you. I know there is no secret that is too hard for you to understand. This was what I dreamed. Tell me what it means. ¹⁰These are the visions I saw while I was lying in my bed: I looked, and there in front of me was a tree. It was standing in the middle of the earth. The tree was very tall. ¹¹The tree grew large and strong. The top of the tree touched the sky. It could be seen from anywhere on earth. ¹²The leaves of the tree were beautiful. It had plenty of good fruit on it. On the tree was food for everyone. The wild animals found shelter under the tree. And the birds lived in its branches. Every animal ate from it.

¹³"I was looking at those things in the vision while lying on my bed. And

then I saw a holy angel coming down from heaven. ¹⁴He spoke very loudly. He said, 'Cut down the tree, and cut off its branches. Strip off its leaves. Scatter its fruit around. Let the animals that are under the tree run away. Let the birds that were in its branches fly away. ¹⁵But let the stump and its roots stay in the ground. Put a band of iron and bronze around it. Let it stay in the field with the grass around it.

"'Let the man become wet with dew. Let him live among the animals and plants of the earth. ¹⁶Let him not think like a man any longer. Let him have the mind of an animal for seven years.

¹⁷"'Messengers gave this command. The holy ones declared the sentence. This is so all the people may know that the Most High God rules over the kingdoms of men. God gives those kingdoms to anyone he wants. And he chooses people to rule them who are not proud.'

¹⁸"That is what I, King Nebuchadnezzar, dreamed. Now Daniel, called Belteshazzar, tell me what the dream means. None of the wise men in my kingdom can explain it to me. But you can, because the spirit of the holy gods is in you."

¹⁹Then Daniel (also called Belteshazzar) was very quiet for a while. His thoughts made him afraid. So the king said, "Belteshazzar, do not let the dream or its meaning make you afraid."

Then Daniel, called Belteshazzar, answered the king. He said, "My master, I wish the dream were about your enemies. And I wish its meaning were for those who are against you! ²⁰You saw a tree in your dream. The tree grew large and strong. Its top touched the sky. It could be seen from all over the earth. ²¹Its leaves were beautiful, and it had plenty of fruit. The fruit gave food for everyone. It was a home for the wild animals. And its branches were nesting places for the birds. That is the tree you saw. ²²My king, you are that tree! You have become great and powerful. You are like the tall tree that touched the sky. And your power reaches to the far parts of the earth.

²³"My king, you saw a holy angel coming down from heaven. He said, 'Cut down the tree and destroy it. But

leave the stump and its roots in the ground. Put a band of iron and bronze around it. Leave it in the field with the grass. Let him become wet with dew. He will live like a wild animal for seven years.'

²⁴"This is the meaning of the dream, my king. The Most High God has commanded these things to happen to my master the king: ²⁵You will be forced away from people. You will live among the wild animals. People will feed you grass like an ox. And dew from the sky will make you wet. Seven years will pass, and then you will learn this lesson: The Most High God is ruler over the kingdoms of men. And the Most High God gives those kingdoms to anyone he wants.

²⁶"The stump of the tree and its roots were to be left in the ground. This means your kingdom will be given back to you. This will happen when you learn that heaven rules your kingdom. ²⁷So, my king, please accept my advice. I advise you to stop sinning and do what is right. Stop doing wicked things and be kind to poor people. Then you might continue to be successful."

²⁸All these things happened to King Nebuchadnezzar. ²⁹Twelve months after the dream, King Nebuchadnezzar was walking on the roof[n] of his palace in Babylon. ³⁰And he said, "Look at Babylon. I built this great city. It is my palace. I built this great place by my power to show how great I am."

³¹The words were still in his mouth when a voice came from heaven. The voice said, "King Nebuchadnezzar, these things will happen to you: Your royal power has been taken away from you. ³²You will be forced away from people. You will live with the wild animals. You will be fed grass like an ox. Seven years will pass before you learn this lesson: The Most High God rules over the kingdoms of men. And the Most High God gives those kingdoms to anyone he wants."

³³Those things happened quickly. Nebuchadnezzar was forced to go away from people. He began eating grass like an ox. He became wet from dew. His hair grew long like the feath-

ers of an eagle. And his nails grew long like the claws of a bird.

³⁴Then at the end of that time, I, Nebuchadnezzar, looked up toward heaven. And I could think correctly again. Then I gave praise to the Most High God. I gave honor and glory to him who lives forever.

> God's rule is forever.
> His kingdom continues for all
>   time.
> ³⁵People on earth
>   are not truly important.
> God does what he wants
>   with the powers of heaven
>   and the people on earth.
> No one can stop his powerful hand.
>   No one can question the things
>   he does.

³⁶So, at that time I could think correctly again. And God gave back my great honor and power as king. The people who advise me and the royal family came to me for help again. I became king again. And I became even greater and more powerful than before. ³⁷Now I, Nebuchadnezzar, give praise and honor and glory to the King of heaven. Everything he does is right. He is always fair. And he is able to make proud people humble.

5 King Belshazzar gave a big banquet for 1,000 royal guests. And he drank wine with them. ²As Belshazzar was drinking his wine, he gave an order to his servants. He told them to bring the gold and silver cups that his ancestor Nebuchadnezzar had taken from the Temple[d] in Jerusalem. King Belshazzar wanted his royal guests to drink from those cups. He also wanted his wives and his slave women[d] to drink from them. ³So they brought the gold cups. They had been taken from the Temple of God in Jerusalem. And the king and his royal guests, his wives and his slave women drank from them. ⁴As they were drinking, they praised their gods. Those gods were made from gold, silver, bronze, iron, wood and stone.

⁵Then suddenly a person's hand appeared. The fingers wrote words on the plaster on the wall. This was near the lampstand in the royal palace. The king watched the hand as it wrote.

⁶King Belshazzar was very fright-

4:29 roof In Bible times houses were built with flat roofs. The roof was used for drying things such as flax and fruit. And it was used as an extra room, as a place for worship and as a place to sleep in the summer.

ened. His face turned white, and his knees knocked together. He could not stand up because his legs were too weak. [7]The king called for the magicians and wise men to be brought to him. He said to the wise men of Babylon, "I will give a reward to anyone who can read this writing and explain it. I will give him purple clothes fit for a king. I will put a gold chain around his neck. And I will make him the third highest ruler in the kingdom."

[8]So all the king's wise men came in. But they could not read the writing. And they could not tell the king what it meant. [9]King Belshazzar became even more afraid. His face became even whiter. His royal guests were confused.

[10]Then the king's mother came into the banquet room. She had heard the voices of the king and his royal guests. She said, "My king, live forever! Don't be afraid! Don't let your face be white with fear! [11]There is a man in your kingdom who has the spirit of the holy gods in him. In the days of your father, this man showed understanding, knowledge and wisdom. He was like the gods in these things. Your father, King Nebuchadnezzar, put this man in charge of all the wise men. He ruled over all the fortune-tellers, magicians and wise men. [12]The man I am talking about is named Daniel. The king gave him the name Belteshazzar. He was very smart, and he had knowledge and understanding. He could explain dreams and secrets. He could answer very hard problems. Call for Daniel. He will tell you what the writing on the wall means."

[13]So they brought Daniel to the king. The king said to him, "Is your name Daniel? Are you one of the captives my father the king brought from Judah? [14]I have heard that the spirit of the gods is in you. And I have heard that you are very smart and have knowledge and understanding. [15]The wise men and magicians were brought to me to read this writing on the wall. I wanted those men to explain to me what it means. But they could not explain it. [16]I have heard that you are able to explain what things mean. And you can find the answers to hard problems. Read this writing on the wall and explain it to me. If you can, I will give you purple clothes fit for a king. And I will put a gold chain around your neck. And you will become the third highest ruler in the kingdom."

[17]Then Daniel answered the king, "You may keep your gifts for yourself. Or you may give those rewards to someone else. I will read the writing on the wall for you. And I will explain to you what it means.

[18]"My king, the Most High God made your father Nebuchadnezzar a great, important and powerful king. [19]God made him very important. So all the people, nations and those who spoke every language were very afraid of Nebuchadnezzar. If he wanted a person to die, he put that person to death. And if he wanted a person to live, he let that person live. If he wanted to promote a person, he promoted him. And if he wanted a person to be unimportant, he made him unimportant.

[20]"But Nebuchadnezzar became too proud and stubborn. So he was taken off his royal throne. His glory was taken away. [21]Then Nebuchadnezzar was forced away from people. His mind became like the mind of an animal. He lived with the wild donkeys and was fed grass like an ox. He became wet with dew. These things happened to him until he learned his lesson: The Most High God rules over the kingdoms of men. And the Most High God sets anyone he wants over those kingdoms.

[22]"But, Belshazzar, you already knew these things. You are a descendant[d] of Nebuchadnezzar. But still you have not been sorry for what you have done. [23]Instead, you have turned against the Lord of heaven. You ordered the drinking cups from the Temple of the Lord to be brought to you. Then you and your royal guests drank wine from them. Your wives and your slave women also drank wine from them. You praised the gods of silver, gold, bronze, iron, wood and stone. They are not really gods. They cannot see or hear or understand anything. But you did not honor God. He is the One who has power over your life and everything you do. [24]So God sent the hand that wrote on the wall.

[25]"These are the words that were written on the wall: 'Mene, mene, tekel, parsin.'

[26]"This is what these words mean: Mene: God has counted the days until your kingdom will end. [27]Tekel: You have been weighed on the scales and found not good enough. [28]Parsin: Your kingdom is being divided. It will be given to the Medes and the Persians."

[29]Then Belshazzar gave an order for

Daniel to be dressed in purple clothes. A gold chain was put around his neck. And he was announced to be the third highest ruler in the kingdom. [30]That very same night Belshazzar, king of the Babylonian people, was killed. [31]A man named Darius the Mede became the new king. Darius was 62 years old.

6 Darius thought it would be a good idea to choose 120 governors. They would rule through all of his kingdom. [2]And he chose three men as supervisors over those 120 governors. Daniel was one of these three supervisors. The king set up these men so that he would not be cheated. [3]Daniel showed that he could do the work better than the other supervisors and the governors. Because of this, the king planned to put Daniel in charge of the whole kingdom. [4]So the other supervisors and the governors tried to find reasons to accuse Daniel. But he went on doing the business of the government. And they could not find anything wrong with him. So they could not accuse him of doing anything wrong. Daniel was trustworthy. He was not lazy and did not cheat the king. [5]Finally these men said, "We will never find any reason to accuse Daniel. But we must find something to complain about. It will have to be about the law of his God."

[6]So the supervisors and the governors went as a group to the king. They said: "King Darius, live forever! [7]The supervisors, assistant governors, governors, the people who advise you and the captains of the soldiers have all agreed on something. We think the king should make this law that everyone would have to obey: No one should pray to any god or man except to you, our king. This should be done for the next 30 days. Anyone who doesn't obey will be thrown into the lions' den. [8]Now, our king, make the law. Write it down so it cannot be changed. The laws of the Medes and Persians cannot be canceled." [9]So King Darius made the law and had it written.

[10]When Daniel heard that the new law had been written, he went to his house. He went to his upstairs room. The windows of that room opened toward Jerusalem. Three times each day Daniel got down on his knees and prayed. He prayed and thanked God, just as he always had done.

[11]Then those men went as a group and found Daniel. They saw him praying and asking God for help. [12]So they went to the king. They talked to him about the law he had made. They said, "Didn't you write a law that says no one may pray to any god or man except you, our king? Doesn't it say that anyone who disobeys during the next 30 days will be thrown into the lions' den?"

The king answered, "Yes, I wrote that law. And the laws of the Medes and Persians cannot be canceled."

[13]Then those men spoke to the king. They said, "Daniel is one of the captives from Judah. And he is not paying attention to the law you wrote. Daniel still prays to his God three times every day." [14]The king became very upset when he heard this. He decided he had to save Daniel. He worked until sunset trying to think of a way to save him.

[15]Then those men went as a group to the king. They said, "Remember, our king, the law of the Medes and Persians. It says that no law or command given by the king can be changed."

[16]So King Darius gave the order. They brought Daniel and threw him into the lions' den. The king said to Daniel, "May the God you serve all the time save you!" [17]A big stone was brought. It was put over the opening of the lions' den. Then the king used his signet[d] ring to put his special seal[d] on the rock. And he used the rings of his royal officers to put their seals on the rock also. This showed that no one could move that rock and bring Daniel out. [18]Then King Darius went back to his palace. He did not eat that night. He did not have any entertainment brought to entertain him. And he could not sleep.

[19]The next morning King Darius got up at dawn. He hurried to the lions' den. [20]As he came near the den, he was worried. He called out to Daniel. He said, "Daniel, servant of the living God! Has your God that you always worship been able to save you from the lions?"

[21]Daniel answered, "My king, live forever! [22]My God sent his angel to close the lions' mouths. They have not hurt me, because my God knows I am innocent. I never did anything wrong to you, my king."

[23]King Darius was very happy. He told his servants to lift Daniel out of the lions' den. So they lifted him out and did not find any injury on him. This was because Daniel had trusted in his God.

[24]Then the king gave a command. The men who had accused Daniel were

brought to the lions' den and thrown into it. Their wives and children were also thrown into it. The lions grabbed them before they hit the floor of the den. And the lions crushed their bones.

²⁵Then King Darius wrote a letter. It was to all people and all nations, to those who spoke every language in the world:

I wish you great wealth.

²⁶I am making a new law. This law is for people in every part of my kingdom. All of you must fear and respect the God of Daniel.

Daniel's God is the living God.
He lives forever.
His kingdom will never be
　　destroyed.
His rule will never end.
²⁷God rescues and saves people.
God does mighty miracles[d]
in heaven and on earth.
God saved Daniel
from the power of the lions.

²⁸So Daniel was successful during the time that Darius was king. This was also the time that Cyrus the Persian was king.

7 In Belshazzar's first year as king of Babylon, Daniel had a dream. He saw visions as he was lying on his bed. Daniel wrote down what he had dreamed.

²Daniel said: "I saw my vision at night. In the vision the wind was blowing from all four directions. These winds made the sea very rough. ³I saw four huge animals come up from the sea. Each animal was different from the others.

⁴"The first animal looked like a lion. But it had wings like an eagle. I watched this animal until its wings were torn off. It was lifted from the ground so that it stood up on two feet like a man. And it was given the mind of a man.

⁵"And then I saw a second animal before me. It looked like a bear. It was raised up on one of its sides. And it had three ribs in its mouth between its teeth. It was told, 'Get up and eat all the meat you want!'

⁶"After that, I looked, and there before me was another animal. This animal looked like a leopard. And the leopard had four wings on its back. The wings looked like a bird's wings. This animal

had four heads. It was given power to rule.

⁷"After that, in my vision at night I continued looking. There in front of me was a fourth animal. This animal looked cruel and terrible and very strong. It had large iron teeth. It crushed and ate what it killed. Then it walked on whatever was left. This fourth animal was different from all the animals I had seen before it. It had ten horns.

⁸"While I was thinking about the horns, another horn grew up among them. It was a little horn. It had eyes like a person's eyes. It also had a mouth. And the mouth was bragging. The little horn pulled out three of the other horns.

⁹"As I looked,
thrones were put in their places.
　And God, who has been alive
　　forever, sat on his throne.
His clothes were white like snow.
　And the hair on his head was
　　white like wool.
His throne was made from fire.
　And the wheels of his throne
　　were blazing with fire.
¹⁰A river of fire was flowing
　from in front of him.
Many thousands of angels were
　　serving him.
　Millions of angels stood before
　　him.
Court was ready to begin.
　And the books were opened.

¹¹"I kept on looking because the little horn was bragging. I kept watching until finally the fourth animal was killed. Its body was destroyed, and it was thrown into the burning fire. ¹²(The power and rule of the other animals had been taken from them. But they were permitted to live for a certain period of time.)

¹³"In my vision at night I looked. There in front of me was someone who looked like a human being. He was coming with clouds in the sky. He came near God, who has been alive forever. And he was led to God. ¹⁴The one who looked like a human being was given the power to rule. He was also given glory and royal power. All peoples, nations and men who spoke every language will serve him. His rule will last forever. His kingdom will never be destroyed.

¹⁵"I, Daniel, was worried. The visions that went through my mind frightened me. ¹⁶I came near one of those standing there. I asked him what all this meant.

"So he told me. He explained to me what these things meant. ¹⁷He said, 'The four great animals are four kingdoms. Those four kingdoms will come from the earth. [18]But the people who belong to the Most High God will receive the power to rule. And they will have the power to rule forever. They will have it from now on.'

[19]"Then I wanted to know what the fourth animal meant. It was different from all the other animals. It was very terrible. It had iron teeth and bronze claws. It was the animal that crushed and ate what it killed. And it walked on whatever was left. [20]I also wanted to know about the ten horns on its head. And I wanted to know about the little horn that grew there. It had pulled out three of the other ten horns. It looked greater than the others. And it had eyes and a mouth that kept bragging. [21]As I watched, the little horn began making war against God's people. And the horn kept killing them [22]until God, who has been alive forever, came. He judged in favor of the people who belong to the Most High God. And the time came for them to receive the power to rule.

[23]"And he explained this to me: 'The fourth animal is a fourth kingdom that will come on the earth. It will be different from all the other kingdoms. It will destroy people all over the world. It will walk on and crush the whole earth. [24]The ten horns are ten kings who will come from this fourth kingdom. After those ten kings are gone, another king will come. He will be different from the kings who ruled before him. He will defeat three of the other kings. [25]This king will say things against the Most High God. And he will hurt and kill God's people. He will try to change times and laws that have already been set. The people that belong to God will be in that king's power for three and one-half years.

[26]"'But the court will decide what should happen. And the power of the king will be taken away. His kingdom will be completely destroyed. [27]Then the people who belong to the Most High God will have the power to rule. They will rule over all the kingdoms under heaven with power and greatness. Their power to rule will last forever. And people from all the other kingdoms will respect and serve them.'

[28]"And that was the end of the dream. I, Daniel, was very afraid. My face became very white from fear. But I kept everything to myself."

8 During the third year Belshazzar was king, I saw this vision. This was after the other one. [2]In this vision I saw myself in the capital city of Susa. Susa is in the area of Elam. I was standing by the Ulai River. [3]I looked up, and I saw a male sheep standing beside the river. It had two long horns. But one horn was longer than the other. The long horn was newer than the other horn. [4]I watched the male sheep charge to the west. He also charged to the north and the south. No animal could stand before him. And none could save another animal from his power. He did whatever he wanted. And he became very powerful.

[5]While I was thinking about this, I saw a male goat come from the west. This goat had one large horn that was easy to see. It was between his eyes. He crossed over the whole earth. But his feet did not touch the ground. [6]That goat charged the male sheep with the two horns. This was the male sheep I had seen standing by the river. The goat was very angry. [7]I watched the goat attack the male sheep. It broke the sheep's two horns. The sheep could not stop it. The goat knocked the sheep to the ground. Then the goat walked all over him. No one was able to save the sheep from the goat. [8]So the male goat became very great. But when he was strong, his big horn broke off. Then four horns grew in place of the one big horn. Those four horns were easy to see. They pointed in four different directions.

[9]Then a little horn grew from one of those four horns. It became very big. It grew to the south and the east and toward the beautiful land of Judah. [10]That little horn grew until it reached to the sky. It even threw some of the army of heaven to the ground. And it walked on them. [11]That little horn became very strong against God, the commander of heaven's armies. It stopped the daily sacrifices that were offered to the commander. The place where people worshiped the commander was pulled down. [12]There was a turning away from God. Because of this the people stopped the daily sacrifices. It was like throwing truth down to the ground. The horn was successful in everything it did.

[13]Then I heard one angel speaking. Another angel asked the first one, "How long will the things in this vision last? The vision is about the daily sacrifices. It is about the turning away from God that brings destruction. It is about the

Temple[d] being pulled down. It is about the army of heaven being walked on."

[14]He said to me, "This will happen for 2,300 evenings and mornings. Then the holy place will be repaired."

[15]I, Daniel, saw this vision. And I tried to understand what it meant. Then someone who looked like a man suddenly stood before me. [16]And I heard a man's voice calling from the Ulai River: "Gabriel, explain the vision to this man."

[17]Gabriel came to where I was standing. When he came close to me, I was very afraid. I bowed facedown on the ground. But Gabriel said to me, "Human being, understand that this vision is about the time of the end."

[18]While Gabriel was speaking, I fell into a deep sleep. My face was on the ground. Then he touched me and lifted me to my feet. [19]He said, "Now, I will explain the vision to you. I will tell you what will happen later, in the time of God's anger. Your vision was about the set time of the end.

[20]"You saw a male sheep with two horns. Those horns are the kings of Media and Persia. [21]The male goat is the king of Greece. The big horn between its eyes is the first king. [22]After that horn broke, four horns grew in its place. Those four horns are four kingdoms. Those four kingdoms will come from the nation of the first king. But they will not be as strong as the first king.

[23]"When the end comes near for those kingdoms, a bold and cruel king will come. This king will tell lies. This will happen when many people have turned against God. [24]This king will be very powerful. But his power will not come from himself. He will cause terrible destruction. He will be successful in everything he does. He will destroy powerful people and even God's people. [25]This king will use his wisdom to make lies successful. He will think that he is very important. He will destroy many people without warning. He will try to fight even God, the Prince of princes! But that cruel king will be destroyed. And it will not be human power that destroys him.

[26]"The vision that has been shown to you about those times is true. But seal up the vision. Those things won't happen for a long time."

[27]I, Daniel, became very weak. I was sick for several days after that vision. Then I got up and went back to work for the king. But I was very upset about the

vision. I didn't understand what it meant.

9 These things happened during the first year Darius son of Xerxes was king. He was a descendant[d] of the Medes. [2]During Darius' first year as king, I, Daniel, was reading the Scriptures.[d] In them I saw what the Lord told Jeremiah. He said Jerusalem would be an empty desert for 70 years.

[3]Then I turned to the Lord God. I prayed to him and asked him for help. I did not eat any food. To show how sad I was I put on rough cloth and sat in ashes. [4]I prayed to the Lord my God. I told him about all of my sins. I said, "Lord, you are a great God. You cause fear and wonder. You keep your agreement of love with all who love you and obey your commands.

[5]"But we have sinned and done wrong. We have been wicked and turned against you. We have not obeyed your commands and laws. [6]We did not listen to your servants, the prophets. They spoke for you to our kings, our leaders and our ancestors. They spoke to all the people of the land.

[7]"Lord, you are good and right. But we are full of shame today. The people of Judah and Jerusalem and all the people of Israel are ashamed. People near and far whom you scattered among many nations are ashamed. We were not loyal to you. [8]Lord, we are all ashamed. Our kings and leaders and our fathers are ashamed. This is because we have sinned against you.

[9]"But, Lord our God, you show us mercy. You forgive us even though we have turned against you. [10]We have not obeyed the Lord our God. We have not obeyed the teachings he gave us through his servants, the prophets. [11]All the people of Israel have disobeyed your teachings. They all have turned away and refused to obey you. So you brought on us the curses and promises of punishment written in the Teachings of Moses, the servant of God. These things have happened to us because we sinned against you.

[12]"God said these things would happen to us and our leaders. And he made them happen. You brought on us a great disaster. Nothing has ever been done here on earth like what was done to Jerusalem. [13]All this disaster came to us just as it is written in the Teachings of Moses. But we still have not stopped sinning. We still do not pay attention to

your truth. [14]The Lord was ready to bring the disaster on us. This is because he is right in everything he does. But we still have not obeyed him.

[15]"Lord our God, you used your power and brought us out of Egypt. Because of that, your name is known even today. Lord, we have sinned. We have done wrong. [16]Lord, you do the right things. So do not be angry with Jerusalem. Jerusalem is your city on your holy hill. All this has happened because of our sins and the evil things done by our ancestors. So now people all around insult and make fun of Jerusalem and your people.

[17]"Now, our God, hear my prayers. I am your servant. Listen to my prayer for help. Do good things for your holy place that is in ruins. Do this for your sake. [18]My God, pay attention and hear me. Open your eyes and see all the terrible things that have happened to us. See what has happened to the city that is called by your name. We do not ask these things because we are good. We ask because of your mercy. [19]Lord, listen! Lord, forgive! Lord, hear us and do something! For your sake, don't wait! Your city and your people are called by your name."

[20]I was saying those things in my prayer to the Lord, my God. I was confessing my sins and the sins of the people of Israel. I was praying for God's holy hill. [21]While I was still praying, Gabriel came to me. Gabriel was the person I had seen in my last vision. He came flying quickly to me about the time of the evening sacrifice. [22]Gabriel said to me, "Daniel, I have come to give you wisdom and to help you understand. [23]When you first started praying, an answer was given. And I came to tell you, because God loves you very much. So think about the message and understand the vision.

[24]"God has ordered 490 years for your people and your holy city. These years are ordered for these reasons: to stop people from turning against God; to put an end to sin; to take away evil; to bring in goodness that continues forever; to make the vision and prophecy[d] come true; and to appoint a most holy place. [25]"Learn and understand these things. A command will come to rebuild Jerusalem. The time from this command until the appointed leader comes will be 49 years and 434 years. Jerusalem will be rebuilt with streets and a trench around

it. But it will be built in times of trouble. [26]After the 434 years the appointed leader will be killed. He will have nothing. The people of the leader who is to come will destroy the city. They will also destroy the holy place. That end will come like a flood. War will continue until the end. God has ordered that place to be completely destroyed. [27]That leader will make an agreement with many people for 7 years. He will put a stop to offerings and sacrifices after 3½ years. And the horrible thing that destroys will be placed on the highest point of the Temple.[d] But God has ordered him to be destroyed!"

10 During Cyrus' third year as king of Persia, Daniel learned about these things. (Daniel's other name is Belteshazzar.) The message was true. It was about a great war. But Daniel understood it, because it was explained to him in a vision.

[2]At that time I, Daniel, was very sad for three weeks. [3]I did not eat any fancy food. I did not eat any meat or drink any wine. I did not use any perfumed oil. I did not do any of these things for three weeks.

[4]On the twenty-fourth day of the first month, I was standing beside the great Tigris River. [5]While standing there, I looked up. And I saw a man dressed in linen clothes. A belt made of fine gold was wrapped around his waist. [6]His body was like shiny yellow quartz. His face was bright like lightning, and his eyes were like fire. His arms and legs were shiny like polished bronze. His voice sounded like the roar of a crowd.

[7]I, Daniel, was the only person who saw the vision. The men with me did not see it. But they were badly frightened. They were so afraid they ran away and hid. [8]So I was left alone, watching this great vision. I lost my strength. My face turned white like a dead person, and I was helpless. [9]Then I heard the man in the vision speaking. As I listened, I fell into a deep sleep. My face was on the ground.

[10]Then a hand touched me and set me on my hands and knees. I was so afraid that I was shaking. [11]The man in the vision said to me, "Daniel, God loves you very much. Think very carefully about the words I will speak to you. Stand up because I have been sent to you." And when he said this, I stood up. I was still shaking.

[12]Then the man said to me, "Daniel,

do not be afraid. Some time ago you decided to try to get understanding. You wanted to be humble before God. Since that time God has listened to you. And I came to you because you have been praying. [13]But the prince of Persia has been fighting against me for 21 days. Then Michael, one of the most important angels, came to help me. He came because I had been left there with the king of Persia. [14]Now I have come to you, Daniel. I will explain to you what will happen to your people. The vision is about a time in the future."

[15]While he was speaking to me, I bowed facedown. I could not speak. [16]Then one who looked like a man touched my lips. I opened my mouth and started to speak. I said to the one standing in front of me, "Master, I am upset and afraid. It is because of what I saw in the vision. I feel helpless. [17]Master, I am Daniel your servant. How can I talk with you! My strength is gone, and it is hard for me to breathe."

[18]The one who looked like a man touched me again. And he gave me strength. [19]He said, "Daniel, don't be afraid. God loves you very much. Peace be with you. Be strong now, be strong."

When he spoke to me, I became stronger. Then I said, "Master, speak, since you have given me strength."

[20]So then he said, "Daniel, do you know why I have come to you? Soon I must go back to fight against the prince of Persia. When I go, the prince of Greece will come. [21]But before I go, I must first tell you what is written in the Book of Truth. No one stands with me against them except Michael. He is the angel ruling over your people.

11 "In the first year Darius the Mede was king, I stood up to support Michael, in his fight against the prince of Persia.

[2]"Now then, Daniel, I tell you the truth: Three more kings will rule in Persia. Then a fourth king will come. He will be much richer than all the kings of Persia before him. He will use his riches to get power. And he will stir up everyone against the kingdom of Greece. [3]Then a mighty king will come. He will rule with great power. He will do anything he wants. [4]After that king has come, his kingdom will be broken up. It will be divided out toward the four parts of the world. His kingdom will not go to his descendants.[d] And it will not have the power that he had. This is because

his kingdom will be pulled up and given to other people.

[5]"The king of the South will become strong. But one of his commanders will become even stronger. He will begin to rule his own kingdom with great power. [6]Then after a few years, the king of the South and the commander will become friends. The daughter of the king of the South will marry the king of the North. She will do this to bring peace. But she will not keep her power. And his family will not last. She, her husband, her child and those who brought her to that country will be killed.

[7]"But a person from her family will become king of the South. He will attack the armies of the king of the North. He will go into that king's strong, walled city. He will fight and win. [8]He will take their gods and their metal idols. He will also take their valuable things made of silver and gold. He will take those things to Egypt. Then he will not bother the king of the North for a few years. [9]Next, the king of the North will attack the king of the South. But he will be beaten back to his own country.

[10]"The sons of the king of the North will prepare for war. They will get a large army together. That army will move through the land very quickly, like a powerful flood. Later, that army will come back and fight. They will fight all the way to the strong, walled city of the king of the South. [11]Then the king of the South will become very angry. He will march out to fight against the king of the North. The king of the North will have a large army. But he will lose the battle. [12]The soldiers will be carried away. So the king of the South will be very proud. And he will kill thousands of soldiers from the northern army. But he will not continue to be successful. [13]The king of the North will gather another army. That army will be larger than the first one. After several years he will attack. That army will be very large, and it will have plenty of weapons.

[14]"In those times many people will be against the king of the South. Some of your own people who love to fight will turn against the king of the South. They will think it is time for God's promises to come true. But it will not be the time yet. And they will fail. [15]Then the king of the North will come. He will build dirt roads to the tops of the city walls. And he will capture a strong, walled city. The southern army will not have the power

to fight back. Even their best soldiers will not be strong enough to stop the northern army. [16]The king of the North will do whatever he wants. No one will be able to stand against him. He will gain power and control in the beautiful land of Israel. And he will have the power to destroy it. [17]The king of the North will decide to use all his power to fight against the king of the South. He will make an agreement with the king of the South. The king of the North will give one of his daughters as a wife to the king of the South. He will do that so he can defeat the king of the South. But those plans will not succeed or help him. [18]Then the king of the North will turn his attention to other places. He will take many cities along the coast of the Mediterranean Sea. But a commander will put an end to the pride of the king of the North. The commander will turn that pride back on him. [19]After that happens the king of the North will go back to the strong, walled cities of his own country. But he will lose his power. That will be the end of him.

[20]"The next king of the North will send out a tax collector. He will then have plenty of money. In a few years that ruler will be killed. But he will not die in anger or in a battle.

[21]"That ruler will be followed by a very cruel and hated man. He will not have the honor of being from a king's family. He will attack the kingdom when the people feel safe. He will take power by lying to the people. [22]He will sweep away in defeat large and powerful armies. He will even defeat a prince who made an agreement. [23]Many nations will make agreements with that cruel and hated ruler. But he will lie to them. He will gain much power. But only a few people will support him. [24]The richest areas will feel safe. But that cruel and hated ruler will attack them. And he will succeed where his ancestors did not. He will take things from the countries he defeated. And he will give those things to his followers. He will plan to defeat and destroy strong cities. He will be successful, but only for a short time.

[25]"That very cruel and hated ruler will have a large army. He will use it to stir up his strength and courage. He will attack the king of the South. The king of the South will get a large and very powerful army and get ready for war. But the people who are against him will make secret plans. And the king of the South

will be defeated. [26]There were people who were supposed to be good friends of the king of the South. But they will try to destroy him. His army will be swept away in defeat. Many of his soldiers will be killed in battle. [27]Those two kings will want to hurt each other. They will sit at the same table and lie to each other. But it will not do either one any good. This is because God has set a time for their end to come. [28]The king of the North will go back to his own country with much wealth. Then he will decide to go against the holy agreement. He will do what he planned. Then he will go back to his own country.

[29]"At the right time the king of the North will attack the king of the South again. But this time he will not be successful as he was before. [30]Ships from the west will come and fight against the king of the North. He will see those ships coming and be afraid. Then he will return and show his anger against God's people who obey the holy agreement. He will be good to those who have stopped obeying the holy agreement. [31]"The king of the North will send his army. They will make the Temple[d] in Jerusalem unclean.[d] They will stop the people from offering the daily sacrifice. Then they will set up the horrible thing that destroys. [32]The king of the North will tell lies to God's people. Those who have not obeyed God will be ruined. But there will be some who know God and obey him. They will be strong and fight back.

[33]"Those who are wise will help the others understand what is happening. But some of them will be killed with swords. Some will be burned or taken captive. Some of them will have their homes and things taken away. These things will continue for many days. [34]When the wise ones are suffering, they will get a little help. Many who join the wise ones will not love God. [35]Some of the wise ones will be killed. But the hard times must come. This is so they can be made stronger and purer. They will be without faults until the time of the end comes. Then, at the right time the end will come.

[36]"The king of the North will do whatever he wants. He will brag about himself. He will praise himself and think he is even better than a god. He will say things against the God of gods that no one has ever heard. He will be successful until all the bad things have hap-

pened. What God has planned to happen will happen. [37]That king of the North will not care about the gods his ancestors worshiped. He won't care about the god that women worship. He won't care about any god. Instead, he will make himself more important than any god. [38]The king of the North will worship power and strength. His ancestors did not love power as he will. He will honor the god of power with gold and silver, expensive jewels and gifts. [39]That king will attack strong, walled cities. He will do it with the help of a foreign god. He will give much honor to the people who join him. He will make them rulers in charge of many other people. He will make those rulers pay him for the land they rule.

[40]"At the time of the end, the king of the South will fight a battle against the king of the North. The king of the North will attack him. He will attack with chariots and soldiers on horses and many large ships. He will invade many countries and sweep through their lands like a flood. [41]The king of the North will attack the beautiful land of Judah. He will defeat many countries. But Edom, Moab and the leaders of Ammon will be saved from him. [42]The king of the North will show his power in many countries. Egypt will not escape. [43]The king will get treasures of gold and silver. And he will get all the riches of Egypt. The Libyan and Nubian people will obey him. [44]But the king of the North will hear news from the east and the north. And it will make him afraid and angry. He will go to destroy completely many nations. [45]He will set up his royal tents. They will be between the sea and the beautiful mountain where the Temple[d] is built. But, finally, his end will come. There will not be anyone to help him when he dies.

12 "Daniel, at that time Michael, the great prince, will stand up. (He is the one who protects your people.) There will be a time of much trouble. It will be the worst time since nations have been on earth. But your people will be

saved. Everyone whose name is written in God's book will be saved. [2]Many people who have already died will live again. Some of them will wake up to have life forever. But some will wake up to find shame and disgrace forever. [3]The wise people will shine like the brightness of the sky. Those who teach others to live right will shine like stars forever and ever.

[4]"But you, Daniel, close up the book and seal it. These things will happen at the time of the end. Many people will go here and there to find true knowledge."

[5]Then I, Daniel, looked, and I saw two other men. One was standing on my side of the river. And the other was standing on the far side. [6]The man who was dressed in linen was standing over the water in the river. One of the two men spoke to him. He asked, "How long will it be before these amazing things come true?"

[7]The man dressed in linen who stood over the water raised his hands toward heaven. And I heard him make a promise. He used the name of God who lives forever. He said, "It will be for three and one-half years. The power of the holy people will finally be broken. Then all these things will come true."

[8]I heard the answer, but I did not really understand. So I asked, "Master, what will happen after all these things come true?"

[9]He answered, "Go your way, Daniel. The message is closed up and sealed until the time of the end. [10]Many people will be made clean,[d] pure and spotless. But the wicked will continue to be wicked. And those wicked people will not understand these things. But the wise people will understand them.

[11]"The daily sacrifice will be stopped. There will be 1,290 days from that time. Then the horrible thing that destroys will be set up. [12]Those who wait for the end of the 1,335 days will be happy. [13]"As for you, Daniel, go your way till the end. You will get your rest when you die. And at the end you will rise from the dead to get your reward."

The Book of
HOSEA

1 The Lord spoke his word to Hosea son of Beeri. This was during the time that Uzziah, Jotham, Ahaz and Hezekiah were kings of Judah. During part of this time Jeroboam son of Jehoash was king of Israel.

² The Lord said to him, "Go, and marry a woman who will be unfaithful to you. She will give you children whose fathers are other men. Do this because people in this country have acted like an unfaithful wife toward the Lord." ³ So Hosea married Gomer daughter of Diblaim. Gomer became pregnant and gave birth to Hosea's son.

⁴ The Lord said to Hosea, "Name him Jezreel. This is because soon I will punish the family of Jehu for the people they killed at Jezreel. Then I will put an end to the kingdom of Israel. ⁵ And I will also break the power of Israel's army in the Valley of Jezreel."

⁶ Gomer became pregnant again and gave birth to a daughter. The Lord said to Hosea, "Name her Lo-Ruhamah.ⁿ This is because I will not pity Israel anymore. I will no longer forgive them. ⁷ But I will show pity to the people of Judah. I will save them. I will not use bows or swords, horses or horsemen, or weapons of war to save them. I, the Lord their God, will save them."

⁸ After Gomer had finished nursing Lo-Ruhamah, she became pregnant again. And she gave birth to another son. ⁹ The Lord said, "Name him Lo-Ammiⁿ because you are not my people. And I am not your God.

¹⁰ "But the people of Israel will become like the grains of sand of the sea. You cannot measure or count them. Now it is said to Israel, 'You are not my people.' But later they will be called 'children of the living God.' ¹¹ Then the people of Judah and Israel will be joined together again. They will choose one leader for themselves. And again they will grow in their land. The day of Jezreel, when God plants, will be truly great.

2 "Your brothers and your sisters will be called 'my people' and 'you have been shown love.'

² "Plead with your mother.ⁿ
Plead with her because she no
longer acts like a wife to me.
And I am not treated like her
husband.
Tell her to stop acting like a
prostitute.ᵈ
Tell her to stop behaving like an
unfaithful wife.
³ If she refuses, I will strip her
naked.
I will leave her bare like the day
she was born.
I will make her dry like a desert.
I will make her like a land
without water.
I will kill her with thirst.
⁴ I will not take pity on her children.
They are the children of an
unfaithful wife.
⁵ Their mother has acted like a
prostitute.
The one who became pregnant
with them has acted
disgracefully.
She said, 'I will chase after my
lovers.ⁿ
They give me food and water.
They give me wool and linen.
They give me wine and olive oil.'
⁶ So I will block her road with
thornbushes.
I will build a wall around her
so she cannot find her way.
⁷ She will run after her lovers.
But she won't catch up to them.
She will look for them.
But she won't find them.
Then she will say, 'I will go back to
my first husband.ⁿ
Life was better for me then than
it is now.'
⁸ But she has not accepted that I was
the one
who gave her grain, wine and oil.
I gave her much silver and gold.
But she used it to make statues of
Baal.ᵈ
⁹ "So I will take away my grain at
harvest time.
And I will take away my wine
when it is ready.
I will take back my wool and linen.

1:6 Lo-Ruhamah This name in Hebrew means "not pitied." **1:9 Lo-Ammi** This name in Hebrew means "not my people." **2:2 mother** This refers to the nation of Israel here. **2:5 lovers** This refers to the nations surrounding Israel, who led Israel to worship false gods. **2:7 husband** This refers to God here.

I gave her those things to cover
    her nakedness.
[10] So I will show her nakedness to her
    lovers.
No one will save her from my
    punishment.
[11] I will put an end to all her
    celebrations:
    her yearly festivals, her New
        Moon[d] festivals and her
        Sabbaths.[d]
    I will stop all of her special
        feasts.
[12] I will destroy her vines and fig
        trees.
    She said they were her pay from
        her lovers.
    I will turn them into a forest.
        Wild animals will eat those
        plants.
[13] I will punish her for all the times
        she burned incense[d] to the Baals.
    She put on her rings and jewelry.
        Then she went chasing after her
        lovers.
    But she has forgotten me!"
        says the Lord.

[14] "So I am going to attract her.
    I will lead her into the desert
        and speak tenderly to her.
[15] Then I will give her back her
        vineyards.
    And I will make the Valley of
        Achor[n] a door of hope.
    Then she will respond as when she
        was young,
        as when she came out of Egypt.

[16] The Lord says, "Then she will call
        me 'my husband.'
    She will no longer call me 'my
        baal.'[n]
[17] I will never let her say the names of
        Baal again.
    Then people won't use their
        names anymore.
[18] At that time I will make an
        agreement for them.
    It will be with the wild animals,
        the birds and the crawling
        things.
    I will remove from the land
        the bow and the sword and the
        weapons of war.
    Then my people will live in
        safety.

[19] And I will make you my promised
        bride forever.
    I will be good and fair.
    I will show you my love and
        mercy.
[20] I will be true to you as my promised
        bride.
    Then you will accept that I am
        the Lord.

[21] "And at that time I will answer
        you," says the Lord.
    "I will speak to the skies.
    And they will give rain to the
        earth.
[22] The earth will produce grain, wine
        and oil.
    Much will grow because my
        people are called Jezreel—God
        plants.
[23] I will plant my people in the land.
    I will show pity to the one I had
        called 'not shown pity.'
    I will say, 'You are my people'
        to those I had called 'not my
        people.'
    And they will say to me, 'You are
        our God.'"

3 The Lord said to me, "Go, show your love to your wife again. She has had other lovers and has been unfaithful to you. But you must keep on loving her the way the Lord loves the people of Israel. This is true even though the Israelites worship other gods. They love to eat the raisin cakes."[n]

[2] So I bought Gomer for six ounces of silver and about ten bushels of barley. [3] Then I told her, "You must wait for me for many days. You must not be a prostitute.[d] You must not be any other man's lover. I, in turn, will wait for you."

[4] In the same way Israel will live many days without a king or leader. They will not have sacrifices or holy stone pillars. They will be without the holy vest[d] or an idol. [5] After this, the people of Israel will return to the Lord their God. They will follow the Lord and the king from David's family. In the last days they will come to the Lord. And he will bless them.

4 People of Israel, listen to the Lord's message.
    The Lord says he has this
        against you who live in this
        country:

2:15 **Achor** This name in Hebrew means "trouble." It refers here to punishment as the way to blessing. 2:16 **baal** Another Hebrew word for husband. But it was the same word as the false god Baal. 3:1 **raisin cakes** This food may have been used in the feasts that honored false gods.

"The people are not true, not loyal
to God.
They do not even know him.
[2]They curse. They lie. They kill.
They steal.
They are guilty of adultery.[d]
They break all my laws.
One murder follows another.
[3]Because of this the land dries up,
and all its people are dying off.
Even the wild animals are dying.
Even the birds of the air and the
fish of the sea are dying.

[4]"No one should accuse
or blame another person.
Don't blame the people, you
priests,
when they quarrel with you.
[5]You will be ruined one of these
days.
And your prophets[d] will be
ruined with you one of these
nights.
I will also destroy your mother, the
nation of Israel.
[6]My people will be destroyed
because they have no knowledge.
You priests have refused to learn.
So I will refuse to let you be
priests to me.
You have forgotten the teachings of
your God.
So I will reject your children.
[7]The more priests there are,
the more they sin against me.
I will take away their honor
and give them nothing but
shame.
[8]The priests live off the sin offerings
of the people.
So they want the people to sin
more and more.
[9]The priests are as wrong as the
people.
I will punish them both for what
they have done.
I will repay them for the wrong
they have done.

[10]"They will eat
but not have enough.
They will have sexual relations
with the prostitutes.[d]
But they will not have children.
This is because they left the Lord.
[11]"Sexual sins, old wine and new
wine

take away my people's ability to
understand.
[12]My people ask wooden idols for
advice.
They ask those sticks of wood to
advise them!
Like prostitutes, they have chased
after other gods.
They have left their own God.
[13]They make sacrifices on the tops of
the mountains.
They burn offerings on the hills,
under oaks, poplars and other
trees.
They think the shade under those
trees is nice.
So your daughters become
prostitutes.
And your daughters-in-law are
guilty of adultery.[d]

[14]"But I will not punish your
daughters
when they become prostitutes.
I will not punish your
daughters-in-law
for their sins of adultery.
I will not punish them
because you yourselves have
sexual relations with
prostitutes.
You offer sacrifices with the temple
prostitutes.
You foolish people are destroying
yourselves.

[15]"Israel, you act like a prostitute.
But don't let Judah be guilty.
Don't go to sacrifice at Gilgal.
Don't go up to give offerings at
Beth Aven.[n]
Don't use the Lord's name to make
promises.
Don't say, 'As surely as the Lord
lives . . .'
[16]The people of Israel are stubborn
like a stubborn young cow.
How then can the Lord feed them
like lambs in a meadow?
[17]Israel has chosen to worship idols.
So, let them.
[18]Her rulers get drunk.
Then they give themselves to
being prostitutes.
They love these disgraceful
things.
[19]They will be swept away as by a
whirlwind.
Their sacrifices will bring them
only shame.

4:15 **Gilgal . . . Beth Aven** Cities in Israel where people worshiped false gods.

5 "Listen, you priests.
  Pay attention, people of Israel.
Listen, royal family.
  You will all be judged.
You have been like a trap at
    Mizpah.
  You have been like a net spread
    out at Mount Tabor.
²You have done many bad things.
  So I will punish you all.
³I know all about Israel.
  What they have done is not
    hidden from me.
They all act like prostitutes.ᵈ
  Israel has made itself unclean.ᵈ

⁴"And those bad things they have
    done
  keep them from returning to their
    God.
They are determined to be
    unfaithful to me.
  They do not know the Lord.
⁵Israel's pride testifies against them.
  The people of Israel will stumble
    because of their sin.
The people of Judah will also
    stumble with them.
⁶The people will come to worship
    the Lord.
  They will come with their sheep
    and cattle.
But they will not be able to find
    him,
  because he has left them.
⁷They have not been true to the
    Lord.
  Their children do not belong to
    him.
So their false worship
  will destroy them and their land.

⁸"Blow the horn in Gibeah.
  Blow the trumpet in Ramah.
Give the warning at Beth Aven.
  Be first into battle, people of
    Benjamin.
⁹A time of punishment is coming.
  Israel will be destroyed.
I warn the tribesᵈ of Israel
  that this will surely happen.
¹⁰The leaders of Judah are like
    thieves.
  They try to steal the property of
    others.
My punishment will overwhelm
    them
  like a flood of water.
¹¹Israel will be crushed by the
    punishments,

because they decided to follow
    idols.
¹²I will destroy Israel
  as a moth destroys clothing.
I will destroy Judah
  as rot destroys wood.

¹³"Israel saw how weak she was.
  Judah saw the wounds she
    suffered.
So Israel turned to Assyria for help.
  She sent to the great king of
    Assyria for help.
But he cannot heal you.
  He cannot cure your wound.
¹⁴I will be like a lion to Israel.
  I will be like a young lion to
    Judah.
I will attack them
  and tear them to pieces.
I will drag them off,
  and no one will be able to save
    them.
¹⁵Then I will go back to my place
  until the people admit they are
    guilty.
At that time they must look for me.
  In their trouble they must turn to
    me."

6 You people say,
  "Come, let's go back to the Lord.
He has hurt us, but he will heal us.
  He has wounded us, but he will
    bandage our wounds.
²In a short while he will put new life
    in us.
  We will not have to wait long for
    him to raise us up.
Then we may live in his presence.
³Let's learn about the Lord.
  Let's try hard to know who he is.
He will come to us
  as surely as the dawn comes.
The Lord will come to us like the
    rain,
  like the spring rain that waters
    the ground."

⁴The Lord says, "Israel, what should
    I do with you?
  Judah, what should I do with
    you?
Your faithfulness is like a morning
    mist.
  It lasts only as long as the dew in
    the morning.
⁵I have warned you by my prophetsᵈ
  that I will kill you and destroy
    you.
My judgments will flash forth
  like lightning against you.

⁶I want faithful love
    more than I want animal
        sacrifices.
I want people to know me
    more than I want burnt offerings.
⁷But you have broken the agreement
    as Adam did.
    You have been unfaithful to me.
⁸Gilead is full of people who do evil.
    It is covered with bloody
        footprints.
⁹Some of the priests are like
    robbers waiting in ambush.
They murder people on the way to
    Shechem.ⁿ
    They do wicked crimes.
¹⁰I have seen horrible things in
    Israel.
The people are unfaithful to God,
    and Israel has become unclean.ᵈ

¹¹"Judah, I have set a time to punish
    you also.

"I would like to give my people
    back their riches.
7 I would like to heal Israel.
    But their sin can be seen by
        everyone.
    The wickedness of Israel is too
        well-known.
They cheat one another.
    They break into other peoples'
        houses.
    There are robberies in the streets.
²It never enters their minds
    that I remember all their wicked
        deeds.
The bad things they do are all
    around,
    and I can see their sins clearly.

³"They make the king happy with
    their wickedness.
    They make their rulers glad with
        their lies.
⁴But all of them are traitors.
    They are like an oven heated by a
        baker.
While he mixes the dough,
    he does not stir up the flame.
⁵They hold a festival day for the
    king.
    On that day the rulers become
        drunk with wine.
    The king joins in with those who
        had made evil plans.
⁶They approach him with murder in
    mind.
    Their hearts are like a hot oven.
All night long its fire is low.

When morning comes, it is
    fanned into flame.
⁷So all these people are as hot as an
    oven.
    Like a fire they destroy their
        rulers.
Their kings fall one after another.
    And no one calls on me.

⁸"Israel mixes with other nations.
    Israel is useless like a pancake
        cooked only on one side.
⁹Foreign nations are using up
    Israel's strength.
    And Israel doesn't even know it.
Israel is weak and feeble, like an
    old man.
    And they don't even know it.
¹⁰Israel's pride will cause their
    defeat.
    They have had many troubles.
But they still do not turn to the
    Lord their God.
    They do not look to him for help.
¹¹Israel has become like a silly
    pigeon.
    The people have no
        understanding.
First they call to Egypt for help.
    Then they run for help to
        Assyria.
¹²When they go, I will catch them
    as men catch birds in a net.
Then I will punish them
    as I have warned them.
¹³How terrible for them because they
    left me!
    They will be destroyed because
        they turned against me.
I want to save them.
    But they have spoken lies against
        me.
¹⁴They do not call to me from their
    hearts.
    They just lie on their beds and
        cry.
They come together to ask for grain
    and new wine.
    But they really turn away from
        me.
¹⁵I trained them and gave them
    strength.
    But they have made evil plans
        against me.
¹⁶They did not turn to the Most High
    God.
    They are like a crooked bow that
        does not shoot straight.
Their leaders brag about their
    strength.

6:9 Shechem A city of safety where men could go for protection.

But they will be killed with
swords.
Then the people in Egypt
will laugh at them.

8 "Put the trumpet to your lips and
give the warning!
The enemy swoops down on my
people like an eagle.
The Israelites have broken my
agreement.
They have turned against my
teachings.
²They cry out to me,
'Our God, we in Israel know you!'
³But Israel has rejected what is
good.
So the enemy chases them.
⁴They chose their own kings
without asking my permission.
They chose their own leaders,
men I did not know.
They made their silver and gold
into idols.
For all this they will be
destroyed.
⁵I hate that calf-shaped idol.
I am very angry with the people.
How long will they remain
unclean?d
⁶The idol is something a craftsman
made.
It is not God.
Israel's calf-shaped idol
will surely be smashed to pieces.

⁷"Israel's foolish plans are like
planting the wind.
But they will harvest a
whirlwind.
Her plans are like a stalk with no
head of grain.
It produces nothing.
Even if it produces something,
other nations would eat it.
⁸Israel is destroyed.
The people are mixed among the
other nations.
They have become useless to me.
⁹Like a wild donkey,
Israel has run to Assyria.
Israel has hired other nations to
protect her.
¹⁰Although Israel is mixed among the
nations,
I will gather them together.
They will become weaker and
weaker
as they suffer under the great
king of Assyria.

¹¹"The more altars Israel built to
remove sin,
the more they have become altars
for sinning.
¹²They reject the many teachings I
have written for them.
They act as if the teachings were
strange and foreign to them.
¹³The Israelites offer sacrifices to me
and eat the meat.
But the Lord is not pleased with
them.
He remembers the evil they have
done.
And he will punish them for their
sins.
They will be slaves again as they
were in Egypt.
¹⁴The people of Israel have forgotten
their Maker.
They trust in the palaces they
have built.
And Judah trusts in her many
strong, walled cities.
But I will send fire on their cities
and destroy their strong towers."

9 Israel, do not rejoice.
Don't celebrate as the other
nations do.
You have been unfaithful to your
God.
You love the grain on your
threshing⁴ floors.
So you worship the gods who
supposedly gave it.
²But there won't be enough grain to
feed the people.
And there won't be enough wine
to go around.
³The Israelites will not stay in the
Lord's land.
Israel will return to being
captives as they were in Egypt.
In Assyria they will eat food that
they are not allowed to eat.
⁴The Israelites will not give
offerings of wine to the Lord.
Their sacrifices will not please
him.
Their sacrifices will be like food
that is eaten at a funeral.
It is unclean,d and everyone who
eats it becomes unclean.
Their food will only satisfy their
hunger.
They cannot sacrifice it in the
Temple.d
⁵What will you do then on the day of
feasts

and on the festival days of the
Lord?
[6]Even if the people are not
destroyed,
Egypt will take them as captives.
They will be buried in Memphis.[n]
Weeds will grow over their silver
treasures.
Thorns will grow over their
houses.
[7]Let Israel know this.
The time of punishment has
come.
The time to pay for your sins has
come.
You have sinned very much,
and your hatred is great.
You think the prophet[d] is a fool.
You say the spiritual man is
crazy.
[8]The prophet is God's watchman
to warn Israel of danger.
But everywhere he goes you set
traps for him.
You treat him as an enemy in
God's own land.
[9]The men of Israel have become as
sinful
as the men of Gibeah[n] were.
The Lord will remember the evil
things they have done.
He will punish them for their
sins.
[10]"When I found Israel,
it was like finding grapes in the
desert.
Your ancestors were like
finding the first figs on the tree.
But when they came to Baal Peor,
they began worshiping an idol.
They became as disgusting as the
thing they worshiped.
[11]Israel's glory will fly away like a
bird.
There will be no more
pregnancies, no more births,
no more babies.
[12]But even if the Israelites bring up
children,
I will take them all away.
How terrible it will be for them
when I turn away from them!
[13]I have seen Israel, like Tyre,
given a pleasant place.
But the people of Israel will soon
bring out
their children to be killed."

[14]Lord, give them what they should
have.
What will you give them?
Make their women unable to
have children.
Give them breasts that cannot
feed their babies.

[15]"The Israelites were wicked in
Gilgal,
so I began to hate them there.
Because of the sinful things they
have done,
I will force them to leave my
land.
I will no longer love them.
Their leaders have turned against
me.
[16]Israel is like a sick plant.
Its root is dying, and it has no
fruit.
So the people will have no more
children.
And if they did, I would kill the
children they love."

[17]God will reject them,
because they have not obeyed
him.
They will wander among the
nations.

10 Israel is like a vine
that produced plenty of fruit.
As the people became richer,
they built more altars for idols.
As their land became better,
they put up better stone pillars to
honor false gods.
[2]Their heart was false.
Now they must pay for their
guilt.
The Lord will break down their
altars.
He will destroy their holy stone
pillars.

[3]Then the Israelites will say, "We
have no king,
because we didn't honor the
Lord.
But even if we had one,
he couldn't do anything for us."
[4]They make many false promises.
They make agreements they
don't keep.
So people sue each other in court.
They are like poisonous weeds
growing in a plowed field.

9:6 Memphis A city in Egypt famous for its tombs.
caused a civil war. See Judges 19–21.

9:9 Gibeah The sins of the men of Gibeah

[5]The people from Israel are worried
about
the calf-shaped idol at Beth Aven.
The people and the priests will cry
because their glorious idol is
gone.
[6]It will be carried off as a payment
that was demanded
to the great king of Assyria.
Israel will be disgraced.
The people will be ashamed of
trusting that idol.
[7]The king of Israel will be carried off
like a chip of wood floating on
the water.
[8]The places of worship at Beth Aven
will be destroyed.
They are where Israel sins.
Thorns and weeds will grow up
and cover their altars.
Then they will say to the
mountains, "Cover us!"
And they will say to the hills,
"Fall on us!"

[9]"Israel, you have sinned since the
time of Gibeah.[n]
The people there have continued
sinning.
But war will surely overwhelm
them,
because of the evil they have
done there.
[10]When I am ready,
I will come to punish them.
Armies will come together against
them.
They will be punished for their
many sins.
[11]Israel is like a well-trained young
cow
that likes to thresh[d] grain.
But I will put a yoke[d] on her neck.
I will make Israel work hard in
the field.
Judah will plow.
Israel will break up the ground.
[12]I said, 'Break new ground.
Plant what is right.
Then you will harvest good things
from your loyalty to me.
It is time for you to turn back to
me, the Lord.
Do it until I come and pour out
my goodness on you.'
[13]But you have planted evil.
So you have harvested trouble.
You have trusted in your own
power
and your many soldiers.

Now you must live with the result
of your lies.
[14]So your armies will hear the noise
of battle.
And all your strong, walled cities
will be destroyed.
It will be like the time King
Shalman
destroyed Beth Arbel in battle.
Mothers and children were
crushed to the ground together.
[15]The same will happen to you,
people of Bethel,
because you did so much evil.
When that time comes,
the king of Israel will die.

11

"When Israel was a child, I loved
him.
And I called my son out of
Egypt.
[2]But the more I called to the people
of Israel,
the further they went from me.
They offered sacrifices to the
Baals.[d]
They burned incense[d] to the
idols.
[3]But it was I who taught Israel to
walk.
I took them by the arms.
But they did not understand
that I had healed them.
[4]I led them with cords of human
kindness,
with ties of love.
I lifted the yoke[d] from their neck.
I bent down and fed them.

[5]"The Israelites will become
captives again, as they were in
Egypt.
The king of Assyria will become
their king.
This is because they refuse to
turn to God.
[6]War will sweep through their cities.
It will destroy them,
because of their wicked plans.
[7]My people have made up their
minds
to turn away from me.
The prophets[d] call them to turn to
me.
But none of them honors me at
all.

[8]"Israel, I don't want to give you up.
I don't want to go away and leave
you.

10:9 **Gibeah** The sins of the men of Gibeah caused a civil war. See Judges 19–21.

I don't want to make you like
Admah.
I don't want to treat you like
Zeboiim.[n]
My heart beats for you.
My love for you stirs up my pity.
[9]I won't punish you in my anger.
I won't destroy Israel again.
I am God and not man.
I am the Holy One, and I am
among you.
I will not come against you in
anger.
[10]I will call for my people like
a lion calling for its young.
My children will come and follow
me.
They will hurry to me from the
west.
[11]They will come swiftly
like birds from a captivity like
Egypt was,
and like doves from Assyria.
I will settle them again in their
homes,"
says the Lord.

[12]Israel has surrounded me with lies.
The people of Israel have made
their secret plans.
And Judah turns against God,
the faithful Holy One.

12 What Israel does is as useless as
chasing the wind,
as dangerous as being in a
windstorm.
They tell more and more lies
and do more and more violence.
They make agreements with Assyria,
and they send a gift of olive oil to
Egypt.
[2]The Lord also has some things
against Judah.
He will punish Israel for what
they have done.
He will give them what they
deserve.
[3]Their ancestor Jacob held on to his
brother's heel
while the two of them were being
born.
When Jacob grew to be a man,
he wrestled with God.
[4]He wrestled with the angel and
won.
Jacob cried and asked for his
blessing.
Later, God met with him at Bethel
and spoke with him there.

[5]He is the Lord God of heaven's
armies.
He wants to be remembered as
the Lord.
[6]Like Jacob you must return to him.
You must be loyal and true to
him.
You must do what is honest and
just.
You must always trust in him as
your God.

[7]The merchants use dishonest
scales.
They like to cheat people.
[8]The people of Israel brag that they
are rich.
They think that because they are
rich
no one will learn about their sins.

[9]"But I am the Lord your God.
I brought you out of Egypt.
I will make you live in tents again
as you used to do in the desert.
[10]I spoke to the prophets[d]
and gave them many visions.
Through them, I taught my
lessons to you."

[11]The people of Gilead are evil.
They are worth nothing.
People sacrifice bulls at Gilgal.
But their altars will become like
piles of stone in a plowed field.
[12]Your ancestor Jacob fled to
Northwest Mesopotamia.
There he worked to get a wife.
He tended sheep to pay for her.
[13]Later the Lord used a prophet
to bring Jacob's descendants[d] out
of Egypt.
The Lord used a prophet
to take care of the Israelites.
[14]But the Israelites made the Lord
angry.
They killed other people.
They deserve to die for their
crimes.
The Lord will make them pay
for the disgraceful things they
have done.

13 People used to fear the tribe[d] of
Ephraim.
They were important people in
Israel.
But they sinned by worshiping
Baal.[d]
So they must die.

²But they keep on sinning more and
more.
They make idols of their silver.
Those idols are cleverly made.
They are the work of a
craftsman.
Yet the people of Israel say to each
other,
"Kiss those calf idols and
sacrifice to them."
³So those people will be like the
morning dew.
They will disappear like the
morning mist.
They will be like chaff^d blown from
the threshing^d floor.
They will vanish away like smoke
rising from a chimney.

⁴"I have been the Lord their God
since they were in the land of
Egypt.
They have really known no other
God except me.
I am the one who has saved
them.
⁵I cared for them in the desert
where it was hot and dry.
⁶I gave them food, and they became
full and satisfied.
But then they became proud and
forgot me.
⁷That is why I will be like a lion to
them.
I will be like a leopard waiting by
the road.
⁸I will attack like a bear robbed of
her cubs.
I will rip their bodies open.
I will devour them like a lion.
I will tear them apart like a wild
animal.

⁹"Israel, I will destroy you
for turning against me, your
helper.
¹⁰What good are your kings and your
leaders now?
Can they save you in any of your
towns?
You asked for them, saying,
'Give us a king and leaders.'
¹¹So I gave you kings, but only in
anger.
And I took them away in my
great anger.
¹²The sins of Israel are on record.
They are filed away, waiting for
punishment.

¹³Israel has a chance to live again,
but the people are too foolish to
take it.
They are like an unborn baby
who won't come out of its
mother's womb.
¹⁴So I will not save them from the
place where the dead are.
I will not rescue them from
death.
I will call on death to hurt them.
I will call on the place where the
dead are to destroy them.
I will show them no mercy.
¹⁵Israel has become important
among the nations.
But the Lord will send a
destroyer from the east.
He will come like a wind from the
desert
that dries up all the springs and
wells of water.
He will destroy all their treasures,
everything of value.
¹⁶The nation of Israel will be
punished,
because it fought against God.
The people of Israel will die by the
sword.
Their children will be torn to
pieces.
And their pregnant women will
be ripped open."

14 Israel, return to the Lord your
God.
Your sins have caused your
ruin.
²Come back to the Lord
and say these words to him:
"Take away all our sin
and kindly receive us.
Then we will give you the praise we
promised you.
³Assyria cannot save us.
We will not trust in our horses.
We will not say again, 'Our gods,'
to the things our hands have
made.
You show mercy to us, who are
like orphans."

⁴The Lord says,
"I will forgive them for leaving me.
I will love them freely.
I am not angry with them
anymore.
⁵I will be like the dew to Israel.
It will blossom like a lily.
Like the cedar trees in Lebanon,
its roots will be firm.

6The people will be like spreading
    branches.
  They will be like the beautiful
    olive trees.
  They will be like the
    sweet-smelling cedars in
    Lebanon.
7The people of Israel will again live
    under my protection.
  They will grow like the grain.
  They will bloom like a vine.
  They will be as famous as the
    wine of Lebanon.
8Israel, have nothing to do with
    idols.

I, the Lord, am the one who
    answers your prayers.
  I am the one who watches over
    you.
I am like a green pine tree.
  Your blessings come from me."

9A wise person will know these
    things.
  An understanding person will
    take them to heart.
The Lord's ways are right.
  Good people live by following
    them,
  but those who turn against God
    die because of them.

The Book of
JOEL

1 The Lord spoke his word to Joel son
of Pethuel:

2Older leaders, listen to this
    message.
  Listen to me, all you people who
    live in the land.
Nothing like this has ever
    happened during your lifetime.
Nothing like this has ever
    happened during your fathers'
    lifetimes.
3Tell your children about these
    things.
  And let your children tell their
    children.
  And let your grandchildren tell
    their children.
4What the cutting locusts have not
    eaten,
  the swarming locusts have eaten.
And what the swarming locusts
    have left,
  the hopping locusts have eaten.
And what the hopping locusts have
    left,
  the destroying locusts[n] have
    eaten.

5Drunks, wake up and cry!
  All of you people who drink
    wine, cry!
Cry because your sweet wine
    has been taken away from you.
6A powerful nation has come into
    my land.

It has too many soldiers to count.
  It has teeth like a lion.
  And it has fangs like a female
    lion.
7That army has eaten my
    grapevines.
  It has destroyed my fig trees.
  It has eaten the bark off my trees
    and left the branches white.

8Cry as a young woman cries
    when the man she was going to
    marry is killed.
9There will be no more grain or
    drink offerings
  to offer in the Temple[d] of the
    Lord.
Because of this, the priests,
    the servants of the Lord, cry.
10The fields are ruined.
  Even the ground is dried up.
The grain is destroyed.
  The new wine is dried up.
  And the olive oil runs out.
11Be sad, farmers.
  Cry loudly, you who grow grapes.
Cry for the wheat and the barley.
  Cry because the harvest in the
    field is lost.
12The vines have become dry.
  And the fig trees are dying.
The pomegranate[d] trees, the date
    palm trees and the apple trees
    have dried up.

1:4 cutting . . . locusts These are different names for an insect like a large grasshopper. The locust can quickly destroy trees, plants and crops. In this destruction by locusts, Joel sees a warning. God will cause this type of destruction when he punishes his people.

All the trees in the field have
died.
And the happiness of the people
has died, too.
[13]Priests, put on your rough cloth
and cry to show your sadness.
Servants of the altar, cry out
loud.
Servants of my God,
sleep in your rough cloth to show
your sadness.
Cry because there will be no more
grain or drink offerings
to offer in the Temple of your
God.
[14]Call the people together.
Tell them there will be a time to
give up food.
Bring together the older leaders
and everyone who lives in the
land.
Bring them to the Temple of the
Lord your God.
And cry out to the Lord.
[15]This will be a terrible day!
The Lord's day of judging is near.
At that time punishment will come
like an attack from God
All-Powerful.

[16]Our food is taken away
while we watch.
Joy and happiness are gone
from the Temple of our God.
[17]We planted seeds,
but they lie dry and dead in the
dirt.
Our barns are empty and falling
down.
The storerooms for grain have
been broken down.
This is because the grain has
dried up.
[18]The animals are hungry and
groaning!
The herds of cattle wander
around confused.
They have no grass to eat.
Even the flocks of sheep suffer.
[19]Lord, I am calling to you for help.
Fire has burned up the open
pastures.
Flames have burned all the trees
in the field.
[20]Wild animals also need your help.

The water in the streams has
dried up.
Fire has burned up the open
pastures.

2 Blow the trumpet in Jerusalem.
Shout a warning on my holy
mountain.
Let all the people who live in the
land shake with fear.
The Lord's day of judging is
coming.
The Lord's day of judging is near.
[2]It will be a dark, gloomy day.
It will be a cloudy and black day.
Like the light at sunrise,
the great and powerful army will
spread over the mountains.
There has never been anything like
it before.
And there will never be anything
like it again.

[3]The army destroys the land
like a burning fire.
The land in front of them is like the
garden of Eden.
The land behind them is like an
empty desert.
Nothing will escape them.
[4]They look like horses.
They run like war horses.
[5]Listen to them!
It is like the noise of chariots
rumbling over the mountains.
It is like the noise of crackling
flames
burning dry stalks.
They are like a powerful army lined
up for battle.
[6]Before this army, nations shake
with fear.
Their faces become pale.

[7]The army charges ahead like
soldiers.
They climb over the walls like
warriors.
They all march straight ahead.
They do not move off their path.
[8]They do not run into each other.
Each one walks in line.
They charge through all efforts to
stop them
and stay in line.
[9]They run into the city.
They run along the tops of the
walls.
They climb into the houses.
They enter through windows like
a thief.
[10]Before them, earth and sky shake.

The sun and the moon become
  dark,
  and the stars stop shining.
[11] The Lord calls out orders loudly
  as he leads his army.
That army obeys his commands.
  It is very large and powerful.
The Lord's day of judging
  is an overwhelming and terrible
   day.
No one can stand up against it.

[12] The Lord says, "Now, come back to
  me with all your heart.
Go without food, and cry and be
  sad."

[13] Tearing your clothes is not enough
  to show you are sad.
Let your heart be broken.
Come back to the Lord your God.
  He is kind and shows mercy.
He doesn't become angry quickly.
  He has great love.
He would rather forgive than
  punish.
[14] Who knows? Maybe the Lord will
  change his mind
and leave behind a blessing for
  you.
Then you may give grain and drink
  offerings
to the Lord your God.

[15] Blow the trumpet in Jerusalem.
  Call for a special time of going
   without food.
Call for a special meeting.
[16] Bring the people together.
  Make the meeting holy for the
   Lord.
Bring together the older leaders.
  Bring together the children,
   even babies that still feed at their
    mothers' breasts.
The bridegroom should come from
  his room.
The bride should come from her
  bedroom.
[17] The priests, the Lord's servants,
  should cry.
They should cry between the
  altar and entrance to the
   Temple.[d]
They should say, "Lord, have mercy
  on your people.
Don't let them be put to shame.
Don't let other nations make fun
  of them.

Don't let people in other nations
  ask,
  'Where is their God?'"

[18] Then the Lord became concerned
  about his land.
He felt sorry for his people.
[19] The Lord said to them:
  "I will send you grain, wine and
   olive oil.
You will have plenty.
No more will I shame you
  among the nations.
[20] I will force the army from the north
  to leave your land.
I will force them into a dry,
  empty land.
Their soldiers in front will be
  forced into the Dead Sea.[d]
And those in the rear will be
  forced into the Mediterranean
   Sea.
Their bodies will rot and stink
  because they did horrible things."

[21] But, land, don't be afraid.
  Be happy and full of joy
because the Lord has begun to do
  wonderful things.
[22] Wild animals, don't be afraid.
  The open pastures will grow
   grass.
The trees will grow fruit.
  The fig trees and the vines will
   grow much fruit.
[23] So be happy, people of Jerusalem.
  Be joyful in the Lord your God.
He will do what is right
  and will give you rain.
He will send the early rain
  and the late rain for you, as
   before.
[24] And the threshing[d] floors will be
  full of wheat.
And the barrels will overflow
  with wine and olive oil.

[25] "I sent my great army against you.
  Those swarming locusts and the
   hopping locusts,
the destroying locusts and the
  cutting locusts[n] ate your crops.
But I will pay you back
  for those years of trouble.
[26] Then you will have plenty to eat.
  You will be full.
You will praise the name of the
  Lord your God.
He has done miracles[d] for you.

2:25 swarming . . . locusts These are different names for an insect like a large grasshopper. The locust can quickly destroy trees, plants and crops. In this destruction by locusts, Joel sees a warning. God will cause this type of destruction when he punishes his people.

My people will never again be
shamed.
²⁷Then you will know that I am
among the people of Israel.
You will know that I am the Lord
your God.
There is no other God.
My people will never be shamed
again.

²⁸"After this,
I will give my Spirit[d] freely to all
kinds of people.
Your sons and daughters will
prophesy.[d]
Your old men will dream dreams.
Your young men will see visions.
²⁹At that time I will give my Spirit
even to servants, both men and
women.
³⁰I will show miracles
in the sky and on the earth:
blood, fire and thick smoke.
³¹The sun will become dark.
The moon will become red as
blood.
And then the Lord's
overwhelming and terrible day
of judging will come.
³²Then anyone who asks the Lord for
help
will be saved.
Even on Mount Zion[d] and in
Jerusalem
there will be people who will be
saved.
This will happen just as the Lord
has said.
Those left alive after the day of
punishment
are the people whom the Lord
called.

3 "In those days and at that time,
I will give Judah and Jerusalem
back their riches.
²I will also gather all the nations
together.
I will bring them down into the
Valley Where the Lord Judges.
And there I will judge them.
Those nations scattered my own
people, Israel.
They forced my people to live in
other nations.
They divided up my land.
³They threw lots[d] for my people.
They traded boys for prostitutes.[d]

And they sold girls to buy wine
to drink.

⁴"Tyre and Sidon and all of you regions of Philistia! What do you have
against me? Are you punishing me for
something I did? Or are you doing something to hurt me? Then I will quickly do
to you what you have done to me. ⁵You
took my silver and gold. You took my
precious treasures and put them in your
temples. ⁶You sold the people of Judah
and Jerusalem to the Greeks. That way
you could send them far from their land.
⁷"You sent my people to that faraway
place. But I will bring them back. And I
will do to you what you have done to
them. ⁸I will sell your sons and daughters to the people of Judah. Then they
will sell them to the Sabean people far
away." The Lord said this.

⁹Announce this among the nations:
Prepare for war!
Wake up the soldiers!
Let all the men of war come near
and attack.
¹⁰Make your plows into swords.
Make spears from your hooks for
trimming trees.
Let the weak say,
"I am strong."
¹¹All of you nations, hurry.
Come together in that place.
Lord, send your strong soldiers
to gather the nations.

¹²"Wake up, nations.
Come to the Valley Where the
Lord Judges.
There I will sit to judge
all the nations on every side.
¹³Cut them down like grain
because the harvest is ripe with
sin.
Come, walk on them as you would
walk on grapes,
because the winepress[d] is full.
The barrels are full of their sins
and spilling over.
These people are so evil!"

¹⁴There are many people
in the Valley of Decision.[n]
The Lord's day of judging is near
in the Valley of Decision.
¹⁵The sun and the moon will become
dark.
The stars will stop shining.

3:14 Valley of Decision This is like the name "the Valley Where the Lord Judges" in 3:2 and
3:12.

[16]The Lord will roar like a lion from
Jerusalem.
His loud voice will sound like a
growl from Jerusalem.
And the sky and the earth will
shake.
But the Lord will be a safe place for
his people.
He will be a strong place of
safety for the people of Israel.

[17]"Then you will know that I am the
Lord your God.
I stay in my holy Mount Zion.[d]
Jerusalem will become holy.
Strangers will never take over
that city again.

[18]"On that day the mountains will be
covered with grapes for sweet
wine.

The hills will be covered with
cows to give milk.
And water will flow through all
the ravines of Judah.
A fountain will flow from the
Temple[d] of the Lord.
It will give water to the valley of
acacia trees.
[19]But Egypt will become empty.
And Edom will become an empty
desert.
This is because they were cruel to
the people of Judah.
They killed innocent people in
the land of Judah.
[20]But there will always be people
living in Judah.
And people will live in Jerusalem
from now on.
[21]Egypt and Edom killed my people.
So I will definitely punish them."

The Lord lives in Jerusalem!

The Book of
AMOS

1 Amos was one of the shepherds from
the town of Tekoa. God showed him
this vision about Israel. It was at the
time Uzziah was king of Judah and Jeroboam son of Jehoash was king of Israel.
This happened two years before the
earthquake.
  [2]Amos said,
"The Lord will roar like a lion from
Jerusalem.
His loud voice will sound like a
growl from Jerusalem.
The green pastures of the
shepherds will become dry.
Even Mount Carmel will dry up."
[3]This is what the Lord says:
"For the many crimes Damascus is
doing,
I will punish them.
They beat the people of Gilead
with threshing[d] boards that had
iron teeth.
[4]So I will send fire upon the house
of Hazael.
That fire will destroy the strong
towers of Ben-Hadad.
[5]I will break down the gate of
Damascus.
I will destroy the king who is in
the Valley of Aven.

I will also destroy the king of Beth
Eden.
The people of Aram will be taken
captive to the country of Kir,"
says the Lord.
[6]This is what the Lord says:
"For the many crimes Gaza is doing,
I will punish them.
They sold all the people of one area
as slaves to Edom.
[7]So I will send a fire on the walls of
Gaza.
That fire will destroy the city's
strong towers.
[8]I will destroy the king of the city of
Ashdod.
I will destroy the king of the city
of Ashkelon.
Then I will turn against the people
of the city of Ekron.
I will punish the Philistines until
they are all dead," says the
Lord God.
[9]This is what the Lord says:
"For the many crimes Tyre is doing,
I will punish them.
They sold all the people of one area
as slaves to Edom.
They forgot the brotherly
agreement they had made with
Israel.

[10]So I will send fire on the walls of
Tyre.
That fire will destroy the city's
strong towers."

[11]This is what the Lord says:
"For the many crimes Edom is
doing,
I will punish them.
They hunted down their brothers,
the Israelites, with the sword.
They showed them no mercy.
The people of Edom were
continually angry.
And they did not hold back their
great anger.

[12]So I will send fire on the city of
Teman.
That fire will even destroy the
strong towers of Bozrah.'"[n]

[13]This is what the Lord says:
"For the many crimes Ammon is
doing,
I will punish them.
They ripped open the pregnant
women in Gilead.
They did this so they could take
over that land
and make their own country
larger.

[14]So I will send fire on the walls of
Rabbah.
That fire will destroy the city's
strong towers.
It will come during a day of battle.
There will be strong winds on a
stormy day.

[15]Then their king and leaders will be
captured.
They will all be taken away
together," says the Lord.

2This is what the Lord says:
"For the many crimes Moab is
doing,
I will punish them.
They burned the bones of the
king of Edom into lime.

[2]So I will send fire on Moab.
And it will destroy the strong
towers of the city of Kerioth.
The people of Moab will die in a
great noise.
They will die in the middle of
sounds of war and trumpets.

[3]So I will bring an end to the king of
Moab.
And I will kill all its leaders with
him," says the Lord.

[4]This is what the Lord says:

"For the many crimes Judah is
doing,
I will punish them.
They rejected the teachings of the
Lord.
They did not keep his commands.
Their ancestors followed false
gods.
And Judah followed those same
gods.

[5]So I will send fire on Judah.
It will destroy the strong towers
of Jerusalem."

[6]This is what the Lord says:
"For the many crimes Israel is
doing,
I will punish them.
For silver they sell people who have
done nothing wrong.
They sell poor people for the
price of a pair of sandals.

[7]They walk on poor people
as if they were dirt.
They refuse to be fair to those
who are suffering.
Fathers and sons have sexual
relations with the same
woman.
By doing this they ruin my holy
name.

[8]As they worship at their altars,
they lie down on clothes taken
from poor people.
They make people pay money as
punishment.
With that money they buy wine
to drink in the house of their
god.

[9]"But it was I who destroyed the
Amorites before them.
The Amorites were tall like cedar
trees and as strong as oaks.
But I destroyed them completely.

[10]It was I who brought you from the
land of Egypt.
For 40 years I led you through the
desert.
I led you so I could give you the
land of the Amorites.

[11]I made some of your sons to be
prophets.[d]
I made some of your young men
to be Nazirites.[d]
People of Israel, isn't this true?"
says the Lord.

[12]"But you made the Nazirites drink
wine.

1:12 Teman . . . Bozrah Teman was in northern Edom, and Bozrah was in southern Edom. So
this means the whole country will be destroyed.

You told the prophets not to
prophesy my message.
[13]Now I will crush you
as a wagon loaded with grain
crushes anything beneath it.
[14]No one will escape, not even the
fastest runner.
Strong men will not be strong
enough.
Warriors will not be able to save
themselves.
[15]Soldiers with bows and arrows will
not stand and fight.
Even soldiers who run quickly
will not get away.
Soldiers on horses will not
escape alive.
[16]At that time even the bravest
warriors
will run away without their
armor," says the Lord.

3 Listen to this message that the Lord
has spoken against you, people of Israel. The message is against the whole
nation the Lord brought out of Egypt.
[2]"I have chosen only you
out of all the families of the
earth.
So I will punish you
for all your sins."

[3]Two people will not walk together
unless they have agreed to do
this.
[4]A lion in the forest will roar
when he has caught an animal.
He does not growl in his den
when he has caught nothing.
[5]A bird will not fall into a trap
where there is no bait.
The trap will not spring shut
if there is nothing to catch.
[6]When a trumpet blows a warning,
the people tremble.
When trouble comes to a city,
the Lord has caused it.
[7]Before the Lord God does anything,
he tells his servants the
prophets.[d]
[8]The lion has roared!
Who wouldn't be afraid?
The Lord God has spoken,
and I must prophesy his
message.

[9]Announce this to the strong towers
of Ashdod.
Announce it to the strong cities
of Egypt:
"Come to the mountains of
Samaria.

There you will see great
confusion.
You will see people hurting
others."

[10]"The people don't know how to do
what is right," says the Lord.
"Their strong cities are filled
with treasures they took by
force from others."

[11]So this is what the Lord God says:
"An enemy will take over the land.
He will pull down your strong
towers.
He will take the treasures you hid
in your strong cities."

[12]This is what the Lord says:
"A shepherd might save from a
lion's mouth
only two leg bones or a scrap of
an ear of his sheep.
In the same way only a few
Israelites will be saved.
These people now sit on their
beds in Samaria.
They sit on their couches."

[13]"You nations, listen to what I say
against the family of Israel. You are my
witnesses against them," says the Lord
God, the God of heaven's armies.

[14]"The people of Israel sinned, and I
will punish them.
I will also destroy the altars at
Bethel.
The corners of the altar will be cut
off,
and they will fall to the ground.
[15]I will tear down the winter house,
together with the summer house.
The houses decorated with ivory
will be destroyed.
And the great houses will come
to an end," says the Lord.

4 Listen to this message, you rich
women on the Mountain of
Samaria.
You take things from the poor
and crush people who are in
need.
You tell your husbands,
"Bring us money so we can
drink!"
[2]The Lord God has promised this:
"It is certain that I am a holy
God.
So it is certain that the time will
come

when some of you will be taken
away by hooks.
The rest of you will be taken
away with fishhooks.
[3]You will go straight out of the city
through holes in the walls.
And you will be thrown on the
garbage dump," says the Lord.

[4]"Go to the city of Bethel and sin.
Go to Gilgal and sin even more.
Offer your sacrifices every
morning.
Bring one-tenth of your crops on
the third day.
[5]Offer bread made with yeast as a
sacrifice to show your thanks.
And brag about the offerings you
bring to show thanks to the
Lord.
Brag about these things, Israelites.
This is what you love to do," says
the Lord God.

[6]"I did not give you any food to eat.
There was not enough food in
any of your towns.
But you did not come back to
me," says the Lord.
[7]"I held back the rain from you
three months before harvest
time.
Then I let it rain on one city
but not on another.
Rain fell on one field,
but another field got none and
dried up.
[8]People weak from thirst went from
town to town for water.
But they could not get enough
water to drink.
But you still did not come back to
me," says the Lord.
[9]"I made your crops die from
disease and mildew.[d]
I destroyed your gardens and
your vineyards.
Locusts[d] ate your fig trees and olive
trees.
But you still did not come back to
me," says the Lord.
[10]"I sent disasters against you,
as I did to Egypt.
I killed your young men with
swords.
I also killed your horses.
I made you smell the stink from all
the dead bodies.
But you still did not come back to
me," says the Lord.

[11]"I destroyed some of you
as I destroyed Sodom and
Gomorrah.
You were like a burning stick
pulled from a fire.
But you still have not come back
to me," says the Lord.

[12]"So this is what I will do to you,
Israel.
And because I will do this to you,
get ready to meet your God,
Israel."

[13]He is the one who makes the
mountains.
He creates the wind.
He makes his thoughts known to
man.
He changes the dawn into
darkness.
He walks over the mountains of
the earth.
His name is the Lord God of
heaven's armies.

5 Listen to this funeral song that I sing
about you, people of Israel.
[2]"Israel has fallen.
It will not rise up again.
It was left alone in the land.
There is no one to lift it up."

[3]This is what the Lord God says:
"If 1,000 soldiers leave a city,
only 100 will return.
If 100 soldiers leave a city,
only 10 will return."

[4]This is what the Lord says to the nation of Israel:
"Come to me and live.
[5] But do not look in Bethel.
Do not go to Gilgal,
and do not go down to
Beersheba.
The people of Gilgal will be taken
away as captives.
And Bethel will become
nothing."
[6]Come to the Lord and live.
If you don't, he will destroy the
descendants[d] of Joseph as a
fire would.
The fire will burn.
But there will be no one to put it
out for Bethel.
[7]You change the justice of the courts
into something unfair.
You reject what is right.
[8]God is the one who made the star
groups Pleiades and Orion.

He changes darkness into the
morning light.
And he changes the day into the
dark night.
He calls for the waters of the sea
to pour out on the earth.
The Lord is his name.
⁹He destroys the protected city.
And he ruins the strong, walled
city.

¹⁰You hate those who speak in court
against evil.
And you hate those who tell the
truth.
¹¹You walk on poor people.
You force them to give you grain.
You have built fancy houses of cut
stone.
But you will not live in them.
You have planted beautiful
vineyards.
But you will not drink the wine
from them.
¹²It is because I know your many
crimes.
I know your terrible sins.
You hurt people who do right.
You accept money to do wrong.
You keep the poor from getting
justice in court.
¹³In such times the wise man will
keep quiet,
because it is a bad time.

¹⁴Try to do good, not evil.
Then you will live.
And the Lord God of heaven's
armies will be with you
just as you say he is.
¹⁵Hate evil and love good.
Be fair in the courts.
Maybe the Lord God of heaven's
armies will be kind
to the people of Joseph who are
left alive.

¹⁶This is what the Lord, the Lord God
of heaven's armies, says:
"People will be crying in all the
public places.
They will be saying, 'Oh, no!' in
the streets.
They will call the farmers to
come and weep.
They will pay people to cry out
loud for them.
¹⁷People will be crying in all the
vineyards.
This is because I will pass among
you to punish you," says the
Lord.

¹⁸How terrible it will be for you who
want
the Lord's day of judging to
come.
Why do you want that day to come?
It will bring darkness for you, not
light.
¹⁹It will be like a man who runs from
a lion
and meets a bear.
It will be like him going into his
house
and putting his hand on the wall.
And then a snake bites him.
²⁰So the Lord's day of judging will
bring darkness, not light.
It will be a time of sadness, not
joy.

²¹The Lord says, "I hate your feasts.
I cannot stand your religious
meetings.
²²You offer me burnt offerings and
grain offerings.
But I won't accept them.
You bring the best fellowship
offerings.
But I will ignore them.
²³Take the noise of your songs away
from here!
I won't listen to the music of your
harps.
²⁴But let justice flow like a river.
Let goodness flow like a stream
that never stops.

²⁵"People of Israel, you did not bring
me sacrifices and offerings
while you traveled in the desert
for 40 years.
²⁶But now you will have to carry with
you
your king, the false god Sakkuth,
and Kaiwan your idol
and the idols of your other star
gods you have made.
²⁷This is because I will send you
away as captives beyond
Damascus,"
says the Lord. His name is God of
heaven's armies.

6 How terrible it will be for you who
have it easy in Jerusalem.
How terrible for you who live on
Mount Samaria and feel safe.
You think you are important people
of the best nation in the world.
The Israelites come to you for
help.

²Go look at the city of Calneh.
   From there go to the great city
      Hamath.
   Go down to Gath of the
      Philistines.
   Are you better than these
      kingdoms?
   Are their lands larger than yours?
³You put off the day of punishment.
   But you bring near the day when
      you can do evil to others.
⁴You lie on beds decorated with
      ivory.
   You stretch out on your couches.
   You eat tender lambs
      and fattened calves.
⁵You play your harps.
   Like David, you compose songs
      on musical instruments.
⁶You drink wine by the bowlful.
   You use the best perfumed
      lotions.
   But you are not sad over the
      ruin of Israel, Joseph's
      descendants.ᵈ
⁷So you will be some of the first
      ones taken as slaves.
   Your feasting and lying around
      will come to an end.

⁸The Lord God made this promise.
The Lord God of heaven's armies says:
   "I hate the pride of the people of
      Israel.
   I hate their strong towers.
   So I will let the enemy take the city
      and everything in it."

⁹At that time there might be ten people left alive in a house. But they will
also die. ¹⁰A relative and one who is to
prepare bodies for burial may come to
get the bodies. One of them will take the
bodies out to burn them. He will call to
the other and ask, "Are there any other
dead bodies with you?"

That person will answer, "No."

Then the one who asked will say,
"Hush! We must not speak the name of
the Lord."

¹¹The Lord has given the command.
   The large house will be broken
      into pieces.
   And the small house will be
      broken into bits.
¹²Horses do not run on rocks.
   People do not plow rocks with
      oxen.

But you have changed fairness into
      poison.
   You have changed what is right
      into something wrong.
¹³You are happy that the town of Lo
      Debarⁿ was taken.
   You say, "We have taken
      Karnaimⁿ by our own
      strength."

¹⁴The Lord God of heaven's armies
      says,
   "Israel, I will bring a nation
      against you.
   It will bring trouble for you from
      Lebo Hamath in the north
   to the valley south of the Dead
      Sea."ᵈ

7 This is what the Lord God showed
me: He was forming a swarm of lo-
custs.ᵈ This was after the king had taken
his share of the first crop. The second
crop had just begun growing. ²The locusts ate all the crops in the country.
After that I said, "Lord God, forgive us,
I beg you! No one in Israel could live
through this. Israel is too small already!"

³So the Lord felt sorry about this.
"This will not happen," said the Lord.

⁴This is what the Lord God showed
me: The Lord God was calling for fire to
come to punish. The fire dried up the
deep water and destroyed the land.
⁵Then I cried out, "Lord God, stop, I beg
you! No one in Israel could live through
this. Israel is too small already."

⁶So the Lord felt sorry about this.
"This will not happen either," said the
Lord God.

⁷This is what the Lord showed me:
The Lord stood by a straight wall. He
had a plumb lineᵈ in his hand. ⁸The Lord
said to me, "Amos, what do you see?"

I said, "A plumb line."

Then the Lord said, "See, I will put a
plumb line among my people Israel to
show how crooked they are. I will not
feel sorry for them any longer.

⁹"The places where Isaac's
      descendantsᵈ worship will be
      destroyed.
   Israel's holy places will be turned
      into ruins.
   And I will attack King
      Jeroboam's family with the
      sword."

6:13 Lo Debar This name means "nothing at all." **6:13 Karnaim** This name means "horns," a symbol of strength.

[10]So Amaziah, a priest at Bethel, sent this message to Jeroboam king of Israel: "Amos is making evil plans against you with the people of Israel. He has been speaking so much that this land can't hold all his words. [11]Amos has said this:

'Jeroboam will die by the sword,
and the people of Israel will be
taken as captives
out of their own country.'"

[12]Then Amaziah said to Amos, "Seer,[d] go, run away to Judah. Do your prophesying[d] and earn your living there. [13]But don't prophesy anymore here at Bethel. This is King Jeroboam's holy place. This is Israel's temple."

[14]Then Amos answered Amaziah, "I do not make my living as a prophet. And I am not a member of a group of prophets. I make my living as a shepherd. And I take care of sycamore trees. [15]But the Lord took me away from tending the sheep. He said to me, 'Go, prophesy to my people, the Israelites.' [16]So listen to the Lord's message. You tell me,
'Don't prophesy against Israel.
And stop prophesying against the
descendants of Isaac.'

[17]"Because you have said this, the Lord says:
'Your wife will become a prostitute[d]
in the city.
Your sons and daughters will be
killed with swords.
Other people will take your land
and divide it among
themselves.
And you will die in a foreign
country.
The people of Israel will definitely
be taken
from their own land as
captives.'"

8 This is what the Lord showed me: a basket of ripe fruit. [2]The Lord said to me, "Amos, what do you see?"

I said, "A basket of fruit from the end of the harvest."

Then the Lord said to me, "An end has come for my people, the Israelites. I will not overlook their sins anymore.

[3]"On that day the palace songs will become funeral songs," says the Lord God. "There will be dead bodies thrown everywhere! Silence!"

[4]Listen to me you who walk on helpless people.

You are trying to destroy the
poor people of this country.
[5]Your businessmen say,
"When will the New Moon[d] Festival
be over
so we can sell grain?
When will the Sabbath[d] be over
so we can bring out wheat to
sell?
We can charge them more
and give them less.
We can change the scales to
cheat the people.
[6]We will buy poor people for silver.
And we will buy needy people for
the price of a pair of sandals.
We will even sell the wheat that
was swept up from the floor."

[7]The Lord used his name, the Pride of Jacob, to make a promise. He said, "I will never forget what these people did.
[8]The whole land will shake because
of it.
Everyone who lives in the land
will cry for those who died.
The whole land will rise like the
Nile.
It will be shaken, and then it will
fall
like the Nile River in Egypt."

[9]The Lord God says:
"At that time I will cause the sun to
go down at noon.
I will make the earth dark on a
clear day.
[10]I will change your festivals into
days of crying for the dead.
All your songs will become songs
of sadness.
I will make all of you wear rough
cloth to show your sadness.
You will shave your heads to
show sadness.
I will make that day like the crying
for the death of an only son.
Its end will be very painful."

[11]The Lord God says: "The days are
coming
when I will cause a time of
hunger in the land.
The people will not be hungry for
bread or thirsty for water.
But they will be hungry for words
from the Lord.
[12]People will wander from the
Mediterranean Sea to the Dead
Sea.[d]
They will wander from the north
to the east.

They will search for the word of the
Lord.
But they won't find it.
[13] At that time the beautiful young
women and the young men
will become weak from thirst.
[14] They made promises by the idol in
Samaria.
They said, 'As surely as the god
of Dan lives . . .'
And they said, 'As surely as the
god of Beersheba[n] lives, we
promise . . .'
So they will fall
and never get up again."

9 I saw the Lord standing by the altar.
He said:
"Smash the top of the pillars
so that even the bottom of the
doors will shake.
Make the pillars fall on the people's
heads.
Anyone left alive I will kill with a
sword.
Not one person will get away.
No one will escape.
[2] If they dig down as deep as where
the dead are,
I will pull them up from there.
If they climb up into the skies,
I will bring them down from
there.
[3] If they hide at the top of Mount
Carmel,
I will find them and take them
away.
If they try to hide from me at the
bottom of the sea,
I will command a snake to bite
them.
[4] If they are captured and taken
away by their enemies,
I will command the sword to kill
them.
I will keep watch over them.
But I will keep watch to give them
trouble, not to do them good."

[5] The Master, the Lord of heaven's
armies, will touch the land.
And the land will shake.
Then everyone who lives in the
land will cry for the dead.
The whole land will rise like the
Nile River.
It will fall like the river of Egypt.
[6] The Lord built his upper rooms
above the skies.

He sets their foundations on the
earth.
He calls for the waters of the sea.
He pours them out on the land.
The Lord is his name.

[7] The Lord says this:
"Israel, you are no different to me
than the people of Cush.
I brought Israel out of the land of
Egypt.
I also brought the Philistines
from Crete
and the Arameans from Kir.
[8] I, the Lord God, am watching the
sinful kingdom Israel.
I will destroy Israel
from the earth's surface.
But I will not completely destroy
Jacob's descendants,"[d] says the
Lord.
[9] "I am giving the command
to scatter the nation of Israel
among all nations.
It will be like someone sifting flour.
A person shakes flour through a
sifter.
The good flour falls through, but
not the bad clumps.
[10] Sinners among my people
will die by the sword.
All of them say,
'Nothing bad will happen to us.'

[11] "The kingdom of David is like a
fallen tent.
But in that day I will set it up
again
and mend its broken places.
I will rebuild its ruins.
I will rebuild it as it was before.
[12] Then Israel will take over what is
left of Edom
and the other nations that belong
to me,"
says the Lord.
And he will make it happen.

[13] The Lord says, "The time is coming
when there will be plenty of
food.
A person will still be harvesting his
crops
when it's time to plow again.
A person will still be taking the
juice from his grapes
when it's time to plant again.
Sweet wine will drip from the
mountains.

8:14 **Dan . . . Beersheba** Dan was the city farthest north in Israel, and Beersheba was the city
farthest south.

And it will pour from the hills.
[14]I will bring my people Israel back
　　from captivity.
　They will build the ruined cities
　　again.
　And they will live in them.
　They will plant vineyards and drink
　　the wine from them.

They will plant gardens and eat
　their fruit.
[15]I will plant my people on their land.
　And they will not be pulled out
　　again
　from the land which I have given
　　them,"
　says the Lord your God.

The Book of
OBADIAH

This is the vision of Obadiah.

This is what the Lord God says
about Edom:[a]
　We have heard a message from the
　　Lord.
　A messenger has been sent
　　among the nations, saying
　"Let's go attack Edom!"

[2]"Look, I have made you only a
　　small nation.
　Others do not respect you.
[3]But your pride has fooled you.
　You live in the hollow places of
　　the cliff.
　Your home is up high.
　And you say to yourself,
　'No one can bring me down to
　　the ground.'
[4]You fly high like the eagle.
　You make your nest among the
　　stars.
　But I will bring you down from
　　there," says the Lord.
[5]"You will really be ruined!
　It would be better if thieves come to
　　you,
　if robbers come by night.
　They would steal only enough for
　　themselves.
　Workers come and pick the grapes
　　from your vines.
　But they would leave a few
　　grapes behind.
[6]But you, Edom, will really lose
　　everything!
　People will find even your hidden
　　treasures!
[7]All the people who are your friends
　　will force you out of the land.
　The people who are at peace with
　　you
　will trick you and defeat you.

They eat your bread with you now.
　But they are planning a trap for
　　you.
　And you will not notice it."

[8]The Lord says, "On that day
　I will surely destroy the wise men
　　from Edom.
　I will destroy these men of
　　understanding from the
　　mountains of Edom.
[9]Then, city of Teman, your mighty
　　men will be afraid.
　And everyone from the
　　mountains of Edom will be
　　killed.
[10]You did violence against your
　　relatives, the people of Israel.
　So you will be covered with
　　shame.
　You will be destroyed forever.
[11]You stood aside without helping
　　while strangers carried Israel's
　　treasures away.
　Foreigners entered Israel's city
　　gate.
　They threw lots[d] to decide what
　　part of Jerusalem they would
　　take.
　At that time you were like one of
　　those foreigners.

[12]"Do not laugh at your brothers'
　　trouble.
　Do not be happy when people
　　destroy Judah.
　Do not brag about the cruel things
　　done to them.
[13]Do not enter the city gate of my
　　people
　in their time of trouble.
　Do not laugh at their problems
　　in their time of trouble.
　Do not take their treasures

1 Edom The Edomites were the people who came from Esau, Jacob's twin brother. They were
enemies of the Israelites.

in their time of trouble.
¹⁴Do not stand at the crossroads
   to destroy those who are trying
     to escape.
Do not capture those who escape
   alive
     in a time of trouble.

¹⁵"The Lord's day of judging is
   coming soon
     to all the nations.
You did evil things to other people.
   Those same things will happen to
     you.
   They will come back upon your
     own head.
¹⁶Because you joined the nations in
   robbing my Temple,^d
   you drank my anger.
So all the nations will drink my
   anger.
   They will be punished so much
     that they will disappear.
¹⁷But on Mount Zion^d some will be
   left alive.
   The mountain will be a holy
     place.
The people of Jacob will take back
   their land.
   They will take it from those who
     took it from them.
¹⁸The people of Jacob, the Israelites,
   will be like a fire.
   And the people of Joseph will be
     like a flame.
But the people of Esau, the

Edomites, will be like dry
   stalks.
The people of Jacob will set these
   stalks on fire.
They will burn up the Edomites.
   Then there will be no one left of
     the people of Esau."
This will happen because the Lord
   has said it.

¹⁹Then God's people will regain
   southern Judah from Edom,
   the mountain of Esau.
They will take back the western
   mountain slopes
   from the Philistines.
They will regain the lands of
   Ephraim and Samaria.
   And Benjamin will take over
     Gilead.
²⁰People from Israel once were
   forced to leave their homes.
But at that time they will take the
   land of the Canaanites.
They will take it all the way to
   Zarephath.
People from Judah were once
   forced to leave Jerusalem
   and live in Sepharad.
But at that time they will take back
   the cities of southern Judah.
²¹Powerful warriors will go up on
   Mount Zion.
   There they will rule the people
     living on Edom's mountain.
   And the kingdom will belong to
     the Lord.

The Book of
JONAH

1 The Lord spoke his word to Jonah son of Amittai: ²"Get up, go to the great city of Nineveh and preach against it. I see the evil things they do."

³But Jonah got up to run away from the Lord. He went to the city of Joppa. There he found a ship that was going to the city of Tarshish. Jonah paid for the trip and went aboard. He wanted to go to Tarshish to run away from the Lord.

⁴But the Lord sent a great wind on the sea. This wind made the sea very rough. So the ship was in danger of breaking apart. ⁵The sailors were afraid. Each man cried to his own god. The men began throwing the cargo into the sea.

This would make the ship lighter so it would not sink.

But Jonah had gone down into the ship to lie down. He fell fast asleep. ⁶The captain of the ship came and said, "Why are you sleeping? Get up! Pray to your god! Maybe your god will pay attention to us. Maybe he will save us!"

⁷Then the men said to each other, "Let's throw lots^d to see who caused these troubles to happen to us."

So the men threw lots. The lot showed that the trouble had happened because of Jonah. ⁸Then the men said to Jonah, "Tell us what you have done. Why has this terrible thing happened to us? What is your job? Where do you come from?

What is your country? Who are your people?"

[9] Then Jonah said to them, "I am a Hebrew. I fear the Lord, the God of heaven. He is the God who made the sea and the land."

[10] Then the men were very afraid. They asked Jonah, "What terrible thing did you do?" They knew Jonah was running away from the Lord because Jonah had told them.

[11] The wind and the waves of the sea were becoming much stronger. So the men said to Jonah, "What should we do to you to make the sea calm down?"

[12] Jonah said to them, "Pick me up, and throw me into the sea. Then it will calm down. I know it is my fault that this great storm has come on you."

[13] Instead, the men tried to row the ship back to the land. But they could not. The wind and the waves of the sea were becoming much stronger.

[14] So the men cried to the Lord, "Lord, please don't let us die because of taking this man's life. Please don't think we are guilty of killing an innocent man. Lord, you have caused all this to happen. You wanted it this way." [15] Then the men picked up Jonah and threw him into the sea. So the sea became calm. [16] Then they began to fear the Lord very much. They offered a sacrifice to the Lord. They also made promises to him.

[17] And the Lord caused a very big fish to swallow Jonah. Jonah was in the stomach of the fish three days and three nights.

2 While Jonah was in the stomach of the fish, he prayed to the Lord his God. Jonah said,

[2] "I was in danger.
  So I called to the Lord,
    and he answered me.
I was about to die.
  So I cried to you,
    and you heard my voice.
[3] You threw me into the sea.
  I went down, down into the deep sea.
The water was all around me.
  Your powerful waves flowed over me.
[4] I said, 'I was driven out of your presence.
  But I hope to see your Holy Temple[d] again.'
[5] The waters of the sea closed over me.
  I was about to die.
The deep sea was all around me.

Seaweed wrapped around my head.
[6] I went down to where the mountains of the sea start to rise.
  I thought I was locked in this prison forever.
But you saved me from death,
  Lord my God.
[7] "When my life had almost gone,
  I remembered the Lord.
Lord, I prayed to you.
  And you heard my prayers in your Holy Temple.

[8] "People who worship useless idols
  give up their loyalty to you.
[9] Lord, I will praise and thank you
  while I give sacrifices to you.
I will make promises to you.
  And I will do what I promise.
Salvation comes from the Lord!"

[10] Then the Lord spoke to the fish. And the fish spit Jonah out of its stomach onto the dry land.

3 Then the Lord spoke his word to Jonah again. The Lord said, [2] "Get up. Go to the great city Nineveh. Preach against it what I tell you."

[3] So Jonah obeyed the Lord. He got up and went to Nineveh. It was a very large city. It took a person three days just to walk across it. [4] Jonah entered the city. When he had walked for one day, he preached to the people. He said, "After 40 days, Nineveh will be destroyed!"

[5] The people of Nineveh believed in God. They announced they would stop eating for a while. They put on rough cloth to show how sad they were. All the people in the city wore the cloth. People from the most important to the least important did this.

[6] When the king of Nineveh heard this news, he got up from his throne. He took off his robe. He covered himself with rough cloth and sat in ashes to show how upset he was.

[7] He made an announcement and sent it through the city. The announcement said:

By command of the king and his important men: No person or animal should eat anything. No herd or flock will be allowed to taste anything. Do not let them eat food or drink water. [8] But every person and animal should be covered with rough cloth. People should cry loudly to God. Everyone must turn away from his evil life. Everyone must stop doing harm. [9]Maybe God will change his mind. Maybe he will stop being angry. Then we will not die.

[10]God saw what the people did. He saw that they stopped doing evil things. So God changed his mind and did not do what he had warned. He did not punish them.

4 But Jonah was very unhappy that God did not destroy the city. He was angry. [2]He complained to the Lord and said, "I knew this would happen. I knew it when I was still in my own country. It is why I quickly ran away to Tarshish. I knew that you are a God who is kind and shows mercy. You don't become angry quickly. You have great love. I knew you would rather forgive than punish them. [3]So now I ask you, Lord, please kill me. It is better for me to die than to live."

[4]Then the Lord said, "Do you think it is right for you to be angry?"

[5]Jonah went out and sat down east of the city. There he made a shelter for himself. And he sat there in the shade. He was waiting to see what would hap-pen to the city. [6]The Lord made a plant grow quickly up over Jonah. This made a cool place for him to sit. And it helped him to be more comfortable. Jonah was very pleased to have the plant for shade. [7]The next day the sun rose. And God sent a worm to attack the plant. Then the plant died.

[8]When the sun was high in the sky, God sent a hot east wind to blow. The sun became very hot on Jonah's head. And he became very weak. He wished he were dead. Jonah said, "It is better for me to die than to live."

[9]But God said this to Jonah: "Do you think it is right for you to be angry be-cause of the plant?"

Jonah answered, "It is right for me to be angry! I will stay angry until I die!"

[10]And the Lord said, "You showed concern for that plant. But you did not plant it or make it grow. It appeared in the night, and the next day it died. [11]Then surely I can show concern for the great city Nineveh. There are many animals in that city. And there are more than 120,000 people living there. Those people simply do not know right from wrong!"

The Book of
MICAH

1 Jotham, Ahaz and Hezekiah were kings of Judah. During the time they were kings, the word of the Lord came to Micah, who was from Moresheth. He saw these visions about Samaria and Je-rusalem.

[2]Hear this, all you nations.
  Listen, all you who live on the earth.
The Lord God will come from his Holy Temple.[d]
  He will come as a witness against you.
[3]See, the Lord is coming out of his place in heaven.
  He is coming down to walk on the tops of the mountains.
[4]The mountains will melt under him like wax in a fire.
  The valleys will crack open
    as if split by water raging down a mountain.
[5]This is because of Jacob's sin.

It is because of the sins of the nation of Israel.
Who is responsible for Jacob's sin? Samaria!
Who is responsible for Judah's worshiping idols?
  Jerusalem!

[6]"So I will make Samaria a pile of ruins in the open country.
  It will be like a place for planting vineyards.
I will pour Samaria's stones down into the valley.
  And I will destroy her down to her foundations.
[7]All her idols will be broken into pieces.
  All the gifts to her idols will be burned with fire.
  I will destroy all her idols.
This is because Samaria earned her money by being unfaithful to me.
  So this money will be carried off

by other people who are not
faithful to me.''

[8]I will moan and cry because of this
evil.
I will go around barefoot and
without clothes.
I will cry loudly like the wild dogs.
I will cry like the ostriches.
[9]I will do this because Samaria's
wound cannot be healed.
Her destruction will spread to
Judah.
It will reach the city gate of my
people.
It will come all the way to
Jerusalem.
[10]Don't tell it in Gath.[n]
Don't cry in Acco.[n]
Cry and roll in the dust
at Beth Ophrah.[n]
[11]Pass on your way, naked and
ashamed,
you who live in Shaphir.[n]
Those who live in Zaanan[n]
won't come out to help you.
The people in Beth Ezel[n] will cry.
But they will not give you any
support.
[12]Those who live in Maroth[n]
will be anxious for good news to
come.
This is because trouble will come
from the Lord.
It will come all the way to the
gate of Jerusalem.
[13]You people living in Lachish,[n]
harness the fastest horse to the
chariot.
Jerusalem's sins started in you.
This is because you followed in
Israel's sins.
[14]So you must give farewell gifts
to Moresheth[n] in Gath.
The houses in Aczib[n] will be false
help
to the kings of Israel.
[15]I will bring an enemy against you
who live in Mareshah.[n]
He will take what you own.
The leaders Israel brags about
will hide in the cave at Adullam.

[16]Cut off your hair to show you are
sad.
Cry for the children you love.
Make yourself bald like the eagle,
because your children will be
forced to live in a foreign land.

2 How terrible it will be for people
who plan wickedness.
They lie on their beds and make
evil plans.
When the morning light comes, they
do the things they planned.
They do them just because they
have the power to do so.
[2]They want fields; so they take
them.
They want houses; so they take
them.
They cheat a man and take his
house.
They cheat a man and take his
property.

[3]That is why the Lord says:
"Look, I am planning trouble
against such people.
You won't be able to save
yourselves.
You will no longer walk proudly,
because it will be a terrible time.
[4]At that time people will make fun
of you.
They will sing this sad song
about you:
'We are completely ruined.
The Lord has taken away our
land.
Yes, he has taken our land away
from us.
He has divided our fields among
our enemies!'"
[5]So you will have no land for people
to measure.
They will not throw lots[d] to
divide the land among the
Lord's people.

[6]People say, "Don't prophesy[d] to us!
Don't say those bad things about
us!
Nothing like that will happen to
us!"

1:10 **Gath** This name sounds like the Hebrew word for "tell." 1:10 **Acco** This name sounds
like the Hebrew word for "cry." 1:10 **Beth Ophrah** This name means "house of dust."
1:11 **Shaphir** This name means "beautiful." 1:11 **Zanaan** This name sounds like the Hebrew
word for "come out." 1:11 **Beth Ezel** This name means "house by the side of another,"
suggesting help or support. 1:12 **Maroth** This name sounds like the Hebrew word for "sad"
or "miserable." 1:13 **Lachish** This name sounds like the Hebrew word for "horses." 1:14 **Moresheth** This may be a wordplay on the word "engaged," referring to a farewell gift to a bride.
1:14 **Aczib** This name means "lie" or "trick." 1:15 **Mareshah** This name sounds like the
Hebrew word for a person who captures other cities and lands.

⁷But I must say this, people of Jacob.
    The Lord is becoming angry
      about what you have done.
  If you lived right,
    I could say nice words to you.
⁸But recently, my people have
    become my enemy.
  You take the coats from people
    who pass by.
  They think they are safe.
    But you rob them
  as if they were prisoners of war.
⁹You've forced the women of my
    people
    from their nice houses.
  You've taken my glory
    from their children forever.
¹⁰Get up and leave.
  This is not your promised place
    of rest anymore.
  You have made this place unclean.ᵈ
    It is doomed to destruction.
¹¹But you people want a false prophet
    who will tell you nothing but lies.
  You want one who promises to
    prophesy good things for you
  if you give him wine and beer.
    He's just the prophet for you.

¹²"Yes, people of Jacob, I will bring
    all of you together.
  I will bring together all those left
    alive in Israel.
  I'll put them together like sheep in
    a pen,
  like a flock in its pasture.
    Then the place will be filled with
      many people.
¹³Someone will open the way and
    lead the people out.
  The people will break through
    the gate and leave the city
    where they were held captive.
  Their king will go out in front of
    them.
    The Lord will lead his people."

3 Then I said,
  "Listen, leaders of the people of
    Jacob.
    Listen, you rulers of the nation of
      Israel.
  You should know how to decide
    cases fairly.
²   But you hate good and love evil.
  You skin my people alive.
    You tear the flesh off their bones.
³You are destroying my people.
    You skin them and break their
      bones.
  You chop them up in pieces
    like meat to put in the pot.

⁴Then you will pray to the Lord.
    But he won't answer you.
  He will hide his face from you,
    because you have done evil."

⁵The Lord says this about the prophetsᵈ who teach his people the wrong way
of living:
    "If someone gives these prophets
      food to eat,
    they shout, 'Peace!'
  But if he doesn't give them food,
    they prepare for war against him.
⁶So it will become like night to the
    prophets.
  They won't have any visions from
    the Lord.
  It will become dark for them.
    They won't be able to tell what
      will happen in the future.
  The sun is about to set for the
    prophets.
    Their days will become dark.
⁷The seersᵈ will be ashamed.
    The people who see the future
      will be embarrassed.
  Yes, all of them will cover their
    mouths.
    This is because there will be no
      answer from God."

⁸But the Lord's Spiritᵈ has filled me
    with power and strength to
      preach fairness.
  I will tell the people of Jacob how
    they have turned against God.
  I will tell the people of Israel how
    they have done wrong.
⁹Leaders of Jacob and rulers of
    Israel,
    listen to me.
  You hate fairness.
    You destroy what is right.
¹⁰You build Jerusalem by murdering
    people.
  You build it with the sins you do.
¹¹The judges in Jerusalem take
    money
    to decide who wins in court.
  The priests in Jerusalem only teach
    for pay.
    The prophetsᵈ only look into the
      future when they get paid.
  But yet those leaders say,
    "The Lord is with us.
    Nothing bad will happen to us."
¹²Because of you,
    Jerusalem will be plowed like a
      field.
  Jerusalem will become a pile of
    rocks.

The hill on which the Temple[d] stands will be covered with bushes.

4 In the last days
the mountain on which the Lord's Temple[d] stands
will become the most important of all mountains.
It will be raised above the hills.
People from other nations will come streaming to it.
[2]Many nations will come and say,
"Come, let us go up to the mountain of the Lord.
Let us go to the Temple of the God of Jacob!
Then God will teach us his ways.
And we will obey his teachings."
The Lord's teachings will go out from Jerusalem.
The word of the Lord will go out from Jerusalem.
[3]The Lord will settle arguments among many nations.
He will decide between strong nations that are far away.
Then the nations will make their swords into plows.
They will make their spears into hooks for trimming trees.
Nations will no longer fight other nations.
They will not even train for war anymore.
[4]Everyone will sit under his own vine and fig tree.
No one will make them afraid.
This is because the Lord of heaven's armies has said it.
[5]All other nations follow their own gods.
But we will follow the Lord our God forever and ever.

[6]The Lord says, "At that time,
I will bring back to me the crippled.
I will bring back to Jerusalem those who were sent away.
I will bring back to me those who were hurt.
[7]I will keep alive those who were crippled.
I will make a strong nation of those who were sent away.
The Lord will be their king in Mount Zion[d] forever.
[8]And you, watchtower of the flocks,[n] strong city of Jerusalem,
you will be a kingdom as in the past.
Jerusalem, the right to rule will come again to you."

[9]Now, why do you cry so loudly?
Is your king gone?
Have you lost your leader?
You are in pain like a woman trying to give birth.
[10]People of Jerusalem, be in pain.
Be like a woman trying to give birth.
Now you must leave the city and live in the field.
You will go to Babylon.
But you will be saved from that place.
The Lord will go there and take you back from your enemies.

[11]But now many nations have come to fight against you.
They say, "Let's destroy Jerusalem and be proud we have defeated her."
[12]But they don't know what the Lord is thinking.
They don't understand his plan for them.
He will crush them like a bundle of grain on the threshing[d] floor.

[13]"Get up and crush them, people of Jerusalem.
I will make you strong as if you had horns of iron.
I will make you strong as if you had hoofs of bronze.
You will beat many nations into small pieces.
You will give their wealth to the Lord.
You will give their treasure to the Lord of all the earth."

5 So, strong city, gather your soldiers together.
We are surrounded and attacked.
The enemy will swing his club.
He will hit the leader of Israel in the face.

[2]"But you, Bethlehem Ephrathah, are one of the smallest towns in Judah.
But from you will come one who will rule Israel for me.
He comes from very old times, from days long ago."

4:8 watchtower . . . flocks This probably means a part of Jerusalem. The leaders would be like shepherds in a tower watching their sheep.

³The Lord will leave his people in
  Babylon
    until Jerusalem, who is in labor,
      gives birth to her children.
  Then his brothers who are in
    captivity will return.
    They will come back to the
      people of Israel living in Judah.
⁴Then the ruler of Israel will stand
    and take care of his people.
  He will lead them with the Lord's
    power.
  He will lead them in the
    wonderful name of the Lord
    his God.
  They will live in safety.
    And his greatness will be known
      all over the earth.
⁵ He will bring peace.

  The Assyrian army will come into
    our country.
    They will destroy our large
      houses.
  But we will choose seven or eight
    leaders.
    They will shepherd our people.
⁶They will destroy the Assyrians
    with their swords.
    They will conquer the land of
      Assyria with their swords
      drawn.
  The Assyrians will come into our
    land.
    They will come within our
      borders.
  But the leaders of Israel
    will save us from them.

⁷Then the people of Jacob who are
    left alive
    will be like dew from the Lord to
      many people.
  They will be like rain which does
    not wait for man.
  They will be like showers which
    do not wait for human beings.
⁸Those left alive of Jacob's people
    will be scattered among the
      nations.
  They will be among many
    peoples.
  They will be like a lion among the
    animals of the forest.
  They will be like a young lion
    going through the flock.
  He steps on what is in his way.
    No one can save the nations from
      God's people.
⁹So you will raise your fist in victory
    over your enemies,
    and you will destroy them.

¹⁰The Lord says, "At that time,
    I will take your horses from you.
    I will destroy your chariots.
¹¹I will destroy the walled cities in
    your country.
    I will tear down all your
      defenses.
¹²You will no longer be able to do
    witchcraft.ᵈ
    You will not have anyone who
      can tell the future.
¹³I will destroy your statues of false
    gods.
    I will tear down the stone pillars
      you worship.
    You will no longer worship
      what your hands have made.
¹⁴I will destroy the Asherahᵈ idols.
    I will destroy your cities.
¹⁵Some people won't obey me.
    I will show my anger and punish
      them."

6 Now hear what the Lord says:
    "Get up; plead your case in front of
      the mountains.
    Let the hills hear your story.
²Mountains, listen to the Lord's
    complaint.
    Foundations of the earth, listen to
      the Lord.
  The Lord has a complaint against
    his people.
    He will prove that Israel is
      wrong."

³The Lord says, "My people, did I do
    something wrong to you?
  How did I make you tired of me?
    Tell me.
⁴I brought you from the land of
    Egypt.
  I freed you from slavery.
  I sent Moses, Aaron and Miriam
    to you.
⁵My people, remember
    the evil plans of Balak king of
      Moab.
  Remember what Balaam son of
    Beor told Balak.
  Remember what happened from
    Acacia to Gilgal.
  Then you will know the Lord
    does what is right!"

⁶You say, "What can I bring with me
    when I come before the Lord?
  What can I bring
    when I bow before God on high?
  Should I come before the Lord with
    burnt offerings,
    with year-old calves?

⁷Will the Lord be pleased with 1,000
male sheep?
Will he be pleased with 10,000
rivers of oil?
Should I give my first child for the
evil I have done?
Should I give my very own child
for my sin?"
⁸The Lord has told you what is good.
He has told you what he wants
from you:
Do what is right to other people.
Love being kind to others.
And live humbly, trusting your
God.

⁹The voice of the Lord shouts to the
city.
The wise person honors the Lord.
So pay attention to the rod of
punishment.
Pay attention to the One who
threatens to punish.
¹⁰Can the Lord forget that the wicked
still hide
treasures they have stolen?
Do they still cheat others?
I curse their false measure!
¹¹Can I forgive people who cheat
others
with wrong weights and scales?
¹²The rich men in the city
still do cruel things.
The people still tell lies.
They do not tell the truth.
¹³So I have started to punish you.
I will destroy you because of your
sins.
¹⁴You will eat, but you won't become
full.
You will still be hungry and empty.
You will store up but save nothing.
What you store up the sword will
destroy.
¹⁵You will plant,
but you won't harvest.
You will squeeze your olives.
But you won't get any oil from
them to put on your skin.
You will crush the grapes.
But you will not drink the wine.
¹⁶This is because you obey the
wicked laws of King Omri.
You do all the evil that Ahab's
family does.
You follow their teachings.
So I will let you be destroyed.
The people in your city will be
laughed at.

Other nations will make fun of
you.

7 Poor me! I am like a hungry man.
And all the summer fruit has been
picked.
There are no grapes left to eat.
There are none of the early figs I
love.
²All of the faithful people are gone.
There is not one good person left
in this country.
Everyone is waiting to kill
someone.
Everyone is trying to trap his
brother.
³People are good at doing evil with
both hands.
Rulers ask for money.
And judges' decisions are bought
for a price.
Rich people make their wishes
known.
They all join in their evil plans.
⁴Even the best of them is like a
thornbush.
Even the nicest of them is worse
than a thornbush.
Your watchmenⁿ warned you about
this day.
Now it has come.
Now you will be punished.
Your punishment will amaze you.
⁵Don't trust your neighbor.
Don't even trust a friend.
Be careful what you say,
even to your wife.
⁶A son will not honor his father.
A daughter will turn against her
mother.
A daughter-in-law will fight with
her mother-in-law.
A person's enemies will be
members of his own family.

⁷Israel says, "I will look to the Lord
for help.
I will wait for God to save me.
My God will hear me.
⁸Enemy, don't laugh at me.
I have fallen, but I will get up
again.
I sit in the shadow of trouble now.
But the Lord will be a light for
me.
⁹I sinned against the Lord.
So he was angry with me.
But he will defend my case in court.
He will do what is right for me.

7:4 watchmen Another name for a prophet. The prophets were like guards who stood on a
city's wall. They watched for trouble coming from far away.

Then he will bring me out into the
light.
I will see him set things right.
[10]Then my enemies will see this,
and they will be ashamed.
My enemies said to me,
'Where is the Lord your God?'
Now I will laugh at them.
They will fall down defeated, like
the mud people walk on."

[11]The time will come when your
walls will be built again.
At that time your country will
grow.
[12]Your people will come back to your
land.
They will come from Assyria and
the cities of Egypt.
They will come from the countries
between the river of Egypt and
the Euphrates River.
They will come from the countries
between the Mediterranean Sea
in the west and the mountains
in the east.
[13]The rest of the earth will be ruined.
This is because of what the
people who lived in it did.

[14]So shepherd your people with your
stick.
Tend the flock of people who
belong to you.
That flock now lives alone in the
desert.
But there is fertile pasture nearby.
Let them feed in Bashan and Gilead
as they did long ago.

[15]The Lord says, "I did many miracles[d]
when I brought you out of Egypt.
I will show you more miracles
like that."

[16]The nations will see those miracles.
Then they will no longer brag
about their power.
They will be amazed and put their
hands over their mouths.
They will refuse to listen.
[17]They will crawl in the dust like a
snake.
They will shake with fear.
They will crawl on the ground
like insects crawling from their
holes.
They will come trembling to you,
Lord our God.
They will tremble in fear before
you.
[18]There is no God like you.
You forgive people who are guilty
of sin.
You don't look at the sins of your
people
who are left alive.
You, Lord, will not stay angry
forever.
You enjoy being kind.
[19]Lord, you will have mercy on us
again.
You will conquer our sins.
You will throw away all our sins
into the deepest sea.
[20]You will be true to the people of
Jacob!
You will be kind to the people of
Abraham.
You will do what you promised
to our ancestors long ago.

The Book of
NAHUM

1 This is the message for the city of
Nineveh.[n] This is the vision of Nahum, who was from the town of Elkosh.

[2]The Lord is a jealous God who
gives punishment.
The Lord punishes wicked people
and is filled with anger.
The Lord punishes those who are
against him.

He stays angry with his enemies.
[3]The Lord does not become angry
quickly.
His power is great.
The Lord will not let the guilty go
unpunished.
Where the Lord goes, whirlwinds
and storms show his power.
The clouds are the dust that his
feet kick up.

1:1 **Nineveh** The capital city of the country of Assyria. Nahum uses Nineveh to stand for all of
Assyria.

[4]The Lord speaks to the sea and
   makes it dry.
He dries up all the rivers.
The areas of Bashan and Carmel
   dry up.
And the flowers of Lebanon die.
[5]He shakes the mountains
   and makes the hills melt away.
The earth trembles when he comes.
   The world and all who live in it
   shake with fear.
[6]No one can stay alive when the
   Lord is angry with him.
No one can survive his strong
   anger.
His anger is poured out like fire.
He smashes rocks that are in his
   path.

[7]The Lord is good.
   He gives protection in times of
   trouble.
He knows who trusts in him.
[8]But he will completely destroy the
   city of Nineveh.
   An army will come like a rushing
   flood.
The Lord will chase his enemies
   until he kills them.

[9]The Lord will completely destroy
   the plans that are made against
   him.
   Trouble will not come a second
   time.
[10]Those people will be like tangled
   thorns
   or like people drunk from their
   wine.
They will be destroyed quickly
   like dry weeds.
[11]Someone has come from Nineveh.
   He makes evil plans against the
   Lord.
And he gives wicked advice.

[12]This is what the Lord says:
   "Assyria is strong and has many
   people.
   But it will be defeated and
   brought to an end.
Judah, I have punished you, my
   people.
   But I will punish you no more.
[13]Now I will free you from their
   control.
   And I will tear away the chains
   with which they hold you."

[14]The Lord has given you this
   command, Nineveh:
   "You will not have descendants[d]
   to carry on your name.
I will destroy the idols and metal
   images
   that are in the temple of your
   gods.
I will dig your grave
   because you are wicked."

[15]Look, there on the hills,
   someone is bringing good news!
   He is announcing peace!
Celebrate your feasts, people of
   Judah.
   And do what you promised to
   God.
The wicked will not attack you
   again.
   They have been completely
   destroyed.

2 The destroyer[n] is coming to attack
   you, Nineveh.
Guard the defenses.
Watch the road.
Get ready.
Gather all your strength!
[2]Destroyers have destroyed God's
   people
   and ruined their vines.
But the Lord will make the people
   of Jacob
   and the people of Israel great
   again.

[3]The shields of the soldiers are red.
   The army is dressed in red.
The metal on the chariots flashes
   when they are ready to attack.
   Their horses are excited.
[4]The chariots race through the
   streets.
   They rush back and forth
   through the city squares.
They look like torches.
   They run like lightning.

[5]He[n] calls his officers.
   But they fall down on the way.
They hurry to the city wall.
   The shield is put into place.
[6]The river gates are thrown open.
   And the palace is destroyed.
[7]It has been announced that the
   people of Nineveh
   will be captured and carried
   away.
The slave girls moan like doves.

2:1 destroyer The Babylonians, the Scythians and the Medes destroyed Nineveh.   **2:5 He** This
probably means the king of Assyria.

They beat their breasts because
they are sad.
[8] Nineveh is like a pool.
And its water is draining away.
"Stop! Stop!" the people yell.
But no one turns back.
[9] Take the silver!
Take the gold!
There is no end to the treasure.
There is wealth of every kind.
[10] Nineveh is robbed, ruined and
destroyed.
The people lose their courage.
Their knees knock with fear.
Stomachs ache. And everyone's
face grows pale from fright.

[11] Where is the lions'[n] den?
Where do they feed their young?
Where did the lion, lioness and
cubs go?
Where were they not afraid?
[12] The lion killed enough for his cubs.
He killed it for his mate.
He filled his cave with the animals
he caught.
He filled his den with what he
had killed.

[13] "I am against you, Nineveh,"
says the Lord of heaven's armies.
"I will burn up your chariots in
smoke.
And I will kill your young lions
with a sword.
I will stop you from hunting
down others on the earth.
Your messengers' voices
will no longer be heard."

3 How terrible it will be for the city
which has killed so many.
It is full of lies.
It is full of stolen things from other
countries.
It is always hurting or killing
somebody.
[2] Hear the sound of whips.
Listen to the wheels.
Hear horses galloping
and chariots bouncing along!
[3] Soldiers on horses are charging.
Their swords are shining.
Their spears are gleaming!
There are many bodies.
Dead people are piled up.
There are too many to count.
People fall over the dead bodies.
[4] The city was like a prostitute.[d]
She was charming and a lover of
magic.

She made nations slaves with her
evil ways
and her witchcraft.[d]

[5] "I am against you, Nineveh," says
the Lord of heaven's armies.
"I will pull your dress up over
your face.
I will show the nations your
nakedness.
And I will show the kingdoms
your shame.
[6] I will throw dirt on you.
I will make a fool of you.
People will see you and make fun
of you.
[7] Everyone who sees you will run
away and say,
'Nineveh is in ruins. Who will cry
for her?'
Nineveh, I cannot find anyone to
comfort you."

[8] Nineveh, you are no better than
Thebes.[n]
She sits by the Nile River
with water all around her.
The river was her defense.
The waters were like a wall
around her.
[9] Cush and Egypt gave her endless
strength.
Put and Libya supported her.
[10] But Thebes was captured.
And she went into captivity.
Her small children were beaten to
death
at every street corner.
Lots[d] were thrown for her
important men.
And all of her leaders were put in
chains.

[11] Nineveh, you will be drunk, too.
You will hide.
You will look for a place safe
from the enemy.
[12] All your defenses are like fig trees
with ripe fruit.
When the tree is shaken, the figs
fall into the mouth of the eater.
[13] Look at your soldiers.
They are all women!
The gates of your land
are wide open for your enemies.
Fire has burned the bars of those
gates.

[14] Get enough water before the attack
begins.
Make your defenses strong!

2:11 **lions'** The symbol of Assyria was the lion.   3:8 **Thebes** A great city in Egypt.

Make the bricks.
Mix the mortar.
Repair the wall!
[15]There the fire will burn you up.
The sword will kill you.
Like grasshoppers eating crops,
the battle will completely
destroy you.
Grow in number like hopping
locusts.[d]
Grow in number like swarming
locusts!
[16]Your traders are more than the
stars in the sky.
But like locusts, they strip the
land and then fly away.
[17]Your guards are like locusts.
Your officers are like swarms of
locusts

that settle in the walls on a cold
day.
But when the sun comes up they fly
away.
And no one knows where they
have gone.
[18]King of Assyria, your rulers are
asleep.
Your important men lie down to
rest.
Your people have been scattered on
the mountains.
And there is no one to bring
them back.
[19]Nothing can heal your wound.
Your injury will not heal.
Everyone who hears about you
applauds
because everyone has felt your
endless cruelty.

The Book of
HABAKKUK

1 This is the message that was given to
Habakkuk the prophet.[d]

[2]Lord, I continue to ask for help.
How long will you ignore me?
I cry out to you about violence,
but you do not save us!
[3]Why do you let me see wrong
things?
Why do you put up with evil?
People are destroying things and
hurting others while I am
looking.
They are arguing and fighting.
[4]People are not forced to obey the
teachings.
No one receives a fair trial.
Evil people gain while good people
lose.
The judges no longer make fair
decisions.

[5]"You and your people, look at the
nations!
Watch them and be amazed.
I will do something in your lifetime
that will amaze you.
You won't believe it even when
you are told about it.
[6]I will use the Babylonian people to
punish the evil people.
The Babylonians are cruel and
powerful fighters.
They march across the earth.

They take lands that don't belong
to them.
[7]The Babylonians frighten other
people.
They do what they want to do.
They are good only to
themselves.
[8]Their horses are faster than
leopards
and more cruel than wolves at
sunset.
Their horse soldiers attack quickly.
They come from places that are
far away.
They attack quickly, like an eagle
swooping down for food.
[9] They all come to fight.
Their armies march quickly like a
whirlwind in the desert.
Their prisoners are as many as
the grains of sand.
[10]The Babylonian soldiers laugh at
kings.
They make fun of rulers.
They laugh at all the strong, walled
cities.
They build dirt roads up to the
top of the walls.
They capture the cities.
[11]Then they leave like the wind and
move on.
They are guilty of worshiping
their own strength."

¹²Lord, you are the Lord who lives
    forever.
  You are my God, my holy God.
  You will not let those who trust
    you die.
  Lord, you have chosen the
    Babylonians to punish people.
  Our Rock,ᵈ you created them to
    punish the people.
¹³Your eyes are too good to look at
    evil.
  You cannot stand to see people
    do wrong.
  So how can you put up with those
    evil people?
  How can you be quiet when
    wicked people defeat people
    who are better than they are?
¹⁴You treat people like fish in the sea.
  You treat them like sea animals
    without a leader.
¹⁵The enemy catches all of them with
    hooks.
  He catches them in his net.
  He drags them in.
  He is glad that he has caught
    them.
¹⁶The enemy offers sacrifices to his
    net.
  He burns incenseᵈ to worship it.
  This is because his net lets him live
    like a rich man.
  His net lets him enjoy the best
    food.
¹⁷Will he keep on taking riches with
    his net?
  Will he go on destroying people
    without showing mercy?

2 I will stand like a guard to watch.
    I will stand on the tower.
  I will wait to see what the Lord will
    say to me.
  I will wait to learn how to answer
    his complaint.

²The Lord answered me:
  "Write down what I show you.
  Write it clearly on stone tablets
    so whoever reads it can run to
    tell others.
³It is not yet time for the message to
    come true.
  But that time is coming soon.
  The message will come true.
  It may seem like a long time before
    it happens.
  But be patient and wait for it.
  These things will happen.
  They will not be delayed.
⁴See, the nation that is evil and
    trusts in itself will fail.

  But those who do right because
    they trust in God will live.

⁵"Wine can trick a person.
  In the same way the Babylonians
    are fooled by their pride.
  Their desire for wealth is like a
    grave's desire for death.
  They always want more and
    more.
  And, like death, they collect other
    nations for themselves.
  They make them their own
    people.
⁶But all the nations the Babylonians
    have hurt will laugh at them.
  They will make fun of the
    Babylonians.
  They will say, 'How terrible it will
    be for the nation that steals
    many things.
  How long will that nation get rich
    by forcing others to pay them?'

⁷"One day the people you have
    taken money from will turn
    against you.
  They will realize what is
    happening and make you
    shake with fear.
  Then they will hurt you.
⁸You have stolen from many nations.
  So the people who are left will
    take much from you.
  This is because you have killed
    many people.
  You have destroyed countries and
    cities and everyone in them.

⁹"How terrible it will be for the
    nation that becomes rich by
    doing wrong.
  They do those things to live in a
    safe place.
  They think they will be safe from
    harm.
¹⁰You have made plans to destroy
    many people.
  This has made your own houses
    ashamed of you.
  Because of it, you will lose your
    lives.
¹¹The stones of the walls will cry out
    against you.
  Even the wooden boards that
    support the roof will agree that
    you are wrong.

¹²"How terrible it will be for the
    nation that kills people to build
    a city.

How terrible for that nation that
wrongs others to start a town.
[13]The Lord of heaven's armies will
send fire
to destroy what those people
have built.
All the nations' work will be for
nothing.
[14]Then people everywhere will know
the Lord's greatness.
This news will spread like water
covering the sea.

[15]"How terrible for the nation that
becomes angry and makes
others suffer.
In anger they knock other people
to the ground.
And they treat them as if they are
naked and drunk.
[16]You Babylonians will receive the
Lord's anger, not respect.
This anger will be like a cup of
poison in the Lord's right hand.
You will taste this anger and fall to
the ground like a drunk person.
You will drink from this cup.
You will receive disgrace, not
respect.
[17]You hurt many people in Lebanon.
Now you will be hurt.
You killed many animals there.
And now you must be afraid.
You will be afraid because of what
you did
to those cities and the people
who lived in them.

[18]"An idol does no good, because a
man made it.
It is only a statue that teaches
lies.
The person who made it expects his
own work to help him.
But it can't even speak!
[19]How terrible it will be for the
nation that says to a wooden
statue, 'Come to life!'
How terrible it will be when this
nation says to a stone that
cannot speak, 'Get up!'
These things cannot tell them what
to do.
That idol is only a statue covered
with gold and silver.
There is no life in it.

[20]The Lord is in his Holy Temple.[d]
So all the earth should be silent
in his presence."

3 This is the prayer of Habakkuk the
prophet,[d] on shigionoth.[d]

[2]Lord, I have heard the news about
you.
Lord, I am amazed at the
powerful things you have done.
Do great things once again in our
time.
Make those things happen again
in our own days.
Even when you are angry,
remember to be gentle with us.

[3]God is coming from Teman in the
south.
The Holy One comes from Mount
Paran.[n]   *Selah*[d]
The Lord's greatness covers the
heavens.
His praise fills the earth.
[4]He is like a bright light.
Rays of light shine from his
hand.
And there he hides his power.
[5]Sickness goes before him,
and fever follows behind him.
[6]The Lord stands and shakes the
earth.
He looks, and the nations shake
with fear.
The mountains, which stood for
ages, break into pieces.
The old hills fall down.
God has always done this.

[7]I saw that the tents of Cushan were
in trouble.
The tents of Midian trembled.
[8]Lord, were you angry at the rivers?
Were you angry at the streams?
Were you angry with the sea
when you rode your horses and
chariots to victory?[n]
[9]You uncovered your bow.
You commanded many arrows to
be brought to you.   *Selah*
You split the earth with rivers.
[10]   The mountains saw you and
shook with fear.
The rushing water flowed by.
The sea made a loud noise,
and its waves rose high.
[11]The sun and moon stood still in the
sky.

3:3 Teman . . . Paran God is seen as again coming from the direction of Mount Sinai. He came from Sinai when he rescued his people from Egypt. **3:8 sea . . . victory** This is probably talking about the Israelites crossing the Red Sea.

They stopped when they saw the
flash of your flying arrows.
They stopped when they saw the
gleam of your shining spear.
[12] In anger you marched on the earth.
In anger you punished the
nations.
[13] You came to save your people.
You came to save your chosen
one.
You crushed the leader of the
wicked ones.
You took everything away from
them.   *Selah*
[14] With the enemy's own spear you
stabbed the leader of his army.
His soldiers rushed out like a
storm to scatter us.
They were happy as if
they were robbing the poor
people in secret.
[15] But you marched through the sea
with your horses,
stirring the great waters.

[16] I hear these things, and my body
trembles.

My lips tremble when I hear the
sound.
My bones feel weak.
My legs shake.

But I will wait patiently for the day
of disaster.
That day is coming to the people
who attack us.
[17] Fig trees may not grow figs.
There may be no grapes on the
vines.
There may be no olives growing on
the trees.
There may be no food growing in
the fields.
There may be no sheep in the pens.
There may be no cattle in the
barns.
[18] But I will still be glad in the Lord.
I will rejoice in God my Savior.
[19] The Lord God gives me my
strength.
He makes me like a deer, which
does not stumble.
He leads me safely on the steep
mountains.

For the director of music. On my
stringed instruments.

The Book of
ZEPHANIAH

1 This is the message of the Lord that
came through Zephaniah. It came
while Josiah son of Amon was king of
Judah. Zephaniah was the son of Cushi,
who was the son of Gedaliah. Gedaliah
was the son of Amariah, who was the
son of Hezekiah.

[2] "I will destroy everything
on earth," says the Lord.
[3] "I will destroy the people and
animals.
I will destroy the birds in the air
and the fish of the sea.
I will ruin the evil people.
I will remove all the people from
the earth," says the Lord.

[4] "I will punish Judah
and all the people living in
Jerusalem.
I will remove from this place

all signs of Baal[d] and his priests.
[5] I will destroy those who worship
the stars from the roofs.[n]
I will destroy those who worship
and make promises
by both the Lord and the god
Molech.[d]
[6] I will destroy those who turned
away from the Lord.
They quit following the Lord and
consulting him.
[7] Be silent before the Lord God.
His day for judging people is
coming soon.
The Lord has prepared to sacrifice
Judah.
He has appointed the invited
guests to feast on Judah.
[8] On that day the Lord will sacrifice
Judah.

1:5 roofs In Bible times houses were built with flat roofs. The roof was used for drying things
such as flax and fruit. And it was used as an extra room, as a place for worship and as a place
to sleep in the summer.

I, the Lord, will punish the
  princes and the king's sons.
And I will punish all
  those who wear foreign clothes.
[9]On that day I will punish those who
    worship Dagon,[d]
  I will punish those who hurt
    others
  and tell lies in the temples of
    their gods.

[10]"On that day this will happen,"
    says the Lord.
  "A cry will be heard at the Fish
    Gate.
  A wail will come from the new
    area of the city.
  A loud crash will echo from the
    hills.
[11]The people living in the market
    area will wail.
  All the merchants will be dead.
  All the silver traders will be
    gone.
[12]At that time I, the Lord, will search
    Jerusalem with lamps.
  I will punish those who are
    settled and satisfied with
    themselves.
  They are like wine left to settle.
  They think, 'The Lord never does
    anything.
  He won't help us or punish us.'
[13]Their wealth will be stolen.
  Their houses will be destroyed.
  They may build houses,
    but they will never live in them.
  They may plant vineyards,
    but they will never drink any
    wine from them.

[14]"The Lord's day of judging is
    coming soon.
  That great day is near and
    coming fast.
  The cry will be very sad on that
    day.
  Even soldiers will cry.
[15]That day will be a day of anger.
  It will be a day of terror and
    trouble.
  It will be a day of destruction and
    ruin.
  It will be a day of darkness and
    gloom.
  It will be a day of clouds and
    blackness.
[16]It will be a day of alarms and battle
    cries.
  'Attack the strong, walled cities!
  Attack the corner towers!'
[17]I will make life hard on the people.

They will walk around like blind
    men.
  This is because they have sinned
    against the Lord.
  Their blood will be poured out like
    dust.
  And their bodies will be dumped
    like trash.
[18]On that day God will show his
    anger.
  Then neither their silver nor gold
    will save them.
  The Lord's anger will be like fire.
  And the whole world will be
    burned up.
  Suddenly he will bring an end
    to everyone on earth."

2 Gather together,
    you unwanted people.
[2]Do it before it's too late.
  Do it before you are blown away
    like chaff.[d]
  Do it before the Lord's terrible
    anger reaches you.
  Do it before the day of the Lord's
    anger comes to you.
[3]All you who are not proud, come to
    the Lord.
  You who obey his laws, come to
    him.
  Do what is right. Learn to be
    humble.
  Maybe you will escape
    on the day the Lord shows his
    anger.

[4]No one will be left in the city of
    Gaza.
  The city of Ashkelon will be
    destroyed.
  Ashdod will be empty by noon.
  And the people of Ekron will be
    chased away.
[5]How terrible it will be for you who
    live by the Mediterranean Sea,
    you Philistines!
  This message from the Lord is for
    you,
  people of Canaan, land of the
    Philistines.

"I will destroy you.
  No one will be left."
[6]You live in the land by the
    Mediterranean Sea.
  It will be a place for shepherds
    and sheep.
[7]Your land will belong to the
    descendants[d] of Judah who are
    left alive.

There they will let their sheep eat
grass.
At night they will sleep
in the houses of Ashkelon.
The Lord their God will come to be
with them.
He will give them back their
riches.

[8]"I heard the country of Moab insult
my people.
The country of Ammon
threatened to take their land."
[9]So the Lord of heaven's armies, the
God of Israel, says,
"As surely as I live,
Moab will be destroyed like Sodom.
Ammon will be destroyed like
Gomorrah.[n]
Their land will be covered with
weeds and salt.
It will be destroyed forever.
Those of my people who are left
alive will take whatever they
want from them.
Those who are left from my
nation will take their land."

[10]This is what Moab and Ammon get
for being proud.
This will happen because they
insulted and made fun of the
people of the Lord of heaven's
armies.
[11]Those people will be afraid of the
Lord.
He will destroy all the gods of the
earth.
Then those people in faraway
places
will worship the Lord in their
own countries.

[12]"You Cushites also
will be killed by my sword."
[13]Then the Lord will turn against the
north
and punish Assyria.
He will destroy Nineveh.
It will be dry like a desert.
[14]Sheep and goats will lie down
there.
Wild animals will live there.
The owls and crows will sit
on the stone pillars that are left
standing.
Their calls will be heard through
the windows.
Trash will be in the doorways.
The wooden boards of the
buildings will be gone.

[15]This is the happy and safe city.
It thinks there is no one else as
strong as it is.
But that city will be destroyed.
Only animals will stay there.
Those who pass by will make fun
and shake their fists.

3 How terrible it will be for Jerusalem
that hurts its own people.
It's a wicked, stubborn city.
[2]Her people don't listen.
They can't be taught to do right.
They don't trust the Lord.
They don't worship their God.
[3]Their officers are like roaring lions.
Their rulers are like hungry
wolves that attack in the
evening.
In the morning nothing is left of
those they attacked.
[4]Their prophets[d] are proud.
They cannot be trusted.
Their priests don't respect holy
things.
They break God's teachings.
[5]But the Lord is good, and he is
there in that city.
He does no wrong.
Every morning he governs the
people fairly.
Every day he can be trusted by
his people.
But evil people are not ashamed
of the bad things they do.

[6]"I have destroyed other nations.
Their towers have fallen.
I made their streets empty.
No one goes there anymore.
Their cities are ruined.
No one lives there anymore.
[7]I said, 'Maybe now Jerusalem will
respect me.
Maybe now my people will let me
teach them to do right.'
Then the place where they lived
would not be destroyed.
Then I would not have punished
them.
They got up early in order to do
evil.
Everything they did was bad.
[8]Just wait," says the Lord.
"Some day I will hold court and
be the judge.
I will gather nations.
I will assemble kingdoms.
I will pour out my anger on them.
My anger will be very strong.

2:9 **Sodom . . . Gomorrah** Two cities God destroyed because the people were so evil.

My anger will be like fire.
And the whole world will be
burned up.

⁹"Then I will make the people of all
nations speak a pure language.
All of them will speak the name
of the Lord.
And they will worship me
together.

¹⁰People will come from where the
Nile River begins.
My scattered people will come
with gifts for me.

¹¹Then Jerusalem will not be
ashamed
of the wrongs done against me.
I will remove from this city
those who like to brag.
There will never be any more proud
people
on my holy mountain in
Jerusalem.

¹²Only the meek and humble will
stay in my city.
And they will trust in the Lord.

¹³Those who are left alive of Israel
won't do wrong.
They won't tell lies.
They won't trick people with
their words.
They will be like sheep that eat and
lie down.
No one will bother them."

¹⁴Sing, Jerusalem.
Israel, shout for joy!
Jerusalem, be happy.
Rejoice with all your heart.

¹⁵The Lord has stopped punishing
you.
He has sent your enemies away.
The King of Israel, the Lord, is with
you.
You will never again be afraid of
being harmed.

¹⁶On that day Jerusalem will be told,
"Don't be afraid, city of
Jerusalem.
Don't be so discouraged that you
can't do anything.

¹⁷The Lord your God is with you.
The mighty One will save you.
The Lord will be happy with you.
You will rest in his love.
He will sing and be joyful about
you."

¹⁸"I will take away the sadness
planned for you.
It would have made you very
ashamed.

¹⁹At that time I will punish
all those who harmed you.
I will save my people who are hurt.
I will gather my people who are
scattered.
I will give them praise and honor
in every place where they were
disgraced.

²⁰At that time I will gather you.
At that time I will bring you back
home.
I will give you honor and praise
from people everywhere.
That will happen when I give you
back your riches.
You will see this with your own
eyes," says the Lord.

The Book of
HAGGAI

1 The prophet[d] Haggai spoke the word
of the Lord to Zerubbabel and to
Joshua. Zerubbabel son of Shealtiel was
governor of Judah. Joshua son of Jehozadak was high priest. This message
came in the second year that Darius was
king of Persia. It came on the first day
of the sixth month of that year. This was
the message:

²"This is what the Lord of heaven's
armies says: 'The people say the right
time has not come to rebuild the Temple[d]
of the Lord.'"

³Then Haggai the prophet spoke the

word of the Lord: ⁴"The Temple is still
in ruins. Is it right for you to be living in
fancy houses?"

⁵This is why the Lord of heaven's armies says: "Think about what you have
done. ⁶You have planted much, but you
harvest little. You eat, but you do not
become full. You drink, but you are still
thirsty. You put on clothes, but you are
not warm enough. You earn money, but
then you lose it all. It is as if you put it
into a purse full of holes."

⁷This is what the Lord of heaven's armies says: "Think about what you have

done. ⁸Go up to the mountains. Bring back wood and build the Temple. Then I will be pleased with it and be honored," says the Lord. ⁹The Lord of heaven's armies says: "You look for much, but you find little. When you bring it home, I destroy it. Why? Because you are busy working on your own houses. But my house is still in ruins! ¹⁰Because of what you have done, the sky holds back its rain. And the ground holds back its crops. ¹¹I have called for a dry time in the land. There will be no rain in the mountains for the grain, new wine and olive oil. It will be a dry time for the plants which the earth produces. It will be a dry time for men and farm animals. The dry time will make your hard work useless."

¹²Zerubbabel was the son of Shealtiel. And Joshua, the high priest, was the son of Jehozadak. Zerubbabel and Joshua obeyed the Lord their God. And they obeyed the message from Haggai the prophet. All the rest of the people who were left alive also obeyed. This was because they realized that the Lord their God had sent Haggai. And they feared the Lord.

¹³The Lord sent a message to Haggai, the Lord's messenger. Haggai gave this message to the people. He said: "The Lord says, 'I am with you.'" ¹⁴The Lord made Zerubbabel and Joshua excited about building the Temple. Zerubbabel son of Shealtiel was the governor of Judah. Joshua son of Jehozadak was the high priest. The Lord made all the rest of the people who were left alive excited, too. They came and worked on the Temple of their God, the Lord of heaven's armies. ¹⁵They began on the twenty-fourth day of the sixth month. This was in the second year that Darius was king of Persia.

2 The Lord spoke his word through Haggai the prophet⁴ on the twenty-first day of the seventh month. This is what the Lord said: ²"Speak to Zerubbabel son of Shealtiel, governor of Judah. Speak also to Joshua son of Jehozadak, the high priest. And speak to the rest of the people who were left alive. Say: ³'Do any of you who are still alive remember how beautiful the Temple⁴ was before it was destroyed? What does it look like now? The truth is it means nothing to you!' ⁴But the Lord says: 'Zerubbabel, be brave. Joshua son of Jehozadak, the high priest, be brave. And all you people who live in the land, be brave,' says the

Lord. 'Work, because I am with you,' says the Lord of heaven's armies. ⁵'I made a promise to you when you came out of Egypt. My Spirit⁴ is still with you. So don't be afraid.'

⁶"This is what the Lord of heaven's armies says: 'In a short time I will shake the heavens and earth once again. And I will shake the sea and the dry land. ⁷I will shake all the nations. All the nations will bring their wealth. Then I will fill this Temple with glory,' says the Lord of heaven's armies. ⁸'The silver is mine, and the gold is mine,' says the Lord of heaven's armies. ⁹'The new Temple will be more beautiful than the one that was destroyed,' says the Lord of heaven's armies. 'And in this place I will give peace to the people,' says the Lord of heaven's armies."

¹⁰The Lord spoke his word to Haggai the prophet. This was on the twenty-fourth day of the ninth month. It was in the second year that Darius was king of Persia. This is what the Lord said: ¹¹"This is what the Lord of heaven's armies says: 'Ask the priests what the teachings say. ¹²A person might carry meat made holy for the Lord in the fold of his clothes. And that fold might touch bread, cooked food, wine, olive oil or some other food. Will the thing the fold touches be made holy for the Lord, too?'"

The priests answered, "No."

¹³Then Haggai said, "A person who touches a dead body will become unclean.⁴ If he touches any of these foods, will it become unclean, too?"

The priests answered, "Yes. It would become unclean."

¹⁴Then Haggai answered, "The Lord says this: 'This is also true for the people of this nation. They are unclean, and everything they do with their hands is unclean to me. If these people offer something at the altar to me, it is also unclean.

¹⁵"'Think about this from now on! Think about how it was before you started piling stones on top of stones. Think about how it was before you started building the Temple of the Lord. ¹⁶A person used to come to a pile of grain expecting to find 20 basketfuls. But there were only 10. And a person used to come to the wine vat to take out 50 jarfuls. But only 20 were there. ¹⁷I destroyed your work with diseases, mildew⁴ and hail. But you still did not come to me.' The Lord says this. ¹⁸'It is the

twenty-fourth day of the ninth month. On this day the people finished working on the foundation of the Temple of the Lord. From now on, think about these things: [19]Do you have seeds for your crops already in the barn? No! Your vines and trees are not giving fruit yet, either. You don't have any figs, pomegranates[d] or olives yet. But from now on I will bless you!' "

[20]Then the Lord spoke his word a second time to Haggai. It was on the twenty-fourth day of the month. This is what the Lord said: [21]"Tell Zerubbabel,

the governor of Judah: 'I am going to shake the heavens and the earth. [22]I will destroy the foreign kingdoms. I will take away the power of the kingdoms of the nations. I will destroy the chariots and their riders. The horses will fall with their riders. People will kill each other with swords.' [23]The Lord of heaven's armies says this: 'On that day I will take you, Zerubbabel son of Shealtiel, my servant.' The Lord says this: 'I will make you important like my signet[d] ring. This is because I have chosen you!' says the Lord of heaven's armies."

The Book of
ZECHARIAH

1 It was the eighth month of the second year Darius was king of Persia. The Lord spoke his word to the prophet[d] Zechariah son of Berekiah. Berekiah was the son of Iddo. The Lord said:

[2]"The Lord was very angry with your ancestors. [3]So tell the people: This is what the Lord of heaven's armies says: Return to me, and I will return to you. [4]Don't be like your ancestors. In the past the prophets spoke to them. They said: This is what the Lord of heaven's armies says: 'Stop your evil ways and evil actions.' But they wouldn't listen or pay attention to me, says the Lord. [5]Your ancestors are dead. And those prophets didn't live forever. [6]I commanded my words and laws to my servants the prophets. They preached to your ancestors, who returned to me. They said, 'The Lord of heaven's armies did as he said he would. He punished us for the way we lived and for what we did.'"

[7]It was on the twenty-fourth day of the eleventh month, which is called Shebat. It was Darius's second year as king. The Lord spoke his word to the prophet[d] Zechariah son of Berekiah. Berekiah was the son of Iddo.

[8]During the night I had a vision. I saw a man riding a red horse. He was standing among some myrtle trees in the ravine. Behind him were red, brown and white horses.

[9]I asked, "What are these, sir?"

The angel who was talking with me answered. He said, "I'll show you what they are."

[10]Then the man standing among the myrtle trees explained. He said, "They are the ones the Lord sent through all the earth."

[11]Then they spoke to the Lord's angel. He was standing among the myrtle trees. They said, "We have gone through all the earth. Everything is calm and quiet."

[12]Then the Lord's angel asked, "Lord of heaven's armies, how long before you show mercy to Jerusalem and the cities of Judah? You have been angry with them for 70 years now." [13]Then the Lord answered the angel who was talking with me. His words were comforting and good.

[14]Then the angel told me, "Announce this: This is what the Lord of heaven's armies says: 'I have a strong love for Jerusalem. [15]And I am very angry with the nations that feel so safe. I was only a little angry, but they made things worse for my people.'

[16]"So this is what the Lord says: 'I will return to Jerusalem with mercy. My Temple[d] will be rebuilt,' says the Lord of heaven's armies. 'And the measuring line will be used to rebuild Jerusalem.'

[17]"Also announce: This is what the Lord of heaven's armies says: 'My towns will be rich again. I will comfort Jerusalem again. I will still choose Jerusalem.'"

[18]Then I looked up and saw four animal horns. [19]I asked the angel who was talking with me, "What are these?"

He said, "These are the strong nations that scattered the people of Judah, Israel and Jerusalem."

[20] Then the Lord showed me four craftsmen. [21] I asked, "What are they coming to do?"

He answered, "They have come to scare and throw down the horns. Those horns scattered the people of Judah. No one could even lift up his head. The horns stand for the strong nations that attacked the people of Judah and scattered them."

2 Then I looked up. And I saw a man holding a line for measuring things. [2] I asked him, "Where are you going?"

He said to me, "I am going to measure Jerusalem. I will see how wide and how long it is."

[3] Then the angel who was talking with me left. And another angel came out to meet him. [4] The second angel said to him, "Run and tell that young man this: 'Jerusalem will become a city without walls because there will be so many people and cattle in it. [5] I will be a wall of fire around it,' says the Lord. 'And I will be the glory within it.'

[6] "Hurry! Run away from Babylon. I have scattered you in all directions," says the Lord.

[7] "Hurry, people of Jerusalem! Escape from Babylon." [8] This is what the Lord of heaven's armies says: "Whoever hurts you hurts what is precious to me."

So the Lord will honor me. And he will send me to speak against those nations who scattered you. [9] "I will raise my hand against them. Their slaves will rob them."

Then you will know that the Lord of heaven's armies sent me.

[10] "Shout and be glad, Jerusalem. I am coming, and I will live among you," says the Lord. [11] "At that time people from many nations will come to the Lord. And they will become my people. I will live among you. And you will know that the Lord of heaven's armies has sent me to you. [12] Judah will be the Lord's special part of the holy land. And Jerusalem will be his chosen city again. [13] Be silent, everyone. The Lord is coming out of the holy place where he lives."

3 Then he showed me Joshua the high priest. He was standing in front of the Lord's angel. And Satan was standing by Joshua's right side to accuse him. [2] The Lord said to Satan, "The Lord says you are guilty, Satan. The Lord who has chosen Jerusalem says you are guilty. This man was like a burning stick pulled from the fire."

[3] Joshua was standing in front of the angel. And Joshua was wearing dirty clothes. [4] Then the angel spoke to those standing near him. He said, "Take those dirty clothes off Joshua."

Then the angel said to Joshua, "Look, I have taken away your sin. And I am giving you new clothes."

[5] Then I said, "Put a clean turban on his head." So they put a clean turban on his head. They also dressed him while the Lord's angel stood there.

[6] Then the Lord's angel said to Joshua, "This is what the Lord of heaven's armies says: [7] 'Do as I tell you and serve me. Then you will be in charge of my Temple.[d] You will take care of my courtyards. And I will let you be with these angels who are standing here.

[8] "'Listen, high priest Joshua and the people with you. You stand for things that will happen. I am going to bring my servant called the Branch. [9] Look, I put this stone in front of Joshua. The stone has seven sides. I will carve a message on it,' says the Lord of heaven's armies. 'And in one day I will take away the sin of this land.'

[10] "The Lord of heaven's armies says, 'In that day, each of you will invite your neighbor to join you. And you will sit together under your own grapevine and under your own fig tree.'"

4 Then the angel who was talking with me came back. He woke me up as if I had been asleep. [2] He asked me, "What do you see?"

I said, "I see a solid gold lampstand. There is a bowl at the top. And there are seven lamps. There are also seven places for wicks. [3] There are two olive trees by it. One is on the right of the bowl. And one is on the left."

[4] I asked the angel who talked with me, "Sir, what are these?"

[5] The angel said, "Don't you know what they are?"

"No, sir," I said.

[6] Then he told me, "This is the message from the Lord to Zerubbabel: 'You will not succeed by your own strength or power. The power will come from my Spirit,'[d] says the Lord of heaven's armies.

[7] "No mountain can stand in Zerubbabel's way. It will be flattened. Then he will bring out the topmost stone. There will be shouts of 'It's beautiful! It's beautiful!'"

[8] Then the Lord spoke his word to me again. He said: [9] "Zerubbabel has laid the foundation of this Temple.[d] He will

also complete it. Then you will know that the Lord of heaven's armies has sent me to you.

10"The people should not think that small beginnings are unimportant. They will be happy when they see Zerubbabel with tools, building the Temple.

"(These seven lamps stand for the eyes of the Lord. They look back and forth across the earth.)"

11Then I asked the angel, "What are the two olive trees on the right and left of the lampstand?"

12I also asked him, "What are the two branches full of olives? The olive oil flows through the two gold pipes to the lamps."

13He answered, "Don't you know what they are?"

"No, sir," I said.

14So he said, "They stand for two men. They have been appointed to serve the Lord of all the earth."

5 I looked up again. And I saw a flying scroll.

2The angel asked me, "What do you see?"

I answered, "I see a flying scroll. It is 30 feet long and 15 feet wide."

3And he said to me, "This is the curse that will go all over the land. One side says every thief will be sent away. The other side says everyone who makes false promises will be sent away. 4The Lord of heaven's armies says, 'I will send it to the houses of thieves. I will also send it to those who use my name to make false promises. The scroll will stay in that person's house. And it will destroy the house with its wood and stones.'"

5Then the angel who was talking with me came forward. He said to me, "Look up and see what is coming."

6I asked, "What is it?"

He answered, "It is a measuring basket." He also said, "It stands for the people's sins in all the land."

7Then the lid made of lead was raised. There was a woman sitting in the basket. 8The angel said, "The woman stands for wickedness." Then he pushed her back into the basket. And he put the lid back down.

9Then I looked up. I saw two women. They had wind in their wings. Their wings were like those of a stork. They lifted up the basket into the sky.

10I spoke to the angel who was talking

with me. I asked, "Where are they taking the basket?"

11He answered, "They are going to Babylonia. They will build a temple for it. When the temple is ready, they will set the basket there in its place."

6 I looked up again. I saw four chariots coming from between two mountains. They were mountains of bronze. 2Red horses pulled the first chariot. Black horses pulled the second chariot. 3White horses pulled the third chariot. And strong, spotted horses pulled the fourth chariot. 4I spoke to the angel who was talking with me. I asked, "What are these, sir?"

5He said, "These are going to the four directions on earth. They have just come from the presence of the Lord of the whole world. 6The chariot pulled by the black horses will go north. The white horses will go west. And the spotted horses will go south."

7The powerful horses were trying to go through all the earth. So he said, "Go through all the earth." And they did.

8Then he called to me, "Look. The horses that went north have calmed the Lord's anger that came from there to punish."

9The Lord spoke his word to me. He said: 10"Heldai, Tobijah and Jedaiah were captives in Babylon. Get silver and gold from them. Go that same day to the house of Josiah son of Zephaniah. 11Make the silver and gold into a crown. And put it on the head of Joshua son of Jehozadak. Joshua is the high priest. 12Tell him this is what the Lord of heaven's armies says: 'There is a man whose name is the Branch. He will branch out from where he is. He will build the Temple*d* of the Lord. 13One man*n* will build the Temple of the Lord. And the other*n* will receive the honor of a king. One man will sit on his throne and rule. And the other will be a priest on his throne. And these two men will work together in peace.' 14The crown will be kept in the Temple of the Lord. It will remind Heldai, Tobijah, Jedaiah and Josiah son of Zephaniah of God's king. 15People living far away will come and build the Temple of the Lord. Then you will know the Lord of heaven's armies has sent me to you. This will happen if you completely obey the Lord your God."

6:13 One man This probably refers to Zerubbabel.   **6:13 other** This probably refers to Joshua.

7 It was the fourth year of King Darius's rule. It was on the fourth day of the ninth month, which is called Kislev. The Lord spoke his word to Zechariah. ²The city of Bethel sent Sharezer, Regem-Melech and their men to ask the Lord a question. ³They went to the prophets[d] and priests. They were at the Temple[d] of the Lord of heaven's armies. The men said, "For years the fifth month of each year has been a special time for us. We have shown our sadness and gone without food in this month. Should we continue to do this?"

⁴The Lord of heaven's armies spoke his word to me. He said, ⁵"Tell the priests and the people in the country this: 'For 70 years you went without food and cried in the fifth and seventh months. But that was not really for me. ⁶And when you ate and drank, it was really for yourselves. ⁷The Lord used the earlier prophets to say the same thing. Jerusalem and the surrounding towns were at peace and wealthy then. People lived in the southern area and the western mountain slopes.'"

⁸And the Lord spoke his word to Zechariah again: ⁹"This is what the Lord of heaven's armies says: 'Do what is right and fair. Be kind and merciful to each other. ¹⁰Don't hurt widows and orphans, foreigners or the poor. Don't even think of doing evil to somebody else.'

¹¹"But they refused to pay attention. They were stubborn and would not listen. ¹²They made their hearts as hard as rock. They would not listen to the teachings of the Lord of heaven's armies. And they would not hear his words through the earlier prophets. So the Lord of heaven's armies became very angry.

¹³"The Lord of heaven's armies says, 'When I called to them, they would not listen. So when they called to me, I would not listen. ¹⁴I scattered them like a hurricane to other countries. These were countries they did not know. This good land was left so ruined that no one could live there.'"

8 The Lord of heaven's armies spoke his word to me again. ²This is what the Lord of heaven's armies says: "I have a very strong love for Jerusalem. My strong love for her is like a fire burning in me."

³This is what the Lord says: "I will return to Jerusalem. I will live in Jerusalem. Then it will be called the City of Truth. And the mountain of the Lord of heaven's armies will be called the Holy Mountain."

⁴This is what the Lord of heaven's armies says: "Old men and old women will again sit along Jerusalem's streets. Each will carry a cane because of his age. ⁵And the streets will be filled with boys and girls playing."

⁶This is what the Lord of heaven's armies says: "Those who are left alive then may think it is too difficult to happen. But it is not too difficult for me," says the Lord of heaven's armies. ⁷This is what the Lord of heaven's armies says: "I will save my people from countries in the east and west. ⁸I will bring them back. And they will live in Jerusalem. They will be my people. And I will be their good and loyal God."

⁹This is what the Lord of heaven's armies says: "Be strong, you who are hearing these words today. The prophets spoke these words when the foundation was laid for the building of the Temple.[d] ¹⁰Before that time there was no money to hire men or animals. People could not safely come and go because of the enemies. I had turned everyone against his neighbor. ¹¹But I will not do to these people who are left alive what I did in the past," says the Lord of heaven's armies. ¹²"Their seeds will come up. Their grapevines will have fruit. The ground will give good crops. And the sky will send rain. I will give all this to those who are left alive. ¹³Judah and Israel, your names have been used as curses. But I will save you. And you will be a blessing. So don't be afraid. Be strong."

¹⁴This is what the Lord of heaven's armies says: "Your ancestors made me angry. So I planned to punish you. I had no mercy," says the Lord of heaven's armies. ¹⁵"But now I am planning to do good to Jerusalem and Judah. So don't be afraid. ¹⁶But do these things: Tell each other the truth. In the courts judge with truth and complete fairness. ¹⁷Do not make plans to hurt your neighbors. And don't make false promises. I hate all these things," says the Lord.

¹⁸The Lord of heaven's armies spoke his word to me again. ¹⁹This is what the Lord of heaven's armies says: "You have special days when you give up eating. These days are in the fourth, fifth, seventh and tenth months. Those days will become good, joyful, happy feasts in Judah. But you must love truth and peace."

²⁰This is what the Lord of heaven's ar-

mies says: "Many people from many cities will still come to Jerusalem. [21]People from one city will say to those from another city, 'We are going to pray to the Lord. We want to ask the Lord of heaven's armies for help. Come and go with us.' [22]Many people and powerful nations will come to Jerusalem. They will worship the Lord of heaven's armies. They will pray to the Lord."

[23]This is what the Lord of heaven's armies says: "At that time, ten men from different countries with different languages will come. They will take hold of one Jew by his coat. They will say to him, 'Let us go with you. We have heard that God is with you.'"

9 This message is the word of the Lord.

The message is against the land of
   Hadrach.
   And it is against the city of
     Damascus.
The tribes[d] of Israel and all people
   belong to the Lord.
[2]The Lord's message is also against
   the city of Hamath, which is on
   the border of the land of
   Hadrach.
   The Lord's message is against
     Tyre and Sidon, with their skill.
[3]Tyre has built a strong, walled city.
   The people have piled up silver
     like dust.
   They have as much gold as mud
     in the streets.
[4]But the Lord will take away all she
   has.
   He will destroy her power on the
     sea.
   That city will be destroyed by
     fire.
[5]The city of Ashkelon will see it and
   be afraid.
   The people of Gaza will shake
     with fear.
   And the people of Ekron will lose
     hope.
   No king will be left in Gaza.
   And no one will live in Ashkelon
     anymore.
[6]Foreigners will live in Ashdod.
   And I will destroy the pride of
     the Philistines.
[7]I will stop them from drinking
   blood.
   They will not eat any other
     forbidden food.
   Those left alive will belong to God.
   They will be leaders in Judah.

   And Ekron will become part of
     my people like the Jebusites.
[8]I will protect my Temple[e]
   from armies who come and go.
No one will hurt my people again
   because now I am guarding it.

[9]Rejoice, people of Jerusalem.
   Shout for joy, people of
     Jerusalem.
Your king is coming to you.
   He does what is right, and he
     saves.
   He is gentle and riding on a
     donkey.
   He is on the colt of a donkey.
[10]I will take away the chariots from
   Ephraim
   and the horses from Jerusalem.
   The bows used in war will be
     broken.
The king will talk to the nations
   about peace.
   His kingdom will go from sea to
     sea,
   and from the Euphrates River to
     the ends of the earth.

[11]My people, I made an agreement
   with you
   and sealed it with the blood of
     sacrifices.
Because of this, I will set your
   prisoners free from captivity,
   which is like a dry pit.
[12]You prisoners who have hope,
   return to your place of safety.
Today I am telling you
   that I will give you back twice as
     much as before.
[13]I will use Judah like a bow.
   And Ephraim will be like the
     arrows.
Jerusalem, I will use your men
   to fight the men of Greece.
   I will make you like the sword of
     a warrior.

[14]Then the Lord will appear to them.
   He will shoot his arrows like
     lightning.
The Lord God will blow the
   trumpet.
   And he will march in the storms
     of the south.
[15]The Lord of heaven's armies will
   protect them.
   They will destroy the enemy with
     slingshots.
They will drink and shout like
   drunk men.
   They will be filled like a bowl

used for sprinkling blood at the
corners of the altar.
[16]On that day the Lord their God will
save them
  as if his people were sheep.
They will shine in his land
  like jewels in a crown.
[17]They will be so pretty and
beautiful.
  The young men will grow strong
on the grain.
  And the young women will grow
strong on new wine.

10 Ask the Lord for rain in the
springtime.
  The Lord makes the clouds.
He sends the showers.
  And he gives everyone green
fields.
[2]Idols tell lies.
  Fortune-tellers see false visions.
They tell about false dreams.
  The comfort they give is worth
nothing.
So the people are like lost sheep.
  They are abused because there is
no shepherd.

[3]The Lord says, "I am angry at my
shepherds.
  I will punish the leaders.
I, the Lord of heaven's armies, will
care
  for my flock, which is the people
of Judah.
I will make them like my proud
war horses.
[4]From Judah will come the
cornerstone[d]
  and the tent peg.
From him will come the battle
bow.
  From him will come every ruler.
[5]They will be like soldiers
marching to battle through
muddy streets.
  The Lord is with them.
So they will fight and defeat the
horsemen.

[6]"I will strengthen the people of
Judah.
  And I will save the people of
Joseph.
I will bring them back
  because I care for them.
It will be as though
  I had never left them.
I am the Lord their God,

and I will answer their calls for
help.
[7]The people of Ephraim will be
strong like soldiers.
  They will be glad as when they
have drunk wine.
Their children will see it and
rejoice.
  They will be happy in the Lord.
[8]I will call my people
  and gather them together.
I will save them.
  And there will be as many of
them as there used to be.
[9]I have scattered them among the
nations.
  But in those faraway places, they
will remember me.
They and their children will live
and return.
[10]I will bring them back from Egypt.
  I will gather them from Assyria.
I will bring them to Gilead and
Lebanon.
  There won't be enough room in
the land for them all.
[11]They will come through their sea of
trouble.
  The waves of the sea will be
calm.
  And the Nile River will dry up.
I will defeat Assyria's pride.
  I will destroy Egypt's power over
other countries.
[12]I will make my people strong.
  And they will live as I say," says
the Lord.

11 Lebanon, open your gates
  so fire may burn your cedar
trees.[n]
[2]Cry, pine trees, because the cedar
has fallen.
  The tall trees are ruined.
Cry, oaks in Bashan,
  because the mighty forest has
been cut down.
[3]Listen to the shepherds crying.
  Their rich pastures are destroyed.
Listen to the lions roaring.
  The thick bushes near the Jordan
River are ruined.

[4]This is what the Lord my God says:
"Feed the sheep that are about to be
killed. [5]Their buyers kill them and are
not punished. Those who sell them say,
'Praise the Lord. I am rich.' Even the
shepherds don't feel sorry for their
sheep. [6]Even I don't feel sorry anymore

11:1 trees In this poem, trees, bushes and animals stand for leaders of countries around Judah.

for the people of this country," says the Lord. "I will let everyone be under the power of his neighbor and king. They will bring trouble to the country. And I will not stop them."

[7] So I fed the sheep about to be killed, particularly the weakest ones. Then I took two sticks. I called one Favor. I called the other Union. And I fed the sheep. [8] In one month I got rid of three shepherds. The flock hated me, and I got impatient with them. [9] I said, "I will no longer take care of you like a shepherd. Let those that are dying die. Let those that are to be destroyed be destroyed. Let those that are left eat each other."

[10] Then I broke the stick named Favor. This broke the agreement God made with his people. [11] That day it was broken. Those weak sheep were watching me. They knew this message was from the Lord.

[12] Then I said, "If you want to pay me, then pay me. If not, then don't." So they paid me 30 pieces of silver.

[13] The Lord said to me, "Throw the money to the potter." That is how little they thought I was worth.[n] So I threw the money to the potter in the Temple[d] of the Lord.

[14] Then I broke the second stick named Union. This broke the tie between Judah and Israel.

[15] Then the Lord said to me, "Become a foolish shepherd again. [16] I am going to get a new shepherd for the country. He will not care for the dying sheep. He will not look for the young ones. He will not heal the injured ones. He will not feed the healthy. But he will eat the best sheep and tear off their hoofs.

[17] "How terrible it will be for the
useless shepherd.
He abandoned the flock.
May war destroy his power and
wisdom.
May his power become useless.
May his wisdom be taken away."

12 This message is the word of the Lord to Israel. The Lord stretched out the skies. He laid the foundations of the earth. He put man's spirit in him. And the Lord says this: [2] "I will make Jerusalem like a cup of poison to the nations around her. They will come and attack Jerusalem and Judah. [3] One day all the nations on earth will come to-gether to attack Jerusalem. But I will make Jerusalem like a heavy rock. Anyone who tries to move it will get hurt. [4] At that time I will scare every horse. And its rider will panic," says the Lord. "I will watch over Judah. But I will blind all the horses of the enemies. [5] Then the leaders of Judah will say to themselves, 'The people of Jerusalem are strong. This is because the Lord of heaven's armies are their God.'

[6] "At that time I will make the leaders of Judah like a fire burning a stack of wood. They will be like a fire burning straw. They will destroy all the people around them left and right. But Jerusalem will remain safe.

[7] "The Lord will save the people of Judah first. Then the people in Jerusalem, David's city, won't have more honor than Judah. [8] At that time the Lord will protect the people in Jerusalem. Then even the weakest of them will be strong like David. And the family of David will be like God. They will be like an angel of the Lord leading the people. [9] At that time I will go to destroy all the nations that attack Jerusalem.

[10] "I will give David's family and people in Jerusalem a spirit of kindness and mercy. They will look at me, the one they have stabbed. And they will cry like someone crying over the death of an only child. They will be as sad as someone who has lost a firstborn[d] son. [11] At that time there will be much crying in Jerusalem. It will be like the crying for Hadad Rimmon in the plain of Megiddo. [12] The land will cry. Each family will cry alone. The family of David and their wives will cry. The family of Nathan and their wives will cry. [13] The family of Levi and their wives will cry. The family of Shimei and their wives will cry. [14] And all the rest of the families and their wives will cry.

13 "At that time a fountain will be opened. It will be for David's descendants[d] and for the people of Jerusalem. It will cleanse them of their sins and wrongs."

[2] The Lord of heaven's armies says, "At that time I will get rid of the names of the idols from the land. No one will remember them anymore. I will also remove the prophets[d] and unclean[d] spirits. [3] A person might continue to prophesy. If he does, his own father and mother

---

11:13 worth This was a small amount. It was about the price paid for a slave.

will tell him, 'You have told lies using the Lord's name. So you must die.' When he prophesies, his own parents should stab him.

⁴"At that time the prophets will be ashamed of their visions and prophecies. They won't wear the prophet's clothes made of hair to trick people. ⁵They will say, 'I am not a prophet. I am a farmer. I have been a farmer since I was young.' ⁶But someone will ask, 'What are the deep cuts on your body?' And he will answer, 'I was hurt at my friend's house.'

⁷"Sword, hit the shepherd.
　　Attack the man who is my
　　　friend,"
　　says the Lord of heaven's armies.
　"Kill the shepherd,
　　and the sheep will scatter.
　I will punish the little ones."
⁸The Lord says, "Two-thirds of the
　　people
　through all the land will die.
　And one-third will be left.
⁹I will test the ones left with fire.
　I will purify them like silver.
　I will test them like gold.
Then they will call on me.
　And I will answer them.
I will say, 'You are my people.'
　And they will say, 'The Lord is
　　our God.'"

14 The Lord's day of judging is coming. The wealth you have taken will be divided among you.

²I will bring all the nations together to fight Jerusalem. They will capture the city and rob the houses. The women will be attacked. Half the people will be taken away as captives. But the rest won't be taken from the city.

³Then the Lord will go to war against those nations. He will fight as in a day of battle. ⁴On that day he will stand on the Mount of Olives,ᵈ east of Jerusalem. The Mount of Olives will split in two. A deep valley will run east and west. Half the mountain will move north. And half will move south. ⁵You will run through this mountain valley to the other side. You will run as you ran from the earthquake. That was when Uzziah was king of Judah. Then the Lord my God will come. And all the holy ones will be with him.

⁶On that day there will be no light, cold or frost. ⁷There will be no other day like it. The Lord knows when it will

come. There will be no day or night. Even at evening it will still be light.

⁸At that time fresh water will flow from Jerusalem. Half of it will flow east to the Dead Sea.ᵈ And half of it will flow west to the Mediterranean Sea. It will flow summer and winter.

⁹Then the Lord will be king over the whole world. At that time there will be only one Lord. And his name will be the only name.

¹⁰All the land south of Jerusalem from Geba to Rimmon will be turned into a plain. Jerusalem will be raised up. But it will stay in the same place. The city will reach from the Benjamin Gate to the First Gate to the Corner Gate. It will go from the Tower of Hananel to the king's winepresses.ᵈ ¹¹People will live there. It will never be destroyed again. Jerusalem will be safe.

¹²But the Lord will punish the nations that fought against Jerusalem. He will bring a terrible disease on them. Their flesh will rot away while they are still standing up. Their eyes will rot in their sockets. And their tongues will rot in their mouths. ¹³At that time the Lord will cause panic. Everybody will grab his neighbor. They will attack each other. ¹⁴The people of Judah will fight in Jerusalem. And the wealth of the nations around them will be collected. There will be much gold, silver and clothes. ¹⁵A similar disease will strike the horses, mules, camels and donkeys. All the animals in the camps will have the disease.

¹⁶Some of the people who came to fight Jerusalem will be left alive. They will come back to Jerusalem year after year. They will come to worship the King, the Lord of heaven's armies. They will celebrate the Feastᵈ of Shelters. ¹⁷Some people from the nations might not go to Jerusalem. They might not worship the King, the Lord of heaven's armies. Then rain will not fall on their land. ¹⁸The Egyptians might not go to Jerusalem. They might not celebrate the Feast of Shelters. Then the Lord will send them the same terrible disease the other nations got. ¹⁹This will be the punishment. It will be for Egypt and any nation which does not go to celebrate the Feast of Shelters.

²⁰At that time the horses' bells will have written on them: Holy to the Lord. The cooking pots in the Templeᵈ of the Lord will be like the holy altar bowls.

²¹Every pot in Jerusalem and Judah will be holy to the Lord of heaven's armies. And everyone who offers sacrifices will be able to cook in them. At that time there will not be any traders in the Temple of the Lord of heaven's armies.

The Book of
MALACHI

1 This message is the word of the Lord. It is given to Israel through Malachi. ²The Lord said, "I love you."

But you ask, "How have you loved us?"

The Lord said, "Esau and Jacob were brothers. I loved Jacob, ³but I hated Esau. I destroyed his mountain country. I left his land to the wild dogs of the desert."

⁴The people of Edom might say, "We were destroyed. But we will go back and rebuild the ruins."

But the Lord of heaven's armies says, "If they rebuild them, I will destroy them. People will say, 'Edom is the Wicked Country. The Lord is always angry with the Edomites.' ⁵You will see these things with your own eyes. You will say, 'The Lord is great, even outside the borders of Israel!'"

⁶The Lord of heaven's armies says, "A child honors his father. A servant honors his master. I am a father. So why don't you honor me? I am a master. So why don't you respect me? You priests do not respect me.

"But you ask, 'How have we shown you disrespect?'

⁷"You have shown it by bringing unclean[d] sacrifices to my altar.

"But you ask, 'What makes them unclean?'

"They are unclean because you don't show respect for my altar. ⁸You bring blind animals as sacrifices, and that is wrong. You bring crippled and sick animals. That is wrong. Try giving them to your governor. Would he be pleased with you? He wouldn't accept you," says the Lord of heaven's armies.

⁹"Now ask God to be kind to you. But he won't accept you with such offerings," says the Lord of heaven's armies. ¹⁰"I wish one of you would close the Temple[d] doors. Then you would not light useless fires on my altar! I am not pleased with you. I will not accept your gifts," says the Lord of heaven's armies. ¹¹"From the east to the west I will be honored among the nations. Everywhere they will bring incense[d] and clean offerings to me. I will be honored among the nations," says the Lord of heaven's armies.

¹²"But you don't honor me. You say about the Lord's altar, 'It is unclean. The food has no worth.' ¹³You say, 'We are tired of doing this.' And you sniff at it in disgust," says the Lord of heaven's armies.

"And you bring hurt, crippled and sick animals. You bring them as gifts. But I won't accept them from you," says the Lord. ¹⁴"The cheat will be cursed. He has an animal in his flock. He promises to offer it. But then he offers me an animal that has something wrong with it. I am a great king," says the Lord of heaven's armies. "I am feared by all the nations.

2 "Priests, this command is for you. ²Listen to me. Pay attention to what I say. Honor my name," says the Lord of heaven's armies. "If you don't, I will send a curse on you. I will curse your blessings. I have already cursed them because you don't pay attention to what I say.

³"I will punish your descendants.[d] I will smear your faces with the garbage from your feasts. And you will be thrown away with it. ⁴Then you will know why I am giving you this command. It is so that my agreement with Levi will continue," says the Lord of heaven's armies. ⁵"My agreement for priests was with the tribe[d] of Levi. I promised them life and peace. And I gave these to them so they would honor me. They did honor me and fear me. ⁶They taught the true teachings. They spoke no lies. With peace and honesty they did what I said they should do. They kept many people from sinning.

⁷"A priest should teach what he knows. People should learn the teachings from him because he is the messenger of the Lord of heaven's armies. ⁸But you priests have stopped obeying me.

With your teachings you have caused many people to do wrong. You have broken the agreement with the tribe[d] of Levi!" says the Lord of heaven's armies. [9]"You have not been careful to do what I say. You take sides in court cases. So I have caused you to be hated and disgraced in front of everybody."

[10]We all have the same father. The same God made us. So why do people break their promises to each other? They don't respect the agreement that our ancestors made with God. [11]The people of Judah have broken their promises. They have done something God hates in Israel and Jerusalem. The people of Judah did not respect the Temple[d] that the Lord loves. The men of Judah married the women who worship foreign gods. [12]The man who does this might bring offerings to the Lord of heaven's armies. But the Lord will still separate him from the community of Israel.

[13]This is another thing you do. You cover the Lord's altar with your tears. You cry and moan because the Lord does not accept your offerings. He is not pleased with what you bring. [14]You ask, "Why?" It is because the Lord sees how you treated the wife you married when you were young. You broke your promise with her. She was your partner. You promised yourself to her. [15]God made husbands and wives to become one body and one spirit for his purpose. This is so they would have children who are true to God. So be careful. Do not break your promise with the wife you married when you were young.

[16]The Lord God of Israel says, "I hate divorce. And I hate people who do cruel things as easily as they put on clothes," says the Lord of heaven's armies. So be careful. And do not break your trust.

[17]You have tired the Lord with what you say.

You ask, "How have we tired him?"

You did it by saying, "God thinks anyone who does evil is good. And he is pleased with them." Or you asked, "Where is the God who is fair?"

3 The Lord of heaven's armies says, "I will send my messenger. He will prepare the way for me to come. Suddenly, the Lord you are looking for will come to his Temple.[d] The messenger of the agreement, whom you want, will come." [2]No one can live through that time. No one can survive when he comes. He will be like a purifying fire. He will be like laundry soap. [3]He will be like someone who heats and purifies silver. He will purify the Levites. He will make them pure like gold and silver. Then they will bring offerings to the Lord in the right way. [4]And he will accept the offerings from Judah and Jerusalem. It will be as it was in the past. [5]The Lord of heaven's armies says, "Then I will come to you and judge you. I will testify against those who take part in evil magic, adultery[d] and lying. I will testify against those who cheat workers of their pay and who cheat widows and orphans. And I will testify against those who are unfair to foreigners. These people do not respect me.

[6]"I am the Lord. I do not change. So you descendants[d] of Jacob have not been destroyed. [7]Like your ancestors before you, you have disobeyed my rules. You have not kept them. Return to me. Then I will return to you," says the Lord of heaven's armies.

"But you ask, 'How can we return?'

[8]"Should a man rob God? But you rob me.

"You ask, 'How have we robbed you?'

"You have robbed me in your offerings and the tenth of your crops. [9]So a curse is on you because the whole nation has robbed me. [10]Bring to the storehouse a tenth of what you gain. Then there will be food in my house. Test me in this," says the Lord of heaven's armies. "I will open the windows of heaven for you. I will pour out more blessings than you have room for. [11]I will stop the insects so they won't eat your crops. The grapes won't fall from your vines before they are ready to pick," says the Lord of heaven's armies. [12]"All the nations will call you blessed. You will have a pleasant country," says the Lord of heaven's armies.

[13]The Lord says, "You have said terrible things about me.

"But you ask, 'What have we said about you?'

[14]"You have said, 'It is useless to serve God. It did no good to obey his laws. And it did no good to show the Lord of heaven's armies that we are sorry for what we did. [15]So we say that proud people are happy. Evil people succeed. They challenge God and get away with it.'"

[16]Then those who honored the Lord spoke with each other. The Lord listened and heard them. The names of those who honored the Lord and respected

him were written in a book. The Lord will remember them.

[17]The Lord of heaven's armies says, "They belong to me. On that day they will be my very own. A father shows mercy to his son who serves him. In the same way I will show mercy to my people. [18]You will again see the difference between good and evil people. You will see the difference between those who serve God and those who don't.

4 "There is a day coming that will be like a hot furnace. All the proud and evil people will be like straw. On that day they will be completely burned up. Not a root or branch will be left," says the Lord of heaven's armies. [2]"But for you who honor me, goodness will shine on you like the sun. There will be healing in its rays. You will jump around, like calves freed from their stalls. [3]Then you will crush the wicked. They will be like ashes under your feet. I will do this on that day," says the Lord of heaven's armies.

[4]"Remember the teaching of Moses my servant. I gave those laws and rules to him at Mount Sinai. They are for all the Israelites.

[5]"But I will send Elijah the prophet[d] to you. He will come before that great and terrible day of the Lord's judging. [6]Elijah will help fathers love their children. And he will help the children love their fathers. Otherwise, I will come and put a curse on the land."

The
NEW
TESTAMENT

The Gospel According to
MATTHEW

1 This is the family history of Jesus Christ. He came from the family of David. David came from the family of Abraham.

[2] Abraham was the father[n] of Isaac.
Isaac was the father of Jacob.
Jacob was the father of Judah and his brothers.
[3] Judah was the father of Perez and Zerah.
(Their mother was Tamar.)
Perez was the father of Hezron.
Hezron was the father of Ram.
[4] Ram was the father of Amminadab.
Amminadab was the father of Nahshon.
Nahshon was the father of Salmon.
[5] Salmon was the father of Boaz.
(Boaz's mother was Rahab.)
Boaz was the father of Obed.
(Obed's mother was Ruth.)
Obed was the father of Jesse.
[6] Jesse was the father of King David.
David was the father of Solomon.
(Solomon's mother had been Uriah's wife.)
[7] Solomon was the father of Rehoboam.
Rehoboam was the father of Abijah.
Abijah was the father of Asa.
[8] Asa was the father of Jehoshaphat.
Jehoshaphat was the father of Jehoram.
Jehoram was the ancestor of Uzziah.
[9] Uzziah was the father of Jotham.
Jotham was the father of Ahaz.
Ahaz was the father of Hezekiah.
[10] Hezekiah was the father of Manasseh.
Manasseh was the father of Amon.
Amon was the father of Josiah.
[11] Josiah was the grandfather of Jehoiachin and his brothers.
(This was at the time that the people were taken to Babylon.)
[12] After they were taken to Babylon:
Jehoiachin was the father of Shealtiel.
Shealtiel was the grandfather of Zerubbabel.
[13] Zerubbabel was the father of Abiud.

Abiud was the father of Eliakim.
Eliakim was the father of Azor.
[14] Azor was the father of Zadok.
Zadok was the father of Akim.
Akim was the father of Eliud.
[15] Eliud was the father of Eleazar.
Eleazar was the father of Matthan.
Matthan was the father of Jacob.
[16] Jacob was the father of Joseph.
Joseph was the husband of Mary, and Mary was the mother of Jesus.
Jesus is called the Christ.[d]

[17] So there were 14 generations from Abraham to David. And there were 14 generations from David until the time when the people were taken to Babylon. And there were 14 generations from the time when the people were taken to Babylon until Christ was born.

[18] The mother of Jesus Christ was Mary. And this is how the birth of Jesus came about. Mary was engaged to marry Joseph. But before they married, she learned that she was going to have a baby. She was pregnant by the power of the Holy Spirit.[d] [19] Mary's husband, Joseph, was a good man. He did not want to disgrace her in public, so he planned to divorce her secretly.

[20] While Joseph thought about this, an angel of the Lord came to him in a dream. The angel said, "Joseph, descendant[d] of David, don't be afraid to take Mary as your wife. The baby in her is from the Holy Spirit. [21] She will give birth to a son. You will name the son Jesus.[n] Give him that name because he will save his people from their sins."

[22] All this happened to make clear the full meaning of what the Lord had said through the prophet:[d] [23] "The virgin[d] will be pregnant. She will have a son, and they will name him Immanuel."[n] This name means "God is with us."

[24] When Joseph woke up, he did what the Lord's angel had told him to do. Joseph married Mary. [25] But he did not have sexual relations with her until she gave birth to the son. And Joseph named the son Jesus.

2 Jesus was born in the town of Bethlehem in Judea during the time when Herod was king. After Jesus was born, some wise men from the east came to

---

1:2 father "Father" in Jewish lists of ancestors can sometimes mean grandfather or more distant relative. **1:21 Jesus** The name Jesus means "salvation." **1:23 "The virgin . . . Immanuel."** Quotation from Isaiah 7:14.

Jerusalem. [2]They asked, "Where is the baby who was born to be the king of the Jews? We saw his star in the east. We came to worship him."

[3]When King Herod heard about this new king of the Jews, he was troubled. And all the people in Jerusalem were worried too. [4]Herod called a meeting of all the leading priests and teachers of the law. He asked them where the Christ[d] would be born. [5]They answered, "In the town of Bethlehem in Judea. The prophet[d] wrote about this in the Scriptures:[d]

[6]'But you, Bethlehem, in the land of
Judah,
    you are important among the
    rulers of Judah.
A ruler will come from you.
    He will be like a shepherd for my
    people, the Israelites.'" *Micah 5:2*

[7]Then Herod had a secret meeting with the wise men from the east. He learned from them the exact time they first saw the star. [8]Then Herod sent the wise men to Bethlehem. He said to them, "Go and look carefully to find the child. When you find him, come tell me. Then I can go worship him too."

[9]The wise men heard the king and then left. They saw the same star they had seen in the east. It went before them until it stopped above the place where the child was. [10]When the wise men saw the star, they were filled with joy. [11]They went to the house where the child was and saw him with his mother, Mary. They bowed down and worshiped the child. They opened the gifts they brought for him. They gave him treasures of gold, frankincense,[d] and myrrh.[d] [12]But God warned the wise men in a dream not to go back to Herod. So they went home to their own country by a different way.

[13]After they left, an angel of the Lord came to Joseph in a dream. The angel said, "Get up! Take the child and his mother and escape to Egypt. Herod will start looking for the child to kill him. Stay in Egypt until I tell you to return."

[14]So Joseph got up and left for Egypt during the night with the child and his mother. [15]Joseph stayed in Egypt until Herod died. This was to make clear the full meaning of what the Lord had said through the prophet.[d] The Lord said, "I called my son out of Egypt."[n]

[16]When Herod saw that the wise men had tricked him, he was very angry. So he gave an order to kill all the baby boys in Bethlehem and in all the area around Bethlehem who were two years old or younger. This was in keeping with the time he learned from the wise men. [17]So what God had said through the prophet[d] Jeremiah came true:

[18]"A sound was heard in Ramah.
    It was painful crying and much
    sadness.
Rachel cries for her children,
    and she cannot be comforted,
    because her children are dead."
Jeremiah 31:15

[19]After Herod died, an angel of the Lord came to Joseph in a dream. This happened while Joseph was in Egypt. [20]The angel said, "Get up! Take the child and his mother and go to Israel. The people who were trying to kill the child are now dead."

[21]So Joseph took the child and his mother and went to Israel. [22]But he heard that Archelaus was now king in Judea. Archelaus became king when his father Herod died. So Joseph was afraid to go there. After being warned in a dream, he went to the area of Galilee. [23]He went to a town called Nazareth and lived there. And so what God had said through the prophets[d] came true: "He will be called a Nazarene."[n]

3 About that time John the Baptist[d] came and began preaching in the desert area of Judea. [2]John said, "Change your hearts and lives because the kingdom of heaven is coming soon." [3]John the Baptist is the one Isaiah the prophet[d] was talking about. Isaiah said:

"This is a voice of a man
    who calls out in the desert:
'Prepare the way for the Lord.
    Make the road straight for him.'"
Isaiah 40:3

[4]John's clothes were made from camel's hair. He wore a leather belt around his waist. For food, he ate locusts[d] and wild honey. [5]Many people went to hear John preach. They came from Jerusalem and all Judea and all the area around the Jordan River. [6]They told of the sins they had done, and John baptized them in the Jordan River.

[7]Many of the Pharisees[d] and Sadducees[d] came to the place where John was baptizing people. When John saw them,

2:15 "I called . . . Egypt." Quotation from Hosea 11:1.   **2:23 Nazarene** A person from the city of Nazareth, a name probably meaning "branch" (see Isaiah 11:1).

he said: "You are all snakes! Who warned you to run away from God's anger that is coming? ⁸You must do the things that show that you have really changed your hearts and lives. ⁹And don't think that you can say to yourselves, 'Abraham is our father.' I tell you that God could make children for Abraham from these rocks. ¹⁰The ax is now ready to cut down the trees. Every tree that does not produce good fruit will be cut down and thrown into the fire.ⁿ

¹¹"I baptize you with water to show that your hearts and lives have changed. But there is one coming later who is greater than I am. I am not good enough to carry his sandals. He will baptize you with the Holy Spiritᵈ and with fire. ¹²He will come ready to clean the grain. He will separate the good grain from the chaff.ᵈ He will put the good part of the grain into his barn. And he will burn the chaff with a fire that cannot be put out.'"

¹³At that time Jesus came from Galilee to the Jordan River. He came to John and wanted John to baptize him. ¹⁴But John tried to stop him. John said, "Why do you come to me to be baptized? I should be baptized by you!"

¹⁵Jesus answered, "Let it be this way for now. We should do all things that are right." So John agreed to baptize Jesus.

¹⁶Jesus was baptized and came up out of the water. Heaven opened, and he saw God's Spiritᵈ coming down on him like a dove. ¹⁷And a voice spoke from heaven. The voice said, "This is my Son and I love him. I am very pleased with him."

4 Then the Spiritᵈ led Jesus into the desert to be tempted by the devil. ²Jesus ate nothing for 40 days and nights. After this, he was very hungry. ³The devil came to Jesus to tempt him. The devil said, "If you are the Son of God, tell these rocks to become bread."

⁴Jesus answered, "It is written in the Scriptures,ᵈ 'A person does not live only by eating bread. But a person lives by everything the Lord says.'"ⁿ

⁵Then the devil led Jesus to the holy city of Jerusalem. He put Jesus on a very high place of the Temple.ᵈ ⁶The devil said, "If you are the Son of God, jump off. It is written in the Scriptures,

'He has put his angels in charge of
  you.
They will catch you with their
  hands.
And you will not hit your foot on a
  rock.'"   *Psalm 91:11-12*

⁷Jesus answered him, "It also says in the Scriptures, 'Do not test the Lord your God.'"ⁿ

⁸Then the devil led Jesus to the top of a very high mountain. He showed Jesus all the kingdoms of the world and all the great things that are in those kingdoms. ⁹The devil said, "If you will bow down and worship me, I will give you all these things."

¹⁰Jesus said to the devil, "Go away from me, Satan! It is written in the Scriptures, 'You must worship the Lord your God. Serve only him!'"ⁿ

¹¹So the devil left Jesus. And then some angels came to Jesus and helped him.

¹²Jesus heard that John had been put in prison. So Jesus went back to Galilee. ¹³He left Nazareth and went and lived in Capernaum, a town near Lake Galilee. Capernaum is in the area near Zebulun and Naphtali. ¹⁴Jesus did this to make true what the prophetᵈ Isaiah said:

¹⁵"Land of Zebulun and land of
   Naphtali
  are on the way to the sea.
They are along the Jordan River.
  This is Galilee where the
   non-Jewish people live.
¹⁶These people who live in darkness
  will see a great light.
They live in a place that is very
   dark.
  But a light will shine on them."
        Isaiah 9:1-2

¹⁷From that time Jesus began to preach, saying, "Change your hearts and lives, because the kingdom of heaven is coming soon."

¹⁸Jesus was walking by Lake Galilee. He saw two brothers, Simon (called Peter) and Simon's brother Andrew. The brothers were fishermen, and they were fishing in the lake with a net. ¹⁹Jesus said, "Come follow me. I will make you fishermen for men." ²⁰At once Simon and Andrew left their nets and followed him.

²¹Jesus continued walking by Lake

3:10 The ax . . . fire. This means that God is ready to punish his people who do not obey him. **3:12 He will . . . out.** This means that Jesus will come to separate the good people from the bad people, saving the good and punishing the bad. **4:4 'A person . . . says.'** Quotation from Deuteronomy 8:3. **4:7 'Do . . . God.'** Quotation from Deuteronomy 6:16. **4:10 'You . . . him!'** Quotation from Deuteronomy 6:13.

Galilee. He saw two other brothers, James and John, the sons of Zebedee. They were in a boat with their father Zebedee, preparing their nets to catch fish. Jesus told them to come with him. [22] At once they left the boat and their father, and they followed Jesus.

[23] Jesus went everywhere in Galilee. He taught in the synagogues[d] and preached the Good News[d] about the kingdom of heaven. And he healed all the people's diseases and sicknesses. [24] The news about Jesus spread all over Syria, and people brought all the sick to him. These sick people were suffering from different kinds of diseases and pain. Some were suffering very great pain, some had demons,[d] some were epileptics,[n] and some were paralyzed. Jesus healed all of them. [25] Many people followed him. They came from Galilee, the Ten Towns,[n] Jerusalem, Judea, and the land across the Jordan River.

5 Jesus saw the crowds who were there. He went up on a hill and sat down. His followers came to him. [2] Jesus taught the people and said:

[3] "Those people who know they have
     great spiritual needs are happy.
The kingdom of heaven belongs
     to them.
[4] Those who are sad now are happy.
     God will comfort them.
[5] Those who are humble are happy.
     The earth will belong to them.
[6] Those who want to do right more
     than anything else are happy.
     God will fully satisfy them.
[7] Those who give mercy to others are
     happy.
     Mercy will be given to them.
[8] Those who are pure in their
     thinking are happy.
     They will be with God.
[9] Those who work to bring peace are
     happy.
     God will call them his sons.
[10] Those who are treated badly for
     doing good are happy.
The kingdom of heaven belongs
     to them.

[11] "People will say bad things about you and hurt you. They will lie and say all kinds of evil things about you because you follow me. But when they do these things to you, you are happy. [12] Re-joice and be glad. You have a great re-ward waiting for you in heaven. People did the same evil things to the prophets[d] who lived before you.

[13] "You are the salt of the earth. But if the salt loses its salty taste, it cannot be made salty again. It is good for nothing. It must be thrown out for people to walk on.

[14] "You are the light that gives light to the world. A city that is built on a hill cannot be hidden. [15] And people don't hide a light under a bowl. They put the light on a lampstand. Then the light shines for all the people in the house. [16] In the same way, you should be a light for other people. Live so that they will see the good things you do. Live so that they will praise your Father in heaven.

[17] "Don't think that I have come to de-stroy the law of Moses or the teaching of the prophets.[d] I have not come to destroy their teachings but to do what they said. [18] I tell you the truth. Nothing will disap-pear from the law until heaven and earth are gone. The law will not lose even the smallest letter or the smallest part of a letter until all has happened. [19] Whoever refuses to obey any command and teaches other people not to obey that command will be the least important in the kingdom of heaven. But whoever obeys the law and teaches other people to obey the law will be great in the king-dom of heaven. [20] I tell you that you must do better than the teachers of the law and the Pharisees.[d] If you are not better than they are, you will not enter the kingdom of heaven.

[21] "You have heard that it was said to our people long ago, 'You must not mur-der anyone.'[n] Anyone who murders an-other will be judged.' [22] But I tell you, if you are angry with your brother, you will be judged. And if you say bad things to your brother, you will be judged by the Jewish council. And if you call your brother a fool, then you will be in danger of the fire of hell.

[23] "So when you offer your gift to God at the altar, and you remember that your brother has something against you, [24] leave your gift there at the altar. Go and make peace with him. Then come and offer your gift.

[25] "If your enemy is taking you to

4:24 epileptics People with a disease that causes them sometimes to lose control of their bodies, and maybe faint, shake strongly, or not be able to move. **4:25 Ten Towns** In Greek, called "Decapolis." It was an area east of Lake Galilee that once had ten main towns. **5:21 You . . . anyone.** Quotation from Exodus 20:13; Deuteronomy 5:17.

court, become friends with him quickly. You should do that before you go to court. If you don't become his friend, he might turn you over to the judge. And the judge might give you to a guard to put you in jail. [26] I tell you that you will not leave that jail until you have paid everything you owe.

[27] "You have heard that it was said, 'You must not be guilty of adultery.'[n] [28] But I tell you that if anyone looks at a woman and wants to sin sexually with her, then he has already done that sin with the woman in his mind. [29] If your right eye causes you to sin, then take it out and throw it away. It is better to lose one part of your body than to have your whole body thrown into hell. [30] If your right hand causes you to sin, then cut it off and throw it away. It is better to lose one part of your body than for your whole body to go into hell.

[31] "It was also said, 'Anyone who divorces his wife must give her a written divorce paper.'[n] [32] But I tell you that anyone who divorces his wife is causing his wife to be guilty of adultery.[d] The only reason for a man to divorce his wife is if she has sexual relations with another man. And anyone who marries that divorced woman is guilty of adultery.

[33] "You have heard that it was said to our people long ago, 'When you make a promise, don't break your promise. Keep the promises that you make to the Lord.'[n] [34] But I tell you, never make an oath. Don't make an oath using the name of heaven, because heaven is God's throne. [35] Don't make an oath using the name of the earth, because the earth belongs to God. Don't make an oath using the name of Jerusalem, because that is the city of the great King. [36] And don't even say that your own head is proof that you will keep your oath. You cannot make one hair on your head become white or black. [37] Say only 'yes' if you mean 'yes,' and say only 'no' if you mean 'no.' If you must say more than 'yes' or 'no,' it is from the Evil One.

[38] "You have heard that it was said, 'An eye for an eye, and a tooth for a tooth.'[n] [39] But I tell you, don't stand up against an evil person. If someone slaps you on the right cheek, then turn and let him slap the other cheek too. [40] If someone

wants to sue you in court and take your shirt, then let him have your coat too. [41] If a soldier forces you to go with him one mile, then go with him two miles. [42] If a person asks you for something, then give it to him. Don't refuse to give to a person who wants to borrow from you.

[43] "You have heard that it was said, 'Love your neighbor[n] and hate your enemies.' [44] But I tell you, love your enemies. Pray for those who hurt you. [45] If you do this, then you will be true sons of your Father in heaven. Your Father causes the sun to rise on good people and on bad people. Your Father sends rain to those who do good and to those who do wrong. [46] If you love only the people who love you, then you will get no reward. Even the tax collectors do that. [47] And if you are nice only to your friends, then you are no better than other people. Even people without God are nice to their friends. [48] So you must be perfect, just as your Father in heaven is perfect.

6 "Be careful! When you do good things, don't do them in front of people to be seen by them. If you do that, then you will have no reward from your Father in heaven.

[2] "When you give to the poor, don't be like the hypocrites.[d] They blow trumpets before they give so that people will see them. They do that in the synagogues[d] and on the streets. They want other people to honor them. I tell you the truth. Those hypocrites already have their full reward. [3] So when you give to the poor, give very secretly. Don't let anyone know what you are doing. [4] Your giving should be done in secret. Your Father can see what is done in secret, and he will reward you.

[5] "When you pray, don't be like the hypocrites.[d] They love to stand in the synagogues[d] and on the street corners and pray loudly. They want people to see them pray. I tell you the truth. They already have their full reward. [6] When you pray, you should go into your room and close the door. Then pray to your Father who cannot be seen. Your Father can see what is done in secret, and he will reward you.

[7] "And when you pray, don't be like those people who don't know God. They

---

5:27 'You . . . adultery.' Quotation from Exodus 20:14; Deuteronomy 5:18. **5:31 'Anyone . . . divorce paper.'** Quotation from Deuteronomy 24:1. **5:33 'When . . . Lord.'** Quotation from Leviticus 19:12; Numbers 30:2; Deuteronomy 23:21. **5:38 'An eye . . . tooth.'** Quotation from Exodus 21:24; Leviticus 24:20; Deuteronomy 19:21. **5:43 Love your neighbor** Quotation from Leviticus 19:18.

continue saying things that mean nothing. They think that God will hear them because of the many things they say. [8]Don't be like them. Your Father knows the things you need before you ask him. [9]So when you pray, you should pray like this:

'Our Father in heaven,
we pray that your name will always
    be kept holy.
[10]We pray that your kingdom will
    come.
We pray that what you want will be
    done,
    here on earth as it is in heaven.
[11]Give us the food we need for each
    day.
[12]Forgive the sins we have done,
    just as we have forgiven those
    who did wrong to us.
[13]Do not cause us to be tested;
    but save us from the Evil One.'

[14]Yes, if you forgive others for the things they do wrong, then your Father in heaven will also forgive you for the things you do wrong. [15]But if you don't forgive the wrongs of others, then your Father in heaven will not forgive the wrong things you do.

[16]"When you give up eating,[n] don't put on a sad face like the hypocrites.[d] They make their faces look strange to show people that they are giving up eating. I tell you the truth, those hypocrites already have their full reward. [17]So when you give up eating, comb your hair and wash your face. [18]Then people will not know that you are giving up eating. But your Father, whom you cannot see, will see you. Your Father sees what is done in secret, and he will reward you.

[19]"Don't store treasures for yourselves here on earth. Moths and rust will destroy treasures here on earth. And thieves can break into your house and steal the things you have. [20]So store your treasure in heaven. The treasures in heaven cannot be destroyed by moths or rust. And thieves cannot break in and steal that treasure. [21]Your heart will be where your treasure is.

[22]"The eye is a light for the body. If your eyes are good, then your whole body will be full of light. [23]But if your eyes are evil, then your whole body will be full of darkness. And if the only light you have is really darkness, then you have the worst darkness.

[24]"No one can be a slave to two masters. He will hate one master and love the other. Or he will follow one master and refuse to follow the other. So you cannot serve God and money at the same time.

[25]"So I tell you, don't worry about the food you need to live. And don't worry about the clothes you need for your body. Life is more important than food. And the body is more important than clothes. [26]Look at the birds in the air. They don't plant or harvest or store food in barns. But your heavenly Father feeds the birds. And you know that you are worth much more than the birds. [27]You cannot add any time to your life by worrying about it.

[28]"And why do you worry about clothes? Look at the flowers in the field. See how they grow. They don't work or make clothes for themselves. [29]But I tell you that even Solomon with his riches was not dressed as beautifully as one of these flowers. [30]God clothes the grass in the field like that. The grass is living today, but tomorrow it is thrown into the fire to be burned. So you can be even more sure that God will clothe you. Don't have so little faith! [31]Don't worry and say, 'What will we eat?' or 'What will we drink?' or 'What will we wear?' [32]All the people who don't know God keep trying to get these things. And your Father in heaven knows that you need them. [33]The thing you should want most is God's kingdom and doing what God wants. Then all these other things you need will be given to you. [34]So don't worry about tomorrow. Each day has enough trouble of its own. Tomorrow will have its own worries.

[7]"Don't judge other people, and you will not be judged. [2]You will be judged in the same way that you judge others. And the forgiveness you give to others will be given to you.

[3]"Why do you notice the little piece of dust that is in your brother's eye, but you don't notice the big piece of wood that is in your own eye? [4]Why do you say to your brother, 'Let me take that little piece of dust out of your eye'? Look at yourself first! You still have that big piece of wood in your own eye. [5]You are a hypocrite![d] First, take the wood out of your own eye. Then you will see clearly

---

6:16 give up eating This is called "fasting." The people would give up eating for a special time of prayer and worship to God. It was also done to show sadness.

enough to take the dust out of your brother's eye.

⁶"Don't give holy things to dogs. Don't throw your pearls before pigs. Pigs will only trample on them. And the dogs will only turn to attack you.

⁷"Continue to ask, and God will give to you. Continue to search, and you will find. Continue to knock, and the door will open for you. ⁸Yes, everyone who continues asking will receive. He who continues searching will find. And he who continues knocking will have the door opened for him.

⁹"What would you do if your son asks for bread? Which of you would give him a stone? ¹⁰Or if your son asks for a fish, would you give him a snake? ¹¹Even though you are bad, you know how to give good gifts to your children. So surely your heavenly Father will give good things to those who ask him.

¹²"Do for other people the same things you want them to do for you. This is the meaning of the law of Moses and the teaching of the prophets.ᵈ

¹³"Enter through the narrow gate. The road that leads to hell is a very easy road. And the gate to hell is very wide. Many people enter through that gate. ¹⁴But the gate that opens the way to true life is very small. And the road to true life is very hard. Only a few people find that road.

¹⁵"Be careful of false prophets.ᵈ They come to you and look gentle like sheep. But they are really dangerous like wolves. ¹⁶You will know these people because of the things they do. Good things don't come from bad people, just as grapes don't come from thornbushes. And figs don't come from thorny weeds. ¹⁷In the same way, every good tree produces good fruit. And bad trees produce bad fruit. ¹⁸A good tree cannot produce bad fruit. And a bad tree cannot produce good fruit. ¹⁹Every tree that does not produce good fruit is cut down and thrown into the fire. ²⁰You will know these false prophets by what they produce.

²¹"Not everyone who says that I am his Lord will enter the kingdom of heaven. The only people who will enter the kingdom of heaven are those who do the things that my Father in heaven wants. ²²On the last day many people will say to me, 'You are our Lord! We

spoke for you. And through you we forced out demonsᵈ and did many miracles.'ᵈ ²³Then I will tell them clearly, 'Get away from me, you who do evil. I never knew you.'

²⁴"Everyone who hears these things I say and obeys them is like a wise man. The wise man built his house on rock. ²⁵It rained hard and the water rose. The winds blew and hit that house. But the house did not fall, because the house was built on rock. ²⁶But the person who hears the things I teach and does not obey them is like a foolish man. The foolish man built his house on sand. ²⁷It rained hard, the water rose, and the winds blew and hit that house. And the house fell with a big crash."

²⁸When Jesus finished saying these things, the people were amazed at his teaching. ²⁹Jesus did not teach like their teachers of the law. He taught like a person who had authority.

8 When Jesus came down from the hill, great crowds followed him. ²Then a man sick with a harmful skin disease came to Jesus. The man bowed down before him and said, "Lord, you have the power to heal me if you want."

³Jesus touched the man and said, "I want to heal you. Be healed!" And immediately the man was healed from his skin disease. ⁴Then Jesus said to him, "Don't tell anyone about what happened. But go and show yourself to the priest.ⁿ And offer the gift that Moses commandedⁿ for people who are made well. This will show people that you are healed."

⁵Jesus went to the city of Capernaum. When he entered the city, an army officer came to Jesus and begged for help. ⁶The officer said, "Lord, my servant is at home in bed. He can't move his body and is in much pain."

⁷Jesus said to the officer, "I will go and heal him."

⁸The officer answered, "Lord, I am not good enough for you to come into my house. All you need to do is command that my servant be healed, and he will be healed. ⁹I myself am a man under the authority of other men. And I have soldiers under my command. I tell one soldier, 'Go,' and he goes. I tell another soldier, 'Come,' and he comes. I say to my servant, 'Do this,' and my servant obeys me.

8:4 show . . . priest The law of Moses said a priest must say when a Jew who had a harmful skin disease was well.   **8:4 Moses commanded** Read about this in Leviticus 14:1-32.

[10] When Jesus heard this, he was amazed. He said to those who were with him, "I tell you the truth. This man has more faith than any other person I have found, even in Israel. [11] Many people will come from the east and from the west. They will sit and eat with Abraham, Isaac, and Jacob in the kingdom of heaven. [12] And those people who should have the kingdom will be thrown outside into the darkness. In that place people will cry and grind their teeth with pain."

[13] Then Jesus said to the officer, "Go home. Your servant will be healed just as you believed he would." And at that same time his servant was healed.

[14] Jesus went to Peter's house. There Jesus saw that Peter's mother-in-law was in bed with a high fever. [15] Jesus touched her hand, and the fever left her. Then she stood up and began to serve Jesus.

[16] That evening people brought to Jesus many who had demons.[d] Jesus spoke and the demons left them. Jesus healed all the sick. [17] He did these things to make come true what Isaiah the prophet[d] said:

"He took our suffering on him.
And he felt our pain for us."

Isaiah 53:4

[18] When Jesus saw the crowd around him, he told his followers to go to the other side of the lake. [19] Then a teacher of the law came to Jesus and said, "Teacher, I will follow you any place you go."

[20] Jesus said to him, "The foxes have holes to live in. The birds have nests to live in. But the Son of Man[d] has no place where he can rest his head."

[21] Another man, one of Jesus' followers, said to Jesus, "Lord, let me go and bury my father first."

[22] But Jesus said to him, "Follow me, and let the people who are dead bury their own dead."

[23] Jesus got into a boat, and his followers went with him. [24] A very bad storm arose on the lake. The waves covered the boat. But Jesus was sleeping. [25] The followers went to Jesus and woke him. They said, "Lord, save us! We will drown!"

[26] Jesus answered, "Why are you afraid? You don't have enough faith." Then Jesus got up and gave a command

to the wind and the sea. The wind stopped, and the sea became very calm.

[27] The men were amazed. They said, "What kind of man is this? Even the wind and the sea obey him!"

[28] Jesus arrived at the other side of the lake in the country of the Gadarene[n] people. There, two men came to Jesus. They had demons[d] in them. These men lived in the burial caves. They were so dangerous that people could not use the road by those caves. [29] The two men came to Jesus and shouted, "What do you want with us, Son of God? Did you come here to punish us before the right time?"

[30] Near that place there was a large herd of pigs feeding. [31] The demons begged Jesus, "If you make us leave these men, please send us into that herd of pigs."

[32] Jesus said to them, "Go!" So the demons left the men and went into the pigs. Then the whole herd of pigs ran down the hill into the lake and were drowned. [33] The men who were caring for the pigs ran away and went into town. They told about all of this and what had happened to the men who had demons. [34] Then the whole town went out to see Jesus. When they saw him, they begged him to leave their area.

9 Jesus got into a boat and went back across the lake to his own town. [2] Some people brought to Jesus a man who was paralyzed. The man was lying on his mat. Jesus saw that these people had great faith, so he said to the paralyzed man, "Be happy, young man. Your sins are forgiven."

[3] Some of the teachers of the law heard this. They said to themselves, "This man speaks as if he were God—that is blasphemy!"[n]

[4] Jesus knew what they were thinking. So he said, "Why are you thinking evil thoughts? [5] Which is easier: to tell this paralyzed man, 'Your sins are forgiven,' or to tell him, 'Stand up and walk'? [6] But I will prove to you that the Son of Man[d] has power on earth to forgive sins." Then Jesus said to the paralyzed man, "Stand up. Take your mat and go home." [7] And the man stood up and went home. [8] The people saw this and were amazed. They praised God for giving power like this to men.

[9] When Jesus was leaving, he saw a

8:28 Gadarene From Gadara, an area southeast of Lake Galilee. **9:3 blasphemy** Saying things against God.

man named Matthew. Matthew was sitting in the tax office. Jesus said to him, "Follow me." And Matthew stood up and followed Jesus.

[10]Jesus had dinner at Matthew's house. Many tax collectors and "sinners" came and ate with Jesus and his followers. [11]The Pharisees[d] saw this and asked Jesus' followers, "Why does your teacher eat with tax collectors and 'sinners'?"

[12]Jesus heard the Pharisees ask this. So he said, "Healthy people don't need a doctor. Only the sick need a doctor. [13]Go and learn what this means: 'I want faithful love more than I want animal sacrifices.'[n] I did not come to invite good people. I came to invite sinners."

[14]Then the followers of John[n] came to Jesus. They said to Jesus, "We and the Pharisees[d] often give up eating.[n] But your followers don't. Why?"

[15]Jesus answered, "The friends of the bridegroom are not sad while he is with them. But the time will come when the bridegroom will leave them. Then his friends are sad, and they will give up eating.

[16]"When someone sews a patch over a hole in an old coat, he never uses a piece of cloth that is not yet shrunk. If he does, the patch will shrink and pull away from the coat. Then the hole will be worse. [17]Also, people never pour new wine into old leather bags for holding wine. If they do, the old bags will break. The wine will spill, and the wine bags will be ruined. But people always pour new wine into new wine bags. Then the wine and the wine bags will continue to be good."

[18]While Jesus was saying these things, a ruler of the synagogue[d] came to him. The ruler bowed down before Jesus and said, "My daughter has just died. But come and put her with your hand, and she will live again."

[19]So Jesus stood up and went with the ruler. Jesus' followers went too.

[20]Then a woman who had been bleeding for 12 years came behind Jesus and touched the edge of his coat. [21]She was thinking, "If I can touch his coat, then I will be healed."

[22]Jesus turned and saw the woman. He said, "Be happy, dear woman. You are made well because you believed." And the woman was healed at once.

[23]Jesus continued along with the ruler and went into the ruler's house. Jesus saw people there who play music for funerals. And he saw many people there crying. [24]Jesus said, "Go away. The girl is not dead. She is only asleep." But the people laughed at Jesus. [25]After the crowd had been put outside, Jesus went into the girl's room. He took her hand, and she stood up. [26]The news about this spread all around the area.

[27]When Jesus was leaving there, two blind men followed him. They cried out, "Show kindness to us, Son of David!"[n]

[28]Jesus went inside, and the blind men went with him. He asked the men, "Do you believe that I can make you see again?"

They answered, "Yes, Lord."

[29]Then Jesus touched their eyes and said, "You believe that I can make you see again. So this will happen." [30]Then the men were able to see. But Jesus warned them very strongly, saying, "Don't tell anyone about this." [31]But the blind men left and spread the news about Jesus all around that area.

[32]When the two men were leaving, some people brought another man to Jesus. This man could not talk because he had a demon[d] in him. [33]Jesus forced the demon to leave the man. Then the man who couldn't talk was able to speak. The crowd was amazed and said, "We have never seen anything like this in Israel."

[34]But the Pharisees[d] said, "The leader of demons is the one that gives him power to force demons out."

[35]Jesus traveled through all the towns and villages. He taught in their synagogues[d] and told people the Good News[d] about the kingdom. And he healed all kinds of diseases and sicknesses. [36]He saw the crowds of people and felt sorry for them because they were worried and helpless. They were like sheep without a shepherd. [37]Jesus said to his followers, "There are many people to harvest, but there are only a few workers to help harvest them. [38]God owns the harvest. Pray to him that he will send more workers to help gather his harvest."[n]

10 Jesus called his 12 followers together. He gave them power to drive out evil spirits and to heal every kind of disease and sickness. [2]These are the names of the 12 apostles:[d] Simon (also called Peter) and his brother Andrew; James son of Zebedee, and his brother John; [3]Philip and Bartholomew; Thomas and Matthew, the tax collector; James son of Alphaeus, and Thaddaeus; [4]Simon the Zealot[d] and Judas Iscariot. Judas is the one who turned against Jesus.

[5]These 12 men he sent out with the following order: 'Don't go to the non-Jewish people. And don't go into any town where the Samaritans[d] live. [6]But go to the people of Israel. They are like sheep that are lost. [7]When you go, preach this: 'The kingdom of heaven is coming soon.' [8]Heal the sick. Give dead people life again. Heal those who have harmful skin diseases. Force demons[d] to leave people. I give you these powers freely. So help other people freely. [9]Don't carry any money with you—gold or silver or copper. [10]Don't carry a bag. Take for your trip only the clothes and sandals you are wearing. Don't take a walking stick. A worker should be given the things he needs.

[11]"When you enter a city or town, find some worthy person there and stay in his home until you leave. [12]When you enter that home, say, 'Peace be with you.' [13]If the people there welcome you, let your peace stay there. But if they don't welcome you, take back the peace you wished for them. [14]And if a home or town refuses to welcome you or listen to you, then leave that place. Shake its dust off your feet.[n] [15]I tell you the truth. On the Judgment Day it will be worse for that town than for the towns of Sodom and Gomorrah."

[16]"Listen! I am sending you out, and you will be like sheep among wolves. So be as smart as snakes. But also be like doves and do nothing wrong. [17]Be careful of people. They will arrest you and take you to court. They will whip you in their synagogues.[d] [18]Because of me you will be taken to stand before governors and kings. You will tell them and the non-Jewish people about me. [19]When you are arrested, don't worry about what to say or how you should say it. At that time you will be given the things to say. [20]It will not really be you speaking. The Spirit of your Father will be speaking through you.

[21]"Brothers will turn against their own brothers and give them over to be killed. Fathers will turn against their own children and give them to be killed. Children will fight against their own parents and have them killed. [22]All people will hate you because you follow me. But the person who continues strong until the end will be saved. [23]When you are treated badly in one city, go to another city. I tell you the truth. You will not finish going through all the cities of Israel before the Son of Man[d] comes.

[24]"A student is not better than his teacher. A servant is not better than his master. [25]A student should be satisfied to become like his teacher. A servant should be satisfied to become like his master. If the head of the family is called Beelzebul,[d] then the other members of the family will be called worse names!

[26]"So don't be afraid of those people. Everything that is hidden will be shown. Everything that is secret will be made known. [27]I tell you these things in the dark, but I want you to tell them in the light. I speak these things only to you, but you should tell them to everyone. [28]Don't be afraid of people. They can only kill the body. They cannot kill the soul. The only one you should fear is the One who can destroy the body and the soul in hell. [29]When birds are sold, two small birds cost only a penny. But not even one of the little birds can die without your Father's knowing it. [30]God even knows how many hairs are on your head. [31]So don't be afraid. You are worth much more than many birds.

[32]"If anyone stands before other people and says he believes in me, then I will say that he belongs to me. I will say this before my Father in heaven. [33]But if anyone stands before people and says he does not believe in me, then I will say that he does not belong to me. I will say this before my Father in heaven.

[34]"Don't think that I have come to bring peace to the earth. I did not come to bring peace, but a sword. [35]I have come to make this happen:

'A son will be against his father,
　a daughter will be against her
　　mother,

a daughter-in-law will be against her mother-in-law.

36 A person's enemies will be members of his own family.'

Micah 7:6

37"Whoever loves his father or mother more than he loves me is not worthy to be my follower. Whoever loves his son or daughter more than he loves me is not worthy to be my follower. 38Whoever is not willing to die on a cross and follow me is not worthy of me. 39Whoever tries to hold on to his life will give up true life. Whoever gives up his life for me will hold on to true life. 40Whoever accepts you also accepts me. And whoever accepts me also accepts the One who sent me. 41Whoever meets a prophet[d] and accepts him will receive the reward of a prophet. And whoever accepts a good man because that man is good will receive the reward of a good man. 42Whoever helps one of these little ones because they are my followers will truly get his reward. He will get his reward even if he only gave my follower a cup of cold water."

11 Jesus finished telling these things to his 12 followers. Then he left there and went to the towns in Galilee to teach and preach.

2John the Baptist[d] was in prison, but he heard about the things Christ was doing. So John sent some of his followers to Jesus. 3They asked Jesus, "Are you the man who John said was coming, or should we wait for another one?"

4Jesus answered, "Go back to John and tell him about the things you hear and see: 5The blind can see. The crippled can walk. People with harmful skin diseases are healed. The deaf can hear. The dead are raised to life. And the Good News[d] is told to the poor. 6The person who does not lose faith because of me is blessed."

7As John's followers were leaving, Jesus began talking to the people about John. Jesus said, "What did you go out to the desert to see? A reed[n] blown by the wind? No. 8Really, what did you go out to see? A man dressed in fine clothes? No. Those people who wear fine clothes live in kings' palaces. 9So what did you go out to see? A prophet?[d] Yes, and I tell you, John is more than a

prophet. 10This was written about John in the Scriptures:[d]

'I will send my messenger ahead of you.

He will prepare the way for you.'

Malachi 3:1

11I tell you the truth: John the Baptist is greater than any other man who has ever lived. But even the least important person in the kingdom of heaven is greater than John. 12Since the time John the Baptist came until now, the kingdom of heaven has been going forward in strength. People using force have been trying to take the kingdom. 13All the prophets and the law of Moses spoke until the time John came. They told about the things that would happen. 14And if you will believe the things the law and the prophets said, then you will believe that John is Elijah. The law and the prophets said he would come. 15You people who hear me, listen!

16"What can I say about the people who live today? What are they like? They are like children sitting in the marketplace. One group calls to the other,

17'We played music for you, but you did not dance;

we sang a sad song, but you did not cry.'

18John came, and he did not eat like other people or drink wine. And people say, 'He has a demon.'[d] 19The Son of Man[d] came, eating and drinking wine, and people say, 'Look at him! He eats too much and drinks too much. He is a friend of tax collectors and "sinners."' But wisdom is proved to be right by the things it does."

20Then Jesus criticized the cities where he did most of his miracles.[d] He criticized them because the people there did not change their lives and stop sinning. 21Jesus said, "How terrible for you, Korazin! How terrible for you, Bethsaida! I did many miracles in you. If those same miracles had happened in Tyre and Sidon,[n] then the people there would have changed their lives a long time ago. They would have worn rough cloth and put ashes on themselves to show that they had changed. 22But I tell you, on the Judgment Day it will be worse for you than for Tyre and Sidon. 23And you, Capernaum,[n] will you be lifted up to heaven? No. You will be thrown down

---

11:7 reed It means that John was not weak like grass blown by the wind. **11:21 Tyre and Sidon** Towns where wicked people lived. **11:21, 23 Korazin . . . Bethsaida . . . Capernaum** Towns by Lake Galilee where Jesus preached to the people.

to the depths. I did many miracles in you. If those same miracles had happened in Sodom,[n] its people would have stopped sinning, and it would still be a city today. [24]But I tell you it will be worse for you on the Judgment Day than for Sodom."

[25]Then Jesus said, "I thank you, Father, Lord of heaven and earth. I praise you because you have hidden these things from the people who are wise and smart. But you have shown them to those who are like little children. [26]Yes, Father, this is what you really wanted.

[27]"My Father has given me all things. No one knows the Son—only the Father knows the Son. And no one knows the Father—only the Son knows the Father. And the only people who will know about the Father are those whom the Son chooses to tell.

[28]"Come to me, all of you who are tired and have heavy loads. I will give you rest. [29]Accept my work and learn from me. I am gentle and humble in spirit. And you will find rest for your souls. [30]The work that I ask you to accept is easy. The load I give you to carry is not heavy."

12 About that same time, Jesus was walking through some fields of grain on a Sabbath[d] day. His followers were with him, and they were hungry. So they began to pick the grain and eat it. [2]The Pharisees[d] saw this, and they said to Jesus, "Look! Your followers are doing something that is against the Jewish law to do on the Sabbath day."

[3]Jesus answered, "Have you not read what David did when he and the people with him were hungry? [4]David went into God's house. He and those with him ate the bread that was made holy for God. It was against the law for them to eat that bread. Only the priests were allowed to eat it. [5]And have you not read in the law of Moses that on every Sabbath day the priests in the Temple[d] break this law about the Sabbath day? But the priests are not wrong for doing that. [6]I tell you that there is something here that is greater than the Temple. [7]The Scripture[d] says, 'I want faithful love more than I want animal sacrifices.'[n] You don't really know what those words mean. If you understood them, you would not judge those who have done nothing wrong.

[8]"The Son of Man[d] is Lord of the Sabbath day."

[9]Jesus left there and went into their synagogue.[d] [10]In the synagogue, there was a man with a crippled hand. Some Jews there were looking for a reason to accuse Jesus of doing wrong. So they asked him, "Is it right to heal on the Sabbath[d] day?"[n]

[11]Jesus answered, "If any of you has a sheep, and it falls into a ditch on the Sabbath day, then you will take the sheep and help it out of the ditch. [12]Surely a man is more important than a sheep. So the law of Moses allows people to do good things on the Sabbath day."

[13]Then Jesus said to the man with the crippled hand, "Let me see your hand." The man put his hand out, and the hand became well again, the same as the other hand. [14]But the Pharisees[d] left and made plans to kill Jesus.

[15]Jesus knew what the Pharisees[d] were doing, so he left that place. Many people followed him, and he healed all who were sick. [16]But Jesus warned the people not to tell who he was. [17]He did these things to make come true what Isaiah the prophet[d] had said:

[18]"Here is my servant whom I have chosen.
I love him, and I am pleased with him.
I will put my Spirit[d] in him.
Then he will tell how I will judge all people fairly.
[19]He will not argue or shout.
No one will hear his voice in the streets.
[20]He will not break a crushed blade of grass.
He will not put out even a weak flame.
He will continue until he makes fair judgment win the victory.
[21] In him will the nations find hope."   *Isaiah 42:1-4*

[22]Then some people brought a man to Jesus. This man was blind and could not talk, because he had a demon.[d] Jesus healed the man, and the man could talk and see. [23]All the people were amazed. They said, "Perhaps this man is the Son of David!"[d]

[24]The Pharisees[d] heard the people say-

11:23 Sodom City that God destroyed because the people were so evil. **12:7 'I . . . sacrifices.'** Quotation from Hosea 6:6. **12:10 "Is it right . . . day?"** It was against Jewish law to work on the Sabbath day.

ing this. The Pharisees said, "Jesus uses the power of Beelzebul[d] to force demons out of people. Beelzebul is the ruler of demons."

[25]Jesus knew what the Pharisees were thinking. So he said to them, "Every kingdom that is fighting against itself will be destroyed. And every city that is divided will fall. And every family that is divided cannot succeed. [26]So if Satan forces out his own demons, then Satan is divided, and his kingdom will not continue. [27]You say that I use the power of Satan when I force out demons. If that is true, then what power do your people use when they force out demons? So your own people prove that you are wrong. [28]But if I use the power of God's Spirit[d] to force out demons, this shows that the kingdom of God has come to you.

[29]"If anyone wants to enter a strong man's house and steal his things, first he must tie up the strong man. Then he can steal the things from the strong man's house.

[30]"If anyone is not with me, then he is against me. He who does not work with me is working against me. [31]So I tell you, people can be forgiven for every sin they do. And people can be forgiven for every bad thing they say. But if anyone speaks against the Holy Spirit, then he will not be forgiven. [32]Anyone who says things against the Son of Man[d] can be forgiven. But anyone who says things against the Holy Spirit will not be forgiven. He will not be forgiven now or in the future.

[33]"If you want good fruit, you must make the tree good. If your tree is not good, then it will have bad fruit. A tree is known by the kind of fruit it produces. [34]You snakes! You are evil people! How can you say anything good? The mouth speaks the things that are in the heart. [35]A good person has good things in his heart. And so he speaks the good things that come from his heart. But an evil person has evil in his heart. So he speaks the evil things that come from his heart. [36]And I tell you that people will have to explain about every careless thing they have said. This will happen on the Judgment Day. [37]The words you have said will be used to judge you. Some of your words will prove you right, but some of your words will prove you guilty."

[38]Then some of the Pharisees[d] and teachers of the law answered Jesus. They said, "Teacher, we want to see you work a miracle[d] as a sign."

[39]Jesus answered, "Evil and sinful people are the ones who want to see a miracle for a sign. But no sign will be given to them. The only sign will be what happened to the prophet[d] Jonah. [40]Jonah was in the stomach of the big fish for three days and three nights. In the same way, the Son of Man[d] will be in the grave three days and three nights. [41]And on the Judgment Day the men from Nineveh[n] will stand up with you people who live today. They will show that you are guilty because when Jonah preached to them, they were sorry and changed their lives. And I tell you that someone greater than Jonah is here! [42]On the Judgment Day, the Queen of the South[n] will stand up with you people who live today. She will show that you are guilty because she came from far away to listen to Solomon's wise teaching. And I tell you that someone greater than Solomon is here!

[43]"When an evil spirit comes out of a man, it travels through dry places looking for a place to rest. But it finds no place to rest. [44]So the spirit says, 'I will go back to the home I left.' When the spirit comes back to the man, the spirit finds the home still empty. The home is swept clean and made neat. [45]Then the evil spirit goes out and brings seven other spirits even more evil than it is. Then all the spirits go into the man and live there. And that man has even more trouble than he had before. It is the same way with the evil people who live today."

[46]While Jesus was talking to the people, his mother and brothers stood outside. They wanted to talk to him. [47]Someone told Jesus, "Your mother and brothers are waiting for you outside. They want to talk to you."

[48]He answered, "Who is my mother? Who are my brothers?" [49]Then he pointed to his followers and said, "See! These people are my mother and my brothers. [50]My true brothers and sisters and mother are those who do the things that my Father in heaven wants."

12:41 Nineveh The city where Jonah preached to warn the people. Read Jonah 3. **12:42 Queen of the South** The Queen of Sheba. She traveled 1,000 miles to learn God's wisdom from Solomon. Read 1 Kings 10:1-13.

13 That same day Jesus went out of the house and sat by the lake. ²Large crowds gathered around him. So Jesus got into a boat and sat, while the people stayed on the shore. ³Then Jesus used stories to teach them many things. He said: "A farmer went out to plant his seed. ⁴While he was planting, some seed fell by the road. The birds came and ate all that seed. ⁵Some seed fell on rocky ground, where there wasn't enough dirt. That seed grew very fast, because the ground was not deep. ⁶But when the sun rose, the plants dried up because they did not have deep roots. ⁷Some other seed fell among thorny weeds. The weeds grew and choked the good plants. ⁸Some other seed fell on good ground where it grew and became grain. Some plants made 100 times more grain. Other plants made 60 times more grain, and some made 30 times more grain. ⁹You people who hear me, listen!"

¹⁰The followers came to Jesus and asked, "Why do you use stories to teach the people?"

¹¹Jesus answered, "Only you can know the secret truths about the kingdom of heaven. Other people cannot know these secret truths. ¹²The person who has something will be given more. And he will have all he needs. But the person who does not have much, even what he has will be taken from him. ¹³This is why I use stories to teach the people: They see, but they don't really see. They hear, but they don't really understand. ¹⁴So they show that the things Isaiah said about them are true:

'You will listen and listen, but you
   will not understand.
You will look and look, but you
   will not learn.
¹⁵For these people have become
   stubborn.
They do not hear with their ears.
And they have closed their eyes.
Otherwise they might really
   understand
what they see with their eyes
and hear with their ears.
They might really understand in
   their minds.
If they did this, they would come
   back to me and be forgiven.'
              Isaiah 6:9-10

¹⁶But you are blessed. You understand the things you see with your eyes. And you understand the things you hear with

your ears. ¹⁷I tell you the truth. Many prophets[d] and good people wanted to see the things that you now see. But they did not see them. And many prophets and good people wanted to hear the things that you now hear. But they did not hear them.

¹⁸"So listen to the meaning of that story about the farmer. ¹⁹What is the seed that fell by the road? That seed is like the person who hears the teaching about the kingdom but does not understand it. The Evil One comes and takes away the things that were planted in that person's heart. ²⁰And what is the seed that fell on rocky ground? That seed is like the person who hears the teaching and quickly accepts it with joy. ²¹But he does not let the teaching go deep into his life. He keeps it only a short time. When trouble or persecution comes because of the teaching he accepted, then he quickly gives up. ²²And what is the seed that fell among the thorny weeds? That seed is like the person who hears the teaching but lets worries about this life and love of money stop that teaching from growing. So the teaching does not produce fruit[n] in that person's life. ²³But what is the seed that fell on the good ground? That seed is like the person who hears the teaching and understands it. That person grows and produces fruit, sometimes 100 times more, sometimes 60 times more, and sometimes 30 times more."

²⁴Then Jesus told them another story. He said, "The kingdom of heaven is like a man who planted good seed in his field. ²⁵That night, when everyone was asleep, his enemy came and planted weeds among the wheat. Then the enemy went away. ²⁶Later, the wheat grew and heads of grain grew on the wheat plants. But at the same time the weeds also grew. ²⁷Then the man's servants came to him and said, 'You planted good seed in your field. Where did the weeds come from?' ²⁸The man answered, 'An enemy planted weeds.' The servants asked, 'Do you want us to pull up the weeds?' ²⁹The man answered, 'No, because when you pull up the weeds, you might also pull up the wheat. ³⁰Let the weeds and the wheat grow together until the harvest time. At harvest time I will tell the workers this: First gather the weeds and tie them together to be

13:22 produce fruit To produce fruit means to have in your life the good things God wants.

burned. Then gather the wheat and bring it to my barn.'"

[31]Then Jesus told another story: "The kingdom of heaven is like a mustard seed. A man plants the seed in his field. [32]That seed is the smallest of all seeds. But when it grows, it is one of the largest garden plants. It becomes a tree, big enough for the wild birds to come and make nests in its branches."

[33]Then Jesus told another story: "The kingdom of heaven is like yeast that a woman mixes into a big bowl of flour. The yeast makes all the dough rise."

[34]Jesus used stories to tell all these things to the people. He always used stories to teach people. [35]This is as the prophet[d] said:

"I will speak using stories;
I will tell things that have been
    secret since the world was
    made."   *Psalm 78:2*

[36]Then Jesus left the crowd and went into the house. His followers came to him and said, "Explain to us the meaning of the story about the weeds in the field."

[37]Jesus answered, "The man who planted the good seed in the field is the Son of Man.[d] [38]The field is the world. And the good seed are all of God's children in the kingdom. The weeds are those people who belong to the Evil One. [39]And the enemy who planted the bad seed is the devil. The harvest time is the end of the world. And the workers who gather are God's angels.

[40]"The weeds are pulled up and burned in the fire. It will be this way at the end of the world. [41]The Son of Man will send out his angels. They will gather out of his kingdom all who cause sin and all who do evil. [42]The angels will throw them into the blazing furnace. There the people will cry and grind their teeth with pain. [43]Then the good people will shine like the sun in the kingdom of their Father. You people who hear me, listen!

[44]"The kingdom of heaven is like a treasure hidden in a field. One day a man found the treasure, and then he hid it in the field again. The man was very happy to find the treasure. He went and sold everything that he owned to buy that field.

[45]"Also, the kingdom of heaven is like a man looking for fine pearls. [46]One day he found a very valuable pearl. The man went and sold everything he had to buy that pearl.

[47]"Also, the kingdom of heaven is like a net that was put into the lake. The net caught many different kinds of fish. [48]When it was full, the fishermen pulled the net to the shore. They sat down and put all the good fish in baskets. Then they threw away the bad fish. [49]It will be this way at the end of the world. The angels will come and separate the evil people from the good people. [50]The angels will throw the evil people into the blazing furnace. In that place the people will cry and grind their teeth with pain."

[51]Jesus asked his followers, "Do you understand all these things?"

They answered, "Yes, we understand."

[52]Then Jesus said to them, "So every teacher of the law who has been taught about the kingdom of heaven is like the owner of a house. He has both new things and old things saved in his house. And he brings out both those new things and old things."

[53]When Jesus finished teaching with these stories, he left there. [54]He went to the town where he grew up. He taught the people in the synagogue,[d] and they were amazed. They said, "Where did this man get this wisdom and this power to do miracles?[d] [55]He is only the son of the carpenter. And his mother is Mary. His brothers are James, Joseph, Simon and Judas. [56]And all his sisters are here with us. So where does this man get all these things?" [57]And the people refused to accept Jesus.

But Jesus said to them, "A prophet[d] is honored everywhere except in his own town or in his own home."

[58]The people there did not believe in Jesus. So Jesus did not do many miracles there.

14 At that time Herod, the ruler of Galilee, heard the reports about Jesus. [2]So Herod said to his servants, "Jesus is really John the Baptist.[d] He has risen from death. That is why he is able to do these miracles."[d]

[3]Sometime before this, Herod had arrested John, tied him up, and put him into prison. Herod did this because of Herodias. Herodias was the wife of Philip, Herod's brother. [4]Herod arrested John because he told Herod: "It is not right for you to have Herodias." [5]Herod wanted to kill John, but he was afraid of the people. They believed that John was a prophet.[d]

[6]On Herod's birthday, the daughter of Herodias danced for Herod and his

guests. Herod was very pleased with her, [7]so he promised he would give her anything she wanted. [8]Herodias told her daughter what to ask for. So she said to Herod, "Give me the head of John the Baptist here on a platter." [9]King Herod was very sad. But he had promised to give her anything she wanted, and the people eating with him had heard his promise. So Herod ordered that what she asked for be done. [10]He sent men to the prison to cut off John's head. [11]And the men brought John's head on a platter and gave it to the girl. She took it to her mother, Herodias. [12]John's followers came and got his body and buried it. Then they went and told Jesus what happened.

[13]When Jesus heard what happened to John, Jesus left in a boat. He went to a lonely place by himself. But when the crowds heard about it, they followed him on foot from the towns. [14]When Jesus arrived, he saw a large crowd. He felt sorry for them and healed those who were sick.

[15]Late that afternoon, his followers came to Jesus and said, "No one lives in this place. And it is already late. Send the people away so they can go to the towns and buy food for themselves."

[16]Jesus answered, "They don't need to go away. You give them some food to eat."

[17]The followers answered, "But we have only five loaves of bread and two fish."

[18]Jesus said, "Bring the bread and the fish to me." [19]Then he told the people to sit down on the grass. He took the five loaves of bread and the two fish. Then he looked to heaven and thanked God for the food. Jesus divided the loaves of bread. He gave them to his followers, and they gave the bread to the people. [20]All the people ate and were satisfied. After they finished eating, the followers filled 12 baskets with the pieces of food that were not eaten. [21]There were about 5,000 men there who ate, as well as women and children.

[22]Then Jesus made his followers get into the boat. He told them to go ahead of him to the other side of the lake. Jesus stayed there to tell the people they could go home. [23]After he said good-bye to them, he went alone up into the hills to pray. It was late, and Jesus was there

alone. [24]By this time, the boat was already far away on the lake. The boat was having trouble because of the waves, and the wind was blowing against it.

[25]Between three and six o'clock in the morning, Jesus' followers were still in the boat. Jesus came to them. He was walking on the water. [26]When the followers saw him walking on the water, they were afraid. They said, "It's a ghost!" and cried out in fear.

[27]But Jesus quickly spoke to them. He said, "Have courage! It is I! Don't be afraid."

[28]Peter said, "Lord, if that is really you, then tell me to come to you on the water."

[29]Jesus said, "Come."

And Peter left the boat and walked on the water to Jesus. [30]But when Peter saw the wind and the waves, he became afraid and began to sink. He shouted, "Lord, save me!"

[31]Then Jesus reached out his hand and caught Peter. Jesus said, "Your faith is small. Why did you doubt?"

[32]After Peter and Jesus were in the boat, the wind became calm. [33]Then those who were in the boat worshiped Jesus and said, "Truly you are the Son of God!"

[34]After they crossed the lake, they came to the shore at Gennesaret. [35]The people there saw Jesus and knew who he was. So they told people all around there that Jesus had come. They brought all their sick to him. [36]They begged Jesus to let them just touch the edge of his coat to be healed. And all the sick people who touched it were healed.

15 Then some Pharisees[d] and teachers of the law came to Jesus from Jerusalem. They asked him, [2]"Why do your followers not obey the rules given to us by the great people who lived before us? Your followers don't wash their hands before they eat!"

[3]Jesus answered, "And why do you refuse to obey God's command so that you can follow those rules you have? [4]God said, 'Honor your father and mother.'[n] And God also said, 'Anyone who says cruel things to his father or mother must be put to death.'[n] [5]But you say that a person can tell his father or mother, 'I have something I could use to help you. But I will not use it for you. I will give it

15:4 'Honor . . . mother.' Quotation from Exodus 20:12; Deuteronomy 5:16.   **15:4** 'Anyone . . . death.' Quotation from Exodus 21:17.

to God.' [6]You teach that person not to
honor his father. You teach that it is not
important to do what God said. You
think that it is more important to follow
the rules you have. [7]You are hypocrites![d]
Isaiah was right when he spoke about
you:

[8]'These people show honor to me
   with words.
But their hearts are far from me.
[9]Their worship of me is worthless.
   The things they teach are nothing
   but human rules they have
   memorized.'"   *Isaiah 29:13*

[10]Jesus called the crowd to him. He
said, "Listen and understand what I am
saying. [11]It is not what a person puts into
his mouth that makes him unclean.[d] It is
what comes out of his mouth that makes
him unclean."

[12]Then his followers came to Jesus
and asked, "Do you know that the Pharisees are angry because of what you
said?"

[13]Jesus answered, "Every plant that
my Father in heaven has not planted
himself will be pulled up by the roots.
[14]Stay away from the Pharisees. They
are blind leaders. And if a blind man
leads another blind man, then both men
will fall into a ditch."

[15]Peter said, "Explain the story to us."

[16]Jesus said, "You still have trouble
understanding? [17]Surely you know that
all the food that enters the mouth goes
into the stomach. Then that food goes
out of the body. [18]But what a person says
with his mouth comes from the way he
thinks. And these are the things that
make him unclean. [19]Out of his mind
come evil thoughts, murder, adultery,[d]
sexual sins, stealing, lying, and saying
bad things against other people. [20]These
things make a person unclean. But eating with unwashed hands does not
make him unclean."

[21]Jesus left that place and went to the
area of Tyre and Sidon. [22]A Canaanite
woman from that area came to Jesus.
The woman cried out, "Lord, Son of David,[d] please help me! My daughter has a
demon,[d] and she is suffering very
much."

[23]But Jesus did not answer the
woman. So the followers came to Jesus
and begged him, "Tell the woman to go
away. She is following us and shouting."

[24]Jesus answered, "God sent me only
to the lost sheep, the people of Israel."

[25]Then the woman came to Jesus
again. She bowed before him and said,
"Lord, help me!"

[26]Jesus answered, "It is not right to
take the children's bread and give it to
the dogs."

[27]The woman said, "Yes, Lord, but
even the dogs eat the pieces of food that
fall from their masters' table."

[28]Then Jesus answered, "Woman, you
have great faith! I will do what you
asked me to do." And at that moment
the woman's daughter was healed.

[29]Then Jesus left that place and went
to the shore of Lake Galilee. He went up
on a hill and sat there.

[30]Great crowds came to Jesus. They
brought their sick with them: the lame,
the blind, the crippled, the dumb and
many others. They put them at Jesus'
feet, and he healed them. [31]The crowd
was amazed when they saw that people
who could not speak were able to speak
again. The crippled were made strong
again. Those who could not walk were
able to walk again. The blind were able
to see again. And they praised the God
of Israel for this.

[32]Jesus called his followers to him and
said, "I feel sorry for these people. They
have been with me three days, and now
they have nothing to eat. I don't want
to send them away hungry. They might
faint while going home."

[33]His followers asked him, "Where
can we get enough bread to feed all
these people? We are far away from any
town."

[34]Jesus asked, "How many loaves of
bread do you have?"

They answered, "We have seven
loaves and a few small fish."

[35]Jesus told the people to sit on the
ground. [36]He took the seven loaves of
bread and the fish and gave thanks to
God for the food. Then Jesus divided the
food and gave it to his followers. They
gave the food to the people. [37]All the
people ate and were satisfied. After this,
the followers filled seven baskets with
the pieces of food that were not eaten.
[38]There were about 4,000 men there who
ate, besides women and children. [39]After
they ate, Jesus told the people to go
home. He got into the boat and went to
the area of Magadan.

16 The Pharisees[d] and Sadducees[d]
came to Jesus. They wanted to
trap him. So they asked him to show
them a miracle[d] to prove that he was
from God.

[2]Jesus answered, "When you see the sunset, you know what the weather will be. If the sky is red, then you say we will have good weather. [3]And in the morning if the sky is dark and red, then you say that it will be a rainy day. You see these signs in the sky, and you know what they mean. In the same way, you see the things that are happening now. But you don't know their meaning. [4]Evil and sinful people ask for a miracle as a sign. But they will have no sign—only the sign of Jonah."[n] Then Jesus left them and went away.

[5]Jesus and his followers went across the lake. But the followers forgot to bring bread. [6]Jesus said to them, "Be careful! Guard against the yeast of the Pharisees[d] and the Sadducees."[d]

[7]The followers discussed the meaning of this. They said, "Did Jesus say this because we forgot to bring bread?"

[8]Jesus knew that they were talking about this. So he asked them, "Why are you talking about not having bread? Your faith is small. [9]You still don't understand? Remember the five loaves of bread that fed the 5,000 people? And remember that you filled many baskets with bread after the people finished eating? [10]And remember the seven loaves of bread that fed the 4,000 people? Remember that you filled many baskets then also? [11]So I was not talking to you about bread. Why don't you understand that? I am telling you to be careful and guard against the yeast of the Pharisees and the Sadducees." [12]Then the followers understood what Jesus meant. He was not telling them to guard against the yeast used in bread. He was telling them to guard against the teaching of the Pharisees and the Sadducees.

[13]Jesus went to the area of Caesarea Philippi. He said to his followers, "I am the Son of Man.[d] Who do the people say I am?"

[14]They answered, "Some people say you are John the Baptist.[d] Others say you are Elijah. And others say that you are Jeremiah or one of the prophets."[d]

[15]Then Jesus asked them, "And who do you say I am?"

[16]Simon Peter answered, "You are the Christ,[d] the Son of the living God."

[17]Jesus answered, "You are blessed, Simon son of Jonah. No person taught you that. My Father in heaven showed you who I am. [18]So I tell you, you are Peter.[n] And I will build my church on this rock. The power of death will not be able to defeat my church. [19]I will give you the keys of the kingdom of heaven. The things you don't allow on earth will be the things that God does not allow. The things you allow on earth will be the things that God allows." [20]Then Jesus warned his followers not to tell anyone that he was the Christ.

[21]From that time on Jesus began telling his followers that he must go to Jerusalem. He explained that the older Jewish leaders, the leading priests, and the teachers of the law would make him suffer many things. And he told them that he must be killed. Then, on the third day, he would be raised from death.

[22]Peter took Jesus aside and began to criticize him. Peter said, "God save you from those things, Lord! Those things will never happen to you!"

[23]Then Jesus said to Peter, "Go away from me, Satan![n] You are not helping me! You don't care about the things of God. You care only about things that men think are important."

[24]Then Jesus said to his followers, "If anyone wants to follow me, he must say 'no' to the things he wants. He must be willing even to die on a cross, and he must follow me. [25]Whoever wants to save his life will give up true life. And whoever gives up his life for me will have true life. [26]It is worth nothing for a man to have the whole world if he loses his soul. He could never pay enough to buy back his soul. [27]The Son of Man[d] will come again with his Father's glory and with his angels. At that time, he will reward everyone for what he has done. [28]I tell you the truth. There are some people standing here who, before they die, will see the Son of Man coming with his kingdom."

17 Six days later, Jesus took Peter, James, and John the brother of James up on a high mountain. They were all alone there. [2]While they watched, Jesus was changed. His face became bright like the sun. And his clothes became white as light. [3]Then two men

---

16:4 sign of Jonah Jonah's three days in the big fish are like Jesus' three days in the tomb. The story about Jonah is in the book of Jonah. **16:18 Peter** The Greek name "Peter," like the Aramaic name "Cephas," means "rock." **16:23 Satan** Name for the devil, meaning "the enemy." Jesus means that Peter was talking like Satan.

were there, talking with him. The men were Moses and Elijah.[n]

[4] Peter said to Jesus, "Lord, it is good that we are here. If you want, I will put three tents here—one for you, one for Moses, and one for Elijah."

[5] While Peter was talking, a bright cloud covered them. A voice came from the cloud. The voice said, "This is my Son and I love him. I am very pleased with him. Obey him!"

[6] The followers with Jesus heard the voice. They were so frightened that they fell to the ground. [7] But Jesus went to them and touched them. He said, "Stand up. Don't be afraid." [8] When the followers looked up, they saw Jesus was now alone.

[9] When Jesus and the followers were coming down the mountain, Jesus commanded them, "Don't tell anyone about the things you saw on the mountain. Wait until the Son of Man[d] has been raised from death. Then you may tell."

[10] The followers asked Jesus, "Why do the teachers of the law say that Elijah must come first, before the Christ[d] comes?"

[11] Jesus answered, "They are right to say that Elijah is coming. And it is true that Elijah will make everything the way it should be. [12] But I tell you, Elijah has already come. People did not know who he was. They did to him everything they wanted to do. It will be the same with the Son of Man. Those same people will make the Son of Man suffer." [13] Then the followers understood that Jesus was talking about John the Baptist.[d]

[14] Jesus and his followers went back to the crowd. A man came to Jesus and bowed before him. [15] The man said, "Lord, please help my son. He has epilepsy[n] and is suffering very much. He often falls into the fire or into the water. [16] I brought him to your followers, but they could not cure him."

[17] Jesus answered, "You people have no faith. Your lives are all wrong. How long must I stay with you? How long must I continue to be patient with you? Bring the boy here." [18] Jesus gave a strong command to the demon[d] inside the boy. Then the demon came out, and the boy was healed.

[19] The followers came to Jesus when he was alone. They said, "Why couldn't we force the demon out?"

[20] Jesus answered, "You were not able to drive out the demon because your faith is too small. I tell you the truth. If your faith is as big as a mustard seed,[n] you can say to this mountain, 'Move from here to there.' And the mountain will move. All things will be possible for you." [21] [n]

[22] Later, the followers met together in Galilee. Jesus said to them, "The Son of Man[d] will be given into the control of some men. [23] They will kill him, but on the third day he will be raised from death." And the followers were filled with sadness.

[24] Jesus and his followers went to Capernaum. There some men came to Peter. They were the men who collected the Temple[d] tax. They asked, "Does your teacher pay the Temple tax?"

[25] Peter answered, "Yes, Jesus pays the tax."

Peter went into the house where Jesus was. Before Peter could speak, Jesus said to him, "The kings on the earth collect different kinds of taxes. But who are the people who pay the taxes? Are they the king's children? Or do others pay the taxes? What do you think?"

[26] Peter answered, "Other people pay the taxes."

Jesus said to Peter, "Then the children of the king don't have to pay taxes. [27] But we don't want to make these tax collectors angry. So go to the lake and fish. After you catch the first fish, open its mouth. Inside its mouth you will find a coin. Take that coin and give it to the tax collectors. That will pay the tax for you and me."

18 At that time the followers came to Jesus and asked, "Who is greatest in the kingdom of heaven?"

[2] Jesus called a little child to him. He stood the child before the followers. [3] Then he said, "I tell you the truth. You must change and become like little children. If you don't do this, you will never enter the kingdom of heaven. [4] The greatest person in the kingdom of heaven is the one who makes himself humble like this child.

[5] "Whoever accepts a little child in my name accepts me. [6] If one of these little

---

17:3 Moses and Elijah Two of the most important Jewish leaders in the past. **17:15 epilepsy** A disease that causes a person sometimes to lose control of his body, and maybe faint, shake strongly, or not be able to move. **17:20 mustard seed** This seed is very small, but the plant grows taller than a man. **17:21 Verse 21** Some Greek copies add verse 21: "That kind of spirit comes out only if you use prayer and give up eating."

children believes in me, and someone causes that child to sin, then it will be very bad for that person. It would be better for him to have a large stone tied around his neck and be drowned in the sea. [7]How terrible for the people of the world because of the things that cause them to sin. Such things will happen. But how terrible for the one who causes them to happen. [8]If your hand or your foot causes you to sin, cut it off and throw it away. It is better for you to have only part of your body but have life forever. That is much better than to have two hands and two feet but be thrown into the fire that burns forever. [9]If your eye causes you to sin, take it out and throw it away. It is better for you to have only one eye but have life forever. That is much better than to have two eyes but be thrown into the fire of hell.

[10]"Be careful. Don't think these little children are worth nothing. I tell you that they have angels in heaven who are always with my Father in heaven. [11] [n]

[12]"If a man has 100 sheep, but 1 of the sheep gets lost, he will leave the other 99 sheep on the hill. He will go to look for the lost sheep. [13]And if he finds it, he is happier about that 1 sheep than about the 99 that were never lost. I tell you the truth. [14]In the same way, your Father in heaven does not want any of these little children to be lost.

[15]"If your brother sins against you, go and tell him what he did wrong. Do this in private. If he listens to you, then you have helped him to be your brother again. [16]But if he refuses to listen, then go to him again and take one or two other people with you. 'Every case may be proved by two or three witnesses.' [n] [17]If he refuses to listen to them, then tell it to the church. If he refuses to listen to the church, then treat him as you would one who does not believe in God. Treat him as if he were a tax collector.

[18]"I tell you the truth. The things you don't allow on earth will be the things God does not allow. The things you allow on earth will be the things that God allows.

[19]"Also, I tell you that if two of you on earth agree about something, then you can pray for it. And the thing you ask for will be done for you by my Father in heaven. [20]This is true because if two or three people come together in my name, I am there with them."

[21]Then Peter came to Jesus and asked, "Lord, when my brother sins against me, how many times must I forgive him? Should I forgive him as many as 7 times?"

[22]Jesus answered, "I tell you, you must forgive him more than 7 times. You must forgive him even if he does wrong to you 70 times 7.

[23]"The kingdom of heaven is like a king who decided to collect the money his servants owed him. [24]So the king began to collect his money. One servant owed him several million dollars. [25]But the servant did not have enough money to pay his master, the king. So the master ordered that everything the servant owned should be sold, even the servant's wife and children. The money would be used to pay the king what the servant owed.

[26]"But the servant fell on his knees and begged, 'Be patient with me. I will pay you everything I owe.' [27]The master felt sorry for his servant. So the master told the servant he did not have to pay. He let the servant go free.

[28]"Later, that same servant found another servant who owed him a few dollars. The servant grabbed the other servant around the neck and said, 'Pay me the money you owe me!'

[29]"The other servant fell on his knees and begged him, 'Be patient with me. I will pay you everything I owe.'

[30]"But the first servant refused to be patient. He threw the other servant into prison until he could pay everything he owed. [31]All the other servants saw what happened. They were very sorry. So they went and told their master all that had happened.

[32]"Then the master called his servant in and said, 'You evil servant! You begged me to forget what you owed. So I told you that you did not have to pay anything. [33]I had mercy on you. You should have had the same mercy on that other servant.' [34]The master was very angry, and he put the servant in prison to be punished. The servant had to stay in prison until he could pay everything he owed.

[35]"This king did what my heavenly Father will do to you if you do not forgive your brother from your heart."

19 After Jesus said all these things, he left Galilee. He went into the area of Judea on the other side of the Jordan River. [2] Large crowds followed Jesus, and he healed them there.

[3] Some Pharisees[d] came to Jesus and tried to trick him. They asked, "Is it right for a man to divorce his wife for any reason he chooses?"

[4] Jesus answered, "Surely you have read in the Scriptures:[d] When God made the world, 'he made them male and female.'[n] [5] And God said, 'So a man will leave his father and mother and be united with his wife. And the two people will become one body.'[n] [6] So the two are not two, but one. God joined the two people together. No person should separate them."

[7] The Pharisees asked, "Why then did Moses give a command for a man to divorce his wife by giving her divorce papers?"

[8] Jesus answered, "Moses allowed you to divorce your wives because you refused to accept God's teaching. But divorce was not allowed in the beginning. [9] I tell you that anyone who divorces his wife and marries another woman is guilty of adultery.[d] The only reason for a man to divorce and marry again is if his first wife has sexual relations with another man."

[10] The followers said to him, "If that is the only reason a man can divorce his wife, then it is better not to marry."

[11] Jesus answered, "Not everyone can accept this truth about marriage. But God has made some able to accept it. [12] There are different reasons why some men cannot marry. Some men were born without the ability to become fathers. Others were made that way later in life by other people. And other men have given up marriage because of the kingdom of heaven. But the person who can marry should accept this teaching about marriage."[n]

[13] Then the people brought their little children to Jesus so that he could put his hands on them[n] and pray for them. When his followers saw this, they told the people to stop bringing their children to Jesus. [14] But Jesus said, "Let the little children come to me. Don't stop them, because the kingdom of heaven belongs to people who are like these children." [15] After Jesus put his hands on the children, he left there.

[16] A man came to Jesus and asked, "Teacher, what good thing must I do to have life forever?"

[17] Jesus answered, "Why do you ask me about what is good? Only God is good. But if you want to have life forever, obey the commands."

[18] The man asked, "Which commands?"

Jesus answered, "'You must not murder anyone. You must not be guilty of adultery.[d] You must not steal. You must not tell lies about your neighbor in court. [19] Honor your father and mother.'[n] Love your neighbor as you love yourself.'"[n]

[20] The young man said, "I have obeyed all these things. What else do I need to do?"

[21] Jesus answered, "If you want to be perfect, then go and sell all the things you own. Give the money to the poor. If you do this, you will have a treasure in heaven. Then come and follow me!"

[22] But when the young man heard this, he became very sad because he was very rich. So he left Jesus.

[23] Then Jesus said to his followers, "I tell you the truth. It will be very hard for a rich person to enter the kingdom of heaven. [24] Yes, I tell you that it is easier for a camel to go through the eye of a needle than for a rich person to enter the kingdom of God."

[25] When the followers heard this, they were very surprised. They asked, "Then who can be saved?"

[26] Jesus looked at them and said, "This is something that men cannot do. But God can do all things."

[27] Peter said to Jesus, "We left everything we had and followed you. So what will we have?"

[28] Jesus said to them, "I tell you the truth. When the new age comes, the Son of Man[d] will sit on his great throne. And all of you who followed me will also sit on 12 thrones. And you will judge the 12 tribes[d] of Israel. [29] And everyone who has left houses, brothers, sisters, father, mother, children, or farms to follow me will get much more than he left. And he

---

19:4 'he made . . . female.' Quotation from Genesis 1:27 or 5:2. **19:5 'So . . . body.'** Quotation from Genesis 2:24. **19:12 But . . . marriage.** This may also mean, "The person who can accept this teaching about not marrying should accept it." **19:13 put his hands on them** Showing that Jesus gave special blessings to these children. **19:18-19 'You . . . mother.'** Quotation from Exodus 20:12-16; Deuteronomy 5:16-20. **19:19 'Love . . . yourself.'** Quotation from Leviticus 19:18.

will have life forever. [30]Many who have the highest place in life now will have the lowest place in the future. And many who have the lowest place now will have the highest place in the future.

20 [1]"The kingdom of heaven is like a man who owned some land. One morning, he went out very early to hire some people to work in his vineyard. [2]The man agreed to pay the workers one silver coin[n] for working that day. Then he sent them into the vineyard to work. [3]About nine o'clock the man went to the marketplace and saw some other people standing there, doing nothing. [4]So he said to them, 'If you go and work in my vineyard, I will pay you what your work is worth.' [5]So they went to work in the vineyard. The man went out again about twelve o'clock and again at three o'clock. Both times he hired people to work in his vineyard. [6]About five o'clock the man went to the marketplace again. He saw others standing there. He asked them, 'Why did you stand here all day doing nothing?' [7]They answered, 'No one gave us a job.' The man said to them, 'Then you can go and work in my vineyard.'

[8]"At the end of the day, the owner of the vineyard said to the boss of all the workers, 'Call the workers and pay them. Start by paying the last people I hired. Then pay all of them, ending with the workers I hired first.'

[9]"The workers who were hired at five o'clock came to get their pay. Each worker received one silver coin. [10]Then the workers who were hired first came to get their pay. They thought they would be paid more than the others. But each one of them also received one silver coin. [11]When they got their silver coin, they complained to the man who owned the land. [12]They said, 'Those people were hired last and worked only one hour. But you paid them the same as you paid us. And we worked hard all day in the hot sun.' [13]But the man who owned the vineyard said to one of those workers, 'Friend, I am being fair to you. You agreed to work for one silver coin. [14]So take your pay and go. I want to give the man who was hired last the same pay that I gave you. [15]I can do what I want with my own money. Are you jealous because I am good to those people?'

[16]"So those who have the last place now will have the first place in the future. And those who have the first place now will have the last place in the future."

[17]Jesus was going to Jerusalem. His 12 followers were with him. While they were on the way, Jesus gathered the followers together and spoke to them privately. He said to them, [18]"We are going to Jerusalem. The Son of Man[d] will be turned over to the leading priests and the teachers of the law. They will say that he must die. [19]They will give the Son of Man to the non-Jewish people. They will laugh at him and beat him with whips, and then they will kill him on a cross. But on the third day after his death, he will be raised to life again."

[20]Then the wife of Zebedee came to Jesus. Her sons were with her. The mother bowed before Jesus and asked him to do something for her.

[21]Jesus asked, "What do you want?"

She said, "Promise that one of my sons will sit at your right side in your kingdom. And promise that the other son will sit at your left side."

[22]But Jesus said, "You don't understand what you are asking. Can you accept the kind of suffering that I must suffer?"[n]

The sons answered, "Yes, we can!"

[23]Jesus said to them, "Truly you will suffer the same things that I will suffer. But I cannot choose who will sit at my right side or my left side. Those places belong to those for whom my Father has prepared them."

[24]The other ten followers heard this and were angry with the two brothers. [25]Jesus called all the followers together. He said, "You know that the rulers of the non-Jewish people love to show their power over the people. And their important leaders love to use all their authority. [26]But it should not be that way among you. If one of you wants to become great, then he must serve the rest of you like a servant. [27]If one of you wants to become first, then he must serve the rest of you like a slave. [28]So it is with the Son of Man.[d] The Son of Man did not come for other people to serve him. He came to serve others. The Son of Man came to give his life to save many people."

20:2 silver coin A Roman denarius. One coin was the average pay for one day's work.
20:22 accept . . . suffer Literally, "drink the cup that I must drink." Jesus used the idea of drinking from a cup to mean accepting the terrible things that would happen to him.

[29]When Jesus and his followers were leaving Jericho, a great many people followed Jesus. [30]There were two blind men sitting by the road. The blind men heard that Jesus was going by, so they shouted, "Lord, Son of David,[d] please help us!"

[31]All the people criticized the blind men. They told them to be quiet. But the blind men shouted more and more, "Lord, Son of David, please help us!"

[32]Jesus stopped and said to the blind men, "What do you want me to do for you?"

[33]They answered, "Lord, we want to be able to see."

[34]Jesus felt sorry for the blind men. He touched their eyes, and at once they were able to see. Then the men followed Jesus.

21 Jesus and his followers were coming closer to Jerusalem. But first they stopped at Bethphage at the hill called the Mount of Olives.[d] From there Jesus sent two of his followers into the town. [2]He said to them, "Go to the town you can see there. When you enter it, you will find a donkey tied there with its colt. Untie them and bring them to me. [3]If anyone asks you why you are taking the donkeys, tell him, 'The Master needs them. He will send them back soon.'" [4]This was to make clear the full meaning of what the prophet[d] said:

[5]"Tell the people of Jerusalem,
  'Your king is coming to you.
He is gentle and riding on a
  donkey.
He is on the colt of a donkey.'"
  Isaiah 62:11; Zechariah 9:9

[6]The followers went and did what Jesus told them to do. [7]They brought the donkey and the colt to Jesus. They laid their coats on the donkeys, and Jesus sat on them. [8]Many people spread their coats on the road before Jesus. Others cut branches from the trees and spread them on the road. [9]Some of the people were walking ahead of Jesus. Others were walking behind him. All the people were shouting,

"Praise[n] to the Son of David![d]
God bless the One who comes in the
  name of the Lord! *Psalm 118:26*
Praise to God in heaven!"

[10]Then Jesus went into Jerusalem. The city was filled with excitement. The people asked, "Who is this man?"

[11]The crowd answered, "This man is Jesus. He is the prophet from the town of Nazareth in Galilee."

[12]Jesus went into the Temple.[d] He threw out all the people who were buying and selling there. He turned over the tables that belonged to the men who were exchanging different kinds of money. And he upset the benches of those who were selling doves. [13]Jesus said to all the people there, "It is written in the Scriptures, 'My Temple will be a house where people will pray.'[n] But you are changing God's house into a 'hideout for robbers.'"[n]

[14]The blind and crippled people came to Jesus in the Temple, and Jesus healed them. [15]The leading priests and the teachers of the law saw that Jesus was doing wonderful things. They saw the children praising him in the Temple. The children were saying, "Praise to the Son of David."[d] All these things made the priests and the teachers of the law very angry.

[16]They asked Jesus, "Do you hear the things these children are saying?"

Jesus answered, "Yes. Haven't you read in the Scriptures, 'You have taught children and babies to sing praises'?"[n]

[17]Then Jesus left and went out of the city to Bethany, where he spent the night.

[18]Early the next morning, Jesus was going back to the city. He was very hungry. [19]He saw a fig tree beside the road. Jesus went to it, but there were no figs on the tree. There were only leaves. So Jesus said to the tree, "You will never again have fruit!" The tree immediately dried up.

[20]His followers saw this and were amazed. They asked, "How did the fig tree dry up so quickly?"

[21]Jesus answered, "I tell you the truth. If you have faith and do not doubt, you will be able to do what I did to this tree. And you will be able to do more. You will be able to say to this mountain, 'Go, mountain, fall into the sea.' And if you have faith, it will happen. [22]If you believe, you will get anything you ask for in prayer."

21:9, 15 Praise Literally, "Hosanna," a Hebrew word used at first in praying to God for help. At this time it was probably a shout of joy used in praising God or his Messiah. **21:13 'My Temple . . . pray.'** Quotation from Isaiah 56:7. **21:13 'hideout for robbers.'** Quotation from Jeremiah 7:11. **21:16 'You . . . praises'** Quotation from the Septuagint (Greek) version of Psalm 8:2.

[23] Jesus went to the Temple.[d] While he was teaching there, the leading priests and the older leaders of the people came to Jesus. They said to him, "Tell us! What authority do you have to do these things? Who gave you this authority?" [24] Jesus answered, "I will ask you a question, too. If you answer me, then I will tell you what authority I have to do these things. [25] Tell me: When John baptized people, did that come from God or from man?"

The priests and the leaders argued about Jesus' question. They said to each other, "If we answer, 'John's baptism was from God,' then Jesus will say, 'Then why didn't you believe John?' [26] But if we say, 'It was from man,' we are afraid of what the people will do because they all believe that John was a prophet."[d]

[27] So they answered Jesus, "We don't know."

Then Jesus said, "Then I won't tell you what authority I have to do these things!

[28] "Tell me what you think about this: There was a man who had two sons. He went to the first son and said, 'Son, go and work today in my vineyard.' [29] The son answered, 'I will not go.' But later the son decided he should go, and he went. [30] Then the father went to the other son and said, 'Son, go and work today in my vineyard.' The son answered, 'Yes, sir, I will go and work.' But he did not go. [31] Which of the two sons obeyed his father?"

The priests and leaders answered, "The first son."

Jesus said to them, "I tell you the truth. The tax collectors and the prostitutes[d] will enter the kingdom of God before you do. [32] John came to show you the right way to live. And you did not believe him. But the tax collectors and prostitutes believed John. You saw this, but you still refused to change and believe him.

[33] "Listen to this story: There was a man who owned a vineyard. He put a wall around the vineyard and dug a hole for a winepress.[d] Then he built a tower. He leased the land to some farmers and left for a trip. [34] Later, it was time for the grapes to be picked. So the man sent his servants to the farmers to get his share of the grapes. [35] But the farmers grabbed the servants, beat one, killed another, and then killed a third servant with stones. [36] So the man sent some other servants to the farmers. He sent more servants than he sent the first time. But the farmers did the same thing to the servants that they had done before. [37] So the man decided to send his son to the farmers. He said, 'The farmers will respect my son.' [38] But when the farmers saw the son, they said to each other, 'This is the owner's son. This vineyard will be his. If we kill him, then his vineyard will be ours!' [39] So the farmers grabbed the son, threw him out of the vineyard, and killed him. [40] So what will the owner of the vineyard do to these farmers when he comes?"

[41] The priests and leaders said, "He will surely kill those evil men. Then he will lease the vineyard to some other farmers. They will give him his share of the crop at harvest time."

[42] Jesus said to them, "Surely you have read this in the Scriptures:[d]

'The stone that the builders did not want
    became the cornerstone.[d]
The Lord did this,
    and it is wonderful to us.'
                                Psalm 118:22-23

[43] "So I tell you that the kingdom of God will be taken away from you. It will be given to people who do the things God wants in his kingdom. [44] The person who falls on this stone will be broken. But if the stone falls on him, he will be crushed."

[45] The leading priests and the Pharisees[d] heard these stories that Jesus told. They knew he was talking about them. [46] They wanted to arrest him. But they were afraid of the people, because the people believed that Jesus was a prophet.[d]

22

Jesus used stories to tell other things to the people. He said, [2] "The kingdom of heaven is like a king who prepared a wedding feast for his son. [3] The king invited some people to the feast. When the feast was ready, the king sent his servants to tell the people to come. But they refused to come to the feast.

[4] "Then the king sent other servants. He said to them, 'Tell those who have been invited that my feast is ready. I have killed my best bulls and calves for the dinner. Everything is ready. Come to the wedding feast.'

[5] "But the people refused to listen to the servants. They went to do other things. One went to work in his field,

and another went to his business. [6]Some of the other people grabbed the servants, beat them, and killed them. [7]The king was very angry. He sent his army to kill the people who had killed his servants. And the army burned their city.

[8]"After that, the king said to his servants, 'The wedding feast is ready. I invited those people, but they were not worthy to come. [9]So go to the street corners and invite everyone you see. Tell them to come to my feast.' [10]So the servants went into the streets. They gathered all the people they could find, both good and bad. And the wedding hall was filled with guests.

[11]"Then the king came in to see all the guests. He saw a man there who was not dressed in the right clothes for a wedding. [12]The king said, 'Friend, how were you allowed to come in here? You are not wearing the right clothes for a wedding.' But the man said nothing. [13]So the king told some servants, 'Tie this man's hands and feet. Throw him out into the darkness. In that place, people will cry and grind their teeth with pain.'

[14]"Yes, many people are invited. But only a few are chosen."

[15]Then the Pharisees[d] left the place where Jesus was teaching. They made plans to trap Jesus with a question. [16]They sent some of their own followers and some men from the group called Herodians.[n] These men said, "Teacher, we know that you are an honest man. We know that you teach the truth about God's way. You are not afraid of what other people think about you. All men are the same to you. [17]So tell us what you think. Is it right to pay taxes to Caesar[d] or not?"

[18]But Jesus knew that these men were trying to trick him. So he said, "You hypocrites![d] Why are you trying to trap me? [19]Show me a coin used for paying the tax." The men showed him a silver coin.[n] [20]Then Jesus asked, "Whose picture is on the coin? And whose name is written on the coin?"

[21]The men answered, "Caesar's."

Then Jesus said to them, "Give to Caesar the things that are Caesar's. And give to God the things that are God's."

[22]The men heard what Jesus said, and they were amazed. They left him and went away.

[23]That same day some Sadducees[d] came to Jesus. (Sadducees believe that no person will rise from death.) The Sadducees asked Jesus a question. [24]They said, "Teacher, Moses told us that a married man might die without having children. Then his brother must marry the widow and have children for him. [25]There were seven brothers among us. The first one married but died. He had no children. So his brother married the widow. [26]Then the second brother also died. The same thing happened to the third brother and all the other brothers. [27]The woman was last to die. [28]But all seven men had married her. So when people rise from death, whose wife will she be?"

[29]Jesus answered, "You don't understand because you don't know what the Scriptures[d] say. And you don't know about the power of God. [30]When people rise from death, there will be no marriage. People will not be married to each other. They will be like the angels in heaven. [31]Surely you have read what God said to you about the rising from death? [32]God said, 'I am the God of Abraham, the God of Isaac, and the God of Jacob.'[n] God is the God of living people, not dead people."

[33]All the people heard this. They were amazed at Jesus' teaching.

[34]The Pharisees[d] learned that the Sadducees[d] could not argue with Jesus' answers to them. So the Pharisees met together. [35]One Pharisee was an expert in the law of Moses. That Pharisee asked Jesus a question to test him. [36]The Pharisee asked, "Teacher, which command in the law is the most important?"

[37]Jesus answered, "'Love the Lord your God with all your heart, soul and mind.'[n] [38]This is the first and most important command. [39]And the second command is like the first: 'Love your neighbor as you love yourself.'[n] [40]All the law and the writings of the prophets[d] depend on these two commands."

[41]While the Pharisees[d] were together, Jesus asked them a question. [42]He asked, "What do you think about the Christ?[d] Whose son is he?"

22:16 Herodians A political group that followed Herod and his family. **22:19 silver coin** A Roman denarius. One coin was the average pay for one day's work. **22:32 'I am . . . Jacob.'** Quotation from Exodus 3:6. **22:37 'Love . . . mind.'** Quotation from Deuteronomy 6:5. **22:39 'Love . . . yourself.'** Quotation from Leviticus 19:18.

The Pharisees answered, "The Christ is the Son of David."[d]

[43]Then Jesus said to them, "Then why did David call him 'Lord'? David was speaking by the power of the Holy Spirit.[d] David said,

[44]'The Lord said to my Lord:
     Sit by me at my right side,
     until I put your enemies under
         your control.'   *Psalm 110:1*

[45]David calls the Christ 'Lord.' So how can he be David's son?"

[46]None of the Pharisees could answer Jesus' question. And after that day no one was brave enough to ask Jesus any more questions.

23

Then Jesus spoke to the crowds and to his followers. Jesus said, [2]"The teachers of the law and the Pharisees[d] have the authority to tell you what the law of Moses says. [3]So you should obey and follow whatever they tell you. But their lives are not good examples for you to follow. They tell you to do things, but they don't do the things themselves. [4]They make strict rules and try to force people to obey them. But they themselves will not try to follow any of those rules.

[5]"The reason they do good things is so other people will see them. They make the boxes[n] of Scriptures[d] that they wear bigger and bigger. And they make their special prayer clothes very long so that people will notice them. [6]Those Pharisees and teachers of the law love to have the most important seats at the feasts. And they love to have the most important seats in the synagogues.[d] [7]They love people to show respect to them in the marketplaces. And they love to have people call them 'Teacher.'

[8]"But you must not be called 'Teacher.' You are all brothers and sisters together. You have only one Teacher. [9]And don't call any person on earth 'Father.' You have one Father. He is in heaven. [10]And you should not be called 'Master.' You have only one Master, the Christ.[d] [11]He who serves you as a servant is the greatest among you. [12]Whoever makes himself great will be made humble. Whoever makes himself humble will be made great.

[13]"How terrible for you, teachers of the law and Pharisees! You are hypocrites![d] You close the door for people to enter the kingdom of heaven. You yourselves don't enter, and you stop others who are trying to enter. [14] [n]

[15]"How terrible for you, teachers of the law and Pharisees! You are hypocrites! You travel across land and sea to find one person who will follow your ways. When you find that person, you make him more fit for hell than you are.

[16]"How terrible for you, teachers of the law and Pharisees! You guide the people, but you are blind. You say, 'If anyone swears by the Temple[d] when he makes a promise, that means nothing. But if anyone swears by the gold that is in the Temple, then he must keep that promise.' [17]You are blind fools! Which is greater: the gold or the Temple? The Temple makes that gold holy. [18]And you say, 'If anyone swears by the altar when he makes a promise, that means nothing. But if he swears by the gift on the altar, then he must keep his promise.' [19]You are blind! Which is greater: the gift or the altar? The altar makes the gift holy. [20]The person who swears by the altar is really using the altar and also everything on the altar. [21]And the person who uses the Temple to make a promise is really using the Temple and also everything in the Temple. [22]The person who uses heaven to make a promise is also using God's throne and the One who sits on that throne.

[23]"How terrible for you, teachers of the law and Pharisees! You are hypocrites! You give to God one-tenth of everything you earn—even your mint, dill, and cummin.[n] But you don't obey the really important teachings of the law—being fair, showing mercy, and being loyal. These are the things you should do, as well as those other things. [24]You guide the people, but you are blind! You are like a person who picks a fly out of his drink and then swallows a camel![n]

23:5 boxes Small leather boxes containing four important Scriptures. Some Jews tied these to the forehead and left arm, probably to show they were very religious.   **23:14 Verse 14** Some Greek copies add verse 14: "How terrible for you, teachers of the law and Pharisees. You are hypocrites. You take away widows' houses, and you make long prayers so that people can see you. So you will have a worse punishment."   **23:23 mint, dill, and cummin** Small plants grown in gardens and used for spices. Only very religious people would be careful enough to give a tenth of these plants.   **23:24 You . . . camel!** Meaning, "You worry about the smallest mistakes but commit the biggest sin."

[25]"How terrible for you, teachers of the law and Pharisees! You are hypocrites! You wash the outside of your cups and dishes. But inside they are full of things that you got by cheating others and pleasing only yourselves. [26]Pharisees, you are blind! First make the inside of the cup clean and good. Then the outside of the cup can be truly clean.

[27]"How terrible for you, teachers of the law and Pharisees! You are hypocrites! You are like tombs that are painted white. Outside, those tombs look fine. But inside, they are full of the bones of dead people, and all kinds of unclean things are there. [28]It is the same with you. People look at you and think you are good. But on the inside you are full of hypocrisy and evil.

[29]"How terrible for you, teachers of the law and Pharisees! You are hypocrites! You build tombs for the prophets.[d] You show honor to the graves of people who lived good lives. [30]And you say, 'If we had lived during the time of our fathers, we would not have helped them kill the prophets.' [31]But you give proof that you are children of those people who murdered the prophets. [32]And you will complete the sin that your fathers started!

[33]"You are snakes! A family of poisonous snakes! You will not escape God. You will all be judged guilty and be sent to hell! [34]So I tell you this: I am sending to you prophets and wise men and teachers. You will kill some of these people. You will nail some of them to crosses. You will beat some of them in your synagogues. You will chase them from town to town. [35]So you will be guilty for the death of all the good people who have been killed on earth. You will be guilty for the murder of that good man Abel. And you will be guilty for the murder of Zechariah[n] son of Berakiah. He was murdered when he was between the Temple and the altar. [36]I tell you the truth. All of these things will happen to you people who are living now.

[37]"Jerusalem, Jerusalem! You kill the prophets[d] and kill with stones those men God sent to you. Many times I wanted to help your people! I wanted to gather them together as a hen gathers her chicks under her wings. But you did not let me. [38]Now your home will be left completely empty. [39]I tell you, you will not see me again until that time when you will say, 'God bless the One who comes in the name of the Lord.'"[n]

24 Jesus left the Temple[d] and was walking away. But his followers came to show him the Temple's buildings. [2]Jesus asked, "Do you see all these buildings? I tell you the truth. Every stone will be thrown down to the ground. Not one stone will be left on another."

[3]Later, Jesus was sitting on the Mount of Olives.[d] His followers came to be alone with him. They said, "Tell us when these things will happen. And what will happen to show us that it is time for you to come again and for the world to end?"

[4]Jesus answered: "Be careful that no one fools you. [5]Many people will come in my name. They will say, 'I am the Christ.'[d] And they will fool many people. [6]You will hear about wars and stories of wars that are coming. But don't be afraid. These things must happen before the end comes. [7]Nations will fight against other nations. Kingdoms will fight against other kingdoms. There will be times when there is no food for people to eat. And there will be earthquakes in different places. [8]These things are like the first pains when something new is about to be born.

[9]"Then men will arrest you and hand you over to be hurt and kill you. They will hate you because you believe in me. [10]At that time, many who believe will lose their faith. They will turn against each other and hate each other. [11]Many false prophets[d] will come and cause many people to believe false things. [12]There will be more and more evil in the world. So most people will stop showing their love for each other. [13]But the person who continues to be strong until the end will be saved. [14]The Good News[d] about God's kingdom will be preached in all the world, to every nation. Then the end will come.

[15]"Daniel the prophet spoke about 'the horrible thing that destroys.'[n] You will see this terrible thing standing in the holy place." (You who read this should understand what it means.) [16]"At that time, the people in Judea should run away to the mountains. [17]If a person

23:35 Abel . . . Zechariah In the Hebrew Old Testament, the first and last men to be murdered. **23:39 'God . . . Lord.'** Quotation from Psalm 118:26. **24:15 'the horrible . . . destroys.'** Mentioned in Daniel 9:27; 12:11 (cf. Daniel 11:31).

is on the roof[n] of his house, he must not go down to get anything out of his house. [18]If a person is in the field, he must not go back to get his coat. [19]At that time, it will be hard for women who are pregnant or have nursing babies! [20]Pray that it will not be winter or a Sabbath[d] day when these things happen and you have to run away. [21]This is because at that time there will be much trouble. There will be more trouble than has ever happened since the beginning of the world. And nothing as bad as that will ever happen again. [22]God has decided to make that terrible time short. If that time were not made short, then no one would go on living. But God will make that time short to help the people he has chosen. [23]At that time, someone might say to you, 'Look, there is the Christ!' Or another person might say, 'There he is!' But don't believe them. [24]False Christs and false prophets will come and perform great things and miracles.[d] They will do these things to the people God has chosen. They will fool them, if that is possible. [25]Now I have warned you about this before it happens.

[26]"If people tell you, 'The Christ is in the desert'—don't go there. If they say, 'The Christ is in the inner room'—don't believe it. [27]When the Son of Man[d] comes, he will be seen by everyone. It will be like lightning flashing in the sky that can be seen everywhere. [28]Wherever there is a dead body, there the vultures will gather.

[29]"Soon after the trouble of those days, this will happen:

'The sun will grow dark.
    And the moon will not give its
        light.
The stars will fall from the sky.
    And everything in the sky will be
        changed.'   *Isaiah 13:10; 34:4*

[30]"At that time, there will be something in the sky that shows the Son of Man is coming. All the peoples of the world will cry. They will see the Son of Man coming on clouds in the sky. He will come with great power and glory. [31]He will use a loud trumpet to send his angels all around the earth. They will gather his chosen people from every part of the world.

[32]"The fig tree teaches us a lesson:

When its branches become green and soft, and new leaves begin to grow, then you know that summer is near. [33]So also, when you see all these things happening, you will know that the time is near, ready to come. [34]I tell you the truth. All these things will happen while the people of this time are still living! [35]The whole world, earth and sky, will be destroyed, but the words I have said will never be destroyed!

[36]"No one knows when that day or time will be. Even the Son and the angels in heaven don't know. Only the Father knows. [37]When the Son of Man[d] comes, it will be the same as what happened during Noah's time. [38]In those days before the flood, people were eating and drinking. They were marrying and giving their children to be married. They were still doing those things until the day Noah entered the boat. [39]They knew nothing about what was happening. But then the flood came, and all those people were destroyed. It will be the same when the Son of Man comes. [40]Two men will be working together in the field. One man will be taken and the other left. [41]Two women will be grinding grain with a hand mill.[n] One woman will be taken and the other will be left.

[42]"So always be ready. You don't know the day your Lord will come. [43]Remember this: If the owner of the house knew what time a thief was coming, then the owner would be ready for him. The owner would watch and not let the thief enter his house. [44]So you also must be ready. The Son of Man will come at a time you don't expect him.

[45]"Who is the wise and trusted servant? The master trusts one servant to give the other servants their food at the right time. [46]When the master comes and finds the servant doing his work, the servant will be very happy. [47]I tell you the truth. The master will choose that servant to take care of everything the master owns. [48]But what will happen if the servant is evil and thinks his master will not come back soon? [49]Then that servant will begin to beat the other servants. He will feast and get drunk with others like him. [50]And the master will come when the servant is not ready and is not expecting him. [51]Then the master

24:17 roof In Bible times houses were built with flat roofs. The roof was used for drying things such as flax and fruit. And it was used as an extra room, as a place for worship and as a place to sleep in the summer.   **24:41 mill** Two large, round, flat rocks used for grinding grain to make flour.

will punish that servant. He will send him away to be among the hypocrites.[d] There people will cry and grind their teeth with pain.

25 "At that time the kingdom of heaven will be like ten girls who went to wait for the bridegroom. They took their lamps with them. [2]Five of the girls were foolish and five were wise. [3]The five foolish girls took their lamps, but they did not take more oil for the lamps to burn. [4]The wise girls took their lamps and more oil in jars. [5]The bridegroom was very late. All the girls became sleepy and went to sleep.

[6]"At midnight someone cried out, 'The bridegroom is coming! Come and meet him!' [7]Then all the girls woke up and got their lamps ready. [8]But the foolish girls said to the wise, 'Give us some of your oil. Our lamps are going out.' [9]The wise girls answered, 'No! The oil we have might not be enough for all of us. Go to the people who sell oil and buy some for yourselves.'

[10]"So the five foolish girls went to buy oil. While they were gone, the bridegroom came. The girls who were ready went in with the bridegroom to the wedding feast. Then the door was closed and locked.

[11]"Later the others came back. They called, 'Sir, sir, open the door to let us in.' [12]But the bridegroom answered, 'I tell you the truth, I don't know you.'

[13]"So always be ready. You don't know the day or the time the Son of Man[d] will come.

[14]"The kingdom of heaven is like a man who was going to another place for a visit. Before he left, he talked with his servants. The man told them to take care of his things while he was gone. [15]He decided how much each servant would be able to care for. He gave one servant five bags of money. He gave another servant two bags of money. And he gave a third servant one bag of money. Then the man left. [16]The servant who got five bags went quickly to invest the money. The five bags of money earned five more. [17]It was the same with the servant who had two bags of money. He invested the money and earned two more. [18]But the servant who got one bag of money went out and dug a hole in the ground. Then he hid his master's money in the hole.

[19]"After a long time the master came home. He asked the servants what they did with his money. [20]The servant who

got five bags of money brought five more bags to the master. The servant said, 'Master, you trusted me to care for five bags of money. So I used your five bags to earn five more.' [21]The master answered, 'You did well. You are a good servant who can be trusted. You did well with small things. So I will let you care for much greater things. Come and share my happiness with me.'

[22]"Then the servant who got two bags of money came to the master. The servant said, 'Master, you gave me two bags of money to care for. So I used your two bags to earn two more.' [23]The master answered, 'You did well. You are a good servant who can be trusted. You did well with small things. So I will let you care for much greater things. Come and share my happiness with me.'

[24]"Then the servant who got one bag of money came to the master. The servant said, 'Master, I knew that you were a hard man. You harvest things you did not plant. You gather crops where you did not sow any seed. [25]So I was afraid. I went and hid your money in the ground. Here is the bag of money you gave me.' [26]The master answered, 'You are a bad and lazy servant! You say you knew that I harvest things I did not plant, and that I gather crops where I did not sow any seed? [27]So you should have put my money in the bank. Then, when I came home, I would get my money back with interest.'

[28]"So the master told his other servants, 'Take the bag of money from that servant and give it to the servant who has ten bags of money. [29]Everyone who uses what he has will get more. He will have much more than he needs. But the one who does not use what he has will have everything taken away from him.' [30]Then the master said, 'Throw that useless servant outside, into the darkness! There people will cry and grind their teeth with pain.'

[31]"The Son of Man[d] will come again in his great glory. All his angels will come with him. He will be King and sit on his great throne. [32]All the people of the world will be gathered before him. Then he will separate them into two groups as a shepherd separates the sheep from the goats. [33]The Son of Man will put the sheep, the good people, on his right and the goats, the bad people, on his left.

[34]"Then the King will say to the good people on his right, 'Come. My Father has given you his blessing. Come and

receive the kingdom God has prepared for you since the world was made. [35]I was hungry, and you gave me food. I was thirsty, and you gave me something to drink. I was alone and away from home, and you invited me into your house. [36]I was without clothes, and you gave me something to wear. I was sick, and you cared for me. I was in prison, and you visited me.'

[37]"Then the good people will answer, 'Lord, when did we see you hungry and give you food? When did we see you thirsty and give you something to drink? [38]When did we see you alone and away from home and invite you into our house? When did we see you without clothes and give you something to wear? [39]When did we see you sick or in prison and care for you?'

[40]"Then the King will answer, 'I tell you the truth. Anything you did for any of my people here, you also did for me.'

[41]"Then the King will say to those on his left, 'Go away from me. God has said that you will be punished. Go into the fire that burns forever. That fire was prepared for the devil and his helpers. [42]I was hungry, and you gave me nothing to eat. I was thirsty, and you gave me nothing to drink. [43]I was alone and away from home, and you did not invite me into your house. I was without clothes, and you gave me nothing to wear. I was sick and in prison, and you did not care for me.'

[44]"Then those people will answer, 'Lord, when did we see you hungry or thirsty? When did we see you alone and away from home? Or when did we see you without clothes or sick or in prison? When did we see these things and not help you?'

[45]"Then the King will answer, 'I tell you the truth. Anything you refused to do for any of my people here, you refused to do for me.'

[46]"These people will go off to be punished forever. But the good people will go to live forever."

26 After Jesus finished saying all these things, he told his followers, [2]"You know that the day after tomorrow is the day of the Passover[d] Feast. On that day the Son of Man[d] will be given to his enemies to be killed on a cross."

[3]Then the leading priests and the older Jewish leaders had a meeting at the palace of the high priest. The high priest's name was Caiaphas. [4]At the meeting, they planned to set a trap to arrest Jesus and kill him. [5]But they said, "We must not do it during the feast. The people might cause a riot."

[6]Jesus was in Bethany. He was at the house of Simon, who had a harmful skin disease. [7]While Jesus was there, a woman came to him. She had an alabaster[d] jar filled with expensive perfume. She poured this perfume on Jesus' head while he was eating.

[8]His followers saw the woman do this and were upset. They asked, "Why waste that perfume? [9]It could be sold for a great deal of money, and the money could be given to the poor."

[10]But Jesus knew what happened. He said, "Why are you troubling this woman? She did a very beautiful thing for me. [11]You will always have the poor with you. But you will not always have me. [12]This woman poured perfume on my body to prepare me for burial. [13]I tell you the truth. The Good News[d] will be told to people in all the world. And in every place where it is preached, what this woman has done will be told. And people will remember her."

[14]Then 1 of the 12 followers went to talk to the leading priests. This was the follower named Judas Iscariot. [15]He said, "I will give Jesus to you. What will you pay me for doing this?" The priests gave Judas 30 silver coins. [16]After that, Judas waited for the best time to give Jesus to the priests.

[17]On the first day of the Feast[d] of Unleavened Bread, the followers came to Jesus. They said, "We will prepare everything for you to eat the Passover[d] Feast. Where do you want to have the feast?"

[18]Jesus answered, "Go into the city to a certain man. Tell him that the Teacher says, 'The chosen time is near. I will have the Passover Feast with my followers at your house.'" [19]The followers did what Jesus told them to do, and they prepared the Passover Feast.

[20]In the evening Jesus was sitting at the table with his 12 followers. [21]They were all eating. Then Jesus said, "I tell you the truth. One of you 12 will turn against me."

[22]This made the followers very sad. Each one said to Jesus, "Surely, Lord, I am not the one who will turn against you. Am I?"

[23]Jesus answered, "The man who has dipped his hand with me into the bowl is the one who will turn against me. [24]The Son of Man[d] will die. The Scrip-

tures[d] say this will happen. But how terrible it will be for the person who gives the Son of Man to be killed. It would be better for him if he had never been born."

[25] Then Judas said to Jesus, "Teacher, surely I am not the one. Am I?" (Judas is the one who would give Jesus to his enemies.)

Jesus answered, "Yes, it is you."

[26] While they were eating, Jesus took some bread. He thanked God for it and broke it. Then he gave it to his followers and said, "Take this bread and eat it. This bread is my body."

[27] Then Jesus took a cup. He thanked God for it and gave it to the followers. He said, "Every one of you drink this. [28] This is my blood which begins the new agreement that God makes with his people. This blood is poured out for many to forgive their sins. [29] I tell you this: I will not drink of this fruit of the vine[n] again until that day when I drink it new with you in my Father's kingdom."

[30] They sang a hymn. Then they went out to the Mount of Olives.[d]

[31] Jesus told the followers, "Tonight you will lose your faith because of me. It is written in the Scriptures:[d]

'I will kill the shepherd,
    and the sheep will scatter.'
                            Zechariah 13:7
[32] But after I rise from death, I will go ahead of you into Galilee."

[33] Peter said, "All the other followers may lose their faith because of you. But I will never lose my faith."

[34] Jesus said, "I tell you the truth. Tonight you will say you don't know me. You will say this three times before the rooster crows."

[35] But Peter said, "I will never say that I don't know you! I will even die with you!" And all the other followers said the same thing.

[36] Then Jesus went with his followers to a place called Gethsemane. He said to them, "Sit here while I go over there and pray." [37] He told Peter and the two sons of Zebedee to come with him. Then Jesus began to be very sad and troubled. [38] He said to Peter and the two sons of Zebedee, "My heart is full of sorrow and breaking with sadness. Stay here with me and watch."

[39] Then Jesus walked a little farther

away from them. He fell to the ground and prayed, "My Father, if it is possible, do not give me this cup[n] of suffering. But do what you want, not what I want."

[40] Then Jesus went back to his followers and found them asleep. Jesus said to Peter, "You men could not stay awake with me for one hour? [41] Stay awake and pray for strength against temptation. Your spirit wants to do what is right. But your body is weak."

[42] Then Jesus went away a second time. He prayed, "My Father, if it is not possible for this painful thing to be taken from me, and if I must do it, then I pray that what you want will be done."

[43] Then Jesus went back to the followers. Again he found them asleep, because their eyes were heavy. [44] So Jesus left them and went away one more time and prayed. This third time he prayed, he said the same thing.

[45] Then Jesus went back to the followers and said, "You are still sleeping and resting? The time has come for the Son of Man[d] to be given to sinful people. [46] Get up. We must go. Here comes the man who has turned against me."

[47] While Jesus was still speaking, Judas came up. Judas was 1 of the 12 followers. He had many people with him. They had been sent from the leading priests and the older leaders of the people. They carried swords and clubs. [48] Judas had planned to give them a signal. He had said, "The man I kiss is Jesus. Arrest him." [49] At once Judas went to Jesus and said, "Greetings, Teacher!" Then Judas kissed him.

[50] Jesus answered, "Friend, do the thing you came to do."

Then the men came and grabbed Jesus and arrested him. [51] When that happened, one of Jesus' followers reached for his sword and pulled it out. The follower struck the servant of the high priest with the sword and cut off his ear.

[52] Jesus said to the man, "Put your sword back in its place. All who use swords will be killed with swords. [53] Surely you know I could ask my Father, and he would give me more than 12 armies of angels. [54] But this thing must happen this way so that it will be as the Scriptures[d] say."

[55] Then Jesus said to the crowd, "You

26:29 fruit of the vine Product of the grapevine; this may also be translated "wine." **26:39 cup** Jesus is talking about the bad things that will happen to him. Accepting these things will be very hard, like drinking a cup of something that tastes very bitter.

came to get me with swords and clubs as if I were a criminal. Every day I sat in the Temple[d] teaching. You did not arrest me there. [56]But all these things have happened so that it will be as the prophets[d] wrote." Then all of Jesus' followers left him and ran away.

[57]Those men who arrested Jesus led him to the house of Caiaphas, the high priest. The teachers of the law and the older Jewish leaders were gathered there. [58]Peter followed Jesus but did not go near him. He followed Jesus to the courtyard of the high priest's house. He sat down with the guards to see what would happen to Jesus.

[59]The leading priests and the Jewish council tried to find something false against Jesus so that they could kill him. [60]Many people came and told lies about him. But the council could find no real reason to kill Jesus. Then two people came and said, [61]"This man said, 'I can destroy the Temple[d] of God and build it again in three days.'"

[62]Then the high priest stood up and said to Jesus, "Aren't you going to answer? Don't you have something to say about their charges against you?" [63]But Jesus said nothing.

Again the high priest said to Jesus, "You must swear to this. I command you by the power of the living God to tell us the truth. Tell us, are you the Christ,[d] the Son of God?"

[64]Jesus answered, "Yes, I am. But I tell you, in the future you will see the Son of Man[d] sitting at the right hand of God, the Powerful One. And you will see him coming in clouds in the sky."

[65]When the high priest heard this, he was very angry. He tore his clothes and said, "This man has said things that are against God! We don't need any more witnesses. You all heard him say these things against God. [66]What do you think?"

The people answered, "He is guilty, and he must die."

[67]Then the people there spit in Jesus' face and beat him with their fists. Others slapped Jesus. [68]They said, "Prove to us that you are a prophet,[d] you Christ! Tell us who hit you!"

[69]At that time, Peter was sitting in the courtyard. A servant girl came to him and said, "You were with Jesus, that man from Galilee."

[70]But Peter said that he was never with Jesus. He said this to all the people there. Peter said, "I don't know what you are talking about."

[71]Then he left the courtyard. At the gate, another girl saw him. She said to the people there, "This man was with Jesus of Nazareth."

[72]Again, Peter said that he was never with Jesus. Peter said, "I swear that I don't know this man Jesus!"

[73]A short time later, some people standing there went to Peter. They said, "We know you are one of those men who followed Jesus. We know this because of the way you talk."

[74]Then Peter began to curse. He said, "May a curse fall on me if I'm not telling the truth. I don't know the man." After Peter said this, a rooster crowed. [75]Then he remembered what Jesus had told him: "Before the rooster crows, you will say three times that you don't know me." Then Peter went outside and cried painfully.

27

[1]Early the next morning, all the leading priests and older leaders of the people decided to kill Jesus. [2]They tied him, led him away, and turned him over to Pilate, the governor.

[3]Judas saw that they had decided to kill Jesus. Judas was the one who gave Jesus to his enemies. When Judas saw what happened, he was very sorry for what he had done. So he took the 30 silver coins back to the priests and the leaders. [4]Judas said, "I sinned. I gave you an innocent man to be killed."

The leaders answered, "What is that to us? That's your problem, not ours."

[5]So Judas threw the money into the Temple.[d] Then he went off and hanged himself.

[6]The leading priests picked up the silver coins in the Temple. They said, "Our law does not allow us to keep this money with the Temple money. This money has paid for a man's death." [7]So they decided to use the coins to buy a field called Potter's Field. This field would be a place to bury strangers who died while visiting Jerusalem. [8]That is why that field is still called the Field of Blood. [9]So the thing came true that Jeremiah the prophet[d] had said: "They took 30 silver coins. That is how little the Israelites thought he was worth. [10]They used those 30 silver coins to buy the potter's field, as the Lord commanded me."[n]

[11]Jesus stood before Pilate the gover-

nor. Pilate asked him, "Are you the King of the Jews?"

Jesus answered, "Yes, I am."

[12] When the leading priests and the older leaders accused Jesus, he said nothing.

[13] So Pilate said to Jesus, "Don't you hear these people accusing you of all these things?"

[14] But Jesus said nothing in answer to Pilate. Pilate was very surprised at this.

[15] Every year at the time of Passover[d] the governor would free one person from prison. This was always a person the people wanted to be set free. [16] At that time there was a man in prison who was known to be very bad. His name was Barabbas. [17] All the people gathered at Pilate's house. Pilate said, "Which man do you want me to free: Barabbas, or Jesus who is called the Christ?"[d] [18] Pilate knew that the people gave Jesus to him because they were jealous.

[19] Pilate said these things while he was sitting on the judge's seat. While he was sitting there, his wife sent a message to him. The message said, "Don't do anything to that man. He is not guilty. Today I had a dream about him, and it troubled me very much."

[20] But the leading priests and older leaders told the crowd to ask for Barabbas to be freed and for Jesus to be killed.

[21] Pilate said, "I have Barabbas and Jesus. Which do you want me to set free for you?"

The people answered, "Barabbas!"

[22] Pilate asked, "What should I do with Jesus, the one called the Christ?"

They all answered, "Kill him on a cross!"

[23] Pilate asked, "Why do you want me to kill him? What wrong has he done?"

But they shouted louder, "Kill him on a cross!"

[24] Pilate saw that he could do nothing about this, and a riot was starting. So he took some water and washed his hands[n] in front of the crowd. Then he said, "I am not guilty of this man's death. You are the ones who are causing it!"

[25] All the people answered, "We will be responsible. We accept for ourselves and for our children any punishment for his death."

[26] Then Pilate freed Barabbas. Pilate told some of the soldiers to beat Jesus with whips. Then he gave Jesus to the soldiers to be killed on a cross.

[27] Pilate's soldiers took Jesus into the governor's palace. All the soldiers gathered around Jesus. [28] They took off his clothes and put a red robe on him. [29] Then the soldiers used thorny branches to make a crown. They put this crown of thorns on Jesus' head. They put a stick in his right hand. Then the soldiers bowed before Jesus and made fun of him. They said, "Hail, King of the Jews!" [30] They spit on Jesus. Then they took his stick and hit him on the head many times. [31] After they finished making fun of Jesus, the soldiers took off the robe and put his own clothes on him again. Then they led Jesus away to be killed on a cross.

[32] The soldiers were going out of the city with Jesus. They forced another man to carry the cross to be used for Jesus. This man was Simon, from Cyrene. [33] They all came to the place called Golgotha. (Golgotha means the Place of the Skull.) [34] At Golgotha, the soldiers gave Jesus wine to drink. This wine was mixed with gall.[n] He tasted the wine but refused to drink it. [35] The soldiers nailed Jesus to a cross. They threw lots[d] to decide who would get his clothes. [36] The soldiers sat there and continued watching him. [37] They put a sign above Jesus' head with the charge against him written on it. The sign read: "THIS IS JESUS, THE KING OF THE JEWS." [38] Two robbers were nailed to crosses beside Jesus, one on the right and the other on the left. [39] People walked by and insulted Jesus. They shook their heads, [40] saying, "You said you could destroy the Temple[d] and build it again in three days. So save yourself! Come down from that cross, if you are really the Son of God!"

[41] The leading priests, the teachers of the law, and the older Jewish leaders were also there. These men made fun of Jesus [42] and said, "He saved other people, but he can't save himself! People say he is the King of Israel! If he is the King, then let him come down now from the cross. Then we will believe in him. [43] He trusts in God. So let God save him now, if God really wants him. He himself said, 'I am the Son of God.' " [44] And in the same way, the robbers who were being killed on crosses beside Jesus also insulted him.

27:24 washed his hands He did this as a sign to show that he wanted no part in what the people did. **27:34 gall** Probably a drink of wine mixed with drugs to help a person feel less pain.

⁴⁵At noon the whole country became dark. This darkness lasted for three hours. ⁴⁶About three o'clock Jesus cried out in a loud voice, "Eli, Eli, lama sabachthani?" This means, "My God, my God, why have you left me alone?"

⁴⁷Some of the people standing there heard this. They said, "He is calling Elijah."

⁴⁸Quickly one of them ran and got a sponge. He filled the sponge with vinegar and tied it to a stick. Then he used the stick to give the sponge to Jesus to drink from it. ⁴⁹But the others said, "Don't bother him. We want to see if Elijah will come to save him."

⁵⁰Again Jesus cried out in a loud voice. Then he died.

⁵¹Then the curtain in the Temple[n] split into two pieces. The tear started at the top and tore all the way down to the bottom. Also, the earth shook and rocks broke apart. ⁵²The graves opened, and many of God's people who had died were raised from death. ⁵³They came out of the graves after Jesus was raised from death. They went into the holy city, and many people saw them.

⁵⁴The army officer and the soldiers guarding Jesus saw this earthquake and everything else that happened. They were very frightened and said, "He really was the Son of God!"

⁵⁵Many women were standing at a distance from the cross, watching. These were women who had followed Jesus from Galilee to care for him. ⁵⁶Mary Magdalene, and Mary the mother of James and Joseph, and the mother of James and John were there.

⁵⁷That evening a rich man named Joseph came to Jerusalem. He was a follower of Jesus from the town of Arimathea. ⁵⁸Joseph went to Pilate and asked to have Jesus' body. Pilate gave orders for the soldiers to give it to Joseph. ⁵⁹Then Joseph took the body and wrapped it in a clean linen cloth. ⁶⁰He put Jesus' body in a new tomb that he had cut in a wall of rock. He rolled a very large stone to block the entrance of the tomb. Then Joseph went away. ⁶¹Mary Magdalene and the other woman named Mary were sitting near the tomb.

⁶²That day was the day called Preparation[d] Day. The next day, the leading priests and the Pharisees[d] went to Pilate.

⁶³They said, "Sir, we remember that while that liar was still alive he said, 'After three days I will rise from death.' ⁶⁴So give the order for the tomb to be guarded closely till the third day. His followers might come and steal the body. Then they could tell the people that he has risen from death. That lie would be even worse than the first one."

⁶⁵Pilate said, "Take some soldiers and go guard the tomb the best way you know." ⁶⁶So they all went to the tomb and made it safe from thieves. They did this by sealing the stone in the entrance and then putting soldiers there to guard it.

28

The day after the Sabbath[d] day was the first day of the week. At dawn on the first day, Mary Magdalene and another woman named Mary went to look at the tomb.

²At that time there was a strong earthquake. An angel of the Lord came down from heaven. The angel went to the tomb and rolled the stone away from the entrance. Then he sat on the stone. ³He was shining as bright as lightning. His clothes were white as snow. ⁴The soldiers guarding the tomb were very frightened of the angel. They shook with fear and then became like dead men.

⁵The angel said to the women, "Don't be afraid. I know that you are looking for Jesus, the one who was killed on the cross. ⁶But he is not here. He has risen from death as he said he would. Come and see the place where his body was. ⁷And go quickly and tell his followers. Say to them: 'Jesus has risen from death. He is going into Galilee. He will be there before you. You will see him there.'" Then the angel said, "Now I have told you."

⁸The women left the tomb quickly. They were afraid, but they were also very happy. They ran to tell Jesus' followers what had happened. ⁹Suddenly, Jesus met them and said, "Greetings." The women came up to Jesus, took hold of his feet, and worshiped him. ¹⁰Then Jesus said to them, "Don't be afraid. Go and tell my brothers to go on to Galilee. They will see me there."

¹¹The women went to tell Jesus' followers. At the same time, some of the soldiers who had been guarding the tomb went into the city. They went to

27:51 curtain in the Temple A curtain divided the Most Holy Place from the other part of the Temple. That was the special building in Jerusalem where God commanded the Jews to worship him.

tell the leading priests everything that had happened. [12]Then the priests met with the older Jewish leaders and made a plan. They paid the soldiers a large amount of money. [13]They said to the soldiers, "Tell the people that Jesus' followers came during the night and stole the body while you were asleep. [14]If the governor hears about this, we will satisfy him and save you from trouble." [15]So the soldiers kept the money and obeyed the priests. And that story is still spread among the Jews even today.

[16]The 11 followers went to Galilee. They went to the mountain where Jesus told them to go. [17]On the mountain they saw Jesus and worshiped him. But some of them did not believe that it was really Jesus. [18]Then Jesus came to them and said, "All power in heaven and on earth is given to me. [19]So go and make followers of all people in the world. Baptize them in the name of the Father and the Son and the Holy Spirit.[d] [20]Teach them to obey everything that I have told you. You can be sure that I will be with you always. I will continue with you until the end of the world."

The Gospel According to

MARK

1 This is the beginning of the Good News[d] about Jesus Christ, the Son of God.[n] [2]as the prophet[d] Isaiah wrote:

"I will send my messenger ahead of
  you.
He will prepare your way."
Malachi 3:1

[3]"There is a voice of a man who
  calls out in the desert:
'Prepare the way for the Lord.
Make the road straight for him.'"
Isaiah 40:3

[4]John was baptizing people in the desert. He preached a baptism of changed hearts and lives for the forgiveness of sins. [5]All the people from Judea and Jerusalem were going out to John. They told about the sins they had done. Then they were baptized by him in the Jordan River. [6]John wore clothes made from camel's hair and had a leather belt around his waist. He ate locusts[d] and wild honey. [7]This is what John preached to the people: "There is one coming later who is greater than I. I am not good enough even to kneel down and untie his sandals. [8]I baptize you with water. But the one who is coming will baptize you with the Holy Spirit."[d]

[9]At that time Jesus came from the town of Nazareth in Galilee to the place where John was. John baptized Jesus in the Jordan River. [10]When Jesus was coming up out of the water, he saw heaven open. The Holy Spirit[d] came down on him like a dove. [11]A voice came

from heaven and said: "You are my Son and I love you. I am very pleased with you."

[12]Then the Spirit sent Jesus into the desert alone. [13]He was in the desert 40 days and was there with the wild animals. While he was in the desert, he was tempted by Satan. Then angels came and took care of him.

[14]After John was put in prison, Jesus went into Galilee and preached the Good News[d] from God. [15]Jesus said, "The right time has come. The kingdom of God is near. Change your hearts and lives and believe the Good News!"

[16]When Jesus was walking by Lake Galilee, he saw Simon[n] and Simon's brother, Andrew. They were fishermen and were throwing a net into the lake to catch fish. [17]Jesus said to them, "Come and follow me. I will make you fishermen for men." [18]So Simon and Andrew immediately left their nets and followed him.

[19]Jesus continued walking by Lake Galilee. He saw two more brothers, James and John, the sons of Zebedee. They were in their boat, preparing their nets to catch fish. [20]Their father Zebedee and the men who worked for him were in the boat with the brothers. When Jesus saw the brothers, he called them to come with him. They left their father and followed Jesus.

[21]Jesus and his followers went to Capernaum. On the Sabbath[d] day Jesus

1:1 **the Son of God** Some Greek copies omit these words.   1:16 **Simon** Simon's other name was Peter.

went to the synagogue[d] and began to teach. [22]The people there were amazed at his teaching. He did not teach like their teachers of the law. He taught like a person who had authority. [23]While he was in the synagogue, a man was there who had an evil spirit in him. The man shouted, [24]"Jesus of Nazareth! What do you want with us? Did you come to destroy us? I know who you are—God's Holy One!"

[25]Jesus said strongly, "Be quiet! Come out of the man!" [26]The evil spirit made the man shake violently. Then the spirit gave a loud cry and came out of him.

[27]The people were amazed. They asked each other, "What is happening here? This man is teaching something new. And he teaches with authority. He even gives commands to evil spirits, and they obey him." [28]And the news about Jesus spread quickly everywhere in the area of Galilee.

[29]Jesus and his followers left the synagogue.[d] They all went at once with James and John to the home of Simon[n] and Andrew. [30]Simon's mother-in-law was sick in bed with a fever. The people there told Jesus about her. [31]So Jesus went to her bed, took her hand, and helped her up. Immediately the fever left her, and she was healed. Then she began serving them.

[32]That night, after the sun went down, the people brought to Jesus all who were sick. They also brought those who had demons[d] in them. [33]The whole town gathered at the door of the house. [34]Jesus healed many who had different kinds of sicknesses. He also forced many demons to leave people. But he would not allow the demons to speak, because they knew who he was.

[35]Early the next morning, Jesus woke and left the house while it was still dark. He went to a place to be alone and pray. [36]Later, Simon and his friends went to look for Jesus. [37]They found him and said, "Everyone is looking for you!"

[38]Jesus answered, "We should go somewhere else, to other towns around here. Then I can preach there too. That is the reason I came." [39]So he traveled everywhere in Galilee. He preached in the synagogues and forced demons to leave people.

[40]A man who had a harmful skin disease came to Jesus. The man fell to his knees and begged Jesus, "I know that you can heal me if you will."

[41]Jesus felt sorry for the man. So he touched him and said, "I want to heal you. Be healed!" [42]At once the disease left the man, and he was healed.

[43]Jesus told the man to go at once. But Jesus warned him strongly, [44]"Don't tell anyone about what I did for you. But go and show yourself to the priest. And offer a gift to God because you have been healed. Offer the gift that Moses commanded.[n] This will show the people that you are healed." [45]The man left there, but he told everyone he saw that Jesus had healed him. So the news about Jesus spread. That is the reason Jesus could not enter a town if people saw him. He stayed in places where nobody lived. But people came from all the towns to wherever he was.

2 A few days later, Jesus came back to Capernaum. The news spread that he was home. [2]So many people gathered to hear him preach that the house was full. There was no place to stand, not even outside the door. Jesus was teaching them. [3]Some people came, bringing a paralyzed man to Jesus. Four of them were carrying the paralyzed man. [4]But they could not get to Jesus because of the crowd. So they went to the roof above Jesus and made a hole in the roof. Then they lowered the mat with the paralyzed man on it. [5]Jesus saw that these men had great faith. So he said to the paralyzed man, "Young man, your sins are forgiven."

[6]Some of the teachers of the law were sitting there. They saw what Jesus did, and they said to themselves, [7]"Why does this man say things like that? He is saying things that are against God. Only God can forgive sins."

[8]At once Jesus knew what these teachers of the law were thinking. So he said to them, "Why are you thinking these things? [9]Which is easier: to tell this paralyzed man, 'Your sins are forgiven,' or to tell him, 'Stand up. Take your mat and walk'? [10]But I will prove to you that the Son of Man[d] has authority on earth to forgive sins." So Jesus said to the paralyzed man, [11]"I tell you, stand up. Take your mat and go home." [12]Immediately the paralyzed man stood up. He took his mat and walked out while everyone was watching him.

1:29 Simon Simon's other name was Peter.   **1:44 Moses commanded** Read about this in Leviticus 14:1-32.

The people were amazed and praised God. They said, "We have never seen anything like this!"

[13] Jesus went to the lake again. A crowd followed him there, and he taught them. [14] While he was walking beside the lake, he saw a tax collector named Levi son of Alphaeus. Levi was sitting in the tax office. Jesus said to him, "Follow me." And Levi stood up and followed Jesus.

[15] Later that day, Jesus ate at Levi's house. There were many tax collectors and "sinners" eating there with Jesus and his followers. Many people like this followed Jesus. [16] The teachers of the law who were Pharisees[d] saw Jesus eating with the tax collectors and "sinners." They asked his followers, "Why does he eat with tax collectors and sinners?"

[17] Jesus heard this and said to them, "Healthy people don't need a doctor. It is the sick who need a doctor. I did not come to invite good people. I came to invite sinners."

[18] One day the followers of John[n] and the Pharisees[d] were giving up eating.[n] Some people came to Jesus and said, "John's followers and the followers of the Pharisees give up eating. But your followers don't. Why?"

[19] Jesus answered, "When there is a wedding, the friends of the bridegroom are not sad while he is with them. They do not give up eating while the bridegroom is still there. [20] But the time will come when the bridegroom will leave them. Then the friends will be sad and will give up eating.

[21] "When a person sews a patch over a hole on an old coat, he never uses a piece of cloth that is not yet shrunk. If he does, the patch will shrink and pull away from the coat. Then the hole will be worse. [22] Also, no one ever pours new wine into old leather bags for holding wine. If he does, the new wine will break the bags, and the wine will be ruined along with the bags for the wine. People always put new wine into new leather bags."

[23] On the Sabbath[d] day, Jesus was walking through some grainfields. His followers were with him and picked some grain to eat. [24] The Pharisees[d] saw this and said to Jesus, "Why are your followers doing what is not lawful on the Sabbath?"

[25] Jesus answered, "You have read what David did when he and those with him were hungry and needed food. [26] It was during the time of Abiathar the high priest. David went into God's house and ate the bread that was made holy for God. The law of Moses says that only priests may eat that bread. But David also gave some of the bread to those who were with him."

[27] Then Jesus said to the Pharisees, "The Sabbath day was made to help people. They were not made to be ruled by the Sabbath day. [28] The Son of Man[d] is Lord even of the Sabbath."

3 Another time when Jesus went into a synagogue.[d] a man with a crippled hand was there. [2] Some people there wanted to see Jesus do something wrong so they could accuse him. They watched him closely to see if he would heal the man on the Sabbath[d] day.

[3] Jesus said to the man with the crippled hand, "Stand up here in front of everyone."

[4] Then Jesus asked the people, "Which is right on the Sabbath day: to do good, or to do evil? Is it right to save a life or to destroy one?" But they said nothing to answer him.

[5] Jesus was angry as he looked at the people. But he felt very sad because they were stubborn. Then he said to the man, "Let me see your hand." The man put his hand out for Jesus, and it was healed. [6] Then the Pharisees[d] left and began making plans with the Herodians[n] about a way to kill Jesus.

[7] Jesus left with his followers for the lake. A large crowd from Galilee followed him. [8] Also many people came from Judea, from Jerusalem, from Idumea, from the lands across the Jordan River, and from the area of Tyre and Sidon. They came because they had heard about all the things Jesus was doing. [9] Jesus saw the crowds. So he told his followers to get a boat ready for him. He wanted the boat so that the many people would not crowd themselves against him. [10] He had healed many people. So all the sick were pushing toward him to touch him. [11] Some had evil spirits in them. When the evil spirits saw Jesus,

2:18 **John** John the Baptist who preached to the Jews about Christ's coming (Mark 1:4-8). 2:18 **giving up eating** This is called "fasting." The people would give up eating for a special time of prayer and worship to God. It was also done to show sadness. 3:6 **Herodians** A political group that followed Herod and his family.

they fell down before him and shouted, "You are the Son of God!" [12]But Jesus strongly commanded the spirits not to tell who he was.

[13]Then Jesus went up on a hill and called some men to come to him. These were the men Jesus wanted, and they went up to him. [14]Jesus chose 12 men and called them apostles.[d] He wanted these 12 to be with him, and he wanted to send them to other places to preach. [15]He also wanted them to have the power to force demons[d] out of people. [16]These are the 12 men he chose: Simon (Jesus gave him the name Peter); [17]James and John, the sons of Zebedee (Jesus gave them the name Boanerges, which means "Sons of Thunder"); [18]Andrew, Philip, Bartholomew, Matthew, Thomas, James the son of Alphaeus, Thaddaeus, Simon the Zealot,[d] [19]and Judas Iscariot. Judas is the one who gave Jesus to his enemies.

[20]Then Jesus went back home. But again a crowd gathered. There were so many people that Jesus and his followers could not eat. [21]His family heard about all these things. They went to get him because people were saying that Jesus was out of his mind.

[22]And the teachers of the law from Jerusalem were saying, "Beelzebul[d] is living inside him! He uses power from the ruler of demons[d] to force demons out."

[23]So Jesus called the people together and used stories to teach them. He said, "Satan will not force his own demons out of people. [24]A kingdom that fights against itself cannot continue. [25]And a family that is divided cannot continue. [26]And if Satan is against himself and fights against his own people, then he cannot continue. And that is the end of Satan. [27]If a person wants to enter a strong man's house and steal his things, first he must tie up the strong man. Then the thief can steal the things from the strong man's house. [28]I tell you the truth. All sins that people do can be forgiven. And all the bad things people say against God can be forgiven. [29]But any person who says bad things against the Holy Spirit[d] will never be forgiven. He is guilty of a sin that continues forever."

[30]Jesus said this because the teachers of the law said that Jesus had an evil spirit inside him.

[31]Then Jesus' mother and brothers arrived. They stood outside and sent someone in to tell him to come out. [32]Many people were sitting around Jesus. They said to him, "Your mother and brothers are waiting for you outside."

[33]Jesus asked, "Who is my mother? Who are my brothers?" [34]Then Jesus looked at those sitting around him. He said, "Here are my mother and my brothers! [35]My true brother and sister and mother are those who do the things God wants."

4 Another time Jesus began teaching by the lake. A great crowd gathered around him. So he got into a boat and went out on the lake. All the people stayed on the shore close to the water. [2]Jesus used many stories to teach them. He said, [3]"Listen! A farmer went out to plant his seed. [4]While the farmer was planting, some seed fell by the road. The birds came and ate all that seed. [5]Some seed fell on rocky ground where there wasn't much dirt. The seed grew very fast there because the ground was not deep. [6]But when the sun rose, the plants withered. The plants died because they did not have deep roots. [7]Some other seed fell among thorny weeds. The weeds grew and choked the good plants. So those plants did not make grain. [8]Some other seed fell on good ground. In the good ground, the seed began to grow. It grew and made a crop of grain. Some plants made 30 times more grain, some 60 times more grain, and some 100 times more grain."

[9]Then Jesus said, "You people who hear me, listen!"

[10]Later, when Jesus was alone, the 12 apostles[d] and others around him asked him about the stories.

[11]Jesus said, "Only you can know the secret truth about the kingdom of God. But to other people I tell everything by using stories. [12]I do this so that:

'They will look and look, but they will not learn.
They will listen and listen, but they will not understand.
If they did learn and understand, they would come back to me and be forgiven.'" *Isaiah 6:9-10*

[13]Then Jesus said to the followers, "Do you understand this story? If you don't, then how will you understand any story? [14]The farmer is like a person who plants God's teaching in people. [15]Sometimes the teaching falls on the road. This is like some people. They hear the teaching of God. But Satan quickly comes and takes away the teaching that was planted in them. [16]Others are like the

seed planted on rocky ground. They hear the teaching and quickly accept it with joy. [17]But they don't allow the teaching to go deep into their lives. They keep it only a short time. When trouble or persecution comes because of the teaching, they quickly give up. [18]Others are like the seed planted among the thorny weeds. They hear the teaching. [19]But then other things come into their lives: worries, the love of money, and wanting all kinds of other things. These things stop the teaching from growing. So that teaching does not produce fruit[n] in their lives. [20]Others are like the seed planted in the good ground. They hear the teaching and accept it. Then they grow and produce fruit—sometimes 30 times more, sometimes 60 times more, and sometimes 100 times more."

[21]Then Jesus said to them, "Do you hide a lamp under a bowl or under a bed? No! You put the lamp on a lampstand. [22]Everything that is hidden will be made clear. Every secret thing will be made known. [23]You people who hear me, listen!

[24]"Think carefully about the things you hear. The way you give to others is the way God will give to you. But God will give you more than you give. [25]The person who has something will be given more. But the person who does not have much, even what he has will be taken from him."

[26]Then Jesus said, "The kingdom of God is like a man who plants seed in the ground. [27]The seed comes up and grows night and day. It doesn't matter whether the man is asleep or awake; the seed still grows. The man does not know how it grows. [28]Without any help, the earth produces grain. First the plant grows, then the head, and then all the grain in the head. [29]When the grain is ready, the man cuts it. This is the harvest time."

[30]Then Jesus said, "How can I show you what the kingdom of God is like? What story can I use to explain it? [31]The kingdom of God is like a mustard seed. The mustard seed is the smallest seed you plant in the ground. [32]But when you plant this seed, it grows and becomes the largest of all garden plants. It produces large branches. Even the wild birds can make nests in it and be protected from the sun."

[33]Jesus used many stories like these to teach them. He taught them all that they could understand. [34]He always used stories to teach them. But when he and his followers were alone together, Jesus explained everything to them.

[35]That evening, Jesus said to his followers, "Come with me across the lake." [36]He and the followers left the people there. They went in the boat that Jesus was already sitting in. There were also other boats with them. [37]A very strong wind came up on the lake. The waves began coming over the sides and into the boat. It was almost full of water. [38]Jesus was at the back of the boat, sleeping with his head on a pillow. The followers went to him and woke him. They said, "Teacher, do you care about us? We will drown!"

[39]Jesus stood up and commanded the wind and the waves to stop. He said, "Quiet! Be still!" Then the wind stopped, and the lake became calm.

[40]Jesus said to his followers, "Why are you afraid? Do you still have no faith?"

[41]The followers were very afraid and asked each other, "What kind of man is this? Even the wind and the waves obey him!"

5 Jesus and his followers went across the lake to the region of the Gerasene people. [2]When Jesus got out of the boat, a man came to him from the caves where dead people were buried. This man, who lived in the caves, had an evil spirit living in him. [3]No one could tie him up, not even with a chain. [4]Many times people had used chains to tie the man's hands and feet. But he always broke the chains off. No one was strong enough to control him. [5]Day and night he would wander around the burial caves and on the hills, screaming and cutting himself with stones. [6]While Jesus was still far away, the man saw him. He ran to Jesus and knelt down before him. [7-8]Jesus said to the man, "You evil spirit, come out of that man."

But the man shouted in a loud voice, "What do you want with me, Jesus, Son of the Most High God? I beg you, promise God that you will not punish me!"

[9]Then Jesus asked the man, "What is your name?"

The man answered, "My name is Legion,[n] because I have many spirits in me." [10]The man begged Jesus again and

---

4:19 produce fruit To produce fruit means to have in your life the good things God wants.
5:9 Legion Means very many. A legion was about 5,000 men in the Roman army.

again not to send the spirits out of that area. [11]A large herd of pigs was eating on a hill near there. [12]The evil spirits begged Jesus, "Send us to the pigs. Let us go into them." [13]So Jesus allowed them to do this. The evil spirits left the man and went into the pigs. Then the herd of pigs rushed down the hill into the lake and were drowned. There were about 2,000 pigs in that herd.

[14]The men who took care of the pigs ran away. They went to the town and to the countryside, telling everyone about this. So people went out to see what had happened. [15]They came to Jesus and saw the man who had had the many evil spirits. The man was sitting there, clothed and in his right mind. The people were frightened. [16]Some people were there who saw what Jesus had done. They told the others what had happened to the man who had the demons[d] living in him. And they also told about the pigs. [17]Then the people began to beg Jesus to leave their area.

[18]Jesus was getting ready to leave in the boat. The man who was freed from the demons begged to go with him. [19]But Jesus would not allow the man to go. Jesus said, "Go home to your family and friends. Tell them how much the Lord has done for you and how he has had mercy on you." [20]So the man left and told the people in the Ten Towns[n] about the great things Jesus had done for him. All the people were amazed.

[21]Jesus went in the boat back to the other side of the lake. There, a large crowd gathered around him. [22]A ruler from the synagogue,[d] named Jairus, came to that place. Jairus saw Jesus and bowed before him. [23]The ruler begged Jesus again and again. He said, "My little daughter is dying. Please come and put your hands on her. Then she will be healed and will live." [24]So Jesus went with the ruler, and many people followed Jesus. They were pushing very close around him.

[25]A woman was there who had been bleeding for the past 12 years. [26]She had suffered very much. Many doctors had tried to help her. She had spent all the money she had, but she was not improving. She was getting worse. [27]When the woman heard about Jesus, she followed him with the people and touched his coat. [28]The woman thought, "If I can even touch his coat, that will be enough to heal me." [29]When she touched his coat, her bleeding stopped. She could feel in her body that she was healed.

[30]At once Jesus felt power go out from him. So he stopped and turned around. Then he asked, "Who touched my clothes?"

[31]The followers said, "There are so many people pushing against you! And you ask, 'Who touched me?'"

[32]But Jesus continued looking around to see who had touched him. [33]The woman knew that she was healed. So she came and bowed at Jesus' feet. Shaking with fear, she told him the whole story. [34]Jesus said to the woman, "Dear woman, you are made well because you believed. Go in peace. You will have no more suffering."

[35]Jesus was still speaking to her when some men came from the house of Jairus, the synagogue ruler. The men said, "Your daughter is dead. There is now no need to bother the teacher."

[36]But Jesus paid no attention to what the men said. He said to the synagogue ruler, "Don't be afraid; only believe."

[37]Jesus let only Peter, James, and John the brother of James go with him to Jairus's house. [38]They came to the house of the synagogue ruler, and Jesus found many people there crying loudly. There was much confusion. [39]Jesus entered the house and said to the people, "Why are you crying and making so much noise? This child is not dead. She is only asleep." [40]But they only laughed at Jesus. He told all the people to leave. Then he went into the room where the child was. He took the child's father and mother and his three followers into the room with him. [41]Then he took hold of the girl's hand and said to her, "Talitha, koum!" (This means, "Little girl, I tell you to stand up!") [42]The girl stood right up and began walking. (She was 12 years old.) The father and mother and the followers were amazed. [43]Jesus gave the father and mother strict orders not to tell people about this. Then he told them to give the girl some food.

6 Jesus left there and went back to his hometown. His followers went with him. [2]On the Sabbath[d] day he taught in the synagogue.[d] Many people heard him and were amazed. They said, "Where

5:20 Ten Towns In Greek, called "Decapolis." It was an area east of Lake Galilee that once had ten main towns.

did this man get these teachings? What is this wisdom that has been given to him? And where did he get the power to work miracles?[d] [3]He is only the carpenter. His mother is Mary. He is the brother of James, Joseph, Judas, and Simon. And his sisters are here with us." The people did not accept Jesus.

[4]Jesus said to them, "Other people give honor to a prophet.[d] But in his own town with his own people and in his own home, a prophet does not receive honor." [5]Jesus was not able to work many miracles there. The only miracles he did were to heal some sick people by putting his hands on them. [6]Jesus was amazed that they had no faith.

Then Jesus went to other villages in that area and taught. [7]He called the 12 followers together and sent them out in groups of 2. He gave them authority over evil spirits. [8]This is what Jesus told them: "Take nothing for your trip except a walking stick. Take no bread, no bag, and no money in your pockets. [9]Wear sandals, and take only the clothes you are wearing. [10]When you enter a house, stay there until you leave that place. [11]If any town refuses to accept you or its people refuse to listen to you, then leave that town. Shake its dust off your feet.[n] This will be a warning to them."

[12]The followers went out and preached to the people to change their hearts and lives. [13]The followers forced many demons[d] out and poured olive oil on many sick people and healed them.

[14]King Herod heard about Jesus, because Jesus was now well-known. Some people said, "He is John the Baptist.[d] He is risen from death. That is the reason he can work these miracles."[d]

[15]Others said, "He is Elijah."[n]

Other people said, "Jesus is a prophet.[d] He is like the prophets who lived long ago."

[16]Herod heard all these things about Jesus. He said, "I killed John by cutting off his head. Now he has been raised from death!"

[17]Herod himself had ordered his soldiers to arrest John, and John was put in prison. Herod did this to please his wife, Herodias. Herodias was the wife of Philip, Herod's brother. But then Herod married her. [18]John told Herod that it was not lawful for him to be married to his brother's wife. [19]So Herodias hated

John and wanted to kill him. But she could not because of Herod. [20]Herod was afraid to kill John because he knew John was a good and holy man. So Herod protected John. Also, Herod enjoyed listening to John preach. But John's preaching always bothered him.

[21]Then the perfect time came for Herodias to cause John's death. It happened on Herod's birthday. Herod gave a dinner party for the most important government leaders, the commanders of his army, and the most important people in Galilee. [22]The daughter of Herodias came to the party and danced. When she danced, Herod and the people eating with him were very pleased.

So King Herod said to the girl, "I will give you anything you want." [23]He promised her, "Anything you ask for I will give to you. I will even give you half of my kingdom."

[24]The girl went to her mother and asked, "What should I ask the king to give me?"

Her mother answered, "Ask for the head of John the Baptist."[d]

[25]Quickly the girl went back to the king. She said to him, "Please give me the head of John the Baptist. Bring it to me now on a platter."

[26]The king was very sad. But he had promised to give the girl anything she wanted. And the people eating there with him had heard his promise. So Herod could not refuse what she asked. [27]Immediately the king sent a soldier to bring John's head. The soldier went and cut off John's head in the prison [28]and brought it back on a platter. He gave it to the girl, and the girl gave it to her mother. [29]John's followers heard about what happened. So they came and got John's body and put it in a tomb.

[30]The apostles[d] that Jesus had sent out to preach returned. They gathered around him and told him about all the things they had done and taught. [31]Crowds of people were coming and going. Jesus and his followers did not even have time to eat. He said to them, "Come with me. We will go to a quiet place to be alone. There we will get some rest."

[32]So they went in a boat alone to a place where there were no people. [33]But many people saw them leave and recognized them. So people from all the towns ran to the place where Jesus was

---

6:11 Shake . . . feet. A warning. It showed that they were finished talking to these people.
6:15 Elijah A man who spoke for God. He lived hundreds of years before Christ.

going. They got there before Jesus arrived. [34]When he landed, he saw a great crowd waiting. Jesus felt sorry for them, because they were like sheep without a shepherd. So he taught them many things.

[35]It was now late in the day. Jesus' followers came to him and said, "No one lives in this place. And it is already very late. [36]Send the people away. They need to go to the farms and towns around here to buy some food to eat."

[37]But Jesus answered, "You give them food to eat."

They said to him, "We can't buy enough bread to feed all these people! We would all have to work a month to earn enough money to buy that much bread!"

[38]Jesus asked them, "How many loaves of bread do you have now? Go and see."

When they found out, they came to him and said, "We have five loaves and two fish."

[39]Then Jesus said to the followers, "Tell all the people to sit in groups on the green grass." [40]So all the people sat in groups. They sat in groups of 50 or groups of 100. [41]Jesus took the five loaves and two fish. He looked up to heaven and thanked God for the bread. He divided the bread and gave it to his followers for them to give to the people. Then he divided the two fish among them all. [42]All the people ate and were satisfied. [43]The followers filled 12 baskets with the pieces of bread and fish that were not eaten. [44]There were about 5,000 men there who ate.

[45]Then Jesus told his followers to get into the boat and go to Bethsaida on the other side of the lake. Jesus said that he would come later. He stayed there to tell the people they could go home. [46]After sending them away, he went into the hills to pray.

[47]That night, the boat was in the middle of the lake. Jesus was alone on the land. [48]He saw the followers working hard to row the boat because the wind was blowing against them. At some time between three and six o'clock in the morning, Jesus came to them, walking on the water. He continued walking until he was almost past the boat. [49]But when his followers saw him walking on the water, they thought he was a ghost and cried out. [50]They all saw him and were terrified. But Jesus spoke to them and said, "Have courage! It is I! Do not be

afraid." [51]Then he got into the boat with them. And the wind became calm. The followers were greatly amazed. [52]They had seen Jesus make more bread from the five loaves. But they did not understand what it meant. Their minds were closed.

[53]When they had crossed the lake, they came to shore at Gennesaret. They tied the boat there. [54]When they got out of the boat, the people saw Jesus and immediately recognized him. [55]They ran to tell others everywhere in that area that Jesus was there. They brought sick people on mats to every place Jesus went. [56]Jesus went into towns and cities and farms around that area. And everywhere he went, the people brought the sick to the marketplaces. They begged him to let them just touch the edge of his coat. And all who touched him were healed.

7 Some Pharisees[d] and some teachers of the law came from Jerusalem. They gathered around Jesus. [2]They saw that some of Jesus' followers ate food with hands that were not clean.[d] ("Not clean" means that they did not wash their hands in the way the Pharisees said people must. [3]The Pharisees and all the Jews never eat before washing their hands in this special way. They do this to follow the teaching given to them by their great people who lived before them. [4]And when the Jews buy something in the market, they never eat it until they wash it in a special way. They also follow other rules of their great people who lived before them. They follow rules about the washing of cups, pitchers, and pots.)

[5]The Pharisees and the teachers of the law said to Jesus, "Your followers don't follow the rules given to us by our great people who lived before us. Your followers eat their food with hands that are not clean. Why do they do this?"

[6]Jesus answered, "You are all hypocrites![d] Isaiah was right when he spoke about you. Isaiah wrote,

'These people show honor to me
    with words.
But their hearts are far from me.
[7]Their worship of me is worthless.
The things they teach are nothing
    but human rules they have
    memorized.'   *Isaiah 29:13*
[8]You have stopped following the commands of God. Now you only follow the teachings of men."

[9]Then Jesus said to them: "You think

you are clever! You ignore the commands of God so that you can follow your own teachings!' [10]Moses said, 'Honor your father and mother.'[n] Then Moses also said, 'Anyone who says cruel things to his father or mother must be put to death.'[n] [11]But you teach that a person can say to his father or mother, 'I have something I could use to help you. But I will not use it for you. I will give it to God.' [12]You are telling that person that he does not have to do anything for his father or mother. [13]So you are teaching that it is not important to do what God said. You think that it is more important to follow your own rules, which you teach people. And you do many things like that."

[14]Jesus called the people to him again. He said, "Every person should listen to me and understand what I am saying. [15]There is nothing a person puts into his body that makes him unclean. A person is made unclean by the things that come out of him." [16] [n]

[17]When Jesus left the people and went inside, his followers asked him about this story. [18]Jesus said, "Do you still have trouble understanding? Surely you know that nothing that enters a man from the outside can make him unclean. [19]Food does not go into a person's mind. Food goes into his stomach. Then that food goes out of his body." (When Jesus said this, he meant that there is no food that is unclean for people to eat.)

[20]And Jesus said, "The things that come out of a man are the things that make him unclean. [21]All these evil things begin inside a person, in his mind: evil thoughts, sexual sins, stealing, murder, adultery,[d] [22]selfishness, doing bad things to other people, lying, doing sinful things, jealousy, saying bad things about people, pride, and foolish living. [23]All these evil things come from within a person. These things make a person unclean."

[24]Jesus left that place and went to the area around Tyre. He went into a house and did not want anyone to know he was there. But Jesus could not stay hidden. [25]A woman heard that he was there. Her little daughter had an evil spirit in her. So the woman quickly came to Jesus and fell at his feet. [26]She was not Jewish.

She was Greek, born in Phoenicia, in Syria. She begged Jesus to force the demon[d] out of her daughter. [27]Jesus told the woman: "It is not right to take the children's bread and give it to the dogs. First let the children eat all they want."

[28]She answered, "That is true, Lord. But the dogs under the table can eat the pieces of food that the children don't eat."

[29]Then Jesus said, "That is a very good answer. You may go. The demon has left your daughter."

[30]The woman went home and found her daughter lying in bed. The demon was gone.

[31]Then Jesus left the area around Tyre. He went through Sidon to Lake Galilee, to the area of the Ten Towns.[n] [32]While he was there, some people brought a man to him. This man was deaf and could not talk. The people begged Jesus to put his hand on the man to heal him.

[33]Jesus led the man away from the crowd, to be alone with him. Jesus put his fingers in the man's ears. Then Jesus spit and touched the man's tongue. [34]Jesus looked up to heaven and took a deep breath. He said to the man, "Ephphatha!" (This means, "Be opened.") [35]When Jesus did this, the man was able to hear. He was also able to use his tongue, and he spoke clearly.

[36]Jesus commanded the people not to tell anyone about what happened. But the more he commanded them, the more they told about it. [37]They were really amazed. They said, "Jesus does everything well. He makes the deaf hear! And those who can't talk—Jesus makes them able to speak."

8 Another time there was a great crowd with Jesus. They had nothing to eat. So Jesus called his followers to him. He said, [2]"I feel sorry for these people. They have been with me for three days, and now they have nothing to eat. [3]I cannot send them home hungry. If they leave without eating, they will faint on the way home. Some of them live a long way from here."

[4]Jesus' followers answered, "But we are far away from any towns. Where can we get enough bread to feed all these people?"

7:10 'Honor your father and mother.' Quotation from Exodus 20:12; Deuteronomy 5:16. **7:10 'Anyone . . . death.'** Quotation from Exodus 21:17. **7:16 Verse 16** Some Greek copies add verse 16: "You people who hear me, listen!" **7:31 Ten Towns** In Greek, called "Decapolis." It was an area east of Lake Galilee that once had ten main towns.

[5]Jesus asked, "How many loaves of bread do you have?"

They answered, "We have seven loaves."

[6]Jesus told the people to sit on the ground. Then he took the seven loaves and gave thanks to God. Jesus divided the bread and gave the pieces to his followers. He told them to pass out the bread to the people, and they did so. [7]The followers also had a few small fish. Jesus gave thanks for the fish and told his followers to give the fish to the people. [8]All the people ate and were satisfied. Then the followers filled seven baskets with the pieces of food that were not eaten. [9]There were about 4,000 men who ate. After they had eaten, Jesus told them to go home. [10]Then he went in a boat with his followers to the area of Dalmanutha.

[11]The Pharisees[d] came to Jesus and asked him questions. They wanted to trap him. So they asked Jesus to do a miracle[d] to show that he was from God. [12]Jesus sighed deeply. He said, "Why do you people ask for a miracle as proof? I tell you the truth. No miracle will be given to you." [13]Then Jesus left the Pharisees. He went in the boat to the other side of the lake.

[14]The followers had only one loaf of bread with them in the boat. They had forgotten to bring more bread. [15]Jesus warned them, "Be careful! Guard against the yeast of the Pharisees[d] and the yeast of Herod."

[16]Among themselves, his disciples discussed the meaning of this. They said, "He said this because we have no bread."

[17]Jesus knew what his followers were talking about. So he asked them, "Why are you talking about having no bread? You still don't see or understand? Are your minds closed? [18]You have eyes, but you don't really see. You have ears, but you don't really listen. Remember what I did before, when we did not have enough bread? [19]I divided five loaves of bread for 5,000 people. Remember how many baskets you filled with pieces of food that were not eaten?"

They answered, "We filled 12 baskets."

[20]"And remember that I divided seven loaves of bread for 4,000 people. Remember how many baskets you filled with pieces of food that were not eaten?"

They answered, "We filled 7 baskets."

[21]Then Jesus said to them, "You remember these things I did, but you still don't understand?"

[22]Jesus and his followers came to Bethsaida. Some people brought a blind man to Jesus and begged him to touch the man. [23]So Jesus took the blind man's hand and led him out of the village. Then he spit on the man's eyes. He put his hands on the blind man and asked, "Can you see now?"

[24]The man looked up and said, "Yes, I see people, but they look like trees walking around."

[25]Again Jesus put his hands on the man's eyes. Then the man opened his eyes wide. His eyes were healed, and he was able to see everything clearly. [26]Jesus told him to go home, saying, "Don't go into the town."

[27]Jesus and his followers went to the towns around Caesarea Philippi. While they were traveling, Jesus asked them, "Who do people say I am?"

[28]They answered, "Some people say you are John the Baptist.[d] Others say you are Elijah.[n] And others say that you are one of the prophets."[d]

[29]Then Jesus asked, "Who do you say I am?"

Peter answered, "You are the Christ."[d]

[30]Jesus ordered his followers, "Don't tell anyone who I am."

[31]Then Jesus began to teach them that the Son of Man[d] must suffer many things. He taught that the Son of Man would not be accepted by the older Jewish leaders, the leading priests, and the teachers of the law. He taught that the Son of Man must be killed and then rise from death after three days. [32]Jesus told them plainly what would happen. Then Peter took Jesus aside and began to criticize him. [33]But Jesus turned and looked at his followers. Then he criticized Peter and said, "Go away from me, Satan![n] You don't care about the things of God. You care only about things men think are important."

[34]Then Jesus called the crowd to him, along with his followers. He said, "If anyone wants to follow me, he must say 'no' to the things he wants. He must be willing to die on a cross, and he must follow me. [35]Whoever wants to save his

8:28 **Elijah** A man who spoke for God. He lived hundreds of years before Christ. **8:33 Satan** Name for the devil meaning "the enemy." Jesus means that Peter was talking like Satan.

life will give up true life. But whoever gives up his life for me and for the Good News[d] will have true life forever. [36]It is worth nothing for a person to have the whole world, if he loses his soul. [37]A person could never pay enough to buy back his soul. [38]The people who live now are living in a sinful and evil time. If anyone is ashamed of me and my teaching, then I will be ashamed of him. I will be ashamed of him when I come with the glory of my Father and the holy angels."

9 Then Jesus said to the people, "I tell you the truth. Some of you standing here will see the kingdom of God come with power before you die."

[2]Six days later Jesus took Peter, James, and John and went up on a high mountain. They were all alone there. While these followers watched, Jesus was changed. [3]His clothes became shining white, whiter than any person could make them. [4]Then two men appeared, talking with Jesus. The men were Moses and Elijah.[n]

[5]Peter said to Jesus, "Teacher, it is good that we are here. We will put three tents here—one for you, one for Moses, and one for Elijah." [6]Peter did not know what to say, because he and the others were so frightened.

[7]Then a cloud came and covered them. A voice came from the cloud. The voice said, "This is my Son, and I love him. Obey him!"

[8]Then Peter, James, and John looked around, but they saw only Jesus there alone with them.

[9]As Jesus and his followers were walking back down the mountain, he commanded them, "Don't tell anyone about the things you saw on the mountain. Wait till the Son of Man[d] rises from death. Then you may tell."

[10]So the followers obeyed Jesus and said nothing about what they had seen. But they discussed what Jesus meant about rising from death.

[11]They asked Jesus, "Why do the teachers of the law say that Elijah must come first?"

[12]Jesus answered, "They are right to say that Elijah must come first. Elijah makes all things the way they should be. But why does the Scripture[d] say that the Son of Man will suffer much and that people will treat him as if he were nothing? [13]I tell you that Elijah has already come. And people did to him whatever

they wanted to do. The Scriptures said this would happen to him."

[14]Then Jesus, Peter, James, and John went to the other followers. They saw a great crowd around them. The teachers of the law were arguing with them. [15]But when the crowd saw Jesus, they were surprised and ran to welcome him.

[16]Jesus asked, "What are you arguing about with the teachers of the law?"

[17]A man answered, "Teacher, I brought my son to you. He has a spirit from the devil in him. This spirit stops him from talking. [18]The spirit attacks him and throws him on the ground. My son foams at the mouth, grinds his teeth, and becomes very stiff. I asked your followers to force the evil spirit out, but they couldn't."

[19]Jesus answered, "You people don't believe! How long must I stay with you? How long must I go on being patient with you? Bring the boy to me!"

[20]So the followers brought him to Jesus. As soon as the evil spirit saw Jesus, it attacked the boy. He fell down and rolled on the ground, foaming from his mouth.

[21]Jesus asked the boy's father, "How long has this been happening?"

The father answered, "Since he was very young. [22]The spirit often throws him into a fire or into water to kill him. If you can do anything for him, please have pity on us and help us."

[23]Jesus said to the father, "You said, 'If you can!' All things are possible for him who believes."

[24]Immediately the father cried out, "I do believe! Help me to believe more!"

[25]Jesus saw that a crowd was running there to see what was happening. So he spoke to the evil spirit, saying, "You deaf and dumb spirit—I command you to come out of this boy and never enter him again!"

[26]The evil spirit screamed and caused the boy to fall on the ground again. Then the spirit came out. The boy looked as if he were dead. And many people said, "He is dead!" [27]But Jesus took hold of the boy's hand and helped him to stand up.

[28]Jesus went into the house. His followers were alone with him there. They said, "Why couldn't we force that evil spirit out?"

[29]Jesus answered, "That kind of spirit can only be forced out by prayer."

9:4 Moses and Elijah Two of the most important Jewish leaders in the past.

30 Then Jesus and his followers left that place and went through Galilee. Jesus did not want anyone to know where he was 31 because he wanted to teach his followers alone. He said to them, "The Son of Man[d] will be given to men who will kill him. After three days, he will rise from death." 32 But the followers did not understand what Jesus meant. And they were afraid to ask.

33 Jesus and his followers went to Capernaum and went into a house there. Then Jesus said to them, "What were you arguing about on the road?" 34 But the followers did not answer, because their argument on the road was about which one of them was the greatest.

35 Jesus sat down and called the 12 apostles[d] to him. He said, "If anyone wants to be the most important, then he must be last of all and servant of all."

36 Then Jesus took a small child and had him stand among them. He took the child in his arms and said, 37 "If anyone accepts children like these in my name, then he is also accepting me. And if he accepts me, then he is also accepting the One who sent me."

38 Then John said, "Teacher, we saw a man using your name to force demons[d] out of a person. We told him to stop, because he does not belong to our group."

39 Jesus said, "Don't stop him. Anyone who uses my name to do powerful things will not say evil things about me. 40 He who is not against us is with us. 41 I tell you the truth. If anyone helps you by giving you a drink of water because you belong to the Christ,[d] then he will truly get his reward.

42 "If one of these little children believes in me, and someone causes that child to sin, then it will be very bad for him. It would be better for him to have a large stone tied around his neck and be drowned in the sea. 43 If your hand causes you to sin, cut it off. It is better for you to lose part of your body but have life forever. That is much better than to have two hands and go to hell. In that place the fire never goes out. 44 n 45 If your foot causes you to sin, cut it off. It is better for you to lose part of your body but have life forever. That is much better than to have two feet and be thrown into hell. 46 n 47 If your eye causes you to sin, take it out. It is better for you to have only one eye but have life forever. That is much better than to have two eyes and be thrown into hell. 48 In hell the worm does not die; the fire is never stopped. 49 Every person will be salted with fire.

50 "Salt is good. But if the salt loses its salty taste, then you cannot make it salty again. So, be full of goodness. And have peace with each other."

10 Then Jesus left that place. He went into the area of Judea and across the Jordan River. Again, crowds came to him. And Jesus taught them as he always did.

2 Some Pharisees[d] came to Jesus and tried to trick him. They asked, "Is it right for a man to divorce his wife?"

3 Jesus answered, "What did Moses command you to do?"

4 They said, "Moses allowed a man to write out divorce papers and send her away."[n]

5 Jesus said, "Moses wrote that command for you because you refused to accept God's teaching. 6 But when God made the world, 'he made them male and female.'[n] 7 'So a man will leave his father and mother and be united with his wife. 8 And the two people will become one body.'[n] So the people are not two, but one. 9 God has joined the two people together. So no one should separate them."

10 Later, the followers and Jesus were in the house. They asked Jesus again about the question of divorce. 11 He answered, "Anyone who divorces his wife and marries another woman is guilty of adultery[d] against her. 12 And the woman who divorces her husband and marries another man is also guilty of adultery."

13 Some people brought their small children to Jesus so he could touch them. But his followers told the people to stop bringing their children to him. 14 When Jesus saw this, he was displeased. He said to them, "Let the little children come to me. Don't stop them. The kingdom of God belongs to people who are like these little children. 15 I tell you the truth. You must accept the kingdom of God as a little child accepts things, or you will never enter it." 16 Then

9:44 Verse 44 Some Greek copies of Mark add verse 44, which is the same as verse 48. **9:46 Verse 46** Some Greek copies of Mark add verse 46, which is the same as verse 48. **10:4 "Moses . . . away."** Quotation from Deuteronomy 24:1. **10:6 'he made . . . female.'** Quotation from Genesis 1:27. **10:7-8 'So . . . body.'** Quotation from Genesis 2:24.

Jesus took the children in his arms. He put his hands on them and blessed them.

¹⁷ Jesus started to leave, but a man ran to him and fell on his knees before Jesus. The man asked, "Good teacher, what must I do to get the life that never ends?"

¹⁸ Jesus answered, "Why do you call me good? No one is good except God alone. ¹⁹ You know the commands: 'You must not murder anyone. You must not be guilty of adultery.ᵈ You must not steal. You must not tell lies about your neighbor in court. You must not cheat. Honor your father and mother.'ᵃ

²⁰ The man said, "Teacher, I have obeyed all these commands since I was a boy."

²¹ Jesus looked straight at the man and loved him. Jesus said, "There is still one more thing you need to do. Go and sell everything you have, and give the money to the poor. You will have a reward in heaven. Then come and follow me."

²² He was very sad to hear Jesus say this, and he left. The man was sad because he was very rich.

²³ Then Jesus looked at his followers and said, "How hard it will be for those who are rich to enter the kingdom of God!"

²⁴ The followers were amazed at what Jesus said. But he said again, "My children, it is very hard to enter the kingdom of God! ²⁵ And it will be very hard for a rich person to enter the kingdom of God. It would be easier for a camel to go through the eye of a needle!"

²⁶ The followers were even more amazed and said to each other, "Then who can be saved?"

²⁷ Jesus looked straight at them and said, "This is something that men cannot do. But God can do it. God can do all things."

²⁸ Peter said to Jesus, "We left everything to follow you!"

²⁹ Jesus said, "I tell you the truth. Everyone who has left his home, brothers, sisters, mother, father, children, or fields for me and for the Good Newsᵈ ³⁰ will get a hundred times more than he left. Here in this world he will have more homes, brothers, sisters, mothers, children, and fields. And with those things, he will also suffer for his

belief. But in the age that is coming he will have life forever. ³¹ Many who have the highest place now will have the lowest place in the future. And those who have the lowest place now will have the highest place in the future."

³² Jesus and the people with him were on the road to Jerusalem. Jesus was leading the way. The followers were amazed, but those who followed behind them were afraid. Jesus took the 12 apostlesᵈ aside and talked with them alone. He told them what would happen in Jerusalem. ³³ He said, "We are going to Jerusalem. The Son of Manᵈ will be given to the leading priests and teachers of the law. They will say that he must die. They will give him to the non-Jewish people, ³⁴ who will laugh at him and spit on him. They will beat him with whips and kill him. But on the third day after his death, he will rise to life again."

³⁵ Then James and John, sons of Zebedee, came to Jesus. They said, "Teacher, we want to ask you to do something for us."

³⁶ Jesus asked, "What do you want me to do for you?"

³⁷ They answered, "You will have glory in your kingdom. Let one of us sit at your right, and let one of us sit at your left."

³⁸ Jesus said, "You don't understand what you are asking. Can you drink the cup that I must drink? And can you be baptized with the same kind of baptism that I must have?"ⁿ

³⁹ They answered, "Yes, we can!"

Jesus said to them, "You will drink the same cup that I will drink. And you will be baptized with the same baptism that I must have. ⁴⁰ But I cannot choose who will sit at my right or my left. These places are for those for whom they are prepared."

⁴¹ The ten followers heard this. They began to be angry with James and John.

⁴² Jesus called all the followers together. He said, "The non-Jewish people have men they call rulers. You know that those rulers love to show their power over the people. And their important leaders love to use all their authority. ⁴³ But it should not be that way among you. If one of you wants to become great, then he must serve you like a servant. ⁴⁴ If one of you wants to become the

most important, then he must serve all of you like a slave. [45]In the same way, the Son of Man[d] did not come to be served. He came to serve. The Son of Man came to give his life to save many people."

[46]Then they came to the town of Jericho. As Jesus was leaving there with his followers and a large crowd, a blind beggar named Bartimaeus (son of Timaeus) was sitting by the road. [47]He heard that Jesus from Nazareth was walking by. The blind man cried out, "Jesus, Son of David,[d] please help me!"

[48]Many people scolded the blind man and told him to be quiet. But he shouted more and more, "Son of David, please help me!"

[49]Jesus stopped and said, "Tell the man to come here."

So they called the blind man. They said, "Cheer up! Get to your feet. Jesus is calling you." [50]The blind man stood up quickly. He left his coat there and went to Jesus.

[51]Jesus asked him, "What do you want me to do for you?"

The blind man answered, "Teacher, I want to see again."

[52]Jesus said, "Go. You are healed because you believed." At once the man was able to see again, and he followed Jesus on the road.

11 Jesus and his followers were coming closer to Jerusalem. They came to the towns of Bethphage and Bethany near the Mount of Olives.[d] There Jesus sent two of his followers. [2]He said to them, "Go to the town you see there. When you enter it, you will find a colt tied which no one has ever ridden. Untie it and bring it here to me. [3]If anyone asks you why you are doing this, tell him, 'The Master needs the colt. He will send it back soon.'"

[4]The followers went into the town. They found a colt tied in the street near the door of a house, and they untied it. [5]Some people were standing there and asked, "What are you doing? Why are you untying that colt?" [6]The followers answered the way Jesus told them to answer. And the people let them take the colt.

[7]The followers brought the colt to Jesus. They put their coats on the colt,

and Jesus sat on it. [8]Many people spread their coats on the road. Others cut branches in the fields and spread the branches on the road. [9]Some of the people were walking ahead of Jesus. Others were following him. All of them were shouting,

"Praise[n] God!
God bless the One who comes in
    the name of the Lord!
                                    Psalm 118:26
[10]God bless the kingdom of our
    father David!
That kingdom is coming!
Praise to God in heaven!"

[11]Jesus entered Jerusalem and went into the Temple.[d] When he had looked at everything, and since it was already late, he went out to Bethany with the 12 apostles.[d]

[12]The next day as Jesus was leaving Bethany, he was hungry. [13]He saw a fig tree in leaf. So he went to the tree to see if it had any figs on it. But he found no figs, only leaves. It was not the right season for figs to grow. [14]So Jesus said to the tree, "May no one ever eat fruit from you again." Jesus' followers heard him say this.

[15]Jesus returned to Jerusalem and went into the Temple.[d] He began to throw out those who were buying and selling things there. He overturned the tables that belonged to the men who were exchanging different kinds of money. And he turned over the benches of the men who were selling doves. [16]Jesus refused to allow anyone to carry goods through the Temple courts. [17]Then Jesus taught the people. He said, "It is written in the Scriptures,[d] 'My Temple will be a house where people from all nations will pray.'[n] But you are changing God's house into a 'hideout for robbers.'"[n]

[18]The leading priests and the teachers of the law heard all this. They began trying to find a way to kill Jesus. They were afraid of him because all the people were amazed at his teaching. [19]That night, Jesus and his followers left the city.

[20]The next morning, Jesus was passing by with his followers. They saw the fig tree, and it was dry and dead, even to the roots. [21]Peter remembered the tree

11:9 Praise Literally, "Hosanna," a Hebrew word used at first in praying to God for help, but at this time it was probably a shout of joy used in praising God or his Messiah. **11:17 'My Temple . . . pray.'** Quotation from Isaiah 56:7. **11:17 'hideout for robbers.'** Quotation from Jeremiah 7:11.

and said to Jesus, "Teacher, look! Yesterday, you cursed the fig tree. Now it is dry and dead!"

²²Jesus answered, "Have faith in God. ²³I tell you the truth. You can say to this mountain, 'Go, mountain, fall into the sea.' And if you have no doubts in your mind and believe that the thing you say will happen, then God will do it for you. ²⁴So I tell you to ask for things in prayer. And if you believe that you have received those things, then they will be yours. ²⁵When you are praying, and you remember that you are angry with another person about something, then forgive him. If you do this, then your Father in heaven will also forgive your sins." ²⁶ n

²⁷Jesus and his followers went again to Jerusalem. Jesus was walking in the Temple.^d The leading priests, the teachers of the law, and the older Jewish leaders came to him. ²⁸They said to him, "Tell us! What authority do you have to do these things? Who gave you this authority?"

²⁹Jesus answered, "I will ask you one question. You answer it. Then I will tell you whose authority I use to do these things. ³⁰Tell me: When John baptized people, was that from God or from man? Answer me!"

³¹They argued about Jesus' question. They said to each other, "If we answer, 'John's baptism was from God,' then Jesus will say, 'Then why didn't you believe John?' ³²But if we say, 'From man,' then the people will be against us." (These leaders were afraid of the people. All the people believed that John was a prophet.^d)

³³So the leaders answered Jesus, "We don't know."

Jesus said, "Then I will not tell you what authority I use to do these things."

12 Jesus used stories to teach the people. He said, "A man planted a vineyard. He put a wall around it and dug a hole for a winepress.^d Then he built a tower. He leased the vineyard to some farmers and left for a trip. ²Later, it was time for the grapes to be picked. So the man sent a servant to the farmers to get his share of the grapes. ³But the farmers grabbed the servant and beat him. They sent him away with nothing. ⁴Then the man sent another servant. They hit him on the head and showed

no respect for him. ⁵So the man sent another servant. They killed this servant. The man sent many other servants. The farmers beat some of them and killed others.

⁶"The man had one person left to send, his son whom he loved. He sent him last of all, saying, 'The farmers will respect my son.'

⁷"But they said to each other, 'This is the owner's son. This vineyard will be his. If we kill him, then it will be ours.' ⁸So they took the son, killed him, and threw him out of the vineyard.

⁹"So what will the man who owns the vineyard do? He will go to the vineyard and kill those farmers. Then he will give the vineyard to other farmers. ¹⁰Surely you have read this Scripture:^d

'The stone that the builders did not
      want
    became the cornerstone.^d
¹¹The Lord did this,
    and it is wonderful to us.'"

Psalm 118:22-23

¹²The Jewish leaders knew that the story was about them. So they wanted to find a way to arrest Jesus, but they were afraid of the people. So the leaders left him and went away.

¹³Later, the Jewish leaders sent some Pharisees^d and some men from the group called Herodiansⁿ to Jesus. They wanted to catch Jesus saying something wrong. ¹⁴They came to him and said, "Teacher, we know that you are an honest man. You are not afraid of what other people think about you. All men are the same to you. And you teach the truth about God's way. Tell us: Is it right to pay taxes to Caesar?^d Should we pay them, or not?"

¹⁵But Jesus knew what these men were really trying to do. He said, "Why are you trying to trap me? Bring me a silver coin. Let me see it." ¹⁶They gave Jesus a coin, and he asked, "Whose picture is on the coin? And whose name is written on it?"

They answered, "Caesar's."

¹⁷Then Jesus said to them, "Give to Caesar the things that are Caesar's. And give to God the things that are God's." The men were amazed at what Jesus said.

¹⁸Then some Sadducees^d came to Jesus. (Sadducees believe that no person will rise from death.) The Sadducees asked

---

11:26 Verse 26 Some early Greek copies add verse 26: "But if you don't forgive other people, then your Father in heaven will not forgive your sins." **12:13 Herodians** A political group that followed Herod and his family.

Jesus a question. [19]They said, "Teacher, Moses wrote that a man's brother might die. He leaves a wife but no children. Then that man must marry the widow and have children for the dead brother. [20]There were seven brothers. The first brother married but died. He had no children. [21]So the second brother married the widow. But he also died and had no children. The same thing happened with the third brother. [22]All seven brothers married her and died. None of the brothers had any children. The woman was last to die. [23]But all seven brothers had married her. So at the time people rise from death, whose wife will the woman be?"

[24]Jesus answered, "Why did you make this mistake? Is it because you don't know what the Scriptures[d] say? Or is it because you don't know about the power of God? [25]When people rise from death, there will be no marriage. People will not be married to each other but will be like angels in heaven. [26]Surely you have read what God said about people rising from death. In the book in which Moses wrote about the burning bush,[n] it says that God told Moses this: 'I am the God of Abraham, the God of Isaac, and the God of Jacob.'[n] [27]God is the God of living people, not dead people. You Sadducees are wrong!"

[28]One of the teachers of the law came to Jesus. He heard Jesus arguing with the Sadducees[d] and the Pharisees.[d] He saw that Jesus gave good answers to their questions. So he asked Jesus, "Which of the commands is most important?"

[29]Jesus answered, "The most important command is this: 'Listen, people of Israel! The Lord our God, he is the only Lord. [30]Love the Lord your God. Love him with all your heart, all your soul, all your mind, and all your strength.'[n] [31]The second most important command is this: 'Love your neighbor as you love yourself.'[n] These two commands are the most important commands."

[32]The man answered, "That was a good answer, Teacher. You were right when you said these things. God is the only Lord, and there is no other God besides him. [33]One must love God with all his heart, all his mind, and all his strength. And one must love his neigh-

bor as he loves himself. These commands are more important than all the animals and sacrifices we offer to God."

[34]Jesus saw that the man answered him wisely. So Jesus said to him, "You are close to the kingdom of God." And after that, no one was brave enough to ask Jesus any more questions.

[35]Jesus was teaching in the Temple.[d] He asked, "Why do the teachers of the law say that the Christ[d] is the son of David? [36]David himself, speaking by the Holy Spirit,[d] said:

'The Lord said to my Lord:
    Sit by me at my right side,
    until I put your enemies under
      your control.'   *Psalm 110:1*

[37]David himself calls the Christ 'Lord.' So how can the Christ be David's son?" The large crowd listened to Jesus with pleasure.

[38]Jesus continued teaching. He said, "Beware of the teachers of the law. They like to walk around wearing clothes that look important. And they love for people to show respect to them in the marketplaces. [39]They love to have the most important seats in the synagogues.[d] And they love to have the most important seats at the feasts. [40]They cheat widows and steal their homes. Then they try to make themselves look good by saying long prayers. God will punish these people terribly."

[41]Jesus sat near the Temple[d] money box where people put their gifts. He watched the people put in their money. Many rich people gave large sums of money. [42]Then a poor widow came and gave two very small copper coins. These coins were not worth even a penny.

[43]Jesus called his followers to him. He said, "I tell you the truth. This poor widow gave only two small coins. But she really gave more than all those rich people. [44]The rich have plenty; they gave only what they did not need. This woman is very poor. But she gave all she had. And she needed that money to help her live."

13 Jesus was leaving the Temple.[d] One of his followers said to him, "Look, Teacher! This Temple has beautiful buildings with very big stones."

[2]Jesus said, "Do you see all these great buildings? Every stone will be

12:26 burning bush Read Exodus 3:1-12 in the Old Testament.   **12:26 'I am . . . Jacob.'** Quotation from Exodus 3:6.   **12:29-30 'Listen . . . strength.'** Quotation from Deuteronomy 6:4-5.   **12:31 'Love . . . yourself.'** Quotation from Leviticus 19:18.

thrown to the ground. Not one stone will be left on another."

[3]Later, Jesus was sitting on the Mount of Olives.[d] He was alone with Peter, James, John, and Andrew. They could all see the Temple. They asked Jesus, [4]"Tell us, when will all these things happen? And what will show us that the time has come for them to happen?"

[5]Jesus said to them: "Be careful that no one fools you. [6]Many people will come and use my name. They will say, 'I am the One.' And they will fool many. [7]You will hear about wars and stories of wars that are coming. But don't be afraid. These things must happen before the end comes. [8]Nations will fight against other nations. Kingdoms will fight against other kingdoms. There will be times when there is no food for people to eat. And there will be earthquakes in different places. These things are like the first pains when something new is about to be born.

[9]"You must be careful. People will arrest you and take you to court. They will beat you in their synagogues.[d] You will be forced to stand before kings and governors, to tell them about me. This will happen to you because you follow me. [10]But before these things happen, the Good News[d] must be told to all people. [11]When you are arrested and judged, don't worry about what you should say. Say the things God gives you to say at that time. It will not really be you speaking. It will be the Holy Spirit.[d]

[12]"Brothers will turn against their own brothers and give them over to be killed. Fathers will turn against their own children and give them over to be killed. Children will fight against their own parents and cause their parents to be killed. [13]All people will hate you because you follow me. But the person who continues to be strong until the end will be saved.

[14]"You will see 'the horrible thing that destroys.'[n] You will see this thing standing in the place where it should not be." (You who read this should understand what it means.) "At that time, the people in Judea should run away to the mountains. [15]If a person is on the roof[n] of his house, he must not go down to take anything out of his house. [16]If a person is in

the field, he must not go back to get his coat. [17]At that time, it will be hard for women who are pregnant or have nursing babies. [18]Pray that these things will not happen in winter. [19]This is because those days will be full of trouble. There will be more trouble than there has ever been since the beginning, when God made the world. And nothing as bad will ever happen again. [20]God has decided to make that terrible time short. If that time were not made short, then no one would go on living. But God will make that time short to help his special people whom he has chosen. [21]At that time, someone might say to you, 'Look, there is the Christ!'[d] Or another person might say, 'There he is!' But don't believe them. [22]False Christs and false prophets[d] will come and perform great wonders and miracles.[d] They will do these things to the people God has chosen. They will do these things to try to fool them, if that is possible. [23]So be careful. For I have warned you about all this before it happens.

[24]"During the days after this trouble comes,

'The sun will grow dark.
    And the moon will not give its
        light.
[25]The stars will fall from the sky.
    And everything in the sky will be
        changed.'   *Isaiah 13:10; 34:4*

[26]"Then people will see the Son of Man[d] coming in clouds with great power and glory. [27]The Son of Man will send his angels all around the earth. They will gather his chosen people from every part of the earth.

[28]"The fig tree teaches us a lesson: When its branches become green and soft, and new leaves begin to grow, then you know that summer is near. [29]So also when you see all these things happening, then you will know that the time is near, ready to come. [30]I tell you the truth. All these things will happen while the people of this time are still living. [31]The whole world, earth and sky, will be destroyed, but the words I have said will never be destroyed.

[32]"No one knows when that day or time will be. The Son and the angels in heaven don't know. Only the Father knows. [33]Be careful! Always be ready!

13:14 'the horrible . . . destroys.' Mentioned in Daniel 9:27; 12:11 (cf. Daniel 11:31). **13:15 roof** In Bible times houses were built with flat roofs. The roof was used for drying things such as flax and fruit. And it was used as an extra room, as a place for worship and as a place to sleep in the summer.

You don't know when that time will be. [34]It is like a man who goes on a trip. He leaves his house and lets his servants take care of it. He gives each servant a special job to do. One servant has the work of guarding the door. The man tells this servant always to be watchful. This is what I am now telling you. [35]You must always be ready. You don't know when the owner of the house will come back. He might come in the evening, or at midnight, or in the early morning, or when the sun rises. [36]He might come back quickly. If you are always ready, then he will not find you sleeping. [37]I tell you this, and I say this to everyone: 'Be ready!'"

14 It was now only two days before the Passover[d] and the Feast[d] of Unleavened Bread. The leading priests and teachers of the law were trying to find a way to use some trick to arrest Jesus and kill him. [2]But they said, "We must not do it during the feast. The people might cause a riot."

[3]Jesus was in Bethany. He was at dinner in the house of Simon, who had a harmful skin disease. While Jesus was there, a woman came to him. She had an alabaster[d] jar filled with very expensive perfume, made of pure nard.[d] The woman opened the jar and poured the perfume on Jesus' head.

[4]Some of those who were there saw this and became angry. They complained to each other, saying, "Why waste that perfume? [5]It was worth a full year's work. It could be sold, and the money could be given to the poor." They spoke to the woman sharply.

[6]Jesus said, "Don't bother the woman. Why are you troubling her? She did a beautiful thing for me. [7]You will always have the poor with you. You can help them anytime you want. But you will not always have me. [8]This woman did the only thing she could do for me. She poured perfume on my body. She did this before I die to prepare me for burial. [9]I tell you the truth. The Good News[d] will be told to people in all the world. And in every place it is preached, what this woman has done will be told. And people will remember her."

[10]One of the 12 followers, Judas Iscariot, went to talk to the leading priests. Judas offered to give Jesus to them. [11]The leading priests were pleased about this. They promised to pay Judas money.

So he waited for the best time to give Jesus to them.

[12]It was now the first day of the Feast[d] of Unleavened Bread. This was a time when the Jews always sacrificed the Passover[d] lambs. Jesus' followers came to him. They said, "We will go and prepare everything for the Passover Feast. Where do you want to eat the feast?"

[13]Jesus sent two of his followers and said to them, "Go into the city. A man carrying a jar of water will meet you. Follow him. [14]He will go into a house. Tell the owner of the house, 'The Teacher asks that you show us the room where he and his followers can eat the Passover Feast.' [15]The owner will show you a large room upstairs. This room is ready. Prepare the food for us there."

[16]So the followers left and went into the city. Everything happened as Jesus had said. So they prepared the Passover Feast.

[17]In the evening, Jesus went to that house with the 12. [18]While they were all eating, Jesus said, "I tell you the truth. One of you will give me to my enemies—one of you eating with me now."

[19]The followers were very sad to hear this. Each one said to Jesus, "I am not the one, am I?"

[20]Jesus answered, "The man who is against me is 1 of the 12. He is the 1 who dips his bread into the bowl with me. [21]The Son of Man[d] must go and die. The Scriptures[d] say this will happen. But how terrible it will be for the person who gives the Son of Man to be killed. It would be better for that person if he had never been born."

[22]While they were eating, Jesus took some bread. He thanked God for it and broke it. Then he gave it to his followers and said, "Take it. This bread is my body."

[23]Then Jesus took a cup. He thanked God for it and gave it to the followers. All the followers drank from the cup.

[24]Then Jesus said, "This is my blood which begins the new agreement that God makes with his people. This blood is poured out for many. [25]I tell you the truth. I will not drink of this fruit of the vine[n] again until that day when I drink it new in the kingdom of God."

[26]They sang a hymn and went out to the Mount of Olives.[q]

[27]Then Jesus told the followers, "You

14:25 fruit of the vine Product of the grapevine; this may also be translated "wine."

will all lose your faith in me. It is written in the Scriptures:[d]

'I will kill the shepherd,
and the sheep will scatter.'

Zechariah 13:7

[28]But after I rise from death, I will go ahead of you into Galilee."

[29]Peter said, "All the other followers may lose their faith. But I will not."

[30]Jesus answered, "I tell you the truth. Tonight you will say you don't know me. You will say this three times before the rooster crows twice."

[31]But Peter answered strongly, "I will never say that I don't know you! I will even die with you!" And all the other followers said the same thing.

[32]Jesus and his followers went to a place called Gethsemane. He said to his followers, "Sit here while I pray." [33]Jesus told Peter, James, and John to come with him. Then Jesus began to be very sad and troubled. [34]He said to them, "I am full of sorrow. My heart is breaking with sadness. Stay here and watch."

[35]Jesus walked a little farther away from them. Then he fell on the ground and prayed. He prayed that, if possible, he would not have this time of suffering. [36]He prayed, "Abba,[n] Father! You can do all things. Let me not have this cup[n] of suffering. But do what you want, not what I want."

[37]Then Jesus went back to his followers. He found them asleep. He said to Peter, "Simon, why are you sleeping? You could not stay awake with me for one hour? [38]Stay awake and pray that you will not be tempted. Your spirit wants to do what is right, but your body is weak."

[39]Again Jesus went away and prayed the same thing. [40]Then he went back to the followers. Again he found them asleep because their eyes were very heavy. And they did not know what to say to Jesus.

[41]After Jesus prayed a third time, he went back to his followers. He said to them, "You are still sleeping and resting? That's enough! The time has come for the Son of Man[d] to be given to sinful people. [42]Get up! We must go. Here comes the man who has turned against me."

[43]While Jesus was still speaking, Judas came up. Judas was 1 of the 12 fol-

lowers. He had many people with him. They were sent from the leading priests, the teachers of the law, and the older Jewish leaders. Those with Judas had swords and clubs.

[44]Judas had planned a signal for them. He had said, "The man I kiss is Jesus. Arrest him and guard him while you lead him away." [45]So Judas went to Jesus and said, "Teacher!" and kissed him. [46]Then the men grabbed Jesus and arrested him. [47]One of the followers standing near drew his sword. He struck the servant of the high priest with the sword and cut off his ear.

[48]Then Jesus said, "You came to get me with swords and clubs as if I were a criminal. [49]Every day I was with you teaching in the Temple.[d] You did not arrest me there. But all these things have happened to make the Scriptures[d] come true." [50]Then all of Jesus' followers left him and ran away.

[51]A young man, wearing only a linen cloth, was following Jesus. The people also grabbed him. [52]But the cloth he was wearing came off, and he ran away naked.

[53]The people who arrested Jesus led him to the house of the high priest. All the leading priests, the older Jewish leaders, and the teachers of the law were gathered there. [54]Peter followed far behind and entered the courtyard of the high priest's house. There he sat with the guards, warming himself by the fire.

[55]The leading priests and all the Jewish council tried to find something that Jesus had done wrong so they could kill him. But the council could find no proof against him. [56]Many people came and told false things about him. But all said different things—none of them agreed.

[57]Then some men stood up and lied about Jesus. They said, [58]"We heard this man say, 'I will destroy this Temple[d] that men made. And three days later, I will build another Temple—a Temple not made by men.'" [59]But even the things these men said did not agree.

[60]Then the high priest stood before them and said to Jesus, "Aren't you going to answer the charges these men bring against you?" [61]But Jesus said nothing. He did not answer.

The high priest asked Jesus another

14:36 **Abba** Name that a child called his father. 14:36 **cup** Jesus is talking about the bad things that will happen to him. Accepting these things will be very hard, like drinking a cup of something that tastes very bitter.

question: "Are you the Christ,[d] the Son of the blessed God?"

[62] Jesus answered, "I am. And in the future you will see the Son of Man[d] sitting at the right side of the Powerful One. And you will see the Son of Man coming on clouds in the sky."

[63] When the high priest heard this, he was very angry. He tore his clothes and said, "We don't need any more witnesses! [64] You all heard him say these things against God. What do you think?"

They all said that Jesus was guilty and should be killed. [65] Some of the people there spit at Jesus. They covered his eyes and hit him with their fists. They said, "Prove that you are a prophet!"[d] Then the guards led Jesus away and beat him.

[66] Peter was still in the courtyard when a servant girl of the high priest came there. [67] She saw Peter warming himself at the fire. She looked closely at him.

Then the girl said, "You were with Jesus, that man from Nazareth."

[68] But Peter said that he was never with Jesus. He said, "I don't know or understand what you are talking about." Then Peter left and went toward the entrance of the courtyard.[n]

[69] The servant girl saw Peter there. Again she said to the people who were standing there, "This man is one of those who followed Jesus." [70] Again Peter said that it was not true.

A short time later, some people were standing near Peter. They said, "We know you are one of those who followed Jesus. You are from Galilee, too."

[71] Then Peter began to curse. He said, "I swear that I don't know this man you're talking about!"

[72] As soon as Peter said this, the rooster crowed the second time. Then Peter remembered what Jesus had told him: "Before the rooster crows twice, you will say three times that you don't know me." Then Peter was very sad and began to cry.

15 Very early in the morning, the leading priests, the older Jewish leaders, the teachers of the law, and all the Jewish council decided what to do with Jesus. They tied him, led him away, and turned him over to Pilate, the governor.

[2] Pilate asked Jesus, "Are you the king of the Jews?"

Jesus answered, "Yes, I am."

[3] The leading priests accused Jesus of many things. [4] So Pilate asked Jesus another question. He said, "You can see that these people are accusing you of many things. Why don't you answer?"

[5] But Jesus still said nothing. Pilate was very surprised at this.

[6] Every year at the Passover[d] time the governor would free one person from prison. He would free any person the people wanted him to free. [7] At that time, there was a man named Barabbas in prison. He was a rebel and had committed murder during a riot. [8] The crowd came to Pilate and asked him to free a prisoner as he always did.

[9] Pilate asked them, "Do you want me to free the king of the Jews?" [10] Pilate knew that the leading priests had given Jesus to him because they were jealous of Jesus. [11] And the leading priests had persuaded the people to ask Pilate to free Barabbas, not Jesus.

[12] Pilate asked the crowd again, "So what should I do with this man you call the king of the Jews?"

[13] They shouted, "Kill him on a cross!"

[14] Pilate asked, "Why? What wrong has he done?"

But they shouted louder and louder, "Kill him on a cross!"

[15] Pilate wanted to please the crowd. So he freed Barabbas for them. And Pilate told the soldiers to beat Jesus with whips. Then he gave Jesus to the soldiers to be killed on a cross.

[16] Pilate's soldiers took Jesus into the governor's palace (called the Praetorium). They called all the other soldiers together. [17] They put a purple robe on Jesus. Then they used thorny branches to make a crown. They put it on his head. [18] Then they called out to him, "Hail, King of the Jews!" [19] The soldiers beat Jesus on the head many times with a stick. They also spit on him. Then they made fun of him by bowing on their knees and worshiping him. [20] After they finished making fun of him, the soldiers took off the purple robe and put his own clothes on him again. Then they led Jesus out of the palace to be killed on a cross.

[21] There was a man from Cyrene coming from the fields to the city. The man was Simon, the father of Alexander and Rufus. The soldiers forced Simon to carry the cross for Jesus. [22] They led Jesus

14:68 Verse 68 Many Greek copies add: "And the rooster crowed."

to the place called Golgotha. (Golgotha means the Place of the Skull.) [2]At Golgotha the soldiers tried to give Jesus wine to drink. This wine was mixed with myrrh.[d] But he refused to drink it. [24]The soldiers nailed Jesus to a cross. Then they divided his clothes among themselves. They threw lots[d] to decide which clothes each soldier would get.

[25]It was nine o'clock in the morning when they nailed Jesus to the cross. [26]There was a sign with the charge against Jesus written on it. The sign read: "THE KING OF THE JEWS." [27]They also put two robbers on crosses beside Jesus, one on the right, and the other on the left. [28] [n] [29]People walked by and insulted Jesus. They shook their heads, saying, "You said you could destroy the Temple[d] and build it again in three days. [30]So save yourself! Come down from that cross!"

[31]The leading priests and the teachers of the law were also there. They made fun of Jesus just as the other people did. They said among themselves, "He saved other people, but he can't save himself. [32]If he is really the Christ,[d] the king of Israel, then let him come down from the cross now. We will see this, and then we will believe in him." The robbers who were being killed on the crosses beside Jesus also insulted him.

[33]At noon the whole country became dark. This darkness lasted for three hours. [34]At three o'clock Jesus cried in a loud voice, "Eloi, Eloi, lama sabachthani." This means, "My God, my God, why have you left me alone?"

[35]Some of the people standing there heard this. They said, "Listen! He is calling Elijah."

[36]One man there ran and got a sponge. He filled the sponge with vinegar and tied it to a stick. Then he used the stick to give the sponge to Jesus to drink from it. The man said, "We should wait now and see if Elijah will come to take him down from the cross."

[37]Then Jesus cried in a loud voice and died.

[38]When Jesus died, the curtain in the Temple[n] split into two pieces. The tear started at the top and tore all the way to the bottom. [39]The army officer that was standing there before the cross saw what happened when Jesus died. The officer said, "This man really was the Son of God!"

[40]Some women were standing at a distance from the cross, watching. Some of these women were Mary Magdalene, Salome, and Mary the mother of James and Joseph. (James was her youngest son.) [41]These were the women who followed Jesus in Galilee and cared for him. Many other women were also there who had come with Jesus to Jerusalem.

[42]This was Preparation[d] Day. (That means the day before the Sabbath[d] day.) It was becoming dark. [43]A man named Joseph from Arimathea was brave enough to go to Pilate and ask for Jesus' body. Joseph was an important member of the Jewish council. He was one of the people who wanted the kingdom of God to come. [44]Pilate wondered if Jesus was already dead. Pilate called the army officer who guarded Jesus and asked him if Jesus had already died. [45]The officer told Pilate that he was dead. So Pilate told Joseph he could have the body. [46]Joseph bought some linen cloth, took the body down from the cross and wrapped it in the linen. He put the body in a tomb that was cut in a wall of rock. Then he closed the tomb by rolling a very large stone to cover the entrance. [47]And Mary Magdalene and Mary the mother of Joseph saw the place where Jesus was laid.

16 The day after the Sabbath[d] day, Mary Magdalene, Mary the mother of James, and Salome bought some sweet-smelling spices to put on Jesus' body. [2]Very early on that day, the first day of the week, the women were on their way to the tomb. It was soon after sunrise. [3]They said to each other, "There is a large stone covering the entrance of the tomb. Who will move the stone for us?"

[4]Then the women looked and saw that the stone was already moved. The stone was very large, but it was moved away from the entrance. [5]The women entered the tomb and saw a young man wearing a white robe. He was sitting on the right side, and the women were afraid.

[6]But the man said, "Don't be afraid. You are looking for Jesus from Nazareth, the one who was killed on a cross.

15:28 Verse 28 Some Greek copies add verse 28: "And the Scripture came true that says, 'They put him with criminals.'" **15:38 curtain in the Temple** A curtain divided the Most Holy Place from the other part of the Temple. That was the special building in Jerusalem where God commanded the Jews to worship him.

He has risen from death. He is not here. Look, here is the place they laid him. [7]Now go and tell his followers and Peter, 'Jesus is going into Galilee. He will be there before you. You will see him there as he told you before.'"

[8]The women were confused and shaking with fear. They left the tomb and ran away. They did not tell anyone about what happened, because they were afraid.[n]

[9]Jesus rose from death early on the first day of the week. He showed himself first to Mary Magdalene. One time in the past, he had forced seven demons[d] to leave Mary. [10]After Mary saw Jesus, she went and told his followers. They were very sad and were crying. [11]But Mary told them that Jesus was alive. She said that she had seen him, but the followers did not believe her.

[12]Later, Jesus showed himself to two of his followers while they were walking in the country. But Jesus did not look the same as before. [13]These followers went back to the others and told them what had happened. Again, the followers did not believe them.

[14]Later Jesus showed himself to the 11 followers while they were eating. He criticized them because they had little faith. They were stubborn and refused to believe those who had seen him after he had risen from death.

[15]Jesus said to the followers, "Go everywhere in the world. Tell the Good News[d] to everyone. [16]Anyone who believes and is baptized will be saved. But he who does not believe will be judged guilty. [17]And those who believe will be able to do these things as proof: They will use my name to force demons[d] out of people. They will speak in languages they never learned. [18]They will pick up snakes without being hurt. And they will drink poison without being hurt. They will touch the sick, and the sick will be healed."

[19]After the Lord Jesus said these things to the followers, he was carried up into heaven. There, Jesus sat at the right side of God. [20]The followers went everywhere in the world and told the Good News to people. And the Lord helped them. The Lord proved that the Good News they told was true by giving them power to work miracles.[d]

The Gospel According to
LUKE

1 To Theophilus:
Many have tried to give a history of the things that happened among us. [2]They have written the same things that we learned from others—the people who saw those things from the beginning and served God by telling people his message. [3]I myself studied everything carefully from the beginning, your Excellency.[n] I thought I should write it out for you. So I put it in order in a book. [4]I write these things so that you can know that what you have been taught is true.

[5]During the time Herod ruled Judea, there was a priest named Zechariah. He belonged to Abijah's group.[n] Zechariah's wife came from the family of Aaron. Her name was Elizabeth. [6]Zechariah and Elizabeth truly did what God

said was good. They did everything the Lord commanded and told people to do. They were without fault in keeping his law. [7]But Zechariah and Elizabeth had no children. Elizabeth could not have a baby; and both of them were very old.

[8]Zechariah was serving as a priest before God for his group. It was his group's time to serve. [9]According to the custom of the priests, he was chosen to go into the Temple[d] of the Lord and burn incense.[d] [10]There were a great many people outside praying at the time the incense was offered. [11]Then, on the right side of the incense table, an angel of the Lord came and stood before Zechariah. [12]When he saw the angel, Zechariah was confused and frightened. [13]But the angel said to him, "Zechariah, don't be afraid. Your prayer has been heard by God.

16:8 Verse 8 Some early Greek copies end the book with verse 8. **1:3 Excellency** This word was used to show respect to an important person like a king or ruler. **1:5 Abijah's group** The Jewish priests were divided into 24 groups. See 1 Chronicles 24.

Your wife, Elizabeth, will give birth to a son. You will name him John. [14]You will be very happy. Many people will be happy because of his birth. [15]John will be a great man for the Lord. He will never drink wine or beer. Even at the time John is born, he will be filled with the Holy Spirit.[d] [16]He will help many people of Israel return to the Lord their God. [17]He himself will go first before the Lord. John will be powerful in spirit like Elijah. He will make peace between fathers and their children. He will bring those who are not obeying God back to the right way of thinking. He will make people ready for the coming of the Lord."

[18]Zechariah said to the angel, "How can I know that what you say is true? I am an old man, and my wife is old, too."

[19]The angel answered him, "I am Gabriel. I stand before God. God sent me to talk to you and to tell you this good news. [20]Now, listen! You will not be able to talk until the day these things happen. You will lose your speech because you did not believe what I told you. But these things will really happen."

[21]Outside, the people were still waiting for Zechariah. They were surprised that he was staying so long in the Temple. [22]Then Zechariah came outside, but he could not speak to them. So they knew that he had seen a vision in the Temple. Zechariah could not speak. He could only make signs to them. [23]When his time of service as a priest was finished, he went home.

[24]Later, Zechariah's wife, Elizabeth, became pregnant. She did not go out of her house for five months. Elizabeth said, [25]"Look what the Lord has done for me! My people were ashamed[n] of me, but now the Lord has taken away that shame."

[26-27]During Elizabeth's sixth month of pregnancy, God sent the angel Gabriel to a virgin[d] who lived in Nazareth, a town in Galilee. She was engaged to marry a man named Joseph from the family of David. Her name was Mary. [28]The angel came to her and said, "Greetings! The Lord has blessed you and is with you."

[29]But Mary was very confused by what the angel said. Mary wondered, "What does this mean?"

[30]The angel said to her, "Don't be afraid, Mary, because God is pleased

with you. [31]Listen! You will become pregnant. You will give birth to a son, and you will name him Jesus. [32]He will be great, and people will call him the Son of the Most High. The Lord God will give him the throne of King David, his ancestor. [33]He will rule over the people of Jacob forever. His kingdom will never end."

[34]Mary said to the angel, "How will this happen? I am a virgin!"

[35]The angel said to Mary, "The Holy Spirit[d] will come upon you, and the power of the Most High will cover you. The baby will be holy. He will be called the Son of God. [36]Now listen! Elizabeth, your relative, is very old. But she is also pregnant with a son. Everyone thought she could not have a baby, but she has been pregnant for six months. [37]God can do everything!"

[38]Mary said, "I am the servant girl of the Lord. Let this happen to me as you say!" Then the angel went away.

[39]Mary got up and went quickly to a town in the mountains of Judea. [40]She went to Zechariah's house and greeted Elizabeth. [41]When Elizabeth heard Mary's greeting, the unborn baby inside Elizabeth jumped. Then Elizabeth was filled with the Holy Spirit.[d] [42]She cried out in a loud voice, "God has blessed you more than any other woman. And God has blessed the baby which you will give birth to. [43]You are the mother of my Lord, and you have come to me! Why has something so good happened to me? [44]When I heard your voice, the baby inside me jumped with joy. [45]You are blessed because you believed what the Lord said to you would really happen."

[46]Then Mary said,

"My soul praises the Lord;
[47] my heart is happy because God is my Savior.
[48]I am not important, but God has shown his care for me, his servant girl.
From now on, all people will say that I am blessed,
[49] because the Powerful One has done great things for me.
His name is holy.
[50]God will always give mercy to those who worship him.
[51]God's arm is strong.
He scatters the people who are proud

1:25 **ashamed** The Jews thought it was a disgrace for women not to have children.

and think great things about themselves.

[52] God brings down rulers from their thrones,
and he raises up the humble.

[53] God fills the hungry with good things,
but he sends the rich away with nothing.

[54] God has helped his people Israel who serve him.
He gave them his mercy.

[55] God has done what he promised to our ancestors,
to Abraham and to his children forever."

[56] Mary stayed with Elizabeth for about three months and then returned home.

[57] When it was time for Elizabeth to give birth, she had a boy. [58] Her neighbors and relatives heard how good the Lord was to her, and they rejoiced.

[59] When the baby was eight days old, they came to circumcise[d] him. They wanted to name him Zechariah because this was his father's name. [60] But his mother said, "No! He will be named John."

[61] The people said to Elizabeth, "But no one in your family has this name!" [62] Then they made signs to his father, "What would you like to name him?"

[63] Zechariah asked for something to write on. Then he wrote, "His name is John." Everyone was surprised. [64] Then Zechariah could talk again. He began to praise God. [65] And all their neighbors became alarmed. In all the mountains of Judea people continued talking about all these things. [66] The people who heard about these things wondered about them. They thought, "What will this child be?" They said this because the Lord was with him.

[67] Then Zechariah, John's father, was filled with the Holy Spirit.[d] He told the people what would happen:

[68] "Let us thank the Lord, the God of Israel.
God has come to help his people and has given them freedom.

[69] God has given us a powerful Savior from the family of God's servant David.

[70] God said that he would do this.
He said it through his holy prophets[d] who lived long ago.

[71] God will save us from our enemies

and from the power of all those who hate us.

[72] God said he would give mercy to our fathers.
And he remembered his holy promise.

[73] God promised Abraham, our father,
[74] that he would free us from the power of our enemies,
so that we could serve him without fear.

[75] We will be righteous and holy before God as long as we live.

[76] "Now you, child, will be called a prophet of the Most High God.
You will go first before the Lord to prepare the people for his coming.

[77] You will make his people know that they will be saved.
They will be saved by having their sins forgiven.

[78] With the loving mercy of our God,
a new day from heaven will shine upon us.

[79] God will help those who live in darkness,
in the fear of death.
He will guide us into the path that goes toward peace."

[80] And so the child grew up and became strong in spirit. John lived away from other people until the time when he came out to preach to Israel.

2 At that time, Augustus Caesar[d] sent an order to all people in the countries that were under Roman rule. The order said that they must list their names in a register. [2] This was the first registration[n] taken while Quirinius was governor of Syria. [3] And everyone went to their own towns to be registered.

[4] So Joseph left Nazareth, a town in Galilee. He went to the town of Bethlehem in Judea. This town was known as the town of David. Joseph went there because he was from the family of David. [5] Joseph registered with Mary because she was engaged to marry him. (Mary was now pregnant.) [6] While Joseph and Mary were in Bethlehem, the time came for her to have the baby. [7] She gave birth to her first son. There were no rooms left in the inn. So she wrapped the baby with cloths and laid him in a box where animals are fed.

[8] That night, some shepherds were in the fields nearby watching their sheep. [9] An angel of the Lord stood before them.

2:2 registration Census. A counting of all the people and the things they own.

The glory of the Lord was shining around them, and suddenly they became very frightened. [10]The angel said to them, "Don't be afraid, because I am bringing you some good news. It will be a joy to all the people. [11]Today your Savior was born in David's town. He is Christ,[d] the Lord. [12]This is how you will know him: You will find a baby wrapped in cloths and lying in a feeding box."

[13]Then a very large group of angels from heaven joined the first angel. All the angels were praising God, saying:

[14]"Give glory to God in heaven,
and on earth let there be peace to
the people who please God."

[15]Then the angels left the shepherds and went back to heaven. The shepherds said to each other, "Let us go to Bethlehem and see this thing that has happened. We will see this thing the Lord told us about."

[16]So the shepherds went quickly and found Mary and Joseph. [17]And the shepherds saw the baby lying in a feeding box. Then they told what the angels had said about this child. [18]Everyone was amazed when they heard what the shepherds said to them. [19]Mary hid these things in her heart; she continued to think about them. [20]Then the shepherds went back to their sheep, praising God and thanking him for everything that they had seen and heard. It was just as the angel had told them.

[21]When the baby was eight days old, he was circumcised,[d] and he was named Jesus. This name had been given by the angel before the baby began to grow inside Mary.

[22]The time came for Mary and Joseph to do what the law of Moses taught about being made pure.[n] They took Jesus to Jerusalem to present him to the Lord. [23]It is written in the law of the Lord: "Give every firstborn[d] male to the Lord."[n] [24]Mary and Joseph also went to offer a sacrifice, as the law of the Lord says: "You must sacrifice two doves or two young pigeons."[n]

[25]A man named Simeon lived in Jerusalem. He was a good man and very religious. He was waiting for the time when God would help Israel. The Holy Spirit[d] was in him. [26]The Holy Spirit told Simeon that he would not die before he saw

the Christ[d] promised by the Lord. [27]The Spirit led Simeon to the Temple.[d] Mary and Joseph brought the baby Jesus to the Temple to do what the law said they must do. [28]Then Simeon took the baby in his arms and thanked God:

[29]"Now, Lord, you can let me, your
servant,
die in peace as you said.
[30]I have seen your Salvation[n] with my
own eyes.
[31]   You prepared him before all
people.
[32]He is a light for the non-Jewish
people to see.
He will bring honor to your
people, the Israelites."

[33]Jesus' father and mother were amazed at what Simeon had said about him. [34]Then Simeon blessed them and said to Mary, "Many in Israel will fall and many will rise because of this child. He will be a sign from God that many people will not accept. [35]The things they think in secret will be made known. And the things that will happen will make your heart sad, too."

[36]Anna, a prophetess,[d] was there at the Temple.[d] She was from the family of Phanuel in the tribe[d] of Asher. Anna was very old. She had once been married for seven years. [37]Then her husband died and she lived alone. She was now 84 years old. Anna never left the Temple. She worshiped God by going without food and praying day and night. [38]She was standing there at that time, thanking God. She talked about Jesus to all who were waiting for God to free Jerusalem.

[39]Joseph and Mary finished doing everything that the law of the Lord commanded. Then they went home to Nazareth, their own town in Galilee. [40]The little child began to grow up. He became stronger and wiser, and God's blessings were with him.

[41]Every year Jesus' parents went to Jerusalem for the Passover[d] Feast. [42]When Jesus was 12 years old, they went to the feast as they always did. [43]When the feast days were over, they went home. The boy Jesus stayed behind in Jerusalem, but his parents did not know it. [44]Joseph and Mary traveled for a whole day. They thought that Jesus was with them

2:22 **pure** The law of Moses said that 40 days after a Jewish woman gave birth to a baby, she must be cleansed by a ceremony at the Temple. Read Leviticus 12:2–8. 2:23 **"Give . . . Lord."** Quotation from Exodus 13:2. 2:24 **"You . . . pigeons."** Quotation from Leviticus 12:8. 2:30 **Salvation** Simeon was talking about Jesus. The name Jesus means "salvation."

in the group. Then they began to look for him among their family and friends, ⁴⁵but they did not find him. So they went back to Jerusalem to look for him there. ⁴⁶After three days they found him. Jesus was sitting in the Temple[d] with the religious teachers, listening to them and asking them questions. ⁴⁷All who heard him were amazed at his understanding and wise answers. ⁴⁸When Jesus' parents saw him, they were amazed. His mother said to him, "Son, why did you do this to us? Your father and I were very worried about you. We have been looking for you."

⁴⁹Jesus asked, "Why did you have to look for me? You should have known that I must be where my Father's work is!" ⁵⁰But they did not understand the meaning of what he said.

⁵¹Jesus went with them to Nazareth and obeyed them. His mother was still thinking about all that had happened. ⁵²Jesus continued to learn more and more and to grow physically. People liked him, and he pleased God.

3 It was the fifteenth year of the rule of Tiberius Caesar.[d] These men were under Caesar: Pontius Pilate was the ruler of Judea. Herod was the ruler of Galilee. Philip, Herod's brother, was the ruler of Iturea and Trachonitis. And Lysanias was the ruler of Abilene. ²Annas and Caiaphas were the high priests. At this time, a command from God came to John son of Zechariah. John was living in the desert. ³He went all over the area around the Jordan River and preached to the people. He preached a baptism of changed hearts and lives for the forgiveness of their sins. ⁴As it is written in the book of Isaiah the prophet:[d]

"This is a voice of a man
    who calls out in the desert:
'Prepare the way for the Lord.
    Make the road straight for him.
⁵Every valley should be filled in.
    Every mountain and hill should
      be made flat.
Roads with turns should be made
    straight,
    and rough roads should be made
      smooth.
⁶And all people will know about the
    salvation of God!'"   *Isaiah 40:3-5*

⁷Crowds of people came to be baptized by John. He said to them, "You poisonous snakes! Who warned you to run away from God's anger that is coming? ⁸You must do the things that will show that you really have changed your hearts. Don't say, 'Abraham is our father.' I tell you that God can make children for Abraham from these rocks here. ⁹The ax is now ready to cut down the trees. Every tree that does not produce good fruit will be cut down and thrown into the fire."[n]

¹⁰The people asked John, "What should we do?"

¹¹John answered, "If you have two shirts, share with the person who does not have one. If you have food, share that too."

¹²Even tax collectors came to John to be baptized. They said to John, "Teacher, what should we do?"

¹³John said to them, "Don't take more taxes from people than you have been ordered to take."

¹⁴The soldiers asked John, "What about us? What should we do?"

John said to them, "Don't force people to give you money. Don't lie about them. Be satisfied with the pay you get."

¹⁵All the people were hoping for the Christ[d] to come, and they wondered about John. They thought, "Maybe he is the Christ."

¹⁶John answered everyone, "I baptize you with water, but there is one coming later who can do more than I can. I am not good enough to untie his sandals. He will baptize you with the Holy Spirit[d] and with fire. ¹⁷He will come ready to clean the grain. He will separate the good grain from the chaff.[d] He will put the good part of the grain into his barn. Then he will burn the chaff with a fire that cannot be put out."[n] ¹⁸And John continued to preach the Good News,[d] saying many other things to encourage the people.

¹⁹But John spoke against Herod, the governor, because of his sin with Herodias, the wife of Herod's brother. John also criticized Herod for the many other evil things Herod did. ²⁰So Herod did another evil thing: He put John in prison.

²¹When all the people were being baptized by John, Jesus also was baptized.

3:9 The ax . . . fire. This means that God is ready to punish his people who do not obey him.
3:17 He will . . . out. This means that Jesus will come to separate the good people from the bad people, saving the good and punishing the bad.

While Jesus was praying, heaven opened and [22]the Holy Spirit[d] came down on him. The Spirit was in the form of a dove. Then a voice came from heaven and said, "You are my Son and I love you. I am very pleased with you."

[23]When Jesus began to teach, he was about 30 years old. People thought that Jesus was Joseph's son.

Joseph was the son[n] of Heli.
[24]Heli was the son of Matthat.
Matthat was the son of Levi.
Levi was the son of Melki.
Melki was the son of Jannai.
Jannai was the son of Joseph.
[25]Joseph was the son of Mattathias.
Mattathias was the son of Amos.
Amos was the son of Nahum.
Nahum was the son of Esli.
Esli was the son of Naggai.
[26]Naggai was the son of Maath.
Maath was the son of Mattathias.
Mattathias was the son of Semein.
Semein was the son of Josech.
Josech was the son of Joda.
[27]Joda was the son of Joanan.
Joanan was the son of Rhesa.
Rhesa was the son of Zerubbabel.
Zerubbabel was the grandson of Shealtiel.
Shealtiel was the son of Neri.
[28]Neri was the son of Melchi.
Melchi was the son of Addi.
Addi was the son of Cosam.
Cosam was the son of Elmadam.
Elmadam was the son of Er.
[29]Er was the son of Joshua.
Joshua was the son of Eliezer.
Eliezer was the son of Jorim.
Jorim was the son of Matthat.
Matthat was the son of Levi.
[30]Levi was the son of Simeon.
Simeon was the son of Judah.
Judah was the son of Joseph.
Joseph was the son of Jonam.
Jonam was the son of Eliakim.
[31]Eliakim was the son of Melea.
Melea was the son of Menna.
Menna was the son of Mattatha.
Mattatha was the son of Nathan.
Nathan was the son of David.
[32]David was the son of Jesse.
Jesse was the son of Obed.
Obed was the son of Boaz.
Boaz was the son of Salmon.
Salmon was the son of Nahshon.

[33]Nahshon was the son of Amminadab.
Amminadab was the son of Admin.
Admin was the son of Arni.
Arni was the son of Hezron.
Hezron was the son of Perez.
Perez was the son of Judah.
[34]Judah was the son of Jacob.
Jacob was the son of Isaac.
Isaac was the son of Abraham.
Abraham was the son of Terah.
Terah was the son of Nahor.
[35]Nahor was the son of Serug.
Serug was the son of Reu.
Reu was the son of Peleg.
Peleg was the son of Eber.
Eber was the son of Shelah.
[36]Shelah was the son of Cainan.
Cainan was the son of Arphaxad.
Arphaxad was the son of Shem.
Shem was the son of Noah.
Noah was the son of Lamech.
[37]Lamech was the son of Methuselah.
Methuselah was the son of Enoch.
Enoch was the son of Jared.
Jared was the son of Mahalalel.
Mahalalel was the son of Kenan.
[38]Kenan was the son of Enosh.
Enosh was the son of Seth.
Seth was the son of Adam.
Adam was the son of God.

4 Jesus, filled with the Holy Spirit,[d] returned from the Jordan River. The Spirit led Jesus into the desert [2]where the devil tempted Jesus for 40 days. Jesus ate nothing during that time. When those days were ended, he was very hungry.

[3]The devil said to Jesus, "If you are the Son of God, tell this rock to become bread."

[4]Jesus answered, "It is written in the Scriptures:[d] 'A person does not live only by eating bread.'"[n]

[5]Then the devil took Jesus and showed him all the kingdoms of the world in a moment of time. [6]The devil said to Jesus, "I will give you all these kingdoms and all their power and glory. It has all been given to me, and I can give it to anyone I wish. [7]If you worship me, all will be yours."

[8]Jesus answered, "It is written in the Scriptures: 'You must worship the Lord your God. Serve only him!'"[n]

[9]Then the devil led Jesus to Jerusalem and put him on a high place of the Tem-

---

3:23 son "Son" in Jewish lists of ancestors can sometimes mean grandson or more distant relative. **4:4 'A person . . . bread.'** Quotation from Deuteronomy 8:3. **4:8 'You . . . him!'** Quotation from Deuteronomy 6:13.

ple.[d] He said to Jesus, "If you are the Son of God, jump off! [10]It is written in the Scriptures:

'He has put his angels in charge of you.
They will watch over you.'
Psalm 91:11

[11]'They will catch you with their hands.
And you will not hit your foot on a rock.'"
Psalm 91:12

[12]Jesus answered, "But it also says in the Scriptures: 'Do not test the Lord your God.'"[n]

[13]After the devil had tempted Jesus in every way, he went away to wait until a better time.

[14]Jesus went back to Galilee with the power of the Holy Spirit.[d] Stories about Jesus spread all through the area. [15]He began to teach in the synagogues,[d] and all the people praised him.

[16]Jesus traveled to Nazareth, where he had grown up. On the Sabbath[d] day he went to the synagogue as he always did. Jesus stood up to read. [17]The book of Isaiah the prophet[d] was given to him. He opened the book and found the place where this is written:

[18]"The Spirit of the Lord is in me.
This is because God chose me to tell the Good News[d] to the poor.
God sent me to tell the prisoners of sin that they are free,
and to tell the blind that they can see again. *Isaiah 61:1*
God sent me to free those who have been treated unfairly, *Isaiah 58:6*
[19]   and to announce the time when the Lord will show kindness to his people." *Isaiah 61:2*

[20]Jesus closed the book, gave it back, and sat down. Everyone in the synagogue was watching Jesus closely. [21]He began to speak to them. He said, "While you heard these words just now, they were coming true!"

[22]All the people praised Jesus. They were amazed at the beautiful words he spoke. They asked, "Isn't this Joseph's son?"

[23]Jesus said to them, "I know that you will tell me the old saying: 'Doctor, heal yourself.' You want to say, 'We heard about the things you did in Capernaum. Do those things here in your own town!'" [24]Then Jesus said, "I tell you the

truth. A prophet is not accepted in his own town. [25]What I say is true. During the time of Elijah it did not rain in Israel for three and a half years. There was no food anywhere in the whole country. And there were many widows in Israel during that time. [26]But Elijah was sent to none of those widows. He was sent only to a widow in Zarephath, a town in Sidon. [27]And there were many with a harmful skin disease living in Israel during the time of the prophet Elisha. But none of them were healed except Naaman, who was from the country of Syria."

[28]When all the people in the synagogue heard these things, they became very angry. [29]They got up and forced Jesus out of town. The town was built on a hill. They took Jesus to the edge of the hill and wanted to throw him off. [30]But Jesus walked through the crowd and went on his way.

[31]Jesus went to Capernaum, a city in Galilee. On the Sabbath[d] day, Jesus taught the people. [32]They were amazed at his teaching, because he spoke with authority. [33]In the synagogue[d] there was a man who had an evil spirit from the devil inside him. The man shouted in a loud voice, [34]"Jesus of Nazareth! What do you want with us? Did you come here to destroy us? I know who you are—God's Holy One!"

[35]But Jesus warned the evil spirit to stop. He said, "Be quiet! Come out of the man!" The evil spirit threw the man down to the ground before all the people. Then the evil spirit left the man and did not hurt him.

[36]The people were amazed. They said to each other, "What does this mean? With authority and power he commands evil spirits, and they come out." [37]And so the news about Jesus spread to every place in the whole area.

[38]Jesus left the synagogue[d] and went to Simon's[n] house. Simon's mother-in-law was very sick with a high fever. They asked Jesus to do something to help her. [39]He stood very close to her and commanded the fever to leave. It left her immediately, and she got up and began serving them.

[40]When the sun went down, the people brought their sick to Jesus. They had many different diseases. Jesus put his hands on each sick person and healed

4:12 **'Do . . . God.'** Quotation from Deuteronomy 6:16.   4:38 **Simon** Simon's other name was Peter.

every one of them. [41]Demons[d] came out of many people. The demons would shout, "You are the Son of God." But Jesus gave a strong command for the demons not to speak. They knew Jesus was the Christ.[d]

[42]At daybreak, Jesus went to a place to be alone, but the people looked for him. When they found him, they tried to keep him from leaving. [43]But Jesus said to them, "I must tell the Good News[d] about God's kingdom to other towns, too. This is why I was sent."

[44]Then Jesus kept on preaching in the synagogues[d] of Judea.

5 One day Jesus was standing beside Lake Galilee. Many people were pressing all around him. They wanted to hear the word of God. [2]Jesus saw two boats at the shore of the lake. The fishermen had left them and were washing their nets. [3]Jesus got into one of the boats, the one which belonged to Simon.[n] Jesus asked Simon to push off a little from the land. Then Jesus sat down in the boat and continued to teach the people on the shore.

[4]When Jesus had finished speaking, he said to Simon, "Take the boat into deep water. If you will put your nets in the water, you will catch some fish."

[5]Simon answered, "Master, we worked hard all night trying to catch fish, but we caught nothing. But you say to put the nets in the water; so I will." [6]The fishermen did as Jesus told them. And they caught so many fish that the nets began to break. [7]They called to their friends in the other boat to come and help them. The friends came, and both boats were filled so full that they were almost sinking.

[8-9]The fishermen were all amazed at the many fish they caught. When Simon Peter saw what had happened, he bowed down before Jesus and said, "Go away from me, Lord. I am a sinful man!" [10]James and John, the sons of Zebedee, were amazed too. (James and John were Simon's partners.)

Jesus said to Simon, "Don't be afraid. From now on you will be fishermen for men." [11]When the men brought their boats to the shore, they left everything and followed Jesus.

[12]One time Jesus was in a town where a very sick man lived. The man was covered with a harmful skin disease. When he saw Jesus, he bowed before Jesus and begged him, "Lord, heal me. I know you can if you want to."

[13]Jesus said, "I want to. Be healed!" And Jesus touched the man. Immediately the disease disappeared. [14]Then Jesus said, "Don't tell anyone about what happened. But go show yourself to the priest." And offer a gift to God for your healing as Moses commanded.[n] This will prove to everyone that you are healed."

[15]But the news about Jesus was spreading more and more. Many people came to hear Jesus and to be healed of their sicknesses. [16]But Jesus often slipped away to other places to be alone so that he could pray.

[17]One day Jesus was teaching the people. The Pharisees[d] and teachers of the law were there, too. They had come from every town in Galilee and from Judea and Jerusalem. The Lord was giving Jesus the power to heal people. [18]There was a man who was paralyzed. Some men were carrying him on a mat. They tried to bring him in and put him down before Jesus. [19]But because there were so many people there, they could not find a way to Jesus. So the men went up on the roof and made a hole in the ceiling. They lowered the mat so that the paralyzed man was lying right before Jesus. [20]Jesus saw that these men believed. So he said to the sick man, "Friend, your sins are forgiven."

[21]The Jewish teachers of the law and the Pharisees thought to themselves, "Who is this man? He is saying things that are against God! Only God can forgive sins."

[22]But Jesus knew what they were thinking. He said, "Why do you have thoughts like that in your hearts? [23]Which is easier: to tell this paralyzed man, 'Your sins are forgiven,' or to tell him, 'Stand up and walk'? [24]But I will prove to you that the Son of Man[d] has authority on earth to forgive sins." So Jesus said to the paralyzed man, "I tell you, stand up! Take your mat and go home."

[25]Then the man stood up before the people there. He picked up his mat and went home, praising God. [26]All the people were fully amazed and began to

---

5:3 Simon Simon's other name was Peter.   **5:14 show . . . priest** The law of Moses said a priest must say when a Jew with a harmful skin disease was well.   **5:14 Moses commanded** Read about this in Leviticus 14:1-32.

praise God. They were filled with much respect and said, "Today we have seen amazing things!"

²⁷After this, Jesus went out and saw a tax collector named Levi sitting in the tax office. Jesus said to him, "Follow me!" ²⁸Levi got up, left everything, and followed Jesus.

²⁹Then Levi gave a big dinner for Jesus. The dinner was at Levi's house. At the table there were many tax collectors and other people, too. ³⁰But the Pharisees[d] and the men who taught the law for the Pharisees began to complain to the followers of Jesus. They said, "Why do you eat and drink with tax collectors and 'sinners'?"

³¹Jesus answered them, "Healthy people don't need a doctor. It is the sick who need a doctor. ³²I have not come to invite good people. I have come to invite sinners to change their hearts and lives!"

³³They said to Jesus, "John's followers often give up eating[n] and pray, just as the Pharisees[d] do. But your followers eat and drink all the time."

³⁴Jesus said to them, "When there is a wedding, you cannot make the friends of the bridegroom give up eating while he is still with them. ³⁵But the time will come when he will be taken away from them. Then his friends will give up eating."

³⁶Jesus told them this story: "No one takes cloth off a new coat to cover a hole in an old coat. If he does, he ruins the new coat, and the cloth from the new coat will not be the same as the old cloth. ³⁷People never pour new wine into old leather bags for holding wine. If they do, the new wine will break the bags, and the wine will spill out. Then the leather bags for holding wine will be ruined. ³⁸People always put new wine into new leather bags. ³⁹No one after drinking old wine wants new wine because he says, 'The old wine is better.' "

6 One Sabbath[d] day Jesus was walking through some grainfields. His followers picked the heads of grain, rubbed them in their hands, and ate them. ²Some Pharisees[d] said, "Why are you doing that? It is against the law of Moses to do that on the Sabbath day."

³Jesus answered, "Haven't you read about what David did when he and those with him were hungry? ⁴David went into God's house. He took the bread that was made holy for God and ate it. And he gave some of the bread to the people with him. This was against the law of Moses. It says that only priests can eat that bread." ⁵Then Jesus said to the Pharisees, "The Son of Man[d] is Lord of the Sabbath day."

⁶On another Sabbath[d] day Jesus went into the synagogue[d] and was teaching. A man with a crippled right hand was there. ⁷The teachers of the law and the Pharisees[d] were watching to see if Jesus would heal on the Sabbath day. They wanted to see Jesus do something wrong so that they could accuse him. ⁸But he knew what they were thinking. He said to the man with the crippled hand, "Get up and stand before these people." The man got up and stood there. ⁹Then Jesus said to them, "I ask you, which is it right to do on the Sabbath day: to do good, or to do evil? Is it right to save a life or to destroy one?" ¹⁰Jesus looked around at all of them. He said to the man, "Let me see your hand." The man stretched out his hand, and it was completely healed.

¹¹The Pharisees and the teachers of the law became very angry. They said to each other, "What can we do to Jesus?"

¹²At that time Jesus went off to a mountain to pray. He stayed there all night, praying to God. ¹³The next morning, Jesus called his followers to him. He chose 12 of them, whom he named "apostles."[d] They were ¹⁴Simon (Jesus named him Peter) and Andrew, Peter's brother; James and John, Philip and Bartholomew; ¹⁵Matthew, Thomas, James son of Alphaeus, and Simon (called the Zealot[d]), ¹⁶Judas son of James and Judas Iscariot. This Judas was the one who gave Jesus to his enemies.

¹⁷Jesus and the apostles[d] came down from the mountain. Jesus stood on level ground where there was a large group of his followers. Also, there were many people from all around Judea, Jerusalem, and the seacoast cities of Tyre and Sidon. ¹⁸They all came to hear Jesus teach and to be healed of their sicknesses. He healed those who were troubled by evil spirits. ¹⁹All the people were trying to touch Jesus, because power was coming from him and healing them all!

5:33 give up eating This is called "fasting." The people would give up eating for a special time of prayer and worship to God. It was also done to show sadness.

²⁰Jesus looked at his followers and said,

"Poor people, you are happy,
    because God's kingdom belongs
        to you.
²¹You people who are now hungry
        are happy,
    because you will be satisfied.
You people who are now crying are
        happy,
    because you will laugh with joy.
²²"You are happy when people hate
you and are cruel to you. You are happy
when they say that you are evil because
you belong to the Son of Man.ᵈ ²³At that
time be full of joy, because you have a
great reward in heaven. Their fathers
were cruel to the prophetsᵈ in the same
way these people are cruel to you.
²⁴"But how terrible it will be for you
    who are rich,
    because you have had your easy
        life.
²⁵How terrible it will be for you who
        are full now,
    because you will be hungry.
How terrible it will be for you who
        are laughing now,
    because you will be sad and cry.
²⁶"How terrible when all people say
only good things about you. Their fathers always said good things about the
false prophets.

²⁷"I say to you who are listening to
me, love your enemies. Do good to those
who hate you. ²⁸Ask God to bless those
who say bad things to you. Pray for
those who are cruel to you. ²⁹If anyone
slaps you on one cheek, let him slap the
other cheek too. If someone takes your
coat, do not stop him from taking your
shirt. ³⁰Give to everyone who asks you.
When a person takes something that is
yours, don't ask for it back. ³¹Do for
other people what you want them to do
for you. ³²If you love only those who love
you, should you get some special praise
for doing that? No! Even sinners love
the people who love them! ³³If you do
good only to those who do good to you,
should you get some special praise for
doing that? No! Even sinners do that!
³⁴If you lend things to people, always
hoping to get something back, should
you get some special praise for that? No!
Even sinners lend to other sinners so
that they can get back the same amount!
³⁵So love your enemies. Do good to
them, and lend to them without hoping
to get anything back. If you do these
things, you will have a great reward. You
will be sons of the Most High God. Yes,
because God is kind even to people who
are ungrateful and full of sin. ³⁶Show
mercy just as your father shows mercy.

³⁷"Don't judge other people, and you
will not be judged. Don't accuse others
of being guilty, and you will not be accused of being guilty. Forgive other people, and you will be forgiven. ³⁸Give, and
you will receive. You will be given much.
It will be poured into your hands—more
than you can hold. You will be given so
much that it will spill into your lap. The
way you give to others is the way God
will give to you."

³⁹Jesus told them this story: "Can a
blind man lead another blind man? No!
Both of them will fall into a ditch. ⁴⁰A
student is not better than his teacher.
But when the student has fully learned
all that he has been taught, then he will
be like his teacher.

⁴¹"Why do you notice the little piece
of dust that is in your brother's eye, but
you don't see the big piece of wood that
is in your own eye? ⁴²You say to your
brother, 'Brother, let me take that little
piece of dust out of your eye.' Why do
you say this? You cannot see that big
piece of wood in your own eye! You are
a hypocrite!ᵈ First, take the piece of
wood out of your own eye. Then you will
see clearly to take the dust out of your
brother's eye.

⁴³"A good tree does not produce bad
fruit. Also, a bad tree does not produce
good fruit. ⁴⁴Each tree is known by its
fruit. People don't gather figs from
thornbushes. And they don't get grapes
from bushes. ⁴⁵A good person has good
things saved up in his heart. And so he
brings good things out of his heart. But
an evil person has evil things saved up
in his heart. So he brings out bad things.
A person speaks the things that are in
his heart.

⁴⁶"Why do you call me, 'Lord, Lord,'
but do not do what I say? ⁴⁷Everyone
who comes to me and listens to my
words and obeys ⁴⁸is like a man building
a house. He digs deep and lays his foundation on rock. The floods come, and
the water tries to wash the house away.
But the flood cannot move the house,
because the house was built well. ⁴⁹But
the one who hears my words and does
not obey is like a man who builds his
house on the ground without a foundation. When the floods come, the house
quickly falls down. And that house is
completely destroyed."

7 When Jesus finished saying all these things to the people, he went to Capernaum. [2] In Capernaum there was an army officer. He had a servant who was so sick he was nearly dead. The officer loved the servant very much. [3] When the officer heard about Jesus, he sent some older Jewish leaders to him. The officer wanted the leaders to ask Jesus to come and heal his servant. [4] The men went to Jesus and begged him saying, "This officer is worthy of your help. [5] He loves our people, and he built us a synagogue."[d] [6] So Jesus went with the men. He was getting near the officer's house when the officer sent friends to say, "Lord, you don't need to come into my house. I am not good enough for you to be under my roof. [7] That is why I did not come to you myself. You only need to say the word, and my servant will be healed. [8] I, too, am a man under the authority of other men. And I have soldiers under my command. I tell one soldier, 'Go,' and he goes. And I tell another soldier, 'Come,' and he comes. And I say to my servant, 'Do this,' and my servant obeys me."

[9] When Jesus heard this, he was amazed. He turned to the crowd following him and said, "I tell you, this is the greatest faith I have seen anywhere, even in Israel."

[10] The men who had been sent to Jesus went back to the house. There they found that the servant was healed.

[11] The next day Jesus went to a town called Nain. His followers and a large crowd were traveling with him. [12] When he came near the town gate, he saw a funeral. A mother, who was a widow, had lost her only son. A large crowd from the town was with the mother while her son was being carried out. [13] When the Lord saw her, he felt very sorry for her. Jesus said to her, "Don't cry." [14] He went up to the coffin and touched it. The men who were carrying it stopped. Jesus said, "Young man, I tell you, get up!" [15] And the son sat up and began to talk. Then Jesus gave him back to his mother.

[16] All the people were amazed. They began praising God. They said, "A great prophet[d] has come to us! God is taking care of his people."

[17] This news about Jesus spread through all Judea and into all the places around there.

[18] John's followers told him about all these things. He called for two of his followers. [19] He sent them to the Lord to ask, "Are you the One who is coming, or should we wait for another?"

[20] So the men came to Jesus. They said, "John the Baptist[d] sent us to you with this question: 'Are you the One who is coming, or should we wait for another?'"

[21] At that time, Jesus healed many people of their sicknesses, diseases, and evil spirits. He healed many blind people so that they could see again. [22] Then Jesus said to John's followers, "Go tell John the things that you saw and heard here. The blind can see. The crippled can walk. People with a harmful skin disease are healed. The deaf can hear, and the dead are given life. And the Good News[d] is told to the poor. [23] The person who does not lose faith is blessed!"

[24] When John's followers left, Jesus began to tell the people about John: "What did you go out into the desert to see? A reed[n] blown by the wind? [25] What did you go out to see? A man dressed in fine clothes? No. People who have fine clothes live in kings' palaces. [26] But what did you go out to see? A prophet?[d] Yes, and I tell you, John is more than a prophet. [27] This was written about John:

'I will send my messenger ahead of
    you.
He will prepare the way for you.'
                                    Malachi 3:1

[28] I tell you, John is greater than any other man ever born. But even the least important person in the kingdom of God is greater than John."

[29] (When the people heard this, they all agreed that God's teaching was good. Even the tax collectors agreed. These were people who were already baptized by John. [30] But the Pharisees[d] and teachers of the law refused to accept God's plan for themselves; they did not let John baptize them.)

[31] Then Jesus said, "What shall I say about the people of this time? What are they like? [32] They are like children sitting in the marketplace. One group of children calls to the other group and says,

'We played music for you, but you
    did not dance.
We sang a sad song, but you did
    not cry.'

[33] John the Baptist came and did not eat like other people or drink wine. And you say, 'He has a demon[d] in him.' [34] The Son

---

7:24 **reed** It means that John was not weak like grass blown by the wind.

of Man[d] came eating like other people and drinking wine. And you say, 'Look at him! He eats too much and drinks too much wine! He is a friend of the tax collectors and "sinners"!' [35] But wisdom is shown to be right by the things it does."

[36] One of the Pharisees[d] asked Jesus to eat with him. Jesus went into the Pharisee's house and sat at the table. [37] A sinful woman in the town learned that Jesus was eating at the Pharisee's house. So she brought an alabaster[d] jar of perfume. [38] She stood at Jesus' feet, crying, and began to wash his feet with her tears. She dried his feet with her hair, kissed them many times and rubbed them with the perfume. [39] The Pharisee who asked Jesus to come to his house saw this. He thought to himself, "If Jesus were a prophet,[d] he would know that the woman who is touching him is a sinner!"

[40] Jesus said to the Pharisee, "Simon, I have something to say to you."

Simon said, "Teacher, tell me."

[41] Jesus said, "There were two men. Both men owed money to the same banker. One man owed the banker 500 silver coins.[n] The other man owed the banker 50 silver coins. [42] The men had no money; so they could not pay what they owed. But the banker told the men that they did not have to pay him. Which one of the two men will love the banker more?"

[43] Simon, the Pharisee, answered, "I think it would be the one who owed him the most money."

Jesus said to Simon, "You are right." [44] Then Jesus turned toward the woman and said to Simon, "Do you see this woman? When I came into your house, you gave me no water for my feet. But she washed my feet with her tears and dried my feet with her hair. [45] You did not kiss me, but she has been kissing my feet since I came in! [46] You did not rub my head with oil, but she rubbed my feet with perfume. [47] I tell you that her many sins are forgiven. This is clear because she showed great love. But the person who has only a little to be forgiven will feel only a little love."

[48] Then Jesus said to her, "Your sins are forgiven."

[49] The people sitting at the table began to think to themselves, "Who is this man? How can he forgive sins?"

[50] Jesus said to the woman, "Because you believed, you are saved from your sins. Go in peace."

8 The next day, while Jesus was traveling through some cities and small towns, he preached and told the Good News[d] about God's kingdom. The 12 apostles[d] were with him. [2] There were also some women with him who had been healed of sicknesses and evil spirits. One of the women was Mary, called Magdalene, from whom seven demons[d] had gone out. [3] Also among the women were Joanna, the wife of Chuza (Herod's helper), Susanna, and many other women. These women used their own money to help Jesus and his apostles.

[4] A great crowd gathered. People were coming to Jesus from every town. He told them this story:

[5] "A farmer went out to plant his seed. While he was planting, some seed fell beside the road. People walked on the seed, and the birds ate all this seed. [6] Some seed fell on rock. It began to grow but then died because it had no water. [7] Some seed fell among thorny weeds. This seed grew, but later the weeds choked the good plants. [8] And some seed fell on good ground. This seed grew and made 100 times more grain."

Jesus finished the story. Then he called out, "You people who hear me, listen!"

[9] Jesus' followers asked him, "What does this story mean?"

[10] Jesus said, "You have been chosen to know the secret truths of the kingdom of God. But I use stories to speak to other people. I do this so that:

'They will look, but they may not see.

They will listen, but they may not understand.'   *Isaiah 6:9*

[11] "This is what the story means: The seed is God's teaching. [12] What is the seed that fell beside the road? It is like the people who hear God's teaching, but then the devil comes and takes it away from their hearts. So they cannot believe the teaching and be saved. [13] What is the seed that fell on rock? It is like those who hear God's teaching and accept it gladly. But they don't have deep roots. They believe for a while, but then trouble comes. They stop believing and turn away from God. [14] What is the seed that fell among the thorny weeds? It is

---

7:41 silver coins A Roman denarius. One coin was the average pay for one day's work.

like those who hear God's teaching, but they let the worries, riches, and pleasures of this life keep them from growing. So they never produce good fruit. [15]And what is the seed that fell on the good ground? That is like those who hear God's teaching with a good, honest heart. They obey God's teaching and patiently produce good fruit.

[16]"No one lights a lamp and then covers it with a bowl or hides it under a bed. Instead, he puts the lamp on a lampstand so that those who come in will have enough light to see. [17]Everything that is hidden will become clear. Every secret thing will be made known. [18]So be careful how you listen. The person who has something will be given more. But to the person who has nothing, this will happen: Even what he thinks he has will be taken away from him."

[19]Jesus' mother and brothers came to see him. There was such a crowd that they could not get to him. [20]Someone said to Jesus, "Your mother and your brothers are standing outside. They want to see you."

[21]Jesus answered them, "My mother and my brothers are those who listen to God's teaching and obey it!"

[22]One day Jesus and his followers got into a boat. He said to them, "Come with me across the lake." And so they started across. [23]While they were sailing, Jesus fell asleep. A big storm blew up on the lake. The boat began to fill with water, and they were in danger.

[24]The followers went to Jesus and woke him. They said, "Master! Master! We will drown!"

Jesus got up and gave a command to the wind and the waves. The wind stopped, and the lake became calm. [25]Jesus said to his followers, "Where is your faith?"

The followers were afraid and amazed. They said to each other, "What kind of man is this? He commands the wind and the water, and they obey him!"

[26]Jesus and his followers sailed across the lake from Galilee to the area where the Gerasene people live. [27]When Jesus got out of the boat, a man from the town came to Jesus. This man had demons[d] inside him. For a long time he had worn no clothes. He lived in the burial caves, not in a house. [28]When he saw Jesus, he cried out and fell down before him. The man said with a loud voice, "What do you want with me, Jesus, Son of the Most High God? Please don't punish me!" [29]He said this because Jesus had commanded the evil spirit to come out of him. Many times it had taken hold of him. He had been kept under guard and chained hand and foot. But he had broken his chains and had been driven by the demon out into the desert.

[30]Jesus asked him, "What is your name?"

The man answered, "Legion."[n] (He said his name was "Legion" because many demons were in him.) [31]The demons begged Jesus not to send them into eternal darkness.[n] [32]On the hill there was a large herd of pigs eating. The demons begged Jesus to allow them to go into the pigs. So Jesus allowed them to do this. [33]Then the demons came out of the man and went into the pigs. The herd of pigs ran down the hill and into the lake. All the pigs drowned.

[34]The men who took care of the pigs ran away. They told about this in the town and the countryside. [35]And people went to see what had happened. They came to Jesus and found the man sitting there at Jesus' feet. The man was clothed and in his right mind because the demons were gone. But the people were frightened. [36]The men who saw these things happen told the others all about how Jesus had made the man well. [37]All the people of the Gerasene country asked Jesus to go away. They were all very afraid. So Jesus got into the boat and went back to Galilee.

[38]The man that Jesus had healed begged to go with him. But Jesus sent him away, saying, [39]"Go back home and tell people what God did for you." So the man went all over town telling how much Jesus had done for him.

[40]When Jesus got back to Galilee, a crowd welcomed him. Everyone was waiting for him. [41]A man named Jairus came to Jesus. Jairus was a ruler of the synagogue.[d] He bowed down at Jesus' feet and begged him to come to his house. [42]Jairus had only one daughter. She was 12 years old, and she was dying.

While Jesus was on his way to Jairus' house, the people were crowding all around him. [43]A woman was there who had been bleeding for 12 years. She had

8:30 "Legion" Means very many. A legion was about 5,000 men in the Roman army.　**8:31 eternal darkness** Literally, "the abyss," something like a pit or a hole that has no end.

spent all her money on doctors, but no doctor was able to heal her. [44]The woman came up behind Jesus and touched the edge of his coat. At that moment, her bleeding stopped. [45]Then Jesus said, "Who touched me?"

All the people said they had not touched Jesus. Peter said, "Master, the people are all around you and are pushing against you."

[46]But Jesus said, "Someone did touch me! I felt power go out from me." [47]When the woman saw that she could not hide, she came forward, shaking. She bowed down before Jesus. While all the people listened, she told why she had touched him. Then, she said, she was healed immediately. [48]Jesus said to her, "Dear woman, you are healed because you believed. Go in peace."

[49]While Jesus was still speaking, someone came from the house of the synagogue ruler and said to the ruler, "Your daughter has died! Don't bother the teacher now."

[50]When Jesus heard this, he said to Jairus, "Don't be afraid. Just believe, and your daughter will be well."

[51]Jesus went to the house. He let only Peter, John, James, and the girl's father and mother go inside with him. [52]All the people were crying and feeling sad because the girl was dead. But Jesus said, "Don't cry. She is not dead; she is only sleeping."

[53]The people laughed at Jesus because they knew that the girl was dead. [54]But Jesus took her by the hand and called to her, "My child, stand up!" [55]Her spirit came back into her, and she stood up immediately. Jesus said, "Give her something to eat." [56]The girl's parents were amazed. Jesus told them not to tell anyone about what happened.

9 Jesus called the 12 apostles[d] together. He gave them power to heal sicknesses and power over all demons.[d] [2]Jesus sent the apostles out to tell about God's kingdom and to heal the sick. [3]He said to them, "When you travel, don't take a walking stick. Also, don't carry a bag, or food, or money. Take for your trip only the clothes you are wearing. [4]When you go into a house, stay there until it is time to leave. [5]If the people in the town will not welcome you, go outside the town and shake the dust off of your feet.[n] This will be a warning to them."

[6]So the apostles went out. They traveled through all the towns. They told the Good News[d] and healed people everywhere.

[7]Herod, the governor, heard about all these things that were happening. He was confused because some people said, "John the Baptist[d] is risen from death." [8]Others said, "Elijah has come to us." And still others said, "One of the prophets[d] from long ago has risen from death." [9]Herod said, "I cut off John's head. So who is this man I hear these things about?" And Herod kept trying to see Jesus.

[10]When the apostles[d] returned, they told Jesus all the things they had done on their trip. Then Jesus took them away to a town called Bethsaida. There, Jesus and his apostles could be alone together. [11]But the people learned where Jesus went and followed him. Jesus welcomed them and talked with them about God's kingdom. He healed those who needed to be healed.

[12]Late in the afternoon, the 12 apostles came to Jesus and said, "No one lives in this place. Send the people away. They need to find food and places to sleep in the towns and countryside around here."

[13]But Jesus said to them, "You give them something to eat."

They said, "We have only five loaves of bread and two fish. Do you want us to go buy food for all these people?" [14](There were about 5,000 men there.)

Jesus said to his followers, "Tell the people to sit in groups of about 50 people."

[15]So the followers did this, and all the people sat down. [16]Then Jesus took the five loaves of bread and two fish. He looked up to heaven and thanked God for the food. Then Jesus divided the food and gave it to the followers to give to the people. [17]All the people ate and were satisfied. And there was much food left. Twelve baskets were filled with pieces of food that were not eaten.

[18]One time when Jesus was praying alone, his followers came together there. Jesus asked them, "Who do the people say I am?"

[19]They answered, "Some say you are John the Baptist.[d] Others say you are

9:5 **shake . . . feet** A warning. It showed that they were finished talking to these people.

Elijah.[n] And others say you are one of the prophets[d] from long ago who has come back to life."

[20] Then Jesus asked, "And who do you say I am?"

Peter answered, "You are the Christ[d] from God."

[21] Jesus warned them not to tell anyone. Then he said, [22] "The Son of Man[d] must suffer many things. He will be rejected by the older Jewish leaders, the leading priests, and the teachers of the law. The Son of Man will be killed. But after three days he will be raised from death."

[23] Jesus went on to say to all of them, "If anyone wants to follow me, he must say 'no' to the things he wants. Every day he must be willing even to die on a cross, and he must follow me. [24] Whoever wants to save his life will lose it. And whoever gives his life for me will save it. [25] It is worth nothing for a man to have the whole world, if he himself is destroyed or lost. [26] If anyone is ashamed of me and my teaching, then I[n] will be ashamed of him. I will be ashamed of him at the time I come with my glory and with the glory of the Father and the holy angels. [27] I tell you the truth. Some of you people standing here will see the kingdom of God before you die."

[28] About eight days after Jesus said these things, he took Peter, James, and John and went up on a mountain to pray. [29] While Jesus was praying, his face was changed, and his clothes became shining white. [30] Then two men were talking with Jesus. The men were Moses and Elijah.[n] [31] They appeared in heavenly glory, talking with Jesus about his death which would happen in Jerusalem. [32] Peter and the others were asleep. But they woke up and saw the glory of Jesus. They also saw the two men who were standing with him. [33] When Moses and Elijah were about to leave, Peter said, "Master, it is good that we are here. We will put three tents here—one for you, one for Moses, and one for Elijah." (Peter did not know what he was saying.)

[34] While Peter was saying these things, a cloud came down all around them. Peter, James, and John became afraid when the cloud covered them. [35] A voice came from the cloud. The voice said,

"This is my Son. He is the One I have chosen. Obey him."

[36] When the voice finished speaking, only Jesus was there. Peter, James, and John said nothing. At that time they told no one about what they had seen.

[37] The next day, Jesus, Peter, James, and John came down from the mountain. A large crowd met Jesus. [38] A man in the crowd shouted to Jesus, "Teacher, please come and look at my son. He is the only child I have. [39] An evil spirit comes into my son, and then he shouts. He loses control of himself, and he foams at the mouth. The evil spirit keeps on hurting him and almost never leaves him. [40] I begged your followers to make the evil spirit leave my son, but they could not do it."

[41] Jesus answered, "You people who live now have no faith. Your lives are all wrong. How long must I be with you and be patient with you?" Then Jesus said to the man, "Bring your son here."

[42] While the boy was coming, the demon[n] threw him on the ground. The boy lost control of himself. But Jesus gave a strong command to the evil spirit. Then the boy was healed, and Jesus gave him back to his father. [43] All the people were amazed at the great power of God.

The people were all wondering about the things Jesus did. But he said to his followers, [44] "Don't forget the things I tell you now: The Son of Man[d] will be handed over into the control of men." [45] But the followers did not understand what Jesus meant. The meaning was hidden from them so that they could not understand it. But they were afraid to ask Jesus about what he said.

[46] Jesus' followers began to have an argument about which one of them was the greatest. [47] Jesus knew what they were thinking. So he took a little child and stood the child beside him. [48] Then Jesus said, "If anyone accepts a little child like this in my name, then he accepts me. And when he accepts me, he accepts the One who sent me. He who is least among you all—he is the greatest."

[49] John answered, "Master, we saw someone using your name to force demons[d] out of people. We told him to stop because he does not belong to our group."

[50] Jesus said to him, "Don't stop him.

9:19 Elijah A man who spoke for God. He lived hundreds of years before Christ. 9:26 I Literally, "the Son of Man." 9:30 Moses and Elijah Two of the most important Jewish leaders in the past.

If a person is not against you, then he is for you."

[51] The time was coming near when Jesus would leave and be taken to heaven. He was determined to go to Jerusalem [52] and sent some men ahead of him. The men went into a town in Samaria to make everything ready for Jesus. [53] But the people there would not welcome him because he was going toward Jerusalem. [54] James and John, the followers of Jesus, saw this. They said, "Lord, do you want us to call fire down from heaven and destroy those people?"[n]

[55] But Jesus turned and scolded them.[n] [56] Then he and his followers went to another town.

[57] They were all going along the road. Someone said to Jesus, "I will follow you any place you go."

[58] Jesus answered, "The foxes have holes to live in. The birds have nests to live in. But the Son of Man[d] has no place to rest his head."

[59] Jesus said to another man, "Follow me!"

But the man said, "Lord, first let me go and bury my father."

[60] But Jesus said to him, "Let the people who are dead bury their own dead! You must go and tell about the kingdom of God."

[61] Another man said, "I will follow you, Lord, but first let me go and say goodbye to my family."

[62] Jesus said, "Anyone who begins to plow a field but keeps looking back is of no use in the kingdom of God."

10 After this, the Lord chose 72[n] others. He sent them out in pairs. He sent them ahead of him into every town and place where he planned to go. [2] He said to them, "There are a great many people to harvest. But there are only a few workers to harvest them. God owns the harvest. Pray to God that he will send more workers to help gather his harvest. [3] You can go now. But listen! I am sending you, and you will be like sheep among wolves. [4] Don't carry a purse, a bag, or sandals. Don't stop to talk with people on the road. [5] Before

you go into a house, say, 'Peace be with this house.' [6] If a peaceful man lives there, your blessing of peace will stay with him. If the man is not peaceful, then your blessing of peace will come back to you. [7] Stay in the peaceful house. Eat and drink what the people there give you. A worker should be given his pay. Don't move from house to house. [8] If you go into a town and the people welcome you, eat what they give you. [9] Heal the sick who live there. Tell them, 'The kingdom of God is soon coming to you!' [10] But if you go into a town, and the people don't welcome you, then go out into the streets of that town. Say to them, [11] 'Even the dirt from your town that sticks to our feet we wipe off against you.[n] But remember that the kingdom of God is coming soon.' [12] I tell you, on the Judgment Day it will be worse for the people of that town than for the people of Sodom.[n]

[13] "How terrible for you, Korazin! How terrible for you, Bethsaida! I did many miracles[d] in you. If those same miracles had happened in Tyre and Sidon,[n] those people would have changed their lives and stopped sinning long ago. They would have worn rough cloth and put ashes on themselves to show that they had changed. [14] But on the Judgment Day it will be worse for you than for Tyre and Sidon. [15] And you, Capernaum,[n] will you be lifted up to heaven? No! You will be thrown down to the depths!

[16] "He who listens to you is really listening to me. He who refuses to accept you is really refusing to accept me. And he who refuses to accept me is refusing to accept the One who sent me."

[17] When the 72[n] men came back from their trip, they were very happy. They said, "Lord, even the demons[d] obeyed us when we used your name!"

[18] Jesus said to the men, "I saw Satan falling like lightning from the sky. [19] Listen! I gave you power to walk on snakes and scorpions. I gave you more power than the Enemy has. Nothing will hurt you. [20] You should be happy, but not because the spirits obey you. You should

9:54 Verse 54 Here, some Greek copies add: ". . . as Elijah did." **9:55 Verse 55** Here, some copies add: "And Jesus said, 'You don't know what kind of spirit you belong to. [56] The Son of Man did not come to destroy the souls of men but to save them.'" **10:1 72** Many Greek copies read 70. **10:11 dirt . . . you** A warning. It showed that they were finished talking to these people. **10:12 Sodom** City that God destroyed because the people were so evil. **10:13 Tyre and Sidon** Towns where wicked people lived. **10:13, 15 Korazin . . . Bethsaida . . . Capernaum** Towns by Lake Galilee where Jesus preached to the people. **10:17 72** Many Greek copies read 70.

be happy because your names are written in heaven."

[21]Then the Holy Spirit[d] made Jesus rejoice. He said, "I thank you, Father, Lord of heaven and earth, because you have hidden these things from the people who are wise and smart. But you have shown them to those who are like little children. Yes, Father, you did this because this is what you really wanted.

[22]"My Father has given me all things. No one knows the Son—only the Father knows. And only the Son knows the Father. The only people who will know about the Father are those whom the Son chooses to tell."

[23]Then Jesus turned to his followers and said privately, "You are blessed to see what you now see! [24]I tell you, many prophets[d] and kings wanted to see what you now see. But they did not see these things. And many prophets and kings wanted to hear what you now hear. But they did not hear these things."

[25]Then a teacher of the law stood up. He was trying to test Jesus. He said, "Teacher, what must I do to get life forever?"

[26]Jesus said to him, "What is written in the law? What do you read there?"

[27]The man answered, "Love the Lord your God. Love him with all your heart, all your soul, all your strength, and all your mind."[n] Also, "You must love your neighbor as you love yourself."[n]

[28]Jesus said to him, "Your answer is right. Do this and you will have life forever."

[29]But the man wanted to show that the way he was living was right. So he said to Jesus, "And who is my neighbor?"

[30]To answer this question, Jesus said, "A man was going down the road from Jerusalem to Jericho. Some robbers attacked him. They tore off his clothes and beat him. Then they left him lying there, almost dead. [31]It happened that a Jewish priest was going down that road. When the priest saw the man, he walked by on the other side of the road. [32]Next, a Levite[n] came there. He went over and looked at the man. Then he walked by on the other side of the road. [33]Then a Samaritan[n] traveling down the road came to where the hurt man was lying. He saw the man and felt very sorry for him. [34]The Samaritan went to him and poured olive oil and wine[n] on his wounds and bandaged them. He put the hurt man on his own donkey and took him to an inn. At the inn, the Samaritan took care of him. [35]The next day, the Samaritan brought out two silver coins[n] and gave them to the innkeeper. The Samaritan said, 'Take care of this man. If you spend more money on him, I will pay it back to you when I come again.'"

[36]Then Jesus said, "Which one of these three men do you think was a neighbor to the man who was attacked by the robbers?"

[37]The teacher of the law answered, "The one who helped him."

Jesus said to him, "Then go and do the same thing he did!"

[38]While Jesus and his followers were traveling, Jesus went into a town. A woman named Martha let Jesus stay at her house. [39]Martha had a sister named Mary. Mary was sitting at Jesus' feet and listening to him teach. [40]Martha became angry because she had so much work to do. She went in and said, "Lord, don't you care that my sister has left me alone to do all the work? Tell her to help me!"

[41]But the Lord answered her, "Martha, Martha, you are getting worried and upset about too many things. [42]Only one thing is important. Mary has chosen the right thing, and it will never be taken away from her."

11 One time Jesus was praying in a place. When he finished, one of his followers said to him, "John taught his followers how to pray. Lord, please teach us how to pray, too."

[2]Jesus said to them, "When you pray, say:

'Father, we pray that your name
　　will always be kept holy.
We pray that your kingdom will
　　come.
[3]Give us the food we need for each
　　day.
[4]Forgive us the sins we have done,
　　because we forgive every person
　　who has done wrong to us.
And do not cause us to be tested.'"

10:27 "Love . . . mind." Quotation from Deuteronomy 6:5.　**10:27 "You . . . yourself."** Quotation from Leviticus 19:18.　**10:32 Levite** Levites were men from the tribe of Levi who helped the Jewish priests with their work in the Temple. Read 1 Chronicles 23:24-32.　**10:33 Samaritan** Samaritans were people from Samaria. These people were part Jewish, but the Jews did not accept them as true Jews. Samaritans and Jews hated each other.　**10:34 olive oil and wine** Oil and wine were used like medicine to soften and clean wounds.　**10:35 silver coins** A Roman denarius. One coin was the average pay for one day's work.

5-6Then Jesus said to them, "Suppose one of you went to your friend's house at midnight and said to him, 'A friend of mine has come into town to visit me. But I have nothing for him to eat. Please loan me three loaves of bread.' 7Your friend inside the house answers, 'Don't bother me! The door is already locked. My children and I are in bed. I cannot get up and give you the bread now.' 8I tell you, maybe friendship is not enough to make him get up to give you the bread. But he will surely get up to give you what you need if you continue to ask. 9So I tell you, continue to ask, and God will give to you. Continue to search, and you will find. Continue to knock, and the door will open for you. 10Yes, if a person continues asking, he will receive. If he continues searching, he will find. And if he continues knocking, the door will open for him. 11What would you fathers do if your son asks you for a fish? Would any of you give him a snake? 12Or, if your son asks for an egg, would you give him a scorpion? 13Even though you are bad, you know how to give good things to your children. So surely your heavenly Father knows how to give the Holy Spirit[d] to those who ask him."

14One time Jesus was sending a demon[d] out of a man who could not talk. When the demon came out, the man was able to speak. The people were amazed. 15But some of them said, "Jesus uses the power of Beelzebul[d] to force demons out of people. Beelzebul is the ruler of demons."

16Other people wanted to test Jesus. They asked him to give him a sign from heaven. 17But Jesus knew what they were thinking. So he said to them, "Every kingdom that is divided and fights against itself will be destroyed. And a family that fights against itself will break apart. 18So if Satan is fighting against himself, then how will his kingdom last? You say that I use the power of Beelzebul to force out demons. 19But if I use the power of Beelzebul to force out demons, then by what power do your people force out demons? So your own people prove that you are wrong. 20But if I use the power of God to force out demons, the kingdom of God has come to you!

21"When a strong man with many weapons guards his own house, then the things in his house are safe. 22But suppose a stronger man comes and defeats him. The stronger man will take away the weapons that the first man trusted to keep his house safe. Then the stronger man will do what he wants with the first man's things.

23"If anyone is not with me, he is against me. He who does not work with me is working against me.

24"When an evil spirit comes out of a person, it travels through dry places, looking for a place to rest. But that spirit finds no place to rest. So it says, 'I will go back to the home I left.' 25When the spirit comes back to that person, it finds that home swept clean and made neat. 26Then the evil spirit goes out and brings seven other spirits more evil than itself. Then all the evil spirits go into that person and live there. And he has even more trouble than he had before."

27When Jesus was saying these things, a woman in the crowd spoke out. She said to Jesus, "Your mother is blessed because she gave birth to you and nursed you."

28But Jesus said, "Those who hear the teaching of God and obey it—they are the ones who are truly blessed."

29The crowd grew larger. Jesus said, "The people who live today are evil. They ask for a miracle[d] as a sign from God. But they will have no sign—only the sign of Jonah.[n] 30Jonah was a sign for those people who lived in Nineveh. In the same way the Son of Man[d] will be a sign for the people of this time. 31On the Judgment Day the Queen of the South[n] will stand up with the men who live now. She will show that they are guilty because she came from far away to listen to Solomon's wise teaching. And I tell you that someone greater than Solomon is here! 32On the Judgment Day the men of Nineveh will stand up with the people who live now. And they will show that you are guilty, because when Jonah preached to those people, they changed their hearts and lives. And I tell you that someone greater than Jonah is here!

33"No one takes a light and puts it under a bowl or hides it. Instead, he puts the light on a lampstand so that the people

---

11:29 sign of Jonah Jonah's three days in the big fish are like Jesus' three days in the tomb.
11:31 Queen of the South The Queen of Sheba. She traveled 1,000 miles to learn God's wisdom from Solomon. Read 1 Kings 10:1-3.

who come in can see. [34]Your eye is a light for the body. If your eyes are good, then your whole body will be full of light. But if your eyes are evil, then your whole body will be full of darkness. [35]So be careful! Don't let the light in you become darkness. [36]If your whole body is full of light, and none of it is dark, then you will shine bright, as when a lamp shines on you."

[37]After Jesus had finished speaking, a Pharisee[d] asked Jesus to eat with him. So Jesus went in and sat at the table. [38]But the Pharisee was surprised when he saw that Jesus did not wash his hands[n] before the meal. [39]The Lord said to him, "You Pharisees clean the outside of the cup and the dish. But inside you are full of greed and evil. [40]You are foolish. The same One who made what is outside also made what is inside. [41]So give what is in your cups and dishes to the poor. Then you will be fully clean. [42]But how terrible for you Pharisees! You give God one-tenth of even your mint, your rue, and every other plant in your garden. But you forget to be fair to other people and to love God. These are the things you should do. And you should also continue to do those other things—like giving one-tenth. [43]How terrible for you Pharisees, because you love to get the most important seats in the synagogues.[d] And you love people to show respect to you in the marketplaces. [44]How terrible for you, because you are like hidden graves. People walk on them without knowing it."

[45]One of the teachers of the law said to Jesus, "Teacher, when you say these things, you are insulting us, too."

[46]Jesus answered, "How terrible for you, you teachers of the law! You make strict rules that are very hard for people to obey. But you yourselves don't even try to follow those rules. [47]How terrible for you, because you build tombs for the prophets.[d] But these are the prophets that your fathers killed! [48]And now you show that you approve of what your fathers did. They killed the prophets, and you build tombs for the prophets! [49]This is why in his wisdom God said, 'I will send prophets and apostles[d] to them. Some of my prophets and apostles will be killed, and others will be treated cruelly.' [50]So you who live now will be pun-

ished for the deaths of all the prophets who were killed since the beginning of the world. [51]You will be punished for the killing of Abel and for the killing of Zechariah.[n] Zechariah was killed between the altar and the Temple.[d] Yes, I tell you that you people who live now will be punished for them all.

[52]"How terrible for you, you teachers of the law. You have hidden the key to learning about God. You yourselves would not learn, and you stopped others from learning, too."

[53]When Jesus was leaving, the teachers of the law and the Pharisees[d] began to give him trouble, asking him questions about many things. [54]They were trying to catch Jesus saying something wrong.

12 Many thousands of people had gathered. There were so many people that they were stepping on each other. Before Jesus spoke to them, he said to his followers, "Be careful of the yeast of the Pharisees.[d] They are hypocrites.[d] [2]Everything that is hidden will be shown. Everything that is secret will be made known. [3]The things you say in the dark will be told in the light. The things you have whispered in an inner room will be shouted from the top of the house."

[4]Then Jesus said to the people, "I tell you, my friends, don't be afraid of people. People can kill the body, but after that they can do nothing more to hurt you. [5]I will show you the One to fear. You should fear him who has the power to kill you and also to throw you into hell. Yes, he is the One you should fear. [6]"When five sparrows are sold, they cost only two pennies. But God does not forget any of them. [7]Yes, God even knows how many hairs you have on your head. Don't be afraid. You are worth much more than many sparrows.

[8]"I tell you, if anyone stands before others and says that he believes in me, then I will say that he belongs to me. I will say this before the angels of God. [9]But if anyone stands before others and says he does not believe in me, then I will say that he does not belong to me. I will say this before the angels of God.

[10]"If a person says something against the Son of Man,[d] he can be forgiven. But

---

11:38 wash his hands This was a Jewish religious custom that the Pharisees thought was very important. **11:51 Abel . . . Zechariah** In the Hebrew Old Testament, the first and last men to be murdered.

a person who says bad things against the Holy Spirit[d] will not be forgiven.

[11]"When men bring you into the synagogues[e] before the leaders and other important men, don't worry about how to defend yourself or what to say. [12]At that time the Holy Spirit will teach you what you must say."

[13]One of the men in the crowd said to Jesus, "Teacher, tell my brother to divide with me the property our father left us."

[14]But Jesus said to him, "Who said that I should be your judge or decide how to divide the property between you two?" [15]Then Jesus said to them, "Be careful and guard against all kinds of greed. A man's life is not measured by the many things he owns."

[16]Then Jesus used this story: "There was a rich man who had some land, which grew a good crop of food. [17]The rich man thought to himself, 'What will I do? I have no place to keep all my crops.' [18]Then he said, 'I know what I will do. I will tear down my barns and build bigger ones! I will put all my grain and other goods together in my new barns. [19]Then I can say to myself, I have enough good things stored to last for many years. Rest, eat, drink, and enjoy life!'

[20]"But God said to that man, 'Foolish man! Tonight you will die. So who will get those things you have prepared for yourself?'

[21]"This is how it will be for anyone who stores things up only for himself and is not rich toward God."

[22]Jesus said to his followers, "So I tell you, don't worry about the food you need to live. Don't worry about the clothes you need for your body. [23]Life is more important than food. And the body is more important than clothes. [24]Look at the birds. They don't plant or harvest. They don't save food in houses or barns. But God takes care of them. And you are worth much more than birds. [25]None of you can add any time to your life by worrying about it. [26]If you cannot do even the little things, then why worry about the big things? [27]Look at the wild flowers. See how they grow. They don't work or make clothes for themselves. But I tell you that even Solomon, the great and rich king, was not dressed as beautifully as one of these flowers. [28]God clothes the grass in the field like that. That grass is living today, but tomorrow it will be thrown into the fire. So you know how much more God will

clothe you. Don't have so little faith! [29]Don't always think about what you will eat or what you will drink. Don't worry about it. [30]All the people in the world are trying to get those things. Your Father knows that you need them. [31]The thing you should seek is God's kingdom. Then all the other things you need will be given to you.

[32]"Don't fear, little flock. Your Father wants to give you the kingdom. [33]Sell the things you have and give to the poor. Get for yourselves purses that don't wear out. Get the treasure in heaven that never runs out. Thieves can't steal it in heaven, and moths can't destroy it. [34]Your heart will be where your treasure is.

[35]"Be ready! Be dressed for service and have your lamps shining. [36]Be like servants who are waiting for their master to come home from a wedding party. The master comes and knocks. The servants immediately open the door for him. [37]Those servants will be blessed when their master comes home, because he sees that his servants are ready and waiting for him. I tell you the truth. The master will dress himself to serve and tell the servants to sit at the table. Then the master will serve them. [38]Those servants might have to wait until midnight or later for their master. But they will be happy when he comes in and finds them still waiting.

[39]"Remember this: If the owner of the house knew what time a thief was coming, then the owner would not allow the thief to enter his house. [40]So you also must be ready! The Son of Man[d] will come at a time when you don't expect him!"

[41]Peter said, "Lord, did you tell this story for us or for all people?"

[42]The Lord said, "Who is the wise and trusted servant? Who is the servant the master trusts to give the other servants their food at the right time? [43]When the master comes and finds his servant doing the work he gave him, that servant will be very happy. [44]I tell you the truth. The master will choose that servant to take care of everything the master owns. [45]But what will happen if the servant is evil and thinks that his master will not come back soon? That servant will begin to beat the other servants, men and women. He will eat and drink and get drunk. [46]Then the master will come when that servant is not ready. It will be a time when the servant is not expecting

him. Then the master will cut him in pieces and send him away to be with the others who don't obey.

⁴⁷"The servant who knows what his master wants but is not ready or does not do what the master wants will be beaten with many blows! ⁴⁸But the servant who does not know what his master wants and does things that should be punished will be beaten with few blows. Everyone who has been given much will be responsible for much. Much more will be expected from the one who has been given more."

⁴⁹Jesus continued speaking, "I came to set fire to the world. I wish it were already burning! ⁵⁰I must be baptized with a different kind of baptism.ⁿ I feel very troubled until it is over. ⁵¹Do you think that I came to give peace to the world? No! I came to divide the world! ⁵²From now on, a family with five people will be divided, three against two, and two against three. ⁵³A father and son will be divided: The son will be against his father. The father will be against his son. A mother and her daughter will be divided: The daughter will be against her mother. The mother will be against her daughter. A mother-in-law and her daughter-in-law will be divided: The daughter-in-law will be against her mother-in-law. The mother-in-law will be against her daughter-in-law."

⁵⁴Then Jesus said to the people, "When you see clouds coming up in the west, you say, 'It's going to rain.' And soon it begins to rain. ⁵⁵When you feel the wind begin to blow from the south, you say, 'It will be a hot day.' And you are right. ⁵⁶Hypocrites!ᵈ You can understand the weather. Why don't you understand what is happening now?

⁵⁷"Why can't you decide for yourselves what is right? ⁵⁸When someone is suing you, and you are going with him to court, try hard to settle it on the way. If you don't settle it, he may take you to the judge. The judge might turn you over to the officer. And the officer might throw you into jail. ⁵⁹You will not get out of there until they have taken everything you have."

13 At that time some people were there with Jesus. They told him about what had happened to some people from Galilee. Pilateⁿ killed these people while they were worshiping. He mixed their blood with the blood of the animals they were sacrificing to God. ²Jesus answered, "Do you think this happened to them because they were more sinful than all others from Galilee? ³No, they were not! But if all of you don't change your hearts and lives, then you will be destroyed as they were! ⁴What about those 18 people who died when the tower of Siloam fell on them? Do you think they were more sinful than all the others who live in Jerusalem? ⁵They were not! But I tell you, if you don't change your hearts and lives, then you will all be destroyed too!"

⁶Jesus told this story: "A man had a fig tree planted in his vineyard. He came looking for some fruit on the tree, but he found none. ⁷So the man said to his servant who took care of his vineyard, 'I have been looking for fruit on this tree for three years, but I never find any. Cut it down! Why should it waste the ground?' ⁸But the servant answered, 'Master, let the tree have one more year to produce fruit. Let me dig up the dirt around it and put on some fertilizer. ⁹Maybe the tree will produce fruit next year. If the tree still doesn't produce fruit, then you can cut it down.'"

¹⁰Jesus was teaching in one of the synagoguesᵈ on the Sabbathᵈ day. ¹¹In the synagogue there was a woman who had an evil spirit in her. This spirit had made the woman a cripple for 18 years. Her back was always bent; she could not stand up straight. ¹²When Jesus saw her, he called her over and said, "Woman, your sickness has left you!" ¹³Jesus put his hands on her. Immediately she was able to stand up straight and began praising God.

¹⁴The synagogue leader was angry because Jesus healed on the Sabbath day. He said to the people, "There are six days for work. So come to be healed on one of those days. Don't come for healing on the Sabbath day."

¹⁵The Lord answered, "You people are hypocrites!ᵈ All of you untie your work animals and lead them to drink water every day—even on the Sabbath day! ¹⁶This woman that I healed is our Jewish sister. But Satan has held her for 18 years. Surely it is not wrong for her to be freed from her sickness on a Sabbath day!" ¹⁷When Jesus said this, all the men who were criticizing him were ashamed.

12:50 I . . . baptism. Jesus was talking about the suffering he would soon go through.
13:1 Pilate Pontius Pilate was the Roman governor of Judea from A.D. 26 to A.D. 36.

And all the people were happy for the wonderful things Jesus was doing.

[18] Then Jesus said, "What is God's kingdom like? What can I compare it with? [19] God's kingdom is like the seed of the mustard plant.[n] A man plants this seed in his garden. The seed grows and becomes a tree. The wild birds build nests on its branches."

[20] Jesus said again, "What can I compare God's kingdom with? [21] It is like yeast that a woman mixes into a big bowl of flour. The yeast makes all the dough rise."

[22] Jesus was teaching in every town and village. He continued to travel toward Jerusalem. [23] Someone said to Jesus, "Lord, how many people will be saved? Only a few?"

Jesus said, [24]"Try hard to enter through the narrow door that opens the way to heaven! Many people will try to enter there, but they will not be able. [25] A man gets up and closes the door of his house. You can stand outside and knock on the door. You can say, 'Sir, open the door for us!' But he will answer, 'I don't know you! Where did you come from?' [26] Then you will say, 'We ate and drank with you. You taught in the streets of our town.' [27] But he will say to you, 'I don't know you! Where did you come from? Go away from me! All of you do evil!' [28] You will see Abraham, Isaac, Jacob, and all the prophets[d] in God's kingdom. But you will be thrown outside. Then you will cry and grind your teeth with pain. [29] People will come from the east, west, north, and south. They will sit down at the table in the kingdom of God. [30] Those who have the lowest place in life now will have the highest place in the future. And those who have the highest place now will have the lowest place in the future."

[31] At that time some Pharisees[d] came to Jesus and said, "Go away from here! Herod wants to kill you!"

[32] Jesus said to them, "Go tell that fox Herod, 'Today and tomorrow I am forcing demons[d] out of people and finishing my work of healing. Then, on the third day, I will reach my goal.' [33] Yet I must be on my way today and tomorrow and the next day. Surely it cannot be right for a prophet[d] to be killed anywhere except in Jerusalem.

[34]"Jerusalem, Jerusalem! You kill the prophets. You kill with stones those men that God has sent you. Many times I wanted to help your people. I wanted to gather them together as a hen gathers her chicks under her wings. But you did not let me. [35] Now your home will be left completely empty. I tell you, you will not see me again until that time when you will say, 'God bless the One who comes in the name of the Lord.'"[n]

14 On a Sabbath[d] day, Jesus went to the home of a leading Pharisee[d] to eat with him. The people there were all watching Jesus very closely. [2] A man with dropsy[n] was brought before him. [3] Jesus said to the Pharisees and teachers of the law, "Is it right or wrong to heal on the Sabbath day?" [4] But they would not answer his question. So Jesus took the man, healed him, and sent him away. [5] Jesus said to the Pharisees and teachers of the law, "If your son or ox falls into a well on the Sabbath day, will you not pull him out quickly?" [6] And they could not answer him.

[7] Then Jesus noticed that some of the guests were choosing the best places to sit. So Jesus told this story: [8]"When someone invites you to a wedding feast, don't take the most important seat. The host may have invited someone more important than you. [9] And if you are sitting in the most important seat, the host will come to you and say, 'Give this man your seat.' Then you will begin to move down to the last place. And you will be very embarrassed. [10] So when you are invited, go sit in a seat that is not important. Then the host will come to you and say, 'Friend, move up here to a more important place!' Then all the other guests will respect you. [11] Everyone who makes himself great will be made humble. But the person who makes himself humble will be made great."

[12] Then Jesus said to the man who had invited him, "When you give a lunch or a dinner, don't invite only your friends, brothers, relatives, and rich neighbors. At another time they will invite you to eat with them. Then you will have your reward. [13] Instead, when you give a feast, invite the poor, the crippled, the lame and the blind. [14] Then you will be blessed, because they cannot pay you back. They have nothing. But you will

13:19 mustard plant The seed is very small, but the plant grows taller than a man. **13:35 'God . . . Lord.'** Quotation from Psalm 118:26. **14:2 dropsy** A sickness that causes the body to swell larger and larger.

be rewarded when the good people rise from death."

[15] One of the men sitting at the table with Jesus heard these things. The man said to Jesus, "The people who will eat a meal in God's kingdom are blessed."

[16] Jesus said to him, "A man gave a big banquet and invited many people. [17] When it was time to eat, the man sent his servant to tell the guests, 'Come! Everything is ready!'

[18] "But all the guests said they could not come. Each man made an excuse. The first one said, 'I have just bought a field, and I must go look at it. Please excuse me.' [19] Another man said, 'I have just bought five pairs of oxen; I must go and try them. Please excuse me.' [20] A third man said, 'I just got married; I can't come.' [21] So the servant returned. He told his master what had happened. Then the master became angry and said, 'Go at once into the streets and alleys of the town. Bring in the poor, the crippled, the blind, and the lame.' [22] Later the servant said to him, 'Master, I did what you told me to do, but we still have places for more people.' [23] The master said to the servant, 'Go out to the roads and country lanes. Tell the people there to come. I want my house to be full! [24] None of those men that I invited first will ever eat with me!'"

[25] Large crowds were traveling with Jesus. He turned and said to them, [26] "If anyone comes to me but loves his father, mother, wife, children, brothers, or sisters more than he loves me, then he cannot be my follower. A person must love me more than he loves himself! [27] If anyone is not willing to die on a cross when he follows me, then he cannot be my follower. [28] If you wanted to build a tower, you would first sit down and decide how much it would cost. You must see if you have enough money to finish the job. [29] If you don't do that, you might begin the work, but you would not be able to finish. And if you could not finish it, then all who would see it would laugh at you. [30] They would say, 'This man began to build but was not able to finish!'

[31] "If a king is going to fight against another king, first he will sit down and plan. If the king has only 10,000 men, he will plan to see if he is able to defeat the other king who has 20,000 men. [32] If he cannot defeat the other king, then he will send some men to speak to the other

king and ask for peace. [33] In the same way, you must give up everything you have to follow me. If you don't, you cannot be my follower!

[34] "Salt is a good thing. But if the salt loses its salty taste, then it is worth nothing. You cannot make it salty again. [35] It is no good for the soil or for manure. People throw it away.

"You people who hear me, listen!"

15

Many tax collectors and "sinners" came to listen to Jesus. [2] The Pharisees[d] and the teachers of the law began to complain: "Look! This man welcomes sinners and even eats with them!"

[3] Then Jesus told them this story: [4] "Suppose one of you has 100 sheep, but he loses 1 of them. Then he will leave the other 99 sheep alone and go out and look for the lost sheep. The man will keep on searching for the lost sheep until he finds it. [5] And when he finds it, the man is very happy. He puts it on his shoulders [6] and goes home. He calls to his friends and neighbors and says, 'Be happy with me because I found my lost sheep!' [7] In the same way, I tell you there is much joy in heaven when 1 sinner changes his heart. There is more joy for that 1 sinner than there is for 99 good people who don't need to change.

[8] "Suppose a woman has ten silver coins,[n] but she loses one of them. She will light a lamp and clean the house. She will look carefully for the coin until she finds it. [9] And when she finds it, she will call her friends and neighbors and say, 'Be happy with me because I have found the coin that I lost!' [10] In the same way, there is joy before the angels of God when 1 sinner changes his heart."

[11] Then Jesus said, "A man had two sons. [12] The younger son said to his father, 'Give me my share of the property.' So the father divided the property between his two sons. [13] Then the younger son gathered up all that was his and left. He traveled far away to another country. There he wasted his money in foolish living. [14] He spent everything that he had. Soon after that, the land became very dry, and there was no rain. There was not enough food to eat anywhere in the country. The son was hungry and needed money. [15] So he got a job with one of the citizens there. The man sent the son into the fields to feed pigs. [16] The son was so hungry that he was willing to eat the food the pigs were eating. But

---

15:8 silver coins A Roman denarius. One coin was the average pay for one day's work.

no one gave him anything. [17]The son realized that he had been very foolish. He thought, 'All of my father's servants have plenty of food. But I am here, almost dying with hunger. [18]I will leave and return to my father. I'll say to him: Father, I have sinned against God and have done wrong to you. [19]I am not good enough to be called your son. But let me be like one of your servants.' [20]So the son left and went to his father.

"While the son was still a long way off, his father saw him coming. He felt sorry for his son. So the father ran to him, and hugged and kissed him. [21]The son said, 'Father, I have sinned against God and have done wrong to you. I am not good enough to be called your son.' [22]But the father said to his servants, 'Hurry! Bring the best clothes and put them on him. Also, put a ring on his finger and sandals on his feet. [23]And get our fat calf and kill it. Then we can have a feast and celebrate! [24]My son was dead, but now he is alive again! He was lost, but now he is found!' So they began to celebrate.

[25]"The older son was in the field. As he came closer to the house, he heard the sound of music and dancing. [26]So he called to one of the servants and asked, 'What does all this mean?' [27]The servant said, 'Your brother has come back. Your father killed the fat calf to eat because your brother came home safely!' [28]The older son was angry and would not go in to the feast. So his father went out and begged him to come in. [29]The son said to his father, 'I have served you like a slave for many years! I have always obeyed your commands. But you never even killed a young goat for me to have a feast with my friends. [30]But your other son has wasted all your money on prostitutes.[d] Then he comes home, and you kill the fat calf for him!' [31]The father said to him, 'Son, you are always with me. All that I have is yours. [32]We had to celebrate and be happy because your brother was dead, but now he is alive. He was lost, but now he is found.'"

16 Jesus also said to his followers, "Once there was a rich man. He had a manager to take care of his business. Later, the rich man learned that his manager was cheating him. [2]So he called the manager in and said to him, 'I have heard bad things about you. Give me a report of what you have done with my money. You can't be my manager any longer!' [3]Later, the manager thought to himself, 'What will I do? My master is taking my job away from me! I am not strong enough to dig ditches. I am too proud to beg. [4]I know! I'll do something so that when I lose my job, people will welcome me into their homes.'

[5]"So the manager called in everyone who owed the master any money. He said to the first man, 'How much do you owe my master?' [6]The man answered, 'I owe him 800 gallons of olive oil.' The manager said to him, 'Here is your bill; sit down quickly and make the bill less. Write 400 gallons.' [7]Then the manager said to another man, 'How much do you owe my master?' The man answered, 'I owe him 1,000 bushels of wheat.' Then the manager said to him, 'Here is your bill; you can make it less. Write 800 bushels.' [8]Later, the master praised the dishonest manager for being smart. Yes, worldly people are smarter with their own kind than spiritual people are.

[9]"I tell you, make friends for yourselves using worldly riches. Then, when those things are gone, you will be welcomed in that home that continues forever. [10]Whoever can be trusted with small things can also be trusted with large things. Whoever is dishonest in little things will be dishonest in large things too. [11]If you cannot be trusted with worldly riches, then you will not be trusted with the true riches. [12]And if you cannot be trusted with the things that belong to someone else, then you will not be given things of your own.

[13]"No servant can serve two masters. He will hate one master and love the other. Or he will follow one master and refuse to follow the other. You cannot serve both God and money."

[14]The Pharisees[d] were listening to all these things. They made fun of Jesus because they all loved money. [15]Jesus said to them, "You make yourselves look good in front of people. But God knows what is really in your hearts. The things that are important to people are worth nothing to God.

[16]"God wanted the people to live by the law of Moses and the writings of the prophets.[d] But ever since John[n] came, the Good News[d] about the kingdom of God is being told. Now everyone is trying hard to get into the kingdom. [17]Even the smallest part of a letter in the law

cannot be changed. It would be easier for heaven and earth to pass away.

[18]"If a man divorces his wife and marries another woman, he is guilty of adultery.[d] And the man who marries a divorced woman is also guilty of adultery."

[19]Jesus said, "There was a rich man who always dressed in the finest clothes. He lived in luxury every day. [20]There was also a very poor man named Lazarus, whose body was covered with sores. Lazarus was often placed at the rich man's gate. [21]He wanted to eat only the small pieces of food that fell from the rich man's table. And the dogs would come and lick his sores! [22]Later, Lazarus died. The angels took Lazarus and placed him in the arms of Abraham.[d] The rich man died, too, and was buried. [23]But he was sent to where the dead are and had much pain. The rich man saw Abraham far away with Lazarus in his arms. [24]He called, 'Father Abraham, have mercy on me! Send Lazarus to me so that he can dip his finger in water and cool my tongue. I am suffering in this fire!' [25]But Abraham said, 'My child, remember when you lived? You had all the good things in life, but all the bad things happened to Lazarus. Now Lazarus is comforted here, and you are suffering. [26]Also, there is a big pit between you and us. No one can cross over to help you. And no one can leave there and come here.' [27]The rich man said, 'Then please send Lazarus to my father's house on earth! [28]I have five brothers. Lazarus could warn my brothers so that they will not come to this place of pain.' [29]But Abraham said, 'They have the law of Moses and the writings of the prophets[d] to read; let them learn from them!' [30]The rich man said, 'No, father Abraham! If someone came to them from the dead, they would believe and change their hearts and lives.' [31]But Abraham said to him, 'No! If your brothers won't listen to Moses and the prophets, then they won't listen to someone who comes back from death.'"

[17] Jesus said to his followers, "Things will surely happen that cause people to sin. But how terrible for the one who causes them to happen. [2]It would be better for him to be thrown

into the sea with a large stone around his neck than to cause one of these weak people to sin. [3]So be careful!

"If your brother sins, tell him he is wrong. But if he is sorry and stops sinning, forgive him. [4]If your brother sins against you seven times in one day, but he says that he is sorry each time, then forgive him."

[5]The apostles[d] said to the Lord, "Give us more faith!"

[6]The Lord said, "If your faith is as big as a mustard seed,[n] then you can say to this mulberry tree, 'Dig yourself up and plant yourself in the sea!' And the tree will obey you.

[7]"Suppose one of you has a servant who has been plowing the ground or caring for the sheep. When the servant comes in from working in the field, would you say, 'Come in and sit down to eat'? [8]No, you would say to your servant, 'Prepare something for me to eat. Then get yourself ready and serve me. When I finish eating and drinking, then you can eat.' [9]The servant does not get any special thanks for doing what his master told him to do. [10]It is the same with you. When you do everything you are told to do, you should say, 'We don't deserve any special thanks. We have only done the work we should do.'"

[11]Jesus was on his way to Jerusalem. Traveling from Galilee to Samaria, [12]he came into a small town. Ten men met him there. These men did not come close to Jesus, because they all had a harmful skin disease. [13]But they called to him, "Jesus! Master! Please help us!"

[14]When Jesus saw the men, he said, "Go and show yourselves to the priests."[n]

While the ten men were going, they were healed. [15]When one of them saw that he was healed, he went back to Jesus. He praised God in a loud voice. [16]Then he bowed down at Jesus' feet and thanked him. (This man was a Samaritan.[d]) [17]Jesus asked, "Ten men were healed; where are the other nine? [18]Is this Samaritan the only one who came back to thank God?" [19]Then Jesus said to him, "Stand up and go on your way. You were healed because you believed."

[20]Some of the Pharisees[d] asked Jesus, "When will the kingdom of God come?" Jesus answered, "God's kingdom is

17:6 mustard seed This seed is very small, but the plant grows taller than a man.   17:14 show ... priests The law of Moses said a priest must say when a Jew with a harmful skin disease became well.

coming, but not in a way that you will be able to see with your eyes. [21]People will not say, 'Look, God's kingdom is here!' or, 'There it is!' No, God's kingdom is within you."

[22]Then Jesus said to his followers, "The time will come when you will want very much to see one of the days of the Son of Man.[d] But you will not be able to see it. [23]People will say to you, 'Look, there he is!' or, 'Look, here he is!' Stay where you are; don't go away and search.

[24]"The Son of Man[d] will come again. On the day he comes he will shine like lightning, which flashes across the sky and lights it up from one side to the other. [25]But first, the Son of Man must suffer many things and be rejected by the people of this time. [26]When the Son of Man comes again, it will be as it was when Noah lived. [27]In the time of Noah, people were eating, drinking, and getting married even on the day when Noah entered the boat. Then the flood came and killed all the people. [28]It will be the same as during the time of Lot. Those people were eating, drinking, buying, selling, planting, and building. [29]They were doing these things even on the day Lot left Sodom.[n] Then fire and sulfur rained down from the sky and killed them all. [30]This is exactly how it will be when the Son of Man comes again.

[31]"On that day, if a man is on his roof, he will not have time to go inside and get his things. If a man is in the field, he cannot go back home. [32]Remember what happened to Lot's wife?[n] [33]Whoever tries to keep his life will give up true life. But whoever gives up his life will have true life. [34]At the time when I come again, there may be two people sleeping in one bed. One will be taken and the other will be left. [35]There may be two women grinding grain together. One will be taken and the other will be left." [36] n

[37]The followers asked Jesus, "Where will this be, Lord?"

Jesus answered, "People can always find a dead body by looking for the vultures."

18 Then Jesus used this story to teach his followers that they should always pray and never lose hope. [2]"Once there was a judge in a town. He did not care about God. He also did not care what people thought about him. [3]In that same town there was a widow who kept coming to this judge. She said, 'There is a man who is not being fair to me. Give me my rights!' [4]But the judge did not want to help the widow. After a long time, he thought to himself, 'I don't care about God. And I don't care about what people think. [5]But this widow is bothering me. I will see that she gets her rights, or she will bother me until I am worn out!'"

[6]The Lord said, "Listen to what the bad judge said. [7]God's people cry to him night and day. God will always give them what is right, and he will not be slow to answer them. [8]I tell you, God will help his people quickly! But when the Son of Man[d] comes again, will he find those on earth who believe in him?"

[9]There were some people who thought that they were very good and looked down on everyone else. Jesus used this story to teach them: [10]"One day there was a Pharisee[d] and a tax collector. Both went to the Temple[d] to pray. [11]The Pharisee stood alone, away from the tax collector. When the Pharisee prayed, he said, 'God, I thank you that I am not as bad as other people. I am not like men who steal, cheat, or take part in adultery.[d] I thank you that I am better than this tax collector. [12]I give up eating[n] twice a week, and I give one-tenth of everything I earn!'

[13]"The tax collector stood at a distance. When he prayed, he would not even look up to heaven. He beat on his chest because he was so sad. He said, 'God, have mercy on me. I am a sinner!' [14]I tell you, when this man went home, he was right with God. But the Pharisee was not right with God. Everyone who makes himself great will be made humble. But everyone who makes himself humble will be made great."

[15]Some people brought their small children to Jesus so that he could touch them. When the followers saw this, they told the people not to do this. [16]But Jesus

---

17:29 Sodom City that God destroyed because the people were so evil.   **17:32 Lot's wife** A story about what happened to Lot's wife is found in Genesis 19:15-17, 26.   **17:36 Verse 36** A few Greek copies add verse 36: "Two men will be in the same field. One man will be taken, but the other man will be left behind."   **18:12 give up eating** This is called "fasting." The people would give up eating for a special time of prayer and worship to God. It was also done to show sadness.

called the little children to him and said to his followers, "Let the little children come to me. Don't stop them, because the kingdom of God belongs to people who are like these little children. [17]I tell you the truth. You must accept God's kingdom like a little child, or you will never enter it!"

[18]A Jewish leader asked Jesus, "Good Teacher, what must I do to get the life that continues forever?"

[19]Jesus said to him, "Why do you call me good? Only God is good. [20]You know the commands: 'You must not be guilty of adultery.[d] You must not murder anyone. You must not steal. You must not tell lies about your neighbor in court. Honor your father and mother.' "[n]

[21]But the leader said, "I have obeyed all these commands since I was a boy!"

[22]When Jesus heard this, he said to him, "But there is still one more thing you need to do. Sell everything you have and give the money to the poor. You will have a reward in heaven. Then come and follow me!" [23]But when the man heard this, he became very sad because he was very rich.

[24]When Jesus saw that the man was sad, he said, "It will be very hard for rich people to enter the kingdom of God! [25]It would be easier for a camel to go through the eye of a needle than for a rich person to enter the kingdom of God!"

[26]When the people heard this, they asked, "Then who can be saved?"

[27]Jesus answered, "God can do things that are not possible for men to do!"

[28]Peter said, "Look, we left everything we had and followed you!"

[29]Jesus said, "I tell you the truth. Everyone who has left his house, wife, brothers, parents, or children for God's kingdom [30]will get much more than he left. He will receive many times more in this life. And after he dies, he will live with God forever."

[31]Then Jesus talked to the 12 apostles[d] alone. He said to them, "Listen! We are going to Jerusalem. Everything that God told the prophets[d] to write about the Son of Man[d] will happen! [32]He will be turned over to the non-Jewish people. They will laugh at him, insult him, and spit on him. [33]They will beat him with whips and then kill him. But on the third day after his death, he will rise to life again." [34]The apostles tried to understand this,

but they could not; the meaning was hidden from them.

[35]Jesus was coming near the city of Jericho. There was a blind man sitting beside the road, begging for money. [36]When he heard the people coming down the road, he asked, "What is happening?"

[37]They told him, "Jesus, the one from Nazareth, is coming here."

[38]The blind man cried out, "Jesus, Son of David![d] Please help me!"

[39]The people who were in front, leading the group, told the blind man to be quiet. But the blind man shouted more and more, "Son of David, please help me!"

[40]Jesus stopped and said, "Bring the blind man to me!" When he came near, Jesus asked him, [41]"What do you want me to do for you?"

He said, "Lord, I want to see again."

[42]Jesus said to him, "Then see! You are healed because you believed."

[43]At once the man was able to see, and he followed Jesus, thanking God. All the people who saw this praised God.

19

Jesus was going through the city of Jericho. [2]In Jericho there was a man named Zacchaeus. He was a wealthy, very important tax collector. [3]He wanted to see who Jesus was, but he was too short to see above the crowd. [4]He ran ahead to a place where he knew Jesus would come. He climbed a sycamore tree so he could see Jesus. [5]When Jesus came to that place, he looked up and saw Zacchaeus in the tree. He said to him, "Zacchaeus, hurry and come down! I must stay at your house today."

[6]Zacchaeus came down quickly. He was pleased to have Jesus in his house. [7]All the people saw this and began to complain, "Look at the kind of man Jesus stays with. Zacchaeus is a sinner!"

[8]But Zacchaeus said to the Lord, "I will give half of my money to the poor. If I have cheated anyone, I will pay that person back four times more!"

[9]Jesus said, "Salvation has come to this house today. This man truly belongs to the family of Abraham. [10]The Son of Man[d] came to find lost people and save them."

[11]Jesus traveled closer to Jerusalem. Some of the people thought that God's kingdom would appear soon. [12]Jesus knew that the people thought this, so he

18:20 'You . . . mother.' Quotation from Exodus 20:12-16; Deuteronomy 5:16-20.

told them this story: "A very important man was preparing to go to a country far away to be made a king. Then he planned to return home and rule his people. [13]So the man called ten of his servants together. He gave a bag of money[n] to each servant. He said, 'Do business with this money till I get back.' [14]But the people in the kingdom hated the man. So they sent a group to follow him and say, 'We don't want this man to be our king!'

[15]"But the man became king. When he came home, he said, 'Call those servants who have my money. I want to know how much they earned with it.'

[16]"The first servant came and said, 'Sir, I earned ten bags of money with the one bag you gave me!' [17]The king said to the servant, 'Fine! You are a good servant. I see that I can trust you with small things. So now I will let you rule over ten of my cities.'

[18]"The second servant said, 'Sir, with your one bag of money I earned five bags!' [19]The king said to this servant, 'You can rule over five cities.'

[20]"Then another servant came in. The servant said to the king, 'Sir, here is your bag of money. I wrapped it in a piece of cloth and hid it. [21]I was afraid of you because you are a hard man. You even take money that you didn't earn and gather food that you didn't plant.' [22]Then the king said to the servant, 'You evil servant! I will use your own words to condemn you. You said that I am a hard man. You said that I even take money that I didn't earn and gather food that I didn't plant. [23]If that is true, then you should have put my money in the bank. Then, when I came back, my money would have earned some interest.'

[24]"Then the king said to the men who were watching, 'Take the bag of money away from this servant and give it to the servant who earned ten bags of money.' [25]They said to the king, 'But sir, that servant already has ten bags of money!' [26]The king said, 'The one who uses what he has will get more. But the one who does not use what he has will have everything taken away from him. [27]Now where are my enemies who didn't want me to be king? Bring them here and kill them before me.'"

[28]After Jesus said this, he went on to-

ward Jerusalem. [29]Jesus came near Bethphage and Bethany, towns near the hill called the Mount of Olives.[d] Then he sent out two of his followers. [30]He said, "Go into the town you can see there. When you enter it, you will find a colt tied there. No one has ever ridden this colt. Untie it, and bring it here to me. [31]If anyone asks you why you are taking it, say, 'The Master needs it.'"

[32]The two followers went into town. They found the colt just as Jesus told them. [33]The followers untied it, but the owners of the colt came out. They asked the followers, "Why are you untying our colt?"

[34]The followers answered, "The Master needs it." [35]So they brought it to Jesus. They threw their coats on the colt's back and put Jesus on it. [36]As Jesus rode toward Jerusalem, the followers spread their coats on the road before him.

[37]Jesus was coming close to Jerusalem. He was already near the bottom of the Mount of Olives. The whole crowd of followers was very happy. They began shouting praise to God for all the powerful works they had seen. They said,

[38]"God bless the king who comes in
    the name of the Lord!
There is peace in heaven and glory
    to God!"   *Psalm 118:26*

[39]Some of the Pharisees[d] said to Jesus, "Teacher, tell your followers not to say these things!"

[40]But Jesus answered, "I tell you, if my followers don't say these things, then the stones will cry out."

[41]Jesus came near Jerusalem. He saw the city and began to cry for it. [42]Jesus said to Jerusalem, "I wish you knew today what would bring you peace! But you can't know it, because it is hidden from you. [43]A time is coming when your enemies will build a wall around you and will hold you in on all sides. [44]They will destroy you and all your people. Not one stone of your buildings will be left on another. All this will happen because you did not know the time when God came to save you."

[45]Jesus went into the Temple.[d] He began to throw out the people who were selling things there. [46]He said, "It is written in the Scriptures,[d] 'My Temple will be a house where people will pray.'[n] But

19:13 bag of money One bag of money was a Greek "mina." One mina was enough money to pay a person for working three months.   **19:46 'My Temple . . . pray.'** Quotation from Isaiah 56:7.

you have changed it into a 'hideout for robbers'!"[n]

[47] Jesus taught in the Temple every day. The leading priests, the teachers of the law, and some of the leaders of the people wanted to kill Jesus. [48] But all the people were listening closely to him and were interested in all the things he said. So the leading priests, the teachers of the law, and the leaders did not know how they could kill him.

20 One day Jesus was in the Temple,[d] teaching the people and telling them the Good News.[d] The leading priests, teachers of the law, and older Jewish leaders came up to talk with him. [2] They said, "Tell us! What authority do you have to do these things? Who gave you this authority?"

[3] Jesus answered, "I will ask you a question too. Tell me: [4] When John baptized people, did that come from God or from man?"

[5] The priests, the teachers of the law, and the Jewish leaders all talked about this. They said to each other, "If we answer, 'John's baptism was from God,' then Jesus will say, 'Then why did you not believe John?' [6] But if we say, 'John's baptism was from man,' then all the people will kill us with stones because they believe that John was a prophet."[d] [7] So they answered, "We don't know the answer."

[8] So Jesus said to them, "Then I will not tell you by what authority I do these things!"

[9] Then Jesus told the people this story: "A man planted a vineyard. The man leased the land to some farmers. Then he went away for a long time. [10] Later, it was time for the grapes to be picked. So the man sent a servant to those farmers to get his share of the grapes. But they beat the servant and sent him away with nothing. [11] Then he sent another servant. They beat this servant too. They showed no respect for him and sent him away with nothing. [12] So the man sent a third servant. The farmers hurt this servant badly and threw him out. [13] The owner of the vineyard said, 'What will I do now? I will send my son whom I love very much. Maybe they will respect him!' [14] When they saw the son, they said to each other, 'This is the owner's son. This vineyard will be his. If we kill him, then it will be ours!' [15] So the farmers threw the son out of the vineyard and killed him.

"What will the owner of this vineyard do? [16] He will come and kill those farmers! Then he will give the vineyard to other farmers."

The people heard this story. They said, "No! Let this never happen!"

[17] But Jesus looked at them and said, "Then what does this verse mean:

'The stone that the builders did not want
became the cornerstone'?[d]
Psalm 118:22

[18] Everyone who falls on that stone will be broken. If that stone falls on you, it will crush you!"

[19] The teachers of the law and the priests heard this story that Jesus told. They knew the story was about them. So they wanted to arrest Jesus at once. But they were afraid of what the people would do.

[20] So they waited for the right time to get Jesus. They sent some spies who acted as if they were good men. They wanted to trap Jesus in what he said so they could hand him over to the authority and power of the governor. [21] So the spies asked Jesus, "Teacher, we know that what you say and teach is true. You teach the same to all people. You always teach the truth about God's way. [22] Tell us, is it right that we pay taxes to Caesar[d] or not?"

[23] But Jesus knew that these men were trying to trick him. He said, [24] "Show me a coin. Whose name is on the coin? And whose picture is on it?"

They said, "Caesar's."

[25] Jesus said to them, "Then give to Caesar the things that are Caesar's. And give to God the things that are God's."

[26] The men were amazed at his answer. They could say nothing. They were not able to trap Jesus in anything he said before the people.

[27] Some Sadducees[d] came to Jesus. (Sadducees believe that people will not rise from death.) They asked, [28] "Teacher, Moses wrote that a man's brother might die. He leaves a wife but no children. Then that man must marry the widow and have children for his dead brother. [29] One time there were seven brothers. The first brother married, but died. He had no children. [30] Then the second brother married the widow, and he died. [31] And the third brother married the widow, and he died. The same thing happened with all the

19:46 **'hideout for robbers'** Quotation from Jeremiah 7:11.

other brothers. They all died and had no children. [32]The woman was the last to die. [33]But all seven brothers married her. So when people rise from death, whose wife will the woman be?"

[34]Jesus said to the Sadducees, "On earth, people marry each other. [35]But those who will be worthy to be raised from death and live again will not marry. [36]In that life they are like angels and cannot die. They are children of God, because they have been raised from death. [37]Moses clearly showed that the dead are raised to life. When Moses wrote about the burning bush,[n] he said that the Lord is 'the God of Abraham, the God of Isaac, and the God of Jacob.'[n] [38]God is the God of living people, not dead people. All people are alive to God."

[39]Some of the teachers of the law said, "Teacher, your answer was good." [40]No one was brave enough to ask him another question.

[41]Then Jesus said, "Why do people say that the Christ[d] is the Son of David?[d] [42]In the book of Psalms, David himself says:

'The Lord said to my Lord:
    Sit by me at my right side,
[43]   until I put your enemies under
       your control.'[n]   *Psalm 110:1*

[44]David calls the Christ 'Lord.' But the Christ is also the son of David. How can both these things be true?"

[45]While all the people were listening, Jesus said to his followers, [46]"Be careful of the teachers of the law. They like to walk around wearing clothes that look important. And they love for people to show respect to them in the marketplaces. They love to have the most important seats in the synagogues[d] and at the feasts. [47]But they cheat widows and steal their houses. Then they try to make themselves look good by saying long prayers. God will punish these men very much."

21 Jesus saw some rich people putting their gifts into the Temple[d] money box.[n] [2]Then Jesus saw a poor widow. She put two small copper coins into the box. [3]He said, "I tell you the truth. This poor widow gave only two small coins. But she really gave more than all those rich people. [4]The rich have plenty; they gave only what they

did not need. This woman is very poor, but she gave all she had. And she needed that money to live on."

[5]Some of the followers were talking about the Temple[d] and how it was decorated with beautiful stones and gifts offered to God.

[6]But Jesus said, "The time will come when all that you see here will be destroyed. Every stone will be thrown down to the ground. Not one stone will be left on another!"

[7]Some followers asked Jesus, "Teacher, when will these things happen? What will show us that it is time for them to take place?"

[8]Jesus said, "Be careful! Don't be fooled. Many people will come using my name. They will say, 'I am the Christ'[d] and, 'The right time has come!' But don't follow them. [9]When you hear about wars and riots, don't be afraid. These things must happen first. Then the end will come later."

[10]Then he said to them, "Nations will fight against other nations. Kingdoms will fight against other kingdoms. [11]There will be great earthquakes, sicknesses, and other terrible things in many places. In some places there will be no food for the people to eat. Fearful events and great signs will come from heaven.

[12]"But before all these things happen, people will arrest you and treat you cruelly. They will judge you in their synagogues[d] and put you in jail. You will be forced to stand before kings and governors. They will do all these things to you because you follow me. [13]But this will give you an opportunity to tell about me. [14]Don't worry about what you will say. [15]I will give you the wisdom to say things so that none of your enemies will be able to show that you are wrong. [16]Even your parents, brothers, relatives and friends will turn against you. They will kill some of you. [17]All people will hate you because you follow me. [18]But none of these things can really harm you. [19]You will save yourselves by continuing strong in your faith through all these things.

[20]"When you see armies all around Jerusalem, then you will know that it will soon be destroyed. [21]At that time, people in Judea should run away to the

---

20:37 **burning bush** Read Exodus 3:1-12 in the Old Testament.   20:37 **'the God of . . . Jacob'** These words are taken from Exodus 3:6.   20:43 **until . . . control** Literally, "until I make your enemies a footstool for your feet."   21:1 **money box** A special box in the Jewish place for worship where people put their gifts to God.

mountains. The people in Jerusalem must get out. If you are near the city, don't go in! [22] These are the days of punishment to make come true all that is written in the Scriptures.[d] [23] At that time, it will be hard for women who are pregnant or have nursing babies! Great trouble will come upon this land, and God will be angry with these people. [24] Some will be killed by the sword and taken as prisoners to all nations. Jerusalem will be crushed by non-Jewish people until their time is over.

[25] "Amazing things will happen to the sun, moon, and stars. On earth, nations will be afraid because of the roar and fury of the sea. They will not know what to do. [26] People will be so afraid they will faint. They will wonder what is happening to the whole world. Everything in the sky will be changed. [27] Then people will see the Son of Man[d] coming in a cloud with power and great glory. [28] When these things begin to happen, don't fear. Look up and hold your heads high because the time when God will free you is near!"

[29] Then Jesus told this story: "Look at the fig tree and all the other trees. [30] When their leaves appear, you know that summer is near. [31] In the same way, when you see all these things happening, then you will know that God's kingdom is coming very soon.

[32] "I tell you the truth. All these things will happen while the people of this time are still living! [33] The whole world, earth and sky, will be destroyed; but the words I have said will never be destroyed!

[34] "Be careful! Don't spend your time feasting and drinking. Or don't be too busy with worldly things. If you do that, you will not be able to think straight. And then that day might come when you are not ready. [35] It will close like a trap on all people on earth. [36] So be ready all the time. Pray that you will be strong enough to escape all these things that will happen. And pray that you will be able to stand before the Son of Man."[d]

[37] During the day, Jesus taught the people in the Temple.[d] At night he went out of the city and stayed on the Mount of Olives.[d] [38] Every morning all the people got up early to go to the Temple to listen to him.

22 It was almost time for the Jewish Feast[d] of Unleavened Bread, called the Passover[d] Feast. [2] The leading priests and teachers of the law were trying to find a way to kill Jesus. But they were afraid of the people.

[3] One of Jesus' 12 apostles[d] was named Judas Iscariot. Satan entered Judas, and he went to [4] the leading priests and some of the soldiers who guarded the Temple.[d] He talked to them about a way to give Jesus to them. [5] They were pleased and promised to give Judas money. [6] Judas agreed. Then he waited for the best time to turn Jesus over to them without the crowd knowing it.

[7] The Day of Unleavened[d] Bread came. This was the day the Passover[d] lambs had to be sacrificed. [8] Jesus said to Peter and John, "Go and prepare the Passover meal for us to eat."

[9] They asked, "Where do you want us to prepare it?"

Jesus said to them, [10] "Listen! After you go into the city, you will see a man carrying a jar of water. Follow him into the house that he enters. [11] Tell the person who owns that house, 'The Teacher asks that you please show us the room where he and his followers may eat the Passover meal.' [12] Then he will show you a large room upstairs. This room is ready for you. Prepare the Passover meal there."

[13] So Peter and John left. Everything happened as Jesus had said. So they prepared the Passover meal.

[14] When the time came, Jesus and the apostles[d] were sitting at the table. [15] He said to them, "I wanted very much to eat this Passover[d] meal with you before I die. [16] I will never eat another Passover meal until it is given its true meaning in the kingdom of God."

[17] Then Jesus took a cup. He gave thanks to God for it and said, "Take this cup and give it to everyone here. [18] I will not drink again from the fruit of the vine[n] until God's kingdom comes."

[19] Then Jesus took some bread. He thanked God for it, broke it, and gave it to the apostles. Then Jesus said, "This bread is my body that I am giving for you. Do this to remember me." [20] In the same way, after supper, Jesus took the cup and said, "This cup shows the new agreement that God makes with his people. This new agreement begins with my blood which is poured out for you."[n]

22:18 fruit of the vine Product of the grapevine; this may also be translated "wine." **22:20 Verse 20** A few Greek copies do not have the last part of verse 19 and all of verse 20.

²¹Jesus said, "One of you will turn against me. His hand is by my hand on the table. ²²The Son of Man[d] will do what God has planned. But how terrible it will be for that man who gives the Son of Man to be killed."

²³Then the apostles[d] asked each other, "Which one of us would do that to Jesus?"

²⁴Then the apostles[d] began to argue about which one of them was the most important. ²⁵But Jesus said to them, "The kings of the world rule over their people. Men who have authority over others are called 'very important.' ²⁶But you must not be like that. The greatest among you should be like the youngest, and the leader should be like the servant. ²⁷Who is more important: the one sitting at the table or the one serving him? You think the one at the table is more important. But I am like a servant among you!

²⁸"You men have stayed with me through many struggles. ²⁹My Father has given me the power to rule. I also give you authority to rule with me. ³⁰You will eat and drink at my table in my kingdom. You will sit on thrones and judge the 12 tribes[d] of Israel.

³¹"Satan has asked to test all of you as a farmer tests his wheat. Simon, Simon, ³²I have prayed that you will not lose your faith! Help your brothers be stronger when you come back to me."

³³But Peter said to Jesus, "Lord, I am ready to go to prison with you. I will even die with you!"

³⁴But Jesus said, "Peter, before the rooster crows tonight, you will say you don't know me. You will say this three times!"

³⁵Then Jesus said to the apostles,[d] "When I sent you out without money, a bag, or sandals, did you need anything?"

They said, "No."

³⁶He said to them, "But now if you have money or a bag, carry that with you. If you don't have a sword, sell your coat and buy one. ³⁷The Scripture[d] says, 'He was treated like a criminal.'[n] This scripture must have its full meaning. It was written about me, and it is happening now."

³⁸The followers said, "Look, Lord, here are two swords!"

He said to them, "That's enough."

³⁹⁻⁴⁰Jesus left the city and went to the Mount of Olives.[d] His followers went with him. (Jesus went there often.) He said to his followers, "Pray for strength against temptation."

⁴¹Then Jesus went about a stone's throw away from them. He kneeled down and prayed, ⁴²"Father, if it is what you want, then let me not have this cup[n] of suffering. But do what you want, not what I want." ⁴³Then an angel from heaven appeared to him to help him. ⁴⁴Jesus was full of pain; he prayed even more. Sweat dripped from his face as if he were bleeding. ⁴⁵When he finished praying, he went to his followers. They were asleep. (Their sadness had made them very tired.) ⁴⁶Jesus said to them, "Why are you sleeping? Get up and pray for strength against temptation."

⁴⁷While Jesus was speaking, a crowd came up. One of the 12 apostles[d] was leading them. He was Judas. He came close to Jesus so that he could kiss him.

⁴⁸But Jesus said to him, "Judas, are you using the kiss to give the Son of Man[d] to his enemies?"

⁴⁹The followers of Jesus were standing there too. They saw what was happening. They said to Jesus, "Lord, should we use our swords?" ⁵⁰And one of them did use his sword. He cut off the right ear of the servant of the high priest.

⁵¹Jesus said, "Stop!" Then he touched the servant's ear and healed him.

⁵²Those who came to arrest Jesus were the leading priests, the soldiers who guarded the Temple,[d] and the older Jewish leaders. Jesus said to them, "Why did you come out here with swords and sticks? Do you think I am a criminal? ⁵³I was with you every day in the Temple. Why didn't you try to arrest me there? But this is your time—the time when darkness rules."

⁵⁴They arrested Jesus and took him away. They brought him into the house of the high priest. Peter followed them, but he did not go near Jesus. ⁵⁵The soldiers started a fire in the middle of the courtyard and sat together. Peter sat with them. ⁵⁶A servant girl saw Peter sitting there near the light. She looked closely at Peter's face and said, "This man was also with him!"

22:37 'He . . . criminal.' Quotation from Isaiah 53:12.   **22:42 cup** Jesus is talking about the bad things that will happen to him. Accepting these things will be hard, like drinking a cup of something that tastes very bitter.

⁵⁷But Peter said this was not true. He said, "Girl, I don't know him."

⁵⁸A short time later, another person saw Peter and said, "You are also one of them."

But Peter said, "Man, I am not!"

⁵⁹About an hour later, another man insisted, "It is true! This man was with him. He is from Galilee!"

⁶⁰But Peter said, "Man, I don't know what you are talking about!"

Immediately, while Peter was still speaking, a rooster crowed. ⁶¹Then the Lord turned and looked straight at Peter. And Peter remembered what the Lord had said: "Before the rooster crows tonight, you will say three times that you don't know me." ⁶²Then Peter went outside and cried with much pain in his heart.

⁶³⁻⁶⁴Some men were guarding Jesus. They made fun of him like this: They covered his eyes so that he could not see them. Then they hit him and said, "Prove that you are a prophet,[d] and tell us who hit you!" ⁶⁵The men said many cruel things to Jesus.

⁶⁶When day came, the older leaders of the people, the leading priests, and the teachers of the law came together. They led Jesus away to their highest court. ⁶⁷They said, "If you are the Christ,[d] then tell us that you are!"

Jesus said to them, "If I tell you I am the Christ, you will not believe me. ⁶⁸And if I ask you, you will not answer. ⁶⁹But beginning now, the Son of Man will sit at the right hand of the powerful God."

⁷⁰They all said, "Then are you the Son of God?"

Jesus said to them, "Yes, you are right when you say that I am."

⁷¹They said, "Why do we need witnesses now? We ourselves heard him say this!"

23 Then the whole group stood up and led Jesus to Pilate.[n] ²They began to accuse Jesus. They told Pilate, "We caught this man telling things that were confusing our people. He says that we should not pay taxes to Caesar.[d] He calls himself the Christ,[d] a king."

³Pilate asked Jesus, "Are you the king of the Jews?"

Jesus answered, "Yes, that is right."

⁴Pilate said to the leading priests and the people, "I find nothing wrong with this man."

⁵They said again and again, "But Jesus is making trouble with the people! He teaches all around Judea. He began in Galilee, and now he is here!"

⁶Pilate heard this and asked if Jesus was from Galilee. ⁷If so, Jesus was under Herod's authority. Herod was in Jerusalem at that time; so Pilate sent Jesus to him. ⁸When Herod saw Jesus, he was very glad. He had heard about Jesus and had wanted to meet him for a long time. Herod was hoping to see Jesus work a miracle.[d] ⁹Herod asked Jesus many questions, but Jesus said nothing. ¹⁰The leading priests and teachers of the law were standing there. They were shouting things against Jesus. ¹¹Then Herod and his soldiers made fun of Jesus. They dressed him in a kingly robe and then sent him back to Pilate. ¹²In the past, Pilate and Herod had always been enemies. But on that day they became friends.

¹³Pilate called all the people together with the leading priests and the Jewish leaders. ¹⁴He said to them, "You brought this man to me. You said that he was making trouble among the people. But I have questioned him before you all, and I have not found him guilty of the things you say. ¹⁵Also, Herod found nothing wrong with him; he sent him back to us. Look, he has done nothing for which he should die. ¹⁶So, after I punish him, I will let him go free." ¹⁷ⁿ

¹⁸But all the people shouted, "Kill him! Let Barabbas go free!" ¹⁹(Barabbas was a man who was in prison because he started a riot in the city. He was guilty of murder.)

²⁰Pilate wanted to let Jesus go free. So he told this to the crowd. ²¹But they shouted again, "Kill him! Kill him on a cross!"

²²A third time Pilate said to them, "Why? What wrong has he done? I can find no reason to kill him. So I will have him punished and set him free."

²³But they continued to shout. They demanded that Jesus be killed on the cross. Their yelling became so loud that ²⁴Pilate decided to give them what they wanted. ²⁵They wanted Barabbas to go free, the man who was in jail for starting a riot and for murder. Pilate let Barab-

23:1 Pilate Pontius Pilate was the Roman governor of Judea from A.D. 26 to A.D. 36. **23:17 Verse 17** A few Greek copies add verse 17: "Every year at the Passover Feast, Pilate had to release one prisoner to the people."

bas go free and gave Jesus to them to be killed.

[26] The soldiers led Jesus away. At that time, there was a man coming into the city from the fields. His name was Simon, and he was from the city of Cyrene. The soldiers forced Simon to carry Jesus' cross and walk behind him.

[27] A large crowd of people was following Jesus. Some of the women were sad and crying. [28] But Jesus turned and said to them, "Women of Jerusalem, don't cry for me. Cry for yourselves and for your children too! [29] The time is coming when people will say, 'Happy are the women who cannot have children! Happy are the women who have no babies to nurse.' [30] Then people will say to the mountains, 'Fall on us!' And they will say to the hills, 'Cover us!' [31] If they act like this now when life is good, what will happen when bad times come?"[n]

[32] There were also two criminals led out with Jesus to be killed. [33] Jesus and the two criminals were taken to a place called the Skull. There the soldiers nailed Jesus to his cross. They also nailed the criminals to their crosses, one beside Jesus on the right and the other beside Jesus on the left. [34] Jesus said, "Father, forgive them. They don't know what they are doing."[n]

The soldiers threw lots[d] to decide who would get his clothes. [35] The people stood there watching. The leaders made fun of Jesus. They said, "If he is God's Chosen One, the Christ,[d] then let him save himself. He saved other people, didn't he?"

[36] Even the soldiers made fun of him. They came to Jesus and offered him some vinegar. [37] They said, "If you are the king of the Jews, save yourself!" [38] (At the top of the cross these words were written: "THIS IS THE KING OF THE JEWS.")

[39] One of the criminals began to shout insults at Jesus: "Aren't you the Christ? Then save yourself! And save us too!"

[40] But the other criminal stopped him. He said, "You should fear God! You are getting the same punishment as he is. [41] We are punished justly; we should die. But this man has done nothing wrong!" [42] Then this criminal said to Jesus,

"Jesus, remember me when you come into your kingdom!"

[43] Then Jesus said to him, "Listen! What I say is true: Today you will be with me in paradise!"[n]

[44] It was about noon, and the whole land became dark until three o'clock in the afternoon. [45] There was no sun! The curtain in the Temple[n] was torn into two pieces. [46] Jesus cried out in a loud voice, "Father, I give you my life." After Jesus said this, he died.

[47] The army officer there saw what happened. He praised God, saying, "I know this was a good man!"

[48] Many people had gathered there to watch this thing. When they saw what happened, they returned home. They beat their chests because they were so sad. [49] Those who were close friends of Jesus were there. Some were women who had followed Jesus from Galilee. They all stood far away from the cross and watched.

[50-51] A man from the Jewish town of Arimathea was there, too. His name was Joseph. He was a good, religious man. He wanted the kingdom of God to come. Joseph was a member of the Jewish council, but he had not agreed when the other leaders decided to kill Jesus. [52] Joseph went to Pilate to ask for the body of Jesus. [53] So Joseph took the body down from the cross and wrapped it in cloth. Then he put Jesus' body in a tomb that was cut in a wall of rock. This tomb had never been used before. [54] This was late on Preparation[d] Day. When the sun went down, the Sabbath[d] day would begin.

[55] The women who had come from Galilee with Jesus followed Joseph. They saw the tomb and saw inside where the body of Jesus was laid. [56] Then the women left to prepare perfumes and spices.

On the Sabbath day they rested, as the law of Moses commanded.

24

Very early on the first day of the week, the women came to the tomb where Jesus' body was laid. They brought the spices they had prepared. [2] They found that the stone had been rolled away from the entrance of the tomb. [3] They went in, but they did not find the body of the Lord Jesus. [4] While they were wondering about this, two

23:31 If . . . come? Literally, "If they do these things in the green tree, what will happen in the dry?" 23:34 Verse 34 Some early Greek copies do not have this part of the verse. 23:43 paradise A place where good people go when they die. 23:45 curtain in the Temple A curtain divided the Most Holy Place from the other part of the Temple. This was the special building in Jerusalem where God commanded the Jews to worship him.

men in shining clothes suddenly stood beside them. ⁵The women were very afraid; they bowed their heads to the ground. The men said to the women, "Why are you looking for a living person here? This is a place for the dead. ⁶Jesus is not here. He has risen from death! Do you remember what he said in Galilee? ⁷He said that the Son of Man^d must be given to evil men, be killed on a cross, and rise from death on the third day." ⁸Then the women remembered what Jesus had said.

⁹The women left the tomb and told all these things to the 11 apostles^d and the other followers. ¹⁰These women were Mary Magdalene, Joanna, Mary the mother of James, and some other women. The women told the apostles everything that had happened at the tomb. ¹¹But they did not believe the women. It sounded like nonsense. ¹²But Peter got up and ran to the tomb. He looked in, but he saw only the cloth that Jesus' body had been wrapped in. Peter went away to be alone, wondering about what had happened.

¹³That same day two of Jesus' followers were going to a town named Emmaus. It is about seven miles from Jerusalem. ¹⁴They were talking about everything that had happened. ¹⁵While they were discussing these things, Jesus himself came near and began walking with them. ¹⁶(They were not allowed to recognize Jesus.) ¹⁷Then he said, "What are these things you are talking about while you walk?"

The two followers stopped. Their faces were very sad. ¹⁸The one named Cleopas answered, "You must be the only one in Jerusalem who does not know what just happened there."

¹⁹Jesus said to them, "What are you talking about?"

The followers said, "It is about Jesus of Nazareth. He was a prophet^d from God to all the people. He said and did many powerful things. ²⁰Our leaders and the leading priests gave him up to be judged and killed. They nailed him to a cross. ²¹But we were hoping that he would free the Jews. It is now the third day since this happened. ²²And today some women among us told us some amazing things. Early this morning they went to the tomb, ²³but they did not find his body there. They came and told us that they had seen a vision of angels. The angels said that Jesus was alive! ²⁴So some of our group went to the tomb,

too. They found it just as the women said, but they did not see Jesus."

²⁵Then Jesus said to them, "You are foolish and slow to realize what is true. You should believe everything the prophets said. ²⁶They said that the Christ^d must suffer these things before he enters his glory." ²⁷Then Jesus began to explain everything that had been written about himself in the Scriptures.^d He started with Moses, and then he talked about what all the prophets had said about him.

²⁸They came near the town of Emmaus, and Jesus acted as if he did not plan to stop there. ²⁹But they begged him, "Stay with us. It is late; it is almost night." So he went in to stay with them. ³⁰Jesus sat down with them and took some bread. He gave thanks for the food and divided it. Then he gave it to them. ³¹And then, they were allowed to recognize Jesus. But when they saw who he was, he disappeared. ³²They said to each other, "When Jesus talked to us on the road, it felt like a fire burning in us. It was exciting when he explained the true meaning of the Scriptures."

³³So the two followers got up at once and went back to Jerusalem. There they found the 11 apostles^d and others gathered. ³⁴They were saying, "The Lord really has risen from death! He showed himself to Simon."

³⁵Then the two followers told what had happened on the road. They talked about how they recognized Jesus when he divided the bread.

³⁶While the two followers were telling this, Jesus himself stood among those gathered. He said to them, "Peace be with you."

³⁷They were fearful and terrified. They thought they were seeing a ghost. ³⁸But Jesus said, "Why are you troubled? Why do you doubt what you see? ³⁹Look at my hands and my feet. It is I myself! Touch me. You can see that I have a living body; a ghost does not have a body like this."

⁴⁰After Jesus said this, he showed them his hands and feet. ⁴¹The followers were amazed and very happy. They still could not believe it. Jesus said to them, "Do you have any food here?" ⁴²They gave him a piece of cooked fish. ⁴³While the followers watched, Jesus took the fish and ate it.

⁴⁴He said to them, "Remember when I was with you before? I said that every-

thing written about me must happen—everything in the law of Moses, the books of the prophets,[d] and the Psalms."

[45] Then Jesus opened their minds so they could understand the Scriptures.[d]

[46] He said to them, "It is written that the Christ[d] would be killed and rise from death on the third day. [47-48] You saw these things happen—you are witnesses. You must tell people to change their hearts and lives. If they do this, their sins will be forgiven. You must start at Jerusalem and preach these things in my name to

all nations. [49] Listen! My Father has promised you something; I will send it to you. But you must stay in Jerusalem until you have received that power from heaven."

[50] Jesus led his followers out of Jerusalem almost to Bethany. He raised his hands and blessed them. [51] While he was blessing them, he was separated from them and carried into heaven. [52] They worshiped him and then went back to the city very happy. [53] They stayed in the Temple[d] all the time, praising God.

The Gospel According to

JOHN

1 Before the world began, there was the Word.[n] The Word was with God, and the Word was God. [2] He was with God in the beginning. [3] All things were made through him. Nothing was made without him. [4] In him there was life. That life was light for the people of the world. [5] The Light shines in the darkness. And the darkness has not overpowered the Light.

[6] There was a man named John[n] who was sent by God. [7] He came to tell people about the Light. Through him all people could hear about the Light and believe. [8] John was not the Light, but he came to tell people about the Light. [9] The true Light was coming into the world. The true Light gives light to all.

[10] The Word was in the world. The world was made through him, but the world did not know him. [11] He came to the world that was his own. But his own people did not accept him. [12] But some people did accept him. They believed in him. To them he gave the right to become children of God. [13] They did not become his children in the human way. They were not born because of the desire or wish of some man. They were born of God.

[14] The Word became a man and lived among us. We saw his glory—the glory that belongs to the only Son of the Fa-

ther. The Word was full of grace and truth. [15] John told about him. He said, "This is the One I was talking about. I said, 'The One who comes after me is greater than I am. He was living before me.'"

[16] The Word was full of grace and truth. From him we all received more and more blessings. [17] The law was given through Moses, but grace and truth came through Jesus Christ. [18] No man has ever seen God. But God the only Son is very close to the Father.[n] And the Son has shown us what God is like.

[19] The Jews in Jerusalem sent some priests and Levites to John.[n] The Jews sent them to ask, "Who are you?"

[20] John spoke freely and did not refuse to answer. He said clearly, "I am not the Christ."[d]

[21] So they asked him, "Then who are you? Are you Elijah?"[n]

He answered, "No, I am not Elijah."

Then they asked, "Are you the Prophet?"[n]

He answered, "No, I am not the Prophet."

[22] Then they said, "Who are you? Give us an answer to tell those who sent us. What do you say about yourself?"

[23] John told them in the words of the prophet Isaiah:

1:1 Word The Greek word is "logos," meaning any kind of communication. It could be translated "message." Here, it means Christ. Christ was the way God told people about himself. **1:6 John** John the Baptist, who preached to people about Christ's coming (Matthew 3, Luke 3). **1:18 But . . . Father.** This could be translated, "But the only God is very close to the Father." Also, some Greek copies say, "But the only Son is very close to the Father." **1:19 John** John the Baptist, who preached to people about Christ's coming (Matthew 3, Luke 3). **1:21 Elijah** A man who spoke for God. He lived hundreds of years before Christ. **1:21 Prophet** They probably meant the prophet that God told Moses he would send (Deuteronomy 18:15-19).

"I am the voice of a man
  calling out in the desert:
'Make the road straight for the
  Lord.'"   *Isaiah 40:3*

[24] In the group of Jews who were sent, there were some Pharisees.[d] [25] They said to John: "You say you are not the Christ. You say you are not Elijah or the Prophet. Then why do you baptize people?"

[26] John answered, "I baptize people with water. But there is one here with you that you don't know. [27] He is the One who comes after me. I am not good enough to untie the strings of his sandals."

[28] This all happened at Bethany on the other side of the Jordan River. This is where John was baptizing people.

[29] The next day John saw Jesus coming toward him. John said, "Look, the Lamb of God.[n] He takes away the sins of the world! [30] This is the One I was talking about. I said, 'A man will come after me, but he is greater than I am, because he was living before me.' [31] Even I did not know who he was. But I came baptizing with water so that the people of Israel could know who he is."

[32-33] Then John said, "I did not know who the Christ was. But God sent me to baptize with water. And God told me, 'You will see the Spirit[d] come down and rest on a man. That man is the One who will baptize with the Holy Spirit.'" John said, "I saw the Spirit come down from heaven. The Spirit looked like a dove and rested on him. [34] I have seen this happen. So I tell people: 'He is the Son of God.'"

[35] The next day John[n] was there again with two of his followers. [36] He saw Jesus walking by and said, "Look, the Lamb of God!"[n]

[37] The two followers heard John say this. So they followed Jesus. [38] Jesus turned and saw them following him. He asked, "What do you want?"

They said, "Rabbi, where are you staying?" ("Rabbi" means "Teacher.")

[39] Jesus answered, "Come with me and you will see." So the two men went with Jesus. They saw the place where Jesus was staying and stayed there with him that day. It was then about four o'clock.

[40] These two men followed Jesus after they heard about him from John. One of the men was Andrew. He was Simon Peter's brother. [41] The first thing Andrew did was to find his brother, Simon. He said to Simon, "We have found the Messiah." ("Messiah" means "Christ."[d])

[42] Then Andrew took Simon to Jesus. Jesus looked at Simon and said, "You are Simon son of John. You will be called Cephas." ("Cephas" means "Peter."[n])

[43] The next day Jesus decided to go to Galilee. He found Philip and said to him, "Follow me." [44] Philip was from the town of Bethsaida, where Andrew and Peter lived. [45] Philip found Nathanael and told him, "Remember that Moses wrote in the law about a man who was coming, and the prophets[d] also wrote about him. We have found him. He is Jesus, the son of Joseph. He is from Nazareth."

[46] But Nathanael said to Philip, "Nazareth! Can anything good come from Nazareth?"

Philip answered, "Come and see."

[47] Jesus saw Nathanael coming toward him. He said, "Here is truly a person of Israel. There is nothing false in him."

[48] Nathanael asked, "How do you know me?"

Jesus answered, "I saw you when you were under the fig tree. That was before Philip told you about me."

[49] Then Nathanael said to Jesus, "Teacher, you are the Son of God. You are the King of Israel."

[50] Jesus said to Nathanael, "You believe in me because I told you I saw you under the fig tree. But you will see greater things than that!" [51] And Jesus said to them, "I tell you the truth. You will all see heaven open. You will see 'angels of God going up and coming down'[n] on the Son of Man."

2 Two days later there was a wedding in the town of Cana in Galilee. Jesus' mother was there. [2] Jesus and his followers were also invited to the wedding. [3] When all the wine was gone, Jesus' mother said to him, "They have no more wine."

[4] Jesus answered, "Dear woman, why come to me? My time has not yet come."

[5] His mother said to the servants, "Do whatever he tells you to do."

[6] In that place there were six stone water jars. The Jews used jars like these in

1:29, 36 Lamb of God Name for Jesus. Jesus is like the lambs that were offered for a sacrifice to God. **1:35 John** John the Baptist, who preached to people about Christ's coming (Matthew 3, Luke 3). **1:42 Peter** The Greek name "Peter," like the Aramaic name "Cephas," means "rock." **1:51 'angels . . . down'** These words are from Genesis 28:12.

their washing ceremony.[n] Each jar held about 20 or 30 gallons.

[7]Jesus said to the servants, "Fill the jars with water." So they filled the jars to the top.

[8]Then he said to them, "Now take some out and give it to the master of the feast."

So the servants took the water to the master. [9]When he tasted it, the water had become wine. He did not know where the wine came from. But the servants who brought the water knew. The master of the wedding called the bridegroom [10]and said to him, "People always serve the best wine first. Later, after the guests have been drinking a lot, they serve the cheaper wine. But you have saved the best wine till now."

[11]So in Cana of Galilee, Jesus did his first miracle.[d] There he showed his glory, and his followers believed in him.

[12]Then Jesus went to the town of Capernaum with his mother, brothers and his followers. They all stayed in Capernaum for a few days. [13]But it was almost time for the Jewish Passover[d] Feast. So Jesus went to Jerusalem. [14]In the Temple[d] he found men selling cattle, sheep, and doves. He saw others sitting at tables, exchanging money. [15]Jesus made a whip out of cords. Then he forced all these men, with the sheep and cattle, to leave the Temple. He turned over the tables and scattered the money of the men who were exchanging it. [16]Then he said to those who were selling pigeons, "Take these things out of here! Don't make my Father's house a place for buying and selling!"

[17]When this happened the followers remembered what was written in the Scriptures:[d] "My strong love for your Temple completely controls me."[n]

[18]The Jews said to Jesus, "Show us a miracle[d] for a sign. Prove that you have the right to do these things."

[19]Jesus answered, "Destroy this temple, and I will build it again in three days."

[20]The Jews answered, "Men worked 46 years to build this Temple! Do you really believe you can build it again in three days?"

[21](But the temple Jesus meant was his own body. [22]After Jesus was raised from death, his followers remembered that Jesus had said this. Then they believed the Scripture[d] and the words Jesus said.)

[23]Jesus was in Jerusalem for the Passover Feast. Many people believed in him because they saw the miracles he did. [24]But Jesus did not trust himself to them because he knew them all. [25]He did not need anyone to tell him about people. Jesus knew what was in a person's mind.

3 There was a man named Nicodemus who was one of the Pharisees.[d] He was an important Jewish leader. [2]One night Nicodemus came to Jesus. He said, "Teacher, we know that you are a teacher sent from God. No one can do the miracles[d] you do, unless God is with him."

[3]Jesus answered, "I tell you the truth. Unless one is born again, he cannot be in God's kingdom."

[4]Nicodemus said, "But if a man is already old, how can he be born again? He cannot enter his mother's body again. So how can he be born a second time?"

[5]But Jesus answered, "I tell you the truth. Unless one is born from water and the Spirit,[d] he cannot enter God's kingdom. [6]A person's body is born from his human parents. But a person's spiritual life is born from the Spirit. [7]Don't be surprised when I tell you, 'You must all be born again.' [8]The wind blows where it wants to go. You hear the wind blow. But you don't know where the wind comes from or where it is going. It is the same with every person who is born from the Spirit."

[9]Nicodemus asked, "How can all this be possible?"

[10]Jesus said, "You are an important teacher in Israel. But you still don't understand these things? [11]I tell you the truth. We talk about what we know. We tell about what we have seen. But you don't accept what we tell you. [12]I have told you about things here on earth, but you do not believe me. So surely you will not believe me if I tell you about the things of heaven! [13]The only one who has ever gone up to heaven is the One who came down from heaven—the Son of Man.[d]

[14]"Moses lifted up the snake in the desert.[n] It is the same with the Son of

---

2:6 washing ceremony The Jews washed themselves in special ways before eating, before worshiping in the Temple, and at other special times. **2:17 "My . . . me."** Quotation from Psalm 69:9. **3:14 Moses . . . desert.** The people of Israel were dying from snake bites. God told Moses to put a brass snake on a pole. The people who looked at the snake were healed (Numbers 21:4-9).

Man. The Son of Man must be lifted up too. [15]Then everyone who believes in him can have eternal life.

[16]"For God loved the world so much that he gave his only Son. God gave his Son so that whoever believes in him may not be lost, but have eternal life. [17]God did not send his Son into the world to judge the world guilty, but to save the world through him. [18]He who believes in God's Son is not judged guilty. He who does not believe has already been judged guilty, because he has not believed in God's only Son. [19]People are judged by this fact: I am the Light from God that has come into the world. But men did not want light. They wanted darkness because they were doing evil things. [20]Everyone who does evil hates the light. He will not come to the light because it will show all the evil things he has done. [21]But he who follows the true way comes to the light. Then the light will show that the things he has done were done through God."

[22]After this, Jesus and his followers went into the area of Judea. There Jesus stayed with his followers and baptized people. [23]John was also baptizing in Aenon, near Salim, because there was plenty of water there. People were going there to be baptized. [24](This was before John was put into prison.)

[25]Some of John's followers had an argument with a Jew about religious washing.[n] [26]So they came to John and said, "Teacher, remember the man who was with you on the other side of the Jordan River, the one you spoke about? He is baptizing, and everyone is going to him."

[27]John answered, "A man can get only what God gives him. [28]You yourselves heard me say, 'I am not the Christ.[d] I am only the one God sent to prepare the way for him.' [29]The bride belongs only to the bridegroom. The friend who helps the bridegroom waits and listens for him. He is glad when he hears the bridegroom's voice. That is the same pleasure I have. And my time of joy is now here. [30]He must become greater. And I must become less important.

[31]"The One who comes from above is greater than all. He who is from the earth belongs to the earth and talks about things on the earth. But the One

who comes from heaven is greater than all. [32]He tells what he has seen and heard, but no one accepts what he says. [33]The person who accepts what he says has proven that God is true. [34]God sent him, and he tells the things that God says. God gives him the Spirit[d] fully. [35]The Father loves the Son and has given him power over everything. [36]He who believes in the Son has eternal life. But he who does not obey the Son will never have that life. God's anger stays with him."

4 The Pharisees[d] heard that Jesus was making and baptizing more followers than John. [2](But really Jesus himself did not baptize people. His followers did the baptizing.) Jesus knew that the Pharisees had heard about him. [3]So he left Judea and went back to Galilee. [4]On the way he had to go through the country of Samaria.

[5]In Samaria Jesus came to the town called Sychar. This town is near the field that Jacob gave to his son Joseph. [6]Jacob's well was there. Jesus was tired from his long trip. So he sat down beside the well. It was about noon. [7]A Samaritan[d] woman came to the well to get some water. Jesus said to her, "Please give me a drink." [8](This happened while Jesus' followers were in town buying some food.)

[9]The woman said, "I am surprised that you ask me for a drink. You are a Jew and I am a Samaritan." (Jews are not friends with Samaritans.[n])

[10]Jesus said, "You don't know what God gives. And you don't know who asked you for a drink. If you knew, you would have asked me, and I would have given you living water."

[11]The woman said, "Sir, where will you get that living water? The well is very deep, and you have nothing to get water with. [12]Are you greater than Jacob, our father? Jacob is the one who gave us this well. He drank from it himself. Also, his sons and flocks drank from this well."

[13]Jesus answered, "Every person who drinks this water will be thirsty again. [14]But whoever drinks the water I give will never be thirsty again. The water I give will become a spring of water flowing inside him. It will give him eternal life."

3:25 religious washing The Jews washed themselves in special ways before eating, before worshiping in the Temple, and at other special times. **4:9 Jews . . . Samaritans.** This can also be translated "Jews don't use things that Samaritans have used."

[15]The woman said to him, "Sir, give me this water. Then I will never be thirsty again. And I will not have to come back here to get more water."

[16]Jesus told her, "Go get your husband and come back here."

[17]The woman answered, "But I have no husband."

Jesus said to her, "You are right to say you have no husband. [18]Really you have had five husbands. But the man you live with now is not your husband. You told the truth."

[19]The woman said, "Sir, I can see that you are a prophet.[d] [20]Our fathers worshiped on this mountain. But you Jews say that Jerusalem is the place where people must worship."

[21]Jesus said, "Believe me, woman. The time is coming when you will not have to be in Jerusalem or on this mountain to worship the Father. [22]You Samaritans worship what you don't understand. We Jews understand what we worship. Salvation comes from the Jews. [23]The time is coming when the true worshipers will worship the Father in spirit and truth. That time is now here. And these are the kinds of worshipers the Father wants. [24]God is spirit. Those who worship God must worship in spirit and truth."

[25]The woman said, "I know that the Messiah is coming." (Messiah is the One called Christ.[d]) "When the Messiah comes, he will explain everything to us."

[26]Then Jesus said, "He is talking to you now. I am he."

[27]Just then his followers came back from town. They were surprised because they saw Jesus talking with a woman. But none of them asked, "What do you want?" or "Why are you talking with her?"

[28]Then the woman left her water jar and went back to town. She said to the people, [29]"A man told me everything I have ever done. Come see him. Maybe he is the Christ!" [30]So the people left the town and went to see Jesus.

[31]While the woman was away, the followers were begging him, "Teacher, eat something!"

[32]But Jesus answered, "I have food to eat that you know nothing about."

[33]So the followers asked themselves, "Did somebody already bring Jesus some food?"

[34]Jesus said, "My food is to do what the One who sent me wants me to do. My food is to finish the work that he gave me to do. [35]You say, 'Four more months to wait before we gather the grain.' But I tell you, open your eyes. Look at the fields that are ready for harvesting now. [36]Even now, the one who harvests the crop is being paid. He is gathering crops for eternal life. So now the one who plants can be happy along with the one who harvests. [37]It is true when we say, 'One person plants, but another harvests the crop.' [38]I sent you to harvest a crop that you did not work for. Others did the work, and you get the profit from their work."[n]

[39]Many of the Samaritans in that town believed in Jesus. They believed because of what the woman said: "He told me everything I have ever done." [40]The Samaritans came to Jesus and begged him to stay with them. So he stayed there two days. [41]Many more believed because of the things he said.

[42]They said to the woman, "First we believed in Jesus because of what you told us. But now we believe because we heard him ourselves. We know that this man really is the Savior of the world."

[43]Two days later, Jesus left and went to Galilee. [44](Jesus had said before that a prophet[d] is not respected in his own country.) [45]When Jesus arrived in Galilee, the people there welcomed him. They had seen all the things he did at the Passover[d] Feast in Jerusalem. They had been at the Passover Feast, too.

[46]Jesus went to visit Cana in Galilee again. This is where Jesus had changed the water into wine. One of the king's important officers lived in the city of Capernaum. This man's son was sick. [47]The man heard that Jesus had come from Judea and was now in Galilee. He went to Jesus and begged him to come to Capernaum and heal his son. His son was almost dead. [48]Jesus said to him, "You people must see signs and miracles[d] before you will believe in me."

[49]The officer said, "Sir, come before my child dies."

[50]Jesus answered, "Go. Your son will live."

The man believed what Jesus told him and went home. [51]On the way the man's servants came and met him. They told him, "Your son is well."

4:35-38 Look at . . . their work. As a farmer sends workers to harvest grain, Jesus sends his followers out to bring people to God.

[52] The man asked, "What time did my son begin to get well?"

They answered, "It was about one o'clock yesterday when the fever left him."

[53] The father knew that one o'clock was the exact time that Jesus had said, "Your son will live." So the man and all the people of his house believed in Jesus.

[54] That was the second miracle that Jesus did after coming from Judea to Galilee.

5 Later Jesus went to Jerusalem for a special Jewish feast. [2] In Jerusalem there is a pool with five covered porches. In the Jewish language[n] it is called Bethzatha.[n] This pool is near the Sheep Gate. [3] Many sick people were lying on the porches beside the pool. Some were blind, some were crippled, and some were paralyzed.[n] [5] There was a man lying there who had been sick for 38 years. [6] Jesus saw the man and knew that he had been sick for a very long time. So Jesus asked him, "Do you want to be well?"

[7] The sick man answered, "Sir, there is no one to help me get into the pool when the water starts moving. I try to be the first one into the water. But when I try, someone else always goes in before I can."

[8] Then Jesus said, "Stand up. Pick up your mat and walk." [9] And immediately the man was well. He picked up his mat and began to walk.

The day all this happened was a Sabbath[d] day. [10] So the Jews said to the man who had been healed, "Today is the Sabbath. It is against our law for you to carry your mat on the Sabbath day."

[11] But he answered, "The man who made me well told me, 'Pick up your mat and walk.'"

[12] Then they asked him, "Who is the man who told you to pick up your mat and walk?"

[13] But the man who had been healed did not know who it was. There were many people in that place, and Jesus had left.

[14] Later, Jesus found the man at the Temple.[d] Jesus said to him, "See, you are

well now. But stop sinning or something worse may happen to you!"

[15] Then the man left and went back to the Jews. He told them that Jesus was the one who had made him well.

[16] Jesus was doing this on the Sabbath day. So the Jews began to do bad things to him. [17] But Jesus said to them, "My Father never stops working. And so I work, too."

[18] This made the Jews try harder to kill him. They said, "First Jesus was breaking the law about the Sabbath day. Then he said that God is his own Father! He is making himself equal with God!"

[19] But Jesus said, "I tell you the truth. The Son can do nothing alone. The Son does only what he sees his Father doing. The Son does whatever the Father does. [20] The Father loves the Son, and the Father shows the Son all the things he himself does. But the Father will show the Son greater things than this to do. Then you will all be amazed. [21] The Father raises the dead and gives them life. In the same way, the Son gives life to those he wants to. [22] Also, the Father judges no one. But the Father has given the Son power to do all the judging. [23] God did this so that all people will respect the Son the same way they respect the Father. He who does not respect the Son does not respect the Father. The Father is the One who sent the Son.

[24] "I tell you the truth. Whoever hears what I say and believes in the One who sent me has eternal life. He will not be judged guilty. He has already left death and has entered into life. [25] I tell you the truth. The time is coming and is already here when the dead will hear the voice of the Son of God. And those who hear will have life. [26] Life comes from the Father himself. So the Father has allowed the Son to give life. [27] And the Father has given the Son the power to judge because he is the Son of Man.[d] [28] Don't be surprised at this. A time is coming when all who are dead and in their graves will hear his voice. [29] Then they will come out of their graves. Those who did good will rise and have life forever. But those who did evil will rise to be judged guilty.

[30] "I can do nothing alone. I judge only

5:2 Jewish language Aramaic, the language of the Jews in the first century. **5:2 Bethzatha** Also called Bethsaida or Bethesda, a pool of water north of the Temple in Jerusalem. **5:3 Verse 3** Some Greek copies add "and they waited for the water to move." A few later copies add verse 4: "Sometimes an angel of the Lord came down to the pool and stirred up the water. After the angel did this, the first person to go into the pool was healed from any sickness he had."

the way I am told, so my judgment is right. I don't try to please myself. I try to please the One who sent me.

[31]"If I tell people about myself, then they will not accept what I say about myself. [32]But there is another who tells about me. And I know that the things he says about me are true.

[33]"You have sent men to John. And he has told you about the truth. [34]But I don't need a man to tell about me. I tell you this so that you can be saved. [35]John was like a burning and shining lamp. And you were happy to enjoy his light for a while.

[36]"But I have a proof about myself that is greater than that of John. The things I do are my proof. These are the things my Father gave me to do. They show that the Father sent me. [37]And the Father who sent me has given proof about me himself. You have never heard his voice. You have never seen what he looks like. [38]His teaching does not live in you because you don't believe in the One that the Father sent. [39]You carefully study the Scriptures[d] because you think that they give you eternal life. Those are the same Scriptures that tell about me! [40]But you refuse to come to me to have that life.

[41]"I don't want praise from men. [42]But I know you—I know that you don't have God's love in you. [43]I have come from my Father—I speak for him. But you don't accept me. But when another person comes, speaking only for himself, you will accept him. [44]You like to have praise from each other. But you never try to get the praise that comes from the only God. So how can you believe? [45]Don't think that I will stand before the Father and say that you are wrong. Moses is the one who says that you are wrong. And he is the one that you hoped would save you. [46]If you really believed Moses, you would believe me because Moses wrote about me. [47]But you don't believe what Moses wrote. So how can you believe what I say?"

6 After this, Jesus went across Lake Galilee (or, Lake Tiberias). [2]Many people followed him because they saw the miracles[d] he did to heal the sick. [3]Jesus went up on a hill and there sat down with his followers. [4]It was almost the time for the Jewish Passover[d] Feast.

[5]Jesus looked up and saw a large crowd coming toward him. He said to Philip, "Where can we buy bread for all these people to eat?" [6](Jesus asked Philip this question to test him. Jesus already knew what he planned to do.)

[7]Philip answered, "We would all have to work a month to buy enough bread for each person here to have only a little piece."

[8]Another follower there was Andrew. He was Simon Peter's brother. Andrew said, [9]"Here is a boy with five loaves of barley bread and two little fish. But that is not enough for so many people."

[10]Jesus said, "Tell the people to sit down." This was a very grassy place. There were about 5,000 men who sat down there. [11]Then Jesus took the loaves of bread. He thanked God for the bread and gave it to the people who were sitting there. He did the same with the fish. He gave them as much as they wanted.

[12]They all had enough to eat. When they had finished, Jesus said to his followers, "Gather the pieces of fish and bread that were not eaten. Don't waste anything." [13]So they gathered up the pieces that were left. They filled 12 large baskets with the pieces that were left of the five barley loaves.

[14]The people saw this miracle that Jesus did. They said, "He must truly be the Prophet[n] who is coming into the world."

[15]Jesus knew that the people planned to come and take him by force and make him their king. So he left and went into the hills alone.

[16]That evening Jesus' followers went down to Lake Galilee. [17]It was dark now and Jesus had not yet come to them. The followers got into a boat and started across the lake to Capernaum. [18]By now a strong wind was blowing, and the waves on the lake were getting bigger. [19]They rowed the boat about three or four miles. Then they saw Jesus walking on the water, coming toward the boat. The followers were afraid. [20]But Jesus said to them, "Don't be afraid. It is I." [21]Then they were glad to take him into the boat. At once the boat came to land at the place where they wanted to go.

[22]The next day came. Some people had stayed on the other side of the lake. They knew that Jesus had not gone in the boat with his followers but that they had left without him. And they knew that only one boat had been there. [23]But

---

6:14 Prophet They probably meant the prophet that God told Moses he would send (Deuteronomy 18:15-19).

then some boats came from Tiberias. They landed near the place where the people had eaten the bread after the Lord had given thanks. [24]The people saw that Jesus and his followers were not there now. So they got into boats and went to Capernaum. They wanted to find Jesus.

[25]The people found Jesus on the other side of the lake. They asked him, "Teacher, when did you come here?"

[26]Jesus answered, "Are you looking for me because you saw me do miracles?[d] No! I tell you the truth. You are looking for me because you ate the bread and were satisfied. [27]Earthly food spoils and ruins. So don't work to get that kind of food. But work to get the food that stays good always and gives you eternal life. The Son of Man[d] will give you that food. God the Father has shown that he is with the Son of Man."

[28]The people asked Jesus, "What are the things God wants us to do?"

[29]Jesus answered, "The work God wants you to do is this: to believe in the One that God sent."

[30]So the people asked, "What miracle will you do? If we can see a miracle, then we will believe you. What will you do? [31]Our fathers ate the manna[d] in the desert. This is written in the Scriptures:[d] 'God gave them bread from heaven to eat.'"[n]

[32]Jesus said, "I tell you the truth. Moses was not the one who gave you bread from heaven. But my Father gives you the true bread from heaven. [33]God's bread is the One who comes down from heaven and gives life to the world."

[34]The people said, "Sir, give us this bread always."

[35]Then Jesus said, "I am the bread that gives life. He who comes to me will never be hungry. He who believes in me will never be thirsty. [36]But as I told you before, you have seen me, and still you don't believe. [37]The Father gives me my people. Every one of them will come to me, and I will always accept them. [38]I came down from heaven to do what God wants me to do. I did not come to do what I want to do. [39]I must not lose even one of those that God has given me, but I must raise them up on the last day. This is what the One who sent me wants me to do. [40]Everyone who sees the Son and believes in him has eternal life. I will raise him up on the last day. This is what my Father wants."

[41]The Jews began to complain about Jesus. They complained because he said, "I am the bread that comes down from heaven." [42]The Jews said, "This is Jesus. We know his father and mother. He is only Joseph's son. How can he say, 'I came down from heaven'?"

[43]But Jesus answered, "Stop complaining to each other. [44]The Father is the One who sent me. No one can come to me unless the Father draws him to me. And I will raise him up on the last day. [45]It is written in the prophets,[d] 'God will teach all the people.'[n] Everyone who listens to the Father and learns from him comes to me. [46]No one has seen the Father except the One who is from God. Only he has seen the Father. [47]I tell you the truth. He who believes has eternal life. [48]I am the bread that gives life. [49]Your ancestors ate the manna in the desert. But still they died. [50]Here is the bread that comes down from heaven. If anyone eats this bread, he will never die. [51]I am the living bread that came down from heaven. If anyone eats this bread, he will live forever. This bread is my flesh. I will give my flesh so that the people in the world may have life."

[52]Then the Jews began to argue among themselves. They said, "How can this man give us his flesh to eat?"

[53]Jesus said, "I tell you the truth. You must eat the flesh of the Son of Man. And you must drink his blood. If you don't do this, then you won't have real life in you. [54]He who eats my flesh and drinks my blood has eternal life. I will raise him up on the last day. [55]My flesh is true food. My blood is true drink. [56]Whoever eats my flesh and drinks my blood lives in me, and I live in him. [57]The Father sent me. The Father lives, and I live because of the Father. So he who eats me will live because of me. [58]I am not like the bread our ancestors ate. They ate that bread, but still they died. I am the bread that came down from heaven. He who eats this bread will live forever." [59]Jesus said all these things while he was teaching in the synagogue[d] in Capernaum.

[60]The followers of Jesus heard this. Many of them said, "This teaching is hard. Who can accept it?"

[61]Jesus knew that his followers were

6:31 'God gave . . . eat.' Quotation from Psalm 78:24.   6:45 'God . . . people.' Quotation from Isaiah 54:13.

complaining about this. So he said, "Does this teaching bother you? [62]Then will it also bother you to see the Son of Man[d] going back to the place where he came from? [63]It is not the flesh that gives a person life. It is the spirit that gives life. The words I told you are spirit, and so they give life. [64]But some of you don't believe." (Jesus knew who did not believe. He knew this from the beginning. And he knew who would turn against him.) [65]Jesus said, "That is the reason I said, 'If the Father does not let a person come to me, then he cannot come.'"

[66]After Jesus said this, many of his followers left him. They stopped following him.

[67]Jesus asked the 12 followers, "Do you want to leave, too?"

[68]Simon Peter answered Jesus, "Lord, where would we go? You have the words that give eternal life. [69]We believe in you. We know that you are the Holy One from God."

[70]Then Jesus answered, "I chose all 12 of you. But 1 of you is a devil."

[71]Jesus was talking about Judas, the son of Simon Iscariot. Judas was 1 of the 12. But later he was going to turn against Jesus.

7 After this, Jesus traveled around Galilee. He did not want to travel in Judea, because the Jews there wanted to kill him. [2]It was time for the Jewish Feast[d] of Shelters. [3]So Jesus' brothers said to him, "You should leave here and go to Judea. Then your followers there can see the miracles[d] you do. [4]Anyone who wants to be well known does not hide what he does. If you are doing these things, show yourself to the world." [5](Even Jesus' brothers did not believe in him.)

[6]Jesus said to his brothers, "The right time for me has not yet come. But any time is right for you. [7]The world cannot hate you. But it hates me, because I tell about the evil things it does. [8]So you go to the feast. I will not go now. The right time for me has not yet come." [9]After saying this, Jesus stayed in Galilee.

[10]So Jesus' brothers left to go to the feast. When they had gone, Jesus went, too. But he did not let people see him. [11]At the feast the Jews were looking for him. They said, "Where is that man?"

[12]There was a large crowd of people there. Many of them were whispering to each other about Jesus. Some said, "He is a good man."

Others said, "No, he fools the people." [13]But no one was brave enough to talk about Jesus openly. They were afraid of the Jews.

[14]The feast was about half over. Then Jesus went to the Temple[d] and began to teach. [15]The Jews were amazed. They said, "This man has never studied in school. How did he learn so much?"

[16]Jesus answered, "The things I teach are not my own. My teaching comes from him who sent me. [17]If anyone chooses to do what God wants, then he will know that my teaching comes from God. He will know that this teaching is not my own. [18]He who teaches his own ideas is trying to get honor for himself. But he who tries to bring honor to the one who sent him—that person speaks the truth. There is nothing false in him. [19]Moses gave you the law,[n] but none of you obey that law. Why are you trying to kill me?"

[20]The people answered, "A demon[d] has come into you. We are not trying to kill you."

[21]Jesus said to them, "I did one miracle,[d] and you are all amazed. [22]Moses gave you the law about circumcision.[d] (But really Moses did not give you circumcision. Circumcision came from our ancestors.) And yet you circumcise a baby on a Sabbath[d] day. [23]This shows that a baby can be circumcised on a Sabbath day to obey the law of Moses. So why are you angry at me for healing a person's whole body on the Sabbath day? [24]Stop judging by the way things look! Be fair, and judge by what is really right."

[25]Then some of the people who lived in Jerusalem said, "This is the man they are trying to kill. [26]But he is teaching where everyone can see and hear him. And no one is trying to stop him. Maybe the leaders have decided that he really is the Christ.[d] [27]But we know where this man is from. And when the real Christ comes, no one will know where he comes from."

[28]Jesus was still teaching in the Temple.[d] He cried out, "Yes, you know me, and you know where I am from. But I have not come by my own authority. I was sent by the One who is true. You don't know him. [29]But I know him. I am from him, and he sent me."

7:19 law Moses gave God's people the law that God gave him on Mount Sinai (Exodus 34:29-32).

[30] When Jesus said this, the people tried to take him. But no one was able to touch him. It was not yet the right time. [31] But many of the people believed in Jesus. They said, "When the Christ comes, will he do more miracles[d] than this man has done?"

[32] The Pharisees[d] heard the crowd whispering these things about Jesus. So the leading priests and the Pharisees sent some Temple[d] guards to arrest him. [33] Then Jesus said, "I will be with you a little while longer. Then I will go back to the One who sent me. [34] You will look for me, but you will not find me. And you cannot come where I am."

[35] The Jews said to each other, "Where will this man go so we cannot find him? Will he go to the Greek cities where our people live? Will he teach the Greek people there? [36] This man says, 'You will look for me but you will not find me.' He also says, 'You cannot come where I am.' What does this mean?"

[37] The last day of the feast came. It was the most important day. On that day Jesus stood up and said in a loud voice, "If anyone is thirsty, let him come to me and drink. [38] If a person believes in me, rivers of living water will flow out from his heart. This is what the Scripture[d] says." [39] Jesus was talking about the Holy Spirit.[d] The Spirit had not yet been given because Jesus had not yet been raised to glory. But later, those who believed in Jesus would receive the Spirit.

[40] The people heard these things that Jesus said. Some of them said, "This man really is the Prophet."[n]

[41] Others said, "He is the Christ."[d]

Still others said, "The Christ will not come from Galilee. [42] The Scripture[d] says that the Christ will come from David's family. And the Scripture says that the Christ will come from Bethlehem, the town where David lived." [43] So the people did not agree with each other about Jesus. [44] Some of them wanted to arrest him, but no one was able to touch him.

[45] The Temple[d] guards went back to the leading priests and the Pharisees.[d] The priests and the Pharisees asked, "Why didn't you bring Jesus?"

[46] The Temple guards answered, "The things he says are greater than the words of any man!"

[47] The Pharisees answered, "So Jesus has fooled you too! [48] Have any of the leaders or the Pharisees believed in him? No! [49] But those people, who know nothing about the law, are under God's curse!"

[50] But Nicodemus was there in that group. He was the one who had gone to see Jesus before.[n] Nicodemus said, [51] "Our law does not judge a man without hearing him. We cannot judge him until we know what he has done."

[52] They answered, "Are you from Galilee too? Study the Scriptures.[d] You will learn that no prophet[d] comes from Galilee."

[53] And everyone left and went home.[n]

8 Jesus went to the Mount of Olives.[d] [2] But early in the morning he went back to the Temple.[d] All the people came to Jesus, and he sat and taught them. [3] The teachers of the law and the Pharisees[d] brought a woman there. She had been caught in adultery.[d] They forced the woman to stand before the people. [4] They said to Jesus, "Teacher, this woman was caught having sexual relations with a man who is not her husband. [5] The law of Moses commands that we kill with stones every woman who does this. What do you say we should do?" [6] They were asking this to trick Jesus so that they could have some charge against him.

But Jesus knelt down and started writing on the ground with his finger. [7] They continued to ask Jesus their question. So he stood up and said, "Is there anyone here who has never sinned? The person without sin can throw the first stone at this woman." [8] Then Jesus knelt down again and wrote on the ground.

[9] Those who heard Jesus began to leave one by one. The older men left first, and then the others. Jesus was left there alone with the woman. She was standing before him. [10] Jesus stood up again and asked her, "Woman, all of those people have gone. Has no one judged you guilty?"

[11] She answered, "No one has judged me, sir."

Then Jesus said, "So I also don't judge you. You may go now, but don't sin again."

[12] Later, Jesus talked to the people

7:40 Prophet They probably meant the prophet that God told Moses he would send (Deuteronomy 18:15-19). **7:50 But Nicodemus . . . before.** The story about Nicodemus going and talking to Jesus is in John 3:1-21. **7:53 Verse 53** Some early Greek manuscripts do not contain 7:53–8:11.

again. He said, "I am the light of the world. The person who follows me will never live in darkness. He will have the light that gives life."

[13]But the Pharisees[d] said to Jesus, "When you talk about yourself, you are the only one to say these things are true. We cannot accept these things you say."

[14]Jesus answered, "Yes, I am saying these things about myself, but they are true. I know where I came from. And I know where I am going. You don't know where I came from or where I am going. [15]You judge me the way you would judge any man. I don't judge anyone. [16]But if I judge, my judging is true. When I judge, I am not alone. The Father who sent me is with me. [17]Your own law says that when two witnesses say the same thing, then you must accept what they say. [18]I am one of the witnesses who speaks about myself. And the Father who sent me is my other witness."

[19]They asked, "Where is your father?"

Jesus answered, "You don't know me or my Father. But if you knew me, then you would know my Father, too." [20]Jesus said these things while he was teaching in the Temple.[d] He was near the place where the money that the people give is kept. But no one arrested him. The right time for Jesus had not yet come.

[21]Again, Jesus said to the people, "I will leave you. You will look for me, but you will die in your sins. You cannot come where I am going."

[22]So the Jews asked, "Will Jesus kill himself? Is that why he said, 'You cannot come where I am going'?"

[23]But Jesus said, "You people are from here below. But I am from above. You belong to this world, but I don't belong to this world. [24]So I told you that you would die in your sins. Yes, you will die in your sins if you don't believe that I am he."

[25]They asked, "Then who are you?"

Jesus answered, "I am what I have told you from the beginning. [26]I have many things to say about you and to judge you for. But I tell people only the things I have heard from the One who sent me. And he speaks the truth."

[27]The people did not understand that Jesus was talking to them about the Father. [28]So Jesus said to them, "You will lift up the Son of Man.[d] Then you will know that I am he. You will know that these things I do are not by my own authority. You will know that I say only what the Father has taught me. [29]The

One who sent me is with me. I always do what is pleasing to him. So he has not left me alone." [30]While Jesus was saying these things, many people believed in him.

[31]So Jesus said to the Jews who believed in him, "If you continue to obey my teaching, you are truly my followers. [32]Then you will know the truth. And the truth will make you free."

[33]They answered, "We are Abraham's children. And we have never been slaves. So why do you say that we will be free?"

[34]Jesus answered, "I tell you the truth. Everyone who lives in sin is a slave to sin. [35]A slave does not stay with a family forever, but a son belongs to the family forever. [36]So if the Son makes you free, then you will be truly free. [37]I know you are Abraham's children. But you want to kill me because you don't accept my teaching. [38]I am telling you what my Father has shown me. But you do what your father has told you."

[39]They answered, "Our father is Abraham."

Jesus said, "If you were really Abraham's children, you would do the things that Abraham did. [40]I am a man who has told you the truth which I heard from God. But you are trying to kill me. Abraham did nothing like that. [41]So you are doing the things that your own father did."

But they said, "We are not like children who never knew who their father was. God is our Father. He is the only Father we have."

[42]Jesus said to them, "If God were really your Father, you would love me. I came from God and now I am here. I did not come by my own authority. God sent me. [43]You don't understand what I say because you cannot accept my teaching. [44]Your father is the devil. You belong to him and want to do what he wants. He was a murderer from the beginning. He was against the truth, for there is no truth in him. He is a liar, and he is like the lies he tells. He is the father of lies. [45]But I speak the truth. That is why you don't believe me. [46]Can any of you prove that I am guilty of sin? If I am telling the truth, why don't you believe me? [47]He who belongs to God accepts what God says. But you don't accept what God says, because you don't belong to God."

[48]The Jews answered, "We say you are a Samaritan![d] We say a demon[d] has come into you. Are we not right?"

[49] Jesus answered, "I have no demon in me. I give honor to my Father, but you dishonor me. [50] I am not trying to get honor for myself. There is One who wants this honor for me, and he is the judge. [51] I tell you the truth. If anyone obeys my teaching, he will never die."

[52] The Jews said to Jesus, "Now we know that you have a demon in you! Even Abraham and the prophets[d] died. But you say, 'Whoever obeys my teaching will never die.' [53] Do you think that you are greater than our father Abraham? Abraham died. And the prophets died, too. Who do you think you are?"

[54] Jesus answered, "If I give honor to myself, that honor is worth nothing. The One who gives me honor is my Father. And you say that he is your God. [55] But you don't really know him. I know him. If I said I did not know him, then I would be a liar as you are liars. But I do know him, and I obey what he says. [56] Your father Abraham was very happy that he would see my day. He saw that day and was glad."

[57] The Jews said to him, "What? You have never seen Abraham! You are not even 50 years old!"

[58] Jesus answered, "I tell you the truth. Before Abraham was born, I am!" [59] When Jesus said this, the people picked up stones to throw at him. But Jesus hid himself, and then he left the Temple.[d]

9 As Jesus was walking along, he saw a man who had been born blind. [2] His followers asked him, "Teacher, whose sin caused this man to be born blind— his own sin or his parents' sin?"

[3] Jesus answered, "It is not this man's sin or his parents' sin that made him be blind. This man was born blind so that God's power could be shown in him. [4] While it is daytime, we must continue doing the work of the One who sent me. The night is coming. And no one can work at night. [5] While I am in the world, I am the light of the world."

[6] After Jesus said this, he spit on the ground and made some mud with it. He put the mud on the man's eyes. [7] Then he told the man, "Go and wash in the Pool of Siloam." (Siloam means Sent.) So the man went to the pool. He washed and came back. And he was able to see.

[8] Some people had seen this man begging before. They and the man's neighbors said, "Look! Is this the same man who always sits and begs?"

[9] Some said, "Yes! He is the one." But others said, "No, he's not the same man. He only looks like him."

So the man himself said, "I am the man."

[10] They asked, "What happened? How did you get your sight?"

[11] He answered, "The man named Jesus made some mud and put it on my eyes. Then he told me to go to Siloam and wash. So I went and washed and came back seeing."

[12] They asked him, "Where is this man?"

The man answered, "I don't know."

[13] Then the people took to the Pharisees[d] the man who had been blind. [14] The day Jesus had made mud and healed his eyes was a Sabbath[d] day. [15] So now the Pharisees asked the man, "How did you get your sight?"

He answered, "He put mud on my eyes. I washed, and now I can see."

[16] Some of the Pharisees were saying, "This man does not keep the Sabbath day. He is not from God!"

Others said, "But a man who is a sinner can't do miracles[d] like these." So they could not agree with each other.

[17] They asked the man again, "What do you say about him? It was your eyes he opened."

The man answered, "He is a prophet."[d]

[18] The Jews did not believe that he had been blind and could now see again. So they sent for the man's parents [19] and asked them, "Is this your son? You say that he was born blind. Then how does he see now?"

[20] His parents answered, "We know that this is our son, and we know that he was born blind. [21] But we don't know how he can see now. We don't know who opened his eyes. Ask him. He is old enough to answer for himself." [22] His parents said this because they were afraid of the Jews. The Jews had already decided that anyone who said that Jesus was the Christ[d] would be put out of the synagogue.[d] [23] That is why his parents said, "He is old enough. Ask him."

[24] So for the second time, they called the man who had been blind. They said, "You should give God the glory by telling the truth. We know that this man is a sinner."

[25] He answered, "I don't know if he is a sinner. But one thing I do know. I was blind, and now I can see."

[26] They asked, "What did he do to you? How did he make you see again?"

[27]He answered, "I have already told you that. But you would not listen to me. Why do you want to hear it again? Do you want to become his followers, too?"

[28]Then they insulted him and said, "You are his follower. We are followers of Moses. [29]We know that God spoke to Moses. But we don't even know where this man comes from!"

[30]The man answered, "This is a very strange thing. You don't know where he comes from, and yet he opened my eyes. [31]We all know that God does not listen to sinners. But God listens to anyone who worships and obeys him. [32]Nobody has ever heard of anyone giving sight to a man born blind. [33]If this man were not from God, he could do nothing."

[34]They answered, "You were born full of sin! Are you trying to teach us?" And they threw the man out.

[35]Jesus heard that they had thrown him out. So Jesus found him and said, "Do you believe in the Son of Man?"[d]

[36]He asked, "Who is the Son of Man, sir? Tell me, so I can believe in him!"

[37]Jesus said to him, "You have already seen him. The Son of Man is the one talking with you now."

[38]He said, "Yes, Lord, I believe!" Then the man bowed and worshiped Jesus.

[39]Jesus said, "I came into this world so that the world could be judged. I came so that the blind[n] could see and so that those who see will become blind."

[40]Some of the Pharisees[d] were near Jesus. When they heard him say this, they asked, "What? Are you saying that we are blind, too?"

[41]Jesus said, "If you were really blind, you would not be guilty of sin. But now that you say you can see, your guilt remains."

10 Jesus said, "I tell you the truth. The man who does not enter the sheepfold by the door, but climbs in some other way, is a thief and a robber. [2]The one who enters by the door is the shepherd of the sheep. [3]The man who guards the door opens it for him. And the sheep listen to the voice of the shepherd. He calls his own sheep, using their names, and he leads them out. [4]He brings all of his sheep out. Then he goes ahead of them and leads them. They follow him because they know his voice. [5]But they will never follow a stranger. They will run away from him because they don't know his voice." [6]Jesus told

the people this story, but they did not understand what it meant.

[7]So Jesus said again, "I tell you the truth. I am the door for the sheep. [8]All the people who came before me were thieves and robbers. The sheep did not listen to them. [9]I am the door. The person who enters through me will be saved. He will be able to come in and go out and find pasture. [10]A thief comes to steal and kill and destroy. But I came to give life—life in all its fullness.

[11]"I am the good shepherd. The good shepherd gives his life for the sheep. [12]The worker who is paid to keep the sheep is different from the shepherd who owns them. So when the worker sees a wolf coming, he runs away and leaves the sheep alone. Then the wolf attacks the sheep and scatters them. [13]The man runs away because he is only a paid worker. He does not really care for the sheep.

[14-15]"I am the good shepherd. I know my sheep, as the Father knows me. And my sheep know me, as I know the Father. I give my life for the sheep. [16]I have other sheep that are not in this flock here. I must bring them also. They will listen to my voice, and there will be one flock and one shepherd. [17]The Father loves me because I give my life. I give my life so that I can take it back again. [18]No one takes it away from me. I give my own life freely. I have the right to give my life, and I have the right to take it back. This is what my Father commanded me to do."

[19]Again the Jews did not agree with each other because of these words Jesus said. [20]Many of them said, "A demon[d] has come into him and made him crazy. Why listen to him?"

[21]But others said, "A man who is crazy with a demon does not say things like this. Can a demon open the eyes of the blind?"

[22]The time came for the Feast[d] of Dedication at Jerusalem. This was during the winter. [23]Jesus was walking in the Temple[d] in Solomon's Porch.[d] [24]The Jews gathered around him and said, "How long will you make us wonder about you? If you are the Christ,[d] then tell us plainly."

[25]Jesus answered, "I told you already, but you did not believe. I do miracles[d] in my Father's name. Those miracles show who I am. [26]But you don't believe be-

---

9:39 blind Jesus is talking about people who are spiritually blind, not physically blind.

...cause you are not my sheep. [27]My sheep listen to my voice. I know them, and they follow me. [28]I give them eternal life, and they will never die. And no person can steal them out of my hand. [29]My Father gave my sheep to me. He is greater than all, and no person can steal my sheep out of my Father's hand. [30]The Father and I are one."

[31]Again the Jews picked up stones to kill Jesus. [32]But Jesus said to them, "I have done many good works from the Father. Which of these good works are you killing me for?"

[33]The Jews answered, "We are not killing you for any good work you did. But you say things that are against God. You are only a man, but you say you are the same as God!"

[34]Jesus answered, "It is written in your law that God said, 'I have said you are gods!'[n] [35]This Scripture[d] called those people gods, the people who received God's message. And Scripture is always true. [36]So why do you say that I speak against God because I said, 'I am God's Son'? I am the one God chose and sent into the world. [37]If I don't do what my Father does, then don't believe me. [38]But if I do what my Father does, even though you don't believe in me, believe what I do. Then you will know and understand that the Father is in me and I am in the Father."

[39]They tried to take Jesus again, but he escaped from them.

[40]Then Jesus went back across the Jordan River to the place where John had first baptized. Jesus stayed there, [41]and many people came to him. They said, "John never did a miracle. But everything John said about this man is true." [42]And in that place many believed in Jesus.

11 There was a man named Lazarus who was sick. He lived in the town of Bethany, where Mary and her sister Martha lived. [2]Mary is the woman who later put perfume on the Lord and wiped his feet with her hair. Mary's brother was Lazarus, the man who was now sick. [3]So Mary and Martha sent someone to tell Jesus, "Lord, the one you love is sick."

[4]When Jesus heard this he said, "This sickness will not end in death. It is for the glory of God. This has happened to bring glory to the Son of God." [5]Jesus loved Martha and her sister and Lazarus. [6]But when he heard that Lazarus was sick, he stayed where he was for two more days. [7]Then Jesus said to his followers, "Let us go back to Judea."

[8]The followers said, "But Teacher, the Jews there tried to kill you with stones. That was only a short time ago. Now you want to go back there?"

[9]Jesus answered, "Are there not 12 hours in the day? If anyone walks in the daylight, he will not stumble because he can see by this world's light. [10]But if anyone walks at night he stumbles because there is no light to help him see."

[11]After Jesus said this, he added, "Our friend Lazarus has fallen asleep. But I am going there to wake him."

[12]The followers said, "But Lord, if he can sleep, he will get well."

[13]Jesus meant that Lazarus was dead. But Jesus' followers thought that he meant Lazarus was really sleeping. [14]So then Jesus said plainly, "Lazarus is dead. [15]And I am glad for your sakes that I was not there so that you may believe. But let us go to him now."

[16]Then Thomas (the one called Didymus) said to the other followers, "Let us go, too. We will die with him."

[17]Jesus arrived in Bethany. There he learned that Lazarus had already been dead and in the tomb for four days. [18]Bethany was about two miles from Jerusalem. [19]Many Jews had come there to comfort Martha and Mary about their brother.

[20]Martha heard that Jesus was coming, and she went out to meet him. But Mary stayed at home. [21]Martha said to Jesus, "Lord, if you had been here, my brother would not have died. [22]But I know that even now God will give you anything you ask."

[23]Jesus said, "Your brother will rise and live again."

[24]Martha answered, "I know that he will rise and live again in the resurrection[n] on the last day."

[25]Jesus said to her, "I am the resurrection and the life. He who believes in me will have life even if he dies. [26]And he who lives and believes in me will never die. Martha, do you believe this?"

[27]Martha answered, "Yes, Lord. I believe that you are the Christ,[d] the Son of God. You are the One who was coming to the world."

10:34 'I . . . gods.' Quotation from Psalm 82:6. **11:24 resurrection** Being raised from death to live again.

²⁸After Martha said this, she went back to her sister Mary. She talked to Mary alone. Martha said, "The Teacher is here and he is asking for you." ²⁹When Mary heard this, she got up quickly and went to Jesus. ³⁰Jesus had not yet come into the town. He was still at the place where Martha had met him. ³¹The Jews were with Mary in the house, comforting her. They saw Mary stand and leave quickly. They followed her, thinking that she was going to the tomb to cry there. ³²But Mary went to the place where Jesus was. When she saw him, she fell at his feet and said, "Lord, if you had been here, my brother would not have died."

³³Jesus saw that Mary was crying and that the Jews who came with her were crying, too. Jesus felt very sad in his heart and was deeply troubled. ³⁴He asked, "Where did you bury him?"

"Come and see, Lord," they said.

³⁵Jesus cried.

³⁶So the Jews said, "See how much he loved him."

³⁷But some of them said, "If Jesus healed the eyes of the blind man, why didn't he keep Lazarus from dying?"

³⁸Again Jesus felt very sad in his heart. He came to the tomb. The tomb was a cave with a large stone covering the entrance. ³⁹Jesus said, "Move the stone away."

Martha said, "But, Lord, it has been four days since he died. There will be a bad smell." Martha was the sister of the dead man.

⁴⁰Then Jesus said to her, "Didn't I tell you that if you believed, you would see the glory of God?"

⁴¹So they moved the stone away from the entrance. Then Jesus looked up and said, "Father, I thank you that you heard me. ⁴²I know that you always hear me. But I said these things because of the people here around me. I want them to believe that you sent me." ⁴³After Jesus said this, he cried out in a loud voice, "Lazarus, come out!" ⁴⁴The dead man came out. His hands and feet were wrapped with pieces of cloth, and he had a cloth around his face.

Jesus said to them, "Take the cloth off of him and let him go."

⁴⁵There were many Jews who had come to visit Mary. They saw what Jesus did. And many of them believed in him. ⁴⁶But some of them went to the Pharisees.[d] They told the Pharisees what Jesus had done. ⁴⁷Then the leading priests and Pharisees called a meeting of the Jewish council. They asked, "What should we do? This man is doing many miracles.[d] ⁴⁸If we let him continue doing these things, everyone will believe in him. Then the Romans will come and take away our Temple[d] and our nation."

⁴⁹One of the men there was Caiaphas. He was the high priest that year. Caiaphas said, "You people know nothing! ⁵⁰It is better for one man to die for the people than for the whole nation to be destroyed. But you don't realize this."

⁵¹Caiaphas did not think of this himself. He was high priest that year. So he was really prophesying[d] that Jesus would die for the Jewish nation ⁵²and for God's scattered children. This would bring them all together and make them one.

⁵³That day they started planning to kill Jesus. ⁵⁴So Jesus no longer traveled openly among the Jews. He left there and went to a place near the desert. He went to a town called Ephraim and stayed there with his followers.

⁵⁵It was almost time for the Jewish Passover[d] Feast. Many from the country went up to Jerusalem before the Passover. They went to do the special things to make themselves pure. ⁵⁶The people looked for Jesus. They stood in the Temple and were asking each other, "Is he coming to the Feast? What do you think?" ⁵⁷But the leading priests and the Pharisees had given orders about Jesus. They said that if anyone knew where Jesus was, he must tell them. Then they could arrest Jesus.

12 Six days before the Passover[d] Feast, Jesus went to Bethany, where Lazarus lived. (Lazarus is the man Jesus raised from death.) ²There they had a dinner for Jesus. Martha served the food. Lazarus was one of the people eating with Jesus. ³Mary brought in a pint of very expensive perfume made from pure nard.[d] She poured the perfume on Jesus' feet, and then she wiped his feet with her hair. And the sweet smell from the perfume filled the whole house.

⁴Judas Iscariot, one of Jesus' followers, was there. (He was the one who would later turn against Jesus.) Judas said, ⁵"This perfume was worth 300 silver coins.[n] It should have been sold and the

12:5 silver coins One coin, a denarius, was the average pay for one day's work.

money given to the poor." [6]But Judas did not really care about the poor. He said this because he was a thief. He was the one who kept the money box, and he often stole money from it.

[7]Jesus answered, "Let her alone. It was right for her to save this perfume for today—the day for me to be prepared for burial. [8]The poor will always be with you, but you will not always have me."

[9]A large crowd of Jews heard that Jesus was in Bethany. So they went there to see not only Jesus but also Lazarus. Lazarus was the one Jesus raised from death. [10]So the leading priests made plans to kill Lazarus, too. [11]Because of Lazarus many Jews were leaving them and believing in Jesus.

[12]The next day a great crowd in Jerusalem heard that Jesus was coming there. These were the people who had come to the Passover[d] Feast. [13]They took branches of palm trees and went out to meet Jesus. They shouted,

"Praise[n] God!
God bless the One who comes in the name of the Lord!
God bless the King of Israel!"

Psalm 118:25-26

[14]Jesus found a colt and sat on it. This was as the Scripture[d] says,

[15]"Don't be afraid, people of Jerusalem!
Your king is coming.
He is sitting on the colt of a donkey."   *Zechariah 9:9*

[16]The followers of Jesus did not understand this at first. But after Jesus was raised to glory, they remembered that this had been written about him. And they remembered that they had done these things to him.

[17]There had been many people with Jesus when he raised Lazarus from death and told him to come out of the tomb. Now they were telling others about what Jesus did. [18]Many people went out to meet Jesus, because they had heard about this miracle.[d] [19]So the Pharisees[d] said to each other, "You can see that nothing is going right for us. Look! The whole world is following him."

[20]There were some Greek people, too, who came to Jerusalem to worship at the Passover[d] Feast. [21]They went to Philip. (Philip was from Bethsaida, in Galilee.) They said, "Sir, we would like

to see Jesus." [22]Philip told Andrew. Then Andrew and Philip told Jesus.

[23]Jesus said to them, "The time has come for the Son of Man[d] to receive his glory. [24]I tell you the truth. A grain of wheat must fall to the ground and die. Then it makes many seeds. But if it never dies, it remains only a single seed. [25]The person who loves his life will give up true life. But the person who hates his life in this world will keep true life forever. [26]Whoever serves me must follow me. Then my servant will be with me everywhere I am. My Father will honor anyone who serves me.

[27]"Now I am very troubled. What should I say? Should I say, 'Father, save me from this time'? No, I came to this time so that I could suffer. [28]Father, bring glory to your name!"

Then a voice came from heaven, "I have brought glory to it, and I will do it again."

[29]The crowd standing there heard the voice. They said it was thunder.

But others said, "An angel has spoken to him."

[30]Jesus said, "That voice was for you, not for me. [31]Now is the time for the world to be judged. Now the ruler of this world will be thrown down. [32]I will be lifted up from the earth. And when this happens, I will draw all people toward me." [33]Jesus said this to show how he would die.

[34]The crowd said, "We have heard from the law that the Christ[d] will live forever. So why do you say, 'The Son of Man must be lifted up'? Who is this 'Son of Man'?"

[35]Then Jesus said, "The light will be with you for a little longer. So walk while you have the light. Then the darkness will not catch you. He who walks in the darkness does not know where he is going. [36]So believe in the light while you still have it. Then you will become sons of light." When Jesus had said this, he left and hid himself from them.

[37]Though Jesus had done many miracles[d] before the people, they still did not believe in him. [38]This was to make clear the full meaning of what Isaiah the prophet[d] said:

"Lord, who believed the things we told them?
Who has seen the Lord's power?"

Isaiah 53:1

12:13 Praise Literally, "Hosanna," a Hebrew word used at first in praying to God for help, but at this time it was probably a shout of joy used in praising God or his Messiah.

[39]This is why the people could not believe: Isaiah also said,

[40]"He has blinded their eyes.
He has closed their minds.
This is so that they will not see with
their eyes
nor understand in their minds.
This is so they will not
come back to me and be
forgiven." *Isaiah 6:10*

[41]Isaiah said this because he saw Jesus' glory and spoke about him.

[42]But many people believed in Jesus, even many of the leaders. But because of the Pharisees,[d] they did not say that they believed in him. They were afraid that they would be put out of the synagogue.[d] [43]They loved praise from men more than praise from God.

[44]Then Jesus cried out, "He who believes in me is really believing in the One who sent me. [45]He who sees me sees the One who sent me. [46]I have come as light into the world. I came so that whoever believes in me would not stay in darkness.

[47]"If anyone hears my words and does not obey them, I do not judge him. For I did not come to judge the world, but to save the world. [48]There is a judge for the one who refuses to believe in me and does not accept my words. The word I have taught will be his judge on the last day. [49]The things I taught were not from myself. The Father who sent me told me what to say and what to teach. [50]And I know that eternal life comes from what the Father commands. So whatever I say is what the Father told me to say."

13 It was almost time for the Jewish Passover[d] Feast. Jesus knew that it was time for him to leave this world and go back to the Father. He had always loved those who were his own in the world, and he loved them all the way to the end. [2]Jesus and his followers were at the evening meal. The devil had already persuaded Judas Iscariot to turn against Jesus. (Judas was the son of Simon.) [3]Jesus knew that the Father had given him power over everything. He also knew that he had come from God and was going back to God. [4]So during the meal Jesus stood up and took off his outer clothing. Taking a towel, he wrapped it around his waist. [5]Then he poured water into a bowl and began to wash the follow-

ers' feet. He dried them with the towel that was wrapped around him.

[6]Jesus came to Simon Peter. But Peter said to Jesus, "Lord, are you going to wash my feet?"

[7]Jesus answered, "You don't understand what I am doing now. But you will understand later."

[8]Peter said, "No! You will never wash my feet."

Jesus answered, "If I don't wash your feet, then you are not one of my people."

[9]Simon Peter answered, "Lord, after you wash my feet, wash my hands and my head, too!"

[10]Jesus said, "After a person has had a bath, his whole body is clean. He needs only to wash his feet. And you men are clean,[d] but not all of you." [11]Jesus knew who would turn against him. That is why Jesus said, "Not all of you are clean."

[12]When he had finished washing their feet, he put on his clothes and sat down again. Jesus asked, "Do you understand what I have just done for you? [13]You call me 'Teacher' and 'Lord.' And this is right, because that is what I am. [14]I, your Lord and Teacher, have washed your feet. So you also should wash each other's feet. [15]I did this as an example for you. So you should do as I have done for you. [16]I tell you the truth. A servant is not greater than his master. A messenger is not greater than the one who sent him. [17]If you know these things, you will be happy if you do them.

[18]"I am not talking about all of you. I know those I have chosen. But what the Scripture[d] said must happen: 'The man who ate at my table has now turned against me.'[n] [19]I am telling you this now before it happens. Then when it happens you will believe that I am he. [20]I tell you the truth. Whoever accepts anyone I send also accepts me. And whoever accepts me also accepts the One who sent me."

[21]After Jesus said this, he was very troubled. He said openly, "I tell you the truth. One of you will turn against me."

[22]The followers all looked at each other. They did not know whom Jesus was talking about. [23]One of the followers was sitting[n] next to Jesus. This was the follower Jesus loved. [24]Simon Peter made signs to him to ask Jesus who it was that he was talking about.

[25]That follower leaned closer to Jesus

13:18 'The man . . . me.' Quotation from Psalm 41:9. 13:23 sitting Literally, "lying." The people of that time ate lying down and leaning on one arm.

and asked, "Lord, who is it that will turn against you?"

[26] Jesus answered, "I will dip this bread into the dish. The man I give it to is the man who will turn against me." So Jesus took a piece of bread. He dipped it and gave it to Judas Iscariot, the son of Simon. [27] As soon as Judas took the bread, Satan entered him. Jesus said to Judas, "The thing that you will do—do it quickly!" [28] None of the men at the table understood why Jesus said this to Judas. [29] He was the one who kept the money box. So some of the followers thought that Jesus was telling Judas to buy what was needed for the feast. Or they thought that Jesus wanted Judas to give something to the poor.

[30] Judas accepted the bread Jesus gave him and immediately went out. It was night.

[31] When Judas was gone, Jesus said, "Now the Son of Man[d] receives his glory. And God receives glory through him. [32] If God receives glory through him, then God will give glory to the Son through himself. And God will give him glory quickly."

[33] Jesus said, "My children, I will be with you only a little longer. You will look for me. And what I told the Jews, I tell you now: Where I am going you cannot come.

[34] "I give you a new command: Love each other. You must love each other as I have loved you. [35] All people will know that you are my followers if you love each other."

[36] Simon Peter asked Jesus, "Lord, where are you going?"

Jesus answered, "Where I am going you cannot follow now. But you will follow later."

[37] Peter asked, "Lord, why can't I follow you now? I am ready to die for you!"

[38] Jesus answered, "Will you really die for me? I tell you the truth. Before the rooster crows, you will say three times that you don't know me."

14 Jesus said, "Don't let your hearts be troubled. Trust in God. And trust in me. [2] There are many rooms in my Father's house. I would not tell you this if it were not true. I am going there to prepare a place for you. [3] After I go and prepare a place for you, I will come back. Then I will take you to be with me so that you may be where I am. [4] You

know the way to the place where I am going."

[5] Thomas said to Jesus, "Lord, we don't know where you are going. So how can we know the way?"

[6] Jesus answered, "I am the way. And I am the truth and the life. The only way to the Father is through me. [7] If you really knew me, then you would know my Father, too. But now you do know him, and you have seen him."

[8] Philip said to him, "Lord, show us the Father. That is all we need."

[9] Jesus answered, "I have been with you a long time now. Do you still not know me, Philip? He who has seen me has seen the Father. So why do you say, 'Show us the Father'? [10] Don't you believe that I am in the Father and the Father is in me? The words I say to you don't come from me. The Father lives in me, and he is doing his own work. [11] Believe me when I say that I am in the Father and the Father is in me. Or believe because of the miracles[d] I have done. [12] I tell you the truth. He who believes in me will do the same things that I do. He will do even greater things than these because I am going to the Father. [13] And if you ask for anything in my name, I will do it for you. Then the Father's glory will be shown through the Son. [14] If you ask me for anything in my name, I will do it.

[15] "If you love me, you will do the things I command. [16] I will ask the Father, and he will give you another Helper.[n] He will give you this Helper to be with you forever. [17] The Helper is the Spirit[d] of truth. The world cannot accept him because it does not see him or know him. But you know him. He lives with you and he will be in you.

[18] "I will not leave you all alone like orphans. I will come back to you. [19] In a little while the world will not see me anymore, but you will see me. Because I live, you will live, too. [20] On that day you will know that I am in my Father. You will know that you are in me and I am in you. [21] He who knows my commands and obeys them is the one who loves me. And my Father will love him who loves me. I will love him and will show myself to him."

[22] Then Judas (not Judas Iscariot) said, "But, Lord, why do you plan to show yourself to us, but not to the world?"

[23] Jesus answered, "If anyone loves

14:16 Helper "Counselor," or "Comforter." Jesus is talking about the Holy Spirit.

me, then he will obey my teaching. My Father will love him, and we will come to him and make our home with him. [24]He who does not love me does not obey my teaching. This teaching that you hear is not really mine. It is from my Father, who sent me.

[25]"I have told you all these things while I am with you. [26]But the Helper will teach you everything. He will cause you to remember all the things I told you. This Helper is the Holy Spirit whom the Father will send in my name.

[27]"I leave you peace. My peace I give you. I do not give it to you as the world does. So don't let your hearts be troubled. Don't be afraid. [28]You heard me say to you, 'I am going, but I am coming back to you.' If you loved me, you should be happy that I am going back to the Father because he is greater than I am. [29]I have told you this now, before it happens. Then when it happens, you will believe. [30]I will not talk with you much longer. The ruler of this world is coming. He has no power over me. [31]But the world must know that I love the Father. So I do exactly what the Father told me to do.

"Come now, let us go.

15 "I am the true vine; my Father is the gardener. [2]He cuts off every branch of mine that does not produce fruit. And he trims and cleans every branch that produces fruit so that it will produce even more fruit. [3]You are already clean[d] because of the words I have spoken to you. [4]Remain in me, and I will remain in you. No branch can produce fruit alone. It must remain in the vine. It is the same with you. You cannot produce fruit alone. You must remain in me.

[5]"I am the vine, and you are the branches. If a person remains in me and I remain in him, then he produces much fruit. But without me he can do nothing. [6]If anyone does not remain in me, then he is like a branch that is thrown away. That branch dies. People pick up dead branches, throw them into the fire, and burn them. [7]Remain in me and follow my teachings. If you do this, then you can ask for anything you want, and it will be given to you. [8]You should produce much fruit and show that you are my followers. This brings glory to my Father. [9]I loved you as the Father loved me. Now remain in my love. [10]I have

obeyed my Father's commands, and I remain in his love. In the same way, if you obey my commands, you will remain in my love. [11]I have told you these things so that you can have the same joy I have. I want your joy to be the fullest joy.

[12]"This is my command: Love each other as I have loved you. [13]The greatest love a person can show is to die for his friends. [14]You are my friends if you do what I command you. [15]I don't call you servants now. A servant does not know what his master is doing. But now I call you friends because I have made known to you everything I heard from my Father. [16]You did not choose me; I chose you. And I gave you this work, to go and produce fruit. I want you to produce fruit that will last. Then the Father will give you anything you ask for in my name. [17]This is my command: Love each other.

[18]"If the world hates you, remember that it hated me first. [19]If you belonged to the world, then it would love you as it loves its own. But I have chosen you out of the world. So you don't belong to it. That is why the world hates you. [20]Remember what I told you: A servant is not greater than his master. If people did wrong to me, they will do wrong to you, too. And if they obeyed my teaching, they will obey yours, too. [21]They will do all this to you because of me. They don't know the One who sent me. [22]If I had not come and spoken to them, they would not be guilty of sin. But now they have no excuse for their sin. [23]He who hates me also hates my Father. [24]I did works among them that no one else has ever done. If I had not done those works, they would not be guilty of sin. But now they have seen what I did, and yet they have hated both me and my Father. [25]But this happened so that what is written in their law would be true: 'They hated me for no reason.'[n]

[26]"I will send you the Helper[n] from the Father. He is the Spirit of truth who comes from the Father. When he comes, he will tell about me. [27]And you also must tell people about me because you have been with me from the beginning.

16 "I have told you these things to keep you from giving up. [2]People will put you out of their synagogues.[d] Yes, the time is coming when whoever kills you will think that he is offering

---

15:25 'They . . . reason.' These words could be from Psalm 35:19 or Psalm 69:4.   **15:26 Helper** "Counselor," or "Comforter." Jesus is talking about the Holy Spirit.

service to God. [3]They will do this because they have not known the Father and they have not known me. [4]I have told you these things now. So when the time comes, you will remember that I warned you.

"I did not tell you these things at the beginning, because I was with you then. [5]Now I am going back to the One who sent me. But none of you asks me, 'Where are you going?' [6]Your hearts are filled with sadness because I have told you these things. [7]But I tell you the truth. It is better for you that I go away. When I go away, I will send the Helper[n] to you. If I do not go away, then the Helper will not come. [8]When the Helper comes, he will prove to the people of the world the truth about sin, about being right with God, and about judgment. [9]He will prove to them about sin, because they don't believe in me. [10]He will prove to them that I am right with God, because I am going to the Father. You will not see me anymore. [11]And the Helper will prove to them the truth about judgment, because the ruler of this world is already judged.

[12]"I have many more things to say to you, but they are too much for you now. [13]But when the Spirit[d] of truth comes he will lead you into all truth. He will not speak his own words. He will speak only what he hears and will tell you what is to come. [14]The Spirit of truth will bring glory to me. He will take what I have to say and tell it to you. [15]All that the Father has is mine. That is why I said that the Spirit will take what I have to say and tell it to you.

[16]"After a little while you will not see me. And then after a little while you will see me again."

[17]Some of the followers said to each other, "What does Jesus mean when he says, 'After a little while you will not see me, and then after a little while you will see me again'? And what does he mean when he says, 'Because I am going to the Father'?" [18]They also asked, "What does he mean by 'a little while'? We don't understand what he is saying."

[19]Jesus saw that the followers wanted to ask him about this. So Jesus said to the followers, "Are you asking each other what I meant when I said, 'After a little while you will not see me. And then after a little while you will see me again'? [20]I tell you the truth. You will cry

and be sad, but the world will be happy. You will be sad, but your sadness will become joy. [21]When a woman gives birth to a baby, she has pain, because her time has come. But when her baby is born, she forgets the pain. She forgets because she is so happy that a child has been born into the world. [22]It is the same with you. Now you are sad. But I will see you again and you will be happy. And no one will take away your joy. [23]In that day you will not ask me for anything. I tell you the truth. My Father will give you anything you ask for in my name. [24]You have never asked for anything in my name. Ask and you will receive. And your joy will be the fullest joy.

[25]"I have told you these things, using words that hide the meaning. But the time will come when I will not use words like that to tell you things. I will speak to you in plain words about the Father. [26]In that day you will ask the Father for things in my name. I am saying that I will not need to ask the Father for you. [27]No! The Father himself loves you. He loves you because you have loved me. And he loves you because you have believed that I came from God. [28]I came from the Father into the world. Now I am leaving the world and going back to the Father."

[29]Then the followers of Jesus said, "You are speaking clearly to us now. You are not using words that are hard to understand. [30]We can see now that you know all things. You can answer a person's question even before he asks it. This makes us believe that you came from God."

[31]Jesus answered, "So now you believe? [32]Listen to me. A time is coming when you will be scattered. Each of you will be scattered to his own home. That time is now here. You will leave me. I will be alone. But I am never really alone. Why? Because the Father is with me.

[33]"I told you these things so that you can have peace in me. In this world you will have trouble. But be brave! I have defeated the world!"

17 After Jesus said these things he looked toward heaven. Jesus prayed, "Father, the time has come. Give glory to your Son so that the Son can give glory to you. [2]You gave the Son power over all people so that the Son

16:7 **Helper** "Counselor," or "Comforter." Jesus is talking about the Holy Spirit.

could give eternal life to all those people you have given to him. ³And this is eternal life: that men can know you, the only true God, and that men can know Jesus Christ, the One you sent. ⁴I finished the work you gave me to do. I brought you glory on earth. ⁵And now, Father, give me glory with you. Give me the glory I had with you before the world was made.

⁶"You gave me some men from the world. I have shown them what you are like. Those men belonged to you, and you gave them to me. They have obeyed your teaching. ⁷Now they know that everything you gave me comes from you. ⁸I gave these men the teachings that you gave me. They accepted those teachings. They know that I truly came from you. ⁹I pray for them now. I am not praying for the people in the world. But I am praying for those men you gave me, because they are yours. ¹⁰All I have is yours, and all you have is mine. And my glory is shown through these men. ¹¹Now I am coming to you. I will not stay in the world now. But these men are still in the world. Holy Father, keep them safe. Keep them safe by the power of your name (the name you gave me), so that they will be one, the same as you and I are one. ¹²While I was with them, I kept them safe. I kept them safe by the power of your name—the name you gave me. I protected them. And only one of them, the one who is going to hell, was lost. He was lost so that what was said in the Scripture* would happen.

¹³"I am coming to you now. But I pray these things while I am still in the world. I say these things so that these men can have my joy. I want them to have all of my joy. ¹⁴I have given them your teaching. And the world has hated them. The world hated these men, because they don't belong to the world, the same as I don't belong to the world. ¹⁵I am not asking you to take them out of the world. But I am asking that you keep them safe from the Evil One. ¹⁶They don't belong to the world, the same as I don't belong to the world. ¹⁷Make them ready for your service through your truth. Your teaching is truth. ¹⁸I have sent them into the world, the same as you sent me into the world. ¹⁹I am making myself ready to serve. I do this for them so that they can truly be ready for your service.

²⁰"I pray for these men. But I am also praying for all people who will believe in me because of the teaching of these men. ²¹Father, I pray that all people who believe in me can be one. You are in me and I am in you. I pray that these people can also be one in us, so that the world will believe that you sent me. ²²I have given these people the glory that you gave me. I gave them this glory so that they can be one, the same as you and I are one. ²³I will be in them and you will be in me. So they will be completely one. Then the world will know that you sent me. And the world will know that you loved these people the same as you loved me.

²⁴"Father, I want these people that you have given me to be with me in every place I am. I want them to see my glory. This is the glory you gave me because you loved me before the world was made. ²⁵Father, you are the One who is good. The world does not know you, but I know you. And these people know that you sent me. ²⁶I showed them what you are like. And again I will show them what you are like. Then they will have the same love that you have for me. And I will live in them."

18 When Jesus finished praying, he left with his followers. They went across the Kidron Valley. On the other side there was a garden of olive trees. Jesus and his followers went there.

²Judas knew where this place was, because Jesus met there often with his followers. Judas was the one who turned against Jesus. ³So Judas led a group of soldiers to the garden. Judas also brought some guards from the leading priests and the Pharisees.* They were carrying torches, lanterns, and weapons.

⁴Jesus knew everything that would happen to him. Jesus went out and asked, "Who is it you are looking for?"

⁵The men answered, "Jesus from Nazareth."

Jesus said, "I am Jesus." (Judas, the one who turned against Jesus, was standing there with them.) ⁶When Jesus said, "I am Jesus," the men moved back and fell to the ground.

⁷Jesus asked them again, "Who is it you are looking for?"

They said, "Jesus of Nazareth."

⁸Jesus said, "I told you that I am he. So if you are looking for me, then let these other men go." ⁹This happened so that the words Jesus said before might come true: "I have not lost any of the men you gave me."

¹⁰Simon Peter had a sword. He took

out the sword and struck the servant of the high priest, cutting off his right ear. (The servant's name was Malchus.) [11]Jesus said to Peter, "Put your sword back. Shall I not drink of the cup[n] the Father has given me?"

[12]Then the soldiers with their commander and the Jewish guards arrested Jesus. They tied him [13]and led him first to Annas. Annas was the father-in-law of Caiaphas, the high priest that year. [14]Caiaphas was the one who had told the Jews that it would be better if one man died for all the people.

[15]Simon Peter and another one of Jesus' followers went along after Jesus. This follower knew the high priest. So he went with Jesus into the high priest's courtyard. [16]But Peter waited outside near the door. The follower who knew the high priest came back outside. He spoke to the girl at the door and brought Peter inside. [17]The girl at the door said to Peter, "Aren't you also one of that man's followers?"

Peter answered, "No, I am not!"

[18]It was cold, so the servants and guards had built a fire. They were standing around it and warming themselves. Peter was standing with them, warming himself.

[19]The high priest asked Jesus questions about his followers and his teaching. [20]Jesus answered, "I have spoken openly to everyone. I have always taught in synagogues[d] and in the Temple,[d] where all the Jews come together. I never said anything in secret. [21]So why do you question me? Ask the people who heard my teaching. They know what I said."

[22]When Jesus said this, one of the guards standing there hit him. The guard said, "Is that the way you answer the high priest?"

[23]Jesus answered him, "If I said something wrong, then say what was wrong. But if what I said is true, why do you hit me?"

[24]Then Annas sent Jesus to Caiaphas, the high priest. Jesus was still tied.

[25]Simon Peter was standing and warming himself. They said to him, "Aren't you one of that man's followers?"

Peter denied it and said, "No, I am not."

[26]One of the servants of the high priest was there. This servant was a relative of the man whose ear Peter had cut off. The servant said, "Didn't I see you with him in the garden?"

[27]Again Peter said it wasn't true. Just then a rooster crowed.

[28]Then they led Jesus from Caiaphas' house to the Roman governor's palace. It was early in the morning. The Jews would not go inside the palace. They did not want to make themselves unclean,[n] because they wanted to eat the Passover[d] meal. [29]So Pilate went outside to them. He asked, "What charges do you bring against this man?"

[30]They answered, "He is a criminal. That is why we brought him to you."

[31]Pilate said to them, "Take him yourselves and judge him by your own law."

They answered, "But we are not allowed to put anyone to death." [32](This happened so that what Jesus had said about how he would die would come true.)

[33]Then Pilate went back inside the palace. He called Jesus to him and asked, "Are you the king of the Jews?"

[34]Jesus said, "Is that your own question, or did others tell you about me?"

[35]Pilate answered, "I am not a Jew. It was your own people and their leading priests who brought you before me. What have you done wrong?"

[36]Jesus said, "My kingdom does not belong to this world. If it belonged to this world, my servants would fight so that I would not be given over to the Jews. But my kingdom is from another place."

[37]Pilate said, "So you are a king!"

Jesus answered, "You say that I am a king. That is true. I was born for this: to tell people about the truth. That is why I came into the world. And everyone who belongs to the truth listens to me."

[38]Pilate said, "What is truth?" After he said this, he went out to the Jews again. He said to them, "I can find nothing to charge against this man. [39]But it is your custom that I free one prisoner to you at the time of the Passover. Do you want me to free this 'king of the Jews'?"

[40]They shouted back, "No, not him! Let Barabbas go free!" (Barabbas was a robber.)

18:11 **cup** Jesus is talking about the bad things that will happen to him. Accepting these things will be very hard, like drinking a cup of something that tastes very bitter. 18:28 **unclean** Going into a non-Jewish place would make them unfit to eat the Passover Feast, according to Jewish law.

19 Then Pilate ordered that Jesus be taken away and whipped. [2]The soldiers used some thorny branches to make a crown. They put this crown on Jesus' head and put a purple robe around him. [3]Then they came to Jesus many times and said, "Hail, King of the Jews!" They hit Jesus in the face.

[4]Again Pilate came out and said to them, "Look! I am bringing Jesus out to you. I want you to know that I find nothing I can charge against him." [5]Then Jesus came out, wearing the crown of thorns and the purple robe. Pilate said to the Jews, "Here is the man!"

[6]When the leading priests and the guards saw Jesus they shouted, "Kill him on a cross! Kill him on a cross!"

But Pilate answered, "Take him and nail him to a cross yourselves. I find nothing I can charge against him."

[7]The Jews answered, "We have a law that says he should die, because he said he is the Son of God."

[8]When Pilate heard this, he was even more afraid. [9]He went back inside the palace and asked Jesus, "Where are you from?" But Jesus did not answer him. [10]Pilate said, "You refuse to speak to me? Don't you know that I have power to set you free and power to have you killed on a cross?"

[11]Jesus answered, "The only power you have over me is the power given to you by God. The man who gave me to you is guilty of a greater sin."

[12]After this, Pilate tried to let Jesus go free. But the Jews cried out, "Anyone who makes himself king is against Caesar. If you let this man go free, you are not Caesar's friend."

[13]Pilate heard what the Jews were saying. So he brought Jesus out to the place called The Stone Pavement. (In the Jewish language[n] the name is Gabbatha.) Pilate sat down on the judge's seat there. [14]It was about six o'clock in the morning on Preparation[d] Day of Passover[d] week. Pilate said to the Jews, "Here is your king!"

[15]They shouted, "Take him away! Take him away! Kill him on a cross!"

Pilate asked them, "Do you want me to kill your king on a cross?"

The leading priests answered, "The only king we have is Caesar!"

[16]So Pilate gave Jesus to them to be killed on a cross.

The soldiers took charge of Jesus. [17]Carrying his own cross, Jesus went out to a place called The Place of the Skull. (In the Jewish language[n] this place is called Golgotha.) [18]There they nailed Jesus to the cross. They also put two other men on crosses, one on each side of Jesus with Jesus in the middle. [19]Pilate wrote a sign and put it on the cross. It read: "JESUS OF NAZARETH, THE KING OF THE JEWS." [20]The sign was written in the Jewish language, in Latin, and in Greek. Many of the Jews read the sign, because this place where Jesus was killed was near the city. [21]The leading Jewish priests said to Pilate, "Don't write, 'The King of the Jews.' But write, 'This man said, I am the King of the Jews.'"

[22]Pilate answered, "What I have written, I have written!"

[23]After the soldiers nailed Jesus to the cross, they took his clothes. They divided them into four parts. Each soldier got one part. They also took his long shirt. It was all one piece of cloth, woven from top to bottom. [24]So the soldiers said to each other, "We should not tear this into parts. We should throw lots[d] to see who will get it." This happened to give full meaning to the Scripture:[d]

"They divided my clothes among
     them.
And they threw lots[d] for my
     clothing."   *Psalm 22:18*

So the soldiers did this.

[25]Jesus' mother stood near his cross. His mother's sister was also standing there, with Mary the wife of Clopas, and Mary Magdalene. [26]Jesus saw his mother. He also saw the follower he loved standing there. He said to his mother, "Dear woman, here is your son." [27]Then he said to the follower, "Here is your mother." From that time on, this follower took her to live in his home.

[28]After this, Jesus knew that everything had been done. To make the Scripture[d] come true, he said, "I am thirsty."[n] [29]There was a jar full of vinegar there, so the soldiers soaked a sponge in it. Then they put the sponge on a branch of a hyssop plant and lifted it to Jesus' mouth. [30]Jesus tasted the vinegar. Then

---

19:13, 17 Jewish language Aramaic, the language of the Jews in the first century.   **19:28 "I am thirsty."** Read Psalms 22:15; 69:21.

he said, "It is finished." He bowed his head and died.

[31] This day was Preparation[d] Day. The next day was a special Sabbath[d] day. The Jews did not want the bodies to stay on the cross on the Sabbath day. So they asked Pilate to order that the legs of the men be broken[n] and the bodies be taken away. [32] So the soldiers came and broke the legs of the first man on the cross beside Jesus. Then they broke the legs of the man on the other cross beside Jesus. [33] But when the soldiers came to Jesus, they saw that he was already dead. So they did not break his legs. [34] But one of the soldiers stuck his spear into Jesus' side. At once blood and water came out. [35] (The one who saw this happen has told about it. The things he says are true. He knows that he tells the truth. He told about it so that you also can believe.) [36] These things happened to make the Scripture come true: "Not one of his bones will be broken."[n] [37] And another Scripture said, "They will look at the one they have stabbed."[n]

[38] Later, a man named Joseph from Arimathea asked Pilate if he could take the body of Jesus. (Joseph was a secret follower of Jesus, because he was afraid of the Jews.) Pilate gave his permission. So Joseph came and took Jesus' body away. [39] Nicodemus went with Joseph. Nicodemus was the man who earlier had come to Jesus at night. He brought about 75 pounds of spices. This was a mixture of myrrh[d] and aloes.[d] [40] These two men took Jesus' body and wrapped it with the spices in pieces of linen cloth. (This is how the Jews bury people.) [41] In the place where Jesus was killed, there was a garden. In the garden was a new tomb where no one had ever been buried. [42] The men laid Jesus in that tomb because it was near, and the Jews were preparing to start their Sabbath[d] day.

20 Early on the first day of the week, Mary Magdalene went to the tomb. It was still dark. Mary saw that the large stone had been moved away from the tomb. [2] So Mary ran to Simon Peter and the other follower (the one Jesus loved). Mary said, "They have taken the Lord out of the tomb. We don't know where they have put him."

[3] So Peter and the other follower started for the tomb. [4] They were both running, but the other follower ran faster than Peter. So the other follower reached the tomb first. [5] He bent down and looked in. He saw the strips of linen cloth lying there, but he did not go in. [6] Then following him came Simon Peter. He went into the tomb and saw the strips of linen lying there. [7] He also saw the cloth that had been around Jesus' head. The cloth was folded up and laid in a different place from the strips of linen. [8] Then the other follower, who had reached the tomb first, also went in. He saw and believed. [9] (These followers did not yet understand from the Scriptures[d] that Jesus must rise from death.)

[10] Then the followers went back home. [11] But Mary stood outside the tomb, crying. While she was still crying, she bent down and looked inside the tomb. [12] She saw two angels dressed in white. They were sitting where Jesus' body had been, one at the head and one at the feet.

[13] They asked her, "Woman, why are you crying?"

She answered, "They have taken away my Lord. I don't know where they have put him." [14] When Mary said this, she turned around and saw Jesus standing there. But she did not know that it was Jesus.

[15] Jesus asked her, "Woman, why are you crying? Whom are you looking for?"

Mary thought he was the gardener. So she said to him, "Did you take him away, sir? Tell me where you put him, and I will get him."

[16] Jesus said to her, "Mary."

Mary turned toward Jesus and said in the Jewish language,[n] "Rabboni." (This means Teacher.)

[17] Jesus said to her, "Don't hold me. I have not yet gone up to the Father. But go to my brothers and tell them this: 'I am going back to my Father and your Father. I am going back to my God and your God.'"

[18] Mary Magdalene went and said to the followers, "I saw the Lord!" And she told them what Jesus had said to her.

[19] It was the first day of the week. That evening the followers were together. The doors were locked, because they were afraid of the Jews. Then Jesus

---

19:31 broken The breaking of the men's bones would make them die sooner. **19:36 "Not one . . . broken."** Quotation from Psalm 34:20. The idea is from Exodus 12:46; Numbers 9:12. **19:37 "They . . . stabbed."** Quotation from Zechariah 12:10. **20:16 Jewish language** Aramaic, the language of the Jews in the first century.

came and stood among them. He said, "Peace be with you!" [20] After he said this, he showed them his hands and his side. The followers were very happy when they saw the Lord.

[21] Then Jesus said again, "Peace be with you! As the Father sent me, I now send you." [22] After he said this, he breathed on them and said, "Receive the Holy Spirit.[d] [23] If you forgive anyone his sins, they are forgiven. If you don't forgive them, they are not forgiven."

[24] Thomas (called Didymus) was not with the followers when Jesus came. Thomas was 1 of the 12. [25] The other followers told Thomas, "We saw the Lord."

But Thomas said, "I will not believe it until I see the nail marks in his hands. And I will not believe until I put my finger where the nails were and put my hand into his side."

[26] A week later the followers were in the house again. Thomas was with them. The doors were locked, but Jesus came in and stood among them. He said, "Peace be with you!" [27] Then he said to Thomas, "Put your finger here. Look at my hands. Put your hand here in my side. Stop doubting and believe."

[28] Thomas said to him, "My Lord and my God!"

[29] Then Jesus told him, "You believe because you see me. Those who believe without seeing me will be truly happy."

[30] Jesus did many other miracles[d] before his followers that are not written in this book. [31] But these are written so that you can believe that Jesus is the Christ,[d] the Son of God. Then, by believing, you can have life through his name.

21

Later, Jesus showed himself to his followers by Lake Galilee.[n] This is how it happened: [2] Some of the followers were together. They were Simon Peter, Thomas (called Didymus), Nathanael from Cana in Galilee, the two sons of Zebedee, and two other followers. [3] Simon Peter said, "I am going out to fish."

The other followers said, "We will go with you." So they went out and got into the boat. They fished that night but caught nothing.

[4] Early the next morning Jesus stood on the shore. But the followers did not know that it was Jesus. [5] Then he said to them, "Friends, have you caught any fish?"

They answered, "No."

[6] He said, "Throw your net into the wa-

ter on the right side of the boat, and you will find some." So they did this. They caught so many fish that they could not pull the net back into the boat.

[7] The follower whom Jesus loved said to Peter, "It is the Lord!" When Peter heard him say this, he wrapped his coat around himself. (Peter had taken his clothes off.) Then he jumped into the water. [8] The other followers went to shore in the boat, dragging the net full of fish. They were not very far from shore, only about 100 yards. [9] When the followers stepped out of the boat and onto the shore, they saw a fire of hot coals. There were fish on the fire, and there was bread.

[10] Then Jesus said, "Bring some of the fish that you caught."

[11] Simon Peter went into the boat and pulled the net to the shore. It was full of big fish. There were 153. Even though there were so many, the net did not tear. [12] Jesus said to them, "Come and eat." None of the followers dared ask him, "Who are you?" They knew it was the Lord. [13] Jesus came and took the bread and gave it to them. He also gave them the fish.

[14] This was now the third time Jesus showed himself to his followers after he was raised from death.

[15] When they finished eating, Jesus said to Simon Peter, "Simon son of John do you love me more than these?"

He answered, "Yes, Lord, you know that I love you."

Jesus said, "Take care of my lambs."

[16] Again Jesus said, "Simon son of John do you love me?"

He answered, "Yes, Lord, you know that I love you."

Jesus said, "Take care of my sheep."

[17] A third time he said, "Simon son of John do you love me?"

Peter was hurt because Jesus asked him the third time, "Do you love me?" Peter said, "Lord, you know everything. You know that I love you!"

He said to him, "Take care of my sheep. [18] I tell you the truth. When you were younger, you tied your own belt and went where you wanted. But when you are old, you will put out your hands and someone else will tie them. They will take you where you don't want to go." [19] (Jesus said this to show how Peter would die to give glory to God.) Then Jesus said to Peter, "Follow me!"

²⁰Peter turned and saw that the follower Jesus loved was walking behind them. (This was the follower who had leaned against Jesus at the supper and had said, "Lord, who will turn against you?") ²¹When Peter saw him behind them he asked Jesus, "Lord, what about him?"

²²Jesus answered, "Perhaps I want him to live until I come back. That should not be important to you. You follow me!"

²³So a story spread among the brothers that this follower would not die. But Jesus did not say that he would not die. He only said, "Perhaps I want him to live until I come back. That should not be important to you."

²⁴That follower is the one who is telling these things. He is the one who has now written them down. We know that what he says is true.

²⁵There are many other things that Jesus did. If every one of them were written down, I think the whole world would not be big enough for all the books that would be written.

THE ACTS
of the Apostles

1 To Theophilus,
The first book I wrote was about everything that Jesus did and taught. ²I wrote about the whole life of Jesus, from the beginning until the day he was taken up into heaven. Before this, Jesus talked to the apostlesᵈ he had chosen. With the help of the Holy Spirit,ᵈ Jesus told them what they should do. ³After his death, he showed himself to them and proved in many ways that he was alive. The apostles saw Jesus during the 40 days after he was raised from death. He spoke to them about the kingdom of God. ⁴Once when he was eating with them, he told them not to leave Jerusalem. He said, "The Father has made you a promise which I told you about before. Wait here to receive this promise. ⁵John baptized people with water, but in a few days you will be baptized with the Holy Spirit."

⁶The apostlesᵈ were all together. They asked Jesus, "Lord, are you at this time going to give the kingdom back to Israel?"

⁷Jesus said to them, "The Father is the only One who has the authority to decide dates and times. These things are not for you to know. ⁸But the Holy Spiritᵈ will come to you. Then you will receive power. You will be my witnesses—in Jerusalem, in all of Judea, in Samaria, and in every part of the world."

⁹After he said this, as they were watching, he was lifted up. A cloud hid him from their sight. ¹⁰As he was going, they were looking into the sky. Suddenly, two men wearing white clothes stood beside them. ¹¹They said, "Men of Galilee, why are you standing here looking into the sky? You saw Jesus taken away from you into heaven. He will come back in the same way you saw him go."

¹²Then they went back to Jerusalem from the Mount of Olives.ᵈ (This mountain is about half a mile from Jerusalem.) ¹³When they entered the city, they went to the upstairs room where they were staying. Peter, John, James, Andrew, Philip, Thomas, Bartholomew, Matthew, James son of Alphaeus, Simon (known as the Zealotᵈ), and Judas son of James were there. ¹⁴They all continued praying together. Some women, including Mary the mother of Jesus, and Jesus' brothers were also there with the apostles.

¹⁵During this time there was a meeting of the believers. (There were about 120 of them.) Peter stood up and said, ¹⁶⁻¹⁷"Brothers, in the Scripturesᵈ the Holy Spiritᵈ said through David that something must happen. The Spirit was talking about Judas, one of our own group, who served together with us. The Spirit said that Judas would lead men to arrest Jesus. ¹⁸(Judas bought a field with the money he got for his evil act. But Judas fell to his death, his body burst open, and all his intestines poured out.) ¹⁹Everyone in Jerusalem learned about this. This is why they named the field Akeldama. In their language Akeldama

means "field of blood.") [20] In the book of Psalms, this is written:

'May his place be empty.
Leave no one to live in it.'
Psalm 69:25

And it is also written:

'Let another man replace him as leader.'
Psalm 109:8

[21-22] "So now a man must join us and become a witness of Jesus' being raised from death. He must be one of the men who were part of our group during all the time the Lord Jesus was with us. He must have been with us from the time John began to baptize people until the day when Jesus was taken up from us to heaven."

[23] They put the names of two men before the group. One was Joseph Barsabbas, who was also called Justus. The other was Matthias. [24-25] The apostles prayed, "Lord, you know the minds of everyone. Show us which one of these two you have chosen to do this work. Judas turned away from it and went where he belongs. Lord, show us which one should take his place as an apostle!"[d] [26] Then they used lots[d] to choose between them, and the lots showed that Matthias was the one. So he became an apostle with the other 11.

2 When the day of Pentecost[d] came, they were all together in one place. [2] Suddenly a noise came from heaven. It sounded like a strong wind blowing. This noise filled the whole house where they were sitting. [3] They saw something that looked like flames of fire. The flames were separated and stood over each person there. [4] They were all filled with the Holy Spirit,[d] and they began to speak different languages. The Holy Spirit was giving them the power to speak these languages.

[5] There were some religious Jews staying in Jerusalem who were from every country in the world. [6] When they heard this noise, a crowd came together. They were all surprised, because each one heard them speaking in his own language. [7] They were completely amazed at this. They said, "Look! Aren't all these men that we hear speaking from Galilee?[n] [8] But each of us hears them in his own language. How is this possible? We are from different places: [9] Parthia, Media, Elam, Mesopotamia, Judea, Cappadocia, Pontus, Asia, [10] Phrygia, Pamphylia, Egypt, the areas of Libya near Cyrene, Rome [11] (both Jews and those who had become Jews), Crete and Arabia. But we hear these men telling in our own languages about the great things God has done!" [12] They were all amazed and confused. They asked each other, "What does this mean?"

[13] But others were making fun of them, saying, "They have had too much wine."

[14] But Peter stood up with the 11 apostles.[d] In a loud voice he spoke to the crowd: "My fellow Jews, and all of you who are in Jerusalem, listen to me. Pay attention to what I have to say. [15] These men are not drunk, as you think; it is only nine o'clock in the morning! [16] But Joel the prophet[d] wrote about what is happening here today:

[17] 'God says: In the last days
I will give my Spirit[d] freely to all kinds of people.
Your sons and daughters will prophesy.[d]
Your old men will dream dreams.
Your young men will see visions.
[18] At that time I will give my Spirit even to my servants, both men and women.
And they will prophesy.
[19] I will show miracles[d]
in the sky and on the earth:
blood, fire and thick smoke.
[20] The sun will become dark.
The moon will become red as blood.
And then the great and glorious day of the Lord will come.
[21] Then anyone who asks the Lord for help
will be saved.'
Joel 2:28-32

[22] "Men of Israel, listen to these words: Jesus from Nazareth was a very special man. God clearly showed this to you by the miracles,[d] wonders, and signs God did through him. You all know this, because it happened right here among you. [23] Jesus was given to you, and you killed him. With the help of evil men you nailed him to a cross. But God knew all this would happen. This was God's plan which he had made long ago. [24] God raised Jesus from death. God set him free from the pain of death. Death could not hold him. [25] For David said this about him:

'I keep the Lord before me always.
Because he is close by my side,
I will not be hurt.

2:7 from Galilee The people thought men from Galilee could speak only their own language.

[26]So I am glad, and I rejoice.

    Even my body has hope.
[27]This is because you will not leave
    me in the grave.

    You will not let your Holy One
    rot.
[28]You will teach me God's way to
    live.

    Being with you will fill me with
    joy.'   *Psalm 16:8-11*
[29]"Brothers, I can tell you truly about
David, our ancestor. He died and was
buried. His grave is still here with us
today. [30]David was a prophet[d] and knew
what God had said. God had promised
David that he would make a person from
David's family a king just as he was.[n]
[31]David knew this before it happened.
That is why he said:

    'He was not left in the grave.

    His body did not rot.'
David was talking about the Christ[d] rising from death. [32]So Jesus is the One
who God raised from death! And we are
all witnesses to this. [33]Jesus was lifted
up to heaven and is now at God's right
side. The Father has given the Holy
Spirit[d] to Jesus as he promised. So now
Jesus has poured out that Spirit. This is
what you see and hear. [34]David was not
the one who was lifted up to heaven. But
he said:

    'The Lord said to my Lord:

      Sit by me at my right side,
   35   until I put your enemies under
      your control.'[n]   *Psalm 110:1*
[36]"So, all the people of Israel should
know this truly: God has made Jesus
both Lord and Christ. He is the man you
nailed to the cross!"
[37]When the people heard this, they
were sick at heart. They asked Peter and
the other apostles, "What shall we do?"
[38]Peter said to them, "Change your
hearts and lives and be baptized, each
one of you, in the name of Jesus Christ
for the forgiveness of your sins. And you
will receive the gift of the Holy Spirit.
[39]This promise is for you. It is also for
your children and for all who are far
away. It is for everyone the Lord our God
calls to himself."
[40]Peter warned them with many other
words. He begged them, "Save yourselves from the evil of today's people!"
[41]Then those people who accepted what

Peter said were baptized. About 3,000
people were added to the number of believers that day. [42]They spent their time
learning the apostles' teaching. And
they continued to share, to break
bread,[n] and to pray together.
[43]The apostles[d] were doing many miracles[d] and signs. And everyone felt great
respect for God. [44]All the believers
stayed together. They shared everything. [45]They sold their land and the
things they owned. Then they divided
the money and gave it to those people
who needed it. [46]The believers met together in the Temple[d] every day. They
all had the same purpose. They broke
bread in their homes, happy to share
their food with joyful hearts. [47]They
praised God, and all the people liked
them. More and more people were being
saved every day; the Lord was adding
those people to the group of believers.

3 One day Peter and John went to the
   Temple.[d] It was three o'clock in the
afternoon. This was the time for the
daily prayer service. [2]There, at the Temple gate called Beautiful Gate, was a
man who had been crippled all his life.
Every day he was carried to this gate to
beg. He would ask for money from the
people going into the Temple. [3]The man
saw Peter and John going into the Temple and asked them for money. [4]Peter
and John looked straight at him and
said, "Look at us!" [5]The man looked at
them; he thought they were going to
give him some money. [6]But Peter said,
"I don't have any silver or gold, but I do
have something else I can give you: By
the power of Jesus Christ from Nazareth—stand up and walk!" [7]Then Peter
took the man's right hand and lifted him
up. Immediately the man's feet and ankles became strong. [8]He jumped up,
stood on his feet, and began to walk. He
went into the Temple with them, walking and jumping, and praising God.
[9-10]All the people recognized him. They
knew he was the crippled man who always sat by the Beautiful Gate begging
for money. Now they saw this same man
walking and praising God. The people
were amazed. They could not understand how this could happen.
[11]The man was holding on to Peter and
John. All the people were amazed and

2:30 God . . . was. See 2 Samuel 7:13; Psalm 132:11. 2:35 until . . . control Literally, "until I
make my enemies a footstool for your feet." 2:42 break bread This may mean a meal as in
verse 46, or the Lord's Supper, the special meal Jesus told his followers to eat to remember
him (Luke 22:14-20).

ran to Peter and John at Solomon's Porch.[d] [12]When Peter saw this, he said to them, "Men of Israel, why are you surprised? You are looking at us as if it were our own power that made this man walk. Do you think this happened because we are good? No! [13]The God of Abraham, Isaac and Jacob, the God of our ancestors, gave glory to Jesus, his servant. But you gave him up to be killed. Pilate decided to let him go free. But you told Pilate you did not want Jesus. [14]He was pure and good, but you said you did not want him. You told Pilate to give you a murderer[n] instead of Jesus. [15]And so you killed the One who gives life! But God raised him from death. We are witnesses to this. [16]It was the power of Jesus that made this crippled man well. This happened because we trusted in the power of Jesus. You can see this man, and you know him. He was made completely well because of trust in Jesus. You all saw it happen!

[17]"Brothers, I know you did those things to Jesus because you did not understand what you were doing. Your leaders did not understand either. [18]God said this would happen. He said through the prophets[d] that his Christ[d] would suffer and die. And now God has made these things come true in this way. [19]So you must change your hearts and lives! Come back to God, and he will forgive your sins. [20]Then the Lord will give you times of spiritual rest. He will give you Jesus, the One he chose to be the Christ. [21]But Jesus must stay in heaven until the time comes when all things will be made right again. God told about this time long ago when he spoke through his holy prophets. [22]Moses said, 'The Lord your God will give you a prophet like me. He will be one of your own people. You must obey everything he tells you. [23]Anyone who does not obey him will die, separated from God's people.'[n] [24]Samuel, and all the other prophets who spoke for God after Samuel, told about this time now. [25]You have received what the prophets talked about. You have received the agreement God made with your ancestors. He said to your father Abraham, 'Through your descendants[d] all the nations on the earth will be blessed.'[n] [26]God has raised up his servant and sent him to you first. He sent

Jesus to bless you by turning each of you away from doing evil things."

4 While Peter and John were speaking to the people, a group of men came up to them. There were Jewish priests, the captain of the soldiers that guarded the Temple,[d] and some Sadducees.[d] [2]They were upset because the two apostles[d] were teaching the people. Peter and John were preaching that people will rise from death through the power of Jesus. [3]The Jewish leaders grabbed Peter and John and put them in jail. It was already night, so they kept them in jail until the next day. [4]But many of those who heard Peter and John preach believed the things they said. There were now about 5,000 men in the group of believers.

[5]The next day the Jewish leaders, the older Jewish leaders, and the teachers of the law met in Jerusalem. [6]Annas the high priest, Caiaphas, John, and Alexander were there. Everyone from the high priest's family was there. [7]They made Peter and John stand before them. The Jewish leaders asked them: "By what power or authority did you do this?"

[8]Then Peter was filled with the Holy Spirit.[d] He said to them, "Rulers of the people and you older leaders, [9]are you questioning us about a good thing that was done to a crippled man? Are you asking us who made him well? [10]We want all of you and all the Jewish people to know that this man was made well by the power of Jesus Christ from Nazareth! You nailed him to a cross, but God raised him from death. This man was crippled, but he is now well and able to stand here before you because of the power of Jesus! [11]Jesus is

'the stone[n] that you builders did not want.

It has become the cornerstone.'[d]

Psalm 118:22

[12]Jesus is the only One who can save people. His name is the only power in the world that has been given to save people. And we must be saved through him!"

[13]The Jewish leaders saw that Peter and John were not afraid to speak. They understood that these men had no special training or education. So they were amazed. Then they realized that Peter

---

3:14 murderer Barabbas, the man the Jews asked Pilate to let go free instead of Jesus (Luke 23:18).   **3:22-23 'The Lord . . . people.'** Quotation from Deuteronomy 18:15, 19.   **3:25 'Through . . . blessed.'** Quotation from Genesis 22:18; 26:24.   **4:11 stone** A symbol meaning Jesus.

and John had been with Jesus. [14]They saw the crippled man standing there beside the two apostles. They saw that the man was healed. So they could say nothing against them. [15]The Jewish leaders told them to leave the meeting. Then the leaders talked to each other about what they should do. [16]They said, "What shall we do with these men? Everyone in Jerusalem knows that they have done a great miracle![d] We cannot say it is not true. [17]But we must warn them not to talk to people anymore using that name. Then this thing will not spread among the people."

[18]So they called Peter and John in again. They told them not to speak or to teach at all in the name of Jesus. [19]But Peter and John answered them, "What do you think is right? What would God want? Should we obey you or God? [20]We cannot keep quiet. We must speak about what we have seen and heard." [21-22]The Jewish leaders could not find a way to punish them because all the people were praising God for what had been done. (This miracle was a proof from God. The man who was healed was more than 40 years old!) So the Jewish leaders warned the apostles again and let them go free.

[23]Peter and John left the meeting of Jewish leaders and went to their own group. They told them everything that the leading priests and the older Jewish leaders had said to them. [24]When the believers heard this, they prayed to God with one purpose. They prayed, "Lord, you are the One who made the sky, the earth, the sea, and everything in the world. [25]Our father David was your servant. With the help of the Holy Spirit[d] he said:

'Why are the nations so angry?
    Why are the people making
        useless plans?
[26]The kings of the earth prepare to
    fight.
    Their leaders make plans
        together
  against the Lord
    and against his Christ.'[d]   *Psalm 2:1-2*

[27]These things really happened when Herod, Pontius Pilate, the non-Jewish people, and the Jewish people all came together against Jesus here in Jerusalem. Jesus is your holy Servant. He is the One you made to be the Christ. [28]These people made your plan happen; it happened because of your power and your will. [29]And now, Lord, listen to what they are saying. They are trying to make us afraid! Lord, we are your servants. Help us to speak your word without fear. [30]Help us to be brave by showing us your power; make sick people well, give proofs, and make miracles[d] happen by the power of Jesus, your holy servant."

[31]After they had prayed, the place where they were meeting was shaken. They were all filled with the Holy Spirit,[d] and they spoke God's word without fear.

[32]The group of believers were joined in their hearts, and they had the same spirit. No person in the group said that the things he had were his own. Instead, they shared everything. [33]With great power the apostles[d] were telling people that the Lord Jesus was truly raised from death. And God blessed all the believers very much. [34]They all received the things they needed. Everyone that owned fields or houses sold them. They brought the money [35]and gave it to the apostles. Then each person was given the things he needed.

[36]One of the believers was named Joseph. The apostles called him Barnabas. (This name means "one who encourages.") He was a Levite, born in Cyprus. [37]Joseph owned a field. He sold it, brought the money, and gave it to the apostles.

5 A man named Ananias and his wife Sapphira sold some land. [2]But he gave only part of the money to the apostles.[d] He secretly kept some of it for himself. His wife knew about this, and she agreed to it. [3]Peter said, "Ananias, why did you let Satan rule your heart? You lied to the Holy Spirit.[d] Why did you keep part of the money you received for the land for yourself? [4]Before you sold the land, it belonged to you. And even after you sold it, you could have used the money any way you wanted. Why did you think of doing this? You lied to God, not to men!" [5-6]When Ananias heard this, he fell down and died. Some young men came in, wrapped up his body, carried it out, and buried it. And everyone who heard about this was filled with fear.

[7]About three hours later his wife came in. She did not know what had happened. [8]Peter said to her, "Tell me how much money you got for your field. Was it this much?"

Sapphira answered, "Yes, that was the price."

[9]Peter said to her, "Why did you and

your husband agree to test the Spirit of the Lord? Look! The men who buried your husband are at the door! They will carry you out." [10]At that moment Sapphira fell down by his feet and died. The young men came in and saw that she was dead. They carried her out and buried her beside her husband. [11]The whole church and all the others who heard about these things were filled with fear.

[12]The apostles[d] did many signs and miracles[d] among the people. And they would all meet together on Solomon's Porch.[d] [13]None of the others dared to stand with them. All the people were saying good things about them. [14]More and more men and women believed in the Lord and were added to the group of believers. [15]As Peter was passing by, the people brought their sick into the streets. They put their sick on beds and mats so at least Peter's shadow might fall on them. [16]Crowds came from all the towns around Jerusalem. They brought their sick and those who were bothered by evil spirits. All of them were healed.

[17]The high priest and all his friends (a group called the Sadducees[d]) became very jealous. [18]They took the apostles[d] and put them in jail. [19]But during the night, an angel of the Lord opened the doors of the jail. He led the apostles outside and said, [20]"Go and stand in the Temple.[d] Tell the people everything about this new life." [21]When the apostles heard this, they obeyed and went into the Temple. It was early in the morning, and they began to teach.

The high priest and his friends arrived. They called a meeting of the Jewish leaders and all the important older men of the Jews. They sent some men to the jail to bring the apostles to them. [22]When the men went to the jail, they could not find the apostles. So they went back and told the Jewish leaders about this. [23]They said, "The jail was closed and locked. The guards were standing at the doors. But when we opened the doors, the jail was empty!" [24]Hearing this, the captain of the Temple guards and the leading priests were confused. They wondered, "What will happen because of this?"

[25]Then someone came and told them, "Listen! The men you put in jail are standing in the Temple. They are teaching the people!" [26]Then the captain and his men went out and brought the apos-

tles back. But the soldiers did not use force, because they were afraid that the people would kill them with stones.

[27]The soldiers brought the apostles to the meeting and made them stand before the Jewish leaders. The high priest questioned them. [28]He said, "We gave you strict orders not to go on teaching in that name. But look what you have done! You have filled Jerusalem with your teaching. You are trying to make us responsible for this man's death."

[29]Peter and the other apostles answered, "We must obey God, not men! [30]You killed Jesus. You hung him on a cross. But God, the same God our ancestors had, raised Jesus up from death! [31]Jesus is the One whom God raised to be on his right side. God made Jesus our Leader and Savior. God did this so that all Jews could change their hearts and lives and have their sins forgiven. [32]We saw all these things happen. The Holy Spirit[d] also proves that these things are true. God has given the Spirit to all who obey him."

[33]When the Jewish leaders heard this, they became very angry and wanted to kill them. [34]A Pharisee[d] named Gamaliel stood up in the meeting. He was a teacher of the law, and all the people respected him. He ordered the apostles to leave the meeting for a little while. [35]Then he said to them, "Men of Israel, be careful of what you are planning to do to these men! [36]Remember when Theudas appeared? He said that he was a great man, and about 400 men joined him. But he was killed. And all his followers were scattered. They were able to do nothing. [37]Later, a man named Judas came from Galilee at the time of the registration.[n] He led a group of followers, too. He was also killed, and all his followers were scattered. [38]And so now I tell you: Stay away from these men. Leave them alone. If their plan comes from men, it will fail. [39]But if it is from God, you will not be able to stop them. You might even be fighting against God himself!"

The Jewish leaders agreed with what Gamaliel said. [40]They called the apostles in again. They beat the apostles and told them not to speak in the name of Jesus again. Then they let them go free. [41]The apostles left the meeting full of joy because they were given the honor of suffering disgrace for Jesus. [42]The apostles

---

5:37 registration Census. A counting of all the people and the things they own.

did not stop teaching people. Every day in the Temple and in people's homes they continued to tell the Good News—that Jesus is the Christ.[d]

6 More and more people were becoming followers of Jesus. But during this same time, the Greek-speaking followers had an argument with the other Jewish followers. The Greek-speaking Jews said that their widows were not getting their share of the food that was given out every day. [2]The 12 apostles[d] called the whole group of followers together. They said, "It is not right for us to stop our work of teaching God's word in order to serve tables. [3]So, brothers, choose seven of your own men. They must be men who are good. They must be full of wisdom and full of the Spirit.[d] We will put them in charge of this work. [4]Then we can use all our time to pray and to teach the word of God."

[5]The whole group liked the idea. So they chose these seven men: Stephen (a man with great faith and full of the Holy Spirit), Philip,[n] Procorus, Nicanor, Timon, Parmenas, and Nicolas (a man from Antioch who had become a Jew). [6]Then they put these men before the apostles. The apostles prayed and laid their hands on[n] the men.

[7]The word of God was reaching more and more people. The group of followers in Jerusalem became larger and larger. A great number of the Jewish priests believed and obeyed.

[8]Stephen was richly blessed by God. God gave him the power to do great miracles[d] and signs among the people. [9]But some Jews were against him. They belonged to a synagogue[d] of Free Men[n] (as it was called). (This synagogue was also for Jews from Cyrene and from Alexandria.) Jews from Cilicia and Asia were also with them. They all came and argued with Stephen.

[10]But the Spirit[d] was helping him to speak with wisdom. His words were so strong that they could not argue with him. [11]So they paid some men to say, "We heard him say things against Moses and against God!"

[12]This upset the people, the older Jewish leaders, and the teachers of the law. They came to Stephen, grabbed him and brought him to a meeting of the Jewish

leaders. [13]They brought in some men to tell lies about Stephen. They said, "This man is always saying things against this holy place and the law of Moses. [14]We heard him say that Jesus from Nazareth will destroy this place. He also said that Jesus will change the things that Moses told us to do." [15]All the people in the meeting were watching Stephen closely. His face looked like the face of an angel.

7 The high priest said to Stephen, "Are these things true?"

[2]Stephen answered, "Brothers and fathers, listen to me. Our glorious God appeared to Abraham, our ancestor. Abraham was in Mesopotamia before he lived in Haran. [3]God said to Abraham, 'Leave your country and your relatives. Go to the land I will show you.'[n] [4]So Abraham left the country of Chaldea and went to live in Haran. After Abraham's father died, God sent him to this place where you now live. [5]God did not give Abraham any of this land, not even a foot of it. But God promised that he would give him and his descendants[d] this land. (This was before Abraham had any descendants.) [6]This is what God said to him: 'Your descendants will be strangers in a land they don't own. The people there will make them slaves. And they will do cruel things to them for 400 years. [7]But I will punish the nation where they are slaves. Then your descendants will leave that land. Then they will worship me in this place.'[n] [8]God made an agreement with Abraham; the sign for this agreement was circumcision.[d] And so when Abraham had his son Isaac, Abraham circumcised him when he was eight days old. Isaac also circumcised his son Jacob. And Jacob did the same for his sons, the 12 ancestors[n] of our people.

[9]"These sons became jealous of Joseph. They sold him to be a slave in Egypt. But God was with him. [10]Joseph had many troubles there, but God saved him from all those troubles. The king of Egypt liked Joseph and respected him because of the wisdom that God gave him. The king made him governor of Egypt. He put Joseph in charge of all the people in his palace.

[11]"Then all the land of Egypt and of Canaan became so dry that nothing

---

6:5 Philip Not the apostle named Philip.   **6:6 laid their hands on** Here, doing this showed that these men were given a special work of God.   **6:9 Free Men** Jews who had been slaves or whose fathers had been slaves, but were now free.   **7:3 'Leave . . . you.'** Quotation from Genesis 12:1.   **7:6-7 'Your descendants . . . place.'** Quotation from Genesis 15:13-14 and Exodus 3:12. **7:8 12 ancestors** Important ancestors of the Jews; the leaders of the 12 Jewish tribes.

would grow there. This made the people suffer very much. The sons could not find anything to eat. [12]But when Jacob heard that there was grain in Egypt, he sent his sons, our ancestors, there. This was their first trip to Egypt. [13]Then they went there a second time. This time, Joseph told his brothers who he was. And the king learned about Joseph's family. [14]Then Joseph sent some men to invite Jacob, his father, to come to Egypt. He also invited all his relatives (75 persons altogether). [15]So Jacob went down to Egypt, where he and his sons died. [16]Later their bodies were moved to Shechem and put in a grave there. (It was the same grave that Abraham had bought in Shechem from the sons of Hamor for a sum of money.)

[17]"The number of people in Egypt grew large. There were more and more of our people there. (The promise that God made to Abraham was soon to come true.) [18]Then a new king began to rule Egypt. He did not know who Joseph was. [19]This king tricked our people and was cruel to our ancestors. He forced them to put their babies outside to die. [20]This was the time when Moses was born. He was a fine child. For three months Moses was cared for in his father's house. [21]When they put Moses outside, the king's daughter took him. She raised him as if he were her own son. [22]The Egyptians taught Moses all the things they knew. He was a powerful man in the things he said and did.

[23]"When Moses was about 40 years old, he thought it would be good to visit his brothers, the people of Israel. [24]Moses saw an Egyptian doing wrong to a Jew. So he defended the Jew and punished the Egyptian for hurting him. Moses killed the Egyptian. [25]Moses thought that his fellow Jews would understand that God was using him to save them. But they did not understand. [26]The next day, Moses saw two Jewish men fighting. He tried to make peace between them. He said, 'Men, you are brothers! Why are you hurting each other?' [27]The man who was hurting the other man pushed Moses away. He said, 'Who made you our ruler and judge? [28]Are you going to kill me as you killed the Egyptian yesterday?'[n] [29]When Moses heard

him say this, he left Egypt. He went to live in the land of Midian where he was a stranger. While Moses lived in Midian, he had two sons.

[30]"After 40 years Moses was in the desert near Mount Sinai. An angel appeared to him in the flames of a burning bush. [31]When Moses saw this, he was amazed. He went near to look closer at it. Moses heard the Lord's voice. [32]The Lord said, 'I am the God of your ancestors. I am the God of Abraham, Isaac and Jacob.'[n] Moses began to shake with fear and was afraid to look. [33]The Lord said to him, 'Take off your sandals. You are standing on holy ground. [34]I have seen the troubles my people have suffered in Egypt. I have heard their cries. I have come down to save them. And now, Moses, I am sending you back to Egypt.'[n]

[35]"This Moses was the same man the Jews said they did not want. They had said to him, 'Who made you our ruler and judge?'[n] Moses is the same man God sent to be a ruler and savior, with the help of an angel. This was the angel Moses saw in the burning bush. [36]So Moses led the people out of Egypt. He worked miracles[d] and signs in Egypt, at the Red Sea,[d] and then in the desert for 40 years. [37]This is the same Moses that said to the Jewish people: 'God will give you a prophet[d] like me. He will be one of your own people.'[n] [38]This is the same Moses who was with the gathering of the Jews in the desert. He was with the angel that spoke to him at Mount Sinai, and he was with our ancestors. He received commands from God that give life, and he gave those commands to us.

[39]"But our fathers did not want to obey Moses. They rejected him. They wanted to go back to Egypt again. [40]They said to Aaron, 'Moses led us out of Egypt. But we don't know what has happened to him. So make us gods who will lead us.'[n] [41]So the people made an idol that looked like a calf. Then they brought sacrifices to it. The people were proud of what they had made with their own hands! [42]But God turned against them. He did not try to stop them from worshiping the sun, moon and stars. This is what is written in the book of the prophets: God says,

7:27-28 'Who . . . yesterday?' Quotation from Exodus 2:14. 7:32 'I am . . . Jacob.' Quotation from Exodus 3:6. 7:33-34 'Take . . . Egypt.' Quotation from Exodus 3:5-10. 7:35 'Who . . . judge?' Quotation from Exodus 2:14. 7:37 'God . . . people.' Quotation from Deuteronomy 18:15. 7:40 'Moses . . . us.' Quotation from Exodus 32:1.

'People of Israel, you did not bring
me sacrifices and offerings
while you traveled in the desert
for 40 years.
⁴³But now you will have to carry with
you
the tent to worship the false god
Molech[d]
and the idols of the star god
Rephan that you made to
worship.
This is because I will send you
away beyond Babylon.'

Amos 5:25-27

⁴⁴"The Holy Tent[d] where God spoke
to our fathers was with the Jews in the
desert. God told Moses how to make this
Tent. He made it like the plan God
showed him. ⁴⁵Later, Joshua led our fathers to capture the lands of the other
nations. Our people went in, and God
drove the other people out. When our
people went into this new land, they
took with them this same Tent. They received this Tent from their fathers and
kept it until the time of David. ⁴⁶God was
very pleased with David. He asked God
to let him build a house for him, the God
of Jacob. ⁴⁷But Solomon was the one
who built the Temple.[d]

⁴⁸"But the Most High does not live in
houses that men build with their hands.
This is what the prophet says:
⁴⁹'Heaven is my throne.
The earth is my footstool.
So do you think you can build a
house for me? says the Lord.
There is no place where I need to
rest.
⁵⁰Remember, I made all these
things!'"

Isaiah 66:1-2

⁵¹Stephen continued speaking: "You
stubborn Jewish leaders! You have not
given your hearts to God! You won't listen to him! You are always against what
the Holy Spirit[d] is trying to tell you. Your
ancestors were like this, and you are just
like them! ⁵²Your fathers tried to hurt
every prophet who ever lived. Those
prophets said long ago that the Righteous One would come. But your fathers
killed them. And now you have turned
against the Righteous One and killed
him. ⁵³You received the law of Moses,
which God gave you through his angels.
But you don't obey it!"

⁵⁴When the leaders heard Stephen
saying all these things, they became
very angry. They were so mad that they

were grinding their teeth at Stephen.
⁵⁵But Stephen was full of the Holy
Spirit.[d] He looked up to heaven and saw
the glory of God. He saw Jesus standing
at God's right side. ⁵⁶He said, "Look! I
see heaven open. And I see the Son of
Man[d] standing at God's right side!"

⁵⁷Then they all shouted loudly. They
covered their ears with their hands and
all ran at Stephen. ⁵⁸They took him out
of the city and threw stones at him until
he was dead. The men who told lies
against Stephen left their coats with a
young man named Saul. ⁵⁹While they
were throwing stones, Stephen prayed,
"Lord Jesus, receive my spirit!" ⁶⁰He fell
on his knees and cried in a loud voice,
"Lord, do not hold this sin against
them!" After Stephen said this, he died.

8 Saul agreed that the killing of Stephen was a good thing.
²⁻³Some religious men buried Ste-
phen. They cried very loudly for him.
On that day people began trying to hurt
the church in Jerusalem and make it suffer. Saul was also trying to destroy the
church. He went from house to house.
He dragged out men and women and put
them in jail. All the believers, except the
apostles,[d] went to different places in Judea and Samaria. ⁴And everywhere they
were scattered, they told people the
Good News.[d]

⁵Philip[n] went to the city of Samaria
and preached about the Christ.[d] ⁶The
people there heard Philip and saw the
miracles[d] he was doing. They all listened
carefully to the things he said. ⁷Many of
these people had evil spirits in them. But
Philip made the evil spirits leave them.
The spirits made a loud noise when they
came out. There were also many weak
and crippled people there. Philip healed
them, too. ⁸So the people in that city
were very happy.

⁹But there was a man named Simon
in that city. Before Philip came there,
Simon had practiced magic. He amazed
all the people of Samaria with his
magic. He bragged and called himself a
great man. ¹⁰All the people—the least
important and the most important—
paid attention to what Simon said. They
said, "This man has the power of God,
called 'the Great Power'!" ¹¹Simon had
amazed them with his magic tricks so
long that the people became his followers. ¹²But Philip told them the Good
News[d] about the kingdom of God and

8:5 **Philip** Not the apostle named Philip.

the power of Jesus Christ. Men and women believed Philip and were baptized. [13]Simon himself believed and was baptized. He stayed very close to Philip. When he saw the miracles and the very powerful things that Philip did, Simon was amazed.

[14]The apostles[d] were still in Jerusalem. They heard that the people of Samaria had accepted the word of God. So they sent Peter and John to them. [15]When Peter and John arrived, they prayed that the Samaritan believers might receive the Holy Spirit.[d] [16]These people had been baptized in the name of the Lord Jesus. But the Holy Spirit had not yet entered any of them. [17]Then, when the two apostles began laying their hands on[n] the people, they received the Holy Spirit.

[18]Simon saw that the Spirit was given to people when the apostles laid their hands on them. So he offered the apostles money. [19]He said, "Give me also this power so that when I lay my hands on a person, he will receive the Holy Spirit."

[20]Peter said to him, "You and your money should both be destroyed! You thought you could buy God's gift with money. [21]You cannot share with us in this work. Your heart is not right before God. [22]Change your heart! Turn away from this evil thing you have done. Pray to the Lord. Maybe he will forgive you for thinking this. [23]I see that you are full of bitter jealousy and ruled by sin."

[24]Simon answered, "Both of you pray for me to the Lord. Pray that the things you have said will not happen to me!"

[25]Then the two apostles told the people the things they had seen Jesus do. And after the apostles had given the message of the Lord, they went back to Jerusalem. On the way, they went through many Samaritan towns and preached the Good News to the people.

[26]An angel of the Lord spoke to Philip.[n] The angel said, "Get ready and go south. Go to the road that leads down to Gaza from Jerusalem—the desert road." [27]So Philip got ready and went. On the road he saw a man from Ethiopia, a eunuch.[d] He was an important officer in the service of Candace, the queen of the Ethiopians. He was responsible for taking care of all her money.

He had gone to Jerusalem to worship, and [28]now he was on his way home. He was sitting in his chariot and reading from the book of Isaiah, the prophet.[d] [29]The Spirit[d] said to Philip, "Go to that chariot and stay near it."

[30]So Philip ran toward the chariot. He heard the man reading from Isaiah, the prophet. Philip asked, "Do you understand what you are reading?"

[31]He answered, "How can I understand? I need someone to explain it to me!" Then he invited Philip to climb in and sit with him. [32]The verse of Scripture[d] that he was reading was this:

> "He was like a sheep being led to
> be killed.
> He was quiet, as a sheep is quiet
> while its wool is being cut.
> He said nothing.
> [33] He was shamed and was treated
> unfairly.
> He died without children to
> continue his family.
> His life on earth has ended."
>
> *Isaiah 53:7-8*

[34]The officer said to Philip, "Please tell me, who is the prophet talking about? Is he talking about himself or about someone else?" [35]Philip began to speak. He started with this same Scripture and told the man the Good News[d] about Jesus.

[36]While they were traveling down the road, they came to some water. The officer said, "Look! Here is water! What is stopping me from being baptized?" [37] [n] [38]Then the officer commanded the chariot to stop. Both Philip and the officer went down into the water, and Philip baptized him. [39]When they came up out of the water, the Spirit of the Lord took Philip away; the officer never saw him again. The officer continued on his way home, full of joy. [40]But Philip appeared in a city called Azotus and preached the Good News in all the towns on the way from Azotus to Caesarea.

9 In Jerusalem Saul was still trying to frighten the followers of the Lord by saying he would kill them. So he went to the high priest [2]and asked him to write letters to the synagogues[d] in the city of Damascus. Saul wanted the high priest to give him the authority to find people in Damascus who were followers of

---

8:17 laying their hands on Here, doing this showed that these men were given a special work of God. **8:26 Philip** Not the apostle named Philip. **8:37 Verse 37** Some late copies of Acts add verse 37: "Philip answered, 'If you believe with all your heart, you can.' The officer said, 'I believe that Jesus Christ is the Son of God.'"

Christ's Way. If he found any there, men or women, he would arrest them and bring them back to Jerusalem.

[3] So Saul went to Damascus. As he came near the city, a bright light from heaven suddenly flashed around him. [4] Saul fell to the ground. He heard a voice saying to him, "Saul, Saul! Why are you doing things against me?"

[5] Saul said, "Who are you, Lord?"

The voice answered, "I am Jesus. I am the One you are trying to hurt. [6] Get up now and go into the city. Someone there will tell you what you must do."

[7] The men traveling with Saul stood there, but they said nothing. They heard the voice, but they saw no one. [8] Saul got up from the ground. He opened his eyes, but he could not see. So the men with Saul took his hand and led him into Damascus. [9] For three days Saul could not see, and he did not eat or drink.

[10] There was a follower of Jesus in Damascus named Ananias. The Lord spoke to Ananias in a vision, "Ananias!"

Ananias answered, "Here I am, Lord."

[11] The Lord said to him, "Get up and go to the street called Straight Street. Find the house of Judas.[n] Ask for a man named Saul from the city of Tarsus. He is there now, praying. [12] Saul has seen a vision. In it a man named Ananias comes to him and lays his hands on him. Then he sees again."

[13] But Ananias answered, "Lord, many people have told me about this man and the terrible things he did to your people in Jerusalem. [14] Now he has come here to Damascus. The leading priests have given him the power to arrest everyone who worships you."

[15] But the Lord said to Ananias, "Go! I have chosen Saul for an important work. He must tell about me to non-Jews, to kings, and to the people of Israel. [16] I will show him how much he must suffer for my name."

[17] So Ananias went to the house of Judas. He laid his hands on Saul and said, "Brother Saul, the Lord Jesus sent me. He is the one you saw on the road on your way here. He sent me so that you can see again and be filled with the Holy Spirit."[d] [18] Immediately, something that looked like fish scales fell from Saul's eyes. He was able to see again! Then Saul got up and was baptized. [19] After eating some food, his strength returned.

Saul stayed with the followers of Jesus in Damascus for a few days. [20] Soon he began to preach about Jesus in the synagogues,[d] saying, "Jesus is the Son of God!"

[21] All the people who heard him were amazed. They said, "This is the man who was in Jerusalem. He was trying to destroy those who trust in this name! He came here to do the same thing. He came here to arrest the followers of Jesus and take them back to the leading priests."

[22] But Saul became more and more powerful. His proofs that Jesus is the Christ[d] were so strong that the Jews in Damascus could not argue with him.

[23] After many days, the Jews made plans to kill Saul. [24] They were watching the city gates day and night. They wanted to kill him, but Saul learned about their plan. [25] One night some followers of Saul helped him leave the city. They lowered him in a basket through an opening in the city wall.

[26] Then Saul went to Jerusalem. He tried to join the group of followers, but they were all afraid of him. They did not believe that he was really a follower. [27] But Barnabas accepted Saul and took him to the apostles.[d] Barnabas told them that Saul had seen the Lord on the road. He explained how the Lord had spoken to Saul. Then he told them how boldly Saul had preached in the name of Jesus in Damascus.

[28] And so Saul stayed with the followers. He went everywhere in Jerusalem, preaching boldly in the name of Jesus. [29] He would often talk and argue with the Jews who spoke Greek. But they were trying to kill him. [30] When the brothers learned about this, they took Saul to Caesarea. From there they sent him to Tarsus.

[31] The church everywhere in Judea, Galilee, and Samaria had a time of peace. With the help of the Holy Spirit,[d] the group became stronger. The believers showed that they respected the Lord by the way they lived. Because of this, the group of believers grew larger and larger.

[32] As Peter was traveling through all the area, he visited God's people who lived in Lydda. [33] There he met a paralyzed man named Aeneas. Aeneas had not been able to leave his bed for the past eight years. [34] Peter said to him, "Aeneas, Jesus Christ heals you. Stand up

9:11 Judas This is not either of the apostles named Judas.

and make your bed!" Aeneas stood up immediately. [35]All the people living in Lydda and on the Plain of Sharon saw him. These people turned to the Lord.

[36]In the city of Joppa there was a follower named Tabitha. (Her Greek name, Dorcas, means "a deer.") She was always doing good and helping the poor. [37]While Peter was in Lydda, Tabitha became sick and died. Her body was washed and put in a room upstairs. [38]The followers in Joppa heard that Peter was in Lydda. (Lydda is near Joppa.) So they sent two men to Peter. They begged him, "Hurry, please come to us!" [39]Peter got ready and went with them. When he arrived, they took him to the upstairs room. All the widows stood around Peter, crying. They showed him the shirts and coats that Tabitha had made when she was still alive. [40]Peter sent everyone out of the room. He kneeled and prayed. Then he turned to the body and said, "Tabitha, stand up!" She opened her eyes, and when she saw Peter, she sat up. [41]He gave her his hand and helped her up. Then he called the saints[d] and the widows into the room. He showed them Tabitha; she was alive! [42]People everywhere in Joppa learned about this, and many believed in the Lord. [43]Peter stayed in Joppa for many days with a man named Simon who was a leatherworker.

10 At Caesarea there was a man named Cornelius. He was an officer in the Italian group of the Roman army. [2]Cornelius was a religious man. He and all the other people who lived in his house worshiped the true God. He gave much of his money to the poor and prayed to God often. [3]One afternoon about three o'clock, Cornelius saw a vision clearly. In the vision an angel of God came to him and said, "Cornelius!"

[4]Cornelius stared at the angel. He became afraid and said, "What do you want, Lord?"

The angel said, "God has heard your prayers. He has seen what you give to the poor. And God remembers you. [5]Send some men now to Joppa to bring back a man named Simon. Simon is also called Peter. [6]Simon is staying with a man, also named Simon, who is a leatherworker. He has a house beside the sea." [7]Then the angel who spoke to

Cornelius left. Cornelius called two of his servants and a soldier. The soldier was a religious man who worked for Cornelius. [8]Cornelius explained everything to these three men and sent them to Joppa.

[9]The next day as they came near Joppa, Peter was going up to the roof[n] to pray. It was about noon. [10]Peter was hungry and wanted to eat. But while the food was being prepared, he had a vision. [11]He saw heaven opened and something coming down. It looked like a big sheet being lowered to earth by its four corners. [12]In it were all kinds of animals, reptiles, and birds. [13]Then a voice said to Peter, "Get up, Peter; kill and eat."

[14]But Peter said, "No, Lord! I have never eaten food that is unholy or unclean."[d]

[15]But the voice said to him again, "God has made these things clean. Don't call them 'unholy'!" [16]This happened three times. Then the sheet was taken back to heaven.

[17]While Peter was wondering what this vision meant, the men Cornelius sent had found Simon's house. They were standing at the gate. [18]They asked, "Is Simon Peter staying here?"

[19]Peter was still thinking about the vision. But the Spirit[d] said to him, "Listen! Three men are looking for you. [20]Get up and go downstairs. Go with them and don't ask questions. I have sent them to you."

[21]So Peter went down to the men. He said, "I am the man you are looking for. Why did you come here?"

[22]They said, "A holy angel spoke to Cornelius, an army officer. He is a good man; he worships God. All the Jewish people respect him. The angel told Cornelius to ask you to his house so that he can hear what you have to say." [23]Peter asked the men to come in and spend the night.

The next day Peter got ready and went with them. Some of the brothers from Joppa joined him. [24]On the following day they came to Caesarea. Cornelius was waiting for them. He had called together his relatives and close friends. [25]When Peter entered, Cornelius met him. He fell at Peter's feet and worshiped him. [26]But Peter helped him up, saying, "Stand up! I too am only a man." [27]Peter went on talking with Cornelius

---

10:9 **roof** In Bible times houses were built with flat roofs. The roof was used for drying things such as flax and fruit. And it was used as an extra room, as a place for worship and as a place to sleep in the summer.

as they went inside. There Peter saw many people together. ²⁸He said, "You people understand that it is against our Jewish law for a Jew to associate with or visit anyone who is not a Jew. But God has shown me that I should not call any person 'unholy' or 'unclean.' ²⁹That is why I did not argue when I was asked to come here. Now, please tell me why you sent for me."

³⁰Cornelius said, "Four days ago, I was praying in my house. It was at this same time—three o'clock in the afternoon. Suddenly, there was a man standing before me wearing shining clothes. ³¹He said, 'Cornelius! God has heard your prayer. He has seen what you give to the poor. And God remembers you. ³²So send some men to Joppa and ask Simon Peter to come. Peter is staying in the house of a man, also named Simon, who is a leatherworker. His house is beside the sea.' ³³So I sent for you immediately, and it was very good of you to come. Now we are all here before God to hear everything the Lord has commanded you to tell us."

³⁴Peter began to speak: "I really understand now that to God every person is the same. ³⁵God accepts anyone who worships him and does what is right. It is not important what country a person comes from. ³⁶You know that God has sent his message to the people of Israel. That message is the Good News[d] that peace has come through Jesus Christ. Jesus is the Lord of all people! ³⁷You know what has happened all over Judea. It began in Galilee after John[n] preached to the people about baptism. ³⁸You know about Jesus from Nazareth. God made him the Christ[d] by giving him the Holy Spirit[d] and power. You know how Jesus went everywhere doing good. He healed those who were ruled by the devil, for God was with Jesus. ³⁹We saw all the things that Jesus did in Judea and in Jerusalem. But they killed him by nailing him to a cross. ⁴⁰Yet, on the third day, God raised Jesus to life and caused him to be seen. ⁴¹But he was not seen by all the people. Only the witnesses that God had already chosen saw him, and we are those witnesses. We ate and drank with him after he was raised from death. ⁴²He told us to preach to the people and to tell them that he is the one whom God chose to be the judge of the living and the dead. ⁴³Everyone who be-

lieves in Jesus will be forgiven. God will forgive his sins through Jesus. All the prophets[d] say this is true."

⁴⁴While Peter was still saying this, the Holy Spirit[d] came down on all those who were listening. ⁴⁵The Jewish believers who came with Peter were amazed that the gift of the Holy Spirit had been given even to the non-Jewish people. ⁴⁶These Jewish believers heard them speaking in different languages and praising God. Then Peter said, ⁴⁷"Can anyone keep these people from being baptized with water? They have received the Holy Spirit just as we did!" ⁴⁸So Peter ordered that they be baptized in the name of Jesus Christ. Then they asked Peter to stay with them for a few days.

11 The apostles[d] and the believers in Judea heard that non-Jewish people had accepted God's teaching too. ²But when Peter came to Jerusalem, some Jewish believers argued with him. ³They said, "You went into the homes of people who are not Jews and are not circumcised![d] You even ate with them!"

⁴So Peter explained the whole story to them. ⁵He said, "I was in the city of Joppa. While I was praying, I had a vision. In the vision, I saw something which looked like a big sheet coming down from heaven. It was being lowered to earth by its four corners. It came down very close to me, and ⁶I looked inside it. I saw animals, wild beasts, reptiles, and birds. ⁷I heard a voice say to me, 'Get up, Peter. Kill and eat.' ⁸But I said, 'No, Lord! I have never eaten anything that is unholy or unclean.'[d] ⁹But the voice from heaven answered again, 'God has made these things clean. Don't call them unholy!' ¹⁰This happened three times. Then the whole thing was taken back to heaven. ¹¹Right then three men came to the house where I was staying. They were sent to me from Caesarea. ¹²The Spirit[d] told me to go with them without doubting. These six believers here also went with me. We went to the house of Cornelius. ¹³He told us about the angel he saw standing in his house. The angel said to him, 'Send some men to Joppa and invite Simon Peter to come. ¹⁴He will speak to you. The things he will say will save you and all your family.' ¹⁵When I began my speech, the Holy Spirit came on them just as he came on us at the beginning. ¹⁶Then I remembered the words of the Lord. He

10:37 John John the Baptist, who preached to people about Christ's coming (Matthew 3, Luke 3).

said, 'John baptized in water, but you will be baptized in the Holy Spirit!' [17]God gave to them the same gift that he gave to us who believed in the Lord Jesus Christ. So could I stop the work of God? No!"

[18]When the Jewish believers heard this, they stopped arguing. They praised God and said, "So God is allowing the non-Jewish people also to turn to him and live."

[19]Many of the believers were scattered by the terrible things that happened after Stephen was killed. Some of them went to places as far away as Phoenicia, Cyprus, and Antioch. They were telling the message to others, but only to Jews. [20]Some of these believers were men from Cyprus and Cyrene. When they came to Antioch, they spoke also to Greeks, telling them the Good News[d] about the Lord Jesus. [21]The Lord was helping the believers. And a large group of people believed and turned to the Lord.

[22]The church in Jerusalem heard about all of this, so they sent Barnabas to Antioch. [23-24]Barnabas was a good man, full of the Holy Spirit[d] and full of faith. When he reached Antioch and saw how God had blessed the people, he was glad. He encouraged all the believers in Antioch. He told them, "Never lose your faith. Always obey the Lord with all your hearts." Many people became followers of the Lord.

[25]Then Barnabas went to the city of Tarsus to look for Saul. [26]When he found Saul, he brought him to Antioch. And for a whole year Saul and Barnabas met with the church. They taught many people there. In Antioch the followers were called Christians for the first time.

[27]About that time some prophets[d] came from Jerusalem to Antioch. [28]One of them was named Agabus. He stood up and spoke with the help of the Holy Spirit. He said, "A very hard time is coming to the whole world. There will be no food for people to eat." (This happened when Claudius ruled.) [29]The followers all decided to help their brothers who lived in Judea. Each one planned to send them as much as he could. [30]They gathered the money and gave it to Barnabas and Saul, who brought it to the elders[d] in Judea.

12 During that same time King Herod began to do terrible things to some who belonged to the church. [1]He ordered James, the brother of John, to be killed by the sword. [3]Herod saw that the Jews liked this, so he decided to arrest Peter, too. (This happened during the time of the Feast[d] of Unleavened Bread.)

[4]After Herod arrested Peter, he put him in jail and handed him over to be guarded by 16 soldiers. Herod planned to bring Peter before the people for trial after the Passover[d] Feast. [5]So Peter was kept in jail. But the church kept on praying to God for him.

[6]The night before Herod was to bring him to trial, Peter was sleeping. He was between two soldiers, bound with two chains. Other soldiers were guarding the door of the jail. [7]Suddenly, an angel of the Lord stood there. A light shined in the room. The angel touched Peter on the side and woke him up. The angel said, "Hurry! Get up!" And the chains fell off Peter's hands. [8]The angel said to him, "Get dressed and put on your sandals." And so Peter did this. Then the angel said, "Put on your coat and follow me." [9]So the angel went out, and Peter followed him. Peter did not know if what the angel was doing was real. He thought he might be seeing a vision. [10]They went past the first and the second guard. They came to the iron gate that separated them from the city. The gate opened itself for them. They went through the gate and walked down a street. And the angel suddenly left him. [11]Then Peter realized what had happened. He thought, "Now I know that the Lord really sent his angel to me. He rescued me from Herod and from all the things the Jewish people thought would happen."

[12]When he realized this, he went to the home of Mary. She was the mother of John. (John was also called Mark.) Many people were gathered there, praying. [13]Peter knocked on the outside door. A servant girl named Rhoda came to answer it. [14]She recognized Peter's voice, and she was very happy. She even forgot to open the door. She ran inside and told the group, "Peter is at the door!"

[15]They said to her, "You are crazy!" But she kept on saying that it was true. So they said, "It must be Peter's angel."

[16]Peter continued to knock. When they opened the door, they saw him and were amazed. [17]Peter made a sign with his hand to tell them to be quiet. He explained how the Lord led him out of the jail. And he said, "Tell James and the

other believers what happened." Then he left to go to another place.

[18]The next day the soldiers were very upset. They wondered what had happened to Peter. [19]Herod looked everywhere for Peter but could not find him. So he questioned the guards and ordered that they be killed.

Later Herod moved from Judea and went to the city of Caesarea, where he stayed for a while. [20]Herod was very angry with the people of Tyre and Sidon. But the people of those cities all came in a group to Herod. They were able to get Blastus, the king's personal servant, on their side. They asked Herod for peace because their country got its food from his country.

[21]On a chosen day Herod put on his royal robes. He sat on his throne and made a speech to the people. [22]They shouted, "This is the voice of a god, not a man!" [23]Herod did not give the glory to God. So an angel of the Lord caused him to become sick. He was eaten by worms and died.

[24]God's message continued to spread and reach more and more people.

[25]After Barnabas and Saul finished their task in Jerusalem, they returned to Antioch. John, also called Mark, was with them.

13 In the church at Antioch there were these prophets[d] and teachers: Barnabas, Simeon (also called Niger), Lucius (from the city of Cyrene), Manaen (who had grown up with Herod, the ruler) and Saul. [2]They were all worshiping the Lord and giving up eating.[n] The Holy Spirit[d] said to them, "Give Barnabas and Saul to me to do a special work. I have chosen them for it."

[3]So they gave up eating and prayed. They laid their hands on[n] Barnabas and Saul and sent them out.

[4]Barnabas and Saul were sent out by the Holy Spirit.[d] They went to the city of Seleucia. From there they sailed to the island of Cyprus. [5]When they came to Salamis, they preached the Good News[d] of God in the Jewish synagogues.[d] John Mark was with them to help.

[6]They went across the whole island to Paphos. In Paphos they met a Jew who was a magician. His name was Bar-Jesus. He was a false prophet,[d] [7]who always stayed close to Sergius Paulus, the

governor. Sergius Paulus was a smart man. He asked Barnabas and Saul to come to him, because he wanted to hear the message of God. [8]But Elymas, the magician, was against them. (Elymas is the name for Bar-Jesus in the Greek language.) He tried to stop the governor from believing in Jesus. [9]But Saul was filled with the Holy Spirit. (Saul's other name was Paul.) He looked straight at Elymas [10]and said, "You son of the devil! You are an enemy of everything that is right! You are full of evil tricks and lies. You are always trying to change the Lord's truths into lies! [11]Now the Lord will touch you, and you will be blind. For a time you will not be able to see anything—not even the light from the sun."

Then everything became dark for Elymas. He walked around, trying to find someone to lead him by the hand. [12]When the governor saw this, he believed. He was amazed at the teaching about the Lord.

[13]Paul and those with him sailed away from Paphos. They came to Perga, in Pamphylia. But John Mark left them and returned to Jerusalem. [14]They continued their trip from Perga and went to Antioch, a city in Pisidia. On the Sabbath[d] day they went into the synagogue[d] and sat down. [15]The law of Moses and the writings of the prophets[d] were read. Then the leaders of the synagogue sent a message to Paul and Barnabas: "Brothers, if you have any message that will encourage the people, please speak!"

[16]Paul stood up. He raised his hand and said, "Men of Israel and you other people who worship God, please listen! [17]The God of the people of Israel chose our ancestors. He made the people great during the time they lived in Egypt. He brought them out of that country with great power. [18]And he was patient with them for 40 years in the desert. [19]God destroyed seven nations in the land of Canaan and gave the land to his people. [20]All this happened in about 450 years.

"After this, God gave them judges until the time of Samuel the prophet. [21]Then the people asked for a king. God gave them Saul son of Kish. Saul was from the tribe[d] of Benjamin. He was king for 40 years. [22]After God took him

---

13:2 giving up eating This is called "fasting." The people would give up eating for a special time of prayer and worship to God. It was also done to show sadness.   **13:3 laid their hands on** Here, this was a sign to show that these men were given a special work of God.

away, God made David their king. This is what God said about him: 'I have found David son of Jesse. He is the kind of man I want. He will do all that I want him to do.' ²³So God has brought one of David's descendants[d] to Israel to be their Savior.[d] That descendant is Jesus. And God promised to do this. ²⁴Before Jesus came, John[n] preached to all the people of Israel. He told them about a baptism of changed hearts and lives. ²⁵When he was finishing his work, he said, 'Who do you think I am? I am not the Christ.[d] He is coming later. I am not worthy to untie his sandals.'

²⁶"Brothers, sons in the family of Abraham, and you non-Jews who worship God, listen! The news about this salvation has been sent to us. ²⁷Those who live in Jerusalem and their leaders did not realize that Jesus was the Savior. They did not understand the words that the prophets wrote, which are read every Sabbath[d] day. But they made them come true when they said Jesus was guilty. ²⁸They could not find any real reason for Jesus to die, but they asked Pilate to have him killed. ²⁹They did to him all that the Scriptures[d] had said. Then they took him down from the cross and laid him in a tomb. ³⁰But God raised him up from death! ³¹After this, for many days, the people who had gone with Jesus from Galilee to Jerusalem saw him. They are now his witnesses to the people. ³²We tell you the Good News[d] about the promise God made to our ancestors. ³³We are their children, and God has made this promise come true for us. God did this by raising Jesus from death. We read about this also in Psalm 2:

'You are my Son.
Today I have become your
    Father.'   *Psalm 2:7*

³⁴God raised Jesus from death. He will never go back to the grave and become dust. So God said:

'I will give you the holy and sure
    blessings
that I promised to David.'
                        Isaiah 55:3

³⁵But in another place God says:

'You will not let your Holy One
    rot in the grave.'   *Psalm 16:10*

³⁶David did God's will during his lifetime. Then he died and was buried with his fathers. And his body did rot in the grave! ³⁷But the One God raised from death did not rot in the grave.

³⁸⁻³⁹Brothers, you must understand what we are telling you: You can have forgiveness of your sins through Jesus. The law of Moses could not free you from your sins. But everyone who believes is free from all sins through him. ⁴⁰Be careful! Don't let what the prophets said happen to you:

⁴¹'Listen, you people who doubt!
    You can wonder, and then die.
I will do something in your lifetime
    that will amaze you.
You won't believe it even when
    you are told about it!'"
                        Habakkuk 1:5

⁴²While Paul and Barnabas were leaving the synagogue, the people asked them to tell them more about these things on the next Sabbath. ⁴³After the meeting, many Jews followed Paul and Barnabas from that place. With the Jews there were many who had changed to the Jewish religion and worshiped God. Paul and Barnabas were persuading them to continue trusting in God's kindness.

⁴⁴On the next Sabbath day, almost all the people in the city came to hear the word of the Lord. ⁴⁵Seeing the crowd, the Jews became very jealous. They said insulting things and argued against what Paul said. ⁴⁶But Paul and Barnabas spoke very boldly. They said, "We must speak the message of God to you first. But you refuse to listen. You are judging yourselves not worthy of having eternal life! So we will now go to the people of other nations! ⁴⁷This is what the Lord told us to do. The Lord said:

'I have made you a light for the
    non-Jewish nations.
You will show people all over the
    world the way to be saved.'"
                        Isaiah 49:6

⁴⁸When the non-Jewish people heard Paul say this, they were happy. They gave honor to the message of the Lord. And many of the people believed the message. They were the ones chosen to have life forever.

⁴⁹And so the message of the Lord was spreading through the whole country. ⁵⁰But the Jews stirred up some of the important religious women and the leaders of the city against Paul and Barnabas. They started trouble against Paul and Barnabas and drove them out of their area. ⁵¹So Paul and Barnabas

13:24 John John the Baptist, who preached to people about Christ's coming (Matthew 3, Luke 3).

shook the dust off their feet[n] and went to Iconium. [52]But the followers were filled with joy and the Holy Spirit.[d]

14 In Iconium, Paul and Barnabas went as usual to the Jewish synagogue.[d] They spoke so well that a great many Jews and Greeks believed. [2]But some of the Jews who did not believe excited the non-Jewish people and turned them against the believers. [3]But Paul and Barnabas stayed in Iconium a long time and spoke bravely for the Lord. The Lord showed that their message about his grace was true by giving them the power to work miracles[d] and signs. [4]But some of the people in the city agreed with the Jews. Others believed the apostles.[d] So the city was divided.

[5]Some non-Jewish people, some Jews, and some of their rulers wanted to harm Paul and Barnabas by killing them with stones. [6]When Paul and Barnabas learned about this, they went to Lystra and Derbe, cities in Lycaonia, and to the areas around those cities. [7]They announced the Good News[d] there, too.

[8]In Lystra there sat a man who had been born crippled; he had never walked. [9]This man was listening to Paul speak. Paul looked straight at him and saw that the man believed God could heal him. [10]So he cried out, "Stand up on your feet!" The man jumped up and began walking around. [11]When the crowds saw what Paul did, they shouted in their own Lycaonian language. They said, "The gods have become like men! They have come down to us!" [12]And the people began to call Barnabas "Zeus."[n] They called Paul "Hermes,"[n] because he was the main speaker. [13]The temple of Zeus was near the city. The priest of this temple brought some bulls and flowers to the city gates. The priest and the people wanted to offer a sacrifice to Paul and Barnabas. [14]But when the apostles,[d] Barnabas and Paul, understood what they were about to do, they tore their clothes in anger. Then they ran in among the people and shouted, [15]"Men, why are you doing these things? We are only men, human beings like you! We are bringing you the Good News.[d] We are telling you to turn away from these worthless things and turn to the true living God. He is the One who made the sky, the earth, the sea, and everything that is in them. [16]In the past, God let all the nations do what they wanted. [17]Yet he did things to prove he is real: He shows kindness to you. He gives you rain from heaven and crops at the right times. He gives you food and fills your hearts with joy." [18]Even with these words, they were barely able to keep the crowd from offering sacrifices to them.

[19]Then some Jews came from Antioch and Iconium. They persuaded the people to turn against Paul. And so they threw stones at Paul and dragged him out of town. They thought that they had killed him. [20]But the followers gathered around him, and he got up and went back into the town. The next day, he and Barnabas left and went to the city of Derbe.

[21]Paul and Barnabas told the Good News[d] in Derbe and many became followers. Paul and Barnabas returned to Lystra, Iconium, and Antioch. [22]In those cities they made the followers of Jesus stronger. They helped them to stay in the faith. They said, "We must suffer many things to enter God's kingdom." [23]They chose elders[d] for each church, by praying and giving up eating.[n] These elders were men who had trusted the Lord. So Paul and Barnabas put them in the Lord's care.

[24]Then they went through Pisidia and came to Pamphylia. [25]They preached the message in Perga, and then they went down to Attalia. [26]And from there they sailed away to Antioch. This is where the believers had put them into God's care and had sent them out to do this work. And now they had finished the work.

[27]When they arrived in Antioch, they gathered the church together. Paul and Barnabas told them all about what God had done with them. They told how God had made it possible for the non-Jews to believe! [28]And they stayed there a long time with the followers.

15 Then some men came to Antioch from Judea. They began teaching the non-Jewish brothers: "You cannot be saved if you are not circumcised.[d] Moses taught us to do this." [2]Paul and Barnabas were against this teaching and argued with the men about it. So

---

13:51 shook . . . feet A warning. It showed that they were finished talking to these people. **14:12 "Zeus"** The Greeks believed in many gods. Zeus was their most important god. **14:12 "Hermes"** The Greeks believed he was a messenger for the other gods. **14:23 giving up eating** This is called "fasting." The people would give up eating for a special time of prayer and worship to God. It was also done to show sadness.

the group decided to send Paul, Barnabas, and some other men to Jerusalem. There they could talk more about this with the apostles[d] and elders.[d]

[3]The church helped the men leave on the trip. They went through the countries of Phoenicia and Samaria, telling all about how the non-Jewish people had turned to God. This made all the believers very happy. [4]When they arrived in Jerusalem, the apostles, the elders, and the church welcomed them. Paul, Barnabas, and the others told about all the things that God had done with them. [5]But some of the believers who had belonged to the Pharisee[d] group came forward. They said, "The non-Jewish believers must be circumcised. We must tell them to obey the law of Moses!"

[6]The apostles and the elders gathered to study this problem. [7]There was a long debate. Then Peter stood up and said to them, "Brothers, you know what happened in the early days. God chose me from among you to preach the Good News[d] to the non-Jewish people. They heard the Good News from me, and they believed. [8]God, who knows the thoughts of all men, accepted them. He showed this to us by giving them the Holy Spirit,[d] just as he did to us. [9]To God, those people are not different from us. When they believed, he made their hearts pure. [10]So now why are you testing God? You are putting a heavy load around the necks of the non-Jewish brothers. It is a load that neither we nor our fathers were able to carry. [11]But we believe that we and they too will be saved by the grace of the Lord Jesus!"

[12]Then the whole group became quiet. They listened to Paul and Barnabas speak. Paul and Barnabas told about all the miracles[d] and signs that God did through them among the non-Jewish people. [13]After they finished speaking, James spoke. He said, "Brothers, listen to me. [14]Simon has told us how God showed his love for the non-Jewish people. For the first time he has accepted them and made them his people. [15]The words of the prophets[d] agree with this too:

[16]'After these things I will return.
    The kingdom of David is like a
        fallen tent.
    But I will rebuild it.
    And I will again build its ruins.
    And I will set it up.

[17]Then those people who are left
        alive may ask the Lord for
        help.
    And all people from other
        nations may worship me,
    says the Lord.
    And he will make it happen.
[18] And these things have been
        known for a long time.'
                        Amos 9:11-12

[19]"So I think we should not bother the non-Jewish brothers who have turned to God. [20]Instead, we should write a letter to them. We should tell them these things: Do not eat food that has been offered to idols. (This makes the food unclean.[d]) Do not take part in any kind of sexual sin. Do not taste blood. Do not eat animals that have been strangled. [21]They should not do these things, because there are still men in every city who teach the law of Moses. For a long time the words of Moses have been read in the synagogue[d] every Sabbath[d] day."

[22]The apostles,[d] the elders,[d] and the whole church decided to send some of their men with Paul and Barnabas to Antioch. They chose Judas Barsabbas and Silas, who were respected by the believers. [23]They sent the following letter with them:

From the apostles and elders, your brothers.

To all the non-Jewish brothers in Antioch, Syria and Cilicia:

Dear Brothers,
[24]We have heard that some of our men have come to you and said things that trouble and upset you. But we did not tell them to do this! [25]We have all agreed to choose some men and send them to you. They will be with our dear friends Barnabas and Paul— [26]men who have given their lives to serve our Lord Jesus Christ. [27]So we have sent Judas and Silas with them. They will tell you the same things. [28]It has pleased the Holy Spirit[d] that you should not have a heavy load to carry, and we agree. You need to do only these things: [29]Do not eat any food that has been offered to idols. Do not taste blood. Do not eat any animals that have been strangled. Do not take part in any kind of sexual sin. If you stay away from these things, you will do well.

Good-bye.

[30]So the men left Jerusalem and went to Antioch. There they gathered the church and gave them the letter. [31]When they read it, they were very happy because of the encouraging letter. [32]Judas

and Silas were also prophets,[d] who said many things to encourage the believers and make them stronger. [33]After some time Judas and Silas were sent off in peace by the believers. They went back to those who had sent them. [34] [n]

[35]But Paul and Barnabas stayed in Antioch. They and many others preached the Good News[d] and taught the people the message of the Lord.

[36]After some time, Paul said to Barnabas, "We preached the message of the Lord in many towns. We should go back to all those towns to visit the believers and see how they are doing."

[37]Barnabas wanted to take John Mark with them too. [38]But John Mark had left them at Pamphylia; he did not continue with them in the work. So Paul did not think it was a good idea to take him. [39]Paul and Barnabas had a serious argument about this. They separated and went different ways. Barnabas sailed to Cyprus and took Mark with him. [40]But Paul chose Silas and left. The believers in Antioch put Paul into the Lord's care. [41]And he went through Syria and Cilicia, giving strength to the churches.

16 Paul came to Derbe and Lystra. A follower named Timothy was there. Timothy's mother was Jewish and a believer. His father was a Greek. [2]The brothers in Lystra and Iconium respected Timothy and said good things about him. [3]Paul wanted Timothy to travel with him. But all the Jews living in that area knew that Timothy's father was Greek. So Paul circumcised[d] Timothy to please the Jews. [4]Paul and the men with him traveled from town to town. They gave the decisions made by the apostles[d] and elders[d] in Jerusalem for the people to obey. [5]So the churches became stronger in the faith and grew larger every day.

[6]Paul and the men with him went through the areas of Phrygia and Galatia. The Holy Spirit[d] did not let them preach the Good News[d] in the country of Asia. [7]When they came near the country of Mysia, they tried to go into Bithynia. But the Spirit of Jesus did not let them. [8]So they passed by Mysia and went to Troas. [9]That night Paul had a vision. In the vision, a man from Macedonia came to him. The man stood there and begged, "Come over to Macedonia. Help us!" [10]After Paul had seen the vision, we immediately prepared to leave for Macedonia. We understood that God had called us to tell the Good News to those people.

[11]We left Troas in a ship, and we sailed straight to the island of Samothrace. The next day we sailed to Neapolis.[n] [12]Then we went by land to Philippi, the leading city in that part of Macedonia. It is also a Roman colony.[n] We stayed there for several days.

[13]On the Sabbath[d] day we went outside the city gate to the river. There we thought we would find a special place for prayer. Some women had gathered there, so we sat down and talked with them. [14]There was a woman named Lydia from the city of Thyatira. Her job was selling purple cloth. She worshiped the true God. The Lord opened her mind to pay attention to what Paul was saying. [15]She and all the people in her house were baptized. Then Lydia invited us to her home. She said, "If you think I am truly a believer in the Lord, then come stay in my house." And she persuaded us to stay with her.

[16]Once, while we were going to the place for prayer, a servant girl met us. She had a special spirit[n] in her. She earned a lot of money for her owners by telling fortunes. [17]This girl followed Paul and us. She said loudly, "These men are servants of the Most High God! They are telling you how you can be saved!"

[18]She kept this up for many days. This bothered Paul, so he turned and said to the spirit, "By the power of Jesus Christ, I command you to come out of her!" Immediately, the spirit came out.

[19]The owners of the servant girl saw this. These men knew that now they could not use her to make money. So they grabbed Paul and Silas and dragged them before the city rulers in the marketplace. [20]Here they brought Paul and Silas to the Roman rulers and said, "These men are Jews and are making trouble in our city. [21]They are teaching things that are not right for us as Romans to do."

[22]The crowd joined the attack against them. The Roman officers tore the clothes of Paul and Silas and had them

beaten with rods again and again. [23]Then Paul and Silas were thrown into jail. The jailer was ordered to guard them carefully. [24]When he heard this order, he put them far inside the jail. He pinned down their feet between large blocks of wood.

[25]About midnight Paul and Silas were praying and singing songs to God. The other prisoners were listening to them. [26]Suddenly, there was a big earthquake. It was so strong that it shook the foundation of the jail. Then all the doors of the jail broke open. All the prisoners were freed from their chains. [27]The jailer woke up and saw that the jail doors were open. He thought that the prisoners had already escaped. So he got his sword and was about to kill himself.[n] [28]But Paul shouted, "Don't hurt yourself! We are all here!"

[29]The jailer told someone to bring a light. Then he ran inside. Shaking with fear, he fell down before Paul and Silas. [30]Then he brought them outside and said, "Men, what must I do to be saved?" [31]They said to him, "Believe in the Lord Jesus and you will be saved—you and all the people in your house." [32]So Paul and Silas told the message of the Lord to the jailer and all the people in his house. [33]At that hour of the night the jailer took Paul and Silas and washed their wounds. Then he and all his people were baptized immediately. [34]After this the jailer took Paul and Silas home and gave them food. He and his family were very happy because they now believed in God.

[35]The next morning, the Roman officers sent the police to tell the jailer, "Let these men go free!"

[36]The jailer said to Paul, "The officers have sent an order to let you go free. You can leave now. Go in peace."

[37]But Paul said to the police, "They beat us in public without a trial, even though we are Roman citizens.[n] And they threw us in jail. Now they want to make us go away quietly. No! Let them come themselves and bring us out!"

[38]The police told the Roman officers what Paul said. When the officers heard that Paul and Silas were Roman citizens, they were afraid. [39]So they came and told Paul and Silas they were sorry. They took Paul and Silas out of jail and

asked them to leave the city. [40]So when they came out of the jail, they went to Lydia's house. There they saw some of the believers and encouraged them. Then they left.

17 Paul and Silas traveled through Amphipolis and Apollonia and came to Thessalonica. In that city there was a Jewish synagogue.[d] [2]Paul went into the synagogue as he always did. On each Sabbath[d] day for three weeks, Paul talked with the Jews about the Scriptures.[d] [3]He explained and proved that the Christ[d] must die and then rise from death. He said, "This Jesus I am telling you about is the Christ." [4]Some of the Jews were convinced and joined Paul and Silas. Many of the Greeks who worshiped the true God and many of the important women joined them.

[5]But the Jews became jealous. They got some evil men from the marketplace, formed a mob and started a riot. They ran to Jason's house, looking for Paul and Silas. The men wanted to bring Paul and Silas out to the people. [6]But they did not find them. So they dragged Jason and some other believers to the leaders of the city. The people were yelling, "These men have made trouble everywhere in the world. And now they have come here too! [7]Jason is keeping them in his house. All of them do things against the laws of Caesar.[d] They say that there is another king called Jesus."

[8]When the people and the leaders of the city heard these things, they became very upset. [9]They made Jason and the others put up a sum of money. Then they let the believers go free.

[10]That same night the believers sent Paul and Silas to Berea. There Paul and Silas went to the Jewish synagogue.[d] [11]These Jews were better than the Jews in Thessalonica. They were eager to hear the things Paul and Silas said. These Jews in Berea studied the Scriptures[d] every day to find out if these things were true. [12]So, many of them believed. Many important Greek men and women also believed. [13]But when the Jews in Thessalonica learned that Paul was preaching the word of God in Berea, they came there, too. They upset the people and made trouble. [14]So the believers quickly sent Paul away to the coast. But Silas and Timothy stayed in

---

16:27 kill himself He thought the leaders would kill him for letting the prisoners escape.
16:37 Roman citizens Roman law said that Roman citizens must not be beaten before they had a trial.

Berea. [15]The men who took Paul went with him to Athens. Then they carried a message from Paul back to Silas and Timothy. It said, "Come to me as soon as you can."

[16]Paul was waiting for Silas and Timothy in Athens. He was troubled because he saw that the city was full of idols. [17]In the synagogue,[d] he talked with the Jews and the Greeks who worshiped the true God. He also talked every day with people in the marketplace.

[18]Some of the Epicurean and Stoic philosophers[n] argued with him. Some of them said, "This man doesn't know what he is talking about. What is he trying to say?" Paul was telling them the Good News[d] of Jesus' rising from death. They said, "He seems to be telling us about some other gods." [19]They got Paul and took him to a meeting of the Areopagus.[n] They said, "Please explain to us this new idea that you have been teaching. [20]The things you are saying are new to us. We want to know what this teaching means." [21](All the people of Athens and those from other countries always used their time talking about all the newest ideas.)

[22]Then Paul stood before the meeting of the Areopagus. He said, "Men of Athens, I can see that you are very religious in all things. [23]I was going through your city, and I saw the things you worship. I found an altar that had these words written on it: "TO A GOD WHO IS NOT KNOWN." You worship a god that you don't know. This is the God I am telling you about! [24]He is the God who made the whole world and everything in it. He is the Lord of the land and the sky. He does not live in temples that men build! [25]This God is the One who gives life, breath, and everything else to people. He does not need any help from them. He has everything he needs. [26]God began by making one man. From him came all the different people who live everywhere in the world. He decided exactly when and where they must live. [27]God wanted them to look for him and perhaps search all around for him and find him. But he is not far from any of us: [28]'We live in him. We walk in him. We are in him.' Some of your own poets

have said: 'For we are his children.' [29]We are God's children. So, you must not think that God is like something that people imagine or make. He is not like gold, silver, or rock. [30]In the past, people did not understand God, but God ignored this. But now, God tells everyone in the world to change his heart and life. [31]God has decided on a day that he will judge all the world. He will be fair. He will use a man to do this. God chose that man long ago. And God has proved this to everyone by raising that man from death!"

[32]When the people heard about Jesus being raised from death, some of them laughed. They said, "We will hear more about this from you later." [33]So Paul went away from them. [34]But some of the people believed Paul and joined him. One of those who believed was Dionysius, a member of the Areopagus. Also a woman named Damaris and some others believed.

18

Later, Paul left Athens and went to Corinth. [2]Here he met a Jew named Aquila. Aquila was born in the country of Pontus. But Aquila and his wife, Priscilla, had recently moved to Corinth from Italy. They left Italy because Claudius[n] commanded that all Jews must leave Rome. Paul went to visit Aquila and Priscilla. [3]They were tentmakers, just as he was. He stayed with them and worked with them. [4]Every Sabbath[d] day he talked with the Jews and Greeks in the synagogue.[d] Paul tried to persuade these people to believe in Jesus.

[5]Silas and Timothy came from Macedonia and joined Paul in Corinth. After this, Paul used all his time telling people the Good News.[d] He showed the Jews that Jesus is the Christ.[d] [6]But they would not accept Paul's teaching and said some evil things. So he shook off the dust from his clothes.[n] He said to them, "If you are not saved, it will be your own fault! I have done all I can do! After this, I will go only to non-Jewish people!" [7]Paul left the synagogue and moved into the home of Titius Justus. It was next to the synagogue. This man worshiped the true God. [8]Crispus was the leader of that synagogue. He and all the people living

---

17:18 Epicurean and Stoic philosophers Philosophers were those who searched for truth. Epicureans believed that pleasure, especially pleasures of the mind, were the goal of life. Stoics believed that life should be without feelings of joy or grief. **17:19 Areopagus** A council or group of important leaders in Athens. They were like judges. **18:2 Claudius** The emperor (ruler) of Rome, A.D. 41-54. **18:6 shook . . . clothes** This was a warning. It showed that Paul was finished talking to the Jews.

in his house believed in the Lord. Many others in Corinth also listened to Paul. They too believed and were baptized.

[9]During the night, Paul had a vision. The Lord said to him, "Don't be afraid! Continue talking to people and don't be quiet! [10]I am with you. No one will hurt you because many of my people are in this city." [11]Paul stayed there for a year and a half, teaching God's word to the people.

[12]Gallio became the governor of the country of Southern Greece. At that time, some of the Jews came together against Paul and took him to the court. [13]They said to Gallio, "This man is teaching people to worship God in a way that is against our law!"

[14]Paul was about to say something, but Gallio spoke to the Jews. Gallio said, "I would listen to you Jews if you were complaining about a crime or some wrong. [15]But the things you are saying are only questions about words and names—arguments about your own law. So you must solve this problem yourselves. I don't want to be a judge of these things!" [16]Then Gallio made them leave the court.

[17]Then they all grabbed Sosthenes. (Sosthenes was now the leader of the synagogue.[d]) They beat him there before the court. But this did not bother Gallio.

[18]Paul stayed with the believers for many more days. Then he left and sailed for Syria. Priscilla and Aquila went with him. At Cenchrea, Paul cut off his hair.[n] This showed that he had made a promise to God. [19]Then they went to Ephesus, where Paul left Priscilla and Aquila. While Paul was there, he went into the synagogue[d] and talked with the Jews. [20]When they asked him to stay with them longer, he refused. [21]He left them, but he said, "I will come back to you again if God wants me to." And so he sailed away from Ephesus.

[22]Paul landed at Caesarea. Then he went and gave greetings to the church in Jerusalem. After that, Paul went to Antioch. [23]He stayed there for a while and then left and went through the countries of Galatia and Phrygia. He traveled from town to town in these countries, giving strength to all the followers.

[24]A Jew named Apollos came to Ephesus. He was born in the city of Alexandria. He was an educated man who knew the Scriptures[d] well. [25]He had been taught about the Lord. He was always very excited when he spoke and taught the truth about Jesus. But the only baptism that Apollos knew about was the baptism that John[n] taught. [26]Apollos began to speak very boldly in the synagogue,[d] and Priscilla and Aquila heard him. So they took him to their home and helped him better understand the way of God. [27]Now Apollos wanted to go to the country of Southern Greece, so the believers helped him. They wrote a letter to the followers there, asking them to accept him. These followers had believed in Jesus because of God's grace. When Apollos went there, he helped them very much. [28]He argued very strongly with the Jews before all the people. Apollos clearly proved that the Jews were wrong. Using the Scriptures, he proved that Jesus is the Christ.[d]

19 While Apollos was in Corinth, Paul was visiting some places on the way to Ephesus. There he found some followers. [2]Paul asked them, "Did you receive the Holy Spirit[d] when you believed?"

They said, "We have never even heard of a Holy Spirit!"

[3]So he asked, "What kind of baptism did you have?"

They said, "It was the baptism that John[n] taught."

[4]Paul said, "John's baptism was a baptism of changed hearts and lives. He told people to believe in the One who would come after him. That One is Jesus."

[5]When they heard this, they were baptized in the name of the Lord Jesus. [6]Then Paul laid his hands on them,[n] and the Holy Spirit came upon them. They began speaking different languages and prophesying.[d] [7]There were about 12 men in this group.

[8]Paul went into the synagogue[d] and spoke out boldly for three months. He talked with the Jews and persuaded them to accept the things he said about the kingdom of God. [9]But some of the Jews became stubborn and refused to believe. These Jews said evil things about the Way of Jesus. All the people

18:18 cut . . . hair Jews did this to show that the time of a special promise to God was finished.
18:25; 19:3 John John the Baptist, who preached to people about Christ's coming (Matthew 3, Luke 3). **19:6 laid his hands on them** Here, doing this was a sign to show that Paul had God's authority or power to give these people special powers of the Holy Spirit.

heard these things. So Paul left them and took the followers with him. He went to a place where a man named Tyrannus had a school. There Paul talked with people every day [10]for two years. Because of his work, every Jew and Greek in the country of Asia heard the word of the Lord.

[11]God used Paul to do some very special miracles.[d] [12]Some people took handkerchiefs and clothes that Paul had used and put them on the sick. When they did this, the sick were healed and evil spirits left them.

[13-14]But some Jews also were traveling around and making evil spirits go out of people. The seven sons of Sceva were doing this. (Sceva was a leading Jewish priest.) These Jews tried to use the name of the Lord Jesus to force the evil spirits out. They would say, "By the same Jesus that Paul talks about, I order you to come out!"

[15]But one time an evil spirit said to these Jews, "I know Jesus, and I know about Paul, but who are you?"

[16]Then the man, who had the evil spirit in him, jumped on these Jews. He was much stronger than all of them. He beat them and tore their clothes off, so they ran away from the house. [17]All the people in Ephesus, Jews and Greeks, learned about this. They were filled with fear. And the people gave great honor to the Lord Jesus. [18]Many of the believers began to confess openly and tell all the evil things they had done. [19]Some of them had used magic. These believers brought their magic books and burned them before everyone. Those books were worth about 50,000 silver coins.[n]

[20]So in a powerful way the word of the Lord kept spreading and growing.

[21]After these things, Paul made plans to go to Jerusalem. He planned to go through the countries of Macedonia and Southern Greece, and then on to Jerusalem. He said, "After I have been to Jerusalem, I must also visit Rome." [22]Paul sent Timothy and Erastus, two of his helpers, ahead to Macedonia. He himself stayed in Asia for a while.

[23]But during that time, there was some serious trouble in Ephesus about the Way of Jesus. [24]There was a man named Demetrius, who worked with silver. He made little silver models that looked like

the temple of the goddess Artemis.[n] The men who did this work made much money. [25]Demetrius had a meeting with these men and some others who did the same kind of work. He told them, "Men, you know that we make a lot of money from our business. [26]But look at what this man Paul is doing! He has convinced and turned away many people in Ephesus and in almost all of Asia! He says the gods that men make are not real. [27]There is a danger that our business will lose its good name. But there is also another danger: People will begin to think that the temple of the great goddess Artemis is not important! Her greatness will be destroyed. And Artemis is the goddess that everyone in Asia and the whole world worships."

[28]When the men heard this, they became very angry. They shouted, "Artemis, the goddess of Ephesus, is great!" [29]The whole city became confused. The people grabbed Gaius and Aristarchus. (These two men were from Macedonia and were traveling with Paul.) Then all the people ran to the theater. [30]Paul wanted to go in and talk to the crowd, but the followers did not let him. [31]Also, some leaders of Asia were friends of Paul. They sent him a message, begging him not to go into the theater. [32]Some people were shouting one thing, and some were shouting another. The meeting was completely confused. Most of the people did not know why they had come together. [33]The Jews put a man named Alexander in front of the people. Some of them had told him what to do. Alexander waved his hand because he wanted to explain things to the people. [34]But when they saw that Alexander was a Jew, they all began shouting the same thing. They continued shouting for two hours: "Great is Artemis of Ephesus!"

[35]Then the city clerk made the crowd be quiet. He said, "Men of Ephesus, everyone knows that Ephesus is the city that keeps the temple of the great goddess Artemis. All people know that we also keep her holy stone[n] that fell from heaven. [36]No one can say that this is not true. So you should be quiet. You must stop and think before you do anything. [37]You brought these men here, but they have not said anything evil against our goddess. They have not stolen anything

---

19:19 **50,000 silver coins** Probably drachmas. One coin was enough to pay a man for working one day.　19:24 **Artemis** A Greek goddess that the people of Asia Minor worshiped.　19:35 **holy stone** Probably a meteorite or stone that the people thought looked like Artemis.

from her temple. [38]We have courts of law, and there are judges. Do Demetrius and the men who work with him have a charge against anyone? They should go to the courts! That is where they can argue with each other! [39]Is there something else you want to talk about? It can be decided at the regular town meeting of the people. [40]I say this because some people might see this trouble today and say that we are rioting. We could not explain this because there is no real reason for this meeting." [41]After the city clerk said these things, he told the people to go home.

20 When the trouble stopped, Paul sent for the followers to come to him. He encouraged them and then told them good-bye. Paul left and went to the country of Macedonia. [2]He said many things to strengthen the followers in the different places on his way through Macedonia. Then he went to Southern Greece. [3]He stayed there three months. He was ready to sail for Syria, but some Jews were planning something against him. So Paul decided to go back through Macedonia to Syria. [4]Some men went with him. They were Sopater son of Pyrrhus, from the city of Berea; Aristarchus and Secundus, from the city of Thessalonica; Gaius, from Derbe; and Timothy; and Tychicus and Trophimus, two men from the country of Asia. [5]These men went first, ahead of Paul, and waited for us at Troas. [6]We sailed from Philippi after the Feast[d] of Unleavened Bread and we met them in Troas five days later. We stayed there seven days.

[7]On the first day of the week,[n] we all met together to break bread.[n] Paul spoke to the group. Because he was planning to leave the next day, he kept on talking till midnight. [8]We were all together in a room upstairs, and there were many lamps in the room. [9]A young man named Eutychus was sitting in the window. As Paul continued talking, Eutychus was falling into a deep sleep. Finally, he went sound asleep and fell to the ground from the third floor. When they picked him up, he was dead. [10]Paul went down to Eutychus. He knelt down and put his arms around him. He said, "Don't worry. He is alive now." [11]Then Paul went upstairs again, broke bread,

and ate. He spoke to them a long time, until it was early morning. Then he left. [12]They took the young man home alive and were greatly comforted.

[13]We sailed for the city of Assos. We went first, ahead of Paul. He wanted to join us on the ship there. Paul planned it this way because he wanted to go to Assos by land. [14]When he met us at Assos, we took him aboard and went to Mitylene. [15]The next day, we sailed from Mitylene and came to a place near Chios. The next day, we sailed to Samos. A day later, we reached Miletus. [16]Paul had already decided not to stop at Ephesus. He did not want to stay too long in the country of Asia. He was hurrying to be in Jerusalem on the day of Pentecost,[d] if that was possible.

[17]Now from Miletus Paul sent to Ephesus and called for the elders[d] of the church. [18]When they came to him, he said, "You know about my life from the first day I came to Asia. You know the way I lived all the time I was with you. [19]The Jews plotted against me. This troubled me very much. But you know that I always served the Lord. I never thought of myself first, and I often cried. [20]You know I preached to you, and I did not hold back anything that would help you. You know that I taught you in public and in your homes. [21]I warned both Jews and Greeks to change their lives and turn to God. And I told them all to believe in our Lord Jesus. [22]But now I must obey the Holy Spirit[d] and go to Jerusalem. I don't know what will happen to me there. [23]I know only that in every city the Holy Spirit tells me that troubles and even jail wait for me. [24]I don't care about my own life. The most important thing is that I complete my mission. I want to finish the work that the Lord Jesus gave me—to tell people the Good News[d] about God's grace.

[25]"And now, I know that none of you will ever see me again. All the time I was with you, I was preaching the kingdom of God. [26]So today I can tell you one thing that I am sure of: If any of you should be lost, I am not responsible. [27]This is because I have told you everything God wants you to know. [28]Be careful for yourselves and for all the people God has given you. The Holy Spirit gave

---

20:7 first day of the week Sunday, which for the Jews began at sunset on our Saturday. But if in this part of Asia a different system of time was used, then the meeting was on our Sunday night. **20:7 break bread** Probably the Lord's Supper, the special meal that Jesus told his followers to eat to remember him (Luke 22:14-20).

you the work of caring for this flock. You must be like shepherds to the church of God.[n] This is the church that God bought with his own death. [29]I know that after I leave, some men will come like wild wolves and try to destroy the flock. [30]Also, men from your own group will rise up and twist the truth. They will lead away followers after them. [31]So be careful! Always remember this: For three years I never stopped warning each of you. I taught you night and day. I often cried over you.

[32]"Now I am putting you in the care of God and the message about his grace. That message is able to give you strength, and it will give you the blessings that God has for all his holy people. [33]When I was with you, I never wanted anyone's money or fine clothes. [34]You know that I always worked to take care of my own needs and the needs of those who were with me. [35]I showed you in all things that you should work as I did and help the weak. I taught you to remember the words of Jesus. He said, 'It is more blessed to give than to receive.'"

[36]When Paul had said this, he knelt down with all of them and prayed. [37-38]And they all cried because Paul had said that they would never see him again. They put their arms around him and kissed him. Then they went with him to the ship.

21 We all said good-bye to them and left. We sailed straight to Cos island. The next day, we reached Rhodes, and from Rhodes we went to Patara. [2]There we found a ship that was going to Phoenicia. We went aboard and sailed away. [3]We sailed near the island of Cyprus. We could see it to the north, but we sailed on to Syria. We stopped at Tyre because the ship needed to unload its cargo there. [4]We found some followers in Tyre, and we stayed with them for seven days. Through the Holy Spirit[d] they warned Paul not to go to Jerusalem. [5]When we finished our visit, we left and continued our trip. All the followers, even the women and children, came outside the city with us. We all knelt down on the beach and prayed. [6]Then we said good-bye and got on the ship. The followers went back home.

[7]We continued our trip from Tyre and arrived at Ptolemais. We greeted the believers there and stayed with them for a day. [8]We left Ptolemais and went to the city of Caesarea. There we went into the home of Philip and stayed with him. Philip had the work of telling the Good News.[d] He was one of the seven helpers.[n] [9]He had four unmarried daughters who had the gift of prophesying.[d] [10]After we had been there for some time, a prophet named Agabus arrived from Judea. [11]He came to us and borrowed Paul's belt. Then he used the belt to tie his own hands and feet. He said, "The Holy Spirit says, 'This is how the Jews in Jerusalem will tie up the man who wears this belt. Then they will give him to the non-Jewish people.'"

[12]We all heard these words. So we and the people there begged Paul not to go to Jerusalem. [13]But he said, "Why are you crying and making me so sad? I am ready to be tied up in Jerusalem. And I am ready to die for the Lord Jesus!"

[14]We could not persuade him to stay away from Jerusalem. So we stopped begging him and said, "We pray that what the Lord wants will be done."

[15]After this, we got ready and started on our way to Jerusalem. [16]Some of the followers from Caesarea went with us. They took us to the home of Mnason, a man from Cyprus. Mnason was one of the first followers. They took us to his home so that we could stay with him.

[17]In Jerusalem the believers were glad to see us. [18]The next day, Paul went with us to visit James. All the elders[d] were there, too. [19]Paul greeted them and told them everything that God had done among the non-Jewish people through him. [20]When they heard this, they praised God. Then they said to Paul, "Brother, you can see that many thousands of Jews have become believers. But they think it is very important to obey the law of Moses. [21]These Jews have heard about your teaching. They heard that you tell the Jews who live among non-Jews to leave the law of Moses. They heard that you tell them not to circumcise[d] their children and not to obey Jewish customs. [22]What should we do? The Jewish believers here will learn that you have come. [23]So we will tell you what to do: Four of our men have made a promise to God. [24]Take these men with you and share in their cleansing cere-

20:28 **of God** Some Greek copies say, "of the Lord." 21:8 **helpers** The seven men chosen for a special work described in Acts 6:1-6.

mony.[n] Pay their expenses. Then they can shave their heads.[n] Do this and it will prove to everyone that what they have heard about you is not true. They will see that you follow the law of Moses in your own life. [25]We have already sent a letter to the non-Jewish believers. The letter said: 'Do not eat food that has been offered to idols. Do not taste blood. Do not eat animals that have been strangled. Do not take part in any kind of sexual sin.'"

[26]Then Paul took the four men with him. The next day, he shared in the cleansing ceremony. Then he went to the Temple.[d] Paul announced the time when the days of the cleansing ceremony would be finished. On the last day an offering would be given for each of the men.

[27]The seven days were almost over. But some Jews from Asia saw Paul at the Temple. They caused all the people to be upset, and they grabbed Paul. [28]They shouted, "Men of Israel, help us! This is the man who goes everywhere teaching things that are against the law of Moses, against our people, and against this Temple. And now he has brought some Greek men into the Temple. He has made this holy place unclean!"[d] [29](The Jews said this because they had seen Trophimus with Paul in Jerusalem. Trophimus was a man from Ephesus. The Jews thought that Paul had brought him into the Temple.)

[30]All the people in Jerusalem became very upset. They ran and took Paul and dragged him out of the Temple. The Temple doors were closed immediately. [31]The people were about to kill Paul. Now the commander of the Roman army in Jerusalem learned that there was trouble in the whole city. [32]Immediately he ran to the place where the crowd was gathered. He brought officers and soldiers with him, and the people saw them. So they stopped beating Paul. [33]The commander went to Paul and arrested him. He told his soldiers to tie Paul with two chains. Then he asked, "Who is this man? What has he done wrong?" [34]Some in the crowd were yelling one thing, and some were yelling another. Because of all this confusion and shouting, the commander could not

learn what had happened. So he ordered the soldiers to take Paul to the army building. [35-36]The whole mob was following them. When the soldiers came to the steps, they had to carry Paul. They did this because the people were ready to hurt him. They were shouting, "Kill him!"

[37]The soldiers were about to take Paul into the army building. But he spoke to the commander, "May I say something to you?"

The commander said, "Do you speak Greek? [38]I thought you were the Egyptian who started some trouble against the government not long ago. He led 4,000 killers out to the desert."

[39]Paul said, "No, I am a Jew from Tarsus in the country of Cilicia. I am a citizen of that important city. Please, let me speak to the people."

[40]The commander gave permission, so Paul stood on the steps. He waved with his hand so that the people would be quiet. When there was silence, Paul spoke to them in the Jewish language.[n]

22 Paul said, "Brothers and fathers, listen to me! I will make my defense to you." [2]When the Jews heard him speaking the Jewish language,[n] they became very quiet. Paul said, [3]"I am a Jew. I was born in Tarsus in the country of Cilicia. I grew up in this city. I was a student of Gamaliel.[n] He carefully taught me everything about the law of our ancestors. I was very serious about serving God, just as all of you here today. [4]I hurt the people who followed the Way of Jesus. Some of them were even killed. I arrested men and women and put them in jail. [5]The high priest and the whole council of older Jewish leaders can tell you that this is true. These leaders gave me letters to the Jewish brothers in Damascus. So I was going there to arrest these people and bring them back to Jerusalem to be punished.

[6]"But something happened to me on my way to Damascus. It was about noon when I came near Damascus. Suddenly a bright light from heaven flashed all around me. [7]I fell to the ground and heard a voice saying, 'Saul, Saul, why are you doing things against me?' [8]I asked, 'Who are you, Lord?' The voice

21:24 cleansing ceremony The special things Jews did to end the Nazirite promise. **21:24 shave their heads** The Jews did this to show that their promise was finished. **21:40; 22:2 Jewish language** Aramaic, the language of the Jews in the first century. **22:3 Gamaliel** A very important teacher of the Pharisees, a Jewish religious group (Acts 5:34).

said, 'I am Jesus from Nazareth. I am the One you are trying to hurt.' [9]The men who were with me did not understand the voice. But they saw the light. [10]I said, 'What shall I do, Lord?' The Lord answered, 'Get up and go to Damascus. There you will be told about all the things I have planned for you to do.' [11]I could not see, because the bright light had made me blind. So the men led me into Damascus.

[12]"There a man named Ananias came to me. He was a religious man; he obeyed the law of Moses. All the Jews who lived there respected him. [13]Ananias came to me, stood by me, and said, 'Brother Saul, see again!' Immediately I was able to see him. [14]Ananias told me, 'The God of our fathers chose you long ago. He chose you to know his plan. He chose you to see the Righteous One and to hear words from him. [15]You will be his witness to all people. You will tell them about the things you have seen and heard. [16]Now, why wait any longer? Get up, be baptized, and wash your sins away. Do this, trusting in him to save you.'

[17]"Later, I returned to Jerusalem. I was praying in the Temple,[d] and I saw a vision. [18]I saw the Lord saying to me, 'Hurry! Leave Jerusalem now! The people here will not accept the truth about me.' [19]But I said, 'Lord, they know that in every synagogue[d] I put the believers in jail and beat them. [20]They also know that I was there when Stephen, your witness, was killed. I stood there and agreed that they should kill him. I even held the coats of the men who were killing him!' [21]But the Lord said to me, 'Leave now. I will send you far away to the non-Jewish people.'"

[22]The crowd listened to Paul until he said this. Then they began shouting, "Kill him! Get him out of the world! A man like this should not be allowed to live!" [23]They shouted and threw off their coats.[n] They threw dust into the air.[n]

[24]Then the commander ordered the soldiers to take Paul into the army building and beat him. The commander wanted to make Paul tell why the people were shouting against him like this. [25]So the soldiers were tying him up, preparing to beat him. But Paul said to an offi-

cer there, "Do you have the right to beat a Roman citizen[n] who has not been proven guilty?"

[26]When the officer heard this, he went to the commander and told him about it. The officer said, "Do you know what you are doing? This man is a Roman citizen!"

[27]The commander came to Paul and said, "Tell me, are you really a Roman citizen?"

He answered, "Yes."

[28]The commander said, "I paid a lot of money to become a Roman citizen."

But Paul said, "I was born a citizen."

[29]The men who were preparing to question Paul moved away from him immediately. The commander was frightened because he had already tied Paul, and Paul was a Roman citizen.

[30]The next day the commander decided to learn why the Jews were accusing Paul. So he ordered the leading priests and the Jewish council to meet. The commander took Paul's chains off. Then he brought Paul out and stood him before their meeting.

23 Paul looked at the Jewish council and said, "Brothers, I have lived my life in a good way before God up to this day." [2]Ananias,[n] the high priest, heard this and told the men who were standing near Paul to hit him on his mouth. [3]Paul said to Ananias, "God will hit you too! You are like a wall that has been painted white! You sit there and judge me, using the law of Moses. But you are telling them to hit me, and that is against the law."

[4]The men standing near Paul said to him, "You cannot talk like that to God's high priest! You are insulting him!"

[5]Paul said, "Brothers, I did not know this man was the high priest. It is written in the Scriptures,[d] 'You must not curse a leader of your people.'"[n]

[6]Some of the men in the meeting were Sadducees,[d] and others were Pharisees.[d] So Paul shouted to them, "My brothers, I am a Pharisee and my father was a Pharisee! I am on trial here because I hope that people will rise from death!"

[7]When Paul said this, there was an argument between the Pharisees and the Sadducees. The group was divided. [8](The Sadducees believe that after peo-

22:23 threw off their coats This showed that the Jews were very angry at Paul. **22:23 threw dust into the air** This showed even greater anger. **22:25 Roman citizen** Roman law said that Roman citizens must not be beaten before they had a trial. **23:2 Ananias** This is not the same man named Ananias in Acts 22:12. **23:5 'You . . . people.'** Quotation from Exodus 22:28.

ple die, they cannot live again. The Sadducees also teach that there are no angels or spirits. But the Pharisees believe in them all.) ⁹So there was a great uproar. Some of the teachers of the law, who were Pharisees, stood up and argued, "We find nothing wrong with this man! Maybe an angel or a spirit did speak to him."

¹⁰The argument was beginning to turn into a fight. The commander was afraid that the Jews would tear Paul to pieces. So the commander told the soldiers to go down and take Paul away and put him in the army building.

¹¹The next night the Lord came and stood by Paul. He said, "Be brave! You have told people in Jerusalem about me. You must do the same in Rome also."

¹²In the morning some of the Jews made a plan to kill Paul. They made a promise that they would not eat or drink anything until they had killed him. ¹³There were more than 40 Jews who made this plan. ¹⁴They went and talked to the leading priests and the older Jewish leaders. They said, "We have made a promise to ourselves that we will not eat or drink until we have killed Paul! ¹⁵So this is what we want you to do: Send a message to the commander to bring Paul out to you. Tell him you want to ask Paul more questions. We will be waiting to kill him while he is on the way here."

¹⁶But Paul's nephew heard about this plan. He went to the army building and told Paul about it. ¹⁷Then Paul called one of the officers and said, "Take this young man to the commander. He has a message for him."

¹⁸So the officer brought Paul's nephew to the commander. The officer said, "The prisoner, Paul, asked me to bring this young man to you. He wants to tell you something."

¹⁹The commander led the young man to a place where they could be alone. The commander asked, "What do you want to tell me?"

²⁰The young man said, "The Jews have decided to ask you to bring Paul down to their council meeting tomorrow. They want you to think that they are going to ask him more questions. ²¹But don't believe them! There are more than 40 men who are hiding and waiting to kill Paul. They have all made a promise not to eat or drink until they have killed him! Now they are waiting for you to agree."

²²The commander sent the young man away. He said to him, "Don't tell anyone that you have told me about their plan."

²³Then the commander called two officers. He said to them, "I need some men to go to Caesarea. Get 200 soldiers ready. Also, get 70 horsemen and 200 men with spears. Be ready to leave at nine o'clock tonight. ²⁴Get some horses for Paul to ride. He must be taken to Governor Felix safely." ²⁵And he wrote a letter that said:

²⁶From Claudius Lysias.

To the Most Excellent Governor Felix:

Greetings.

²⁷The Jews had taken this man, and they planned to kill him. But I learned that he is a Roman citizen, so I went with my soldiers and saved him. ²⁸I wanted to know why they were accusing him. So I brought him before their council meeting. ²⁹I learned that the Jews said Paul did some things that were wrong. But these charges were about their own laws. And no charge was worthy of jail or death. ³⁰I was told that some of the Jews were planning to kill Paul. So I sent him to you at once. I also told those Jews to tell you what they have against him.

³¹So the soldiers did what they were told. They took Paul and brought him to the city of Antipatris that night. ³²The next day the horsemen went with Paul to Caesarea. But the other soldiers went back to the army building in Jerusalem. ³³The horsemen came to Caesarea and gave the letter to the governor. Then they turned Paul over to him. ³⁴The governor read the letter. Then he asked Paul, "What area are you from?" He learned that Paul was from Cilicia. ³⁵He said, "I will hear your case when those who are against you come here too." Then the governor gave orders for Paul to be kept under guard in the palace. (This building had been built by Herod.)

24 Five days later Ananias, the high priest, went to the city of Caesarea. With him were some of the older Jewish leaders and a lawyer named Tertullus. They had come to make charges against Paul before the governor. ²Paul was called into the meeting, and Tertullus began to accuse him, saying: "Most Excellent Felix! Our people enjoy much peace because of you, and many wrong things in our country are being made right through your wise help. ³We accept these things always and in every place. And we are thankful for them. ⁴But I do not want to take any more of your time. I beg you to be kind and listen to our few words. ⁵This man is a troublemaker. He makes trouble among the Jews everywhere in the world. He is a leader of the Nazarene[d] group. ⁶Also, he was trying to make the Temple[d] unclean,[d] but we stopped him.[n] ⁸You can decide if all these things are true. Ask him some questions yourself." ⁹The other Jews agreed and said that all of this was true.

¹⁰The governor made a sign for Paul to speak. So Paul said, "Governor Felix, I know that you have been a judge over this nation for a long time. So I am happy to defend myself before you. ¹¹I went to worship in Jerusalem only 12 days ago. You can learn for yourself that this is true. ¹²Those who are accusing me did not find me arguing with anyone in the Temple. I was not stirring up the people. And I was not making trouble in the Temple or in the synagogues[d] or in the city. ¹³They cannot prove the things they are saying against me now. ¹⁴But I will tell you this: I worship the God of our ancestors as a follower of the Way of Jesus. The Jews say that the Way of Jesus is not the right way. But I believe everything that is taught in the law of Moses and that is written in the books of the Prophets.[d] ¹⁵I have the same hope in God that they have—the hope that all people, good and bad, will be raised from death. ¹⁶This is why I always try to do what I believe is right before God and men.

¹⁷"I was away from Jerusalem for several years. I went back there to bring money to my people and to offer sacrifices. ¹⁸I was doing this when they found me in the Temple. I had finished the cleansing ceremony. I had not made any trouble; no people were gathering around me. ¹⁹But some Jews from the country of Asia were there. They should be here, standing before you. If I have really done anything wrong, they are the ones who should accuse me. ²⁰Or ask these Jews here if they found any wrong in me when I stood before the Jewish council in Jerusalem. ²¹But I did say one thing when I stood before them: 'You are

judging me today because I believe that people will rise from death!'"

²²Felix already understood much about the Way of Jesus. He stopped the trial and said, "When commander Lysias comes here, I will decide about your case." ²³Felix told the officer to keep Paul guarded. But he told the officer to give Paul some freedom and to let his friends bring him what he needed.

²⁴After some days Felix came with his wife, Drusilla, who was a Jew. He asked for Paul to be brought to him. He listened to Paul talk about believing in Christ Jesus. ²⁵But Felix became afraid when Paul spoke about things like right living, self-control, and the time when God will judge the world. He said, "Go away now. When I have more time, I will call for you." ²⁶At the same time Felix hoped that Paul would give him some money. So he sent for Paul often and talked with him.

²⁷But after two years, Porcius Festus became governor. Felix was no longer governor, but he had left Paul in prison to please the Jews.

25 Three days after Festus became governor, he went from Caesarea to Jerusalem. ²There the leading priests and the important Jewish leaders made charges against Paul before Festus. ³They asked Festus to do something for them; they wanted him to send Paul back to Jerusalem. (They had a plan to kill Paul on the way.) ⁴But Festus answered, "No! Paul will be kept in Caesarea. I will return there soon myself. ⁵Some of your leaders should go with me. They can accuse the man there in Caesarea, if he has really done something wrong."

⁶Festus stayed in Jerusalem another eight or ten days. Then he went back to Caesarea. The next day he told the soldiers to bring Paul before him. Festus was seated on the judge's seat ⁷when Paul came into the room. The Jews who had come from Jerusalem stood around him. They started making serious charges against Paul. But they could not prove any of them. ⁸This is what Paul said to defend himself: "I have done nothing wrong against the Jewish law, against the Temple,[d] or against Caesar!"[d]

⁹But Festus wanted to please the Jews.

So he asked Paul, "Do you want to go to Jerusalem? Do you want me to judge you there on these charges?"

¹⁰Paul said, "I am standing at Caesar's judgment seat now. This is where I should be judged! I have done nothing wrong to the Jews; you know this is true. ¹¹If I have done something wrong and the law says I must die, I do not ask to be saved from death. But if these charges are not true, then no one can give me to them. No! I want Caesar to hear my case!"

¹²Festus talked about this with the people who advised him. Then he said, "You have asked to see Caesar; so you will go to Caesar!"

¹³A few days later King Agrippa and Bernice came to Caesarea to visit Festus. ¹⁴They stayed there for some time, and Festus told the king about Paul's case. Festus said, "There is a man that Felix left in prison. ¹⁵When I went to Jerusalem, the leading priests and the older Jewish leaders there made charges against him. They wanted me to sentence him to death. ¹⁶But I answered, 'When a man is accused of a crime, Romans do not hand him over just to please someone. The man must be allowed to face his accusers and defend himself against their charges.' ¹⁷So these Jews came here to Caesarea for the trial. And I did not waste time. The next day I sat on the judge's seat and commanded that the man be brought in. ¹⁸The Jews stood up and accused him. But they did not accuse him of any serious crime as I thought they would. ¹⁹The things they said were about their own religion and about a man named Jesus. Jesus died, but Paul said that he is still alive. ²⁰I did not know much about these things; so I did not ask questions. But I asked Paul, 'Do you want to go to Jerusalem and be judged there?' ²¹But he asked to be kept in Caesarea. He wants a decision from the Emperor.ⁿ So I ordered that Paul be held until I could send him to Caesarᵈ in Rome."

²²Agrippa said to Festus, "I would like to hear this man, too."

Festus said, "Tomorrow you will hear him!"

²³The next day Agrippa and Bernice appeared. They dressed and acted like very important people. Agrippa and Bernice, the army leaders, and the important men of Caesarea went into the judgment room. Then Festus ordered the soldiers to bring Paul in. ²⁴Festus said, "King Agrippa and all who are gathered here with us, you see this man. All the Jewish people, here and in Jerusalem, have complained to me about him. They shout that he should not live any longer. ²⁵When I judged him, I could find nothing wrong. I found no reason to order his death. But he asked to be judged by Caesar. So I decided to send him. ²⁶But I have nothing definite to write the Emperor about him. So I have brought you before all of you—especially you, King Agrippa. I hope that you can question him and give me something to write. ²⁷I think it is foolish to send a prisoner to Caesar without telling what the charges are against him."

26 Agrippa said to Paul, "You may now speak to defend yourself."

Then Paul raised his hand and began to speak. ²He said, "King Agrippa, I will answer all the charges that the Jews make against me. I think it is a blessing that I can stand here before you today. ³I am very happy to talk to you, because you know so much about all the Jewish customs and the things that the Jews argue about. Please listen to me patiently.

⁴"All the Jews know about my whole life. They know the way I lived from the beginning in my own country and later in Jerusalem. ⁵They have known me for a long time. If they want to, they can tell you that I was a good Pharisee.ᵈ And the Pharisees obey the laws of the Jewish religion more carefully than any other group of Jewish people. ⁶Now I am on trial because I hope for the promise that God made to our ancestors. ⁷This is the promise that the 12 tribesᵈ of our people hope to receive. For this hope the Jews serve God day and night. My king, the Jews have accused me because I hope for this same promise! ⁸Why do any of you people think it is impossible for God to raise people from death?

⁹"I too thought I ought to do many things against Jesus from Nazareth. ¹⁰And in Jerusalem I did many things against God's people. The leading priests gave me the power to put many of them in jail. When they were being killed, I agreed that it was a good thing. ¹¹In every synagogue,ᵈ I often punished them. I tried to make them say evil things against Jesus. I was so angry

²⁵:²¹ **Emperor** The ruler of the Roman Empire, which was almost all the world.

against them that I even went to other cities to find them and punish them.

[12] "One time the leading priests gave me permission and the power to go to Damascus. [13] On the way there, at noon, I saw a light from heaven. The light was brighter than the sun. It flashed all around me and the men who were traveling with me. [14] We all fell to the ground. Then I heard a voice speaking to me in the Jewish language.[n] The voice said, 'Saul, Saul, why are you doing things against me? You are only hurting yourself by fighting me.' [15] I said, 'Who are you, Lord?' The Lord said, 'I am Jesus. I am the One you are trying to hurt. [16] Stand up! I have chosen you to be my servant. You will be my witness—you will tell people the things that you have seen and the things that I will show you. This is why I have come to you today. [17] I will not let your own people hurt you. And I will keep you safe from the non-Jewish people too. These are the people I am sending you to. [18] I send you to open their eyes that they may turn away from darkness to the light. I send you that they may turn away from the power of Satan and turn to God. Then their sins can be forgiven and they can have a place with those people who have been made holy by believing in me.'

[19] "King Agrippa, after I had this vision from heaven, I obeyed it. [20] I began telling people that they should change their hearts and lives and turn to God. I told them to do things to show that they really had changed. I told this first to those in Damascus, then in Jerusalem and in every part of Judea, and also to the non-Jewish people. [21] This is why the Jews took me and were trying to kill me in the Temple.[d] [22] But God helped me and is still helping me today. With God's help I am standing here today and telling all people what I have seen. But I am saying nothing new. I am saying what Moses and the prophets[d] said would happen. [23] They said that the Christ[d] would die and be the first to rise from death. They said that the Christ would bring light to the Jewish and non-Jewish people."

[24] While Paul was saying these things to defend himself, Festus said loudly, "Paul, you are out of your mind! Too much study has driven you crazy!"

[25] Paul said, "Most Excellent Festus, I am not crazy. My words are true. They are not the words of a foolish man. [26] King Agrippa knows about these things. I can speak freely to him. I know that he has heard about all of these things. They did not happen off in a corner. [27] King Agrippa, do you believe what the prophets[d] wrote? I know you believe!"

[28] King Agrippa said to Paul, "Do you think you can persuade me to become a Christian in such a short time?"

[29] Paul said, "Whether it is a short or a long time, I pray to God that not only you but every person listening to me today would be saved and be like me—except for these chains I have!"

[30] Then King Agrippa, Governor Festus, Bernice, and all the people sitting with them stood up [31] and left the room. They were talking to each other. They said, "There is no reason why this man should die or be put in jail." [32] And Agrippa said to Festus, "We could let this man go free, but he has asked Caesar[d] to hear his case."

27 It was decided that we would sail for Italy. An officer named Julius, who served in the Emperor's[n] army, guarded Paul and some other prisoners. [2] We got on a ship and left. The ship was from the city of Adramyttium and was about to sail to different ports in the country of Asia. Aristarchus, a man from the city of Thessalonica in Macedonia, went with us. [3] The next day we came to Sidon. Julius was very good to Paul. He gave Paul freedom to go visit his friends, who took care of his needs. [4] We left Sidon and sailed close to the island of Cyprus because the wind was blowing against us. [5] We went across the sea by Cilicia and Pamphylia. Then we came to the city of Myra, in Lycia. [6] There the officer found a ship from Alexandria that was going to Italy. So he put us on it.

[7] We sailed slowly for many days. We had a hard time reaching Cnidus because the wind was blowing against us. We could not go any farther that way. So we sailed by the south side of the island of Crete near Salmone. [8] We sailed along the coast, but the sailing was hard. Then we came to a place called Safe Harbors, near the city of Lasea.

[9] But we had lost much time. It was now dangerous to sail, because it was

26:14 Jewish language Aramaic, the language of the Jews in the first century. **27:1 Emperor** The ruler of the Roman Empire, which was almost all the world.

already after the Day of Cleansing.[n] So Paul warned them, [10]"Men, I can see there will be a lot of trouble on this trip. The ship and the things in the ship will be lost. Even our lives may be lost!" [11]But the captain and the owner of the ship did not agree with Paul. So the officer did not believe Paul. Instead, the officer believed what the captain and owner of the ship said. [12]And that harbor was not a good place for the ship to stay for the winter. So most of the men decided that the ship should leave. The men hoped we could go to Phoenix. The ship could stay there for the winter. (Phoenix was a city on the island of Crete. It had a harbor which faced southwest and northwest.)

[13]Then a good wind began to blow from the south. The men on the ship thought, "This is the wind we wanted, and now we have it!" So they pulled up the anchor. We sailed very close to the island of Crete. [14]But then a very strong wind named the "Northeaster" came from the island. [15]This wind took the ship and carried it away. The ship could not sail against it. So we stopped trying and let the wind blow us. [16]We went below a small island named Cauda. Then we were able to bring in the lifeboat, but it was very hard to do. [17]After the men took the lifeboat in, they tied ropes around the ship to hold it together. The men were afraid that the ship would hit the sandbanks of Syrtis.[n] So they lowered the sail and let the wind carry the ship. [18]The next day the storm was blowing us so hard that the men threw out some of the cargo. [19]A day later they threw out the ship's equipment. [20]For many days we could not see the sun or the stars. The storm was very bad. We lost all hope of staying alive—we thought we would die.

[21]The men had gone without food for a long time. Then one day Paul stood up before them and said, "Men, I told you not to leave Crete. You should have listened to me. Then you would not have all this trouble and loss. [22]But now I tell you to cheer up. None of you will die! But the ship will be lost. [23]Last night an angel from God came to me. This is the God I worship. I am his. [24]God's angel

said, 'Paul, do not be afraid! You must stand before Caesar.[d] And God has given you this promise: He will save the lives of all those men sailing with you.' [25]So men, be cheerful! I trust in God. Everything will happen as his angel told me. [26]But we will crash on an island."

[27]On the fourteenth night we were floating around in the Adriatic Sea.[n] The sailors thought we were close to land. [28]They threw a rope into the water with a weight on the end of it. They found that the water was 120 feet deep. They went a little farther and threw the rope in again. It was 90 feet deep. [29]The sailors were afraid that we would hit the rocks, so they threw four anchors into the water. Then they prayed for daylight to come. [30]Some of the sailors wanted to leave the ship, and they lowered the lifeboat. These sailors wanted the other men to think that they were throwing more anchors from the front of the ship. [31]But Paul told the officer and the other soldiers, "If these men do not stay in the ship, your lives cannot be saved!" [32]So the soldiers cut the ropes and let the lifeboat fall into the water.

[33]Just before dawn Paul began persuading all the people to eat something. He said, "For the past 14 days you have been waiting and watching. You have not eaten. [34]Now I beg you to eat something. You need it to stay alive. None of you will lose even one hair off your heads." [35]After he said this, Paul took some bread and thanked God for it before all of them. He broke off a piece and began eating. [36]All the men felt better. They all started eating too. [37](There were 276 people on the ship.) [38]We ate all we wanted. Then we began making the ship lighter by throwing the grain into the sea.

[39]When daylight came, the sailors saw land. They did not know what land it was, but they saw a bay with a beach. They wanted to sail the ship to the beach, if they could. [40]So they cut the ropes to the anchors and left the anchors in the sea. At the same time, they untied the ropes that were holding the rudders. Then they raised the front sail into the wind and sailed toward the beach. [41]But the ship hit a sandbank.

27:9 Day of Cleansing An important Jewish holy day in the fall of the year. This was the time of year that bad storms happened on the sea. **27:17 Syrtis** Shallow area in the sea near the Libyan coast. **27:27 Adriatic Sea** The sea between Greece and Italy, including the central Mediterranean.

The front of the ship stuck there and could not move. Then the big waves began to break the back of the ship to pieces. [42]The soldiers decided to kill the prisoners so that none of them could swim away and escape. [43]But Julius, the officer, wanted to let Paul live. He did not allow the soldiers to kill the prisoners. Instead he ordered everyone who could swim to jump into the water and swim to land. [44]The rest used wooden boards or pieces of the ship. And this is how all the people made it safely to land.

28 When we were safe on land, we learned that the island was called Malta. [2]It was raining and very cold. But the people who lived there were very good to us. They made us a fire and welcomed all of us. [3]Paul gathered a pile of sticks for the fire. He was putting them on the fire when a poisonous snake came out because of the heat and bit him on the hand. [4]The people living on the island saw the snake hanging from Paul's hand. They said to each other, "This man must be a murderer! He did not die in the sea, but Justice[n] does not want him to live." [5]But Paul shook the snake off into the fire. He was not hurt. [6]The people thought that Paul would swell up or fall down dead. The people waited and watched him for a long time, but nothing bad happened to him. So they changed their minds about Paul. Now they said, "He is a god!"

[7]There were some fields around there owned by a very important man on the island. His name was Publius. He welcomed us into his home and was very good to us. We stayed in his house for three days. [8]Publius' father was very sick with a fever and dysentery.[n] But Paul went to him and prayed. Then he put his hands on the man and healed him. [9]After this, all the other sick people on the island came to Paul, and he healed them, too. [10-11]The people on the island gave us many honors. When we were ready to leave, they gave us the things we needed.

We got on a ship from Alexandria. The ship had stayed on the island during the winter. On the front of the ship was the sign of the twin gods.[n] [12]We stopped at Syracuse for three days and then left. [13]From there we sailed to Rhegium. The next day a wind began to blow from the southwest, so we were able to leave. A day later we came to Puteoli. [14]We found some believers there, and they asked us to stay with them for a week. Finally, we came to Rome. [15]The believers in Rome heard that we were there. They came out as far as the Market of Appius[n] and the Three Inns[n] to meet us. When Paul saw them, he was encouraged and thanked God.

[16]Then we arrived at Rome. There, Paul was allowed to live alone. But a soldier stayed with him to guard him.

[17]Three days later Paul sent for the Jewish leaders there. When they came together, he said, "Brothers, I have done nothing against our people. I have done nothing against the customs of our fathers. But I was arrested in Jerusalem and given to the Romans. [18]The Romans asked me many questions. But they could find no reason why I should be killed. They wanted to let me go free, [19]but the Jews there did not want that. So I had to ask to come to Rome to have my trial before Caesar.[d] But I have no charge to bring against my own people. [20]That is why I wanted to see you and talk with you. I am bound with this chain because I believe in the hope of Israel."

[21]The Jews answered Paul, "We have received no letters from Judea about you. None of our Jewish brothers who have come from there brought news about you or told us anything bad about you. [22]We want to hear your ideas. We know that people everywhere are speaking against this religious group."

[23]Paul and the Jews chose a day for a meeting. On that day many more of the Jews met with Paul at the place he was staying. Paul spoke to them all day long, explaining the kingdom of God to them. He tried to persuade them to believe these things about Jesus. He used the law of Moses and the writings of the prophets[d] to do this. [24]Some of the Jews believed what Paul said, but others did not. [25]So they argued, and the Jews were ready to leave. But Paul said one more thing to them: "The Holy Spirit[d] spoke

28:4 Justice The people thought there was a god named Justice who would punish bad people. **28:8 dysentery** A sickness like diarrhea. **28:10-11 twin gods** Statues of Castor and Pollux, gods in old Greek tales. **28:15 Market of Appius** A town about 27 miles from Rome. **28:15 Three Inns** A town about 30 miles from Rome.

the truth to your fathers through Isaiah the prophet. He said,

> [26]'Go to this people and say:
> You will listen and listen, but you
>   will not understand.
> You will look and look, but you will
>   not learn.
> [27]For these people have become
>   stubborn.
> They don't hear with their ears.
> And they have closed their eyes.
> Otherwise, they might really
>   understand
> what they see with their eyes
> and hear with their ears.

They might really understand in
    their minds.
If they did this, they would come
    back to me and be forgiven.'

Isaiah 6:9-10

[28]"I want you Jews to know that God has also sent his salvation to the non-Jewish people. They will listen!" [29] n

[30]Paul stayed two full years in his own rented house. He welcomed all people who came and visited him. [31]He preached about the kingdom of God and taught about the Lord Jesus Christ. He was very bold, and no one tried to stop him from speaking.

The Letter of Paul the Apostle to the
ROMANS

1 From Paul, a servant of Christ Jesus. God called me to be an apostle[d] and chose me to tell the Good News.[d]

[2]God promised this Good News long ago through his prophets.[d] That promise is written in the Holy Scriptures.[d] [3-4]The Good News is about God's Son, Jesus Christ our Lord. As a man, he was born from the family of David. But through the Spirit[d] of holiness he was appointed to be God's Son with great power by rising from death. [5]Through Christ, God gave me the special work of an apostle. This was to lead people of all nations to believe and obey. I do this work for Christ. [6]And you who are in Rome are also called to belong to Jesus Christ.

[7]This letter is to all of you in Rome whom God loves and has called to be his holy people.

May God our Father and the Lord Jesus Christ show you kindness and give you peace.

[8]First I want to say that I thank my God through Jesus Christ for all of you. I thank God because people everywhere in the world are talking about your great faith. [9-10]God knows that every time I pray I always mention you. God is the One I serve with my whole heart by telling the Good News[d] about his Son. I pray that I will be allowed to come to you, and this will happen if God wants it. [11]I want very much to see you, to give you some spiritual gift to make you

strong, [12]I mean that I want us to help each other with the faith that we have. Your faith will help me, and my faith will help you. [13]Brothers, I want you to know that I planned many times to come to you. But this has not been possible. I wanted to come so that I could help you grow spiritually. I wanted to help you as I have helped the other non-Jewish people.

[14]I must serve all people—Greeks and non-Greeks, the wise and the foolish. [15]That is why I want so much to preach the Good News to you in Rome.

[16]I am proud of the Good News. It is the power God uses to save everyone who believes—to save the Jews first, and also to save the non-Jews. [17]The Good News shows how God makes people right with himself. God's way of making people right with him begins and ends with faith. As the Scripture[d] says, "The person who is made right with God by faith will live forever."[n]

[18]God's anger is shown from heaven against all the evil and wrong things that people do. By their own evil lives they hide the truth. [19]God shows his anger because everything that may be known about God has been made clear. Yes, God has clearly shown them everything that may be known about him. [20]There are things about God that people cannot see—his eternal power and all the things that make him God. But

28:29 Verse 29 Some late Greek copies add verse 29: "After Paul said this, the Jews left. They were arguing very much with each other." **1:17 "The person . . . forever."** Quotation from Habakkuk 2:4.

since the beginning of the world those things have been easy to understand. They are made clear by what God has made. So people have no excuse for the bad things they do. ²¹They knew God. But they did not give glory to God, and they did not thank him. Their thinking became useless. Their foolish minds were filled with darkness. ²²They said they were wise, but they became fools. ²³They gave up the glory of God who lives forever. They traded that glory for the worship of idols made to look like earthly people. They traded God's glory for things that look like birds, animals, and snakes.

²⁴People were full of sin, wanting only to do evil. So God let them go their sinful way. They became full of sexual sin, using their bodies wrongly with each other. ²⁵They traded the truth of God for a lie and worshiped and served things that were made by man. But they did not worship and serve the God who made those things. God should be praised forever. Amen.

²⁶Because people did those things, God left them and let them do the shameful things they wanted to do. Women stopped having natural sex and started having sex with other women. ²⁷In the same way, men stopped having natural sex and began wanting each other. Men did shameful things with other men. And in their bodies they received the punishment for those wrongs.

²⁸People did not think it was important to have a true knowledge of God. So God left them and allowed them to have their own worthless thinking. And so those people do the things that they should not do. ²⁹They are filled with every kind of sin, evil, selfishness, and hatred. They are full of jealousy, murder, fighting, lying, and thinking the worst about each other. They gossip ³⁰and say evil things about each other. They hate God. They are rude and conceited and brag about themselves. They invent ways of doing evil. They do not obey their parents. ³¹They are foolish, they do not keep their promises, and they show no kindness or mercy to other people. ³²They know God's law says that those who live like this should die. But they continue to do these evil things. And they also feel that those who do these things are doing right.

2 If you think that you can judge others, then you are wrong. You too are guilty of sin. You judge people, but you do the same bad things they do. So when you judge them, you are really judging yourself guilty. ²God judges those who do wrong things. And we know that God's judging is right. ³You judge those who do wrong, but you do wrong yourselves. Do you think you will be able to escape the judgment of God? ⁴God has been very kind to you, and he has been patient with you. God has been waiting for you to change. But you think nothing of his kindness. Perhaps you do not understand that God is kind to you so that you will change your hearts and lives. ⁵But you are hard and stubborn and refuse to change. So you are making your own punishment greater and greater on the day God shows his anger. On that day all people will see God's right judgments. ⁶God will reward or punish every person for what he has done. ⁷Some people live for God's glory, for honor, and for life that has no end. They live for those things by always continuing to do good. God will give life forever to them. ⁸But other people are selfish and refuse to follow truth. They follow evil. God will give them his punishment and anger. ⁹He will give trouble and suffering to everyone who does evil—to the Jews first and also to the non-Jews. ¹⁰But God will give glory, honor, and peace to everyone who does good—to the Jews first and also to the non-Jews. ¹¹For God judges all people in the same way.

¹²People who have God's law and those who have never heard of the law are all the same when they sin. Those who do not have the law and are sinners will be lost. And, in the same way, people who have the law and are sinners will be judged by the law. ¹³Hearing the law does not make people right with God. The law makes people right with God only if they obey what the law says. ¹⁴(The non-Jews do not have the law. But when they freely do things that the law commands, then they are the law for themselves. This is true even though they do not have the law. ¹⁵They show that in their hearts they know what is right and wrong, just as the law commands. And they also show this by the way they feel about right and wrong. Sometimes their thoughts tell them they did wrong. And sometimes their thoughts tell them they did right.)

[16] All these things will happen on the day when God will judge the secret thoughts of people's hearts. The Good News[d] that I preach says that God will judge everyone through Christ Jesus.

[17] What about you? You call yourself a Jew. You trust in the law of Moses and brag that you are close to God. [18] You know what God wants you to do. And you know the things that are important because you have learned the law. [19] You think you are a guide for the blind and a light for those who are in darkness. [20] You think you can show foolish people what is right and teach those who know nothing. You have the law; so you think you know everything and have all truth. [21] You teach other people. So why don't you teach yourself? You tell others not to steal. But you yourselves steal. [22] You say that others must not take part in adultery.[d] But you yourselves are guilty of that sin. You hate idols. But you steal from temples. [23] You brag about having God's law. But you bring shame to God by breaking his law. [24] It is written in the Scriptures:[d] "The non-Jews speak against God's name because of you Jews."[n]

[25] If you follow the law, then your circumcision[d] has meaning. But if you break the law, then it is as if you were never circumcised. [26] The non-Jews are not circumcised. But if they do what the law says, then it is as if they were circumcised. [27] You Jews have the written law and circumcision, but you break the law. So those who are not circumcised in their bodies, but still obey the law, will show that you are guilty.

[28] A person is not a true Jew if he is only a Jew in his physical body. True circumcision is not only on the outside of the body. [29] A person is a true Jew only if he is a Jew inside. True circumcision is done in the heart by the Spirit,[d] not by the written law. Such a person gets praise from God, not from other people.

3 So, do Jews have anything that other people do not have? Is there anything special about being circumcised? [2] Yes, of course, there is in every way. The most important thing is this: God trusted the Jews with his teachings. [3] It is true that some Jews were not faithful to God. But will that stop God from doing what he promised? [4] No! God will continue to be true even when every person is false. As the Scriptures[d] say:

"So your words may be shown to
    be right.
You are fair when you judge me."
                        Psalm 51:4

[5] When we do wrong, that shows more clearly that God is right. So can we say that God is wrong to punish us? (I am talking as men might talk.) [6] No! If God could not punish us, then God could not judge the world.

[7] A person might say, "When I lie, it really gives God glory, because my lie shows God's truth. So why am I judged a sinner?" [8] It would be the same to say, "We should do evil so that good will come." Some people find fault with us and say that we teach this. Those who say such things about us are wrong, and they should be punished.

[9] So are we Jews better than others? No! We have already said that Jews and non-Jews are the same. They are all guilty of sin. [10] As the Scriptures[d] say:

"There is no one without sin. None!
[11]   There is no one who
        understands.
    There is no one who looks to God
        for help.
[12] All have turned away.
    Together, everyone has become
        evil.
None of them does anything good."
                        Psalm 14:1-3
[13] "Their throats are like open graves.
    They use their tongues for telling
        lies."   *Psalm 5:9*
"Their words are like snake's
    poison."   *Psalm 140:3*
[14]   "Their mouths are full of cursing
        and hate."   *Psalm 10:7*
[15] "They are always ready to kill
        people.
[16]   Everywhere they go they cause
        ruin and misery.
[17] They don't know how to live in
        peace."   *Isaiah 59:7-8*
[18]   "They have no fear of or respect
        for God."   *Psalm 36:1*

[19] The law commands many things. We know that those commands are for those who are under the law. This stops all excuses and brings the whole world under God's judgment, [20] because no one can be made right with God by following the law. The law only shows us our sin.

[21] But God has a way to make people right with him without the law. And God has now shown us that way which the

2:24 **"The non-Jews . . . Jews."** Quotation from Isaiah 52:5; Ezekiel 36:20.

law and the prophets[d] told us about. [22]God makes people right with himself through their faith in Jesus Christ. This is true for all who believe in Christ, because all are the same. [23]All people have sinned and are not good enough for God's glory. [24]People are made right with God by his grace, which is a free gift. They are made right with God by being made free from sin through Jesus Christ. [25]God gave Jesus as a way to forgive sin through faith. And all of this is because of the blood of Jesus' death. This showed that God always does what is right and fair. God was right in the past when he was patient and did not punish people for their sins. [26]And God gave Jesus to show today that God does what is right. God did this so that he could judge rightly and also make right any person who has faith in Jesus.

[27]So do we have a reason to brag about ourselves? No! And why not? It is the way of faith that stops all bragging, not the way of following the law. [28]A person is made right with God through faith, not through what he does to follow the law. [29]Is God only the God of the Jews? Is he not also the God of the non-Jews? [30]Of course he is, for there is only one God. He will make Jews right with him by their faith. And he will also make non-Jews right with him through their faith. [31]So do we destroy the law by following the way of faith? No! Faith causes us to be what the law truly wants.

4 So what can we say about Abraham,[n] the father of our people? What did he learn about faith? [2]If Abraham was made right by the things he did, then he had a reason to brag. But he could not brag before God. [3]The Scripture[d] says, "Abraham believed God. And that faith made him right with God."[n]

[4]When a person works, his pay is not given to him as a gift. He earns the pay he gets. [5]But a person cannot do any work that will make him right with God. So he must trust in God. Then God accepts his faith, and that makes him right with God. God is the One who can make even those who are evil right in his sight. [6]David said the same thing. He said that a person is truly blessed when God does not look at what he has done but accepts him as good:

[7]"Happy are they
     whose sins are forgiven,
     whose wrongs are pardoned.
[8]Happy is the person
     whom the Lord does not consider
     guilty."   *Psalm 32:1-2*

[9]Is this blessing only for those who are circumcised?[d] Or is it also for those who are not circumcised? We have already said that God accepted Abraham's faith, and that faith made him right with God. [10]So how did this happen? Did God accept Abraham before or after he was circumcised? God accepted him before his circumcision. [11]Abraham was circumcised later to show that God accepted him. His circumcision was proof that he was right with God through faith before he was circumcised. So Abraham is the father of all those who believe but are not circumcised. He is the father of all believers who are accepted as being right with God. [12]And Abraham is also the father of those who have been circumcised. But it is not their circumcision that makes him their father. He is their father only if they live following the faith that our father Abraham had before he was circumcised.

[13]Abraham[n] and his descendants[d] received the promise that they would get the whole world. But Abraham did not receive that promise through the law. He received it because he was right with God through his faith. [14]If people could receive what God promised by following the law, then faith is worthless. And God's promise to Abraham is worthless, [15]because the law can only bring God's anger. But if there is no law, then there is nothing to disobey.

[16]So people receive God's promise by having faith. This happens so that the promise can be a free gift. And if the promise is a free gift, then all of Abraham's children can have that promise. The promise is not only for those people that live under the law of Moses. It is for anyone who lives with faith like Abraham. He is the father of us all. [17]As it is written in the Scriptures:[d] "I am making you a father of many nations."[n] This is true before God. Abraham believed in God—the God who gives life to the dead and decides that things will happen that have not yet happened.

[18]There was no hope that Abraham

4:1, 13 **Abraham** Most respected ancestor of the Jews. Every Jew hoped to see Abraham. 4:3 **"Abraham . . . God."** Quotation from Genesis 15:6. 4:17 **"I . . . nations,"** Quotation from Genesis 17:5.

would have children. But Abraham believed God and continued hoping. And that is why he became the father of many nations. As God told him, "Your descendants will also be too many to count."[n] [19]Abraham was almost 100 years old, much past the age for having children. Also, Sarah could not have children. Abraham thought about all this. But his faith in God did not become weak. [20]He never doubted that God would keep his promise. Abraham never stopped believing. He grew stronger in his faith and gave praise to God. [21]Abraham felt sure that God was able to do the thing that God promised. [22]So, "God accepted Abraham's faith, and that made him right with God."[n] [23]Those words ("God accepted Abraham's faith") were written not only for Abraham. [24]They were written also for us. God will accept us also because we believe. We believe in the One who raised Jesus our Lord from death. [25]Jesus was given to die for our sins. And he was raised from death to make us right with God.

5 We have been made right with God because of our faith. So we have peace with God through our Lord Jesus Christ. [2]Through our faith, Christ has brought us into that blessing of God's grace that we now enjoy. And we are happy because of the hope we have of sharing God's glory. [3]And we also have joy with our troubles because we know that these troubles produce patience. [4]And patience produces character, and character produces hope. [5]And this hope will never disappoint us, because God has poured out his love to fill our hearts. God gave us his love through the Holy Spirit,[f] whom God has given to us. [6]Christ died for us while we were still weak. We were living against God, but at the right time, Christ died for us. [7]Very few people will die to save the life of someone else. Although perhaps for a good man someone might possibly die. [8]But Christ died for us while we were still sinners. In this way God shows his great love for us.

[9]We have been made right with God by the blood of Christ's death. So through Christ we will surely be saved from God's anger. [10]I mean that while we were God's enemies, God made friends with us through the death of his Son. Surely, now that we are God's friends,

God will save us through his Son's life. [11]And not only that, but now we are also very happy in God through our Lord Jesus Christ. Through Jesus we are now God's friends again.

[12]Sin came into the world because of what one man did. And with sin came death. And this is why all men must die—because all men sinned. [13]Sin was in the world before the law of Moses. But God does not judge people guilty of sin if there is no law. [14]But from the time of Adam to the time of Moses, everyone had to die. Adam died because he sinned by not obeying God's command. But even those who did not sin in the same way had to die.

Adam was like the One who was coming in the future. [15]But God's free gift is not like Adam's sin. Many people died because of the sin of that one man. But the grace that they received from God was much greater. Many people received God's gift of life by the grace of the one man, Jesus Christ. [16]After Adam sinned once, he was judged guilty. But the gift of God is different. God's free gift came after many sins. And the gift makes people right with God. [17]One man sinned, and so death ruled all people because of that one man. But now some people accept God's full grace and the great gift of being made right with him. They will surely have true life and rule through the one man, Jesus Christ.

[18]So one sin of Adam brought the punishment of death to all people. But in the same way, one good act that Christ did makes all people right with God. And that brings true life for all. [19]One man disobeyed God, and many became sinners. But in the same way, one man obeyed God, and many will be made right. [20]The law came to make people have more sin. But when people had more sin, God gave them more of his grace. [21]Sin once used death to rule us. But God gave people more of his grace so that grace could rule by making people right with him. And this brings life forever through Jesus Christ our Lord.

6 So do you think that we should continue sinning so that God will give us more and more grace? [2]No! We died to our old sinful lives. So how can we continue living with sin? [3]Did you forget that all of us became part of Christ when we were baptized? We shared his death in our baptism. [4]So when we were baptized, we were buried with Christ and shared his death. We were buried with him so that we could live a new life, just as Christ was raised from death by the wonderful power of the Father.

[5]Christ died, and we have been joined with Christ by dying too. So we will also be joined with him by rising from death as he did. [6]We know that our old life died with Christ on the cross. This was so that our sinful selves would have no power over us, and we would not be slaves to sin. [7]Anyone who has died is made free from sin's control.

[8]If we died with Christ, we know that we will also live with him. [9]Christ was raised from death. And we know that he cannot die again. Death has no power over him now. [10]Yes, when Christ died, he died to defeat the power of sin one time—enough for all time. He now has a new life, and his new life is with God. [11]In the same way, you should see yourselves as being dead to the power of sin and alive with God through Christ Jesus.

[12]So, do not let sin control you in your life here on earth. You must not be ruled by the things your sinful self makes you want to do. [13]Do not offer the parts of your body to serve sin. Do not use your bodies as things to do evil with, but offer yourselves to God. Be like people who have died and now live. Offer the parts of your body to God to be used for doing good. [14]Sin will not be your master, because you are not under law but under God's grace.

[15]So what should we do? Should we sin because we are under grace and not under law? No! [16]Surely you know that when you give yourselves like slaves to obey someone, then you are really slaves of that person. The person you obey is your master. You can follow sin, or obey God. Sin brings spiritual death. But obeying God makes you right with him. [17]In the past you were slaves to sin—sin controlled you. But thank God, you fully obeyed the things that were taught to you. [18]You were made free from sin, and now you are slaves to goodness. [19]I use this example because this is hard for you to understand. In the past you offered the parts of your body to be slaves to sin and evil. You lived only for evil. In the same way now you must give yourselves to be slaves of

goodness. Then you will live only for God.

[20]In the past you were slaves to sin, and goodness did not control you. [21]You did evil things, and now you are ashamed of them. Those things only bring death. [22]But now you are free from sin and have become slaves of God. This brings you a life that is only for God. And this gives you life forever. [23]When someone sins, he earns what sin pays—death. But God gives us a free gift—life forever in Christ Jesus our Lord.

7Brothers, all of you understand the law of Moses. So surely you know that the law rules over a person only while he is alive. [2]For example, a woman must stay married to her husband as long as he is alive. But if her husband dies, then she is free from the law of marriage. [3]But if she marries another man while her husband is still alive, the law says she is guilty of adultery.[d] But if her husband dies, then the woman is free from the law of marriage. So if she marries another man after her husband dies, she is not guilty of adultery.

[4]In the same way, my brothers, your old selves died, and you became free from the law through the body of Christ. Now you belong to someone else. You belong to the One who was raised from death. We belong to Christ so that we can be used in service to God. [5]In the past, we were ruled by our sinful selves. The law made us want to do sinful things. And those sinful things we wanted to do controlled our bodies, so that the things we did were only bringing us death. [6]In the past, the law held us like prisoners. But our old selves died, and we were made free from the law. So now we serve God in a new way, not in the old way with written rules. Now we serve God in the new way, with the Spirit.[d]

[7]You might think that I am saying that sin and the law are the same thing. That is not true. But the law was the only way I could learn what sin meant. I would never have known what it means to want something wrong if the law had not said, "You must not want to take your neighbor's things."[n][8] And sin found a way to use that command and cause me to want every kind of wrong thing. So sin came to me because of that command. But without the law, sin has no power. [9]I was alive without the law be-

7:7 "You . . . things." Quotation from Exodus 20:13, 15-17.

fore I knew the law. But when the law's command came to me, then sin began to live. [10]And I died because of sin. The command was meant to bring life, but for me that command brought death. [11]Sin found a way to fool me by using the command. Sin used the command to make me die.

[12]So the law is holy, and the command is holy and right and good. [13]Does this mean that something that is good brought death to me? No! Sin used something that is good to bring death to me. This happened so that I could see what sin is really like. The command was used to show that sin is something very evil.

[14]We know that the law is spiritual. But I am not spiritual. Sin rules me as if I were its slave. [15]I do not understand the things I do. I do not do the good things I want to do. And I do the bad things I hate to do. [16]And if I do not want to do the bad things I do, then that means that I agree that the law is good. [17]But I am not really the one who is doing these bad things. It is sin living in me that does these things. [18]Yes, I know that nothing good lives in me—I mean nothing good lives in the part of me that is earthly and sinful. I want to do the things that are good. But I do not do them. [19]I do not do the good things that I want to do. I do the bad things that I do not want to do. [20]So if I do things I do not want to do, then I am not the one doing those things. It is sin living in me that does those bad things.

[21]So I have learned this rule: When I want to do good, evil is there with me. [22]In my mind, I am happy with God's law. [23]But I see another law working in my body. That law makes war against the law that my mind accepts. That other law working in my body is the law of sin, and that law makes me its prisoner. [24]What a miserable man I am! Who will save me from this body that brings me death? [25]God will. I thank him for saving me through Jesus Christ our Lord!

So in my mind I am a slave to God's law. But in my sinful self I am a slave to the law of sin.

8 So now, those who are in Christ Jesus are not judged guilty. [2]I am not judged guilty because in Christ Jesus the law of the Spirit[d] that brings life made me free. It made me free from the law that brings sin and death. [3]The law

was without power, because the law was made weak by our sinful selves. But God did what the law could not do. He sent his own Son to earth with the same human life that others use for sin. He sent his Son to be an offering to pay for sin. So God used a human life to destroy sin. [4]He did this so that we could be right as the law said we must be. Now we do not live following our sinful selves, but we live following the Spirit.

[5]Those who live following their sinful selves think only about things that their sinful selves want. But those who live following the Spirit are thinking about the things that the Spirit wants them to do. [6]If a person's thinking is controlled by his sinful self, then there is death. But if his thinking is controlled by the Spirit, then there is life and peace. [7]This is true because if a person's thinking is controlled by his sinful self, then he is against God. He refuses to obey God's law. And really he is not able to obey God's law. [8]Those people who are ruled by their sinful selves cannot please God.

[9]But you are not ruled by your sinful selves. You are ruled by the Spirit, if that Spirit of God really lives in you. But if anyone does not have the Spirit of Christ, then he does not belong to Christ. [10]Your body will always be dead because of sin. But if Christ is in you, then the Spirit gives you life, because Christ made you right with God. [11]God raised Jesus from death. And if God's Spirit is living in you, then he will also give life to your bodies that die. God is the One who raised Christ from death. And he will give life through his Spirit that lives in you.

[12]So, my brothers, we must not be ruled by our sinful selves. We must not live the way our sinful selves want. [13]If you use your lives to do the wrong things your sinful selves want, then you will die spiritually. But if you use the Spirit's help to stop doing the wrong things you do with your body, then you will have true life.

[14]The true children of God are those who let God's Spirit lead them. [15]The Spirit that we received is not a spirit that makes us slaves again to fear. The Spirit that we have makes us children of God. And with that Spirit we say, "Father, dear Father."[n] [16]And the Spirit himself joins with our spirits to say that we are

8:15 **"Father, dear Father."** Literally, "Abba, Father." Jewish children called their fathers "Abba."

God's children. [17]If we are God's children, then we will receive the blessings God has for us. We will receive these things from God together with Christ. But we must suffer as Christ suffered, and then we will have glory as Christ has glory.

[18]We have sufferings now. But the sufferings we have now are nothing compared to the great glory that will be given to us. [19]Everything that God made is waiting with excitement for the time when God will show the world who his children are. The whole world wants very much for that to happen. [20]Everything that God made was changed to become useless. This was not by its own wish. It happened because God wanted it. But there was this hope: [21]that everything God made would be set free from ruin. There was hope that everything God made would have the freedom and glory that belong to God's children.

[22]We know that everything God made has been waiting until now in pain, like a woman ready to give birth. [23]Not only the world, but we also have been waiting with pain inside us. We have the Spirit[d] as the first part of God's promise. So we are waiting for God to finish making us his own children. I mean we are waiting for our bodies to be made free. [24]We were saved, and we have this hope. If we see what we are waiting for, then that is not really hope. People do not hope for something they already have. [25]But we are hoping for something that we do not have yet. We are waiting for it patiently.

[26]Also, the Spirit helps us. We are very weak, but the Spirit helps us with our weakness. We do not know how to pray as we should. But the Spirit himself speaks to God for us, even begs God for us. The Spirit speaks to God with deep feelings that words cannot explain. [27]God can see what is in people's hearts. And he knows what is in the mind of the Spirit, because the Spirit speaks to God for his people in the way that God wants.

[28]We know that in everything God works for the good of those who love him. They are the people God called, because that was his plan. [29]God knew them before he made the world. And God decided that they would be like his Son. Then Jesus would be the firstborn[n] of many brothers. [30]God planned for

them to be like his Son. And those he planned to be like his Son, he also called. And those he called, he also made right with him. And those he made right, he also glorified.

[31]So what should we say about this? If God is with us, then no one can defeat us. [32]God let even his own Son suffer for us. God gave his Son for us all. So with Jesus, God will surely give us all things. [33]Who can accuse the people that God has chosen? No one! God is the One who makes them right. [34]Who can say that God's people are guilty? No one! Christ Jesus died, but that is not all. He was also raised from death. And now he is on God's right side and is begging God for us. [35]Can anything separate us from the love Christ has for us? Can troubles or problems or sufferings? If we have no food or clothes, if we are in danger, or even if death comes—can any of these things separate us from Christ's love? [36]As it is written in the Scriptures:[d]

"For you we are in danger of death
    all the time.
People think we are worth no
    more than sheep to be killed."
Psalm 44:22

[37]But in all these things we have full victory through God who showed his love for us. [38-39]Yes, I am sure that nothing can separate us from the love God has for us. Not death, not life, not angels, not ruling spirits, nothing now, nothing in the future, no powers, nothing above us, nothing below us, or anything else in the whole world will ever be able to separate us from the love of God that is in Christ Jesus our Lord.

9 I am in Christ, and I am telling you the truth. I do not lie. My feelings are ruled by the Holy Spirit,[d] and they tell me that I am not lying. [2]I have great sorrow and always feel much sadness for the Jewish people. [3]I wish I could help my Jewish brothers, my people. I would even wish that I were cursed and cut off from Christ if that would help them. [4]They are the people of Israel. They were God's chosen children. They have the glory of God and the agreements that God made between himself and his people. God gave them the law of Moses and the right way of worship. And God gave his promises to them. [5]They are the descendants[d] of our great ancestors, and they are the earthly fam-

8:29 firstborn Here this probably means that Christ was the first in God's family to share God's glory.

ily of Christ. Christ is God over all. Praise him forever![n] Amen.

[6]I do not mean that God failed to keep his promise to them. But only some of the people of Israel are truly God's people.[n] [7]And only some of Abraham's[n] descendants are true children of Abraham. But God said to Abraham: "The descendants I promised you will be from Isaac."[n] [8]This means that not all of Abraham's descendants are God's true children. Abraham's true children are those who become God's children because of the promise God made to Abraham. [9]God's promise to Abraham was this: "At the right time I will return, and Sarah will have a son." [10]And that is not all. Rebekah also had sons. And those sons had the same father, our father Isaac. [11-12]But before the two boys were born, God told Rebekah, "The older will serve the younger."[n] This was before the boys had done anything good or bad. God said this before they were born so that the one chosen would be chosen because of God's own plan. He was chosen because he was the one God wanted to call, not because of anything he did. [13]As the Scripture[d] says, "I loved Jacob, but I hated Esau."[n]

[14]So what should we say about this? Is God unfair? In no way. [15]God said to Moses, "I will show kindness to anyone I want to show kindness. I will show mercy to anyone I want to show mercy."[n] [16]So God will choose the one he decides to show mercy. And his choice does not depend on what people want or try to do. [17]The Scripture says to the king of Egypt: "I made you king so I might show my power in you. In this way my name will be talked about in all the earth."[n] [18]So God shows mercy where he wants to show mercy. And he makes stubborn the people he wants to make stubborn.

[19]So one of you will ask me: "If God controls the things we do, then why does he blame us for our sins? Who can fight his will?" [20]Do not ask that. You are only human. And human beings have no right to question God. An object cannot tell the person who made it, "Why did you make me like this?" [21]The man who

makes a jar can make anything he wants to make. He can use the same clay to make different things. He can make one thing for special use and another thing for daily use.

[22]It is the same way with what God has done. God wanted to show his anger and to let people see his power. But God patiently stayed with those people he was angry with—people who were ready to be destroyed. [23]God waited with patience so that he could make known his rich glory. He wanted to give that glory to the people who receive his mercy. He has prepared these people to have his glory, and [24]we are those people whom God called. He called us from the Jews and from the non-Jews. [25]As the Scripture says in Hosea:

"I will say, 'You are my people'
    to those I had called 'not my
      people.'
And I will show my love
    to those people I did not love."
               Hosea 2:1, 23

[26]"Now it is said to Israel,
    'You are not my people.'
But later they will be called
    'children of the living God.'"
               Hosea 1:10

[27]And Isaiah cries out about Israel:
"There are so many people of
    Israel.
They are like the grains of sand
    by the sea.
But only a few of them will be
    saved.
[28]   For the Lord will quickly and
    completely punish the people
    on the earth."   *Isaiah 10:22-23*

[29]It is as Isaiah said:
"The Lord of heaven's armies
    allowed a few of our descendants
    to live.
Otherwise we would have been
    completely destroyed
like the cities of Sodom and
    Gomorrah."[n]   *Isaiah 1:9*

[30]So what does all this mean? It means this: the non-Jews were not trying to make themselves right with God. But they were made right with God because of their faith. [31]And the people of Israel

---

9:5 Christ . . . forever! This can also mean, "May God, who rules over all things, be praised forever!" **9:6 God's people** Literally, "Israel," the people God chose to bring his blessings to the world. **9:7 Abraham** Most respected ancestor of the Jews. Every Jew hoped to see Abraham. **9:7 "The descendants . . . Isaac."** Quotation from Genesis 21:12. **9:9 "At . . . son."** Quotation from Genesis 18:10, 14. **9:11-12 "The older . . . younger."** Quotation from Genesis 25:23. **9:13 "I . . . Esau."** Quotation from Malachi 1:2-3. **9:15 "I . . . mercy."** Quotation from Exodus 33:19. **9:17 "I . . . earth."** Quotation from Exodus 9:16. **9:29 Sodom and Gomorrah** Two cities that God destroyed because the people were so evil.

tried to follow a law to make themselves right with God. But they did not succeed, [32]because they tried to make themselves right by the things they did. They did not trust in God to make them right. They fell over the stone that causes people to fall. [33]As it is written in the Scripture:

"I will put in Jerusalem a stone that
   causes people to stumble.
It is a rock that makes them fall.
Anyone who trusts in him will not
   be disappointed."

Isaiah 8:14; 28:16

10 Brothers, the thing I want most is for all the Jews to be saved. That is my prayer to God. [2]I can say this about them: They really try to follow God. But they do not know the right way. [3]They did not know the way that God makes people right with him. And they tried to make themselves right in their own way. So they did not accept God's way of making people right. [4]Christ ended the law, so that everyone who believes in him may be right with God.

[5]Moses writes about being made right by following the law. He says, "A person who does these things will have life forever because of them."[n] [6]But this is what the Scripture says about being made right through faith: "Don't say to yourself, 'Who will go up into heaven?'" (That means, "Who will go up to heaven to get Christ and bring him down to earth?") [7]"And do not say, 'Who will go down into the world below?'" (That means, "Who will go down to get Christ and bring him up from death?") [8]This is what the Scripture says: "God's teaching is near you; it is in your mouth and in your heart."[n] That is the teaching of faith that we tell. [9]If you use your mouth to say, "Jesus is Lord," and if you believe in your heart that God raised Jesus from death, then you will be saved. [10]We believe with our hearts, and so we are made right with God. And we use our mouths to say that we believe, and so we are saved. [11]As the Scripture says, "Anyone who trusts in him will never be disappointed."[n] [12]That Scripture says "anyone" because there is no difference between Jew and non-Jew. The same Lord is the Lord of all and gives many blessings to all who trust in him. [13]The

Scripture says, "Anyone who asks the Lord for help will be saved."[n]

[14]But before people can trust in the Lord for help, they must believe in him. And before they can believe in the Lord, they must hear about him. And for them to hear about the Lord, someone must tell them. [15]And before someone can go and tell them, he must be sent. It is written, "How beautiful is the person who comes to bring good news."[n]

[16]But not all the Jews accepted the good news. Isaiah said, "Lord, who believed what we told them?"[n] [17]So faith comes from hearing the Good News.[d] And people hear the Good News when someone tells them about Christ.

[18]But I ask: Didn't people hear the Good News? Yes, they heard—as the Scripture says:

"Their message went out through
   all the world.
It goes everywhere on earth."

Psalm 19:4

[19]Again I ask: Didn't the people of Israel understand? Yes, they did understand. First, Moses says:

"I will use those who are not a
   nation to make you jealous.
I will use a nation that does not
   understand to make you
   angry."   *Deuteronomy 32:21*

[20]Then Isaiah is bold enough to say:

"I was found by those who were
   not asking me for help.
I made myself known to people
   who were not looking for me."

Isaiah 65:1

[21]But about Israel God says,

"All day long I stood ready to
   accept
people who disobey and are
   stubborn."   *Isaiah 65:2*

11 So I ask: Did God throw out his people? No! I myself am an Israelite. I am from the family of Abraham, from the tribe[d] of Benjamin. [2]God chose the Israelites to be his people before they were born. And God did not leave his people. Surely you know what the Scripture[d] says about Elijah, how he prayed to God against the people of Israel. Elijah said, [3]"They have killed your prophets,[d] and they have destroyed your altars. I am the only prophet left. And now they are trying to kill me, too."[n] [4]But what answer did God give Elijah? He said, "But I have left 7,000 people in Israel. Those 7,000 have never bowed down before Baal.'"[n] [5]It is the same now. There are a few people that God has chosen by his grace. [6]And if God chose them by grace, then it is not for the things they have done. If they could be made God's people by what they did, then God's gift of grace would not really be a gift.

[7]So this is what has happened: The people of Israel tried to be right with God. But they did not succeed. But the ones God chose did become right with him. The others became hard and refused to listen to God. [8]As it is written in the Scriptures:[d]

"God gave the people a dull mind
so they could not understand."
Isaiah 29:10
"God closed their eyes so they
could not see,
and God closed their ears so they
could not hear.
This continues until today."
Deuteronomy 29:4

[9]And David says:

"Let their own feasts trap them and
cause their ruin.
Let their feasts cause them to sin
and be paid back.
[10]Let their eyes be closed so they
cannot see.
Let their backs be forever weak
from troubles."
Psalm 69:22-23

[11]So I ask: When the Jews fell, did that fall destroy them? No! But their mistake brought salvation to the non-Jews. This took place to cause the Jews to be jealous. [12]The Jews' mistake brought rich blessings for the world. And what the Jews lost brought rich blessings for the non-Jewish people. So surely the world will get much richer blessings when enough Jews become the kind of people God wants.

[13]Now I am speaking to you who are not Jews. I am an apostle[d] to the non-Jews. So while I have that work, I will do the best I can. [14]I hope I can make my own people jealous. That way, maybe I can help some of them to be saved. [15]God turned away from the Jews. When that happened, God became friends with the other people in the world. So

when God accepts the Jews, then surely that will bring to them life after death.

[16]If the first piece of bread is offered to God, then the whole loaf is made holy. If the roots of a tree are holy, then the tree's branches are holy too.

[17]Some of the branches from an olive tree have been broken off, and the branch of a wild olive tree has been joined to that first tree. You non-Jews are the same as that wild branch, and you now share the strength and life of the first tree, the Jews. [18]So do not brag about those branches that were broken off. You have no reason to brag. Why? You do not give life to the root. The root gives life to you. [19]You will say, "Branches were broken off so that I could be joined to their tree." [20]That is true. But those branches were broken off because they did not believe. And you continue to be part of the tree only because you believe. Do not be proud, but be afraid. [21]If God did not let the natural branches of that tree stay, then he will not let you stay if you don't believe.

[22]So you see that God is kind, but he can also be very strict. God punishes those who stop following him. But God is kind to you, if you continue following in his kindness. If you do not continue following him, you will be cut off from the tree. [23]And if the Jews will believe in God again, then God will accept the Jews back again. God is able to put them back where they were. [24]It is not natural for a wild branch to be part of a good tree. But you non-Jews are like a branch cut from a wild olive tree. And you were joined to a good olive tree. But those Jews are like a branch that grew from the good tree. So surely they can be joined to their own tree again.

[25]I want you to understand this secret truth, brothers. This truth will help you understand that you do not know everything. The truth is this: Part of Israel has been made stubborn. But that will change when many non-Jews have come to God. [26]And that is how all Israel will be saved. It is written in the Scriptures:

"The Savior will come from
Jerusalem;
he will take away all evil from
the family of Jacob.[n]

11:3 "They . . . too." Quotation from 1 Kings 19:10, 14. **11:4 "But . . . Baal."** Quotation from 1 Kings 19:18. **11:26 Jacob** Father of the 12 family groups of Israel, the people God chose to be his people.

²⁷And I will make this agreement
  with those people
when I take away their sins."

Isaiah 59:20-21; 27:9

²⁸The Jews refuse to accept the Good
News,ᵈ so they are God's enemies. This
has happened to help you non-Jews. But
the Jews are still God's chosen people,
and God loves them very much. He loves
them because of the promises he made
to their ancestors. ²⁹God never changes
his mind about the people he calls and
the things he gives them. ³⁰At one time
you refused to obey God. But now you
have received mercy, because those people refused to obey. ³¹And now the Jews
refuse to obey, because God showed
mercy to you. But this happened so that
they also can receive mercy from God.
³²All people have refused to obey God.
God has given them all over to their
stubborn ways, so that God can show
mercy to all.

³³Yes, God's riches are very great!
God's wisdom and knowledge have no
end! No one can explain the things God
decides. No one can understand God's
ways. ³⁴As the Scriptureᵈ says,

"Who has known the mind of the
  Lord?
Who has been able to give the
  Lord advice?"   *Isaiah 40:13*
³⁵"No one has ever given God
  anything
that he must pay back."   *Job 41:11*
³⁶Yes, God made all things. And everything continues through God and for
God. To God be the glory forever! Amen.

12 So brothers, since God has shown
us great mercy, I beg you to offer
your lives as a living sacrifice to him.
Your offering must be only for God and
pleasing to him. This is the spiritual way
for you to worship. ²Do not change yourselves to be like the people of this world.
But be changed within by a new way of
thinking. Then you will be able to decide
what God wants for you. And you will
be able to know what is good and pleasing to God and what is perfect. ³God has
given me a special gift. That is why I
have something to say to everyone
among you. Do not think that you are
better than you are. You must see yourself as you really are. Decide what you
are by the amount of faith God has given
you. ⁴Each one of us has a body, and
that body has many parts. These parts
all have different uses. ⁵In the same way,

we are many, but in Christ we are all
one body. Each one is a part of that body.
And each part belongs to all the other
parts. ⁶We all have different gifts. Each
gift came because of the grace that God
gave us. If one has the gift of prophecy,ᵈ
he should use that gift with the faith he
has. ⁷If one has the gift of serving, he
should serve. If one has the gift of teaching, he should teach. ⁸If one has the gift
of encouraging others, he should encourage. If one has the gift of giving to
others, he should give freely. If one has
the gift of being a leader, he should try
hard when he leads. If one has the gift of
showing kindness to others, that person
should do so with joy.

⁹Your love must be real. Hate what is
evil. Hold on to what is good. ¹⁰Love
each other like brothers and sisters.
Give your brothers and sisters more
honor than you want for yourselves.
¹¹Do not be lazy but work hard. Serve
the Lord with all your heart. ¹²Be joyful
because you have hope. Be patient when
trouble comes. Pray at all times. ¹³Share
with God's people who need help. Bring
strangers in need into your homes.

¹⁴Wish good for those who do bad
things to you. Wish them well and do
not curse them. ¹⁵Be happy with those
who are happy. Be sad with those who
are sad. ¹⁶Live together in peace with
each other. Do not be proud, but make
friends with those who seem unimportant. Do not think how smart you are.

¹⁷If someone does wrong to you, do
not pay him back by doing wrong to
him. Try to do what everyone thinks is
right. ¹⁸Do your best to live in peace with
everyone. ¹⁹My friends, do not try to
punish others when they wrong you.
Wait for God to punish them with his
anger. It is written: "I am the One who
punishes; I will pay people back,'" says
the Lord. ²⁰But you should do this:

"If your enemy is hungry, feed him;
  if your enemy is thirsty, give him
    a drink.
Doing this will be like pouring
  burning coals on his head."

Proverbs 25:21-22
²¹Do not let evil defeat you. Defeat evil
by doing good.

13 All of you must obey the government rulers. No one rules unless
God has given him the power to rule.
And no one rules now without that
power from God. ²So if anyone is

12:19 "I . . . back" Quotation from Deuteronomy 32:35.

against the government, he is really against what God has commanded. And so he brings punishment on himself. [3]Those who do right do not have to fear the rulers. But people who do wrong must fear them. Do you want to be unafraid of the rulers? Then do what is right, and the ruler will praise you. [4]He is God's servant to help you. But if you do wrong, then be afraid. The ruler has the power to punish; he is God's servant to punish those who do wrong. [5]So you must obey the government. You must obey not only because you might be punished, but because you know it is the right thing to do.

[6]And this is also why you pay taxes. Rulers are working for God and give their time to their work. [7]Pay everyone, then, what you owe him. If you owe any kind of tax, pay it. Show respect and honor to them all.

[8]Do not owe people anything. But you will always owe love to each other. The person who loves others has obeyed all the law. [9]The law says, "You must not be guilty of adultery.[d] You must not murder anyone. You must not steal. You must not want to take your neighbor's things."[n] All these commands and all others are really only one rule: "Love your neighbor as you love yourself."[n] [10]Love never hurts a neighbor. So loving is obeying all the law.

[11]I say this because we live in an important time. Yes, it is now time for you to wake up from your sleep. Our salvation is nearer now than when we first believed. [12]The "night"[n] is almost finished. The "day"[n] is almost here. So we should stop doing things that belong to darkness and take up the weapons used for fighting in the light. [13]Let us live in a right way, like people who belong to the day. We should not have wild parties or get drunk. There should be no sexual sins of any kind, no fighting or jealousy. [14]But clothe yourselves with the Lord Jesus Christ. Forget about satisfying your sinful self.

14 Do not refuse to accept into your group someone who is weak in faith. And do not argue with him about opinions. [2]One person believes that he can eat all kinds of food.[n] But if another man's faith is weak, then he believes he can eat only vegetables. [3]The one who knows that he can eat any kind of food must not feel that he is better than the one who eats only vegetables. And the person who eats only vegetables must not think that the one who eats all foods is wrong. God has accepted him. [4]You cannot judge another man's servant. His own master decides if he is doing well or not. And the Lord's servant will do well because the Lord helps him do well.

[5]One person thinks that one day is more important than another. And someone else thinks that every day is the same. Each one should be sure in his own mind. [6]The person who thinks one day is more important than other days is doing that for the Lord. And the one who eats all kinds of food is doing that for the Lord. Yes, he gives thanks to God for that food. And the man who refuses to eat some foods does that for the Lord, and he gives thanks to God. [7]For we do not live or die for ourselves. [8]If we live, we are living for the Lord. And if we die, we are dying for the Lord. So living or dying, we belong to the Lord.

[9]That is why Christ died and rose from death to live again. He did this so that he would be Lord over both the dead and the living. [10]So why do you judge your brother in Christ? And why do you think that you are better than he is? We will all stand before God, and he will judge us all. [11]Yes, it is written in the Scriptures:[d]

"Everyone will bow before me;
  everyone will say that I am God.
As surely as I live, these things will
  happen, says the Lord."
                              Isaiah 45:23

[12]So each of us will have to answer to God for what he has done.

[13]So we should stop judging each other. We must make up our minds not to do anything that will make a Christian brother sin. [14]I am in the Lord Jesus, and I know that there is no food that is wrong to eat. But if a person believes that something is wrong, then that thing is wrong for him. [15]If you hurt your brother's faith because of something you eat, then you are not really following the way of love. Do not destroy his

---

13:9 "You . . . things." Quotation from Exodus 20:13-15, 17. **13:9 "Love . . . yourself."** Quotation from Leviticus 19:18. **13:12 "night"** This is used as a symbol of the sinful world we live in. This world will soon end. **13:12 "day"** This is used as a symbol of the good time that is coming, when we will be with God. **14:2 all . . . food** The Jewish law said there were some foods Jews should not eat. When Jews became Christians, some of them did not understand they could now eat all foods.

faith by eating food that he thinks is wrong. Christ died for him. [16]Do not allow what you think is good to become what others say is evil. [17]In the kingdom of God, eating and drinking are not important. The important things are living right with God, peace, and joy in the Holy Spirit.[d] [18]Anyone who serves Christ by living this way is pleasing God and will be accepted by other people.

[19]So let us try to do what makes peace and helps one another. [20]Do not let the eating of food destroy the work of God. All foods are all right to eat, but it is wrong to eat food that causes someone else to sin. [21]It is better not to eat meat or drink wine or do anything that will cause your brother to sin.

[22]Your beliefs about these things should be kept secret between you and God. A person is blessed if he can do what he thinks is right without feeling guilty. [23]But if he eats something without being sure that it is right, then he is wrong because he did not believe that it was right. And if he does anything without believing that it is right, then it is a sin.

15 We who are strong in faith should help those who are weak. We should help them with their weaknesses, and not please only ourselves. [2]Let each of us please his neighbor for his good, to help him be stronger in faith. [3]Even Christ did not live to please himself. It was as the Scriptures[d] said: "When people insult you, it hurts me."[n] [4]Everything that was written in the past was written to teach us, so that we could have hope. That hope comes from the patience and encouragement that the Scriptures give us. [5]Patience and encouragement come from God. And I pray that God will help you all agree with each other the way Christ Jesus wants. [6]Then you will all be joined together, and you will give glory to God the Father of our Lord Jesus Christ. [7]Christ accepted you, so you should accept each other. This will bring glory to God. [8]I tell you that Christ became a servant of the Jews. This was to show that God's promises to the Jewish ancestors are true. [9]And he also did this so that the non-Jews could give glory to God for the mercy he gives to them. It is written in the Scriptures:

"So I will praise you among the
    non-Jewish people.
I will sing praises to your
    name."   *Psalm 18:49*

[10]The Scripture also says,

"Be happy, you non-Jews, together
    with God's people."
         Deuteronomy 32:43

[11]Again the Scripture says,

"All you non-Jews, praise the Lord.
All you people, sing praises to
    him."   *Psalm 117:1*

[12]And Isaiah says,

"A new king will come from Jesse's
    family.[n]
He will come to rule over the
    non-Jews;
and the non-Jews will have hope
    because of him."   *Isaiah 11:10*

[13]I pray that the God who gives hope will fill you with much joy and peace while you trust in him. Then your hope will overflow by the power of the Holy Spirit.[d]

[14]My brothers, I am sure that you are full of goodness. I know that you have all the knowledge you need and that you are able to teach each other. [15]But I have written to you very openly about some things that I wanted you to remember. I did this because God gave me this special gift: [16]to be a minister of Christ Jesus to the non-Jewish people. I served God by teaching his Good News,[d] so that the non-Jewish people could be an offering that God would accept—an offering made holy by the Holy Spirit.[d]

[17]So I am proud of what I have done for God in Christ Jesus. [18]I will not talk about anything I did myself. I will talk only about what Christ has done through me in leading the non-Jewish people to obey God. They have obeyed God because of what I have said and done. [19]And they have obeyed God because of the power of miracles[d] and the great things they saw, and the power of the Holy Spirit. I preached the Good News from Jerusalem all the way around to Illyricum. And so I have finished that part of my work. [20]I always want to preach the Good News in places where people have never heard of Christ. I do this because I do not want to build on the work that someone else has already started. [21]But it is written in the Scriptures:[d]

15:3 "When . . . me." Quotation from Psalm 69:9.   **15:12 Jesse's family** Jesse was the father of David, king of Israel. Jesus was from their family.

"Those who were not told about
  him will see,
and those who have not heard
  about him will understand."
Isaiah 52:15

[22]That is why many times I was
stopped from coming to you. [23]Now I
have finished my work here. Since for
many years I have wanted to come to
you, [24]I hope to visit you on my way to
Spain. I will enjoy being with you, and
you can help me on my trip. [25]Now I am
going to Jerusalem to help God's people. [26]The believers in Macedonia and
Southern Greece were happy to give
their money to help the poor among
God's people at Jerusalem. [27]They were
happy to do this, and really they owe it
to them. These non-Jews have shared
in the Jews' spiritual blessings. So they
should use their material possessions to
help the Jews. [28]I must be sure that the
poor in Jerusalem get the money that
has been given for them. After I do this,
I will leave for Spain and stop and visit
you. [29]I know that when I come to you, I
will bring Christ's full blessing.

[30]Brothers, I beg you to help me in my
work by praying for me to God. Do this
because of our Lord Jesus and the love
that the Holy Spirit[d] gives us. [31]Pray that
I will be saved from the non-believers in
Judea. And pray that this help I bring
to Jerusalem will please God's people
there. [32]Then, if God wants me to, I will
come to you. I will come with joy, and
together you and I will have a time of
rest. [33]The God who gives peace be with
you all. Amen.

16 I recommend to you our sister
Phoebe. She is a helper[n] in the
church in Cenchrea. [2]I ask you to accept
her in the Lord in the way God's people
should. Help her with anything she
needs because she has helped me and
many other people too.

[3]Give my greetings to Priscilla and
Aquila, who work together with me in
Christ Jesus. [4]They risked their own
lives to save my life. I am thankful to
them, and all the non-Jewish churches
are thankful to them as well. [5]Also, greet
for me the church that meets at their
house.

Greetings to my dear friend Epenetus.
He was the first person in the country
of Asia to follow Christ. [6]Greetings to
Mary, who worked very hard for you.

[7]Greetings to Andronicus and Junias,
my relatives, who were in prison with
me. The apostles feel they are very important. They were believers in Christ
before I was. [8]Greetings to Ampliatus,
my dear friend in the Lord. [9]Greetings
to Urbanus. He is a worker together
with me for Christ. And greetings to my
dear friend Stachys. [10]Greetings to Apel-
les. He was tested and proved that he
truly loves Christ. Greetings to all those
who are in the family of Aristobulus.
[11]Greetings to Herodion, my relative.
Greetings to all those in the family of
Narcissus who belong to the Lord.
[12]Greetings to Tryphena and Tryphosa.
Those women work very hard for the
Lord. Greetings to my dear friend Per-
sis. She also has worked very hard for
the Lord. [13]Greetings to Rufus who is a
special person in the Lord. Greetings to
his mother, who has been a mother to
me also. [14]Greetings to Asyncritus, Phle-
gon, Hermes, Patrobas, Hermas, and all
the brothers who are with them. [15]Greet-
ings to Philologus and Julia, Nereus and
his sister, and Olympas. And greetings
to all God's people with them. [16]Greet
each other with a holy kiss. All of
Christ's churches send greetings to you.

[17]Brothers, I ask you to look out for
those who cause people to be against
each other and who upset other people's
faith. They are against the true teaching you learned. Stay away from them.
[18]For such people are not serving our
Lord Christ. They are only doing what
pleases themselves. They use fancy talk
and fine words to fool the minds of those
who do not know about evil. [19]All the
believers have heard that you obey. So I
am very happy because of you. But I
want you to be wise in what is good and
innocent in what is evil.

[20]The God who brings peace will soon
defeat Satan and give you power over
him.

The grace of our Lord Jesus be with
you.

[21]Timothy, a worker together with me,
sends greetings, as well as Lucius, Jason, and Sosipater, my relatives.

[22]I am Tertius, and I am writing this
letter from Paul. I send greetings to you
in the Lord.

[23]Gaius is letting me and the whole
church here use his home. He also sends

16:1 helper Literally, "deaconess." This might mean the same as one of the special women
helpers in 1 Timothy 3:11.

greetings to you, as do Erastus and our brother Quartus. Erastus is the city treasurer here. 24 n

25Glory to God! God is the One who can make you strong in faith by the Good News[d] that I tell people and by the message about Jesus Christ. The message about Christ is the secret truth that

was hidden for long ages past, but is now made known. 26It has been made clear through the writings of the prophets.[d] And by the command of the eternal God it is made known to all nations, that they might believe and obey.

27To the only wise God be glory forever through Jesus Christ! Amen.

The First Letter of Paul the Apostle to the
CORINTHIANS

1 From Paul. I was called to be an apostle[d] of Christ Jesus because that is what God wanted. Also from Sosthenes, our brother in Christ.

2To the church of God in Corinth, to those people who have been made holy in Christ Jesus. You were called to be God's holy people with all people everywhere who trust in the name of the Lord Jesus Christ—their Lord and ours:

3Grace and peace to you from God our Father and the Lord Jesus Christ.

4I always thank my God for you because of the grace that God has given you in Christ Jesus. 5In Jesus you have been blessed in every way, in all your speaking and in all your knowledge. 6The truth about Christ has been proved in you. 7So you have every gift from God while you wait for our Lord Jesus Christ to come again. 8Jesus will keep you strong until the end. He will keep you strong, so that there will be no wrong in you on the day our Lord Jesus Christ comes again. 9God is faithful. He is the One who has called you to share life with his Son, Jesus Christ our Lord.

10I beg you, brothers, in the name of our Lord Jesus Christ. I beg that all of you agree with each other, so that you will not be divided into groups. I beg that you be completely joined together by having the same kind of thinking and the same purpose. 11My brothers, some people from Chloe's family have told me that there are arguments among you. 12This is what I mean: One of you says, "I follow Paul"; another says, "I follow Apollos"; another says, "I follow Peter"; and another says, "I follow Christ." 13Christ cannot be divided into different

groups! Did Paul die on the cross for you? No! Were you baptized in the name of Paul? No! 14I am thankful that I did not baptize any of you except Crispus and Gaius. 15I am thankful, because now no one can say that you were baptized in my name. 16(I also baptized the family of Stephanas. But I do not remember that I myself baptized any others.) 17Christ did not give me the work of baptizing people. He gave me the work of preaching the Good News,[d] and he sent me to preach the Good News without using words of worldly wisdom. If I used worldly wisdom to tell the Good News, the cross[n] of Christ would lose its power.

18The teaching about the cross seems foolish to those who are lost. But to us who are being saved it is the power of God. 19It is written in the Scriptures:[d]

"I will cause the wise men to lose
    their wisdom.
I will make the wise men unable
    to understand."   *Isaiah 29:14*

20Where is the wise person? Where is the educated person? Where is the philosopher[n] of our times? God has made the wisdom of the world foolish. 21The world did not know God through its own wisdom. So God chose to use the message that sounds foolish to save those who believe it. 22The Jews ask for miracles[d] as proofs. The Greeks want wisdom. 23But we preach Christ on the cross. This is a big problem to the Jews. And it seems foolish to the non-Jews. 24But Christ is the power of God and the wisdom of God to those people God has called—Jews and Greeks. 25Even the foolishness of God is wiser than men.

16:24 Verse 24 Some Greek copies add verse 24: "The grace of our Lord Jesus Christ be with all of you. Amen."   **1:17 cross** Paul uses the cross as a picture of the gospel, the story of Christ's death and rising from death to pay for men's sins. The cross, or Christ's death, was God's way to save men.   **1:20 philosopher** Philosophers were those who searched for truth.

Even the weakness of God is stronger than men.

26Brothers, look at what you were when God called you. Not many of you were wise in the way the world judges wisdom. Not many of you had great influence. Not many of you came from important families. 27But God chose the foolish things of the world to shame the wise. He chose the weak things of the world to shame the strong. 28And he chose what the world thinks is not important. He chose what the world hates and thinks is nothing. He chose these to destroy what the world thinks is important. 29God did this so that no man can brag before him. 30It is God who has made you part of Christ Jesus. Christ has become wisdom for us from God. Christ is the reason we are right with God and have freedom from sin; Christ is the reason we are holy. 31So, as the Scripture[d] says, "If a person brags, he should brag only about the Lord."[n]

2 Dear brothers, when I came to you, I did not come as a proud man. I preached God's truth, but not with fancy words or a show of great learning. 2I decided that while I was with you I would forget about everything except Jesus Christ and his death on the cross. 3When I came to you, I was weak and shook with fear. 4My teaching and my speaking were not with wise words that persuade people. But the proof of my teaching was the power that the Spirit[d] gives. 5I did this so that your faith would be in God's power, not in the wisdom of a man.

6Yet I speak wisdom to those who are mature. But this wisdom is not from this world or of the rulers of this world. (These rulers are losing their power.) 7But I speak God's secret wisdom, which he has kept hidden. God planned this wisdom for our glory, before the world began. 8None of the rulers of this world understood it. If they had, they would not have killed the Lord of glory on a cross. 9But as it is written in the Scriptures:[d]

"No one has ever seen this.
No one has ever heard about it.
No one has ever imagined
  what God has prepared for those
  who love him." *Isaiah 64:4*
10But God has shown us these things through the Spirit.

The Spirit knows all things, even the deep secrets of God. 11It is like this: No one knows the thoughts that another person has. Only a person's spirit that lives in him knows his thoughts. It is the same with God. No one knows the thoughts of God. Only the Spirit of God knows God's thoughts. 12We did not receive the spirit of the world, but we received the Spirit that is from God. We received this Spirit so that we can know all that God has given us. 13When we speak, we do not use words taught to us by the wisdom that men have. We use words taught to us by the Spirit. We use spiritual words to explain spiritual things. 14A person who is not spiritual does not accept the gifts that come from the Spirit of God. That person thinks they are foolish. He cannot understand the Spirit's gifts, because they can only be judged spiritually. 15But the spiritual person is able to judge all things. Yet no one can judge him. The Scripture says:

16"Who has known the mind of the
    Lord?
  Who has been able to teach
    him?" *Isaiah 40:13*
But we have the mind of Christ.

3 Brothers, in the past I could not talk to you as I talk to spiritual people. I had to talk to you as I would to people of the world—babies in Christ. 2The teaching I gave you was like milk, not solid food. I did this because you were not ready for solid food. And even now you are not ready. 3You are still not spiritual. You have jealousy and arguing among you. This shows that you are not spiritual. You are acting like people of the world. 4One of you says, "I follow Paul," and another says, "I follow Apollos." When you say things like this, you are acting like worldly people.

5Is Apollos important? No! Is Paul important? No! We are only servants of God who helped you believe. Each one of us did the work God gave us to do. 6I planted the seed of the teaching in you, and Apollos watered it. But God is the One who made the seed grow. 7So the one who plants is not important, and the one who waters is not important. Only God is important, because he is the One who makes things grow. 8The one who plants and the one who waters have the same purpose. And each will be rewarded for his own work. 9We are workers together for God. And you are like a farm that belongs to God.

1:31 "If . . . Lord." Quotation from Jeremiah 9:24.

And you are a house that belongs to God. [10]Like an expert builder I built the foundation of that house. I used the gift that God gave me to do this. Others are building on that foundation. But everyone should be careful how he builds. [11]The foundation has already been built. No one can build any other foundation. The foundation that has already been laid is Jesus Christ. [12]Anyone can build on that foundation, using gold, silver, jewels, wood, grass, or straw. [13]But the work that each person does will be clearly seen, because the Day[n] will make it plain. That Day will appear with fire, and the fire will test every man's work. [14]If the building that a man puts on the foundation still stands, he will get his reward. [15]But if his building is burned up, he will suffer loss. The man will be saved, but it will be as if he escaped from a fire.

[16]You should know that you yourselves are God's temple. God's Spirit[d] lives in you. [17]If anyone destroys God's temple, God will destroy him, because God's temple is holy. You yourselves are God's temple.

[18]Do not fool yourselves. If anyone among you thinks he is wise in this world, he should become a fool. Then he can become truly wise, [19]because the wisdom of this world is foolishness to God. It is written in the Scriptures,[d] "He catches wise men in their own clever traps."[n] [20]It is also written in the Scriptures, "The Lord knows what people think. He knows they are just a puff of wind."[n] [21]So you should not brag about men. All things are yours: [22]Paul, Apollos and Peter; the world, life, death, the present, and the future—all these things are yours. [23]And you belong to Christ, and Christ belongs to God.

4 This is what people should think about us: We are servants of Christ. We are the ones God has trusted with his secret truths. [2]A person who is trusted with something must show that he is worthy of that trust. [3]I do not care if I am judged by you or if I am judged by any human court. I do not even judge myself. [4]I know of no wrong that I have done. But this does not make me innocent. The Lord is the One who judges me. [5]So do not judge before the right time; wait until the Lord comes. He will

bring to light things that are now hidden in darkness. He will make known the secret purposes of people's hearts. Then God will give everyone the praise he should get.

[6]Brothers, I have used Apollos and myself as examples. I did this so that you could learn from us the meaning of the words, "Follow only what is written in the Scriptures."[d] Then you will not be proud of one man and hate another. [7]Who says that you are better than others? Everything you have was given to you. And if this is so, why do you brag as if you got these things by your own power?

[8]You think you have everything you need. You think you are rich. You think you have become kings without us. I wish you really were kings! Then we could be kings together with you. [9]But it seems to me that God has given me and the other apostles[d] the last place. We are like men sentenced to die. We are like a show for the whole world to see—angels and people. [10]We are fools for Christ's sake. But you think you are very wise in Christ. We are weak, but you think you are strong. You receive honor, but we are hated. [11]Even now we still do not have enough to eat or drink or enough clothes. We are often beaten. We have no homes. [12]We work hard with our own hands for our food. People curse us, but we bless them. They hurt us, and we accept it. [13]They say evil things against us, but we say only kind things to them. Even today, we are treated as though we are the garbage of the world—the dirt of the earth.

[14]I am not trying to make you feel ashamed. I am writing this to give you a warning as if you were my own dear children. [15]For though you may have 10,000 teachers in Christ, you do not have many fathers. Through the Good News[d] I became your father in Christ Jesus. [16]So I beg you, please be like me. [17]That is why I am sending Timothy to you. He is my son in the Lord. I love Timothy, and he is faithful. He will help you remember the way I live in Christ Jesus. This way of life is what I teach in all the churches everywhere.

[18]Some of you have become proud, thinking that I will not come to you again. [19]But I will come very soon if the

Lord wants me to. Then I will see what those who are proud can do, not what they say. [20]I want to see this because the kingdom of God is not talk but power. [21]Which do you want: that I come to you with punishment, or that I come to you with love and gentleness?

5 Now, it is actually being said that there is sexual sin among you. And it is of such a bad kind that it does not happen even among those who do not know God. A man there has his father's wife. [2]And still you are proud of yourselves! You should have been filled with sadness. And the man who did that sin should be put out of your group. [3]My body is not there with you, but I am with you in spirit. And I have already judged the man who did that sin. I judged him just as I would if I were really there. [4]Meet together as the people of our Lord Jesus. I will be with you in spirit, and you will have the power of our Lord Jesus with you. [5]Then give this man to Satan, so that his sinful self[n] will be destroyed. And then his spirit can be saved on the day of the Lord.

[6]Your bragging is not good. You know the saying, "Just a little yeast makes the whole batch of dough rise." [7]Take out all the old yeast so that you will be a new batch of dough. And you really are new dough without yeast. For Christ, our Passover[d] lamb, was killed to cleanse us. [8]So let us continue our feast, but not with the bread that has the old yeast. That old yeast is the yeast of sin and wickedness. But let us eat the bread that has no yeast. This is the bread of goodness and truth.

[9]I wrote to you in my letter that you should not associate with those who take part in sexual sin. [10]But I did not mean that you should not associate with the sinful people of this world. People of the world do take part in sexual sin, or they are selfish and they cheat each other, or they worship idols. But to get away from them you would have to leave this world. [11]I am writing to tell you that the person you must not associate with is this: anyone who calls himself a brother in Christ but who takes part in sexual sin, or is selfish, or worships idols, or lies about others, or gets drunk, or cheats people. Do not even eat with someone like that.

[12-13]It is not my business to judge those who are not part of the church. God will judge them. But you must judge the people who are part of the church. The Scripture[d] says, "You must get rid of the evil person among you."[n]

6 When one of you has something against a brother in Christ, why do you go to the judges in the law courts? Those people are not right with God. So why do you let them decide who is right? You should be ashamed! Why do you not let God's people decide who is right? [2]Surely you know that God's people will judge the world. So if you are to judge the world, then surely you are able to judge small things as well. [3]You know that in the future we will judge angels. So surely we can judge things in this life. [4]So if you have disagreements that must be judged, why do you take them to those who are not part of the church? They mean nothing to the church. [5]I say this to shame you. Surely there is someone among you wise enough to judge a complaint between two brothers in Christ. [6]But now one brother goes to court against another brother. And you let men who are not believers judge their case!

[7]The lawsuits that you have against each other show that you are already defeated. It would be better for you to let someone wrong you! It would be better for you to let someone cheat you! [8]But you yourselves do wrong and cheat! And you do this to your own brothers in Christ!

[9-10]Surely you know that the people who do wrong will not receive God's kingdom. Do not be fooled. These people will not receive God's kingdom: those who sin sexually, or worship idols, or take part in adultery,[d] or men who have sexual relations with other men, or steal, or are selfish, or get drunk, or lie about others, or cheat. [11]In the past, some of you were like that. But you were washed clean. You were made holy. And you were made right with God in the name of the Lord Jesus Christ and by the Spirit of our God.

[12]"I am allowed to do all things." But all things are not good for me to do. "I am allowed to do all things." But I must not do those things that will make me their slave. [13]"Food is for the stomach, and the stomach for food." Yes. But God will destroy them both. The body is not

---

5:5 sinful self Literally, "flesh." This could also mean his body.   **5:12-13 "You . . . you."** Quotation from Deuteronomy 17:7; 19:19; 22:21, 24; 24:7.

for sexual sin. The body is for the Lord, and the Lord is for the body. [14]By God's power God raised the Lord Jesus from death. And God will also raise us from death. [15]Surely you know that your bodies are parts of Christ himself. So I must never take parts of Christ and join them to a prostitute![d] [16]It is written in the Scriptures,[d] "The two people will become one body."[n] So you should know that a man who joins himself with a prostitute becomes one with her in body. [17]But the one who joins himself with the Lord is one with the Lord in spirit.

[18]So run away from sexual sin. Every other sin that a man does is outside his body. But the one who sins sexually sins against his own body. [19]You should know that your body is a temple for the Holy Spirit.[d] The Holy Spirit is in you. You have received the Holy Spirit from God. You do not own yourselves. [20]You were bought by God for a price. So honor God with your bodies.

7 Now I will discuss the things you wrote to me about. It is good for a man not to marry. [2]But sexual sin is a danger. So each man should have his own wife. And each woman should have her own husband. [3]The husband should give his wife all that she should have as his wife. And the wife should give her husband all that he should have as her husband. [4]The wife does not have power over her own body. Her husband has the power over her body. And the husband does not have power over his own body. His wife has the power over his body. [5]Do not refuse to give your bodies to each other. But you might both agree to stay away from sexual relations for a time. You might do this so that you can give your time to prayer. Then come together again. This is so that Satan cannot tempt you in your weakness. [6]I say this to give you permission. It is not a command. [7]I wish everyone were like me. But each person has his own gift from God. One has one gift, another has another gift.

[8]Now for those who are not married and for the widows I say this: It is good for them to stay single as I am. [9]But if they cannot control their bodies, then they should marry. It is better to marry than to burn with sexual desire.

[10]Now I give this command for the married people. (The command is not from me; it is from the Lord.) A wife should not leave her husband. [11]But if she does leave, she must not marry again. Or she should go back to her husband. Also the husband should not divorce his wife.

[12]For all the others I say this (I am saying this, not the Lord): A brother in Christ might have a wife who is not a believer. If she will live with him, he must not divorce her. [13]And a woman might have a husband who is not a believer. If he will live with her, she must not divorce him. [14]The husband who is not a believer is made holy through his believing wife. And the wife who is not a believer is made holy through her believing husband. If this were not true, then your children would not be clean.[d] But now your children are holy.

[15]But if the person who is not a believer decides to leave, let him leave. When this happens, the brother or sister in Christ is free. God called us to a life of peace. [16]Wives, maybe you will save your husband; and husbands, maybe you will save your wife. You do not know now what will happen later.

[17]But each one should continue to live the way God has given him to live—the way he was when God called him. This is a rule I make in all the churches. [18]If a man was already circumcised[d] when he was called, he should not change his circumcision. If a man was without circumcision when he was called, he should not be circumcised. [19]It is not important if a man is circumcised or not circumcised. The important thing is obeying God's commands. [20]Each one should stay the way he was when God called him. [21]If you were a slave when God called you, do not let that bother you. But if you can be free, then become free. [22]The person who was a slave when the Lord called him is free in the Lord. He belongs to the Lord. In the same way, the one who was free when he was called is now Christ's slave. [23]You all were bought for a price. So do not become slaves of men. [24]Brothers, in your new life with God each one of you should continue the way you were when you were called.

[25]Now I write about people who are not married. I have no command from the Lord about this, but I give my opinion. And I can be trusted, because the Lord has given me mercy. [26]This is a time of trouble. So I think that it is good

6:16 **"The two . . . body."** Quotation from Genesis 2:24.

for you to stay the way you are. [27] If you have a wife, then do not try to become free from her. If you are not married, then do not try to find a wife. [28] But if you decide to marry, this is not a sin. And it is not a sin for a girl who has never married to get married. But those who marry will have trouble in this life. And I want you to be free from this trouble.

[29] Brothers, this is what I mean: We do not have much time left. So starting now, those who have wives should use their time to serve the Lord as if they had no wives. [30] Those who are sad should live as if they are not sad. Those who are happy should live as if they are not happy. Those who buy things should live as if they own nothing. [31] Those who use the things of the world should live as if those things are not important to them. You should live like this, because this world, the way it is now, will soon be gone.

[32] I want you to be free from worry. A man who is not married is busy with the Lord's work. He is trying to please the Lord. [33] But a man who is married is busy with things of the world. He is trying to please his wife. [34] He must think about two things—pleasing his wife and pleasing the Lord. A woman who is not married or a girl who has never married is busy with the Lord's work. She wants to give herself fully—body and soul—to the Lord. But a married woman is busy with things of the world. She is trying to please her husband. [35] I am saying this to help you. I am not trying to limit you. But I want you to live in the right way. And I want you to give yourselves fully to the Lord without giving your time to other things.

[36] A man might think that he is not doing the right thing with the girl he is engaged to. The girl might be almost past the best age to marry. So he might feel that he should marry her. He should do what he wants. They should get married. It is no sin. [37] But another man might be more sure in his mind. There may be no need for marriage, so he is free to do what he wants. If he has decided in his own heart not to marry, he is doing the right thing. [38] So the man who marries his girl does right. And the man who does not marry does even better.

[39] A woman must stay with her husband as long as he lives. If the husband

dies, she is free to marry any man she wants. But she must marry in the Lord. [40] The woman is happier if she does not marry again. This is my opinion, and I believe that I have God's Spirit.

8 Now I will write about meat that is sacrificed to idols. We know that "we all have knowledge." Knowledge puffs you up with pride, but love builds up. [2] Whoever thinks he knows something does not yet know anything as he should. [3] But he who loves God is known by God.

[4] So this is what I say about eating meat sacrificed to idols: We know that an idol is really nothing in the world. And we know that there is only one God. [5] It is really not important if there are things called gods, in heaven or on earth. (And there are many things that people call "gods" and "lords.") [6] But for us there is only one God. He is our Father. All things came from him, and we live for him. And there is only one Lord—Jesus Christ. All things were made through Jesus, and we also have life through him.

[7] But not all people know this. Until now, some people have had the habit of worshiping idols. So now when they eat meat, they still feel as if it belongs to an idol. They are not sure that it is right to eat this meat. When they eat it, they feel guilty. [8] But food will not make us closer to God. Refusing to eat does not make us less pleasing to God. And eating does not make us better in God's sight.

[9] But be careful with your freedom. Your freedom may cause those who are weak in faith to fall into sin. [10] You have "knowledge," so you might eat in an idol's temple.[n] Someone who is weak in faith might see you eating there. This would encourage him to eat meat sacrificed to idols. But he really thinks it is wrong. [11] So this weak brother is ruined because of your "knowledge." And Christ died for this brother. [12] When you sin against your brothers in Christ like this and cause them to do what they feel is wrong, you are also sinning against Christ. [13] So if the food I eat makes my brother fall into sin, I will never eat meat again. I will stop eating meat, so that I will not cause my brother to sin.

9 I am a free man. I am an apostle.[a] I have seen Jesus our Lord. You people are all an example of my work in the Lord. [2] Others may not accept me as an

---

8:10 idol's temple Building where a false god is worshiped.

apostle, but surely you accept me. You are proof that I am an apostle in the Lord.

[3] Some people want to judge me. So this is the answer I give them: [4] Do we not have the right to eat and drink? [5] Do we not have the right to bring a believing wife with us when we travel? The other apostles, the Lord's brothers, and Peter all do this. [6] And are Barnabas and I the only ones who must work to earn our living? [7] No soldier ever serves in the army and pays his own salary. No one ever plants a vineyard without eating some of the grapes himself. No person takes care of a flock of sheep without drinking some of the milk himself.

[8] This is not only what men think. God's law says the same thing. [9] Yes, it is written in the law of Moses: "When an ox is working in the grain, do not cover its mouth and keep it from eating."[n] When God said this, was he thinking only about oxen? No. [10] He was really talking about us. Yes, that Scripture[d] was written for us. The one who plows and the one who works in the grain should hope to get some of the grain for their work. [11] We planted spiritual seed among you. So we should be able to harvest from you some things for this life. Surely this is not asking too much. [12] Other men have the right to get something from you. So surely we have this right, too. But we do not use this right. No, we put up with everything ourselves so that we will not stop anyone from obeying the Good News[d] of Christ. [13] Surely you know that those who work at the Temple[d] get their food from the Temple. And those who serve at the altar get part of what is offered at the altar. [14] It is the same with those who tell the Good News. The Lord has commanded that those who tell the Good News should get their living from this work.

[15] But I have not used any of these rights. And I am not writing this now to get anything from you. I would rather die than to have my reason for bragging taken away. [16] Telling the Good News is not my reason for bragging. Telling the Good News is my duty—something I must do. And how bad it will be for me if I do not tell the Good News. [17] If I preach because it is my own choice, I should get a reward. But I have no choice. I must tell the Good News. I am only doing the duty that was given to me. [18] So

what reward do I get? This is my reward: that when I tell the Good News I can offer it freely. In this way I do not use my right to be paid in my work for the Good News.

[19] I am free. I belong to no man. But I make myself a slave to all people. I do this to help save as many people as I can. [20] To the Jews I became like a Jew. I did this to help save the Jews. I myself am not ruled by the law. But to those who are ruled by the law I became like a person who is ruled by the law. I did this to help save those who are ruled by the law. [21] To those who are without the law I became like a person who is without the law. I did this to help save those people who are without the law. (But really, I am not without God's law—I am ruled by Christ's law.) [22] To those who are weak, I became weak so that I could help save them. I have become all things to all people. I did this so that I could save some of them in any way possible. [23] I do all this because of the Good News. I do it so that I can share in the blessings of the Good News.

[24] You know that in a race all the runners run. But only one gets the prize. So run like that. Run to win! [25] All those who compete in the games use strict training. They do this so that they can win a crown. That crown is an earthly thing that lasts only a short time. But our crown will continue forever. [26] So I do not run without a goal. I fight like a boxer who is hitting something—not just the air. [27] It is my own body that I hit. I make it my slave. I do this so that I myself will not be rejected after I have preached to others.

10 Brothers, I want you to know what happened to our ancestors who followed Moses. They were all under the cloud, and they all went through the sea. [2] They were all baptized as followers of Moses in the cloud and in the sea. [3] They all ate the same spiritual food. [4] And they all drank the same spiritual drink. They drank from that spiritual rock that was with them. That rock was Christ. [5] But God was not pleased with most of them. They died in the desert.

[6] And these things that happened are examples for us. They should stop us from wanting evil things as those people did. [7] Do not worship idols, as some of them did. It is written in the Scriptures:[d] "The people sat down to eat and drink.

Then they got up and sinned sexually."[n] [8]We should not take part in sexual sins, as some of them did. In one day 23,000 of them died because of their sins. [9]We should not test the Lord as some of them did. They were killed by snakes. [10]And do not complain as some of them did. They were killed by the angel that destroys.

[11]The things that happened to those people are examples. And they were written down to be warnings for us. For we live in a time when all these things of the past have reached their goal. [12]So anyone who thinks he is standing strong should be careful not to fall. [13]The only temptations that you have are the temptations that all people have. But you can trust God. He will not let you be tempted more than you can stand. But when you are tempted, God will also give you a way to escape that temptation. Then you will be able to stand it.

[14]So, my dear friends, stay away from worshiping idols. [15]I am speaking to you, as to intelligent people; judge for yourselves what I say. [16]We give thanks for the cup of blessing.[n] It is a sharing in the blood of Christ's death. And the bread that we break is a sharing in the body of Christ. [17]There is one loaf of bread. And we are many people. But we all share from that one loaf. So we are really one body.

[18]Think about the people of Israel: Do not those who eat the sacrifices share in the altar? [19]I do not mean that the food sacrificed to an idol is something important. And I do not mean that an idol is anything at all. [20]But I say that what is sacrificed to idols is offered to demons,[d] not to God. And I do not want you to share anything with demons. [21]You cannot drink the cup of the Lord and the cup of demons, too. You cannot share in the Lord's table and the table of demons, too. [22]Do we want to make the Lord jealous? We are not stronger than he is, are we?

[23]"We are allowed to do all things." Yes. But all things are not good for us to do. "We are allowed to do all things." Yes. But not all things help others grow stronger. [24]No one should try to do what will help only himself. He should try to do what is good for others.

[25]Eat any meat that is sold in the meat market. Do not ask questions about the meat to see if it is something you think is wrong to eat. [26]You can eat it, "because the earth and everything on it belong to the Lord."[n]

[27]Someone who is not a believer may invite you to eat with him. If you want to go, eat anything that is put before you. Do not ask questions to see if it is something you think might be wrong to eat. [28]But if anyone says to you, "That food was offered to idols," then do not eat it. Do not eat it because of that person who told you and because eating it would be something that might be thought wrong. [29]I don't mean that you think it is wrong. But the other person might think it is wrong. My own freedom should not be judged by what someone else thinks. [30]I eat the meal with thankfulness. And I do not want to be criticized because of something I thank God for.

[31]So if you eat, or if you drink, or if you do anything, do everything for the glory of God. [32]Never do anything that might make others do wrong—Jews, Greeks, or God's church. [33]I do the same thing. I try to please everybody in every way. I am not trying to do what is good for me. I try to do what is good for the most people. I do this so that they can be saved.

11

Follow my example, as I follow the example of Christ.

[2]I praise you because you remember me in everything. You follow closely the teachings that I gave you. [3]But I want you to understand this: The head of every man is Christ. And the head of a woman is the man.[n] And the head of Christ is God. [4]Every man who prophesies[d] or prays with his head covered brings shame to his head. [5]But every woman who prays or prophesies should have her head covered. If her head is not covered, she brings shame to her head. She is the same as a woman who has her head shaved. [6]If a woman does not cover her head, it is the same as cutting off all her hair. But it is shameful for a woman to cut off her hair or to shave her head. So she should cover her head. [7]But a man should not cover his head, because he is made like God and is God's glory. But woman is man's glory.

10:7 "The people . . . sexually." Quotation from Exodus 32:6. **10:16 cup of blessing** The cup of the fruit of the vine that Christians thank God for and drink at the Lord's Supper. **10:26 "because . . . Lord"** Quotation from Psalms 24:1; 50:12; 89:11. **11:3 the man** This could also mean "her husband."

[8] Man did not come from woman, but woman came from man. [9] And man was not made for woman. Woman was made for man. [10] So that is why a woman should have her head covered with something to show that she is under authority. And also she should do this because of the angels. [11] But in the Lord the woman is important to the man, and the man is important to the woman. [12] This is true because woman came from man, but also man is born from woman. Really, everything comes from God. [13] Decide this for yourselves: Is it right for a woman to pray to God without something on her head? [14] Even nature itself teaches you that wearing long hair is shameful for a man. [15] But wearing long hair is a woman's honor. Long hair is given to the woman to cover her head. [16] Some people may still want to argue about this. But I would add that neither we nor the churches of God accept any other practice.

[17] In the things I tell you now I do not praise you. Your meetings hurt you more than they help you. [18] First, I hear that when you meet together as a church you are divided. And I believe some of this. [19] (It is necessary for there to be differences among you. That is the way to make it clear which of you are really doing right.) [20] When you all come together, you are not really eating the Lord's Supper.[n] [21] This is because when you eat, each person eats without waiting for the others. Some people do not get enough to eat, while others have too much to drink. [22] You can eat and drink in your own homes! It seems that you think God's church is not important. You embarrass those who are poor. What should I tell you? Should I praise you for doing this? I do not praise you.

[23] The teaching that I gave you is the same teaching that I received from the Lord: On the night when Jesus was handed over to be killed, he took bread [24] and gave thanks for it. Then he broke the bread and said, "This is my body; it is for you. Do this to remember me." [25] In the same way, after they ate, Jesus took the cup. He said, "This cup shows the new agreement from God to his people. This new agreement begins with the blood of my death. When you drink this, do it to remember me." [26] Every time you eat this bread and drink this cup, you show others about the Lord's death until he comes.

[27] So a person should not eat the bread or drink the cup of the Lord in a way that is not worthy of it. If he does he is sinning against the body and the blood of the Lord. [28] Everyone should look into his own heart before he eats the bread and drinks the cup. [29] If someone eats the bread and drinks the cup without recognizing the body, then he is judged guilty by eating and drinking. [30] That is why many in your group are sick and weak. And many have died. [31] But if we judged ourselves in the right way, then God would not judge us. [32] But when the Lord judges us, he punishes us to show us the right way. He does this so that we will not be destroyed along with the world.

[33] So my brothers, when you come together to eat, wait for each other. [34] If anyone is too hungry, he should eat at home. Do this so that your meeting together will not bring God's judgment on you. I will tell you what to do about the other things when I come.

12 Now, brothers, I want you to understand about spiritual gifts. [2] You remember the lives you lived before you were believers. You let yourselves be influenced and led away to worship idols—things that have no life. [3] So I tell you that no one who is speaking with the help of God's Spirit says, "Jesus be cursed." And no one can say, "Jesus is Lord," without the help of the Holy Spirit.[d]

[4] There are different kinds of gifts; but they are all from the same Spirit. [5] There are different ways to serve; but all these ways are from the same Lord. [6] And there are different ways that God works in people; but all these ways are from the same God. God works in us all in everything we do. [7] Something from the Spirit can be seen in each person, to help everyone. [8] The Spirit gives one person the ability to speak with wisdom. And the same Spirit gives another the ability to speak with knowledge. [9] The same Spirit gives faith to one person. And that one Spirit gives another gifts of healing. [10] The Spirit gives to another person the power to do miracles,[d] to another the ability to prophesy.[d] And he gives to another the ability to know the difference between good and evil spirits. The Spirit gives one person the ability to

11:20 Lord's Supper The meal Jesus told his followers to eat to remember him (Luke 22:14-20).

speak in different kinds of languages and to another the ability to interpret those languages. [11]One Spirit, the same Spirit, does all these things. The Spirit decides what to give each person.

[12]A person's body is only one thing, but it has many parts. Yes, there are many parts to a body, but all those parts make only one body. Christ is like that too. [13]Some of us are Jews, and some of us are Greeks. Some of us are slaves, and some of us are free. But we were all baptized into one body through one Spirit.[d] And we were all made to share in the one Spirit.

[14]And a person's body has more than one part. It has many parts. [15]The foot might say, "I am not a hand. So I am not part of the body." But saying this would not stop the foot from being a part of the body. [16]The ear might say, "I am not an eye. So I am not part of the body." But saying this would not make the ear stop being a part of the body. [17]If the whole body were an eye, the body would not be able to hear. If the whole body were an ear, the body would not be able to smell anything. [18-19]If each part of the body were the same part, there would be no body. But truly God put the parts in the body as he wanted them. He made a place for each one of them. [20]And so there are many parts, but only one body.

[21]The eye cannot say to the hand, "I don't need you!" And the head cannot say to the foot, "I don't need you!" [22]No! Those parts of the body that seem to be weaker are really very important. [23]And the parts of the body that we think are not worth much are the parts that we give the most care to. And we give special care to the parts of the body that we want to hide. [24]The more beautiful parts of our body need no special care. But God put the body together and gave more honor to the parts that need it. [25]God did this so that our body would not be divided. God wanted the different parts to care the same for each other. [26]If one part of the body suffers, then all the other parts suffer with it. Or if one part of our body is honored, then all the other parts share its honor.

[27]All of you together are the body of Christ. Each one of you is a part of that body. [28]And in the church God has given a place first to apostles,[d] second to prophets,[d] and third to teachers. Then God has given a place to those who do miracles,[d] those who have gifts of healing, those who can help others, those who are able to lead, and those who can speak in different languages. [29]Not all are apostles. Not all are prophets. Not all are teachers. Not all do miracles. [30]Not all have gifts of healing. Not all speak in different languages. Not all interpret those languages. [31]But you should truly want to have the greater gifts.

And now I will show you the best way of all.

13 I may speak in different languages of men or even angels. But if I do not have love, then I am only a noisy bell or a ringing cymbal. [2]I may have the gift of prophecy;[d] I may understand all the secret things of God and all knowledge; and I may have faith so great that I can move mountains. But even with all these things, if I do not have love, then I am nothing. [3]I may give everything I have to feed the poor. And I may even give my body as an offering to be burned. But I gain nothing by doing these things if I do not have love.

[4]Love is patient and kind. Love is not jealous, it does not brag, and it is not proud. [5]Love is not rude, is not selfish, and does not become angry easily. Love does not remember wrongs done against it. [6]Love is not happy with evil, but is happy with the truth. [7]Love patiently accepts all things. It always trusts, always hopes, and always continues strong.

[8]Love never ends. There are gifts of prophecy,[d] but they will be ended. There are gifts of speaking in different languages, but those gifts will end. There is the gift of knowledge, but it will be ended. [9]These things will end, because this knowledge and these prophecies we have are not complete. [10]But when perfection comes, the things that are not complete will end. [11]When I was a child, I talked like a child; I thought like a child; I made plans like a child. When I became a man, I stopped those childish ways. [12]It is the same with us. Now we see as if we are looking into a dark mirror. But at that time, in the future, we shall see clearly. Now I know only a part. But at that time I will know fully, as God has known me. [13]So these three things continue forever: faith, hope and love. And the greatest of these is love.

14 Love, then, is what you should try for. And you should truly want to have the spiritual gifts. And the gift you should want most is to be able to prophesy.[d] [2]I will explain why. One who has the gift of speaking in a different language is not speaking to people. He is speaking to God. No one understands him—he is speaking secret things through the Spirit.[d] [3]But one who prophesies is speaking to people. He gives people strength, encouragement, and comfort. [4]The one who speaks in a different language is helping only himself. But the one who prophesies is helping the whole church. [5]I would like all of you to have the gift of speaking in different kinds of languages. But more, I want you to prophesy. The person who prophesies is greater than the one who can only speak in different languages—unless someone is there who can explain what he says. Then the whole church can be helped.

[6]Brothers, will it help you if I come to you speaking in different languages? No! It will help you only if I bring you a new truth or some knowledge, or some prophecy, or some teaching. [7]It is the same as with non-living things that make sounds—like a flute or a harp. If different musical notes are not made clear, you will not know what song is being played. Each note must be played clearly for you to be able to understand the tune. [8]And in a war, if the trumpet does not sound clearly, the soldiers will not know it is time to prepare for fighting. [9]It is the same with you. The words you speak with your tongue must be clear. Unless you speak clearly, no one can understand what you are saying. You will be talking in the air! [10]It is true that there are many kinds of speech in the world. And they all have meaning. [11]So unless I understand the meaning of what someone says to me, I am a stranger to him, and he is a stranger to me. [12]It is the same with you. You want spiritual gifts very much. So try most to have the gifts that help the church grow stronger.

[13]The one who has the gift of speaking in a different language should pray that he can also interpret what he says. [14]If I pray in a different language, my spirit is praying, but my mind does nothing. [15]So what should I do? I will pray with my spirit, but I will also pray with my mind. I will sing with my spirit, but I will also sing with my mind. [16]You might be praising God with your spirit. But a person there without understanding cannot say "Amen"[n] to your prayer of thanks. He

does not know what you are saying. [17]You may be thanking God in a good way, but the other person is not helped.

[18]I thank God that my gift of speaking in different kinds of languages is greater than any of yours. [19]But in the church meetings I would rather speak five words that I understand than thousands of words in a different language. I would rather speak with my understanding, so that I can teach others.

[20]Brothers, do not think like children. In evil things be like babies. But in your thinking you should be like full-grown men. [21]It is written in the Scriptures:[d]

"I will use strange words and
        foreign languages
    to speak to these people.
But even then they will not listen."
                        Isaiah 28:11-12

That is what the Lord says. [22]So the gift of speaking in different kinds of languages is a proof for those who do not believe, not for those who believe. And prophecy is for people who believe, not for those who do not believe. [23]Suppose the whole church meets together and everyone speaks in different languages. If some people come in who are without understanding or do not believe, they will say you are crazy. [24]But suppose everyone is prophesying and someone comes in who does not believe or is without understanding. If everyone is prophesying, his sin will be shown to him, and he will be judged by all that he hears. [25]The secret things in his heart will be made known. So he will bow down and worship God. He will say, "Truly, God is with you."

[26]So, brothers, what should you do? When you meet together, one person has a song. Another has a teaching. Another has a new truth from God. Another speaks in a different language, and another person interprets that language. The purpose of all these things should be to help the church grow strong. [27]When you meet together, if anyone speaks in a different language, then it should be only two, or not more than three, who speak. They should speak one after the other. And someone else should interpret what they say. [28]But if there is no interpreter, then anyone who speaks in a different language should be quiet in the church meeting. He should speak only to himself and to God.

[29]And only two or three prophets[d] should speak. The others should judge what they say. [30]And if a message from God comes to another person who is sitting, then the first speaker should stop. [31]You can all prophesy one after the other. In this way all the people can be taught and encouraged. [32]The spirits of prophets are under the control of the prophets themselves. [33]God is not a God of confusion but a God of peace.

This is true in all the churches of God's people. [34]Women should keep quiet in the church meetings. They are not allowed to speak. They must be under control. This is also what the law of Moses says. [35]If there is something the women want to know, they should ask their own husbands at home. It is shameful for a woman to speak in the church meeting. [36]Did God's teaching come from you? Or are you the only ones who have received that teaching?

[37]If anyone thinks that he is a prophet or that he has a spiritual gift, then he should understand that what I am writing to you is the Lord's command. [38]If that person does not know this, then he is not known by God.

[39]So my brothers, you should truly want to prophesy. And do not stop people from using the gift of speaking in different kinds of languages. [40]But let everything be done in a way that is right and orderly.

15 Now, brothers, I want you to remember the Good News[d] I brought to you. You received this Good News, and you continue strong in it. [2]And you are saved by this Good News. But you must continue believing what I told you. If you do not, then you believed for nothing.

[3]I passed on to you what I received. And this was the most important: that Christ died for our sins, as the Scriptures[d] say; [4]that he was buried and was raised to life on the third day as the Scriptures say; [5]and that he showed himself to Peter and then to the twelve apostles.[d] [6]After that, Jesus showed himself to more than 500 of the believers at the same time. Most of them are still living today. But some have died. [7]Then Jesus showed himself to James and later to all the apostles. [8]Last of all he showed himself to me—as to a person not born at the normal time. [9]All the other apostles are greater than I am. This is be-

cause I persecuted the church of God. And this is why I am not even good enough to be called an apostle. [10]But God's grace has made me what I am. And his grace to me was not wasted. I worked harder than all the other apostles. (But I was not really the one working. It was God's grace that was with me.) [11]So then it is not important if I preached to you or if the other apostles preached to you. We all preach the same thing, and this is what you believed.

[12]It is preached that Christ was raised from death. So why do some of you say that people will not be raised from death? [13]If no one will ever be raised from death, then Christ was not raised from death. [14]And if Christ was not raised, then our preaching is worth nothing. And your faith is worth nothing. [15]And also, we will be guilty of lying about God. Because we have preached about him by saying that he raised Christ from death. And if people are not raised from death, then God never raised Christ from death. [16]If the dead are not raised, Christ has not been raised either. [17]And if Christ has not been raised, then your faith is for nothing; you are still guilty of your sins. [18]And also, those in Christ who have already died are lost. [19]If our hope in Christ is for this life only, we should be pitied more than anyone else in the world.

[20]But Christ has truly been raised from death—the first one and proof that those who are asleep in death will also be raised. [21]Death comes to everyone because of what one man did. But the rising from death also happens because of one man. [22]In Adam all of us die. In the same way, in Christ all of us will be made alive again. [23]But everyone will be raised to life in the right order. Christ was first to be raised. When Christ comes again, those who belong to him will be raised to life. [24]Then the end will come. Christ will destroy all rulers, authorities, and powers. And he will give the kingdom to God the Father. [25]Christ must rule until God puts all enemies under Christ's control. [26]The last enemy to be destroyed will be death. [27]The Scripture[d] says, "God put all things under his control."[n] When it says that "all things" are put under him, it is clear that this does not include God himself. God is the one putting everything under Christ's

---

15:27 "God put . . . control." Quotation from Psalm 8:6.

control. [28] After everything has been put under Christ, then the Son himself will be put under God. God is the One who put all things under Christ. And Christ will be put under God, so that God will be the complete ruler over everything.

[29] If the dead are never raised, then what will people do who are baptized for those who have died? If the dead are not raised at all, why are people baptized for them?

[30] And what about us? Why do we put ourselves in danger every hour? [31] I die every day. That is true, brothers, just as it is true that I brag about you in Christ Jesus our Lord. [32] If I fought wild animals in Ephesus only for human reasons, I have gained nothing. If the dead are not raised, then, "Let us eat and drink, because tomorrow we will die."[n]

[33] Do not be fooled: "Bad friends will ruin good habits." [34] Come back to your right way of thinking and stop sinning. I say this to shame you—some of you do not know God.

[35] But someone may ask, "How are the dead raised? What kind of body will they have?" [36] Those are stupid questions. When you plant something, it must die in the ground before it can live and grow. [37] And when you plant it, what you plant does not have the same "body" that it will have later. What you plant is only a seed, maybe wheat or something else. [38] But God gives it a body that he has planned for it. And God gives each kind of seed its own body. [39] All things made of flesh are not the same kinds of flesh: People have one kind of flesh, animals have another kind, birds have another, and fish have another. [40] Also there are heavenly bodies and earthly bodies. But the beauty of the heavenly bodies is one kind. The beauty of the earthly bodies is another kind. [41] The sun has one kind of beauty. The moon has another beauty, and the stars have another. And each star is different in its beauty.

[42] It is the same with the dead who are raised to life. The body that is "planted" will ruin and decay. But that body is raised to a life that cannot be destroyed. [43] When the body is "planted," it is without honor. But it is raised in glory. When the body is "planted," it is weak. But when it is raised, it has power. [44] The body that is "planted" is a physical body. When it is raised, it is a spiritual body.

There is a physical body. And there is also a spiritual body. [45] It is written in the Scriptures:[d] "The first man became a living person."[n] But the last Adam became a spirit that gives life. [46] The spiritual man did not come first. It was the physical man who came first; then came the spiritual. [47] The first man came from the dust of the earth. The second man came from heaven. [48] People belong to the earth. They are like the first man of earth. But those people who belong to heaven are like the man of heaven. [49] We were made like the man of earth. So we will also be made like the man of heaven.

[50] I tell you this, brothers: Flesh and blood cannot have a part in the kingdom of God. A thing that will ruin cannot have a part in something that never ruins. [51] But listen, I tell you this secret: We will not all die, but we will all be changed. [52] It will only take a second. We will be changed as quickly as an eye blinks. This will happen when the last trumpet sounds. The trumpet will sound and those who have died will be raised to live forever. And we will all be changed. [53] This body that will ruin must clothe itself with something that will never ruin. And this body that dies must clothe itself with something that will never die. [54] So this body that ruins will clothe itself with that which never ruins. And this body that dies will clothe itself with that which never dies. When this happens, then this Scripture will be made true:

"Death is destroyed forever in
  victory."   *Isaiah 25:8*
[55] "Death, where is your victory?
  Death, where is your power to
  hurt?"   *Hosea 13:14*

[56] Death's power to hurt is sin. The power of sin is the law. [57] But we thank God! He gives us the victory through our Lord Jesus Christ.

[58] So my dear brothers, stand strong. Do not let anything change you. Always give yourselves fully to the work of the Lord. You know that your work in the Lord is never wasted.

15:32 "Let us . . . die." Quotation from Isaiah 22:13; 56:12. **15:45** "The first . . . person." Quotation from Genesis 2:7.

16 Now I will write about the collection of money for God's people. Do the same thing that I told the Galatian churches to do: [2] On the first day of every week, each one of you should put aside as much money as you can from what you are blessed with. You should save it up, so that you will not have to collect money after I come. [3] When I arrive, I will send some men to take your gift to Jerusalem. These will be men who you all agree should go. I will send them with letters of introduction. [4] If it seems good for me to go also, these men will go along with me.

[5] I plan to go through Macedonia. So I will come to you after I go through there. [6] Maybe I will stay with you for a time. I might even stay all winter. Then you can help me on my trip, wherever I go. [7] I do not want to come to see you now, because I would have to leave to go other places. I hope to stay a longer time with you if the Lord allows it. [8] But I will stay at Ephesus until Pentecost. [d] [9] I will stay, because a good opportunity for a great and growing work has been given to me now. And there are many people working against me.

[10] Timothy might come to you. Try to make him feel comfortable with you. He is working for the Lord just as I am. [11] So none of you should refuse to accept Timothy. Help him on his trip in peace, so that he can come back to me. I am expecting him to come back with the brothers.

[12] Now about our brother Apollos: I strongly encouraged him to visit you with the other brothers. But he was sure that he did not want to go now. But when he has the opportunity, he will go to you.

[13] Be careful. Continue strong in the faith. Have courage, and be strong. [14] Do everything in love.

[15] You know that the family of Stephanas were the first believers in Southern Greece. They have given themselves to the service of God's people. I ask you, brothers, [16] to follow the leading of people like these and anyone else who works and serves with them.

[17] I am happy that Stephanas, Fortunatus, and Achaicus have come. You are not here, but they have filled your place. [18] They have given rest to my spirit and to yours. You should recognize the value of men like these.

[19] The churches in the country of Asia send greetings to you. Aquila and Priscilla greet you in the Lord. Also the church that meets in their house greets you. [20] All the brothers here send greetings. Give each other a holy kiss when you meet.

[21] I am Paul, and I am writing this greeting with my own hand.

[22] If anyone does not love the Lord, then let him be separated from God—lost forever!

Come, O Lord!

[23] The grace of the Lord Jesus be with you.

[24] My love be with all of you in Christ Jesus.

The Second Letter of Paul the Apostle to the

CORINTHIANS

1 From Paul, an apostle [d] of Christ Jesus. I am an apostle because that is what God wanted.

Also from Timothy our brother in Christ.

To the church of God in Corinth, and to all of God's people in the whole country of Southern Greece:

[2] Grace and peace to you from God our Father and the Lord Jesus Christ.

[3] Praise be to the God and Father of our Lord Jesus Christ. God is the Father who is full of mercy. And he is the God of all comfort. [4] He comforts us every time we have trouble, so that we can comfort others when they have trouble. We can comfort them with the same comfort that God gives us. [5] We share in the many sufferings of Christ. In the same way, much comfort comes to us through Christ. [6] If we have troubles, it is for your comfort and salvation. If we have comfort, then you also have comfort. This helps you to accept patiently the same sufferings that we have. [7] Our hope for you is strong. We know that you share in our sufferings. So we know that you also share in the comfort we receive.

[8] Brothers, we want you to know about

the trouble we suffered in the country of Asia. We had great burdens there that were greater than our own strength. We even gave up hope for life. ⁹Truly, in our own hearts we believed that we would die. But this happened so that we would not trust in ourselves. It happened so that we would trust in God, who raises people from death. ¹⁰God saved us from these great dangers of death. And he will continue to save us. We have put our hope in him, and he will save us again. ¹¹And you can help us with your prayers. Then many people will give thanks for us—that God blessed us because of their many prayers.

¹²This is what we are proud of, and I can say with all my heart that it is true: In all the things we have done in the world, we have done everything with an honest and pure heart from God. And this is even more true in what we have done with you. We did this by God's grace, not by the kind of wisdom the world has. ¹³For we write to you only what you can read and understand. And I hope that ¹⁴as you have understood some things about us, you may come to know everything about us. Then you can be proud of us, as we will be proud of you on the day our Lord Jesus Christ comes again.

¹⁵I was very sure of all this. That is why I made plans to visit you first. Then you could be blessed twice. ¹⁶I planned to visit you on my way to Macedonia. Then I planned to visit you again on my way back. I wanted to get help from you for my trip to Judea. ¹⁷Do you think that I made these plans without really thinking? Or maybe you think I make plans as the world does, so that I say "Yes, yes," and at the same time "No, no."

¹⁸But if you can believe God, then you can believe that what we tell you is never both "Yes" and "No." ¹⁹The Son of God, Jesus Christ, that Silas and Timothy and I preached to you, was not "Yes" and "No." In Christ it has always been "Yes." ²⁰The "Yes" to all of God's promises is in Christ. And that is why we say "Amen"ⁿ through Christ to the glory of God. ²¹And God is the One who makes you and us strong in Christ. God made us his chosen people. ²²He put his mark on us to show that we are his. And he put his Spiritᵈ in our hearts to be a guarantee for all he has promised.

²³I tell you this, and I ask God to be my witness that this is true: The reason I did not come back to Corinth was that I did not want to punish or hurt you. ²⁴I do not mean that we are trying to control your faith. You are strong in faith. But we are workers with you for your own happiness.

2 So I decided that my next visit to you would not be another visit to make you sad. ²If I make you sad, who will make me happy? Only you can make me happy—you whom I made sad. ³I wrote you a letter for this reason: that when I came to you I would not be made sad by the people who should make me happy. I felt sure of all of you. I felt sure that you would share my joy. ⁴When I wrote to you before, I was very troubled and unhappy in my heart. I wrote with many tears. I did not write to make you sad, but to let you know how much I love you.

⁵Someone there among you has caused sadness. He caused this not to me, but to all of you—I mean he caused sadness to all in some way. (I do not want to make it sound worse than it really is.) ⁶The punishment that most of you gave him is enough for him. ⁷But now you should forgive him and comfort him. This will keep him from having too much sadness and giving up completely. ⁸So I beg you to show him that you love him. ⁹This is why I wrote to you. I wanted to test you and see if you obey in everything. ¹⁰If you forgive someone, I also forgive him. And what I have forgiven—if I had anything to forgive—I forgave it for you, and Christ was with me. ¹¹I did this so that Satan would not win anything from us. We know very well what Satan's plans are.

¹²I went to Troas to preach the Good Newsᵈ of Christ. The Lord gave me a good opportunity there. ¹³But I had no peace because I did not find my brother Titus there. So I said good-bye and went to Macedonia.

¹⁴But thanks be to God, who always leads us in victory through Christ. God uses us to spread his knowledge everywhere like a sweet-smelling perfume. ¹⁵Our offering to God is this: We are the sweet smell of Christ among those who are being saved and among those who are being lost. ¹⁶To those who are lost, we are the smell of death that brings death. But to those who are being saved, we are the smell of life that brings life.

1:20 "Amen" When a person says "Amen," it means he agrees with the things that were said.

So who is able to do this work? [17]We do not sell the word of God for a profit as many other people do. But in Christ we speak the truth before God. We speak as men sent from God.

3 Are we starting to brag about ourselves again? Do we need letters of introduction to you or from you, like some other people? [2]You yourselves are our letter, written on our hearts. It is known and read by everyone. [3]You show that you are a letter from Christ that he sent through us. This letter is not written with ink, but with the Spirit[d] of the living God. It is not written on stone tablets.[n] It is written on human hearts.

[4]We can say this, because through Christ we feel sure before God. [5]I do not mean that we are able to say that we can do this work ourselves. It is God who makes us able to do all that we do. [6]God made us able to be servants of a new agreement from himself to his people. This new agreement is not a written law. It is of the Spirit. The written law brings death, but the Spirit gives life.

[7]The law that brought death was written in words on stone. It came with God's glory. Moses' face was so bright with glory that the people of Israel could not continue to look at his face. And that glory later disappeared. [8]So surely the new way that brings the Spirit has even more glory. [9]That law judged people guilty of sin, but it had glory. So surely the new way that makes people right with God has much greater glory. [10]That old law had glory. But it really loses its glory when it is compared to the much greater glory of this new way. [11]If that law which disappeared came with glory, then this new way which continues forever has much greater glory.

[12]We have this hope, so we are very brave. [13]We are not like Moses. He put a covering over his face so that the people of Israel would not see it. The glory was disappearing, and Moses did not want them to see it end. [14]But their minds were closed. Even today that same covering hides the meaning when they read the old agreement. That covering is taken away only through Christ. [15]But even today, when they read the law of Moses, there is a covering over their minds. [16]But when a person changes and follows the Lord, that covering is taken away. [17]The Lord is the Spirit. And

where the Spirit of the Lord is, there is freedom. [18]Our faces, then, are not covered. We all show the Lord's glory, and we are being changed to be like him. This change in us brings more and more glory. And it comes from the Lord, who is the Spirit.

4 God, with his mercy, gave us this work to do. So we don't give up. [2]But we have turned away from secret and shameful ways. We use no trickery, and we do not change the teaching of God. We teach the truth plainly. This is how we show everyone who we are. And this is how they can know in their hearts what kind of people we are before God. [3]The Good News[d] that we preach may be hidden. But it is hidden only to those who are lost. [4]The devil who rules this world has blinded the minds of those who do not believe. They cannot see the light of the Good News—the Good News about the glory of Christ, who is exactly like God. [5]We do not preach about ourselves. But we preach that Jesus Christ is Lord; and we preach that we are your servants for Jesus. [6]God once said, "Let the light shine out of the darkness!" And this is the same God who made his light shine in our hearts. He gave us light by letting us know the glory of God that is in the face of Christ.

[7]We have this treasure from God. But we are only like clay jars that hold the treasure. This shows that this great power is from God, not from us. [8]We have troubles all around us, but we are not defeated. We do not know what to do, but we do not give up. [9]We are persecuted, but God does not leave us. We are hurt sometimes, but we are not destroyed. [10]We carry the death of Jesus in our own bodies, so that the life of Jesus can also be seen in our bodies. [11]We are alive, but for Jesus we are always in danger of death. This is so that the life of Jesus can be seen in our bodies that die. [12]So death is working in us, but life is working in you.

[13]It is written in the Scriptures,[d] "I believed, so I spoke."[n] Our faith is like this, too. We believe, and so we speak. [14]God raised the Lord Jesus from death. And we know that God will also raise us with Jesus. God will bring us together with you, and we will stand before him. [15]All these things are for you. And so the grace of God is being given to more and

---

3:3 stone tablets Meaning the law of Moses that was written on stone tablets (Exodus 24:12; 25:16). **4:13 "I . . . spoke."** Quotation from Psalm 116:10.

2 CORINTHIANS 4:16   1018   *Living by Faith*

more people. This will bring more and more thanks to God for his glory.

[16] So we do not give up. Our physical body is becoming older and weaker, but our spirit inside us is made new every day. [17] We have small troubles for a while now, but they are helping us gain an eternal glory. That glory is much greater than the troubles. [18] So we set our eyes not on what we see but on what we cannot see. What we see will last only a short time. But what we cannot see will last forever.

[5] We know that our body—the tent we live in here on earth—will be destroyed. But when that happens, God will have a house for us to live in. It will not be a house made by men. It will be a home in heaven that will last forever. [2] But now we are tired of this body. We want God to give us our heavenly home. [3] It will clothe us, and we will not be naked. [4] While we live in this body, we have burdens, and we complain. We do not want to be naked. We want to be clothed with our heavenly home. Then this body that dies will be fully covered with life. [5] This is what God made us for. And he has given us the Spirit[d] to be a guarantee for this new life.

[6] So we always have courage. We know that while we live in this body, we are away from the Lord. [7] We live by what we believe, not by what we can see. [8] So I say that we have courage. And we really want to be away from this body and be at home with the Lord. [9] Our only goal is to please God. We want to please him whether we live here or there. [10] For we must all stand before Christ to be judged. Each one will receive what he should get—good or bad—for the things he did when he lived in the earthly body.

[11] We know what it means to fear the Lord. So we try to help people accept the truth. God knows what we really are. And I hope that in your hearts you know, too. [12] We are not trying to prove ourselves to you again. But we are telling you about ourselves, so you will be proud of us. Then you will have an answer for those who are proud about things that can be seen. They do not care about what is in the heart. [13] If we are out of our minds, it is for God. If we have our right mind, then it is for you. [14] The love of Christ controls us. Because we know that One died for all. So all have died. [15] Christ died for all so that those who live would not continue to

live for themselves. He died for them and was raised from death so that they would live for him.

[16] From this time on we do not think of anyone as the world does. It is true that in the past we thought of Christ as the world thinks. But we no longer think of him in that way. [17] If anyone belongs to Christ, then he is made new. The old things have gone; everything is made new! [18] All this is from God. Through Christ, God made peace between us and himself. And God gave us the work of bringing everyone into peace with him. [19] I mean that God was in Christ, making peace between the world and himself. In Christ, God did not hold the world guilty of its sins. And he gave us this message of peace. [20] So we have been sent to speak for Christ. It is as if God is calling to you through us. We speak for Christ when we beg you to be at peace with God. [21] Christ had no sin. But God made him become sin. God did this for us so that in Christ we could become right with God.

[6] We are workers together with God. So we beg you: Do not let the grace that you received from God be for nothing. [2] God says,

"I heard your prayers at the right
        time,
    and I gave you help on the day of
        salvation."   *Isaiah 49:8*

I tell you that the "right time" is now. The "day of salvation" is now.

[3] We do not want anyone to find anything wrong with our work. So we do nothing that will be a problem for anyone. [4] But in every way we show that we are servants of God: in accepting many hard things, in troubles, in difficulties, and in great problems. [5] We are beaten and thrown into prison. Men become upset and fight us. We work hard, and sometimes we get no sleep or food. [6] We show that we are servants of God by living a pure life, by our understanding, by our patience, and by our kindness. We show this by the Holy Spirit,[d] by true love, [7] by speaking the truth, and by God's power. We use our right living to defend ourselves against everything. [8] Some people honor us, but other people shame us. Some people say good things about us, but other people say bad things. Some people say we are liars, but we speak the truth. [9] We are not known, but we are well-known. We seem to be dying, but look—we continue to live. We are punished, but we are not

killed. [10]We have much sadness, but we are always rejoicing. We are poor, but we are making many people rich in faith. We have nothing, but really we have everything.

[11]We have spoken freely to you in Corinth. We have opened our hearts to you. [12]Our feelings of love for you have not stopped. It is you that have stopped your feelings of love for us. [13]I speak to you as if you were my children. Do to us as we have done—open your hearts to us.

[14]You are not the same as those who do not believe. So do not join yourselves to them. Good and bad do not belong together. Light and darkness cannot share together. [15]How can Christ and Belial, the devil, have any agreement? What can a believer have together with a non-believer? [16]The temple of God cannot have any agreement with idols. And we are the temple of the living God. As God said: "I will live with them and walk with them. And I will be their God. And they will be my people."[n]

[17]"Leave those people,
    and make yourselves pure, says
        the Lord.
Touch nothing that is unclean,[d]
    and I will accept you."

Isaiah 52:11; Ezekiel 20:34, 41

[18]"I will be your father,
    and you will be my sons and
        daughters,
    says the Lord All-Powerful."

2 Samuel 7:14; 7:8

7 Dear friends, we have these promises from God. So we should make ourselves pure—free from anything that makes body or soul unclean. We should try to become perfect in the way we live, because we respect God.

[2]Open your hearts to us. We have not done wrong to anyone. We have not ruined the faith of any person, and we have cheated no one. [3]I do not say this to blame you. I told you before that we love you so much that we would live or die with you. [4]I feel very sure of you. I am very proud of you. You give me much comfort. And in all of our troubles I have great joy.

[5]When we came into Macedonia, we had no rest. We found trouble all around us. We had fighting on the outside and fear on the inside. [6]But God comforts those who are troubled. And God comforted us when Titus came. [7]We were

comforted by his coming and also by the comfort that you gave him. Titus told us about your wish to see me. He told us that you are very sorry for what you did. And he told me about your great care for me. When I heard this, I was much happier.

[8]Even if the letter I wrote you made you sad, I am not sorry I wrote it. I know it made you sad, and I was sorry for that. But it made you sad only for a short time. [9]Now I am happy, but not because you were made sad. I am happy because your sorrow made you change your hearts. You became sad in the way God wanted you to. So you were not hurt by us in any way. [10]Being sorry in the way God wants makes a person change his heart and life. This leads to salvation, and we cannot be sorry for that. But the kind of sorrow the world has will bring death. [11]You had the kind of sorrow God wanted you to have. Now see what this sorrow has brought you: It has made you very serious. It made you want to prove that you were not wrong. It made you angry and afraid. It made you want to see me. It made you care. It made you want the right thing to be done. You proved that you were not guilty in any part of the problem. [12]I wrote that letter, but not because of the one who did the wrong. And it was not written because of the person who was hurt. But I wrote the letter so that you could see, before God, the great care that you have for us. [13]That is why we were comforted.

We were very comforted. And we were even happier to see that Titus was so happy. All of you made him feel much better. [14]I bragged to Titus about you. And you showed that I was right. Everything that we said to you was true. And you have proved that what we bragged about to Titus is true. [15]And his love for you is stronger when he remembers that you were all ready to obey. You welcomed him with respect and fear. [16]I am very happy that I can trust you fully.

8 And now, brothers, we want you to know about the grace that God gave the churches in Macedonia. [2]They have been tested by great troubles. And they are very poor. But they gave much because of their great joy. [3]I can tell you that they gave as much as they were able. They gave even more than they could afford. No one told them to do it. [4]But they asked us again and again—

they begged us to let them share in this service for God's people. ⁵And they gave in a way that we did not expect: They first gave themselves to the Lord and to us. This is what God wants. ⁶So we asked Titus to help you finish this special work of grace. He is the one who started this work. ⁷You are rich in everything—in faith, in speaking, in knowledge, in truly wanting to help, and in the love you learned from us. And so we want you to be rich also in this gift of giving.

⁸I am not commanding you to give. But I want to see if your love is true love. I do this by showing you that others really want to help. ⁹You know the grace of our Lord Jesus Christ. You know that Christ was rich, but for you he became poor. Christ did this so that by his being poor you might become rich.

¹⁰This is what I think you should do: Last year you were the first to want to give. And you were the first who gave. ¹¹So now finish the work that you started. Then your "doing" will be equal to your "wanting to do." Give from what you have. ¹²If you want to give, your gift will be accepted. Your gift will be judged by what you have, not by what you do not have. ¹³We do not want you to have troubles while other people are at ease. We want everything to be equal. ¹⁴At this time you have plenty. What you have can help others who are in need. Then later, when they have plenty, they can help you when you are in need. Then all will be equal. ¹⁵As it is written in the Scriptures,ᵈ "The person who gathered more did not have too much. The person who gathered less did not have too little."ᵐ

¹⁶I thank God because he gave Titus the same love for you that I have. ¹⁷Titus accepted what we asked him to do. He wanted very much to go to you. This was his own idea. ¹⁸We are sending with him the brother who is praised by all the churches. This brother is praised because of his service in preaching the Good News.ᵈ ¹⁹Also, this brother was chosen by the churches to go with us when we deliver this gift of money. We are doing this service to bring glory to the Lord and to show that we really want to help.

²⁰We are being careful so that no one will criticize us about the way we are handling this large gift. ²¹We are trying

to do what is right. We want to do what the Lord accepts as right and also what people think is right.

²²Also, we are sending with them our brother who is always ready to help. He has proved this to us in many ways. And he wants to help even more now because he has much faith in you.

²³Now about Titus—he is my partner who is working with me to help you. And about the other brothers—they are sent from the churches, and they bring glory to Christ. ²⁴So show these men that you really have love. Show them why we are proud of you. Then all the churches can see it.

9 I really do not need to write to you about this help for God's people. ²I know that you want to help. I have been bragging about this to the people in Macedonia. I have told them that you in Southern Greece have been ready to give since last year. And your wanting to give has made most of them here ready to give also. ³But I am sending the brothers to you. I do not want our bragging about you in this to be for nothing. I want you to be ready, as I said you would be. ⁴If any of the people from Macedonia come with me and find that you are not ready, we will be ashamed. We will be ashamed that we were so sure of you. (And you will be ashamed, too!) ⁵So I thought that I should ask these brothers to go to you before we come. They will finish getting in order the gift you promised. Then the gift will be ready when we come, and it will be a gift you wanted to give—not a gift that you hated to give.

⁶Remember this: The person who plants a little will have a small harvest. But the person who plants a lot will have a big harvest. ⁷Each one should give, then, what he has decided in his heart to give. He should not give if it makes him sad. And he should not give if he thinks he is forced to give. God loves the person who gives happily. ⁸And God can give you more blessings than you need. Then you will always have plenty of everything. You will have enough to give to every good work. ⁹It is written in the Scriptures:ᵈ

"He gives freely to the poor.
The things he does are right and
will continue forever."
Psalm 112:9

¹⁰God is the One who gives seed to the farmer. And he gives bread for food. And God will give you all the seed you need and make it grow. He will make a great harvest from your goodness. ¹¹God will make you rich in every way so that you can always give freely. And your giving through us will cause many to give thanks to God. ¹²This service that you do helps the needs of God's people. It is also bringing more and more thanks to God. ¹³This service you do is a proof of your faith. Many people will praise God because of it. They will praise God because you follow the Good News^d of Christ—the gospel you say you believe. They will praise God because you freely share with them and with all others. ¹⁴And when they pray, they will wish they could be with you. They will feel this because of the great grace that God has given you. ¹⁵Thanks be to God for his gift that is too wonderful to explain.

10 I, Paul, am begging you with the gentleness and the kindness of Christ. Some people say that I am easy on you when I am with you and strict when I am away. ²They think that we live in a worldly way. I plan to be very strict against them when I come. I beg you that when I come I will not need to use that same strictness with you. ³We do live in the world. But we do not fight in the same way that the world fights. ⁴We fight with weapons that are different from those the world uses. Our weapons have power from God. These weapons can destroy the enemy's strong places. We destroy men's arguments. ⁵And we destroy every proud thing that raises itself against the knowledge of God. We capture every thought and make it give up and obey Christ. ⁶We are ready to punish anyone there who does not obey. But first we want you to obey fully.

⁷You must look at the facts before you. If anyone feels sure that he belongs to Christ, then he must remember that we belong to Christ just as he does. ⁸It is true that we brag freely about the authority the Lord gave us. But he gave us this authority to strengthen you, not to hurt you. So I will not be ashamed of the bragging we do. ⁹I don't want you to think that I am trying to scare you with my letters. ¹⁰Some people say, "Paul's letters are powerful and sound important. But when he is with us, he is weak.

And his speaking is nothing." ¹¹They should know this: We are not there with you now, so we say these things in letters. But when we are there with you, we will show the same authority that we show in our letters.

¹²We do not dare to put ourselves in the same group with those who think that they are very important. We do not compare ourselves to them. They use themselves to measure themselves, and they judge themselves by what they themselves are. This shows that they know nothing. ¹³But we will not brag about things outside the work that was given us to do. We will limit our bragging to the work that God gave us. And this work includes our work with you. ¹⁴We are not bragging too much. We would be bragging too much if we had not already come to you. But we have come to you with the Good News^d of Christ. ¹⁵We limit our bragging to the work that is ours. We do not brag in the work other men have done. We hope that your faith will continue to grow. And we hope that you will help our work to grow much larger. ¹⁶We want to tell the Good News in the areas beyond your city. We do not want to brag about work that has already been done in another man's area. ¹⁷But, "If a person brags, he should brag only about the Lord."^n ¹⁸It is not the one who says he is good who is accepted but the one that the Lord thinks is good.

11 I wish you would be patient with me even when I am a little foolish. But you are already doing that. ²I am jealous over you. And this jealousy comes from God. I promised to give you to Christ. He must be your only husband. I want to give you to Christ to be his pure bride. ³But I am afraid that your minds will be led away from your true and pure following of Christ. This might happen just as Eve was tricked by the snake with his evil ways. ⁴You are very patient with anyone who comes to you and preaches a different Jesus than the one we preached. You are very willing to accept a spirit or Good News that is different from the Spirit^d and Good News^d that you received from us.

⁵I do not think that those "great apostles" are any better than I am. ⁶I may not be a trained speaker, but I do have knowledge. We have shown this to you clearly in every way.

10:17 "If a person . . . Lord." Quotation from Jeremiah 9:24.

⁷I preached God's Good News to you without pay. I made myself unimportant to make you important. Do you think that was wrong? ⁸I accepted pay from other churches. I took their money so that I could serve you. ⁹If I needed something when I was with you, I did not trouble any of you. The brothers who came from Macedonia gave me all that I needed. I did not allow myself to depend on you in any way. And I will never depend on you. ¹⁰No one in Southern Greece will stop me from bragging about that. I say this with the truth of Christ in me. ¹¹And why do I not depend on you? Do you think it is because I do not love you? No. God knows that I love you.

¹²And I will keep on doing what I am doing now. I will continue because I want to stop those people from having a reason to brag. They would like to say that the work they brag about is the same as ours. ¹³Such men are not true apostles.ᵈ They are workers who lie. And they change themselves to look like apostles of Christ. ¹⁴This does not surprise us. Even Satan changes himself to look like an angel of light.ⁿ ¹⁵So it does not surprise us if Satan's servants also make themselves look like servants who work for what is right. But in the end they will be punished for the things they do.

¹⁶I tell you again: No one should think that I am a fool. But if you think that I am a fool, then accept me as you would accept a fool. Then I can brag a little, too. ¹⁷I brag because I feel sure of myself. But I am not talking as the Lord would talk. I am bragging like a fool. ¹⁸Many people are bragging about their lives in the world. So I will brag, too. ¹⁹You are wise, so you will gladly be patient with fools! ²⁰You are even patient with someone who orders you around and uses you! You are patient with those who trick you, or think they are better than you, or hit you in the face! ²¹It is shameful to me to say this, but we were too "weak" to do those things to you!

But if anyone else is brave enough to brag, then I also will be brave and brag. (I am talking like a fool.) ²²Are they Hebrews?ⁿ So am I. Are they Israelites? So am I. Are they from Abraham's family?

So am I. ²³Are they serving Christ? I am serving him more. (I am crazy to talk like this.) I have worked much harder than they. I have been in prison more often. I have been hurt more in beatings. I have been near death many times. ²⁴Five times the Jews have given me their punishment of 39 lashes with a whip. ²⁵Three different times I was beaten with rods. One time they tried to kill me with stones. Three times I was in ships that were wrecked, and one of those times I spent the night and the next day in the sea. ²⁶I have gone on many travels. And I have been in danger from rivers, from thieves, from my own people, the Jews, and from those who are not Jews. I have been in danger in cities, in places where no one lives, and on the sea. And I have been in danger with false brothers. ²⁷I have done hard and tiring work, and many times I did not sleep. I have been hungry and thirsty. Many times I have been without food. I have been cold and without clothes. ²⁸Besides all this, there is on me every day the load of my concern for all the churches. ²⁹I feel weak every time someone is weak. I feel upset every time someone is led into sin.

³⁰If I must brag, I will brag about the things that show I am weak. ³¹God knows that I am not lying. He is the God and Father of the Lord Jesus Christ, and he is to be praised forever. ³²When I was in Damascus, the governor under King Aretas wanted to arrest me. So he put guards around the city. ³³But my friends put me in a basket. Then they put the basket through a hole in the wall and lowered me down. So I escaped from the governor.

12 I must continue to brag. It will do no good, but I will talk now about visions and revelationsⁿ from the Lord. ²I know a man in Christ who was taken up to the third heaven. This happened 14 years ago. I do not know whether the man was in his body or out of his body. But God knows. ³⁻⁴And I know that this man was taken up to paradise.ⁿ I don't know if he was in his body or away from his body. But he heard things he is not able to explain. He heard things that no man is allowed to tell. ⁵I will brag about a man like that. But I will not brag about

---

11:14 angel of light Messenger from God. The devil fools people so that they think he is from God. **11:22 Hebrews** A name for the Jews that some Jews were very proud of. **12:1 revelations** Revelation is making known a truth that was hidden. **12:3-4 paradise** A place where good people go when they die.

myself, except about my weaknesses. [6]But if I wanted to brag about myself, I would not be a fool. I would not be a fool, because I would be telling the truth. But I will not brag about myself. I do not want people to think more of me than what they see me do or hear me say.

[7]But I must not become too proud of the wonderful things that were shown to me. So a painful problem[n] was given to me. This problem is a messenger from Satan. It is sent to beat me and keep me from being too proud. [8]I begged the Lord three times to take this problem away from me. [9]But the Lord said to me, "My grace is enough for you. When you are weak, then my power is made perfect in you." So I am very happy to brag about my weaknesses. Then Christ's power can live in me. [10]So I am happy when I have weaknesses, insults, hard times, sufferings, and all kinds of troubles. All these things are for Christ. And I am happy, because when I am weak, then I am truly strong.

[11]I have been talking like a fool. But you made me do it. You are the ones who should say good things about me. I am worth nothing, but those "great apostles" are not worth any more than I am! [12]When I was with you, I did what proves that I am an apostle[d]—signs, wonders, and miracles.[d] And I did these things with much patience. [13]So you received everything that the other churches have received. Only one thing was different: I was not a burden to you. Forgive me for this!

[14]I am now ready to visit you the third time. And I will not be a burden to you. I want nothing from you, I only want you. Children should not have to save up to give to their parents. Parents should save to give to their children. [15]So I am happy to give everything I have for you. I will even give myself for you. If I love you more, will you love me less?

[16]It is clear that I was not a burden to you. But you think that I was tricky and used lies to catch you. [17]Did I cheat you by using any of the men I sent to you? No, you know I did not. [18]I asked Titus to go to you. And I sent our brother with him. Titus did not cheat you, did he? No, you know that Titus and I did the same thing and with the same spirit.

[19]Do you think that we have been defending ourselves to you all this time? We have been speaking in Christ and before God. You are our dear friends. And everything that we do is to make you stronger. [20]I do this because I am afraid that when I come, you will not be what I want you to be. And I am afraid that I will not be what you want me to be. I am afraid that among you there may be arguing, jealousy, anger, selfish fighting, evil talk, gossip, pride, and confusion. [21]I am afraid that when I come to you again, my God will make me ashamed before you. I may be saddened by many of those who have sinned. I may be saddened because they have not changed their hearts and have not turned away from their sexual sins and from the shameful things they have done.

13 I will come to you for the third time. And remember, "Every case must be proved by two or three witnesses."[a] [2]When I was with you the second time, I gave a warning to those who had sinned. Now I am away from you, and I give a warning to all the others. When I come to you again, I will not be easy with them. [3]You want proof that Christ is speaking through me. My proof is that he is not weak among you, but he is powerful. [4]It is true that he was weak when he was killed on the cross. But he lives now by God's power. It is true that we are weak in Christ. But for you we will be alive in Christ by God's power.

[5]Look closely at yourselves. Test yourselves to see if you are living in the faith. You know that Christ Jesus is in you—unless you fail the test. [6]But I hope you will see that we ourselves have not failed the test. [7]We pray to God that you will not do anything wrong. It is not important to see that we have passed the test. But it is important that you do what is right, even if it seems that we have failed. [8]We cannot do anything against the truth, but only for the truth. [9]We are happy to be weak, if you are strong. And we pray that you will grow stronger and stronger. [10]I am writing this while I am away from you. I am writing so that when I come I will not have to be harsh in my use of authority. The Lord gave me this authority to use to make you stronger, not to destroy you.

[11]Now, brothers, I say good-bye. Try

12:7 painful problem Literally, "thorn in the flesh." **13:1 "Every . . . witnesses."** Quotation from Deuteronomy 19:15.

to be perfect. Do what I have asked you to do. Agree with each other, and live in peace. Then the God of love and peace will be with you.

[12] Give each other a holy kiss when you greet each other. [13] All of God's holy people send greetings to you.

[14] The grace of the Lord Jesus Christ, the love of God, and the fellowship of the Holy Spirit[d] be with you all.

The Letter of Paul the Apostle to the
GALATIANS

1 From Paul, an apostle.[d] I was not chosen to be an apostle by men. I was not sent from men. It was Jesus Christ and God the Father who made me an apostle. God is the One who raised Jesus from death.

[2] This letter is also from all the brothers who are with me.

To the churches in Galatia.[n]

[3] I pray that God our Father and the Lord Jesus Christ will be good to you and give you peace. [4] Jesus gave himself for our sins to free us from this evil world we live in. This is what God the Father wanted. [5] The glory belongs to God forever and ever. Amen.

[6] A short time ago God called you to follow him. He called you by his grace that came through Christ. But now I am amazed at you! You are already turning away and believing something different than the Good News.[d] [7] Really, there is no other Good News. But some people are confusing you and want to change the Good News of Christ. [8] We preached to you the Good News. So if we ourselves, or even an angel from heaven, preach to you something different than the Good News, he should be condemned! [9] I said this before. Now I say it again: You have already accepted the Good News. If anyone tells you another way to be saved, he should be condemned!

[10] Do you think I am trying to make people accept me? No! God is the One I am trying to please. Am I trying to please men? If I wanted to please men, I would not be a servant of Christ.

[11] Brothers, I want you to know that the Good News[d] I preached to you was not made by men. [12] I did not get it from men, nor did any man teach it to me. Jesus Christ showed it to me.

[13] You have heard about my past life. I belonged to the Jewish religion. I hurt the church of God very much and tried to destroy it. [14] I was becoming a leader in the Jewish religion. I did better than most other Jews of my age. I tried harder than anyone else to follow the old rules. These rules were the customs handed down by our ancestors.

[15] But God had special plans for me even before I was born. So he called me through his grace that I might [16] tell the Good News about his Son to the non-Jewish people. So God showed me about his Son. When God called me, I did not get advice or help from any man. [17] I did not go to Jerusalem to see those who were apostles[d] before I was. But, without waiting, I went away to Arabia and later went back to Damascus.

[18] After three years I went to Jerusalem to meet Peter and stayed with him for 15 days. [19] I met no other apostles, except James, the brother of the Lord. [20] God knows that these things I write are not lies. [21] Later, I went to the areas of Syria and Cilicia.

[22] In Judea the churches in Christ had never met me. [23] They had only heard this about me: "This man was trying to hurt us. But now he is preaching the same faith that he once tried to destroy." [24] And these believers praised God because of me.

2 After 14 years, I went to Jerusalem again, this time with Barnabas. I also took Titus with me. [2] I went because God showed me that I should go. I met with those men who were the leaders of the believers. When we were alone, I told them the Good News[d] that I preach to the non-Jewish people. I did not want my past work and the work I am now doing to be wasted. [3] Titus was with me. But Titus was not forced to be circumcised,[d] even though he was a Greek. [4] We talked about this problem because some false brothers had come into our group

1:2 Galatia Probably the same country where Paul preached and began churches on his first missionary trip. Read the book of Acts, chapters 13 and 14.

secretly. They came in like spies to find out about the freedom we have in Christ Jesus. They wanted to make us slaves. [5]But we did not agree with anything those false brothers wanted! We wanted the truth of the Good News to continue for you.

[6]Those men who seemed to be important did not change the Good News that I preach. (It doesn't matter to me if they were "important" or not. To God all men are the same.) [7]But these leaders saw that God had given me special work, just as he had to Peter. God gave Peter the work of telling the Good News to the Jews. But God gave me the work of telling the Good News to the non-Jewish people. [8]God gave Peter the power to work as an apostle[d] for the Jewish people. But he also gave me the power to work as an apostle for those who are not Jews. [9]James, Peter, and John, who seemed to be the leaders, saw that God had given me this special grace. So they accepted Barnabas and me. They said, "Paul and Barnabas, we agree that you should go to the people who are not Jews. We will go to the Jews." [10]They asked us to do only one thing—to remember to help the poor. And this was something that I really wanted to do.

[11]When Peter came to Antioch, I was against him because he was wrong. [12]This is what happened: When Peter first came to Antioch, he ate with the non-Jewish people. But then some Jewish men were sent from James. When they arrived, Peter stopped eating with the non-Jewish people and separated himself from them. He was afraid of the Jews who believe that all non-Jewish people must be circumcised.[d] [13]So Peter was a hypocrite.[d] The other Jewish believers joined with him and were hypocrites, too. Even Barnabas was influenced by what these Jewish believers did. [14]I saw what they did. They were not following the truth of the Good News.[d] So I spoke to Peter in front of them all. I said: "Peter, you are a Jew, but you are not living like a Jew. You are living like the non-Jewish people. So why do you now try to force the non-Jewish people to live like Jews?"

[15]We were not born as non-Jewish "sinners," but we were born as Jews. [16]Yet we know that a person is not made right with God by following the law. No! It is trusting in Jesus Christ that makes

a person right with God. So we, too, have put our faith in Christ Jesus, that we might be made right with God. And we are right with God because we trusted in Christ—not because we followed the law. For no one can be made right with God by following the law.

[17]We Jews came to Christ to be made right with God. So it is clear that we were sinners too. Does this mean that Christ makes us sinners? No! [18]But I would really be wrong to begin teaching again those things of the Law of Moses that I gave up. [19]I stopped living for the law. It was the law that put me to death. I died to the law so that I can now live for God. I was put to death on the cross with Christ. [20]I do not live anymore—it is Christ living in me. I still live in my body, but I live by faith in the Son of God. He loved me and gave himself to save me. [21]This gift is from God, and it is very important to me. If the law could make us right with God, then Christ did not have to die.

3 You people in Galatia were told very clearly about the death of Jesus Christ on the cross. But you were very foolish. You let someone trick you. [2]Tell me this one thing: How did you receive the Holy Spirit?[d] Did you receive the Spirit by following the law? No! You received the Spirit because you heard the Good News[d] and believed it. [3]You began your life in Christ by the Spirit. Now do you try to continue it by your own power? That is foolish. [4]You have experienced many things. Were all those experiences wasted? I hope not! [5]Does God give you the Spirit because you follow the law? No! Does God work miracles[d] among you because you follow the law? No! God gives you his Spirit and works miracles among you because you heard the Good News and believed it.

[6]The Scriptures[d] say the same thing about Abraham: "Abraham believed God, and God accepted Abraham's faith, and that faith made him right with God."[n] [7]So you should know that the true children of Abraham are those who have faith. [8]The Scriptures told what would happen in the future. They said that God would make the non-Jewish people right through their faith. This Good News was told to Abraham beforehand, as the Scripture says: "All na-

---

3:6 **"Abraham . . . God."** Quotation from Genesis 15:6.

tions will be blessed through you.'"[n] [9]Abraham believed this, and because he believed, he was blessed. It is the same today. All who believe today are blessed just as Abraham was blessed. [10]But those who depend on following the law to make them right are under a curse because the Scriptures say, "Anyone will be cursed who does not always obey what is written in the Book of the Law!'"[n] [11]So it is clear that no one can be made right with God by the law. The Scriptures say, "He who is right with God by faith will live." [12]The law does not use faith. It says, "A person who does these things will live forever because of them.'"[n] [13]So the law put a curse on us, but Christ took away that curse. He changed places with us and put himself under that curse. It is written in the Scriptures, "Everyone whose body is displayed on a tree[n] is cursed." [14]Christ did this so that God's blessing promised to Abraham might come to the non-Jews. This blessing comes through Jesus Christ. Jesus died so that we could have the Spirit that God promised and receive this promise by believing.

[15]Brothers, let me give you an example: Think about an agreement that a person makes with another person. After that agreement is accepted by both people, no one can stop that agreement or add anything to it. [16]God made promises to Abraham and his descendant.[d] God did not say, "and to your descendants." That would mean many people. But God said, "and to your descendant." That means only one person; that person is Christ. [17]This is what I mean: God had an agreement with Abraham and promised to keep it. The law, which came 430 years later, cannot change God's promise to Abraham. [18]Can following the law give us what God promised? No! If this is so, it is not God's promise that brings us the blessings. Instead God freely gave his blessings to Abraham through the promise he had made.

[19]So what was the law for? The law was given to show the wrong things people do. It continued until the special descendant of Abraham came. God's promise was about this descendant. The law was given through angels who used Moses for a mediator[n] to give the law to men. [20]But a mediator is not needed when there is only one side. And God is only one.

[21]Does this mean that the law is against God's promises? Never! If there were a law that could give men life, then we could be made right by following that law. [22]But this is not true, because the Scriptures[d] showed that the whole world is bound by sin. This was so that the promise would be given through faith. And it is given to people who believe in Jesus Christ.

[23]Before this faith came, we were all held prisoners by the law. We had no freedom until God showed us the way of faith that was coming. [24]So the law was our master until Christ came. After Christ came, we could be made right with God through faith. [25]Now the way of faith has come, and we no longer live under the law.

[26-27]You were all baptized into Christ, and so you were all clothed with Christ. This shows that you are all children of God through faith in Christ Jesus. [28]Now, in Christ, there is no difference between Jew and Greek. There is no difference between slaves and free men. There is no difference between male and female. You are all the same in Christ Jesus. [29]You belong to Christ. So you are Abraham's descendants.[d] You get all of God's blessings because of the promise that God made to Abraham.

4 I want to tell you this: While the one who will inherit his father's property is still a child, he is no different from a slave. It does not matter that the child owns everything. [2]While he is a child, he must obey those who are chosen to care for him. But when the child reaches the age set by his father, he is free. [3]It is the same for us. We were once like children. We were slaves to the useless rules of this world. [4]But when the right time came, God sent his Son. His Son was born of a woman and lived under the law. [5]God did this so that he could buy freedom for those who were under the law. His purpose was to make us his children.

[6]And you are God's children. That is why God sent the Spirit of his Son into your hearts. The Spirit[d] cries out, "Fa-

---

3:8 "All . . . you." Quotation from Genesis 12:3. **3:10 "Anyone . . . Law!"** Quotation from Deuteronomy 27:26. **3:12 "A person . . . them."** Quotation from Leviticus 18:5. **3:13 displayed on a tree** Deuteronomy 21:22-23 says that when a person was killed for doing wrong, his body was hung on a tree to show shame. Paul means that the cross of Jesus was like that. **3:19 mediator** A person who helps one person talk to or give something to another person.

ther, dear Father.'"[n] [7]So now you are not a slave; you are God's child, and God will give you what he promised, because you are his child.

[8]In the past you did not know God. You were slaves to gods that were not real. [9]But now you know the true God. Really, it is God who knows you. So why do you turn back to those weak and useless rules you followed before? Do you want to be slaves to those things again? [10]You still follow teachings about special days, months, seasons, and years. [11]I am afraid for you. I fear that my work for you has been wasted.

[12]Brothers, I was like you; so I beg you to become like me. You were very good to me before. [13]You remember that I came to you the first time because I was sick. That was when I preached the Good News[d] to you. [14]Though my sickness was a trouble for you, you did not hate me or make me leave. But you welcomed me as an angel from God, as if I were Jesus Christ himself! [15]You were very happy then. Where is that joy now? I remember that you would have taken out your eyes and given them to me if that were possible. [16]Now am I your enemy because I tell you the truth?

[17]Those people[n] are working hard to persuade you. But this is not good for you. They want to persuade you to turn against us. They want you to follow only them. [18]It is good for people to show interest in you, but only if their purpose is good. This is always true. It is true when I am with you and when I am away. [19]My little children, again I feel pain for you as a mother feels when she gives birth. I will feel this until you truly become like Christ. [20]I wish I could be with you now. Then maybe I could change the way I am talking to you. Now I do not know what to do about you.

[21]Some of you people still want to be under the law of Moses. Tell me, do you know what the law says? [22]The Scriptures[d] say that Abraham had two sons. The mother of one son was a slave woman. The mother of the other son was a free woman. [23]Abraham's son from the slave woman was born in the normal human way. But the son from the free woman was born because of the promise God made to Abraham.

[24]This makes a picture for us. The two women are like the two agreements between God and men. One agreement is the law that God made on Mount Sinai.[n] The people who are under this agreement are like slaves. The mother named Hagar is like that agreement. [25]She is like Mount Sinai in Arabia and is a picture of the earthly Jewish city of Jerusalem. This city is a slave, and all its people, the Jews, are slaves to the law. [26]But the heavenly Jerusalem which is above is like the free woman. She is our mother. [27]It is written in the Scriptures:

"Be happy, Jerusalem.
 You are like a woman who never
  gave birth to children.
Start singing and shout for joy.
 You never felt the pain of giving
  birth to children.
But you will have more children
 than the woman who has a
  husband." *Isaiah 54:1*

[28]My brothers, you are God's children because of his promise, as Isaac was then. [29]The son who was born in the normal way treated the other son badly. It is the same today. [30]But what does the Scripture say? "Throw out the slave woman and her son! The son of the free woman will receive everything his father has. But the son of the slave woman will receive nothing."[n] [31]So, my brothers, we are not children of the slave woman. We are children of the free woman.

[5] We have freedom now because Christ made us free. So stand strong. Do not change and go back into the slavery of the law. [2]Listen! I am Paul. I tell you that if you go back to the law by being circumcised,[d] then Christ is no good for you. [3]Again, I warn every man: If you allow yourselves to be circumcised, then you must follow all the law. [4]If you try to be made right with God through the law, then your life with Christ is over—you have left God's grace. [5]But we hope to be made right with God through faith, and we wait for this hope anxiously with the Spirit's[d] help. [6]When we are in Christ Jesus, it is not important if we are circumcised or not. The important thing is faith—the kind of faith that works through love.

[7]You were running a good race. You were obeying the truth. Who stopped

---

4:6 "Father, dear Father" Literally, "Abba, Father." Jewish children called their fathers "Abba."   **4:17 Those people** They are the false teachers who were bothering the believers in Galatia (Galatians 1:7).   **4:24 Mount Sinai** Mountain in Arabia where God gave his laws to Moses (Exodus 19 and 20).   **4:30 "Throw . . . nothing."** Quotation from Genesis 21:10.

you from following the true way? [8]Whatever way he used did not come from the One who chose you. [9]Be careful! "Just a little yeast makes the whole batch of dough rise." [10]But I trust in the Lord that you will not believe those different ideas. Someone is confusing you with such ideas. And he will be punished, whoever he is.

[11]My brothers, I do not teach that a man must be circumcised. If I teach circumcision, then why am I still being treated badly? If I still taught circumcision, my preaching about the cross would not be a problem. [12]I wish the people who are bothering you would castrate[n] themselves!

[13]My brothers, God called you to be free. But do not use your freedom as an excuse to do the things that please your sinful self. Serve each other with love. [14]The whole law is made complete in this one command: "Love your neighbor as you love yourself."[n] [15]If you go on hurting each other and tearing each other apart, be careful! You will completely destroy each other.

[16]So I tell you: Live by following the Spirit.[d] Then you will not do what your sinful selves want. [17]Our sinful selves want what is against the Spirit. The Spirit wants what is against our sinful selves. The two are against each other. So you must not do just what you please. [18]But if you let the Spirit lead you, you are not under the law.

[19]The wrong things the sinful self does are clear: being sexually unfaithful, not being pure, taking part in sexual sins, [20]worshiping false gods, doing witchcraft,[d] hating, making trouble, being jealous, being angry, being selfish, making people angry with each other, causing divisions among people, [21]having envy, being drunk, having wild and wasteful parties, and doing other things like this. I warn you now as I warned you before: Those who do these things will not be in God's kingdom. [22]But the Spirit gives love, joy, peace, patience, kindness, goodness, faithfulness, [23]gentleness, self-control. There is no law that says these things are wrong. [24]Those who belong to Christ Jesus have crucified their own sinful selves. They have given up their old selfish feelings and

the evil things they wanted to do. [25]We get our new life from the Spirit. So we should follow the Spirit. [26]We must not be proud. We must not make trouble with each other. And we must not be jealous of each other.

6 Brothers, someone in your group might do something wrong. You who are spiritual should go to him and help make him right again. You should do this in a gentle way. But be careful! You might be tempted to sin, too. [2]Help each other with your troubles. When you do this, you truly obey the law of Christ. [3]If anyone thinks that he is important when he is really not important, he is only fooling himself. [4]He should not compare himself with others. Each person should judge his own actions. Then he can be proud for what he himself has done. [5]Each person must be responsible for himself.

[6]Anyone who is learning the teaching of God should share all the good things he has with his teacher.

[7]Do not be fooled: You cannot cheat God. A person harvests only what he plants. [8]If he plants to satisfy his sinful self, his sinful self will bring him eternal death. But if he plants to please the Spirit,[d] he will receive eternal life from the Spirit. [9]We must not become tired of doing good. We will receive our harvest of eternal life at the right time. We must not give up! [10]When we have the opportunity to help anyone, we should do it. But we should give special attention to those who are in the family of believers.

[11]I am writing this myself. See what large letters I use. [12]Some men are trying to force you to be circumcised.[d] They do these things so that the Jews will accept them. They are afraid that they will be treated badly if they follow only the cross of Christ.[n] [13]Those who are circumcised do not obey the law themselves, but they want you to be circumcised. Then they can brag about what they forced you to do. [14]I hope I will never brag about things like that. The cross of our Lord Jesus Christ is my only reason for bragging. Through the cross of Jesus my world was crucified and I died to the world. [15]It is not important if a man is circumcised or not circumcised. The

---

5:12 castrate To cut off part of the male sex organ. Paul uses this word because it is similar to "circumcision." Paul wanted to show that he is very upset with the false teachers.
5:14 "Love . . . yourself." Quotation from Leviticus 19:18.   **6:12 cross of Christ** Paul uses the cross as a picture of the gospel, the story of Christ's death from death to pay for men's sins. The cross, or Christ's death, was God's way to save men.

important thing is being the new people God has made. [16]Peace and mercy to those who follow this rule—to all of God's people.

[17]So do not give me any more trouble.

I have scars on my body. These show[n] I belong to Christ Jesus.

[18]My brothers, I pray that the grace of our Lord Jesus Christ will be with your spirit. Amen.

The Letter of Paul the Apostle to the
EPHESIANS

1 From Paul, an apostle[d] of Christ Jesus. I am an apostle because that is what God wanted.

To God's holy people living in Ephesus, believers in Christ Jesus.

[2]Grace and peace to you from God our Father and the Lord Jesus Christ.

[3]Praise be to the God and Father of our Lord Jesus Christ. In Christ, God has given us every spiritual blessing in heaven. [4]In Christ, he chose us before the world was made. In his love he chose us to be his holy people—people without blame before him. [5]And before the world was made, God decided to make us his own children through Jesus Christ. That was what he wanted and what pleased him. [6]This brings praise to God because of his wonderful grace. God gave that grace to us freely, in Christ, the One he loves. [7]In Christ we are set free by the blood of his death. And so we have forgiveness of sins because of God's rich grace. [8]God gave us that grace fully and freely. God, with full wisdom and understanding, [9]let us know his secret purpose. This was what God wanted, and he planned to do it through Christ. [10]His goal was to carry out his plan when the right time came. He planned that all things in heaven and on earth would be joined together in Christ as the head.

[11]In Christ we were chosen to be God's people. God had already chosen us to be his people, because that is what he wanted. And God is the One who makes everything agree with what he decides and wants. [12]We are the first people who hoped in Christ. And we were chosen so that we would bring praise to God's glory. [13]So it is with you. You heard the true teaching—the Good News[d] about your salvation. When you heard it, you believed in Christ. And in Christ, God put his special mark on you by giving

you the Holy Spirit[d] that he had promised. [14]That Holy Spirit is the guarantee that we will get what God promised for his people. This will bring full freedom to the people who belong to God, to bring praise to God's glory.

[15-16]That is why I always remember you in my prayers and always thank God for you. I have always done this since the time I heard about your faith in the Lord Jesus and your love for all God's people. [17]I always pray to the God of our Lord Jesus Christ—to the glorious Father. I pray that he will give you a spirit that will make you wise in the knowledge of God—the knowledge that he has shown you. [18]I pray that you will have greater understanding in your heart. Then you will know the hope that God has chosen to give us. I pray that you will know that the blessings God has promised his holy people are rich and glorious. [19]And you will know that God's power is very great for us who believe. That power is the same as the great strength [20]God used to raise Christ from death and put him at his right side in heaven. [21]God made Christ more important than all rulers, authorities, powers, and kings. Christ is more important than anything in this world or in the next world. [22]God put everything under his power. And God made him the head over everything for the church. [23]The church is Christ's body. The church is filled with Christ, and Christ fills everything in every way.

2 In the past your spiritual lives were dead because of your sins and the things you did wrong against God. [2]Yes, in the past you lived the way the world lives. You followed the ruler of the evil powers that are above the earth. That same spirit is now working in those who refuse to obey God. [3]In the past all of us lived like them. We lived trying to please

---

6:17 These show Many times Paul was beaten and whipped by people who were against him because he was teaching about Christ. The scars were from these beatings.

our sinful selves. We did all the things our bodies and minds wanted. We should have suffered God's anger because of the way we were. We were the same as all other people.

[4] But God's mercy is great, and he loved us very much. [5] We were spiritually dead because of the things we did wrong against God. But God gave us new life with Christ. You have been saved by God's grace. [6] And he raised us up with Christ and gave us a seat with him in the heavens. He did this for those of us who are in Christ Jesus. [7] He did this so that for all future time he could show the very great riches of his grace. He shows that grace by being kind to us in Christ Jesus. [8] I mean that you have been saved by grace because you believe. You did not save yourselves. It was a gift from God. [9] You cannot brag that you are saved by the work you have done. [10] God has made us what we are. In Christ Jesus, God made us new people so that we would do good works. God had planned in advance those good works for us. He had planned for us to live our lives doing them.

[11] You were born non-Jews. You are the people the Jews call "uncircumcised."[n] Those who call you "uncircumcised" call themselves "circumcised."[d] (Their circumcision is only something they themselves do on their bodies.) [12] Remember that in the past you were without Christ. You were not citizens of Israel. And you had no part in the agreements[n] with the promise that God made to his people. You had no hope, and you did not know God. [13] Yes, at one time you were far away from God. But now in Christ Jesus you are brought near to God through the blood of Christ's death. [14] Because of Christ we now have peace. Christ made both Jews and non-Jews one people. They were separated as if there were a wall between them. But Christ broke down that wall of hate by giving his own body. [15] The Jewish law had many commands and rules. But Christ ended that law. Christ's purpose was to make the two groups of people become one new people in him. By doing this Christ would make peace. [16] Through the cross Christ ended the hatred between the two groups. And after Christ made the two groups to be one

body, he wanted to bring them back to God. Christ did this with his death on the cross. [17] Christ came and preached peace to you non-Jews who were far away from God. And he preached peace to those Jews who were near to God. [18] Yes, through Christ we all have the right to come to the Father in one Spirit.[d]

[19] So now you non-Jews are not visitors or strangers. Now you are citizens together with God's holy people. You belong to God's family. [20] You believers are like a building that God owns. That building was built on the foundation of the apostles[d] and prophets.[d] Christ Jesus himself is the most important stone[n] in that building. [21] That whole building is joined together in Christ. And Christ makes it grow and become a holy temple in the Lord. [22] And in Christ you, too, are being built together with the Jews. You are being built into a place where God lives through the Spirit.

3 So I, Paul, am a prisoner of Christ Jesus. I am a prisoner for you who are not Jews. [2] Surely you know that God gave me this work through his grace to help you. [3] God let me know his secret plan. He showed it to me. I have already written a little about this. [4] And if you read what I wrote, then you can see that I truly understand the secret truth about the Christ.[d] [5] People who lived in other times were not told that secret truth. But now, through the Spirit,[d] God has shown that secret truth to his holy apostles[d] and prophets.[d] [6] This is that secret truth: that the non-Jews will receive what God has for his people, just as the Jews will. The non-Jews are together with the Jews as part of the same body. And they share together in the promise that God made in Christ Jesus. The non-Jews have all of this because of the Good News.[d]

[7] By God's special gift of grace, I became a servant to tell that Good News. God gave me that grace through his power. [8] I am the least important of all God's people. But God gave me this gift—to tell the non-Jewish people the Good News about the riches of Christ. Those riches are too great to understand fully. [9] And God gave me the work of telling all people about the plan for God's secret truth. That secret truth has been hidden in God since the beginning

---

2:11 uncircumcised People not having the mark of circumcision as the Jews have. **2:12 agreements** The agreements that God gave to his people in the Old Testament. **2:20 most important stone** Literally, "cornerstone." The first and most important stone in a building.

of time. God is the One who created everything. [10]His purpose was that through the church all the rulers and powers in the heavenly world will now know God's wisdom, which has so many forms. [11]This agrees with the purpose God had since the beginning of time. And God carried out his plan through Christ Jesus our Lord. [12]In Christ we can come before God with freedom and without fear. We can do this through faith in Christ. [13]So I ask you not to become discouraged because of the sufferings I am having for you. My sufferings bring honor to you.

[14]So I bow in prayer before the Father. [15]Every family in heaven and on earth gets its true name from him. [16]I ask the Father in his great glory to give you the power to be strong in spirit. He will give you that strength through his Spirit.[d] [17]I pray that Christ will live in your hearts because of your faith. I pray that your life will be strong in love and be built on love. [18]And I pray that you and all God's holy people will have the power to understand the greatness of Christ's love. I pray that you can understand how wide and how long and how high and how deep that love is. [19]Christ's love is greater than any person can ever know. But I pray that you will be able to know that love. Then you can be filled with the fullness of God.

[20]With God's power working in us, God can do much, much more than anything we can ask or think of. [21]To him be glory in the church and in Christ Jesus for all time, forever and ever. Amen.

4 I am in prison because I belong to the Lord. God chose you to be his people. I tell you now to live the way God's people should live. [2]Always be humble and gentle. Be patient and accept each other with love. [3]You are joined together with peace through the Spirit.[d] Do all you can to continue together in this way. Let peace hold you together. [4]There is one body and one Spirit. And God called you to have one hope. [5]There is one Lord, one faith, and one baptism. [6]There is one God and Father of everything. He rules everything. He is everywhere and in everything.

[7]Christ gave each one of us a special gift. Each one received what Christ wanted to give him. [8]That is why it says in the Scriptures,[d]

"When he went up to the heights,
    he led a parade of captives.
And he gave gifts to people."

Psalm 68:18

[9]When it says, "He went up," what does it mean? It means that he first came down to the earth. [10]So Jesus came down, and he is the same One who went up. He went up above all the heavens. Christ did that to fill everything with himself. [11]And Christ gave gifts to men—he made some to be apostles,[d] some to be prophets,[d] some to go and tell the Good News,[d] and some to have the work of caring for and teaching God's people. [12]Christ gave those gifts to prepare God's holy people for the work of serving. He gave those gifts to make the body of Christ stronger. [13]This work must continue until we are all joined together in the same faith and in the same knowledge about the Son of God. We must become like a mature person—we must grow until we become like Christ and have all his perfection.

[14]Then we will no longer be babies. We will not be tossed about like a ship that the waves carry one way and then another. We will not be influenced by every new teaching we hear from men who are trying to fool us. Those men make plans and try any kind of trick to fool people into following the wrong path. [15]No! We will speak the truth with love. We will grow up in every way to be like Christ, who is the head. [16]The whole body depends on Christ. And all the parts of the body are joined and held together. Each part of the body does its own work. And this makes the whole body grow and be strong with love.

[17]In the Lord's name, I tell you this. I warn you: Do not continue living like those who do not believe. Their thoughts are worth nothing. [18]They do not understand. They know nothing, because they refuse to listen. So they cannot have the life that God gives. [19]They have lost their feeling of shame. And they use their lives for doing evil. More and more they want to do all kinds of evil things. [20]But the things you learned in Christ were not like this. [21]I know that you heard about him, and you are in him; so you were taught the truth. Yes, the truth is in Jesus. [22]You were taught to leave your old self—to stop living the evil way you lived before. That old self becomes worse and worse because people are fooled by the evil things they want to do. [23]But you were taught to be made new

in your hearts. [24]You were taught to become a new person. That new person is made to be like God—made to be truly good and holy.

[25]So you must stop telling lies. Tell each other the truth because we all belong to each other in the same body.[n] [26]When you are angry, do not sin. And do not go on being angry all day. [27]Do not give the devil a way to defeat you. [28]If a person is stealing, he must stop stealing and start working. He must use his hands for doing something good. Then he will have something to share with those who are poor.

[29]When you talk, do not say harmful things. But say what people need— words that will help others become stronger. Then what you say will help those who listen to you. [30]And do not make the Holy Spirit[d] sad. The Spirit is God's proof that you belong to him. God gave you the Spirit to show that God will make you free when the time comes. [31]Do not be bitter or angry or mad. Never shout angrily or say things to hurt others. Never do anything evil. [32]Be kind and loving to each other. Forgive each other just as God forgave you in Christ.

5 You are God's children whom he loves. So try to be like God. [2]Live a life of love. Love other people just as Christ loved us. Christ gave himself for us—he was a sweet-smelling offering and sacrifice to God.

[3]But there must be no sexual sin among you. There must not be any kind of evil or greed. Those things are not right for God's holy people. [4]Also, there must be no evil talk among you. You must not speak foolishly or tell evil jokes. These things are not right for you. But you should be giving thanks to God. [5]You can be sure of this: No one will have a place in the kingdom of Christ and of God if he does sexual sins, or does evil things, or is greedy. Anyone who is greedy is serving a false god.

[6]Do not let anyone fool you by telling you things that are not true. These things will bring God's anger on those who do not obey him. [7]So have no part with them. [8]In the past you were full of darkness, but now you are full of light in the Lord. So live like children who belong to the light. [9]Light brings every kind of goodness, right living, and truth. [10]Try to learn what pleases the Lord. [11]Do not do the things that people in

darkness do. That brings nothing good. But do good things to show that the things done in darkness are wrong. [12]It is shameful even to talk about what those people do in secret. [13]But the light makes all things easy to see. [14]And everything that is made easy to see can become light. This is why it is said:

"Wake up, sleeper!
   Rise from death,
   and Christ will shine on you."

[15]So be very careful how you live. Do not live like those who are not wise. Live wisely. [16]I mean that you should use every chance you have for doing good, because these are evil times. [17]So do not be foolish with your lives. But learn what the Lord wants you to do. [18]Do not be drunk with wine. That will ruin you spiritually. But be filled with the Spirit.[d] [19]Speak to each other with psalms, hymns, and spiritual songs. Sing and make music in your hearts to the Lord. [20]Always give thanks to God the Father for everything, in the name of our Lord Jesus Christ.

[21]Be willing to obey each other. Do this because you respect Christ.

[22]Wives, be under the authority of your husbands, as of the Lord. [23]The husband is the head of the wife, as Christ is the head of the church. The church is Christ's body—Christ is the Savior of the body. [24]The church is under the authority of Christ. So it is the same with you wives. You should be under the authority of your husbands in everything.

[25]Husbands, love your wives as Christ loved the church. Christ died for the church [26]to make it belong to God. Christ used the word to make the church clean by washing it with water. [27]Christ died so that he could give the church to himself like a bride in all her beauty. He died so that the church could be pure and without fault, with no evil or sin or any other wrong thing in it. [28]And husbands should love their wives in the same way. They should love their wives as they love their own bodies. The man who loves his wife loves himself. [29]No person ever hates his own body, but feeds and takes care of it. And that is what Christ does for the church, [30]because we are parts of his body. [31]The Scripture says, "So a man will leave his father and mother and be united with his wife. And the two people will become one

---

4:25 Tell . . . body. Quotation from Zechariah 8:16.

body."[n] [32]That secret truth is very important—I am talking about Christ and the church. [33]But each one of you must love his wife as he loves himself. And a wife must respect her husband.

6 Children, obey your parents the way the Lord wants. This is the right thing to do. [2]The command says, "Honor your father and mother."[n] This is the first command that has a promise with it. [3]The promise is: "Then everything will be well with you, and you will have a long life on the earth."[n]

[4]Fathers, do not make your children angry, but raise them with the training and teaching of the Lord.

[5]Slaves, obey your masters here on earth with fear and respect. And do that with a heart that is true, just as you obey Christ. [6]You must do more than obey your masters to please them only while they are watching you. You must obey them as you are obeying Christ. With all your heart you must do what God wants. [7]Do your work, and be happy to do it. Work as if you were serving the Lord, not as if you were serving only men. [8]Remember that the Lord will give a reward to everyone, slave or free, for doing good.

[9]Masters, in the same way, be good to your slaves. Do not say things to scare them. You know that the One who is your Master and their Master is in heaven. And that Master treats everyone alike.

[10]Finally, be strong in the Lord and in his great power. [11]Wear the full armor of God. Wear God's armor so that you can fight against the devil's evil tricks. [12]Our fight is not against people on earth. We are fighting against the rulers and authorities and the powers of this world's

darkness. We are fighting against the spiritual powers of evil in the heavenly world. [13]That is why you need to get God's full armor. Then on the day of evil you will be able to stand strong. And when you have finished the whole fight, you will still be standing. [14]So stand strong, with the belt of truth tied around your waist. And on your chest wear the protection of right living. [15]And on your feet wear the Good News[d] of peace to help you stand strong. [16]And also use the shield of faith. With that you can stop all the burning arrows of the Evil One. [17]Accept God's salvation to be your helmet. And take the sword of the Spirit[d]—that sword is the teaching of God. [18]Pray in the Spirit at all times. Pray with all kinds of prayers, and ask for everything you need. To do this you must always be ready. Never give up. Always pray for all God's people.

[19]Also pray for me. Pray that when I speak, God will give me words so that I can tell the secret truth of the Good News without fear. [20]I have the work of speaking that Good News. I am doing that now, here in prison. Pray that when I preach the Good News I will speak without fear, as I should.

[21]I am sending to you Tychicus, our brother whom we love. He is a faithful servant of the Lord's work. He will tell you everything that is happening with me. Then you will know how I am and what I am doing. [22]That is why I am sending him. I want you to know how we are. I am sending him to encourage you.

[23]Peace and love with faith to you from God the Father and the Lord Jesus Christ. [24]God's grace to all of you who love our Lord Jesus Christ with love that never ends.

The Letter of Paul the Apostle to the
PHILIPPIANS

1 From Paul and Timothy, servants of Jesus Christ.

To all of God's holy people in Christ Jesus who live in Philippi. And to your elders[d] and deacons.[d]

[2]Grace and peace to you from God our Father and the Lord Jesus Christ.

[3]I thank God every time I remember you. [4]And I always pray for all of you with joy. [5]I thank God for the help you gave me while I preached the Good News.[d] You helped from the first day you believed until now. [6]God began doing a good work in you. And he will continue

5:31 "So . . . body." Quotation from Genesis 2:24.   **6:2 "Honor . . . mother."** Quotation from Exodus 20:12; Deuteronomy 5:16.   **6:3 "Then . . . earth."** Quotation from Exodus 20:12; Deuteronomy 5:16.

it until it is finished when Jesus Christ comes again. I am sure of that.

⁷And I know that I am right to think like this about all of you. I am sure because I have you in my heart. All of you share in God's grace with me. You share in God's grace with me while I am in prison, while I am defending the Good News, and while I am proving the truth of the Good News. ⁸God knows that I want to see you very much. I love all of you with the love of Christ Jesus.

⁹This is my prayer for you: that your love will grow more and more; that you will have knowledge and understanding with your love; ¹⁰that you will see the difference between good and bad and choose the good; that you will be pure and without wrong for the coming of Christ; ¹¹that you will do many good things with the help of Christ to bring glory and praise to God.

¹²Brothers, I want you to know that what has happened to me has helped to spread the Good News.ᵈ ¹³I am in prison because I am a believer in Christ. All the palace guards and everyone else knows this. ¹⁴I am still in prison, but most of the believers feel better about it now. And so they are much braver about telling the Good News about Christ.

¹⁵It is true that some preach about Christ because they are jealous and bitter. But others preach about Christ because they want to help. ¹⁶They preach because they have love, and they know that God gave me the work of defending the Good News. ¹⁷But others preach about Christ because they are selfish. Their reason for preaching is wrong. They want to make trouble for me in prison.

¹⁸But I do not care if they make trouble for me. The important thing is that they are preaching about Christ. They should do it for the right reasons. But I am happy even if they do it for wrong reasons. And I will continue to be happy. ¹⁹You are praying for me, and the Spirit of Jesus Christ helps me. So I know that this trouble will bring my freedom. ²⁰The thing I want and hope for is that I will not fail Christ in anything. I hope that I will have the courage now, as always, to show the greatness of Christ in my life here on earth. I want to do that if I die or if I live. ²¹To me the only important thing about living is Christ. And even death would be profit for me. ²²If I continue living in the body, I will be able to work for the Lord. But what should I

choose—living or dying? I do not know. ²³It is hard to choose between the two. I want to leave this life and be with Christ. That is much better. ²⁴But you need me here in my body. ²⁵I know that you need me, and so I know that I will stay with you. I will help you grow and have joy in your faith. ²⁶You will be very happy in Christ Jesus when I am with you again.

²⁷Be sure that you live in a way that brings honor to the Good News of Christ. Then whether I come and visit you or am away from you, I will hear good things about you. I will hear that you continue strong with one purpose and that you work together as a team for the faith of the Good News. ²⁸And you will not be afraid of those who are against you. All of these things are proof from God that you will be saved and that your enemies will be lost. ²⁹God gave you the honor both of believing in Christ and suffering for Christ. Both these things bring glory to Christ. ³⁰When I was with you, you saw the struggles I had. And you hear about the struggles I am having now. You yourselves are having the same kind of struggles.

2 Does your life in Christ give you strength? Does his love comfort you? Do we share together in the Spirit?ᵈ Do you have mercy and kindness? ²If so, make me very happy by having the same thoughts, sharing the same love, and having one mind and purpose. ³When you do things, do not let selfishness or pride be your guide. Be humble and give more honor to others than to yourselves. ⁴Do not be interested only in your own life, but be interested in the lives of others.

⁵In your lives you must think and act like Christ Jesus.
⁶Christ himself was like God in everything.
He was equal with God.
But he did not think that being equal with God was something to be held on to.
⁷He gave up his place with God and made himself nothing.
He was born to be a man and became like a servant.
⁸And when he was living as a man, he humbled himself and was fully obedient to God.
He obeyed even when that caused his death—death on a cross.
⁹So God raised Christ to the highest place.
God made the name of Christ greater than every other name.

[10]God wants every knee to bow to Jesus—
everyone in heaven, on earth, and under the earth.
[11]Everyone will say, "Jesus Christ is Lord"
and bring glory to God the Father.

[12]My dear friends, you have always obeyed. You obeyed God when I was with you. It is even more important that you obey now while I am not with you. Keep on working to complete your salvation, and do it with fear and trembling. [13]Yes, God is working in you to help you want to do what pleases him. Then he gives you the power to do it.

[14]Do everything without complaining or arguing. [15]Then you will be innocent and without anything wrong in you. You will be God's children without fault. But you are living with crooked and mean people all around you. Among them you shine like stars in the dark world. [16]You offer to them the teaching that gives life. So when Christ comes again, I can be happy because my work was not wasted. I ran in the race and won.

[17]Your faith makes you offer your lives as a sacrifice in serving God. Perhaps I will have to offer my own blood with your sacrifice. But if that happens, I will be happy and full of joy with all of you. [18]You also should be happy and full of joy with me.

[19]I hope in the Lord Jesus to send Timothy to you soon. I will be happy to learn how you are. [20]I have no other person like Timothy. He truly cares for you. [21]Other people are interested only in their own lives. They are not interested in the work of Christ Jesus. [22]You know the kind of person Timothy is. You know that he has served with me in telling the Good News,[d] as a son serves his father. [23]I plan to send him to you quickly when I know what will happen to me. [24]I am sure that the Lord will help me to come to you soon.

[25]Epaphroditus is my brother in Christ. He works and serves with me in the army of Christ. When I needed help, you sent him to me. I think now that I must send him back to you [26]because he wants very much to see all of you. He is worried because you heard that he was sick. [27]Yes, he was sick, and nearly died. But God helped him and me too, so that I would not have more sadness. [28]So I want very much to send him to you. When you see him, you can be happy. And I can stop worrying about you. [29]Welcome him in the Lord with much joy. Give honor to people like Epaphroditus. [30]He should be honored because he almost died for the work of Christ. He put his life in danger so that he could help me. This was help that you could not give me.

3 My brothers, be full of joy in the Lord. It is no trouble for me to write the same things to you again, and it will help you to be more ready. [2]Be careful of those who do evil. They are like dogs. They demand to cut[n] the body. [3]But we are the ones who are truly circumcised.[d] We worship God through his Spirit.[d] We are proud to be in Christ Jesus. And we do not trust in ourselves or anything we can do. [4]Even if I am able to trust in myself, still I do not. If anyone thinks that he has a reason to trust in himself, he should know that I have greater reason for trusting in myself. [5]I was circumcised eight days after my birth. I am from the people of Israel and the tribe[d] of Benjamin. I am a Hebrew, and my parents were Hebrews. The law of Moses was very important to me. That is why I became a Pharisee.[d] [6]I was so enthusiastic that I tried to hurt the church. No one could find fault with the way I obeyed the law of Moses. [7]At one time all these things were important to me. But now I think those things are worth nothing because of Christ. [8]Not only those things, but I think that all things are worth nothing compared with the greatness of knowing Christ Jesus my Lord. Because of Christ, I have lost all those things. And now I know that all those things are worthless trash. This allows me to have Christ [9]and to belong to him. Now that I belong to Christ, I am right with God and this being right does not come from my following the law. It comes from God through faith. God uses my faith in Christ to make me right with him. [10]All I want is to know Christ and the power of his rising from death. I want to share in Christ's sufferings and become like him in his death. [11]If I have those things, then I have hope that I myself will be raised from death.

[12]I do not mean that I am already as God wants me to be. I have not yet reached that goal. But I continue trying to reach it and to make it mine. Christ

3:2 **cut** The word in Greek is like the word "circumcise," but it means "to cut completely off."

wants me to do that. That is the reason Christ made me his. [13]Brothers, I know that I have not yet reached that goal. But there is one thing I always do: I forget the things that are past. I try as hard as I can to reach the goal that is before me. [14]I keep trying to reach the goal and get the prize. That prize is mine because God called me through Christ to the life above.

[15]All of us who have grown spiritually to be mature should think this way, too. And if there are things you do not agree with, God will make them clear to you. [16]But we should continue following the truth we already have.

[17]Brothers, all of you should try to follow my example and to copy those who live the way we showed you. [18]Many people live like enemies of the cross of Christ. I have often told you about them, and it makes me cry to tell you about them now. [19]The way they live is leading them to destruction. Instead of serving God, they do whatever their bodies want. They do shameful things, and they are proud of it. They think only about earthly things. [20]But our homeland is in heaven, and we are waiting for our Savior, the Lord Jesus Christ, to come from heaven. [21]He will change our simple bodies and make them like his own glorious body. Christ can do this by his power. With that power he is able to rule all things.

4 My dear brothers, I love you and want to see you. You bring me joy and make me proud of you. Continue following the Lord as I have told you.

[2]I ask Euodia and Syntyche to agree in the Lord. [3]And because you serve faithfully with me, my friend, I ask you to help these women to do this. They served with me in telling people the Good News.[n] They served together with Clement and others who worked with me. Their names are written in the book of life.[n]

[4]Be full of joy in the Lord always. I will say again, be full of joy.

[5]Let all men see that you are gentle and kind. The Lord is coming soon. [6]Do not worry about anything. But pray and ask God for everything you need. And when you pray, always give thanks. [7]And God's peace will keep your hearts

and minds in Christ Jesus. The peace that God gives is so great that we cannot understand it.

[8]Brothers, continue to think about the things that are good and worthy of praise. Think about the things that are true and honorable and right and pure and beautiful and respected. [9]And do what you learned and received from me. Do what I told you and what you saw me do. And the God who gives peace will be with you.

[10]I am very happy in the Lord that you have shown your care for me again. You continued to care about me, but there was no way for you to show it. [11]I am telling you this, but it is not because I need anything. I have learned to be satisfied with the things I have and with everything that happens. [12]I know how to live when I am poor. And I know how to live when I have plenty. I have learned the secret of being happy at any time in everything that happens. I have learned to be happy when I have enough to eat and when I do not have enough to eat. I have learned to be happy when I have all that I need and when I do not have the things I need. [13]I can do all things through Christ because he gives me strength.

[14]But it was good that you helped me when I needed help. [15]You people in Philippi remember when I first preached the Good News[d] there. When I left Macedonia, you were the only church that gave me help. [16]Several times you sent me things I needed when I was in Thessalonica. [17]Really, it is not that I want to receive gifts from you. But I want you to have the good that comes from giving. [18]And now I have everything, and more. I have all I need because Epaphroditus brought your gift to me. Your gift is like a sweet-smelling sacrifice offered to God. God accepts that sacrifice, and it pleases him. [19]My God will use his wonderful riches in Christ Jesus to give you everything you need. [20]Glory to our God and Father forever and ever! Amen.

[21]Greet each of God's people in Christ. God's people who are with me send greetings to you. [22]All of God's people greet you. And those believers from the palace of Caesar[d] greet you, too.

[23]The grace of the Lord Jesus Christ be with you all.

4:3 book of life God's book that has the names of all God's chosen people (Revelation 3:5; 21:27).

The Letter of Paul the Apostle to the
COLOSSIANS

1 From Paul, an apostle[d] of Christ Jesus. I am an apostle because that is what God wanted.

Also from Timothy, our brother.

[2] To the holy and faithful brothers in Christ that live in Colosse. Grace and peace from God our Father.

[3] In our prayers for you we always thank God, the Father of our Lord Jesus Christ. [4] We thank God because we have heard about the faith you have in Christ Jesus and the love you have for all of God's people. [5] You have this faith and love because of your hope, and what you hope for is saved for you in heaven. You learned about this hope when you heard the true teaching, the Good News[d] [6] that was told to you. Everywhere in the world that Good News is bringing blessings and is growing. This has happened with you, too, since you heard the Good News and understood the truth about the grace of God. [7] You learned about God's grace from Epaphras, whom we love. Epaphras works together with us and is a faithful servant of Christ for us. [8] He also told us about the love you have from the Holy Spirit.[d]

[9] Since the day we heard this about you, we have continued praying for you. We ask God that you will know fully what God wants. We pray that you will also have great wisdom and understanding in spiritual things. [10] Then you will live the kind of life that honors and pleases the Lord in every way. You will produce fruit in every good work and grow in the knowledge of God. [11] Then God will strengthen you with his own great power. And you will not give up when troubles come, but you will be patient. [12] Then you will joyfully give thanks to the Father. He has made you able to have all that he has prepared for his people who live in the light. [13] God made us free from the power of darkness, and he brought us into the kingdom of his dear Son. [14] The Son paid for our sins, and in him we have forgiveness.

[15] No one has seen God, but Jesus is exactly like him. Christ ranks higher than all the things that have been made. [16] Through his power all things were made—things in heaven and on earth, things seen and unseen, all powers, authorities, lords, and rulers. All things were made through Christ and for Christ. [17] Christ was there before anything was made. And all things continue because of him. [18] He is the head of the body. (The body is the church.) Everything comes from him. And he is the first one who was raised from death. So in all things Jesus is most important. [19] God was pleased for all of himself to live in Christ. [20] And through Christ, God decided to bring all things back to himself again—things on earth and things in heaven. God made peace by using the blood of Christ's death on the cross.

[21] At one time you were separated from God. You were God's enemies in your minds because the evil deeds you did were against God. [22] But now Christ has made you God's friends again. He did this by his death while he was in the body, that he might bring you into God's presence. He brings you before God as people who are holy, with no wrong in you, and with nothing that God can judge you guilty of. [23] And Christ will do this if you continue to believe in the Good News[d] you heard. You must continue strong and sure in your faith. You must not be moved away from the hope that Good News gave you. That same Good News has been told to everyone in the world. I, Paul, help in preaching that Good News.

[24] I am happy in my sufferings for you. There are many things that Christ must still suffer through his body, the church. I am accepting my part of these things that must be suffered. I accept these sufferings in my body. I suffer for his body, the church. [25] I became a servant of the church because God gave me a special work to do that helps you. My work is to tell fully the teaching of God. [26] This teaching is the secret truth that was hidden since the beginning of time. It was hidden from everyone, but now it is made known to God's holy people. [27] God decided to let his people know this rich and glorious truth which he has for all people. This truth is Christ himself, who is in you. He is our only hope for glory. [28] So we continue to preach Christ to all men. We use all wisdom to warn and to teach everyone. We are trying to

bring each one into God's presence as a mature person in Christ. [29]To do this, I work and struggle, using Christ's great strength that works so powerfully in me.

2 I want you to know that I am trying very hard to help you. And I am trying to help those in Laodicea and others who have never seen me. [2]I want them to be strengthened and joined together with love. I want them to be rich in the strong belief that comes from understanding. I mean I want you to know fully God's secret truth. That truth is Christ himself. [3]And in him all the treasures of wisdom and knowledge are safely kept.

[4]I say this so that no one can fool you by arguments that seem good, but are false. [5]I am not there with you, but my heart is with you. I am happy to see your good lives and your strong faith in Christ.

[6]As you received Christ Jesus the Lord, so continue to live in him. [7]Keep your roots deep in him and have your lives built on him. Be strong in the faith, just as you were taught. And always be thankful.

[8]Be sure that no one leads you away with false ideas and words that mean nothing. Those ideas come from men. They are the worthless ideas of this world. They are not from Christ. [9]All of God lives in Christ fully (even when Christ was on earth). [10]And in him you have a full and true life. He is ruler over all rulers and powers.

[11]In Christ you had a different kind of circumcision.[d] That circumcision was not done by hands. I mean, you were made free from the power of your sinful self. That is the kind of circumcision Christ does. [12]When you were baptized, you were buried with Christ and you were raised up with Christ because of your faith in God's power. That power was shown when he raised Christ from death. [13]You were spiritually dead because of your sins and because you were not free from the power of your sinful self. But God made you alive with Christ. And God forgave all our sins. [14]We owed a debt because we broke God's laws. That debt listed all the rules we failed to follow. But God forgave us that debt. He took away that debt and nailed it to the cross. [15]God defeated the spiritual rulers and powers. With the cross God won the victory and defeated

them. He showed the world that they were powerless.

[16]So do not let anyone make rules for you about eating and drinking or about a religious feast, a New Moon[d] Festival, or a Sabbath[d] day. [17]In the past, these things were like a shadow of what was to come. But the new things that were coming are found in Christ. [18]Some enjoy acting as if they were humble and love to worship angels. They are always talking about the visions they have seen. Do not let them tell you that you are wrong. They are full of foolish pride because of their human way of thinking. [19]They do not keep themselves under the control of Christ, the head. The whole body depends on Christ. Because of him all the parts of the body care for each other and help each other. This strengthens the body and holds it together. And so the body grows in the way God wants.

[20]You died with Christ and were made free from the worthless rules of the world. So why do you act as if you still belong to this world? I mean, why do you follow rules like these: [21]"Don't eat this," "Don't taste that," "Don't touch that thing"? [22]These rules are talking about earthly things that are gone as soon as they are used. They are only man-made commands and teachings. [23]These rules seem to be wise. But they are only part of a man-made religion. They make people pretend not to be proud and make them punish their bodies. But they do not really control the evil desires of the sinful self.

3 You were raised from death with Christ. So aim at what is in heaven, where Christ is sitting at the right hand of God. [2]Think only about the things in heaven, not the things on earth. [3]Your old sinful self has died, and your new life is kept with Christ in God. [4]Christ is your life. When he comes again, you will share in his glory.

[5]So put all evil things out of your life: sexual sinning, doing evil, letting evil thoughts control you, wanting things that are evil, and always selfishly wanting more and more. This really means living to serve a false god. [6]These things make God angry.[n] [7]In your evil life in the past, you also did these things.

[8]But now put these things out of your life: anger, bad temper, doing or saying things to hurt others, and using evil

---

3:6 **These ... angry.** Some Greek copies add: "against the people who do not obey God."

words when you talk. [8]Do not lie to each other. You have left your old sinful life and the things you did before. [10]You have begun to live the new life. In your new life you are being made new. You are becoming like the One who made you. This new life brings you the true knowledge of God. [11]In the new life there is no difference between Greeks and Jews. There is no difference between those who are circumcised[d] and those who are not circumcised, or people that are foreigners, or Scythians.[n] There is no difference between slaves and free people. But Christ is in all believers. And Christ is all that is important.

[12]God has chosen you and made you his holy people. He loves you. So always do these things: Show mercy to others; be kind, humble, gentle, and patient. [13]Do not be angry with each other, but forgive each other. If someone does wrong to you, then forgive him. You forgive each other because the Lord forgave you. [14]Do all these things; but most important, love each other. Love is what holds you all together in perfect unity. [15]Let the peace that Christ gives control your thinking. You were all called together in one body[n] to have peace. Always be thankful. [16]Let the teaching of Christ live in you richly. Use all wisdom to teach and strengthen each other. Sing psalms, hymns, and spiritual songs with thankfulness in your hearts to God. [17]Everything you say and everything you do should all be done for Jesus your Lord. And in all you do, give thanks to God the Father through Jesus.

[18]Wives, be under the authority of your husbands. This is the right thing to do in the Lord.

[19]Husbands, love your wives, and be gentle to them.

[20]Children, obey your parents in all things. This pleases the Lord.

[21]Fathers, do not nag your children. If you are too hard to please, they may want to stop trying.

[22]Slaves, obey your masters in all things. Do not obey just when they are watching you, to gain their favor. But serve them honestly, because you respect the Lord. [23]In all the work you are doing, work the best you can. Work as if you were working for the Lord, not for men. [24]Remember that you will receive your reward from the Lord, which he

promised to his people. You are serving the Lord Christ. [25]But remember that anyone who does wrong will be punished for that wrong. And the Lord treats everyone the same.

4 Masters, give the things that are good and fair to your slaves. Remember that you have a Master in heaven.

[2]Continue praying and keep alert. And when you pray, always thank God. [3]Also pray for us. Pray that God will give us an opportunity to tell people his message. Pray that we can preach the secret truth that God has made known about Christ. I am in prison because I preach this truth. [4]Pray that I can speak in a way that will make it clear as I should.

[5]Be wise in the way you act with people who are not believers. Use your time in the best way you can. [6]When you talk, you should always be kind and wise. Then you will be able to answer everyone in the way you should.

[7]Tychicus is my dear brother in Christ. He is a faithful minister and servant with me in the Lord. He will tell you all the things that are happening to me. [8]That is why I am sending him. I want you to know how we are. I am sending him to encourage you. [9]I send him with Onesimus. Onesimus is a faithful and dear brother in Christ. He is one of your group. They will tell you all that has happened here.

[10]Aristarchus greets you. He is a prisoner with me. And Mark, the cousin of Barnabas, also greets you. (I have already told you what to do about Mark. If he comes, welcome him.) [11]Jesus, who is called Justus, also greets you. These are the only Jewish believers who work with me for the kingdom of God. They have been a comfort to me.

[12]Epaphras also greets you. He is a servant of Jesus Christ. And he is from your group. He always prays for you. He prays that you will grow to be spiritually mature and have everything that God wants for you. [13]I know that he has worked hard for you and the people in Laodicea and in Hierapolis. [14]Demas and our dear friend Luke, the doctor, greet you.

[15]Greet the brothers in Laodicea. And greet Nympha and the church that meets in her house. [16]After this letter is read to you, be sure that it is also read to the church in Laodicea. And you read

3:11 **Scythians** The Scythians were known as very wild and cruel people. 3:15 **body** The spiritual body of Christ, meaning the church or his people.

the letter that I wrote to Laodicea. ¹⁷Tell Archippus, "Be sure to do the work the Lord gave you."

¹⁸I, Paul, greet you and write this with my own hand. Remember me in prison. God's grace be with you.

The First Letter of Paul the Apostle to the
THESSALONIANS

1 From Paul, Silas, and Timothy.
To the church in Thessalonica, the church in God the Father and the Lord Jesus Christ. May God's grace and peace be yours.

²We always remember you when we pray and thank God for all of you. ³When we pray to God our Father, we always thank him for the things you have done because of your faith. And we thank him for the work you have done because of your love. And we thank him that you continue to be strong because of your hope in our Lord Jesus Christ.

⁴Brothers, God loves you. And we know that he has chosen you to be his. ⁵We brought the Good News[d] to you. But we did not use only words. We brought the Good News with power, with the Holy Spirit,[d] and with sure knowledge that it is true. Also you know how we lived when we were with you. We lived that way to help you. ⁶And you became like us and like the Lord. You suffered much, but still you accepted the teaching with the joy that comes from the Holy Spirit. ⁷So you became an example to all the believers in Macedonia and Southern Greece. ⁸The Lord's teaching spread from you in Macedonia and Southern Greece. And your faith in God has become known everywhere. So we do not need to say anything about your faith. ⁹People everywhere are telling about the good way you accepted us when we were there with you. They tell about how you stopped worshiping idols and changed to serving the living and true God. ¹⁰And you changed to wait for God's Son to come from heaven. God raised that Son from death. He is Jesus, who saves us from God's angry judgment that is sure to come.

2 Brothers, you know that our visit to you was not a failure. ²Before we came to you, we suffered in Philippi. People there insulted us. You know about that. And when we came to you, many people were against us. But our God helped us to be brave and to tell you his Good News.[d] ³Our message was a message to encourage you. We were not trying to lie. We had no evil plan. We were not trying to trick you. ⁴But we speak the Good News because God tested us and trusted us to do it. When we speak, we are not trying to please men. But we are trying to please God, who tests our hearts. ⁵You know that we never tried to influence you by saying nice things about you. We were not trying to get your money. We had no selfishness to hide from you. God knows that this is true. ⁶We were not looking for praise from you or anyone else. We are apostles[d] of Christ. When we were with you, we could have used our authority to make you do things.

⁷But we were very gentle with you. We were like a mother caring for her little children. ⁸Because we loved you, we were happy to share God's Good News with you. But not only that, we were also happy to share even our own lives with you. ⁹Brothers, I know that you remember how hard we worked. We worked night and day so that we would not burden any of you while we preached God's Good News to you.

¹⁰When we were with you, we lived in a holy and right way, without fault. You know that this is true, and God knows that this is true. ¹¹You know that we treated each of you as a father treats his own children. ¹²We strengthened you, we comforted you, and we told you to live good lives for God. It is God who calls you to his glorious kingdom.

¹³Also, we always thank God because of the way you accepted his message. You heard his message from us, and you accepted it as the word of God, not the words of men. And it really is God's message. And that message works in you who believe. ¹⁴Brothers, you have been like God's churches in Christ that

are in Judea.[n] God's people suffered bad things from the other Jews there. And you suffered the same bad things from the people of your own country. [15]Those Jews killed both the Lord Jesus and the prophets.[d] And they forced us to leave that country. They do not please God. They are against all people. [16]They try to stop us from teaching the non-Jews so that they may be saved. But those Jews are adding more and more sins to the sins they already have. The anger of God has come to them at last.

[17]Brothers, we were separated from you for a short time, but our thoughts were still with you. We wanted very much to see you, and tried very hard to do so. [18]I, Paul, tried to come many times, but Satan stopped us. [19]For you are our hope, our joy, and the crown we will be proud of when our Lord Jesus Christ comes. [20]Truly you are our glory and our joy.

3 We could not come to you, but it was very hard to wait any longer. So we decided to stay in Athens alone [2]and send Timothy to you. Timothy is our brother, who works with us for God. He helps us tell people the Good News[d] about Christ. We sent Timothy to strengthen and comfort you in your faith. [3]We sent him so that none of you would be upset by these troubles we have now. You yourselves know that we must have these troubles. [4]Even when we were with you, we told you that we all would have to suffer. And you know that it has happened the way we said. [5]This is why I sent Timothy to you, so that I could know about your faith. I sent him when I could not wait any longer. I was afraid that the devil had tempted you, and then our hard work would have been wasted.

[6]But Timothy now has come back to us from you and has brought us good news about your faith and love. He told us that you always remember us in a good way. He told us that you want to see us just as much as we want to see you. [7]So, brothers, we are comforted about you, because of your faith. We have much trouble and suffering, but still we are comforted. [8]For our life is really full if you stand strong in the Lord. [9]We have so much joy before our God because of you, and we thank him for you. But we cannot thank him

enough for all the joy we feel. [10]And we continue praying with all our heart for you night and day. We pray that we can see you again and give you all the things you need to make your faith strong.

[11]We pray that our God and Father and our Lord Jesus will prepare the way for us to come to you. [12]We pray that the Lord will make your love grow more and more for each other and for all people. We pray that you will love others as we love you and [13]that your hearts will be made strong. Then you will be holy and without fault before our God and Father when our Lord Jesus comes with all his holy people.

4 Brothers, now I have some other things to tell you. We taught you how to live in a way that will please God. And you are living that way. Now we ask you and encourage you in the Lord Jesus to live that way more and more. [2]You know what we told you to do by the authority of the Lord Jesus. [3]God wants you to be holy and to stay away from sexual sins. [4]He wants each one of you to learn how to take a wife[n] in a way that is holy and honorable. [5]Don't use your body for sexual sin. The people who do not know God use their bodies for that. [6]So do not wrong your brother or cheat him in this way. The Lord will punish people who do those things. We have already told you and warned you about that. [7]God called us to be holy and does not want us to live in sin. [8]So the person who refuses to obey this teaching is refusing to obey God, not man. And God is the One who gives us his Holy Spirit.[d]

[9]We do not need to write to you about having love for your brothers and sisters in Christ. God has already taught you to love each other. [10]And truly you do love the brothers in all of Macedonia. Brothers, now we encourage you to love them more and more.

[11]Do all you can to live a peaceful life. Take care of your own business. Do your own work. We have already told you to do these things. [12]If you do, then people who are not believers will respect you. And you will not have to depend on others for what you need.

[13]Brothers, we want you to know about those who have died. We do not want you to be sad as others who have no hope. [14]We believe that Jesus died

2:14 **Judea** The Jewish land where Jesus lived and taught and where the church first began.
4:4 **learn . . . wife** This might also mean "learn to control your own body."

and that he rose again. So, because of Jesus, God will bring together with Jesus those who have died. ¹⁵What we tell you now is the Lord's own message. We who are living now may still be living when the Lord comes again. We who are living at that time will be with the Lord, but not before those who have already died. ¹⁶The Lord himself will come down from heaven. There will be a loud command with the voice of the archangel[n] and with the trumpet call of God. And those who have died and were in Christ will rise first. ¹⁷After that, those who are still alive at that time will be gathered up with them. We will be taken up in the clouds to meet the Lord in the air. And we will be with the Lord forever. ¹⁸So comfort each other with these words.

5 Now, brothers, we do not need to write to you about times and dates. ²You know very well that the day the Lord comes again will be a surprise like a thief that comes in the night. ³People will say, "We have peace and we are safe." At that time they will be destroyed quickly, as pains come quickly to a woman having a baby. And those people will not escape. ⁴But you, brothers, are not living in darkness. And so that day will not surprise you like a thief. ⁵You are all people who belong to the light. You belong to the day. We do not belong to the night or to darkness. ⁶So we should not be like other people. We should not be sleeping, but we should be awake and have self-control. ⁷Those who sleep, sleep at night. Those who get drunk, get drunk at night. ⁸But we belong to the day; so we should control ourselves. We should wear faith and love to protect us. And the hope of salvation should be our helmet. ⁹God did not choose us to suffer his anger, but to have salvation through our Lord Jesus Christ. ¹⁰Jesus died for us so that we can live together with him. It is not important if we are alive or dead when Jesus comes. ¹¹So comfort each other and give each other strength, just as you are doing now.

¹²Now, brothers, we ask you to respect those people who work hard with you, who lead you in the Lord and teach you. ¹³Respect them with a very special love because of the work they do with you.

Live in peace with each other. ¹⁴We ask you, brothers, to warn those who do not work. Encourage the people who are afraid. Help those who are weak. Be patient with every person. ¹⁵Be sure that no one pays back wrong for wrong. But always try to do what is good for each other and for all people.

¹⁶Always be happy. ¹⁷Never stop praying. ¹⁸Give thanks whatever happens. That is what God wants for you in Christ Jesus.

¹⁹Do not stop the work of the Holy Spirit.[d] ²⁰Do not treat prophecy[d] as if it were not important. ²¹But test everything. Keep what is good. ²²And stay away from everything that is evil.

²³We pray that God himself, the God of peace, will make you pure, belonging only to him. We pray that your whole self—spirit, soul, and body—will be kept safe and be without wrong when our Lord Jesus Christ comes. ²⁴The One who calls you will do that for you. You can trust him.

²⁵Brothers, please pray for us. ²⁶Give all the brothers a holy kiss when you meet. ²⁷I tell you by the authority of the Lord to read this letter to all the brothers. ²⁸The grace of our Lord Jesus Christ be with you.

The Second Letter of Paul the Apostle to the
THESSALONIANS

1 From Paul, Silas, and Timothy.
To the church in Thessalonica in God our Father and the Lord Jesus Christ.

²Grace and peace to you from God the Father and the Lord Jesus Christ.

³We must always thank God for you. And we should do this because it is right. It is right because your faith is growing more and more. And the love that every one of you has for each other is also growing. ⁴So we brag about you to the other churches of God. We tell them about the way you continue to be strong and have faith. You are being

4:16 **archangel** The leader among God's angels or messengers.

treated badly and are suffering many troubles, but you continue with strength and faith.

[5]This is proof that God is right in his judgment. God wants you to be worthy of his kingdom. Your suffering is for that kingdom. [6]And God will do what is right. He will give trouble to those who trouble you. [7]And he will give peace to you people who are troubled and to us also. God will give us this help when the Lord Jesus is shown to us from heaven with his powerful angels. [8]He will come from heaven with burning fire to punish those who do not know God. He will punish those who do not obey the Good News[d] of our Lord Jesus Christ. [9]Those people will be punished with a destruction that continues forever. They will not be allowed to be with the Lord, and they will be kept away from his great power. [10]This will happen on the day when the Lord Jesus comes to receive glory with his holy people. And all the people who have believed will be amazed at Jesus. You will be in that group of believers because you believed what we told you.

[11]That is why we always pray for you. We ask our God to help you live the good way that he called you to live. The goodness you have makes you want to do good, and the faith you have makes you work. We pray that with his power God will help you do these things more and more. [12]We pray all this so that the name of our Lord Jesus Christ can have glory in you. And you can have glory in him. That glory comes from the grace of our God and the Lord Jesus Christ.

2 Brothers, we have something to say about the coming of our Lord Jesus Christ. We want to talk to you about that time when we will meet together with him. [2]Do not become easily upset in your thinking or afraid if you hear that the day of the Lord has already come. Someone may say this in a prophecy[d] or in a message. Or you may read it in a letter that someone tells you came from us. [3]Do not let any person fool you in any way. That day of the Lord will not come until the turning away from God happens. And that day will not come until the Man of Evil appears. He belongs to hell. [4]He is against anything called God or anything that people worship. And the Man of Evil puts himself above anything called God or anything that

people worship. And that Man of Evil even goes into God's Temple[d] and sits there. Then he says that he is God.

[5]I told you when I was with you that all this would happen. Do you not remember? [6]And you know what is stopping that Man of Evil now. He is being stopped now so that he will appear at the right time. [7]The secret power of evil is already working in the world now. But there is one who is stopping that power. And he will continue to stop it until he is taken out of the way. [8]Then that Man of Evil will appear. And the Lord Jesus will kill him with the breath that comes from his mouth and will destroy him with the glory of his coming. [9]The Man of Evil will come by the power of Satan. He will have great power, and he will do many different false miracles,[d] signs, and wonders. [10]He will use every kind of evil to trick those who are lost. They are lost because they refused to love the truth. (If they loved the truth, they would be saved.) [11]But they refused to love the truth; so God sends them something powerful that leads them away from the truth. He sends them that power so they will believe something that is not true. [12]So all those who do not believe the truth will be judged guilty. They did not believe the truth, and they enjoyed doing evil.

[13]Brothers, the Lord loves you. God chose you from the beginning to be saved. So we must always thank God for you. You are saved by the Spirit[d] that makes you holy and by your faith in the truth. [14]God used the Good News[d] that we preached to call you to be saved. He called you so that you can share in the glory of our Lord Jesus Christ. [15]So, brothers, stand strong and continue to believe the teachings we gave you. We taught you those things in our speaking and in our letter to you.

[16-17]We pray that the Lord Jesus Christ himself and God our Father will comfort you and strengthen you in every good thing you do and say. God loved us. Through his grace he gave us a good hope and comfort that continues forever.

3 And now, brothers, pray for us. Pray that the Lord's teaching will continue to spread quickly. And pray that people will give honor to that teaching, just as happened with you. [2]And pray that we will be protected from bad and evil people. (Not all people believe in the Lord.)

[3]But the Lord is faithful. He will give you strength and protect you from the Evil One. [4]The Lord makes us feel sure that you are doing the things we told you. And we know that you will continue to do those things. [5]We pray that the Lord will lead your hearts into God's love and Christ's patience.

[6]Brothers, by the authority of our Lord Jesus Christ we command you to stay away from any believer who refuses to work. People who refuse to work are not following the teaching that we gave them. [7]You yourselves know that you should live as we live. We were not lazy when we were with you. [8]And when we ate another person's food, we always paid for it. We worked and worked so that we would not be a trouble to any of you. We worked night and day. [9]We had the right to ask you to help us. But we worked to take care of ourselves so that we would be an example for you to follow. [10]When we were with you, we gave you this rule: "If anyone will not work, he will not eat."

[11]We hear that some people in your group refuse to work. They do nothing. And they busy themselves in other people's lives. [12]We command those people to work quietly and earn their own food. In the Lord Jesus Christ we beg them to do this. [13]Brothers, never become tired of doing good.

[14]If anyone does not obey what we tell you in this letter, then remember who he is. Do not associate with him. Then maybe he will feel ashamed. [15]But do not treat him as an enemy. Warn him as a brother.

[16]We pray that the Lord of peace will give you peace at all times and in every way. May the Lord be with all of you.

[17]I am Paul, and I end this letter now in my own handwriting. All my letters have this to show they are from me. This is the way I write.

[18]May our Lord Jesus Christ show all of you his grace.

The First Letter of Paul the Apostle to
TIMOTHY

1 From Paul, an apostle[d] of Christ Jesus, by the command of God our Savior and Christ Jesus our hope.

[2]To Timothy, a true son to me because you believe.

Grace, mercy, and peace from God the Father and Christ Jesus our Lord.

[3]I want you to stay in Ephesus. I asked you to do that when I went into Macedonia. Some people there in Ephesus are teaching false things. Stay there so that you can command them to stop. [4]Tell them not to spend their time on stories that are not true and on long lists of names in family histories. These things only bring arguments; they do not help God's work. God's work is done by faith. [5]The purpose of this command is for people to have love. To have this love they must have a pure heart, they must do what they know is right, and they must have true faith. [6]Some people have wandered away from these things. They talk about things that are worth nothing. [7]They want to be teachers of the law, but they do not know what they are talking about. They do not even understand what they say they are sure about.

[8]We know that the law is good if a man uses it right. [9]We also know that the law is not made for good men. The law is made for people who are against the law and for those who refuse to follow the law. It is for people who are against God and are sinful, who are not holy and have no religion, who kill their fathers and mothers, who murder, [10]who take part in sexual sins, men who have sexual relations with other men, those who sell slaves, who tell lies, who speak falsely, and who do anything against the true teaching of God. [11]That teaching is part of the Good News[e] that God gave me to tell. That glorious Good News is from the blessed God.

[12]I thank Christ Jesus our Lord because he trusted me and gave me this work of serving him. And he gives me strength. [13]In the past I spoke against Christ and persecuted him and did all kinds of things to hurt him. But God showed mercy to me because I did not know what I was doing. I did those things when I did not believe. [14]But the grace of our Lord was fully given to me.

And with that grace came the faith and love that are in Christ Jesus.

[15]What I say is true, and you should fully accept it: Christ Jesus came into the world to save sinners. And I am the worst of those sinners. [16]But I was given mercy. I was given mercy so that in me Christ Jesus could show that he has patience without limit. And he showed his patience with me, the worst of all sinners. Christ wanted me to be an example for those who would believe in him and have life forever. [17]Honor and glory to the King that rules forever! He cannot be destroyed and cannot be seen. Honor and glory forever and ever to the only God. Amen.

[18]Timothy, you are like a son to me. I am giving you a command that agrees with the prophecies[d] that were given about you in the past. I tell you this so that you can follow those prophecies and fight the good fight of faith. [19]Continue to have faith and do what you know is right. Some people have not done this. Their faith has been destroyed. [20]Hymenaeus and Alexander are men who have done that. I have given them to Satan so that they will learn not to speak against God.

2 First, I tell you to pray for all people. Ask God for the things people need, and be thankful to him. [2]You should pray for kings and for all who have authority. Pray for the leaders so that we can have quiet and peaceful lives—lives full of worship and respect for God. [3]This is good, and it pleases God our Savior. [4]God wants all people to be saved. And he wants everyone to know the truth. [5]There is only one God. And there is only one way that people can reach God. That way is through Jesus Christ, who is also a man. [6]Jesus gave himself to pay for the sins of all people. Jesus is proof that God wants all people to be saved. And that proof came at the right time. [7]That is why I was chosen to tell the Good News[d] and was chosen to be an apostle.[d] (I am telling the truth. I am not lying.) I was chosen to teach the non-Jewish people to believe and to know the truth.

[8]I want men everywhere to pray. These men who lift up their hands in prayer must be holy. They must not be men who become angry and have arguments.

[9]I also want women to wear clothes that are right for them. They should dress with respect and right thinking. They should not use fancy braided hair or gold or pearls or expensive clothes to make themselves beautiful. [10]But they should make themselves beautiful by doing good deeds. Women who say they worship God should make themselves beautiful in that way.

[11]A woman should learn by listening quietly and being fully ready to obey. [12]I do not allow a woman to teach a man or to have authority over a man. She must remain silent. [13]For Adam was made first; Eve was made later. [14]Also, Adam was not the one who was tricked by the devil. It was the woman who was tricked and became a sinner. [15]But women will be saved through having children. They will be saved if they continue in faith, love, holiness, and self-control.

3 What I say is true: If anyone wants to become an elder,[d] he is wanting a good work. [2]An elder must be so good that people cannot rightly criticize him. He must have only one wife. He must have self-control and be wise. He must be respected by other people and must be ready to help people by accepting them into his home. He must be a good teacher. [3]He must not drink too much wine, and he must not be a man who likes to fight. He must be gentle and peaceful. He must not love money. [4]He must be a good leader of his own family so that his children obey him with full respect. [5](If a man does not know how to be a leader over his own family, he will not be able to take care of God's church.) [6]But an elder must not be a new believer. A new believer might be too proud of himself. Then he would be judged guilty for his pride just as the devil was. [7]An elder must also have the respect of people who are not in the church. Then he will not be criticized by others and caught in the devil's trap.

[8]In the same way, deacons[d] must be men that people can respect. They must not say things they do not mean. They must not use their time drinking too much wine, and they must not be men who are always trying to get rich by cheating others. [9]They must follow the faith that God made known to us and always do what they know is right. [10]You should test those men first. If you find nothing wrong in them, then they can serve as deacons. [11]In the same way, the

women[n] must have the respect of other people. They must not be women who repeat evil gossip about other people. They must have self-control and be women who can be trusted in everything. [12]Deacons must have only one wife. They must be good leaders of their children and their own families. [13]Those who serve well as deacons are making an honorable place for themselves. And they will feel very sure of their faith in Christ Jesus.

[14]I hope I can come to you soon. But I am writing these things to you now. [15]Then, even if I cannot come soon, you will know about the things that people must do in the family of God. That family is the church of the living God, the support and foundation of the truth. [16]Without doubt, the secret of our life of worship is great:

> He was shown to us in a human body,
>
> proved right by the Spirit,[d]
> and seen by angels.
>
> He was preached to the nations,
> believed in by the world,
> and taken to heaven in glory.

4 The Holy Spirit[d] clearly says that in the later times some people will stop believing the true faith. They will obey spirits that lie and will follow the teachings of demons.[d] [2]Such teachings come from hypocrites,[d] men who cannot see what is right and what is wrong. It is as if their understanding were destroyed by a hot iron. [3]They tell people that it is wrong to marry. And they tell people that there are some foods that must not be eaten. But God made those foods, and the people who believe and who know the truth can eat those foods with thanks. [4]Everything that God made is good. Nothing that God made should be refused if it is accepted with thanks to God. [5]Everything God made is made holy by what God has said and by prayer.

[6]Tell these things to the brothers. This will show that you are a good servant of Christ Jesus. You will show that you are made strong by the words of faith and good teaching that you have been following. [7]People tell silly stories that do not agree with God's truth. Do not follow what those stories teach. But teach yourself only to serve God. [8]Training

your body helps you in some ways, but serving God helps you in every way. Serving God brings you blessings in this life and in the future life, too. [9]What I say is true, and you should fully accept it. [10]For this is why we work and struggle: We hope in the living God. He is the Savior of all people. And in a very special way, he is the Savior of all who believe in him.

[11]Command and teach these things. [12]You are young, but do not let anyone treat you as if you were not important. Be an example to show the believers how they should live. Show them with your words, with the way you live, with your love, with your faith, and with your pure life. [13]Continue to read the Scriptures[d] to the people, strengthen them, and teach them. Do these things until I come. [14]Remember to use the gift that you have. That gift was given to you through a prophecy[d] when the group of elders[d] laid their hands on[n] you. [15]Continue to do those things. Give your life to doing them. Then everyone can see that your work is progressing. [16]Be careful in your life and in your teaching. Continue to live and teach rightly. Then you will save yourself and those people who listen to you.

5 Do not speak angrily to an older man, but talk to him as if he were your father. Treat younger men like brothers. [2]Treat older women like mothers, and younger women like sisters. Always treat them in a pure way.

[3]Take care of widows who are all alone. [4]But if a widow has children or grandchildren, the first thing they need to learn is to do their duty to their own family. When they do this, they will be repaying their parents or grandparents. That pleases God. [5]If a widow is all alone and without help, then she puts her hope in God and prays night and day for God's help. [6]But the widow who uses her life to please herself is really dead while she is still living. [7]Tell the believers there to do these things so that no one can say they are doing wrong. [8]A believer should take care of his own relatives, especially his own family. If he does not do that, he has turned against the faith. He is worse than a person who does not believe in God.

[9]To be on your list of widows, a

3:11 women This might mean the wives of the deacons, or it might mean women who serve in the same way as deacons. **4:14 laid their hands on** A sign to show that Timothy was being given a special work of God.

woman must be 60 years old or older. She must have been faithful to her husband. [10]She must be known as a woman who has done good works. By this, I mean good works such as raising her children, accepting visitors in her home, washing the feet of God's people, helping those in trouble, and using her life to do all kinds of good deeds.

[11]But do not put younger widows on that list. After they give themselves to Christ, they are often pulled away from him by their physical needs. And then they want to marry again. [12]And they will be judged for not doing what they first promised to do. [13]Also, those younger widows begin to waste their time going from house to house. They begin to gossip and busy themselves with other people's lives. They say things that they should not say. [14]So I want the younger widows to marry, have children, and take care of their homes. If they do this, then no enemy will have any reason to criticize them. [15]But some of the younger widows have already turned away to follow Satan.

[16]If any woman who is a believer has widows in her family, then she should care for them herself. The church should not have to care for them. Then the church will be able to care for the widows who have no living family.

[17]The elders[d] who lead the church well should receive great honor. Those who work hard by speaking and teaching especially should receive great honor. [18]For the Scripture[d] says, "When an ox is working in the grain, do not cover its mouth to keep it from eating."[n] And the Scripture also says, "A worker should be given his pay."[n]

[19]Do not listen to someone who accuses an elder, unless there are two or three other persons who say he did wrong. [20]Tell those who keep on sinning that they are wrong. Do this in front of the whole church so that the others will have a warning.

[21]Before God and Jesus Christ and the chosen angels, I command you to do these things. Be careful to do them without showing favor to anyone.

[22]Think carefully before you lay your hands on[n] anyone for the Lord's service. Do not share in the sins of others. Keep yourself pure.

[23]Timothy, you stop drinking only water and drink a little wine. This will help your stomach, and you will not be sick so often.

[24]The sins of some people are easy to see even before they are judged. But the sins of others are seen only later. [25]So also good deeds are easy to see. But even when they are not easy to see, they cannot stay hidden.

6 All who are slaves should show full respect to their masters. Then no one will speak against God's name and our teaching. [2]Some slaves have masters who are believers. This means they are all brothers. But the slaves should not show their masters any less respect. They should serve their masters even better, because they are helping believers they love.

You must teach and preach these things. [3]If anyone has a different teaching, he does not accept the true teaching of our Lord Jesus Christ. And that teaching shows him the true way to serve God. [4]The person who teaches falsely is full of pride and understands nothing. He is sick with a love for arguing and fighting about words. And that brings jealousy, making trouble, insults, and evil mistrust. [5]And that also brings arguments from men who have evil minds. They have lost the truth. They think that serving God is a way to get rich.

[6]It is true that serving God makes a person very rich, if he is satisfied with what he has. [7]When we came into the world, we brought nothing. And when we die, we can take nothing out. [8]So, if we have food and clothes, we will be satisfied with that. [9]Those who want to become rich bring temptation to themselves. They are caught in a trap. They begin to want many foolish things that will hurt them, things that ruin and destroy people. [10]The love of money causes all kinds of evil. Some people have left the true faith because they want to get more and more money. But they have caused themselves much sorrow.

[11]But you are a man of God. So you should stay away from all those things. Try to live in the right way, serve God, have faith, love, patience, and gentleness. [12]Keeping your faith is like running a race. Try as hard as you can to win. Be sure you receive the life that continues forever. You were called to have that life. And you confessed the

5:18 **"When . . . eating."** Quotation from Deuteronomy 25:4.   5:18 **"A worker . . . pay."** Quotation from Luke 10:7.   5:22 **lay your hands on** A sign of giving authority or power to another person.

great truth about Christ in a way that many people heard. [13]Before God and Christ Jesus I give you a command. Christ Jesus confessed that same great truth when he stood before Pontius Pilate. And God gives life to everything. Now I tell you: [14]Do the things you were commanded to do. Do them without wrong or blame until the time when our Lord Jesus Christ comes again. [15]God will make that happen at the right time. He is the blessed and only Ruler. He is the King of all kings and the Lord of all lords. [16]God is the only One who never dies. He lives in light so bright that men cannot go near it. No one has ever seen God, or can see him. May honor and power belong to God forever. Amen.

[17]Give this command to those who are rich with things of this world. Tell them not to be proud. Tell them to hope in God, not their money. Money cannot be trusted, but God takes care of us richly. He gives us everything to enjoy. [18]Tell the rich people to do good and to be rich in doing good deeds. Tell them to be happy to give and ready to share. [19]By doing that, they will be saving a treasure for themselves in heaven. That treasure will be a strong foundation. Their future life can be built on that treasure. Then they will be able to have the life that is true life.

[20]Timothy, God has trusted you with many things. Keep those things safe. Stay away from people who say foolish things that are not from God. Stay away from those who argue against the truth. They use something they call "knowledge," but it is really not knowledge. [21]They say that they have that "knowledge," but they have left the true faith.

God's grace be with you.

The Second Letter of Paul the Apostle to
TIMOTHY

1 From Paul, an apostle[d] of Christ Jesus by the will of God. God sent me to tell about the promise of life that is in Christ Jesus.

[2]To Timothy, a dear son to me. Grace, mercy, and peace to you from God the Father and Christ Jesus our Lord.

[3]I always remember you in my prayers, day and night. And I thank God for you in these prayers. He is the God my ancestors served. And I serve him, doing what I know is right. [4]I remember that you cried for me. And I want very much to see you so that I can be filled with joy. [5]I remember your true faith. That kind of faith first belonged to your grandmother Lois and to your mother Eunice. And I know that you now have that same faith. [6]That is why I remind you to use the gift God gave you. God gave you that gift when I laid my hands on[n] you. Now let it grow, as a small flame grows into a fire. [7]God did not give us a spirit that makes us afraid. He gave us a spirit of power and love and self-control.

[8]So do not be ashamed to tell people about our Lord Jesus. And do not be ashamed of me. I am in prison for the Lord. But suffer with me for the Good News.[d] God gives us the strength to do that. [9]God saved us and made us his holy people. That was not because of anything we did ourselves but because of what he wanted and because of his grace. That grace was given to us through Christ Jesus before time began. [10]It was not shown to us until our Savior Christ Jesus came. Jesus destroyed death. And through the Good News, he showed us the way to have life that cannot be destroyed. [11]I was chosen to tell that Good News and to be an apostle[d] and a teacher. [12]And I suffer now because I tell the Good News. But I am not ashamed. I know Jesus, the One I have believed in. And I am sure that he is able to protect what he has trusted me with until that Day.[n] [13]Follow the true teachings you heard from me. Follow them as an example of the faith and love we have in Christ Jesus. [14]Protect the truth that you were given. Protect it with the help of the Holy Spirit[n] who lives in us.

[15]You know that everyone in the country of Asia has left me, even Phygelus and Hermogenes. [16]I pray that the Lord will show mercy to the family of Onesiphorus. He has often helped me and

---

1:6 laid . . . on A sign to show that Paul had power from God to give Timothy a special blessing.
1:12 Day The day Christ will come to judge all people and take his people to live with him.

was not ashamed that I was in prison. [17]When he came to Rome, he looked for me until he found me. [18]I pray that the Lord will allow Onesiphorus to have mercy from the Lord on that Day. You know how many ways Onesiphorus helped me in Ephesus.

2 Timothy, you are like a son to me. Be strong in the grace that we have in Christ Jesus. [2]You and many others have heard what I have taught. You should teach the same thing to some people you can trust. Then they will be able to teach it to others. [3]Share in the troubles that we have. Accept them like a true soldier of Christ Jesus. [4]A soldier wants to please his commanding officer, so he does not waste his time doing the things that most people do. [5]If an athlete is running in a race, he must obey all the rules in order to win. [6]The farmer who works hard should be the first person to get some of the food that he grew. [7]Think about these things that I am saying. The Lord will give you the ability to understand all these things.

[8]Remember Jesus Christ. He is from the family of David. After Jesus died, he was raised from death. This is the Good News[d] that I preach, [9]and I am suffering because of that Good News. I am even bound with chains like a criminal. But God's teaching is not in chains. [10]So I patiently accept all these troubles. I do this so that those whom God has chosen can have the salvation that is in Christ Jesus. With that salvation comes glory that never ends.

[11]This teaching is true:
If we died with him,
  then we will also live with him.
[12]If we accept suffering,
  then we will also rule with him.
If we refuse to accept him,
  then he will refuse to accept us.
[13]If we are not faithful,
  he will still be faithful,
  because he cannot be false to
    himself.

[14]Continue teaching these things. And warn people before God not to argue about words. Arguing about words does not help anyone, and it ruins those who listen. [15]Do the best you can to be the kind of person that God will accept, and give yourself to him. Be a worker who is not ashamed of his work—a worker who uses the true teaching in the right way. [16]Stay away from those who talk about useless worldly things. That kind of talk will lead a person more and more away from God. [17]Their evil teaching will spread like a sickness inside the body. Hymenaeus and Philetus are men like that. [18]They have left the true teaching. They say that the rising from death of all men has already taken place. And those two men are destroying the faith of some people. [19]But God's strong foundation continues to stand. These words are written on that foundation: "The Lord knows those who belong to him."[n] And also these words are written on that foundation, "Everyone who says that he believes in the Lord must stop doing wrong."

[20]In a large house there are things made of gold and silver. But also there are things made of wood and clay. Some things are used for special purposes, and others are made for ordinary jobs. [21]If anyone makes himself clean[d] from evil things, he will be used for special purposes. He will be made holy, and the Master can use him. He will be ready to do any good work.

[22]Stay away from the evil things young people love to do. Try hard to live right and to have faith, love, and peace. Work for these things together with those who have pure hearts and who trust in the Lord. [23]Stay away from foolish and stupid arguments. You know that such arguments grow into bigger arguments. [24]And a servant of the Lord must not quarrel! He must be kind to everyone. He must be a good teacher. He must be patient. [25]The Lord's servant must gently teach those who do not agree with him. Maybe God will let them change their hearts so that they can accept the truth. [26]The devil has trapped them and causes them to do what he wants. But maybe they can wake up and free themselves from the devil's trap.

3 Remember this! There will be many troubles in the last days. [2]In those times people will love only themselves and money. They will brag and be proud. They will say evil things against others. They will not obey their parents. People will not be thankful or be the kind of people God wants. [3]They will not have love for others. They will refuse to forgive others and will speak bad things. They will not control themselves. They will be cruel and will hate what is good. [4]In the last days, people will turn against their friends. They will do foolish things without thinking. They will be conceited and proud. They will love pleasure. They will not love God. [5]They will continue to act as if they serve God, but they will not really serve God. Stay away from those people. [6]Some of them go into homes and get control of weak women who are full of sin. They are led to sin by the many evil desires they have. [7]Those women always try to learn new teachings, but they are never able to understand the truth fully. [8]Just as Jannes and Jambres were against Moses, these people are against the truth. They are people whose thinking has been confused. They have failed in trying to follow the faith. [9]But they will not be successful in what they do. Everyone will see that they are foolish. That is what happened to Jannes and Jambres.

[10]But you know all about me. You know what I teach and the way I live. You know my goal in life. You know my faith, my patience, and my love. You know that I never stop trying. [11]You know how I have been hurt and have suffered. You know all that happened to me in Antioch, Iconium, and Lystra. You know the hurts I suffered in those places. But the Lord saved me from all those troubles. [12]Everyone who wants to live the way God wants, in Christ Jesus, will be hurt. [13]People who are evil and cheat other people will go from bad to worse. They will fool others, but they will also be fooling themselves.

[14]But you should continue following the teachings that you learned. You know that these teachings are true. And you know you can trust those who taught you. [15]You have known the Holy Scriptures[d] since you were a child. The Scriptures are able to make you wise. And that wisdom leads to salvation through faith in Christ Jesus. [16]All Scripture is given by God and is useful for teaching and for showing people what is wrong in their lives. It is useful for correcting faults and teaching how to live right. [17]Using the Scriptures, the person who serves God will be ready and will have everything he needs to do every good work.

4 Before God and Jesus Christ I give you a command. Christ Jesus is the One who will judge all who are living and all who have died. Jesus has a kingdom, and he is coming again. So I give you this command: [2]Preach the Good News.[d] Be ready at all times. Tell people what they need to do, tell them when they are wrong, and encourage them. Do these things with great patience and careful teaching. [3]The time will come when people will not listen to the true teaching. They will find more and more teachers who are pleasing to them, teachers who say the things they want to hear. [4]They will stop listening to the truth. They will begin to follow the teaching in false stories. [5]But you should control yourself at all times. When troubles come, accept them. Do the work of telling the Good News. Do all the duties of a servant of God.

[6]My life is being given as an offering to God. The time has come for me to leave this life. [7]I have fought the good fight. I have finished the race. I have kept the faith. [8]Now, a crown is waiting for me. I will get that crown for being right with God. The Lord is the judge who judges rightly, and he will give me the crown on that Day.[n] He will give that crown not only to me but to all those who have waited with love for him to come again.

[9]Do your best to come to me as soon as you can. [10]Demas loved this world too much. He left me and went to Thessalonica. Crescens went to Galatia. And Titus went to Dalmatia. [11]Luke is the only one still with me. Get Mark and bring him with you when you come. He can help me in my work here. [12]I sent Tychicus to Ephesus.

[13]When I was in Troas, I left my coat there with Carpus. So when you come, bring it to me. Also, bring my books, particularly the ones written on parchment.[n]

[14]Alexander the metalworker did many harmful things against me. The Lord will punish him for the things he did. [15]You should be careful that he does not hurt you too. He fought strongly against our teaching.

[16]The first time I defended myself, no one helped me. Everyone left me. I pray that God will forgive them. [17]But the Lord stayed with me. He gave me strength so that I could fully tell the Good News[d] to the non-Jews. The Lord

4:8 Day The day Christ will come to judge all people and take his people to live with him.
4:13 parchment Something like paper made from the skins of sheep and used for writing on.

wanted all the non-Jews to hear it. So I was saved from the lion's mouth. [18]The Lord will save me when anyone tries to hurt me. The Lord will bring me safely to his heavenly kingdom. Glory forever and ever be the Lord's. Amen.

[19]Greet Priscilla and Aquila and the family of Onesiphorus. [20]Erastus stayed in Corinth. And I left Trophimus sick in Miletus. [21]Try as hard as you can to come to me before winter.

Eubulus sends greetings to you. Also Pudens, Linus, Claudia, and all the brothers in Christ greet you.

[22]The Lord be with your spirit. Grace be with you.

The Letter of Paul the Apostle to
TITUS

1 From Paul, a servant of God and an apostle[d] of Jesus Christ. I was sent to help the faith of God's chosen people. I was sent to help them to know the truth. And that truth shows people how to serve God. [2]That faith and that knowledge come from our hope for life forever. God promised that life to us before time began, and God does not lie. [3]At the right time God let the world know about that life through preaching. He trusted me with that work, and I preached because God our Savior commanded me to.

[4]To Titus. You are like a true son to me in the faith we share.

Grace and peace to you from God the Father and Christ Jesus our Savior.

[5]I left you in Crete so that you could finish doing the things that still needed to be done. I left you there also so that you could choose men to be elders[d] in every town. [6]To be an elder, a man must not be guilty of doing wrong. He must have only one wife. His children must be believers. They must not be known as children who are wild and who do not obey. [7]An elder has the job of taking care of God's work. So he must not be guilty of doing wrong. He must not be a man who is proud and selfish or who becomes angry quickly. He must not drink too much wine. He must not be a person who likes to fight. And he must not be a person who always tries to get rich by cheating people. [8]An elder must be ready to help others by accepting them into his home. He must love what is good. He must be wise. He must live right. He must be holy. And he must be able to control himself. [9]An elder must faithfully follow the truth just as we teach it. He must be able to help people by using true and right teaching. And he must be able to show those who are

against the true teaching that they are wrong.

[10]There are many people who refuse to obey—people who talk about worthless things and lead others into the wrong way. I am talking mostly about those who say that all non-Jews must be circumcised.[d] [11]These people must be stopped from talking. They are destroying whole families by teaching things that they should not teach. They teach them only to cheat people and make money. [12]Even one of their own prophets from Crete said, "Cretan people are always liars. They are evil animals and lazy people who do nothing but eat." [13]The words that prophet said are true. So tell those people that they are wrong. You must be strict with them. Then they will become strong in the faith [14]and stop accepting Jewish stories. And they will stop following the commands of others who do not accept the truth. [15]To those who are pure, all things are pure. But to those who are full of sin and do not believe, nothing is pure. The thinking of those people has become evil and their knowledge of what is right has been ruined. [16]They say they know God, but the evil things they do show that they do not accept God. They are terrible people, they refuse to obey, and they are useless for doing anything good.

2 You must tell everyone what they must do to follow the true teaching. [2]Teach older men to have self-control, to be serious, and to be wise. They should be strong in faith, strong in love, and strong in patience.

[3]Also, teach older women to be holy in the way they live. Teach them not to speak against others or have the habit of drinking too much wine. They should teach what is good. [4]In that way they can teach younger women to love their

husbands and children. [5]They can teach younger women to be wise and pure, to take care of their homes, to be kind, and to obey their husbands. Then no one will be able to criticize the teaching God gave us.

[6]In the same way, tell young men to be wise. [7]You should do good deeds to be an example in every way for young men. When you teach, be honest and serious. [8]And when you speak, speak the truth so that you cannot be criticized. Then anyone who is against you will be ashamed because there is nothing bad that he can say against us.

[9]And tell slaves to obey their masters at all times. They should try to please them and not argue with them. [10]They should not steal from them. And they should show their masters that they can be trusted. Slaves should do these things so that in everything they do, they will show that the teaching of God our Savior is good.

[11]That is the way we should live, because God's grace has come. That grace can save every person. [12]It teaches us not to live against God and not to do the evil things the world wants to do. That grace teaches us to live on earth now in a wise and right way—a way that shows that we serve God. [13]We should live like that while we are waiting for the coming of our great God and Savior Jesus Christ. He is our great hope, and he will come with glory. [14]He gave himself for us; he died to free us from all evil. He died to make us pure people who belong only to him—people who are always wanting to do good things.

[15]Tell everyone these things. You have full authority. So use that authority to strengthen the people and tell them what they should do. And do not let anyone treat you as if you were not important.

3 Remind the believers to do these things: to be under the authority of rulers and government leaders, to obey them and be ready to do good, [2]to speak no evil about anyone, to live in peace with all, to be gentle and polite to all people.

[3]In the past we were foolish people, too. We did not obey, we were wrong, and we were slaves to many things our bodies wanted and enjoyed. We lived doing evil and being jealous. People hated us and we hated each other. [4]But then the kindness and love of God our Savior was shown. [5]He saved us because of his mercy, not because of good deeds we did to be right with God. He saved us through the washing that made us new people. He saved us by making us new through the Holy Spirit. [6]God poured out to us that Holy Spirit fully through Jesus Christ our Savior. [7]We were made right with God by His grace. And God gave us the Spirit so that we could receive the life that never ends. That is what we hope for.

[8]This teaching is true. And I want you to be sure that the people understand these things. Then those who believe in God will be careful to use their lives for doing good. These things are good and will help all people.

[9]Stay away from those who have foolish arguments, who talk about useless family histories, who make trouble and fight about what the law of Moses teaches. Those things are worth nothing and will not help anyone. [10]If someone causes arguments, then give him a warning. If he continues to cause arguments, warn him again. If he still continues causing arguments, then do not be around him. [11]You know that such a person is evil and sinful. His sins prove that he is wrong.

[12]I will send Artemas and Tychicus to you. When I send them, try hard to come to me at Nicopolis. I have decided to stay there this winter. [13]Zenas the lawyer and Apollos will be traveling from there. Do all that you can to help them on their way. Be sure that they have everything they need. [14]Our people must learn to use their lives for doing good deeds. They should do good to those in need. Then our people will not have useless lives.

[15]All who are with me greet you. Greet those who love us in the faith.

Grace be with you all.

The Letter of Paul the Apostle to
PHILEMON

From Paul, a prisoner of Jesus Christ, and from Timothy, our brother.

To Philemon, our dear friend and worker with us; [2]to Apphia, our sister; to Archippus, a worker with us; and to the church that meets in your home.

[3]Grace and peace to you from God our Father and the Lord Jesus Christ.

[4]I remember you in my prayers. And I always thank my God for you. [5]I hear about the love you have for all God's holy people and the faith you have in the Lord Jesus. [6]I pray that the faith you share will make you understand every blessing that we have in Christ. [7]My brother, you have shown love to God's people. You have made them feel happy. This has given me great joy and comfort.

[8]There is something that you should do. And because of your love in Christ, I feel free to order you to do it. [9]But because I love you, I am asking you instead. I, Paul, am an old man now, and a prisoner for Christ Jesus. [10]I am asking you a favor for my son Onesimus. He became my son while I was in prison. [11]In the past he was useless to you. But now he has become useful for both you and me.

[12]I am sending him back to you, and with him I am sending my own heart. [13]I wanted to keep him with me to help me while I am in prison for the Good News.[d] By helping me he would be serving you. [14]But I did not want to do anything without asking you first. Then any favor you do for me will be because you want to do it, not because I forced you to do it.

[15]Onesimus was separated from you for a short time. Maybe that happened so that you could have him back forever— [16]not to be a slave, but better than a slave, to be a loved brother. I love him very much. But you will love him even more. You will love him as a man and as a brother in the Lord.

[17]If you think of me as your friend, then accept Onesimus back. Welcome him as you would welcome me. [18]If Onesimus has done anything wrong to you, charge that to me. If he owes you anything, charge that to me. [19]I, Paul, am writing this with my own hand. I will pay back anything Onesimus owes. And I will say nothing about what you owe me for your own life. [20]So, my brother, I ask that you do this for me in the Lord. Comfort my heart in Christ. [21]I write this letter, knowing that you will do what I ask you and even more.

[22]Also, please prepare a room for me to stay in. I hope that God will answer your prayers and I will be able to come to you.

[23]Epaphras is a prisoner with me for Christ Jesus. He sends greetings to you. [24]And also Mark, Aristarchus, Demas, and Luke send greetings. They are workers together with me.

[25]The grace of our Lord Jesus Christ be with your spirit.

The Letter to the
HEBREWS

1 In the past God spoke to our ancestors through the prophets.[d] He spoke to them many times and in many different ways. [2]And now in these last days God has spoken to us through his Son. God has chosen his Son to own all things. And he made the world through the Son. [3]The Son reflects the glory of God. He is an exact copy of God's nature. He holds everything together with his powerful word. The Son made people clean from their sins. Then he sat down at the right side of God, the Great One in heaven. [4]The Son became much greater than the angels. And God gave him a name that is much greater than theirs.

[5]This is because God never said to any of the angels,

"You are my Son.
Today I have become your
Father."   *Psalm 2:7*

Nor did God say of any angel,

"I will be his Father,
and he will be my Son."
                              2 Samuel 7:14

[6]And when God brings his firstborn Son into the world, he says,

"Let all God's angels worship
him."ⁿ *Psalm 97:7*

[7]This is what God said about the angels:

"God makes his angels become like
winds.

He makes his servants become
like flames of fire." *Psalm 104:4*

[8]But God said this about his Son:

"God, your throne will last forever
and ever.

You will rule your kingdom with
fairness.

[9]You love what is right and hate evil.

So God has chosen you to rule
those with you.

Your God has given you much
joy." *Psalm 45:6-7*

[10]God also says,

"Lord, in the beginning you made
the earth.

And your hands made the skies.

[11]They will be destroyed, but you will
remain.

They will all wear out like
clothes.

[12]You will fold them like a coat.

And, like clothes, you will
change them.

But you never change.

And your life will never end."
Psalm 102:25-27

[13]And God never said this to an angel:

"Sit by me at my right side

until I put your enemies under your
control."ⁿ *Psalm 110:1*

[14]All the angels are spirits who serve
God and are sent to help those who will
receive salvation.

2 So we must be more careful to follow
what we were taught. Then we will
not be pulled away from the truth. [2]The
teaching that God spoke through angels
was shown to be true. And anyone who
did not follow it or obey it received the
punishment he earned. [3]The salvation
that was given to us is very great. So
surely we also will be punished if we live
as if this salvation were not important. It
was the Lord himself who first told
about this salvation. And those who
heard him proved to us that this salvation is true. [4]God also proved it by using
wonders, great signs, and many kinds
of miracles.ᵈ And he proved it by giving
people gifts through the Holy Spirit,ᵈ
just as he wanted.

[5]God did not choose angels to be the
rulers of the new world that was coming.
It is that future world we have been talking about. [6]It is written somewhere in
the Scriptures,ᵈ

"Why is man important to you?

Why do you take care of the son
of man?ⁿ

[7]For a short time you made him
lower than the angels.

But you crowned him with glory
and honor.

[8] You put all things under his
control." *Psalm 8:4-6*

If God put everything under his control,
there was nothing left that he did not
rule. But we do not yet see him ruling
over everything. [9]But we see Jesus! For
a short time he was made lower than the
angels. But now we see him wearing a
crown of glory and honor because he
suffered and died. Because of God's
grace, he died for everyone.

[10]God is the One who made all things.
And all things are for his glory. God
wanted to have many sons share his
glory. So God made perfect the One who
leads people to salvation. He made
Jesus a perfect Savior through Jesus'
suffering.

[11]Jesus, who makes people holy, and
those who are made holy are from the
same family. So he is not ashamed to
call them his brothers. [12]He says,

"Then, I will tell my fellow
Israelites about you.

I will praise you when your
people meet to worship you."
Psalm 22:22

[13]He also says,

"I will trust in God." *Isaiah 8:17*

And he also says,

"I am here. And with me are the
children that God has given
me." *Isaiah 8:18*

[14]These children are people with
physical bodies. So Jesus himself became like them and had the same experiences they have. He did this so that, by
dying, he could destroy the one who has
the power of death. That one is the devil.
[15]Jesus became like men and died so that
he could free them. They were like
slaves all their lives because of their fear
of death. [16]Clearly, it is not angels that
Jesus helps, but the people who are from

1:6 "Let . . . him." These words are found in Deuteronomy 32:43 in the Septuagint, the Greek
version of the Old Testament, and in a Hebrew copy among the Dead Sea Scrolls. **1:13 until . . .
control** Literally, "until I make your enemies a footstool for your feet." **2:6 son of man** This
can mean any, but the name "Son of Man" is often used to mean Jesus. When Jesus became a
man, he showed what God planned for all people to be.

Abraham."[n] [17] For this reason Jesus had to be made like his brothers in every way. He became like men so that he could be their merciful and faithful high priest in service to God. Then Jesus could bring forgiveness for their sins. [18] And now he can help those who are tempted. He is able to help because he himself suffered and was tempted.

3 So all of you, holy brothers, should think about Jesus. You were all called by God. God sent Jesus to us, and he is the high priest of our faith. [2] And Jesus was faithful to God as Moses was. Moses did everything God wanted him to do in God's family. [3] A man who is the head of a family receives more honor than others in the family. It is the same with Jesus. Jesus should have more honor than Moses. [4] Every family has its head, but God is the head of everything. [5] Moses was faithful in God's family as a servant. He told what God would say in the future. [6] But Christ is faithful as a Son who is the head of God's family. And we are God's family if we hold on to our faith and are proud of the great hope we have.

[7] So it is as the Holy Spirit[d] says:

"Today listen to what he says.
[8]   Do not be stubborn as in the past
         when you turned against God.
   There you tested God in the desert.
[9]   For 40 years in the desert your
         ancestors saw the things I did.
       But they tested me and my
         patience.
[10] I was angry with them.
       I said, 'They are not loyal to me.
       They have not understood my
         ways.'
[11] So I was angry and made a
         promise.
       'They will never enter my land of
         rest.'"[n]   *Psalm 95:7-11*

[12] So brothers, be careful that none of you has an evil, unbelieving heart. This will stop you from following the living God. [13] But encourage each other every day. Do this while it is "today."[n] Help each other so that none of you will become hardened because of sin and its tricks. [14] We all share in Christ. This is true if we keep till the end the sure faith

we had in the beginning. [15] This is what the Scripture[d] says:

"Today listen to what he says.
   Do not be stubborn as in the past
     when you turned against God."
                      Psalm 95:7-8

[16] Who heard God's voice and was against him? It was all those people Moses led out of Egypt. [17] And whom was God angry with for 40 years? He was angry with those who sinned, who died in the desert. [18] And whom was God talking to when he promised that they would never enter and have his rest? He was talking to those who did not obey him. [19] So we see that they were not allowed to enter and have God's rest because they did not believe.

4 Now God has left us that promise that we may enter and have his rest. Let us be very careful, then, so that none of you will fail to get that rest. [2] The Good News[d] was preached to us just as it was to them. But the teaching they heard did not help them. They heard it but did not accept it with faith. [3] We who have believed are able to enter and have God's rest. As God has said,

"So I was angry and made a
         promise.
   'They will never enter my land of
         rest.'"   *Psalm 95:11*

But God's work was finished from the time he made the world. [4] Somewhere in the Scriptures[d] he talked about the seventh day of the week: "And on the seventh day God rested from all his work."[n] [5] And again in the Scripture God said, "They will never enter my land of rest." [6] It is still true that some people will enter and have God's rest. But those who first heard the way to be saved did not enter. They did not enter because they did not obey. [7] So God planned another day, called "today." He spoke about that day through David a long time later. It is the same Scripture used before:

"Today listen to what he says.
   Do not be stubborn." *Psalm 95:7-8*

[8] We know that Joshua[n] did not lead the people into that rest. We know this because God spoke later about another day. [9] This shows that the seventh-day rest[n] for God's people is still coming. [10] For anyone who enters and has God's

---

2:16 Abraham Most respected ancestor of the Jews. Every Jew hoped to see Abraham. **3:11 rest** A place of rest God promised to give his people. **3:13 "today"** This word is taken from verse 7. It means that it is important to do these things now. **4:4 "And . . . work."** Quotation from Genesis 2:2. **4:8 Joshua** After Moses died, Joshua became leader of the Jewish people. Joshua led them into the land that God promised to give them. **4:9 seventh-day rest** Literally, "sabbath rest," meaning a sharing in the rest that God began after he created the world.

rest will rest from his work as God did. [11]So let us try as hard as we can to enter God's rest. We must try hard so that no one will be lost by following the example of those who refused to obey.

[12]God's word is alive and working. It is sharper than a sword sharpened on both sides. It cuts all the way into us, where the soul and the spirit are joined. It cuts to the center of our joints and our bones. And God's word judges the thoughts and feelings in our hearts. [13]Nothing in all the world can be hidden from God. Everything is clear and lies open before him. And to him we must explain the way we have lived.

[14]We have a great high priest who has gone into heaven. He is Jesus the Son of God. So let us hold on to the faith we have. [15]For our high priest is able to understand our weaknesses. When he lived on earth, he was tempted in every way that we are, but he did not sin. [16]Let us, then, feel free to come before God's throne. Here there is grace. And we can receive mercy and grace to help us when we need it.

5 Every high priest is chosen from among men. He is given the work of going before God for them. He must offer gifts and sacrifices for sins. [2]He himself is weak. So he is able to be gentle with those who do not understand and who are doing wrong things. [3]Because he is weak the high priest must offer sacrifices for his own sins. And then he offers sacrifices for the sins of the people.

[4]To be a high priest is an honor. But no one chooses himself for this work. He must be called by God as Aaron[n] was. [5]So also Christ did not choose himself to have the honor of being a high priest. But God chose him. God said to him,

"You are my Son;
   today I have become your
     Father."   *Psalm 2:7*
[6]And in another Scripture[d] God says,

"You are a priest forever,
   a priest like Melchizedek."[n]
               Psalm 110:4
[7]While Jesus lived on earth, he prayed to God and asked God for help. He prayed with loud cries and tears to the One who could save him from death.

And his prayer was heard because he left it all up to God. [8]Even though Jesus was the Son of God, he learned to obey by what he suffered. [9]And he became our perfect high priest. He gives eternal salvation to all who obey him. [10]And God made Jesus high priest, a priest like Melchizedek.

[11]We have much to say about this. But it is hard to explain because you are so slow to understand. [12]You have had enough time so that by now you should be teachers. But you need someone to teach you again the first lessons of God's message. You still need the teaching that is like milk. You are not ready for solid food. [13]Anyone who lives on milk is still a baby. He knows nothing about right teaching. [14]But solid food is for those who are grown up. They have practiced in order to know the difference between good and evil.

6 So let us go on to grown-up teaching. Let us not go back over the beginning lessons we learned about Christ. We should not start over again with teaching about turning from acts that lead to death and about believing in God. [2]We should not return to the teaching of baptisms,[n] of laying on of hands,[n] of the raising of the dead and eternal judgment. [3]And we will go on to grown-up teaching if God allows.

[4]Some people cannot be brought back again to a changed life. They were once in God's light. They enjoyed heaven's gift, and they shared in the Holy Spirit.[d] [5]They found out how good God's word is, and they received the powers of his new world. [6]And then they fell away from Christ! It is not possible to keep on bringing them back to a changed life again. For they are nailing the Son of God to a cross again and are shaming him in front of others.

[7]Some people are like land that gets plenty of rain. The land produces a good crop for those who work it, and it receives God's blessings. [8]Other people are like land that grows thorns and weeds and is worthless. It is in danger of being cursed by God. It will be destroyed by fire.

[9]Dear friends, we are saying this to you. But we really expect better things from you that will lead to your salvation.

5:4 Aaron Aaron was the first Jewish high priest. He was Moses' brother.   **5:6 Melchizedek** A priest and king who lived in the time of Abraham. (Read Genesis 14:17-24.)   **6:2 baptisms** The word here may refer to Christian baptism, or it may refer to the Jewish ceremonial washings. **6:2 laying . . . hands** Putting the hands on people showed that they were being given some special work or some spiritual gift or blessing.

[10]God is fair. He will not forget the work you did and the love you showed for him by helping his people. And he will remember that you are still helping them. [11]We want each of you to go on with the same hard work all your lives. Then you will surely get what you hope for. [12]We do not want you to become lazy. Be like those who have faith and patience. They will receive what God has promised.

[13]God made a promise to Abraham. And as there is no one greater than God, he used himself when he swore to Abraham. [14]He said, "I will surely bless you and give you many descendants."[n] [15]Abraham waited patiently for this to happen. And he received what God promised.

[16]People always use the name of someone greater than themselves when they swear. The oath proves that what they say is true. And this ends all arguing about what they say. [17]God wanted to prove that his promise was true. He wanted to prove this to those who would get what he promised. He wanted them to understand clearly that his purposes never change. So God proved his promise by also making an oath. [18]These two things cannot change. God cannot lie when he makes a promise, and he cannot lie when he makes an oath. These things encourage us who came to God for safety. They give us strength to hold on to the hope we have been given. [19]We have this hope as an anchor for the soul, sure and strong. It enters behind the curtain in the Most Holy Place in heaven. [20]Jesus has gone in there ahead of us and for us. He has become the high priest forever, a priest like Melchizedek.[n]

7 Melchizedek[n] was the king of Salem and a priest for the Most High God. He met Abraham when Abraham was coming back after defeating the kings. When they met, Melchizedek blessed Abraham. [2]And Abraham gave Melchizedek a tenth of everything he had brought back from the battle. First, Melchizedek's name means "king of goodness." Also, he is king of Salem, which means "king of peace." [3]No one knows who Melchizedek's father or mother was.[n] No one knows where he came from. And no one knows when he was

born or when he died. Melchizedek is like the Son of God; he continues being a priest forever.

[4]You can see that Melchizedek was very great. Abraham, the great father, gave Melchizedek a tenth of everything that Abraham won in battle. [5]Now the law says that those in the tribe[d] of Levi who become priests must get a tenth from the people. The priests collect it from their own people, even though the priests and the people are both from the family of Abraham. [6]Melchizedek was not from the tribe of Levi. But he got a tenth from Abraham. And he blessed Abraham, the man who had God's promises. [7]And everyone knows that the more important person blesses the less important person. [8]Those priests get a tenth, but they are only men who live and then die. But Melchizedek, who got a tenth from Abraham, continues living, as the Scripture[d] says. [9]It is Levi who gets a tenth from the people. But we might even say that when Abraham paid Melchizedek a tenth, then Levi also paid it. [10]Levi was not yet born. But Levi was in the body of his ancestor Abraham when Melchizedek met Abraham.

[11]The people were given the law[n] based on a system of priests from the tribe of Levi. But they could not be made spiritually perfect through that system of priests. So there was a need for another priest to come. I mean a priest like Melchizedek, not Aaron. [12]And when a different kind of priest comes, the law must be changed, too. [13]We are saying these things about Christ. He belonged to a different tribe. No one from that tribe ever served as a priest at the altar. [14]It is clear that our Lord came from the tribe of Judah. And Moses said nothing about priests belonging to that tribe.

[15]And this becomes even more clear. We see that another priest comes, who is like Melchizedek.[n] [16]He was not made a priest by human rules and laws. He became a priest through the power of his life, which continues forever. [17]In the Scriptures,[d] this is said about him:

"You are a priest forever,
   a priest like Melchizedek."

Psalm 110:4

6:14 "I . . . descendants." Quotation from Genesis 22:17. **6:20; 7:1, 15 Melchizedek** A priest and king who lived in the time of Abraham. (Read Genesis 14:17-24.) **7:3 No . . . was** Literally, "Melchizedek was without father, without mother, without genealogy." **7:11 The . . . law** This refers to the people of Israel who were given the law of Moses.

[18]The old rule is now set aside because it was weak and useless. [19]The law of Moses could not make anything perfect. But now a better hope has been given to us. And with this hope we can come near to God.

[20]Also, it is important that God made an oath when he made Jesus high priest. When the others became priests, there was no oath. [21]But Christ became a priest with God's oath. God said:

"The Lord has made a promise
and will not change his mind.
'You are a priest forever.'"

Psalm 110:4

[22]So this means that Jesus is the guarantee of a better agreement[n] from God to his people.

[23]Also, when one of the other priests died, he could not continue being a priest. So there were many priests. [24]But Jesus lives forever. He will never stop serving as priest. [25]So he is always able to save those who come to God through him. He can do this, because he always lives, ready to help those who come before God.

[26]So Jesus is the kind of high priest that we need. He is holy; he has no sin in him. He is pure and not influenced by sinners. And he is raised above the heavens. [27]He is not like the other priests. They had to offer sacrifices every day, first for their own sins, and then for the sins of the people. But Christ does not need to do that. He offered his sacrifice only once and for all time. Christ offered himself! [28]The law chooses high priests who are men with all their weaknesses. But the word of God's oath came later than the law. It made God's Son to be the high priest. And that Son has been made perfect forever.

8 Here is the point of what we are saying: We do have a high priest who sits on the right side of God's throne in heaven. [2]Our high priest serves in the Most Holy Place. He serves in the true place of worship that was made by God, not by men. [3]Every high priest has the work of offering gifts and sacrifices to God. So our high priest must also offer something to God. [4]If our high priest were now living on earth, he would not be a priest. I say

this because there are already priests here who follow the law by offering gifts to God. [5]The work that they do as priests is only a copy of what is in heaven. For when Moses was ready to build the Holy Tent,[d] God warned him: "Be very careful to make everything by the plan I showed you on the mountain."[n] [6]But the priestly work that has been given to Jesus is much greater than the work that was given to the other priests. In the same way, the new agreement that Jesus brought from God to his people is much greater than the old one. And the new agreement is based on promises of better things.

[7]If there was nothing wrong with the first agreement,[n] there would be no need for a second agreement. [8]But God found something wrong with his people. He says:

"The time is coming, says the Lord,
when I will make a new
agreement.
It will be with the people of Israel
and the people of Judah.
[9]It will not be like the agreement
I made with their ancestors.
That was when I took them by the
hand
to bring them out of Egypt.
But they broke that agreement,
and I turned away from them,
says the Lord.
[10]In the future I will make this
agreement
with the people of Israel, says the
Lord.
I will put my teachings in their
minds.
And I will write them on their
hearts.
I will be their God,
and they will be my people.
[11]People will no longer have to teach
their neighbors and relatives to
know the Lord.
This is because all will know me,
from the least to the most
important.
[12]I will forgive them for the wicked
things they did.
I will not remember their sins
anymore." *Jeremiah 31:31-34*

7:22 agreement God gives a contract or agreement to his people. For the Jews, this agreement was the law of Moses. But now God has given a better agreement to his people through Christ. **8:5 "Be . . . mountain."** Quotation from Exodus 25:40. **8:7 first agreement** The contract God gave the Jewish people when he gave them the law of Moses.

[13]God called this a new agreement, so he has made the first agreement old. And anything that is old and worn out is ready to disappear.

9 The first agreement[n] had rules for worship. And it had a man-made place for worship. [2]The Holy Tent[d] was set up for this. The first area in the Tent was called the Holy Place. In it were the lamp and the table with the bread that was made holy for God. [3]Behind the second curtain was a room called the Most Holy Place. [4]In it was a golden altar for burning incense.[d] Also there was the Holy Box[d] that held the old agreement. The Holy Box was covered with gold. Inside this Holy Box was a golden jar of manna[d] and Aaron's rod—the rod that once grew leaves. Also in it were the stone tablets of the old agreement. [5]Above the Holy Box were the creatures with wings that showed God's glory. The wings of the creatures reached over the lid. But we cannot tell everything about these things now.

[6]Everything in the Tent was made ready in this way. Then the priests went into the first room every day to do their worship. [7]But only the high priest could go into the second room, and he did that only once a year. He could never enter the inner room without taking blood with him. He offered that blood to God for himself and for the people's sins. These were sins people did without knowing that they were sinning. [8]The Holy Spirit[d] uses this to show that the way into the Most Holy Place was not open. This was while the system of the old Holy Tent was still being used. [9]This is an example for the present time. It shows that the gifts and sacrifices offered cannot make the worshiper perfect in his heart. [10]These gifts and sacrifices were only about food and drink and special washings. They were rules for the body, to be followed until the time of God's new way.

[11]But Christ has come as the high priest of the good things we now have. The tent he entered is greater and more perfect. It is not made by men. It does not belong to this world. [12]Christ entered the Most Holy Place only once—and for all time. He did not take with him the blood of goats and calves. His sacrifice was his own blood. He entered the Most Holy Place and set us free from sin forever. [13]The blood of goats and bulls and the ashes of a cow are sprinkled on the people who are unclean[d] and this makes their bodies clean again.

[14]How much more is done by the blood of Christ. He offered himself through the eternal Spirit[n] as a perfect sacrifice to God. His blood will make our hearts clean from useless acts. We are made pure so that we may serve the living God.

[15]So Christ brings a new agreement from God to his people. Those who are called by God can now receive the blessings that God has promised. These blessings will last forever. They can have those things because Christ died so that the people who lived under the first agreement could be set free from sin.

[16]When there is a will,[n] it must be proven that the man who wrote that will is dead. [17]A will means nothing while the man is alive. It can be used only after he dies. [18]This is why even the first agreement could not begin without blood to show death. [19]First, Moses told all the people every command in the law. Next he took the blood of calves and mixed it with water. Then he used red wool and a branch of the hyssop plant to sprinkle the blood and water on the book of the law and on all the people. [20]He said, "This is the blood which begins the agreement that God commanded you to obey."[n] [21]In the same way, Moses sprinkled the blood on the Holy Tent[d] and over all the things used in worship. [22]The law says that almost everything must be made clean by blood. And sins cannot be forgiven without blood to show death.

[23]So the copies of the real things in heaven had to be made clean[d] by animal sacrifices. But the real things in heaven need much better sacrifices. [24]For Christ did not go into the Most Holy Place made by men. It is only a copy of the real one. He went into heaven itself. He is there now before God to help us. [25]The high priest enters the Most Holy Place once every year. He takes with him blood that is not his own blood. But Christ did not go into heaven to offer

9:1 first agreement The contract God gave the Jewish people when he gave them the law of Moses. **9:14 Spirit** This refers to the Holy Spirit; to Christ's own spirit; or to the spiritual and eternal nature of his sacrifice. **9:16 will** A legal document that shows how a person's money and property are to be distributed at the time of his death. This is the same word in Greek as "agreement" in verse 15. **9:20 "This . . . obey."** Quotation from Exodus 24:8.

himself many times. [26]Then he would have had to suffer many times since the world was made. But Christ came only once and for all time. He came at just the right time to take away all sin by sacrificing himself. [27]Everyone must die once. After a person dies, he is judged. [28]So Christ was offered as a sacrifice one time to take away the sins of many people. And he will come a second time, but not to offer himself for sin. He will come again to bring salvation to those who are waiting for him.

10 The law is only an unclear picture of the good things coming in the future. It is not a perfect picture of the real things. The people under the law offered the same sacrifices every year. These sacrifices can never make perfect those who come near to worship God. [2]If the law could make them perfect, the sacrifices would have already stopped. The worshipers would be made clean, and they would no longer feel guilty for their sins. [3]These sacrifices remind them of their sins every year, [4]because it is not possible for the blood of bulls and goats to take away sins.

[5]So when Christ came into the world, he said:

"You do not want sacrifices and offerings.
But you have prepared a body for me.
[6]You do not ask for burnt offerings and offerings to take away sins.
[7]Then I said, 'Look, I have come.
It is written about me in the book.
My God, I have come to do what you want.'" *Psalm 40:6-8*

[8]In this Scripture[d] he first said, "You do not want sacrifices and offerings. You do not ask for burnt offerings and offerings to take away sins." (These are all sacrifices that the law commands.) [9]Then he said, "Here I am. I have come to do what you want." So God ends the first system of sacrifices so that he can set up the new system. [10]Jesus Christ did what God wanted him to do. And because of this, we are made holy through the sacrifice of his body. Christ made this sacrifice only once, and for all time.

[11]Every day the priests stand and do their religious service. Again and again they offer the same sacrifices. But those sacrifices can never take away sins. [12]But Christ offered one sacrifice for sins, and it is good forever. Then he sat down at the right side of God. [13]And now Christ waits there for his enemies to be put under his power. [14]With one sacrifice he made perfect forever those who are being made holy.

[15]The Holy Spirit[d] also tells us about this. First he says:

[16]"In the future I will make this agreement[n]
with the people of Israel, says the Lord.
I will put my teachings in their hearts.
And I will write them on their minds." *Jeremiah 31:33*
[17]Then he says:
"Their sins and the evil things they do—
I will not remember anymore." *Jeremiah 31:34*
[18]And when these have been forgiven, there is no more need for a sacrifice for sins.

[19]So, brothers, we are completely free to enter the Most Holy Place. We can do this without fear because of the blood of Jesus' death. [20]We can enter through a new way that Jesus opened for us. It is a living way. It leads through the curtain—Christ's body. [21]And we have a great priest over God's house. [22]So let us come near to God with a sincere heart and a sure faith. We have been cleansed and made free from feelings of guilt. And our bodies have been washed with pure water. [23]Let us hold firmly to the hope that we have confessed. We can trust God to do what he promised.

[24]Let us think about each other and help each other to show love and do good deeds. [25]You should not stay away from the church meetings, as some are doing. But you should meet together and encourage each other. Do this even more as you see the Day[n] coming.

[26]If we decide to go on sinning after we have learned the truth, there is no longer any sacrifice for sins. [27]There is nothing but fear in waiting for the judgment and the angry fire that will destroy all those who live against God. [28]Any

10:16 agreement God gives a contract or agreement to his people. For the Jews, this agreement was the law of Moses. But now God has given a better agreement to his people through Christ. **10:25 Day** The day Christ will come to judge all people and take his people to live with him.

person who refused to obey the law of Moses was found guilty from the proof given by two or three witnesses. He was put to death without mercy. [29]So what do you think should be done to a person who does not respect the Son of God? He looks at the blood of the agreement, the blood that made him holy, as no different from other men's blood. He insults the Spirit[d] of God's grace. Surely he should have a much worse punishment. [30]We know that God said, "I will punish those who do wrong. I will repay them."[*] And he also said, "The Lord will judge his people."[n 31]It is a terrible thing to fall into the hands of the living God.

[32]Remember those days in the past when you first learned the truth. You had a hard struggle with many sufferings, but you continued strong. [33]Sometimes you were hurt and persecuted before crowds of people. And sometimes you shared with those who were being treated that way. [34]You helped the prisoners. And you even had joy when all that you owned was taken from you. You were joyful because you knew that you had something better and more lasting.

[35]So do not lose the courage that you had in the past. It has a great reward. [36]You must hold on, so you can do what God wants and receive what he has promised. [37]For in a very short time,

"The One who is coming will come.
    He will not be late.
[38]The person who is right with me
    will have life because of his faith.
But if he turns back with fear,
    I will not be pleased with him."

Habakkuk 2:3-4

[39]But we are not those who turn back and are lost. We are people who have faith and are saved.

11 Faith means being sure of the things we hope for. And faith means knowing that something is real even if we do not see it. [2]People who lived in the past became famous because of faith.

[3]It is by faith we understand that the whole world was made by God's command. This means that what we see was made by something that cannot be seen.

[4]It was by faith that Abel offered God a better sacrifice than Cain did. God said he was pleased with the gifts Abel offered. So God called Abel a good man because of his faith. Abel died, but through his faith he is still speaking.

[5]It was by faith that Enoch was taken to heaven. He never died. He could not be found, because God had taken him away. Before he was taken, the Scripture[d] says that he was a man who truly pleased God. [6]Without faith no one can please God. Anyone who comes to God must believe that he is real and that he rewards those who truly want to find him.

[7]It was by faith Noah heard God's warnings about things that he could not yet see. He obeyed God and built a large boat to save his family. By his faith, Noah showed that the world was wrong. And he became one of those who are made right with God through faith.

[8]It was by faith Abraham obeyed God's call to go to another place that God promised to give him. He left his own country, not knowing where he was to go. [9]It was by faith that he lived in the country God promised to give him. He lived there like a visitor who did not belong. He lived in tents with Isaac and Jacob, who had received that same promise from God. [10]Abraham was waiting for the city[n] that has real foundations—the city planned and built by God.

[11]He was too old to have children, and Sarah was not able to have children. It was by faith that Abraham was made able to become a father. Abraham trusted God to do what he had promised. [12]This man was so old that he was almost dead. But from him came as many descendants as there are stars in the sky. They are as many as the grains of sand on the seashore that cannot be counted.

[13]All these great men died in faith. They did not get the things that God promised his people. But they saw them coming far in the future and were glad. They said that they were like visitors and strangers on earth. [14]When people say such things, then they show that they are looking for a country that will be their own country. [15]If they had been thinking about that country they had left, they could have gone back. [16]But those men were waiting for a better country—a heavenly country. So God is

10:30 "I . . . them." Quotation from Deuteronomy 32:35.   10:30 "The Lord . . . people." Quotation from Deuteronomy 32:36; Psalm 135:14.   11:10 city The spiritual "city" where God's people live with him. Also called "the heavenly Jerusalem." (See Hebrews 12:22.)

not ashamed to be called their God. For he has prepared a city for them.

[17] It was by faith that Abraham offered his son Isaac as a sacrifice. God made the promises to Abraham. But God tested him. And Abraham was ready to offer his own son as a sacrifice. [18] God had said, "The descendants I promised you will be from Isaac."[n] [19] Abraham believed that God could raise the dead. And really, it was as if Abraham got Isaac back from death.

[20] It was by faith that Isaac blessed the future of Jacob and Esau. [21] It was by faith that Jacob blessed each one of Joseph's sons. He did this while he was dying. Then he worshiped as he leaned on the top of his walking stick.

[22] It was by faith that Joseph spoke about the Israelites leaving Egypt while he was dying. He told them what to do with his body.

[23] It was by faith that Moses' parents hid him for three months after he was born. They saw that Moses was a beautiful baby. And they were not afraid to disobey the king's order.

[24] It was by faith that Moses, when he grew up, refused to be called the son of the king of Egypt's daughter. [25] He chose to suffer with God's people instead of enjoying sin for a short time. [26] He thought that it was better to suffer for the Christ[d] than to have all the treasures of Egypt. He was looking only for God's reward. [27] It was by faith that Moses left Egypt. He was not afraid of the king's anger. Moses continued strong as if he could see the God that no one can see. [28] It was by faith that Moses prepared the Passover[d] and spread the blood on the doors. It was spread so that the one who brings death would not kill the firstborn[d] sons of Israel.

[29] It was by faith that the people crossed the Red Sea as if it were dry land. The Egyptians also tried to do it, but they were drowned.

[30] It was by faith that the walls of Jericho fell. They fell after the people had marched around the walls of Jericho for seven days.

[31] It was by faith that Rahab, the prostitute,[d] welcomed the spies and was not killed with those who refused to obey God.

[32] Do I need to give more examples? I do not have time to tell you about Gideon, Barak, Samson, Jephthah, David, Samuel, and the prophets.[d] [33] Through their faith they defeated kingdoms. They did what was right and received what God promised. They shut the mouths of lions, [34] stopped great fires and were saved from being killed with swords. They were weak, and yet were made strong. They were powerful in battle and defeated other armies. [35] Women received their dead relatives raised back to life. Others were tortured and refused to accept their freedom. They did this so that they could be raised from death to a better life. [36] Some were laughed at and beaten. Others were tied and put into prison. [37] They were killed with stones and they were cut in half. They were killed with swords. Some wore the skins of sheep and goats. They were poor, abused, and treated badly. [38] The world was not good enough for them! They wandered in deserts and mountains, living in caves and holes in the earth.

[39] All these people are known for their faith. But none of them received what God had promised. [40] God planned to give us something better. Then they would be made perfect, but only together with us.

12 So we have many people of faith around us. Their lives tell us what faith means. So let us run the race that is before us and never give up. We should remove from our lives anything that would get in the way. And we should remove the sin that so easily catches us. [2] Let us look only to Jesus. He is the one who began our faith, and he makes our faith perfect. Jesus suffered death on the cross. But he accepted the shame of the cross as if it were nothing. He did this because of the joy that God put before him. And now he is sitting at the right side of God's throne. [3] Think about Jesus. He held on patiently while sinful men were doing evil things against him. Look at Jesus' example so that you will not get tired and stop trying.

[4] You are struggling against sin, but your struggles have not yet caused you to be killed. [5] You have forgotten his encouraging words for his sons:

"My son, don't think the Lord's
    discipline of you is worth
    nothing.
And don't stop trying when the
    Lord corrects you.

11:18 "The descendants . . . Isaac." Quotation from Genesis 21:12.

[6]"The Lord corrects those he loves.
And he punishes everyone he
accepts as his child."

Proverbs 3:11-12

[7]So accept your sufferings as if they were a father's punishment. God does these things to you as a father punishing his sons. All sons are punished by their fathers. [8]If you are never punished (and every son must be punished), you are not true children and not really sons. [9]We have all had fathers here on earth who punished us. And we respected our fathers. So it is even more important that we accept punishment from the Father of our spirits. If we do this, we will have life. [10]Our fathers on earth punished us for a short time. They punished us the way they thought was best. But God punishes us to help us, so that we can become holy as he is. [11]We do not enjoy punishment. Being punished is painful. But later, after we have learned from being punished, we have peace, because we start living in the right way.

[12]You have become weak. So make yourselves strong again. [13]Live in the right way so that you will be saved and your weakness will not cause you to be lost.

[14]Try to live in peace with all people. And try to live lives free from sin. If anyone's life is not holy, he will never see the Lord. [15]Be careful that no one fails to get God's grace. Be careful that no one becomes like a bitter weed growing among you. A person like that can ruin all of you. [16]Be careful that no one takes part in sexual sin. And be careful that no person is like Esau and never thinks about God. Esau was the oldest son, and he would have received everything from his father. But Esau sold all that for a single meal. [17]You remember that after Esau did this, he wanted to get his father's blessing. He wanted this blessing so much that he cried. But his father refused to give him the blessing, because Esau could find no way to change what he had done.

[18]You have not come to a mountain that can be touched and that is burning with fire. You have not come to darkness, sadness and storms. [19]You have not come to the noise of a trumpet or to the sound of a voice. When the people of Israel heard the voice, they begged not to have to hear another word. [20]They did not want to hear the command: "If anything, even an animal, touches the mountain, it must be put to death with stones."[n] [21]What they saw was so terrible that Moses said, "I am shaking with fear."[n]

[22]But you have not come to that kind of place. The new place you have come to is Mount Zion.[n] You have come to the city of the living God, the heavenly Jerusalem. You have come to thousands of angels gathered together with joy. [23]You have come to the meeting of God's firstborn[n] children. Their names are written in heaven. You have come to God, the judge of all people. And you have come to the spirits of good people who have been made perfect. [24]You have come to Jesus, the One who brought the new agreement from God to his people. You have come to the sprinkled blood[n] that has a better message than the blood of Abel.[n]

[25]So be careful and do not refuse to listen when God speaks. They refused to listen to him when he warned them on earth. And they did not escape. Now God is warning us from heaven. So it will be worse for us if we refuse to listen to him. [26]When he spoke before, his voice shook the earth. But now he has promised, "Once again I will shake not only the earth but also the heavens."[n] [27]The words "once again" clearly show us that everything that was made will be destroyed. These are the things that can be shaken. And only the things that cannot be shaken will remain.

[28]So let us be thankful because we have a kingdom that cannot be shaken. We should worship God in a way that pleases him. So let us worship him with respect and fear, [29]because our God is like a fire that burns things up.

13 Keep on loving each other as brothers in Christ. [2]Remember to welcome strangers into your homes. Some people have done this and have welcomed angels without knowing it. [3]Do not forget those who are in prison.

12:20 "If . . . stones." Quotation from Exodus 19:12-13.   **12:21 "I . . . fear."** Quotation from Deuteronomy 9:19.   **12:22 Mount Zion** Another name for Jerusalem, here meaning the spiritual city of God's people.   **12:23 firstborn** The first son born in a Jewish family was given the most important place in the family and received special blessings. All of God's children are like that.   **12:24 sprinkled blood** The blood of Jesus' death.   **12:24 Abel** The son of Adam and Eve, who was killed by his brother Cain (Genesis 4:8).   **12:26 "Once . . . heavens."** Quotation from Haggai 2:6, 21.

Remember them as if you were in prison with them. Remember those who are suffering as if you were suffering with them. [4]Marriage should be honored by everyone. Husband and wife should keep their marriage pure. God will judge guilty those who take part in sexual sins. [5]Keep your lives free from the love of money. And be satisfied with what you have. God has said,

"I will never leave you;
    I will never forget you."

Deuteronomy 31:6

[6]So we can feel sure and say,

"I will not be afraid because the
    Lord is my helper.
People can't do anything to me."

Psalm 118:6

[7]Remember your leaders. They taught God's message to you. Remember how they lived and died, and copy their faith. [8]Jesus Christ is the same yesterday, today, and forever. [9]Do not let all kinds of strange teachings lead you into the wrong way. Your hearts should be strengthened by God's grace, not by obeying rules about foods. Obeying such rules does not help anyone. [10]We have a sacrifice. But the priests who serve in the Holy Tent[d] cannot eat from it. [11]The high priest carries the blood of animals into the Most Holy Place. There he offers this blood for sins. But the bodies of the animals are burned outside the camp. [12]So Jesus also suffered outside the city. He died to make his people holy with his own blood. [13]So let us go to Jesus outside the camp. We should accept the same shame that Jesus had.

[14]Here on earth we do not have a city that lasts forever. But we are looking for the city that we will have in the future. [15]So through Jesus let us always offer our sacrifice to God. This sacrifice is our praise, coming from lips that speak his name. [16]Do not forget to do good to others. And share with them what you have. These are the sacrifices that please God.

[17]Obey your leaders and be under their authority. These men are watching you because they are responsible for your souls. Obey them so that they will do this work with joy, not sadness. It will not help you to make their work hard.

[18]Continue praying for us. We feel sure about what we are doing, because we always want to do the right thing. [19]And I beg you to pray that God will send me back to you soon.

[20-21]I pray that the God of peace will give you every good thing you need so that you can do what he wants. God is the One who raised from death our Lord Jesus, the Great Shepherd of the sheep. God raised him because of the blood of his death. His blood began the agreement that God made with his people. And this agreement is eternal. I pray that God, through Christ, will do in us what pleases him. And to Jesus Christ be glory forever and ever. Amen.

[22]My brothers, I beg you to listen patiently to this message I have written to encourage you. This letter is not very long. [23]I want you to know that our brother Timothy has been let out of prison. If he arrives soon, we will both come to see you.

[24]Greet all your leaders and all of God's people. Those from Italy send greetings to you.

[25]God's grace be with you all.

The Letter of
JAMES

1 From James, a servant of God and of the Lord Jesus Christ. To all of God's people who are scattered everywhere in the world:

Greetings.

[2]My brothers, you will have many kinds of troubles. But when these things happen, you should be very happy. [3]You know that these things are testing your faith. And this will give you patience. [4]Let your patience show itself perfectly in what you do. Then you will be perfect and complete. You will have everything you need. [5]But if any of you needs wisdom, you should ask God for it. God is generous. He enjoys giving to all people, so God will give you wisdom. [6]But when you ask God, you must believe. Do not doubt God. Anyone who doubts is like a

wave in the sea. The wind blows the wave up and down. [7-8]He who doubts is thinking two different things at the same time. He cannot decide about anything he does. A person like that should not think that he will receive anything from the Lord.

[9]If a believer is poor, he should be proud because God has made him spiritually rich. [10]If he is rich, he should be proud because God has shown him that he is spiritually poor. The rich person will die like a wild flower in the grass. [11]The sun rises and becomes hotter and hotter. The heat makes the plants very dry, and the flower falls off. The flower was beautiful, but now it is dead. It is the same with a rich person. While he is still taking care of his business, he will die.

[12]When a person is tempted and still continues strong, he should be happy. After he has proved his faith, God will reward him with life forever. God promised this to all people who love him. [13]When someone is being tempted, he should not say, "God is tempting me." Evil cannot tempt God, and God himself does not tempt anyone. [14]It is the evil that a person wants that tempts him. His own evil desire leads him away and holds him. [15]This desire causes sin. Then the sin grows and brings death.

[16]My dear brothers, do not be fooled about this. [17]Every good action and every perfect gift is from God. These good gifts come down from the Creator of the sun, moon, and stars. God does not change like their shifting shadows. [18]God decided to give us life through the word of truth. He wanted us to be the most important of all the things he made.

[19]My dear brothers, always be willing to listen and slow to speak. Do not become angry easily. [20]Anger will not help you live a good life as God wants. [21]So put out of your life every evil thing and every kind of wrong you do. Don't be proud but accept God's teaching that is planted in your hearts. This teaching can save your souls.

[22]Do what God's teaching says; do not just listen and do nothing. When you only sit and listen, you are fooling yourselves. [23]A person who hears God's teaching and does nothing is like a man looking in a mirror. [24]He sees his face, then goes away and quickly forgets what he looked like. [25]But the truly happy person is the one who carefully studies God's perfect law that makes people free. He continues to study it. He listens to God's teaching and does not forget what he heard. Then he obeys what God's teaching says. When he does this, it makes him happy.

[26]A person might think he is religious. But if he says things he should not say, then he is just fooling himself. His "religion" is worth nothing. [27]Religion that God accepts is this: caring for orphans or widows who need help; and keeping yourself free from the world's evil influence. This is the kind of religion that God accepts as pure and good.

2 My dear brothers, you are believers in our glorious Lord Jesus Christ. So never think that some people are more important than others. [2]Suppose someone comes into your church meeting wearing very nice clothes and a gold ring. At the same time a poor man comes in wearing old, dirty clothes. [3]You show special attention to the one wearing nice clothes. You say, "Please, sit here in this good seat." But you say to the poor man, "Stand over there," or "Sit on the floor by my feet!" [4]What are you doing? You are making some people more important than others. With evil thoughts you are deciding which person is better.

[5]Listen, my dear brothers! God chose the poor in the world to be rich with faith. He chose them to receive the kingdom God promised to people who love him. [6]But you show no respect to the poor man. And you know that it is the rich who are always trying to control your lives. And they are the ones who take you to court. [7]They are the ones who say bad things against Jesus, who owns you.

[8]One law rules over all other laws. This royal law is found in the Scriptures:[d] "Love your neighbor as you love yourself."[n] If you obey this law, then you are doing right. [9]But if you are treating one person as if he were more important than another, then you are sinning. That royal law proves that you are guilty of breaking God's law. [10]A person might follow all of God's law. But if he fails to obey even one command, he is guilty of breaking all the commands in that law. [11]God said, "You must not be guilty of

adultery."[dn] The same God also said, "You must not murder anyone."[n] So if you do not take part in adultery, but you murder someone, then you are guilty of breaking all of God's law. [12]You will be judged by the law that makes people free. You should remember this in everything you say and do. [13]Yes, you must show mercy to others, or God will not show mercy to you when he judges you. But the person who shows mercy can stand without fear when he is judged.

[14]My brothers, if someone says he has faith, but does nothing, his faith is worth nothing. Can faith like that save him? [15]A brother or sister in Christ might need clothes or might need food. [16]And you say to him, "God be with you! I hope you stay warm and get plenty to eat." You say this, but you do not give that person the things he needs. Unless you help him, your words are worth nothing. [17]It is the same with faith. If faith does nothing, then that faith is dead, because it is alone.

[18]Someone might say, "You have faith, but I do things. Show me your faith! Your faith does nothing. I will show you my faith by the things I do." [19]You believe there is one God. Good! But the demons[d] believe that, too! And they shake with fear.

[20]You foolish person! Must you be shown that faith that does nothing is worth nothing? [21]Abraham is our father. He was made right with God by the things he did. He offered his son Isaac to God on the altar. [22]So you see that Abraham's faith and the things he did worked together. His faith was made perfect by what he did. [23]This shows the full meaning of the Scripture[d] that says: "Abraham believed God, and God accepted Abraham's faith, and that faith made him right with God."[n] And Abraham was called "God's friend."[n] [24]So you see that a person is made right with God by the things he does. He cannot be made right by faith only.

[25]Another example is Rahab, who was a prostitute.[d] But she was made right with God by something she did: She helped the spies for God's people. She welcomed them into her home and helped them escape by a different road.

[26]A person's body that does not have a spirit is dead. It is the same with faith. Faith that does nothing is dead!

3 My brothers, not many of you should become teachers. You know that we who teach will be judged more strictly than others. [2]We all make many mistakes. If there were a person who never said anything wrong, he would be perfect. He would be able to control his whole body, too. [3]We put bits into the mouths of horses to make them obey us. We can control their whole bodies. [4]It is the same with ships. A ship is very big, and it is pushed by strong winds. But a very small rudder controls that big ship. The man who controls the rudder decides where the ship will go. The ship goes where the man wants. [5]It is the same with the tongue. It is a small part of the body, but it brags about doing great things.

A big forest fire can be started with only a little flame. [6]And the tongue is like a fire. It is a whole world of evil among the parts of our bodies. The tongue spreads its evil through the whole body. It starts a fire that influences all of life. The tongue gets this fire from hell. [7]People can tame every kind of wild animal, bird, reptile, and fish, and they have tamed them. [8]But no one can tame the tongue. It is wild and evil. It is full of poison that can kill. [9]We use our tongues to praise our Lord and Father, but then we curse people. And God made them like himself. [10]Praises and curses come from the same mouth! My brothers, this should not happen. [11]Do good and bad water flow from the same spring? [12]My brothers, can a fig tree make olives? Can a grapevine make figs? No! And a well full of salty water cannot give good water.

[13]Is there anyone among you who is truly wise and understanding? Then he should show his wisdom by living right. He should do good things without being proud. A wise person does not brag. [14]But if you are selfish and have bitter jealousy in your hearts, you have no reason to brag. Your bragging is a lie that hides the truth. [15]That kind of "wisdom" does not come from God. That "wisdom" comes from the world. It is not spiritual. It is from the devil. [16]Where

2:11 **"You . . . adultery."** Quotation from Exodus 20:14 and Deuteronomy 5:18.   2:11 **"You . . . anyone."** Quotation from Exodus 20:13 and Deuteronomy 5:17.   2:23 **"Abraham . . . God."** Quotation from Genesis 15:6.   2:23 **"God's friend."** These words about Abraham are found in 2 Chronicles 20:7 and Isaiah 41:8.

there is jealousy and selfishness, there will be confusion and every kind of evil. [17]But the wisdom that comes from God is like this: First, it is pure. Then it is also peaceful, gentle, and easy to please. This wisdom is always ready to help those who are troubled and to do good for others. This wisdom is always fair and honest. [18]When people work for peace in a peaceful way, they receive the good result of their right-living.

4 Do you know where your fights and arguments come from? They come from the selfish desires that make war inside you. [2]You want things, but you do not have them. So you are ready to kill and are jealous of other people. But you still cannot get what you want. So you argue and fight. You do not get what you want because you do not ask God. [3]Or when you ask, you do not receive because the reason you ask is wrong. You want things only so that you can use them for your own pleasures.

[4]So, you people are not loyal to God! You should know that loving the world is the same as hating God. So if a person wants to be a friend of the world, he makes himself God's enemy. [5]Do you think the Scripture[d] means nothing? It says, "The Spirit[d] that God made to live in us wants us for himself alone."[n] [6]But God gives us even more grace, as the Scripture says,

"God is against the proud,
but he gives grace to the
humble."   *Proverbs 3:34*

[7]So give yourselves to God. Stand against the devil, and the devil will run away from you. [8]Come near to God, and God will come near to you. You are sinners. So clean sin out of your lives. You are trying to follow God and the world at the same time. Make your thinking pure. [9]Be sad, cry, and weep! Change your laughter into crying. Change your joy into sadness. [10]Don't be too proud before the Lord, and he will make you great.

[11]Brothers, do not say bad things about each other. If you say bad things about your brother in Christ or judge him, then you are saying bad things about the law he follows. You are also judging the law he follows. And when you are judging the law, you are not a follower of the law. You have become a judge! [12]God is the only One who makes laws, and he is the only Judge. He is the

only One who can save and destroy. So it is not right for you to judge your neighbor.

[13]Some of you say, "Today or tomorrow we will go to some city. We will stay there a year, do business, and make money." [14]But you do not know what will happen tomorrow! Your life is like a mist. You can see it for a short time, but then it goes away. [15]So you should say, "If the Lord wants, we will live and do this or that." [16]But now you are proud and you brag. All of this bragging is wrong. [17]And when a person knows the right thing to do, but does not do it, then he is sinning.

5 You rich people, listen! Cry and be very sad because of the trouble that will come to you. [2]Your riches will rot, and your clothes will be eaten by moths. [3]Your gold and silver will rust, and rust will be a proof that you were wrong. It will eat your bodies like fire. You saved your treasure for the last days. [4]Men worked in your fields, but you did not pay them. They harvested your crops and are crying out against you. Now the Lord of heaven's armies has heard their cries. [5]Your life on earth was full of rich living. You pleased yourselves with everything you wanted. You made yourselves fat, like an animal ready to be killed. [6]You showed no mercy to the innocent man. You murdered him. He cannot stand against you.

[7]Brothers, be patient until the Lord comes again. A farmer is patient. He waits for his valuable crop to grow from the earth. He waits patiently for it to receive the first rain and the last rain. [8]You, too, must be patient. Do not give up hope. The Lord is coming soon. [9]Brothers, do not complain against each other. If you do not stop complaining, you will be judged guilty. And the Judge is ready to come! [10]Brothers, follow the example of the prophets[d] who spoke for the Lord. They suffered many hard things, but they were patient. [11]We say they are happy because they were able to do this. You have heard about Job's patience. You know that after all his trouble, the Lord helped him. This shows that the Lord is full of mercy and is kind.

[12]My brothers, it is very important that you not use an oath when you make a promise. Don't use the name of heaven, earth, or anything else to prove

4:5 "The Spirit . . . alone." These words may be from Exodus 20:5.

what you say. When you mean yes, say only "yes." When you mean no, say only "no." Do this so that you will not be judged guilty.

[13]If one of you is having troubles, he should pray. If one of you is happy, he should sing praises. [14]If one of you is sick, he should call the church's elders.[d] The elders should pour oil on him[n] in the name of the Lord and pray for him. [15]And the prayer that is said with faith will make the sick person well. The Lord will heal him. And if he has sinned, God will forgive him. [16]Confess your sins to each other and pray for each other. Do this so that God can heal you. When a good man prays, great things happen. [17]Elijah was a man just like us. He prayed that it would not rain. And it did not rain on the land for three and a half years! [18]Then Elijah prayed again. And the rain came down from the sky, and the land grew crops again.

[19]My brothers, one of you may wander away from the truth. And someone may help him come back. [20]Remember this: Anyone who brings a sinner back from the wrong way will save that sinner's soul from death. By doing this, that person will cause many sins to be forgiven.

The First Letter of
PETER

1 From Peter, an apostle[d] of Jesus Christ.

To God's chosen people who are away from their homes. You are scattered all around the countries of Pontus, Galatia, Cappadocia, Asia, and Bithynia. [2]God planned long ago to choose you by making you his holy people. Making you holy is the Spirit's[d] work. God wanted you to obey him and to be made clean by the blood of the death of Jesus Christ. Grace and peace be yours more and more.

[3]Praise be to the God and Father of our Lord Jesus Christ. God has great mercy, and because of his mercy he gave us a new life. He gave us a living hope because Jesus Christ rose from death. [4]Now we hope for the blessings God has for his children. These blessings are kept for you in heaven. They cannot be destroyed or be spoiled or lose their beauty. [5]God's power protects you through your faith, and it keeps you safe until your salvation comes. That salvation is ready to be given to you at the end of time. [6]This makes you very happy. But now for a short time different kinds of troubles may make you sad. [7]These troubles come to prove that your faith is pure. This purity of faith is worth more than gold. Gold can be proved to be pure by fire, but gold will ruin. But the purity of your faith will bring you praise and glory and honor when Jesus Christ comes again. [8]You have not seen Christ, but still you love him. You cannot see him now, but you believe in him. You are filled with a joy that cannot be explained. And that joy is full of glory. [9]Your faith has a goal, to save your souls. And you are receiving that goal—your salvation.

[10]The prophets[d] searched carefully and tried to learn about this salvation. They spoke about the grace that was coming to you. [11]The Spirit[d] of Christ was in the prophets. And the Spirit was telling about the sufferings that would happen to Christ and about the glory that would come after those sufferings. The prophets tried to learn about what the Spirit was showing them. They tried to learn when those things would happen and what the world would be like at that time. [12]It was shown to them that their service was not for themselves. It was for you. They were serving you when they told about the truths you have now heard. The men who preached the Good News[d] to you told you those things. They did it with the help of the Holy Spirit that was sent from heaven. These are truths that even the angels want very much to know about.

[13]So prepare your minds for service and have self-control. All your hope should be for the gift of grace that will be yours when Jesus Christ comes again. [14]In the past you did not understand, so you did the evil things you

---

5:14 **pour oil on him** Oil was used like medicine, so that is probably how the believers used it.

wanted. But now you are children of God who obey. So do not live as you lived in the past. [15]But be holy in all that you do, just as God is holy. God is the One who called you. [16]It is written in the Scriptures:[c] "You must be holy, because I am holy."[n]

[17]You pray to God and call him Father. And this Father judges each man's work equally. So while you are here on earth, you should live with respect for God. [18]You know that in the past you were living in a worthless way. You got that way of living from the people who lived before you. But you were saved from that useless life. You were bought, but not with something that ruins like gold or silver. [19]You were bought with the precious blood of the death of Christ, who was like a pure and perfect lamb. [20]Christ was chosen before the world was made. But he was shown to the world in these last times for you. [21]You believe in God through Christ. God raised Christ from death and gave him glory. So your faith and your hope are in God.

[22]Now you have made yourselves pure by obeying the truth. Now you can have true love for your brothers. So love each other deeply with all your heart. [23]You have been born again. This new life did not come from something that dies, but from something that cannot die. You were born again through God's living message that continues forever. [24]The Scripture says,

"All people are like the grass.
　And all their strength is like the
　　flowers of the field.
　The grass dies and the flowers fall.
[25]But the word of the Lord will live
　forever." *Isaiah 40:6-8*
And this is the word that was preached to you.

2 So then, get rid of all evil and all lying. Do not be a hypocrite.[d] Do not be jealous or speak evil of others. Put all these things out of your life. [2]As newborn babies want milk, you should want the pure and simple teaching. By it you can grow up and be saved. [3]For you have already examined and seen how good the Lord is.

[4]The Lord Jesus is the "stone"[n] that lives. The people of the world did not want this stone. But he was the stone God chose. To God he was worth much.

So come to him. [5]You also are like living stones. Let yourselves be used to build a spiritual temple—to be holy priests who offer spiritual sacrifices to God. He will accept those sacrifices through Jesus Christ. [6]The Scripture[d] says:

"I will put a stone in the ground in
　Jerusalem.
　Everything will be built on this
　　important and precious rock.
　Anyone who trusts in him
　　will never be disappointed."
Isaiah 28:16
[7]This stone is worth much to you who believe. But to the people who do not believe, he is

"the stone that the builders did not
　want.
　It has become the cornerstone."[d]
Psalm 118:22
[8]To people who do not believe, he is
"a stone that causes people to
　stumble.
　It is a rock that makes them fall."
Isaiah 8:14
They stumble because they do not obey what God says. This is what God planned to happen to them.

[9]But you are chosen people. You are the King's priests. You are a holy nation. You are a nation that belongs to God alone. God chose you to tell about the wonderful things he has done. He called you out of darkness into his wonderful light. [10]At one time you were not God's people. But now you are his people. In the past you had never received mercy. But now you have received God's mercy.

[11]Dear friends, you are like visitors and strangers in this world. So I beg you to stay away from the evil things your bodies want to do. These things fight against your soul. [12]People who do not believe are living all around you. They might say that you are doing wrong. So live good lives. Then they will see the good things you do, and they will give glory to God on the day when Christ comes again.

[13]Obey the people who have authority in this world. Do this for the Lord. Obey the king, who is the highest authority. [14]And obey the leaders who are sent by the king. They are sent to punish those who do wrong and to praise those who do right. [15]So when you do good, you stop foolish people from saying stupid things about you. This is what God

---

1:16 "You must be . . . holy." Quotation from Leviticus 11:45; 19:2; 20:7. **2:4 "stone"** The most important stone in God's spiritual temple or house (his people).

wants. [16]Live as free men. But do not use your freedom as an excuse to do evil. Live as servants of God. [17]Show respect for all people. Love the brothers and sisters of God's family. Respect God. Honor the king.

[18]Slaves, accept the authority of your masters. Do this with all respect. You should obey masters who are good and kind, and you should obey masters who are bad. [19]A person might have to suffer even when he has done nothing wrong. But if he thinks of God and bears the pain, this pleases God. [20]If you are punished for doing wrong, there is no reason to praise you for bearing punishment. But if you suffer for doing good, and you are patient, then that pleases God. [21]That is what you were called to do. Christ suffered for you. He gave you an example to follow. So you should do as he did.

[22]"He did no sin.
　　He never lied."   *Isaiah 53:9*
[23]People insulted Christ, but he did not insult them in return. Christ suffered, but he did not threaten. He let God take care of him. God is the One who judges rightly. [24]Christ carried our sins in his body on the cross. He did this so that we would stop living for sin and start living for what is right. And we are healed because of his wounds. [25]You were like sheep that went the wrong way. But now you have come back to the Shepherd and Protector of your souls.

3 In the same way, you wives should accept the authority of your husbands. Then, if some husbands have not obeyed God's teaching, they will be persuaded to believe. You will not need to say a word to them. They will be persuaded by the way their wives live. [2]Your husbands will see the pure lives that you live with your respect for God. [3]It is not fancy hair, gold jewelry, or fine clothes that should make you beautiful. [4]No, your beauty should come from within you—the beauty of a gentle and quiet spirit. This beauty will never disappear, and it is worth very much to God. [5]It was the same with the holy women who lived long ago and followed God. They made themselves beautiful in this way. They accepted the authority of their husbands. [6]Sarah obeyed Abraham, her husband, and called him her master. And you women are true children of Sarah if you always do what is right and are not afraid.

[7]In the same way, you husbands should live with your wives in an understanding way. You should show respect to them. They are weaker than you. But God gives them the same blessing that he gives you—the grace that gives true life. Do this so that nothing will stop your prayers.

[8]Finally, all of you should live together in peace. Try to understand each other. Love each other as brothers. Be kind and humble. [9]Do not do wrong to a person to pay him back for doing wrong to you. Or do not insult someone to pay him back for insulting you. But ask God to bless that person. Do this, because you yourselves were called to receive a blessing. [10]The Scripture[d] says,

"A person must do these things
　　to enjoy life and have many,
　　　happy days.
He must not say evil things.
　　He must not tell lies.
[11]He must stop doing evil and do good.
　　He must look for peace and work for it.
[12]The Lord sees the good people.
　　He listens to their prayers.
But the Lord is against
　　those who do evil."   *Psalm 34:12-16*
[13]If you are always trying to do good, no one can really hurt you. [14]But you may suffer for doing right. Even if that happens, you are blessed.

"Don't be afraid of the things they fear.
　　Do not dread those things.
[15]But respect Christ as the holy Lord in your hearts."   *Isaiah 8:12-13*
Always be ready to answer everyone who asks you to explain about the hope you have. [16]But answer in a gentle way and with respect. Always feel that you are doing right. Then, those who speak evil of your good life in Christ will be made ashamed. [17]It is better to suffer for doing good than for doing wrong. Yes, it is better, if that is what God wants. [18]Christ himself died for you. And that one death paid for your sins. He was not guilty, but he died for those who are guilty. He did this to bring you all to God. His body was killed, but he was made alive in the spirit. [19]And in the spirit he went and preached to the spirits in prison. [20]These were the spirits who refused to obey God long ago in the time of Noah. God was waiting patiently for them while Noah was building the

boat. Only a few people—eight in all—were saved by water. [21]That water is like baptism that now saves you—not the washing of dirt from the body, but the promise made to God from a good heart. And this is because Jesus Christ was raised from death. [22]Now Jesus has gone into heaven and is at God's right side. He rules over angels, authorities, and powers.

4Christ suffered while he was in his body. So you should strengthen yourselves with the same way of thinking Christ had. The person who has suffered in his body is finished with sin. [2]Strengthen yourselves so that you will live your lives here on earth doing what God wants, not doing the evil things that people want. [3]In the past you wasted too much time doing what the non-believers like to do. You were guilty of sexual sins and had evil desires. You were getting drunk, you had wild and drunken parties, and you did wrong by worshiping idols. [4]Non-believers think it is strange that you do not do the many wild and wasteful things that they do. And so they insult you. [5]But they will have to explain about what they have done. They must explain to God who is ready to judge the living and the dead. [6]The Good News[d] was preached to those who are now dead. By their dying, they were judged like all men. But the Good News was preached to them so that they could live in the spirit as God lives.

[7]The time is near when all things will end. So keep your minds clear, and control yourselves. Then you will be able to pray. [8]Most importantly, love each other deeply. Love has a way of not looking at others' sins. [9]Open your homes to each other, without complaining. [10]Each of you received a spiritual gift. God has shown you his grace in giving you different gifts. And you are like servants who are responsible for using God's gifts. So be good servants and use your gifts to serve each other. [11]Anyone who speaks should speak words from God. The person who serves should serve with the strength that God gives. You should do these things so that in everything God will be praised through Jesus Christ. Power and glory belong to him forever and ever. Amen.

[12]My friends, do not be surprised at the painful things you are now suffer-

ing. These things are testing your faith. So do not think that something strange is happening to you. [13]But you should be happy that you are sharing in Christ's sufferings. You will be happy and full of joy when Christ comes again in glory. [14]When people insult you because you follow Christ, then you are blessed. You are blessed because the glorious Spirit,[d] the Spirit of God, is with you. [15]Do not suffer for murder, theft, or any other crime, nor because you trouble other people. [16]But if you suffer because you are a Christian, then do not be ashamed. You should praise God because you wear that name. [17]It is time for judgment to begin, and it will begin with God's family. If that judging begins with us, what will happen to those people who do not obey the Good News[d] of God?

[18]"It is very hard for a good person
  to be saved.
Then the wicked person and
  the sinner will surely be lost!"[n]

[19]So then those who suffer as God wants them to should trust their souls to him. God is the One who made them, and they can trust him. So they should continue to do what is right.

5Now I have something to say to the elders[d] in your group. I am also an elder. I myself have seen Christ's sufferings. And I will share in the glory that will be shown to us. I beg you to [2]take care of God's flock, his people, that you are responsible for. Watch over it because you want to, not because you are forced to do it. That is how God wants it. Do it because you are happy to serve, not because you want money. [3]Do not be like a ruler over people you are responsible for. Be good examples to them. [4]Then when Christ, the Head Shepherd, comes, you will get a crown. This crown will be glorious, and it will never lose its beauty.

[5]In the same way, younger men should be willing to be under older men. And all of you should be very humble with each other.

"God is against the proud,
  but he gives grace to the
    humble."   *Proverbs 3:34*

[6]So be humble under God's powerful hand. Then he will lift you up when the right time comes. [7]Give all your worries to him, because he cares for you.

4:18 "It . . . lost!" Quotation from Proverbs 11:31 in the Septuagint, the Greek version of the Old Testament.

⁸Control yourselves and be careful! The devil is your enemy. And he goes around like a roaring lion looking for someone to eat. ⁹Refuse to give in to the devil. Stand strong in your faith. You know that your Christian brothers and sisters all over the world are having the same sufferings you have.

¹⁰Yes, you will suffer for a short time. But after that, God will make everything right. He will make you strong. He will support you and keep you from falling. He is the God who gives all grace. He called you to share in his glory in Christ.

That glory will continue forever. ¹¹All power is his forever and ever. Amen.

¹²I wrote this short letter with the help of Silas. I know that he is a faithful brother in Christ. I wrote to comfort and encourage you. I wanted to tell you that this is the true grace of God. Stand strong in that grace.

¹³The church in Babylon sends you greetings. They were chosen the same as you. Mark, my son in Christ, also greets you. ¹⁴Give each other a kiss of Christian love when you meet.

Peace to all of you who are in Christ.

The Second Letter of
PETER

1 From Simon Peter, a servant and apostleᵈ of Jesus Christ.

To you who have received a faith as valuable as ours. You received that faith because our God and Savior Jesus Christ is fair and does what is right.

²Grace and peace be given to you more and more. You will have grace and peace because you truly know God and Jesus our Lord.

³Jesus has the power of God. His power has given us everything we need to live and to serve God. We have these things because we know him. Jesus called us by his glory and goodness. ⁴Through his glory and goodness, he gave us the very great and rich gifts he promised us. With those gifts you can share in being like God. And so the world will not ruin you with its evil desires.

⁵Because you have these blessings, you should try as much as you can to add these things to your lives: to your faith, add goodness; and to your goodness, add knowledge; ⁶and to your knowledge, add self-control; and to your self-control, add the ability to hold on; and to your ability to hold on, add service for God; ⁷and to your service for God, add kindness for your brothers and sisters in Christ; and to this kindness, add love. ⁸If all these things are in you and are growing, they will help you never to be useless. They will help your knowledge of our Lord Jesus Christ make your lives better. ⁹But if anyone does not have these things, he cannot see clearly. He is blind. He has forgotten

that he was made clean from his past sins.

¹⁰My brothers, God called you and chose you to be his. Try hard to show that you really are God's chosen people. If you do all these things, you will never fall. ¹¹And you will be given a very great welcome into the kingdom of our Lord and Savior Jesus Christ. That kingdom continues forever.

¹²You know these things, and you are very strong in the truth. But I will always help you to remember these things. ¹³I think it is right for me to help you remember while I am still living here on earth. ¹⁴I know that I must soon leave this body. Our Lord Jesus Christ has shown me that. ¹⁵I will try the best I can to help you remember these things always. I want you to be able to remember them even after I am gone.

¹⁶We have told you about the powerful coming of our Lord Jesus Christ. What we told you were not just smart stories that someone invented. But we saw the greatness of Jesus with our own eyes. ¹⁷Jesus heard the voice of God, the Greatest Glory. That was when Jesus received honor and glory from God the Father. The voice said, "This is my Son, and I love him. I am very pleased with him." ¹⁸We heard that voice. It came from heaven while we were with Jesus on the holy mountain.

¹⁹This makes us more sure about the message the prophetsᵈ gave. And it is good for you to follow closely what they said. Their message is like a light shining in a dark place. That light shines

until the day begins and the morning star rises in your hearts. [20]Most of all, you must understand this: No prophecy in the Scriptures[d] ever comes from the prophet's own interpretation. [21]No prophecy ever came from what a man wanted to say. But men led by the Holy Spirit[d] spoke words from God.

2 There used to be false prophets[d] among God's people, just as there are now. And you will have some false teachers in your group. They will secretly teach things that are wrong— teachings that will cause people to be lost. They will even refuse to accept the Master, Jesus, who bought their freedom. And so they will quickly destroy themselves. [2]Many will follow their evil ways and say evil things about the Way of truth. [3]Those false teachers only want your money. So they will use you by telling you what is not true. But God has already judged them guilty. And they will not escape the One who will destroy them.

[4]When angels sinned, God did not let them go free without punishment. God sent them to hell and put them in caves of darkness. They are being held there to be judged. [5]And God punished the evil people who lived long ago. He brought a flood to the world that was full of people who were against him. But God saved Noah and seven other people with him. Noah was a man who preached about being right with God. [6]And God also punished the evil cities of Sodom and Gomorrah.[n] He burned those cities until there was nothing left but ashes. He made those cities an example to show what will happen to those who are against God. [7]But God saved Lot from those cities. Lot, a good man, was troubled because of the dirty lives of evil people. [8](Lot was a good man, but he lived with evil people every day. His good heart was hurt by the evil things that he saw and heard.) [9]And so the Lord knows how to save those who serve him. He will save them when troubles come. And the Lord will hold evil people and punish them, while waiting for the Judgment Day. [10]That punishment is especially for those who live by doing the evil things their sinful selves want, and for those who hate the Lord's authority.

These false teachers do anything they want and brag about it. They are not afraid to say bad things about the glorious angels. [11]The angels are much stronger and more powerful than false teachers. But even the angels do not accuse them with insults before the Lord. [12]But these men say bad things about what they do not understand. They are like animals that act without thinking. These animals are born to be caught and killed. And, like wild animals, these false teachers will be destroyed. [13]They have caused many people to suffer; so they themselves will suffer. That is their pay for what they have done. They take pleasure in doing evil things openly. So they are like dirty spots and stains among you. They bring shame to you in the meals that you eat together. [14]Every time they look at a woman they want her. Their desire for sin is never satisfied. They lead weak people into the trap of sin. They have taught their hearts to be selfish. God will punish them. [15]These false teachers left the right road and lost their way. They followed the way that Balaam went. Balaam was the son of Beor, who loved being paid for doing wrong. [16]But a donkey told Balaam that he was sinning. And the donkey is an animal that cannot talk. But the donkey spoke with a man's voice and stopped the prophet's crazy thinking.

[17]Those false teachers are like rivers that have no water. They are like clouds blown by a storm. A place in the blackest darkness has been kept for them. [18]They brag with words that mean nothing. By their evil desires they lead people into the trap of sin. They lead away people who are just beginning to escape from other people who live in error. [19]They promise them freedom, but they themselves are not free. They are slaves of things that will be destroyed. For a person is a slave of anything that controls him. [20]They were made free from the evil in the world by knowing our Lord and Savior Jesus Christ. But if they return to evil things and those things control them, then it is worse for them than it was before. [21]Yes, it would be better for them to have never known the right way. That would be better than to know the right way and then to turn away from the holy teaching that was given to them. [22]What they did is like this true saying: "A dog eats what it throws up."[n] And, "After a pig

---

2:6 Sodom and Gomorrah Two cities God destroyed because the people were so evil. **2:22 "A dog . . . up."** Quotation from Proverbs 26:11.

is washed, it goes back and rolls in the mud."

3 My friends, this is the second letter I have written to you. I wrote both letters to you to help your honest minds remember something. [2] I want you to remember the words that the holy prophets[d] spoke in the past. And remember the command that our Lord and Savior gave us through your apostles.[d] [3] It is important for you to understand what will happen in the last days. People will laugh at you. They will live doing the evil things they want to do. [4] They will say, "Jesus promised to come again. Where is he? Our fathers have died. But the world continues the way it has been since it was made." [5] But they do not want to remember what happened long ago. God spoke and made heaven and earth. He made the earth from water and with water. [6] Then the world was flooded and destroyed with water. [7] And that same word of God is keeping heaven and earth that we have now. They are being kept to be destroyed by fire. They are being kept for the Judgment Day and the destruction of all who are against God.

[8] But do not forget this one thing, dear friends: To the Lord one day is as a thousand years, and a thousand years is as one day. [9] The Lord is not slow in doing what he promised—the way some people understand slowness. But God is being patient with you. He does not want anyone to be lost. He wants everyone to change his heart and life.

[10] But the day the Lord comes again

will be a surprise, like a thief. The skies will disappear with a loud noise. Everything in the skies will be destroyed by fire. And the earth and everything in it will be burned up.[n] [11] In that way everything will be destroyed. So what kind of people should you be? You should live holy lives and serve God. [12] You should wait for the day of God and look forward to its coming. When that day comes, the skies will be destroyed with fire, and everything in the skies will melt with heat. [13] But God made a promise to us. And we are waiting for what he promised—a new heaven and a new earth where goodness lives.

[14] Dear friends, we are waiting for this to happen. So try as hard as you can to be without sin and without fault. Try to be at peace with God. [15] Remember that we are saved because our Lord is patient. Our dear brother Paul told you the same thing when he wrote to you with the wisdom that God gave him. [16] Paul writes about this in all his letters. Sometimes there are things in Paul's letters that are hard to understand. And some people explain these things falsely. They are ignorant and weak in faith. They also falsely explain the other Scriptures.[d] But they are destroying themselves by doing that.

[17] Dear friends, you already know about this. So be careful. Do not let those evil people lead you away by the wrong they do. Be careful so that you will not fall from your strong faith. [18] But grow in the grace and knowledge of our Lord and Savior Jesus Christ. Glory be to him now and forever! Amen.

The First Letter of
JOHN

1 We write you now about something that has always existed.

We have heard.

We have seen with our own eyes.

We have watched,

and we have touched with our hands.

We write to you about the Word[n] that gives life. [2] He who gives life was shown to us. We saw him, and we can give

proof about it. And now we tell you that he has life that continues forever. The one who gives this life was with God the Father. God showed him to us. [3] Now we tell you what we have seen and heard because we want you to have fellowship with us. The fellowship we share together is with God the Father and his Son, Jesus Christ. [4] We write this to you so that you can be full of joy with us.

3:10 will be burned up Many Greek copies say, "will be found." One copy says, "will disappear." **1:1 Word** The Greek word is "logos," meaning any kind of communication. It could be translated "message." Here, it means Christ. Christ was the way God told people about himself.

[5]Here is the message we have heard from God and now tell to you: God is light,[n] and in him there is no darkness at all. [6]So if we say that we have fellowship with God, but we continue living in darkness, then we are liars. We do not follow the truth. [7]God is in the light. We should live in the light, too. If we live in the light, we share fellowship with each other. And when we live in the light, the blood of the death of Jesus, God's Son, is making us clean from every sin.

[8]If we say that we have no sin, we are fooling ourselves, and the truth is not in us. [9]But if we confess our sins, he will forgive our sins. We can trust God. He does what is right. He will make us clean from all the wrongs we have done. [10]If we say that we have not sinned, then we make God a liar. We do not accept God's true teaching.

[2] My dear children, I write this letter to you so that you will not sin. But if anyone does sin, we have Jesus Christ to help us. He is the Righteous One. He defends us before God the Father. [2]Jesus is the way our sins are taken away. And Jesus is the way that all people can have their sins taken away, too.

[3]If we obey what God has told us to do, then we are sure that we truly know God. [4]If someone says, "I know God!" but does not obey God's commands, then he is a liar. The truth is not in him. [5]But if someone obeys God's teaching, then God's love has truly arrived at its goal in him. This is how we know that we are following God: [6]Whoever says that God lives in him must live as Jesus lived.

[7]My dear friends, I am not writing a new command to you. It is the same command you have had since the beginning. It is the teaching you have already heard. [8]But I am writing a new command to you. This command is true; you can see its truth in Jesus and in yourselves. The darkness is passing away, and the true light is already shining.

[9]Someone says, "I am in the light."[n] But if he hates his brother, he is still in the darkness. [10]Whoever loves his brother lives in the light, and there is nothing in him that will cause him to do wrong. [11]But whoever hates his brother is in darkness. He lives in darkness and does not know where he is going. The darkness has made him blind.

[12]I write to you, dear children,
 because your sins are forgiven
  through Christ.
[13]I write to you, fathers,
 because you know the One who
  existed from the beginning.
 I write to you, young men,
 because you have defeated the
  Evil One.
[14]I write to you, children,
 because you know the Father.
 I write to you, fathers,
 because you know the One who
  existed from the beginning.
 I write to you, young men,
 because you are strong;
  the word of God lives in you,
 and you have defeated the Evil
  One.

[15]Do not love the world or the things in the world. If anyone loves the world, the love of the Father is not in him. [16]These are the evil things in the world: wanting things to please our sinful selves, wanting the sinful things we see, being too proud of the things we have. But none of those things comes from the Father. All of them come from the world. [17]The world is passing away. And everything that people want in the world is passing away. But the person who does what God wants lives forever.

[18]My dear children, the end is near! You have heard that the Enemy of Christ[d] is coming. And now many enemies of Christ are already here. So we know that the end is near. [19]Those enemies of Christ were in our group. But they left us. They did not really belong with us. If they were really part of our group, then they would have stayed with us. But they left. This shows that none of them really belonged with us.

[20]You have the gift[n] that the Holy One gave you. So you all know the truth. [21]Why do I write to you? Do I write because you do not know the truth? No, I write this letter because you do know the truth. And you know that no lie comes from the truth.

[22]So who is the liar? It is the person who says Jesus is not the Christ. A person who says Jesus is not the Christ is the enemy of Christ. He does not believe in the Father or in his Son. [23]If anyone

1:5; 2:9 light This word is used to show what God is like. It means goodness or truth. **2:20 gift** This might mean the Holy Spirit. Or it might mean teaching or truth as in verse 24.

does not believe in the Son, he does not have the Father. But whoever accepts the Son has the Father, too.

²⁴Be sure that you continue to follow the teaching that you heard from the beginning. If you continue in that teaching, you will stay in the Son and in the Father. ²⁵And this is what the Son promised to us—life forever.

²⁶I am writing this letter about those people who are trying to lead you the wrong way. ²⁷Christ gave you a special gift. You still have this gift in you. So you do not need any other teacher. The gift he gave you teaches you about everything. This gift is true, not false. So continue to live in Christ, as his gift taught you.

²⁸Yes, my dear children, live in him. If we do this, we can be without fear on the day when Christ comes back. We will not need to hide and be ashamed when he comes. ²⁹You know that Christ is righteous. So you know that all who do what is right are God's children.

3 The Father has loved us so much! He loved us so much that we are called children of God. And we really are his children. But the people in the world do not understand that we are God's children, because they have not known him. ²Dear friends, now we are children of God. We have not yet been shown what we will be in the future. But we know that when Christ comes again, we will be like him. We will see him as he really is. ³Christ is pure. And every person who has this hope in Christ keeps himself pure like Christ.

⁴When a person sins, he breaks God's law. Yes, sinning is the same as living against God's law. ⁵You know that Christ came to take away sins. There is no sin in Christ. ⁶So the person who lives in Christ does not go on sinning. If he goes on sinning, he has never really understood Christ and has never known him.

⁷Dear children, do not let any person lead you the wrong way. Christ is righteous. To be like Christ, a person must do what is right. ⁸The devil has been sinning since the beginning. Anyone who continues to sin belongs to the devil. The Son of God came for this purpose: to destroy the devil's work.

⁹When God makes someone his child, that person does not go on sinning. The

new life God gave that person stays in him. So he is not able to go on sinning, because he has become a child of God. ¹⁰So we can see who God's children are and who the devil's children are. Those who do not do what is right are not children of God. And anyone who does not love his brother is not a child of God.

¹¹This is the teaching you have heard from the beginning: We must love each other. ¹²Do not be like Cain who belonged to the Evil One. Cain killed his brother. He killed his brother because the things Cain did were evil, and the things his brother did were good.

¹³Brothers, do not be surprised when the people of this world hate you. ¹⁴We know that we have left death and have come into life. We know this because we love our brothers in Christ. Whoever does not love is still in death. ¹⁵Everyone who hates his brother is a murderer.ᵇ And you know that no murderer has eternal life in him. ¹⁶This is how we know what real love is: Jesus gave his life for us. So we should give our lives for our brothers. ¹⁷Suppose a believer is rich enough to have all that he needs. He sees his brother in Christ who is poor and does not have what he needs. What if the believer does not help the poor brother? Then the believer does not have God's love in his heart. ¹⁸My children, our love should not be only words and talk. Our love must be true love. And we should show that love by what we do.

¹⁹⁻²⁰This is the way we know that we belong to the way of truth. When our hearts make us feel guilty, we can still have peace before God. God is greater than our hearts, and he knows everything.

²¹My dear friends, if we do not feel that we are doing wrong, we can be without fear when we come to God. ²²And God gives us the things we ask for. We receive these things because we obey God's commands, and we do what pleases him. ²³This is what God commands: that we believe in his Son, Jesus Christ, and that we love each other, just as he commanded. ²⁴The person who obeys God's commands lives in God. And God lives in him. How do we know that God lives in us? We know because of the Spiritᵈ whom God gave us.

3:15 Everyone . . . murderer. If a person hates his brother in Christ, then in his mind he has killed his brother. Jesus taught about this sin to his followers (Matthew 5:21-26).

4 My dear friends, many false prophets[d] are in the world now. So do not believe every spirit. But test the spirits to see if they are from God. [2]This is how you can know God's Spirit:[c] One spirit says, "I believe that Jesus is the Christ who came to earth and became a man." That Spirit is from God. [3]Another spirit refuses to say this about Jesus. That spirit is not from God but is the spirit of the Enemy of Christ. You have heard that the Enemy of Christ is coming. And now he is already in the world.

[4]My dear children, you belong to God. So you have defeated them because God's Spirit, who is in you, is greater than the devil, who is in the world. [5]And they belong to the world. What they say is from the world, and the world listens to them. [6]But we are from God, and those who know God listen to us. But those who are not from God do not listen to us. That is how we know the Spirit that is true and the spirit that is false.

[7]Dear friends, we should love each other, because love comes from God. The person who loves has become God's child and knows God. [8]Whoever does not love does not know God, because God is love. [9]This is how God showed his love to us: He sent his only Son into the world to give us life through him. [10]True love is God's love for us, not our love for God. God sent his Son to be the way to take away our sins.

[11]That is how much God loved us, dear friends! So we also must love each other. [12]No one has ever seen God. But if we love each other, God lives in us. If we love each other, God's love has reached its goal. It is made perfect in us.

[13]We know that we live in God and God lives in us. We know this because God gave us his Spirit.[c] [14]We have seen that the Father sent his Son to be the Savior of the world. That is what we teach. [15]If someone says, "I believe that Jesus is the Son of God," then God lives in him. And he lives in God. [16]And so we know the love that God has for us, and we trust that love.

God is love. Whoever lives in love lives in God, and God lives in him. [17]If God's love is made perfect in us, then we can be without fear on the day God judges us. We will be without fear, because in this world we are like him. [18]Where God's love is, there is no fear, because God's perfect love takes away fear. It is punishment that makes a person fear. So love is not made perfect in the person who has fear.

[19]We love because God first loved us. [20]If someone says, "I love God," but hates his brother, he is a liar. He can see his brother, but he hates him. So he cannot love God, whom he has never seen. [21]And God gave us this command: Whoever loves God must also love his brother.

5 Everyone who believes that Jesus is the Christ[d] is God's child. The person who loves the Father also loves the Father's children. [2]How do we know that we love God's children? We know because we love God and we obey his commands. [3]Loving God means obeying his commands. And God's commands are not too hard for us. [4]Everyone who is a child of God has the power to win against the world. It is our faith that wins the victory against the world. [5]So the one who wins against the world is the person who believes that Jesus is the Son of God.

[6]Jesus Christ is the One who came with water[n] and with blood.[n] He did not come by water only. He came by both water and blood. And the Spirit[d] says that this is true. The Spirit is the truth. [7]So there are three witnesses that tell us about Jesus: [8]the Spirit, the water, and the blood. These three witnesses agree. [9]We believe people when they say something is true. But what God says is more important. And he has told us the truth about his own Son. [10]Anyone who believes in the Son of God has the truth that God told us. Anyone who does not believe makes God a liar. He does not believe what God told us about his Son. [11]This is what God told us: God has given us eternal life, and this life is in his Son. [12]Whoever has the Son has life. But the person who does not have the Son of God does not have life.

[13]I write this letter to you who believe in the Son of God. I write so that you will know that you have eternal life now. [14]We can come to God with no doubts. This means that when we ask God for things (and those things agree with what God wants for us), then God cares about what we say. [15]God listens to us every time we ask him. So we know that

---

5:6 water This probably means the water of Jesus' baptism.   **5:6 blood** This probably means the blood of Jesus' death.

he gives us the things that we ask from him.

[16] Suppose someone sees his brother in Christ sinning (sin that does not lead to eternal death). That person should pray for his brother who is sinning. Then God will give the brother life. I am talking about people whose sin does not lead to eternal death. There is sin that leads to death. I do not mean that a person should pray about that sin. [17] Doing wrong is always sin. But there is sin that does not lead to eternal death.

[18] We know that anyone who is God's child does not continue to sin. The Son of God keeps him safe, and the Evil One cannot hurt him. [19] We know that we belong to God. But the Evil One controls the whole world. [20] And we know that the Son of God has come and has given us understanding. Now we can know God, the One who is true. And our lives are in that true God and in his Son, Jesus Christ. He is the true God, and he is eternal life. [21] So, dear children, keep yourselves away from false gods.

The Second Letter of
JOHN

From the Elder.[n] To the chosen lady[n] and to her children:

I love all of you in the truth.[n] Also, all those who know the truth love you. [2] We love you because of the truth—the truth that lives in us and will be with us forever.

[3] Grace, mercy, and peace will be with us from God the Father and from his Son, Jesus Christ. And may we have these blessings in truth and love.

[4] I was very happy to learn about some of your children. I am happy that they are following the way of truth, as the Father commanded us. [5] And now, dear lady, I tell you: We should all love each other. This is not a new command. It is the same command we have had from the beginning. [6] And loving means living the way he commanded us to live. And God's command is this: that you live a life of love. You have heard this command from the beginning.

[7] Many false teachers are in the world now. They refuse to say that Jesus Christ came to earth and became a man. Anyone who refuses to say this is a false teacher and an enemy of Christ. [8] Be careful! Do not lose the reward that you have worked for. Be careful, so that you will receive your full reward.

[9] A person must continue to follow only the teaching of Christ. If he goes beyond Christ's teaching, then he does not have God. But if he continues following the teaching of Christ, then he has both the Father and the Son. [10] If someone comes to you, but does not bring this teaching, then do not accept him into your house. Do not welcome him. [11] If you accept him, you are helping him with his evil work.

[12] I have much to say to you, but I do not want to use paper and ink. Instead, I hope to come visit you. Then we can be together and talk. That will make us very happy. [13] The children of your chosen sister[n] send you their love.

1 **Elder** This is probably John the apostle. "Elder" means an older man. It can also mean a special leader in the church (as in Titus 1:5). 1 **lady** This might mean a woman. Or, in this letter, it might mean a church. If it is a church, then "her children" would be the people of the church. 1 **truth** The truth or "Good News" about Jesus Christ that joins all believers together. 13 **sister** Sister of the "lady" in verse 1. This might be another woman or another church.

The Third Letter of
JOHN

From the Elder.[n]
To my dear friend Gaius whom I love in the truth:[n]

[2] My dear friend, I know your soul is doing well. I pray that you are doing fine in every way and that your health is good. [3] Some brothers in Christ came and told me about the truth in your life. They said that you are following the way of truth. This made me very happy. [4] It always gives me the greatest joy when I hear that my children are following the way of truth.

[5] My dear friend, it is good that you continue to help the brothers. You are helping those that you do not even know! [6] These brothers told the church about the love you have. Please help them to continue their trip. Help them in a way that will please God. [7] They started out on their trip to serve Christ. They did not accept any help from those who are not believers. [8] So we should help these brothers. And when we do, we share in their work for the truth.

[9] I wrote a letter to the church. But Diotrephes will not listen to what we say. He always wants to be their leader. [10] When I come, I will talk about what Diotrephes is doing. He lies and says evil things about us. But that is not all he does. He refuses to help those who are working to serve Christ. He also stops those who want to help the brothers and puts them out of the church.

[11] My dear friend, do not follow what is bad; follow what is good. He who does what is good is from God. But he who does evil has never known God.

[12] Everyone says good things about Demetrius. And the truth agrees with what they say. Also, we say good about him. And you know that what we say is true.

[13] I have many things I want to tell you, but I do not want to use pen and ink. [14] I hope to visit you soon. Then we can be together and talk. [15] Peace to you. The friends here with me send their love. Please give our love to each one of the friends there.

The Letter of
JUDE

From Jude, a servant of Jesus Christ and a brother of James.

To all who have been called by God. God the Father loves you, and you have been kept safe in Jesus Christ.

[2] All mercy, peace, and love be yours.

[3] Dear friends, I wanted very much to write to you about the salvation we all share together. But I felt the need to write to you about something else: I want to encourage you to fight hard for the faith that God gave his holy people. God gave this faith once, and it is good for all time. [4] Some people have secretly entered your group. They have already been judged guilty for the things they are doing. Long ago the prophets[d] wrote about these people. They are against God. They have used the grace of our God in the wrong way—to do sinful things. They refuse to accept Jesus Christ, our only Master and Lord.

[5] I want to remind you of some things that you already know: Remember that the Lord saved his people by bringing them out of the land of Egypt. But later the Lord destroyed all those who did not believe. [6] And remember the angels who had power but did not keep it. They left their own home. So the Lord has kept these angels in darkness. They are bound with everlasting chains, to be judged on the great day. [7] Also remember the cities of Sodom and Gomorrah[n] and the other towns around them. They acted as the angels who did not obey God. Their towns were full of sexual sin and men having sexual relations with men. They suffer the punishment of eternal fire, as an example for all to see.

---

1 Elder This is probably John the apostle. "Elder" means an older man. It can also mean a special leader in the church (as Titus 1:5). **1 truth** The truth or "Good News" about Jesus Christ that joins all believers together. **7 Sodom and Gomorrah** Two cities God destroyed because the people were so evil.

[8]It is the same with these people who have entered your group. They are guided by dreams. They make themselves dirty with sin. They reject God's authority and say bad things against the glorious angels. [9]Not even the archangel[n] Michael did this. He argued with the devil about who would have the body of Moses. Michael did not dare to accuse the devil with insults. He said, "The Lord punish you." [10]But these people say bad things about what they do not understand. They do understand some things. But they understand them not by thinking, but by feeling, the way dumb animals understand things. And these are the very things that destroy them. [11]It will be bad for them. They have followed the way that Cain went. To make money, they have given themselves to doing the wrong that Balaam did. They have fought against God as Korah did. And like Korah, they will be destroyed. [12]They are like dirty spots in the special meals you share together. They eat with you and have no fear. They take care of only themselves. They are clouds without rain. The wind blows them around. They are trees that have no fruit when it is time and are pulled out of the ground. So they are dead two times. [13]They are like wild waves in the sea. These people do shameful things in the same way waves make foam. They are like stars that wander in the sky. A place in the blackest darkness has been kept for them forever.

[14]Enoch, the seventh descendant[d] from Adam, said this about these people: "Look, the Lord is coming with thousands and thousands of his holy angels. [15]The Lord will judge every person. He is coming to judge everyone and to punish all who are against God. He will punish them for all the evil they have done against him. And he will punish the sinners who are against God. He will punish them for all the evil things they have said against him."

[16]These people always complain and blame others. They always do the evil things they want to do. They brag about themselves. The only reason they say good things about other people is to get what they want.

[17]Dear friends, remember what the apostles[d] of our Lord Jesus Christ said before. [18]They said to you, "In the last times there will be people who laugh about God. They will do only what they want to do—things that are against God." [19]These are the people who divide you. They do only what their sinful selves want. They do not have the Spirit.[d]

[20]But dear friends, use your most holy faith to build yourselves up strong. Pray with the Holy Spirit. [21]Keep yourselves in God's love. Wait for the Lord Jesus Christ with his mercy to give you life forever.

[22]Show mercy to people who have doubts. [23]Save them. Take them out of the fire. Show mercy mixed with fear to others. Hate even their clothes which are dirty from sin.

[24]God is strong and can help you not to fall. He can bring you before his glory without any wrong in you and give you great joy. [25]He is the only God. He is the One who saves us. To him be glory, greatness, power, and authority through Jesus Christ our Lord for all time past, now, and forever. Amen.

THE REVELATION
of Jesus Christ

1 This is the revelation[n] of Jesus Christ. God gave this revelation to Jesus, to show his servants what must soon happen. And Jesus sent his angel to show it to his servant John. [2]John has told everything that he has seen. It is the truth that Jesus Christ told him; it is the message from God. [3]The one who reads the words of God's message is happy. And the people who hear this message and do what is written in it are happy. The time is near when all of this will happen.

[4]From John,

To the seven churches in the country of Asia:

Grace and peace to you from the One who is and was and is coming, and from

9 **archangel** The leader among God's angels or messengers.　1:1 **revelation** A making known of truth that has been hidden.

the seven spirits before his throne, [5] and from Jesus Christ. Jesus is the faithful witness. He is first among those raised from death. He is the ruler of the kings of the earth.

He is the One who loves us. And he is the One who made us free from our sins with the blood of his death. [6] He made us to be a kingdom of priests who serve God his Father. To Jesus Christ be glory and power forever and ever! Amen.

[7] Look, Jesus is coming with the clouds! Everyone will see him, even those who stabbed him. And all peoples of the earth will cry loudly because of him. Yes, this will happen! Amen.

[8] The Lord God says, "I am the Alpha and the Omega.[n] I am the One who is and was and is coming. I am the All-Powerful."

[9] I am John, and I am your brother in Christ. We are together in Jesus, and we share in these things: in suffering, in the kingdom, and in patience. I was on the island of Patmos[n] because I had preached God's message and the truth about Jesus. [10] On the Lord's day the Spirit[d] took control of me. I heard a loud voice behind me that sounded like a trumpet. [11] The voice said, "Write what you see and send that book to the seven churches: to Ephesus, Smyrna, Pergamum, Thyatira, Sardis, Philadelphia, and Laodicea."

[12] I turned to see who was talking to me. When I turned, I saw seven golden lampstands. [13] I saw someone among the lampstands who was "like a Son of Man."[n] He was dressed in a long robe. He had a gold band around his chest. [14] His head and hair were white like wool, as white as snow. His eyes were like flames of fire. [15] His feet were like bronze that glows hot in a furnace. His voice was like the noise of flooding water. [16] He held seven stars in his right hand. A sharp two-edged sword came out of his mouth. He looked like the sun shining at its brightest time.

[17] When I saw him, I fell down at his feet like a dead man. He put his right hand on me and said, "Do not be afraid! I am the First and the Last. [18] I am the One who lives. I was dead, but look: I am alive forever and ever! And I hold the keys of death and where the dead

are. [19] So write the things you see, what is now and what will happen later. [20] Here is the hidden meaning of the seven stars that you saw in my right hand and the seven golden lampstands that you saw: The seven lampstands are the seven churches. The seven stars are the angels of the seven churches.

2 "Write this to the angel of the church in Ephesus:

"The One who holds the seven stars in his right hand and walks among the seven golden lampstands says this to you. [2] I know what you do. You work hard, and you never give up. I know that you do not accept evil people. You have tested those who say that they are apostles[d] but really are not. You found that they are liars. [3] You continue to serve me. You have suffered troubles for my name, and you have not given up.

[4] "But I have this against you: You have left the love you had in the beginning. [5] So remember where you were before you fell. Change your hearts and do what you did at first. If you do not change, I will come to you. I will take away your lampstand from its place. [6] But there is something you do that is right: You hate what the Nicolaitans[n] do, as much as I.

[7] "Every person who has ears should listen to what the Spirit[d] says to the churches. To him who wins the victory I will give the right to eat the fruit from the tree of life. This tree is in the garden of God.

[8] "Write this to the angel of the church in Smyrna:

"The One who is the First and the Last says this to you. He is the One who died and came to life again. [9] I know your troubles. I know that you are poor, but really you are rich! I know the bad things that some people say about you. They say they are Jews, but they are not true Jews. They are a synagogue[d] that belongs to Satan. [10] Do not be afraid of what will happen to you. I tell you, the devil will put some of you in prison to test you. You will suffer for ten days. But be faithful, even if you have to die. If you are faithful, I will give you the crown of life.

[11] "Everyone who has ears should listen to what the Spirit[d] says to the

---

1:8 Alpha and the Omega The first and last letters in the Greek alphabet. This means "the beginning and the end." **1:9 Patmos** A small island in the Aegean Sea, near the coast of Asia Minor (modern Turkey). **1:13 "like . . . Man"** "Son of Man" is a name Jesus called himself. It showed he was God's Son, but he was also a man. See dictionary. **2:6 Nicolaitans** This is the name of a religious group that followed false beliefs and ideas.

churches. He who wins the victory will not be hurt by the second death.

[12]"Write this to the angel of the church in Pergamum:

"The One who has the sharp two-edged sword says this to you. [13]I know where you live. You live where Satan has his throne. But you are true to me. You did not refuse to tell about your faith in me even during the time of Antipas. Antipas was my faithful witness who was killed in your city. Your city is where Satan lives.

[14]"But I have a few things against you: You have some there who follow the teaching of Balaam. Balaam taught Balak how to cause the people of Israel to sin. They sinned by eating food offered to idols and by taking part in sexual sins. [15]You also have some who follow the teaching of the Nicolaitans.[n] [16]So change your hearts and lives! If you do not, I will come to you quickly and fight against them with the sword that comes out of my mouth.

[17]"Everyone who has ears should listen to what the Spirit[d] says to the churches!

"I will give the hidden manna[d] to everyone who wins the victory. I will also give him a white stone with a new name written on it. No one knows this new name except the one who receives it.

[18]"Write this to the angel of the church in Thyatira:

"The Son of God is saying these things. He is the One who has eyes that blaze like fire and feet like shining bronze. He says this to you: [19]I know what you do. I know about your love, your faith, your service, and your patience. I know that you are doing more now than you did at first. [20]But I have this against you: You let that woman Jezebel do what she wants. She says that she is a prophetess.[d] But she is leading my people away with her teaching. Jezebel leads them to take part in sexual sins and to eat food that is offered to idols. [21]I have given her time to change her heart and turn away from her sin. But she does not want to change. [22]And so I will throw her on a bed of suffering. And all those who take part in adultery[d] with her will suffer greatly. I will do this now if they do not turn away from the wrongs she does. [23]I will also kill her followers. Then all the churches will

know that I am the One who knows what people feel and think. And I will repay each of you for what you have done.

[24]"But others of you in Thyatira have not followed her teaching. You have not learned what some call Satan's deep secrets. This is what I say to you: I will not put any other load on you. [25]Only continue the way you are until I come.

[26]"I will give power to everyone who wins the victory and continues to the end to do what I want. I will give him power over the nations:

[27]'You will make them obey you by
　　punishing them with an iron
　　rod.
　You will break them into pieces
　　like pottery.'　　*Psalm 2:9*

[28]This is the same power I received from my Father. I will also give him the morning star. [29]Everyone who has ears should listen to what the Spirit[d] says to the churches.

3 "Write this to the angel of the church in Sardis:

"The One who has the seven spirits and the seven stars says this to you. I know what you do. People say that you are alive, but really you are dead. [2]Wake up! Make yourselves stronger while you still have something left and before it dies completely. I have found that what you are doing is not good enough for my God. [3]So do not forget what you have received and heard. Obey it. Change your hearts and lives! You must wake up, or I will come to you and surprise you like a thief. And you will not know when I will come. [4]But you have a few there in Sardis who have kept themselves clean. They will walk with me. They will wear white clothes, because they are worthy. [5]He who wins the victory will be dressed in white clothes like them. I will not take away his name from the book of life. I will say that he belongs to me before my Father and before his angels. [6]Everyone who has ears should listen to what the Spirit[d] says to the churches.

[7]"Write this to the angel of the church in Philadelphia:

"The One who is holy and true says this to you. He holds the key of David. When he opens something, it cannot be closed. And when he closes something, it cannot be opened. [8]I know what you do. I have put an open door before you,

---

2:15 **Nicolaitans** This is the name of a religious group that followed false beliefs and ideas.

and no one can close it. I know that you have a little strength. But you have followed my teaching. And you were not afraid to speak my name. [9]Listen! There is a synagogue[d] that belongs to Satan. Those in this synagogue say they are Jews, but they are liars. They are not true Jews. I will make them come before you and bow at your feet. They will know that I have loved you. [10]You have followed my teaching about not giving up. So I will keep you from the time of trouble that will come to the whole world. This trouble will test those who live on earth.

[11]"I am coming soon. Continue the way you are now. Then no one will take away your crown. [12]I will make the one who wins the victory a pillar in the temple of my God. He will never have to leave it. I will write on him the name of my God and the name of the city of my God. This city is the new Jerusalem.[n] It comes down out of heaven from my God. I will also write on him my new name. [13]Every person who has ears should listen to what the Spirit[d] says to the churches.

[14]"Write this to the angel of the church in Laodicea:

"The Amen[n] is the One who is the faithful and true witness. He is the ruler of all that God has made. He says this to you: [15]I know what you do. You are not hot or cold. I wish that you were hot or cold! [16]But you are only warm—not hot, not cold. So I am ready to spit you out of my mouth. [17]You say you are rich. You think you have become wealthy and do not need anything. But you do not know that you are really miserable, pitiful, poor, blind, and naked. [18]I advise you to buy gold from me—gold made pure in fire. Then you can be truly rich. Buy from me clothes that are white. Then you can cover your shameful nakedness. Buy from me medicine to put on your eyes. Then you can truly see.

[19]"I correct and punish those whom I love. So be eager to do right. Change your hearts and lives. [20]Here I am! I stand at the door and knock. If anyone hears my voice and opens the door, I will come in and eat with him. And he will eat with me.

[21]"He who wins the victory will sit with me on my throne. It was the same with me. I won the victory and sat down with my Father on his throne. [22]Everyone who has ears should listen to what the Spirit[d] says to the churches."

4 After this I looked, and there before me was an open door in heaven. And I heard the same voice that spoke to me before. It was the voice that sounded like a trumpet. The voice said, "Come up here, and I will show you what must happen after this." [2]Then the Spirit[d] took control of me. There before me was a throne in heaven. Someone was sitting on the throne. [3]The One who sat on the throne looked like precious stones, like jasper and carnelian. All around the throne was a rainbow the color of an emerald. [4]Around the throne there were 24 other thrones. There were 24 elders[n] sitting on the 24 thrones. The elders were dressed in white, and they had golden crowns on their heads. [5]Lightning flashes and noises of thunder came from the throne. Before the throne there were seven lamps burning. These lamps are the seven spirits of God. [6]Also before the throne there was something that looked like a sea of glass. It was clear like crystal.

Around the throne, on each side, there were four living things. These living things had eyes all over them, in front and in back. [7]The first living thing was like a lion. The second was like a calf. The third had a face like a man. The fourth was like a flying eagle. [8]Each of these four living things had six wings. The living things were covered all over with eyes, inside and out. Day and night they never stop saying:

"Holy, holy, holy is the Lord God
   All-Powerful.
He was, he is, and he is coming."

[9]These living things give glory and honor and thanks to the One who sits on the throne. He is the One who lives forever and ever. And every time the living things do this, [10]the 24 elders bow down before the One who sits on the throne. The elders worship him who lives forever and ever. They put their crowns down before the throne and say:

[11]"Our Lord and God! You are
   worthy
to receive glory and honor and
   power.

3:12 Jerusalem This name is used to mean the spiritual city God built for his people. **3:14 Amen** Used here as a name for Jesus, it means to agree fully that something is true. **4:4 24 elders** Elder means "older." Here the elders probably represent God's people.

You made all things.
Everything existed and was made
because you wanted it."

5 Then I saw a scroll in the right hand of the One sitting on the throne. The scroll had writing on both sides. It was kept closed with seven seals. [2]And I saw a powerful angel. He called in a loud voice, "Who is worthy to break the seals and open the scroll?" [3]But there was no one in heaven or on earth or under the earth who could open the scroll or look inside it. [4]I cried and cried because there was no one who was worthy to open the scroll or look inside. [5]But one of the elders said to me, "Do not cry! The Lion[d] from the tribe[d] of Judah has won the victory. He is David's descendant.[d] He is able to open the scroll and its seven seals."

[6]Then I saw a Lamb standing in the center of the throne with the four living things around it. The elders were also around the Lamb. The Lamb looked as if he had been killed. He had seven horns and seven eyes. These are the seven spirits of God that were sent into all the world. [7]The Lamb came and took the scroll from the right hand of the One sitting on the throne. [8]After he took the scroll, the four living things and the 24 elders bowed down before the Lamb. Each one of them had a harp. Also, they were holding golden bowls full of incense.[d] These bowls of incense are the prayers of God's holy people. [9]And they all sang a new song to the Lamb:

"You are worthy to take the scroll
and to open its seals,
because you were killed;
and with the blood of your death
you bought men for God
from every tribe, language,
people, and nation.
[10]You made them to be a kingdom of
priests for our God.
And they will rule on the earth."

[11]Then I looked, and I heard the voices of many angels. The angels were around the throne, the four living things, and the elders. There were thousands and thousands of angels—there were 10,000 times 10,000. [12]The angels said in a loud voice:

"The Lamb who was killed is
worthy
to receive power, wealth, wisdom
and strength,
honor, glory, and praise!"

[13]Then I heard every living thing in heaven and on earth and under the earth and in the sea. I heard every thing in all these places, saying:

"All praise and honor and glory
and power
forever and ever
to the One who sits on the throne
and to the Lamb!"

[14]The four living things said, "Amen!" And the elders bowed down and worshiped.

6 Then I watched while the Lamb opened the first of the seven seals. I heard one of the four living things speak with a voice like thunder. It said, "Come!" [2]I looked and there before me was a white horse. The rider on the horse held a bow, and he was given a crown. And he rode out, defeating the enemy. He rode out to win the victory.

[3]The Lamb opened the second seal. Then I heard the second living thing say, "Come!" [4]Then another horse came out. This was a red horse. Its rider was given power to take away peace from the earth. He was given power to make people kill each other. And he was given a big sword.

[5]The Lamb opened the third seal. Then I heard the third living thing say, "Come!" I looked, and there before me was a black horse. Its rider held a pair of scales in his hand. [6]Then I heard something that sounded like a voice. It came from where the four living things were. The voice said, "A quart of wheat for a day's pay. And three quarts of barley for a day's pay. And do not damage the olive oil and wine!"

[7]The Lamb opened the fourth seal. Then I heard the voice of the fourth living thing say, "Come!" [8]I looked, and there before me was a pale horse. Its rider was named death. Hades[n] was following close behind him. They were given power over a fourth of the earth. They were given power to kill people by war, by starving them, by disease, and by the wild animals of the earth.

[9]The Lamb opened the fifth seal. Then I saw some souls under the altar. They were the souls of those who had been killed because they were faithful to God's message and to the truth they had received. [10]These souls shouted in a loud voice, "Holy and true Lord, how long until you judge the people of the earth and punish them for killing us?" [11]Then

5:5 **Lion** Here refers to Christ. 6:8 **Hades** The unseen world where the dead are.

each one of these souls was given a white robe. They were told to wait a short time longer. There were still some of their brothers in the service of Christ who must be killed as they were. They were told to wait until all of this killing was finished.

[12]Then I watched while the Lamb opened the sixth seal. There was a great earthquake. The sun became black like rough black cloth. The full moon became red like blood. [13]The stars in the sky fell to the earth like figs falling from a fig tree when the wind blows. [14]The sky disappeared. It was rolled up like a scroll. And every mountain and island was moved from its place.

[15]Then all people hid in caves and behind the rocks on the mountains. There were the kings of the earth, the rulers, the generals, the rich people and the powerful people. Everyone, slave and free, hid himself. [16]They called to the mountains and the rocks, "Fall on us. Hide us from the face of the One who sits on the throne. Hide us from the anger of the Lamb! [17]The great day for their anger has come. Who can stand against it?"

7 After this I saw four angels standing at the four corners of the earth. The angels were holding the four winds of the earth. They were stopping the wind from blowing on the land or on the sea or on any tree. [2]Then I saw another angel coming from the east. This angel had the seal of the living God. He called out in a loud voice to the four angels. These were the four angels that God had given power to harm the earth and the sea. He said to the four angels, [3]"Do not harm the land or the sea or the trees before we put the sign on the people who serve our God. We must put the sign on their foreheads." [4]Then I heard how many people were marked with the sign. There were 144,000. They were from every tribe[d] of the people of Israel.

[5]From the tribe of Judah 12,000 were marked with the sign,

from the tribe of Reuben 12,000,
from the tribe of Gad 12,000,
[6]from the tribe of Asher 12,000,
from the tribe of Naphtali 12,000,
from the tribe of Manasseh 12,000,
[7]from the tribe of Simeon 12,000,
from the tribe of Levi 12,000,

from the tribe of Issachar 12,000,
[8]from the tribe of Zebulun 12,000,
from the tribe of Joseph 12,000,
from the tribe of Benjamin 12,000.

[9]Then I looked, and there was a great number of people. There were so many people that no one could count them. They were from every nation, tribe,[d] people, and language of the earth. They were all standing before the throne and before the Lamb. They wore white robes and had palm branches in their hands. [10]They were shouting in a loud voice, "Salvation belongs to our God, who sits on the throne, and to the Lamb." [11]The elders[n] and the four living things were there. All the angels were standing around them and the throne. The angels bowed down on their faces before the throne and worshiped God. [12]They were saying, "Amen! Praise, glory, wisdom, thanks, honor, power, and strength belong to our God forever and ever. Amen!"

[13]Then one of the elders asked me, "Who are these people in white robes? Where did they come from?"

[14]I answered, "You know who they are, sir."

And the elder said, "These are the people who have come out of the great suffering. They have washed their robes[n] with the blood of the Lamb. Now they are clean and white. [15]And they are before the throne of God. They worship God day and night in his temple. And the One who sits on the throne will protect them. [16]Those people will never be hungry again. They will never be thirsty again. The sun will not hurt them. No heat will burn them. [17]For the Lamb at the center of the throne will be their shepherd. He will lead them to springs of water that give life. And God will wipe away every tear from their eyes."

8 The Lamb opened the seventh seal. Then there was silence in heaven for about half an hour. [2]And I saw the seven angels who stand before God. They were given seven trumpets.

[3]Another angel came and stood at the altar. This angel had a golden pan for incense.[d] The angel was given much incense to offer with the prayers of all God's holy people. The angel put this offering on the golden altar before the throne. [4]The smoke from the incense

---

7:11 elders Elder means "older." Here the elders probably represent God's people.
7:14 washed their robes This means they believed in Jesus so that their sins could be forgiven by Christ's blood.

went up from the angel's hand to God. It went up with the prayers of God's people. [5]Then the angel filled the incense pan with fire from the altar and threw it on the earth. There were flashes of lightning, thunder and loud noises, and an earthquake.

[6]Then the seven angels who had the seven trumpets prepared to blow them.

[7]The first angel blew his trumpet. Then hail and fire mixed with blood was poured down on the earth. And a third of the earth and all the green grass and a third of the trees were burned up.

[8]The second angel blew his trumpet. Then something that looked like a big mountain burning with fire was thrown into the sea. And a third of the sea became blood. [9]And a third of the living things in the sea died, and a third of the ships were destroyed.

[10]The third angel blew his trumpet. Then a large star, burning like a torch, fell from the sky. It fell on a third of the rivers and on the springs of water. [11]The name of the star is Wormwood.[n] And a third of all the water became bitter. Many people died from drinking the water that was bitter.

[12]The fourth angel blew his trumpet. Then a third of the sun and a third of the moon and a third of the stars were hit. So a third of them became dark. A third of the day was without light.

[13]While I watched, I heard an eagle that was flying high in the air. The eagle said with a loud voice, "Trouble! Trouble! Trouble for those who live on the earth! The trouble will begin with the sounds of the trumpets that the other three angels are about to blow."

9 Then the fifth angel blew his trumpet. And I saw a star fall from the sky to the earth. The star was given the key to the deep hole that leads down to the bottomless pit. [2]Then it opened the bottomless pit. Smoke came up from the hole like smoke from a big furnace. The sun and sky became dark because of the smoke from the hole. [3]Then locusts[d] came down to the earth out of the smoke. They were given the power to sting like scorpions.[n] [4]They were told not to harm the grass on the earth or any plant or tree. They could harm only the people who did not have the sign of God on their foreheads. [5]These locusts

were given the power to cause pain to the people for five months. But they were not given the power to kill anyone. And the pain they felt was like the pain that a scorpion gives when it stings a person. [6]During those days people will look for a way to die, but they will not find it. They will want to die, but death will run away from them.

[7]The locusts looked like horses prepared for battle. On their heads they wore things that looked like crowns of gold. Their faces looked like human faces. [8]Their hair was like women's hair, and their teeth were like lions' teeth. [9]Their chests looked like iron breastplates. The sound their wings made was like the noise of many horses and chariots hurrying into battle. [10]The locusts had tails with stingers like scorpions. The power they had to hurt people for five months was in their tails. [11]The locusts had a king who was the angel of the bottomless pit His name in the Hebrew language is Abaddon. In the Greek language his name is Apollyon.[n]

[12]The first great trouble is past. There are still two other great troubles that will come.

[13]The sixth angel blew his trumpet. Then I heard a voice coming from the horns on the golden altar that is before God. [14]The voice said to the sixth angel who had the trumpet, "Free the four angels who are tied at the great river Euphrates." [15]These four angels had been kept ready for this hour and day and month and year. They were freed to kill a third of all people on the earth. [16]I heard how many troops on horses were in their army. There were 200,000,000.

[17]In my vision I saw the horses and their riders. They looked like this: They had breastplates that were fiery red, dark blue, and yellow like sulfur. The heads of the horses looked like heads of lions. The horses had fire, smoke, and sulfur coming out of their mouths. [18]A third of all the people on earth were killed by these three terrible things coming out of the horses' mouths: the fire, the smoke, and the sulfur. [19]The horses' power was in their mouths and also in their tails. Their tails were like snakes that have heads to bite and hurt people.

[20]The other people on the earth were not killed by these terrible things. But

---

8:11 Wormwood Name of a very bitter plant, used here to give the idea of bitter sorrow. **9:3 scorpions** A scorpion is an insect that stings with a bad poison. **9:11 Abaddon . . . Apollyon** Both names mean "Destroyer."

they still did not change their hearts and turn away from what they had made with their own hands. They did not stop worshiping demons[d] and idols made of gold, silver, bronze, stone, and wood—things that cannot see or hear or walk. [21]These people did not change their hearts and turn away from murder or evil magic, from their sexual sins or stealing.

10 Then I saw another powerful angel coming down from heaven. He was dressed in a cloud and had a rainbow around his head. His face was like the sun, and his legs were like poles of fire. [2]The angel was holding a small scroll open in his hand. He put his right foot on the sea and his left foot on the land. [3]He shouted loudly like the roaring of a lion. When he shouted, the voices of seven thunders spoke. [4]The seven thunders spoke, and I started to write. But then I heard a voice from heaven. The voice said, "Do not write what the seven thunders said. Keep these things secret."

[5]Then the angel I saw standing on the sea and on the land raised his right hand to heaven. [6]He made a promise by the power of the One who lives forever and ever. He is the One who made the skies and all that is in them. He made the earth and all that is in it, and he made the sea and all that is in it. The angel said, "There will be no more waiting! [7]In the days when the seventh angel is ready to blow his trumpet, God's secret plan will be finished. This plan is the Good News[d] God told to his servants, the prophets."[d]

[8]Then I heard the same voice from heaven again. The voice said to me, "Go and take the open scroll that is in the angel's hand. This is the angel that is standing on the sea and on the land."

[9]So I went to the angel and asked him to give me the little scroll. He said to me, "Take the scroll and eat it. It will be sour in your stomach. But in your mouth it will be sweet as honey." [10]So I took the little scroll from the angel's hand and I ate it. In my mouth it tasted sweet as honey. But after I ate it, it was sour in my stomach. [11]Then I was told, "You must prophesy[d] again about many peoples, nations, languages, and kings."

11 Then I was given a measuring stick like a rod. I was told, "Go and measure the temple[n] of God and the altar, and count the number of people worshiping there. [2]But do not measure the yard outside the temple. Leave it alone. It has been given to the people who are not Jews. They will walk on the holy city for 42 months. [3]And I will give power to my two witnesses to prophesy[d] for 1,260 days. They will be dressed in rough cloth to show how sad they are."

[4]These two witnesses are the two olive trees and the two lampstands that stand before the Lord of the earth. [5]If anyone tries to hurt the witnesses, fire comes from their mouths and kills their enemies. Anyone who tries to hurt them will die like this. [6]These witnesses have the power to stop the sky from raining during the time they are prophesying. They have power to make the waters become blood. They have power to send every kind of trouble to the earth. They can do this as many times as they want.

[7]When the two witnesses have finished telling their message, the beast will fight against them. This is the beast that comes up from the bottomless pit. He will defeat them and kill them. [8]The bodies of the two witnesses will lie in the street of the great city. This city is named Sodom[n] and Egypt. These names for the city have a special meaning. It is the city where the Lord was killed. [9]Men from every race of people, tribe,[d] language, and nation will look at the bodies of the two witnesses for three and a half days. They will refuse to bury them. [10]People who live on the earth will be happy because these two are dead. They will have parties and send each other gifts. They will do these things because these two prophets brought much suffering to those who live on the earth.

[11]But after three and a half days, God put the breath of life into the two prophets again. They stood on their feet. Everyone who saw them was filled with fear. [12]Then the two prophets heard a loud voice from heaven say, "Come up here!" And they went up into heaven in a cloud. Their enemies watched them go.

[13]At that same time there was a great earthquake. A tenth of the city was destroyed. And 7,000 people were killed in

---

11:1 temple God's house—the place where God's people worship and serve him. Here, John sees it pictured as the special building in Jerusalem where God commanded the Jews to worship him.   **11:8 Sodom** City that God destroyed because the people were so evil.

the earthquake. Those who did not die were very afraid. They gave glory to the God of heaven.

[14]The second great trouble is finished. The third great trouble is coming soon.

[15]Then the seventh angel blew his trumpet. And there were loud voices in heaven. The voices said:

"The power to rule the world
now belongs to our Lord and his Christ.[d]
And he will rule forever and ever."

[16]Then the 24 elders[n] bowed down on their faces and worshiped God. These are the elders who sit on their thrones before God. [17]They said:

"We give thanks to you, Lord God All-Powerful.
You are the One who is and who was.
We thank you because you have used your great power
and have begun to rule!
[18]The people of the world were angry;
but now is the time for your anger.
Now is the time for the dead to be judged.
It is time to reward your servants the prophets[d]
and to reward your holy people,
all who respect you, great and small.
It is time to destroy those who destroy the earth!"

[19]Then God's temple[n] in heaven was opened. The Holy Box[d] that holds the agreement that God gave to his people could be seen in his temple. Then there were flashes of lightning, noises, thunder, an earthquake, and a great hailstorm.

12And then a great wonder appeared in heaven: There was a woman who was clothed with the sun. The moon was under her feet. She had a crown of 12 stars on her head. [2]The woman was pregnant. She cried out with pain because she was about to give birth. [3]Then another wonder appeared in heaven: There was a giant red dragon. He had seven heads and seven crowns on each head. He also had ten horns. [4]The dragon's tail swept a third of the stars out of the sky and threw them

down to the earth. The dragon stood in front of the woman who was ready to give birth to a baby. He wanted to eat the woman's baby as soon as it was born. [5]The woman gave birth to a son. He will rule all the nations with an iron scepter.[d] But her child was taken up to God and to his throne. [6]The woman ran away into the desert to a place God prepared for her. There she would be taken care of for 1,260 days.

[7]Then there was a war in heaven. Michael[n] and his angels fought against the dragon. The dragon and his angels fought back. [8]But the dragon was not strong enough. He and his angels lost their place in heaven. [9]He was thrown down out of heaven. (The giant dragon is that old snake called the devil or Satan. He leads the whole world the wrong way.) The dragon with his angels was thrown down to the earth.

[10]Then I heard a loud voice in heaven say:

"The salvation and the power and the kingdom of our God
and the authority of his Christ[d] have now come.
They have come because the accuser of our brothers has been thrown out.
He accused our brothers day and night before our God.
[11]And our brothers defeated him by the blood of the Lamb's death
and by the truth they preached.
They did not love their lives so much
that they were afraid of death.
[12]So be happy, you heavens
and all who live there!
But it will be terrible for the earth and the sea,
because the devil has come down to you!
He is filled with anger.
He knows that he does not have much time."

[13]The dragon saw that he had been thrown down to the earth. So he hunted down the woman who had given birth to the son. [14]But the woman was given the two wings of a great eagle. Then she could fly to the place that was prepared for her in the desert. There she would be taken care of for three and a half

11:16 24 elders Elder means "older." Here the elders probably represent God's people. **11:19 temple** God's house—the place where God's people worship and serve him. John sees the heavenly temple pictured to be like the Temple of God's people in the Old Testament. **12:7 Michael** The archangel—leader among God's angels or messengers (Jude 9).

years. There she would be away from the snake. [15]Then the snake poured water out of its mouth like a river. He poured the water toward the woman, so that the flood would carry her away. [16]But the earth helped her. The earth opened its mouth and swallowed the river that came from the mouth of the dragon. [17]Then the dragon was very angry at the woman. He went off to make war against all her other children. Her children are those who obey God's commands and have the truth that Jesus taught.

[18]And the dragon stood on the seashore.

13 Then I saw a beast coming up out of the sea. It had ten horns and seven heads. There was a crown on each horn. A name against God was written on each head. [2]This beast looked like a leopard, with feet like a bear's feet. He had a mouth like a lion's mouth. The dragon gave the beast all of his power and his throne and great authority. [3]One of the heads of the beast looked as if it had been wounded and killed. But this death wound was healed. The whole world was amazed and followed the beast. [4]People worshiped the dragon because he had given his power to the beast. And they also worshiped the beast. They asked, "Who is as powerful as the beast? Who can make war against him?"

[5]The beast was allowed to say proud words and words against God. He was allowed to use his power for 42 months. [6]He used his mouth to speak against God. He spoke against God's name, against the place where God lives, and against all those who live in heaven. [7]He was given power to make war against God's holy people and to defeat them. He was given power over every tribe,[d] people, language, and nation. [8]All who live on earth will worship the beast. These are all the people since the beginning of the world whose names are not written in the Lamb's book of life. The Lamb is the One who was killed.

[9]If anyone has ears, he should listen:
[10]If anyone is to be a prisoner,
then he will be a prisoner.
If anyone is to be killed with the sword,
then he will be killed with the sword.

This means that God's holy people must have patience and faith.

[11]Then I saw another beast coming up out of the earth. He had two horns like a lamb, but he talked like a dragon. [12]This beast stands before the first beast and uses the same power that the first beast has. He uses this power to make everyone living on earth worship the first beast. The first beast was the one that had the death wound that was healed. [13]The second one does great miracles.[d] He even makes fire come down from heaven to earth while people are watching. [14]This second beast fools those who live on earth. He fools them by the miracles he has been given the power to do. He does these miracles to serve the first beast. The second beast ordered people to make an idol to honor the first beast. This was the one that was wounded by the sword but did not die. [15]The second beast was given power to give life to the idol of the first one. Then the idol could speak and order all who did not worship it to be killed. [16]The second animal also forced all people, small and great, rich and poor, free and slave, to have a mark on their right hand or on their forehead. [17]No one could buy or sell without this mark. This mark is the name of the beast or the number of his name. [18]Whoever has understanding can find the meaning of the number. This requires wisdom. This number is the number of a man. His number is 666.

14 Then I looked, and there before me was the Lamb. He was standing on Mount Zion.[n] There were 144,000 people with him. They all had his name and his Father's name written on their foreheads. [2]And I heard a sound from heaven like the noise of flooding water and like the sound of loud thunder. The sound I heard was like people playing harps. [3]And they sang a new song before the throne and before the four living things and the elders. The only ones who could learn the new song were the 144,000 who had been saved from the earth. No one else could learn the song. [4]These 144,000 are the ones who did not do sinful things with women. They kept themselves pure. They follow the Lamb every place he goes. These 144,000 were saved from among the people of the earth. They are the first people to be offered to God and the Lamb. [5]They

14:1 Mount Zion Another name for Jerusalem, here meaning the spiritual city of God's people. **14:3 elders** Elder means "older." Here the elders probably represent God's people.

were not guilty of telling lies. They are without fault.

[6]Then I saw another angel flying high in the air. The angel had the eternal Good News[d] to preach to those who live on earth—to every nation, tribe,[d] language, and people. [7]The angel said in a loud voice, "Fear God and give him praise. The time has come for God to judge all people. Worship God. He made the heavens, the earth, the sea, and the springs of water."

[8]Then the second angel followed the first angel and said, "She is destroyed! The great city of Babylon is destroyed! She made all the nations drink the wine of her adultery[d] and of God's anger."

[9]A third angel followed the first two angels. This third angel said in a loud voice: "It will be bad for the person who worships the beast and his idol and gets the beast's mark on the forehead or on the hand. [10]He will drink the wine of God's anger. This wine is prepared with all its strength in the cup of God's anger. He will be put in pain with burning sulfur before the holy angels and the Lamb. [11]And the smoke from their burning pain will rise forever and ever. There will be no rest, day or night, for those who worship the beast and his idol or who get the mark of his name." [12]This means that God's holy people must be patient. They must obey God's commands and keep their faith in Jesus.

[13]Then I heard a voice from heaven. It said, "Write this: From now on, the dead who were in the Lord when they died are happy."

The Spirit[d] says, "Yes, that is true. They will rest from their hard work. The reward of all they have done stays with them."

[14]I looked and there before me was a white cloud. Sitting on the white cloud was One who looked like a Son of Man.[n] He had a gold crown on his head and a sharp sickle[n] in his hand. [15]Then another angel came out of the temple. This angel called to the One who was sitting on the cloud, "Take your sickle and gather from the earth. The time to harvest has come. The fruit of the earth is ripe." [16]So the One that was sitting on the cloud swung his sickle over the earth. And the earth was harvested.

[17]Then another angel came out of the temple in heaven. This angel also had a sharp sickle. [18]And then another angel came from the altar. This angel has power over the fire. This angel called to the angel with the sharp sickle. He said, "Take your sharp sickle and gather the bunches of grapes from the earth's vine. The earth's grapes are ripe." [19]The angel swung his sickle over the earth. He gathered the earth's grapes and threw them into the great winepress[d] of God's anger. [20]The grapes were crushed in the winepress outside the city. And blood flowed out of the winepress. It rose as high as the heads of the horses for a distance of 200 miles.

15 Then I saw another wonder in heaven. It was great and amazing. There were seven angels bringing seven troubles. These are the last troubles, because after these troubles God's anger is finished.

[2]I saw what looked like a sea of glass mixed with fire. All of those who had won the victory over the beast and his idol and over the number of his name were standing by the sea. They had harps that God had given them. [3]They sang the song of Moses, the servant of God, and the song of the Lamb:

"You do great and wonderful
    things,   *Psalm 111:2*
Lord God, the God of heaven's
    armies.   *Amos 3:13*
Everything the Lord does is right
    and true,   *Psalm 145:17*
    King of the nations.
[4]Everyone will respect you, Lord.
                  Jeremiah 10:7
    They will honor you.
Only you are holy.
All people will come
    and worship you.   *Psalm 86:9, 10*
This is because he is a faithful God
    who does no wrong.
    He is right and fair."
               Deuteronomy 32:4

[5]After this I saw the temple (the Tent[d] of the Agreement) in heaven. The temple was opened. [6]And the seven angels bringing the seven troubles came out of the temple. They were dressed in clean, shining linen. They wore golden bands tied around their chests. [7]Then one of the four living things gave seven golden bowls to the seven angels. The bowls were filled with the anger of God, who

14:14 Son of Man "Son of Man" is a name Jesus called himself. It showed he was God's Son, but he was also a man. See dictionary. **14:14 sickle** A farming tool with a curved blade. It was used to harvest grain.

lives forever and ever. [8]The temple was filled with smoke from the glory and the power of God. No one could enter the temple until the seven troubles of the seven angels were finished.

16 Then I heard a loud voice from the temple. The voice said to the seven angels, "Go and pour out the seven bowls of God's anger on the earth."

[2]The first angel left. He poured out his bowl on the land. Then ugly and painful sores came upon all those who had the mark of the beast and who worshiped his idol.

[3]The second angel poured out his bowl on the sea. Then the sea became blood like that of a dead man. Every living thing in the sea died. [4]The third angel poured out his bowl on the rivers and the springs of water. And they became blood. [5]Then I heard the angel of the waters say to God:

"Holy One, you are the One who is
    and who was.
You are right to decide to punish
    these evil people.
[6]They have spilled the blood of your
    holy people and your
    prophets.[d]
Now you have given them blood
    to drink as they deserve."

[7]And I heard the altar say:

"Yes, Lord God All-Powerful,
    the way you punish evil people is
    right and fair."

[8]The fourth angel poured out his bowl on the sun. The sun was given power to burn the people with fire. [9]They were burned by the great heat, and they cursed the name of God. God is the One who had control over these troubles. But the people refused to change their hearts and lives and give glory to God.

[10]The fifth angel poured out his bowl on the throne of the beast. And darkness covered the beast's kingdom. People bit their tongues because of the pain. [11]They cursed the God of heaven because of their pain and the sores they had. But they refused to change their hearts and turn away from the evil things they did.

[12]The sixth angel poured out his bowl on the great river Euphrates. The water in the river was dried up. This prepared the way for the kings from the east to come. [13]Then I saw three evil spirits that

looked like frogs. They came out of the mouth of the dragon, out of the mouth of the beast, and out of the mouth of the false prophet.[d] [14]These evil spirits are the spirits of demons.[d] They have power to do miracles.[d] They go out to the kings of the whole world. They go out to gather the kings for battle on the great day of God All-Powerful.

[15]"Listen! I will come as a thief comes! Happy is the person who stays awake and keeps his clothes with him. Then he will not have to go without clothes and be ashamed because he is naked."

[16]Then the evil spirits gathered the kings together to the place that is called Armageddon[n] in the Hebrew language.

[17]The seventh angel poured out his bowl into the air. Then a loud voice came out of the temple from the throne. The voice said, "It is finished!" [18]Then there were flashes of lightning, noises, thunder, and a big earthquake. This was the worst earthquake that has ever happened since people have been on earth. [19]The great city split into three parts. The cities of the nations were destroyed. And God did not forget to punish Babylon the Great. He gave that city the cup filled with the wine of his terrible anger. [20]Every island disappeared, and there were no more mountains. [21]Giant hailstones fell on people from the sky. The hailstones weighed about 100 pounds each. People cursed God because of the hail. This trouble was a terrible thing.

17 One of the seven angels came and spoke to me. This was one of the angels that had the seven bowls. He said, "Come, and I will show you the punishment that will be given to the famous prostitute.[d] She is the one sitting over many waters. [2]The kings of the earth sinned sexually with her. And the people of the earth became drunk from the wine of her sexual sin."

[3]Then the angel carried me away by the Spirit[d] to the desert. There I saw a woman sitting on a red beast. He was covered with names against God written on him. He had seven heads and ten horns. [4]The woman was dressed in purple and red. She was shining with the gold, jewels, and pearls she was wearing. She had a golden cup in her hand. This cup was filled with evil things and

16:16 Armageddon This word means "Hill of Megiddo," where many battles were fought long ago.

the uncleanness of her sexual sin. [5]She had a title written on her forehead. This title has a hidden meaning. This is what was written:

THE GREAT BABYLON

MOTHER OF PROSTITUTES

AND THE EVIL THINGS OF THE EARTH

[6]I saw that the woman was drunk. She was drunk with the blood of God's holy people. She was drunk with the blood of those who were killed because of their faith in Jesus.

When I saw the woman, I was fully amazed. [7]Then the angel said to me, "Why are you amazed? I will tell you the hidden meaning of this woman and the beast she rides—the one with seven heads and ten horns. [8]The beast that you saw was once alive. He is not alive now. But he will be alive and come up out of the bottomless pit and go away to be destroyed. The people who live on earth will be amazed when they see the beast. They will be amazed because he was once alive, is not alive now, but will come again. These are the people whose names have never been written in the book of life since the beginning of the world.

[9]"You need a wise mind to understand this. The seven heads on the beast are the seven hills where the woman sits. They are also seven kings. [10]Five of the kings have already died. One of the kings lives now. And the last king is coming. When he comes, he will stay only a short time. [11]The beast that was once alive but is not alive now is an eighth king. This eighth king also belongs to the first seven kings. And he will go away to be destroyed.

[12]"The ten horns you saw are ten kings. These ten kings have not yet begun to rule. But they will receive power to rule with the beast for one hour. [13]All ten of these kings have the same purpose. And they will give their power and authority to the beast. [14]They will make war against the Lamb. But the Lamb will defeat them, because he is Lord of lords and King of kings. He will defeat them with his chosen and faithful followers—the people that he has called."

[15]Then the angel said to me, "You saw the water where the prostitute sits. These waters are the many peoples, the different races, nations, and languages. [16]The beast and the ten horns you saw will hate the prostitute. They will take everything she has and leave her naked.

They will eat her body and burn her with fire. [17]God made the ten horns want to carry out his purpose: They agreed to give the beast their power to rule. They will rule until what God has said is completed. [18]The woman you saw is the great city that rules over the kings of the earth."

18 Then I saw another angel coming down from heaven. This angel had great power. The angel's glory made the earth bright. [2]The angel shouted in a powerful voice:

"The great city of Babylon is
    destroyed!
  She has become a home for
      demons.[d]
She has become a city for every
      evil spirit,
  a city for every unclean[d] and
      hated bird.
[3]All the peoples of the earth have
      drunk
  the strong wine of her sexual sin.
The kings of the earth have sinned
      sexually with her,
  and the businessmen of the world
      have grown rich from the great
      wealth of her luxury."

[4]Then I heard another voice from heaven say:

"Come out of that city, my people,
  so that you will not share in her
      sins.
  Then you will not receive the
      terrible things that will happen
      to her.
[5]The city's sins are piled up as high
      as the sky.
  God has not forgotten the wrongs
      she has done.
[6]Give that city the same as she gave
      to others.
  Pay her back twice as much as
      she did.
Prepare wine for her that is twice
      as strong
  as the wine she prepared for
      others.
[7]She gave herself much glory and
      rich living.
  Give her that much suffering and
      sadness.
She says to herself, 'I am a queen
      sitting on my throne.
  I am not a widow; I will never be
      sad.'
[8]So these terrible things will come
      to her in one day:
  death, crying, and great hunger.

She will be destroyed by fire,
  because the Lord God who
    judges her is powerful."

[9]The kings of the earth who sinned sexually with her and shared her wealth will see the smoke from her burning. Then they will cry and weep because of her death. [10]They will be afraid of her suffering and stand far away. They will say:

"Terrible! How terrible, great city,
  powerful city of Babylon!
Your punishment has come in one
    hour!"

[11]And the businessmen of the earth will cry and weep for her. They will be sad because now there is no one to buy the things they sell. [12]They sell gold, silver, jewels, pearls, fine linen cloth, purple cloth, silk, and red cloth. They sell all kinds of citron wood and all kinds of things made from ivory, expensive wood, bronze, iron, and marble. [13]They also sell cinnamon, spice, incense,[d] myrrh,[d] frankincense,[d] wine, and olive oil; fine flour, wheat, cattle, sheep, horses, and carriages. They sell the bodies and souls of men.

[14]They will say,
"Babylon, the good things you
    wanted are gone from you.
All your rich and fancy things have
    disappeared.
You will never have them again."

[15]The businessmen will be afraid of her suffering and stand far away from her. These are the men who became rich from selling those things to her. The men will cry and be sad. [16]They will say:

"Terrible! How terrible for the great
    city!
She was dressed in fine linen,
    purple and red cloth.
She was shining with gold,
    jewels, and pearls!
[17]All these riches have been
    destroyed in one hour!"

Every sea captain, all those who travel on ships, the sailors, and all the people who earn money from the sea stood far away from Babylon. [18]They saw the smoke from her burning. They said loudly, "There was never a city like this great city!" [19]They threw dust on their heads and cried to show how sad they were. They said:

"Terrible! How terrible for the great
    city!
All the people who had ships on the
    sea
  became rich because of her
    wealth!
But she has been destroyed in one
    hour!"
[20]Be happy because of this, heaven!
  Be happy, God's holy people and
    apostles[d] and prophets![d]
God has punished her because of
    what she did to you."

[21]Then a powerful angel picked up a stone like a large stone for grinding grain. The angel threw the stone into the sea and said:

"That is how the great city of
    Babylon will be thrown down.
  The city will never be found
    again.
[22]The music of people playing harps
    and other instruments, flutes
    and trumpets,
  will never be heard in you again.
No workman doing any job
  will ever be found in you again.
The sound of grinding grain
  will never be heard in you again.
[23]The light of a lamp
  will never shine in you again.
The voices of a bridegroom and
    bride
  will never be heard in you again.
Your businessmen were the world's
    great men.
  All the nations were tricked by
    your magic.
[24]She is guilty of the death
  of the prophets and God's holy
    people
  and of all who have been killed
    on earth."

19

After this I heard what sounded like a great many people in heaven. They were saying:

"Hallelujah![n]
Salvation, glory, and power belong
  to our God.
[2] His judgments are true and right.
Our God has punished the
    prostitute.[d]
  She is the one who made the
    earth evil with her sexual sin.
God has punished the prostitute to
  pay her for the death of his
    servants."

19:1 Hallelujah This means "praise God!"

³Again they said:
"Hallelujah!
She is burning, and her smoke will
rise forever and ever."
⁴Then the 24 elders[n] and the four living things bowed down. They worshiped
God, who sits on the throne. They said:
"Amen, Hallelujah!"
⁵Then a voice came from the throne:
"Praise our God, all you who serve
him!
Praise our God, all you who honor
him, both small and great!"
⁶Then I heard what sounded like a
great many people. It sounded like the
noise of flooding water and like loud
thunder. The people were saying:
"Hallelujah!
Our Lord God rules. He is the
All-Powerful.
⁷Let us rejoice and be happy
and give God glory!
Give God glory, because the
wedding of the Lamb has
come.
And the Lamb's bride has made
herself ready.
⁸Fine linen was given to the bride
for her to wear.
The linen was bright and clean."
(The fine linen means the good things
done by God's holy people.)
⁹Then the angel said to me, "Write
this: Those who are invited to the wedding meal of the Lamb are happy!" Then
the angel said, "These are the true
words of God."
¹⁰Then I bowed down at the angel's
feet to worship him. But he said to me,
"Do not worship me! I am a servant like
you and your brothers who have the
truth of Jesus. Worship God! Because
the truth about Jesus is the spirit that
gives all prophecy."[d]
¹¹Then I saw heaven open. There before me was a white horse. The rider on
the horse is called Faithful and True. He
is right when he judges and makes war.
¹²His eyes are like burning fire, and on
his head are many crowns. He has a
name written on him, but he is the only
one who knows the name. No other person knows the name. ¹³He is dressed in
a robe dipped in blood. His name is the
Word of God. ¹⁴The armies of heaven
were following him on white horses.
They were dressed in fine linen, white
and clean. ¹⁵A sharp sword comes out of
the rider's mouth. He will use this sword

to defeat the nations. He will rule them
with a scepter[d] of iron. He will crush out
the wine in the winepress[d] of the terrible
anger of God All-Powerful. ¹⁶On his robe
and on his leg was written this name:
"KING OF KINGS AND LORD OF LORDS."
¹⁷Then I saw an angel standing in the
sun. The angel called with a loud voice
to all the birds flying in the sky, "Come
together for the great feast of God.
¹⁸Come together so that you can eat the
bodies of kings and generals and famous men. Come to eat the bodies of the
horses and their riders and the bodies
of all people—free, slave, small, and
great."
¹⁹Then I saw the beast and the kings
of the earth. Their armies were gathered
together to make war against the rider
on the horse and his army. ²⁰But the
beast was captured and with him the
false prophet.[d] This false prophet was
the one who did the miracles[d] for the
beast. The false prophet had used these
miracles to trick those who had the
mark of the beast and worshiped his
idol. The false prophet and the beast
were thrown alive into the lake of fire
that burns with sulfur. ²¹Their armies
were killed with the sword that came
out of the mouth of the rider on the
horse. All the birds ate the bodies until
they were full.

20 I saw an angel coming down from
heaven. He had the key to the bottomless pit. He also held a large chain
in his hand. ²The angel grabbed the
dragon, that old snake who is the devil.
The angel tied him up for 1,000 years.
³Then he threw him into the bottomless
pit and closed it and locked it over him.
The angel did this so that he could not
trick the people of the earth anymore
until the 1,000 years were ended. After
1,000 years he must be set free for a
short time.
⁴Then I saw some thrones and people
sitting on them. They had been given
the power to judge. And I saw the souls
of those who had been killed because
they were faithful to the truth of Jesus
and the message from God. They had
not worshiped the beast or his idol. They
had not received the mark of the beast
on their foreheads or on their hands.
They came back to life and ruled with
Christ for 1,000 years. ⁵(The others that
were dead did not live again until the
1,000 years were ended.) This is the first

raising of the dead. [6]Blessed and holy are those who share in this first raising of the dead. The second death has no power over them. They will be priests for God and for Christ. They will rule with him for 1,000 years.

[7]When the 1,000 years are over, Satan will be set free from his prison. [8]He will go out to trick the nations in all the earth—Gog and Magog. Satan will gather them for battle. There will be so many people that they will be like sand on the seashore. [9]And Satan's army marched across the earth and gathered around the camp of God's people and the city that God loves. But fire came down from heaven and burned them up. [10]And Satan, who tricked them, was thrown into the lake of burning sulfur with the beast and the false prophet.[d] There they will be punished day and night forever and ever.

[11]Then I saw a great white throne and the One who was sitting on it. Earth and sky ran away from him and disappeared. [12]And I saw the dead, great and small, standing before the throne. And the book of life was opened. There were also other books opened. The dead were judged by what they had done, which was written in the books. [13]The sea gave up the dead who were in it. Death and Hades[n] gave up the dead who were in them. Each person was judged by what he had done. [14]And Death and Hades were thrown into the lake of fire. This lake of fire is the second death. [15]And if anyone's name was not found written in the book of life, he was thrown into the lake of fire.

21 Then I saw a new heaven and a new earth. The first heaven and the first earth had disappeared. Now there was no sea. [2]And I saw the holy city coming down out of heaven from God. This holy city is the new Jerusalem.[n] It was prepared like a bride dressed for her husband. [3]I heard a loud voice from the throne. The voice said, "Now God's home is with men. He will live with them, and they will be his people. God himself will be with them and will be their God. [4]He will wipe away every tear from their eyes. There will be no more death, sadness, crying, or pain. All the old ways are gone."

[5]The One who was sitting on the throne said, "Look! I am making everything new!" Then he said, "Write this, because these words are true and can be trusted."

[6]The One on the throne said to me: "It is finished! I am the Alpha and the Omega,[n] the Beginning and the End. I will give free water from the spring of the water of life to anyone who is thirsty. [7]Anyone who wins the victory will receive this. And I will be his God, and he will be my son. [8]But those who are cowards, who refuse to believe, who do evil things, who kill, who sin sexually, who do evil magic, who worship idols, and who tell lies—all these will have a place in the lake of burning sulfur. This is the second death."

[9]One of the seven angels came to me. This was one of the angels who had the seven bowls full of the seven last troubles. He said, "Come with me. I will show you the bride, the wife of the Lamb." [10]The angel carried me away by the Spirit[d] to a very large and high mountain. He showed me the holy city, Jerusalem. It was coming down out of heaven from God. [11]It was shining with the glory of God. It was shining bright like a very expensive jewel, like a jasper. It was clear as crystal. [12]The city had a great high wall with 12 gates. There were 12 angels at the gates. On each gate was written the name of 1 of the 12 tribes[d] of Israel. [13]There were three gates on the east, three on the north, three on the south, and three on the west. [14]The walls of the city were built on 12 foundation stones. On the stones were written the names of the 12 apostles[d] of the Lamb.

[15]The angel who talked with me had a measuring rod made of gold. He had this rod to measure the city, its gates, and its wall. [16]The city was built in a square. Its length was equal to its width. The angel measured the city with the rod. The city was 12,000 stadia[n] long, 12,000 stadia wide, and 12,000 stadia high. [17]The angel also measured the wall. It was 144 cubits[n] high, by man's measurement. That was the measurement the angel was using. [18]The wall was made of jasper. The city was made of pure gold, as pure as glass. [19]The foundation stones

20:13 Hades Where the dead are. **21:2 new Jerusalem** The spiritual city where God's people live with him. **21:6 Alpha and the Omega** The first and last letters in the Greek alphabet. This means "the beginning and the end." **21:16 stadia** One stadion was a distance of about 200 yards. It was one-eighth of a Roman mile. **21:17 cubits** A cubit is about half a yard, the length from the elbow to the tip of the little finger.

of the city walls had every kind of jewel in them. The first cornerstone was jasper, the second was sapphire, the third was chalcedony, the fourth was emerald, [20]the fifth was onyx, the sixth was carnelian, the seventh was chrysolite, the eighth was beryl, the ninth was topaz, the tenth was chrysoprase, the eleventh was jacinth, and the twelfth was amethyst. [21]The 12 gates were 12 pearls. Each gate was made from a single pearl. The street of the city was made of pure gold. The gold was clear as glass.

[22]I did not see a temple in the city. The Lord God All-Powerful and the Lamb are the city's temple. [23]The city does not need the sun or the moon to shine on it. The glory of God is its light, and the Lamb is the city's lamp. [24]By its light the people of the world will walk. The kings of the earth will bring their glory into it. [25]The city's gates will never be shut on any day, because there is no night there. [26]The greatness and the honor of the nations will be brought into it. [27]Nothing unclean[d] will ever enter the city. No one who does shameful things or tells lies will ever go into it. Only those whose names are written in the Lamb's book of life will enter the city.

22 Then the angel showed me the river of the water of life. The river was shining like crystal. It flows from the throne of God and of the Lamb [2]down the middle of the street of the city. The tree of life was on each side of the river. It produces fruit 12 times a year, once each month. The leaves of the tree are for the healing of all people. [3]Nothing that God judges guilty will be in that city. The throne of God and of the Lamb will be there. And God's servants will worship him. [4]They will see his face, and his name will be written on their foreheads. [5]There will never be night again. They will not need the light of a lamp or the light of the sun. The Lord God will give them light. And they will rule like kings forever and ever.

[6]The angel said to me, "These words are true and can be trusted. The Lord is the God of the spirits of the prophets.[d] He sent his angel to show his servants the things that must happen soon."

[7]"Listen! I am coming soon! He who

obeys the words of prophecy in this book will be happy."

[8]I am John. I am the one who heard and saw these things. When I heard and saw them, I bowed down to worship at the feet of the angel who showed these things to me. [9]But the angel said to me, "Do not worship me! I am a servant like you and your brothers the prophets. I am a servant like all those who obey the words in this book. Worship God!"

[10]Then the angel told me, "Do not keep secret the words of prophecy in this book. The time is near for all this to happen. [11]Whoever is doing evil, let him continue to do evil. Whoever is unclean, let him continue to be unclean. Whoever is doing right, let him continue to do right. Whoever is holy, let him continue to be holy."

[12]"Listen! I am coming soon! I will bring rewards with me. I will repay each one for what he has done. [13]I am the Alpha and the Omega,[n] the First and the Last, the Beginning and the End.

[14]"Those who wash their robes[n] will be blessed. They will have the right to eat the fruit from the tree of life. They may go through the gates into the city. [15]Outside the city are the evil people, those who do evil magic, who sin sexually, who murder, who worship idols, and who love lies and tell lies.

[16]"I, Jesus, have sent my angel to tell you these things for the churches. I am the descendant[d] from the family of David. I am the bright morning star."

[17]The Spirit[d] and the bride say, "Come!" Everyone who hears this should also say, "Come!" If anyone is thirsty, let him come; whoever wishes it may have the water of life as a free gift.

[18]I warn everyone who hears the words of the prophecy of this book: If anyone adds anything to these words, God will give him the troubles written about in this book. [19]And if anyone takes away from the words of this book of prophecy, God will take away his share of the tree of life and of the holy city, which are written about in this book.

[20]Jesus is the One who says that these things are true. Now he says, "Yes, I am coming soon."

Amen. Come, Lord Jesus!

[21]The grace of the Lord Jesus be with all. Amen.

22:13 Alpha and the Omega The first and last letters in the Greek alphabet. This means "the beginning and the end." **22:14 wash their robes** This means they believed in Jesus so that their sins could be forgiven by Christ's blood.

DICTIONARY

A

Aaron (AIR-ohn) was the older brother of Moses. He often spoke for Moses. Only men from Aaron's family could be priests. (Exodus 4–40; Numbers 1–25)

Abba (AB-uh) was a child's word for "father" in the Aramaic language. Early Christians used this word in speaking to God. This shows how close we can feel to him. (Mark 14:36; Romans 8:15; Galatians 4:6)

Abib (ah-BEEB) means "young ears of grain." It is the first month of the Jewish calendar and about the time of year as our March or April. It is also called Nisan. (Exodus 13:4; 34:18; Deuteronomy 16:1)

Abraham (AY-brah-ham) was the most respected man in the Jewish nation. The Jews called him "father Abraham." He was known for his great faith. (Genesis 12–25; John 8:39; Romans 4:1, 16; Hebrews 11:11-12)

Adam (AD-um) means "out of the earth." He was the first man God created. He was made from the dust of the ground. (Genesis 1–4; 1 Corinthians 15:45)

adultery (ah-DUL-ter-ee) is breaking a marriage promise by having sexual relations with someone other than your husband or wife. (Exodus 20:14; Mark 10:11-12; John 8:3-5)

agreement (uh-GREE-ment) is a contract or promise. It is sometimes called a covenant. God made agreements with his people. One agreement was the "law of Moses." God has given a new agreement to his people through Christ in the New Testament. Hebrews 8–10 explains the differences between the two agreements. (Genesis 9:9-17; Hebrews 9:15-22)

Agrippa (uh-GRIP-pah) See "Herod Agrippa II."

alabaster (AL-a-bas-ter) is a bright-colored stone with streaks or stripes through it. Perfume was often kept in beautiful containers made of alabaster. (Matthew 26:7; Luke 7:37)

alamoth (AL-a-moth) was probably a musical word. It may mean "like a flute" or "high-pitched." (Psalm 46)

aloes (AL-ohs) were oils from sweet-smelling sap of certain trees. They were used for perfume, medicine and to prepare bodies for burial. (Numbers 24:6; John 19:39)

altar (ALL-ter) was a place where sacrifices, gifts or prayers were offered to God. Altars were often made of dirt, grass or rocks piled up in the shape of a table on which the gift could be placed. (Genesis 8:20; 22:9; 1 Kings 18:30-35; Matthew 5:23-24; James 2:21)

amen (AY-MEN or AH-MEN) is a Hebrew word for "that is right." A person says "amen" to show he agrees with what has been said. (1 Chronicles 16:36; Nehemiah 5:13; 8:6; Psalm 106:48; 1 Corinthians 14:16; Revelation 7:11-12)

Anak/Anakites (A-nak/AN-uh-kites) The Anakites were named for their ancestor Anak. They were a group of people who lived in Canaan when the Israelites arrived. They were known as large, mean, fighting people. (Numbers 13:22, 28, 33; Deuteronomy 1:28; 2:10-11; 9:2; Joshua 11:21-22)

Andrew (AN-droo) was a fisherman and the brother of the apostle Peter. Andrew was also 1 of the 12 apostles of Jesus. (Mark 1:16-18; 3:14-19; John 1:40-44; Acts 1:13)

angel (AIN-jel) is a Greek word that means "messenger." Angels are heavenly beings. They can sometimes look like people. God used angels to help his people and to announce important events. (Genesis 21:17; 22:11-15; Matthew 25:41; Luke 2:8-15; Hebrews 1:14; 12:22; 13:2; 2 Peter 2:4)

Annas (AN-us) was a high priest of the Jews during Jesus' lifetime. He served as the high priest in Jerusalem from A.D. 7 to 14. (Luke 3:2; John 18:12-23; Acts 4:6) See also "priest."

apostle (uh-POS-'l) is a Greek word that means "someone who is sent off." Jesus gave the name to the 12 men he chose as his special followers. He sent them to tell the good news about him to the whole world. Later, after Judas killed himself, Matthias became an apostle. Paul was also called an apostle. (Matthew 10:1-4; Mark 3:14-19; Acts 1:2-26; 1 Corinthians 15:8-10)

Aquila (AK-wi-lah) was a Jewish Christian from the city of Rome. He and his wife Priscilla (or Prisca) worked as tentmakers and traveled with Paul. When they were at home in Rome or working in Ephesus, the Christians worshiped in their home. (Acts 18:2-3, 18, 26; Romans 16:3-5; 1 Corinthians 16:19)

Aramaic (AIR-uh-MAY-ik) was the language of the people in the nation of Aram. The Jews in the country of Palestine started speaking Aramaic when they were taken as slaves by the Babylonian people. Jesus probably spoke Aramaic. (2 Kings 18:26-28; John 19:20)

ark, Noah's In this Bible it is called Noah's boat. (Genesis 6:13-14; 1 Peter 3:20)

Ark of the Covenant See "Box of the Agreement with the Lord."

Asherah (ah-SHIR-ah) was the name of a false goddess of the people of Canaan. She was thought to be the wife of the false god Baal. (Judges 3:7; 1 Kings 15:13; 2 Kings 21:7; 2 Chronicles 15:16)

Ashtoreth (ASH-toh-reth) was the name of a false goddess of the Canaanites. (Judges 2:13; 1 Samuel 7:3; 12:10; 1 Kings 11:5, 33)

Augustus Caesar (aw-GUS-tus SEE-zer) or Caesar Augustus was the first Roman emperor. He was the ruler when Jesus was born. He was a nephew to the famous Julius Caesar. (Luke 2:1-2)

B

Baal was a false god of the Canaanites. (1 Kings 18:17-40; Jeremiah 11:13)

Babylonians (bab-e-LONE-e-unz) were the people from Babylonia. This was a land east of Israel. Their largest city was Babylon. When Nebuchadnezzar was their king, they took many of the people of Judah to Babylonia as captives. The Babylonians were sometimes called Chaldeans. (2 Kings 25:4-26; 2 Chronicles 36; Daniel 1–4)

balm was an oil from a plant used as a medicine to comfort and heal sore skin. (Genesis 37:25; Jeremiah 51:8)

Baptist (BAP-tist) means "someone who baptizes." John, a relative of Jesus, was called this because he baptized many people. (Matthew 3:11)

baptize (BAP-tize) is from a Greek word that in New Testament times meant to dip or immerse. Baptism as practiced by Christians was in water. Baptism reminds us of Jesus' death, burial and rising to live again. It shows our death to sin and our being raised to new life with Christ. (Acts 2:38, 41; 8:36-39; 10:47; 16:15, 33; 18:8; Romans 6:3-4)

Barabbas (bah-RAB-us) means "son of a father." He was a robber who had murdered someone in Jerusalem. He was in jail when Jesus was on trial. It was the time of year when a criminal would be freed from prison. The people cried out to have Barabbas freed and Jesus killed on the cross. Pilate, the Roman governor, did as they demanded. (Matthew 27:16-26; Mark 15:6-11)

Barnabas (BAR-nah-bus) means "one who encourages." The apostles gave this name to Joseph because he helped others. Barnabas, who was from Cyprus, often traveled with Paul to teach about Jesus. The journeys of Barnabas with Paul are told in Acts 13–15. (Acts 4:36-37; 11:22-26)

Bartholomew (bar-THOL-oh-mew) was 1 of the 12 apostles of Jesus. He may also have been called Nathanael. (Matthew 10:2-3; Luke 6:13-15; John 1:43-50)

beatitude (bee-AT-i-tyood) means "blessed" or "happy." This name is often used for Jesus' teaching in Matthew 5:3-12 and Luke 6:20-22. In these verses Jesus described a blessed or happy person.

Beelzebul (bee-EL-ze-bull), also spelled Beelzebub, came from the name Baal-Zebub. This was the name of the false god of the Philistines. In the New Testament, Beelzebul is a name sometimes used for the devil. (Matthew 12:24; Mark 3:22-23)

Bel was a false god of the Babylonians. (Jeremiah 50:2)

believers (be-LEE-vers) is a word used in the New Testament to describe the followers of Jesus. (Acts 2:41-47; 5:14)

Bethlehem (BETH-le-hem) means "house of bread." It is a small town five miles from Jerusalem in the country of Judea. It was the hometown of King David in the Old Testament. Jesus was born there. (1 Samuel 16:4; Matthew 2:1; Luke 2:15-18)

Bible (BY-bul) means "the book." The Bible is a group of books and letters that Christians accept as the word of God. It is divided into two parts. The Old Testament contains 39 books, and the New Testament contains 27 books. See also "Scriptures."

blasphemy (BLAS-feh-mee) is saying things against God. Jesus was often accused of blasphemy because he said he was the Son of God. The people who accused him did not understand that he really was God's Son. (Matthew 9:3; 26:65; John 10:36)

blessing (BLES-ing) is a good gift from God to his people. (Luke 6:28; 24:50-51; Acts 3:26; Hebrews 6:7; 1 Peter 3:9)

Box of the Agreement with the Lord *or* **Holy Box** is often called Ark of the Covenant. It was a special box made of acacia wood and gold. Gold creatures with wings covered the top. Inside were the stone tablets where the Ten Commandments were written. Later, a pot of manna and Aaron's walking stick were also put into the Box. It was to remind the people of Israel of God's promise to be with them. In this Bible it is also called the Holy Box or the Holy Box of God. (Exodus 25:10-22; 26:34; Joshua 3:1-17; 2 Chronicles 35:3; Hebrews 9:4)

bread that shows we are in God's presence is also called Bread of the Presence, or showbread. It was a group of 12 loaves of bread that were kept on the table in the Holy Tent and later in the Temple. This special bread reminded the people that they were always in God's presence. (Exodus 25:30; Leviticus 24:5-9; Luke 6:14)

C

Caesar (SEE-zer) was the name of a famous Roman family. In New Testament times it was used as the title of the Roman emperors. (Luke 2:1; 3:1; 20:22-25) See "Augustus Caesar."

Caiaphas (KAY-uh-fus) was the Jewish high priest from A.D. 18 to 36. He was one of those who planned to kill Jesus. (Matthew 26:57-68; John 11:49-53; 18:12-28)

calamus (KAH-lah-mus) is a sweet-tasting plant stalk probably like sugar cane. (Exodus 30:23; Jeremiah 6:20; Ezekiel 27:19)

capital is the top of a pillar. This top part of the pillar was usually decorated with beautiful carvings. (1 Kings 7:16-20; 2 Kings 25:17; Amos 9:1)

cassia (CASH-ah) is a pleasant-smelling powder. Its odor is like that of the cinnamon plant. (Exodus 30:24; Psalm 45:8)

centurion (sen-TUR-ree-un) was a Roman army officer who commanded 100 soldiers. (Matthew 8:5; 7:12)

Cephas (SEE-fus) See "Peter."

chaff (CHAF) is the husk of a head of grain. Farmers must separate it from the good part of the grain. In Bible times they tossed the grain and chaff together into the air. Since the chaff is lighter, the wind blew it away and the good grain fell back to the threshing floor. (Job 21:18; Psalms 1:4; 35:5; Isaiah 29:5; 41:2) See "threshing."

chariot (CHAIR-e-ut) was a fast, two-wheeled cart usually pulled by two horses. It was used for battles, traveling and parades. (Genesis 46:29; Exodus 14:6; Acts 8:28-31)

Chemosh (KEE-mosh) was the name of a false god of the Moabites. (Numbers 21:29; Jeremiah 48:46)

Christ (KRYST) means "anointed (or chosen) one" in Greek. In Hebrew the word is "Messiah." Jesus is the Christ. He was chosen by God to save people from their sins. (Mark 8:29; 14:61-62; Luke 23:2; Acts 2:36; 17:3; 18:28)

Christian (KRIS-chun) means "belonging to Christ." Christ's followers are called Christians. (Acts 11:26; 26:28; 1 Peter 4:16)

church in the New Testament means a group of Christians. In those times the church often met in someone's home. (Matthew 16:18; Acts 2:47; 14:27; Romans 16:5)

circumcision (SIR-kum-SIH-zhun) This means to cut off the foreskin of the male sex organ. Each Jewish baby boy was circumcised on the eighth day after he was born. This act was done as a sign of the agreement God had made with his people, the Jews. Because of this, the Jews sometimes are called "the circumcision" and non-Jews are called "the uncircumcision." (Leviticus 12:3; John 7:22; Acts 7:8)

clean is used to describe the state of a person, animal or action that is pleasing to God. God called some animals clean and said they could be eaten. People who had not touched or eaten anything God said was unclean were called clean. Or, if they did not have a disease that made them unclean, they were called clean. They could live and serve God normally. (Genesis 7:2; Leviticus 20:25; Deuteronomy 14:3-20) See "unclean."

Cleansing, Day of is also called the Day of Atonement. It was the most special day of the year for the Israelites. No one worked or ate on that day. This was the one day of the year when the high priest could go into the Most Holy Place. Animals were sacrificed for the sins of the people. This was a sign to the people that they were cleansed from their sins for a year. Jews still celebrate this day today. It is called Yom Kippur. (Leviticus 16:1-34; 25:9)

confess (kun-FES) means to admit that something is true. The New Testament teaches a believer to confess that Jesus is the Son of God. Christians are also told to confess their sins, to admit that they have done wrong. (Romans 10:9-10; Philippians 2:11; 1 John 1:9)

coral (KOR-al) is a type of limestone that forms in the ocean. Coral is usually a rich red or deep pink color. It is used to make jewelry. (Job 28:18; Ezekiel 27:16)

cornerstone This was the most important stone at a corner in the base of a building. The cornerstone had to be perfect so the building's walls would be straight. The other stones were fitted against the cornerstone. Jesus is called the cornerstone of the new law. (Joshua 6:26; Job 38:6; Ephesians 2:20)

council (KOWN-s'l), or meeting, was the highest Jewish court in the days of Jesus. Its proper name was the "Sanhedrin." The men of the council sat in a half circle to hear the people who came to speak to them. The trials of Jesus and Stephen were held in front of this council. (Matthew 26:57-68; Acts 6:13-15)

covenant (KUV-eh-nant) See "agreement."

cross refers to a cruel way of killing criminals in New Testament times. The person was tied or nailed to two rough beams of wood nailed together in the shape of an "x" or a "t." Then, he was left hanging in a public place to die. Jesus was killed by the Roman soldiers this way. In the New Testament the word "cross" is often used to remind us that Christ's death on the cross was God's way of saving us from our sins. (John 19:17-31; 1 Corinthians 1:18-25; Galatians 6:12; Ephesians 2:15-16)

cud An animal that chews the cud chews its food and swallows it. Then it chews it a second time. (Leviticus 11:3)

D

Dagon (DAY-gon) was one of the false gods of the Philistines. (Judges 16:23; 1 Samuel 5:2-7; 1 Chronicles 10:10)

Daniel (DAN-yel) was a Hebrew captive taken to Babylon as a young man. He told Nebuchadnezzar what his dream meant. God also made him able to tell Belshazzar what the strange handwriting on the wall meant. When he was about 80 years old, Daniel was put in the lions' den by King Darius. But God saved him. (Daniel 1–6)

David (DAY-vid) was Israel's greatest king. Jesus is called the "Son of David" because he was born to members of David's family. (1 Sam-

uel 1:16-31; Luke 1:69; 2:4; 18:38;
Acts 2:29-31; 13:22)

deacon (DEE-kun) is a Greek word
meaning "servant." Deacons are
people chosen to serve the church
in special ways. The men named
in Acts 6:1-6 may have been the
first deacons. Deacons are described in 1 Timothy 3:8-13.

Dead Sea is a large lake at the
south end of the Jordan River.
The Jordan and several small
streams flow into it. But it has
no outlet. And it is so salty that
nothing lives in it. It is about 50
miles long and 10 miles wide. In
Bible days it was often called the
Salt Sea, the Eastern Sea or the
Sea of the Arabah. (Genesis 14:3;
Numbers 34:3, 12; Joshua 3:16)

demon (DEE-mun) was an evil
spirit from the devil. Sometimes
a demon lived in a person. But
Jesus has more power than demons and could make them come
out of people. (Deuteronomy 32:17;
Psalm 106:37; Matthew 12:22; Luke
8:26-39)

descendants (de-SEN-dants) are
family members who are born to
a person and his children. They
would include grandchildren, great-
grandchildren, great-great-grandchildren and so on. (Genesis 12:7;
Leviticus 21:21; Romans 4:18)

devil (DEV-'l) means "one who accuses." In the New Testament, the
devil is often called Satan or Beelzebul. He is a spirit and the enemy of God and man. (Matthew

4:1-11; John 13:2; Ephesians 4:27;
6:10-17) See "Beelzebul."

disciple (dih-SYE-p'l) See "follower."

E

Edom (E-dum) means "red." Edom
was also called Esau, the older son
of Isaac. The land where Esau's descendants lived was named Edom.
It was south of the Dead Sea. Seir
is another name for the land of
Edom. (Genesis 25:30; 36:8; 2 Samuel 8:14; Psalm 137:7; Ezekiel
25:12-14; Obadiah 10-14)

elder (EL-der) means "older." In
the Old Testament this Bible uses
elders, older leaders, to describe a
special group of men who led God's
people. In the New Testament elders are appointed leaders in the
church. (Numbers 11:16; Acts
20:17-38; 1 Timothy 3:1-7; 1 Peter 5:1-4)

Elijah (e-LIE-juh) was a man who
spoke for God in the Old Testament. He was a prophet about
800 years before Jesus was born.
(1 Kings 17–21; 2 Kings 1; 2; Matthew 16:14; 17:3-4; 27:47; Luke
1:17; James 5:17)

ephod (EF-ahd) See "vest, holy."

epistle (e-PIS-'l) is a Greek word
meaning "letter." Many books of
the New Testament were actually
letters written to Christians in various cities. Some of these letters
are Ephesians, Galatians, Romans,
1 and 2 Corinthians, Philippians
and Colossians. (Colossians 4:16;

1 Thessalonians 5:27; 2 Thessalonians 3:17; 2 Peter 3:16)

Esau (E-saw) See "Edom."

eternal life (e-TER-nul LIFE) is the new kind of life promised to those who follow Jesus. It is living with a new help from God. It is also life that will never end. (John 3:16; 4:14; Galatians 2:20; 1 John 5:11-15)

eunuch (U-nuk) is a man who cannot have sexual relations. In the Bible eunuchs were often high officers in royal palaces or armies. (2 Kings 9:32; Esther 2:3; Isaiah 56:3-5; Acts 8:26-40)

Eutychus (YOU-ti-cus) means "lucky." Eutychus was a young man in the city of Troas. As he was sitting in an upstairs window listening to Paul preach, he went to sleep. He fell out of the window and died. But Paul, by God's power, brought him back to life. (Acts 20:7-12)

Ezra (EZ-ra) was the leader of a group of Israelites who were allowed to return to Jerusalem from Babylon. He taught them to worship and serve God correctly. (Ezra 7–10; Nehemiah 8; 9)

F

faith (FAYTH) is belief and trust. People who have great faith in God do what he says to do, even when they do not understand why. They do it because they believe in him and trust him. Faith in Jesus means believing he is the Son of God and trusting in him. (2 Chronicles 20:20; Isaiah 7:9; Habakkuk 2:4; Matthew 8:10; Luke 8:24-25; Romans 4:16-22; 5:1-2; Ephesians 4:13; Hebrews 11)

fasting (FAST-ing) means giving up food for a while. People sometimes fast during a special time of prayer and worship to God. Jesus fasted for 40 days before he began preaching. It was also done to show sadness. (2 Samuel 12:16-22; Ezra 8:23; Matthew 4:1-11; 6:16-18; 9:14-15; Acts 12:2-3; 14:23)

feast (FEEST) is a special meal and celebration for a certain purpose. There were many different feasts in Bible times.

Feast of Dedication was an eight-day celebration for the Jews. It was a way of being thankful that the Temple had been cleansed again. This was done in 164 B.C. after the Greeks had spoiled and ruined it. The celebration is called Hanukkah today by the Jews. (John 10:22)

Feast of Harvest See "Feast of Weeks."

Feast of Shelters is also called the Feast of Booths or Feast of Tabernacles. The people gathered fruit and lived in tent-like shelters for a week. This feast reminded them of how God had taken care of them when the Israelites left Egypt and lived in tents in the wilderness. (Exodus 23:14-17; Deuteronomy 16:13-17)

Feast of Unleavened Bread was also called Passover. It was held to remember how God helped the Israelites in Egypt. He saved them from the one that brings death that passed over their families. And God led them out of slavery. For seven days they ate bread made without yeast and did only certain types of work. (Exodus 12:14-20; Numbers 28:16-25; Deuteronomy 16:1-8) See "Passover Feast."

Feast of Weeks was also called Pentecost, the Feast of Harvest and the Day of Firstfruits. It was held seven weeks and one day after Passover. This was a feast of thanksgiving for the summer harvest. (Exodus 34:22; Leviticus 23:15-22; Numbers 28:26-31; Deuteronomy 16:9-12; Acts 2) See "Pentecost."

Felix (FEE-lix) was the Roman governor of Judea from A.D. 52 to 54. He was a cruel ruler. He kept the apostle Paul in prison for two years to please the Jews who hated Jesus and Paul. His full name was Marcus Antonius Felix. (Acts 23:24–24:27)

fellowship (FEL-o-ship) is sharing friendship and love with others. Christians have a very special fellowship with God and his people. (Acts 2:42; 1 John 1:3-7)

Festus (FES-tus) was the governor of Judea after Felix. His full name was Porcius (POR-shus) Festus. He allowed Paul to go to Rome to be tried by Caesar. (Acts 24:27–25:27; 26:24-32)

firstborn (FIRST-born) is the oldest child in a family. The son born first to a Jewish family received a double share of his father's wealth. Then he became the leader of the family when his father died. The Israelite people were called God's firstborn because he gave them special privileges. Jesus was also called God's firstborn Son. He is now ruling over all creation. (Genesis 35:23; Exodus 4:22; Psalm 89:27; Romans 8:29; Colossians 1:18; Hebrews 1:6)

firstfruits (FIRST-fruits) were the first and best crops and animals the Israelites raised. They were to give these to God. This showed that they knew everything really belonged to God. (Exodus 34:22-26; Leviticus 23:9-21; Numbers 28:26; Deuteronomy 18:4)

flax (FLAKS) is a plant used to make clothing and ropes. The inside of the plant was combed and spun into thread. Then it was woven into cloth. (Exodus 9:31; Joshua 2:6; Proverbs 31:13; Isaiah 19:9)

follower (FAHL-o-wer) is a person who is learning from someone. Jesus' followers are those who believe and obey his teaching. Another word for "follower" is "disciple." During his ministry, Jesus chose 12 special followers and made them his apostles. (Matthew 15:32-39; John 19:38; Acts 6:1-7; 11:26)

forgiveness (for-GIV-ness) means to be pardoned and not punished for a wrong thing done. A sinner who is sorry for his sin and stops doing that sin will be forgiven when he comes to God. That person will not be punished. Christians are also to forgive others for wrong things done to them. (Genesis 50:17; Psalms 19:12; 32:1-5; 51:1-17; Matthew 6:12-15; 9:2-8; 18:21-22; Acts 8:22; Romans 4:7; 1 John 1:9)

frankincense (FRANK-in-sense) is a very expensive, sweet-smelling perfume. It comes from inside the terebinth tree that grows in the country of Arabia. Some wise men gave frankincense to Jesus when he was born. (Exodus 30:34; Matthew 2:11; Revelation 18:13)

G

Gabriel (GAY-bree-el) is God's angel who announced that John the Baptist and Jesus would be born. (Luke 1:11-20, 26-35)

Galilee (GAL-i-lee) was the country between the Jordan River and the Mediterranean Sea. It had lots of water and trees, and the land was good for growing grains like wheat and barley. Jesus grew up in the city of Nazareth in Galilee and, so, was often called "the Galilean." (Matthew 4:23-25; 21:11; John 2:1-2; 7:1, 9, 41)

Galilee, Lake (GAL-i-lee) is also called the "Sea of Galilee." It is really a lake 13 miles long and about 8 miles wide. Storms often come up very quickly on this lake. Jesus spent much time around Lake Galilee. (Matthew 4:18-22; 8:23-27; 14:22-36; John 6:1-2, 16-21)

gazelle (guh-ZEL) is an animal of the antelope family. It is known for its beauty and speed. It is usually about two feet tall and three feet long. (Deuteronomy 12:15, 22; 2 Samuel 2:18; Proverbs 6:5)

Gentiles (JEN-tiles) means "nations." The Jews called anyone who was not a Jew a Gentile. The Jews thought all non-Jewish people were enemies. The Good News of Jesus is for all people, both Jews and non-Jewish people. (Acts 10:44-48; 11:18; 13:46-48; Romans 1:5; 11:11-13; Ephesians 3:6-8)

Gethsemane (geth-SEM-uh-nee) was a garden of olive trees just outside Jerusalem. It was at the bottom of the Mount of Olives. The night before Jesus was killed, he prayed in this garden. Jesus was there when Judas brought the soldiers to arrest him. (Matthew 26:36-50; Mark 14:32)

gittith (GIT-tith) is probably a musical word and may be a kind of musical instrument. (Psalms 8; 81; 84)

God is the One who made the world and everything in it. He is a spirit and does not have a body as man does. But people can know what God is like because he sent Jesus into the world to show them. God hates evil, but he loves his people

---

so much that he let his Son die for them. God is the wisest and most powerful being in the universe. He has always been alive, and he will always be alive. He is love. Christians are called "children of God" because they have been given a spirit like God. (Genesis 1:1; Psalm 139:7-12; Isaiah 44:6; Matthew 5:9; John 4:24; 14:9; Romans 1:18; 5:8-11; 8:16; 11:36; Hebrews 1:1-4; 1 John 4:7-12)

Golgotha (GOL-guh-thuh) is an Aramaic word meaning "skull." The Latin word for it is "Calvary." This is the hill where Jesus was killed on the cross by the Roman soldiers. It may have been called "the place of the skull" because many people died there. Or it may have been called that because the hill looks like a giant skull. (Matthew 27:32-35; Mark 15:22-24; John 19:17-18)

Good News is also called the gospel. In the New Testament, the Good News is that Jesus died for us on the cross, was buried in a tomb and came back to life. Because he did these things for us, we can be saved. That is good news. (Mark 1:1; Acts 20:24; Colossians 1:21-23; 2 Timothy 1:10) See "gospel."

gospel (GOS-p'l) means "good news." It refers to Jesus' life, death and rising to live again. The first four books of the New Testament are called the Gospels because they tell the good news of

what Jesus has done for us. (Philippians 1:5, 7, 12; 2 Thessalonians 1:8) See "Good News."

grace is God's kindness and love shown to us, even though we do not deserve them. Part of God's grace is his forgiveness. He forgives us for the wrong things we do. He even let Jesus take the punishment for our sins. (John 1:14; Acts 15:11; Romans 5:1-2, 8; 1 Corinthians 15:10; 2 Corinthians 6:1-2; Ephesians 2:4-5, 8; Titus 3:3-7; Hebrews 4:16)

Greek is the language of the people of Greece. The New Testament was first written in the Greek language. Also, a person from the country of Greece is called a Greek. (John 19:20; Acts 14:1; 16:1, 3; 21:37; Colossians 3:11)

H

Hades (HAY-deez) is where the dead, both good and bad, are. (Acts 2:27, 31; Revelation 1:18)

heart in the Bible usually means the mind or feelings. It is not talking about the physical heart that pumps blood through the body. (Deuteronomy 30:10-17; Psalm 26:2; Proverbs 15:13-15; Mark 12:30; Luke 2:19; 6:45; 12:34; Acts 2:46)

heaven (HEV-'n) is the home of God. In the New Testament it is said to be a place where there is no pain, no crying, no sadness, no night and no death. Jesus showed us his love by leaving heaven and coming to earth to die on a cross. God's people will live in heaven with him forever. (John 3:13; 6:38-40; Acts 7:56; 2 Corinthians 5:1-10; 1 Peter 1:4; Revelation 21:4)

Hebrews (HEE-brooz) is another name for the Jewish people. The book of Hebrews is a letter written to Jewish Christians. (2 Corinthians 11:22; Philippians 3:5; Hebrews)

heir (AIR) is the person who is supposed to inherit what belongs to a relative. The heir usually receives these things when the relative dies. Because through Christ we can be adopted children of God, Christians are heirs of God's riches. (Genesis 15:3-4; 2 Samuel 14:7; Galatians 4:1)

hell is the home of the devil. It is the place of punishment forever for those who turn against God. Hell is described in the New Testament as a place of fire, pain, sorrow and sadness. (Matthew 23:33; 25:41; 2 Peter 2:4, 9; Revelation 20:14-15; 21:8)

Herod (HEH-rud) was the name of four different rulers in the New Testament:

Herod I (Herod the Great) was king of the country of Palestine from the year 40 B.C. until about 4 B.C. He tried to kill the baby Jesus because Jesus was called a "king." Herod thought Jesus was an earthly king and would take away his throne. (Matthew 2:1-16; Luke 1:5)

Herod Antipas was the son of Herod I. He had John the Baptist's head cut off. Later, Jesus was sent to this man for trial. He ruled from the year 4 B.C. to about A.D. 39. (Matthew 14:1; Mark 6:14; Luke 23:6)

Herod Agrippa I was the king of Palestine for about three years (A.D. 41–44). He was the grandson of Herod I. He had the apostle James killed and the apostle Peter arrested. He did it to please the Jews who hated Jesus' followers. Later, this man was eaten by worms and died because he let the people treat him like a god. (Acts 12:1-21)

Herod Agrippa II was king of Palestine from the year A.D. 48 to 93. He was a great-grandson to Herod I. He heard the apostle Paul speak. He sent Paul to Caesar for trial. (Acts 25:13, 26; 26:1-32)

higgaion (hig-GI-on) is probably a musical word. It seems to mean "to meditate." So it may mean a time to think quietly during a song. (Psalm 9:16)

high priest was the most important religious leader of the Jewish people. He was often as important as the king. Caiaphas was the high priest when Jesus was killed. Annas was another high priest at that time. (Matthew 26:3, 57; Acts 23:2-5)

holy (HO-lee) means pure, belonging to and willing to serve God. God's people are called "holy peo-

ple." (Exodus 3:5; 22:31; 31:13;
1 Corinthians 1:2; Ephesians 1:4;
Philemon 4; 1 Peter 1:15-16)

Holy Place This was a room in the
Holy Tent and the Temple. The
priests came to this room every
day to burn candles and incense to
the Lord. Each week fresh loaves
of bread were placed on the table
there. A curtain separated the
Holy Place from the Most Holy
Place. (Exodus 26:31-35; 31:11;
Leviticus 6:30) See "bread that
shows we are in God's presence."

Holy Spirit (HO-lee SPIH-rit) is
one of the three persons of God.
The other two persons are God the
Father and God the Son (Jesus).
The Holy Spirit helped the apostles do miracles. He led men to
write God's word. The Holy Spirit
lives in Christians today. He is
also called the Spirit of Christ,
the Spirit of God, and the Comforter. (Genesis 1:2; John 3:5-8;
16:13; Acts 2:1-4; 5:32; Romans
5:5; 8:9-16; 2 Peter 1:20-21)

Holy Tent See "Meeting Tent."

hypocrite (HIP-oh-krit) comes from
the word for an actor on a stage.
In the Bible it is a person who acts
as if he is good but isn't. (Matthew 6:2, 5, 16; 7:3-5; Luke 13:15-
17)

I

idol (EYE-d'l) is a false god. The
non-Jewish people often worshiped
statues they made from wood,
stone or metal. They worshiped

these idols instead of the true God
of heaven. (Leviticus 19:4; 2 Kings
17:12-17; Acts 7:40-43; 17:16-23;
1 Thessalonians 1:9)

incense (IN-senz) was a spice burned
to make a sweet smell. This was
done by the priests in the Meeting
Tent and the Temple. A special
altar was used to burn incense as
worship to God. Since the smoke
seemed to go up to God, this reminded people of prayer. (Exodus
30:1-10, 34-38; Psalm 141:2; Luke
1:9; Revelation 8:3-4)

Isaac (EYE-zak) means "laughter."
He was the son of Abraham and
Sarah. He was named Isaac because Sarah laughed when the
angel told her she would have a
baby. She thought she was too old.
God tested Abraham by asking
him to offer Isaac as a sacrifice
on an altar. When God saw that
Abraham would obey him, he saved
Isaac's life. (Genesis 21–26; Mark
12:26; Hebrews 11:17-20)

Isaiah (i-ZAY-uh) was one of the
great prophets of the Old Testament. He often gave God's message to King Hezekiah. (2 Kings
19; 20; Isaiah 6–9; 53)

Israel (IZ-rah-el) is a Hebrew word
that means "he who wrestles with
God." When Jacob struggled with
an angel at Bethel, God named him
Israel. The 12 tribes of the Jewish
nation were descendants of Jacob. They were called Israelites.
(Exodus 3:16-18; Psalm 73:1;
Luke 1:68; Acts 2:36; 5:33-36)

J

Jacob (JAY-cub) was one of the sons of Isaac. He was the father of the 12 tribes of God's chosen people. He had 12 sons, and each son was the head of a tribe. (Genesis 25–36; Matthew 1:2; 8:11; John 4:6)

Jacob's Portion (JAY-cubs POR-shun) is a name for God. It means that God cares for Jacob's people, the Israelites. (Jeremiah 10:16; 51:19)

James was the name of several men in the New Testament:

James, the son of Zebedee, was an apostle of Jesus and a brother of the apostle John. He was killed by Herod Agrippa I. (Matthew 10:2; Mark 10:35, 41; Acts 12:2)

James, the son of Alphaeus, was also one of Jesus' apostles. He may have been a cousin to Jesus. (Matthew 10:3)

James, the brother of Jesus, was a respected leader in the church in Jerusalem. He probably wrote the book of James in the New Testament. (Matthew 13:55; John 7:5; Acts 12:17; 21:18; Galatians 1:19)

Jeremiah (jer-eh-MY-ah) was a prophet who warned the people of Judah. He told them they were disobeying God and would be punished. He had a very difficult life, but he stayed faithful to God. He lived to see Jerusalem destroyed and the people taken to Babylon. (2 Chronicles 35:25; 36:21-22; Jeremiah 1; 2; 20:1-6; 28:5; 36–40)

Jerusalem (jeh-ROO-suh-lem) is sometimes called "Zion" or the "City of David." It was the greatest city of the country of Palestine. It was the center of the Jewish religion because the Temple was there. Jesus was killed on the cross near Jerusalem. The city was destroyed by the Roman army in the year A.D. 70. Later, it was rebuilt in the same place by the Moslems and is a great city today in the Middle East. (2 Samuel 5:5-6; 2 Chronicles 36:14, 19; Ezra 1:1-11; Luke 2:22-45; 13:34; 24:13, 18, 33, 47, 49; Acts 2:5, 14) See "Zion."

Jesus (JEE-zus) means "savior." He is the Son of God. He was born to Mary, a young Jewish woman. Mary was told by the angel Gabriel that she would have a baby boy. She was to name him "Jesus" because he would save his people from their sins. He is also called "Christ" and "Messiah." He lived a perfect life and never sinned. But he was killed by Roman soldiers on a cross near Jerusalem. Then, he came back to life and now lives in heaven with his father, God. He is one of the three persons of God. The other two persons are God the Father, and God the Holy Spirit. (Matthew 1:21; Luke 2:21; 3:23; John 20:19; Acts 1:19, 36; 4:10; Philippians 2:10-11) See "Christ" and "Messiah."

Jesus was a common name among Jewish people, so there

were other less important men in the New Testament named Jesus, too. (Colossians 4:11)

Jew (JOO) at first meant someone from the tribe of Judah. Judah was 1 of Jacob's 12 sons and the head of 1 of the 12 tribes of Israel. Later, the word Jew meant any person in any of the 12 tribes (Hebrews 1–13). A person who is not a Jew is called a Gentile or non-Jew. Jesus was a Jew. (Ezra 4:12; Matthew 2:2; 28:11-15; Acts 2:5; Romans 1:16; 10:12)

John was the name of several men in the New Testament:

John the Baptist was Jesus' relative and the son of Elizabeth and Zechariah the priest. He lived in the desert and ate locusts and wild honey. He preached that the Savior, Jesus, was coming soon. Jesus came to John the Baptist to be baptized in the Jordan River. Herod Antipas had John killed by cutting off his head. (Matthew 3:1-17; 11:11-13; 14:3-12; Luke 1:13-17)

John, the apostle, was one of the sons of Zebedee. He and his brother James were fishermen. He wrote the Gospel of John, the books of 1, 2 and 3 John and probably Revelation. He is sometimes referred to as "the one Jesus loved." John, Peter and James were Jesus' closest friends. (Mark 1:19-20; 9:2; 14:33-34; Acts 3:1-11; Revelation 1:1-4, 9)

John Mark See Mark.

Jordan (JOR-d'n) is the only large river in the country of Palestine. It runs about 75 miles from Mount Hermon to the Dead Sea. It also makes two lakes—Lake Huleh and Lake Galilee. Jesus was baptized in the Jordan River near the city of Jericho. (Joshua 3:11-17; 2 Kings 5:10, 14; Matthew 3:5-17)

Joseph (JOZ-uf) was the name of several men in the Bible.

Joseph, the son of Jacob, was 1 of the 12 sons of Israel. His two sons, Ephraim and Manasseh, each started a tribe. (Genesis 37–50; Exodus 1:5-8; 13:19; Acts 7:10-14)

Joseph of Nazareth was the husband of Mary, Jesus' mother. He was a carpenter. He may have died when Jesus was a young man because he is not mentioned after Jesus' childhood. The New Testament says he was "a good man." (Matthew 1:18-24; 2:13-23)

Joseph of Arimathea took the body of Jesus down from the cross and buried it in a tomb he had dug for himself. He was a member of the Jewish religious court called the Sanhedrin. He was probably a Christian. (Matthew 27:57-60; Mark 15:43-46)

Jubilee (JOO-bih-lee) was a Jewish celebration that took place every fifty years. Israelites were to do three things: (1) give the soil a rest and not farm, (2) free Israelite slaves, and (3) return land and houses to the first owners or their children. (Leviticus 25)

Judas Iscariot (JOO-dus is-CARE-ee-ut) was the apostle who turned against Jesus and handed him over to the Roman soldiers to be killed. For this he was paid only 30 pieces of silver, the price of a slave. Later, Judas killed himself. (Matthew 26:47-50; 27:3-5; John 13:26-30)

Jude (JOOD) was possibly a brother of Jesus and James. In Jesus' early ministry, Jude did not believe Jesus was the Son of God. Later, he believed and became a leader in Christ's church. He wrote the book of Jude in the New Testament. (John 7:5; Jude)

Judea (joo-DEE-uh) was the land of the Jews. It was a district in the country of Palestine. Both Jerusalem and Bethlehem were cities in Judea. John the Baptist began his preaching in the desert of Judea. (Matthew 2:1; Luke 1:5; 2:4; Acts 1:8)

judges (JUHG-es) were the leaders of Israel before Israel had kings. A judge decided who was guilty in court, led the army in battle and was in charge of the government, like a governor. Israel had 15 judges in all. (Judges 2:16-19; 1 Samuel 7:15-17)

Judgment Day (JUJ-ment DAY) is the day Christ will judge all people. He will take his followers to live with him forever in heaven. Those who have followed the devil will be sent to live with him in hell forever. (Matthew 11:20-24; Hebrews 9:27-28; 2 Peter 2:9-10; 3:7)

L

lamb (LAM) is an animal that the Jews often offered as a sacrifice (gift) to God. Since Jesus died as a sacrifice for us, he is called the Lamb of God that takes away the sins of the world. (Genesis 4:4; 22:7; Exodus 12:3-13; John 1:29, 36; 1 Corinthians 5:7)

Lazarus (LAZ-uh-rus) was the name of two men in the New Testament:

Lazarus of Bethany was a brother to Mary and Martha. He was also a very dear friend of Jesus. When he died, Jesus brought him back to life. (John 11:1-45; 12:1-11)

Lazarus, the beggar, was the name of a person in a story Jesus told his followers. (Luke 16:19-31)

leprosy (LEH-prah-see) is a name for some bad skin diseases. A person with leprosy was called a leper and had to live outside the city. When other people came by, the lepers had to warn them by crying out, "Unclean! Unclean!" (Leviticus 13:45-46; 2 Kings 5:1-27; 2 Chronicles 26:19-23; Matthew 8:1-3; Luke 17:11-19)

Leviathan (lee-VI-ah-than) was the name for a sea monster. Some people think it was a crocodile.

(Job 3:8; 41:1; Psalm 74:14; Isaiah 27:1)

Levites (LEE-vites) were descendants of Levi, one of Jacob's sons. The priests all came from this tribe. But not all Levites were priests. Those who were not priests worked in the Meeting Tent or Temple in other ways. (Exodus 32:25-29; Numbers 1:47-53; 8:5-26; Deuteronomy 10:8-9; 18:1-8; 1 Kings 12:31; Luke 10:32)

lid on the Holy Box is also called the mercy seat. This was the beautiful gold lid on the Box of the Agreement. It had a gold creature with wings on each end of it. This Holy Box was kept in the Most Holy Place of the Meeting Tent and later in the Temple. (Exodus 25:17-22; 26:34; Leviticus 16:2, 14-16; Hebrews 9:5)

locust (LO-cust) is an insect that looks like a grasshopper. Locusts travel in large groups. They eat crops and other green plants. Locusts were sometimes eaten as food. (Exodus 10:4-19; Deuteronomy 28:38-42; Joel 1:4; Matthew 3:4)

lord means "master" or one who is in control. Jesus is called Lord because he rules over all the world and universe. Christians let Jesus be the Lord of their lives. (Acts 2:36; 21:12-14; Romans 10:9; 1 Corinthians 6:11; Colossians 3:17-24)

Lord's Prayer is the name often given to the model prayer Jesus

taught his followers. (Matthew 6:9-13; Luke 11:1-4)

Lord's Supper is the meal Jesus' followers eat to remember how he died for them. The bread reminds us of his body. The fruit of the vine reminds us of his blood. The Lord's Supper also shows that Jesus came back to life and now lives in heaven with God. (Matthew 26:26-30; Luke 22:14-20; 1 Corinthians 10:17; 11:23-32)

lots were sticks, stones or pieces of bone thrown like dice to decide something. Often God controlled the result of the lots to let the people know what he wanted them to do. (Numbers 26:55-56; Proverbs 18:18; Jonah 1:7; Luke 1:9; 23:34; Acts 1:26)

Luke was a non-Jewish doctor who often traveled with the apostle Paul. He was a very educated man. He wrote the books of Luke and Acts in the New Testament. Luke tells many acts of Jesus that are not told in the other three Gospels. (Colossians 4:14; 2 Timothy 4:11)

lyre (LIRE) is a musical instrument with strings. It is similar to a harp, but smaller. (2 Samuel 6:5; 1 Chronicles 15:16-28; Psalms 33:2; 144:9; 150:3)

M

mahalath (mah-HAY-lath), or mahalath leannoth, was probably a musical word. It may have been the name of a tune, or it may mean to dance and shout. (Psalms 53; 88)

manna (MAN-ah) means "what is it?" It was the white, sweet-tasting food God gave the people of Israel in the wilderness. It appeared on the ground during the night so they could gather it in the morning. (Exodus 16:13-35; Numbers 11:7-9; Joshua 5:12; Hebrews 9:4)

Marduk (MAR-dook) was a false god of the Babylonians. (Jeremiah 50:2)

Mark, sometimes called John Mark, was a cousin to Barnabas. Mark traveled with Paul and Barnabas on part of their first missionary journey. He also wrote the Gospel of Mark. Christians met in the home of Mark's mother, Mary, to pray for Peter to be freed from prison. (Acts 12:12, 25; 13:5, 13; 15:36-41; Colossians 4:10; 2 Timothy 4:11)

Martha (MAR-thuh) was the sister of Mary and Lazarus. They lived in the village of Bethany, which is very near Jerusalem. Jesus often stayed in their home when he was in that area. Martha and her brother and sister loved Jesus very much. (Luke 10:38-41; John 11:1-39; 12:12)

martyr (MAR-ter) is a Greek word that means "witness." Being a witness means telling what you know about something. Later, martyr came to mean a person who was killed for being a wit-ness. Stephen was the first Christian martyr. He was killed because he told people that Jesus is the Son of God. It is believed that all the apostles, except one, were martyrs for being witnesses about Jesus. (Acts 7:54-60; 12:2; 22:20; Revelation 2:13)

Mary is the name of several women in the New Testament:

Mary, the mother of Jesus, was a Jewish woman whom God chose to give birth to his only Son. This was a great honor and blessing from God. She married a man named Joseph. Mary stood at the foot of the cross when Jesus was killed. (Matthew 1:18-25; Luke 1:27-45; John 19:25-27)

Mary Magdalene was from the town of Magdala. She was a follower of Jesus. She watched the men put Jesus' body in the tomb. She was the first person to see Jesus after he came back to life. (Matthew 27:56, 61; Mark 15:40, 47; 16:1, 9; John 20:1-18)

Mary of Bethany was the sister of Martha and Lazarus. She was a dear friend of Jesus. Mary sat at Jesus' feet and listened to him teach. One time she poured some expensive perfume on his feet and dried them with her hair. (Luke 10:39-42)

maskil (MAS-kil) is probably a description of the kind of song that some of the Psalms were. It appears with 13 of the Psalms. (Psalms 32; 42; 44; 45)

Matthew (MATH-you), also called Levi, was a tax collector. He was 1 of Jesus' 12 apostles. He wrote the Gospel of Matthew. (Matthew 9:9-10; 10:3)

medium (MEED-ee-um) means "go-between." This is a person who tries to help living people talk to the spirits of dead people. (Leviticus 19:31; Deuteronomy 18:11; 1 Samuel 28:3-9; 2 Kings 23:24; Isaiah 8:19-20)

Meeting Tent is often called the Tabernacle or Holy Tent. This was the special tent where the Israelites worshiped God. It was used from the time they left Egypt until Solomon built the Temple in Jerusalem. This tent was kept in the middle of their camp to remind them that God was always with them. (Exodus 25–27; 39:32–40:36; Numbers 8; 2 Chronicles 1:3-13; 5:5)

Melchizedek (mel-KIZ-ih-dek) means "king of righteousness." He was a priest and king who worshiped God in the time of Abraham. Jesus is now the Christian's king and high priest. In this way, Jesus is a priest and a king like Melchizedek. (Genesis 14:17-24; Hebrews 5:4-10; 7:1-17)

mercy (MUR-see) is kindness and forgiveness. God had mercy on us. He sent his only Son, Jesus, to die on the cross for our sins. We, too, are taught to have mercy on other people. God says he will be as merciful to us as we are to others. (Genesis 43:14; 2 Samuel 24:14; Matthew 5:7; Romans 11:32; James 2:13; 5:11; 1 Peter 2:10)

mercy seat See "lid on the Holy Box."

Messiah (muh-SYE-uh) is a Hebrew word for "appointed one" or "one chosen by God." The Greek word for Messiah is "Christ." Christians believe that Jesus is the Messiah or Christ. (John 1:41; 4:25)

miktam (MIK-tam) is probably a description of what kind of song some of the Psalms were. It may mean that it is a sad song or a song about danger. (Psalms 16; 56–60)

mildew (MIL-doo) is a growth that appears on things that have been damp for a long time. (Leviticus 13:47-59; 14:33-54)

minister (MIN-i-ster) means "servant." It also means one who lives serving God and others. Christians are taught to minister to each other and to non-Christians. (Romans 15:16)

miracle (MEER-ih-k'l) is a Latin word that means "wonderful thing." It is a great event which can be done only by God's help. Miracles are special signs to show God's power. In the Old Testament God used miracles to rescue his people. Jesus did miracles to prove that he was God's Son. The Bible tells us of many miracles. The sick were healed, the blind were given sight, the crippled were able to walk and people could speak languages they had never studied. Sometimes people were even brought back to life after they had died. The best miracle was Jesus' coming back to life after he was killed on the cross. (Nehemiah 9:17; Psalm 77:11, 14; Matthew 28:5-7; Luke 23:8; John 2:1-11; 3:2; 20:30-31; Acts 4:16-22; 8:13)

Molech (MO-lek) was a false god of the Canaanite people. Those who worshiped Molech often sacrificed their own children to him by burning them on altars. (Leviticus 18:21; 20:1-5; 2 Kings 23:10; Jeremiah 32:35)

mortar (MORE-tar) has two meanings:

It can be a stone bowl where grain is ground into flour by pounding. Manna was ground up this way. (Numbers 11:8; Proverbs 27:22)

Mortar is also the sticky material that holds bricks together. It was often made of mud or clay. (Genesis 11:3; Exodus 1:14; Isaiah 41:25)

Moses (MO-zez) in Hebrew means "saved from the water." Moses led God's people out of the land of Egypt where they had been slaves for 400 years. Moses wrote the first five books of the Old Testament. On Mount Sinai God gave to Moses the law for the Israelite people. It is called "the law of Moses." (Exodus 2–40; Numbers 1–26; Deuteronomy 27–34; John 1:17, 45; 3:14; Hebrews 11:23-24; Revelation 15:3)

Most Holy Place was the inner and most special room in the Meeting Tent and the Temple. The Box of the Agreement was kept here. Only the high priest could come into this room, and he could enter only once a year. This was when he sprinkled blood on the lid of the Holy Box to remind the people that their sins needed to be forgiven. (Exodus 26:33-34; Leviticus 16:2-20; 1 Kings 6:16-35; Hebrews 9:3-25)

Mount of Olives is a hill covered with olive trees near Jerusalem. The garden of Gethsemane is on one side of the Mount of Olives. Jesus was praying there when the Roman soldiers came to arrest him. Some of the same olive trees that were in the garden when Jesus was on earth may still be there today. (2 Samuel 15:30; Luke 22:39-52; Acts 1:12)

Mount Zion (ZI-on) at first meant one of the hills on which Jerusalem was built. Later Zion became another name for the whole city of Jerusalem. In the New Testament, Zion is also used as a name for heaven. (Psalms 48:2, 11; 74:2; 78:68; Obadiah 17; Hebrews 12:22)

myrrh (MUR) was a sweet-smelling liquid taken from certain trees and shrubs. It was used as a perfume and as a pain reliever. It was one of the gifts the wise men gave Jesus when he was born. (Genesis 37:25; 43:11; Proverbs 7:17; Matthew 2:11; Mark 15:23; John 19:39)

N

nard was an expensive perfume. It cost so much because it had to be imported from India. (Song of Solomon 4:13; Mark 14:3; John 12:3)

Nazarene (NAZ-uh-reen) is a person from the town of Nazareth. Jesus grew up in Nazareth and was called a Nazarene. Sometimes Christians also were called Nazarenes, since they followed Jesus. (Matthew 2:23; Acts 24:5)

Nazirite (NAZ-e-rite) was a Jewish person who made a special promise to God. He was to serve God by following special rules. Samson and Samuel were Nazirites. (Numbers 6:1-21; Judges 13:7; 16:17)

Nebo (NEE-boh) was the name of a Babylonian god. He was thought to be the god of writing and the son of Bel. (Isaiah 46:1)

Nebo was also the name of the mountain where Moses died, as well as a town nearby. (Numbers 32:3; Deuteronomy 34:1; Isaiah 15:2)

Nehemiah (nee-uh-MY-uh) was a servant of King Artaxerxes I of Persia. He got permission to take a group of Jews back to Jerusalem to rebuild its walls. Nehemiah was such a good leader that they finished the job even though they had many difficulties. (Nehemiah 1–12)

Nephilim (NEF-eh-lim) were a group of people who were famous for being large and strong. The ten spies who were afraid to enter Canaan had seen the Nephilim who lived there. (Genesis 6:4; Numbers 13:33)

New Moon was a Jewish feast held on the first day of the month. It was celebrated with animal sacrifices and the blowing of trumpets. It was a way for the Israelites to dedicate the month to the Lord. (Numbers 10:10; 28:14; 1 Samuel 20:5, 24; Psalm 81:3; Ezekiel 46:3-6; Colossians 2:16)

Noah (NO-uh) and his family were the only people of their time who served God. So God told them about the great flood that was coming. They built a large boat (often called an ark) about 450 feet long. Noah's family and every kind of animal were saved to start the world all over again. (Genesis 6–9; 1 Peter 3:20)

P

parable (PARE-uh-b'l) is a story that teaches a lesson by comparing two things. Jesus often used parables to teach the people. Some examples of parables can be found in Mark 12:1-12; Luke 10:29-37 and Luke 15:1-31.

Passover Feast (PASS-o-ver FEEST) was an important holy day for the Jews in the spring of each year. They ate a special meal on this day to remind them that God had freed them from being slaves in Egypt. Jesus was killed at Passover time. (Exodus 12:27; Numbers 9; Joshua 5:10; Matthew 26:2, 17-19)

Paul is the Roman name for "Saul." Saul was a Jew, born in the city of Tarsus. He studied under Gamaliel, a famous teacher of God's law. At first, Paul tried to destroy Christ's church by putting Christians in jail and killing them. But Jesus appeared to him and changed his life completely. He was then called Paul. And he became an apostle and a great servant of God. He traveled to many countries, teaching about Jesus. Paul wrote many of the books of the New Testament as letters to Christians in different cities, such as Romans, Colossians and Corinthians. (Acts 7:58-60; 9:1-31; Philippians 3:5-7)

Pentecost (PEN-tee-cost) means "fifty." Pentecost was a Jewish feast day celebrating the summer harvest. It took place 50 days after the Passover Feast. The apostles began telling the Good News on Pentecost after Jesus died. (Acts 2; 20:16; 1 Corinthians 16:8)

persecute (PUR-seh-cute) means to hurt people. Christians in the New Testament times were often persecuted. Saul persecuted Christians by dragging them from their homes, putting them in jail and killing them. (Matthew 5:11-12; Acts 8:1-4; Galatians 6:12; 1 Peter 3:13-15)

Peter (PEE-ter) was a fisherman. He and his brother, Andrew, were the first two apostles Jesus chose. He was first named Simon, but Jesus changed his name to Cephas, which means "rock" in Aramaic. In Greek the name is Peter. Peter, James and John were Jesus' closest friends. Peter was the first to tell the Good News of Jesus to the non-Jewish people. Later in his life Peter wrote the New Testament books of 1 and 2 Peter. He probably died as a martyr for Christ. (Matthew 14:25-33; 16:13-18; Mark 14:27-39; Luke 22:54-62; John 20:1-6; Acts 3:1-26; 10:1-48)

pharaoh (FAY-row) was the title given to the kings of Egypt. The word first meant "great house," meaning the palace where the king lived. Later it became the title of the king who lived in the great house. Pharaoh is also called "king of Egypt." (Genesis 40–47; Exodus 1–14; 2 Kings 23:29)

Pharisees (FARE-uh-seez) means "the separate people." They were a Jewish religious group who followed the religious laws and customs very strictly. Jesus often spoke against the Pharisees for their religious teachings and traditions. Many of the Pharisees did not like Jesus because he did not follow all of their rules. (Matthew 5:20; 23:23-36; Mark 7:1-13; Luke 18:9-14)

Philip (FIL-ip) was the name of several men in the New Testament:

Philip, the apostle, was from the city of Bethsaida and was a friend of Peter and Andrew. He brought Nathanael to Jesus. (Matthew 10:2-3; John 1:43-48; 12:21; 14:8-9)

Philip, the evangelist, was a Greek-speaking Jew. He was one of the seven men chosen to serve in the church in Jerusalem. Later, he preached the Good News in many places. (Acts 6:1-6; 8:5-40; 21:8-9)

Philip, the tetrarch (ruler), was the son of Herod I and Cleopatra. He built the city of Caesarea Philippi. (Luke 3:1)

Philistines (FIL-ih-steens) were Israel's enemies for many years. They had five strong cities near the Mediterranean Sea: Ashdod, Ashkelon, Ekron, Gath and Gaza. They worshiped several false gods. They were finally defeated by the Egyptians. (Judges 15; 16; 1 Samuel 4:1-10; 6; 7; 17; 18; 1 Chronicles 18:1)

plumb line (PLUM LINE) is a string with a rock or other weight on one end. People used it to see if a wall was straight. The plumb line was sometimes used to mean that God was checking to see if his people were living right. This is just as they checked to see if a wall was built right. (2 Kings 21:13; Amos 7:7-8)

pomegranate (PAHM-gran-it) is a red fruit about the size of an apple. It has many seeds. Each seed has a pocket of sweet juice around it. (Exodus 28:33; 39:24; Numbers 13:23; Deuteronomy 8:8; 1 Samuel 14:2)

Pontius Pilate (PON-shus PIE-lut) means "armed with a spear." Pilate was the Roman governor of Judea from A.D. 26 to 36. The Jews who wanted Jesus killed brought him to Pilate. He did not find Jesus guilty of any crime. But Pilate allowed the Jews to crucify Jesus because he was afraid of the people. (Luke 13:1; 23:1-52; Acts 3:13; 4:27; 1 Timothy 6:13)

Preparation Day (prep-a-RAY-shun-DAY) was the day before the Sabbath day. On that day the Jews prepared or got everything ready for the Sabbath. (Luke 23:54; John 19:14, 31)

priest (PREEST) in the Old Testament was a servant of God who worked in the Meeting Tent or Temple. Priests helped the people offer their gifts and sacrifices to God. Jesus is the Christian's high priest. He brings man and God together. Because of this all Christians are now priests. (Leviticus 21; 22; Hebrews 7:26-28; 1 Peter 2:5, 9; Revelation 1:5-6) See "high priest."

Priscilla (prih-SIL-uh) See "Aquila."

prophecy (PRAH-feh-see) means "message." It is God speaking through chosen people called prophets. The Old Testament has many prophecies about the Savior who was to come into the world. Jesus was the answer to these prophecies. (Ezekiel 12:26-28; 2 Peter 1:20-21; Revelation 22:18-19) See "prophet."

prophesy (PRAH-fes-sy) is to speak a prophecy. See "prophecy."

prophet (PRAH-fet) means "messenger" or one who speaks for someone else. With God's help, a prophet was able to tell the people God's message correctly. Sometimes prophets told what would happen in the future. A woman who spoke God's message was called a prophetess (2 Kings 22:14; Luke 2:36). Several books of the Old Testament were written by prophets, including Jeremiah, Amos, Jonah and Micah. (2 Kings 6:12-16; 17:12-13; Matthew 2:5-6; Luke 16:29-31; 24:25-27; Romans 1:2; 1 Corinthians 12:28-29; 1 Peter 1:10-12)

prophetess See "prophet."

prostitute (PRAH-sti-toot) is a person who sells his or her body for sexual relations with someone to whom he or she is not married. This is a sin. In the Old Testament God's people often worshiped other gods. God said this was acting like a prostitute. (Genesis 38:15; Exodus 34:15-16; Proverbs 23:27; Jeremiah 3:1-6; Hosea 3:3; 1 Corinthians 6:15)

proverbs (PRAH-verbs) are wise sayings. They are usually short so they can be easily remembered. The Old Testament book of Proverbs contains many wise sayings. They tell how to live a good and happy life. (book of Proverbs)

psalm (SAHM) means "song." The book of Psalms is like a songbook. The Jews sang many of these psalms, particularly at special times. There are many musical directions in the Psalms, such as the tune or the instruments to be used. (book of Psalms)

Q

Queen Goddess is another name for Ishtar, a goddess of the Babylonians. During Jeremiah's time some of the Israelites worshiped her. (Jeremiah 7:18; 44:17-25)

R

Rahab (RAY-hab) was the name of a make-believe dragon. In a well-known story, Rahab looked strong but was defeated. Egypt was sometimes called Rahab to show that it would be defeated as Rahab was. (Job 9:13; 26:12; Psalms 87:4; 89:10; Isaiah 30:7; 51:9)

Rahab was also the name of a woman in Jericho. She hid the Israelite spies and helped them escape. (Joshua 2:1-3; 6:17-25; Matthew 1:5; Hebrews 11:31; James 2:25)

Rapha (RAY-fa) was a leader of a group of people in Canaan. They may have been giants. The descendants of Rapha are called Rephaites. (Genesis 14:5; Deuteronomy 2:11; 2 Samuel 21:16-22)

Red Sea is sometimes called the Sea of Reeds. It is a large body of water between Africa and Arabia. At the northern end it has two parts, one on each side of the Sinai Peninsula. God used a miracle to divide these waters on the northern end on the west side. Then the Israelites could walk across on dry land and escape from Egypt. (Exodus 13:17–15:22; Joshua 2:10; 4:23; Psalm 106:7-22)

repent (ree-PENT) means being sorry for doing something wrong and not continuing to do that wrong thing. To repent is to "change your heart and life." (2 Chronicles 32:26; Matthew 3:2; 4:17; Mark 1:15; Luke 15:7, 10; Acts 2:38; 3:19)

Rephaites See "Rapha."

resurrection (REZ-uh-REK-shun) is a dead person's coming back to life. In the New Testament several people came back to life with God's help. Some of them were Lazarus (John 11:38-45), Tabitha (Acts 9:36-42), the widow's son in the town of Nain (Luke 7:11-17), and Eutychus (Acts 20:8-12). Jesus, the Son of God, came back to life after being dead three days. This was the most important resurrection. His resurrection from death means we can be saved and live in heaven forever. (Matthew 28:1-

10; 1 Corinthians 15; 1 Peter 3:21-22)

revelation (rev-uh-LAY-shun) means to show plainly something that has been hidden. The last book in the New Testament is called the Revelation of Jesus Christ. God showed the apostle John what to write to Christians to give them hope and faith even though they were being persecuted. (2 Corinthians 12:1; Revelation 1:1-3)

Rock is often used as a name for God. A large rock is strong and a good place to hide. God is strong and protects us from our enemies. (Genesis 49:24; Deuteronomy 32:4, 15, 18, 30; 2 Samuel 22:32, 47; Psalm 18:2, 31, 46)

S

Sabbath (SAB-uth) means "rest." It was the seventh day of the Jewish week, their day of worship to God. The Jews were not allowed to work on this day. Some Jews became angry with Jesus because he healed people on the Sabbath. They thought this was breaking the Old Testament law of the Sabbath. (Exodus 16:23-30; 20:8-11; Matthew 12:9-14; Luke 6:1-11; Acts 18:4; Colossians 2:16-17)

Sadducees (SAD-you-seez) were a Jewish religious group. They were rich and important men. They believed that only the first five books of the Old Testament were true. They did not believe in angels or life after death (resurrection). The

Sadducees lost their power and importance after Jerusalem was destroyed by the Romans about the year A.D. 70. (Matthew 22:23-33; Acts 4:1-2; 5:17-18; 23:6-9)

safety, city of is sometimes called City of Refuge. In Bible times, someone who had accidentally killed another person could go to a city of safety for protection. As long as the person was in a city of safety, the dead person's relative could not punish him. There were six cities of safety. (Numbers 35:6-34; Joshua 20)

saffron (SAF-ron) is a purple flower. Parts of it are used as a spice. (Song of Solomon 4:14)

saint is another word for Christian. God has set Christians apart to serve him. They live to please God and be like him—pure and holy. (Acts 9:13, 32, 41; 26:10; Romans 1:7; 1 Corinthians 1:2; Ephesians 1:1)

Samaritan (suh-MEHR-ih-t'n) was a person from the area of Samaria in Palestine. Samaria was between Galilee and Judea. These people were only part Jewish, so the Jews did not accept them. They hated the Samaritans. But Jesus showed love and concern for the Samaritans. One story that Jesus told is known as the story of "the good Samaritan." (Luke 10:30-37; John 4:1-42)

Samuel (SAM-you-el) was the last judge in Israel. God used him to choose both Saul and David as kings. (1 Samuel 1–3; 7–16)

Sanhedrin (san-HEE-drin) See "council."

Satan (SAY-t'n) in Hebrew means "enemy." It is a name for the devil, the enemy of God and man. (1 Chronicles 21:1; Job 1:6-9; Matthew 4:10; Luke 10:18-19; Acts 5:3; 26:18) See "devil."

Saul (SAWL) in the Old Testament was the first king of Israel (1 Samuel 9–31). Saul in the New Testament was a man whose name was changed to Paul. See "Paul."

savior (SAVE-yor) is someone who saves people from danger. The name Jesus means "savior." Jesus is the Savior of the people of this world. His life, death and resurrection made it possible for people to be saved from death and punishment for their sins. (Luke 2:11; John 4:42; Ephesians 5:23; Philippians 3:20; Titus 1:4; 1 John 4:14)

scepter (SEP-tur) is a wand or a rod that the king holds. It is a sign of his power. Some are long and thin. Others are short and flat like a paddle. Some of them are highly decorated with gold. (Esther 4:11; 5:2; 8:4; Psalm 2:9)

scribe is a Hebrew word that means to write, to count and to put in order. In New Testament times scribes were men who wrote copies of the Scriptures. They were very careful when they copied the words of God. To be sure they had not made a mistake in copying, they would count the number of letters on each line they wrote. Scribes were educated, and some of them served as secretaries, royal assistants and teachers. (Nehemiah 8:1; Jeremiah 36:26; Matthew 7:29; 15:1-9; 23:1-36; Luke 22:2)

Scriptures (SCRIP-churs) means "writing." They are the special writings of God's word for man. When the word "Scriptures" is used in the New Testament, it usually means the Old Testament. Later, it came to mean the whole Bible. (Daniel 9:2; Luke 24:27, 32, 45; Acts 8:32-35; 17:2, 11; 2 Timothy 3:16; 2 Peter 1:20; 3:16) See "Bible."

scroll is a long roll of paper used for writing. In Bible times books were written on scrolls. These scrolls were rolled up from each end to the middle. They were made of papyrus (a plant) or parchment (an animal skin). Some scrolls were as long as 35 feet. (Numbers 5:23; Isaiah 8:1; Jeremiah 36; Luke 4:17-20; 2 Timothy 4:13; Revelation 5:1-5)

Sea of Galilee See "Galilee, Lake."

seal was a tool with a design or picture carved on it. Kings pressed this seal into wax which would be placed on important papers to close them. It was like a person's signature. If the seal was broken, it showed that someone else had looked at the papers. A seal also showed who owned something. Sometimes these seals were worn as rings. (1 Kings 21:8; Esther 8:8; 2 Corinthians 1:22) See "signet ring."

seer was another name for prophet. (1 Samuel 9:9) See "prophet."

Selah (SEE-lah) is probably a musical direction and is used in the Psalms. It may mean to pause. The word was not intended to be spoken when reading the Psalm. (Psalms 3; 4; 9; 24)

sheminith (SHEM-e-nith) means "on the eighth." It is probably a musical word in the Psalms that means an octave. It may mean to use an instrument with eight strings. (1 Chronicles 15:21; Psalms 6; 12)

shepherd (SHEP-'rd) is a person who cares for and protects sheep. A shepherd loves his sheep and gives them food and water. He guides them to a quiet place to rest. He protects the sheep from wolves and other wild animals. A good shepherd will even die trying to protect his sheep.

Jesus is called the Good Shepherd because he loves and cares for his followers who are often called sheep. Jesus was willing to die for his followers to save them. (Psalm 23; Mark 6:34; John 10:1-30; 1 Peter 2:25; 5:4)

shiggaion/shigionoth (shi-GY-on/shi-gi-O-noth) could be musical words meaning a sad song. (Psalm 7; Habakkuk 3:1)

signet ring (SIG-net ring) was a ring worn by a king or other important person. It had his seal on it. He would stamp things with this ring to show that he owned them. The stamp was like a signature. (Genesis 41:42; Esther 3:10; 8:2-10; Daniel 6:17) See "seal."

Silas (SY-lus) is sometimes called Silvanus. He was a teacher in the church in Jerusalem who often traveled with Paul. He became one of Paul's most trusted helpers. He may have written down some of Peter and Paul's letters for them. (Acts 15:22, 30–17:16; 18:5; 1 Thessalonians 1:1; 1 Peter 5:12)

Simeon (SIM-ee-un) is a name that means "God has heard." He was 1 of the 12 sons of Israel. (Genesis 29:33; 35:23)

Another Simeon was a godly man who lived in Jerusalem. When he saw the baby Jesus in the Temple, he knew that this child would save his people from their sins. He held the baby Jesus in his arms and said a prayer of thanks to God. (Luke 2:25-35)

Simon (SY-mun), sometimes called Simeon, is a name that means "God has heard." The apostle Peter was first named Simon. Other men named Simon are also mentioned in the New Testament:

Simon of Cyrene carried the cross of Jesus to the hill of Calvary. (Matthew 27:32)

Simon, the magician, tried to buy the power of the Holy Spirit to do miracles. (Acts 8:9-24)

Simon, the Zealot, was 1 of the 12 apostles. (Matthew 10:4)

Simon, the brother of Jesus (Matthew 13:55)

sin is a word, thought or act against the law of God. Sin is doing something God said not to do, or it could be not doing something he said to do. Jesus came to save us from being punished for our sins. (Psalm 32:2; Romans 3:23; 5:12; 1 Corinthians 15:3; Galatians 1:4; Hebrews 4:15-16; 1 John 1:8-10; 2:1-2)

Solomon (SOL-o-mon) was a son of David. He took his father's place as king. He was famous for his wisdom and for building the Temple in Jerusalem. (1 Kings 1–11; 2 Chronicles 1–11)

Solomon's Porch (SOL-o-mon's PORCH) was a covered courtyard on the east side of the Temple. People gathered here to sell animals and exchange money. Others met to discuss the Law of Moses. (1 Kings 7:6; John 10:23; Acts 3:11; 5:12)

Son of David was a name the Jews used for the Christ who was to save the world. This was because the Savior was to come from the family of King David. Jesus was the "Son of David." (Matthew 9:27; 20:30; 21:9)

Son of Man was a name Jesus called himself. It showed that he was God's Son, but he was also a man. This title for Jesus comes from "one who looked like a human being" in Daniel 7:13-14. There Daniel prophesies about Jesus. (Matthew 24:30; 26:64; Mark 13:26; 14:62; Luke 21:27; 22:69)

sorcery (SOR-sir-ee) means trying to put magical spells on people or harming them by some kind of magic. The Bible warns against doing this. (Leviticus 19:26; Deuteronomy 18:14; 2 Kings 17:17)

soul (SOLE) is what makes a person alive. Sometimes the Bible writers used words like heart and soul to mean a person's whole being or the person himself. (Deuteronomy 4:29; Psalm 108:1; Matthew 10:28)

Spirit See "Holy Spirit."

spirit (SPIH-rit) is the part of man that was made to be like God because God is spirit. The New Testament also talks about evil spirits. (Isaiah 26:9; John 4:23-24; James 2:24-26) See "demons," "Holy Spirit" and "soul."

Stephen (STEE-ven) was one of the seven men chosen to serve the church in Jerusalem. The New Testament says he was a man who had much faith. He was able to do miracles. Stephen was the first martyr for Christ. The Jews killed him by throwing stones at him because he taught that Jesus was the Son of God. (Acts 6:5-15; 7:54-60; 22:20)

synagogue (SIN-uh-gog) is a Greek word that means "a meeting." By the first century, the Jews met in synagogues to read and study the Scriptures. The building was also used as the Jewish court and as a school. Both Jesus and Paul often went to the Jewish synagogues to teach and discuss the Scriptures. (Matthew 4:23; Luke 4:16-17; Acts 15:21; 17:1, 10)

Syria (SEER-ee-uh) is a Hebrew word that means "plain." In New Testament times, it was the area north of Galilee and east of the Mediterranean Sea. Damascus was its capital city. In Old Testament times, this country was called Aram. (1 Kings 11:25; 2 Kings 5:1; Matthew 4:24; 15:23)

T

tabernacle (TAB-er-NAK'l) See "Meeting Tent."

tambourine (tam-buh-REEN) is a musical instrument that is beaten to keep rhythm. (Exodus 15:20; 1 Samuel 18:6; Psalm 81:2)

tax collector was a Jew hired by the Romans to collect taxes. Most people did not like tax collectors because they worked for the Romans and often cheated people. The apostle Matthew was a tax collector before he became an apostle. Zacchaeus was also a tax collector. (Matthew 9:10-11; 10:3; Luke 5:27; 19:1-8)

temple (TEM-p'l) is a building where people worship their gods. God told the Jewish people to worship him at the Temple in Jerusalem. This Temple had been built by King Solomon. It was later destroyed by the Babylonians. It was rebuilt by Zerubbabel. This Temple was destroyed by a Roman general, Pompey. Herod built a third Temple which was used in Jesus' time. (2 Chronicles 2–7; Ezra 3:10-12; Mark 11:15-17; Acts 7:47; 19:27)

The New Testament also speaks of a Christian's body as a temple. That is because God's Spirit lives in the Christian. (Acts 7:48; 19:27; 1 Corinthians 6:19)

temptation (temp-TAY-shun) is the devil's trying to get us to do something wrong. God has promised to help us when we are tempted, so we can choose to do the right thing. (Matthew 4:1-11; 1 Corinthians 10:13; Hebrews 2:18; 4:15-16; James 1:12-14)

Tent See "Meeting Tent."

testament (TES-tuh-ment) See "agreement."

Thaddaeus (THAD-ee-us) was 1 of the 12 apostles. Little else is known about him. (Matthew 10:3; Mark 3:18)

Thomas (TOM-us), or Didymus, is a name that means "twin." He was 1 of Jesus' 12 apostles. His courage and love for Jesus are shown in John 11:16. Sometimes people call him "doubting Thomas." The other apostles told him Jesus had been raised from death. But Thomas did not believe it until he saw Jesus himself. (John 14:5-7; 20:24-29; 21:2)

threshing floor was a place where farmers separated grain from chaff. This was done by beating the stalks on the hard ground. Then they would throw it in the air and let the wind blow the chaff away. (Genesis 50:10; Judges 6:11; 2 Samuel 24:16-24) See "chaff."

Thummim (THUM-im) The Urim and Thummim were something attached to the holy vest of the high priest. They may have been gems. They were used in some way to find out what God wanted the Israelites to do. (Exodus 28:30; Leviticus 8:8; Deuteronomy 33:8)

Tiberius Caesar (tie-BEER-ee-us SEE-zur) was the Roman emperor during the last half of Jesus' life. He ruled from A.D. 14 to 37. The city of Tiberias was named for him. (Luke 3:1)

Timothy (TIM-oh-thee) means "one who honors God." Timothy was a close friend and helper of the apostle Paul. He was the son of a Greek father and Jewish Christian mother. His mother Eunice and his grandmother Lois taught him the Scriptures. Paul wrote two letters, called 1 and 2 Timothy, to him. (Acts 16:1-3; 17:13-16; 1 Corinthians 4:17; 1 Thessalonians 3:1-6; 2 Timothy 1:2-5)

tithe (TIETH) means "tenth." In the Old Testament the Jewish people were told to give one-tenth of what they earned to God. (Leviticus 27:30-32; Malachi 3:8; Luke 11:42; 18:12)

Titus (TIE-tus) was a trusted friend and helper of the apostle Paul. He often traveled with or for Paul. Paul wrote the book of Titus to him while Titus was on the island of Crete. (2 Corinthians 2:13; 7:6-7, 13-15; 8:6, 16, 23; Titus 1:4-5)

tomb (TOOM) is a place where a dead person's body is buried. Some tombs were underground. More often, in biblical times they were dug out of the side of a huge rock or mountain. A large stone was then rolled in front of the tomb to seal it. (Genesis 50:5; Luke 23:53-55; 24:1-2; John 20:1-9; 11:38-41)

transfiguration (tranz-fig-you-RAY-shun) means "to change." Jesus was transfigured in front of Peter, James and John. Jesus had taken them up on a mountain with him. There his face and clothes began to shine brightly. God spoke to the apostles. He said that Jesus is his Son and that they should obey only him. (Matthew 17:1-9)

tribe was all the descendants of a certain person. The 12 tribes of Israel were the descendants of the 12 sons of Jacob, who was later named Israel. (Genesis 49:28; Joshua 3:12; 7:14)

U

uncircumcised See "circumcision."

unclean is used to describe the state of a person, animal or action that was not pleasing to God. In the Old Testament God said certain animals were unclean. They

were not to be eaten. If a person disobeyed this (or some other rule about being clean), that person was called unclean. He could not serve God until he was made clean again. (Genesis 7:2; Leviticus 11–15; Romans 14:14) See "clean."

unleavened bread (un-LEV-'nd bread) is bread made without yeast. This kind of bread is like a flat, thin cracker because it does not rise when it is baked. God told the Jews to use unleavened bread for the Passover Feast. (Exodus 12:20; Matthew 26:17-29; Mark 14:12-25)

Unleavened Bread, Day of was the first day of the Feast of Unleavened Bread or Passover. (Luke 22:7)

Urim (YOUR-im) See "Thummim."

V

vest, holy is often called the "ephod. This was a special type of clothing for the priests in the Old Testament. The holy vest for the high priest had gold and gems on it. The Urim and Thummim were attached to the holy vest. (Exodus 25; 28; 39) See "Thummim."

virgin (VUR-jin) is a woman or girl who has not had sexual relations. (Genesis 24:16; Deuteronomy 22:15-28; Isaiah 7:14; Matthew 1:23; Luke 1:34)

vision (VIZ-zhun) is like a dream. A vision may come to a person when he is awake or asleep. God used visions to tell people what he wanted them to do, to teach them something or to let them know something that was going to happen. Peter had a vision of a sheet filled with animals. (Genesis 15:1; Daniel 2:19; Acts 9:10-12; 10:3-19; 11:5; 16:9-10; 18:9)

W

winepress was a pit where grapes were mashed to get the juice out. People stepped on the grapes. The juice ran out into another container. The winepress is sometimes used to describe how God will punish people. When they sinned terribly, God would allow enemy armies to defeat them as if they were grapes crushed in a winepress. (Deuteronomy 15:14; Judges 6:11; Lamentations 1:15)

wise men, or "magi," was a name for men who studied the stars. Some wise men followed a star from the East and brought gifts to Jesus when he was born. (Matthew 2:1-12)

witchcraft means using the power of the devil to do magic. (Deuteronomy 18:10; 2 Chronicles 33:6; Galatians 5:20)

witness (WIT-ness) is someone who tells what he has seen or what he knows. The apostles were witnesses for Christ because they told people that Jesus is the Son of God. (Acts 1:8, 22; 2:32; 22:14-15)

woman, slave is also called a concubine. She was a woman who may have been captured by a man during a war. Or he may have bought her as a slave. She was like a second-class wife whose main purpose was to have children for him. (Genesis 36:12; 2 Chronicles 11:21)

word in the Bible often means God's message to us in the Scriptures. (1 Peter 1:24-25; 1 John 2:14) Jesus is called the "Word" because he shows us what God is like. (John 1:1-5, 14)

Y

yoke is a wooden frame that fits on the necks of animals to hold them together while working. Two oxen were often yoked together to pull a farmer's plow. The word yoke is also used to mean the work a person is to do. (Deuteronomy 21:3; 2 Chronicles 10:4-11; Matthew 11:29)

Z

Zealots (ZEL-ots) were a group of Jewish men who were also called "Enthusiasts." They hated the Romans for controlling their home country and planned to force them out. Simon, the apostle, was a Zealot. (Luke 6:15; Acts 1:13)

Zion (ZY-on) was a hill inside the city of Jerusalem. Later, the name Zion, or Sion, was used to mean all of Jerusalem. In the New Testament, Mount Zion is sometimes even used as a name for heaven. (Hebrews 12:22; Revelation 14:1)

WHERE DO I FIND IT?

WHAT GOD PROMISES ABOUT . . .

The Bible contains many wonderful promises that God has made to us. Below are just a few of them. You might want to see what other promises you can find. One reason God's promises are special is that "the Lord will keep his promises" (Psalm 145:13).

Doing Good

We must not become tired of doing good. We will receive our harvest of eternal life at the right time. We must not give up!
Galatians 6:9

You are young, but do not let anyone treat you as if you were not important. Be an example to show the believers how they should live. Show them with your words, with the way you live, with your love, with your pure life. . . . . Then you will save yourself and those people who listen to you.
1 Timothy 4:12, 16

Forgiveness

If we confess our sins, he will forgive our sins. We can trust God. He does what is right. He will make us clean from all the wrongs we have done.
1 John 1:9

Giving

God loves the person who gives happily. And God can give you more blessings than you need. Then you will always have plenty of everything.
2 Corinthians 9:7-8

Helping Me

God is our protection and our strength:
He always helps in times of trouble.
Psalm 46:1

The Lord is close to the brokenhearted.
He saves those whose spirits have been crushed.
Psalm 34:18

You can be sure that I will be with you always. I will continue with you until the end of the world.
Matthew 28:20

The Lord is my shepherd.
I have everything I need.
Psalm 23:1

Remember the Lord in everything you do.
And he will give you success.
Proverbs 3:6

With God's power working in us, God can do much, much more than anything we can ask or think of.

Ephesians 3:20

Yes, God is working in you to help you want to do what pleases him. Then he gives you the power to do it.

Philippians 2:13

I can do all things through Christ because he gives me strength.

Philippians 4:13

My Faith

Remember that I commanded you to be strong and brave. So don't be afraid. The Lord your God will be with you everywhere you go.

Joshua 1:9

I tell you the truth. If your faith is as big as a mustard seed, you can say to this mountain, "Move from here to there." And the mountain will move. All things will be possible for you.

Matthew 17:20

Jesus said to her, "I am the resurrection and the life. He who believes in me will have life even if he dies. And he who lives and believes in me will never die."

John 11:25-26

In Christ we can come before God with freedom and without fear. We can do this through faith in Christ.

Ephesians 3:12

Everyone who is a child of God has the power to win against the world. It is our faith that wins the victory against the world. So the one who wins against the world is the person who believes that Jesus is the Son of God.

1 John 5:4-5

My Happiness

Do what the Lord says is good and right. Then things will go well for you.

Deuteronomy 6:18

Those people who know they have great spiritual needs are happy.
The kingdom of heaven belongs to them.
Those who are sad now are happy.
God will comfort them.
Those who are humble are happy.
The earth will belong to them.
Those who want to do right more than anything else are happy.
God will fully satisfy them.
Those who give mercy to others are happy.
Mercy will be given to them.
Those who are pure in their thinking are happy.
They will be with God.
Those who work to bring peace are happy.
God will call them his sons.

Those who are treated badly for
doing good are happy.
The kingdom of heaven
belongs to them.
Matthew 5:3-10

My Obedience

Honor your father and your mother.
Then you will live a long time in
the land.
Exodus 20:12

Jesus said, "Those who hear the
teaching of God and obey it—they
are the ones who are truly blessed."
Luke 11:28

Children, obey your parents the
way the Lord wants. This is the
right thing to do. . . . "Then everything will be well with you, and
you will have a long life on the
earth."
Ephesians 6:1, 3

My Prayers

The Lord listens when I pray to
him.
Psalm 4:3

When a good man prays, great
things happen.
James 5:16

Salvation

God will soon save those who
respect him.
And his greatness will be seen
in our land.
Psalm 85:9

For God loved the world so much
that he gave his only Son. God
gave his Son so that whoever believes in him may not be lost, but
have eternal life.
John 3:16

Jesus said, "Don't let your hearts
be troubled. Trust in God. And
trust in me. There are many rooms
in my Father's house. . . . I am
going there to prepare a place for
you. After I go and prepare a
place for you, I will come back.
Then I will take you to be with me
so that you may be where I am."
John 14:1-3

Wisdom

The Lord says, "I will make you
wise. I will show you where
to go.
I will guide you and watch
over you."
Psalm 32:8

Listen to advice and accept
correction.
Then in the end you will be
wise.
Proverbs 19:20

But if any of you needs wisdom,
you should ask God for it. God is
generous. He enjoys giving to all
people, so God will give you wisdom.
James 1:5

MEMORY VERSES FOR MY LIFE

Always be humble and gentle. Be patient and accept each other with love.

Ephesians 4:2

A friend loves you all the time.
Proverbs 17:17

But I tell you, love your enemies. Pray for those who hurt you.
Matthew 5:44

Do what is right to other people.
Love being kind to others.
And live humbly, trusting your God.
Micah 6:8

Do for other people what you want them to do for you.
Luke 6:31

Depend on the Lord.
Trust him, and he will take care of you.
Psalm 37:5

Being afraid of people can get you into trouble.
But if you trust the Lord, you will be safe.
Proverbs 29:25

Do not worry about anything. But pray and ask God for everything you need.
Philippians 4:6

My child, do not reject the Lord's discipline.
And don't become angry when he corrects you.
The Lord corrects those he loves just as a father corrects the child that he likes.
Proverbs 3:11-12

Give all your worries to him, because he cares for you.
1 Peter 5:7

A gentle answer will calm a person's anger.
But an unkind answer will cause more anger.
Proverbs 15:1

Children, obey your parents the way the Lord wants. This is the right thing to do.
Ephesians 6:1

Those who work to bring peace are happy.
God will call them his sons.
Matthew 5:9

Serve the Lord with joy.
Come before him with singing. . . .
Come into his city with songs of thanksgiving.
Come into his courtyards with songs of praise.
Thank him, and praise his name.
Psalm 100:2, 4

If someone does wrong to you, do not pay him back by doing wrong to him. Try to do what everyone thinks is right. Do your best to live in peace with everyone.

Romans 12:17-18

Praise the Lord!
Thank the Lord because he is good.
His love continues forever.
Psalm 106:1

Do not be bitter or angry or mad. Never shout angrily or say things to hurt others. Never do anything evil. Be kind and loving to each other. Forgive each other just as God forgave you in Christ.

Ephesians 4:31-32

Happy is the person
whose sins are forgiven,
whose wrongs are pardoned.
Psalm 32:1

Be happy with those who are happy.
Romans 12:15

Wait for the Lord's help.
Be strong and brave
and wait for the Lord's help.
Psalm 27:14

Be full of joy in the Lord always. I will say again, be full of joy.
Philippians 4:4

But the people who trust the Lord
will become strong again.
They will be able to rise up as an
eagle in the sky.
They will run without needing
rest.
They will walk without
becoming tired.
Isaiah 40:31

Come to me, all of you who are tired and have heavy loads. I will give you rest.

Matthew 11:28

Finally, be strong in the Lord and in his great power.
Ephesians 6:10

Those who want to do right more
than anything else are happy.
God will fully satisfy them.
Matthew 5:6

If you love me, you will do the things I command.
John 14:15

Do not let evil defeat you. Defeat evil by doing good.
Romans 12:21

Your word is like a lamp for my
feet and a light for my way.
Psalm 119:105

The only temptations that you have are the temptations that all people have. But you can trust God. He will not let you be tempted more than you can stand. But when you are tempted, God will also give you a way to escape that temptation. Then you will be able to stand it.

1 Corinthians 10:13

When a person is tempted and still continues strong, he should be happy. After he has proved his faith, God will reward him with life forever. God promised this to all people who love him.

James 1:12

Dear children, do not let any person lead you the wrong way. Christ is righteous. To be like Christ, a person must do what is right.

1 John 3:7

You must choose for yourselves today. You must decide whom you will serve. . . . As for me and my family, we will serve the Lord.

Joshua 24:15

We know that in everything God works for the good of those who love him. They are the people God called, because that was his plan.

Romans 8:28

We have troubles all around us, but we are not defeated. We do not know what to do, but we do not give up.

2 Corinthians 4:8

The Lord is kind and shows mercy.
He does not become angry
   quickly but is full of love.
Psalm 145:8

[Jesus] said to them, "Let the little children come to me. Don't stop them. The kingdom of God belongs to people who are like these little children."

Mark 10:14

God, examine me and know my heart.
Test me and know my thoughts.
See if there is any bad thing in me.
Lead me in the way you set long
   ago.
Psalm 139:23-24

I showed you in all things that you should work as I did and help the weak. I taught you to remember the words of Jesus. He said, "It is more blessed to give than to receive."

Acts 20:35

Always remember what you have
   been taught.
Don't let go of it.
Keep safe all that you have learned.
   It is the most important thing in
   your life.
Proverbs 4:13

Love is patient and kind. Love is not jealous, it does not brag, and it is not proud.

1 Corinthians 13:4

Continue to ask, and God will give to you. Continue to search, and you will find. Continue to knock, and the door will open for you.

Matthew 7:7

All people have sinned and are not good enough for God's glory.

Romans 3:23

I give you a new command: Love each other. You must love each other as I have loved you. All people will know that you are my followers if you love each other.

John 13:34-35

I can do all things through Christ because he gives me strength.

Philippians 4:13

Forget about the wrong things people do to you. You must not try to get even. Love your neighbor as you love yourself.

Leviticus 19:18

Everything you say and everything you do should all be done for Jesus your Lord. And in all you do, give thanks to God the Father through Jesus.

Colossians 3:17

Love the Lord your God with all your heart, soul and strength.

Deuteronomy 6:5

Be kind and loving to each other. Forgive each other just as God forgave you in Christ.

Ephesians 4:32

But if we confess our sins, he will forgive us our sins. We can trust God. He does what is right. He will make us clean from all the wrongs we have done.

1 John 1:9

May the Lord bless you and keep you.
May the Lord show you his
    kindness.
    May he have mercy on you.
May the Lord watch over you
    and give you peace.

Numbers 6:24-26

The Names of God

God is much bigger and greater than anything or anyone we could ever imagine. No name can describe all that He is and all that He does. So God chose to show us who He is through the many different names for God that we find in the Bible. Here are just some of them:

The Great Shepherd of the Sheep (Psalm 23:1; Hebrews 13:20)
The Word of God (Revelation 19:13)
Wonderful Counselor (Isaiah 9:6)
Prince of Peace (Isaiah 9:6)
God Most High (Genesis 14:19)
God Who Sees Me (Genesis 16:13)
Father, Dear Father (Romans 8:15)
The Righteous One (1 John 2:1)
The Beginning and the End (Revelation 22:13)
The One Who Gives Life (Acts 3:15)
The Bright Morning Star (Revelation 22:16)
The Helper (John 14:26)
The Savior (Luke 2:11; Romans 11:26)
Faithful and True (Revelation 19:11)
Our Great Hope (Titus 2:13)
I AM WHO I AM (Exodus 3:14)
Christ, the Lord (Luke 2:11)
King of Kings and Lord of Lords (1 Timothy 6:15; Revelation 19:16)
The True Light (John 1:9)
The Light of the World (John 8:12)
Love (1 John 4:8)
Master (Luke 5:5)
The Potter (Isaiah 64:8)
The Rock (1 Corinthians 10:4)
The Way and the Truth and the Life (John 14:6)
The Word (John 1:1)

The Disciples

Jesus had many followers while He was on earth, but a few men became His special group of disciples. The disciples spent a lot of time living, eating, working, and walking with Jesus. All that time together prepared them to teach people far and wide about how Jesus is the Son of God. After Jesus died, rose again, and went up into heaven, the Holy Spirit filled the disciples and helped them with the important job of spreading the Good News to the world.

Peter

Andrew

James, son of Zebedee

John, son of Zebedee

James, son of Alphaeus

Philip

Bartholomew

Matthew

Thomas

Thaddaeus

Simon

Judas Iscariot

Judas died after he betrayed Jesus. Matthias was chosen to replace Judas and to join the disciples in telling others about Jesus.

The Miracles of Jesus

Jesus did many miracles. He helped people by healing not only their sick bodies but also their souls. Each of His miracles showed God's glory and proved that Jesus is the Son of God.

Changing water into wine (John 2:1–11)
Healing an officer's son (John 4:46–54)
Casting out demons (Mark 1:21–28; Matthew 8:28–32)
Healing Peter's mother-in-law (Luke 4:38–39)
Filling nets with fish (Luke 5:3–11)
Healing the bleeding woman (Mark 5:25–34)
Healing Jairus's daughter (Luke 8:41–42, 49–56)
Healing lepers (Matthew 8:1–3; Luke 17:11–19)
Healing the soldier's servant (Matthew 8:5–13)
Making the paralyzed man walk (Mark 2:1–12)
Healing the man with the crippled hand (Luke 6:6–10)
Bringing the widow's son back to life (Luke 7:11–17)
Calming the wind and the waves (Matthew 8:23–27)
Healing the sick man by the pool (John 5:1–17)
Feeding more than 5,000 people (Mark 6:35–44)
Walking on water (John 6:16–21)
Freeing the girl from a demon (Matthew 15:21–28)
Healing the man who could not hear or speak (Mark 7:31–37)
Feeding more than 4,000 people (Matthew 15:29–39)
Healing the blind man in Bethsaida (Mark 8:22–26)
Healing the man who was born blind (John 9)
Freeing the boy from a demon (Matthew 17:14–20)
Catching a fish with a coin in its mouth (Matthew 17:24–27)
Bringing Lazarus back to life (John 11:1–44)
Healing blind Bartimaeus (Mark 10:46–52)
Drying up the fig tree (Matthew 21:18–22)
Healing the man whose ear was cut off (Luke 22:47–51)
Coming back to life Himself (Matthew 28, Mark 16, Luke 24, John 20)
Filling nets with fish after His resurrection (John 21:4–11)

Kids in the Bible

One time Jesus' disciples thought the children in the crowd were getting in the way, so they tried to make the children leave Him alone. "Stop!" Jesus said. "Let the little children come to me." As the boys and girls came, He blessed each of them. Children are very important to Jesus!

Paul says the same thing in 1 Timothy 4:12. Even though you aren't grown up yet, you are still special. God can do mighty work through you! Take a look at these children of the Bible and how their lives made a difference.

Samuel — As a boy, Samuel heard God's voice and obeyed (1 Samuel 3:1–19).

David — As a young shepherd, David killed the giant Goliath (1 Samuel 17).

Josiah — He was crowned king at age eight and led the people of Israel to follow God (2 Kings 22).

Joash — He became king when he was seven and repaired God's temple (2 Kings 11–12).

Naaman's servant girl — She told Naaman about a prophet who could heal him and change his life (2 Kings 5).

Jesus — He listened and taught in the temple when He was only twelve years old (Luke 2:42–52).

Children coming to Jesus — Jesus gave them His blessings (Matthew 19:13–14).

Boy with five loaves and two fish — He shared his lunch and helped Jesus feed more than 5,000 people (John 6:1–14).

Rhoda — This servant girl opened the door for Peter and was among the first to hear how an angel had freed him from prison (Acts 12:12–19).

Timothy — He was raised by a godly mom and grandmother and grew up to love and serve God (2 Timothy 1:5–8).

Caspian Sea

Persian Gulf

Mount Ararat?

Nineveh

Nuzi

Tigris River

Babylon

Euphrates River

Erech

Ur

MESOPOTAMIA

Haran

Carchemish

PADAN
ARAM

Mari

Ebla

Ugarit

HITTITES

Damascus

Hazor

Dothan

Shechem

Dead
Sea

CANAAN

Beersheba

Mediterranean Sea

Mount Sinai

Red
Sea

On

Memphis

EGYPT

ABRAHAM'S JOURNEY

Possible route
that Abraham followed.

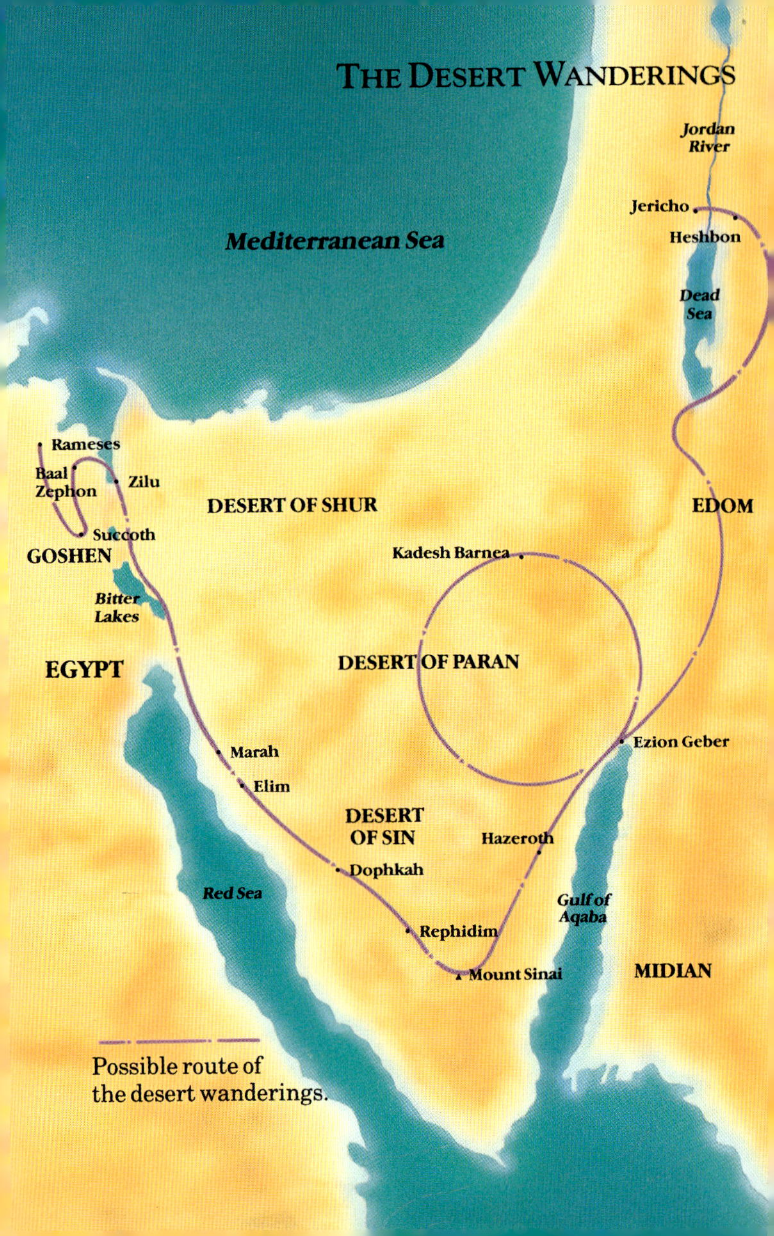

THE DESERT WANDERINGS

Jordan River

Mediterranean Sea

Jericho
Heshbon

Dead Sea

Rameses
Baal Zephon • Zilu
DESERT OF SHUR
EDOM
Succoth
GOSHEN
Kadesh Barnea •

Bitter Lakes

EGYPT
DESERT OF PARAN

Ezion Geber
Marah
Elim
DESERT OF SIN
Hazeroth
Dophkah
Red Sea
Gulf of Aqaba
Rephidim
Mount Sinai
MIDIAN

Possible route of
the desert wanderings.

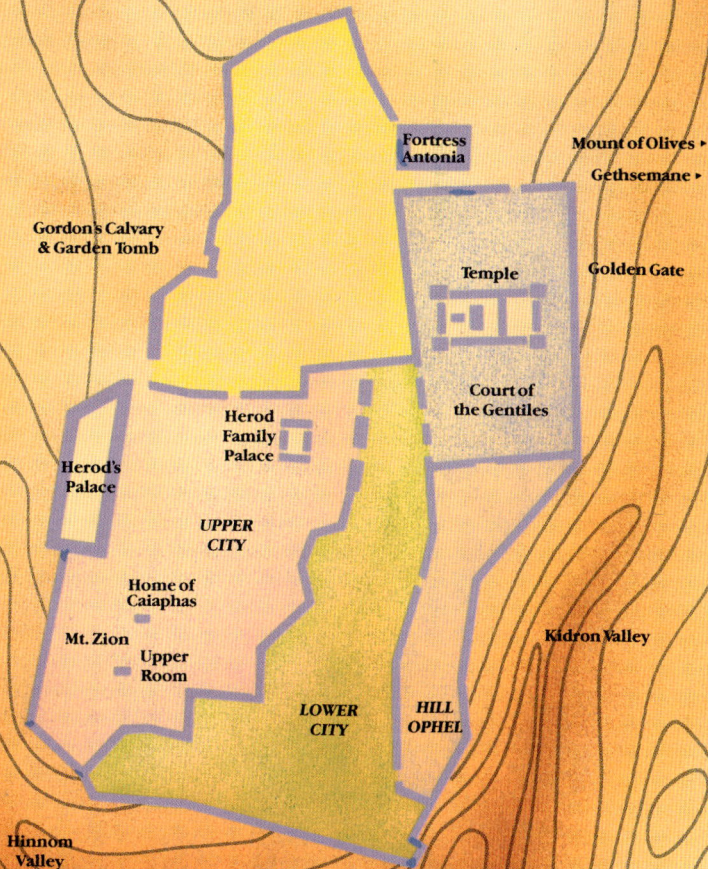

JESUS' LAST WEEK IN JERUSALEM

Fortress Antonia

Mount of Olives ▸

Gethsemane ▸

Gordon's Calvary & Garden Tomb

Temple

Golden Gate

Court of the Gentiles

Herod Family Palace

Herod's Palace

UPPER CITY

Home of Caiaphas

Mt. Zion

Upper Room

Kidron Valley

LOWER CITY

HILL OPHEL

Hinnom Valley

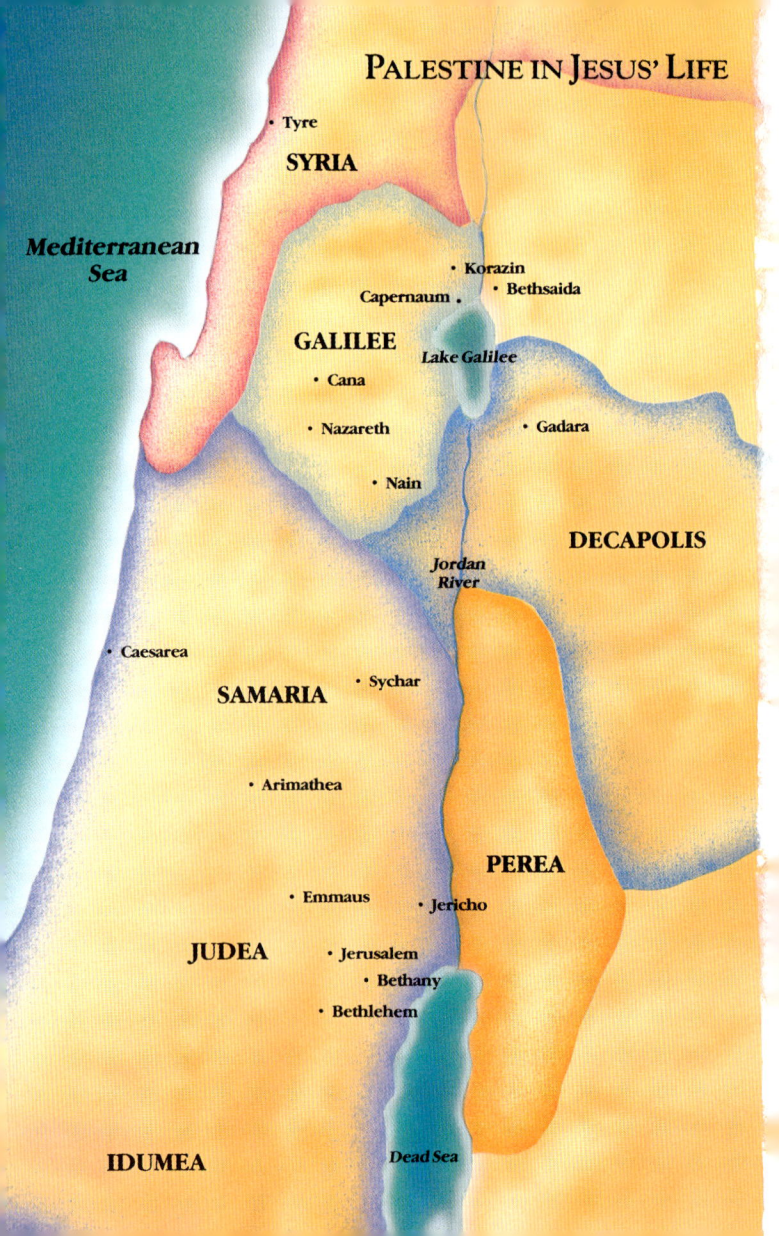

PALESTINE IN JESUS' LIFE

Tyre •

SYRIA

Mediterranean
Sea

Korazin •
Capernaum • • Bethsaida

GALILEE

Lake Galilee

Cana •

Nazareth • • Gadara

Nain •

DECAPOLIS

Jordan
River

Caesarea •

SAMARIA • Sychar

Arimathea •

PEREA

Emmaus • • Jericho

JUDEA • Jerusalem
• Bethany

Bethlehem •

IDUMEA Dead Sea